AN
ANALYTICAL CONCORDANCE
TO THE
REVISED STANDARD VERSION
OF THE
NEW TESTAMENT

AN ANALYTICAL CONCORDANCE TO THE REVISED STANDARD VERSION OF THE NEW TESTAMENT

BY

CLINTON MORRISON

THE WESTMINSTER PRESS
PHILADELPHIA

COPYRIGHT © 1979 THE WESTMINSTER PRESS

All rights reserved—no part of this book may be reproduced in any form without permission in writing from the publisher, except by a reviewer who wishes to quote brief passages in connection with a review in magazine or newspaper.

The Bible text in this publication is from the Revised Standard Version of the Bible, copyrighted 1946, 1952, © 1971, 1973 by the Division of Christian Education of the National Council of the Churches of Christ in the U.S.A., and is used by permission.

First edition

Published by The Westminster Press®
Philadelphia, Pennsylvania

PRINTED IN THE UNITED STATES OF AMERICA

9 8 7 6 5 4 3 2 1

Library of Congress Cataloging in Publication Data

Morrison, Clinton, 1924–
An analytical concordance to the Revised Standard Version of the New Testament.

Includes index.
1. Bible. N.T.—Concordances, English—Revised standard. I. Title.
BS2305.M67 225.5′204 77-26210
ISBN 0-664-20773-1

JEAN

CLINTON GREGORY

AMY

CONTENTS

PREFACE

In the last hundred years there have been great advances in Biblical scholarship, one being the establishment of a much sounder text of the Greek New Testament. During this same period, however, the study of Greek has greatly declined, even among students for the ministry, leaving many of those charged with preaching and teaching in the church increasingly dependent upon the English versions alone. Modern translators, of course, have had access to a reliable Greek text, and this fact is one of the most important—although commonly overlooked—characteristics of modern versions. But in the absence of a modern analytical concordance there has been no means by which the English reader could identify the Greek underlying modern versions and thus no sound way of enlarging or discriminating material for study.

Although with some effort modern versions can be used with the old analytical concordances of Young and Strong, which are based on the Authorized (King James) Version, the result is subjection once more to an unreliable Greek text; one might as well return to the King James Version.

My colleague, Dean Floyd V. Filson, sometime member of the Standard Bible Committee, and Dean Luther A. Weigle, its chairman, were of one mind on the urgent need for a modern analytical concordance. This present work, which began with their enthusiastic support, owes its completion in no small measure to their sustained encouragement.

In this revival of the analytical concordance, I hope to have maintained what has proven useful, to have improved what was awkward, and to have added a few aids to study. Only use can determine whether I have succeeded. As was the case with the Revised Standard Version itself, this Concordance will benefit from the comments and criticism of careful users, both as to what they find to be defects and what they propose as improvements. I hope, especially now that the RSV will be revised periodically, that the Concordance likewise can be shaped to its most useful form and attain to the precision that is necessary in a basic tool of Bible study.

This work could not have been produced without the help and encouragement of many persons. The chairmen of the Standard Bible Committee have been the source of much essential information and of unfailing and generous support. Dean Luther A. Weigle provided notes on the Greek text base which he had prepared in cooperation with Professors Henry J. Cadbury and Millar Burrows. He also provided information on early changes in the RSV. Professor Herbert G. May provided for me well in advance the substance of the second edition of the RSV New Testament. Professor Bruce M. Metzger reviewed hundreds of textual questions related to the Greek text base.

I am greatly indebted to McCormick Theological Seminary and Louisville Presbyterian Theological Seminary—each granted me a full year's sabbatical leave to work on this project. I am also indebted to the Association of Theological Schools and the Advanced Religious Studies Foundation for fellowships.

Louisville Seminary, in the persons of Presidents Albert C. Winn and C. Ellis Nelson and Business Manager Kenneth R. Hougland, has provided support and encouragement in many forms from able assistants to xerography. All who participated cannot be named, but it would be unjust not to acknowledge the contribution of those who carried major responsibilities in the project: Student assistants Richard McLean, Lewis Donelson, and Robert E. Tedrow skillfully carried out diverse tasks of verification, insertion of RSV footnote entries and revisions, and the collation of compact entries. Dora Boyer turned countless slips of paper and file cards into thousands of pages of manuscript.

The design and style of the Concordance benefited from the suggestions of Professors Gregory T. Armstrong, Leander E. Keck, Donald G. Miller, and Thomas A. Schafer, and Mrs. Ella Oelrich. Professors F. Wilbur Gingrich, Robert Morgenthaler, and Sherman E. Johnson kindly responded to lexical and critical queries. Professor George R. Edwards reviewed many textual questions and Appendix I.

The pronunciations supplied for the proper nouns were much improved by the complete review and counsel of Dr. Lewis A. Briner. Among several persons who provided special help and encouragement, I must give hearty thanks to Wilbur Ruggles and Helen Hawley.

The Westminster Press has devoted to this work the extraordinary resources of its editors and staff. In particular I must mention Dr. Paul L. Meacham, Religious Book Editor, for the courage to undertake a work of this kind and for his encouragement; and Carl Helmich, whose grasp of the work as a whole and in detail, together with his keen eye and sound judgment, has contributed greatly to the integrity, accuracy, and usefulness of the final product.

Finally, to my family I owe more than is seemly to print, not only for their support throughout but for their own participation over several years, at times as a full-time job, collating and verifying unnumbered data in sundry classes and combinations, even to the reading of the proofs. Thus it is also their work beyond the page of dedication.

If after so much assistance from so many there yet remain errors or infelicities, they will surely be my own.

CLINTON MORRISON, JR.

Louisville Presbyterian Theological Seminary
May 7, 1977

EXPLANATORY NOTES

INTRODUCTION

A concordance is an alphabetical index of the words in a book or a body of literature in which each occurrence is presented in its immediate context. It is used primarily to find something—perhaps a single saying that we may faintly remember or all that a single author has written about a given matter. The context line is useful for finding one particular instance among many or for distinguishing several uses with a common element. The purpose of a concordance is to provide the user precise, efficient, and—if it is unabridged—comprehensive access to the literature covered. The Bible concordance has been a basic aid to Bible study for generations, used by scholars, pastors, church school teachers, and the general public.

The Purpose of This Analytical Concordance

Professional Biblical scholars are expected to deal directly with the Greek text of the New Testament, but most persons must rely upon the translated Bible alone. The purpose of an analytical concordance is to help the English reader to exercise the optimum precision and discrimination in the study of Scripture. It also makes accessible relevant material that otherwise would be unknown. The present work is an analytical concordance to the Revised Standard Version of the New Testament, Second Edition, which is an English translation from the original Greek.

An ordinary concordance to the Revised Standard Version will enable one to find every use of "church" in the RSV New Testament, but it will not mention six other passages that anyone doing careful study will want to take into account. The word "church" translates only the Greek word EKKLĒSIA—the transliterated Greek in the Analytical Concordance is often of interest in itself—but not every instance of EKKLĒSIA is translated "church." EKKLĒSIA is also translated "assembly" (four times) and "congregation" (twice). By making this known, the Analytical Concordance makes possible a comprehensive study not ordinarily accessible to the English reader.

The Analytical Concordance also enables precision. It will not be adequate for us simply to turn to "assembly" in an ordinary RSV concordance to further our study of EKKLĒSIA, for the seven uses of "assembly" in the RSV represent three different Greek words. In addition to EKKLĒSIA, one is a very general term for a large number (PLĒTHOS); the other, SYNAGŌGĒ! Only an analytical concordance can show the English reader which passages use which term. And if we wish to pursue these ideas further—whether for careful study or simply out of fascination—we will find that the general term (PLĒTHOS) is also rendered "body," "bundle," "company," "many," "mob," while SYNAGŌGĒ is otherwise always translated "synagogue."

This Analytical Concordance has provided some additional detail that is new. For example, under "church" we will see that in 1 Cor 5.12 the word is used "contextually." That is to say, "church" here is implied by the context; it translates no Greek word as such.

Yet its explicit expression makes for clarity and good English idiom.

The manifold benefits of the Analytical Concordance are easily discovered with use. But a warning should be recorded. Precisely because such a concordance will greatly increase the range of our Bible study, we must be cautioned against undisciplined conclusions and novel interpretation beyond our depth. The language of the New Testament is far more complex than mere vocabulary, and the art of interpretation requires wide learning and exact skills. The Analytical Concordance will serve each person at his or her own level of scholarship, and will provide a stimulus and tool for growth; but it will not make an authority of a zealot.

Why the RSV Was Chosen

The Revised Standard Version was chosen for this Analytical Concordance for several reasons. (*a*) It is a modern version. The great increase in Bible translation in this generation is adequate testimony to the need for and the importance of the Bible in contemporary language. (*b*) The policy of periodic revision of the RSV assures its continuing currency in idiom as well as in scholarship. (*c*) In its tradition as well as in the makeup of its sponsoring body and translating committee, the RSV represents a church version, not the work of an individual scholar or a private publisher. (*d*) Of the several modern versions, its style of translation is most compatible with the kind of analysis required for this work and with the kind of Biblical study that this Analytical Concordance will make possible. (*e*) The Revised Standard Version is an excellent basis, or point of reference, for the English reader to use when comparing various modern versions of the Bible.

ORGANIZATION AND USE OF THE CONCORDANCE

These Explanatory Notes, together with the various tables that follow, will help persons consulting the Concordance to make full and precise use of it. A thorough understanding of the details is, of course, neither possible nor necessary before one actually begins to use the Concordance. To assist the reader in visualizing the organization of this work, examples are provided. **Boldface numbers** refer to lines on the page of examples entitled "Explanatory Notes Illustrated."

The Analytical Concordance is composed of two principal parts, the Concordance proper, or text, and the Index-Lexicon. The Concordance text is arranged according to English words in alphabetical order; the Index-Lexicon is arranged according to transliterated Greek words in alphabetical order.

First of all, and emphatically, it should be said that this Concordance does not presuppose a knowledge of New Testament Greek. The regular appearance of Greek words on the subtitle lines—in both Greek and English (i.e., Roman) letters—is to assist in the essential function to be described below, but in no instance is it assumed that one will "know" these Greek words. Here and there, Greek words may appear as special notes to those who can use them, but they should in no way intimidate or distract anyone.

Titles in the Concordance Text

In the Concordance proper, every entry begins with an English title in capital letters (**1, 8, 18**). This is the word or phrase from the RSV New Testament that is dealt with in everything that follows, up to the next title. These titles are given only in lexical form. That is, a person studying "go" will not have to look up "went," "gone," and "going" as well. Such an arrangement would be not only inconvenient but artificial. The user of this Concordance will find among the titles not only GO but also GO ABOARD, GO ABOUT, GO ABROAD, GO ACROSS, GO AHEAD (**31, 58, 61**). This distribution is important. On the one hand it serves to break up an otherwise exceedingly long entry into clearly distinct ideas; on the other hand it displays these ideas as they represent corresponding distinctions in the Greek vocabulary. Thus a title may take an inflected form if in that form (e.g., in its plural) it has a different meaning than in the usual lexical form (see PRINCIPALITIES).

The English personal pronouns are ordinarily given according to number and gender, but not case. That is, under I, WE, YOU, HE, SHE, IT, and THEY all other personal pronouns are found. Thus "me" is under I; "her" under SHE; "their" under THEY. Exceptions to this practice will be noted by cross-reference at these headings to ensure full access to every entry.

When one English word serves more than one English part of speech, this is differentiated not in the title, but in the subtitles. Thus under STONE may be found the noun, the adjective, and the verb, under separate subtitles (**31, 32, 35, 49**).

Titles comprised of more than one word should not be taken to represent every occurrence of these words together. For example, the title GREAT, VERY will cover only instances in which the underlying Greek cannot be further broken down—instances in which a Greek word means something more than merely "great." In other instances, when the New Testament authors do as we do, and use one word for "very" and another for "great," these words will be found under their respective titles, not under GREAT, VERY (**58-60; 49-51**). This explanation illustrates the general principle of the analysis, which is to break down the RSV English as far as possible, but no further than the Greek will allow. In some cases (see below, at the heading "Idiomatically") this means taking a whole Greek clause as the minimal base for a whole English clause.

If a known title is not found in alphabetical order, it should be sought in a nearby grouping of two or more titles that begin with the same word. For example, CALL UPON is not found after CALL TOGETHER, but with CALL ON at the head of a combined entry. COME BY is not found in alphabetical order after COME, BE TO, but with COME BACK at the head of a combined entry (**77-78**). In a few instances of extreme dislocation, cross-references have been provided.

The Subtitle Line

Under every title there is ordinarily at least one subtitle line, which is comprised of three major parts: a definition of the Greek word, the Greek word itself, and a transliteration of the Greek word into English (i.e., Roman) letters (**19, 32**). The sequence of subtitles is determined by the alphabetical order of the transliterated Greek words (**32, 35, 37**).

The *definition* preceding the Greek word on the subtitle line must be accorded no greater significance than is appropriate. It offers to the user a "second eye" for perspective—serving, for example, to clarify the part of speech of the title word. The same definition ordinarily appears on the subtitle line at every occurrence of the particular Greek word (**37, 68; 19, 25**), so it does not have the versatility necessary to bear full lexical responsibility, and should not be expected to bear it. This subtitle line definition should, however, be a useful supplement to the range of meaning displayed in the Index-Lexicon.

The definitions on the subtitle lines are not original but are derived from the leading general and New Testament Greek lexicons.[1] When interested in fuller definition of a given word, one should look first to the work of the RSV translators as it is summarized in the Index-Lexicon (**89 ff.**), noting both the range of meaning and the most frequent translations. The fullest understanding will come from the study of a word's use throughout the RSV New Testament. It is the special service of the Analytical Concordance to enable one to do this kind of study. Usage, after all, is what governs any lexicon's definitions.

The *Greek word* in Greek letters ordinarily is spelled as in the Bauer-Arndt-Gingrich lexicon. The method of *transliteration* and the pronunciation of Greek words is set forth in the table "Transliteration."

In addition to the three major items already mentioned, the subtitle line may carry a variety of other clarifying or helpful data. Indications of voice or tense within the subtitle definition (**62**) are occasionally necessary because of the nature of Greek lexicography; their omission would be misleading. Ordinarily, however, grammatical references appear in parentheses between the Greek and its transliteration (**11, 68**) and refer only to the usage that follows, not to the basic subtitle definition. A fuller explanation will be found in Appendix I, Part Two: Grammatical Terms. See the table "Signs and Symbols" for the interpretation of other matter that appears on the subtitle line.

Context Lines

Context lines are provided for all major Greek words (nouns, verbs, adjectives, adverbs) with few exceptions—e.g., the occur-

[1]Definitions given on the subtitle lines are derived from *A Greek-English Lexicon*, by Henry George Liddell and Robert Scott, revised by Henry Stuart Jones, Oxford University Press, 1940; and *A Greek-English Lexicon of the New Testament and Other Early Christian Literature*, by William F. Arndt and F. Wilbur Gingrich, The University of Chicago Press, 1957—a translation and adaptation of Walter Bauer's *Wörterbuch*. The spelling of English words in the definitions conforms to *Webster's Third New International Dictionary* (G. & C. Merriam Co., 1961).

rences of "be" based on EỊMI are given in compact form (**27-29**). The context line serves a variety of purposes, not all of which are mutually agreeable. It should include enough of the context to enable the user to identify a passage already known and to discern common formulas and the associations of major words and ideas. It should also be intelligible and, if possible, should reflect the line of thought integral to its use. To achieve optimum value, ellipses (. .) have been employed within context lines (**23, 80, 88**). One way of showing the context is to indicate whether the words cited are a quotation, a parenthetical expression, a question, or an exclamation. This is indicated in every instance by the appropriate mark, but when one of these marks begins or ends a context line, that does not necessarily represent its exact location in the RSV (**13, 23, 38**). Ordinarily a line is given for every occurrence of the title word in a verse (**47-48**).

Symbols Used on Context Lines

A variety of symbols appear from time to time on context lines. They are not essential to the basic function of the Concordance, but an understanding of the symbols will save time and supply additional and more precise information. It is important, however, to know that a context line preceded by a square bracket represents an entry from the RSV footnotes (**17, 20**), and that the table "Signs and Symbols" is the place to find an interpretation of any other symbol not immediately understandable.

Despite the great care given to the selection of the context lines, the Concordance user is cautioned against basing judgments of any consequence solely upon a survey of context lines. Ellipses, for example, may be suited to one purpose but work to the disadvantage of another, and seldom can a single line do justice to the whole context affecting a word's meaning.

Compact Entries

A work as comprehensive as this will embrace a number of words not likely to be studied except by the specialist. Compact entries—i.e., book, chapter, and verse only (**29**)—have been used for these, and also for some words of undoubted importance that cannot be profitably displayed in context lines.

"Idiomatically"

After the regular entries, and under the heading IDIOMATICALLY, are listed instances in which the RSV translates the Greek freely. Among the Greek and English words in a given idiom, some may, in their own right, be capable of simple identification. But the English title word cannot simply be identified with a corresponding Greek word; the full statement seems best suited to account for the English. The transliterated Greek in brackets at the end of the IDIOMATICALLY entry is, thus, by definition, merely the closest association to be made between the title word and the Greek, and it is offered solely for the purpose of allowing the user to consult the Index-Lexicon and to follow up the nearest possible associations with the word or idea at hand (**55**). Where such a correlation is considered impossible, the English is classed as "contextual" and the Greek as "not translated." The designation "Idiomatically" thus has its roots in the process of analysis and does not necessarily relate to idiomatic usage in Greek or in English alone.

"Contextually"

The heading CONTEXTUALLY presents substantial English usage that lacks a clear Greek base (**16-17; 56-57**). This is a service to the person who may be intent upon a particular theme or study and would be unable otherwise to find certain passages if only those instances were provided that rest upon specific Greek words. This section embraces not only genuine contextual use, but the English expression of what is present in Greek moods, tenses, and other nonlexical forms. As this listing serves only a "finding" function, verses that are listed otherwise under the same title are ordinarily not also listed among the "contextual" entries.

The Index-Lexicon

The Index-Lexicon follows the text of the Concordance proper, beginning on p. 661. Under each transliterated Greek word (**89, 101**), all English translations of it found in the RSV are listed alphabetically. This Greek-English arrangement is an index to the Concordance. At the same time it is a lexicon, for it displays various meanings of the Greek from actual use. Where the English words are set in italic type (**103**), their corresponding Concordance entry is compact (book, chapter, and verse only).

Each translated meaning that occurs more than once is followed by its frequency in parentheses (**91**). Figures not in parentheses are subtitle numbers (**95**). The table "Signs and Symbols" will aid in the understanding of other information provided in the Index-Lexicon.

Grammatical terms in the Index-Lexicon are the same as those on the corresponding subtitle line in the Concordance text (**92**). Entries so marked, and especially those prefaced by the symbol § (**95**), should be particularly noted, for they cannot be considered as ordinary definitions of the Greek. They derive their meaning from combination with other words or through particular grammatical and syntactical circumstances described in Appendix I. When a given Greek word appears only in circumstances of this sort, a definition in brackets is provided in the Index-Lexicon to compensate for the lack of a simple definition on the subtitle lines in the Concordance (**108**).

Following the alphabetical list is the heading IDIOMATICALLY (**97**), under which reference is made to all idiomatic use, by title word and italic letter (**98**). Finally there is listed every instance in which the Greek word is NOT TRANSLATED (**99**). This circumstance is not common and entails no loss of meaning; it is usually necessary in order to avoid violating English idiom. In a number of instances, especially for those Greek words that are mostly given compact entry, there is a single section with the heading IDIOMATICALLY OR NOT TRANSLATED. This is an especially suitable means of handling a number of instances in which precise discrimination would be far more perplexing than useful.

The Cross-Reference Function

The cross-reference function, from which all other uses of the Analytical Concordance follow naturally, is based upon the following simple observations: (*a*) The English titles in the text are the very English words listed in the Index-Lexicon. (*b*) The Greek title words in the Index-Lexicon are the very transliterated Greek words that appear at the right end of subtitle lines (and at the end of IDIOMATICALLY entries) in the Concordance text. (*c*) The sequence of subtitles in the text is determined by the alphabetical order of their respective transliterated Greek words.

When this basic relationship of the two parts of the work is understood, its total contents become available for use.

The Analysis

This Concordance is based upon an analysis of the RSV New Testament that relates the RSV English to the original Greek. The procedure was based in the Greek and includes every Greek word in the New Testament except the four most common ones: ὁ/HO ("the"); καί/KAI ("and," "even," etc.); δέ/DE ("but," "and," etc.); αὐτός/AUTOS ("self"; "he," "she," "it," etc.). Together, these four words represent about 37,000 occurrences, more than a quarter of New Testament usage. (Those who wish to study these words should consult Kurt Aland's *Vollständige Konkordanz zum griechischen Neuen Testament*, Vol. II.)

Basing the analysis in the Greek has served to eliminate from the Concordance a number of English "function words" such as "will" and "have" as indicators of tenses, "in" and "to" expressing Greek cases, "should" and "may" expressing moods, etc.; there are no Greek lexical equivalents in these instances. On the other hand, no word, however common (e.g., "in," "is," "but"), is omitted if it represents the translation of any but the four Greek words cited above.

The analysis resulted in four kinds of association of the RSV English and the Greek: (*a*) simple identification, such as is common to lexicons; (*b*) meanings that arise from usage, for which standard grammatical terms are appropriate explanations; (*c*) meanings derived from word combination, paraphrase, and special usage, which are described in Appendix I; (*d*) liberal paraphrase and idiomatic translation. The remainder was considered as Greek not translated, or as contextual use of the English.

It would be misleading to suggest that there is a clear distinction between adjacent categories. The need for simplicity and consistency for the benefit of the user was in constant tension with the urge to explain everything, to let the Concordance display the learning stored in the lexicons and grammars that relates to the actual cases presented. The zigzag path between two extremes will of course represent too much clutter for some and too much simplicity for others. If withal it has avoided untenable word association and gross error, the serious user of the Concordance probably will be able to get on with his or her study with some benefit.

The Greek Text

The Greek text underlying the Revised Standard Version has never been formally established by the Committee. Early in the preparation of this Concordance, Dean Luther A. Weigle, then chairman of the Standard Bible Committee, made available notes (see the Preface) on several hundred textual problems, indicating the Greek readings that probably were followed. Scores of other cases have arisen in the course of the analysis and have been carefully studied. In two dozen instances it was decided to indicate variant readings for the Greek text base. These, of course, are in addition to the RSV footnotes dealing with the Greek text. It is important to state that the text base displayed in this work remains unofficial and errors are thus the responsibility of the author.

EXPLANATORY NOTES ILLUSTRATED

ANY MAN

1. *no one, nothing:* οὐδείς (+neg.) OUDEIS

Jn 18.31 "not lawful . . to put any man to death

2. *anyone, any:* τὶς TIS II

Mt 16.24 "If any man would come after me

Also Mk **8**.34; Lk **9**.23

Mk [7.16 "*If any man has ears to hear, let him hear*‡

ANYTHING

1. *one:* εἷς (neut.+neg.) HEIS

Jn 1. 3 without him was not anything made

4. *all, every, whole:* πᾶς (subst. neut.) PAS

[a]+πρᾶγμα ὅ ἐάν A.1.f [b]pl.

Mt 18.19 [a]"if two of you agree on earth about a.

Eph 5.13 [b]when anything is exposed by the light

5.13(14) anything that becomes visible is light

CONTEXTUALLY

Mk [7. 4 (*they do not eat a. from the market*†[0]

BAPTIZE

1. *dip, plunge, baptize:* βαπτίζω BAPTIZŌ

Mk [1. 4 John *was baptizing* in the wilderness†‡

1. 9 Jesus . . was baptized by John in the Jordan

[7. 4 (do not eat unless they *baptize* themselves‡

Lk 7.29 (tax collectors . . , having been baptized

BAPTIZER

1. *dip, plunge, baptize:* βαπτίζω (subst. part.) BAPTIZŌ

Mk 1. 4 John the b. appeared[c] in the wilderness†‡

BE

4. *be:* εἰμί EIMI

Mt **1**.19, 20; **2**.2, 6, 9, 18; **3**.3, 4, 11[2], 15, 17; **4**.3, 6, 18; **5**.3, 10, 11, 13, 14, 21, 22[3], 34, 35[2], 37, 48; **6**.4, [13‡, 21[2], 22[3]

BEAR (*See also* NAME OF, BEAR THE; WITNESS, BEAR)

1. *bring, carry up:* ἀναφέρω ANAPHERŌ

Heb 9.28 offered once to bear the sins of many

1 Pet 2.24 He himself bore our sins in his body[g]†

2. *bear:* ἄρκος ARKOS*
Rev 13. 2 its feet were like a bear's
3. *lift up, carry:* βαστάζω BASTAZŌ
Lk 11.27 "Blessed is the womb that bore you!
4. *give:* δίδωμι DIDŌMI [A.6.a.5]
1 Tim 2. 6 testimony to which was borne at the . . time
9. *bring, bear:* φέρω PHERŌ
Mt 7.18a "A sound tree cannot bear evil fruit
Var. POIEŌ
Heb 13.13 go forth . . and bear the abuse he endured[0]
10. *bear, wear:* φορέω PHOREŌ
Rom 13. 4 he does not bear the sword in vain
1 Cor 15.49 we have borne the image of the man of dust,
we shall[a] also b. the image‡
11. *do, make:* ποιέω POIEŌ
Mt 3. 8 "Bear fruit that befits repentance
Lk 13. 9 " 'if it bears fruit next year, well and good
Also variant to: Mt 7.18a
IDIOMATICALLY
a. Gal 1.15 before I was born ἐκ κοιλίας μητρός μου
[KOILIA; MĒTĒR]
CONTEXTUALLY
Jn 8.43 "It is because you cannot bear to hear

BEAR FRUIT
1. *bear fruit:* καρποφορέω KARPOPHOREŌ
Col 1. 6 ⟨the gospel⟩ is bearing fruit and growing

BEAR WITH
1. *bear up, endure* (mid.): ἀνέχω ANECHŌ
Mt 17.17 "How long am I to bear with you?
Lk 9.41 "how long am I to . . bear with you?
2. *bear with another's mood:* τροποφορέω TROPOPHOREŌ*
Acts 13.18 "he bore with[m] them in the wilderness‡

BEARER
1. *lift up, carry:* βαστάζω (subst. part.) BASTAZŌ
Lk 7.14 the bearers stood still

BELOVED
3. *beloved:* ἀγαπητός AGAPĒTOS
Mt 3.17 "This is my beloved Son[ht]

BRIEFLY
3. *concisely, quickly:* συντόμως SYNTOMŌS*
Mk [16.[end] *they reported briefly to Peter*‡
Acts 24. 4 "I beg you . . to hear us briefly

COME BACK

COME BY
2. *come, go:* ἔρχομαι ERCHOMAI
Acts 5.15 as Peter came by . . his shadow might fall
2 Cor 1.16 I wanted to . . come back to you

CYRENE: sīˈrēnē II,D-4
1. *Cyrene:* Κυρήνη
Acts 2.10 "parts of Libya belonging to Cyrene

85 2. *of Cyrene:* Κυρηναῖος [A.3.a.2]
86 Mt 27.32 they came upon a man of C., Simon
87 **CYRENIAN:** Κυρηναῖος (*See also* CYRENE 2)
88 Acts 6. 9 belonged to . . synagogue . . of the Cyrenians

INDEX-LEXICON

89 **ECHŌ** ἔχω
90 §be (50)+
91 bear (4)
92 devoid of (*neg. part.*)
93 §(obliged, be 1)
94 §remember 4[b] (2)
95 §require 3
96 (take [*imper.*]†)
97 IDIOMATICALLY
98 able, be *a*; present *b*
99 NOT TRANSLATED
100 Jn **19.**10
101 **MĒ** μή
102 never (12)
103 *not* (522)
104 §*As the negative in:*
105 abstain 2 (Rom **14.**3[2], 6a)
106 beware 3[a]
107 **PHILOSTORGOS** φιλόστοργος
108 [*affectionate, devoted*]
109 §love
110 **SABBATON** σάββατον
111 sabbath (58)†
112 week (10)

SIGNS AND SYMBOLS

Sign or Symbol	*Explanation*	*Line Number in "Explanatory Notes Illustrated"*
II,C-4	map II, coordinates C and 4	**82**
+	plus, with	**12**
(gen.)	a grammatical note (e.g., the English meaning or form is influenced by the *genitive case* of the Greek). See Appendix I, Part Two: Grammatical Terms	**11, 62, 68**
*	all occurrences of this Greek word are listed in this entry	**35, 65**
A.1.b.2	an analytical note. See Appendix I, Part One: English Paraphrase	**12, 39**
[b]	a technical note, placed under a subtitle, applies to all references so marked (beginning a context line or following a compact entry of chapter and verse alone)	**12-14**
1.14(15)	the Greek verse division is added parenthetically when it differs from the RSV. See Nestle, *Novum Testamentum Graece*, 25th edition	**15**
[end]	the "short ending" of Mark	**75**
" '	the following words are designated a quotation in the RSV, but the marks do not necessarily indicate the true beginning of the quotation	**5, 51, 64**
(	the following words are parenthetical in the RSV, but the mark does not necessarily indicate the true beginning of the parenthesis	**23**
? !	the preceding words are designated a question or exclamation in the RSV, but the marks do not necessarily indicate the true end of the sentence	**38, 64**
[*b*]	footnote reference as it appears in the RSV	**34, 66**
⟨will⟩	words enclosed in angle brackets are introduced out of sequence or from outside the verse to clarify the context line	**60**
. .	one or more words are omitted: an ellipsis	**23, 80, 88**
[2]	the frequency of occurrence at the place cited. Used in compact entries—book, chapter, and verse alone	**29, 30**

°	a different translation is provided by an earlier edition of the RSV. Refer to Appendix II, Former Readings of the RSV New Testament	**17, 44**
†	a footnote in the RSV provides an *alternate translation* or definition of the Greek	**34**
‡	a footnote in the RSV provides the translation of an *alternate Greek text*	**66**
†‡	a footnote in the RSV provides an alternate translation of the Greek, influenced by an alternate Greek reading in the context	**26**
†	a footnote in the RSV provides an alternate translation, affecting this word only secondarily. No context line is provided in this case; see the RSV footnote	**72**
‡	a footnote in the RSV provides the translation of an alternate Greek text of a minor character, influencing only the form of the Greek and the English. No context line is provided in this case; see the RSV footnote	**47-48**
[*italics*	words from the RSV footnote are in italics	**17, 75**
[†	an alternate translation of the Greek from the RSV footnote ("Or . . .")	**17**
[‡	the translation of an alternate Greek text from the RSV footnote ("Other ancient authorities read . . .")	**7, 22, 30, 75**
[†‡	an alternate translation of the Greek, influenced by an alternate Greek reading elsewhere in the context; from the RSV footnote	**20**

INDEX-LEXICON

§	not an ordinary meaning of the Greek. The corresponding Concordance entry will usually refer to a note in Appendix I, Part One: English Paraphrase	**90, 104**
italics	the corresponding Concordance entry is compact, listing references only by book, chapter, and verse	**103**
2	subtitle number, given to help locate a Concordance entry that is under another Greek word. The figure is unenclosed	**95, 105**
2[a]	subtitle number with designation of a pertinent note at the place cited	**94**
(3)	the frequency of translation (always in parentheses)	**91, 103**
+	at least once this word is used in an RSV footnote to translate an alternate Greek text, or in a variant reading. These instances appear in the Concordance but are not counted	**90**
(tell)	the enclosed word appears only in one or more RSV footnotes or in a variant reading, as explained at + above	**93**
†	at least once this word is used in an RSV footnote to provide an alternate translation. These instances appear in the Concordance but are not counted	**111**
(angel †)	the enclosed word appears only in one or more RSV footnotes, as explained at † above	**96**

PRONUNCIATION SYMBOLS

- **ə** banana, collect, abut, humdrum
- **ᵊ** immediately preceding \l\ or \n\, as in battle, mitten
- **ər** operation, further, urger
- **a** mat, map, mad, snap
- **ā** day, fade, date
- **ä** bother, cot, and, with most American speakers, father, cart
- **au̇** now, loud, out
- **b** baby, rib
- **ch** chin (\t\+\sh\)
- **d** did, adder
- **e** bet, bed, peck
- **ē** beat, easy
- **f** fifty, cuff
- **g** go, big, gift
- **h** hat, ahead
- **i** tip, banish, active
- **ī** site, side, buy (\ä\+\i\)
- **j** job, gem, edge (\d\+\zh\)
- **k** kin, cook, ache
- **k̲** German ich, Buch
- **l** lily, pool
- **m** murmur, dim
- **n** no, own
- **ŋ** sing, ink
- **ō** bone, know, beau
- **ȯ** saw, all, gnaw
- **ȯi** coin, destroy
- **p** pepper, lip
- **r** red, car, rarity
- **s** source, less
- **sh** shy, mission, machine
- **t** tie, attack
- **th** thin, ether
- **ü** rule, youth
- **u̇** pull, wood, book
- **ue̅** French rue, German fühlen
- **v** vivid
- **w** we, away
- **y** yard, young
- **yü** youth, union, cue, few
- **yu̇** curable, fury
- **z** zone, raise
- **zh** vision
- **ˈ** mark preceding a syllable with primary (strongest) stress
- **ˌ** mark preceding a syllable with secondary (next-strongest) stress
- **( )** indicate that what is symbolized between is present in some utterances but not in others
- **** slant line used to mark beginning and end of a phonetic transcription

The system of indicating pronunciation is used by permission. From *Webster's New Collegiate Dictionary* © 1976 by G. & C. Merriam Co., Publishers of the Merriam-Webster Dictionaries.

TRANSLITERATION

The following equivalents have been used in the transliteration of the Greek words of the New Testament. It is not necessary to know or to refer to this table in order to use the Concordance, but persons who wish to use the Index-Lexicon for the translation of Greek words encountered in their other reading should learn to transliterate accurately. The pronunciation of New Testament Greek varies for many reasons. The sounds shown here are agreeable to many standard works (alternate sounds are shown for O and EI). Accent is simply by emphasis upon the accented vowel.

The Greek "breathing" mark appears upon all initial vowels and diphthongs (and initial rho). It appears in transliteration and pronunciation as follows: The "smooth breathing" (') is neither transliterated nor sounded. The "rough breathing" (ʽ) is transliterated by prefixing the letter H and is pronounced \h\.

Greek Letter		English Transliteration	Name	Sound
Α	α	A	alpha	ä
Β	β	B	beta	b
Γ	γ	G	gamma	g[1]
Δ	δ	D	delta	d
Ε	ε	E	epsilon	e
Ζ	ζ	Z	zeta	z[2], dz
Η	η	Ē	eta	ā
Θ	θ	TH	theta	th
Ι	ι	I	iota	i, ē
Κ	κ	K	kappa	k
Λ	λ	L	lambda	l
Μ	μ	M	mu	m
Ν	ν	N	nu	n
Ξ	ξ	X	xi	ks
Ο	ο	O	omicron	\ä\ *or* \ȯ\ *or* \ō\
Π	π	P	pi	p
Ρ	ρ	R[3]	rho	r
Σ	σ ς	S	sigma	s
Τ	τ	T	tau	t
Υ	υ	Y[4]	upsilon	ue̅
Φ	φ	PH	phi	f
Χ	χ	CH	chi	ḵ
Ψ	ψ	PS	psi	ps
Ω	ω	Ō	omega	ō

Greek Diphthong	English Transliteration	Sound
αι	AI	ī
αυ	AU	aů
ει	EI	\ā\ *or* \ī\
ευ	EU	yü
οι	OI	ȯi
ου	OU	ü
υι	UI	wē
ᾳ	A	ä
ῃ	Ē	ā
ῳ	Ō	ō

[1]Gamma before κ, γ, or χ is pronounced \ŋ\.

[2]Zeta is pronounced \z\ only when it is the initial sound of a word.

[3]Initial rho always bears the rough breathing (ʽΡ, ῥ) and is transliterated RH.

[4]Upsilon in diphthongs is transliterated U.

ABBREVIATIONS

GENERAL

absol.	absolute	interrog.	interrogative
acc.	accusative	intrans.	intransitive
act.	active	Lat.	Latin
adv.	adverb; adverbial	masc.	masculine
aor.	aorist	mid.	middle
2 aor.	second aorist	neg.	negative
appos.	appositive	neut.	neuter
Aram.	Aramaic	nom.	nominative
art.	article; articular	obj.	object
attr.	attributive	om.	omits
cf.	compare	opt.	optative
comp.	comparative	part.	participle
dat.	dative	pass.	passive
def.	definite	perf.	perfect
dep.	deponent	periphr.	periphrastic
e.g.	for example	pl.	plural
emph.	emphatic	pluperf.	pluperfect
fem.	feminine	pred.	predicate; predicative
gen.	genitive	prep.	preposition
Gr.	Greek	pres.	present
Heb.	Hebrew	s.	someone; something; somewhere
hort.	hortatory	sg.	singular
i.e.	that is	subj.	subjunctive
imper.	imperative	subst.	substantive
imperf.	imperfect	superl.	superlative
impers.	impersonal	var.	variant reading
ind.	indicative	voc.	vocative
indef.	indefinite	w.	who; which; what
inf.	infinitive		

NEW TESTAMENT BOOKS

Mt	Matthew
Mk	Mark
Lk	Luke
Jn	John
Acts	Acts of the Apostles
Rom	Romans
1 Cor	1 Corinthians
2 Cor	2 Corinthians
Gal	Galatians
Eph	Ephesians
Phil	Philippians
Col	Colossians
1 Th	1 Thessalonians
2 Th	2 Thessalonians
1 Tim	1 Timothy
2 Tim	2 Timothy
Tit	Titus
Phm	Philemon
Heb	Hebrews
Jas	James
1 Pet	1 Peter
2 Pet	2 Peter
1 Jn	1 John
2 Jn	2 John
3 Jn	3 John
Jude	Jude
Rev	Revelation

AN
ANALYTICAL CONCORDANCE
TO THE
REVISED STANDARD VERSION
OF THE
NEW TESTAMENT

A

A
AN
1. There is no indefinite article in Greek. English idiom often requires the use of "a" or "an" when the Greek definite article is not used.
2. *one:* εἷς HEIS
Mt **5.**18[2]; 8.19; **21.**19, 24; **26.**69
Mk **11.**29; **12.**42
Jn **20.7**
Rev 8.13; **9.**13; **18.**21a; **19.**17

AARON: Ἀαρών 'erən
Lk 1. 5 of the daughters of Aaron . . , Elizabeth
Acts 7.40 "saying to Aaron, 'Make for us gods
Heb 5. 4 he is called by God, just as Aaron was
7.11 rather than . . after the order of A.
9. 4 ark . . contained . . Aaron's rod that budded

ABADDON: Ἀβαδδών ə'badᵊn
Rev 9.11 angel of the bottomless pit; his name . . A.

ABANDON
1. *let go, leave, forgive:* ἀφίημι APHIĒMI
Rev 2. 4 " 'you have abandoned the love you had
2. *leave behind:* ἐγκαταλείπω EGKATALEIPŌ
Acts 2.27 " 'thou wilt not abandon my soul to Hades
2.31 "he was not abandoned to Hades
3. *pour out:* ἐκχέω EKCHEŌ
[a]pass. *abandon oneself*
Jude .11 [a]they . . abandon themselves for . . gain
4. *take away, strip off:* περιαιρέω PERIAIREŌ
Acts 27.20 all hope . . was at last abandoned

ABASE
1. *lower, humble:* ταπεινόω TAPEINOŌ
2 Cor 11. 7 Did I commit a sin in abasing myself?
Phil 4.12 I know how to be abased

ABBA: 'äbə
1. *father* (Aram.): ἀββά ABBA*
Mk 14.36 And he said, "Abba, Father
Rom 8.15 When we cry, "Abba! Father!
Gal 4. 6 the Spirit . . crying, "Abba! Father!

ABEL: Ἄβελ 'ābəl
Mt 23.35 "from the blood of innocent A.
Lk 11.51 "from the blood of A.
Heb 11. 4 By faith A. offered to God a . . sacrifice
12.24 speaks more graciously than the blood of A.

ABHOR
1. *loathe, be sick:* βδελύσσομαι BDELYSSOMAI
Rom 2.22 You who abhor idols, do you rob temples?

ABIATHAR: Ἀβιαθάρ ə'bīəthər
Mk 2.26 "A. was high priest, and ate the bread

ABIDE
1. *return; behave* (pass.): ἀναστρέφω ANASTREPHŌ
Mt [17.22 As they *abode* in Galilee‡
2. *stay in, stand by:* ἐμμένω EMMENŌ
Gal 3.10 "one who does not abide by . . the law
3. *stay, wait:* μένω MENŌ
Jn 5.38 "you do not have his word abiding in you
6.56 "He who eats my flesh . . abides in me
15. 4 "Abide in me, and I in you
15. 4 "branch cannot bear fruit . . unless it abides
15. 4 "neither can you, unless you abide in me
15. 5 "He who abides in me, and I in him
15. 6 "If a man does not abide in me
15. 7 "If you abide in me, and my words abide in you, ask whatever you will
15. 9 "so have I loved you; abide in my love
15.10 "you will abide in my love, just as I . . abide in his love
15.16 "I chose you . . that your fruit should abide
1 Cor 13.13 So faith, hope, love abide, these three
Heb 10.34 a better possession and an abiding one
1 Pet 1.23 the living and abiding word of God
1.25 "the word of the Lord abides for ever
1 Jn 2. 6 he who says he abides in him ought to walk
2.10 who loves his brother abides in the light
2.14 the word of God abides in you
2.17 he who does the will of God abides for ever
2.24 Let what you heard . . abide in you
2.24 If what you heard . . abides in you
2.24 you will abide in the Son and . . Father
2.27 the anointing . . abides in you
2.27 as it has taught you, abide in him
2.28 little children, abide in him
3. 6 No one who abides in him sins
3. 9 God's[f] nature abides in him
3.14 He who does not love abides in death[0]
3.15 no murderer has eternal life abiding in him
3.17 how does God's love abide in him?
3.24 who keep his commandments abide in him
3.24 we know that he abides in us, by the Spirit
4.12 if we love one another, God abides in us
4.13 By this we know that we abide in him
4.15 Whoever confesses . . , God abides in him
4.16 he who abides in love abides in God, and God abides in him
2 Jn . 2 because of the truth which abides in us
. 9 who . . does not abide in the doctrine of Christ
. 9 he who abides in the doctrine

ABIJAH: Ἀβιά ə'bījə
Mt 1. 7 Rehoboam the father of A.
1. 7 A. the father of Asa[b]
Lk 1. 5 Zechariah,[b] of the division of A.

ABILENE: Ἀβιληνή ˌabəˈlēnē I,E-1
Lk 3. 1 Lysanias tetrarch of A.

ABILITY (*See also* DISTINGUISH, ABILITY TO)
1. *power, ability:* δύναμις DYNAMIS
Mt 25.15 "he gave . . to each according to his ability
IDIOMATICALLY
a. Acts 11.29 every one according to his ability
καθὼς εὐπορεῖτό τις [EUPOREŌ*]

ABIUD: Ἀβιούδ əˈbīəd
Mt 1.13 Zerubbabel the father of A.
1.13 A. the father of Eliakim

ABLAZE, SET
1. *kindle:* ἀνάπτω ANAPTŌ
Jas 3. 5 a forest is set ablaze by a small fire!

ABLE
1. *possible, strong:* δυνατός DYNATOS
Lk 14.31 "take counsel whether he is able
Rom 4.21 convinced that God was able to do
2 Tim 1.12 I am sure that he is able to guard
Tit 1. 9 so that he may be able to give instruction
Heb 11.19 God was able to raise men
Jas 3. 2 a perfect man, able to bridle the . . body
2. *enough:* ἱκανός HIKANOS
2 Tim 2. 2 faithful men who will be able to teach

ABLE, BE
1. *be able:* δύναμαι DYNAMAI
Mt 3. 9 "able from these stones to raise up children
9.28 "Do you believe that I am able to do this?
19.12 "He who is able to receive this, let him
20.22 "Are you able to drink the cup that I am to drink?" They said to him, "We are able
22.46 no one was able to answer him a word
26.61 " 'I am able to destroy the temple of God
Mk 3.25 "that house will not be able to stand
4.33 he spoke . . as they were able to hear it
9.39 "no one . . in my name will be able . . to speak
10.38 "Are you able to drink the cup that I drink?
10.39 they said to him, "We are able
Lk 3. 8 "able from these stones to raise up children
12.26 "If . . you are not a. . . , why . . anxious?
16.26 " 'that those who would . . may not be able
21.15 "none of your adversaries will be able
Jn 10.29 "no one is able to snatch them
Acts 5.39 "if it is of God, you will not be able!
20.32 "the word of his grace, which is able
24. 8 "you will be able to learn from him
Rom 8.39 able to separate us from the love of God
15.14 able to instruct one another
16.25 Now to him who is able to strengthen
1 Cor 2.14 unspiritual[e] man is not a. to understand
10.13 that you may be able to endure
2 Cor 1. 4 that we may be able to comfort
Eph 3.20 to him who . . is able to do . . abundantly
6.11 able to stand against the wiles of the devil
6.13 be able to withstand in the evil day
2 Tim 3.15 writings . . able to instruct you for salvation
Heb 2.18 he is able to help those who are tempted
5. 7 who was able to save him from death
7.25 able . . to save those who draw near to God
Jas 1.21 word, which is able to save your souls
4.12 he who is able to save and to destroy
Jude .24 who is able to keep you from falling
Rev 3. 8 " 'an open door, which no one is able to shut
5. 3 no one . . was able to open the scroll
2. *be strong:* δυνατέω DYNATEŌ
Rom 14. 4 the Master is able to make him stand
2 Cor 9. 8 God is a. to provide you . . every blessing
3. *have, hold:* ἔχω ECHŌ
Eph 4.28 be able to give to those in need
2 Pet 1.15 that . . you may be able . . to recall these
4. *be strong, prevail:* ἰσχύω ISCHYŌ
Mk 9.18 "your disciples . . were not able
Lk 13.24 "many . . will seek . . and will not be able
14.29 "when he . . is not able to finish
14.30 " 'This man . . was not able to finish
Lk 20.26 they were not able . . to catch him
Jn 21. 6 they were not able to haul it in
Acts 15.10 "a yoke . . we have ⟨not⟩ been able to bear
IDIOMATICALLY
a. 2 Cor 5.12 so that you may be able to answer
ἵνα ἔχητε πρός [ECHŌ]

ABLUTION
1. *dipping in water, baptism:* βαπτισμός BAPTISMOS
Heb 6. 2 instruction[k] about ablutions
9.10 various ablutions, regulations for the body

ABOARD (*See* TAKE ABOARD)

ABOARD, GO
1. *go up, come up:* ἀναβαίνω ANABAINŌ
Jn 21.11 Peter went aboard and hauled the net
2. *go upon, mount, board:* ἐπιβαίνω EPIBAINŌ
Acts 21. 2 we went aboard, and set sail

ABOLISH
1. *take up, kill:* ἀναιρέω ANAIREŌ
Heb 10. 9 abolishes the first . . to establish the second
2. *put down, destroy:* καταλύω KATALYŌ
Mt 5.17 "not . . to abolish the law and the prophets
5.17 "not to abolish them but to fulfil
3. *make ineffective, hinder:* καταργέω KATARGEŌ
Eph 2.15 abolishing in his flesh the law
2 Tim 1.10 Christ Jesus, who abolished death

ABOMINATION
1. *loathsome thing:* βδέλυγμα BDELYGMA
Lk 16.15 "an abomination in the sight of God
Rev 17. 4 a golden cup full of abominations
17. 5 "mother . . of earth's abominations
21.27 one who practices abomination or falsehood

ABOUND
1. *abound:* περισσεύω PERISSEUŌ
Rom 3. 7 if . . truthfulness abounds to his glory
5.15 the free gift . . abounded for many
15.13 so that . . you may abound in hope
1 Cor 15.58 always abounding in the work of the Lord
2 Cor [1. 5 *as the sufferings of Christ abound for us, so . . our comfort abounds through Christ*†
Phil 1. 9 my prayer that your love may abound
4.12 I know how to abound
Col 2. 7 abounding in thanksgiving
1 Th 3.12 Lord make you increase and abound in love
2. *be more, cause to increase:* πλεονάζω PLEONAZŌ
Rom 6. 1 Are we to . . sin that grace may abound?
2 Pet 1. 8 if these things are yours and abound

ABOUND ALL THE MORE
1. *be present in excess:* ὑπερπερισσεύω HYPERPERISSEUŌ
Rom 5.20 sin increased, grace abounded all the more

ABOUT
1. *already, now:* ἤδη ĒDĒ
Jn 7.14 About the middle of the feast Jesus went
2. *into, to, for:* εἰς (+acc.) EIS
Mt **6.34**
3. *in, at, by:* ἐν (+dat.) EN
Acts **25.5**
2 Cor **8.20**
Gal **4.20**
4. *on, at:* ἐπί (+dat.) EPI
except [a]+acc. [b]+gen.
Mk **5.21**[a]; **6.52**; **12.26**[b]
Lk **20.37**[b]
1 Th **3.7**
2 Th **3.4**[a]
Rev **10.11**
5. *as, so:* ὡς HŌS
Mk **5.13**; **8.9**
Lk **1.56**; **8.42**
Jn **1.39**; **4.6**; **6.10**, 19; **11.18**; **19.14**, 39; **21.8**
Acts **4.4**; **5.7**, 36; **13.18**, 19(20); **19.34**; **27.**[37‡
Rev **8.1**
6. *as if:* ὡσεί HŌSEI
Mt **14.21**
Lk **3.23**; **9.14**[2]; **9.28**; **22.41**, 59; **23.44**
Acts **1.15**; **2.41**; **10.3**; **19.7**, 34

7. *over, for the sake of:* ὑπέρ (+gen.) HYPER
2 Cor **8**.24; **9**.2, 3; **12**.8
Phil **1**.7
8. *in accordance with, for:* κατά (+acc.) KATA
Acts **12**.1; **16**.25; **19**.23; **27**.27
Rom **9**.9
9. *as far as:* μέχρι MECHRI [D.2]
Acts 10.30 "Four days ago, about this hour
10. *about, concerning:* περί (+gen.) PERI
except [a]+acc.
Mt **6**.28; **16**.11; **18**.19; **19**.17; **20**.3[a], 5[a], 6[a], 9[a]; **21**.45; **27**.46[a]
Mk **3**.8[a], 32[a], 34[a]; **4**.10[a]; **5**.27; **6**.48[a]; 8.30; **9**.14[a]; **10**.10
Lk **2**.33; **9**.9, 45; **10**.41[a]; **12**.26; **13**.8[a]; **16**.2; **22**.37, 49[a]; **23**.8; **24**.4, 14, 44
Jn **1**.22; **7**.12, 32, 39; **8**.5‡, 26; **9**.17; **10**.41; **18**.19, 34
Acts **5**.24; **8**.12, 34[3]; **9**.13; **10**.3[a], 9[a]; **15**.2; **17**.32; **18**.15; **19**.8, [39‡; **21**.21, 24; **22**.6[2a], 18; **23**.11, 20, 29; **24**.8, 25; **25**.15, 19[2], 24, 26; **26**.26; **28**.21[2], 23, 31
Rom **15**.14
2 Cor **9**.1
1 Tim **1**.7
Heb **5**.11; **7**.14
1 Pet **1**.10; **5**.7
1 Jn **2**.26, 27
Jude .9
11. *somewhere, about:* πού POU II
Rom 4.19 he was about a hundred years old
12. *to, with, against:* πρός (+acc.) PROS
Mt **13**.2
Mk **1**.33; **2**.2, 13; **4**.1
Gal **2**.14

ABOUT, BE
1. *be about to:* μέλλω (+inf.) MELLŌ
Mt 2.13 "Herod is about to search for the child
Lk 10. 1 place where he himself was about to come
21. 7 "the sign when this is about to take place
Jn 6.15 they were about to come and take him
Acts 3. 3 Peter and John about to go into the temple
12. 6 when Herod was about to bring him out
16.27 the jailer . . was about to kill himself
18.14 when Paul was about to open his mouth
20. 3 as he was about to set sail for Syria
21.37 Paul was about to be brought
22.26 "What are you about to do?
22.29 those who were about to examine him
23.27 "This man . . was about to be killed
27. 2 about to sail to the ports along the coast
27.33 As day was about to dawn
Heb 8. 5 when Moses was about to erect the tent[n]
Rev 2.10 Do not fear what you are about to suffer
2.10 devil is about to throw some . . into prison
8.13 "which the three angels are about to blow
10. 4 I was about to write, but I heard a voice
12. 4 woman who was about to bear a child

ABOVE
1. *above, upward:* ἄνω ANŌ
[a]subst. neut. pl.
Jn 8.23 [a]"You are from below, I am from above
Acts 2.19 " 'wonders in the heaven above
Gal 4.26 the Jerusalem above is free
Col 3. 1 seek the things that are above
3. 2 Set your minds on things that are above
2. *higher, above:* ἀνώτερος (neut.) ANŌTEROS
Heb 10. 8 When he said above, "Thou hast neither
3. *above:* ἐπάνω EPANŌ
Jn 3.31 He who comes . . is above all
3.31 he who comes from heaven is above all
4. *on, at:* ἐπί (+dat.) EPI
except [a]+gen.
Eph **4**.6[a]
Col **3**.14
5. *where, wherever:* ὅπου HOPOU [B.2.a.2]
Mk **2**.4
6. *over, more than:* ὑπέρ (+acc.) HYPER
Mt **10**.24[2]
Lk **6**.40
Phil **2**.9
7. *above:* ὑπεράνω HYPERANŌ
Heb 9. 5 above it were the cherubim of glory
8. *before:* πρό (+gen.) PRO
Jas **5**.12
1 Pet **4**.8

ABOVE ALL
1. *especially:* μάλιστα MALISTA
2 Tim 4.13 bring . . above all the parchments

ABOVE, FAR
1. *above:* ὑπεράνω HYPERANŌ
Eph 1.21 far above all rule and authority
4.10 (also ascended far above all the heavens

ABOVE, FROM
1. *from above, anew:* ἄνωθεν ANŌTHEN
Jn [3. 3 "unless one is born *from above*†
[3. 7 " 'You must be born *from above*†
3.31 who comes from above is above all
19.11 "power over me . . given you from above
Jas 1.17 every perfect gift is from above
3.15 This wisdom is not . . from above
3.17 the wisdom from above is first pure

ABRAHAM: Ἀβραάμ ˈābrəˌham
Mt 1. 1 Jesus Christ, the son of David, the son of A.
1. 2 A. was the father of Isaac
1.17 the generations from A. to David
3. 9 " 'We have A. as our father
3. 9 "from these stones to raise up children to A.
8.11 "many will . . sit at table with A.
22.32 " 'I am the God of A.
Mk 12.26 " 'I am the God of A.
Lk 1.55 "he spoke to our fathers, to A.
1.73 "which he swore to our father A.
3. 8 " 'We have A. as our father
3. 8 "from these stones to raise up children to A.
3.34 Isaac, the son of A.
13.16 "this woman, a daughter of A.
13.28 "A. and Isaac and Jacob
16.22 "carried . . to Abraham's bosom
16.23 "saw A. far off and Lazarus in his bosom
16.24 " 'Father A., have mercy upon me
16.25 "A. said, 'Son, remember
16.29 "A. said, 'They have Moses and the prophets
16.30 " 'No, father A. . . . , they will repent
19. 9 "salvation . . , since he also is a son of A.
20.37 "he calls the Lord the God of A.
Jn 8.33 "We are descendants of A.
8.37 "I know that you are descendants of A.
8.39 "A. is our father
8.39 "If you were Abraham's children, you would do what A. did
8.40 "this is not what A. did
8.52 "A. died, as did the prophets
8.53 "Are you greater than our father A.?
8.56 "Your father A. rejoiced
8.57 "have you seen A.?[u]
8.58 "before A. was, I am
Acts 3.13 "The God of A. and of Isaac
3.25 "the covenant . . God gave . . , saying to A.
7. 2 "The God of glory appeared to our father A.
7.16 "laid in the tomb that A. had bought
7.17 "the promise . . God had granted to A.
7.32 " 'the God of your fathers, the God of A.
13.26 "Brethren, sons of the family of A.
Rom 4. 1 What then shall we say about[e] A.?
4. 2 if A. was justified by works
4. 3 "A. believed God, and it was reckoned
4. 9 faith was reckoned to A. as righteousness
4.12 the faith which our father A. had before
4.13 promise to A. and his descendants
4.16 the faith of A., . . father of us all
9. 7 not all are children of A.
11. 1 I myself am an Israelite, a descendant of A.
2 Cor 11.22 Are they descendants of A.? So am I
Gal 3. 6 A. "believed God and it was reckoned to him

Gal 3. 7 men of faith . . are the sons of A.
3. 8 scripture . . preached the gospel . . to A.
3. 9 men of faith are blessed with A.
3.14 in Christ Jesus the blessing of A. might come
3.16 promises were made to A.
3.18 God gave it to A. by a promise
3.29 then you are Abraham's offspring, heirs
4.22 it is written that A. had two sons
Heb 2.16 he is concerned . . with the descendants of A.
6.13 God made a promise to A.
7. 1 Melchizedek . . met A. returning
7. 2 to him A. apportioned a tenth part
7. 4 A. the patriarch gave him a tithe
7. 5 these also are descended from A.
7. 6 this man . . received tithes from A.
7. 9 Levi himself . . paid tithes through A.
11. 8 By faith A. obeyed when he was called
11.17 By faith A. . . offered up Isaac
Jas 2.21 Was not A. our father justified by works?
2.23 "A. believed God, and it was reckoned
1 Pet 3. 6 Sarah obeyed A., calling him lord
CONTEXTUALLY
Acts 7. 8 "Abraham became the father of Isaac
Heb 6.15 Abraham,[m] having patiently endured†

ABROAD (*See* GO ABROAD; SCATTER ABROAD; SPREAD ABROAD)

ABSENCE
1. *absence:* ἀπουσία APOUSIA*
Phil 2.12 in my absence, work out your own salvation
2. *deficiency, need:* ὑστέρημα HYSTERĒMA
1 Cor 16.17 they have made up for your absence

ABSENCE OF, IN THE
1. *without, apart from:* ἄτερ ATER
Lk 22. 6 betray him . . in the absence of the multitude

ABSENT
ABSENT, BE
1. *be away from:* ἄπειμι APEIMI I
[a]part.
1 Cor 5. 3 [a]though absent in body I am present in spirit
2 Cor 10.11 [a]what we say by letter when absent
13. 2 [a]I warn them now while absent
Phil 1.27 whether I come . . or am absent
Col 2. 5 I am absent in body, yet . . with you

ABSTAIN
ABSTAIN FROM
1. *be distant:* ἀπέχω (mid.) APECHŌ
Acts 15.20 "abstain from the pollutions of idols
15.29 "abstain from what has been sacrificed
1 Th 4. 3 abstain from unchastity
5.22 abstain from every form of evil
1 Pet 2.11 abstain from the passions of the flesh
2. *eat:* ἐσθίω (neg.) ESTHIŌ
Rom 14. 3 not . . despise him who abstains
14. 3 let not him who abstains pass judgment
14. 6 while he who abstains, abstains in honor of the Lord
3. *guard, observe:* φυλάσσω (mid.) PHYLASSŌ
Acts 21.25 "abstain from what has been sacrificed

ABSTINENCE
1. *be distant:* ἀπέχω (mid. inf.) APECHŌ
1 Tim 4. 3 abstinence from foods which God created

ABUNDANCE
1. *excess:* ὑπερβολή HYPERBOLĒ
2 Cor 12. 7 elated by the abundance of revelations
2. *abundance, surplus:* περισσεία PERISSEIA
Rom 5.17 those who receive the a. of grace . . reign
2 Cor 8. 2 their abundance of joy . . overflowed
3. *superfluity:* περίσσευμα PERISSEUMA
Mt 12.34 "out of the abundance of the heart
Lk 6.45 "out of the abundance of the heart
2 Cor 8.14 your abundance . . should supply their want
8.14 their abundance may supply your want
4. *abound:* περισσεύω PERISSEUŌ
[a]subst. part. [b]inf.
Mk 12.44 [a]"they all contributed out of . . abundance
Lk 12.15 [b]"life does not consist in the abundance
Lk 21. 4 [a]"they all contributed out of . . abundance
Phil 4.12 [b]I have learned the secret of . . abundance

ABUNDANCE, HAVE
ABUNDANCE, PROVIDE IN
1. *abound:* περισσεύω PERISSEUŌ
[a]pass.
Mt 13.12 [a]"who has . . will have abundance
25.29 [a]" 'every one who has . . will have abundance
2 Cor 9. 8 God is able to provide . . in abundance, so that you . . may provide in abundance

ABUNDANT
1. *still more:* περισσοτέρως PERISSOTERŌS [A.4.a]
2 Cor 2. 4 the abundant love that I have for you

ABUNDANTLY
1. *superfluous, extraordinary:* περισσός (neut.) PERISSOS
Jn 10.10 "they may have life, and have it abundantly

ABUNDANTLY, FAR MORE
1. *superabundantly:* ὑπερεκπερισσοῦ HYPEREKPERISSOU
Eph 3.20 far more a. than all that we ask

ABUNDANTLY, GROW
1. *increase exceedingly:* ὑπεραυξάνω HYPERAUXANŌ*
2 Th 1. 3 because your faith is growing abundantly

ABUNDANTLY, SHARE
1. *abound:* περισσεύω PERISSEUŌ [A.6.c.3]
2 Cor 1. 5 as we share abundantly in Christ's sufferings, so through Christ we share abundantly†

ABUSE
1. *blaspheme, slander:* βλασφημέω BLASPHĒMEŌ
1 Pet 4. 4 They are surprised . . and they abuse you
2. *threaten, disparage, mistreat:* ἐπηρεάζω EPĒREAZŌ
Lk 6.28 "pray for those who abuse you
3. *speak against:* καταλαλέω KATALALEŌ
1 Pet 3.16 keep your conscience clear . . when . . abused
4. *reproach:* ὀνειδισμός ONEIDISMOS
Heb 10.33 publicly exposed to abuse and affliction
11.26 abuse suffered for the Christ
13.13 let us . . bear the abuse he endured

ABUSIVE
1. *blasphemous, slanderous:* βλάσφημος BLASPHĒMOS
2 Tim 3. 2 men will be . . proud, arrogant, abusive

ABYSS
1. *abyss, underworld:* ἄβυσσος ABYSSOS
Lk 8.31 not to command them . . into the abyss
Rom 10. 7 "Who will descend into the abyss?

ACCENT
1. *speech, dialect:* λαλιά LALIA
Mt 26.73 "for your accent betrays you

ACCEPT
1. *receive favorably:* ἀποδέχομαι APODECHOMAI
Acts 24. 3 "we accept this with all gratitude
2. *receive, accept:* δέχομαι DECHOMAI
Mt 11.14 "if you are willing to accept it, he is Elijah
2 Cor 6. 1 accept the grace of God
8.17 he not only accepted our appeal
11. 4 a different gospel from the one you accepted
11.16 accept me as a fool, so that I too may boast
1 Th 2.13 you accepted it not as the word of men
3. *receive, take:* λαμβάνω LAMBANŌ
2 Cor 11. 8 I robbed other churches by accepting support
3 Jn . 7 they . . accepted nothing from the heathen
4. *accept, receive:* παραδέχομαι PARADECHOMAI
Mk 4.20 "who hear the word and accept it
Acts 16.21 "not lawful for us Romans to accept
22.18 " 'they will not accept your testimony
5. *accept, expect:* προσδέχομαι PROSDECHOMAI
Acts 24.15 "a hope in God which these . . accept
Heb 10.34 you joyfully accepted the plundering
11.35 were tortured, refusing to accept release
CONTEXTUALLY
Heb 11. 4 bearing witness by accepting his gifts

ACCEPTABLE
1. *welcome, pleasing:* ἀπόδεκτος APODEKTOS*
1 Tim 2. 3 it is acceptable in the sight of God
5. 4 this is acceptable in the sight of God

2. *welcome:* δεκτός DEKTOS*
Lk 4.19 "the acceptable year of the Lord
4.24 "no prophet is a. in his own country
Acts 10.35 "who . . does what is right is acceptable
2 Cor 6. 2 "At the acceptable time I have listened
Phil 4.18 a sacrifice acceptable and pleasing
3. *pleasing:* εὐάρεστος EUARESTOS
Rom 12. 1 present your bodies . . holy and acceptable
12. 2 the will of God, what is good and acceptable
14.18 who thus serves Christ is acceptable to God
4. *acceptably:* εὐαρέστως EUARESTŌS* [A.4.a]
Heb 12.28 let us offer to God acceptable worship
5. *welcome:* εὐπρόσδεκτος EUPROSDEKTOS*
Rom 15.16 the Gentiles may be acceptable
15.31 that my service . . may be acceptable
2 Cor 6. 2 Behold, now is the acceptable time
8.12 acceptable according to what a man has
1 Pet 2. 5 spiritual sacrifices acceptable to God
CONTEXTUALLY
Heb 11. 4 a more acceptable sacrifice than Cain

ACCEPTANCE
1. *reception, approval:* ἀποδοχή APODOCHĒ*
1 Tim 1.15 The saying is . . worthy of full acceptance
4. 9 The saying is . . worthy of full acceptance
2. *acquisition:* πρόσλημψις PROSLĒMPSIS*
Rom 11.15 what will their acceptance mean but life?

ACCEPTED
1. *approved:* δόκιμος DOKIMOS
2 Cor 10.18 man who commends himself . . is ⟨not⟩ a.

ACCESS
1. *approach:* προσαγωγή PROSAGŌGĒ*
Rom 5. 2 Through him we have obtained access[g]
Eph 2.18 through him we both have access
3.12 we have boldness and confidence of access

ACCOMPANIED BY, BE
1. *lead around, go about:* περιάγω PERIAGŌ
1 Cor 9. 5 the right to be accompanied by a wife[n]

ACCOMPANY
1. *go with:* ἔρχομαι σύν ERCHOMAI [A.6.a.4]
Acts 11.12 "six brethren . . accompanied me
2. *go out with:* ἐξέρχομαι σύν EXERCHOMAI [A.6.a.4]
Acts 16. 3 Paul wanted Timothy to accompany him
3. *follow closely, understand:* παρακολουθέω PARAKOLOUTHEŌ
Mk 16.17 "And these signs will accompany those[k]‡
4. *go with:* πορεύομαι σύν POREUOMAI [A.6.a.4]
Acts 10.20 "accompany them without hesitation
1 Cor 16. 4 If . . I . . go . . they will accompany me
5. *come together:* συμπορεύομαι SYMPOREUOMAI
Lk 14.25 great multitudes accompanied him
6. *follow along with:* συνέπομαι SYNEPOMAI*
Acts 20. 4 Sopater of Beroea . . accompanied him
7. *come together:* συνέρχομαι SYNERCHOMAI
Acts 1.21 "men who have accompanied us
10.23 brethren from Joppa accompanied him

ACCOMPLISH
1. *operate, be effective:* ἐνεργέω ENERGEŌ
Eph 1.11 purpose of him who accomplishes all
1.20 accomplished in Christ when he raised him
2. *fill full, complete:* πληρόω PLĒROŌ
Lk 9.31 his departure . . to a. at Jerusalem
3. *fulfill:* πληροφορέω PLĒROPHOREŌ
Lk 1. 1 a narrative of the things . . accomplished
4. *bring to an end:* συντελέω SYNTELEŌ
Mk 13. 4 "when will . . these . . be accomplished?
5. *make perfect, complete:* τελειόω TELEIOŌ
Jn 4.34 "My food is . . to accomplish his work
5.36 "works . . granted me to accomplish
17. 4 "accomplished the work . . thou gavest me
Acts 20.24 "if only I may accomplish . . the ministry
6. *finish, fulfill:* τελέω TELEŌ
Lk 12.50 "constrained until it is accomplished!
18.31 "everything . . will be accomplished

ACCOMPLISHED, BE
1. *come to be, happen, be:* γίνομαι GINOMAI
Mt 5.18 "not a dot . . until all is accomplished

ACCORD (*See also* YOUR *a*)
1. *agreement:* συμφώνησις SYMPHŌNĒSIS*
2 Cor 6.15 What accord has Christ with Belial?[i]
CONTEXTUALLY
Jn 5.19 "Son can do nothing of his own accord
7.28 "I have not come of my own accord
8.42 "I came not of my own accord
10.18 "I lay it down of my own accord
11.51 He did not say this of his own accord
18.34 "Do you say this of your own accord?

ACCORD, IN FULL
1. *united in mind:* σύμψυχος SYMPSYCHOS*
Phil 2. 2 being in full accord and of one mind

ACCORD, OF ITS OWN
ACCORD, OF ONE'S OWN
1. *by free choice:* αὐθαίρετος AUTHAIRETOS
2 Cor 8.17 he is going to you of his own accord
2. *acting of one's own will:* αὐτόματος AUTOMATOS
Acts 12.10 iron gate . . opened . . of its own accord

ACCORD, TO ONE
ACCORD, WITH ONE
1. *together, with one mind:* ὁμοθυμαδόν HOMOTHYMADON
Acts 1.14 with one a. devoted themselves to prayer
8. 6 multitudes with one accord gave heed
15.25 "seemed good . . , having come to one a.[o]

ACCORD WITH, IN
1. *in accordance with, for:* κατά (+acc.) KATA
Rom **15.5**
2 Th **3.6**

ACCORDANCE WITH, IN
1. *in accordance with, for:* κατά (+acc.) KATA
1 Cor **15.3**, 4
1 Tim **1.11**, 18

ACCORDING TO
1. *from, out of:* ἐκ (+gen.) EK
Jn **8.44**
2. *as, so:* ὡς HŌS
Rom **12.3**
3. *in accordance with, for:* κατά (+acc.) KATA
Mt **2.16**; **9.29**; **25.15**
Mk **7.5**
Lk **1.9**, 38; **2.22**, 24, 27, 29, 39, 42; **23.56**
Jn **8.15**
Acts **7.44**; **22.3**, 12; **23.3**, 31; **24.**[6‡, 14; **26.5**
Rom **1.3**, 4; **2.6**, 16; **4.1**; **8.4**², 5², 12, 13, 27, 28; **9.5**; **12.6**; **16.25**², 26
1 Cor **1.26**; **3.8**, 10; **12.8**
2 Cor **8.3**
Gal **1.4**, [11†; **3.29**; **4.23**, 29²
Eph **1.5**, 7, 9, 11², 19; **3.7**, 11, 16; **4.7**
Phil **4.19**
Col **1.11**, 25; **2.8**³, 22
2 Th **1.12**
2 Tim **1.1**
Heb **2.4**; **7.16**; **8.4**, 5; **9.9**; **10.8**
Jas **2.8**
1 Pet **1.17**; **4.19**
2 Pet **3.13**, 15
1 Jn **5.14**
4. *as, insofar as:* καθό KATHO
2 Cor 8.12 acceptable according to what a man has, not according to what he has not
5. *to, with, against:* πρός (+acc.) PROS
Lk **12.47**
2 Cor **5.10**
IDIOMATICALLY
a. Acts 11.29 according to his ability καθὼς εὐπορεῖτό τις [KATHŌS]
CONTEXTUALLY
Acts **2.23**; **15.1**

ACCORDINGLY
1. *therefore then:* ἄρα οὖν ARA II [A.5]
Rom 7. 3 Accordingly, she will be called an adulteress
2. *therefore:* διό DIO
Phm . 8 Accordingly, though I am bold enough

3. *so, therefore:* οὖν OUN
Rom **7.3**
CONTEXTUALLY
2 Cor 8. 6 Accordingly we have urged Titus

ACCORDS WITH, WHICH
1. *in accordance with, for:* κατά (+acc.) KATA [B.1.a.2]
1 Tim **6.3**
Tit **1.1**

ACCOUNT
1. *word, reckoning:* λόγος LOGOS
Mt 12.36 "render account for every careless word
Lk 16. 2 " 'Turn in the account of your stewardship
Rom 14.12 each of us shall give account of himself
Heb 13.17 your leaders . . will have to give account
1 Pet 4. 5 they will give account to him
2. *do, make:* ποιέω POIEŌ
Acts 20.24 "I do not account my life of . . value
IDIOMATICALLY
a. 1 Pet 3.15 to any one who calls you to account παντὶ τῷ αἰτοῦντι ὑμᾶς λόγον [LOGOS]
CONTEXTUALLY
Lk 1. 3 to write an orderly account for you
Heb 6. 6 since they crucify . . on their own account

ACCOUNT, CALL TO
1. *examine closely:* ἀνακρίνω ANAKRINŌ
1 Cor 14.24 an unbeliever . . is called to account by all

ACCOUNT, CHARGE TO ONE'S
1. *reckon, impute:* ἐλλογέω ELLOGEŌ
Phm .18 charge that to my account

ACCOUNT, OF NO
1. *treat with contempt:* ἐξουθενέω (pass. part.) EXOUTHENEŌ
2 Cor 10.10 "his speech of no account

ACCOUNT OF, ON
ACCOUNT, ON S.'S
1. *from:* ἀπό (+gen.) APO
Lk **19.3**
2. *because of:* διά (+acc.) DIA
Mt **13.21**
Mk **4.17**
Jn **11.42**; **12.9**, 11; **15.21**
Phil **1.24**
Col **3.6**; **4.3**
2 Pet **3.**[9‡
Rev **1.9**
3. *on, at:* ἐπί (+acc.) EPI
Rev **1.7**
4. *for the sake of:* ἕνεκα HENEKA
Mt 5.11 "evil against you falsely on my account
Lk 6.22 "revile you . . on account of the Son of man!
2 Cor 7.12 not on a. of the one who did the wrong, nor on a. of the one who suffered

ACCOUNTABLE
1. *answerable:* ὑπόδικος HYPODIKOS*
Rom 3.19 whole world may be held accountable

ACCOUNTED WORTHY, BE
1. *consider worthy:* καταξιόω (pass.) KATAXIOŌ
Lk 20.35 "are a. worthy to attain to that age

ACCOUNTS
1. *word, reckoning:* λόγος LOGOS
Mt 18.23 "king who wished to settle accounts
25.19 "the master . . came and settled accounts

ACCREDIT
1. *test, approve:* δοκιμάζω DOKIMAZŌ
1 Cor 16. 3 whom you accredit . . to carry your gift

ACCUMULATE
1. *heap up:* ἐπισωρεύω EPISŌREUŌ*
2 Tim 4. 3 accumulate for themselves teachers

ACCURATE, RATHER
1. *precisely:* ἀκριβῶς (comp.) AKRIBŌS [A.4.a]
Acts 24.22 Felix, having a rather accurate knowledge

ACCURATELY
1. *precisely:* ἀκριβῶς AKRIBŌS
[a]comp.
Lk [1. 3 having followed all things *accurately*†
Acts 18.25 taught accurately . . concerning Jesus
18.26 [a]expounded to him . . more accurately

ACCURSED
1. *something dedicated:* ἀνάθεμα ANATHEMA [A.1.b.4]
1 Cor 16.22 If . . one has no love . . let him be accursed
Gal 1. 8 if . . a gospel contrary . . let him be accursed
1. 9 If . . a gospel contrary . . let him be accursed
2. *accursed:* ἐπάρατος EPARATOS*
Jn 7.49 who do not know the law, are accursed
3. *curse:* κατάρα (gen.) KATARA
2 Pet 2.14 trained in greed. Accursed children!
4. *accursed thing:* κατάθεμα KATATHEMA* [A.1.b.5]
Rev 22. 3 no more be anything accursed

ACCURSED AND CUT OFF
1. *something dedicated:* ἀνάθεμα ANATHEMA [A.1.b.4]
Rom 9. 3 wish that I myself were a. and cut off

ACCUSATION
1. *call, accuse:* ἐγκαλέω EGKALEŌ [B.2.a.1]
Acts 26. 2 "defense . . against . . accusations of the Jews
2. *accusation:* κατηγορία KATĒGORIA
Jn 18.29 "What accusation do you bring?

ACCUSATION AGAINST
1. *accuse:* κατηγορέω (inf.) KATĒGOREŌ
Lk 6. 7 might find an accusation against him

ACCUSATION, MAKE AN
1. *accuse:* κατηγορέω KATĒGOREŌ
Acts 24.19 "they ought to be here . . to make an a.

ACCUSATION, ROB BY FALSE
1. *oppress, defraud:* συκοφαντέω SYKOPHANTEŌ
Lk 3.14 "Rob no one by violence or by false a.

ACCUSE
1. *call, accuse:* ἐγκαλέω EGKALEŌ
Acts 23.28 "the charge on which they accused him
23.29 "accused about questions of their law
26. 7 "for this hope I am accused by Jews!
2. *accuse:* κατηγορέω KATĒGOREŌ
Mt 12.10 they asked . . so that they might accuse him
27.12 when he was accused by the chief priests
Mk 3. 2 watched . . that they might accuse him
15. 3 chief priests accused him of many things
Lk 23. 2 they began to accuse him
23.10 the scribes stood by . . accusing him
Jn 5.45 "Do not think that I shall accuse you
5.45 "it is Moses who accuses you
Acts 22.30 the real reason why the Jews accused him
24. 2 Tertullus began to accuse him
24. 8 "everything of which we accuse him
25. 5 "if . . anything wrong . . let them accuse him
Rom 2.15 thoughts accuse or perhaps excuse them
Rev 12.10 "accuses them day and night before our God

ACCUSED
1. *accuse:* κατηγορέω (subst. pass. part.) KATĒGOREŌ
Acts 25.16 "before the accused met the accusers

ACCUSER
1. *opponent:* ἀντίδικος ANTIDIKOS
Mt 5.25 "Make friends quickly with your accuser
5.25 "lest your accuser hand you over
Lk 12.58 "As you go with your accuser . . settle
2. *accuser:* κατήγωρ KATĒGŌR*
Rev 12.10 "accuser of our brethren has been thrown
3. *prosecutor:* κατήγορος KATĒGOROS*
Acts 23.30 "ordering his accusers also to state
23.35 "I will hear you when your accusers arrive
[24. 8 "*commanding his accusers to come*‡
25.16 "the accused met the accusers face to face
25.18 "accusers . . brought no charge in his case

ACCUSTOMED, BE
1. *be accustomed:* εἴωθα EIŌTHA
Mt 27.15 governor was accustomed to release . . one

ACCUSTOMED, BEING
1. *custom, practice:* συνήθεια (dat.) SYNĒTHEIA
1 Cor 8. 7 being hitherto accustomed to idols

ACHAIA: Ἀχαΐα əˈkā(y)ə II,D-3
Acts 18.12 when Gallio was proconsul of A.

Acts 18.27 when he wished to cross to A.
19.21 Paul resolved . . to pass through . . A.
Rom 15.26 A. . . to make some contribution for the poor
1 Cor 16.15 household of Stephanas . . first converts in A.
2 Cor 1. 1 all the saints who are in the whole of A.
9. 2 A. has been ready since last year
11.10 shall not be silenced in the regions of A.
1 Th 1. 7 an example to all the believers . . in A.
1. 8 the word of the Lord sounded forth . . in . . A.

ACHAICUS: Ἀχαϊκός ə'kāəkəs
1 Cor 16.17 I rejoice at the coming of . . A.

ACHIM: Ἀχίμ 'ākim
Mt 1.14 Zadok the father of A., and A. the father of Eliud

ACKNOWLEDGE
1. *learn to know, recognize:* ἐπιγινώσκω EPIGINŌSKŌ
1 Cor 14.37 acknowledge . . a command of the Lord
2. *confess, acknowledge:* ὁμολογέω HOMOLOGEŌ
Mt 10.32 "who acknowledges me before men, I also will acknowledge before my Father
Lk 12. 8 "who acknowledges me before men, the Son of man also will acknowledge
Acts 23. 8 the Pharisees acknowledge them all
Heb 11.13 acknowledged that they were strangers
13.15 the fruit of lips that acknowledge his name
2 Jn . 7 not acknowledge . . Christ in the flesh
IDIOMATICALLY
a. Rom 1.28 they did not see fit to acknowledge God οὐκ ἐδοκίμασαν τὸν θεὸν ἔχειν ἐν ἐπιγνώσει [EPIGNŌSIS]

ACKNOWLEDGE AUTHORITY
1. *receive, recognize:* ἐπιδέχομαι EPIDECHOMAI
3 Jn . 9 D. . . does not acknowledge my authority

ACKNOWLEDGING
1. *confession, agreement:* ὁμολογία (gen.) HOMOLOGIA
2 Cor 9.13 obedience in acknowledging the gospel

ACQUAINTANCE
1. *known, knowable:* γνωστός (subst.) GNŌSTOS
Lk 2.44 sought him among their . . acquaintances
23.49 acquaintances . . stood at a distance

ACQUAINTED WITH, BE
1. *know:* οἶδα OIDA
2 Tim 3.15 have been a. with the sacred writings

ACQUIRE
IDIOMATICALLY
a. Eph 1.14 the guarantee . . until we acquire possession of it ἀρραβὼν . . εἰς ἀπολύτρωσιν τῆς περιποιήσεως [APOLYTRŌSIS]

ACQUIT
1. *justify, vindicate:* δικαιόω DIKAIOŌ
1 Cor 4. 4 but I am not thereby acquitted

ACQUITTAL
1. *justification:* δικαίωσις DIKAIŌSIS
Rom 5.18 act of righteousness leads to acquittal

ACROSS (*See also* SAIL ACROSS)
1. *in, at, by:* ἐν (+dat.) EN [B.1.b]
Acts **27.27**
2. *on the other side, beyond:* πέραν PERAN
Mt 4.15 "toward the sea, across the Jordan
Jn 6.17 started across the sea to Capernaum
10.40 He went away again across the Jordan
18. 1 across the Kidron valley . . was a garden

ACT (*See also* APPOINT TO ACT; IMMORALLY, ACT; MERCY, DO ACTS OF; RIGHTEOUSNESS, ACT OF; SHAMELESS ACTS)
1. *return; behave* (pass.): ἀναστρέφω ANASTREPHŌ
Heb 13.18 clear conscience, desiring to act honorably
2. *work, deed:* ἔργον ERGON [A.1.e]
Jas 1.25 being . . a doer that acts
3. *walk, behave:* περιπατέω PERIPATEŌ
2 Cor 10. 2 who suspect us of acting in worldly fashion
12.18 Did we not act in the same spirit?
4. *do, make:* ποιέω POIEŌ
ᵃὃ ποιεῖ A.6.a.4
Lk 12.47 "servant who knew . . but did not . . act
Acts 9.36 ᵃfull of good works and acts of charity
1 Tim 1.13 mercy because I had acted ignorantly
Jas 2.12 act as . . judged under the law of liberty
5. *do, practice:* πράσσω PRASSŌ
Acts 3.17 "I know that you acted in ignorance
17. 7 "acting against the decrees of Caesar
IDIOMATICALLY
a. Jn 8.4 "this woman has been caught in the act of adultery[r]‡ αὕτη ἡ γυνὴ κατείληπται ἐπ' αὐτοφώρῳ μοιχευομένη [AUTOPHŌROS]

ACT INSINCERELY WITH
1. *pretend to agree with:* συνυποκρίνομαι SYNYPOKRINOMAI*
Gal 2.13 with him the rest . . acted insincerely

ACTION
1. *achieve:* κατεργάζομαι KATERGAZOMAI [B.2.a.1]
Rom 7.15 I do not understand my own actions

ACTIVE
1. *effective, active:* ἐνεργής ENERGĒS
Heb 4.12 the word of God is living and active

ACTIVE ALONG WITH, BE
1. *work together with:* συνεργέω SYNERGEŌ
Jas 2.22 faith was active along with his works

ACTIVITY
1. *operation, activity:* ἐνέργεια ENERGEIA
2 Th 2. 9 coming . . by the activity of Satan

ACTUALLY
1. *actually:* ὅλως HOLŌS
1 Cor 5. 1 actually reported that there is immorality
2. *happen:* συμβαίνω SYMBAINŌ [A.6.e]
Acts 21.35 he was actually carried by the soldiers

ADAM: Ἀδάμ 'adəm
Lk 3.38 Adam, the son of God
Rom 5.14 death reigned from Adam to Moses
5.14 not like the transgression of Adam
1 Cor 15.22 as in Adam all die
15.45 "first man Adam became a living being
15.45 last Adam became a life-giving spirit
1 Tim 2.13 Adam was formed first, then Eve
2.14 Adam was not deceived, but the woman
Jude .14 the seventh generation from Adam

ADD

ADD TO
1. *add to a will:* ἐπιδιατάσσομαι EPIDIATASSOMAI*
Gal 3.15 no one annuls . . a man's will,[g] or adds to it
2. *lay on, add:* ἐπιτίθημι EPITITHĒMI
Rev 22.18 if any one adds to them, God will add to him the plagues described in this book
3. *say, speak:* ἐρῶ ERŌ
Heb 10. 9 then he added, "Lo, I have come
4. *add, counsel with* (mid.): προσανατίθημι PROSANATITHĒMI
Gal 2. 6 those . . who were of repute added nothing
5. *put to, add, continue:* προστίθημι PROSTITHĒMI
Mt 6.27 "which of you . . can add one cubit?
Lk 3.20 ⟨Herod⟩ added this to them all
12.25 "which of you . . can add a cubit?
Acts 2.41 added that day about three thousand souls
2.47 the Lord added to their number
5.14 believers were added to the Lord
11.24 a large company was added to the Lord
Gal 3.19 law . . was added because of transgressions
CONTEXTUALLY
Heb 10.17 then he adds, "I will remember . . no more

ADDI: Ἀδδί 'ad,ī
Lk 3.28 Melchi, the son of A., the son of Cosam

ADDICTED
1. *hold to, be intent on:* προσέχω (part.) PROSECHŌ
1 Tim 3. 8 Deacons . . not addicted to much wine

ADDRESS
1. *reply:* ἀποκρίνομαι APOKRINOMAI
Acts 3.12 when Peter saw it he addressed the people
Rev 7.13 one of the elders addressed me
2. *speak out:* ἀποφθέγγομαι APOPHTHEGGOMAI
Acts 2.14 Peter . . addressed them, "Men of Judea
3. *discuss:* διαλέγομαι DIALEGOMAI
Heb 12. 5 the exhortation which addresses you

4. *speak, talk:* λαλέω LALEŌ
1 Cor 3. 1 could not address you as spiritual men
Eph 5.19 addressing one another in psalms
5. *say, speak:* λέγω LEGŌ [B.2.d.1]
Heb 7.21 but this one was addressed with an oath
6. *call to, address:* προσφωνέω PROSPHŌNEŌ
Lk 23.20 Pilate addressed them once more
Acts 22. 2 he addressed them in . . Hebrew

ADHERENT
1. *walk, behave:* περιπατέω (subst. part.) PERIPATEŌ
Heb 13. 9 foods . . have not benefited their adherents
CONTEXTUALLY
Rom 4.14 If it is the adherents of the law
4.16 not only to the adherents of the law

ADJURE
1. *make s. swear:* ἐνορκίζω ENORKIZŌ*
1 Th 5.27 I adjure you . . that this letter be read
2. *exorcise:* ἐξορκίζω EXORKIZŌ*
Mt 26.63 "I adjure you by the living God, tell us
3. *make s. swear:* ὁρκίζω HORKIZŌ*
Mk 5. 7 "I adjure you by God, do not torment
Acts 19.13 "I adjure you by . . Jesus

ADMIN: Ἀδμίν 'admin
Lk 3.33 Amminadab, the son of A., the son of Arni

ADMINISTER
1. *do a service, minister:* διακονέω DIAKONEŌ
2 Cor 8.20 this liberal gift which we are administering

ADMINISTRATOR
1. *steering, government:* κυβέρνησις KYBERNĒSIS* [C.2]
1 Cor 12.28 then healers, helpers, administrators

ADMISSION, SECRETLY GAIN
1. *slip in, penetrate:* παρεισδύνω PAREISDYNŌ
Jude . 4 admission has been secretly gained

ADMIT
1. *confess, acknowledge:* ὁμολογέω HOMOLOGEŌ
Acts 24.14 "I a. . . that according to the Way
2. *accept, receive:* παραδέχομαι PARADECHOMAI
1 Tim 5.19 Never a. any charge against an elder except

ADMONISH
1. *admonish, warn:* νουθετέω NOUTHETEŌ
Acts 20.31 "I did not cease night or day to admonish
1 Cor 4.14 write . . to admonish you as my . . children
Col 3.16 teach and admonish one another⁰
1 Th 5.12 respect those who . . admonish you
5.14 brethren, admonish the idlers

ADMONISHING
1. *admonition, warning:* νουθεσία NOUTHESIA
Tit 3.10 after admonishing him once or twice

ADOPT
1. *take up, kill:* ἀναιρέω (mid.) ANAIREŌ
Acts 7.21 "Pharaoh's daughter adopted him

ADOPTION AS SONS
1. *adoption as a son:* υἱοθεσία HUIOTHESIA
Rom 8.23 as we wait for adoption as sons
Gal 4. 5 that we might receive adoption as sons

ADORN
1. *prepare, adorn:* κοσμέω KOSMEŌ
Mt 23.29 "adorn the monuments of the righteous
Lk 21. 5 some spoke of the temple, how it was adorned
1 Tim 2. 9 women should adorn themselves modestly
Tit 2.10 may adorn the doctrine of God our Savior
1 Pet 3. 5 holy women . . used to adorn themselves
Rev 21. 2 as a bride adorned for her husband
21.19 The foundations . . of the city were adorned

ADORNING
1. *world, world order:* κόσμος KOSMOS
1 Pet 3. 3 Let not yours be the outward adorning

ADRAMYTTIUM: Ἀδραμυττηνός ,adrə'mitēəm II,E-3
Acts 27. 2 embarking in a ship of A.

ADRIA: Ἀδρίας 'ādrēə II,C-2
Acts 27.27 we were drifting across the sea of Adria

ADRIFT
CONTEXTUALLY
2 Cor 11.25 a night and a day I have been a. at sea

ADULTERER
1. *adulterer:* μοιχός MOICHOS
Lk 18.11 " 'not like other men . . unjust, adulterers
1 Cor 6. 9 neither the immoral . . nor adulterers

ADULTERESS
1. *adulteress:* μοιχαλίς MOICHALIS
Rom 7. 3 adulteress if she lives with another man
7. 3 if her husband dies . . she is not an a.
2. *commit adultery:* μοιχεύω (pass. inf.) MOICHEUŌ [A.6.d]
Mt 5.32 "divorces his wife . . makes her an a.

ADULTEROUS
1. *adulteress:* μοιχαλίς (attr.) MOICHALIS
Mt 12.39 "An evil and adulterous generation
16. 4 "An evil and adulterous generation
Mk 8.38 "this adulterous and sinful generation
2. *adulterer:* μοιχός (pl.) MOICHOS
Heb 13. 4 God will judge the immoral and adulterous

ADULTERY
1. *adulteress:* μοιχαλίς MOICHALIS [C.2]
2 Pet 2.14 eyes full of adultery, insatiable for sin
2. *adultery:* μοιχεία MOICHEIA*
Mt 15.19 "evil thoughts, murder, adultery, fornication
Mk 7.21 "fornication, theft, murder, adultery
Jn 8. 3 a woman who had been caught in adultery[r]‡
IDIOMATICALLY
a. Jn 8.4 "this woman has been caught in the act of adultery[r]‡ αὕτη ἡ γυνὴ κατείληπται ἐπ' αὐτοφώρῳ μοιχευομένη [MOICHEUŌ]

ADULTERY, COMMIT
1. *commit adultery with:* μοιχάω (pass.) MOICHAŌ*
Mt 5.32 marries a divorced woman commits a.
19. 9 "divorces . . and marries . . commits a.[k]‡
[19. 9 "*who marries a divorced woman commits a.*‡
Mk 10.11 "Whoever divorces . . marries . . commits a.
10.12 "if she . . marries another, she commits a.
2. *commit adultery:* μοιχεύω MOICHEUŌ
Mt 5.27 "You have heard . . 'You shall not commit a.
5.28 "committed adultery with her in his heart
[19. 9 "whoever divorces . . *makes her commit a.*‡
19.18 "You shall not commit adultery
Mk 10.19 "commandments: . . 'Do not commit adultery
Lk 16.18 "who divorces . . and marries . . commits a.
16.18 "marries a woman divorced . . commits a.
18.20 "commandments: 'Do not commit a.
Rom 2.22 who say that one must not commit adultery, do you commit adultery?
13. 9 commandments, "You shall not commit a.
Jas 2.11 who said, "Do not commit adultery
2.11 If you do not commit adultery
Rev 2.22 " 'those who commit adultery with her

ADVANCE (*See also* ARRANGE IN ADVANCE)
1. *for progress:* εἰς προκοπήν PROKOPĒ [B.1.a.2]
Phil 1.12 has really served to advance the gospel
2. *make progress, advance:* προκόπτω PROKOPTŌ
Gal 1.14 I advanced in Judaism beyond many

ADVANCED
1. *go before:* προβαίνω (perf. part.) PROBAINŌ
Lk 1. 7 because . . both were advanced in years
1.18 "my wife is advanced in years

ADVANTAGE
1. *help, profit:* ὠφέλεια ŌPHELEIA
Jude .16 flattering people to gain advantage
2. *superfluous, extraordinary:* περισσός (subst. neut.) PERISSOS
Rom 3. 1 Then what advantage has the Jew?
3. *useful:* σύμφορος (subst. neut.) SYMPHOROS
1 Cor 10.33 not seeking my own advantage

ADVANTAGE, BE OF
1. *help, aid:* ὠφελέω ŌPHELEŌ
Gal 5. 2 Christ will be of no advantage to you

ADVANTAGE, IT IS TO S.'S
1. *bring together, be useful:* συμφέρω (impers.+dat.) SYMPHERŌ
Jn 16. 7 "it is to your advantage that I go away

ADVANTAGE, OF NO
1. *unprofitable:* ἀλυσιτελής ALYSITELĒS*
Heb 13.17 that would be of no advantage to you

ADVANTAGE OF, TAKE
ADVANTAGE OVER, GAIN THE
1. *receive, take:* λαμβάνω LAMBANŌ
2 Cor 11.20 if a man . . takes advantage of you
2. *defraud:* πλεονεκτέω PLEONEKTEŌ
2 Cor 2.11 keep Satan from gaining the a. over us
7. 2 we have taken advantage of no one
12.17 Did I take advantage of you?
12.18 Did Titus take advantage of you?

ADVERSARY
1. *opponent:* ἀντίδικος ANTIDIKOS
Lk 18. 3 " 'Vindicate me against my adversary
1 Pet 5. 8 Your adversary the devil prowls around
2. *be opposed:* ἀντίκειμαι (subst. part.) ANTIKEIMAI
Lk 13.17 all his adversaries were put to shame
21.15 "none of your adversaries will . . withstand
1 Cor 16. 9 a wide door . . and there are many adversaries
3. *opposite, opposed:* ὑπεναντίος (subst.) HYPENANTIOS
Heb 10.27 fire which will consume the adversaries

ADVICE
1. *judgment, opinion, purpose:* γνώμη GNŌMĒ
2 Cor 8.10 in this matter I give my advice

ADVICE, TAKE
1. *persuade:* πείθω (pass.) PEITHŌ
Acts 5.40(39) they took his advice . . and let them go

ADVISABLE
1. *worthy:* ἄξιος AXIOS
1 Cor 16. 4 If it seems advisable that I should go also

ADVISE
1. *give counsel:* τιθέναι βουλήν BOULĒ [A.6.a.4]
Acts 27.12 the majority advised to put to sea
2. *advise, recommend:* παραινέω PARAINEŌ
Acts 27. 9 As . . time had been lost, . . Paul advised

ADVOCATE
1. *proclaim, announce:* καταγγέλλω KATAGGELLŌ
Acts 16.21 "They advocate customs . . not lawful for us
2. *intercessor, advocate:* παράκλητος PARAKLĒTOS
1 Jn 2. 1 we have an advocate . . , Jesus Christ

AENEAS: Αἰνέας i'nēəs
Acts 9.33 A., who had been bedridden for eight years
9.34 "A., Jesus Christ heals you; rise

AENON: Αἰνών 'ēnən
Jn 3.23 John also was baptizing at A.

AFAR, FROM
1. *from afar:* μακρόθεν MAKROTHEN
[a]+ἀπό
Mt 27.55 [a]many women there, looking on from afar
Mk 5. 6 [a]when he saw Jesus from afar, he ran
15.40 [a]also women looking on from afar
2. *distantly, from afar:* πόρρωθεν PORRŌTHEN
Heb 11.13 having seen it and greeted it from afar

AFFAIR (*See also* YOUR OWN AFFAIRS)
CONTEXTUALLY
1 Cor 7.32 anxious about the affairs of the Lord
7.33 anxious about worldly affairs
7.34 anxious about the affairs of the Lord
7.34 anxious about worldly affairs
Col 4. 7 will tell you all about my affairs
1 Th 4.11 to live quietly, to mind your own affairs

AFFECTION
1. *inward parts* (pl.): σπλάγχνον SPLAGCHNON
2 Cor 6.12 you are restricted in your own affections
Phil 1. 8 I yearn for you . . with the a. of Christ
2. 1 if there is . . any affection and sympathy

AFFECTION, BROTHERLY
1. *brotherly love:* φιλαδελφία PHILADELPHIA
Rom 12.10 love one another with brotherly affection
2 Pet 1. 7 godliness with brotherly affection, and brotherly affection with love

AFFECTIONATELY DESIROUS, BE
1. *desire, long for:* ὁμείρομαι HOMEIROMAI*
1 Th 2. 8 being affectionately desirous of you

AFFIRM
1. *say, speak:* λέγω LEGŌ
Eph 4.17 this I affirm and testify in the Lord
2. *say, assert:* φάσκω PHASKŌ
Acts 24. 9 Jews also . . affirming that all this was so

AFFLICT
1. *squeeze, oppress:* θλίβω THLIBŌ
2 Cor 1. 6 If we are afflicted, it is for your comfort
4. 8 We are afflicted in every way . . not crushed
7. 5 we were afflicted at every turn
2 Th 1. 6 just to repay . . those who afflict you
1. 7 grant rest . . to you who are afflicted
2. *raise affliction:* θλῖψιν ἐγείρειν THLIPSIS [A.6.a.4]
Phil 1.17 thinking to afflict me in my imprisonment

AFFLICTED
1. *disturb:* ὀχλέω (pass. part.) OCHLEŌ*
Acts 5.16 those afflicted with unclean spirits
2. *hold together, impel:* συνέχω (pass. part.) SYNECHŌ
Mt 4.24 those afflicted with various diseases
3. *squeeze, oppress:* θλίβω (pass. part.) THLIBŌ
1 Tim 5.10 as one who has . . relieved the afflicted
Heb 11.37 they were . . destitute, afflicted, ill-treated

AFFLICTION
1. *affliction, oppression:* θλῖψις THLIPSIS
Acts 7.10 "rescued him out of all his afflictions
7.11 "a famine . . and great affliction
20.23 "in every city . . afflictions await me
2 Cor 1. 4 who comforts us in all our affliction
1. 4 to comfort those who are in any affliction
1. 8 the affliction we experienced in Asia
2. 4 much affliction and anguish of heart
4.17 momentary affliction is preparing for us
6. 4 great endurance, in afflictions, hardships
7. 4 With all our affliction, I am overjoyed
8. 2 in a severe test of affliction
Col 1.24 what is lacking in Christ's afflictions
1 Th 1. 6 you received the word in much affliction
3. 3 no one be moved by these afflictions
3. 7 in . . affliction we have been comforted
2 Th 1. 4 the afflictions which you are enduring
1. 6 God deems it just to repay with affliction
Heb 10.33 publicly exposed to abuse and affliction
Jas 1.27 visit . . widows in their affliction

AFFLICTION, SUFFER
1. *squeeze, oppress:* θλίβω (pass.) THLIBŌ
1 Th 3. 4 we told you . . that we were to suffer a.

AFLAME, BE
1. *set on fire:* πυρόω (pass.) PYROŌ
1 Cor 7. 9 better to marry than to be aflame

AFRAID
1. *vile, cowardly:* δειλός DEILOS
Mt 8.26 "Why are you afraid, O men of little faith?
Mk 4.40 "Why are you afraid? Have you no faith?

AFRAID, BE
1. *be cowardly:* δειλιάω DEILIAŌ*
Jn 14.27 "Let not your hearts . . be afraid
2. *terrify:* φοβέω (pass.) PHOBEŌ
Mt 2.22 he was afraid to go there
9. 8 they were afraid, and they glorified God
14.30 when he saw the wind,[n] he was afraid
21.26 "we are afraid of the multitude
25.25 " 'I was afraid . . and hid your talent
28. 5 the angel said . . "Do not be afraid
28.10 Jesus said . . "Do not be afraid
Mk 5.15 saw the demoniac . . and they were afraid
9.32 and they were afraid to ask him
10.32 and those who followed were afraid
11.32 they were afraid of the people

Mk 16. 8 said nothing . . for they were afraid
Lk 1.13 "Do not be afraid, Zechariah
1.30 "Do not be afraid, Mary
2.10 angel said to them, "Be not afraid
5.10 Jesus said to Simon, "Do not be afraid
8.25 they were afraid, and they marveled
8.35 found the man . . and they were afraid
9.34 they were afraid as they entered the cloud
9.45 were afraid to ask him about this saying
19.21 " 'I was a. . . because you are a severe man
Jn 6.20 "It is I; do not be afraid
19. 8 When Pilate heard . . he was the more afraid
Acts 5.26 they were afraid of being stoned
9.26 they were all afraid of him
16.38 magistrates . . were afraid when they heard
18. 9 "Do not be afraid, but speak
22.29 the tribune also was afraid
23.10 tribune, afraid that Paul would be torn
27.24 " 'Do not be afraid, Paul
Rom 13. 4 if you do wrong, be afraid
2 Cor 11. 3 I am a. . . your thoughts will be led astray
Gal 4.11 I am a. I have labored over you in vain
Heb 11.23 they were not afraid of the king's edict
11.27 he left Egypt, not being afraid
13. 6 "The Lord is my helper, I will not be afraid
3. *tremble, be afraid:* τρέμω TREMŌ
2 Pet 2.10 are not afraid to revile the glorious ones

AFRAID, EXCEEDINGLY
1. *terrified:* ἔκφοβος EKPHOBOS
Mk 9. 6 they were exceedingly afraid

AFTER
1. *through:* διά (+gen.) DIA [B.1.b]
Mk **2.1**
Acts **24.17**
Gal **2.1**
2. *say, speak:* εἶπον (part.) EIPON [A.6.a.7]
Jn 21.19 And after this he said to him
3. *from, out of:* ἐκ (+gen.) EK
Jn **6.66**
4. *in, at, by:* ἐν (+dat.) EN [B.1.b]
Rom **4.10**[2]
5. *since:* ἐπειδή EPEIDĒ
Lk 7. 1 After he had ended all his sayings
6. *on, at:* ἐπί (+acc.) EPI
[a]+dat.
Lk **1.59**[a]; **15.4**
7. *as, so:* ὡς HŌS [B.3.b.4]
Jn **7.10**
Acts **19.21**
8. *when, whenever:* ὅταν HOTAN [B.2.a.2]
1 Cor **15.24**; **16.5**
9. *latter, behind, later:* ὕστερος (neut.+gen.) HYSTEROS
Mt 22.27 "After them all, the woman died
10. *in accordance with, for:* κατά (+acc.) KATA
Acts **13.22**
Col **3.10**
Heb **5.6**, 10; **6.20**; **7.11**[2], 17
11. *after:* μετά (+acc.) META
Mt **1.12**; **17.1**; **24.29**; **25.19**; **26.2**, 32, 73; **27.53**, 62, 63
Mk **1.14**; 8.31; **9.2**, 31; **10.34**; **13.24**; **14.28**, 70; **16.12**‡, 19‡, [end‡
Lk **1.24**; **2.46**; **5.27**; **9.28**; **10.1**; **12.4**, 5; **22.20**‡
Jn **2.12**; **3.22**; **4.43**; **5.1**, [4‡; **6.1**; **7.1**; **11.7**; **13.27**; **19.28**, 38; **21.1**
Acts **1.3**; **5.37**; **7.4**, 5, 7; **10.37**, 41; **12.4**; **13.15**, 20, 25; **15.13**, 16, 36; **18.1**; 19.4, 21; **20.1**, 6, 29; **21.15**; **24.1**, 24; **25.1**; **28.11**, 13, 17
1 Cor **11.25**
Gal **1.18**
Tit **3.10**
Heb **8.10**; **9.27**; **10.15**, 16, 26
2 Pet **1.15**
Rev **4.1**[2]; **7.1**, 9; **11.11**; **15.5**; **18.1**; **19.1**; **20.3**
12. *behind, backward:* ὀπίσω OPISŌ
Mt **3.11**; **16.24**
Mk **1.7**; **8.34**
Lk **9.23**; **14.27**; **19.14**; **21.8**
Jn **1.15**, 27, 30; **12.19**
Acts **5.37**; **20.30**
1 Tim **5.15**
Rev **12.15**
13. *behind:* ὄπισθεν OPISTHEN
Mt 15.23 "Send her away, for she is crying after us
14. *late in the day:* ὀψέ (+gen.) OPSE
Mt 28. 1 after the sabbath, toward the dawn
IDIOMATICALLY
a. Acts **19.21** [PLĒROŌ]

AFTER THAT
1. *no longer, no more:* οὐκέτι (+neg.) OUKETI
Mk 12.34 after that no one dared to ask him any

AFTER THE LIKENESS OF
1. *in accordance with, for:* κατά (+acc.) KATA
Eph 4.24 nature, created after the likeness of God

AFTERWARD
1. *after a time:* μετὰ χρόνον CHRONOS [B.1.a.1]
Heb 4. 7 saying through David so long afterward
2. *second:* δεύτερος (subst. neut.) DEUTEROS
Jude . 5 he[b] who saved . . afterward destroyed those
3. *latter, behind, later:* ὕστερος (neut.) HYSTEROS
Mt 4. 2 he fasted . . and afterward he was hungry
21.29 "but afterward he repented and went
21.32 "you did not afterward repent and believe
21.37 "Afterward he sent his son to them
25.11 "Afterward the other maidens came also
Mk 16.14 Afterward he appeared to the eleven[k]‡
Lk 20.32 "Afterward the woman also died
Jn 13.36 "you shall follow afterward
4. *after these things:* μετὰ ταῦτα META [B.1.a.1]
[a]μετὰ . . ἔτη [b]μετὰ τοσοῦτον χρόνον
Lk **17.8**; **18.4**
Jn **5.14**; **13.7**
Gal **3.17**[a]
Heb **4.7**[b]
5. *thereafter:* μετέπειτα METEPEITA*
Heb 12.17 afterward . . he was rejected

AFTERWARD, SOON
1. *in the next:* ἐν τῷ ἑξῆς HEXĒS [B.1.a.1]
Lk 7.11 Soon afterward[y] he went to a city
2. *in the next:* ἐν τῷ καθεξῆς KATHEXĒS [B.1.a.1]
Lk 8. 1 Soon afterward, he went on through

AFTERWARD, THOSE WHO CAME
1. *in a row, in order:* καθεξῆς (subst. pl.) KATHEXĒS
Acts 3.24 "Samuel and those who came afterward

AGABUS: Ἄγαβος 'agəbəs
Acts 11.28 A. stood up and foretold . . famine
21.10 a prophet named A. came down

AGAIN
1. *but:* ἀλλά ALLA
Rom **10.19**
2. *from now on:* ἀπ' ἄρτι ARTI [B.1.a.1]
Mt 23.39 "I tell you, you will not see me again
26.29 "I shall not drink again of this fruit
3. *even yet:* καὶ ἔτι ETI [A.4.e]
2 Cor 1.10 our hope that he will deliver us again
4. *no longer, no more:* μηκέτι (+neg.) MĒKETI
Mt 21.19 "May no fruit ever come from you again!
Mk 11.14 "May no one ever eat fruit from you again
5. *no longer, no more:* οὐκέτι (+neg.) OUKETI
Mk 14.25 "I shall not drink again of the fruit
Lk [22.16 "I shall *never* eat it *again* until‡
Rev 18.14 "lost to thee, never to be found again!
6. *again, back:* πάλιν PALIN
Mt 4. 7 "Again it is written, 'You shall not tempt
4. 8 Again, the devil took him to a . . mountain
5.33 "Again you have heard that it was said
13.45 "Again, the kingdom of heaven is like
13.47 "Again, the kingdom of heaven is like
18.19 "Again I say . . if two of you agree
19.24 "Again I tell you, it is easier for a camel
20. 5 "Going out again about the sixth hour
21.36 "Again he sent other servants

Mt 22. 1 again Jesus spoke . . in parables
22. 4 "Again he sent other servants, saying
26.42 Again, for the second time, he went away
26.43 again he came and found them sleeping
26.44 So, leaving them again, he went away
26.72 And again he denied it with an oath
27.50 Jesus cried again with a loud voice
Mk 2.13 He went out again beside the sea
3. 1 Again he entered the synagogue
3.20 and the crowd came together again
4. 1 Again he began to teach beside the sea
5.21 when Jesus had crossed again in the boat
7.14 And he called the people to him again
8. 1 when again a great crowd had gathered
8.13 getting into the boat again he departed
8.25 again he laid his hands upon his eyes
10. 1 and crowds gathered to him again; and again, as his custom was, he taught them
10.10 disciples asked him again about this
10.24 Jesus said to them again, "Children
10.32 taking the twelve again, he began to tell
11.27 And they came again to Jerusalem
12. 4 Again he sent to them another servant
14.39 And again he went away and prayed
14.40 again he came and found them sleeping
14.61 Again the high priest asked him
14.69 the maid . . began again to say
14.70 But again he denied it
14.70 again the bystanders said to Peter
15. 4 Pilate a. asked him, "Have you no answer?
15.12 And Pilate again said to them
15.13 And they cried out again, "Crucify him
Lk 6.43 "nor again does a bad tree bear good fruit
13.20 again he said, "To what shall I compare?
Jn 1.35 The next day again John was standing
4. 3 he left Judea and departed again to G.
4.13 "who drinks of this water will thirst a.
4.46 So he came again to Cana in Galilee
6.15 Jesus withdrew again to the mountain
8. 2 Early . . he came again to the temple[r]‡
8.12 Again Jesus spoke to them, saying
8.21 Again he said to them, "I go away
9.15 The Pharisees again asked him how
9.17 So they again said to the blind man
9.27 "Why do you want to hear it again?
10. 7 So Jesus again said to them, "Truly
10.17 "lay down my life, that I may take it a.
10.18 "and I have power to take it again
10.19 There was again a division among the Jews
10.31 The Jews took up stones again to stone him
10.39 Again they tried to arrest him
10.40 He went away again across the Jordan
11. 7 "Let us go into Judea again
11. 8 "and are you going there again?
11.38 Jesus, deeply moved a., came to the tomb
12.28 "I have glorified it, and I will . . again
12.39 For Isaiah again said
14. 3 "I will come again and will take you
16.16 "again a little while, and you will see me
16.17 " 'a. a little while, and you will see me
16.19 " 'a. a little while, and you will see me
16.22 "but I will see you again
16.28 again, I am leaving the world and going
18. 7 A. he asked them, "Whom do you seek?
18.27 Peter again denied it
18.33 Pilate entered the praetorium again
18.38 he went out to the Jews again
18.40 They cried out again, "Not this man
19. 4 Pilate went out again, and said . . "See
19. 9 he entered the praetorium again
19.37 And again another scripture says
20.21 Jesus said . . again, "Peace be with you
20.26 his disciples were again in the house
21. 1 After this Jesus revealed himself again
Acts 10.15 And the voice came to him again
11.10 "all was drawn up again into heaven
17.32 "We will hear you again about this
27.28 a little farther on they sounded again
Rom 11.23 God has the power to graft them in a.
15.10 again it is said, "Rejoice, O Gentiles
15.11 and a., "Praise the Lord, all Gentiles
1 Cor 3.20 a., "The Lord knows that the thoughts
7. 5 come together again, lest Satan tempt you
12.21 nor again the head to the feet
2 Cor 3. 1 Are we beginning to commend . . again?
5.12 not commending ourselves to you again
12.21 I fear that when I come again
13. 2 if I come again I will not spare them
Gal 1. 9 As we have said . . so now I say again
1.17 and again I returned to Damascus
2. 1 I went up again to Jerusalem
2.18 But if I build up again those things
4. 9 how can you turn back again to the weak?
4.19 with whom I am again in travail
5. 1 do not submit again to a yoke of slavery
5. 3 I testify again to every man
Phil 1.26 because of my coming to you again
2.28 that you may rejoice at seeing him a.
4. 4 Rejoice . . ; again I will say, Rejoice
Heb 1. 5 Or again, "I will be to him a father
1. 6 And again, when he brings the firstborn
2.13 again, "I will put my trust in him
2.13 again, "Here am I, and the children
4. 5 And again in this place he said
4. 7 again he sets a certain day, "Today
5.12 you need some one to teach you again
6. 1 not laying again a foundation
6. 4(6) to restore again to repentance
10.30 And again, "The Lord will judge his people
Jas 5.18 he prayed again and the heaven gave rain
2 Pet 2.20 if . . they are again entangled in them
Rev 10. 8 the voice . . spoke to me again, saying, "Go
10.11 "You must a. prophesy about many peoples

IDIOMATICALLY
a. Phil 4.16 you sent me help[f] once and again *καὶ ἅπαξ καὶ δὶς τὴν χρείαν μοι ἐπέμψατε* [DIS]
b. 1 Th 2.18 I, Paul, again and again *ἐγὼ μὲν Παῦλος καὶ ἅπαξ καὶ δίς* [HAPAX; DIS]

AGAIN, NEVER
AGAIN, NOT

1. *no longer, no more: μηκέτι* MĒKETI
Mk 9.25 "come out . . and never enter him again
Jn 8.11 "go, and do not sin again[r]‡
2. *no longer, no more: οὐκέτι* OUKETI
Rom 6. 9 Christ being raised . . will never die again

AGAINST

1. *opposite: ἀπέναντι* APENANTI
Acts 17. 7 "all acting against the decrees of Caesar
2. *from: ἀπό* (+gen.) APO
Lk **18.**3
1 Jn **3.**17
3. *into, to, for: εἰς* (+acc.) EIS
Mt **18.**15, 21
Mk **3.**29
Lk **12.**10^{2}; **15.**18, 21; **17.**4; **22.**65
Acts **6.**11; **9.**1; **23.**30; **25.**8^{3}
1 Cor **6.**18; **8.**12^{2}
Heb **12.**3
4. *from, out of: ἐκ* (+gen.) EK
Rev **18.**20
5. *before: ἔμπροσθεν* EMPROSTHEN
Mt 23.13 "you shut the kingdom of heaven a. men
6. *opposite, contrary: ἐναντίος* ENANTIOS
[a]A.3.d.1
Mt 14.24 [a]the wind was against them
Mk 6.48 the wind was against them
Acts 27. 4 [a]the winds were against us
28.17 [a]"I had done nothing against the people
7. *on, at: ἐπί* (+acc.) EPI
except [a]+dat.
Mt **10.**21; **12.**26; **24.**7; **26.**55
Mk **3.**24, 25, 26; **10.**11; **13.**8^{2}, 12; **14.**48; **15.**46
Lk **9.**5; **11.**17, 18; **12.**52^{2a}, 53^{2a}, 53^{4}; **14.**31; **21.**10^{2}; **22.**52^{2}

Jn **13**.18
Acts **4**.27; **7**.54; **8**.1; **13**.50, 51
Rom **1**.18; **4**.18[a]
2 Cor **1**.23; **10**.2
2 Th **2**.4
1 Pet **3**.12
Rev **7**.1
8. *down from, against:* κατά (+gen.) KATA
Mt **5**.11, 23; **10**.35[3]; **12**.14, 25[2], 30, 32[2]; **26**.59; **27**.1
Mk **3**.6; **9**.40; **11**.25; **14**.55, 56, 57
Lk **9**.50; **11**.23; **23**.14
Acts **4**.26; **6**.13; **14**.2; **21**.28; **24**.1; **25**.2, 15, 27
Rom **8**.31, 33; **11**.2
1 Cor **4**.6
2 Cor **13**.8
Gal **3**.21; **5**.17[2], 23
Col **2**.14
1 Tim **5**.19
Jas **5**.9
1 Pet **2**.11
Jude .15
Rev **2**.4, 14, 20
9. *not:* μή MĒ [A.4.c]
Rom **2**.21
10. *with:* μετά (+gen.) META
1 Cor **6**.6
Rev **2**.16; **12**.7; **13**.4; **19**.19[2]
11. *about, concerning:* περί (+gen.) PERI
Acts **26**.2
12. *to, with, against:* πρός (+acc.) PROS
Mt **4**.6
Mk **12**.12
Lk **4**.11; **5**.30; **20**.19
Acts **6**.1; **9**.29; **19**.38; **23**.30; **24**.19; **26**.14
1 Cor **6**.1
Eph **6**.11, 12[5]
Col **3**.13
Heb **12**.4
Rev **13**.6

AGATE
1. *chalcedony:* χαλκηδών CHALKĒDŌN*
Rev 21.19 foundations . . adorned . . , the third a.

AGE
1. *age:* αἰών AIŌN
Mt 12.32 "will not be forgiven, either in this age
13.39 "the harvest is the close of the age
13.40 "so will it be at the close of the age
13.49 "So it will be at the close of the age
24. 3 "your coming and . . the close of the age
28.20 "I am with you . . to the close of the age
Mk 10.30 "in the age to come eternal life
Lk 18.30 "in the age to come eternal life
20.34 "The sons of this age marry
20.35 "attain to that a. and to the resurrection
1 Cor 1.20 Where is the debater of this age?
2. 6 it is not a wisdom of this age
2. 6 the rulers of this age, who are doomed
2. 7 wisdom . . God decreed before the ages
2. 8 None of the rulers of this a. understood
3.18 one . . wise in this age, let him become a fool
10.11 upon whom the end of the ages has come
Gal 1. 4 to deliver us from the present evil age
Eph 1.21 every name that is named . . in this age
2. 7 in the coming ages . . riches of his grace
3. 9 the mystery hidden for ages in[d] God
Col 1.26 mystery hidden for ages and generations[c]†
1 Tim 1.17 King of ages, immortal, invisible
Heb 6. 5 the powers of the age to come
9.26 he has appeared . . at the end of the age
Rev 15. 3 "true are thy ways, O King of the ages![i]‡
2. *time, period:* χρόνος CHRONOS
[a]+αἰωνίων
Rom 16.25 the mystery . . kept . . for long ages
2 Tim 1. 9 [a]grace . . in Christ Jesus ages ago
Tit 1. 2 [a]eternal life . . promised ages ago
3. *time, opportunity:* καιρός KAIROS
Heb 9. 9 (which is symbolic for the present age
11.11 to conceive, . . when . . past the age
IDIOMATICALLY
a. Lk 2.36 she was of a great age αὕτη προβεβηκυῖα ἐν ἡμέραις πολλαῖς [HĒMERA; PROBAINŌ]
b. Jn 9.21, 23 "he is of age ἡλικίαν ἔχει [HĒLIKIA]
c. Heb 11.11 even when she was past the age καὶ παρὰ καιρὸν ἡλικίας [HĒLIKIA]
CONTEXTUALLY
Mk 5.42 (she was twelve years of age[o]
Lk 3.23 Jesus . . was about thirty years of age
8.42 daughter, about twelve years of age
1 Tim 5. 9 if she is not less than sixty years of age

AGE, S. OF ONE'S OWN
1. *a contemporary:* συνηλικιώτης SYNĒLIKIOTĒS*
Gal 1.14 advanced . . beyond many of my own age

AGE, OLD
1. *old age:* γῆρας GĒRAS*
Lk 1.36 "Elizabeth in her old age has also conceived

AGENT
1. *servant:* διάκονος DIAKONOS
Gal 2.17 is Christ then an agent of sin?

AGITATOR
1. *one who causes strife:* κινῶν στάσεις (subst. part.) KINEŌ [A.6.a.4]
Acts 24. 5 "an agitator among all the Jews

AGLOW, BE
1. *boil, seethe:* ζέω ZEŌ
Rom 12.11 be aglow with the Spirit

AGO (*See also* YEAR AGO, A)
1. *from:* ἀπό (+gen.) APO [B.1.a.5]
Acts 10.30 "Four days ago, about this hour
2. *before:* πρό (+gen.) PRO [B.1.a.5]
2 Cor 12. 2 a man in Christ who fourteen years ago
2 Tim 1. 9 grace which he gave . . ages ago
Tit 1. 2 in hope . . which God . . promised ages ago

AGO, LONG
1. *for a long time:* ἔκπαλαι EKPALAI
2 Pet 3. 5 heavens existed long ago
2. *long ago:* πάλαι PALAI
Mt 11.21 "they would have repented long ago
Lk 10.13 "they would have repented long ago
Jude . 4 long ago . . designated for . . condemnation

AGONY
1. *agony:* ἀγωνία AGŌNIA*
Lk [22.44 *being in . . agony he prayed more earnestly*‡

AGREE
1. *agree:* ἐξομολογέω EXOMOLOGEŌ
Lk 22. 6 So he agreed, and sought . . to betray him
2. *be the same:* ἴσος εἶναι ISOS [B.2.a.1]
Mk 14.56 their witness did not agree
14.59 not even so did their testimony agree
3. *say the same thing:* τὸ αὐτὸ λέγειν LEGŌ [B.2.a.1]
1 Cor 1.10 I appeal . . that all of you agree
4. *think the same thing:* τὸ αὐτὸ φρονεῖν PHRONEŌ [B.2.a.1]
2 Cor 13.11 agree with one another, live in peace
Phil 4. 2 I entreat Syntyche to agree in the Lord
5. *come to, approach:* προσέρχομαι PROSERCHOMAI
1 Tim 6. 3 agree with the sound words of our Lord
6. *assent, approve:* σύμφημι SYMPHĒMI*
Rom 7.16 I agree that the law is good
7. *sound together, harmonize with:* συμφωνέω SYMPHŌNEŌ
Mt 18.19 "if two of you agree . . about anything
20. 2 "agreeing with the laborers for a denarius
20.13 " 'did you not agree with me for a denarius?
Acts 5. 9 "agreed together to tempt the Spirit
15.15 "with this the words of the prophets agree
8. *put together:* συντίθημι (mid.) SYNTITHĒMI
Jn 9.22 for the Jews had already agreed
Acts 23.20 "Jews have agreed to ask you to bring Paul
IDIOMATICALLY
a. 1 Jn 5.8 these three agree οἱ τρεῖς εἰς τὸ ἕν εἰσιν [HEIS]

AGREEMENT
1. *approval:* συγκατάθεσις SYGKATATHESIS*

2 Cor 6.16 What agreement has the temple of God?
2. *harmonious:* σύμφωνος (subst.) SYMPHŌNOS*
1 Cor 7. 5 Do not refuse . . except . . by agreement

AGRIPPA: Ἀγρίππας ə'gripə
Acts 25.13 A. the king and Bernice arrived at Caesarea
25.22 A. said . . "I should like to hear the man
25.23 A. and Bernice came with great pomp
25.24 "King A. and all who are present with us
25.26 "I have brought him before you, . . King A.
26. 1 A. said to Paul, "You have permission
26. 2 "before you, King A., I . . make my defense
26.19 "O King A., I was not disobedient
26.27 "King A., do you believe the prophets?
26.28 A. said . . "you think to make me a Christian!
26.32 A. said . . "This man could have been . . free

AGROUND, RUN
1. *bring* (ships) *to shore:* ἐπικέλλω EPIKELLŌ*
Acts 27.41 striking a shoal[e] they ran the vessel a.

AH
1. *ha!:* ἔα EA*
Lk 4.34 "Ah![m] What have you to do with us?†
2. *behold, look!:* ἴδε IDE
Jn 16.29 "Ah, now you are speaking plainly!

AHA
1. *aha!* (Lat. *vah*): οὐά OUA
Mk 15.29 "Aha! You who would destroy the temple

AHAZ: Ἀχάζ 'āhaz
Mt 1. 9 Jotham the father of A.
1. 9 A. the father of Hezekiah

AHEAD (*See also* PRO- *entries*)
AHEAD OF
AHEAD, WHAT LIES
1. *before:* ἔμπροσθεν EMPROSTHEN
[a]subst. neut. pl.
Lk 19.28 when he had said this, he went on ahead
Phil 3.13 [a]straining forward to what lies ahead
2. *before the face:* πρὸ προσώπου PRO; PROSŌPON [B.1.b]
Lk 9.52 And he sent messengers ahead of him
10. 1 sent them on ahead of him, two by two

AID, GIVE
1. *set over, direct:* προΐστημι (mid.) PROISTĒMI
Rom 12. 8 he who gives aid, with zeal

AID, WITH
1. *do a service, minister:* διακονέω (part.) DIAKONEŌ
Rom 15.25 I am going to Jerusalem with aid

AILMENT
1. *weakness, sickness:* ἀσθένεια ASTHENEIA
Gal 4.13 because of a bodily a. that I preached
1 Tim 5.23 use a little wine for . . your frequent ailments

AIM
1. *end, goal:* τέλος TELOS
1 Tim 1. 5 the aim of our charge is love

AIM AT
1. *pursue:* διώκω DIŌKŌ
1 Tim 6.11 you, man of God, . . aim at righteousness
2 Tim 2.22 aim at righteousness, faith, love, and peace
2. *foresee, provide:* προνοέω PRONOEŌ
2 Cor 8.21 we aim at what is honorable

AIM IN LIFE
1. *presentation, purpose:* πρόθεσις PROTHESIS
2 Tim 3.10 you have observed . . my aim in life

AIM, MAKE IT ONE'S
1. *seek after honor:* φιλοτιμέομαι PHILOTIMEOMAI
2 Cor 5. 9 we make it our aim to please him

AIM, MAKE S. ONE'S
1. *pursue:* διώκω DIŌKŌ
1 Cor 14. 1 Make love your aim, and earnestly desire

AIMLESSLY
1. *secretly, uncertainly:* ἀδήλως ADĒLŌS*
1 Cor 9.26 Well, I do not run aimlessly

AIR
1. *air:* ἀήρ AĒR*
Acts 22.23 cried out and . . threw dust into the air
1 Cor 9.26 I do not box as one beating the air
14. 9 you will be speaking into the air
Eph 2. 2 the prince of the power of the air
1 Th 4.17 in the clouds to meet the Lord in the air
Rev 9. 2 the sun and the air were darkened
16.17 angel poured his bowl into the air
2. *heaven, sky:* οὐρανός OURANOS
Mt 6.26 "birds of the air . . neither sow nor reap
8.20 "birds of the air have nests; but the Son
13.32 "birds of the air come and make nests
Mk 4.32 "birds of the air can make nests in its shade
Lk 8. 5 "the birds of the air devoured it
9.58 "birds of the air have nests; but the Son
13.19 "birds of the air made nests in its branches
Acts 10.12 animals and reptiles and birds of the air
11. 6 "reptiles and birds of the air

AIRS, PUT ON
1. *raise, lift:* ἐπαίρω (pass.) EPAIRŌ
2 Cor 11.20 you bear it if a man . . puts on airs

AKELDAMA: Ἀκελδαμάχ ə'keldəmə
Acts 1.19 "(was called . . Akeldama . . Field of Blood

ALABASTER FLASK
1. *vase* (made of alabaster): ἀλάβαστρος ALABASTROS
Mt 26. 7 a woman came . . with an alabaster flask[o]
Mk 14. 3 a woman came with an alabaster flask[o]
Lk 7.37 a woman . . brought an alabaster flask

ALARM
1. *fear:* φόβος PHOBOS
2 Cor 7.11 what indignation, what alarm, what longing!

ALARMED
1. *terrified:* ἔμφοβος EMPHOBOS
Acts 24.25 Felix was alarmed and said, "Go away

ALARMED, BE
1. *make a disturbance:* θορυβέω (pass.) THORYBEŌ
Acts 20.10 "Do not be alarmed, for his life is in him
2. *terrify:* θροέω (pass.) THROEŌ
Mt 24. 6 "rumors . . ; see that you are not alarmed
Mk 13. 7 "when you hear of wars . . do not be alarmed

ALAS
1. *woe, alas:* οὐαί OUAI
Mt 24.19 "alas for those who are with child!
Mk 13.17 "alas for those who are with child!
Lk 21.23 "Alas for those who are with child!
Rev 18.10 "Alas! alas! thou great city, . . Babylon!
18.16 "Alas, alas, for the great city!
18.19 "Alas, alas, for the great city!

ALERT, BE
1. *be awake, watch:* γρηγορέω GRĒGOREŌ
Acts 20.31 "Therefore be alert, remembering

ALERT, KEEP
1. *keep watch:* ἀγρυπνέω AGRYPNEŌ
Eph 6.18 To that end keep alert

ALEXANDER: Ἀλέξανδρος ˌalig'zandər
[1]son of Simon of Cyrene [2]kinsman of the high priest Annas
[3]Jew of Ephesus [4]false Christian teacher
Mk 15.21 [1]Simon of Cyrene, . . the father of A.
Acts 4. 6 [2]John and A. . . of the high-priestly family
19.33 [3]Some of the crowd prompted A.
19.33 [3]A. motioned . . to make a defense
1 Tim 1.20 [4]A., whom I have delivered to Satan
2 Tim 4.14 [4]A. the coppersmith did me great harm

ALEXANDRIA: ˌalig'zandrēə II,E-5
1. *an Alexandrian:* Ἀλεξανδρεύς [B.3.b.4]
Acts 18.24 a Jew named Apollos, a native of A.
2. *Alexandrian:* Ἀλεξανδρῖνος [A.3.a.2]
Acts 27. 6 a ship of A. sailing for Italy
28.11 we set sail in a ship . . of A.

ALEXANDRIAN: Ἀλεξανδρεύς (*See also* ALEXANDRIA 1)
Acts 6. 9 some . . Alexandrians . . arose and disputed

ALIEN
1. *foreign:* πάροικος (subst.) PAROIKOS
Acts 7. 6 "his posterity would be aliens in a land
1 Pet 2.11 I beseech you as aliens and exiles

ALIENATED, BE
1. *estrange, alienate:* ἀπαλλοτριόω (pass.) APALLOTRIOŌ
Eph 2.12 you were . . alienated from . . Israel
4.18 they are . . alienated from the life of God

ALIGHT
1. *come, go:* ἔρχομαι ERCHOMAI
Mt 3.16 the Spirit of God descending . . and alighting

ALIKE
1. *with one:* ἀπὸ μιᾶς HEIS [B.3.b.2]
Lk 14.18 "they all alike began to make excuses
CONTEXTUALLY
Rom 14. 5 while another man esteems all days alike

ALIVE
1. *live:* ζάω (part.) ZAŌ
Acts 1. 3 presented himself alive after his passion
9.41 calling the saints . . he presented her alive
20.12 they took the lad away alive
Rom 6.11 consider yourselves . . alive to God in C.
Rev 19.20 thrown alive into the lake of fire
2. *life:* ζωή (pred.) ZOĒ
Rom 8.10 spirits are alive because of righteousness
CONTEXTUALLY
Mt 6.30 "grass of the field, which today is alive

ALIVE AGAIN, BE
1. *come to life again:* ἀναζάω ANAZAŌ
Lk 15.24 " 'this my son was dead, and is alive again

ALIVE, BE
1. *be:* εἰμί EIMI
Lk 12.28 "clothes the grass which is alive . . today
2. *stay, wait:* μένω MENŌ
1 Cor 15. 6 brethren . ., most of whom are still alive
3. *live:* ζάω ZAŌ
Mt 27.63 "impostor said, while he was still alive
Mk 16.11 when they heard that he was alive[k]‡
Lk 15.32 " 'this your brother was dead, and is alive
24.23 "angels . . said that he was alive
Acts 25.19 "Jesus, . . whom Paul asserted to be alive
Rom 7. 3 adulteress . . while her husband is alive
7. 9 I was once alive apart from the law
1 Th 4.15 we who are alive . . shall not precede
4.17 we who are alive . . shall be caught up
Heb 9.17 as long as the one who made it is alive
Rev 1.18 "I died, and behold, I am alive
3. 1 " 'you have the name of being alive

ALIVE, KEEP
1. *preserve alive:* ζῳογονέω ZŌOGONEŌ
Acts 7.19 "infants, that they might not be kept alive

ALIVE, MAKE
1. *make alive:* ζῳοποιέω ZŌOPOIEŌ
1 Cor 15.22 in Christ shall all be made alive
Gal 3.21 if a law . . which could make alive
1 Pet 3.18 put to death . . but made alive
CONTEXTUALLY
Eph 2. 1 And you he made alive, when you were dead

ALIVE TOGETHER WITH, MAKE S.
1. *make alive together with:* συζωοποιέω SYZŌOPOIEŌ*
Eph 2. 5 ⟨God⟩ made us alive together with Christ
Col 2.13 you . . God made alive together with him

ALL (*See also* ABOVE ALL; ALONG, ALL; LEFT ALL ALONE, BE; MORE, ALL THE; MOST OF ALL; NOT AT ALL; NOTHING AT ALL; ONCE FOR ALL; ROUND, ALL)
1. *quite all:* ἅπας HAPAS
Mt 6.32 "Father knows that you need them all
24.39 "the flood came and swept them all away
28.11 told . . all that had taken place
Mk 1.27 they were all amazed
11.32 all held that John was a real prophet
16.15 "Go into all the world and preach[k]‡
Lk 3.21 when all the people were baptized
4. 6 "To you I will give all this authority
4.40 all those who had any that were sick
5.26 And amazement seized them all
8.37 all the people . . asked him to depart
9.15 And they . . made them all sit down
Lk 19.48 for all the people hung upon his words
20. 6 "if . . 'From men,' all the people will stone us
Jn 4.25 "Messiah . . will show us all things
Acts 2.44 all who believed were together
4.31 they were all filled with the Holy Spirit
5.16 the sick and . . afflicted . . were all healed
11.10 "all was drawn up again into heaven
16. 3 they all knew that his father was a Greek
16.28 "Do not harm yourself, for we are all here
16.33 he was baptized at once, with all his family
27.33 Paul urged them all to take some food
Eph 6.13 be able . . having done all, to stand
Jas 3. 2 we all make many mistakes
2. *each:* ἕκαστος (+pl. vb.) HEKASTOS
Rev 20.13 all were judged by what they had done
3. *whole, entire:* ὅλος HOLOS
Mt 1.22 All this took place to fulfil . . the prophet
4.23 he went about all Galilee, teaching
4.24 his fame spread throughout all Syria
9.26 the report . . went through all that district
9.31 spread his fame through all that district
13.33 "hid in . . meal, till it was all leavened
14.35 they sent round to all that region
20. 6 " 'Why do you stand here idle all day?
22.37 "You shall love the Lord your God with all your heart, and with all your soul, and with all your mind
22.40 "depend all the law and the prophets
26.56 "all this has taken place, that the scriptures
Mk 1.28 his fame . . throughout all the . . region
1.39 he went throughout all Galilee, preaching
12.30 " 'you shall love the Lord your God with all your heart, and with all your soul, and with all your mind, and with all your strength
12.33 "love him with all the heart, and with all the understanding, and with all the strength
Lk 1.65 talked about through all the hill country
4.14 a report . . through all the . . country
5. 5 "we toiled all night and took nothing!
[8.43 *spent all her living upon physicians*‡
10.27 "love the Lord your God with all your heart, and with all your soul, and with all your strength, and with all your mind
13.21 "leaven . . hid . . till it was all leavened
23. 5 "teaching throughout all Judea
Jn 4.53 he himself believed, and all his household
Acts 2. 2 a sound . . filled all the house
2.47 having favor with all the people
7.10 "governor . . over all his household
7.11 "famine throughout all Egypt and Canaan
[8.37 "*If you believe with all your heart*‡
9.31 church throughout all Judea and Galilee
9.42 known throughout all Joppa
10.37 "word . . proclaimed throughout all Judea
11.28 a great famine over all the world
13.49 word . . spread throughout all the region
18. 8 Crispus . . believed . . with all his household
19.27 "whom all Asia and the world worship
21.30 all the city was aroused
21.31 all Jerusalem was in confusion
Rom 1. 8 your faith is proclaimed in all the world
8.36 "we are being killed all the day long
10.21 "All day long I have held out my hands
Heb [3. 2 Moses . . was faithful in *all* God's house‡
3. 5 Moses was faithful in all God's house
4. *as great as, how great:* ὅσος (pl.) HOSOS
2 Cor 1.20 all the promises of God find their Yes
2 Tim 1.18 well know all the service he rendered
5. *all, every, whole:* πᾶς PAS
Mt 1.17 all the generations from Abraham
2. 3 the king . . was troubled, and all Jerusalem
2. 4 all the chief priests and scribes of the people
2.16 he . . killed all the male children in Bethlehem and in all that region
3. 5 all Judea and all the region about the Jordan
3.15 "fitting for us to fulfil all righteousness
4. 8 devil . . showed him all the kingdoms

Mt 4. 9 "All these . . if you will . . worship me
4.24 brought him all the sick, those afflicted
5.15 "a lamp . . gives light to all in the house
5.18 "not an iota . . until all is accomplished
6.29 "even Solomon in all his glory
6.32 "the Gentiles seek all these things
6.33 "all these things shall be yours as well
8.16 he . . healed all who were sick
8.34 all the city came out to meet Jesus
9.35 Jesus went about all the cities
10.22 "hated by all for my name's sake
10.30 "the hairs of your head are all numbered
11.13 "all the prophets and the law prophesied
11.27 "All things have been delivered to me
11.28 "Come to me, all who labor
12.15 many followed him, and he healed them all
12.23 all the people were amazed
13.32 "the smallest of all seeds
13.34 All this Jesus said . . in parables
13.41 "his angels . . will gather . . all causes of sin
13.44 "in his joy he goes and sells all that he has
13.46 "sold all that he had and bought it
13.51 "Have you understood all this?
13.56 "are not all his sisters with us?
13.56 "Where then did this man get all this?
14.20 they all ate and were satisfied
14.35 they . . brought to him all that were sick
15.37 they all ate and were satisfied
17.11 "Elijah does come, and he is to restore all
18.25 "ordered him to be sold, with . . all . . he had
18.31 "reported . . all that had taken place
18.32 " 'wicked servant! I forgave you all that debt
18.34 "to the jailers,[h] till he should pay all
19.11 "Not all men can receive this saying
19.20 "All these I have observed
19.26 "with God all things are possible
21.10 all the city was stirred
21.12 Jesus . . drove out all who sold and bought
21.26 "all hold that John was a prophet
22.10 " 'servants . . gathered all whom they found
22.27 "After them all, the woman died
22.28 "to which . . ? For they all had her
23. 5 "They do all their deeds to be seen by men
23. 8 "you are all brethren
23.27 "full of . . bones and all uncleanness
23.35 "all the righteous blood shed on earth
23.36 "all this will come upon this generation
24. 2 "You see all these, do you not?
24. 8 "all this is but the beginning
24. 9 "hated by all nations for my name's sake
24.14 "this gospel . . a testimony to all nations
24.30 "all the tribes of the earth will mourn
24.33 "when you see all these things, you know
24.34 "not pass away till all these things take place
24.47 "he will set him over all his possessions
25. 5 "they all slumbered and slept
25. 7 "all those maidens . . trimmed their lamps
25.31 "Son of man . . and all the angels with him
25.32 "Before him will be . . all the nations
26. 1 Jesus . . finished all these sayings
26.27 "Drink of it, all of you
26.31 "You will all fall away because of me
26.33 "Though they all fall away because of you
26.35 And so said all the disciples
26.52 "all who take the sword will perish
26.56 all the disciples forsook him and fled
26.70 he denied it before them all
27. 1 all the chief priests . . took counsel
27.22 They all said, "Let him be crucified
27.25 all . . answered, "His blood be on us
27.45 darkness over all the land[m]
28.18 "All authority . . has been given to me
28.19 "make disciples of all nations, baptizing
28.20 "observe all that I have commanded
Mk 1. 5 all the country of Judea, and all the people of Jerusalem
1.32 they brought to him all who were sick
Mk 2.12 he . . went out before them all
2.12 they were all amazed and glorified God
2.13 all the crowd gathered about him
3.28 all sins will be forgiven the sons of men
4.13 "will you understand all the parables?
4.31 "a grain of mustard seed, . . smallest of all
4.32 "it . . becomes the greatest of all shrubs
5.20 and all men marveled
5.26 spent all that she had, and . . grew worse
5.40 he put them all outside
6.30 apostles . . told him all that they had done
6.33 they ran there on foot from all the towns
6.39 he commanded them all to sit down
6.41 he divided the two fish among them all
6.42 they all ate and were satisfied
6.50 they all saw him, and were terrified
7. 3 (all the Jews, do not eat unless they wash
7.14 "Hear me, all of you, and understand
7.19 (Thus he declared all foods clean
7.23 "All these evil things come from within
7.37 "He has done all things well
9.12 "Elijah does come first to restore all things
9.15 all the crowd . . were greatly amazed
9.23 "All things are possible to him who believes
9.35 "If any one would be first, he must be last of all and servant of all
10.20 "all these I have observed from my youth
10.27 "all things are possible with God
10.44 "first among you must be slave of all
11.17 " 'house of prayer for all the nations
11.18 all the multitude was astonished
12.22 "Last of all the woman also died
12.28 "Which commandment is the first of all?
12.33 "to love . . is . . more than all . . sacrifices
12.43 "this poor widow has put in more than all
12.44 "all contributed out of their abundance
13. 4 "when . . are all to be accomplished?
13.10 "gospel must . . be preached to all nations
13.13 "you will be hated by all for my . . sake
13.23 "I have told you all things beforehand
13.30 "will not pass away before all these things
13.37 "And what I say to you I say to all: Watch
14.23 he gave it to them, and they all drank of it
14.27 Jesus said . . "You will all fall away
14.29 "Even though they all fall away, I will not
14.31 they all said the same
14.36 "Father, all things are possible to thee
14.50 they all forsook him, and fled
14.53 all the chief priests . . were assembled
14.64 all condemned him as deserving death
[16.[end] *they reported . . all . . they had been told*‡
Lk 1. 3 having followed all things closely[a]
1. 6 walking in all the commandments
1.48 "all generations will call me blessed
1.63 "His name is John." And . . all marveled
1.65 fear came on all their neighbors
1.65 all these things were talked about
1.66 all who heard them laid them up
1.71 "saved . . from the hand of all who hate us
1.75 "before him all the days of our life
2. 1 that all the world should be enrolled
2. 3 all went to be enrolled
2.10 "news . . which will come to all the people
2.18 all who heard it wondered
2.19 Mary kept all these things . . in her heart
2.20 praising God for all they had heard and seen
2.31 "prepared in the presence of all peoples
2.38 spoke of him to all who were looking
2.47 all who heard him were amazed
2.51 mother kept all these things in her heart
3. 3 into all the region about the Jordan
3. 6 "all flesh shall see the salvation of God
3.15 all men questioned in their hearts
3.16 John answered them all
3.19 all the evil things that Herod had done
3.20 ⟨Herod⟩ added this to them all
4. 5 the devil . . showed him all the kingdoms

Lk 4. 7 "If you . . worship me, it shall all be yours
4.15 he taught . . , being glorified by all
4.20 eyes of all in the synagogue were fixed
4.22 all spoke well of him, and wondered
4.25 "there came a great famine over all the land
4.28 all in the synagogue were filled with wrath
4.36 they were all amazed
5. 9 he was astonished, and all . . with him
6.10 he looked around on them all
6.17 multitude of people from all Judea
6.19 all the crowd sought to touch him
6.19 power came forth . . and healed them all
6.26 "Woe to you, when all speak well of you
7. 1 After he had ended all his sayings
7.16 Fear seized them all
7.17 through . . all the surrounding country
7.18 disciples of John told him . . all these things
7.29 (all the people . . justified God
7.35 "wisdom is justified by all her children
8.40 they were all waiting for him
8.45 When all denied it, Peter[c] said, "Master
8.47 she . . declared in the presence of all
8.52 all were weeping and bewailing her
9. 1 power and authority over all demons
9. 7 Herod . . heard of all that was done
9.13 "to go and buy food for all these people
9.17 And all ate and were satisfied
9.23 he said to all . . "let him . . take up his cross
9.43 all were astonished at the majesty of God
9.43 they were all marveling at everything
9.48 "he who is least among you all is . . great
10.19 "authority . . over all the power of the enemy
10.22 "All things have been delivered to me
11.50 "blood of all . . prophets . . may be required
12. 7 "the hairs of your head are all numbered
12.15 "Take heed, and beware of all covetousness
12.18 " 'I will store all my grain and my goods
12.27 "even Solomon in all his glory
12.30 "all the nations . . seek these things
12.41 "telling this parable for us or for all?
12.44 "he will set him over all his possessions
13. 2 "worse sinners than all the other Galileans?
13. 3 "unless you repent you will all . . perish
13. 4 "worse offenders than all the others?
13. 5 "unless you repent you will all . . perish
13.17 all his adversaries were put to shame
13.17 all the people rejoiced at all the glorious things that were done by him
13.27 " 'depart . . , all you workers of iniquity!
13.28 "when you see . . all the prophets
14.10 "you will be honored in the presence of all
14.18 "all alike began to make excuses
14.29 "all who see it begin to mock him
14.33 "whoever . . does not renounce all . . he has
15. 1 sinners were all drawing near to hear him
15.13 "the younger son gathered all he had
15.31 " 'Son, . . all that is mine is yours
16.14 Pharisees . . heard all this, and . . scoffed
16.26 " 'besides all this . . a great chasm . . fixed
17.10 "when you have done all that is commanded
17.27 "the flood came and destroyed them all
17.29 "fire and sulphur . . destroyed them all
18.12 " 'I give tithes of all that I get
18.21 "All these I have observed from my youth
18.22 "Sell all that you have and distribute
18.43 all the people . . gave praise to God
19. 7 when they saw it they all murmured
19.37 praise God . . for all the mighty works
20.38 "not God of the dead . . for all live to him
20.45 in the hearing of all the people he said
21. 3 "this poor widow has put in more than all
21. 4 "all contributed out of their abundance
21. 4 "she . . put in all the living that she had
21.12 "before all this they will . . persecute you
21.17 "hated by all for my name's sake
21.22 "vengeance, to fulfil all that is written
21.24 "they will . . be led captive among all nations

Lk 21.29 "Look at the fig tree, and all the trees
21.32 "will not pass away till all has taken place
21.35 "upon all who dwell upon . . earth
21.36 "watch at all times, praying
21.36 "escape all these things that will take place
21.38 all the people came to him in the temple
22.70 they all said, "Are you the Son of God?
23.48 all the multitudes who assembled . . returned
23.49 all his acquaintances . . saw these things
24. 9 returning from the tomb they told all this to the eleven and to all the rest
24.14 about all these things that had happened
24.19 "prophet . . before God and all the people
24.21 "besides all this, it is now the third day
24.25 "all that the prophets have spoken!
24.27 beginning with Moses and all the prophets
24.27 he interpreted . . in all the scriptures
24.47 "preached in his name to all nations[z]

Jn 1. 3 all things were made through him
1. 7 that all might believe through him
1.16 from his fulness have we all received
2.15 he drove them all . . out of the temple
2.25(24) because he knew all men
3.26 "baptizing, and all are going to him
3.31 who comes from above is above all
3.31 who comes from heaven is above all
3.35 Father . . has given all things into his hand
4.29 "a man who told me all that I ever did
4.39 "He told me all that I ever did
4.45 Galileans . . , having seen all that he had done
5.20 "Father loves the Son, and shows him all
5.22 "Father . . has given all judgment to the Son
5.23 "that all may honor the Son
5.28 "all who are in the tombs will hear
6.37 "All that the Father gives me will come
6.39 "lose nothing of all that he has given me
6.45 " 'they shall all be taught by God
7.21 "I did one deed, and you all marvel
8. 2 all the people came to him[r]‡
10. 4 "When he has brought out all his own
10. 8 "All who came before me are thieves
10.29 "My Father . . is greater than all
12.32 "I . . will draw all men to myself
13. 3 Father had given all things into his hands
13.11 why he said, "You are not all clean
13.18 "I am not speaking of you all
13.35 "all men will know that you are my disciples
14.26 "Holy Spirit . . will teach you all things
14.26 "bring to . . remembrance all . . I have said
15.15 "all that I have heard from my Father
15.21 "all this they will do to you on my account
16.13 "Spirit . . will guide you into all the truth
16.15 "All that the Father has is mine
16.30 "we know that you know all things
17. 2 "thou hast given him power over all flesh, to give eternal life to all
17.10 "all mine are thine, and thine are mine
17.21 "that they may all be one
18. 4 Jesus, knowing all that was to befall him
18.20 "the temple, where all Jews come together
19.28 Jesus, knowing that all was now finished

Acts 1. 1 I have dealt with all that Jesus began
1. 8 "you shall be my witnesses in . . all Judea
1.14 All these . . devoted themselves to prayer
1.18 "(he burst . . and all his bowels gushed out
1.19 "(known to all the inhabitants of Jerusalem
1.21 "who have accompanied us . . all the time
1.24 "Lord, who knowest the hearts of all men
2. 1 they were all together in one place
2. 4 they were all filled with the Holy Spirit
2. 7 "Are not all these . . speaking Galileans?
2.12 all were amazed and perplexed
2.14 "all who dwell in Jerusalem, . . give ear
2.17 " 'I will pour out my Spirit upon all flesh
2.32 "Jesus God raised up, . . we all are witnesses
2.36 "Let all the house of Israel . . know
2.39 "For the promise is to you . . and to all

Acts 2.44 all who believed were together
2.45 they . . distributed ⟨their possessions⟩ . . to all
3. 9 all the people saw him walking
3.11 all the people ran together to them
3.16 "perfect health in the presence of you all
3.18 "what God foretold by . . all the prophets
3.21 "time for establishing all that God spoke
3.24 all the prophets who have spoken
3.25 " 'all the families of the earth be blessed
4.10 "be it known to you all, and to all the people of Israel
4.16 "manifest to all the inhabitants of Jerusalem
4.21 all . . praised God for what had happened
4.29 "to speak thy word with all boldness
4.33 great grace was upon them all
5. 5 great fear came upon all who heard
5.11 great fear came . . upon all who heard
5.12 all together in Solomon's Portico
5.17 the high priest . . and all who were with him
5.20 "Go . . and speak to the people all the words
5.21 high priest . . called . . all the senate
5.34 Gamaliel, . . held in honor by all
5.36 "all who followed him were dispersed
5.37 "all who followed him were scattered
6.15 all who sat in the council saw
7.10 "rescued him out of all his afflictions
7.14 "Jacob his father and all his kindred
7.22 "Moses was instructed in all the wisdom
7.50 " 'Did not my hand make all these things?
8. 1 they were all scattered throughout
8.10 They all gave heed to him
8.27 Ethiopian . . in charge of all her treasure
8.40 Philip . . preached the gospel to all the towns
9.14 "to bind all who call upon thy name
9.21 all who heard him were amazed
9.26 they were all afraid of him
9.32 Peter went here and there among them all
9.35 all the residents of Lydda . . saw him
9.39 All the widows stood beside him
9.40 Peter put them all outside and knelt down
10. 2 a devout man . . with all his household
10.33 "we are all here present in the sight of God
10.33 all that you have been commanded
10.36 "Jesus Christ (he is Lord of all
10.38 "healing all that were oppressed
10.39 "we are witnesses to all that he did
10.41 "not to all the people but to us
10.43 "To him all the prophets bear witness
10.44 Spirit fell on all who heard the word
11.14 " 'will be saved, . . and a. your household
11.23 he exhorted them all to remain faithful
12.11 "all that the Jewish people were expecting
13.10 "you enemy of all righteousness, full of all deceit and villainy
13.22 " 'David . . , who will do all my will
13.24 "repentance to all the people
13.29 "they had fulfilled all that was written
14.15 "earth and the sea and all that is in them
14.16 allowed all the nations . . their own ways
15. 3 they gave great joy to all the brethren
15.12 all the assembly kept silence
15.17 " 'all the Gentiles . . called by my name
16.26 immediately all the doors were opened
16.32 they spoke . . to all that were in his house
17. 7 "they are all acting against . . Caesar
17.11 they received the word with all eagerness
17.21 all the Athenians and the foreigners
17.25 "he himself gives to all men life
17.26 "men to live on all the face of the earth
17.30 "commands all men everywhere to repent
17.31 "he has given assurance to all men
18. 2 Claudius had commanded all the Jews
18.17 they all seized Sosthenes . . and beat him
18.23 went . . strengthening all the disciples
19. 7 There were about twelve of them in all
19.10 all the residents of Asia heard the word
19.17 this became known to all residents

Acts 19.17 fear fell upon them all
19.19 books . . and burned them in the sight of all
19.26 "at Ephesus but . . throughout all Asia
19.34 all . . cried out, "Great is Artemis!
20.18 "I lived among you all the time
20.19 "serving the Lord with all humility
20.25 "all you among whom I have gone
20.26 "I am innocent of the blood of all of you
20.28 "Take heed to yourselves and . . all the flock
20.32 "inheritance among all . . who are sanctified
20.35 "In all things I have shown you
20.36 he knelt down and prayed with them all
20.37 they all wept and embraced Paul
21. 5 they all . . brought us on our way
21.18 all the elders were present
21.20 "those who have believed . . are all zealous
21.21 "you teach all the Jews . . among the Gentiles
21.24 "Thus all will know . . about you
21.27 Jews from Asia . . stirred up all the crowd
22. 3 "I am a Jew . . zealous for God as you all are
22.10 " 'you will be told all that is appointed
22.12 "Ananias, . . well spoken of by all the Jews
22.15 " 'you will be a witness for him to all men
22.30 commanded . . all the council to meet
23. 1 "I have lived . . in all good conscience
24. 3 "we accept this with all gratitude
24. 5 "an agitator among all the Jews
25.24 "King Agrippa and all who are present
26. 2 "my defense . . against all the accusations
26. 3 "you are especially familiar with all customs
26. 4 "My . . life . . is known by all the Jews
26.11 "I punished them . . in all the synagogues
26.14 "when we had all fallen to the ground
26.20 "throughout all the country of Judea
26.29 "I would to God that . . all who hear me
27.20 all hope of our being saved was . . abandoned
27.24 " 'God has granted you all those who sail
27.35 in the presence of all he broke it
27.36 all were encouraged and ate some food
27.37 (in all two hundred and seventy-six[d]
27.44 And so it was that all escaped to land
28. 2 the natives . . welcomed us all
28.30 he . . welcomed all who came to him

Rom 1. 5 obedience of faith . . among all the nations
1. 7 To all God's beloved in Rome
1. 8 I thank my God . . for all of you
1.18 wrath . . is revealed . . against all ungodliness
3. 9 all men . . are under the power of sin
3.12 "All have turned aside, . . no one does good
3.22 righteousness of God . . for all who believe
3.23 all have sinned and fall short
4.11 the father of all who believe
4.16 promise . . guaranteed to all his descendants
4.16 faith of Abraham, . . father of us all
5.12 as sin came . . so death spread to all men because all men sinned
5.18 as one . . trespass led to condemnation for all . . , so one . . act . . leads to . . life for all
8.32 He who . . gave him up for us all, will he not also give us all things with him?
8.37 in all these things we are . . conquerors
9. 5 God who is over all be blessed for ever[n]
9. 6 not all . . descended from Israel belong
9. 7 not all are children of Abraham
9.17 "name . . proclaimed in all the earth
10.12 the same Lord is Lord of all and bestows his riches upon all who call upon him
10.16 they have not all obeyed the gospel
10.18 "Their voice has gone out to all the earth
11.26 all Israel will be saved
11.32 God has consigned all men to disobedience, that he may have mercy upon all
11.36 For from him . . and to him are all things
12. 4 all the members do not have the same
12.17 what is noble in the sight of all
12.18 If possible . . live peaceably with all
13. 7 Pay all of them their dues

Rom 14. 5 another man esteems all days alike
14.10 we shall all stand before the judgment seat
15.11 "Praise the Lord, all Gentiles, and let all the peoples praise him
15.13 the God of hope fill you with all joy
15.14 full of goodness, filled with all knowledge
15.33 The God of peace be with you all
16. 4 all the churches of the Gentiles give thanks
16.15 all the saints who are with them
16.16 All the churches of Christ greet you
16.19 your obedience is known to all
[16.24 *The grace of . . Christ be with you all*‡
16.26 ⟨mystery⟩ made known to all nations
1 Cor 1. 2 saints . . with all . . who . . call on . . our Lord
1. 5 you were enriched in him with all speech and all knowledge
1.10 I appeal . . that all of you agree
2.15 The spiritual man judges all things
3.21 all things are yours
3.22 whether . . life or death . . , all are yours
4.13 we . . are now . . the offscouring of all things
6.12 "All things are lawful for me," but not all things are helpful. "All things are lawful for me," but I will not be enslaved
7. 7 I wish that all were as I myself am
7.17 This is my rule in all the churches
8. 1 we know . . "all of us possess knowledge
8. 6 the Father, from whom are all things
8. 6 Christ, through whom are all things
8. 7 However, not all possess this knowledge
9.19 though I am free from all men, I have made myself a slave to all
9.22 I have become all things to all men, that I might . . save some
9.23 I do it all for the sake of the gospel
9.24 in a race all the runners compete
9.25 athlete exercises self-control in all things
10. 1 our fathers were all under the cloud, and all passed through the sea
10. 2 all were baptized into Moses
10. 3 all ate the same supernatural[o] food
10. 4 all drank the same supernatural[o] drink
10.17 we all partake of the one bread
10.23 "All things are lawful," but not all things are helpful. "All things are lawful," but not all things build up
10.31 do all to the glory of God
10.33 I try to please all men in everything I do
11.12 (all things are from God
12. 6 God who inspires them all in every one
12.11 All these are inspired by one . . Spirit
12.12 all the members of the body . . are one
12.13 we were all baptized into one body
12.13 all were made to drink of one Spirit
12.19 If all were a single organ
12.26 If one member suffers, all suffer together; if one member is honored, all rejoice
12.29 Are all apostles? Are all prophets? Are all teachers? Do all work miracles?
12.30 Do all possess gifts of healing? Do all speak with tongues? Do all interpret?
13. 2 if I . . understand all mysteries and all knowledge, and if I have all faith
13. 3 If I give . . all I have, . . but have not love
13. 7 Love bears all things, believes all things, hopes all things, endures all things
14. 5 Now I want you all to speak in tongues
14.18 I speak in tongues more than you all
14.23 If . . all speak in tongues
14.24 if all prophesy, . . an unbeliever . . is convicted by all, . . called to account by all
14.26 Let all things be done for edification
14.31 you can all prophesy one by one, so that all may learn and all be encouraged
14.33 As in all the churches of the saints
14.40 all things should be done decently
15. 7 he appeared . . then to all the apostles
1 Cor 15. 8 Last of all . . he appeared also to me
15.19 we are of all men most to be pitied
15.22 as in Adam all die, so also in Christ shall all be made alive
15.25 until he has put all his enemies under
15.27 "For God[z] has put all things in subjection
15.27 "All things are put in subjection
15.27 he is excepted who put all things under
15.28 When all things are subjected to him
15.28 the Son . . put all things under him
15.39 not all flesh is alike
15.51 We shall not all sleep, but we shall all be changed
16.14 Let all that you do be done in love
16.20 All the brethren send greetings
16.24 My love be with you all in Christ
2 Cor 1. 1 To the church of God . . , with all the saints
1. 3 Blessed be the God . . of all comfort
1. 4 ⟨God⟩ comforts us in all our affliction
2. 3 I felt sure of all of you, that my joy would be the joy of you all
2. 5 if any one has caused pain . . to you all
3. 2 our letter . . to be . . read by all men
3.18 we all . . are being changed into his likeness
4.15 it is all for your sake
5.10 we must all appear before the judgment
5.14 one has died for all; therefore all have died
5.15 he died for all, that those . . might live
5.18 All this is from God, who . . reconciled us
7. 4 With all our affliction, I am overjoyed
7.13 his mind has been set at rest by you all
7.15 he remembers the obedience of you all
8. 7 as you excel . . in all earnestness
8.18 who is famous among all the churches
9.13 your contribution . . for all others
11. 6 we have made this plain . . in all things
11.28 my anxiety for all the churches
12.12 The signs . . were performed . . in all patience
12.19 all for your upbuilding, beloved
13. 2 all the others . . I warn . . now while absent
13.13(12) All the saints greet you
13.14(13) the Holy Spirit be with you all
Gal 1. 2 all the brethren who are with me
2.14 I said to Cephas before them all
3. 8 "In you shall all the nations be blessed
3.10 "every one who does not abide by all things
3.22 scripture consigned all things to sin
3.26 you are all sons of God, through faith
3.28 you are all one in Christ Jesus
4. 1 the heir . . is the owner of all the estate
6. 6 Let him . . share all good things
6.10 let us do good to all men
Eph 1. 9(8) known to us in all wisdom and insight
1.10 a plan . . to unite all things in him
1.11 who accomplishes all things
1.15 your love[c] toward all the saints
1.21 far above all rule and authority
1.22 he has put all things under his feet
1.22 head over all things for the church
1.23 the fulness of him who fills all in all
2. 3 Among these we all once lived
3. 8 I am the very least of all the saints
3. 9 God who created all things
3.18 to comprehend with all the saints
3.19 be filled with all the fulness of God
3.20 more abundantly than all that we ask
3.21 glory . . to all generations, for ever
4. 2 with all lowliness and meekness
4. 6 one God and Father of us all, who is above all and through all and in all
4.10 (ascended far above all the heavens, that he might fill all things
4.13 until we all attain to . . mature manhood
4.31 Let all bitterness . . be put away from you, with all malice
5. 3 all impurity . . must not even be named
5. 9 (light is found in all that is good

Eph 6.16 besides all these taking the shield
6.16 you can quench all the flaming darts
6.18 Pray at all times in the Spirit, with all prayer and supplication
6.18 keep alert with all perseverance, making supplication for all the saints
6.24 Grace be with all who love our Lord Jesus
Phil 1. 1 To all the saints in Christ Jesus
1. 3 I thank my God in all my remembrance
1. 4 in every prayer of mine for you all
1. 7 right for me to feel thus about you all
1. 7 you are all partakers with me of grace
1. 8 how I yearn for you all
1. 9 love may abound . . , with . . all discernment
1.13 it has become known . . to all the rest
1.25 I shall remain and continue with you all
2.14 Do all things without grumbling
2.17 I am glad and rejoice with you all
2.21 all look after their own interests
2.26 he has been longing for you all
2.29 receive him in the Lord with all joy
3. 8 I have suffered the loss of all things
3.21 the power . . to subject all things to himself
4. 5 Let all men know your forbearance
4. 7 peace . . , which passes all understanding
4.12 in any and all circumstances
4.13 I can do all things in him
4.22 All the saints greet you
Col 1. 4 the love which you have for all the saints
1. 9 knowledge . . in all spiritual wisdom
1.11 May you be strengthened with all power
1.11 for all endurance and patience with joy
1.15 the first-born of all creation
1.16 in him all things were created
1.16 all things were created through him
1.17 He is before all things, and in him all things hold together
1.19 in him all the fulness of God
1.20 to reconcile to himself all things
1.28 teaching every man in all wisdom
2. 2 to have all the riches of . . understanding
2. 3 in whom are hid all the treasures of wisdom
2.10 the head of all rule and authority
2.13 having forgiven us all our trespasses
2.22 (things which all perish as they are used
3. 8 put them all away: anger, wrath
3.11 Here there cannot be Greek and Jew, . . but Christ is all, and in all
3.14 above all these put on love
3.16 admonish one another in all wisdom
4. 7 Tychicus will tell you all about my affairs
4.12 fully assured in all the will of God
1 Th 1. 2 We give thanks to God always for you all
1. 7 an example to all the believers
2.15 who . . displease God and oppose all men
3. 7 in all our distress and affliction
3. 9 all the joy which we feel for your sake
3.12 love to one another and to all men
3.13 coming of our Lord Jesus with all his saints
4. 6 the Lord is an avenger in all these things
4.10 you do love all the brethren
5. 5 you are all sons of light
5.14 help the weak, be patient with them all
5.15 do good to one another and to all
5.18 give thanks in all circumstances
5.26 Greet all the brethren with a holy kiss
5.27 that this letter be read to all the brethren
2 Th 1. 4 your . . faith in all your persecutions
1.10 marveled at in all who have believed
2. 9 the lawless one . . will be with all power
2.10 with all wicked deception
2.12 so that all may be condemned
3. 2 for not all have faith
3.16 may the Lord of peace himself give you peace at all times in all ways. The Lord be with you all
3.18 grace of our Lord . . be with you all
1 Tim 2. 1 First of all, then, I urge that . . thanksgivings be made for all men
2. 2 kings and all who are in high positions
2. 4 who desires all men to be saved
2. 6 gave himself as a ransom for all
2.11 learn in silence with all submissiveness
3.11 women . . must be . . faithful in all things
4.10 God, who is the Savior of all men
4.15 so that all may see your progress
5. 2 ⟨treat⟩ women like sisters, in all purity
5.20 rebuke them in the presence of all
6. 1 all who are under the yoke of slavery
6.10 love of money is the root of all evils
6.13 God who gives life to all things
2 Tim 1.15 all who are in Asia turned away
3. 9 their folly will be plain to all
3.11 from them all the Lord rescued me
3.12 all who desire to live a godly life
3.16 All scripture is inspired by God[d]†
4. 8 all who have loved his appearing
4.16 At my first defense . . all deserted me
4.17 that all the Gentiles might hear
4.21 Linus and Claudia and all the brethren
Tit 1.15 To the pure all things are pure
2. 7 Show yourself in all respects a model
2.11 grace of God . . for the salvation of all men
2.14 gave himself . . to redeem us from all iniquity
2.15 exhort and reprove with all authority
3. 2 show perfect courtesy toward all men
3.15 All who are with me send greetings
3.15 Grace be with you all
Phm . 5 your love . . toward . . all the saints
. 6 all the good that is ours in Christ
Heb 1. 2 a Son, . . the heir of all things
1. 6 "Let all God's angels worship him
1.11 "they will all grow old like a garment
1.14 Are they not all ministering spirits?
2.10 for whom and by whom all things exist
2.11 who are sanctified have all one origin
3. 4 (the builder of all things is God
3.16 Was it not all those who left Egypt?
4. 4 "God rested . . from all his works
4.13 all are open and laid bare
5. 9 the source of eternal salvation to all
6.16 in all their disputes an oath is final
8.11 "they shall not teach . . for all shall know me
9.19 declared by Moses to all the people
9.19 sprinkled . . the book . . and all the people
9.21 all the vessels used in worship
11.13 These all died in faith
11.39 all these, . . well attested by their faith
12. 8 discipline, in which all have participated
12.11 all discipline seems painful
12.14 Strive for peace with all men
12.23 a judge who is God of all
13. 4 Let marriage be held in honor among all
13.18 desiring to act honorably in all things
13.24 Greet all your leaders and all the saints
13.25 Grace be with all of you. Amen
Jas 1. 2 Count it all joy, my brethren
1. 5 God, who gives to all men generously
1. 8 double-minded man, unstable in all his ways
1.21 put away all filthiness and rank growth
2.10 whoever . . fails . . has become guilty of all
4.16 All such boasting is evil
5.12 above all, my brethren, do not swear
1 Pet 1.15 be holy yourselves in all your conduct
1.24 "All flesh is like grass and all its glory like the flower of grass
2. 1 put away all malice and all guile and insincerity and envy and all slander
2.17 Honor all men. Love the brotherhood
2.18 be submissive . . with all respect
3. 8 Finally, all of you, have unity of spirit
4. 7 The end of all things is at hand
4. 8 Above all hold unfailing your love
5. 5 Clothe yourselves, all of you

1 Pet 5. 7 Cast all your anxieties on him
5.10 the God of all grace . . strengthen[m] you
5.14 Peace to all of you that are in Christ
2 Pet 1. 3 His divine power has granted . . all things
3. 4 "all things have continued as they were
3. 9 wishing . . that all should reach repentance
3.11 Since all these things are . . to be dissolved
3.16 speaking of this . . in all his letters
1 Jn 1. 7 blood of Jesus . . cleanses us from all sin
1. 9 cleanse us from all unrighteousness
2.16 all . . in the world . . is not of the Father
2.19 might be plain that they all are not of us
2.20 anointed by the Holy One, . . you all know[d]‡
5.17 All wrongdoing is sin
2 Jn . 1 also all who know the truth
3 Jn . 2 I pray that all may go well with you
Jude .15 "to execute judgment on all, and to convict all the ungodly of all their deeds . . and of all the harsh things
.25 before all time and now and for ever
Rev 1. 7 all tribes of the earth will wail
2.23 " 'all the churches shall know that I am he
4.11 "for thou didst create all things
5. 6 spirits of God sent out into all the earth
5.13 the sea, and all therein
7.11 all the angels stood round the throne
8. 3 prayers of all the saints upon the . . altar
8. 7 all green grass was burnt up
12. 5 a male child . . to rule all the nations
13. 8 all who dwell on earth will worship it
13.12 exercises all the authority of the first beast
13.16 it causes all . . to be marked on the . . hand
14. 8 "Babylon . . , who made all nations drink
15. 4 "All nations shall come and worship thee
18. 3 "all nations have drunk[k] the wine
18.12 all kinds of scented wood, all articles of ivory, all articles of costly wood
18.14 "all thy dainties . . are lost to thee!
18.17 all shipmasters and seafaring men
18.17 all whose trade is on the sea
18.19 "the great city where all . . grew rich!
18.23 "all nations were deceived by thy sorcery
18.24 "the blood . . of all who have been slain
19. 5 "Praise our God, all you his servants
19.17 with a loud voice he called to all the birds
19.18 "the flesh of all men, both free and slave
19.21 all the birds were gorged with their flesh
21. 5 "Behold, I make all things new
21. 8 "all liars . . shall be in the lake that burns
22.21 grace . . be with all the saints[t]‡

IDIOMATICALLY
a. Mk 10.48 he cried out all the more *ὁ . . πολλῷ μᾶλλον ἔκραζεν* [MALLON]
b. Lk 18.39 he cried out all the more *αὐτὸς . . πολλῷ μᾶλλον ἔκραζεν* [MALLON]
c. Heb 10.12 when Christ[w] had offered for all time a single sacrifice for sins *οὗτος . . μίαν ὑπὲρ ἁμαρτιῶν προσενέγκας θυσίαν εἰς τὸ διηνεκές* [DIĒNEKĒS]
d. Heb 10.14 he has perfected for all time *τετελείωκεν εἰς τὸ διηνεκές* [DIĒNEKĒS]
e. Heb 10.25 all the more as you see the Day *τοσούτῳ μᾶλλον ὅσῳ βλέπετε . . τὴν ἡμέραν* [TOSOUTOS]

CONTEXTUALLY
Rev 7. 9 multitude . . from all tribes and peoples

ALL, AT
1. *origin, rule:* ἀρχή (acc.) ARCHĒ
Jn [8.25 "*Why do I talk to you at all?*†
2. *actually:* ὅλως HOLŌS
a+neg.
Mt 5.34 aBut I say to you, Do not swear at all
1 Cor 6. 7 To have lawsuits at all . . is defeat
15.29 aIf the dead are not raised at all
3. *on the whole:* καθόλου (neg.) KATHOLOU*
Acts 4.18 charged them not to speak or teach at all
4. *in all ways, assuredly:* πάντως (+neg.) PANTŌS
Rom 3. 9 No, not at all
1 Cor 5.10 not at all meaning the immoral
16.12 it was not at all his will[b]
5. *anyone, any:* τὶς (neut.) TIS II
Acts 25.8
Phm .18

ALL KINDS OF
ALL MANNER OF
1. *all, every, whole:* πᾶς PAS
Mt 5.11 "when men . . utter all kinds of evil
Acts 10.12 In it were all kinds of animals
Rom 1.29 filled with all manner of wickedness
7. 8 sin . . wrought . . all kinds of covetousness

ALL MEANS, BY
1. *in all ways, assuredly:* πάντως PANTŌS
1 Cor 9.22 that I might by all means save some

ALL OF THEM
1. *both:* ἀμφότεροι (subst. pl.) AMPHOTEROI
Acts 19.16 the man . . mastered all of them

ALL OVER
1. *whole, entire:* ὅλος HOLOS [A.3.b.2]
Jn 13.10 "but he is clean all over

ALL SIDES, ON
1. *from every side:* πάντοθεν PANTOTHEN
Heb 9. 4 covered on all sides with gold

ALL THAT
1. *all who:* ὅσος (neut. pl.) HOSOS
Mt 13.44 "sells all that he has and buys that field
Mk 3. 8 multitude, hearing all that he did, came
Acts 14.27 declared all that God had done with them
15. 4 they declared all that God had done
Rev 1. 2 bore witness . . even to all that he saw

ALL THE WAY TO
1. *even unto:* ἄχρι καί ACHRI [B.3.b.4]
2 Cor 10.14 the first to come all the way to you

ALL, THEM
1. *both:* ἀμφότεροι (subst. acc. pl.) AMPHOTEROI
Acts 23. 8 the Pharisees acknowledge them all

ALL THIS
1. *so large, so many:* τοσοῦτος TOSOUTOS
Rev 18.17 all this wealth has been laid waste

ALL WHO
1. *as great as, how great:* ὅσος (pl.) HOSOS
Mk 3.10 all who had diseases pressed upon him
Jn 2.12 to all who received him . . he gave power
Acts 4. 6 all who were of the high-priestly family
Rom 2.12 All who have sinned without the law
2.12 all who have sinned under the law
6. 3 all . . who have been baptized into Christ
8.14 all who are led by the Spirit of God
Gal 3.10 all who rely on works of the law
6.16 Peace . . upon all who walk by this rule
Col 2. 1 all who have not seen my face
1 Tim 6. 1 all who are under the yoke of slavery
Heb 2.15 deliver all those who . . were subject
Rev 18.17 all whose trade is on the sea

ALLEGORICALLY
1. *spiritually:* πνευματικῶς PNEUMATIKŌS
Rev 11. 8 city which is allegorically[d] called Sodom†

ALLEGORY
1. *interpret allegorically:* ἀλληγορέω (subst. pass. part.) ALLĒGOREŌ*
Gal 4.24 an allegory: these women are . . covenants

ALLOTTED
1. *command:* προστάσσω (perf. pass. part.) PROSTASSŌ
Acts 17.26 "allotted periods and the boundaries

ALLOTTED, BE
1. *obtain by lot:* λαγχάνω LAGCHANŌ
Acts 1.17 "he . . was allotted his share in . . ministry

ALLOW
1. *let go, leave, forgive:* ἀφίημι APHIĒMI
Mt 23.13 nor allow those who would . . to go in
Mk 5.37 allowed no one to follow him except Peter
11.16 he would not allow any one to carry anything

2. *give:* δίδωμι DIDŌMI
Rev 9. 5 they were allowed to torture them
13. 5 beast . . was allowed to exercise authority
13. 7 it was allowed to make war on the saints‡
13.14 the signs which it is allowed to work
13.15 it was allowed to give breath to the image
16. 8 it was allowed to scorch men with fire

3. *permit:* ἐάω EAŌ
Lk 4.41 he . . would not allow them to speak
Acts 14.16 "he allowed all the nations . . their own ways
16. 7 but the Spirit of Jesus did not allow them
28. 4 "justice has not allowed him to live

4. *permit:* ἐπιτρέπω EPITREPŌ
Mt 19. 8 "Moses allowed you to divorce your wives
Mk 10. 4 "Moses allowed . . a certificate of divorce
Acts 28.16 Paul was allowed to stay by himself

5. *it is allowed, it is possible:* ἔξεστι EXESTI [A.6.C.3]
Mt 20.15 " 'Am I not allowed to do what I choose?

ALLOW TO GO ON
1. *permit to go farther:* προσεάω PROSEAŌ*
Acts 27. 7 the wind did not allow us to go on

ALMIGHTY
1. *all-powerful:* παντοκράτωρ PANTOKRATŌR*
2 Cor 6.18 "I will be a father . . , says the Lord Almighty
Rev 1. 8 says the Lord God . . , the Almighty
4. 8 "Holy . . is the Lord God Almighty
11.17 "We give thanks to thee, . . God Almighty
15. 3 "Great . . are thy deeds, . . God the Almighty!
16. 7 I heard . . "Yea, Lord God the Almighty!
16.14 the great day of God the Almighty
19. 6 "Hallelujah! . . our God the Almighty reigns
19.15 fury of the wrath of God the Almighty
21.22 the Lord God the Almighty and the Lamb

ALMOST
1. *nearly:* σχεδόν SCHEDON*
Acts 13.44 almost the whole city gathered together
19.26 "almost throughout all Asia
Heb 9.22 almost everything is purified with blood

ALMOST, BE
1. *be about to:* μέλλω (+inf.) MELLŌ
Acts 21.27 the seven days were almost completed

ALMS
1. *mercy, kind deed:* ἐλεημοσύνη (sg. or pl.) ELEĒMOSYNĒ
Mt 6. 2 "when you give alms, sound no trumpet
6. 3 "when you give alms
6. 4 "so that your alms may be in secret
Lk 11.41 "give for alms those things which are within
12.33 "Sell your possessions, and give alms
Acts 3. 2 a man . . was . . at that gate . . to ask alms
3. 3 Seeing Peter and John . . , he asked for alms
3.10 one who sat for alms at the Beautiful Gate
10. 2 man who . . gave alms liberally
10. 4 "your alms have ascended as a memorial
10.31 " 'your alms have been remembered
24.17 "I came to bring to my nation alms

ALOES
1. *bitter aloes:* ἀλόη ALOĒ*
Jn 19.39 Nicodemus . . came bringing . . aloes

ALONE
1. *one:* εἷς HEIS
Mk 2. 7 "Who can forgive sins but God alone?
10.18 "No one is good but God alone
Lk 18.19 "No one is good but God alone

2. *only, alone:* μόνος MONOS
[a]κατὰ μόνας [b]neut.
Mt 4. 4 " 'Man shall not live by bread alone
14.23 When evening came, he was there alone
18.15 "tell him . . between you and him alone
Mk 4.10 [a]And when he was alone
6.47 he was alone on the land
Lk 4. 4 " 'Man shall not live by bread alone
9.18 [a]it happened that as he was praying alone
9.36 Jesus was found alone
10.40 "my sister has left me to serve alone
Jn 6.22 his disciples had gone away alone
Jn 8. 9 Jesus was left alone with the woman[r]‡
8.16 "not I alone that judge, but I and he[s]
8.29 "he has not left me alone
12.24 unless a grain . . dies, it remains alone
16.32 "when you . . will leave me alone; yet I am not alone, for the Father is with me
Rom 4.23 [b]words . . written not for his sake alone
11. 3 "I alone am left, and they seek my life
Gal 6. 4 his reason to boast will be in himself alone
1 Th 3. 1 willing to be left behind at Athens alone
1 Tim 6.16 ⟨the Lord⟩ alone has immortality
2 Tim 4.11 Luke alone is with me
Jas 2.24 [b]a man is justified . . not by faith alone
Rev 15. 4 "thou alone art holy

ALONE, BE LEFT ALL
1. *make single:* μονόω (pass.) MONOŌ*
1 Tim 5. 5 who is a real widow, and is left all alone

ALONE, LET
1. *let go, leave, forgive:* ἀφίημι APHIĒMI
Mt 15.14 "Let them alone; they are blind guides
Mk 14. 6 "Let her alone; why do you trouble her?
Lk 13. 8 "Let it alone . . this year also, till I dig
Jn 12. 7 "Let her alone, let her keep it
Acts 5.38 "keep away . . and let them alone

ALONE, LET ONE
1. *ha!* ἔα EA
Lk [4.34 *Let us alone!* What have you to do with us?†

ALONG (*See also* PARA- *entries*)
1. *in, at, by:* ἐν (+dat.) EN
Lk **9.57**

2. *in accordance with, for:* κατά (+acc.) KATA
Acts **8.36**

3. *more than, by:* παρά (+acc.) PARA
Mt **13.**4, 19; **15.**29
Mk **4.**4, 15
Lk **8.**5, 12

ALONG, ALL
1. *long ago:* πάλαι PALAI
2 Cor 12.19 Have you been thinking all along?

ALONG WITH
1. *at the same time:* ἅμα (prep.) HAMA
Mt 13.29 " 'root up the wheat along with them

2. *with:* μετά (+gen.) META
Mt **22.**16
2 Tim **2.**22

3. *with:* σύν (+dat.) SYN
Acts **21.**24; **23.**15
1 Cor **11.**32

ALOUD (*See also* CRY ALOUD)
1. *say, speak:* λέγω (part.) LEGŌ
Rev 18.15(16) merchants . . will stand . . weeping . . a.

CONTEXTUALLY
Rev 1. 3 Blessed is he who reads aloud the words

ALPHA
1. *alpha, first:* ἄλφα ALPHA*
Rev 1. 8 "I am the Alpha and the Omega
21. 6 "I am the Alpha and the Omega
22.13 "I am the Alpha and the Omega

ALPHAEUS: Ἁλφαῖος 'alfēəs
Mt 10. 3 James the son of Alphaeus, and Thaddaeus[z]
Mk 2.14 he saw Levi the son of Alphaeus
3.18 James the son of Alphaeus, and Thaddaeus
Lk 6.15 James the son of Alphaeus, and Simon
Acts 1.13 James the son of Alphaeus and Simon

ALREADY (*See also* PRO- *entries*)
1. *already, now:* ἤδη ĒDĒ
Mt 5.28 "already committed adultery . . in his heart
17.12 "I tell you that Elijah has already come
Mk 4.37 so that the boat was already filling
11.11 as it was already late, he went . . to Bethany
15.44 Pilate wondered if he were already dead
15.44 asked . . whether he was already dead[j]‡
Lk 12.49 "would that it were already kindled!
21.30 "the summer is already near

Jn 3.18 who does not believe is condemned already
4.35 "the fields are already white for harvest
9.22 for the Jews had already agreed
9.27 "I have told you already
11.17 already . . in the tomb four days
13. 2 devil had already put it into . . Judas
15. 3 "You are already made clean by the word
19.33 they . . saw that he was already dead
Acts 4. 3 arrested them . . , for it was already evening
27. 9 the voyage was already dangerous because the fast had already gone by
1 Cor 4. 8 Already you are filled! Already you have become rich!
5. 3 I have already pronounced judgment
Phil 3.12 Not that I have already obtained this or am already perfect
2 Th 2. 7 lawlessness is already at work
1 Tim 5.15 some have already strayed after Satan
2 Tim 2.18 that the resurrection is past already
4. 6 already on the point of being sacrificed
1 Jn 2. 8 the true light is already shining
4. 3 spirit of antichrist . . is in the world already

ALREADY DONE, WORK

1. *ready, prepared:* ἕτοιμος (subst. neut. pl.) HETOIMOS
2 Cor 10.16 without boasting of work already done

ALSO

1. *in like manner:* ὡσαύτως HŌSAUTŌS
1 Tim 2. 9 also . . adorn themselves modestly
2. *and, even, indeed:* καί KAI
3. *and, both . . . and:* τέ TE
Acts **19**.18; **23**.24

ALSO, HE

1. *and that one:* κἀκεῖνος KAKEINOS
Lk 20.11 "him also they beat and . . sent . . away
Acts 5.37 "Judas the Galilean arose . . ; he also perished
2 Tim 2.12 if we deny him, he also will deny us

ALSO, I

1. *and I:* κἀγώ KAGŌ
[a]also I
Mt 10.32 I also will acknowledge
10.33 "whoever denies me . . I also will deny
21.24 "I also will ask you a question
21.24 "I also will tell you by what authority
Lk 1. 3 it seemed good to me also . . to write
20. 3 "I also will ask you a question
Acts 8.19 "Give me also this power
1 Cor 15. 8 [a]Last of all . . he appeared also to me
16. 4 If . . I should go also, they will accompany
2 Cor 2.10 Any one whom you forgive, I also forgive
11.21 I also dare to boast of that
Gal 4.12 I also have become as you are
Rev 2. 6 " 'works of the Nicolaitans . . I also hate

ALTAR

1. *raised platform, stand:* βωμός BŌMOS*
Acts 17.23 "I found also an altar with this inscription
2. *altar:* θυσιαστήριον THYSIASTĒRION
Mt 5.23 "if you are offering your gift at the altar
5.24 "leave your gift there before the altar and go
23.18 " 'If any one swears by the altar, it is nothing
23.19 "which is greater, the gift or the altar?
23.20 "he who swears by the altar, swears by it
23.35 "murdered between the sanctuary and the a.
Lk 1.11 an angel . . on the right side of the altar
11.51 "perished between . . altar and . . sanctuary
Rom 11. 3 "they have demolished thy altars
1 Cor 9.13 who serve at the altar share in . . offerings
10.18 those who eat ⟨are⟩ partners in the altar
Heb 7.13 from which . . no one has . . served at the a.
13.10 altar from which those . . have no right
Jas 2.21 he offered his son Isaac upon the altar
Rev 6. 9 I saw under the altar the souls
8. 3 another angel came and stood at the altar
8. 3 the golden altar before the throne
8. 5 censer . . filled . . with fire from the altar
9.13 a voice from . . the golden altar
Rev 11. 1 "measure . . the altar and those who worship
14.18 another angel came out from the altar
16. 7 I heard the altar cry, "Yea, Lord God!

ALTAR OF INCENSE

1. *censer, altar of incense:* θυμιατήριον THYMIATĒRION*
Heb 9. 4 the golden altar of incense and the ark

ALTERED

1. *another, different:* ἕτερος HETEROS
Lk 9.29 praying, . . his countenance was altered

ALTHOUGH

1. *even if:* εἰ καί EI [A.5.a]
2 Cor 7.12 So although I wrote to you
2. *if indeed, since:* εἴπερ EIPER
1 Cor 8. 5 although there may be so-called gods
3. *although:* καίπερ KAIPER
Heb 5. 8 Although . . a Son, he learned obedience
4. *and yet:* καίτοι KAITOI
Heb 4. 3 although his works were finished
5. *and yet:* καίτοιγε KAITOIGE*
Jn 4. 2 (although Jesus himself did not baptize
6. *indeed, on the one hand:* μέν MEN
Rom **8**.10

ALWAYS

1. *always:* ἀεί AEI*
Acts 7.51 "you always resist the Holy Spirit
2 Cor 4.11 we are always being given up to death
6.10 sorrowful, yet always rejoicing
Tit 1.12 "Cretans are always liars, evil beasts
Heb 3.10 " 'They always go astray
1 Pet 3.15 Always be prepared to make a defense
2 Pet 1.12 I intend always to remind you
2. *always:* πάντοτε PANTOTE
Mt 26.11 "you always have the poor with you, but you will not always have me
Mk 14. 7 "you always have the poor with you . . but you will not always have me
Lk 15.31 " 'Son, you are always with me
18. 1 he told them . . they ought always to pray
Jn 6.34 "Lord give us this bread always
7. 6 "your time is always here
8.29 "I always do what is pleasing to him
11.42 "I knew that thou hearest me always
12. 8 "The poor you always have with you, but you do not always have me
18.20 "I have always taught in synagogues
Rom 1. 9(10) I mention you always in my prayers
1 Cor 1. 4 I give thanks to God[a] always for you
15.58 be steadfast, immovable, always abounding
2 Cor 2.14 God . . always leads us in triumph
4.10 always carrying . . the death of Jesus
5. 6 we are always of good courage
9. 8 so that you may always have much of
Gal 4.18 it is always good to be made much of
Eph 5.20 always . . giving thanks in . . our Lord Jesus
Phil 1. 4 always in every prayer . . with joy
1.20 with full courage now as always
2.12 beloved, as you have always obeyed
4. 4 Rejoice in the Lord always
Col 1. 3 We always thank God . . when we pray
4. 6 Let your speech always be gracious
4.12 Epaphras, . . always remembering you
1 Th 1. 2 We give thanks to God always for you all
2.16 as a. to fill up the measure of their sins
3. 6 you always remember us kindly
4.17 so we shall always be with the Lord
5.15 always seek to do good to one another
5.16 Rejoice always
2 Th 1. 3 We are bound to give thanks . . always
1.11 To this end we always pray for you
2.13 we are bound to give thanks . . always
Phm . 4 I thank my God always . . in my prayers
Heb 7.25 he always lives to make intercession
3. *all, every, whole:* πᾶς PAS
[a]διὰ παντός *through everything* B.1.a.1
[b]πάσας τὰς ἡμέρας *all days* B.3.b.4
[c]ἐν πᾶσιν (sg. or pl.) *in all* B.1.a.1

Mt 18.10 [a]"in heaven their angels always behold
28.20 [b]"lo, I am with you always, to the close
Acts 2.25 [a]" 'I saw the Lord always before me
24.16 [a]"I a. take pains to have a clear conscience
2 Tim 4. 5 [c]As for you, always be steady, endure
CONTEXTUALLY
Mk 5. 5 he was always crying out
2 Cor 1.19 but in him it is always Yes

AMAZE

AMAZED, BE

1. *astonish:* ἐκθαμβέω EKTHAMBEŌ
Mk 16. 5 entering the tomb, .. they were amazed
16. 6 "Do not be amazed; you seek Jesus
2. *wonder greatly:* ἐκθαυμάζω EKTHAUMAZŌ*
Mk 12.17 they were amazed at him
3. *displace, amaze:* ἐξίστημι EXISTĒMI
[a]aor.=intrans.
Mt 12.23 all the people were amazed
Mk 2.12 he rose .. so that they were all amazed
Lk 2.47 all who heard him were amazed
8.56 [a]her parents were amazed
24.22 "some women of our company amazed us
Acts 2. 7 they were amazed and wondered
2.12 all were amazed and perplexed
8. 9 Simon .. amazed the nation of Samaria
8.11 he had amazed them with his magic
8.13 Simon .. seeing signs .. was amazed
9.21 all who heard him were amazed
10.45 [a]were amazed, because .. Holy Spirit
12.16 [a]they saw him and were amazed
4. *be astounded:* θαμβέω (pass.) THAMBEŌ*
Mk 1.27 they were all amazed
10.24 the disciples were amazed at his words
10.32 and they were amazed
5. *there is amazement:* γίνεται θάμβος THAMBOS [B.3.a.2]
Lk 4.36 they were all amazed and said

AMAZED, BE GREATLY

1. *astonish:* ἐκθαμβέω (pass.) EKTHAMBEŌ
Mk 9.15 all the crowd .. were greatly amazed

AMAZEMENT

1. *displacement, ecstasy:* ἔκστασις EKSTASIS
Mk 5.42 they were .. overcome with amazement
Lk 5.26 And amazement seized them all
Acts 3.10 they were filled with wonder and amazement

AMBASSADOR

1. *old man:* πρεσβύτης PRESBYTĒS
Phm . 9 I, Paul, an ambassador[a] and now a prisoner†

AMBASSADOR, BE AN

1. *be the elder, represent:* πρεσβεύω PRESBEUŌ*
2 Cor 5.20 So we are ambassadors for Christ
Eph 6.20 I am an ambassador in chains

AMBITION (*See* SELFISH AMBITION)

AMBITION, MAKE IT ONE'S

1. *seek after honor:* φιλοτιμέομαι PHILOTIMEOMAI
Rom 15.20 thus making it my ambition to preach

AMBUSH

1. *lying in wait:* ἐνέδρα ENEDRA*
Acts 23.16 Now the son .. heard of their ambush
25. 3 planning an ambush to kill him on the way

AMBUSH, LIE IN

1. *lie in wait:* ἐνεδρεύω ENEDREUŌ
Acts 23.21 "more than forty of their men lie in ambush

AMEN

1. *truly* (Heb.): ἀμήν AMĒN
Mt [6.13 *"power and the glory, for ever. Amen*‡
Mk 16.20 confirmed the message by the signs .. Amen[k]‡
Rom 1.25 the Creator, who is blessed for ever! Amen
9. 5 God .. be blessed for ever.[n] Amen
11.36 To him be glory for ever. Amen
15.33 The God of peace be with you all. Amen
[16.24 *grace .. be with you all. Amen*‡
16.27 glory .. through Jesus Christ! Amen
1 Cor 14.16 how can .. an outsider[x] say the "Amen"?
16.24 love be with you all in Christ Jesus. Amen
2 Cor 1.20 why we utter the Amen through him
Gal 1. 5 to whom be the glory for ever .. Amen
6.18 grace .. be with your spirit, brethren. Amen
Eph 3.21 to him be glory .. for ever and ever. Amen
Phil 4.20 be glory for ever and ever. Amen
1 Tim 1.17 honor and glory for ever and ever.[b] Amen
6.16 be honor and eternal dominion. Amen
2 Tim 4.18 be the glory for ever and ever. Amen
Heb 13.21 to whom be glory for ever and ever. Amen
13.25 Grace be with all of you. Amen
1 Pet 4.11 glory and dominion for ever .. Amen
5.11 To him be the dominion for ever .. Amen
2 Pet 3.18 To him be the glory .. Amen
Jude .25 glory, majesty .. for ever. Amen
Rev 1. 6 glory and dominion for ever .. Amen
1. 7 Even so. Amen
3.14 " 'words of the Amen, the faithful .. witness
5.14 the four living creatures said, "Amen!
7.12 "Amen! Blessing and glory .. be to our God for ever and ever! Amen
19. 4 worshiped .., saying, "Amen. Hallelujah!
22.20 "Surely I am coming soon." Amen
22.21 grace .. be with all the saints.[t] Amen

AMEND

1. *correct afterward:* ἐπιδιορθόω (mid.) EPIDIORTHOŌ*
Tit 1. 5 that you might amend what was defective

AMETHYST

1. *amethyst:* ἀμέθυστος AMETHYSTOS*
Rev 21.20 eleventh jacinth, the twelfth amethyst

AMMINADAB: Ἀμιναδάβ ə'minə,dab
Mt 1. 4 Ram[a] the father of Amminadab
1. 4 Amminadab the father of Nahshon
Lk 3.33 Amminadab, the son of Admin

AMON: Ἀμών 'amən
Mt [1.10 Manasseh the father of *Amon*‡
[1.10 *Amon* the father of Josiah‡

AMONG

1. *through:* διά (+gen.) DIA
2 Cor **8.18**
2. *into, to, for:* εἰς (+acc.) EIS
Mt **13.22**
Mk **4.7**, 18
Lk **8.14**; **10.36**; **21.24**; **22.17**
Jn **6.9**; **21.23**
Acts **4.17**; **14.14**; **19.30**; **20.29**
Rom **16.6**
2 Cor **8.6**
Rev **6.15**
3. *from, out of:* ἐκ (+gen.) EK
Lk **11.11**
Jn **12.20**
Acts **27.22**
2 Tim **3.6**
4. *in, at, by:* ἐν (+dat.) EN
Mt **2.6**; **4.23**; **11.11**; **16.7**, 8; **20.26**², 27; **26.5**; **27.56**
Mk **5.3**, 5; **6.4**; **10.43**², 44; **15.40**
Lk **1.1**, 25, [28‡, 42; **2.14**; **7.16**, 28, 49; **8.27**; **9.46**, 48; **16.15**; **22.24**, 26
Jn **1.14**; **7.12**, 43; **9.16**; **10.19**; **11.54**; **15.24**
Acts **1.17**; **4.12**, 34; **5.12**; **6.8**; **12.18**; **13.26**; **15.7**, 12, 22; **17.34**; **18.11**; **20.25**, 32; **21.19**, 20; **24.21**; **25.5**, 6; **26.4**, 18; **28.**[29‡
Rom **1.5**, 13²; 24; **2.24**; **8.29**; **12.3**; **15.9**; **16.7**
1 Cor **1.6**, 10, 11; **2.2**, 6; **3.3**, 18; **5.1**²; **6.5**; **11.18**, 19²; **14.25**
2 Cor **1.19**; **2.15**²; **10.15**; **12.12**
Gal **1.14**, 16; **2.2**; **3.5**
Eph **2.3**; **5.3**
Phil **2.5**, 15
Col **1.6**, 27
1 Th **5.12**, 13
1 Tim **3.16**
Heb **13.4**
Jas **2.4**; **3.6**, 13; **4.1**; **5.13**, 14, 19
1 Pet **2.12**; **5.1**
2 Pet **2.1**², 8
1 Jn **4.9**

5. *on, at:* ἐπί (+acc.) EPI
Acts **1.**21
6. *in accordance with, for:* κατά (+acc.) KATA
Acts **21.**21
7. *in a circle, round about:* κύκλῳ KYKLŌ [B.2.d.1]
Mk **6.**6
8. *middle, in the middle:* μέσος MESOS
[a]ἀνὰ μέσον [b]ἐν μέσῳ
[c]εἰς τὸ μέσον *among s.*
Mt **13.**25[a]
Lk **2.**46[b]; **8.**7[b]; **22.**27[b], 55; **24.**36[b]
Jn **1.**26; **20.**19[c], 26[c]
Acts **1.**15[b]; **17.**33; **23.**10; **27.**21[b]
1 Th **2.**7[b]
Rev **2.**1[b]; **5.**6[b]
9. *with:* μετά (+gen.) META
Mk **15.**7
Lk **24.**5
Jn **6.**43
Acts **20.**18
10. *beside, with:* παρά (+dat.) PARA
Mt **22.**25; **28.**15
Col **4.**16
Rev **2.**13
11. *to, with, against:* πρός (+acc.) PROS
Mk **1.**27
Jn **6.**52
Acts **28.**25
1 Cor **16.**10
1 Th **1.**9
2 Th **3.**1
IDIOMATICALLY
a. Mt **10.**5 [HODOS]

AMONG, FROM
1. *from, out of:* ἐκ (+gen.) EK
Acts **6.**3; **10.**45; **15.**22; **20.**30
1 Cor **5.**13
Heb **5.**1

AMOS: 'Αμώς 'āməs
Mt 1.10 Manasseh the father of Amos[c]‡
1.10 Amos[c] the father of Josiah‡
Lk 3.25 Mattathias, the son of Amos

AMPHIPOLIS: 'Αμφίπολις am'fipələs II,D-2
Acts 17. 1 they had passed through Amphipolis

AMPLE
1. *many, great:* πολύς POLYS
Lk 12.19 " 'Soul, you have ample goods laid up

AMPLE, HAVE
1. *abound:* περισσεύω PERISSEUŌ [A.6.c.3]
Phil 1.26 so that . . you may have ample cause to glory

AMPLIATUS: 'Αμπλιᾶτος ˌamplē'ātəs
Rom 16. 8 Ampliatus, my beloved in the Lord

ANANIAS: 'Ανανίας ˌanə'nīəs
[1]of Jerusalem [2]of Damascus [3]high priest
Acts 5. 1 [1]Ananias with his wife Sapphira
5. 3 [1]"A., why has Satan filled your heart?
5. 5 [1]When A. heard these words, he . . died
9.10 [2]a disciple at Damascus named A.
9.10 [2]The Lord said to him in a vision, "A.
9.12 [2]"he has seen a man named A. come in
9.13 [2]A. answered, "Lord, I have heard
9.17 [2]So A. departed and entered the house
22.12 [2]"A., a devout man according to the law
23. 2 [3]the high priest A. commanded
24. 1 [3]the high priest A. came down

ANCESTOR
1. *father:* πατήρ PATĒR
Heb 7.10 he was still in the loins of his ancestor

ANCHOR
1. *anchor:* ἄγκυρα AGKYRA*
Acts 27.29 they let out four anchors . . and prayed
27.30 under pretense of laying out anchors
27.40 they cast off the anchors and left them
Heb 6.19 this as a sure and steadfast anchor

ANCHOR, WEIGH
1. *lift, carry away:* αἴρω AIRŌ
Acts 27.13 they weighed anchor and sailed along Crete

ANCIENT
1. *from the beginning, old:* ἀρχαῖος ARCHAIOS
2 Pet 2. 5 if he did not spare the ancient world
Rev 12. 9 the great dragon . . , that ancient serpent
20. 2 the dragon, that ancient serpent, . . the Devil

AND
1. *but, and:* δέ DE
2. *or, than:* ἤ Ē
Mt **5.**17
Rom **4.**13
1 Pet **3.**3
3. *for:* γάρ GAR
Mt **6.**32
Acts **8.**39
Rev **21.**25
4. *that, because:* ὅτι HOTI
Jn **1.**16
5. *and, even, indeed:* καί KAI
6. *yes:* ναί NAI
Phil 4. 3 And I ask you also, true yokefellow
7. *nor, and not:* οὐδέ (+neg.) OUDE
Mt **6.**20
8. *so, therefore:* οὖν OUN
Jn **4.**52
9. *with:* σύν (+dat.) SYN
Acts **16.**32
10. *and, both . . . and:* τέ TE
Mt **28.**12
Lk **2.**16; **12.**45; **14.**26; **21.**11; **24.**20
Acts **2.**33, 37, 40, 46; **4.**13, 33; **5.**19, 35, 42; **6.**7, 12, 13; **7.**26; **8.**3, 13, 31, 38; **9.**3, 15, 18, 29; **10.**28, 33; **11.**21, 26; **12.**6, 17; **13.**4, 46, 52; **14.**11, 13; **15.**4, 5, 32; **16.**13; **17.**4, 26; **19.**2, 3, 6, 11, 12, 27, 29; **20.**7; **21.**18, 20, 31; **22.**7, 8, 23; **23.**5, 28; **24.**5, 10, 27; **25.**2, 16; **26.**4, 11, 14, 16, 20, 30; **27.**3, 5, 20, 21, 29; **28.**2, 23
Rom **2.**19; **14.**8; **16.**26
Eph **3.**19
Heb **6.**5; **9.**1; **12.**2
Jude .6

AND HE
1. *and that one:* κἀκεῖνος KAKEINOS
Mk **12.**5
Lk **11.**7; **22.**12
Jn **7.**29

AND I
1. *and I:* κἀγώ KAGŌ
Mt **11.**28; **16.**18
Lk **2.**48; **11.**9; **19.**23; **22.**29[0]
Jn **1.**34; **5.**17; **6.**44, 54, 56, 57; **8.**26; **10.**15, 27, 28, 38; **12.**32; **14.**16, 20, 21; **15.**4, 5; **16.**32; **17.**6, 11, 21, 26; **20.**15
Acts **22.**13, 19
Rom **11.**3
1 Cor **2.**3; **7.**40
2 Cor **12.**20
Gal **6.**14
Phil **2.**28
Heb **8.**9
Jas **2.**18[2]

AND IF
1. *even if:* κἄν KAN
Mk **16.**18‡
Lk **13.**9
1 Cor **13.**2[2], 3
Jas **5.**15

AND THERE
1. *and there:* κἀκεῖ KAKEI
Mt **5.**23; **28.**10
Mk **1.**35
Jn **11.**54
Acts **14.**7; **22.**10; **25.**20

2. *and from there:* κἀκεῖθεν KAKEITHEN
Acts 28.15 And the brethren there . . came . . to meet us

AND THEY
1. *anyone who, whoever:* ὅστις HOSTIS
Col 4.11 and they have been a comfort to me
2. *and that one:* κἀκεῖνος KAKEINOS
Mk **12.**4; **16.**13‡
Acts **18.**19

AND THIS
1. *anyone who, whoever:* ὅστις HOSTIS
Acts 11.28 and this took place in . . days of Claudius
2. *and that one:* κἀκεῖνος KAKEINOS
Mt **15.**18

ANDREW: 'Ανδρέας 'andrü
Mt 4.18 he saw . . Peter and A. his brother
10. 2 Peter, and Andrew his brother
Mk 1.16 he saw Simon and A. . . casting a net
1.29 entered the house of Simon and A.
3.18 A., and Philip, and Bartholomew
13. 3 John and A. asked him privately
Lk 6.14 Peter, and A. his brother
Jn 1.40 A., Simon Peter's brother
1.44 Bethsaida, the city of A. and Peter
6. 8 One of his disciples, A., . . Peter's brother
12.22 Philip went and told A.; A. went with Philip and they told Jesus
Acts 1.13 Peter and John and James and A.

ANDRONICUS: 'Ανδρόνικος ˌandrəˈnīkəs, anˈdränikəs
Rom 16. 7 Andronicus and Junias, my kinsmen

ANEW (*See also* ANA- *entries*)
1. *from above, anew:* ἄνωθεν ANŌTHEN
Jn 3. 3 "Truly, . . unless one is born anew[e]†
3. 7 "I said to you, 'You must be born anew[e]†

ANGEL
1. *messenger, angel:* ἄγγελος AGGELOS
Mt 1.20 an angel of the Lord appeared to him
1.24 the angel of the Lord commanded him
2.13 an angel of the Lord appeared to Joseph
2.19 an angel of the Lord appeared in a dream
4. 6 " 'He will give his angels charge of you
4.11 angels came and ministered to him
13.39 "the reapers are angels
13.41 "The Son of man will send his angels
13.49 "angels will . . separate . . evil
16.27 "the Son of man is to come with his angels
18.10 "their angels . . behold the face of my Father
22.30 "in the resurrection they . . are like angels[s]
24.31 "his angels . . will gather his elect
24.36 "no one knows, not even the angels
25.31 "the Son of man . . and all the angels
25.41 " 'eternal fire . . for the devil and his angels
26.53 "more than twelve legions of angels
28. 2 angel of the Lord descended from heaven
28. 5 the angel said . . "Do not be afraid
Mk 1.13 and the angels ministered to him
8.38 "when he comes . . with the holy angels
12.25 "when they rise . . they . . are like angels
13.27 "he will send . . angels, and gather his elect
13.32 "no one knows, not even the angels
Lk 1.11 there appeared to him an angel
1.13 a. said . . , "Do not be afraid, Zechariah
1.18 Zechariah said to the a., "How shall I know?
1.19 the angel answered . . "I am Gabriel
1.26 the angel Gabriel was sent from God
1.30 the angel said to her, "Do not be afraid
1.34 Mary said to the a., "How shall this be?
1.35 angel said . . "The Holy Spirit will come
1.38 the angel departed from her
2. 9 angel of the Lord appeared to them
2.10 angel said to them, "Be not afraid
2.13 with the angel . . the heavenly host praising
2.15 angels went away from them into heaven
2.21 Jesus, the name given by the angel
4.10 " 'He will give his angels charge of you
9.26 "of the Father and of the holy angels
Lk 12. 8 "will acknowledge before the angels of God
12. 9 "denied before the angels of God
15.10 "there is joy before the angels of God
16.22 "The poor man . . was carried by the angels
[22.43 *an angel from heaven, strengthening him*‡
24.23 "they had even seen a vision of angels
Jn 1.51 "will see heaven opened, and the angels
[5. 4 *an angel . . went down . . into the pool*‡
12.29 Others said, "An angel has spoken
20.12 she saw two angels in white
Acts 5.19 an angel of the Lord opened the prison
6.15 his face was like the face of an angel
7.30 "an angel appeared to him in the wilderness
7.35 "the angel that appeared to him in the bush
7.38 "the angel who spoke to him at Mount Sinai
7.53 "the law as delivered by angels
8.26 an angel of the Lord said to Philip
10. 3 he saw clearly in a vision an angel
10. 7 "When the angel who spoke . . had departed
10.22 "Cornelius . . was directed by a holy angel
11.13 "he told us how he had seen the angel
12. 7 behold, an angel of the Lord appeared
12. 8 the angel said to him, "Dress yourself
12. 9 what was done by the angel was real
12.10 immediately the angel left him
12.11 "his angel . . rescued me from . . Herod
12.15 They said, "It is his angel!
12.23 an angel of the Lord smote him
23. 8 Sadducees say that there is no . . angel
23. 9 "What if a spirit or an angel spoke to him?
27.23 "this very night there stood by me an angel
Rom 8.38 neither death, nor life, nor angels
1 Cor 4. 9 we have become a spectacle . . to angels
6. 3 know that we are to judge angels?
11.10 a veil[r] on her head, because of the angels
13. 1 the tongues of men and of angels
2 Cor 11.14 Satan disguises himself as an angel of light
Gal 1. 8 if we, or an angel from heaven, should preach
3.19 the law . . was ordained by angels
4.14 you . . received me as an angel of God
Col 2.18 self-abasement and worship of angels
2 Th 1. 7 Jesus is revealed . . with his mighty angels
1 Tim 3.16 He[h] was . . seen by angels, . . taken up in glory
5.21 In the presence . . of the elect angels
Heb 1. 4 as much superior to angels as the name
1. 5 to what angel did God ever say?
1. 6 "Let all God's angels worship him
1. 7 Of the angels he says, "Who makes his angels winds, and his servants flames of fire
1.13 to what angel has he ever said?
2. 2 if the message declared by angels was valid
2. 5 not to angels . . God subjected the world
2. 7 "didst make him . . lower than the angels
2. 9 Jesus . . made lower than the angels
2.16 it is not with angels that he is concerned
12.22 you have come . . to innumerable angels
13. 2 some have entertained angels unawares
1 Pet 1.12 things into which angels long to look
3.22 at the right hand of God, with angels
2 Pet 2. 4 if God did not spare the angels
2.11 angels . . do not pronounce . . judgment
Jude . 6 angels that did not keep their own position
Rev 1. 1 sending his angel to his servant John
1.20 "the angels of the seven churches
2. 1 "To the angel of the church in Ephesus
2. 8 "to the angel of the church in Smyrna
2.12 "to the angel of the church in Pergamum
2.18 "to the angel of the church in Thyatira
3. 1 "to the angel of the church in Sardis
3. 5 " 'I will confess his name . . before his angels
3. 7 "to the angel of the church in Philadelphia
3.14 "to the angel of the church in Laodicea
5. 2 I saw a strong angel proclaiming
5.11 I heard . . the voice of many angels
7. 1 four angels standing at the four corners
7. 2 I saw another angel ascend from the . . sun
7. 2 the four angels who had . . power to harm

Rev 7.11 all the angels . . worshiped God
8. 2 the seven angels who stand before God
8. 3 another angel came and stood at the altar
8. 4 incense . . from the hand of the angel
8. 5 the angel took the censer and filled it
8. 6 the seven angels . . made ready to blow
8. 8 The second angel blew his trumpet
8.10 The third angel blew his trumpet
8.12 The fourth angel blew his trumpet
8.13 "trumpets which the three angels . . blow!
9. 1 the fifth angel blew his trumpet
9.11 the angel of the bottomless pit
9.13 the sixth angel blew his trumpet
9.14 to the sixth angel who had the trumpet, "Release the four angels who are bound
9.15 the four angels were released
10. 1 I saw another mighty angel coming
10. 5 the angel . . lifted up his right hand to heaven
10. 7 the trumpet call . . by the seventh angel
10. 8 "the scroll . . in the hand of the angel
10. 9 I went to the angel and told him
10.10 little scroll from the hand of the angel
11.15 the seventh angel blew his trumpet
12. 7 Michael and his angels fighting
12. 7 and the dragon and his angels fought
12. 9 his angels were thrown down with him
14. 6 I saw another angel flying in midheaven
14. 8 Another angel, a second, followed
14. 9 another angel, a third, followed
14.10 "in the presence of the holy angels
14.15 another angel came out of the temple
14.17 another angel came out of the temple
14.18 another angel came out from the altar
14.19 the angel swung his sickle on the earth
15. 1 I saw . . seven angels with seven plagues
15. 6 the seven angels with the seven plagues
15. 7 gave the seven angels seven golden bowls
15. 8 the seven plagues of the seven angels
16. 1 a loud voice . . telling the seven angels
16. 5 I heard the angel of water
17. 1 one of the seven angels who had the . . bowls
17. 7 But the angel said to me, "Why marvel?
18. 1 another angel . . having great authority
18.21 a mighty angel took up a stone
19.17 I saw an angel standing in the sun
20. 1 I saw an angel coming down from heaven
21. 9 Then came one of the seven angels
21.12 at the gates twelve angels
21.17 a man's measure, that is, an angel's
22. 6 "God . . has sent his angel to show
22. 8 I fell down . . at the feet of the angel
22.16 "I Jesus have sent my angel to you

2. *age:* αἰών AIŌN
Col [1.26 the mystery hidden *from angels and men*†

CONTEXTUALLY
Rev 8. 7 The first angel blew his trumpet
16. 2 the first angel went and poured his bowl
16. 8 fourth angel poured his bowl on the sun
16.10 fifth angel poured his bowl on the throne
16.12 sixth a. poured his bowl on the . . river
16.17 seventh a. poured his bowl into the air
19. 9 And the a. said[l] to me, "Write this†

ANGEL, EQUAL TO AN

1. *like an angel:* ἰσάγγελος ISAGGELOS*
Lk 20.36 "equal to angels and . . sons of God

ANGER

1. *wrath, anger:* ὀργή ORGĒ
Mk 3. 5 he looked around at them with anger
Eph 4.31 Let all . . anger . . be put away from you
Col 3. 8 put them all away: anger, wrath
1 Tim 2. 8 pray, lifting holy hands without anger
Jas 1.19 be quick to hear, . . slow to anger
1.20 anger of man does not work . . righteousness
Rev 14.10 "wrath, poured . . into the cup of his anger

2. *provocation, anger:* παροργισμός PARORGISMOS*
Eph 4.26 not let the sun go down on your anger

3. *strong feeling, wrath:* θυμός THYMOS
2 Cor 12.20 there may be quarreling, jealousy, anger
Gal 5.20 sorcery, enmity, strife, jealousy, anger
Heb 11.27 not being afraid of the anger of the king

ANGER, IN

1. *make angry:* ὀργίζω (pass. part.) ORGIZŌ
Mt 18.34 "in anger his lord delivered him to . . jailers[h]
Lk 14.21 "the householder in anger said to his servant

ANGER, PROVOKE TO

1. *make angry:* παροργίζω PARORGIZŌ
Eph 6. 4 do not provoke your children to anger

ANGRY, BE

1. *be full of black bile:* χολάω CHOLAŌ*
Jn 7.23 "are you angry . . because on the sabbath?

2. *make angry:* ὀργίζω (pass.) ORGIZŌ
Mt 5.22 "who is angry with his brother[i] shall be liable
22. 7 "king was angry, and he sent his troops
Lk 15.28 "But he was angry and refused to go in
Eph 4.26 Be angry but do not sin
Rev 12.17 the dragon was angry with the woman

3. *make angry, provoke:* θυμομαχέω THYMOMACHEŌ*
Acts 12.20 Herod was angry with the people of Tyre

ANGRY, MAKE

1. *make angry:* παροργίζω PARORGIZŌ
Rom 10.19 "with a foolish nation I will make you angry

ANGUISH

1. *pain, distress:* ὀδύνη ODYNĒ
Rom 9. 2 I have great sorrow and unceasing anguish

2. *work, stress, pain:* πόνος PONOS
Rev 16.10 men gnawed their tongues in anguish

3. *conflict, distress:* συνοχή SYNOCHĒ
2 Cor 2. 4 I wrote you out of . . anguish of heart

4. *affliction, oppression:* θλῖψις THLIPSIS
Jn 16.21 "no longer remembers the anguish, for joy

ANGUISH, BE IN

1. *cause pain:* ὀδυνάω (pass.) ODYNAŌ
Lk 16.24 " 'send Lazarus . . for I am in anguish
16.25 " 'he is comforted . . and you are in anguish

ANGUISH, IN

1. *question by torture, torment:* βασανίζω (pres. pass. part.) BASANIZŌ
Rev 12. 2 she cried out . . in anguish for delivery

ANIMAL

1. *beast:* κτῆνος KTĒNOS
1 Cor 15.39 one kind for men, another for animals

2. *four-footed:* τετράπους (subst.) TETRAPOUS*
Acts 10.12 In it were all kinds of animals and reptiles
11. 6 "I observed animals and beasts of prey
Rom 1.23 images resembling . . animals or reptiles

3. *living being:* ζῷον ZŌON
Heb 13.11 those animals . . burned outside the camp
2 Pet 2.12 irrational animals, creatures of instinct
Jude .10 know by instinct as irrational animals do

ANKLE

1. *ankle:* σφυδρόν SPHYDRON*
Acts 3. 7 his feet and ankles were made strong

ANNA: Ἄννα 'anə
Lk 2.36 prophetess, Anna, the daughter of Phanuel

ANNAS: Ἄννας 'anəs
Lk 3. 2 high-priesthood of Annas and Caiaphas
Jn 18.13 First they led him to Annas
18.24 Annas then sent him bound to Caiaphas
Acts 4. 6 Annas the high priest and Caiaphas

ANNOUNCE

1. *report:* ἀναγγέλλω ANAGGELLŌ
1 Pet 1.12 announced to you by those who preached

2. *bring good news* (mid.): εὐαγγελίζω (act.) EUAGGELIZŌ
Rev 10. 7 mystery . . as he announced to his servants

ANNOUNCE BEFOREHAND

1. *foretell:* προκαταγγέλλω PROKATAGGELLŌ
Acts 7.52 "who announced beforehand the coming

ANNOYED

ANNOYED, BE

1. *be disturbed:* διαπονέομαι DIAPONEOMAI*
[a]part.
Acts 4. 2 [a]annoyed because they were teaching
16.18 Paul was annoyed . . and said to the spirit

ANNUL

1. *cancel:* ἀκυρόω AKYROŌ
Gal 3.17 the law . . does not annul a covenant
2. *deny, nullify:* ἀθετέω ATHETEŌ
Gal 3.15 no one annuls even a man's will[g]

ANOINT

1. *anoint with oil:* ἀλείφω ALEIPHŌ*
Mt 6.17 "when you fast, anoint your head
Mk 6.13 anointed with oil many that were sick
16. 1 spices, so that they might . . anoint him
Lk 7.38 kissed his feet, and anointed them
7.46 "You did not anoint my head with oil, but she has anointed my feet
Jn 11. 2 It was Mary who anointed the Lord
12. 3 Mary . . anointed the feet of Jesus
Jas 5.14 Let . . the elders . . pray . . , anointing him
2. *rub, anoint:* χρίω CHRIŌ
Lk 4.18 "anointed me to preach good news
Acts 4.27 "Jesus, whom thou didst anoint
10.38 "God anointed Jesus of Nazareth
Heb 1. 9 "therefore God . . has anointed thee
3. *rub, put on:* ἐγχρίω EGCHRIŌ*
Rev 3.18 " 'buy . . salve to anoint your eyes
4. *smear:* ἐπιχρίω EPICHRIŌ*
Jn 9. 6 anointed the man's eyes with the clay
9.11 "Jesus made clay and anointed my eyes
5. *rub with ointment:* μυρίζω MYRIZŌ*
Mk 14. 8 "she has anointed my body beforehand

ANOINTED

1. *anointed:* χριστός CHRISTOS
Acts 4.26 " 'against the Lord and . . his Anointed[e]†

ANOINTED, BE

1. *unction, anointing:* χρῖσμα CHRISMA [B.3.a.5]
1 Jn 2.20 But you have been anointed by the Holy One

ANOINTING

1. *unction, anointing:* χρῖσμα CHRISMA
1 Jn 2.27 anointing . . from him abides in you
2.27 his anointing teaches you about everything

ANOTHER

1. *other, another:* ἄλλος ALLOS
Mt 2.12 they departed . . by another way
8. 9 "I say . . to another, 'Come,' and he comes
13.24 Another parable he put before them
13.31 Another parable he put before them
13.33 He told them another parable
19. 9 "whoever divorces . . and marries another‡
21.33 "Hear another parable
26.71 another maid saw him
[27.49 *another . . pierced his side*‡
Mk 10.11 "Whoever divorces . . and marries another
10.12 "if she divorces . . and marries another
12. 4 "he sent to them another servant
12. 5 "he sent another, and him they killed
14.58 " 'I will build another, not made with hands
Lk 7. 8 "I say . . to another, 'Come,' and he comes
7.20 " 'Are you he . . or shall we look for another?
22.59 another insisted, saying, . . "this man also
Jn 4.37 " 'One sows and another reaps
5. 7 "while I am going another steps down
5.32 "another . . bears witness to me
5.43 "if another comes . . him you will receive
14.16 "he will give you another Counselor
18.15 Peter followed Jesus, . . so did another
21.18 "another will gird you and carry you
Acts 19.32 Now some cried one thing, some a.
21.34 Some . . shouted one thing, some a.
1 Cor 3.10 another man is building upon it
12. 8 to another the utterance of knowledge
12. 9 to another gifts of healing
12.10 to another the working of miracles, to another prophecy, to another the ability to distinguish between spirits . . to another the interpretation of tongues
14.30 If a revelation is made to another
15.39 not all flesh is alike, but there is one kind for men, another for animals, another for birds, and another for fish
15.41 another glory of the moon, and another glory of the stars
2 Cor 11. 4 another Jesus than . . we preached
Gal 1. 7 not that there is another gospel
Heb 4. 8 God[i] would not speak . . of another day
Rev 6. 4 out came another horse, bright red
7. 2 Then I saw another angel ascend
8. 3 another angel came and stood at the altar
10. 1 I saw another mighty angel
12. 3 another portent appeared in heaven
13.11 another beast which rose out of the earth
14. 6 I saw another angel flying in midheaven
14. 8 Another angel, . . saying, "Fallen, fallen
14. 9 another angel, a third, followed
14.15 another angel came out of the temple
14.17 another angel came out of the temple
14.18 another angel came out from the altar
15. 1 I saw another portent in heaven
18. 1 I saw another angel
18. 4 I heard another voice from heaven
20.12 another book was opened, . . the book of life
2. *glory:* δόξα DOXA [A.1.g]
2 Cor 3.18 from one degree of glory to another
3. *another, different:* ἕτερος HETEROS
Mt 8.21 Another of the disciples said
11. 3 "Are you he . . or shall we look for another?
Mk 16.12 appeared in another form to two of them[k]‡
Lk 6. 6 On another sabbath . . he entered the synag.
9.56 And they went on to another village
9.59 To another he said, "Follow me
9.61 Another said, "I will follow you, . . but
14.19 "another said, . . 'have me excused
14.20 "another said, 'I have married a wife
14.31 "what king, going to encounter another king?
16. 7 "to another, 'And how much do you owe?
16.18 "who divorces his wife and marries another
19.20 "another came, saying, 'Lord, here
20.11 "he sent another servant
Jn 19.37 again another scripture says
Acts 1.20 "it is written . . 'His office let another take
7.18 "another king who had not known Joseph
12.17 he departed and went to another place
13.35 "he says also in another psalm
17. 7 "there is another king, Jesus
Rom 2. 1 no excuse . . when you judge another
7. 3 adulteress if she lives with another man . . and if she marries another man she is not
7. 4 you may belong to another
7.23 I see in my members another law at war
1 Cor 3. 4 another, "I belong to Apollos
4. 6 puffed up in favor of one against another
12. 9 to another faith by the same Spirit
12.10 to another various kinds of tongues
15.40 the glory of the terrestrial is another
Heb 5. 6 he says also in another place
7.11 what further need . . for another priest?
7.13 belonged to another tribe
7.15 another priest . . in . . likeness of Melchizedek
Jas 2.25 she . . sent them out another way
4. *who, which, what:* ὅς HOS [B.3.b.5]
Mt **13.23**²; **21.35**²; **22.5**; **25.15**²
Rom **9.21**; **14.5**
1 Cor **11.21**
5. *stone:* λίθος LITHOS [A.1.g]
Mt 24. 2 "there will not be left . . one stone upon a.
Mk 13. 2 "there will not be left . . one stone upon a.
Lk 19.44 "they will not leave one stone upon a.
21. 6 "there shall not be left . . one stone upon a.

6. *again, back:* πάλιν PALIN [A.4.a]
2 Cor 2. 1 not to make you another painful visit
IDIOMATICALLY
a. Mt 26.22 to say to him one after another λέγειν αὐτῷ εἷς ἕκαστος [HEKASTOS]
b. 1 Cor 7.7 one of one kind and one of another ὁ μὲν οὕτως, ὁ δὲ οὕτως [HOUTŌS]

ANOTHER MAN'S
1. *other, another:* ἄλλος ALLOS
1 Cor 10.29 determined by another man's scruples
2. *foreign:* ἀλλότριος ALLOTRIOS
Rom 15.20 lest I build on another man's foundation
1 Tim 5.22 Do not . . participate in another man's sins

ANOTHER NATION, ONE OF
1. *of another tribe:* ἀλλόφυλος (subst.) ALLOPHYLOS*
Acts 10.28 "unlawful . . to visit any one of another n.

ANOTHER, OF
1. *foreign:* ἀλλότριος ALLOTRIOS
Rom 14. 4 judgment on the servant of another?

ANOTHER, ONE
1. *one another:* ἀλλήλων ALLĒLŌN
Mt 24.10 "then many will . . betray one another, and hate one another
25.32 "he will separate them one from another
Mk 4.41 said to one another, "Who then is this?
8.16 they discussed it with one another
9.34 they had discussed with one another
9.50 "be at peace with one another
15.31 chief priests mocked him to one another
Lk 2.15 the shepherds said to one another
4.36 said to one another, "What is this word?
6.11 they . . discussed with one another
7.32 "like children . . calling to one another
8.25 saying to one another, "Who then is this
12. 1 so many . . that they trod upon one another
Jn 4.33 the disciples said to one another
5.44 "you . . who receive glory from one another
11.56 saying to one another . . "What do you think?
13.14 "you . . ought to wash one another's feet
13.22 disciples looked at one another, uncertain
13.34 "A new commandment . . that you love one a.
13.34 "as I have loved you, . . love one another
13.35 "if you have love for one another
15.12 "commandment, that you love one another
15.17 "This I command you, to love one another
16.17 his disciples said to one another
19.24 said to one another, "Let us not tear it
Acts 4.15 they conferred with one another
19.38 "let them bring charges against one another
21. 5(6) we prayed and bade one another farewell
26.31 withdrawn, they said to one another
28. 4 to one another . . "this man is a murderer
Rom 1.27 consumed with passion for one another
12. 5 individually members one of another
12.10 love one another with brotherly affection; outdo one another in showing honor
12.16 Live in harmony with one another
13. 8 except to love one another
14.13 no more pass judgment on one another
15. 5 to live in such harmony with one another
15. 7 Welcome one another, therefore
15.14 you . . are . . able to instruct one another
16.16 Greet one another with a holy kiss
1 Cor 7. 5 Do not refuse one another except
11.33 wait for one another
12.25 have the same care for one another
16.20 Greet one another with a holy kiss
2 Cor 13.12 Greet one another with a holy kiss
Gal 5.13 through love be servants of one another
5.15 if you . . devour one another take heed that you are not consumed by one another
5.26 no self-conceit, nor provoking of one another, no envy of one another
6. 2 Bear one another's burdens
Eph 4. 2 patience, forbearing one another in love
4.25 for we are members one of another
Eph 4.32 be kind to one another
5.21 Be subject to one another out of reverence
Col 3. 9 Do not lie to one another
3.13 forbearing one another and . . forgiving
1 Th 3.12 abound in love to one another
4. 9 taught by God to love one another
4.18 comfort one another with these words
5.11 Therefore encourage one another
5.15 always seek to do good to one another
2 Th 1. 3 love . . for one another is increasing
Tit 3. 3 hated by men and hating one another
Heb 10.24 stir up one another to love and good works
Jas 4.11 Do not speak evil against one another
5. 9 Do not grumble . . against one another
5.16 confess your sins to one another, and pray for one another
1 Pet 1.22 love one another earnestly from the heart
4. 9 Practice hospitality . . to one another
5. 5 with humility toward one another
5.14 Greet one another with the kiss of love
1 Jn 1. 7 we have fellowship with one another
3.11 that we should love one another
3.23 love one another, just as he has commanded
4. 7 let us love one another; for love is of God
4.11 we also ought to love one another
4.12 if we love one another, God abides in us
2 Jn . 5 commandment . . that we love one another
Rev 6. 4 so that men should slay one another
2. *himself:* ἑαυτοῦ HEAUTOU
Mt 21.25 they argued with one another
Mk [10.26 they . . said *to one another*‡
11.31 they argued with one another
12. 7 "those tenants said to one another
16. 3 to one another, "Who will roll . . the stone?
Lk 20. 5 they discussed it with one another
22.23 they began to question one another
Jn 7.35 The Jews said to one another
12.19 Pharisees then said to one another
1 Cor 6. 7 To have lawsuits at all with one another
2 Cor 10.12 measure themselves by one another, and compare themselves with one another
Eph 4.32 forgiving one another, as God . . forgave
5.19 addressing one another in psalms
Col 3.16 teach and admonish one another
Heb 3.13 exhort one another every day
1 Pet 4. 8 hold unfailing your love for one another
4.10 employ it for one another, as good stewards
IDIOMATICALLY
a. Acts 2.12 saying to one another ἄλλος πρὸς ἄλλον λέγοντες [ALLOS]
b. 1 Th 5.11 build one another up οἰκοδομεῖτε εἷς τὸν ἕνα [HEIS]

ANOTHER WAY, BY
1. *from another place:* ἀλλαχόθεν ALLACHOTHEN*
Jn 10. 1 "he . . climbs in by another way

ANOTHER'S
1. *foreign:* ἀλλότριος ALLOTRIOS
[a]subst.
Lk 16.12 [a]"faithful in that which is another's
2 Cor 10.16 work already done in another's field

ANSWER
ANSWER, GIVE
ANSWER, MAKE

(a'd = answered)

1. *reply:* ἀποκρίνομαι APOKRINOMAI
Mt 3.15 Jesus a'd . . "Let it be so now
4. 4 he a'd, " 'Man shall not live by bread alone
8. 8 centurion a'd . . "Lord, I am not worthy
11. 4 Jesus a'd . . "Go and tell John
12.39 he a'd . . "no sign shall be given
13.11 he a'd . . "To you it has been given
13.37 He a'd, "He who sows . . is the Son of man
14.28 Peter a'd . . "Lord, . . bid me come
15. 3 He a'd . . "And why do you transgress?
15.13 He a'd, "Every plant . . will be rooted up
15.23 he did not answer her a word

Mt 15.24 He a'd, "I was sent only to the lost sheep
15.26 he a'd, "It is not fair
15.28 Jesus a'd . . "O woman, great is your faith!
16. 2 He a'd . . "When it is evening, you say
16.17 Jesus a'd . . "Blessed are you, Simon!
17.17 Jesus a'd, "O faithless . . generation
19. 4 He a'd, "Have you not read?
20.22 Jesus a'd, "You do not know what
21.21 Jesus a'd . . "Truly, . . if you have faith
21.24 Jesus a'd . . "I also will ask you
21.27 they a'd . . "We do not know
21.29 "he a'd, 'I will not'; but . . repented
21.30 "he a'd, 'I go, sir,' but did not go
22.29 Jesus a'd . . "You are wrong
22.46 no one was able to answer him a word
24. 2 he a'd . . "You see all these
24. 4 Jesus a'd . . "Take heed
25.26 "master a'd . . 'You wicked . . servant!
25.37 "the righteous will answer him, 'Lord
25.40 "King will answer . . 'Truly, I say to you
25.44 "will answer, 'Lord, when did we see thee?
25.45 "he will answer . . 'you did it not to me
26.23 He a'd, "He who has dipped . . in the dish
26.62 "Have you no answer to make?
26.66 They a'd, "He deserves death
27.12 when he was accused . . , he made no answer
27.14 he gave . . no answer . . to a single charge
27.25 people a'd, "His blood be on us!
Mk 6.37 he a'd . . "You give them something
7.28 she a'd . . " . . even the dogs under the table
8. 4 disciples a'd . . "How can one feed these men?
8.29 Peter a'd . . "You are the Christ
9.17 a'd . . "Teacher, I brought my son to you
9.19 a'd . . "O faithless generation, how long?
10. 3 He a'd . . "What did Moses command you?
11.22 Jesus a'd . . "Have faith in God
11.29 "answer me, and I will tell you
11.30 ⟨"I will ask you a question⟩ . . Answer me
11.33 they a'd . . "We do not know
12.28 seeing that he a'd them well
12.29 Jesus a'd, "The first is, 'Hear, O Israel
12.34 Jesus saw that he a'd wisely
14.40 they did not know what to answer him
14.60 "Have you no answer to make?
14.61 he was silent and made no answer
15. 2 he a'd . . , "You have said so
15. 4 "Have you no answer to make?
15. 5 Jesus made no further answer
15. 9 he a'd . . , "Do you want me to release?
Lk 1.19 angel a'd . . "I am Gabriel
3.11 he a'd . . "He who has two coats
3.16 John a'd . . "I baptize you with water
4. 4 a'd . . " 'Man shall not live by bread alone
4. 8 Jesus a'd . . " 'You shall worship the Lord
4.12 Jesus a'd . . " 'You shall not tempt the Lord
5. 5 Simon a'd, "Master, we toiled all night!
5.22 he a'd . . "Why do you question?
5.31 Jesus a'd . . "Those . . have no need
6. 3 Jesus a'd, "Have you not read?
7.22 he a'd . . "Go and tell John
7.40 Jesus answering said to him, "Simon
7.43 Simon a'd, "The one . . whom he forgave
8.50 Jesus a'd . . "Do not fear
9.19 they a'd, "John the Baptist
9.20 Peter a'd, "The Christ of God
9.41 Jesus a'd, "O faithless . . generation
9.49 John a'd, "Master, we saw a man
10.27 he a'd, "You shall love the Lord
10.28 "You have a'd right; do this
10.41 Lord a'd . . "Martha, . . you are anxious
11. 7 "he will answer . . 'Do not bother me
11.45 One . . a'd . . "you reproach us also
13. 2 a'd . . "Do you think . . these . . were worse?
13. 8 "he a'd . . 'Let it alone, sir, this year
13.15 Lord a'd . . "You hypocrites!
13.25 " 'Lord, open to us.' He will answer
15.29 "he a'd his father, 'Lo, . . I have served you
Lk 17.20 he a'd . . "The kingdom . . is not coming
19.40 He a'd, "I tell you, if these were silent
20. 3 He a'd . . "I also will ask you
20. 7 they a'd that they did not know
20.39 some of the scribes a'd, "Teacher
22.68 "if I ask you, you will not answer
23. 3 he a'd him, "You have said so
23. 9 but he made no answer
24.18 Cleopas a'd . . "Are you the only visitor?
Jn 1.21 "Are you the prophet?" . . he a'd, "No
1.26 John a'd . . "I baptize with water
1.48 Jesus a'd . . "Before Philip called . . I saw you
1.49 N. a'd . . "Rabbi, you are the Son of God!
1.50 Jesus a'd . . "Because I said to you?
2.19 Jesus a'd . . "Destroy this temple
3. 3 Jesus a'd . . "Truly, truly, I say to you
3. 5 Jesus a'd, "Truly, truly, I say to you
3.10 Jesus a'd . . "Are you a teacher of Israel?
3.27 John a'd, "No one can receive anything
4.10 Jesus a'd . . "If you knew the gift of God
4.17 woman a'd . . "I have no husband
5. 7 sick man a'd . . "Sir, I have no man
5.11 he a'd . . "The man who healed me said
5.17 Jesus a'd . . "My Father is working still
6. 7 Philip a'd . . "Two hundred denarii
6.26 Jesus a'd . . "Truly, truly, I say to you
6.29 Jesus a'd . . "This is the work of God
6.43 Jesus a'd . . "Do not murmur
6.68 Peter a'd . . "Lord, to whom shall we go?
6.70 Jesus a'd . . "Did I not choose you?
7.16 Jesus a'd . . "My teaching is not mine
7.20 people a'd, "You have a demon!
7.21 Jesus a'd . . "I did one deed
7.46 officers a'd, "No man . . spoke like this man!
7.47 Pharisees a'd . . "Are you led astray . . also?
8.14 Jesus a'd, "Even if I do bear witness
8.19 Jesus a'd, "You know neither me nor
8.33 a'd . . "We are descendants of Abraham
8.34 Jesus a'd . . "Truly, truly, I say to you
8.39 They a'd . . "Abraham is our father
8.48 Jews a'd . . "Are we not right in saying?
8.49 Jesus a'd, "I have not a demon
8.54 Jesus a'd, "If I glorify myself
9. 3 Jesus a'd, "It was not that this man sinned
9.11 He a'd, "The man called Jesus made clay
9.20 parents a'd, "We know . . this is our son
9.25 a'd, "Whether he is a sinner, I do not know
9.27 He a'd . . "I have told you already
9.30 man a'd, "Why, this is a marvel!
9.34 They a'd . . "You were born in utter sin
9.36 a'd . . "who is he, sir, that I may believe?
10.25 Jesus a'd . . "I told you
10.32 Jesus a'd . . "I have shown you many
10.33 Jews a'd . . "It is not for a good work
10.34 Jesus a'd . . "Is it not written in your law?
11. 9 Jesus a'd, "Are there not twelve hours?
12.23 Jesus a'd . . "The hour has come
12.30 Jesus a'd, "This voice has come
12.34 crowd a'd . . "We have heard from the law
13. 7 a'd . . "What I am doing you do not know
13. 8 Jesus a'd . . "If I do not wash you
13.26 Jesus a'd . . "to whom I shall give this morsel
13.36 Jesus a'd, "Where I am going you cannot
13.38 Jesus a'd, "Will you lay down your life?
14.23 Jesus a'd . . "If a man loves me
16.31 Jesus a'd . . "Do you now believe?
18. 5 They a'd . . "Jesus of Nazareth
18. 8 Jesus a'd, "I told you that I am he
18.20 Jesus a'd . . "I have spoken openly
18.22 "Is that how you answer the high priest?
18.23 Jesus a'd . . "If I have spoken wrongly
18.30 a'd . . "If this man were not an evildoer
18.34 Jesus a'd, "Do you say this?
18.35 Pilate a'd, "Am I a Jew?
18.36 Jesus a'd, "My kingship is not of this world
18.37 Jesus a'd, "You say that I am a king
19. 7 Jews a'd . . "We have a law

Jn 19.11 Jesus a'd.. "You would have no power
19.15 chief priests a'd.. "no king but Caesar
19.22 Pilate a'd, "What I have written
20.28 Thomas a'd.. "My Lord and my God!
21. 5 They answered him, "No
Acts 4.19 Peter and John a'd.. "Whether it is right
5.29 apostles a'd, "We must obey God
8.24 Simon a'd, "Pray for me
9.13 Ananias a'd, "Lord, I have heard.. about
11. 9 "voice a'd.. 'What God has cleansed
19.15 evil spirit a'd.. "Jesus I know, and Paul
21.13 Paul a'd, "What are you doing, weeping?
22. 8 "I a'd, 'Who are you, Lord?
22.28 tribune a'd, "I bought this citizenship
25.12 Festus.. a'd, "You have appealed
25.16 "I a'd.. that it was not the custom
Col 4. 6 know how you ought to answer

2. *decision, answer:* ἀπόκρισις APOKRISIS*
Lk 2.47 all.. were amazed at.. his answers
20.26 marveling at his answer they were silent
Jn 1.22 "Who are you? Let us have an answer
19. 9 But Jesus gave no answer

3. *defend oneself, speak in defense:* ἀπολογέομαι APOLOGEOMAI
Lk 12.11 "do not be anxious how.. to answer
21.14 "not to meditate beforehand how to answer

4. *listen, obey:* ὑπακούω HYPAKOUŌ
Acts 12.13 a maid named Rhoda came to answer

5. *say, affirm:* φημί PHĒMI
Lk 7.40 he answered, "What is it, Teacher?

CONTEXTUALLY
Mt 21.24 "and if you tell me the answer
2 Cor 1.11 granted us in answer to many prayers

ANSWER BACK

1. *answer again:* ἀνταποκρίνομαι ANTAPOKRINOMAI
Rom 9.20 who are you, a man, to answer back?

ANTICHRIST

1. *antichrist:* ἀντίχριστος ANTICHRISTOS*
1 Jn 2.18 antichrist is coming, so now many antichrists have come
2.22 antichrist.. denies the Father and the Son
4. 3 spirit of antichrist.. is in the world already
2 Jn . 7 such a one is the deceiver and the antichrist

ANTIOCH: Ἀντιόχεια 'antē,äk II,G-3; F-3

[1]in Syria [2]in Pisidia
Acts 11.19 [1]those.. traveled as far as A.
11.20 [1]men of Cyprus and Cyrene,.. coming to A.
11.22 [1]they sent Barnabas to A.
11.26 [1]he brought him to A.
11.26 [1]in A... disciples were.. called Christians
11.27 [1]prophets came down.. to A.
13. 1 [1]at A. there were prophets and teachers
13.14 [2]they.. came to Antioch of Pisidia
14.19 [2]Jews came there from A. and Iconium
14.21 [2]they returned to Lystra and to.. A.
14.26 [1]from there they sailed to A.
15.22 [1]send them to A. with Paul and Barnabas
15.23 [1]"to the brethren who are.. in A.
15.30 [1]sent off, they went down to A.
15.35 [1]Paul and Barnabas remained in A.
18.22 [1]then went down to A.
Gal 2.11 [1]when Cephas came to A. I opposed him
2 Tim 3.11 [2]my sufferings.. at Antioch

ANTIOCH, OF: Ἀντιοχεύς
Acts 6. 5 Nicolaus, a proselyte of Antioch

ANTIPAS: Ἀντιπᾶς 'antəpəs
Rev 2.13 " 'A. my witness,.. who was killed

ANTIPATRIS: Ἀντιπατρίς an'tipətrəs I,B-4; II,F-4
Acts 23.31 took Paul and brought him.. to A.

ANXIETIES, FREE FROM

1. *free from care:* ἀμέριμνος AMERIMNOS
1 Cor 7.32 I want you to be free from anxieties

ANXIETY

1. *anxious mind, cares:* μέριμνα MERIMNA
2 Cor 11.28 my anxiety for all the churches
1 Pet 5. 7 Cast all your anxieties on him

ANXIETY, HAVE

1. *be anxious, care for:* μεριμνάω MERIMNAŌ
Phil 4. 6 Have no anxiety about anything

ANXIETY, WITH

1. *weigh down:* βαρέω (pres. pass. part.) BAREŌ
2 Cor 5. 4 still in this tent, we sigh with anxiety

ANXIOUS, BE

1. *be anxious, care for:* μεριμνάω MERIMNAŌ
Mt 6.25 "do not be anxious about your life
6.27 "which.. being anxious can add one cubit?
6.28 "And why are you anxious about clothing?
6.31 "do not be anxious, saying, 'What?
6.34 "do not be anxious about tomorrow, for tomorrow will be anxious for itself
10.19 "When they deliver you.., do not be.. a.
Lk 10.41 "Martha, Martha, you are anxious
12.11 "before.. the rulers.. do not be anxious
12.22 "do not be anxious about your life
12.25 "which.. being anxious can add a cubit?
12.26 "why are you anxious about the rest?
1 Cor 7.32 The unmarried man is anxious
7.33 married man is anxious about worldly affairs
7.34 the unmarried woman or girl[z] is anxious
7.34 the married woman is anxious
Phil 2.20 who will be genuinely anxious

ANXIOUS BEFOREHAND, BE

1. *take thought before:* προμεριμνάω PROMERIMNAŌ*
Mk 13.11 "do not be anxious beforehand

ANXIOUS, LESS

1. *free from anxiety:* ἄλυπος (comp.) ALYPOS*
Phil 2.28 to send him.. that I may be less anxious

ANXIOUS MIND, BE OF

1. *worry:* μετεωρίζομαι METEŌRIZOMAI*
Lk 12.29 "do not seek.. nor be of anxious mind

ANXIOUSLY

1. *cause pain:* ὀδυνάω (pass. part.) ODYNAŌ
Lk 2.48 "I have been looking.. anxiously

ANY

1. *no one:* μηδείς (+neg.) MĒDEIS
Acts 10.28 "I should not call any man common
1 Cor 1. 7 you are not lacking in any spiritual gift
2 Th 2. 3 Let no one deceive you in any way

2. *no one, nothing:* οὐδείς (+neg.) OUDEIS
Lk 20.40 no longer dared to ask him any question
Acts 8.16 it had not yet fallen on any of them
1 Cor 9.15 I.. made no use of any of these rights

3. *all, every, whole:* πᾶς PAS
Mt 19. 3 "Is it lawful to divorce.. for any cause?
1 Cor 11. 4 Any man who prays or prophesies
11. 5 any woman who prays or prophesies
15.10 I worked harder than any of them
2 Cor 1. 4 to comfort those who are in any affliction
11. 9 refrain from burdening you in any way
13. 1 Any charge must be sustained
Phil 4.12 in any and all circumstances I have learned
2 Th 3. 6 keep away from any brother.. in idleness
2 Tim 2.21 ready for any good work
Tit 1.16 unfit for any good deed
3. 1 be ready for any honest work
Heb 4.12 sharper than any two-edged sword
Rev 7. 1 that no wind might blow.. against any tree
7.16 "the sun.. nor any scorching heat
9. 4 not to harm.. any green growth or any tree
18.22 "a craftsman of any craft.. no more

4. *who? what?:* τίς TIS I
Lk 17. 7 "Will a. one of you, who has a servant

5. *anyone, any:* τὶς TIS II
Jn 7.48 "Have any of the authorities.. believed?
20.23 "If you forgive the sins of any
20.23 "if you retain the sins of any
21. 5 Jesus said.. "Children, have you any fish?
Acts 2.45 distributed them to all, as any had need
4.32 that any of the things which he possessed

Acts 4.35 distribution was made . . as any had need
9. 2 if he found any belonging to the Way
13.15 "if you have any word of exhortation
25.16 "to give up any one before the accused
27.42 lest any should swim away and escape
Rom 13. 9 and any other commandment, are summed
1 Cor 7.12 if any brother has a wife . . an unbeliever
7.13 If any woman has a husband . . an unbeliever
14.27 If any speak in a tongue, let there be . . two
2 Cor 12.17 through any of those whom I sent to you
Gal 5. 6 nor uncircumcision is of any avail
6. 1 if a man is overtaken in any trespass
Phil 2. 1 So if there is any encouragement in Christ, any incentive of love, any participation in the Spirit, any affection and sympathy
3. 4 If any other man thinks he has reason
4. 8 if there is any excellence
1 Th 2. 9 that we might not burden any of you
2 Th 3. 8 we did not eat a. one's bread without paying
1 Tim 5.16 If a. believing woman[l] has relatives
Heb 3.12 lest there be in a. of you an evil . . heart
4. 1 let us fear lest any of you be judged
Jas 1. 5 If a. of you lacks wisdom, let him ask God
5.12 do not swear . . with any other oath
5.13 Is any cheerful? Let him sing praise
5.14 Is any among you sick? . . call . . the elders
2 Pet 3. 9 not wishing that any should perish

IDIOMATICALLY
a. Lk 6.4 "which it is not lawful for any but the priests to eat οὓς οὐκ ἔξεστιν φαγεῖν εἰ μὴ μόνους τοὺς ἱερεῖς [MONOS]

ANY, IF
1. *whoever:* ὃς ἄν HOS [B.3.b.4]
Mk 6.11 "and if any place will not receive you

ANY LONGER
1. *no longer, no more:* μηκέτι (+neg.) MĒKETI
Acts 25.24 "he ought not to live any longer

ANY MAN
1. *no one, nothing:* οὐδείς (+neg.) OUDEIS
Jn 18.31 "not lawful . . to put any man to death
2. *anyone, any:* τὶς TIS II
Mt 16.24 "If any man would come after me
Also Mk **8.34**; Lk **9.23**
Mk 4.23 "If any man has ears to hear, let him hear
[7.16 *"If any man has ears to hear, let him hear*‡
Jn 7.17 "if any man's will is to do his will
1 Cor 3.14 If the work which any man has built
3.15 If any man's work is burned up
Eph 2. 9 lest any man should boast
Phil 3. 4 If any other man thinks he has reason
Tit 1. 6 if any man is blameless

ANY MORE
1. *still, yet:* ἔτι (+neg.) ETI
Lk 20.36 "for they cannot die any more
Rev 7.16 "they shall . . neither thirst any more
21.4 "neither shall there be . . pain any more
2. *no longer, no more:* μηκέτι (+neg.) MĒKETI
Lk 8.49 "do not trouble the Teacher any more
3. *no longer, no more:* οὐκέτι (+neg.) OUKETI
Mt 22.46 nor . . dare to ask him any more questions
Mk 5. 3 no one could bind him any more
Rev 18.11 no one buys their cargo any more

ANY, NOT
1. *no one:* μηδείς MĒDEIS
2 Th 3.11 some of you are . . not doing any work
2. *no one, nothing:* οὐδείς OUDEIS [A.4.c]
[a]οὐθείς
Lk 23.14 [a]"I did not find . . guilty of any . . charges
Acts 27.34 "not a hair is to perish from . . any of you

ANY ONE
ANY ONE WHO
1. *man, mankind:* ἄνθρωπος ANTHRŌPOS
Rom 14.20 wrong for any one to make others fall
2. *each:* ἕκαστος (subst.) HEKASTOS
Eph 6. 8 whatever good any one does
3. *whoever:* ὃς ἄν/ἐάν HOS [B.3.b.4]
[a]ὅς
Mt **11.27**; **21.**[44‡
Lk **10.22**; **20.18**
Acts **8.19**
Rom **6.16**[a]
2 Cor **2.10**[a]
4. *no one:* μηδείς (+neg.) MĒDEIS
Mk 1.44 "See that you say nothing to any one
Acts 4.17 "warn them to speak no more to any one
2 Cor 6. 3 We put no obstacle in any one's way
5. *no one, nothing:* οὐδείς (+neg.) OUDEIS
[a]οὐθείς
Mk 9. 8 they no longer saw any one . . but Jesus
16. 8 they said nothing to any one
Lk 8.43 woman . . could not be healed by any one
Jn 8.33 "have never been in bondage to any one
1 Cor 9.15 rather die than have any one deprive me
2 Cor 11. 9 [a]in want, I did not burden any one
6. *all, every, whole:* πᾶς PAS
Mt 13.19 "When any one hears the word
1 Pet 3.15 be prepared to make a defense to any one
1 Jn 3.15 Any one who hates his brother
5.18 any one born of God does not sin
2 Jn . 9 Any one who . . does not abide in the doctrine
7. *anyone, any:* τὶς TIS II
[a]+ἄν
Mt **12.19**; **21.3**; **22.46**; **24.23**
Mk **9.30**, 35; **11.3**, 16; **13.21**
Lk **14.8**, 26; **19.8**, 31
Jn **4.33**; **6.46**, 51; **7.37**; **8.51**, 52; **9.22**, 31, 32; **10.9**; **11.9**, 10, 57; **12.26**[2], 47; **13.20**[a]
Acts **10.47**; **19.38**; **24.12**
Rom **8.9**
1 Cor **1.15**, 16; **3.12**, 17, 18; **5.11**; **7.18**[2], 36; **8.2**, 10; **11.16**, 34; **14.37**, 38; **16.22**
2 Cor **2.5**; **5.17**; **10.7**; **11.21**
Gal. **1.9**; **6.3**
2 Th **3.8**, 10, 14
1 Tim **1.8**; **3.1**; **5.8**; **6.3**
2 Tim **2.21**
Jas **1.23**, 26; **3.2**; **5.13**, 19
1 Jn **2.1**, 15, 27; **4.20**; **5.16**
2 Jn .10
Rev **3.20**; **11.5**[2]; **13.9**, 10[2]; **14.9**; **20.15**; **22.18**, 19

ANY ONE, IF
1. *whoever:* ὃς ἄν HOS [B.3.b.4]
Mt **10.14**; **15.5**; **23.16**[2], 18[2]
1 Jn **3.17**
2. *anyone who, whoever:* ὅστις HOSTIS
Mt 5.39 "if any one strikes you on the right cheek
5.41 "if any one forces you to go one mile

ANY ONE, NO . . .
ANY ONE, NOT
1. *no one, nothing:* οὐδείς OUDEIS
Mk 7.24 he . . would not have any one know
1 Cor 3.11 no other foundation can any one lay

ANYBODY
IDIOMATICALLY
a. 2 Tim 3.7 ⟨weak women⟩ who will listen to anybody ⟨γυναικάρια⟩ πάντοτε μανθάνοντα [PANTOTE; A.4.d]

ANYTHING
ANY THING
1. *one:* εἷς (neut.+neg.) HEIS
Jn 1. 3 without him was not anything made
2. *no one:* μηδείς (neut.+neg.) MĒDEIS
Rom 13. 8 Owe no one anything, except to love
Phil 1.28 not frightened in anything by . . opponents
3. *no one, nothing:* οὐδείς (+neg.) OUDEIS
Mk 7.12 "you no longer permit him to do anything
9.29 "cannot be driven out by anything but
Lk 9.36 told no one in those days anything
Jn 3.27 "No one can receive anything except
Acts 20.20 "I did not shrink from declaring . . anything
4. *all, every, whole:* πᾶς (subst. neut.) PAS
[a]+πρᾶγμα ὃ ἐάν A.1.f [b]pl.

Mt 18.19 a"if two of you agree on earth about a.
Acts 10.14 "I have never eaten anything..unclean
Rom 14. 2 bOne believes he may eat anything
1 Cor 9.12 bendure a. rather than put an obstacle
Eph 5.13 bwhen anything is exposed by the light
5.13(14) anything that becomes visible is light
Rev 22. 3 There shall no more be anything accursed
5. *vessel, tackle:* σκεῦος (+neg.) SKEUOS
Mk 11.16 not allow any one to carry anything
6. *who? what?:* τίς TIS I
Lk **19.48**
7. *anyone, any:* τις TIS II
Mt **21.3**
Mk **8.23**; **9.22**; **11.13**, 25; **13.15**; **16.18**‡
Lk **19.8**; **22.35**; **24.41**
Jn **1.46**; **14.14**; **16.23**
Acts **17.25**; **19.39**; **24.19**; **25.5**, 11
Rom **8.39**; **15.18**
1 Cor **3.7**; **6.12**; **10.19**²; **14.35**
2 Cor **2.10**; **3.5**; **13.8**
Gal. **6.15**
Eph **5.27**
Phil **3.15**; **4.8**
1 Th **1.8**
1 Tim **6.7**
Phm .18
Jas **1.7**
1 Jn **5.14**
CONTEXTUALLY
Mt 5.37 "a. more than this comes from evil[l]
Mk 4.22 "nor is anything secret
[7. 4 (*they do not eat a. from the market*†[0]
Lk 8.17 "nor a. secret that shall not be known
11. 7 "'I cannot get up and give you anything
11. 8 "though he will not get up and give him a.
15.16 "and no one gave him anything
Rom 14.21 or do a. that makes your brother stumble
1 Th 5. 1 you have no need to have a. written to you

ANYTHING, NEITHER...
ANYTHING, NO...
ANYTHING, NOT
1. *no one:* μηδείς (neut.) MĒDEIS [A.4.c]
Phil 4. 6 Have no anxiety about anything
2. *no one, nothing:* οὐδείς OUDEIS
Mt 5.13 "It is no longer good for anything
1 Cor 4. 4 I am not aware of a. against myself
7.19 neither circumcision counts for anything

APART
1. *by oneself, privately:* κατ' ἰδίαν IDIOS [B.1.a.1]
Mt 14.13 Jesus..withdrew..to a lonely place apart
17. 1 Jesus..led them up a high mountain apart
Mk 9. 2 Jesus..led them up a high mountain apart
Lk 9.10 he took them and withdrew apart

APART FROM
1. *separately, apart from:* χωρίς CHŌRIS
Jn 15. 5 "apart from me you can do nothing
Rom 3.21 righteousness..manifested apart from law
3.28 justified by faith apart from works
4. 6 God reckons righteousness apart from works
7. 8 Apart from the law sin lies dead
7. 9 I was once alive apart from the law
2 Cor 11.28 apart from other things, there is .. pressure
Heb 11.40 apart from us they should not be..perfect
Jas 2.18 Show me your faith apart from your works
2.20 that faith apart from works is barren
2.26 as the body apart from the spirit is dead, so faith apart from works is dead

APART, SET
1. *separate, appoint:* ἀφορίζω APHORIZŌ
Acts 13. 2 "Set apart for me Barnabas and Saul
Rom 1. 1 Paul,..set apart for the gospel of God
Gal 1.15 he who had set me apart before I was born

APELLES: Ἀπελλῆς ə'pelēz
Rom 16.10 Greet Apelles, who is approved in Christ

APOLLONIA: Ἀπολλωνία ˌapə'lōnēə II,D-3
Acts 17. 1 when they had passed through..A.

APOLLOS: Ἀπολλῶς ə'päləs
Acts 18.24 Jew named A., a native of Alexandria
19. 1 While Apollos was at Corinth, Paul passed
1 Cor 1.12 "I belong to Paul," or "I belong to A.
3. 4 when one says.."I belong to Apollos
3. 5 What then is Apollos? What is Paul?
3. 6 I planted, Apollos watered
3.22 whether Paul or A..., all are yours
4. 6 I have applied all this to myself and A.
16.12 As for..A., I..urged him to visit you
Tit 3.13 speed Zenas..and A. on their way

APOLLYON: Ἀπολλύων ə'pälyən
Rev 9.11 angel of the bottomless pit..called A.[b]†

APOLOGIZE TO
1. *call to, exhort, comfort:* παρακαλέω PARAKALEŌ
Acts 16.39 they came and apologized to them

APOSTASY, COMMIT
1. *fall to the side:* παραπίπτω PARAPIPTŌ*
Heb 6. 6 if they then commit apostasy

APOSTLE
1. *ambassador, messenger:* ἀπόστολος APOSTOLOS
Mt 10. 2 The names of the twelve apostles are these
Mk [3.14 twelve, *whom also he named apostles*‡
6.30 apostles returned to Jesus, and told him all
Lk 6.13 chose..twelve, whom he named apostles
9.10 On their return the apostles told him
11.49 "'I will send them prophets and apostles
17. 5 The apostles said.."Increase our faith!
22.14 he sat at table, and the apostles with him
24.10 women..who told this to the apostles
Acts 1. 2 after..commandment..to the apostles
1.26 he was enrolled with the eleven apostles
2.37 said to Peter and the rest of the apostles
2.42 devoted themselves to the apostles' teaching
2.43 signs were done through the apostles
4.33 with..power the apostles gave..testimony
4.35 laid it at the apostles' feet
4.36 Joseph..surnamed by..apostles Barnabas
4.37 money and laid it at the apostles' feet
5. 2 only..part and laid it at the apostles' feet
5.12 wonders were done..by..the apostles
5.18 they arrested the apostles
5.29 apostles answered, "We must obey God
5.40 they..called in the apostles,..beat them
6. 6 These they set before the apostles
8. 1 they were all scattered..except the apostles
8.14 when the apostles..heard that Samaria
8.18 Spirit was given through..apostles' hands
9.27 Barnabas..brought him to the apostles
11. 1 apostles..heard that the Gentiles..received
14. 4 some sided with..the apostles
14.14 apostles Barnabas and Paul..tore
15. 2 to go up to Jerusalem to the apostles
15. 4 welcomed by the church and the apostles
15. 6 apostles and the elders were gathered
15.22 seemed good to the apostles and..elders
15.23 "brethren, both the apostles and the elders
16. 4 decisions..by the apostles and elders
Rom 1. 1 Paul,..called to be an apostle
11.13 as I am an apostle to the Gentiles
16. 7 they are men of note among the apostles
1 Cor 1. 1 Paul,..an apostle of Christ Jesus
4. 9 apostles..., like men sentenced to death
9. 1 Am I not free? Am I not an apostle?
9. 2 If to others I am not an apostle
9. 5 other apostles and..brothers of the Lord
12.28 first apostles, second prophets, third teachers
12.29 Are all apostles? Are all prophets?
15. 7 appeared to James, then to all the apostles
15. 9 I am the least of the apostles, unfit to be called an apostle
2 Cor 1. 1 Paul, an apostle of Christ Jesus
11. 5 not..inferior to these superlative apostles

2 Cor 11.13 disguising themselves as apostles
12.11 not . . inferior to these superlative apostles
12.12 signs of a true apostle were performed
Gal 1. 1 Paul an apostle—not from men
1.17 those who were apostles before me
1.19 none of the other apostles except James
Eph 1. 1 Paul, an apostle of Christ Jesus
2.20 foundation of the apostles and prophets
3. 5 revealed to his holy apostles and prophets
4.11 some should be apostles, some prophets
Col 1. 1 Paul, an apostle of Christ Jesus
1 Th 2. 6 we might have made demands as apostles
1 Tim 1. 1 Paul, an apostle of Christ Jesus
2. 7 I was appointed a preacher and apostle
2 Tim 1. 1 Paul, an apostle of Christ Jesus
1.11 I was appointed a preacher and apostle
Tit 1. 1 Paul, . . an apostle of Jesus Christ
Heb 3. 1 Jesus, the apostle and high priest
1 Pet 1. 1 Peter, an apostle of Jesus Christ
2 Pet 1. 1 Simeon[x] Peter, . . apostle of Jesus Christ
3. 2 commandment . . through your apostles
Jude .17 predictions of the apostles of our Lord Jesus
Rev 2. 2 "'those who call themselves apostles
18.20 "Rejoice . . , O saints and apostles!
21.14 the twelve names of the twelve apostles

APOSTLE, FALSE
1. *false ambassador:* ψευδαπόστολος PSEUDAPOSTOLOS*
2 Cor 11.13 such men are false apostles

APOSTLESHIP
1. *mission, office of apostle:* ἀποστολή APOSTOLĒ
Acts 1.25 "the place in this ministry and apostleship
Rom 1. 5 we have received grace and apostleship
1 Cor 9. 2 you are the seal of my apostleship

APPAREL
1. *clothing:* ἐσθής ESTHĒS
Lk 23.11 arraying him in gorgeous apparel
24. 4 two men stood by them in dazzling apparel
Acts 10.30 "a man stood before me in bright apparel
2. *clothing:* ἱματισμός HIMATISMOS
Acts 20.33 "I coveted no one's silver or . . apparel
3. *dress, dignity:* καταστολή KATASTOLĒ*
1 Tim 2. 9 adorn themselves . . in seemly apparel

APPARELED, BE
1. *clothing:* ἱματισμός HIMATISMOS [B.1.a.2]
Lk 7.25 those who are gorgeously appareled

APPEAL
APPEAL, HEED AN
APPEAL, MAKE AN
1. *question, pledge:* ἐπερώτημα EPERŌTĒMA*
1 Pet 3.21 an appeal to God for a clear conscience
2. *call to, exhort, comfort:* παρακαλέω PARAKALEŌ
[a]pass. imper.
Mt 26.53 "think that I cannot appeal to my Father?
Rom 12. 1 I appeal to you therefore, brethren
15.30 I appeal to you, brethren, by our Lord
16.17 I appeal to you, brethren, to take note
1 Cor 1.10 I appeal to you, brethren, by the name
2 Cor 5.20 God making his appeal through us
13.11 [a]Mend your ways, heed my appeal
Phm . 9 for love's sake I prefer to appeal to you
.10 I appeal to you for my child, Onesimus
Heb 13.22 appeal to you, brethren, bear with my word
Jude . 3 necessary to write appealing to you
3. *exhortation, comfort:* παράκλησις PARAKLĒSIS
2 Cor 8.17 he not only accepted our appeal
1 Th 2. 3 our appeal does not spring from error

APPEAL TO
1. *call, surname:* ἐπικαλέω (mid.) EPIKALEŌ
Acts 25.11 "I appeal to Caesar
25.12 "You have appealed to Caesar
25.21 "Paul had appealed to be kept in custody
25.25 "as he himself appealed to the emperor
26.32 "set free if he had not appealed to Caesar
28.19 "I was compelled to appeal to Caesar

APPEAR
1. *cause to appear:* ἀναφαίνω (pass.) ANAPHAINŌ
Lk 19.11 supposed . . the kingdom . . was to appear
2. *manifest, make clear:* ἐμφανίζω (pass.) EMPHANIZŌ
Mt 27.53 out of the tombs . . they . . appeared to many
Heb 9.24 Christ has entered . . to a. . . on our behalf
3. *stand by:* ἐφίστημι EPHISTĒMI
Lk 2. 9 angel of the Lord appeared to them
Acts 12. 7 an angel of the Lord appeared
4. *appear:* ἐπιφαίνω EPIPHAINŌ
[a]aor. pass.
Acts 27.20 when neither sun nor stars appeared
Tit 2.11 [a]the grace of God has appeared for . . all men
3. 4 [a]when the goodness . . of God . . appeared
5. *come, go:* ἔρχομαι ERCHOMAI
Jn 7.27 "when the Christ appears, no one will know
7.31 "When the Christ appears, will he do more?
6. *come to be, happen, be:* γίνομαι GINOMAI
Mk 1. 4 John the baptizer appeared[c]†‡
7. *see, perceive:* ὁράω (pass.) HORAŌ
Mt 17. 3 there appeared to them Moses and Elijah
Mk 9. 4 there appeared to them Elijah with Moses
Lk 1.11 there appeared to him an angel of the Lord
9.31 appeared in glory and spoke
[22.43 *there appeared to him an angel*‡
24.34 "The Lord . . has appeared to Simon!
Acts 2. 3 there appeared to them tongues as of fire
7. 2 "The God of glory appeared to our father
7.26 "appeared to them as they were quarreling
7.30 "an angel appeared to him in the wilderness
7.35 "angel that appeared . . in the bush
9.17 "Jesus, who appeared to you . . , has sent me
13.31 "for many days he appeared to . . witnesses
16. 9 "a vision appeared to Paul in the night
26.16 "I have appeared . . to appoint you to serve
26.16 "the things . . in which I will appear
1 Cor 15. 5 he appeared to Cephas, then to the twelve
15. 6 he appeared to more than five hundred
15. 7 appeared to James, then to all the apostles
15. 8 Last of all . . he appeared also to me
Heb 9.28 Christ . . will appear a second time
Rev 12. 1 a great portent appeared in heaven
12. 3 another portent appeared in heaven
8. *be seen:* ὀπτάνομαι OPTANOMAI*
Acts 1. 3 appearing to them during forty days
9. *arrive, stand by:* παραγίνομαι PARAGINOMAI
Heb 9.11 when Christ appeared as a high priest
10. *bring to light, shine:* φαίνω (pass.) PHAINŌ
Mt 1.20 an angel of the Lord appeared to him
2. 7 ascertained . . what time the star appeared
2.13 an angel of the Lord appeared to Joseph
2.19 angel of the Lord appeared in a dream
13.26 "when the plants came up . . weeds appeared
23.27 "tombs, which outwardly appear beautiful
23.28 "So you also outwardly appear righteous
24.30 "then will appear the sign of the Son of man
Mk 16. 9 he appeared first to Mary Magdalene[k]‡
Lk 9. 8 ⟨said⟩ by some that Elijah had appeared
2 Cor 13. 7 not that we may appear to have met the test
Heb 11. 3 made out of things which do not appear
Jas 4.14 you are a mist that appears for a little
1 Pet 4.18 "where will the impious and sinner appear?
11. *make manifest, make known:* φανερόω (pass.) PHANEROŌ
Mk 16.12 he appeared . . to two of them . . walking[k]‡
16.14 he appeared to the eleven themselves[k]‡
2 Cor 5.10 we must all appear before the judgment
Col 3. 4 When Christ who is our life appears, then you also will appear with him in glory
Heb 9.26 he has appeared once for all at the end
1 Jn 2.28 abide in him, so that when he appears
3. 2 it does not yet appear what we shall be
3. 2 when he appears we shall be like him
3. 5 he appeared to take away sins
3. 8 Son of God appeared . . to destroy the works
12. *make over to; pretend to* (mid.): προσποιέω PROSPOIEŌ*
Lk 24.28 He appeared to be going further

IDIOMATICALLY
a. Rev 4.3 he who sat there appeared like jasper
ὁ καθήμενος ὅμοιος ὁράσει λίθῳ ἰάσπιδι [HORASIS]

APPEAR LATER
1. *follow close upon:* ἐπακολουθέω EPAKOLOUTHEŌ
1 Tim 5.24 the sins of others appear later

APPEARANCE
APPEARANCES
1. *form, semblance:* εἰδέα EIDEA*
Mt 28. 3 His appearance was like lightning
2. *form, appearance:* εἶδος EIDOS
Lk 9.29 appearance of his countenance was altered
3. *word, reckoning:* λόγος LOGOS
Col 2.23 appearance of wisdom in promoting rigor
4. *face, appearance:* ὄψις OPSIS
Jn 7.24 "Do not judge by appearances
5. *face, person:* πρόσωπον PROSŌPON
Mt 16. 3 "how to interpret the appearance of the sky‡
Lk 12.56 "how to interpret the appearance of earth
IDIOMATICALLY
a. Rev 9.7 In appearance the locusts were like horses
καὶ τὰ ὁμοιώματα τῶν ἀκρίδων ὅμοιοι ἵπποις [HOMOIŌMA]

APPEARING
1. *appearance:* ἐπιφάνεια EPIPHANEIA*
2 Th 2. 8 Jesus will slay him . . by his appearing
1 Tim 6.14 until the appearing of our Lord Jesus
2 Tim 1.10 manifested through the appearing of . . Jesus
4. 1 I charge you . . by his appearing
4. 8 all who have loved his appearing
Tit 2.13 the appearing of the glory of our . . God

APPEARS TO BE, WHAT
1. *as, so:* ὡς HŌS [B.3.b.4]
Rev 15. 2 I saw what appeared to be a sea of glass

APPETITES
1. *body cavity, belly:* κοιλία KOILIA [C.2]
Rom 16.18 such persons . . serve . . their own appetites[z]†

APPHIA: Ἀπφία 'afēə, 'apfēə
Phm . 2 ⟨to Philemon⟩ and A. our sister

APPIUS, FORUM OF: 'apēəs II,B-2
1. *forum of Appius:* Ἀππίου φόρον PHORON*
Acts 28.15 they . . came as far as the Forum of A.

APPLY
1. *change the form:* μετασχηματίζω METASCHĒMATIZŌ
1 Cor 4. 6 I have applied all this to myself and Apollos

APPLY ONESELF TO
1. *set over, direct:* προΐστημι (mid.) PROISTĒMI
Tit 3. 8 careful to apply themselves to good deeds[d]
3.14 learn to apply themselves to good deeds[d]†

APPOINT
1. *lift up and show:* ἀναδείκνυμι ANADEIKNYMI
Lk 10. 1 the Lord appointed seventy[g] others
2. *stretch out the hand (to elect):* χειροτονέω CHEIROTONEŌ*
Acts 14.23 when they had appointed elders
2 Cor 8.19 he has been appointed by the churches
3. *command:* διαταγή DIATAGĒ [A.1.a]
Rom 13. 2 he . . resists what God has appointed
4. *appoint, direct:* διατάσσω DIATASSŌ
Lk 3.13 "Collect no more than is appointed you
5. *determine, appoint:* ὁρίζω HORIZŌ
Acts 17.31 "judge . . by a man whom he has appointed
6. *set in order, appoint:* καθίστημι KATHISTĒMI
Acts 6. 3 "seven men . . whom we may appoint
Tit 1. 5 appoint elders in every town as I directed
Heb 7.28 the law appoints men in their weakness
8. 3 every high priest is appointed to offer gifts
7. *appoint by lot:* κληρόω KLĒROŌ*
Eph 1.12(11) appointed to live for . . his glory
8. *do, make:* ποιέω POIEŌ
Mk 3.14 he appointed twelve,[k] to be with him
[3.16 *So he appointed the twelve*‡[o]
Heb 3. 2 He was faithful to him who appointed him
9. *produce; select* (mid.): προχειρίζω PROCHEIRIZŌ*
Acts 3.20 "the Christ appointed for you, Jesus
22.14 "'The God of our fathers appointed you
26.16 "'to appoint you to serve and bear witness
10. *appoint, assign:* τάσσω TASSŌ
Acts 15. 2 appointed to go up to Jerusalem
22.10 "'you will be told all that is appointed for you
28.23 When they had appointed a day for him
11. *lay, put:* τίθημι (act. or mid.) TITHĒMI
Jn 15.16 "but I chose you and appointed you
1 Cor 12.28 God has appointed . . first apostles
1 Tim 1.12 he judged me faithful by appointing me
2. 7 For this I was appointed a preacher
2 Tim 1.11 For this gospel I was appointed a preacher
Heb 1. 2 a Son, whom he appointed the heir
CONTEXTUALLY
Heb 5. 5 but was appointed by him who said to him

APPOINT TO ACT
1. *set in order, appoint:* καθίστημι KATHISTĒMI
Heb 5. 1 every high priest . . is appointed to act

APPOINTED (*See also* TIME, APPOINTED)
1. *ordered:* τακτός TAKTOS*
Acts 12.21 On an appointed day Herod . . took his seat

APPOINTED, BE
1. *be laid away:* ἀπόκειμαι APOKEIMAI
Heb 9.27 it is appointed for men to die once

APPORTION
1. *take apart, divide:* διαιρέω DIAIREŌ
1 Cor 12.11 Spirit, who apportions to each . . as he wills
2. *divide, distribute:* μερίζω MERIZŌ
2 Cor 10.13 the limits God has apportioned us
Heb 7. 2 to him Abraham apportioned a tenth

APPROACH
1. *approach:* ἐγγίζω EGGIZŌ
Lk 12.33 "the heavens . . , where no thief approaches
Acts 9. 3 he approached Damascus

APPROVAL
1. *praise, approval:* ἔπαινος EPAINOS
Rom 13. 3 do . . good, and you will receive his approval
IDIOMATICALLY
a. 1 Pet 2.20 you have God's approval τοῦτο χάρις παρὰ θεῷ [CHARIS]

APPROVAL, RECEIVE
1. *bear witness, testify:* μαρτυρέω (pass.) MARTYREŌ
Heb 11. 2 the men of old received divine approval
11. 4 Abel . . received approval as righteous

APPROVE
1. *test, approve:* δοκιμάζω DOKIMAZŌ
Rom 2.18 ⟨if you⟩ approve what is excellent
14.22 to judge himself for what he approves
Phil 1.10 that you may approve what is excellent
1 Th 2. 4 just as we have been approved by God
2. *consent:* συνευδοκέω SYNEUDOKEŌ
Acts 22.20 "'I also was standing by and approving
Rom 1.32 they not only do them but approve

APPROVED
1. *approved:* δόκιμος DOKIMOS
Rom 14.18 who . . serves Christ is . . approved by men
16.10 Greet Apelles, who is approved in Christ
2 Tim 2.15 present yourself to God as one approved
IDIOMATICALLY
a. 1 Pet 2.19 For one is approved if τοῦτο γὰρ χάρις εἰ . . τις [CHARIS]

APRON
1. *apron:* σιμικίνθιον SIMIKINTHION*
Acts 19.12 aprons were carried away from his body

APT (*See* TEACHER, APT)

AQUILA: Ἀκύλας 'akwilə, ə'kwilə
Acts 18. 2 a Jew named A., a native of Pontus
18.18 Paul . . sailed . . with . . Priscilla and A.
18.26 when Priscilla and A. heard him
Rom 16. 3 Greet Prisca and A., my fellow workers
1 Cor 16.19 A. and Prisca . . send you hearty greetings
2 Tim 4.19 Greet Prisca and Aquila

ARABIA: Ἀραβία ə'rābēə II,G-5
Gal 1.17 I went . . into A.; . . I returned to Damascus
4.25 Now Hagar is Mount Sinai in A.[i]

ARABIAN: Ἄραψ
Acts 2.11 "Cretans and Arabians, we hear them

ARCHANGEL
1. *archangel:* ἀρχάγγελος ARCHAGGELOS*
1 Th 4.16 a cry of command, with the archangel's call
Jude . 9 archangel Michael, contending with the devil

ARCHELAUS: Ἀρχέλαος ˌärkəˈlāəs
Mt 2.22 he heard that A. reigned over Judea

ARCHIPPUS: Ἄρχιππος ärˈkipəs
Col 4.17 to A., "See that you fulfil the ministry
Phm . 2 Apphia.. and A. our fellow soldier

AREOPAGITE: Ἀρεοπαγίτης
Acts 17.34 believed, among them Dionysius the A.

AREOPAGUS: Ἄρειος πάγος ˌarēˈäpəgəs
Acts 17.19 they.. brought him to the Areopagus
17.22 Paul, standing in the middle of the A.

ARETAS: Ἀρέτας ˈarətəs
2 Cor 11.32 governor under King A. guarded.. Damascus

ARGUE
1. *discuss:* διαλέγομαι DIALEGOMAI
Acts 17. 2 Paul.. argued with them
17.17 he argued in the synagogue with the Jews
18. 4 he argued in the synagogue every sabbath
18.19 into the synagogue and argued with the Jews
19. 8 arguing and pleading about the kingdom
19. 9 argued daily in the hall of Tyrannus[r]
24.25 he argued about justice and self-control
2. *calculate, argue:* διαλογίζομαι DIALOGIZOMAI
Mt 21.25 ⟨elders⟩ argued with one another
Mk 11.31 ⟨scribes⟩ argued with one another
3. *examine together with, dispute:* συζητέω SYZĒTEŌ
Mk 8.11 Pharisees came and began to argue with him
9.14 disciples.. and scribes arguing with them

ARGUMENT
1. *calculation, argument:* διαλογισμός DIALOGISMOS
Lk 9.46 an argument arose among them
2. *reasoning:* λογισμός LOGISMOS
2 Cor 10. 5 We destroy arguments and every.. obstacle

ARIMATHEA: Ἀριμαθαία ˌarəməˈthēə I,C-4
Mt 27.57 rich man from A., named Joseph,.. a disciple
Mk 15.43 Joseph of A., a.. member of the council
Lk 23.50(51) a man named Joseph from.. A.
Jn 19.38 Joseph of A... asked Pilate

ARISE
1. *raise up, rise:* ἀνίστημι ANISTĒMI
Mt 12.41 "men of Nineveh will arise at the judgment
Mk 7.24 he arose and went away to the region of Tyre
9.27 Jesus.. lifted him up, and he arose
Lk 1.39 Mary arose and went with haste into.. Judah
4.38 he arose.. and entered Simon's house
11.32 "men of Nineveh will arise at the judgment
15.18 "'I will arise and go to my father
15.20 "And he arose and came to his father
23. 1 the whole company of them arose
Acts 5.36 "Theudas arose.. but he was slain
5.37 "After him Judas the Galilean arose
6. 9 some.. arose and disputed with Stephen
7.18 "there arose over Egypt another king
20.30 "from among your own selves will arise men
Eph 5.14 "Awake, O sleeper, and arise from the dead
Heb 7.11 need.. for another priest to arise
7.15 priest arises in the likeness of Melchizedek
2. *raise:* ἐγείρω (pass.) EGEIRŌ
[a]act. imper.
Mt 9.25 took her by the hand, and the girl arose
12.42 "queen of the South will arise
24.11 "many false prophets will arise
24.24 "false Christs and false prophets will arise
Mk 5.41 [a]"Little girl, I say to you, arise
13.22 "False Christs and false prophets will arise
Lk 7.14 "Young man, I say to you, arise
7.16 "A great prophet has arisen among us!
8.54 [a]he called, saying, "Child, arise
11.31 "queen of the South will arise at.. judgment
Acts 9. 8 Saul arose from the ground
3. *enter, go into:* εἰσέρχομαι EISERCHOMAI
Lk 9.46 argument arose.. as to.. the greatest
4. *come to be, happen, be:* γίνομαι GINOMAI
Mt 8.24 there arose a great storm on the sea
13.21 "persecution arises on account of the word
Mk 4.17 "persecution arises on account of the word
4.37 And a great storm of wind arose
Lk 6.48 "when a flood arose, the stream broke
15.14 "a great famine arose in that country
22.24 A dispute also arose among them
Jn 3.25 discussion arose between John's disciples
Acts 8. 1 great persecution arose against the church
11.19 the persecution that arose over Stephen
15.39 And there arose a sharp contention
19.23 there arose no little stir concerning the Way
23. 7 dissension arose between the Pharisees
23. 9 Then a great clamor arose
2 Pet 2. 1 But false prophets also arose
Rev 12. 7 Now war arose in heaven

ARISTARCHUS: Ἀρίσταρχος ˌarəˈstärkəs
Acts 19.29 Gaius and A.,.. Paul's companions in travel
20. 4 Thessalonians, A. and Secundus
27. 2 we put to sea, accompanied by A.
Col 4.10 A. my fellow prisoner greets you
Phm .24 Mark, A... and Luke, my fellow workers

ARISTOBULUS: Ἀριστόβουλος əˌristəˈbyüləs, ˌarisˈtäbyüləs
Rom 16.10 Greet those who belong to the family of A.

ARK
1. *box, chest:* κιβωτός KIBŌTOS*
[1]Noah's [2]of the covenant
Mt 24.38 [1]"until the day when Noah entered the ark
Lk 17.27 [1]"until the day when Noah entered the ark
Heb 9. 4 [2]ark of the covenant covered.. with gold
11. 7 [1]Noah, being warned.., constructed an ark
1 Pet 3.20 [1]during the building of the ark
Rev 11.19 [2]ark of his covenant was seen

ARM
1. *bent arm:* ἀγκάλη AGKALĒ*
Lk 2.28 took him up in his arms and blessed God
2. *arm:* βραχίων BRACHIŌN*
Lk 1.51 "He has shown strength with his arm
Jn 12.38 "has the arm of the Lord been revealed?
Acts 13.17 "with uplifted arm he led them out
3. *get ready, equip:* ὁπλίζω HOPLIZŌ*
1 Pet 4. 1 Since.. Christ suffered.., arm yourselves

ARMAGEDDON: Ἁρμαγεδών ˌärməˈgedᵊn
Rev 16.16 assembled . . at the place . . called . . A.

ARMED, FULLY
1. *equip, arm fully:* καθοπλίζω (mid. part.) KATHOPLIZŌ*
Lk 11.21 "When.. fully armed.. his goods are in peace

ARMOR
1. *tool, weapon:* ὅπλον (pl.) HOPLON
Rom 13.12 Let us.. put on the armor of light
2. *full armor:* πανοπλία PANOPLIA
Lk 11.22 "one stronger.. takes away his armor

ARMOR, WHOLE
1. *full armor:* πανοπλία PANOPLIA
Eph 6.11 Put on the whole armor of God
6.13 take the whole armor of God

ARMS, TAKE IN ONE'S
1. *take in one's arms:* ἐναγκαλίζομαι ENAGKALIZOMAI*
Mk 9.36 he took a child.. in his arms
10.16 he took them in his arms and blessed them

ARMY
1. *soldiers' quarters, company:* παρεμβολή PAREMBOLĒ
Heb 11.34 ⟨prophets who⟩ put foreign armies to flight
2. *army:* στράτευμα STRATEUMA
Rev 19.14 armies of heaven, arrayed in fine linen
19.19 the kings of the earth with their armies gathered to make war against.. his army
3. *encamped army:* στρατόπεδον STRATOPEDON*
Lk 21.20 "Jerusalem surrounded by armies

ARNI: Ἀρνί 'ärnī
Lk 3.33 Admin, the son of Arni, the son of Hezron

AROMA
1. *sweet smell:* εὐωδία EUŌDIA
2 Cor 2.15 we are the aroma of Christ to God

AROUND (*See also* PERI- *entries*)
1. *in a circle, round about:* κύκλῳ KYKLŌ
Rev 5.11 I heard around the throne . . the voice
2. *about, around:* περί (+acc.) PERI
Mt **3.**4; **8.**18
Mk **1.**6
3. *all around:* πέριξ PERIX*
Acts 5.16 people . . from the towns around Jerusalem

AROUSE
1. *stir up, arouse:* διεγείρω DIEGEIRŌ
2 Pet 1.13 right . . to arouse you by way of reminder
3. 1 I . . aroused your . . mind by way of reminder
2. *move, remove:* κινέω KINEŌ
Acts 21.30 all the city was aroused
CONTEXTUALLY
Rom 7. 5 sinful passions, aroused by the law

ARPHAXAD: Ἀρφαξάδ är'fagzəd
Lk 3.36 Cainan, the son of A., the son of Shem

ARRANGE
1. *appoint, direct:* διατάσσω DIATASSŌ
Acts 20.13 we set sail . . for so he had arranged
2. *lay, put:* τίθημι (mid.) TITHĒMI
1 Cor 12.18 God arranged the organs in the body

ARRANGE IN ADVANCE
1. *complete beforehand:* προκαταρτίζω PROKATARTIZŌ*
2 Cor 9. 5 brethren to . . arrange in advance for this gift

ARRANGEMENT
CONTEXTUALLY
Heb 9. 9 According to this a., gifts and sacrifices

ARRAY
1. *throw around, put on:* περιβάλλω PERIBALLŌ
Mt 6.29 "Solomon . . was not arrayed like one of these
Lk 12.27 "Solomon . . was not arrayed like one of these
23.11 Herod . . arraying him in gorgeous apparel
Jn 19. 2 soldiers . . arrayed him in a purple robe
Rev 17. 4 woman was arrayed in purple and scarlet

ARRAY, SET ONESELF IN
1. *place beside, stand before:* παρίστημι PARISTĒMI
Acts 4.26 " 'kings of the earth set themselves in array

ARRAYED
1. *put on, clothe:* ἐνδύω (perf. mid. part.) ENDYŌ
Rev 19.14 armies of heaven, arrayed in fine linen
2. *prepare, get ready:* ἑτοιμάζω (perf. pass. part.) HETOIMAZŌ
Rev 9. 7 locusts were like horses arrayed for battle

ARREST
1. *put hands upon:* ἐπιβάλλειν χεῖρας CHEIR; EPIBALLŌ [B.2.a.1]
Acts 4. 3 arrested them and put them in custody
5.18 they arrested the apostles
2. *take, lay hold of:* ἐπιλαμβάνομαι EPILAMBANOMAI
Acts 21.33 the tribune came up and arrested him
3. *seize, hold fast:* κρατέω KRATEŌ
Mt 21.46 when they tried to arrest him, they feared
26. 4 took counsel . . in order to arrest Jesus
Mk 12.12 they tried to arrest him, but feared
14. 1 seeking how to arrest him by stealth
4. *give up, allow:* παραδίδωμι PARADIDŌMI
Mt 4.12 when he heard that John had been arrested
Mk 1.14 after John was arrested, Jesus came
5. *take hold of:* πιάζω PIAZŌ
Jn 7.30 So they sought to arrest him
7.32 Pharisees sent officers to arrest him
7.44 Some of them wanted to arrest him, but
8.20 he taught . . but no one arrested him
10.39 they tried to arrest him, but he escaped
11.57 orders . . so that they might arrest him
6. *gather, seize, conceive:* συλλαμβάνω SYLLAMBANŌ
Acts 1.16 "Judas . . was guide to those who arrested
12. 3 he proceeded to arrest Peter also

ARRIVE
1. *stand by:* ἐφίστημι EPHISTĒMI
Acts 11.11 "At that very moment three men arrived
2. *come, go:* ἔρχομαι ERCHOMAI
2 Tim 3. 7 can never arrive at a knowledge of the truth
3 Jn . 3 some of the brethren arrived and testified
3. *come to be, happen, be:* γίνομαι GINOMAI
Acts 13. 5 When they arrived at Salamis
27. 7 We . . arrived with difficulty off Cnidus
2 Tim 1.17 but when he arrived in Rome he searched
4. *come down to, arrive:* καταντάω KATANTAŌ
Acts 21. 7 from Tyre, we arrived at Ptolemais
25.13 Agrippa the king and Bernice arrived
28.13 from there we . . arrived at Rhegium
5. *sail toward land:* καταπλέω KATAPLEŌ*
Lk 8.26 arrived at the country of the Gerasenes[a]
6. *go down, come to:* κατέρχομαι KATERCHOMAI
Acts 18. 5 Silas and Timothy arrived from Macedonia
7. *arrive, stand by:* παραγίνομαι PARAGINOMAI
Lk 11. 6 " 'friend of mine has arrived on a journey
Acts 14.27 when they arrived, they gathered the church
17.10 they arrived . . went into . . synagogue
18.27 When he arrived, he greatly helped those
23.35 "I will hear you when your accusers arrive
1 Cor 16. 3 And when I arrive, I will send those

ARROGANCE
1. *false pretension:* ἀλαζονεία (pl.) ALAZONEIA
Jas 4.16 As it is, you boast in your arrogance

ARROGANT
1. *self-willed, surly:* αὐθάδης AUTHADĒS
Tit 1. 7 a bishop . . must not be arrogant
2. *arrogant:* ὑπερήφανος HYPERĒPHANOS
2 Tim 3. 2 men will be lovers of self, . . arrogant
3. *puff up:* φυσιόω (perf. pass. part.) PHYSIOŌ
1 Cor 4.19 not the talk of these arrogant people

ARROGANT, BE
1. *puff up:* φυσιόω (pass.) PHYSIOŌ
1 Cor 4.18 Some are arrogant
5. 2 And you are arrogant!
13. 5(4) ⟨Love⟩ is not arrogant or rude

ART (*See also* MAGIC ARTS)
1. *art, skill:* τέχνη TECHNĒ
Acts 17.29 "a representation by the art . . of man

ARTEMAS: Ἀρτεμᾶς 'ärtəməs
Tit 3.12 When I send A. . . , do your best to come

ARTEMIS: Ἄρτεμις 'ärtəməs
Acts 19.24 Demetrius . . made silver shrines of A.
19.27 "temple of the great goddess A.
19.28 "Great is A. of the Ephesians!
19.34 "Great is A. of the Ephesians!
19.35 "Ephesus . . is temple keeper of the great A.

ARTICLE
1. *vessel, tackle:* σκεῦος SKEUOS
Rev 18.12 ⟨no one buys their cargo . .⟩ all articles of ivory, all articles of costly wood

AS
1. *until when:* ἄχρι οὗ ACHRI [A.4.e]
Acts **27.**33
2. *if, since:* εἰ EI [B.2.d.1]
1 Tim 5.10 attested . . as one who . . brought up children
3. *be:* εἰμί (inf.) EIMI
Lk 22.24 which . . was to be regarded as the greatest
4. *into, to, for:* εἰς (+acc.) EIS
Mt **24.**14
Lk **9.**5
Acts **7.**21; **10.**4
Rom **2.**26; **4.**3, 5, 9, 22; **9.**8
2 Cor **11.**13, 14
Gal **3.**6; **5.**13
Eph **1.**10
Heb **11.**8
Jas **2.**23
5. *in, at, by:* ἐν (+dat.) EN [B.1.a.2]
Mt **13.**4

Mk 4.4
Lk 2.43; 8.5, 42; 9.18, 29, 33, 34; 10.38; 11.27; 17.14; 18.35
Acts 9.3; 11.15; 26.7
1 Cor 11.18

6. *since:* ἐπειδή EPEIDĒ
1 Cor 15.21 For as by a man came death

7. *what, such as:* οἷος HOIOS
Mk 9.3
Rom 9.6
1 Cor 15.48[2]

8. *like, similar:* ὅμοιος HOMOIOS
Rev 21.18

9. *who, which, what:* ὅς HOS [B.3.b.4]
1 Cor 7.36
1 Tim 2.10

10. *as, so:* ὡς HŌS
Mt 1.24; 5.48; 6.10, 12; 7.29; 8.13; 10.16[3]; 15.28; 17.2, 20; 18.33; 19.19; 20.14; 22.39; 24.38; 26.19, 39, 55; 27.65; 28.3, 15
Mk 1.22[2]; 4.26; 7.6; 10.1; 12.31, 33; 14.48
Lk 3.4, 22, 23; 6.22; 7.12; 9.[54‡; 10.3, 27; 11.36; 12.58; 15.19, [21‡, 25; 17.6; 22.26[2], 27, 52; 23.14, 26
Jn 1.14, 32; 8.7‡; 15.6; 20.11
Acts 2.15; 3.22; 7.37, 51; 8.32, 36; 11.17; 13.25, 33; 16.4; 17.15, 28; 22.5; 23.11; 25.10, 14
Rom 1.21; 3.7; 5.18; 8.36; 9.25, 27; 13.9, 13; 15.24
1 Cor 3.1[3], 5, 15; 4.1, 7, 13, 14; 7.7, 8, 25; 8.7; 9.5, 20[2], 21, 26; 10.15; 14.33; 16.10
2 Cor 1.7; 2.17[2]; 3.1, 5; 6.4, 8, 9[3], 10[3], 13; 9.5[2]; 10.14; 11.3, 15, 16, 17; 13.2
Gal 1.9; 4.12, 14; 5.14; 6.10
Eph 3.5; 5.1, 8, 15[2], 22, 23, 24, 28, 33; 6.5, 6[2], 7, 20
Phil 1.20; 2.12, 15, 22
Col 2.6, 20; 3.12, 18, 22, 23; 4.4
1 Th 2.6; 5.6
2 Th 3.15[2]
1 Tim 5.1
2 Tim 2.3; 3.9
Tit 1.5, 7
Phm .16, 17
Heb 3.5, 6, 8, 11, 15; 4.3; 6.19; 11.9, 12, 27; 12.5, 7, 27; 13.3, 17
Jas 2.8, 9, 12
1 Pet 1.14; 2.11, 12, 13, 14, 16[3]; 3.6, 7; 4.10, 11[2], 12, 15, 16; 5.3, 12
2 Pet 1.19; 2.1; 3.8[2], 9, 16[2]
1 Jn 1.7; 2.27
2 Jn .5
Jude .10
Rev 1.14[2], 15, 17; 2.27[2]; 3.21; 5.6; 6.1, 11, 12, 13; 10.9, 10; 16.21; 17.12; 18.6; 21.2, 21; 22.1

11. *as if:* ὡσεί HŌSEI
Rom 6.13 as men . . brought from death to life

12. *as great as, how great:* ὅσος HOSOS
[a]ἐφ' ὅσον [b]with τοσοῦτος [c]καθ' ὅσον
Mt 25.40[a], 45[a]
Heb 1.4[b]; 3.3[c]; 8.6
Rev 18.7

13. *just as:* ὥσπερ HŌSPER
Mt 6.2, 7; 12.40; 18.17; 24.27, 37; 25.14, 32
Lk 17.24
Jn 5.21, 26
Acts 3.17
Rom 5.12, 19, 21; 6.4
1 Cor 8.5; 10.7; 11.12; 15.22; 16.1
2 Cor 8.7
Gal 4.29
1 Th 5.3
Heb 4.10; 7.27; 9.25
Jas 2.26

14. *as though it were:* ὡσπερεί HŌSPEREI*
1 Cor 15.8

15. *that, because:* ὅτι HOTI
Jn 19.42

16. *in accordance with, for:* κατά (+acc.) KATA
Rom 4.4[2]
1 Pet 1.15

17. *just as:* καθά KATHA*
Mt 27.10

18. *just as:* καθάπερ KATHAPER
Rom 3. 4 though every man be false, as it is written
9.13 As it is written, "Jacob I loved, but Esau
10.15 As it is written, "How beautiful are the feet!
11. 8 as it is written, "God gave them . . stupor
12. 4 as in one body we have many members
1 Cor 10.10 nor grumble, as some of them did
2 Cor 1.14 as you have understood in part
1 Th 3. 6 long to see us, as we long to see you
3.12 abound in love . . as we do to you

19. *as, insofar as:* καθό KATHO
Rom 8.26 we do not know how to pray as we ought

20. *as, just as:* καθώς KATHŌS
Mt 21.6; 26.24; 28.6
Mk 1.2; 4.33; 9.13; 14.16, 21; 15.8; 16.7
Lk 1.55, 70; 2.20, 23; 5.14; 6.31; 11.1, 30; 17.26, 28; 19.32; 22.13, 29; 24.39
Jn 1.23; 3.14; 5.30; 6.31, 57; 7.38; 8.28; 10.15; 12.14, 50; 13.15, 33; 14.27, 31; 15.4, 9, 12; 17.11, 14, 16, 18; 19.40; 20.21
Acts 2.4, 22; 7.17, 42, 48; 15.15; 22.3
Rom 1.17; 2.24; 3.8, 10; 4.17; 8.36; 9.29, 33; 11.26; 15.3, 7, 9, 21
1 Cor 1.31; 2.9; 4.17; 5.7; 8.2; 10.6, 7, 8, 9; 11.1; 12.11, 18; 14.34; 15.38
2 Cor 1.5, 14; 6.16; 8.5, 6, 15; 9.3, 7, 9; 10.7; 11.12
Gal 5.21
Eph 3.3; 4.17, 21, 32; 5.2, 3, 25, 29
Phil 2.12; 3.17
Col 1.6, 7; 3.13
1 Th 2.2, 5, 13, 14; 4.1, 6, 11, 13
2 Th 1.3; 3.1
1 Tim 1.3
Heb 3.7; 4.3; 5.6; 10.25; 11.12
1 Pet 4.10
2 Pet 1.14
1 Jn 2.18; 3.2, 3, 7; 4.17
2 Jn .6
3 Jn .3

21. *so far as, as:* καθότι KATHOTI
Acts 2.45 distributed them to all, as any had need
4.35 distribution . . to each as any had need

22. *about, concerning:* περί (+gen.) PERI
Rom 8.[3†

23. *in the manner in which:* ὃν τρόπον (acc.) TROPOS
[a]καθ' ὃν τρόπον B.1.a.1
Mt 23.37
Lk 13.34
Acts 1.11; 7.28; 27.25[a]
2 Tim 3.8

IDIOMATICALLY
a. Heb 5.15 [HOMOIOTĒS]
b. 1 Cor 16.2 [HOSTIS]

AS FOR

1. *whether, or:* εἴτε EITE
1 Cor 13. 8 as for prophecies, they will pass away; as for tongues, they will cease; as for knowledge, it will pass away
2 Cor 8.23 As for Titus, he is my partner
8.23 as for our brethren, they are messengers[j]

2. *for:* γάρ GAR [A.5.b]
Acts 7.40

AS FOR YOU

1. *you, thou:* σύ SY
2 Tim 3.14; 4.5
Tit 2.1

AS IF

1. *as, so:* ὡς HŌS
Rom 9.32; 1 Cor 5.3; Heb 11.29

AS IT IS

1. *thus, so:* οὕτως HOUTŌS
2 Pet 3. 4 "all things have continued as they were

2. *in accordance with, for:* κατά (+acc.) KATA
Phil 1.20

3. *now:* νῦν NYN
1 Cor 7.14 unclean, but as it is they are holy
12.18 But as it is, God arranged the organs
12.20 As it is, there are many parts, yet one body
2 Cor 7. 9 As it is, I rejoice,.. because you were grieved
Heb 2. 8 As it is, we do not yet see
8. 6 as it is, Christ[o] has obtained a ministry
11.16 But as it is, they desire a better country
Jas 4.16 As it is, you boast in your arrogance
4. *now:* νυνί NYNI
Heb 9.26 But as it is, he has appeared once for all

AS, JUST (*See* JUST AS)

AS OF
1. *as if:* ὡσεί HŌSEI
Acts 2. 3 there appeared to them tongues as of fire

AS OFTEN AS
1. *as many times as:* ὁσάκις HOSAKIS*
[a]+ἐάν
1 Cor 11.25 [a]"Do this, as often as you drink it
11.26 [a]For as often as you eat this bread
Rev 11. 6 [a]power.. to smite.. as often as they desire

AS ONE IS
1. *thus, so:* οὕτως HOUTŌS
1 Cor 7.26 well for a person to remain as he is
7.40 she is happier if she remains as she is

AS SOON AS
1. *when, as soon as:* ὡς ἄν HŌS [A.4.e]
Phil 2.23 just as soon as I see how it will go
IDIOMATICALLY
a. Mt 24.32; Mk 13.28 "as soon as its branch becomes tender ὅταν ἤδη ὁ κλάδος αὐτῆς γένηται ἁπαλός [ĒDĒ; HOTAN]
b. Mk 15.1 as soon as it was morning εὐθὺς πρωΐ [EUTHYS II]
c. Lk 21.30 "as soon as they come out in leaf ὅταν προβάλωσιν ἤδη [ĒDĒ; HOTAN]

AS, SUCH (*See* SUCH AS)

AS THOUGH
1. *as, so:* ὡς HŌS
Acts **3**.12; **23**.15, 20; 1 Cor **4**.18; **7**.29, 30, 31
IDIOMATICALLY
a. Rom 9.6 But it is not as though οὐχ οἷον δὲ ὅτι [HOIOS]

AS TO
1. *in accordance with, for:* κατά (+acc.) KATA
Phil **3**.5, 6[2]
2. *about, concerning:* περί (+gen.) PERI
1 Cor **8**.4; 1 Th. **5**.1

AS WELL AS
1. *as, just as:* καθώς KATHŌS
Rom 1.13 among you as well as among the rest
Heb 5. 3 for his.. sins as well as for.. the people

AS S. WOULD HAVE
1. *in accordance with, for:* κατά (+acc.) KATA
1 Pet [5. 2 but willingly, *as God would have you*‡

ASA: Ἀσάφ 'āsə
Mt 1. 7 Abijah the father of Asa[b]†
1. 8 Asa[b] the father of Jehoshaphat†

ASCEND
1. *go up, come up:* ἀναβαίνω ANABAINŌ
Jn 1.51 "angels of God ascending and descending
3.13 "No one has ascended into heaven but he
6.62 "if you were to see the Son of man ascending
20.17 "I have not yet ascended to the Father
20.17 "I am ascending to my Father
Acts 2.34 "David did not ascend into the heavens
10. 4 "your alms have ascended as a memorial
Rom 10. 6 "Who will ascend into heaven?
Eph 4. 8 "When he ascended on high he led a host
4. 9 ("He ascended," what does it mean?
4.10 (He who descended is he who also ascended
Rev 7. 2 Then I saw another angel ascend
11. 7 the beast that ascends from the.. pit
17. 8 "The beast.. is to ascend from the.. pit

ASCERTAIN
1. *make exact:* ἀκριβόω AKRIBOŌ*
Mt 2. 7 Herod.. ascertained from ⟨the wise men⟩
2.16 time.. ascertained from the wise men
2. *learn to know, recognize:* ἐπιγινώσκω EPIGINŌSKŌ
Acts 24.11 "As you may ascertain, it is not more

ASHAMED, BE
ASHAMED OF, BE
1. *be ashamed:* αἰσχύνομαι AISCHYNOMAI
Lk 16. 3 " 'I am ashamed to beg
Phil 1.20 I shall not be at all ashamed
1 Pet 4.16 as a Christian, let him not be ashamed
2. *put to shame:* ἐντρέπω (pass.) ENTREPŌ
2 Th 3.14 that he may be ashamed
3. *be ashamed of:* ἐπαισχύνομαι EPAISCHYNOMAI*
Mk 8.38 "whoever is ashamed of me.., of him will the Son of man also be ashamed
Lk 9.26 "whoever is ashamed of me.., of him will the Son of man be ashamed
Rom 1.16 For I am not ashamed of the gospel
6.21 the things of which you are now ashamed
2 Tim 1. 8 Do not be ashamed then of testifying
1.12 not ashamed, for I know whom I.. believed
1.16 he was not ashamed of my chains
Heb 2.11 he is not ashamed to call them brethren
11.16 God is not ashamed to be called their God

ASHAMED, HAVING NO NEED TO BE
1. *having no cause for shame:* ἀνεπαίσχυντος ANEPAISCHYNTOS*
2 Tim 2.15 workman who has no need to be ashamed

ASHAMED, MAKE
1. *put to shame:* ἐντρέπω ENTREPŌ
1 Cor 4.14 I do not write this to make you ashamed

ASHER: Ἀσήρ 'ashər
Lk 2.36 a prophetess, Anna,.. of the tribe of A.
Rev 7. 6 twelve thousand of the tribe of A.

ASHES
1. *ashes:* σποδός SPODOS*
Mt 11.21 "repented long ago in sackcloth and ashes
Lk 10.13 "repented.., sitting in sackcloth and ashes
Heb 9.13 if the sprinkling.. with the ashes.. sanctifies

ASHES, TURN TO
1. *burn to ashes:* τεφρόω TEPHROŌ*
2 Pet 2. 6 turning.. Sodom and Gomorrah to ashes

ASHORE
1. *to the seashore:* ἐπὶ τὸν αἰγιαλόν AIGIALOS [B.1.a.1]
Mt 13.48 when it was full, men drew it ashore
2. *to land:* εἰς τὴν γῆν GĒ [B.1.a.1]
Jn 21.11 Simon Peter.. hauled the net ashore

ASHORE, BRING
1. *expel, drive on shore:* ἐξωθέω EXŌTHEŌ
Acts 27.39 planned if possible to bring the ship ashore

ASHORE, GO
1. *go out:* ἐξέρχομαι EXERCHOMAI
Mt 14.14 As he went ashore he saw a great throng
Mk 6.34 As he went ashore he saw a great throng[o]

ASIA: Ἀσία 'āzhə II,E-3
Acts 2. 9 "residents of Mesopotamia.. and A.
6. 9 those from Cilicia and Asia, arose
16. 6 forbidden by the Holy Spirit to speak.. in A.
19.10 residents of Asia heard the word of the Lord
19.22 having sent.. his helpers,.. he.. stayed in A.
19.26 "throughout all A. this Paul has persuaded
19.27 "Artemis.., whom all A... worship
20.16 that he might not have to spend time in A.
20.18 "from the first day.. I set foot in A.
21.27 Jews from A... stirred.. the crowd
24.18 "Jews from Asia ⟨ought to be here⟩
27. 2 a ship.. about to sail.. along the coast of A.
Rom 16. 5 Epaenetus,.. the first convert in A.
1 Cor 16.19 The churches of Asia send greetings
2 Cor 1. 8 the affliction we experienced in Asia
2 Tim 1.15 all who are in A. turned away from me
1 Pet 1. 1 To the exiles of the Dispersion in.. A.
Rev 1. 4 John to the seven churches that are in A.

ASIAN: Ἀσιανός
Acts 20. 4 the Asians, Tychicus and Trophimus

ASIARCH: Ἀσιάρχης
Acts 19.31 some of the Asiarchs also . . sent to him

ASIDE (*See also* LAY ASIDE)
1. *by oneself, on the side:* παρ' ἑαυτῷ HEAUTOU [B.1.a.1]
1 Cor 16. 2 each of you is to put something aside
2. *by oneself, privately:* κατ' ἰδίαν IDIOS [B.1.a.1]
Mt 20.17 he took the twelve disciples aside
3. *out of the middle:* ἐκ τοῦ μέσου MESOS [B.1.a.1]
Col 2.14 this he set aside, nailing it to the cross

ASIDE, GO
1. *withdraw:* ἀναχωρέω ANACHŌREŌ
Acts 23.19 tribune . . going aside asked him privately

ASIDE, SET
1. *abolition, rejection:* ἀθέτησις ATHETĒSIS [B.3.a.2]
Heb 7.18 a former commandment is set aside

ASIDE, TURN
1. *turn away:* ἐκκλίνω EKKLINŌ
Rom 3.12 "All have turned aside
2. *go by the side of:* παραβαίνω PARABAINŌ
Acts 1.25 "ministry . . from which Judas turned aside

ASK
ASK FOR
1. *ask, request:* αἰτέω (act. or mid.) AITEŌ
Mt 6. 8 "Father knows what you need before you ask
7. 7 "Ask, and it will be given you
7. 8 "every one who asks receives
7. 9 "what man . . , if his son asks him for bread?
7.10 "if he asks for a fish, will give . . serpent?
7.11 "Father ⟨will⟩ give . . to those who ask!
14. 7 promised . . whatever she might ask
18.19 "if two . . agree . . about anything they ask
20.20 mother of the sons of Zebedee . . asked him
20.22 "You do not know what you are asking
21.22 "whatever you ask in prayer, you will receive
27.20 ask for Barabbas and destroy Jesus
27.58 He . . asked for the body of Jesus
Mk 6.22 "Ask me for whatever you wish
6.23 "Whatever you ask me, I will give you
6.24 "What shall I ask?" . . "The head of John
6.25 she . . asked, . . "I want . . the head of John
10.35 "do for us whatever we ask of you
10.38 "You do not know what you are asking
11.24 "whatever you ask in prayer, believe
15. 8 to ask Pilate to do as he was wont
15.43 Joseph of A. . . asked for the body of Jesus
Lk 1.63 he asked for a writing tablet, and wrote
11. 9 "Ask, and it will be given you
11.10 "every one who asks receives
11.11 "What father . . , if his son asks for[l] a fish,
11.12 "or if he asks for an egg, . . a scorpion?
11.13 "the Holy Spirit to those who ask!
23.25 He released the man . . whom they asked for
23.52 This man . . asked for the body of Jesus
Jn 4. 9 "How is it that you . . ask a drink of me?
4.10 "If you knew . . , you would have asked
11.22 "whatever you ask from God, God will give
14.13 "Whatever you ask in my name, I will do
14.14 "if you ask[g] . . in my name, I will do it
15. 7 "ask whatever you will, and it shall be
15.16 "that whatever you ask . . , he may give it
16.23 "if you ask anything of the Father, he will
16.24 "Hitherto you have asked nothing in my name; ask, and you will receive
16.26 "In that day you will ask in my name
Acts 3. 2 to ask alms of those who entered the temple
3.14 "you . . asked for a murderer to be granted
9. 2 asked him for letters to the synagogues
12.20 people of Tyre . . asked for peace
13.21 "they asked for a king; . . God gave them
13.28 "yet they asked Pilate to have him killed
25. 3 asking . . to have the man sent to Jerusalem
25.15 "elders . . asking for sentence against him
Eph 3.13 So I ask you not to[e] lose heart
3.20 more abundantly than all that we ask
Col 1. 9 we have not ceased to pray . . , asking
Jas 1. 5 If any of you lacks wisdom, let him ask God
1. 6 let him ask in faith, with no doubting
4. 2 You do not have, because you do not ask
4. 3 You ask and do not receive, because you ask wrongly
1 Jn 3.22 we receive from him whatever we ask
5.14 if we ask anything according to his will
5.15 he hears us in whatever we ask
5.16 he will ask, and God[i] will give him life
2. *pray, beg:* δέομαι DEOMAI
Rom 1.10 asking that . . I may now . . succeed
3. *say, speak:* εἶπον EIPON
Mk 9.18 "I asked your disciples to cast it out
Acts 8.30 Philip . . asked, "Do you understand?
4. *consult, ask a question:* ἐπερωτάω EPERŌTAŌ
Mt 12.10 asked . . "Is it lawful to heal on the sabbath?
16. 1 they asked him to show them a sign
17.10 disciples asked . . "why do the scribes say?
27.11 governor asked him, "Are you the King?
Mk 5. 9 Jesus[o] asked him, "What is your name?
7. 5 scribes asked him, "Why do your disciples?
7.17 his disciples asked him about the parable
8.23 he asked him, "Do you see anything?
8.27 he asked . . "Who do men say that I am?
8.29 he asked . . "But who do you say that I am?
9.11 they asked . . "Why do the scribes say?
9.16 he asked them, "What are you discussing?
9.21 Jesus[h] asked . . "How long has he had this?
9.28 disciples asked . . "Why could we not?
9.32 they were afraid to ask him
9.33 he asked them, "What were you discussing?
10. 2 Pharisees . . asked, "Is it lawful . . to divorce?
10.10 in the house the disciples asked him again
10.17 asked him, "Good Teacher, what must I do?
12.28 asked him, "Which commandment is . . first?
13. 3 Peter and J. . . asked him privately
14.60 high priest . . asked . . "Have you no answer?
14.61 high priest asked . . "Are you the Christ?
15. 2 Pilate asked . . "Are you . . King of the Jews?
15. 4 Pilate again asked . . "Have you no answer?
15.44 Pilate . . asked . . whether he was . . dead[i]
Lk 3.10 multitudes asked . . "What then shall we do?
3.14 Soldiers . . asked . . "what shall we do?
6. 9 "I ask you, is it lawful on the sabbath?
8. 9 disciples asked him what this parable meant
8.30 Jesus . . asked . . "What is your name?
9.18 asked . . "Who do . . people say that I am?
17.20 asked . . when the kingdom . . was coming
18.18 ruler asked . . "what shall I do to inherit . . life?
18.40 when he came near, ⟨Jesus⟩ asked him
20.21 They asked him, "Teacher, we know
21. 7 they asked him, "Teacher, when will this be?
22.64 asked him, "Prophesy! Who . . struck you?
23. 6 asked whether the man was a Galilean
Jn 9.23 his parents said, "He is of age, ask him
18. 7 Again he asked them, "Whom do you seek?
Acts 23.34 he asked to what province he belonged
Rom 10.20 "shown myself to those who did not ask
1 Cor 14.35 let them ask their husbands at home
5. *say, speak:* ἐρῶ ERŌ
1 Cor 15.35 some one will ask, "How are the dead raised?
6. *ask, question, beg:* ἐρωτάω ERŌTAŌ
Mt 16.13 asked . . "Who do men say . . Son of man is?
19.17 "Why do you ask me about what is good?
21.24 Jesus answered . . "I also will ask you
Mk 4.10 the twelve asked him concerning the parables
8. 5 he asked them, "How many loaves?
Lk 5. 3 he asked him to put out . . from the land
7. 3 asking him to come and heal his slave
7.36 One of the Pharisees asked him to eat
8.37 the Gerasenes[a] asked him to depart
9.45 they were afraid to ask him about this
11.37 a Pharisee asked him to dine with him
14.32 "he sends an embassy and asks terms
19.31 "If any one asks you, 'Why are you untying?

Lk 20. 3 He answered . . "I also will ask you
22.68 "if I ask you, you will not answer
23. 3 Pilate asked . . "Are you . . King of the Jews?
Jn 1.19 Jews sent priests . . to ask . . "Who are you?
1.21 they asked him . . "Are you Elijah?
1.25 They asked . . "Then why are you baptizing?
4.40 the Samaritans . . asked him to stay
5.12 They asked him, "Who is the man?
8. 7 as they continued to ask . . , he stood up[r]‡
9. 2 his disciples asked . . "Rabbi, who sinned?
9.15 asked him how he had received his sight
9.19 asked them, "Is this your son?
9.21 "Ask him; he is of age
16. 5 "none of you asks me, 'Where are you going?
16.19 Jesus knew that they wanted to ask him
16.23 "In that day you will ask nothing of me
16.26 "In that day you will ask in my name
18.21 "Why do you ask me? Ask those who have heard me
19.31 Jews asked . . that their legs might be broken
19.38 Joseph . . asked . . that he might take
Acts 1. 6 they asked . . "Lord, will you at this time?
3. 3 Seeing Peter and John . . , he asked for alms
10.48 they asked him to remain for some days
16.39 they . . asked them to leave the city
18.20 they asked him to stay for a longer period
23.18 "Paul . . asked me to bring this . . man to you
23.20 "Jews have agreed to ask you to bring Paul
Phil 4.3 I ask you also, . . help these women
7. *examine well:* ἐξετάζω EXETAZŌ
Jn 21.12 none of the disciples dared ask him
8. *say, speak:* λέγω LEGŌ
Jn 18.26 One . . asked, "Did I not see you?
Acts 25.20 "I asked whether he wished to go
Rom 10.18 But I ask, have they not heard?
10.19 Again I ask, did Israel not understand?
11. 1 I ask . . has God rejected his people?
11.11 I ask, have they stumbled so as to fall?
9. *recall, summon:* μετακαλέω (mid.) METAKALEŌ
Acts 10.32 "'Send . . to Joppa and ask for Simon
10. *ask for, decline:* παραιτέομαι PARAITEOMAI
Mk 15. 6 to release . . one . . for whom they asked[0]
11. *call to, exhort, comfort:* παρακαλέω PARAKALEŌ
Acts 28.20 "I have asked . . because of the hope of Israel
12. *inquire about, learn:* πυνθάνομαι PYNTHANOMAI
Lk 15.26 "he called one of the servants and asked
Jn 4.52 he asked . . the hour when he began to mend
Acts 10.18 to ask whether Simon . . was lodging there
10.29 "I ask then why you sent for me
23.19 tribune . . asked him privately, "What is it?
13. *seek, desire:* ζητέω ZĒTEŌ
Mt 12.46 brothers stood outside, asking to speak
[12.47 "*standing outside, asking to speak to you*‡
Mk 3.32 "your brothers[l] are outside, asking for you
Jn 16.19 "Is this what you are asking yourselves?
IDIOMATICALLY
a. Gal. 3.2 Let me ask you only this τοῦτο μόνον θέλω μαθεῖν ἀφ' ὑμῶν [MANTHANŌ]
CONTEXTUALLY
Lk [11.11 *or if he asks for* a fish†‡

ASK A QUESTION
1. *consult, ask a question:* ἐπερωτάω EPERŌTAŌ
Mt 22.23 Sadducees . . asked him a question
22.35 lawyer, asked him a question, to test him
22.41 Jesus asked them a question
22.46 nor . . dare to ask him any more questions
Mk 11.29 Jesus said . . "I will ask you a question
12.18 Sadducees . . asked him a question
12.34 no one dared to ask him any question
Lk 2.46 in the temple . . asking them questions
20.28(27) they asked him a question . . "Teacher
20.40 no longer dared to ask him any question

ASK AGAIN
1. *demand back:* ἀπαιτέω APAITEŌ
Lk 6.30 "of him . . do not ask ⟨your goods⟩ again

ASK LEAVE
1. *ask, request:* αἰτέω (mid.) AITEŌ
Acts 7.46 "⟨David⟩ asked leave to find a habitation

ASLEEP
1. *sleep, be asleep:* καθεύδω (part.) KATHEUDŌ
Mk 4.38 he was in the stern, asleep on the cushion
13.36 "lest he come . . and find you asleep

ASLEEP, BE
1. *sleep, be asleep:* καθεύδω KATHEUDŌ
Mt 8.24 there arose a . . storm . . but he was asleep
Mk 14.37 he said to Peter, "Simon, are you asleep?
2. *put to sleep:* κοιμάω (pass.) KOIMAŌ
Mt 28.13 "'His disciples came . . while we were asleep
1 Th 4.13 not . . ignorant . . concerning those who are a.
3. *doze, be half asleep:* νυστάζω NYSTAZŌ
2 Pet 2. 3 their destruction has not been asleep

ASLEEP, FALL
1. *fall asleep:* ἀφυπνόω APHYPNOŌ*
Lk 8.23 as they sailed he fell asleep
2. *put to sleep:* κοιμάω (pass.) KOIMAŌ
Mt 27.52 saints who had fallen asleep were raised
Jn 11.11 "Our friend Lazarus has fallen asleep
11.12 "if he has fallen asleep, he will recover
Acts 7.60 when he had said this, he fell asleep
13.36 "David . . fell asleep . . and saw corruption
1 Cor 15. 6 alive, though some have fallen asleep
15.18 who have fallen asleep in Christ have perished
15.20 first fruits of those who have fallen asleep
1 Th 4.14 with him those who have fallen asleep
4.15 not precede those who have fallen asleep
2 Pet 3. 4 "ever since the fathers fell asleep

ASP
1. *Egyptian cobra:* ἀσπίς ASPIS*
Rom 3.13 "The venom of asps is under their lips

ASPIRE
1. *reach, stretch:* ὀρέγω (mid.) OREGŌ
1 Tim 3. 1 If . . one aspires to the office of bishop
2. *seek after honor:* φιλοτιμέομαι PHILOTIMEOMAI
1 Th 4.11 to aspire to live quietly . . and to work

ASS
1. *beast for the yoke:* ὑποζύγιον HYPOZYGION*
Mt 21. 5 "on a colt, the foal of an ass
2 Pet 2.16 a dumb ass spoke with human voice
2. *ass, donkey:* ὄνος ONOS*
Mt 21. 2 "you will find an ass tied, and a colt with her
21. 5 "humble, and mounted on an ass
21. 7 they brought the ass and the colt
Lk 13.15 "on the sabbath untie . . his ass?
[14. 5 "Which of you, having *an ass* or an ox?‡[0]
Jn 12.15 "king is coming, sitting on an ass's colt!

ASS, YOUNG
1. *little donkey:* ὀνάριον ONARION*
Jn 12.14 Jesus found a young ass and sat upon it

ASSAIL
1. *come upon:* ἐπέρχομαι EPERCHOMAI
Lk 11.22 "when one stronger than he assails him

ASSASSIN
1. *dagger man* (Lat. *sicarius*): σικάριος SIKARIOS*
Acts 21.38 "led the four thousand men of the Assassins

ASSEMBLE
1. *come together with:* συμπαραγίνομαι SYMPARAGINOMAI*
Lk 23.48 multitudes who assembled to see the sight
2. *bring together:* συνάγω SYNAGŌ
[a]pass.
Mt 2. 4 assembling all the chief priests and scribes
28.12 [a]when they had assembled with the elders
1 Cor 5. 4 [a]When . . assembled, and my spirit is present
Rev 16.14 demonic spirits . . go . . to assemble ⟨kings⟩
16.16 they assembled them at . . Armageddon
3. *come together:* συνέρχομαι SYNERCHOMAI
1 Cor 11.18 when you assemble as a church
14.23 If, therefore, the whole church assembles

ASSEMBLED, BE
1. *come together:* συνέρχομαι SYNERCHOMAI
Mk 14.53 elders and the scribes were assembled

ASSEMBLING
1. *gathering together:* ἐπισυναγωγή EPISYNAGŌGĒ
2 Th 2. 1 concerning . . our assembling to meet him

ASSEMBLY (*See also* ELDERS, ASSEMBLY OF)
1. *assembly, church:* ἐκκλησία EKKLĒSIA
Acts 19.32 the assembly was in confusion
19.39 "it shall be settled in the regular assembly
19.41 when he . . said this, he dismissed the a.
Heb 12.23 the assembly[z] of the first-born
2. *multitude, mass:* πλῆθος PLĒTHOS
Acts 15.12 all the assembly kept silence
23. 7 the assembly was divided
3. *meeting, meeting place:* συναγωγή SYNAGŌGĒ
Jas 2. 2 if a man . . comes into your assembly

ASSERT
1. *say, assert:* φάσκω PHASKŌ
Acts 25.19 "Jesus, . . whom Paul asserted to be alive

ASSERTIONS, MAKE
1. *affirm, be positive:* διαβεβαιόομαι DIABEBAIOOMAI
1 Tim 1. 7 things about which they make assertions

ASSIGN
1. *arrange:* διατίθημι (mid.) DIATITHĒMI
Lk 22.29 "and I assign to you, as my Father assigned to me, a kingdom[0]
2. *give:* δίδωμι DIDŌMI
1 Cor 3. 5 you believed, as the Lord assigned
3. *divide, distribute:* μερίζω MERIZŌ
Rom 12. 3 measure of faith which God has assigned
1 Cor 7.17 lead the life which the Lord has assigned

ASSIST
1. *help:* ἐπαρκέω EPARKEŌ
1 Tim 5.16 If . . relatives . . are widows . . assist them; let the church . . assist . . real widows
2. *servant, helper:* ὑπηρέτης HYPĒRETĒS [A.1.d]
Acts 13. 5 they had John to assist them

ASSOCIATE
ASSOCIATE WITH
1. *join, unite:* κολλάω (pass.) KOLLAŌ
Acts 10.28 "how unlawful . . for a Jew to associate with
2. *partaking with:* συμμέτοχος SYMMETOCHOS [B.3.a.2]
Eph 5. 7 Therefore do not associate with them
3. *mix up together:* συναναμείγνυμι (pass.) SYNANAMEIGNYMI
1 Cor 5. 9 not to associate with immoral men
5.11 not to associate with any . . brother . . guilty
4. *lead away with:* συναπάγω (pass.) SYNAPAGŌ
Rom 12.16 associate with the lowly;[s] never be conceited†

ASSOS: Ἄσσος 'as,äs II,E-3
Acts 20.13 going ahead . . we set sail for A.
20.14 when he met us at A., we took him

ASSUMING THAT
1. *since indeed:* εἴ γε EI [B.3.b.4]
Eph 3. 2 a. that you . . heard of the stewardship
4.21 assuming that you have heard about him

ASSURANCE
1. *foundation, reality, confidence:* ὑπόστασις HYPOSTASIS
Heb 11. 1 faith is the assurance of things hoped for
2. *trust, faith:* πίστις PISTIS
Acts 17.31 "assurance to all men by raising him

ASSURANCE, FULL
1. *certainty:* πληροφορία PLĒROPHORIA
Heb 6.11 realizing the full assurance of hope
10.22 draw near . . in full assurance of faith

ASSURED
1. *certainty:* πληροφορία PLĒROPHORIA [A.1.b.1]
Col 2. 2 all the riches of assured understanding

ASSURED, FULLY
1. *fulfill:* πληροφορέω (perf. pass. part.) PLĒROPHOREŌ
Col 4.12 stand mature and fully assured in all

ASSUREDLY
1. *safely, with certainty:* ἀσφαλῶς ASPHALŌS
Acts 2.36 "know a. . . God has made him . . Lord

ASTONISHED, BE
1. *expel, amaze:* ἐκπλήσσω (pass.) EKPLĒSSŌ*
Mt 7.28 crowds were astonished at his teaching
13.54 he taught . . so that they were astonished
19.25 the disciples . . were greatly astonished
22.33 they were astonished at his teaching
Mk 1.22 they were astonished at his teaching
6. 2 many who heard him were astonished
7.37 they were astonished beyond measure
10.26 they were exceedingly astonished
11.18 multitude was astonished at his teaching
Lk 2.48 when they saw him they were astonished
4.32 they were astonished at his teaching
9.43 all were astonished at the majesty of God
Acts 13.12 proconsul believed, . . for he was astonished
2. *marvel, admire:* θαυμάζω THAUMAZŌ
Lk 11.38 was astonished . . that he did not first wash
Gal 1. 6 I am astonished that you are . . deserting
IDIOMATICALLY
a. Lk 5.9 For he was astonished θάμβος γὰρ περιέσχεν αὐτόν [THAMBOS]

ASTONISHMENT
1. *displacement, ecstasy:* ἔκστασις EKSTASIS
Mk 16. 8 astonishment had come upon them

ASTOUND
1. *displace, amaze:* ἐξίστημι EXISTĒMI
Mk 6.51 wind ceased. And they were . . astounded

ASTOUNDED
1. *amazed:* ἔκθαμβος EKTHAMBOS*
Acts 3.11 all the people ran together . . , astounded

ASTRAY, GO
1. *cause to wander:* πλανάω (pass.) PLANAŌ
Mt 18.12 "If . . one . . has gone astray, does he not . . go in search of the one that went astray?
18.13 "the ninety-nine that never went astray
Heb 3.10 "'They always go astray in their hearts
2 Pet 2.15 they have gone astray

ASTRAY, LEAD
1. *lead away:* ἀπάγω APAGŌ
1 Cor 12. 2 you were led astray to dumb idols
2. *lead astray:* ἀποπλανάω APOPLANAŌ
Mk 13.22 "False Christs . . will arise . . to lead astray
3. *entice, destroy:* φθείρω PHTHEIRŌ
2 Cor 11. 3 your thoughts will be led astray
4. *cause to wander:* πλανάω PLANAŌ
Mt 24. 4 "Take heed that no one leads you astray
24. 5 "they will lead many astray
24.11 "false prophets will . . lead many astray
24.24 "false Christs . . will arise . . to lead astray
Mk 13. 5 "Take heed that no one leads you astray
13. 6 "saying, 'I am he!' . . they will lead . . astray
Lk 21. 8 "'Take heed that you are not led astray
Jn 7.12 "No, he is leading the people astray
7.47 "Are you led astray, you also?
Tit 3. 3 we ourselves were once . . led astray

ASUNDER, PUT
1. *separate, divide:* χωρίζω CHŌRIZŌ
Mt 19. 6 "God has joined . . let not man put asunder
Mk 10. 9 "God has joined . . let not man put asunder

ASYNCRITUS: Ἀσύγκριτος ə'siŋkrətəs
Rom 16.14 Greet Asyncritus, Phlegon, Hermes

AT
1. *until:* ἄχρι ACHRI
Phil **1.6**
2. *from:* ἀπό (+gen.) APO
Acts **23.23**
3. *through:* διά (+gen.) DIA
[a]+acc.
Jn **3.29**[a]
Acts **5.19**
4. *into, to, for:* εἰς (+acc.) EIS
Mt **6.26**; **12.41**; **14.34**

Mk **6**.53
Lk **4**.23; **8**.26; **9**.61; **11**.32; **14**.1
Jn **13**.22; **19**.13
Acts **3**.4[2]; **6**.15; **8**.40; **9**.2, 28; **11**.6; **13**.9; **18**.22; **20**.6, 14, 15, 16; **21**.3, 7, 13; **23**.11; **24**.11; **25**.4, 13, 15; **27**.3; **28**.12, 13, 23
2 Cor **3**.7
1 Th **2**.[16†
2 Tim **3**.7
Tit **3**.12
Rev **16**.16
5. *from, out of:* ἐκ (+gen.) EK
Mt **20**.21[2], 23[2]; **22**.44; **25**.33[2], 34, 41; **26**.64
Mk **10**.37[2], 40[2]; **12**.36; **14**.62; **16**.19‡
Lk **11**.31; **20**.42; **22**.69
Acts **2**.25, 34; **7**.55, 56
Heb **1**.13
Rev **8**.13
6. *before:* ἔμπροσθεν EMPROSTHEN
Rev **19**.10; **22**.8
7. *in, at, by:* ἐν (+dat.) EN
Mt **6**.5; **8**.6, 13; **11**.6, 25; **12**.1, 41, 42; **13**.30, 40, 49, 57; **14**.1; **18**.1; **23**.6; **24**.41, 45, 50; **26**.6, 55
Mk **2**.1; **6**.3; **12**.39; **14**.3
Lk **7**.23; **9**.31; **11**.31, 32; **12**.42, 46; **13**.1, 31; **14**.14; **19**.5; **20**.19, 46; **21**.36; **23**.12
Jn **2**.1, 11, 23; **3**.23; **4**.45, 46; **6**.39 *var. om.*, 40 *var. om.*, 44; **7**.11; **10**.22; **12**.20; **18**.39; **21**.20
Acts **1**.6; **5**.4; **7**.13, 20, 29, 36, 38; **8**.14; **9**.10, 13, 19, 27, 36; **10**.1; **11**.15; **13**.1, 5; **14**.1, 8; **16**.2, 4; **17**.13, 16; **18**.18; **19**.1; **20**.5, [15‡; **21**.11; **22**.3; **25**.24; **26**.4, 20; **28**.30†
Rom **3**.26; **8**.34; **11**.5; **15**.26; **16**.1
1 Cor **1**.2; **11**.34; **14**.35; **15**.23, 32, 52
2 Cor **1**.1; **7**.5, 11; **8**.14; **11**.26, 32
Eph **1**.1, 20; **6**.18
Phil **1**.1; **2**.10
Col **1**.2; **2**.1; **3**.1; **4**.15
1 Th **2**.2, 19; **3**.1, 13; **5**.23
1 Tim **1**.3
2 Tim **1**.18; **3**.11[3]; **4**.13, 16, 20[2]
Heb **1**.3; **8**.1; **10**.12; **12**.2
1 Pet **1**.7, 13; **3**.22; **5**.13
2 Pet **3**.14
1 Jn **2**.28
Rev **11**.13; **18**.19; **20**.8
8. *on, at:* ἐπί (+dat.) EPI
except [a]+gen. [b]+acc.
Mt **1**.11[a]; **5**.23[b]; **7**.28; **9**.9[b]; **22**.33; **24**.33
Mk **1**.22; **2**.14[b]; **3**.5; **10**.22, 24; **11**.18; **12**.17; **13**.29
Lk **1**.14, 29; **2**.33, 47; **4**.22, 32; **5**.5, 9, 27[b]; **9**.43[2]; **13**.17; **20**.26; **22**.30[a]; **24**.22[b]
Jn **6**.21[a]; **8**.7[b]‡, 59[b]
Acts **3**.1[b], 10[2], 12; **5**.9, 23[a]; **10**.25[b]; **11**.11[b]; **13**.12; **15**.31
1 Cor **13**.6; **16**.17
2 Cor **7**.13
Heb **9**.17, 26; **10**.28
1 Pet **1**.20[a]
Rev **3**.20[b]; **7**.1[b]; **8**.3[a]; **9**.14; **21**.12
9. *when:* ὅτε HOTE [B.2.a.2]
Mk **1**.32
Lk **2**.21
10. *under:* ὑπό (+acc.) HYPO
Acts **5**.21
11. *in accordance with, for:* κατά (+acc.) KATA
except [a]+gen.
Mt **20**.11[a]; **27**.15
Mk **15**.6
Lk **23**.[17‡
Jn **5**.[4‡
Acts **8**.[26†
Rom **5**.6
Heb **12**.10
12. *more than, by:* παρά (+acc.) PARA
Mt **15**.30
Lk **7**.38; **8**.35, 41; **17**.16
Acts **4**.35; **5**.2; **7**.58; **22**.3
Also variant to: Acts **4**.37
13. *about, concerning:* περί (+gen.) PERI
Mt **20**.24
Mk **10**.41
Lk **2**.18
Jn **6**.41, 61
14. *before:* πρό (+gen.) PRO
Acts **12**.14
Jas **5**.9
15. *to, with, against:* πρός (+acc.) PROS
except [a]+dat.
Mt **26**.18
Mk **5**.22; **7**.25; **11**.1, 4; **14**.54
Lk **10**.39; **16**.20; **19**.29, 37[a]
Jn **11**.32; **18**.16[a]; **20**.12[2a]
Acts **3**.2, 10; **4**.37 (*Var.* PARA); **5**.10
Rev **1**.17

AT ALL
1. *origin, rule:* ἀρχή (acc.) ARCHĒ
Jn [8.25 "*Why do I talk to you at all?*†
2. *actually:* ὅλως HOLŌS
[a]+neg.
Mt 5.34 [a]"But I say to you, Do not swear at all
1 Cor 6. 7 To have lawsuits at all . . is defeat
15.29 [a]If the dead are not raised at all
3. *on the whole:* καθόλου (neg.) KATHOLOU*
Acts 4.18 charged them not to speak or teach at all
4. *in all ways, assuredly:* πάντως (+neg.) PANTŌS
Rom 3. 9 No, not at all
1 Cor 5.10 not at all meaning the immoral
16.12 it was not at all his will[b]
5. *anyone, any:* τὶς (neut.) TIS II
Acts **25**.8
Phm .18

AT ANY TIME
1. *each time, always:* ἑκάστοτε HEKASTOTE*
2 Pet 1.15 able at any time to recall these things

AT S.'S HANDS
AT THE HANDS OF
1. *by:* ὑπό (+gen.) HYPO
Mt **17**.12
2 Cor **11**.24

ATHENIAN: Ἀθηναῖος (*See also* ATHENS 2)
Acts 17.21 Athenians . . spent their time . . telling

ATHENS: 'athənz II,D-3
1. *Athens:* Ἀθῆναι
Acts 17.15 conducted Paul . . as far as A.
17.16 at A., his spirit was provoked within him
18. 1 After this he left A. and went to Corinth
1 Th 3. 1 we were willing to be left behind at A.
2. *Athenian, one of Athens:* Ἀθηναῖος [A.3.a.2]
Acts 17.22 "Men of A. . . you are very religious

ATHLETE
1. *fight, contend:* ἀγωνίζομαι (subst. part.) AGŌNIZOMAI
1 Cor 9.25 Every athlete exercises self-control
IDIOMATICALLY
a. 2 Tim 2.5 An athlete is not crowned unless ἐὰν δὲ καὶ ἀθλῇ τις, οὐ στεφανοῦται ἐὰν μή [ATHLEŌ]

ATTACK
1. *stand by:* ἐφίστημι EPHISTĒMI
Acts 17. 5 Jews . . attacked the house of Jason
2. *lay on, add:* ἐπιτίθημι (mid.) EPITITHĒMI
Acts 18.10 "I am with you, and no man shall attack
3. *break:* ῥήγνυμι RHĒGNYMI
Mt 7. 6 "lest they trample them . . and turn to a.

ATTACK UPON, MAKE AN
1. *rise up against:* κατεφίσταμαι KATEPHISTAMAI*
Acts 18.12 the Jews made a united attack upon Paul

ATTAIN
1. *catch:* καταλαμβάνω KATALAMBANŌ
Rom 9.30 Gentiles . . have attained it . . through faith
2. *come down to, arrive:* καταντάω KATANTAŌ
Acts 26. 7 "to which our twelve tribes hope to attain
Eph 4.13 until we all attain to the unity of the faith
Phil 3.11 that . . I may attain the resurrection

3. *come first, arrive:* φθάνω PHTHANŌ
Phil 3.16 let us hold true to what we have attained
4. *happen, attain:* τυγχάνω TYGCHANŌ
Lk 20.35 "accounted worthy to attain to that age

ATTAINABLE
CONTEXTUALLY
Heb 7.11 Now if perfection had been attainable

ATTALIA: 'Αττάλεια ˌatəˈlīə II,F-3
Acts 14.25 they went down to Attalia

ATTEMPT
1. *impulse, effort:* ὁρμή HORMĒ
Acts 14. 5 an attempt was made . . to molest them
2. *undergo trial:* πεῖραν λαμβάνειν PEIRA [B.2.a.1]
Heb 11.29 when they attempted . . were drowned
3. *tempt, try:* πειράζω PEIRAZŌ
Acts 9.26 he attempted to join the disciples
16. 7 they attempted to go into Bithynia

ATTEND
1. *follow close upon:* ἐπακολουθέω EPAKOLOUTHEŌ
Mk 16.20 confirmed . . by the signs that attended it[k]‡
2. *persist in:* προσκαρτερέω PROSKARTEREŌ
[a]+ἐν
Acts 2.46 [a]day by day, attending the temple
Rom 13. 6 the authorities are . . attending to this
CONTEXTUALLY
2 Cor 3. 8 the dispensation of the Spirit be attended

ATTEND TO
1. *hold to, be intent on:* προσέχω PROSECHŌ
1 Tim 4.13 attend to the public reading of scripture

ATTEND TO NEEDS
1. *serve:* ὑπηρετέω HYPĒRETEŌ
Acts 24.23 none . . prevented from attending to his needs

ATTENDANT
1. *servant:* διάκονος DIAKONOS
Mt 22.13 "the king said to the attendants, 'Bind him
2. *servant, helper:* ὑπηρέτης HYPĒRETĒS
Lk 4.20 gave ⟨the book⟩ back to the attendant

ATTENTION, PAY
ATTENTION TO, PAY
1. *look at, consider:* ἐπιβλέπω EPIBLEPŌ
Jas 2. 3 you pay attention to . . the fine clothing
2. *care:* μέλει MELEI [A.6.e]
Acts 18.17 But Gallio paid no attention to this
3. *persuade:* πείθω (pass.) PEITHŌ
Acts 27.11 centurion paid more attention to the captain
4. *hold to, be intent on:* προσέχω PROSECHŌ
Heb 2. 1 Therefore we must pay . . closer attention
2 Pet 1.19 You will do well to pay attention to this

ATTENTION UPON, FIX ONE'S
1. *hold upon, aim at:* ἐπέχω EPECHŌ
Acts 3. 5 he fixed his attention upon them

ATTEST
1. *point out:* ἀποδείκνυμι APODEIKNYMI
Acts 2.22 "Jesus of Nazareth, a man attested to you
2. *confirm, establish:* βεβαιόω BEBAIOŌ
Heb 2. 3 attested to us by those who heard him
3. *bear witness, testify:* μαρτυρέω MARTYREŌ
Heb 11. 5 Enoch . . was attested as having pleased God

ATTESTED, BE WELL
1. *bear witness, testify:* μαρτυρέω (pass.) MARTYREŌ
1 Tim 5.10 must be well attested for her good deeds

ATTESTED, WELL
1. *bear witness, testify:* μαρτυρέω (pass. part.) MARTYREŌ
Heb 11.39 though well attested by their faith

ATTIRE
1. *clothing:* ἱματισμός HIMATISMOS
1 Tim 2. 9 modestly . . , not with . . costly attire

AUDIENCE HALL
1. *audience room:* ἀκροατήριον AKROATĒRION*
Acts 25.23 Agrippa and Bernice . . entered the a. hall

AUGUSTAN
1. *venerable, august:* σεβαστός SEBASTOS
Acts 27. 1 a centurion of the Augustan Cohort

AUGUSTUS: Αὐγοῦστος əˈgəstəs
Lk 2. 1 a decree went out from Caesar Augustus

AUTHOR
1. *founder, leader:* ἀρχηγός ARCHĒGOS
Acts 3.15 "killed the Author of life, whom God raised

AUTHORITY
1. *origin, rule:* ἀρχή ARCHĒ
Lk 20.20 deliver him . . to . . a. . . of the governor
2. *ruler:* ἄρχων ARCHŌN
Jn 7.26 "authorities really know . . this is the Christ?
7.48 "Have any of the authorities . . believed?
12.42 many even of the authorities believed
3. *command:* ἐπιταγή EPITAGĒ
Tit 2.15 exhort and reprove with all authority
4. *authority, power:* ἐξουσία EXOUSIA
Mt 7.29 who had authority, and not as their scribes
8. 9 "I am a man under authority
9. 6 "Son of man has authority . . to forgive sins
9. 8 glorified God, who had given such authority
10. 1 gave them authority over unclean spirits
21.23 "By what authority are you doing these things, and who gave you this authority?
21.24 "then I also will tell you by what authority
21.27 "Neither will I tell you by what authority
28.18 "All authority in heaven and on earth
Mk 1.22 he taught them as one who had authority
1.27 "With authority he commands . . spirits
2.10 "know that the Son of man has authority
3.15 have authority to cast out demons
6. 7 gave them authority over the unclean spirits
11.28 "By what authority are you doing these things, or who gave you this authority?
11.29 "and I will tell you by what authority
11.33 "Neither will I tell you by what authority
Lk 4. 6 "To you I will give all this authority
4.32 for his word was with authority
4.36 "with authority and power he commands
5.24 "know that the Son of man has authority
7. 8 "I am a man set under authority
9. 1 called the twelve . . and gave them . . a.
10.19 "Behold, I have given you authority
12.11 "they bring you before . . the authorities
19.17 "you shall have authority over ten cities
20. 2 "Tell us by what authority you do these things, or who it is that gave you this a.
20. 8 "Neither will I tell you by what authority
Jn 5.27 "given him authority to execute judgment
Acts 1. 7 "times . . fixed by his own authority
9.14 "he has authority from the chief priests
26.10 "by authority from the chief priests
26.12 "with the authority . . of the chief priests
Rom 13. 1 be subject to the governing authorities
13. 1 For there is no authority except from God
13. 2 who resists the authorities resists . . God
1 Cor 15.24 destroying every rule and every authority
2 Cor 10. 8 if I boast a little too much of our authority
13.10 not . . be severe in my use of the authority
Eph 1.21 far above all rule and authority
Col 1.16 all things . . , whether thrones or . . authorities
2.10 who is the head of all rule and authority
Tit 3. 1 be submissive to rulers and authorities
1 Pet 3.22 with . . authorities, and powers subject to him
Jude .25 to the only God . . be glory . . and authority
Rev 12.10 "and the authority of his Christ have come
13. 2 to it the dragon gave his . . great authority
13. 4 dragon . . had given his authority to the beast
13. 5 the beast . . was allowed to exercise authority
13. 7 authority was given it over every tribe
13.12 exercises all the authority of the first beast
17.12 "they are to receive authority as kings
17.13 "These . . give over . . authority to the beast
18. 1 another angel . . having great authority
5. *ruling power, lordship:* κυριότης KYRIOTĒS
2 Pet 2.10 especially those who . . despise authority
Jude . 8 these men . . defile the flesh, reject authority

CONTEXTUALLY
Jn 5.30 "I can do nothing on my own authority
7.17 "whether I am speaking on my own a.
7.18 "He who speaks on his own authority
8.28 "I do nothing on my own authority
14.10 "I do not speak on my own authority
16.13 "for he will not speak on his own authority
Rom 13. 6 for the authorities are ministers of God

AUTHORITY, ACKNOWLEDGE
1. *receive, recognize:* ἐπιδέχομαι EPIDECHOMAI
3 Jn . 9 D... does not acknowledge my authority

AUTHORITY, CITY
1. *civic magistrate:* πολιτάρχης POLITARCHĒS*
Acts 17. 6 dragged.. before the city authorities
17. 8 the city authorities were disturbed

AUTHORITY, MAN OF
1. *possible, strong:* δυνατός (subst.) DYNATOS
Acts 25. 5 "let the men of authority.. go.. with me

AUTHORITY, ONE WHO IS IN
1. *authority, power:* ἐξουσία EXOUSIA [C.2]
Rom 13. 3 fear of him who is in authority

AUTHORITY OVER, EXERCISE
1. *exercise authority over:* κατεξουσιάζω KATEXOUSIAZŌ*
Mt 20.25 "great men exercise authority over them
Mk 10.42 "great men exercise authority over them

AUTHORITY OVER, HAVE
1. *have authority over:* αὐθεντέω AUTHENTEŌ*
1 Tim 2.12 no woman.. to have authority over men

AUTHORITY OVER, ONE IN
1. *exercise authority over:* ἐξουσιάζω (subst. part.) EXOUSIAZŌ
Lk 22.25 "those in authority over them

AUTHORITY, WITH S.'S
1. *in accordance with, for:* κατά (+acc.) KATA [B.3.b.4]
2 Cor **11.17**

AUTUMN, IN LATE
1. *autumnal:* φθινοπωρινός PHTHINOPŌRINOS* [A.3.d.1]
Jude .12 fruitless trees in late autumn, twice dead

AVAIL, BE OF
1. *be strong, prevail:* ἰσχύω ISCHYŌ
Gal 5. 6 neither.. nor uncircumcision is of any avail
2. *help, aid:* ὠφελέω ŌPHELEŌ
Jn 6.63 "spirit.. gives life, the flesh is of no avail

AVAIL ONESELF OF THE OPPORTUNITY
1. *make use of, act:* χράομαι (imper.) CHRAOMAI
1 Cor 7.21 avail yourself of the opportunity†

AVENGE
1. *avenge, punish:* ἐκδικέω EKDIKEŌ
Rom 12.19 Beloved, never avenge yourselves
Rev 6.10 "how long before thou wilt.. avenge?
19. 2 "he has avenged .. the blood of his servants
2. *make vengeance:* ποιεῖν ἐκδίκησιν EKDIKĒSIS [B.2.a.1]
Acts 7.24 "avenged him by striking the Egyptian

AVENGER
1. *avenging:* ἔκδικος (subst.) EKDIKOS
1 Th 4. 6 Lord is an avenger in all these things

AVOID (*See also* QUARRELING *a*)
1. *turn away from:* ἀποτρέπω (mid.) APOTREPŌ*
2 Tim 3. 5 Avoid such people
2. *turn away:* ἐκκλίνω EKKLINŌ
Rom 16.17 take note of those.. ; avoid them
3. *turn out of course:* ἐκτρέπω (pass.) EKTREPŌ
1 Tim 6.20 Avoid.. godless chatter and contradictions
4. *not:* μή MĒ [A.4.c]
2 Tim 2.14 charge them.. to avoid disputing
5. *stand around:* περιΐστημι (mid.) PERIISTĒMI
2 Tim 2.16 Avoid such godless chatter
Tit 3. 9 avoid stupid controversies, genealogies

AVOID, TO
1. *because of:* διά (+acc.) DIA [B.1.a.2]
Rom 13. 5 subject, not only to avoid God's wrath

AWAIT
1. *expect anxiously:* ἀπεκδέχομαι APEKDECHOMAI
Phil 3.20 we await a Savior, the Lord Jesus
2. *stay, wait:* μένω MENŌ
Acts 20.23 "in every city.. afflictions await me
3. *accept, expect:* προσδέχομαι PROSDECHOMAI
Tit 2.13 awaiting our blessed hope, the appearing

AWAKE
1. *raise:* ἐγείρω (imper.) EGEIRŌ
Eph 5.14 "Awake, O sleeper, and arise from the dead
2. *be awake, watch:* γρηγορέω GRĒGOREŌ
[a]part.
Lk 12.37 [a]"servants whom the master finds awake
Rev 3. 2 " 'Awake, and strengthen what remains
3. 3 " 'If you will not a., I will come like a thief
16.15 [a]("Blessed is he who is awake!

AWAKE, KEEP
1. *be awake, watch:* γρηγορέω GRĒGOREŌ
Mt [26.38 "remain here, and *keep awake* with me†
[26.40 "could you not *keep awake*.. one hour?†
[26.41 "*Keep awake* and pray†
Mk [14.34 "remain here, and *keep awake*†
[14.37 "Could you not *keep awake* one hour?†
[14.38 "*Keep awake* and pray†
1 Th 5. 6 let us keep awake and be sober

AWAKE OUT OF SLEEP
1. *awaken from sleep:* ἐξυπνίζω EXYPNIZŌ*
Jn 11.11 "but I go to awake him out of sleep

AWAKEN
1. *stir up, arouse:* διεγείρω (pass.) DIEGEIRŌ
Mk 4.39 he awoke and rebuked the wind
Lk 8.24 he awoke and rebuked the wind

AWARD
1. *give up, return:* ἀποδίδωμι APODIDŌMI
2 Tim 4. 8 Lord.. will award to me on that Day

AWARE, BE
AWARE OF, BE
1. *know:* οἶδα OIDA
2 Tim 1.15 You are aware that all.. turned away
2. *know as a witness, be conscious:* σύνοιδα SYNOIDA
1 Cor 4. 4 I am not aware of anything against myself

AWARE OF
AWARE OF, BEING
1. *know, understand:* γινώσκω (aor. part.) GINŌSKŌ
Mt 12.15 Jesus, aware of this, withdrew from there
16. 8 Jesus, a. of this, said, "O men of little
22.18 Jesus, aware of their malice, said, "Why?
26.10 Jesus, aware of this, said .. "Why do you?
Mk 8.17 being aware of it, Jesus said.. "Why do you?

AWAY
1. *from that place:* ἐκεῖθεν EKEITHEN
Mt 19.15 he laid his hands on them and went away
2. *hence:* ἐντεῦθεν ENTEUTHEN
Jn 2.16 "Take these things away
3. *outside:* ἔξω EXŌ
Mt 13.48 "sorted the good.. but threw away the bad
Lk 14.35 "men throw it away

AWAY, BE
AWAY FROM, BE
1. *be away from:* ἄπειμι APEIMI I
2 Cor 10. 1 I.. am.. bold to you when I am away!
13.10 I write this while I am away from you
2. *be abroad:* ἐκδημέω EKDĒMEŌ*
[a]+ἀπό [b]+ἐκ
2 Cor 5. 6 [a]in the body we are away from the Lord
5. 8 [b]we would rather be away from the body
5. 9 whether we are at home or away

AWAY FROM
1. *outside:* ἔξω EXŌ
Lk 13.33 " 'prophet.. perish away from Jerusalem

AWAY WITH
1. *lift, carry away:* αἴρω (imper.) AIRŌ
Lk 23.18 "Away with this man, and release to us B.
Jn 19.15 They cried out, "Away with him, away with him, crucify him!
Acts 21.36 people followed, crying, "Away with him!
22.22 "Away with such a fellow from the earth!

AWE
1. *fear, alarm:* δέος DEOS*
Heb 12.28 let us . . worship, with reverence and awe
2. *fear:* φόβος PHOBOS
Mk 4.41 filled with awe, and said . . "Who then is this?
Lk 5.26 glorified God and were filled with awe

AWE, BE FILLED WITH
AWE, STAND IN
1. *terrify:* φοβέω (pass.) PHOBEŌ
[a]φοβεῖσθαι σφόδρα SPHODRA A.6.c.1
[b]φοβεῖσθαι φόβον μέγαν PHOBOS A.6.a.6
Mt 17. 6 [a]the disciples . . were filled with awe
27.54 [a]they were filled with awe
Mk 4.41 [b]And they were filled with awe
Rom 11.20 So do not become proud, but stand in awe

AXE
1. *axe:* ἀξίνη AXINĒ*
Mt 3.10 "now the axe is laid to the root of the trees
Lk 3. 9 "now the axe is laid to the root of the trees

AZOR: Ἀζώρ 'āzȯr
Mt 1.13 Eliakim the father of Azor
1.14 Azor the father of Zadok

AZOTUS: Ἄζωτος ə'zōtəs I,B-5
Acts 8.40 Philip was found at Azotus

B

BAAL: Βάαλ 'bā(ə)l
Rom 11. 4 "men who have not bowed the knee to Baal

BABBLER
1. *picking up seeds; gossip* (subst.): σπερμολόγος SPERMOLOGOS*
Acts 17.18 "What would this babbler say?

BABE
1. *infant:* βρέφος BREPHOS
Lk 1.41 the babe leaped in her womb
1.44 "the babe in my womb leaped for joy
2.12 "you will find a babe wrapped in swaddling
2.16 found . . the babe lying in a manger
1 Pet 2. 2 Like . . babes, long for . . spiritual milk
2. *childlike, childish:* νήπιος (subst.) NĒPIOS
Mt 11.25 "thou hast . . revealed them to babes
21.16 " 'Out of the mouth of babes and sucklings
Lk 10.21 "thou hast . . revealed them to babes
1 Cor 3. 1 as men of the flesh, as babes in Christ
1 Th [2. 7 But we were *babes* among you‡

BABE, BE A
1. *be as a babe:* νηπιάζω NĒPIAZŌ*
1 Cor 14.20 be babes in evil, but in thinking be mature

BABYLON: Βαβυλών 'babələn
Mt 1.11 at the time of the deportation to B.
1.12 after the deportation to B.
1.17 from David to the deportation to B.
1.17 from the deportation to B. to the Christ
Acts 7.43 " 'I will remove you beyond B.
1 Pet 5.13 She who is at B. . . sends you greetings
Rev 14. 8 "Fallen, fallen is B. the great
16.19 God remembered great B.
17. 5 "B. the great, mother of harlots
18. 2 "Fallen, fallen is B. the great!
18.10 "alas! thou great city . . mighty city, B.!
18.21 "So shall B. the great city be thrown

BACK (*See also* DRAW BACK; GIVE BACK; HOLD BACK)
1. *back* (any wide surface): νῶτος NŌTOS*
Rom 11.10 "bend their backs for ever
2. *behind, backward:* ὀπίσω OPISŌ
[a]εἰς τὰ ὀπίσω B.1.a.1
Mt 24.18 "let him who is in the field not turn back
Mk 13.16 [a]"let him who is in the field not turn back
Lk 9.62 [a]"No one who . . looks b. is fit for . . kingdom
17.31 [a]"let him who is in the field not turn back
Jn 6.66 [a]After this many of his disciples drew back
18. 6 [a]they drew back and fell to the ground
3. *again, back:* πάλιν PALIN
Mk 11. 3 " 'The Lord . . will send it back
Jn 20.10 the disciples went back to their homes
Rom 8.15 the spirit of slavery to fall back into fear
2 Cor 1.16 to come back to you from Macedonia

BACK, BRING
1. *turn about, return:* ἐπιστρέφω EPISTREPHŌ
Jas 5.19 if . . some one brings him back
5.20 whoever brings back a sinner from . . error

BACK, KEEP
1. *withhold:* ἀφυστερέω APHYSTEREŌ*
Jas 5. 4 wages . . which you kept back by fraud
2. *put aside for oneself* (mid.): νοσφίζω NOSPHIZŌ
Acts 5. 2 he kept back some of the proceeds
5. 3 "to keep back part of the proceeds

BACK, ON THE
1. *behind:* ὄπισθεν OPISTHEN
Rev 5. 1 a scroll written within and on the back

BAD
1. *evil, bad:* κακός KAKOS
Rom 13. 3 rulers are . . a terror . . to bad ⟨conduct⟩
1 Cor 15.33 "Bad company ruins good morals
2. *cheap, mean, bad:* φαῦλος PHAULOS
Rom 9.11 they . . had done nothing either good or bad
3. *sick, base, evil:* πονηρός PONĒROS
Mt 22.10 "gathered all . . both bad and good
4. *rotten, bad:* σαπρός SAPROS
Mt 7:17 "the bad tree bears evil fruit
7.18 "nor can a bad tree bear good fruit
12.33 "make the tree bad, and its fruit bad; for the tree is known by its fruit
13.48 "sorted the good . . but threw away the bad
Lk 6.43 "For no good tree bears bad fruit, nor again does a bad tree bear good fruit
CONTEXTUALLY
2 Tim 3.13 impostors will go on from bad to worse

BAG
1. *leather pouch, knapsack:* πήρα PĒRA*
Mt 10.10 "no bag for your journey, nor two tunics
Mk 6. 8 no bread, no bag, no money in their belts
Lk 9. 3 "Take nothing for your journey, . . nor bag
10. 4 "Carry no purse, no bag, no sandals
22.35 "When I sent you out with no purse or bag
22.36 "now, let him who has . . a bag ⟨take it⟩

BALAAM: Βαλαάμ 'bāləm
2 Pet 2.15 they have followed the way of B.
Jude .11 "abandon themselves . . to Baalam's error
Rev 2.14 " 'hold the teaching of B., who taught Balak

BALAK: Βαλάκ 'bālak
Rev 2.14 " 'the teaching of Balaam, who taught B.

BALANCE
1. *yoke, crossbar:* ζυγός ZYGOS
Rev 6. 5 its rider had a balance in his hand

BAND OF SOLDIERS
1. *cohort, tactical unit:* σπεῖρα SPEIRA
Jn 18. 3 Judas, procuring a band of soldiers
18.12 the band of soldiers . . seized Jesus

BANDAGE
1. *swathing band, bandage:* κειρία KEIRIA*
Jn 11.44 The dead man came out . . with bandages

BANISH
1. *turn back, turn away:* ἀποστρέφω APOSTREPHŌ
Rom 11.26 "he will banish ungodliness from Jacob

BANK
1. *pole, palisade:* χάραξ CHARAX*
Lk 19.43 "enemies will cast up a bank about you
2. *table:* τράπεζα TRAPEZA
Lk 19.23 " 'Why . . not put my money into the bank?

BANK, STEEP
1. *cliff, crag:* κρημνός KRĒMNOS*
Mt 8.32 whole herd rushed down the steep bank

Mk 5.13 the herd . . rushed down the steep bank
Lk 8.33 the herd rushed down the steep bank

BANKER

1. *money changer:* τραπεζίτης TRAPEZITĒS*
Mt 25.27 " 'invested my money with the bankers

BANQUET

1. *meal, dinner:* δεῖπνον DEIPNON
Mk 6.21 Herod on his birthday gave a banquet
Lk 14.12 "When you give a dinner or a banquet
14.16 "A man once gave a great banquet
14.17 "at the time for the banquet he sent
14.24 " 'none of those men . . shall taste my b.

BAPTISM

1. *baptism:* βάπτισμα BAPTISMA*
Mt 3. 7 Pharisees and Sadducees coming for baptism
21.25 "The baptism of John, whence was it?
Mk 1. 4 John . . preaching a baptism of repentance
10.38 "the baptism with which I am baptized
10.39 "with the baptism . . you will be baptized
11.30 "Was the baptism of John from heaven?
Lk 3. 3 a baptism of repentance for . . forgiveness
7.29 (baptized with the baptism of John
12.50 "I have a baptism to be baptized with
20. 4 "Was the baptism of John from heaven?
Acts 1.22 "beginning from the baptism of John
10.37 "after the baptism which John preached
13.24 "John had preached a baptism of repentance
18.25 he knew only the baptism of John
19. 3 They said, "Into John's baptism
19 4 John baptized with the b. of repentance
Rom 6. 4 buried therefore with him by baptism
Eph 4. 5 one Lord, one faith, one baptism
Col 2.12 you were buried with him in baptism
1 Pet 3.21 Baptism . . saves you . . as an appeal to God

BAPTIST: 'baptəst

1. *one that dips, baptizer:* βαπτιστής BAPTISTĒS*
Mt 3. 1 John the B., preaching in the wilderness
11.11 "no one greater than John the B.
11.12 "From the days of John the B. until now
14. 2 " 'This is John the B., he has been raised
14. 8 "Give me the head of John the Baptist
16.14 "Some say John the B., others say Elijah
17.13 he was speaking to them of John the B.
Mk 6.25 "give me . . the head of John the B.
8.28 "John the B.; and others say, Elijah
Lk 7.20 "John the B. has sent us to you
7.33 "John the B. has come eating no bread
9.19 "John the Baptist; but others say, Elijah

BAPTIZE

1. *dip, plunge, baptize:* βαπτίζω BAPTIZŌ
Mt 3. 6 they were baptized by him in the river Jordan
3.11 "I baptize you with water for repentance, but he . . will baptize you with the Holy Spirit
3.13 Jesus came . . to John, to be baptized
3.14 "I need to be baptized by you
3.16 when Jesus was baptized . . he saw the Spirit
28.19 "Go therefore and make disciples . . baptizing
Mk [1. 4 John *was baptizing* in the wilderness†‡
1. 5 they were baptized . . in the river Jordan
1. 8 "I have baptized you with water; but he will baptize you with the Holy Spirit
1. 9 Jesus . . was baptized by John in the Jordan
[7. 4 (do not eat unless they *baptize* themselves‡
10.38 "Are you able . . to be baptized with the baptism with which I am baptized?
10.39 "with the baptism with which I am baptized, you will be baptized
16.16 He who . . is baptized will be saved[k]‡
Lk 3. 7 multitudes . . came out to be baptized
3.12 Tax collectors also came to be baptized
3.16 "I baptize you with water; but he . . will baptize you with the Holy Spirit
3.21 when all the people were baptized, and when Jesus also had been baptized
7.29 (tax collectors . . , having been baptized
7.30 (Pharisees . . , not having been baptized
12.50 "I have a baptism to be baptized with
Jn 1.25 "Then why are you baptizing?
1.26 "I baptize with water
1.28 beyond the Jordan, where John was baptizing
1.31 "for this I came baptizing with water
1.33 "he who sent me to baptize with water said . . 'this is he who baptizes with the . . Spirit
3.22 Jesus . . remained with them and baptized
3.23 John also was baptizing at Aenon . . and people came and were baptized
3.26 "here he is, baptizing, and all are going
4. 1 Jesus . . baptizing more disciples than John
4. 2 (although Jesus himself did not baptize
10.40 the place where John at first baptized
Acts 1. 5 "John baptized with water, but . . you shall be baptized with the Holy Spirit
2.38 "Repent, and be baptized every one of you
2.41 those who received his word were baptized
8.12 believed Philip . . and . . were baptized
8.13 Simon . . being baptized . . continued
8.16 they had only been baptized in the name
8.36 "What is to prevent my being baptized?[h]
8.38 they both went down . . and he baptized him
9.18 Then he rose and was baptized
10.47 "Can any one forbid water for baptizing?
10.48 he commanded them to be baptized
11.16 " 'John baptized with water, but you shall be baptized with the Holy Spirit
16.15 she was baptized, with her household
16.33 he was baptized at once, with all his family
18. 8 many . . believed and were baptized
19. 3 "Into what then were you baptized?
19. 4 "John baptized with the b. of repentance
19. 5 On hearing this, they were baptized
22.16 "why do you wait? Rise and be baptized
Rom 6. 3 all of us who have been baptized into Christ Jesus were baptized into his death
1 Cor 1.13 were you baptized in the name of Paul?
1.14 thankful[b] that I baptized none . . except
1.15 lest . . say that you were baptized in my name
1.16 (I did b. . . the household of Stephanas
1.16 (whether I baptized any one else
1.17 For Christ did not send me to baptize
10. 2 all were baptized into Moses in the cloud
12.13 we were all baptized into one body
15.29 being baptized on behalf of the dead
15.29 why are people baptized on their behalf?
Gal 3.27 as many . . as were baptized into Christ

BAPTIZER

1. *dip, plunge, baptize:* βαπτίζω (subst. part.) BAPTIZŌ
Mk 1. 4 John the b. appeared[c] in the wilderness†‡
6.14 "John the baptizer has been raised
6.24 "The head of John the baptizer

BARABBAS: Βαραββᾶς bə'rabəs
Mt 27.16 they had . . a notorious prisoner, called B.[k]
27.17 "Whom do you want me to release . . , B.?[k]
27.20 elders persuaded the people to ask for B.
27.21 "Which of the two . . ?" And they said, "B.
27.26 released . . B., . . having scourged Jesus
Mk 15. 7 among the rebels . . was a man called B.
15.11 to have him release for them B.
15.15 Pilate, wishing to satisfy . . released . . B.
Lk 23.18 "Away with this man, and release to us B.
Jn 18.40 They cried out . . "Not this man, but B.!" Now B. was a robber

BARACHIAH: Βαραχίας ˌbarə'kīə
Mt 23.35 "the blood of Zechariah the son of B.

BARAK: Βαράκ 'berək
Heb 11.32 For time would fail me to tell of . . B.

BARBARIAN

1. *non-Greek, foreign:* βάρβαρος (subst.) BARBAROS
Rom 1.14 I am under obligation . . to barbarians
Col 3.11 Here there cannot be Greek and . . barbarian

BARE
1. *naked, bare:* γυμνός GYMNOS
1 Cor 15.37 what you sow is . . a bare kernel

BARE, BE LAID
1. *twist the neck of; be laid open* (pass.): τραχηλίζω TRACHĒLIZŌ*
Heb 4.13 all are open and laid bare to . . him

BARELY
1. *barely:* ὀλίγως OLIGŌS*
2 Pet 2.18 they entice . . men who have barely escaped

BAR-JESUS: Βαριησοῦς ˌbär'jēzəs
Acts 13. 6 a Jewish false prophet, named B.

BAR-JONA: Βαριωνᾶ ˌbär'jōnə
Mt 16.17 "Blessed are you, Simon B.

BARLEY
1. *barley:* κριθή KRITHĒ*
Rev 6. 6 "three quarts of barley for a denarius[a]
2. *made from barley:* κρίθινος KRITHINOS*
Jn 6. 9 "a lad here who has five barley loaves
6.13 twelve baskets . . from the five barley loaves

BARN
1. *storehouse:* ἀποθήκη APOTHĒKĒ
Mt 6.26 "they neither . . reap nor gather into barns
13.30 " 'gather the wheat into my barn
Lk 12.18 " 'I will pull down my barns, and build larger
12.24 "they have neither storehouse nor barn

BARNABAS: Βαρναβᾶς 'bärnəbəs
Acts 4.36 Joseph . . surnamed by the apostles B.
9.27 B. . . brought him to the apostles
11.22 News . . came . . and they sent B. to Antioch
11.30 sending it to the elders by . . B. and Saul
12.25 B. and Saul returned from[k] Jerusalem
13. 1 at Antioch there were prophets . . , B.
13. 2 "Set apart for me B. and Saul
13. 7 Sergius Paulus . . summoned B. and Saul
13.43 converts to Judaism followed Paul and B.
13.46 Paul and B. spoke out boldly
13.50 stirred up persecution against Paul and B.
14.12 B. they called Zeus, and Paul . . Hermes
14.14 when the apostles B. and Paul heard of it
14.20 next day he went on with B. to Derbe
15. 2 Paul and B. had no small dissension
15. 2 Paul and B. . . were . . to go up to Jerusalem
15.12 all the assembly . . listened to B. and Paul
15.22 to . . send them to Antioch with Paul and B.
15.25 "to you with our beloved B. and Paul
15.35 Paul and B. remained in Antioch, teaching
15.36 Paul said to B., "Come, let us return
15.37 B. wanted to take with them John
15.39 B. took Mark with him and sailed away
1 Cor 9. 6 is it only B. and I who have no right?
Gal 2. 1 I went up again to Jerusalem with B.
2. 9 gave to me and B. the right hand
2.13 B. was carried away by their insincerity
Col 4.10 A. . . greets you, and Mark the cousin of B.
CONTEXTUALLY
Acts 11.25 So B. went to Tarsus to look for Saul

BARRACKS
1. *soldiers' quarters, company:* παρεμβολή PAREMBOLĒ
Acts 21.34 ordered him to be brought into the barracks
21.37 about to be brought into the barracks
22.24 commanded him to be brought into the b.
23.10 commanded . . to . . bring him into the b.
23.16 he . . entered the barracks and told Paul
23.32 on the morrow they returned to the barracks

BARREN
1. *idle:* ἀργός ARGOS
Jas 2.20 faith apart from works is barren
2. *barren:* στεῖρος STEIROS*
Lk 1. 7 no child, because Elizabeth was barren
1.36 "Elizabeth . . who was called barren
23.29 "they will say, 'Blessed are the barren!
Gal 4.27 "Rejoice, O barren one who does not bear

BARRENNESS
1. *death:* νέκρωσις NEKRŌSIS
Rom 4.19 he considered the b. of Sarah's womb

BARSABBAS: Βαρσαββᾶς bär'sabəs, 'bärsəbəs
Acts 1.23 Joseph called B. . . and Matthias
15.22 They sent Judas called B., and Silas

BARTHOLOMEW: Βαρθολομαῖος bär'thŏləmyü
Mt 10. 3 Philip and B.; Thomas and Matthew
Mk 3.18 Andrew, and Philip, and B., and Matthew
Lk 6.14 James and John, and Philip, and B.
Acts 1.13 Andrew, Philip and Thomas, B.

BARTIMAEUS: Βαρτιμαῖος ˌbärtə'mēəs
Mk 10.46 B. . . was sitting by the roadside

BASE
1. *counterfeit, worthless:* ἀδόκιμος ADOKIMOS
Rom 1.28 God gave them up to a base mind
2. *shameful:* αἰσχρός AISCHROS
Tit 1.11 teaching for base gain
3. *sick, base, evil:* πονηρός PONĒROS
1 Tim 6. 4 envy, dissension, slander, base suspicions
CONTEXTUALLY
Rom 9.31 righteousness which is based on law

BASED ON
1. *from, out of:* ἐκ (+gen.) EK
Rom 9.32 but as if it were based on works
10. 5 righteousness which is based on the law
10. 6 But the righteousness based on faith says
Phil 3. 9 not having a righteousness . . based on law

BASIN
1. *washing vessel:* νιπτήρ NIPTĒR*
Jn 13. 5 Then he poured water into a basin

BASIS OF, ON THE
1. *from, out of:* ἐκ (+gen.) EK
Rom 11. 6 it is no longer on the basis of works

BASKET
1. *basket:* κόφινος KOPHINOS*
Mt 14.20 they took up twelve baskets full
16. 9 "Do you not remember . . how many baskets?
Mk 6.43 they took up twelve baskets full
8.19 "how many baskets full of broken pieces?
Lk 9.17 they took up . . twelve baskets of . . pieces
Jn 6.13 they . . filled twelve baskets with fragments
2. *braid, basket:* σαργάνη SARGANĒ*
2 Cor 11.33 I was let down in a basket . . and escaped
3. *large basket, hamper:* σπυρίς SPYRIS*
Mt 15.37 they took up seven baskets full of . . pieces
16.10 "⟨Do you not remember⟩ how many baskets?
Mk 8. 8 broken pieces left over, seven baskets full
8.20 "how many baskets full of broken pieces?
Acts 9.25 disciples . . let him down . . in a basket

BATHE
1. *wash:* λούω (mid.) LOUŌ
Jn 13.10 "He who has bathed does not need to wash

BATTALION
1. *cohort, tactical unit:* σπεῖρα SPEIRA
Mt 27.27 gathered the whole battalion before him
Mk 15.16 they called together the whole battalion

BATTLE
1. *fight, war:* πόλεμος POLEMOS
1 Cor 14. 8 who will get ready for battle?
Rev 9. 7 locusts were like horses arrayed for battle
9. 9 chariots with horses rushing into battle
16.14 to assemble ⟨the kings⟩ for battle
20. 8 Gog and Magog, to gather them for battle

BAY
1. *bosom, lap:* κόλπος KOLPOS
Acts 27.39 they noticed a bay with a beach

BE
1. *make use of, act:* χράομαι CHRAOMAI [B.2.d.2]
2 Cor 3.12 we have such a hope, we are very bold
13.10 that . . I may not have to be severe
2. *one must:* δεῖ (+inf.) DEI
Acts 9. 6 "you will be told what you are to do

3. *have, hold:* ἔχω ECHŌ
In the following passages, ECHŌ is used in combination with other Greek words. The constructions are usually stated explicitly under the associated word (e.g., for "be sick" see SICK, BE).

Mt 1.18 she was found to be with child
8.16 he . . healed all who were sick
9.12 "but those who are sick ⟨have need⟩
14.35 brought to him all that were sick
24.19 "alas for those who are with child!
Mk 1.32 they brought to him all who were sick
1.34 And he healed many who were sick
2.17 "but those who are sick ⟨have need⟩
2.25 "what David did, when he was in need
5.23 "My little daughter is at the point of death
8.17 "Are your hearts hardened?
13.17 "alas for those who are with child
Lk 5.31 "but those who are sick ⟨have need⟩
7. 2 who was sick and at the point of death
21.23 "Alas for those who are with child
[23.17 *he was obliged to release one man*‡
Jn 5. 5 who had been ill for thirty-eight years
5. 6 he had been lying there a long time
8.57 "You are not yet fifty years old
9.21 "Ask him; he is of age
9.23 "He is of age, ask him
11.17 had already been in the tomb four days
Acts 7. 1 the high priest said, "Is this so?
12.15 But she insisted that it was so
15.36 "Come, let us . . see how they are
17.11 examining . . to see if these things were so
21.13 "I am ready . . even to die
21.23 "We have four men who are under a vow
23.29 "he was . . charged with nothing deserving
24. 9 Jews also . . affirming that all this was so
1 Cor 12.23 parts are treated with greater modesty
2 Cor 10. 6 being ready to punish . . disobedience
10.15 our hope is that as your faith increases
12.14 for the third time I am ready to come
Gal 4.27 the children of her that is married
6. 4 then his reason to boast will be in himself
Phil 1.23 My desire is to depart
1 Th 4.12 that you may . . be dependent on nobody
1 Tim 3. 7 he must be well thought of by outsiders
5.25 when they are not ⟨conspicuous⟩
Phm . 8 though I am bold enough in Christ
Heb 12. 1 Therefore, since we are surrounded
12.28 Therefore let us be grateful for receiving
1 Pet 4. 5 to him who is ready to judge the living
2 Pet 2.16 but was rebuked for his own transgression
1 Jn 2.20 you have been anointed by the Holy One
Rev 9.11 in Greek he is called Apollyon[b]
12. 2 she was with child and she cried out
12.12 "because he knows that his time is short!
13.14 the beast which was wounded by the sword
17.13 These are of one mind

4. *be:* εἰμί EIMI

Mt **1.**19, 20; **2.**2, 6, 9, 18; **3.**3, 4, 11^2, 15, 17; **4.**3, 6, 18; **5.**3, 10, 11, 13, 14, 21, 22^3, 34, 35^2, 37, 48; **6.**4, [13‡, 21^2, 22^3, 23^3, 25, 30; **7.**11, 12, 13, 14, 15, 27; **8.**8, 9, 26, 27, 30; **9.**5, 15, 19, 36; **10.**2, 11, 13^2, 15, 20, 22, 24, 26, 30, 31, 37^2, 38; **11.**3, 6, 10, 11, 14, 16, 22, 24, 29, 30; **12.**4, 5, 6, 8, 23, 27, 30^2, 34, 40^2, 45, 48^2, 50; **13.**20, 22, 23, 31, 32^2, 33, 37, 38^2, 39^3, 40, 44, 45, 46, 47, 49, 52, 55, 56, 57; **14.**2, 15, 21, 23, 24, 26, 27, 28, 33; **15.**14, 16, 20, 26, 38; **16.**13, 15, 16, 17, 18, 19^2, 20, 23, 28; **17.**4^2, 5, 17, 26; **18.**1, 4, 8, 9, 14, 17, 18^2, 20^2; **19.**6, 10, 12^3, 17, 21, 24, 26, 30; **20.**1, 4, 15, 16, 23, 26, 27; **21.**10, 11, 25, 33, 38, 42; **22.**8^2, 14, 16, 23, 25, 28, 30, 32^2, 38, 42, 45; **23.**8, 11, 16, 17, 18, 28, 31; **24.**3, 5, 6, 7, 9, 21, 26, 27, 28, 33, 37, 38, 39, 40, 45; **25.**2, 21, 23, 24, 35, 36, 43; **26.**18, 22, 24, 25, 26, 28, 38, 39, 43, 48, 63, 68, 69, 71, 73; **27.**6, 11, 24, 37, 40, 42, 43, 46, 54, 55, 56, 61, 62, 64; **28.**3, 6, 20

Mk **1.**6, 7, 11, 13^2, 16, 23, 24, 27, 33, 45; **2.**1, 6, 9, 15, 18, 19, 26, 28; **3.**1, 11, 14, 17, 29, 33, 35; **4.**1, 15, 16, 18^2, 20, 21, 22, 26, 31, 36^2, 38, 40, 41; **5.**5, 9, 11, 14, 18, 21, 34, 40, 42; **6.**3^2, 4, 15, 31, 34, 35, 44, 47, 48, 50, 52, 55; **7.**2, 4, 11, 15^2, 18, 26, 27, 34; **8.**9, 27, 29^2; **9.**1, 4, 5^2, 7, 19, 35, 40, 42, 43, 45, 47; **10.**8, 24, 25, 29, 31, 32^2, 40, 43, 44, 47; **11.**11, 13, 30, 32; **12.**7^2, 11, 14, 18, 20, 23, 25, 27, 28, 29^2, 31, 32^2, 33, 34, 35, 37; **13.**4, 6, 8^2, 11, 13, 19, 25, 28, 29; **14.**1, 2, 3, 4, 14, 22, 24, 34, 35, 40, 44, 49, 54, 61, 62, 66, 67, 68, 69, 70^2; **15.**2, 7, 16, 25, 39, 40, 41, 42^2, 43; **16.**4, 6

Lk **1.**6, 7^2, 10, 15, 18, 19, 20, 21, 29, 32, 33, 34, 36, 45, 61, 63, 66^2, 80; **2.**4, 5, 6, 7, 8, 11, 25^2, 26, 36, 40, 44, 49, 51; **3.**15, 16, 22, 23^2; **4.**3, 7, 9, 16, 17, 20, 22, 24, 25, 27, 31, 32, 33, 34, 38, 41^2, 44; **5.**1, 3, 8, 10^2, 12, 17^3, 18, 21, 23, 29, 34, 39; **6.**3, 5, 6^2, 20, 22, 32, 33, 34, 35^3, 36, 40^2, 47, 48, 49; **7.**2, 4, 6, 8, 12^2, 19, 20, 23, 25, 27, 28^2, 31, 32, 37, 39^2, 49; **8.**2, 11^2, 12, 14, 15, 17, 21, 25, 26, 30, 32, 38, 40; **9.**9, 12, 14, 18^2, 20, 27, 32, 33^2, 35, 38, 41, 45, 46, 48, 50^2, 53, 55, 62; **10.**6, 12, 14, 22^2, 29, 42; **11.**1, 7, 8, 14^2, 19, 21, 23^2, 29, 30, 34^4, 35, 36, 41, 44, 48; **12.**1, 2, 6, 20, 23, 34^2, 35, 38, 42, 52, 55; **13.**10, 11, 14, 18, 19, 21, 30^4; **14.**1, 2, 8, 14, 17, 22, 26, 27, 31, 32, 33, 35; **15.**1, 7, 19, 21, 24^2, 25, 31^2, 32; **16.**1, 8, 10^2, 15, 17, 19; **17.**1, 10, 16, 21, 24, 26, 30, 31, 34, 35, 36; **18.**2, 3, 9, 11, 23, 25, 27, 29, 34; **19.**2, 3^2, 9, 11, 21, 22, 46, 47; **20.**2, 4, 6^2, 14, 17, 20, 27, 29, 33, 36^2, 38, 41, 44; **21.**7, 8, 11^2, 17, 22, 23, 24, 25, 30, 31, 37; **22.**3, 11, 19, 23, 27, 28, 33, 38, 49, 53^2, 56, 58^2, 59^2, 64, 67, 69, 70^3; **23.**2, 3, 6, 7, 12, 35, 37, 38, 39, 40, 43, 44, 47, 53, 54; **24.**[6‡, 6, 10, 13, 21, 29, 38, 39, 44, 53

Jn **1.**1^3, 2, 4^2, 8, 9, 10, 15^2, 18, 19^2, 20, 21^3, 22, 24, 25, 27, 28, 30^2, 33, 34, 39, 40, 42, 44, 47, 48, 49^2; **2.**1, 6, 13, 17, 23, 24, 25; **3.**1, 2, 4, 6^2, 8, 10, 13, 19^2, 21, 23^2, 24, 26, 27, 28^2, 29, 31^3, 33; **4.**6^2, 10, 11, 12, 18, 19, 20, 22, 23, 26, 29, 34, 35^2, 37, 42, 46; **5.**1, 2, 5, 9, 10, 12, 13^2, 15, 25, 27, 30, 31, 32^2, 35, 39, 45; **6.**4, 9^2, 10, 14, 20, 22, 24, 29, 31, 33, 35, 39, 40, 41, 42, 45^2, 46, 48, 50, 51^2, 55^2, 58, 60, 62, 63^2, 64^3, 65, 69, 70; **7.**2, 6, 7, 11, 12^2, 16, 17, 18^2, 22, 25, 26, 28, 33, 34, 36, 39, 40, 41, 42, 49, 50, 52; **8.**10‡, 12, 13, 14, 16^2, 17, 18, 19, 23^4, 24, 25, 26, 28, 29, 31, 33, 34, 36, 37, 39^2, 42, 44^4, 47^2, 48, 50, 53, 54^3, 55, 58; **9.**4, 5^2, 8^2, 9^3, 12, 14, 16^2, 17, 18, 19, 20, 24^2, 25^2, 28^2, 30, 31, 33, 36, 37, 40, 41; **10.**1, 2, 7, 8, 9, 11, 12^2, 13, 14, 16, 21, 23(22), 24, 29, 30, 33, 34^2, 36, 41; **11.**1, 2, 4, 6, 9, 10, 15, 18, 21, 25, 27, 30, 31, 32^2, 38, 49, 51, 55, 57; **12.**1, 2, 3, 6, 9, 14, 16, 17, 20, 26^2, 31, 34, 35, 50; **13.**5, 10^2, 11, 13, 16, 17, 19, 23, 24, 25, 26, 30, 33, 35; **14.**2, 3^2, 6, 9, 16, 17, 21, 24, 28; **15.**1^2, 3, 5, 11, 12, 14, 19^2, 20, 27; **16.**4, 15, 17, 24, 32^2; **17.**3, 6, 7, 9, 10, 11^3, 12, 14^2, 16^2, 17, 19, 21^2, 22, 24^2, 26; **18.**1, 5, 6, 8, 10, 13^2, 14, 15, 17^2, 18^2, 25^3, 28, 30, 33, 35, 36^3, 37^3, 38, 40; **19.**9, 11, 12, 14^2, 20^2, 21, 23, 24, 31^2, 35, 38, 40, 41^2, 42; **20.**1, 7, 14, 15, 19, 24, 26, 30, 31; **21.**2, 4, 7^3, 8, 11, 12^2, 18, 20, 24^2, 25

Acts **1.**7, 8, 10, 12, 13, 15, 17, 19, 20; **2.**1, 2, 3, 5, 7, 13, 14, 15, 16, 17, 21, 24, 25, 29, 39, 44; **3.**15, 23, 25; **4.**3, 6, 10, 11, 12^2, 13^2, 19, 22, 31, 32^2, 33, 34; **5.**12, 25, 32, 36, 38, 39; **6.**2; **7.**2, 6, 9, 12, 20, 22, 26, 33, 37, 38; **8.**1, 9, 10, 21, 23, 26, 28, 32, [37‡; **9.**5^2, 9, 10, 15, 20, 21, 22, 26, 33, 36^2, 38^2, 39; **10.**4, 6, 21, 24, 26, 28, 30, 35, 36, 38, 42; **11.**1, 5, 11, 17, 20, 21, 24, 28; **12.**3, 5, 6, 9, 12, 15, 18, 19, 20; **13.**1, 7, 11, 25^3, 31, 33, 38, 46, 48; **14.**12, 13, 15, 26; **15.**32; **16.**1, 3, 9, 12, 13, 15, 17, 28, 38; **17.**1, 3, 7, 11, 16, 18, 28, 29; **18.**3^2, 5, 7, 10, 12, 14, 15^2, 25, 28; **19.**1, 2, 4, 7, 14, 15, 16, 26, 31, 32, 34, 35^2, 38; **20.**8^2, 10, 13, 26, 34, 35; **21.**3, 8, 20, 22, 24, 28, 29, 33, 38, 39; **22.**3^2, 5, 8^2, 9, 15, 20, 26, 27, 29^2; **23.**5, 6^2, 8, 13, 15, 19, 21, 27, 30; **24.**10, 15, 24; **25.**5, 10, 11, 13, 14, 16; **26.**3, 15^2, 26, 29; **27.**4, 8, 9, 10, 22, 25, 37; **28.**3, 4, 5, 6, 28

Rom **1.**7, 9, 12, 14, 16, 19, 20, 22, 25; **2.**1, 14, 19, 28; **3.**8, 9, 10, 18, 22, 26; **4.**10, 15, 16^2, 18, 21; **5.**6, 8, 10, 13^2, 14; **6.**5, 14, 15, 16, 17, 20^2; **7.**3^2, 14^2, 18; **8.**8, 9, 12, 14, 16, 24, 28, 29, 34; **9.**3, 4, 5, 7, 20, 27^2; **10.**6, 7, 8^2, 12; **11.**1, 13, 25; **12.**5; **13.**1^2, 3, 4^2, 6; **14.**4, 8, 17, 23; **15.**14, 16, 27; **16.**5, 7

1 Cor **1.**2, 10^2, 11, 18^2, 25, 28^2; **2.**14; **3.**3^2, 4, 5^2, 7, 8, 9^2, 11, 16, 17^2, 18, 19, 20, 21; **4.**3, 4, 8; **5.**2, 7^2, 11; **6.**2, 7, 11, 15, 18, 19^2; **7.**7, 9, 14^2, 22^2, 25, 32, 34, 36, 39, 40; **8.**5^2, 7, 10; **9.**1^2, 2^3, 3, 18, 19, 20, 21; **10.**1, 4, 16^2, 17, 18, 19^2, 22; **11.**3, 5, 7, 13, 14, 15, 19, 20, 24, 25, 27; **12.**2, 4, 5, 6, 12^2, 15, 16, 19, 22, 25, 27; **13.**2, 11; **14.**9, 10, 11, 12, 14, 22, 25, 28, 33, 35, 37^2; **15.**9^2, 10^2, 12, 13, 17, 19, 28, 44^2, 58; **16.**12, 15, 22

2 Cor **1.1**^{2}, 12; **2.3**, 9, 15, 17; **3.2**, 3, 5, 17; **4.3**^{2}, 4; **5.4**, 19; **6.16**^{3}, 18^{2}; **7.3**; **8.9**; **9.1**, 3, 5; **10.7**, 18; **11.10**, 19, 22^{3}, 23, 31; **12.6**, 10, 11; **13.9**, 11
Gal **1.7**^{2}, 8, 9, 10, 11, 22; **2.3**, 6^{2}, 9; **3.3**, 7, 10, 16, 20, 21, 25, 26, 28, 29; **4.1**^{2}, 2, 3^{2}, 6, 7, 8, 21, 24^{3}, 25, 26^{2}, 28, 31; **5.3**, 10, 18, 19, 22, 23; **6.3**^{2}, 17
Eph **1.1**, 4, 14, 18, 23; **2.1**, 3, 4, 5^{2}, 8, 10, 12, 13, 14, 19^{2}, 20; **3.6**, 13; **4.10**, 14, 15, 18^{2}, 21, 25; **5.5**, 8, 10, 12, 13(14), 16, 18, 23, 27, 30, 32; **6.1**, 2, 3, 9^{2}
Phil **1.1**, 7^{2}, 10, 23, 28; **2.6**, 13, 26, 28; **3.3**; **4.8**, 9, 11^{2}
Col **1.6**, 7, 15, 17, 18^{2}, 21, 24, 27; **2.3**, 5, 10, 13, 17, 23; **3.1**, 5, 25; **4.9**, 11
1 Th **2.13**, 14, 20; **3.4**; **4.3**, 9, 17; **5.4**, 5^{2}
2 Th **1.3**; **2.4**, 5; **3.3**, 10, 17
1 Tim **1.5**, 7, 15; **2.2**; **3.2**, 12, 15, 16; **4.6**, 8^{2}, 10; **5.4**, 8, 24; **6.1**, 2^{2}, 5, 6, 10, 18
2 Tim **1.6**, 12; **2.2**, 17, 19, 20, 21, 24; **3.2**, 6, 9, 17; **4.11**^{2}
Titus **1.6**, 7, 9, 10, 13, 16; **2.2**; **3.1**, 3, 8, 9, 11, 14
Phm .14
Heb **1.5**^{3}, 10, 12, 14; **2.6**, 14, 15; **3.2**, 6, 12; **4.13**; **5.5**, 8, 12 13, 14; **7.2**, 5, 10, 11, 23; **8.4**^{2}, 6, 7, 10^{2}, 12; **9.11**, 15; **10.10**, 20, 39; **11.1**, 13, 16, 38; **12.8**^{2}, 21; **13.3**, 15
Jas **1.4**, 17, 18, 19, 23, 24, 25, 26, 27; **2.17**, 19, 20, 26^{2}; **3.4**, 5, 15, 17; **4.4**^{2}, 11, 12^{2}, 14, 16, 17; **5.3**, 11, 12, 17
1 Pet **1.16**, 21, 25; **2.15**, 25; **3.3**, 4, 20, 22; **5.12**
2 Pet **1.9**, 13, 14, 17, 18; **2.1**, 11, 17, 21; **3.4**, 7, 16
1 Jn **1.1**, 2, 4, 5^{3}, 7, 8, 9, 10; **2.4**, 5, 7, 8, 9^{2}, 10, 11, 14, 15, 16^{2}, 18^{2}, 19^{3}, 21, 22^{3}, 25, 27^{2}, 29; **3.1**, 2^{4}, 3, 4, 5, 7^{2}, 8, 10^{2}, 11, 12^{2}, 15, 19, 20, 23; **4.1**, 2, 3^{3}, 4^{2}, 5, 6^{2}, 7, 8, 10, 12, 15, 16, 17^{2}, 18(17), 20; **5.1**, 3^{2}, 4, 5^{2}, 6, 7(6)^{2}, 8(7), 9^{2}, 11^{2}, 14, 16, 17^{2}, 19, 20^{2}
2 Jn .2, 3, 6^{2}, 7, 12
3 Jn .11, 12
Jude .12, 16, 18, 19
Rev **1.4**^{2}, 8^{3}, 17, 18, 19, 20^{2}; **2.2**, 7, 9^{3}, 23; **3.1**, 4, 9^{2}, 15^{2}, 16, 17^{2}; **4.5**, 8^{2}, 11; **5.6**, 8, 9, 12; **7.13**, 14, 15; **9.19**; **10.6**, 9, 10; **11.4**, 17; **13.2**, 10, 18^{2}; **14.4**^{2}, 5, 8, 12; **16.5**^{2}, 6, 14, 21; **17.4**, 8^{4}, 9, 10^{2}, 11^{3}, 12, 14, 15, 18; **18.7**, 23; **19.8**, 9, 10^{2}; **20.2**, 6, 12, 14; **21.1**, 3^{2}, 4^{2}, 5, 7^{2}, 8, 16, 17, 22, 25; **22.3**^{2}, 5, 9, 10, 16

5. *come to be, happen, be:* γίνομαι GINOMAI
Mt **5.45**; **8.26**; **10.16**, 25; **11.26**; **14.15**; **16.2**‡; **19.8**; **20.26**; **23.26**; **24.20**, 21^{2}, 44; **25.6**; **26.5**, 6, 20, 54; **27.45**, 57; **28.2**
Mk **1.**[4†‡; **4.10**, 11, 22, 39; **6.26**; **9.6**, 26, 33; **10.43**, 44; **13.19**^{2}; **14.17**; **15.33**; **16.10**‡
Lk **1.2**, 5, 38; **2.2**, 13, 42; **4.42**; **6.13**, 36, 49; **8.24**; **10.21**; **12.40**; **13.2**, 4; **15.10**; **16.11**, 12; **17.26**, 28; **19.17**, 19; **20.14**, 33; **22.**[44‡; **23.44**; **24.5**, 19, 22, 37
Jn **1.6**; **2.1**; **3.9**; **5.**[4‡, 6, 9, 14; **6.17**, 21; **7.43**; **8.58**; **9.22**; **10.16**, 19, 22; **12.42**; **14.22**; **20.27**
Acts **1.16**; **7.38**; **8.8**; **9.19**; **12.23**; **15.7**; **16.26**, 35; **19.21**; **20.16**; **21.40**; **23.12**; **24.25**; **25.15**; **26.19**; **27.36**, 39, 42, 44
Rom **1.3**; **3.4**; **6.5**; **10.20**; **11.5**, 6, 34; **12.16**; **15.16**, 31; **16.2**, 7
1 Cor **2.3**; **4.16**; **7.36**; **9.27**; **10.6**, 7, 20; **11.1**, 19; **13.1**; **14.20**^{2}, 25; **15.10**, 37, 58
2 Cor **1.18**, 19^{2}; **6.14**; **8.14**; **12.11**
Gal **3.24**
Eph **4.32**; **5.1**, 17; **6.3**
Phil **2.15**
Col **1.18**; **3.15**; **4.11**
1 Th **2.1**, 7; **3.5**
2 Th **2.7**
1 Tim **5.9**
2 Tim **3.9**
Heb **2.2**; **6.12**; **7.12**, 23; **9.22**; **10.33**; **11.24**
Jas **1.22**, 25; **3.10**; **5.2**
1 Pet **1.15**; **3.6**, 13; **5.3**
2 Pet **1.16**, 20
3 Jn .8
Rev. **1.9**, 10; **2.10**; **4.2**; **6.12**; **8.1**, 5; **11.13**^{2}, 15, 19; **16.10**, 18^{3}

6. *find:* εὑρίσκω HEURISKŌ [A.6.e]
Rev 12. 8 there was no longer any place for them

7. *as, so:* ὡς HŌS [B.3.b.4]
Mt **14.5**

8. *be, exist, belong to:* ὑπάρχω HYPARCHŌ
Lk **8.41**; **9.48**; **11.13**; **16.14**, 23; **23.50**
Acts **2.30**; **4.34**; **5.4**; **8.16**; **10.12**; **16.3**, 20, 37; **17.24**, 27, 29; **19.36**, 40; **21.20**; **22.3**; **27.12**, 21; **28.7**, 18
Rom **4.19**
1 Cor **7.26**; **11.7**, 18; **12.22**
2 Cor **8.17**; **12.16**
Gal **1.14**
Phil **2.6**; **3.20**
Jas **2.15**
2 Pet **1.8**; **2.19**; **3.11**

9. *say, speak:* λέγω (pass.) LEGŌ
Rev 8.11 The name of the star is Wormwood

10. *be about to:* μέλλω (+inf.) MELLŌ
Mt **11.14**; **16.27**; **17.22**; **20.22**
Mk **10.32**; **13.4**
Lk **9.31**, 44; **19.4**, 11
Jn **6.71**; **7.39**; **12.4**, 33; **18.32**
Acts **26.2**
Rom **8.18**
1 Th **3.4**
1 Tim **1.16**
2 Tim **4.1**
Heb **1.14**; **11.8**
Jas **2.12**
1 Pet **5.1**
2 Pet **2.6**
Rev **1.19**; **6.11**; **12.5**; **17.8**

11. *cause:* παρέχω PARECHŌ [A.6.a.5]
Acts 22. 2 when they heard . . they were the more quiet

12. *be present:* πάρειμι PAREIMI
2 Cor 11. 8 when I was with you and . . in want

13. *do, make:* ποιέω POIEŌ [A.6.a.5]
Acts **10.33**
2 Cor **11.25**
Phil **4.14**
Jude .3
Rev **17.17**

IDIOMATICALLY
a. Lk 24.21 "it is now the third day τρίτην ταύτην ἡμέραν ἄγει [AGŌ]
b. Heb 8.7 there would have been no occasion for a second οὐκ ἂν δευτέρας ἐζητεῖτο τόπος [ZĒTEŌ]
c. 1 Pet 3.17 if that should be God's will εἰ θέλοι τὸ θέλημα τοῦ θεοῦ [THELŌ]

BE BEFORE THIS

1. *exist before:* προϋπάρχω PROYPARCHŌ
Lk 23.12 for before this they had been at enmity

BE THAT, CAN IT

1. *perhaps, never:* μήποτε (interrog.) MĒPOTE
Jn 7.26 "Can it be that the authorities . . know?

BE, THERE (THERE IS)

1. *there is:* ἔνι ENI*
1 Cor **6.5**
Gal **3.28**^{3}
Col **3.11**
Jas **1.17**

BE UNDER

1. *have, hold:* ἔχω ECHŌ [A.6.a.2]
1 Cor 7.37 in his heart, being under no necessity

IDIOMATICALLY
a. Acts 21.23 "We have four men who are under a vow εἰσὶν ἡμῖν ἄνδρες τέσσαρες εὐχὴν ἔχοντες ἀφ' ἑαυτῶν [HEAUTOU]

BE WITH

1. *wait for, stay with:* προσμένω PROSMENŌ
Mt 15.32 "they have been with me now three days
Mk 8. 2 "they have been with me now three days
2. *be with:* σύνειμι SYNEIMI I*
Lk 9.18 the disciples were with him
Acts 22.11 "I was led . . by those who were with me

BE WITHIN

1. *be in:* ἔνειμι ENEIMI*
Lk 11.41 "give . . those things which are within

BEACH

1. *seashore:* αἰγιαλός AIGIALOS

Mt 13. 2 the whole crowd stood on the beach
Jn 21. 4 day was breaking, Jesus stood on the beach
Acts 21. 5 kneeling down on the beach we prayed
27.39 they noticed a bay with a beach
27.40 they made for the beach

BEAR (*See also* NAME OF, BEAR THE; WITNESS, BEAR)
1. *bring, carry up:* ἀναφέρω ANAPHERŌ
Heb 9.28 offered once to bear the sins of many
1 Pet 2.24 He himself bore our sins in his body[g]†
2. *bear:* ἄρκος ARKOS*
Rev 13. 2 its feet were like a bear's
3. *lift up, carry:* βαστάζω BASTAZŌ
Mt 8.17 "He took our infirmities and bore our diseases
20.12 "'who have borne the burden of the day
Lk 11.27 "Blessed is the womb that bore you!
14.27 "Whoever does not bear his own cross
Jn 16.12 "but you cannot bear them now
19.17 they took Jesus . . bearing his own cross
Acts 15.10 "yoke . . neither . . have been able to bear
Rom 15. 1 strong ought to bear with the . . weak
Gal 5.10 he . . troubling you will bear his judgment
6. 2 Bear one another's burdens
6. 5 each man will have to bear his own load
6.17 I bear on my body the marks of Jesus
Rev 2. 2 "'I know . . how you cannot bear evil men
4. *give:* δίδωμι DIDŌMI [A.6.a.5]
1 Tim 2. 6 testimony to which was borne at the . . time
5. *have, hold:* ἔχω ECHŌ
2 Tim 2.19 God's . . foundation . . bearing this seal
Rev 6. 9 souls . . slain . . for the witness they had borne
12.17 those who . . bear testimony to Jesus
16. 2 men who bore the mark of the beast
6. *carry out:* ἐκφέρω EKPHERŌ
Heb 6. 8 if it bears thorns . . it is worthless
7. *beget, bear:* γεννάω GENNAŌ
Lk 1.13 "Elizabeth will bear you a son . . John
23.29 "'Blessed are the . . wombs that never bore!
8. *bear witness, testify:* μαρτυρέω MARTYREŌ [A.6.a.6]
Jn 5.32 "testimony which he bears to me is true
1 Jn 5.10 testimony that God has borne to his Son
9. *bring, bear:* φέρω PHERŌ
Mt 7.18a "A sound tree cannot bear evil fruit
Var. POIEŌ
Jn 12.24 "if it dies, it bears much fruit
15. 2 "branch . . that bears no fruit, he takes away
15. 2 "every branch that does bear fruit he prunes, that it may bear more fruit
15. 4 "the branch cannot bear fruit by itself
15. 5 "He who abides in me . . bears much fruit
15. 8 "bear much fruit, and so . . be my disciples
15.16 "you should go and bear fruit
Heb 13.13 go forth . . and bear the abuse he endured[o]
2 Pet 1.17 voice was borne . . by the Majestic Glory
1.18 we heard this voice borne from heaven
Also variant to: Mt **7.**18b
10. *bear, wear:* φορέω PHOREŌ
Rom 13. 4 he does not bear the sword in vain
1 Cor 15.49 we have borne the image of the man of dust, we shall[a] also b. the image‡
11. *do, make:* ποιέω POIEŌ
Mt 3. 8 "Bear fruit that befits repentance
3.10 "every tree . . that does not bear good fruit
7.17 "every sound tree bears good fruit, but the bad tree bears evil fruit
7.18b "nor can a bad tree bear good fruit
Var. PHERŌ
7.19 "Every tree that does not bear good fruit
13.26 "when the plants came up and bore grain
Lk 3. 8 "Bear fruits that befit repentance
3. 9 "every tree . . that does not bear good fruit
6.43 "For no good tree bears bad fruit, nor again does a bad tree bear good fruit
13. 9 "'if it bears fruit next year, well and good
Also variant to: Mt **7.**18a
12. *endure, bear:* στέγω STEGŌ
1 Cor 13. 7 Love bears all things, believes all things
13. *bear, bring forth:* τίκτω TIKTŌ
Mt 1.21 "she will bear a son . . you shall call . . Jesus
1.23 "a virgin shall conceive and bear a son
1.25 knew her not until she had borne a son
2. 2 "he who has been born king of the Jews
Lk 1.31 "you will conceive . . and bear a son
2.11 "to you is born this day . . a Savior
Gal 4.27 "Rejoice, O barren one who does not bear
Rev 12. 4 woman who was about to bear a child
12.13 the woman who had borne the male child
IDIOMATICALLY
a. Gal 1.15 before I was born ἐκ κοιλίας μητρός μου [KOILIA; MĒTĒR]
CONTEXTUALLY
Jn 8.43 "It is because you cannot bear to hear

BEAR ANEW
1. *regenerate:* ἀναγεννάω ANAGENNAŌ*
[a]A.6.e
1 Pet 1. 3 [a]we have been born anew to a living hope
1.23 You have been born anew

BEAR, CAN
1. *endure, bear:* στέγω (+neg.) STEGŌ
1 Th 3. 1 when we could bear it no longer
3. 5 when I could bear it no longer, I sent

BEAR CHILDREN
1. *beget, bear:* γεννάω GENNAŌ
Gal 4.24 Sinai, bearing children for slavery
2. *beget or bear children:* τεκνογονέω TEKNOGONEŌ*
1 Tim 5.14 younger widows marry, bear children

BEAR FALSE WITNESS
1. *be a false witness:* ψευδομαρτυρέω PSEUDOMARTYREŌ*
Mt 19.18 "You shall not bear false witness
Mk 10.19 "'Do not bear false witness
14.56 many bore false witness against him
14.57 some . . bore false witness against him
Lk 18.20 "'Do not bear false witness

BEAR FRUIT
1. *bear fruit:* καρποφορέω KARPOPHOREŌ
Mt 13.23 "he indeed bears fruit, and yields
Mk 4.20 "bear fruit, thirtyfold and sixtyfold
Rom 7. 4 raised . . that we may bear fruit for God
7. 5 passions . . to bear fruit for death
Col 1. 6 ⟨the gospel⟩ is bearing fruit and growing
1.10 bearing fruit in every good work

BEAR, HARD TO
1. *intolerable:* δυσβάστακτος DYSBASTAKTOS*
Mt 23. 4 "They bind heavy burdens, hard to bear[u]‡
Lk 11.46 "you load men with burdens hard to bear

BEAR IT
1. *bear up, endure* (mid.): ἀνέχω ANECHŌ
2 Cor 11.20 you bear it if a man makes slaves of you

BEAR TESTIMONY
1. *for testimony:* εἰς μαρτύριον MARTYRION [B.1.a.2]
Mt 10.18 "before governors . . to bear testimony
Mk 13. 9 "before governors . . to bear testimony
Lk 21.13 "a time for you to bear testimony

BEAR UP
1. *lift, carry away:* αἴρω AIRŌ
Mt 4. 6 "'On their hands they will bear you up
Lk 4.11 "'On their hands they will bear you up
2. *lift up, carry:* βαστάζω BASTAZŌ
Rev 2. 3 "'you are enduring patiently and bearing up

BEAR WITH
1. *bear up, endure* (mid.): ἀνέχω ANECHŌ
Mt 17.17 "How long am I to bear with you?
Mk 9.19 "How long am I to bear with you?
Lk 9.41 "how long am I to . . bear with you?
Acts 18.14 "I should . . bear with you, O Jews
2 Cor 11. 1 I wish you would bear with me in a little foolishness. Do bear with me!
11.19 you gladly bear with fools, being wise!
Heb 13.22 bear with my word of exhortation
2. *bear with another's mood:* τροποφορέω TROPOPHOREŌ*
Acts 13.18 "he bore with[m] them in the wilderness‡

BEARER
1. *lift up, carry:* βαστάζω (subst. part.) BASTAZŌ
Lk 7.14 the bearers stood still

BEARING CHILDREN
1. *childbearing:* τεκνογονία TEKNOGONIA*
1 Tim 2.15 woman . . saved through bearing children[c]†

BEAST
1. *beast:* κτῆνος KTĒNOS
Lk 10.34 "then he set him on his own beast
2. *wild animal:* θηρίον THĒRION
Tit 1.12 "Cretans are always liars, evil beasts
Heb 12.20 "If even a beast touches the mountain
Jas 3. 7 every kind of beast . . can be tamed
Rev 11. 7 the beast . . will make war upon them
13. 1 I saw a beast rising out of the sea
13. 2 the beast that I saw was like a leopard
13. 3 whole earth followed the beast with wonder
13. 4 dragon . . had given his authority to the beast, and they worshiped the beast, saying, "Who is like the beast?
13.11 another beast which rose out of the earth
13.12 exercises all the authority of the first beast
13.12 its inhabitants worship the first beast
13.14 signs . . in the presence of the beast
13.14 bidding them make an image for the beast
13.15 to give breath to the image of the beast so that the image of the beast should even speak
13.15 would not worship the image of the beast
13.17 the mark, that is, the name of the beast
13.18 reckon the number of the beast
14. 9 "If any one worships the beast and its image
14.11 "worshipers of the beast and its image
15. 2 who had conquered the beast and its image
16. 2 men who bore the mark of the beast
16.10 poured his bowl on the throne of the beast
16.13 issuing from . . the mouth of the beast
17. 3 I saw a woman sitting on a scarlet beast
17. 7 "I will tell you the mystery of . . the beast
17. 8 "The beast that you saw was, and is not
17. 8 "the beast . . was and is not and is to come
17.11 "the beast that was and is not
17.12 "kings for one hour, together with the beast
17.13 "These . . give . . authority to the beast
17.16 "they and the beast will hate the harlot
17.17 "giving over their royal power to the beast
19.19 I saw the beast and the kings of the earth
19.20 the beast was captured
19.20 who had received the mark of the beast
20. 4 souls . . who had not worshiped the beast
20.10 where the beast and the false prophet were
CONTEXTUALLY
Rev 13. 5 And the beast was given a mouth

BEAST OF PREY
1. *wild animal:* θηρίον THĒRION
Acts 11. 6 "I observed animals and beasts of prey

BEAST, SLAIN
1. *victim, sacrifice:* σφάγιον SPHAGION*
Acts 7.42 "'Did you offer to me slain beasts?

BEAST, WILD
1. *wild animal:* θηρίον THĒRION
Mk 1.13 he was with the wild beasts
Rev 6. 8 to kill . . by wild beasts of the earth

BEASTS, FIGHT WITH
1. *fight with wild beasts:* θηριομαχέω THĒRIOMACHEŌ*
1 Cor 15.32 if . . I fought with beasts at Ephesus?

BEAT
1. *question by torture, torment:* βασανίζω BASANIZŌ
Mt 14.24 the boat . . was . . beaten by the waves
2. *skin, flay:* δέρω DERŌ
Mt 21.35 "tenants . . beat one, killed another
Mk 12. 3 "took him and beat him, and sent him away
12. 5 "some they beat and some they killed
13. 9 "you will be beaten in synagogues
20.10 "the tenants beat him, and sent him away
20.11 "another servant . . also they beat
Mk 22.63 the men . . mocked him and beat him
Acts 5.40 they beat ⟨the apostles⟩ and charged them
16.37 "They have beaten us publicly, . . citizens
22.19 "'Lord, . . I . . beat those who believed
1 Cor 9.26 I do not box as one beating the air
3. *throw upon:* ἐπιβάλλω EPIBALLŌ
Mk 4.37 the waves beat into the boat
4. *slap, buffet:* κολαφίζω KOLAPHIZŌ
1 Pet 2.20 if when you do wrong and are beaten
5. *lay on blows:* πληγὰς ἐπιτιθέναι PLĒGĒ [B.2.a.1]
Lk 10.30 "robbers, who stripped him and beat him
6. *strike, beat:* τύπτω TYPTŌ
Mt 24.49 "begins to beat his fellow servants
Lk 12.45 "begins to beat the menservants
18.13 "beat his breast, saying, 'God, be merciful!
23.48 returned home beating their breasts
Acts 18.17 they all seized Sosthenes . . and beat him
21.32 when they saw . . they stopped beating Paul

BEAT AGAINST
1. *strike against:* προσκόπτω PROSKOPTŌ
Mt 7.27 "the winds blew and beat against that house

BEAT UPON
1. *fall down at, strike against:* προσπίπτω PROSPIPTŌ
Mt 7.25 "the winds blew and beat upon that house

BEAT WITH RODS
1. *beat with a rod:* ῥαβδίζω RHABDIZŌ*
Acts 16.22 gave orders to beat them with rods
2 Cor 11.25 Three times I have been beaten with rods

BEATING
1. *blow, stroke:* πληγή PLĒGĒ
[a]pl.
Lk 12.48 [a]"he who . . did what deserved a beating
2 Cor 6. 5 beatings, imprisonments, tumults, labors
11.23 countless beatings, and often near death

BEATING, RECEIVE A
1. *skin, flay:* δέρω (pass.) DERŌ
Lk 12.47 "that servant . . shall receive a severe beating
12.48 "he . . shall receive a light beating

BEAUTIFUL
1. *refined, good:* ἀστεῖος ASTEIOS*
Acts 7.20 "Moses . . was beautiful before God
Heb 11.23 they saw that the child was beautiful
2. *seasonable, youthful, fair:* ὡραῖος HŌRAIOS*
Mt 23.27 "hypocrites! . . you . . appear beautiful
Acts 3. 2 gate of the temple . . called Beautiful
3.10 sat . . at the Beautiful Gate of the temple
Rom 10.15 "beautiful are the feet of those who preach!
3. *good, beautiful:* καλός KALOS
Mt 26.10 "For she has done a beautiful thing to me
Mk 14. 6 "She has done a beautiful thing to me

BEAUTY
1. *goodly appearance:* εὐπρέπεια EUPREPEIA*
Jas 1.11 its flower falls, and its beauty perishes
2. *honor, value:* τιμή TIMĒ
Rom 9.21 one . . for beauty and another for menial use?

BECAUSE
1. *for which* (reason): ἀνθ' ὧν ANTI [B.1.a.1]
Lk 1.20 "because you did not believe my words
19.44 "because you did not know the time
Acts 12.23 because he did not give God the glory
2 Th 2.10 because they refused to love the truth
2. *because of:* διά (+acc.) DIA
Mt **24.12**
Lk **2.4**; **6.48**‡; **8.6**; **9.7**; **11.8**[2]; **18.5**; **19.11**; **23.8**
Jn **2.25**
Acts **4.2**; **8.11**; **12.20**; **18.2**, 3; **21.34**; **27.4**, 9; **28.18**
Rom **3.25**
Phil **1.7**
Heb **7.23**, 24
Jas **4.2**
3. *because, since:* διότι DIOTI
Lk 2. 7 because there was no place . . in the inn
21.28 "because your redemption is drawing near
Acts 22.18 "'because they will not accept your testimony
Rom 8.21 because the creation itself will be set free

1 Cor 15. 9 because I persecuted the church of God
Phil 2.26 because you heard that he was ill
1 Th 2. 8 because you had become very dear to us
2.18 because we wanted to come to you
4. 6 because the Lord is an avenger in all these
Heb 11. 5 not found, because God had taken him
11.23 because . . the child was beautiful
Jas 4. 3 do not receive, because you ask wrongly
4. *since, otherwise:* ἐπεί EPEI
Mt 18.32 " 'I forgave you . . because you besought me
21.46 because they held him to be a prophet
Jn 13.29 because Judas had the money box
5. *since:* ἐπειδή EPEIDĒ
Acts 14.12 because he was the chief speaker
6. *for:* γάρ GAR
Mt **7**.25; **14**.4
Mk **11**.18
Lk **6**.[48‡; **20**.36
Jn **3**.19
Rom **1**.19; **2**.1
2 Pet **1**.21
7. *on account of which:* οὗ εἵνεκεν HENEKA [B.1.a.1]
Lk 4.18 "because he has anointed me to preach
8. *who, which, what:* ὅς HOS [B.1.a.1]
[a]ἀνθ' ὧν [b]οὗ εἵνεκεν [c]ἐφ' ᾧ [d]ἐν ᾧ
Lk **1**.20[a]; **4**.18[b]; **19**.44[a]
Acts **12**.23[a]
Rom **5**.12[c]
Phil **3**.12[c]
2 Th **2**.10[a]
Heb **2**.18[d]
9. *that, because:* ὅτι HOTI
Mt **2**.18; **9**.36; **11**.20; **13**.13; **14**.5; **15**.32; **20**.7; **23**.13
Mk **1**.34; **4**.29; **6**.17, 34; **8**.2; **9**.38, 41; **16**.14‡
Lk **4**.41; **9**.49, 53; **13**.2, 14; **14**.14; **15**.27; **17**.9; **19**.3, 17, 21
Jn **1**.50; **2**.25; **3**.18, 23; **5**.16, 18, 27, 30, 39; **6**.2, 26[2], 41; **7**.1, 7[2], 23, 30; **8**.20, 37, 43, 44, 45; **9**.22; **10**.13, 17, 26, 33, 36; **11**.9, 10; **12**.6, 11, 41; **14**.12, 17, 19, 28; **15**.19, 21, 27; **16**.3, 4, 6, 9, 10, 11, 17, 21, 27; **17**.14; **18**.18; **19**.7; **20**.13, 29; **21**.17
Acts **2**.6; **6**.1; **8**.20; **10**.45; **17**.18
Rom **1**.8; **5**.5; **6**.15; **8**.21, 27†; **9**.7, 32; **10**.9; **14**.23
1 Cor **2**.14; **3**.13; **4**.9; **9**.10; **10**.17; **11**.2, 17; **12**.15, 16; **15**.15; **16**.17
2 Cor **3**.14; **7**.9[2], 13, 16; **11**.7, 11
Gal **2**.11, 16; **4**.6
Eph **5**.16, 30
2 Th **1**.3, 10; **2**.13; **3**.9
1 Tim **1**.12, 13; **4**.10
Phm .7
Jas **1**.10
1 Pet **2**.21; **4**.14
1 Jn **2**.8†, 11, 12, 13[3], 14[2], 21[2]; **3**.9, 12, 14, 22; **4**.13, 17, 19; **5**.7(6), 10
Rev **3**.10, 16; **8**.11; **11**.10; **17**.8
10. *so far as, as:* καθότι KATHOTI
Lk 1. 7 no child, because Elizabeth was barren
Acts 2.24 "because it was not possible . . to be held
17.31 "because he has fixed a day

BECAUSE OF

1. *from:* ἀπό (+gen.) APO
Acts **11**.19; **22**.11; **28**.3
2. *on account of:* χάριν CHARIN
Gal 3.19 It was added because of transgressions
3. *because of:* διά (+acc.) DIA
[a]+gen.
Mt **13**.58; **14**.9; **17**.20
Mk **2**.4; **3**.9; **6**.6, 26
Lk **5**.19
Jn **4**.39, 41, 42; **6**.57[2]; **10**.19; **19**.42
Acts **4**.21; **16**.3; **21**.35
Rom **2**.24; **6**.19; **8**.10[2]; **15**.15
1 Cor **7**.2; **11**.10
2 Cor **3**.7; **9**.14
Gal **2**.4; **4**.13
Eph **4**.18; **5**.6
Phil **1**.26[a]; **3**.8
Col **1**.5
1 Th **5**.13
Heb **2**.9; **3**.19; **4**.6; **5**.3; **7**.18
2 Pet **2**.2; **3**.12
2 Jn .2
4. *from, out of:* ἐκ (+gen.) EK
Rom **9**.11(12)[2]
Eph **2**.9
Tit **3**.5
5. *in, at, by:* ἐν (+dat.) EN
Mt **26**.31, 33
Gal **1**.24
2 Pet **1**.4
6. *on, at:* ἐπί (+dat.) EPI
Acts **20**.38
1 Cor **1**.4
7. *for the sake of:* ἕνεκα HENEKA
Acts 28.20 "because of the hope of Israel . . I am bound
2 Cor 3.10 because of the splendor that surpasses it

BECKON

1. *nod assent, signify by a nod:* κατανεύω KATANEUŌ*
Lk 5. 7 beckoned to their partners in the other boat
2. *nod, beckon:* νεύω NEUŌ
Jn 13.24 Peter beckoned to him and said, "Tell us

BECOME (*See also, e.g.,* FATHER OF, BECOME THE; FUTILE, BECOME; POOR, BECOME)

1. *be:* εἰμί EIMI
[a]+εἰς
Mt 19. 5 [a]" 'and the two shall become one
Mk 10. 8 [a]" 'and the two shall become one
1 Cor 6.16 becomes one body with her . . "The two shall become one flesh
6.17 [a]becomes one spirit with him
Eph 5.31 [a]"and the two shall become one flesh
Heb 7.15 This becomes even more evident
2. *come to be, happen, be:* γίνομαι GINOMAI
[a]+εἰς
Mt 4. 3 "command these stones to become loaves
12.45 "the last state of that man becomes worse
13.32 "when it has grown it . . becomes a tree
17. 2 his garments became white as light
18. 3 "unless you turn and become like children
21.42 [a]" 'stone . . has become the head of the corner
23.15 "and when he becomes a proselyte
24.32 "as soon as its branch becomes tender
28. 4 the guards . . became like dead men
Mk 1.17 "I will make you become fishers of men
4.32 "it . . becomes the greatest of all shrubs
6.14 for Jesus'[s] name had become known
9. 3 and his garments became glistening
12.10 [a]" 'stone . . has become the head of the corner
13.28 "as soon as its branch becomes tender
Lk 4. 3 "command this stone to become bread
6.16 Judas Iscariot, who became a traitor
9.29 his raiment became dazzling white
11.26 "the last state of that man becomes worse
11.30 "For as Jonah became a sign to . . Nineveh
13.19 [a]"it grew and became a tree
18.23 But when he heard this he became sad
20.17 [a]" 'stone . . has become the head of the corner
22.26 "let the greatest . . become as the youngest
[22.44 *his sweat became like . . drops of blood*‡
23.12 Herod and Pilate became friends
Jn 1.12 power to become children of God
1.14 Word became flesh and dwelt among us
2. 9 steward . . tasted the water now become wine
4.14 "the water . . will become in him a spring
9.27 "Do you . . want to become his disciples?
9.39 "that those who see may become blind
12.36 "that you may become sons of light
Acts 1.19 it became known to all the inhabitants
1.20 " 'Let his habitation become desolate
1.22 "one . . must become with us a witness
4.11 [a]"stone . . has become the head of the corner
7.13 "Joseph's family became known to Pharaoh

Acts 7.29 "Moses fled, and became an exile
7.40 " 'we do not know what has become of him
9.42 it became known throughout all Joppa
10.10 he became hungry and desired something
12.18 stir . . over what had become of Peter
19.17 this became known to all residents
23.10 when the dissension became violent
26.29 "that . . all . . might become such as I am
Rom 2.25 your circumcision becomes uncircumcision
4.18 that he . . become the father of many nations
7.13 through the commandment . . become sinful
11. 9 [a]"Let their table become a snare and a trap
15. 8 Christ became a servant to the circumcised
1 Cor 3.13 each man's work will become manifest
3.18 let him become a fool that he may become wise
4. 9 we have become a spectacle to the world
4.13 we have become . . as the refuse of the world
7.23 do not become slaves of men
8. 9 lest . . liberty . . become a stumbling block
9.20 To the Jews I became as a Jew
9.22 To the weak I became weak
9.22 I have become all things to all men
13.11 when I became a man
15.45 [a]"first man Adam became a living being
2 Cor 5.21 that . . we . . become the righteousness of God
Gal 3.13 Christ . . having become a curse for us
4.12 Brethren, I beseech you, become as I am
4.16 Have I then become your enemy?
Phil 1.13 it has become known throughout the . . guard
2. 8 he . . became obedient unto death
Col 1.23 of which I, Paul, became a minister
1.25 ⟨church⟩ of which I became a minister
1 Th 1. 6 And you became imitators of us
1. 7 you became an example to all . . believers
2. 8 because you had become very dear to us
2.14 you . . became imitators of the churches
1 Tim 2.14 the woman . . became a transgressor
Tit 3. 7 that we might . . become heirs in hope
Heb 1. 4 having become as much superior to angels
2.17 so that he might become a . . high priest
5. 9 he became the source of eternal salvation
5.11 since you have become dull of hearing
6. 4 have become partakers of the Holy Spirit
6.20 having become a high priest for ever
7.16 who has become a priest
7.21(20) Those who formerly became priests
11. 7 Noah . . became an heir of the righteousness
11.34 ⟨who⟩ became mighty in war
Jas 2. 4 have you not . . become judges?
2.10 whoever . . fails . . has become guilty of all
2.11 you have become a transgressor of the law
3. 1 Let not many of you become teachers
1 Pet 2. 7 [a]"stone . . has become the head of the corner
2 Pet 1. 4 may . . become partakers of the divine nature
2.20 the last state has become worse for them
Rev 6.12 and the sun became black as sackcloth, the full moon became like blood
8. 9(8) a third of the sea became blood
8.11 [a]A third of the waters became wormwood
11.15 "has become the kingdom of our Lord
16. 3 it became like the blood of a dead man
16. 4 the fountains . . became blood
18. 2 "It has become a dwelling place of demons

CONTEXTUALLY
1 Cor 9.21 I became as one outside the law

BECOMINGLY

1. *with grace and dignity:* εὐσχημόνως EUSCHĒMONŌS
Rom 13.13 let us conduct ourselves becomingly

BED (*See also* YOUR *b*)

1. *bed, bedstead:* κλινάριον KLINARION*
Acts 5.15 laid ⟨the sick⟩ on beds and pallets
2. *bed, couch:* κλίνη KLINĒ
Mt 9. 2 they brought . . a paralytic, lying on his bed
9. 6 "Rise, take up your bed and go home
Mk 4.21 "Is a lamp . . to be put . . under a bed?
Mk [7. 4 (the washing of cups and pots . . *and beds*‡
7.30 the child lying in bed, and the demon gone
Lk 5.18 bringing on a bed a man . . paralyzed
8.16 "No one . . puts ⟨a lamp⟩ under a bed
17.34 "there will be two in one bed
3. *pallet, stretcher:* κλινίδιον KLINIDION*
Lk 5.19 let him down with his bed through the tiles
5.24 "rise, take up your bed and go home
4. *marriage bed:* κοίτη KOITĒ
Lk 11. 7 " 'my children are with me in bed

CONTEXTUALLY
Acts 9.34 "Jesus Christ heals you; rise . . make your b.

BED, MARRIAGE

1. *marriage bed:* κοίτη KOITĒ
Heb 13. 4 let the marriage bed be undefiled

BEDECK

1. *make golden:* χρυσόω CHRYSOŌ*
Rev 17. 4 The woman was . . bedecked with gold
18.16 "alas, for the great city . . bedecked with gold!

BEDRIDDEN, BE

1. *lie on a mattress:* κατακεῖσθαι ἐπὶ κραβάττου KATAKEIMAI; KRABATTOS [B.3.b.4]
Acts 9.33 Aeneas . . had been bedridden for eight years

BEELZEBUL: βεεζεβούλ bē'elzib,əl
Mt 10.25 "they have called the master of the house B.
12.24 "It is only by B., the prince of demons
12.27 "if I . . by B., by whom do your sons cast?
Mk 3.22 "He is possessed by Beelzebul
Lk 11.15 "He casts out demons by B., the prince
11.18 "you say that I cast out demons by B.
11.19 "if I . . by B., by whom do your sons cast?

BEFALL

1. *come upon:* ἔρχομαι ἐπί ERCHOMAI [A.6.a.4]
Jn 18. 4 knowing all that was to befall him
2. *come to be, happen, be:* γίνομαι GINOMAI
Jn 5.14 "Sin no more, that nothing worse b. you
2 Tim 3.11 what befell me at Antioch, at Iconium
3. *happen:* συμβαίνω SYMBAINŌ
Acts 20.19 "serving . . with trials which befell me

BEFALL, WHAT SHALL

1. *meet together, happen:* συναντάω (subst. part. neut. pl.) SYNANTAŌ
Acts 20.22 "to Jerusalem . . not knowing what shall b. me

BEFIT

1. *be fitting:* πρέπω PREPŌ
1 Tim 2.10 as befits women who profess religion
Tit 2. 1 teach what befits sound doctrine

BEFITS, AS

1. *worthily:* ἀξίως AXIŌS
Rom 16. 2 receive her in the Lord as befits the saints
3 Jn . 6 send them on . . as befits God's service

BEFITS, THAT

1. *worthy:* ἄξιος AXIOS
Mt 3. 8 "Bear fruit that befits repentance
Lk 3. 8 "Bear fruits that befit repentance

BEFORE

1. *until:* ἄχρι ACHRI
Rom **5.13**
2. *opposite:* ἀπέναντι APENANTI
Rom 3.18 "no fear of God before their eyes
3. *from:* ἀπό (+gen.) APO
Rev **13.8**
4. *through:* διά (+gen.) DIA
2 Tim **2.2**
5. *into, to, for:* εἰς (+acc.) EIS
Acts **6.12**; **9.21**; **22.30**
6. *before:* ἔμπροσθεν EMPROSTHEN
Mt **5.16**, 24; **6.1**, 2; **7.6**; **10.32**[2], 33[2]; **11.10**, [26†; **17.2**; **25.32**; **26.70**; **27.11**, 29
Mk **2.12**; **9.2**
Lk **5.19**; **7.27**; **10.**[21†; **12.8**[2]; **14.2**; **19.27**; **21.36**
Jn **1.15**, 30; **3.28**; **10.4**; **12.37**
Acts **10.4**
2 Cor **5.10**

Gal **2**.14
1 Th **1**.3; **2**.19; **3**.9, 13
1 Jn **3**.19
7. *in, at, by:* ἐν (+dat.) EN [B.1.b]
Mt **14.**6
Jn **8.**9‡
Acts **5.**27
Rom **4**.10², 12
8. *in the presence of:* ἔναντι ENANTI*
Lk **1.**8
Acts **8.**21
9. *opposite, facing:* ἐναντίον ENANTION
Lk **1.**6; **24.**19
Acts **7.**10; **8.**32
10. *face to face, before:* ἐνώπιον ENŌPION
Lk **1.**15, 17, 75, 76; **5.**18, 25; **12.**6, 9²; **15.**10, 18, 21; **16.**15; **23.**14; **24.**43
Acts **2.**25; **4.**10; **6.**6; **9.**15; **10.**30, 31; **19.**9
Gal **1.**20
2 Tim **2.**14
Heb **4.**13
Jas **4.**10
3 Jn .6
Rev **1.**4; **2.**14; **3.**5², 8, 9; **4.**5, 6, 10²; **5.**8; **7.**9², 11, 15; **8.**2, 3, 4; **9.**13; **11.**4; **11.**16; **12.**4, 10; **14.**3²; **20.**12
11. *on, at:* ἐπί (+gen.) EPI
except [a]+acc.
Mt **10.**18[a]; **27.**27[a]
Mk **13.**9
Lk **12.**11[a], 58[a]; **21.**12[a]; **23.**1[a]
Acts **9.**21[a]; **10.**17[a]; **16.**19[a]; **17.**6[a]; **18.**12[a]; **23.**30; **24.**[8‡[a], 19, 20, 21; **25.**9, 10, 26; **26.**2
1 Cor **6.**1, 6
2 Cor **7.**14
1 Tim **6.**13
12. *until, when:* ἕως HEŌS
[a]ἕως ἄν B.3.b.4
Mt **10.**23; **16.**28[a]
Mk **9.**1[a]
Lk **9.**27[a]
1 Cor **4.**5[a]
13. *opposite:* κατέναντι KATENANTI
Mt 27.24 he .. washed his hands before the crowd
14. *opposite, before:* κατενώπιον KATENŌPION
Eph 1. 4 that we should be holy .. before him
Col 1.22 to present you holy .. before him
15. *as far as:* μέχρι MECHRI
[a]μέχρις οὗ A.5.a
Mk 13.30 [a]"not .. before all these things take place
16. *in the midst:* ἐν μέσῳ MESOS [B.1.b]
[a]ἐν τῷ μέσῳ B.3.b.2
Mt **14.**6[a]
Jn **8.**9‡
17. *after:* μετά (+acc.) META
[a]B.1.b [b]neg.
Mk **14.**1[a]; Acts **1.**5[b]
18. *not, no:* οὐ OU [A.4.c]
Rev **6.**10
19. *beside, with:* παρά (+dat.) PARA
Rom **2.**13
Gal **3.**11
Jas **1.**27
2 Pet **2.**11
20. *before:* πρίν PRIN*
[a]πρὶν ἤ
Mt **1.**18[a]; **26.**34, 75
Mk **14.**30[a], 72
Lk **2.**26[a]; **22.**61
Jn **4.**49; **8.**58; **14.**29
Acts **2.**20; **7.**2[a]; **25.**16[a]
21. *before:* πρό (+gen.) PRO
[a]πρὸ προσώπου
Mt **5.**12; **6.**8; **8.**29; **11.**10; **24.**38
Mk **1.**2
Lk **2.**21; **7.**27; **11.**38; **21.**12; **22.**15
Jn **1.**48; **5.**7; **10.**8; **11.**55; **12.**1; **13.**1, 19; **17.**5, 24
Acts **5.**36; **12.**6; **13.**24[a]; **23.**15
Rom **16.**7
1 Cor **2.**7; **4.**5
Gal **1.**17; **2.**12; **3.**23
Eph **1.**4
Col **1.**17
2 Tim **4.**21
Heb **11.**5
1 Pet **1.**20
Jude .25
22. *to, with, against:* πρός (+acc.) PROS
Mt **27.**62
Acts **22.**1
Rom **4.**2
2 Cor **12.**21
Eph **3.**14
1 Jn **3.**21
23. *face, person:* πρόσωπον PROSŌPON [B.1.a.1]
[a]+ἀπό [b]+πρό [c]+εἰς
Acts **7.**45[a]; **13.**24[b]
2 Cor **8.**24[c]
24. *earlier:* πρότερος (neut.) PROTEROS
[a]+art.
Jn **6.**62[a]; **7.**50; **9.**8[a]
25. *first, foremost:* πρῶτος (+gen.) PRŌTOS
[a]neut.
Jn **1.**15, 30; **15.**18[a]

BEFORE THE PRESENCE OF

1. *opposite, before:* κατενώπιον KATENŌPION
Jude .24 before the presence of his glory

BEFOREHAND (*See also* PRO- *entries*)

1. *take before, go before:* προλαμβάνω PROLAMBANŌ [B.2.d.1]
Mk 14. 8 she has anointed my body beforehand

BEG

1. *pray, beg:* δέομαι DEOMAI
Lk 8.38 The man .. begged that he might be with him
9.38 "Teacher, I beg you to look upon my son
9.40 "I begged your disciples to cast it out
Acts 21.39 "I beg you, let me speak to the people
26. 3 "I beg you to listen to me patiently
2 Cor 8. 4 begging us .. for the favor of taking part
10. 2 I beg .. I may not have to show boldness
2. *beg as a mendicant:* ἐπαιτέω EPAITEŌ*
Lk 16. 3 " 'What shall I do .. ? .. I am ashamed to beg
18.35 blind man was .. by the roadside begging
3. *ask, question, beg:* ἐρωτάω ERŌTAŌ
Mt 15.23 disciples .. begged him .. "Send her away
Mk 7.26 begged him to cast the demon out
Lk 16.27 " 'Then I beg you, father, to send him
Jn 4.47 he .. begged him to .. heal his son
2 Th 2. 1 concerning the coming of our Lord .. we beg
2 Jn . 5 I beg you, lady .. that we love one another
4. *call to, exhort, comfort:* παρακαλέω PARAKALEŌ
Mt 8.31 demons begged .. "send us away into the herd
8.34 they begged him to leave their neighborhood
Mk 5.10 he begged him eagerly not to send them
5.12 they begged him, "Send us to the swine
5.17 they began to beg Jesus[p]
5.18 begged him that he might be with him
8.22 brought .. blind man .. begged him to touch
Lk 8.31 begged him not to command them to depart
8.32 they begged him to let them enter these
Acts 13.42 begged that these things might be told
19.31 begged him not to venture into the theater
21.12 begged him not to go up to Jerusalem
24. 4 "I beg you .. to hear us briefly
2 Cor 2. 8 I beg you to reaffirm your love for him
Eph 4. 1 I .. beg you to lead a life worthy
5. *ask besides, be a beggar:* προσαιτέω PROSAITEŌ*
Jn 9. 8 "Is not this the man who used to .. beg?

BEG FROM

1. *ask, request:* αἰτέω AITEŌ
Mt 5.42 "Give to him who begs from you
Lk 6.30 "Give to every one who begs from you

BEGET

1. *beget, bear:* γεννάω GENNAŌ

Lk [3.22 "*today I have begotten thee*‡
Acts 13.33 " 'my Son, today I have begotten thee
Heb 1. 5 "my Son, today I have begotten thee
Also Heb **5.5**

BEGGAR

1. *beggar:* προσαίτης PROSAITĒS*
Mk 10.46 Bartimaeus, a blind beggar
Jn 9. 8 those who had seen him before as a beggar

BEGGARLY

1. *poor, beggarly:* πτωχός PTŌCHOS
Gal 4. 9 weak and beggarly elemental spirits

BEGIN

1. *rule; begin* (mid.): ἄρχω ARCHŌ
Mt 4.17 Jesus began to preach, saying, "Repent
11. 7 Jesus began to speak . . concerning John
11.20 he began to upbraid the cities
12. 1 they began to pluck heads of grain and to eat
14.30 beginning to sink he cried out
16.21 Jesus began to show his disciples
16.22 Peter took him and began to rebuke him
18.24 "When he began the reckoning
20. 8 " 'pay . . their wages, beginning with the last
24.49 "begins to beat his fellow servants
26.22 began to say to him . . "Is it I, Lord?
26.37 he began to be sorrowful and troubled
26.74 he began to invoke a curse on himself
Mk 1.45 he went out and began to talk freely
2.23 his disciples began to pluck heads of grain
4. 1 he began to teach beside the sea
5.17 they began to beg Jesus[p] to depart
5.20 he went away and began to proclaim
6. 2 he began to teach in the synagogue
6. 7 he . . began to send them out two by two
6.34 he began to teach them many things
6.55 began to bring sick people on their pallets
8.11 The Pharisees came and began to argue
8.31 began to teach . . that the Son . . must suffer
8.32 Peter took him, and began to rebuke him
10.28 Peter began to say . . "Lo, we have
10.32 he began to tell . . what was to happen
10.41 they began to be indignant at James
10.47 he began to cry out . . "Jesus, Son of David!
11.15 he . . began to drive out those who sold
12. 1 he began to speak to them in parables
13. 5 Jesus began to say to them, "Take heed
14.19 They began to be sorrowful
14.33 he . . began to be greatly distressed
14.65 some began to spit on him . . and to strike
14.69 the maid . . began again . . "This man is one
14.71 he began to invoke a curse on himself
15. 8 the crowd . . began to ask Pilate
15.18 they began to salute him, "Hail!
Lk 3. 8 "do not begin to say . . 'We have Abraham
3.23 Jesus, when he began his ministry
4.21 began to say . . "scripture has been fulfilled
5.21 Pharisees began to question . . "Who is this?
7.15 dead man sat up, and began to speak
7.24 he began to speak . . concerning John
7.38 she began to wet his feet with her tears
7.49 began to say . . "Who is this?
9.12 Now the day began to wear away
11.29 he began to say, "This . . is an evil generation
11.53 the Pharisees began to press him hard
12. 1 he began to say . . "Beware of the leaven
12.45 "if that servant . . begins to beat
13.25 "you will begin . . to knock . . saying, 'Lord
13.26 "you will begin to say, 'We ate and drank
14. 9 "then you will begin . . to take the lowest
14.18 "all alike began to make excuses
14.29 "all who see it begin to mock him
14.30 " 'This man began . . and was not able
15.14 "famine arose . . he began to be in want
15.24 "they began to make merry
19.37 the whole multitude . . began to rejoice
19.45 he . . began to drive out those who sold
20. 9 he began to tell the people this parable
Lk 21.28 "when these things begin to take place, look
22.23 they began to question . . which of them it was
23. 2 they began to accuse him
23.30 "they will begin to say to the mountains
24.27 beginning with Moses . . he interpreted
24.47 "preached . . to all . . beginning from Jerusalem
Jn 8. 9 one by one, beginning with the eldest[r]‡
13. 5 he . . began to wash the disciples' feet
Acts 1. 1 I have dealt with all . . Jesus began to do
1.22 "beginning from the baptism of John
2. 4 began to speak in other tongues
8.35 beginning with this scripture he told him
10.37 "beginning from Galilee after the baptism
11. 4 Peter began and explained to them in order
11.15 "As I began to speak, the Holy Spirit fell
18.26 began to speak boldly in the synagogue
24. 2 Tertullus began to accuse him
27.35 he took bread, . . broke it and began to eat
2 Cor 3. 1 Are we beginning to commend ourselves?
1 Pet 4.17 judgment . . begin with the household of God

2. *make a beginning:* ἐνάρχομαι ENARCHOMAI*
Gal 3. 3 Having begun with the Spirit
Phil 1. 6 he who began a good work in you

3. *grow toward daylight:* ἐπιφώσκω EPIPHŌSKŌ
Lk 23.54 the sabbath was beginning[s]†

4. *come to be, happen, be:* γίνομαι GINOMAI
Mt 27.24 Pilate saw that . . a riot was beginning

5. *begin before:* προενάρχομαι PROENARCHOMAI
2 Cor 8.10 you began not only to do but to desire

6. *first, foremost:* πρῶτος PRŌTOS [B.3.b.2]
1 Pet 4.17 if it begins with us, what will be the end?

IDIOMATICALLY

a. Acts 28.2 because it had begun to rain διὰ τὸν ὑετὸν τὸν ἐφεστῶτα [EPHISTĒMI]

CONTEXTUALLY

Lk 5. 7 filled . . boats, so that they began to sink
Jn 9.32 "Never since the world began has it been
Acts 27.18 they began next day to throw the cargo
Rev 11.17 "taken thy great power and begun to reign

BEGIN WITH, TO

1. *first, foremost:* πρῶτος (neut.) PRŌTOS
Rom 3. 2 To begin with, the Jews are entrusted

BEGINNING

1. *origin, rule:* ἀρχή ARCHĒ
Mt 19. 4 "from the beginning . . male and female
19. 8 "from the beginning it was not so
24. 8 "all this is but the b. of the birth-pangs
24.21 "such as has not been from the beginning
Mk 1. 1 The beginning of the gospel of Jesus Christ
10. 6 "from the beginning . . 'male and female
13. 8 "this is but the beginning of the birth-pangs
13.19 "tribulation as has not been from the b.
Lk 1. 2 who from the beginning were eyewitnesses
Jn 1. 1 In the beginning was the Word
1. 2 He was in the beginning with God
8.25 "what I have told you from the beginning[t]†
8.44 "He was a murderer from the beginning
15.27 "you have been with me from the beginning
16. 4 "I did not say these things . . from the b.
Acts 11.15 "Spirit fell . . just as on us at the beginning
26. 4 "My . . life . . spent from the beginning
Phil 4.15 in the beginning of the gospel
Col 1.18 he is the beginning, the first-born
2 Th 2.13 God chose you from the beginning[b]‡
Heb 1.10 "Lord, didst found the earth in the b.
7. 3 He . . has neither beginning of days nor end
2 Pet 3. 4 all things . . as . . from the beginning
1 Jn 1. 1 That which was from the beginning
2. 7 commandment . . you had from the beginning
2.13 you know him who is from the beginning
2.14 you know him who is from the beginning
2.24 Let what you heard from the b. abide
2.24 If what you heard from the b. abides
3. 8 the devil has sinned from the beginning
3.11 message . . you . . heard from the beginning
2 Jn . 5 from the b., that we love one another

2 Jn . 6 from the beginning, that you follow love
Rev 3.14 " 'the Amen, .. the beginning of .. creation
21. 6 "I am .. the beginning and the end
22.13 "I am .. the beginning and the end

BEGINNING, ALREADY MAKE A
1. *begin before:* προενάρχομαι PROENARCHOMAI
2 Cor 8. 6 Titus .. had already made a beginning

BEGONE
1. *go away:* ὑπάγω (imper.) HYPAGŌ
Mt 4.10 Then Jesus said to him, "Begone, Satan!

BEGRUDGE
IDIOMATICALLY
a. Mt 20.15 " 'Or do you begrudge my generosity?[n]†
ἢ ὁ ὀφθαλμός σου πονηρός ἐστιν ὅτι ἐγὼ ἀγαθός εἰμι;
[PONĒROS]

BEGUILE
1. *cause to wander:* πλανάω PLANAŌ
Rev 2.20 " 'Jezebel .. is .. beguiling my servants

BEGUILING SPEECH
1. *persuasive argument:* πιθανολογία PITHANOLOGIA*
Col 2. 4 that no one .. delude you with b. speech

BEHALF OF, ON
BEHALF, ON S.'S
1. *over, for the sake of:* ὑπέρ (+gen.) HYPER
Rom 15.30 your prayers to God on my behalf
1 Cor 15.29 being baptized on behalf of the dead
15.29 why are people baptized on their behalf?
2 Cor 1.11 that many will give thanks on our behalf
5.20 We beseech you on behalf of Christ
12. 5 On behalf of this man I will boast, but on my own behalf I will not boast
Eph 3. 1 a prisoner .. on behalf of you Gentiles
Col 1. 7 faithful minister of Christ on our[a] behalf
Phm .13 that he might serve me on your behalf
Heb 5. 1 to act on behalf of men in relation to God
6.20 Jesus .. as a forerunner on our behalf
9.24 in the presence of God on our behalf
CONTEXTUALLY
Acts 24. 2 "introduced on behalf of this nation

BEHAVE
1. *return; behave* (pass.): ἀναστρέφω ANASTREPHŌ
2 Cor 1.12 we have behaved in the world .. with holiness
1 Tim 3.15 how one ought to behave in .. the church
2. *walk, behave:* περιπατέω PERIPATEŌ
1 Cor 3. 3 are you not .. behaving like ordinary men?

BEHAVE PROPERLY, NOT
1. *behave disgracefully:* ἀσχημονέω ASCHĒMONEŌ
1 Cor 7.36 thinks that he is not behaving properly

BEHAVIOR
1. *behavior:* ἀναστροφή ANASTROPHĒ
1 Pet 3. 1 won .. by the behavior of their wives
3. 2 they see your reverent and chaste behavior
3.16 who revile your good behavior in Christ
2. *condition:* κατάστημα KATASTĒMA*
Tit 2. 3 Bid the older women .. to be reverent in b.

BEHAVIOR IS, ONE'S
1. *come to be, happen, be:* γίνομαι GINOMAI [A.6.e]
1 Th 2.10 how .. blameless was our behavior to you

BEHEAD
1. *behead:* ἀποκεφαλίζω APOKEPHALIZŌ*
Mt 14.10 he .. had John beheaded in the prison
Mk 6.16 "John, whom I beheaded, has been raised
6.27 He went and beheaded him in the prison
Lk 9. 9 "John I beheaded; but who is this?
2. *cut off with an ax:* πελεκίζω PELEKIZŌ*
Rev 20. 4 the souls .. beheaded for their testimony

BEHIND (*See also* LEAVE BEHIND)
1. *after:* μετά (+acc.) META
Heb **9.3**
2. *behind, backward:* ὀπίσω OPISŌ
Mt 16.23 said to Peter, "Get behind me, Satan!
Mk 8.33 rebuked Peter, .. "Get behind me, Satan!
Lk 7.38 standing behind him at his feet, weeping
Phil 3.13 forgetting what lies behind and straining
Rev 1.10 I heard behind me a loud voice
3. *behind:* ὄπισθεν OPISTHEN
Mt 9.20 came up behind him and touched the fringe
Mk 5.27 She .. came up behind him in the crowd
Lk 8.44 came up behind him, and touched the fringe
23.26 they seized one .. to carry it behind Jesus
Rev 4. 6 creatures, full of eyes in front and behind
CONTEXTUALLY
Heb 6.19 enters .. the inner shrine b. the curtain

BEHIND, STAY
1. *be patient under, stand firm:* ὑπομένω HYPOMENŌ
Lk 2.43 boy Jesus stayed behind in Jerusalem

BEHOLD
1. *see, look:* βλέπω BLEPŌ
Mt 18.10 "their angels .. behold the face of my Father
Rev 17. 8 dwellers .. will marvel to behold the beast
2. *see, perceive:* εἶδον EIDON
Acts 13.41 " 'Behold, you scoffers, and wonder
3. *behold, look!:* ἴδε IDE
Mk 15.35 "Behold, he is calling Elijah
Jn 1.29 "Behold, the Lamb of God!
1.36 "Behold, the Lamb of God!
1.47 "Behold, an Israelite indeed!
19.14 He said to the Jews, "Behold your King![o]
19.26 "Woman, behold, your son!
19.27 said to the disciple, "Behold, your mother!
4. *behold!:* ἰδού IDOU
Mt 1.20 behold, an angel of the Lord appeared
1.23 "Behold, a virgin shall conceive and bear
2. 1 behold, wise men from the East came
2.13 behold, an angel of the Lord appeared
2.19 behold, an angel of the Lord appeared
3.16 behold, the heavens were opened[g]
4.11 behold, angels came and ministered
8. 2 behold, a leper came to him and knelt
8.24 behold, there arose a great storm on the sea
8.29 behold, they cried out, "What have you?
8.32 behold, the whole herd rushed down
8.34 behold, all the city came out to meet Jesus
9. 2 behold, they brought to him a paralytic
9. 3 b., some .. said .. "This man is blaspheming
9.10 behold, many .. sinners came and sat
9.18 behold, a ruler came in and knelt
9.20 behold, a woman .. touched the fringe
9.32 behold, a dumb demoniac was brought
10.16 "Behold, I send you out as sheep
11. 8 "Behold, those who wear soft raiment
11.10 " 'Behold, I send my messenger
11.19 " 'Behold, a glutton and a drunkard!
12.10 behold .. a man with a withered hand
12.18 "Behold, my servant whom I have chosen
12.41 "behold, something greater than Jonah is here
12.42 "behold, something greater than Solomon
12.46 behold, his mother .. stood outside, asking
15.22 behold, a Canaanite woman .. came out
17. 3 behold, there appeared .. Moses and Elijah
19.16 behold, one came .. to him, saying, "Teacher
20.18 "Behold, we are going up to Jerusalem
20.30 behold, two blind men sitting by the roadside
21. 5 "Behold, your king is coming to you
22. 4 " 'Behold, I have made ready my dinner
23.38 "Behold, your house is forsaken
25. 6 " 'Behold, the bridegroom! Come out
26.45 "Behold, the hour is at hand
26.51 behold, one of those who were with Jesus
27.51 behold, the curtain of the temple was torn
28. 2 behold, there was a great earthquake
28. 7 "behold, he is going before you to Galilee
28. 9 behold, Jesus met them
28.11 behold, some of .. guard went into the city
Mk 1. 2 "Behold, I send my messenger
10.33 "Behold, we are going up to Jerusalem
Lk 1.20 "behold, you will be .. unable to speak
1.31 "behold, you will conceive in your womb
1.36 "behold .. Elizabeth .. has also conceived
1.38 "Behold, I am the handmaid of the Lord

Lk 1.44 "behold . . the babe in my womb leaped
1.48 "behold . . all generations will call me blessed
2.10 "behold, I bring you good news
2.34 "B., this child is set for the fall and rising
2.48 "B., your father and I have been looking
5.18 behold, men were bringing on a bed
6.23 "behold, your reward is great in heaven
7.12 behold, a man who had died was . . carried
7.25 "Behold, those who . . live in luxury
7.27 " 'Behold, I send my messenger
7.34 " 'Behold, a glutton and a drunkard!
7.37 behold, a woman of the city . . a sinner
9.30 behold, ⟨Moses and Elijah⟩ talked with him
9.38 behold, a man . . cried, "Teacher, I beg you
9.39 "behold, a spirit seizes him
10. 3 "behold, I send you out as lambs
10.19 "Behold, I have given you authority
10.25 behold, a lawyer . . put him to the test
11.31 "behold, something greater than Solomon
11.32 "b., something greater than Jonah is here
11.41 "behold, everything is clean for you
13.30 "behold, some are last who will be first
13.32 " 'B., I cast out demons . . today
13.35 "Behold, your house is forsaken
14. 2 behold, there was a man . . who had dropsy
17.21 "behold, the kingdom . . is in the midst . . [z]
18.31 "Behold, we are going up to Jerusalem
19. 8 "Behold, Lord, the half of my goods I give
22.10 "Behold, when you have entered the city
22.21 "behold, the hand of him who betrays me
22.31 "Simon, behold, Satan demanded . . you[k]
23.14 "behold, I did not find this man guilty
23.15 "B., nothing deserving death . . done by him
23.29 "behold, the days are coming
24. 4 behold, two men stood by them . . dazzling
24.49 "behold, I send the promise of my Father
Jn 12.15 "behold, your king is coming!
19. 5 Pilate said to them, "Behold the man![o]
Acts 1.10 behold, two men stood by them in white
7.56 "Behold, I see the heavens opened
8.27 behold, an Ethiopian, a eunuch, a minister
9.11 "a man of Tarsus . . behold, he is praying
10.17 b., the men that were sent by Cornelius
10.19 "Behold, three men are looking for you
10.30 "b., a man stood before me in bright apparel
12. 7 behold, an angel of the Lord appeared
13.11 "behold, the hand of the Lord is upon you
13.46 "behold, we turn to the Gentiles
20.22 "behold, I am going to Jerusalem
20.25 "behold . . you . . will see my face no more
Rom 9.33 "Behold, I am laying in Zion a stone
2 Cor 5.17 behold, the new has come
6. 2 Behold, now is the acceptable time
6. 2 behold, now is the day of salvation
6. 9 as dying, and behold, we live
Jas 5. 4 Behold, the wages of the laborers . . cry out
5. 7 Behold, the farmer waits for . . fruit
5. 9 behold, the Judge is . . at the doors
5.11 Behold, we call those happy
1 Pet 2. 6 "Behold, I am laying in Zion a stone
Jude .14 "Behold, the Lord came with his holy myriads
Rev 1. 7 Behold, he is coming with the clouds
1.18 "behold, I am alive for evermore
2.10 " 'Behold, the devil is about to throw some
2.22 " 'Behold, I will throw her on a sickbed
3. 8 " 'Behold, . . I set before you an open door
3. 9 " 'Behold, I will make those . . —behold, I will make them come
3.20 " 'Behold, I stand at the door and knock
6. 2 behold, a white horse, and its rider
6. 5 behold, a black horse, and its rider
6. 8 b., a pale horse, . . its rider's name . . Death
6.12 behold, there was a great earthquake
7. 9 I looked, and behold, a great multitude
9.12 behold, two woes are still to come
11.14 behold, the third woe is soon to come
12. 3 behold, a great red dragon
Rev 19.11 behold, a white horse!
21. 3 "Behold, the dwelling of God is with men
21. 5 "Behold, I make all things new
22. 7 "behold, I am coming soon
22.12 "Behold I am coming soon

5. *show as in a mirror:* κατοπτρίζω (mid.) KATOPTRIZŌ*
2 Cor 3.18 beholding[d] the glory of the Lord†

6. *behold:* θεάομαι THEAOMAI
Mt 11. 7 "What did you go out . . to behold?
Lk 7.24 "What did you go out . . to behold?
Jn 1.14 we have beheld his glory

7. *look at, observe:* θεωρέω THEŌREŌ
Mk 3.11 whenever the unclean spirits beheld him
Jn 17.24 "to behold my glory which thou hast given

BEING (*See* HUMAN BEING)

BEING, A

1. *life, soul, self:* ψυχή PSYCHĒ
Rom 2. 9 for every human being who does evil
1 Cor 15.45 "The first man Adam became a living being

BEING, HAVE ONE'S

1. *be:* εἰμί EIMI
Acts 17.28 " 'In him we live . . and have our being

BELIAL: βελιάρ 'bĕlēəl
2 Cor 6.15 What accord has Christ with Belial?[i]†

BELIEF

1. *trust, faith:* πίστις PISTIS
2 Th 2.13 to be saved, through . . belief in the truth

BELIEVE

1. *believe, trust:* πιστεύω PISTEUŌ*
Mt 8.13 "Go; be it done for you as you have believed
9.28 "Do you believe that I am able?
18. 6 "one of these little ones who believe in me
21.25 " 'Why then did you not believe him?
21.32 "John came . . and you did not believe him, but . . harlots believed him; and even when you saw it, you did not . . believe him
24.23 " 'There he is!' do not believe it
24.26 "if they say . . 'Lo . .' do not believe it
27.42 "let him come down . . and we will believe
Mk 1.15 "repent, and believe in the gospel
5.36 "Do not fear, only believe
9.23 "All things are possible to him who believes
9.24 "I believe; help my unbelief!
9.42 "one of these little ones who believe in me
11.23 "whoever . . believes . . , it will be done
11.24 "whatever you ask in prayer, believe
11.31 " 'Why then did you not believe him?
13.21 " 'Look, there he is!' do not believe it
15.32 "come down . . that we may see and believe
16.13 told the rest, but they did not believe[k]‡
16.14 upbraided . . because they had not believed[k]‡
16.16 "He who believes . . will be saved[k]‡
16.17 "signs will accompany those who believe[k]‡
Lk 1.20 "because you did not believe my words
1.45 "blessed is she who believed
8.12 "they may not believe and be saved
8.13 "they believe for a while and . . fall away
8.50 "Do not fear; only believe
20. 5 " 'Why did you not believe him?
22.67 "If I tell you, you will not believe
24.25 "slow of heart to believe . . the prophets!
Jn 1. 7 that all might believe through him
1.12 to all who . . believed . . he gave power
1.50 "Because I said . . I saw you . . , do you b.?
2.11 his disciples believed in him
2.22 remembered . . and . . believed the scripture
2.23 many believed . . when they saw the signs
3.12 "If . . earthly things . . you do not believe, how can you believe . . heavenly things?
3.15 "that whoever believes . . may have . . life[h]
3.16 whoever believes in him should not perish
3.18 who believes in him is not condemned; he who does not believe is condemned already, because he has not believed
3.36 He who believes in the Son has eternal life

Jn 4.21 "Woman, believe me, the hour is coming
4.39 Many Samaritans from that city believed
4.41 many more believed because of his word
4.42 "we believe, .. we have heard for ourselves
4.48 "Unless you see signs .. you will not believe
4.50 man believed the word that Jesus spoke
4.53 "Your son will live"; and he .. believed
5.24 "he who hears my word and believes
5.38 "you do not believe him whom he has sent
5.44 "can you believe, who receive glory?
5.46 "If you believed Moses, you would believe me, for he wrote of me
5.47 "But if you do not believe his writings, how will you believe my words?
6.29 "This is the work of God, that you believe
6.30 "what sign do you do, that we may .. believe?
6.35 "he who believes in me shall never thirst
6.36 "you have seen me and yet do not believe
6.40 "that .. one who .. believes .. have .. life
6.47 "he who believes has eternal life
6.64 "there are some of you that do not believe
6.64 Jesus knew .. who .. did not believe
6.69 "we have believed, and have come to know
7. 5 "even his brothers did not believe
7.31 many of the people believed in him
7.38 "who believes in me, as[q] the scripture .. said†
7.39 who believed .. were to receive .. the Spirit
7.48 "Have any .. authorities .. believed in him?
8.24 "you will die in your sins unless you believe
8.30 As he spoke thus, many believed in him
8.31 to the Jews who had believed in him
8.45 "I tell the truth, you do not believe me
8.46 "If I tell the truth, why do you not believe?
9.18 Jews did not believe that he had been blind
9.35 "Do you believe in the Son of man?[v]
9.36 "who is he, sir, that I may believe in him?
9.38 "Lord, I believe"; and he worshiped him
10.25 "I told you, and you do not believe
10.26 "do not believe, because you do not belong
10.37 "If .. not .., then do not believe me
10.38 "if I do them, even though you do not believe me, believe the works
10.42 many believed in him there
11.15 "I was not there, so that you may believe
11.25 "who believes .. though he die .. shall .. live
11.26 "whoever .. believes in me shall never die. Do you believe this?
11.27 "I believe that you are the Christ
11.40 "if you would b. you would see the glory
11.42 "they may believe that thou didst send me
11.45 Many .. Jews .. believed in him
11.48 "If we let him go on .. every one will believe
12.11 many of the Jews were .. believing
12.36 "While you have the light, b. in the light
12.37 yet they did not believe in him
12.38 "Lord, who has believed our report?
12.39 Therefore they could not believe
12.42 many .. authorities believed in him
12.44 "He who believes in me, believes not in me but in him who sent me
12.46 "whoever believes .. not remain in darkness
13.19 "when it does take place you may believe
14. 1 "Let not your hearts be troubled; believe[e] in God, believe also in me
14.10 "Do you not believe .. I am in the Father?
14.11 "Believe me that I am in the Father .. or else believe me for the sake of the works
14.12 "he who believes in me will .. do .. greater
14.29 "I have told you .. so that .. you may b.
16. 9 "because they do not believe in me
16.27 "you .. believed that I came from the Father
16.30 "by this we believe that you came from God
16.31 Jesus answered .. "Do you now believe?
17. 8 "believed that thou didst send me
17.20 "who believe in me through their word
17.21 "world may believe that thou hast sent me
19.35 he tells the truth—that you also may believe

Jn 20. 8 the other disciple .. saw and believed
20.25 "Unless I see .. I will not believe
20.29 "believed because you have seen me? Blessed are those who have not seen .. yet b.
20.31 these are written that you may believe .. and .. believing .. have life in his name

Acts 2.44 all who believed were together
4. 4 many of those who heard the word believed
4.32 those who believed were of one heart
8.12 they believed Philip as he preached
8.13 Even Simon himself believed
[8.37 *"If you believe with all your heart*‡
[8.37 *"I b. . . Jesus Christ is the Son of God*‡
9.26 they did not believe that he was a disciple
9.42 many believed in the Lord
10.43 "who believes in him receives forgiveness
11.17 "gift .. he gave to us when we believed
11.21 a great number that believed turned
13.12 Then the proconsul believed
13.39 "one that believes is freed from everything
13.41 " 'a deed you will never believe
13.48 many .. ordained to eternal life believed
14. 1 so spoke that a great company believed
14.23 to the Lord in whom they believed
15. 7 "Gentiles should hear the word .. and believe
15.11 "we believe that we shall be saved
16.31 "B. in the Lord Jesus, and you will be saved
16.34 he rejoiced .. that he had believed in God
17.12 Many of them therefore believed
17.34 But some men joined him and believed
18. 8 Crispus .. believed .., with all his household
18. 8 many .. Corinthians hearing Paul believed
18.27 those who through grace had believed
19. 2 "receive the .. Spirit when you believed?
19. 4 "John baptized .., telling the people to b.
21.20 "thousands .. among the Jews .. believed
21.25 "as for the Gentiles who have believed
22.19 " 'I .. beat those who believed in thee
24.14 "believing everything laid down by the law
26.27 "King Agrippa, do you believe the prophets? I know that you believe

Rom 3.22 righteousness of God .. for all who believe
4. 3 "Abraham believed God
4.11 to make him the father of all who believe
4.17 the presence of the God in whom he believed
4.18 In hope he believed against hope
4.24 It will be reckoned to us who believe
6. 8 believe that we shall also live with him
9.33 "who believes in him will not be put to shame
10. 9 believe in your heart that God raised him
10.10 man believes .. and so is justified
10.11 "No one who believes .. will be put to shame
10.14 him in whom they have not believed
10.14 And how are they to believe in him?
10.16 "who has believed what he has heard?
13.11 nearer .. now than when we first believed
14. 2 One believes he may eat anything
15.13 fill you with all joy and peace in believing

1 Cor 1.21 through .. folly .. to save those who believe
3. 5 Servants through whom you believed
11.18 that there are divisions .. I partly believe
13. 7 Love bears all things, believes all things
15. 2 you are saved .. unless you believed in vain
15.11 so we preach and so you believed

2 Cor 4.13 he .. wrote, "I believed, and so I spoke," we too believe, and so we speak

Gal 2.16 even we have believed in Christ Jesus
3. 6 Abraham "believed God
3.22 what was promised .. given to those who b.

Eph 1.13 you also, who .. have believed in him
1.19 greatness of his power in us who believe

Phil 1.29 not only believe in him but also suffer

1 Th 4.14 since we believe that Jesus died and rose

2 Th 1.10 marveled at in all who .. believed, because our testimony to you was believed
2.11 delusion, to make them b. what is false
2.12 all may be condemned who did not b.

1 Tim 1.16 an example to those who were to believe
3.16 believed on in the world, taken up in glory
2 Tim 1.12 I know whom I have believed
Tit 3. 8 those who have believed in God
Heb 4. 3 we who have believed enter that rest
11. 6 must believe that he exists and . . rewards
Jas 2.19 You believe that God is one; you do well. Even the demons believe—and shudder
2.23 "Abraham believed God
1 Pet 1. 8 though you do not now see him you[c] believe
2. 6 "he who believes . . will not be put to shame
2. 7 To you . . who believe, he is precious
1 Jn 3.23 his commandment, that we should believe
4. 1 Beloved, do not believe every spirit
4.16 we know and believe the love God has
5. 1 who believes that Jesus is the Christ
5. 5 he who believes that Jesus is the Son
5.10 who believes in the Son . . has the testimony
5.10 who does not believe God has made him a liar, because he has not believed
5.13 to you who believe . . , that you may know
Jude . 5 destroyed those who did not believe

BELIEVE, FIRMLY
1. *make trustworthy:* πιστόω (pass.) PISTOŌ*
2 Tim 3.14 what you . . have firmly believed

BELIEVE, NOT
1. *disbelieve, be faithless:* ἀπιστέω APISTEŌ
Mk 16.11 when they heard . . , they would not believe[k]‡
16.16 "he who does not b. will be condemned[k]‡
Lk 24.11 seemed . . an idle tale, and they did not b.
1 Pet 2. 7 but for those who do not believe

BELIEVER
1. *believe, trust:* πιστεύω (subst. part.) PISTEUŌ
Acts 5.14 believers were added to the Lord
15. 5 "some believers . . belonged to the . . Pharisees
19.18 Many . . who were now believers came
1 Cor 14.22 tongues are a sign not for believers
14.22 prophecy is . . for believers
1 Th 1. 7 an example to all the believers
2.10 blameless was our behavior to you believers
2.13 the word of God . . at work in you believers
2. *faithful, trustworthy:* πιστός (subst.) PISTOS
Acts 10.45 believers from among the circumcised
16. 1 Timothy, the son of a Jewish . . believer
2 Cor 6.15 a believer in common with an unbeliever
1 Tim 4.12 set the believers an example in speech
6. 2 those who benefit . . are believers
Tit 1. 6 if . . his children are believers

BELIEVES, ONE WHO
1. *faithful, trustworthy:* πιστός (subst.) PISTOS
1 Tim 4. 3 those who believe and know the truth
4.10 Savior of all . . especially of those who believe

BELIEVING
1. *faithful, trustworthy:* πιστός PISTOS
Jn 20.27 "do not be faithless, but believing
1 Tim 6. 2 Those who have believing masters

BELIEVING MAN
BELIEVING WOMAN
1. *faithful, trustworthy:* πιστός (subst.) PISTOS
1 Tim 5.16 If any believing woman[l] has relatives‡
[5.16 If any believing *man or woman* has relatives‡
[5.16 If any believing *man* has relatives‡

BELLY
1. *body cavity, belly:* κοιλία KOILIA
Mt 12.40 "Jonah was . . in the belly of the whale
Lk [15.16 "would gladly have *filled his belly*‡
Phil 3.19 their god is the belly

BELONG
BELONG TO
1. *from:* ἀπό (+gen.) APO [B.1.a.2]
Acts **12.1**; **15.5**
2. *have, hold:* ἔχω (pass.) ECHŌ
Heb 6. 9 better things that belong to salvation
3. *be:* εἰμί EIMI [A.6.a.5]
[a]+ἐκ
Mt 19.14 "to such belongs the kingdom of heaven
Mk 10.14 "to such belongs the kingdom of God
Lk 18.16 "to such belongs the kingdom of God
23. 7 [a]that he belonged to Herod's jurisdiction
Jn 3.31 [a]who is of the earth belongs to the earth
10.26 [a]"you do not belong to my sheep
Acts 9. 2 if he found any belonging to the Way
23.34 [a]he asked to what province he belonged
27.23 "an angel of the God to whom I belong
Rom 8. 9 does not have the Spirit . . does not belong
1 Cor 1.12 each one of you says, "I belong to Paul
3. 4 For when one says, "I belong to Paul
12.15 [a]"I do not belong to the body
12.16 [a]"I do not belong to the body
2 Cor 4. 7 the transcendent power belongs to God
1 Th 5. 8 since we belong to the day, let us be sober
1 Pet 4.11 To him belong glory and dominion for ever
Rev 17.11 [a]"it is an eighth but . . belongs to the seven
4. *come to be, happen, be:* γίνομαι (+dat.) GINOMAI
Rom 7. 4 so that you may belong to another
5. *be, exist, belong to:* ὑπάρχω HYPARCHŌ
Acts 4.37 sold a field which belonged to him
6. *participate in, share:* μετέχω METECHŌ
Heb 7.13 the one . . belonged to another tribe
CONTEXTUALLY
Lk 14. 1 a ruler who belonged to the Pharisees
Acts 6. 9 some of those who belonged to . . synagogue
12. 1 violent hands upon some who belonged
15. 5 believers who belonged to the party
28. 7 were lands belonging to the chief man
Rom 1. 6 who are called to belong to Jesus Christ
9. 4 and to them b. the sonship, the glory
9. 5 to them belong the patriarchs
9. 6 not all . . descended from Israel belong
16.10 Greet those who belong to the family
16.11 who belong to the family of Narcissus
1 Cor 1.12 What I mean is that each one of you says . . "I belong to Apollos," or "I belong to Cephas," or "I belong to Christ
3. 4 For when one says . . "I belong to Apollos
15.23 then at his coming those who b. to Christ
Eph 4. 4 the one hope that belongs to your call
Col 2.17 but the substance belongs to Christ
2.20 as if you still belonged to the world
Rev 7.10 "Salvation belongs to our God
19. 1 "glory and power belong to our God

BELONGING (*See* OTHERS, BELONGING TO)

BELONGING TO
BELONGS TO, WHICH
1. *in accordance with, for:* κατά (+acc.) KATA [B.3.b.4]
Acts **2.10**; Eph **4.22**

BELONGS TO ME, WHAT
BELONGS TO YOU, WHAT
1. *my, mine:* ἐμός (subst. neut. pl.) EMOS
Mt 20.15 " 'do what I choose with what belongs to me
2. *your, thy:* σός (subst. neut.) SOS
Mt 20.14 " 'Take what belongs to you, and go

BELOVED
1. *love:* ἀγαπάω (perf. pass. part.) AGAPAŌ
Rom 9.25 "and he who was not beloved I will call 'my beloved
Eph 1. 6 grace . . bestowed on us in the Beloved
Col 3.12 as God's chosen ones, holy and beloved
1 Th 1. 4 we know, brethren beloved by God
2 Th 2.13 brethren beloved by the Lord
Jude . 1 To those who are called, beloved in God
Rev 20. 9 camp of the saints and the beloved city
2. *love:* ἀγάπη (gen.) AGAPĒ
Col 1.13 the kingdom of his beloved Son
3. *beloved:* ἀγαπητός AGAPĒTOS
Mt 3.17 "This is my beloved Son[h]†
12.18 "my beloved with whom my soul is . . pleased
17. 5 "This is my beloved Son[w]†
Mk 1.11 "Thou art my beloved Son[d]†
9. 7 "This is my beloved Son;[g] listen to him†
12. 6 "He had still one other, a beloved son

Lk 3.22 "Thou art my beloved Son[j]‡
[9.35 "This is my Son, my *Beloved*‡
20.13 " 'I will send my beloved son
Acts 15.25 "with our beloved Barnabas and Paul
Rom 1. 7 To all God's beloved in Rome . . saints
11.28 as regards election they are beloved
12.19 Beloved, never avenge yourselves
16. 5 Greet my beloved Epaenetus
16. 8 Greet Ampliatus, my beloved
16. 9 Greet . . my beloved Stachys
16.12 Greet the beloved Persis
1 Cor 4.14 admonish you as my beloved children
4.17 Timothy, my beloved and faithful child
10.14 my beloved, shun the worship of idols
15.58 my beloved brethren, be steadfast
2 Cor 7. 1 beloved, let us cleanse ourselves
12.19 speaking . . for your upbuilding, beloved
Eph 5. 1 imitators of God, as beloved children
6.21 Tychicus the beloved brother
Phil 2.12 my beloved, as you have always obeyed
4. 1 stand firm thus in the Lord, my beloved
Col 1. 7 Epaphras our beloved fellow servant
4. 7 Tychicus is a beloved brother
4. 9 Onesimus, the faithful and beloved brother
4.14 Luke the beloved physician and Demas
1 Tim 6. 2 those . . are believers and beloved
2 Tim 1. 2 To Timothy, my beloved child
Phm . 1 To Philemon our beloved fellow worker
.16 more than a slave, as a beloved brother
Heb 6. 9 yet in your case, beloved, we feel sure
Jas 1.16 Do not be deceived, my beloved brethren
1.19 Know this, my beloved brethren
2. 5 Listen, my beloved brethren
1 Pet 2.11 Beloved, I beseech you as aliens
4.12 Beloved, do not be surprised at the . . ordeal
2 Pet 1.17 "This is my beloved Son[d]†
3. 1 second letter . . written to you, beloved
3. 8 do not ignore this one fact, beloved
3.14 Therefore, beloved . . be zealous
3.15 our beloved brother Paul wrote to you
3.17 beloved . . beware lest you be carried away
1 Jn 2. 7 Beloved . . no new commandment, but an old
3. 2 Beloved, we are God's children now
3.21 Beloved, if our hearts do not condemn us
4. 1 Beloved, do not believe every spirit
4. 7 Beloved, let us love one another
4.11 Beloved, if God so loved us, we also ought
3 Jn . 1 The elder to the beloved Gaius
. 2 Beloved, I pray that all may go well
. 5 Beloved, it is a loyal thing you do
.11 Beloved, do not imitate evil but . . good
Jude . 3 Beloved . . contend for the faith
.17 you must remember, beloved
.20 beloved, build yourselves up on your . . faith

BELOW
1. *downward, below:* κάτω KATŌ
[a]subst. neut. pl.
Mk 14.66 as Peter was below in the courtyard
Jn 8.23 [a]"You are from below, I am from above

BELT
1. *girdle, belt:* ζώνη ZŌNĒ
Mt 10. 9 "Take no gold . . in your belts
Mk 6. 8 to take nothing . . in their belts

BEND
1. *bend forward, stoop:* κύπτω KYPTŌ
Jn 8. 6 Jesus bent down and wrote with his finger[r]‡
2. *bend down:* συγκάμπτω SYGKAMPTŌ*
Rom 11.10 bend their backs for ever

BEND DOWN
1. *stoop, bend down:* κατακύπτω KATAKYPTŌ
Jn 8. 8 once more he bent down and wrote[r]‡

BEND OVER
1. *fall upon:* ἐπιπίπτω EPIPIPTŌ
Acts 20.10 Paul . . bent over him, and embracing him

BENEATH
1. *downward, below:* κάτω KATŌ
Acts 2.19 "I will show . . signs on the earth beneath

BENEFACTOR
1. *benefactor:* εὐεργέτης EUERGETĒS*
Lk 22.25 "those in authority . . are called benefactors

BENEFIT
1. *lay hold of, help* (mid.): ἀντιλαμβάνω ANTILAMBANŌ
1 Tim 6. 2 those who benefit by their service
2. *help, aid:* ὠφελέω ŌPHELEŌ
1 Cor 14. 6 how . . benefit . . unless I bring . . revelation?
Heb 4. 2 message which they heard did not benefit
13. 9 foods . . have not benefited their adherents
3. *useful:* σύμφορος (subst. neut.) SYMPHOROS
1 Cor 7.35 I say this for your own benefit
CONTEXTUALLY
1 Cor 9.11 if we reap your material benefits

BENEFIT, FOR S.'S
1. *because of:* διά (+acc.) DIA
1 Cor 4. 6 I have applied all this . . for your b.

BENEFIT, WANT SOME
1. *profit, gratify:* ὀνίνημι (aor. mid. opt.) ONINĒMI*
Phm .20 I want some benefit from you in the Lord

BENEVOLENCE
1. *righteousness, justice:* δικαιοσύνη DIKAIOSYNĒ
2 Cor [9. 9 "his *benevolence* endures for ever†
[9.10 He . . will . . increase the harvest of your *b.*†

BENJAMIN: Βενιαμείν 'benjəmən
Acts 13.21 "Saul . . a man of the tribe of B.
Rom 11. 1 an Israelite, . . a member of the tribe of B.
Phil 3. 5 of the people of Israel, of the tribe of B.
Rev 7. 8 twelve thousand sealed out of the tribe of B.

BENT OVER, BE
1. *bend forward:* συγκύπτω SYGKYPTŌ*
Lk 13.11 a woman . . of infirmity . . ; she was bent over

BEOR: Βεώρ 'bēôr
2 Pet 2.15 Balaam, the son of B., who loved gain

BEREFT, BE
1. *bereave:* ἀπορφανίζω (pass.) APORPHANIZŌ*
1 Th 2.17 bereft of you, brethren, for a short time
2. *defraud:* ἀποστερέω (pass.) APOSTEREŌ
1 Tim 6. 5 are depraved . . and bereft of the truth

BERNICE: Βερνίκη bər'nēs
Acts 25.13 Agrippa the king and B. arrived at C.
25.23 Agrippa and B. came with great pomp
26.30 the king rose, and the governor and B.

BEROEA: bə'rēə II,D-3
1. *Beroea:* Βέροια
Acts 17.10 sent Paul and Silas away by night to B.
17.13 word of God was proclaimed by Paul at B.
2. *of Beroea:* Βεροιαῖος
Acts 20. 4 Sopater of B. . . accompanied him

BERYL
1. *gem of sea-green color:* βήρυλλος BĒRYLLOS
Rev 21.20 the eighth beryl, the ninth topaz

BESEECH
1. *pray, beg:* δέομαι DEOMAI
Lk 5.12 a man full of leprosy . . besought him
8.28 "I beseech you, do not torment me
2 Cor 5.20 We beseech you on behalf of Christ
Gal 4.12 Brethren, I beseech you, become as I am
2. *ask, question, beg:* ἐρωτάω ERŌTAŌ
Lk 4.38 they besought him for her
Jn 4.31 disciples besought him . . "Rabbi, eat
1 Th 4. 1 brethren, we beseech and exhort you
5.12 we beseech you . . to respect those
3. *call to, exhort, comfort:* παρακαλέω PARAKALEŌ
Mt 8. 5 a centurion came . . beseeching him
14.36 besought him that they might . . touch
18.29 "his fellow servant fell down and besought
18.32 " 'I forgave you . . because you besought me
Mk 1.40 a leper came to him beseeching him
5.23 besought him . . "My little daughter
6.56 besought him that they might touch

Mk 7.32 besought him to lay his hand upon him
Lk 7. 4 besought him earnestly .. "He is worthy
8.41 he besought him to come to his house
Acts 16. 9 a man of Macedonia .. beseeching him
16.15 with her household, she besought us
2 Cor 12. 8 Three times I besought the Lord
1 Pet 2.11 I beseech you as aliens .. to abstain

BESET WITH, BE
1. *lie around, wear:* περίκειμαι PERIKEIMAI
Heb 5. 2 he himself is beset with weakness

BESIDE (*See also* PARA- *entries*)
BESIDES
1. *separately, apart from:* χωρίς CHŌRIS
Mt 14.21 five thousand men, besides women and child.
15.38 four thousand men, besides women .. children
2. *in, at, by:* ἐν (+dat.) EN
Lk **16.26**
Eph **6.16**
3. *on, at:* ἐπί (+acc.) EPI
except [a]+dat.
Jn **4.6**[a]
2 Cor **7.13**[a]
Rev **15.2**
4. *more than, by:* παρά (+acc.) PARA
Mt **13.1**
Mk **2.13**; **4.1**; **5.21**
5. *to, with, against:* πρός (+acc.) PROS
Mk **4.1**
Acts **5.10**
6. *with:* σύν (+dat.) SYN
Lk **24.21**
Acts **4.14**
CONTEXTUALLY
Mt **27.19**; Rom **13.11**

BESIDE ONESELF, BE
1. *displace, amaze:* ἐξίστημι EXISTĒMI
Mk 3.21 saying, "He is beside himself
2 Cor 5.13 if we are beside ourselves, it is for God

BESIDES THAT
1. *at the same time:* ἅμα HAMA
1 Tim 5.13 Besides that, they learn to be idlers

BESIDES THIS
1. *then, next:* εἶτα EITA
Heb 12. 9 Besides this, we have had earthly fathers

BEST
1. *first, foremost:* πρῶτος PRŌTOS
Lk 15.22 " 'Bring quickly the best robe
IDIOMATICALLY
a. Tit 3.13 Do your best to speed Z... and A. on their way
Z... καὶ A. σπουδαίως πρόπεμψον [SPOUDAIŌS]

BEST, DO ONE'S
1. *be eager:* σπουδάζω SPOUDAZŌ
2 Tim 2.15 Do your best to present yourself to God
4. 9 Do your best to come to me soon
4.21 Do your best to come before winter
Tit 3.12 do your best to come to me at Nicopolis

BEST FOR S., IT IS
1. *bring together, be useful:* συμφέρω (impers. +dat.)
SYMPHERŌ
2 Cor 8.10 it is best for you now to complete

BEST SEAT
1. *first seat:* πρωτοκαθεδρία PRŌTOKATHEDRIA*
Mt 23. 6 "love .. the best seats in the synagogues
Mk 12.39 "⟨like⟩ the best seats in the synagogues
Lk 11.43 "Pharisees, .. you love the best seat
20.46 "scribes .. love .. the best seats

BEST, THINK
1. *consider worthy:* ἀξιόω AXIOŌ
Acts 15.38 Paul thought best not to take ⟨Mark⟩

BESTOW (*See also* RICHES, BESTOW ONE'S)
1. *impart:* ἀπονέμω APONEMŌ*
1 Pet 3. 7 husbands, .. bestowing honor on the woman
2. *give graciously:* χαρίζομαι CHARIZOMAI
Lk 7.21 on many .. blind he bestowed sight
1 Cor 2.12 might understand the gifts bestowed on us
Phil 2. 9 bestowed on him the name .. above every n.

BESTOW, FREELY
1. *show grace:* χαριτόω CHARITOŌ [A.6.a.6]
Eph 1. 6 grace which he freely bestowed on us

BETHANY: Βηθανία 'bethənē I,C-5
[a]I,D-5
Mt 21.17 he went out of the city to B. and lodged
26. 6 when Jesus was at B. in the house of Simon
Mk 11. 1 when they drew near to Jerusalem .. and B.
11.11 as it was already late, he went out to B.
11.12 when they came from B., he was hungry
14. 3 while he was at B. in the house of Simon
Lk 19.29 he drew near to Bethphage and B.
24.50 Then he led them out as far as B.
Jn 1.28 [a]B. beyond the Jordan .. John was baptizing
11. 1 a .. man was ill, Lazarus of B.
11.18 B. was near Jerusalem, about two miles[y]
12. 1 Jesus came to B., where Lazarus was

BETHESDA: Βηθεσδά bə'thezdə
Jn [5. 2 by the Sheep Gate a pool .. called *B.*‡

BETHLEHEM: Βηθλέεμ 'bethli,hem I,C-5
Mt 2. 1 when Jesus was born in B. of Judea
2. 5 "In B. of Judea; for so it is written
2. 6 " 'And you, O B., in the land of Judah
2. 8 he sent them to B... "Go and search
2.16 Herod .. killed all the male children in B.
Lk 2. 4 to the city of David, which is called B.
2.15 "Let us go over to B. and see this thing
Jn 7.42 "Christ is descended from David .. from B.

BETHPHAGE: Βηθφαγή 'bethfə,jē, 'beth,fāj I,C-5
Mt 21. 1 came to B., to the Mount of Olives
Mk 11. 1 they drew near to .. B. and Bethany
Lk 19.29 he drew near to B. and Bethany,

BETHSAIDA: Βηθσαϊδά(ν) beth'sāədə I,D-3
Mt 11.21 "Woe to you, Chorazin! woe to you, B.!
Mk 6.45 go before him to the other side, to B.
8.22 And they came to Bethsaida
Lk 9.10 he .. withdrew apart to a city called B.
10.13 "Woe to you, Chorazin! woe to you, B.!
Jn 1.44 Philip was from B., the city of Andrew
[5. 2 by the Sheep Gate a pool .. called B.‡
12.21 Philip, who was from B. in Galilee

BETHZATHA: Βηθζαθά beth'zāthə
Jn 5. 2 by the Sheep Gate a pool .. called B.[j]‡

BETRAY
1. *make evident:* δῆλον ποιεῖν DĒLOS [B.2.a.1]
Mt 26.73 "your accent betrays you
2. *give up, allow:* παραδίδωμι PARADIDŌMI
Mt 10. 4 Judas Iscariot, who betrayed him
24.10 "many will fall away,[y] and betray
26.16 he sought an opportunity to betray him
26.21 "I say to you, one of you will betray me
26.23 "who has dipped his hand .. will betray me
26.24 "by whom the Son of man is betrayed!
26.25 Judas, who betrayed him, said, "Is it I?
26.45 "the Son of man is betrayed
27. 4 "I have sinned in betraying innocent blood
Mk 3.19 Judas Iscariot, who betrayed him
14.10 Judas .. went .. in order to betray him
14.11 he sought an opportunity to betray him
14.18 "I say to you, one of you will betray me
14.21 "by whom the Son of man is betrayed
14.41 "the Son of man is betrayed
Lk 22. 4 he .. conferred .. how he might betray him
22. 6 he .. sought an opportunity to betray him
22.21 "behold, the hand of him who betrays me
22.22 "woe to that man by whom he is betrayed!
22.48 "Judas, would you betray the Son of man?
Jn 6.64 Jesus knew .. who .. would betray him[o]
6.71 Judas .. one of the twelve, was to betray
12. 4 Judas .. (he who was to betray him
13. 2 into the heart of Judas .. to betray him
13.11 he knew who was to betray him
13.21 "I say to you, one of you will betray me

Jn 18. 2 Judas, who betrayed him, .. knew the place
18. 5 Judas, who betrayed him
21.20 "Lord, who is .. going to betray you?
1 Cor 11.23 the night when he was betrayed took bread
3. *betrayer, traitor:* προδότης (+gen.) PRODOTĒS [B.3.a.2]
Acts 7.52 "Righteous One, whom you have .. betrayed

BETRAYER

1. *give up, allow:* παραδίδωμι (subst. part.) PARADIDŌMI
Mt 26.46 "see, my betrayer is at hand
26.48 "the betrayer had given them a sign
27. 3 Judas, his betrayer .. repented
Mk 14.42 "see, my betrayer is at hand
14.44 the betrayer had given them a sign

BETROTH

1. *join, betroth:* ἁρμόζω (mid.) HARMOZŌ*
2 Cor 11. 2 I betrothed you to Christ

BETROTHED

BETROTHED, BE

1. *court, betroth:* μνηστεύω (pass.) MNĒSTEUŌ*
[a]perf. pass. part.
[b]subst. perf. pass. part.
Mt 1.18 Mary had been betrothed to Joseph
Lk 1.27 [a]a virgin betrothed to .. Joseph
2. 5 [b]Mary, his betrothed, who was with child
2. *maiden, girl:* παρθένος PARTHENOS
1 Cor 7.36 not behaving properly toward his b.[z]†
7.37 to keep her as his betrothed,[z] he will do well†
7.38 he who marries his betrothed[z] does well†

BETTER

1. *good, useful:* χρηστός CHRĒSTOS [A.3.f]
Lk [5.39 " 'The old is *better*‡
2. *over:* ὑπέρ (adv.) HYPER
2 Cor 11.23 Are they servants .. ? I am a better one
3. *good, beautiful:* καλός KALOS [A.3.f]
[a]καλὸν μᾶλλον MALLON
Mt 18. 8 "it is better for you to enter life maimed
18. 9 "better for you to enter life with one eye
26.24 "better for that man if he had not been born
Mk 9.42 [a]"better .. if .. he were thrown into the sea
9.43 "it is better for you to enter life maimed
9.45 "it is better for you to enter life lame
9.47 "better for you to enter .. with one eye
14.21 "better for that man if he had not been born
4. *better, stronger:* κρείσσων KREISSŌN
1 Cor 7. 9 better to marry than to be aflame
7.38 who refrains from marriage will do better
11.17 you come together .. not for the better
Phil 1.23 to depart and be with Christ .. is far better
Heb 6. 9 in your case .. we feel sure of better things
7.19 a better hope is introduced
7.22 Jesus the surety of a better covenant
8. 6 the covenant he mediates is better, since it is enacted on better promises
9.23 purified .. heavenly things .. with b. sacrifices
10.34 you yourselves had a better possession
11.16 they desire a better country
11.35 they might rise again to a better life
11.40 God had foreseen something better for us
1 Pet 3.17 it is better to suffer for doing right
2 Pet 2.21 better .. never to have known .. righteousness
CONTEXTUALLY
Rom 14. 5 One .. esteems one day as b. than another

BETTER, ALL THE

1. *more, rather:* μᾶλλον MALLON
1 Tim 6. 2 rather they must serve all the better

BETTER, BE

1. *carry through, differ:* διαφέρω DIAPHERŌ
Gal 4. 1 the heir .. is no better than a slave
2. *be better* (impers.): λυσιτελέω LYSITELEŌ*
Lk 17. 2 "be better for him if .. cast into the sea
3. *help, aid:* ὠφελέω (pass.) ŌPHELEŌ
Mk 5.26 she .. was no better but rather grew worse

BETTER, IT IS

1. *bring together, be useful:* συμφέρω (impers.) SYMPHERŌ
Mt 5.29 "it is b. that you lose one of your members
5.30 "it is b. that you lose one of your members
18. 6 "it would be better .. to be drowned

BETTER OF, GET THE

1. *receive, take:* λαμβάνω LAMBANŌ
2 Cor 12.16 you say ⟨I⟩ got the better of you by guile

BETTER OFF, BE

1. *abound:* περισσεύω PERISSEUŌ
Cor 8. 8 We are .. no better off if we do

BETTER OFF, BE ANY

1. *project, excel:* προέχω (mid. interrog.) PROECHŌ*
Rom 3. 9 Are we Jews any better off?[c]†

BETTER THAN

1. *be above:* ὑπερέχω (part.) HYPERECHŌ
Phil 2. 3 count others better than yourselves

BETWEEN

1. *from, out of:* ἐκ (+gen.) EK
Jn **3**.25
Phil **1**.23
2. *middle, in the middle:* μέσος MESOS
[a]διὰ μέσον [b]neut. [c]ἀνὰ μέσον [d]ἐν μέσῳ
Lk 17.11 [a]passing along between Samaria and Galilee
Jn 19.18 [b]crucified .. two others .. and Jesus b. them
1 Cor 6. 5 [c]wise enough to decide between members
Rev 5. 6 [d]between the throne and the .. creatures
3. *between:* μεταξύ METAXY
Mt 18.15 "tell him .. between you and him alone
23.35 "murdered between .. sanctuary and .. altar
Lk 11.51 "perished between .. altar and .. sanctuary
16.26 " 'between us and you a great chasm
Acts 12. 6 Peter was sleeping between two soldiers
15. 9 "made no distinction between us and them
IDIOMATICALLY
a. Jn 3.25 Now a discussion arose between John's disciples and a Jew Ἐγένετο οὖν ζήτησις ἐκ τῶν μαθητῶν Ἰωάννου μετὰ Ἰουδαίου [META]

BEWAIL

1. *cut, strike:* κόπτω (mid.) KOPTŌ
Lk 8.52 all were weeping and bewailing her
23.27 women who bewailed and lamented him

BEWARE

1. *see, look:* βλέπω (imper.) BLEPŌ
Mk 8.15 "beware of the leaven of the Pharisees
12.38 "Beware of the scribes, who like .. long robes
Acts 13.40 "Beware .. what is said in the prophets
2. *guard, observe:* φυλάσσω (mid.) PHYLASSŌ
Lk 12.15 "Take heed, and beware of all covetousness
2 Tim 4.15 Beware .., for he strongly opposed our message
2 Pet 3.17 beware lest you be carried away with .. error
3. *hold to, be intent on:* προσέχω (+ἀπό) PROSECHŌ
[a]–ἀπό, +μή [b]+ἑαυτοῖς
Mt 6. 1 [a]"Beware of practicing .. piety before men
7.15 "Beware of false prophets
10.17 "Beware of men; for they will deliver you
16. 6 "beware of the leaven of the Pharisees
16.11 "Beware of the leaven of the Pharisees
16.12 beware .. the teaching of the Pharisees
Lk 12. 1 [b]"Beware of the leaven of the Pharisees
20.46 "Beware of the scribes, who like .. long robes

BEWILDERED, BE

1. *confound:* συγχέω (pass.) SYGCHEŌ
Acts 2. 6 were b., because each .. heard .. his own

BEWITCH

1. *bewitch:* βασκαίνω BASKAINŌ*
Gal 3. 1 foolish Galatians! Who has bewitched you?

BEYOND (*See also* LIMIT, BEYOND *a, b*)

1. *separately, apart from:* χωρίς CHŌRIS
Heb 7. 7 beyond dispute that the inferior is blessed
2. *beyond:* ἐπέκεινα EPEKEINA*
Acts 7.43 " 'I will remove you beyond Babylon
3. *over, more than:* ὑπέρ (+acc.) HYPER
1 Cor 10.13 not .. tempted beyond your strength
Gal 1.14 advanced .. beyond many of my own age

4. *beyond:* ὑπερέκεινα HYPEREKEINA
2 Cor 10.16 that we may preach . . in lands beyond you
5. *more than, by:* παρά (+acc.) PARA
2 Cor 8.3
Heb 1.9
6. *on the other side, beyond:* πέραν PERAN
Mt 4.25 crowds followed . . from beyond the Jordan
19. 1 the region of Judea beyond the Jordan
Mk 3. 8 from beyond the Jordan and . . about Tyre
10. 1 region of Judea and beyond the Jordan
Jn 1.28 b. the Jordan, where John was baptizing
3.26 "who was with you beyond the Jordan

BEYOND MEASURE
1. *to excess:* καθ' ὑπερβολήν HYPERBOLĒ [B.1.b]
Rom 7.13 that sin . . might become sinful b. measure
2. *beyond all measure:* ὑπερπερισσῶς HYPERPERISSŌS*
Mk 7.37 they were astonished beyond measure

BEYOND THAT
1. *remaining, left:* λοιπός (neut.) LOIPOS
1 Cor 1.16 (Beyond that, I do not know

BID (*See also* FAREWELL, BID)
1. *say, speak:* εἶπον EIPON
Lk 9.54 "to bid fire come down from heaven?
12.13 "bid my brother divide the inheritance
2. *say, speak:* ἐρῶ ERŌ
Jn 12.50 "I say as the Father has bidden me
3. *order, command:* κελεύω KELEUŌ
Mt 14.28 "Lord, if it is you, bid me come to you
4. *say, speak:* λέγω LEGŌ
Rom 12. 3 by the grace given to me I bid every one
Rev 13.14 bidding them make an image for the beast
5. *advise, recommend:* παραινέω PARAINEŌ
Acts 27.22 "I now bid you take heart
CONTEXTUALLY
Tit 2. 2 Bid the older men be temperate
2. 3 B. the older women likewise to be reverent
2. 9 B. slaves to be submissive to . . masters

BIER
1. *coffin:* σορός SOROS*
Lk 7.14 touched the bier, and . . said . . "arise

BILL
1. *letter, document:* γράμμα (pl.) GRAMMA
Lk 16. 6 " 'Take your bill . . and write fifty
16. 7 " 'Take your bill, and write eighty

BIND
1. *bind, tie:* δέω DEŌ
Mt 12.29 "unless he first binds the strong man
13.30 " 'Gather the weeds first and bind them
14. 3 Herod had seized John and bound him
16.19 "whatever you bind on earth shall be bound in heaven
18.18 "whatever you bind on earth shall be bound in heaven
22.13 " 'Bind him hand and foot, and cast him
27. 2 they bound him and led him away
Mk 3.27 "unless he first binds the strong man
5. 3 no one could bind him any more
5. 4 he had often been bound with fetters
6.17 seized John, and bound him in prison
15. 1 they bound Jesus and led him away
Lk 13.16 whom Satan bound for eighteen years
Jn 11.44 his hands and feet bound with bandages
18.12 the officers . . seized Jesus and bound him
18.24 Annas then sent him bound to Caiaphas
19.40 They took the body of Jesus, and bound it
Acts 9. 2 might bring them bound to Jerusalem
9.14 "to bind all who call upon thy name
9.21 to bring . . bound before the chief priests
12. 6 Peter was . . bound with two chains
20.22 "going to Jerusalem, bound in the Spirit
21.11 took Paul's girdle and bound his own feet
21.11 " 'So shall the Jews at Jerusalem bind
21.33 ordered him to be bound with . . chains
22.29 he realized . . that he had bound him
Rom 7. 2 a married woman is bound by law
1 Cor 7.27 Are you bound to a wife?
7.39 A wife is bound to her husband
Rev 9.14 "angels who are bound at the great river
20. 2 he seized the dragon . . and bound him
2. *put in chains:* δεσμεύω DESMEUŌ*
Mt 23. 4 "They bind heavy burdens, hard to bear[u]
Lk 8.29 he was . . bound with chains and fetters
Acts 22. 4 persecuted . . , binding . . both men and women

BIND BY AN OATH
BIND STRICTLY BY AN OATH
1. *bind by a curse:* ἀναθεματίζω ANATHEMATIZŌ
[a]+ἀναθέματι C.3
Acts 23.12 bound themselves by an oath neither to eat
23.14 [a]"have strictly bound ourselves by an o.
23.21 "bound themselves by an oath neither to eat

BIND TOGETHER
1. *that which binds together:* σύνδεσμος SYNDESMOS [B.3.a.1]
Col 3.14 binds everything together in . . harmony

BIND UP
1. *bind on, bind fast:* καταδέω KATADEŌ*
Lk 10.34 "bound up his wounds, pouring on oil

BINDING ON, BE
1. *be lord, rule:* κυριεύω KYRIEUŌ
Rom 7. 1 the law is binding on a person

BIRD
1. *bird:* ὄρνεον ORNEON*
Rev 18. 2 "a haunt of every foul and hateful bird
19.17 to all the birds that fly in midheaven
19.21 all the birds were gorged with their flesh
2. *bird:* πετεινόν PETEINON*
Mt 6.26 "Look at the birds of the air
8.20 "birds of the air have nests; but the Son
13. 4 "birds came and devoured them
13.32 "birds of the air come and make nests
Mk 4. 4 "the birds came and devoured it
4.32 "birds of the air can make nests in its shade
Lk 8. 5 "the birds of the air devoured it
9.58 "birds of the air have nests; but the Son
12.24 "Of . . more value are you than the birds!
13.19 "birds of the air made nests in its branches
Acts 10.12 In it were all kinds of animals and . . birds
11. 6 "I observed animals . . and birds of the air
Rom 1.23 images resembling mortal man or birds
Jas 3. 7 every kind of beast and bird . . can be tamed
3. *flying, winged:* πτηνός (subst.) PTĒNOS*
1 Cor 15.39 not all flesh is alike . . one kind for . . birds

BIRTH (*See also* NOBLE BIRTH, OF)
1. *origin, birth:* γένεσις GENESIS
Mt 1.18 birth of Jesus Christ[f] took place in this way
Lk 1.14 "many will rejoice at his birth
Jas [3. 6 setting on fire the *wheel of birth*†
2. *the hour of birth:* γενετή GENETĒ*
Jn 9. 1 he saw a man blind from his birth
3. *kind, race, family:* γένος GENOS
Mk 7.26 the woman was . . Syrophoenician by birth
4. *nature, kind:* φύσις PHYSIS
Gal 2.15 Jews by birth and not Gentile sinners
IDIOMATICALLY
a. Mt 19.12 "there are eunuchs who have been so from birth εἰσὶν . . εὐνοῦχοι οἵτινες ἐκ κοιλίας μητρὸς ἐγεννήθησαν οὕτως [GENNAŌ]
b. Acts 3.2 a man lame from birth τὶς ἀνὴρ χωλὸς ἐκ κοιλίας μητρὸς αὐτοῦ ὑπάρχων [KOILIA]
c. Acts 14.8 he was a cripple from birth χωλὸς ἐκ κοιλίας μητρὸς αὐτοῦ [KOILIA]

BIRTH, IN ONE'S PANGS OF
1. *suffer birth pangs:* ὠδίνω (part. fem.) ŌDINŌ
Rev 12. 2 she cried out in her pangs of birth

BIRTH OF THE CHILD
1. *childbearing:* τεκνογονία TEKNOGONIA
1 Tim [2.15 will be saved *by the birth of the child*†

BIRTH TO, GIVE
1. *beget, bear:* γεννάω GENNAŌ
Lk 1.57 Elizabeth . . gave birth to a son

2. *bear, bring forth:* τίκτω TIKTŌ
Lk 2. 7 she gave birth to her first-born son
Jas 1.15 Then desire . . gives birth to sin

BIRTHDAY
1. *birthday celebration:* γενέσια GENESIA*
Mt 14. 6 when Herod's birthday came
Mk 6.21 Herod on his birthday gave a banquet

BIRTH-PANGS
1. *birth pangs, suffering:* ὠδίν ŌDIN
Mt 24. 8 "but the beginning of the birth-pangs[o]
Mk 13. 8 "this is but the beginning of the birth-pangs[o]

BIRTHRIGHT
1. *birthright:* πρωτοτόκια PRŌTOTOKIA*
Heb 12.16 like Esau, who sold his birthright

BISHOP
1. *overseer, guardian:* ἐπίσκοπος EPISKOPOS
Phil 1. 1 saints . . at Philippi, with the bishops[b]†
1 Tim 3. 2 a bishop must be above reproach
Tit 1. 7 a bishop . . must be blameless

BISHOP, OFFICE OF
1. *visitation, office of bishop:* ἐπισκοπή EPISKOPĒ
1 Tim 3. 1 If any one aspires to the office of b.

BIT
1. *bit and bridle:* χαλινός CHALINOS
Jas 3. 3 we put bits into the mouths of horses

BITE
1. *bite:* δάκνω DAKNŌ*
Gal 5.15 if you bite and devour one another

BITHYNIA: Βιθυνία bəˈthinēə II,F-3
Acts 16. 7 they attempted to go into B.
1 Pet 1. 1 To the exiles of the Dispersion in . . B.

BITTER
1. *sharp, bitter:* πικρός PIKROS
Jas 3.14 if you have bitter jealousy . . in your hearts

BITTER, MAKE
1. *make sharp, embitter:* πικραίνω PIKRAINŌ
Rev 8.11 men died . . because ⟨the water⟩ was made b.
10.10 my stomach was made bitter

BITTER TO, BE
1. *make sharp, embitter:* πικραίνω PIKRAINŌ
Rev 10. 9 "eat; it will be bitter to your stomach

BITTERLY
1. *harshly, bitterly:* πικρῶς PIKRŌS*
Mt 26.75 Peter remembered . . and wept bitterly
Lk 22.62 And he went out and wept bitterly

BITTERNESS
1. *bitterness:* πικρία PIKRIA*
Acts 8.23 "I see that you are in the gall of bitterness
Rom 3.14 "Their mouth is full of . . bitterness
Eph 4.31 Let all bitterness and wrath . . be put away
Heb 12.15 See . . that no "root of b." spring up

BLACK
1. *black:* μέλας MELAS
Mt 5.36 "you cannot make one hair white or black
Rev 6. 5 I saw, and behold, a black horse
6.12 the sun became black as sackcloth

BLADE
1. *grass, fodder:* χόρτος CHORTOS
Mk 4.28 "The earth produces . . first the blade

BLAME
1. *find fault with:* μωμάομαι MŌMAOMAI
2 Cor 8.20 no one should blame us

BLAMELESS
1. *innocent:* ἄκακος AKAKOS
Heb 7.26 such a high priest, holy, blameless
2. *blameless:* ἄμεμπτος AMEMPTOS
Lk 1. 6 in all . . ordinances of the Lord blameless
Phil 2.15 that you may be blameless and innocent
3. 6 as to righteousness . . blameless
3. *blamelessly:* ἀμέμπτως AMEMPTŌS* [A.4.a]
1 Th 2.10 righteous and blameless was our behavior
5.23 blameless at the coming of our Lord
4. *unblemished:* ἄμωμος AMŌMOS
Eph 1. 4 we should be holy and blameless before him
Col 1.22 to present you holy and blameless
5. *blameless:* ἀνέγκλητος ANEGKLĒTOS
1 Tim 3.10 if . . blameless let them serve as deacons
Tit 1. 6 if any man is blameless
1. 7 a bishop . . must be blameless
6. *giving no offense:* ἀπρόσκοπος APROSKOPOS
Phil 1.10 pure and blameless for the day of Christ

BLASPHEME
1. *blaspheme, slander:* βλασφημέω BLASPHĒMEŌ
Mt 9. 3 scribes said . . "This man is blaspheming
Mk 3.29 "whoever blasphemes . . the Holy Spirit
Lk 12.10 "he who blasphemes against the Holy Spirit
Jn 10.36 "do you say . . 'You are blaspheming'?
Acts 26.11 "I . . tried to make them blaspheme
Rom 2.24 "The name of God is blasphemed
1 Tim 1.20 that they may learn not to blaspheme
Jas 2. 7 Is it not they who blaspheme?
Rev 13. 6 blaspheming his name and his dwelling
2. *blasphemous, slanderous:* βλάσφημος BLASPHĒMOS [A.6.a.3]
1 Tim 1.13 I formerly blasphemed and persecuted

BLASPHEMER
1. *blaspheme, slander:* βλασφημέω (subst. part.) BLASPHĒMEŌ
Acts 19.37 "neither sacrilegious nor blasphemers

BLASPHEMOUS
1. *slander, profane speech:* βλασφημία BLASPHĒMIA
[a]gen. [b]A.1.b.3
Rev 13. 1 [a]a blasphemous name upon its heads
13. 5 [b]uttering haughty and blasphemous words
17. 3 [a]beast . . full of blasphemous names
2. *blasphemous, slanderous:* βλάσφημος BLASPHĒMOS
Acts 6.11 "heard him speak blasphemous words

BLASPHEMY
1. *blaspheme, slander:* βλασφημέω BLASPHĒMEŌ [A.6.a.2]
Mk 2. 7 "It is blasphemy! Who can forgive sins?
2. *slander, profane speech:* βλασφημία BLASPHĒMIA
Mt 12.31 "every sin and blasphemy will be forgiven men, but the blasphemy against the Spirit
26.65 "You have now heard his blasphemy
Mk 3.28 "will be forgiven . . whatever blasphemies
14.64 "You have heard his blasphemy
Lk 5.21 "Who is this that speaks blasphemies?
Jn 10.33 "we stone you . . for blasphemy
Rev 13. 6 it opened its mouth to utter blasphemies

BLASPHEMY, UTTER
1. *blaspheme, slander:* βλασφημέω BLASPHĒMEŌ
[a]+βλασφημία A.6.a.6
Mt 26.65 "He has uttered blasphemy
Mk 3.28 [a]"whatever blasphemies they utter

BLAST
1. *voice, sound:* φωνή PHŌNĒ
Rev 8.13 "at the blasts of the other trumpets

BLASTUS: Βλάστος ˈblastəs
Acts 12.20 having persuaded B. . . they asked for peace

BLAZE
1. *kindle, burn:* καίω KAIŌ
Heb 12.18 not . . to what may be touched, a blazing fire
Rev 8.10 a great star fell . . blazing like a torch

BLEACH
1. *make white:* λευκαίνω LEUKAINŌ
Mk 9. 3 white, as no fuller . . could bleach them

BLEMISH
1. *disgrace:* μῶμος MŌMOS*
2 Pet 2.13 They are blots and blemishes
2. *spot, reef:* σπιλάς SPILAS*
Jude .12 These are blemishes[d] on your love feasts†

BLEMISH, WITHOUT
1. *blameless:* ἀμώμητος AMŌMĒTOS*
2 Pet 3.14 be zealous to be found . . without . . blemish
2. *unblemished:* ἄμωμος AMŌMOS
Eph 5.27 that she might be holy and without blemish
Phil 2.15 that you may be . . children . . without b.
Heb 9.14 Christ, who . . offered himself without b.

1 Pet 1.19 like that of a lamb without blemish
Jude .24 who is able .. to present you without blemish

BLESS

1. *bless:* ἐνευλογέω ENEULOGEŌ
Acts 3.25 " 'shall .. families of the earth be blessed
2. *praise, bless:* εὐλογέω EULOGEŌ
Mt 14.19 blessed, and broke and gave the loaves
26.26 Jesus took bread, and blessed, and broke it
Mk 6.41 blessed, and broke the loaves, and gave
8. 7 a few small fish; and having blessed them
14.22 took bread, and blessed, and broke it
Lk 1.64 his tongue loosed, .. he spoke, blessing God
2.28 took him up in his arms and blessed God
2.34 Simeon blessed them and said to Mary
6.28 "bless those who curse you
9.16 blessed and broke them, and gave them
24.30 took the bread and blessed, and broke it
24.50 lifting up his hands he blessed them
24.51 he blessed them, he parted from them
24.53 continually in the temple blessing God
Acts 3.26 "God .. sent him .. to bless you
Rom 12.14 Bless those who persecute you; bless and do not curse them
1 Cor 4.12 When reviled, we bless
10.16 The cup .. which we bless, is .. participation[q]
14.16 Otherwise, if you bless[w] with the spirit†
Gal 3. 9 men of faith are blessed with Abraham
Eph 1. 3 God .., who has blessed us in Christ
Heb 6.14 "Surely I will bless you
7. 1 Melchizedek .. blessed him
7. 6 blessed him who had the promises
7. 7 the inferior is blessed by the superior
11.21 By faith Jacob, when dying, blessed each
Jas 3. 9 With it we bless the Lord and Father
1 Pet 3. 9 bless, for to this you have been called
Also variant to: Acts **3.25**
3. *bless:* κατευλογέω KATEULOGEŌ*
Mk 10.16 he took them .. and blessed them

BLESS IN

1. *bless:* ἐνευλογέω ENEULOGEŌ
Gal 3. 8 "In you shall all the nations be blessed

BLESSED

1. *praise, bless:* εὐλογέω (pass. part.) EULOGEŌ
Mt 21. 9 "B. is he who comes in the name of the Lord!
Also Mt **23.39**; Mk **11.9**; Lk **13.35**; Jn **12.13**
25.34 " 'Come, O blessed of my Father, inherit
Mk 11.10 "B. is the kingdom of our father David
Lk [1.28 *"Blessed are you among women!*‡
1.42 "Blessed are you among women, and blessed is the fruit of your womb!
19.38 "Blessed is the King who comes in the name!
2. *praised, blessed:* εὐλογητός EULOGĒTOS*
Mk 14.61 "Are you the Christ, the Son of the Blessed?
Lk 1.68 "Blessed be the Lord God of Israel
Rom 1.25 the Creator, who is blessed for ever! Amen
9. 5 who is over all be blessed for ever.[n] Amen
2 Cor 1. 3 Blessed be the God and Father of our Lord
11.31 God .., who is blessed for ever
Eph 1. 3 Blessed be the God and Father of our Lord
1 Pet 1. 3 Blessed be the God and Father of our Lord!
3. *blessed, happy:* μακάριος MAKARIOS
Mt 5. 3 "Blessed are the poor in spirit
5. 4 "Blessed are those who mourn
5. 5 "Blessed are the meek
5. 6 "Blessed are those who hunger and thirst
5. 7 "Blessed are the merciful
5. 8 "Blessed are the pure in heart
5. 9 "Blessed are the peacemakers
5.10 "Blessed are those who are persecuted
5.11 "Blessed are you when men revile you
11. 6 "blessed is he who takes no offense at me
13.16 "blessed are your eyes, for they see
16.17 "Blessed are you, Simon Bar-Jona!
24.46 "Blessed is that servant .. so doing
Lk 1.45 "blessed is she who believed
6.20 "Blessed are you poor
Lk 6.21 "Blessed are you that hunger now
6.21 "Blessed are you that weep now
6.22 "Blessed are you when men hate you!
7.23 "blessed is he who takes no offense at me
10.23 "B. are the eyes which see what you see!
11.27 "Blessed is the womb that bore you!
11.28 "Blessed rather are those who hear the word!
12.37 "Blessed are those servants .. awake
12.38 "If .. so, blessed are those servants!
12.43 "Blessed is that servant .. so doing
14.14 "blessed, because they cannot repay you
14.15 "Blessed is he .. in the kingdom of God!
23.29 "they will say, 'Blessed are the barren!
Jn 13.17 "blessed are you if you do them
20.29 "Blessed are those who .. yet believe
Acts 20.35 " 'more blessed to give than to receive
Rom 4. 7 "B. .. those whose iniquities are forgiven
4. 8 "b. is the man against whom the Lord
1 Tim 1.11 glorious gospel of the blessed God
6.15 the blessed and only Sovereign
Tit 2.13 awaiting our blessed hope .. Jesus Christ
Jas 1.12 Blessed is the man who endures trial
1.25 a doer .. shall be blessed in his doing
1 Pet 3.14 even if you .. suffer .. you will be blessed
4.14 If .. reproached for .. Christ, you are blessed
Rev 1. 3 Blessed is he who reads .. the prophecy
14.13 "Blessed are the dead who die in the Lord
16.15 ("Blessed is he who is awake!
19. 9 "Blessed are those .. invited to the .. supper
20. 6 Blessed and holy is he who shares!
22. 7 Blessed is he who keeps .. the prophecy
22.14 Blessed are those who wash their robes[s]

BLESSED, CALL

1. *bless, call happy:* μακαρίζω MAKARIZŌ
Lk 1.48 "all generations will call me blessed

BLESSING (*See also* SURE BLESSINGS)

1. *grace, favor, gratitude:* χάρις CHARIS
2 Cor 9. 8 God is able to provide you with every b.
2. *gift, favor bestowed:* χάρισμα CHARISMA
2 Cor 1.11 blessing granted us in answer to .. prayers
3. *praise, blessing, gift:* εὐλογία EULOGIA
Rom 15.29 I shall come in .. the blessing[y] of Christ
1 Cor 10.16 The cup of blessing which we bless
Gal 3.14 in Christ Jesus the blessing of Abraham
Eph 1. 3 blessed us .. with every spiritual blessing
Heb 6. 7 For land .. receives a blessing from God
12.17 when he desired to inherit the blessing
Jas 3.10 From the same mouth come b. and cursing
1 Pet 3. 9 bless .. that you may obtain a blessing
Rev 5.12 "to receive .. honor and glory and blessing!
5.13 "to the Lamb be blessing and honor!
7.12 "Amen! Blessing and glory and wisdom!
4. *blessing:* μακαρισμός MAKARISMOS
Rom 4. 6 David pronounces a blessing
4. 9 In this blessing .. only upon the circumcised?
CONTEXTUALLY
Rom 15.27 to share in their spiritual blessings
15.27 of service to them in material blessings
1 Cor 9.23 that I may share in its blessings

BLESSINGS, INVOKE

1. *praise, bless:* εὐλογέω EULOGEŌ
Heb 11.20 Isaac invoked future blessings on Jacob

BLESSINGS, SURE

1. *faithful, sure:* πιστός (subst. neut. pl.) PISTOS
Acts 13.34 " 'I will give you the .. sure blessings of David

BLIND

1. *make blind:* τυφλόω TYPHLOŌ*
Jn 12.40 "He has blinded their eyes .. lest they .. see
2 Cor 4. 4 the god of this world has blinded the minds
1 Jn 2.11 the darkness has blinded his eyes
2. *blind:* τυφλός TYPHLOS*
Mt 9.27 two blind men followed him, crying aloud
9.28 the blind men came to him
11. 5 "the blind receive their sight

Mt 12.22 a blind and dumb demoniac was brought
15.14 "Let them alone; they are blind guides. And if a blind man leads a blind man, both will fall into a pit
15.30 crowds . . bringing . . the maimed, the blind
15.31 the lame walking, and the blind seeing
20.30 two blind men sitting by the roadside
21.14 the blind and the lame came to him
23.16 "Woe to you, blind guides
23.17 "You blind fools! For which is greater?
23.19 "You blind men! For which is greater?
23.24 "You blind guides, straining out a gnat!
23.26 "You blind Pharisee! first cleanse the inside
Mk 8.22 some people brought to him a blind man
8.23 he took the blind man by the hand
10.46 Bartimaeus, a blind beggar . . by the roadside
10.49 they called the blind man
10.51 the blind man said . . "let me receive my sight
Lk 4.18 "proclaim . . recovering of sight to the blind
6.39 "Can a blind man lead a blind man? Will they not both fall?
7.21 on many . . blind he bestowed sight
7.22 "blind receive their sight, the lame walk
14.13 "invite the poor, . . the lame, the blind
14.21 "bring in the poor . . and blind and lame
18.35 blind man was sitting by the roadside
Jn 5. 3 a multitude of invalids, blind, lame
9. 1 he saw a man blind from his birth
9. 2 "who sinned . . that he was born blind?
9.13 the man who had formerly been blind
9.17 they again said to the blind man
9.18 Jews did not believe that he had been blind
9.19 "your son, who you say was born blind
9.20 "We know . . that he was born blind
9.24 they called the man who had been blind
9.25 "though I was blind, now I see
9.32 "opened the eyes of a man born blind
9.39 "that those who see may become blind
9.40 they said to him, "Are we also blind?
9.41 "If you were blind, . . no guilt
10.21 "Can a demon open the eyes of the blind?
11.37 "he who opened the eyes of the blind man
Acts 13.11 "you shall be blind and unable to see the sun
Rom 2.19 if . . you are a guide to the blind
2 Pet 1. 9 whoever lacks these things is blind
Rev 3.17 " 'you are wretched, pitiable, poor, blind

BLINDFOLD

1. *cover all around:* περικαλύπτω PERIKALYPTŌ
Lk 22.64 they also blindfolded him and asked him

BLOCK, STUMBLING

1. *offense, obstacle:* πρόσκομμα PROSKOMMA
Rom 14.13 never to put a stumbling block . . in the way
1 Cor 8. 9 lest this liberty . . become a stumbling block
2. *stumbling block, trap:* σκάνδαλον SKANDALON
1 Cor 1.23 Christ crucified, a stumbling block
Gal 5.11 the stumbling block of the cross
Rev 2.14 " 'to put a stumbling block before . . Israel

BLOOD

1. *blood:* αἷμα HAIMA
Mt 16.17 "flesh and blood has not revealed this
23.30 " 'shedding the blood of the prophets
23.35 "upon you may come all the righteous blood . . from the blood of innocent Abel to the blood of Zechariah
26.28 "this is my blood of the[a] covenant
27. 4 "I have sinned in betraying innocent blood
27. 6 "the pieces of silver . . are blood money
27. 8 that field has been called the Field of Blood
27.24 "I am innocent of this man's blood[l]
27.25 "His blood be on us and . . our children!
[27.49 *out came water and blood*‡
Mk 5.25 woman . . had a flow of b. . . twelve years
14.24 "This is my blood of the[c] covenant
Lk 8.43 woman . . had a flow of blood . . twelve years[b]
8.44 immediately her flow of blood ceased
11.50 "the blood of all the prophets, shed
11.51 "from the blood of Abel to the blood of Zechariah
13. 1 Galileans whose blood Pilate had mingled
22.20 "cup . . is the new covenant in my blood[j]‡
[22.44 *his sweat became like great drops of blood*‡
Jn 1.13 born, not of blood nor . . will of the flesh
6.53 "unless you . . drink his b., you have no life
6.54 "he who . . drinks my blood has eternal life
6.55 "my blood is drink indeed
6.56 "He who . . drinks my blood abides in me
19.34 pierced . . there came out blood and water
Acts 1.19 "(the field was called . . Field of Blood
2.19 " 'signs on the earth . . blood, and fire
2.20 " 'the moon ⟨shall be turned⟩ into blood
5.28 "intend to bring this man's blood upon us
15.20 "write to them to abstain from . . blood
15.29 "abstain from . . blood
18. 6 "Your blood be upon your heads!
20.26 "I am innocent of the blood of all of you
20.28 "obtained with the blood of his own Son[w]
21.25 "they should abstain from . . blood
22.20 " 'the blood of Stephen thy witness
Rom 3.15 "Their feet are swift to shed blood
3.25 put forward as an expiation by his blood
5. 9 we are now justified by his blood
1 Cor 10.16 a participation[q] in the blood of Christ
11.25 "cup is the new covenant in my blood
11.27 guilty of profaning the body and blood
15.50 flesh and blood cannot inherit the kingdom
Gal 1.16 I did not confer with flesh and blood
Eph 1. 7 we have redemption through his blood
2.13 brought near in the blood of Christ
6.12 not contending against flesh and blood
Col 1.20 making peace by the blood of his cross
Heb 2.14 the children share in flesh and blood
9. 7 b. which he offers for himself and . . people
9.12 taking[s] not the blood of goats . . but his own blood, thus securing . . redemption
9.13 sprinkling of defiled persons with the blood
9.14 much more shall the blood of Christ
9.18 covenant was not ratified without blood
9.19 he took the blood of calves and goats
9.20 "This is the blood of the covenant
9.21 sprinkled with . . b. . . tent[p] and . . vessels
9.22 almost everything is purified with blood
9.25 high priest enters . . yearly with blood
10. 4 impossible . . blood of bulls . . take away sins
10.19 we have confidence . . by the blood of Jesus
10.29 profaned the blood of the covenant
11.28 he kept the Passover and sprinkled . . blood
12. 4 not yet resisted to . . shedding your blood
12.24 sprinkled blood that speaks . . graciously
13.11 animals whose blood is brought
13.12 to sanctify the people through his . . blood
13.20 by the blood of the eternal covenant
1 Pet 1. 2 sanctified . . for sprinkling with his blood
1.19 the precious blood of Christ
1 Jn 1. 7 the blood of Jesus his Son cleanses us
5. 6 This is he who came by water and blood, . . not with the water only but with . . blood
5. 8 the Spirit, the water, and the blood
Rev 1. 5 who . . freed us from our sins by his blood
5. 9 "by thy blood didst ransom men for God
6.10 "thou wilt judge and avenge our blood
6.12 the full moon became like blood
7.14 "washed their robes . . in . . blood of the Lamb
8. 7 hail and fire, mixed with blood
8. 9(8) a third of the sea became blood
11. 6 they have power . . to turn them into blood
12.11 "conquered him by the blood of the Lamb
14.20 blood flowed from the wine press
16. 3 it became like the blood of a dead man
16. 4 the rivers and . . fountains . . became blood
16. 6 "men have shed the blood of saints . . and thou hast given them blood to drink

Rev 17. 6 the woman, drunk with the blood of the saints and the blood of the martyrs of Jesus
18.24 "in her was found the blood . . of saints
19. 2 "avenged on her the blood of his servants
19.13 He is clad in a robe dipped in[m] blood

BLOOD, THE SHEDDING OF
1. *the shedding of blood:* αἱματεκχυσία HAIMATEKCHYSIA*
Heb 9.22 without . . shedding of blood . . no forgiveness

BLOT
1. *stain, blemish:* σπίλος SPILOS
2 Pet 2.13 They are blots and blemishes, reveling

BLOT OUT
1. *wipe out:* ἐξαλείφω EXALEIPHŌ
Acts 3.19 "Repent . . that your sins may be blotted out
Rev 3. 5 " 'not blot his name out of the book of life

BLOW
1. *blow, stroke:* πληγή PLĒGĒ
Acts 16.23 when they had inflicted many blows
2. *blow, breathe:* πνέω PNEŌ
Mt 7.25 "the winds blew and beat upon that house
7.27 "winds blew and beat against that house
Lk 12.55 " 'when you see the south wind blowing
Jn 3. 8 "The wind[f] blows where it wills
6.18 sea rose because a . . wind was blowing
Rev 7. 1 that no wind might blow on earth or sea
3. *stroke, slap:* ῥάπισμα RHAPISMA
Mk 14.65 the guards received him with blows
4. *sound a trumpet:* σαλπίζω SALPIZŌ [A.6.a.5]
Rev 8. 6 the seven angels . . made ready to blow
8.13 "trumpets which . . angels are about to blow!

BLOW GENTLY
1. *blow gently:* ὑποπνέω HYPOPNEŌ*
Acts 27.13 when the south wind blew gently

BLOW ONE'S TRUMPET
1. *sound a trumpet:* σαλπίζω SALPIZŌ
Rev 8. 7 The first angel blew his trumpet
8. 8 The second angel blew his trumpet
8.10 The third angel blew his trumpet
8.12 The fourth angel blew his trumpet
9. 1 the fifth angel blew his trumpet
9.13 the sixth angel blew his trumpet
11.15 the seventh angel blew his trumpet

BOANERGES: Βοανηργές ˌbōəˈnərjēz
Mk 3.17 he surnamed B., that is, sons of thunder

BOARD (*See* TAKE ON BOARD)

BOARD, GO ON
1. *step in, embark:* ἐμβαίνω EMBAINŌ
[a]+εἰς
Acts 21. 6 [a]Then we went on board the ship

BOARD, PUT ON
1. *take into, put on board:* ἐμβιβάζω EMBIBAZŌ*
Acts 27. 6 found a ship . . and put us on board
2. *lay on, add:* ἐπιτίθημι (mid.) EPITITHĒMI
Acts 28.10 they put on board whatever we needed

BOAST
1. *boast:* αὐχέω AUCHEŌ*
Jas 3. 5 the tongue is a little member and boasts
2. *exult over:* κατακαυχάομαι KATAKAUCHAOMAI
Rom 11.18 if you do boast, remember . . the root
Jas 3.14 do not boast and be false to the truth
3. *boast:* καυχάομαι KAUCHAOMAI
Rom 2.17 if you call yourself a Jew . . and boast
2.23 You who boast in the law, do you dishonor?
1 Cor 1.29 so that no human being might boast
1.31 therefore, as it is written, "Let him who boasts, boast of the Lord
3.21 So let no one boast of men
4. 7 If then you received it, why do you boast?
2 Cor 9. 2 your readiness, of which I boast about you
10. 8 if I boast a little too much of our authority
10.13 we will not boast beyond limit
10.15 We do not boast beyond limit
10.16 preach . . without boasting of . . another's
10.17 "Let him who boasts, boast of the Lord
2 Cor 11.12 claim of those . . in their boasted mission
11.16 accept me as a fool, so that I too may boast
11.18 (since many boast of worldly things, I too will boast
11.30 If I must boast, I will boast of the things that show my weakness
12. 1 I must boast; there is nothing to be gained
12. 5 On behalf of this man I will boast, but on my own behalf I will not boast
12. 6 if I wish to boast, I shall not be a fool
12. 9 I will . . gladly boast of my weaknesses
Eph 2. 9 not . . works, lest any man should boast
Jas 1. 9 Let the lowly . . boast in his exaltation
4.16 As it is, you boast in your arrogance
4. *boasting:* καύχησις KAUCHĒSIS
2 Cor 1.12 boast is . . the testimony of our conscience
11.10 this boast of mine shall not be silenced
CONTEXTUALLY
2 Cor 11.21 whatever any one dares to boast of
11.21 I also dare to boast of that

BOAST ABOUT, SOMETHING TO
1. *object of boasting, boast:* καύχημα KAUCHĒMA
Rom 4. 2 he has something to boast about

BOAST, LOUD
1. *excessive:* ὑπέρογκος (subst. neut.) HYPEROGKOS
2 Pet 2.18 uttering loud boasts of folly

BOAST OF
1. *pride oneself on:* ἐγκαυχάομαι EGKAUCHAOMAI*
2 Th 1. 4 we ourselves boast of you in the churches

BOAST, ONE'S REASON TO
1. *object of boasting, boast:* καύχημα KAUCHĒMA
Gal 6. 4 his reason to boast will be in himself

BOAST OVER
1. *exult over:* κατακαυχάομαι KATAKAUCHAOMAI
Rom 11.18 do not boast over the branches

BOASTER
IDIOMATICALLY
a. Jude .16 These are grumblers . . loud-mouthed boasters
οὗτοί εἰσιν γογγυσταὶ . . καὶ τὸ στόμα αὐτῶν λαλεῖ ὑπέρογκα [LALEŌ]

BOASTFUL
1. *boaster:* ἀλαζών (pred.) ALAZŌN
Rom 1.30 haters of God, insolent, haughty, boastful
2. *boasting:* καύχησις (gen.) KAUCHĒSIS
2 Cor 11.17 (I say . . in this boastful confidence

BOASTFUL, BE
1. *boast, brag:* περπερεύομαι PERPEREUOMAI*
1 Cor 13. 4 love is not jealous or boastful

BOASTING

BOASTING, GROUND FOR
1. *object of boasting, boast:* καύχημα KAUCHĒMA
1 Cor 5. 6 Your boasting is not good
9.15 than . . deprive me of my ground for boasting
9.16 the gospel . . gives me no ground for boasting
2 Cor 9. 3 that our boasting . . may not prove vain
2. *boasting:* καύχησις KAUCHĒSIS
Rom 3.27 Then what becomes of our boasting?
2 Cor 7.14 our boasting before Titus has proved true
8.24 give proof . . of our boasting about you
1 Th 2.19 what is our . . crown of boasting?
Jas 4.16 All such boasting is evil

BOAT
1. *boat, small ship:* πλοιάριον PLOIARION*
Mk 3. 9 he told his disciples to have a boat ready
Jn 6.22 saw that there had been only one boat there
6.24 got into the boats and went to Capernaum
21. 8 other disciples came in the boat
Also variants to: Lk **5**.2; Jn **6**.23
2. *boat, ship:* πλοῖον PLOION
Mt 4.21 in the boat with Zebedee their father
4.22 they left the boat and their father
8.23 he got into the boat, his disciples followed
8.24 the boat was being swamped by the waves
9. 1 getting into a boat he crossed over

Mt 13. 2 he got into a boat and sat there
14.13 Jesus . . withdrew from there in a boat
14.22 he made the disciples get into the boat
14.24 the boat . . was many furlongs distant
14.29 Peter got out of the boat and walked
14.32 they got into the boat, the wind ceased
14.33 those in the boat worshiped him
15.39 sending away the crowds, he got into the boat
Mk 1.19 James . . and John . . in their boat mending
1.20 they left their father Zebedee in the boat
4. 1 he got into a boat and sat in it on the sea
4.36 they took him . . in the boat. And other boats were with him[0]
4.37 the waves beat into the boat, so that the boat was already filling
5. 2 when he had come out of the boat
5.18 as he was getting into the boat
5.21 when Jesus had crossed again in the boat
6.32 they went . . in the boat to a lonely place
6.45 he made his disciples get into the boat
6.47 evening came, the boat was out on the sea
6.51 he got into the boat . . and the wind ceased
6.54 they got out of the boat, immediately
8.10 he got into the boat with his disciples
8.14 they had only one loaf with them in the boat
Lk 5. 2 he saw two boats by the lake
Var. PLOIARION
5. 3 Getting into one of the boats . . he sat down and taught the people from the boat
5. 7 beckoned to their partners in the other boat . . And they came and filled both the boats
5.11 when they had brought their boats to land
8.22 One day he got into a boat with his disciples
8.37 so he got into the boat and returned
Jn 6.17 ⟨his disciples⟩ got into a boat
6.19 they saw Jesus . . drawing near to the boat
6.21 they were glad to take him into the boat, and immediately the boat was at the land
6.22 Jesus had not entered the boat
6.23 boats from Tiberias came near the place
Var. PLOIARION
21. 3 They went out and got into the boat
21. 6 "Cast . . on the right side of the boat
3. *tub, light boat:* σκάφη SKAPHĒ*
Acts 27.16 we managed with difficulty to secure the boat
27.30 sailors . . lowered the boat into the sea
27.32 soldiers cut away the ropes of the boat
CONTEXTUALLY
Mk 8.13 getting into the b. again he departed

BOAZ: [a]Βόες [b]Βόος 'bōaz
Mt 1. 5 [a]Salmon the father of Boaz by Rahab, and Boaz the father of Obed by Ruth
Lk 3.32 [b]Obed, the son of Boaz, the son of Sala

BODILY
1. *fleshly:* σάρκινος SARKINOS
Heb 7.16 a priest, not according to . . bodily descent
2. *flesh, body:* σάρξ (gen.) SARX
Gal 4.13 because of a bodily ailment that I preached
3. *body:* σῶμα (gen.) SŌMA
2 Cor 10.10 his bodily presence is weak
Eph 4.16 each part . . makes bodily growth . . in love
4. *bodily:* σωματικός SŌMATIKOS*
Lk 3.22 Holy Spirit descended . . in bodily form
1 Tim 4. 8 bodily training is of some value
5. *corporeally:* σωματικῶς SŌMATIKŌS*
Col 2. 9 in him the . . fulness of deity dwells bodily

BODY
1. *skin, body surface:* χρώς CHRŌS*
Acts 19.12 handkerchiefs . . were carried . . from his body
2. *limb; corpse:* κῶλον KŌLON*
Heb 3.17 not . . those who sinned, whose bodies fell?
3. *multitude, mass:* πλῆθος PLĒTHOS
Acts 6. 2 the twelve summoned the body of . . disciples
4. *fall, fallen body:* πτῶμα PTŌMA
Mt 14.12 ⟨John's⟩ disciples came and took the body
24.28 "Wherever the body is, there the eagles[z]
Mk 6.29 ⟨John's⟩ disciples . . came and took his body
15.45 he granted the body to Joseph
5. *flesh, body:* σάρξ SARX
2 Cor 7. 1 let us cleanse . . every defilement of body
7. 5 our bodies had no rest but we were afflicted
Eph 2. 3 following the desires of body and mind
Col 2. 5 though . . absent in body, yet I am with you
Heb 9.10 regulations for the body
1 Pet 3.21 not as a removal of dirt from the body
6. *tent, habitation:* σκήνωμα SKĒNŌMA
2 Pet 1.13 right, as long as I am in this body[c]†
1.14 the putting off of my body[c] will be soon†
7. *vessel, tackle:* σκεῦος SKEUOS
1 Th [4. 4 know how *to control his own body*†[0]
8. *body:* σῶμα SŌMA
Mt 5.29 "than that your whole body be thrown
5.30 "than that your whole body go into hell[k]
6.22 "The eye is the lamp of the body
6.22 "your whole body will be full of light
6.23 "your whole body will be full of darkness
6.25 "do not be anxious . . about your body . . Is not . . the body more than clothing?
10.28 "do not fear those who kill the body
10.28 fear him who can destroy . . soul and body
26.12 "pouring this ointment on my body
26.26 "Take, eat; this is my body
27.52 many bodies of the saints . . were raised
27.58 He went to Pilate and asked for the body
27.59 Joseph took the body, and wrapped it
Mk 5.29 she felt in her body that she was healed
14. 8 "she has anointed my body beforehand
14.22 "Take; this is my body
15.43 Joseph . . asked for the body of Jesus
Lk 11.34 "Your eye is the lamp of your body; . . sound, your whole body is full of light; . . not sound, your body is full of darkness
11.36 "If then your whole body is full of light
12. 4 "do not fear those who kill the body
12.22 "do not be anxious . . about your body
12.23 "the body ⟨is⟩ more than clothing
17.37 "Where the body is, there the eagles[c]
22.19 "This is my body which is given for you
23.52 This man . . asked for the body of Jesus
23.55 The women . . saw . . how his body was laid
24. 3 they did not find the body[t]
24.23 "did not find his body
Jn 2.21 he spoke of the temple of his body
19.31 prevent . . bodies from remaining on the cross
19.38 that he might take away the body of Jesus . . ⟨Joseph⟩ came and took away his body
19.40 They took the body of Jesus, and bound it
20.12 angels . . where the body of Jesus had lain
Acts 9.40 turning to the body he said, "Tabitha, rise
Rom 1.24 dishonoring of their bodies among themselves
4.19 his own body, which was as good as dead
6. 6 that the sinful body might be destroyed
6.12 Let not sin . . reign in your mortal bodies
7. 4 died to the law through the body of Christ
7.24 Who will deliver me from this body of death?
8.10 although your bodies are dead because of sin
8.11 will give life to your mortal bodies
8.13 put to death the deeds of the body
8.23 we wait for . . the redemption of our bodies
12. 1 present your bodies as a living sacrifice
12. 4 as in one body we have many members
12. 5 we, though many, are one body in Christ
1 Cor 5. 3 though absent in body I am present in spirit
6.13 The body is not meant for immorality, but for the Lord, and the Lord for the body
6.15 that your bodies are members of Christ?
6.16 who joins . . to a prostitute becomes one body
6.18 other sin . . is outside the body
6.18 immoral man sins against his own body
6.19 your body is a temple of the Holy Spirit
6.20 So glorify God in your body
7. 4 the wife does not rule over her own body

1 Cor 7. 4 the husband does not rule over his own body
7.34 how to be holy in body and spirit
9.27 I pommel my body and subdue it
10.16 is it not a participation[q] in the body?
10.17 we who are many are one body
11.24 "This is my body which is for[s] you
11.27 guilty of profaning the body and blood
11.29 one who eats .. without discerning the body
12.12 as the body is one and has many members, and all the members of the body, though many, are one body, so it is with Christ
12.13 we were all baptized into one body
12.14 the body does not consist of one member
12.15 "not a hand, I do not belong to the body
12.15 not make it any less a part of the body
12.16 "not an eye, I do not belong to the body
12.16 not make it any less a part of the body
12.17 If the whole body were an eye
12.18 God arranged the organs in the body
12.19 If all were a single organ, where .. the body?
12.20 there are many parts, yet one body
12.22 parts of the body which seem to be weaker
12.23 parts of the body .. less honorable
12.24 But God has so composed the body
12.25 there may be no discord in the body
12.27 Now you are the body of Christ
13. 3 if I deliver my body to be burned[v]
15.35 "With what kind of body do they come?
15.37 what you sow is not the body which is to be
15.38 God gives it a body as he has chosen, and to each kind of seed its own body
15.40 There are celestial bodies and there are terrestrial bodies
15.44 It is sown a physical body, it is raised a spiritual body. If there is a physical body, there is also a spiritual

2 Cor 4.10 carrying in the body the death of Jesus, so .. the life of Jesus may .. be .. in our bodies
5. 6 at home in the body .. away from the Lord
5. 8 we would rather be away from the body
5.10 according to what he has done in the body
12. 2 caught up .. whether in the body or out of the body I do not know, God knows
12. 3 caught up .. whether in the body or out of the body I do not know, God knows

Gal 6.17 I bear on my body the marks of Jesus

Eph 1.23 his body, the fulness of him who fills all
2.16 might reconcile us both to God in one body
4. 4 There is one body and one Spirit
4.12 for building up the body of Christ
4.16 whole body, joined and knit together
5.23 Christ is the head of the church, his body
5.28 should love their wives as their own bodies
5.30 because we are members of his body

Phil 1.20 always Christ will be honored in my body
3.21 who will change our lowly body to be like his glorious body

Col 1.18 He is the head of the body, the church
1.22 he has now reconciled in his body all flesh
1.24 for the sake of his body, that is, the church
2.11 circumcised .. putting off the body of flesh
2.19 Head, from whom the whole body .. grows
2.23 severity to the body .. of no value
3.15 to which .. you were called in the one body

1 Th 5.23 may your .. soul and body be kept sound

Heb 10. 5 "a body hast thou prepared for me
10.10 sanctified through the .. body of Jesus Christ
10.22 with .. our bodies washed with pure water
13. 3 Remember .. since you also are in the body
13.11 bodies of those animals .. are burned outside

Jas 2.16 without .. things needed for the body
2.26 the body apart from the spirit is dead
3. 2 able to bridle the whole body also
3. 3 we guide their whole bodies
3. 6 The tongue .. staining the whole body

1 Pet 2.24 He himself bore our sins in his body

Jude . 9 Michael .. disputed about the body of Moses

IDIOMATICALLY
a. Mk 14.51 with nothing but a linen cloth about his body
περιβεβλημένος σινδόνα ἐπὶ γυμνοῦ [GYMNOS]

CONTEXTUALLY
Jn 7.23 "I made a man's whole body well

BODY, DEAD

1. *fall, fallen body:* πτῶμα PTŌMA
Rev 11. 8 their dead bodies will lie in the street
11. 9 nations gaze at their dead bodies

BODY, IN A

1. *together with one mind:* ὁμοθυμαδόν HOMOTHYMADON
Acts 12.20 they came to him in a body

BODY, MEMBER OF THE SAME

1. *united in one body:* σύσσωμος (subst.) SYSSŌMOS*
Eph 3. 6 Gentiles .. members of the same body

BOLD

1. *venturous man:* τολμητής (appos.) TOLMĒTĒS*
2 Pet 2.10 Bold and wilful, they are not afraid

BOLD, BE

1. *act boldly:* ἀποτολμάω APOTOLMAŌ*
Rom 10.20 Isaiah is so bold as to say
2. *outspokenness:* παρρησία PARRĒSIA [B.2.d.2]
[a]+χράομαι *act with boldness*
[b]+ἔχω *have boldness*
2 Cor 3.12 [a]Since we have .. hope, we are very bold
Phm . 8 [b]I am bold enough in Christ to command
3. *have confidence:* θαρρέω THARREŌ
2 Cor 10. 1 I who am .. bold .. when .. away!
4. *dare:* τολμάω TOLMAŌ
Phil 1.14 much more bold to speak the word of God

BOLDLY

1. *without fear:* ἀφόβως APHOBŌS
Jude .12 they boldly carouse together
2. *in boldness:* ἐν παρρησίᾳ PARRĒSIA [B.1.a.1]
Eph 6.19 boldly .. proclaim the mystery of the gospel

BOLDLY, DECLARE
BOLDLY, PREACH
BOLDLY, SPEAK
BOLDLY, SPEAK OUT

1. *speak freely:* παρρησιάζομαι PARRĒSIAZOMAI
Acts 9.27 at Damascus he had preached boldly
9.29(28) preaching boldly in the name of the Lord
13.46 Paul and Barnabas spoke out boldly
14. 3 remained for a long time, speaking boldly
18.26 began to speak boldly in the synagogue
19. 8 entered the synagogue and .. spoke boldly
Eph 6.20 that I may declare it boldly, as I ought

BOLDLY, VERY

1. *more boldly:* τολμηροτέρως TOLMĒROTERŌS*
Rom 15.15 I have written to you very boldly

BOLDNESS

1. *outspokenness:* παρρησία PARRĒSIA
Acts 4.13 saw the boldness of Peter and John
4.29 "to speak thy word with all boldness
4.31 spoke the word of God with boldness
Eph 3.12 in whom we have boldness .. through .. faith

BOLDNESS, SHOW

1. *have confidence:* θαρρέω THARREŌ
2 Cor 10. 2 that .. I may not have to show boldness

BOND

1. *note of indebtedness:* χειρόγραφον CHEIROGRAPHON*
Col 2.14 having canceled the bond .. against us
2. *bond:* δεσμός DESMOS
Lk 8.29 (bound with chains .. he broke the bonds
13.16 "loosed from this bond on the sabbath day
3. *that which binds together:* σύνδεσμος SYNDESMOS
Acts 8.23 "you are in .. the bond of iniquity
Eph 4. 3 unity of the Spirit in the bond of peace

BONDAGE

1. *bondage, slavery:* δουλεία DOULEIA
Rom 8.21 creation .. will be set free from .. bondage
Heb 2.15 through fear of death .. subject to .. bondage

BONDAGE, BE IN
1. *serve, be a slave:* δουλεύω DOULEUŌ
Jn 8.33 "We . . have never been in b. to any one
Gal 4. 8 Formerly . . you were in b. to beings

BONDAGE, BRING INTO
1. *enslave:* καταδουλόω KATADOULOŌ
Gal 2. 4 that they might bring us into bondage

BONDS, IN
1. *bind, tie:* δέω (perf. pass. part.) DEŌ
Acts 22. 5 bring them in bonds . . to be punished

BONE
1. *bone:* ὀστέον OSTEON
Mt 23.27 "you are . . tombs . . full of dead men's bones
Lk 24.39 "a spirit has not flesh and bones
Jn 19.36 "Not a bone of him shall be broken

BOOK
1. *book, document:* βιβλίον BIBLION
Lk 4.17 there was given to him the book
4.17 He opened the book and found the place
4.20 he closed the book, and gave it back
Jn 20.30 many other signs . . not written in this book
21.25 world itself could not contain the books
Gal 3.10 "does not abide by all things . . in the book
2 Tim 4.13 bring the cloak . . , also the books
Heb 9.19 sprinkled both the book . . and . . the people
10. 7 " 'it is written of me in the roll of the book
Rev 1.11 "Write what you see in a book
13. 8 written . . in the book of life of the Lamb
17. 8 "names . . not . . written in the book of life
20.12 I saw the dead . . before the throne, and books were opened. Also another book was opened . . And the dead were judged by . . the books
21.27 only those . . written in the Lamb's book
22. 7 Blessed is he who keeps the words . . of this b.
22. 9 "those who keep the words of this book
22.10 "Do not seal up the words of . . this book
22.18 who hears the words of . . this book
22.18 the plagues described in this book
22.19 if any one takes away from . . the book
22.19 the tree . . and . . city . . described in this book
2. *scroll, book:* βίβλος BIBLOS*
Mt 1. 1 book of the genealogy of Jesus Christ
Mk 12.26 "have you not read in the book of Moses?
Lk 3. 4 As it is written in the book . . of Isaiah
20.42 "David himself says in the Book of Psalms
Acts 1.20 "it is written in the book of Psalms
7.42 "as . . written in the book of the prophets
19.19 brought their books together and burned
Phil 4. 3 whose names are in the book of life
Rev 3. 5 "not blot his name out of the book of life
20.15 if . . one's name was not . . in the book of life
3. *word, reckoning:* λόγος LOGOS
Acts 1. 1 In the first book, O Theophilus

BOOTH
1. *tent, booth:* σκηνή SKĒNĒ
Mt 17. 4 "if you wish, I will make three booths here
Mk 9. 5 "Master[f] . . let us make three booths
Lk 9.33 "Master . . let us make three booths

BORN
1. *beget, bear:* γεννάω (pass. part.) GENNAŌ
Jn 9.32 "opened the eyes of a man born blind
2 Pet 2.12 like . . animals . . born to be caught
1 Jn 5.18 any one born of God does not sin
2. *begotten, born:* γεννητός GENNĒTOS*
Mt 11.11 "among those born of women . . no one greater
Lk 7.28 among those born of women none is greater
3. *come to be, happen, be:* γίνομαι (part.) GINOMAI
Gal 4. 4 God sent forth his Son, born of woman, born under the law
CONTEXTUALLY
1 Cor 11.12 "so man is now born of woman
Phil 3. 5 a Hebrew born of Hebrews

BORN, BE
1. *beget, bear:* γεννάω (pass.) GENNAŌ
Mt 1.16 Mary, of whom Jesus was born
2. 1 when Jesus was born in Bethlehem
2. 4 inquired . . where the Christ was to be born
26.24 "better for that man if he had not been born
Mk 14.21 "better for that man if he had not been born
Lk 1.35 "child to be born[d] will be called holy
Jn 1.13 were born, not of blood nor of the will
3. 3 "unless one is born anew,[e] he cannot
3. 4 "How can a man be born when he is old? Can he enter a second time . . and be born?
3. 5 "unless one is born of water and the Spirit
3. 6 "That which is born of the flesh is flesh, and that which is born of the Spirit is spirit[f]
3. 7 "I said to you, 'You must be born anew[e]
3. 8 "so . . with every one who is born of the Spirit
8.41 "We were not born of fornication
9. 2 "who sinned . . that he was born blind?
9.19 "Is this your son, who . . was born blind?
9.20 "We know . . that he was born blind
9.34 "You were born in utter sin
16.21 "for joy that a child[j] is born into the world
18.37 "I am a king. For this I was born
Acts 7.20 "At this time Moses was born
22. 3 "I am a Jew, born at Tarsus
22.28 Paul said, "But I was born a citizen
Rom 9.11 though they were not yet born
Gal 4.23 son of the slave was born
4.29 he who was born according to the flesh
Heb 11.12 from one man . . were born descendants
11.23 Moses, when he was born, was hid
1 Jn 2.29 every one who does right is born of him
3. 9 No one born of God commits sin; . . he cannot sin because he is[g] born of God
4. 7 he who loves is born of God
5. 4 whatever is born of God overcomes the world
5.18 but He who was born of God keeps him
2. *come to be, happen, be:* γίνομαι GINOMAI
Phil 2. 7 servant,[d] being born in the likeness of men
Heb 11.12 from one man . . were born descendants

BORN, ONE UNTIMELY
1. *miscarriage:* ἔκτρωμα EKTRŌMA*
1 Cor 15. 8 Last of all, as to one untimely born

BORROW
1. *lend:* δανείζω (mid.) DANEIZŌ
Mt 5.42 "do not refuse him who would borrow

BOSOM
1. *bosom, lap:* κόλπος KOLPOS
Lk 16.22 "carried by . . angels to Abraham's bosom
16.23 "Abraham far off and Lazarus in his bosom
Jn 1.18 who is in the bosom of the Father

BOTH
1. *both:* ἀμφότεροι AMPHOTEROI
Mt 9.17 "both ⟨wine and wineskins⟩ are preserved
13.30 " 'Let both grow together until the harvest
15.14 "if a blind man leads . . both will fall
Lk 1. 6 they were both righteous before God
1. 7 because . . both were advanced in years
5. 7 they came and filled both the boats
6.39 "Will they not both fall into a pit?
7.42 "they could not pay, he forgave them both
Acts 8.38 they both went down into the water
Eph 2.14 he is our peace, who has made us both one
2.16 reconcile us both to God in one body
2.18 we both have access in one Spirit
2. *the two together:* οἱ δύο ὁμοῦ HOMOU [B.3.b.4]
Jn 20. 4 They both ran, but the other disciple outran
3. *and, both . . . and:* τέ TE
Mt **22.**10
Lk **22.**66
Acts **2.**10(11); **4.**27; **5.**14; **8.**12; **10.**39; **14.**1, 5; **15.**3; **19.**10, 17; **20.**21; **22.**4; **24.**15; **25.**24; **26.**22, 23; **28.**23
Rom **1.**12, 14²; **3.**9
1 Cor **1.**24
Phil **1.**7
Heb **9.**19
Rev **19.**18

BOTHER
1. *give trouble:* κόπον παρέχειν KOPOS [B.2.a.1]
Lk 11. 7 " 'Do not bother me; the door is now shut
18. 5 " 'this widow bothers me, I will vindicate her

BOTTOM
IDIOMATICALLY
a. Mt 27.51 the curtain of the temple was torn in two, from top to bottom τὸ καταπέτασμα τοῦ ναοῦ ἐσχίσθη ἀπ' ἄνωθεν ἕως κάτω εἰς δύο [KATŌ]
b. Mk 15.38 the curtain of the temple was torn in two, from top to bottom τὸ καταπέτασμα τοῦ ναοῦ ἐσχίσθη εἰς δύο ἀπ' ἄνωθεν ἕως κάτω [KATŌ]
c. Jn 19.23 woven from top to bottom ἐκ τῶν ἄνωθεν ὑφαντὸς δι' ὅλου [HOLOS]

BOTTOMLESS PIT
1. *abyss, underworld:* ἄβυσσος ABYSSOS
Rev 9. 1 the key of the shaft of the bottomless pit
9. 2 he opened the shaft of the bottomless pit
9.11 as king . . the angel of the bottomless pit
11. 7 beast . . ascends from the bottomless pit
17. 8 "beast . . is to ascend from the bottomless pit
20. 1 in his hand the key of the bottomless pit

BOUND
1. *debtor:* ὀφειλέτης (pred.) OPHEILETĒS
Gal 5. 3 he is bound to keep the whole law

BOUND, BE
1. *enslave:* δουλόω (pass.) DOULOŌ
1 Cor 7.15 in such a case the brother . . is not bound
2. *ought, owe:* ὀφείλω OPHEILŌ
Mt 23.16 " 'if any one swears by the gold . . he is bound
23.18 " 'if any one swears by the gift . . he is bound
2 Th 1. 3 We are bound to give thanks to God
2.13 we are bound to give thanks to God
Heb 5. 3 he is bound to offer sacrifice for his own sins

BOUND WITH, BE
1. *lie around, wear:* περίκειμαι PERIKEIMAI
Acts 28.20 "because of the hope of Israel . . I am bound

BOUNDARY
1. *fixed boundary:* ὁροθεσία HOROTHESIA*
Acts 17.26 "determined . . boundaries of their habitation

BOUNTIFULLY
1. *in abundance:* ἐπ' εὐλογίαις EULOGIA [B.1.a.1]
2 Cor 9. 6 he who sows bountifully will also reap bountifully

BOW
1. *bend:* κάμπτω KAMPTŌ*
Rom 11. 4 "men who have not bowed the knee to Baal
14.11 "every knee shall bow to me
Eph 3.14 I bow my knees before the Father
Phil 2.10 at the name . . every knee should bow
2. *incline:* κλίνω KLINŌ
Lk 24. 5 frightened and bowed their faces
Jn 19.30 he bowed his head and gave up his spirit
3. *prow* (of ship): πρῷρα PRŌRA*
Acts 27.30 pretense of laying out anchors from the bow
27.41 they ran the vessel aground; the bow stuck
4. *bow* (for archery): τόξον TOXON*
Rev 6. 2 a white horse, and its rider had a bow

BOW DOWN
1. *prostrate oneself before:* προσκυνέω PROSKYNEŌ
Rev 3. 9 " 'I will make them come and bow down

BOW IN WORSHIP
1. *prostrate oneself before:* προσκυνέω PROSKYNEŌ
Heb 11.21 Jacob . . blessed each . . , bowing in worship

BOWELS
1. *inward parts:* σπλάγχνον (pl.) SPLAGCHNON
Acts 1.18 "(he burst open . . and . . his bowels gushed

BOWL
1. *pan, bowl:* φιάλη PHIALĒ*
Rev 5. 8 elders . . each . . with golden bowls
15. 7 gave the seven angels seven golden bowls
16. 1 "pour out on the earth the seven bowls
16. 2 first angel went and poured his bowl
16. 3 second angel poured his bowl into the sea
16. 4 The third angel poured his bowl
16. 8 The fourth angel poured his bowl
16.10 The fifth angel poured his bowl
16.12 The sixth angel poured his bowl
16.17 The seventh angel poured his bowl
17. 1 one of the . . angels who had the seven bowls
21. 9 one of the . . angels who had the seven bowls
2. *vessel, tackle:* σκεῦος SKEUOS
Jn 19.29 A bowl full of vinegar stood there

BOX
1. *spar, fight:* πυκτεύω PYKTEUŌ*
1 Cor 9.26 I do not box as one beating the air

BOX, MONEY
1. *money box:* γλωσσόκομον GLŌSSOKOMON*
Jn 12. 6 as he had the money box
13.29 because Judas had the money box

BOY
1. *child, servant:* παῖς PAIS
Mt 17.18 the boy was cured instantly
Lk 2.43 the boy Jesus stayed behind in Jerusalem
9.42 But Jesus . . healed the boy
CONTEXTUALLY
Mk 9.20 And they brought the boy to him
9.20 immediately it convulsed the boy
9.26 and the boy was like a corpse

BRACKISH
1. *sharp, bitter:* πικρός (subst. neut.) PIKROS
Jas 3.11 the same opening fresh water and brackish

BRAIDED HAIR
1. *anything twined:* πλέγμα (pl.) PLEGMA*
1 Tim 2. 9 not with braided hair or gold or pearls

BRAIDING
1. *braiding:* ἐμπλοκή EMPLOKĒ*
1 Pet 3. 3 Let not yours be . . braiding of hair

BRAMBLE BUSH
1. *thornbush:* βάτος BATOS I
Lk 6.44 "nor are grapes picked from a bramble bush

BRANCH
1. *palm leaf:* βαΐον BAION*
Jn 12.13 they took branches of palm trees
2. *shoot:* κλάδος KLADOS*
Mt 13.32 "birds . . come and make nests in its branches
21. 8 crowd . . cut branches . . and spread them
24.32 "as soon as its branch becomes tender
Mk 4.32 "⟨mustard⟩ puts forth large branches
13.28 "as soon as its branch becomes tender
Lk 13.19 "birds of the air made nests in its branches
Rom 11.16 if the root is holy, so are the branches
11.17 if some of the branches were broken off
11.18 do not boast over the branches
11.19 "Branches were broken off
11.21 if God did not spare the natural branches
3. *vine twig, branch:* κλῆμα KLĒMA*
Jn 15. 2 "Every branch of mine that bears no fruit
15. 4 "As the branch cannot bear fruit by itself
15. 5 "I am the vine, you are the branches
15. 6 "he is cast forth as a branch and withers
CONTEXTUALLY
Rom 11.24 will these natural branches be grafted

BRANCH, LEAFY
1. *bed of straw, leaves:* στιβάς STIBAS*
Mk 11. 8 others spread leafy branches

BRANCH, PALM
1. *date palm tree, palm frond:* φοῖνιξ PHOINIX
Rev 7. 9 clothed in white robes, with palm branches

BREAD
1. *bread, loaf of bread:* ἄρτος (sg. or pl.) ARTOS
Mt 4. 4 " 'Man shall not live by bread alone
6.11 "Give us this day our daily bread[m]
7. 9 "if his son asks him for bread
12. 4 "how ⟨David⟩ ate the bread of the Presence
15.26 "It is not fair to take the children's bread

Mt 15.33 "Where are we to get bread enough?
16. 5 they had forgotten to bring any bread
16. 7 "We brought no bread
16. 8 "why . . discuss . . that you have no bread?
16.11 "that I did not speak about bread? Beware
16.12 not . . to beware of the leaven of bread
26.26 Jesus took bread, and blessed, and broke it
Mk 2.26 "⟨David⟩ ate the bread of the Presence
6. 8 take nothing for their journey . . no bread
6.37 "Shall we go and buy . . bread, and give it?
7.27 "it is not right to take the children's bread
8. 4 "How can one feed these men with bread?
8.14 they had forgotten to bring bread
8.16 "they discussed . . , saying, "We have no b.
8.17 "Why . . discuss . . that you have no bread?
14.22 "he took bread, and blessed, and broke it
Lk 4. 3 "command this stone to become bread
4. 4 " 'Man shall not live by bread alone
6. 4 "⟨David⟩ ate the bread of the Presence
7.33 "John . . has come eating no bread
9. 3 "Take nothing for your journey, no . . bread
11. 3 "Give us each day our daily bread[k]
[11.11 "What father . . if his son asks for *bread*‡
14.15 "Blessed is he who shall eat bread!
15.17 " 'How many . . have bread enough!
22.19 he took bread, and when he had given thanks
24.30 he took the bread and blessed, and broke it
24.35 known . . in the breaking of the bread
Jn 6. 5 "How are we to buy bread?
6. 7 "would not buy enough bread for each
6.23 the place where they ate the bread
6.31 " 'He gave them bread from heaven to eat
6.32 "not Moses who gave you the bread . . ; my Father gives you the true bread
6.33 "bread of God . . comes down from heaven
6.34 "Lord give us this bread always
6.35 Jesus said . . "I am the bread of life
6.41 "I am the bread . . from heaven
6.48 "I am the bread of life
6.50 "This is the bread . . from heaven
6.51 "I am the living bread . . from heaven; if any one eats of this bread, he will live . . ; the bread which I shall give . . is my flesh
6.58 "This is the bread . . from heaven
6.58 "he who eats this bread will live
13.18 " 'He who ate my bread has lifted his heel
21. 9 a charcoal fire . . with fish . . and bread
21.13 Jesus came and took the bread and gave it
Acts 2.42 devoted themselves to . . breaking of bread
2.46 day by day . . breaking bread in their homes
20. 7 we were gathered together to break bread
20.11 when Paul . . had broken bread and eaten
27.35 he took bread, and giving thanks to God
1 Cor 10.16 bread which we break, is . . participation[q]
10.17 Because . . one bread, we . . are one body, for we all partake of the one bread
11.23 Jesus . . when he was betrayed took bread
11.26 as you eat this bread . . you proclaim
11.27 Whoever . . eats the b. . . in an unworthy
11.28 so eat of the bread and drink of the cup
2 Cor 9.10 He who supplies . . bread for food
2 Th 3. 8 did not eat any one's bread without paying
Heb 9. 2 in which were . . bread of the Presence[q]†

BREAD, LOAF OF

1. *bread, loaf of bread:* ἄρτος ARTOS
Mt 4. 3 "these stones to become loaves of bread

BREAD, UNLEAVENED

1. *unleavened:* ἄζυμος (subst. masc.) AZYMOS
Mt 26.17 on the first day of Unleavened Bread
Mk 14. 1 two days before . . the feast of U. Bread
14.12 "on the first day of Unleavened Bread
Lk 22. 1 feast of Unleavened Bread drew near
22. 7 Then came the day of Unleavened Bread
Acts 12. 3 during the days of Unleavened Bread
20. 6 after the days of Unleavened Bread
1 Cor 5. 8 celebrate . . with the u. bread of sincerity

BREADTH

1. *width:* πλάτος PLATOS
Eph 3.18 to comprehend . . what is the breadth
Rev 21.16 its length the same as its breadth
21.16 length and breadth and height are equal

BREAK

1. *break through:* διαρήγνυμι DIARĒGNYMI
Lk 5. 6 their nets were breaking
8.29 (he broke the bonds and was driven
2. *break in pieces:* κατάγνυμι KATAGNYMI*
Mt 12.20 "he will not break a bruised reed
Jn 19.31 Jews asked . . that their legs might be broken
19.32 soldiers came and broke the legs of the first
19.33 he was . . dead, they did not break his legs
3. *snap off, break in pieces:* κατακλάω KATAKLAŌ*
Mk 6.41 broke the loaves, and gave them
Lk 9.16 taking the five loaves . . he . . broke them
4. *break off:* κλάω KLAŌ*
Mt 14.19 taking the five loaves . . he . . broke . . them
15.36 he took the seven loaves and . . broke them
26.26 Jesus took bread, and blessed, and broke it
Mk 8. 6 took the seven loaves, and . . broke them
8.19 "I broke the five loaves
14.22 he took bread, and blessed, and broke it
Lk 22.19 "he took bread, and . . he broke it
24.30 he took the bread and blessed, and broke it
Acts 2.46 breaking bread in their homes
20. 7 we were gathered together to break bread
20.11 when Paul had . . broken bread and eaten
27.35 he took bread, and . . he broke it
1 Cor 10.16 bread which we break, is . . participation[q]
11.24 when he had given thanks, he broke it
[11.24 "my body which is *broken* for you‡
5. *break up, unbind:* λύω LYŌ
Jn 5.18 to kill him, because he . . broke the sabbath
7.23 that the law of Moses may not be broken
10.35 "(and scripture cannot be broken
Acts 13.43 the meeting of the synagogue broke up
27.41 the stern was broken up by the surf
Rev 5. 2 "Who is worthy to . . break its seals?
6. *transgressor:* παραβάτης PARABATĒS [B.2.d.2]
Rom 2.25 but if you break the law
7. *break in pieces, crush:* συνθρύπτω SYNTHRYPTŌ*
Acts 21.13 "What are you doing, . . breaking my heart?
8. *shatter, grind:* συντρίβω SYNTRIBŌ
Mk 14. 3 she broke the flask and poured it
Jn 19.36 "Not a bone of him shall be broken

IDIOMATICALLY

a. Jn 21.4 Just as day was breaking πρωΐας δὲ ἤδη γινομένης [PRŌIA]

BREAK AGAINST

1. *dash against:* προσρήσσω PROSRĒSSŌ*
Lk 6.48 "the stream broke against that house
6.49 "house . . against which the stream broke

BREAK DOWN

1. *throw upon:* ἐπιβάλλω EPIBALLŌ
Mk 14.72 Peter . . broke down and wept
2. *break up, unbind:* λύω LYŌ
Eph 2.14 he . . has broken down the dividing wall

BREAK FORTH

1. *break:* ῥήγνυμι RHĒGNYMI
Gal 4.27 "break forth . . you who are not in travail

BREAK IN
BREAK INTO

1. *dig through:* διορύσσω DIORYSSŌ*
Mt 6.19 "earth . . where thieves break in and steal
6.20 "heaven, where . . thieves do not break in
24.43 "not have let his house be broken into
Lk 12.39 "not have left his house to be broken into

BREAK IN PIECES

1. *shatter, grind:* συντρίβω SYNTRIBŌ
Mk 5. 4 the fetters he broke in pieces
Rev 2.27 " 'as when earthen pots are broken in pieces

BREAK OFF
1. *break off:* ἐκκλάω EKKLAŌ*
Rom 11.17 if some of the branches were broken off
11.19 You will say, "Branches were broken off
11.20 broken off because of their unbelief

BREAK ONE'S WORD TO
1. *deny, nullify:* ἀθετέω ATHETEŌ
Mk 6.26 king . . did not want to break his word to her

BREAK TO PIECES
1. *crush together:* συνθλάω SYNTHLAŌ*
Mt [21.44 *"he . . will be broken to pieces*‡
Lk 20.18 "one who falls . . will be broken to pieces

BREAKFAST, FINISHED
1. *eat morning or noon meal:* ἀριστάω (aor.) ARISTAŌ
Jn 21.15 When they had finished breakfast

BREAKFAST, HAVE
1. *eat morning or noon meal:* ἀριστάω ARISTAŌ
Jn 21.12 Jesus said . . "Come and have breakfast

BREAKING
1. *fracture:* κλάσις KLASIS*
Lk 24.35 known . . in the breaking of the bread
Acts 2.42 the breaking of bread and the prayers
2. *digression, transgression:* παράβασις PARABASIS
Rom 2.23 do you dishonor God by breaking the law?

BREAKS, ONE WHO
1. *transgressor:* παραβάτης PARABATĒS
Rom 2.27 condemn you who . . break the law

BREAST
1. *bosom, lap:* κόλπος KOLPOS
Jn 13.23 One . . lying close to the breast of Jesus
2. *woman's breast:* μαστός (sg. or pl.) MASTOS*
Lk 11.27 "Blessed . . the breasts that you sucked!
23.29 " 'Blessed . . breasts that never gave suck!
Rev 1.13 with a golden girdle round his breast
3. *chest:* στῆθος STĒTHOS*
Lk 18.13 tax collector . . beat his breast
23.48 all . . returned home beating their breasts
Jn 13.25 lying thus, close to the breast of Jesus
21.20 disciple . . who had lain close to his breast
Rev 15. 6 their breasts girded with golden girdles

BREASTPLATE
1. *coat of mail, chest:* θώραξ THŌRAX
Eph 6.14 put on the breastplate of righteousness
1 Th 5. 8 put on the breastplate of faith and love
Rev 9. 9 they had scales like iron breastplates
9.17 riders wore breastplates the color of fire

BREATH
1. *wind, breath, spirit:* πνεῦμα PNEUMA
2 Th 2. 8 Lord Jesus will slay him with the breath
Rev 11.11 breath of life from God entered them
13.15 it was allowed to give breath to the image
2. *wind, breath:* πνοή PNOĒ
Acts 17.25 "gives to all men life and breath

BREATHE
1. *blow, breathe:* ἐμπνέω EMPNEŌ*
Acts 9. 1 Saul, still breathing threats and murder

BREATHE ON
1. *blow upon:* ἐμφυσάω EMPHYSAŌ*
Jn 20.22 he breathed on them, and said . . "Receive

BREATHE ONE'S LAST
1. *breathe out, expire:* ἐκπνέω EKPNEŌ*
Mk 15.37 uttered a loud cry, and breathed his last
15.39 centurion . . saw that he . . breathed his last
Lk 23.46 having said this he breathed his last

BREED
1. *beget, bear:* γεννάω GENNAŌ
2 Tim 2.23 senseless controversies . . breed quarrels

BRETHREN, HAVE LOVE OF THE
1. *loving one's brother:* φιλάδελφος PHILADELPHOS* [A.3.e.2]
1 Pet 3. 8 all of you, have . . love of the brethren

BRETHREN, LOVE OF THE
1. *brotherly love:* φιλαδελφία PHILADELPHIA
1 Th 4. 9 concerning love of the brethren
1 Pet 1.22 for a sincere love of the brethren

BRIDE
1. *woman, wife:* γυνή GYNĒ
Rev 19. 7 "his Bride has made herself ready
2. *bride, young wife:* νύμφη NYMPHĒ
Mt [25. 1 "went to meet the bridegroom *and the bride*‡
Jn 3.29 "He who has the bride is the bridegroom
Rev 18.23 "the voice of bridegroom and bride
21. 2 I saw the holy city . . prepared as a bride
21. 9 "Come, I will show you the Bride
22.17 The Spirit and the Bride say, "Come
3. *maiden, girl:* παρθένος PARTHENOS
2 Cor 11. 2 I betrothed you to Christ . . as a pure bride

BRIDEGROOM
1. *bridegroom:* νυμφίος NYMPHIOS*
Mt 9.15 "as long as the bridegroom is with them?
9.15 "days . when the bridegroom is taken away
25. 1 "who . . went to meet the bridegroom[c]
25. 5 "bridegroom was delayed, they all . . slept
25. 6 " 'Behold, the bridegroom! Come
25.10 "while they went . . the bridegroom came
Mk 2.19 "fast while the bridegroom is with them?
2.19 "as they have the bridegroom . . they cannot
2.20 "days . . when the bridegroom is taken away
Lk 5.34 "fast while the bridegroom is with them?
5.35 "days . . when the bridegroom is taken away
Jn 2. 9 steward of the feast called the bridegroom
3.29 "He who has the bride is the bridegroom
3.29 "the friend of the bridegroom . . rejoices greatly at the bridegroom's voice
Rev 18.23 "the voice of bridegroom and bride

BRIDLE
1. *guide with bit and bridle:* χαλιναγωγέω CHALINAGŌGEŌ*
Jas 1.26 If any one . . does not bridle his tongue
3. 2 perfect man, able to bridle the whole body
2. *bit and bridle:* χαλινός CHALINOS
Rev 14.20 blood flowed . . high as a horse's bridle

BRIEFLY
1. *with a few* (words): διὰ βραχέων BRACHYS [B.3.b.2; B.1.a.1]
Heb 13.22 for I have written to you briefly
2. *few, little:* ὀλίγος OLIGOS [B.3.b.2; B.1.a.1]
Eph 3. 3 as I have written briefly
1 Pet 5.12 I have written briefly
3. *concisely, quickly:* συντόμως SYNTOMŌS*
Mk [16.[end] *they reported briefly to Peter*‡
Acts 24. 4 "I beg you . . to hear us briefly

BRIGHT (*See also* RED, BRIGHT)
1. *bright, radiant:* λαμπρός LAMPROS
Acts 10.30 "a man stood before me in bright apparel
Rev 15. 6 seven angels . . robed in pure bright linen
19. 8 "clothed with fine linen, bright and pure
22. 1 the water of life, bright as crystal
22.16 "I Jesus . . am . . the bright morning star
2. *shining, bright:* φωτεινός PHŌTEINOS
Mt 17. 5 lo, a bright cloud overshadowed them
Lk 11.36 "If . . full of light . . it will be wholly bright

BRIGHT, MAKE
1. *shine, illuminate:* φωτίζω PHŌTIZŌ
Rev 18. 1 earth was made bright with his splendor

BRIGHTER
1. *beyond the brightness:* ὑπὲρ τὴν λαμπρότητα LAMPROTĒS [B.1.a.1]
Acts 26.13 "light from heaven, b. than the sun

BRIGHTNESS
1. *glory:* δόξα DOXA
Acts 22.11 I could not see because of the brightness
2 Cor 3. 7 not look at Moses' face because of its b.

BRIM
IDIOMATICALLY
a. Jn 2.7 they filled them up to the brim ἐγέμισαν αὐτὰς ἕως ἄνω [ANŌ]

BRING (*See also, e.g.,* LIGHT, BRING TO)
1. *lead, bring:* ἄγω AGŌ
Mt 21. 2 "an ass . . and a colt with her; . . bring them
21. 7 they brought the ass and the colt
Mk 13.11 "when they b. you to trial
Lk 4.40 who had any that were sick . . brought them
10.34 "brought him to an inn, and took care of him
18.40 Jesus . . commanded him to be brought
19.27 " 'as for these enemies . . , bring them here
19.30 "you will find a colt . . bring it here
19.35 they brought it . . and . . set Jesus upon it
23. 1 whole company . . brought him before Pilate
Jn 1.42 He brought him to Jesus
7.45 "Why did you not bring him?
8. 3 the Pharisees brought a woman[r]‡
9.13 brought . . the man who had . . been blind
10.16 "I must bring them also, and they will heed
19. 4 "See, I am bringing him out to you
19.13 he brought Jesus out and sat down
Acts 5.21 sent to the prison to have them brought
5.26 captain with the officers . . brought them
5.27 they . . brought them . . before the council
6.12 they . . brought him before the council
9. 2 he might bring them bound to Jerusalem
9.21 "he has come here . . to bring them bound
9.27 Barnabas . . brought him to the apostles
11.26 he brought him to Antioch
13.23 "God has brought to Israel a Savior, Jesus
17.15 brought him as far as Athens
17.19 brought him to the Areopagus
18.12 brought him before the tribunal
19.37 "you have brought these men here
21.16 bringing us to the house of Mnason
21.34 ordered him to be brought into the barracks
22. 5 to . . bring them in bonds to Jerusalem
23.10 soldiers to . . bring him into the barracks
23.18 brought him to the tribune and said, "Paul . . asked me to bring this young man
23.31 took Paul and brought him . . to Antipatris
25. 6 he . . ordered Paul to be brought
25.17 ordered the man to be brought in
25.23 by command of Festus Paul was brought in
1 Th 4.14 God will b. . . those who have fallen asleep
2 Tim 4.11 Get Mark and bring him with you
Heb 2.10 bringing many sons to glory
2. *lead away:* ἀπάγω APAGŌ
Lk 21.12 you will be brought before kings
3. *throw, put:* βάλλω BALLŌ
Mt 10.34 "Do not think that I . . bring peace on earth; I have not come to bring peace, but a sword
4. *have, hold:* ἔχω ECHŌ
Mt 15.30 bringing with them the lame, the maimed
5. *carry in:* εἰσφέρω EISPHERŌ
Lk 12.11 "when they bring you before the synagogues
Acts 17.20 "you bring some strange things to our ears
6. *throw out:* ἐκβάλλω EKBALLŌ
Mt 12.20 "till he brings justice to victory
7. *carry out:* ἐκφέρω EKPHERŌ
Lk 15.22 " 'Bring quickly the best robe
8. *come to be, happen, be:* γίνομαι GINOMAI [A.6.a.5]
Rom 7.13 Did that which is good . . bring death to me?
Eph 2.13 you . . have been brought near in the blood
9. *lead down, bring home:* κατάγω KATAGŌ
Lk 5.11 when they had brought their boats to land
10. *put in order, make:* καταρτίζω (mid.) KATARTIZŌ
Mt 21.16 " 'thou has brought perfect praise
11. *achieve:* κατεργάζομαι KATERGAZOMAI
Rom 4.15 the law brings wrath
12. *bring, carry off:* κομίζω KOMIZŌ
Lk 7.37 a woman . . brought an alabaster flask
13. *speak, talk:* λαλέω LALEŌ
1 Cor 14. 6 unless I bring you some revelation
14. *receive, take:* λαμβάνω LAMBANŌ
Mt 16. 5 they had forgotten to bring any bread
16. 7 "We brought no bread
Mk 8.14 they had forgotten to bring bread
15. *send for:* μεταπέμπω (mid.) METAPEMPŌ
Acts 10. 5 "bring one Simon who is called Peter
11.13 " 'Send to Joppa and bring Simon
16. *take, receive:* παραλαμβάνω PARALAMBANŌ
Mt 12.45 "he goes and brings with him seven other
Lk 11.26 "he goes and brings seven other spirits
17. *show, offer, cause:* παρέχω PARECHŌ
Acts 16.16 slave girl . . brought her owners much gain
19.24 brought no little business to the craftsmen
18. *place beside, stand before:* παρίστημι PARISTĒMI
2 Cor 4.14 will . . bring us with you into his presence
19. *carry around:* περιφέρω PERIPHERŌ
Mk 6.55 began to bring sick people on their pallets
20. *bring, bear:* φέρω PHERŌ
Mt 14.11 his head was brought on a platter and . . the girl . . brought it to her mother
14.18 he said, "Bring them here to me
17.17 "Bring him here to me
Mk 1.32 they brought to him all who were sick
2. 3 they came, bringing to him a paralytic
6.27 king sent a soldier . . to bring his head
6.28 brought his head on a platter . . to the girl
7.32 they brought to him a man who was deaf
8.22 some people brought to him a blind man
9.17 "Teacher, I brought my son to you
9.19 "O faithless generation . . Bring him to me
9.20 they brought the boy to him
11. 2 "find a colt tied . . ; untie it and bring it
11. 7 they brought the colt to Jesus
12.15 "Bring me a coin,[x] and let me look at it
12.16 they brought one. And he said . . "Whose?
15.22 brought him to the place called Golgotha
Lk 5.18 bringing on a bed a man who was paralyzed
15.23 " 'bring the fatted calf and kill it
Jn 4.33 "Has any one brought him food?
18.29 "What accusation do you bring?
19.39 N. . . came bringing a mixture of myrrh
21.10 "Bring some of the fish . . you have . . caught
Acts 4.34 brought the proceeds of what was sold
4.37 sold a field . . and brought the money
5. 2 brought . . and laid it at the apostles' feet
5.16 bringing the sick and those afflicted
14.13 brought oxen and garlands to the gates
25.18 "they brought no charge in his case
2 Tim 4.13 When you come, bring the cloak
2 Jn .10 If any one . . does not bring this doctrine
Rev 21.24 the kings of the earth shall bring their glory
21.26 they shall bring . . the glory . . of the nations
21. *do, make:* ποιέω POIEŌ
Acts 24.17 "I came to bring to my nation alms
22. *send forth, escort:* προπέμπω PROPEMPŌ
Acts 20.38 they brought him to the ship
23. *bring to:* προσάγω PROSAGŌ
Lk 9.41 "Bring your son here
24. *bring to, present:* προσφέρω PROSPHERŌ
Mt 25.20 "came . . , bringing five talents more
IDIOMATICALLY
a. Rev 22.12 "Behold, I am coming soon, bringing my recompense Ἰδοὺ ἔρχομαι ταχύ, καὶ ὁ μισθός μου μετ' ἐμοῦ [META]
CONTEXTUALLY
Rom 1. 5 to bring about the obedience of faith
5.16 judgment . . brought condemnation
5.16 gift following many . . brings justification
16.26 to bring about the obedience of faith

BRING AGAIN
1. *lead up, bring back:* ἀνάγω ANAGŌ
Heb 13.20 who brought again from the dead our Lord

BRING AGAINST
1. *bring down, sink:* καταφέρω KATAPHERŌ
Acts 25. 7 bringing against him many serious charges

BRING ASHORE
1. *expel, drive on shore:* ἐξωθέω EXŌTHEŌ
Acts 27.39 planned if possible to bring the ship ashore

BRING BACK
1. *turn about, return:* ἐπιστρέφω EPISTREPHŌ

Jas 5.19 if . . some one brings him back
5.20 whoever brings back a sinner from . . error
2. *turn, return:* στρέφω STREPHŌ
Mt 27. 3 repented and brought back the thirty pieces

BRING BEFORE
1. *lead forward:* προάγω PROAGŌ
[a]+ἐπί
Acts 25.26 [a]"brought him before you . . , King Agrippa

BRING CHARGES
BRING CHARGES AGAINST
BRING A CHARGE
1. *bring charges, accuse:* διαβάλλω DIABALLŌ
Lk 16. 1 "charges were brought to him
2. *call, accuse:* ἐγκαλέω EGKALEŌ
Acts 19.38 "let them bring charges against one another
Rom 8.33 Who shall bring any c. against God's elect?
3. *accuse:* κατηγορέω KATĒGOREŌ
Mk 15. 4 "many charges they bring against you
Jn 8. 6 have some charge to bring against him[r]‡
Acts 28.19 "though I had no charge to bring

BRING DOWN
1. *make to go down:* καταβιβάζω KATABIBAZŌ*
Mt 11.23 "You shall be brought down to Hades
Lk 10.15 "You shall be brought down to Hades
2. *lead down, bring home:* κατάγω KATAGŌ
Acts 9.30 they brought him down to Caesarea
22.30 brought Paul down and set him before them
23.15 "give notice . . to bring him down to you
23.20 "to ask you to bring Paul down to the council
23.28 "I brought him down to their council
Rom 10. 6 "Who will ascend . . ?" (. . to b. Christ down

BRING FORTH
1. *give birth to:* ἀποκυέω APOKYEŌ*
Jas 1.15 sin when . . full-grown brings forth death
1.18 Of his own will he brought us forth
2. *sprout, produce:* βλαστάνω BLASTANŌ
Jas 5.18 the earth brought forth its fruit
3. *give:* δίδωμι DIDŌMI
Mt 13. 8 "Other seeds . . brought forth grain
Mk 4. 8 "other seeds . . brought forth grain
4. *throw out:* ἐκβάλλω EKBALLŌ
Mt 12.35 "The good man . . brings forth good, and the evil man . . brings forth evil
5. *bear, bring forth:* τίκτω TIKTŌ
Heb 6. 7 land . . brings forth vegetation useful
Rev 12. 4 devour her child when she brought it forth
12. 5 she brought forth a male child

BRING FORTH FRUIT
1. *bear fruit:* καρποφορέω KARPOPHOREŌ
Lk 8.15 "hearing the word, . . bring forth fruit

BRING FORTH PLENTIFULLY
1. *bear well, be fruitful:* εὐφορέω EUPHOREŌ*
Lk 12.16 "land of a rich man brought forth plentifully

BRING GOOD NEWS
1. *bring good news* (mid.): εὐαγγελίζω EUAGGELIZŌ
Lk 1.19 "I was sent . . to bring you this good news
2.10 "I bring you good news of a great joy
8. 1 bringing the good news of the kingdom
Acts 13.32 "we bring you the good news
14.15 "bring you good news, that you should turn
1 Th 3. 6 Timothy . . has brought us the good news

BRING IN
BRING INTO
1. *lead in:* εἰσάγω EISAGŌ*
Lk 2.27 when the parents brought in the child Jesus
14.21 " 'bring in the poor and maimed and blind
22.54 bringing him into the high priest's house
Jn 18.16 spoke to the maid . . and brought Peter in
Acts 7.45 "fathers in turn brought it in with Joshua
9. 8 led him . . and brought him into Damascus
21.28 "he also brought Greeks into the temple
21.29 supposed . . Paul . . brought him into . . temple
21.37 about to be brought into the barracks
22.24 commanded him . . brought into the barracks
Heb 1. 6 when he brings the first-born into the world
2. *carry in:* εἰσφέρω EISPHERŌ
Lk 5.18 sought to bring him in . . before Jesus[q]
5.19 finding no way to bring him in
1 Tim 6. 7 we brought nothing into the world
Heb 13.11 whose blood is brought into the sanctuary

BRING IN, SECRETLY
1. *admit secretly:* παρεισάγω PAREISAGŌ*
2 Pet 2. 1 false teachers . . will secretly b. in . . heresies

BRING ON ONE'S WAY
1. *send forth, escort:* προπέμπω PROPEMPŌ
Acts 21. 5 they all . . brought us on our way

BRING OUT
1. *lead up, bring back:* ἀνάγω ANAGŌ
Acts 12. 4 after the Passover to bring him out
2. *throw out:* ἐκβάλλω EKBALLŌ
Mt 13.52 "householder who brings out . . what is new
Jn 10. 4 "When he has brought out all his own
3. *lead out:* ἐξάγω EXAGŌ
Acts 5.19 an angel . . brought them out
12.17 how the Lord had brought him out
4. *lead forward:* προάγω PROAGŌ
Acts 12. 6 when Herod was about to bring him out
16.30 ⟨the jailer⟩ brought them out
17. 5 seeking to bring them out to the people

BRING TO
1. *bring to, come near:* προσάγω PROSAGŌ
Mt 18.24 "one was brought to him who owed him
Acts 16.20 they had brought them to the magistrates
1 Pet 3.18 Christ . . died[h] . . that he might b. us to God
2. *bring to, present:* προσφέρω PROSPHERŌ
Mt 4.24 brought him all the sick, those afflicted
8.16 That evening they brought to him many
9. 2 they brought to him a paralytic
9.32 a dumb demoniac was brought to him
12.22 dumb demoniac was brought to him
14.35 they . . brought to him all that were sick
17.16 "I brought him to your disciples
19.13 Then children were brought to him
22.19 they brought him a coin[r]
Mk 10.13 they were bringing children to him
Lk 18.15 they were bringing even infants to him
23.14 "You brought me this man as . . perverting

BRING TO REMEMBRANCE
1. *remind:* ὑπομιμνῄσκω HYPOMIMNĒSKŌ
Jn 14.26 "Spirit . . will . . b. to your remembrance

BRING TOGETHER
1. *bring together, be useful:* συμφέρω SYMPHERŌ
Acts 19.19 brought their books t. and burned them

BRING UP
1. *lead up, bring back:* ἀνάγω ANAGŌ
Lk 2.22 they brought him up to Jerusalem
Acts 16.34 Then he brought them up into his house
Rom 10. 7 "Who will descend . . ?" (. . to bring Christ up
2. *bring up, educate:* ἀνατρέφω ANATREPHŌ*
Acts 7.20 Moses . . was brought up for three months
7.21 Pharaoh's daughter . . brought him up
22. 3 "I am a Jew . . brought up in this city
3. *nourish, rear:* ἐκτρέφω EKTREPHŌ
Eph 6. 4 Fathers, . . bring them up in the discipline
4. *remind:* ὑπομιμνῄσκω HYPOMIMNĒSKŌ
3 Jn .10 I will bring up what he is doing
5. *feed, nourish:* τρέφω TREPHŌ
Lk 4.16 Nazareth, where he had been brought up

BRING UP AGAINST
1. *accuse:* κατηγορέω KATĒGOREŌ
Acts 24.13 Neither . . what they . . bring up against me

BRING UP CHILDREN
1. *rear children:* τεκνοτροφέω TEKNOTROPHEŌ*
1 Tim 5.10 one who has brought up children

BRING UPON
1. *bring on:* ἐπάγω EPAGŌ*
Acts 5.28 "intend to bring this man's blood upon us
2 Pet 2. 1 bringing upon themselves swift destruction
2. 5 he brought a flood upon . . the ungodly

BRING WITH ONE
1. *take along with one:* συμπαραλαμβάνω SYMPARALAMBANŌ
Acts 12.25 their mission, bringing with them John

BRINGS NO REGRET, THAT
1. *not to be regretted:* ἀμεταμέλητος AMETAMELĒTOS
2 Cor 7.10 godly grief . . that . . brings no regret

BROAD
1. *width:* πλάτος (+gen.) PLATOS
Rev 20. 9 they marched up over the broad earth

BROAD, MAKE
1. *widen, make broad:* πλατύνω PLATYNŌ
Mt 23. 5 for they make their phylacteries broad

BROILED
1. *roasted, baked:* ὀπτός OPTOS*
Lk 24.42 They gave him a piece of broiled fish

BROKEN PIECE
1. *fragment, piece:* κλάσμα KLASMA
Mt 14.20 twelve baskets full of the broken pieces
15.37 seven baskets full of the broken pieces
Mk 6.43 twelve baskets full of broken pieces
8. 8 broken pieces left over, seven baskets full
8.19 "how many baskets . . of broken pieces?
8.20 "how many baskets full of broken pieces?
Lk 9.17 twelve baskets of broken pieces

BRONZE
1. *copper, brass, bronze:* χαλκός CHALKOS
Rev 18.12 all articles of costly wood, bronze
2. *of copper, bronze, or brass:* χαλκοῦς CHALKOUS*
Rev 9.20 idols of gold and silver and bronze

BRONZE, BURNISHED
1. *fine brass or bronze:* χαλκολίβανον CHALKOLIBANON*
Rev 1.15 his feet were like burnished bronze
2.18 " 'whose feet are like burnished bronze

BRONZE, VESSEL OF
1. *copper vessel, kettle:* χαλκίον CHALKION*
Mk 7. 4 (the washing of . . vessels of bronze[x]

BROOD
1. *offspring:* γέννημα (pl.) GENNĒMA*
Mt 3. 7 "You brood of vipers! Who warned you?
12.34 "You brood of vipers! how can you?
23.33 "You serpents, you brood of vipers
Lk 3. 7 "You brood of vipers! Who warned you?
2. *nest of young birds:* νοσσιά NOSSIA*
Lk 13.34 "How often . . as a hen gathers her brood
3. *nestling, chick:* νοσσίον (pl.) NOSSION*
Mt 23.37 "How often . . as a hen gathers her brood

BROTHER (*See also* TWIN BROTHERS)
1. *brother:* ἀδελφός ADELPHOS
Mt 1. 2 Jacob the father of Judah and his brothers
1.11 the father of Jechoniah and his brothers
4.18 two brothers, Simon who is called Peter and Andrew his brother, casting a net
4.21 he saw two other brothers, James the son of Zebedee and John his brother
5.22 "every one who is angry with his brother[i]
5.22 "whoever insults[j] his brother shall be liable
5.23 "if . . your brother has something against you
5.24 "go; first be reconciled to your brother
5.47 "if you salute only your brethren
7. 3 "see the speck that is in your brother's eye
7. 4 "to your brother, 'Let me take the speck out
7. 5 "to take the speck out of your brother's eye
10. 2 Peter, and Andrew his brother; James . . and John his brother
10.21 "Brother will deliver up brother to death, and the father his child
12.46 his mother and his brothers stood outside
[12.47 "*your brothers are standing outside*‡
12.48 "Who is my mother, and who . . my brothers?
12.49 "Here are my mother and my brothers!
12.50 "whoever does the will . . is my brother
13.55 "are not his brothers James and Joseph?
14. 3 Herodias, his brother Philip's wife[l]
17. 1 Peter and James and John his brother
Mt 18.15 "If your brother sins against you
18.15 If he listens . . you have gained your brother
18.21 "how often shall my brother sin against me?
18.35 "if you do not forgive your brother
19.29 "every one who has left houses or brothers
20.24 they were indignant at the two brothers
22.24 " 'his brother must marry the widow, and raise up children for his brother
22.25 "Now there were seven brothers among us
22.25 "died, and . . left his wife to his brother
23. 8 "you have one teacher, and . . are all brethren
25.40 " 'to one of the least of these my brethren
28.10 "Do not be afraid; go and tell my brethren
Mk 1.16 Simon and Andrew the brother of Simon
1.19 he saw James . . and John his brother
3.17 James . . and John the brother of James
3.31 his mother and his brothers came
3.32 "Your mother and . . brothers[l] are outside
3.33 "Who are my mother and my brothers?
3.34 "Here are my mother and my brothers!
3.35 "Whoever does the will of God is my brother
5.37 James and John the brother of James
6. 3 "the son of Mary and brother of James
6.17 Herodias, his brother Philip's wife
6.18 "It is not lawful . . to have your brother's wife
10.29 "no one who has left house or brothers
10.30 "a hundredfold now . . houses and brothers
12.19 "if a man's brother dies and leaves a wife . . the man[y] must . . raise up children for his b.
12.20 "There were seven brothers; the first . . died
13.12 "brother will deliver up brother to death, and the father his child
Lk 3. 1 Herod . . and his brother Philip . . of . . Ituraea
3.19 reproved . . for Herodias, his brother's wife
6.14 Peter, and Andrew his brother
6.41 "the speck that is in your brother's eye?
6.42 "how can you say to your brother, 'Brother, let me take out the speck'?
6.42 "to take out the speck . . in your brother's eye
8.19 his mother and his brothers came to him
8.20 "Your mother and your brothers
8.21 "my brothers are those who hear the word
12.13 "bid my brother divide the inheritance
14.12 "do not invite your friends or your brothers
14.26 "If any one . . does not hate his . . brothers
15.27 " 'Your brother has come
15.32 " 'this your brother was dead, and is alive
16.28 " 'I have five brothers, . . warn them
17. 3 "if your brother sins, rebuke him
18.29 "no man who has left . . brothers or parents
20.28 "if a man's brother dies, having a wife
20.28 "must . . raise up children for his brother
20.29 "seven brothers; the first took a wife
21.16 "You will be delivered up . . by . . brothers
22.32 "turned again, strengthen your brethren
Jn 1.40 Andrew, Simon Peter's brother
1.41 He first found his brother Simon
2.12 he went . . with his mother and his brothers
6. 8 Andrew, Simon Peter's brother
7. 3 his brothers said . . "go to Judea
7. 5 even his brothers did not believe in him
7.10 after his brothers had gone . . to the feast
11. 2 It was Mary . . whose brother Lazarus was ill
11.19 to console them concerning their brother
11.21 "my brother would not have died
11.23 "Your brother will rise again
11.32 "my brother would not have died
20.17 "go to my brethren and say . . I am ascending
21.23 The saying spread . . among the brethren
Acts 1.14 the mother of Jesus, and with his brothers
1.15 Peter stood up among the brethren
1.16 "Brethren, the scripture had to be fulfilled
2.29 "Brethren, . . David . . died and was buried
2.37 "Brethren, what shall we do?
3.17 "brethren, . . you acted in ignorance
3.22 " 'God will raise . . from your brethren
6. 3 "brethren, pick out . . seven men

Acts 7. 2 Stephen said: "Brethren and fathers, hear
7.13 "made himself known to his brothers
7.23 "it came into his heart to visit his brethren
7.25 "supposed that his brethren understood
7.26 " 'brethren, why do you wrong each other?
7.37 " 'God will raise . . from your brethren
9.17 "Brother Saul, the Lord Jesus . . has sent me
9.30 when the brethren knew . . , they brought him
10.23 brethren from Joppa accompanied him
11. 1 the apostles and the brethren . . in Judea
11.12 "These six brethren also accompanied me
11.29 "to send relief to the brethren . . in Judea
12. 2 He killed James the brother of John
12.17 "Tell this to James and to the brethren
13.15 "Brethren, if you have any word . . say it
13.26 "Brethren, sons of the family of Abraham
13.38 "brethren, . . through this man forgiveness
14. 2 poisoned their minds against the brethren
15. 1 some . . from Judea . . were teaching the brethren
15. 3 they gave great joy to all the brethren
15. 7 "Brethren, you know that in the early days
15.13 James replied, "Brethren, listen to me
15.22 leading men among the brethren
15.23 "brethren, both the apostles and the elders, to the brethren . . of the Gentiles
15.32 Judas and Silas . . exhorted the brethren
15.33 they were sent off in peace by the brethren
15.36 Paul said . . "Come, let us . . visit the brethren
15.40 being commended by the brethren
16. 2 well spoken of by the brethren at Lystra
16.40 when they had seen the brethren
17. 6 they dragged Jason and some of the brethren
17.10 brethren immediately sent Paul and Silas
17.14 the brethren immediately sent Paul off
18.18 took leave of the brethren . . for Syria
18.27 the brethren encouraged him, and wrote
21. 7 greeted the brethren and stayed with them
21.17 the brethren received us gladly
21.20 "You see, brother, how many . . Jews
22. 1 "Brethren and fathers, hear the defense
22. 5 From them . . letters to the brethren
22.13 " 'Brother Saul, receive your sight
23. 1 Paul, looking intently . . , said, "Brethren
23. 5 "I did not know, brethren, . . the high priest
23. 6 "Brethren, I am a Pharisee
28.14 we found brethren, and were invited to stay
28.15 brethren . . came as far as the Forum
28.17 "Brethren, . . I was delivered prisoner
28.21 "none of the brethren . . has reported . . you

Rom 1.13 brethren, . . I have often intended to come
7. 1 brethren . . those who know the law
7. 4 my brethren, you have died to the law
8.12 brethren, we are debtors, not to the flesh
8.29 the first-born among many brethren
9. 3 cut off from Christ for . . my brethren
10. 1 Brethren, my . . prayer . . is that they may
11.25 understand this mystery, brethren
12. 1 I appeal to you therefore, brethren
14.10 Why do you pass judgment on your brother? Or you, why do you despise your brother?
14.13 hindrance in the way of a brother
14.15 If your brother is being injured
14.21 anything that makes your brother stumble[v]
15.14 I . . am satisfied about you, my brethren
15.30 I appeal to you, brethren, by our Lord
16.14 Greet . . the brethren who are with them
16.17 I appeal to you, brethren, to take note
16.23 Erastus . . and our brother Quartus, greet you[b]

1 Cor 1. 1 Paul . . and our brother Sosthenes
1.10 I appeal to you, brethren, by the name
1.11 there is quarreling among you, my brethren
1.26 For consider your call, brethren
2. 1 brethren, I did not come . . in lofty words
3. 1 I, brethren, could not address you
4. 6 all this . . for your benefit, brethren
5.11 who bears the name of brother if he is guilty

1 Cor 6. 6 brother goes to law against brother, and that before unbelievers?
6. 8 you . . wrong . . even your own brethren
7.12 if any brother has a wife . . an unbeliever
7.15 in such a case the brother . . is not bound
7.24 brethren, in whatever state each was called
7.29 brethren, the . . time has grown very short
8.11 destroyed, the brother for whom Christ died
8.12 Thus, sinning against your brethren
8.13 if food is a cause of my brother's falling, I will never eat meat, lest . . my brother . . fall
9. 5 other apostles and the brothers of the Lord
10. 1 brethren, . . our fathers . . passed through
11.33 brethren, when you come together to eat
12. 1 Now concerning spiritual gifts,[x] brethren
14. 6 brethren, if I come . . speaking in tongues
14.20 Brethren, do not be children in . . thinking
14.26 What then, brethren? When you come
14.39 brethren, earnestly desire to prophesy
15. 1 brethren, in what terms I preached
15. 6 to more than five hundred brethren
15.31 I protest, brethren, by my pride in you!
15.50 brethren: flesh and blood cannot inherit
15.58 brethren, be steadfast, immovable
16.11 I am expecting him with the brethren
16.12 our brother Apollos, I strongly urged him to visit you with the other brethren
16.15 Now, brethren, you know . . Stephanas
16.20 All the brethren send greetings

2 Cor 1. 1 Paul . . and Timothy our brother
1. 8 do not . . be ignorant, brethren
2.13 I did not find my brother Titus there
8. 1 know, brethren, about the grace of God
8.18 we are sending the brother who is famous
8.22 with them we are sending our brother
8.23 as for our brethren, they are messengers[j]
9. 3 I am sending the brethren
9. 5 urge the brethren to go on to you before me
11. 9 my needs were supplied by the brethren
12.18 I urged Titus to go, and sent the brother
13.11 Finally, brethren, farewell

Gal 1. 2 all the brethren . . To the churches of Galatia
1.11 I would have you know, brethren
1.19 apostles except James the Lord's brother
3.15 To give a human example, brethren
4.12 Brethren, I beseech you, become as I am
4.28 we,[j] brethren, . . are children of promise
4.31 brethren, we are not children of the slave
5.11 if I, brethren, still preach circumcision
5.13 For you were called to freedom, brethren
6. 1 Brethren, . . restore him in . . gentleness
6.18 grace . . be with your spirit, brethren

Eph 6.21 Tychicus the beloved brother
6.23 Peace be to the brethren, and love

Phil 1.12 know, brethren, that what has happened
1.14 the brethren have been made confident
2.25 send to you Epaphroditus my brother
3. 1 my brethren, rejoice in the Lord
3.13 Brethren, . . I have ⟨not⟩ made it my own
3.17 Brethren, join in imitating me
4. 1 brethren, whom I love and long for
4. 8 Finally, brethren, whatever is true
4.21 The brethren who are with me greet you

Col 1. 1 Paul . . and Timothy our brother
1. 2 To the saints and faithful brethren
4. 7 Tychicus . . he is a beloved brother
4. 9 Onesimus, the faithful and beloved brother
4.15 my greetings to the brethren at Laodicea

1 Th 1. 4 we know, brethren beloved by God
2. 1 For you yourselves know, brethren
2. 9 you remember our labor and toil, brethren
2.14 you, brethren, became imitators
2.17 since we were bereft of you, brethren
3. 2 Timothy, our brother and God's servant
3. 7 brethren, . . we have been comforted
4. 1 brethren, we beseech and exhort you
4. 6 that no man . . wrong his brother in this

1 Th 4.10 indeed you do love all the brethren . . But we exhort you, brethren, to do . . more
4.13 we would not have you ignorant, brethren
5. 1 as to the times and the seasons, brethren
5. 4 you are not in darkness, brethren
5.12 we beseech you, brethren, to respect
5.14 exhort you, brethren, admonish the idle
5.25 Brethren, pray for us
5.26 Greet all the brethren with a holy kiss
5.27 that this letter be read to all the brethren
2 Th 1. 3 thanks to God always for you, brethren
2. 1 we beg you, brethren, ⟨not to be . . shaken⟩
2.13 thanks to God always for you, brethren
2.15 So then, brethren, stand firm
3. 1 Finally, brethren, pray for us
3. 6 Now we command you, brethren . . keep away from any brother . . in idleness
3.13 Brethren, do not be weary in well-doing
3.15 warn him as a brother
1 Tim 4. 6 put these instructions before the brethren
5. 1 treat younger men like brothers
6. 2 believing masters . . are brethren
2 Tim 4.21 Linus and Claudia and all the brethren
Phm . 1 Paul . . and Timothy our brother
. 7 comfort from your love, my brother
.16 more than a slave, as a beloved brother
.20 Yes, brother, I want some benefit from you
Heb 2.11 he is not ashamed to call them brethren
2.12 "I will proclaim thy name to my brethren
2.17 he had to be made like his brethren
3. 1 holy brethren, who share in a heavenly call
3.12 Take care, brethren
7. 5 to . . take tithes from . . their brethren
8.11 " 'they shall not teach . . every one his brother
10.19 brethren, since we have confidence
13.22 brethren, bear with my word of exhortation
13.23 our brother Timothy has been released
Jas 1. 2 Count it all joy, my brethren
1. 9 Let the lowly brother boast in his exaltation
1.16 Do not be deceived, my beloved brethren
1.19 Know this, my beloved brethren
2. 1 My brethren, show no partiality
2. 5 Listen, my beloved brethren
2.14 What does it profit, my brethren?
2.15 If a brother or sister is ill-clad
3. 1 Let not many . . become teachers, . . brethren
3.10 My brethren, this ought not to be so
3.12 Can a fig tree, my brethren, yield olives?
4.11 not speak evil against one another, brethren. He that speaks evil against a brother or judges his brother, speaks evil against the law
5. 7 Be patient, . . brethren, until the coming
5. 9 not grumble, brethren, against one another
5.10 As an example . . , brethren, take
5.12 above all, my brethren, do not swear
5.19 My brethren, if any one among you wanders
1 Pet 5.12 Silvanus, a faithful brother
2 Pet 1.10 Therefore, brethren, be the more zealous
3.15 our beloved brother Paul wrote to you
1 Jn 2. 9 He who . . hates his brother is in the darkness
2.10 He who loves his brother abides in the light
2.11 he who hates his brother is in the darkness
3.10 nor he who does not love his brother
3.12 Cain . . murdered his brother . . Because . . his brother's ⟨deeds were⟩ righteous
3.13 Do not wonder, brethren
3.14 life, because we love the brethren
3.15 who hates his brother is a murderer
3.16 to lay down our lives for the brethren
3.17 if any one . . sees his brother in need
4.20 "I love God," and hates his brother
4.20 does not love . . brother . . cannot[h] love God
4.21 he who loves God should love his brother
5.16 If any one sees his brother . . sin
3 Jn . 3 I . . rejoiced when . . the brethren arrived
. 5 when you render . . service to the brethren
.10 refuses . . to welcome the brethren
Jude . 1 Jude, . . brother of James
Rev 1. 9 I John, your brother, who share with you
6.11 their fellow servants and their brethren
12.10 "accuser of our brethren has been thrown
19.10 "fellow servant with you and your brethren
22. 9 "with you and your brethren the prophets

2. *another, different:* ἕτερος (subst.) HETEROS
1 Cor 6. 1 When one . . has a grievance against a brother

BROTHER, FALSE

1. *false brother:* ψευδάδελφος PSEUDADELPHOS*
2 Cor 11.26 danger from false brethren
Gal 2. 4 false brethren secretly brought in

BROTHERHOOD

1. *brotherhood:* ἀδελφότης ADELPHOTĒS*
1 Pet 2.17 Love the brotherhood. Fear God
5. 9 suffering is required of your brotherhood

IDIOMATICALLY

a. 1 Cor 6.5 between members of the brotherhood ἀνὰ μέσον τοῦ ἀδελφοῦ αὐτοῦ [ADELPHOS]

BROTHERLY AFFECTION

1. *brotherly love:* φιλαδελφία PHILADELPHIA
Rom 12.10 love one another with brotherly affection
2 Pet 1. 7 godliness with brotherly affection, and brotherly affection with love

BROTHERLY LOVE

1. *brotherly love:* φιλαδελφία PHILADELPHIA
Heb 13. 1 Let brotherly love continue

BROUGHT IN, BE

1. *come, go:* ἔρχομαι ERCHOMAI
Mk 4.21 "Is a lamp brought in to be put under?

BROUGHT IN, SECRETLY

1. *introduced secretly, smuggled in:* παρείσακτος PAREISAKTOS*
Gal 2. 4 false brethren secretly brought in

BROW

1. *eyebrow, edge:* ὀφρῦς OPHRYS*
Lk 4.29 led him to the brow of the hill

BRUISE

1. *cut down, weary:* κατακόπτω KATAKOPTŌ*
Mk 5. 5 he was . . bruising himself with stones

BRUISED

1. *shatter, grind:* συντρίβω (perf. pass. part.) SYNTRIBŌ
Mt 12.20 "he will not break a bruised reed

BUD

1. *sprout, produce:* βλαστάνω BLASTANŌ
Heb 9. 4 ark . . contained . . Aaron's rod that budded

BUFFET

1. *slap, buffet:* κολαφίζω KOLAPHIZŌ
1 Cor 4.11 we are ill-clad and buffeted and homeless

BUGLE

1. *war trumpet, trumpet call:* σάλπιγξ SALPIGX
1 Cor 14. 8 if the bugle gives an indistinct sound

BUILD

1. *prepare, construct:* κατασκευάζω KATASKEUAZŌ
Heb 3. 4 (For every house is built by some one
1 Pet 3.20 during the building of the ark
2. *build, edify:* οἰκοδομέω OIKODOMEŌ
Mt 7.24 "wise man who built his house upon the rock
7.26 "man who built his house upon the sand
16.18 "on this rock[t] I will build my church
21.33 "a householder who . . built a tower
23.29 "you build the tombs of the prophets
26.61 " 'able to destroy the temple . . and to build it
27.40 "who would destroy the temple and build it!
Mk 12. 1 "built a tower, and let it out to tenants
14.58 " 'destroy this temple . . and . . build another
15.29 "who would destroy the temple and build it
Lk 4.29 the hill on which their city was built
6.48 "he is like a man building a house
6.48 "because it had been well built[w]‡
6.49 "like a man who built a house on the ground
7. 5 "he built us our synagogue
11.47 "you build the tombs of the prophets
11.48 "they killed them, and you build their tombs

Lk 12.18 " 'I will pull down my barns, and build larger
14.28 "which of you, desiring to build a tower?
14.30 " 'began to build, and was not able to finish
17.28 "they sold, they planted, they built
Jn 2.20 "forty-six years to build this temple
Acts 7.47 "Solomon who built a house for him
7.49 " 'What house will you build for me?
9.31 church . . was built up . . and . . multiplied
20.32 "his grace, which is able to build you up
Rom 15.20 lest I build on another man's foundation
1 Cor 8. 1 "Knowledge" puffs up, but love builds up
10.23 not all things build up
Gal 2.18 if I build up again those things
1 Th 5.11 build one another up, just as you are doing
1 Pet 2. 5 be yourselves built into a spiritual house

BUILD ON
BUILD UP
BUILD UP ON
BUILD UPON

1. *build on:* ἐποικοδομέω EPOIKODOMEŌ*
1 Cor 3.10 another man is building upon ⟨foundation⟩. Let each . . take care how he builds upon it
3.12 if any one builds on the foundation
3.14 work . . any man has built on the foundation
Eph 2.20 built upon the foundation of the apostles
Col 2. 7 ⟨live⟩ rooted and built up in him
Jude .20 beloved, build yourselves up on your . . faith

BUILDER

1. *prepare, construct:* κατασκευάζω (subst. part.) KATASKEUAZŌ
Heb 3. 3 builder of a house has more honor
3. 4 the builder of all things is God
2. *build, edify:* οἰκοδομέω (subst. part.) OIKODOMEŌ
Mt 21.42 " 'The very stone which the builders rejected
Also Mk **12.**10; Lk **20.**17; 1 Pet **2.**7
3. *builder:* οἰκοδόμος OIKODOMOS*
Acts 4.11 "stone which was rejected by you builders
4. *craftsman, artisan:* τεχνίτης TECHNITĒS
Heb 11.10 the city . . whose builder and maker is God

BUILDER, MASTER

1. *master builder:* ἀρχιτέκτων ARCHITEKTŌN*
1 Cor 3.10 like a . . master builder I laid a foundation

BUILDING
BUILDING UP

1. *building, edification:* οἰκοδομή OIKODOMĒ
Mt 24. 1 to point out . . the buildings of the temple
Mk 13. 1 "Look, Teacher . . what wonderful buildings!
13. 2 "Do you see these great buildings?
1 Cor 3. 9 you are God's field, God's building
14.12 strive to excel in building up the church
2 Cor 5. 1 we have a building from God, . . eternal
10. 8 which the Lord gave for building you up
13.10 the Lord has given me for building up
Eph 4.12 for building up the body of Christ

BUILT, BE

1. *material:* ἐνδώμησις ENDŌMĒSIS* [A.1.a]
Rev 21.18 The wall was built of jasper
2. *build together with:* συνοικοδομέω (pass.) SYNOIKODOMEŌ*
Eph 2.22 you also are built into it for a dwelling

BULL

1. *bull:* ταῦρος TAUROS
Heb 9.13 if the sprinkling . . with the blood of . . bulls
10. 4 that the blood of bulls . . take away sins

BULWARK

1. *support:* ἑδραίωμα HEDRAIŌMA*
1 Tim 3.15 the church . . pillar and bulwark of the truth

BUNDLE

1. *package:* δέσμη DESMĒ*
Mt 13.30 " 'bind them in bundles to be burned
2. *a considerable number:* τι πλῆθος PLĒTHOS [B.3.b.4]
Acts 28. 3 Paul had gathered a bundle of sticks

BURDEN

1. *weigh down:* βαρέω BAREŌ
1 Tim 5.16 let the church not be burdened
2. *weight:* βάρος BAROS
Mt 20.12 " 'who have borne the burden of the day
Acts 15.28 "upon you no greater burden than these
Gal 6. 2 Bear one another's burdens
Rev 2.24 " 'I do not lay upon you any other burden
3. *weigh down:* ἐπιβαρέω EPIBAREŌ
1 Th 2. 9 that we might not burden any of you
2 Th 3. 8 that we might not burden any of you
4. *weigh down:* καταβαρέω KATABAREŌ*
2 Cor 12.16 granting that I myself did not burden you
5. *be a burden:* καταναρκάω KATANARKAŌ
2 Cor 11. 9 in want, I did not burden any one
12.13 that I myself did not burden you
6. *burden, load:* φορτίον PHORTION
Mt 11.30 "my yoke is easy, and my burden is light
23. 4 "They bind heavy burdens, hard to bear[u]
Lk 11.46 "you load men with burdens hard to bear
11.46 "you yourselves do not touch the burdens
7. *heap up:* σωρεύω SŌREUŌ
2 Tim 3. 6 capture weak women, burdened with sins

IDIOMATICALLY
a. 2 Cor 8.13 I do not mean that others should be eased and you burdened οὐ γὰρ ἵνα ἄλλοις ἄνεσις, ὑμῖν θλῖψις [THLIPSIS]

BURDEN, BE A

1. *be a burden:* καταναρκάω KATANARKAŌ
2 Cor 12.14 I will not be a burden

BURDENING

IDIOMATICALLY
a. 2 Cor 11.9 I refrained . . from burdening you ἀβαρῆ ἐμαυτὸν ὑμῖν ἐτήρησα [ABARĒS*]

BURDENSOME

1. *heavy, severe:* βαρύς BARYS
1 Jn 5. 3 his commandments are not burdensome

BURIAL

1. *preparation for burial:* ἐνταφιασμός ENTAPHIASMOS
Jn 12. 7 "let her keep it for the day of my burial
2. *prepare for burial:* ἐνταφιάζω ENTAPHIAZŌ [A.6.b]
Jn 19.40 as is the burial custom of the Jews
3. *bone:* ὀστέον (pl.) OSTEON
Heb 11.22 gave directions concerning his burial[x]†

BURIAL, PREPARE FOR

1. *prepare for burial:* ἐνταφιάζω ENTAPHIAZŌ
Mt 26.12 "she has done it to prepare me for burial

BURN (*See also* INCENSE, BURN)

1. *kindle:* ἐμπίμπρημι EMPIMPRĒMI*
Mt 22. 7 "sent his troops and . . burned their city
2. *kindle, burn:* καίω KAIŌ
Lk 12.35 "Let . . your lamps ⟨be⟩ burning
24.32 "Did not our hearts burn within us?[c]
Jn 5.35 "He was a burning and shining lamp
15. 6 "the branches are gathered . . and burned
1 Cor 13. 3 If I deliver my body to be burned[v]‡
Rev 4. 5 before the throne burn seven torches
8. 8 a great mountain, burning with fire
19.20 lake of fire that burns with sulphur
21. 8 "lake that burns with fire and sulphur
3. *burn completely:* κατακαίω KATAKAIŌ
Mt 3.12 "chaff he will b. with unquenchable fire
13.30 " 'bind them in bundles to be burned
13.40 "weeds are gathered and burned with fire
Lk 3.17 "chaff he will burn with . . fire
Acts 19.19 brought their books . . and burned them
1 Cor 3.15 If any man's work is burned up
Heb 13.11 animals . . are burned outside the camp
2 Pet 3.10 the earth . . will be burned up
Rev 18. 8 "she shall be burned with fire
4. *burning:* καῦσις KAUSIS* [B.1.a.2]
Heb 6. 8 if it bears thorns . . its end is to be burned

BURN UP

1. *burn completely:* κατακαίω KATAKAIŌ
Rev 8. 7 a third of the earth was burnt up, and a third of the trees were burnt up, and all green grass was burnt up

Rev 17.16 "the beast will . . burn her up with fire

BURNING

1. *fire, flame:* πῦρ (gen.) PYR
Rom 12.20 "you will heap burning coals upon his head
2. *burning, proving by fire:* πύρωσις PYRŌSIS
Rev 18. 9 when they see the smoke of her burning
18.18 they saw the smoke of her burning

BURNISHED BRONZE

1. *fine brass or bronze:* χαλκολίβανον CHALKOLIBANON*
Rev 1.15 his feet were like burnished bronze
2.18 " 'whose feet are like burnished bronze

BURNT OFFERING

1. *whole burnt offering:* ὁλοκαύτωμα HOLOKAUTŌMA
Heb 10. 6 "in burnt offerings . . thou hast . . no pleasure
10. 8 "nor taken pleasure in . . burnt offerings

BURNT OFFERING, WHOLE

1. *whole burnt offering:* ὁλοκαύτωμα HOLOKAUTŌMA
Mk 12.33 "much more than all whole burnt offerings

BURST

1. *break:* ῥήγνυμι RHĒGNYMI
Mt 9.17 "the skins burst, and the wine is spilled
Mk 2.22 "if he does, the wine will burst the skins
Lk 5.37 "the new wine will burst the skins

BURST OPEN

1. *burst open:* λακάω LAKAŌ*
Acts 1.18 "(falling headlong[b] he burst open

BURY

1. *gather in:* συγκομίζω SYGKOMIZŌ*
Acts 8. 2 Devout men buried Stephen
2. *burial:* ταφή TAPHĒ* [B.1.a.2]
Mt 27. 7 the potter's field, to bury strangers in
3. *bury:* θάπτω THAPTŌ*
Mt 8.21 "let me first go and bury my father
8.22 "leave the dead to bury their own dead
14.12 disciples . . took the body and buried it
Lk 9.59 "let me first go and bury my father
9.60 "Leave the dead to bury their own dead
16.22 "The rich man also died and was buried
Acts 2.29 "David . . both died and was buried
5. 6 young men . . carried him out and buried him
5. 9 "those that have buried your husband
5.10 they carried her out and buried her
1 Cor 15. 4 that he was buried, that he was raised

BURY WITH

1. *bury together:* συνθάπτω SYNTHAPTŌ*
Rom 6. 4 We were buried . . with him by baptism
Col 2.12 you were buried with him in baptism

BURYING

1. *preparation for burial:* ἐνταφιασμός ENTAPHIASMOS
Mk 14. 8 "she has anointed my body . . for burying

BUSH

1. *thornbush:* βάτος BATOS I
Mk 12.26 "in the passage about the bush
Lk 20.37 "in the passage about the bush
Acts 7.30 "angel appeared . . in a . . fire in a bush
7.35 "the angel that appeared to him in the bush

BUSH, BRAMBLE

1. *thornbush:* βάτος BATOS I
Lk 6.44 "nor are grapes picked from a bramble bush

BUSHEL

1. *modios* (a dry measure): μόδιος MODIOS*
Mt 5.15 "Nor do men . . put it under a bushel
Mk 4.21 "Is a lamp . . to be put under a bushel?
Lk 11.33 "No one . . puts it . . under a bushel

BUSINESS

1. *commerce, trade:* ἐμπορία EMPORIA*
Mt 22. 5 "made light of it and went off . . to his b.
2. *function, business:* ἐργασία ERGASIA
Acts 19.24 Demetrius . . brought no little business
19.25 "from this business we have our wealth
3. *thing, deed:* πρᾶγμα PRAGMA
1 Th [4. 6 that no man . . *defraud . . in business*†

BUSINESS, AT ONE'S

1. *sit down:* κάθημαι (part.) KATHĒMAI
Jn 2.14 he found . . money-changers at their business

BUSYBODY

1. *meddlesome, curious:* περίεργος (subst.) PERIERGOS
1 Tim 5.13 they learn to be . . gossips and busybodies

BUSYBODY, BE A

1. *be a busybody, meddle:* περιεργάζομαι PERIERGAZOMAI*
2 Th 3.11 some of you are . . mere busybodies

BUT

1. *but:* ἀλλά ALLA
Mt **4**.4; **5**.15, 17, 39; **6**.13, 18; **7**.21; **8**.4, 8; **9**.12, 13, 17, 18, 24; **10**.20, 34; **13**.21; **15**.11; **16**.12, 17, 23; **17**.12; **18**.22; **19**.6; **20**.23, 26, 28; **21**.21; **22**.30, 32; **24**.6; **26**.39; **27**.24
Mk **1**.44, 45; **2**.17², 22‡; **3**.26, 27, 29; **4**.17; **5**.19, 26, 39; **6**.9, 52; **7**.5, 15, 19, 25; **8**.33; **9**.13, 22, 37; **10**.8, 27, 40, 43, 45; **11**.23, 32; **12**.14, 25, 27; **13**.7, 11², 20, 24; **14**.28, 36, 49; **16**.7
Lk **5**.14, 31, 32, 38; **6**.27; **7**.7; **8**.16, 27, 52; [**9**.56‡; **11**.33, 42; **12**.51; **13**.3, 5; **14**.10, 13; **16**.30; **18**.13; **20**.21, 38; **21**.9; **22**.36, 42, 53; [**24**.5(6)‡
Jn **1**.8, 13, 31, 33; **3**.8, 16, 17, 28, 36; **4**.23; **5**.18, 22, 24, 30, 34, 42; **6**.9, 22, 26, 27, 36, 38, 39, 64; **7**.10, 16, 22, 24, 44, 49; **8**.12, 16, 26, 28, 42, 49, 55; **9**.3, 9, 31; **10**.1, 5, 8, 18, 26, 33; **11**.11, 15, 30, 42, 51, 52, 54; **12**.6, 9, 16, 42, 44, 47; **13**.9, 10²; **14**.24, 31; **15**.16, 19, 21; **16**.4, 6, 12, 13, 20, 25, 33; **17**.9, 15, 20; **18**.28, 40; **19**.21, 24, 34; **20**.7, 27; **21**.8, 23
Acts **1**.4, 8; **2**.16; **4**.17, 32; **5**.4, 13; **7**.39; **9**.6; **10**.35, 41; **13**.25; **15**.11, 20; **18**.9, 21; **19**.26, 27; **20**.24; **21**.13, 24; **26**.16, 20, 25, 29; **27**.10
Rom **1**.21, 32; **2**.13, 29; **3**.27; **4**.2, 4, 10, 12, 13, 16, 20, 24; **5**.11, 15; **6**.13, 14, 15; **7**.15, 17, 19, 20; **8**.4, 15, 20, 23, 26, 32; **9**.7, 8, 10, 11(12), 16, 24, 32; **10**.2, 8, 16, 18; **11**.4, 11, 18, 20; **12**.2, 3, 16, 19, 21; **13**.3, 5, 14; **14**.13, 17, 20; **15**.3, 21; **16**.4, 18
1 Cor **1**.17, 27; **2**.4, 5, 7, 9, 12, 13; **3**.1, 6; **4**.4, 14, 19, 20; **5**.8; **6**.6, 8, 11, 12², 13; **7**.4², 7, 10, 19, 21, 35; **9**.12, 21, 27; **10**.13, 23², 24, 33; **11**.8, 9, 17; **12**.14, 24, 25; **14**.2, 17, 22², 33, 34; **15**.10, 35, 37, 39, 40, 46²
2 Cor **1**.9, 12, 13, 19; **2**.4, 5, 17; **3**.3², 6, 14; **4**.2, 5, 8², 9², 18; **5**.4, 12, 15; **6**.4; **7**.5, 6, 7, 9, 12, 14; **8**.5, 8, 10, 14(13), 19, 21; **9**.12; **10**.4, 12, 13, 18; **11**.17; **12**.14²; **13**.3, 4², 7
Gal **1**.1, 8, 12, 17; **2**.3, 7, 14; **3**.16, 22; **4**.2, 7, 14, 17, 23, 29, 30, 31; **5**.6, 13; **6**.13, 15
Eph **1**.21; **2**.19; **4**.29; **5**.4, 15, 17, 18, 29; **6**.4, 6, 12
Phil **1**.20, 29; **2**.3, 4, 7, 12, 27²; **3**.7, 9; **4**.6, 17
Col **3**.11, 22
1 Th **1**.5, 8; **2**.2, 4², 7, 8, 13; **4**.7, 8; **5**.6, 9, 15
2 Th **2**.12; **3**.8, 9, 15
1 Tim **1**.13, 16; **2**.10; **3**.3; **4**.12; **5**.1, 13, 23; **6**.17
2 Tim **1**.7, 8, 9, 12, 17; **2**.9, 20, 24; **3**.9; **4**.3, 8
Tit **1**.8; **2**.10; **3**.5
Phm .14, 16
Heb **2**.16; **3**.13; **4**.2; **5**.4, 5; **7**.16; **9**.24; **10**.3, 25, 39; **11**.13; **12**.22, 26; **13**.14
Jas **1**.25, 26; **2**.18; **3**.15; **4**.11
1 Pet **1**.15, 19, 23; **2**.16, 18, 20, 25; **3**.4, 14, 21; **4**.2, 13; **5**.2², 3
2 Pet **1**.16, 21; **2**.4, 5; **3**.9²
1 Jn **2**.2, 7, 16, 19², 21; **3**.18; **4**.1, 10, 18; **5**.6, 18
2 Jn .1, 5, 8, 12
3 Jn .9, 11, 13
Jude .6, 9
Rev **2**.4, 9², 14, 20; **3**.9; **9**.5; **10**.7, 9; **17**.12; **20**.6
2. *but, and:* δέ DE
3. *if not, except:* ἐὰν μή EAN MĒ
Gal **2**.16
4. *if not, unless:* εἰ μή EI MĒ
Mt **12**.4; **17**.8; **21**.19; **24**.36
Mk **2**.7, 26; **9**.8, 29; **10**.18; **11**.13
Lk **5**.21; **6**.4; **18**.19
Jn **3**.13; **14**.6; **17**.12; **19**.15
Rom **11**.15; **14**.14
1 Cor **8**.4

2 Cor **2**.2
Gal **1**.7
Eph **4**.9
Heb **3**.18
1 Jn **2**.22; **5**.5
Rev **19**.12
5. *except, outside:* ἐκτός EKTOS
Acts 26.22 "saying nothing but what . . Moses said
6. *for:* γάρ GAR
Gal **2**.18
Phil **3**.20
1 Pet **4**.15
7. *not:* μή MĒ
Acts **4**.20
8. *yet, nevertheless:* μέντοι MENTOI
Jn 4.27 but none said, "What do you wish?
20. 5 he saw . . but he did not go in
2 Tim 2.19 But God's firm foundation stands
9. *so, therefore:* οὖν OUN
Acts **23**.21
Rom **6**.21; **10**.14
1 Cor **14**.11
10. *but, however, except:* πλήν PLĒN
Mt **11**.22, 24; **18**.7; **26**.64
Mk **12**.32
Lk **6**.24, 35; **10**.14; **11**.41; **17**.1; **19**.27; **22**.21, 22; **23**.28
11. *and, both . . . and:* τέ TE
Acts **4**.14; **17**.14; **24**.23; **26**.10

BUT I
1. *and I:* κἀγώ KAGŌ
Acts **10**.28
1 Cor **3**.1

BUT NOT
1. *nor, and not:* οὐδέ OUDE
Mk 16.13 but they did not believe them[k]‡

BUT ONLY
1. *but:* ἀλλά ALLA
Mt **19**.11
Jn **4**.2
1 Cor **3**.7
2 Cor **13**.8
2. *if not, except:* ἄν (=ἐάν) μή AN [B.3.b.4]
Jn 5.19 "but only what he sees the father doing
3. *if not, except:* εἰ μή EI MĒ
Mk 13.32 "not even the angels . . but only the Father
Lk 4.26 "to none of them but only to Zarephath
4.27 "none . . was cleansed, but only Naaman
Rev 9. 4 but only those . . who have not the seal
21.27 but only those . . in the Lamb's book of life
4. *but, however, except:* πλήν PLĒN
Acts 27.22 "no loss of life . . but only of the ship

BUT THEY
1. *and that one:* κἀκεῖνος KAKEINOS
Mk **16**.11‡

BUY
1. *buy in the market:* ἀγοράζω AGORAZŌ
Mt 13.44 "sells all that he has and buys that field
13.46 "sold all that he had and bought it
14.15 "send the crowds away to . . buy food
21.12 Jesus . . drove out all who sold and bought
25. 9 " 'go rather . . and buy for yourselves
25.10 "they went to buy, the bridegroom came
27. 7 bought with them the potter's field
Mk 6.36 "send them . . to . . buy . . something to eat
6.37 "Shall we go and buy . . bread?
11.15 drive out . . those who bought in the temple
15.46 he bought a linen shroud, and . . wrapped him
16. 1 bought spices . . that they might . . anoint
Lk 9.13 "unless we are to go and buy food
14.18 "to make excuses. . . 'I have bought a field
14.19 " 'I have bought five yoke of oxen
17.28 "in the days of Lot—they ate, . . they bought
22.36 "let him who has no sword . . buy one
Jn 4. 8 his disciples had gone . . to buy food
6. 5 "How are we to buy bread?
13.29 "Buy what we need for the feast
1 Cor 6.20 you were bought with a price
7.23 You were bought with a price
7.30 those who buy as though they had no goods
2 Pet 2. 1 denying the Master who bought them
Rev 3.18 " 'buy from me gold refined by fire
13.17 no one can buy . . unless he has the mark
18.11 no one buys their cargo any more
2. *acquire, get:* κτάομαι KTAOMAI
Acts 1.18 "(this man bought a field with the reward
22.28 "I bought this citizenship for a large sum
3. *purchase, bargain:* ὠνέομαι ŌNEOMAI*
Acts 7.16 "laid in the tomb that Abraham had bought
CONTEXTUALLY
Jn 6. 7 "would not buy enough bread for each

BY
1. *from:* ἀπό (+gen.) APO
Mt **7**.16, 20; **11**.19; **27**.9
Lk **7**.35; **8**.29, 43, 46; **9**.22; **17**.25
Jn **15**.4
Acts **2**.22; **4**.36; **15**.4, 33; **20**.9
Rom **15**.15
2 Cor **7**.13
Jas **1**.13
1 Jn **2**.20
Jude .23
Rev **9**.18; **12**.6
2. *through:* διά (+gen.) DIA
[a]+acc.
Mt **1**.22; **2**.5, 12, 15, 17, 23; **3**.3; **4**.14; **7**.13[2]; **8**.17; **11**.2; **12**.17; **13**.35; **18**.7; **21**.4; **24**.15; **26**.24; **27**.9
Mk **6**.2; **14**.21; **16**.20‡
Lk **1**.70; **13**.24; **17**.1; **18**.31; **22**.22
Jn **10**.1, 2, 9; **11**.4; **14**.6; **15**.3[a]
Acts **1**.16; **2**.16, 23; **3**.18, 21; **4**.25; **5**.12; **7**.25; **10**.36; **11**.28, 30; **12**.9; **14**.3; **15**.7, 27; **17**.10; **18**.28; **19**.11; **23**.31; **24**.2
Rom **1**.12; **2**.12, 16, 23; **3**.25, 31; **5**.9, 10, 19[2]; **6**.4[2]; **7**.5, 11; **8**.3, 20[a]; **10**.17; **12**.1, 3; **14**.15; **15**.4[2], 30[2], 32; **16**.18
1 Cor **1**.1, 9, 10; **6**.14; **15**.2, 21[2]; **16**.3
2 Cor **1**.1; **5**.7[2]; **8**.5, 8; **10**.1, 11
Gal **3**.18, 19; **6**.14†
Eph **1**.1; **4**.16
Phil **1**.20[2]
Col **1**.1, 20, 22; **2**.8
2 Th **2**.2[3], 15[2]
1 Tim **2**.10, [15†; **4**.5, 14
2 Tim **1**.1, 14
Tit **3**.5
Heb **2**.2, 3, 10; **5**.12, 14[a]; **9**.26; **11**.7, 39; **12**.11, 15; **13**.11
1 Pet **1**.7, 12; **2**.14; **3**.1; **5**.12
2 Pet **1**.4
1 Jn **5**.6
Rev **4**.11[a]; **12**.11[2a], 12[a]; **13**.14[a]; **21**.24
3. *into, to, for:* εἰς (+acc.) EIS
Mt **5**.35
4. *from, out of:* ἐκ (+gen.) EK
Mt **1**.3, 5[2], 6; **12**.33, 37[2]
Lk **6**.44
Jn **3**.34; **6**.65
Rom **1**.4, [17†; **3**.20; **4**.2; **5**.1; **9**.10
1 Cor **7**.5; **9**.14
2 Cor **2**.17; **13**.4[2]
Gal **2**.16[4]; **3**.2[2], 5[2], 8, [11†, 18[2], 24; **4**.22[2]; **5**.5
Heb **10**.38; **11**.35
Jas **2**.18, 21, 22, 24[2], 25; **3**.13
1 Pet **4**.11
1 Jn **3**.24; **4**.6
Rev **2**.11; **3**.18; **9**.18; **18**.[3†[‡], 19; **20**.12
5. *in, at, by:* ἐν (+dat.) EN
Mt **5**.34, 35, 36; **9**.34‡; **12**.24, 27[2], 28; [**17**.21‡; **21**.23, 24, 27; **22**.43†; **23**.16[2], 18[2], 20[3], 21[3], 22[3]; **26**.52
Mk **3**.22; **9**.29; **11**.28, 29, 33; **12**.36†; **14**.1
Lk **2**.27†; **4**.1; **11**.15, 18, 19[2], 20; **20**.2, 8; **21**.19
Jn **13**.35; **15**.8; **16**.30
Acts **1**.3, 7; **4**.7[2], 9, 10[2], 12; **11**.14; **13**.39(38), 39

Rom **1**.10, 18; **3**.25; **5**.9, 10; **10**.5; **15**.13, 16, 19²
1 Cor **2**.13; **4**.6; **6**.2, 4; **8**.11; **12**.3², 9², 13; **14**.21²
2 Cor **1**.12²; **6**.6, 12; **7**.6, 7²; **10**.12; **11**.3
Gal **2**.20; **3**.11, 12, 14; **5**.4
Eph **3**.5, [9†; **4**.14²
Col **2**.11
1 Th **3**.3; **4**.15
2 Th **1**.11
1 Tim **1**.18
Heb **1**.1, 2; **4**.11; **10**.10, 19, 29; **11**.2; **13**.20
1 Pet **1**.2, 5, 11, 22; **2**.2
1 Jn **2**.3, 5; **3**.10, 16, 19, 24; **4**.2, 13; **5**.2
Jude .10
Rev **1**.5; **5**.9; **9**.20; **10**.6; **18**.23; **19**.20, 21

6. *on, at:* ἐπί (+dat.) EPI
except ᵃ+gen.
Mt **4**.4²; **18**.16ᵃ; **21**.19ᵃ
Lk **4**.4
Jn **5**.2; **21**.1ᵃ
2 Cor **9**.13; **13**.1ᵃ
Heb **11**.4

7. *by:* ὑπό (+gen.) HYPO
Mt **2**.16; **3**.6, 13, 14; **4**.1²; **5**.13; **6**.2; **8**.24; **10**.22; **11**.7, 27; **14**.8, 24; **19**.12; **20**.23; **22**.31; **23**.7; **24**.9; **27**.12
Mk **1**.5, 9, 13; **2**.3; **8**.31; **13**.13; **16**.11‡
Lk **2**.21, 26; **3**.7, 19; **4**.2, 15; **7**.24, 30; **8**.14; **9**.7, 8; **10**.22; **13**.17; **14**.8²; **16**.22; **17**.20; **21**.16, 17, 20, 24; **23**.8
Jn **14**.21
Acts **2**.24; **4**.11; **8**.6; **10**.17, 22², 33, 38, 41, 42; **12**.5; **13**.4, 45; **15**.3, 40; **16**.2, 4, 6, 14; **17**.13, 25; **20**.3; **21**.35; **22**.11, 12; **23**.10, 27²; **24**.26; **25**.14; **26**.6, 7; **27**.41
Rom **12**.21; **13**.1; **15**.24
1 Cor **1**.11; **2**.12, 15; **4**.3²; **6**.12; **7**.25; **8**.3; **10**.9, 10, 29; **11**.32; **14**.24²
2 Cor **1**.4; **2**.6; **3**.2, 3; **5**.4; **8**.19; **12**.11
Gal **1**.11; **3**.17; **4**.9; **5**.15
Eph **2**.11; **5**.13
Phil **1**.28
Col **2**.18
1 Th **1**.4; **2**.4
2 Th **2**.13
2 Tim **2**.26
Heb **2**.3; **3**.4; **5**.4, 10; **7**.7; **9**.19; **11**.23; **12**.5
Jas **1**.14; **2**.9; **3**.4², 6
1 Pet **2**.4
2 Pet **1**.17, 21; **2**.7, 17
Jude .12
Rev **6**.8, 13

8. *in accordance with, for:* κατά (+acc.) KATA
except ᵃ+gen.
Mt **26**.63ᵃ
Mk **6**.40²
Lk **10**.31
Jn **7**.24; **8**.9‡; **10**.3; **18**.31; **19**.7
Acts **28**.16
Rom **2**.5, 7
Gal **2**.2
Eph **3**.3, 7, 20
Phil **3**.21
2 Th **2**.9
1 Tim **1**.1
Tit **1**.3
Phm .14
Heb **6**.13²ᵃ, 16ᵃ; **7**.16
Jas **2**.17
1 Pet **1**.3
Rev **20**.12, 13

9. *receive, take:* λαμβάνω (part.) LAMBANŌ
Acts **26**.10

10. *by:* νή NĒ*
1 Cor 15.31 I protest, brethren, by my pride in you

11. *more than, by:* παρά (+acc.) PARA
ᵃ+gen. ᵇ+dat.
Mt **4**.18; **18**.19ᵃ
Mk **1**.16
Lk **5**.1, 2
Jn **19**.25ᵇ
Acts **26**.8ᵇ
Heb **11**.12
2 Jn .4ᵃ

12. *with:* σύν (+dat.) SYN
Acts **7**.35

IDIOMATICALLY
a. 2 Cor **4**.1† [KATHŌS]

BY ITSELF

1. *separately, apart from:* χωρίς CHŌRIS
Jn 20. 7 rolled up in a place by itself

BY MEANS OF

1. *through:* διά (+gen.) DIA
Mk **16**.[end‡
2 Pet **3**.5
2. *from, out of:* ἐκ (+gen.) EK
Lk **16**.9
3. *in, at, by:* ἐν (+dat.) EN
Rev **9**.19²

BY S.'S SIDE

1. *beside, with:* παρά (+dat.) PARA
Lk **9**.47

BY WAY OF

1. *through:* διά (+gen.) DIA
Rom **15**.28
2. *in, at, by:* ἐν (+dat.) EN
2 Pet **1**.13; **3**.1
3. *as, so:* ὡς HŌS
Rom **15**.15
4. *in accordance with, for:* κατά (+acc.) KATA
1 Cor **7**.6

BYSTANDER

1. *there:* ἐκεῖ (+art.) EKEI
Mt 26.71 another maid . . said to the bystanders
2. *stand, set:* ἵστημι (subst. perf. part.) HISTĒMI
ᵃ+ἐκεῖ A.4.e
Mt 26.73 After a little while the bystanders came
27.47 ᵃbystanders . . said, "This man is calling
3. *place beside, stand before:* παρίστημι (subst. part.) PARISTĒMI
Mk 14.69 to the bystanders, "This man is one
14.70 bystanders said to Peter, "Certainly
15.35 bystanders . . said . . "he is calling Elijah

C

CAESAR: Καῖσαρ 'sēzər

Mt 22.17 "Is it lawful to pay taxes to Caesar, or not?
22.21 They said, "Caesar's." Then he said to them, "Render therefore to C. the things that are Caesar's
Mk 12.14 "Is it lawful to pay taxes to Caesar?
12.16 "Whose likeness . . ?" They said . . "Caesar's
12.17 "Render to Caesar the things that are Caesar's, and to God . . that are God's
Lk 2. 1 a decree went out from Caesar Augustus
3. 1 fifteenth year of the reign of Tiberius C.
20.22 "Is it lawful for us to give tribute to C.?
20.24 "Whose likeness . . has it?" They said, "C.'s
20.25 "render to Caesar the things that are Caesar's, and to God . . that are God's
23. 2 "forbidding us to give tribute to Caesar
Jn 19.12 "you are not C.'s friend; every one who makes himself a king sets himself against C.
19.15 "We have no king but Caesar
Acts 17. 7 "all acting against the decrees of Caesar
25. 8 "Neither against the law . . nor against C.
25.10 "I am standing before Caesar's tribunal
25.11 "no one can give me up . . I appeal to Caesar
25.12 Then Festus . . answered, "You have appealed to C.; to C. you shall go
25.21 "to be held until I could send him to C.
26.32 "free if he had not appealed to Caesar

Acts 27.24 " 'Paul; you must stand before Caesar
28.19 "I was compelled to appeal to Caesar
Phil 4.22 saints . . , especially those of C.'s household

CAESAREA: Καισάρεια ˌsesəˈrēə I,B-4; II,F-4
Acts 8.40 Philip . . preached . . till he came to Caesarea
9.30 to Caesarea, and sent him off to Tarsus
10. 1 At C. there was a man named Cornelius
10.24 entered Caesarea. Cornelius was expecting
11.11 "three men arrived . . , sent to me from C.
12.19 he went down from Judea to C.
18.22 When he had landed at C.
21. 8 On the morrow we . . came to Caesarea
21.16 some . . disciples from C. went with us
23.23 "two hundred spearmen to go as far as C.
23.33 they came to C. and delivered the letter
25. 1 Festus . . went up to Jerusalem from C.
25. 4 Festus replied that Paul was being kept at C.
25. 6 he went . . to C. . . and ordered Paul
25.13 Agrippa the king and Bernice arrived at C.

CAESAREA PHILIPPI: Καισάρεια ἡ Φιλίππου ˌsesəˈrēə fəˈlipī, ˈfiləˌpī I, D-2
Mt 16.13 Jesus came into . . Caesarea Philippi
Mk 8.27 Jesus went . . to the villages of C. Philippi

CAIAPHAS: Καϊάφας ˈkāəfəs
Mt 26. 3 the high priest, who was called Caiaphas
26.57 those who had seized Jesus led him to C.
Lk 3. 2 the high-priesthood of Annas and C.
Jn 11.49 C., who was high priest that year
18.13 to Annas; for he was the father-in-law of C.
18.14 It was Caiaphas who had given counsel
18.24 Annas then sent him bound to Caiaphas
18.28 they led Jesus from the house of Caiaphas
Acts 4. 6 Annas the high priest and Caiaphas

CAIN: Κάϊν ˈkān
Heb 11. 4 a more acceptable sacrifice than Cain
1 Jn 3.12 not be like Cain who was of the evil one
Jude .11 Woe . . ! For they walk in the way of Cain

CAINAN: Καϊνάμ ˈkānən, ˌkāˈīnən
Lk 3.36 Cainan, the son of Arphaxad
3.37 Cainan, ⟨the son of Enos⟩

CALAMITY
1. *distress, difficulty:* στενοχωρία STENOCHŌRIA
2 Cor 6. 4 through great endurance, in . . calamities
12.10 I am content with weaknesses, . . calamities

CALF
1. *calf, young bull:* μόσχος MOSCHOS
Lk 15.23 " 'bring the fatted calf and kill it
15.27 " 'your father has killed the fatted calf
15.30 " 'you killed for him the fatted calf!
Heb 9.12 not the blood of . . calves but his own
9.19 Moses . . took the blood of calves and goats

CALF, FAT
1. *fed up, fatted:* σιτιστός (subst. neut.) SITISTOS*
Mt 22. 4 " 'fat calves are killed, and . . ready

CALF, MAKE A
1. *make a calf:* μοσχοποιέω MOSCHOPOIEŌ*
Acts 7.41 "they made a calf . . and offered a sacrifice

CALL (*See also* BLESSED, CALL; COMMON, CALL; HAPPY, CALL; TRUMPET CALL)
1. *say, speak:* εἶπον EIPON
Jn 10.35 "If he called them gods to whom the word
2. *call, surname:* ἐπικαλέω EPIKALEŌ
Mt 10.25 "If they have called the master . . Beelzebul
Acts 10. 5 "bring one Simon who is called Peter
10.18 whether Simon . . called Peter was . . there
10.32 " 'to Joppa and ask for Simon . . called Peter
11.13 " 'to Joppa and bring Simon called Peter
15.17 " 'all the Gentiles . . called by my name
2 Cor 1.23 But I call God to witness against me
Heb 11.16 God is not ashamed to be called their God
3. *say, speak:* ἐρῶ ERŌ
Jn 15.15 "but I have called you friends
4. *call, name:* καλέω KALEŌ
Mt 1.21 "bear a son, and you shall call his name Jesus
1.23 "his name shall be called Emmanuel
1.25 and he called his name Jesus
2.15 "Out of Egypt have I called my son
2.23 "He shall be called a Nazarene
4.21 two other brothers . . and he called them
5. 9 "peacemakers . . shall be called sons of God
5.19 "Whoever . . relaxes . . these . . shall be called
5.19 "but he who does them . . shall be called great
9.13 "not to call the righteous, but sinners
20. 8 " 'Call the laborers and pay them
21.13 " 'My house shall be called . . house of prayer
22. 3 "to call those . . invited to the marriage
22.43 "How is it . . that David . . calls him Lord?
22.45 "If David . . calls him Lord, how is he his son?
23. 7 "⟨they love⟩ being called rabbi by men
23. 8 "you are not to be called rabbi
23. 9 "call no man your father on earth
23.10 "Neither be called masters, for you have one
25.14 "a man . . called his servants
27. 8 that field has been called the Field of Blood
Mk 1.20 he called them; and they left their father
2.17 "I came not to call the righteous, but sinners
3.31 his mother . . sent to him and called him
11.17 " 'My house shall be called a house of prayer
Lk 1.13 "a son, and you shall call his name John
1.31 "a son, and you shall call his name Jesus
1.32 "He will be . . called the Son of the Most High
1.35 "the child to be born[d] will be called holy
1.36 "sixth month with her who was called barren
1.60 "Not so; he shall be called John
1.61 "None of your kindred is called by this
1.62 inquiring what he would have him called
1.76 "you, child, will be called the prophet
2. 4 the city of David, which is called Bethlehem
2.21 when . . circumcised, he was called Jesus
2.23 ("Every male . . shall be called holy
5.32 "not . . to call the righteous, but sinners
6.15 Simon who was called the Zealot
6.46 "Why do you call me 'Lord, Lord'?
7.11 he went to a city called Nain
8. 2 some women . . : Mary, called Magdalene
9.10 withdrew apart to a city called Bethsaida
10.39 ⟨Martha⟩ had a sister called Mary
15.19 " ' "no longer worthy to be called your son
15.21 " 'no longer worthy to be called your son[v]
19.13 "Calling ten of his servants
19.29 at the mount that is called Olivet
20.44 "David . . calls him Lord; so how is he his son?
21.37 lodged on the mount called Olivet
22. 3 Satan entered into Judas called Iscariot
22.25 "those in authority . . are called benefactors
23.33 the place which is called The Skull
Jn 1.42 "Simon . . shall be called Cephas . .[c]
Acts 1.12 mount called Olivet . . near Jerusalem
1.19 "(field was called . . Akeldama . . Field of Blood
1.23 Joseph called Barsabbas
3.11 the portico called Solomon's
4.18 called them and charged them not to speak
8.10 "power of God which is called Great
9.11 "go to the street called Straight
13. 1 prophets . . Simeon who was called Niger
14.12 Barnabas they called Zeus, and Paul . . Hermes
15.22 They sent Judas called Barsabbas
15.37 to take with them John called Mark
24. 2 he was called, Tertullus began to accuse
27. 8 we came to a place called Fair Havens
27.14 a tempestuous wind, called the northeaster
27.16 under the lee of a small island called Cauda[b]
28. 1 learned that the island was called Malta
Rom 4.17 calls into existence . . things that do not exist
8.30 whom he predestined he also called; . . whom he called he also justified
9.11 not because of works but . . of his call
9.24 even us whom he has called
9.25 "Those . . I will call 'my people

Rom 9.26 "will be called 'sons of the living God
1 Cor 1. 9 God is faithful, by whom you were called
7.15 For God has called us[l] to peace
7.17 the life . . in which God has called him
7.18 at the time of his call already circumcised?
7.18 at the time of his call uncircumcised?
7.20 remain in the state in which he was called
7.21 Were you a slave when called?
7.22 who was called in the Lord as a slave
7.22 who was free when called is a slave of Christ
7.24 in whatever state each was called, . . remain
15. 9 I am . . unfit to be called an apostle
Gal 1. 6 him who called you in the grace of Christ
1.15 he who . . called me through his grace
5. 8 This . . is not from him who calls you
5.13 For you were called to freedom, brethren
Eph 4. 1 life . . to which you have been called
4. 4 just as you were called to the one hope
Col 3.15 the peace . . to which indeed you were called
1 Th 2.12 a life worthy of God, who calls you
4. 7 God has not called us for uncleanness
5.24 He who calls you is faithful
2 Th 2.14 To this he called you through our gospel
1 Tim 6.12 the eternal life to which you were called
2 Tim 1. 9 who saved us and called us
Heb 2.11 not ashamed to call them brethren
3.13 every day, as long as it is called "today
5. 4 he is called by God, just as Aaron was
9.15 so that those who are called may receive
11. 8 Abraham obeyed when he was called to go
Jas 2.23 ⟨Abraham⟩ was called the friend of God
1 Pet 1.15 as he who called you is holy, be holy
2. 9 declare the . . deeds of him who called you
2.21 For to this you have been called
3. 6 Sarah obeyed Abraham, calling him lord
3. 9 bless, for to this you have been called
5.10 God of all grace, who has called you
2 Pet 1. 3 him who called us to[b] his own glory
1 Jn 3. 1 that we should be called children of God
Rev 1. 9 I John . . was on the island called Patmos
11. 8 city which is allegorically[d] called Sodom
12. 9 ancient serpent, who is called the Devil
16.16 place . . called in Hebrew Armageddon
19.11 He who sat upon it is called Faithful
19.13 name by which he is called is The Word

5. *call, position:* κλῆσις KLĒSIS
[a]A.1.a
Rom 11.29 gifts and the call of God are irrevocable
1 Cor 1.26 consider your call, brethren
Eph 1.18 [a]the hope to which he has called you
4. 4 you were called to the one hope
Phil 3.14 prize of the upward call of God in Christ
2 Th 1.11 God . . make you worthy of his call
Heb 3. 1 brethren, who share in a heavenly call
2 Pet 1.10 be . . zealous to confirm your call

6. *cry out, shout:* κράζω KRAZŌ
Rev 7. 2 angel . . called with a loud voice
14.15 angel . . calling with a loud voice to him
19.17 with a loud voice he called to all the birds

7. *say, speak:* λέγω LEGŌ
Mt 1.16 Jesus . . , who is called Christ
2.23 went and dwelt in a city called Nazareth
4.18 Simon who is called Peter
9. 9 man called Matthew sitting at the tax office
10. 2 apostles . . : first, Simon, who is called Peter
13.55 "Is not his mother called Mary?
26. 3 the high priest, who was called Caiaphas
26.14 one of the twelve, who was called Judas
26.36 Jesus went . . to a place called Gethsemane
27.16 a notorious prisoner, called Barabbas[k]
27.17 "Barabbas[k] or Jesus who is called Christ?
27.22 "what shall I do with Jesus . . called Christ?
27.33 they came to a place called Golgotha
Mk 10.18 Jesus said . . "Why do you call me good?
12.37 "David himself calls him Lord
15. 7 there was a man called Barabbas
15.12 "man whom you call the King of the Jews
Lk 18.19 Jesus said . . "Why do you call me good?
20.37 "Moses . . calls the Lord the God of Abraham
22. 1 the feast . . called the Passover
22.47 man called Judas, one of the twelve
Jn 4. 5 a city of Samaria, called Sychar
4.25 "Messiah is coming (he who is called Christ
5.18 because he . . called God his own Father
9.11 "The man called Jesus made clay
11.16 Thomas, called the Twin
11.54 to a town called Ephraim
15.15 "No longer do I call you servants[h]
19.13 sat down . . at a place called The Pavement
19.17 place called the place of a skull, which is called in Hebrew Golgotha
20.24 Thomas, . . called the Twin
Acts 3. 2 that gate of the temple . . called Beautiful
6. 9 synagogue of . . Freedmen (as it was called
10.28 "I should not call any man common
24.14 "the Way, which they call a sect
Eph 2.11 Gentiles . . called the uncircumcision by what is called the circumcision
Col 4.11 Jesus who is called Justus
Heb 9. 2 the outer one . . is called the Holy Place
9. 3 a tent[p] called the Holy of Holies
11.24 Moses . . refused to be called . . son
Rev 2. 2 " 'those who call themselves apostles
2.20 " 'Jezebel, who calls herself a prophetess
2.24 " 'what some call the deep things of Satan
6.16 calling to the . . rocks, "Fall on us

8. *voice, sound:* φωνή PHŌNĒ
1 Th 4.16 Lord himself . . with the archangel's call
Rev 10. 7 days of the trumpet call to be sounded

9. *call, make a sound:* φωνέω PHŌNEŌ
Mt 20.32 Jesus stopped and called them
27.47 "This man is calling Elijah
Mk 9.35 he sat down and called the twelve
10.49 Jesus stopped and said, "Call him." And they called the blind man, saying . . "Take heart; rise, he is calling you
15.35 "Behold, he is calling Elijah
Lk 8.54 he called, saying, "Child, arise
16. 2 "he called him . . 'What is this that I hear?
19.15 "he commanded these . . to be called
Jn 1.48 "Before Philip called you . . I saw you
2. 9 steward of the feast called the bridegroom
4.16 "Go, call your husband, and come here
9.18 until they called the parents of the man
9.24 for the second time they called the man
10. 3 "he calls his own sheep by name and leads
11.28 she went and called her sister Mary
11.28 "The Teacher is here and is calling for you
12.17 when he called Lazarus out of the tomb
13.13 "You call me Teacher and Lord
18.33 Pilate entered . . and called Jesus
Acts 9.41 calling the saints . . he presented her alive
10. 7 ⟨Cornelius⟩ called two of his servants
10.18 called out to ask whether Simon . . was
Rev 14.18 angel . . called with a loud voice

10. *call on, summon:* προσκαλέω (mid.) PROSKALEŌ
Lk 15.26 "he called one of the servants and asked
Acts 13. 2 "the work to which I have called them
16.10 God had called us to preach the gospel
23.17 Paul called one of the centurions
23.18 "Paul the prisoner called me and asked me
23.23 Then he called two of the centurions

11. *call to, address:* προσφωνέω PROSPHŌNEŌ
Lk 6.13 he called his disciples, and chose
13.12 when Jesus saw her, he called her

IDIOMATICALLY

a. 1 Pet 3.15 be prepared to make a defense to any one who calls you to account ἕτοιμοι . . ἀεὶ πρὸς ἀπολογίαν παντὶ τῷ αἰτοῦντι ὑμᾶς λόγον [AITEŌ]

CONTEXTUALLY

Mk 15.22 to the place called Golgotha
Acts 13. 9 But Saul, who is also called Paul
Rev 13.10 Here is a call for . . endurance and faith
14.12 Here is a call for the endurance

CALL FOR
1. *ask, request:* αἰτέω AITEŌ
Acts 16.29 he called for lights and rushed in
2. *call on, summon:* προσκαλέω (mid.) PROSKALEŌ
Jas 5.14 Let him call for the elders of the church

CALL IN
1. *call in, invite:* εἰσκαλέομαι EISKALEOMAI*
Acts 10.23 So he called them in to be his guests
2. *call on, summon:* προσκαλέω (mid.) PROSKALEŌ
Acts 5.40 when they had called in the apostles

CALL ON
CALL UPON
1. *call, surname:* ἐπικαλέω (mid.) EPIKALEŌ
Acts 2.21 " 'whoever calls on the name of the Lord
9.14 "to bind all who call upon thy name
9.21 "those who called on this name
22.16 "Rise and be baptized, . . calling on his name
Rom 10.12 his riches upon all who call upon him
10.13 "one who calls upon the name of the Lord
10.14 But how are men to call upon him?
1 Cor 1. 2 those who in every place call on the name
2 Tim 2.22 who call upon the Lord from a pure heart

CALL ONESELF
1. *name:* ἐπονομάζω (pass.) EPONOMAZŌ
Rom 2.17 you call yourself a Jew and rely upon the law

CALL OUT
1. *cry out, shout:* κράζω KRAZŌ
Rev 10. 3 called out with a loud voice, like a lion
10. 3 when he called out, the . . thunders sounded
18. 2 he called out with a mighty voice
2. *call, make a sound:* φωνέω PHŌNEŌ
Lk 8. 8 he called out, "He who has ears to hear
16.24 "he called out, 'Father Abraham

CALL TO
1. *call to, address:* προσφωνέω PROSPHŌNEŌ
Mt 11.16 like children . . calling to their playmates
Lk 7.32 "like children . . calling to one another

CALL TO ACCOUNT
1. *examine closely:* ἀνακρίνω ANAKRINŌ
1 Cor 14.24 an unbeliever . . is called to account by all

CALL TO ONE
1. *summon* (mid.): μετακαλέω METAKALEŌ
Acts 7.14 "Joseph sent and called to him Jacob
20.17 he . . called to him the elders of the church
2. *call on, summon:* προσκαλέω (mid.) PROSKALEŌ
Mt 10. 1 he called to him his twelve disciples
15.10 he called the people to him and said . . "Hear
15.32 Then Jesus called his disciples to him
18. 2 calling . . a child he put him in the midst
20.25 Jesus called them to him
Mk 3.13 called to him those whom he desired
3.23 he called them . . and said . . in parables
6. 7 called to him the twelve, and began to send
7.14 he called the people to him again
8. 1 he called his disciples to him
8.34 And he called to him the multitude
10.42 Jesus called them to him
12.43 he called his disciples to him
Lk 7.19 John, calling to him two of his disciples
18.16 But Jesus called them to him
Acts 2.39 "every one . . the Lord our God calls to him

CALL TOGETHER
1. *convene:* συγκαλέω (act. or mid.) SYGKALEŌ*
Mk 15.16 they called together the whole battalion
Lk 9. 1 called the twelve together and gave . . power
15. 6 "calls together his friends and his neighbors
15. 9 "calls together her friends and neighbors
23.13 Pilate then called together the chief priests
Acts 5.21 high priest . . called together the council
10.24 Cornelius . . called together his kinsmen
28.17 he called together the local leaders

CALL UPON (*See* CALL ON)

CALLED
1. *call, surname:* ἐπικαλέω (pass. part.) EPIKALEŌ
Mt [10. 3 James . . and *Lebbaeus called Thaddaeus*‡
2. *call by name:* ἐπιλέγω (pass. part.) EPILEGŌ
Jn 5. 2 a pool, in Hebrew called Bethzatha[j]
3. *invited, chosen:* κλητός KLĒTOS*
Mt 22.14 "many are called, but few are chosen
Rom 1. 1 Paul, . . called to be an apostle
1. 6 who are called to belong to Jesus Christ
1. 7 To all God's beloved . . , called to be saints
8.28 God works for good[k] with those . . called
1 Cor 1. 1 Paul, called by the will of God
1. 2 sanctified in Christ Jesus, called to be saints
1.24 those who are called, both Jews and Greeks
Jude . 1 To those who are called, beloved in God
Rev 17.14 "those with him are called and chosen

IDIOMATICALLY
a. Mk 14.32 a place which was called Gethsemane
χωρίον οὗ τὸ ὄνομα Γ. [ONOMA]

CALLED, BE
1. *negotiate, order:* χρηματίζω (pass.) CHRĒMATIZŌ
Acts 11.26 in Antioch . . were . . called Christians
Rom 7. 3 Accordingly, she will be called an adulteress

CALLED, FALSELY
1. *falsely called:* ψευδώνυμος PSEUDŌNYMOS*
1 Tim 6.20 contradictions . . falsely called knowledge

CALLING
1. *call, position:* κλῆσις KLĒSIS
Eph 4. 1 lead a life worthy of the calling
2 Tim 1. 9 called us with a holy calling

CALLOUS, BECOME
1. *become callous:* ἀπαλγέω APALGEŌ*
Eph 4.19 they have become callous and . . greedy

CALM
1. *calmness:* γαλήνη GALĒNĒ*
Mt 8.26 rebuked . . the sea; and there was . . calm
Mk 4.39 wind ceased, and there was a great calm
Lk 8.24 they ceased, and there was a calm

CAMEL
1. *camel:* κάμηλος KAMĒLOS*
Mt 3. 4 John wore a garment of camel's hair
19.24 "a camel to go through the eye of a needle
23.24 "straining out a gnat and swallowing a camel!
Also Mk **10.25**; Lk **18.25**
Mk 1. 6 John was clothed with camel's hair

CAMP
1. *soldiers' quarters, company:* παρεμβολή PAREMBOLĒ
Heb 13.11 those animals . . are burned outside the camp
13.13 let us go forth to him outside the camp
Rev 20. 9 surrounded the camp of the saints

CAN
1. (particle): ἄν AN
Lk 17. 6 "you could say to this sycamine tree
2. *be able:* δύναμαι DYNAMAI
Mt 6.24 "No one can serve two masters
6.27 "by being anxious can add one cubit?
8. 2 "Lord, if you will, you can make me clean
9.15 "Can the wedding guests mourn?
10.28 "who can destroy both soul and body
12.29 "how can one enter a strong man's house?
12.34 "how can you speak good, when you are evil?
17.16 "your disciples . . could not heal him
17.19 "Why could we not cast it out?
19.25 astonished, saying, "Who then can be saved?
Mk 1.40 "If you will, you can make me clean
1.45 Jesus[g] could no longer openly enter a town
2. 4 could not get near him because of the crowd
2. 7 "Who can forgive sins but God alone?
2.19 "Can the wedding guests fast?
3.20 crowd . . so that they could not even eat
3.23 "How can Satan cast out Satan?
3.27 "no one can enter a strong man's house
4.32 "birds of the air can make nests in its shade
5. 3 no one could bind him any more
6. 5 he could do no mighty work there
6.19 wanted to kill him. But she could not

Mk 7.15 "nothing outside a man . . can defile him
7.24 yet he could not be hid
8. 4 "How can one feed these men . . here?
9. 3 as no fuller on earth could bleach them
9.22 "if you can do anything, have pity
9.23 Jesus said to him, "If you can!
9.28 "Why could we not cast it out?
10.26 "Then who can be saved?
14. 7 "whenever you will, you can do good to them
Lk 1.22 when he came out, he could not speak
5.12 "if you will, you can make me clean
5.21 "Who can forgive sins but God only?
5.34 "Can you make wedding guests fast?
6.39 "Can a blind man lead a blind man?
6.42 "how can you say to your brother?
8.19 they could not reach him for the crowd
9.40 "to cast it out, but they could not
12.25 "which . . by being anxious can add a cubit?
13.11 she . . could not fully straighten herself
16. 2 " 'you can no longer be steward
16.13 "No servant can serve two masters
18.26 "Then who can be saved?
19. 3 could not, on account of the crowd
Jn 1.46 "Can anything good come out of Nazareth?
3. 2 "no one can do these signs that you do
3. 4 "How can a man be born when he is old?
3. 4 "Can he enter . . into his mother's womb?
3. 9 Nicodemus said . . "How can this be?
3.27 "No one can receive . . except what is given
5.19 "the Son can do nothing of his own accord
5.30 "I can do nothing on my own authority
5.44 "How can you believe?
6.44 "No one can come to me unless
6.52 "How can this man give us his flesh?
6.60 "This is a hard saying; who can listen to it?
6.65 "no one can come to me unless it is granted
9. 4 "night comes, when no one can work
9.16 "How can . . a sinner do such signs?
9.33 "If . . not from God, he could do nothing
10.21 "Can a demon open the eyes of the blind?
11.37 "Could not he who opened the eyes?
12.39 Therefore they could not believe
15. 5 "for apart from me you can do nothing
Acts 8.31 "How can I, unless some one guides me?
10.47 "Can any one forbid water for baptizing?
13.39 "you could not be freed by the law of Moses
19.40 "no cause that we can give to justify this
21.34 he could not learn the facts
24.13 "Neither can they prove to you
25.11 "no one can give me up to them. I appeal
26.32 "This man could have been set free
27.12 that somehow they could reach Phoenix
27.15 the ship . . could not face the wind
27.43 He ordered those who could swim
1 Cor 3. 1 could not address you as spiritual men
3.11 For no other foundation can any one lay
7.21 if you can gain your freedom
12. 3 no one can say "Jesus is Lord" except
14.31 you can all prophesy one by one
2 Cor 3. 7 Israelites could not look at Moses' face
Gal 3.21 for if a law . . could make alive
Eph 3. 4 you can perceive my insight
6.16 you can quench all the flaming darts
1 Th 3. 9 what thanksgiving can we render to God?
1 Tim 6.16 whom no man has ever seen or can see
2 Tim 3. 7 can never arrive at a knowledge of the truth
Heb 5. 2 He can deal gently with the ignorant
10. 1 the law . . can never . . make perfect
10.11 sacrifices, which can never take away sins
Jas 2.14 Can his faith save him?
3. 8 no human being can tame the tongue
3.12 Can a fig tree, my brethren, yield olives?
Rev 6.17 "who can stand before it?
7. 9 multitude which no man could number
13. 4 "who can fight against ⟨the beast⟩?
13.17 no one can buy . . unless he has the mark
14. 3 No one could learn that song except
Rev 15. 8 no one could enter the temple until

3. *possible, strong:* δυνατός (+inf.) DYNATOS
Acts 11.17 "who was I that I could withstand God?

4. *have, hold:* ἔχω ECHŌ [A.6.a.5]
Mt 18.25 "as he could not pay, his lord ordered
Mk 14. 8 "she has done what she could
Lk 7.42 "When they could not pay, he forgave

5. *be strong, prevail:* ἰσχύω ISCHYŌ
Mt 8.28 so fierce that no one could pass that way
26.40 "So, could you not watch[h] . . one hour?
Mk 14.37 "Could you not watch[d] one hour?
Lk 6.48 "the stream . . could not shake ⟨that house⟩
8.43 woman who . . could not be healed by any
14. 6 they could not reply to this
Acts 6.10 they could not withstand the wisdom
25. 7 serious charges which they could not prove
Phil 4.13 I can do all things in him

6. *know:* οἶδα OIDA
Mt 27.65 "make it as secure as you can[p]†

IDIOMATICALLY
a. Rom 7.18 I can will what is right τὸ γὰρ θέλειν παράκειταί μοι . . τὸ καλόν [PARAKEIMAI]
b. 2 Cor 2.13 but my mind could not rest οὐκ ἔσχηκα ἄνεσιν τῷ πνεύματί μου [ECHŌ]

CONTEXTUALLY
Mt 19.11 "Not all men can receive this saying
Acts 19.36 "these things cannot be contradicted
Rom 11.10 "be darkened so that they cannot see
1 Cor 6. 5 Can it be that there is no man among you
7. 9 But if they cannot exercise self-control
Tit 2. 8 sound speech that cannot be censured
Heb 9. 5 Of these things we cannot now speak

CANA: Κανά 'kānə I,C-3
Jn 2. 1 there was a marriage at Cana in Galilee
2.11 the first of his signs, Jesus did at Cana
4.46 So he came again to Cana in Galilee
21. 2 Nathanael of Cana in Galilee

CANAAN: Χανάαν 'kānən
Acts 7.11 "a famine throughout all Egypt and Canaan
13.19 "destroyed seven nations in the land of C.

CANAANITE: Χαναναῖος
Mt 15.22 a Canaanite woman . . cried, "Have mercy

CANANAEAN: Καναναῖος
Mt 10. 4 Simon the Cananaean, and Judas Iscariot
Mk 3.18 Thaddaeus, and Simon the Cananaean

CANCEL
1. *wipe out:* ἐξαλείφω EXALEIPHŌ
Col 2.14 having canceled the bond . . against us

CANDACE: Κανδάκη 'kandəsē, kan'dāsē
Acts 8.27 a eunuch, a minister of the Candace

CANNOT
1. *impossible, weak:* ἀδύνατος (subst.) ADYNATOS [A.1.a]
Rom 8. 3 God has done what the law . . could not do

2. *not be able:* οὐ δύναμαι DYNAMAI [B.3.b.4]
[a]μή [b]οὐδείς [c]οὐδέ [d]οὔτε *cannot either*
Mt 5.14 "a city set on a hill cannot be hid
5.36 "you cannot make one hair white or black
6.24 "You cannot serve God and mammon[z]
7.18 "A sound tree cannot bear evil fruit
10.28 [a]"who kill the body but cannot kill the soul
16. 3 "you cannot interpret the signs of the times‡
26.42 "if this cannot pass unless I drink it
26.53 "Do you think that I cannot appeal?
27.42 "He saved others; he cannot save himself
Mk 2.19 "they have the bridegroom . . , they cannot
3.24 "divided . . that kingdom cannot stand
3.26 "Satan . . is divided, he cannot stand
7.18 "whatever goes into a man . . cannot defile
9.29 [b]"cannot be driven out by anything but
15.31 "He saved others; he cannot save himself
Lk 11. 7 " 'I cannot get up and give you anything
14.20 " 'I married a wife, and . . cannot come
14.26 "he cannot be my disciple
14.27 "Whoever does not . . cannot be my disciple
14.33 "whoever . . does not . . cannot be my disciple

Lk 16.13 "You cannot serve God and mammon[a]
20.36 [c]"they cannot die any more
Jn 3. 3 "he cannot see the kingdom of God
3. 5 "unless . . born of water . . he cannot enter
7. 7 "world cannot hate you, but it hates me
7.34 "where I am you cannot come
7.36 " 'Where I am you cannot come
8.21 "where I am going, you cannot come
8.22 " 'Where I am going, you cannot come
8.43 "because you cannot bear to hear my word
10.35 "(scripture cannot be broken
13.33 " 'Where I am going you cannot come
13.36 "Where I am going you cannot follow
13.37 "Lord, why cannot I follow you now?
14.17 "Spirit of truth . . the world cannot receive
15. 4 "the branch cannot bear fruit by itself
16.12 "but you cannot bear them now
Acts 4.16 "a notable sign . . and we cannot deny it
4.20 "we cannot but speak of what we have seen
15. 1 "Unless . . circumcised . . you cannot be saved
27.31 [c]"Unless these . . stay . . you cannot be saved
Rom 8. 7 mind . . set on the flesh . . cannot ⟨submit⟩
8. 8 who are in the flesh cannot please God
1 Cor 10.21 cannot drink the cup of the Lord
10.21 cannot partake of the table of the Lord
12.21 eye cannot say . . "I have no need of you
15 50 flesh and blood cannot inherit the kingdom
2 Cor 13. 8 we cannot do anything against the truth
1 Tim 5.25 good deeds . . cannot remain hidden
6. 7 [c]we cannot take anything out of the world
2 Tim 2.13 remains faithful . . he cannot deny himself
Heb 9. 9 [a]sacrifices are offered which cannot perfect
Jas 4. 2 you covet[d] and cannot obtain
1 Jn 3. 9 he cannot sin because he is[g] born of God
4.20 does not love . . brother . . cannot[h] love God
Rev 2. 2 " 'you cannot bear evil men
9.20 [d]which cannot either see or hear or walk

3. *not have:* οὐκ ἔχειν ECHŌ [B.3.b.4]
Lk 14.14 "because they cannot repay you
4. *not:* μή MĒ [A.4.c]
Rom 11.10 "darkened so that they cannot see
Heb 12.27 that what cannot be shaken may remain
5. *not, no:* οὐ OU [A.4.c]
[a]οὐκ ἔστιν
Rom **7.18**
1 Cor **7.9**
Phil **1.22**
Col **3.11**
Heb **9.5**[a]

IDIOMATICALLY
a. Acts 14.8 there was a man . . who could not use his feet
τὶς ἀνὴρ ἀδύνατος . . τοῖς ποσίν [ADYNATOS]

CANNOT BE, IT
1. *be possible:* ἐνδέχομαι (impers. + neg.) ENDECHOMAI
Lk 13.33 " 'it cannot be . . away from Jerusalem

CAPERNAUM: Καφαρναούμ kə'pərnēəm I,D-3
Mt 4.13 leaving Nazareth he went and dwelt in C.
8. 5 As he entered C., a centurion came forward
11.23 "And you, C., will you be exalted in heaven?
17.24 When they came to C., the collectors . . said
Mk 1.21 And they went into Capernaum
2. 1 when he returned to C. . . it was reported
9.33 And they came to Capernaum
Lk 4.23 " 'what we . . heard you did at C., do here
4.31 he went down to C., a city of Galilee
7. 1 After he had ended . . he entered C.
10.15 "you, C., will you be exalted to heaven?
Jn 2.12 After this he went down to C.
4.46 at C. . . was an official whose son was ill
6.17 ⟨disciples⟩ started across the sea to C.
6.24 they . . went to C., seeking Jesus
6.59 he said in the synagogue, as . . at C.

CAPPADOCIA: Καππαδοκία ,kapə'dōsh(ē)ə II,G-3
Acts 2. 9 "residents of Mesopotamia, Judea and C.
1 Pet 1. 1 To the exiles of the Dispersion in . . C.

CAPTAIN
CAPTAIN, CHIEF
1. *captain over a thousand:* χιλίαρχος CHILIARCHOS
Jn 18.12 soldiers and their captain . . seized Jesus
Acts [24. 7 "*the chief captain Lysias came*‡
Rev 19.18 "to eat the flesh of kings, . . of captains
2. *steersman, pilot:* κυβερνήτης KYBERNĒTĒS
Acts 27.11 centurion paid more attention to the captain
3. *leader, magistrate:* στρατηγός STRATĒGOS
Acts 4. 1 priests and the captain of the temple
5.24 captain of the temple and the chief priests
5.26 captain with the officers . . brought them

CAPTIVE
1. *captive:* αἰχμάλωτος AICHMALŌTOS*
Lk 4.18 "to proclaim release to the captives

CAPTIVE, HOLD
1. *hold fast, restrain:* κατέχω KATECHŌ
Rom 7. 6 dead to that which held us captive

CAPTIVE, LEAD
CAPTIVE, MAKE
CAPTIVE, TAKE
1. *captivity:* αἰχμαλωσία AICHMALŌSIA [B.1.a.1]
Rev 13.10 If any one is to be taken captive
2. *take prisoner:* αἰχμαλωτίζω AICHMALŌTIZŌ
Lk 21.24 "they will . . be led captive among all nations
Rom 7.23 making me captive to the law of sin
2 Cor 10. 5 take every thought captive to obey Christ

CAPTIVES, A HOST OF
1. *captivity:* αἰχμαλωσία AICHMALŌSIA [C.2]
Eph 4. 8 "When he ascended . . he led a host of c.

CAPTIVITY
1. *captivity:* αἰχμαλωσία AICHMALŌSIA
Rev 13.10 If . . one is to be taken . . to captivity he goes

CAPTURE
1. *take prisoner:* αἰχμαλωτίζω AICHMALŌTIZŌ
2 Tim 3. 6 capture weak women, burdened with sins
2. *take hold of:* πιάζω PIAZŌ
Rev 19.20 the beast was captured
3. *gather, seize, conceive:* συλλαμβάνω SYLLAMBANŌ
Mt 26.55 "Have you come . . to capture me?
Mk 14.48 "Have you come out . . to capture me?
4. *take captive:* ζωγρέω ZŌGREŌ
2 Tim 2.26 after being captured by him to do his will[c]

CARE
1. *look upon, visit:* ἐπισκέπτομαι EPISKEPTOMAI
Heb 2. 6 "son of man, that thou carest for him
2. *care:* μέλει MELEI [A.6.c.3]
Mt 22.16 "you are true . . and care for no man
Mk 4.38 "Teacher, do you not care if we perish?
12.14 "you are true, and care for no man
Lk 10.40 "do you not care that my sister has left me?
Jn 10.13 "a hireling . . cares nothing for the sheep
12. 6 he said, not that he cared for the poor
1 Pet 5. 7 he cares about you

CARE, EARNEST
1. *zeal, haste:* σπουδή SPOUDĒ
2 Cor 8.16 God . . puts the same earnest care for you

CARE FOR
1. *take care of:* ἐπιμελέομαι EPIMELEOMAI
1 Tim 3. 5 how can he care for God's church?
2. *tend, herd, govern:* ποιμαίνω POIMAINŌ
Acts 20.28 "made you overseers, to care for the church[o]
3. *bring nourishment, sustain:* τροφοφορέω TROPHOPHOREŌ
Acts [13.18 "he *cared for* them in the wilderness‡

CARE, HAVE
1. *be anxious, care for:* μεριμνάω MERIMNAŌ
1 Cor 12.25 members . . have . . care for one another

CARE OF, TAKE
1. *take care of:* ἐπιμελέομαι EPIMELEOMAI
Lk 10.34 "brought him to an inn, and took care of him
10.35 " 'Take care of him; . . I will repay you
2. *warm, cherish:* θάλπω THALPŌ
1 Th 2. 7 like a nurse taking care of her children

CARE, TAKE
1. *see, look:* βλέπω (imper.) BLEPŌ
1 Cor 3.10 Let each man take care how he builds
8. 9 take c. lest this . . become a stumbling block
Heb 3.12 Take care . . lest there be . . an evil . . heart

CARE WHAT ONE DOES, TAKE
1. *take heed to oneself:* προσέχειν ἑαυτῷ PROSECHŌ [B.2.d.1]
Acts 5.35 "Men of Israel, take care what you do

CARED FOR, BE
1. *receive attention:* ἐπιμελείας τυγχάνειν EPIMELEIA*; TYGCHANŌ [B.2.d.2]
Acts 27. 3 to go to his friends and be cared for

CAREFUL, BE
1. *consider, give heed:* φροντίζω PHRONTIZŌ*
Tit 3. 8 may be careful to apply . . to good deeds[d]
2. *consider, look out for:* σκοπέω SKOPEŌ
Lk 11.35 "be careful lest the light in you be darkness

CAREFULLY
1. *precisely:* ἀκριβῶς AKRIBŌS
Eph 5.15 Look carefully then how you walk

CARELESS
1. *idle:* ἀργός ARGOS
Mt 12.36 "account for every careless word they utter

CARES
1. *anxious mind, cares:* μέριμνα (sg. or pl.) MERIMNA
Mt 13.22 "cares of the world . . delight in riches
Mk 4.19 "cares of the world, . . delight in riches
Lk 8.14 "they are choked by the cares and riches
21.34 "drunkenness and cares of this life

CARGO (*See also* THROW CARGO OVERBOARD)
1. *cargo:* γόμος GOMOS*
Acts 21. 3 there the ship was to unload its cargo
Rev 18.11 no one buys their cargo any more
18.12 cargo of gold, silver, jewels and pearls
2. *burden, load:* φορτίον PHORTION
Acts 27.10 "loss, not only of the cargo . . but . . lives

CARNAL
1. *fleshly:* σάρκινος SARKINOS
Rom 7.14 I am carnal, sold under sin

CARNELIAN
1. *Sardian stone:* σάρδιον SARDION*
Rev 4. 3 he . . appeared like jasper and carnelian
21.20 the fifth onyx, the sixth carnelian

CAROUSE
1. *feast together:* συνευωχέομαι SYNEUŌCHEOMAI*
2 Pet 2.13 reveling in their dissipation,[g] carousing
Jude .12 blemishes[d] . . as they boldly carouse together

CAROUSING
1. *revelry:* κῶμος (pl.) KŌMOS
Gal 5.21 envy,[k] drunkenness, carousing, and the like
2. *drinking party:* πότος POTOS*
1 Pet 4. 3 passions, drunkenness, revels, carousing

CARPENTER
1. *woodworker, builder:* τέκτων TEKTŌN*
Mt 13.55 "Is not this the carpenter's son?
Mk 6. 3 "Is not this the carpenter, the son of Mary?

CARPUS: Κάρπος 'kärpəs
2 Tim 4.13 the cloak that I left with Carpus at Troas

CARRIED AWAY BY, BE
CARRIED AWAY WITH, BE
1. *lead away with:* συναπάγω (pass.) SYNAPAGŌ
Gal 2.13 Barnabas was c. away by their insincerity
2 Pet 3.17 lest you be carried away with the error

CARRY
1. *lift, carry away:* αἴρω AIRŌ
Mt 27.32 this man they compelled to carry his cross
Mk 2. 3 bringing . . a paralytic carried by four men
15.21 compelled . . Simon . . to carry his cross
Jn 5.10 "not lawful for you to carry your pallet
2. *carry away:* ἀποφέρω APOPHERŌ
Lk 16.22 "carried by . . angels to Abraham's bosom
1 Cor 16. 3 I will send those . . to c. your gift to Jerusalem
3. *lift up, carry:* βαστάζω BASTAZŌ
Mt 3.11 "whose sandals I am not worthy to carry
Mk 14.13 "man carrying a jar of water will meet you
Lk 10. 4 "Carry no purse, no bag, no sandals
22.10 "a man carrying a jar of water will meet you
Jn 20.15 "Sir, if you have carried him away, tell me
Acts 3. 2 a man lame from birth was being carried
9.15 "chosen . . to c. my name before the Gentiles
21.35 he was actually carried by the soldiers
Rev 17. 7 "beast with seven heads . . that carries her
4. *carry around:* περιφέρω PERIPHERŌ
2 Cor 4.10 carrying in the body the death of Jesus
Eph 4.14 carried about with every wind of doctrine
5. *bring, bear:* φέρω PHERŌ
Lk 23.26 seized . . Simon . . to carry ⟨the cross⟩
Jn 21.18 "another will gird you and carry you
CONTEXTUALLY
Acts 27.43 kept them from carrying out their purpose

CARRY ALONG
1. *carry away:* παραφέρω PARAPHERŌ
Jude .12 waterless clouds, carried along by winds

CARRY AWAY
1. *carry away:* ἀποφέρω APOPHERŌ
Acts 19.12 aprons were carried away . . to the sick
Rev 17. 3 he carried me away in the Spirit
21.10 in the Spirit he carried me away

CARRY BACK
1. *transpose, change:* μετατίθημι METATITHĒMI
Acts 7.16 "they were carried back to Shechem

CARRY ON (*See also* WAR, CARRY ON A)
1. *do a service, minister:* διακονέω DIAKONEŌ
2 Cor 8.19 gracious work which we are carrying on

CARRY OUT
1. *carry out:* ἐκκομίζω EKKOMIZŌ*
Lk 7.12 a man who had died was being carried out
2. *carry out:* ἐκφέρω EKPHERŌ
Acts 5. 6 rose . . and carried him out and buried him
5. 9 "Hark, . . they will carry you out
5.10 they carried her out and buried her
5.15 they . . carried out the sick into the streets
3. *do, make:* ποιέω POIEŌ
Rev 17.17 "into their hearts to carry out his purpose

CARRY THROUGH
1. *carry through, differ:* διαφέρω DIAPHERŌ
Mk 11.16 to carry anything through the temple

CARRY UP
1. *bring, carry up:* ἀναφέρω ANAPHERŌ
Lk 24.51 he . . was carried up into heaven[a]‡
1 Pet [2.24 He himself *carried up* our sins†

CARVE
1. *carve upon:* ἐντυπόω ENTYPOŌ*
2 Cor 3. 7 dispensation of death, carved . . on stone

CASE
1. *charge, cause:* αἰτία AITIA
Mt 19.10 "If such is the case of a man with his wife
2. *lawsuit, lawcourt:* κριτήριον KRITĒRION
1 Cor 6. 2 are you incompetent to try trivial cases?
6. 4 If then you have such cases, why?
3. *part, share:* μέρος MEROS
2 Cor 3.10 in this case, what once had splendor
9. 3 may not prove vain in this case
CONTEXTUALLY
Mt 13.23 "in one c. a hundredfold . . another sixty
Acts 23.15 "you were going to determine his case
24.22 "I will decide your case
25.14 Festus laid Paul's case before the king
25.18 "they brought no charge in his case
1 Cor 7.15 in such a c. the brother or sister
2 Cor 4. 4 In their case the god of this world
Tit 3.14 so as to help cases of urgent need
Heb 6. 9 in your case, beloved, we feel sure
1 Pet 2.12 in c. they speak against you as wrongdoers

CASE BEFORE, LAY ONE'S
1. *manifest, make clear:* ἐμφανίζω EMPHANIZŌ
Acts 24. 1 They laid before the governor their case

CASE, IN

CASE, IN ONE

1. *who, which, what:* ὅς HOS
[a]ὃ μέν A.5.a [b]ἐν ᾧ B.1.b
Mt **13.23**[a]
1 Pet **2.12**[b]

CASE, IN THAT

1. *then:* ἄρα ARA II
Gal 5.11 In that case . . the cross has been removed

CAST (*See also* LOTS, CAST)

1. *throw, put:* βάλλω BALLŌ
Mt 4.18 Peter . . casting a net into the sea
17.27 "cast a hook, and take the first fish
21.21 " 'Be taken up and cast into the sea
27.35 divided his garments . . by casting lots
Mk 9.22 "it has often cast him into the fire
11.23 " 'Be taken up and cast into the sea
15.24 divided his garments . . casting lots
Lk 12.49 "I came to cast fire upon the earth
23.34 And they cast lots to divide his garments
Jn 15. 6 "he is cast forth as a branch and withers
19.24 "for my clothing they cast lots
21. 6 "Cast the net on the right side
21. 6 cast it and . . were not able to haul it in
1 Jn 4.18 perfect love casts out fear
Rev 4.10 they cast their crowns before the throne
12. 4 His tail swept . . and cast them to the earth
2. *give:* δίδωμι DIDŌMI
Acts 1.26 they cast lots . . and the lot fell on Matthias
3. *throw out:* ἐκβάλλω EKBALLŌ
Mt 22.13 " 'cast him into the outer darkness
25.30 "cast the . . servant into . . outer darkness
4. *throw in:* ἐμβάλλω EMBALLŌ*
Lk 12. 5 "fear him who . . has power to cast into hell[m]
5. *throw, cast out:* ῥίπτω RHIPTŌ
Lk 17. 2 "better . . if . . he were cast into the sea

CAST A NET

1. *throw around:* ἀμφιβάλλω AMPHIBALLŌ*
Mk 1.16 he saw Simon . . casting a net in the sea

CAST AGAINST

1. *bring down, sink:* καταφέρω KATAPHERŌ
Acts 26.10 "I cast my vote against them

CAST INTO HELL

1. *cast into Tartarus:* ταρταρόω TARTAROŌ*
2 Pet 2. 4 if God . . cast them into hell[f]†

CAST OFF

1. *put away:* ἀποτίθημι (mid.) APOTITHĒMI
Rom 13.12 Let us then cast off the works of darkness
2. *take away, strip off:* περιαιρέω PERIAIREŌ
Acts 27.40 cast off the anchors and left them in the sea

CAST ON

1. *throw upon:* ἐπιρίπτω EPIRIPTŌ
[a]+ἐπί
1 Pet 5. 7 [a]Cast all your anxieties on him

CAST OUT

1. *throw out:* ἐκβάλλω EKBALLŌ
[a]+ἐκ [b]+ἔξω
Mt 7.22 " 'did we not . . cast out demons in your name?
8.16 he cast out the spirits with a word
8.31 "If you cast us out, send us . . into the herd
9.33 when the demon had been cast out
9.34 "He c. out demons by the prince of demons[a]‡
10. 1 authority . . to cast . . out ⟨unclean spirits⟩
10. 8 "cleanse lepers, cast out demons
12.24 "by Beelzebul . . this man casts out demons
12.26 "if Satan casts out Satan, he is divided
12.27 "if I cast out demons by Beelzebul, by whom do your sons cast them out?
12.28 "if . . by the Spirit of God . . I cast out demons
17.19 "Why could we not cast it out?
21.39 [b]" 'took him and cast him out of the vineyard
Mk 1.34 he healed . . and cast out many demons
1.39 throughout all Galilee . . casting out demons
3.15 have authority to cast out demons
3.22 "by Beelzebul . . he casts out the demons
3.23 "How can Satan cast out Satan?
6.13 they cast out many demons, and anointed
7.26 [a]she begged him to cast the demon out
9.18 "I asked your disciples to cast it out
9.28 "Why could we not cast it out?
9.38 "a man casting out demons in your name[k]
12. 8 [b]"took him . . and cast him out of the vineyard
16. 9 from whom he had cast out . . demons[k]‡
16.17 "in my name they will cast out demons[k]‡
Lk 6.22 "when men . . cast out your name as evil!
9.40 "I begged your disciples to cast it out
9.49 "a man casting out demons in your name
11.14 "casting out a demon that was dumb
11.15 "He casts out demons by Beelzebul
11.18 "you say that I c. out demons by Beelzebul
11.19 "if I cast out demons by Beelzebul, by whom do your sons cast them out?
11.20 "if . . by . . finger of God . . I cast out demons
13.32 "tell that fox, 'Behold, I cast out demons
20.12 "this one they wounded and cast out
20.15 [b]"cast him out of the vineyard and killed him
Jn 6.37 [b]"him who comes to me I will not cast out
9.34 [b]"would you teach us?" . . they cast him out
9.35 [b]Jesus heard that they had cast him out
12.31 [b]"now shall the ruler of this world be c. out
Acts 7.58 [b]they cast him out of the city and stoned
16.37 "do they now cast us out secretly? No!
Gal 4.30 "Cast out the slave and her son
2. *throw, cast out:* ῥίπτω RHIPTŌ
Acts 27.19 the third day they cast out . . the tackle

CAST UP

1. *put in beside:* παρεμβάλλω PAREMBALLŌ*
Lk 19.43 "your enemies will cast up a bank about you

CAST UP THE FOAM OF

1. *foam up:* ἐπαφρίζω EPAPHRIZŌ*
Jude .13 waves . . casting up the foam of their . . shame

CATCH

1. *prey:* ἄγρα AGRA*
Lk 5. 4 "let down your nets for a catch
5. 9 he was astonished . . at the catch of fish
2. *grasp, seize:* δράσσομαι DRASSOMAI*
1 Cor 3.19 "He catches the wise in their craftiness
3. *take, lay hold of:* ἐπιλαμβάνομαι EPILAMBANOMAI
Mt 14.31 caught him, saying . . "O man of little faith
Lk 20.26 not able . . to catch him by what he said
4. *catch:* καταλαμβάνω KATALAMBANŌ
Jn 8. 3 woman who had been caught in adultery[r]‡
8. 4 "has been caught in the act of adultery[r]‡
5. *take hold of:* πιάζω PIAZŌ
Jn 21. 3 but that night they caught nothing
21.10 "Bring some of the fish . . you have . . caught
6. *snatch and carry away with:* συναρπάζω SYNARPAZŌ
Acts 27.15 when the ship was caught . . we gave way
7. *hunt, catch:* θηρεύω THĒREUŌ*
Lk 11.54 to catch at something he might say
8. *take captive:* ζωγρέω ZŌGREŌ
Lk 5.10 "henceforth you will be catching men

CATCH UP

1. *seize, snatch up:* ἁρπάζω HARPAZŌ
Acts 8.39 the Spirit of the Lord caught up Philip
2 Cor 12. 2 a man in Christ . . caught up to . . heaven
12. 3(4) this man was caught up into Paradise
1 Th 4.17 we . . shall be caught up together with them
Rev 12. 5 her child was caught up to God

CATTLE

1. *beast:* κτῆνος (pl.) KTĒNOS
Rev 18.13 flour and wheat, cattle and sheep
2. *animals:* θρέμμα THREMMA*
Jn 4.12 "Jacob . . and his sons, and his cattle

CAUDA: Καῦδα 'kōdə II,D-4
Acts 27.16 under the lee of . . island called Cauda[b]‡

CAUGHT, TO BE

1. *capture:* ἅλωσις HALŌSIS* [B.1.a.2]
2 Pet 2.12 creatures of instinct, born to be caught

CAUSE (*See also* FALL, CAUSE TO; FALLING, BE A CAUSE OF S.'S; GLORY, CAUSE TO; PAIN, CAUSE; RUIN OF, CAUSE THE; SIN, CAUSE OF; SIN, CAUSE S. TO; STUMBLING, CAUSE FOR; TROUBLE, CAUSE)
1. *charge, cause:* αἰτία AITIA
Mt 19. 3 "lawful to divorce one's wife for any cause?
2. *responsible:* αἴτιος (subst. neut.) AITIOS
Acts 19.40 "no cause . . to justify this commotion
3. *origin, occasion:* ἀφορμή APHORMĒ
2 Cor 5.12 giving you cause to be proud of us
4. *do in order that:* ποιεῖν ἵνα POIEŌ [B.2.a.1]
Rev 13.15 cause those who would not . . to be slain
13.16 causes all . . to be marked on the right hand

CAUSE, WITHOUT
CAUSE, WITHOUT A
1. *freely, as a gift:* δωρεάν DŌREAN
Jn 15.25 " 'They hated me without a cause
2. *without purpose:* εἰκῇ EIKĒ
Mt [5.22 "who is angry with his brother *w. cause*‡

CAUSES, WHAT
1. *whence, from what:* πόθεν POTHEN
Jas 4. 1 What causes wars, and what causes fightings among you?

CAUTION
1. *command:* διαστέλλω (mid.) DIASTELLŌ
Mk 8.15 he cautioned them, saying, "Take heed

CAVALRY
1. *of a horse:* ἱππικός (subst. neut.) HIPPIKOS*
Rev 9.16 of . . troops of cavalry . . twice ten thousand

CAVE
1. *hole, opening:* ὀπή OPĒ
Heb 11.38 in dens and caves of the earth
2. *grotto, cave:* σπήλαιον SPĒLAION
Jn 11.38 Jesus . . came to the tomb; it was a cave
Rev 6.15 every one . . hid in the caves

CEASE
1. *have rest:* ἀνάπαυσιν ἔχειν ANAPAUSIS [B.2.a.1]
Rev 4. 8 four living creatures . . never cease to sing
2. *leave an interval:* διαλείπω DIALEIPŌ*
Lk 7.45 "she has not ceased to kiss my feet
3. *be quiet, be at rest:* ἡσυχάζω HĒSYCHAZŌ
Acts 21.14 when he would not be persuaded, we ceased
4. *stand, set:* ἵστημι (2 aor.) HISTĒMI
Lk 8.44 immediately her flow of blood ceased
5. *stop, rest:* καταπαύω KATAPAUŌ
Heb 4.10 whoever enters . . ceases from his labors
6. *grow weary, abate:* κοπάζω KOPAZŌ*
Mt 14.32 they got into the boat, the wind ceased
Mk 4.39 "Peace! Be still!" And the wind ceased
6.51 he got into the boat . . and the wind ceased
7. *cease, stop:* παύω (mid.) PAUŌ
Lk 5. 4 when he had ceased speaking
8.24 the wind and the raging waves . . ceased
11. 1 He was praying . . and when he ceased
Acts 5.42 they did not cease teaching
6.13 "This man never ceases to speak . . against
20. 1 uproar ceased, Paul sent for the disciples
20.31 "I did not cease night or day to admonish
1 Cor 13. 8 as for tongues, they will cease
Eph 1.16 I do not cease to give thanks for you
Col 1. 9 we have not ceased to pray for you
Heb 10. 2 would they not have ceased to be offered?
1 Pet 4. 1 whoever has suffered . . has ceased from sin
8. *dry up:* ξηραίνω (pass.) XĒRAINŌ
Mk 5.29 immediately the hemorrhage ceased

CEASING, WITHOUT
1. *unceasingly:* ἀδιαλείπτως ADIALEIPTŌS
Rom 1. 9 without c. I mention you . . in my prayers

CELEBRATE THE FESTIVAL
1. *celebrate a festival:* ἑορτάζω HEORTAZŌ*
1 Cor 5. 8 Let us, therefore, celebrate the festival

CELESTIAL
1. *heavenly:* ἐπουράνιος EPOURANIOS
1 Cor 15.40 There are celestial bodies and . . terrestrial
15.40 glory of . . c. is one, . . terrestrial . . another

CELL
1. *room, prison:* οἴκημα OIKĒMA*
Acts 12. 7 a light shone in the cell

CELLAR
1. *a hidden place:* κρύπτη KRYPTĒ*
Lk 11.33 "No one . . puts ⟨a lamp⟩ in a cellar

CENCHREAE: Κεγχρεαί 'seŋkrēə, seŋ'krēə II,D-3
Acts 18.18 At C. he cut his hair, for he had a vow
Rom 16. 1 Phoebe, a deaconess of the church at C.

CENSER
1. *frankincense, censer:* λιβανωτός LIBANŌTOS*
Rev 8. 3 angel . . stood . . with a golden censer
8. 5 angel took the censer and filled it with fire

CENSURED, THAT CANNOT BE
1. *not to be condemned:* ἀκατάγνωστος AKATAGNŌSTOS*
Tit 2. 8 sound speech that cannot be censured

CENSUS
1. *register, list:* ἀπογραφή APOGRAPHĒ
Acts 5.37 "Judas . . arose in the days of the census

CENTURION
1. *leader of a hundred:* ἑκατοντάρχης HEKATONTARCHĒS*
Mt 8. 5 a centurion came forward to him
8. 8 centurion answered . . "Lord, I am not worthy
8.13 to the centurion . . "Go; be it done for you
27.54 c. . . said, "Truly . . the Son[x] of God!
Lk 7. 2 centurion had a slave . . dear[x] to him
7. 6 c. sent friends . . "do not trouble
23.47 the centurion saw . . he praised God
Acts 10. 1 Cornelius, a c. of . . the Italian Cohort
10.22 "Cornelius, a centurion, an upright . . man
21.32 He at once took soldiers and centurions
22.25 Paul said to the centurion . . "Is it lawful?
22.26 c. said . . "What are you about to do?
23.17 Paul called one of the centurions
23.23 he called two of the centurions
24.23 Then he gave orders to the centurion
27. 1 they delivered Paul . . to a centurion
27. 6 centurion found a ship of Alexandria
27.11 centurion paid more attention to . . captain
27.31 said to the c. . . "Unless these men stay
27.43 the centurion, wishing to save Paul
2. *centurion* (Lat.): κεντυρίων KENTYRIŌN*
Mk 15.39 c. . . "Truly this man was the Son[x] of God!
15.44 summoning the centurion, he asked him
15.45 learned from the c. that he was dead

CEPHAS: Κηφᾶς 'sēfəs
Jn 1.42 "You shall be called Cephas
1 Cor 1.12 "I belong to Cephas," or "I . . to Christ
3.22 whether Paul or Apollos or Cephas
9. 5 right to be accompanied by a wife,[n] as . . C.?
15. 5 he appeared to Cephas, then to the twelve
Gal 1.18 I went up to Jerusalem to visit Cephas
2. 9 grace that was given to me, James and C.
2.11 when C. came to Antioch I opposed him
2.14 I said to C. . . "If you . . live like a Gentile

CERTAIN (*See also* SEASON, CERTAIN)
1. *clear:* δῆλος DĒLOS
1 Tim [6. 7 *it is c. that* we cannot take anything‡
2. *anyone, any:* τὶς TIS II
Lk **7.41**; **11.1**; **18.2**
Acts **13.6**; **25.19**
Heb **4.7**

CERTAIN MAN
1. *anyone, any:* τὶς TIS II
Jn **11.1**
Gal **2.12**

CERTAIN ONE
1. *such a one, so and so:* δεῖνα DEINA*
Mt 26.18 "Go into the city to a certain one[o]

CERTAIN PERSON
1. *anyone, any:* τὶς TIS II
1 Tim **1.3**, **6**, **19**

CERTAINLY
1. *of a truth:* ἐπ' ἀληθείας ALĒTHEIA [B.1.a.1]
Lk 22.59 "Certainly this man also was with him
2. *truly:* ἀληθῶς ALĒTHŌS
Mt 26.73 "Certainly you are also one of them
Mk 14.70 "Certainly you are one of them
3. *but:* ἀλλά ALLA
Rom 6. 5 we shall certainly be united with him
4. *actually, really:* ὄντως ONTŌS
Lk 23.47 "Certainly this man was innocent!
5. *in all ways, assuredly:* πάντως PANTŌS
Acts 21.22 "They will certainly hear

CERTAINLY NOT
1. *may it not be:* μὴ γένοιτο MĒ; GINOMAI [B.3.b.8]
Gal 2.17 is Christ . . an agent of sin? Certainly not!
3.21 against the promises of God? Certainly not!

CERTIFICATE
1. *document, book:* βιβλίον BIBLION
Mt 19. 7 "Why then . . a certificate of divorce?
Mk 10. 4 "allowed a man to write a certificate

CERTIFICATE OF DIVORCE
1. *divorce, bill of divorce:* ἀποστάσιον APOSTASION
Mt 5.31 " 'let him give her a certificate of divorce

CHAFF
1. *chaff:* ἄχυρον ACHYRON*
Mt 3.12 "chaff he will burn with unquenchable fire
Lk 3.17 "chaff he will burn with unquenchable fire

CHAIN
1. *bond:* δεσμός DESMOS
Acts 26.29 "such as I am—except for these chains
Heb 11.36 Others suffered mocking . . and even chains
Jude . 6 angels . . kept by him in eternal chains
2. *chain:* ἅλυσις HALYSIS*
Mk 5. 3 no one could bind him . . even with a chain
5. 4 often been bound with fetters and chains, but the chains he wrenched apart
Lk 8.29 kept under guard, and bound with chains
Acts 12. 6 Peter was . . bound with two chains
12. 7 the chains fell off his hands
21.33 ordered him to be bound with two chains
28.20 "because of . . hope . . I am bound with this c.
Eph 6.20 for which I am an ambassador in chains
2 Tim 1.16 he was not ashamed of my chains
Rev 20. 1 the key of the . . pit and a great chain

CHALDEAN: Χαλδαῖος
Acts 7. 4 "he departed from . . the Chaldeans

CHAMBER, UPPER
1. *upper story, spare room:* ὑπερῷον HYPERŌON
Acts 20. 8 lights in the upper chamber where we were

CHAMBERLAIN
1. *one in charge of the bedchamber:* ὁ ἐπὶ τοῦ κοιτῶνος KOITŌN [B.1.a.1]
Acts 12.20 persuaded Blastus, the king's chamberlain

CHANCE
1. *coincidence:* συγκυρία SYGKYRIA*
Lk 10.31 "by chance a priest was going down that road
2. *place:* τόπος TOPOS
Heb 12.17 rejected, for he found no chance to repent

CHANCE THAT, ON THE
1. *if, since:* εἰ EI
Acts 27.12 on the c. that . . they could reach Phoenix

CHANCE TO BE THERE
1. *happen to be present:* παρατυγχάνω PARATYGCHANŌ*
Acts 17.17 argued . . with those who chanced to be t.

CHANGE
1. *change:* ἀλλάσσω ALLASSŌ
Acts 6.14 "change the customs which Moses delivered
1 Cor 15.51 We shall not all sleep, but . . be changed
15.52 dead will be raised . . we shall be changed
Gal 4.20 I could wish . . to change my tone
Heb 1.12 "they will be changed[c] . . thou art the same
2. *change the form:* μετασχηματίζω METASCHĒMATIZŌ
Phil 3.21 will change our lowly body to be like his
3. *change of position:* μετάθεσις METATHESIS
Heb 7.12 necessarily a change in the law as well
4. *transpose, change:* μετατίθημι METATITHĒMI
Heb 7.12 when there is a change in the priesthood
5. *turn, change:* τροπή TROPĒ
Jas 1.17 no variation or shadow due to change[a]†‡

CHANGE ONE'S MIND
1. *change, alter:* μεταβάλλω (mid.) METABALLŌ*
Acts 28. 6 no misfortune . . they changed their minds
2. *regret, repent:* μεταμέλομαι METAMELOMAI
Heb 7.21 "The Lord . . will not change his mind

CHANGED, BE
1. *transform:* μεταμορφόω (pass.) METAMORPHOŌ
2 Cor 3.18 we all . . are being changed into his likeness

CHARACTER (*See also* UNCHANGEABLE CHARACTER, THE)
1. *test, proof:* δοκιμή DOKIMĒ
Rom 5. 4 endurance produces character, and character produces hope

CHARCOAL FIRE
1. *burning charcoal:* ἀνθρακιά ANTHRAKIA*
Jn 18.18 officers had made a charcoal fire
21. 9 a charcoal fire there, with fish lying on it

CHARGE
1. *charge, cause:* αἰτία AITIA
Mt 27.37 over his head they put the charge
Mk 15.26 inscription of the charge against him
Acts 23.28 "to know the charge on which they accused
25.18 "they brought no charge in his case of such
25.27 "unreasonable . . not to indicate the charges
2. *accusation:* αἰτίωμα AITIŌMA*
Acts 25. 7 bringing against him many serious charges
3. *bear witness to:* διαμαρτύρομαι DIAMARTYROMAI
1 Tim 5.21 I charge you to keep these rules
2 Tim 2.14 charge . . to avoid disputing about words
4. 1 I charge you in the presence of God
4. *command:* διαστέλλω (mid.) DIASTELLŌ
Mk 5.43 strictly charged . . that no one should know
7.36 he charged them to tell no one; but the more he charged . . the more . . they proclaimed
9. 9 he charged them to tell no one
5. *call, accuse:* ἐγκαλέω EGKALEŌ
Acts 19.40 "in danger of being charged with rioting
6. *command:* ἐντολή ENTOLĒ
Jn 10.18 "charge I have received from my Father
7. *rebuke:* ἐπιτιμάω EPITIMAŌ
Mk 8.30 charged them to tell no one about him
Lk 9.21 charged . . them to tell this to no one
8. *authority, power:* ἐξουσία EXOUSIA [B.2.d.1]
Mk 13.34 "leaves home and puts his servants in charge
9. *accusation:* κατηγορία KATĒGORIA
1 Tim 5.19 Never admit any charge against an elder
Tit 1. 6 not . . to the charge of being profligate
10. *reckon, count:* λογίζομαι LOGIZOMAI
2 Tim 4.16 May it not be charged against them!
11. *call to witness:* μαρτύρομαι MARTYROMAI
1 Th 2.11(12) like a father . . we exhorted . . and charged
12. *command, order:* παραγγελία PARAGGELIA
Acts 16.24 Having received this charge, he put them
1 Tim 1. 5 the aim of our charge is love
1.18 This charge I commit to you, Timothy
13. *give orders:* παραγγέλλω PARAGGELLŌ
Mt 10. 5 twelve Jesus sent out, charging them
Mk 6. 8 charged them to take nothing
Lk 5.14 charged him to tell no one
8.56 he charged them to tell no one
Acts 1. 4 charged them not to depart from Jerusalem
4.18 charged them not to speak or teach at all
5.28 "We strictly charged you not to teach
5.40 charged them not to speak in the name
15. 5 "charge them to keep the law of Moses
16.18 "I charge you in the name of Jesus
16.23 charging the jailer to keep them safely
23.22 dismissed the young man, charging him
1 Th 4.11 work with your hands, as we charged
1 Tim 1. 3 charge . . not to teach any different doctrine
6.14(13) I charge you to keep the commandment

1 Tim 6.17 charge them not to be haughty
14. *say, affirm:* φημί PHĒMI
Rom 3. 8 some . . slanderously charge us with saying
15. *word, saying:* ῥῆμα RHĒMA
Mt 27.14 no answer, not even to a single charge
2 Cor 13. 1 charge must be sustained by the evidence
IDIOMATICALLY
a. Lk 23.14 I did not find this man guilty of any of your charges ἐγὼ . . οὐθὲν εὗρον ἐν τῷ ἀνθρώπῳ τούτῳ αἴτιον ὧν κατηγορεῖτε [KATĒGOREŌ]
b. Acts 13.28 Though they could charge him with nothing deserving death καὶ μηδεμίαν αἰτίαν θανάτου εὑρόντες [AITIA]
c. Acts 25.11 if there is nothing in their charges against me εἰ . . οὐδέν ἐστιν ὧν οὗτοι κατηγοροῦσίν μου [KATĒGOREŌ]
CONTEXTUALLY
Acts 25. 9 "and there be tried on these charges
1 Pet 5. 2 the flock of God that is your charge[k]

CHARGE, ALREADY
1. *accuse beforehand:* προαιτιάομαι PROAITIAOMAI*
Rom 3. 9 I . . a. charged that all . . are under . . sin†

CHARGE, BRING A
CHARGES AGAINST, BRING
CHARGES, BRING
1. *bring charges, accuse:* διαβάλλω DIABALLŌ
Lk 16. 1 "charges were brought to him
2. *call, accuse:* ἐγκαλέω EGKALEŌ
Acts 19.38 "let them bring charges against one another
Rom 8.33 Who shall bring any c. against God's elect?
3. *accuse:* κατηγορέω KATĒGOREŌ
Mk 15. 4 "many charges they bring against you
Jn 8. 6 have some charge to bring against him[r]‡
Acts 28.19 "though I had no charge to bring

CHARGE, FREE OF
1. *without expense:* ἀδάπανος ADAPANOS*
1 Cor 9.18 I may make the gospel free of charge

CHARGE, GIVE
1. *command:* ἐντέλλω (mid.) ENTELLŌ
Mt 4. 6 " 'He will give his angels charge of you
Lk 4.10 " 'He will give his angels charge of you
2. *give orders:* παραγγέλλω PARAGGELLŌ
1 Cor 7.10 To the married I give charge

CHARGE, JOIN IN THE
1. *join in attacking:* συνεπιτίθεμαι SYNEPITITHEMAI*
Acts 24. 9 The Jews also joined in the charge

CHARGE LAID AGAINST ONE
1. *accusation:* ἔγκλημα EGKLĒMA
Acts 25.16 "concerning the charge laid against him

CHARGE OF, IN
1. *on, at:* ἐπί (+gen.) EPI
Acts 8.27

CHARGE, STERNLY
1. *admonish, be deeply moved:* ἐμβριμάομαι EMBRIMAOMAI
Mt 9.30 And Jesus sternly charged them
Mk 1.43 he sternly charged him, and sent him away

CHARGE, STRICTLY
1. *rebuke:* ἐπιτιμάω EPITIMAŌ
Mt 16.20 strictly charged the disciples to tell no one

CHARGE, THOSE IN ONE'S
1. *lot, share:* κλῆρος (pl.) KLĒROS
1 Pet 5. 3 not . . domineering over those in your charge

CHARGED
1. *having a charge against one:* ἔχων ἔγκλημα EGKLĒMA [B.2.a.1]
Acts 23.29 "but charged with nothing deserving death

CHARIOT
1. *chariot:* ἅρμα HARMA*
Acts 8.28 seated in his chariot, he was reading
8.29 to Philip, "Go up and join this chariot
8.38 he commanded the chariot to stop
Rev 9. 9 wings . . like the noise of many chariots
2. *chariot:* ῥέδη RHEDĒ*
Rev 18.13 sheep, horses and chariots, and slaves

CHARITY
1. *mercy, kind deed:* ἐλεημοσύνη ELEĒMOSYNĒ
Acts 9.36 Tabitha . . was full of . . acts of charity

CHASM
1. *chasm:* χάσμα CHASMA*
Lk 16.26 " 'between us and you a great chasm

CHASTE
1. *pure:* ἁγνός HAGNOS
Tit 2. 5 be sensible, chaste, domestic, kind
1 Pet 3. 2 your reverent and chaste behavior
2. *maiden, girl, virgin:* παρθένος (pred.) PARTHENOS
Rev 14. 4 they are chaste[h] . . who follow the Lamb†

CHASTEN
1. *discipline, educate:* παιδεύω PAIDEUŌ
1 Cor 11.32 chastened[u] . . that we . . not be condemned
Rev 3.19 " 'whom I love, I reprove and chasten

CHASTISE
1. *whip, flog:* μαστιγόω MASTIGOŌ
Heb 12. 6 Lord . . chastises every son whom he receives
2. *discipline, educate:* παιδεύω PAIDEUŌ
Lk 23.16 "I will therefore chastise him
23.22 "therefore chastise him and release him

CHATTER
1. *empty talking:* κενοφωνία KENOPHŌNIA*
1 Tim 6.20 Avoid the godless c. and contradictions
2 Tim 2.16 Avoid such godless chatter

CHECK
CONTEXTUALLY
Col 2.23 they are of no value in checking†

CHEEK
1. *jaw, cheek:* σιαγών SIAGŌN*
Mt 5.39 "if any one strikes you on the right cheek
Lk 6.29 "To him who strikes you on the cheek

CHEER, BE OF GOOD
1. *have confidence:* θαρρέω THARREŌ
Jn 16.33 "you have tribulation; but be of good cheer

CHEERED, BE
1. *be of good courage:* εὐψυχέω EUPSYCHEŌ*
Phil 2.19 that I may be cheered by news of you

CHEERFUL
1. *merry, gracious:* ἱλαρός HILAROS*
2 Cor 9. 7 for God loves a cheerful giver

CHEERFUL, BE
1. *be of good cheer:* εὐθυμέω EUTHYMEŌ
Jas 5.13 Is any cheerful? Let him sing praise

CHEERFULLY
1. *cheerfully:* εὐθύμως EUTHYMŌS*
Acts 24.10 "I cheerfully make my defense

CHEERFULNESS
1. *gaiety, graciousness:* ἱλαρότης HILAROTĒS*
Rom 12. 8 who does acts of mercy, with cheerfulness

CHERISH
1. *warm, cherish:* θάλπω THALPŌ
Eph 5.29 cherishes it, as Christ does the church

CHERUB
1. *cherub:* χερούβ CHEROUB*
Heb 9. 5 cherubim . . overshadowing the mercy seat

CHIEF
1. *first, foremost:* πρῶτος PRŌTOS
Acts 28. 7 chief man of the island, named Publius
IDIOMATICALLY
a. Acts 14.12 because he was the chief speaker ἐπειδὴ αὐτὸς ἦν ὁ ἡγούμενος τοῦ λόγου [HĒGEOMAI]

CHIEF CAPTAIN
1. *captain over a thousand:* χιλίαρχος CHILIARCHOS
Acts [24. 7 *"the chief captain Lysias came*‡

CHIEF PRIEST
1. *chief priest:* ἀρχιερεύς ARCHIEREUS
Always plural
Mt 2. 4 assembling all the chief priests and scribes
16.21 suffer many things from the . . chief priests

Mt 20.18 “will be delivered to . . chief priests
21.15 chief priests . . saw the wonderful things
21.23 chief priests . . said, “By what authority?
21.45 When the chief priests . . heard his parables
26. 3 the chief priests . . gathered in the palace
26.14 Judas Iscariot, went to the chief priests
26.47 a great crowd . . from the chief priests
26.59 chief priests . . sought false testimony
27. 1 chief priests . . took counsel against Jesus
27. 3 brought back . . silver to the chief priests
27. 6 chief priests, taking the pieces of silver
27.12 when he was accused by the chief priests
27.20 chief priests . . persuaded the people
27.41 also the chief priests . . mocked him
27.62 chief priests . . gathered before Pilate
28.11 some of the guard . . told the chief priests
Mk 8.31 must . . be rejected by . . chief priests
10.33 “Son of man . . delivered to . . chief priests
11.18 chief priests . . sought . . to destroy him
11.27 chief priests . . and the elders came to him
14. 1 chief priests . . were seeking how to . . kill him
14.10 Judas Iscariot . . went to the chief priests
14.43 crowd with swords . . from the chief priests
14.53 chief priests and . . scribes were assembled
14.55 chief priests . . sought testimony against Jesus
15. 1 chief priests . . held a consultation
15. 3 chief priests accused him of many things
15.10 chief priests had delivered him up
15.11 the chief priests stirred up the crowd
15.31 also the chief priests mocked him
Lk 9.22 “be rejected by the elders and chief priests
19.47 The chief priests . . sought to destroy him
20. 1 chief priests and the scribes . . came up
20.19 chief priests tried to lay hands on him
22. 2 chief priests and the scribes were seeking how
22. 4 conferred with the chief priests and officers
22.52 chief priests and officers of the temple
22.66 assembly . . both chief priests and scribes
23. 4 Pilate said to the chief priests
23.10 chief priests and the scribes stood by
23.13 Pilate then called together the chief priests
24.20 “chief priests and rulers delivered him up
Jn 7.32 chief priests and Pharisees sent officers
7.45 officers then went back to the chief priests
11.47 chief priests . . gathered the council
11.57 chief priests . . had given orders
12.10 c. priests planned to put Lazarus . . to death
18. 3 officers from the chief priests . . went there
18.35 “chief priests have handed you over to me
19. 6 chief priests . . cried out, “Crucify him!
19.15 chief priests answered, “We have no king
19.21 chief priests of the Jews . . said to Pilate
Acts 4.23 reported what the chief priests . . said
5.24 chief priests heard these words
9.14 “he has authority from the chief priests
9.21 “to bring them . . before the chief priests
22.30 commanded the chief priests . . to meet
23.14 they went to the chief priests and elders
25. 2 chief priests . . informed him against Paul
25.15 “chief priests . . gave information about him
26.10 “by authority from the chief priests
26.12 “with the authority . . of the chief priests

CHIEF SHEPHERD

1. *chief shepherd:* ἀρχιποίμην ARCHIPOIMĒN*
1 Pet 5. 4 when the chief Shepherd is manifested

CHIEF TAX COLLECTOR

1. *chief tax collector:* ἀρχιτελώνης ARCHITELŌNĒS*
Lk 19. 2 Zacchaeus . . a chief tax collector, and rich

CHILD

1. *man, mankind:* ἄνθρωπος ANTHRŌPOS
Jn 16.21 “a child[j] is born into the world†
2. *beget, bear:* γεννάω (subst. perf. pass. part.) GENNAŌ
1 Jn 5. 1 one who loves the parent loves the child
3. *son:* υἱός HUIOS
Mt 23.15 “twice as much a child of hell[w] as yourselves
Rev 12. 5 a male child . . who is to rule all the nations
4. *childlike, childish:* νήπιος (subst.) NĒPIOS
Rom 2.20 corrector of the foolish, a teacher of children
1 Cor 13.11 When I was a child, I spoke like a child, I thought like a child, I reasoned like a child
Gal 4. 1 the heir, as long as he is a child
4. 3 So with us; when we were children
Eph 4.14 so that we may no longer be children
Heb 5.13 unskilled in the word . . for he is a child
5. *young child:* παιδίον PAIDION
Mt 2. 8 “Go and search diligently for the child
2. 9 star . . came to rest . . where the child was
2.11 they saw the child with Mary his mother
2.13 “take the child and his mother . . to Egypt
2.13 “Herod is about to search for the child
2.14 took the child and his mother by night
2.20 “Rise, take the child and his mother
2.20 “those who sought the child's life are dead
2.21 he rose and took the child and his mother
11.16 “this generation . . like children
14.21 five thousand . . besides women and children
15.38 four thousand . . besides women and children
18. 2 calling . . a child he put him in the midst
18. 3 “unless you turn and become like children
18. 4 “Whoever humbles himself like this child
18. 5 “Whoever receives one such child
19.13 Then children were brought to him
19.14 “Let the children come . . and do not hinder
Mk 5.39 “The child is not dead but sleeping
5.40 took the child's father and mother . . in where the child was
7.27 he said to her, “Let the children first be fed
7.30 child lying in bed, and the demon gone
9.24 father of the c. cried out[i] . . “I believe
9.36 took a child, and put him in the midst
9.37 “Whoever receives one such child
10.13 they were bringing children to him
10.14 “Let the children come to me
10.15 “receive the kingdom of God like a child
Lk 1.59 they came to circumcise the child
1.66 “What then will this child be?
1.76 “you, child, will be called the prophet
1.80 child grew and became strong in spirit
2.17 the saying . . told them concerning this c.
2.27 parents brought in the child Jesus
2.40 the child grew and became strong
7.32 “like children sitting in the market place
9.47 took a child and put him by his side
9.48 “Whoever receives this c. in my name
11. 7 “ ‘my children are with me in bed
18.16 “Let the children come to me
18.17 “receive the kingdom of God like a child
Jn 4.49 “Sir, come down before my child dies
16.21 “when she is delivered of the child
21. 5 “Children, have you any fish?
1 Cor 14.20 do not be children in your thinking
Heb 2.13 “Here am I, and the children God has given
2.14 Since . . the children share in flesh and blood
11.23 they saw that the child was beautiful
1 Jn 2.13 I write . . you, children, because you know
2.18 Children, it is the last hour
6. *child, servant:* παῖς PAIS
Mt 21.15 children crying out in the temple
Lk 8.51 father and mother of the child
8.54 he called, saying, “Child, arise
Acts [3.13 “God . . glorified his *child* Jesus†
[3.26 “God, having raised up his *child*†
[4.25 “thy *child*, didst say by the Holy Spirit†
[4.27 “gathered together against thy holy *child*†
[4.30 “through the name of thy holy *child*†
7. *child:* τέκνον TEKNON
Mt 2.18 “Rachel weeping for her children
3. 9 “ ‘able from these stones to raise up children
7.11 “how to give good gifts to your children
10.21 “the father ⟨will deliver up⟩ his child
10.21 “children will rise against parents
[11.19 “Yet wisdom is justified by her *children*‡
15.26 “It is not fair to take the children's bread

Mt 18.25 "to be sold, with his wife and children
19.29 "left . . sisters or father or mother or children
22.24 " 'If a man dies, having no children
23.37 "would . . have gathered your children!
27.25 "His blood be on us and on our children!
Mk 7.27 "Let the children first be fed, for it is not right to take the children's bread
10.24 "Children, how hard it is[r] to enter!
10.29 "left . . children or lands, for my sake
10.30 "who will not receive . . children and lands
12.19 "dies and leaves a wife, but leaves no child
13.12 "father ⟨will deliver up⟩ his child
13.12 "children will rise against parents
Lk 1. 7 no child, because Elizabeth was barren
1.17 "turn the hearts . . to the children
3. 8 " 'able from these stones to raise up children
7.35 "wisdom is justified by all her children
11.13 "how to give good gifts to your children
13.34 "would . . have gathered your children!
14.26 "hate his own . . wife and children
18.29 "left . . brothers or parents or children
19.44 "dash you . . and your children within you
20.31 "likewise all seven left no children and died
23.28 "weep for yourselves and for your children
Jn 1.12 he gave power to become children of God
8.39 "If you were Abraham's children
11.52 gather into one the children of God
Acts 2.39 "promise is to you and to your children
7. 5 "to his posterity . . though he had no child
13.33 "this he has fulfilled to us their children
21. 5 all, with wives and children, brought us
21.21 "telling them not to circumcise their children
Rom 8.16 witness . . that we are children of God
8.17 if children, then heirs, heirs of God
8.21 glorious liberty of the children of God
9. 7 not all are children of Abraham
9. 8 it is not the children of the flesh who are the children of God, but the children of the promise
1 Cor 4.14 to admonish you as my beloved children
4.17 Timothy, my . . faithful child in the Lord
7.14 Otherwise, your children would be unclean
2 Cor 6.13 In return—I speak as to children
12.14 children ought not to lay up for their parents, but parents for their children
Gal 4.25 Jerusalem . . in slavery with her children
4.27 "children of the desolate one are . . more
4.28 we,[j] brethren, like Isaac, are children
4.31 brethren, we are not children of the slave
Eph 2. 3 we were by nature children of wrath
5. 1 imitators of God, as beloved children
5. 8 walk as children of light
6. 1 Children, obey your parents in the Lord
6. 4 do not provoke your children to anger
Phil 2.15 you may be blameless . . children of God
Col 3.20 Children, obey your parents
3.21 Fathers, do not provoke your children
1 Th 2. 7 like a nurse taking care of her children
2.11 like a father with his children, we exhorted
1 Tim 1. 2 Timothy, my true child in the faith
3. 4 keeping his children submissive
3.12 let them manage their children . . well
5. 4 If a widow has children or grandchildren
2 Tim 1. 2 To Timothy, my beloved child
Tit 1. 4 Titus, my true child in a common faith
1. 6 if . . his children are believers
Phm .10 I appeal to you for my child, Onesimus
1 Pet 1.14 As obedient children . . not . . conformed
3. 6 you are now her children if you do right
2 Pet 2.14 hearts trained in greed. Accursed children!
1 Jn 3. 1 that we should be called children of God
3. 2 Beloved, we are God's children now
3.10 it may be seen who are the children of God, and who are the children of the devil
5. 2 we know that we love the children of God
2 Jn . 1 elder to the elect lady and her children
. 4 some of your children following the truth
2 Jn .13 children of your elect sister greet you
3 Jn . 4 to hear that my children follow the truth
Rev 2.23 " 'I will strike her children dead
12. 4 devour her child when she brought it forth
12. 5 her child was caught up to God

IDIOMATICALLY

a. Mt 1.18 she was found to be with child *εὑρέθη ἐν γαστρὶ ἔχουσα* [GASTĒR]
b. Mt 24.19 "alas for those who are with child *οὐαὶ . . ταῖς ἐν γαστρὶ ἐχούσαις* [GASTĒR]
Also Mk **13.**17; Lk **21.**23
c. 1 Th 5.3 as travail comes upon a woman with child *ὥσπερ ἡ ὠδὶν τῇ ἐν γαστρὶ ἐχούσῃ* [GASTĒR]
d. Rev 12.2 she was with child and she cried out *ἐν γαστρὶ ἔχουσα, καὶ κράζει* [GASTĒR]

CONTEXTUALLY

Lk 1.35 "the c. to be born[d] will be called holy
2.34 "this c. is set for the fall and rising
9.38 "look upon my son, for he is my only c.
Rev 12. 4 the woman who was about to bear a child
12.13 the woman who had borne the male child

CHILD, BE A

1. *beget, bear:* *γεννάω* (perf. pass.) GENNAŌ
1 Jn 5. 1 Every one who believes . . is a child of God

CHILD, BIRTH OF THE

1. *childbearing:* *τεκνογονία* TEKNOGONIA
1 Tim [2.15 will be saved *by the birth of the child*†

CHILD, LITTLE

1. *little child:* *τεκνίον* TEKNION*
Jn 13.33 "Little children, yet a little while . . with you
Gal 4.19 little children . . I am again in travail!
1 Jn 2. 1 little children, I am writing this to you
2.12 little children, . . your sins are forgiven
2.28 now, little children, abide in him
3. 7 Little children, let no one deceive you
3.18 Little children, let us not love in word
4. 4 Little children, you are of God
5.21 Little children, keep yourselves from idols

CHILD, MALE

1. *child, servant:* *παῖς* PAIS
Mt 2.16 he sent and killed all the male children

CHILD, WITH

1. *pregnant:* *ἔγκυος* EGKYOS*
Lk 2. 5 with Mary . . who was with child

CHILDHOOD

1. *infant:* *βρέφος* BREPHOS [C.2]
2 Tim 3.15 from childhood you have been acquainted

CHILDHOOD, FROM

1. *from a child:* *παιδιόθεν* PAIDIOTHEN*
[a] + *ἐκ*
Mk 9.21 [a]"How long . . ?" . . he said, "From childhood

CHILDISH

1. *childlike, childish:* *νήπιος* NĒPIOS
1 Cor 13.11 I became a man, I gave up childish ways

CHILDREN (*See also* ILLEGITIMATE CHILDREN)

1. *seed, offspring:* *σπέρμα* (pl.) SPERMA
Mt 22.24 " 'raise up children for his brother
Also Mk **12.**19; Lk **20.**28
22.25 "having no c. left his wife to his brother
Mk 12.20 "when he died left no children
12.21 "second . . died, leaving no children
12.22 "and the seven left no children
Rom 9.29 "If the Lord . . had not left us children

CHILDREN, BEAR

1. *beget, bear:* *γεννάω* GENNAŌ
Gal 4.24 Sinai, bearing children for slavery
2. *beget or bear children:* *τεκνογονέω* TEKNOGONEŌ*
1 Tim 5.14 younger widows marry, bear children

CHILDREN, BEARING

1. *childbearing:* *τεκνογονία* TEKNOGONIA*
1 Tim 2.15 woman . . saved through bearing children[c]†

CHILDREN, BRING UP

1. *rear children:* *τεκνοτροφέω* TEKNOTROPHEŌ*
1 Tim 5.10 one who has brought up children

CHILDREN, HAVE NO
1. *be childless:* ἄτεκνος εἶναι ATEKNOS [B.3.b.4]
Lk 20.28 "brother dies, having a wife but no children

CHILDREN, LOVE ONE'S
1. *loving one's children:* φιλότεκνος PHILOTEKNOS* [A.6.a.3]
Tit 2. 4 young women to love their . . children

CHILDREN, WITHOUT
1. *childless:* ἄτεκνος ATEKNOS
Lk 20.29 "took a wife, and died without children

CHIOS: Χίος 'kī,äs II,E-3
Acts 20.15 we came the following day opposite Chios

CHLOE: Χλόη 'klōē
1 Cor 1.11 reported to me by Chloe's people

CHOICE, MAKE
1. *choose:* ἐκλέγομαι EKLEGOMAI
Acts 15. 7 "in the early days God made choice

CHOKE
1. *choke, drown:* ἀποπνίγω APOPNIGŌ
Mt 13. 7 "the thorns grew up and choked them
Lk 8. 7 "thorns grew with it and choked it
2. *press closely, choke:* συμπνίγω SYMPNIGŌ
Mt 13.22 "cares . . , delight in riches choke the word
Mk 4. 7 "thorns grew up and choked it
4.19 "cares . . , delight in riches . . choke the word
Lk 8.14 "as they go on their way they are choked

CHOOSE
1. *wish, will:* βούλομαι BOULOMAI
Mt 11.27 "any . . to whom the Son chooses to reveal
Lk 10.22 "any . . to whom the Son chooses to reveal
2. *choose:* ἐκλέγομαι EKLEGOMAI
Mk 13.20 "for the sake of the elect, whom he chose
Lk 6.13 called his disciples, and chose . . twelve
9.35 "This is my Son, my Chosen[d]‡
10.42 "Mary has chosen the good portion
14. 7 marked how they chose the places of honor
Jn 6.70 "Did I not choose you, the twelve?
13.18 "I know whom I have chosen
15.16 "You did not choose me, but I chose you and appointed you
15.19 "I chose you out of the world
Acts 1. 2 the apostles whom he had chosen
1.24 "which one of these two thou hast chosen
6. 5 they chose Stephen, a man full of faith
13.17 "God of this people Israel chose our fathers
15.22 to choose men . . and send them to Antioch
15.25 "to choose men and send them to you
1 Cor 1.27 God chose what is foolish in the world
1.27 God chose what is weak in the world
1.28 God chose what is low and despised
Eph 1. 4 he chose us in him before the foundation
Jas 2. 5 Has not God chosen those who are poor?
3. *choice, election:* ἐκλογή EKLOGĒ [A.1.e]
1 Th 1. 4 we know . . that he has chosen you
4. *call by name:* ἐπιλέγω (mid.) EPILEGŌ
Acts 15.40 Paul chose Silas and departed
5. *choose* (mid.): αἱρέω HAIREŌ*
Phil 1.22 which I shall choose I cannot tell
2 Th 2.13 God chose you from the beginning[b]
Heb 11.25 choosing rather to share ill-treatment
6. *choose:* αἱρετίζω HAIRETIZŌ*
Mt 12.18 "my servant whom I have chosen
7. *receive, take:* λαμβάνω LAMBANŌ
Heb 5. 1 every high priest chosen from among men
8. *elect beforehand:* προχειροτονέω PROCHEIROTONEŌ*
Acts 10.41 "us who were chosen by God as witnesses
9. *will, wish:* θέλω THELŌ
Mt 20.14 " 'I choose to give to this last as . . to you
20.15 " 'what I choose with what belongs to me?
1 Cor 12.18 God arranged the organs . . as he chose
15.38 God gives it a body as he has chosen
Col 1.27 God chose to make known how great

CHORAZIN: Χοραζίν kō'rāzən I,D-3
Mt 11.21 "Woe to you, C.! woe to you, Bethsaida!
Lk 10.13 "Woe to you, C.! woe to you, Bethsaida!

CHOSEN
1. *select, choice:* ἐκλεκτός EKLEKTOS
Mt 22.14 "many are called, but few are chosen
Lk 23.35 "if he is the Christ . . his Chosen One!
Col 3.12 as God's chosen ones, holy and beloved
1 Pet 1. 2(1) chosen and destined by God the Father
2. 4 that living stone . . in God's sight chosen
2. 6 "a cornerstone chosen and precious
2. 9 you are a chosen race, a royal priesthood
Rev 17.14 "those with him are called and chosen
2. *choice, selection:* ἐκλογή EKLOGĒ
[a]gen. [b]B.1.a.1
Acts 9.15 [a]"Go, for he is a chosen instrument of mine
Rom 11. 5 [b]there is a remnant, chosen by grace

CHOSEN, LIKEWISE
1. *chosen together with:* συνεκλεκτός SYNEKLEKTOS*
1 Pet 5.13 She who is at Babylon . . likewise chosen

CHRIST
1. *anointed:* χριστός (subst.) CHRISTOS
(J. C. = Jesus Christ)
Mt 1. 1 The book of the genealogy of J. C.
1.16 Mary, of whom Jesus was born . . called C.
1.17 from . . deportation . . to the C. fourteen
1.18 the birth of J. C.[f] took place in this way
2. 4 inquired . . where the C. was to be born
11. 2 when John heard . . about the deeds of the C.
16.16 "You are the C., the Son of the living God
16.20 charged . . to tell no one that he was the C.
22.42 "What do you think of the C.? Whose son?
23.10 "for you have one master, the Christ
24. 5 "many will come . . saying, 'I am the C.
24.23 "if any one says . . 'Lo, here is the C.!
26.63 "I adjure you . . tell us if you are the C.
26.68 "Prophesy to us, you Christ! Who is it?
27.17 "Barabbas[k] or Jesus who is called C.?
27.22 "what shall I do with Jesus who is called C.?
Mk 1. 1 The beginning of the gospel of J. C.
8.29 Peter answered him, "You are the C.
9.41 "water . . because you bear the name of C.
12.35 "scribes say . . C. is the son of David
13.21 "if any one says . . 'Look, here is the C.!
14.61 "Are you the C., the Son of the Blessed?
15.32 "Let the C., the King of Israel, come down
Lk 2.11 "born this day . . a Savior . . C. the Lord
2.26 not . . before he had seen the Lord's C.
3.15 questioned . . whether . . he were the C.
4.41 because they knew that he was the C.
9.20 Peter answered, "The Christ of God
20.41 "say that the Christ is David's son?
22.67 "If you are the Christ, tell us
23. 2 "saying that he himself is C. a king
23.35 "let him save himself, if he is the C.!
23.39 "Are you not the Christ? Save yourself!
24.26 "necessary that the C. should suffer?
24.46 "written, that the Christ should suffer
Jn 1.17 grace and truth came through J. C.
1.20 confessed, "I am not the Christ
1.25 "why . . baptizing, if . . neither the Christ?
1.41 "We have found the Messiah" (. . Christ
3.28 "I am not the C., but . . sent before him
4.25 "Messiah is coming (he who is called Christ
4.29 "Can this be the Christ?
7.26 "authorities . . know . . this is the Christ?
7.27 "C. . . no one will know where he comes from
7.31 "When the C. appears, will he do more signs?
7.41 "This is the C." But some said, "Is the C. to come from Galilee?
7.42 "C. is descended from David
9.22 "if any one should confess him to be C.
10.24 "If you are the Christ, tell us plainly
11.27 "I believe . . you are the C., the Son of God
12.34 "We have heard . . that the C. remains
17. 3 "know thee . . and J. C. whom thou hast sent
20.31 that you may believe that Jesus is the C.
Acts 2.31 "he foresaw . . the resurrection of the C.
2.36 "God . . made him . . Lord and C., this Jesus

Acts 2.38 "be baptized . . in the name of J. C.
3. 6 "in the name of J. C. of Nazareth, walk
3.18 "God foretold . . that his C. should suffer
3.20 "send the Christ appointed for you, Jesus
4.10 "by the name of J. C. . . this man is . . well
[4.26 " 'against the Lord and . . his *Christ*†
5.42 did not cease . . preaching Jesus as the C.
8. 5 Philip . . proclaimed to them the Christ
8.12 good news about . . the name of J. C.
[8.37 *"that Jesus Christ is the Son of God*‡
9.22 Saul . . proving that Jesus was the C.
9.34 "Aeneas, J. C. heals you; rise
10.36 "preaching good news of peace by J. C.
10.48 to be baptized in the name of J. C.
11.17 "when we believed in the Lord J. C.
15.26 "risked their lives for . . our Lord J. C.
16.18 "I charge you in the name of J. C.
17. 3 it was necessary for the Christ to suffer
17. 3 "This Jesus, whom I proclaim . . is the C.
18. 5 testifying . . that the C. was Jesus
18.28 in public, showing . . that the C. was Jesus
20.21 "testifying . . of faith in our Lord J. C.
24.24 heard ⟨Paul⟩ speak upon faith in C. J.
26.23 "the C. must suffer, and . . proclaim light
28.31 teaching about the Lord J. C. quite openly

Rom 1. 1 Paul, a servant[a] of Jesus Christ
1. 4 by his resurrection . . J. C. our Lord
1. 6 yourselves . . called to belong to J. C.
1. 7 peace from God . . and the Lord J. C.
1. 8 I thank my God through J. C. for . . you
2.16 God judges the secrets of men by C. J.
3.22 righteousness of God through faith in J. C.
3.24 through the redemption which is in C. J.
5. 1 peace with God through our Lord J. C.
5. 6 at the right time C. died for the ungodly
5. 8 while we were yet sinners C. died for us
5.11 We also rejoice . . through our Lord J. C.
5.15 grace of that one man J. C. abounded
5.17 righteousness . . through the one man J. C.
5.21 righteousness . . through J. C. our Lord
6. 3 all of us who have been baptized into C. J.
6. 4 so that as C. was raised . . we too might
6. 8 if we have died with C., we shall . . live
6. 9 Christ being raised . . will never die again
6.11 consider yourselves . . alive to God in C. J.
6.23 the free gift of God is eternal life in C. J.
7. 4 died to the law through the body of C.
7.25 Thanks be to God through J. C. our Lord!
8. 1 There is . . no condemnation . . in C. J.
8. 2 Spirit of life in C. J. has set me free
8. 9 one who does not have the Spirit of C.
8.10 if Christ is in you . . your spirits are alive
8.11 he who raised Christ Jesus . . will give life
8.17 heirs with C., provided we suffer with him
8.34 Is it C. J., who died, yes, who was raised?
8.35 Who shall separate us from the love of C.?
8.39 separate us from the love of God in C. J.
9. 1 I am speaking the truth in Christ
9. 3 I could wish . . I . . were . . cut off from C.
9. 5 of their race, according to the flesh, is . . C.†
10. 4 Christ is the end of the law
10. 6 "Who will ascend . ." (. . to bring C. down
10. 7 "Who will descend . ." (. . to bring C. up
10.17 what is heard comes by the preaching of C.
12. 5 so we, though many, are one body in C.
13.14 put on the Lord Jesus Christ
14. 9 to this end Christ died and lived again
14.15 not . . cause the ruin of one for whom C. died
14.18 who thus serves C. is acceptable to God
15. 3 Christ did not please himself
15. 5 live . . in accord with Christ Jesus
15. 6 God and Father of our Lord J. C.
15. 7 Welcome . . as Christ has welcomed you
15. 8 C. became a servant to the circumcised
15.16 a minister of C. J. to the Gentiles
15.17 In C. J., then, I have reason to be proud
15.18 speak of . . what C. has wrought through me

Rom 15.19 I have fully preached the gospel of C.
15.20 preach . . not where C. has . . been named
15.29 I shall come in . . the blessing[y] of Christ
15.30 I appeal to you . . by our Lord J. C.
16. 3 Prisca and Aquila, my fellow workers in C. J.
16. 5 Epaenetus, . . the first convert in Asia for C.
16. 7 Andronicus and Junias . . were in C. before
16. 9 Urbanus, our fellow worker in Christ
16.10 Greet Apelles, who is approved in Christ
16.16 All the churches of Christ greet you
16.18 such persons do not serve our Lord Christ
16.20 The grace of our Lord J. C. be with you[a]‡
[16.24 *The grace of our Lord Jesus Christ*‡
16.25 my gospel and the preaching of J. C.
16.27 glory for evermore through Jesus Christ!

1 Cor 1. 1 Paul, called . . to be an apostle of C. J.
1. 2 To the church of God . . sanctified in C. J.
1. 2 who . . call on the name of our Lord J. C.
1. 3 peace from God . . and the Lord J. C.
1. 4 grace of God which was given you in C. J.
1. 6 testimony to C. was confirmed among you
1. 7 wait for the revealing of our Lord J. C.
1. 8 guiltless in the day of our Lord J. C.
1. 9 called into the fellowship of his Son, J. C.
1.10 I appeal . . by the name of our Lord J. C.
1.12 "I belong to Cephas," or "I belong to C.
1.13 Is C. divided? Was Paul crucified for you?
1.17 C. did not send me to baptize but to preach . . lest the cross of Christ be emptied
1.23 we preach C. crucified, a stumbling block
1.24 C. the power . . and the wisdom of God
1.30 He is the source of your life in C. J.
2. 2 I decided to know nothing . . except J. C.
2.16 But we have the mind of Christ
3. 1 as men of the flesh, as babes in Christ
3.11 no . . foundation can any . . lay than . . J. C.
3.23 you are Christ's; and Christ is God's
4. 1 one should regard us, as servants of C.
4.10 We are fools for Christ's sake, but you are wise in Christ
4.15 you have countless guides in Christ . . I became your father in C. J. through the gospel
4.17 to remind you of my ways in Christ
5. 7 Christ, our paschal lamb, has been sacrificed
6.11 justified in the name of the Lord J. C.
6.15 your bodies are members of Christ
6.15 Shall I therefore take the members of C.?
7.22 who was free when called is a slave of C.
8. 6 one Lord, J. C., through whom are all things
8.11 brother for whom Christ died
8.12 wounding . . conscience . . , you sin against C.
9.12 obstacle in the way of the gospel of C.
9.21 outside the law . . but under the law of C.
10. 4 supernatural[o] Rock which followed . . was C.
[10. 9 We must not put *Christ* to the test‡
10.16 participation[q] in the blood of Christ
10.16 participation[q] in the body of Christ
11. 1 Be imitators of me, as I am of Christ
11. 3 the head of every man is Christ . . and the head of Christ is God
12.12 though many, are one body, so it is with C.
12.27 you are the body of C. and . . members of it
15. 3 Christ died for our sins
15.12 if C. is preached as raised from the dead?
15.13 then Christ has not been raised
15.14 if C. has not been raised . . faith is in vain
15.15 we testified of God that he raised Christ
15.16 if . . not . . then C. has not been raised
15.17 If C. has not been raised . . faith is futile
15.18 Then those . . in Christ have perished
15.19 If for this life only we have hoped in C.
15.20 C. has been raised from the dead
15.22 so also in C. shall all be made alive
15.23 C. the first fruits, then at his coming those who belong to C.
15.31 my pride in you which I have in C. J.
15.57 God . . gives . . the victory through . . J. C.

1 Cor 16.24 My love be with you all in C. J. Amen
2 Cor 1. 1 Paul, an apostle of Christ Jesus
1. 2 peace from God . . and the Lord J. C.
1. 3 Blessed be the God . . of our Lord J. C.
1. 5 we share abundantly in Christ's sufferings, so through Christ . . in comfort too[a]
1.19 J. C., whom we preached among you
1.21 God who establishes us with you in Christ
2.10 forgiven . . for your sake in the presence of C.
2.12 to Troas to preach the gospel of C.
2.14 God, who in C. always leads us in triumph
2.15 we are the aroma of Christ to God
2.17 in the sight of God we speak in Christ
3. 3 you are a letter from C. delivered by us
3. 4 confidence that we have through C.
3.14 only through Christ is it taken away
4. 4 light of the gospel of the glory of C.
4. 5 what we preach is not ourselves, but J. C.
4. 6 the glory of God in the face of Christ
5.10 appear before the judgment seat of Christ
5.14 the love of Christ controls us
5.16 we once regarded C. from a human . . view
5.17 if any one is in C., he is a new creation[g]
5.18 God . . through C. reconciled us to himself
5.19 in Christ God was reconciling[h] the world
5.20 we are ambassadors for C.
5.20 on behalf of Christ, be reconciled to God
6.15 What accord has Christ with Belial?[i]
8. 9 you know the grace of our Lord J. C.
8.23 messengers[j] of the churches, the glory of C.
9.13 acknowledging the gospel of Christ
10. 1 by the meekness and gentleness of C.
10. 5 take every thought captive to obey Christ
10. 7 If any one is confident that he is Christ's
10. 7 as he is Christ's, so are we
10.14 first to come . . to you with the gospel of C.
11. 2 I betrothed you to C. . . as a pure bride
11. 3 led astray from a . . pure devotion to Christ
11.10 As the truth of Christ is in me
11.13 disguising themselves as apostles of C.
11.23 Are they servants of C.? I am a better
12. 2 man in C. . . caught up to . . heaven
12. 9 that the power of Christ . . rest upon me
12.10 For the sake of Christ . . I am content
12.19 we have been speaking in Christ
13. 3 proof that Christ is speaking in me
13. 5 Do you not realize that J. C. is in you?
13.14 The grace of the Lord Jesus Christ
Gal 1. 1 Paul an apostle . . through J. C. and God
1. 3 peace from God . . and our Lord J. C.
1. 6 deserting him who called you in . . C.
1. 7 some who . . want to pervert the gospel of C.
1.10 I should not be a servant[a] of Christ
1.12 it came through a revelation of J. C.
1.22 I was still not known . . to the churches of C.
2. 4 freedom which we have in C. J.
2.16 through faith in J. C. . . we have believed in C. J., in order to be justified by faith in C.
2.17 if . . to be justified in C., we . . were found to be sinners, is C. . . an agent of sin?
2.20 I have been crucified with C.; it is no longer I who live, but C. . . in me
2.21 if . . the law, then Christ died to no purpose
3. 1 before whose eyes J. C. was . . portrayed
3.13 C. redeemed us from the curse of the law
3.14 in C. J. the blessing of Abraham
3.16 "And to your offspring," which is Christ
3.22 what was promised to faith in J. C.
3.24 the law was our custodian until C.
3.26 in Christ Jesus you are all sons of God
3.27 as many of you as were baptized into Christ have put on Christ
3.28 you are all one in Christ Jesus
3.29 if you are C.'s, then you are Abraham's
4.14 you . . received me as an angel . . as C. J.
4.19 again in travail until C. be formed in you!
5. 1 For freedom Christ has set us free
Gal 5. 2 Christ will be of no advantage to you
5. 4 You are severed from Christ
5. 6 in C. J. neither circumcision nor uncirc.
5.24 who belong to C. J. have crucified the flesh
6. 2 Bear one another's burdens . . the law of C.
6.12 not be persecuted for the cross of C.
6.14 to glory except in the cross of our Lord J. C.
6.18 grace of our Lord J. C. be with your spirit
Eph 1. 1 Paul, an apostle of Christ Jesus
1. 1 To the saints who are also faithful[a] in C. J.
1. 2 peace from God . . and the Lord J. C.
1. 3 Blessed be the God . . of our Lord J. C., who has blessed us in Christ
1. 5 destined us . . to be his sons through J. C.
1. 9(10) according to his purpose . . set forth in C.
1.12 who first hoped in C. have been destined
1.17 God of our Lord J. C., the Father of glory
1.20 accomplished in C. when he raised him
2. 5 made us alive together with Christ
2. 6 sit . . in the heavenly places in C. J.
2. 7 kindness toward us in Christ Jesus
2.10 we are his workmanship, created in C. J.
2.12 you were . . separated from C., alienated
2.13 in C. J. you who once were far off have been brought near in the blood of Christ
2.20 foundation . . , C. J. . . being the cornerstone
3. 1 I, Paul, a prisoner for C. J.
3. 4 my insight into the mystery of Christ
3. 6 partakers of the promise in C. J.
3. 8 to preach . . the unsearchable riches of Christ
3.11 purpose which he has realized in C. J.
3.17 C. . . in your hearts through faith
3.19 the love of C. which surpasses knowledge
3.21 to him be glory in the church and in C. J.
4. 7 according to the measure of C.'s gift
4.12 building up the body of Christ
4.13 measure of the stature of the fulness of C.
4.15 we are to grow up in every way . . into C.
4.20 You did not so learn Christ!
4.32 tenderhearted . . as God in C. forgave you
5. 2 as C. loved us and gave himself . . for us
5. 5 inheritance in the kingdom of C. and of God
5.14 "Awake . . and Christ shall give you light
5.20 thanks in the name of our Lord Jesus Christ
5.21 subject . . out of reverence for Christ
5.23 husband is . . head . . as C. is . . of the church
5.24 As the church is subject to C., so let wives
5.25 your wives, as Christ loved the church
5.29 cherishes it, as Christ does the church
5.32 This mystery . . refers to Christ
6. 5 trembling, in singleness of heart, as to Christ
6. 6 as servants[f] of C., doing the will of God
6.23 Peace . . from God . . and the Lord J. C.
6.24 Grace be with all who love our Lord J. C.
Phil 1. 1 Paul and Timothy, servants[a] of C. J.
1. 1 To all the saints in C. J.
1. 2 peace from God . . and the Lord J. C.
1. 6 bring it to completion at the day of J. C.
1. 8 I yearn . . with the affection of C. J.
1.10 be pure and blameless for the day of C.
1.11 fruits of righteousness . . through J. C.
1.13 known . . that my imprisonment is for C.
1.15 Some indeed preach C. from envy
1.17 the former proclaim C. out of partisanship
1.18 Christ is proclaimed; and in that I rejoice
1.19 through . . help of the Spirit of J. C.
1.20 as always C. will be honored in my body
1.21 For to me to live is C. . . to die is gain
1.23 My desire is to depart and be with Christ
1.26 in me you . . have ample cause to glory in C. J.
1.27 manner of life be worthy of the gospel of C.
1.29 for the sake of C. you should . . also suffer
2. 1 if there is any encouragement in C.
2. 5 Have this mind . . which is yours in C. J.
2.11 every tongue confess that J. C. is Lord
2.16 that in the day of Christ I may be proud
2.21 their own interests, not those of J. C.

Phil 2.30 he nearly died for the work of Christ
3. 3 we . . worship God in spirit,[e] and glory in C. J.
3. 7 gain I had, I counted as loss for . . C.
3. 8 the . . worth of knowing C. J. my Lord
3. 8 loss of all . . in order that I may gain C.
3. 9 not . . based on law, but . . through faith in C.
3.12 I press . . because C. J. has made me his own
3.14 prize of the upward call of God in C. J.
3.18 many . . live as enemies of the cross of C.
3.20 we await a Savior, the Lord J. C.
4. 7 peace of God . . keep . . minds in C. J.
4.19 God will supply every need of yours . . in C. J.
4.21 Greet every saint in Christ Jesus
4.23 grace of the Lord J. C. be with your spirit
Col 1. 1 Paul, an apostle of Christ Jesus
1. 2 To the saints and faithful brethren in C.
1. 3 thank God, the Father of our Lord J. C.
1. 4 we have heard of your faith in C. J.
1. 7 Epaphras . . is a faithful minister of Christ
1.24 complete what is lacking in C.'s afflictions
1.27 this mystery, which is Christ in you
1.28 that we may present every man mature in C.
2. 2 the knowledge of God's mystery, of C.
2. 5 to see . . the firmness of your faith in C.
2. 6 As . . you received C. J. the Lord, so live
2. 8 to the elemental spirits . . not . . Christ
2.11 body of flesh in the circumcision of C.
2.17 the substance belongs to Christ
2.20 If with C. you died to the elemental spirits
3. 1 If then you have been raised with C., seek the things . . above, where C. is
3. 3 have died, and your life is hid with C.
3. 4 When Christ who is our life appears
3.11 ⟨not⟩ slave, free man, but C. is all, and in all
3.15 let the peace of Christ rule in your hearts
3.16 Let the word of Christ dwell in you
3.24 you are serving the Lord Christ
4. 3 a door . . to declare the mystery of C.
4.12 Epaphras . . a servant[g] of Christ Jesus
1 Th 1. 1 in God the Father and the Lord J. C.
1. 3 steadfastness of hope in our Lord J. C.
2. 6 might have made demands as apostles of C.
2.14 imitators of the churches of God in C. J.
3. 2 Timothy . . God's servant in the gospel of C.
4.16 the dead in Christ will rise first
5. 9 obtain salvation through our Lord J. C.
5.18 this is the will of God in C. J. for you
5.23 blameless at the coming of our Lord J. C.
5.28 grace of our Lord J. C. be with you
2 Th 1. 1 in God our Father and the Lord J. C.
1. 2 peace from God . . and the Lord J. C.
1.12 grace of our God and the Lord J. C.
2. 1 concerning the coming of our Lord J. C.
2.14 you may obtain the glory of our Lord J. C.
2.16 may our Lord J. C. himself . . ⟨comfort⟩
3. 5 the love of God and . . steadfastness of C.
3. 6 in the name of our Lord J. C. . . keep away
3.12 we command and exhort in the Lord J. C.
3.18 grace of our Lord J. C. be with you
1 Tim 1. 1 Paul, an apostle of C. J. by command of God our Savior and of C. J. our hope
1. 2 peace from God . . and C. J. our Lord
1.12 C. J. our Lord . . judged me faithful
1.14 faith and love that are in C. J.
1.15 C. J. came into the world to save sinners
1.16 that in me . . J. C. might display his . . patience
2. 5 there is one mediator . . the man C. J.
3.13 confidence in the faith which is in C. J.
4. 6 you will be a good minister of C. J.
5.11 wanton against C. they desire to marry
5.21 In the presence of God and of C. J.
6. 3 the sound words of our Lord Jesus Christ
6.13 presence of God who gives life . . and of C. J.
6.14 until the appearing of our Lord J. C.
2 Tim 1. 1 Paul, an apostle of C. J. by the will of God according to the promise . . which is in C. J.
1. 2 peace from God . . and C. J. our Lord
2 Tim 1. 9 in virtue of his . . grace . . in Christ Jesus
1.10 through the appearing of our Savior C. J.
1.13 in the faith and love which are in C. J.
2. 1 son, be strong in the grace that is in C. J.
2. 3 Share in suffering as a good soldier of C. J.
2. 8 Remember J. C., risen from the dead
2.10 salvation in C. J. with its eternal glory
3.12 all who desire to live a godly life in C. J.
3.15 for salvation through faith in C. J.
4. 1 C. J. who is to judge the living and the dead
Tit 1. 1 Paul . . an apostle of Jesus Christ
1. 4 peace from God . . and C. J. our Savior
2.13 glory of our great God and Savior[c] J. C.
3. 6 poured out . . richly through J. C. our Savior
Phm . 1 Paul, a prisoner for Christ Jesus
. 3 peace from God . . and the Lord J. C.
. 6 the good that is ours in Christ
. 8 bold enough in Christ to command you
. 9 Paul . . a prisoner also for Christ Jesus
.20 Yes, brother . . Refresh my heart in Christ
.23 Epaphras, my fellow prisoner in C. J.
.25 grace of the Lord J. C.
Heb 3. 6 Christ was faithful over God's[f] house as a son
3.14 we share in Christ, if only we hold . . firm
5. 5 Christ did not exalt himself to . . high priest
6. 1 leave the elementary doctrine of C.
9.11 when Christ appeared as a high priest
9.14 how much more shall the blood of C.
9.24 For C. has entered . . into heaven itself
9.28 C. . . will appear a second time, . . to save
10.10 through the offering of the body of J. C.
11.26 considered abuse suffered for the C.
13. 8 J. C. is the same yesterday and today
13.21 through J. C.; to whom be glory for ever
Jas 1. 1 a servant of God and of the Lord J. C.
2. 1 as you hold the faith of our Lord J. C.
1 Pet 1. 1 Peter, an apostle of Jesus Christ
1. 2 sanctified . . for obedience to J. C.
1. 3 the God and Father of our Lord J. C.!
1. 3 living hope through the resurrection of J. C.
1. 7 glory and honor at the revelation of J. C.
1.11 person or time . . indicated by the Spirit of C. . . when predicting the sufferings of C.
1.13 grace . . coming . . at the revelation of J. C.
1.19 precious blood of C., like that of a lamb
2. 5 sacrifices acceptable to God through J. C.
2.21 called, because Christ also suffered for you
3.15 in your hearts reverence Christ as Lord
3.16 who revile your good behavior in Christ
3.18 For Christ also died[h] for sins once for all
3.21 saves you . . through the resurrection of J. C.
4. 1 Since . . Christ suffered in the flesh[i]
4.11 that . . God may be glorified through J. C.
4.13 rejoice . . as you share Christ's sufferings
4.14 If you are reproached for the name of C.
5. 1 elder and a witness of the sufferings of C.
5.10 called you to his eternal glory in C.
5.14 Peace to all of you that are in Christ
2 Pet 1. 1 Simeon[x] Peter, a servant and apostle of J. C.
1. 1 righteousness of our God and Savior J. C.[a]
1. 8 unfruitful in the knowledge of our Lord J. C.
1.11 eternal kingdom of our Lord and Savior J. C.
1.14 soon, as our Lord J. C. showed me
1.16 power and coming of our Lord J. C.
2.20 knowledge of our Lord and Savior J. C.
3.18 knowledge of our Lord and Savior J. C.
1 Jn 1. 3 fellowship is with . . his Son J. C.
2. 1 we have an advocate with the Father, J. C.
2.22 the liar . . denies that Jesus is the Christ
3.23 we should believe in the name of his Son J. C.
4. 2 Spirit of God . . confesses . . J. C.
5. 1 who believes that Jesus is the Christ
5. 6 he who came by water and blood, J. C.
5.20 we are in him who is true, in his Son J. C.
2 Jn . 3 peace . . from God . . and from J. C.
. 7 not acknowledge the coming of J. C.
. 9 who . . does not abide in the doctrine of C.

Jude . 1 Jude, a servant of J. C... To those who are ..kept for J. C.
. 4 who .. deny our only Master and Lord, J. C.[a]
.17 predictions of the apostles of our Lord J. C.
.21 wait for the mercy of our Lord J. C.
.25 to .. God, our Savior through J. C.
Rev 1. 1 revelation of J. C., which God gave him
1. 2 bore witness .. to the testimony of J. C.
1. 5 from Jesus Christ the faithful witness
11.15 "kingdom of our Lord and of his Christ
12.10 "salvation .. and the authority of his Christ
20. 4 reigned with Christ a thousand years
20. 6 priests of God and of Christ .. shall reign
CONTEXTUALLY
Heb 8. 6 as it is, C.[o] has obtained a ministry†
10. 5 when Christ[v] came into the world†
10.12 when Christ[w] had offered for all time†

CHRIST, FALSE
1. *false Christ:* ψευδόχριστος PSEUDOCHRISTOS*
Mt 24.24 "false Christs and false prophets will arise
Mk 13.22 "False Christs and false prophets will arise

CHRISTIAN
1. *Christian:* χριστιανός CHRISTIANOS*
Acts 11.26 for the first time called Christians
26.28 "you think to make me a Christian!
1 Pet 4.16 if one suffers as a Christian, let him .. glorify

CHRYSOLITE
1. *topaz:* χρυσόλιθος CHRYSOLITHOS*
Rev 21.20 the seventh chrysolite, the eighth beryl

CHRYSOPRASE
1. *chrysoprase:* χρυσόπρασος CHRYSOPRASOS*
Rev 21.20 the ninth topaz, the tenth chrysoprase

CHURCH
1. *assembly, church:* ἐκκλησία EKKLĒSIA
Mt 16.18 "on this rock[t] I will build my church
18.17 "If he refuses to listen .. tell .. the church
18.17 "if he refuses to listen even to the church
Acts 5.11 great fear came upon the whole church
8. 1 great persecution arose against the church
8. 3 Saul was ravaging the church
9.31 the church .. had peace and was built up
11.22 News .. came to .. the church in Jerusalem
11.26 they met with[j] the church, and taught
12. 1 some who belonged to the church
12. 5 earnest prayer .. was made to God by the c.
13. 1 in the church at Antioch .. were prophets
14.23 they .. appointed elders .. in every church
14.27 they gathered the church together
15. 3 being sent on their way by the church
15. 4 they were welcomed by the church
15.22 it seemed good to .. the whole church
15.41 he went .. strengthening the churches
16. 5 churches were strengthened in the faith
18.22 at Caesarea, he .. greeted the church
20.17 he .. called to him the elders of the church
20.28 "overseers, to care for the church of God[v]
Rom 16. 1 Phoebe, .. of the church at Cenchreae
16. 4 all the churches of the Gentiles give thanks
16. 5 greet also the church in their house
16.16 All the churches of Christ greet you
16.23 Gaius, who is host .. to the whole church
1 Cor 1. 2 To the church of God which is at Corinth
4.17 as I teach them everywhere in every church
6. 4 those who are least esteemed by the church
7.17 This is my rule in all the churches
10.32 Give no offense .. to the church of God
11.16 we recognize no other .. nor do the churches
11.18 when you assemble as a church
11.22 Or do you despise the church of God?
12.28 God has appointed in the c. first apostles
14. 4 he who prophesies edifies the church
14. 5 interprets, so that the church may be edified
14.12 strive to excel in building up the church
14.19 in church .. rather .. words with my mind
1 Cor 14.23 If, therefore, the whole church assembles
14.28 let each of them keep silence in church
14.33 As in all the churches of the saints
14.34 women should keep silence in the churches
14.35 shameful for a woman to speak in church
15. 9 because I persecuted the church of God
16. 1 as I directed the churches of Galatia
16.19 churches of Asia send greetings. Aquila and Prisca .. with the church in their house
2 Cor 1. 1 To the church of God which is at Corinth
8. 1 the grace of God .. shown in the churches
8.18 brother .. famous among all the churches
8.19 appointed by the churches to travel
8.23 they are messengers[j] of the churches
8.24 So give proof, before the churches
11. 8 I robbed other churches .. to serve you
11.28 my anxiety for all the churches
12.13 less favored than the rest of the churches
Gal 1. 2 To the churches of Galatia
1.13 I persecuted the church of God violently
1.22 still not known by sight to the churches
Eph 1.22 the head over all things for the church
3.10 through the church the .. wisdom of God
3.21 glory in the church and in Christ Jesus
5.23 as Christ is the head of the church
5.24 As the church is subject to Christ, so .. wives
5.25 love your wives, as Christ loved the church
5.27 might present the church .. in splendor
5.29 cherishes it, as Christ does the church
5.32 mystery .. refers to Christ and the church
Phil 3. 6 as to zeal a persecutor of the church
4.15 no church entered into partnership .. except
Col 1.18 He is the head of the body, the church
1.24 for the sake of his body, .. the church
4.15 to Nympha and the church in her house
4.16 read also in the church of the Laodiceans
1 Th 1. 1 To the church of the Thessalonians
2.14 imitators of the churches of God
2 Th 1. 1 To the church of the Thessalonians
1. 4 we ourselves boast of you in the churches
1 Tim 3. 5 how can he care for God's church?
3.15 the household of God .. the church
5.16 let the church not be burdened
Phm . 2 Archippus .. and the church in your house
Jas 5.14 Let him call for the elders of the church
3 Jn . 6 testified to your love before the church
. 9 I have written something to the church
.10 stops .. and puts them out of the church
Rev 1. 4 John to the seven churches .. in Asia
1.11 "Write what you see .. to the seven churches
1.20 "stars are the angels of the seven churches
1.20 "seven lampstands are the seven churches
2. 1 "To the angel of the c. in Ephesus
2. 7 "hear what the Spirit says to the churches
Also Rev **2.**11, 17, 29; **3.**6, 13, 22
2. 8 "to the angel of the c. in Smyrna
2.12 "to the angel of the c. in Pergamum
2.18 "to the angel of the c. in Thyatira
2.23 " 'churches shall know that I am he
3. 1 "to the angel of the c. in Sardis
3. 7 "to the angel of the c. in Philadelphia
3.14 "to the angel of the c. in Laodicea
22.16 "this testimony for the churches
CONTEXTUALLY
1 Cor 5.12 Is it not those inside the church?

CHUZA: Χουζᾶς 'kyüzə
Lk 8. 3 Joanna, the wife of Chuza, Herod's steward

CILICIA: Κιλικία sə'lish(ē)ə II,G-3
Acts 6. 9 those from C... arose and disputed
15.23 "to the brethren .. of the Gentiles in .. C.
15.41 he went through Syria and C.
21.39 "I am a Jew, from Tarsus in Cilicia
22. 3 "I am a Jew, born at Tarsus in Cilicia
23.34 When he learned that he was from C.
27. 5 sea which is off Cilicia and Pamphylia
Gal 1.21 I went into the regions of Syria and C.

CINNAMON
1. *cinnamon:* κιννάμωμον KINNAMŌMON*
Rev 18.13 cinnamon, spice, incense, myrrh

CIRCUIT, MAKE A
1. *go about:* περιέρχομαι PERIERCHOMAI
Acts 28.13 we made a circuit and arrived at Rhegium

CIRCUMCISE
1. *cut around:* περιτέμνω PERITEMNŌ
Lk 1.59 they came to circumcise the child
2.21 when . . circumcised, he was called Jesus
Jn 7.22 "you circumcise a man upon the sabbath
Acts 7. 8 "Abraham . . circumcised him
15. 1 "circumcised according to the custom
15. 5 "It is necessary to circumcise them
16. 3 Paul . . took him and circumcised him
21.21 "telling them not to circumcise their children
1 Cor 7.18 Was any one . . already circumcised?
Gal 2. 3 Titus . . not compelled to be circumcised
6.12 would compel you to be circumcised
6.13 they desire to have you circumcised
Col 2.11 In him also you were circumcised

CIRCUMCISED
1. *foreskin, uncircumcision:* ἀκροβυστία AKROBYSTIA
[a]B.1.a.2 [b]dat.
Rom 4.10 [ab]Was it before . . he had been circumcised?
4.10 [ab]It was . . before he was circumcised
4.11 [a]who believe without being circumcised
4.12 [ab]Abraham had before he was circumcised
2. *cutting around:* περιτομή PERITOMĒ
[a]C.2 [b]B.1.a.2 [c]A.3.b.4
Acts 10.45 [a]believers from among the circumcised
Rom 3.30 [a]he will justify the circumcised
4. 9 [a]blessing pronounced . . upon the circumcised?
4.10 [b]Was it . . after he had been circumcised? It was not after . . he was circumcised
4.12 [a]the father of the circumcised who are not merely circumcised
15. 8 [a]Christ became a servant to the c.
Gal 2. 7 [a]entrusted with the gospel to the c.
2. 8 [a](worked through Peter for . . the circumcised
2. 9 [a]they ⟨should go⟩ to the circumcised
Phil 3. 5 [c]circumcised on the eighth day
Col 3.11 [a]circumcised and uncircumcised

CIRCUMCISION
1. *cutting around:* περιτομή PERITOMĒ
Jn 7.22 "Moses gave you circumcision
7.23 "If on the sabbath . . circumcision
Acts 7. 8 "he gave him the covenant of circumcision
11. 2 the circumcision party criticized him
Rom 2.25 Circumcision indeed is of value if you obey
2.25 your circumcision becomes uncircumcision
2.26 his uncircumcision . . as circumcision?
2.27 you who have . . circumcision
2.28 nor is true circumcision . . external
2.29 real circumcision is a matter of the heart
3. 1 what is the value of circumcision?
4.11 He received circumcision as a sign
1 Cor 7.19 neither circumcision counts for anything
Gal 2.12 drew back . . fearing the circumcision party
5. 6 in Christ Jesus neither circumcision
5.11 if I, brethren, still preach circumcision
6.15 neither circumcision counts for anything
Eph 2.11 circumcision, which is made in the flesh
Phil 3. 3 we are the true circumcision, who worship
Col 2.11 a circumcision made without hands
2.11 in the circumcision of Christ
4.11 the only men of the circumcision
Tit 1.10 deceivers, especially the circumcision party

CIRCUMCISION, RECEIVE
1. *cut around:* περιτέμνω (pass.) PERITEMNŌ
Gal 5. 2 that if you receive circumcision
5. 3 to every man who receives circumcision
6.13 even those who receive circumcision do not

CIRCUMCISION, REMOVE THE MARKS OF
1. *draw the prepuce forward:* ἐπισπάομαι EPISPAOMAI*
1 Cor 7.18 not seek to remove the marks of c.

CIRCUMCISION, SEEK
1. *cut around:* περιτέμνω (pass.) PERITEMNŌ
1 Cor 7.18 Let him not seek circumcision

CIRCUMSTANCE
CONTEXTUALLY
Phil 4.12 in any and all circumstances I have learned
1 Th 5.18 give thanks in all circumstances

CITIZEN (*See also* ROMAN CITIZEN)
1. *citizen, fellow citizen:* πολίτης POLITĒS
Lk 15.15 "joined himself to one of the citizens
19.14 "citizens hated him and sent an embassy
Acts 21.39 "from Tarsus . . a citizen of no mean city
CONTEXTUALLY
Acts 16.37 "beaten us . . who are Roman citizens
16.38 heard that they were Roman citizens
22.25 "Is it lawful . . to scourge . . a Roman c.?
22.26 "For this man is a Roman citizen
22.27 "Tell me, are you a Roman citizen?
22.28 Paul said, "But I was born a citizen
22.29 he realized that Paul was a Roman c.
23.27 "having learned that he was a Roman c.

CITIZEN, FELLOW
1. *fellow citizen:* συμπολίτης SYMPOLITĒS*
Eph 2.19 you are fellow citizens with the saints

CITIZENSHIP
1. *citizenship, body of citizens:* πολιτεία POLITEIA
Acts 22.28 "I bought this citizenship for a large sum

CITY
1. *city, city-state:* πόλις POLIS
Mt 2.23 went and dwelt in a city called Nazareth
4. 5 the devil took him to the holy city
5.14 "A city set on a hill cannot be hid
5.35 "Jerusalem . . is the city of the great King
8.33 herdsmen fled, and going into the city
8.34 all the city came out to meet Jesus
9. 1 crossed over and came to his own city
9.35 Jesus went about all the cities . . teaching
11. 1 he went on . . to . . preach in their cities
11.20 Then he began to upbraid the cities
12.25 "no city . . divided against itself will stand
21.10 entered Jerusalem, all the city was stirred
21.17 he went out of the city to Bethany
21.18 returning to the city, he was hungry
22. 7 "The king was angry . . and burned their city
26.18 "Go into the city to a certain one
27.53 they went into the holy city and appeared
28.11 some of the guard went into the city
Mk 1.33 the whole city was gathered together
5.14 herdsmen fled, and told it in the city
6.56 wherever he came, in villages, cities
11.19 evening . . they[u] went out of the city
14.13 "Go into the city, and a man carrying a jar
14.16 disciples set out and went to the city
Lk 1.26 to a city of Galilee named Nazareth
1.39 into the hill country, to a city of Judah
2. 3 all went to be enrolled, each to his own city
2. 4 Joseph also went up . . from the city of Nazareth, to Judea, to the city of David
2.11 "born this day in the city of David
2.39 they returned . . to their own city, Nazareth
4.29 they rose up and put him out of the city
4.29 the hill on which their city was built
4.31 down to Capernaum, a city of Galilee
4.43 "I must preach . . to the other cities also
5.12 While he was in one of the cities
7.11 he went to a city called Nain
7.12 As he drew near to the gate of the city
7.12 a large crowd from the city was with her
7.37 a woman of the city, who was a sinner
8. 1 he went on through cities and villages
8.27 a man from the city who had demons
8.34 told it in the city and in the country
8.39 proclaiming throughout the whole city
9.10 withdrew apart to a city called Bethsaida

Lk 14.21 " 'Go out quickly to the streets .. of the city
18. 2 "In a certain city there was a judge
18. 3 "a widow in that city who kept coming
19.17 " 'you shall have authority over ten cities
19.19 " 'And you are to be over five cities
19.41 drew near and saw the city he wept over it
22.10 "Behold, when you have entered the city
23.19 for an insurrection started in the city
24.49 "in the city, until you are clothed with power
Jn 1.44 Bethsaida, the city of Andrew
4. 5 he came to a city of Samaria, called Sychar
4. 8 gone away into the city to buy food
4.28 left her water jar, and went .. into the city
4.30 They went out of the city
4.39 Samaritans from that city believed in him
19.20 Jesus was crucified .. near the city
Acts 4.27 "in this city there were gathered together
7.58 cast him out of the city and stoned him
8. 5 Philip went down to a city of Samaria
8. 8 So there was much joy in that city
8. 9 Simon .. had .. practiced magic in the city
9. 6 "rise and enter the city, and you will be told
10. 9 as they were .. coming near the city
11. 5 "I was in the city of Joppa praying
12.10 to the iron gate leading into the city
13.44 almost the whole city gathered together
13.50 Jews incited .. the leading men of the city
14. 4 the people of the city were divided
14. 6 Lystra and Derbe, cities of Lycaonia
14.13 Zeus, whose temple was in front of the city
14.19 stoned Paul and dragged him out of the city
14.20 he rose up and entered the city
14.21 they .. preached the gospel to that city
15.21 "Moses has .. in every city those who preach
15.36 "let us .. visit the brethren in every city
16. 4 went on their way through the cities
16.12 Philippi .. the leading city .. of Macedonia
16.12 We remained in this city some days
16.14 Lydia, from the city of Thyatira
16.20 "These .. Jews .. are disturbing our city
16.39 they .. asked them to leave the city
17. 5 gathered a crowd, set the city in an uproar
17.16 he saw that the city was full of idols
18.10 "for I have many people in this city
19.29 So the city was filled with the confusion
19.35 "the city of the Ephesians is temple keeper
20.23 "Holy Spirit testifies to me in every city
21. 5 on our way till we were outside the city
21.29 seen Trophimus .. with him in the city
21.30 Then all the city was aroused
21.39 "from Tarsus .. a citizen of no mean city
22. 3 "born at Tarsus .. but brought up in this city
24.12 "the temple .. the synagogues, or .. the city
25.23 tribunes and the prominent men of the city
26.11 "I persecuted them even to foreign cities
27. 8 Fair Havens, near .. the city of Lasea
Rom 16.23 Erastus, the city treasurer
2 Cor 11.26 danger in the city, danger in the wilderness
11.32 guarded the city of Damascus .. to seize me
Heb 11.10 city .. whose builder and maker is God
11.16 God .. has prepared for them a city
12.22 Mount Zion and .. the city of the living God
13.14 here we have no lasting city
2 Pet 2. 6 cities of Sodom and Gomorrah to ashes
Jude . 7 surrounding cities .. likewise acted immorally
Rev 3.12 " 'the name of the city of my God
11. 2 "they will trample over the holy city
11. 8 great city .. allegorically[d] called Sodom
11.13 earthquake, and a tenth of the city fell
14.20 wine press was trodden outside the city
16.19 The great city was split into three parts, and the cities of the nations fell
17.18 "the woman that you saw is the great city
18.10 "Alas! alas! thou great city, thou mighty city, Babylon!
18.16 "Alas, alas, for the great city!
18.18 "What .. was like the great city?
Rev 18.19 "Alas, alas, for the great city!
18.21 "So shall Babylon the great city be thrown
20. 9 camp of the saints and the beloved city
21. 2 I saw the holy city, new Jerusalem
21.10 showed me the holy city Jerusalem
21.14 wall of the city had twelve foundations
21.15 measuring rod of gold to measure the city
21.16 The city lies foursquare .. ; and he measured the city with his rod
21.18 the city was pure gold, clear as glass
21.19 foundations of the wall of the city
21.21 the street of the city was pure gold
21.23 the city has no need of sun or moon
22.14 they may enter the city by the gates
22.19 will take away his share in the .. holy city

CONTEXTUALLY
Lk 21.21 "let those who are inside the c. depart
Rev 21.22 And I saw no temple in the city
22. 2 through the middle of the street of the c.

CITY AUTHORITY

1. *civic magistrate:* πολιτάρχης POLITARCHĒS*
Acts 17. 6 dragged .. before the city authorities
17. 8 the city authorities were disturbed

CIVILIAN

1. *everyday life, livelihood:* βίος (gen.) BIOS
2 Tim 2. 4 gets entangled in civilian pursuits

CLAD IN

CLAD IN, BE

1. *throw around, put on:* περιβάλλω PERIBALLŌ
[a]+ἐν [b]part.
Rev 3. 5 [a]" 'He .. shall be clad .. in white garments
4. 4 [ab]elders, clad in white garments
19.13 [b]He is clad in a robe dipped in[m] blood

CLAIM

1. *origin, occasion:* ἀφορμή APHORMĒ
[a]A.1.d
2 Cor 11.12 [a]in order to undermine the claim of those who would like to claim
2. *reckon, count:* λογίζομαι LOGIZOMAI
2 Cor 3. 5 Not .. competent .. to claim anything
3. *say, assert:* φάσκω PHASKŌ
Rom 1.22 Claiming to be wise, they became fools
IDIOMATICALLY
a. Jn 8.53 "Who do you claim to be? τίνα σεαυτὸν ποιεῖς; [POIEŌ]

CLAIM, RIGHTFUL

1. *authority, power:* ἐξουσία EXOUSIA
1 Cor 9.12 If others share this rightful c. upon you

CLAMOR

1. *shouting:* κραυγή KRAUGĒ
Acts 23. 9 Then a great clamor arose
Eph 4.31 clamor and slander be put away from you

CLANG

1. *wail loudly:* ἀλαλάζω ALALAZŌ
1 Cor 13. 1 I am a noisy gong or a clanging cymbal

CLASS

1. *reckon in, select:* ἐγκρίνω EGKRINŌ*
2 Cor 10.12 Not that we venture to class .. ourselves

CLAUDA: Κλαῦδα 'klôdə
Acts [27.16 a small island called *Clauda*‡

CLAUDIA: Κλαυδία 'klôdēə
2 Tim 4.21 Eubulus sends greetings .. as do .. C.

CLAUDIUS: Κλαύδιος 'klôdēəs (*See also* LYSIAS, CLAUDIUS)
Acts 11.28 this took place in the days of Claudius
18. 2 C. .. commanded all the Jews to leave Rome

CLAY

1. *earth, mud:* πηλός PĒLOS*
Jn 9. 6 he spat on the ground and made clay .. and anointed the man's eyes with the clay
9.11 "Jesus made clay and anointed my eyes
9.14 a sabbath day when Jesus made the clay
9.15 "He put clay on my eyes .. and I see
Rom 9.21 Has the potter no right over the clay?

CLEAN (*See also* SPRINKLE CLEAN)
1. *pure:* καθαρός KATHAROS
Mt 23.26 "that the outside also may be clean
27.59 wrapped it in a clean linen shroud
Lk 11.41 "behold, everything is clean for you
Jn 13.10 "He who has bathed . . is clean all over; and you[x] are clean, but not every one of you
13.11 why he said, "You are not all clean
15. 3 "You are already made clean by the word
Rom 14.20 Everything is indeed clean

CLEAN, BE

CLEAN, DECLARE

CLEAN, MAKE
1. *cleanse:* καθαρίζω KATHARIZŌ
[a]pass.
Mt 8. 2 "Lord, if you will, you can make me clean
8. 3 [a]"I will; be clean
Mk 1.40 "If you will, you can make me clean
1.41 [a]"I will; be clean
1.42 leprosy left him, and he was made clean
7.19 (Thus he declared all foods clean
Lk 5.12 "Lord, if you will, you can make me clean
5.13 [a]"I will; be clean

CLEANSE
1. *cleanse:* καθαρίζω KATHARIZŌ
Mt 8. 3 "immediately his leprosy was cleansed
10. 8 "raise the dead, cleanse lepers
11. 5 "lepers are cleansed and the deaf hear
23.25 "for you cleanse the outside of the cup
23.26 "blind Pharisee! first cleanse the inside
Lk 4.27 "many lepers . . ; and none . . was cleansed
7.22 "the lame walk, lepers are cleansed
11.39 "Pharisees cleanse the outside of the cup
17.14 as they went they were cleansed
17.17 "Were not ten cleansed? Where are the nine?
Acts 10.15 "What God has cleansed
11. 9 " 'What God has cleansed
15. 9 "cleansed their hearts by faith
2 Cor 7. 1 beloved, let us cleanse ourselves
Eph 5.26 might sanctify her, having cleansed her
Heb 10. 2 If the worshipers had once been cleansed
Jas 4. 8 Cleanse your hands, you sinners
1 Jn 1. 7 the blood of Jesus his Son cleanses us
1. 9 will . . cleanse us from all unrighteousness

CLEANSE OUT
1. *clean out:* ἐκκαθαίρω EKKATHAIRŌ
1 Cor 5. 7 Cleanse out the old leaven

CLEANSED, THAT ONE WAS
1. *purification:* καθαρισμός KATHARISMOS [A.l.e]
2 Pet 1. 9 forgotten that he was cleansed from his . . sins

CLEANSING
1. *purification:* καθαρισμός KATHARISMOS
Mk 1.44 "for your cleansing what Moses commanded
Lk 5.14 "make an offering for your cleansing

CLEAR (*See also* OMEN, CLEAR)
1. *good:* ἀγαθός AGATHOS
1 Pet 3.16 keep your conscience clear
3.21 an appeal to God for a clear conscience
2. *giving no offense:* ἀπρόσκοπος APROSKOPOS
Acts 24.16 "I . . take pains to have a clear conscience
3. *purge thoroughly:* διακαθαίρω DIAKATHAIRŌ*
Lk 3.17 "winnowing fork . . to clear his threshing floor
4. *purge thoroughly:* διακαθαρίζω DIAKATHARIZŌ*
Mt 3.12 "he will clear his threshing floor
5. *good, beautiful:* καλός KALOS
Heb 13.18 we are sure that we have a clear conscience
6. *pure:* καθαρός KATHAROS
1 Tim 3. 9 mystery of the faith with a clear conscience
2 Tim 1. 3 God whom I serve with a clear conscience
Rev 21.18 the city was pure gold, clear as glass

CLEAR AS CRYSTAL
1. *be clear as crystal:* κρυσταλλίζω (part.) KRYSTALLIZŌ*
Rev 21.11 jewel, like a jasper, clear as crystal

CLEAR, MAKE
1. *make manifest, make known:* φανερόω PHANEROŌ
Col 4. 4 that I may make it clear, as I ought

CLEAR, MAKE IT
1. *manifest, make clear:* ἐμφανίζω EMPHANIZŌ
Heb 11.14 people who speak thus make it clear

CLEAR ONESELF, EAGERNESS TO
1. *speech in defense:* ἀπολογία APOLOGIA
2 Cor 7.11 what eagerness to clear yourselves!

CLEARLY (*See also* SEE CLEARLY)
1. *openly:* φανερῶς PHANERŌS
Acts 10. 3 he saw clearly in a vision an angel
2. *more clearly:* τηλαυγῶς TĒLAUGŌS*
Mk 8.25 he . . was restored, and saw everything clearly
IDIOMATICALLY
a. Rom 1.20 his invisible nature . . has been clearly perceived τὰ . . ἀόρατα αὐτοῦ . . νοούμενα καθορᾶται [NOEŌ]

CLEARLY SEEN, BE
1. *make manifest, make known:* φανερόω (pass.) PHANEROŌ
Jn 3.21 that it may be clearly seen that his deeds

CLEMENT: Κλήμης 'klemənt
Phil 4. 3 labored . . with me in the gospel . . with C.

CLEOPAS: Κλεοπᾶς 'klēəpəs
Lk 24.18 Then one of them, named C., answered

CLERK, TOWN
1. *secretary, registrar:* γραμματεύς GRAMMATEUS
Acts 19.35 when the town clerk had quieted the crowd

CLEVER
1. *intelligent, wise:* συνετός SYNETOS
1 Cor 1.19 "the cleverness of the clever I will thwart

CLEVERLY DEVISED
1. *make wise, instruct:* σοφίζω (perf. pass. part.) SOPHIZŌ
2 Pet 1.16 we did not follow cleverly devised myths

CLEVERNESS
1. *intelligence, understanding:* σύνεσις SYNESIS
1 Cor 1.19 "the cleverness of the clever I will thwart

CLIMB IN

CLIMB UP
1. *go up, come up:* ἀναβαίνω ANABAINŌ
Lk 19. 4 he . . climbed up into a sycamore tree
Jn 10. 1 "he who . . climbs in by another way

CLING
1. *join, unite:* κολλάω (pass.) KOLLAŌ
Lk 10.11 " 'the dust of your town that clings to our feet
2. *seize, hold fast:* κρατέω KRATEŌ
Acts 3.11 he clung to Peter and John

CLINGS SO CLOSELY, WHICH
1. *easily entrapping:* εὐπερίστατος EUPERISTATOS*
Heb 12. 1 lay aside . . sin which clings so closely

CLOAK
1. *outer garment:* ἱμάτιον (sg. or pl.) HIMATION
Mt 5.40 "let him have your cloak as well
2. *thick upper garment:* φαιλόνης PHAILONĒS*
2 Tim 4.13 When you come, bring the cloak
3. *pretense, excuse:* πρόφασις PROPHASIS
1 Th 2. 5 we never used . . a cloak for greed

CLOAK, PURPLE
1. *purple dye, purple cloth:* πορφύρα PORPHYRA
Mk 15.17 they clothed him in a purple cloak
15.20 they stripped him of the purple cloak

CLOPAS: Κλωπᾶς 'klōpəs
Jn 19.25 Mary the wife of C., and Mary Magdalene

CLOSE
1. *necessary:* ἀναγκαῖος ANAGKAIOS
Acts 10.24 Cornelius . . called . . his . . close friends
2. *nearer:* ἆσσον ASSON*
Acts 27.13 sailed along Crete, close inshore
3. *close the eyes:* καμμύω KAMMYŌ*
Mt 13.15 " 'eyes they have closed, lest they . . perceive
Acts 28.27 " 'eyes they have closed; lest they . . perceive
4. *shut:* κλείω KLEIŌ
1 Jn 3.17 if any . . sees his brother . . yet closes his heart
5. *fold, roll up:* πτύσσω PTYSSŌ*
Lk 4.20 he closed the book, and gave it back

6. *completion, end:* συντέλεια SYNTELEIA
Mt 13.39 "the harvest is the close of the age
13.40 "so will it be at the close of the age
13.49 "So it will be at the close of the age
24. 3 "the sign . . of the close of the age?
28.20 "I am with you always, to the close of the age
CONTEXTUALLY
Jn 19.42 as the tomb was c. at hand, they laid J.

CLOSE TO
1. *in, at, by:* ἐν (+dat.) EN
Jn **13.**23
2. *on, at:* ἐπί (+acc.) EPI
Jn **13.**25; **21.**20

CLOSELY (*See also* CLINGS SO CLOSELY, WHICH; LOOK CLOSELY AT)
1. *precisely:* ἀκριβῶς AKRIBŌS
[a]comp.
Lk 1. 3 followed all things closely[a] for some time past†
Acts 23.20 [a]"to inquire somewhat more closely about him

CLOSER, THE
1. *still more:* περισσοτέρως PERISSOTERŌS
Heb 2. 1 we must pay the closer attention

CLOTH
1. *strip of cloth, patch:* ῥάκος RHAKOS*
Mt 9.16 "piece of unshrunk cloth on an old garment
Mk 2.21 "piece of unshrunk cloth on an old garment
2. *napkin, towel:* σουδάριον SOUDARION
Jn 11.44 his face wrapped with a cloth

CLOTH, LINEN
1. *linen cloth:* ὀθόνιον OTHONION*
Lk [24.12 *Peter . . saw the linen cloths by themselves*‡
Jn 19.40 took the body . . bound it in linen cloths
20. 5 he saw the linen cloths lying there
20. 6 Then Simon . . saw the linen cloths lying
20. 7 napkin . . not lying with the linen cloths
2. *fine cloth, linen:* σινδών SINDŌN
Mk 14.51 nothing but a linen cloth about his body
14.52 he left the linen cloth and ran away naked

CLOTHE
1. *clothe:* ἀμφιάζω AMPHIAZŌ*
Lk 12.28 "if God so clothes the grass
2. *put around, clothe in:* ἀμφιέννυμι AMPHIENNYMI*
Mt 6.30 "if God so clothes the grass of the field
11. 8 "To see a man[a] clothed in soft raiment?
Lk 7.25 "A man clothed in soft clothing?
3. *dress:* ἱματίζω HIMATIZŌ*
Mk 5.15 demoniac . . clothed and in his right mind
Lk 8.35 sitting at the feet of Jesus, clothed
4. *throw around, put on:* περιβάλλω PERIBALLŌ
Mt 25.36 " 'I was naked and you clothed me
25.38 " 'when did we see thee . . naked and c.?
25.43 " 'I was . . naked and you did not clothe me
Rev 3.18 " 'buy . . white garments to clothe you
7. 9 multitude . . clothed in white robes
7.13 "Who are these, clothed in white robes?
11. 3 "to prophesy . . days, clothed in sackcloth
12. 1 a woman clothed with the sun
18.16 "great city that was clothed in fine linen!
19. 8 "granted her to be clothed with fine linen

CLOTHE IN
1. *put on, clothe:* ἐνδιδύσκω ENDIDYSKŌ
Mk 15.17 they clothed him in a purple cloak

CLOTHE ONESELF
1. *wear s. constantly:* ἐγκομβόομαι EGKOMBOOMAI*
1 Pet 5. 5 Clothe yourselves, all of you

CLOTHED
1. *put on, clothe:* ἐνδύω (mid. part.) ENDYŌ
Rev 1.13 a son of man, clothed with a long robe

CLOTHED, BE
1. *put on, clothe:* ἐνδύω (mid.) ENDYŌ
Mk 1. 6 John was clothed with camel's hair
Lk 24.49 "until you are clothed with power

CLOTHED, BE FURTHER
1. *put on over:* ἐπενδύομαι EPENDYOMAI
2 Cor 5. 4 that we would be further clothed

CLOTHED IN, BE
1. *put on, clothe:* ἐνδιδύσκω (mid.) ENDIDYSKŌ
Lk 16.19 "a rich man, who was clothed in purple

CLOTHES
1. *outer garment:* ἐπενδύτης EPENDYTĒS*
Jn 21. 7 he put on his clothes, for he was stripped
2. *outer garment:* ἱμάτιον (pl.) HIMATION
Mt 27.31 put his own clothes on him, and led him
Mk 15.20 put his own clothes on him. And they led
Lk 8.27 for a long time he had worn no clothes

CLOTHING
1. *garment:* ἔνδυμα ENDYMA
Mt 6.25 "Is not life more than . . clothing?
6.28 "why are you anxious about clothing?
7.15 "false prophets . . in sheep's clothing
Lk 12.23 "the body ⟨is⟩ more than clothing
2. *clothing:* ἐσθής ESTHĒS
Jas 2. 2 if a man . . in fine clothing comes . . and a poor man in shabby clothing also comes in
2. 3 the one who wears the fine clothing
3. *outer garment:* ἱμάτιον HIMATION
Lk 7.25 "A man clothed in soft clothing?[o]
1 Pet 3. 3 Let not yours be . . wearing of fine clothing[o]
4. *clothing:* ἱματισμός HIMATISMOS
Jn 19.24 "for my clothing they cast lots
5. *covering:* σκέπασμα SKEPASMA*
1 Tim 6. 8 but if we have food and clothing

CLOTHS, WRAP IN SWADDLING
1. *swathe:* σπαργανάω SPARGANOŌ*
Lk 2. 7 she . . wrapped him in swaddling cloths
2.12 "a babe wrapped in swaddling cloths

CLOUD
1. *cloud:* νεφέλη NEPHELĒ*
Mt 17. 5 a bright c. overshadowed them, . . voice from the c. said, "This is my . . Son[w]
24.30 "the Son of man coming on the clouds
26.64 "the Son of man . . coming on the clouds
Mk 9. 7 a cloud overshadowed them, and a voice came out of the cloud, "This is my . . Son[g]
13.26 "the Son of man coming in clouds
14.62 "the Son of man . . coming with the clouds
Lk 9.34 a cloud came and overshadowed them; and they were afraid as they entered the cloud
9.35 out of the cloud, saying, "This is my Son
12.54 "When you see a cloud rising in the west
21.27 "the Son of man coming in a cloud
Acts 1. 9 he was lifted up, and a cloud took him
1 Cor 10. 1 our fathers were all under the cloud
10. 2 all were baptized into Moses in the cloud
1 Th 4.17 we . . shall be caught up . . in the clouds
Jude .12 waterless clouds, carried along by winds
Rev 1. 7 Behold, he is coming with the clouds
10. 1 another mighty angel . . wrapped in a cloud
11.12 they went up to heaven in a cloud
14.14 lo, a white cloud, and seated on the cloud one like a son of man
14.15 calling . . to him who sat upon the cloud
14.16 he who sat upon the cloud swung his sickle
2. *cloud:* νέφος NEPHOS*
Heb 12. 1 we are surrounded by . . a cloud of witnesses

CLUB
1. *tree, wood:* ξύλον XYLON
Mt 26.47 a great crowd with swords and clubs
26.55 "with swords and clubs to capture me
Also Mk **14.**48; Lk **22.**52
Mk 14.43 with him a crowd with swords and clubs

CLUSTER
1. *bunch of grapes:* βότρυς BOTRYS*
Rev 14.18 "gather the clusters . . for its grapes are ripe

CNIDUS: Κνίδος 'nīdəs II,E-3
Acts 27. 7 We sailed slowly . . and arrived . . off Cnidus

COAL
1. *coal, charcoal:* ἄνθραξ ANTHRAX*
Rom 12.20 "you will heap burning coals upon his head

COAST
CONTEXTUALLY
Acts 27. 2 to the ports along the coast of Asia

COAST ALONG
1. *sail along:* παραλέγομαι PARALEGOMAI
Acts 27. 8 Coasting along . . we came to . . Fair Havens

COAT
1. *outer garment:* ἱμάτιον HIMATION
Lk 6.29 "from him who takes away your coat[o]
2. *tunic, undergarment:* χιτών CHITŌN
Mt 5.40 "if any one would . . take your coat
Lk 3.11 "who has two coats, let him share

COCK
1. *cock:* ἀλέκτωρ ALEKTŌR*
Mt 26.34 "before the cock crows, you will deny me
26.74 immediately the cock crowed
26.75 "Before the cock crows, you will deny me
Mk 14.30 "before the cock crows twice, you will deny
[14.68 *and the cock crowed*‡
14.72 immediately the cock crowed a second time
14.72 "Before the cock crows twice, you will deny
Lk 22.34 "the cock will not crow . . until you . . deny
22.60 "while he was still speaking, the cock crowed
22.61 "Before the cock crows . . you will deny me
Jn 13.38 "cock will not crow, till you have denied
18.27 Peter . . denied it; and . . the cock crowed

COCKCROW
1. *cockcrow:* ἀλεκτοροφωνία ALEKTOROPHŌNIA*
Mk 13.35 "will come, in the evening . . or at cockcrow

CODE (*See* OLD CODE)

CODE, WRITTEN
1. *letter, document:* γράμμα GRAMMA
Rom 2.27 you who have the written code
7. 6 we serve not under the old written code
2 Cor 3. 6 not in a written code but in the Spirit; for the written code kills

COHORT
1. *cohort, tactical unit:* σπεῖρα SPEIRA
Acts 10. 1 a centurion of . . the Italian Cohort
21.31 word came to the tribune of the cohort
27. 1 a centurion of the Augustan Cohort

COIN
1. *denarius:* δηνάριον DĒNARION
Mt 22.19 they brought him a coin[r]†
Mk 12.15 "Bring me a coin,[x] and let me look at it†
Lk 20.24 "Show me a coin.[f] "Whose likeness . . has it?†
2. *drachma:* δραχμή DRACHMĒ
Lk 15. 8 "what woman . . if she loses one coin?
15. 9 " 'for I have found the coin which I had lost
3. *fragment, coin:* κέρμα KERMA*
Jn 2.15 poured out the coins of the money-changers

COIN, COPPER
1. *thin, small:* λεπτός LEPTOS [B.3.b.2]
Mk 12.42 a poor widow . . put in two copper coins
Lk 21. 2 he saw a poor widow put in two copper coins

COIN, SILVER
1. *drachma:* δραχμή DRACHMĒ
Lk 15. 8 "what woman, having ten silver coins[t]?

COLD
1. *cold:* ψῦχος PSYCHOS*
Jn 18.18 made a charcoal fire, because it was cold
Acts 28. 2 because it had begun to rain and was cold
2 Cor 11.27 often without food, in cold and exposure
2. *cold:* ψυχρός PSYCHROS
Rev 3.15 " 'you are neither cold nor hot. Would that you were cold or hot!
3.16 " 'you are lukewarm, . . neither cold nor hot

COLD, GROW
1. *blow, cool:* ψύχω (pass.) PSYCHŌ*
Mt 24.12 "most men's love will grow cold

COLD WATER
1. *cold:* ψυχρός PSYCHROS [B.3.b.2]
Mt 10.42 "whoever gives . . even a cup of cold water

COLLECT
1. *do, practice:* πράσσω PRASSŌ
Lk 3.13 "Collect no more than is appointed you
19.23 " 'I should have collected it with interest

COLLECTOR
1. *receive, take:* λαμβάνω (subst.) LAMBANŌ
Mt 17.24 collectors of the half-shekel tax

COLLECTOR, CHIEF TAX
1. *chief tax collector:* ἀρχιτελώνης ARCHITELŌNĒS*
Lk 19. 2 Zacchaeus . . a chief tax collector, and rich

COLLECTOR, TAX
1. *farmer or collector of taxes:* τελώνης TELŌNĒS*
Mt 5.46 "Do not even the tax collectors do the same?
9.10 many tax collectors and sinners came
9.11 "Why . . eat with tax collectors?
10. 3 Matthew the tax collector
11.19 " 'a friend of tax collectors and sinners!
18.17 "let him be to you as . . a tax collector
21.31 "tax collectors . . go into the kingdom
21.32 "tax collectors and . . harlots believed him
Mk 2.15 many tax collectors . . sitting with Jesus
2.16 he was eating with . . tax collectors
2.16 "Why does he eat[i] with tax collectors?
Lk 3.12 Tax collectors also came to be baptized
5.27 saw a tax collector, named Levi
5.29 tax collectors and others sitting at table[r]
5.30 "Why do you eat . . with tax collectors?
7.29 (the tax collectors justified God
7.34 " 'a friend of tax collectors and sinners!
15. 1 tax collectors . . were all drawing near
18.10 "one a Pharisee . . the other a tax collector
18.11 " 'that I am not like . . this tax collector
18.13 "the tax collector, standing far off

COLONY
1. *colony* (Lat.): Κολωνία KOLŌNIA*
Acts 16.12 Philippi . . the leading city . . and a . . colony

COLOR OF FIRE, THE
1. *of fire, fiery:* πύρινος PYRINOS*
Rev 9.17 riders wore breastplates the color of fire

COLOR OF SULPHUR, THE
1. *sulphurous, yellow:* θειώδης THEIŌDĒS*
Rev 9.17 riders wore breastplates the c. . . of sulphur

COLOSSAE: Κολοσσαί kə'läsē II,E-3
Col 1.2 To the . . faithful brethren . . at Colossae

COLT
1. *foal, colt, or filly:* πῶλος PŌLOS*
Mt 21. 2 "you will find an ass tied, and a colt with her
21. 5 "mounted . . on a colt, the foal of an ass
21. 7 they brought the ass and the colt
Mk 11. 2 "immediately . . you will find a colt tied
11. 4 they . . found a colt tied at the door
11. 5 "What are you doing, untying the colt?
11. 7 they brought the colt to Jesus
Lk 19.30 "on entering you will find a colt tied
19.33 as they were untying the colt, its owners said to them, "Why are you untying the colt?
19.35 throwing their garments on the colt
Jn 12.15 "your king is coming, sitting on an ass's colt!

COME (*See also* AFTERWARD, THOSE WHO CAME; EARS, COME TO THE; FULLY, COME; FULNESS OF LIFE, COME TO; GOOD NEWS COMES TO ONE; HELP OF S., COME TO THE; KNOW, COME TO; LIFE, COME TO; RUNNING TOGETHER, COME; SIGHT OF, COME IN; VIOLENTLY, COME)
1. *come on:* ἄγε AGE*
Jas 4.13 Come now, you who say, "Today
5. 1 Come now, you rich, weep and howl
2. *go up, come up:* ἀναβαίνω ANABAINŌ
Acts 7.23 "it came into his heart to visit his brethren
21.31 word came to the tribune of the cohort
3. *go away:* ἀπέρχομαι APERCHOMAI
Mk 3.13 called . . whom he desired; and they came

4. *so! indeed!:* δή DĒ
Acts 15.36 "Come, let us return and visit
5. *come on:* δεῦρο DEURO
Mt 19.21 "sell what you possess . . and come, follow me
Mk 10.21 "sell what you have . . and come, follow me
Lk 18.22 "Sell all . . you have . . and come, follow me
Jn 11.43 with a loud voice, "Lazarus, come out
Acts 7.34 "now come, I will send you to Egypt
Rev 17. 1 "Come, I will show you the judgment
21. 9 "Come, I will show you the Bride
6. *come hither:* δεῦτε DEUTE
Mt 11.28 "C. to me, all who labor and are heavy laden
21.38 " 'This is the heir; come, let us kill him
22. 4 " 'come to the marriage feast
25.34 " 'Come, O blessed of my Father, inherit
28. 6 "Come, see the place where he[q] lay
Mk 6.31 "Come away by yourselves
12. 7 " 'This is the heir; come, let us kill him
Jn 4.29 "Come, see a man who told me all
21.12 "Come and have breakfast
Rev 19.17 "Come, gather for the great supper of God
7. *pass through:* διέρχομαι DIERCHOMAI
Jn 4.15 "that I may not thirst, nor come here to draw
Acts 9.38 "Please come to us without delay
8. *raise:* ἐγείρω (imper.) EGEIRŌ
Mk 3. 3 he said to the man . . "Come here
Lk 6. 8 he said to the man . . "Come and stand here
9. *be:* εἰμί EIMI [A.6.a.5]
Mt 5.37 "anything more than this comes from evil[l]
Mk 13.33 "you do not know when the time will come
Lk 2.10 "joy which will come to all the people
13.25 " 'I do not know where you come from
13.27 " 'I do not know where you come from
Jn 1.46 "anything good come out of Nazareth?
2. 9 and did not know where it came from
7.27 "we know where this man comes from
7.27 "no one will know where he comes from
7.28 "you know where I come from?
7.29 "I come from him, and he sent me
9.29 "we do not know where he comes from
9.30 "You do not know where he comes from
Rom 15.12 "The root of Jesse shall come
1 Cor 7. 5 but then come together again
2 Tim 4. 3 time is coming when people will not endure
10. *enter, go into:* εἰσέρχομαι EISERCHOMAI
Mt 8. 8 "Lord, I am not worthy to have you come
Lk 1.28 And he came to her and said, "Hail!
7. 6 "I am not worthy to have you come
11. *go into, enter:* εἰσπορεύομαι EISPOREUOMAI
Mk 6.56 wherever he came, in villages, cities
Acts 28.30 welcomed all who came to him
12. *place in, be present:* ἐνίστημι (act. or mid.) ENISTĒMI
2 Th 2. 2 that the day of the Lord has come
2 Tim 3. 1 in the last days there will come . . stress
13. *come upon:* ἐπέρχομαι EPERCHOMAI
Eph 2. 7 in the coming ages . . riches of his grace
14. *stand by:* ἐφίστημι EPHISTĒMI
2 Tim 4. 6 the time of my departure has come
15. *travel:* ἐπιπορεύομαι EPIPOREUOMAI*
Lk 8. 4 people from town after town came to him
16. *come, go:* ἔρχομαι ERCHOMAI
Mt 2. 2 "we . . have come to worship him
2. 8 "that I too may come and worship him
2. 9 till it came to rest . . where the child was
3. 7 "to flee from the wrath to come
3.11 "who is coming after me is mightier than I
3.14 "I need . . and do you come to me?
5.17 "Think not that I have come to abolish
5.17 "have come not to abolish them but to fulfil
5.24 "then come and offer your gift
6.10 "Thy kingdom come, Thy will be done
7.15 "Beware of false prophets, who come
7.25 "the floods came, and the winds blew
7.27 "the floods came, and the winds blew
8. 7 "I will come and heal him
8. 9 "to one, 'Go,' and he goes, and to another, 'Come,' and he comes
Mt 8.28 he came . . to the country of the Gadarenes[t]
8.29 "Have you come here to torment us?
9. 1 crossed over and came to his own city
9.10 many tax collectors and sinners came
9.13 "I came not to call the righteous
9.15 "days will come . . then they will fast
9.18 "come and lay your hand on her
9.23 when Jesus came to the ruler's house
10.13 "let your peace come upon it
10.23 "not . . before the Son of man comes
10.34 "not . . that I have come to bring peace . .; I have not come to bring peace, but a sword
10.35 "have come to set a man against his father
11. 3 "Are you he who is come, or . . another?
11.14 "he is Elijah who is to come
11.18 "John came neither eating nor drinking
11.19 "the Son of man came eating and drinking
12.42 "queen of the South . . came . . to hear . . Solomon
12.44 "when he comes he finds it empty, swept
13. 4 "the birds came and devoured them
13.19 "the evil one comes and snatches away
13.25 "his enemy came and sowed weeds
13.32 "birds of the air come and make nests
13.54 coming to his own country he taught them
14.25 he came to them, walking on the sea
14.28 "Lord, if it is you, bid me come to you
14.29 He said, "Come." So Peter . . walked on the water and came to Jesus
14.34 they came to land at Gennesaret
15.25 she came and knelt . . saying, "Lord, help
16.13 Jesus came into . . Caesarea Philippi
16.24 "If any man would come after me
16.27 "Son of man is to come with his angels
16.28 "see the Son of man coming in his kingdom
17.10 "the scribes say that first Elijah must come
17.11 "Elijah does come, and he is to restore all
17.12 "Elijah has . . come, and they did not know
17.14 when they came to the crowd
17.24 When they came to Capernaum
17.25 when he came home, Jesus spoke
18. 7 "it is necessary that temptations come
18. 7 "woe to . . by whom the temptation comes!
[18.11 *"the Son of man came to save the lost*‡
19.14 Jesus said, "Let the children come to me
20. 9 "those hired about the eleventh hour came
20.10 "first came . .; each . . received a denarius
20.28 "the Son of man came not to be served
21. 1 came to Bethphage . . the Mount of Olives
21. 5 "Behold, your king is coming to you
21. 9 "he who comes in the name of the Lord!
21.32 "John came . . in the way of righteousness
21.40 "When . . the owner of the vineyard comes
22. 3 "those who were invited . . would not come
23.35 "upon you may come all the righteous blood
23.39 " 'he who comes in the name of the Lord
24. 5 "many will come in my name
24.30 "the Son of man coming on the clouds
24.39 "they did not know until the flood came
24.42 "not know . . what day your Lord is coming
24.43 "part of the night the thief was coming
24.44 "be ready; for the Son of man is coming
24.46 "his master when he comes will find
25.10 "while they went . . the bridegroom came
25.11 "the other maidens came also
25.19 "the master of those servants came
25.27 " 'at my coming I should have received
25.31 "When the Son of man comes in his glory
25.36 " 'I was in prison and you came to me
26.40 he came . . and found them sleeping
26.43 again he came and found them sleeping
26.45 Then he came to the disciples
26.47 While he was still speaking, Judas came
26.64 "Son of man . . coming on the clouds
27.33 they came to a place called Golgotha
27.49 "let us see whether Elijah will come
27.57 there came a rich man from Arimathea

Mt 28.13 " 'His disciples came by night and stole him
Mk 1. 7 "After me comes he who is mightier
1. 9 In those days Jesus came from Nazareth
1.14 after John was arrested, Jesus came
1.24 "Have you come to destroy us?
1.40 a leper came to him beseeching him
1.45 people came to him from every quarter
2. 3 they came, bringing to him a paralytic
2.17 "I came not to call the righteous, but sinners
2.18 Pharisees were fasting; and people came
2.20 "days will come . . and then they will fast
3. 8 multitude, hearing all that he did, came
3.31 his mother and his brothers came
4. 4 "the birds came and devoured it
4.15 "Satan . . comes and takes away the word
4.22 "⟨nothing⟩ secret, except to come to light
5. 1 They came to the other side of the sea
5.14 people came to see what . . had happened
5.15 they came to Jesus, and saw the demoniac
5.22 Then came one of the rulers . . , Jairus
5.23 "Come and lay your hands on her
5.27 She . . came up behind him . . and touched
5.33 the woman . . came in fear and trembling
5.35 there came from the ruler's house some
5.38 they came to the house of the ruler
6. 1 He . . came to his own country
6.29 his disciples . . came and took his body
6.31 many were coming and going
6.48 he came to them, walking on the sea
6.53 they came to land at Gennesaret
7. 1 scribes, who had come from Jerusalem
7.25 a woman . . came and fell down at his feet
8.22 they came to Bethsaida
8.34 "If any man would come after me
8.38 "when he comes in the glory of his Father
9. 1 "not . . before they see the kingdom . . come
9.11 "scribes say that first Elijah must come
9.12 "Elijah does come first to restore all things
9.13 "But I tell you that Elijah has come
9.14 when they came to the disciples, they saw
9.33 they came to Capernaum
10.14 "Let the children come to me
10.30 "receive . . in the age to come eternal life
10.45 "the Son of man also came not to be served
10.46 they came to Jericho
10.50 he sprang up and came to Jesus
11. 9 "he who comes in the name of the Lord!
11.10 "Blessed is the kingdom . . that is coming!
11.13 when he came to it, he found nothing
11.15 they came to Jerusalem
11.27 they came again to Jerusalem
11.27 scribes and the elders came to him
12. 9 "He will come and destroy the tenants
12.14 they came and said to him, "Teacher
12.18 Sadducees came to him . . and they asked
12.42 poor widow came, and put in two . . coins
13. 6 "Many will come in my name
13.26 see the Son of man coming in clouds
13.35 "when the master of the house will come
13.36 "lest he come suddenly and find you
14. 3 a woman came with an alabaster flask
14.17 when . . evening he came with the twelve
14.37 he came and found them sleeping
14.40 again he came and found them sleeping
14.41 And he came the third time
14.41 "It is enough; the hour has come
14.45 when he came, he went up to him at once
14.62 "Son of man . . coming with the clouds
14.66 one of the maids of the high priest came
15.21 Simon of Cyrene, who was coming in
15.36 "let us see whether Elijah will come
Lk 1.43 "why . . the mother of my Lord should come?
1.59 on the eighth day they came to circumcise
2.27 inspired . . he came into the temple
2.51 he went . . with them and came to Nazareth
3.12 Tax collectors also came to be baptized
3.16 "he who is mightier than I is coming

Lk 4.16 he came to Nazareth
4.34 "Have you come to destroy us?
4.42 the people sought him and came to him
5. 7 beckoned to their partners . . to come . .
And they came and filled both the boats
5.17 teachers . . had come from every village
5.32 "I have not come to call the righteous
5.35 "days will come . . then they will fast
6.17(18) multitude . . who came to hear him
6.47 "Every one who comes to me and hears
7. 3 asking him to come and heal his slave
7. 7 "I did not presume to come to you
7. 8 "I say to one, 'Go,' and he goes; and to another, 'Come,' and he comes
7.19 "Are you he who is to come?
7.20 " 'Are you he who is to come?
7.33 "John the Baptist has come eating no bread
7.34 "Son of man has come eating and drinking
8.12 "the devil comes and takes away the word
8.17 "nor anything . . that shall not . . come to light
8.35 they came to Jesus, and found the man
8.41 there came a man named Jairus
8.47 the woman . . came trembling, and falling
8.49 a man from the ruler's house came
8.51 when he came to the house
9.23 "If any man would come after me
9.26 "when he comes in his glory
[9.55(56) *"the Son of man came not to destroy*‡
10. 1 sent . . where he himself was about to come
10.32 "likewise a Levite, when he came to the place
10.33 "a Samaritan . . came to where he was
11. 2 "hallowed be thy name. Thy kingdom come
11.25 "when he comes he finds it swept
11.31 "she came from the ends of the earth
12.36 "open to him at once when he comes
12.37 "the master finds awake when he comes
12.38 "If he comes in the second watch
12.39 "known at what hour the thief was coming
12.40 "Son of man is coming at an unexpected hour
12.43 "whom his master when he comes will find
12.45 " 'My master is delayed in coming
12.49 "I came to cast fire upon the earth!
12.54 "you say at once, 'A shower is coming
13. 6 "he came seeking fruit on it and found none
13. 7 " 'these three years I have come seeking fruit
13.14 "come on those days and be healed
13.35 " 'he who comes in the name of the Lord!
14. 9 "he who invited you both will come and say
14.10 "so that when your host comes he may say
14.17 " 'Come; for all is now ready
14.20 " 'I have married a wife, and . . I cannot come
14.26 "If any one comes to me and does not hate
14.27 "Whoever does not . . come after me
14.31 "to meet him who comes against him
15. 6 "he comes home, he calls together his friends
15.17 "But when he came to himself he said
15.20 "And he arose and came to his father
15.25 "as he came and drew near to the house
15.30 " 'But when this son of yours came
16.21 "the dogs came and licked his sores
16.28 " 'warn them, lest they also come into this
17. 1 "Temptations to sin[z] are sure to come; but woe to him by whom they come!
17.20 asked . . when the kingdom . . was coming
17.20 "The kingdom . . is not coming with signs
17.22 "The days are coming when you will desire
17.27 "the flood came and destroyed them all
18. 3 "a widow in that city who kept coming
18. 5 " 'she will wear me out by . . continual coming
18. 8 "when the Son . . comes, will he find faith?
18.16 "Let the children come to me
18.30 "receive . . in the age to come eternal life
19. 5 "when Jesus came to the place
19.10 "Son of man came to seek . . the lost
19.13 " 'Trade with these till I come
19.18 "the second came, saying, 'Lord
19.20 "Then another came, saying, 'Lord

Lk 19.23 " 'at my coming I should have . . interest
19.38 "who comes in the name of the Lord!
20.16 "He will come and destroy those tenants
21. 6 "days will come when there shall not be left
21. 8 " 'for many will come in my name
21.27 "they will see the Son of man coming
22. 7 Then came . . day of Unleavened Bread
22.18 "not drink . . until the kingdom . . comes
22.45 he came to the disciples and found them
23.26 Simon . . who was coming in from the country
23.29 "For behold, the days are coming
23.33 they came to the place . . called The Skull
23.42 "Jesus, remember me when you come
Jn 1. 7 He came for testimony, to bear witness
1. 9 true light . . was coming into the world
1.11 He came to his own home
1.15 (" 'He who comes after me ranks before me
1.27 "even he who comes after me
1.29 The next day he saw Jesus coming
1.30 " 'After me comes a man who ranks before
1.31 "for this I came baptizing with water
1.39 He said to them, "Come and see." They came and saw where he was staying
1.46 Philip said to him, "Come and see
1.47 Jesus saw Nathanael coming to him
3. 2 This man came to Jesus[d] by night and said . . "you are a teacher come from God
3. 8 "you do not know whence it comes
3.19 the light has come into the world
3.20 who does evil . . does not come to the light
3.21 who does what is true comes to the light
3.26 they came to John
3.31 who comes from above is above all; . . he who comes from heaven is above all
4. 5 So he came to a city of Samaria
4. 7 There came a woman of Samaria to draw
4.16 "Go, call your husband, and come here
4.21 "Woman, believe me, the hour is coming
4.23 "But the hour is coming, and now is
4.25 "I know that Messiah is coming
4.25 "when he comes, he will show us all things
4.27 Just then his disciples came
4.30 out of the city ⟨they⟩ were coming to him
4.35 " 'yet four months, then comes the harvest
4.40 when the Samaritans came to him
4.45 when he came . . the Galileans welcomed him
4.46 So he came again to Cana in Galilee
4.54 when he had come from Judea to Galilee
5.24 "he does not come into judgment
5.25 "truly . . the hour is coming, and now is
5.28 "the hour is coming when all . . will hear
5.40 "yet you refuse to come to me
5.43 "I have come in my Father's name
5.43 "if another comes in his own name
6. 5 a multitude was coming to him
6.14 "the prophet who is to come into the world!
6.15 about to come and take him by force
6.17 dark, and Jesus had not yet come to them
6.23 boats from Tiberias came near the place
6.35 "he who comes to me shall not hunger
6.37 "him who comes to me I will not cast out
6.44 "No one can come . . unless the Father . . draws
6.45 "one who has heard . . the Father comes to me
6.65 "no one can come to me unless it is granted
7.28 "I have not come of my own accord
7.30 because his hour had not yet come
7.34 "where I am you cannot come
7.36 " 'Where I am you cannot come
7.37 "If any one thirst, let him come to me
7.41 "Is the Christ to come from Galilee?
7.42 "Christ . . comes from Bethlehem
8. 2 in . . morning he came again to the temple[r]‡
8. 2 people came to him . . he . . taught them[r]‡
8.14 "I know whence I have come and whither . . but you do not know whence I come
8.20 because his hour had not yet come
8.21 "where I am going, you cannot come
Jn 8.22 " 'Where I am going, you cannot come
8.42 "I came not of my own accord, but he sent
9. 4 "night comes, when no one can work
9.39 "For judgment I came into this world
10. 8 "All who came before me are thieves
10.10 "The thief comes only to steal and kill . . ; I came that they may have life
10.12 "hireling . . sees the wolf coming and leaves
10.41 many came to him
11.17 Jesus came, he found that Lazarus[z]
11.19 the Jews had come to Martha and Mary
11.20 Martha heard that Jesus was coming
11.27 "the Son . . who is coming into the world
11.30 Jesus had not yet come to the village
11.32 Mary . . came where Jesus was and saw him
11.34 They said to him, "Lord, come and see
11.38 Jesus, deeply moved . . came to the tomb
11.45 Jews . . who had come with Mary . . believed
11.48 "the Romans will come and destroy both
11.56 "That he will not come to the feast?
12. 1 Jesus came to Bethany, where Lazarus was
12. 9 When the great crowd . . learned . . , they came
12.12 a great crowd who had come to the feast heard that Jesus was coming
12.13 "who comes in the name of the Lord!
12.15 "king is coming, sitting on an ass's colt!
12.23 "The hour has come for the Son of man
12.27 "for this purpose I have come to this hour
12.28 a voice came . . "I have glorified it
12.46 "I have come as light into the world
12.47 "for I did not come to judge the world
13. 1 Jesus knew that his hour had come
13. 6 He came to Simon Peter
13.33 " 'Where I am going you cannot come
14. 3 "I will come again and will take you
14. 6 "no one comes to the Father, but by me
14.18 "I will not leave you desolate: I will come
14.23 "If a man loves me . . we will come to him
14.28 " 'I go away, and I will come to you
14.30 "for the ruler of this world is coming
15.22 "If I had not come and spoken to them
15.26 "when the Counselor comes
16. 2 "the hour is coming when whoever kills you
16. 4 "when their hour comes you may remember
16. 7 "the Counselor will not come to you
16. 8 "when he comes, he will convince[z] the world
16.13 "the Spirit of truth comes, he will guide . . and . . declare . . the things that are to come
16.21 "she has sorrow, because her hour has come
16.25 "the hour is coming when I shall . . tell
16.28 "from . . Father ⟨I⟩ have come into the world
16.32 "The hour is coming, indeed it has come, when you will be scattered
17. 1 "Father, the hour has come; glorify thy Son
17.11 "I am coming to thee
17.13 "now I am coming to thee
18.37 "for this I have come into the world
19. 3 they came up to him, saying, "Hail, King!
19.32 soldiers came and broke the legs of the first
19.33 came to Jesus and saw that he was . . dead
19.38 So he came and took away his body
19.39 Nicodemus . . who had . . come to him by night, came bringing a mixture of myrrh
20. 1 Mary Magdalene came to the tomb early
20. 6 Then Simon Peter came, following him
20.19 Jesus came and stood among them
20.24 Thomas . . was not with them when Jesus came
20.26 Jesus came and stood among them
21. 8 the other disciples came in the boat
21.13 Jesus came and took the bread
21.22 "If it is my will that he remain until I come
21.23 "If it is my will that he remain until I come
Acts 1.11 "This Jesus . . will come in the same way
2.20 " 'before the day of the Lord comes
3.19 "that times of refreshing may come
7.11 "there came a famine throughout all Egypt

Acts 8.27 eunuch . . had come to Jerusalem to worship
8.36 along the road they came to some water
8.40 Philip . . preached . . till he came to Caesarea
9.17 "appeared . . on the road by which you came
9.21 "he has come here for this purpose
10.29 "I came without objection
11. 5 "a great sheet . . came down to me
11.20 on coming to Antioch spoke to the Greeks[i]
12.10 came to the iron gate leading into the city
13.13 Paul . . came to Perga in Pamphylia
13.25 " 'I am not he . . but after me one is coming
14.24 through Pisidia, and came to Pamphylia
16. 7 when they had come opposite Mysia
16.37 "let them come themselves and take us out
16.39 so they came and apologized to them
17. 1 they came to Thessalonica
17.13 they came there too, stirring up . . crowds
17.15 command for Silas and Timothy to come
18. 2 Aquila . . of Pontus, lately come from Italy
19. 1 Paul passed through . . and came to Ephesus
19. 4 "the one who was to come after him
19. 6 "the Holy Spirit came on them
19.18 those who were now believers came
19.27 "this trade of ours may come into disrepute
20. 2 he came to Greece
20. 6 in five days we came to them at Troas
20.14 we took him on board and came
20.15 the day after that we came to Miletus
21. 1 we came by a straight course to Cos
21. 8 we departed and came to Caesarea
21.11 coming to us he took Paul's girdle
21.22 "They will . . hear that you have come
22.11 led by the hand ⟨I⟩ . . came into Damascus
22.13 "⟨Ananias⟩ came to me, and . . said . . 'Brother
[24. 8 *"commanding his accusers to c. before you*‡
25.23 Agrippa and Bernice came with great pomp
27. 8 we came to a place called Fair Havens
28.13 on the second day we came to Puteoli
28.14 And so we came to Rome
28.15 brethren . . came as far as the Forum
28.23 they came to him at his lodging

Rom 1.10 by God's will I may . . succeed in coming
1.13 I have often intended to come to you
3. 8 why not do evil that good may come?
7. 9 when the commandment came, sin revived
15.22 so often . . hindered from coming to you
15.23 I have longed for many years to come to you
15.29 I know that when I come to you I shall come in . . the blessing[y] of Christ
15.32 by God's will I may come to you with joy

1 Cor 2. 1 When I came to you . . I did not come proclaiming . . in lofty words or wisdom
4. 5 before the time, before the Lord comes
4.18 as though I were not coming to you
4.19 I will come to you soon, if the Lord wills
4.21 Shall I come to you with a rod?
11.26 you proclaim the Lord's death until he comes
11.34 I will give directions when I come
13.10 when the perfect comes
14. 6 if I come to you speaking in tongues
15.35 "With what kind of body do they come?
16. 2 contributions . . not be made when I come
16.10 When Timothy comes . . put him at ease
16.12 it was not at all his will[b] to come now. He will come when he has opportunity

2 Cor 1.15 I wanted to come to you first
1.23 to spare you . . I refrained from coming
2. 3 that when I came I might not suffer pain
2.12 When I came to Troas to preach
7. 5 even when we came into Macedonia
9. 4 lest if some Macedonians come with me
11. 4 if some one comes and preaches another Jesus
11. 9 brethren who came from Macedonia
12.14 the third time I am ready to come to you
12.20 I fear that perhaps I may come and find
12.21 when I come again my God may humble me
13. 1 This is the third time I am coming to you

2 Cor 13. 2 if I come again I will not spare them

Gal 2.11 when Cephas came to Antioch I opposed
2.12 before certain men came from James
2.12 when they came he drew back
3.19 law . . was added . . till the offspring . . come
3.23 before faith came, we were . . under . . law
3.25 now that faith has come, we are no longer
4. 4 when the time had fully come, God sent

Eph 2.17 he came and preached peace to you
5. 6 because of these . . the wrath of God comes

Phil 1.27 whether I come and see you or am absent
2.24 shortly I myself shall come also

Col 3. 6 the wrath of God is coming[f]
4.10 (if he comes to you, receive him

1 Th 1.10 Jesus . . delivers us from the wrath to come
2.18 because we wanted to come to you
3. 6 now that Timothy has come to us
5. 2 the day of the Lord will come like a thief

2 Th 1.10 when he comes on that day to be glorified
2. 3 unless the rebellion comes first

1 Tim 1.15 Christ Jesus came into the world to save
2. 4 to come to the knowledge of the truth
3.14 I hope to come to you soon
4.13 Till I come, attend to the . . scripture

2 Tim 4. 9 Do your best to come to me soon
4.13 When you come, bring the cloak
4.21 Do your best to come before winter

Tit 3.12 do your best to come to me at Nicopolis

Heb 8. 8 "The days will come, says the Lord
10.37 "the coming one . . shall not tarry
13.23 with whom I shall see you if he comes

2 Pet 3. 3 scoffers will come in the last days

1 Jn 2.18 you have heard that antichrist is coming
4. 2 that Jesus Christ has come in the flesh
4. 3 you heard that ⟨antichrist⟩ was coming
5. 6 This is he who came by water and blood

2 Jn . 7 the coming of Jesus Christ in the flesh
.10 If any one comes to you

3 Jn .10 if I come, I will bring up

Jude .14 "the Lord came with his holy myriads

Rev 1. 4 who is and who was and who is to come
1. 7 Behold, he is coming with the clouds
1. 8 who is and who was and who is to come
2. 5 " 'I will come . . and remove your lampstand
2.16 " 'I will come . . soon and war against them
3.10 " 'trial which is coming on the whole world
3.11 " 'I am coming soon; hold fast
4. 8 "Lord God . . who was and is and is to come!
6. 1 as with a voice of thunder, "Come!
6. 3 heard . . second living creature say, "Come!
6. 5 heard . . third living creature say, "Come!
6. 7 heard . . fourth living creature say, "Come!
6.17 "the great day of their wrath has come
7.13 "whence have they come?
7.14 "have come out of the great tribulation
8. 3 another angel came and stood at the altar
9.12 behold, two woes are still to come
11.14 behold, the third woe is soon to come
11.18 "The nations raged, but thy wrath came
14. 7 "for the hour of his judgment has come
14.15 "for the hour to reap has come
16.15 ("Lo, I am coming like a thief!
17. 1 Then one of the seven angels . . came
17.10 "the other has not yet come, and when he comes he must remain only a little while
18.10 "In one hour has thy judgment come
19. 7 "the marriage of the Lamb has come
21. 9 Then came one of the seven angels
22. 7 behold, I am coming soon
22.12 "Behold, I am coming soon
22.17 The Spirit and the Bride say, "Come." And let him who hears say, "Come." And let him who is thirsty come
22.20 "Surely I am coming soon." Amen. Come, Lord Jesus!

17. *go out:* ἐξέρχομαι EXERCHOMAI

Mt 12.44 " 'return to my house from which I came

Mt 24.27 "as the lightning comes from the east
Mk 8.11 The Pharisees came and began to argue
11.12 they came from Bethany, he was hungry
Lk 11.24 " 'return to my house from which I came
Jn 13. 3 had come from God and was going to God
16.27 "believed that I came from the Father
16.30 "by this we believe that you came from God
17. 8 "know in truth that I came from thee
Jas 3.10 From the same mouth come blessing
Rev 19. 5 from the throne came a voice

18. *come to be, happen, be:* *γίνομαι* GINOMAI
Mt 14. 6 But when Herod's birthday came
14.23 When evening came, he was there alone
20. 8 "And when evening came, the owner .. said
21.19 "May no fruit ever come from you again!
26. 2 "after two days the Passover is coming
27. 1 When morning came .. elders .. took counsel
Mk 1.11 and a voice came from heaven
4.35 On that day, when evening had come
6.21 an opportunity came .. on his birthday
6.47 when evening came, the boat was out
9. 7 and a voice came out of the cloud
11.19 And when evening came they[u] went out
15.33 And when the sixth hour had come
15.42 And when evening had come
Lk 1.44 "when the voice of your greeting came
1.65 And fear came on all their neighbors
3. 2 the word of God came to John
3.22 and a voice came from heaven
4.25 when there came a great famine
5.12 there came a man full of leprosy
9.34 a cloud came and overshadowed them
9.35 And a voice came out of the cloud
19. 9 "Today salvation has come to this house
22.14 And when the hour came, he sat at table
22.40 And when he came to the place he said
22.66 When day came, the assembly .. gathered
Jn 1.17 grace and truth came through Jesus Christ
6.16 When evening came, his disciples went
6.25 "Rabbi, when did you come here?
10.35 "to whom the word of God came
12.30 "This voice has come for your sake
Acts 2. 2 suddenly a sound came from heaven
2.43 And fear came upon every soul
5. 5 And great fear came upon all who heard
5.11 And great fear came upon the whole church
5.36 "all who followed .. came to nothing
7.31 "the voice of the Lord came
10.13 And there came a voice to him
12.11 And Peter came to himself, and said
12.18 Now when day came, there was .. stir
15.25 "good .. having come to one accord[o]
21.17 When we had come to Jerusalem
21.35 And when he came to the steps
27.27 When the fourteenth night had come
27.29 they .. prayed for day to come
28. 6 they .. saw no misfortune come to him
Rom 11.25 hardening has come upon part of Israel
2 Cor 3. 7 Now if the dispensation of death .. came
5.17 behold, the new has come
Gal 3.14 that .. the blessing of Abraham might come
3.17 the law, which came .. years afterward
1 Th 1. 5 our gospel came to you not only in word
Heb 9.11 priest of the good things that have come[r]‡
1 Pet 4.12 the fiery ordeal which comes upon you
1 Jn 2.18 so now many antichrists have come
2 Jn .12 but I hope to come to see you
Rev 12.10 "the power and .. authority .. have come
16. 2 foul and evil sores came upon the men

19. *have come, be present:* *ἥκω* HĒKŌ
[a]pres.
Mt 8.11 "many will come from east and west
23.36 "all this will come upon this generation
24.14 and then the end will come
24.50 "master of that servant will come on a day
Mk 8. 3 [a]"some of them have come a long way
Lk 12.46 "master of that servant will come on a day
13.29 "men will come from east and west
15.27 [a]" 'Your brother has come
19.43 "the days shall come upon you
Jn 2. 4 [a]"My hour has not yet come
4.47 [a]he heard that Jesus had come from Judea
6.37 "All that the Father gives me will come
Rom 11.26 "The Deliverer will come from Zion
Heb 10. 7 [a]" 'Lo, I have come to do thy will, O God
10. 9 [a]"Lo, I have come to do thy will
10.37 "one shall come and shall not tarry
2 Pet 3.10 day of the Lord will come like a thief
1 Jn 5.20 [a]know that the Son of God has come
Rev 2.25 " 'hold fast what you have, until I come
3. 3 " 'If .. not awake, I will come like a thief, .. you will not know at what hour I will come
3. 9 " 'behold, I will make them come
15. 4 "All nations shall come and worship thee
18. 8 "so shall her plagues come in a single day

20. *come down to, arrive:* *καταντάω* KATANTAŌ
Acts 16. 1 And he came also to Derbe and to Lystra
18.19 they came to Ephesus, and he left them
18.24 Jew named Apollos .. came to Ephesus
20.15 we came the following day opposite Chios
1 Cor 10.11 upon whom the end of the ages has come

21. *go down, come to:* *κατέρχομαι* KATERCHOMAI
Acts 27. 5 we came to Myra in Lycia

22. *arrive, stand by:* *παραγίνομαι* PARAGINOMAI
Mt 2. 1 wise men from the East came to Jerusalem
3. 1 In those days came John the Baptist
3.13 Then Jesus came from Galilee to the Jordan
Mk 14.43 Judas came .. and with him a crowd
Lk 7. 4 when they came to Jesus, they besought
7.20 when the men had come to him
8.19 his mother and brothers came to him
12.51 "think that I have come to give peace?
14.21 "the servant came and reported this
19.16 "The first came .. saying, 'Lord, your pound
22.52 elders, who had come out against him
Jn 3.23 people came and were baptized
8. 2 in the morning he came again to the temple[r]‡
Acts 5.21 high priest came and .. called .. the council
5.22 officers came, they did not find them
5.25 some one came and told them
9.26 when he had come to Jerusalem
9.39 when he had come, they took him
10.33 "you have been kind enough to come
11.23 he came and saw the grace of God
13.14 they .. came to Antioch of Pisidia
15. 4 When they came to Jerusalem
20.18 when they came to him
24.17 "I came to bring to my nation alms
24.24 Felix came with his wife Drusilla
25. 7 when he had come, the Jews .. stood about
28.21 "none .. coming here has reported .. evil

23. *be present:* *πάρειμι* PAREIMI
[a]pres.
Mt [26.50 [a]"*do that for which you have come*†
Jn 7. 6 [a]"My time has not yet come
Acts 12.20 people of Tyre .. came to him in a body
17. 6 [a]"These men .. have come here also
2 Cor 13.10 when I come I may not have to be severe
Col 1. 6 [a]⟨the gospel⟩ which has come to you

24. *pass by, transgress:* *παρέρχομαι* PARERCHOMAI
Lk 12.37 "master finds awake when he comes
17. 7 " 'Come at once and sit down at table
Acts [24. 7 *But the chief captain Lysias came*‡

25. *place beside, stand before:* *παρίστημι* PARISTĒMI
Mk 4.29 "sickle, because the harvest has come

26. *bring, bear:* *φέρω* (pass.) PHERŌ
1 Pet 1.13 hope fully upon the grace that is coming
2 Pet 1.21 no prophecy ever came by .. impulse of man

27. *come first, arrive:* *φθάνω* PHTHANŌ
Mt 12.28 "then the kingdom of God has come upon you
Lk 11.20 "then the kingdom of God has come upon you
1 Th 2.16 God's wrath has come upon them at last![b]

28. *fill, satisfy:* *πίμπλημι* (pass.) PIMPLĒMI
Lk 1.57 time came for Elizabeth to be delivered

Lk 2. 6 time came for her to be delivered
2.22 time came for their purification
29. *come to, approach:* προσέρχομαι PROSERCHOMAI
Mt 4. 3 the tempter came and said to him, "If
4.11 angels came and ministered to him
13.10 disciples came and said to him, "Why?
13.27 "the servants[j] of the householder came
14.12 disciples came and took the body
15.12 Then the disciples came and said to him
15.23 his disciples came and begged him
16. 1 Sadducees came, and to test him . . asked
17. 7 But Jesus came and touched them
24. 1 his disciples came to point out to him
28. 2 angel . . descended from heaven and came
28. 9 they came up and took hold of his feet
28.18 Jesus came and said . . "All authority
Mk 1.31 he came and took her by the hand
Lk 7.14 he came and touched the bier
9.12 twelve came and said . . "Send the crowd
9.42 While he was coming, the demon tore him
13.31 Pharisees came, and said . . "Get away
Acts 12.13 a maid named Rhoda came to answer
22.27 the tribune came and said . . "Tell me
28. 9 people . . who had diseases also came
30. *fill completely:* συμπληρόω (pass.) SYMPLĒROŌ
Acts 2. 1 When the day of Pentecost had come
CONTEXTUALLY
Mk 7. 4 (when they come from the market place
Lk 20.10 "When the time came, he sent a servant
22.47 While he was . . speaking, there came a crowd
Jn 1. 8 but came to bear witness to the light
5.44 "the glory that comes from the only God
6.69 "we have believed, and have c. to know
Acts 10.15 And the voice came to him again
Rom 10.17 So faith comes from what is heard, and what is heard comes by the preaching
11.11 salvation has come to the Gentiles
15.27 for if the Gentiles have come to share
1 Cor 15.21 For as by a man came death, by a man has come also the resurrection of the dead
15.24 Then comes the end, when he delivers
Gal 1.12 it came through a revelation of Jesus
3.24 the law was our custodian until Christ came
4. 9 now that you have come to know God
Phil 1.11 fruits of righteousness which c. through
2 Th 2. 3 for that day will not come
2 Tim 2.25 will repent and come to know the truth
Heb 13.24 Those who come from Italy send . . greetings
1 Pet 4.17 For the time has come for judgment

COME BACK
COME BY

1. *go back, return:* ἐπανέρχομαι EPANERCHOMAI
Lk 10.35 " 'I will repay you when I come back
2. *come, go:* ἔρχομαι ERCHOMAI
Lk 24.23 "did not find his body; and they came back
Jn 9. 7 he went and washed and came back seeing
Acts 5.15 as Peter came by . . his shadow might fall
2 Cor 1.16 I wanted to . . come back to you

COME, BE THE FIRST TO

1. *come first, arrive:* φθάνω PHTHANŌ
2 Cor 10.14 we were the first to come all the way to you

COME, BE TO

1. *be present:* πάρειμι PAREIMI
Rev 17. 8 "because it was and is not and is to come

COME DOWN

1. *come down, go down:* καταβαίνω KATABAINŌ
Mt 8. 1 When he came down from the mountain
17. 9 as they were coming down the mountain
27.40 "If you are the Son of God, come down
27.42 "let him come down now from the cross
Mk 3.22 scribes who came down from Jerusalem
9. 9 as they were coming down the mountain
15.30 "save yourself . . come down from the cross!
15.32 "Let the Christ . . come down now
Lk 6.17 he came down with them and stood
8.23 a storm of wind came down on the lake
Lk 9.54 "do you want us to bid fire come down?
17.31 "let him . . not come down to take them away
19. 5 "Zacchaeus, make haste and come down
19. 6 So he made haste and came down
Jn 4.47 begged him to come down and heal his son
4.49 "Sir, come down before my child dies
6.33 "bread of God is that which comes down
6.38 "I have come down from heaven
6.41 "I am the bread which came down
6.42 " 'I have come down from heaven
6.50 "bread which comes down from heaven
6.51 "bread which came down from heaven
6.58 "bread which came down from heaven
Acts 7.34 " 'I have come down to deliver them
8.15 ⟨Peter⟩ came down and prayed for them
14.11 "The gods have come down to us
24. 1 high priest Ananias came down
24.22 "When Lysias the tribune comes down
Jas 1.17 perfect gift . . coming down from the Father
Rev 3.12 " 'the new Jerusalem which comes down
10. 1 another mighty angel coming down
12.12 "devil has come down to you in great wrath!
13.13 great signs, even making fire come down
18. 1 another angel coming down
20. 1 an angel coming down from heaven
20. 9 but fire came down from heaven[n]
21. 2 the holy city . . coming down out of heaven
21.10 the holy city Jerusalem coming down
2. *go down, come to:* κατέρχομαι KATERCHOMAI
Lk 9.37 they had come down from the mountain
Acts 9.32 he came down also to the saints
11.27 prophets came down from Jerusalem
15. 1 men came down from Judea . . teaching
21.10 a prophet named Agabus came down
Jas 3.15 not such as comes down from above

COME FORTH

1. *go out:* ἐκπορεύομαι EKPOREUOMAI
Jn 5.29 "⟨all who are in the tombs will⟩ come forth
2. *go out, go forth:* ἐξέρχομαι EXERCHOMAI
Lk 6.19 power came forth from him and healed them
3. *have come, be present:* ἥκω HĒKŌ
Jn 8.42 "I proceeded and came forth from God

COME FORWARD
COME FORWARD TO

1. *go out:* ἐξέρχομαι EXERCHOMAI
Jn 18. 4 Jesus, knowing all . . came forward
2. *stand, set:* ἵστημι (aor. pass.) HISTĒMI
Acts 27.21 Paul then came forward among them
3. *come to, approach:* προσέρχομαι PROSERCHOMAI
Mt 8. 5 a centurion came forward to him
25.20 "who had received the five . . came forward
25.22 "who had the two talents came forward
25.24 "He . . who had . . one talent came forward
26.60 they found none, though many false witnesses came forward. At last two came forward
4. *approach:* προσπορεύομαι PROSPOREUOMAI*
Mk 10.35 sons of Zebedee, came forward to him

COME FROM

1. *go out:* ἐκπορεύομαι EKPOREUOMAI
Mk 7.21 "For from within . . come evil thoughts
7.23 "All these evil things come from within
2. *go out:* ἐξέρχομαι EXERCHOMAI
Mt 2. 6 " 'from you shall come a ruler
Jn 16.28 "I came from the Father
Rev 9. 3 from the smoke came locusts on the earth

COME HOME

1. *unloose, return:* ἀναλύω ANALYŌ
Lk 12.36 waiting for their master to come home

COME IN
COME INTO

1. *enter, go into:* εἰσέρχομαι EISERCHOMAI
Mt 9.18 behold, a ruler came in and knelt
22.11 "when the king came in to look at the guests
Mk 6.22 Herodias' daughter came in and danced

Mk 6.25 she came in immediately with haste
Lk 7.45 "from the time I came in she has not ceased
14.23 " 'Go out . . and compel people to come in
17. 7 "when he has come in from the field
Acts 5. 7 After . . about three hours his wife came in
5.10 When the . . men came in they found her
9.12 "he has seen a man named Ananias come in
10. 3 in a vision an angel of God coming in
20.29 "fierce wolves will come in among you
28.16 when we came into Rome, Paul was allowed
Rom 5.12 as sin came into the world through one man
11.25 until the full number of the Gentiles come in
Heb 10. 5 when Christ[v] came into the world
Jas 2. 2 if a man with gold rings . . comes into your assembly, and a poor man . . also comes in
Rev 3.20 " 'I will come in to him and eat with him

2. *go upon, mount, board:* ἐπιβαίνω EPIBAINŌ
Acts 25. 1 when Festus had come into his province

3. *come in:* παρεισέρχομαι PAREISERCHOMAI
Rom 5.20 Law came in, to increase the trespass

COME NEAR

1. *approach:* ἐγγίζω EGGIZŌ
Lk 10. 9 " 'kingdom of God has come near to you
10.11 " 'the kingdom of God has come near
18.40 when he came near, he asked him
21.20 "know that its desolation has come near
Acts 10. 9 as they were . . coming near the city
23.15 "ready to kill him before he comes near

COME ON
COME UPON

1. *have, hold:* ἔχω ECHŌ
Mk 16. 8 astonishment had come upon them

2. *come in besides:* ἐπεισέρχομαι EPEISERCHOMAI*
Lk 21.35 "it will come upon all who dwell

3. *come upon:* ἐπέρχομαι EPERCHOMAI
Lk 1.35 "The Holy Spirit will come upon you
21.26 "foreboding of what is coming on the world
Acts 1. 8 "when the Holy Spirit has come upon you
8.24 "Pray . . that nothing . . may come upon me
13.40 "lest there come upon you what is said
Jas 5. 1 the miseries that are coming upon you

4. *stand by:* ἐφίστημι EPHISTĒMI
Lk 21.34 "lest . . that day come upon you suddenly
Acts 4. 1 priests and . . Sadducees came upon them
6.12 they came upon him and seized him
23.27 "I came upon them with the soldiers
1 Th 5. 3 sudden destruction will come upon them

5. *find:* εὑρίσκω HEURISKŌ
Mt 18.28 "he . . came upon one of his fellow servants
27.32 they came upon a man of Cyrene, Simon
Acts 13. 6 they came upon a certain magician

COME, OUR LORD

1. *our Lord, come!* (Aram.): μαράνα θᾶ MARANATHA*
1 Cor 16.22 let him be accursed. Our Lord, come![c]†

COME OUT
COME OUT FROM
COME OUT OF

1. *go out:* ἐκπορεύομαι EKPOREUOMAI
[a]+ἐκ
Mt 15.11 [a]"what comes out of the mouth, this defiles
15.18 [a]"what comes out of the mouth . . defiles
[17.21 *"never comes out except by prayer*‡
Mk 7.15 [a]"things which come out of a man . . defile
7.20 [a]"What comes out of a man is what defiles
13. 1 [a]as he came out of the temple
Lk 3. 7 multitudes that came out to be baptized
Acts 19.12 the evil spirits came out of them
Eph 4.29 [a]Let no evil talk come out of your mouths

2. *go out:* ἐξέρχομαι EXERCHOMAI
[a]+ἐκ [b]+ἀπό [c]+ἔξω [d]+ἐκ μέσου
Mt 8.28 [a]two demoniacs . . coming out of the tombs
8.32 they came out and went into the swine
8.34 all the city came out to meet Jesus
13.49 "angels will come out and separate the evil
15.19 [a]"out of the heart come evil thoughts
15.22 Canaanite woman from that region came out
17.18 [b]the demon came out of him
25. 6 " 'the bridegroom! Come out to meet him
26.55 "Have you come out as against a robber?
[27.49 *pierced his side, and out came water*‡
27.53 [a]coming out of the tombs after . . resurrection
Mk 1.25 [a]"Be silent, and come out of him!
1.26 [a]the unclean spirit . . came out of him
1.38 "for that is why I came out
5. 2 [a]when he had come out of the boat
5. 8 [a]"Come out of the man, you unclean spirit!
5.13 the unclean spirits came out
9.25 [a]"You dumb and deaf spirit, . . c. out of him
9.26 it came out, and the boy was like a corpse
14.48 "Have you come out as against a robber?
Lk 1.22 when he came out, he could not speak
4.35 [b]"Be silent, and come out of him!
4.35 [b]he came out of him
4.36 "the unclean spirits . . come out
4.41 [b]demons also came out of many, crying
8.29 [b]commanded the . . spirit to c. out of the man
8.33 [b]Then the demons came out of the man
15.28 "His father came out and entreated him
22.39 he came out, and went, as was his custom
22.52 "Have you come out as against a robber?
Jn 11.44 dead man came out, his hands . . bound
19. 5 [c]Jesus came out, wearing the crown
19.34 at once there came out blood and water
20. 3 Peter then came out with the other disciple
Acts 7. 7 " 'after that they shall come out and worship
8. 7 For unclean spirits came out of many
16.18 [b]"I charge you in the name of Jesus Christ to come out of her." And it came out
16.36 "now therefore come out and go in peace
28. 3 a viper came out because of the heat
2 Cor 6.17 [d]"come out from them, and be separate
Rev 6. 4 out came another horse, bright red
14.15 [a]another angel came out of the temple
14.17 [a]another angel came out of the temple
14.18 [a]another angel came out from the altar
15. 6 [a]out of the temple came the seven angels
16.17 [a]a loud voice came out of the temple
18. 4 [a]"Come out of her, my people
20. 8 ⟨Satan⟩ will come out to deceive the nations

COME OUT IN LEAF

1. *put forward:* προβάλλω PROBALLŌ
Lk 21.30 "as soon as they come out in leaf

COME OVER

1. *stride, go through:* διαβαίνω DIABAINŌ
Acts 16. 9 "Come over to Macedonia and help us

COME THERE

1. *come upon:* ἐπέρχομαι EPERCHOMAI
Acts 14.19 Jews came there from Antioch

COME, THINGS TO (*See* COME, W. IS TO)

COME TO

1. *have, hold:* ἔχω ECHŌ
Mk 3.26 "he cannot stand but is coming to an end

2. *enter, go into:* εἰσέρχομαι EISERCHOMAI
Lk 8.41 he besought him to come to his house
Acts 16.15 "Lord, come to my house and stay
23.33 came to Caesarea and delivered the letter

3. *come to be, happen, be:* γίνομαι GINOMAI
Acts 4. 4 number . . came to about five thousand
5.24 wondering what this would come to

4. *come to, approach:* προσέρχομαι PROSERCHOMAI
Mt 5. 1 when he sat down his disciples came to him
8. 2 a leper came to him and knelt before him
9.14 Then the disciples of John came to him
9.28 the blind men came to him
13.36 his disciples came to him
14.15 it was evening, the disciples came to him
15. 1 scribes came to Jesus from Jerusalem
15.30 great crowds came to him
17.19 the disciples came to Jesus privately
18. 1 At that time the disciples came to Jesus
21.14 the blind and the lame came to him
22.23 The same day Sadducees came to him

Mt 24. 3 the disciples came to him privately
26.17 disciples came to Jesus, saying, "Where?
Mk 6.35 when it grew late, his disciples came to him
Lk 20.27 There came to him some Sadducees
Jn 12.21 ⟨some Greeks⟩ came to Philip
Heb 12.18 have not come to what may be touched
12.22 But you have come to Mount Zion
1 Pet 2. 4 Come to him, to that living stone

COME, TO

1. *be about to:* μέλλω (attr. part.) MELLŌ
Mt 3. 7 "to flee from the wrath to come
12.32 "either in this age or in the age to come
Lk 3. 7 "to flee from the wrath to come
1 Tim 4. 8 present life and also for the life to come
Heb 2. 5 God subjected the world to come
6. 5 the powers of the age to come
[9.11 a high priest of the good things *to come*‡
10. 1 shadow of the good things to come

COME TO PASS

1. *come to be, happen, be:* γίνομαι GINOMAI
Mk 11.23 "what he says will come to pass
Lk 1.20 "until the day that these things come to p.
Acts 26.22 "what . . Moses said would come to pass
1 Cor 15.54 then shall come to pass the saying
1 Th 3. 4 just as it has come to pass

COME TOGETHER

1. *bring together:* συνάγω (pass.) SYNAGŌ
Mt 22.34 Pharisees heard . . , they came together
2. *assemble:* σύνειμι SYNEIMI II*
Lk 8. 4 when a great crowd came together
3. *come together:* συνέρχομαι SYNERCHOMAI
Mt 1.18 before they came together she was found
Mk 3.20 the crowd came together again
Jn 18.20 "temple, where all Jews come together
Acts 1. 6 when they had come together, they asked
2. 6 at this sound the multitude came together
16.13 spoke to . . women who had c. together
19.32 did not know why they had come together
25.17 "When therefore they came together here
1 Cor 11.17 you come together . . for the worse
11.33 when you come together to eat, wait
11.34 lest you come together to be condemned
14.26 you come together, each . . has a hymn

COME UP

1. *go up, come up:* ἀναβαίνω ANABAINŌ
Mt 17.27 "take the first fish that comes up
Mk 1.10 he came up out of the water, immediately
15. 8 crowd came up and began to ask Pilate
Acts 8.31 he invited Philip to come up and sit
8.39 when they came up out of the water
Rev 4. 1 "Come up hither, and I will show you
11.12 a loud voice . . "Come up hither!
2. *sprout, produce:* βλαστάνω BLASTANŌ
Mt 13.26 "the plants came up and bore grain
3. *bring near, approach:* ἐγγίζω EGGIZŌ
Acts 21.33 the tribune came up and arrested him
4. *stand by:* ἐφίστημι EPHISTĒMI
Lk 2.38 coming up at that very hour she gave thanks
20. 1 as he was teaching . . , scribes . . came up
5. *come to, approach:* προσέρχομαι PROSERCHOMAI
Mt 8.19 scribe came up and said . . "Teacher
9.20 woman . . came up behind him and touched
17.14 man came up to him and kneeling . . said
18.21 Peter came up and said . . "Lord, how often?
19. 3 Pharisees came up . . asking, "Is it lawful?
19.16 one came up . . saying, "Teacher
20.20 mother of the sons of Zebedee came up
21.23 elders of the people came up to him
26. 7 woman came up . . with an alabaster flask
26.49 he came up to Jesus . . and . . kissed him
26.50 they came up and laid hands on Jesus
26.69 in the courtyard . . a maid came up to him
26.73 bystanders came up and said to Peter
Mk 10. 2 Pharisees came up and . . asked, "Is it lawful?
12.28 one of the scribes came up and heard them
Lk 8.44 came up behind him, and touched the fringe
Lk 23.36 soldiers also mocked him, coming up

COME UP WITH

1. *go up with:* συναναβαίνω SYNANABAINŌ*
Mk 15.41 many other women who came up with him
Acts 13.31 "those who came up with him from Galilee

COME UPON (*See* COME ON)

COME, W. IS TO

COME, THINGS TO

1. *be about to:* μέλλω (subst. part.) MELLŌ
[a]neut. pl.
Rom 5.14 who was a type of the one who was to come
8.38 [a]nor things to come, nor powers
Eph 1.21 this age but also in that which is to come
Col 2.17 These are only a shadow of what is to come
Heb 13.14 we seek the city which is to come

COME WITH

1. *come together:* συνέρχομαι SYNERCHOMAI
Lk 23.55 who had come with him from Galilee
Jn 11.33 Jews who came with her also weeping
Acts 10.45 believers . . who came with Peter

COMFORT

1. *call to, exhort, comfort:* παρακαλέω PARAKALEŌ
Mt 5. 4 "those who mourn . . shall be comforted
Lk 16.25 " 'now he is comforted here
Acts 20.12 they . . were not a little comforted
2 Cor 1. 4 ⟨God⟩ who comforts us in all our affliction, so that we may be able to comfort
1. 4 with which we . . are comforted by God
1. 6 if we are comforted, it is for your comfort
2. 7 rather turn to forgive and comfort him
7. 6 God, who comforts the downcast, comforted us by the coming of Titus
7. 7 the comfort with which he was comforted
7.13 Therefore we are comforted
1 Th 3. 7 we have been comforted about you
4.18 comfort one another with these words
2 Th 2.17 comfort your hearts and establish them
2. *exhortation, comfort:* παράκλησις PARAKLĒSIS
Acts 9.31 walking . . in the comfort of the Holy Spirit
2 Cor 1. 3 Father of mercies and God of all comfort
1. 4 those . . in any affliction, with the comfort
1. 5 so through Christ we share . . in comfort too[a]
1. 6 If . . afflicted, it is for your comfort
1. 6 comfort . . you experience when you . . endure
1. 7 you will also share in our comfort
7. 4 great pride in you; I am filled with comfort
7. 7 by his coming but also by the comfort
7.13 besides our own comfort we rejoiced
2 Th 2.16 eternal comfort and good hope through grace
Phm . 7 I have derived much joy and comfort
3. *exhortation, consolation:* παρηγορία PARĒGORIA*
Col 4.11 they have been a comfort to me

COMING

1. *entrance:* εἴσοδος EISODOS
Acts 13.24 "Before his coming John had preached
2. *coming:* ἔλευσις ELEUSIS*
Acts 7.52 "who announced beforehand the coming
3. *be present:* πάρειμι PAREIMI [B.2.a.2]
Acts 10.21 "what is the reason for your coming?
4. *presence, arrival:* παρουσία PAROUSIA
Mt 24. 3 "what will be the sign of your coming?
24.27 "so will be the coming of the Son of man
24.37 "so will be the coming of the Son of man
24.39 "so will be the coming of the Son of man
1 Cor 15.23 "at his coming those who belong to Christ
16.17 I rejoice at the coming of Stephanas
2 Cor 7. 6 God . . comforted us by the coming of Titus
7. 7 not only by his coming but . . the comfort
Phil 1.26 because of my coming to you again
1 Th 2.19 before our Lord Jesus at his coming
3.13 at the coming of our Lord Jesus
4.15 we who . . are left until the coming
5.23 kept sound and blameless at the coming
2 Th 2. 1 concerning the coming of our Lord Jesus
2. 8 Lord Jesus will slay him . . by . . his coming

2 Th 2. 9 The coming of the lawless one
Jas 5. 7 Be patient . . until the coming of the Lord
5. 8 for the coming of the Lord is at hand
2 Pet 1.16 the power and coming of our Lord Jesus
3. 4 "Where is the promise of his coming?
3.12 hastening[i] the coming of the day of God
1 Jn 2.28 not shrink from him . . at his coming

COMMAND

1. *appoint, direct:* διατάσσω DIATASSŌ
Lk 17. 9 "because he did what was commanded
17.10 "when you have done all that is commanded
Acts 18. 2 Claudius had commanded all the Jews
1 Cor 9.14 Lord commanded that those who proclaim
2. *say, speak:* εἶπον EIPON
Mt 4. 3 "command these stones to become loaves
20.21 "Command that these two sons . . sit
Mk 8. 7 he commanded . . these . . be set before them
Lk 4. 3 "command this stone to become bread
19.15 "commanded these servants . . to be called
3. *command:* ἐντέλλω (mid.) ENTELLŌ
Mt 15. 4 "God commanded, 'Honor your father
17. 9 Jesus commanded them, "Tell no one
19. 7 "Why then did Moses command one?
28.20 "observe all that I have commanded
Mk 10. 3 "What did Moses command you?
13.34 "commands the doorkeeper to . . watch
Jn 8. 5 "Moses commanded us to stone such[r]‡
15.14 "if you do what I command you
15.17 "This I command you, to love one another
Acts 13.47 "For so the Lord has commanded us
Heb 9.20 "covenant which God commanded you
4. *command:* ἐντολή ENTOLĒ
[a]ἐντολὴν διδόναι DIDŌMI [b]ἐντολὴν λαμβάνειν LAMBANŌ
Lk 15.29 " 'I never disobeyed your command
Jn 14.31 [a]"I do as the Father has commanded me
Acts 17.15 receiving a c. for Silas and Timothy
1 Cor 14.37 what I am writing to you is a command
Tit 1.14 to Jewish myths or to commands of men
1 Jn 3.23 [a]love one another, just as he has commanded
2 Jn . 4 [b]just as we have been commanded
5. *command:* ἐπιταγή EPITAGĒ
Rom 16.26 the command of the eternal God
1 Cor 7. 6 by way of concession, not of command
7.25 I have no command of the Lord
2 Cor 8. 8 I say this not as a command
1 Tim 1. 1 an apostle of Christ Jesus by command
Tit 1. 3 been entrusted by command of God
6. *enjoin, order:* ἐπιτάσσω EPITASSŌ
Mk 1.27 "With authority he commands
6.39 he commanded them all to sit down
9.25 "I command you, come out of him
Lk 4.36 "with authority and power he commands
8.25 "Who then is this, that he commands?
8.31 begged him not to command them to depart
14.22 " 'Sir, what you commanded has been done
Acts 23. 2 Ananias commanded those . . to strike him
Phm . 8 I am bold enough in Christ to command
7. *order, command:* κελεύω KELEUŌ
[a]gen. absol.
Mt 14. 9 he commanded it to be given
Lk 18.40 Jesus . . commanded him to be brought
Acts 4.15 when they had commanded them to go
8.38 And he commanded the chariot to stop
22.24 tribune commanded him to be brought
22.30 he . . commanded . . the council to meet
23.10 commanded the soldiers to go down
23.35 he commanded him to be guarded
[24. 8 *"commanding his accusers to come*‡
25.21 "I commanded him to be held
25.23 [a]by command of Festus Paul was brought
8. *give orders:* παραγγέλλω PARAGGELLŌ
Mt 15.35 commanding the crowd to sit down
Mk 8. 6 he commanded the crowd to sit down
Lk 8.29 he had commanded the unclean spirit
9.21 he charged and commanded them
Acts 10.42 "he commanded us to preach to the people
Acts 17.30 "he commands all men everywhere to repent
2 Th 3. 4 do the things which we command
3. 6 we command you . . in the name of our Lord
3.12 such persons we command and exhort
1 Tim 4.11 Command and teach these things
5. 7 Command this, so that they may be
9. *command:* προστάσσω PROSTASSŌ
Mt 1.24 he did as the angel of the Lord commanded
8. 4 "offer the gift that Moses commanded
Mk 1.44 "offer . . what Moses commanded
Lk 5.14 "make an offering . . as Moses commanded
Acts 10.33 "all that you have been commanded
10.48 he commanded them to be baptized

IDIOMATICALLY
a. 1 Th 4.12 so that you may command the respect of outsiders ἵνα περιπατῆτε εὐσχημόνως πρὸς τοὺς ἔξω [PERIPATEŌ]

COMMAND, CRY OF

1. *order, call:* κέλευσμα KELEUSMA*
1 Th 4.16 Lord . . will descend . . with a cry of command

COMMAND, GIVE

1. *give orders:* παραγγέλλω PARAGGELLŌ
2 Th 3.10 when . . with you, we gave . . this command

COMMANDMENT

1. *command, injunction:* ἐντολή ENTOLĒ
Mt 5.19 "one of the least of these commandments
15. 3 "why do you transgress the commandment?
19.17 "If you would . . keep the commandments
22.36 "which is the great commandment?
22.38 "This is the great and first commandment
22.40 "On these two commandments depend all
Mk 7. 8 "You leave the commandment of God
7. 9 "rejecting the commandment of God!
10. 5 "For your hardness . . he wrote you this c.
10.19 "You know the commandments
12.28 "Which commandment is the first of all?
12.31 "There is no other commandment greater
Lk 1. 6 walking in all the commandments
18.20 "You know the commandments
23.56 rested according to the commandment
Jn 12.49 "the Father . . has . . given me c.
12.50 "his commandment is eternal life
13.34 "A new commandment I give . . you, . . love
14.15 "love me, you will keep my commandments
14.21 "He who has my commandments and keeps
15.10 "keep my commandments, you will abide
15.10 "I have kept my Father's commandments
15.12 "This is my commandment . . love
Rom 7. 8 finding opportunity in the commandment
7. 9 when the commandment came, sin revived
7.10 the very commandment . . proved to be death
7.11 finding opportunity in the commandment
7.12 law is holy, and the commandment is holy
7.13 that sin . . through the commandment
13. 9 and any other commandment, are summed
1 Cor 7.19 keeping the commandments of God
Eph 2.15 abolishing . . the law of commandments
6. 2 (this is the first commandment
1 Tim 6.14 keep the commandment unstained
Heb 7. 5 a commandment in the law to take tithes
7.18 a former commandment is set aside
9.19 every commandment of the law . . declared
2 Pet 2.21 turn back from the holy commandment
3. 2 the holy prophets and the commandment
1 Jn 2. 3 know him, if we keep his commandments
2. 4 but disobeys his commandments is a liar
2. 7 I am writing you no new commandment, but an old commandment which you had . . ; the old commandment is the word
2. 8 I am writing you a new commandment
3.22 because we keep his commandments
3.23 this is his c., . . believe . . and love
3.24 who keep his commandments abide in him
4.21 this commandment we have from him
5. 2 we love God and obey his commandments
5. 3 this is . . love . . keep his commandments

1 Jn 5. 3 his commandments are not burdensome
2 Jn . 5 as though . . writing . . a new commandment
. 6 love, that we follow his commandments; this is the commandment, . . love
Rev 12.17 war on . . those who keep the commandments
14.12 saints, those who keep the commandments
[22.14 those who *do his commandments*‡

COMMANDMENT, GIVE
1. *command:* ἐντέλλω (mid.) ENTELLŌ
Acts 1. 2 after he had given commandment

COMMEND
1. *approve, praise:* ἐπαινέω EPAINEŌ
Lk 16. 8 "master commended the dishonest steward
1 Cor 11. 2 I commend you because you remember me
11.17 in the following . . I do not commend you
11.22 Shall I commend you in this? No
2. *give up, allow:* παραδίδωμι PARADIDŌMI
Acts 14.26 to Antioch, where they had been commended
15.40 departed, being commended by the brethren
3. *place before:* παρατίθημι (mid.) PARATITHĒMI
Acts 20.32 "now I commend you to God
4. *place beside, stand before:* παρίστημι PARISTĒMI
1 Cor 8. 8 Food will not commend us to God
5. *stand with, commend:* συνίστημι SYNISTĒMI
Rom 16. 1 I commend to you our sister Phoebe
2 Cor 3. 1 Are we beginning to commend ourselves?
4. 2 c. ourselves to every man's conscience
5.12 We are not commending ourselves
6. 4 as servants of God we commend ourselves
10.12 some of those who commend themselves
10.18 not the man who commends himself . . but the man whom the Lord commends
12.11 I ought to have been commended by you

COMMENDATION
1. *praise, approval:* ἔπαινος EPAINOS
1 Cor 4. 5 every man will receive his commendation

COMMISSION
1. *rub, anoint:* χρίω CHRIŌ
2 Cor 1.21 it is God who . . has commissioned us
2. *stewardship:* ἐπιτροπή EPITROPĒ*
Acts 26.12 "with the . . commission of the chief priests
3. *stewardship, management:* οἰκονομία OIKONOMIA
1 Cor 9.17 I am entrusted with a commission

COMMISSIONED
CONTEXTUALLY
2 Cor 2.17 as commissioned by God . . we speak

COMMIT (*See also* ADULTERY, COMMIT; FORNICATION, COMMIT; UNGODLY WAY, COMMIT IN SUCH AN)
1. *give:* δίδωμι DIDŌMI
Rev 20. 4 those to whom judgment was committed
2. *work, do:* ἐργάζομαι ERGAZOMAI
Jas 2. 9 if you show partiality, you commit sin
3. *sin:* ἁμαρτάνω HAMARTANŌ [A.6.a.6]
1 Jn 5.16 committing what is not a mortal sin
4. *achieve:* κατεργάζομαι KATERGAZOMAI
Rom 1.27 men committing shameless acts with men
5. *give up, allow:* παραδίδωμι PARADIDŌMI
Acts 8. 3 dragged off . . and committed them to prison
Rom 6.17 standard . . to which you were committed
2 Pet 2. 4 committed them to pits of nether gloom
6. *place before:* παρατίθημι (mid.) PARATITHĒMI
Lk 12.48 "to whom men commit much
23.46 "into thy hands I commit my spirit!
Acts 14.23 they committed them to the Lord
1 Tim 1.18 This charge I commit to you, Timothy
7. *do, make:* ποιέω POIEŌ
Mk 15. 7 rebels . . who had committed murder
Jn 8.34 "every one who commits sin is a slave to sin
1 Cor 6.18 Every other sin which a man commits
2 Cor 11.7 "Did I commit a sin in abasing myself
Jas 5.15 committed sins, he will be forgiven
1 Pet 2.22 He committed no sin; no guile
1 Jn 3. 4 who commits sin is guilty of lawlessness
3. 8 He who commits sin is of the devil
3. 9 No one born of God commits sin
8. *do, practice:* πράσσω PRASSŌ
Acts 25.11 "If . . I . . have committed anything

COMMIT APOSTASY
1. *fall to the side:* παραπίπτω PARAPIPTŌ*
Heb 6. 6 if they then commit apostasy

COMMON (*See also* GOOD, THE COMMON; MAN, THAT IS COMMON TO)
1. *used by the public:* δημόσιος DĒMOSIOS
Acts 5.18 put them in the common prison
2. *private individual, layman:* ἰδιώτης (attr.) IDIŌTĒS
Acts 4.13 they were uneducated, common men
3. *common, profane:* κοινός KOINOS
Acts 10.14 "I have never eaten anything . . common
10.28 "I should not call any man common
11. 8 " 'nothing c. . . has . . entered my mouth
Tit 1. 4 Titus, my true child in a common faith
Jude . 3 write to you of our common salvation
IDIOMATICALLY
a. 2 Cor 6.15 what has a believer in common with an unbeliever? τίς μερὶς πιστῷ μετὰ ἀπίστου; [MERIS]

COMMON, CALL
1. *make common, defile:* κοινόω KOINOŌ
Acts 10.15 "God . . cleansed, you must not call common
11. 9 " 'God . . cleansed you must not call common

COMMON, IN
1. *common, profane:* κοινός (neut. pl.) KOINOS
Acts 2.44 all who believed . . had all things in c.
4.32 they had everything in common

COMMONWEALTH
1. *citizenship, body of citizens:* πολιτεία POLITEIA
Eph 2.12 alienated from the commonwealth of Israel
2. *citizen, corporate body:* πολίτευμα POLITEUMA*
Phil 3.20 our commonwealth is in heaven

COMMOTION
1. *seditious meeting:* συστροφή SYSTROPHĒ
Acts 19.40 "no cause . . to justify this commotion

COMMUNION
1. *fellowship, sharing:* κοινωνία KOINŌNIA
1 Cor [10.16 cup . . is . . *c.* in the blood of Christ†
[10.16 bread . . is . . *c.* in the body of Christ†

COMPANION IN TRAVEL
1. *traveling companion:* συνέκδημος SYNEKDĒMOS
Acts 19.29 who were Paul's companions in travel

COMPANY (*See also* BEFORE 16[a]; ENJOY COMPANY)
1. *association:* ὁμιλία (pl.) HOMILIA*
1 Cor 15.33 "Bad company ruins good morals
2. *group eating together:* κλισία KLISIA*
Lk 9.14 "sit down in companies, about fifty each
3. *crowd, populace:* ὄχλος OCHLOS
Lk 5.29 there was a large company of tax collectors
Acts 1.15 (c. . . was . . about a hundred and twenty
11.24 a large company was added to the Lord
4. *multitude, mass:* πλῆθος PLĒTHOS
Lk 23. 1 whole company . . brought him before Pilate
Acts 4.32 the company of those who believed
14. 1 so spoke that a great company believed
5. *group of travelers:* συνοδία SYNODIA*
Lk 2.44 supposing him to be in the company
IDIOMATICALLY
a. Mk 6.39 all to sit down by companies ἀνακλιθῆναι πάντας συμπόσια συμπόσια [SYMPOSION*]
CONTEXTUALLY
Lk 24.22 "some women of our c. amazed us
Acts 13.13 Now Paul and his company set sail

COMPANY, BE REFRESHED IN S.'S
1. *rest with:* συναναπαύομαι (+dat.) SYNANAPAUOMAI*
Rom 15.32 that . . I may . . be refreshed in your company

COMPANY OF PEOPLE
1. *crowd, populace:* ὄχλος OCHLOS
Acts 11.26 taught a large company of people
19.26 "turned away a considerable c. of people

COMPARE
1. *make like, compare:* ὁμοιόω HOMOIOŌ
Mt 11.16 "But to what shall I compare this generation?

Mt 13.24 "kingdom . . compared to a man who sowed
18.23 "kingdom . . compared to a king
22. 2 "kingdom . . compared to a . . marriage feast
25. 1 "kingdom . . compared to ten maidens
Mk 4.30 "With what can we compare the kingdom?
Lk 7.31 "To what . . compare . . this generation?
13.18 "And to what shall I compare it?
13.20 "To what shall I compare the kingdom?
2. *combine, explain:* συγκρίνω SYGKRINŌ
1 Cor [2.13 *comparing spiritual things*†
2 Cor 10.12 Not that we . . compare ourselves with some
10.12 But when they . . compare themselves

COMPARING, WORTH
1. *worthy:* ἄξιος AXIOS
Rom 8.18 not worth comparing with the glory

COMPARISON, BEYOND ALL
IDIOMATICALLY
a. 2 Cor 4.17 an eternal weight of glory beyond all comparison καθ' ὑπερβολὴν εἰς ὑπερβολὴν αἰώνιον βάρος δόξης [HYPERBOLĒ]

COMPASSION
1. *bowels of mercy:* σπλάγχνα οἰκτιρμοῦ OIKTIRMOS [A.1.f]
Col 3.12 Put on then . . compassion, kindness

COMPASSION, HAVE
COMPASSION ON, HAVE
1. *have pity on:* οἰκτίρω OIKTIRŌ*
Rom 9.15 For he says to Moses . . "I will have compassion on whom I have compassion
2. *feel pity:* σπλαγχνίζομαι SPLAGCHNIZOMAI
Mt 9.36 he saw the crowds, he had compassion
14.14 he had compassion on them, and healed
15.32 "I have compassion on the crowd
Mk 6.34 and he had compassion on them
8. 2 "I have compassion on the crowd
Lk 7.13 the Lord saw her, he had compassion on her
10.33 "when he saw him, he had compassion
15.20 "his father saw him and had compassion
3. *sympathize with:* συμπαθέω SYMPATHEŌ
Heb 10.34 you had compassion on the prisoners

COMPASSIONATE
1. *merciful:* πολύσπλαγχνος POLYSPLAGCHNOS*
Jas 5.11 how the Lord is compassionate and merciful

COMPEL
1. *press into service:* ἀγγαρεύω AGGAREUŌ
Mt 27.32 this man they compelled to carry his cross
Mk 15.21 they compelled a passer-by, Simon of Cyrene
2. *compel:* ἀναγκάζω ANAGKAZŌ
[a]pres. *would compel*
Lk 14.23 " 'Go out . . and compel people to come in
Acts 28.19 "I was compelled to appeal to Caesar
Gal 2. 3 Titus . . was not compelled to be circumcised
2.14 "how can you ⟨a Jew⟩ compel the Gentiles?
6.12 [a]those . . would compel you to be circumcised

COMPETE
1. *contend:* ἀθλέω ATHLEŌ
2 Tim 2. 5 unless he competes according to the rules
2. *run, move quickly:* τρέχω TRECHŌ
1 Cor 9.24 in a race all the runners compete

COMPETENCE
1. *sufficiency, fitness:* ἱκανότης HIKANOTĒS*
2 Cor 3. 5 our competence is from God[0]

COMPETENT
1. *enough:* ἱκανός HIKANOS
2 Cor 3. 5 Not that we are c. of ourselves[0]

COMPETENT, MAKE
1. *make sufficient, qualify:* ἱκανόω HIKANOŌ
2 Cor 3. 6 who has made us competent to be ministers[0]

COMPILE
1. *set in order:* ἀνατάσσομαι ANATASSOMAI*
Lk 1. 1 many have undertaken to compile

COMPLAIN
1. *say, speak:* λέγω LEGŌ [A.6.a.5]
Phil 4.11 Not that I complain of want

COMPLAINT
1. *word, reckoning:* λόγος LOGOS
Acts 19.38 "craftsmen with him have a complaint
2. *blame:* μομφή MOMPHĒ*
Col 3.13 if one has a complaint against another

COMPLETE
1. *fill up:* ἀναπληρόω ANAPLĒROŌ
Phil 2.30 risking his life to complete your service to me
2. *fill up:* ἀνταναπληρόω ANTANAPLĒROŌ*
Col 1.24 in my flesh I complete what is lacking
3. *exactly fitted, perfect:* ἄρτιος ARTIOS*
2 Tim 3.17 that the man of God may be complete
4. *finish, complete:* ἐπιτελέω EPITELEŌ
Rom 15.28 When therefore I have completed this
2 Cor 8. 6 complete among you this gracious work
8.10(11) to complete what a year ago you began
8.11 desiring it . . matched by your completing it
5. *complete, whole:* ὁλόκληρος HOLOKLĒROS
Jas 1. 4 that you may be perfect and complete
6. *fill full, complete:* πληρόω PLĒROŌ
2 Cor 10. 6 when your obedience is complete
Phil 2. 2 complete my joy by being of the same mind
1 Jn 1. 4 writing this that our[a] joy may be complete
2 Jn .12 so that our joy may be complete
Rev 6.11 number . . complete, who were to be killed
7. *bring to an end:* συντελέω SYNTELEŌ
Acts 21.27 the seven days were almost completed
8. *make perfect, complete:* τελειόω TELEIOŌ
Jas 2.22 faith was completed by works
IDIOMATICALLY
a. Lk 14.28 "whether he has enough to complete it?
εἰ ἔχει εἰς ἀπαρτισμόν; [APARTISMOS*]

COMPLETELY
IDIOMATICALLY
a. 1 Th [2.16 God's wrath has come upon them *completely*†
ἔφθασεν . . ἐπ' αὐτοὺς ἡ ὀργὴ εἰς τέλος [TELOS]

COMPLETION, BRING TO
1. *finish, complete:* ἐπιτελέω EPITELEŌ
Phil 1. 6 he who began . . will bring it to completion

COMPOSE
1. *mix, compose:* συγκεράννυμι SYGKERANNYMI
1 Cor 12.24 But God has so composed the body[0]

COMPREHEND
1. *know, understand:* γινώσκω GINŌSKŌ
1 Cor 2.11 no one comprehends the thoughts of God
2. *catch:* καταλαμβάνω (mid.) KATALAMBANŌ
Eph 3.18 power to comprehend with all the saints

COMPULSION
1. *force, necessity:* ἀνάγκη ANAGKĒ
2 Cor 9. 7 not reluctantly or under compulsion
Phm .14 that . . goodness might not be by compulsion

COMRADE
1. *sharing in:* μέτοχος (subst.) METOCHOS
Heb 1. 9 "anointed thee . . beyond thy comrades

CONCEAL
1. *hide:* παρακαλύπτω PARAKALYPTŌ*
Lk 9.45 concealed . . that they should not perceive it

CONCEIT
1. *vanity:* κενοδοξία KENODOXIA*
Phil 2. 3 Do nothing from selfishness or conceit
2. *inflation, pride:* φυσίωσις PHYSIŌSIS*
2 Cor 12.20 slander, gossip, conceit, and disorder

CONCEIT, BE PUFFED UP WITH
CONCEIT, BE SWOLLEN WITH
1. *be crazy, be conceited:* τυφόομαι TYPHOOMAI
1 Tim 3. 6 he may be puffed up with conceit
6. 4 he is puffed up with conceit
2 Tim 3. 4 swollen with conceit, lovers of pleasure

CONCEITED
1. *wise according to oneself:* φρόνιμος παρ' ἑαυτῷ PHRONIMOS [B.2.a.1]
Rom 12.16 never be conceited

CONCEITS
CONTEXTUALLY
Rom 11.25 Lest you be wise in your own conceits

CONCEIVE
1. *go up, come up:* ἀναβαίνω ANABAINŌ [B.2.d.3]
1 Cor 2. 9 "nor the heart of man conceived
2. *gather, seize, conceive:* συλλαμβάνω SYLLAMBANŌ
Lk 1.24 Elizabeth conceived, and .. hid herself
1.31 "behold, you will conceive in your womb
1.36 "Elizabeth in her old age has also conceived
2.21 called Jesus .. before he was conceived
Jas 1.15 desire when it has conceived gives birth
IDIOMATICALLY
a. Mt 1.23 "a virgin shall conceive ἡ παρθένος ἐν γαστρὶ ἕξει [GASTĒR]
b. Rom 9.10 when Rebecca had conceived children by one man 'Ρ. ἐξ ἑνὸς κοίτην ἔχουσα [KOITĒ]
c. Heb 11.11 Sarah .. received power to conceive Σ. δύναμιν εἰς καταβολὴν σπέρματος ἔλαβεν [SPERMA]

CONCEIVED, BE
1. *beget, bear:* γεννάω (pass.) GENNAŌ
Mt 1.20 "that which is conceived .. is of the .. Spirit

CONCERN
1. *think, set one's mind on:* φρονέω (inf.) PHRONEŌ
Phil 4.10 you have revived your concern for me

CONCERNED, BE
1. *take, lay hold of:* ἐπιλαμβάνομαι EPILAMBANOMAI
Heb 2.16 not with angels that he is concerned
2. *care:* μέλει MELEI [A.6.c.3]
1 Cor 9. 9 Is it for oxen that God is concerned?
3. *think, set one's mind on:* φρονέω PHRONEŌ
Phil 4.10 you were indeed concerned for me

CONCERNING
1. *into, to, for:* εἰς (+acc.) EIS
Acts **2**.25
Rom **4**.20
2. *on, at:* ἐπί (+dat.) EPI
Acts **4**.9
3. *over, for the sake of:* ὑπέρ (+gen.) HYPER
Rom **9**.27
2 Th **2**.1
4. *about, concerning:* περί (+gen.) PERI
Mt **11**.7
Lk **1**.4; **2**.17; **3**.15; **4**.14; **5**.15; **7**.17, 24; **24**.19, 27
Jn **11**.19
Acts **1**.16; **18**.25; **19**.23; **25**.16
Rom **1**.3
1 Cor **7**.1, 25; **8**.1; **12**.1; **16**.1
Col **4**.10
1 Th **1**.9; **4**.9, 13
Heb **11**.7, 22
1 Jn **1**.1
CONTEXTUALLY
Mk **4**.10
Rom **7**.2
Heb **7**.16

CONCESSION
1. *forbearance:* συγγνώμη SYGGNŌMĒ*
1 Cor 7. 6 by way of concession, not of command

CONCILIATE, TRY TO
1. *call to, exhort, comfort:* παρακαλέω PARAKALEŌ
1 Cor 4.13 when slandered, we try to conciliate

CONCLUDE
1. *bring together, infer, teach:* συμβιβάζω SYMBIBAZŌ
Acts 16.10 concluding that God had called us to preach

CONDEMN
1. *condemn:* καταδικάζω KATADIKAZŌ*
Mt 12. 7 "would not have condemned the guiltless
12.37 "by your words you will be condemned
Lk 6.37 "condemn not, and you will not be condemned; forgive, and you will be forgiven
Jas 5. 6 You have condemned .. the righteous man
2. *condemn:* καταγινώσκω KATAGINŌSKŌ
1 Jn 3.20 whenever our hearts condemn us
1 Jn 3.21 Beloved, if our hearts do not condemn us
3. *condemn:* κατακρίνω KATAKRINŌ*
Mt 12.41 "men of Nineveh will .. condemn it
12.42 "queen of the South will .. condemn it
20.18 "they will condemn him to death
27. 3 Judas .. saw that he was condemned
Mk 10.33 "they will condemn him to death
14.64 all condemned him as deserving death
16.16 "he who does not believe will be condemned[r]‡
Lk 11.31 "queen of the South will .. condemn them
11.32 "men of Nineveh will .. condemn it
Jn 8.10 "Has no one condemned you?[r]‡
8.11 "Neither do I condemn you; go[r]‡
Rom 2. 1 in passing judgment .. you c. yourself
8. 3 God .. condemned sin in the flesh
8.34 who is to condemn? Is it Christ Jesus?
14.23 But he who has doubts is condemned
1 Cor 11.32 not be condemned along with the world
Heb 11. 7 by this he condemned the world
2 Pet 2. 6 he condemned them to extinction
4. *to judgment:* πρὸς κατάκρισιν KATAKRISIS [B.1.a.2]
2 Cor 7. 3 I do not say this to condemn you
5. *to judgment:* εἰς κρίμα KRIMA [B.1.a.2]
Lk 24.20 "delivered him .. to be condemned to death
1 Cor 11.34 lest you come together to be condemned
6. *judge, decide:* κρίνω KRINŌ
Lk 19.22 "He said to him, 'I will condemn you!
Jn 3.17 God sent the Son .. not to condemn
3.18 who believes in him is not condemned; he who does not believe is condemned
Acts 13.27 "fulfilled these by condemning him
Rom 2.27 physically uncircumcised .. will condemn you
3. 7 why am I still being condemned as a sinner?
2 Th 2.12 so that all may be condemned

CONDEMNATION
1. *punishment:* κατάκριμα KATAKRIMA*
Rom 5.16 judgment .. brought condemnation
5.18 one man's trespass led to condemnation
8. 1 There is therefore now no condemnation
2. *judgment:* κατάκρισις KATAKRISIS
2 Cor 3. 9 if .. in the dispensation of condemnation
3. *judgment:* κρίμα KRIMA
Mt [23.14 *"you will receive the greater c.*‡
Mk 12.40 "They will receive .. condemnation
Lk 20.47 "They will receive .. condemnation
23.40 "you are under the same .. condemnation
Rom 3. 8 Their condemnation is just
1 Tim 3. 6 fall into the condemnation of the devil[f]
5.12 they incur condemnation for having violated
2 Pet 2. 3 their condemnation has not been idle
Jude . 4 long ago .. designated for this condemnation
4. *judgment:* κρίσις KRISIS
Jas 5.12 that you .. not fall under condemnation

CONDEMNED, STAND
1. *condemn:* καταγινώσκω (pluperf. pass. periphr.) KATAGINŌSKŌ
Gal 2.11 I opposed him .. because he stood condemned

CONDITION
1. *flesh, body:* σάρξ SARX
Gal 4.14 though my condition was a trial to you
CONTEXTUALLY
1 Cor [7.21 *make use of your present condition instead*†

CONDUCT
1. *way of life:* ἀγωγή AGŌGĒ*
2 Tim 3.10 Now you have observed my .. conduct
2. *behavior:* ἀναστροφή ANASTROPHĒ
1 Tim 4.12 set the believers an example in .. conduct
1 Pet 1.15 be holy yourselves in all your conduct
2.12 Maintain good conduct among the Gentiles
3. *work, deed:* ἔργον ERGON
Rom 13. 3 rulers are not a terror to good conduct
4. *set in order, appoint:* καθίστημι KATHISTĒMI
Acts 17.15 Those who conducted Paul brought him
IDIOMATICALLY
a. Rom 1.28 improper conduct ποιεῖν τὰ μὴ καθήκοντα [POIEŌ]

CONDUCT ONESELF
1. *return; behave* (pass.): ἀναστρέφω ANASTREPHŌ
1 Pet 1.17 conduct yourselves with fear throughout
2. *walk, behave:* περιπατέω PERIPATEŌ
Rom 13.13 let us conduct ourselves becomingly
Col 4. 5 C. yourselves wisely toward outsiders

CONFER
1. *add, counsel with* (mid.): προσανατίθημι PROSANATITHĒMI
Gal 1.16 I did not confer with flesh and blood
2. *talk with:* συλλαλέω SYLLALEŌ
Lk 22. 4 conferred with the chief priests and officers
Acts 25.12 when he had conferred with his council
3. *throw together, compare:* συμβάλλω SYMBALLŌ
Acts 4.15 they conferred with one another

CONFESS
1. *agree:* ἐξομολογέω (mid.) EXOMOLOGEŌ
Mt 3. 6 baptized . . confessing their sins
Mk 1. 5 baptized . . confessing their sins
Acts 19.18 believers came, confessing and divulging
Rom [14.11 "every tongue shall *confess* to God†
Phil 2.11 every tongue confess . . Jesus Christ is Lord
Jas 5.16 confess your sins to one another, and pray
2. *confess, acknowledge:* ὁμολογέω HOMOLOGEŌ
Jn 1.20 He confessed, he did not deny, but confessed, "I am not the Christ
9.22 if any one should confess him to be Christ
12.42 for fear . . they did not confess it
Rom 10. 9 if you confess . . that Jesus is Lord
10.10 he confesses with his lips and so is saved
1 Jn 1. 9 If we confess our sins, he . . will forgive
2.23 He who confesses the Son has the Father
4. 2 every spirit which confesses . . is of God
4. 3 every spirit which does not confess Jesus
4.15 Whoever confesses that Jesus is the Son
Rev 3. 5 " 'I will confess his name before my Father

CONFESSES, ONE
1. *admittedly:* ὁμολογουμένως HOMOLOGOUMENŌS* [A.4.e]
1 Tim 3.16 Great indeed, we confess, is the mystery

CONFESSION
1. *confession, agreement:* ὁμολογία HOMOLOGIA
[a]ὡμολόγησας . . ὁμολογίαν
1 Tim 6.12 [a]when you made the good confession
6.13 Christ Jesus who . . made the good confession
Heb 3. 1 apostle and high priest of our confession
4.14 let us hold fast our confession
10.23 Let us hold fast the confession of our hope

CONFIDENCE
1. *foundation, reality, confidence:* ὑπόστασις HYPOSTASIS
2 Cor 11.17 (but as a fool, in this boastful confidence
Heb 3.14 if only we hold our first confidence firm
2. *outspokenness:* παρρησία PARRĒSIA
2 Cor 7. 4 I have great confidence in you
1 Tim 3.13 deacons gain . . great confidence in the faith
Heb 3. 6 if we hold fast our confidence and pride
4.16 Let us then with confidence draw near
10.19 confidence to enter the sanctuary
10.35 do not throw away your confidence
1 Jn 2.28 when he appears we may have confidence
3.21 we have confidence before God
4.17 that we may have confidence for the day
5.14 this is the confidence which we have in him
3. *trust, boldness:* πεποίθησις PEPOITHĒSIS
2 Cor 3. 4 Such is the confidence that we have
8.22 because of his great confidence in you
10. 2 to show boldness with such confidence
Eph 3.12 we have boldness and confidence of access

CONFIDENCE, HAVE
CONFIDENCE, HAVE REASON FOR
1. *persuade:* πείθω (perf.) PEITHŌ
Gal 5.10 I have confidence in the Lord that
Phil 3. 4 he has reason for confidence in the flesh
2 Th 3. 4 we have confidence in the Lord about you
2. *faithful, trustworthy:* πιστός (subst.) PISTOS [A.1.a]
1 Pet 1.21 Through him you have confidence in God

3. *have confidence:* θαρρέω THARREŌ
2 Cor 7.16 because I have perfect confidence in you

CONFIDENCE, PUT
1. *persuade:* πείθω (perf.) PEITHŌ
Phil 3. 3 we . . put no confidence in the flesh

CONFIDENCE, REASON FOR
1. *trust, boldness:* πεποίθησις PEPOITHĒSIS
Phil 3. 4 I . . have reason for confidence in the flesh

CONFIDENT
1. *persuade:* πείθω (perf. part.) PEITHŌ
Phm .21 Confident of your obedience, I write

CONFIDENT, BE
1. *foundation, reality, confidence:* ὑπόστασις HYPOSTASIS [B.1.a.2]
2 Cor 9. 4 humiliated . . for being so confident
2. *persuade oneself:* πείθειν ἑαυτῷ (perf.) PEITHŌ
2 Cor 10. 7 [a]If any one is confident that he is Christ's

CONFIDENT, MAKE
1. *persuade:* πείθω PEITHŌ
Phil 1.14 brethren have been made confident

CONFIDENTLY
1. *with confidence:* μετὰ παρρησίας PARRĒSIA [B.1.a.1]
Acts 2.29 "I may say . . c. of the patriarch David
2. *have confidence:* θαρρέω (part.) THARREŌ
Heb 13. 6 confidently say, "The Lord is my helper

CONFINE
1. *guard, keep:* φρουρέω PHROUREŌ
Gal 3.23 before faith came, we were confined

CONFIRM
1. *confirm, establish:* βεβαιόω BEBAIOŌ
Mk 16.20 Lord . . confirmed the message by the signs[k]‡
Rom 15. 8 to confirm the promises . . to the patriarchs
1 Cor 1. 6 as the testimony to Christ was confirmed
2. *make firm:* βέβαιον ποιεῖν BEBAIOS [B.2.a.1]
2 Pet 1.10 be the more zealous to confirm your call
3. *stand, set:* ἵστημι HISTĒMI
Mt 18.16 "that every word may be confirmed

CONFIRMATION
1. *confirmation:* βεβαίωσις BEBAIŌSIS*
Phil 1. 7 defense and confirmation of the gospel
Heb 6.16 an oath is final for confirmation

CONFLICT
1. *struggle:* ἀγών AGŌN
Phil 1.30 engaged in the same conflict

CONFLICTING
1. *between one another:* μεταξὺ ἀλλήλων METAXY [B.1.a.1]
Rom 2.15 their c. thoughts accuse or . . excuse

CONFORM TO
1. *correct, mold after:* συσχηματίζω SYSCHĒMATIZŌ*
Rom 12. 2 Do not be conformed to this world[q]
1 Pet 1.14 do not be conformed to the passions

CONFORMED
1. *of the same shape as:* σύμμορφος SYMMORPHOS
Rom 8.29 he also predestined to be conformed

CONFOUND
1. *confuse:* συγχέω SYGCHEŌ
Acts 9.22 Saul increased . . and confounded the Jews

CONFUSION
1. *instability:* ἀκαταστασία AKATASTASIA
1 Cor 14.33 God is not a God of confusion but of peace
2. *mixture, confusion:* σύγχυσις SYGCHYSIS*
Acts 19.29 the city was filled with the confusion

CONFUSION, BE IN
1. *confound:* συγχέω (pass.) SYGCHEŌ
Acts 19.32 for the assembly was in confusion
21.31 word . . that all Jerusalem was in confusion

CONFUTE
1. *refute conclusively:* διακατελέγχομαι DIAKATELEGCHOMAI*
Acts 18.28 he powerfully confuted the Jews in public
2. *expose, test, refute:* ἐλέγχω ELEGCHŌ
Tit 1. 9 able . . to confute those who contradict it

CONGREGATION
1. *assembly, church:* ἐκκλησία EKKLĒSIA
Acts 7.38 "in the congregation in the wilderness
Heb 2.12 "in the midst of the c. I will praise thee
2. *multitude, mass:* πλῆθος PLĒTHOS
Acts 15.30 having gathered the congregation together
19. 9 speaking evil . . before the congregation

CONJUGAL RIGHTS
1. *debt, one's due:* ὀφειλή OPHEILĒ
1 Cor 7. 3 should give to his wife her c. rights

CONNECTION
CONTEXTUALLY
Heb 7.14 in c. with that tribe Moses said nothing

CONQUER
1. *prevail against:* καταγωνίζομαι KATAGŌNIZOMAI*
Heb 11.33 who through faith conquered kingdoms
2. *conquer, prevail:* νικάω NIKAŌ
Rev 2. 7 " 'To him who conquers I will grant to eat
2.11 " 'He who conquers shall not be hurt
2.17 " 'To him who conquers I will give . . manna
2.26 " 'who conquers and who keeps my works
3. 5 " 'who conquers shall be clad . . in white
3.12 " 'He who conquers, I will make him a pillar
3.21 " 'He who conquers, I will grant . . to sit
3.21 " 'I . . conquered and sat . . with my Father
5. 5 "the Root of David, has conquered
6. 2 a crown was given to him, and he went out conquering and to conquer
11. 7 beast . . will . . conquer them and kill them
12.11 "they have conquered him by the blood
13. 7 it was allowed . . to conquer them[f]‡
15. 2 those who had conquered the beast
17.14 "the Lamb will conquer them, for he is Lord
21. 7 "He who conquers shall have this heritage

CONQUEROR, BE MORE THAN
1. *prevail completely over:* ὑπερνικάω HYPERNIKAŌ*
Rom 8.37 in all these . . we are more than conquerors

CONSCIENCE
1. *conscience, consciousness:* συνείδησις SYNEIDĒSIS
Acts 23. 1 "I have lived . . in all good conscience
24.16 "I . . take pains to have a clear conscience
Rom 2.15 their conscience also bears witness
9. 1 my conscience bears me witness
13. 5 be subject . . also for the sake of conscience
1 Cor 8. 7 their conscience, being weak, is defiled
8.10 not . . encouraged, if his conscience is weak?
8.12 wounding their conscience when it is weak
10.25 without . . question on the ground of c.
10.27 without . . question on the ground of c.
10.28 (for conscience' sake ⟨do not eat it⟩
10.29 (I mean his conscience, not yours
2 Cor 1.12 our boast is . ., the testimony of our conscience
4. 2 commend ourselves to every . . conscience
5.11 I hope it is known also to your conscience
1 Tim 1. 5 love that issues from . . a good conscience
1.19 holding faith and a good conscience
3. 9 mystery of the faith with a clear conscience
4. 2 liars whose consciences are seared
2 Tim 1. 3 God whom I serve with a clear conscience
Tit 1.15 their . . minds and consciences are corrupted
Heb 9. 9 sacrifices . . which cannot perfect the c.
9.14 blood of Christ . . purify your[t] conscience
10.22 sprinkled clean from an evil conscience
13.18 we are sure that we have a clear conscience
1 Pet 3.16 keep your conscience clear
3.21 an appeal to God for a clear conscience

CONSCIOUSNESS
1. *conscience, consciousness:* συνείδησις SYNEIDĒSIS
Heb 10. 2 no longer have any consciousness of sin

CONSECRATE
1. *make sacred:* ἁγιάζω HAGIAZŌ
Jn 10.36 "him whom the Father consecrated and sent
17.19 "for their sake I consecrate myself, that they also may be consecrated in truth
1 Cor 7.14 the unbelieving husband is consecrated
7.14 wife is consecrated through her husband
1 Tim 4. 5 then it is consecrated by the word of God
2 Tim 2.21 he will be a vessel for noble use, consecrated

CONSENT
1. *allow him:* ἀφιέναι αὐτόν APHIĒMI [B.2.a.1]
Mt 3.15 "Let it be so now . ." Then he consented
2. *judgment, opinion, purpose:* γνώμη GNŌMĒ
Phm .14 to do nothing without your consent
3. *agree with:* συγκατατίθημι (mid.) SYGKATATITHĒMI*
Lk 23.51 who had not consented to their purpose
4. *consent:* συνευδοκέω SYNEUDOKEŌ
Lk 11.48 "you are witnesses and consent
Acts 8. 1 Saul was consenting to his death
1 Cor 7.12 if . . she consents to live with him
7.13 If . . he consents to live with her

CONSEQUENTLY
1. *therefore:* διό DIO
Heb 10. 5 Consequently, when Christ[v] came
2. *whence, where:* ὅθεν HOTHEN
Heb 7.25 Consequently he is able for all time to save

CONSIDER (*See also* WORTHY, CONSIDER)
1. *sum up, consider:* ἀναλογίζομαι ANALOGIZOMAI*
Heb 12. 3 Consider him who endured from sinners
2. *examine carefully:* ἀναθεωρέω ANATHEŌREŌ
Heb 13. 7 consider the outcome of their life
3. *see, look:* βλέπω (imper.) BLEPŌ
1 Cor 1.26 consider your call, brethren
10.18 Consider the people of Israel[a]
4. *have, hold:* ἔχω ECHŌ
Phm .17 if you consider me your partner, receive
5. *look about:* εἶδον περί EIDON [B.2.a.1]
Acts 15. 6 elders were gathered together to consider
6. *ponder, consider:* ἐνθυμέομαι ENTHYMEOMAI
Mt 1.20 as he considered this, behold, an angel
7. *think, lead:* ἡγέομαι HĒGEOMAI
Heb 11.11 Sarah . . considered him faithful
11.26 He considered abuse suffered for the Christ
8. *observe well:* καταμανθάνω KATAMANTHANŌ*
Mt 6.28 "Consider the lilies of the field
9. *consider, perceive:* κατανοέω KATANOEŌ
Lk 12.24 "Consider the ravens: they neither sow
12.27 "Consider the lilies, how they grow
Rom 4.19 when he considered his own body
Heb 3. 1 c. Jesus, the apostle and high priest
10.24 consider how to stir up one another
10. *reckon, count:* λογίζομαι LOGIZOMAI
Rom 6.11 you also must consider yourselves dead
8.18 I consider . . the sufferings of this present
Phil 3.13 I do not consider . . I have made it my own
Heb 11.19 He considered that God was able to raise

CONSIDER IN ONE'S MIND
1. *calculate, argue:* διαλογίζομαι DIALOGIZOMAI
Lk 1.29 considered in her mind what sort of greeting

CONSIDERABLE
1. *enough:* ἱκανός HIKANOS
Acts 19.26 "Paul . . turned away a c. company

CONSIDERATELY
1. *with knowledge:* κατὰ γνῶσιν GNŌSIS [B.1.a.1]
1 Pet 3. 7 live considerately with your wives

CONSIDERATION FOR, OUT OF
1. *because of:* διά (+acc.) DIA
1 Cor **10.28**

CONSIGN
1. *enclose, close:* συγκλείω SYGKLEIŌ
Rom 11.32 God . . consigned all men to disobedience
Gal 3.22 the scripture consigned all things to sin

CONSIST
CONTEXTUALLY
1 Cor 4.20 kingdom of God does not consist in talk

CONSIST IN
CONSIST OF
1. *be:* εἰμί EIMI [A.6.a.5]
Lk 12.15 "life does not consist in the abundance

1 Cor 12.14 the body does not consist of one member

CONSOLATION

1. *exhortation, comfort:* παράκλησις PARAKLĒSIS
   Lk 2.25 Simeon . . looking for the consolation of Israel
   6.24 "you have received your consolation
2. *encouragement, consolation:* παραμυθία PARAMYTHIA*
   1 Cor 14. 3 speaks to men for their . . consolation

CONSOLE

1. *call to, exhort, comfort:* παρακαλέω PARAKALEŌ
   Mt 2.18 "Rachel weeping . . refused to be consoled
2. *encourage, support:* παραμυθέομαι PARAMYTHEOMAI
   Jn 11.19 many of the Jews had come . . to console them
   11.31 the Jews . . in the house, consoling her

CONSPICUOUS

1. *clear, foreseen:* πρόδηλος PRODĒLOS
   1 Tim 5.24 The sins of some men are conspicuous
   5.25 So also good deeds are conspicuous

CONSPIRACY

1. *conspiracy, plot:* συνωμοσία SYNŌMOSIA*
   Acts 23.13 more than forty who made this conspiracy

CONSTANT, BE

1. *persist in:* προσκαρτερέω PROSKARTEREŌ
   Rom 12.12 be patient in tribulation, be c. in prayer

CONSTANTLY

1. *unceasing:* ἀδιάλειπτος (neut.) ADIALEIPTOS
   2 Tim 1. 3 I remember you constantly in my prayers
2. *unceasingly:* ἀδιαλείπτως ADIALEIPTŌS
   1 Th 1. 2 constantly mentioning you in our prayers
   2.13 we also thank God constantly for this
   5.17 pray constantly
3. *through everything:* διὰ παντός PAS [B.1.a.1]
   Acts 10. 2 devout man who . . prayed constantly to God

CONSTRAIN

1. *do by force, compel:* παραβιάζομαι PARABIAZOMAI
   Lk 24.29 they constrained him, saying, "Stay

CONSTRAINED, BE

1. *hold together, impel:* συνέχω (pass.) SYNECHŌ
   Lk 12.50 "I am constrained until it is accomplished!

CONSTRAINT, BY

1. *by force:* ἀναγκαστῶς ANAGKASTŌS*
   1 Pet 5. 2 Tend the flock of God . . not by constraint

CONSTRUCT

1. *prepare, construct:* κατασκευάζω KATASKEUAZŌ
   Heb 11. 7 By faith Noah . . constructed an ark

CONSULTATION

1. *counsel, plan:* συμβούλιον SYMBOULION
   Mk 15. 1 the whole council held a consultation

CONSUME

1. *use up:* ἀναλίσκω ANALISKŌ*
   Lk 9.54 "bid fire come down . . and consume them[e]
   Gal 5.15 take heed that you are not consumed
2. *make unseen, destroy:* ἀφανίζω APHANIZŌ
   Mt 6.19 "on earth, where moth and rust[o] consume
   6.20 "where neither moth nor rust[o] consumes
3. *eat:* ἐσθίω ESTHIŌ
   Heb 10.27 fire which will consume the adversaries
4. *use up, spend:* καταναλίσκω KATANALISKŌ*
   Heb 12.29 for our God is a consuming fire
5. *devour, eat up:* κατεσθίω KATESTHIŌ
   Jn 2.17 "Zeal for thy house will consume me
   Rev 11. 5 fire . . consumes their foes
   20. 9 fire came down . . and consumed them

CONSUMED, BE

1. *burn out:* ἐκκαίω (pass.) EKKAIŌ*
   Rom 1.27 were consumed with passion for one another

CONTAIN

1. *make room for, hold, go:* χωρέω CHŌREŌ
   Jn 21.25 world itself could not contain the books

CONTEXTUALLY
   Heb 9. 4 ark . . , which contained a golden urn

CONTEMPT, HOLD UP TO

1. *make an example:* παραδειγματίζω PARADEIGMATIZŌ*
   Heb 6. 6 crucify . . and hold him up to contempt

CONTEMPT, TREAT WITH

1. *hold valueless:* ἐξουδενέω EXOUDENEŌ*
   Mk 9.12 "that he should . . be treated with contempt
2. *treat with contempt:* ἐξουθενέω EXOUTHENEŌ
   Lk 23.11 his soldiers treated him with contempt

CONTEND

1. *differentiate, decide:* διακρίνω (mid.) DIAKRINŌ
   Jude . 9 archangel Michael, contending with the devil
2. *fight:* διαμάχομαι DIAMACHOMAI*
   Acts 23. 9 some . . scribes . . stood up and contended
3. *contend with:* ἐπαγωνίζομαι EPAGŌNIZOMAI*
   Jude . 3 appealing to you to contend for the faith
4. *fight:* πάλη PALĒ* [A.6.a.3]
   Eph 6.12 For we are not contending against flesh

CONTENT

1. *suffice, satisfy:* ἀρκέω (pass. part.) ARKEŌ
   3 Jn .10 not c. with that, he refuses . . to welcome
2. *self-reliant:* αὐτάρκης AUTARKĒS*
   Phil 4.11 in whatever state I am, to be content

CONTENT, BE

1. *suffice, satisfy:* ἀρκέω (pass.) ARKEŌ
   Lk 3.14 "be content with your wages
   1 Tim 6. 8 with these we shall be content
   Heb 13. 5 be content with what you have
2. *be well pleased:* εὐδοκέω EUDOKEŌ
   2 Cor 12.10 I am content with weaknesses, insults

CONTENTION, SHARP

1. *irritation, provoking:* παροξυσμός PAROXYSMOS
   Acts 15.39 there arose a sharp contention

CONTENTIOUS

1. *fond of victory, contentious:* φιλόνεικος PHILONEIKOS*
   1 Cor 11.16 If any one is disposed to be contentious

CONTENTMENT

1. *self-sufficiency:* αὐτάρκεια AUTARKEIA
   1 Tim 6. 6 great gain in godliness with contentment

CONTINUAL

1. *end, goal:* τέλος TELOS [B.1.a.1]
   Lk 18. 5 " 'she will wear me out by her c. coming

CONTINUALLY

1. *through everything:* διὰ παντός PAS [B.1.a.1]
   Lk 24.53 continually in the temple blessing God
   Heb 9. 6 priests go continually into the outer tent[p]
   13.15 let us continually offer up a sacrifice

IDIOMATICALLY
   a. Heb 10.1 by the same sacrifices which are continually offered ταῖς αὐταῖς θυσίαις ἃς προσφέρουσιν εἰς τὸ διηνεκές [DIĒNEKĒS]

CONTINUE

1. *persist, persevere:* διαμένω DIAMENŌ
   Lk 22.28 "You are those who have continued with me
   2 Pet 3. 4 "all things have continued as they were
2. *continue:* διατελέω DIATELEŌ*
   Acts 27.33 "continued in suspense and without food
3. *stay in, stand by:* ἐμμένω EMMENŌ
   Acts 14.22 exhorting them to continue in the faith
   Heb 8. 9 "they did not continue in my covenant
4. *continue, remain:* ἐπιμένω EPIMENŌ
   Jn 8. 7 as they continued to ask him, he stood up[r]‡
   Acts 12.16 But Peter continued knocking
   Rom 6. 1 to continue in sin that grace may abound?
   11.22 provided you continue in his kindness
   Col 1.23 provided that you continue in the faith
5. *come to be, happen, be:* γίνομαι GINOMAI
   Acts 19.10 This continued for two years
6. *stay, wait:* μένω MENŌ
   Jn 8.31 "If you continue in my word
   8.35 "slave does not continue in the house for ever; the son continues for ever
   Rom 9.11 God's purpose of election might continue
   1 Tim 2.15 if she continues[d] in faith and love†
   2 Tim 3.14 continue in what you have learned
   Heb 7. 3 he continues a priest for ever
   7.24 because he continues for ever
   13. 1 Let brotherly love continue

1 Jn 2.19 they would have continued with us
7. *stay beside, endure:* παραμένω PARAMENŌ
Phil 1.25 I shall remain and continue with you all
Heb 7.23 prevented by death from continuing in office
8. *persist in:* προσκαρτερέω PROSKARTEREŌ
Acts 8.13 being baptized he continued with Philip
9. *wait for, stay with:* προσμένω PROSMENŌ
Acts 13.43 urged them to continue in the grace of God
1 Tim 5. 5 real widow . . continues in supplications
CONTEXTUALLY
2 Cor 11.12 And what I do I will continue to do

CONTINUE ALL NIGHT
1. *pass the night:* διανυκτερεύω DIANYKTEREUŌ*
Lk 6.12 all night he continued in prayer

CONTINUE STEADFASTLY
1. *persist in:* προσκαρτερέω PROSKARTEREŌ
Col 4. 2 Continue steadfastly in prayer

CONTRADICT
1. *speak against:* ἀντεῖπον ANTEIPON
Lk 21.15 "none . . will be able to . . contradict
2. *speak against:* ἀντιλέγω ANTILEGŌ
Acts 13.45 contradicted what was spoken by Paul
Tit 1. 9 able . . to confute those who contradict it

CONTRADICTED, NOT TO BE
1. *not to be opposed:* ἀναντίρρητος ANANTIRRĒTOS*
Acts 19.36 "that these things cannot be contradicted

CONTRADICTION
1. *opposition:* ἀντίθεσις ANTITHESIS*
1 Tim 6.20 Avoid the godless chatter and contradictions

CONTRARY
1. *speak against:* ἀντιλέγω (part.) ANTILEGŌ
Rom 10.21 "to a disobedient and contrary people

CONTRARY, BE
1. *be opposed:* ἀντίκειμαι ANTIKEIMAI
1 Tim 1.10 whatever else is contrary to sound doctrine

CONTRARY, ON THE
1. *but:* ἀλλά ALLA
Rom **3.31**
1 Cor **15.10**
2. *much more:* πολλῷ μᾶλλον MALLON; POLYS [A.4.b]
[a]+ἀλλά
1 Cor 12.22 [a]On the c., the . . weaker are indispensable
3. *on the other hand:* τοὐναντίον TOUNANTION
Gal 2. 7 but on the contrary, when they saw
1 Pet 3. 9 not return evil . . but on the contrary bless

CONTRARY TO
1. *more than, by:* παρά (+acc.) PARA
Acts **18.13**
Gal **1.8**, 9

CONTRARY TO THE LAW
1. *transgress the law:* παρανομέω (part.) PARANOMEŌ
Acts 23. 3 "contrary to the law you order me . . struck?

CONTRIBUTE
1. *throw, put:* βάλλω BALLŌ
Mk 12.43 "more than all those who are contributing
12.44 "they all contributed out of their abundance
Lk 21. 4 "they all contributed out of their abundance
2. *share:* μεταδίδωμι METADIDŌMI
Rom 12. 8 he who contributes, in liberality

CONTRIBUTE TO
1. *share in:* κοινωνέω KOINŌNEŌ
Rom 12.13 Contribute to the needs of the saints

CONTRIBUTION
1. *fellowship, sharing:* κοινωνία KOINŌNIA
Rom 15.26 contribution for the poor among the saints
2 Cor 9.13 generosity of your contribution for them
2. *collection:* λογεία LOGEIA*
1 Cor 16. 1 concerning the contribution for the saints
16. 2 so that contributions need not be made

CONTRIVE
1. *lay, put:* τίθημι (mid.) TITHĒMI
Acts 5. 4 "How is it that you have contrived this?

CONTROL
1. *authority, power:* ἐξουσία EXOUSIA
1 Cor 7.37 having his desire under control
2. *acquire, get:* κτάομαι KTAOMAI
1 Th [4. 4 know how *to control his own body*†[0]
3. *hold together, impel:* συνέχω SYNECHŌ
2 Cor 5.14 For the love of Christ controls us

CONTROL ONESELF
1. *be of sound mind:* σωφρονέω SŌPHRONEŌ
Tit 2. 6 urge the younger men to c. themselves

CONTROL, OUTSIDE S.'S
1. *not made subject:* ἀνυπότακτος ANYPOTAKTOS
Heb 2. 8 he left nothing outside his control

CONTROVERSY
1. *what is sought, question:* ζήτημα ZĒTĒMA
Acts 26. 3 "all customs and controversies of the Jews
2. *seeking, controversy:* ζήτησις ZĒTĒSIS
1 Tim 6. 4 he has a morbid craving for controversy
2 Tim 2.23 Have nothing to do with . . controversies
Tit 3. 9 avoid stupid controversies, genealogies

CONVERSATION
1. *word, reckoning:* λόγος (pl.) LOGOS
Lk 24.17 "What is this c. . . you are holding?

CONVERSE
1. *speak to:* ὁμιλέω HOMILEŌ
Acts 20.11 he conversed with them a long while
24.26 he sent for him often and conversed

CONVERSION
1. *turning about:* ἐπιστροφή EPISTROPHĒ*
Acts 15. 3 reporting the conversion of the Gentiles

CONVERT
1. *proselyte, convert:* προσήλυτος PROSĒLYTOS
Acts 13.43 Jews and devout converts to Judaism

CONVERT, FIRST
1. *firstfruits:* ἀπαρχή APARCHĒ
Rom 16. 5 Epaenetus, . . the first convert in Asia
1 Cor 16.15 household of Stephanas . . the first converts
2 Th [2.13 God chose you *as the first converts*‡

CONVERT, RECENT
1. *newly planted:* νεόφυτος (subst.) NEOPHYTOS*
1 Tim 3. 6 He must not be a recent convert

CONVICT
1. *expose, test, refute:* ἐλέγχω ELEGCHŌ
Jn 8.46 "Which of you convicts me of sin?
[16. 8 "when he comes, he will *convict* the world†[0]
1 Cor 14.24 if all prophesy . . he is convicted by all
Jas 2. 9 if you show partiality, you . . are convicted
Jude .15 "to convict all the ungodly of all their deeds

CONVICTION
1. *testing, conscience:* ἔλεγχος ELEGCHOS*
Heb 11. 1 faith is . . the conviction of things not seen
2. *certainty:* πληροφορία PLĒROPHORIA
1 Th 1. 5 in the Holy Spirit and with full conviction

CONVINCE
1. *test, refute:* ἐλέγχω ELEGCHŌ
Jn 16. 8 "he will convince[x] the world†[0]
2 Tim 4. 2 in season and out of season, convince
Jude .22 And convince some, who doubt
2. *persuade:* πείθω PEITHŌ
Lk 16.31 " 'neither . . convinced if some one should rise
20. 6 "they are convinced that John was a prophet
Acts 28.23 trying to convince them about Jesus
28.24 some were convinced by what he said

CONVINCED
1. *persuade:* πείθω (perf. part.) PEITHŌ
Phil 1.25 Convinced of this, I know that I shall

CONVINCED, BE
1. *think within oneself:* δοκεῖν ἑαυτῷ DOKEŌ [B.2.a.1]
Acts 26. 9 "was convinced that I ought to do . . things

CONVINCED, BE FULLY
CONVINCED, FULLY
1. *fulfill:* πληροφορέω (pass.) PLĒROPHOREŌ
[a]part.

Rom 4.21 [a]fully convinced that God was able
14. 5 every one be fully convinced in his . . mind

CONVINCED, BECAUSE ONE IS
1. *judge, decide:* κρίνω (part.) KRINŌ
2 Cor 5.14 because we are convinced that one has died

CONVINCINGLY (*See* MORE CONVINCINGLY)

CONVULSE
1. *tear, attack:* σπαράσσω SPARASSŌ*
Mk 1.26 unclean spirit, convulsing him and crying
9.26 crying out and convulsing him terribly
Lk 9.39 "it convulses him till he foams, and shatters
2. *tear in pieces:* συσπαράσσω SYSPARASSŌ*
Mk 9.20 spirit . . immediately . . convulsed the boy
Lk 9.42 the demon tore him and convulsed him

COOL
1. *cool, become cold:* καταψύχω KATAPSYCHŌ*
Lk 16.24 " 'send Lazarus to . . cool my tongue

COPPER
1. *copper, brass, bronze:* χαλκός CHALKOS
Mt 10. 9 "Take no gold . . nor copper in your belts
2. *thin, small:* λεπτός LEPTOS [B.3.b.2]
Lk 12.59 "till you have paid the very last copper

COPPER COIN
1. *thin, small:* λεπτός LEPTOS [B.3.b.2]
Mk 12.42 a poor widow . . put in two copper coins
Lk 21. 2 he saw a poor widow put in two copper coins

COPPERSMITH
1. *coppersmith, smith:* χαλκεύς CHALKEUS*
2 Tim 4.14 Alexander the c. did me great harm

COPY
1. *corresponding:* ἀντίτυπος (subst.) ANTITYPOS
Heb 9.24 a sanctuary made with hands, a copy
2. *example, pattern:* ὑπόδειγμα HYPODEIGMA
Heb 8. 5 They serve a copy . . of the . . sanctuary
9.23 necessary for the copies . . to be purified

CORBAN: 'kȯr,ban
1. *gift* (Heb.): κορβᾶν KORBAN*
Mk 7.11 " 'Corban' (that is, given to God[z]

CORD
1. *small rope, cord:* σχοινίον SCHOINION
Jn 2.15 making a whip of cords, he drove them

CORINTH: Κόρινθος 'kȯrənth II,D-3
Acts 18. 1 he left Athens and went to Corinth
19. 1 While Apollos was at Corinth
1 Cor 1. 2 To the church of God which is at C.
2 Cor 1. 1 To the church of God which is at C.
1.23 to spare you . . I refrained from coming to C.
2 Tim 4.20 Erastus remained at Corinth

CORINTHIAN: Κορίνθιος
Acts 18. 8 many . . Corinthians hearing Paul believed
2 Cor 6.11 Our mouth is open to you, Corinthians

CORNELIUS: Κορνήλιος kȯr'nēlyəs
Acts 10. 1 At Caesarea there was a man named C.
10. 3 God coming in and saying to him, "C.
10.17 men . . sent by C. . . stood before the gate
10.22 "C., a centurion, an upright . . man
10.24 C. . . had called together his kinsmen
10.25 When Peter entered, Cornelius met him
10.30 C. said, "Four days ago . . this hour
10.31 " 'Cornelius, your prayer has been heard

CORNER
1. *origin, rule:* ἀρχή ARCHĒ
Acts 10.11 a great sheet, let down by four corners
11. 5 "a great sheet, let down . . by four corners
2. *angle, corner:* γωνία GŌNIA*
Mt 6. 5 "hypocrites . . stand . . at . . street corners
21.42 " 'stone . . has become the head of the corner
Also Mk **12.**10; Lk **20.**17; Acts **4.**11; 1 Pet **2.**7
Acts 26.26 "this was not done in a corner
Rev 7. 1 four angels standing at the four corners
20. 8 nations . . at the four corners of the earth

CORNERSTONE
1. *at the extreme angle:* ἀκρογωνιαῖος (subst.) AKROGŌNIAIOS*
Eph 2.20 Christ Jesus himself being the cornerstone
1 Pet 2. 6 "a cornerstone chosen and precious

CORPSE
1. *dead:* νεκρός (subst.) NEKROS
Mk 9.26 it came out, and the boy was like a corpse

CORRECT
1. *discipline, educate:* παιδεύω PAIDEUŌ
2 Tim 2.25 correcting his opponents with gentleness

CORRECTION
1. *correcting:* ἐπανόρθωσις EPANORTHŌSIS*
2 Tim 3.16 scripture is . . profitable . . for correction

CORRECTOR
1. *teacher, instructor:* παιδευτής PAIDEUTĒS
Rom 2.20 corrector of the foolish, a teacher of children

CORRESPOND TO
1. *be:* εἰμί EIMI [A.6.a.4]
2 Cor 11.15 Their end will correspond to their deeds
2. *correspond to:* συστοιχέω SYSTOICHEŌ*
Gal 4.25 Hagar . . corresponds to . . Jerusalem

CORRESPONDS TO, WHICH
1. *corresponding:* ἀντίτυπος ANTITYPOS
1 Pet 3.21 Baptism, which corresponds to this

CORRUPT
1. *destroy, corrupt:* καταφθείρω (perf. pass. part.) KATAPHTHEIRŌ*
2 Tim 3. 8 men of corrupt mind and counterfeit faith
2. *stain, defile:* μιαίνω MIAINŌ
[a]subst. perf. part.
Tit 1.15 [a]but to the corrupt . . nothing is pure; their . . minds and consciences are corrupted
3. *entice, destroy:* φθείρω PHTHEIRŌ
2 Cor 7. 2 we have corrupted no one
Eph 4.22 your old nature which . . is corrupt
Rev 19. 2 "great harlot who corrupted the earth

CORRUPTION
1. *destruction, corruption:* διαφθορά DIAPHTHORA*
Acts 2.27 " 'nor let thy Holy One see corruption
2.31 "nor did his flesh see corruption
13.34 "raised him . ., no more to return to c.
13.35 " 'not let thy Holy One see corruption
13.36 "David . . fell asleep . . and saw corruption
13.37 "he whom God raised up saw no corruption
2. *destruction:* φθορά PHTHORA
Gal 6. 8 he . . will from the flesh reap corruption
2 Pet 1. 4 that . . you may escape from the corruption
2.19 they themselves are slaves of corruption

COS: Κῶς 'käs II,E-3
Acts 21. 1 we came by a straight course to Cos

COSAM: Κωσάμ 'kōsəm
Lk 3.28 Addi, the son of C., the son of Elmadam

COST
1. *expenditure:* δαπάνη DAPANĒ*
Lk 14.28 "not first sit down and count the cost?

COST, WITHOUT
1. *freely, as a gift:* δωρεάν DŌREAN
2 Cor 11. 7 I preached God's gospel without cost

COSTLY
1. *very expensive:* πολυτελής POLYTELĒS
1 Tim 2. 9 not with braided hair or . . costly attire
2. *very valuable:* πολύτιμος POLYTIMOS
Jn 12. 3 Mary took a pound of costly ointment
3. *held in honor, costly:* τίμιος (superl.) TIMIOS
Rev 18.12 all articles of costly wood, bronze

COSTLY, VERY
1. *very expensive:* πολυτελής POLYTELĒS
Mk 14. 3 flask of ointment of pure nard, very costly

COULD (*See* CAN)

COUNCIL (*See also* ELDERS, COUNCIL OF)
1. *counsel, plan:* συμβούλιον SYMBOULION
Acts 25.12 Festus . . conferred with his council
2. *meeting, council:* συνέδριον SYNEDRION*
Mt 5.22 "whoever insults[j] . . liable to the council
10.17 "they will deliver you up to councils

Mt 26.59 the chief priests and the whole council
Mk 13. 9 "they will deliver you up to councils
14.55 whole council sought testimony against Jesus
15. 1 the whole council held a consultation
Lk 22.66 they led him away to their council
Jn 11.47 the Pharisees gathered the council
Acts 4.15 commanded them to go . . out of the council
5.21 high priest . . called together the council
5.27 they set them before the council
5.34 a Pharisee in the council named Gamaliel
5.41 they left . . the council, rejoicing
6.12 brought him before the council
6.15 council saw that his face was like . . an angel
22.30 commanded . . all the council to meet
23. 1 Paul, looking intently at the council
23. 6 Paul . . cried out in the council, "Brethren
23.15 "You therefore, along with the council
23.20 "to bring Paul down to the council tomorrow
23.28 "I brought him down to their council
24.20 "found when I stood before the council

COUNCIL, MEMBER OF THE

1. *councillor:* βουλευτής BOULEUTĒS*
Mk 15.43 Joseph of A., a . . member of the council
Lk 23.50 Joseph . . a member of the council

COUNSEL

1. *will, purpose:* βουλή BOULĒ
Acts 13.36 "after he had served the counsel of God
20.27 "declaring to you the whole counsel of God
Eph 1.11 according to the counsel of his will
2. *advise, recommend:* συμβουλεύω SYMBOULEUŌ
Rev 3.18 " 'I counsel you to buy from me gold
3. *counsel, plan:* συμβούλιον SYMBOULION
Mt 12.14 Pharisees went out and took counsel
22.15 the Pharisees went and took counsel
27. 1 elders . . took counsel against Jesus
27. 7 took counsel, and bought . . the potter's field
28.12 when they had . . taken counsel, they gave
Mk 3. 6 Pharisees . . immediately held counsel

COUNSEL, GIVE

1. *advise, recommend:* συμβουλεύω SYMBOULEUŌ
Jn 18.14 Caiaphas who had given counsel to the Jews

COUNSEL, TAKE

1. *deliberate, plan* (mid.): βουλεύω BOULEUŌ
Lk 14.31 "what king . . will not . . first . . take counsel
Jn 11.53 from that day on they took counsel

COUNSEL TOGETHER, TAKE

1. *advise, recommend:* συμβουλεύω (mid.) SYMBOULEUŌ
Mt 26. 4 took counsel together . . to arrest Jesus

COUNSELOR

1. *intercessor, advocate:* παράκλητος PARAKLĒTOS
Jn 14.16 "another Counselor, to be with you for ever
14.26 "the Counselor, the Holy Spirit
15.26 "when the Counselor comes, . . the Spirit
16. 7 "if . . not . . the Counselor will not come
2. *adviser:* σύμβουλος SYMBOULOS*
Rom 11.34 "who has been his counselor?

COUNT (*See also* WORTHY, COUNT)

1. *be:* εἰμί EIMI [A.6.a.5]
1 Cor 7.19 neither circumcision counts for anything
Gal 6.15 neither circumcision counts for anything
2. *reckon, impute:* ἐλλογέω ELLOGEŌ
Rom 5.13 sin is not counted where there is no law
3. *think, lead:* ἡγέομαι HĒGEOMAI
Phil 2. 3 in humility c. others better than yourselves
2. 6 did not count equality with God
3. 7 whatever gain I had, I counted as loss
3. 8 I count everything as loss
3. 8 count them . . refuse . . that I may gain
Jas 1. 2 Count it all joy . . when you meet . . trials
2 Pet 2.13 They count it pleasure to revel in . . daytime
3. 9 Lord is not slow . . as some count slowness
3.15 count the forbearance . . as salvation
4. *reckon, count:* λογίζομαι LOGIZOMAI
Acts 19.27 "danger . . that . . Artemis may c. for nothing
2 Cor 5.19 reconciling[h] . . not counting their trespasses
10. 2 with such confidence as I count on showing
5. *count, reckon:* ψηφίζω PSĒPHIZŌ
Lk 14.28 "which . . does not first . . count the cost?
6. *reckon, count up:* συμψηφίζω SYMPSĒPHIZŌ*
Acts 19.19 they counted the value of them

COUNTED WORTHY, BE

1. *consider worthy:* καταξιόω (pass.) KATAXIOŌ
Acts 5.41 were counted worthy to suffer dishonor

COUNTENANCE

1. *face, person:* πρόσωπον PROSŌPON
Lk 9.29 appearance of his countenance was altered

COUNTENANCE FALLS, ONE'S

1. *have a gloomy look:* στυγνάζω STYGNAZŌ
Mk 10.22 At that saying his countenance fell

COUNTERFEIT

1. *counterfeit, worthless:* ἀδόκιμος ADOKIMOS
2 Tim 3. 8 of corrupt mind and counterfeit faith

COUNTLESS

1. *exceedingly:* ὑπερβαλλόντως HYPERBALLONTŌS* [A.4.a]
2 Cor 11.23 countless beatings, and often near death
2. *numberless:* μυρίος MYRIOS*
1 Cor 4.15 though you have countless guides in Christ

COUNTRY

1. *field:* ἀγρός AGROS
Mk 5.14 herdsmen fled, and told it . . in the country
6.36 "send them away, to go into the country
6.56 wherever he came, in villages . . or country
15.21 Simon of Cyrene . . coming . . from the c.
16.12 appeared . . to two . . walking into the c.[k]‡
Lk 8.34 herdsmen . . fled, and told it . . in the country
9.12 "into the villages and country round about
23.26 Simon of Cyrene . . coming . . from the c.
2. *country, place:* χώρα CHŌRA
Mt 2.12 they departed to their own country
8.28 to the country of the Gadarenes[t]
Mk 1. 5 there went out . . all the country of Judea
5. 1 to the country of the Gerasenes[n]
5.10 begged . . not to send them out of the country
Lk 8.26 arrived at the country of the Gerasenes[a]
15.13 "took his journey into a far country
15.14 "a great famine arose in that country
15.15 "joined . . one of the citizens of that country
19.12 "A nobleman went into a far country
21.21 "let not those . . in the country enter
Jn 11.54 Jesus . . went from there to the country
11.55 many went up from the c. to Jerusalem
Acts 10.39 "all that he did . . in the country of the Jews
12.20 their country depended on the king's
26.20 "throughout all the country of Judea
3. *desolate place:* ἔρημος τόπος ERĒMOS [A.1.f]
Mk 1.45 so that Jesus[g] . . was out in the country
4. *part, share:* μέρος (pl.) MEROS
Acts 19. 1 Paul passed through the upper country
5. *fatherland:* πατρίς PATRIS
Jn 4.44 a prophet has no honor in his own country
CONTEXTUALLY
Heb 11.16 But as it is, they desire a better c.

COUNTRY, GO INTO ANOTHER

1. *be away, go abroad:* ἀποδημέω APODĒMEŌ
Mt 21.33 "householder . . went into another country
Mk 12. 1 "A man . . went into another country
Lk 20. 9 "A man . . went into another country

COUNTRY, HILL

1. *hilly:* ὀρεινός OREINOS* [B.3.b.2]
Lk 1.39 Mary . . went with haste into the hill country
1.65 talked about through all the hill country

COUNTRY, ONE'S OWN

1. *fatherland:* πατρίς PATRIS
Mt 13.54 coming to his own country he taught them
13.57 "not without honor except in his own c.
Mk 6. 1 He went away . . to his own country
6. 4 "not without honor, except in his own country
Lk 4.23 " 'do here also in your own country
4.24 "no prophet is acceptable in his own country

COUNTRY, SURROUNDING
1. *around a place:* περίχωρος PERICHŌROS [B.3.b.2]
Lk 4.14 report . . went . . through all the s. country
7.17 report . . spread through . . all the s. country
8.37 people of the s. country of the Gerasenes[a]
Acts 14. 6 fled to Lystra and . . the s. country

COUNTRYMAN
1. *countryman:* συμφυλέτης SYMPHYLETĒS*
1 Th 2.14 suffered . . from your own countrymen

COURAGE
1. *outspokenness:* παρρησία PARRĒSIA
Phil 1.20 with full courage . . Christ will be honored
2. *courage:* θάρσος THARSOS*
Acts 28.15 Paul thanked God and took courage

COURAGE, BE OF GOOD
1. *have confidence:* θαρρέω THARREŌ
2 Cor 5. 6 So we are always of good courage
5. 8 We are of good courage

COURAGE, HAVE
1. *speak freely:* παρρησιάζομαι PARRĒSIAZOMAI
1 Th 2. 2 we had courage . . to declare . . the gospel

COURAGE, LOSE
1. *relax:* ἐκλύω (pass.) EKLYŌ
Heb 12. 5 "do not . . lose courage when . . punished

COURAGE, TAKE
1. *have confidence:* θαρρέω THARREŌ
Acts 23.11 the Lord . . said, "Take courage
2. *dare:* τολμάω TOLMAŌ
Mk 15.43 Joseph of A. . . took c. and went to Pilate

COURAGEOUS, BE
1. *act in a manly way:* ἀνδρίζομαι ANDRIZOMAI*
1 Cor 16.13 stand firm in your faith, be courageous

COURSE
1. *age:* αἰών AIŌN
Eph 2. 2 following the course of this world
2. *course, race:* δρόμος DROMOS
Acts 13.25 "as John was finishing his course
20.24 "if only I may accomplish my course

COURSE, BY A STRAIGHT
1. *run a straight course:* εὐθυδρομέω (part.) EUTHYDROMEŌ
Acts 21. 1 we came by a straight course to Cos

COURSE, FINISH ONE'S
1. *make perfect, complete:* τελειόω (pass.) TELEIOŌ
Lk 13.32 " 'the third day I finish my course

COURT (*See also* KING'S COURT)
1. *pertaining to the market:* ἀγοραῖος (subst.) AGORAIOS
Acts 19.38 "courts are open, and there are proconsuls
2. *courtyard, court:* αὐλή AULĒ
Jn 18.15 he entered the court of the high priest
Rev 11. 2 "do not measure the court outside
3. *day, tribunal:* ἡμέρα HĒMERA
1 Cor 4. 3 judged by you or by any human court
4. *lawsuit, lawcourt:* κριτήριον (pl.) KRITĒRION
Jas 2. 6 is it not they who drag you into court?
CONTEXTUALLY
Mt 5.25 "while you are going with him to court

COURT, MEMBER OF THE
1. *brought up together with:* σύντροφος (subst.) SYNTROPHOS*
Acts 13. 1 Manaen a member of the court of Herod

COURTESY
1. *gentleness:* πραΰτης PRAYTĒS
Tit 3. 2 to show perfect courtesy toward all men

COURTIER
1. *great man:* μεγιστάν MEGISTAN
Mk 6.21 Herod . . gave a banquet for his courtiers

COURTYARD
1. *court, courtyard:* αὐλή AULĒ
Mt 26.58 Peter followed . . as far as the courtyard
26.69 Peter was sitting outside in the courtyard
Mk 14.54 Peter . . followed . . right into the courtyard
14.66 Peter was below in the courtyard
Lk 22.55 kindled a fire in the . . courtyard

COUSIN
1. *cousin:* ἀνεψιός ANEPSIOS*
Col 4.10 Mark the cousin of Barnabas

COVENANT
1. *covenant:* διαθήκη DIATHĒKĒ
Mt 26.28 "this is my blood of the[g] covenant
Mk 14.24 "This is my blood of the[c] covenant
Lk 1.72 "to remember his holy covenant
22.20 "cup . . is the new covenant in my blood[j]‡
Acts 3.25 "sons of the prophets and of the covenant
7. 8 "he gave him the covenant of circumcision
Rom 9. 4 to them belong the . . covenants
11.27 "this will be my covenant with them
1 Cor 11.25 "This cup is the new covenant
2 Cor 3. 6 to be ministers of a new covenant
3.14 when they read the old covenant
Gal [3.15 no one annuls even a man's *covenant*†
3.17 does not annul a covenant previously ratified
4.24 allegory: these women are two covenants
Eph 2.12 strangers to the covenants of promise
Heb 7.22 makes Jesus the surety of a better covenant
8. 6 the covenant he mediates is better
8. 8 "I will establish a new covenant with . . Israel
8. 9 "not like the covenant . . with their fathers . . for they did not continue in my covenant
8.10 "This is the covenant that I will make
9. 4 ⟨Holy of Holies⟩ having . . the ark of the covenant . . and the tables of the covenant
9.15 he is the mediator of a new covenant
9.15 transgressions under the first covenant[u]†
9.20 "This is the blood of the covenant
10.16 "This is the covenant that I will make
10.29 profaned the blood of the covenant
12.24 Jesus, the mediator of a new covenant
13.20 by the blood of the eternal covenant
Rev 11.19 the ark of his covenant was seen within
CONTEXTUALLY
Heb 8. 7 For if that first c. had been faultless
8.13 In speaking of a new covenant
9. 1 even the first c. had regulations
9.18 first c. was not ratified without blood

COVER
1. *cover over:* ἐπικαλύπτω EPIKALYPTŌ*
Rom 4. 7 "Blessed are those . . whose sins are covered
2. *cover, hide:* καλύπτω KALYPTŌ
Mt 10.26 "nothing is covered that will not be revealed
Lk 8.16 "No one after lighting a lamp covers it
23.30 "to say to . . the hills, 'Cover us
Jas 5.20 save his soul . . cover a multitude of sins
1 Pet 4. 8 since love covers a multitude of sins
3. *cover up:* κατακαλύπτω (mid.) KATAKALYPTŌ
1 Cor 11. 7 a man ought not to cover his head
4. *cover all around:* περικαλύπτω PERIKALYPTŌ
Mk 14.65 began to spit on him, and to cover his face
Heb 9. 4 ark of the covenant covered . . with gold
IDIOMATICALLY
a. 1 Cor 11. 4 Any man who prays . . with his head covered πᾶς ἀνὴρ προσευχόμενος . . κατὰ κεφαλῆς ἔχων [KATA]

COVER UP
1. *bury, hide:* κρύπτω KRYPTŌ
Mt 13.44 "which a man found and covered up
2. *cover completely:* συγκαλύπτω SYGKALYPTŌ*
Lk 12. 2 "covered up that will not be revealed

COVERING
1. *what is thrown around, covering:* περιβόλαιον PERIBOLAION
1 Cor 11.15 her hair is given to her for a covering

COVET
1. *desire, long for:* ἐπιθυμέω EPITHYMEŌ
Acts 20.33 "I coveted no one's silver or gold
Rom 7. 7 the law . . said, "You shall not covet
13. 9 "You shall not steal, You shall not covet
2. *strive after, be jealous:* ζηλόω ZĒLOŌ
Jas 4. 2 you covet[d] and cannot obtain

COVET, WHAT IT IS TO
1. *desire, yearning:* ἐπιθυμία EPITHYMIA
Rom 7. 7 I should not have known what it is to covet

COVETING
1. *greediness:* πλεονεξία PLEONEXIA
Mk 7.22 coveting, wickedness, deceit

COVETOUS, ONE WHO IS
1. *one who is greedy:* πλεονέκτης PLEONEKTĒS
Eph 5. 5 no . . one who is c. . . has any inheritance

COVETOUSNESS
1. *desire, yearning:* ἐπιθυμία EPITHYMIA
Rom 7. 8 sin . . wrought in me . . covetousness
2. *greediness:* πλεονεξία PLEONEXIA
Lk 12.15 "Take heed, and beware of all covetousness
Rom 1.29 wickedness, evil, covetousness, malice
Eph 5. 3 fornication and all impurity or covetousness
Col 3. 5 covetousness, which is idolatry

COWARDLY
1. *vile, cowardly:* δειλός DEILOS
Rev 21. 8 the cowardly, the faithless, the polluted

CRAFT
1. *art, skill:* τέχνη TECHNĒ
Rev 18.22 "a craftsman of any craft . . no more

CRAFTILY WITH, DEAL
1. *outwit by sophisms:* κατασοφίζομαι KATASOPHIZOMAI*
Acts 7.19 "He dealt craftily with our race

CRAFTINESS
1. *cunning, trickery:* πανουργία PANOURGIA
Lk 20.23 But he perceived their craftiness
1 Cor 3.19 "He catches the wise in their craftiness
Eph 4.14 their craftiness in deceitful wiles

CRAFTSMAN
1. *craftsman, artisan:* τεχνίτης TECHNITĒS
Acts 19.24 brought no little business to the craftsmen
19.38 "If . . the craftsmen . . have a complaint
Rev 18.22 "a craftsman of any craft . . no more

CRAFTY
1. *ready to do anything:* πανοῦργος PANOURGOS*
2 Cor 12.16 I was crafty, you say, and got the better

CRAVE
1. *reach, stretch:* ὀρέγω (mid.) OREGŌ
1 Tim 6.10 through this craving . . some have wandered

CRAVING, HAVE A MORBID
1. *be sick, suffer:* νοσέω NOSEŌ*
1 Tim 6. 4 he has a morbid craving for controversy

CREATE
1. *put in order, make:* καταρτίζω KATARTIZŌ
Heb 11. 3 world was created by the word of God
2. *make, establish:* κτίζω KTIZŌ
Mk 13.19 "from . . the creation which God created
1 Cor 11. 9 (Neither was man created for woman
Eph 2.10 we are his workmanship, created in Christ
2.15 he might create in himself one new man
3. 9 hidden . . in[d] God who created all things
4.24 the new . . created after the likeness of God
Col 1.16 for in him all things were created . . —all things were created through him
1 Tim 4. 3 foods which God created to be received
Rev 4.11 "Worthy art thou . . for thou didst create all . . and by thy will they . . were created
10. 6 who created heaven and what is in it
3. *do, make:* ποιέω POIEŌ
Rom 16.17 take note of those who create dissensions
Heb 1. 2 Son . . through whom . . he created the world

CREATED
1. *creation, creature:* κτίσμα KTISMA [A.1.b.5]
1 Tim 4. 4 everything created by God is good

CREATION
1. *founding, creation:* κτίσις KTISIS
Mk 10. 6 "from . . creation . . 'male and female
13.19 "from the beginning of the creation
16.15 "preach the gospel to the whole creation[k]‡
Rom 1.20 Ever since the creation of the world
8.19 For the creation waits with eager longing
8.20 for the creation was subjected to futility
8.21 creation itself will be set free from . . bondage
8.22 the whole creation has been groaning
8.39 nor depth, nor anything else in all creation
2 Cor 5.17 if any one is in Christ, he is a new creation[o]†
Gal 6.15 nor uncircumcision, but a new creation
Col 1.15 image of . . God, the first-born of all creation
Heb 9.11 more perfect tent[p] . . (not of this creation
2 Pet 3. 4 "as they were from the beginning of creation
Rev 3.14 " 'the Amen . . the beginning of God's c.
CONTEXTUALLY
Rom 8.23 not only the c., but we ourselves . . groan

CREATOR
1. *founder, creator:* κτίστης KTISTĒS*
1 Pet 4.19 entrust their souls to a faithful Creator
2. *make, establish:* κτίζω (subst. part.) KTIZŌ
Rom 1.25 served the creature rather than the Creator
Col 3.10 renewed . . after the image of its creator

CREATURE (*See also* INSTINCT, CREATURE OF; UNFAITHFUL CREATURE)
1. *creation, creature:* κτίσμα KTISMA
Jas 1.18 we . . a kind of first fruits of his creatures
Rev 5.13 I heard every creature in heaven
2. *founding, creation:* κτίσις KTISIS
Rom 1.25 worshiped and served the creature
2 Cor [5.17 if any one is in Christ, he is a new *creature*†
Col 1.23 gospel . . preached to every creature
Heb 4.13 before him no creature is hidden
3. *wild animal:* θηρίον THĒRION
Acts 28. 4 When the natives saw the creature hanging
28. 5 He . . shook off the creature into the fire

CREATURE, LIVING
1. *creation, creature:* κτίσμα KTISMA
Rev 8. 9 third of the living creatures in the sea died
2. *living being:* ζῷον ZŌON
Rev 4. 6 round the throne . . four living creatures
4. 7 the first living creature like a lion
4. 7 the second living creature like a ox
4. 7 third l. creature with the face of a man
4. 7 the fourth l. creature like a flying eagle
4. 8 four living creatures . . never cease to sing
4. 9 whenever the living creatures give glory
5. 6 between the throne and the four l. creatures
5. 8 the four living creatures . . fell down
5.11 around the throne and the living creatures
5.14 the four living creatures said, "Amen!
6. 1 I heard one of the four living creatures
6. 3 I heard the second living creature
6. 5 I heard the third living creature
6. 6 in the midst of the four living creatures
6. 7 I heard the voice of the fourth living creature
7.11 the elders and the four living creatures
14. 3 they sing . . before the four living creatures
15. 7 one of the . . living creatures gave . . bowls
19. 4 the four living creatures . . worshiped God

CREATURE, SEA
1. *of the sea:* ἐνάλιος (subst.) ENALIOS*
Jas 3. 7 every kind of . . sea creature, can be tamed

CREDIT
1. *grace, favor, gratitude:* χάρις CHARIS
Lk 6.32 "If you love those . . what credit is that?
6.33 "if you do . . to those . . what credit is that?
6.34 "if you lend to those . . what credit is that?
2. *rumor, report, fame:* κλέος KLEOS*
1 Pet 2.20 For what credit is it, if when you do wrong?
3. *word, reckoning:* λόγος LOGOS
Phil 4.17 the fruit which increases to your credit

CREDITOR
1. *money lender:* δανειστής DANEISTĒS*
Lk 7.41 "A certain creditor had two debtors

CRESCENS: Κρήσκης 'kresəns
2 Tim 4.10 Crescens has gone to Galatia[e]

CRETAN: Κρής
Acts 2.11 "Cretans.., we hear..in our own tongues
Tit 1.12 "Cretans are always liars, evil beasts

CRETE: Κρήτη ˈkrēt II,D-4
Acts 27. 7 we sailed under the lee of Crete
27.12 they could reach Phoenix, a harbor of C.
27.13 they weighed anchor and sailed along C.
27.21 "Men, you..should not have set sail from C.
Tit 1. 5 This is why I left you in Crete

CRIME
1. *charge, cause:* αἰτία AITIA
Jn 18.38 he..told them, "I find no crime in him
19. 4 "know that I find no crime in him
19. 6 "Take him.., I find no crime in him
2. *responsible:* αἴτιος (subst. neut.) AITIOS
Lk 23. 4 Pilate said.."I find no crime in this man
23.22 "I have found..no crime deserving death
3. *misdeed, villainy:* ῥᾳδιούργημα RHADIOURGĒMA*
Acts 18.14 Gallio said.., "If it were a..vicious crime

CRIMINAL
1. *doing ill, mischievous:* κακοῦργος (subst.) KAKOURGOS*
Lk 23.32 Two.., who were criminals, were led away
23.33 they crucified him, and the criminals
23.39 One of the criminals..railed at him
2 Tim 2. 9 I am..wearing fetters like a criminal

CRIPPLE
1. *a weak man:* ἄνθρωπος ἀσθενής ASTHENĒS [A.1.f]
Acts 4. 9 "concerning a good deed done to a cripple
2. *lame:* χωλός (subst.) CHŌLOS
Acts 14. 8 a cripple from birth, who had never walked

CRISPUS: Κρίσπος ˈkrispəs
Acts 18. 8 C., the ruler of the synagogue, believed
1 Cor 1.14 I baptized none of you except Crispus

CRITICIZE
1. *differentiate, decide:* διακρίνω (mid.) DIAKRINŌ
Acts 11. 2 the circumcision party criticized him

CROOKED
1. *crooked, unjust:* σκολιός SKOLIOS
Lk 3. 5 "the crooked shall be made straight
Acts 2.40 "Save yourselves from this c. generation
Phil 2.15 be blameless..in..a crooked..generation

CROOKED, MAKE
1. *twist about:* διαστρέφω DIASTREPHŌ
Acts 13.10 "stop making crooked the straight paths

CROPS
1. *fruit:* καρπός (pl.) KARPOS
Lk 12.17 " 'for I have nowhere to store my crops
2 Tim 2. 6 ought to have the first share of the crops

CROSS
1. *stride, go through:* διαβαίνω DIABAINŌ
Heb 11.29 By faith the people crossed the Red Sea
2. *go over, pass through:* διαπεράω DIAPERAŌ
Lk 16.26 " 'none may cross from there to us
Acts 21. 2 having found a ship crossing to Phoenicia
3. *pass through:* διέρχομαι DIERCHOMAI
Acts 18.27 when he wished to cross to Achaia
4. *upright pale, stake:* σταυρός STAUROS*
Mt 10.38 "who does not take his cross and follow me
16.24 "let him deny himself and take up his cross
Also Mk **8**.34; Lk **9**.23
27.32 this man they compelled to carry his cross
27.40 "If you are.., come down from the cross
27.42 "let him come down now from the cross
Mk 15.21 compelled..Simon..to carry his cross
15.30 "come down from the cross!
15.32 "come down now from the cross
Lk 14.27 "Whoever does not bear his own cross
23.26 laid on him the c., to carry it behind Jesus
Jn 19.17 they took Jesus..bearing his own cross
19.19 wrote a title and put it on the cross
19.25 standing by the cross..were his mother
19.31 in order to prevent..remaining on the cross
1 Cor 1.17 lest the cross of Christ be emptied
1.18 the word of the cross is folly to those
Gal 5.11 the stumbling block of the cross
6.12 that they..not be persecuted for the cross
6.14 to glory except in the cross of our Lord
Eph 2.16 might reconcile us both..through the cross
Phil 2. 8 obedient..even death on a cross
3.18 many..live as enemies of the cross of Christ
Col 1.20 making peace by the blood of his cross
2.14 this he set aside, nailing it to the cross
Heb 12. 2 who for the joy..endured the cross

CROSS AGAIN

CROSS OVER
1. *go over, pass through:* διαπεράω DIAPERAŌ
Mt 9. 1 getting into a boat he crossed over
14.34 when they had crossed over, they came
Mk 5.21 when Jesus had crossed again in the boat
6.53 when they had crossed over, they came

CROW
1. *call, make a sound:* φωνέω PHŌNEŌ
Mt 26.34 "before the cock crows, you will deny me
26.74 And immediately the cock crowed
26.75 "Before the cock crows, you will deny me
Mk 14.30 "before the cock crows twice, you will deny
[14.68 *and the cock crowed*‡
14.72 immediately the cock crowed a second time
14.72 "Before the cock crows twice, you will deny
Lk 22.34 "cock will not crow..until..three times
22.60 while he was..speaking, the cock crowed
22.61 "Before the cock crows..you will deny
Jn 13.38 "cock will not crow, till you have denied
18.27 at once the cock crowed

CROWD
1. *people, popular assembly:* δῆμος DĒMOS
Acts 19.30 Paul wished to go in among the crowd
2. *crowd, populace:* ὄχλος OCHLOS
Mt 4.25 great crowds followed him from Galilee
5. 1 Seeing the crowds, he went up
7.28 crowds were astonished at his teaching
8. 1 When he came..great crowds followed him
8.18 when Jesus saw great crowds around him
9. 8 When the crowds saw it, they were afraid
9.23 Jesus..saw..the crowd making a tumult
9.25 the crowd..outside, he went in
9.33 dumb man spoke;..the crowds marveled
9.36 he saw the crowds, he had compassion
11. 7 Jesus began to speak to the crowds
13. 2 great crowds gathered about him
13. 2 and the whole crowd stood on the beach
13.34 this Jesus said to the crowds in parables
13.36 left the crowds and went into the house
14.13 when the crowds heard it, they followed
14.15 "send the crowds away to go into the villages
14.19 Then he ordered the crowds to sit down
14.19 the disciples gave them to the crowds
14.22 while he dismissed the crowds
14.23 after he had dismissed the crowds
15.30 great crowds came..bringing..the lame
15.32 "I have compassion on the crowd
15.33 "bread enough..to feed so great a crowd
15.35 commanding the crowd to sit down
15.36 the disciples gave them to the crowds
15.39 sending away the crowds, he got into the boat
17.14 they came to the crowd, a man came up
19. 2 large crowds followed him, and he healed
20.29 out of Jericho, a great crowd followed him
20.31 The crowd rebuked.., telling them
21. 8 Most of the crowd spread their garments
21. 9 crowds that went before him..shouted
21.11 crowds said, "This is the prophet Jesus
22.33 when the c. heard it, they were astonished
23. 1 Then said Jesus to the crowds
26.47 Judas came..and with him a great crowd
26.55 At that hour Jesus said to the crowds
27.15 to release for the crowd any one prisoner
27.24 washed his hands before the crowd
Mk 2. 4 could not get near..because of the crowd
2.13 all the crowd gathered about him

Mk 3. 9 a boat ready for him because of the crowd
3.20 the crowd came together again
3.32 a crowd was sitting about him
4. 1 a very large crowd gathered about him
4. 1 the whole crowd was beside the sea
4.36 leaving the crowd, they took him
5.21 a great crowd gathered about him
5.24 a great crowd followed him
5.27 She . . came up behind him in the crowd
5.30 Jesus . . turned about in the crowd
5.31 "You see the crowd pressing around you
6.45 to Bethsaida, while he dismissed the crowd
8. 1 when again a great crowd had gathered
8. 2 "I have compassion on the crowd
8. 6 he commanded the crowd to sit down
8. 6 they set them before the crowd
9.14 they saw a great crowd about them
9.15 all the crowd . . were greatly amazed
9.17 one of the crowd answered him, "Teacher
9.25 Jesus saw that a crowd came running
10. 1 crowds gathered to him again
14.43 Judas came . . and with him a crowd
15. 8 crowd came up and began to ask
15.11 chief priests stirred up the crowd
15.15 So Pilate, wishing to satisfy the crowd
Lk 5.19 finding no way . . because of the crowd
6.17 stood on a level place, with a great crowd
6.19 all the crowd sought to touch him
7.11 disciples and a great crowd went with him
7.12 a large crowd from the city was with her
7.24 to speak to the crowds concerning John
8. 4 when a great crowd came together
8.19 they could not reach him for the crowd
8.40 Jesus returned, the crowd welcomed him
9.11 the crowds learned it, they followed him
9.12 the twelve . . said . . "Send the crowd away
9.16 gave them . . to set before the crowd
9.37 next day . . a great crowd met him
9.38 a man from the crowd cried, "Teacher
11.27 a woman in the crowd raised her voice
11.29 crowds were increasing, he began to say
19. 3 could not ⟨see⟩ on account of the crowd
22.47 there came a crowd, and . . Judas
Jn 5.13 Jesus had withdrawn, as there was a crowd
7.32 Pharisees heard the crowd thus muttering
7.49 "this crowd, who do not know the law
12. 9 great crowd . . learned that he was there
12.12 a great crowd who had come to the feast
12.17 crowd . . with him when he called Lazarus
12.18 the crowd went to meet him
12.29 The crowd . . said that it had thundered
12.34 crowd answered him, "We have heard
Acts 14.11 when the crowds saw what Paul had done
16.22 The crowd joined in attacking them
17.13 stirring up and inciting the crowds
19.33 Some of the crowd prompted Alexander
19.35 when the town clerk had quieted the crowd
21.27 Jews . . stirred up all the crowd
21.34 Some in the crowd shouted one thing
21.35 because of the violence of the crowd
24.12 "they did not find me . . stirring up a crowd
24.18 "they found me purified . . without any crowd

CROWD, GATHER A

1. *form a mob:* ὀχλοποιέω OCHLOPOIEŌ*
Acts 17. 5 the Jews . . gathered a crowd

CROWN

1. *confer honor:* στεφανόω STEPHANOŌ*
2 Tim 2. 5 athlete is not crowned unless he competes
Heb 2. 7 "thou hast crowned him with glory
2. 9 Jesus . . crowned with glory and honor
2. *crown, prize:* στέφανος STEPHANOS
Mt 27.29 a crown of thorns they put . . on his head
Mk 15.17 a crown of thorns they put . . on him
Jn 19. 2 soldiers plaited a crown of thorns
19. 5 Jesus came . . wearing the crown of thorns
Phil 4. 1 my brethren . . my joy and crown
1 Th 2.19 our hope or joy or crown of boasting
2 Tim 4. 8 Henceforth there is laid up for me the crown
Jas 1.12 he will receive the crown of life
1 Pet 5. 4 you will obtain the unfading crown of glory
Rev 2.10 " 'I will give you the crown of life
3.11 " 'hold fast . . that no one may seize your c.
4. 4 elders, clad in white . . with golden crowns
4.10 they cast their crowns before the throne
6. 2 a crown was given to him, and he went out
9. 7 what looked like crowns of gold
12. 1 on her head a crown of twelve stars
14.14 like a son of man, with a golden crown

CRUCIFY

1. *crucify again:* ἀνασταυρόω ANASTAUROŌ*
Heb 6. 6 crucify the Son of God on their own account
2. *fix to, crucify:* προσπήγνυμι PROSPĒGNYMI*
Acts 2.23 "you crucified and killed by . . lawless men
3. *crucify:* σταυρόω STAUROŌ*
Mt 20.19 "to be mocked and scourged and crucified
23.34 "some of whom you will kill and crucify
26. 2 "Son of man will be delivered . . to be crucified
27.22 They all said, "Let him be crucified
27.23 they shouted . . "Let him be crucified
27.26 scourged Jesus, delivered him to be crucified
27.31 led him away to crucify him
27.35 when they had crucified him
27.38 two robbers were crucified with him
28. 5 "I know . . you seek Jesus who was crucified
Mk 15.13 they cried out again, "Crucify him
15.14 they shouted all the more, "Crucify him
15.15 he delivered him to be crucified
15.20 they led him out to crucify him
15.24 they crucified him, and divided his garments
15.25 the third hour . . they crucified him
15.27 with him they crucified two robbers
16. 6 "you seek Jesus . . , who was crucified
Lk 23.21 they shouted out, "Crucify, crucify him!
23.23 loud cries that he should be crucified
23.33 there they crucified him, and the criminals
24. 7 "be crucified, and on the third day rise
24.20 "condemned to death, and crucified
Jn 19. 6 they cried out, "Crucify him, crucify him! Pilate said to them, "Take him yourselves and crucify him
19.10 "I have power . . to crucify you
19.15 "Away with him . . crucify him!" Pilate said to them, "Shall I crucify your King?
19.16 handed him over to them to be crucified
19.18 There they crucified him
19.20 Jesus was crucified . . near the city
19.23 When the soldiers had crucified Jesus
19.41 where he was crucified there was a garden
Acts 2.36 "this Jesus whom you crucified
4.10 "Jesus Christ of Nazareth, whom you crucified
1 Cor 1.13 Was Paul crucified for you?
1.23 preach Christ crucified, a stumbling block
2. 2 except Jesus Christ and him crucified
2. 8 they would not have crucified the Lord
2 Cor 13. 4 he was crucified in weakness, but lives
Gal 3. 1 Christ was publicly portrayed as crucified
5.24 those who belong . . have crucified the flesh
6.14 the world has been crucified to me
Rev 11. 8 Egypt, where their Lord was crucified

CRUCIFY WITH

1. *crucify together with:* συσταυρόω SYSTAUROŌ*
Mt 27.44 robbers who were crucified with him
Mk 15.32 Those who were crucified with him
Jn 19.32 the other who had been crucified with him
Rom 6. 6 our old self was crucified with him
Gal 2.20 I have been crucified with Christ

CRUMB

1. *a very little bit:* ψιχίον PSICHION*
Mt 15.27 "yet even the dogs eat the crumbs
Mk 7.28 "even the dogs . . eat the children's crumbs

CRUSH

1. *weigh down:* βαρέω BAREŌ

2 Cor 1. 8 we were so utterly, unbearably crushed
2. *crush, destroy:* λικμάω LIKMAŌ*
Mt [21.44 "*when it falls on .. one, it will crush him*‡
Lk 20.18 "when it falls on any one it will crush him
3. *crowd, cramp:* στενοχωρέω STENOCHŌREŌ
2 Cor 4. 8 afflicted in every way, but not crushed
4. *shatter, grind:* συντρίβω SYNTRIBŌ
Rom 16.20 the God of peace will soon crush Satan
5. *squeeze, oppress:* θλίβω THLIBŌ
Mk 3. 9 a boat ready .. lest they should crush him

CRY (*See also* COMMAND, CRY OF)
1. *cry out:* ἀναβοάω ANABOAŌ*
Mt 27.46 Jesus cried with a loud voice, "Eli, Eli
Var. BOAŌ
2. *cry aloud, shout:* βοάω BOAŌ
Mt 3. 3 "The voice of one crying in the wilderness
Also Mk **1**.3; Lk **3**.4
Mk 15.34 Jesus cried with a loud voice, "Eloi, Eloi
Lk 9.38 a man from the crowd cried, "Teacher
18. 7 "vindicate his elect, who cry to him
18.38 he cried, "Jesus .. have mercy on me!
Jn 1.23 "voice of one crying in the wilderness
Acts 8. 7 spirits came out .. crying with a loud voice
17. 6 before the city authorities, crying
Also variant to: Mt **27**.46
3. *loud cry:* βοή BOĒ*
Jas 5. 4 cries of the harvesters have reached
4. *say, speak:* ἐρῶ ERŌ
Rev 19. 3 Once more they cried, "Hallelujah!
5. *cry aloud:* κραυγάζω KRAUGAZŌ
Lk 4.41 demons also came out of many, crying
Var. KRAZŌ
Jn 11.43 he cried with a loud voice, "Lazarus
12.13 went out to meet him, crying, "Hosanna!
6. *shouting:* κραυγή KRAUGĒ
Mt 25. 6 "there was a cry, 'Behold, the bridegroom!
Lk 1.42 she exclaimed with a loud cry, "Blessed
Heb 5. 7 Jesus[j] offered up prayers .. with loud cries
7. *cry out, shout:* κράζω KRAZŌ
Mt 15.22 a Canaanite woman .. cried, "Have mercy
15.23 "Send her away, for she is crying after us
27.50 Jesus cried again with a loud voice
Jn 1.15 (John bore witness .. and cried, "This was he
Acts 7.60 he knelt down and cried with a loud voice
14.14 rushed out among the multitude, crying
16.17 She followed Paul and us, crying, "These
19.32 Now some cried one thing, some another
21.36 mob .. followed, crying, "Away with him!
Rom 8.15 When we cry, "Abba! Father!
Gal 4. 6 God has sent the Spirit .. crying, "Abba!
Also variant to: Lk **4**.41
8. *say, speak:* λέγω LEGŌ
Rev 8.13 I heard an eagle crying with a loud voice
16. 7 I heard the altar cry, "Yea, Lord God
19. 1 a great multitude .. crying, "Hallelujah!
19. 5 a voice crying, "Praise our God
19. 6 I heard .. the voice .. crying, "Hallelujah!
9. *voice, sound:* φωνή PHŌNĒ
Mk 15.37 And Jesus uttered a loud cry
Lk 23.23 loud cries that he should be crucified
10. *call, make a sound:* φωνέω PHŌNEŌ
Mk 1.26 unclean spirit, convulsing him and crying
Lk 23.46 Jesus, crying .. said, "Father, into thy hands
Acts 16.28 Paul cried .. "Do not harm yourself

CRY ALOUD
1. *cry aloud:* κραυγάζω KRAUGAZŌ
Mt 12.19 "He will not wrangle or cry aloud
2. *cry out, shout:* κράζω KRAZŌ
Mt 9.27 two blind men followed him, crying aloud

CRY OUT
1. *cry out:* ἀνακράζω ANAKRAZŌ*
Mk 1.24(23) he cried out, "What .. to do with us?
6.49 they thought it was a ghost, and cried out
Lk 4.33 who had .. an unclean demon .. cried out
8.28 When he saw Jesus, he cried out
23.18 all cried out together, "Away with this man
2. *cry aloud:* κραυγάζω KRAUGAZŌ
Jn 18.40 They cried out again, "Not this man!
19. 6 they cried out, "Crucify him, crucify him!
19.12 Jews cried out .. "you are not Caesar's friend
19.15 cried out, "Away with him .. crucify him!
Acts 22.23 they cried out and waved their garments
3. *cry out, shout:* κράζω KRAZŌ
Mt 8.29 they cried out, "What have you to do with us?
14.26 "It is a ghost!" And they cried out for fear
14.30 he cried out, "Lord, save me
20.30 two blind men .. cried out,[o] "Have mercy!
20.31 they cried out the more, "Lord, have mercy!
21.15 children crying out .. "Hosanna to the Son!
Mk 3.11 unclean spirits .. cried out, "You are the Son
5. 5 among the tombs .. he was .. crying out
5. 7 crying out .. "What have you to do with me?
9.24 cried out[i] .. "I believe; help my unbelief!
9.26 crying out and convulsing him terribly
10.47 he began to cry out .. "Jesus, Son of David!
10.48 he cried out all the more, "Son of David!
11. 9 those who followed cried out, "Hosanna!
15.13 they cried out again, "Crucify him
[15.39 he thus *cried out and* breathed his last‡
Lk 9.39 "spirit seizes him, and he suddenly cries out
18.39 he cried out all the more, "Son of David!
19.40 "the very stones would cry out
Jn 12.44 Jesus cried out .. "He who believes in me
Acts 7.57 they cried out with a loud voice
19.28 cried out, "Great is Artemis of the Ephesians!
19.34 cried out, "Great is Artemis of the Ephesians!
21.28 crying out, "Men of Israel, help!
23. 6 he cried out in the council, "Brethren
24.21 "I cried out while standing among them
Rom 9.27 Isaiah cries out concerning Israel
Jas 5. 4 cries of the harvesters have reached
Rev 6.10 they cried out .. "O Sovereign Lord
7.10 crying out .. "Salvation belongs to our God!
12. 2 she cried out in her pangs of birth
18.18 cried out as they saw the smoke
18.19 crying out, "Alas, alas, for the great city!

CRYING
1. *shouting:* κραυγή KRAUGĒ
Rev 21. 4 "neither .. mourning nor crying nor pain

CRYSTAL
1. *rock crystal:* κρύσταλλος KRYSTALLOS*
Rev 4. 6 there is as it were a sea of glass, like crystal
22. 1 river of the water of life, bright as crystal

CRYSTAL, CLEAR AS
1. *be clear as crystal:* κρυσταλλίζω (part.) KRYSTALLIZŌ*
Rev 21.11 jewel, like a jasper, clear as crystal

CUBIT
1. *forearm, cubit:* πῆχυς PĒCHYS
Mt 6.27 "which .. can add one cubit to his .. life?[p]
Lk 12.25 "which of you .. can add a cubit to his .. life?[n]
Rev 21.17 its wall, a hundred and forty-four cubits

CULTIVATE
1. *till, plow:* γεωργέω GEŌRGEŌ*
Heb 6. 7 those for whose sake it is cultivated

CULTIVATED OLIVE TREE
1. *garden olive tree:* καλλιέλαιος KALLIELAIOS*
Rom 11.24 grafted .. into a cultivated olive tree

CUMI: 'kü,mī
1. *stand up* (Aram.): κοῦμ KOUM*
Mk 5.41 he said to her, "Talitha cumi

CUMMIN
1. *cummin:* κύμινον KYMINON*
Mt 23.23 "you tithe the mint and dill and cummin

CUNNING
1. *dice-playing, trickery:* κυβεία KYBEIA*
Eph 4.14 by the cunning of men, by their craftiness
2. *cunning, trickery:* πανουργία PANOURGIA
2 Cor 4. 2 we refuse to practice cunning or to tamper
11. 3 serpent deceived Eve by his cunning

CUP
1. *drinking vessel:* ποτήριον POTĒRION*
Mt 10.42 "whoever gives . . even a cup of cold water
20.22 "Are you able to drink the cup that I am?
20.23 "You will drink my cup
23.25 "for you cleanse the outside of the cup
23.26 "first cleanse the inside of the cup
26.27 he took a cup, and when he had given thanks
26.39 "let this cup pass from me
Mk 7. 4 (the washing of cups and pots and vessels
9.41 "whoever gives you a cup of water
10.38 "Are you able to drink the cup that I drink?
10.39 "The cup that I drink you will drink
14.23 he took a cup, and when he had given thanks
14.36 "remove this cup from me
Lk 11.39 "Pharisees cleanse the outside of the cup
22.17 took a cup, and when he had given thanks
22.20 likewise the cup . . saying, "This cup . . is the new covenant in my blood[j]‡
22.42 "remove this cup from me
Jn 18.11 "shall I not drink the cup . . given me?
1 Cor 10.16 The cup of blessing which we bless
10.21 You cannot drink the cup of the Lord and the cup of demons
11.25 also the cup, after supper, saying, "This cup is the new covenant in my blood
11.26 as often as you . . drink the cup, you proclaim
11.27 Whoever . . drinks the cup of the Lord
11.28 so eat of the bread and drink of the cup
Rev 14.10 "poured unmixed into the cup of his anger
16.19 make her drain the cup of the fury
17. 4 holding . . a golden cup full of abominations
18. 6 "double draught for her in the cup she mixed

CURE
1. *treat, heal:* ἰάομαι IAOMAI
Lk 9.11 he . . cured those who had need of healing
2. *remedy, healing:* ἴασις IASIS
Lk 13.32 " 'I cast out demons and perform cures
3. *serve, treat medically:* θεραπεύω THERAPEUŌ
Mt 17.18 the boy was cured instantly
Lk 6.18 those . . troubled with . . spirits were cured
7.21 In that hour he cured many of diseases
9. 1 he . . gave them power . . to cure diseases
Jn 5.10 the Jews said to the man who was cured
Acts 28. 9 who had diseases also came and were cured

CURSE
1. *blaspheme, slander:* βλασφημέω BLASPHĒMEŌ
Rev 16. 9 they cursed the name of God
16.11 cursed the God of heaven for their pain
16.21 till men cursed God for the plague
2. *curse:* κατάρα KATARA
Gal 3.10 all who rely on works . . are under a curse
3.13 Christ redeemed us from the curse of the law, having become a curse for us
3. *curse:* καταράομαι KATARAOMAI*
Mt 25.41 " 'Depart from me, you cursed
Mk 11.21 "The fig tree which you cursed has withered
Lk 6.28 "bless those who curse you
Rom 12.14 Bless those . . and do not curse them
Jas 3. 9 With it we bless the Lord and . . curse men

CURSE ON ONESELF, INVOKE A
1. *bind by a curse:* ἀναθεματίζω ANATHEMATIZŌ
Mk 14.71 he began to invoke a curse on himself
2. *bind by a curse, curse:* καταθεματίζω KATATHEMATIZŌ*
Mt 26.74 he began to invoke a curse on himself

CURSED
1. *something dedicated:* ἀνάθεμα ANATHEMA [A.1.b.4]
1 Cor 12. 3 no one . . by the Spirit . . says "Jesus be c.!
2. *accursed:* ἐπικατάρατος EPIKATARATOS*
Gal 3.10 "Cursed be every one who does not abide
3.13 "Cursed be every one who hangs on a tree

CURSED, BEING
1. *curse:* κατάρα KATARA
Heb 6. 8 it is worthless and near to being cursed

CURSES
1. *vow, curse:* ἀρά ARA I*
Rom 3.14 "Their mouth is full of curses

CURSING
1. *curse:* κατάρα KATARA
Jas 3.10 From the same . . come blessing and cursing

CURTAIN
1. *curtain, veil:* καταπέτασμα KATAPETASMA*
Mt 27.51 the curtain of the temple was torn in two
Also Mk **15**.38; Lk **23**.45
Heb 6.19 the inner shrine behind the curtain
9. 3 Behind the second curtain stood a tent[p]
10.20 way . . opened for us through the curtain

CUSHION
1. *pillow, cushion:* προσκεφάλιον PROSKEPHALION*
Mk 4.38 he was in the stern, asleep on the cushion

CUSTODIAN
1. *boy's attendant, leader:* παιδαγωγός PAIDAGŌGOS
Gal 3.24 the law was our custodian until Christ
3.25 we are no longer under a custodian

CUSTODY
1. *safekeeping:* τήρησις TĒRĒSIS
Acts 4. 3 arrested them and put them in custody

CUSTODY, KEEP IN
1. *keep, observe:* τηρέω TĒREŌ
Acts 24.23 that he should be kept in custody
25.21 "Paul had appealed to be kept in custody

CUSTOM
1. *accustom:* ἐθίζω (subst. perf. pass. part.) ETHIZŌ*
Lk 2.27 to do . . according to the custom of the law
2. *be accustomed:* εἴωθα (subst. perf. part.) EIŌTHA
Lk 4.16 as his custom was, on the sabbath day
Acts 17. 2 Paul went in, as was his custom
3. *custom, habit:* ἔθος ETHOS
Lk 1. 9 according to the custom of the priesthood
2.42 they went up according to custom
22.39 he came out, and went, as was his custom
Jn 19.40 as is the burial custom of the Jews
Acts 6.14 "that this Jesus . . will change the customs
15. 1 "circumcised according to the custom
16.21 "They advocate customs . . not lawful for us
21.21 "telling them not to . . observe the customs
25.16 "it was not the custom of the Romans
26. 3 "you are especially familiar with all customs
28.17 "nothing against the people or the customs
4. *custom, practice:* συνήθεια SYNĒTHEIA
Jn 18.39 "a custom that I should release one man

CUSTOM, BE ONE'S
1. *be accustomed:* εἴωθα EIŌTHA
Mk 10. 1 as his custom was, he taught them

CUT
1. *cut short, clip:* κείρω KEIRŌ
Acts 18.18 At Cenchreae he cut his hair
2. *cut, strike:* κόπτω KOPTŌ
Mt 21. 8 cut branches . . and spread them on the road
Mk 11. 8 branches which they had cut from the fields

CUT AWAY
1. *cut off:* ἀποκόπτω APOKOPTŌ
Acts 27.32 the soldiers cut away the ropes of the boat

CUT, BE
1. *be pierced, be stunned:* κατανύσσομαι KATANYSSOMAI*
Acts 2.37 when they heard . . they were c. to the heart

CUT DOWN
CUT FROM
1. *cut out, cut off:* ἐκκόπτω EKKOPTŌ
Mt 3.10 "that does not bear good fruit is cut down
Also Mt **7**.19; Lk **3**.9
Lk 13. 7 " 'seeking fruit . . I find none. Cut it down
13. 9 " 'but if not, you can cut it down
Rom 11.24 you have been cut from . . a wild olive tree

CUT IN PIECES
1. *cut in two:* διχοτομέω DICHOTOMEŌ
Mt [24.51 "⟨the master⟩ will *cut him in pieces*†
Lk [12.46 "the master . . will *cut him in pieces*†

CUT OFF
1. *take away:* ἀφαιρέω APHAIREŌ
Mt 26.51 one . . drew his sword, . . and cut off his ear
Mk 14.47 one . . drew his sword, . . and cut off his ear
Lk 22.50 one of them struck . . and c. off his right ear
2. *cut off:* ἀποκόπτω APOKOPTŌ
Mk 9.43 "if your hand causes you to sin,[l] cut it off
9.45 "if your foot causes you to sin,[l] cut it off
Jn 18.10 Simon . . drew . . and cut off his right ear
18.26 the man whose ear Peter had cut off
3. *cut out, cut off:* ἐκκόπτω EKKOPTŌ
Mt 5.30 "if your . . hand causes . . sin, c. it off
18. 8 "if your hand . . causes . . sin,[z] c. it off
Rom 11.22 otherwise you too will be cut off

CUT OFF, ACCURSED AND
1. *something dedicated:* ἀνάθεμα ANATHEMA [A.1.b.4]
Rom 9. 3 that I . . were accursed and cut off

CUT OFF ONE'S HAIR
1. *cut short, clip:* κείρω (mid.) KEIRŌ
1 Cor 11. 6 then she should cut off her hair

CYCLE
1. *wheel:* τροχός TROCHOS*
Jas 3. 6 tongue . . setting on fire the cycle of nature[b]†

CYMBAL
1. *cymbal:* κύμβαλον KYMBALON*
1 Cor 13. 1 I am a noisy gong or a clanging cymbal

CYPRUS: 'sīprəs II,F-4
1. *one of Cyprus:* Κύπριος
Acts 4.36 Barnabas . . a Levite, a native of Cyprus
11.20 men of Cyprus . . , preaching the Lord
21.16 bringing us to the house of Mnason of C.
2. *Cyprus:* Κύπρος
Acts 11.19 traveled as far as Phoenicia and C.
13. 4 from there they sailed to Cyprus
15.39 Barnabas took Mark with him . . to C.
21. 3 When we had come in sight of Cyprus
27. 4 we sailed under the lee of Cyprus

CYRENE: sī'rēnē II,D-4
1. *Cyrene:* Κυρήνη
Acts 2.10 "parts of Libya belonging to Cyrene
2. *of Cyrene:* Κυρηναῖος [A.3.a.2]
Mt 27.32 they came upon a man of C., Simon
Mk 15.21 they compelled a passer-by, Simon of C.
Lk 23.26 they seized one Simon of Cyrene
Acts 11.20 there were some of them, men of . . Cyrene
13. 1 Symeon . . called Niger, Lucius of Cyrene

CYRENIAN: Κυρηναῖος (*See also* CYRENE 2)
Acts 6. 9 belonged to . . synagogue . . of the Cyrenians

D

DAILY
1. *for the day, for the morrow:* ἐπιούσιος EPIOUSIOS*
Mt 6.11 "Give us this day our daily bread[m]†
Lk 11. 3 "Give us each day our daily bread[k]†
2. *for the day, daily:* ἐφήμερος EPHĒMEROS*
Jas 2.15 If a brother or sister is . . in lack of daily food
3. *every day:* καθ' ἡμέραν HĒMERA [B.1.a.1]
Lk 9.23 "let him . . take up his cross daily
19.47 he was teaching daily in the temple
Acts 3. 2 a man . . whom they laid daily at that gate
16. 5 they increased in numbers daily
17.11 Jews were . . examining the scriptures daily
19. 9 argued daily in the hall of Tyrannus[r]
2 Cor 11.28 daily pressure upon me of my anxiety
Heb 7.27 those high priests, to offer sacrifices daily
10.11 every priest stands daily at his service
4. *daily:* καθημερινός KATHĒMERINOS*
Acts 6. 1 widows . . neglected in . . daily . . distribution

DAINTIES
1. *rich, bright:* λιπαρός (subst. neut. pl.) LIPAROS*
Rev 18.14 "all thy dainties and . . splendor are lost!

DALMANUTHA: Δαλμανουθά ˌdalmə'nüthə
Mk 8.10 went to the district of Dalmanutha[a]‡

DALMATIA: Δαλματία dal'māsh(ē)ə II,C-2
2 Tim 4.10 Crescens has gone to Galatia,[e] Titus to D.

DAMARIS: Δάμαρις 'damərəs
Acts 17.34 some . . believed, among them . . Damaris

DAMASCUS: də'maskəs I,E-2; II,G-4
1. *Damascene, of Damascus:* Δαμασκηνός
2 Cor 11.32 governor under King Aretas guarded . . D.
2. *Damascus:* Δαμασκός
Acts 9. 2 letters to the synagogues at Damascus
9. 3 as he journeyed he approached D.
9. 8 they led him by the hand . . into D.
9.10 a disciple at D. named Ananias
9.19 several days he was with the disciples at D.
9.22 confounded the Jews who lived in D.
9.27 how at D. he had preached boldly
22. 5 "I journeyed to D. to take those
22. 6 "As I . . drew near to D., about noon
22.10 " 'Rise, and go into Damascus
22.11 "I was led by the hand . . into D.
26.12 "I journeyed to D. with the authority
26.20 "declared first to those at Damascus
2 Cor 11.32 At D. the governor . . guarded the city
Gal 1.17 again I returned to Damascus

DANCE
1. *dance:* ὀρχέομαι ORCHEOMAI*
Mt 11.17 " 'We piped to you, and you did not dance
14. 6 daughter of Herodias danced
Mk 6.22 Herodias' daughter came in and danced
Lk 7.32 " 'We piped to you, and you did not dance
2. *play like a child, dance:* παίζω PAIZŌ*
1 Cor 10. 7 "sat down to eat . . and rose up to dance

DANCING
1. *dance:* χορός CHOROS*
Lk 15.25 "his elder son . . heard music and dancing

DANGER
1. *hazard, risk:* κίνδυνος KINDYNOS
2 Cor 11.26 on frequent journeys, in danger from rivers, danger from robbers, danger from my own people, danger from Gentiles, danger in the city, danger in the wilderness, danger at sea, danger from false brethren

DANGER, BE IN
DANGER, THERE IS
1. *be daring, run a risk:* κινδυνεύω KINDYNEUŌ
[a]A.6.e
Lk 8.23 filling with water, and were in danger
Acts 19.27 [a]"there is danger . . that this trade of ours
19.40 "are in danger of being charged with rioting

DANGEROUS
1. *prone to fall, precarious:* ἐπισφαλής EPISPHALĒS*
Acts 27. 9 the voyage was already dangerous

DANIEL: Δανιήλ 'danyəl
Mt 24.15 "desolating sacrilege spoken of by . . Daniel

DARE
1. *dare:* τολμάω TOLMAŌ
Mt 22.46 nor . . did any one dare to ask him
Mk 12.34 after that no one dared to ask him
Lk 20.40 no longer dared to ask him any question
Jn 21.12 none of the disciples dared ask him
Acts 5.13 None of the rest dared join them
7.32 "Moses trembled and did not dare to look
Rom 5. 7 for a good man one will dare even to die
1 Cor 6. 1 does he dare go to law before the unrighteous?
2 Cor 11.21 whatever any one dares to boast of . . I also dare to boast of that

DARK
1. *dry, miserable:* αὐχμηρός AUCHMĒROS*
2 Pet 1.19 as to a lamp shining in a dark place
2. *dark, obscure:* σκοτεινός SKOTEINOS
Lk 11.36 "body is full of light, having no part dark

3. *darkness, gloom:* σκοτία SKOTIA
Mt 10.27 "I tell you in the dark, utter in the light
Lk 12. 3 "whatever you have said in the dark
Jn 6.17 It was now dark, and Jesus had not yet come
20. 1 to the tomb early, while it was still dark

DARKEN

1. *make dark:* σκοτίζω SKOTIZŌ*
Mt 24.29 "the sun will be darkened
Mk 13.24 "But in those days . . the sun will be darkened
Lk [23.45 while the sun *was darkened*‡
Rom 1.21 their senseless minds were darkened
11.10 let their eyes be darkened
Rev 8.12 a third of their light was darkened
2. *darken, blind:* σκοτόω SKOTOŌ
Eph 4.18 they are darkened in their understanding
Rev 9. 2 the sun and the air were darkened

DARKNESS

1. *darkness:* γνόφος GNOPHOS*
Heb 12.18 a blazing fire, and darkness, and gloom
2. *darkness, gloom:* σκοτία SKOTIA
Mt 4.16 "people who sat in darkness have seen
Jn 1. 5 The light shines in the darkness, and the darkness has not overcome it
8.12 "who follows me will not walk in darkness
12.35 "Walk . . lest the darkness overtake you
12.35 "who walks in the darkness does not know
12.46 "whoever believes . . may not remain in d.
1 Jn 1. 5 God is light and in him is no darkness
2. 8 because[b] the darkness is passing away
2. 9 who . . hates his brother is in the darkness
2.11 he who hates his brother is in the darkness and walks in the darkness . . the darkness has blinded his eyes
3. *darkness:* σκότος SKOTOS*
Mt 6.23 "If then the light in you is darkness, how great is the darkness!
8.12 "thrown into the outer darkness
22.13 " 'cast him into the outer darkness
25.30 " 'cast the . . servant into the outer darkness
27.45 there was darkness over all the land[m]
Mk 15.33 there was darkness over the whole land[h]
Lk 1.79 "give light to those who sit in darkness
11.35 "be careful lest the light in you be darkness
22.53 "this is your hour, and the power of darkness
23.44 there was darkness over the whole land[q]
Jn 3.19 men loved darkness rather than light
Acts 2.20 the sun shall be turned into darkness
13.11 Immediately . . darkness fell upon him
26.18 " 'that they may turn from darkness to light
Rom 2.19 a light to those who are in darkness
13.12 then cast off the works of darkness
1 Cor 4. 5 to light the things now hidden in darkness
2 Cor 4. 6 "Let light shine out of darkness
6.14 what fellowship has light with darkness?
Eph 5. 8 you were darkness, but now you are light
5.11 Take no part in . . works of darkness
6.12 world rulers of this present darkness
Col 1.13 He has delivered us from . . darkness
1 Th 5. 4 you are not in darkness, brethren
5. 5 we are not of the night or of darkness
1 Pet 2. 9 who called you out of darkness into . . light
2 Pet 2.17 for them the nether gloom of darkness
1 Jn 1. 6 If we say . . while we walk in darkness
Jude .13 for whom the nether gloom of darkness

DARKNESS, FULL OF

1. *dark, obscure:* σκοτεινός SKOTEINOS
Mt 6.23 "your whole body will be full of darkness
Lk 11.34 "your body is full of darkness

DARKNESS, IN

1. *darken, blind:* σκοτόω (perf. pass. part.) SKOTOŌ
Rev 16.10 its kingdom was in darkness

DART

1. *missile, arrow:* βέλος BELOS*
Eph 6.16 quench all the flaming darts

DASH DOWN

1. *break:* ῥήγνυμι RHĒGNYMI
Mk 9.18 "wherever it seizes him, it dashes him down

DASH TO THE GROUND

1. *dash to the ground:* ἐδαφίζω EDAPHIZŌ*
Lk 19.44 "⟨enemies will⟩ dash you to the ground

DATE SET, THE

1. *a fixed time:* προθεσμία PROTHESMIA*
Gal 4. 2 he is under guardians . . until the date set

DAUGHTER

1. *daughter:* θυγάτηρ THYGATĒR*
Mt 9.18 "My daughter has just died; but come
9.22 "daughter, your faith has made you well
10.35 "to set . . a daughter against her mother
10.37 "he who loves . . daughter more than me
14. 6 the daughter of Herodias danced
15.22 "my daughter is . . possessed by a demon
15.28 her daughter was healed instantly
21. 5 "Tell the daughter of Zion, Behold
Mk 5.34 "Daughter, your faith has made you well
5.35 "Your daughter is dead
6.22 Herodias' daughter came in and danced
7.26 begged him to cast the demon out of her d.
7.29 "the demon has left your daughter
Lk 1. 5 he had a wife of the daughters of Aaron
2.36 prophetess, Anna, the daughter of Phanuel
8.42 an only daughter, about twelve years of age
8.48 "Daughter, your faith has made you well
8.49 "Your daughter is dead
12.53 "divided . . mother against daughter and daughter against her mother
13.16 "this woman, a daughter of Abraham
23.28 "Daughters of Jerusalem, do not weep for me
Jn 12.15 "Fear not, daughter of Zion; behold
Acts 2.17 " 'your daughters shall prophesy
7.21 "Pharaoh's daughter adopted him
21. 9 "he had four unmarried daughters
2 Cor 6.18 "you shall be my sons and daughters
Heb 11.24 refused to be called the son of Pharaoh's d.

DAUGHTER, LITTLE

1. *little daughter:* θυγάτριον THYGATRION*
Mk 5.23 "My little daughter is at the point of death
7.25 woman, whose little daughter was possessed

DAUGHTER-IN-LAW

1. *bride, young wife:* νύμφη NYMPHĒ
Mt 10.35 "daughter-in-law against her mother-in-law
Lk 12.53 "mother-in-law against her daughter-in-law
12.53 "daughter-in-law against her mother-in-law

DAVID: Δαυίδ 'dāvәd
Mt 1. 1 genealogy of Jesus Christ, the son of D.
1. 6 Jesse the father of David the king
1. 6 David was the father of Solomon
1.17 the generations from Abraham to David
1.17 from David to the deportation to Babylon
1.20 "Joseph, son of David, do not fear
9.27 "Have mercy on us, Son of David
12. 3 "Have you not read what David did
12.23 "Can this be the Son of David?
15.22 "Have mercy on me, O Lord, Son of David
20.30 "Have mercy on us, Son of David!
20.31 "Lord, have mercy on us, Son of David!
21. 9 "Hosanna to the Son of David!
21.15 "Hosanna to the Son of David!
22.42 They said to him, "The son of David
22.43 "How is it . . that David . . calls him Lord?
22.45 "If David thus calls him Lord
Mk 2.25 "Have you never read what David did?
10.47 "Jesus, Son of David, have mercy on me!
10.48 "Son of David, have mercy on me!
11.10 "Blessed is the kingdom of our father David!
12.35 "that the Christ is the son of David
12.36 "D. . . declared, 'The Lord said to my Lord
12.37 "D. . . calls him Lord; so how is he his son?
Lk 1.27 betrothed to . . Joseph, of the house of D.
1.32 "the throne of his father David

Lk 1.69 "in the house of his servant David
2. 4 to Judea, to the city of D., . . Bethlehem, because he was of the . . lineage of D.
2.11 "to you is born this day in the city of D.
3.31 Nathan, the son of David
6. 3 "Have you not read what David did?
18.38 "Jesus, Son of David, have mercy on me!
18.39 "Son of David, have mercy on me!
20.41 "can they say that the Christ is D.'s son?
20.42 "David himself says in the Book of Psalms
20.44 "David thus calls him Lord
Jn 7.42 "that the Christ is descended from David
7.42 "Bethlehem, the village where David was
Acts 1.16 "spoke beforehand by the mouth of D.
2.25 "David says . . 'I saw the Lord always
2.29 "David . . both died and was buried
2.34 "David did not ascend into the heavens
4.25 "by the mouth of our father David
7.45 "So it was until the days of David
13.22 "he raised up David to be their king
13.22 " 'I have found in D. . . a man after my heart
13.34 " 'the holy and sure blessings of David
13.36 "David . . served the counsel of God
15.16 " 'I will rebuild the dwelling of David
Rom 1. 3 his Son, who was descended from D.
4. 6 D. pronounces a blessing upon the man
11. 9 D. says, "Let their feast become a snare
2 Tim 2. 8 Jesus Christ, . . descended from David
Heb 4. 7 saying through David so long afterward
11.32 time would fail me to tell of David
Rev 3. 7 " 'the true one, who has the key of David
5. 5 "the Root of David, has conquered
22.16 "I am the root and the offspring of David

DAWN

1. *make to rise:* ἀνατέλλω ANATELLŌ
Mt 4.16 "for those . . light has dawned
2. *shine through:* διαυγάζω DIAUGAZŌ*
2 Pet 1.19 pay attention . . until the day dawns
3. *grow toward daylight:* ἐπιφώσκω (subst. part.) EPIPHŌSKŌ
Mt 28. 1 the dawn of the first day of the week
4. *come to be, happen, be:* γίνομαι GINOMAI [A.6.a.5]
Acts 27.33 day was about to dawn, Paul urged them

DAWN, AT

1. *dawn, about daybreak:* ὄρθρος (gen.) ORTHROS
Lk 24. 1 the first day of the week, at early dawn

DAWN UPON

1. *look upon, visit:* ἐπισκέπτομαι EPISKEPTOMAI
Lk 1.78 "the day shall dawn upon[f] us from on high†‡

DAY (*See also* FOLLOWING DAY, THE; NEXT DAY; PREPARATION, DAY OF; SABBATH, THE DAY BEFORE THE; SECOND DAY, ON THE)

1. *rising, east:* ἀνατολή ANATOLĒ
Lk 1.78 "when the day shall dawn upon[f] us†
2. *day, tribunal:* ἡμέρα HĒMERA
[a]καθ' ἡμέραν [b]+σήμερον
Mt 2. 1 when Jesus was born . . in the days of Herod
3. 1 In those days came John the Baptist
4. 2 he fasted forty days and forty nights
6.34 "Let . . trouble be sufficient for the day
7.22 "On that day many will say to me, 'Lord
9.15 "days . . when the bridegroom is taken away
10.15 "more tolerable on the day of judgment
11.12 "From the days of John the Baptist
11.22 "it shall be more tolerable on the day
11.24 "more tolerable on the day of judgment
12.36 "I tell you, on the day of judgment
12.40 "Jonah was three days and three nights
12.40 "Son of man . . three days and three nights
13. 1 That same day Jesus went out of the house
15.32 "they have been with me now three days
16.21 be killed, and on the third day be raised
17. 1 after six days Jesus took with him Peter
17.23 "he will be raised on the third day
20. 2 "agreeing . . for a denarius[m] a day
20. 6 " 'Why do you stand here idle all day?
20.12 " 'who have borne the burden of the day
Mt 20.19 "he will be raised on the third day
22.23 The same day Sadducees came to him
22.46 nor from that day did any one . . ask
23.30 " 'If we had lived in the days of our fathers
24.19 "those who give suck in those days!
24.22 "if those days had not been shortened
24.22 "those days will be shortened
24.29 "after the tribulation of those days
24.36 "But of that day and hour no one knows
24.37 "As were the days of Noah
24.38 "For as in those days before the flood . . until the day when Noah entered the ark
24.42 "Watch . . for you do not know on what day
24.50 "master of that servant will come on a day
25.13 "you know neither the day nor the hour
26. 2 "after two days the Passover is coming
26.29 "until that day when I drink it new
26.55 [a]"Day after day I sat in the temple teaching
26.61 " 'destroy . . and to build it in three days
27.40 "would destroy . . and build it in three days
27.63 " 'After three days I will rise again
27.64 "sepulchre . . made secure until the third day
28.15 [b]story . . spread among the Jews to this day
Mk 1. 9 In those days Jesus came from Nazareth
1.13 he was in the wilderness forty days
2. 1 returned to Capernaum after some days
2.20 "days will come, when the bridegroom is taken . . and then they will fast in that day
4.27 "should sleep and rise night and day
4.35 On that day, when evening had come
5. 5 Night and day among the tombs
8. 1 In those days, when again a great crowd
8. 2 "crowd . . have been with me now three days
8.31 killed, and after three days rise again
9. 2 after six days Jesus took with him Peter
9.31 "killed, after three days he will rise
10.34 "kill him; and after three days he will rise
13.17 "those who give suck in those days!
13.19 "in those days there will be such tribulation
13.20 "if the Lord had not shortened the days
13.20 "for . . the elect . . he shortened the days
13.24 "But in those days, after that tribulation
13.32 "But of that day or that hour no one knows
14. 1 It was now two days before the Passover
14.12 "on the first day of Unleavened Bread
14.25 "until that day when I drink it new
14.49 [a]"Day after day I was with you
14.58 " 'and in three days I will build another
15.29 "would destroy . . and build it in three days
Lk 1. 5 In the days of Herod, king of Judea
1.20 "silent and unable to speak until the day
1.24 After these days . . Elizabeth conceived
1.25 "the days when he looked on me
1.39 In those days Mary arose and went
1.59 on the eighth day they came to circumcise
1.75 "in holiness . . before him all the days
1.80 he was in the wilderness till the day
2. 1 In those days a decree went out
2.21 at the end of eight days . . circumcised
2.37 fasting and prayer night and day
2.44 they went a day's journey
2.46 After three days they found him
4. 2 forty days in the wilderness, tempted
4. 2 he ate nothing in those days
4.16 went to the synagogue . . on the sabbath day
4.25 "many widows . . in the days of Elijah
4.42 when it was day he departed
5.17 On one of those days, as he was teaching
5.35 "days will come, when the bridegroom is taken . . and . . they will fast in those days
6.12 In these days he went out . . to pray
6.13 when it was day, he called his disciples
6.23 "Rejoice in that day, and leap for joy
8.22 One day he got into a boat with his disciples
9.12 Now the day began to wear away
9.22 "killed, and on the third day be raised
9.28 about eight days after these sayings

Lk 9.36 told no one in those days anything
9.37 On the next day, when they had come
9.51 When the days drew near for him
10.12 "it shall be more tolerable on that day
11. 3 "Give us each day our daily bread[k]
12.46 "the master . . will come on a day
13.14 "There are six days . . ; come on those . . and be healed, and not on the sabbath day
13.16 "loosed from this bond on the sabbath day
14. 5 "not . . pull him out on a sabbath day
15.13 "Not many days later, the younger son
16.19 "who feasted sumptuously every day
17. 4 "if he sins against you seven times in the day
17.22 "The days are coming when you will desire to see one of the days of the Son of man
17.24 "so will the Son of man be in his day[a]‡
17.26 "As it was in the days of Noah, so will it be in the days of the Son of man
17.27 "until the day when Noah entered the ark
17.28 "Likewise as it was in the days of Lot
17.29 "the day when Lot went out from Sodom
17.30 "on the day when the Son of man
17.31 "On that day, let him . . not come down
18. 7 "his elect, who cry to him day and night?
18.33 "on the third day he will rise
19.43 "For the days shall come upon you
20. 1 One day, as he was teaching the people
21. 6 "days will come when there shall not be left
21.22 "for these are days of vengeance
21.23 "for those who give suck in those days
21.34 "and that day come upon you suddenly
21.37 every day he was teaching in the temple
22. 7 Then came the day of Unleavened Bread
22.53 [a]"with you day after day in the temple
22.66 When day came, the assembly . . gathered
23.12 friends with each other that very day
23.29 "behold, the days are coming
23.54 It was the day of Preparation
24. 7 "crucified, and on the third day rise
24.13 That very day two of them were going
24.18 "things that have happened . . in these days
24.21 "it is now the third day since this
24.29 "evening and the day is now far spent
24.46 "on the third day rise from the dead

Jn 1.39 they stayed with him that day
2. 1 On the third day there was a marriage
2.12 there they stayed for a few days
2.19 "in three days I will raise it up
2.20 "will you raise it up in three days?
4.40 he stayed there two days
4.43 After the two days he departed
5. 9 Now that day was the sabbath
6.39 "lose nothing . . but raise it up at the last day
6.40 "I will raise him up at the last day
6.44 "I will raise him up at the last day
6.54 "I will raise him up at the last day
7.37 On the last day of the feast
8.56 "rejoiced that he was to see my day
9. 4 "We must work . . while it is day
9.14 Now it was a sabbath day
11. 6 he stayed two days longer in the place
11. 9 "Are there not twelve hours in the day?
11. 9 "in the day, he does not stumble
11.17 already been in the tomb four days
11.24 "I know that he will rise . . at the last day
11.53 from that day on they took counsel
12. 1 Six days before the Passover
12. 7 "let her keep it for the day of my burial
12.48 "word . . will be his judge on the last day
14.20 "In that day you will know
16.23 "In that day you will ask nothing of me
16.26 "In that day you will ask in my name
19.31 Since it was the day of Preparation
20.19 On the evening of that day
20.26 Eight days later . . Thomas was with them

Acts 1. 2 until the day when he was taken up
1. 3 appearing to them during forty days
1. 5 "before many days you shall be baptized
1.15 In those days Peter stood up
1.22 "until the day when he was taken up
2. 1 When the day of Pentecost had come
2.15 "it is only the third hour of the day
2.17 " 'in the last days it shall be, God declares
2.18 " 'in those days I will pour out my Spirit
2.20 " 'before the day of the Lord comes
2.29 "his tomb is with us to this day
2.41 were added that day about three thousand
2.46 [a]day by day, attending the temple
2.47 added to their number day by day
3.24 "prophets . . also proclaimed these days
5.36 "before these days Theudas arose
5.37 "Judas the Galilean arose in the days
5.42 every day . . they did not cease teaching
6. 1 in these days . . disciples were increasing
7. 8 "circumcised him on the eighth day
7.26 "on the following day he appeared to them
7.41 "they made a calf in those days
7.45 "So it was until the days of David
8. 1 on that day a great persecution arose
9. 9 for three days he was without sight
9.19 For several days he was with the disciples
9.23 When many days had passed
9.24 watching the gates day and night
9.37 In those days she fell sick and died
9.43 he stayed in Joppa for many days
10. 3 the ninth hour of the day he saw clearly
10.30 "Four days ago, about this hour
10.40 "God raised him on the third day
10.48 they asked him to remain for some days
11.27 in these days prophets came down
12. 3 during the days of Unleavened Bread
12.18 when day came, there was no small stir
12.21 On an appointed day Herod put on
13.14 on the sabbath day . . into the synagogue
13.31 "for many days he appeared to those
13.41 " 'for I do a deed in your days
15. 7 "in the early days God made choice
15.36 after some days Paul said to Barnabas
16.12 We remained in this city some days
16.13 on the sabbath day we went outside
16.18 this she did for many days
16.35 when it was day, the magistrates sent
17.17 in the market place every day
17.31 "he has fixed a day on which he will judge
18.18 After this Paul stayed many days longer
20. 6 we sailed . . after the days of Unleavened Bread, and in five days we came to . . Troas, where we stayed for seven days
20.16 to be at Jerusalem . . on the day of Pentecost
20.18 "from the first day . . in Asia
20.26 [b]"I testify to you this day that I am innocent
20.31 "I did not cease night or day to admonish
21. 4 we stayed there for seven days
21. 5 when our days there were ended
21. 7 we . . stayed with them for one day
21.10 While we were staying for some days
21.15 After these days we made ready
21.26 the next day he purified himself
21.26 the days of purification would be fulfilled
21.27 the seven days were almost completed
23. 1 "in all good conscience up to this day
23.12 When it was day, the Jews made a plot
24. 1 after five days . . Ananias came
24.11 "it is not more than twelve days since
24.24 After some days Felix came
25. 1 after three days he went up to Jerusalem
25. 6 not more than eight or ten days
25.13 when some days had passed, Agrippa
25.14 as they stayed there many days
26. 7 "as they earnestly worship night and day
26.22 "To this day I have had . . help . . from God
27. 7 We sailed slowly for a number of days
27.20 sun nor stars appeared for many a day
27.29 they . . prayed for day to come

Acts 27.33 As day was about to dawn, Paul urged them . . "Today is the fourteenth day
27.39 when it was day, they did not recognize
28. 7 entertained us hospitably for three days
28.12 at Syracuse, we stayed there for three days
28.13 after one day a south wind sprang up
28.14 invited to stay with them for seven days
28.17 After three days he called . . the . . leaders
28.23 When they had appointed a day for him
Rom 2. 5 wrath for yourself on the day of wrath
2.16 on that day when . . God judges
8.36 "we are being killed all the day long
10.21 "All day long I have held out my hands
11. 8 [b]"a spirit of stupor . . down to this very day
13.12 night is far gone, the day is at hand
13.13 conduct ourselves becomingly as in the day
14. 5 One . . esteems one day as better . . another man esteems all days alike
14. 6 He who observes the day, observes it
1 Cor 1. 8 guiltless in the day of our Lord Jesus Christ
3.13 for the Day will disclose it
5. 5 that his spirit may be saved in the day
10. 8 twenty-three thousand fell in a single day
15. 4 he was raised on the third day
15.31 I protest, brethren . . I die every day!
2 Cor 1.14 proud . . on the day of the Lord Jesus
3.14 [b]to this day . . that same veil remains
6. 2 "helped you on the day of salvation
6. 2 behold, now is the day of salvation
Gal 1.18 I . . remained with him fifteen days
4.10 You observe days, and months, and seasons!
Eph 4.30 you were sealed for the day of redemption
5.16 because the days are evil
6.13 be able to withstand in the evil day
Phil 1. 5 partnership in the gospel from the first day
1. 6 completion at the day of Jesus Christ
1.10 be pure and blameless for the day of Christ
2.16 that in the day of Christ I may be proud
Col 1. 6 bearing fruit . . from the day you heard
1. 9 from the day we heard . . we have not ceased
1 Th 2. 9 we worked night and day
3.10 praying earnestly night and day
5. 2 the day of the Lord will come like a thief
5. 4 for that day to surprise you like a thief
5. 5 all sons of light and sons of the day
5. 8 since we belong to the day, let us be sober
2 Th 1.10 when he comes on that day to be glorified
2. 2 that the day of the Lord has come
3. 8 we worked night and day
1 Tim 5. 5 in supplications . . night and day
2 Tim 1. 4(3) I long night and day to see you
1.12 he is able to guard until that Day
1.18 grant him to find mercy . . on that Day
3. 1 in the last days there will come . . stress
4. 8 judge, will award to me on that Day
Heb 1. 2 in these last days he has spoken . . by a Son
3. 8 "on the day of testing in the wilderness
3.13 "exhort one another every day
4. 4 "And God rested on the seventh day
4. 7 again he sets a certain day, "Today
4. 8 God[i] would not speak . . of another day
5. 7 In the days of his flesh, Jesus[j] offered
7. 3 neither beginning of days nor end of life
8. 8 "The days will come, says the Lord
8. 9 "on the day when I took them by the hand
8.10 "after those days, says the Lord
10.16 "after those days, says the Lord
10.25 as you see the Day drawing near
10.32 But recall the former days
11.30 they had been encircled for seven days
Jas 5. 3 You have laid up treasure[e] for the last days
5. 5 fattened your hearts in a day of slaughter
1 Pet 2.12 glorify God on the day of visitation
3.10 "He that would love life and see good days
3.20 God's patience waited in the days of Noah
2 Pet 1.19 pay attention . . until the day dawns
2 Pet 2. 8 (he was vexed in his righteous soul day after day with their lawless deeds
2. 9 punishment until the day of judgment
3. 3 will come in the last days with scoffing
3. 7 kept until the day of judgment
3. 8 with the Lord one day is as a thousand years, and a thousand years as one day
3.10 day of the Lord will come like a thief
3.12 "hastening[i] the coming of the day of God
3.18 both now and to the day of eternity
1 Jn 4.17 confidence for the day of judgment
Jude . 6 until the judgment of the great day
Rev 1.10 I was in the Spirit on the Lord's day
2.10 " 'for ten days you will have tribulation
2.13 " 'even in the days of Antipas my witness
4. 8 day and night they never cease to sing
6.17 "the great day of their wrath has come
7.15 "serve him day and night within his temple
8.12 a third of the day was kept from shining
9. 6 in those days men will seek death
9.15 held ready for the hour, the day
10. 7 in the days of the trumpet call
11. 3 "one thousand two hundred and sixty days
11. 6 during the days of their prophesying
11. 9 For three days and a half men . . gaze
11.11 after the three and a half days a breath
12. 6 one thousand two hundred and sixty days
12.10 "accuses them day and night before our God
14.11 "they have no rest, day or night
16.14 battle on the great day of God
18. 8 "shall her plagues come in a single day
20.10 they will be tormented day and night
21.25 its gates shall never be shut by day

IDIOMATICALLY
a. Mt 14.15 "the day is now over *ἡ ὥρα ἤδη παρῆλθεν* [HŌRA]
b. Jn 21.4 Just as day was breaking *πρωΐας δὲ ἤδη γινομένης* [PRŌIA]
c. Acts 20.15 the day after that we came to Miletus *τῇ . . ἐχομένῃ ἤλθομεν εἰς Μίλητον* [ECHŌ]

CONTEXTUALLY
Mt 26.17 on the first day of Unleavened Bread
Mk 16. 9 early on the first day of the week[k]‡
Lk 13.32 "and the third day I finish my course
Acts 1.12 a sabbath day's journey away
11.28 this took place in the days of Claudius
27.19 third d. they cast out with their own hands
2 Th 2. 3 for that day will not come
Heb 4. 4 he has . . spoken of the seventh day

DAY, A NIGHT AND A

1. *a night and a day: νυχθήμερον* NYCHTHĒMERON*
2 Cor 11.25 a night and a day I have been adrift

DAY, BEFORE

1. *at night: ἔννυχος* ENNYCHOS* [A.4.b]
Mk 1.35 in the morning, a great while before day

DAY, EVERY

IDIOMATICALLY
a. 2 Cor 4.16 is being renewed every day *ἀνακαινοῦται ἡμέρᾳ καὶ ἡμέρᾳ* [HĒMERA]

DAY, NEXT
DAY, ON THE FOLLOWING
DAY, ON THE NEXT
DAY, THE FOLLOWING

1. *tomorrow: αὔριον* AURION
Lk 10.35 "the next day he took out two denarii[i]
2. *have, hold: ἔχω* (part.) ECHŌ [B.3.b.2]
Lk 13.33 " 'I must go . . the day following
3. *tomorrow: ἐπαύριον* EPAURION [B.3.b.4]
Mt 27.62 Next day, that is, after . . Preparation
Mk 11.12 On the following day, when they came
Jn 1.29 The next day he saw Jesus coming
1.35 The next day again John was standing
1.43 The next day Jesus decided to go
6.22 On the next day the people who remained
12.12 The next day a great crowd . . heard
Acts 10. 9 The next day, as they were on their journey
10.23 The next day he rose and went off

Acts 10.24 on the following day they entered Caesarea
14.20 on the next day he went on with Barnabas
25. 6 next day he took his seat on the tribunal

4. *on the following:* τῇ ἐπιούσῃ EPEIMI [B.3.b.2]
Acts 16.11 the following day to Neapolis
20.15 we came the following day opposite Chios
21.18 On the following day Paul went in

5. *another, different:* ἕτερος HETEROS [B.3.b.2]
Acts 20.15 the next day we touched at Samos
27. 3 The next day we put in at Sidon

6. *next:* ἑξῆς HEXĒS [B.3.b.2]
Lk [7.11 *Next day* he went to a city‡
Acts 21. 1 we came . . the next day to Rhodes
25.17 "on the next day took my seat
27.18 they began next day to throw the cargo

DAY, ON THE EIGHTH

1. *eight days old:* ὀκταήμερος OKTAĒMEROS*
Phil 3. 5 circumcised on the eighth day

DAY, ON THE SECOND

1. *on the second day:* δευτεραῖος (pl.) DEUTERAIOS*
Acts 28.13 on the second day we came to Puteoli

DAY, THIS

1. *today:* σήμερον SĒMERON
[a]B.3.b.2 [b]+ἡμέρα
Mt 6.11 "Give us this day our daily bread[m]
11.23 [a]"it would have remained until this day
27. 8 [a]called the Field of Blood to this day
28.15 [b]story . . spread among the Jews to this day
Lk 2.11 "to you is born this day in the city of David
22.34 "the cock will not crow this day, until
Acts 20.26 [b]"I testify . . this day that I am innocent
22. 3 "being zealous for God as you all are this day
24.21 " 'I am on trial before you this day
26.29 "all who hear me this day
Rom 11. 8 [b]"a spirit of stupor . . down to this very day
2 Cor 3.14 [b]for to this day, when they read
3.15 [a]to this day whenever Moses is read

DAYBREAK

1. *light of the sun, dawn:* αὐγή AUGĒ*
Acts 20.11 conversed . . until daybreak, and . . departed
2. *dawn, about daybreak:* ὄρθρος ORTHROS
Acts 5.21 they entered the temple at daybreak

DAYS, FOUR

1. *for four days:* τεταρταῖος TETARTAIOS [A.3.b.3]
Jn 11.39 "an odor, for he has been dead four days

DAYS, PASS ONE'S

1. *draw through, live:* διάγω DIAGŌ
Tit 3. 3 passing our days in malice and envy

DAYS, WRITE IN FORMER

1. *write before:* προγράφω PROGRAPHŌ
Rom 15. 4 whatever was written in former days

DAYSPRING

1. *rising, east:* ἀνατολή ANATOLĒ
Lk [1.78 *whereby the dayspring will visit*†

DAYTIME

1. *day, tribunal:* ἡμέρα HĒMERA
2 Pet 2.13 count it pleasure to revel in the daytime

DAZZLING

1. *lighten, gleam:* ἀστράπτω (part.) ASTRAPTŌ
Lk 24. 4 two men stood by them in dazzling apparel
2. *flash like lightning:* ἐξαστράπτω (part.) EXASTRAPTŌ*
Lk 9.29 his raiment became dazzling white

DEACON

1. *servant:* διάκονος DIAKONOS
Phil 1. 1 at Philippi, with the bishops[b] and deacons
1 Tim 3. 8 Deacons likewise must be serious
3.12 Let deacons be the husband of one wife

DEACON, SERVE AS

1. *do a service, minister:* διακονέω DIAKONEŌ
1 Tim 3.10 if . . blameless let them serve as deacons
3.13 those who serve well as deacons gain

DEACONESS

1. *servant:* διάκονος (fem.) DIAKONOS
Rom 16. 1 a deaconess of the church at Cenchreae

DEAD

1. *dead:* νεκρός NEKROS
Mt 8.22 "leave the dead to bury their own dead
10. 8 "Heal the sick, raise the dead
11. 5 "deaf hear, and the dead are raised up
14. 2 "he has been raised from the dead
17. 9 "the Son of man is raised from the dead
22.31 "as for the resurrection of the dead
22.32 "He is not God of the dead, but of the living
23.27 "within they are full of dead men's bones
27.64 "tell the people, 'He has risen from the dead
28. 4 trembled and became like dead men
28. 7 "he has risen from the dead
Mk 6.14 "John . . has been raised from the dead
9. 9 until the Son . . have risen from the dead
9.10 what the rising from the dead meant
12.25 "when they rise from the dead
12.26 "as for the dead being raised
12.27 "He is not God of the dead, but of the living
Lk 7.15 dead man sat up, and began to speak
7.22 "the deaf hear, the dead are raised up
9. 7 that John had been raised from the dead
9.60 "Leave the dead to bury their own dead; but as for you, go and proclaim
15.24 " 'this my son was dead, and is alive again
15.32 " 'for this your brother was dead, and is alive
16.30 " 'if some one goes to them from the dead
16.31 " 'if some one should rise from the dead
20.35 "attain to . . the resurrection from the dead
20.37 "that the dead are raised . . Moses showed
20.38 "he is not God of the dead, but of the living
24. 5 "Why . . seek the living among the dead?[u]
24.46 "on the third day rise from the dead
Jn 2.22 When . . he was raised from the dead
5.21 "For as the Father raises the dead
5.25 "the dead will hear the voice of the Son
12. 1 whom Jesus . . raised from the dead
12. 9 Lazarus, whom he . . raised from the dead
12.17 when he . . raised him from the dead
20. 9 scripture, that he must rise from the dead
21.14 after he was raised from the dead
Acts 3.15 "whom God raised from the dead
4. 2 proclaiming . . resurrection from the dead
4.10 "whom God raised from the dead
5.10 they found her dead, and . . buried her
10.41 "with him after he rose from the dead
10.42 "to be judge of the living and the dead
13.30 "But God raised him from the dead
13.34 "he raised him from the dead
17. 3 Christ to suffer and to rise from the dead
17.31 "assurance . . by raising him from the dead
17.32 heard of the resurrection of the dead
20. 9 he fell . . and was taken up dead
23. 6 "the hope and the resurrection of the dead
24.21 " 'With respect to . . resurrection of the dead
26. 8 "incredible . . that God raises the dead?
26.23 "by being the first to rise from the dead
28. 6 to swell up or suddenly fall down dead
Rom 1. 4 by his resurrection from the dead
4.17 "God . . who gives life to the dead
4.24 that raised from the dead Jesus our Lord
6. 4 as Christ was raised from the dead
6. 9 Christ being raised from the dead
6.11 you also must consider yourselves dead
7. 4 to him who has been raised from the dead
7. 8 Apart from the law sin lies dead
8.10 your bodies are dead because of sin
8.11 who raised Jesus from the dead
8.11 who raised Christ Jesus from the dead
8.34 Christ Jesus . . who was raised from the dead
10. 7 "(to bring Christ up from the dead
10. 9 believe . . God raised him from the dead
11.15 acceptance mean but life from the dead?
14. 9 Lord both of the dead and of the living

1 Cor 15.12 Christ is preached as raised from the dead
15.12 say . . there is no resurrection of the dead?
15.13 if there is no resurrection of the dead
15.15 if it is true that the dead are not raised
15.16 if the dead are not raised, then Christ has not
15.20 Christ has been raised from the dead
15.21 by a man has come . . resurrection of the dead
15.29 being baptized on behalf of the dead
15.29 If the dead are not raised at all, why?
15.32 If the dead are not raised, "Let us eat
15.35 one will ask, "How are the dead raised?
15.42 So is it with the resurrection of the dead
15.52 the dead will be raised imperishable
2 Cor 1. 9 rely . . on God who raises the dead
Gal 1. 1 the Father, who raised him from the dead
Eph 1.20 Christ when he raised him from the dead
2. 1 you were dead through the trespasses
2. 5 when we were dead through our trespasses
5.14 "Awake, O sleeper, and arise from the dead
Phil 3.11 may attain the resurrection from the dead
Col 1.18 the beginning, the first-born from the dead
2.12 God, who raised him from the dead
2.13 who were dead in trespasses
1 Th 1.10 his Son . . whom he raised from the dead
4.16 the dead in Christ will rise first
2 Tim 2. 8 Jesus Christ, risen from the dead
4. 1 who is to judge the living and the dead
Heb 6. 1 of repentance from dead works
6. 2 resurrection of the dead, and . . judgment
9.14 purify your[t] conscience from dead works
11.19 able to raise men even from the dead
11.35 Women received their d. by resurrection
13.20 brought again from the d. our Lord Jesus
Jas 2.17 So faith by itself . . is dead
2.26 as the body apart from the spirit is dead, so faith apart from works is dead
1 Pet 1. 3 resurrection of Jesus Christ from the dead
1.21 God, who raised him from the dead
4. 5 ready to judge the living and the dead
4. 6 gospel was preached even to the dead
Rev 1. 5 Jesus Christ . . the first-born of the dead
1.17 I fell at his feet as though dead
3. 1 " 'I know your works; . . you are dead
11.18 " 'the time for the dead to be judged
14.13 "Blessed are the dead who die in the Lord
16. 3 it became like the blood of a dead man
20. 5 rest of the dead did not come to life
20.12 I saw the dead, great and small
20.12 the dead were judged by what was written
20.13 the sea gave up the dead in it, Death and Hades gave up the dead in them

2. *die, finish:* τελευτάω (perf. part.) TELEUTAŌ
Jn 11.39 Martha, the sister of the dead man
3. *die:* θνήσκω (perf. part.) THNĒSKŌ
Jn 11.44 The dead man came out
CONTEXTUALLY
Mk 15.45 when he learned . . that he was dead
Jn 11.39 "for he has been dead four days

DEAD, AS GOOD AS
1. *make dead:* νεκρόω (perf. pass. part.) NEKROŌ
Rom 4.19 his own body, which was as good as dead
Heb 11.12 from one man, and him as good as dead

DEAD, BE
1. *die:* ἀποθνήσκω (aor.) APOTHNĒSKŌ
Mt 9.24 "the girl is not dead but sleeping
Mk 5.35 "daughter is dead. Why trouble the Teacher?
5.39 "The child is not dead but sleeping
9.26 most of them said, "He is dead
15.44 asked . . whether he was already dead[j]†‡
Lk 8.52 "for she is not dead but sleeping
8.53 they laughed . . knowing that she was dead
Jn 11.14 Jesus told them . . "Lazarus is dead
Rom 7. 6 now we are . . dead to that which held us
Jude .12 trees in late autumn, twice dead, uprooted
2. *die:* θνήσκω (perf.) THNĒSKŌ
Mt 2.20 "those who sought the child's life are dead
Mk 15.44 Pilate wondered if he were already dead
Lk 8.49 "Your daughter is dead
Jn 19.33 came . . and saw that he was already dead
Acts 14.19 dragged him . . supposing that he was dead
25.19 "dispute . . about one Jesus, who was dead
1 Tim 5. 6 she who is self-indulgent is dead

DEAD BODY
1. *fall, fallen body:* πτῶμα PTŌMA
Rev 11. 8 their dead bodies will lie in the street
11. 9 nations gaze at their dead bodies

DEAD, HALF
1. *half dead:* ἡμιθανής HĒMITHANĒS*
Lk 10.30 "robbers . . departed, leaving him half dead

DEAD, STRIKE
IDIOMATICALLY
a. Rev 2.23 " 'I will strike her children dead τὰ τέκνα αὐτῆς ἀποκτενῶ ἐν θανάτῳ [APOKTEINŌ]

DEADLY
1. *fatal:* θανάσιμος THANASIMOS
Mk 16.18 if they drink any deadly thing[k]‡
2. *death-bringing:* θανατηφόρος THANATĒPHOROS*
Jas 3. 8 the tongue . . full of deadly poison
3. *death:* θάνατος THANATOS [A.1.b.5]
2 Cor 1.10 he delivered us from so deadly a peril

DEAF
1. *blunt, deaf, mute:* κωφός KŌPHOS
Mt 11. 5 "the deaf hear, and the dead are raised up
Mk 7.32 brought to him a man who was deaf
7.37 "he even makes the deaf hear
9.25 "dumb and deaf spirit, . . come out
Lk 7.22 "the deaf hear, the dead are raised up

DEAL (*See also* TRULY, DEAL)
1. *make use of, act:* χράομαι CHRAOMAI
1 Cor 7.31 who deal . . as though they had no dealings
2. *do, make:* ποιέω (mid.) POIEŌ
Acts 1. 1 I have dealt with all that Jesus began
CONTEXTUALLY
2 Cor 13. 3 He is not weak in dealing with you
13. 4 but in dealing with you we shall live
Heb 9.10 but deal only with food and drink

DEAL CRAFTILY WITH
1. *outwit by sophisms:* κατασοφίζομαι KATASOPHIZOMAI*
Acts 7.19 "He dealt craftily with our race

DEAL GENTLY
1. *feel moderately:* μετριοπαθέω METRIOPATHEŌ*
Heb 5. 2 He can deal gently with the ignorant

DEAL WITH, NOT TO
1. *separately, apart from:* χωρίς CHŌRIS
Heb 9.28 not to deal with sin but to save

DEALER
1. *sell:* πωλέω (subst. part.) PŌLEŌ
Mt 25. 9 " 'go rather to the dealers and buy

DEALING WITH, IN
1. *into, to, for:* εἰς (+acc.) EIS
Lk **16.8**
2 Cor **13.3**, 4

DEALINGS WITH, HAVE
1. *make full use of:* καταχράομαι KATACHRAOMAI
1 Cor 7.31 as though they had no dealings with it
2. *make use of, have dealings with:* συγχράομαι SYGCHRAOMAI*
Jn 4. 9 Jews have no dealings with Samaritans

DEAR
1. *honored, valuable:* ἔντιμος ENTIMOS
Lk 7. 2 a slave who was dear[x] to him†

DEAR, VERY
1. *beloved:* ἀγαπητός AGAPĒTOS
1 Th 2. 8 because you had become very dear to us

DEATH
1. *destruction, killing:* ἀναίρεσις ANAIRESIS*
Acts 8. 1 Saul was consenting to his death
2. *die:* ἀποθνήσκω APOTHNĒSKŌ [B.2.d.1]
Jn 4.47 he was at the point of death

Rev 3. 2 " 'what remains and is on the point of death
3. *underworld:* ᾅδης HADĒS
Mt 16.18 "death[u] shall not prevail against it
4. *dead:* νεκρός (subst. pl.) NEKROS [C.2]
Rom 6.13 men who have been brought from d. to life
Heb 9.17 For a will[u] takes effect only at death
5. *death:* νέκρωσις NEKRŌSIS
2 Cor 4.10 carrying in the body the death of Jesus
6. *die, finish:* τελευτάω (inf.) TELEUTAŌ
Lk 7. 2 who was sick and at the point of death
7. *completion, end, death:* τελευτή TELEUTĒ*
Mt 2.15 remained there until the death of Herod
8. *death:* θάνατος THANATOS
Mt 4.16 "who sat in the region and shadow of death
10.21 "Brother will deliver up brother to death
16.28 "not taste death before they see the Son
20.18 "they will condemn him to death
26.38 "My soul is very sorrowful, even to death
26.66 They answered, "He deserves death
Mk 9. 1 "some . . here who will not taste death
10.33 "they will condemn him to death
13.12 "brother will deliver up brother to death
14.34 "My soul is very sorrowful, even to death
14.64 all condemned him as deserving death
Lk 1.79 "those who sit in . . the shadow of death
2.26 not see death before he had seen the . . Christ
9.27 "not taste d. before they see the kingdom
22.33 "ready to go with you to prison and to death
23.15 "nothing deserving death has been done
23.22 "I have found . . no crime deserving death
24.20 "to be condemned to death, and crucified
Jn 5.24 "who . . believes . . has passed from death
8.51 "keeps my word, he will never see death
8.52 " 'keeps my word, he will never taste death
11. 4 "This illness is not unto death
11.13 Jesus had spoken of his death
12.33 to show by what death he was to die
18.32 to show by what death he was to die
21.19 (to show by what death he was to glorify
Acts 2.24 "having loosed the pangs of death
13.28 "charge him with nothing deserving death
22. 4 "I persecuted this Way to the death
23.29 "charged with nothing deserving death
25.11 "I do not seek to escape death
25.25 "he had done nothing deserving death
26.31 "doing nothing to deserve death
28.18 "there was no reason for the death penalty
Rom 5.10 reconciled to God by the death of his Son
5.12 as sin came . . through one man and death through sin, and so death spread to all
5.14 Yet death reigned from Adam to Moses
5.17 death reigned through that one man
5.21 as sin reigned in death, grace also might
6. 3 all of us . . were baptized into his death
6. 4 We were buried . . by baptism into death
6. 5 if we have been united with him in a death
6. 9 death no longer has dominion over him
6.16 slaves . . of sin, which leads to death
6.21 The end of those things is death
6.23 For the wages of sin is death
7. 5 sinful passions . . were at work . . for death
7.10 the very commandment . . proved to be death
7.13 Did that which is good . . bring death to me? By no means! It was sin, working death
7.24 Who will deliver me from this body of death?
8. 2 free from the law of sin and death
8. 6 To set the mind on the flesh is death
8.38 I am sure that neither death, nor life
1 Cor 3.22 world or life or death . ., all are yours
11.26 proclaim the Lord's death until he comes
15.21 For as by a man came death
15.26 last enemy to be destroyed is death
15.54 "Death is swallowed up in victory
15.55 "O death, where is thy victory? O death, where is thy sting?
15.56 The sting of death is sin
2 Cor 1. 9 felt . . we had received the sentence of death
2.16 to one a fragrance from death to death, to the other . . from life to life
3. 7 dispensation of death, carved . . on stone
4.11 we are always being given up to death
4.12 So death is at work in us, but life in you
7.10 but worldly grief produces death
11.23 countless beatings, and often near death
Phil 1.20 honored . . whether by life or by death
2. 8 he humbled himself and became obedient unto death, even death on a cross
2.27 Indeed he was ill, near to death
3.10 becoming like him in his death
Col 1.22 now reconciled . . all flesh by his death
2 Tim 1.10 Savior Christ Jesus, who abolished death
Heb 2. 9 crowned . . because of the suffering of death, so . . he might taste death for every one
2.14 that through death he might destroy him who has the power of death, . . the devil
2.15 deliver all those who through fear of death
5. 7 who was able to save him from death
7.23 because they were prevented by death
9.15 a death has occurred which redeems
9.16 the death of the one . . must be established
11. 5 taken up so that he should not see death
Jas 1.15 sin when . . full-grown brings forth death
5.20 will save his soul from death
1 Jn 3.14 we have passed out of death into life
3.14 He who does not love abides in death
Rev 1.18 "I have the keys of Death and Hades
2.10 " 'Be faithful unto death
2.11 " 'shall not be hurt by the second death
6. 8 its rider's name was Death
9. 6 men will seek death and will not find it; they will long to die, and death will fly
12.11 "they loved not their lives even unto death
20. 6 Over such the second death has no power
20.13 Death and Hades gave up the dead in them
20.14 Then Death and Hades were thrown
20.14 This is the second death, the lake of fire
21. 4 "and death shall be no more
21. 8 "the lake that burns . . is the second death

IDIOMATICALLY
a. Mk 5.23 "My little daughter is at the point of death
τὸ θυγάτριόν μου ἐσχάτως ἔχει [ESCHATŌS*]

CONTEXTUALLY
Rom 6.10 The death he died he died to sin, once

DEATH, HAVE S. PUT TO
DEATH, PUT TO

1. *take up, kill:* ἀναιρέω ANAIREŌ
Lk 22. 2 scribes were seeking how to put him to death
23.32 led away to be put to death with him
Acts 10.39 "put him to death by hanging him on a tree
26.10 "when they were put to death
2. *lead away:* ἀπάγω APAGŌ
Acts 12.19 ordered that they should be put to death
3. *kill:* ἀποκτείνω APOKTEINŌ
Mt 14. 5 though he wanted to put him to death
24. 9 "they will . . put you to death
Jn 11.53 they took counsel how to put him to death
12.10 planned to put Lazarus also to death
18.31 "not lawful for us to put any man to death
4. *destroy utterly:* ἀπόλλυμι APOLLYMI
Mt 21.41 "He will put those . . to a miserable death
5. *make dead:* νεκρόω NEKROŌ
Col 3. 5 Put to death . . what is earthly in you
6. *give up, allow:* παραδίδωμι PARADIDŌMI
Rom 4.25 who was put to death for our trespasses
7. *put to death:* θανατόω THANATOŌ
Mt 10.21 "children will . . have them put to death
26.59 that they might put him to death
27. 1 counsel against Jesus to put him to death
Mk 13.12 "children will . . have them put to death
14.55 testimony . . to put him to death
Lk 21.16 "some of you they will put to death
Rom 8.13 if by the Spirit you put to death the deeds
1 Pet 3.18 being put to death in the flesh

DEATH, SENTENCED TO
1. *condemned to death:* ἐπιθανάτιος EPITHANATIOS*
1 Cor 4. 9 apostles . . like men sentenced to death

DEBATE
1. *seeking, controversy:* ζήτησις ZĒTĒSIS
Acts 15. 2 no small dissension and debate
15. 7 after . . much debate, Peter rose

DEBATER
1. *disputant:* συζητητής SYZĒTĒTĒS*
1 Cor 1.20 Where is the debater of this age?

DEBAUCHERY
1. *profligacy, dissipation:* ἀσωτία ASŌTIA
Eph 5.18 drunk with wine, for that is debauchery
2. *marriage bed:* κοίτη (pl.) KOITĒ [C.1]
Rom 13.13 conduct ourselves becomingly . . not in d.

DEBT
1. *loan:* δάνειον DANEION*
Mt 18.27 "the lord . . forgave him the debt
2. *debt, one's due:* ὀφειλή OPHEILĒ
Mt 18.32 " 'wicked servant! I forgave you . . that debt
3. *debt:* ὀφείλημα OPHEILĒMA
Mt 6.12 "And forgive us our debts
4. *ought, owe:* ὀφείλω (subst. pass. part. neut.) OPHEILŌ
Mt 18.30 "in prison till he should pay the debt
18.34 "to the jailers,[h] till he should pay all his debt

DEBT, IN
1. *debtor:* ὀφειλέτης (pred.) OPHEILETĒS
Rom 15.27 indeed they are in debt to them

DEBTOR
1. *debtor:* χρεοφειλέτης CHREOPHEILETĒS*
Lk 7.41 "A certain creditor had two debtors
16. 5 "summoning his master's debtors
2. *debtor:* ὀφειλέτης OPHEILETĒS
Mt 6.12 "As we also have forgiven our debtors
Rom 8.12 brethren, we are debtors, not to the flesh

DECAPOLIS: Δεκάπολις di'kapələs I,D-3
Mt 4.25 crowds followed . . from Galilee and the D.
Mk 5.20 he . . began to proclaim in the D.
7.31 he . . went . . through the region of the D.

DECAY
1. *destruction:* φθορά PHTHORA
Rom 8.21 creation itself will be set free from . . decay

DECEIT
1. *trick, fraud, pleasure:* ἀπάτη APATĒ
Col 2. 8 makes a prey of you by . . empty deceit
2. *cunning:* δόλος DOLOS
Mk 7.22 "wickedness, deceit, licentiousness
Acts 13.10 "You son of the devil, . . full of all deceit
Rom 1.29 Full of envy, murder, strife, deceit

DECEITFUL
1. *trick, fraud, pleasure:* ἀπάτη (gen.) APATĒ
Eph 4.22 corrupt through deceitful lusts
2. *treacherous:* δόλιος DOLIOS*
2 Cor 11.13 such men are . . deceitful workmen
3. *wandering, deceit:* πλάνη (gen.) PLANĒ
Eph 4.14 by their craftiness in deceitful wiles
4. *leading astray:* πλάνος PLANOS
1 Tim 4. 1 giving heed to deceitful spirits

DECEITFULNESS
1. *trick, fraud, pleasure:* ἀπάτη APATĒ
Heb 3.13 hardened by the deceitfulness of sin

DECEIVE
1. *cheat:* ἀπατάω APATAŌ*
Eph 5. 6 Let no one deceive you with . . words
1 Tim 2.14 Adam was not deceived, but the woman
Jas 1.26 If any one . . deceives his heart
2. *deal treacherously with:* δολιόω DOLIOŌ*
Rom 3.13 "they use their tongues to deceive
3. *deceive:* ἐξαπατάω EXAPATAŌ*
Rom 7.11 sin . . deceived me and by it killed me
16.18 by fair and flattering words they deceive
1 Cor 3.18 Let no one deceive himself
2 Cor 11. 3 as the serpent deceived Eve
2 Th 2. 3 Let no one deceive you in any way
1 Tim 2.14 but the woman was deceived
4. *cheat, defraud:* παραλογίζομαι PARALOGIZOMAI
Jas 1.22 not hearers only, deceiving yourselves
5. *deceive:* φρεναπατάω PHRENAPATAŌ*
Gal 6. 3 when he is nothing, he deceives himself
6. *cause to wander:* πλανάω PLANAŌ
1 Cor 6. 9 Do not be deceived
15.33 Do not be deceived
Gal 6. 7 Do not be deceived; God is not mocked
2 Tim 3.13 from bad to worse, deceivers and deceived
Jas 1.16 Do not be deceived, my beloved brethren
1 Jn 1. 8 If we say we have no sin, we d. ourselves
2.26 I write . . about those who would deceive you
3. 7 let no one deceive you
Rev 13.14 it deceives those who dwell on earth
18.23 "all nations were deceived by thy sorcery
19.20 worked the signs by which he deceived
20. 3 should deceive the nations no more
20. 8 will come out to deceive the nations
20.10 the devil who had deceived them

DECEIVER
1. *soul deceiver:* φρεναπάτης PHRENAPATĒS*
Tit 1.10 empty talkers and deceivers
2. *cause to wander:* πλανάω (subst. part.) PLANAŌ
2 Tim 3.13 from bad to worse, deceivers and deceived
Rev 12. 9 Satan, the deceiver of the whole world
3. *leading astray:* πλάνος (subst.) PLANOS
2 Jn . 7 deceivers have gone out into the world
. 7 such a one is the deceiver and the antichrist

DECENTLY
1. *with grace and dignity:* εὐσχημόνως EUSCHĒMONŌS
1 Cor 14.40 all things should be done decently

DECEPTION
1. *trick, fraud, pleasure:* ἀπάτη APATĒ
2 Th 2.10 deception for those who are to perish

DECIDE
1. *discern, decide:* διαγινώσκω DIAGINŌSKŌ
Acts 24.22 "When Lysias . . comes . . I will decide
2. *differentiate, decide:* διακρίνω DIAKRINŌ
1 Cor 6. 5 no man . . wise enough to decide
3. *know, understand:* γινώσκω GINŌSKŌ
Lk 16. 4 " 'I have decided what to do
4. *judge, decide:* κρίνω KRINŌ
Acts 3.13 "when he had decided to release him
20.16 Paul had decided to sail past Ephesus
25.25 "as he . . appealed . . I decided to send him
27. 1 when it was decided that we should sail
Rom 14.13 decide never to put a stumbling block
1 Cor 2. 2 I decided to know nothing among you
Tit 3.12 I have decided to spend the winter there
5. *will, wish:* θέλω THELŌ
Jn 1.43 next day Jesus decided to go to Galilee
CONTEXTUALLY
Mk 15.24 to decide what each should take

DECISION
1. *distinguishing, deciding:* διάγνωσις DIAGNŌSIS*
Acts 25.21 "in custody for the decision of the emperor
2. *decree, decision:* δόγμα DOGMA
Acts 16. 4 delivered . . decisions . . reached
IDIOMATICALLY
a. Mk 14.64 "What is your decision? τί ὑμῖν φαίνεται; [PHAINŌ]

DECLARE
1. *report:* ἀναγγέλλω ANAGGELLŌ
Jn 16.13 "the Spirit of truth . . will declare to you
16.14 "he will take what is mine and declare it
16.15 "he will take what is mine and declare it
Acts 14.27 gathered the church together and declared
15. 4 they declared all that God had done
20.20 "I did not shrink from declaring to you
20.27 "I did not shrink from declaring to you
2. *bring tidings:* ἀπαγγέλλω APAGGELLŌ
Lk 8.47 falling down before him ⟨she⟩ declared
Acts 26.20 "declared first to those at Damascus

1 Cor 14.25 he will worship God and declare
3. *reply:* ἀποκρίνομαι APOKRINOMAI
Acts 10.46 Peter declared, ⟨Can any one forbid?⟩
4. *set out in detail:* διηγέομαι DIĒGEOMAI
Lk 8.39 "Return to your home, and declare
Acts 9.27 Barnabas . . declared . . he had seen the Lord
5. *say, speak:* εἶπον EIPON
Mt 11.25 Jesus declared, "I thank thee, Father
26.33 Peter declared . . "Though they all fall
Mk 12.36 "David . . declared, 'The Lord said
6. *tell in detail:* ἐκδιηγέομαι EKDIĒGEOMAI
Acts 13.41 " 'you will never believe, if one declares it
7. *bear witness:* ἐπιμαρτυρέω EPIMARTYREŌ*
1 Pet 5.12 declaring that this is the true grace of God
8. *make known, proclaim:* ἐξαγγέλλω EXAGGELLŌ
1 Pet 2. 9 that you may declare the wonderful deeds
9. *confess, acknowledge:* ὁμολογέω HOMOLOGEŌ
Mt 7.23 "then will I declare to them, 'I never knew
10. *speak, talk:* λαλέω LALEŌ
Jn 8.26 "I declare to the world what I have heard
Acts 11.14 " 'he will declare to you a message
Col 4. 3 to declare the mystery of Christ
1 Th 2. 2 to declare to you the gospel of God
Tit 2.15 Declare these things; exhort and reprove
Heb 2. 2 if the message declared by angels was valid
2. 3 It was declared at first by the Lord
9.19 every commandment . . declared by Moses
11. *say, speak:* λέγω LEGŌ
Acts 2.17 " 'in the last days it shall be, God declares
1 Th 4.15 this we declare to you by the word

DECLARE BOLDLY
1. *speak freely:* παρρησιάζομαι PARRĒSIAZOMAI
Eph 6.20 that I may declare it boldly, as I ought

DECLARE CLEAN
1. *cleanse:* καθαρίζω KATHARIZŌ
Mk 7.19 (Thus he declared all foods clean

DECLINE
1. *nod assent:* ἐπινεύω (neg.) EPINEUŌ*
Acts 18.20 When they asked him . . he declined

DECORATION
1. *putting on:* περίθεσις PERITHESIS*
1 Pet 3. 3 Let not yours be . . decoration of gold

DECREASE
1. *make less:* ἐλαττόω (pass.) ELATTOŌ
Jn 3.30 "He must increase, but I must decrease[i]

DECREE
1. *ordinance, justification:* δικαίωμα DIKAIŌMA
Rom 1.32 Though they know God's decree
2. *decree, decision:* δόγμα DOGMA
Lk 2. 1 a decree went out from Caesar Augustus
Acts 17. 7 "they are all acting against the decrees
3. *determine beforehand:* προορίζω PROORIZŌ
1 Cor 2. 7 which God decreed before the ages

DEDICATION, FEAST OF THE
1. *feast of consecration:* ἐγκαίνια EGKAINIA*
Jn 10.22 It was the feast of the Dedication

DEED (*See also* RIGHTEOUS DEED; WONDERFUL DEEDS)
1. *work, deed:* ἔργον ERGON
Mt 11. 2 John heard . . about the deeds of the Christ
11.19 "Yet wisdom is justified by her deeds[e]‡
23. 5 "They do all their deeds to be seen
Lk 11.48 "you . . consent to the deeds of your fathers
24.19 "a prophet mighty in deed and word
Jn 3.19 loved darkness . . because . . deeds were evil
3.20 lest his deeds should be exposed
3.21 that his deeds have been wrought in God
7.21 "I did one deed, and you all marvel
Acts 7.22 "he was mighty in his words and deeds
13.41 " 'I do a deed in your days, a deed you will never believe, if one declares it to you
26.20 "perform deeds worthy of their repentance
Rom 15.18 to win obedience . . by word and deed
2 Cor 11.15 Their end will correspond to their deeds
Col 1.21 hostile in mind, doing evil deeds
3.17 whatever you do, in word or deed
1 Tim 2.10 by good deeds, as befits women who profess
5.10 well attested for her good deeds
5.25 also good deeds are conspicuous
6.18 rich in good deeds, liberal and generous
2 Tim 4.14 the Lord will requite him for his deeds
Tit 1.16 they deny him by their deeds; they are . . disobedient, unfit for any good deed
2. 7 Show yourself . . a model of good deeds
2.14 a people . . who are zealous for good deeds
3. 5 saved us, not because of deeds done by us
3. 8 apply themselves to good deeds[d]
3.14 to apply themselves to good deeds[d]†
1 Pet 1.17 who judges each . . according to his deeds
2.12 they may see your good deeds
2 Pet 2. 8 (vexed . . with their lawless deeds
1 Jn 3.12 Because his own deeds were evil
3.18 let us . . love . . in deed and in truth
Jude .15 "convict . . the ungodly of all their deeds
Rev 14.13 "for their deeds follow them!
15. 3 "Great and wonderful are thy deeds!
16.11 cursed . . and did not repent of their deeds
18. 6 "repay her double for her deeds
2. *thing, deed:* πρᾶγμα PRAGMA
Acts 5. 4 "contrived this deed in your heart?
3. *do, practice:* πράσσω PRASSŌ [B.2.a.1]
Lk 23.41 "receiving the due reward of our deeds
4. *practice, act:* πρᾶξις PRAXIS
Lk 23.51 not consented to their purpose and deed
Rom 8.13 if . . you put to death the deeds of the body

DEED, GOOD
1. *good deed:* εὐεργεσία EUERGESIA
Acts 4. 9 "concerning a good deed done to a cripple

DEEM
CONTEXTUALLY
2 Th 1. 6 since indeed God deems it just to repay

DEEP (*See also* WORDS, TOO DEEP FOR)
1. *depth:* βάθος BATHOS
Lk 5. 4 "Put out into the deep
2. *deepen, go down deep:* βαθύνω BATHYNŌ* [A.6.c.2]
Lk 6.48 "who dug deep, and laid the foundation
3. *deep:* βαθύς BATHYS
Jn 4.11 "the well is deep
Acts 20. 9 He sank into a deep sleep as Paul talked
Rev 2.24 " 'what some call the deep things of Satan

DEEPLY (*See* MOVED, DEEPLY; SIGH DEEPLY)

DEFAME
1. *slander, blaspheme:* βλασφημέω BLASPHĒMEŌ
1 Tim 6. 1 that the name of God . . not be defamed

DEFEAT
1. *defeat:* ἥττημα HĒTTĒMA
1 Cor 6. 7 To have lawsuits . . is defeat for you

DEFEATED, BE
1. *be strong, prevail:* ἰσχύω (neg.) ISCHYŌ
Rev 12. 8 but they were defeated

DEFECTIVE
1. *leave, be incomplete:* λείπω (part.) LEIPŌ
Tit 1. 5 you might amend what was defective

DEFEND
1. *guard oneself against:* ἀμύνομαι AMYNOMAI*
Acts 7.24 "he defended the oppressed man

DEFEND ONESELF
1. *defend oneself, speak in defense:* ἀπολογέομαι APOLOGEOMAI
2 Cor 12.19 that we have been defending ourselves

DEFENSE
1. *speech in defense:* ἀπολογία APOLOGIA
Acts 22. 1 "hear the defense which I now make
25.16 "had opportunity to make his defense
1 Cor 9. 3 my defense to those who would examine me
Phil 1. 7 defense and confirmation of the gospel
1.16 I am put here for the defense of the gospel
2 Tim 4.16 At my first defense . . all deserted me
1 Pet 3.15 Always be prepared to make a defense

DEFENSE, MAKE A
DEFENSE, MAKE ONE'S
DEFENSE, SAY IN ONE'S
1. *defend oneself, speak in defense:* ἀπολογέομαι APOLOGEOMAI
Acts 19.33 Alexander motioned .. wishing to make a d.
24.10 "I cheerfully make my defense
25. 8 Paul said in his defense
26. 1 Then Paul .. made his defense
26. 2 "I am to make my defense today
26.24 as he thus made his defense

DEFILE
1. *make common, defile:* κοινόω KOINOŌ
Mt 15.11 "not what goes into the mouth defiles a man, but what comes out .. this defiles a man
15.18 "what comes out of the mouth .. defiles
15.20 "These are what defile a man; but to eat with unwashed hands does not defile
Mk 7.15 "nothing outside a man .. can defile him; but the things which come out .. defile him[a]
7.18 "whatever goes .. from outside cannot defile
7.20 "What comes out of a man is what defiles
7.23 "come from within, and they defile a man
Acts 21.28 "he has defiled this holy place
Heb 9.13 sprinkling of defiled persons with the blood
2. *stain, defile:* μιαίνω MIAINŌ
Jn 18.28 so that they might not be defiled
Heb 12.15 by it the many become defiled
Jude . 8 these men in their dreamings defile the flesh
3. *stain, defile:* μολύνω MOLYNŌ
1 Cor 8. 7 their conscience, being weak, is defiled
Rev 14. 4 have not defiled themselves with women

DEFILED
1. *common, profane:* κοινός KOINOS
Mk 7. 2 some of his disciples ate with hands defiled
7. 5 "your disciples .. eat with hands defiled

DEFILEMENT
1. *stain, pollution:* μίασμα MIASMA*
2 Pet 2.20 escaped the defilements of the world
2. *pollution, defilement:* μολυσμός MOLYSMOS*
2 Cor 7. 1 let us cleanse ourselves from every defilement

DEFILING
1. *pollution:* μιασμός (gen.) MIASMOS*
2 Pet 2.10 who indulge in the lust of defiling passion

DEFINITE
1. *certain, safe:* ἀσφαλής ASPHALĒS
Acts 25.26 "nothing definite to write to my lord
2. *determine, appoint:* ὁρίζω (pass. part.) HORIZŌ
Acts 2.23 "delivered up according to the definite plan

DEFRAUD
1. *defraud:* ἀποστερέω APOSTEREŌ
Mk 10.19 " 'Do not bear false witness, Do not defraud
1 Cor 6. 7 Why not rather be defrauded?
6. 8 But you yourselves wrong and defraud
2. *defraud:* πλεονεκτέω PLEONEKTEŌ
1 Th [4. 6 that no man .. *defraud .. in business*†
3. *oppress, defraud:* συκοφαντέω SYKOPHANTEŌ
Lk 19. 8 "if I have defrauded any one of anything

DEGRADING
1. *disgrace, dishonor:* ἀτιμία ATIMIA [A.1.b.4]
1 Cor 11.14 for a man to wear long hair is degrading

DEGREE
CONTEXTUALLY
2 Cor 3.18 changed .. from one d. of glory to another

DEGREE, OF LOW
1. *low, poor, humble:* ταπεινός TAPEINOS
Lk 1.52 "he has .. exalted those of low degree

DEITY
1. *divine:* θεῖος (subst. neut.) THEIOS
Acts 17.29 "not to think that the Deity is like gold
2. *divine nature:* θειότης THEIOTĒS*
Rom 1.20 namely, his eternal power and deity
3. *divinity:* θεότης THEOTĒS*
Col 2. 9 in him the whole fulness of deity dwells

DEJECTION
1. *dejection:* κατήφεια KATĒPHEIA*
Jas 4. 9 Let .. your joy ⟨be turned⟩ to dejection

DELAY
1. *delay:* ἀναβολή ANABOLĒ*
Acts 25.17 "I made no delay, but .. took my seat
2. *spend time, linger:* χρονίζω (art. inf.) CHRONIZŌ
Lk 1.21 wondered at his delay in the temple
3. *time, period:* χρόνος CHRONOS
Rev 10. 6 that there should be no more delay

DELAY LONG
1. *be patient, persevere:* μακροθυμέω MAKROTHYMEŌ
Lk 18. 7 "Will he delay long over them?

DELAY, WITHOUT
1. *shrink from, hesitate:* ὀκνέω (neg. part.) OKNEŌ*
Acts 9.38 "Please come to us without delay

DELAYED, BE
1. *delay, loiter:* βραδύνω BRADYNŌ
1 Tim 3.15 if I am delayed, you may know
2. *spend time, linger:* χρονίζω CHRONIZŌ
Mt 24.48 " 'My master is delayed
25. 5 "the bridegroom was delayed
Lk 12.45 " 'My master is delayed in coming

DELIBERATELY
1. *willingly, deliberately:* ἑκουσίως HEKOUSIŌS
Heb 10.26 For if we sin deliberately after .. the truth
2 *will, wish:* θέλω (part.) THELŌ
2 Pet 3. 5 They deliberately ignore this fact

DELIGHT
1. *trick, fraud, pleasure:* ἀπάτη APATĒ
Mt 13.22 "and the delight in riches choke the word
Mk 4.19 "cares of the world, and the delight in riches
2. *rejoice together:* συνήδομαι SYNĒDOMAI*
Rom 7.22 For I delight in the law of God

DELIVER
1. *give up, deliver:* ἀναδίδωμι ANADIDŌMI*
Acts 23.33 delivered the letter to the governor
2. *set free:* ἀπαλλάσσω APALLASSŌ
Heb 2.15 deliver all those who through fear of death
3. *do a service, minister:* διακονέω DIAKONEŌ
2 Cor 3. 3 a letter from Christ delivered by us
4. *give freely, deliver:* ἐπιδίδωμι EPIDIDŌMI
Acts 15.30 they delivered the letter
5. *take out:* ἐξαιρέω (mid.) EXAIREŌ
Acts 7.34 " 'I have come down to deliver them
26.17 " 'delivering you from the people
Gal 1. 4 to deliver us from the present evil age
6. *give up, allow:* παραδίδωμι PARADIDŌMI
Mt 11.27 "All things have been delivered to me
17.22 "The Son of man is to be delivered
18.34 "And in anger his lord delivered him
20.18 "the Son of man will be delivered
20.19 "deliver him to the Gentiles to be mocked
25.20 " 'Master, you delivered to me five talents
25.22 " 'Master, you delivered to me two talents
26.15 "What will you give me if I deliver him?
27. 2 delivered him to Pilate the governor
27.26 scourged Jesus, delivered him to be crucified
Mk 9.31 "The Son of man will be delivered
10.33 "the Son of man will be delivered
10.33 "they will .. deliver him to the Gentiles
15. 1 led him away and delivered him to Pilate
15.15 he delivered him to be crucified
Lk 1. 2 just as they were delivered to us by those
4. 6 "it has been delivered to me, and I give it
9.44 "for the Son of man is to be delivered
10.22 "All things have been delivered to me
18.32 "For he will be delivered to the Gentiles
24. 7 "the Son of man must be delivered
Jn 19.11 "he who delivered me .. has the greater sin
Acts 6.14 "the customs which Moses delivered to us
12. 4 delivered him to four squads of soldiers
16. 4 they delivered to them .. the decisions
21.11 " 'deliver him into the hands of the Gentiles

Acts 22. 4 delivering to prison both men and women
27. 1 they delivered Paul and .. other prisoners
28.17 "I was delivered prisoner from Jerusalem
1 Cor 5. 5 you are to deliver this man to Satan
11. 2 even as I have delivered them to you
11.23 I received .. what I also delivered to you
13. 3 if I deliver my body to be burned[v]
15. 3 I delivered to you as of first importance
15.24 when he delivers the kingdom to God
1 Tim 1.20 whom I have delivered to Satan
2 Pet 2.21 the holy commandment delivered to them
Jude . 3 the faith which was once for all delivered
7. *save, rescue:* ῥύομαι RHYOMAI
Mt 6.13 "But deliver us from evil[n]
27.43 "let God deliver him now, if he desires him
Lk 1.74 "we, being delivered from .. our enemies
Rom 7.24 Who will d. me from this body of death?
15.31 that I .. be delivered from the unbelievers
2 Cor 1.10 he delivered us from so deadly a peril, and he will deliver us; on him we have set our hope that he will deliver us again
Col 1.13 delivered us from the dominion of darkness
1 Th 1.10 Jesus who delivers us from the wrath
2 Th 3. 2 delivered from wicked and evil men
8. *close with a seal, certify:* σφραγίζω (mid.) SPHRAGIZŌ [A.6.a.5]
Rom 15.28 have delivered .. what has been raised[x]†

DELIVER UP

1. *give up, allow:* παραδίδωμι PARADIDŌMI
Mt 10.17 "for they will deliver you up to councils
10.19 "When they deliver you up
10.21 "Brother will deliver up brother to death
24. 9 "Then they will deliver you up to tribulation
26. 2 "the Son of man will be delivered up
27.18 out of envy that they had delivered him up
Mk 13. 9 "they will deliver you up to councils
13.11 "bring you to trial and deliver you up
13.12 "brother will deliver up brother to death
15.10 the chief priests had delivered him up
Lk 20.20 so as to deliver him up to .. the governor
21.12 "delivering you up to the synagogues
21.16 "delivered up even by parents
23.25 Jesus he delivered up to their will
24.20 "delivered him up to be condemned
Acts 3.13 "Jesus, whom you delivered up and denied

DELIVERANCE

1. *salvation, preservation:* σωτηρία SŌTĒRIA
Acts 7.25 "giving them deliverance by his hand
Phil 1.19 this will turn out for my deliverance

DELIVERED

1. *command:* διαταγή DIATAGĒ [B.1.a.2]
Acts 7.53 "who received the law as d. by angels

DELIVERED, BE

1. *bear, bring forth:* τίκτω TIKTŌ
Lk 1.57 time came for Elizabeth to be delivered
2. 6 the time came for her to be delivered

DELIVERED OF, BE

1. *bear, beget:* γεννάω GENNAŌ
Jn 16.21 "when she is delivered of the child

DELIVERED UP

1. *given up:* ἔκδοτος EKDOTOS*
Acts 2.23 "delivered up according to the definite plan

DELIVERER

1. *redeemer:* λυτρωτής LYTRŌTĒS*
Acts 7.35 "God sent as both ruler and deliverer
2. *save, rescue:* ῥύομαι (subst. part.) RHYOMAI
Rom 11.26 "The Deliverer will come from Zion

DELIVERY

1. *bear, bring forth:* τίκτω (inf.) TIKTŌ
Rev 12. 2 she cried out .. in anguish for delivery

DELUDE

1. *cheat, defraud:* παραλογίζομαι PARALOGIZOMAI
Col 2. 4 that no one may delude you

DELUGE

1. *inundate, flood:* κατακλύζω KATAKLYZŌ*
2 Pet 3. 6 the world that then existed was deluged

DELUSION

1. *wandering, deceit:* πλάνη PLANĒ
2 Th 2.11 God sends upon them a strong delusion

DEMAND

1. *request:* αἴτημα AITĒMA
Lk 23.24 that their demand should be granted
2. *ask, request:* αἰτέω (act. or mid.) AITEŌ
Lk 12.48 "of him .. they will demand the more
23.23 demanding .. that he should be crucified
1 Cor 1.22 Jews demand signs and Greeks seek wisdom

DEMAND, LEGAL

1. *decree, decision:* δόγμα DOGMA
Col 2.14 canceled the bond .. with its legal demands

DEMAND TO HAVE

1. *ask for s. from:* ἐξαιτέω (mid.) EXAITEŌ*
Lk 22.31 "Satan demanded to have you[k]

DEMANDS

IDIOMATICALLY
a. 1 Th 2.6(7) though we might have made demands
δυνάμενοι ἐν βάρει εἶναι [BAROS]

DEMAS: Δημᾶς 'dēməs
Col 4.14 Luke .. and Demas greet you
2 Tim 4.10 Demas, in love with this present world
Phm .24 Demas, and Luke, my fellow workers

DEMETRIUS: Δημήτριος də'mētrēəs
[a]the silversmith [b]another
Acts 19.24 [a]a man named Demetrius, a silversmith
19.38 [a]"D. and the craftsmen .. have a complaint
3 Jn .12 [b]Demetrius has testimony from every one

DEMOLISH

1. *dig down, destroy utterly:* κατασκάπτω KATASKAPTŌ*
Rom 11. 3 "they have demolished thy altars

DEMON

1. *god, evil spirit:* δαίμων DAIMŌN*
Mt 8.31 demons begged him, "If you cast us out
2. *demon, divine power:* δαιμόνιον DAIMONION
Mt 7.22 " 'did we not .. cast out demons?
9.33 when the demon had been cast out
9.34 Pharisees said, "He casts out demons by the prince of demons[a]‡
10. 8 "cleanse lepers, cast out demons
11.18 "they say, 'He has a demon
12.24 "by Beelzebul, the prince of demons, that this man casts out demons
12.27 "if I cast out demons by Beelzebul?
12.28 "by the Spirit of God that I cast out demons
17.18 the demon came out of him
Mk 1.34 he .. cast out many demons; and he would not permit the demons to speak
1.39 he went .. casting out demons
3.15 have authority to cast out demons
3.22 "by Beelzebul .. by the prince of demons he casts out the demons
6.13 they cast out many demons
7.26 she begged him to cast the demon out
7.29 "the demon has left your daughter
7.30 found the child .. and the demon gone
9.38 "we saw a man casting out demons
16. 9 M. M., from whom he .. cast out .. demons[k]‡
16.17 "in my name they will cast out demons[k]‡
Lk 4.32 who had the spirit of an unclean demon
4.35 when the demon had thrown him down
4.41 demons also came out of many
7.33 "you say, 'He has a demon
8. 2 Mary .. from whom seven demons had gone
8.27 a man from the city who had demons
8.29 (driven by the demon into the desert
8.30 for many demons had entered him
8.33 Then the demons came out of the man
8.35 the man from whom the demons had gone
8.38 The man from whom the demons had gone

Lk 9. 1 gave them . . authority over all demons
9.42 demon tore him and convulsed him
9.49 "a man casting out demons in your name
10.17 "Lord, even the demons are subject to us!
11.14 he was casting out a demon that was dumb; when the demon had gone out
11.15 "He casts out demons by Beelzebul, the prince of demons
11.18 "you say . . I cast out demons by Beelzebul
11.19 "if I cast out demons by Beelzebul
11.20 "by . . God that I cast out demons
13.32 "tell that fox, 'Behold, I cast out demons
Jn 7.20 "You have a demon!
8.48 "you are a Samaritan and have a demon
8.49 Jesus answered, "I have not a demon
8.52 "Now we know that you have a demon
10.20 "He has a demon, and he is mad
10.21 "Can a demon open the eyes of the blind?
1 Cor 10.20 what pagans sacrifice they offer to demons
10.20 not want you to be partners with demons
10.21 cup of the Lord and the cup of demons
10.21 table of the Lord and the table of demons
1 Tim 4. 1 some will . . heed . . doctrines of demons
Jas 2.19 Even the demons believe—and shudder
Rev 9.20 worshiping demons and idols of gold
18. 2 "Babylon . . a dwelling place of demons

DEMON, BE POSSESSED BY A

1. *be possessed by a demon:* δαιμονίζομαι DAIMONIZOMAI
Mt 15.22 "daughter is severely possessed by a demon

DEMON, ONE WHO HAS A

1. *be possessed by a demon:* δαιμονίζομαι (subst. part.) DAIMONIZOMAI
Jn 10.21 "not the sayings of one who has a demon

DEMONIAC

1. *be possessed by a demon:* δαιμονίζομαι (subst. part.) DAIMONIZOMAI
Mt 4.24 demoniacs, epileptics, and paralytics
8.28 two demoniacs met him
8.33 what had happened to the demoniacs
9.32 a dumb demoniac was brought to him
12.22 dumb demoniac was brought to him
Mk 5.15 saw the demoniac sitting there, clothed
5.16 told what had happened to the demoniac

DEMONIC

1. *demon, divine power:* δαιμόνιον (gen. pl.) DAIMONION
Rev 16.14 they are demonic spirits, performing signs

DEMONS, ONE WHO IS POSSESSED WITH

1. *be possessed by a demon:* δαιμονίζομαι (subst. part.) DAIMONIZOMAI
Mt 8.16 many who were possessed with demons
Mk 1.32 all who were . . possessed with demons
5.18 who had been possessed with demons
Lk 8.36 who had been possessed with demons

DEMONSTRATION

1. *showing forth:* ἀπόδειξις APODEIXIS*
1 Cor 2. 4 demonstration of the Spirit and of power

DEN

1. *grotto, cave:* σπήλαιον SPĒLAION
Mt 21.13 "but you make it a den of robbers
Mk 11.17 "you have made it a den of robbers
Lk 19.46 "you have made it a den of robbers
Heb 11.38 wandering . . in dens and caves of the earth

DENARIUS

1. *denarius:* δηνάριον DĒNARION
Mt 18.28 "servants who owed him a hundred denarii[g]
20. 2 "agreeing with the laborers for a denarius[m]
20. 9 "each of them received a denarius
20.10 "each of them also received a denarius
20.13 " 'did you not agree with me for a denarius?
Mk 6.37 "Shall we go and buy two hundred denarii[u]?
14. 5 "sold for more than three hundred denarii[b]
Lk 7.41 "two debtors; one owed five hundred denarii
10.35 "the next day he took out two denarii[i]
Jn 6. 7 "Two hundred denarii[l] would not
12. 5 "Why . . not sold for three hundred denarii[b]?
Rev 6. 6 "A quart of wheat for a denarius,[a] and three quarts of barley for a denarius[a]

DENOUNCE

1. *slander, blaspheme:* βλασφημέω BLASPHĒMEŌ
1 Cor 10.30 why am I denounced because of that?

DENY

1. *lift, carry away:* αἴρω AIRŌ
Acts 8.33 "In his humiliation justice was denied him
2. *deny utterly:* ἀπαρνέομαι APARNEOMAI*
Mt 16.24 "let him deny himself and take up his cross
26.34 "you will deny me three times
26.35 "Even if I must die . . I will not deny you
26.75 "you will deny me three times
Mk 8.34 "let him deny himself and take up his cross
14.30 "you will deny me three times
14.31 "If I must die . . I will not deny you
14.72 "you will deny me three times
Lk 12. 9 "he . . will be denied before the angels
22.34 "until you three times deny
22.61 "you will deny me three times
3. *deny:* ἀρνέομαι ARNEOMAI
Mt 10.33 "whoever denies me before men, I also will deny before my Father
26.70 he denied it before them all
26.72 again he denied it with an oath
Mk 14.68 he denied it, saying, "I neither know
14.70 But again he denied it
Lk 8.45 When all denied it, Peter[c] said, "Master!
9.23 "let him deny himself and take up his cross
12. 9 "he who denies me before men
22.57 he denied it, saying, "Woman, I do not
Jn 1.20 he did not deny, but confessed
13.38 "till you have denied me three times
18.25 He denied it and said, "I am not
18.27 Peter again denied it
Acts 3.13 "Jesus, whom you delivered up and denied
3.14 "you denied the Holy and Righteous One
4.16 "a notable sign . . and we cannot deny it
2 Tim 2.12 if we deny him, he also will deny us
2.13 for he cannot deny himself
3. 5 denying the power of ⟨religion⟩
Tit 1.16 they deny him by their deeds
2 Pet 2. 1 denying the Master who bought them
1 Jn 2.22 Who . . denies that Jesus is the Christ?
2.22 antichrist . . denies the Father and the Son
2.23 No one who denies the Son has the Father
Jude . 4 persons who . . deny our only Master
Rev 2.13 " 'you did not deny my faith
3. 8 " 'kept my word and have not denied

DEPART

DEPART FROM

1. *withdraw:* ἀναχωρέω ANACHŌREŌ
Mt 2.12 they departed to their own country
2.13 when they had departed, behold, an angel
2.14 he rose . . and departed to Egypt
9.24 "Depart; for the girl is not dead but sleeping
27. 5 he departed . . and hanged himself
2. *unloose, return:* ἀναλύω ANALYŌ
Phil 1.23 My desire is to depart and be with Christ
3. *go away:* ἀπέρχομαι APERCHOMAI
Mt 16. 4 So he left them and departed
27.60 he rolled a great stone . . and departed
28. 8 they departed quickly from the tomb
Mk 5.17 they began to beg Jesus[p] to depart
8.13 getting into the boat again he departed
Lk 1.38 And the angel departed from her
8.31 begged him not to command them to depart
8.37 all the people . . asked him to depart
10.30 "robbers, who stripped him and . . departed
Jn 4. 3 he left Judea and departed again to Galilee
12.36 When Jesus had said this, he departed
Acts 9.17 So Ananias departed and entered the house
10. 7 When the angel who spoke to him . . departed
[28.29 *the Jews departed, holding . . dispute*‡
4. *depart, withdraw from:* ἀφίστημι APHISTĒMI
Lk 2.37 She did not depart from the temple

Lk 4.13 the devil . . departed from him
13.27 " 'depart from me . . workers of iniquity!
1 Tim 4. 1 some will depart from the faith
2 Tim 2.19 "depart from iniquity
5. *go from:* ἀποχωρέω APOCHŌREŌ
Mt 7.23 " 'depart from me, you evildoers
6. *loose from, dismiss:* ἀπολύω (mid.) APOLYŌ
Acts 28.25 as they disagreed . . , they departed
7. *separate, divide:* χωρίζω (pass.) CHŌRIZŌ
Acts 1. 4 charged them not to d. from Jerusalem
8. *depart:* ἐκχωρέω EKCHŌREŌ*
Lk 21.21 "let those who are inside the city depart
9. *go out:* ἔξειμι EXEIMI
Acts 17.15 receiving a command . . , they departed
20. 7 intending to depart on the morrow
10. *go out:* ἐξέρχομαι EXERCHOMAI
[a]+ἀπό [b]+ἐκεῖθεν [c]+ἐκ
Mt 10.11 "stay with him until you depart
Lk 4.42 when it was day he departed
5. 8 [a]"Depart from me, for I am a sinful man
9. 4 [b]"stay there, and from there depart
9. 6 departed and went through the villages
Jn 4.43 [b]After the two days he departed
Acts 7. 3 [c]" 'Depart from your land
7. 4 [c]"he departed from the land
12.17 he departed and went to another place
15.40 Paul chose Silas and departed
16.40 they exhorted them and departed
18.23 he departed and went from place to place
20. 1 Paul . . departed for Macedonia
20.11 conversed with them . . and so departed
21. 5 we departed and went on our journey
21. 8 we departed and came to Caesarea
11. *pass over:* μεταβαίνω METABAINŌ
Jn 13. 1 his hour had come to depart
12. *go, walk:* πορεύομαι POREUOMAI
Mt 25.41 " 'Depart from me, you cursed
Acts 22.21 " 'Depart; for I will send you far away

DEPART, LET
1. *loose from, dismiss:* ἀπολύω APOLYŌ
Lk 2.29 "now lettest thou thy servant depart

DEPARTURE
1. *loosing, departure:* ἀνάλυσις ANALYSIS*
2 Tim 4. 6 the time of my departure has come
2. *arrival, departure:* ἄφιξις APHIXIS*
Acts 20.29 "after my departure fierce wolves will come
3. *going out:* ἔξοδος EXODOS
Lk 9.31 spoke of his departure
2 Pet 1.15 after my departure you may . . recall

DEPEND
1. *hang up:* κρεμάννυμι (mid.) KREMANNYMI
Mt 22.40 "On these two . . depend all the law
CONTEXTUALLY
Rom 4.16 That is why it depends on faith
9.16 So it depends not upon man's will
12.18 so far as it depends upon you
Phil 3. 9 righteousness . . that depends on faith

DEPENDENT, BE
1. *have need:* χρείαν ἔχειν CHREIA [B.3.a.5]
1 Th 4.12 so that you may . . be dependent on nobody

DEPORTATION
1. *captivity, migration:* μετοικεσία METOIKESIA*
Mt 1.11 at the time of the deportation to Babylon
1.12 after the deportation to Babylon
1.17 from David to the deportation to Babylon
1.17 from the deportation . . to the Christ

DEPOSE
1. *take down, destroy:* καθαιρέω KATHAIREŌ
Acts 19.27 "she may even be deposed

DEPRAVED
1. *destroy utterly:* διαφθείρω (perf. pass. part.) DIAPHTHEIRŌ
1 Tim 6. 5 among men who are depraved in mind

DEPRIVE
1. *empty, make void:* κενόω KENOŌ
1 Cor 9.15 rather die than have any one deprive me

DEPTH
1. *depth:* βάθος BATHOS
Mt 13. 5 "sprang up, since they had no depth of soil
Mk 4. 5 "sprang up, since it had no depth of soil
Rom 8.39 nor height, nor depth, nor anything else
11.33 O the depth of the riches and wisdom!
Eph 3.18 breadth and length and height and depth
2. *high sea:* πέλαγος PELAGOS
Mt 18. 6 "to be drowned in the depth of the sea

DEPTHS
1. *depth:* βάθος (pl.) BATHOS
1 Cor 2.10 everything, even the depths of God

DERBE: 'dərbē II,F-3
1. *from Derbe:* Δερβαῖος
Acts 20. 4 Gaius of Derbe, and Timothy
2. *Derbe:* Δέρβη
Acts 14. 6 fled to Lystra and Derbe, cities of Lycaonia
14.20 next day he went on with Barnabas to D.
16. 1 he came also to Derbe and to Lystra

DERIDE
1. *slander, blaspheme:* βλασφημέω BLASPHĒMEŌ
Mt 27.39 those who passed by derided him
Mk 15.29 those who passed by derided him

DERIVE
1. *have, hold:* ἔχω ECHŌ
Phm . 7 For I have derived much joy and comfort

DESCEND
1. *make to rise:* ἀνατέλλω ANATELLŌ
Heb 7.14 our Lord was descended from Judah
2. *come out of the loins:* ἐξέρχεσθαι ἐκ τῆς ὀσφύος EXERCHOMAI; OSPHYS [C.1]
Heb 7. 5 these also are descended from Abraham
3. *come down, go down:* καταβαίνω KATABAINŌ
Mt 3.16 he saw the Spirit of God descending
28. 2 angel of the Lord descended from heaven
Mk 1.10 Spirit descending upon him like a dove
Lk 3.22 Spirit descended upon him in bodily form
Jn 1.32 "I saw the Spirit descend as a dove
1.33 " 'on whom you see the Spirit descend
1.51 "angels of God ascending and descending
3.13 "he who descended from heaven
Acts 10.11 heaven opened, and something descending
11. 5 "something descending, like a great sheet
Rom 10. 7 "Who will descend into the abyss?
Eph 4. 9 (he had also descended into the lower parts
4.10 (He who descended is he who also ascended
1 Th 4.16 the Lord himself will descend from heaven
CONTEXTUALLY
Rom 9. 6 not all who are descended from Israel

DESCENDANT
DESCENDANTS
1. *son:* υἱός HUIOS
Heb 7. 5 descendants of Levi
2. *seed, offspring:* σπέρμα SPERMA
[a]ἐκ σπέρματος B.1.a.1
Jn 8.33 "We are descendants of Abraham
8.37 "you are descendants of Abraham
Rom 4.13 Abraham and his descendants
4.16 guaranteed to all his descendants
4.18 "So shall your descendants be
9. 7 because they are his descendants
9. 7 "Through Isaac shall your descendants be
9. 8 children of the promise are . . descendants
11. 1 [a]I myself am . . a descendant of Abraham
2 Cor 11.22 Are they descendants of Abraham?
Heb 2.16 concerned . . with . . descendants of Abraham
11.18 "Through Isaac shall your descendants
IDIOMATICALLY
a. Acts 2.30 "set one of his descendants ἐκ καρποῦ τῆς ὀσφύος αὐτοῦ καθίσαι [KARPOS; OSPHYS]
CONTEXTUALLY
Heb 11.12 from one man . . were born descendants

DESCENDED
1. *of the seed:* ἐκ σπέρματος SPERMA [B.1.a.2]
Jn 7.42 "the Christ is descended from David

Rom 1. 3 Son, who was descended from David
2 Tim 2. 8 Jesus Christ, . . descended from David

DESCENT
1. *steep ground, way down:* καταβασις KATABASIS*
Lk 19.37 at the descent of the Mount of Olives
CONTEXTUALLY
Heb 7.16 a legal requirement concerning bodily d.

DESCRIBE
1. *set out in detail:* διηγέομαι DIĒGEOMAI
Acts 8.33 "Who can describe his generation?
12.17 "motioning . . he described to them
2. *write:* γράφω GRAPHŌ
Rev 22.18 the plagues described in this book
22.19 tree of life and . . holy city . . described in this

DESERT
1. *leave behind:* ἐγκαταλείπω EGKATALEIPŌ
2 Tim 4.10 Demas . . has deserted me and gone
4.16 At my first defense . . all deserted me
2. *desert, solitude:* ἐρημία ERĒMIA
Mt 15.33 "are we to get bread enough in the desert?
Mk 8. 4 "can one feed these men . . in the desert?
Heb 11.38 wandering over deserts and mountains
3. *lonely, desolate:* ἔρημος (subst. fem.) ERĒMOS
Lk 8.29 (driven by the demon into the desert
Acts 8.26 This is a desert road
4. *change from:* μετατίθημι ἀπό (mid.) METATITHĒMI [A.6.a.4]
Gal 1. 6 so quickly deserting him who called you

DESERVE
1. *consider worthy:* ἀξιόω AXIOŌ
Heb 10.29 How much worse . . will be deserved?
2. *worthy:* ἄξιος AXIOS
[a]A.6.a.3 [b]A.3.d.2
Mt 10.10 [a]"for the laborer deserves his food
Lk 10. 7 [a]"the laborer deserves his wages
Acts 26.31 [b]"nothing to deserve death or imprisonment
Rom 1.32 [a]those who do such things deserve to die
1 Tim 5.18 [a]"The laborer deserves his wages
3. *liable, guilty:* ἔνοχος ENOCHOS [A.6.a.3]
Mt 26.66 "He deserves death
Mk 14.64 all condemned him as deserving death

DESERVES, AS S.
1. *in accordance with, for:* κατά (+acc.) KATA [B.3.b.4]
Rev 2.23

DESERVES, FOR WHICH ONE
1. *worthy:* ἄξιος AXIOS
Acts 25.11 "anything for which I deserve to die

DESERVES, WHAT
1. *worthy:* ἄξιος (subst.) AXIOS
Lk 12.48 "did what deserved a beating

DESERVING
1. *worthy:* ἄξιος AXIOS
Lk 23.15 "nothing deserving death has been done
Acts 23.29 "charged with nothing deserving death
25.25 "he had done nothing deserving death
CONTEXTUALLY
Lk 23.22 "in him no crime deserving death

DESIGN
1. *mind, thought, purpose:* νόημα NOĒMA
2 Cor 2.11 we are not ignorant of his designs

DESIGNATE
1. *determine, appoint:* ὁρίζω HORIZŌ
Rom 1. 4 designated Son of God in power
2. *address, call by name:* προσαγορεύω PROSAGOREUŌ*
Heb 5.10 designated by God a high priest

DESIGNATED, BE
1. *write before:* προγράφω (pass.) PROGRAPHŌ
Jude . 4 were designated for this condemnation

DESIRE
1. *consider worthy:* ἀξιόω AXIOŌ
Acts 28.22 "we desire to hear from you
2. *wish, will:* βούλομαι BOULOMAI
Acts 22.30 desiring to know the real reason why
23.28 "desiring to know the charge
1 Tim 2. 8 I desire then that . . men should pray
1 Tim 6. 9 who desire to be rich fall into temptation
Tit 3. 8 I desire you to insist on these things
Heb 6.17 God desired to show more convincingly
Jude . 5 Now I desire to remind you
3. *desire, long for:* ἐπιθυμέω EPITHYMEŌ
[a]ἡ σάρξ ἐπιθυμεῖ B.2.d.2
Lk 16.21 "desired to be fed . . from the rich man's table
17.22 "you will desire to see one of the days
22.15 "I have earnestly desired to eat this
Gal 5.17 [a]the desires of the flesh are against the Spirit
1 Tim 3. 1 he desires a noble task
Heb 6.11 we desire each . . to show . . earnestness
Jas 4. 2 You desire and do not have; so you kill
4. *one who longs for:* ἐπιθυμητής EPITHYMĒTĒS* [A.6.a.3]
1 Cor 10. 6 warnings . . not to desire evil as they did
5. *desire, yearning:* ἐπιθυμία EPITHYMIA
[a]B.1.a.2
Mk 4.19 "the desire for other things
Jn 8.44 "your will is to do your father's desires
Rom 13.14 [a]make no provision . . to gratify its desires
Gal 5.16 do not gratify the desires of the flesh
5.24 the flesh with its passions and desires
Phil 1.23 My desire is to depart and be with Christ
Col 3. 5 passion, evil desire, and covetousness
1 Th 2.17 we endeavored . . with great desire to see you
1 Tim 6. 9 hurtful desires that plunge men into ruin
Jas 1.14 lured and enticed by his own desire
1.15 desire . . gives birth to sin
6. *satisfaction, goodwill:* εὐδοκία EUDOKIA
Rom 10. 1 my . . desire . . is that they may be saved
7. *reach, stretch:* ὀρέγω (mid.) OREGŌ
Heb 11.16 as it is, they desire a better country
8. *will, desire:* θέλημα THELĒMA
1 Cor 7.37 having his desire under control
Eph 2. 3 following the desires of body and mind
9. *will, wish:* θέλω THELŌ
Mt 9.13 " 'I desire mercy, and not sacrifice
12. 7 " 'I desire mercy, and not sacrifice
15.28 "Be it done for you as you desire
27.43 "let God deliver him now, if he desires him
Mk 3.13 called to him those whom he desired
Lk 5.39 "no one after drinking old wine desires new
8.20 "standing outside, desiring to see you
10.24 "many . . desired to see what you see
10.29 he, desiring to justify himself
14.28 "which of you, desiring to build a tower?
23. 8 for he had long desired to see him
23.20 Pilate . ., desiring to release Jesus
Jn 17.24 "Father, I desire that they . . be with me
Acts 10.10 hungry and desired something to eat
24.27 desiring to do the Jews a favor
Rom 9.22 God, desiring to show his wrath
1 Cor 14.35 If . . they desire to know, let them ask
2 Cor 8.10 what a year ago you began . . to desire
8.11 that . . desiring it may be matched
Gal 4.21 Tell me, you who desire to be under law
6.13 they desire to have you circumcised
1 Tim 1. 7 desiring to be teachers of the law
2. 4 who desires all men to be saved
5.11 wanton against Christ they desire to marry
2 Tim 3.12 all who desire to live a godly life in Christ
Heb 10. 5 "offerings thou hast not desired
10. 8 "Thou hast neither desired nor taken pleasure
12.17 when he desired to inherit the blessing
13.18 desiring to act honorably in all things
Rev 11. 6 to smite the earth . . as often as they desire
22.17 let him who desires take the water of life
10. *seek, desire:* ζητέω ZĒTEŌ
2 Cor 13. 3 you desire proof that Christ is speaking in me
CONTEXTUALLY
1 Cor 7.15 if . . unbelieving partner desires to separate

DESIRE, EARNESTLY
1. *strive for, hasten:* σπεύδω SPEUDŌ
2 Pet [3.12 *earnestly desiring* . . the day of God†
2. *strive after, be jealous:* ζηλόω ZĒLOŌ
1 Cor 12.31 earnestly desire the higher gifts

1 Cor 14. 1 earnestly desire the spiritual gifts
14.39 brethren, earnestly desire to prophesy

DESIROUS, BE AFFECTIONATELY

1. *desire, long for:* ὁμείρομαι HOMEIROMAI*
1 Th 2. 8 being affectionately desirous of you

DESOLATE

1. *strip bare, lay waste:* ἐρημόω (perf. pass. part.) ERĒMOŌ
Rev 17.16 "they will make her desolate and naked
2. *desolate, lonely:* ἔρημος ERĒMOS
Mt 23.38 "your house is forsaken and desolate[z]‡
Acts 1.20 " 'Let his habitation become desolate
Gal 4.27 "children of the desolate one are many
3. *without parents, neglected:* ὀρφανός ORPHANOS
Jn 14.18 "I will not leave you desolate

DESOLATING

1. *desolation:* ἐρήμωσις (gen.) ERĒMŌSIS
Mt 24.15 "So when you see the desolating sacrilege
Mk 13.14 "when you see the desolating sacrilege

DESOLATION

1. *desolation:* ἐρήμωσις ERĒMŌSIS
Lk 21.20 "know that its desolation has come near

DESPAIR

DESPAIR, BE DRIVEN TO

1. *be in great doubt:* ἐξαπορέω (pass.) EXAPOREŌ
2 Cor 1. 8 so . . crushed that we despaired of life itself
4. 8 perplexed, but not driven to despair

DESPAIR OF

1. *hope to receive back:* ἀπελπίζω APELPIZŌ
Lk [6.35 "lend, *despairing of no man*†‡

DESPISE

1. *spit out:* ἐκπτύω EKPTYŌ*
Gal 4.14 you did not scorn or despise me
2. *treat with contempt:* ἐξουθενέω EXOUTHENEŌ
Lk 18. 9 they were righteous and despised others
Rom 14. 3 Let not him who eats d. him who abstains
14.10 why do you despise your brother?
1 Cor 1.28 God chose what is low and despised
16.11 So let no one despise him
1 Th 5.20 do not despise prophesying
3. *look down upon, despise:* καταφρονέω KATAPHRONEŌ
Mt 6.24 "devoted to the one and despise the other
18.10 "See that you do not despise one of these
Lk 16.13 "devoted to the one and despise the other
1 Cor 11.22 Or do you despise the church of God?
1 Tim 4.12 Let no one despise your youth
Heb 12. 2 endured the cross, despising the shame
2 Pet 2.10 indulge in the lust . . and despise authority

DESTINE

1. *foreknow:* προγινώσκω PROGINŌSKŌ
1 Pet 1.20 He was destined before the foundation
2. *determine beforehand:* προορίζω PROORIZŌ
Eph 1. 5 He destined us in love[b] to be his sons
3. *lay, put:* τίθημι (act. or mid.) TITHĒMI
1 Th 5. 9 God has not destined us for wrath
1 Pet 2. 8 they disobey . . as they were destined to do

DESTINED

1. *according to prediction:* κατὰ πρόγνωσιν PROGNŌSIS [B.1.a.1]
1 Pet 1. 2 chosen and destined by God the Father
2. *determine beforehand:* προορίζω (part.) PROORIZŌ
Eph 1.12(11) destined . . to live for . . his glory

DESTITUTE

1. *lack, fail:* ὑστερέω (pass. part.) HYSTEREŌ
Heb 11.37 destitute, afflicted, ill-treated

DESTROY

1. *lift, carry away:* αἴρω AIRŌ
Jn 11.48 "the Romans will come and destroy both
2. *destroy utterly:* ἀπόλλυμι APOLLYMI
Mt 2.13 "Herod is about . . to destroy him
9.17 "wine is spilled, and the skins are destroyed
10.28 "fear him who can d. both soul and body
12.14 counsel against him, how to destroy him
22. 7 "The king . . destroyed those murderers
27.20 to ask for Barabbas and destroy Jesus
Mk 1.24 "Have you come to destroy us?
Mk 3. 6 counsel . . against him, how to destroy him
9.22 "often cast him into the fire . . to destroy him
11.18 the scribes . . sought a way to destroy him
12. 9 "He will come and destroy the tenants
Lk 4.34 "Have you come to destroy us?
5.37 "the skins will be destroyed
6. 9 "to save life or to destroy it?
[9.55(56) *"the Son of man came not to destroy*‡
17.27 "the flood came and destroyed them all
17.29 "fire and sulphur . . destroyed them all
19.47 the principal men . . sought to destroy him
20.16 "He will come and destroy those tenants
Jn 10.10 "The thief comes only to . . destroy
1 Cor 1.19 "I will destroy the wisdom of the wise
8.11 this weak man is destroyed
10. 9 some of them . . were destroyed by serpents
10.10 some of them did and were destroyed
2 Cor 4. 9 struck down, but not destroyed
Jas 4.12 who is able to save and to destroy
Jude . 5 destroyed those who did not believe
3. *destroy utterly:* διαφθείρω DIAPHTHEIRŌ
Lk 12.33 "the heavens . . where . . no moth destroys
Rev 8. 9 a third of the ships were destroyed
11.18 "for destroying the destroyers of the earth
4. *destroy utterly:* ἐξολεθρεύω EXOLETHREUŌ*
Acts 3.23 " 'that does not listen . . shall be destroyed
5. *put down, destroy:* καταλύω KATALYŌ
Mt 26.61 " 'I am able to destroy the temple of God
27.40 "You who would destroy the temple
Mk 14.58 " 'I will destroy this temple
15.29 "You who would destroy the temple
Acts 6.14 "Jesus of Nazareth will destroy this place
Rom 14.20 Do not . . destroy the work of God
2 Cor 5. 1 if the earthly tent we live in is destroyed
6. *make ineffective, hinder:* καταργέω KATARGEŌ
Rom 6. 6 that the sinful body might be destroyed
1 Cor 6.13 God will destroy both one and the other
15.24 after destroying every rule and . . authority
15.26 last enemy to be destroyed is death
2 Th 2. 8 Jesus will . . destroy him by his appearing
Heb 2.14 that through death he might destroy him
7. *take down, destroy:* καθαιρέω KATHAIREŌ
Acts 13.19 "when he had destroyed seven nations
2 Cor 10. 5 We destroy arguments
8. *pulling down:* καθαίρεσις KATHAIRESIS [B.1.a.2]
2 Cor 10. 4 divine power to destroy strongholds
9. *break up, unbind:* λύω LYŌ
Jn 2.19 "Destroy this temple, and . . I will raise it
1 Jn 3. 8 to destroy the works of the devil
10. *entice, destroy:* φθείρω PHTHEIRŌ
1 Cor 3.17 If any one destroys God's temple, God will destroy him
2 Pet 2.12 destroyed in the same destruction
Jude .10 by those things . . they are destroyed
11. *destroy, plunder:* πορθέω PORTHEŌ
Gal 1.13 persecuted the church . . and tried to destroy
1.23 "preaching the faith he once tried to destroy

DESTROYED, BE

1. *destruction:* ἀπώλεια APŌLEIA [B.2.b.1]
Heb 10.39 those who shrink back and are destroyed

DESTROYER

1. *one who destroys:* ἀπολλύων APOLLYŌN
Rev [9.11 angel of the . . pit . . called *Destroyer*†
2. *destroy utterly:* διαφθείρω (subst. part.) DIAPHTHEIRŌ
Rev 11.18 "for destroying the destroyers of the earth
3. *destroy:* ὀλοθρεύω (subst. part.) OLOTHREUŌ*
Heb 11.28 that . . destroyer of . . first-born might not
4. *destroyer:* ὀλοθρευτής OLOTHREUTĒS*
1 Cor 10.10 some . . were destroyed by the Destroyer

DESTROYING

1. *pulling down:* καθαίρεσις KATHAIRESIS
2 Cor 10. 8 authority . . not for destroying you

DESTRUCTION

1. *destruction:* ἀπώλεια APŌLEIA
Mt 7.13 "the way is easy,[q] that leads to destruction
Rom 9.22 vessels of wrath made for destruction

Phil 1.28 clear omen to them of their destruction
3.19 Their end is destruction
1 Tim 6. 9 desires that plunge men into . . destruction
2 Pet 2. 1 bringing upon themselves swift destruction
2. 3 their destruction has not been asleep
3. 7 kept until the day of . . destruction
3.16 unstable twist to their own destruction
2. *destruction, death:* ὄλεθρος OLETHROS
1 Cor 5. 5 deliver this man to Satan for . . destruction
1 Th 5. 3 sudden destruction will come upon them
2 Th 1. 9 suffer the punishment of eternal destruction
3. *destruction:* φθορά PHTHORA
2 Pet 2.12 will be destroyed in the same destruction

DESTRUCTIVE
1. *destruction:* ἀπώλεια (gen.) APŌLEIA
2 Pet 2. 1 will secretly bring in destructive heresies

DETAIL
IDIOMATICALLY
a. Heb 9. 5 we cannot now speak in detail οὐκ ἔστιν νῦν λέγειν κατὰ μέρος [MEROS]

DETAIN
1. *hinder, oppose:* ἐγκόπτω EGKOPTŌ
Acts 24. 4 "to detain you no further, . . hear

DETERMINE
1. *discern, decide:* διαγινώσκω DIAGINŌSKŌ
Acts 23.15 "to determine his case more exactly
2. *judgment, opinion:* γνώμη GNŌMĒ [B.3.a.2]
Acts 20.3 determined to return through Macedonia
3. *determine, appoint:* ὁρίζω HORIZŌ
Lk 22.22 "Son of man goes as it has been determined
Acts 11.29 disciples determined . . to send relief
17.26 "having determined allotted periods
4. *judge, decide:* κρίνω KRINŌ
1 Cor 7.37 determined . . to keep . . his betrothed[z]
10.29 determined by another man's scruples

DETESTABLE
1. *disgusting:* βδελυκτός BDELYKTOS*
Tit 1.16 they are detestable, disobedient, unfit

DEVIL
1. *slanderous:* διάβολος (subst.) DIABOLOS
Mt 4. 1 Jesus was led . . to be tempted by the devil
4. 5 the devil took him to the holy city
4. 8 devil took him to a very high mountain
4.11 devil left him, and behold, angels came
13.39 "the enemy who sowed them is the devil
25.41 " 'the eternal fire prepared for the devil
Lk 4. 2 in the wilderness, tempted by the devil
4. 3 devil said . . "If you are the Son of God
4. 5(6) the devil took him up, and showed him
4.13 when the devil had ended every temptation
8.12 "the devil comes and takes away the word
Jn 6.70 "twelve, and one of you is a devil
8.44 "You are of your father the devil
13. 2 devil had already put it into the heart
Acts 10.38 "all that were oppressed by the devil
13.10 "You son of the devil, you enemy
Eph 4.27 give no opportunity to the devil
6.11 able to stand against the wiles of the devil
1 Tim 3. 6 fall into the condemnation of the devil[f]†
3. 7 fall into . . the snare of the devil[f]†
2 Tim 2.26 escape from the snare of the devil
Heb 2.14 who has the power of death, . . the devil
Jas 4. 7 Resist the devil and he will flee from you
1 Pet 5. 8 Your adversary the devil prowls around
1 Jn 3. 8 He who commits sin is of the devil; for the devil has sinned from the beginning
3. 8 to destroy the works of the devil
3.10 who are the children of the devil
Jude . 9 Michael, contending with the devil
Rev 2.10 " 'the devil is about to throw some
12. 9 ancient serpent, who is called the Devil
12.12 "devil has come down . . in great wrath!
20. 2 that ancient serpent, who is the Devil
20.10 the devil who had deceived them

DEVILISH
1. *like a demon:* δαιμονιώδης DAIMONIŌDĒS*
Jas 3.15 earthly, unspiritual, devilish

DEVISED, CLEVERLY
1. *make wise, instruct:* σοφίζω (perf. pass. part.) SOPHIZŌ
2 Pet 1.16 we did not follow cleverly devised myths

DEVOID OF
1. *have, hold:* ἔχω (neg. part.) ECHŌ
Jude .19 worldly people, devoid of the Spirit

DEVOTE
1. *appoint, assign:* τάσσω TASSŌ
1 Cor 16.15 devoted themselves to . . the saints

DEVOTE ONESELF
1. *follow close upon:* ἐπακολουθέω EPAKOLOUTHEŌ
1 Tim 5.10 devoted herself to doing good
2. *persist in:* προσκαρτερέω PROSKARTEREŌ
Acts 1.14 devoted themselves to prayer
2.42 devoted themselves to . . apostles' teaching
6. 4 "we will devote ourselves to prayer
3. *have leisure, study, be empty:* σχολάζω SCHOLAZŌ
1 Cor 7. 5 that you may devote yourselves to prayer

DEVOTED TO, BE
1. *hold against:* ἀντέχω (mid.) ANTECHŌ
Mt 6.24 "be devoted to the one . . despise the other
Lk 16.13 "be devoted to the one . . despise the other

DEVOTION
1. *constant:* εὐπάρεδρος (subst.) EUPAREDROS*
1 Cor 7.35 your undivided devotion to the Lord

DEVOTION, RIGOR OF
1. *self-chosen religion:* ἐθελοθρησκία ETHELOTHRĒSKIA*
Col 2.23 wisdom in promoting rigor of devotion

DEVOTION, PURE
1. *purity:* ἁγνότης HAGNOTĒS
2 Cor 11. 3 a sincere and pure devotion to Christ

DEVOTION, SINCERE
1. *simplicity, liberality:* ἁπλότης HAPLOTĒS
2 Cor 11. 3 a sincere and pure devotion to Christ

DEVOUR
1. *eat:* ἐσθίω ESTHIŌ
Rev 17.16 "devour her flesh and burn her up
2. *swallow:* καταπίνω KATAPINŌ
1 Pet 5. 8 roaring lion, seeking some one to devour
3. *devour, eat up:* κατεσθίω KATESTHIŌ
Mt 13. 4 "birds came and devoured them
[23.14 *"you devour widows' houses*‡
Mk 4. 4 "birds came and devoured it
12.40 "who devour widows' houses
Lk 8. 5 "the birds of the air devoured it
15.30 " 'devoured your living with harlots!
20.47 "who devour widows' houses
Gal 5.15 if you bite and devour one another
Rev 12. 4 that he might devour her child

DEVOUT
1. *discreet, reverent:* εὐλαβής EULABĒS*
Lk 2.25 Simeon . . was righteous and devout
Acts 2. 5 devout men from every nation under heaven
8. 2 Devout men buried Stephen
22.12 "Ananias, a devout man according to the law
2. *reverent:* εὐσεβής EUSEBĒS
Acts 10. 2 a devout man who feared God
10. 7 "two of his servants and a devout soldier
3. *worship, honor:* σέβω (mid. part.) SEBŌ
Acts 13.43 many Jews and devout converts
13.50 the Jews incited the devout women
17. 4 a great many of the devout Greeks
17.17 he argued . . with . . the devout persons

DIADEM
1. *headband, crown:* διάδημα DIADĒMA*
Rev 12. 3 and seven diadems upon his heads
13. 1 ten diadems upon its horns
19.12 on his head are many diadems

DIE
1. *be taken away:* ἀπογίνομαι APOGINOMAI*
1 Pet 2.24 that we might die to sin and live

2. *die:* ἀποθνήσκω APOTHNĒSKŌ
Mt 22.24 " 'If a man dies, having no children
22.27 "After them all, the woman died
26.35 "Even if I must die with you, I will not
Mk 12.19 "if a man's brother dies and leaves a wife
12.20 "when he died left no children
12.21 "the second took her, and died
12.22 "Last of all the woman also died
Lk 8.42 an only daughter . . and she was dying
16.22 "poor man died and was carried
16.22 "rich man also died and was buried
20.28 "if a man's brother dies, having a wife
20.29 "took a wife, and died without children
20.31 "likewise all seven left no children and died
20.32 "Afterward the woman also died
20.36 "they cannot die any more
Jn 4.49 "Sir, come down before my child dies
6.49 "fathers ate the manna . . and they died
6.50 "that a man may eat of it and not die
6.58 "not such as the fathers ate and died
8.21 "you will seek me and die in your sin
8.24 "I told you that you would die in your sins, for you will die . . unless you believe
8.52 "Abraham died, as did the prophets
8.53 "Are you greater than . . Abraham who died? And the prophets died!
11.16 "Let us also go, that we may die with him
11.21 "my brother would not have died
11.25 "though he die, yet shall he live
11.26 "whoever . . believes in me shall never die
11.32 "my brother would not have died
11.37 "not . . have kept this man from dying?
11.50 "that one man should die for the people
11.51 he prophesied that Jesus should die
12.24 "unless a grain of wheat . . dies
12.24 "but if it dies, it bears much fruit
12.33 to show by what death he was to die
18.14 expedient that one man should die
18.32 to show by what death he was to die
19. 7 "by that law he ought to die
21.23 "that this disciple was not to die; yet Jesus did not say . . that he was not to die
Acts 7. 4 "after his father died, God removed him
9.37 In those days she fell sick and died
21.13 "ready . . to be imprisoned . . even to die
25.11 "anything for which I deserve to die
Rom 5. 6 at the right time Christ died
5. 7 one will hardly die for a righteous man
5. 7 for a good man one will dare even to die
5. 8 while we were yet sinners Christ died for us
5.15 if many died through one man's trespass
6. 2 How can we who died to sin still live in it?
6. 7 he who has died is freed from sin
6. 8 But if we have died with Christ
6. 9 Christ . . will never die again
6.10 The death he died he died to sin, once for all, but the life he lives he lives to God
7. 2 if her husband dies she is discharged
7. 3 But if her husband dies she is free
7. 9(10) commandment came, . . and I died
8.13 if you live according to the flesh you will die
8.34 Is it Christ Jesus, who died?
14. 7 none of us dies to himself
14. 8 If we live, we live to the Lord, and if we die, we die to the Lord; so then, whether we live or whether we die, we are the Lord's
14. 9 to this end Christ died and lived again
14.15 the ruin of one for whom Christ died
1 Cor 8.11 the brother for whom Christ died
9.15 rather die than have any one deprive me
15. 3 Christ died for our sins
15.22 as in Adam all die
15.31 I die every day!
15.32 "Let us eat and drink, for tomorrow we die
15.36 does not come to life unless it dies
2 Cor 5.14 we are convinced that one has died for all; therefore all have died
2 Cor 5.15 he died . . that those who live might live
5.15 who for their sake died and was raised
6. 9 as dying, and behold, we live
Gal 2.19 For I through the law died to the law
2.21 then Christ died to no purpose
Phil 1.21 to live is Christ, and to die is gain
Col 2.20 If with Christ you died to the . . spirits
3. 3 you have died, and your life is hid
1 Th 4.14 we believe that Jesus died and rose
5.10 died for us so that . . we might live
Heb 9.27 it is appointed for men to die once
10.28 who has violated the law of Moses dies
11. 4 died, but through his faith he is still speaking
11.13 These all died in faith
11.21 By faith Jacob, when dying, blessed each
1 Pet 3.18 Christ also died[h] for sins once for all‡
Rev 8. 9 third of the living creatures in the sea died
8.11 many men died of the water
9. 6 they will long to die, and death will fly
14.13 "Blessed are the dead who die in the Lord
16. 3 every living thing died that was in the sea

3. *swoon, expire:* ἐκψύχω EKPSYCHŌ*
Acts 5. 5 Ananias . . fell down and died
5.10 she fell down at his feet and died
12.23 he was eaten by worms and died

4. *put to sleep:* κοιμάω (pass.) KOIMAŌ
1 Cor 7.39 If the husband dies, she is free
11.30 That is why many of you . . have died[t]†

5. *become dead:* γίνεσθαι νεκρός NEKROS [A.6.a.3]
Rev 1.18 "I died, and behold, I am alive for evermore
2. 8 " 'the first and the last, who died and came

6. *die, finish:* τελευτάω TELEUTAŌ
Mt 2.19 when Herod died . . an angel . . appeared
9.18 "My daughter has just died
15. 4 " 'who speaks evil of father . . let him . . die
22.25 "the first married, and died
Mk 7.10 " 'who speaks evil of father . . let him . . die
9.48 "where their worm does not die
Also Mk **9.** [44‡, [46‡
Acts 2.29 "David . . both died and was buried
7.15 "Jacob . . died, himself and our fathers

7. *put to death:* θανατόω (pass.) THANATOŌ
Rom 7. 4 my brethren, you have died to the law

8. *death:* θάνατος THANATOS
[a]A.1.d [b]A.6.c.1
Rom 1.32 [a]those who do such things deserve to die
Phil 2.30 [b]he nearly died for the work of Christ

9. *die:* θνήσκω THNĒSKŌ
Lk 7.12 a man who had died was being carried out

DIE TOGETHER
1. *die together with:* συναποθνήσκω SYNAPOTHNĒSKŌ
2 Cor 7. 3 to die together and to live together

DIE WITH
1. *die together with:* συναποθνήσκω SYNAPOTHNĒSKŌ
Mk 14.31 "If I must die with you, I will not deny
2 Tim 2.11 If we have died with him, we shall also live

DIFFER
1. *carry through, differ:* διαφέρω DIAPHERŌ
1 Cor 15.41 star differs from star in glory

DIFFERENCE, MAKE A
1. *carry through, differ:* διαφέρω DIAPHERŌ
Gal 2. 6 (what they were makes no difference to me

DIFFERENT
1. *kind, race, family:* γένος (gen. pl.) GENOS
1 Cor 14.10 doubtless many different languages
2. *another, different:* ἕτερος HETEROS
2 Cor 11. 4 if you receive a different spirit
11. 4 if you accept a different gospel
Gal 1. 6 turning to a different gospel

DIFFERENT DOCTRINE, TEACH A
1. *teach false doctrine:* ἑτεροδιδασκαλέω HETERODIDASKALEŌ
1 Tim 1. 3 charge . . not to teach any different doctrine

DIFFERENT IN, SEE S.
1. *differentiate, decide:* διακρίνω DIAKRINŌ
1 Cor 4. 7 who sees anything different in you?

DIFFERS, THAT
1. *different, excellent:* διάφορος DIAPHOROS [A.3.d.3]
Rom 12. 6 gifts that differ according to the grace

DIFFICULTY
1. *stumbling block, trap:* σκάνδαλον SKANDALON
Rom 16.17 who create dissensions and difficulties•

DIFFICULTY, WITH
1. *barely, hardly:* μόλις MOLIS
Acts 27. 7 arrived with difficulty off Cnidus
27. 8 Coasting along it with difficulty
27.16 managed with difficulty to secure the boat

DIG
1. *burrow, dig up:* ὀρύσσω ORYSSŌ*
Mt 21.33 "householder who . . dug a wine press in it
25.18 "dug in the ground and hid . . money
Mk 12. 1 "dug a pit for the wine press
2. *dig, cultivate:* σκάπτω SKAPTŌ*
Lk 6.48 "a man building a house, who dug deep
13. 8 " 'till I dig about it and put on manure
16. 3 " 'I am not strong enough to dig

DIGNIFIED
1. *well ordered, modest:* κόσμιος KOSMIOS
1 Tim 3. 2 dignified, hospitable, an apt teacher

DILIGENTLY
1. *precisely:* ἀκριβῶς AKRIBŌS
Mt 2. 8 "Go and search diligently for the child
2. *carefully:* ἐπιμελῶς EPIMELŌS*
Lk 15. 8 "seek diligently until she finds it

DILL
1. *dill:* ἄνηθον ANĒTHON*
Mt 23.23 "you tithe the mint and dill and cummin

DIMLY
1. *in a riddle:* ἐν αἰνίγματι AINIGMA* [B.1.a.1]
1 Cor 13.12 For now we see in a mirror dimly

DINE
1. *eat morning or noon meal:* ἀριστάω ARISTAŌ
Lk 11.37 a Pharisee asked him to dine with him
2. *eat bread:* ἐσθίειν ἄρτον ESTHIŌ [B.2.a.1]
Lk 14. 1 when he went to dine at the house of a ruler

DINNER
1. *breakfast, luncheon:* ἄριστον ARISTON*
Mt 22. 4 " 'Behold, I have made ready my dinner
Lk 11.38 he did not first wash before dinner
14.12 "When you give a dinner or a banquet
CONTEXTUALLY
1 Cor 10.27 If one of the unbelievers invites you to d.

DIONYSIUS: Διονύσιος ˌdīə'nish(ē)əs
Acts 17.34 some . . believed, among them Dionysius

DIOTREPHES: Διοτρέφης dī'ätrəfēz
3 Jn . 9 Diotrephes, who likes to put himself first

DIP
1. *dip:* βάπτω BAPTŌ*
Lk 16.24 " 'send Lazarus to dip . . his finger in water
Jn 13.26 "this morsel when I have dipped it." So when he had dipped the morsel, he gave it
Rev 19.13 He is clad in a robe dipped in[m] blood‡
2. *dip in:* ἐμβάπτω EMBAPTŌ*
Mt 26.23 "who has dipped his hand in the dish
Mk 14.20 "one who is dipping bread into the dish

DIRECT (*See also* GAZE, DIRECT ONE'S)
1. *wish, will:* βούλομαι BOULOMAI
Jas 3. 4 wherever the will of the pilot directs
2. *negotiate, order:* χρηματίζω CHRĒMATIZŌ
Acts 10.22 "directed by a holy angel to send for you
3. *appoint, direct:* διατάσσω DIATASSŌ
Lk 8.55 directed that something . . be given her
Acts 7.44 "he who spoke to Moses directed him
1 Cor 16. 1 as I directed the churches of Galatia
Tit 1. 5 appoint elders in every town as I directed
4. *teach:* διδάσκω DIDASKŌ
Mt 28.15 did as they were directed
5. *direct, guide:* κατευθύνω KATEUTHYNŌ
1 Th 3.11 may our God . . direct our way to you
2 Th 3. 5 May the Lord direct your hearts
6. *put in order:* συντάσσω SYNTASSŌ*
Mt 21. 6 disciples . . did as Jesus had directed them
26.19 disciples did as Jesus had directed them
27.10 "for the potter's field, as the Lord directed
7. *appoint, assign:* τάσσω (mid.) TASSŌ
Mt 28.16 mountain to which Jesus had directed them

DIRECT VOYAGE, MAKE A
1. *run a straight course:* εὐθυδρομέω EUTHYDROMEŌ
Acts 16.11 we made a direct voyage to Samothrace

DIRECTIONS, GIVE
1. *appoint, direct:* διατάσσω DIATASSŌ
1 Cor 11.34 I will give directions when I come
2. *command* (mid.): ἐντέλλω ENTELLŌ
Heb 11.22 gave directions concerning his burial[x]

DIRT
1. *filth:* ῥύπος RHYPOS*
1 Pet 3.21 not as a removal of dirt from the body

DISADVANTAGE, BE AT A
1. *project, excel:* προέχω (pass.) PROECHŌ
Rom [3. 9 Are we Jews *at any disadvantage?*†

DISAGREE
1. *be at variance:* ἀσύμφωνος εἶναι ASYMPHŌNOS* [A.6.a.3]
Acts 28.25 as they disagreed among themselves

DISAPPOINT
1. *put to shame, dishonor:* καταισχύνω KATAISCHYNŌ
Rom 5. 5 hope does not disappoint us

DISARM
1. *strip off:* ἀπεκδύομαι APEKDYOMAI
Col 2.15 He disarmed the principalities and powers

DISBELIEVE
1. *disobey:* ἀπειθέω APEITHEŌ
Acts 19. 9 some were stubborn and disbelieved
2. *disbelieve, be faithless:* ἀπιστέω APISTEŌ
Lk 24.41 they still disbelieved for joy
Acts 28.24 while others disbelieved

DISCERN
1. *examine closely:* ἀνακρίνω ANAKRINŌ
1 Cor 2.14 gifts of the Spirit . . spiritually discerned
2. *differentiate, decide:* διακρίνω DIAKRINŌ
1 Cor 11.29 without discerning the body

DISCERNING
1. *able to discern:* κριτικός KRITIKOS*
Heb 4.12 discerning the thoughts . . of the heart

DISCERNMENT
1. *sense perception:* αἴσθησις AISTHĒSIS*
Phil 1. 9 love may abound . . with . . all discernment

DISCHARGE
1. *make ineffective, hinder:* καταργέω KATARGEŌ
Rom 7. 2 if her husband dies she is discharged
7. 6 now we are discharged from the law

DISCIPLE
1. *learner, pupil:* μαθητής MATHĒTĒS*
Mt 5. 1 when he sat down his disciples came to him
8.21 Another of the disciples said . . "Lord
8.23 his disciples followed him
9.10 sinners . . sat down with Jesus and his disciples
9.11 Pharisees . . said to his disciples
9.14 disciples of John came . . saying, "Why do we . . fast,[w] but your disciples do not fast?
9.19 Jesus . . followed him, with his disciples
9.37 to his disciples, "The harvest is plentiful
10. 1 he called to him his twelve disciples
10.24 "A disciple is not above his teacher
10.25 "for the disciple to be like his teacher
10.42 "a cup of cold water because he is a disciple
11. 1 finished instructing his twelve disciples
11. 2 John . . sent word by his disciples
12. 1 his disciples were hungry
12. 2 "your disciples are doing what is not lawful
12.49 stretching . . his hand toward his disciples
13.10 disciples came and said to him
13.36 his disciples came to him, saying

Mt 14.12 his disciples came and took the body
14.15 When it was evening, the disciples came
14.19 gave the loaves to the disciples, and the disciples gave them to the crowds
14.22 he made the disciples get into the boat
14.26 disciples saw him walking on the sea
15. 2 "Why do your disciples transgress?
15.12 the disciples came and said to him
15.23 his disciples came and begged him
15.32 Jesus called his disciples to him
15.33 the disciples said to him, "Where?
15.36 gave them to the disciples, and the disciples gave them to the crowds
16. 5 When the disciples reached the other side
16.13 asked his disciples, "Who do men say?
16.20 strictly charged the disciples to tell no one
16.21 Jesus began to show his disciples
16.24 Jesus told his disciples, "If any . . come
17. 6 When the disciples heard this, they fell
17.10 disciples asked . . "Then why do the scribes?
17.13 disciples understood that he was speaking
17.16 "I brought him to your disciples
17.19 the disciples came to Jesus privately
18. 1 the disciples came to Jesus, saying
19.10 disciples said . . "it is not expedient to marry
19.13 The disciples rebuked the people
19.23 Jesus said to his disciples, "Truly
19.25 the disciples . . were greatly astonished
20.17 he took the twelve disciples aside
21. 1 then Jesus sent two disciples
21. 6 disciples went and did as Jesus had directed
21.20 When the disciples saw it they marveled
22.16 they sent their disciples to him
23. 1 Then said Jesus . . to his disciples
24. 1 his disciples came to point out to him
24. 3 disciples came to him privately
26. 1 he said to his disciples
26. 8 when the disciples saw it, they were indignant
26.17 the disciples came to Jesus, saying
26.18 " 'passover at your house with my disciples
26.19 disciples did as Jesus had directed them
26.20 he sat at table with the twelve disciples[e]‡
26.26 gave it to the disciples and said, "Take
26.35 so said all the disciples
26.36 said to his disciples, "Sit here
26.40 he came to the disciples
26.45 came to the disciples and said
26.56 all the disciples forsook him and fled
27.64 "lest his disciples go and steal him away
28. 7 "go quickly and tell his disciples
28. 8 they departed . . and ran to tell his disciples
28.13 " 'His disciples came by night and stole him
28.16 the eleven disciples went to Galilee
Mk 2.15 sinners . . with Jesus and his disciples
2.16 said to . . disciples, "Why . . with . . sinners?
2.18 John's disciples . . were fasting; and people . . said . . "Why do John's disciples and the disciples of the Pharisees fast, but your disciples do not fast?
2.23 his disciples began to pluck heads of grain
3. 7 Jesus withdrew with his disciples
3. 9 told his disciples to have a boat ready
4.34 his own disciples he explained everything
5.31 disciples said to him, "You see the crowd
6. 1 his disciples followed him
6.29 disciples . . came and took his body
6.35 disciples . . said, "This is a lonely place
6.41 gave ⟨the loaves⟩ to the disciples
6.45 made his disciples get into the boat
7. 2 some . . disciples ate with hands defiled
7. 5 "your disciples . . eat with hands defiled
7.17 disciples asked him about the parable
8. 1 he called his disciples to him
8. 4 disciples answered . . "How . . feed these men?
8. 6 gave ⟨the loaves⟩ to his disciples
8.10 he got into the boat with his disciples
8.27 Jesus went . . with his disciples
Mk 8.27 on the way he asked his disciples
8.33 seeing his disciples, he rebuked Peter
8.34 he called . . the multitude with his disciples
9.14 when they came to the disciples
9.18 "I asked your disciples to cast it out
9.28 "disciples asked . . "Why could we not?
9.31 for he was teaching his disciples
10.10 in the house the disciples asked him again
10.13 the disciples rebuked them
10.23 said to his disciples, "How hard it will be!
10.24 disciples were amazed at his words
10.46 he was leaving Jericho with his disciples
11. 1 he sent two of his disciples
11.14 his disciples heard it
12.43 he called his disciples to him
13. 1 one of his disciples said to him, "Look!
14.12 disciples said . . "Where will you have us go?
14.13 he sent two . . disciples . . "Go into the city
14.14 " 'to eat the passover with my disciples
14.16 disciples set out and went to the city
14.32 said to . . disciples, "Sit here, while I pray
16. 7 "go, tell his disciples and Peter
Lk 5.30 scribes murmured against his disciples
5.33 "so do the disciples of the Pharisees
6. 1 disciples plucked and ate . . heads of grain
6.13 called his disciples, and chose . . twelve
6.17 came . . with a great crowd of his disciples
6.20 he lifted up his eyes on his disciples
6.40 "A disciple is not above his teacher
7.11 disciples and a great crowd went with him
7.18 disciples of John told him of all these things
7.19 John, calling to him two of his disciples
8. 9 disciples asked him what this parable meant
8.22 One day he got into a boat with his disciples
9.14 said to his disciples, "Make them sit down
9.16 gave ⟨the loaves⟩ to the disciples
9.18 he was praying . . disciples were with him
9.40 "I begged your disciples to cast it out
9.43 all marveling . . he said to his disciples
9.54 when his disciples James and John saw
10.23 turning to the disciples he said privately
11. 1 one of his disciples said . . "teach us to pray, as John taught his disciples
12. 1 he began to say to his disciples . . "Beware
12.22 said to his disciples . . "do not be anxious
14.26 "he cannot be my disciple
14.27 "Whoever does not . . cannot be my disciple
14.33 "whoever . . does not . . cannot be my disciple
16. 1 said to . . disciples, "There was a rich man
17. 1 said to his disciples, "Temptations . . come
17.22 said to the disciples, "The days are coming
18.15 when the disciples saw it, they rebuked
19.29 at . . Olivet, he sent two of the disciples
19.37 disciples began to rejoice and praise God
19.39 "Teacher, rebuke your disciples
20.45 in the hearing of all . . he said to his disciples
22.11 " 'to eat the passover with my disciples
22.39 to the Mount . . ; the disciples followed him
22.45 from prayer, he came to the disciples
Jn 1.35 John . . standing with two of his disciples
1.37 The two disciples heard him say this
2. 2 Jesus also was invited . . with his disciples
2.11 his disciples believed in him
2.12 he went down . . with . . his disciples
2.17 disciples remembered that it was written
2.22 disciples remembered . . he had said this
3.22 Jesus and his disciples went into . . Judea
3.25 discussion arose between John's disciples
4. 1 baptizing more disciples than John
4. 2 (did not baptize, but only his disciples
4. 8 his disciples had gone away into the city
4.27 Just then his disciples came
4.31 disciples besought him . . "Rabbi, eat
4.33 disciples said . . "Has any . . brought . . food?
6. 3 there sat down with his disciples
6. 8 One of his disciples, Andrew
6.12 told his disciples, "Gather . . fragments

Jn 6.16 his disciples went down to the sea
6.22 not entered the boat with his disciples
6.22 his disciples had gone away alone
6.24 Jesus was not there, nor his disciples
6.60 disciples . . said, "This is a hard saying
6.61 his disciples murmured at it
6.66 After this many . . disciples drew back
7. 3 "that your disciples may see the works
8.31 "you are truly my disciples
9. 2 disciples asked him, "Rabbi, who sinned?
9.27 "Do you too want to become his disciples?
9.28 "You are his disciple, but we are disciples of Moses
11. 7 he said to the disciples, "Let us go
11. 8 disciples said to him, "Rabbi
11.12 disciples said . . "Lord, . . he will recover
11.54 there he stayed with the disciples
12. 4 Judas Iscariot, one of his disciples
12.16 His disciples did not understand this
13. 5 began to wash the disciples' feet
13.22 disciples looked at one another, uncertain
13.23 One of his disciples, whom Jesus loved
13.35 "all men will know that you are my disciples
15. 8 "so prove to be my disciples
16.17 Some . . disciples said . . "What is this?
16.29 disciples said . . "now you are speaking plainly!
18. 1 went . . with his disciples across the Kidron
18. 1 garden, which he and his disciples entered
18. 2 Jesus often met there with his disciples
18.15 Peter followed . . and so did another disciple
18.15 this disciple was known to the high priest
18.16 other disciple . . known to the high priest
18.17 "Are not you . . one of this man's disciples?
18.19 questioned Jesus about his disciples
18.25 "Are not you also one of his disciples?
19.26 disciple whom he loved standing near
19.27 said to the disciple, "Behold, your mother!
19.27 the disciple took her to his own home
19.38 Joseph of Arimathea, who was a disciple
20. 2 other disciple, the one whom Jesus loved
20. 3 Peter then came out with the other disciple
20. 4 the other disciple outran Peter
20. 8 other disciple, who reached the tomb first
20.10 the disciples went back to their homes
20.18 Mary M. went and said to the disciples
20.19 doors being shut where the disciples were
20.20 disciples were glad . . they saw the Lord
20.25 disciples told him, "We have seen
20.26 his disciples were again in the house
20.30 other signs in the presence of the disciples
21. 1 Jesus revealed himself . . to the disciples
21. 2 Peter . . and two others of his disciples
21. 4 yet the disciples did not know
21. 7 disciple whom Jesus loved said to Peter
21. 8 the other disciples came in the boat
21.12 none of the disciples dared ask him
21.14 Jesus was revealed to the disciples
21.20 the disciple whom Jesus loved
21.23 that this disciple was not to die
21.24 the disciple who is bearing witness

Acts 6. 1 when the disciples were increasing
6. 2 twelve summoned the body of the disciples
6. 7 number of the disciples multiplied
9. 1 threats and murder against the disciples
9.10 a disciple at Damascus named Ananias
9.19 he was with the disciples at Damascus
9.25 his disciples took him by night
9.26 he attempted to join the disciples
9.26 they did not believe that he was a disciple
9.38 disciples, hearing that Peter was there
11.26 disciples were . . first . . called Christians
11.29 disciples determined . . to send relief
13.52 the disciples were filled with joy
14.20 when the disciples gathered about him
14.22 strengthening the souls of the disciples
14.28 remained no little time with the disciples
15.10 "a yoke upon the neck of the disciples
16. 1 A disciple was there, named Timothy
18.23 strengthening all the disciples
18.27 wrote to the disciples to receive him
19. 1 There he found some disciples
19. 9 taking the disciples with him
19.30 the disciples would not let him
20. 1 Paul sent for the disciples
20.30 "to draw away the disciples after them
21. 4 having sought out the disciples
21.16 some of the disciples from Caesarea
21.16 Mnason of Cyprus, an early disciple

2. *woman disciple:* *μαθήτρια* MATHĒTRIA*
Acts 9.36 at Joppa a disciple named Tabitha

DISCIPLE, BE A

1. *be a pupil, make disciples:* *μαθητεύω* (pass.) MATHĒTEUŌ
Mt 27.57 Joseph, who also was a disciple of Jesus

DISCIPLE, FELLOW

1. *fellow disciple:* *συμμαθητής* SYMMATHĒTĒS*
Jn 11.16 Thomas . . said to his fellow disciples

DISCIPLES, MAKE

1. *be a pupil, make disciples:* *μαθητεύω* MATHĒTEUŌ
Mt 28.19 "Go . . and make disciples of all nations
Acts 14.21 When they . . had made many disciples

DISCIPLINE

1. *teaching, training:* *παιδεία* PAIDEIA
Eph 6. 4 bring them up in the discipline . . of the Lord
Heb 12. 5 "not regard lightly . . discipline of the Lord
12. 7 for discipline that you have to endure
12. 8 If you are left without discipline
12.11 discipline seems painful rather than pleasant

2. *discipline, educate:* *παιδεύω* PAIDEUŌ
Heb 12. 6 Lord disciplines him whom he loves
12. 7 son . . whom his father does not discipline
12.10 they disciplined us for a short time

3. *teacher, instructor:* *παιδευτής* PAIDEUTĒS [A.1.d]
Heb 12. 9 we have had . . fathers to discipline us

DISCLOSE

1. *disclose, show:* *δηλόω* DĒLOŌ
1 Cor 3.13 the Day will disclose it

2. *reveal, inform:* *μηνύω* MĒNYŌ
Acts 23.30 "⟨a plot⟩ was disclosed to me

3. *make manifest, make known:* *φανερόω* PHANEROŌ
Rom 16.26 disclosed and . . made known to all
1 Cor 4. 5 Lord . . will disclose . . purposes of the heart

DISCLOSED

1. *visible, known:* *φανερός* PHANEROS
1 Cor 14.25 the secrets of his heart are disclosed

DISCORD

1. *division, split:* *σχίσμα* SCHISMA
1 Cor 12.25 that there may be no discord in the body

DISCOURAGED, BECOME

1. *be disheartened:* *ἀθυμέω* ATHYMEŌ*
Col 3.21 lest they become discouraged

DISCREDIT

1. *slander, blaspheme:* *βλασφημέω* BLASPHĒMEŌ
Tit 2. 5 that the word of God may not be discredited

DISCUSS

DISCUSS TOGETHER

1. *talk with:* *διαλαλέω* DIALALEŌ
Lk 6.11 discussed . . what they might do to Jesus

2. *discuss:* *διαλέγομαι* DIALEGOMAI
Mk 9.34 they had discussed . . who was the greatest

3. *calculate, argue:* *διαλογίζομαι* DIALOGIZOMAI
Mt 16. 7 they discussed it among themselves
16. 8 "why do you discuss among yourselves?
Mk 8.16 they discussed it with one another
8.17 "Why . . discuss . . that you have no bread?
9.33 "What were you discussing on the way?

4. *compute, reason:* *συλλογίζομαι* SYLLOGIZOMAI*
Lk 20. 5 they discussed it with one another

5. *examine together with, dispute:* *συζητέω* SYZĒTEŌ
Mk 9.16 "What are you discussing with them?
Lk 24.15 While they were . . discussing together

DISCUSSION
1. *seeking, controversy:* ζήτησις ZĒTĒSIS
Jn 3.25 discussion arose between John's disciples

DISCUSSION, VAIN
1. *idle talk:* ματαιολογία MATAIOLOGIA*
1 Tim 1. 6 wandered away into vain discussion

DISEASE
1. *weakness, sickness:* ἀσθένεια ASTHENEIA
Acts 28. 9 who had diseases also came and were cured
2. *whip, plague:* μάστιξ MASTIX
Mk 3.10 all who had diseases pressed upon him
5.29 she felt . . that she was healed of her disease
5.34 "go in peace, and be healed of your disease
3. *disease:* νόσημα NOSĒMA
Jn [5. 4 *healed of whatever disease he had*‡
4. *sickness, disease:* νόσος NOSOS*
Mt 4.23 healing every disease and every infirmity
4.24 those afflicted with various diseases
8.17 "He took our infirmities and bore our diseases
9.35 healing every disease and every infirmity
10. 1 gave them authority . . to heal every disease
Mk 1.34 many who were sick with various diseases
Lk 4.40 any that were sick with various diseases
6.17 came . . to be healed of their diseases
7.21 In that hour he cured many of diseases
9. 1 authority over all demons and . . diseases
Acts 19.12 diseases left them and . . evil spirits came out

DISEASED, BE
1. *be weak, be sickly:* ἀσθενέω ASTHENEŌ
Jn 6. 2 which he did on those who were diseased

DISFIGURE
1. *make unseen, destroy:* ἀφανίζω APHANIZŌ
Mt 6.16 "hypocrites . . disfigure their faces

DISGRACEFUL
1. *shameful:* αἰσχρός AISCHROS
1 Cor 11. 6 disgraceful for a woman to be shorn
2. *shame:* αἰσχύνη (gen.) AISCHYNĒ
2 Cor 4. 2 We have renounced disgraceful . . ways

DISGUISE ONESELF
1. *change the form:* μετασχηματίζω (mid.) METASCHĒMATIZŌ
2 Cor 11.13 disguising themselves as apostles
11.14 even Satan disguises himself as an angel
11.15 his servants also disguise themselves

DISH
1. *platter:* πίναξ PINAX
Lk 11.39 "Pharisees cleanse the outside of the . . dish
2. *bowl:* τρύβλιον TRYBLION*
Mt 26.23 "He who has dipped his hand in the dish
Mk 14.20 "one who is dipping bread into the dish

DISHONEST
1. *wrongdoing, injustice:* ἀδικία (gen.) ADIKIA
Lk 16. 8 "master commended the dishonest steward
2. *unjust, unrighteous:* ἄδικος ADIKOS
Lk 16.10 he who is dishonest in a very little is dishonest also in much

DISHONOR
1. *hold in no honor, insult:* ἀτιμάζω ATIMAZŌ
Jn 8.49 "I honor my Father, and you dishonor me
Rom 1.24 dishonoring . . their bodies among themselves
2.23 do you dishonor God by breaking the law?
Jas 2. 6 you have dishonored the poor man
2. *dishonor, disgrace:* ἀτιμία ATIMIA
1 Cor 15.43 sown in dishonor, it is raised in glory
2 Cor 6. 8 in honor and dishonor, in ill repute and good
3. *put to shame, dishonor:* καταισχύνω KATAISCHYNŌ
1 Cor 11. 4 who prays . . head covered dishonors his head
11. 5 prays . . head unveiled dishonors her head

DISHONOR, SUFFER
1. *hold in no honor, insult:* ἀτιμάζω (pass.) ATIMAZŌ
Acts 5.41 worthy to suffer dishonor for the name

DISHONORABLE
1. *dishonor, disgrace:* ἀτιμία (gen.) ATIMIA
Rom 1.26 God gave them up to dishonorable passions

DISMAL, LOOK
1. *be sad looking:* γίνεσθαι σκυθρωπός SKYTHRŌPOS [A.6.a.3]
Mt 6.16 "And when you fast, do not look dismal

DISMISS
1. *loose from, dismiss:* ἀπολύω APOLYŌ
Mt 14.22 while he dismissed the crowds
14.23 after he had dismissed the crowds
Mk 6.45 while he dismissed the crowd
Acts 19.41 he had said this, he dismissed the assembly
23.22 the tribune dismissed the young man

DISOBEDIENCE
1. *disobedience:* ἀπείθεια APEITHEIA*
Rom 11.30 mercy because of their disobedience
11.32 consigned all men to disobedience
Eph 2. 2 now at work in the sons of disobedience
5. 6 wrath . . comes upon the sons of disobedience
Col [3. 6 wrath . . is coming *upon the sons of d.*‡
Heb 4. 6 failed to enter because of disobedience
4.11 that no one fall by . . disobedience
2. *unwillingness to hear:* παρακοή PARAKOĒ*
Rom 5.19 by one man's disobedience many . . sinners
2 Cor 10. 6 ready to punish every disobedience
Heb 2. 2 every transgression or disobedience

DISOBEDIENT
1. *not made subject:* ἀνυπότακτος ANYPOTAKTOS
1 Tim 1. 9 law is . . for the . . disobedient
2. *disobey:* ἀπειθέω (part.) APEITHEŌ
Rom 10.21 "to a disobedient and contrary people
3. *disobedient:* ἀπειθής APEITHĒS*
Lk 1.17 "turn . . the disobedient to . . wisdom
Acts 26.19 "I was not disobedient to the . . vision
Rom 1.30 inventors of evil, disobedient to parents
2 Tim 3. 2 disobedient to their parents, ungrateful
Tit 1.16 they are detestable, disobedient
3. 3 we ourselves were once foolish, disobedient

DISOBEDIENT, BE
1. *disobey:* ἀπειθέω APEITHEŌ
Rom 11.30 you were once disobedient to God
11.31 they have now been disobedient
Heb 3.18 but to those who were disobedient
11.31 not perish with those who were disobedient

DISOBEY
1. *disobey:* ἀπειθέω APEITHEŌ
1 Pet 2. 8 "they stumble because they disobey
2. *pass by, transgress:* παρέρχομαι PARERCHOMAI
Lk 15.29 " 'I never disobeyed your command
3. *keep, observe:* τηρέω (neg.) TĒREŌ
1 Jn 2. 4 who says "I know him" but disobeys

DISORDER
1. *instability:* ἀκαταστασία AKATASTASIA
2 Cor 12.20 there may be . . conceit, and disorder
Jas 3.16 there will be disorder and every vile practice

DISOWN
1. *deny:* ἀρνέομαι ARNEOMAI
1 Tim 5. 8 he has disowned the faith

DISPATCH, WITH
1. *cut short:* συντέμνω (part.) SYNTEMNŌ*
Rom 9.28 "will execute his sentence . . with . . dispatch

DISPENSATION
1. *service:* διακονία DIAKONIA
2 Cor 3. 7 dispensation of death, carved . . on stone
3. 8 the dispensation of the Spirit
3. 9 if . . splendor in the d. of condemnation
3. 9 d. of righteousness must far exceed

DISPERSE
1. *loose from one another:* διαλύω DIALYŌ*
Acts 5.36 "all who followed him were dispersed

DISPERSION
1. *scattering:* διασπορά DIASPORA*
Jn 7.35 "Does he intend to go to the Dispersion?
Jas 1. 1 To the twelve tribes in the Dispersion
1 Pet 1. 1 To the exiles of the Dispersion

DISPLAY
1. *show, display:* ἐνδείκνυμι (mid.) ENDEIKNYMI
1 Tim 1.16 Christ might display his perfect patience

DISPLEASE
1. *please:* ἀρέσκω (neg.) ARESKŌ
1 Th 2.15 displease God and oppose all men

DISPOSAL
1. *authority, power:* ἐξουσία EXOUSIA
Acts 5. 4 "was it not at your disposal?

DISPOSED, BE
1. *think, suppose:* δοκέω DOKEŌ
1 Cor 11.16 If any one is disposed to be contentious
2. *will, wish:* θέλω THELŌ
1 Cor 10.27 If . . you are disposed to go, eat

DISPOSSESS
1. *holding back, possession:* κατάσχεσις KATASCHESIS [B.1.a.2]
Acts 7.45 "when they dispossessed the nations

DISPUTE
1. *contradiction, dispute:* ἀντιλογία ANTILOGIA
Heb 6.16 in all their disputes an oath is final
7. 7 beyond d. . . the inferior . . by the superior
2. *separation:* διάκρισις DIAKRISIS
Rom 14. 1 welcome him, but not for disputes
3. *discuss:* διαλέγομαι DIALEGOMAI
Acts 24.12 "they did not find me disputing
Jude . 9 Michael . . disputed about the body of Moses
4. *quarrel, fight:* μάχομαι MACHOMAI
Jn 6.52 Jews then disputed among themselves
5. *love of victory:* φιλονεικία PHILONEIKIA*
Lk 22.24 A dispute also arose among them
6. *examine together with, dispute:* συζητέω SYZĒTEŌ
Mk 12.28 heard them disputing with one another
Acts 6. 9 some . . arose and disputed with Stephen
9.29 disputed against the Hellenists
7. *dispute, discussion:* συζήτησις SYZĒTĒSIS
Acts [28.29 *holding much dispute among themselves*‡

DISPUTE ABOUT WORDS
1. *fight about words:* λογομαχέω LOGOMACHEŌ*
2 Tim 2.14 to avoid disputing about words
2. *war about words:* λογομαχία LOGOMACHIA*
1 Tim 6. 4 craving . . for disputes about words

DISPUTE, POINT OF
1. *what is sought, question:* ζήτημα ZĒTĒMA
Acts 25.19 "they had certain points of dispute

DISQUALIFIED
1. *counterfeit, worthless:* ἀδόκιμος ADOKIMOS
1 Cor 9.27 lest . . I myself should be disqualified

DISQUALIFY
1. *give judgment against:* καταβραβεύω KATABRABEUŌ*
Col 2.18 Let no one disqualify you

DISREGARD
1. *deny, nullify:* ἀθετέω ATHETEŌ
1 Th 4. 8 whoever disregards this, disregards not man but God
2. *despise:* περιφρονέω PERIPHRONEŌ*
Tit 2.15 Let no one disregard you

DISREPUTE
1. *refutation, discredit:* ἀπελεγμός APELEGMOS*
Acts 19.27 "trade of ours may come into disrepute

DISREPUTE, HELD IN
1. *unhonored, dishonored:* ἄτιμος ATIMOS
1 Cor 4.10 You are held in honor, but we in disrepute

DISRESPECTFUL, BE
1. *look down upon, despise:* καταφρονέω KATAPHRONEŌ
1 Tim 6. 2 must not be disrespectful . . rather . . serve

DISSENSION
1. *dissension:* διχοστασία DICHOSTASIA*
Rom 16.17 who create dissensions and difficulties
Gal 5.20 selfishness, dissension, party spirit
2. *strife, rivalry:* ἔρις ERIS
[a]sg.
1 Tim 6. 4 envy, dissension, slander, base suspicions
Tit 3. 9 [a]controversies, genealogies, dissensions
3. *division, split:* σχίσμα SCHISMA
1 Cor 1.10 I appeal . . that there be no dissensions
4. *standing, uprising:* στάσις STASIS
Acts 15. 2 Paul and Barnabas had no small dissension
23. 7 a dissension arose between the Pharisees
23.10 when the dissension became violent

DISSIPATION
1. *trick, fraud, pleasure:* ἀπάτη APATĒ
2 Pet 2.13 reveling in their dissipation,[g] carousing‡
2. *intoxication:* κραιπάλη KRAIPALĒ*
Lk 21.34 "hearts be weighed down with dissipation

DISSOLVE
1. *break up, unbind:* λύω LYŌ
2 Pet 3.10 the elements will be dissolved with fire
3.11 all these things are thus to be dissolved
3.12 the heavens will be kindled and dissolved!

DISTANCE
IDIOMATICALLY
a. Lk 15.20 "But while he was yet at a distance ἔτι δὲ αὐτοῦ μακρὰν ἀπέχοντος [APECHŌ; MAKRAN]

DISTANCE, AT A
1. *from afar:* μακρόθεν MAKROTHEN
[a]ἀπὸ μακρόθεν
Mt 26.58 [a]But Peter followed him at a distance
Mk 14.54 [a]Peter had followed him at a distance
Lk 22.54 Peter followed at a distance
23.49 [a]the women who had followed . . stood at a d.
2. *distantly, from afar:* πόρρωθεν PORRŌTHEN
Lk 17.12 met by ten lepers, who stood at a distance

DISTANCE, AT SOME
1. *far:* μακράν MAKRAN
Mt 8.30 swine . . feeding at some distance from them

DISTANCE, IN THE
1. *from afar:* μακρόθεν MAKROTHEN
[a]ἀπὸ μακρόθεν
Mk 11.13 [a]seeing in the distance a fig tree in leaf

DISTANT, BE
1. *be distant:* ἀπέχω APECHŌ
Mt 14.24 the boat . . was many furlongs distant‡

DISTINCT
1. *distinction:* διαστολή DIASTOLĒ [A.1.b.5]
1 Cor 14. 7 If . . instruments . . do not give distinct notes

DISTINCTION
1. *distinction:* διαστολή DIASTOLĒ
Rom 3.22 For there is no distinction
10.12 no distinction between Jew and Greek

DISTINCTION, MAKE A
DISTINCTIONS, MAKE
1. *differentiate, decide:* διακρίνω DIAKRINŌ
[a]pass.
Acts 11.12 "Spirit told me . . making no distinction
15. 9 "he made no distinction between us and them
Jas 2. 4 [a]have you not made distinctions?

DISTINGUISH
1. *separation:* διάκρισις DIAKRISIS [B.1.a.2]
Heb 5.14 trained by practice to distinguish good

DISTINGUISH, ABILITY TO
1. *separation:* διάκρισις DIAKRISIS
1 Cor 12.10 the ability to distinguish between spirits

DISTRACTED, BE
1. *divert, disturb:* περισπάω (pass.) PERISPAŌ*
Lk 10.40 Martha was distracted with much serving

DISTRESS
1. *force, necessity:* ἀνάγκη ANAGKĒ
Lk 21.23 "great distress shall be upon the earth
1 Cor 7.26 in view of the present[m] distress
1 Th 3. 7 in . . our distress . . we have been comforted
2. *subdue, oppress:* καταπονέω KATAPONEŌ
2 Pet 2. 7 greatly distressed by the licentiousness
3. *distress, difficulty:* στενοχωρία STENOCHŌRIA
Rom 2. 9 distress for every human being
8.35 tribulation, or distress, or persecution

4. *conflict, distress:* συνοχή SYNOCHĒ
Lk 21.25 "upon the earth distress of nations

DISTRESS, IN
1. *question by torture, torment:* βασανίζω (pass. part.) BASANIZŌ
Mt 8. 6 "paralyzed at home, in terrible distress

DISTRESSED, BE
1. *be dismayed, be anxious:* ἀδημονέω ADĒMONEŌ
Phil 2.26 he has . . been distressed because you
2. *grieve, cause pain:* λυπέω (pass.) LYPEŌ
Mt 17.23 they were greatly distressed
18.31 "they were greatly distressed

DISTRESSED, BE GREATLY
1. *astonish:* ἐκθαμβέω (pass.) EKTHAMBEŌ
Mk 14.33 to be greatly distressed and troubled

DISTRIBUTE
1. *distribute:* διαδίδωμι DIADIDŌMI
Lk 18.22 "Sell all that you have and distribute
Jn 6.11 distributed them to those who were seated
Acts 4.35 distribution was made . . as any had need
2. *divide:* διαμερίζω DIAMERIZŌ
Acts 2. 3 distributed and resting on each one
2.45 sold their . . goods . . distributed them to all

DISTRIBUTED
IDIOMATICALLY
a. Heb 2.4 by gifts of the Holy Spirit distributed πνεύματος ἁγίου μερισμοῖς [MERISMOS]

DISTRIBUTION
1. *service:* διακονία DIAKONIA
Acts 6. 1 widows were neglected in the . . distribution

DISTRICT
1. *earth, land:* γῆ GĒ
Mt 9.26 report . . went through all that district
9.31 spread his fame through all that district
2. *boundary:* ὅριον (pl.) HORION
Acts 13.50 Jews . . drove them out of their district
3. *part, portion:* μερίς MERIS
Acts 16.12 leading city of the district[x] of Macedonia
4. *part, share:* μέρος (pl.) MEROS
Mt 2.22 he withdrew to the district of Galilee
15.21 withdrew to the district of Tyre
16.13 into the district of Caesarea Philippi
Mk 8.10 went to the district of Dalmanutha[d]

DISTRUST
1. *distrust, faithlessness:* ἀπιστία APISTIA
Rom 4.20 No distrust made him waver

DISTURB
1. *throw into confusion:* ἐκταράσσω EKTARASSŌ*
Acts 16.20 "These . . Jews . . are disturbing our city
2. *trouble, disturb:* ταράσσω TARASSŌ
Acts 17. 8 the city authorities were disturbed

DIVERSE
1. *diversified:* ποικίλος POIKILOS
Heb 13. 9 Do not be led away by diverse . . teachings

DIVIDE
1. *distribute:* διαδίδωμι DIADIDŌMI
Lk 11.22 "one stronger than he . . divides his spoil
2. *take apart, divide:* διαιρέω DIAIREŌ
Lk 15.12 "he divided his living between them
3. *divide:* διαμερίζω DIAMERIZŌ
Mt 27.35 they divided his garments among them
Mk 15.24 crucified him, and divided his garments
Lk 11.17 "Every kingdom divided against itself
11.18 "if Satan also is divided against himself
12.52 "in one house there will be five divided
12.53 "they will be divided, father against son
22.17 "Take this, and divide it
23.34 And they cast lots to divide his garments
4. *divide, distribute:* μερίζω (act. or mid.) MERIZŌ
Mt 12.25 "Every kingdom divided against itself
12.25 "house divided against itself will stand
12.26 "Satan . . is divided against himself
Mk 3.24 "If a kingdom is divided against itself
3.25 "And if a house is divided against itself
3.26 "if Satan . . is divided, he cannot stand
6.41 he divided the two fish among them all
Lk 12.13 "bid my brother divide the inheritance
1 Cor 1.13 Is Christ divided?
7.34 his interests are divided
5. *divide, split:* σχίζω SCHIZŌ
Acts 14. 4 the people of the city were divided
23. 7 the assembly was divided
IDIOMATICALLY
a. Lk 11.17 "a divided household falls[0] οἶκος ἐπὶ οἶκον πίπτει [EPI]

DIVIDER
1. *divider, distributor:* μεριστής MERISTĒS*
Lk 12.14 "Man, who made me a judge or divider?

DIVIDING WALL
1. *dividing wall:* μεσότοιχον MESOTOICHON*
Eph 2.14 he . . has broken down the dividing wall

DIVINATION, SPIRIT OF
1. *spirit of divination:* πύθων PYTHŌN*
[a]+ πνεῦμα B.3.b.6
Acts 16.16 [a]slave girl who had a spirit of divination

DIVINE
1. *divine:* θεῖος THEIOS
2 Pet 1. 3 His divine power has granted to us all
1. 4 partakers of the divine nature
2. *God:* θεός (gen. or dat.) THEOS
Rom 3.25(26) in his divine forbearance he had passed
2 Cor 10. 4 divine power to destroy strongholds
11. 2 I feel a divine jealousy for you
Col 1.25 a minister according to the divine office
1 Tim 1. 4 speculations rather than . . divine training[a]
CONTEXTUALLY
Heb 11. 2 the men of old received divine approval

DIVINITY
1. *demon, divine power:* δαιμόνιον DAIMONION
Acts 17.18 "seems to be a preacher of foreign divinities

DIVISION
1. *division, dissension:* διαμερισμός DIAMERISMOS*
Lk 12.51 "to give peace . . ? No . . but rather division
2. *division for the daily service:* ἐφημερία EPHĒMERIA*
Lk 1. 5 priest . . Zechariah,[b] of . . division of Abijah
1. 8 when his division was on duty
3. *dividing:* μερισμός MERISMOS
Heb 4.12 piercing to the division of soul and spirit
4. *division, split:* σχίσμα SCHISMA
Jn 7.43 there was a division among the people
9.16 There was a division among them
10.19 again a division among the Jews
1 Cor 11.18 I hear that there are divisions among you

DIVISIONS, SET UP
1. *mark off by dividing:* ἀποδιορίζω APODIORIZŌ*
Jude .19 who set up divisions, worldly people

DIVORCE
1. *let go, leave, forgive:* ἀφίημι APHIĒMI
1 Cor 7.11 the husband should not divorce his wife
7.12 he should not divorce her
7.13 she should not divorce him
2. *loose from, dismiss:* ἀπολύω APOLYŌ
Mt 1.19 Joseph . . resolved to divorce her quietly
5.31 " 'Whoever divorces his wife, let him give
5.32 "every one who divorces his wife
19. 3 "Is it lawful to divorce one's wife?
19. 8 "Moses allowed you to divorce your wives
19. 9 "whoever divorces his wife . . and marries
Mk 10. 2 "Is it lawful for a man to divorce?
10.11 "Whoever divorces his wife and marries
10.12 "if she divorces her husband and marries
Lk 16.18 "Every one who divorces his wife
3. *divorce, bill of divorce:* ἀποστάσιον APOSTASION
Mt 19. 7 "Why . . give a certificate of divorce?
Mk 10. 4 "Moses allowed . . a certificate of divorce

DIVORCE, CERTIFICATE OF
1. *divorce, bill of divorce:* ἀποστάσιον APOSTASION
Mt 5.31 " 'let him give her a certificate of divorce

DIVORCED WOMAN
1. *loose from, dismiss:* ἀπολύω (subst. perf. pass. part. fem.) APOLYŌ
Mt 5.32 "whoever marries a divorced woman
[19. 9 "*he who marries a divorced woman*‡
Lk 16.18 "he who marries a woman divorced

DIVULGE
1. *report:* ἀναγγέλλω ANAGGELLŌ
Acts 19.18 confessing and divulging their practices

DO (*See also, e.g.,* GOOD, DO; RIGHT, DO)
1. *do a service, minister:* διακονέω DIAKONEŌ [A.6.a.6]
Heb 6.10 in serving the saints, as you still do
2. *show, display:* ἐνδείκνυμι ENDEIKNYMI
2 Tim 4.14 the coppersmith did me great harm
3. *work, do:* ἐργάζομαι ERGAZOMAI
Mt 26.10 "she has done a beautiful thing to me
Mk 14. 6 "She has done a beautiful thing to me
Jn 6.28 "to be doing the works of God
Acts 10.35 "any one who . . does what is right
13.41 " 'I do a deed . . you will never believe
Rom 2.10 peace for every one who does good
13.10 Love does no wrong to a neighbor
1 Cor 16.10 he is doing the work of the Lord
Gal 6.10 let us do good to all men
4. *work, deed:* ἔργον ERGON [A.1.a]
[a]A.6.a.3
Mt 23. 3 "but not what they do
Jn 8.39 "you would do what Abraham did
8.40 "this is not what Abraham did
2 Cor 10.11 [a]what we say by letter . . we do when present
Rev 20.12 dead were judged . . by what they had done
20.13 all were judged by what they had done
22.12 "to repay every one for what he has done
5. *come to be, happen, be:* γίνομαι GINOMAI [A.6.e]
Lk 4.23 " 'what we . . heard you did at Capernaum
Eph 5.12 the things that they do in secret
6. *put down:* κατατίθημι KATATITHĒMI [A.6.a.5]
Acts 24.27 desiring to do the Jews a favor, Felix
25. 9 Festus, wishing to do the Jews a favor
7. *achieve:* κατεργάζομαι KATERGAZOMAI
Rom 2. 9 distress for . . human being who does evil
7.17 it is no longer I that do it, but sin
7.18 I can will what is right, but I cannot do it
7.20 it is no longer I that do it, but sin
1 Cor 5. 4(3) on the man who has done such a thing
Eph 6.13 and having done all, to stand
1 Pet 4. 3 suffice for doing what the Gentiles like
8. *show, offer, cause:* παρέχω (mid.) PARECHŌ
Lk 7. 4 "He is worthy to have you do this for him
9. *walk, behave:* περιπατέω PERIPATEŌ [B.3.b.7]
Eph 4.17 you must no longer live as the Gentiles do
1 Th 4. 1 learned . . to live . . , just as you are doing
10. *do, make:* ποιέω POIEŌ
Mt 1.24 he did as the angel of the Lord commanded
5.19 "he who does them . . shall be called great
5.46 "Do not even the tax collectors do the same?
5.47 "what more are you doing than others? Do not even the Gentiles do the same?
6. 2 "sound no trumpet . . as the hypocrites
6. 3 "not . . know what your right hand is doing
7.12 "whatever you wish that men would do to you, do so to them
7.21 "but he who does the will of my Father
7.22 " 'did we not . . do many mighty works?
7.24 "who hears these words . . and does them
7.26 "who hears these words . . and does not do
8. 9 "I say . . to my slave, 'Do this,' and he does
9.28 "Do you believe . . I am able to do this?
12. 2 "Look, your disciples are doing what is not lawful to do on the sabbath
12. 3 "Have you not read what David did?
12.12 "it is lawful to do good on the sabbath
12.50 "whoever does the will of my Father
13.28 " 'An enemy has done this
13.58 he did not do many mighty works there
17.12 "they . . did to him whatever they pleased
Mt 18.35 "my heavenly Father will do to every one
19.16 "Teacher, what good deed must I do?
20. 5 "the ninth hour, he did the same
20.15 " 'Am I not allowed to do what I choose?
20.32 "What do you want me to do for you?
21. 6 disciples went and did as Jesus had directed
21.15 scribes saw the wonderful things that he did
21.21 "have faith and never doubt, you will . . do
21.23 "By what authority are you doing these?
21.24 "by what authority I do these things
21.27 "by what authority I do these things
21.31 "Which of the two did the will of his father?
21.36 "they did the same to them
21.40 "what will he do to those tenants?
23. 5 "They do all their deeds to be seen by men
23.23 "these you ought to have done
24.46 "whom his master . . will find so doing
25.40 " 'as you did it to one of the least of these my brethren, you did it to me
25.45 " 'as you did it not to one of the least of these, you did it not to me
26.12 "she has done it to prepare me for burial
26.13 "what she has done will be told in memory
26.19 disciples did as Jesus had directed
27.22 "Then what shall I do with Jesus?
27.23 "Why, what evil has he done?
28.15 they . . did as they were directed
Mk 2.24 "why are they doing what is not lawful?
2.25 "Have you never read what David did?
3. 4 "Is it lawful on the sabbath to do good?
3. 8 hearing all that he did, came to him
3.35 "Whoever does the will of God is my brother
5.19 "tell them how much the Lord has done
5.20 how much Jesus had done for him
5.32 he looked around to see who had done it
6. 5 he could do no mighty work there
6.30 told him all that they had done and taught
7.12 "you no longer permit him to do anything
7.13 "And many such things you do
7.37 "He has done all things well
9.13 "they did to him whatever they pleased
9.39 "no one who does a mighty work
10.17 "what must I do to inherit eternal life?
10.35 "do for us whatever we ask of you
10.36 "What do you want me to do for you?
10.51 "What do you want me to do for you?
11. 3 " 'Why are you doing this?
11. 5 "What are you doing, untying the colt?
11.28 "By what authority are you doing these?
11.28 "who gave you this authority to do them?
11.29 "I will tell you by what authority I do these
11.33 "by what authority I do these things
12. 9 "What will the owner of the vineyard do?
14. 7 "whenever you will, you can do good to them
14. 8 "She has done what she could
14. 9 "what she has done will be told in memory
15. 8 as he was wont to do for them
15.12 "Then what shall I do with the man?
15.14 "Why, what evil has he done?
Lk 1.25 "Thus the Lord has done to me
1.49 "he who is mighty has done great things
2.27 to do for him according to the custom
3.10 "What then shall we do?
3.11 "he who has food, let him do likewise
3.12 "Teacher, what shall we do?
3.14 "And we, what shall we do?
3.19 all the evil things that Herod had done
4.23 " 'what we have heard . . do here also
5. 6 when they had done this, they enclosed
6. 2 "Why are you doing what is not lawful to do on the sabbath?
6. 3 "Have you not read what David did?
6.10 he did so, and his hand was restored
6.11 discussed . . what they might do to Jesus
6.23 "for so their fathers did to the prophets
6.26 "so their fathers did to the false prophets
6.27 "do good to those who hate you

Lk 6.31 "And as you wish that men would do to you, do so to them
6.33 "For even sinners do the same
6.46 "Why do you . . not do what I tell you?
6.47 "who . . hears my words and does them
6.49 "he who hears and does not do them
7. 8 "I say . . to my slave, 'Do this,' and he does it
8.21 "those who hear the word of God and do it
8.39 "declare how much God has done for you
8.39 how much Jesus had done for him
9.10 apostles told him what they had done
9.43 all marveling at everything he did
[9.54 "to bid fire come down . . *as Elijah did*‡
10.25 "what shall I do to inherit eternal life?
10.28 "do this, and you will live
10.37 Jesus said to him, "Go and do likewise
11.42 "these you ought to have done
12. 4 "have no more that they can do
12.17 "he thought to himself, 'What shall I do?
12.18 " 'I will do this: I will pull down my barns
12.43 "when he comes will find so doing
12.48 "he . . did what deserved a beating
16. 3 "steward said to himself, 'What shall I do?
16. 4 " 'I have decided what to do
17. 9 "Does he thank the servant because he did?
17.10 "when you have done all that is commanded
17.10 " 'we have only done what was our duty
18.18 "what shall I do to inherit eternal life?
18.41 "What do you want me to do for you?
19.48 they did not find anything they could do
20. 2 "by what authority you do these things
20. 8 "by what authority I do these things
20.13 " 'What shall I do? I will send my . . son
20.15 "What then will the owner . . do?
22.19 "Do this in remembrance of me‡
23.22 "Why, what evil has he done?
23.31 "if they do this when the wood is green
23.34 "they know not what they do[n]‡
Jn 2. 5 "Do whatever he tells you
2.11 first of his signs, Jesus did at Cana
2.18 "What sign . . for doing this?
2.23 when they saw the signs which he did
3. 2 "Rabbi, . . no one can do . . signs that you do
3.21 he who does what is true
4.29 "a man who told me all that I ever did
4.34 "My food is to do the will of him
4.39 "He told me all that I ever did
4.45 all that he had done in Jerusalem
4.54 now the second sign that Jesus did
5.16 because he did this on the sabbath
5.19 "I say to you, the Son can do nothing of his own accord, but only what he sees the Father doing; for whatever he does, that the Son does likewise
5.20 "shows him all that he himself is doing
5.29 "come forth, those who have done good
5.30 "I can do nothing on my own authority
5.36 "works which I am doing, bear me witness
6. 2 they saw the signs which he did
6. 6 he himself knew what he would do
6.14 people saw the sign which he had done
6.28 they said to him, "What must we do?
6.30 "Then what sign do you do?
6.38 "I have come . . not to do my own will
7. 3 "see the works you are doing
7. 4 "If you do these things, show yourself
7.17 "if any man's will is to do his will
7.21 "I did one deed, and you all marvel
7.31 "When the Christ appears, will he do more signs than this man has done?
7.51 "without first . . learning what he does
8.28 "I do nothing on my own authority
8.29 "I always do what is pleasing to him
8.38 "you do what you have heard
8.39 "you would do what Abraham did
8.40 "this is not what Abraham did
8.41 "You do what your father did
Jn 8.44 "your will is to do your father's desires
9.16 "How can . . a sinner do such signs?
9.26 They said to him, "What did he do to you?
9.31 "if any one . . does his will . . God listens
9.33 "If . . not from God, he could do nothing
10.25 "works that I do . . bear witness to me
10.37 "If I am not doing the works of my Father
10.38 "if I do them . . believe the works
10.41 "John did no sign
11.45 Jews . . who . . had seen what he did, believed
11.46 told them what Jesus had done
11.47 "What are we to do?
12.16 remembered . . this . . had been done to him
12.18 they heard he had done this sign
12.37 Though he had done so many signs
13. 7 "What I am doing you do not know now
13.12 "Do you know what I have done to you?
13.15 "an example, that you also should do as I have done to you
13.17 "blessed are you if you do them
13.27 Jesus said to him, "What you are going to do, do quickly
14.10 "Father who dwells in me does his works
14.12 "he who believes in me will also do the works that I do; and greater works than these will he do
14.13 "Whatever you ask . . I will do it
14.14 "if you ask[g] . . in my name, I will do it
14.31 "I do as the Father has commanded me
15. 5 "apart from me you can do nothing
15.14 "if you do what I command you
15.15 "does not know what his master is doing
15.21 "all this they will do to you on my account
15.24 "If I had not done among them the works which no one else did
16. 3 "will do this because they have not known
17. 4 "the work which thou gavest me to do
18.35 "what have you done?
19.25(24) So the soldiers did this
20.30 Now Jesus did many other signs
21.25 also many other things which Jesus did
Acts 1. 1 all that Jesus began to do and teach
2.22 "signs which God did through him
2.37 "Brethren, what shall we do?
4. 7 "by what name did you do this?
4.16 "What shall we do with these men?
4.28 "to do whatever . . thy plan had predestined
6. 8 Stephen . . did great wonders and signs
8. 6 heard him and saw the signs which he did
9. 6 "you will be told what you are to do
9.13 "how much evil he has done to thy saints
10.39 "we are witnesses to all that he did
11.30 they did so, sending it to the elders
12. 8 "Dress yourself . . " And he did so
13.22 " 'David . . who will do all my will
14.11 "the crowds saw what Paul had done
14.15 "Men, why are you doing this?
14.27 declared all that God had done with them
15. 4 declared all that God had done with them
15.12 they related what signs . . God had done
16.18 this she did for many days
16.30 "Men, what must I do to be saved?
19.11 God did extraordinary miracles
19.14 Seven sons of . . Sceva were doing this
21.13 "What are you doing, weeping?
21.19 he related . . the things that God had done
21.23 "Do therefore what we tell you
21.33 He inquired . . what he had done
22.10 "And I said, 'What shall I do, Lord?
22.10 " 'told all that is appointed for you to do
22.26 "What are you about to do?
26.10 "I did so in Jerusalem
28.17 "I had done nothing against the people
Rom 1.32 they not only do them but approve
2. 3 you judge . . and yet do them yourself
2.14 When Gentiles . . do by nature what the law
3. 8 why not do evil that good may come?

Rom 3.12 "no one does good, not even one
4.21 God was able to do what he had promised
7.15 I do the very thing I hate
7.16 if I do what I do not want
7.19 I do not do the good I want
7.20 Now if I do what I do not want
7.21 when I want to do right, evil lies close
12.20 "by so doing you will heap burning coals
13. 3 Then do what is good
13. 4 if you do wrong, be afraid
1 Cor 7.36 let him do as he wishes: let them marry
7.37 to keep . . his betrothed,[z] he will do well
7.38 he who marries his betrothed[z] does well; . . he who refrains from marriage will do better
9.23 I do it all for the sake of the gospel
10.31 whether you eat or drink, or whatever you do, do all to the glory of God
11.24 "Do this in remembrance of me
11.25 "Do this, as often as you drink it
16. 1 as I directed . . so you also are to do
2 Cor 8.10 you began not only to do but to desire
11.12 what I do I will continue to do, in order to undermine the claim of those
13. 7 we pray God that you may not do wrong . . but that you may do what is right
Gal 2.10 which very thing I was eager to do
3.10 "abide by all things . . in the . . law, . . do them
3.12 "He who does them shall live by them
5.17 prevent you from doing what you would
Eph 3.20 able to do far more abundantly
6. 6 servants[f] of Christ, doing the will of God
6. 8 whatever good any one does
6. 9 Masters, do the same to them, and forbear
Phil 2.14 Do all things without grumbling
Col 3.17 whatever you do, in word or deed
1 Th 4.10 we exhort you, brethren, to do so more
5.11 build one another up, just as you are doing
5.24 He who calls you is faithful, and . . will do it
2 Th 3. 4 we have confidence . . that you are doing and will do the things which we command
1 Tim 4.16 by so doing you will save . . yourself
5.21 doing nothing from partiality
2 Tim 4. 5 do the work of an evangelist
Tit 3. 5 not because of deeds done by us
Phm .14 to do nothing without your consent
.21 knowing that you will do even more
Heb 6. 3 this we will do if God permits[l]‡
7.27 he did this once for all
10. 7 " 'Lo, I have come to do thy will, O God
10. 9 "Lo, I have come to do thy will
10.36 so that you may do the will of God
13. 6 "not . . afraid; what can man do to me?
13.17 Let them do this joyfully, and not sadly
13.19 do this in order that I may be restored
13.21 that you may do his will
Jas 2. 8 If you . . fulfil the . . law . . you do well
2.19 You believe that God is one; you do well
4.15 "we shall live and we shall do this or that
4.17 Whoever knows what is right to do and fails to do it, for him it is sin
1 Pet 3.11 "let him turn away from evil and do right
3.12 "But . . against those that do evil
2 Pet 1.10 for if you do this you will never fall
1.19 You will do well to pay attention
1 Jn 2.17 who does the will of God abides for ever
2.29 every one who does right is born of him
3. 7 He who does right is righteous
3.10 whoever does not do right is not of God
3.22 because we . . do what pleases him
3 Jn . 5 Beloved, it is a loyal thing you do
. 6 You will do well to send them on
.10 I will bring up what he is doing
Rev 2. 5 " 'Remember . . repent and do the works
22.11 "Let . . the righteous still do right
[22.14 Blessed are those who *do his commandments*‡

11. *do, practice:* πράσσω PRASSŌ
Lk 22.23 to question . . which . . would do this
23.15 "nothing deserving death has been done
23.41 "this man has done nothing wrong
Jn 3.20 every one who does evil hates the light
5.29 "those who have done evil, to . . judgment
Acts 5.35 "take care what you do with these men
15.29 "you will do well. Farewell
19.36 "be quiet and do nothing rash
25.25 "he had done nothing deserving death
26. 9 "I ought to do many things in opposing
26.26 "for this was not done in a corner
26.31 "doing nothing to deserve death
Rom 1.32 those who do such things deserve to die
2. 1 you, the judge, are doing the very same
2. 2 judgment . . falls upon those who do such
2. 3 when you judge those who do such things
7.15 For I do not do what I want
7.19 the evil I do not want is what I do
9.11 not yet born and had done nothing
1 Cor 5. 2 Let him who has done this be removed
9.17 if I do this of my own will
2 Cor 5.10 according to what he has done
Gal 5.21 those who do such things shall not inherit
Eph 6.21 how I am and what I am doing
Phil 4. 9 What you have . . seen in me, do

IDIOMATICALLY
a. Jn 12.19 "You see that you can do nothing θεωρεῖτε ὅτι οὐκ ὠφελεῖτε οὐδέν [ŌPHELEŌ]
b. Heb 4.13 with whom we have to do πρὸς ὃν ἡμῖν ὁ λόγος [LOGOS]

For "do" as an auxiliary verb, see the other words concerned (e.g., do EVIL, do GOOD, do HARM, do WRONG). The common English use of "do" in questions and negations and for emphasis has no counterpart in Greek and therefore is omitted.

DO WITH, HAVE NOTHING TO

1. *ask for, decline:* παραιτέομαι (imper.) PARAITEOMAI
1 Tim 4. 7 Have n. to do with godless and silly myths
2 Tim 2.23 Have n. to do with stupid . . controversies
Tit 3.10 have nothing more to do with him

DO WITH, HAVE TO

1. *have, hold:* ἔχω ECHŌ
1 Jn 4.18 For fear has to do with punishment
2. *mix up together:* συναναμείγνυμι (pass.) SYNANAMEIGNYMI
2 Th 3.14 have nothing to do with him

DOCTRINE (*See also* TEACH A DIFFERENT DOCTRINE)

1. *teaching:* διδαχή DIDACHĒ
Rom 16.17 in opposition to the doctrine . . taught
2 Jn . 9 who . . does not abide in the d. of Christ
. 9 he who abides in the doctrine has both
.10 If any one . . does not bring this doctrine
2. *teaching:* διδασκαλία DIDASKALIA
Mt 15. 9 " 'teaching as doctrines the precepts of men
Mk 7. 7 " 'teaching as doctrines the precepts of men
Eph 4.14 carried about with every wind of doctrine
Col 2.22 according to human precepts and doctrines
1 Tim 1.10 whatever else is contrary to sound doctrine
4. 1 giving heed to . . doctrines of demons
4. 6 good doctrine which you have followed
Tit 1. 9 able to give instruction in sound doctrine
2. 1 teach what befits sound doctrine
2.10 that . . they may adorn the doctrine of God
3. *word, reckoning:* λόγος LOGOS
Heb 6. 1 let us leave the elementary doctrine[0]

DOER

1. *maker, poet:* ποιητής POIĒTĒS
Rom 2.13 the doers of the law who will be justified
Jas 1.22 be doers of the word, and not hearers only
1.23 a hearer of the word and not a doer
1.25 being no hearer that forgets but a doer
4.11 you are not a doer of the law but a judge

DOES WRONG, ONE WHO

1. *doing evil:* κακοποιός (subst.) KAKOPOIOS
1 Pet 2.14 sent . . to punish those who do wrong

DOG

1. *little dog, puppy:* κυνάριον KYNARION*
Mt 15.26 "It is not fair to . . throw it to the dogs

Mt 15.27 "even the dogs eat the crumbs that fall
Mk 7.27 "it is not right to . . throw it to the dogs
7.28 "yet even the dogs under the table eat
2. *dog:* κύων KYŌN*
Mt 7. 6 "Do not give dogs what is holy
Lk 16.21 "the dogs came and licked his sores
Phil 3. 2 Look out for the dogs
2 Pet 2.22 The dog turns back to his own vomit
Rev 22.15 Outside are the dogs and sorcerers

DOING
1. *work, deed:* ἔργον ERGON
[a]A.1.a
1 Tim 5.10 [a]devoted herself to doing good
Rev 2.22 " 'unless they repent of her doings
2. *making, creation:* ποίησις POIĒSIS*
Jas 1.25 he shall be blessed in his doing

DOING, BE S.'S
1. *come to be, happen, be:* γίνομαι GINOMAI [B.2.d.1]
Mt 21.42 "this was the Lord's doing, and . . marvelous
Mk 12.11 "this was the Lord's doing, and . . marvelous

DOMESTIC
1. *working at home:* οἰκουργός OIKOURGOS*
Tit 2. 5 be sensible, chaste, domestic, kind

DOMINEER
1. *dominate completely:* κατακυριεύω KATAKYRIEUŌ
1 Pet 5. 3 not as domineering over . . your charge

DOMINION
1. *kingdom, reign:* βασιλεία BASILEIA
Rev 17.18 "city which has dominion over the kings
2. *authority, power:* ἐξουσία EXOUSIA
Col 1.13 delivered us from the dominion of darkness
3. *strength, sovereignty:* κράτος KRATOS
1 Tim 6.16 To him be honor and eternal dominion
1 Pet 4.11 To him belong glory and dominion
5.11 To him be the dominion for ever and ever
Jude .25 be glory, majesty, dominion
Rev 1. 6 to him be glory and dominion for ever
4. *ruling power, lordship:* κυριότης KYRIOTĒS
Eph 1.21 above all rule and authority and . . dominion
Col 1.16 all things . . whether thrones or dominions

DOMINION OVER, HAVE
1. *be lord, rule:* κυριεύω KYRIEUŌ
Rom 6. 9 death no longer has dominion over him
6.14 sin will have no dominion over you

DONE

DONE, BE
1. *come to be, happen, be:* γίνομαι GINOMAI
[a]part.
Mt 6.10 "Thy kingdom come, Thy will be done
8.13 "be it done for you as you have believed
9.29 "According to your faith be it done to you
11.20 where . . his mighty works had been done
11.21 [a]"if the mighty works done in you had been done in Tyre and Sidon
11.23 [a]"if the mighty works done in you had been done in Sodom
15.28 "Be it done for you as you desire
18.19 "it will be done for them by my Father
21.21 "if you say . . 'Be taken up . .' it will be done
26.42 "My Father, . . thy will be done
Mk 5.33 knowing what had been done to her
Lk 9. 7 Herod . . heard of all that was done
10.13 [a]"if the mighty works done in you had been done in Tyre and Sidon
13.17 the glorious things that were done by him
14.22 " 'Sir, what you commanded has been done
22.42 "not my will, but thine, be done[l]
23. 8 [a]hoping to see some sign done by him
Jn 15. 7 "ask . . and it shall be done for you
Acts 2.43 signs were done through the apostles
5.12 wonders were done among the people
12. 9 did not know that what was done . . was real
14. 3 granting signs . . to be done by their hands
21.14 we . . said, "The will of the Lord be done
1 Cor 14.26 Let all things be done for edification
14.40 all things should be done decently
16.14 Let all that you do be done in love
Rev 16.17 a loud voice . . saying, "It is done!
21. 6 "It is done! I am the Alpha and the Omega

DONE, WHAT S. HAS
1. *practice, act:* πρᾶξις PRAXIS
Mt 16.27 "he will repay . . man for what he has done

DOOMED, BE
1. *one must:* δεῖ DEI
Rev 11. 5 thus he is doomed to be killed

DOOMED TO PASS AWAY, BE
1. *make ineffective, hinder:* καταργέω (pass.) KATARGEŌ
1 Cor 2. 6 rulers . . who are doomed to pass away

DOOR
1. *door:* θύρα THYRA
Mt 6. 6 "go into your room and shut the door
25.10 "bridegroom came . . and the door was shut
27.60 he rolled a great stone to the door
Mk 1.33 whole city was gathered . . about the door
2. 2 no longer room . . even about the door
11. 4 they . . found a colt tied at the door
15.46 he rolled a stone against the door
16. 3 "Who will roll . . the stone . . from the door?
Lk 11. 7 " 'Do not bother me; the door is now shut
13.24 "Strive to enter by the narrow door
13.25 "householder has risen up and shut the door
13.25 "you will begin to . . knock at the door
Jn 10. 1 "he who does not enter . . by the door
10. 2 "he who enters by the door is the shepherd
10. 7 "I am the door of the sheep
10. 9 "I am the door; if any one enters by me
18.16 Peter stood outside at the door
20.19 doors being shut where the disciples were
20.26 The doors were shut, but Jesus came
Acts 5. 9 "Hark, the feet of those . . at the door
5.19 angel of the Lord opened the prison doors
5.23 "We found . . sentries standing at the doors
12. 6 sentries before the door were guarding
12.13 when he knocked at the door of the gateway
14.27 he . . opened a door of faith to the Gentiles
16.26 immediately all the doors were opened
16.27 jailer . . saw that the prison doors were open
1 Cor 16. 9 a wide door for effective work has opened
2 Cor 2.12 a door was opened for me in the Lord
Col 4. 3 pray . . that God may open to us a door
Jas 5. 9 behold, the Judge is . . at the doors
Rev 3. 8 " 'Behold, I have set before you an open door
3.20 " 'Behold, I stand at the door and knock; if any one hears my voice and opens the door
4. 1 lo, in heaven an open door!

DOOR, MAID WHO KEEPS THE

DOOR, WHO KEEPS THE

DOORKEEPER
1. *doorkeeper:* θυρωρός THYRŌROS
[a]fem. [b]appos.
Mk 13.34 "commands the doorkeeper to . . watch
Jn 18.16 [a]spoke to the maid who kept the door
18.17 [b]maid who kept the door said to Peter

DOOR TO, BE NEXT
1. *border on:* συνομορέω SYNOMOREŌ*
Acts 18. 7 his house was next door to the synagogue

DORCAS: Δορκάς 'dòrkəs
Acts 9.36 a disciple named Tabitha, which means D.
9.39 garments which D. made while . . with them

DOT
1. *horn, hook:* κεραία KERAIA*
Mt 5.18 "not a dot, will pass from the law
Lk 16.17 "than for one dot of the law to become void

DOUBLE
1. *second:* δεύτερος DEUTEROS
2 Cor 1.15 that you might have a double pleasure[b]
2. *double:* διπλοῦς DIPLOUS
1 Tim 5.17 elders . . worthy of double honor

Rev 18. 6 "repay her double for her deeds; mix a double draught for her

DOUBLE MIND, MAN OF

1. *double-minded:* δίψυχος (subst.) DIPSYCHOS
   Jas 4. 8 purify your hearts, you men of double mind

DOUBLE-MINDED

1. *double-minded:* δίψυχος DIPSYCHOS
   Jas 1. 8 double-minded man, unstable in all his ways

DOUBLE-TONGUED

1. *double-tongued:* δίλογος DILOGOS*
   1 Tim 3. 8 be serious, not double-tongued

DOUBT

1. *differentiate, decide:* διακρίνω (mid. or aor. pass.) DIAKRINŌ
   Mt 21.21 "if you have faith and never doubt
   Mk 11.23 "whoever . . does not doubt in his heart
   Rom 14.23 But he who has doubts is condemned
   Jas 1. 6 ask in faith, with no doubting, for he who doubts is like a wave of the sea
   Jude .22 convince some, who doubt
2. *doubt:* διστάζω DISTAZŌ*
   Mt 14.31 "O man of little faith, why did you doubt?
   28.17 they worshiped him; but some doubted

DOUBT, NO

1. *in all ways, assuredly:* πάντως PANTŌS
   Acts 28. 4 "No doubt this man is a murderer

DOUBTLESS

1. *in all ways, assuredly:* πάντως PANTŌS
   Lk 4.23 "Doubtless you will quote . . this proverb
2. *happen, attain:* τυγχάνω TYGCHANŌ [B.3.b.8]
   1 Cor 14.10 There are doubtless many . . languages

DOUGH

CONTEXTUALLY
   Rom 11.16 If the d. offered as first fruits is holy

DOVE

1. *dove:* περιστερά PERISTERA
   Mt 3.16 the Spirit of God descending like a dove
   10.16 "wise as serpents and innocent as doves
   Mk 1.10 Spirit descending upon him like a dove
   Lk 3.22 descended . . in bodily form, as a dove
   Jn 1.32 "I saw the Spirit descend as a dove

DOWN (*See also* GO DOWN; LET DOWN)

1. *down from, against:* κατά (+gen.) KATA
   Mt **8.32**
   Mk **5.13**
   Lk **8.33**
2. *downward, below:* κάτω KATŌ
   Mt 4. 6 "If . . the Son of God, throw yourself down
   Lk 4. 9 "If . . the Son of God, throw yourself down
   Jn 8. 6 Jesus bent down and wrote with his finger"‡
   Acts 20. 9 being overcome by sleep, he fell down

DOWNCAST

1. *low, poor, humble:* ταπεινός TAPEINOS
   2 Cor 7. 6 God, who comforts the downcast

DRAG

1. *bring, lead:* ἄγω AGŌ
   Mt 10.18 "you will be dragged before governors
2. *draw, drag:* ἕλκω HELKŌ
   Acts 16.19 seized Paul and Silas and dragged them
   21.30 they seized Paul and dragged him out
   Jas 2. 6 is it not they who drag you into court?
3. *pull down, drag:* κατασύρω KATASYRŌ*
   Lk 12.58 "lest he drag you to the judge
4. *draw, sweep:* σύρω SYRŌ
   Jn 21. 8 dragging the net full of fish
   Acts 8. 3 he dragged off men and women . . to prison
   14.19 stoned Paul and dragged him out of the city
   17. 6 dragged Jason . . before the city authorities

DRAG WITH ONE

1. *snatch and carry away with:* συναρπάζω SYNARPAZŌ
   Acts 19.29 dragging with them Gaius and Aristarchus

DRAGON

1. *dragon, serpent:* δράκων DRAKŌN*
   Rev 12. 3 behold, a great red dragon
   Rev 12. 4 the dragon stood before the woman
   12. 7 Michael and his angels fighting . . the dragon; and the dragon and his angels fought
   12. 9 the great dragon was thrown down
   12.13 the dragon saw that he had been thrown
   12.16 the river which the dragon had poured
   12.17 the dragon was angry with the woman
   13. 2 to it the dragon gave his power
   13. 4 Men worshiped the dragon
   13.11 it spoke like a dragon
   16.13 issuing from the mouth of the dragon
   20. 2 he seized the dragon, that ancient serpent

DRAIN

IDIOMATICALLY
   a. Rev 16.19 to make her drain the cup of the fury δοῦναι αὐτῇ τὸ ποτήριον τοῦ οἴνου τοῦ θυμοῦ [DIDŌMI]

DRAUGHT

CONTEXTUALLY
   Rev 18. 6 "mix a double draught for her in the cup

DRAW

1. *draw up:* ἀναβιβάζω ANABIBAZŌ*
   Mt 13.48 "men drew it ashore and . . sorted
2. *draw water:* ἀντλέω ANTLEŌ
   Jn 2. 9 (servants who had drawn the water knew
   4. 7 woman of Samaria ⟨came⟩ to draw water
   4.15 "that I may not thirst, nor come here to draw
3. *draw away:* ἀποσπάω APOSPAŌ
   Mt 26.51 drew his sword, and struck the slave
4. *come to be, happen, be:* γίνομαι GINOMAI [A.6.a.5]
   Jn 6.19 they saw Jesus . . drawing near to the boat
5. *draw, drag:* ἕλκω HELKŌ
   Jn 6.44 "unless the Father who sent me draws him
   12.32 "and I . . will draw all men to myself
   18.10 Simon Peter, having a sword, drew it
6. *draw, pull:* σπάω (mid.) SPAŌ*
   Mk 14.47 one of those who stood by drew his sword
   Acts 16.27 drew . . sword and was about to kill himself

IDIOMATICALLY
   a. Jn 6.66 many of his disciples drew back πολλοὶ τῶν μαθητῶν αὐτοῦ ἀπῆλθον εἰς τὰ ὀπίσω [APERCHOMAI]
   b. Jn 18.6 they drew back and fell to the ground ἀπῆλθαν εἰς τὰ ὀπίσω καὶ ἔπεσαν χαμαί [APERCHOMAI]

DRAW AWAY

1. *depart, withdraw from:* ἀφίστημι APHISTĒMI
   Acts 5.37 "drew away some of the people after him
2. *draw away:* ἀποσπάω APOSPAŌ
   Acts 20.30 "to draw away the disciples after them

DRAW BACK

1. *draw back:* ὑποστέλλω HYPOSTELLŌ
   Gal 2.12 when they came he drew back

DRAW NEAR
DRAW NEAR TO

1. *approach:* ἐγγίζω EGGIZŌ
   Mt 21. 1 when they drew near to Jerusalem
   21.34 "When the season of fruit drew near
   Mk 11. 1 when they drew near to Jerusalem
   Lk 7.12 As he drew near to the gate of the city
   15. 1 sinners were all drawing near to hear him
   15.25 "as he came and drew near to the house
   18.35 As he drew near to Jericho, a blind man
   19.29 When he drew near to Bethphage
   19.37 As he was now drawing near
   19.41 when he drew near and saw the city
   21.28 "because your redemption is drawing near
   22. 1 feast of Unleavened Bread drew near
   22.47 He drew near to Jesus to kiss him
   24.15 Jesus himself drew near
   24.28 So they drew near to the village
   Acts 7.17 "But as the time of the promise drew near
   22. 6 "As I . . drew near to Damascus
   Heb 7.19 hope . . through which we draw near to God
   10.25 as you see the Day drawing near
   Jas 4. 8 Draw near to God and he will draw near to you

2. *come to, approach:* *προσέρχομαι* PROSERCHOMAI
Acts 7.31 "as he drew near to look, the voice . . came
Heb 4.16 Let us then . . draw near to the throne
7.25 to save those who draw near to God
10. 1 never . . make perfect those who draw near
10.22 let us draw near with a true heart
11. 6 whoever would draw near to God
3. *fill completely:* *συμπληρόω* (pass.) SYMPLĒROŌ
Lk 9.51 days drew near for him to be received up

DRAW OUT
1. *draw water:* *ἀντλέω* ANTLEŌ
Jn 2. 8 "draw some out, and take it to the steward

DRAW UP
1. *pull up:* *ἀνασπάω* ANASPAŌ
Acts 11.10 "all was drawn up again into heaven

DRAW WITH, S. TO
1. *bucket for drawing water:* *ἄντλημα* ANTLĒMA*
Jn 4.11 "Sir, you have nothing to draw with

DREAM
1. *dream:* *ἐνυπνιάζομαι* ENYPNIAZOMAI
Acts 2.17 " 'your old men shall dream dreams
2. *dream:* *ἐνύπνιον* ENYPNION*
Acts 2.17 " 'your old men shall dream dreams
3. *dream:* *ὄναρ* ONAR*
Mt 1.20 an angel . . appeared to him in a dream
2.12 being warned in a dream not to return
2.13 an angel . . appeared to Joseph in a dream
2.19 an angel . . appeared in a dream to Joseph
2.22 being warned in a dream he withdrew
27.19 "I have suffered much over him . . in a dream

DREAMING, IN ONE'S
1. *dream:* *ἐνυπνιάζομαι* (part.) ENYPNIAZOMAI
Jude . 8 these men in their dreamings defile the flesh

DRESS
1. *throw around, put on:* *περιβάλλω* PERIBALLŌ
Mk 16. 5 a young man . . dressed in a white robe

DRESS ONESELF
1. *gird:* *ζώννυμι* (mid.) ZŌNNYMI
Acts 12. 8 "Dress yourself and put on your sandals

DRIFT
1. *carry through, differ:* *διαφέρω* DIAPHERŌ
Acts 27.27 as we were drifting across the sea of Adria

DRIFT AWAY
1. *flow by:* *παραρρέω* PARARREŌ*
Heb 2. 1 closer attention . . lest we drift away

DRINK
1. *wine:* *οἶνος* OINOS
Tit 2. 3 not to be slanderers or slaves to drink
2. *drink:* *πίνω* PINŌ*
[a]inf. as a noun
Mt 6.25 "do not be anxious . . what you shall drink
6.31 "anxious, saying . . 'What shall we drink?
11.18 "For John came neither eating nor drinking
11.19 "Son of man came eating and drinking
20.22 "Are you able to drink the cup that I am to drink?" They said to him, "We are able
20.23 He said to them, "You will drink my cup
24.38 "they were eating and drinking, marrying
24.49 "eats and drinks with the drunken
26.27 saying, "Drink of it, all of you
26.29 "I shall not drink again of this fruit of the vine until that day when I drink it new
26.42 "if this cannot pass unless I drink it
27.34 offered him wine to drink, mingled with gall; . . when he tasted it, he would not drink it
Mk [2.16 "Why . . eat *and drink* with tax collectors?‡
10.38 "Are you able to drink the cup that I drink, or to be baptized with the baptism?
10.39 And Jesus said to them, "The cup that I drink you will drink
14.23 he gave it to them . . they all drank of it
14.25 "I shall not drink again of the fruit of the vine until that day when I drink it new
16.18 "if they drink any deadly thing[k]‡
Lk 1.15 "and he shall drink no wine
5.30 "Why do you . . drink with tax collectors?
5.33 "disciples of John fast . . but yours eat and d.
5.39 "no one after drinking old wine desires new
7.33 "the Baptist has come . . drinking no wine
7.34 "Son of man has come eating and drinking
10. 7 "eating and drinking what they provide
12.19 " 'take your ease, eat, drink, be merry
12.29 "do not seek . . what you are to drink
12.45 "begins . . to eat and drink and get drunk
13.26 " 'We ate and drank in your presence
17. 8 " 'serve me, till I eat and drink; and afterward you shall eat and drink
17.27 "They ate, they drank, they married
17.28 "they ate, they drank, they bought
22.18 "from now on I shall not drink of the fruit
22.30 "that you may eat and drink at my table
Jn 4. 7 [a]Jesus said to her, "Give me a drink
4. 9 [a]"How is it that you, a Jew, ask a drink?
4.10 [a]"who . . is saying to you, 'Give me a drink
4.12 "Jacob . . drank from it himself, and his sons
4.13 "Every one who drinks of this . . will thirst
4.14 "whoever drinks of the water . . I shall give
6.53 "unless you . . drink his blood . . no life
6.54 "who eats my flesh and drinks my blood
6.56 "who eats my flesh and drinks my blood
7.37 "If any . . thirst, let him come . . and drink†
18.11 "shall I not drink the cup?
Acts 9. 9 for three days he . . neither ate nor drank
23.12 bound . . by an oath neither to eat nor drink
23.21 "bound . . by an oath neither to eat nor drink
Rom 14.21 it is right not to eat meat or drink wine
1 Cor 9. 4 [a]not have the right to our food and drink?
10. 4 all drank the same supernatural[o] drink
10. 4 they drank from the supernatural[o] Rock
10. 7 "The people sat down to eat and drink
10.21 You cannot drink the cup of the Lord
10.31 whether you eat or drink, or whatever
11.22 you . . have houses to eat and drink in
11.25 "Do this, as often as you drink it
11.26 For as often as you . . drink the cup
11.27 Whoever . . eats the bread or drinks the cup
11.28 Let a man examine himself, and so . . drink
11.29 any one who . . drinks without discerning the body eats and drinks judgment
15.32 "Let us eat and drink, for tomorrow we die
Heb 6. 7 land which has drunk the rain
Rev 14.10 "also shall drink the wine of God's wrath
16. 6 "thou hast given them blood to drink
18. 3 "all nations have drunk[k] the wine‡
3. *drink:* *πόμα* POMA*
1 Cor 10. 4 all drank the same supernatural[o] drink
Heb 9.10 but deal only with food and drink
4. *drinking, drink:* *πόσις* POSIS*
Jn 6.55 "my blood is drink indeed
Rom 14.17 the kingdom . . is not food and drink
Col 2.16 judgment . . in questions of food and drink

DRINK FREELY
1. *be drunk:* *μεθύω* METHYŌ
Jn 2.10 "when men have drunk freely, then the poor

DRINK, GIVE
DRINK, GIVE S. TO
DRINK, MAKE TO
1. *water, give to drink:* *ποτίζω* POTIZŌ
Mt 25.35 " 'I was thirsty and you gave me drink
25.37 " 'Lord, when did we . . give thee drink?
25.42 " 'I was thirsty and you gave me no drink
27.48 vinegar . . and gave it to him to drink
Mk 9.41 "whoever gives you a cup of water to drink
15.36 vinegar . . and gave it to him to drink
Rom 12.20 "if your enemy . . is thirsty, give him drink
1 Cor 12.13 all were made to drink of one Spirit
Rev 14. 8 "she who made all nations drink the wine

DRINK, STRONG
1. *fermented liquor:* *σίκερα* SIKERA*
Lk 1.15 "he shall drink no wine nor strong drink

DRINK WATER
1. *drink water:* ὑδροποτέω HYDROPOTEŌ*
1 Tim 5.23 No longer drink only water

DRINK WITH
1. *drink together:* συμπίνω SYMPINŌ*
Acts 10.41 "who ate and drank with him after he rose

DRIVE (*See also* DESPAIR, BE DRIVEN TO)
1. *drive away:* ἀπελαύνω APELAUNŌ*
Acts 18.16 he drove them from the tribunal
2. *drive:* ἐλαύνω ELAUNŌ
Lk 8.29 (driven by the demon into the desert
Jas 3. 4 ships . . are driven by strong winds
2 Pet 2.17 These are . . mists driven by a storm
3. *bring, bear:* φέρω PHERŌ
Acts 27.15 we gave way to it and were driven
27.17 they lowered the gear, and so were driven

DRIVE OUT
1. *throw out:* ἐκβάλλω EKBALLŌ
Mt 21.12 Jesus . . drove out all who sold and bought
Mk 1.12 Spirit . . drove him out into the wilderness
11.15 to drive out those who sold . . in the temple
Lk 19.45 he . . began to drive out those who sold
Jn 2.15 making a whip . . he drove them all . . out
Acts 13.50 the Jews . . drove them out of their district
2. *chase away:* ἐκδιώκω EKDIŌKŌ*
1 Th 2.15 who killed . . the prophets, and drove us out
3. *lift up, remove:* ἐξαίρω EXAIRŌ*
1 Cor 5.13 "Drive out the wicked . . from among you

DRIVEN BY THE WIND, BE
1. *be driven by the wind* (pass.): ἀνεμίζω ANEMIZŌ*
Jas 1. 6 sea that is driven and tossed by the wind

DRIVEN OUT, BE
1. *go out:* ἐξέρχομαι EXERCHOMAI
Mk 9.29 "This kind cannot be driven out

DROOP
1. *disregard, slacken:* παρίημι (pass.) PARIĒMI
Heb 12.12 Therefore lift your drooping hands

DROP
1. *come down, go down:* καταβαίνω KATABAINŌ
Rev 16.21 hailstones . . dropped on men from heaven
2. *drop, clot:* θρόμβος THROMBOS*
Lk [22.44 *his sweat became like great drops of blood*‡

DROPSY, WHO HAS
1. *suffering from dropsy:* ὑδρωπικός HYDRŌPIKOS*
Lk 14. 2 a man before him who had dropsy

DROWN
1. *choke, drown:* ἀποπνίγω APOPNIGŌ
Lk 8.33 the herd rushed down . . were drowned
2. *swallow:* καταπίνω KATAPINŌ
Heb 11.29 but the Egyptians . . were drowned
3. *choke, drown:* πνίγω PNIGŌ
Mk 5.13 the herd . . rushed down . . and were drowned

DROWNED, BE
1. *throw into the sea, drown:* καταποντίζω (pass.) KATAPONTIZŌ
Mt 18. 6 "better for him . . to be drowned in the . . sea

DRUNK
1. *be drunk:* μεθύω (part.) METHYŌ
Rev 17. 6 woman, drunk with the blood of the saints

DRUNK, BE
1. *be drunk:* μεθύω METHYŌ
Acts 2.15 "these men are not drunk, as you suppose
1 Cor 11.21 one is hungry and another is drunk
1 Th 5. 7 those who get drunk are drunk at night

DRUNK, BECOME
DRUNK, GET
1. *make drunk:* μεθύσκω (pass.) METHYSKŌ*
Lk 12.45 "begins . . to eat and drink and get drunk
Eph 5.18 do not get drunk . . for that is debauchery
1 Th 5. 7 those who get drunk are drunk at night
Rev 17. 2 "dwellers on earth have become drunk

DRUNKARD
1. *drunkard:* μέθυσος METHYSOS*
1 Cor 5.11 an idolater, reviler, drunkard, or robber
6.10 nor thieves, nor the greedy, nor drunkards
2. *wine drinker:* οἰνοπότης OINOPOTĒS*
Mt 11.19 " 'Behold, a glutton and a drunkard!
Lk 7.34 " 'Behold, a glutton and a drunkard!
3. *addicted to wine:* πάροινος (subst.) PAROINOS*
1 Tim 3. 3 no drunkard, not violent but gentle
Tit 1. 7 he must not be arrogant . . or a drunkard

DRUNKEN
1. *be drunk:* μεθύω (part.) METHYŌ
Mt 24.49 "eats and drinks with the drunken

DRUNKENNESS
1. *strong drink, drunkenness:* μέθη METHĒ*
Lk 21.34 "dissipation and drunkenness and cares
Rom 13.13 not in reveling and drunkenness
Gal 5.21 envy,[k] drunkenness, carousing, and the like
2. *drunkenness:* οἰνοφλυγία (pl.) OINOPHLYGIA*
1 Pet 4. 3 licentiousness, passions, drunkenness

DRUSILLA: Δρούσιλλα drü'silə
Acts 24.24 Felix came with his wife D. . . a Jewess

DRY
1. *withered, dry:* ξηρός XĒROS
Lk 23.31 "what will happen when it is dry?
Heb 11.29 crossed the Red Sea as if on dry land

DRY UP
1. *dry up:* ξηραίνω XĒRAINŌ
Rev 16.12 Euphrates, and its water was dried up

DUE (*See also* REWARD, DUE; TIME, DUE)
1. *which is necessary:* ἦν δεῖ DEI [B.2.a.1]
Rom 1.27 receiving . . the due penalty for their error
2. *one's own:* ἴδιος IDIOS
Gal 6. 9 for in due season we shall reap
3. *debt:* ὀφείλημα OPHEILĒMA [B.1.a.2]
Rom 4. 4 his wages are . . reckoned . . as his due
IDIOMATICALLY
a. Rev 16.6 "It is their due! ἄξιοί εἰσιν [AXIOS]
CONTEXTUALLY
Rom 13. 7 Pay . . taxes to whom taxes are due, revenue to whom revenue is due, respect to whom respect is due, honor to whom honor is due
Jas 1.17 no variation or shadow due to change[a]

DUE TO
1. *because of:* διά (+acc.) DIA
Eph **4**.18

DUES
1. *debt, one's due:* ὀφειλή (pl.) OPHEILĒ
Rom 13. 7 Pay all of them their dues

DULL
1. *dull, slothful:* νωθρός NŌTHROS
Heb 5.11 you have become dull of hearing

DULL, GROW
1. *fatten, make dull:* παχύνω (pass.) PACHYNŌ*
Mt 13.15 " 'this people's heart has grown dull
Acts 28.27 " 'this people's heart has grown dull

DUMB
1. *speechless:* ἄλαλος ALALOS*
Mk 7.37 "he even makes . . the dumb speak
9.17 "I brought my son . . for he has a dumb spirit
9.25 "You dumb and deaf spirit, . . come out
2. *voiceless:* ἄφωνος APHŌNOS
Acts 8.32 "As . . a lamb before its shearer is dumb
1 Cor 12. 2 you were led astray to dumb idols
2 Pet 2.16 a dumb ass spoke with human voice
3. *blunt, deaf, mute:* κωφός KŌPHOS
Mt 9.32 behold, a dumb demoniac was brought
9.33 dumb man spoke; . . the crowds marveled
12.22 a blind and dumb demoniac was brought
12.22 he healed him, so that the dumb man spoke
15.30 bringing with them . . the blind, the dumb
15.31 when they saw the dumb speaking
Lk 1.22 he made signs to them and remained dumb

Lk 11.14 casting out a demon that was dumb
11.14 dumb man spoke, and the people marveled

DUNGHILL

1. *dunghill, rubbish heap:* κοπρία KOPRIA*
Lk 14.35 "fit neither for the land nor for the dunghill

DURING

1. *through:* διά (+gen.) DIA
Acts **1**.3
2. *in, at, by:* ἐν (+dat.) EN
Mt **26**.5
Mk **14**.2
Acts **1**.21; **13**.17
Phm .13
3. *come to be, happen, be:* γίνομαι (gen. absol.) GINOMAI
Jn 13. 2 during supper, when the devil had already

IDIOMATICALLY
a. Rom 7.1 the law is binding . . only during his life
ὁ νόμος κυριεύει . . ἐφ' ὅσον χρόνον ζῇ [CHRONOS]

CONTEXTUALLY
Acts **12**.3
1 Pet **3**.20
Rev **11**.6

DUST

1. *dust:* χοῦς CHOUS*
Mk 6.11 "when you leave, shake off the dust
Rev 18.19 threw dust on their heads, as they wept
2. *dust raised:* κονιορτός KONIORTOS*
Mt 10.14 "shake off the dust from your feet
Lk 9. 5 "shake off the dust from your feet
10.11 " 'Even the dust of your town . . we wipe off
Acts 13.51 they shook off the dust from their feet
22.23 they cried out and . . threw dust into the air

DUST, OF

1. *of earth:* χοϊκός CHOIKOS*
1 Cor 15.47 first man was from the earth, a man of dust
15.48 As was the man of dust, so are those who are of the dust
15.49 we have borne the image of the man of dust

DUTY (*See also* RITUAL DUTY)

1. *need, want:* χρεία CHREIA
Acts 6. 3 "whom we may appoint to this duty

IDIOMATICALLY
a. Lk 1.8 when his division was on duty ἐν τῇ τάξει τῆς ἐφημερίας αὐτοῦ [TAXIS]
b. Lk 17.10 " 'we have only done what was our duty
ὃ ὠφείλομεν ποιῆσαι πεποιήκαμεν [OPHEILŌ]

CONTEXTUALLY
1 Tim 4.15 Practice these duties . . that all may see
6. 2 Teach and urge these duties

DUTY, RELIGIOUS

1. *show piety toward:* εὐσεβέω (inf.) EUSEBEŌ
1 Tim 5. 4 let them . . learn their religious duty to

DWELL

1. *be:* εἰμί EIMI
Rom 7.23 of sin which dwells in my members
2. *encamp, rest:* κατασκηνόω KATASKĒNOŌ
Acts 2.26 " 'moreover my flesh will dwell in hope
3. *sit down:* κάθημαι KATHĒMAI
Lk 21.35 "all who dwell upon . . the whole earth
Rev 14. 6 to proclaim to those who dwell on earth
4. *dwell, settle:* κατοικέω KATOIKEŌ
Mt 2.23 he . . dwelt in a city called Nazareth
4.13 he went and dwelt in Capernaum
12.45 "with him seven other spirits . . dwell there
23.21 "swears by it and by him who dwells in it
Lk 11.26 "brings seven . . spirits . . and they . . dwell
13. 4 "than . . others who dwelt in Jerusalem?
Acts 2. 5 there were dwelling in Jerusalem Jews
2.14 "Men of Judea . . all who dwell in Jerusalem
7.48 "the Most High does not dwell in houses
Eph 3.17 Christ . . dwell in your hearts through faith
Col 1.19 all the fulness of God was pleased to dwell
2. 9 in him the whole fulness of deity dwells
2 Pet 3.13 a new earth in which righteousness dwells
Rev 2.13 " 'where you dwell, where Satan's throne is
2.13 " 'killed among you, where Satan dwells
3.10 to try those who dwell upon the earth
6.10 "avenge . . on those who dwell upon the earth
8.13 "Woe . . to those who dwell on the earth!
11.10 those who dwell on the earth will rejoice
11.10 a torment to those who dwell on the earth
13. 8 all who dwell on earth will worship it
13.14 it deceives those who dwell on earth
5. *stay, wait:* μένω MENŌ
Jn 14.10 "Father who dwells in me does his works
14.17 "he dwells with you, and will be in you
6. *dwell:* οἰκέω OIKEŌ
Rom 7.18 I know that nothing good dwells within me
7.20 no longer I . . but sin which dwells within me
8. 9 if . . the Spirit of God dwells in you
8.11 If the Spirit of him . . dwells in you
1 Cor 3.16 know . . God's Spirit dwells in you?
1 Tim 6.16 who alone . . dwells in unapproachable light
7. *encamp, settle:* σκηνόω SKĒNOŌ
Jn 1.14 Word became flesh and dwelt among us
Rev 12.12 "O heaven and you that dwell therein!
13. 6 blaspheming . . those who dwell in heaven
21. 3 "He will dwell with them

DWELL IN
DWELL WITHIN

1. *dwell in:* ἐνοικέω ENOIKEŌ
Rom 7.17 no longer I . . but sin which dwells within me
8.11 through his Spirit which dwells in you
Col 3.16 Let the word of Christ dwell in you
2 Tim 1. 5 faith that dwelt first in your grandmother
1.14 by the Holy Spirit who dwells within us

DWELL, MAKE TO

1. *settle, establish:* κατοικίζω KATOIKIZŌ*
Jas 4. 5 "spirit which he has made to dwell in us

DWELLER

1. *dwell, settle:* κατοικέω (subst. part.) KATOIKEŌ
Rev 17. 2 "dwellers on earth have become drunk
17. 8 "dwellers on earth . . will marvel

DWELLING (*See also* HIRED DWELLING)

1. *dwelling place:* οἰκητήριον OIKĒTĒRION*
2 Cor 5. 2 long to put on our heavenly dwelling
Jude . 6 the angels that . . left their proper dwelling
2. *tent, booth:* σκηνή SKĒNĒ
Acts 15.16 " 'I will rebuild the dwelling of David
Rev 13. 6 blaspheming his name and his dwelling
21. 3 "Behold, the dwelling of God is with men

DWELLING PLACE

1. *dwelling place:* κατοικητήριον KATOIKĒTĒRION*
Eph 2.22 a dwelling place of God in the Spirit
Rev 18. 2 "It has become a dwelling place of demons

DYSENTERY

1. *dysentery:* δυσεντέριον DYSENTERION*
Acts 28. 8 Publius lay sick with fever and dysentery

E

EACH

1. *at the rate of:* ἀνά (+acc.) ANA
Lk 9.14 "sit down in companies, about fifty each
Jn 2. 6 each holding twenty or thirty gallons
2. *each:* ἕκαστος HEKASTOS
[a]ἀνὰ εἷς ἕκαστος
Mt 25.15 "to each according to his ability
Mk 13.34 "servants in charge, each with his work
Lk 2. 3 to be enrolled, each to his own city
6.44 "each tree is known by its own fruit
13.15 "Does not each of you on the sabbath?
Jn 7.53 They went each to his own house[r]‡
19.23 four parts, one for each soldier
Acts 2. 3 distributed and resting on each one
2. 6 each one heard them . . in his own language
4.35 distribution . . to each as any had need
17.27 "Yet he is not far from each one of us

Rom 12. 3 each according to the measure of faith
14.12 So each of us shall give account of himself
15. 2 let each of us please his neighbor
1 Cor 3. 5 believed, as the Lord assigned to each
3. 8 each shall receive . . according to his labor
7. 7 each has his own special gift from God
7.24 in whatever state each was called
12. 7 each is given . . manifestation of . . Spirit
12.18 God arranged . . each one . . as he chose
15.23 each in his own order: Christ the first
16. 2 each of you is to put something aside
Eph 4. 7 grace was given to each of us
4.16 when each part is working properly
1 Th 2.11 we exhorted each one of you
Heb 11.21 blessed each of the sons of Joseph
1 Pet 4.10 As each has received a gift, employ it
Rev 2.23 "'to each of you as your works deserve
5. 8 fell down . . each holding a harp
6.11 they were each given a white robe
21.21 [a]each of the gates made of a single pearl
22. 2 yielding its fruit each month

3. *who? what?:* τίς TIS I
Mk 15.24

IDIOMATICALLY
a. 1 Cor 14.27 and each in turn καὶ ἀνὰ μέρος [ANA]
b. Rev 4.8 each of them with six wings ἓν καθ' ἓν αὐτῶν ἔχων ἀνὰ πτέρυγας ἕξ [ANA]

CONTEXTUALLY
1 Cor 14.28 let each of them keep silence in church

EACH KIND OF

1. *each:* ἕκαστος HEKASTOS
1 Cor 15.38 to each kind of seed its own body

EACH MAN
EACH OF THEM
EACH OF US
EACH OF YOU
EACH ONE
EACH PERSON

1. *at the rate of:* ἀνά (+acc.) ANA [A.4.d]
Mt 20. 9 "each of them received a denarius
20.10 "each of them also received a denarius

2. *each:* ἕκαστος (subst.) HEKASTOS
Jn 6. 7 "enough . . for each of them to get a little
Acts 2. 8 "each of us in his own native language
1 Cor 1.12 each one . . says, "I belong to Paul
3.10 Let each man take care how he builds
3.13 each man's work will become manifest
3.13 what sort of work each one has done
7. 2 each man should have his own wife
11.21 each one goes ahead with his own meal
12.11 apportions to each one . . as he wills
14.26 each one has a hymn, a lesson
2 Cor 5.10 that each one may receive good or evil
9. 7 Each one must do as he has made
Gal 6. 4 let each one test his own work
6. 5 each man will have to bear his own load
Eph 5.33 let each one of you love his wife
Phil 2. 4 each of you look . . to . . interests of others
1 Th 4. 4 each one of you know how to take a wife
Heb 6.11 we desire each one of you to show
Jas 1.14 each person is tempted when he is lured
1 Pet 1.17 Father . . who judges each one impartially

EACH OTHER

1. *one another:* ἀλλήλων ALLĒLŌN
[a]B.1.a.1
Lk 23.12 friends with each other that very day
24.14 talking with each other about all these
24.17 "conversation . . with each other as you walk
24.32 to each other, "Did not our hearts burn?
Acts 7.26 "'why do you wrong each other?
15.39 they separated from each other
Rom 1.12 [a]encouraged by each other's faith
Gal 5.17 these are opposed to each other

2. *himself:* ἑαυτοῦ HEAUTOU
[a]αὑτοῦ
Lk 23.12 [a]they had been at enmity with each other
Col 3.13 forgiving each other; as the Lord has

EACH WOMAN

1. *each:* ἕκαστος (subst. fem.) HEKASTOS
1 Cor 7. 2 each woman her own husband

EAGER (*See also* EXPECTATION, EAGER; LONGING, EAGER)

1. *ready, eager:* πρόθυμος PROTHYMOS
Rom 1.15 so I am eager to preach the gospel

2. *be eager:* σπουδάζω (part.) SPOUDAZŌ
Eph 4. 3 eager to maintain the unity of the Spirit

3. *zealous admirer:* ζηλωτής (pred.) ZĒLŌTĒS
1 Cor 14.12 since you are eager for manifestations

IDIOMATICALLY
a. Jude .3 being very eager to write πᾶσαν σπουδὴν ποιούμενος γράφειν [SPOUDĒ]

EAGER, BE

1. *be eager:* σπουδάζω SPOUDAZŌ
Gal 2.10 which very thing I was eager to do

EAGER, THE MORE

1. *earnestly, with haste:* σπουδαίως (comp.) SPOUDAIŌS [A.4.a]
Phil 2.28 I am the more eager to send him

EAGERLY (*See also* WAIT, EAGERLY)

1. *many, great:* πολύς (neut. pl.) POLYS
Mk 5.10 begged him eagerly not to send them

2. *zealously:* προθύμως PROTHYMŌS*
1 Pet 5. 2 not for shameful gain but eagerly

3. *earnestly, with haste:* σπουδαίως SPOUDAIŌS
2 Tim 1.17 he searched for me eagerly and found me

EAGERLY, ENDEAVOR

1. *be eager:* σπουδάζω SPOUDAZŌ
1 Th 2.17 we endeavored the more eagerly

EAGERNESS (*See also* CLEAR ONESELF, EAGERNESS TO)

1. *willingness, goodwill:* προθυμία PROTHYMIA
Acts 17.11 they received the word with all eagerness

EAGLE

1. *eagle:* ἀετός AETOS*
Mt 24.28 "there the eagles[z] will be gathered together†
Lk 17.37 "there the eagles[c] will be gathered together†
Rev 4. 7 fourth living creature like a flying eagle
8.13 I heard an eagle crying with a loud voice
12.14 given the two wings of the great eagle

EAR

1. *hearing, report:* ἀκοή AKOĒ
Mk 7.35 And his ears were opened
Acts 17.20 "you bring some strange things to our ears
1 Cor 12.17 If the whole body were an ear
2 Tim 4. 3 people . . having itching ears

2. *little ear:* ὠτάριον ŌTARION*
Mk 14.47 struck the slave . . and cut off his ear
Jn 18.10 struck the . . slave and cut off his right ear

3. *the external ear:* ὠτίον ŌTION*
Mt 26.51 struck the slave . . and cut off his ear
Lk 22.51 And he touched his ear and healed him
Jn 18.26 the man whose ear Peter had cut off

4. *ear:* οὖς OUS
Mt 11.15 "He who has ears to hear,[d] let him hear
13. 9 "He who has ears,[h] let him hear
13.15 "'their ears are heavy of hearing
13.15 "'lest they . . hear with their ears
13.16 "blessed are . . your ears, for they hear
13.43 "He who has ears, let him hear
Mk 4. 9 "He who has ears to hear, let him hear
4.23 "If any man has ears to hear, let him hear
[7.16 "*If any man has ears to hear*‡
7.33 he put his fingers into his ears
8.18 "having ears do you not hear?
Lk 1.44 "when . . your greeting came to my ears
8. 8 "He who has ears to hear, let him hear
9.44 "Let these words sink into your ears
14.35 "He who has ears to hear, let him hear
22.50 struck the slave . . and cut off his right ear
Acts 7.51 "people, uncircumcised in heart and ears
7.57 stopped their ears and rushed together
11.22 News . . came to the ears of the church

Acts 28.27 " 'their ears are heavy of hearing
28.27 " 'lest they should . . hear with their ears
Rom 11. 8 "God gave them . . ears that should not hear
1 Cor 2. 9 "What no eye has seen, nor ear heard
12.16 if the ear should say . . "I do not belong
Jas 5. 4 cries . . have reached the ears of the Lord
1 Pet 3.12 "his ears are open to their prayer
Rev 2. 7 " 'He who has an ear, let him hear
Also Rev **2**.11, 17, 29; **3**.6, 13, 22
13. 9 If any one has an ear, let him hear

5. *ear of grain:* στάχυς STACHYS
Mk 4.28 "first the blade, then the ear, then the full grain in the ear

EAR TO, GIVE

1. *pay attention to:* ἐνωτίζομαι ENŌTIZOMAI*
Acts 2.14 "Men of Judea . . give ear to my words

EARLY

1. *from the beginning, old:* ἀρχαῖος ARCHAIOS
Acts 15. 7 "in the early days God made choice
15.21 "from early generations . . those who preach
21.16 Mnason of Cyprus, an early disciple
2. *deep:* βαθύς BATHYS
Lk 24. 1 at early dawn, they went to the tomb
3. *early, early in the day:* πρωΐ PRŌI
Mk 16. 2 very early on the first day of the week
16. 9 early on the first day of the week[k]‡
Jn 18.28 It was early. They . . did not enter
20. 1 Mary Magdalene came to the tomb early

EARLY IN THE MORNING

1. *at daybreak:* ὀρθρινός ORTHRINOS* [A.3.b.1]
Lk 24.22 "at the tomb early in the morning
2. *dawn, about daybreak:* ὄρθρος (gen.) ORTHROS
Jn 8. 2 Early in the morning he came again[r]‡

IDIOMATICALLY

a. Mt 20.1 "who went out early in the morning *ὅστις ἐξῆλθεν ἅμα πρωΐ* [PRŌI]
b. Lk 21.38 early in the morning all the people came to him *πᾶς ὁ λαὸς ὤρθριζεν πρὸς αὐτόν* [ORTHRIZŌ*]

EARLY RAIN

1. *early:* πρόϊμος PROIMOS* [B.3.b.2]
Jas 5. 7 patient . . until it receives the early . . rain

EARN

IDIOMATICALLY

a. 2 Th 3.12 to earn their own living *τὸν ἑαυτῶν ἄρτον ἐσθίωσιν* [ESTHIŌ]

EARNEST

1. *earnestly:* ἐκτενῶς EKTENŌS [A.4.a]
Acts 12. 5 earnest prayer for him was made to God
2. *earnest:* σπουδαῖος SPOUDAIOS
2 Cor 8.22 brother whom we have . . found earnest

EARNEST CARE

1. *zeal, haste;* σπουδή SPOUDĒ
2 Cor 8.16 God . . puts the same earnest care for you

EARNEST, MORE

1. *earnest:* σπουδαῖος (comp.) SPOUDAIOS
2 Cor 8.22 who is now more earnest than ever

EARNEST, VERY

1. *earnest:* σπουδαῖος (comp.) SPOUDAIOS
2 Cor 8.17 being himself very earnest he is going to you

EARNESTLY (*See also* DESIRE, EARNESTLY)

1. *zeal, earnestness:* ἐκτένεια EKTENEIA* [B.1.a.1]
Acts 26. 7 "they earnestly worship night and day
2. *earnestly:* ἐκτενῶς EKTENŌS
1 Pet 1.22 love one another earnestly from the heart
3. *desire earnestly:* ἐπιθυμίᾳ ἐπιθυμεῖν EPITHYMIA [C.3]
Lk 22.15 "I have earnestly desired to eat this
4. *superabundantly:* ὑπερεκπερισσοῦ HYPEREKPERISSOU
1 Th 3.10 praying earnestly night and day
5. *with much exhortation:* μετὰ πολλῆς παρακλήσεως PARAKLĒSIS [B.1.a.1]
2 Cor 8. 4 begging us earnestly for the favor
6. *earnestly, with haste:* σπουδαίως SPOUDAIŌS
Lk 7. 4 they besought him earnestly

EARNESTLY, MORE

1. *earnestly:* ἐκτενῶς (comp.) EKTENŌS
Lk [22.44 *being in an agony he prayed more earnestly*‡

EARNESTLY, REMEMBER

1. *contend on behalf of:* ἀγωνίζομαι ὑπέρ AGŌNIZOMAI [A.6.a.5]
Col 4.12 always remembering you e. in his prayers

EARNESTLY, THE MORE

1. *still more:* περισσοτέρως PERISSOTERŌS
Heb 13.19 I urge you the more earnestly to do this

EARNESTNESS

1. *zeal, haste:* σπουδή SPOUDĒ
2 Cor 7.11 what earnestness this . . grief has produced!
8. 7 as you excel . . in all earnestness
8. 8 to prove by the earnestness of others
Heb 6.11 show the same earnestness

EARS, COME TO THE

1. *hear:* ἀκούω (pass.) AKOUŌ
[a]+ εἰς τὰ ὦτα
Mt 28.14 "if this comes to the governor's ears
Acts 11.22 [a]News . . came to the ears of the church

EARTH

1. *earth, land:* γῆ GĒ
Mt 5. 5 "the meek . . shall inherit the earth
5.13 "You are the salt of the earth
5.18 "till heaven and earth pass away
5.35 "or by the earth, for it is his footstool
6.10 "be done, On earth as it is in heaven
6.19 "Do not lay up . . treasures on earth
9. 6 "the Son of man has authority on earth
10.34 "not . . to bring peace on earth
11.25 "Father, Lord of heaven and earth
12.40 "three nights in the heart of the earth
12.42 "she came from the ends of the earth
16.19 "whatever you bind on earth shall be bound
16.19 "whatever you loose on earth
17.25 "From whom do kings of the earth take toll?
18.18 "whatever you bind on earth shall be bound
18.18 "whatever you loose on earth
18.19 "if two of you agree on earth
23. 9 "call no man your father . . on earth
23.35 "all the righteous blood shed on earth
24.30 "all the tribes of the earth will mourn
24.35 "Heaven and earth will pass away
[27.45 there was darkness over all the *earth*†
27.51 the earth shook, and the rocks were split
28.18 "All authority in heaven and on earth
Mk 2.10 "the Son of man has authority on earth
4.28 "The earth produces of itself
4.31 "the smallest of all the seeds on earth
9. 3 white, as no fuller on earth could bleach
13.27 "four winds, from the ends of the earth
13.31 "Heaven and earth will pass away
[15.33 there was darkness over the whole *earth*†
Lk 2.14 "and on earth peace among men!
5.24 "the Son of man has authority on earth
10.21 "Father, Lord of heaven and earth
11.31 "she came from the ends of the earth
12.49 "I came to cast fire upon the earth
12.51 "that I have come to give peace on earth?
12.56 "how to interpret the appearance of earth
16.17 "easier for heaven and earth to pass away
18. 8 "will he find faith on earth?
21.23 "great distress shall be upon the earth
21.25 "upon the earth distress of nations
21.33 "Heaven and earth will pass away
21.35 "who dwell upon the face of the . . earth
[23.44 there was darkness over the whole *earth*†
Jn 3.31 He who comes from above is above all; he who is of the earth belongs to the earth, and of the earth he speaks
12.24 "unless a grain . . falls into the earth
12.32 "when I am lifted up from the earth
17. 4 "I glorified thee on earth
Acts 1. 8 "my witnesses . . to the end of the earth
2.19 " 'I will show . . signs on the earth beneath

Acts 3.25 “ ‘all the families of the earth be blessed
4.24 “Lord, who didst make the . . earth
4.26 “ ‘kings of . . earth set themselves in array
7.49 “ ‘Heaven is my throne . . earth my footstool
8.33 “his life is taken up from the earth
10.11 let down by four corners upon the earth
13.47 “ ‘that you may bring salvation to . . earth
14.15 “a living God who made . . the earth
17.24 “God . . being Lord of heaven and earth
17.26 “to live on all the face of the earth
22.22 “Away with such a fellow from the earth!
Rom 9.17 “name . . proclaimed in all the earth
9.28 “execute his sentence upon the earth
10.18 “Their voice has gone out to all the earth
1 Cor 8. 5 so-called gods in heaven or on earth
10.26 “the earth is the Lord’s, and everything in it
15.47 The first man was from the earth
Eph 1.10 things in heaven and things on earth
3.15 every family in heaven and on earth
4. 9 descended into the lower parts of the earth
6. 3 “that you may live long on the earth
Col 1.16 all things . . in heaven and on earth
1.20 all things, whether on earth or in heaven
3. 2 not on things that are on earth
Heb 1.10 “Thou, Lord, didst found the earth
8. 4 if . . on earth, he would not be a priest
11.13 they were strangers and exiles on the earth
11.38 in dens and caves of the earth
12.25 refused him who warned them on earth
12.26 His voice then shook the earth . . “Yet once more I will shake not only the earth
Jas 5. 5 You have lived on the earth in luxury
5. 7 farmer waits for the . . fruit of the earth
5.12 do not swear . . by heaven or by earth
5.17 it did not rain on the earth
5.18 the earth brought forth its fruit
2 Pet 3. 5 an earth formed out of water
3. 7 heavens and earth . . stored up for fire
3.10 the earth . . will be burned up
3.13 a new earth in which righteousness dwells
Rev 1. 5 Jesus Christ . . the ruler of kings on earth
1. 7 all tribes of the earth will wail
3.10 “ ‘to try those who dwell upon the earth
5. 3 no one in heaven or on earth or under the earth was able to open the scroll
5. 6 seven spirits . . sent out into all the earth
5.10 “they shall reign on earth
5.13 every creature in heaven and on earth and under the earth and in the sea
6. 4 permitted to take peace from the earth
6. 8 given power over a fourth of the earth, to kill . . by wild beasts of the earth
6.10 “judge . . those who dwell upon the earth
6.13 the stars of the sky fell to the earth
6.15 Then the kings of the earth . . hid
7. 1 standing at the four corners of the earth, holding back the four winds of the earth, that no wind might blow on earth or sea
7. 2 angels who had . . power to harm earth
7. 3 “Do not harm the earth or the sea
8. 5 angel . . threw ⟨the censer⟩ on the earth
8. 7 hail and fire . . fell on the earth; and a third of the earth was burnt up
8.13 “woe to those who dwell on the earth!
9. 1 I saw a star fallen from heaven to earth
9. 3 Then . . came locusts on the earth
9. 3 like the power of scorpions of the earth
9. 4 not to harm the grass of the earth
10. 6 who created . . the earth and what is in it
11. 4 trees . . stand before the Lord of the earth
11. 6 to smite the earth with every plague
11.10 those who dwell on the earth will rejoice
11.10 torment to those who dwell on the earth
11.18 “destroying the destroyers of the earth
12. 4 His tail . . cast ⟨the stars⟩ to the earth
12. 9 he was thrown down to the earth
12.12 “But woe to you, O earth and sea!
Rev 12.13 he had been thrown down to the earth
12.16 the earth came to the help of the woman, and the earth . . swallowed the river
13. 3 the whole earth followed the beast
13. 8 all who dwell on earth will worship it
13.11 another beast which rose out of the earth
13.12 makes the earth . . worship the first beast
13.13 making fire come down . . to earth
13.14 it deceives those who dwell on earth
14. 3 who had been redeemed from the earth
14. 6 to proclaim to those who dwell on earth
14. 7 “worship him who made heaven and earth
14.15 “the harvest of the earth is fully ripe
14.16 he . . swung his sickle on the earth, and the earth was reaped
14.18 “gather the clusters . . of the earth
14.19 the angel swung his sickle on the earth and gathered the vintage of the earth
16. 1 “pour out on the earth the seven bowls
16. 2 first angel . . poured his bowl on the earth
16.18 never . . since men were on the earth
17. 2 “kings of the e. . . committed fornication
17. 2 “the dwellers on earth have become drunk
17. 5 mother . . of earth’s abominations
17. 8 “dwellers on earth . . will marvel
17.18 “dominion over the kings of the earth
18. 1 earth was made bright with his splendor
18. 3 “kings of the e. . . committed fornication
18. 3 “merchants of the earth have grown rich
18. 9 kings of the e. . . committed fornication
18.11 merchants of the earth weep and mourn
18.23 “merchants were . . great men of the earth
18.24 “blood . . of all . . slain on earth
19. 2 “the great harlot who corrupted the earth
19.19 the kings of the earth with their armies
20. 8 nations . . at the four corners of the earth
20. 9 they marched up over the broad earth
20.11 from his presence earth . . fled away
21. 1 I saw a new heaven and a new earth; for the first heaven and the first earth had passed
21.24 kings of the earth shall bring their glory

EARTH, ON

1. *of the earth:* ἐπίγειος EPIGEIOS
Phil 2.10 every knee should bow . . on earth

EARTH, UNDER THE

1. *subterranean:* καταχθόνιος KATACHTHONIOS*
Phil 2.10 every knee . . on earth and under the earth

EARTHEN

1. *of pottery:* κεραμικός KERAMIKOS*
Rev 2.27 “ ‘when earthen pots are broken in pieces
2. *made of clay:* ὀστράκινος OSTRAKINOS
2 Cor 4. 7 we have this treasure in earthen vessels

EARTHENWARE

1. *earthen vessels:* σκεύη ὀστράκινα OSTRAKINOS [A.1.f]
2 Tim 2.20 vessels of gold . . and earthenware

EARTHLY

1. *of the earth:* ἐπίγειος EPIGEIOS
Jn 3.12 “If I have told you earthly things
2 Cor 5. 1 if the earthly tent we live in is destroyed
Phil 3.19 with minds set on earthly things
Jas 3.15 This wisdom is . . earthly, unspiritual, devilish
2. *of the world:* κοσμικός KOSMIKOS
Heb 9. 1 first covenant had . . an earthly sanctuary
3. *fleshly:* σαρκικός SARKIKOS
2 Cor 1.12 godly sincerity, not by earthly wisdom
4. *flesh, body:* σάρξ SARX
[a]κατὰ σάρκα B.1.a.1 [b]gen.
Eph 6. 5 [a]those who are your earthly masters
Col 3.22 [a]Slaves, obey . . your earthly masters
Heb 12. 9 [b]Besides this, we have had earthly fathers

IDIOMATICALLY

a. Col 3.5 Put to death . . what is earthly in you νεκρώσατε . . τὰ μέλη τὰ ἐπὶ τῆς γῆς [GĒ]

EARTHQUAKE
1. *shaking, earthquake:* σεισμός SEISMOS
Mt 24. 7 "famines and earthquakes in various places
27.54 the centurion . . saw the earthquake
28. 2 behold, there was a great earthquake
Mk 13. 8 "there will be earthquakes in various places
Lk 21.11 "there will be great earthquakes
Acts 16.26 suddenly there was a great earthquake
Rev 6.12 behold, there was a great earthquake
8. 5 flashes of lightning, and an earthquake
11.13 at that hour there was a great earthquake
11.13 people were killed in the earthquake
11.19 peals of thunder, an earthquake
16.18 peals of thunder, and a great earthquake
16.18 so great was that earthquake

EASE
IDIOMATICALLY
a. 2 Cor 8.13 I do not mean that others should be eased
οὐ γὰρ ἵνα ἄλλοις ἄνεσις [ANESIS]

EASE, AT
1. *without fear:* ἀφόβως APHOBŌS [A.4.b]
1 Cor 16.10 see that you put him at ease among you

EASE, TAKE ONE'S
1. *make to cease, cause to rest:* ἀναπαύω (mid.) ANAPAUŌ
Lk 12.19 " 'take your ease, eat, drink, be merry

EASIER
1. *easy:* εὔκοπος (comp.) EUKOPOS*
Mt 9. 5 "which is easier . . 'Your sins are forgiven'?
Also Mk **2**.9; Lk **5**.23
19.24 "it is easier for a camel to go through
Also Mk **10**.25; Lk **18**.25
Lk 16.17 "easier for heaven and earth to pass away

EAST
1. *rising, east:* ἀνατολή (sg. or pl.) ANATOLĒ
[a]+ἡλίου
Mt 2. 1 behold, wise men from the East
2. 2 "For we have seen his star in the East
2. 9 the star which they had seen in the East
8.11 "many will come from east and west
24.27 "as the lightning comes from the east
Mk [16.end *Jesus . . sent out . . from east to west*‡
Lk 13.29 "men will come from east and west
Rev [16.12 [a]to prepare . . for the kings from the east
21.13 on the east three gates

EASY
1. *good, useful:* χρηστός CHRĒSTOS
Mt 11.30 "my yoke is easy, and my burden is light
2. *wide:* εὐρύχωρος EURYCHŌROS*
Mt 7.13 "the gate is wide and the way is easy[q]

EAT
1. *eat:* βιβρώσκω BIBRŌSKŌ*
Jn 6.13 fragments . . left by those who had eaten
2. *eatable:* βρώσιμος BRŌSIMOS* [A.3.d.2]
Lk 24.41 "Have you anything here to eat?
3. *dine:* δειπνέω DEIPNEŌ
Rev 3.20 " 'I will come in to him and eat with him
4. *eat:* ἐσθίω ESTHIŌ
Mt 6.25 "what you shall eat or what you shall drink
6.31 "anxious, saying, 'What shall we eat?
9.11 "Why does your teacher eat with . . sinners?
11.18 "For John came neither eating nor drinking
11.19 "the Son of man came eating
12. 1 they began to pluck heads of grain and to eat
12. 4 "he . . ate the bread of the Presence, which it was not lawful for him to eat
14.16 "you give them something to eat
14.20 And they all ate and were satisfied
14.21 those who ate were about five thousand
15. 2 "they do not wash . . when they eat
15.20 "to eat with unwashed hands does not defile
15.27 "yet even the dogs eat the crumbs
15.32 "they . . have nothing to eat
15.37 they all ate and were satisfied
15.38 Those who ate were four thousand men
24.49 "⟨servant⟩ eats and drinks with the drunken
Mt 26.17 "prepare for you to eat the passover
26.21 as they were eating, he said, "Truly
26.26 as they were eating, Jesus took bread . . and said, "Take, eat; this is my body
Mk 1. 6 Now John . . ate locusts and wild honey
2.16 they saw that he was eating with sinners
2.16 "Why does he eat[i] with tax collectors?
2.26 "he . . ate the bread of the Presence, . . not lawful for any but the priests to eat
3.20 so that they could not even eat
5.43 told them to give her something to eat
6.31 "they had no leisure even to eat
6.36 "to . . buy themselves something to eat
6.37 "You give them something to eat
6.37 "Shall we . . give it to them to eat?
6.42 they all ate and were satisfied
6.44 those who ate . . were five thousand men
7. 2 some . . disciples ate with hands defiled
7. 3 (the Jews, do not eat unless they wash
7. 4 (they do not eat unless they purify[w]
7. 5 "your disciples . . eat with hands defiled
7.28 "even the dogs . . eat the children's crumbs
8. 1 when . . they had nothing to eat
8. 2 "because they . . have nothing to eat
8. 8 they ate, and were satisfied
11.14 "May no one ever eat fruit from you again
14.12 "prepare for you to eat the passover
14.14 " 'where I am to eat the passover
14.18 they were at table eating
14.18 "one who is eating with me
14.22 as they were eating, he took bread
Lk 4. 2 And he ate nothing in those days
5.30 "Why do you eat and drink with . . sinners?
5.33 "disciples of John fast . . but yours eat
6. 1 his disciples plucked and ate some . . grain
6. 4 "he . . ate the bread of the Presence, . . not lawful for any but the priests to eat
7.33 "For John . . has come eating no bread
7.34 "The Son of man has come eating
7.36 One of the Pharisees asked him to eat
8.55 something should be given her to eat
9.13 "You give them something to eat
9.17 And all ate and were satisfied
10. 7 "eating and drinking what they provide
10. 8 "eat what is set before you
12.19 "take your ease, eat, drink, be merry
12.22 "do not be anxious . . what you shall eat
12.29 "do not seek what you are to eat
12.45 "servant . . begins . . to eat and drink
13.26 " 'We ate and drank in your presence
14.15 "who shall eat . . in the kingdom of God!
15.16 "fed on[u] the pods that the swine ate
15.23 " 'let us eat and make merry
17. 8 " 'serve me, till I eat and drink; and afterward you shall eat and drink
17.27 "They ate, they drank, they married
17.28 "they ate, they drank, they bought
22. 8 "prepare the passover . . that we may eat it
22.11 " 'where I am to eat the passover
22.15 "I have . . desired to eat this passover
22.16 "I shall not eat it[i] until it is fulfilled
22.30 "that you may eat and drink at my table
24.43 he took it and ate before them
Jn 4.31 disciples besought him, saying, "Rabbi, eat
4.32 "food to eat of which you do not know
6. 5 "buy bread, so that these people may eat
6.23 near the place where they ate the bread
6.26 "because you ate your fill of the loaves
6.31 "Our fathers ate the manna
6.31 " 'He gave them bread from heaven to eat
6.49 "Your fathers ate the manna . . and . . died
6.50 "a man may eat of it and not die
6.51 "if any one eats of this bread, he will live
6.52 "can this man give us his flesh to eat?
6.53 "unless you eat the flesh of the Son
6.58 "not such as the fathers ate and died
18.28 so that they . . might eat the passover

Acts 9. 9 for three days he . . neither ate nor drank
10.13 "Rise, Peter; kill and eat
10.14 "I have never eaten anything that is common
11. 7 " 'Rise, Peter; kill and eat
23.12 bound . . by an oath neither to eat nor drink
23.21 "bound . . by an oath neither to eat nor drink
27.35 he took bread . . he broke it and began to eat
Rom 14. 2 One believes he may eat anything, while the weak man eats only vegetables
14. 3 Let not him who eats despise him
14. 3 not . . pass judgment on him who eats
14. 6 He also who eats, eats in honor of the Lord, since he gives thanks to God
14.20 wrong . . to make others fall by what he eats
14.21 it is right not to eat meat
14.23 he who has doubts is condemned, if he eats
1 Cor 8. 7 some . . eat food as really offered to an idol
8. 8 We are no worse off if we do not eat
8.10 might he not be encouraged . . to eat food?
8.13 I will never eat meat, lest
9. 7 Who plants . . without eating any . . fruit?
10. 3 all ate the same supernatural[o] food
10. 7 "The people sat down to eat and drink
10.18 are not those who eat . . sacrifices partners?
10.25 Eat whatever is sold in the meat market
10.27 eat whatever is set before you
10.29 (⟨for conscience' sake⟩ do not eat it
10.31 whether you eat . . do all to the glory of God
11.20 it is not the Lord's supper that you eat
11.21 in eating, each one goes ahead
11.22 Do you not have houses to eat and drink in?
11.26 as often as you eat this bread and drink
11.27 Whoever . . eats the bread or drinks the cup
11.28 so eat of the bread and drink of the cup
11.29 any one who eats . . without discerning . . eats and drinks judgment upon himself
11.33 when you come together to eat, wait
11.34 if any one is hungry, let him eat at home
15.32 "Let us eat and drink, for tomorrow we die
2 Th 3. 8 we did not eat any one's bread
3.10 If any one will not work, let him not eat
Heb 13.10 those who serve . . have no right to eat
Jas 5. 3 their rust . . will eat your flesh like fire
Rev 2. 7 " 'I will grant to eat of the tree of life
2.14 " 'they might eat food sacrificed to idols
2.20 " 'to eat food sacrificed to idols
10.10 when I had eaten . . my stomach was . . bitter
19.18 "to eat the flesh of kings, . . of captains

5. *taste:* γεύομαι GEUOMAI
Acts 10.10 he . . desired something to eat
20.11 when Paul had . . eaten, he conversed

6. *devour, eat up:* κατεσθίω KATESTHIŌ
Rev 10. 9 "Take it and eat; it will be bitter
10.10 I took the little scroll . . and ate it

7. *receive in addition:* προσλαμβάνω (mid.) PROSLAMBANŌ
Acts 27.36 they all . . ate some food themselves

8. *gnaw, munch:* τρώγω TRŌGŌ*
Mt 24.38 "before the flood they were eating
Jn 6.54 "he who eats my flesh . . has eternal life
6.56 "He who eats my flesh . . abides in me
6.57 "he who eats me will live because of me
6.58 "who eats this bread will live for ever
13.18 " 'He who ate my bread has lifted his heel

IDIOMATICALLY
a. Acts 27.38 And when they had eaten enough *κορεσθέντες δὲ τροφῆς* [TROPHĒ]
b. 2 Tim 2.17 their talk will eat its way *ὁ λόγος αὐτῶν . . νομὴν ἕξει* [NOMĒ]

CONTEXTUALLY
1 Cor 8. 4 as to the eating of food offered to idols

EAT ONE'S FILL
1. *fill quite full:* ἐμπίμπλημι (pass.) EMPIMPLĒMI
Jn 6.12 when they had eaten their fill

EAT WITH
1. *eat salt with, bring together:* συναλίζω SYNALIZŌ
Acts [1. 4 while *eating* with them he charged them†

2. *eat together:* συνεσθίω SYNESTHIŌ*
Lk 15. 2 "receives sinners and eats with them
Acts 10.41 "witnesses, who ate and drank with him
11. 3 "Why did you . . eat with them?
1 Cor 5.11 not even to eat with such a one
Gal 2.12 he ate with the Gentiles

EATEN BY WORMS
1. *eaten by worms:* σκωληκόβρωτος SKŌLĒKOBRŌTOS*
Acts 12.23 he was eaten by worms and died

EATS, WHAT ONE
1. *food:* βρῶμα BRŌMA
Rom 14.15 If . . injured by what you eat
14.15 Do not let what you eat cause the ruin

EBER: Ἔβερ 'ēbər
Lk 3.35 Peleg, the son of E., the son of Shelah

ECLIPSED, BE
1. *fail, cease:* ἐκλείπω EKLEIPŌ
Lk [23.45 while *the sun was eclipsed*†

EDGE
1. *mouth:* στόμα STOMA
Lk 21.24 "they will fall by the edge of the sword
Heb 11.34 escaped the edge of the sword

EDICT
1. *ordinance, edict:* διάταγμα DIATAGMA*
Heb 11.23 they were not afraid of the king's edict

EDIFICATION
1. *building, edification:* οἰκοδομή OIKODOMĒ
1 Cor 14.26 Let all things be done for edification

EDIFY
1. *build, edify:* οἰκοδομέω OIKODOMEO
1 Cor 14. 4 He who speaks in a tongue edifies himself, but he who prophesies edifies the church
14.17 but the other man is not edified
2. *building, edification:* οἰκοδομή OIKODOMĒ
[a]B.1.a.2
[b]οἰκοδομὴν λαμβάνειν *receive edification* A.6.a.4
Rom 15. 2 [a]let each . . please his neighbor . . to edify him
1 Cor 14. 5 [b]so that the church may be edified

EDIFYING
1. *building, edification:* οἰκοδομή OIKODOMĒ
Eph 4.29 only such as is good for edifying

EDUCATE
1. *discipline, educate:* παιδεύω PAIDEUŌ
Acts 22. 3 "at the feet of Gamaliel, educated

EFFECT
1. *work, deed:* ἔργον ERGON
Jas 1. 4 let steadfastness have its full effect

IDIOMATICALLY
a. Acts 23.25 And he wrote a letter to this effect *γράψας ἐπιστολὴν ἔχουσαν τὸν τύπον τοῦτον* [TYPOS]

CONTEXTUALLY
Lk 18. 1 to the effect that they ought . . to pray
Rom 5.16 not like the e. of that one man's sin

EFFECT, TAKE
1. *steady, firm:* βέβαιος BEBAIOS [A.6.a.3]
Heb 9.17 a will[u] takes effect only at death

EFFECT, TO THE
1. *as, so:* ὡς HŌS
2 Th 2.2

EFFECT, TO THIS
1. *thus, so:* οὕτως HOUTŌS
Acts 7. 6 "God spoke to this effect

EFFECTIVE, MAKE
1. *operate, be effective:* ἐνεργέω ENERGEŌ
Gal [5. 6 but faith *made effective* through love†[o]

EFFECTIVE WORK, FOR
1. *effective, active:* ἐνεργής ENERGĒS
1 Cor 16. 9 a wide door for effective work has opened

EFFECTS, IN ITS
1. *operate, be effective:* ἐνεργέω (pass. part.) ENERGEŌ
Jas 5.16 prayer . . has great power in its effects

EFFORT
1. *function, business:* ἐργασία ERGASIA
Lk 12.58 "make an effort to settle with him on the way
IDIOMATICALLY
a. 2 Pet 1.5 make every effort σπουδὴν πᾶσαν παρεισενέγκαντες [PAREISPHERŌ*; SPOUDĒ]

EGG
1. *egg:* ᾠόν ŌON*
Lk 11.12 "or if he asks for an egg

EGYPT: Αἴγυπτος 'ējəpt II,E-5
Mt 2.13 "flee to Egypt, and remain there
2.14 he rose and . . departed to Egypt
2.15 "Out of Egypt have I called my son
2.19 appeared in a dream to Joseph in Egypt
Acts 2.10 "Pamphylia, Egypt and the parts of Libya
7. 9 "the patriarchs . . sold him into Egypt
7.10 "before Pharaoh, king of Egypt, who made him governor over Egypt
7.11 "there came a famine throughout all Egypt
7.12 "Jacob heard that there was grain in Egypt
7.15 "Jacob went down into Egypt
7.17 "the people grew and multiplied in Egypt
7.18 "till there arose over Egypt another king
7.34 " 'ill-treatment of my people that are in E.
7.34 " 'now come, I will send you to Egypt
7.36 "performed wonders and signs in Egypt
7.39 "in their hearts they turned to Egypt
7.40 " 'Moses who led us out from the land of E.
13.17 "during their stay in the land of Egypt
Heb 3.16 Was it not all those who left Egypt?
8. 9 "to lead them out of the land of Egypt
11.26 greater wealth than the treasures of E.
11.27 By faith he left Egypt, not being afraid
Jude . 5 he[b] who saved a people out of . . E.
Rev 11. 8 the great city . . called Sodom and Egypt

EGYPTIAN: Αἰγύπτιος
Acts 7.22 "in all the wisdom of the Egyptians
7.24 "he . . avenged him by striking the E.
7.28 " 'to kill me as you killed the E.?
21.38 "Are you not the Egyptian, then?
Heb 11.29 but the Egyptians . . were drowned

EIGHT
1. *eight:* ὀκτώ OKTŌ
Lk 2.21 end of eight days . . he was circumcised
9.28 about eight days after . . he took . . Peter
Jn 20.26 Eight days later . . Thomas was with them
Acts 9.33 Aeneas . . bedridden for eight years
25. 6 stayed . . not more than eight or ten days
1 Pet 3.20 the ark, in which . . eight . . were saved

EIGHTEEN
1. *ten and eight:* δέκα καὶ ὀκτώ OKTŌ; DEKA [A.3.c]
Lk 13.16 "whom Satan bound for eighteen years
2. *eighteen:* δεκαοκτώ DEKAOKTŌ
Lk 13. 4 "eighteen upon whom the tower in Siloam fell
13.11 a spirit of infirmity for eighteen years

EIGHTH
1. *eighth:* ὄγδοος OGDOOS
Lk 1.59 on the eighth day they came to circumcise
Acts 7. 8 "circumcised him on the eighth day
Rev 17.11 "an eighth but it belongs to the seven
21.20 the eighth beryl, the ninth topaz

EIGHTH DAY, ON THE
1. *eight days old:* ὀκταήμερος OKTAĒMEROS*
Phil 3. 5 circumcised on the eighth day

EIGHTY
1. *eighty:* ὀγδοήκοντα OGDOĒKONTA
Lk 16. 7 " 'Take your bill, and write eighty

EIGHTY-FOUR
1. *eighty-four:* ὀγδοήκοντα τέσσαρες OGDOĒKONTA; TESSARES [A.3.c]
Lk 2.37 a widow till she was eighty-four

EITHER (*See also* SIDE, ON EITHER)
1. *or, than:* ἤ Ē
[a]ἤτοι*
Mt 6.24; 12.33
Lk 16.13
Rom 6.16[a]
2. *whether, or:* εἴτε EITE
2 Th 2.15 either by word of mouth or by letter
3. *and not:* μήτε MĒTE
Mt 5.34 "Do not swear at all, either by heaven
2 Th 2. 2 not . . excited, either by spirit or by word
1 Tim 1. 7 e. what they are saying or the things
Jas 5.12 not swear, either by heaven or by earth
4. *and not:* οὔτε OUTE [A.4.c]
[a]+neg. [b]+ποτέ [c]οὔτε δύναται
Mt 12.32 [a]either in this age or in the age to come
Acts 24.12 "either in the temple or in the synagogues
1 Th 2. 5 [b]we never used either . . flattery . . or a cloak
Rev 9.20 [c]idols . . which cannot either see or hear
CONTEXTUALLY
Rom 9.11
1 Jn 3.6

ELAMITE: Ἐλαμίτης
Acts 2. 9 Parthians and Medes and Elamites

ELAPSE
1. *fill full, complete:* πληρόω (pass.) PLĒROŌ
Acts 24.27 when two years had elapsed, Felix

ELATED, BE TOO
1. *exalt oneself:* ὑπεραίρομαι HYPERAIROMAI
2 Cor 12. 7 to keep me from being too elated
12. 7 a thorn . . to keep me from being too elated

ELDER
1. *greater:* μείζων MEIZŌN
Rom 9.12 "The elder will serve the younger
2. *elder, older:* πρεσβύτερος PRESBYTEROS
Mt 15. 2 "transgress the tradition of the elders
16.21 suffer many things from the elders
21.23 elders of the people came up to him
26. 3 elders of the people gathered in the palace
26.47 great crowd . . from . . the elders of the people
26.57 where . . the elders had gathered
27. 1 the elders of the people took counsel
27. 3 brought back the . . silver to the . . elders
27.12 when he was accused by the . . elders
27.20 elders persuaded . . to ask for Barabbas
27.41 chief priests, with the . . elders, mocked him
28.12 when they had assembled with the elders
Mk 7. 3 (observing the tradition of the elders
7. 5 "according to the tradition of the elders
8.31 Son of man must . . be rejected by the elders
11.27 in the temple . . the elders came to him
14.43 a crowd . . from . . the scribes and the elders
14.53 elders and the scribes were assembled
15. 1 elders . . and . . council held a consultation
Lk 7. 3 he sent to him elders of the Jews
9.22 "Son of man must . . be rejected by the elders
15.25 "Now his elder son was in the field
20. 1 as he was teaching . . the elders came up
22.52 elders, who had come out against him
Acts 4. 5 elders and scribes were gathered together
4. 8 "Rulers of the people and elders
4.23 they . . reported what . . the elders had said
6.12 they stirred up the people and the elders
11.30 they did so, sending it to the elders
14.23 when they had appointed elders
15. 2 to Jerusalem to the apostles and the elders
15. 4 welcomed by the church and the . . elders
15. 6 apostles and . . elders were gathered together
15.22 it seemed good to the . . elders
15.23 "brethren, both the apostles and the elders
16. 4 the decisions . . reached by the . . elders
20.17 sent to Ephesus and called to him the elders
21.18 all the elders were present
23.14 they went to the chief priests and elders
24. 1 Ananias came down with some elders
25.15 "elders of the Jews gave information
1 Tim 5.17 elders who rule . . worthy of double honor
5.19 Never admit . . charge against an elder except
Tit 1. 5 appoint elders in every town as I directed

Jas 5.14 Let him call for the elders of the church
1 Pet 5. 1 I exhort the elders among you
5. 5 you . . younger be subject to the elders
2 Jn . 1 The elder to the elect lady
3 Jn . 1 The elder to the beloved Gaius
Rev 4. 4 twenty-four elders, clad in white
4.10 twenty-four elders fall down before him
5. 5 one of the elders said to me, "Weep not
5. 6 among the elders, I saw a Lamb standing
5. 8 twenty-four elders . . before the Lamb
5.11 I heard around . . the elders the voice
5.14 the elders fell down and worshiped
7.11 all the angels stood . . round the elders
7.13 Then one of the elders addressed me
11.16 the twenty-four elders . . fell on their faces
14. 3 they sing a new song before . . the elders
19. 4 the twenty-four elders . . fell down

ELDER, FELLOW
1. *fellow elder:* *συμπρεσβύτερος* SYMPRESBYTEROS*
1 Pet 5. 1 I exhort the elders . . as a fellow elder

ELDERS, ASSEMBLY OF
ELDERS, COUNCIL OF
1. *council of elders:* *πρεσβυτέριον* PRESBYTERION*
Lk 22.66 the assembly of the elders . . gathered
Acts 22. 5 "whole council of elders bear me witness
1 Tim 4.14 the c. of elders laid their hands upon you[o]

ELDEST
1. *elder, older:* *πρεσβύτερος* PRESBYTEROS
Jn 8. 9 they went away . . beginning with the eldest[r]‡

ELEAZAR: 'Ελεάζαρ ˌelē'āzər
Mt 1.15 Eliud the father of Eleazar, and Eleazar the father of Matthan

ELECT
1. *select, choice:* *ἐκλεκτός* EKLEKTOS
Mt 24.22 "for . . the elect those days will be shortened
24.24 "to lead astray, if possible, even the elect
24.31 "will gather his elect from the four winds
Mk 13.20 "for . . the elect . . he shortened the days
13.22 "to lead astray, if possible, the elect
13.27 "he will send out . . and gather his elect
Lk 18. 7 "will not God vindicate his elect?
Rom 8.33 Who shall . . charge . . God's elect?
1 Tim 5.21 In the presence . . of the elect angels
2 Tim 2.10 I endure . . for the sake of the elect
Tit 1. 1 to further the faith of God's elect
2 Jn . 1 The elder to the elect lady
.13 children of your elect sister greet you
2. *choice, selection:* *ἐκλογή* (pl.) EKLOGĒ
Rom 11. 7 Israel failed . . The elect obtained it

ELECTION
1. *choice, selection:* *ἐκλογή* EKLOGĒ
Rom 9.11 that God's purpose of election . . continue
11.28 as regards election they are beloved
2 Pet 1.10 be . . zealous to confirm your . . election

ELEMENT
1. *element:* *στοιχεῖον* STOICHEION
2 Pet 3.10 the elements will be dissolved with fire
3.12 the elements will melt with fire!

ELEMENTAL SPIRIT
1. *element:* *στοιχεῖον* STOICHEION
Gal 4. 3 we were slaves to the elemental spirits
4. 9 turn back again to the . . elemental spirits
Col 2. 8 prey . . according to the elemental spirits
2.20 If . . you died to the elemental spirits

ELEMENTARY
1. *origin, rule:* *ἀρχή* (gen.) ARCHĒ
Heb 6. 1 let us leave the elementary doctrine

ELEVEN
1. *eleven:* *ἕνδεκα* HENDEKA*
Mt 28.16 Now the eleven disciples went to Galilee
Mk 16.14 Afterward he appeared to the eleven[k]‡
Lk 24. 9 they told all this to the eleven
24.33 they found the eleven gathered together
Acts 1.26 Matthias . . was enrolled with the eleven
2.14 Peter, standing with the eleven

ELEVENTH
1. *eleventh:* *ἑνδέκατος* HENDEKATOS*
Mt 20. 6 "about the eleventh hour he went out
20. 9 "those hired about the eleventh hour came
Rev 21.20 the eleventh jacinth

ELI: 'ēlī, 'ālē
1. *my God* (Aram.): *ἠλί* ĒLI*
Mt 27.46 Jesus cried with a loud voice, "Eli, Eli, lama sabachthani?

ELIAKIM: 'Ελιακίμ i'līəkim
Mt 1.13 Abiud the father of Eliakim, and Eliakim the father of Azor
3.30 Jonam, the son of Eliakim

ELIEZER: 'Ελιέζερ ˌelī'ēzər
Lk 3.29 Joshua, the son of Eliezer

ELIJAH: 'Ηλίας i'lījə
Mt 11.14 "he is Elijah who is to come
16.14 "others say Elijah, and others Jeremiah
17. 3 there appeared to them Moses and Elijah
17. 4 "one for Moses and one for Elijah
17.10 "why . . that first Elijah must come?
17.11 "Elijah does come, and he is to restore
17.12 "I tell you that Elijah has already come
27.47 "This man is calling Elijah
27.49 "let us see whether Elijah will come
Mk 6.15 others said, "It is Elijah
8.28 "and others say, Elijah
9. 4 there appeared to them Elijah with Moses
9. 5 "one for Moses and one for Elijah
9.11 "Why . . that first Elijah must come?
9.12 "Elijah does come first to restore all things
9.13 "But I tell you that Elijah has come
15.35 "Behold, he is calling Elijah
15.36 "let us see whether Elijah will come
Lk 1.17 "will go before him in the . . power of Elijah
4.25 "widows in Israel in the days of Elijah
4.26 "Elijah was sent to none . . but . . Zarephath
9. 8 by some that Elijah had appeared
9.19 "but others say, Elijah
9.30 two men talked with him, Moses and Elijah
9.33 "one for Moses and one for Elijah
[9.54 "to bid fire come down . . *as Elijah did*‡
Jn 1.21 "What then? Are you Elijah?
1.25 "if . . neither the Christ, nor Elijah
Rom 11. 2 know what the scripture says of Elijah
Jas 5.17 Elijah was . . of like nature with ourselves

ELISHA: 'Ελισαῖος i'līshə
Lk 4.27 "lepers . . in the time of . . Elisha

ELIUD: 'Ελιούδ i'līəd
Mt 1.14 Achim the father of Eliud
1.15 Eliud the father of Eleazar

ELIZABETH: 'Ελισάβετ i'lizəbəth
Lk 1. 5 Zechariah[b] . . had a wife . . , Elizabeth
1. 7 no child, because Elizabeth was barren
1.13 "your wife Elizabeth will bear you a son
1.24 his wife Elizabeth conceived
1.36 "Elizabeth . . has also conceived a son
1.40 she entered . . and greeted Elizabeth
1.41 when Elizabeth heard the greeting of Mary
1.41 Elizabeth was filled with the . . Spirit
1.57 time came for Elizabeth to be delivered

ELMADAM: 'Ελμαδάμ el'mādəm
Lk 3.28 Cosam, the son of Elmadam

ELOI: 'ēlōī, 'ālōī
1. *my God* (Aram.): *ἐλωΐ* ELŌI*
Mk 15.34 Jesus cried with a loud voice, "Eloi, Eloi, lama sabachthani?

ELOQUENT
1. *eloquent, learned:* *λόγιος* LOGIOS*
Acts 18.24 Apollos . . was an eloquent man
2. *word, reckoning:* *λόγος* (gen.) LOGOS
1 Cor 1.17 to preach . . , not with eloquent wisdom

ELSE
1. *other, another:* ἄλλος (+neg.) ALLOS
Jn 15.24 "works which no one else did
Acts 4.12 "there is salvation in no one else
1 Cor 1.16 (whether I baptized any one else
2. *if not, except:* εἰ μή EI MĒ
Jn 14.11 "or else believe me for . . the works
3. *another, different:* ἕτερος HETEROS
Acts 8.34 "about himself or about some one else?
Rom 8.39 nor anything else in all creation
1 Tim 1.10 whatever else is contrary to . . doctrine
CONTEXTUALLY
Acts 24.20 "Or else let these men themselves say
1 Cor 7.11 (or else be reconciled to her husband

ELSE, SOME ONE
1. *another, different:* ἕτερος (subst. indef.) HETEROS
Lk 22.58 a little later some one else saw him

ELYMAS: Ἐλύμας 'eləməs
Acts 13. 8 Elymas the magician . . withstood them

EMBARK IN
1. *go upon, mount, board:* ἐπιβαίνω EPIBAINŌ
Acts 27. 2 embarking in a ship of Adramyttium

EMBASSY
1. *age, embassy:* πρεσβεία PRESBEIA*
Lk 14.32 "he sends an embassy and asks terms
19.14 "his citizens . . sent an embassy

EMBODIMENT
1. *form, appearance:* μόρφωσις MORPHŌSIS
Rom 2.20 in the law the embodiment of knowledge

EMBRACE
1. *fall upon the neck:* ἐπιπίπτειν ἐπὶ τὸν τράχηλον EPIPIPTŌ; TRACHĒLOS [B.2.a.1]
Lk 15.20 "his father . . ran and embraced him
Acts 20.37 they all wept and embraced Paul
2. *gather together:* συμπεριλαμβάνω SYMPERILAMBANŌ*
Acts 20.10 Paul . . bent over him, and embracing him

EMERALD
1. *emerald-green:* σμαράγδινος SMARAGDINOS*
Rev 4. 3 a rainbow that looked like an emerald
2. *emerald:* σμάραγδος SMARAGDOS*
Rev 21.19 the third agate, the fourth emerald

EMINENT
1. *select, choice:* ἐκλεκτός EKLEKTOS
Rom 16.13 Greet Rufus, eminent in the Lord
2. *honored, valuable:* ἔντιμος ENTIMOS
[a]comp.
Lk 14. 8 [a]"lest a more eminent man . . be invited

EMMANUEL: Ἐμμανουήλ i'manyüəl
Mt 1.23 "his name shall be called Emmanuel

EMMAUS: Ἐμμαοῦς e'māəs I,B-5
Lk 24.13 two of them were going to . . Emmaus

EMPEROR
1. *king:* βασιλεύς BASILEUS
1 Pet 2.13 whether . . to the emperor as supreme
2.17 Fear God. Honor the emperor
2. *venerable, august:* σεβαστός (subst.) SEBASTOS
Acts 25.21 "kept . . for the decision of the emperor
25.25 "as he himself appealed to the emperor

EMPLOY
EMPLOYED, BE
1. *do a service, minister:* διακονέω DIAKONEŌ
1 Pet 4.10 employ it for one another
2. *work, do:* ἐργάζομαι ERGAZOMAI [A.6.e]
1 Cor 9.13 those who are employed in the temple

EMPTY
1. *empty, make void:* κενόω KENOŌ
1 Cor 1.17 lest the cross of Christ be emptied
Phil 2. 7 emptied himself, taking . . form of a servant[d]
2. *empty, vain:* κενός KENOS
Lk 1.53 "the rich he has sent empty away
Eph 5. 6 no one deceive you with empty words
Col 2. 8 philosophy and empty deceit
3. *have leisure, study, be empty:* σχολάζω (part.) SCHOLAZŌ
Mt 12.44 "when he comes he finds it empty, swept

EMPTY PHRASES, HEAP UP
1. *babble:* βατταλογέω BATTALOGEŌ*
Mt 6. 7 "in praying do not heap up empty phrases

EMPTY TALKER
1. *talking idly:* ματαιολόγος (subst.) MATAIOLOGOS*
Tit 1.10 many insubordinate men, empty talkers

EMPTY-HANDED
1. *empty, vain:* κενός KENOS
Mk 12. 3 "sent him away empty-handed
Lk 20.10 "sent him away empty-handed
20.11 "sent him away empty-handed

ENABLE
1. *be able:* δύναμαι DYNAMAI [A.6.a.5]
Phil 3.21 which enables him . . to subject all things

ENACTED, BE
1. *frame laws:* νομοθετέω (pass.) NOMOTHETEŌ
Heb 8. 6 since it is enacted on better promises

ENCIRCLE
1. *surround, encircle:* κυκλόω KYKLOŌ
Heb 11.30 walls of Jericho . . encircled for seven days

ENCLOSE
1. *enclose, close:* συγκλείω SYGKLEIŌ
Lk 5. 6 they enclosed a great shoal of fish

ENCOUNTER
1. *throw together, compare:* συμβάλλω SYMBALLŌ
Lk 14.31 "going to encounter another king in war

ENCOURAGE
1. *build, edify:* οἰκοδομέω OIKODOMEŌ
1 Cor 8.10 might he not be encouraged, if . . weak?
2. *call to, exhort, comfort:* παρακαλέω PARAKALEŌ
1 Cor 14.31 prophesy . . so that all may . . be encouraged
Eph 6.22 that he may encourage your hearts
Col 2. 2 that their hearts may be encouraged
4. 8 that he may encourage your hearts
1 Th 5.11 Therefore encourage one another
Heb 10.25 encouraging one another
3. *encourage, support:* παραμυθέομαι PARAMYTHEOMAI
1 Th 2.11 we . . encouraged you and charged you
5.14 encourage the fainthearted
4. *urge on:* προτρέπω (mid.) PROTREPŌ*
Acts 18.27 the brethren encouraged him

ENCOURAGED
1. *cheerful, spirited:* εὔθυμος EUTHYMOS*
Acts 27.36 they all were encouraged and ate

ENCOURAGED, BE MUTUALLY
1. *appeal together:* συμπαρακαλέω (pass.) SYMPARAKALEŌ*
Rom 1.12 that we may be mutually encouraged

ENCOURAGEMENT
1. *exhortation, comfort:* παράκλησις PARAKLĒSIS
Acts 4.36 Barnabas (which means, Son of e.
Rom 15. 4 by the encouragement of the scriptures
15. 5 God of steadfastness and encouragement
1 Cor 14. 3 speaks to men for their . . encouragement
Phil 2. 1 if . . any encouragement in Christ
Heb 6.18 strong encouragement to seize the hope

ENCOURAGEMENT, GIVE
1. *call to, exhort, comfort:* παρακαλέω PARAKALEŌ
Acts 20. 2 When he . . had given them much e.

END
1. *end, extremity:* ἄκρον AKRON
Mt 24.31 "from one end of heaven to the other
Mk 13.27 "four winds, from the ends of the earth to the ends of heaven
Lk 16.24 " 'to dip the end of his finger in water
2. *fail, cease:* ἐκλείπω EKLEIPŌ
Heb 1.12 "thy years will never end
3. *finish, complete:* ἐπιτελέω EPITELEŌ
Gal 3. 3 are you now ending with the flesh?
4. *last, extreme:* ἔσχατος ESCHATOS
Acts 1. 8 "in . . Samaria and to the end of the earth
Pet 1.20 at the end of the times for your sake

5. *complete, furnish:* ἐξαρτίζω EXARTIZŌ [A.6.c.3]
Acts 21. 5 when our days there were ended
6. *end, limit:* πέρας PERAS
Mt 12.42 "she came from the ends of the earth
Lk 11.31 "she came from the ends of the earth
Rom 10.18 "their words to the ends of the world
7. *fill, satisfy:* πίμπλημι PIMPLĒMI
Lk 1.23 when his time of service was ended
8. *fall, fail:* πίπτω PIPTŌ
1 Cor 13. 8 Love never ends
9. *fill full, complete:* πληρόω PLĒROŌ
Lk 7. 1 After he had ended all his sayings
10. *completion, end:* συντέλεια SYNTELEIA
Heb 9.26 once for all at the end of the age
11. *bring to an end:* συντελέω SYNTELEŌ
Lk 4. 2 when they were ended, he was hungry
4.13 when the devil had ended every temptation
12. *make perfect, complete:* τελειόω TELEIOŌ
Lk 2.43 when the feast was ended
13. *finish, fulfill:* τελέω TELEŌ
Rev 15. 1 with them the wrath of God is ended
15. 8 until the seven plagues . . were ended
20. 3 till the thousand years were ended
20. 5 until the thousand years were ended
20. 7 when the thousand years are ended
14. *end, goal:* τέλος TELOS
Mt 10.22 "he who endures to the end will be saved
24. 6 "this must take place, but the end is not yet
24.13 "he who endures to the end will be saved
24.14 "then the end will come
26.58 he sat with the guards to see the end
Mk 3.26 "he . . is coming to an end
13. 7 "this must take place, but the end is not yet
13.13 "he who endures to the end will be saved
Lk 1.33 "of his kingdom there will be no end
21. 9 "the end will not be at once
Jn 13. 1 his own . . he loved . . to the end
Rom 6.21 The end of those things is death
6.22 sanctification and its end, eternal life
10. 4 For Christ is the end of the law
1 Cor 1. 8 who will sustain you to the end, guiltless
10.11 upon whom the end of the ages has come
15.24 the end, when he delivers the kingdom
2 Cor 3.13 that the Israelites might not see the end
11.15 Their end will correspond to their deeds
Phil 3.19 Their end is destruction
Heb [3. 6 if we hold fast . . *firm to the end*‡
3.14 if only we hold . . firm to the end
6. 8 its end is to be burned
6.11 realizing . . assurance of hope until the end
7. 3 neither beginning of days nor end of life
1 Pet 4. 7 The end of all things is at hand
4.17 what will be the end of those?
Rev 2.26 " 'He . . who keeps my works until the end
21. 6 "I am . . the beginning and the end
22.13 "I am . . the beginning and the end
IDIOMATICALLY
a. Lk 2.21 at the end of eight days ὅτε ἐπλήσθησαν ἡμέραι ὀκτώ [PIMPLĒMI]
CONTEXTUALLY
Rom 14. 9 For this e. Christ died and lived again
Eph 6.18 To that e. keep alert with all perseverance
2 Th 1.11 To this end we always pray for you
1 Tim 4.10 For to this end we toil and strive[j]

END, BRING TO AN
1. *kill:* ἀποκτείνω APOKTEINŌ
Eph 2.16 thereby bringing the hostility to an end

END OF ONE'S LIFE, AT THE
1. *die, finish:* τελευτάω (part.) TELEUTAŌ
Heb 11.22 By faith Joseph, at the end of his life

ENDEAVOR EAGERLY
1. *be eager:* σπουδάζω SPOUDAZŌ
1 Th 2.17 we endeavored the more eagerly

ENDEAVOR, IN ONE'S
1. *seek, desire:* ζητέω (part.) ZĒTEO
Gal 2.17 if, in our endeavor to be justified in Christ

ENDLESS
1. *boundless:* ἀπέραντος APERANTOS*
1 Tim 1. 4 occupy themselves with . . endless genealogies

ENDOWMENT
1. *giving, gift:* δόσις DOSIS
Jas 1.17 Every good endowment . . is from above

ENDURANCE
ENDURANCE, PATIENT
1. *endurance:* ὑπομονή HYPOMONĒ
Lk 21.19 "By . . endurance you will gain your lives
Rom 5. 3 knowing that suffering produces endurance
5. 4 endurance produces character
2 Cor 6. 4 through great endurance, in afflictions
Col 1.11 for all endurance and patience with joy
Heb 10.36 For you have need of endurance
Rev 1. 9 I John . . share . . the patient endurance
2. 2 " 'I know . . your patient endurance
2.19 " 'I know your . . patient endurance
3.10 " 'you . . kept my word of patient endurance
13.10 Here is a call for the endurance
14.12 Here is a call for the endurance

ENDURE (*See also* SUFFERING, ENDURE)
1. *bear up, endure* (mid.): ἀνέχω ANECHŌ
1 Cor 4.12 when persecuted, we endure
2 Th 1. 4 the afflictions which you are enduring
2 Tim 4. 3 people will not endure sound teaching
2. *be patient under, stand firm:* ὑπομένω HYPOMENŌ
Mt 10.22 "he who endures to the end will be saved
24.13 "he who endures to the end will be saved
Mk 13.13 "he who endures to the end will be saved
1 Cor 13. 7 Love . . endures all things
2 Tim 2.10 I endure everything for . . the elect
2.12 if we endure, we shall also reign
Heb 10.32 you endured a hard struggle
12. 2 Jesus . . who . . endured the cross
12. 3 who endured from sinners such hostility
12. 7 for discipline that you have to endure
Jas 1.12 Blessed is the man who endures trial
3. *bear up, endure:* ὑποφέρω HYPOPHERŌ*
1 Cor 10.13 temptation . . you may be able to endure
2 Tim 3.11 at Lystra, what persecutions I endured
1 Pet 2.19 he endures pain while suffering unjustly
4. *be steadfast:* καρτερέω KARTEREŌ*
Heb 11.27 he endured as seeing him who is invisible
5. *stay, wait:* μένω MENŌ
Jn 6.27 "food which endures to eternal life
2 Cor 9. 9 "his righteousness[k] endures for ever
6. *bring, bear:* φέρω PHERŌ
Rom 9.22 God . . has endured with much patience
Heb 12.20 they could not endure the order
7. *be transient:* πρόσκαιρος εἶναι PROSKAIROS [A.6.a.3]
Mt 13.21 "he . . endures for a while, and . . falls away[l]
Mk 4.17 "they have no root . . but endure . . a while
8. *endure, bear:* στέγω STEGŌ
1 Cor 9.12 we e. anything rather than put an obstacle
CONTEXTUALLY
Heb 13.13 let us . . bear the abuse he endured⁰

ENDURE PATIENTLY
1. *endurance:* ὑπομονή HYPOMONĒ
[a]B.1.a.2 [b]B.3.a.5
2 Cor 1. 6 [a]when you patiently e. the same sufferings
Rev 2. 3 [b]" 'I know you are enduring patiently
2. *be patient, persevere:* μακροθυμέω MAKROTHYMEŌ
Heb 6.15 Abraham,[m] having patiently endured

ENEMY
1. *be opposed:* ἀντίκειμαι (subst. part.) ANTIKEIMAI
1 Tim 5.14 give the enemy no occasion to revile us
2. *hated, hostile:* ἐχθρός (subst.) ECHTHROS
Mt 5.43 " 'love your neighbor and hate your enemy
5.44 "But I say to you, Love your enemies
13.25 "his enemy came and sowed weeds
13.28 "He said . . 'An enemy has done this
13.39 "the enemy who sowed them is the devil
22.44 " 'till I put thy enemies under thy feet
Mk 12.36 " 'till I put thy enemies under thy feet

Lk 1.71 "that we . . be saved from our enemies
1.74 "delivered from the hand of our enemies
6.27 "But I say to you . . Love your enemies
6.35 "love your enemies, and do good
10.19 "authority . . over . . the power of the enemy
19.27 " 'enemies . . who did not want me to reign
19.43 "your enemies will cast up a bank
20.43 " 'till I make thy enemies a stool for thy feet
Acts 2.35 " 'till I make thy enemies a stool for thy feet
13.10 "you enemy of all righteousness
Rom 5.10 if while we were enemies we were reconciled
11.28 As regards the gospel they are enemies
12.20 "if your enemy is hungry, feed him
1 Cor 15.25 until he has put all his enemies under
15.26 last enemy to be destroyed is death
Gal 4.16 Have I then become your enemy?
Phil 3.18 many . . live as enemies of the cross
2 Th 3.15 Do not look on him as an enemy
Heb 1.13 "till I make thy enemies a stool for thy feet
10.13 until his enemies should be made a stool
Jas 4. 4 friend of the world . . an enemy of God

ENERGY

1. *operation, activity:* ἐνέργεια ENERGEIA
Col 1.29 the energy which he mightily inspires

ENFORCE

1. *work, do:* ἐργάζομαι ERGAZOMAI
Heb 11.33 who through faith . . enforced justice

ENGAGE

1. *put together:* συντίθημι (mid.) SYNTITHĒMI
Lk 22. 5 they . . engaged to give him money

ENGAGED IN, BE

1. *have, hold:* ἔχω ECHŌ
Phil 1.30 ⟨suffer,⟩ engaged in the same conflict

ENJOY

1. *pleasure:* ἀπόλαυσις APOLAUSIS*
[a]B.1.a.2
1 Tim 6.17 [a]God . . furnishes us with everything to enjoy
2. *have, hold:* ἔχω ECHŌ [A.6.a.5]
Heb 11.25 rather . . than . . enjoy the . . pleasures of sin
3. *happen, attain:* τυγχάνω TYGCHANŌ
Acts 24. 2 "through you we enjoy much peace

ENJOY COMPANY

1. *fill quite full:* ἐμπίμπλημι (pass.) EMPIMPLĒMI
Rom 15.24 once I have enjoyed your company

ENLARGE GREATLY

1. *make large, extol:* μεγαλύνω MEGALYNŌ
2 Cor 10.15 our field . . may be greatly enlarged

ENLIGHTEN

1. *shine, illuminate:* φωτίζω PHŌTIZŌ
Jn 1. 9 true light that enlightens every man
Eph 1.18 the eyes of your hearts enlightened
Heb 6. 4 those who have once been enlightened
10.32 after you were enlightened, you endured

ENLIGHTENED

1. *according to knowledge:* κατὰ ἐπίγνωσιν EPIGNŌSIS [B.1.a.1]
Rom 10. 2 they have a zeal . . but it is not e.

ENLIST

1. *enlist soldiers:* στρατολογέω STRATOLOGEŌ*
2 Tim 2. 4 to satisfy the one who enlisted him

ENMITY

1. *hostility:* ἔχθρα ECHTHRA
Lk 23.12 before this they had been at enmity
Gal 5.20 idolatry, sorcery, enmity, strife
Jas 4. 4 friendship with the world is e. with God

ENOCH: Ἑνώχ ˈēnək
Lk 3.37 Methuselah, the son of E., the son of Jared
Heb 11. 5 By faith Enoch was taken up
Jude .14 Enoch . . prophesied, saying, "Behold

ENOS: Ἐνώς ˈēnəs
Lk 3.38 Enos, the son of Seth, the son of Adam

ENOUGH (*See also* STRONG ENOUGH, BE)

1. *sufficient:* ἀρκετός ARKETOS
Mt 10.25 "it is enough . . to be like his teacher
2. *self-sufficiency:* αὐτάρκεια AUTARKEIA
2 Cor 9. 8 so that you may always have enough
3. *enough:* ἱκανός HIKANOS
Lk 22.38 And he said to them, "It is enough
2 Cor 2. 6 this punishment by the majority is enough
4. *many, great:* πολύς POLYS
Phm . 8 I am bold enough . . to command you
5. *so large, so many:* τοσοῦτος TOSOUTOS
Mt 15.33 "Where are we to get bread enough?

IDIOMATICALLY

a. Jn 6.7 "Two hundred denarii[l] would not buy enough bread διακοσίων δηναρίων ἄρτοι οὐκ ἀρκοῦσιν [ARKEŌ]
b. Acts 27.38 And when they had eaten enough κορεσθέντες δὲ τροφῆς [KORENNYMI]
c. 1 Cor 6.5 Can it be that there is no man among you wise enough to decide? οὕτως οὐκ ἔνι ἐν ὑμῖν οὐδεὶς σοφός, ὃς δυνήσεται διακρῖναι; [DYNAMAI]

CONTEXTUALLY

Lk 16. 3 " 'I am not strong enough to dig
1 Cor 14.17 For you may give thanks well enough

ENOUGH AND TO SPARE, HAVE

1. *abound:* περισσεύω PERISSEUŌ
Lk 15.17 " 'servants have bread enough and to spare

ENOUGH, BE

1. *receive in full:* ἀπέχω (impers.) APECHŌ
Mk 14.41 "It is enough; the hour has come
2. *suffice, satisfy:* ἀρκέω ARKEŌ
Mt 25. 9 " 'Perhaps there will not be enough . . for you

ENRAGED, BE

1. *infuriate, saw through:* διαπρίω (pass.) DIAPRIŌ*
Acts 5.33 When they heard . . they were enraged
7.54 when they heard . . they were enraged
2. *be full of rage:* γίνεσθαι πλήρης θυμοῦ THYMOS [A.6.a.3]
Acts 19.28 When they heard . . they were enraged

ENRICH

1. *make wealthy:* πλουτίζω PLOUTIZŌ
1 Cor 1. 5 you were enriched in him with all speecn
2 Cor 9.11 You will be enriched in every way

ENROLL

1. *register:* ἀπογράφω APOGRAPHŌ*
Lk 2. 1 that all the world should be enrolled
2. 3 all went to be enrolled
2. 5 to be enrolled with Mary, his betrothed
Heb 12.23 first-born who are enrolled in heaven
2. *recount, enlist:* καταλέγω KATALEGŌ*
1 Tim 5. 9 Let a widow be enrolled

ENROLLED WITH, BE

1. *be reckoned along with:* συγκαταψηφίζομαι SYGKATAPSĒPHIZOMAI*
Acts 1.26 Matthias . . was enrolled with the eleven

ENROLLMENT

1. *register, list:* ἀπογραφή APOGRAPHĒ
Lk 2. 2 This was the first enrollment

ENSLAVE

1. *enslave:* δουλόω DOULOŌ
Acts 7. 6 "aliens . . who would enslave them
2 Pet 2.19 to that he is enslaved
2. *enslave:* ἐξουσιάζω EXOUSIAZŌ
1 Cor 6.12 I will not be enslaved by anything

ENSLAVED, BE

1. *serve, be a slave:* δουλεύω DOULEUŌ
Rom 6. 6 we might no longer be enslaved to sin

ENTANGLE

1. *entrap:* παγιδεύω PAGIDEUŌ*
Mt 22.15 Pharisees . . took counsel how to entangle him

ENTANGLED, BE

ENTANGLED, GET

1. *be entangled* (pass.): ἐμπλέκω EMPLEKŌ
2 Tim 2. 4 No soldier . . gets e. in civilian pursuits
2 Pet 2.20 they are again entangled in ⟨defilements⟩

ENTER (*See also* PARTNERSHIP WITH, ENTER INTO; VIOLENTLY, ENTER)

1. *enter, go into:* εἰσέρχομαι EISERCHOMAI
Mt 5.20 "you will never enter the kingdom

Mt 7.13 "Enter by the narrow gate
7.13 "those who enter by it are many
7.21 "Not every one . . shall enter the kingdom
8. 5 As he entered Capernaum, a centurion came
10. 5 "enter no town of the Samaritans
10.11 "whatever town or village you enter
10.12 "As you enter the house, salute it
12. 4 "how he entered the house of God
12.29 "how can one enter a strong man's house?
12.45 "spirits more evil . . enter and dwell there
18. 3 "you will never enter the kingdom
18. 8 "it is better for you to enter life maimed
18. 9 "it is better for you to enter life
19.17 "If you would enter life, keep
19.23 "hard for a rich man to enter the kingdom
19.24 "for a rich man to enter the kingdom
21.10 when he entered Jerusalem
21.12 Jesus entered the temple of God[p]
23.13 "for you neither enter yourselves, nor allow those who would enter to go in[v]
24.38 "the day when Noah entered the ark
Mk 1.21 he entered the synagogue and taught
1.45 Jesus[g] could no longer . . enter a town
2.26 "how he entered the house of God
3. 1 Again he entered the synagogue
3.27 "no one can enter a strong man's house
5.12 "Send us to the swine, let us enter them
5.13 the unclean spirits . . entered the swine
5.39 when he had entered, he said to them
6.10 "Where you enter a house, stay there
7.17 when he had entered the house
7.24 he entered a house
8.26 "Do not even enter the village
9.25 "come out . . and never enter him again
9.28 when he had entered the house
9.43 "it is better for you to enter life maimed
9.45 "it is better for you to enter life lame
9.47 "it is better for you to enter the kingdom
10.15 "whoever does not . . shall not enter it
10.23 "How hard . . to enter the kingdom of God!
10.24 "how hard . . to enter the kingdom of God!
10.25 "than for a rich man to enter the kingdom
11.11 he entered Jerusalem
11.15 he entered the temple
13.15 "let him . . not . . enter his house
14.14 "wherever he enters, say to the householder
16. 5 entering the tomb, they saw a young man
Lk 1. 9 it fell to him by lot to enter the temple
1.40 she entered the house of Zechariah
4.38 he arose and . . entered Simon's house
6. 4 "how he entered the house of God
6. 6 when he entered the synagogue and taught
7. 1 After he had ended . . he entered Capernaum
7.44 "I entered your house, you gave me no water
8.30 for many demons had entered him
8.32 they begged him to let them enter these
8.33 the demons . . entered the swine
8.51 he permitted no one to enter
9. 4 "whatever house you enter, stay there
9.34 they were afraid as they entered the cloud
9.52 entered a village of the Samaritans
10. 5 "Whatever house you enter . . say, 'Peace!
10. 8 "Whenever you enter a town
10.10 "whenever you enter a town
10.38 he entered a village
11.26 "they enter and dwell there
11.52 "you did not enter yourselves, and you hindered those who were entering
13.24 "Strive to enter by the narrow door; for many, I tell you, will seek to enter
17.12 as he entered . . he was met by ten lepers
17.27 "the day when Noah entered the ark
18.17 "whoever does not . . shall not enter it
18.25 "it is easier . . than . . to enter the kingdom
19. 1 He entered Jericho and was passing through
19.45 he entered the temple
21.21 "let not those . . enter it
Lk 22.10 "when you have entered the city
Jn 3. 5 "he cannot enter the kingdom of God
10. 1 "he who does not enter the sheepfold
10. 2 "he who enters by the door is the shepherd
10. 9 "if any one enters by me
18. 1 there was a garden, which he . . entered
18.28 They themselves did not enter
18.33 "Pilate entered the praetorium again
19. 9 he entered the praetorium again
Acts 1.13 when they had entered, they went up
3. 8 he stood and walked and entered
5.21 they entered the temple at daybreak
9. 6 "rise and enter the city
9.17 So Ananias departed and entered the house
10.24 the following day they entered Caesarea
10.25 When Peter entered, Cornelius met him
11. 8 " 'nothing . . unclean has ever entered
11.12 "we entered the man's house
14. 1 at Iconium they entered . . the . . synagogue
14.20 he rose up and entered the city
14.22 we must enter the kingdom of God
19. 8 he entered the synagogue
21. 8 we entered the house of Philip
23.16 so he went and entered the barracks
25.23 they entered the audience hall
1 Cor 14.23 If . . outsiders or unbelievers enter
14.24 if . . an unbeliever or outsider enters
Heb 3.11 " 'They shall never enter my rest
3.18 that they should never enter his rest
3.19 unable to enter because of unbelief
4. 1 promise of entering his rest remains
4. 3 we who have believed enter that rest
4. 3 " 'They shall never enter my rest
4. 5 "They shall never enter my rest
4. 6 it remains for some to enter it
4. 6 failed to enter because of disobedience
4.10 whoever enters God's rest also ceases
4.11 Let us therefore strive to enter that rest
9.25 high priest enters the Holy Place yearly
Rev 11.11 breath of life from God entered them
15. 8 no one could enter the temple
21.27 nothing unclean shall enter it
22.14 they may enter the city by the gates

2. *entrance:* εἴσοδος EISODOS [B.1.a.2]
Heb 10.19 confidence to enter the sanctuary

3. *go into, enter:* εἰσπορεύομαι EISPOREUOMAI
Mk 7.19 "since it enters . . his stomach
11. 2 "as you enter it you will find a colt
Lk 8.16 "that those who enter may see the light
11.33 "that those who enter may see the light
18.24 "hard . . to enter the kingdom of God!
19.30 "on entering you will find a colt tied
22.10 "Behold, when you have entered the city
Acts 3. 2 to ask alms of those who entered the temple
8. 3 Saul . . entering house after house

4. *go into:* ἔρχομαι εἰς ERCHOMAI [A.6.a.4]
Mt 8.14 when Jesus entered Peter's house
9.28 When he entered the house
12. 9 he . . entered their synagogue
19. 1 Jesus . . entered the region of Judea
21.23 when he entered the temple
Mk 1.29 entered the house of Simon and Andrew‡
14.38 "that you may not enter into temptation

5. *set over, direct:* προΐστημι (mid.) PROISTĒMI
Tit [3.14 learn to *enter honorable occupations*†

ENTER IN

1. *go into, enter:* εἰσπορεύομαι EISPOREUOMAI
Mk 4.19 "cares . . enter in and choke the word

ENTER INTO

1. *enter, go into:* εἰσέρχομαι EISERCHOMAI
Mt 25.21 " 'enter into the joy of your master
25.23 " 'enter into the joy of your master
26.41 "may not enter into temptation
Lk 22. 3 Satan entered into Judas called Iscariot
22.40 "Pray . . you may not enter into temptation
22.46 "pray . . you may not enter into temptation

Lk 24.26 that .. Christ should .. enter into his glory
Jn 3. 4 "enter .. into his mother's womb?
4.38 "you have entered into their labor
13.27 Then .. Satan entered into him
Heb 6.19 a hope that enters into the inner shrine
9.12 he entered once for all into the Holy Place
9.24 Christ has entered .. into heaven itself

ENTER WITH
1. *enter along with:* συνεισέρχομαι SYNEISERCHOMAI*
Jn 6.22 Jesus had not entered .. with his disciples
18.15 he entered the court .. along with Jesus

ENTERTAIN
1. *receive as a guest, surprise:* ξενίζω XENIZŌ
Acts 28. 7 Publius, who .. entertained us hospitably
Heb 13. 2 some have entertained angels unawares

ENTICE
1. *lure:* δελεάζω DELEAZŌ*
Jas 1.14 when he is .. enticed by his own desire
2 Pet 2.14 They entice unsteady souls
2.18 they entice with licentious passions

ENTIRE
1. *all, every, whole:* πᾶς PAS
Tit 2.10 show entire and true fidelity

ENTIRELY
1. *in all ways, assuredly:* πάντως PANTŌS
1 Cor 9.10 Does he not speak entirely for our sake?

ENTRANCE
1. *entrance:* εἴσοδος EISODOS
2 Pet 1.11 an entrance into the eternal kingdom

ENTRAP
1. *catch:* ἀγρεύω AGREUŌ*
Mk 12.13 Pharisees .. to entrap him in his talk

ENTREAT
1. *ask for, decline:* παραιτέομαι PARAITEOMAI
Heb 12.19 whose words made the hearers entreat
2. *call to, exhort, comfort:* παρακαλέω PARAKALEŌ
Lk 15.28 "His father came out and entreated him
Acts 9.38 sent two men to him entreating him
2 Cor 6. 1 we entreat you not to accept .. in vain
10. 1 I, Paul, myself entreat you
Phil 4. 2 I entreat Euodia and I entreat Syntyche to agree in the Lord

ENTRUST
1. *give up, allow:* παραδίδωμι PARADIDŌMI
Mt 25.14 "entrusted to them his property
2. *place before:* παρατίθημι (mid.) PARATITHĒMI
2 Tim 2. 2 entrust to faithful men .. to teach
1 Pet 4.19 let those who suffer .. entrust their souls
3. *believe, trust:* πιστεύω PISTEUŌ
Lk 16.11 " 'who will entrust to you the true riches?
Rom 3. 2 Jews are entrusted with the oracles
1 Cor 9.17 I am entrusted with a commission
Gal 2. 7 I had been entrusted with the gospel
1 Th 2. 4 approved .. to be entrusted with the gospel
1 Tim 1.11 gospel .. with which I have been entrusted
Tit 1. 3 preaching with which I have been entrusted
4. *lay, put:* τίθημι (mid.) TITHĒMI*
2 Cor 5.19 entrusting to us the message of reconciliation

ENTRUSTED, WHAT HAS BEEN
ENTRUSTS, WHAT S.
1. *anything entrusted, deposit:* παραθήκη PARATHĒKĒ*
1 Tim 6.20 guard what has been entrusted to you
2 Tim 1.12 to guard .. what has been entrusted to me[a]
[1.12 to guard .. *what I have entrusted to him*†
1.14 the truth that has been entrusted

ENVY
1. *be jealous, resent:* φθονέω PHTHONEŌ* [A.6.a.5]
Gal 5.26 Let us have .. no envy of one another
2. *envy, jealousy:* φθόνος PHTHONOS
Mt 27.18 out of envy .. they .. delivered him up
Mk 15.10 out of envy .. the chief priests .. delivered him
Rom 1.29 Full of envy, murder, strife, deceit
Gal 5.21 envy,[k] drunkenness, carousing, and the like
Phil 1.15 Some .. preach Christ from envy
1 Tim 6. 4 disputes .. which produce envy
Tit 3. 3 passing our days in malice and envy
1 Pet 2. 1 So put away all malice and .. envy
3. *evil eye:* ὀφθαλμὸς πονηρός PONĒROS [A.1.f]
Mk 7.22 "envy, slander, pride, foolishness

EPAENETUS: Ἐπαίνετος i'pēnətəs
Rom 16. 5 Greet my beloved Epaenetus

EPAPHRAS: Ἐπαφρᾶς 'epəfras
Col 1. 7 Epaphras our beloved fellow servant
4.12 E., who is one of yourselves, a servant[g]
Phm .23 Epaphras, my fellow prisoner

EPAPHRODITUS: Ἐπαφρόδιτος i,pafrə'dītəs
Phil 2.25 necessary to send to you E.
4.18 having received from E. the gifts

EPHESIAN: Ἐφέσιος (*See also* EPHESUS 1)
Acts 19.28 "Great is Artemis of the Ephesians!
19.34 "Great is Artemis of the Ephesians!
19.35 city of the Ephesians is temple keeper
21.29 they had .. seen Trophimus the Ephesian

EPHESUS: 'efəsəs II,E-3
1. *Ephesian:* Ἐφέσιος [A.3.a.2]
Acts 19.35 he said, "Men of Ephesus
2. *Ephesus:* Ἔφεσος
Acts 18.19 they came to Ephesus, and he left them
18.21 he set sail from Ephesus
18.24 Apollos .. came to Ephesus
19. 1 Paul passed through .. and came to Ephesus
19.17 this became known to all residents of E.
19.26 "not only at E. but almost .. all Asia
20.16 Paul had decided to sail past Ephesus
20.17 from Miletus he sent to Ephesus
1 Cor 15.32 What .. if .. I fought with beasts at Ephesus?
16. 8 But I will stay in Ephesus until Pentecost
Eph [1. 1 To the saints who are *at Ephesus*‡
1 Tim 1. 3 remain at Ephesus that you may charge
2 Tim 1.18 all the service he rendered at Ephesus
4.12 Tychicus I have sent to Ephesus
Rev 1.11 "Write .. and send it .. to Ephesus
2. 1 "To the angel of the church in Ephesus

EPHPHATHA: 'efəthə
1. *be opened* (Aram.): ἐφφαθά EPHPHATHA
Mk 7.34 "Ephphatha," that is, "Be opened

EPHRAIM: Ἐφραίμ 'ēfrēəm I,C-5
Jn 11.54 Jesus .. went .. to a town called Ephraim

EPICUREAN: Ἐπικούρειος
Acts 17.18 Some .. Epicurean and Stoic philosophers

EPILEPTIC, AN
EPILEPTIC, BE AN
1. *be moonstruck:* σεληνιάζομαι SELĒNIAZOMAI
[a]subst. part.
Mt 4.24 [a]demoniacs, epileptics, and paralytics
17.15 "have mercy .. for he is an epileptic

EQUAL
1. *one:* εἷς HEIS
1 Cor 3. 8 He who plants and he who waters are equal
2. *equal, same:* ἴσος ISOS
Mt 20.12 " 'you have made them equal to us
Jn 5.18 making himself equal with God
Rev 21.16 its .. breadth and height are equal

EQUAL STANDING, OF
1. *equal in honor or value:* ἰσότιμος ISOTIMOS*
2 Pet 1. 1 a faith of equal standing with ours

EQUAL TO AN ANGEL
1. *like an angel:* ἰσάγγελος ISAGGELOS*
Lk 20.36 "because they are equal to angels

EQUALITY
1. *being equal:* τὸ εἶναι ἴσα ISOS [B.2.a.1]
Phil 2. 6 did not count equality .. to be grasped
2. *equality:* ἰσότης ISOTĒS
2 Cor 8.14(13) as a matter of e. .. supply their want
8.14 that there may be equality

EQUIP
1. *complete, furnish:* ἐξαρτίζω EXARTIZŌ
2 Tim 3.17 complete, equipped for every good work
2. *restoration, training:* καταρτισμός KATARTISMOS* [B.1.a.2]
Eph 4.12 to equip the saints for . . ministry[o]
3. *put in order, make:* καταρτίζω KATARTIZŌ
Heb 13.21 equip you with everything good

EQUIPMENT
1. *preparation, equipment:* ἑτοιμασία HETOIMASIA*
Eph 6.15 the equipment of the gospel of peace

ER: Ἤρ 'ər
Lk 3.28 Elmadam, the son of Er

ERASTUS: Ἔραστος i'rastəs
Acts 19.22 two of his helpers, Timothy and Erastus
Rom 16.23 Erastus, the city treasurer
2 Tim 4.20 Erastus remained at Corinth

ERECT
1. *finish, complete:* ἐπιτελέω EPITELEŌ
Heb 8. 5 when Moses was about to erect the tent[n]

ERROR
1. *fault of ignorance:* ἀγνόημα AGNOĒMA*
Heb 9. 7 he offers . . for the errors of the people
2. *wandering, deceit:* πλάνη PLANĒ
Rom 1.27 receiving . . the due penalty for their error
1 Th 2. 3 our appeal does not spring from error
Jas 5.20 brings . . a sinner from the error of his way
2 Pet 2.18 escaped from those who live in error
3.17 carried away with the error of lawless men
1 Jn 4. 6 the spirit of truth and the spirit of error
Jude .11 abandon themselves . . to Balaam's error

ESAU: Ἠσαῦ 'ēsȯ
Rom 9.13 "Jacob I loved, but Esau I hated
Heb 11.20 Isaac invoked future blessings on . . Esau
12.16 immoral or irreligious like Esau

ESCAPE
ESCAPE FROM
1. *come to one's senses:* ἀνανήφω ANANĒPHŌ*
2 Tim 2.26 they may escape from the . . devil
2. *flee from:* ἀποφεύγω APOPHEUGŌ*
2 Pet 1. 4 you may escape from the corruption
2.18 barely escaped from those who live in error
2.20 after they have escaped the defilements
3. *get away from:* διαφεύγω DIAPHEUGŌ*
Acts 27.42 lest any should swim away and escape
4. *save, preserve:* διασῴζω (pass.) DIASŌZŌ
Acts 27.44 so it was that all escaped to land
28. 1 After we had escaped, we then learned
28. 4 "Though he has escaped from the sea
5. *flee away:* ἐκφεύγω EKPHEUGŌ
Lk 21.36 "that you may have strength to escape
Acts 16.27 supposing that the prisoners had escaped
Rom 2. 3 Do you suppose, O man, . . you will escape?
2 Cor 11.33 I was let down in a basket . . and escaped
1 Th 5. 3 destruction . . and there will be no escape
Heb 2. 3 how shall we escape if we neglect such?
12.25 if they did not escape when they refused him
6. *go out:* ἐξέρχομαι EXERCHOMAI
[a]+ ἐκ
Jn 10.39 [a]he escaped from their hands
7. *flee, avoid:* φεύγω PHEUGŌ
Mt 23.33 "You serpents, . . how are you to escape?
Acts 27.30 as the sailors were seeking to escape
Heb 11.34 escaped the edge of the sword

ESCAPE ONE'S NOTICE
1. *escape notice:* λανθάνω LANTHANŌ
Acts 26.26 "none of these things has escaped his notice

ESCAPE, SEEK TO
1. *ask for, decline:* παραιτέομαι PARAITEOMAI
Acts 25.11 "I do not seek to escape death

ESCAPE, WAY OF
1. *way out:* ἔκβασις EKBASIS
1 Cor 10.13 God . . will also provide the way of escape

ESLI: Ἑσλί 'eslī
Lk 3.25 Nahum, the son of Esli

ESPECIALLY
1. *especially:* μάλιστα MALISTA
Acts 25.26 "especially before you, King Agrippa
26. 3 "you are especially familiar with all customs
Gal 6.10 especially to . . the household of faith
Phil 4.22 especially those of Caesar's household
1 Tim 4.10 Savior . . especially of those who believe
5. 8 provide . . especially for his own family
5.17 especially those who labor in preaching
Tit 1.10 especially the circumcision party
Phm .16 as a beloved brother, especially to me
2 Pet 2.10 especially those who indulge in the lust
2. *more, rather:* μᾶλλον MALLON
1 Cor 14. 1 desire . . especially that you may prophesy
CONTEXTUALLY
3 Jn . 5 service to the brethren, e. to strangers

ESTABLISH
1. *establish, confirm:* βεβαιόω BEBAIOŌ
2 Cor 1.21 it is God who establishes us with you
Col 2. 7 established in the faith, just as you
2. *stand, set:* ἵστημι HISTĒMI
Rom 10. 3 seeking to establish their own . . righteousness
Heb 10. 9 "abolishes the first . . to establish the second
3. *bring, bear:* φέρω PHERŌ
Heb 9.16 the one who made it must be established
4. *support, fix:* στηρίζω STĒRIZŌ
1 Th 3. 2 to establish you in your faith
3.13 that he may establish your hearts
2 Th 2.17 comfort your hearts and establish them
Jas 5. 8 Establish your hearts
1 Pet 5.10 restore, establish, and strengthen[m] you
2 Pet 1.12 established in the truth that you have
5. *bring to an end:* συντελέω SYNTELEŌ
Heb 8. 8 "when I will establish a new covenant

ESTABLISHED, BE
1. *stand, set:* ἵστημι (perf.) HISTĒMI
1 Cor 7.37 whoever is firmly established

ESTABLISHING
1. *restoration:* ἀποκατάστασις APOKATASTASIS*
Acts 3.21 "time for establishing all that God spoke

ESTATE
CONTEXTUALLY
Gal 4. 1 though he is the owner of all the estate

ESTATE, LOW
1. *humiliation, low estate:* ταπείνωσις TAPEINŌSIS
Lk 1.48 "regarded the low estate of his handmaiden

ESTEEM
1. *think, lead:* ἡγέομαι HĒGEOMAI
1 Th 5.13 to esteem them very highly in love
2. *judge, decide:* κρίνω KRINŌ
Rom 14. 5 One man esteems one day as better . . another man esteems all days alike

ESTEEM LEAST
1. *treat with contempt:* ἐξουθενέω EXOUTHENEŌ
1 Cor 6. 4 those . . least esteemed by the church

ESTRANGED, BE
1. *estrange, alienate:* ἀπαλλοτριόω (pass.) APALLOTRIOŌ
Col 1.21 you, who once were estranged

ETERNAL
1. *everlasting:* ἀΐδιος AIDIOS*
Rom 1.20 his eternal power and deity
Jude . 6 angels . . kept by him in eternal chains
2. *age:* αἰών (gen. pl.) AIŌN
Eph 3.11 the eternal purpose . . in Christ Jesus
3. *eternal:* αἰώνιος AIŌNIOS
Mt 18. 8 "to be thrown into the eternal fire
19.16 "what . . must I do, to have eternal life?
19.29 "will . . inherit eternal life
25.41 " 'the eternal fire prepared for the devil
25.46 "they will go . . into eternal punishment, but the righteous into eternal life
Mk 3.29 "guilty of an eternal sin
10.17 "what must I do to inherit eternal life?
10.30 "receive . . in the age to come eternal life

Mk [16.end *sacred . . proclamation of eternal salvation*‡
Lk 10.25 "what shall I do to inherit eternal life?
16. 9 "receive you into the eternal habitations
18.18 "what shall I do to inherit eternal life?
18.30 "receive . . in the age to come eternal life
Jn 3.15 "whoever believes . . may have eternal life[h]
3.16 whoever believes . . should . . have eternal life
3.36 who believes in the Son has eternal life
4.14 "water welling up to eternal life
4.36 "He who reaps . . gathers fruit for eternal life
5.24 "he who . . believes . . has eternal life
5.39 "you think that in them you have e. life
6.27 "food which endures to eternal life
6.40 "who . . believes in him should have e. life
6.47 "he who believes has eternal life
6.54 "who . . drinks my blood has eternal life
6.68 "You have the words of eternal life
10.28 "I give them eternal life
12.25 "he . . will keep it for eternal life
12.50 "his commandment is eternal life
17. 2 "eternal life to all . . thou hast given him
17. 3 "this is eternal life, that they know thee
Acts 13.46 "judge yourselves unworthy of eternal life
13.48 as many as were ordained to eternal life
Rom 2. 7 to those . . he will give eternal life
5.21 grace . . might reign . . to eternal life
6.22 sanctification and its end, eternal life
6.23 the free gift of God is eternal life
16.26 the command of the eternal God
2 Cor 4.17 for us an eternal weight of glory
4.18 the things that are unseen are eternal
5. 1 a building . . eternal in the heavens
Gal 6. 8 he . . will from the Spirit reap eternal life
2 Th 1. 9 the punishment of eternal destruction
2.16 God . . who . . gave us eternal comfort
1 Tim 1.16 who were to believe in him for eternal life
6.12 take hold of the eternal life
6.16 To him be honor and eternal dominion
2 Tim 2.10 salvation . . with its eternal glory
Tit 1. 2 in hope of eternal life
3. 7 become heirs in hope of eternal life
Heb 5. 9 he became the source of eternal salvation
6. 2 instruction[k] about . . eternal judgment
9.12 thus securing an eternal redemption
9.14 through the eternal Spirit offered himself
9.15 receive the promised eternal inheritance
13.20 by the blood of the eternal covenant
1 Pet 5.10 called you to his eternal glory in Christ
2 Pet 1.11 an entrance into the eternal kingdom
1 Jn 1. 2 proclaim to you the eternal life
2.25 what he has promised us,[e] eternal life
3.15 no murderer has eternal life . . in him
5.11 God gave us eternal life
5.13 know that you have eternal life
5.20 This is the true God and eternal life
Jude . 7 undergoing a punishment of eternal fire
.21 wait for the mercy . . unto eternal life
Rev 14. 6 another angel . . with an eternal gospel

ETERNITY
1. *age:* αἰών AIŌN
2 Pet 3.18 both now and to the day of eternity

ETHIOPIAN: Αἰθίοψ
Acts 8.27 behold, an Ethiopian, a eunuch, a minister of the Candace, queen of the Ethiopians

EUBULUS: Εὔβουλος yü'byüləs
2 Tim 4.21 Eubulus sends greetings to you

EUNICE: Εὐνίκη 'yünəs
2 Tim 1. 5 faith . . that dwelt . . in . . your mother E.

EUNUCH
1. *eunuch:* εὐνοῦχος EUNOUCHOS*
Mt 19.12 "there are eunuchs . . from birth, and . . eunuchs . . made . . by men, and . . eunuchs who have made themselves
Acts 8.27 an Ethiopian, a eunuch, a minister
8.34 the eunuch said to Philip, "About whom?
8.36 the eunuch said, "See, here is water!
8.38 both went down . . , Philip and the eunuch
8.39 the eunuch saw him no more

EUNUCH, MAKE A
1. *castrate:* εὐνουχίζω EUNOUCHIZŌ*
Mt 19.12 "who have been made eunuchs by men
19.12 "who have made themselves eunuchs

EUODIA: Εὐοδία yü'ōdēə
Phil 4. 2 I entreat Euodia and I entreat Syntyche

EUPHRATES: Εὐφράτης yü'frātēz II,G-3
Rev 9.14 "angels . . bound at the great river Euphrates
16.12 poured his bowl on the great river E.

EUTYCHUS: Εὔτυχος 'yütəkəs
Acts 20. 9 Eutychus was sitting in the window

EVACUATE
1. *throw out:* ἐκβάλλω EKBALLŌ
Mt [15.17 "passes into the stomach, and *is evacuated*†

EVACUATED, BE
1. *go out:* ἐκπορεύομαι EKPOREUOMAI
Mk [7.19 "enters . . his stomach, and so *is evacuated*†

EVANGELIST
1. *bringer of good tidings:* εὐαγγελιστής EUAGGELISTĒS*
Acts 21. 8 the house of Philip the evangelist
Eph 4.11 some evangelists, some pastors and teachers
2 Tim 4. 5 do the work of an evangelist

EVE: Εὕα 'ēv
2 Cor 11. 3 as the serpent deceived Eve
1 Tim 2.13 For Adam was formed first, then Eve

EVEN
1. *still, yet:* ἔτι ETI
Lk 1.15 "even from his mother's womb
1 Cor 3. 2 and even yet you are not ready
Heb 7.15 This becomes even more evident
11.36 suffered . . even chains and imprisonment
2. *until:* ἕως HEŌS
Mk 6.23 "even half of my kingdom
Rom 3.12 "no one does good, not even one
3. *nevertheless, also:* ὅμως HOMŌS
1 Cor 14. 7 even lifeless instruments, such as the flute
Gal 3.15 no one annuls even a man's will[g]
4. *and, even, indeed:* καί KAI
5. *even if:* κἄν KAN
Mk 5.28 "If I touch even his garments
6.56 touch even the fringe of his garment
6. *and not, nor:* μηδέ (+neg.) MĒDE
Mk 3.20 so that they could not even eat
7. *only, alone:* μόνος (neut.) MONOS
Mt 10.42 "even a cup of cold water
8. *nor, and not:* οὐδέ OUDE
Mk 5. 3 no one could bind him . . even with a chain
6.31 they had no leisure even to eat
Lk 18.13 "not even lift up his eyes to heaven
9. *and, both . . . and:* τέ TE
2 Cor **10.8**

EVEN AS
1. *just as:* ὥσπερ HŌSPER
Mt 20.28 "even as the Son of man came
2. *as, just as:* καθώς KATHŌS
Lk 6.36 "even as your Father is merciful
Jn 5.23 "even as they honor the Father
13.34 "love one another; even as I have loved you
17.21 "even as thou, Father, art in me
17.22 "that they may be one even as we are one
17.23 "loved them even as thou hast loved me
Acts 7.44 "even as he who spoke to Moses directed
1 Cor 1. 6 even as the testimony . . was confirmed
11. 2 traditions even as I have delivered them
13.12 even as I have been fully understood
Eph 1. 4 even as he chose us in him

EVEN IF
1. *if:* ἐάν EAN
Jn 8.16 "even if I do judge, my judgment is true
Gal 1. 8 even if we, or an angel from heaven, . . preach

2. *even if:* κἄν KAN
Mt 21.21 "even if you say to this mountain
26.35 "Even if I must die . . I will not deny you
Jn 8.14 "Even if I do bear witness to myself
2 Cor 11.16 but even if you do, accept me as a fool
Heb 12.20 "If even a beast touches the mountain

EVEN, NEVER (*See* NEVER EVEN)

EVEN, NOT (*See* NOT EVEN)

EVEN SO
1. *thus, so:* οὕτως HOUTŌS
Eph 5.28 Even so husbands should love their wives
1 Th 4.14 even so . . God will bring . . those
2. *yes:* ναί NAI
Rev 1. 7 the earth will wail . . Even so. Amen

EVEN SO I
1. *and I:* κἀγώ KAGŌ
Jn 20.21 "even so I send you

EVEN THE OTHER
1. *and that one:* κἀκεῖνος KAKEINOS
Rom 11.23 And even the others, if they do not persist

EVEN TO
1. *until:* ἕως HEŌS
[a]ἕως καὶ εἰς
Mt 26.38 "My soul is very sorrowful, even to death
Mk 14.34 "My soul is very sorrowful, even to death
Lk 23. 5 "from Galilee even to this place
Acts 26.11 [a]"I persecuted them even to foreign cities

EVENING
1. *evening:* ἑσπέρα HESPERA*
Lk 24.29 "Stay with us, for it is toward evening
Acts 4. 3 for it was already evening
28.23 he expounded . . from morning till evening
2. *late in the day:* ὀψέ OPSE [A.4.d]
Mk 11.19 when evening came they[u] went out
3. *late:* ὄψιος (subst. fem.) OPSIOS*
Mt 8.16 That evening they brought to him many
14.15 When it was evening, the disciples came
14.23 When evening came, he was there alone
16. 2 "When it is evening, you say‡
20. 8 "when evening came, the owner . . said
26.20 When it was evening, he sat at table
27.57 When it was evening, there came . . Joseph
Mk 1.32 That evening . . they brought to him all
4.35 when evening had come, he said to them
6.47 when evening came . . he was alone
14.17 when it was evening he came
15.42 when evening had come, ⟨Joseph . . went⟩
Jn 6.16 When evening came, his disciples went
20.19 On the evening of that day, the first day

EVENING, IN THE
1. *late in the day:* ὀψέ OPSE
Mk 13.35 "the master . . will come, in the evening

EVER
1. *not yet:* οὐδέπω (+neg.) OUDEPŌ
Jn 19.41 tomb where no one had ever been laid
2. *not yet:* οὔπω (+neg.) OUPŌ
Mk 11. 2 "a colt . . on which no one has ever sat
3. *ever yet:* πώποτε PŌPOTE
Lk 19.30 "a colt . . on which no one has ever yet sat
Jn 1.18 No one has ever seen God
1 Jn 4.12 No man has ever seen God
4. *at some time, once:* ποτέ POTE II
Eph 5.29 no man ever hates his own flesh
Heb 1. 5 to what angel did God ever say?
1.13 to what angel has he ever said?
2 Pet 1.21 no prophecy ever came by . . man
IDIOMATICALLY
a. Mt 21.19 "May no fruit ever come from you again! *οὐ μηκέτι ἐκ σοῦ καρπὸς γένηται εἰς τὸν αἰῶνα* [AIŌN]
b. Mk 11.14 "May no one ever eat fruit from you again *μηκέτι εἰς τὸν αἰῶνα ἐκ σοῦ μηδεὶς καρπὸν φάγοι* [AIŌN]
CONTEXTUALLY
Jn 4.29 "see a man who told me all that I ever did
4.39 "He told me all that I ever did
Acts 5.14 more than ever believers were added
1 Cor 12. 3 no one . . by the Spirit . . ever says "Jesus
2 Cor 8.22 who is now more earnest than ever
1 Tim 6.16 whom no man has ever seen or can see
Heb 7.13 from which no one has ever served

EVER, FOR
EVER, FOR EVER AND
1. *eternal:* αἰώνιος (neut.) AIŌNIOS
Phm .15 that you might have him back for ever
IDIOMATICALLY
[a]*εἰς τὸν αἰῶνα for ever* [AIŌN]
[b]*εἰς τοὺς αἰῶνας for ever* [AIŌN]
[c]*εἰς αἰῶνα for ever* [AIŌN]
[d]*εἰς πάντας τοὺς αἰῶνας for ever and ever* [AIŌN]
[e]*εἰς τοὺς αἰῶνας τῶν αἰώνων for ever and ever* [AIŌN]
[f]*τοῦ αἰῶνος τῶν αἰώνων for ever and ever* [AIŌN]
[g]*εἰς τὸν αἰῶνα τοῦ αἰῶνος for ever and ever* [AIŌN]
[h]*εἰς αἰῶνας αἰώνων for ever and ever* [AIŌN]
[i]*εἰς τὸ διηνεκές for ever* [DIĒNEKĒS]
[j]*διὰ παντός for ever* [PAS]
[k]*εἰς τέλος for ever* [TELOS]
Mt [6.13 [b]"*the power and the glory, for ever*‡
Lk 1.33 [b]"he will reign over the house of Jacob for ever
1.55 [a]"to Abraham and to his posterity for ever
Jn 6.51 [a]"if any one eats . . he will live for ever
6.58 [a]"who eats this bread will live for ever
8.35 [a]"The slave does not continue in the house for ever; the son continues for ever
12.34 [a]"the Christ remains for ever
14.16 [a]"another Counselor . . with you for ever
Rom 1.25 [b]the Creator, who is blessed for ever!
9. 5 [b]God who is over all be blessed for ever[n]
11.10 [j]"bend their backs for ever
11.36 [b]To him be glory for ever
2 Cor 9. 9 [a]"his righteousness[k] endures for ever
11.31 [b]he who is blessed for ever
Gal 1. 5 [e]to whom be the glory for ever and ever
Eph 3.21 [f]to him be glory . . for ever and ever
Phil 4.20 [e]To our God . . be glory for ever and ever
1 Th [2.16 [k]God's wrath has come upon them *for ever*†
1 Tim 1.17 [e]honor and glory for ever and ever[b]†
2 Tim 4.18 [e]To him be the glory for ever and ever
Heb 1. 8 [g]"Thy throne, O God,[a] is for ever and ever
5. 6 [a]"Thou art a priest for ever
6.20 [a]for ever after the order of Melchizedek
7. 3 [i]he continues a priest for ever
7.17 [a]"for ever, after the order of Melchizedek
7.21 [a]" 'Thou art a priest for ever
7.24 [a]his priesthood . . continues for ever
7.28 [a]a Son who has been made perfect for ever
13. 8 [b]Christ is the same . . today and for ever
13.21 [e]to whom be glory for ever and ever
1 Pet 1.25 [a]"the word of the Lord abides for ever
4.11 [e]glory and dominion for ever and ever
5.11 [e]To him be the dominion for ever and ever
1 Jn 2.17 [a]he who does the will of God abides for ever
2 Jn . 2 [a]the truth . . will be with us for ever
Jude .13 [c]gloom . . has been reserved for ever
.25 [d]before all time and now and for ever
Rev 1. 6 [e]glory and dominion for ever and ever
4. 9 [e]to him . . who lives for ever and ever
4.10 [e]him who lives for ever and ever
5.13 [e]"glory and might for ever and ever!
7.12 [e]"might be to our God for ever and ever!
10. 6 [e]by him who lives for ever and ever
11.15 [e]"he shall reign for ever and ever
14.11 [h]"their torment goes up for ever and ever
15. 7 [e]God who lives for ever and ever
19. 3 [e]"The smoke . . goes up for ever and ever
20.10 [e]day and night for ever and ever
22. 5 [e]they shall reign for ever and ever

EVER, NO . . .
1. *never:* οὐδέποτε OUDEPOTE
Jn 7.46 "No man ever spoke like this man!

EVER, NOTHING . . .
1. *never:* οὐδέποτε OUDEPOTE
Acts 11. 8 " 'n. . . unclean has ever entered my mouth

EVER SINCE
1. *from:* ἀπό (+gen.) APO
[a]ἀφ' ἧς B.3.b.2
Rom **1.20**
2 Pet **3.4**[a]

EVER YET
1. *not yet:* οὔπω (+neg.) OUPŌ
Lk 23.53 where no one had ever yet been laid

EVERMORE, FOR
IDIOMATICALLY
[a]εἰς τοὺς αἰῶνας τῶν αἰώνων [AIŌN]
Rom 16.27 [a]to . . God be glory for evermore
Rev 1.18 [a]"behold I am alive for evermore

EVERY
1. *each:* ἕκαστος HEKASTOS
Lk 4.40 he laid his hands on every one of them
Acts 20.31 "to admonish every one with tears
21.26 offering presented for every one of them
Col 4. 6 how you ought to answer every one
2 Th 1. 3 because . . the love of every one of you
Heb 3.13 exhort one another every day
2. *all, every, whole:* πᾶς PAS
[a]+ὃς ἐάν
Mt 3.10 "every tree . . that does not bear good fruit
4. 4 " 'by every word . . from the mouth of God
4.23 he went about . . healing every disease and every infirmity among the people
7.17 "every sound tree bears good fruit
7.19 "Every tree that does not bear good fruit
9.35 Jesus went about . . healing every disease and every infirmity
10. 1 gave them authority . . to heal every disease and every infirmity
12.25 "Every kingdom divided against itself
12.31 "every sin and blasphemy will be forgiven
12.36 "for every careless word they utter
13.47 "a net which . . gathered fish of every kind
13.52 "every scribe . . trained for the kingdom
15.13 "Every plant . . my . . Father has not planted
18.16 "that every word may be confirmed
Mk [9.49 "*and every sacrifice will be salted*‡
Lk 2.23 "Every male that opens the womb
3. 5 "Every valley shall be filled, and every mountain and hill shall be brought low
3. 9 "every tree . . that does not bear good fruit
4.13 when the devil had ended every temptation
4.37 reports of him went out into every place
5.17 Pharisees . . from every village of Galilee
10. 1 two by two, into every town and place
11.17 "Every kingdom divided against itself
11.42 "you tithe mint and rue and every herb
Jn 1. 9 The true light that enlightens every man
2.10 "Every man serves the good wine first
15. 2 "Every branch of mine that bears no fruit
15. 2 "every branch that does bear fruit
Acts 2. 5 devout men from every nation
2.43 And fear came upon every soul
3.23 " 'every soul that does not listen
5.42 every day in the temple and at home
10.35 "in every nation any one who fears him
13.27 "the prophets which are read every sabbath
15.21 "for he is read every sabbath
15.36 "let us . . visit the brethren in every city
17.17 he argued . . in the market place every day
17.22 "in every way you are very religious
17.26 "he made from one every nation
18. 4 he argued in the synagogue every sabbath
Rom 2. 9 distress for every human being who does evil
3. 2 Much in every way
3. 4 Let God be true though every man be false
3.19 so that every mouth may be stopped
13. 1 Let every person be subject
14.11 "every knee shall bow to me, and every tongue shall give praise[u] to God
1 Cor 1. 2 who in every place call on the name
1. 5 in every way you were enriched
4.17 my ways . . as I teach them . . in every church
6.18 [a]Every other sin which a man commits
9.25 Every athlete exercises self-control
11. 3 the head of every man is Christ
15.24 he delivers the kingdom . . after destroying every rule and every authority and power
15.30 Why am I in peril every hour?
16.16 be subject . . to every fellow worker
2 Cor 4. 2 commend . . to every man's conscience
4. 8 afflicted in every way, but not crushed
6. 4 we commend ourselves in every way
7. 1 cleanse ourselves from every defilement
7. 5 we were afflicted at every turn
7.11 "At every point . . guiltless in the matter
9. 8 with every blessing in abundance
9. 8 provide in abundance for every good work
9.11 You will be enriched in every way
10. 5 We destroy . . every proud obstacle . . and take every thought captive
10. 6 ready to punish every disobedience
11. 6 in every way we have made this plain
Gal 5. 3 I testify again to every man
Eph 1. 3 blessed us . . with every spiritual blessing
1.21 above every name that is named
3.15 from whom every family . . is named
4.14 carried about with every wind of doctrine
4.15 we are to grow up in every way into him
4.16 joined and knit together by every joint
4.19 to practice every kind of uncleanness
Phil 1. 4 in every prayer of mine for you all
1.18 in every way . . Christ is proclaimed
2. 9 the name which is above every name
2.10 that . . every knee should bow, in heaven
2.11 every tongue confess . . Jesus Christ is Lord
4.19 God will supply every need of yours
4.21 Greet every saint in Christ Jesus
Col 1.10 bearing fruit in every good work
1.23 preached to every creature under heaven
1.28 Him we proclaim, warning every man and teaching every man in all wisdom, that we may present every man mature
1 Th 5.22 abstain from every form of evil
2 Th 1.11 that . . God . . may fulfil every good resolve
2. 4 who opposes . . every so-called god
2.17 establish them in every good work
3.17 This is the mark in every letter of mine
1 Tim 2. 2 godly and respectful in every way
2. 8 that in every place the men should pray
3. 4 submissive and respectful in every way
4. 8 godliness is of value in every way
5.10 devoted . . to doing good in every way
2 Tim [3.16 *Every scripture inspired by God*†
3.17 complete, equipped for every good work
4.18 Lord will rescue me from every evil
Tit 2. 9 to give satisfaction in every respect
Heb 2. 2 every transgression . . received . . retribution
2.17 made like his brethren in every respect
3. 4 (For every house is built by some one
4.15 one who in every respect has been tempted
5. 1 every high priest chosen from among men
8. 3 every high priest is appointed to offer
9.19 every commandment of the law
10.11 every priest stands daily at his service
12. 1 let us also lay aside every weight
12. 6 the Lord . . chastises every son
Jas 1.17 Every good endowment and every perfect gift is from above
1.19 Let every man be quick to hear
3. 7 every kind of beast . . can be tamed
3.16 there will be disorder and every vile practice
1 Pet 2.13 Be subject . . to every human institution[f]
2 Pet 1. 5 every effort to supplement your faith
1 Jn 4. 1 Beloved, do not believe every spirit

1 Jn 4. 2 every spirit which confesses
4. 3 every spirit which does not confess Jesus
Rev 1. 7 he is coming . . and every eye will see him
5. 9 "from every tribe and tongue and people
5.13 I heard every creature in heaven
6.14 every mountain and island was removed
7. 4 out of every tribe of the sons of Israel
7. 9 from every nation, from all tribes
7.17 "God will wipe away every tear
11. 6 to smite the earth with every plague
13. 7 authority was given it over every tribe
14. 6 to every nation and tribe and tongue
16. 3 every living thing died that was in the sea
16.20 every island fled away
18. 2 "a haunt of every foul spirit, a haunt of every foul and hateful bird
21. 4 "he will wipe away every tear
21.19 foundations . . adorned with every jewel

IDIOMATICALLY
a. 3 Jn .15 Greet the friends, every one of them ἀσπάζου τοὺς φίλους κατ' ὄνομα [ONOMA]

CONTEXTUALLY
Lk 21.37 every day he was teaching in the temple
1 Cor 16. 2 On the first day of every week

EVERY DAY

IDIOMATICALLY
a. 2 Cor 4.16 is being renewed every day ἀνακαινοῦνται ἡμέρᾳ καὶ ἡμέρᾳ [HĒMERA]

EVERY MAN

1. *each:* ἕκαστος (subst.) HEKASTOS
Mt 16.27 "will repay every man for what he has done
Jn 16.32 "scattered, every man to his home
Rom 2. 6 to every man according to his works
1 Cor 4. 5 every man will receive his commendation

EVERY ONE

1. *each:* ἕκαστος (subst.) HEKASTOS
Mt 18.35 "my . . Father will do to every one of you
Acts 2.38 "be baptized every one of you
3.26 "turning every one . . from your wickedness
11.29 every one according to his ability
Rom 14. 5 Let every one be fully convinced
1 Cor 7.17 let every one lead the life . . assigned
7.20 Every one should remain in the state
Eph 4.25 let every one speak the truth
Heb 8.11 "they shall not teach every one his fellow or every one his brother
Rev 22.12 "to repay every one for what he has done

2. *all, every, whole:* πᾶς PAS [B.2.d.1]
[a]+ὃς ἄν
Mt 5.22 "every one who is angry with his brother[i]
5.28 "every one who looks at a woman lustfully
5.32 "every one who divorces his wife
7. 8 "For every one who asks receives
7.21 "Not every one who says to me, 'Lord
7.24 "Every one then who hears these words
7.26 "every one who hears these words of mine
10.32 "every one who acknowledges me
19.29 "every one who has left houses
25.29 " 'to every one who has will more be given
Mk 1.37 "Every one is searching for you
9.49 "For every one will be salted with fire[0]
Lk 6.30 "Give to every one who begs from you
6.40 "every one when he is fully taught
6.47 "Every one who comes to me and hears
11. 4 "we ourselves forgive every one
11.10 "every one who asks receives
12. 8 [a]"every one who acknowledges me
12.10 "every one who speaks . . against the Son
12.48 "Every one to whom much is given
14.11 "For every one who exalts himself
16.16 "every one enters it violently
16.18 "Every one who divorces his wife
18.14 "every one who exalts himself
19.26 " 'to every one who has will more be given
20.18 "Every one who falls on that stone
Jn 3. 8 "with every one who is born of the Spirit
3.20 every one who does evil hates the light
4.13 "Every one who drinks of this . . will thirst
6.40 "every one who sees the Son and believes
6.45 "Every one who has heard and learned
8.34 "every one who commits sin is a slave to sin
11.48 "every one will believe in him
13.10 "you[x] are clean, but not every one of you[0]
18.37 "Every one who is of the truth hears
19.12 "every one who makes himself a king
Acts 10.43 "every one who believes in him receives
13.39 "by him every one that believes is freed
16.26 every one's fetters were unfastened
Rom 1.16 for salvation to every one who has faith
2.10 peace for every one who does good
10. 4 that every one who has faith . . be justified
10.13 [a]"e. one who calls upon the name of the Lord
12. 3 by the grace given to me I bid every one
1 Cor 12. 6 God who inspires them all in every one
15.28 that God may be everything to every one
Gal 3.10 "Cursed be every one who does not abide
3.13 "Cursed be every one who hangs on a tree
2 Tim 2.19 "Let every one who names the name
2.24 kindly to every one, an apt teacher
Heb 2. 9 that . . he might taste death for every one
5.13 every one who lives on milk is unskilled
1 Jn 2.29 be sure that every one who does right
3. 3 every one who thus hopes in him
3. 4 Every one who commits sin is guilty
5. 1 Every one who believes . . Jesus is the Christ
5. 1 every one who loves the parent
3 Jn .12 Demetrius has testimony from every one
Rev 6.15 every one, slave and free, hid in the caves
22.15 every one who loves . . falsehood
22.18 I warn every one who hears the words

3. *anyone, any:* τὶς TIS II
Acts **11.29**

CONTEXTUALLY
Rev 13. 8 every one whose name has not been written

EVERY ONE WHO

1. *as great as, how great:* ὅσος (pl.) HOSOS
[a]+ἄν
Acts 2.39 [a]"every one whom the Lord our God calls

2. *anyone who, whoever:* ὅστις HOSTIS
Mt 7.26 "every one who hears these words of mine
Rev 1. 7 every one who pierced him

EVERY QUARTER, FROM

1. *from every side:* πάντοθεν PANTOTHEN
Mk 1.45 people came to him from every quarter

EVERY SIDE, ON

1. *from every side:* πάντοθεν PANTOTHEN
Lk 19.43 "enemies will . . hem you in on every side

EVERY WAY, IN

1. *in every way:* πάντῃ PANTĒ*
Acts 24. 3 "in every way . . we accept this

EVERYTHING

1. *quite all:* ἅπας (neut. pl.) HAPAS
Mk 8.25 he . . saw everything clearly
Acts 10. 8 having related everything to them

2. *all, every, whole:* πᾶς (neut.) PAS
[a]τὰ πάντα [b]+ὅσα
Mt 8.33 The herdsmen fled, and . . told everything
18.26 " 'I will pay you everything
19.27 "Lo, we have left everything
22. 4 " 'calves are killed, and everything is ready
23.20 "he who swears . . by everything on it
Mk 4.11 [a]"for those outside everything is in parables
4.34 privately . . he explained everything
10.28 "Lo, we have left everything
11.11 when he had looked round at everything
12.44 [b]"but she . . has put in everything
Lk 2.39 when they had performed everything
5.11 they left everything and followed him
5.28 he left everything . . and followed
9.43 they were all marveling at everything
11.41 "behold, everything is clean for you

Lk 15.14 "when he had spent everything
18.31 "e. . . written . . will be accomplished
24.44 "everything written . . must be fulfilled
Jn 10.41 [b]"everything that John said . . was true
17. 7 [b]"everything . . given me is from thee
21.17 "Lord, you know everything
Acts 4.24 "earth and the sea and everything in them
4.32 they had everything in common
13.39 "one that believes is freed from everything
17.24 "who made the world and everything in it
17.25 [a]"life and breath and everything
24. 8 "everything of which we accuse him
24.14 "believing everything laid down by the law
Rom 8.28 in everything God works for good[k]†‡
14.20 Everything is indeed clean
1 Cor 2.10 For the Spirit searches everything
10.33 I try to please all men in everything I do
11. 2 because you remember me in everything
15.28 that God may be everything to every one
2 Cor 2. 9 whether you are obedient in everything
6.10 having nothing . . yet possessing everything
7.14 as everything we said to you was true
8. 7 Now as you excel in everything
9. 8 that you may . . have enough of everything
Eph 5.20 for everything giving thanks
5.24 let wives also be subject in everything
6.21 Tychicus . . will tell you everything
Phil 3. 8 Indeed I count everything as loss
4. 6 in everything by prayer and supplication
Col 1.18 that in everything he might be pre-eminent
3.17 do everything in the name of the Lord
3.20 obey your parents in everything
3.22 Slaves, obey in everything . . your . . masters
4. 9 They will tell you of everything
1 Th 5.21 test everything; hold fast what is good
1 Tim 4. 4 everything created by God is good
6.17 God . . furnishes us with everything to enjoy
2 Tim 2. 7 grant you understanding in everything
2.10 I endure everything for . . the elect
Tit 2.10 that in everything they may adorn . . doctrine
Heb 2. 8 [a]"putting everything in subjection
2. 8 in putting everything in subjection
2. 8 we do not yet see everything in subjection
7. 2 [a]apportioned a tenth part of everything
8. 5 "make everything according to the pattern
9.22 almost everything is purified with blood
13.21 ⟨may God⟩ equip you with everything good
1 Pet 4.11 that in everything God may be glorified
1 Jn 2.27 as his anointing teaches you about e.
3.20 God . . knows everything

3. *fullness:* πλήρωμα PLĒRŌMA
1 Cor 10.26 "the earth is the Lord's, and everything in it

CONTEXTUALLY
Col 3.14 love, which binds everything together

EVERYWHERE

1. *everywhere:* πανταχῇ PANTACHĒ*
Acts 21.28 "the man who is teaching men everywhere

2. *altogether, everywhere:* πανταχοῦ PANTACHOU*
Mk 1.28 at once his fame spread everywhere
16.20 they went forth and preached everywhere[k]‡
Lk 9. 6 preaching . . and healing everywhere
Acts 17.30 "he commands all men everywhere to repent
24. 3 "everywhere we accept this with . . gratitude
28.22 "everywhere it is spoken against
1 Cor 4.17 my ways . . as I teach them everywhere

3. *in every place:* ἐν παντὶ τόπῳ PAS; TOPOS [B.1.a.1]
2 Cor 2.14 fragrance of the knowledge of him e.
1 Th 1. 8 your faith . . has gone forth everywhere

EVIDENCE

1. *evidence:* ἔνδειγμα ENDEIGMA*
2 Th 1. 5 This is evidence of the righteous judgment

2. *testimony, proof:* μαρτύριον MARTYRION
Jas 5. 3 their rust will be evidence against you

3. *mouth:* στόμα STOMA [C.2]
Mt 18.16 "by the evidence of two or three witnesses
2 Cor 13. 1 by the evidence of two or three witnesses

CONTEXTUALLY
1 Tim 5.19 on the e. of two or three witnesses

EVIDENT

1. *clear:* δῆλος DĒLOS
Gal 3.11 it is evident that no man is justified

2. *visible:* κατάδηλος KATADĒLOS*
Heb 7.15 This becomes even more evident

3. *clear, foreseen:* πρόδηλος PRODĒLOS
Heb 7.14 it is evident that our Lord was descended

EVIL
EVIL ONE

1. *badness:* κακία KAKIA
1 Cor 14.20 be babes in evil, but in thinking be mature
1 Pet 2.16 without . . freedom as a pretext for evil

2. *evil, bad:* κακός KAKOS
Mt 27.23 "Why, what evil has he done?
Also Mk **15.**14; Lk **23.**22
Mk 7.21 "For from within . . come evil thoughts
Lk 16.25 " 'Lazarus in like manner evil things
Acts 9.13 "I have heard . . how much evil he has done
Rom 1.30 inventors of evil, disobedient
2. 9 distress for every human being who does evil
3. 8 why not do evil that good may come?
7.19 evil I do not want is what I do
7.21 evil lies close at hand
12.17 Repay no one evil for evil, but take thought for what is noble
12.21 Do not be overcome by evil, but overcome evil with good
16.19 guileless as to what is evil
1 Cor 10. 6 warnings . . not to desire evil as they did
Col 3. 5 impurity, passion, evil desire
1 Th 5.15 See that none of you repays evil for evil, but always seek to do good
1 Tim 6.10 love of money is the root of all evils
Tit 1.12 "Cretans are always liars, evil beasts
Heb 5.14 trained . . to distinguish good from evil
Jas 1.13 God cannot be tempted with evil
3. 8 a restless evil, full of deadly poison
1 Pet 3. 9 Do not return evil for evil or reviling for reviling
3.10 "let him keep his tongue from evil
3.11 "let him turn away from evil and do right
3.12 "the Lord is against those that do evil
3 Jn .11 do not imitate evil but imitate good
Rev 2. 2 " 'I know . . how you cannot bear evil men

3. *badly, ill:* κακῶς KAKŌS [A.4.a]
Acts 23. 5 " 'You shall not speak evil of a ruler

4. *cheap, mean, bad:* φαῦλος PHAULOS
Jn 3.20 one who does evil hates the light
5.29 "who have done evil, to the resurrection
2 Cor 5.10 that each one may receive good or evil
Tit 2. 8 put to shame, having nothing evil to say

5. *wickedness:* πονηρία PONĒRIA
Rom 1.29 wickedness, evil, covetousness, malice
1 Cor 5. 8 the leaven of malice and evil

6. *sick, base, evil:* πονηρός PONĒROS
[a]comp.
Mt 5.11 "when men . . utter . . evil against you
5.37 "anything more than this comes from evil[l]†
[5.37 "anything more . . comes from *the evil one*†
5.39 "Do not resist one who is evil
5.45 "he makes his sun rise on the evil
6.13 "But deliver us from evil[n]†
[6.13 "But deliver us from *the evil one*†
7.11 "If you then, who are evil, know how
7.17 "the bad tree bears evil fruit
7.18 "A sound tree cannot bear evil fruit
9. 4 "Why do you think evil in your hearts?
12.34 "how can you speak good, when you are evil?
12.35 "The good man out of his good treasure brings forth good, and the evil man out of his evil treasure brings forth evil
12.39 "An evil . . generation seeks for a sign
12.45 [a]"seven other spirits more evil than himself
12.45 "So shall it be also with this evil generation

Mt 13.19 "the evil one comes and snatches away
13.38 "the weeds are the sons of the evil one
13.49 "will . . separate the evil from the righteous
15.19 "out of the heart come evil thoughts
16. 4 "An evil . . generation seeks for a sign
[20.15 " '*is your eye evil because I am good?*†
Mk 7.23 "All these evil things come from within
Lk 3.19 reproved by him for . . all the evil things
6.22 "when they . . cast out your name as evil
6.45 "The good man . . produces good, and the evil man out of his evil treasure produces evil
7.21 he cured many of . . evil spirits
8. 2 women who had been healed of evil spirits
11.13 "If you then, who are evil, know how
11.26 [a]"seven other spirits more evil than himself
11.29 "This generation is an evil generation
Jn 3.19 because their deeds were evil
7. 7 "I testify of it that its works are evil
17.15 "keep them from the evil one[k]†
[17.15 "keep them from *evil*†
Acts 19.12 the evil spirits came out of them
19.13 those who had evil spirits
19.15 the evil spirit answered them
19.16 the man in whom the evil spirit
25.18 "no charge . . of such evils as I supposed
28.21 "none . . here . . spoken any evil about you
Rom 12. 9 Let love be genuine; hate what is evil
Gal 1. 4 deliver us from the present evil age
Eph 5.16 because the days are evil
6.13 able to withstand in the evil day
6.16 quench all the . . darts of the evil one
Col 1.21 hostile in mind, doing evil deeds
1 Th 5.22 abstain from every form of evil
2 Th 3. 2 be delivered from wicked and evil men
3. 3 he will . . guard you from evil[d]†
[3. 3 he will . . guard you from *the evil one*†
2 Tim 3.13 while evil men . . go on from bad to worse
4.18 Lord will rescue me from every evil
Heb 3.12 an evil, unbelieving heart
10.22 clean from an evil conscience
Jas 2. 4 judges with evil thoughts?
4.16 All such boasting is evil
1 Jn 2.13 you have overcome the evil one
2.14 you have overcome the evil one
3.12 like Cain who was of the evil one
3.12 Because his own deeds were evil
5.18 the evil one does not touch him
5.19 whole world is in the power of the evil one
3 Jn .10 prating against me with evil words
Rev 16. 2 foul and evil sores came upon the men

7. *rotten, bad:* *σαπρός* SAPROS
Eph 4.29 Let no evil talk come out of your mouths

EVIL AGAINST, SPEAK

1. *speak against:* *καταλαλέω* KATALALEŌ
Jas 4.11 Do not speak evil against one another . . He that speaks evil against a brother . . speaks evil against the law

EVIL, DO

1. *do wrong, do harm:* *κακοποιέω* KAKOPOIEŌ
3 Jn .11 he who does evil has not seen God

EVIL OF, SPEAK

1. *blaspheme, slander:* *βλασφημέω* BLASPHĒMEŌ
Tit 3. 2 to speak evil of no one
2. *revile, abuse:* *κακολογέω* KAKOLOGEŌ*
Mt 15. 4 " 'He who speaks evil of father or mother
Mk 7.10 " 'He who speaks evil of father or mother
9.39 "soon after to speak evil of me
Acts 19. 9 some were . . speaking evil of the Way

EVIL, SPEAK OF S. AS

1. *blaspheme, slander:* *βλασφημέω* BLASPHĒMEŌ
Rom 14.16 not let your good be spoken of as evil

EVILDOER

1. *do wrong, harm:* *ἀδικέω* (subst. part.) ADIKEŌ
Rev 22.11 "Let the evildoer still do evil

2. *lawlessness:* *ἀνομία* ANOMIA [B.2.a.1]
[a]*ὁ ἐργαζόμενος τὴν ἀνομίαν one who works lawlessness*
[b]*ὁ ποιῶν τὴν ἀνομίαν one who does lawlessness*
Mt 7.23 [a]" 'depart from me, you evildoers
13.41 [b]"gather . . all causes of sin and all evildoers
3. *one who does evil:* *κακὸν ποιῶν* KAKOS [B.2.a.1]
Jn 18.30 "If this man were not an evildoer

EVIL-WORKER

1. *evil worker:* *κακὸς ἐργάτης* KAKOS; ERGATĒS [B.2.a.1]
Phil 3. 2 look out for the evil-workers

EXACTION

1. *greediness:* *πλεονεξία* PLEONEXIA
2 Cor 9. 5 not as an exaction but as a willing gift

EXACTLY, MORE

1. *precisely:* *ἀκριβῶς* AKRIBŌS
Acts 23.15 "to determine his case more exactly

EXALT

1. *extol, honor:* *δοξάζω* DOXAZŌ
Heb 5. 5 So also Christ did not exalt himself
1 Pet 1. 8 rejoice with unutterable and exalted joy
2. *exalt, lift high:* *ὑψόω* HYPSOŌ
Mt 11.23 "Capernaum, will you be exalted in heaven?
23.12 "whoever exalts himself will be humbled, . . whoever humbles himself will be exalted
Lk 1.52 "he has . . exalted those of low degree
10.15 "Capernaum, will you be exalted to heaven?
14.11 "one who exalts himself will be humbled, . . he who humbles himself will be exalted
18.14 "one who exalts himself will be humbled, . . he who humbles himself will be exalted
Acts 2.33 "exalted at the right hand of God
5.31 "God exalted him at his right hand
2 Cor 11. 7 abasing myself so that you might be exalted
Jas 4.10 Humble yourselves . . and he will exalt you
1 Pet 5. 6 Humble yourselves . . that . . he may e. you

EXALT, HIGHLY

1. *exalt exceedingly:* *ὑπερυψόω* HYPERYPSOŌ*
Phil 2. 9 Therefore God has highly exalted him

EXALT ONESELF

1. *exalt oneself:* *ὑπεραίρομαι* HYPERAIROMAI
2 Th 2. 4 exalts himself against every so-called god

EXALTATION

1. *height:* *ὕψος* HYPSOS
Jas 1. 9 Let the lowly . . boast in his exaltation

EXALTED

1. *high, proud:* *ὑψηλός* HYPSĒLOS
Lk 16.15 "exalted among men is an abomination

EXALTED ABOVE

1. *high, proud:* *ὑψηλός* (comp.+gen.) HYPSĒLOS
Heb 7.26 a high priest . . exalted above the heavens

EXAMINE

1. *examine closely:* *ἀνακρίνω* ANAKRINŌ
Lk 23.14 "examining him . . I did not find . . guilty
Acts 4. 9 "examined today concerning a good deed
12.19 he examined the sentries
17.11 these Jews were . . examining the scriptures
24. 8 "examining him yourself you will . . learn
28.18 "When they had examined me
1 Cor 9. 3 my defense to those who would examine me
2. *examination:* *ἀνάκρισις* ANAKRISIS* [B.3.a.2; A.6.e]
Acts 25.26 "after we have examined him
3. *inquire of:* *ἀνετάζω* ANETAZŌ*
Acts 22.24 ordered him to be examined by scourging
22.29 those who were about to examine him
4. *test, approve:* *δοκιμάζω* DOKIMAZŌ
Lk 14.19 " 'I have . . oxen, and I go to e. them
1 Cor 11.28 Let a man examine himself
5. *tempt, try:* *πειράζω* PEIRAZŌ
2 Cor 13. 5 Examine yourselves, to see whether

EXAMPLE

1. *pattern, image:* *δεῖγμα* DEIGMA*
Jude . 7 example by undergoing a punishment
2. *example, pattern:* *ὑπόδειγμα* HYPODEIGMA
Jn 13.15 I have given you an example

Jas 5.10 As an example of suffering and patience
2 Pet 2. 6 an example to those who were to be ungodly
3. *model:* ὑπογραμμός HYPOGRAMMOS*
1 Pet 2.21 Christ . . suffered . . leaving you an example
4. *model, pattern:* ὑποτύπωσις HYPOTYPŌSIS
1 Tim 1.16 his perfect patience for an example
5. *footsteps:* ἴχνος (pl.) ICHNOS
Rom 4.12 who . . follow the example of the faith
6. *pattern:* τύπος TYPOS
Phil 3.17 so live as you have an example in us
1 Th 1. 7 so that you became an example to all
2 Th 3. 9 to give you in our conduct an example
1 Tim 4.12 set the believers an example in speech
1 Pet 5. 3 being examples to the flock
IDIOMATICALLY
a. Gal 3.15 To give a human example, brethren Ἀδελφοί, κατὰ ἄνθρωπον λέγω [LEGŌ]

EXAMPLE, MAKE AN
1. *make an example:* δειγματίζω DEIGMATIZŌ
Col 2.15 He . . made a public example of them

EXCEED
1. *abound:* περισσεύω PERISSEUŌ
Mt 5.20 "unless your righteousness exceeds that
2 Cor 3. 9 righteousness must far exceed it
2. *more:* πλείων PLEIŌN [A.6.a.3]
Rev 2.19 " 'your latter works exceed the first

EXCEEDINGLY (*See also* AFRAID, EXCEEDINGLY; SORRY, EXCEEDINGLY)
1. *even more:* περισσῶς PERISSŌS
Mk 10.26 they were exceedingly astonished
2 *very, very much:* σφόδρα SPHODRA
Mt 2.10 they rejoiced exceedingly

EXCEL
1. *abound:* περισσεύω PERISSEUŌ
1 Cor 14.12 strive to excel in building up the church
2 Cor 8. 7 Now as you excel in everything . . excel in this gracious work also

EXCELLENCE
1. *goodness, excellence:* ἀρετή ARETĒ
Phil 4. 8 if there is any excellence
2 Pet 1. 3 called us to[b] his own glory and excellence

EXCELLENCY, HIS
1. *most excellent:* κράτιστος (subst.) KRATISTOS
Acts 23.26 "his Excellency the governor Felix

EXCELLENT
1. *good, beautiful:* καλός KALOS
Tit 3. 8 these are excellent and profitable

EXCELLENT, MORE
1. *different, excellent:* διάφορος (comp.) DIAPHOROS
Heb 1. 4 name he has obtained is more excellent
8. 6 a ministry which is as much more excellent
2. *to excess:* καθ' ὑπερβολήν HYPERBOLĒ [B.1.a.1]
1 Cor 12.31 I will show you a . . more excellent way

EXCELLENT, MOST
1. *most excellent:* κράτιστος (voc.) KRATISTOS
Lk 1. 3 you, most excellent Theophilus
Acts 24. 2(3) "your provision, most excellent Felix
26.25 "I am not mad, most excellent Festus

EXCELLENT, WHAT IS
1. *carry through, differ:* διαφέρω (subst. part. neut. pl.) DIAPHERŌ
Rom 2.18 approve what is excellent
Phil 1.10 that you may approve what is excellent

EXCEPT
EXCEPT FOR
1. *but:* ἀλλά ALLA
Mk 4.22 "nor . . secret, except to come to light
2. *or, than:* ἤ Ē
Acts **24.**21
3. *if not, unless:* ἐὰν μή EAN MĒ
Mk 4.22 "nothing hid, except to be made manifest
Jn 3.27 "No one can receive . . except what is given
4. *if not, except:* εἰ μή EI MĒ
[a]+μόνον [b]+ἐκτός

Mt 5.13 "no longer good . . except to be thrown out
11.27 "no one knows the Son except the Father, and no one knows the Father except the Son
12.39 "except the sign of the prophet Jonah
13.57 "not without honor except in his own country
16. 4 "no sign . . except the sign of Jonah
[17.21 *"never . . except by prayer and fasting‡*
Mk 5.37 he allowed no one . . except Peter
6. 4 "not without honor, e. in his own country
6. 5 no mighty work . . except . . upon a few sick
6. 8 [a]nothing for their journey except a staff
Lk 8.51 no one to enter with him, except Peter
10.22 "no one knows . . Son . . except the Father, or . . the Father . . except the Son
11.29 "no sign . . except the sign of Jonah
17.18 "no one . . except this foreigner
Jn 6.46 "except him who is from God
13.10 "not need to wash, except for his feet[c]‡
Acts 11.19 [a]speaking the word to none except Jews
Rom 13. 1 there is no authority except from God
13. 8 except to love one another
1 Cor 1.14 baptized none of you except Crispus
2. 2 to know nothing . . except Jesus Christ
2.11 except the spirit of the man
2.11 no one . . except the Spirit of God
12. 3 no one . . except by the Holy Spirit
2 Cor 12. 5 I will not boast, except of my weaknesses
12.13 except that I myself did not burden you
Gal 1.19 none . . except James the Lord's brother
6.14 except in the cross of our Lord Jesus
Phil 4.15 no church . . except you only
1 Tim 5.19 [b]Never admit any charge . . except on . . evidence
Rev 2.17 " 'no one knows except him who receives it
14. 3 No one could learn that song except
5. *other than:* ἕτερος ἤ HETEROS [B.3.b.4]
Acts 17.21 spent their time in nothing except telling
6. *not:* μή MĒ [A.4.c]
Mt 19. 9 "whoever divorces . . except for unchastity[j]
7. *not, no:* οὐ OU [A.4.c]
Rom **15.**18
8. *besides, except for:* παρεκτός PAREKTOS
Mt 5.32 "except on the ground of unchastity
Acts 26.29 "such as I am—except for these chains
9. *but, however, except:* πλήν PLĒN
Acts 8. 1 all scattered . . except the apostles
20.23 "except that the Holy Spirit testifies

EXCEPT PERHAPS
1. *unless indeed:* εἰ μήτι MĒTI [B.3.b.4]
1 Cor 7. 5 except perhaps by agreement for a season

EXCEPTED
IDIOMATICALLY
a. 1 Cor 15.27 it is plain that he is excepted who . . δῆλον ὅτι ἐκτὸς τοῦ . . [EKTOS]

EXCESSIVE
1. *more, greater:* περισσότερος PERISSOTEROS
2 Cor 2. 7 overwhelmed by excessive sorrow

EXCHANGE
1. *change:* ἀλλάσσω ALLASSŌ
Rom 1.23 exchanged the glory of the immortal God
2. *change, exchange:* μεταλλάσσω METALLASSŌ*
Rom 1.25 they exchanged the truth about God
1.26 women exchanged natural relations
3. *send to one another:* πέμπειν ἀλλήλοις PEMPŌ [B.2.a.1]
Rev 11.10 make merry and exchange presents

EXCITED, BE
1. *terrify:* θροέω (pass.) THROEŌ
2 Th 2. 2 be . . excited, either by spirit or by word

EXCLAIM
1. *shout:* ἀναφωνέω ANAPHŌNEŌ*
Lk 1.42 she exclaimed with a loud cry, "Blessed

EXCLUDE
1. *separate, appoint:* ἀφορίζω APHORIZŌ
Lk 6.22 "when they exclude you and revile you

2. *shut out:* ἐκκλείω EKKLEIŌ
Rom 3.27 boasting? It is excluded

EXCLUSION
CONTEXTUALLY
2 Th 1. 9 shall suffer . . eternal destruction and e.

EXCUSE
1. *defend oneself, speak in defense:* ἀπολογέομαι APOLOGEOMAI
Rom 2.15 thoughts accuse or perhaps excuse them
2. *pretense, excuse:* πρόφασις PROPHASIS
Jn 15.22 "they have no excuse for their sin

EXCUSE, HAVE NO
1. *be inexcusable:* ἀναπολόγητος εἶναι ANAPOLOGĒTOS [A.6.a.3]
Rom 2. 1 Therefore you have no excuse, O man

EXCUSE, WITHOUT
1. *inexcusable:* ἀναπολόγητος ANAPOLOGĒTOS
Rom 1.20 So they are without excuse

EXCUSED
1. *ask for, decline:* παραιτέομαι (perf. pass. part.) PARAITEOMAI
Lk 14.18 " 'I pray you, have me excused
14.19 " 'I pray you, have me excused

EXCUSES, MAKE
1. *ask for, decline:* παραιτέομαι PARAITEOMAI
Lk 14.18 "all alike began to make excuses

EXECUTE
1. *do, make:* ποιέω POIEŌ
Jn 5.27 "authority to execute judgment
Rom 9.28 "the Lord will execute his sentence
Jude .15 "to execute judgment on all
IDIOMATICALLY
a. Rom 13.4 he is the servant of God to execute his wrath
θεοῦ . . διάκονός ἐστιν ἔκδικος εἰς ὀργὴν [EKDIKOS]

EXERCISE (*See also* AUTHORITY OVER, EXERCISE; LORDSHIP OVER, EXERCISE; OVERSIGHT, EXERCISE; SELF-CONTROL, EXERCISE)
1. *do, make:* ποιέω POIEŌ
Rev 13. 5 it was allowed to exercise authority
13.12 exercises all the authority of the first beast

EXERTION
1. *run, move quickly:* τρέχω (subst. part.) TRECHŌ
Rom 9.16 depends not upon man's . . exertion

EXHIBIT
1. *point out:* ἀποδείκνυμι APODEIKNYMI
1 Cor 4. 9 God has exhibited us apostles

EXHORT
1. *call to, exhort, comfort:* παρακαλέω PARAKALEŌ
Acts 2.40 he . . exhorted them . . "Save yourselves
11.23 he exhorted them all to remain faithful
14.22 exhorting them to continue in the faith
15.32 exhorted the brethren with many words
16.40 they exhorted them and departed
20. 1 having exhorted them took leave
Rom 12. 8 he who exhorts, in his exhortation
1 Th 2.11 we exhorted each one of you
3. 2 we sent Timothy . . to exhort you
4. 1 we beseech and exhort you
4.10 we exhort you, brethren, to do so more
5.14 we exhort you, brethren, admonish
2 Th 3.12 such persons we . . exhort in the Lord
1 Tim 5. 1 exhort him as you would a father
2 Tim 4. 2 convince, rebuke, and exhort
Tit 2.15 exhort and reprove with all authority
Heb 3.13 But exhort one another every day
1 Pet 5. 1 So I exhort the elders among you
5.12 I have written briefly to you, exhorting

EXHORTATION
1. *call to, exhort, comfort:* παρακαλέω PARAKALEŌ [B.2.a.2]
Lk 3.18 with many . . exhortations, he preached
2. *exhortation, comfort:* παράκλησις PARAKLĒSIS
Acts 13.15 "if you have any word of exhortation
15.31 they rejoiced at the exhortation
Rom 12. 8 who exhorts, in his exhortation
Heb 12. 5 have you forgotten the exhortation?
13.22 bear with my word of exhortation

EXILE
1. *sojourning:* παρεπίδημος (subst.) PAREPIDĒMOS*
Heb 11.13 they were strangers and exiles
1 Pet 1. 1 To the exiles of the Dispersion
2.11 as aliens and exiles to abstain
2. *sojourn:* παροικία PAROIKIA
1 Pet 1.17 throughout the time of your exile
3. *foreign:* πάροικος (subst.) PAROIKOS
Acts 7.29 "Moses . . became an exile in . . Midian

EXIST
1. *be:* εἰμί EIMI
Rom 4.17 into existence . . things that do not exist
13. 1 those that exist have been instituted
Heb 11. 6 believe that he exists and that he rewards
2 Pet 3. 5 that by the word of God heavens existed
Rev 4.11 "by thy will they existed
CONTEXTUALLY
1 Cor 8. 6 the Father, . . for whom we exist
8. 6 Lord, Jesus Christ, . . through whom we exist
Heb 2.10 he, for whom and by whom all things exist
Jas 3.16 where jealousy and selfish ambition exist
2 Pet 3. 6 world that then existed was deluged
3. 7 the heavens and earth that now exist

EXISTENCE
IDIOMATICALLY
a. Rom 4.17 calls into e. the things that do not exist
καλοῦντος τὰ μὴ ὄντα ὡς ὄντα [EIMI]

EXODUS
1. *going out:* ἔξοδος EXODOS
Heb 11.22 mention of the exodus of the Israelites

EXORCIST
1. *exorcist:* ἐξορκιστής EXORKISTĒS*
Acts 19.13 some of the itinerant Jewish exorcists

EXPECT
1. *think, suppose:* δοκέω DOKEŌ
Mt 24.44 "coming at an hour you do not expect
2. *wait for:* ἐκδέχομαι EKDECHOMAI
1 Cor 16.11 for I am expecting him with the brethren
3. *hope for, expect:* ἐλπίζω ELPIZŌ
2 Cor 8. 5 and this, not as we expected
4. *wait for, expect:* προσδοκάω PROSDOKAŌ
Mt 24.50 "on a day when he does not expect him
Lk 12.46 "on a day when he does not expect him
Acts 3. 5 expecting to receive something
10.24 Cornelius was expecting them
IDIOMATICALLY
a. Acts 28. 6 They waited, expecting him to swell up
οἱ δὲ προσεδόκων αὐτὸν μέλλειν πίμπρασθαι [MELLŌ]

EXPECT IN RETURN
1. *hope to receive back:* ἀπελπίζω APELPIZŌ*
Lk 6.35 "lend, expecting nothing in return[v]†‡

EXPECTATION, BE IN
1. *wait for, expect:* προσδοκάω PROSDOKAŌ
Lk 3.15 As the people were in expectation

EXPECTATION, EAGER
1. *earnest expectation:* ἀποκαραδοκία APOKARADOKIA
Phil 1.20 it is my eager expectation and hope

EXPECTING, WHAT S. IS
1. *expectation:* προσδοκία (+gen.) PROSDOKIA
Acts 12.11 "all that the Jewish people were expecting

EXPEDIENT, IT IS
1. *bring together, be useful:* συμφέρω (impers.) SYMPHERŌ
Mt 19.10 "it is not expedient to marry
Jn 11.50 "expedient . . that one man should die
18.14 expedient that one man should die

EXPENSE
1. *contract, rent:* μίσθωμα MISTHŌMA*
Acts 28.30 he lived there . . at his own expense[h]†
2. *salary, pay:* ὀψώνιον OPSŌNION
1 Cor 9. 7 Who serves as a soldier at his own e.?

EXPENSES, PAY
IDIOMATICALLY
a. Acts 21.24 "pay their expenses δαπάνησον ἐπ' αὐτοῖς [DAPANAŌ]

EXPENSIVE, VERY
1. *very costly:* βαρύτιμος BARYTIMOS*
Mt 26. 7 alabaster flask of very e. ointment

EXPERIENCE
1. *operate, be effective:* ἐνεργέω ENERGEŌ [A.6.e]
2 Cor 1. 6 experience when you patiently endure
2. *come to be, happen, be:* γίνομαι GINOMAI [A.6.e]
2 Cor 1. 8 the affliction we experienced in Asia
3. *suffer, experience:* πάσχω PASCHŌ
Gal 3. 4 Did you experience . . in vain?
CONTEXTUALLY
1 Pet 5. 9 the same e. of suffering is required

EXPIATION
1. *sin offering:* ἱλασμός HILASMOS*
1 Jn 2. 2 he is the expiation for our sins
4.10 his Son to be the expiation for our sins
2. *means of expiation:* ἱλαστήριον HILASTĒRION
Rom 3.25 whom God put forward as an expiation

EXPIATION, MAKE
1. *conciliate, expiate:* ἱλάσκομαι HILASKOMAI
Heb 2.17 make e. for the sins of the people

EXPLAIN
1. *lay open, explain:* διανοίγω DIANOIGŌ
Acts 17. 3 explaining . . that it was necessary
2. *show plainly:* διασαφέω DIASAPHEŌ
Mt 13.36 "Explain to us the parable of the weeds
3. *set out, expound:* ἐκτίθημι EKTITHĒMI
Acts 11. 4 Peter . . explained to them in order
4. *loose, explain, solve:* ἐπιλύω EPILYŌ
Mk 4.34 privately . . he explained everything
5. *point out:* φράζω PHRAZŌ*
Mt 15.15 "Explain the parable to us

EXPLAIN, HARD TO
1. *hard to interpret:* δυσερμήνευτος DYSERMĒNEUTOS*
Heb 5.11 much to say which is hard to explain

EXPLOIT
1. *travel, be a merchant:* ἐμπορεύομαι EMPOREUOMAI
2 Pet 2. 3 they will exploit you with false words

EXPOSE
1. *make exposed:* ποιεῖν ἔκθετον EKTHETOS* [A.6.a.4]
Acts 7.19 "forced our fathers to expose their infants
2. *set out, expound:* ἐκτίθημι EKTITHĒMI
Acts 7.21 "when he was exposed
3. *expose, test, refute:* ἐλέγχω ELEGCHŌ
Jn 3.20 lest his deeds should be exposed
Eph 5.11 Take no part . . but instead expose them
5.13 when anything is exposed by the light
IDIOMATICALLY
a. Rev 16.15 ("that he may not . . be seen exposed! ἵνα μὴ . . βλέπωσιν τὴν ἀσχημοσύνην αὐτοῦ [ASCHĒMOSYNĒ]

EXPOSE, PUBLICLY
1. *be on the stage, put to shame:* θεατρίζω THEATRIZŌ*
Heb 10.33 being publicly exposed to abuse

EXPOSURE
1. *nakedness:* γυμνότης GYMNOTĒS
2 Cor 11.27 often without food, in cold and exposure

EXPOUND
1. *set out, expound:* ἐκτίθημι EKTITHĒMI
Acts 18.26 expounded to him the way of God
28.23 he expounded the matter to them

EXPRESS (*See* PRIDE, EXPRESS)

EXPRESSLY
1. *explicitly:* ῥητῶς RHĒTŌS*
1 Tim 4. 1 Spirit expressly says . . some will depart

EXTEND
1. *be more, cause to increase:* πλεονάζω PLEONAZŌ
2 Cor 4.15 as grace extends to more and more

EXTERNAL
1. *visible, known:* φανερός PHANEROS
Rom 2.28 nor is true circumcision something external

EXTINCTION
1. *destruction, ruin:* καταστροφή KATASTROPHĒ
2 Pet 2. 6 he condemned them to extinction

EXTOL
1. *make large, extol:* μεγαλύνω MEGALYNŌ
Acts 10.46 speaking in tongues and extolling God
19.17 name of the Lord Jesus was extolled

EXTORTION
1. *robbery, plunder:* ἁρπαγή HARPAGĒ
Mt 23.25 "they are full of extortion and rapacity
Lk 11.39 "inside you are full of extortion

EXTORTIONER
1. *robbing:* ἅρπαξ (subst.) HARPAX
Lk 18.11 " 'not like other men, extortioners, unjust

EXTRAORDINARY
1. *happen, attain:* τυγχάνω (neg. part.) TYGCHANŌ
Acts 19.11 And God did extraordinary miracles

EXTREME
1. *to the depths:* κατὰ βάθους BATHOS [B.1.a.2]
2 Cor 8. 2 their extreme poverty . . overflowed

EXTREMELY, SO
1. *still more:* περισσοτέρως PERISSOTERŌS
Gal 1.14 so extremely zealous was I for the traditions

EXULT
1. *rejoice greatly:* ἀγαλλιάω AGALLIAŌ
Rev 19. 7 Let us . . exult and give him the glory

EYE
1. *sight, eye:* ὄμμα OMMA*
Mt 20.34 Jesus in pity touched their eyes
Mk 8.23 when he had spit on his eyes
2. *eye:* ὀφθαλμός OPHTHALMOS
Mt 5.29 "If your right eye causes you to sin
5.38 "You have heard that it was said, 'An eye for an eye and a tooth for a tooth
6.22 "The eye is the lamp of the body. So, if your eye is sound, your whole body will be
6.23 "but if your eye is not sound
7. 3 "Why do you see the speck . . in your brother's eye, . . not . . log . . in your own eye?
7. 4 " 'Let me take the speck out of your eye,' when there is the log in your own eye?
7. 5 "take the log out of your own eye, and then . . the speck out of your brother's eye
9.29 Then he touched their eyes
9.30 And their eyes were opened
13.15 " 'their eyes they have closed, lest they should perceive with their eyes
13.16 "blessed are your eyes, for they see
17. 8 they lifted up their eyes, they saw no one
18. 9 "if your eye causes you to sin,[z] pluck it out
18. 9 "with two eyes to be thrown into . . hell[b]
[20.15 " '*is your eye evil because I am good?*†
20.33 "Lord, let our eyes be opened
21.42 " 'it is marvelous in our eyes
26.43 sleeping, for their eyes were heavy
Mk 8.18 "Having eyes do you not see?
8.25 he laid his hands upon his eyes
9.47 "if your eye causes you to sin,[l] pluck it out
9.47 "than with two eyes to be thrown into hell[m]
12.11 " 'it is marvelous in our eyes
14.40 sleeping, for their eyes were very heavy
Lk 2.30 "mine eyes have seen thy salvation
4.20 eyes of all in the synagogue were . . on him
6.20 he lifted up his eyes on his disciples
6.41 "Why . . the speck that is in your brother's eye, but . . not . . the log . . in your own eye?
6.42 " 'let me take out the speck . . in your eye
6.42 "you . . do not see the log . . in your own eye
6.42 "take the log out of your own eye
6.42 "the speck that is in your brother's eye

Lk 10.23 "Blessed are the eyes which see what you see!
11.34 "Your eye is the lamp of your body; when your eye is sound, your . . body is
16.23 "he lifted up his eyes, and saw Abraham
18.13 "would not . . lift up his eyes to heaven
19.42 "But now they are hid from your eyes
24.16 their eyes were kept from recognizing him
24.31 And their eyes were opened
Jn 4.35 "I tell you, lift up your eyes, and see
6. 5 Lifting up his eyes, . . seeing . . a multitude
9. 6 anointed the man's eyes with the clay
9.10 "Then how were your eyes opened?
9.11 "Jesus made clay and anointed my eyes
9.14 Jesus made the clay and opened his eyes
9.15 "He put clay on my eyes . . and I see
9.17 "he has opened your eyes
9.21 "nor do we know who opened his eyes
9.26 "How did he open your eyes?
9.30 "You do not know . . yet he opened my eyes
9.32 "opened the eyes of a man born blind
10.21 "Can a demon open the eyes of the blind?
11.37 "he who opened the eyes of the blind man
11.41 Jesus lifted up his eyes and said, "Father
12.40 "He has blinded their eyes . . lest they should see with their eyes
17. 1 he lifted up his eyes to heaven
Acts 9. 8 his eyes were opened, he could see nothing
9.18 something like scales fell from his eyes
9.40 "Tabitha, rise." And she opened her eyes
26.18 " 'to open their eyes, that they may turn
28.27 " 'their eyes they have closed; lest they should perceive with their eyes
Rom 3.18 "There is no fear of God before their eyes
11. 8 "God gave them . . eyes that should not see
11.10 let their eyes be darkened
1 Cor 2. 9 "What no eye has seen, nor ear heard
12.16 "I am not an eye, I do not belong
12.17 If the whole body were an eye
12.21 The eye cannot say to the hand
15.52 in a moment, in the twinkling of an eye
Gal 3. 1 before whose eyes . . Christ was . . portrayed
4.15 you would have plucked out your eyes
Eph 1.18 the eyes of your hearts enlightened
Heb 4.13 all are open and laid bare to the eyes
1 Pet 3.12 "eyes of the Lord are upon the righteous
2 Pet 2.14 eyes full of adultery, insatiable for sin
1 Jn 1. 1 which we have seen with our eyes
2.11 because the darkness has blinded his eyes
2.16 lust of the flesh and the lust of the eyes
Rev 1. 7 every eye will see him
1.14 his eyes were like a flame of fire
2.18 " 'Son of God, who has eyes like a flame
3.18 " 'to anoint your eyes, that you may see
4. 6 creatures, full of eyes in front and behind
4. 8 creatures . . full of eyes all round and within
5. 6 seven eyes, . . the seven spirits of God
7.17 "wipe away every tear from their eyes
19.12 His eyes are like a flame of fire
21. 4 "wipe away every tear from their eyes

3. *hole:* τρῆμα TRĒMA*
Mt 19.24 "a camel . . through the eye of a needle
Lk 18.25 "a camel . . through the eye of a needle

4. *hole:* τρυμαλιά TRYMALIA*
Mk 10.25 "a camel . . through the eye of a needle

IDIOMATICALLY
a. 2 Cor 10.7 Look at what is before your eyes Τὰ κατὰ πρόσωπον βλέπετε [PROSŌPON]

EYE, WITH ONE

1. *one-eyed:* μονόφθαλμος MONOPHTHALMOS*
Mt 18. 9 "better for you to enter life with one eye
Mk 9.47 "better for you to enter . . with one eye

EYESERVICE

1. *eye-service:* ὀφθαλμοδουλία OPHTHALMODOULIA*
Eph 6. 6 not in the way of eyeservice
Col 3.22 not with eyeservice, as men-pleasers

EYEWITNESS

1. *eyewitness:* αὐτόπτης AUTOPTĒS*
Lk 1. 2 eyewitnesses and ministers of the word

2. *spectator:* ἐπόπτης EPOPTĒS*
2 Pet 1.16 we were eyewitnesses of his majesty

F

FACE

1. *look in the face:* ἀντοφθαλμέω ANTOPHTHALMEŌ*
Acts 27.15 the ship . . could not face the wind

2. *face, appearance:* ὄψις OPSIS
Jn 11.44 his face wrapped with a cloth
Rev 1.16 his face was like the sun shining

3. *face, person:* πρόσωπον PROSŌPON
Mt 6.16 "hypocrites . . disfigure their faces
6.17 "when you fast . . wash your face
11.10 " 'I send my messenger before thy face
17. 2 his face shone like the sun
17. 6 the disciples . . fell on their faces
18.10 "their angels . . behold the face of my Father
26.39 going a little farther he fell on his face
26.67 Then they spat in his face
Mk 1. 2 "I send my messenger before thy face
14.65 some began . . to cover his face
Lk 5.12 when he saw Jesus, he fell on his face
7.27 " 'I send my messenger before thy face
9.51 he set his face to go to Jerusalem
9.53 his face was set toward Jerusalem
17.16 he fell on his face at Jesus' feet
21.35 "who dwell upon the face of the . . earth
24. 5 they . . bowed their faces to the ground
Acts 6.15 his face was like the face of an angel
17.26 "to live on all the face of the earth
20.25 "all you . . will see my face no more
20.38 that they should see his face no more
25.16 "the accused met the accusers face to face
1 Cor 13.12 now we see . . dimly, but then face to face
14.25 falling on his face, he will worship God
2 Cor 3. 7 Israelites could not look at Moses' face
3.13 like Moses, who put a veil over his face
3.18 with unveiled face, beholding[d] the glory
4. 6 the glory of God in the face of Christ
10. 1 humble when face to face with you
11.20 if a man . . strikes you in the face
Gal 2.11 I opposed him to his face
Col 2. 1 all who have not seen my face
1 Th 3.10 that we may see you face to face
Jas 1.23 who observes his natural face in a mirror
1 Pet 3.12 "the face of the Lord is against those
Rev 4. 7 third . . creature with the face of a man
6.16 "hide us from the face of him
7.11 they fell on their faces before the throne
9. 7 In appearance the locusts were like horses . . ; their faces were like human faces
10. 1 his face was like the sun
11.16 twenty-four elders . . fell on their faces
22. 4 they shall see his face

4. *mouth:* στόμα STOMA [C.2]
2 Jn .12 I hope to . . talk with you face to face
3 Jn .14 we will talk together face to face

IDIOMATICALLY
a. 1 Th 2.17 we endeavored . . to see you face to face ἐσπουδάσαμεν τὸ πρόσωπον ὑμῶν ἰδεῖν [PROSŌPON]

CONTEXTUALLY
1 Th 2. 2 to declare . . in the f. of great opposition

FACING (*See also* HUNGER, FACING)

1. *opposite, contrary:* ἐναντίος ENANTIOS [B.1.a.1]
Mk 15.39 the centurion, who stood facing him

FACING PLENTY

1. *feed, fatten:* χορτάζω (inf.) CHORTAZŌ
Phil 4.12 the secret of facing plenty and hunger

FACT (*See also* THAT, AS FOR THE FACT; THAT, THE FACT)
CONTEXTUALLY
2 Pet 3. 5 They deliberately ignore this fact

FACT, IF IN
1. *if indeed, since:* εἴπερ EIPER
Rom 8. 9 if in fact the Spirit of God dwells in you[0]

FACT, IN
1. *now:* νυνί NYNI
1 Cor 15.20 But in fact Christ has been raised

FACT, ONE
1. *one:* εἷς (neut.) HEIS
2 Pet 3. 8 do not ignore this one fact, beloved

FACTION
1. *sect, opinion:* αἵρεσις HAIRESIS
1 Cor 11.19 there must be factions among you

FACTIOUS
1. *selfish ambition:* ἐριθεία ERITHEIA [B.1.a.1]
Rom 2. 8 who are factious and do not obey the truth
2. *factious:* αἱρετικός HAIRETIKOS*
Tit 3.10 As for a man who is factious

FACTS
1. *certain, safe:* ἀσφαλής (subst. neut.) ASPHALĒS
Acts 21.34 as he could not learn the facts

FACULTY
1. *sense organ:* αἰσθητήριον AISTHĒTĒRION*
Heb 5.14 those who have their faculties trained

FADE
FADE AWAY
1. *make ineffective, hinder:* καταργέω (pass.) KATARGEŌ
2 Cor 3. 7 its brightness, fading as this was
3.11 if what faded away came with splendor
3.13 might not see the end of the fading splendor
2. *wither:* μαραίνω (pass.) MARAINŌ*
Jas 1.11 So will the rich man fade away

FAIL
1. *let go:* ἀνίημι ANIĒMI
Heb 13. 5 "I will never fail you nor forsake you
2. *fail, cease:* ἐκλείπω EKLEIPŌ
Lk 16. 9 "so that when it fails they may receive you
22.32 "prayed . . that your faith may not fail
23.45 while the sun's light failed[r]†‡
3. *fall out:* ἐκπίπτω EKPIPTŌ
Rom 9. 6 not as though the word of God had failed
4. *leave behind, fail:* ἐπιλείπω EPILEIPŌ*
Heb 11.32 time would fail me to tell of Gideon
5. *lack, fail:* ὑστερέω HYSTEREŌ
Heb 4. 1 lest any of you be judged to have failed
6. *put down, destroy:* καταλύω (pass.) KATALYŌ
Acts 5.38 "if . . this undertaking is of men, it will fail
7. *not:* μή MĒ [A.4.c]
Jas 4.17 Whoever knows . . and fails to do it
8. *not, no:* οὐ OU [A.4.c]
Mt 16.11 "How is it that you fail to perceive?
Rom 11. 7 Israel failed to obtain what it sought
Heb 4. 6 failed to enter because of disobedience
9. *stumble, fall:* πταίω PTAIŌ
Jas 2.10 whoever . . fails in one point

FAIL, THAT DOES NOT
1. *unfailing:* ἀνέκλειπτος ANEKLEIPTOS* [A.3.d.3]
Lk 12.33 "treasure in the heavens that does not fail

FAIL TO MEET THE TEST
FAILED, HAVE
1. *be worthless:* ἀδόκιμος εἶναι ADOKIMOS [A.6.a.3]
2 Cor 13. 5 unless indeed you fail to meet the test!
13. 6 you will find out that we have not failed
13. 7 though we may seem to have failed

FAIL TO OBTAIN
1. *lack, fail:* ὑστερέω HYSTEREŌ
Heb 12.15 See . . that no one fail to obtain the grace

FAILING
1. *weakness:* ἀσθένημα ASTHENĒMA*
Rom 15. 1 bear with the failings of the weak

FAILURE
1. *defeat:* ἥττημα HĒTTĒMA
Rom 11.12 if their failure means riches for the Gentiles

FAINT
1. *stop breathing:* ἀποψύχω APOPSYCHŌ*
Lk 21.26 "men fainting with fear
2. *relax:* ἐκλύω (pass.) EKLYŌ
Mt 15.32 "lest they faint on the way
Mk 8. 3 "they will faint on the way

FAINTHEARTED
1. *fainthearted:* ὀλιγόψυχος OLIGOPSYCHOS*
1 Th 5.14 encourage the fainthearted
IDIOMATICALLY
a. Heb 12.3 so that you may not grow weary or fainthearted ἵνα μὴ κάμητε ταῖς ψυχαῖς ὑμῶν ἐκλυόμενοι [EKLYŌ; PSYCHĒ]

FAIR
1. *good, beautiful:* καλός KALOS
Mt 15.26 "not fair to take the children's bread

FAIR HAVENS: II,E-4
1. *good harbor:* Καλοὶ λιμένες KALOS; LIMĒN
Acts 27. 8 we came to a place called Fair Havens

FAIR WEATHER
1. *fair weather:* εὐδία EUDIA*
Mt 16. 2 "you say, 'It will be fair weather‡

FAIR WORDS
1. *fair speaking:* χρηστολογία CHRĒSTOLOGIA*
Rom 16.18 by fair and flattering words they deceive

FAIRLY
1. *equality:* ἰσότης ISOTĒS [A.1.c.1]
Col 4. 1 treat your slaves . . fairly

FAITH
1. *trust, faith:* πίστις PISTIS
Mt 8.10 "not even[s] in Israel have I found such faith
9. 2 when Jesus saw their faith
9.22 "your faith has made you well
9.29 "According to your faith be it
15.28 "O woman, great is your faith!
17.20 "if you have faith as a . . mustard seed
21.21 "if you have faith and never doubt
23.23 "justice and mercy and faith
Mk 2. 5 when Jesus saw their faith
4.40 "Have you no faith?
5.34 "Daughter, your faith has made you well
10.52 "your faith has made you well
11.22 "Have faith in God
Lk 5.20 when he saw their faith
7. 9 "not even in Israel have I found such faith
7.50 "Your faith has saved you
8.25 "Where is your faith?
8.48 "Daughter, your faith has made you well
17. 5 The apostles said . . "Increase our faith!
17. 6 "If you had faith as a . . mustard seed
17.19 "your faith has made you well
18. 8 "will he find faith on earth?
18.42 "your faith has made you well
22.32 "prayed . . that your faith may not fail
Acts 3.16 "by faith in his name
3.16 "the faith which is through Jesus[d]
6. 5 a man full of faith and of the Holy Spirit
6. 7 priests were obedient to the faith
11.24 full of the Holy Spirit and of faith
13. 8 to turn away the proconsul from the faith
14. 9 he had faith to be made well
14.22 exhorting them to continue in the faith
14.27 how he had opened a door of faith
15. 9 "he . . cleansed their hearts by faith
16. 5 churches were strengthened in the faith
20.21 "testifying . . of faith in our Lord Jesus
24.24 Felix . . heard him speak upon faith in Christ
26.18 " 'those who are sanctified by faith in me
Rom 1. 5 to bring about the obedience of faith
1. 8 your faith is proclaimed in all the world
1.12 encouraged by each other's faith

Rom 1.17 the righteousness of God is revealed through faith for faith; as it is written, "He who through faith is righteous[b]
3.22 the righteousness of God through faith
3.25 expiation . . to be received by faith
3.26 he justifies him who has faith in Jesus
3.27 No, but on the principle of faith
3.28 justified by faith apart from works
3.30 justify . . on the ground of their faith and the uncircumcised through their faith
3.31 Do we . . overthrow the law by this faith?
4. 5 his faith is reckoned as righteousness
4. 9 faith was reckoned . . as righteousness
4.11 the righteousness which he had by faith
4.12 also follow the example of the faith
4.13 but through the righteousness of faith
4.14 faith is null and the promise is void
4.16 That is why it depends on faith
4.16 those who share the faith of Abraham
4.19 He did not weaken in faith
4.20 he grew strong in his faith
5. 1 since we are justified by faith
[5. 2 we . . obtained access *by f.* to this grace‡
9.30 righteousness through faith
9.32 they did not pursue it through faith
10. 6 righteousness based on faith says
10. 8 (the word of faith which we preach
10.17 So faith comes from what is heard
11.20 you stand fast only through faith
12. 3 each according to the measure of faith
12. 6 if prophecy, in proportion to our faith
14. 1 As for the man who is weak in faith
14.22 The faith that you have, keep
14.23 he does not act from faith; . . whatever does not proceed from faith is sin[w]
16.26 to bring about the obedience of faith
1 Cor 2. 5 that . . faith . . not rest in the wisdom of men
12. 9 to another faith by the same Spirit
13. 2 and if I have all faith
13.13 So faith, hope, love abide, these three
15.14 then . . your faith is in vain
15.17 If . . not . . raised, your faith is futile
16.13 Be watchful, stand firm in your faith
2 Cor 1.24 Not that we lord it over your faith; . . for you stand firm in your faith
4.13 Since we have the same spirit of faith
5. 7 for we walk by faith, not by sight
8. 7 Now as you excel in everything—in faith
10.15 our hope is that as your faith increases
13. 5 whether you are holding to your faith
Gal 1.23 "He . . is now preaching the faith
2.16 justified[d] . . through faith in Jesus Christ
2.16 to be justified by faith in Christ
2.20 the life I now live in the flesh I live by faith
3. 2 by works of the law, or by . . faith?
3. 5 by works of the law, or by . . faith?
3. 7 men of faith . . the sons of Abraham
3. 8 God would justify the Gentiles by faith
3. 9 men of faith are blessed with Abraham
3.11 "who through faith is righteous shall live[f]
3.12 the law does not rest on faith
3.14 the promise of the Spirit through faith
3.22 what was promised to faith in Jesus
3.23 before faith came, we were . . kept under restraint until faith should be revealed
3.24 that we might be justified by faith
3.25 But now that faith has come
3.26 you are all sons of God, through faith
5. 5 through the Spirit, by faith, we wait
5. 6 faith working[x] through love
6.10 those who are of the household of faith
Eph 1.15 I have heard of your faith in the Lord Jesus
2. 8 you have been saved through faith
3.12 confidence of access through our faith
3.17 Christ . . in your hearts through faith
4. 5 one Lord, one faith, one baptism
4.13 until we all attain to . . the faith
Eph 6.16 besides all these . . the shield of faith
6.23 Peace . . and love with faith
Phil 1.25 your progress and joy in the faith
1.27 striving . . for the faith of the gospel
2.17 the sacrificial offering of your faith
3. 9 that which is through faith in Christ, the righteousness from God that depends on faith
Col 1. 4 we have heard of your faith in Christ
1.23 provided that you continue in the faith
2. 5 the firmness of your faith in Christ
2. 7 established in the faith
2.12 raised with him through faith
1 Th 1. 3 your work of faith and labor of love
1. 8 your faith in God has gone forth
3. 2 to establish you in your faith
3. 5 I sent that I might know your faith
3. 6 brought us the good news of your faith
3. 7 comforted . . through your faith
3.10 supply what is lacking in your faith
5. 8 the breastplate of faith and love
2 Th 1. 3 because your faith is growing abundantly
1. 4 for your steadfastness and faith
1.11 every good resolve and work of faith
3. 2 for not all have faith
1 Tim 1. 2 Timothy, my true child in the faith
1. 4 the divine training[a] that is in faith
1. 5 a good conscience and sincere faith
1.14 faith and love that are in Christ Jesus
1.19 holding faith and a good conscience
1.19 have made shipwreck of their faith
2. 7 teacher of the Gentiles in faith and truth
2.15 if she continues[d] in faith and love
3. 9 they must hold the mystery of the faith
3.13 also great confidence in the faith
4. 1 some will depart from the faith
4. 6 nourished on the words of the faith
4.12 conduct, in love, in faith, in purity
5. 8 he has disowned the faith
6.10 some have wandered away from the faith
6.11 godliness, faith, love, steadfastness
6.12 Fight the good fight of the faith
6.21 missed the mark as regards the faith
2 Tim 1. 5 I am reminded of your sincere faith
1.13 faith and love which are in Christ Jesus
2.18 They are upsetting the faith of some
2.22 aim at righteousness, faith, love
3. 8 corrupt mind and counterfeit faith
3.10 my faith, my patience, my love
3.15 salvation through faith in Christ Jesus
4. 7 I have kept the faith
Tit 1. 1 to further the faith of God's elect
1. 4 my true child in a common faith
1.13 they may be sound in the faith
2. 2 sound in faith, in love
3.15 Greet those who love us in the faith
Phm . 5 I hear of your love and of the faith
. 6 your faith may promote the knowledge
Heb 4. 2 did not meet with faith in the hearers[h]
6. 1 foundation . . of faith toward God
6.12 who through faith and patience
10.22 a true heart in full assurance of faith
10.38 "my righteous one shall live by faith
10.39 who have faith and keep their souls
11. 1 faith is the assurance of things hoped for
11. 3 By f. we understand . . the world was created
11. 4 By faith Abel offered . . acceptable sacrifice
11. 5 By faith Enoch was taken up
11. 6 without faith it is impossible to please him
11. 7 By faith Noah, being warned by God
11. 7 the righteousness which comes by faith
11. 8 By faith Abraham obeyed
11. 9 By faith he sojourned in the land
11.11 By faith Sarah herself received power
11.13 These all died in faith
11.17 By faith Abraham . . offered up Isaac
11.20 By faith Isaac invoked future blessings
11.21 By faith Jacob . . blessed each of the sons

Heb 11.22 By f. Joseph . . made mention of the exodus
11.23 By faith Moses . . was hid for three months
11.24 By faith Moses . . refused
11.27 By faith he left Egypt, not being afraid
11.28 By faith he kept the Passover
11.29 By faith the people crossed the Red Sea
11.30 By faith the walls of Jericho fell down
11.31 By faith Rahab the harlot did not perish
11.33 who through faith conquered kingdoms
11.39 though well attested by their faith
12. 2 the pioneer and perfecter of our faith
13. 7 Remember . . and imitate their faith
Jas 1. 3 your faith produces steadfastness
1. 6 let him ask in faith
2. 1 no partiality as you hold the faith
2. 5 rich in faith and heirs of the kingdom
2.14 What . . if a man says he has faith but has not works? Can his faith save him?
2.17 faith by itself, if it has no works
2.18 "You have faith and I have works." Show me your faith apart from your works
2.18 I by my works will show you my faith
2.20 that faith apart from works is barren
2.22 faith was active along with his works, and faith was completed by works
2.24 justified by works and not by faith alone
2.26 so faith apart from works is dead
5.15 prayer of faith will save the sick man
1 Pet 1. 5 guarded through faith for a salvation
1. 7 the genuineness of your faith
1. 9 the outcome of your faith . . salvation
1.21 your faith and hope are in God[d]
5. 9 Resist him, firm in your faith
2 Pet 1. 1 obtained a faith of equal standing
1. 5 supplement your faith with virtue
1 Jn 5. 4 victory that overcomes the world, our faith
Jude . 3 appealing to you to contend for the faith
.20 build yourselves up on your . . faith
Rev 2.13 " 'you did not deny my faith
2.19 " 'your works, your love and faith
13.10 the endurance and faith of the saints
14.12 who keep . . the faith of Jesus

CONTEXTUALLY
Rom 4.22 That is why his f. was "reckoned to him

FAITH, HAVE

1. *believe, trust:* πιστεύω PISTEUŌ
Mt 21.22 "you will receive, if you have faith
Acts 27.25 "take heart, men, for I have faith
Rom 1.16 salvation to every one who has faith
10. 4 every one who has faith may be justified

FAITH, LITTLE

1. *littleness of faith:* ὀλιγοπιστία OLIGOPISTIA*
Mt 17.20 "Because of your little faith

FAITH, OF LITTLE

1. *of little faith:* ὀλιγόπιστος OLIGOPISTOS*
Mt 6.30 "much more clothe you, O men of little faith
8.26 "Why are you afraid, O men of little faith?
14.31 "O man of little faith, why did you doubt?
16. 8 "O men of little faith, why do you discuss?
Lk 12.28 "much more . . clothe you, O men of little f.!

FAITH, WHO HAD

1. *faithful, trustworthy:* πιστός (attr.) PISTOS
Gal 3. 9 blessed with Abraham who had faith

FAITHFUL (*See also* REMAIN FAITHFUL)

1. *faithful, trustworthy:* πιστός PISTOS
Mt 24.45 "Who then is the faithful and wise servant?
25.21 " 'Well done, good and faithful servant; you have been faithful over a little
25.23 " 'Well done, good and faithful servant; you have been faithful over a little
Lk 12.42 "Who then is the faithful and wise steward?
16.10 "He who is faithful in a very little is faithful also in much
16.11 " 'If then you have not been faithful
16.12 "if you have not been faithful in that
Lk 19.17 " 'you have been faithful in a very little
Acts 16.15 "If you have judged me to be faithful
1 Cor 1. 9 God is faithful, by whom you were called
4.17 Timothy, my beloved and faithful child
10.13 God is faithful, and he will not let you
2 Cor 1.18 As surely as God is faithful
Eph 1. 1 To the saints who are also faithful[a]
6.21 Tychicus the . . faithful minister
Col 1. 2 To the saints and faithful brethren
1. 7 Epaphras . . is a faithful minister of Christ
4. 7 Tychicus . . is a . . faithful minister
4. 9 Onesimus, the faithful . . brother
1 Th 5.24 He who calls you is faithful
2 Th 3. 3 the Lord is faithful; he will strengthen you
1 Tim 1.12 he judged me faithful by appointing me
3.11 women likewise must be . . faithful in all
2 Tim 2. 2 entrust to faithful men
2.13 if we are faithless, he remains faithful
Heb 2.17 a merciful and faithful high priest
3. 2 faithful to him who appointed him
3. 5 Moses was faithful in all God's house
10.23 he who promised is faithful
11.11 considered him faithful who had promised
1 Pet 4.19 entrust their souls to a faithful Creator
5.12 Silvanus, a faithful brother
1 Jn 1. 9 he is faithful and just, and will forgive
Rev 1. 5 Jesus Christ the faithful witness
2.10 " 'Be faithful unto death
2.13 " 'Antipas my witness, my faithful one
3.14 " 'the Amen, the faithful and true witness
17.14 "called and chosen and faithful
19.11 He who sat upon it is called Faithful

CONTEXTUALLY
Heb 3. 6 but Christ was faithful over God's[f] house

FAITHFULNESS

1. *trust, faith:* πίστις PISTIS
Rom 3. 3 nullify the faithfulness of God
Gal 5.22 patience, kindness, goodness, faithfulness

FAITHLESS

1. *unfaithful, incredible:* ἄπιστος APISTOS
Mt 17.17 "O faithless and perverse generation
Mk 9.19 "O faithless generation, how long?
Lk 9.41 "O faithless and perverse generation
Jn 20.27 "do not be faithless, but believing
Rev 21. 8 "the cowardly, the faithless, the polluted
2. *faithless:* ἀσύνθετος ASYNTHETOS*
Rom 1.31 foolish, faithless, heartless, ruthless

FAITHLESS, BE

1. *disbelieve, be faithless:* ἀπιστέω APISTEŌ
2 Tim 2.13 if we are faithless, he remains faithful

FAITHLESSNESS

1. *distrust, faithlessness:* ἀπιστία APISTIA
Rom 3. 3 Does their faithlessness nullify?

FALL (*See also* ASLEEP, FALL; LOT, FALL TO ONE BY; SICK, FALL)

1. *throw, put:* βάλλω (pass.) BALLŌ
Rev 8. 7 hail and fire, mixed with blood, which fell
2. *wet, rain:* βρέχω BRECHŌ [A.6.a.5]
Rev 11. 6 that no rain . . fall during . . prophesying
3. *be:* εἰμί (+ἐπί) EIMI [A.6.a.5]
Rom 2. 2 judgment of God rightly falls upon those
4. *fall out:* ἐκπίπτω EKPIPTŌ
Jas 1.11 its flower falls, and its beauty perishes
1 Pet 1.24 "grass withers, and the flower falls
5. *fall in:* ἐμπίπτω EMPIPTŌ*
Mt 12.11 "if he has one sheep and it falls
Lk 6.39 "Will they not both fall into a pit?
10.36 "the man who fell among the robbers
1 Tim 3. 6 he may . . fall into the condemnation
3. 7 he may fall into reproach
6. 9 who desire to be rich fall into temptation
Heb 10.31 to fall into the hands of the living God
6. *come, go:* ἔρχομαι ERCHOMAI [A.6.a.5]
Heb 6. 7 the rain that often falls upon it
7. *come to be, happen, be:* γίνομαι GINOMAI [A.6.a.5]
Acts 1.18 "(falling headlong[b] he burst open†

Acts 10.10 he fell into a trance
8. *come down, go down:* καταβαίνω KATABAINŌ
Mt 7.25 "the rain fell, and the floods came
7.27 "the rain fell, and the floods came
9. *fall, drop:* καταπίπτω KATAPIPTŌ
Lk 8. 6 "And some fell on the rock
Acts 26.14 "when we had all fallen to the ground
10. *fall, fail:* πίπτω PIPTŌ
Mt 7.25 "that house . . did not fall
7.27 "the winds blew and . . that house . . fell
10.29 "not one of them will fall to the ground
13. 4 "some seeds fell along the path
13. 5 "Other seeds fell on rocky ground
13. 7 "Other seeds fell upon thorns
13. 8 "Other seeds fell on good soil
15.14 "both will fall into a pit
15.27 "crumbs that fall from their masters' table
17. 6 the disciples . . fell on their faces
17.15 "often he falls into the fire
18.26 servant fell on his knees, imploring him
[21.44 "*he who falls on this stone*‡
[21.44 "*when it falls on any one*‡
24.29 "the stars will fall from heaven
26.39 going a little farther he fell on his face
Mk 4. 4 "some seed fell along the path
4. 5 "Other seed fell on rocky ground
4. 7 "Other seed fell among thorns
4. 8 "other seeds fell into good soil
5.22 seeing him, he fell at his feet
9.20 he fell on the ground and rolled about
13.25 "the stars will be falling from heaven
14.35 going a little farther, he fell on the ground
Lk 5.12 "when he saw Jesus, he fell on his face
8. 5 "as he sowed, some fell along the path
8. 7 "And some fell among thorns
8. 8 "some fell into good soil and grew
8.14 "as for what fell among the thorns
8.41 falling at Jesus' feet he besought him
10.18 "I saw Satan fall like lightning from heaven
11.17 "a divided household falls
13. 4 "eighteen upon whom the tower in Siloam fell
14. 5 "an ox that has fallen into a well
16.21 "what fell from the rich man's table
17.16 he fell on his face at Jesus' feet
20.18 "Every one who falls on that stone
20.18 "when it falls on any one it will crush him
21.24 "they will fall by the edge of the sword
23.30 "they will . . say to the mountains, 'Fall on us
Jn 11.32 Mary . . fell at his feet, saying . . "Lord
12.24 "unless a grain of wheat falls into the earth
18. 6 they drew back and fell to the ground
Acts 1.26 the lot fell on Matthias
9. 4 he fell to the ground and heard a voice
13.11 Immediately . . darkness fell upon him
15.16 " 'the dwelling of David, which has fallen
22. 7 "I fell to the ground and heard a voice
Rom 11.11 I ask, have they stumbled so as to fall?
11.22 severity toward those who have fallen
14. 4 before his own master . . he stands or falls
1 Cor 10. 8 twenty-three thousand fell in a single day
10.12 take heed lest he fall
14.25 falling on his face, he will worship God
Heb 3.17 whose bodies fell in the wilderness
4.11 that no one fall by the same . . disobedience
Jas 5.12 that you . . not fall under condemnation
Rev 1.17 I fell at his feet as though dead
2. 5 " 'Remember . . from what you have fallen
6.13 stars of the sky fell to the earth
6.16 "Fall on us and hide us
7.11 they fell on their faces before the throne
8.10 a great star fell from heaven . . and it fell on a third of the rivers
9. 1 I saw a star fallen from heaven
11.13 a tenth of the city fell
11.16 twenty-four elders . . fell on their faces
16.19 the cities of the nations fell
17.10 "seven kings, five of whom have fallen
Rev [18. 3 "for all nations have *fallen by* the wine‡
11. *stumble, fall:* πταίω PTAIŌ
2 Pet 1.10 if you do this you will never fall
12. *falling, fall:* πτῶσις PTŌSIS*
Mt 7.27 "great was the fall of it
Lk 2.34 "child is set for the fall and rising of many
13. *fall together:* συμπίπτω SYMPIPTŌ*
Lk 6.49 "the stream broke, and immediately it fell
IDIOMATICALLY
a. Rom 14.20 wrong for any one to make others fall by what he eats κακὸν τῷ ἀνθρώπῳ τῷ διὰ προσκόμματος ἐσθίοντι [PROSKOMMA]

FALL AMONG
1. *fall in with, encounter:* περιπίπτω (+dat.) PERIPIPTŌ
Lk 10.30 "he fell among robbers, who stripped him

FALL AWAY
1. *depart, withdraw from:* ἀφίστημι APHISTĒMI
Lk 8.13 "they . . in time of temptation fall away
Heb 3.12 leading you to fall away from . . God
2. *fall out:* ἐκπίπτω EKPIPTŌ
Gal 5. 4 you have fallen away from grace
3. *cause to stumble, offend:* σκανδαλίζω (pass.) SKANDALIZŌ
Mt 13.21 "immediately he falls away[i]†
24.10 "then many will fall away[y]†
26.31 "You will all fall away because of me
26.33 "Though they all fall away because of you, I will never fall away
Mk 4.17 "immediately they fall away[m]†
14.27 "You will all fall away
14.29 "Even though they all fall away
Jn 16. 1 "to you to keep you from falling away

FALL, CAUSE TO
1. *cause to stumble, offend:* σκανδαλίζω SKANDALIZŌ
1 Cor 8.13 lest I cause my brother to fall

FALL DOWN
1. *come down, go down:* καταβαίνω KATABAINŌ
Lk [22.44 *great drops of blood falling down*‡
2. *fall, drop:* καταπίπτω KATAPIPTŌ
Acts 28. 6 expecting him to . . suddenly fall down dead
3. *fall, fail:* πίπτω PIPTŌ
Mt 2.11 they fell down and worshiped him
4. 9 "if you will fall down and worship me
18.29 "So his fellow servant fell down
Acts 5. 5 When Ananias heard . . he fell down and died
5.10 she fell down at his feet and died
10.25 Cornelius met him and fell down at his feet
20. 9 he fell down from the third story
Heb 11.30 By faith the walls of Jericho fell down
Rev 4.10 twenty-four elders fall down before him
5. 8 elders fell down before the Lamb
5.14 the elders fell down and worshiped
19. 4 living creatures fell down and worshiped
19.10 Then I fell down at his feet to worship
22. 8 I fell down to worship at the feet

FALL DOWN AT
FALL DOWN BEFORE
1. *fall down at:* προσπίπτω PROSPIPTŌ
Mk 3.11 unclean spirits . . fell down before him
5.33 the woman . . fell down before him
7.25 a woman . . fell down at his feet
Lk 5. 8 Simon Peter . . fell down at Jesus' knees
8.28 he cried out and fell down before him
8.47 falling down before him declared
Acts 16.29 trembling . . he fell down before Paul

FALL FROM
1. *fall from:* ἀποπίπτω APOPIPTŌ*
Acts 9.18 something like scales fell from his eyes

FALL, MAKE TO
1. *cause to stumble, offend:* σκανδαλίζω SKANDALIZŌ
2 Cor 11.29 Who is made to fall, and I am not indignant?

FALL OFF
1. *fall out:* ἐκπίπτω EKPIPTŌ
Acts 12. 7 the chains fell off his hands

FALL ON
FALL UPON
1. *fall upon:* ἐπιπίπτω (+ἐπί) EPIPIPTŌ
Lk 1.12 he saw him, and fear fell upon him
Acts 8.16 it had not yet fallen on any of them
10.44 the Holy Spirit fell on all who heard
11.15 "the Holy Spirit fell on them just as on us
19.17 fear fell upon them all
Rom 15. 3 "those who reproached thee fell on me
Rev 11.11 great fear fell on those who saw them
2. *overshadow, darken:* ἐπισκιάζω EPISKIAZŌ
Acts 5.15 that . . his shadow might fall on some

FALL SHORT OF
1. *lack, fail:* ὑστερέω (pass.) HYSTEREŌ
Rom 3.23 all . . fall short of the glory of God

FALL, THAT WILL MAKE ONE
1. *stumbling block, trap:* σκάνδαλον (gen.) SKANDALON
Rom 9.33 "a rock that will make them fall
1 Pet 2. 8 "a rock that will make them fall

FALL TO
1. *throw upon:* ἐπιβάλλω EPIBALLŌ
Lk 15.12 " 'the share of property that falls to me

FALL UPON (*See* FALL ON)

FALLEN
IDIOMATICALLY
a. Rev. 14.8 *and* 18.2 "Fallen, fallen is Babylon the great ἔπεσεν ἔπεσεν Βαβυλὼν ἡ μεγάλη [PIPTŌ]

FALLING
IDIOMATICALLY
a. Jude .24 to keep you from falling φυλάξαι ὑμᾶς ἀπταίστους [APTAISTOS*]

FALLING, BE A CAUSE OF S.'S
1. *cause to stumble, offend:* σκανδαλίζω SKANDALIZŌ
1 Cor 8.13 if food is a cause of my brother's falling

FALLS, ONE'S COUNTENANCE
1. *have a gloomy look:* στυγνάζω STYGNAZŌ
Mk 10.22 At that saying his countenance fell

FALSE
1. *fabricated:* πλαστός PLASTOS*
2 Pet 2. 3 they will exploit you with false words
2. *false, lying:* ψευδής PSEUDĒS
Acts 6.13 ⟨they⟩ set up false witnesses
Rev 2. 2 " 'you . . found them to be false
3. *liar, cheat:* ψεύστης PSEUSTĒS [A.1.b.4]
Rom 3. 4 Let God be true though . . man be false

FALSE ACCUSATION, ROB BY
1. *oppress, defraud:* συκοφαντέω SYKOPHANTEŌ
Lk 3.14 "Rob no one . . by false accusation

FALSE APOSTLE
1. *false ambassador:* ψευδαπόστολος PSEUDAPOSTOLOS*
2 Cor 11.13 such men are false apostles

FALSE, BE
1. *lie, be false:* ψεύδομαι PSEUDOMAI
Jas 3.14 do not boast and be false to the truth

FALSE BROTHER
1. *false brother:* ψευδάδελφος PSEUDADELPHOS*
2 Cor 11.26 danger from false brethren
Gal 2. 4 false brethren secretly brought in

FALSE CHRIST
1. *false Christ:* ψευδόχριστος PSEUDOCHRISTOS*
Mt 24.24 "false Christs and false prophets will arise
Mk 13.22 "False Christs and false prophets will arise

FALSE PROPHET
1. *false prophet:* ψευδοπροφήτης PSEUDOPROPHĒTĒS*
Mt 7.15 "Beware of false prophets
24.11 "many false prophets will arise
24.24 "false Christs and false prophets will arise
Mk 13.22 "False Christs and false prophets will arise
Lk 6.26 "so their fathers did to the false prophets
Acts 13. 6 a Jewish false prophet, named Bar-Jesus
2 Pet 2. 1 false prophets also arose among the people
1 Jn 4. 1 many false prophets have gone out
Rev 16.13 from the mouth of the false prophet
Rev 19.20 the false prophet who . . worked the signs
20.10 where the beast and the false prophet were

FALSE, PROVE
1. *lie, be false:* ψεύδομαι PSEUDOMAI
Heb 6.18 impossible that God should prove false

FALSE TEACHER
1. *false teacher:* ψευδοδιδάσκαλος PSEUDODIDASKALOS*
2 Pet 2. 1 there will be false teachers among you

FALSE TESTIMONY
1. *false witness, perjury:* ψευδομαρτυρία PSEUDOMARTYRIA
Mt 26.59 the whole counsel sought false testimony

FALSE, WHAT IS
1. *lie, falsehood:* ψεῦδος PSEUDOS
2 Th 2.11 to make them believe what is false

FALSE WITNESS
1. *false witness, perjury:* ψευδομαρτυρία PSEUDOMARTYRIA
Mt 15.19 "fornication, theft, false witness, slander
2. *false witness:* ψευδόμαρτυς PSEUDOMARTYS
Mt 26.60 many false witnesses came forward

FALSE WITNESS, BEAR
1. *be a false witness:* ψευδομαρτυρέω PSEUDOMARTYREŌ*
Mt 19.18 "You shall not bear false witness
Mk 10.19 " 'Do not bear false witness
14.56 many bore false witness against him
14.57 some . . bore false witness against him
Lk 18.20 " 'Do not bear false witness

FALSEHOOD
1. *wrongdoing, injustice:* ἀδικία ADIKIA
Jn 7.18 "in him there is no falsehood
2. *lie, falsehood:* ψεῦδος PSEUDOS
Eph 4.25 putting away falsehood
Rev 21.27 one who practices abomination or falsehood
22.15 one who loves and practices falsehood
3. *lie:* ψεῦσμα PSEUSMA*
Rom 3. 7 through my falsehood God's truthfulness

FALSELY
1. *lie, be false:* ψεύδομαι (part.) PSEUDOMAI
Mt 5.11 "utter all kinds of evil against you falsely

FALSELY CALLED
1. *falsely called:* ψευδώνυμος PSEUDŌNYMOS*
1 Tim 6.20 contradictions . . falsely called knowledge

FALSELY, SWEAR
1. *swear falsely:* ἐπιορκέω EPIORKEŌ*
Mt 5.33 " 'You shall not swear falsely

FAME
1. *hearing, report:* ἀκοή AKOĒ
Mt 4.24 his fame spread throughout all Syria
14. 1 Herod . . heard about the fame of Jesus
Mk 1.28 at once his fame spread everywhere

FAME, SPREAD S.'S
1. *spread widely, make known:* διαφημίζω DIAPHĒMIZŌ
Mt 9.31 they went away and spread his fame

FAMILIAR
1. *one who knows:* γνώστης GNŌSTĒS* [A.1.b.4]
Acts 26. 3 "you are especially familiar with all customs

FAMILY
1. *kind, race, family:* γένος GENOS
Acts 4. 6 who were of the high-priestly family
7.13 "Joseph's family became known to Pharaoh
13.26 "Brethren, sons of the family of Abraham
2. *house, household:* οἶκος OIKOS
1 Tim 5. 4 religious duty to their own family
Tit 1.11 they are upsetting whole families
3. *family, lineage:* πατριά PATRIA
Acts 3.25 " 'all the families of the earth be blessed
Eph 3.15 from whom every family . . is named
IDIOMATICALLY
a. Mk 3.21 And when his family heard it καὶ ἀκούσαντες οἱ παρ' αὐτοῦ [PARA]
CONTEXTUALLY
Rom 16.10 who belong to the f. of Aristobulus
16.11 who belong to the f. of Narcissus

FAMILY, ONE'S OWN
1. *of the house:* οἰκεῖος (subst. pl.) OIKEIOS
1 Tim 5. 8 especially for his own family

FAMINE
1. *famine, hunger:* λιμός LIMOS
Mt 24. 7 "there will be famines and earthquakes
Mk 13. 8 "in various places, there will be famines
Lk 4.25 "there came a great famine over all the land
15.14 "a great famine arose in that country
21.11 "in various places famines and pestilences
Acts 7.11 "there came a famine throughout all Egypt
11.28 a great famine over all the world
Rom 8.35 persecution, or famine, or nakedness
Rev 6. 8 to kill with sword and with famine
18. 8 "pestilence and mourning and famine

FAMOUS
1. *praise, approval:* ἔπαινος EPAINOS [A.1.b.4]
2 Cor 8.18 we are sending the brother who is famous

FAR (*See also* ABOVE, FAR; ABUNDANTLY, FAR MORE; GREATER, FAR; MORE, FAR; SPENT, BE FAR)
1. *far:* μακράν MAKRAN
[a]+ἀπέχειν
Mk 12.34 "You are not far from the kingdom
Lk 7. 6 [a]he was not far from the house
Jn 21. 8 they were not far from the land
Acts 17.27 "Yet he is not far from each one of us
2. *far, long:* μακρός MAKROS
Lk 15.13 "took his journey into a far country
19.12 "A nobleman went into a far country
3. *much more:* πολλῷ μᾶλλον MALLON; POLYS [A.4.e]
2 Cor 3. 9 righteousness must far exceed it
Phil 1.23 to . . be with Christ, for that is far better
4. *far off, at a distance:* πόρρω PORRŌ
[a]+ἀπέχειν
Mt 15. 8 [a]" 'their heart is far from me
Mk 7. 6 [a]" 'their heart is far from me
IDIOMATICALLY
a. Rom 1.13 (but thus far have been prevented καὶ ἐκωλύθην ἄχρι τοῦ δεῦρο [DEURO]
CONTEXTUALLY
Rom 12.18 so far as it depends upon you

FAR AS, AS
1. *until:* ἄχρι ACHRI
Acts 13. 6 through the whole island as far as Paphos
28.15 came as far as the Forum of Appius
2. *until:* ἕως HEŌS
Mt 24.27 "lightning . . shines as far as the west
26.58 as far as the courtyard of the high priest
Lk 24.50 he led them out as far as Bethany
Acts 11.19 Stephen traveled as far as Phoenicia
17.15 conducted Paul . . as far as Athens
23.23 "spearmen to go as far as Caesarea
3. *as far as:* μέχρι MECHRI
Rom 15.19 as f. round as Illyricum I have . . preached

FAR AS, IN SO
1. *as, insofar as:* καθό KATHO
1 Pet 4.13 in so far as you share Christ's sufferings

FAR AWAY
1. *far:* μακράν MAKRAN
Acts 22.21 " 'I will send you far away to the Gentiles

FAR, BE
1. *be distant:* ἀπέχω APECHŌ
[a]+πόρρω [b]+μακράν
Mt 15. 8 [a]" 'their heart is far from me
Mk 7. 6 [a]" 'their heart is far from me
Lk 7. 6 [b]he was not far from the house

FAR BE IT
1. *may it not be:* μὴ γένοιτο GINOMAI [B.3.b.8]
Gal 6.14 far be it from me to glory except in the cross

FAR GONE, BE
1. *make progress, advance:* προκόπτω (aor.) PROKOPTŌ
Rom 13.12 the night is far gone, the day is at hand

FAR OFF
1. *far:* μακράν MAKRAN
[a]εἰς μακράν
Acts 2.39 [a]"to all that are far off
Eph 2.13 you who once were far off
2.17 preached peace to you who were far off
2. *from afar:* μακρόθεν MAKROTHEN
[a]ἀπὸ μακρόθεν
Lk 16.23 [a]"he . . saw Abraham far off
18.13 "the tax collector, standing far off
Rev 18.10 they will stand far off, in fear
18.15 merchants . . will stand far off, in fear
18.17 all whose trade is on the sea, stood far off

FARE
1. *come to be, happen, be:* γίνομαι GINOMAI
Rom 9.29 "we would have fared like Sodom

FAREWELL
1. *rejoice:* χαίρω (imper.) CHAIRŌ
2 Cor 13.11 Finally, brethren, farewell
2. *strengthen:* ῥώννυμι (pass. imper.) RHŌNNYMI*
Acts 15.29 "you will do well. Farewell

FAREWELL, BID
1. *take leave of:* ἀπασπάζομαι APASPAZOMAI*
Acts 21. 5(6) we prayed and bade one another farewell

FAREWELL, SAY
1. *part from* (mid.): ἀποτάσσω APOTASSŌ
Lk 9.61 "let me first say farewell to those

FARM
1. *field:* ἀγρός AGROS
Mt 22. 5 "one to his farm, another to his business

FARMER
1. *farmer, tenant:* γεωργός GEŌRGOS
2 Tim 2. 6 It is the hard-working farmer who ought
Jas 5. 7 the farmer waits for the . . fruit

FARTHER (*See* LITTLE FARTHER, A)

FASHION (*See* WORLDLY FASHION, IN A)

FAST
1. *fasting, hunger:* νηστεία NĒSTEIA
Acts 27. 9 the fast had already gone by
2. *fast, abstain from:* νηστεύω NĒSTEUŌ*
Mt 4. 2 he fasted forty days and forty nights
6.16 "when you fast, do not look dismal
6.16 "that their fasting may be seen by men
6.17 "when you fast, anoint your head
6.18 "that your fasting may not be seen by men
9.14 "Why do we and the Pharisees fast,[w] but your disciples do not fast?
9.15 "days will come . . and then they will fast
Mk 2.18 Pharisees were fasting; and people . . said . . "Why do . . Pharisees fast, but your disciples do not fast?
2.19 "Can the wedding guests fast while the bridegroom is with them? . . they cannot fast
2.20 "then they will fast in that day
Lk 5.33 "The disciples of John fast often
5.34 "Can you make wedding guests fast?
5.35 "then they will fast in those days
18.12 " 'I fast twice a week, I give tithes
Acts 13. 2 While they were worshiping . . and fasting
13. 3 after fasting and praying they . . sent them

FAST, HOLD
1. *hold upon, aim at:* ἐπέχω EPECHŌ
Phil 2.16 holding fast the word of life
2. *hold fast, restrain:* κατέχω KATECHŌ
Lk 8.15 "who, hearing the word, hold it fast
1 Cor 15. 2 by which you are saved, if you h. it fast
1 Th 5.21 test everything; hold fast what is good
Heb 3. 6 if we hold fast our confidence and pride
10.23 Let us hold fast the confession of our hope
3. *join, unite:* κολλάω (pass.) KOLLAŌ
Rom 12. 9 hold fast to what is good
4. *seize, hold fast:* κρατέω KRATEŌ
Mk 7. 8 "You . . hold fast the tradition of men
Col 2.19 not holding fast to the Head

Heb 4.14 let us hold fast our confession
Rev 2.13 " 'you hold fast my name
2.25 " 'only hold fast what you have
3.11 " 'hold fast what you have

FAST, STAND

1. *stand, place:* ἵστημι HISTĒMI
[a]2 aor.
1 Pet 5.12 [a]the true grace of God; stand fast in it
2. *stand:* στήκω STĒKŌ
Gal 5. 1 stand fast, therefore, and do not submit
1 Th 3. 8 we live, if you stand fast in the Lord

FASTEN

1. *fortify:* ἀσφαλίζω (mid.) ASPHALIZŌ
Acts 16.24 he . . fastened their feet in the stocks
2. *hang up:* κρεμάννυμι KREMANNYMI
Mt 18. 6 "a great millstone fastened round his neck

FASTEN ON

1. *fasten on, take hold of:* καθάπτω KATHAPTŌ*
Acts 28. 3 a viper . . fastened on his hand

FASTING

1. *fasting, hunger:* νηστεία NĒSTEIA
Mt [17.21 "*never . . except by prayer and fasting*‡
Mk [9.29 "cannot . . by anything but prayer *and f.*‡
Lk 2.37 worshiping with fasting and prayer
Acts 14.23 with prayer and fasting, they committed

FAT CALF

1. *fed up, fatted:* σιτιστός (subst. neut.) SITISTOS*
Mt 22. 4 " 'fat calves are killed . . everything is ready

FATHER

1. *father:* πατήρ PATĒR
Mt 2.22 Archelaus reigned . . in place of his f. Herod
3. 9 " 'We have Abraham as our father
4.21 in the boat with Zebedee their father
4.22 they left the boat and their father
5.16 "give glory to your Father who is in heaven
5.45 "that you may be sons of your Father
5.48 "as your heavenly Father is perfect
6. 1 "you will have no reward from your Father
6. 4 "your Father who sees in secret
6. 6 "pray to your Father who is in secret; and your Father . . will reward you
6. 8 "for your Father knows what you need
6. 9 "Our Father who art in heaven
6.14 "your heavenly Father also will forgive you
6.15 "neither will your Father forgive
6.18 "by your Father who is in secret; and your Father . . will reward you
6.26 "yet your heavenly Father feeds them
6.32 "your . . Father knows that you need them
7.11 "how much more will your Father!
7.21 "he who does the will of my Father
8.21 "Lord, let me first go and bury my father
10.20 "the Spirit of your Father speaking
10.21 "the father ⟨will deliver up⟩ his child
10.29 "not one . . without your Father's will
10.32 "I . . will acknowledge before my Father
10.33 "I also will deny before my Father
10.35 "come to set a man against his father
10.37 "He who loves father or mother more
11.25 "I thank thee, Father, Lord of heaven
11.26 "yea, Father, for such was thy . . will[f]
11.27 "delivered to me by my Father; . . no one knows the Son except the Father, and no one knows the Father except the Son
12.50 "whoever does the will of my Father
13.43 "in the kingdom of their Father
15. 4 " 'Honor your father and your mother,' and, 'He who speaks evil of father or mother
15. 5 " 'If any one tells his father
15. 5 " 'he need not honor his father
15.13 "which my heavenly Father has not planted
16.17 "but my Father who is in heaven
16.27 "with his angels in the glory of his Father
18.10 "face of my Father who is in heaven[c]
Mt 18.14 "So it is not the will of my[d] Father
18.19 "it will be done for them by my Father
18.35 "my heavenly Father will do to every one
19. 5 " 'a man shall leave his father and mother
19.19 "Honor your father and mother
19.29 "every one who has left . . father or mother
20.23 "for whom it has been prepared by my Father
21.31 "Which of the two did the will of his father?
23. 9 "call no man your father on earth, for you have one Father, who is in heaven
23.30 " 'in the days of our fathers
23.32 "Fill up, then, the measure of your fathers
24.36 "no one knows . . but the Father only
25.34 " 'Come, O blessed of my Father
26.29 "new with you in my Father's kingdom
26.39 "My Father, if it be possible
26.42 "My Father, if this cannot pass unless
26.53 "that I cannot appeal to my Father?
28.19 "the name of the Father and of the Son
Mk 1.20 they left their father Zebedee in the boat
5.40 he . . took the child's father and mother
7.10 " 'Honor your father and your mother'; and, 'He who speaks evil of father or mother
7.11 " 'If a man tells his father or his mother
7.12 "to do anything for his father or mother
8.38 "when he comes in the glory of his Father
9.21 Jesus[h] asked his father, "How long?
9.24 the father of the child cried out[i]
10. 7 " 'a man shall leave his father and mother
10.19 " 'Honor your father and mother
10.29 "no one who has left . . mother or father
11.10 "the kingdom of our father David
11.25 "your Father also who is in heaven
[11.26 "*neither will your Father . . forgive*‡
13.12 "the father ⟨will deliver⟩ his child
13.32 "no one knows . . but only the Father
14.36 "Abba, Father, all things are possible
15.21 Simon of Cyrene, . . the father of . . Rufus
Lk 1.17 "to turn the hearts of the fathers
1.32 "the throne of his father David
1.55 "as he spoke to our fathers, to Abraham
1.59 would have named him . . after his father
1.62 they made signs to his father
1.67 his father . . was filled with the Holy Spirit
1.72 "perform the mercy promised to our fathers
1.73 "which he swore to our father Abraham
2.33 his father and his mother marveled
2.48 "your father and I have been looking
2.49 "I must be in my Father's house
3. 8 " 'We have Abraham as our father
6.23 "for so their fathers did to the prophets
6.26 "so their fathers did to the false prophets
6.36 "even as your Father is merciful
8.51 the father and mother of the child
9.26 "when he comes in . . the glory of the Father
9.42 Jesus . . gave him back to his father
9.59 "Lord, let me first go and bury my father
10.21 "I thank thee, Father, Lord of heaven
10.21 "yea, Father, for such was thy gracious will[h]
10.22 "delivered to me by my Father; and no one knows who the Son is except the Father, or who the Father is except the Son
11. 2 "Father, hallowed be thy name
11.11 "What father . . will . . give him a serpent?
11.13 "how much more will the heavenly Father!
11.47 "the prophets whom your fathers killed
11.48 "you . . consent to the deeds of your fathers
12.30 "your Father knows that you need them
12.32 "for it is your Father's good pleasure
12.53 "they will be divided, father against son and son against father
14.26 "If any . . does not hate his own father
15.12 "the younger of them said to his father, 'Father, give me the share of property
15.17 " 'How many of my father's hired servants!
15.18 " 'I will . . go to my father, and I will say to him, "Father, I have sinned

Lk 15.20 "he arose and came to his father
15.20 "his father saw him and had compassion
15.21 " 'Father, I have sinned against heaven
15.22 "the father said to his servants
15.27 " 'your father has killed the fatted calf
15.28 "His father came out and entreated him
15.29 "he answered his father . . 'I have served
16.24 " 'Father Abraham, have mercy upon me
16.27 " 'Then I beg you, father, to send him to my father's house
16.30 " 'No, father Abraham
18.20 " 'Honor your father and mother
22.29 "my Father assigned to me a kingdom
22.42 "Father, if thou art willing
23.34 "Father, forgive them; for they know not‡
23.46 "Father, into thy hands I commit my spirit!
24.49 "I send the promise of my Father upon you

Jn 1.14 glory as of the only Son from the Father
1.18 who is in the bosom of the Father
2.16 "my Father's house a house of trade
3.35 the Father loves the Son
4.12 "Are you greater than our father Jacob?
4.20 "Our fathers worshiped on this mountain
4.21 "when . . you worship the Father
4.23 "worship the Father in spirit and truth, for such the Father seeks to worship him
4.53 "The father knew that was the hour
5.17 "My Father is working still, and I am
5.18 he . . also called God his own Father
5.19 "only what he sees the Father doing
5.20 "For the Father loves the Son
5.21 "For as the Father raises the dead
5.22 "The Father judges no one
5.23 "even as they honor the Father
5.23 "does not honor the Father
5.26 "For as the Father has life in himself
5.36 "works which the Father has granted me . . bear . . witness that the Father has sent me
5.37 "the Father . . has himself borne witness
5.43 "I have come in my Father's name
5.45 "not . . that I shall accuse you to the Father
6.27 "on him has God the Father set his seal
6.31 "Our fathers ate the manna
6.32 "my Father gives you the true bread
6.37 "All that the Father gives me will come
6.40 "this is the will of my Father
6.42 "Jesus, . . whose father and mother we know
6.44 "the Father who sent me draws him
6.45 "who has . . learned from the Father
6.46 "Not that any one has seen the Father except him . . ; he has seen the Father
6.49 "Your fathers ate the manna
6.57 "As the living Father sent me, and I live because of the Father
6.58 "not such as the fathers ate and died
6.65 "unless it is granted him by the Father
7.22 "(not . . from Moses, but from the fathers
[8.16 "but I and *the Father* who sent me‡
8.18 "the Father who sent me bears witness
8.19 "Where is your Father?
8.19 "You know neither me nor my Father
8.19 "you would know my Father also
8.27 he spoke to them of the Father
8.28 "speak thus as the Father taught me
8.38 "what I have seen with my Father
8.38 "what you have heard from your father
8.39 "Abraham is our father
8.41 "You do what your father did
8.41 "we have one Father, even God
8.42 "If God were your Father, you would love
8.44 "You are of your father the devil, and your will is to do your father's desires
8.44 "for he is a liar and the father of lies
8.49 "I honor my Father, and you dishonor me
8.53 Are you greater than our f. Abraham?
8.54 "it is my Father who glorifies me
8.56 "Your father Abraham rejoiced

Jn 10.15 "as the Father knows me and I know the Father; and I lay down my life
10.17 "For this reason the Father loves me
10.18 "this charge I have . . from my Father
10.25 "The works that I do in my Father's name
10.29 "My Father, who has given them to me[w]
10.29 "to snatch them out of the Father's hand
10.30 "I and the Father are one
10.32 "many good works from the Father
10.36 "whom the Father consecrated and sent
10.37 "If I am not doing the works of my Father
10.38 "understand that the Father is in me and I am in the Father
11.41 "Father, I thank thee . . thou hast heard
12.26 "the Father will honor him
12.27 "say . . 'Father, save me from this hour'?
12.28 "Father, glorify thy name
12.49 "the Father who sent me
12.50 "I say as the Father has bidden me
13. 1 his hour . . to depart . . to the Father
13. 3 Father had given all things into his hands
14. 2 "In my Father's house are many rooms
14. 6 "no one comes to the Father, but by me
14. 7 "you would have known my Father also
14. 8 "Lord, show us the Father
14. 9 "He who has seen me has seen the Father; how can you say, 'Show us the Father'?
14.10 "Do you not believe that I am in the Father and the Father in me?
14.10 "Father who dwells in me
14.11 "Believe me that I am in the Father and the Father in me
14.12 "because I go to the Father
14.13 "that the Father . . be glorified in the Son
14.16 "And I will pray the Father
14.20 "you will know that I am in my Father
14.21 "who loves me will be loved by my Father
14.23 "my Father will love him
14.24 "not mine but the Father's who sent me
14.26 "Holy Spirit, whom the Father will send
14.28 "because I go to the Father; for the Father is greater than I
14.31 "I do as the Father has commanded me
14.31 "may know that I love the Father
15. 1 "my Father is the vinedresser
15. 8 "By this my Father is glorified
15. 9 "As the Father has loved me
15.10 "just as I have kept my Father's
15.15 "all that I have heard from my Father
15.16 "whatever you ask the Father in my name
15.23 "He who hates me hates my Father also
15.24 "hated both me and my Father
15.26 "I shall send to you from the Father, even the Spirit . . who proceeds from the Father
16. 3 "they have not known the Father
16.10 "because I go to the Father
16.15 "All that the Father has is mine
16.17 " 'because I go to the Father
16.23 "if you ask anything of the Father
16.25 "but ⟨I⟩ tell you plainly of the Father
16.26 "not . . that I shall pray the Father for you
16.27 "for the Father himself loves you
16.27 "you . . believed that I came from the Father
16.28 "I came from the Father and . . I am . . going to the Father
16.32 "I am not alone, for the Father is with me
17. 1 "Father, the hour has come
17. 5 "Father, glorify thou me
17.11 "Holy Father, keep them in thy name
17.21 "even as thou, Father, art in me
17.24 "Father, I desire that they . . be with me
17.25 "Father, the world has not known thee
18.11 "the cup which the Father has given me
20.17 "I have not yet ascended to the Father; . . I am ascending to my Father and your Father, to my God and your God
20.21 "As the F. has sent me . . I send you

Acts 1. 4 "to wait for the promise of the Father
1. 7 "seasons which the Father has fixed
2.33 "received from the Father the promise
3.13 "God of our fathers, glorified his servant[c]
3.25 "covenant which God gave to your fathers
4.25 "by the mouth of our father David
5.30 "God of our fathers raised Jesus
7. 2 "Brethren and fathers, hear me . . God . . appeared to our father Abraham
7. 4 "after his father died, God removed him
7.11 "our fathers could find no food
7.12 "he sent forth our fathers the first time
7.14 "Joseph . . called to him Jacob his father
7.15 "he died, himself and our fathers
7.19 "forced our fathers to expose their infants
7.20 "brought up . . in his father's house
7.32 " 'I am the God of your fathers
7.38 "This is he who was . . with our fathers
7.39 "Our fathers refused to obey him
7.44 "Our fathers had the tent of witness
7.45 "Our fathers . . brought it in with Joshua
7.45 "nations . . God thrust out before our fathers
7.51 "As your fathers did, so do you
7.52 "did not your fathers persecute?
13.17 "God of this people Israel chose our fathers
13.32 "what God promised to the fathers
13.36 "David . . was laid with his fathers
15.10 "neither our fathers nor we
16. 1 his father was a Greek
16. 3 they all knew that his father was a Greek
22. 1 "Brethren and fathers, hear the defense
22.14 " 'God of our fathers appointed you
26. 6 "promise made by God to our fathers
28. 8 the father of Publius lay sick
28.25 "saying to your fathers through Isaiah
Rom 1. 7 peace from God our Father
4.11 the father of all who believe
4.12 the father of the circumcised
4.12 faith which our father Abraham had
4.16 for he is the father of us all
4.17 "I have made you the father of many nations
4.18 that he should become the father of many
6. 4 raised . . by the glory of the Father
8.15 When we cry, "Abba! Father!
15. 6 glorify the God and Father of our Lord
1 Cor 1. 3 peace from God our Father
4.15 you do not have many fathers
5. 1 a man is living with his father's wife
8. 6 for us there is one God, the Father
10. 1 our fathers were all under the cloud
15.24 he delivers the kingdom to God the Father
2 Cor 1. 2 peace from God our Father
1. 3 Blessed be the God and Father of our Lord Jesus Christ, the Father of mercies
6.18 "I will be a father to you
11.31 God and Father of the Lord Jesus
Gal 1. 1 Jesus Christ and God the Father
1. 3 God the Father and our Lord Jesus
1. 4 according to . . will of our God and Father
4. 2 until the date set by the father
4. 6 Spirit of his Son . . crying, "Abba! Father!
Eph 1. 2 peace from God our Father
1. 3 God and Father of our Lord Jesus Christ
1.17 God of our Lord . . , the Father of glory
2.18 access in one Spirit to the Father
3.14 I bow my knees before the Father
4. 6 God and Father of us all
5.20 giving thanks . . to God the Father
5.31 "a man shall leave his father
6. 2 "Honor your father and mother
6. 4 Fathers, do not provoke your children
6.23 love with faith, from God the Father
Phil 1. 2 peace from God our Father
2.11 to the glory of God the Father
2.22 how as a son with a father he has served
4.20 To our God and Father be glory
Col 1. 2 peace from God our Father
Col 1. 3 the Father of our Lord Jesus Christ
1.12 giving thanks to the Father
3.17 thanks to God the Father through him
3.21 Fathers, do not provoke your children
1 Th 1. 1 To the church . . in God the Father
1. 3 remembering before our God and Father
2.11 like a father with his children
3.11 Now may our God and Father himself
3.13 in holiness before our God and Father
2 Th 1. 1 To the church . . in God our Father
1. 2 peace from God the Father
2.16 God our Father, who loved us
1 Tim 1. 2 peace from God the Father
5. 1 exhort him as you would a father
2 Tim 1. 2 peace from God the Father
Tit 1. 4 peace from God the Father
Phm . 3 peace from God our Father
Heb 1. 1 God spoke of old to our fathers
1. 5 "I will be to him a father
3. 9 "your fathers put me to the test
8. 9 "covenant that I made with their fathers
12. 7 son . . whom his father does not discipline
12. 9 we have had earthly fathers
12. 9 subject to the Father of spirits
Jas 1.17 coming down from the Father of lights
1.27 undefiled before God and the Father
2.21 Was not Abraham our father justified?
3. 9 With it we bless the Lord and Father
1 Pet 1. 2 chosen and destined by God the Father
1. 3 Blessed be the God and Father!
1.17 if you invoke as Father him who judges
2 Pet 1.17 glory from God the Father
3. 4 "ever since the fathers fell asleep
1 Jn 1. 2 life which was with the Father
1. 3 our fellowship is with the Father
2. 1 we have an advocate with the Father
2.13 I am writing to you, fathers
2.13 because you know the Father
2.14 I write to you, fathers
2.15 love for the Father is not in him
2.16 is not of the Father but is of the world
2.22 he who denies the Father and the Son
2.23 No one who denies the Son has the Father. He who confesses . . has the Father
2.24 then you will abide . . in the Father
3. 1 See what love the Father has given
4.14 Father has sent his Son as the Savior
2 Jn . 3 peace . . with us, from God the Father and from Jesus Christ the Father's Son
. 4 we have been commanded by the Father
. 9 he . . has both the Father and the Son
Jude . 1 beloved in God the Father
Rev 1. 6 priests to his God and Father
2.27 " 'I . . received power from my Father
3. 5 " 'I will confess his name before my Father
3.21 " 'sat down with my Father on his throne
14. 1 Father's name written on their foreheads

2. *ancestor, parent* (subst.): πρόγονος PROGONOS
2 Tim 1. 3 God whom I serve . . as did my fathers

FATHER, BECOME S.'S
FATHER OF, BECOME THE

1. *beget, bear:* γεννάω GENNAŌ
Acts 7. 8 "Abraham became the father of Isaac
7.29 "he became the father of two sons
1 Cor 4.15 I became your father in Christ Jesus
Phm .10 Onesimus, whose father I have become

FATHER, INHERITED FROM ONE'S

1. *inherited from one's father:* πατροπαράδοτος PATROPARADOTOS*
1 Pet 1.18 futile ways inherited from your fathers

FATHER, MURDERER OF

1. *one who slays his father, parricide:* πατρολῴας PATROLŌAS*
1 Tim 1. 9 the law is . . for murderers of fathers

FATHER OF, BE THE
1. *beget, bear:* γεννάω GENNAŌ
Mt 1. 2 Abraham was the father of Isaac, and Isaac the father of Jacob, and Jacob the father of Judah
1. 3 Judah the father of Perez . . , Perez the father of Hezron, and Hezron the father of Ram[a]
1. 4 Ram[a] the father of Amminadab, and Amminadab the father of Nahshon, and Nahshon the father of Salmon
1. 5 Salmon the father of Boaz . . , and Boaz the father of Obed by Ruth, and Obed the father of Jesse
1. 6 Jesse the father of David the king. And David was the father of Solomon
1. 7 Solomon the father of Rehoboam, and Rehoboam the father of Abijah, and Abijah the father of Asa[b]
1. 8 Asa[b] the father of Jehoshaphat, and Jehoshaphat the father of Joram, and Joram the father of Uzziah
1. 9 Uzziah the father of Jotham, and Jotham the father of Ahaz, and Ahaz the father of Hezekiah
1.10 Hezekiah the father of Manasseh, and Manasseh the father of Amos,[c] and Amos[c] the father of Josiah
1.11 Josiah the father of Jechoniah
1.12 Jechoniah was the father of Shealtiel,[d] and Shealtiel[d] the father of Zerubbabel
1.13 Zerubbabel the father of Abiud, and Abiud the father of Eliakim, and Eliakim the father of Azor
1.14 Azor the father of Zadok, and Zadok the father of Achim, and Achim the father of Eliud
1.15 Eliud the father of Eleazar, and Eleazar the father of Matthan, and Matthan the father of Jacob
1.16 Jacob the father of Joseph

FATHER, WITHOUT
1. *without father:* ἀπάτωρ APATŌR*
Heb 7. 3 He is without father or mother

FATHER-IN-LAW
1. *father-in-law:* πενθερός PENTHEROS*
Jn 18.13 Annas . . was the father-in-law of Caiaphas

FATHERS, OF ONE'S
1. *paternal:* πατρικός PATRIKOS*
Gal 1.14 zealous . . for the traditions of my fathers
2. *of one's father:* πατρῷος PATRŌOS*
Acts 22. 3 "strict manner of the law of our fathers
24.14 "I worship the God of our fathers
28.17 "nothing against . . the customs of our fathers

FATHOM
1. *fathom* (6 feet): ὀργυιά ORGUIA*
Acts 27.28 sounded and found twenty fathoms; . . sounded again and found fifteen fathoms

FATTED
1. *fattened:* σιτευτός SITEUTOS*
Lk 15.23 " 'bring the fatted calf and kill it
15.27 " 'your father has killed the fatted calf
15.30 " 'you killed for him the fatted calf!

FATTEN
1. *feed, nourish:* τρέφω TREPHŌ
Jas 5. 5 you have fattened your hearts

FAULT, FIND
1. *blame, censure:* μέμφομαι MEMPHOMAI*
Rom 9.19 "Why does he still find fault?
Heb 8. 8 For he finds fault with them
2. *find fault with:* μωμάομαι MŌMAOMAI
2 Cor 6. 3 no fault may be found with our ministry

FAULT, TELL S. HIS
1. *expose, test, refute:* ἐλέγχω ELEGCHŌ
Mt 18.15 "go and tell him his fault

FAULTLESS
1. *blameless:* ἄμεμπτος AMEMPTOS
Heb 8. 7 if that first covenant had been faultless

FAVOR
1. *grace, favor, gratitude:* χάρις CHARIS
Lk 1.30 "for you have found favor with God
2.40 and the favor of God was upon him
2.52 increased . . in favor with God and man
Acts 2.47 having favor with all the people
7.10 "gave him favor . . before Pharaoh
7.46 "who found favor in the sight of God
24.27 desiring to do the Jews a favor
25. 3 asking as a favor to have the man sent
25. 9 Festus, wishing to do the Jews a favor
2 Cor [1.15 that you might have a double *favor*‡
8. 4 begging us earnestly for the favor
2. *prejudgment:* πρόκριμα PROKRIMA*
1 Tim 5.21 keep these rules without favor

FAVOR OF, IN
1. *over, for the sake of:* ὑπέρ (+gen.) HYPER
1 Cor 4. 6 none . . puffed up in favor of one

FAVOR OF, SEEK THE
1. *persuade:* πείθω PEITHŌ
Gal 1.10 Am I . . seeking the favor of men, or of God?

FAVORED IN, BE LESS
1. *be inferior to, be defeated:* ἡττάομαι HĒTTAOMAI
2 Cor 12.13 For in what were you less favored?

FAVORED ONE
1. *bestow favor:* χαριτόω (subst. perf. pass. part.) CHARITOŌ
Lk 1.28 "O favored one, the Lord is with you![c]

FEAR
FEAR, HAVE
1. *terrify:* φοβέω (pass.) PHOBEŌ
[a]+φόβον C.3
Mt 1.20 "do not fear to take Mary your wife
10.26 "So have no fear of them
10.28 "do not fear those who kill the body . . ; rather fear him who can destroy both
10.31 "Fear not, therefore; you are of more value
14. 5 he feared the people
14.27 "Take heart, it is I; have no fear
17. 7 "Rise, and have no fear
21.46 they feared the multitudes
Mk 5.33 woman . . came in fear and trembling
5.36 "Do not fear, only believe
6.20 Herod feared John
6.50 "Take heart, it is I; have no fear
11.18 for they feared him
12.12 they tried to arrest him, but feared
Lk 1.50 "his mercy is on those who fear him
8.50 "Do not fear; only believe
12. 4 "do not fear those who kill the body
12. 5 "I will warn you whom to fear: fear him who . . has power . . ; yes, I tell you, fear him!
12. 7 "Fear not; you are of more value
12.32 "Fear not, little flock
18. 2 "a judge who neither feared God
18. 4 " 'Though I neither fear God
20.19 but they feared the people
22. 2 for they feared the people
23.40 "Do you not fear God?
Jn 9.22 because they feared the Jews
12.15 "Fear not, daughter of Zion
Acts 10. 2 a devout man who feared God
10.35 "one who fears him and does what is right
13.16 "Men of Israel, and you that fear God
13.26 "those among you that fear God
27.17 fearing that they should run on the Syrtis
27.29 fearing that we might run on the rocks
Rom 13. 3 Would you have no fear of him?
2 Cor 12.20 I fear that perhaps I may come
Gal 2.12 fearing the circumcision party
Col 3.22 in singleness of heart, fearing the Lord
Heb 4. 1 let us fear lest any of you be judged
1 Pet 2.17 Honor all men. . . Fear God

1 Pet 3.14 ᵃHave no fear of them, nor be troubled
1 Jn 4.18 he who fears is not perfected in love
Rev 1.17 "Fear not, I am the first and the last
2.10 " 'Do not fear what you are about to suffer
11.18 "those who fear thy name, . . small and great
14. 7 "Fear God and give him glory
15. 4 "Who shall not fear and glorify thy name?
19. 5 "you who fear him, small and great

2. *fear:* φόβος PHOBOS
Mt 14.26 "they cried out for fear
28. 4 for fear of him the guards trembled
28. 8 they departed . . with fear and great joy
Lk 1.12 fear fell upon him
1.65 fear came on all their neighbors
2. 9 and they were filled with fear
7.16 Fear seized them all
8.37 they were seized with great fear
21.26 "men fainting with fear
Jn 7.13 for fear of the Jews no one spoke openly
19.38 Joseph of A. . . for fear of the Jews
20.19 doors being shut . . for fear of the Jews
Acts 2.43 fear came upon every soul
5. 5 great fear came upon all who heard
5.11 great fear came upon the whole church
9.31 walking in the fear of the Lord
19.17 fear fell upon them all
Rom 3.18 "There is no fear of God before their eyes
8.15 the spirit of slavery to fall back into fear
1 Cor 2. 3 in much fear and trembling
2 Cor 5.11 knowing the fear of the Lord
7. 1 make holiness perfect in the fear of God
7. 5 fighting without and fear within
7.15 the fear . . with which you received him
Eph 6. 5 be obedient . . with fear and trembling
Phil 2.12 work out your own salvation with fear
1 Tim 5.20 so that the rest may stand in fear
Heb 2.15 through fear of death . . subject to . . bondage
1 Pet 1.17 conduct yourselves with fear
3.14 Have no fear of them, nor be troubled
1 Jn 4.18 There is no fear in love, but perfect love casts out fear. For fear has to do with punishment
Jude .23 on some have mercy with fear
Rev 11.11 great fear fell on those who saw
18.10 stand far off, in fear of her torment
18.15 stand far off, in fear of her torment

IDIOMATICALLY
a. Heb 12.21 Moses said, "I tremble with fear Μωϋσῆς εἶπεν· ἔκφοβός εἰμι καὶ ἔντρομος [EKPHOBOS]

CONTEXTUALLY
Acts 16.29 trembling with f. he fell down before Paul
2 Cor 12.21 I fear that when I come again

FEAR, BE FILLED WITH
1. *terrify:* φοβέω (pass.) PHOBEŌ
ᵃφοβεῖσθαι φόβον μέγαν A.6.a.6
Lk 2. 9 ᵃand they were filled with fear

FEAR, GODLY
1. *discretion, reverence:* εὐλάβεια EULABEIA
Heb 5. 7 he was heard for his godly fear

FEAR OF, FOR
1. *because of:* διά (+acc.) DIA
Jn **12.**42

FEAR THAT, FOR
1. *not:* μή MĒ
1 Th 3. 5 for fear that . . the tempter had tempted

FEAR, WITHOUT
1. *without fear:* ἀφόβως APHOBŌS
Lk 1.74 "that we . . might serve him without fear
Phil 1.14 bold to speak the word of God without fear

FEARFUL
1. *great:* μέγας MEGAS
Rev 16.21 cursed God . . , so fearful was that plague
2. *fearful, terrible:* φοβερός PHOBEROS
Heb 10.27 a fearful prospect of judgment
10.31 a fearful thing to fall into the hands

FEAST (*See also* LOVE FEAST)
1. *meal, dinner:* δεῖπνον DEIPNON
Mt 23. 6 "they love the place of honor at feasts
Mk 12.39 "the places of honor at feasts
Lk 20.46 "the places of honor at feasts
2. *reception, banquet:* δοχή DOCHĒ*
Lk 5.29 Levi made him a great feast
14.13 "when you give a feast, invite the poor
3. *gladden:* εὐφραίνω (pass.) EUPHRAINŌ
Lk 16.19 "a rich man . . who feasted sumptuously
4. *feast, festival:* ἑορτή HEORTĒ
Mt 26. 5 they said, "Not during the feast
27.15 at the feast the governor was accustomed
Mk 14. 2 they said, "Not during the feast
15. 6 at the feast he used to release . . one
Lk 2.41 every year at the feast of the Passover
2.43(42) when the feast was ended
22. 1 feast of Unleavened Bread drew near
Jn 2.23 he was in Jerusalem at the Passover feast
4.45 all . . he had done in Jerusalem at the feast, for they too had gone to the feast
5. 1 After this there was a feast of the Jews
6. 4 the Passover, the feast of the Jews
7. 8 "Go to the feast yourselves; I am not[o] going up to this feast
7.10 his brothers had gone up to the feast
7.11 Jews were looking for him at the feast
7.14 the middle of the feast Jesus went up
7.37 On the last day of the feast
11.56 "That he will not come to the feast?
12.12 a great crowd who had come to the feast
12.20 those who went up to worship at the feast
13. 1 before the feast of the Passover
13.29 "Buy what we need for the feast

CONTEXTUALLY
Mk 14. 1 the feast of Unleavened Bread

FEAST, MARRIAGE
1. *wedding, wedding celebration:* γάμος GAMOS
Mt 22. 2 "a king who gave a marriage feast
22. 3 "who were invited to the marriage feast
22. 4 " 'come to the marriage feast
22. 9 " 'invite to the marriage feast as many
25.10 "went in with him to the marriage feast
Lk 12.36 "to come home from the marriage feast
14. 8 "When . . invited . . to a marriage feast

FEAST OF TABERNACLES
1. *setting up of tents:* σκηνοπηγία SKĒNOPĒGIA*
Jn 7. 2 Jews' feast of Tabernacles was at hand

FEAST OF THE DEDICATION
1. *feast of consecration:* ἐγκαίνια EGKAINIA*
Jn 10.22 It was the feast of the Dedication

FEAST, STEWARD OF THE
1. *headwaiter:* ἀρχιτρίκλινος ARCHITRIKLINOS*
Jn 2. 8 "take it to the steward of the feast
2. 9 the steward of the feast tasted the water
2. 9 s. of the feast called the bridegroom

FEED
1. *feed, tend:* βόσκω BOSKŌ
Mt 8.30 a herd of many swine was feeding
Mk 5.11 a great herd of swine was feeding
Lk 8.32 a large herd of swine was feeding
15.15 "sent him into his fields to feed swine
Jn 21.15 "Feed my lambs
21.17 "Feed my sheep
2. *feed, fatten:* χορτάζω CHORTAZŌ
Mt 15.33 "bread enough . . to feed so great a crowd?
Mk 7.27 "Let the children first be fed
8. 4 "How can one feed these men?
Lk 15.16 "he would gladly have fed on[u] the pods‡
16.21 "fed with what fell from the rich man's table
3. *water, give to drink:* ποτίζω POTIZŌ
1 Cor 3. 2 I fed you with milk, not solid food
4. *give food by hand:* ψωμίζω PSŌMIZŌ
Rom 12.20 "if your enemy is hungry, feed him
5. *feed, nourish:* τρέφω TREPHŌ

Mt 6.26 "yet your heavenly Father feeds them
25.37 " 'Lord, when did we . . feed thee?
Lk 12.24 "yet God feeds them

FEEL (*See also* GRIEF, FEEL; SATISFACTION ONE FEELS; SURE, FEEL)
1. *know, understand:* γινώσκω GINŌSKŌ
Mk 5.29 she felt in her body that she was healed
2. *think, set one's mind on:* φρονέω PHRONEŌ
Phil 1. 7 It is right for me to feel thus
IDIOMATICALLY
a. 2 Cor 1.9 we felt that we had received the sentence αὐτοὶ ἐν ἑαυτοῖς τὸ ἀπόκριμα . . ἐσχήκαμεν [HEAUTOU]
b. 2 Cor 11.2 I feel a divine jealousy for you ζηλῶ γὰρ ὑμᾶς θεοῦ ζήλῳ [ZĒLOŌ]
c. 1 Th 3.9 for all the joy which we feel ἐπὶ πάσῃ τῇ χαρᾷ ᾗ χαίρομεν [CHAIRŌ]

FEEL AFTER
1. *grope after, feel:* ψηλαφάω PSĒLAPHAŌ
Acts 17.27 "that they might feel after him

FELIX: Φῆλιξ 'fēliks
Acts 23.24 "bring him safely to Felix the governor
23.26 "to his Excellency the governor Felix
24. 2(3) "by your provision, most excellent Felix
24.22 Felix, having . . knowledge of the Way
24.24 Felix came with his wife Drusilla
24.25 Felix was alarmed and said, "Go away
24.27 Felix was succeeded by Porcius Festus; and . . Felix left Paul in prison
25.14 "There is a man left prisoner by Felix

FELL FROM THE SKY, SACRED STONE THAT
1. *fallen from heaven:* διοπετής (subst. neut.) DIOPETĒS* [D.1]
Acts 19.35 "the sacred stone that fell from the sky[s]

FELLOW (*See also* PESTILENT FELLOW)
1. *man, husband:* ἀνήρ ANĒR
Acts 17. 5 some wicked fellows of the rabble
2. *citizen, fellow citizen:* πολίτης POLITĒS
Heb 8.11 "they shall not teach every one his fellow
CONTEXTUALLY
Mt 26.61 "This fellow said, 'I am able to destroy
Acts 22.22 "Away with such a f. from the earth!

FELLOW CITIZEN
1. *fellow citizen:* συμπολίτης SYMPOLITĒS*
Eph 2.19 you are fellow citizens with the saints

FELLOW DISCIPLE
1. *fellow disciple:* συμμαθητής SYMMATHĒTĒS*
Jn 11.16 Thomas . . said to his fellow disciples

FELLOW ELDER
1. *fellow elder:* συμπρεσβύτερος SYMPRESBYTEROS*
1 Pet 5. 1 I exhort the elders . . as a fellow elder

FELLOW HEIR
1. *inheriting with:* συγκληρονόμος (subst.) SYGKLĒRONOMOS
Rom 8.17 fellow heirs with Christ
Eph 3. 6 how the Gentiles are fellow heirs

FELLOW JEWS
IDIOMATICALLY
a. Rom 11.14 in order to make my fellow Jews jealous εἴ πως παραζηλώσω μου τὴν σάρκα [SARX]

FELLOW PRISONER
1. *fellow prisoner:* συναιχμάλωτος SYNAICHMALŌTOS*
Rom 16. 7 my kinsmen and my fellow prisoners
Col 4.10 Aristarchus my fellow p. greets you
Phm .23 Epaphras, my fellow p. in Christ Jesus

FELLOW SERVANT
1. *fellow slave:* σύνδουλος SYNDOULOS*
Mt 18.28 "came upon one of his fellow servants
18.29 "So his fellow servant fell down
18.31 "fellow servants saw what had taken place
18.33 " 'had mercy on your fellow servant
24.49 "begins to beat his fellow servants
Col 1. 7 Epaphras our beloved fellow servant
4. 7 faithful minister and fellow servant
Rev 6.11 the number of their fellow servants
Rev 19.10 "I am a fellow servant with you
22. 9 "I am a fellow servant with you

FELLOW SOLDIER
1. *fellow soldier:* συστρατιώτης SYSTRATIŌTĒS*
Phil 2.25 fellow worker and fellow soldier
Phm . 2 Archippus our fellow soldier

FELLOW WORKER
1. *work together with:* συνεργέω (subst. part.) SYNERGEŌ
1 Cor 16.16 be subject . . to every fellow worker
2. *helper, fellow worker:* συνεργός SYNERGOS
Rom 16. 3 Prisca and Aquila, my fellow workers
16. 9 Urbanus, our fellow worker in Christ
16.21 Timothy, my fellow worker
1 Cor 3. 9 For we are God's fellow workers
2 Cor 8.23 Titus . . is my . . fellow worker
Phil 2.25 Epaphroditus my . . fellow worker
4. 3 Clement and the rest of my fellow workers
Col 4.11 my fellow workers for the kingdom
Phm . 1 To Philemon our beloved fellow worker
.24 Demas, and Luke, my fellow workers
3 Jn . 8 fellow workers in the truth

FELLOWSHIP
1. *fellowship, sharing:* κοινωνία KOINŌNIA
Acts 2.42 the apostles' teaching and fellowship
1 Cor 1. 9 you were called into the fellowship
2 Cor 6.14 what fellowship has light with darkness?
13.14(13) fellowship of[n] the Holy Spirit†
Gal 2. 9 the right hand of fellowship
1 Jn 1. 3 that you may have fellowship with us; and our fellowship is with the Father
1. 6 If we say we have fellowship with him
1. 7 we have fellowship with one another

FEMALE
1. *female:* θῆλυς THĒLYS
Mt 19. 4 "made them male and female
Mk 10. 6 " 'God made them male and female
Gal 3.28 there is neither male nor female

FERVENT, BE
1. *boil, seethe:* ζέω ZEŌ
Acts 18.25 being fervent in spirit, he spoke

FERVENTLY
IDIOMATICALLY
a. Jas 5.17 Elijah . . prayed fervently Ἠλίας . . προσευχῇ προσηύξατο [PROSEUCHĒ; C.3]

FESTAL GATHERING
1. *festal assembly:* πανήγυρις PANĒGYRIS*
Heb 12.22 innumerable angels in festal gathering[†]

FESTIVAL
1. *feast, festival:* ἑορτή HEORTĒ
Lk [23.17 *obliged to release one man . . at the f.*‡
Col 2.16 a festival or a new moon or a sabbath

FESTIVAL, CELEBRATE THE
1. *celebrate a festival:* ἑορτάζω HEORTAZŌ*
1 Cor 5. 8 Let us, therefore, celebrate the festival

FESTUS, PORCIUS: Πόρκιος Φῆστος 'pôrshəs 'festəs
Acts 24.27 Felix was succeeded by Porcius Festus
25. 1 when Festus had come into his province
25. 4 Festus replied that Paul was . . at Caesarea
25. 9 Festus, wishing to do the Jews a favor
25.12 Festus . . answered, "You have appealed
25.13 Agrippa . . arrived . . to welcome Festus
25.14 Festus laid Paul's case before the king
25.22 Agrippa said to Festus, "I should
25.23 by command of Festus Paul was brought
25.24 Festus said, "King Agrippa and all
26.24 Festus said . . "Paul, you are mad
26.25 "I am not mad, most excellent Festus
26.32 Agrippa said to Festus, "This man

FETTER
1. *bind, tie:* δέω DEŌ
2 Tim 2. 9 But the word of God is not fettered
2. *bond:* δεσμός DESMOS
Acts 16.26 every one's fetters were unfastened
Col 4.18 Remember my fetters

2 Tim 2. 9 I am suffering and wearing fetters
3. *shackle:* πέδη PEDĒ*
Mk 5. 4 he had often been bound with fetters . . and the fetters he broke in pieces
Lk 8.29 (he was . . bound with chains and fetters

FEVER
1. *burning heat, fever:* πυρετός PYRETOS*
Mt 8.15 he touched her hand, and the fever left
Mk 1.31 he . . lifted her up, and the fever left
Lk 4.38 Simon's mother-in-law . . with a high fever
4.39 he . . rebuked the fever, and it left her
Jn 4.52 "at the seventh hour the fever left him
Acts 28. 8 Publius lay sick with fever and dysentery

FEVER, WITH A
1. *be feverish:* πυρέσσω (part.) PYRESSŌ*
Mt 8.14 his mother-in-law lying sick with a f.
Mk 1.30 Simon's mother-in-law lay sick with a f.

FEW
1. *few, little:* ὀλίγος OLIGOS
Mt 7.14 "those who find it are few
9.37 "but the laborers are few
15.34 "Seven, and a few small fish
22.14 "many are called, but few are chosen
Mk 6. 5 laid his hands upon a few sick people
8. 7 they had a few small fish
Lk 10. 2 "but the laborers are few
[10.42 "*few things are* needful‡
13.23 "Lord, will those who are saved be few?
Acts 17. 4 Greeks and not a few of the leading women
17.12 a few Greek women of high standing
1 Pet 3.20 the ark, in which a few . . were saved
Rev 2.14 " 'I have a few things against you
3. 4 " 'you have still a few names in Sardis

FEW, A
1. *many, great:* πολύς (neg. pl.) POLYS
Jn 2.12 there they stayed for a few days

FIDELITY
1. *trust, faith:* πίστις PISTIS
Tit 2.10 to show entire and true fidelity

FIELD
1. *field:* ἀγρός AGROS
Mt 6.28 "Consider the lilies of the field
6.30 "if God so clothes the grass of the field
13.24 "a man who sowed good seed in his field
13.27 " 'did you not sow good seed in your field?
13.31 "grain of mustard seed . . sowed in his field
13.36 "the parable of the weeds of the field
13.38 "the field is the world
13.44 "kingdom . . is like treasure hidden in a field
13.44 "sells all that he has and buys that field
24.18 "let him who is in the field not turn back
24.40 "Then two men will be in the field
27. 7 bought with them the potter's field
27. 8 that field has been called the Field of Blood
27.10 "they gave them for the potter's field
Mk 11. 8 leafy branches . . cut from the fields
13.16 "let him who is in the field not turn back
Lk 12.28 "grass which is alive in the field today
14.18 "first said to him, 'I have bought a field
15.15 "sent him into his fields to feed swine
15.25 "his elder son was in the field
17. 7 "when he has come in from the field
17.31 "let him who is in the field not turn back
[17.36 "*Two men will be in the field*‡
Acts 4.37 sold a field which belonged to him
2. *country, place:* χώρα CHŌRA
Jn 4.35 "see how the fields are already white
Jas 5. 4 the laborers who mowed your fields
3. *place, district:* χωρίον CHŌRION
Jn 4. 5 the field that Jacob gave to . . Joseph
Acts 1.18 "(man bought a field with the reward
1.19 "(the field was called in their language Akeldama, that is, Field of Blood
4. *field:* γεώργιον GEŌRGION*
1 Cor 3. 9 you are God's field, God's building
5. *province, rule:* κανών KANŌN
2 Cor 10.15 that . . our field . . may be . . enlarged
10.16 work already done in another's field

FIELD, BE OUT IN THE
1. *live out of doors:* ἀγραυλέω AGRAULEŌ*
Lk 2. 8 there were shepherds out in the field

FIERCE
1. *savage:* ἀνήμερος ANĒMEROS*
2 Tim 3. 3 profligates, fierce, haters of good
2. *heavy, severe:* βαρύς BARYS
Acts 20.29 "after my departure fierce wolves will come
3. *difficult, dangerous:* χαλεπός CHALEPOS
Mt 8.28 so fierce that no one could pass that way
4. *great:* μέγας MEGAS
Rev 16. 9 men were scorched by the fierce heat

FIERY ORDEAL
1. *burning, proving by fire:* πύρωσις PYRŌSIS
1 Pet 4.12 do not be surprised at the fiery ordeal

FIFTEEN
1. *fifteen:* δεκαπέντε DEKAPENTE
Acts 27.28 they sounded . . and found fifteen fathoms
Gal 1.18 I . . remained with him fifteen days

FIFTEENTH
1. *fifteenth:* πεντεκαιδέκατος PENTEKAIDEKATOS*
Lk 3. 1 fifteenth year of the reign of Tiberius

FIFTH
1. *five, fifth:* ε′ E
Acts [19. 9 argued . . *from the fifth hour to the tenth*‡
2. *fifth:* πέμπτος PEMPTOS*
Rev 6. 9 he opened the fifth seal
9. 1 the fifth angel blew his trumpet
16.10 The fifth angel poured his bowl
21.20 the fifth onyx

FIFTY
1. *five myriads, fifty thousand:* μυριάδας πέντε PENTE [A.3.c.2]
Acts 19.19 it came to fifty thousand pieces of silver
2. *fifty:* πεντήκοντα PENTĒKONTA
[a]κατὰ πεντήκοντα
Mk 6.40 [a]they sat down in groups . . by fifties
Lk 7.41 "two debtors; one owed . . fifty ⟨denarii⟩
9.14 "sit down in companies, about fifty each
16. 6 " 'sit down quickly and write fifty
Jn 8.57 "You are not yet fifty years old
Acts 13.19(20) "for about four hundred and fifty years

FIFTY-THREE
1. *fifty-three:* πεντήκοντα τρεῖς PENTĒKONTA; TREIS [A.3.c]
Jn 21.11 a hundred and fifty-three of them

FIG
1. *fig:* σῦκον SYKON*
Mt 7.16 "Are . . figs ⟨gathered⟩ from thistles?
Mk 11.13 for it was not the season for figs
Lk 6.44 "figs are not gathered from thorns
Jas 3.12 Can . . a grapevine ⟨yield⟩ figs?

FIG TREE
1. *fig tree:* συκῆ SYKĒ*
Mt 21.19 seeing a fig tree by the wayside
21.19 And the fig tree withered at once
21.20 "How did the fig tree wither at once?
21.21 "do what has been done to the fig tree
24.32 "From the fig tree learn its lesson
Mk 11.13 seeing in the distance a fig tree in leaf
11.20 they saw the fig tree withered away
11.21 "The fig tree which you cursed has withered
13.28 "From the fig tree learn its lesson
Lk 13. 6 "A man had a fig tree planted
13. 7 " 'I have come seeking fruit on this fig t.
21.29 "Look at the fig tree, and all the trees
Jn 1.48 "when you were under the fig tree
1.50 "I saw you under the fig tree
Jas 3.12 Can a fig tree, my brethren, yield olives?
Rev 6.13 as the fig tree sheds its winter fruit

FIGHT
1. *struggle:* ἀγών AGŌN
1 Tim 6.12 Fight the good fight of the faith
2 Tim 4. 7 I have fought the good fight
2. *fight, contend:* ἀγωνίζομαι AGŌNIZOMAI
Jn 18.36 "my servants would fight
1 Tim 6.12 Fight the good fight of the faith
2 Tim 4. 7 I have fought the good fight
3. *quarrel, fight:* μάχομαι MACHOMAI
Jas 4. 2 so you fight and wage war
4. *fight, make war:* πολεμέω POLEMEŌ
Rev 12. 7 Michael . . fighting against the dragon; and the dragon and his angels fought
13. 4 "who can fight against ⟨the beast⟩?

FIGHT WITH BEASTS
1. *fight with wild beasts:* θηριομαχέω THĒRIOMACHEŌ*
1 Cor 15.32 if . . I fought with beasts at Ephesus

FIGHTING
1. *battle, fighting:* μάχη MACHĒ
[a]pl.
2 Cor 7. 5 [a]fighting without and fear within
Jas 4. 1 what causes fightings among you?

FIGURATIVELY SPEAKING
1. *in a parable:* ἐν παραβολῇ PARABOLĒ [B.1.a.2]
Heb 11.19 figuratively speaking, he did receive him

FIGURE
1. *figure, proverb:* παροιμία PAROIMIA
Jn 10. 6 This figure Jesus used with them
16.25 "I have said this to you in figures; . . I shall no longer speak . . in figures
16.29 "you are speaking plainly, not in any figure!
2. *pattern, image:* τύπος TYPOS
Acts 7.43 " 'figures which you made to worship

FIGUREHEAD
IDIOMATICALLY
a. Acts 28.11 with the Twin Brothers as figurehead παρασήμῳ Διοσκούροις [PARASĒMOS*]

FILL
1. *feed, fatten:* χορτάζω CHORTAZŌ
[a]A.6.c.2
Jn 6.26 [a]"because you ate your fill of the loaves
Jas 2.16 "Go in peace, be warmed and filled
2. *fill quite full:* ἐμπίμπλημι EMPIMPLĒMI
Lk 1.53 "he has filled the hungry with good things
3. *fill full:* γεμίζω GEMIZŌ*
Mk 4.37 the boat was already filling
15.36 filling a sponge full of vinegar
Lk 14.23 " 'that my house may be filled
[15.16 "gladly have *filled his belly with* . . pods‡
Jn 2. 7 "Fill the jars with water." And they filled them up to the brim
6.13 they . . filled twelve baskets with fragments
Rev 8. 5 the angel took the censer and filled it
15. 8 the temple was filled with smoke
4. *fill full:* μεστόω MESTOŌ*
Acts 2.13 "They are filled with new wine
5. *fill, satisfy:* πίμπλημι PIMPLĒMI
Mt 22.10 " 'wedding hall was filled with guests
27.48 took a sponge, filled it with vinegar
Lk 1.15 "he will be filled with the Holy Spirit
1.41 Elizabeth . . filled with the Holy Spirit
1.67 Zechariah was filled with the Holy Spirit
4.28 all . . were filled with wrath
5. 7 they came and filled both the boats
5.26 they glorified God and were filled with awe
6.11 they were filled with fury
Acts 2. 4 they were all filled with the Holy Spirit
3.10 they were filled with wonder
4. 8 Peter, filled with the Holy Spirit
4.31 they were all filled with the Holy Spirit
5.17 high priest rose up . . filled with jealousy
9.17 "that you . . be filled with the Holy Spirit
13. 9 Saul . . , filled with the Holy Spirit
13.45 they were filled with jealousy
19.29 the city was filled with the confusion
6. *fill full, complete:* πληρόω PLĒROŌ
Lk 3. 5 "Every valley shall be filled
Jn 12. 3 the house was filled with the fragrance
16. 6 "sorrow has filled your hearts
Acts 2. 2 a mighty wind, and it filled all the house
5. 3 "why has Satan filled your heart to lie
5.28 "yet here you have filled Jerusalem
13.52 the disciples were filled with joy
Rom 1.29 filled with all manner of wickedness
15.13 the God of hope fill you with all joy
15.14 you . . are . . filled with all knowledge
2 Cor 7. 4 I am filled with comfort
Eph 1.23 the fulness of him who fills all in all
3.19 that you . . be filled with all the fulness
4.10 (that he might fill all things
5.18 be filled with the Spirit
Phil 1.11 filled with the fruits of righteousness
4.18 I am filled, having received . . the gifts
Col 1. 9 that you may be filled with the knowledge
2 Tim 1. 4 that I may be filled with joy
IDIOMATICALLY
a. Mt 17.6 they . . were filled with awe ἐφοβήθησαν σφόδρα [SPHODRA]
Also Mt **27.54**
b. Mk 4.41 they were filled with awe ἐφοβήθησαν φόβον μέγαν [MEGAS]
c. Lk 2.9 they were filled with fear ἐφοβήθησαν φόβον μέγαν [MEGAS]

FILL, EAT ONE'S
1. *fill quite full:* ἐμπίμπλημι (pass.) EMPIMPLĒMI
Jn 6.12 when they had eaten their fill

FILL UP
1. *fill full, complete:* πληρόω PLĒROŌ
Mt 23.32 "Fill up, then, the measure of your fathers

FILL UP THE MEASURE OF
1. *fill up:* ἀναπληρόω ANAPLĒROŌ
1 Th 2.16 to fill up the measure of their sins

FILL WITH WATER
1. *fill completely:* συμπληρόω (pass.) SYMPLĒROŌ
Lk 8.23 they were filling with water

FILLED
1. *fill:* κορέννυμι (perf. pass. part.) KORENNYMI
1 Cor 4. 8 Already you are filled!
2. *fill full, complete:* πληρόω (pass. part.) PLĒROŌ
Lk 2.40 child . . became strong, filled with wisdom

FILTHINESS
1. *indecency:* αἰσχρότης AISCHROTĒS*
Eph 5. 4 Let there be no filthiness, nor silly talk
2. *dirt, filth:* ῥυπαρία RHYPARIA*
Jas 1.21 put away all filthiness and rank growth

FILTHY
1. *dirty:* ῥυπαρός RHYPAROS
Rev 22.11 "Let . . the filthy still be filthy

FILTHY, BE
1. *defile, pollute:* ῥυπαίνω (pass.) RHYPAINŌ*
Rev 22.11 "Let . . the filthy still be filthy

FINAL
1. *end, limit:* πέρας (pred.) PERAS
Heb 6.16 in all their disputes an oath is final

FINALLY
1. *last, extreme:* ἔσχατος (neut.) ESCHATOS
Mk 12. 6 "beloved son; finally he sent him to them
2. *remaining, left:* λοιπός (neut.) LOIPOS
2 Cor 13.11 Finally, brethren, farewell
Eph 6.10 Finally, be strong in the Lord
Phil 3. 1 Finally, my brethren, rejoice in the Lord
4. 8 Finally, brethren, whatever is true
1 Th 4. 1 Finally, brethren, we beseech and exhort
2 Th 3. 1 Finally, brethren, pray for us
3. *end, goal:* τέλος TELOS
[a]τὸ τέλος (acc.)
1 Pet 3. 8 [a]Finally, all of you, have unity of spirit

FIND (*See also* FAULT, FIND)
1. *find out:* ἀνευρίσκω ANEURISKŌ
Lk 2.16 they . . found Mary and Joseph, and the babe
2. *find:* εὑρίσκω HEURISKŌ
Mt 1.18 she was found to be with child
2. 8 "when you have found him bring me word
7. 7 "seek, and you will find
7. 8 "he who seeks finds
7.14 "those who find it are few
8.10 not even[s] in Israel have I found such faith
10.39 "He who finds his life will lose it, and he who loses his life for my sake will find it
11.29 "you will find rest for your souls
12.43 "he passes . . seeking rest, but he finds none
12.44 "when he comes he finds it empty
13.44 "treasure . . which a man found
13.46 "on finding one pearl of great value
16.25 "whoever loses his life . . will find it
17.27 "you will find a shekel; take that
18.13 "truly, I say to you, he rejoices over it
20. 6 "he went out and found others standing
21. 2 "immediately you will find an ass tied
21.19 he . . found nothing on it but leaves
22. 9 " 'invite to the . . feast as many as you find
22.10 "gathered all whom they found
24.46 "whom his master . . will find so doing
26.40 he came . . and found them sleeping
26.43 again he came and found them sleeping
26.60 ⟨sought false testimony⟩ but . . found none
Mk 1.37 they found him and said to him
7.30 she . . found the child lying in bed
11. 2 "immediately . . you will find a colt tied
11. 4 they . . found a colt tied at the door
11.13 he went to see if he could find anything . . When he came to it, he found . . leaves
13.36 "lest he come suddenly and find you
14.16 the disciples . . found it as he had told
14.37 he came and found them sleeping
14.40 again he came and found them sleeping
14.55 sought testimony . . but they found none
Lk 1.30 "Mary, . . you have found favor with God
2.12 "you will f. a babe wrapped in swaddling
2.45 when they did not find him, they returned
2.46 they found him in the temple
4.17 He . . found the place where it was written
5.19 finding no way to bring him in
6. 7 that they might find an accusation
7. 9 "not even in Israel have I found such faith
7.10 they found the slave well
8.35 they . . found the man . . sitting . . clothed
9.36 Jesus was found alone
11. 9 "seek, and you will find
11.10 "he who seeks finds
11.24 "finding none he says, 'I will return
11.25 "when he comes he finds it swept
12.37 "servants whom the master finds awake
12.38 "If he comes . . and finds them so
12.43 "whom his master . . will find so doing
13. 6 "he came seeking fruit on it and found none
13. 7 " 'seeking fruit . . and I find none
15. 4 "after the one which is lost, until he finds it
15. 5 "when he has found it
15. 6 " 'Rejoice . . for I have found my sheep
15. 8 "does ⟨she⟩ not . . seek . . until she finds it?
15. 9 "when she has found it, she calls
15. 9 " 'for I have found the coin which I had lost
15.24 " 'he was lost, and is found
15.32 " 'he was lost, and is found
17.18 "Was no one found to return?
18. 8 "will he find faith on earth?
19.30 "entering you will find a colt tied
19.32 those . . went away and found it
19.48 they did not find anything they could do
22.13 they . . found it as he had told them
22.45 he . . found them sleeping for sorrow
23. 2 "We found this man perverting our nation
23. 4 "I find no crime in this man
Lk 23.14 "I did not find this man guilty
23.22 "I have found in him no crime
24. 2 they found the stone rolled away
24. 3 they did not find the body[t]
24.23 "did not find his body
24.24 "found it just as the women had said
24.33 they found the eleven gathered together
Jn 1.41 He first found his brother Simon
1.41 "We have found the Messiah
1.43 he found Philip and said . . "Follow me
1.45 Philip found Nathanael, and said to him, "We have found him
2.14 In the temple he found those
5.14 Jesus found him in the temple
6.25 they found him on the other side
7.34 "seek me and you will not find me
7.35 "Where . . that we shall not find him?
7.36 " 'You will seek me and . . not find me
9.35 having found him he said, "Do you believe?
10. 9 "go in and out and find pasture
11.17 found . . Lazarus[x] . . already . . in the tomb
12.14 Jesus found a young ass
18.38 "I find no crime in him
19. 4 "know that I find no crime in him
19. 6 "Take him . . for I find no crime in him
21. 6 "Cast . . and you will find some
Acts 4.21 finding no way to punish them
5.10 they found her dead
5.22 they did not find them in the prison
5.23 "We found the prison securely locked . . but when we opened it we found no one
5.39 "You might even be found opposing God!
7.11 "our fathers could find no food
7.46 "who found favor in the sight of God and asked leave to find a habitation
8.40 Philip was found at Azotus
9. 2 if he found any belonging to the Way
9.33 There he found a man named Aeneas
10.27 he went in and found many persons
11.26 when he had found him, he brought him
12.19 sought for him and could not find him
13.22 " 'I have found in David the son of Jesse
17. 6 when they could not find them
17.23 "I found also an altar with this inscription
17.27 "in the hope that they might . . find him
18. 2 And he found a Jew named Aquila
19. 1 There he found some disciples
19.19 they . . found it came to fifty thousand
21. 2 having found a ship crossing to Phoenicia
23. 9 "We find nothing wrong in this man
23.29 "I found that he was accused
24. 5 "we have found this man a pestilent fellow
24.12 "they did not find me disputing
24.18 "they found me purified in the temple
24.20 "say what wrongdoing they found
27. 6 centurion found a ship of Alexandria
27.28 they sounded and found twenty fathoms; a little farther . . they . . found fifteen
28.14 There we found brethren
Rom 7.21 So I find it to be a law
10.20 "I have been found by those
1 Cor 4. 2 that they be found trustworthy
15.15 even found to be misrepresenting God
2 Cor 2.13 because I did not find my brother Titus
5. 3 so that . . we may not be found naked
9. 4 lest if some . . find that you are not ready
12.20 I may come and find you not what I wish, and . . you may find me not what you wish
Gal 2.17 if . . we ourselves were found to be sinners
Phil 2. 8 found in human form he humbled himself
3. 9 found in him, not having a righteousness
2 Tim 1.17 he searched for me eagerly and found me
1.18 the Lord grant him to find mercy
Heb 4.16 that we may receive mercy and find grace
11. 5 not found, because God had taken him
12.17 for he found no chance to repent
1 Pet 2.22 no guile was found on his lips

2 Pet 3.14 be zealous to be found by him without spot
2 Jn .4 I rejoiced .. to find some of your children
Rev 2.2 " 'tested those .. and found them to be false
3.2 " 'I have not found your works perfect
5.4 no one was found worthy to open the scroll
9.6 men will seek death and will not find it
14.5 in their mouth no lie was found
16.20 no mountains were to be found
18.14 "lost to thee, never to be found again!
18.21 "Babylon .. shall be found no more
18.22 "a craftsman .. shall be found in thee no more
18.24 "in her was found the blood of prophets
20.11 no place was found for them
20.15 if any one's name was not found written

3. *catch:* καταλαμβάνω (mid.) KATALAMBANŌ
Acts 25.25 "I found that he had done nothing

4. *receive, take:* λαμβάνω LAMBANŌ
Rom 7.8 sin, finding opportunity .., wrought in me
7.11 sin, finding opportunity .., deceived me

IDIOMATICALLY
a. Jude .3 I found it necessary to write ἀνάγκην ἔσχον γράψαι [ECHŌ]

CONTEXTUALLY
1 Cor 5.1 a kind that is not found .. among pagans
2 Cor 1.20 the promises of God f. their Yes in him
Eph 5.9 (fruit of light is found in all that is good

FIND A PLACE
1. *make room for, hold, go:* χωρέω CHŌREŌ
Jn 8.37 "because my word finds no place in you

FIND OUT
1. *learn to know, recognize:* ἐπιγινώσκω EPIGINŌSKŌ
Acts 22.24 to find out why they shouted thus
2. *examine well:* ἐξετάζω EXETAZŌ
Mt 10.11 "find out who is worthy in it
3. *know, understand:* γινώσκω GINŌSKŌ
Mk 6.38 when they had found out, they said, "Five
1 Cor 4.19 I will find out not the talk of these
2 Cor 13.6 hope you will find out .. we have not failed

FINE (*See also* FLOUR, FINE; LINEN, FINE)
1. *good, beautiful:* καλός KALOS
Mt 13.45 "like a merchant in search of fine pearls
2. *well, rightly:* καλῶς KALŌS [A.4.a]
Mk 7.9 "You have a fine way of rejecting
3. *bright, radiant:* λαμπρός LAMPROS
Jas 2.2 if a man .. in fine clothing comes
2.3 the one who wears the fine clothing

CONTEXTUALLY
1 Pet 3.3 Let not yours be .. wearing of fine clothing[o]

FINGER
1. *finger:* δάκτυλος DAKTYLOS*
Mt 23.4 "not move them with their finger
Mk 7.33 he put his fingers into his ears
Lk 11.20 "by the finger of God .. I cast out demons
11.46 "not touch .. with one of your fingers
16.24 " 'send Lazarus to dip the end of his finger
Jn 8.6 Jesus bent down and wrote with his finger[r]‡
8.8 once more he .. wrote with his finger[r]‡
20.25 "place my finger in the mark of the nails
20.27 "Put your finger here, and see my hands

FINISH (*See also* BREAKFAST, FINISHED)
1. *finish, complete:* διανύω DIANYŌ*
Acts 21.7 When we had finished the voyage
2. *accomplish:* ἐκτελέω EKTELEŌ*
Lk 14.29 "when he .. is not able to finish
14.30 " 'began .. and was not able to finish
3. *fill full, complete:* πληρόω PLĒROŌ
Acts 13.25 "as John was finishing his course
4. *finish, fulfill:* τελέω TELEŌ
Mt 7.28 when Jesus finished these sayings
11.1 when Jesus had finished instructing
13.53 when Jesus had finished these parables
19.1 when Jesus had finished these sayings
26.1 When Jesus had finished all these sayings
Jn 19.28 Jesus, knowing that all was now finished
19.30 he said, "It is finished
2 Tim 4.7 I have finished the race
Rev 11.7 when they have finished their testimony

FINISH ONE'S COURSE
1. *make perfect, complete:* τελειόω (pass.) TELEIOŌ
Lk 13.32 " 'the third day I finish my course

FINISH SPEAKING
1. *be silent, keep silent:* σιγάω (aor.) SIGAŌ
Acts 15.13 After they finished speaking, James replied

FINISHED, BE
1. *come to be, happen, be:* γίνομαι (aor.) GINOMAI
Heb 4.3 although his works were finished

FIRE
1. *light:* φῶς PHŌS
Mk 14.54 Peter .. was .. warming himself at the fire
2. *fire, flame:* πῦρ PYR
Mt 3.10 "cut down and thrown into the fire
3.11 "he will baptize you .. with fire
3.12 "he will burn with unquenchable fire
5.22 "shall be liable to the hell[k] of fire
7.19 "cut down and thrown into the fire
13.40 "weeds are gathered and burned with fire
13.42 "throw them into the furnace of fire
13.50 "throw them into the furnace of fire
17.15 "for often he falls into the fire
18.8 "than .. be thrown into the eternal fire
18.9 "than .. be thrown into the hell[b] of fire
25.41 " 'Depart from me .. into the eternal fire
Mk 9.22 "it has often cast him into the fire
9.43 "than .. go to hell,[m] to the unquenchable fire[n]
9.48 "where .. the fire is not quenched
Also Mk 9. [44‡, [46‡
9.49 "For every one will be salted with fire[o]
Lk 3.9 "cut down and thrown into the fire
3.16 "he will baptize you .. with fire
3.17 "he will burn with unquenchable fire
9.54 "to bid fire come down from heaven
12.49 "I came to cast fire upon the earth
17.29 "fire and sulphur rained from heaven
22.55 when they had kindled a fire
Jn 15.6 "thrown into the fire and burned
Acts 2.3 appeared to them tongues as of fire
2.19 " 'blood, and fire, and vapor of smoke
7.30 "an angel .. in a flame of fire in a bush
28.5 shook off the creature into the fire
1 Cor 3.13 it will be revealed with fire, and the fire will test what sort of work
3.15 saved, but only as through fire
2 Th 1.7(8) revealed from heaven .. in flaming fire
Heb 1.7 "Who makes .. his servants flames of fire
10.27 fury of fire which will consume
11.34 ⟨who⟩ quenched raging fire
12.18 a blazing fire, and darkness, and gloom
12.29 our God is a consuming fire
Jas 3.5 a forest is set ablaze by a small fire!
3.6 And the tongue is a fire
5.3 their rust .. will eat your flesh like fire†
1 Pet 1.7 gold which .. is tested by fire
2 Pet 3.7 heavens and earth .. stored up for fire
Jude .7 undergoing a punishment of eternal fire
.23 by snatching them out of the fire
Rev 1.14 his eyes were like a flame of fire
2.18 " 'who has eyes like a flame of fire
3.18 " 'buy from me gold refined by fire
4.5 before the throne .. seven torches of fire
8.5 filled it with fire from the altar
8.7 there followed hail and fire
8.8 a great mountain, burning with fire
9.17 fire and smoke and sulphur
9.18 by the fire and smoke and sulphur
10.1 his legs like pillars of fire
11.5 fire pours from their mouth
13.13 even making fire come down from heaven
14.10 "tormented with fire and sulphur
14.18 "the angel who has power over fire
15.2 a sea of glass mingled with fire
16.8 it was allowed to scorch men with fire

Rev 17.16 "devour her flesh and burn her up with fire
18. 8 "she shall be burned with fire
19.12 His eyes are like a flame of fire
19.20 thrown alive into the lake of fire
20. 9 but fire came down from heaven[n]
20.10 devil . . was thrown into the lake of fire
20.14 Death . . thrown into the lake of fire. This is the second death, the lake of fire
20.15 he was thrown into the lake of fire
21. 8 "lake that burns with fire and sulphur

3. *fire, burning heap:* πυρά PYRA*
Acts 28. 2 they kindled a fire and welcomed us all
28. 3 Paul . . put them on the fire

FIRE, CHARCOAL

1. *burning charcoal:* ἀνθρακιά ANTHRAKIA*
Jn 18.18 officers had made a charcoal fire
21. 9 a charcoal fire there, with fish lying on it

FIRE, SET ON

1. *set on fire, burn:* φλογίζω PHLOGIZŌ*
Jas 3. 6 the tongue is a fire . . setting on fire the cycle of nature,[b] and set on fire by hell[c]

FIRE, THE COLOR OF

1. *of fire, fiery:* πύρινος PYRINOS*
Rev 9.17 the riders wore breastplates the color of fire

FIRE, WITH

1. *heat, burn up:* καυσόω (pass. part.) KAUSOŌ*
2 Pet 3.10 the elements will be dissolved with fire
3.12 the elements will melt with fire!

FIRM

1. *steady, firm:* βέβαιος BEBAIOS
Heb [3. 6 if we hold fast . . *firm to the end*‡
3.14 hold our first confidence firm to the end
2. *strong, firm:* στερεός STEREOS
2 Tim 2.19 But God's firm foundation stands
1 Pet 5. 9 Resist him, firm in your faith

FIRM, HOLD

1. *hold against:* ἀντέχω (mid.) ANTECHŌ
Tit 1. 9 he must hold firm to the sure word

FIRM, STAND

1. *stand, set:* ἵστημι (perf.) HISTĒMI
2 Cor 1.24 for you stand firm in your faith

FIRMLY

1. *steadfast, firm:* ἑδραῖος HEDRAIOS [A.3.b.1]
1 Cor 7.37 whoever is firmly established in his heart

FIRMNESS

1. *steadfastness:* στερέωμα STEREŌMA*
Col 2. 5 the firmness of your faith in Christ

FIRST (*See also* COME, BE THE FIRST TO; SPEAK FIRST)

1. *origin, rule:* ἀρχή ARCHĒ
[a]ἀρχὴν λαβοῦσα
Jn 2.11 the first of his signs, Jesus did
6.64 Jesus knew from the first who those were
Heb 2. 3 [a]It was declared at first by the Lord
3.14 if only we hold our first confidence firm
5.12 the first principles of God's word
2. *one:* εἷς (attr.) HEIS
Rev 9.12 The first woe has passed
3. *earlier:* πρότερος (neut.) PROTEROS
2 Cor 1.15 I wanted to come to you first
Heb 7.27 sacrifices daily, first for his own sins
4. *first, foremost:* πρῶτος PRŌTOS
[a]neut.
Mt 5.24 [a]"first be reconciled to your brother
6.33 [a]"seek first his kingdom and his righteousness
7. 5 [a]"first take the log out of your own eye
8.21 [a]"Lord, let me first go and bury my father
10. 2 first, Simon, who is called Peter
12.29 [a]"how . . , unless he first binds the strong man?
12.45 "the last state . . worse than the first
13.30 [a]" 'Gather the weeds first and bind
17.10 [a]"scribes say that first Elijah must come
17.27 "take the first fish that comes up
19.30 "But many that are first will be last, and the last first
Mt 20. 8 " 'beginning with the last, up to the first
20.10 "when the first came, they thought
20.16 "So the last will be first, and the first last
20.27 "whoever would be first . . must be your slave
21.28 "he went to the first and said, 'Son, go
21.31 "Which . . ?" They said, "The first
21.36 "he sent other servants, more than the first
22.25 "the first married, and died
22.38 "This is the . . first commandment
23.26 [a]"first cleanse the inside of the cup
26.17 on the first day of Unleavened Bread
27.64 "the last fraud will be worse than the first
Mk 3.27 [a]"unless he first binds the strong man
4.28 [a]"first the blade, then the ear
7.27 [a]"Let the children first be fed
9.11 [a]"scribes say that first Elijah must come
9.12 [a]"Elijah does come first to restore all things
9.35 "If any one would be first, he must be last
10.31 "But many that are first will be last, and the last first
10.44 "first among you must be slave of all
12.20 "seven brothers; the first took a wife
12.28 "Which commandment is the first of all?
12.29 "The first is, 'Hear, O Israel
13.10 [a]"the gospel must first be preached to all
14.12 on the first day of Unleavened Bread
16. 9 early on the first day of the week[k]‡
16. 9 [a]he appeared first to Mary Magdalene[k]‡
Lk 2. 2 This was the first enrollment
6.42 [a]"first take the log out of your own eye
9.59 [a]"let me first go and bury my father
9.61 [a]"but let me first say farewell
10. 5 [a]"first say, 'Peace be to this house!
11.26 "last state . . becomes worse than the first
11.38 [a]he did not first wash before dinner
12. 1 [a]to his disciples first, "Beware of the leaven
13.30 "some are last who will be first, and some are first who will be last
14.18 "The first said . . 'I have bought a field
14.28 [a]"which . . does not first . . count the cost?
14.31 [a]"not sit down first and take counsel
16. 5 "he said to the first, 'How much?
17.25 [a]"But first he must suffer many things
19.16 "The first came before him, saying, 'Lord
20.29 "the first took a wife, and died
21. 9 [a]"for this must first take place
Jn 1.41 [a]He first found his brother Simon
2.10 [a]"Every man serves the good wine first
[5. 4 *whoever stepped in first . . was healed*‡
7.51 [a]"without first giving him a hearing
8. 7 "Let him . . be the first to throw a stone[r]‡
10.40 [a]the place where John at first baptized
12.16 [a]disciples did not understand this at first
18.13 [a]First they led him to Annas
19.32 soldiers . . broke the legs of the first
19.39 [a]Nicodemus . . who had at f. come . . by night
20. 4 other disciple . . reached the tomb first
20. 8 disciple, who reached the tomb first
Acts 1. 1 In the first book, O Theophilus
3.26 [a]"sent him to you first, to bless you
7.12 [a]"he sent forth our fathers the first time
12.10 passed the first and the second guard
13.46 [a]"word of God should be spoken first to you
15.14 [a]"how God first visited the Gentiles
20.18 "the first day that I set foot in Asia
26.20 [a]"declared first to those at Damascus
26.23 "being the first to rise from the dead
27.43 to throw themselves overboard first
Rom 1. 8 [a]F., I thank my God through Jesus Christ
1.16 [a]to the Jew first and also to the Greek
2. 9 [a]the Jew first and also the Greek
2.10 [a]the Jew first and also the Greek
10.19 First Moses says, "I will make you jealous
1 Cor 11.18 [a]in the first place, when you assemble
12.28 [a]first apostles, second prophets
14.30 let the first be silent
15.45 "first man Adam became a living being

1 Cor 15.46 [a]it is not the spiritual which is first
15.47 The first man was from the earth
2 Cor 8. 5 [a]first they gave themselves to the Lord
Eph 6. 2 (this is the first commandment
Phil 1. 5 partnership . . from the first day until now
1 Th 4.16 [a]the dead in Christ will rise first
2 Th 2. 3 [a]unless the rebellion comes first
1 Tim 2. 1 [a]First of all, then, I urge . . supplications
2.13 For Adam was formed first
3.10 [a]let them also be tested first
5. 4 [a]let them first learn their religious duty
5.12 having violated their first pledge
2 Tim 1. 5 [a]faith that dwelt first in your grandmother
2. 6 [a]ought to have the first share of the crops
4.16 At my first defense
Heb 7. 2 [a]He is first . . king of righteousness
8. 7 if that first covenant had been faultless
8.13 he treats the first as obsolete
9. 1 even the first covenant had regulations
9.15 transgressions under the first covenant[u]
9.18 f. covenant was not ratified without blood
10. 9 abolishes the first . . to establish the second
Jas 3.17 [a]the wisdom from above is first pure
2 Pet 1.20 [a]First of all you must understand this
2.20 last state . . worse for them than the first
3. 3 [a]First of all you must understand this
1 Jn 4.19 We love, because he first loved us
Rev 1.17 "Fear not, I am the first and the last
2. 4 " 'abandoned the love you had at first
2. 5 " 'do the works you did at first
2. 8 " 'The words of the first and the last
2.19 " 'your latter works exceed the first
4. 1 the first voice . . like a trumpet
4. 7 the first living creature like a lion
8. 7 The first angel blew his trumpet
13.12 authority of the first beast
13.12 its inhabitants worship the first beast
16. 2 first angel . . poured his bowl on the earth
20. 5 This is the first resurrection
20. 6 who shares in the first resurrection
21. 1 for the first heaven and the first earth had passed away
21.19 the first was jasper, the second sapphire
22.13 "I am . . the first and the last

IDIOMATICALLY

a. the first day of the week μία (τῶν) σαββάτων
[a]μία σαββάτου
Mt **28.**1; Mk **16.**2; Lk **24.**1; Jn **20.**1, 19; Acts **20.**7; 1 Cor **16.**2[a] [HEIS]

b. 1 Cor 15.3 I delivered to you as of first importance
παρέδωκα . . ὑμῖν ἐν πρώτοις [PRŌTOS]

CONTEXTUALLY

Rom 13.11 nearer . . now than when we first believed

FIRST, AT

1. *earlier:* πρότερος (neut.) PROTEROS
Gal 4.13 I preached the gospel to you at first

FIRST CONVERT

1. *firstfruits:* ἀπαρχή APARCHĒ
Rom 16. 5 Epaenetus . . the first convert in Asia
1 Cor 16.15 household of Stephanas . . the first converts
2 Th [2.13 God chose you *as the first converts*‡

FIRST FRUITS

1. *firstfruits:* ἀπαρχή APARCHĒ
Rom 8.23 who have the first fruits of the Spirit
11.16 the dough offered as first fruits is holy
1 Cor 15.20 Christ . . the first fruits of those . . asleep
15.23 each in . . order: Christ the first fruits
Jas 1.18 a kind of first fruits of his creatures
Rev 14. 4 redeemed from mankind as first fruits

FIRST HOPE

1. *hope before, expect:* προελπίζω PROELPIZŌ*
Eph 1.12 we who first hoped in Christ

FIRST, LIKE TO PUT ONESELF

1. *wish to be first:* φιλοπρωτεύω PHILOPRŌTEUŌ*
3 Jn . 9 Diotrephes, who likes to put himself first

FIRST, SECOND

1. *second s. after the first:* δευτερόπρωτος DEUTEROPRŌTOS*
Lk [6. 1 On *the second first* sabbath‡

FIRST TIME, FOR THE

1. *primarily:* πρώτως PRŌTŌS*
Acts 11.26 for the first time called Christians

FIRST-BORN

1. *firstborn:* πρωτότοκος PRŌTOTOKOS*
Lk 2. 7 she gave birth to her first-born son
Rom 8.29 the first-born among many brethren
Col 1.15 the first-born of all creation
1.18 the first-born from the dead
Heb 1. 6 he brings the first-born into the world
11.28 the Destroyer of the first-born
12.23 the assembly[z] of the first-born
Rev 1. 5 the first-born of the dead

FISH

1. *fish:* ἁλιεύω (inf.) HALIEUŌ*
Jn 21. 3 Peter said . . "I am going fishing

2. *fish:* ἰχθύς ICHTHYS*
Mt 7.10 "Or if he asks for a fish
14.17 "only five loaves here and two fish
14.19 taking the five loaves and the two fish
15.36 he took the seven loaves and the fish
17.27 "take the first fish that comes up
Mk 6.38 "Five, and two fish
6.41 taking the five loaves and the two fish
6.41 he divided the two fish among them
6.43 full of broken pieces and of the fish
Lk 5. 6 they enclosed a great shoal of fish
5. 9 astonished . . at the catch of fish
9.13 "no more than five loaves and two fish
9.16 taking the five loaves and the two fish
11.11 "if his son asks for[l] a fish, will instead of a fish give him a serpent?
24.42 They gave him a piece of broiled fish
Jn 21. 6 not able to haul . . the quantity of fish
21. 8 dragging the net full of fish
21.11 hauled the net . . full of large fish
1 Cor 15.39 another for birds, and another for fish

3. *fish:* ὀψάριον OPSARION*
Jn 6. 9 "five barley loaves and two fish
6.11 he distributed . . also the fish
21. 9 a charcoal fire there, with fish lying on it
21.10 "Bring some of the fish
21.13 Jesus came . . and gave . . them . . the fish

4. *fish:* προσφάγιον PROSPHAGION*
Jn 21. 5 "Children, have you any fish?

CONTEXTUALLY

Mt 13.47 "and gathered fish of every kind

FISH, SMALL

1. *little fish:* ἰχθύδιον ICHTHYDION*
Mt 15.34 "Seven, and a few small fish
Mk 8. 7 they had a few small fish

FISHER
FISHERMAN

1. *fisherman:* ἁλιεύς HALIEUS*
Mt 4.18 casting a net . . for they were fishermen
4.19 "I will make you fishers of men
Mk 1.16 casting a net . . for they were fishermen
1.17 "I will make you become fishers of men
Lk 5. 2 the fishermen had gone out of them

FIT

1. *suitable:* εὔθετος EUTHETOS
Lk 9.62 "No one who . . looks back is fit
14.35 "fit neither for the land nor for the dunghill

FIT, SEE

1. *test, approve:* δοκιμάζω DOKIMAZŌ
Rom 1.28 they did not see fit to acknowledge God

FITS THE OCCASION, AS

1. *need, want:* χρεία (gen.) CHREIA
Eph 4.29 no evil talk . . but only such . . as fits the o.

FITTING
1. *worthy:* ἄξιος AXIOS
2 Th 1. 3 fitting, because your faith is growing

FITTING, BE
1. *be proper:* ἀνήκω (impers.) ANĒKŌ
Eph 5. 4 nor levity, which are not fitting
Col 3.18 subject to your husbands, as is fitting
2. *one must:* δεῖ DEI
Lk 15.32 " 'It was fitting to make merry
3. *be fitting:* πρέπω PREPŌ
Mt 3.15 "Let it be so now, for thus it is fitting
Eph 5. 3 as is fitting among saints
Heb 2.10 was fitting that he . . should make . . perfect
7.26 was fitting that we . . have such a high priest

FIVE
1. *five:* πέντε PENTE
Mt 14.17 "only five loaves here and two fish
14.19 taking the five loaves and the two fish
16. 9 "Do you not remember the five loaves?
25. 2 "Five of them were foolish, and five were wise
25.15 "to one he gave five talents[d]
25.16 "He who had received the five talents . . made five talents more
25.20 "he who had received the five talents came forward, bringing five talents more, saying . . 'you delivered to me five talents; here I have made five talents more
Mk 6.38 "Five ⟨loaves⟩ and two fish
6.41 taking the five loaves and the two fish
8.19 "When I broke the five loaves
Lk 1.24 for five months she hid herself
9.13 "no more than five loaves and two fish
9.16 taking the five loaves and the two fish
12. 6 "five sparrows sold for two pennies
12.52 "five divided, three against two
14.19 " 'I have bought five yoke of oxen
16.28 " 'I have five brothers
19.18 " 'your pound has made five pounds
19.19 " 'you are to be over five cities
Jn 4.18 "you have had five husbands
5. 2 a pool . . which has five porticoes
6. 9 "a lad here who has five barley loaves
6.13 fragments from the five barley loaves
Acts 4. 4 many . . believed; . . about five thousand
20. 6 in five days we came to them at Troas
24. 1 after five days . . Ananias came
1 Cor 14.19 rather speak five words with my mind
Rev 9. 5 allowed to torture them for five months
9 10 power of hurting men for five months
17.10 "seven kings, five of whom have fallen

FIVE HUNDRED
1. *five hundred:* πεντακόσιοι PENTAKOSIOI*
Lk 7.41 "one owed five hundred denarii
1 Cor 15. 6 to more than five hundred brethren

FIVE THOUSAND
1. *five thousand:* πεντακισχίλιοι PENTAKISCHILIOI*
Mt 14.21 f. thousand men, besides women and children
16. 9 "remember the five loaves of the f. thousand?
Mk 6.44 those who ate . . were five thousand men
8.19 "I broke the five loaves for the five t.
Lk 9.14 there were about five thousand men
Jn 6.10 men sat down, in number about five t.

FIVE TIMES
1. *five times:* πεντάκις PENTAKIS*
2 Cor 11.24 Five times I have received . . forty lashes

FIX (*See also* ATTENTION UPON, FIX ONE'S)
1. *stand, set:* ἵστημι HISTĒMI
Acts 17.31 "fixed a day on which he will judge
2. *support, fix:* στηρίζω STĒRIZŌ
Lk 16.26 " 'between us . . a great chasm has been fixed
3. *lay, put:* τίθημι (mid.) TITHĒMI
Acts 1. 7 "seasons which the Father has fixed

FIXED, BE
1. *look intently at:* ἀτενίζω ATENIZŌ
Lk 4.20 the eyes of all . . were fixed on him

FLAG
1. *idle, troublesome:* ὀκνηρός OKNĒROS [A.6.a.3]
Rom 12.11 Never flag in zeal, be aglow with the Spirit

FLAME
1. *flame:* φλόξ PHLOX
Lk 16.24 " 'for I am in anguish in this flame
Acts 7.30 "in a flame of fire in a bush
Heb 1. 7 "Who makes . . his servants flames of fire
Rev 1.14 his eyes were like a flame of fire
2.18 " 'who has eyes like a flame of fire
19.12 His eyes are like a flame of fire

FLAMING
1. *flame:* φλόξ (gen.) PHLOX
2 Th 1. 7(8) with his mighty angels in flaming fire
2. *set on fire:* πυρόω (perf. pass. part.) PYROŌ
Eph 6.16 can quench all the flaming darts

FLASH (*See also* LIGHTNING, FLASH OF)
1. *lighten, gleam:* ἀστράπτω ASTRAPTŌ
Lk 17.24 "as the lightning flashes and lights up
2. *flash around:* περιαστράπτω PERIASTRAPTŌ
Acts 9. 3 suddenly a light from heaven flashed

FLASK

FLASK, ALABASTER
1. *vessel:* ἀγγεῖον AGGEION*
Mt 25. 4 "but the wise took flasks of oil
2. *vase* (made of alabaster): ἀλάβαστρος ALABASTROS*
Mt 26. 7 alabaster flask of very expensive ointment[o]
Mk 14. 3 a woman came with an alabaster flask of ointment . . and she broke the flask[o]
Lk 7.37 brought an alabaster flask of ointment

FLATTER
IDIOMATICALLY
a. Jude .16 flattering people to gain advantage θαυμάζοντες πρόσωπα ὠφελείας χάριν [PROSŌPON; THAUMAZŌ]

FLATTERING WORDS
1. *praise, blessing, gift:* εὐλογία EULOGIA
Rom 16.18 by . . flattering words they deceive

FLATTERY
1. *flattery:* κολακεία KOLAKEIA*
1 Th 2. 5 For we never used either words of flattery

FLEE

FLEE FOR REFUGE
1. *flee for refuge:* καταφεύγω KATAPHEUGŌ*
Acts 14. 6 they learned of it and fled to Lystra
Heb 6.18 we who have fled for refuge
2. *flee, avoid:* φεύγω PHEUGŌ
Mt 2.13 "flee to Egypt, and remain there till I tell
3. 7 "Who warned you to flee from the wrath?
8.33 The herdsmen fled, . . going into the city
10.23 "flee to the next ⟨town⟩
24.16 "let those . . in Judea flee to the mountains
26.56 all the disciples forsook him and fled
Mk 5.14 The herdsmen fled, and told it
13.14 "let those . . in Judea flee to the mountains
14.50 they all forsook him, and fled
16. 8 they went out and fled from the tomb
Lk 3. 7 "Who warned you to flee from the wrath?
8.34 they fled, and told it in the city
21.21 "let those . . in Judea flee to the mountains
Jn 10. 5 "they will not follow, but they will flee
10.12 "a hireling . . leaves the sheep and flees
Acts 7.29 "Moses fled, and became an exile
Jas 4. 7 Resist the devil and he will flee from you
Rev 12. 6 the woman fled into the wilderness
16.20 every island fled away
20.11 earth and sky fled away
CONTEXTUALLY
Jn 10.13 "He flees because he is a hireling

FLEE OUT OF
1. *flee away:* ἐκφεύγω EKPHEUGŌ
Acts 19.16 they fled out of that house naked

FLEETING
1. *temporary:* πρόσκαιρος PROSKAIROS
Heb 11.25 rather . . than . . the fleeting pleasures of sin

FLESH

1. *flesh, body:* σάρξ SARX
Mt 16.17 “flesh and blood has not revealed this
19. 5 “ ‘and the two shall become one flesh[0]
19. 6 “So they are no longer two but one flesh[0]
26.41 “the spirit . . is willing, but the flesh is weak
Mk 10. 8 “ ‘and the two shall become one flesh[0]
10. 8 “So they are no longer two but one flesh[0]
14.38 “the spirit . . is willing, but the flesh is weak
Lk 3. 6 “all flesh shall see the salvation of God
24.39 “for a spirit has not flesh and bones
Jn 1.13 born, not . . of the will of the flesh
1.14 Word became flesh and dwelt among us
3. 6 “That which is born of the flesh is flesh, and
that which is born of the Spirit is spirit[f]
6.51 “the bread which I shall give . . is my flesh
6.52 “can this man give us his flesh to eat?
6.53 “unless you eat the flesh of the Son
6.54 “who eats my flesh and drinks my blood
6.55 “For my flesh is food indeed
6.56 “He who eats my flesh . . abides in me
6.63 “the spirit . . gives life, the flesh is of no avail
8.15 “You judge according to the flesh
17. 2 “thou hast given him power over all flesh
Acts 2.17 “ ‘I will pour out my Spirit upon all flesh
2.26 “ ‘moreover my flesh will dwell in hope
2.31 “nor did his flesh see corruption
Rom 1. 3 from David according to the flesh
4. 1 our forefather according to the flesh
7. 5 While we were living in the flesh
7.18 nothing good dwells . . in my flesh
7.25 with my flesh I serve the law of sin
8. 3 the law, weakened by the flesh
8. 3 his own Son in the likeness of sinful flesh
8. 3 he condemned sin in the flesh
8. 4 who walk not according to the flesh
8. 5 those who live according to the flesh set their
minds on the things of the flesh
8. 6 To set the mind on the flesh is death
8. 7 mind that is set on the flesh is hostile
8. 8 those . . in the flesh cannot please God
8. 9 But you are not in the flesh
8.12 we are debtors, not to the flesh, to live ac-
cording to the flesh
8.13 if you live according to the flesh you will die
9. 5 of their race, according to the flesh
9. 8 not the children of the flesh
13.14 make no provision for the flesh
1 Cor 5. 5 to Satan for the destruction of the flesh
6.16 “The two shall become one flesh[0]
15.39 For not all flesh is alike
15.50 f. and blood cannot inherit the kingdom
2 Cor 4.11 the life of Jesus . . in our mortal flesh
12. 7 a thorn was given me in the flesh
Gal 1.16 I did not confer with flesh and blood
2.20 the life I now live in the flesh I live by faith
3. 3 are you now ending with the flesh?
4.23 son of the slave was born according to the f.
4.29 he who was born according to the flesh
5.13 not . . as an opportunity for the flesh
5.16 do not gratify the desires of the flesh
5.17 desires of the flesh are against the Spirit, and
the desires of the Spirit are against the flesh
5.19 the works of the flesh are plain
5.24 have crucified the flesh with its passions
6. 8 he who sows to his own flesh will from the
flesh reap corruption
6.12 to make a good showing in the flesh
6.13 that they may glory in your flesh
Eph 2. 3 once lived in the passions of our flesh
2.11 you Gentiles in the flesh
2.11 circumcision, which is made in the flesh
2.15 abolishing in his flesh the law
5.29 no man ever hates his own flesh
5.31 “and the two shall become one flesh[0]
6.12 not contending against flesh and blood
Phil 1.22 If it is to be life in the flesh
1.24 to remain in the flesh is more necessary
3. 3 we . . put no confidence in the flesh
3. 4 I . . have reason for confidence in the flesh
3. 4 he has reason for confidence in the flesh
Col 1.22 he has now reconciled in his body all flesh
1.24 in my flesh I complete what is lacking
2.11 by putting off the body of flesh
2.13 the uncircumcision of your flesh
2.23 checking the indulgence of the flesh[e]
1 Tim 3.16 He[h] was manifested in the flesh
Phm .16 both in the flesh and in the Lord
Heb 2.14 the children share in flesh and blood
5. 7 In the days of his flesh, Jesus[j]
9.13 sanctifies for the purification of the flesh
10.20 way which he opened . . through his flesh
Jas 5. 3 their rust . . will eat your flesh like fire
1 Pet 1.24 “All flesh is like grass
3.18 being put to death in the flesh
4. 1 Christ suffered in the flesh[i]
4. 1 whoever has suffered in the flesh
4. 2 live for the rest of the time in the flesh
4. 6 though judged in the flesh like men
2 Pet 2.18 with licentious passions of the flesh
1 Jn 2.16 lust of the flesh and the lust of the eyes
4. 2 that Jesus Christ has come in the flesh
2 Jn . 7 the coming of Jesus Christ in the flesh
Jude . 8 these men in their dreamings defile the flesh
.23 hating . . the garment spotted by the flesh[e]
Rev 17.16 “devour her flesh and burn her up
19.18 “to eat the flesh of kings, the flesh of cap-
tains, the flesh of mighty men, the flesh of
horses and their riders, and the flesh of all
men, both free and slave, both small and
great
19.21 all the birds were gorged with their flesh

FLESH, OF THE

1. *fleshly:* σαρκικός SARKIKOS
1 Cor 3. 3 for you are still of the flesh. For while there
is jealousy . . are you not of the flesh?
1 Pet 2.11 abstain from the passions of the flesh
2. *fleshly:* σάρκινος SARKINOS
1 Cor 3. 1 as men of the flesh, as babes in Christ

FLESH, THOSE WHO MUTILATE THE

1. *incision, mutilation:* κατατομή KATATOMĒ* [C.2]
Phil 3. 2 look out for those who mutilate the flesh

FLIGHT

1. *escape, flight:* φυγή PHYGĒ*
Mt 24.20 “Pray that your flight may not be in winter

FLIGHT, PUT TO

1. *incline:* κλίνω KLINŌ
Heb 11.34 put foreign armies to flight

FLOCK

1. *flock:* ποίμνη POIMNĒ
Mt 26.31 “ ‘the sheep of the flock will be scattered
Lk 2. 8 keeping watch over their flock by night
Jn 10.16 “there shall be one flock, one shepherd
1 Cor 9. 7 tends a flock without getting some . . milk
2. *flock:* ποίμνιον POIMNION*
Lk 12.32 “Fear not, little flock
Acts 20.28 “Take heed . . to all the flock
20.29 “wolves will come . . not sparing the flock
1 Pet 5. 2 Tend the flock of God that is your charge[k]
5. 3 being examples to the flock

FLOG

1. *whip, flog:* μαστιγόω MASTIGOŌ
Mt 10.17 “they will . . flog you in their synagogues

FLOOD

1. *deluge, flood:* κατακλυσμός KATAKLYSMOS*
Mt 24.38 “before the flood they were eating
24.39 “they did not know until the flood came
Lk 17.27 “the flood came and destroyed them all
2 Pet 2. 5 when he brought a flood upon the world
2. *flood tide:* πλήμμυρα PLĒMMYRA*
Lk 6.48 “when a flood arose, the stream broke

3. *river, stream:* ποταμός POTAMOS
Mt 7.25 "the floods came, and the winds blew
7.27 "the floods came, and the winds blew
IDIOMATICALLY
a. Rev 12.15 to sweep her away with the flood ἵνα αὐτὴν ποταμοφόρητον ποιήσῃ [POTAMOPHORĒTOS*]

FLOOR, THRESHING
1. *threshing floor:* ἅλων HALŌN*
Mt 3.12 "he will clear his threshing floor
Lk 3.17 "to clear his threshing floor

FLOUR
1. *flour:* ἄλευρον ALEURON*
Mt 13.33 "like leaven . . hid in three measures of flour⁰
Lk 13.21 "like leaven . . hid in three measures of flour⁰

FLOUR, FINE
1. *finest wheat flour:* σεμίδαλις SEMIDALIS*
Rev 18.13 wine, oil, fine flour and wheat

FLOW
1. *stream, flow:* ῥέω RHEŌ*
Jn 7.38 " 'Out of his heart shall flow rivers
2. *stream, flowing:* ῥύσις RHYSIS*
Mk 5.25 a woman who had had a flow of blood
Lk 8.43 a woman who had had a flow of blood
8.44 immediately her flow of blood ceased

FLOW FROM
1. *go out:* ἐκπορεύομαι EKPOREUOMAI
Rev 22. 1 water of life . . flowing from the throne
2. *go out:* ἐξέρχομαι EXERCHOMAI
Rev 14.20 blood flowed from the wine press

FLOWER
1. *flower:* ἄνθος ANTHOS*
Jas 1.10 like the flower of the grass he will pass away
1.11 its flower falls, and its beauty perishes
1 Pet 1.24 "all its glory like the flower of grass. The grass withers, and the flower falls

FLUTE
1. *flute:* αὐλός AULOS*
1 Cor 14. 7 lifeless instruments, such as the flute

FLUTE PLAYER
1. *flute player:* αὐλητής AULĒTĒS*
Mt 9.23 when Jesus . . saw the flute players
Rev 18.22 the sound of . . flute players

FLY
1. *fly, rush:* πέτομαι PETOMAI*
Rev 4. 7 fourth living creature like a flying eagle
8.13 an eagle crying . . as it flew in midheaven
12.14 that she might fly from the serpent
14. 6 I saw another angel flying in midheaven
19.17 all the birds that fly in midheaven
2. *flee, avoid:* φεύγω PHEUGŌ
Rev 9. 6 they will long to die, and death will fly

FOAL
1. *son:* υἱός HUIOS
Mt 21. 5 "on a colt, the foal of an ass

FOAM
1. *foam:* ἀφρίζω APHRIZŌ*
Mk 9.18 "he foams and grinds his teeth
9.20 he fell . . foaming at the mouth
2. *with foam:* μετὰ ἀφροῦ APHROS* [B.1.a.2]
Lk 9.39 "it convulses him till he foams

FOAM OF, CAST UP THE
1. *foam up:* ἐπαφρίζω EPAPHRIZŌ*
Jude .13 waves . . casting up the foam of their . . shame

FOE
1. *hated, hostile:* ἐχθρός (subst.) ECHTHROS
Mt 10.36 "a man's foes will be . . of his own household
Rev 11. 5 fire . . consumes their foes
11.12 in the sight of their foes they went up

FOLD
1. *court, courtyard:* αὐλή AULĒ
Jn 10.16 "other sheep, that are not of this fold

FOLLOW
1. *follow, obey:* ἀκολουθέω AKOLOUTHEŌ*
Mt 4.20 they left their nets and followed him
4.22 they left the boat . . and followed him
4.25 great crowds followed him from Galilee
8. 1 great crowds followed him
8.10 Jesus . . said to those who followed
8.19 "Teacher, I will follow you wherever you go
8.22 "Follow me, and leave the dead
8.23 he got into the boat, his disciples followed
9. 9 he said to ⟨Matthew⟩, "Follow me." And he rose and followed him
9.19 Jesus rose and followed him
9.27 two blind men followed him
10.38 "who does not . . follow me is not worthy
12.15 many followed him, and he healed them
14.13 they followed him on foot from the towns
16.24 "let him deny himself . . and follow me
19. 2 large crowds followed him, and he healed
19.21 "sell what you possess and . . follow me
19.27 "Lo, we have . . followed you
19.28 "you who have followed me
20.29 a great crowd followed him
20.34 they received their sight and followed him
21. 9 the crowds . . that followed him shouted
26.58 Peter followed him at a distance
27.55 many women . . who had followed Jesus
Mk 1.18 they left their nets and followed him
2.14 he said to ⟨Levi⟩, "Follow me." And he rose and followed him
2.15 there were many who followed him
3. 7 a great multitude from Galilee followed
5.24 a great crowd followed him
6. 1 his disciples followed him
8.34 "let him deny himself . . and follow me
9.38 "because he was not following us
[9.38 "we saw a man . . *who does not follow us*‡
10.21 "sell what you have . . and come, follow me
10.28 "Lo, we have . . followed you
10.32 those who followed were afraid
10.52 he received his sight and followed him
11. 9 those who followed cried out, "Hosanna!
14.13 "a man . . will meet you; follow him
14.54 Peter had followed him at a distance
15.41 followed him, and ministered to him
Lk 5.11 they left everything and followed him
5.27 he said to ⟨Levi⟩, "Follow me
5.28 he left everything . . and followed him
7. 9 Jesus . . said to the multitude that followed
9.11 When the crowds learned it, they followed
9.23 "let him deny himself . . and follow me
9.49 "because he does not follow with us
9.57 "I will follow you wherever you go
9.59 To another he said, "Follow me
9.61 Another said, "I will follow you, Lord
18.22 "Sell all that you have and . . follow me
18.28 "Lo, we have . . followed you
18.43 he received his sight and followed him
22.10 "follow him into the house which he enters
22.39 the disciples followed him
22.54 Peter followed at a distance
23.27 there followed him a great multitude
Jn 1.37 The two disciples . . followed Jesus
1.38 Jesus turned, and saw them following
1.40 One of the two who . . followed him
1.43 he found Philip and said . . "Follow me
6. 2 a multitude followed him
8.12 "who follows . . will not walk in darkness
10. 4 "the sheep follow him
10. 5 "A stranger they will not follow
10.27 "I know them, and they follow me
11.31 Jews . . saw Mary rise . . and . . they followed
12.26 If any one serves me, he must follow
13.36 "Where I am going you cannot follow me now; but you shall follow afterward
13.37 "Lord, why cannot I follow you now?
18.15 Simon Peter followed Jesus

Jn 20. 6 Simon Peter came, following him
21.19 after this he said to him, "Follow me
21.20 Peter . . saw following them the disciple
21.22 Jesus said to him . . "Follow me!
Acts 12. 8 "Wrap your mantle around you and f. me
12. 9 he went out and followed him
13.43 many Jews . . followed Paul and Barnabas
21.36 the mob of the people followed
1 Cor 10. 4 supernatural° Rock which followed them
Rev 6. 8 Hades followed him
14. 4 it is these who follow the Lamb
14. 8 Another angel, a second, followed
14. 9 another angel, a third, followed
14.13 "for their deeds follow them!
19.14 the armies of heaven . . followed him
2. *go away after:* ἀπέρχομαι ὀπίσω APERCHOMAI [A.6.a.4]
Mk 1.20 they left their father . . and followed him
3. *come after:* δεῦτε ὀπίσω DEUTE [A.6.a.4]
Mt 4.19 "Follow me, and I will make you fishers
Mk 1.17 "Follow me and I will make you . . fishers
4. *pursue:* διώκω DIŌKŌ
Lk 17.23 "Do not go, do not follow them
5. *have, hold:* ἔχω ECHŌ [A.6.a.5]
2 Tim 1.13 Follow the pattern of . . sound words
6. *be:* εἰμί EIMI
Lk 22.49 when those . . saw what would follow
7. *follow:* ἐξακολουθέω EXAKOLOUTHEŌ*
2 Pet 1.16 we did not follow cleverly devised myths
2. 2 many will follow their licentiousness
2.15 they have followed the way of Balaam
8. *come to be, happen, be:* γίνομαι GINOMAI
Rev 8. 7 there followed hail and fire
9. *follow after:* κατακολουθέω KATAKOLOUTHEŌ*
Lk 23.55 women . . from Galilee followed
Acts 16.17 She followed Paul and us, crying
10. *follow closely, understand:* παρακολουθέω PARAKOLOUTHEŌ
Lk 1. 3 having followed all things closely[a]
1 Tim 4. 6 the good doctrine which you have followed
11. *persuade:* πείθω (pass.) PEITHŌ
Acts 5.36 "all who followed him were dispersed
5.37 "all who followed him were scattered
12. *walk:* περιπατέω PERIPATEŌ [A.6.a.4]
[a]+ἐν [b]+κατά
2 Jn . 4 [a]to find . . your children following the truth
. 6 [b]love, that we follow his commandments
. 6 [a]commandment . . that you follow love
3 Jn . 3 [a]as indeed you do follow the truth
. 4 [a]to hear that my children follow the truth
13. *do, make:* ποιέω POIEŌ
Eph 2. 3 following the desires of body and mind
14. *go according to:* πορεύομαι κατά POREUOMAI [A.6.a.4]
2 Pet 3. 3 scoffing, following their own passions
Jude .16 malcontents, following their own passions
.18 "following their own ungodly passions
15. *agree with, walk by:* στοιχέω (+dat.) STOICHEŌ
Rom 4.12 also follow the example of the faith
16. *follow along with:* συνακολουθέω SYNAKOLOUTHEŌ*
[a]+μετά [b]+dat.
Mk 5.37 [a]no one to follow him except Peter
14.51 [b]a young man followed him
Lk 23.49 [b]the women who had followed him
IDIOMATICALLY
a. Rev 13.3 the whole earth followed the beast with wonder
ἐθαυμάσθη ὅλη ἡ γῆ ὀπίσω τοῦ θηρίου [OPISŌ]

FOLLOW IN
1. *follow close upon:* ἐπακολουθέω EPAKOLOUTHEŌ
1 Pet 2.21 that you should follow in his steps

FOLLOWING
1. *come on:* ἔπειμι (part.) EPEIMI
Acts 7.26 "on the following day he appeared
23.11 following night the Lord stood by him
2. *from, out of:* ἐκ (+gen.) EK [B.1.a.2]
Rom 5.16 the judgment following one trespass
5.16 the free gift following many trespasses
3. *in accordance with, for:* κατά (+acc.) KATA
Eph **2.2**[2]
CONTEXTUALLY
Acts 15.23 with the following letter: "The brethren

FOLLOWING DAY, ON THE
FOLLOWING DAY, THE
1. *have, hold:* ἔχω (part.) ECHŌ [B.3.b.2]
Lk 13.33 " 'I must go . . the day following
2. *tomorrow:* ἐπαύριον EPAURION [B.3.b.4]
Mk 11.12 On the following day, when they came
Acts 10.24 on the following day they entered C.
3. *on the following:* τῇ ἐπιούσῃ EPEIMI [B.3.b.2]
Acts 16.11 the following day to Neapolis
20.15 we came the following day opposite Chios
21.18 On the following day Paul went in

FOLLY
1. *want of understanding:* ἄνοια ANOIA
2 Tim 3. 9 for their folly will be plain to all
2. *vanity, emptiness:* ματαιότης MATAIOTĒS
2 Pet 2.18 uttering loud boasts of folly, they entice
3. *foolishness:* μωρία MŌRIA*
1 Cor 1.18 the word of the cross is folly
1.21 it pleased God through the folly . . we preach
1.23 Christ crucified . . folly to Gentiles
2.14 the gifts . . of God . . are folly to him
3.19 the wisdom of this world is folly with God

FOOD
1. *food:* βρῶμα (sg. or pl.) BRŌMA
Mt 14.15 "send the crowds . . to . . buy food
Mk 7.19 (Thus he declared all foods clean
Lk 3.11 "he who has food, let him do likewise
9.13 "unless we are to go and buy food
Jn 4.34 "My food is to do the will of him
Rom 14.20 Do not, for the sake of food
1 Cor 3. 2 I fed you with milk, not solid food
6.13 "Food is meant for the stomach and the stomach for food
8. 8 Food will not commend us to God
8.13 if food is a cause of my brother's falling
10. 3 all ate the same supernatural° food
1 Tim 4. 3 who . . enjoin abstinence from foods
Heb 9.10 food and drink and various ablutions
13. 9 foods . . have not benefited their adherents
2. *eating, food:* βρῶσις BRŌSIS
Jn 4.32 he said to them, "I have food to eat
6.27 "Do not labor for the food which perishes, but for the food which endures
6.55 "my flesh is food indeed
Rom 14.17 the kingdom of God is not food
1 Cor 8. 4 as to the eating of food offered to idols
2 Cor 9.10 He who supplies . . bread for food
Col 2.16 questions of food and drink
3. *fodder, food:* χόρτασμα CHORTASMA*
Acts 7.11 "our fathers could find no food
4. *sustenance:* διατροφή DIATROPHĒ*
1 Tim 6. 8 if we have food and clothing
5. *eat:* ἐσθίω (inf.) ESTHIŌ
Mt 25.35 " 'I was hungry and you gave me food
25.42 " 'I was hungry and you gave me no food
Jn 4.33 "Has any one brought him food?
1 Cor 9. 4 Do we not have the right to our food?
6. *table:* τράπεζα TRAPEZA [C.2]
Acts 16.34 he brought them . . and set food before them
7. *nourishment:* τροφή TROPHĒ
Mt 3. 4 his food was locusts and wild honey
6.25 "Is not life more than food?
10.10 "for the laborer deserves his food
24.45 "to give them . . food at the proper time
Lk 12.23 "For life is more than food
Jn 4. 8 his disciples had gone . . to buy food
Acts 2.46 they partook of food with glad . . hearts
9.19 took food and was strengthened
14.17 "satisfying your hearts with food
27.33 Paul urged them all to take some food
27.34 "I urge you to take some food
27.36 all were encouraged and ate some food
Heb 5.12 You need milk, not solid food
5.14 But solid food is for the mature

Jas 2.15 If a brother . . is . . in lack of daily food
CONTEXTUALLY
Acts 23.14 "to taste no f. till we have killed Paul
1 Cor 8. 1 concerning food offered to idols
8. 7 some . . eat f. as . . offered to an idol
8.10 might . . be encouraged . . to eat food offered
10.19 That food offered to idols is anything
Rev 2.14 " 'that they might eat f. sacrificed
2.20 " 'and to eat food sacrificed to idols

FOOD, DEPEND ON FOR
1. *feed, nourish:* τρέφω (pass.) TREPHŌ
Acts 12.20 depended on the king's country for food

FOOD FROM, GET ONE'S
1. *eat:* ἐσθίω ESTHIŌ
1 Cor 9.13 those . . get their food from the temple

FOOD, PORTION OF
1. *ration of grain:* σιτομέτριον SITOMETRION*
Lk 12.42 "to give them their portion of food

FOOD, WITHOUT
1. *lack of food, lack of appetite:* ἀσιτία ASITIA [A.1.e]
Acts 27.21 As they had been long without food
2. *without food:* ἄσιτος ASITOS*
Acts 27.33 "you have continued . . without food
3. *in times of hunger:* ἐν νηστείαις NĒSTEIA [B.1.b]
2 Cor 11.27 in hunger and thirst, often without f.

FOOL
1. *foolish:* ἄφρων (subst.) APHRŌN
Lk 11.40 "You fools! Did not he . . make the inside?
12.20 "But God said to him, 'Fool!
2 Cor 11.16 even if you do, accept me as a fool
11.19 For you gladly bear with fools!
12. 6 if I wish to boast, I shall not be a fool
12.11 I have been a fool! You forced me
2. *in foolishness:* ἐν ἀφροσύνῃ APHROSYNĒ [B.1.a.1]
2 Cor 11.17 (as a fool, in this boastful confidence
11.21 I am speaking as a fool
3. *dull, stupid:* μωρός (subst.) MŌROS
Mt 5.22 "whoever says, 'You fool!' shall be liable
23.17 "You blind fools! For which is greater?
1 Cor 3.18 become a fool that he may become wise
4.10 We are fools for Christ's sake

FOOL, BECOME A
1. *make foolish:* μωραίνω (pass.) MŌRAINŌ
Rom 1.22 Claiming to be wise, they became fools

FOOLISH
1. *unintelligent:* ἀνόητος ANOĒTOS
Lk 24.25 "O foolish men, and slow of heart!
Rom 1.14 I am under obligation . . to the foolish
Gal 3. 1 O foolish Galatians!
3. 3 Are you so foolish?
Tit 3. 3 For we ourselves were once foolish
2. *foolish:* ἄφρων APHRŌN
Rom 2.20 a corrector of the foolish
1 Cor 15.36 You foolish man!
2 Cor 11.16 I repeat, let no one think me foolish
Eph 5.17 do not be foolish, but understand
1 Pet 2.15 silence the ignorance of foolish men
3. *unintelligible, senseless:* ἀσύνετος ASYNETOS
Rom 1.31 foolish, faithless, heartless, ruthless
10.19 "with a foolish nation I will make you angry
4. *dull, stupid:* μωρός MŌROS
Mt 7.26 "foolish man who built . . upon the sand
25. 2 "Five of them were foolish
25. 3 "when the foolish took their lamps
25. 8 "the foolish said . . 'Give us . . oil
1 Cor 1.27 God chose what is foolish in the world

FOOLISH, MAKE
1. *make foolish:* μωραίνω MŌRAINŌ
1 Cor 1.20 Has not God made foolish the wisdom?

FOOLISHNESS
1. *folly:* ἀφροσύνη APHROSYNĒ
Mk 7.22 "envy, slander, pride, foolishness
2 Cor 11. 1 bear with me in a little foolishness
2. *dull, stupid:* μωρός (subst. neut.) MŌROS
1 Cor 1.25 the foolishness of God is wiser than men

FOOT
1. *foot, base:* βάσις BASIS*
Acts 3. 7 his feet and ankles were made strong
2. *footstool:* ὑποπόδιον HYPOPODION [C.2]
[a]sg.
Jas 2. 3 [a]"Stand there," or, "Sit at my feet
3. *leg with the foot, foot:* πούς POUS
Mt 4. 6 " 'lest you strike your foot against a stone
7. 6 "lest they trample them under foot
10.14 "shake off the dust from your feet
15.30 they put them at his feet
18. 8 "if your hand or your foot causes you to sin[g]
18. 8 "with . . two feet . . into the eternal fire
22.13 " 'Bind him hand and foot, and cast him
22.44 " 'Sit at my right hand
28. 9 they . . took hold of his feet and worshiped
Mk 5.22 seeing him, he fell at his feet
6.11 "shake off the dust that is on your feet
7.25 a woman . . came and fell down at his feet
9.45 "if your foot causes you to sin,[l] cut it off
9.45 "with two feet to be thrown into hell[m, n]
12.36 " 'till I put thy enemies under thy feet
Lk 1.79 "to guide our feet into the way of peace
4.11 " 'lest you strike your foot against a stone
7.38 standing behind him at his feet, weeping, she began to wet his feet with her tears, and . . kissed his feet, and anointed them
7.44 "you gave me no water for my feet, but she has wet my feet with her tears
7.45 "she has not ceased to kiss my feet
7.46 "she has anointed my feet with ointment
8.35 sitting at the feet of Jesus, clothed
8.41 falling at Jesus' feet he besought him
9. 5 "shake off the dust from your feet
10.11 " 'Even the dust . . that clings to our feet
10.39 Mary, who sat at the Lord's feet
15.22 "the father said . . 'put . . shoes on his feet
17.16 he fell on his face at Jesus' feet
20.43 "I make thy enemies a stool for thy feet
24.39 "See my hands and my feet
[24.40 *he showed them his hands and his feet*‡
Jn 11. 2 It was Mary who . . wiped his feet
11.32 Mary . . fell at his feet, saying . . "Lord
11.44 his hands and feet bound with bandages
12. 3 Mary . . anointed the feet of Jesus and wiped his feet with her hair
13. 5 he . . began to wash the disciples' feet
13. 6 Peter said . . "Lord, do you wash my feet?
13. 8 "You shall never wash my feet
13. 9 "not my feet only but also my hands!
13.10 "not need to wash, except for his feet[c]‡
13.12 When he had washed their feet
13.14 "If I then . . have washed your feet, you also ought to wash one another's feet
20.12 she saw two angels . . one at the feet
Acts 2.35 " 'I make thy enemies a stool for thy feet
4.35 laid ⟨the proceeds⟩ at the apostles' feet
4.37 laid ⟨the money⟩ at the apostles' feet
5. 2 laid ⟨only a part⟩ at the apostles' feet
5. 9 "feet of those that . . buried your husband
5.10 she fell down at his feet and died
7. 5 "no inheritance . . not even a foot's length
7.33 " 'Take off the shoes from your feet
7.58 laid . . their garments at the feet of . . Saul
10.25 Cornelius . . fell down at his feet
13.25 " 'sandals of whose feet I am not worthy
13.51 they shook off the dust from their feet
14. 8 a man sitting, who could not use his feet
14.10 "Stand upright on your feet
16.24 he . . fastened their feet in the stocks
21.11 he took Paul's girdle and bound his . . feet
22. 3 "brought up . . at the feet of Gamaliel
26.16 " 'rise and stand upon your feet
Rom 3.15 "Their feet are swift to shed blood

Rom 10.15 "beautiful are the feet of those who preach!
16.20 will soon crush Satan under your feet
1 Cor 12.15 If the foot should say .. "I do not belong
12.21 nor .. to the feet, "I have no need of you
15.25 until he .. put all his enemies under his feet
15.27 "God[z] has put all things .. under his feet
Eph 1.22 he has put all things under his feet
6.15 having shod your feet with the equipment
1 Tim 5.10 who has .. washed the feet of the saints
Heb 1.13 "I make thy enemies a stool for thy feet
2. 8 "putting everything .. under his feet
10.13 until his enemies .. be .. a stool for his feet
12.13 make straight paths for your feet
Rev 1.15 his feet were like burnished bronze
1.17 I fell at his feet as though dead
2.18 " 'whose feet are like burnished bronze
3. 9 " 'bow down before your feet
10. 2 he set his right foot on the sea
11.11 they stood up on their feet
12. 1 with the moon under her feet
13. 2 its feet were like a bear's
19.10 I fell down at his feet to worship him
22. 8 I fell down to worship at the feet

FOOT, ON

1. *on foot:* πεζῇ PEZĒ*
Mt 14.13 they followed him on foot from the towns
Mk 6.33 they ran .. on foot from all the towns

FOOT, SET

1. *go upon, mount, board:* ἐπιβαίνω EPIBAINŌ
Acts 20.18 "from the .. day .. I set foot in Asia

FOOT, TREAD UNDER

1. *tread underfoot:* καταπατέω KATAPATEŌ
Mt 5.13 "except to be .. trodden under foot
Lk 8. 5 "some .. was trodden under foot

FOOTSTOOL

1. *footstool:* ὑποπόδιον HYPOPODION
[a]+τῶν ποδῶν
Mt 5.35 [a]"for it is his footstool
Acts 7.49 [a]" 'and earth my footstool

FOR

1. *until:* ἄχρι ACHRI
Acts **13.**11
2. *but:* ἀλλά ALLA
Gal **3.**12
3. *opposite, instead of:* ἀντί (+gen.) ANTI
Mt **5.**38[2]; **17.**27; **20.**28
Mk **10.**45
Rom **12.**17
1 Cor **11.**15
1 Th **5.**15
Heb **12.**2, 16
1 Pet **3.**9[2]
4. *from:* ἀπό (+gen.) APO
Mt **14.**26; **18.**7; **28.**4
Lk **8.**43; **12.**57; **21.**31(30); **22.**45; **24.**41
Jn **21.**6
Rom **15.**23, 24
Eph **3.**9
Col **1.**26†
Heb **5.**7
Rev **14.**20
5. *on account of:* χάριν CHARIN
Tit **1.**11
6. *because of:* διά (+acc.) DIA
[a]+gen.
Mk **2.**27[2]; **5.**4; **7.**29
Lk **8.**19; **23.**19, 25
Jn **1.**31; **7.**13; **10.**17, 32; **12.**27, 30; **16.**21; **19.**38; **20.**19
Acts **10.**21; **28.**20
Rom **1.**26; **4.**24, 25[2]; **7.**7[a]; **13.**6
1 Cor **8.**11; **11.**9[2]
Eph **1.**15
Phil **2.**30
1 Th **2.**13; **3.**5, 7
1 Tim **1.**16
Heb **2.**10
Rev **6.**9[2]; **20.**4[2]
7. *because, since:* διότι DIOTI
Lk **1.**13
Acts **18.**10[2]
Rom **1.**19, 21; **3.**20; **8.**7
1 Pet **1.**24; **2.**6
8. *if, since:* εἰ EI
1 Pet **2.**3
9. *into, to, for:* εἰς (+acc.) EIS
Mt **3.**11; **5.**13; **8.**4; **10.**10; **20.**1; **26.**28; **27.**10
Mk **1.**4, 44; **2.**22‡; **6.**11; **8.**19, 20; **14.**8
Lk **2.**32, 34[2]; **3.**3; **5.**4, 14; **7.**30; **9.**3, 13; **12.**19; **14.**35[2]
Jn **1.**7; **4.**36; **9.**39; **12.**7, 25; **13.**29; **18.**37[2]
Acts **2.**38; **13.**2; **14.**26; **18.**18; **19.**27; **20.**1, 3; **25.**21; **26.**16; **27.**1, 6, 40
Rom **1.**1, 16, 17, 26, 27; **3.**22; **5.**8, 15, 18[2]; **6.**19; **8.**28; **9.**17, 21[2], 22, 23; **13.**4; **14.**1; **15.**2, 4, 7, 26, 31; **16.**5
1 Cor **2.**7; **5.**5; **8.**6; **11.**17[2]; **14.**8; **16.**1
2 Cor **2.**4, 8; **5.**5; **9.**1, 8, 10, 11, 13[2]; **10.**8[2]; **13.**10[2]
Gal **2.**8[2]; **4.**24
Eph **1.**12; **2.**22; **3.**2; **4.**12[2], 30
Phil **1.**10, 16, 19, 25; **3.**14; **4.**[16†‡
Col **1.**4, 11, 16, 25, 29; **4.**8, 11
1 Th **5.**9, 18
2 Th **1.**3
1 Tim **1.**16; **2.**7; **6.**19
2 Tim **1.**11; **2.**20[2], 21[2]; **3.**15; **4.**18
Heb **6.**10, 16; **9.**9; **11.**7; **12.**7
1 Pet **1.**2, 4, 5, 22; **4.**7, 8, 10
Jude .4
Rev **9.**7, 15; **16.**14; **19.**17; **20.**8; **22.**2
10. *from, out of:* ἐκ (+gen.) EK
Mt **20.**2; **26.**42, 44
Jn **9.**24
Acts **9.**33; **24.**10
2 Cor **8.**7
Rev **16.**11, 21
11. *in, at, by:* ἐν (+dat.) EN
Mt **6.**7
Lk **1.**44
Jn **13.**35
Acts **27.**7
Rom **1.**23, 25; **14.**22
1 Cor **11.**13; **15.**19
2 Cor **8.**18
Gal **4.**18
Eph **4.**1
Phil **1.**13
1 Tim **5.**10
2 Tim **2.**9
Jas **5.**3
1 Pet **4.**14
1 Jn **4.**16, 17
12. *since:* ἐπειδή EPEIDĒ
Lk **11.**6
1 Cor **1.**22
Phil **2.**26
13. *on, at:* ἐπί (+acc.) EPI
except [a]+dat.
Mt **3.**7; **19.**9[a]; **26.**[50†
Mk **15.**24
Lk **2.**20[a]; **4.**43; **7.**44; **18.**4; **23.**28[3]
Jn **19.**24
Acts **4.**21[a]; **13.**31; **14.**3[a]; **16.**18; **17.**2; **18.**20; **19.**8, 10, 34; **20.**13; **26.**6[a]; **27.**20, 43
Rom **2.**9; **9.**23
2 Cor **9.**15[a]
Eph **2.**10[a]
Phil **1.**5[a]
1 Th **3.**9[a]; **4.**7[a]
Heb **11.**30; **12.**10
Jas **5.**1[a]
Rev **18.**11; **22.**16[a]
14. *for:* γάρ GAR
Mt **1.**20, 21; **2.**2, 5, 6, 13, 20; **3.**2, 3, 9, 15; **4.**6, 10, 17, 18; **5.**12, 18, 20, 46; **6.**7, 8, 14, 16, 21, 24, 32, 34; **7.**2, 8, 12,

29; 8.9; 9.5, 13, 16, 21, 24; 10.10, 17, 19, 20, 23, 26, 35; 11.13, 18, 30; 12.8, 33, 34, 37, 40, 50; 13.12, 15; 14.3, 24; 15.2, 4, 19; 16.2‡, 3‡, 25, 26, 27; 17.15, 20; 18.7, 10, [11‡, 20; 19.12, 14, 22; 20.1; 21.26, 32; 22.14, 16, 28, 30; 23.3, 5, 8, 9, 13, 17, 19, 39; 24.5, 6, 7, 21, 24, 27, 38; 25.3, 14, 29, 35, 42; 26.9, 10, 11, 28, 31, 43, 52, 73; 27.18, 19, 43; 28.2, 5, 6

Mk 1.16, 22, 38; 2.15; 3.10, 21; 4.22, 25; 5.8, 28; 6.14, 17, 18, 20, 31, 48, 50, 52; 7.3, 10, 21, 27; 8.35, 36, 37, 38; 9.6^{2}, 31, 34, 39, 40, 41, 49; 10.14, 22, 27, 45; 11.13, 18, 32; 12.12, 14, 23, 25, 44; 13.8, 9, 11, 19, 33, 35; 14.2, 5, 7, 40, 56, 70; 15.10; 16.8^{2}

Lk 1.15, 18, 30, 44, 48, 66, 76; 2.10; 3.8; 4.10; 5.9, 39; 6.23^{2}, 26, 32, 33, 38, 43, 44^{2}, 45; 7.5, 6, 8, 33; 8.17, 18, 29^{2}, 40, 46, 52; 9.14, 24, 25, 26, 44, 48, 50, [56‡; 10.7, 24; 11.4, 10, 30; 12.12, 23, 30, 34, 52; 14.24, 28; 16.2, 13, 28; 17.21, 24; 18.16, 23, 25, 32; 19.5, 10, 21, 48; 20.6, 19, 33, 36, 38, 40, 42; 21.4, 8, 9, 15, 23, 26, 35; 22.2, 16, 18, 27, 37^{2}, 59; 23.8, 12, 15, 34‡, 41

Jn 2.25; 3.2, 16, 17, 20, 24, 34^{2}; 4.8, 9, 18, 23, 37, 42, 44, 45, 47; 5.[4‡, 13, 19, 20, 21, 26, 36, 46; 6.6, 27, 33, 40, 55, 64, 71; 7.4, 5, 39; 8.24, 42; 9.22; 12.43, 47; 13.11, 13, 15; 14.30; 16.7, 13, 27; 18.13; 19.6, 31, 36; 20.9, 17; 21.7, 8

Acts 1.20; 2.15, 25, 34, 39; 4.3, 12, 16, 20, 22, 27, 34; 5.26, 36; 6.14; 7.33; 8.7, 16, 21, 23; 9.11, 16; 10.46; 13.8, 27, 36, 47; 15.21, 28; 16.3, 28; 17.20, 23, 28^{2}; 18.3, 18, 28; 19.24, 32, 37, 40; 20.10, 13, 16^{2}, 27; 21.3, 13, 29, 36; 22.22, 26; 23.5, 8, 11, 17, 21; 24.5; 25.27; 26.16, 26^{3}; 27.22, 23, 25; 28.2, 22, 27

Rom 1.9, 11, 16, 17, 18; 2.1, 11, 13, 24, 28; 3.9, 22, 28; 4.2, 3, 15; 5.10, 15, 16, 19; 6.5, 7, 14, 19, 23; 7.1, 11, 15, 18, 19, 22; 8.2, 3, 5, 13, 14, 15, 19, 20, 24^{2}, 26, 38; 9.3, 6, 9, 15, 17, 19, 28; 10.3, 4, 10, 12, 13, 16; 11.15, 21, 23, 24, 29, 32, 34; 12.3, 4, 19, 20; 13.1, 3, 4^{2}, 6^{2}, 8, 11; 14.3, 4, 9, 10, 11, 17; 15.3, 4, 8, 18, 26, 27; 16.2, 18, 19

1 Cor 1.11, 17, 18, 19, 21, 26; 2.2, 8, 10, 11, 14, 16; 3.2, 3^{2}, 4, 9, 11, 13, 17, 19^{2}, 21; 4.7, 9, 15^{2}, 20; 5.3, 7, 12; 6.16; 7.9, 14, 22, 31; 8.5, 10; 9.2, 9, 15, 16^{2}, 17, 19; 10.4, 5, 17, 26, 29; 11.6, 7, 8, 12, 18, 19, 21, 23, 26, 29; 12.12, 13, 14; 13.9, 12; 14.2^{2}, 9, 14, 17, 31, 33, 34, 35; 15.3, 9, 16, 21, 22, 25, 27, 32, 34, 41, 52, 53; 16.5, 7, 9, 10, 11, 18

2 Cor 1.8, 12, 13, 19, 20, 24; 2.1, 2, 4, 9, 11, 17; 3.6, 9, 11, 14; 4.5, 11, 15, 17, 18; 5.1, 4, 7, 10, 13, 14, 6.2, 14, 16; 7.3, 5, 8, 9, 10, 11; 8.9, 12, 21; 9.2, 7; 10.3, 4, 8, 14, 18; 11.2, 4, 9, 13, 14, 19, 20; 12.6, 9, 10, 11^{2}, 13, 14^{2}, 20; 13.4^{2}, 8, 9

Gal 1.11, 12, 13; 2.8, 12, 19, 21; 3.10^{2}, 18, 21, 26, 27, 28; 4.15, 22, [25‡, 25, 27, 30; 5.5, 6, 13, 14, 17^{2}; 6.3, 5, 7, 9, 13, 15, 17

Eph 2.8, 10, 14; 5.6, 8, 9, 12, 13(14), 29; 6.1

Phil 1.8, 19, 21, 23; 2.13; 3.3, 18; 4.11

Col 2.1, 5; 3.3, 20, 25; 4.13

1 Th 1.8, 9; 2.1, 3, 5, 9, 14, 19, 20; 3.3, 4, 9; 4.2, 3, 7, 9, 14, 15; 5.2, 5, 7, 18

2 Th 2.7; 3.2, 7, 10, 11

1 Tim 2.5, 13; 3.13; 4.5, 8, 10, 16; 5.4, 11, 15, 18; 6.7, 10

2 Tim 1.7, 12; 2.7, 13, 16; 3.2, 6, 9; 4.3, 6, 10, 11, 15

Tit 1.7, 10; 2.11; 3.3, 9, 12

Phm .7, 22

Heb 1.5; 2.2, 5, 10, 11, 16, 18; 3.4, 14; 4.2, 3, 4, 8, 10, 12, 15; 5.1, 12, 13^{2}; 6.4, 7, 10, 13; 7.1, 10, 11, 12, 13, 14, 17, 19, 26; 8.3, 7, 8; 9.2, 13, 16, 17, 19, 24; 10.1, 4, 14, 15, 23, 26, 30, 34, 36, 37; 11.2, 6, 10, 14, 16, 26, 27, 32; 12.6, 7, 10, 17^{2}, 18, 20, 25, 29; 13.2, 4, 5, 9, 11, 14, 16, 17^{2}, 18, 22

Jas 1.6, 7, 11, 13, 20, 24; 2.2, 10, 11, 13, 26; 3.2, 7, 16; 4.14

1 Pet 2.19, 20, 21, 25; 3.10, 17; 4.6

2 Pet 1.8, 9, 10, 16, 17; 2.4, 8, 18, 19, 20, 21; 3.4

1 Jn 2.19; 4.20; 5.3

2 Jn .11

3 Jn .3, 7

Jude .4

Rev 1.3; 3.2; 9.19; 13.18; 14.4, 5, 13; 16.14; 17.17; 19.8, 10; 21.1, 22, 23; 22.10

15. *for the sake of:* ἕνεκα HENEKA

Mk 10.29

16. *as, so:* ὡς HŌS [B.3.b.4]

Rev 22.12

17. *so that, therefore:* ὥστε HŌSTE

1 Cor 5.1

18. *that, because:* ὅτι HOTI

Mt 5.3, 4, 5, 6, 7, 8, 9, 10, 12, 34, 35^{2}, 36, 45; 6.5, 7, [13‡; 7.13, 14; 11.21, 23, 26, 29; 12.41, 42; 13.16^{2}; 15.23; 16.17, 23; 17.15; 23.10, 14, 15, 23, 25, 27, 29; 24.42, 44; 25.8, 13

Mk 3.30; 5.9; 8.33; 14.21, 27

Lk 1.37, 48, 49, 68; 2.11, 30; 4.6, 32, 36, 43; 5.8; 6.19, 20, 21^{2}, 24, 25^{2}, 35; 7.39, 47; 8.30, 37, 42; 9.12, 38; 10.13, 21; 11.18, 31, 32, 42, 43, 44, 46, 47, 48, 52; 12.15, 17, 32, 40; 13.24, 31, 33; 14.11, 17; 15.6, 9, 24, 32; 16.8, 15, 24; 18.14; 19.4, 43; 21.22; 22.22; 23.29, 31; 24.29, 39

Jn 1.15, 17, 30; 2.18; 4.22; 5.28, 38; 6.38; 7.8, 29, 39; 8.14, 16, 29, 44; 9.16; 10.4, 5; 11.47; 12.39, 49; 14.17, 28; 15.5, 15^{2}; 16.14, 32; 17.8, 9; 18.2; 19.20

Acts 1.5, 17; 2.25, 27; 4.21; 5.38; 8.33; 9.15; 10.14, 20, 38; 11.8, 24; 13.41; 22.15, 21, 29

Rom 8.29; 11.36

1 Cor 1.25; 11.15

2 Cor 1.5, 7, 8; 2.15; 4.6; 7.8, 14; 8.2, 3, 17; 9.2, 12; 10.10

Gal 3.11, 13; 4.12, 20, 22, 27; 6.8

Eph 2.18; 4.25; 5.23; 6.12

Phil 1.29; 2.30; 4.16

Col 1.16, 19; 2.9

1 Th 1.5; 2.14; 3.8; 4.16; 5.9

2 Th 2.3

1 Tim 4.4; 5.12

2 Tim 1.16

Heb 8.9, 11, 12

Jas 1.12, 23; 3.1; 5.8

1 Pet 1.16; 2.15; 3.9, 12, 18; 4.1, 17; 5.5, 7

1 Jn 2.16; 3.2, 8, 9, 11, 20; 4.1, 4, 7, 8, 18; 5.4, 9

2 Jn .7

Jude .11

Rev 3.4, 17; 4.11; 5.9; 6.17; 7.17; 11.2; 12.10, 12; 13.4; 14.7, 15^{2}, 18; 15.1, 4^{2}; 16.6; 17.14; 18.3, 5, 8, 20, 23; 19.2, 6, 7; 21.4, 5; 22.5

19. *over, for the sake of:* ὑπέρ (+gen.) HYPER

Mt 5.44

Mk 9.40; 14.24

Lk 9.50; 22.19‡, 20‡

Jn 6.51; 10.11, 15; 11.4, 50, 51, 52; 13.37, 38; 15.13; 18.14

Acts 5.41; 8.24; 21.13, 26; 26.1

Rom 5.6, 7^{2}, 8; 8.27, 31, 32, 34; 10.1; 14.15; 15.9; 16.4

1 Cor 1.13; 10.30; 11.24; 12.25; 15.3

2 Cor 1.6^{2}, 7; 5.14, 15, 20; 7.7, 12; 8.16; 9.14; 12.15, 19; 13.8

Gal 1.4; 2.20; 3.13

Eph 1.16; 3.13; 5.2, 20, 25; 6.19, 20

Phil 1.4; 2.13; 4.10

Col 1.9; 2.1; 4.13

2 Th 1.4, 5

1 Tim 2.1, 2, 6

Tit 2.14

Heb 2.9; 5.1; 7.25, 27; 9.7; 10.12

Jas 5.16

1 Pet 2.21; 3.18; 4.[1‡

1 Jn 3.16^{2}

20. *in accordance with, for:* κατά (+acc.) KATA

Mt 16.27; 19.3

Jn 2.6

2 Tim 4.14

Rev 18.6

21. *just as:* καθάπερ KATHAPER

1 Th 2.11

22. *as, just as:* καθώς KATHŌS

Heb 8.5

23. *about, concerning:* περί (+gen.) PERI

except [a]+acc.

Mt 2.8; 9.36; 12.36; 22.16; 26.28

Mk 1.44; 4.19[a]; 12.14

Lk 2.27; 3.19^{2}; 4.38; 5.14; 6.28; 19.37; 22.32

Jn 9.21; 10.13, 33; 12.6; 15.22; 16.26; 17.9^{3}, 20^{2}; 19.24

Acts 8.15; 12.5; 26.7

Rom 1.8; 8.3†

1 Cor 1.4

Eph 6.18

Phil **2**.20
Col **1**.3; **4**.3
1 Th **1**.2; **3**.9; **5**.10, 25
2 Th **1**.3, 11; **2**.13; **3**.1
1 Tim **6**.4[a]
Phm .10
Heb **5**.3; **10**.18, 26; **11**.40; **13**.18
1 Pet **3**.15, 18
1 Jn **2**.2[3]; **4**.10; **5**.16

24. *to, with, against:* πρός (+acc.) PROS
Mt **19**.8; **26**.12
Mk **10**.5
Lk **8**.13; **12**.41[2]; **19**.42
Jn **4**.35; **5**.35
Acts **13**.15; **17**.15
Rom **15**.17
1 Cor **7**.5, 35; **10**.11; **12**.7; **14**.26
2 Cor **2**.16; **7**.8; **8**.19
Gal **2**.5[2]
Eph **4**.12, 29
1 Th **2**.17
1 Tim **1**.16
2 Tim **3**.16[4], 17
Tit **1**.16; **3**.1
Phm .15
Heb **9**.13; **12**.10, 11
Jas **4**.14

IDIOMATICALLY
a. 2 Pet 2.13 suffering wrong for their wrongdoing ἀδικούμενοι μισθὸν ἀδικίας [MISTHOS]

FOR A REASON

1. *opposite, instead of:* ἀντί ANTI
Eph 5.31 "For this r. a man shall leave his father

2. *for the sake of:* χάριν CHARIN [B.1.b]
Eph 3. 1 For this r. I, Paul, a prisoner
3.14 For this reason I bow my knees

3. *for the sake of:* ἕνεκα HENEKA [B.1.b]
Mt 19. 5 "'For this r. a man shall leave his father
Mk 10. 7 "'For this r. a man shall leave his father
Acts 26.21 "For this reason the Jews seized me

FOR, AS

1. *whether, or:* εἴτε EITE
1 Cor 13. 8 as for prophecies, they will pass away; as for tongues, they will cease; as for knowledge, it will pass away
2 Cor 8.23 As for Titus, he is my partner
8.23 as for our brethren, they are messengers[j]

2. *about, concerning:* περί (+gen.) PERI
Mt **22**.31
Mk **12**.26
Acts **21**.25
1 Cor **16**.12

FOR EVER (*See* EVER, FOR)

FOR EVER AND EVER (*See* EVER, FOR EVER AND)

FOR EVERMORE (*See* EVERMORE, FOR)

FOR ONE TO

1. *if:* ἐάν EAN
1 Cor 11.14 for a man to wear long hair is degrading

FOR S.'S SAKE
FOR THE SAKE OF

1. *because of:* διά (+acc.) DIA
Mt **10**.22; **14**.3; **15**.3, 6; **19**.12; **24**.9, 22
Mk **6**.17; **13**.13, 20
Lk **21**.17
Jn **11**.15; **12**.30; **14**.11
Rom **4**.23; **11**.28[2]; **13**.5
1 Cor **4**.10; **9**.10[2], 23
2 Cor **2**.10; **4**.5, 11, 15; **8**.9
Phil **3**.7, 8
1 Th **1**.5; **3**.9
1 Tim **5**.23
2 Tim **2**.10
Phm .9
Heb **1**.14; **6**.7
1 Pet **1**.20; **2**.13; **3**.14
1 Jn **2**.12
Rev **2**.3

2. *for the sake of:* ἕνεκα HENEKA
Mt 5.10 "who are persecuted for righteousness' s.
10.18 "you will be dragged before . . kings for my s.
10.39 "who loses his life for my sake will find it
16.25 "whoever loses his life for my s. will find it
19.29 "who has left houses . . for my name's s.
Mk 8.35 "whoever loses his life for my sake
10.29 "no one who has left house . . for my sake
13. 9 "you will stand before . . kings for my sake
Lk 9.24 "whoever loses his life for my sake
18.29 "for the sake of the kingdom of God
21.12 "brought before kings . . for my name's sake
Rom 8.36 "For thy sake we are being killed
14.20 Do not, for the sake of food, destroy

3. *over, for the sake of:* ὑπέρ (+gen.) HYPER
Jn 17.19 "for their sake I consecrate myself
Acts 9.16 "he must suffer for the sake of my name
15.26 "risked . . for the sake of . . Jesus Christ
Rom 1. 5 obedience . . for the sake of his name
9. 3 cut off . . for the sake of my brethren
2 Cor 5.15 For him who for their sake died
5.21 For our sake he made him to be sin
12.10 For the sake of Christ . . I am content
Phil 1.29 for the sake of Christ you should not only believe in him but also suffer for his sake
Col 1.24 I rejoice in my sufferings for your sake
1.24 for the sake of his body, that is, the church
3 Jn . 7 For they have set out for his sake

IDIOMATICALLY
a. Heb 6.10 the love which you showed for his sake τῆς ἀγάπης ἧς ἐνεδείξασθε εἰς τὸ ὄνομα αὐτοῦ [ONOMA]
b. 1 Jn 2.12 because your sins are forgiven for his sake ὅτι ἀφέωνται ὑμῖν αἱ ἁμαρτίαι διὰ τὸ ὄνομα αὐτοῦ [ONOMA]

CONTEXTUALLY
1 Cor 10.28 (out of consideration . . for conscience' s.
Jude .11 abandon themselves for the sake of gain

FOR THEN

1. *since, otherwise:* ἐπεί EPEI
Rom 3. 6 For then how could God judge the world?

FORBEAR

1. *bear up, endure* (mid.): ἀνέχω ANECHŌ
Eph 4. 2 forbearing one another in love
Col 3.13 forbearing one another and . . forgiving

2. *let go:* ἀνίημι ANIĒMI
Eph 6. 9 Masters, . . forbear threatening

FORBEARANCE

1. *forbearance:* ἀνοχή ANOCHĒ*
Rom 2. 4 the riches of his kindness and forbearance
3.25(26) because in his divine forbearance

2. *fitting, kind:* ἐπιεικής (subst. neut.) EPIEIKĒS
Phil 4. 5 Let all men know your forbearance

3. *patience, forbearance:* μακροθυμία MAKROTHYMIA
2 Cor 6. 6 knowledge, forbearance, kindness
2 Pet 3.15 count the forbearance . . as salvation

FORBEARING

1. *forbearing:* ἀνεξίκακος ANEXIKAKOS*
2 Tim 2.24 the Lord's servant must . . be . . forbearing

FORBEARING, BE

1. *be patient, persevere:* μακροθυμέω MAKROTHYMEŌ
2 Pet 3. 9 The Lord . . is forbearing toward you[h]

FORBID

1. *hinder, prevent, withhold:* κωλύω KŌLYŌ
Mk 9.38 "casting out demons . . and we forbade him
9.39 But Jesus said, "Do not forbid him
Lk 9.49 "casting out demons . . and we forbade him
9.50 Jesus said to him, "Do not forbid him
23. 2 "forbidding us to give tribute to Caesar
Acts 10.47 "Can any one forbid water for baptizing?
16. 6 forbidden . . to speak the word in Asia
1 Cor 14.39 do not forbid speaking in tongues
1 Tim 4. 3 who forbid marriage and enjoin abstinence

FORBID, GOD
IDIOMATICALLY
a. Mt 16.22 "God forbid, Lord! ἵλεώς σοι, κύριε [HILEŌS]
b. Lk 20.16 "God forbid! μὴ γένοιτο [GINOMAI]

FORCE
1. *compel:* ἀναγκάζω ANAGKAZŌ
2 Cor 12.11 "I have been a fool! You forced me
2. *mistreat:* κακόω KAKOŌ
Acts 7.19 "forced our fathers to expose their infants

FORCE, BE IN
1. *be strong, prevail:* ἰσχύω ISCHYŌ
Heb 9.17 is not in force as long as the one . . is alive

FORCE, TAKE BY
1. *seize, snatch up:* ἁρπάζω HARPAZŌ
Mt 11.12 "men of violence take it by force
Jn 6.15 take him by force to make him king
Acts 23.10 take him by force from among them

FORCE TO GO
1. *press into service:* ἀγγαρεύω AGGAREUŌ
Mt 5.41 "if any one forces you to go one mile

FOREBODING
1. *expectation:* προσδοκία PROSDOKIA
Lk 21.26 "fainting with fear and with foreboding

FORE-COURT
1. *vestibule, forecourt:* προαύλιον PROAULION
Mk [14.68 And he went out into the *fore-court*†

FOREFATHER
1. *father:* πατήρ PATĒR
Rom 9.10 children by one man, our forefather Isaac
11.28 beloved for the sake of their forefathers
2. *forefather:* προπάτωρ PROPATŌR*
Rom 4. 1 Abraham, our f. according to the flesh

FOREHEAD
1. *forehead, brow:* μέτωπον METŌPON*
Rev 7. 3 "sealed the servants . . upon their foreheads
9. 4 have not the seal . . upon their foreheads
13.16 marked on the right hand or the forehead
14. 1 Father's name written on their foreheads
14. 9 "a mark on his forehead or on his hand
17. 5 on her forehead was written a name
20. 4 not received its mark on their foreheads
22. 4 his name shall be on their foreheads

FOREIGN
1. *foreign:* ἀλλότριος ALLOTRIOS
Heb 11. 9 as in a foreign land, living in tents
11.34 put foreign armies to flight
2. *outside:* ἔξω EXŌ
Acts 26.11 "I persecuted them even to foreign cities
3. *strange, foreign:* ξένος XENOS
Acts 17.18 "a preacher of foreign divinities

FOREIGNER
1. *of another race:* ἀλλογενής (subst.) ALLOGENĒS*
Lk 17.18 "no one . . to . . give praise . . except this f.?
2. *non-Greek, foreign:* βάρβαρος (subst.) BARBAROS
1 Cor 14.11 I shall be a foreigner to the speaker and the speaker a foreigner to me
3. *another, different:* ἕτερος (subst.) HETEROS
1 Cor 14.21 "by the lips of foreigners will I speak
4. *strange, foreign:* ξένος (subst.) XENOS
Acts 17.21 all the Athenians and the foreigners

FOREKNOW
1. *foreknow:* προγινώσκω PROGINŌSKŌ
Rom 8.29 whom he foreknew he also predestined
11. 2 not rejected his people whom he foreknew

FOREKNOWLEDGE
1. *foreknowledge:* πρόγνωσις PROGNŌSIS
Acts 2.23 "according to the . . foreknowledge of God

FOREMOST
1. *first, foremost:* πρῶτος PRŌTOS
1 Tim 1.15 And I am the foremost of sinners
1.16 in me, as the foremost

FORERUNNER
1. *going before:* πρόδρομος (subst.) PRODROMOS*
Heb 6.20 where Jesus has gone as a forerunner

FORESAIL
1. *foresail:* ἀρτέμων ARTEMŌN*
Acts 27.40 then hoisting the foresail to the wind

FORESEE
1. *foresee:* προβλέπω (mid.) PROBLEPŌ*
Heb 11.40 since God had foreseen something better
2. *foresee:* προεῖδον PROEIDON*
Acts 2.31 "he foresaw and spoke of the resurrection
Gal 3. 8 foreseeing that God would justify

FOREST
1. *forest, wood:* ὕλη HYLĒ*
Jas 3. 5 How great a forest is set ablaze!

FORETELL
1. *foretell:* προκαταγγέλλω PROKATAGGELLŌ
Acts 3.18 "what God foretold by . . all the prophets
2. *indicate, report:* σημαίνω SĒMAINŌ
Acts 11.28 Agabus . . foretold . . a great famine

FOREWARN, SOLEMNLY
IDIOMATICALLY
a. 1 Th 4.6 as we solemnly forewarned you καθὼς καὶ προείπαμεν ὑμῖν καὶ διεμαρτυράμεθα [DIAMARTYROMAI; PROEIPON]

FORFEIT
1. *cause loss:* ζημιόω (pass.) ZĒMIOŌ
Mt 16.26 "if he gains the . . world and forfeits his life
Mk 8.36 "to gain the . . world and forfeit his life
Lk 9.25 "gains the . . world and . . forfeits himself

FORGET
1. *forget altogether:* ἐκλανθάνομαι EKLANTHANOMAI*
Heb 12. 5 have you forgotten the exhortation?
2. *forget, neglect:* ἐπιλανθάνομαι EPILANTHANOMAI
Mt 16. 5 they had forgotten to bring any bread
Mk 8.14 they had forgotten to bring bread
Lk 12. 6 "And not one of them is forgotten
Phil 3.13 forgetting what lies behind and straining
Jas 1.24 he . . at once forgets what he was like
3. *suffer forgetfulness:* λήθην λαμβάνειν LĒTHĒ [A.6.a.4]
2 Pet 1. 9 has forgotten that he was cleansed

FORGETS, THAT
1. *forgetfulness:* ἐπιλησμονή (gen.) EPILĒSMONĒ*
Jas 1.25 being no hearer that forgets but a doer

FORGIVE
1. *let go, leave, forgive:* ἀφίημι APHIĒMI
Mt 6.12 "And forgive us our debts, As we also have forgiven our debtors
6.14 "For if you forgive men their trespasses, your heavenly Father also will forgive you
6.15 "if you do not forgive . . their trespasses, neither will your Father forgive your
9. 2 "Take heart . . ; your sins are forgiven
9. 5 "which is easier . . 'Your sins are forgiven'?
9. 6 "authority on earth to forgive sins
12.31 "every sin . . will be forgiven . . but the blasphemy . . will not be forgiven
12.32 "a word against the Son . . will be forgiven; . . against the Holy Spirit will not be forgiven
18.21 "Lord, how often shall . . I forgive him?
18.27 "the lord . . forgave him the debt
18.32 " 'You wicked servant! I forgave you all
18.35 "if you do not forgive your brother
Mk 2. 5 "My son, your sins are forgiven
2. 7 "Who can forgive sins but God alone?
2. 9 "Which is easier . . 'Your sins are forgiven'?
2.10 "authority on earth to forgive sins
3.28 "all sins will be forgiven the sons of men
4.12 "lest they should turn . . and be forgiven
11.25 "forgive . . anything against any one; so that your Father . . may forgive you
[11.26 *"if you do not forgive, neither will your Father . . forgive your trespasses*‡
Lk 5.20 "Man, your sins are forgiven you

Lk 5.21 “Who can forgive sins but God only?
5.23 “Which . . ‘Your sins are forgiven you’?
5.24 “authority on earth to forgive sins
7.47 “her sins, which are many, are forgiven . . ; but he who is forgiven little, loves little
7.48 “Your sins are forgiven
7.49 “Who is this, who even forgives sins?
11. 4 “forgive us our sins, for we ourselves forgive every one who is indebted to us
12.10 “a word against the Son . . will be forgiven; . . against the Holy Spirit will not be forgiven
17. 3 “if he repents, forgive him
17. 4 “if he . . says, ‘I repent,’ you must forgive
23.34 “Father, forgive them; for they know not‡
Jn 20.23 “If you forgive the sins of any, they are forgiven
Acts 8.22 “that . . intent of your heart . . be forgiven
Rom 4. 7 “those whose iniquities are forgiven
Jas 5.15 if he has . . sins, he will be forgiven
1 Jn 1. 9 he . . will forgive our sins and cleanse us
2.12 because your sins are forgiven

2. *loose from, dismiss:* ἀπολύω APOLYŌ
Lk 6.37 “you will not be condemned; forgive, and you will be forgiven

3. *give graciously:* χαρίζομαι CHARIZOMAI
Lk 7.42 “he forgave them both
7.43 “The one . . to whom he forgave more
2 Cor 2. 7 so you should rather turn to forgive
2.10 Any one whom you forgive, I also . . What I have forgiven, if I have forgiven anything, has been for your sake
12.13 Forgive me this wrong!
Eph 4.32 tenderhearted, forgiving one another, as God in Christ forgave you
Col 2.13 having forgiven us all our trespasses
3.13 forgiving each other; as the Lord has forgiven you

FORGIVENESS

1. *release, forgiveness:* ἄφεσις APHESIS
Mt 26.28 “poured out . . for the forgiveness of sins
Mk 1. 4 baptism . . for the forgiveness of sins
3.29 “never has forgiveness, but is guilty
Lk 1.77 “knowledge . . in the forgiveness of their sins
3. 3 baptism . . for the forgiveness of sins
24.47 “repentance and forgiveness of sins
Acts 2.38 Peter said . . “Repent, and be baptized
5.31 “to give repentance . . and forgiveness of sins
10.43 “who believes . . receives forgiveness
13.38 “forgiveness of sins is proclaimed to you
26.18 “ ‘that they may receive forgiveness
Eph 1. 7 redemption, . . forgiveness of our trespasses
Col 1.14 redemption, the forgiveness of sins
Heb 9.22 without . . blood . . no forgiveness of sins
10.18 Where there is forgiveness of these

FORK, WINNOWING

1. *winnowing shovel:* πτύον PTYON*
Mt 3.12 “His winnowing fork is in his hand
Lk 3.17 “His winnowing fork is in his hand

FORM

1. *form, appearance:* εἶδος EIDOS
Lk 3.22 Holy Spirit descended . . in bodily form
Jn 5.37 “his form you have never seen
1 Th 5.22 abstain from every form of evil

2. *image, likeness:* εἰκών EIKŌN
Heb 10. 1 but a shadow . . instead of the true form

3. *form, shape:* μορφή MORPHĒ*
Mk 16.12 After this he appeared in another form[k]‡
Phil 2. 6 though he was in the form of God
2. 7 emptied himself, taking . . f. of a servant[d]

4. *form, shape:* μορφόω MORPHOŌ*
Gal 4.19 in travail until Christ be formed in you!

5. *form, appearance:* μόρφωσις MORPHŌSIS
2 Tim 3. 5 holding the form of religion

6. *form, mold:* πλάσσω PLASSŌ
1 Tim 2.13 For Adam was formed first, then Eve

7. *form, appearance:* σχῆμα SCHĒMA*
1 Cor 7.31 the form of this world is passing away
Phil 2. 8 found in human form he humbled himself

FORMED

1. *stand with, commend:* συνίστημι (perf. part.) SYNISTĒMI
2 Pet 3. 5 an earth formed out of water

FORMER

1. *at some time, once:* ποτέ POTE II
Gal 1.13 you have heard of my former life in Judaism

2. *lead forward:* προάγω (part.) PROAGŌ
Heb 7.18 a former commandment is set aside

3. *happen before:* προγίνομαι (perf. part.) PROGINOMAI*
Rom 3.25 he had passed over former sins

4. *earlier:* πρότερος PROTEROS
[a]neut.
Eph 4.22 belongs to your former manner of life
Heb 10.32 recall the former days
1 Pet 1.14 [a]the passions of your former ignorance

5. *first, foremost:* πρῶτος PRŌTOS
Rev 21. 4 “for the former things have passed away

CONTEXTUALLY
Phil 1.17 f. proclaim Christ out of partisanship
Heb 7.23 The former priests were many in number

FORMER DAYS, WRITE IN

1. *write before:* προγράφω PROGRAPHŌ
Rom 15. 4 whatever was written in former days

FORMERLY

1. *at some time, once:* ποτέ POTE II
Jn 9.13 the man who had formerly been blind
Phm .11 (Formerly he was useless to you
1 Pet 3.20 who formerly did not obey

2. *earlier:* πρότερος (neut.) PROTEROS
1 Tim 1.13 though I formerly blasphemed
Heb 4. 6 who formerly received the good news

3. *then, formerly:* τότε TOTE
Gal 4. 8 Formerly, when you did not know God

FORNICATION

1. *fornication, unchastity:* πορνεία (sg. or pl.) PORNEIA
Mt 15.19 “murder, adultery, fornication, theft
Mk 7.21 “fornication, theft, murder, adultery
Jn 8.41 “We were not born of fornication
Gal 5.19 works of the flesh are plain: fornication[0]
Eph 5. 3 But f. . . must not . . be named among you[0]
Col 3. 5 Put to death . . what is earthly in you: f.[0]
Rev 17. 2 “the wine of whose fornication
17. 4 the impurities of her fornication
19. 2 “who corrupted the earth with her f.

FORNICATION, COMMIT

1. *fornicate:* πορνεύω PORNEUŌ
Rev 17. 2 “kings of the earth have committed f.
18. 3 “kings of the earth have committed f.
18. 9 kings of the earth, who committed f.

FORNICATOR

1. *brothel-keeper, immoral man:* πόρνος PORNOS
Eph 5. 5 no f. . . has any inheritance in the kingdom[0]
Rev 21. 8 “murderers, fornicators, sorcerers
22.15 sorcerers and fornicators and murderers

FORSAKE

1. *let go, leave, forgive:* ἀφίημι APHIĒMI
Mt 23.38 “your house is forsaken and desolate[x]
26.56 “all the disciples forsook him and fled
Mk 14.50 they all forsook him, and fled
Lk 13.35 “Behold, your house is forsaken

2. *rebellion:* ἀποστασία APOSTASIA [A.1.d]
Acts 21.21 “you teach all the Jews . . to forsake Moses

3. *leave behind:* ἐγκαταλείπω EGKATALEIPŌ
Mt 27.46 “my God, why hast thou forsaken me?
Mk 15.34 “my God, why hast thou forsaken me?
2 Cor 4. 9 persecuted, but not forsaken
Heb 13. 5 “I will never fail you nor forsake you

4. *leave behind:* καταλείπω KATALEIPŌ
2 Pet 2.15 Forsaking the right way they have gone

FORTH (*See also* BRING FORTH FRUIT; COME FORTH; SEND FORTH)
1. *outside:* ἔξω EXŌ
Jn 15. 6 "he is cast forth as a branch and withers

FORTH, BRING
1. *give birth to:* ἀποκυέω APOKYEŌ
Jas 1.15 sin when . . full-grown brings forth death
1.18 Of his own will he brought us forth
2. *sprout, produce:* βλαστάνω BLASTANŌ
Jas 5.18 the earth brought forth its fruit
3. *give:* δίδωμι DIDŌMI
Mt 13. 8 "Other seeds . . brought forth grain
Mk 4. 8 "other seeds . . brought forth grain
4. *throw out:* ἐκβάλλω EKBALLŌ
Mt 12.35 "The good man . . brings forth good, and the evil man . . brings forth evil
5. *bear, bring forth:* τίκτω TIKTŌ
Heb 6. 7 land . . brings forth vegetation useful
Rev 12. 4 devour her child when she brought it forth
12. 5 she brought forth a male child

FORTUNATE
1. *blessed, happy:* μακάριος MAKARIOS
Acts 26. 2 "I think myself fortunate . . , King Agrippa

FORTUNATUS: Φορτουνᾶτος ˌfôrtyüˈnātəs
1 Cor 16.17 Stephanas and Fortunatus and Achaicus

FORTY
1. *forty:* τεσσαράκοντα TESSARAKONTA
Mt 4. 2 he fasted forty days and forty nights, and afterward he was hungry
Mk 1.13 he was in the wilderness forty days
Lk 4. 2 for forty days in the wilderness
Acts 1. 3 appearing to them during forty days
4.22 the man . . was more than forty years old
7.30 "when forty years had passed
7.36 "in the wilderness for forty years
7.42 " 'sacrifices, forty years in the wilderness
13.21 "God gave them Saul . . for forty years
23.13 more than forty who made this conspiracy
23.21 "more than forty of their men lie in ambush
2 Cor 11.24 Five times I have received . . the forty lashes
Heb 3. 9 "fathers . . saw my works for forty years
3.17 with whom was he provoked forty years?

FORTY YEARS
1. *forty years:* τεσσαρακονταετής TESSARAKONTAETĒS*
Acts 7.23 "When he was forty years old
13.18 "about forty years he bore with[m] them

FORTY-FOUR
1. *forty-four:* τεσσαράκοντα τέσσαρες TESSARAKONTA; TESSARES [A.3.c]
Rev 7. 4 a hundred and forty-four thousand sealed
14. 1 a hundred and forty-four thousand
14. 3 the hundred and forty-four thousand
21.17 a hundred and forty-four cubits

FORTY-SIX
1. *forty and six:* τεσσαράκοντα καὶ ἕξ TESSARAKONTA; HEX [A.3.c]
Jn 2.20 "forty-six years to build this temple

FORTY-TWO
1. *forty and two:* τεσσαράκοντα καὶ δύο TESSARAKONTA; DYO [A.3.c]
Rev 11. 2 "trample . . the holy city . . forty-two months
13. 5 to exercise authority for forty-two months

FORUM OF APPIUS: ˈapēəs II,B-2
1. *forum of Appius:* Ἀππίου φόρον PHORON*
Acts 28.15 they . . came as far as the Forum of A.

FORWARD (*See* COME FORWARD; COME FORWARD TO; LOOK FORWARD TO; PUT FORWARD; STRAIN FORWARD)

FOUL
1. *unclean:* ἀκάθαρτος AKATHARTOS
Rev 16.13 I saw . . three foul spirits like frogs
18. 2 "a haunt of every foul spirit, a haunt of every foul and hateful bird
2. *evil, bad:* κακός KAKOS
Rev 16. 2 foul and evil sores came upon the men

FOUL TALK
1. *obscenity:* αἰσχρολογία AISCHROLOGIA*
Col 3. 8 malice, slander, and foul talk

FOUND
1. *found, establish:* θεμελιόω THEMELIOŌ
Mt 7.25 "because it had been founded on the rock
Lk [6.48 "it had been *founded upon the rock*‡
Heb 1.10 "Thou, Lord, didst found the earth

FOUNDATION
1. *throwing down, building:* καταβολή KATABOLĒ
Mt 13.35 "since the foundation of the world
25.34 " 'from the foundation of the world
Lk 11.50 "shed from the foundation of the world
Jn 17.24 "before the foundation of the world
Eph 1. 4 before the foundation of the world
Heb 4. 3 from the foundation of the world
9.26 since the foundation of the world
1 Pet 1.20 before the foundation of the world
Rev 13. 8 before the foundation of the world
17. 8 "from the foundation of the world
2. *foundation:* θεμέλιον THEMELION*
Acts 16.26 foundations of the prison were shaken
3. *foundation:* θεμέλιος THEMELIOS
Lk 6.48 "a man . . laid the foundation upon rock
6.49 "a house . . without a foundation
14.29 "Otherwise, when he has laid a foundation
Rom 15.20 lest I build on another man's foundation
1 Cor 3.10 like a skilled master builder I laid a f.
3.11 no other foundation can any one lay
3.12 if any one builds on the foundation
Eph 2.20 built upon the foundation of the apostles
1 Tim 6.19 laying up . . a good foundation
2 Tim 2.19 But God's firm foundation stands
Heb 6. 1 not laying again a foundation
11.10 the city which has foundations
Rev 21.14 the city had twelve foundations
21.19 foundations of the wall of the city
CONTEXTUALLY
1 Cor 3.14 which any man has built on the foundation

FOUNTAIN
1. *running water, spring:* πηγή PĒGĒ
Rev 8.10 it fell . . on the fountains of water
14. 7 "made heaven . . and the fountains of water
16. 4 the rivers and the fountains of water
21. 6 "from the fountain of the water of life

FOUR
1. *four:* τέσσαρες TESSARES
Mt 24.31 "gather his elect from the four winds
Mk 2. 3 a paralytic carried by four men
13.27 "gather his elect from the four winds
Jn 11.17 already . . in the tomb four days
19.23 the soldiers . . made four parts, one for each
Acts 10.11 let down by four corners upon the earth
11. 5 "let down from heaven by four corners
12. 4 delivered him to four squads of soldiers
21. 9 he had four unmarried daughters
21.23 "We have four men who are under a vow
27.29 they let out four anchors from the stern
Rev 4. 6 four living creatures, full of eyes
4. 8 the four living creatures . . never cease
5. 6 the throne and the four living creatures
5. 8 the four living creatures and the . . elders
5.14 the four living creatures said, "Amen!
6. 1 I heard one of the four living creatures
6. 6 in the midst of the four living creatures
7. 1 I saw four angels standing at the four corners of the earth, holding back the four winds of the earth
7. 2 called with a loud voice to the four angels
7.11 the elders and the four living creatures
9.13 I heard a voice from the four horns
9.14 "Release the four angels who are bound
9.15 the four angels were released
14. 3 they sing . . before the four living creatures
15. 7 one of the four living creatures
19. 4 the four living creatures fell down

Rev 20. 8 nations . . at the four corners of the earth
2. *thirty:* τριάκοντα TRIAKONTA [A.3.c.1]
Jn 6.19 rowed about three or four miles[m]†
IDIOMATICALLY
a. Acts 10.30 "Four days ago, about this hour ἀπὸ τετάρτης ἡμέρας μέχρι ταύτης τῆς ὥρας [TETARTOS]

FOUR DAYS
1. *for four days:* τεταρταῖος TETARTAIOS [A.3.b.3]
Jn 11.39 "an odor, for he has been dead four days

FOUR HUNDRED
1. *four hundred:* τετρακόσιοι TETRAKOSIOI*
Acts 5.36 "men, about four hundred, joined him
7. 6 "ill-treat them four hundred years
13.19(20) "for about four hundred and fifty years

FOUR MONTHS
1. *of four months:* τετράμηνος (subst. fem.) TETRAMĒNOS*
Jn 4.35 " 'There are yet four months

FOUR THOUSAND
1. *four thousand:* τετρακισχίλιοι TETRAKISCHILIOI*
Mt 15.38 Those who ate were four thousand men
16.10 "the seven loaves of the four thousand
Mk 8. 9 there were about four t. people
8.20 "the seven for the four thousand
Acts 21.38 "the four thousand men of the Assassins

FOURFOLD
1. *four times:* τετραπλοῦς TETRAPLOUS*
Lk 19. 8 "I restore it fourfold

FOURSQUARE
1. *with four angles, square:* τετράγωνος TETRAGŌNOS*
Rev 21.16 The city lies foursquare

FOURTEEN
1. *fourteen:* δεκατέσσαρες DEKATESSARES*
Mt 1.17 from Abraham . . fourteen generations
1.17 from David . . fourteen generations
1.17 from the deportation . . fourteen generations
2 Cor 12. 2 a man in Christ . . fourteen years ago
Gal 2. 1 after fourteen years I went up again

FOURTEENTH
1. *fourteenth:* τεσσαρεσκαιδέκατος TESSARESKAIDEKATOS*
Acts 27.27 When the fourteenth night had come
27.33 "Today is the fourteenth day

FOURTH
1. *fourth:* τέταρτος TETARTOS
Mt 14.25 in the fourth watch of the night
Mk 6.48 about the fourth watch of the night
Rev 4. 7 fourth living creature like a flying eagle
6. 7 When he opened the fourth seal, I heard the voice of the fourth living creature
6. 8 power over a fourth of the earth
8.12 The fourth angel blew his trumpet
16. 8 The fourth angel poured his bowl
21.19 the third agate, the fourth emerald

FOX
1. *fox:* ἀλώπηξ ALŌPĒX*
Mt 8.20 "Foxes have holes, and birds . . nests
Lk 9.58 "Foxes have holes, and birds . . nests
13.32 "Go and tell that fox, 'Behold

FRAGMENT
1. *fragment, piece:* κλάσμα KLASMA
Jn 6.12 "Gather up the fragments left over
6.13 filled twelve baskets with fragments

FRAGRANCE
1. *smell, scent:* ὀσμή OSMĒ
Jn 12. 3 the house was filled with . . fragrance
2 Cor 2.14 through us spreads the f. of the knowledge
2.16 to one a fragrance from death to death, to the other a fragrance from life to life

FRAGRANT
1. *sweet smell:* εὐωδία (gen.) EUŌDIA
Phil 4.18 a fragrant offering, a sacrifice acceptable
IDIOMATICALLY
a. Eph 5.2 a fragrant offering and sacrifice to God προσφορὰν καὶ θυσίαν τῷ θεῷ εἰς ὀσμὴν εὐωδίας [EUŌDIA; OSMĒ]

FRANKINCENSE
1. *frankincense:* λίβανος LIBANOS*
Mt 2.11 gold and frankincense and myrrh
Rev 18.13 myrrh, frankincense, wine, oil

FRAUD
1. *wandering, deceit:* πλάνη PLANĒ
Mt 27.64 "the last fraud will be worse than the first
CONTEXTUALLY
Jas 5. 4 wages . . which you kept back by fraud

FREE (*See also* ANXIETIES, FREE FROM; GIFT, FREE; LOVE OF MONEY, FREE FROM; REPROACH, FREE FROM)
1. *loose from, dismiss:* ἀπολύω APOLYŌ
Lk 13.12 "you are freed from your infirmity
2. *justify, vindicate:* δικαιόω DIKAIOŌ
Acts 13.39 "by him every one that believes is freed
13.39 "you could not be freed by the law of Moses
Rom 6. 7 For he who has died is freed from sin
3. *free:* ἐλεύθερος ELEUTHEROS
Mt 17.26 Jesus said to him, "Then the sons are free
Jn 8.33 "you say, 'You will be made free
8.36 "you will be free indeed
Rom 6.20 you were free in regard to righteousness
7. 3 if her husband dies she is free
1 Cor 7.22 he who was free when called is a slave
7.39 If the husband dies, she is free
9. 1 Am I not free? Am I not an apostle?
9.19 For though I am free from all men
12.13 Jews or Greeks, slaves or free
Gal 3.28 there is neither slave nor free
4.22 one by a slave and one by a free woman
4.23 son of the free woman through promise
4.26 But the Jerusalem above is free
4.30 "not inherit with the son of the free woman
4.31 we are . . children . . of the free woman
Eph 6. 8 whether he is a slave or free
Col 3.11 barbarian, Scythian, slave, free man
1 Pet 2.16 Live as free men
Rev 6.15 every one, slave and free, hid in the caves
13.16 both free and slave, to be marked
19.18 "both free and slave, both small and great
4. *break up, unbind:* λύω LYŌ
Rev 1. 5 To him who . . has freed us from our sins

FREE, BE
1. *break up, unbind:* λύω (perf. pass.) LYŌ
1 Cor 7.27 Are you free from a wife?

FREE GIFT (*See* GIFT, FREE)

FREE, MAKE
1. *set free:* ἐλευθερόω ELEUTHEROŌ
Jn 8.32 "the truth will make you free
8.36 "if the Son makes you free, you will be free

FREE OF CHARGE
1. *without expense:* ἀδάπανος ADAPANOS*
1 Cor 9.18 I may make the gospel free of charge

FREE, SET
1. *loose from, dismiss:* ἀπολύω APOLYŌ
Acts 26.32 "This man could have been set free
2. *set free:* ἐλευθερόω ELEUTHEROŌ
Rom 6.18 having been set free from sin
6.22 now that you have been set free from sin
8. 2 Christ Jesus has set me free from the law
8.21 the creation itself will be set free
Gal 5. 1 For freedom Christ has set us free

FREE, TO BE
1. *loosing, divorce:* λύσις LYSIS* [A.1.d]
1 Cor 7.27 Do not seek to be free

FREE WILL
1. *voluntary, willing:* ἑκούσιος (subst.) HEKOUSIOS
Phm .14 but of your own free will

FREE WILL, OF ONE'S OWN
1. *by free choice:* αὐθαίρετος AUTHAIRETOS
2 Cor 8. 3 beyond their means, of their own free w.

FREEDMAN
1. *freedman:* ἀπελεύθερος APELEUTHEROS*
1 Cor 7.22 he . . is a freedman of the Lord
2. *freedman:* Λιβερτῖνος LIBERTINOS*
Acts 6. 9 belonged to the synagogue of the Freedmen

FREEDOM
1. *freedom:* ἐλευθερία ELEUTHERIA
2 Cor 3.17 where the Spirit . . is, there is freedom
Gal 2. 4 slipped in to spy out our freedom
5. 1 For freedom Christ has set us free
5.13 For you were called to freedom . . ; only do not use your freedom as an opportunity
1 Pet 2.16 without using your freedom as a pretext
2 Pet 2.19 They promise them freedom
IDIOMATICALLY
a. 1 Cor 7.21 if you can gain your freedom εἰ καὶ δύνασαι ἐλεύθερος γενέσθαι [ELEUTHEROS]

FREELY (*See also* DRINK FREELY)
1. *speak freely:* παρρησιάζομαι (part.) PARRĒSIAZOMAI
Acts 26.26 "the king knows . . and to him I speak freely
2. *many, great:* πολύς (neut. pl.) POLYS
Mk 1.45 he . . began to talk freely about it

FREELY BESTOW
1. *show grace:* χαριτόω CHARITOŌ [A.6.a.6]
Eph 1. 6 grace which he freely bestowed on us

FREQUENT
1. *often, many times:* πολλάκις POLLAKIS [A.4.a]
2 Cor 11.26 on frequent journeys, in danger
2. *close, frequent:* πυκνός PYKNOS
1 Tim 5.23 use a little wine for . . your frequent ailments

FRESH
1. *sweet, fresh:* γλυκύς GLYKYS
Jas 3.11 pour forth . . fresh water and brackish?
3.12 No more can salt water yield fresh
2. *new, fresh:* καινός KAINOS
Mt 9.17 "new wine is put into fresh wineskins
Mk 2.22 "new wine is for fresh skins[j]‡
Lk 5.38 new wine must be put into fresh wineskins

FRIEND (*See also* HIS FRIENDS; THEIR FRIENDS)
1. *comrade:* ἑταῖρος HETAIROS
Mt 20.13 " 'Friend, I am doing you no wrong
22.12 " 'Friend, how did you get in here?
26.50 "Friend, why are you here?[j]
2. *beloved, dear:* φίλος (subst.) PHILOS*
Mt 11.19 " 'a friend of tax collectors and sinners!
Lk 7. 6 the centurion sent friends to him
7.34 " 'friend of tax collectors and sinners!
11. 5 "Which of you who has a friend?
11. 5 " 'Friend, lend me three loaves
11. 6 " 'a friend of mine has arrived
11. 8 "he will not . . give . . because he is his friend
12. 4 "I tell you, my friends, do not fear those
14.10 " 'Friend, go up higher
14.12 "do not invite your friends or . . brothers
15. 6 "calls together his friends and his neighbors
15. 9 "calls together her friends and neighbors
15.29 " 'that I might make merry with my friends
16. 9 "I tell you, make friends for yourselves
21.16 "brothers and kinsmen and friends
23.12 Herod and Pilate became friends
Jn 3.29 "the friend of the bridegroom
11.11 "Our friend Lazarus has fallen asleep
15.13 "that a man lay down his life for his friends
15.14 "You are my friends if you do
15.15 "but I have called you friends
19.12 Jews cried . . "you are not Caesar's friend
Acts 10.24 Cornelius . . had called . . close friends
19.31 Asiarchs also, who were friends of his
27. 3 gave him leave to go to his friends
Jas 2.23 he was called the friend of God
4. 4 whoever wishes to be a friend of the world
3 Jn .15 The friends greet you. Greet the friends, every one of them
CONTEXTUALLY
Mk 5.19 "Go home to your friends, and tell them

FRIENDLY
1. *with peace:* μετ' εἰρήνης EIRĒNĒ [B.1.a.1]
Heb 11.31 she had given friendly welcome to the spies

FRIENDS, MAKE
1. *be favorable:* εὐνοέω EUNOEŌ*
Mt 5.25 "Make friends quickly with your accuser

FRIENDSHIP
1. *love, friendship:* φιλία PHILIA*
Jas 4. 4 that friendship with the world is enmity

FRIGHTEN
1. *alarm, frighten:* ἐκφοβέω EKPHOBEŌ*
2 Cor 10. 9 I would not seem to be frightening you

FRIGHTENED
1. *terrified:* ἔμφοβος EMPHOBOS
Lk 24. 5 as they were frightened and bowed
24.37 they were startled and frightened
2. *frighten:* πτύρω (part.) PTYRŌ*
Phil 1.28 not frightened . . by your opponents

FRIGHTENED, BE
1. *terrify:* φοβέω (pass.) PHOBEŌ
Jn 6.19 They were frightened

FRINGE
1. *edge, border:* κράσπεδον KRASPEDON*
Mt 9.20 woman . . touched the fringe of his garment
14.36 only touch the fringe of his garment
23. 5 "they make . . their fringes long
Mk 6.56 might touch . . the fringe of his garment
Lk 8.44 touched the fringe of his garment

FRO (*See* TOSSED TO AND FRO)

FROG
1. *frog:* βάτραχος BATRACHOS*
Rev 16.13 three foul spirits like frogs

FROM
1. *from:* ἀπό (+gen.) APO
Mt **1.**17^{3}, 21, 24; **2.**1; **3.**7, 13, 16; **4.**17, 25; **5.**18, 42; **6.**13; **7.**16^{2}, 23; **8.**1, 11, 30; **9.**15, 16; **11.**12, 25, 29; **12.**38; **13.**12; **14.**2, 13, 24‡; **15.**1, 8, 22, 27; **16.**21^{2}; **17.**25^{3}, 26; **18.**35; **19.**1, 4, 8; **21.**8, 11, 43; **22.**46; **23.**34, 35; **24.**21, 27, 29, 31, 32; **25.**28, 29, 32^{2}, 34, 41; **26.**16, 39, 47; **27.**40, 42, 45, 51, 55^{2}, 57, 64; **28.**7, 8
Mk **1.**9; **2.**20, 21; **3.**7^{2}, 22; **4.**25; **5.**6, 17, 35; **6.**33; **7.**1, 4, 6, 33; **8.**11; **10.**6; **11.**12; **12.**34; **13.**19, 27, 28; **14.**35, 36; **15.**21, 30, 32, 38, 40, 45; **16.**8, [^{end}‡
Lk **1.**2, 26, 38, 52, 70; **2.**4, 15, 36; **3.**7; **4.**1, 13; **5.**3, 8, 35, 36^{2}; **6.**13, 17, 29; **7.**6, 45; **8.**2, 12, 18, 35, 37, 38; **9.**5, 33, 37, 38, 45, 54; **10.**21, 30; **11.**50, 51; **13.**15, 16, 27, 29^{2}; **16.**3, 18, 21, 30; **17.**29^{2}; **18.**34; **19.**24, 26, 42; **21.**11; **22.**18, 41, 42, [43‡, 45, 69, 71; **23.**5, 26, 49, 50(51); **24.**2, 9, 13, 47, 51
Jn **1.**44; **3.**2; **6.**38; **7.**42; **8.**44; **10.**5, 18; **11.**53; **12.**21, 36; **13.**3; **15.**27; **16.**22, 30; **18.**28; **19.**27; **21.**8
Acts **1.**4, 11, 12, 22^{2}, 25; **2.**5, 40; **3.**19(20), 24, 26; **5.**38; **6.**9; **8.**10, 26, 33; **9.**8, 13, 18; **10.**23, 37; **11.**11, 27; **12.**19; **13.**8, 13, 14, 29, 31, 39; **14.**15, 19; **15.**1, 18, 38, 39; **16.**11; **17.**2, 27; **18.**2, 5, 6, 16, 21; **19.**9, [9‡, 12; **20.**6, 9, 17, 18; **21.**1, 7, 10, 16, 27; **22.**22, 29; **23.**21, 34; **24.**19; **25.**1, 7; **26.**4, 18, 22; **27.**21, 34; **28.**21, 23^{2}
Rom **1.**7, 18; **5.**9, 14; **6.**7, 18, 22; **7.**2, 3, 6; **8.**2, 21, 35, 39; **9.**3; **11.**26; **15.**19, 31
1 Cor **1.**3; **4.**5; **6.**19; **7.**10, 27; **11.**23
2 Cor **1.**2, 16; **2.**3; **3.**18^{2}; **5.**6, 16; **7.**1; **11.**3, 9
Gal **1.**1, 3; **2.**6, 12; **4.**24; **5.**4
Eph **1.**2; **4.**31; **6.**23
Phil **1.**2, 5, 28
Col **1.**2, 6, 7, 9, 23, [26†; **3.**24
1 Th **1.**8, 9; **2.**6^{2}; **3.**6; **4.**3, 16; **5.**22
2 Th **1.**2, 7, 9^{2}; **2.**13‡; **3.**2, 3, 6
1 Tim **1.**2; **6.**10
2 Tim **1.**2; **2.**19, 21; **3.**15; **4.**4, 18
Tit **1.**4; **2.**14
Phm .3
Heb **3.**12; **4.**3, 4, 10^{2}; **6.**1, 7; **7.**1, 13, 26; **8.**11; **9.**14; **10.**22; **11.**12, 15; **12.**25; **13.**24
Jas **1.**17, 27; **4.**7; **5.**19

1 Pet **1**.12; **3**.10, 11
2 Pet **1**.21‡; **3**.4
1 Jn **1**.1, 5, 7, 9; **2**.7, 13, 14, 24[2], 27, 28; **3**.8, 11, 22; **4**.21; **5**.21
2 Jn .5, 6
3 Jn .7
Jude .14
Rev **1**.4[2], 5; **3**.12; **6**.16[2]; **7**.2; **9**.6; **12**.14; **14**.3, 4; **16**.12, 17; **17**.8; **18**.14, 15; **19**.5; **20**.[9‡, 11; **21**.2, 10; **22**.19

2. *through:* διά (+gen.) DIA
[a]+acc.
Mt **4**.4
Phil **1**.15[2a]
2 Th **2**.2

3. *from, out of:* ἐκ (+gen.) EK
Mt **2**.6; **3**.9, 17; **5**.37; **12**.42; **15**.5; **16**.1; **17**.5, 9; **21**.19, 25[3], 26; **24**.31; **28**.2
Mk **1**.11; **5**.30; **6**.14; **7**.11, 31; **9**.9, 10, 21; **10**.20; **11**.8, 14, 30[2], 31, 32; **12**.25; **13**.25, 27; **16**.3
Lk **1**.15, 71[2], 74, 78; **2**.4; **3**.8, 22; **5**.3, 17; **6**.44[2]; **8**.27; **9**.7; **10**.7, 18; **11**.16; **12**.36; **16**.31; **17**.7, 24; **18**.21; **20**.4[2], 5, 6, 35; **23**.55; **24**.46, 49
Jn **1**.16, 19, 24, 32; **2**.22; **3**.13, 27, 31; **4**.12, 22, 39, 47, 54; **5**.24; **6**.13, 23, 31, 32[2], 33, 41, 42, 50, 51[2], 58, 64; **7**.17, 22[2], 41, 52[2]; **8**.23[2], 42; **9**.1; **10**.32, 39; **11**.55; **12**.1, 9, 17, 27, 28, 32, 34; **13**.4; **16**.4, 28; **17**.15; **18**.3; **19**.23; **20**.1, 9; **21**.14
Acts **2**.2; **3**.2, 15, 22, 23; **4**.2, 10; **7**.3, 4, 37; **9**.3; **10**.41; **11**.5, 9; **12**.11, 25‡; **13**.30, 34; **14**.8; **15**.21, 24, 29; **17**.3, 26, 31, 33; **19**.25; **22**.6, 14; **23**.10; **26**.4, 17[2]; **27**.29, 30[2]; **28**.4[2], 17
Rom **1**.3; **2**.29[2]; **4**.24; **6**.4, 9, 13, 17; **7**.4, 24; **8**.11[2], 34; **9**.6, 24[2]; **10**.7, 9, 17; **11**.15, 24, 26, 36; **13**.11; **14**.23[2]
1 Cor **2**.12; **5**.2; **7**.7; **8**.6; **9**.13, 19; **10**.4; **11**.8[2], 12[2]; **15**.12, 20, 47[2]
2 Cor **1**.10; **2**.16[2]; **3**.1, 5[2]; **5**.1, 8, 18; **11**.26[2]; **12**.6
Gal **1**.1, 4, 8; **3**.13; **5**.8; **6**.8[2]
Eph **1**.20; **3**.15; **4**.16; **5**.14; **6**.6
Phil **3**.9, 11, 20
Col **1**.13, 18; **2**.12, 19; **3**.8; **4**.16
1 Th **1**.10[3]; **2**.3, 6
1 Tim **1**.5
2 Tim **2**.8, 22, 26; **3**.11; **4**.17
Heb **5**.7; **7**.5, 14; **11**.19; **13**.10, 20
Jas **3**.10, 11; **5**.20[2]
1 Pet **1**.3, 18, 21, 22
2 Pet **1**.18; **2**.9, 21
1 Jn **2**.19
Rev **1**.5, 16; **2**.5; **3**.10; **4**.5; **5**.7, 9; **6**.4, 14; **7**.9, 17; **8**.4, 10; **9**.1, 2, 3, 13, 17, 18; **10**.1, 4, 8, 10; **11**.5, 7, 9, 11, 12; **12**.16; **13**.13; **14**.2, 13[2], 20; **15**.8[2]; **16**.1, 13[3], 21; **17**.8; **18**.1, 4; **19**.15, 21; **20**.1, 7, 9†‡; **21**.3, 4, 6; **22**.1

4. *in, at, by:* ἐν (+dat.) EN
2 Cor **11**.26

5. *on, at:* ἐπί (+dat.) EPI
Rom **6**.21
Phm .7

6. *by:* ὑπό (+gen.) HYPO
Rom **13**.1
1 Th **2**.14[2]
Heb **12**.3
3 Jn .12[2]

7. *in accordance with, for:* κατά (+acc.) KATA
Phil **2**.3
1 Tim **5**.21

8. *from among:* ἐκ μέσου MESOS [B.3.b.1]
Mt **13**.49
1 Cor **5**.2
2 Cor **6**.17

9. *not, no:* οὐ OU [A.4.c]
2 Cor **11**.4[2]

10. *from:* παρά (+gen.) PARA
[a]+dat.
Mt **2**.7, 16; **6**.1[a]
Mk **8**.11; **12**.2; **14**.43; **16**.9‡
Lk **1**.45; **2**.1; **6**.19, 34; **8**.49; **11**.16
Jn **1**.6, 14; **5**.34, 41, 44[2]; **6**.45, 46; **7**.29; **8**.26, 38, 40; **9**.16, 33; **10**.18; **15**.15, 26[2]; **16**.27; **17**.7, 8
Acts **2**.33; **3**.5; **7**.16; **9**.14; **17**.9; **20**.24; **22**.5; **24**.8; **26**.10; **28**.22
Gal **1**.12
Eph **6**.8
Phil **4**.18
1 Th **2**.13; **4**.1
2 Th **3**.6
2 Tim **1**.13, 18; **2**.2; **3**.14
Jas **1**.7
2 Pet **1**.17
2 Jn .3[2]
Rev **2**.27; **3**.18

11. *about, around:* περί (+acc.) PERI
2 Tim **2**.18

FROM AMONG (*See* AMONG, FROM)

FROM HERE

1. *hence:* ἐντεῦθεν ENTEUTHEN
Lk 4. 9 "throw yourself down from here
13.31 "Get away from here, for Herod wants

2. *thence, therefore:* ἔνθεν ENTHEN*
Mt 17.20 " 'Move from here to there[0]
Lk 16.26 " 'those who would pass from here to you

FROM THE WORLD

1. *hence:* ἐντεῦθεν ENTEUTHEN
Jn 18.36 "my kingship is not from the world

FROM THERE

1. *from that place:* ἐκεῖθεν EKEITHEN
Mt 4.21 going on from there he saw two . . brothers
9. 9 As Jesus passed on from t., he saw a man
9.27 as Jesus passed on from t., two blind men
11. 1 he went on from there to teach
12. 9 he went on from there, and entered
12.15 Jesus, aware of this, withdrew from there
13.53 he went away from there
14.13 he withdrew from there in a boat
15.21 Jesus went away from there and withdrew
15.29 Jesus went on from there . . along the Sea
Mk 6. 1 He went away from there . . to his own
7.24 from there he arose and went away
Lk 9. 4 "stay there, and from there depart
16.26 " 'none may cross from there to us
Jn 11.54 Jesus . . went from there to the country
Acts 13. 4 from there they sailed to Cyprus
27.12 majority advised to put to sea from there

2. *whence, where:* ὅθεν HOTHEN
Acts 28.13 And from there we made a circuit

3. *and from there:* κἀκεῖθεν KAKEITHEN
Mk **9**.30
Lk **11**.53
Acts **7**.4; **14**.26; **16**.12; **20**.15; **21**.1; **27**.4

FROM WHICH

1. *whence, where:* ὅθεν HOTHEN
Mt 12.44 " 'return to my house from which I came
Lk 11.24 " 'return to my house from which I came

FRONT, BE IN

1. *lead forward:* προάγω PROAGŌ
Lk 18.39 those who were in front rebuked him

FRONT, IN
FRONT OF, IN

1. *before:* ἔμπροσθεν EMPROSTHEN
Acts 18.17 seized . . and beat him in front of the tribunal
Rev 4. 6 creatures, full of eyes in front and behind

2. *before:* πρό (+gen.) PRO
Acts 14.13 whose temple was in front of the city

FRUIT

1. *produce, fruit:* γένημα GENĒMA
Mt 26.29 "I shall not drink again of this fruit
Mk 14.25 "I shall not drink again of the fruit
Lk 22.18 "from now on I shall not drink of the fruit

2. *fruit:* καρπός KARPOS
Mt 3. 8 "Bear fruit that befits repentance
3.10 "every tree . . that does not bear good fruit
7.16 "You will know them by their fruits
7.17 "every sound tree bears good fruit, but the bad tree bears evil fruit

Mt 7.18 "A sound tree cannot bear evil fruit, nor can a bad tree bear good fruit
7.19 "Every tree that does not bear good fruit
7.20 "Thus you will know them by their fruits
12.33 "Either make the tree good, and its fruit good; or make the tree bad, and its fruit bad; for the tree is known by its fruit
21.19 "May no fruit ever come from you again!
21.34 "When the season of fruit drew near, he sent his servants . . to get his fruit
21.41 "who will give him the fruits in their seasons
21.43 "given to a nation producing the fruits of it[q]
Mk 11.14 "May no one ever eat fruit from you again
12. 2 "he sent a servant . . to get . . fruit
Lk 1.42 "blessed is the fruit of your womb!
3. 8 "Bear fruits that befit repentance
3. 9 "every tree . . that does not bear . . fruit
6.43 "For no good tree bears bad fruit, nor . . does a bad tree bear good fruit
6.44 "for each tree is known by its own fruit
13. 6 "he came seeking fruit on it and found none
13. 7 " 'I have come seeking fruit on this fig tree
13. 9 " 'if it bears fruit next year
20.10 "that they . . give him some of the fruit
Jn 4.36 "He who . . gathers fruit for eternal life
12.24 "if it dies, it bears much fruit
15. 2 "Every branch of mine that bears no fruit
15. 2 every branch that does bear fruit he prunes, that it may bear more fruit
15. 4 "the branch cannot bear fruit by itself
15. 5 "he it is that bears much fruit
15. 8 "Father is glorified, that you bear much fruit
15.16 "that you should go and bear fruit and that your fruit should abide
1 Cor 9. 7 plants . . without eating any of its fruit
Gal 5.22 fruit of the Spirit is love, joy, peace
Eph 5. 9 (for the fruit of light is found in all
Phil 1.11 filled with the fruits of righteousness
4.17 I seek the fruit which increases
Heb 12.11 the peaceful fruit of righteousness
13.15 fruit of lips that acknowledge his name
Jas 3.17 wisdom . . full of mercy and good fruits
5. 7 the farmer waits for the precious fruit
5.18 the earth brought forth its fruit
Rev 22. 2 tree of life[r] with its twelve kinds of fruit, yielding its fruit each month

3. *fruit:* ὀπώρα OPŌRA*
Rev 18.14 "The fruit for which thy soul longed

FRUIT, BEAR

FRUIT, BRING FORTH

1. *bear fruit:* καρποφορέω KARPOPHOREŌ
Mt 13.23 "he indeed bears fruit, and yields
Mk 4.20 "bear fruit, thirtyfold and sixtyfold
Lk 8.15 "hearing the word . . bring forth fruit
Rom 7. 4 raised . . that we may bear fruit for God
7. 5 passions . . to bear fruit for death
Col 1. 6 ⟨the gospel⟩ is bearing fruit and growing
1.10 bearing fruit in every good work

FRUIT MATURES, ONE'S

1. *bring fruit to maturity:* τελεσφορέω TELESPHOREŌ*
Lk 8.14 "their fruit does not mature

FRUIT, WINTER

1. *late fig:* ὄλυνθος OLYNTHOS*
Rev 6.13 as the fig tree sheds its winter fruit

FRUITFUL

1. *fruit:* καρπός KARPOS [A.1.b.5]
Phil 1.22 that means fruitful labor for me
2. *fruit-bearing:* καρποφόρος KARPOPHOROS*
Acts 14.17 from heaven rains and fruitful seasons

FRUITLESS

1. *without fruit:* ἄκαρπος AKARPOS
Jude .12 fruitless trees in late autumn, twice dead

FRUITS, FIRST

1. *firstfruits:* ἀπαρχή APARCHĒ
Rom 8.23 who have the first fruits of the Spirit
11.16 the dough offered as first fruits is holy
1 Cor 15.20 Christ . . the first fruits of those . . asleep
15.23 each in . . order: Christ the first fruits
Jas 1.18 a kind of first fruits of his creatures
Rev 14. 4 redeemed from mankind as first fruits

FULFIL

1. *fill up:* ἀναπληρόω ANAPLĒROŌ
Mt 13.14 "With them indeed is fulfilled . . Isaiah
Gal 6. 2 and so fulfil the law of Christ
2. *fill up, fulfill:* ἐκπληρόω EKPLĒROŌ*
Acts 13.33 "this he has fulfilled to us
3. *fulfillment:* ἐκπλήρωσις EKPLĒRŌSIS* [A.1.a]
Acts 21.26 the days of purification would be fulfilled
4. *fill, satisfy:* πίμπλημι (pass.) PIMPLĒMI
Lk 21.22 "vengeance, to fulfil all that is written
5. *fill full, complete:* πληρόω PLĒROŌ
Mt 1.22 to fulfil what the Lord had spoken
2.15 to fulfil what the Lord had spoken
2.17 Then was fulfilled what was spoken
2.23 that what was spoken . . might be fulfilled
3.15 "fitting for us to fulfil all righteousness
4.14 that what was spoken . . might be fulfilled
5.17 "not to abolish them but to fulfil them
8.17 This was to fulfil what was spoken
12.17 This was to fulfil what was spoken
13.35 This was to fulfil what was spoken
21. 4 This took place to fulfil what was spoken
26.54 "how . . should the scriptures be fulfilled?
26.56 "that the scriptures . . might be fulfilled
27. 9 Then was fulfilled what had been spoken
Mk 1.15 "The time is fulfilled
14.49 "But let the scriptures be fulfilled
[15.28 *the scripture was fulfilled which says*‡
Lk 1.20 "words, which will be fulfilled in their time
4.21 "Today this scripture has been fulfilled
21.24 "until the times of the Gentiles are fulfilled
22.16 "until it is fulfilled in the kingdom of God
24.44 "everything written . . must be fulfilled
Jn 12.38 that the word . . might be fulfilled
13.18 "it is that the scripture may be fulfilled
15.25 "It is to fulfil the word that is written
17.12 "that the scripture might be fulfilled
17.13 "that they may have my joy fulfilled
18. 9 This was to fulfil the word
18.32 This was to fulfil the word
19.24 This was to fulfil the scripture
19.36 that the scripture might be fulfilled
Acts 1.16 "the scripture had to be fulfilled
3.18 "what God foretold . . he thus fulfilled
12.25 when they had fulfilled their mission
13.27 "those . . fulfilled these by condemning him
14.26 for the work which they had fulfilled
Rom 8. 4 that the . . law might be fulfilled in us
13. 8 he who loves . . has fulfilled the law
Gal 5.14 the whole law is fulfilled in one word
Col 4.17 "See that you fulfil the ministry
2 Th 1.11 God . . may fulfil every good resolve
Jas 2.23 the scripture was fulfilled
6. *fulfill:* πληροφορέω PLĒROPHOREŌ
2 Tim 4. 5 always be steady . . fulfil your ministry
7. *make perfect, complete:* τελειόω TELEIOŌ
Jn 19.28 said (to fulfil the scripture), "I thirst
8. *finish, fulfill:* τελέω TELEŌ
Lk 22.37 "this scripture must be fulfilled in me
Acts 13.29 "when they had fulfilled all that was written
Jas 2. 8 If you really fulfil the royal law
Rev 10. 7 the mystery of God . . should be fulfilled
17.17 "until the words of God shall be fulfilled

FULFILLING

1. *fullness:* πλήρωμα PLĒRŌMA
Rom 13.10 therefore love is the fulfilling of the law

FULFILMENT

1. *fulfillment:* τελείωσις TELEIŌSIS
Lk 1.45 "believed that there would be[e] a fulfilment
2. *end, goal:* τέλος TELOS
Lk 22.37 "what is written . . has its fulfilment

FULL (*See also* PLĒRO- *entries and* DARKNESS, FULL OF; IDOLS, FULL OF; LIGHT, FULL OF; SORES, BE FULL OF; STRENGTH, FULL; TIME, FULL; USE OF, MAKE FULL)

1. *be full:* γέμω (part.) GEMŌ
Rev 4. 6 four living creatures, full of eyes
5. 8 with golden bowls full of incense
15. 7 golden bowls full of the wrath of God
17. 3 beast . . full of blasphemous names
17. 4 a golden cup full of abominations
21. 9 bowls full of the seven last plagues
2. *whole, entire:* ὅλος HOLOS
Rev 6.12 the full moon became like blood
3. *full:* μεστός MESTOS*
Mt 23.28 "within you are full of hypocrisy
Jn 19.29 A bowl full of vinegar stood there; so they put a sponge full . . to his mouth
21.11 hauled the net ashore, full of large fish
Rom 1.29 Full of envy, murder, strife
15.14 you yourselves are full of goodness
Jas 3. 8 a restless evil, full of deadly poison
3.17 wisdom . . full of mercy and good fruits
2 Pet 2.14 eyes full of adultery, insatiable for sin
4. *all, every, whole:* πᾶς PAS
[a]neut. pl. B.3.b.4
Phil 1.20 with full courage now as always
4.18 [a]I have received full payment, and more
1 Tim 1.15 saying is sure and worthy of full acceptance
4. 9 saying is sure and worthy of full acceptance
5. *full, complete:* πλήρης PLĒRĒS
Mt 14.20 twelve baskets full of the broken pieces
15.37 seven baskets full of the broken pieces
Mk 4.28 "then the full grain in the ear
8.19 "how many baskets full of broken pieces?
Lk 4. 1 Jesus, full of the Holy Spirit, returned
5.12 there came a man full of leprosy
Jn 1.14 the Word . . full of grace and truth
Acts 6. 3 "men of good repute, full of the Spirit
6. 5 Stephen, a man full of faith
6. 8 Stephen, full of grace and power
7.55 full of the Holy Spirit, gazed into heaven
9.36 She was full of good works and acts
11.24 a good man, full of the Holy Spirit
13.10 "full of all deceit and villainy
2 Jn .8 that you . . may win a full reward
6. *fullness:* πλήρωμα PLĒRŌMA [A.1.b.5]
Mk 6.43 twelve baskets full of broken pieces
8.20 "how many baskets full of broken pieces?
7. *many, great:* πολύς POLYS
1 Th 1. 5 our gospel came . . with full conviction
8. *perfect, complete:* τέλειος TELEIOS
Jas 1. 4 let steadfastness have its full effect
CONTEXTUALLY
Mk 8. 8 broken pieces left over, seven baskets f.
15.36 and, filling a sponge full of vinegar
Jn 21. 8 came . . dragging the net full of fish
Rev 1.16 face . . like the sun shining in f. strength

FULL ACCORD, IN

1. *united in mind:* σύμψυχος SYMPSYCHOS*
Phil 2. 2 being in full accord and of one mind

FULL, BE

1. *fill quite full:* ἐμπίμπλημι (pass.) EMPIMPLĒMI
Lk 6.25 "Woe to you that are full now
2. *be full:* γέμω GEMŌ
Mt 23.25 "they are full of extortion and rapacity
23.27 "within they are full of dead men's bones
Lk 11.39 "but inside you are full of extortion
Rom 3.14 "Their mouth is full of curses
Rev 4. 8 creatures . . are full of eyes all round
3. *fill full, complete:* πληρόω (pass.) PLĒROŌ
Mt 13.48 "when it was full, men drew it ashore
Jn 3.29 "therefore this joy of mine is now full
15.11 "I have spoken . . that your joy may be full
16.24 "you will receive, that your joy may be full

FULL INCLUSION

FULL NUMBER

1. *fullness:* πλήρωμα PLĒRŌMA
Rom 11.12 how much more will . . full inclusion mean
11.25 until . . f. number of the Gentiles come in

FULL, MAKE

1. *fill full, complete:* πληρόω PLĒROŌ
Acts 2.28 " 'thou wilt make me full of gladness

FULLER

1. *bleacher, fuller:* γναφεύς GNAPHEUS*
Mk 9. 3 white, as no fuller . . could bleach them

FULL-GROWN, BE

1. *bring to an end:* ἀποτελέω (aor. pass.) APOTELEŌ
Jas 1.15 sin when it is full-grown brings . . death

FULLY (*See also* PLĒRO- *entries and* ARMED, FULLY; RIPE, BE FULLY; UNDERSTAND FULLY)

1. *unto completion:* εἰς τὸ παντελές PANTELĒS [B.1.a.1]
Lk 13.11 she . . could not fully straighten herself
2. *all, every, whole:* πᾶς PAS [A.3.b.1]
Col 1.10 to lead a life . . fully pleasing to him
Jude .5 you were once for all fully informed
3. *finally, completely:* τελείως TELEIŌS*
1 Pet 1.13 set your hope fully upon the grace
4. *unto the end:* ἕως τέλους TELOS [B.1.a.1]
2 Cor 1.13 I hope you will understand fully
IDIOMATICALLY
a. Rom 15.19 so that . . I have fully preached the gospel ὥστε με . . πεπληρωκέναι τὸ εὐαγγέλιον [PLĒROŌ]
b. Gal 4.4 But when the time had fully come ὅτε δὲ ἦλθεν τὸ πλήρωμα τοῦ χρόνου [PLĒRŌMA]
c. 2 Tim 4.17 gave me strength to proclaim the message fully ἐνεδυνάμωσέν με, ἵνα δι' ἐμοῦ τὸ κήρυγμα πληροφορηθῇ [PLĒROPHOREŌ]

FULLY, COME

1. *fill full, complete:* πληρόω PLĒROŌ
Jn 7. 8 "for my time has not yet fully come

FULLY KNOWN, MAKE

1. *fill full, complete:* πληρόω PLĒROŌ
Col 1.25 to make the word of God fully known

FULNESS

1. *fullness:* πλήρωμα PLĒRŌMA
Jn 1.16 from his fulness have we all received
Rom 15.29 in the fulness of the blessing[v] of Christ
Eph 1.10 a plan for the fulness of time
1.23 the fulness of him who fills all in all
3.19 filled with all the fulness of God
4.13 the stature of the fulness of Christ
Col 1.19 all the fulness of God was pleased to dwell
2. 9 in him the whole fulness of deity dwells

FULNESS OF LIFE, COME TO

1. *fill full, complete:* πληρόω (pass. periphr.) PLĒROŌ
Col 2.10 you have come to fulness of life in him

FUNCTION

1. *practice, act:* πρᾶξις PRAXIS
Rom 12. 4 members do not have the same function

FURIOUS

1. *very much:* λίαν LIAN [A.4.a]
Mt 2.16 Then Herod . . was in a furious rage

FURLONG

1. *stade* (200+ yards): στάδιον STADION
Mt 14.24 the boat . . was many furlongs distant‡

FURNACE

1. *oven, furnace:* κάμινος KAMINOS*
Mt 13.42 "throw them into the furnace of fire
13.50 "throw them into the furnace of fire
Rev 1.15 bronze, refined as in a furnace
9. 2 like the smoke of a great furnace

FURNISH

1. *show, offer, cause:* παρέχω PARECHŌ
1 Tim 6.17 God who richly furnishes us with everything

FURNISHED

1. *spread:* στρωννύω (perf. pass. part.) STRŌNNYŌ
Mk 14.15 "a large upper room furnished
Lk 22.12 "a large upper room furnished

FURTHER (*See also* CLOTHED, BE FURTHER; THREATEN, FURTHER)
1. *still, yet:* ἔτι ETI
Lk 22.71 "What further testimony do we need?
Heb 7.11 what further need . . for another priest?
2. *again, back:* πάλιν PALIN
Rom 15.12 further Isaiah says, "The root of Jesse
3. *further:* περαιτέρω PERAITERŌ*
Acts 19.39 "if you seek anything further[t]‡
4. *to a greater* (extent): ἐπὶ πλεῖον PLEIŌN [B.1.a.1; B.3.b.2]
Acts 4.17 "that it may spread no further
24. 4 "But, to detain you no further
5. *far off, at a distance:* πόρρω (comp.) PORRŌ
Lk 24.28 He appeared to be going further
IDIOMATICALLY
a. Mk 15.5 But Jesus made no further answer ὁ δὲ Ἰησοῦς οὐκέτι οὐδὲν ἀπεκρίθη [OUKETI]
b. Heb 12.19 that no further messages be spoken to them μὴ προστεθῆναι αὐτοῖς λόγον [PROSTITHĒMI]

FURTHER, ANY
1. *still, yet:* ἔτι (interrog.) ETI
Mk 5.35 "Why trouble the Teacher any further?

FURTHER, TO
1. *in accordance with, for:* κατά (+acc.) KATA [B.3.b.4]
Tit **1.1**

FURY
1. *want of understanding:* ἄνοια ANOIA
Lk 6.11 But they were filled with fury
2. *be enraged against:* ἐμμαίνομαι (part.) EMMAINOMAI* [A.3.d.1]
Acts 26.11 "in raging fury against them, I persecuted
3. *strong feeling, wrath:* θυμός THYMOS
Rom 2. 8 there will be wrath and fury
Rev 16.19 drain the cup of the fury of his wrath
19.15 wine press of the fury of the wrath of God
4. *zeal, jealousy:* ζῆλος ZĒLOS
Heb 10.27 a fury of fire which will consume

FUTILE
1. *empty, idle, foolish:* μάταιος MATAIOS
1 Cor 3.20 "the thoughts of the wise are futile
15.17 If . . not . . your faith is futile
Tit 3. 9 for they are unprofitable and futile
1 Pet 1.18 you were ransomed from the futile ways

FUTILE, BECOME
1. *bring to naught:* ματαιόω (pass.) MATAIOŌ*
Rom 1.21 they became futile in their thinking

FUTILITY
1. *vanity, emptiness:* ματαιότης MATAIOTĒS
Rom 8.20 the creation was subjected to futility
Eph 4.17 as . . Gentiles . . in the futility of their minds

FUTURE
1. *be about to:* μέλλω (part.) MELLŌ
[a]subst. neut. [b]B.1.a.1
Acts 24.25 he argued about . . future judgment
1 Cor 3.22 [a]the present or the future, all are yours
1 Tim 6.19 [a]a good foundation for the future
Heb 11.20 [ab]Isaac invoked future blessings on Jacob

G

GABBATHA: Γαββαθᾶ 'gabətha
Jn 19.13 called The Pavement, and in Hebrew, G.

GABRIEL: Γαβριήλ 'gābrēəl
Lk 1.19 the angel answered him, "I am G.
1.26 the angel G. was sent from God

GAD: Γάδ 'gad
Rev 7. 5 twelve thousand of the tribe of Gad

GAD ABOUT
1. *go about:* περιέρχομαι PERIERCHOMAI
1 Tim 5.13 gadding about from house to house

GADARENE: Γαδαρηνός
Mt 8.28 the country of the Gadarenes[t]‡
Mk [5. 1 came . . to the country of the *Gadarenes*‡
Lk [8.26 arrived at the country of the *Gadarenes*‡
[8.37 all the people . . of the *Gadarenes*‡

GAIN
1. *on account of:* χάριν CHARIN [B.1.a.2]
Jude .16 flattering people to gain advantage
2. *function, business:* ἐργασία ERGASIA
Acts 16.16 slave girl who . . brought . . much gain
16.19 saw that their hope of gain was gone
3. *come to be, happen, be:* γίνομαι GINOMAI [B.3.a.2]
1 Cor 7.21 But if you can gain your freedom
4. *find:* εὑρίσκω HEURISKŌ
Rom [4. 1 What . . *was gained by* Abraham?‡
5. *gain:* κερδαίνω KERDAINŌ
Mt 16.26 "gains the whole world and forfeits his life
18.15 "you have gained your brother
Mk 8.36 "to gain the whole world and forfeit his life
Lk 9.25 "gains the whole world and loses . . himself
Phil 3. 8 in order that I may gain Christ
Jas 4.13 "spend a year there and trade and get gain
6. *profit, gain:* κέρδος KERDOS*
Phil 1.21 to live is Christ, and to die is gain
3. 7 whatever gain I had, I counted as loss
Tit 1.11 teaching for base gain
7. *acquire, get:* κτάομαι KTAOMAI
Lk 21.19 "By your endurance you will gain your lives
8. *reward, wages:* μισθός MISTHOS
2 Pet 2.15 Balaam . . loved gain from wrongdoing
Jude .11 "abandon themselves for the sake of gain
9. *help, aid:* ὠφελέω (act. or pass.) ŌPHELEŌ
Mt 15. 5 " 'What you would have gained . . is given
27.24 Pilate saw that he was gaining nothing
Mk 7.11 " 'What you would have gained . . is Corban
1 Cor 13. 3 but have not love, I gain nothing
10. *advantage, benefit:* ὄφελος OPHELOS [A.6.a.3]
1 Cor 15.32 What do I gain if . . I fought with beasts?
11. *acquire, save* (mid.): περιποιέω PERIPOIEŌ
Lk 17.33 Whoever seeks to gain his life
1 Tim 3.13 those who serve well as deacons gain
12. *means of gain:* πορισμός PORISMOS
1 Tim 6. 6 There is great gain in godliness
IDIOMATICALLY
a. 2 Cor 12.1 there is nothing to be gained by it οὐ συμφέρον μέν [SYMPHERŌ]

GAIN BY TRADING
1. *gain by trading:* διαπραγματεύομαι DIAPRAGMATEUOMAI*
Lk 19.15 "what they had gained by trading

GAIN, FOR SHAMEFUL
1. *in greed for dishonest gain:* αἰσχροκερδῶς AISCHROKERDŌS
1 Pet 5. 2 not for shameful gain but eagerly

GAIN, GREEDY FOR
1. *greedy for dishonest gain:* αἰσχροκερδής AISCHROKERDĒS*
1 Tim 3. 8 Deacons likewise . . not greedy for gain
Tit 1. 7 bishop . . must not be . . greedy for gain

GAIN, MEANS OF
1. *means of gain:* πορισμός PORISMOS
1 Tim 6. 5 imagining that godliness is a means of gain

GAIUS: Γάϊος 'gā(y)əs
Acts 19.29 dragging with them Gaius
20. 4 Gaius of Derbe, and Timothy
Rom 16.23 Gaius, who is host to me . . , greets you
1 Cor 1.14 I baptized none . . except Crispus and G.
3 Jn . 1 The elder to the beloved Gaius

GALATIA: gə'lāsh(ē)ə II,F-3
1. *Galatia:* Γαλατία
1 Cor 16. 1 as I directed the churches of Galatia
Gal 1. 2 To the churches of Galatia
2 Tim 4.10 Crescens has gone to Galatia[e]‡
1 Pet 1. 1 To the exiles of the Dispersion in . . G.
2. *Galatian:* Γαλατικός [A.3.a.2]
Acts 16. 6 they went through the region of . . G.
18.23 he . . went . . through the region of G.

GALATIAN: Γαλάτης
Gal 3. 1 O foolish Galatians!

GALE
1. *great wind:* ἄνεμος μέγας ANEMOS [A.1.f]
Rev 6.13 as the fig tree . . when shaken by a gale

GALILEAN: Γαλιλαῖος (*See also* GALILEE 2)
Mt 26.69 "You also were with Jesus the Galilean
Mk 14.70 "you are one of them; for you are a G.
Lk 13. 1 Galileans whose blood Pilate had mingled
13. 2 "Do you think that these Galileans were worse sinners than all the other Galileans?
22.59 "this man also . . ; for he is a Galilean
23. 6 he asked whether the man was a G.
Jn 4.45 the Galileans welcomed him
Acts 2. 7 "Are not all these . . Galileans?
5.37 "After him Judas the Galilean arose

GALILEE: 'galə,lē I,C-3
1. *Galilee:* Γαλιλαία
Mt 2.22 he withdrew to the district of Galilee
3.13 Jesus came from Galilee to the Jordan
4.12 when he heard . . he withdrew into G.
4.15 "Galilee of the Gentiles
4.18 As he walked by the Sea of G.
4.23 he went about all Galilee
4.25 great crowds followed him from G.
15.29 Jesus . . passed along the Sea of G.
17.22 As they were gathering[y] in G.
19. 1 he went away from Galilee
21.11 "the prophet Jesus from Nazareth of G.
26.32 "I will go before you to Galilee
27.55 women . . who had followed Jesus from G.
28. 7 "he is going before you to Galilee
28.10 "tell my brethren to go to Galilee
28.16 Now the eleven disciples went to Galilee
Mk 1. 9 Jesus came from Nazareth of Galilee
1.14 Jesus came into Galilee, preaching
1.16 passing along by the Sea of Galilee
1.28 his fame spread . . throughout all . . Galilee
1.39 he went throughout all G., preaching
3. 7 a great multitude from G. followed
6.21 officers and the leading men of G.
7.31 he . . went through Sidon to the Sea of G.
9.30 They . . passed through G.
14.28 "I will go before you to Galilee
15.41 who, when he was in Galilee, followed
16. 7 "he is going before you to G.
Lk 1.26 angel Gabriel was sent . . to a city of G.
2. 4 Joseph also went up from G.
2.39 they returned into G., to . . Nazareth
3. 1 Herod being tetrarch of Galilee
4.14 Jesus returned . . into G.
4.31 Capernaum, a city of Galilee
[4.44 preaching in the synagogues of *Galilee*‡
5.17 Pharisees . . from every village of G.
8.26 country of the Gerasenes[a] . . opposite G.
17.11 passing along between Samaria and G.
23. 5 "throughout all Judea, from G.
23.49 women who had followed him from G.
23.55 women who had come with him from G.
24. 6 "while he was still in G.
Jn 1.43 next day Jesus decided to go to G.
2. 1 there was a marriage at Cana in G.
2.11 the first of his signs . . at Cana in G.
4. 3 he left Judea and departed again to G.
4.43 he departed to G.
4.45 when he came to Galilee
4.46 So he came again to Cana in G.
4.47 Jesus had come from Judea to G.
4.54 when he had come from Judea to G.
6. 1 to the other side of the Sea of G.
7. 1 After this Jesus went about in G.
7. 9 So saying, he remained in G.
7.41 "Is the Christ to come from Galilee?
7.52 They replied, "Are you from G. too?
7.52 no prophet is to rise from G.
12.21 Philip, who was from Bethsaida in G.
Jn 21. 2 Nathanael of Cana in G.
Acts 9.31 the church throughout all Judea and G.
10.37 "throughout all Judea, beginning from G.
13.31 "those who came up with him from G.
2. *Galilean:* Γαλιλαῖος [A.3.a.2]
Acts 1.11 "Men of G., why do you stand looking?

GALL
1. *bile:* χολή CHOLĒ*
Mt 27.34 they offered him wine . . mingled with gall
Acts 8.23 "you are in the gall of bitterness

GALLIO: Γαλλίων 'galēō
Acts 18.12 when G. was proconsul of Achaia
18.14 Gallio said to the Jews
18.17 But Gallio paid no attention to this

GALLON
1. *measure* (10 gallons): μετρητής METRĒTĒS* [A.3.c.1]
Jn 2. 6 holding twenty or thirty gallons

GAMALIEL: Γαμαλιήλ gə'mālyəl
Acts 5.34 a Pharisee in the council named G.
22. 3 a Jew . . brought up . . at the feet of G.

GANGRENE
1. *gangrene:* γάγγραινα GAGGRAINA*
2 Tim 2.17 their talk will eat its way like gangrene

GARDEN
1. *garden, orchard:* κῆπος KĒPOS*
Lk 13.19 "like a grain of mustard seed . . in his garden
Jn 18. 1 garden, which he and his disciples entered
18.26 "Did I not see you in the garden?
19.41 where he was crucified there was a garden, and in the garden a new tomb

GARDENER
1. *gardener:* κηπουρός KĒPOUROS*
Jn 20.15 Supposing him to be the gardener

GARLAND
1. *garland, wreath:* στέμμα STEMMA*
Acts 14.13 the priest . . brought oxen and garlands

GARMENT
1. *tunic, undergarment:* χιτών CHITŌN
Mk 14.63 the high priest tore his garments[0]
Jude .23 hating . . the garment spotted by the flesh[e]
2. *garment:* ἔνδυμα ENDYMA [A.6.a.6]
[a]ἐνδεδῦσθαι ἔνδυμα
Mt 3. 4 John wore a garment of camel's hair
22.11 [a]"a man who had no wedding garment
22.12 " 'how did you get in . . without a wedding g.?
3. *outer garment:* ἱμάτιον HIMATION
Mt 9.16 "unshrunk cloth on an old garment
9.16 "the patch tears away from the garment
9.20 touched the fringe of his garment
9.21 "If I only touch his garment
14.36 might only touch the fringe of his garment
17. 2 his garments became white as light
21. 7 put their garments on them
21. 8 spread their garments on the road
27.35 divided his garments among them
Mk 2.21 "unshrunk cloth on an old garment
5.27 She . . touched his garment
5.28 "If I touch even his garments
5.30 "Who touched my garments?
6.56 touch even the fringe of his garment
9. 3 his garments became glistening
11. 7 threw their garments on ⟨the colt⟩
11. 8 many spread their garments on the road
15.24 they . . divided his garments among them
Lk 5.36 "No one tears a piece from a new garment and puts it upon an old garment
8.44 touched the fringe of his garment
19.35 throwing their garments on the colt
19.36 they spread their garments on the road
23.34 they cast lots to divide his garments
Jn 13. 4 rose from supper, laid aside his garments
13.12 When he had . . taken his garments
19.23 the soldiers . . took his garments
19.24 "They parted my garments among them

Acts 7.58 witnesses laid down their garments
9.39 showing . . garments which Dorcas made
14.14 Barnabas and Paul . . tore their garments
16.22 magistrates tore the garments off them
18. 6 he shook out his garments and said
22.20 " 'keeping the garments of those who killed
22.23 cried out and waved their garments
Heb 1.11 "they will all grow old like a garment
[1.12 "they will be changed *like a garment*‡
Jas 5. 2 your garments are moth-eaten
Rev 3. 4 " 'people who have not soiled their garments
3. 5 " 'clad thus in white garments
3.18 " 'rich, and white garments to clothe you
4. 4 elders, clad in white garments
16.15 ("who is awake, keeping his garments!

GATE

1. *gate:* πύλη PYLĒ
Mt 7.13 "Enter by the narrow gate; for the gate is wide and the way is easy[q]‡
7.14 "the gate is narrow and the way is hard
Lk 7.12 he drew near to the gate of the city
Acts 3.10 who sat for alms at the Beautiful Gate
9.24 watching the gates day and night
12.10 they came to the iron gate
16.13 outside the gate to the riverside
Heb 13.12 Jesus also suffered outside the gate
2. *gateway:* πυλών PYLŌN
Lk 16.20 at his gate lay a poor man named Lazarus
Acts 10.17 men . . sent by Cornelius . . stood before the g.
12.14 in her joy she did not open the gate but . . told that Peter was . . at the gate
14.13 brought oxen and garlands to the gates
Rev 21.12 at the gates twelve angels, and on the gates the names of the twelve tribes
21.13 on the east three gates, on the north three gates, on the south three gates, and on the west three gates
21.15 to measure the city and its gates
21.21 the twelve gates were twelve pearls, each of the gates made of a single pearl
21.25 its gates shall never be shut by day
22.14 they may enter the city by the gates
3. *door:* θύρα THYRA
Mt 24.33 "know that he is near, at the very gates
Mk 13.29 "know that he is near, at the very gates
Acts 3. 2 laid daily at that gate of the temple
21.30 at once the gates were shut

GATE, SHEEP

1. *of sheep:* προβατικός PROBATIKOS* [B.3.b.2]
Jn 5. 2 in Jerusalem by the Sheep Gate a pool

GATEKEEPER

1. *doorkeeper:* θυρωρός THYRŌROS
Jn 10. 3 "To him the gatekeeper opens

GATEWAY

1. *vestibule, forecourt:* προαύλιον PROAULION*
Mk 14.68 And he went out into the gateway[f]†
2. *gateway:* πυλών PYLŌN
Acts 12.13 he knocked at the door of the gateway

GATHER

1. *gather together:* ἐπισυνάγω EPISYNAGŌ
Mt 23.37 "as a hen gathers her brood
24.31 "gather his elect from the four winds
Mk 13.27 "gather his elect from the four winds
2. *receive, take:* λαμβάνω LAMBANŌ
Mt 16. 9 "how many baskets you gathered
16.10 "how many baskets you gathered
3. *gather, collect:* συλλέγω SYLLEGŌ
Mt 7.16 "Are grapes gathered from thorns?
13.28 " 'Then do you want us to . . gather them?
13.29 " 'No; lest in gathering the weeds
13.30 " 'Gather the weeds first and bind them
13.40 "Just as the weeds are gathered and burned
13.41 "his angels . . will gather . . all causes of sin
Lk 6.44 "For figs are not gathered from thorns
4. *come together:* συμπορεύομαι SYMPOREUOMAI
Mk 10. 1 crowds gathered to him again
5. *bring together:* συνάγω SYNAGŌ
[a]pass.
Mt 3.12 "he will . . gather his wheat
6.26 "they neither sow . . nor gather into barns
12.30 "he who does not gather with me scatters
13. 2 [a]great crowds gathered about him
13.30 " 'but gather the wheat into my barn
13.47 "a net which . . gathered fish of every kind
18.20 "two or three are gathered in my name
22.10 "servants . . gathered all whom they found
25.24 " 'gathering where you did not winnow
25.26 " 'gather where I have not winnowed
25.32 "Before him will be gathered all
26. 3 [a]elders of the people gathered in the palace
26.57 [a]where the scribes . . had gathered
27.17 [a]when they had gathered, Pilate said
27.27 they gathered the whole battalion
27.62 [a]the Pharisees gathered before Pilate
Mk 4. 1 [a]a very large crowd gathered about him
5.21 [a]a great crowd gathered about him
Lk 3.17 "to gather the wheat into his granary
11.23 "he who does not gather with me scatters
15.13 "the younger son gathered all he had
Jn 4.36 "He . . gathers fruit for eternal life
11.47 the Pharisees gathered the council
11.52 to gather into one the children of God
15. 6 "branches . . gathered, thrown into the fire
Acts 20. 8 upper chamber where we were gathered
Rev 19.17 [a]"Come, gather for the great supper of God
19.19 armies gathered to make war against him
20. 8 to gather them for battle
6. *come together:* συνέρχομαι SYNERCHOMAI
Lk 5.15 great multitudes gathered to hear
Acts 5.16 people also gathered from the towns
10.27 he went in and found many persons gathered
28.17 when they had gathered, he said to them
7. *collect, unite:* συστρέφω SYSTREPHŌ*
Mt 17.22 As they were gathering[y] in Galilee‡
Acts 28. 3 Paul had gathered a bundle of sticks
8. *gather in:* τρυγάω TRYGAŌ
Rev 14.18 "gather the clusters of the vine
14.19 the angel . . gathered the vintage
CONTEXTUALLY
2 Cor 8.15 "He who gathered much had nothing over, and he who gathered little had no lack

GATHER A CROWD

1. *form a mob:* ὀχλοποιέω OCHLOPOIEŌ*
Acts 17. 5 the Jews . . gathered a crowd

GATHER ABOUT

1. *go to:* ἔρχομαι πρός ERCHOMAI [A.6.a.5]
Mk 2.13 all the crowd gathered about him
2. *surround, encircle:* κυκλόω KYKLOŌ
Acts 14.20 when the disciples gathered about him

GATHER ROUND

1. *surround, encircle:* κυκλόω KYKLOŌ
Jn 10.24 the Jews gathered round him

GATHER TOGETHER

1. *collect:* ἀθροίζω ATHROIZŌ*
Lk 24.33 they found the eleven gathered together
2. *gather together:* ἐπισυνάγω EPISYNAGŌ
Mt 23.37 "would I have gathered your children t.
Mk 1.33 the whole city was gathered together
Lk 12. 1 thousands . . had gathered together
13.34 "would I have gathered your children t.
17.37 "the eagles[c] will be gathered together
3. *bring together:* συνάγω SYNAGŌ
[a]pass.
Mt 22.41 Pharisees were gathered together
24.28 "the eagles[z] will be gathered together
Mk 2. 2 many were gathered together
7. 1 [a]when the Pharisees gathered together
Lk 22.66 [a]the assembly . . gathered together
Acts 4. 5 elders and scribes were gathered together
4.26 " 'the rulers were gathered together

Acts 4.27 "gathered together against thy holy servant[c]
4.31 place in which they were gathered together
13.44 gathered together to hear the word of God
14.27 they gathered the church together
15. 6 the elders were gathered together
15.30 having gathered the congregation together
20. 7 when we were gathered together

4. *gather, assemble:* συναθροίζω SYNATHROIZŌ*
Acts 12.12 were gathered together and were praying
19.25 These he gathered together

GATHER UP

1. *bring together:* συνάγω SYNAGŌ
Jn 6.12 "Gather up the fragments left over
6.13 So they gathered them up

GATHERING, FESTAL

1. *festal assembly:* πανήγυρις PANĒGYRIS*
Heb 12.22 innumerable angels in festal gathering†

GAUL: Γαλλία
2 Tim[4.10 Crescens has gone to *Gaul*‡

GAZA: Γάζα 'gāzə, 'gäzə I,A-6; II,F-4
Acts 8.26 "to the road . . from Jerusalem to Gaza

GAZE
GAZE AT

1. *look intently at:* ἀτενίζω ATENIZŌ
Lk 22.56 a maid, . . gazing at him, said
Acts 1.10 while they were gazing into heaven
6.15 gazing at him, all . . the council saw
7.55 full of the Holy Spirit, gazed into heaven

2. *see, look:* βλέπω BLEPŌ
Rev 11. 9 nations gaze at their dead bodies

GAZE, DIRECT ONE'S

1. *look intently at:* ἀτενίζω ATENIZŌ
Acts 3. 4 Peter directed his gaze at him

GEAR

1. *vessel, tackle:* σκεῦος SKEUOS
Acts 27.17 they lowered the gear, and so were driven

GENEALOGY

1. *pedigree:* γενεαλογία GENEALOGIA*
1 Tim 1. 4 with myths and endless genealogies
Tit 3. 9 avoid stupid controversies, genealogies

2. *origin, birth:* γένεσις GENESIS
Mt 1. 1 book of the genealogy of Jesus Christ

GENEALOGY, HAVE A

1. *trace a pedigree:* γενεαλογέω (pass.) GENEALOGEŌ*
Heb 7. 6 this man who has not their genealogy

GENEALOGY, WITHOUT

1. *of unrecorded descent:* ἀγενεαλόγητος AGENEALOGĒTOS*
Heb 7. 3 without father or mother or genealogy

GENERAL

1. *captain over a thousand:* χιλίαρχος CHILIARCHOS
Rev 6.15 the generals and the rich and the strong

GENERATION

1. *race, generation:* γενεά GENEA*
Mt 1.17 So all the generations from Abraham to David were fourteen generations
1.17 David . . to Babylon fourteen generations
1.17 Babylon to . . Christ fourteen generations
11.16 "to what shall I compare this generation?
12.39 "An evil . . generation seeks for a sign
12.41 "men of Nineveh . . with this generation
12.42 "queen of the South will arise . . with this g.
12.45 "So shall it be also with this evil generation
16. 4 "An evil . . generation seeks for a sign
17.17 "O faithless and perverse generation
23.36 "all this will come upon this generation
24.34 "this generation will not pass away till
Mk 8.12 "Why does this generation seek a sign? Truly . . no sign shall be given to this g.
8.38 "this adulterous and sinful generation
9.19 "O faithless g., how long . . to be with you?
13.30 "this generation will not pass away before
Lk 1.48 "all generations will call me blessed
1.50 "his mercy is on those who fear him from generation to generation
7.31 "To what then shall I compare . . this g.?
9.41 "O faithless and perverse generation
11.29 "This generation is an evil generation; it seeks a sign, but no sign shall be given to it
11.30 "so will the Son of man be to this g.
11.31 "queen . . will arise . . with the men of this g.
11.32 "men of Nineveh will arise . . with this g.
11.50 "blood . . may be required of this g.
11.51 "it shall be required of this generation
16. 8 "more shrewd . . with their own generation
17.25 "he must . . be rejected by this g.
21.32 "this generation will not pass away
Acts 2.40 "Save yourselves from this crooked g.
8.33 "Who can describe his generation?
13.36 "counsel of God in his own generation
14.16 In past generations he allowed all the nations
15.21 "from early generations Moses has had
Eph 3. 5 the sons of men in other generations
3.21 to him be glory . . to all generations
Phil 2.15 in the midst of a crooked . . generation
Col 1.26 mystery hidden for ages and generations[c]†
Heb 3.10 " 'I was provoked with that generation

CONTEXTUALLY
Jude .14 Enoch in the seventh g. from Adam

GENEROSITY

1. *simplicity, liberality:* ἁπλότης HAPLOTĒS
2 Cor 9.11 enriched in every way for great generosity
9.13 by the generosity of your contribution

IDIOMATICALLY
a. Mt 20.15 " 'Or do you begrudge my generosity?[n]† ἢ ὁ ὀφθαλμός σου πονηρός ἐστιν ὅτι ἐγὼ ἀγαθός εἰμι;
[AGATHOS]

GENEROUS

1. *simplicity:* ἀφελότης (+gen.) APHELOTĒS*
Acts 2.46 partook of food with . . generous hearts

2. *held in common, sharing:* κοινωνικός KOINŌNIKOS*
1 Tim 6.18 rich in good deeds, liberal and generous

GENEROUSLY

1. *singly, openly:* ἁπλῶς HAPLŌS*
Jas 1. 5 God, who gives to all men generously

GENNESARET: Γεννησαρέτ gə'nesə,ret I,C-3
Mt 14.34 they came to land at Gennesaret
Mk 6.53 they came to land at Gennesaret
Lk 5. 1 he was standing by the lake of G.

GENTILE

1. *foreign, Gentile:* ἐθνικός ETHNIKOS
Mt 5.47 " 'Do not even the Gentiles do the same?
6. 7 "not heap up . . phrases as the Gentiles do
18.17 "let him be to you as a Gentile

2. *nation, people, Gentile:* ἔθνος ETHNOS
Mt 4.15 "across the Jordan, Galilee of the Gentiles
6.32 "For the Gentiles seek all these things
10. 5 "Go nowhere among the Gentiles
10.18 "bear testimony before . . the Gentiles
12.18 "he shall proclaim justice to the Gentiles
12.21 "in his name will the Gentiles hope
20.19 "deliver him to the Gentiles
20.25 "rulers of the Gentiles lord it over them
Mk 10.33 "deliver him to the Gentiles
10.42 "those who . . rule over the Gentiles
Lk 2.32 "a light for revelation to the Gentiles
18.32 "For he will be delivered to the Gentiles
21.24 "trodden down by the Gentiles, until the times of the Gentiles are fulfilled
22.25 "kings of the Gentiles exercise lordship
Acts 4.25 " 'Why did the Gentiles rage?
4.27 "with the Gentiles and the peoples of Israel
9.15 "to carry my name before the Gentiles
10.45 Spirit . . poured out even on the Gentiles
11. 1 Gentiles also had received the word
11.18 "to . . Gentiles also . . repentance unto life
13.46 "behold, we turn to the Gentiles

Acts 13.47 " 'I . . set you to be a light for . . Gentiles
13.48 the Gentiles heard this, they were glad
14. 2 unbelieving Jews stirred up the Gentiles
14. 5 an attempt was made by both Gentiles
14.27 he had opened a door of faith to the Gentiles
15. 3 reporting the conversion of the Gentiles
15. 7 "that by my mouth the Gentiles should hear
15.12 wonders God had done . . among the Gentiles
15.14 "how God first visited the Gentiles
15.17 " 'Gentiles who are called by my name
15.19 "we should not trouble those of the Gentiles
15.23 "brethren who are of the Gentiles
18. 6 "From now on I will go to the Gentiles
21.11 " 'deliver him into the hands of the Gentiles
21.19 that God had done among the Gentiles
21.21 "you teach . . Jews who are among the G.
21.25 "as for the Gentiles who have believed
22.21 " 'I will send you far away to the Gentiles
26.17 " 'delivering you . . from the Gentiles
26.20 "declared . . also to the Gentiles
26.23 "to the people and to the Gentiles
28.28 "salvation . . has been sent to the Gentiles
Rom 1.13 as well as among the rest of the Gentiles
2.14 When Gentiles who have not the law do
2.24 "God is blasphemed among the Gentiles
3.29 Is he not the God of Gentiles also? Yes, of Gentiles also
9.24 not . . Jews only but also from the Gentiles
9.30 That Gentiles who did not pursue
11.11 salvation has come to the Gentiles
11.12 their failure means riches for the Gentiles
11.13 Now I am speaking to you Gentiles
11.13 as I am an apostle to the Gentiles
11.25 a hardening . . until . . the Gentiles come in
15. 9 that the Gentiles might glorify God
15. 9 "I will praise thee among the Gentiles
15.10 "Rejoice, O Gentiles, with his people
15.11 "Praise the Lord, all Gentiles
15.12 "he who rises to rule the Gentiles; in him shall the Gentiles hope
15.16 a minister of Christ Jesus to the Gentiles . . so that . . the Gentiles may be acceptable
15.18 to win obedience from the Gentiles
15.27 Gentiles . . share in their spiritual blessings
16. 4 all the churches of the Gentiles give thanks
1 Cor 1.23 Christ crucified . . folly to Gentiles
2 Cor 11.26 danger from Gentiles, danger in the city
Gal 1.16 that I might preach him among the Gentiles
2. 2 gospel which I preach among the Gentiles
2. 8 (worked through me also for the Gentiles
2. 9 that we should go to the Gentiles
2.12 before . . men came . . he ate with the Gentiles
2.14 "compel the Gentiles to live like Jews
2.15 Jews by birth and not Gentile sinners
3. 8 God would justify the Gentiles by faith
3.14 blessing of Abraham . . upon the Gentiles
Eph 2.11 at one time you Gentiles in the flesh
3. 1 a prisoner . . on behalf of you Gentiles
3. 6 the Gentiles are fellow heirs
3. 8 grace was given, to preach to the Gentiles
4.17 you must no longer live as the Gentiles do
Col 1.27 great among the Gentiles are the riches
1 Th 2.16 hindering us from speaking to the Gentiles
1 Tim 2. 7 a teacher of the Gentiles in faith
2 Tim 4.17 that all the Gentiles might hear it
1 Pet 2.12 Maintain good conduct among the Gentiles
4. 3 doing what the Gentiles like to do

GENTILE, LIKE A

1. *like a Gentile:* ἐθνικῶς ETHNIKŌS*
Gal 2.14 "If you, though a Jew, live like a Gentile

GENTLE

1. *fitting, kind:* ἐπιεικής EPIEIKĒS
1 Tim 3. 3 not violent but gentle
1 Tit 3. 2 to avoid quarreling, to be gentle
Jas 3.17 first pure, then peaceable, gentle
1 Pet 2.18 not only to the kind and gentle

2. *gentle, kind:* ἤπιος ĒPIOS
1 Th 2. 7 we were gentle[a] among you, like a nurse‡

3. *quiet:* ἡσύχιος HĒSYCHIOS
1 Pet 3. 4 jewel of a gentle and quiet spirit

4. *gentle, meek:* πραΰς PRAYS
Mt 11.29 for I am gentle and lowly in heart

GENTLENESS

1. *reasonableness, goodness:* ἐπιείκεια EPIEIKEIA
2 Cor 10. 1 by the meekness and gentleness of Christ

2. *gentleness:* πραϋπάθεια PRAYPATHEIA*
1 Tim 6.11 aim at . . love, steadfastness, gentleness

3. *gentleness:* πραΰτης PRAYTĒS
1 Cor 4.21 with love in a spirit of gentleness
Gal 5.23 gentleness, self-control
6. 1 restore him in a spirit of gentleness
2 Tim 2.25 correcting his opponents with gentleness
1 Pet 3.15 yet do it with gentleness and reverence

GENTLY, BLOW

1. *blow gently:* ὑποπνέω HYPOPNEŌ*
Acts 27.13 when the south wind blew gently

GENTLY, DEAL

1. *feel moderately:* μετριοπαθέω METRIOPATHEŌ*
Heb 5. 2 He can deal gently with the ignorant

GENUINE

1. *without hypocrisy:* ἀνυπόκριτος ANYPOKRITOS
Rom 12. 9 Let love be genuine; hate what is evil
2 Cor 6. 6 by . . kindness, the Holy Spirit, genuine love

2. *approved:* δόκιμος DOKIMOS
1 Cor 11.19 those who are genuine . . be recognized

3. *true, genuine:* γνήσιος GNĒSIOS
2 Cor 8. 8 to prove . . that your love is genuine

GENUINELY

1. *truly, sincerely:* γνησίως GNĒSIŌS*
Phil 2.20 genuinely anxious for your welfare

GENUINENESS

1. *test, proof:* δοκίμιον DOKIMION
1 Pet 1. 7 genuineness of your faith . . may redound

GERASENE: Γερασηνός
Mt [8.28 the country of the *Gerasenes*‡
Mk 5. 1 came . . to the country of the Gerasenes[n]‡
Lk 8.26 arrived at the country of the Gerasenes[a]‡
8.37 all the people . . of the Gerasenes[a]‡

GERGESENE: Γεργεσηνός
Mt [8.28 the country of the *Gergesenes*‡
Mk [5. 1 came . . to the country of the *Gergesenes*‡
Lk [8.26 arrived at the country of the *Gergesenes*‡
[8.37 all the people . . of the *Gergesenes*‡

GET

1. *take up:* ἀναλαμβάνω ANALAMBANŌ
2 Tim 4.11 Get Mark and bring him with you

2. *have, hold:* ἔχω ECHŌ
Jn 4.11 "where do you get that living water?
Rom 6.21 what return did you get from the things?
6.22 the return you get is sanctification

3. *eat:* ἐσθίω ESTHIŌ
1 Cor 9. 7 without getting some of the milk

4. *find:* εὑρίσκω HEURISKŌ
Lk 9.12 "Send the crowd . . to . . get provisions

5. *go away:* ὑπάγω (imper.) HYPAGŌ
Mt 16.23 "Get behind me, Satan!
Mk 8.33 "Get behind me, Satan!

6. *acquire, get:* κτάομαι KTAOMAI
Lk 18.12 " 'I give tithes of all that I get

7. *receive, take:* λαμβάνω LAMBANŌ
Mt 21.34 "he sent his servants . . to get his fruit
Mk 12. 2 "to get from them some of the fruit
Jn 6. 7 "enough bread for each of them to get a little

8. *make progress, advance:* προκόπτω PROKOPTŌ
2 Tim 3. 9 but they will not get very far

IDIOMATICALLY

a. Lk 13.31 "Get away from here ἔξελθε καὶ πορεύου ἐντεῦθεν [EXERCHOMAI; POREUOMAI]

CONTEXTUALLY

Mt 13.54 "Where did this man get this wisdom?

Mt 13.56 "Where then did this man get all this?
15.33 "Where are we to get bread enough?
Mk 6. 2 "Where did this man get all this?

GET BACK A MEASURE
1. *measure in return:* ἀντιμετρέω (pass.) ANTIMETREŌ*
Lk 6.38 "will be the measure you get back

GET IN
1. *enter, go into:* εἰσέρχομαι EISERCHOMAI
Mt 22.12 " 'Friend, how did you get in here?

GET INTO
1. *go up, come up:* ἀναβαίνω ANABAINŌ
Mt 14.32 they got into the boat, the wind ceased
Mk 6.51 he got into the boat with them
2. *step in, embark:* ἐμβαίνω EMBAINŌ
Mt 8.23 he got into the boat, his disciples followed
9. 1 getting into a boat he crossed over
13. 2 so that he got into a boat and sat there
14.22 he made the disciples get into the boat
15.39 he got into the boat and went
Mk 4. 1 he got into a boat and sat in it
5.18 as he was getting into the boat
6.45 he made his disciples get into the boat
8.10 he got into the boat with his disciples
8.13 getting into the boat again he departed
Lk 5. 3 Getting into one of the boats
8.22 One day he got into a boat with his disciples
8.37 so he got into the boat and returned
Jn 6.17 got into a boat, and started across
6.24 they themselves got into the boats
21. 3 They went out and got into the boat

GET OUT
GET OUT OF
1. *go away, step off from:* ἀποβαίνω APOBAINŌ
Jn 21. 9 When they got out on land
2. *go out:* ἐξέρχομαι EXERCHOMAI
[a]+ ἐκεῖθεν [b]+ ἐκ
Mt 5.26 [a]"you will never get out till you have paid
Mk 6.54 [b]when they got out of the boat
Lk 12.59 [a]"you will never get out till you have paid
Acts 22.18 [b]" 'get quickly out of Jerusalem
3. *come down, go down:* καταβαίνω KATABAINŌ
[a]+ ἀπό
Mt 14.29 [a]So Peter got out of the boat

GET THERE AHEAD OF
1. *go before, go forward:* προέρχομαι PROERCHOMAI
Mk 6.33 they . . got there ahead of them

GET UP
1. *raise up, rise:* ἀνίστημι ANISTĒMI
Mk 5.42 immediately the girl got up and walked
Lk 8.55 her spirit returned, and she got up
11. 7 " 'I cannot get up and give you anything
11. 8 "though he will not get up and give
Acts 12. 7 struck Peter . . saying, "Get up quickly

GETHSEMANE: Γεθσημανί ˌgeth'semənē
Mt 26.36 Jesus went with them to a place called G.
Mk 14.32 they went to a place which was called G.

GHOST
1. *apparition:* φάντασμα PHANTASMA*
Mt 14.26 they were terrified, saying, "It is a ghost!
Mk 6.49 thought it was a ghost, and cried out

GIDEON: Γεδεών 'gidēən
Heb 11.32 time would fail me to tell of Gideon

GIFT (*See also* DISTRIBUTED *a*)
1. *grace, favor, gratitude:* χάρις CHARIS
Rom 4. 4 his wages are not reckoned as a gift
1 Cor 16. 3 send those . . to carry your gift to Jerusalem
2. *gift, favor bestowed:* χάρισμα CHARISMA
Rom 1.11 I may impart to you some spiritual gift
11.29 the gifts and the call of God are irrevocable
12. 6 gifts that differ according to the grace
1 Cor 12. 4 Now there are varieties of gifts
12. 9 to another gifts of healing
12.30 Do all possess gifts of healing?
12.31 But earnestly desire the higher gifts
1 Tim 4.14 Do not neglect the gift you have
2 Tim 1. 6 rekindle the gift of God . . within you
1 Pet 4.10 As each has received a gift, employ it
3. *gift:* δόμα DOMA*
Mt 7.11 "how to give good gifts to your children
Lk 11.13 "how to give good gifts to your children
Eph 4. 8 it is said . . "he gave gifts to men
Phil 4.17 Not that I seek the gift
4. *gift, bounty:* δωρεά DŌREA
Jn 4.10 "If you knew the gift of God
Acts 2.38 "shall receive the g. of the Holy Spirit
8.20 "you thought you could obtain the gift!
10.45 gift of the Holy Spirit had been poured
11.17 "God gave the same gift to them
2 Cor 9.15 Thanks be to God for his . . gift!
Eph 3. 7 minister according to the gift of . . grace
4. 7 according to the measure of Christ's gift
Heb 6. 4 those . . who have tasted the heavenly gift
5. *gift:* δώρημα DŌRĒMA
Jas 1.17 every perfect gift is from above
6. *gift:* δῶρον DŌRON
Mt 2.11 they offered him gifts, gold . . and myrrh
5.23 "if you are offering your gift at the altar
5.24 "leave your gift there before the altar . . and then come and offer your gift
8. 4 "offer the gift that Moses commanded
23.18 " 'if any one swears by the gift . . on the altar
23.19 "which is greater, the gift or the altar that makes the gift sacred?
Lk 21. 1 He . . saw the rich putting their gifts
Eph 2. 8 not your own doing, it is the gift of God
Heb 5. 1 high priest . . to offer gifts and sacrifices
8. 3 high priest is appointed to offer gifts
8. 4 there are priests who offer gifts
9. 9 gifts . . are offered which cannot perfect
11. 4 God bearing witness by accepting his gifts
7. *praise, blessing, gift:* εὐλογία EULOGIA
2 Cor 9. 5 arrange in advance for this gift
8. *honor, value:* τιμή TIMĒ
Acts 28.10 They presented many gifts to us/†
IDIOMATICALLY
a. 1 Cor 4.7 why do you boast as if it were not a gift?
τί καυχᾶσαι ὡς μὴ λαβών; [LAMBANŌ]
b. Eph 4.11 his gifts were that some should be apostles
αὐτὸς ἔδωκεν τοὺς μὲν ἀποστόλους [DIDŌMI]
CONTEXTUALLY
1 Cor 2.12 understand the gifts bestowed on us
2.14 does not receive the gifts of the Spirit
12. 1 Now concerning spiritual gifts[x]†[o]
14. 1 earnestly desire the spiritual gifts
Phil 4.18 having received . . the gifts you sent

GIFT, AS A
1. *freely, as a gift:* δωρεάν DŌREAN
Rom 3.24 they are justified by his grace as a gift

GIFT, FREE
1. *gift, favor bestowed:* χάρισμα CHARISMA
Rom 5.15 But the free gift is not like the trespass
5.16 but the free gift . . brings justification
6.23 free gift of God is eternal life in Christ
2. *gift, bounty:* δωρεά DŌREA
Rom 5.15 grace of God and the free gift in the grace
5.17 who receive . . the free gift of righteousness
3. *gift:* δώρημα DŌRĒMA
Rom 5.16 the free gift is not like . . that one man's sin

GIFT, GIVE A
1. *give up:* προδίδωμι PRODIDŌMI*
Rom 11.35 "Or who has given a gift to him?

GIFT, LIBERAL
1. *abundance:* ἁδρότης HADROTĒS*
2 Cor 8.20 this l. gift which we are administering

GIFT, SPECIAL
GIFT, SPIRITUAL
1. *gift, favor bestowed:* χάρισμα CHARISMA
1 Cor 1. 7 you are not lacking in any spiritual gift
7. 7 each has his own special gift from God

GIFT, WILLING
1. *praise, blessing, gift:* εὐλογία EULOGIA
2 Cor 9. 5 not as an exaction but as a willing gift

GIFTS, HE THAT IS WITHOUT
1. *private individual, layman:* ἰδιώτης IDIŌTĒS
1 Cor [14.16 in the position of *him that is w. gifts*†

GIRD
1. *tie around, put on:* διαζώννυμι DIAZŌNNYMI
Jn 13. 4 rose . . and girded himself with a towel
13. 5 the towel with which he was girded
2. *gird about:* περιζώννυμι (act. or mid.) PERIZŌNNYMI
Lk 12.35 "Let your loins be girded
12.37 "he will gird himself and . . serve them
17. 8 " 'gird yourself and serve me, till I eat
Eph 6.14 having girded your loins with truth
Rev 15. 6 their breasts girded with golden girdles
3. *gird:* ζώννυμι ZŌNNYMI
Jn 21.18 "you were young, you girded yourself
21.18 "when you are old . . another will gird you

GIRD UP
1. *gird up:* ἀναζώννυμι ANAZŌNNYMI*
1 Pet 1.13 Therefore gird up your minds

GIRDLE
1. *girdle, belt:* ζώνη ZŌNĒ
Mt 3. 4 John wore a . . leather girdle
Mk 1. 6 John . . had a leather girdle around his waist
Acts 21.11 coming to us he took Paul's girdle
21.11 " 'shall . . bind the man who owns this girdle
Rev 1.13 with a golden girdle round his breast
15. 6 their breasts girded with golden girdles

GIRL
1. *little girl:* κοράσιον KORASION*
Mt 9.24 "the girl is not dead but sleeping
9.25 took her by the hand, and the girl arose
14.11 his head was . . given to the girl
Mk 5.41 "Little girl, I say to you, arise
5.42 the girl got up and walked
6.22 the king said to the girl, "Ask me
6.28 brought his head . . and gave it to the girl; and the girl gave it to her mother
2. *maiden, girl:* παρθένος PARTHENOS
1 Cor 7.28 if a girl[z] marries she does not sin†
7.34 girl[z] is anxious about the affairs of the Lord†

GIRL, SLAVE
1. *female slave:* παιδίσκη PAIDISKĒ
Acts 16.16 we were met by a slave girl

GIVE (*See also, e.g.*, COMMAND, GIVE ; LEAVE, GIVE ; THANKS, GIVE)
1. *give up, return:* ἀποδίδωμι APODIDŌMI
[a]ἀποδιδόναι λόγον
Mt 21.41 "to . . tenants who will give him the fruits
27.58 Then Pilate ordered it to be given to him
Acts 4.33 the apostles gave their testimony
1 Cor 7. 3 should give to his wife her conjugal rights
Heb 13.17 [a]as men who will have to give account
1 Pet 4. 5 [a]but they will give account to him
2. *give graciously:* χαρίζομαι CHARIZOMAI
Rom 8.32 will he not . . give us all things with him?
Gal 3.18 God gave it to Abraham by a promise
3. *arrange:* διατίθημι (mid.) DIATITHĒMI
Acts 3.25 "the covenant which God gave
4. *give:* δίδωμι DIDŌMI
Mt 4. 9 "All these I will give you, if
5.31 " 'let him give her a certificate of divorce
5.42 "Give to him who begs from you
6.11 "Give us this day our daily bread[m]
7. 6 "Do not give dogs what is holy
7. 7 "Ask, and it will be given you
7.11 "If you . . know how to give good gifts . . more will your Father . . give good things!
9. 8 God, who had given such authority
10. 1 he . . gave them authority over unclean spirits
10. 8 "received without paying, give without pay
10.19 "what you are to say will be given to you
12.39 "but no sign shall be given to it except
Mt 13.11 "To you it has been given to know . . but to them it has not been given
13.12 "to him who has will more be given
14. 7 to give her whatever she might ask
14. 8 "Give me the head of John the Baptist
14. 9 the king . . commanded it to be given
14.11 his head was . . given to the girl
14.16 "you give them something to eat
14.19 he . . gave the loaves to the disciples
15.36 he . . gave them to the disciples
16. 4 "but no sign shall be given to it except
16.19 "I will give you the keys of the kingdom
16.26 "what shall a man give in return for his life?
17.27 "take that and give it to them
19. 7 "Why . . give a certificate of divorce?
19.11 "only those to whom it is given
19.21 "sell what you possess and give to the poor
20. 4 " 'whatever is right I will give you
20.14 " 'to give to this last as I give to you
20.28 "to give his life as a ransom for many
21.23 "who gave you this authority?
21.43 "given to a nation producing . . fruits of it[q]
24.29 "the moon will not give its light
24.45 "to give them . . food at the proper time
25. 8 " 'Give us some of your oil
25.15 "to one he gave five talents[d]
25.28 " 'give it to him who has the ten talents
25.29 " 'to every one who has will more be given
25.35 " 'I was hungry and you gave me food
25.42 " 'I was hungry and you gave me no food
26. 9 "ointment might have been sold . . and given
26.15 "What will you give me if I deliver him?
26.26 Jesus took bread, . . gave it to the disciples
26.27 he gave it to them, saying, "Drink
26.48 the betrayer had given them a sign
27.10 "they gave them for the potter's field
28.12 they gave a sum of money to the soldiers
28.18 "All authority . . has been given to me
Mk 2.26 "also gave it to those who were with him
4.11 "To you has been given the secret
4.25 "to him who has will more be given
5.43 told them to give her something to eat
6. 2 "What is the wisdom given to him?
6. 7 gave them authority over the unclean spirits
6.23 "Whatever you ask me, I will give you
6.25 "give me at once the head of John
6.28 brought his head . . and gave it to the girl; and the girl gave it to her mother
6.37 "You give them something to eat
6.37 "Shall we go and buy . . bread, and give it?
6.41 he . . gave them to the disciples
8. 6 he . . gave them to his disciples
8.12 "no sign shall be given . . this generation
8.37 "what can a man give in return for his life?
10.21 "sell what you have, and give to the poor
10.45 "to give his life as a ransom for many
11.28 "who gave you this authority to do them?
12. 9 "He will . . give the vineyard to others
13.11 "say whatever is given you in that hour
13.24 "the moon will not give its light
14. 5 "ointment might have been sold . . given
14.11 they . . promised to give him money
14.22 gave it to them, and said, "Take
14.23 when he had given thanks he gave it
14.44 the betrayer had given them a sign
Lk 1.32 "God will give to him the throne
1.77 "to give knowledge of salvation
4. 6 "To you I will give all this authority
4. 6 "I give it to whom I will
6. 4 "he . . also gave it to those with him
6.30 "Give to every one who begs
6.38 "give, and it will be given to you; good measure, pressed down
6.38 "For the measure you give . . you get back
7.15 And he gave him to his mother
7.44 "you gave me no water for my feet
7.45 "You gave me no kiss

Lk 8.10 "To you it has been given to know
8.18 "to him who has will more be given
8.55 something should be given her to eat
9. 1 he . . gave them power . . over all demons
9.13 "You give them something to eat
9.16 he . . gave them to the disciples
10.19 "Behold, I have given you authority
10.35 "he . . gave them to the innkeeper
11. 3 "Give us each day our daily bread[k]
11. 7 " 'I cannot get up and give you anything
11. 8 "though he will not get up and give . . , yet . . he will . . give him whatever he needs
11. 9 "Ask, and it will be given you
11.13 "If you . . know how to give good gifts . . , how much more will the . . Father give!
11.29 "no sign shall be given to it except
11.41 "give for alms those things which are within
12.32 "your Father's good pleasure to give
12.33 "Sell your possessions, and give alms
12.42 "to give them their portion of food
12.48 "Every one to whom much is given
12.51 "that I have come to give peace on earth
14. 9 " 'Give place to this man
15.12 " 'Father, give me the share of property
15.16 "no one gave him anything
15.29 " 'yet you never gave me a kid
16.12 "who will give you that which is your own?
17.18 "Was no one found to . . give praise to God?
18.43 people, when they saw it, gave praise to God
19. 8 "the half of my goods I give to the poor
19.13 "he gave them ten pounds[e]
19.15 "servants, to whom he had given the money
19.24 " 'give it to him who has the ten pounds
19.26 " 'to every one who has will more be given
20. 2 "who it is that gave you this authority
20.10 "they should give him some of the fruit
20.16 "He will . . give the vineyard to others
20.22 "Is it lawful for us to give tribute?
21.15 "for I will give you a mouth and wisdom
22. 5 they . . engaged to give him money
22.19 he took bread . . and gave it to them
22.19 "This is my body which is given for you‡
23. 2 "forbidding us to give tribute to Caesar

Jn 1.12 he gave power to become children of God
1.17 the law was given through Moses
3.16 God so loved . . that he gave his only Son
3.27 "except what is given him from heaven
3.34 not by measure that he gives the Spirit
3.35 Father . . has given all things into his hand
4. 5 field that Jacob gave to his son Joseph
4. 7 Jesus said to her, "Give me a drink
4.10 "saying to you, 'Give me a drink
4.10 "he would have given you living water
4.12 "Jacob, who gave us the well
4.14 "the water that I shall give him
4.14 "the water that I shall give him
4.15 "Sir, give me this water
5.22 "Father . . has given . . judgment to the Son
5.27 "⟨Father⟩ has given him authority
6.27 "food . . which the Son of man will give
6.31 " 'He gave them bread from heaven to eat
6.32 "not Moses who gave you the bread . . ; my Father gives you the true bread
6.33 "bread of God . . gives life to the world
6.34 "Lord give us this bread always
6.37 "All that the Father gives me will come
6.39 "lose nothing of all that he has given me
6.51 the bread which I shall give for the life
6.52 "How can this man give us his flesh?
7.19 "Did not Moses give you the law?
7.22 "Moses gave you circumcision
9.24 "Give God the praise
10.28 "I give them eternal life
10.29 "My Father, who has given them to me[w]
11.22 "whatever you ask . . God will give you
11.57 Pharisees had given orders
12. 5 "Why was this . . not . . given to the poor?

Jn 12.49 "Father . . has . . given me commandment
13. 3 Father had given all things into his hands
13.15 "For I have given you an example
13.26 "he to whom I shall give this morsel
13.26 he gave it to Judas
13.29 that he should give something to the poor
13.34 "A new commandment I give to you
14.16 "he will give you another Counselor
14.27 "my peace I give to you; not as the world gives do I give to you. Let not your hearts be troubled
15.16 "whatever you ask . . he may give it to you
16.23 "he will give it to you in my name
17. 2 "since thou hast given him power over all flesh, to give eternal life to all whom thou hast given him
17. 4 "the work which thou gavest me to do
17. 6 "to the men whom thou gavest me
17. 6 "thou gavest them to me
17. 7 "everything that thou hast given me
17. 8 "for I have given them the words which thou gavest me
17. 9 "those whom thou hast given me
17.11 "thy name, which thou hast given me
17.12 "thy name, which thou hast given me
17.14 "I have given them thy word
17.22 "The glory which thou hast given me I have given to them
17.24 "they also, whom thou hast given me
17.24 "my glory which thou hast given me
18. 9 "Of those whom thou gavest me
18.11 "the cup which the Father has given me
19. 9 But Jesus gave no answer
19.11 "unless it had been given you from above
21.13 Jesus . . took the bread and gave it to them

Acts 2. 4 as the Spirit gave them utterance
3. 6 "I give you what I have
3.16 "faith . . has given the man . . perfect health
4.12 "no other name . . given among men
5.31 "Savior, to give repentance to Israel
5.32 "Spirit whom God has given to those
7. 5 "he gave him no inheritance in it . . but promised to give it to him
7. 8 "he gave him the covenant of circumcision
7.10 "gave him favor . . before Pharaoh
7.25 "God was giving them deliverance
7.38 "he received living oracles to give to us
8.18 Simon saw that the Spirit was given
8.19 "Give me also this power
9.41 he gave her his hand and lifted her up
11.17 "If then God gave the same gift to them
12.23 because he did not give God the glory
13.20 "he gave them judges until Samuel
13.21 "God gave them Saul the son of Kish
13.34 " 'I will give you the . . blessings of David
14.17 "he . . gave you from heaven rains
15. 8 "giving them the Holy Spirit
17.25 "he himself gives to all men life
20.32 "to give you the inheritance among all
20.35 " 'more blessed to give than to receive
24.26 he hoped that money would be given him

Rom 4.20 grew strong in his faith as he gave glory
5. 5 the Holy Spirit which has been given to us
11. 8 "God gave them a spirit of stupor
12. 3 by the grace given to me I bid every one
12. 6 according to the grace given to us
14.12 each of us shall give account of himself
15.15 because of the grace given me by God

1 Cor 1. 4 grace of God which was given you in Christ
3.10 the grace of God given to me
7.25 I have no command . . but I give my opinion
11.15 her hair is given to her for a covering
12. 7 To each is given the . . Spirit
12. 8 To one is given . . the utterance of wisdom
12.24 giving the greater honor to the inferior
14. 7 If . . instruments . . do not give distinct notes
14. 8 if the bugle gives an indistinct sound

1 Cor 15.38 God gives it a body as he has chosen
15.57 thanks be to God, who gives us the victory
2 Cor 1.22 he has .. given us his Spirit
5. 5 God, who has given us the Spirit
5.12 giving you cause to be proud of us
5.18 gave us the ministry of reconciliation
8. 5 first they gave themselves to the Lord
8.10 in this matter I give my advice
9. 9 "He scatters abroad, he gives to the poor
10. 8 our authority, which the Lord gave
12. 7 a thorn was given me in the flesh
13.10 authority which the Lord has given me
Gal 1. 4 gave himself for our sins to deliver us
2. 9 the grace that was given to me
2. 9 gave .. the right hand of fellowship
3.21 if a law had been given which could make
3.22 that what was promised .. might be given
4.15 plucked out your eyes and given them
Eph 1.17 that .. God .. give you a spirit of wisdom
3. 2 God's grace that was given to me for you
3. 7 according to the .. grace which was given
3. 8 grace was given, to preach to the Gentiles
4. 7 grace was given to each of us
4. 8 "he gave gifts to men
4.27 give no opportunity to the devil
6.19 that utterance may be given me
Col 1.25 the divine office which was given to me
1 Th 4. 2 what instructions we gave you
4. 8 God, who gives his Holy Spirit to you
2 Th 2.16 who loved us and gave us eternal comfort
3. 9 to give you in our conduct an example
3.16 may the Lord .. give you peace
1 Tim 2. 6 who gave himself as a ransom for all
4.14 gift .. given you by prophetic utterance
5.14 give the enemy no occasion to revile us
2 Tim 1. 7 God did not give us a spirit of timidity
1. 9 grace which he gave us in Christ Jesus
Tit 2.14 who gave himself for us to redeem us
Heb 2.13 "the children God has given me
7. 4 Abraham .. gave him a tithe of the spoils
Jas 1. 5 let him ask God, who gives to all men .. and it will be given him
2.16 without giving them the things needed
4. 6 But he gives more grace
4. 6 "God opposes the proud, but gives grace
5.18 the heaven gave rain
1 Pet 1.21 God, who raised him .. gave him glory
5. 5 "God .. gives grace to the humble
2 Pet 3.15 according to the wisdom given him
1 Jn 3. 1 what love the Father has given us
3.24 by the Spirit which he has given us
4.13 because he has given us of his own Spirit
5.11 God gave us eternal life
5.16 he will ask, and God[i] will give him life
5.20 Son of God .. has given us understanding
Rev 1. 1 revelation of Jesus Christ, which God gave
2.10 " 'I will give you the crown of life
2.17 " 'I will give some of the hidden manna, and I will give him a white stone
2.21 " 'I gave her time to repent
2.23 " 'give to each of you as your works deserve
2.26 " 'I will give him power over the nations
2.28 " 'I will give him the morning star
4. 9 whenever the living creatures give glory
6. 2 a crown was given to him
6. 4 he was given a great sword
6. 8 given power over a fourth of the earth
6.11 they were each given a white robe
7. 2 four angels who had been given power
8. 2 seven trumpets were given to them
8. 3 he was given much incense to mingle
9. 1 he was given the key of the shaft
9. 3 they were given power like .. scorpions
10. 9 I .. told him to give me the little scroll
11. 1 Then I was given a measuring rod
11. 2 "for it is given over to the nations
11.13 the rest .. gave glory to the God of heaven
Rev 12.14 the woman was given the two wings
13. 2 to it the dragon gave his power
13. 4 for he had given his authority to the beast
13. 5 beast was given a mouth uttering
13. 7 authority was given it over every tribe
13.15 it was allowed to give breath to the image
14. 7 "Fear God and give him glory
15. 7 four living creatures gave .. seven .. bowls
16. 6 "thou hast given them blood to drink
16. 9 they did not repent and give him glory
18. 7 "give her a like measure of torment
19. 7 "Let us .. give him the glory
21. 6 "To the thirsty I will give .. water

5. *give freely, deliver:* ἐπιδίδωμι EPIDIDŌMI
Mt 7. 9 "what man .. will give him a stone?
7.10 "Or .. will give him a serpent?
Lk 4.17 there was given to him .. book of .. Isaiah
11.11 "What father .. will .. give him a serpent?
[11.11 "What father .. *will give him a stone?*‡
11.12 "or .. will give him a scorpion?
24.30 he took the bread .. and gave it to them
24.42 They gave him a piece of broiled fish

6. *call, name:* καλέω KALEŌ
Lk 2.21 Jesus, the name given by the angel

7. *say, speak:* λέγω LEGŌ
Acts 5.36 "giving himself out to be somebody
2 Jn .10 do not .. give him any greeting

8. *share:* μεταδίδωμι METADIDŌMI
Eph 4.28 able to give to those in need

9. *give up, allow:* παραδίδωμι PARADIDŌMI
Gal 2.20 Son of God, who .. gave himself for me

10. *show, offer, cause:* παρέχω PARECHŌ
Acts 17.31 "of this he has given assurance

11. *do, make:* ποιέω POIEŌ
Mt 6. 2 "when you give alms, sound no trumpet
6. 3 "when you give alms
22. 2 "a king who gave a marriage feast
Mk 6.21 Herod .. gave a banquet for his courtiers
Lk 14.12 "When you give a dinner or a banquet
14.13 "when you give a feast, invite the poor
14.16 "A man once gave a great banquet
Acts 10. 2 a devout man .. gave alms liberally
15. 3 they gave great joy to all the brethren

12. *water, give to drink:* ποτίζω POTIZŌ
Mt 10.42 "whoever gives to one of these little ones

13. *to, with, against:* πρός (+acc.) PROS [B.1.a.2]
2 Cor 4. 6 to give the light of the knowledge

IDIOMATICALLY
a. Acts 27.34 "it will give you strength τοῦτο γὰρ πρὸς τῆς ὑμετέρας σωτηρίας ὑπάρχει [HYPARCHŌ]
b. Rev 18.20 "for God has given judgment for you against her! ὅτι ἔκρινεν ὁ θεὸς τὸ κρίμα ὑμῶν ἐξ αὐτῆς [KRINŌ]

CONTEXTUALLY
Acts 19.40 "no cause that we can give to justify
Rom 2. 7 to those .. he will give eternal life
5.13 in the world before the law was given
15. 8 in order to confirm the promises given
2 Cor 8. 3 For they gave according to their means
Rev 9.20 did not .. give up worshiping demons

GIVE A GIFT
1. *give up:* προδίδωμι PRODIDŌMI*
Rom 11.35 "Or who has given a gift to him?

GIVE AWAY
1. *give food by hand:* ψωμίζω PSŌMIZŌ
1 Cor 13. 3 If I g. away all I have .. but have not love

GIVE BACK
1. *give up, return:* ἀποδίδωμι APODIDŌMI
Lk 4.20 he closed the book, and gave it back
9.42 Jesus .. gave him back to his father

GIVE ONESELF
1. *lead away with:* συναπάγω (pass.) SYNAPAGŌ
Rom [12.16 *give yourselves to humble tasks*†

GIVE OUT
1. *lack, fail:* ὑστερέω HYSTEREŌ
Jn 2. 3 When the wine gave out[0]

GIVE OVER
1. *give:* δίδωμι DIDŌMI
Rev 17.13 "These .. give over their power
17.17 "giving over .. royal power to the beast
2. *give up, allow:* παραδίδωμι PARADIDŌMI
Acts 7.42 "gave them o. to worship .. host of heaven

GIVE STILL MORE
1. *put to, add, continue:* προστίθημι PROSTITHĒMI
Mk 4.24 "still more will be given you

GIVE UP
1. *let go, leave, forgive:* ἀφίημι APHIĒMI
Rom 1.27 men likewise gave up natural relations
2. *give graciously:* χαρίζομαι CHARIZOMAI
Acts 25.11 "no one can give me up to them. I appeal
25.16 "not the custom .. to give up any
3. *give:* δίδωμι DIDŌMI
Rev 20.13 the sea gave up the dead in it, Death and Hades gave up the dead in them
4. *leave behind:* καταλείπω KATALEIPŌ
Acts 6. 2 "not right that we should give up preaching
5. *make ineffective, hinder:* καταργέω KATARGEŌ
1 Cor 13.11 when .. a man, I gave up childish ways
6. *give up, allow:* παραδίδωμι PARADIDŌMI
Jn 19.30 he bowed his head and gave up his spirit
Rom 1.24 gave them up in the lusts of their hearts
1.26 God gave them up to dishonorable passions
1.28 God gave them up to a base mind
8.32 did not spare his own Son but gave him up
2 Cor 4.11 we are always being given up to death
Eph 4.19 given themselves up to licentiousness
5. 2 Christ loved us and gave himself up for us
5.25 Christ loved the church and gave himself up

GIVE WAY
1. *give freely, deliver:* ἐπιδίδωμι EPIDIDŌMI
Acts 27.15 we gave way to it and were driven

GIVEN TO GOD
1. *gift:* δῶρον DŌRON
Mt 15. 5 " 'What you would have .. is given to God[o]†
Mk 7.11 " 'Corban' (that is, given to God[z]†

GIVER
1. *giver:* δότης DOTĒS*
2 Cor 9. 7 God loves a cheerful giver

GIVING (*See also* LAW, GIVING OF THE)
1. *giving, gift:* δόσις DOSIS
Phil 4.15 partnership with me in giving

GLAD
1. *great joy:* ἀγαλλίασις AGALLIASIS [A.1.b.5]
Acts 2.46 they partook .. with glad .. hearts

GLAD, BE
1. *rejoice greatly:* ἀγαλλιάω (dep.) AGALLIAŌ
1 Pet 4.13 that you may also rejoice and be glad
2. *wish, will:* βούλομαι BOULOMAI
Phm .13 I would have been glad to keep him
3. *rejoice:* χαίρω CHAIRŌ
Mt 5.12 "Rejoice and be glad, for your reward is great
Mk 14.11 they were glad, and promised to give
Lk 15.32 "'It was fitting to make merry and be glad
22. 5 they were glad, and engaged to give
23. 8 When Herod saw Jesus, he was very glad
Jn 8.56 "he saw it and was glad
11.15 "I am glad that I was not there
20.20 disciples were g. when they saw the Lord
Acts 11.23 he .. saw the grace of God, he was glad
13.48 they were glad and glorified the word
2 Cor 13. 9 we are glad when .. you are strong
Phil 2.17 I am glad and rejoice with you all
2.18 you also should be glad and rejoice
1 Pet 4.13 that you may also rejoice and be glad
4. *gladden:* εὐφραίνω (pass.) EUPHRAINŌ
Acts 2.26 " 'therefore my heart was glad
5. *will, wish:* θέλω THELŌ
Jn 6.21 they were glad to take him into the boat

GLAD, MAKE
1. *gladden:* εὐφραίνω EUPHRAINŌ
2 Cor 2. 2 who is there to make me glad?

GLADLY
1. *gladly:* ἀσμένως ASMENŌS*
Acts 21.17 the brethren received us gladly
2. *pleasantly:* ἡδέως HĒDEŌS*
[a]superl.
Mk 6.20 yet he heard him gladly
12.37 the great throng heard him gladly
2 Cor 11.19 "you gladly bear with fools, being wise!
12. 9 [a]I will all the more gladly boast
12.15 [a]I will most gladly spend and be spent

GLADLY, WOULD
1. *desire, long for:* ἐπιθυμέω (imperf.+inf.) EPITHYMEŌ
Lk 15.16 "he would gladly have fed on[u] the pods

GLADNESS
1. *great joy:* ἀγαλλίασις AGALLIASIS
Lk 1.14 "you will have joy and gladness
Heb 1. 9 "anointed thee with the oil of gladness
2. *joy:* εὐφροσύνη EUPHROSYNĒ*
Acts 2.28 "'thou wilt make me full of gladness
14.17 "satisfying your hearts with .. gladness

GLASS
1. *of glass:* ὑάλινος HYALINOS*
Rev 4. 6 there is as it were a sea of glass
15. 2 I saw .. a sea of glass mingled with fire
15. 2 beside the sea of glass with harps
2. *glass, glassware:* ὕαλος HYALOS*
Rev 21.18 the city was pure gold, clear as glass
21.21 the street of the city was pure gold

GLISTENING
1. *glitter:* στίλβω (part.) STILBŌ*
Mk 9. 3 his garments became glistening

GLOOM
GLOOM, NETHER
1. *darkness:* ζόφος ZOPHOS
Heb 12.18 darkness, and gloom, and a tempest
2 Pet 2. 4 committed them to pits of nether gloom
2.17 for them the nether gloom of darkness
Jude . 6 in eternal chains in the nether gloom
.13 for whom the nether gloom of darkness

GLORIFICATION
1. *glory:* δόξα DOXA
1 Cor 2. 7 before the ages for our glorification

GLORIFIED, BE
1. *be glorified:* ἐνδοξάζομαι ENDOXAZOMAI*
2 Th 1.10 he comes on that day to be glorified
1.12 that the name .. may be glorified in you

GLORIFIED WITH, BE
1. *glorify with:* συνδοξάζω (pass.) SYNDOXAZŌ*
Rom 8.17 that we may also be glorified with him

GLORIFY
1. *extol, honor:* δοξάζω DOXAZŌ
Mt 9. 8 they were afraid, and they glorified God
15.31 they glorified the God of Israel
Mk 2.12 they were all amazed and glorified God
Lk 2.20 shepherds returned, glorifying .. God
4.15 he taught .., being glorified by all
5.25 he rose .. and went home, glorifying God
5.26 they glorified God and were filled with awe
7.16 Fear seized them .. and they glorified God
18.43 he .. followed him, glorifying God
Jn 7.39 because Jesus was not yet glorified
8.54 "If I glorify myself, my glory is nothing; it is my Father who glorifies me
11. 4 "that the Son of God may be glorified
12.16 when Jesus was glorified .. they remembered
12.23 "hour .. for the Son of man to be glorified
12.28 "Father, glorify thy name
12.28 "I have glorified it, and I will glorify it again
13.31 "Now is the Son of man glorified, and in him God is glorified

Jn 13.32 "if God is glorified in him, God will also glorify him in himself, and glorify him at once
14.13 "Father may be glorified in the Son
15. 8 "By this my Father is glorified
16.14 "He will glorify me
17. 1 "Father, the hour has come; glorify thy Son that the Son may glorify thee
17. 4 "I glorified thee on earth
17. 5 "now, Father, glorify thou me
17.10 "and I am glorified in them
21.19 (by what death he was to glorify God
Acts 3.13 "God of our fathers, glorified his servant[c]
11.18 And they glorified God
13.48 they were glad and glorified the word
21.20 when they heard it, they glorified God
Rom 8.30 those whom he justified he also glorified
15. 6 with one voice glorify the God and Father
15. 9 that the Gentiles might glorify God
1 Cor 6.20 So glorify God in your body
2 Cor 9.13 you[m] will glorify God by your obedience†
Gal 1.24 they glorified God because of me
1 Pet 2.12 see your good deeds and glorify God
4.11 that in everything God may be glorified
4.16 under that name let him glorify God
Rev 15. 4 "Who shall not fear and glorify thy name?
18. 7 "glorified herself and played the wanton

GLORIOUS

1. *glory:* δόξα (gen.) DOXA
Mt 19.28 "Son of man shall sit on his g. throne
25.31 "then he will sit on his glorious throne
Rom 8.21 the glorious liberty of the children of God
Eph 1. 6 to the praise of his glorious grace
1.18 the riches of his glorious inheritance
Phil 3.21 our lowly body to be like his glorious body
Col 1.11 according to his glorious might
1 Tim 1.11 in accordance with the glorious gospel

2. *glorious, honored:* ἔνδοξος ENDOXOS
Lk 13.17 people rejoiced at all the glorious things

GLORIOUS ONES

1. *glory:* δόξα (subst. pl.) DOXA
2 Pet 2.10 not afraid to revile the glorious ones
Jude . 8 these men . . revile the glorious ones[c]†

GLORY

1. *glory:* δόξα DOXA
Mt 4. 8 the kingdoms . . and the glory of them
[6.13 *"the kingdom and the power and the glory*‡
6.29 "Solomon in all his glory was not
16.27 "to come . . in the glory of his Father
24.30 "coming on the clouds . . with . . great glory
25.31 "When the Son of man comes in his glory
Mk 8.38 "when he comes in the glory of his Father
10.37 "to sit, one at your right hand . . in your g.
13.26 "coming in clouds with . . glory
Lk 2. 9 the glory of the Lord shone around them
2.14 "Glory to God in the highest
2.32 "for glory to thy people Israel
4. 6 "To you I will give . . their glory
9.26 "ashamed when he comes in his glory
9.31 appeared in glory and spoke of his departure
9.32 Peter . . saw his glory and the two men
12.27 "Solomon in all his glory was not
19.38 "Peace in heaven and glory in the highest!
21.27 "coming in a cloud with . . great glory
24.26 "that . . Christ should . . enter into his glory
Jn 1.14 we have beheld his glory, glory as of the only Son from the Father
2.11 Jesus . . manifested his glory
5.41 "I do not receive glory from men
5.44 "you . . who receive glory from one another and do not seek the glory . . from . . God
7.18 "speaks on his own . . seeks his own glory
7.18 but he who seeks the glory of him who sent
8.50 "Yet I do not seek my own glory
8.54 "If I glorify myself, my glory is nothing
11. 4 "This illness . . is for the glory of God
11.40 "that . . you would see the glory of God
Jn 12.41 Isaiah . . saw his glory
17. 5 "glorify . . me . . with the glory which I had
17.22 "The glory which thou hast given me
17.24 "to behold my glory which thou hast given
Acts 7. 2 "God of glory appeared to our father
7.55 But he . . saw the glory of God
12.23 because he did not give God the glory
Rom 1.23 exchanged the glory of the immortal God
2. 7 seek for glory and honor and immortality
2.10 glory and honor and peace for every one
3. 7 God's truthfulness abounds to his glory
3.23 all . . fall short of the glory of God
4.20 strong in his faith as he gave glory to God
5. 2 our hope of sharing the glory of God
6. 4 raised . . by the glory of the Father
8.18 not worth comparing with the glory
9. 4 the sonship, the glory, the covenants
9.23 riches of his glory for the vessels of mercy, which he has prepared beforehand for glory
11.36 To him be glory for ever. Amen
15. 7 Welcome one another . . for the glory of God
16.27 to the only wise God be glory!
1 Cor 2. 8 would not have crucified the Lord of glory
10.31 do all to the glory of God
11. 7 a man . . is the image and glory of God; but woman is the glory of man
15.40 the glory of the celestial is one
15.41 There is one glory of the sun, and another glory of the moon, and another glory of the stars; for star differs from star in glory
15.43 sown in dishonor, it is raised in glory
2 Cor 1.20 we utter the Amen . . to the glory of God
3.18 beholding[d] the glory of the Lord
3.18 changed . . from one degree of glory
4. 4 light of the gospel of the glory of Christ
4. 6 light of the knowledge of the glory of God
4.15 increase thanksgiving, to the glory of God
4.17 preparing for us an eternal weight of glory
8.19 this gracious work . . for the glory of the Lord
8.23 messengers[j] . . the glory of Christ
Gal 1. 5 to whom be the glory for ever and ever
Eph 1.12 to live for the praise of his glory
1.14 to the praise of his glory
1.17 God of our Lord . . , the Father of glory
3.13 I am suffering for you, which is your glory
3.16 according to the riches of his glory
3.21 to him be glory in the church
Phil 1.11 through Jesus Christ, to . . glory . . of God
2.11 confess . . to the glory of God the Father
3.19 they glory in their shame
4.19 according to his riches in glory in Christ
4.20 To our God and Father be glory for ever
Col 1.27 the riches of the glory of this mystery, which is Christ in you, the hope of glory
3. 4 then you also will appear with him in glory
1 Th 2. 6 nor did we seek glory from men
2.12 calls you into his own kingdom and glory
2.20 For you are our glory and joy
2 Th 1. 9 exclusion . . from the glory of his might
2.14 that you may obtain the glory of our Lord
1 Tim 1.17 be honor and glory for ever and ever[b]
3.16 believed on in the world, taken up in glory
2 Tim 2.10 salvation . . with its eternal glory
4.18 To him be the glory for ever and ever
Tit 2.13 appearing of the glory of our great God
Heb 1. 3 He reflects the glory of God
2. 7 "thou hast crowned him with g. and honor[d]
2. 9 Jesus . . crowned with glory and honor
2.10 bringing many sons to glory
3. 3 worthy of . . more glory than Moses
9. 5 above it were the cherubim of glory
13.21 to whom be glory for ever and ever
Jas 2. 1 our Lord Jesus Christ, the Lord of glory
1 Pet 1. 7 redound to praise and glory and honor
1.11 sufferings of Christ and . . subsequent g.
1.21 God, who raised him . . and gave him glory
1.24 "its glory like the flower of grass

1 Pet 4.11 To him belong glory and dominion
4.13 glad when his glory is revealed
4.14 spirit of glory[j] and of God rests upon you
5. 1 as well as a partaker in the glory
5. 4 you will obtain the unfading crown of glory
5.10 called you to his eternal glory in Christ
2 Pet 1. 3 called us to[b] his own glory and excellence
1.17 he received honor and glory from God
1.17 borne to him by the Majestic Glory
3.18 To him be the glory both now
Jude .24 before the presence of his glory
.25 be glory, majesty, dominion
Rev 1. 6 to him be glory and dominion for ever
4. 9 the living creatures give glory and honor
4.11 "Worthy art thou . . to receive glory
5.12 "Worthy is the Lamb . . to receive . . glory!
5.13 "be blessing and honor and glory!
7.12 "Blessing and glory and wisdom!
11.13 gave glory to the God of heaven
14. 7 "Fear God and give him glory
15. 8 filled with smoke from the glory of God
16. 9 they did not repent and give him glory
19. 1 "glory and power belong to our God
19. 7 "rejoice and exult and give him the glory
21.11 ⟨Jerusalem⟩ having the glory of God
21.23 for the glory of God is its light
21.24 kings of the earth shall bring their glory
21.26 they shall bring into it the glory

2. *boast:* καυχάομαι KAUCHAOMAI
1 Cor [13. 3 if I deliver my body *that I may glory*‡
Gal 6.13 that they may glory in your flesh
6.14 far be it from me to glory
Phil 3. 3 worship God in spirit,[e] and glory in Christ

GLORY, CAUSE TO

1. *object of boasting, boast:* καύχημα KAUCHĒMA
Phil 1.26 so that . . you may have ample cause to g.

GLORY, GIVE

1. *extol, honor:* δοξάζω DOXAZŌ
Mt 5.16 "that they may . . give glory to your Father

GLUTTON

1. *belly:* γαστήρ GASTĒR
Tit 1.12 "Cretans are always . . lazy gluttons
2. *glutton:* φάγος PHAGOS*
Mt 11.19 " 'Behold, a glutton and a drunkard!
Lk 7.34 " 'Behold, a glutton and a drunkard!

GNASH

1. *biting, gnashing:* βρυγμός BRYGMOS* [A.6.a.3]
Mt 8.12 "there men will weep and gnash their teeth
Also Mt **13**.42, 50; **22**.13; **24**.51; **25**.30
Lk 13.28 "there you will weep and gnash your teeth

GNAT

1. *gnat, mosquito:* κώνωψ KŌNŌPS*
Mt 23.24 "straining out a g. and swallowing a camel!

GNAW

1. *chew, bite:* μασάομαι MASAOMAI*
Rev 16.10 men gnawed their tongues in anguish

GO (*See also, e.g.,* ALLOW TO GO ON; ASTRAY, GO; LET GO; WELL WITH ONE, GO)

1. *lead, bring:* ἄγω (hort. subj.) AGŌ
Mt 26.46 "Rise, let us be going
Mk 1.38 "Let us go on to the next towns
14.42 "Rise, let us be going
Jn 11. 7 "Let us go into Judea again
11.15 "But let us go to him
11.16 "Let us also go, that we may die with him
14.31 "Rise, let us go hence
2. *go up, come up:* ἀναβαίνω ANABAINŌ
Jn 7. 8 "Go to the feast yourselves
3. *go away:* ἄπειμι APEIMI II*
Acts 17.10 they went into the Jewish synagogue
4. *go away:* ἀπέρχομαι APERCHOMAI
Mt 2.22 he was afraid to go there
5.30 "than that your whole body go into hell[k]
8.19 "Teacher, I will follow you wherever you go
8.21 "Lord, let me first go and bury my father
Mt 8.32 they came out and went into the swine
8.33 going into the city they told everything
9. 7 And he rose and went home
10. 5 "Go nowhere among the Gentiles
13.28 " 'do you want us to go and gather them?
13.46 "went and sold all that he had and bought it
14.15 "send the crowds away to go into the villages
16.21 that he must go to Jerusalem and suffer
18.30 "refused and went and put him in prison
20. 4(5) "So they went
21.29 "but afterward he repented and went
21.30 " 'I go, sir,' but did not go
25.10 "while they went . . the bridegroom came
25.18 "But he . . went and dug in the ground
25.25 " 'I went and hid your talent
26.36 Jesus went with them to . . Gethsemane
27. 5 and he went and hanged himself
28.10 "tell my brethren to go to Galilee
Mk 5.24 And he went with him
6.27(28) He went and beheaded him
6.36 "send them away, to go into the country
6.37 "Shall we go and buy . . bread?
7.30 she went home, and found the child
9.43 "than with two hands to go to hell[m]
14.10 Judas . . went to the chief priests
14.12 "Where will you have us go and prepare?
Lk 1.23 he went to his home
5.14 "go and show yourself to the priest
5.25 he . . went home, glorifying God
7.24 When the messengers of John had gone
9.57 "I will follow you wherever you go
9.59 "let me first go and bury my father
9.60 "as for you, go and proclaim the kingdom
17.23 "Do not go, do not follow them
22.13 And they went, and found it
24.24 "Some of those . . went to the tomb
Jn 4.47 he went and begged him to come down
6. 1 After this Jesus went to the other side
6.68 "Lord, to whom shall we go?
9. 7 he went and washed and came back
9.11 "so I went and washed
11.28 she went and called her sister Mary
11.46 some of them went to the Pharisees
11.54 Jesus . . went from there to the country
12.19 "look, the world has gone after him
Acts 4.15 they had commanded them to go aside
5.26 the captain with the officers went
Rev 10. 9 So I went to the angel and told him
16. 2 first angel went and poured his bowl
18.14 "fruit for which thy soul longed has gone!
5. *come on:* δεῦρο DEURO
Acts 7. 3 " 'go into the land which I will show you
6. *pass through:* διέρχομαι DIERCHOMAI
Acts 20.25 "you among whom I have gone preaching[o]
7. *enter, go into:* εἰσέρχομαι EISERCHOMAI
Mt 26.58 going inside he sat with the guards
Mk 15.43 Joseph . . took courage and went to Pilate
Lk 4.16 he went to the synagogue, as his custom
18.25 "easier for a camel to go through . . a needle
Acts 11. 3 "Why did you go to uncircumcised men?
Heb 6.20 where Jesus has gone as a forerunner
8. *fall out:* ἐκπίπτω EKPIPTŌ
Acts 27.32 cut away the ropes of the boat, and let it go
9. *go out:* ἐκπορεύομαι EKPOREUOMAI
Acts 25. 4 he himself intended to go there shortly
10. *stand by:* ἐφίστημι EPHISTĒMI
Lk 10.40 she went to him and said, "Lord
11. *come, go:* ἔρχομαι ERCHOMAI
Mt 2.11 going into the house they saw the child
2.23 he went and dwelt in . . Nazareth
4.13 he went and dwelt in Capernaum
13.36 he left . . and went into the house
14.12 they went and told Jesus
15.39 he . . went to the region of Magadan
18.31 "they went and reported to their lord
21.19 seeing a fig tree . . he went to it
26.36 Jesus went with them to . . Gethsemane

Mt 27.64 "lest his disciples go and steal him away
28. 1 the other Mary went to see the sepulchre
28.11 some of the guard went into the city
Mk 1.39 he went throughout all Galilee
3.19(20) Then he went home
7.31 he . . went through Sidon to the Sea of G.
8.10 he . . went to the district of Dalmanutha[d]
10. 1 he left there and went to . . Judea
11.13 he went to see if he could find anything
14.16 the disciples set out and went to the city
14.32 they went to a place . . called Gethsemane
15.43 went to Pilate, and asked for the body
16. 1 that they might go and anoint him
16. 2 first day of the week they went to the tomb
Lk 2.16 they went with haste, and found Mary
2.44 they went a day's journey
3. 3 he went into . . the region about the Jordan
14. 1 he went to dine at the house of a ruler
24. 1 at early dawn, they went to the tomb
Jn 3.22 Jesus . . went into the land of Judea
3.26 "all are going to him
4.45 for they too had gone to the feast
5. 7 "while I am going another steps down
6.24 they . . went to Capernaum, seeking Jesus
7.50 Nicodemus, who had gone to him before
11.29 she rose quickly and went to him
12.22 Philip went and told Andrew; Andrew went with Philip and they told Jesus
18. 3 Judas, procuring a band of soldiers . . went
20. 2 So she ran, and went to Simon Peter
20. 3 they went toward the tomb
20.18 Mary Magdalene went . . to the disciples
21. 3 They said to him, "We will go with you
Acts 4.23 they went to their friends and reported
12.12 he went to the house of Mary
13.14 they went into the synagogue
13.51 they . . went to Iconium
18. 1 he left Athens and went to Corinth
18. 7 went to the house of a man named Titius[q]
Gal 1.21 Then I went into the regions of Syria
Heb 11. 8 not knowing where he was to go
Rev 5. 7 he went and took the scroll

12. *go out:* ἐξέρχομαι EXERCHOMAI
Mt 9.26 report . . went through all that district
25. 1 "maidens . . went to meet the bridegroom[c]
Mk 9.30 They went on from there . . through Galilee
Lk 8.35 man from whom the demons had gone
8.38 man from whom the demons had gone
10.10 "go into its streets
Jn 1.43 Jesus decided to go to Galilee
Acts 11.25 Barnabas went to Tarsus
16.13 we went outside the gate to the riverside
16.19 saw that their hope of gain was gone
2 Cor 8.17 he is going to you of his own accord

13. *be on the road:* εἶναι ἐν τῇ ὁδῷ HODOS [B.2.a.1]
Mt 5.25 "while you are going with him to court

14. *go away:* ὑπάγω HYPAGŌ
Mt 5.24 "leave your gift there before the altar and go
5.41 "if any one forces you . . go with him two
8. 4 "go, show yourself to the priest
8.13 "Go; be it done . . as you have believed
8.32 And he said to them, "Go
9. 6 "Rise, take up your bed and go home
13.44 "in his joy he goes and sells all that he has
18.15 "If your brother sins against you, go
19.21 "If you would be perfect, go, sell
20. 4 " 'You go into the vineyard too
20. 7 " 'You go into the vineyard too
20.14 " 'Take what belongs to you, and go
21.28 " 'Son, go and work in the vineyard
26.18 "Go into the city to a certain one
26.24 "The Son of man goes as it is written of him
27.65 "go, make it as secure as you can[p]
28.10 "go and tell my brethren
Mk 1.44 "go, show yourself to the priest
2.11 "rise, take up your pallet and go home
5.19 "Go home to your friends
Mk 5.34 "go in peace, and be healed of your disease
6.31 For many were coming and going
6.33 many saw them going, and knew them
6.38 "How many loaves have you? Go and see
10.21 "You lack one thing; go, sell what you have
11. 2 "Go into the village opposite you
14.13 said to them, "Go into the city
14.21 "the Son of man goes as it is written of him
16. 7 "go, tell his disciples and Peter
Lk 8.42 As he went, the people pressed round
12.58 "As you go with your accuser
17.14 And as they went they were cleansed
19.30 "Go into the village opposite
Jn 3. 8 "you do not know . . whither it goes
4.16 "Go, call your husband, and come here
6.21 at the land to which they were going
7. 3 "Leave here and go to Judea
7.33 "then I go to him who sent me
8.14 "I know . . whither I am going, but you do not know . . whither I am going
8.21 "where I am going, you cannot come
8.22 " 'Where I am going, you cannot come
9. 7 "Go, wash in the pool of Siloam
9.11 "Jesus . . said . . 'Go to Siloam and wash
11. 8 "you are going there again?
11.31 that she was going to the tomb to weep
11.44 "Unbind him, and let him go
12.35 "he . . does not know where he goes
13. 3 knowing . . that he . . was going to God
13.33 " 'Where I am going you cannot come
13.36 "Lord, where are you going?
13.36 "Where I am going you cannot follow
14. 4 "And you know the way where I am going[f]
14. 5 "we do not know where you are going
15.16 "that you should go and bear fruit
16. 5 "I am going to him who sent me; yet none of you asks me, 'Where are you going?
16.10 "righteousness, because I go to the Father
16.17 " 'because I go to the Father
18. 8 "so, if you seek me, let these men go
21. 3 Peter said to them, "I am going fishing
Jas 2.16 "Go in peace, be warmed and filled
1 Jn 2.11 he . . does not know where he is going
Rev 10. 8 "Go, take the scroll which is open
13.10 to captivity he goes
14. 4 who follow the Lamb wherever he goes
16. 1 "Go and pour out . . the seven bowls
17. 8 "The beast . . is to . . go to perdition
17.11 "As for the beast . . it goes to perdition

15. *pass over:* μεταβαίνω METABAINŌ
Lk 10. 7 "do not go from house to house

16. *arrive, stand by:* παραγίνομαι PARAGINOMAI
Acts 23.16 so he went and entered the barracks

17. *pass by:* παραπορεύομαι PARAPOREUOMAI
Mk 2.23 he was going through the grainfields

18. *walk, behave:* περιπατέω PERIPATEŌ
Rev 16.15 ("that he may not go naked and be seen!

19. *go, walk:* πορεύομαι POREUOMAI
Mt 2. 8 "Go and search diligently for the child
2.20 "Rise . . and go to the land of Israel
8. 9 "I say to one, 'Go,' and he goes, and to another, 'Come,' and he comes
9.13 "Go and learn what this means
10. 6 "go rather to the lost sheep of . . Israel
10. 7 "preach as you go
11. 4 "Go and tell John what you hear and see
12. 1 Jesus went through the grainfields
12.45 "he goes and brings . . seven other spirits
17.27 "go to the sea and cast a hook
18.12 "does he not . . go in search of the one?
19.15 he laid his hands on them and went away
21. 2 "Go into the village opposite you
21. 6 disciples went and did as Jesus had directed
22. 9 " 'Go therefore to the thoroughfares
22.15 the Pharisees went and took counsel
25. 9 " 'go rather . . and buy for yourselves
25.16 "He . . went at once and traded with them

Mt 26.14 Judas Iscariot, went to the chief priests
27.66 went and made the sepulchre secure
28. 7 "go quickly and tell his disciples
28.11 While they were going, behold
28.16 the eleven disciples went to Galilee
28.19 "Go . . and make disciples of all nations
Mk 16.10 She went out and told those[k]‡
16.15 "Go into all the world and preach[k]‡
Lk 1.39 Mary arose and went with haste
2. 3 And all went to be enrolled
2.41 his parents went to Jerusalem every year
4.42 he . . went into a lonely place
5.24 "rise, take up your bed and go home
7. 6 And Jesus went with them
7. 8 "I say to one, 'Go,' and he goes; and to another, 'Come,' and he comes
7.11 afterward[y] he went to a city called Nain
7.22 "Go and tell John what you have seen
7.50 "Your faith has saved you; go in peace
8.48 "your faith has made you well; go in peace
9.12 "Send the crowd . . to go into the villages
9.13 "unless we are to go and buy food for all
9.51 he set his face to go to Jerusalem
9.52 messengers . . went and entered a village
9.56 they went on to another village
9.57 they were going along the road
10.37 Jesus said to him, "Go and do likewise
11. 5 "Which . . will go to him at midnight?
11.26 "he goes and brings seven other spirits
13.32 "Go and tell that fox, 'Behold
14.10 "go and sit in the lowest place
14.19 "'I have bought . . and I go to examine
14.31 "what king, going to encounter another
15. 4 "and go after the one which is lost
15.15 "he went and joined himself to one
15.18 "'I will arise and go to my father
16.30 "'if some one goes to them from the dead
17.14 "Go and show yourselves to the priests
19.12 "A nobleman went into a far country
21. 8 "Do not go after them
22. 8 "Go and prepare the passover for us
22.22 "Son of man goes as it has been determined
22.33 "Lord, I am ready to go with you
22.39 he . . went, as was his custom, to the Mount
24.13 That very day two of them were going
24.28 drew near to the village to which they were going. He appeared to be going further
Jn 4.50 Jesus said to him, "Go; your son will live
7.35 "Where does this man intend to go?
7.35 "Does he intend to go to the Dispersion?
7.53 They went each to his own house[r]‡
8. 1 but Jesus went to the Mount of Olives[r]‡
8.11 "go, and do not sin again[r]‡
10. 4 "he goes before them . . the sheep follow
11.11 "I go to awake him out of sleep
14. 2 "I go to prepare a place for you
14. 3 "when I go and prepare a place for you
14.12 "because I go to the Father
14.28 "because I go to the Father
16. 7 "but if I go, I will send him to you
16.28 "again, I am . . going to the Father
20.17 "go to my brethren and say to them
Acts 1.10 they were gazing into heaven as he went
1.11 "same way as you saw him go into heaven
1.25 "Judas turned aside, to go to his own place
5.20 "Go and stand in the temple and speak
8.26 Lord said to Philip, "Rise and go
8.27 he rose and went
8.36 as they went along the road
8.39 the eunuch . . went on his way rejoicing
9.11 "Rise and go to the street called Straight
9.15 "Go, for he is a chosen instrument of mine
12.17 he departed and went to another place
16. 7 they attempted to go into Bithynia
16.16 As we were going to the place of prayer
16.36 "therefore come out and go in peace
18. 6 "From now on I will go to the Gentiles
Acts 19.21 Paul resolved . . to . . go to Jerusalem
20.22 "now, behold, I am going to Jerusalem
22.10 "'Rise, and go into Damascus
23.23 "spearmen to go as far as Caesarea
25.12 "to Caesar you shall go
25.20 "whether he wished to go to Jerusalem
27. 3 Julius . . gave him leave to go to his friends
28.26 "'Go to this people, and say
Rom 15.24 I hope to see you . . as I go to Spain
15.25 I am going to Jerusalem with aid
1 Cor 10.27 If . . you are disposed to go, eat
16. 4 If it seems advisable that I should go also
16. 6 speed me on my journey, wherever I go
1 Tim 1. 3 when I was going to Macedonia
2 Tim 4.10 Demas . . has deserted me and gone
Jas 4.13 "tomorrow we will go into such and such
1 Pet 3.19 he went and preached to the spirits
3.22 ⟨Jesus Christ,⟩ who has gone into heaven

20. *go before, go forward:* προέρχομαι PROERCHOMAI
Mt 26.39 going a little farther he fell on his face
Mk 14.35 going a little farther, he fell on the ground
Lk 1.17 "he will go before him in the spirit

21. *come to, approach:* προσέρχομαι PROSERCHOMAI
Mt 8.25 And they went and woke him
Lk 8.24 And they went and woke him
10.34 "went to him and bound up his wounds

CONTEXTUALLY
1 Cor 4. 6 learn . . not to go beyond what is written[0]
Phil 2.23 as soon as I see how it will go with me

GO ABOARD

1. *go up, come up:* ἀναβαίνω ANABAINŌ
Jn 21.11 Peter went aboard and hauled the net
2. *go upon, mount, board:* ἐπιβαίνω EPIBAINŌ
Acts 21. 2 we went aboard, and set sail

GO ABOUT

1. *pass through:* διέρχομαι DIERCHOMAI
Acts 8. 4 those . . scattered went about preaching
10.38 "how he went about doing good
2. *lead around, go about:* περιάγω PERIAGŌ
Mt 4.23 he went about all Galilee
9.35 Jesus went about all the cities
Mk 6. 6 he went about among the villages
Acts 13.11 he went about seeking people to lead him
3. *go about:* περιέρχομαι PERIERCHOMAI
Heb 11.37 they went about in skins of sheep
4. *walk, behave:* περιπατέω PERIPATEŌ
Mk 12.38 "scribes, who like to go about in long robes
Lk 20.46 "scribes, who like to go about in long robes
Jn 6.66 many . . no longer went about with him
7. 1 After this Jesus went about in Galilee; he would not go about in Judea
11.54 Jesus therefore no longer went about openly

GO ABROAD

1. *pass through:* διέρχομαι DIERCHOMAI
Lk 5.15 so much the more the report went abroad
2. *go out:* ἐκπορεύομαι EKPOREUOMAI
Rev 16.14 demonic spirits . . who go abroad

GO ACROSS

1. *pass through:* διέρχομαι DIERCHOMAI
Mk 4.35 "Let us go across to the other side
Lk 8.22 "Let us go across to the other side

GO AHEAD

1. *lead forward:* προάγω PROAGŌ
2 Jn . 9 one who goes ahead and does not abide
2. *go before, go forward:* προέρχομαι PROERCHOMAI
Acts 20.13 going ahead to the ship, we set sail

GO AHEAD WITH

1. *take before, go before:* προλαμβάνω PROLAMBANŌ
1 Cor 11.21 each one goes ahead with his own meal

GO ASHORE

1. *go out:* ἐξέρχομαι EXERCHOMAI
Mt 14.14 As he went ashore he saw a great throng
Mk 6.34 As he went ashore he saw a great throng[0]

GO ASIDE
1. *withdraw:* ἀναχωρέω ANACHŌREŌ
Acts 23.19 tribune . . going aside asked him privately

GO AWAY
1. *go away:* ἀπέρχομαι APERCHOMAI
Mt 13.25 "his enemy came . . and went away
14.16 Jesus said, "They need not go away
19.22 the young man . . went away sorrowful
22.22 they marveled . . and went away
25.46 "they will go away into eternal punishment
26.42 he went away and prayed, "My Father
26.44 again, he went away and prayed
Mk 5.20 he went away and began to proclaim
6.32 they went away in the boat
7.24 he . . went away to the region of Tyre
10.22 he went away sorrowful
11. 4 they went away, and found a colt tied
12.12 so they left him and went away
14.39 again he went away and prayed
Lk 2.15 When the angels went away from them
8.39 he went away, proclaiming
19.32 So those who were sent went away
22. 4 he went away and conferred
Jn 4. 8 For his disciples had gone away
4.28 woman . . went away into the city
5.15 The man went away and told the Jews
6.22 his disciples had gone away alone
10.40 He went away again across the Jordan
16. 7 "advantage that I go away, for if I do not go away, the Counselor will not come
Gal 1.17 I went away into Arabia
Jas 1.24 he . . goes away and at once forgets
2. *be away, go abroad:* ἀποδημέω APODĒMEŌ
Mt 25.15 "Then he went away
3. *go out:* ἐξέρχομαι EXERCHOMAI
Mt 9.31 they went away and spread his fame
9.32 As they were going away, behold
15.21 Jesus went away . . to . . Tyre and Sidon
Mk 6. 1 He went away . . to his own country
Lk 11.53 As he went away from there
Jn 8. 9 when they heard it, they went away[r]‡
4. *go away:* ὑπάγω HYPAGŌ
Jn 6.67 Jesus said . . "Do you also wish to go away?[o]
8.21 "I go away, and you will seek me
12.11 many of the Jews were going away
14.28 "'I go away, and I will come to you
5. *shift, depart:* μεταίρω METAIRŌ*
Mt 13.53 he went away from there
19. 1 he went away from Galilee
6. *go, walk:* πορεύομαι POREUOMAI
Mt 11. 7 As they went away, Jesus began to speak
24. 1 Jesus left the temple and was going away
Lk 4.30 passing through the midst . . he went away
Acts 24.25 Felix . . said, "Go away for the present

GO BACK
1. *go away:* ἀπέρχομαι APERCHOMAI
Mk 16.13 And they went back and told the rest[k]‡
Jn 20.10 the disciples went back to their homes
2. *come, go:* ἔρχομαι ERCHOMAI
Jn 7.45 officers then went back to the chief priests

GO BEFORE
1. *lead forward:* προάγω PROAGŌ
Mt 2. 9 lo, the star . . went before them
14.22 he made the disciples . . go before him
21. 9 the crowds that went before him
21.31 "harlots go into the kingdom . . before you
26.32 "I will go before you to Galilee
28. 7 "behold, he is going before you to Galilee
Mk 6.45 he made his disciples . . go before him
11. 9 those who went before . . cried . . "Hosanna!
14.28 "I will go before you to Galilee
16. 7 "he is going before you to Galilee
2. *go before, advance:* προπορεύομαι PROPOREUOMAI*
Lk 1.76 "for you will go before the Lord
Acts 7.40 "'Make for us gods to go before us

GO BY
1. *go through:* διαπορεύομαι DIAPOREUOMAI
Lk 18.36 hearing a multitude going by, he inquired
2. *pass by, transgress:* παρέρχομαι PARERCHOMAI
Acts 27. 9 because the fast had already gone by

GO BY LAND
1. *go on foot:* πεζεύω PEZEUŌ*
Acts 20.13 intending himself to go by land

GO DOWN
1. *set:* ἐπιδύω EPIDYŌ*
Eph 4.26 do not let the sun go down on your anger
2. *come down, go down:* καταβαίνω KATABAINŌ
Mt 24.17 "let him . . on the housetop not go down
Mk 13.15 "let him . . on the housetop not go down
Lk 2.51 he went down with them . . to Nazareth
10.30 "A man was going down from Jerusalem
10.31 "a priest was going down that road
18.14 "this man went down to his house
Jn 2.12 After this he went down to Capernaum
4.51 As he was going down, his servants met him
[5. 4 *an angel . . went down at certain seasons*‡
6.16 his disciples went down to the sea
Acts 7.15 "and Jacob went down into Egypt
8.26 "the road that goes down from Jerusalem
8.38 they both went down into the water
10.20 "Rise and go down, and accompany them
10.21 Peter went down to the men
14.25 they went down to Attalia
16. 8 they went down to Troas
18.22 then went down to Antioch
20.10 Paul went down and bent over him
23.10 commanded the soldiers to go down
25. 6 he went down to Caesarea
25. 7 Jews who had gone down from Jerusalem
3. *go down, come to:* κατέρχομαι KATERCHOMAI
Lk 4.31 he went down to Capernaum
Acts 8. 5 Philip went down to a city of Samaria
12.19 he went down from Judea to Caesarea
13. 4 they went down to Seleucia
15.30 they went down to Antioch
18.22 then went down to Antioch

GO DOWN WITH
1. *go down with:* συγκαταβαίνω SYGKATABAINŌ*
Acts 25. 5 "let . . men of authority . . go down with me

GO, FORCE TO
1. *press into service:* ἀγγαρεύω AGGAREUŌ
Mt 5.41 "if any one forces you to go one mile

GO FORTH
1. *go out:* ἐξέρχομαι EXERCHOMAI
Mk 5.30 that power had gone forth from him
16.20 they went forth and preached everywhere[k]‡
Lk 8.46 "power has gone forth from me
Jn 18. 1 he went forth with his disciples
1 Th 1. 8 your faith in God has gone forth
Heb 13.13 let us go forth to him outside the camp

GO HERE AND THERE
1. *pass through:* διέρχομαι DIERCHOMAI
Acts 9.32 Peter went here and there among them all

GO HOME
IDIOMATICALLY
a. Lk [24.12 *he went home*‡ ἀπῆλθεν πρὸς ἑαυτόν [APERCHOMAI]

GO IN
GO INTO
1. *go into, enter:* εἴσειμι EISEIMI
Acts 3. 3 Seeing Peter . . about to go into the temple
21.18 Paul went in with us to James
21.26 Paul . . went into the temple, to give notice
Heb 9. 6 the priests go continually into the outer tent[p]
2. *enter, go into:* εἰσέρχομαι EISERCHOMAI
Mt 6. 6 "when you pray, go into your room
9.25 he went in and took her by the hand
15.11 "not what goes into the mouth defiles
25.10 "those who were ready went in with him
27.53 they went into the holy city and appeared

Lk 7.36 he went into the Pharisee's house
11.37 so he went in and sat at table
15.28 "he was angry and refused to go in
19. 7 "He has gone in to be the guest
24. 3 they went in they did not find the body[t]
24.29 So he went in to stay with them
Jn 10. 9 "he will be saved, and will go in
20. 5 he saw . . but he did not go in
20. 6 Simon Peter . . went into the tomb
20. 8 the other disciple . . also went in
Acts 1.21 "time that the Lord Jesus went in and out
10.27 he went in and found many persons
17. 2 Paul went in, as was his custom
18.19 he himself went into the synagogue
3. *go into, enter:* εἰσπορεύομαι EISPOREUOMAI
Mt 15.17 "whatever goes into the mouth passes
Mk 1.21 they went into Capernaum
5.40 he . . went in where the child was
7.15 "nothing . . by going into him can defile
7.18 "whatever goes into a man from outside
Acts 9.28 went in and out among them at Jerusalem

GO IN AMONG
1. *enter, go into:* εἰσέρχομαι EISERCHOMAI
Acts 19.30 Paul wished to go in among the crowd

GO INTO ANOTHER COUNTRY
1. *be away, go abroad:* ἀποδημέω APODĒMEŌ
Mt 21.33 "householder . . went into another country
Mk 12. 1 "A man . . went into another country
Lk 20. 9 "A man . . went into another country

GO OFF
1. *go away:* ἀπέρχομαι APERCHOMAI
Mt 22. 5 "they made light of it and went off
Rev 12.17 dragon . . went off to make war on the rest
2. *go out:* ἐξέρχομαι EXERCHOMAI
Acts 10.23 The next day he rose and went off

GO ON
1. *go away:* ἀπέρχομαι APERCHOMAI
Acts 23.32 leaving the horsemen to go on with him
Rom 15.28 I shall go on by way of you to Spain
2. *go upon, mount, board:* ἐπιβαίνω EPIBAINŌ
Acts 21. 4 they told Paul not to go on to Jerusalem
3. *come, go:* ἔρχομαι ERCHOMAI
2 Cor 12. 1 I will go on to visions and revelations
4. *go out:* ἐξέρχομαι EXERCHOMAI
Mk 8.27 Jesus went on with his disciples
9.30 They went on from there . . through Galilee
Acts 14.20 he went on with Barnabas to Derbe
16.10 we sought to go on into Macedonia
2 Cor 2.13 I took leave . . and went on to Macedonia
5. *pass over:* μεταβαίνω METABAINŌ
Mt 11. 1 he went on from there to teach and preach
12. 9 he went on . . and entered their synagogue
15.29 Jesus went on from there
6. *bring, bear:* φέρω PHERŌ
Heb 6. 1 let us . . go on to maturity
7. *go, walk:* πορεύομαι POREUOMAI
Lk 19.28 when he had said this, he went on ahead
8. *go before:* προβαίνω PROBAINŌ
Mt 4.21 going on . . he saw two other brothers
Mk 1.19 going on a little farther, he saw James
9. *go before, go forward:* προέρχομαι PROERCHOMAI
Acts 20. 5 went on and were waiting . . at Troas
2 Cor 9. 5 to urge the brethren to go on to you
10. *make progress, advance:* προκόπτω PROKOPTŌ
2 Tim 3.13 impostors will go on from bad to worse

GO ON A JOURNEY
1. *be away, go abroad:* ἀποδημέω APODĒMEŌ
Mt 25.14 "as when a man going on a journey

GO ON, ALLOW TO
1. *permit to go farther:* προσεάω PROSEAŌ*
Acts 27. 7 the wind did not allow us to go on

GO ON ONE'S JOURNEY
1. *go, walk:* πορεύομαι POREUOMAI
Acts 21. 5 we departed and went on our journey

GO ON ONE'S WAY
GO ONE'S WAY
1. *go away:* ὑπάγω HYPAGŌ
Mk 7.29 "For this saying you may go your way
10.52 "Go your way; . . faith has made you well
Lk 10. 3 "Go your way; behold, I send you out
2. *go, walk:* πορεύομαι POREUOMAI
Mt 2. 9 When they had heard . . they went their w.
Lk 8.14 "as they go on their way they are choked
10.38 as they went on their way, he entered
13.33 "'I must go on my way today
17.19 "Rise and go your way
Jn 4.50 man believed . . and went his way

GO ON ONE'S WAY THROUGH
1. *go through:* διαπορεύομαι DIAPOREUOMAI
Lk 13.22 He went on his way through towns
Acts 16. 4 they went on their way through the cities

GO ON THROUGH
1. *travel through:* διοδεύω DIODEUŌ
[a]+κατά
Lk 8. 1 [a]he went on through cities

GO OUT
1. *go away, step off from:* ἀποβαίνω APOBAINŌ
Lk 5. 2 the fishermen had gone out of them
2. *go out of:* ἐκβαίνω EKBAINŌ*
Heb 11.15 that land from which they had gone out
3. *go out:* ἐκπορεύομαι EKPOREUOMAI
Mt 3. 5 Then went out to him Jerusalem
20.29 as they went out of Jericho
Mk 1. 5 went out to him all the country of Judea
11.19 they[u] went out of the city‡
Lk 4.37 reports of him went out into every place
Acts 9.28 So he went in and out among them
4. *go out:* ἔξειμι EXEIMI
Acts 13.42 As they went out, the people begged
5. *go out:* ἐξέρχομαι EXERCHOMAI
[a]+ἐκ [b]+ἀπό [c]+ἔξω
Mt 11. 7 "What did you go out . . to behold?
11. 8 "Why then did you go out?
11. 9 "Why then did you go out?
12.14 the Pharisees went out and took counsel
12.43 [b]"When the unclean spirit has gone out
13. 1 Jesus went out of the house and sat
13. 3 "A sower went out to sow
18.28 "that same servant, as he went out
20. 1 "a householder who went out early
20. 3 "going out about the third hour
20. 5 "Going out again about the sixth hour
20. 6 "about the eleventh hour he went out
21.17 [c]he went out of the city to Bethany
22.10 "those servants went out into the streets
24.26 "if they say to you, 'Lo . . ,' do not go out
26.30 they went out to the Mount of Olives
26.71 when he went out to the porch
26.75 [c]And he went out and wept bitterly
27.32 As they went out, they came upon a man[o]
Mk 1.35 he rose and went out to a lonely place
1.45 he went out and began to talk freely
2.12 he . . went out before them all
2.13 He went out again beside the sea
3. 6 Pharisees went out, and . . held counsel
3.21 they went out to seize him
4. 3 "Listen! A sower went out to sow
6.12 So they went out and preached
6.24 she went out, and said to her mother
11.11 he went out to Bethany with the twelve
14.26 they went out to the Mount of Olives
14.68 [c]And he went out into the gateway[f]
16. 8 they went out and fled from the tomb
Lk 2. 1 a decree went out from Caesar Augustus
4.14 a report concerning him went out
5.27 he went out, and saw a tax collector
6.12 he went out to the mountain to pray
7.24 "What did you go out . . to behold?
7.25 "What then did you go out to see?

Lk 7.26 "What then did you go out to see?
8. 2 from whom seven demons had gone out
8. 5 "A sower went out to sow his seed
8.35 Then people went out to see
11.14 when the demon had gone out
11.24 [b]"When the unclean spirit has gone out
14.18 "'I have bought a field, and I must go out
14.21 "'Go out quickly to the streets and lanes
14.23 "'Go out to the highways and hedges
17.29 "the day when Lot went out from Sodom
21.37 at night he went out and lodged
22.62 [c]And he went out and wept bitterly
Jn 4.30 [a]They went out of the city
8.59 [a]Jesus hid . . and went out of the temple
10. 9 "will go in and out and find pasture
11.31 saw Mary rise quickly and go out
12.13 So they . . went out to meet him
13.30 he immediately went out; and it was night
13.31 When he had gone out, Jesus said
18.16 the other disciple . . went out
18.29 [c]So Pilate went out to them
18.38 Pilate . . went out to the Jews again
19. 4 [c]Pilate went out again, and said . . "See
19.17 Jesus . . went out, bearing his own cross
21. 3 They went out and got into the boat
Acts 1.21 "the Lord Jesus went in and out among us
12. 9 he went out and followed him
12.10 they went out and passed on through
16.40 [b]So they went out of the prison
17.33 Paul went out from among them
Rom 10.18 "Their voice has gone out to all the earth
1 Cor 5.10 [a]you would need to go out of the world
Heb 11. 8 Abraham . . was called to go out to a place . . and he went out, not knowing where
1 Jn 2.19 [a]They went out from us
4. 1 false prophets have gone out into the world
2 Jn . 7 deceivers have gone out into the world
Rev 3.12 [c]"'never shall he go out of it
6. 2 he went out conquering and to conquer

6. *quench, put out:* σβέννυμι (pass.) SBENNYMI
Mt 25. 8 "'for our lamps are going out

GO OVER

1. *go away:* ἀπέρχομαι APERCHOMAI
Mt 8.18 he gave orders to go over to the other side

2. *pass through:* διέρχομαι DIERCHOMAI
Lk 2.15 "Let us go over to Bethlehem

GO THROUGH

1. *go through:* διαπορεύομαι DIAPOREUOMAI
Lk 6. 1 he was going through the grainfields

2. *pass through:* διέρχομαι DIERCHOMAI
Mt 19.24 "for a camel to go through . . a needle
Mk 10.25 "for a camel to go through . . a needle
Lk 9. 6 they . . went through the villages
Acts 13. 6 they had gone through the whole island
15.41 he went through Syria and Cilicia
16. 6 they went through the region of Phrygia
18.23 went . . through . . Galatia and Phrygia
20. 2 When he had gone through these parts

3. *finish, fulfill:* τελέω TELEŌ
Mt 10.23 "you will not have gone through all the towns

GO TO

1. *enter, go into:* εἰσέρχομαι EISERCHOMAI
[a]+εἰς
Mt 2.21 [a]he rose . . and went to the land of Israel

2. *come to, approach:* προσέρχομαι PROSERCHOMAI
Mt 21.28 "he went to the first and said, 'Son
21.30 "he went to the second and said the same
27.58 went to Pilate and asked for the body
Lk 23.52 This man went to Pilate
Acts 9. 1 Saul . . went to the high priest
22.26 "the centurion . . went to the tribune
23.14 they went to the chief priests and elders

GO TO SEE

1. *come to, approach:* προσέρχομαι PROSERCHOMAI
Acts 18. 2 And he went to see them

GO UP

1. *go up, come up:* ἀναβαίνω ANABAINŌ
Mt 3.16 he went up immediately from the water
5. 1 he went up on the mountain
14.23 he went up on the mountain . . to pray
15.29 he went up on the mountain, and sat down
20.17 as Jesus was going up to Jerusalem
20.18 "Behold, we are going up to Jerusalem
Mk 3.13 he went up on the mountain
10.32 were on the road, going up to Jerusalem
10.33 "Behold, we are going up to Jerusalem
Lk 2. 4 Joseph also went up from Galilee
2.42 they went up according to custom
5.19 they went up on the roof and let him down
9.28 went up on the mountain to pray
18.10 "Two men went up into the temple to pray
18.31 "Behold, we are going up to Jerusalem
19.28 went on ahead, going up to Jerusalem
Jn 2.13 Jesus went up to Jerusalem
5. 1 Jesus went up to Jerusalem
7. 8 "I am not[e] going up to this feast
7.10 his brothers had gone up to the feast, then he also went up, not publicly
7.14 Jesus went up into the temple and taught
11.55 went up from the country to Jerusalem
12.20 among those who went up to worship
Acts 1.13 they went up to the upper room
3. 1 going up to the temple at . . hour of prayer
10. 9 Peter went up on the housetop to pray
11. 2 when Peter went up to Jerusalem
15. 2 appointed to go up to Jerusalem
18.22 he went up and greeted the church
20.11 when Paul had gone up and . . eaten
21.12 begged him not to go up to Jerusalem
21.15 we made ready and went up to Jerusalem
24.11 "since I went up to worship at Jerusalem
25. 1 after three days he went up to Jerusalem
25. 9 "Do you wish to go up to Jerusalem?
Gal 2. 1 I went up . . to Jerusalem with Barnabas
2. 2 I went up by revelation
Rev 11.12 loud voice . . saying . . "Come up hither!
11.12 they went up to heaven in a cloud
14.11 "the smoke . . goes up for ever and ever
19. 3 "The smoke from her goes up for ever

2. *go up:* ἀνέρχομαι ANERCHOMAI*
Jn 6. 3 Jesus went up on the mountain
Gal 1.17 nor did I go up to Jerusalem
1.18 after three years I went up to Jerusalem

3. *go away:* ἀπέρχομαι APERCHOMAI
Mk 6.46 he went up on the mountain to pray

4. *go up, climb:* προσαναβαίνω PROSANABAINŌ*
Lk 14.10 "he may say to you, 'Friend, go up higher

5. *come to, approach:* προσέρχομαι PROSERCHOMAI
Acts 8.29 the Spirit said to Philip, "Go up

GO UP TO

1. *come to, approach:* προσέρχομαι PROSERCHOMAI
Mt 17.24 collectors of the . . tax went up to Peter
Mk 14.45 when he came, he went up to him at once

GO WITH

1. *come together:* συμπορεύομαι SYMPOREUOMAI
Lk 7.11 disciples and a . . crowd went with him
24.15 Jesus himself . . went with them

2. *come together:* συνέρχομαι SYNERCHOMAI
Acts 9.39 So Peter rose and went with them
11.12 "the Spirit told me to go with them
15.38 who . . had not gone with them to the work
21.16 disciples from Caesarea went with us

GOAD

1. *sharp point, sting:* κέντρον KENTRON
Acts 26.14 "'It hurts you to kick against the goads

GOAL

1. *goal, end:* σκοπός SKOPOS*
Phil 3.14 I press on toward the goal for the prize

GOAT

1. *kid, goat:* ἐρίφιον ERIPHION*
Mt 25.33 "sheep at his right . . goats at the left
2. *kid, goat:* ἔριφος ERIPHOS
Mt 25.32 "separates the sheep from the goats
3. *goat:* τράγος TRAGOS*
Heb 9.12 taking[s] not the blood of goats
9.13 sprinkling . . with the blood of goats
9.19 he took the blood of calves and goats
10. 4 that the blood of . . goats . . take away sins

GOAT, OF A

1. *of a goat:* αἴγειος AIGEIOS*
Heb 11.37 they went about in skins of . . goats

GOD (*See also* GIVEN TO GOD; REPLY, GOD'S)

1. *God:* θεός THEOS
Mt 1.23 "Emmanuel" (which means, God with us
3. 9 "God is able from these stones to raise up
3.16 Spirit of God descending like a dove
4. 3 "If you are the Son of God, command
4. 4 " 'every word that proceeds from . . God
4. 6 "If you are the Son of G., throw yourself
4. 7 " 'shall not tempt the Lord your God
4.10 " 'You shall worship the Lord your God
5. 8 "the pure in heart . . shall see God
5. 9 "peacemakers . . shall be called sons of God
5.34 "heaven, for it is the throne of God
6.24 "You cannot serve God and mammon[x]
6.30 "if God so clothes the grass of the field
8.29 "What have you to do with us, O Son of G.?
9. 8 glorified G., who had given such authority
12. 4 "how he entered the house of God
12.28 "if . . by the Spirit of G. . . I cast out demons, then the kingdom of G. has come upon you
14.33 "Truly you are the Son of God
15. 3 "you transgress the commandment of G.
15. 4 "God commanded, 'Honor your father
15. 6 "you have made void the word[p] of God
15.31 they glorified the God of Israel
16.16 "the Christ, the Son of the living God
16.23 "you are not on the side of G., but of men
19. 6 "What therefore God has joined together
19.24 "for a rich man to enter the kingdom of G.
19.26 "with God all things are possible
21.12 entered the temple of God[p] and drove‡
21.31 "harlots go into the kingdom of God
21.43 "kingdom of God will be taken . . from you
22.16 "you . . teach the way of God truthfully
22.21 "Render therefore . . to God the things that are God's
22.29 "neither the scriptures nor the power of G.
[22.30 "but are like angels *of God* in heaven‡
22.31 "not read what was said to you by God?
22.32 "⟨have you not read⟩ 'I am the God of Abraham, and the God of Isaac, and the God of Jacob'? He is not God of the dead, but of the living
22.37 "You shall love the Lord your God
23.22 "he . . swears by the throne of God
26.61 " 'I am able to destroy the temple of God
26.63 "I adjure you by the living God, tell us if you are the Christ, the Son of God
27.40 "If you are the Son of God, come down
27.43 "He trusts in God
27.43 "for he said, 'I am the Son of God
27.46 "Eli, Eli, lama sabachthani?" . . "My God, my God, why hast thou forsaken me?
27.54 "Truly this was the Son[x] of God!
Mk 1. 1 gospel of Jesus Christ, the Son of God[a]‡
1.14 Jesus came . . preaching the gospel of G.
1.15 "the kingdom of God is at hand
1.24 "I know who you are, the Holy One of G.
2. 7 "Who can forgive sins but God alone?
2.12 they were all amazed and glorified God
2.26 "how he entered the house of God
3.11 spirits . . cried out, "You are the Son of G.
3.35 "Whoever does . . will of G. is my brother
Mk 4.11 "the secret of the kingdom of God
4.26 "kingdom of G. . . as . . seed . . upon the ground
4.30 "can we compare . . kingdom of God?
5. 7 "Jesus, Son of the Most High God? I adjure you by God, do not torment me
7. 8 "You leave the commandment of God
7. 9 "rejecting the commandment of God
7.13 "void the word of G. through . . tradition
8.33 "For you are not on the side of God
9. 1 "see that the kingdom of God has come
9.47 "better for you to enter the kingdom of G.
10. 9 "What therefore God has joined together
10.14 "for to such belongs the kingdom of God
10.15 "receive the kingdom of God like a child
10.18 "No one is good but God alone
10.23 "hard . . to enter the kingdom of God!
10.24 "hard . . to enter the kingdom of God!
10.25 "a rich man to enter the kingdom of God
10.27 "With men it is impossible, but not with God; for all things are possible with God
11.22 Jesus answered them, "Have faith in God
12.14 "you . . truly teach the way of God
12.17 Jesus said to them, "Render to . . God the things that are God's
12.24 "neither the scriptures nor the power of G.
12.26 "have you not read . . how God said to him, 'I am the God of Abraham, and the God of Isaac, and the God of Jacob'?
12.27 "He is not God of the dead, but of the living
12.29 " 'The Lord our God, the Lord is one
12.30 " 'you shall love the Lord your God
12.34 "are not far from the kingdom of God
13.19 "the creation which God created
14.25 "when I drink it new in the kingdom of G.
15.34 Jesus cried . . "My God, my God, why hast thou forsaken me?
15.39 "Truly this man was the Son[x] of God!
15.43 himself looking for the kingdom of God
16.19 he . . sat down at the right hand of God[k]‡
Lk 1. 6 they were both righteous before God
1. 8 while he was serving as priest before God
1.16 "will turn many . . to the Lord their God
1.19 "Gabriel, who stand in the presence of God
1.26 Gabriel was sent from God to . . Galilee
1.30 "Mary, . . you have found favor with God
1.32 "Lord God will give to him the throne
1.35 "child to be born[d] will be called . . Son of G.
1.37 "with God nothing will be impossible
1.47 "my spirit rejoices in God my Savior
1.64 he spoke, blessing God
1.68 "Blessed be the Lord God of Israel
1.78 "through the tender mercy of our God
2.13 "the heavenly host praising God
2.14 "Glory to God in the highest
2.20 praising God for all they had heard
2.28 took him up in his arms and blessed God
2.38 at that very hour she gave thanks to God
2.40 the favor of God was upon him
2.52 Jesus increased . . in favor with G. and man
3. 2 the word of God came to John
3. 6 "all flesh shall see the salvation of God
3. 8 "God is able from these stones to raise up
3.38 Seth, the son of Adam, the son of God
4. 3 "If you are the Son of God, command
4. 8 " 'You shall worship the Lord your God
4. 9 "If you are . . Son of G., throw yourself
4.12 " 'You shall not tempt the Lord your God
4.34 "I know who you are, the Holy One of G.
4.41 demons . . crying, "You are the Son of G.!
4.43 "the good news of the kingdom of G.
5. 1 people pressed . . to hear the word of G.
5.21 "Who can forgive sins but God only?
5.25 he . . went home, glorifying God
5.26 they glorified God and were filled with awe
6. 4 "how he entered the house of God
6.12 he continued in prayer to God
6.20 "for yours is the kingdom of God

Lk 7.16 Fear seized them . . ; and they glorified God, saying . . "God has visited his people!
7.28 he who is least in the kingdom of God
7.29 (the tax collectors justified God
7.30 (the lawyers rejected the purpose of God
8. 1 the good news of the kingdom of God
8.10 "the secrets of the kingdom of God
8.11 "The seed is the word of God
8.21 "those who hear the word of God
8.28 "Jesus, Son of the Most High God
8.39 "declare how much God has done
9. 2 sent . . out to preach the kingdom of G.
9.11 spoke to them of the kingdom of God
9.20 Peter answered, "The Christ of God
9.27 "before they see the kingdom of God
9.43 all were astonished at the majesty of God
9.60 "go and proclaim the kingdom of God
9.62 "fit for the kingdom of God
10. 9 " 'kingdom of God has come near to you
10.11 " 'the kingdom of God has come near
10.27 "You shall love the Lord your God
11.20 "if . . by the finger of G. . . I cast out demons, then the kingdom of G. has come
11.28 "who hear the word of God and keep it!
11.42 "you . . neglect justice and the love of God
11.49 "Wisdom of G. said, 'I will send . . prophets
12. 6 "not one of them is forgotten before G.
12. 8 "will acknowledge before the angels of G.
12. 9 "will be denied before the angels of G.
12.20 "But God said to him, 'Fool!
12.21 "So is he who . . is not rich toward God
12.24 "Consider the ravens: . . God feeds them
12.28 "But if God so clothes the grass
[12.31 "Instead, seek *God's* kingdom‡
13.13 she was made straight, and she praised G.
13.18 "What is the kingdom of God like?
13.20 "To what shall I compare the kingdom of G.?
13.28 "all the prophets in the kingdom of God
13.29 "sit at table in the kingdom of God
14.15 "who shall eat bread in the kingdom of G.!
15.10 "there is joy before the angels of God
16.13 "You cannot serve God and mammon[a]
16.15 "but God knows your hearts
16.15 "an abomination in the sight of God
16.16 "good news of the kingdom of God
17.15 praising God with a loud voice
17.18 "Was no one found to . . give praise to G.?
17.20 when the kingdom of God was coming
17.20 "kingdom of God is not coming with signs
17.21 "kingdom of G. is in the midst of you[z]
18. 2 "who neither feared God nor regarded man
18. 4 " 'I neither fear God nor regard man
18. 7 "will not God vindicate his elect?
18.11 "Pharisee . . prayed . . 'God, I thank thee
18.13 " 'God, be merciful to me a sinner!
18.16 "for to such belongs the kingdom of God
18.17 "whoever does not receive . . kingdom of G.
18.19 "No one is good but God alone
18.24 "How hard . . to enter the kingdom of G.!
18.25 "rich man to enter the kingdom of G.
18.27 "impossible with men is possible with G.
18.29 "for the sake of the kingdom of God
18.43 he . . followed him, glorifying God; and all the people . . gave praise to God
19.11 that the kingdom of God was to appear
19.37 disciples began to rejoice and praise God
20.21 "you . . truly teach the way of God
20.25 "Then render . . to God the things that are God's
20.36 "because they are . . sons of God
20.37 "the passage about the bush, where he calls the Lord the God of Abraham and the God of Isaac and the God of Jacob
20.38 "he is not G. of the dead, but of the living
21.31 "know that the kingdom of G. is near
22.16 "until it is fulfilled in the kingdom of God
22.18 "until the kingdom of God comes

Lk 22.69 "at the right hand of the power of God
22.70 "Are you the Son of God, then?
23.35 "if he is the Christ of God!
23.40 "Do you not fear God?
23.47 "when the centurion saw . . he praised G.
23.51 he was looking for the kingdom of G.
24.19 "mighty in deed and word before God
24.53 continually in the temple blessing God

Jn 1. 1 the Word was with God, and the Word was God
1. 2 He was in the beginning with God
1. 6 There was a man sent from God
1.12 he gave power to become children of God
1.13 nor of the will of man, but of God
1.18 No one has ever seen God
[1.18 the only *God*, . . he has made him known‡
1.29 "Behold, the Lamb of God!
1.34 "witness that this is the Son of God
1.36 "Behold, the Lamb of God!
1.49 "Rabbi, you are the Son of God!
1.51 "angels of God ascending and descending
3. 2 "you are a teacher come from God
3. 2 "unless God is with him
3. 3 "he cannot see the kingdom of God
3. 5 "he cannot enter the kingdom of God
3.16 G. so loved . . that he gave his . . Son
3.17 God sent the Son into the world
3.18 the name of the only Son of God
3.21 his deeds have been wrought in God
3.33 he . . sets his seal . . that God is true
3.34 For he whom God has sent utters the words of God
3.36 but the wrath of God rests upon him
4.10 "If you knew the gift of God
4.24 "God is spirit, and those who worship
5.18 because he . . called God his own Father, making himself equal with God
5.25 "dead will hear the voice of the Son of G.
5.42 "you have not the love of G. within you
5.44 "glory that comes from the only God
6.27 "on him has God the Father set his seal
6.28 "to be doing the works of God
6.29 "This is the work of God, that you believe
6.33 "bread of God is that which comes down
6.45 " 'they shall all be taught by God
6.46 "Not . . any . . except him who is from God
6.69 "that you are the Holy One of God
7.17 "whether the teaching is from God
8.40 "the truth which I heard from God
8.41 "we have one Father, even God
8.42 "If G. were your Father, you would love
8.42 "for I proceeded and came forth from God
8.47 "He who is of God hears the words of God; the reason why you do not hear them is that you are not of God
8.54 "of whom you say that he is your God
9. 3 "that the works of G. might be . . manifest
9.16 "This man is not from God
9.24 "Give G. the praise; we know . . this man
9.29 "We know that God has spoken to Moses
9.31 "God does not listen to sinners
9.33 "If this man were not from God
[9.35 "Do you believe in the *Son of God?*‡
10.33 "you, being a man, make yourself God
10.34 "Is it not written . . 'I said, you are gods'?
10.35 "If he called them gods to whom the word of God came
10.36 "because I said, 'I am the Son of God
11. 4 "it is for the glory of God, so that the Son of God may be glorified by means of it
11.22 "I know that whatever you ask from God, God will give you
11.27 "you are the Christ, the Son of God
11.40 "you would see the glory of God
11.52 to gather into one the children of God
12.43 praise of men more than . . praise of God
13. 3 he had come from God and was going to God

Jn 13.31 "in him God is glorified
13.32 "if God is glorified in him, God will also glorify him in himself
14. 1 believe[e] in God, believe also in me
16. 2 "will think he is offering service to God
16.30 "by this we believe that you came from God
17. 3 "that they know thee the only true God
19. 7 "he has made himself the Son of God
20.17 "ascending to my Father and your Father, to my God and your God
20.28 "My Lord and my God!
20.31 that Jesus is the Christ, the Son of God
21.19 (by what death he was to glorify God
Acts 1. 3 alive . . speaking of the kingdom of G.
2.11 "telling . . the mighty works of God
2.17 " 'God declares . . I will pour out my Spirit
2.22 "a man attested to you by God with . . signs which God did through him
2.23 "definite plan and foreknowledge of God
2.24 "But God raised him up
2.30 "knowing that G. had sworn with an oath
2.32 "This Jesus God raised up
2.33 "exalted at the right hand of God
2.36 "God has made him both Lord and Christ
2.39 "whom the Lord our God calls to him
2.47 praising God and having favor with all
3. 8 walking and leaping and praising God
3. 9 all . . saw him walking and praising God
3.13 "The God of Abraham . . Isaac and . . Jacob, the God of our fathers, glorified his servant[c]
3.15 "whom God raised from the dead
3.18 "what God foretold by . . all the prophets
3.21 "all that God spoke by . . his holy prophets
3.22 " 'Lord God will raise up for you a prophet
3.25 "covenant which God gave to your fathers
3.26 "God, having raised up his servant[c]
4.10 "whom God raised from the dead
4.19 "Whether it is right in the sight of God to listen to you rather than to God
4.21 all men praised God for what had happened
4.24 they lifted their voices together to God
4.31 spoke the word of God with boldness
5. 4 "You have not lied to men but to God
5.29 "We must obey God rather than men
5.30 "The God of our fathers raised Jesus
5.31 "God exalted him at his right hand
5.32 "the Holy Spirit whom God has given
5.39 "if it is of God, you will not be able
6. 2 "not . . give up preaching the word of God
6. 7 And the word of God increased
6.11 "blasphemous words against Moses and G.
7. 2 "God of glory appeared to . . Abraham
7. 6 "God spoke to this effect
7. 7 " 'I will judge the nation . .' said God
7. 9 "but God was with him
7.17 "which God had granted to Abraham
7.20 "Moses . . was beautiful before God
7.25 "that God was giving them deliverance
7.32 " 'I am the God of your fathers, the God of Abraham . . Isaac and . . Jacob
7.35 "God sent as both ruler and deliverer
7.37 " 'God will raise up for you a prophet
7.40 " 'Make for us gods to go before us
7.42 "G. . . gave them . . to worship . . heaven
7.43 " 'the star of the god Rephan
7.45 "the nations which God thrust out
7.46 "found favor in the sight of God
7.46 "to find a habitation for the God of Jacob
7.55 gazed into heaven and saw the glory of G., and Jesus . . at the right hand of G.
7.56 "Son of man . . at the right hand of God
8.10 "that power of God which is called Great
8.12 good news about the kingdom of God
8.14 that Samaria . . received the word of God
8.20 "thought you could obtain the gift of G.!
8.21 "your heart is not right before God
[8.37 *"I believe that Jesus Christ is the Son of G.*‡
Acts 9.20 "He is the Son of God
10. 2 a devout man who feared God . . and prayed constantly to God
10. 3 "saw clearly in a vision an angel of God
10. 4 "Your prayers . . as a memorial before God
10.15 "What G. has cleansed you must not call
10.28 "God has shown me that I should not call
10.31 " 'your prayer has been heard . . before God
10.33 "we are all here present in the sight of God
10.34 "Truly . . God shows no partiality
10.38 "God anointed Jesus of Nazareth
10.38 "healing all . . for God was with him
10.40 "God raised him on the third day
10.41 "to us who were chosen by God
10.42 "he is the one ordained by God
10.46 speaking in tongues and extolling God
11. 1 Gentiles also had received the word of G.
11. 9 " 'What G. has cleansed you must not call
11.17 "If then God gave the same gift to them . . who was I that I could withstand God?
11.18 When they heard . . they glorified God, saying . . "God has granted repentance
11.23 he came and saw the grace of God
12. 5 prayer . . was made to God by the church
12.22 "The voice of a god, and not of man!
12.23 because he did not give God the glory
12.24 word of God grew and multiplied
13. 5 at Salamis, they proclaimed the word of God
13. 7 Sergius Paulus . . to hear the word of God
13.16 "Men of Israel, and you that fear God
13.17 "The God of this people Israel
13.21 "God gave them Saul the son of Kish
13.23 "God has brought to Israel a Savior
13.26 "those among you that fear God
13.30 "But God raised him from the dead
13.32 "good news that what God promised
13.36 "David . . served the counsel of God
13.37 "he whom God raised up saw no corruption
13.43 urged them to continue in the grace of G.
13.44 gathered together to hear the word of God
13.46 "word of G. should be spoken first to you
13.48 they . . glorified the word of God
14.11 "The gods have come down to us!
14.15 "turn from these vain things to a living God
14.22 through . . tribulations . . the kingdom of G.
14.26 commended to the grace of God
14.27 declared all that God had done with them
15. 4 declared all that God had done with them
15. 7 "God made choice among you
15. 8 "God who knows the heart bore witness
15.10 "why do you make trial of God?
15.12 they related what signs . . God had done
15.14 "how God first visited the Gentiles
15.19 "those of the Gentiles who turn to God
16.10 that God . . called us to preach the gospel
16.14 Lydia . . who was a worshiper of God
16.17 "These men are servants of the Most High G.
16.25 praying and singing hymns to God
16.34 he rejoiced . . that he had believed in G.
17.13 the word of God was proclaimed by Paul
17.23 "this inscription, 'To an unknown god
17.24 "The God who made the world
17.27 "that they should seek God, in the hope
17.29 "Being . . God's offspring, we ought not
17.30 "The times of ignorance God overlooked
18. 7 Titius[q] Justus, a worshiper of God
18.11 teaching the word of God among them
18.13 "to worship God contrary to the law
18.21 "I will return to you if God wills
18.26 they . . expounded to him the way of God
19. 8 pleading about the kingdom of God
19.11 God did extraordinary miracles
19.26 "⟨gods⟩ made with hands are not gods
20.21 "testifying . . of repentance to God
20.24 "testify to the gospel of the grace of God
20.27 "declaring to you the whole counsel of God
20.28 "to care for the church of God[v]‡[0]

Acts 20.32 "now I commend you to God
21.19 one by one the things that God had done
21.20 when they heard it, they glorified God
22. 3 "being zealous for God as you all are
22.14 "'The God of our fathers appointed you
23. 1 "Brethren, I have lived before God
23. 3 Paul said to him, "God shall strike you!
23. 4 "Would you revile God's high priest?
24.14 "I worship the God of our fathers
24.15 "a hope in God . . that . . a resurrection
24.16 "to have a clear conscience toward God
26. 6 "the promise made by God to our fathers
26. 8 "Why . . incredible . . that God raises . . dead?
26.18 " 'from the power of Satan to God
26.20 "that they should repent and turn to God
26.22 "the help that comes from God
26.29 "I would to God . . you . . might become
27.23 "an angel of the God to whom I belong
27.24 " 'God has granted you all those . . with you
27.25 "take heart, men, for I have faith in God
27.35 giving thanks to God in . . presence of all
28. 6 they . . said that he was a god
28.15 Paul thanked God and took courage
28.23 testifying to the kingdom of God
28.28 "salvation of G. . . sent to the Gentiles
28.31 preaching the kingdom of God
Rom 1. 1 Paul . . set apart for the gospel of God
1. 4 designated Son of God in power
1. 7 To all God's beloved in Rome, . . Grace to you and peace from God our Father
1. 8 I thank my God through Jesus Christ
1. 9 God is my witness, whom I serve
1.10 that somehow by God's will I may
1.16 it is the power of God for salvation
1.17 in it the righteousness of G. is revealed
1.18 the wrath of God is revealed
1.19 what can be known about God is plain . . because God has shown it to them
1.21 although they knew God they did not honor him as God or give thanks to him
1.23 exchanged the glory of the immortal God
1.24 G. gave them up in the lusts of their hearts
1.25 they exchanged the truth about God
1.26 For this reason God gave them up
1.28 since they did not see fit to acknowledge God, God gave them up
1.32 God's decree that those . . deserve to die
2. 2 judgment of God rightly falls upon those
2. 3 that . . you will escape . . judgment of God
2. 4 God's kindness is meant to lead you
2. 5 day of wrath when God's . . judgment
2.11 God shows no partiality
2.13 not . . hearers . . who are righteous before G.
2.16 when . . God judges the secrets of men
2.17 you . . boast of your relation to God
2.23 do you dishonor G. by breaking the law?
2.24 "God is blasphemed among the Gentiles
2.29 His praise is not from men but from God
3. 2 Jews are entrusted with the oracles of G.
3. 3 faithlessness nullify . . faithfulness of God?
3. 4 Let G. be true though every man be false
3. 5 wickedness serves to show the justice of G.
3. 5 That G. is unjust to inflict wrath on us?
3. 6 then how could God judge the world?
3. 7 through my falsehood God's truthfulness
3.11 "no one seeks for God
3.18 "no fear of God before their eyes
3.19 the whole world . . held accountable to G.
3.21 righteousness of God has been manifested
3.22 righteousness of God through faith
3.23 all . . fall short of the glory of God
3.25 whom God put forward as an expiation
3.29 is ⟨God⟩ the God of Jews only?
3.30 ⟨of Gentiles also,⟩ since God is one
4. 2 something to boast . . but not before God
4. 3 "Abraham believed God
4. 6 man to whom God reckons righteousness

Rom 4.17 the God in whom he believed
4.20 concerning the promise of God
4.20 he grew strong . . as he gave glory to God
5. 1 peace with G. through our Lord Jesus
5. 2 our hope of sharing the glory of God
5. 5 God's love has been poured into our hearts
5. 8 God shows his love for us
5.10 while . . enemies we were reconciled to God
5.11 we also rejoice in God
5.15 much more have the grace of God
6.10 but the life he lives he lives to God
6.11 dead to sin and alive to God in Christ
6.13 yield yourselves to God . . and your members to God as instruments
6.17 thanks be to G. . . you . . have become obedient
6.22 you have . . become slaves of God
6.23 the free gift of God is eternal life
7. 4 in order that we may bear fruit for God
7.22 I delight in the law of God
7.25 Thanks be to God through Jesus Christ . .! I of myself serve the law of God
8. 3 God has done what the law . . could not
8. 7 mind that is set on the flesh is hostile to God; it does not submit to God's law
8. 8 those who are in the flesh cannot please G.
8. 9 if in fact the Spirit of God dwells in you
8.14 For all who are led by the Spirit of God are sons of God
8.16 bearing witness . . that we are children of G.
8.17 if children, then heirs, heirs of God
8.19 longing for the revealing of the sons of God
8.21 the glorious liberty of the children of God
8.27 intercedes . . according to the will of G.
8.28 in everything God works for good[k]‡
8.31 If God is for us, who is against us?
8.33 Who shall bring any charge against God's elect? It is God who justifies
8.34 who is at the right hand of God[m]
8.39 the love of God in Christ Jesus our Lord
9. 5 God who is over all be blessed for ever[n]†
9. 6 not as though the word of God had failed
9. 8 who are the children of God
9.11 that God's purpose of election . . continue
9.14 Is there injustice on God's part?
9.16 it depends . . upon God's mercy
9.20 who are you . . to answer back to God?
9.22 if God, desiring to show his wrath
9.26 "they will be called 'sons of the living G.
10. 1 my heart's desire and prayer to God
10. 2 zeal for God, but it is not enlightened
10. 3 the righteousness that comes from God
10. 3 they did not submit to God's righteousness
10. 9 that God raised him from the dead
11. 1 has God rejected his people?
11. 2 God has not rejected his people
11. 2 how he pleads with God against Israel
11. 8 "God gave them a spirit of stupor
11.21 God did not spare the natural branches
11.22 Note then . . the severity of God . . but God's kindness to you
11.23 God has the power to graft them in again
11.29 the gifts and the call of G. are irrevocable
11.30 as you were once disobedient to G.
11.32 G. has consigned all . . to disobedience
11.33 O the depth of the . . knowledge of God!
12. 1 I appeal to you . . by the mercies of G.
12. 1 sacrifice, holy and acceptable to G.
12. 2 that you may prove what is the will of G.
12. 3 measure of faith which God has assigned
13. 1 there is no authority except from G., and those that exist have been instituted by G.
13. 2 he . . resists what God has appointed
13. 4 he is God's servant for your good
13. 4 the servant of God to execute his wrath
13. 6 the authorities are ministers of God
14. 3 for God has welcomed him

Rom 14. 6 He also who eats . . gives thanks to God; . . he who abstains . . gives thanks to G.
14.10 all stand before the judgment seat of God
14.11 "every tongue shall give praise[u] to God
14.12 each of us shall give account . . to God
14.17 kingdom of God is not food
14.18 he who thus serves . . is acceptable to God
14.20 Do not . . destroy the work of God
14.22 faith . . keep between yourself and God
15. 5 God of steadfastness and encouragement
15. 6 you may with one voice glorify the G.
15. 7 Christ has welcomed you, for the glory of G.
15. 8 a servant . . to show God's truthfulness
15. 9 that the Gentiles might glorify God
15.13 May the God of hope fill you
15.15 because of the grace given me by God
15.16 priestly service of the gospel of God
15.17 reason to be proud of my work for God
15.30 your prayers to God on my behalf
15.32 that by God's will I may come to you
15.33 The God of peace be with you all
16.20 the God of peace will soon crush Satan
16.26 the command of the eternal God
16.27 to the only wise God be glory!
1 Cor 1. 1 Paul, called by the will of God
1. 2 To the church of God which is at Corinth
1. 3 Grace to you and peace from God
1. 4 I give thanks to God[a] always for you because of the grace of God . . given you
1. 9 G. is faithful, by whom you were called
[1.14 *I thank God* that I baptized none‡
1.18 to us . . it is the power of G.
1.20 Has not G. made foolish . . wisdom?
1.21 in the wisdom of God, the world did not know God through wisdom, it pleased God through the folly of what we preach to save
1.24 to those who are called, . . Christ the power of God and the wisdom of God
1.25 foolishness of God is wiser than men . . weakness of God is stronger than men
1.27 God chose what is foolish in the world
1.27 God chose what is weak in the world
1.28 God chose what is low and despised
1.29 no human . . boast in the presence of G.
1.30 whom God made our wisdom
2. 1 the testimony[c] of God in lofty words
2. 5 that . . faith . . rest . . in the power of God
2. 7 a secret and hidden wisdom of God, which God decreed before the ages
2. 9 "what God has prepared for those who love
2.10 God has revealed to us through the Spirit
2.10 the Spirit searches . . even the depths of God
2.11 no one comprehends the thoughts of God except the Spirit of God
2.12 we . . received . . the Spirit which is from G.
2.12 the gifts bestowed on us by God
2.14 gifts of the Spirit of God . . are folly to him
3. 6 I planted . . but God gave the growth
3. 7 only God who gives the growth
3. 9 For we are God's fellow workers . . ; you are God's field, God's building[0]
3.10 According to the grace of God
3.16 Do you not know that you are God's temple and that God's Spirit dwells in you?
3.17 If any one destroys God's temple, God will destroy him. For God's temple is holy, and that temple you are
3.19 the wisdom of this world is folly with God
3.23 you are Christ's; and Christ is God's
4. 1 stewards of the mysteries of God
4. 5 will receive his commendation from God
4. 9 God has exhibited us apostles as last
4.20 kingdom of God does not consist in talk
5.13 God judges those outside
6. 9 will not inherit the kingdom of God
6.10 will inherit the kingdom of God
6.11 you were justified in . . the Spirit of our G.

1 Cor 6.13 God will destroy both one and the other
6.14 God raised the Lord and will . . raise us
6.19 the Holy Spirit . . which you have from G.
6.20 So glorify God in your body
7. 7 each has his own special gift from God
7.15 For God has called us[l] to peace
7.17 the life . . in which God has called him
7.19 keeping the commandments of God
7.24 there let him remain with God
7.40 I think that I have the Spirit of God
8. 3 if one loves God, one is known by him
8. 4 "there is no God but one
8. 5 although there may be so-called gods . . as indeed there are many "gods
8. 6 yet for us there is one God, the Father
8. 8 Food will not commend us to God
9. 9 Is it for oxen that God is concerned?
9.21 not being without law toward God
10. 5 with most of them God was not pleased
10.13 God . . will not let you be tempted
10.20 they offer to demons and not to God
10.31 do all to the glory of God
10.32 Give no offense . . to the church of God
11. 3 the head of Christ is God
11. 7 since he is the image and glory of God
11.12 (And all things are from God
11.13 to pray to God with her head uncovered
11.16 nor do the churches of God
11.22 do you despise the church of God?
12. 3 no one speaking by the Spirit of God
12. 6 it is the same God who inspires them all
12.18 God arranged the organs in the body
12.24 God has so composed the body
12.28 God has appointed . . first apostles
14. 2 who speaks in a tongue speaks . . to G.
14.18 I thank God that I speak in tongues
14.25 he will worship God and declare that God is really among you
14.28 let each of them . . speak to himself and to G.
14.33 not a God of confusion but of peace
14.36 Did the word of God originate with you?
15. 9 because I persecuted the church of God
15.10 But by the grace of God I am what I am
15.10 it was not I, but the grace of God
15.15 found to be misrepresenting God, because we testified of God that he raised Christ
15.24 when he delivers the kingdom to God
15.28 that God may be everything to every one
15.34 For some have no knowledge of God
15.38 God gives it a body as he has chosen
15.50 flesh . . cannot inherit the kingdom of G.
15.57 thanks be to God, who gives us the victory
2 Cor 1. 1 Paul, an apostle . . by the will of God
1. 1 To the church of God which is at Corinth
1. 2 Grace to you and peace from God
1. 3 Blessed be the God and Father
1. 3 Father of mercies and God of all comfort
1. 4 which we ourselves are comforted by God
1. 9 rely not on ourselves but on God
1.12 not by earthly wisdom but by the grace of G.
1.18 As surely as God is faithful
1.19 the Son of God, Jesus Christ
1.20 promises of God find their Yes in him
1.20 we utter the Amen . . to the glory of G.
1.21 it is God who establishes us
1.23 I call God to witness against me
2.14 But thanks be to God, who . . leads us
2.15 we are the aroma of Christ to God
2.17 not, like so many, peddlers of God's word; but as men . . commissioned by God, in the sight of God we speak in Christ
3. 3 with the Spirit of the living God
3. 4 confidence . . we have . . toward God
3. 5 our competence is from God
4. 2 we refuse . . to tamper with God's word
4. 2 commend ourselves . . in the sight of God
4. 4 god of this world has blinded . . unbelievers

2 Cor 4. 4 Christ, who is the likeness of God
4. 6 it is the God who said, "Let light shine
4. 6 the glory of God in the face of Christ
4. 7 the transcendent power belongs to God
4.15 thanksgiving, to the glory of God
5. 1 we have a building from God
5. 5 He who has prepared us . . is God
5.11 what we are is known to God
5.13 if we are beside ourselves, it is for God
5.18 this is from God, who . . reconciled us
5.19 in Christ God was reconciling[h] the world
5.20 God making his appeal through us
5.20 be reconciled to God
5.21 that . . we . . become the righteousness of G.
6. 1 not to accept the grace of God in vain
6. 4 as servants of G. we commend ourselves
6. 7 truthful speech, and the power of G.
6.16 What agreement has the temple of God with idols? For we are the temple of the living God; as God said . . "I will be their God, and they shall be my people
7. 1 make holiness perfect in the fear of God
7. 6 God, who comforts the downcast
7.12 revealed to you in the sight of God
8. 1 the grace of God which has been shown
8. 5 gave themselves . . to us by the will of G.
8.16 But thanks be to God
9. 7 God loves a cheerful giver
9. 8 God is able to provide you with every blessing
9.11 generosity . . will produce thanksgiving to G.
9.12 overflows in many thanksgivings to God
9.13 you[m] will glorify God by your obedience
9.14 because of the surpassing grace of God
9.15 Thanks be to God for his . . gift!
10. 5 obstacle to the knowledge of God
10.13 the limits God has apportioned us
11. 7 I preached God's gospel without cost
11.11 I do not love you? God knows I do!
11.31 The God and Father of the Lord Jesus
12. 2 I do not know, God knows
12. 3 I do not know, God knows
12.19 It is in the sight of God
12.21 when I come again my G. may humble me
13. 4 crucified . . but lives by the power of G.
13. 4 we shall live with him by the power of G.
13. 7 we pray God that you may not
13.11 God of love and peace will be with you
13.14(13) love of G. and . . fellowship of[n] the . . Spirit
Gal 1. 1 through Jesus Christ and God the F.
1. 3 Grace to you and peace from God
1. 4 according to the will of our God
1.10 seeking the favor of men, or of God?
1.13 I persecuted the church of God violently
1.20 (before God, I do not lie!
1.24 they glorified God because of me
2. 6 (God shows no partiality
2.19 I . . died to the law, that I might live to G.
2.20 I live by faith in the Son of God
2.21 I do not nullify the grace of God
3. 6 Thus Abraham "believed God
3. 8 that God would justify the Gentiles
3.11 no man is justified before God
3.17 a covenant previously ratified by God
3.18 God gave it to Abraham by a promise
3.20 but God is one
3.21 Is the law . . against the promises of G.?
3.26 in Christ Jesus you are all sons of God
4. 4 God sent forth his Son, born of woman
4. 6 God has sent the Spirit of his Son
4. 7 through God you are no longer a slave
4. 8 when you did not know God
4. 8 beings that by nature are no gods
4. 9 now that you have come to know God, or rather to be known by God
4.14 received me as an angel of God
5.21 those . . shall not inherit the kingdom of God
6. 7 Do not be deceived; God is not mocked
Gal 6.16 Peace and mercy . . upon the Israel of G.
Eph 1. 1 Paul, an apostle . . by the will of God
1. 2 Grace to you and peace from God
1. 3 Blessed be the God and Father
1.17 the God of our Lord Jesus Christ
2. 4 But God, who is rich in mercy
2. 8 not your own doing, it is the gift of God
2.10 works, which God prepared beforehand
2.16 might reconcile us both to God
2.19 members of the household of God
2.22 for a dwelling place of God in the Spirit
3. 2 the stewardship of God's grace
3. 7 according to the gift of God's grace
3. 9 the mystery hidden for ages in[d] God
3.10 manifold wisdom of God . . made known
3.19 filled with all the fulness of God
4. 6 one God and Father of us all
4.13 knowledge of the Son of God
4.18 alienated from the life of God
4.24 created after the likeness of God
4.30 do not grieve the Holy Spirit of God
4.32 forgiving . . as God . . forgave you
5. 1 Therefore be imitators of God
5. 2 a fragrant offering and sacrifice to God
5. 5 inheritance in . . kingdom of Christ and of G.
5. 6 because of these . . the wrath of God comes
5.20 giving thanks . . to God the Father
6. 6 doing the will of God from the heart
6.11 Put on the whole armor of God
6.13 Therefore take the whole armor of God
6.17 sword of the Spirit, . . the word of G.
6.23 love with faith, from God the Father
Phil 1. 2 Grace to you and peace from God
1. 3 I thank my God in all my remembrance
1. 8 For God is my witness, how I yearn
1.11 to the glory and praise of God
1.14 to speak the word of God without fear
1.28 your salvation, and that from God
2. 6 though . . in the form of God, did not count equality with God a thing to be grasped
2. 9 Therefore God has highly exalted him
2.11 to the glory of God the Father
2.13 for God is at work in you
2.15 children of God without blemish
2.27 But God had mercy on him
3. 3 who worship God in spirit[e‡]
3. 9 righteousness from G. that depends
3.14 the prize of the upward call of God
3.15 God will reveal that also to you
3.19 their god is the belly
4. 6 let your requests be made known to G.
4. 7 peace of G. . . passes all understanding
4. 9 the God of peace will be with you
4.18 a sacrifice . . pleasing to God
4.19 God will supply every need of yours
4.20 To our God and Father be glory
Col 1. 1 Paul, an apostle . . by the will of God
1. 2 Grace to you and peace from God
1. 3 We always thank God
1. 6 the day you . . understood . . grace of God
1.10 increasing in the knowledge of God
1.15 the image of the invisible God
1.25 to make the word of God fully known
1.27 To them God chose to make known
2. 2 knowledge of God's mystery, of Christ
2.12 through faith in the working of God
2.19 grows with a growth that is from God
3. 1 Christ . . seated at . . right hand of God
3. 3 your life is hid with Christ in God
3. 6 the wrath of God is coming[f]
3.12 as God's chosen ones, holy and beloved
3.16 with thankfulness in your hearts to God
3.17 giving thanks to God the Father
4. 3 that God may open to us a door
4.11 fellow workers for the kingdom of G.
4.12 fully assured in all the will of God
1 Th 1. 1 church of the Thessalonians in God

1 Th 1. 2 We give thanks to God always for you
1. 3 remembering before our God
1. 4 we know, brethren beloved by God
1. 8 your faith in God has gone forth
1. 9 how you turned to God from idols, to serve a living and true God
2. 2 we had courage in our God to declare to you the gospel of God
2. 4 as we have been approved by God . . we speak . . to please God
2. 5 For we never . . , as God is witness
2. 8 to share . . not only the gospel of God
2. 9 we preached to you the gospel of God
2.10 You are witnesses, and God also
2.12 to lead a life worthy of God
2.13 we also thank God constantly for this, that when you received the word of God . . you accepted it . . as the word . . of God
2.14 imitators of the churches of God in Christ
2.15 who . . displease God and oppose all men
3. 2 Timothy . . God's servant in the gospel
3. 9 what . . can we render to God . . for all the joy which we feel . . before our God?
3.11 may our God and Father . . direct our way
3.13 unblamable in holiness before our God
4. 1 to please God, just as you are doing
4. 3 the will of God, your sanctification
4. 5 like heathen who do not know God
4. 7 God has not called us for uncleanness
4. 8 disregards not man but God
4.14 God will bring . . those . . fallen asleep
4.16 with the sound of the trumpet of God
5. 9 God has not destined us for wrath
5.18 this is the will of God in Christ Jesus
5.23 the God of peace . . sanctify you wholly

2 Th 1. 1 God our Father and . . Lord Jesus Christ
1. 2 God the Father and . . Lord Jesus Christ
1. 3 thanks to God always for you, brethren
1. 4 we . . boast of you in the churches of God
1. 5 evidence of the righteous judgment of God
1. 5 worthy of the kingdom of God
1. 6 G. deems it just to repay with affliction
1. 8 upon those who do not know God
1.11 that our God may make you worthy
1.12 according to the grace of our God
2. 4 exalts himself against every so-called god
2. 4 he takes his seat in the temple of God, proclaiming himself to be God
2.11 God sends . . them a strong delusion
2.13 thanks to God always for you, . . because God chose you from the beginning[b]
2.16 God our Father, who loved us
3. 5 Lord direct your hearts to . . love of God

1 Tim 1. 1 Paul, an apostle . . by command of God
1. 2 Grace, mercy, and peace from God
1.11 the glorious gospel of the blessed God
1.17 To . . the only God, be honor and glory
2. 3 it is acceptable in the sight of God
2. 5 For there is one God, and there is one mediator between God and men
3. 5 how can he care for God's church?
3.15 how . . to behave in the household of God, which is the church of the living God
[3.16 *God* was manifested in the flesh‡
4. 3 foods which God created to be received
4. 4 everything created by God is good
4. 5 consecrated by the word of God
4.10 we have our hope set on the living God
5. 4 this is acceptable in the sight of God
5. 5 real widow . . has set her hope on God
5.21 In the presence of God and of Christ
6. 1 that the name of G. . . not be defamed
6.11 as for you, man of God, shun all this
6.13 In the presence of God who gives life
6.17 G. . . richly furnishes us with everything

2 Tim 1. 1 Paul, an apostle . . by the will of God
1. 2 Grace, mercy, and peace from God
1. 3 God whom I serve with a clear conscience
1. 6 rekindle the gift of G. . . within you
1. 7 God did not give us a spirit of timidity
1. 8 suffering . . in the power of God
2. 9 But the word of God is not fettered
[2.14 charge them before *God* to avoid‡
2.15 Do your best to present yourself to God
2.19 But God's firm foundation stands
2.25 God may . . grant that they will repent
3.17 that the man of God may be complete
4. 1 I charge you in the presence of God

Tit 1. 1 Paul, a servant[a] of God and an apostle . . , to further the faith of God's elect
1. 2 eternal life which God . . promised ages ago
1. 3 entrusted by command of God our Savior
1. 4 Grace and peace from God the Father
1. 7 a bishop, as God's steward
1.16 profess to know God, but . . deny him
2. 5 that the word of God may not be discredited
2.10 adorn the doctrine of God our Savior
2.11 grace of God has appeared for . . salvation
2.13 our great God and Savior[c] Jesus Christ
3. 4 loving kindness of God our Savior
3. 8 those who have believed in God

Phm . 3 Grace to you and peace from God
. 4 I thank my God . . when I remember

Heb 1. 1 In many and various ways God spoke
1. 6 "Let all God's angels worship him
1. 8 "Thy throne, O God,[a] is for ever†
1. 9 "therefore God, thy God, has anointed thee with the oil of gladness
2. 4 God also bore witness by signs
2. 9 by the grace of God he might taste death
2.13 "I, and the children God has given me
2.17 high priest in the service of God
3. 4 (but the builder of all things is God
3.12 to fall away from the living God
4. 4 "And God rested on the seventh day
4. 9 a sabbath rest for the people of God
4.10 whoever enters God's rest also ceases from his labors as God did from his
4.12 the word of God is living and active
4.14 a great high priest . . , Jesus, the Son of God
5. 1 to act on behalf of men in relation to God
5. 4 he is called by God, just as Aaron was
5.10 designated by God a high priest
5.12 the first principles of God's word
6. 1 a foundation . . of faith toward God
6. 3 this we will do if God permits[l]
6. 5 tasted the goodness of the word of God
6. 6 since they crucify the Son of God
6. 7 For land . . receives a blessing from God
6.10 God is not so unjust as to overlook
6.13 when God made a promise to Abraham
6.17 God desired to show more convincingly
6.18 impossible that God should prove false
7. 1 Melchizedek, . . of the Most High God
7. 3 resembling the Son of God
7.19 through which we draw near to God
7.25 to save those who draw near to God
8.10 "I will be their God, . . they . . my people
9.14 offered himself without blemish to God
9.14 purify your[t] conscience . . to serve . . God
9.20 "the covenant which God commanded
9.24 to appear in the presence of God
10. 7 " 'Lo, I have come to do thy will, O God
10.12 he sat down at the right hand of God
10.21 a great priest over the house of God
10.29 the man who has spurned the Son of God
10.31 to fall into the hands of the living God
10.36 so that you may do the will of God
11. 3 the world was created by the word of G.
11. 4 Abel offered to G. . . acceptable sacrifice . . , God bearing witness by accepting his gifts
11. 5 not found, because God had taken him
11. 5 he was attested as having pleased God
11. 6 whoever would draw near to God

Heb 11.10 city . . whose builder and maker is G.
11.16 Therefore God is not ashamed to be called their God, for he has prepared for them a city
11.19 considered that God was able to raise men
11.25 ill-treatment with the people of God
11.40 since God had foreseen something better
12. 2 at the right hand of the throne of God
12. 7 God is treating you as sons
12.15 that no one fail to obtain the grace of God
12.22 you have come to . . the city of . . God
12.23 to a judge who is God of all
12.28 let us offer to God acceptable worship
12.29 for our God is a consuming fire
13. 4 God will judge the immoral and adulterous
13. 7 those who spoke to you the word of God
13.15 offer up a sacrifice of praise to God
13.16 for such sacrifices are pleasing to God
13.20 God of peace who brought . . our Lord
Jas 1. 1 servant of God and of the Lord Jesus
1. 5 let him ask God, who gives to all men
1.13 Let no one say . . "I am tempted by God"; for God . . himself tempts no one
1.20 does not work the righteousness of G.
1.27 Religion that is pure . . before God
2. 5 Has not God chosen those who are poor
2.19 You believe that God is one; you do well
2.23 "Abraham believed G., and it was reckoned . ."; and he was called the friend of God
3. 9 men, who are made in the likeness of G.
4. 4 friendship with . . world is enmity with G.
4. 4 friend of the world makes . . enemy of G.
4. 6 "G. opposes the proud, but gives grace
4. 7 Submit yourselves therefore to God
4. 8 Draw near to God . . he will draw near
1 Pet 1. 2 chosen and destined by God the Father
1. 3 Blessed be the God . . of our Lord Jesus!
1. 5 by God's power . . guarded through faith
1.21 Through him you have confidence in God . . so that your faith and hope are in God[d]
1.23 been born . . through the . . word of God
2. 4 rejected . . but in God's sight chosen
2. 5 spiritual sacrifices acceptable to God
2.10 but now you are God's people
2.12 see your good deeds and glorify God
2.15 it is God's will that by doing right
2.16 Live as free men . . but . . as servants of G.
2.17 Love the brotherhood. Fear God
2.19 if, mindful of God, he endures pain
2.20 if . . patiently, you have God's approval
3. 4 which in God's sight is very precious
3. 5 the holy women who hoped in God
3.17 if that should be God's will
3.18 that he might bring us to God
3.20 God's patience waited in the days of Noah
3.21 as an appeal to God for a clear conscience
3.22 who . . is at the right hand of God
4. 2 to live . . by the will of God
4. 6 they might live in the spirit like God
4.10 as good stewards of God's varied grace
4.11 as one who utters oracles of God
4.11 by the strength which God supplies; . . that in everything God may be glorified
4.14 spirit of glory[j] and of G. rests upon you
4.16 under that name let him glorify God
4.17 to begin with the household of God
4.17 those who do not obey the gospel of G.
4.19 who suffer according to God's will
5. 2 Tend the flock of God that is your charge[k]
[5. 2 but willingly, *as God would have you*‡
5. 5 "God opposes the proud, but gives grace
5. 6 Humble yourselves . . under the . . hand of G.
5.10 God of all grace, who has called you
5.12 this is the true grace of God; stand fast in it
2 Pet 1. 1 our God and Savior Jesus Christ[a]†
1. 2 multiplied to you in the knowledge of God
1.17 honor and glory from God the Father
1.21 men moved by the . . Spirit spoke from G.[e]
2 Pet 2. 4 if God did not spare the angels
3. 5 by the word of God heavens existed
3.12 the coming of the day of God
1 Jn 1. 5 God is light and in him is no darkness
2. 5 in him truly love for God is perfected
2.14 the word of God abides in you
2.17 who does the will of God abides for ever
3. 1 that we should be called children of G.
3. 2 Beloved, we are God's children now
3. 8 The reason the Son of God appeared
3. 9 No one born of God commits sin; . . he cannot sin because he is[g] born of G.
3.10 be seen who are the children of God
3.10 whoever does not do right is not of God
3.17 how does God's love abide in him?
3.20 for God is greater than our hearts
3.21 we have confidence before God
4. 1 to see whether they are of God
4. 2 By this you know the Spirit of God: every spirit which confesses . . is of God
4. 3 which does not confess . . is not of God
4. 4 Little children, you are of God
4. 6 We are of God. Whoever knows God listens to us, and he who is not of God does not listen to us
4. 7 Beloved, let us love one another; for love is of God, and he who loves is born of God and knows God
4. 8 He who does not love does not know God; for God is love
4. 9 In this the love of G. was made manifest . . that G. sent his only Son into the world
4.10 not that we loved G. but . . he loved us
4.11 if G. . . loved us, we . . ought to love
4.12 No man has ever seen God; if we love one another, God abides in us
4.15 Whoever confesses that Jesus is the Son of G., God abides in him, and he in G.
4.16 So we know and believe the love God has for us. God is love, and he who abides in love abides in God, and God abides in him
4.20 If any one says, "I love God
4.20 cannot[h] love G. whom he has not seen
4.21 who loves God should love his brother
5. 1 Every one who believes . . is a child of G.
5. 2 we know that we love the children of God, when we love God and obey
5. 3 For this is the love of God
5. 4 whatever is . . of G. overcomes the world
5. 5 who believes that Jesus is the Son of God
5. 9 the testimony of God is greater; for this is the testimony of God
5.10 He who believes in the Son of God
5.10 He who does not believe God
5.10 testimony that God has borne to his Son
5.11 testimony, that God gave us eternal life
5.12 who has not the Son of God has not life
5.13 who believe in the name of the Son of G.
5.18 any one born of God does not sin, but He who was born of God keeps him
5.19 We know that we are of God
5.20 the Son of God has come . . This is the true God and eternal life
2 Jn . 3 peace will be with us, from God the F.
. 9 one who . . does not abide . . does not have G.
3 Jn . 6 send them on . . as befits God's service
.11 He who does good is of God; he who does evil has not seen God
Jude . 1 To those who are called, beloved in G.
. 4 persons who pervert the grace of our G.
[. 5 *God* who saved a people out of . . Egypt‡
.21 keep yourselves in the love of God
.25 to the only God, our Savior . . be glory
Rev 1. 1 The revelation of Jesus . . , which G. gave
1. 2 who bore witness to the word of G.
1. 6 priests to his God and Father
1. 8 "Alpha and the Omega," says the Lord G.

Rev 1. 9 on account of the word of God
2. 7 " 'the tree . . which is in the paradise of G.
2.18 " 'The words of the Son of God
3. 1 " 'who has the seven spirits of God
3. 2 " 'not . . perfect in the sight of my God
3.12 " 'a pillar in the temple of my God; . . I will write on him the name of my God, and the name of the city of my God . . which comes down from my God
3.14 " 'the Amen . . the beginning of God's creation
4. 5 torches . . which are the seven spirits of G.
4. 8 "Holy, holy, holy, is the Lord God!
4.11 "Worthy art thou, our Lord and God
5. 6 eyes, which are the seven spirits of God
5. 9 "by thy blood didst ransom men for God
5.10 "a kingdom and priests to our God
6. 9 who had been slain for the word of G.
7. 2 another angel . . with the seal of . . God
7. 3 "till we have sealed the servants of our G.
7.10 "Salvation belongs to our God!
7.11 fell on their faces . . and worshiped God
7.12 "Blessing . . to our God for ever and ever!
7.15 "they ⟨are⟩ before the throne of God
7.17 "God will wipe away every tear
8. 2 the seven angels who stand before God
8. 4 from the hand of the angel before God
9. 4 the seal of God upon their foreheads
9.13 horns of the golden altar before God
10. 7 the mystery of God, as he announced
11. 1 "Rise and measure the temple of God
11.11 a breath of life from God entered them
11.13 rest . . gave glory to the G. of heaven
11.16 elders who sit on their thrones before G. fell on their faces and worshiped God
11.17 "thanks to thee, Lord God Almighty
11.19 God's temple in heaven was opened
12. 5 her child was caught up to God
12. 6 where she has a place prepared by God
12.10 "the power and the kingdom of our God
12.10 "who accuses them . . before our God
12.17 who keep the commandments of God
13. 6 to utter blasphemies against God
14. 4 redeemed . . as first fruits for God
14. 7 "Fear God and give him glory
14.10 "he . . shall drink the wine of God's wrath
14.12 who keep the commandments of God
14.19 the great wine press of the wrath of G.
15. 1 with them the wrath of God is ended
15. 2 with harps of God in their hands
15. 3 the song of Moses, the servant of God
15. 3 "Great . . are thy deeds, O Lord God!
15. 7 the wrath of God who lives for ever
15. 8 smoke from the glory of God
16. 1 "the seven bowls of the wrath of God
16. 7 I heard the altar cry, "Yea, Lord God
16. 9 they cursed the name of God
16.11 cursed the God of heaven for their pain
16.14 battle on the great day of God
16.19 God remembered great Babylon
16.21 men cursed God for the plague
17.17 "God has put it into their hearts
17.17 "until the words of God shall be fulfilled
18. 5 "God has remembered her iniquities
18. 8 "mighty . . the Lord God who judges her
18.20 "God has given judgment for you!
19. 1 "glory and power belong to our God
19. 4 elders . . fell down and worshiped God
19. 5 "Praise our God, all you his servants
19. 6 "the Lord our God the Almighty reigns
19. 9 "These are true words of God
19.10 "You must not do that! . . Worship God
19.13 which he is called is The Word of God
19.15 fury of the wrath of God the Almighty
19.17 "Come, gather for the great supper of God
20. 4 beheaded . . for the word of God
20. 6 they shall be priests of God
[20. 9 fire came down *from God, out of heaven*‡

Rev [20. 9 fire came down *out of heaven from God*‡
21. 2 coming down out of heaven from God
21. 3 "the dwelling of God is with men . . and God himself will be with them[p]
[21. 3 "will be with them *and be their God*‡
21. 7 "I will be his G. and he shall be my son
21.10 Jerusalem coming down . . from God
21.11 ⟨Jerusalem⟩ having the glory of God
21.22 its temple is the Lord God
21.23 for the glory of God is its light
22. 1 flowing from the throne of God
22. 3 the throne of God . . shall be in it
22. 5 the Lord God will be their light
22. 6 "the God of the spirits of the prophets
22. 9 "You must not do that! . . Worship God
22.18 God will add to him the plagues
22.19 G. will take away his share

CONTEXTUALLY
Mk 10. 6 " 'God made them male and female
Acts 7. 4 "God removed him from there into this land
Rom 3.25 This was to show God's righteousness
4.21 that G. was able to do what he . . promised
5. 9 saved by him from the wrath of God
11. 4 But what is God's reply to him?
11.28 they are enemies of God, for your sake
12.19 but leave it[t] to the wrath of God
13. 5 must be subject . . to avoid God's wrath
1 Cor 15.27 "God[z] has put all things in subjection†
[16.12 it was not at all *God's will for him*†
2 Cor 4. 1 having this ministry by the mercy of God[e]†
Col 1.19 all the fulness of G. was pleased to dwell
2.13 you . . G. made alive together with him
Heb 1. 3 He reflects the glory of God
1. 5 For to what angel did God ever say
2. 5 not to angels . . G. subjected the world
3. 2 Moses also was faithful in[e] God's house
3. 5 Moses was faithful in all God's house
3. 6 Christ was faithful over God's[f] house†
4. 8 G.[i] would not speak later of another day†
8. 5 he was instructed by God, saying
11. 7 By faith Noah, being warned by God
Jas 1.12 which G. has promised . . those who love him
1 Pet 2. 9 you are a chosen race . . God's own people[e]†
1 Jn 3. 9 for God's[f] nature abides in him†
5.16 he will ask, and God[i] will give him life†

GOD FORBID (*See* FORBID, GOD)

GOD, HATER OF

1. *hated of God, hating God:* θεοστυγής (subst.) THEOSTYGĒS*
Rom 1.30 slanderers, haters of God, insolent

GOD, INSPIRED BY

1. *inspired by God:* θεόπνευστος THEOPNEUSTOS*
2 Tim 3.16 All scripture is inspired by God[d]†

GOD, LOVER OF

1. *loving God, pious:* φιλόθεος (subst.) PHILOTHEOS*
2 Tim 3. 4 lovers of pleasure rather than lovers of God

GOD, OPPOSING

1. *fighting against God:* θεομάχος THEOMACHOS*
Acts 5.39 "You might even be found opposing God!

GOD, TAUGHT BY

1. *taught by God:* θεοδίδακτος THEODIDAKTOS*
1 Th 4. 9 taught by God to love one another

GOD, WITHOUT

1. *without God:* ἄθεος ATHEOS*
Eph 2.12 having no hope and without God

GOD, WORSHIPER OF

1. *fearing God, devout:* θεοσεβής (subst.) THEOSEBĒS*
Jn 9.31 "but if any one is a worshiper of God

GODDESS

1. *goddess:* θεά THEA*
Acts 19.27 "the temple of the great goddess Artemis
2. *god:* θεός (fem.) THEOS
Acts 19.37 "nor blasphemers of our goddess

GOD-FEARING
1. *fearing God:* φοβούμενος τὸν θεόν THEOS; PHOBEŌ [B.2.a.1]
Acts 10.22 "Cornelius, a . . God-fearing man

GODLESS
1. *profane, unhallowed:* βέβηλος BEBĒLOS
1 Tim 4. 7 Have nothing to do with godless . . myths
6.20 Avoid the g. chatter and contradictions
2 Tim 2.16 Avoid such godless chatter

GODLINESS
1. *reverence, piety:* εὐσέβεια EUSEBEIA
1 Tim 4. 7 Train yourself in godliness
4. 8 godliness is of value in every way
6. 3 teaching which accords with godliness
6. 5 imagining that godliness is a means of gain
6. 6 great gain in godliness with contentment
6.11 aim at righteousness, godliness, faith
Tit 1. 1 the truth which accords with godliness
2 Pet 1. 3 things that pertain to life and godliness
1. 6 ⟨supplement⟩ steadfastness with godliness
1. 7 ⟨supplement⟩ g. with brotherly affection
3.11 in lives of holiness and godliness

GODLY
1. *reverence, piety:* εὐσέβεια EUSEBEIA [A.1.b.5]
1 Tim 2. 2 godly and respectful in every way
2. *reverent:* εὐσεβής EUSEBĒS
2 Pet 2. 9 how to rescue the godly from trial
3. *in a pious manner:* εὐσεβῶς EUSEBŌS* [A.4.a]
2 Tim 3.12 all who desire to live a godly life
Tit 2.12 to live . . godly lives in this world
4. *God:* θεός THEOS
[a]gen. [b]κατὰ θεόν [B.1.a.1]
2 Cor 1.12 [a]with holiness and godly sincerity
7. 9 [b]a godly grief, so that you suffered no loss
7.10 [b]godly grief produces a repentance
7.11 [b]earnestness this godly grief has produced

GODLY FEAR
1. *discretion, reverence:* εὐλάβεια EULABEIA
Heb 5. 7 he was heard for his godly fear

GOG: Γώγ 'gäg
Rev 20. 8 to deceive the nations . . Gog and Magog

GOING, BE
1. *be about to:* μέλλω (+inf.) MELLŌ
Acts 23.15 "were going to determine his case
23.20 "were going to inquire somewhat

GOING ON A JOURNEY
1. *abroad:* ἀπόδημος APODĒMOS* [A.3.d.3]
Mk 13.34 "It is like a man going on a journey

GOLD
1. *gold:* χρυσίον CHRYSION*
Acts 3. 6 Peter said, "I have no silver and gold
20.33 "I coveted no one's silver or gold
1 Cor 3.12 if any one builds . . with gold, silver
1 Tim 2. 9 not with braided hair or gold
Heb 9. 4 ark . . covered on all sides with gold
1 Pet 1. 7 your faith, more precious than gold
1.18 not . . perishable things such as . . gold
3. 3 braiding of hair, decoration of gold
Rev 3.18 " 'buy from me gold refined by fire
17. 4 The woman was . . bedecked with gold
18.16 "the great city that was . . bedecked with g.
21.18 the city was pure gold, clear as glass
21.21 the street of the city was pure gold
2. *gold:* χρυσός CHRYSOS*
Mt 2.11 gold and frankincense and myrrh
10. 9 "Take no gold, nor silver . . in your belts
23.16 " 'if . . one swears by the gold of the temple
23.17 "For which is greater, the gold or the temple that has made the gold sacred?
Acts 17.29 "ought not to think that the Deity is like g.
Jas 5. 3 Your gold and silver have rusted
Rev 9. 7 what looked like crowns of gold
18.12 cargo of gold, silver, jewels and pearls

GOLD, OF
1. *golden:* χρυσοῦς CHRYSOUS
2 Tim 2.20 there are not only vessels of gold
Rev 9.20 idols of gold and silver and bronze
21.15 he . . had a measuring rod of gold

GOLD RINGS, WITH
1. *with a gold ring:* χρυσοδακτύλιος CHRYSODAKTYLIOS*
Jas 2. 2 man with gold rings and in fine clothing

GOLDEN
1. *golden:* χρυσοῦς CHRYSOUS
Heb 9. 4 having the golden altar of incense
9. 4 a golden urn holding the manna
Rev 1.12 I saw seven golden lampstands
1.13 with a golden girdle round his breast
1.20 "the seven golden lampstands
2. 1 " 'walks among the seven golden lampstands
4. 4 with golden crowns upon their heads
5. 8 with golden bowls full of incense
8. 3 stood at the altar with a golden censer
8. 3 the golden altar before the throne
9.13 from the four horns of the golden altar
14.14 with a golden crown on his head
15. 6 their breasts girded with golden girdles
15. 7 golden bowls full of the wrath of God
17. 4 a golden cup full of abominations

GOLGOTHA: Γολγοθᾶ 'gälgəthə
Mt 27.33 Golgotha (which means the place of a skull
Mk 15.22 Golgotha (which means the place of a skull
Jn 19.17 place of a skull, . . called in Hebrew G.

GOMORRAH: Γόμορρα gə'môrə
Mt 10.15 "the land of Sodom and Gomorrah
Rom 9.29 "we would have fared . . like Gomorrah
2 Pet 2. 6 if by turning . . Gomorrah to ashes
Jude . 7 as . . G. . . , which likewise acted immorally

GONE, BE FAR
1. *make progress, advance:* προκόπτω (aor.) PROKOPTŌ
Rom 13.12 the night is far gone, the day is at hand

GONG
1. *copper, brass, bronze:* χαλκός CHALKOS
1 Cor 13. 1 a noisy gong or a clanging cymbal

GOOD (*See also* CHEER, BE OF GOOD; COURAGE, BE OF GOOD; DEAD, AS GOOD AS; REPUTE, OF GOOD; SEEM GOOD)
1. *good:* ἀγαθός AGATHOS
Mt 5.45 "makes his sun rise on the evil and on the g.
7.11 "If you . . know how to give good gifts . . more will your Father . . give g. things!
7.18 "nor can a bad tree bear good fruit
12.34 "how can you speak good, when you are evil?
12.35 "The good man out of his good treasure brings forth good, and the evil man out of his evil treasure brings forth evil
19.16 "Teacher, what good deed must I do?
19.17 "Why do you ask me about what is good? One there is who is good
[20.15 " '*is your eye evil because I am good?*†
22.10 "all whom they found, both bad and g.
25.21 " 'Well done, good and faithful servant
25.23 " 'Well done, good and faithful servant
Mk 3. 4 "Is it lawful on the sabbath to do good?
10.17 "Good Teacher, what must I do?
10.18 "Why do you call me good? No one is good but God alone
Lk 1.53 "he has filled the hungry with good things
6.45 "The good man out of the good treasure of his heart produces good
8. 8 "some fell into good soil and grew
8.15 "hold it fast in an honest and good heart
10.42 "Mary has chosen the good portion
11.13 "If you . . know how to give good gifts
16.25 " 'you in your lifetime received . . g. things
18.18 "Good Teacher, what shall I do?
18.19 Jesus said to him, "Why do you call me good? No one is good but God alone
19.17 "he said to him, 'Well done, good servant!
23.50 Joseph . . a good and righteous man

Jn 1.46 "Can anything good come out of Nazareth?
5.29 "come forth, those who have done good
7.12 some said, "He is a good man
Acts 9.36 Dorcas . . was full of good works
11.24 a good man, full of the Holy Spirit
23. 1 "I have lived . . in all good conscience
Rom 2.10 honor and peace for . . one who does g.
3. 8 why not do evil that good may come?
5. 7 for a good man one will dare even to die
7.12 the commandment is holy and . . good
7.13 Did that which is good . . bring death . . ? It was sin, working . . through what is good
7.18 I know . . nothing good dwells within me
7.19 For I do not do the good I want
8.28 in everything God works for good[k]
9.11 had done nothing either good or bad
10.15 "those who preach good news!
12. 2 what is good and acceptable and perfect[r]
12. 9 hate what is evil, hold fast to what is g.
12.21 but overcome evil with good
13. 3 rulers are not a terror to good conduct . . Then do what is good
13. 4 he is God's servant for your good
14.16 do not let . . good be spoken of as evil
15. 2 let each . . please his neighbor for his good
16.19 would have you wise as to what is good
2 Cor 5.10 that each one may receive good or evil
9. 8 that you . . provide . . for every good work
Gal 6. 6 Let him who is taught . . share . . good things
6.10 let us do good to all men
Eph 2.10 created in Christ Jesus for good works
4.29 Let . . only such as is good for edifying
6. 8 that whatever good any one does
Phil 1. 6 he who began a good work in you
Col 1.10 bearing fruit in every good work
1 Th 5.15 always seek to do good to one another
2 Th 2.16 eternal comfort and good hope through grace
2.17 establish them in every good work
1 Tim 1. 5 love that issues from . . a good conscience
1.19 holding faith and a good conscience
2.10 by good deeds, as befits women
5.10 who has . . devoted herself to doing good
2 Tim 2.21 he will be . . ready for any good work
3.17 equipped for every good work
Tit 1.16 they are . . unfit for any good deed
Phm . 6 knowledge of all the good that is ours
Heb 9.11 Christ . . a high priest of the g. things
10. 1 law has but a shadow of the good things
13.21 ⟨may God⟩ equip you with everything good
Jas 1.17 Every good endowment . . is from above
3.17 full of mercy and good fruits
1 Pet 3.10 "He that would love life and see good days
3.16 those who revile your good behavior
3 Jn .11 do not imitate evil but imitate good

2. *goodness:* ἀγαθωσύνη (gen.) AGATHŌSYNĒ
2 Th 1.11 that . . God . . may fulfil every good resolve

3. *good, useful:* χρηστός CHRĒSTOS
Lk 5.39 "for he says, 'The old is good[s]‡
1 Cor 15.33 "Bad company ruins good morals

4. *kindness, uprightness:* χρηστότης CHRĒSTOTĒS
Rom 3.12 "no one does good, not even one

5. *do well:* εὖ ποιεῖν EU [A.6.a.5]
Mk 14. 7 "whenever you will, you can do g. to them

6. *good, beautiful:* καλός KALOS
Mt 3.10 "every tree . . that does not bear good fruit
5.16 "that they may see your good works
7.17 "every sound tree bears good fruit
7.18 "nor can a bad tree bear good fruit
7.19 "Every tree that does not bear good fruit
12.33 "Either make the tree good, and its fruit good; or make the tree bad
13. 8 "Other seeds fell on good soil
13.23 "As for what was sown on good soil
13.24 "a man who sowed good seed in his field
13.27 "'did you not sow good seed in your field?
13.37 "He who sows . . g. seed is the Son of man
13.38 "good seed means the sons of the kingdom
Mt 13.48 "men . . sorted the good into vessels
Mk 4. 8 "other seeds fell into good soil
4.20 "those that were sown upon . . good soil
9.50 "Salt is good; . . Have salt in yourselves
Lk 3. 9 "tree . . that does not bear good fruit
6.38 "g. measure, pressed down, shaken together
6.43 "For no good tree bears bad fruit, nor again does a bad tree bear good fruit
8.15 "as for that in the good soil
14.34 "Salt is g.; but if salt has lost its taste
Jn 2.10 "Every man serves the good wine first; . . you have kept the good wine until now
10.11 "I am the good shepherd. The good shepherd lays down his life for the sheep
10.14 "I am the good shepherd; I know my own
10.32 "I have shown you many good works
10.33 "not for a good work that we stone you
Rom 7.16 I agree that the law is good
1 Cor 5. 6 Your boasting is not good
Gal 4.18 For a good purpose it is always good to be made much of
1 Th 5.21 test everything; hold fast what is good
1 Tim 1. 8 we know that the law is good
1.18 that . . you may wage the good warfare
2. 3 This is good, and it is acceptable
3.13 who serve well . . gain a good standing
4. 4 everything created by God is good
4. 6 a good minister of Christ Jesus, nourished on the words . . of the good doctrine
5.10 well attested for her good deeds
5.25 So also good deeds are conspicuous
6.12 Fight the good fight of the faith
6.12 when you made the good confession
6.13 Christ Jesus who . . made the g. confession
6.18 They are . . to be rich in good deeds
6.19 a good foundation for the future
2 Tim 2. 3 Share in suffering as a g. soldier
4. 7 I have fought the good fight
Tit 2. 7 in all respects a model of good deeds
2.14 a people . . who are zealous for good deeds
3. 8 to apply themselves to good deeds[d]
3.14 to apply themselves to good deeds[d]†
Heb 5.14 trained . . to distinguish good from evil
10.24 to stir up one another to . . good works
Jas 3.13 By his good life let him show his works
1 Pet 2.12 Maintain good conduct . . so that . . they may see your good deeds
4.10 as good stewards of God's varied grace

7. *well, rightly:* καλῶς KALŌS [A.4.a]
Mt 12.12 "it is lawful to do good on the sabbath
Lk 6.27 "do good to those who hate you

IDIOMATICALLY
a. Gal 4.17 They make much of you, but for no good purpose ζηλοῦσιν ὑμᾶς οὐ καλῶς [KALŌS]
b. 2 Tim 2.14 which does no good ἐπ' οὐδὲν χρήσιμον [CHRĒSIMOS*]

CONTEXTUALLY
Lk 13. 9 "'And if it bears fruit . . , well and good
1 Cor 9.11 If we have sown spiritual g. among you
10.24 Let no one seek his own good, but the good of his neighbor
Heb 11.12 from one man, and him as good as dead

GOOD, BE

1. *be strong, prevail:* ἰσχύω ISCHYŌ
Mt 5.13 "It is no longer good for anything

GOOD DEED

1. *good deed:* εὐεργεσία EUERGESIA
Acts 4. 9 "a good deed done to a cripple

GOOD, DO

1. *do good, do well:* ἀγαθοεργέω AGATHOERGEŌ*
[a]ἀγαθουργέω
Acts 14.17 [a]"for he did good and gave you . . rains
1 Tim 6.18 They are to do good

2. *do good:* ἀγαθοποιέω AGATHOPOIEŌ
Lk 6. 9 "is it lawful on the sabbath to do good?

Lk 6.33 "And if you do good to those who do good to you, what credit is that to you?
6.35 "love your enemies, and do good
3 Jn .11 He who does good is of God
3. *be a benefactor, do good:* εὐεργετέω EUERGETEŌ*
Acts 10.38 "he went about doing good and healing

GOOD, HATER OF
1. *not loving the good:* ἀφιλάγαθος (subst.) APHILAGATHOS*
2 Tim 3. 3 profligates, fierce, haters of good

GOOD NEWS
IDIOMATICALLY
a. 1 Pet 1.25 That word is the good news which was preached to you τοῦτο δέ ἐστιν τὸ ῥῆμα τὸ εὐαγγελισθὲν εἰς ὑμᾶς [EUAGGELIZŌ]

GOOD NEWS, BRING
GOOD NEWS, PREACH
GOOD NEWS, PREACH THE
GOOD NEWS, TELL
1. *bring good news* (mid.): εὐαγγελίζω EUAGGELIZŌ
[a]pass.
Mt 11.5 [a]"poor have good news preached to them
Lk 1.19 "sent . . to bring you this good news
2.10 "I bring you good news of a great joy
3.18 he preached good news to the people
4.18 "to preach good news to the poor
4.43 "I must preach the good news
7.22 [a]"poor have good news preached to them
8. 1 bringing the good news of the kingdom
16.16 [a]"the g. news of . . kingdom . . is preached
Acts 8.12 believed Philip as he preached good news
8.35 he told him the good news of Jesus
10.36 "preaching good news of peace
13.32 "we bring you the good news
14.15 bring . . good news, that you should turn
Rom 10.15 "those who preach good news
1 Th 3. 6 Timothy . . brought us the good news
1 Pet 1.12 who preached the good news to you

GOOD NEWS COMES TO ONE
GOOD NEWS, RECEIVE THE
1. *bring good news* (mid.): εὐαγγελίζω (pass.) EUAGGELIZŌ
Heb 4. 2 For good news came to us
4. 6 those who . . received the good news

GOOD, ONE'S
1. *bring together, be useful:* συμφέρω (subst. part. neut.) SYMPHERŌ
Heb 12.10 he disciplines us for our good

GOOD ORDER
1. *noble, proper:* εὐσχήμων (subst. neut.) EUSCHĒMŌN
1 Cor 7.35 I say this . . to promote good order
2. *order, rank:* τάξις TAXIS
Col 2. 5 rejoicing to see your good order

GOOD PLEASURE
1. *satisfaction, goodwill:* εὐδοκία EUDOKIA
Phil 2.13 to will and to work for his good pleasure

GOOD PLEASURE, IT IS ONE'S
1. *be well pleased:* εὐδοκέω EUDOKEŌ [A.6.e]
Lk 12.32 "it is your Father's good pleasure

GOOD REPUTE
1. *good repute, good report:* εὐφημία EUPHĒMIA*
2 Cor 6. 8 ⟨we commend ourselves⟩ in . . good repute

GOOD SHOWING, MAKE A
1. *make a good showing:* εὐπροσωπέω EUPROSŌPEŌ*
Gal 6.12 to make a good showing in the flesh

GOOD, TEACH WHAT IS
1. *teaching what is good:* καλοδιδάσκαλος KALODIDASKALOS* [A.6.a.3]
Tit 2. 3 they are to teach what is good

GOOD, THE COMMON
1. *bring together, be useful:* συμφέρω (subst. part. neut.) SYMPHERŌ
1 Cor 12. 7 given . . the Spirit for the common good

GOOD, TO DO
1. *the doing of good:* εὐποιΐα EUPOIIA* [A.1.d]
Heb 13.16 Do not neglect to do good and to share

GOOD, WHAT IS
1. *goodness:* ἀγαθωσύνη AGATHŌSYNĒ
Eph 5. 9 (all that is good and right and true

GOOD WILL
1. *satisfaction, goodwill:* εὐδοκία EUDOKIA
Lk [2.14 "*peace, good will among men*‡
Phil 1.15 others ⟨preach Christ⟩ from good will
2. *goodwill, favor:* εὔνοια EUNOIA*
Eph 6. 7 rendering service with a good will
3. *willingness, goodwill:* προθυμία PROTHYMIA
2 Cor 8.19 this gracious work . . to show our good will

GOODNESS
1. *good:* ἀγαθός (subst. neut.) AGATHOS
Phm .14 that . . g. might not be by compulsion
2. *goodness:* ἀγαθωσύνη AGATHŌSYNĒ
Rom 15.14 that you yourselves are full of goodness
Gal 5.22 peace, patience, kindness, goodness
3. *kindness, uprightness:* χρηστότης CHRĒSTOTĒS
Tit 3. 4 the goodness and loving kindness of God
4. *good, beautiful:* καλός KALOS [A.3.a.4]
Heb 6. 5 tasted the goodness of the word of God

GOODNESS, LOVER OF
1. *loving goodness:* φιλάγαθος (subst.) PHILAGATHOS*
Tit 1. 8 a lover of goodness, master of himself

GOODS
1. *good:* ἀγαθός (subst. neut. pl.) AGATHOS
Lk 12.18 " 'there I will store . . my goods
12.19 " 'Soul, you have ample goods laid up
2. *everyday life, livelihood:* βίος BIOS
1 Jn 3.17 if any one has the world's goods
3. *be, exist, belong to:* ὑπάρχω (subst. neut. pl.) HYPARCHŌ
Lk 11.21 "his goods are in peace
16. 1 "that this man was wasting his goods
19. 8 "half of my goods I give to the poor
4. *property:* ὕπαρξις (pl.) HYPARXIS
Acts 2.45 they sold their possessions and goods
5. *vessel, tackle:* σκεῦος (pl.) SKEUOS
Mt 12.29 "how can one . . plunder his goods?
Mk 3.27 "no one can . . plunder his goods
Lk 17.31 "with his goods in the house
CONTEXTUALLY
Acts 16.14 Lydia, . . a seller of purple goods

GOODS, HAVE
1. *hold fast, restrain:* κατέχω KATECHŌ
1 Cor 7.30 who buy as though they had no goods

GORGE
1. *feed, fatten:* χορτάζω CHORTAZŌ
Rev 19.21 the birds were gorged with their flesh

GORGEOUS
1. *bright, radiant:* λαμπρός LAMPROS
Lk 23.11 arraying him in gorgeous apparel

GORGEOUSLY
1. *glorious, honored:* ἔνδοξος ENDOXOS [A.3.b.1]
Lk 7.25 "those who are gorgeously appareled

GOSPEL
1. *good news:* εὐαγγέλιον EUAGGELION*
Mt 4.23 preaching the gospel of the kingdom
9.35 preaching the gospel of the kingdom
24.14 "gospel of the kingdom will be preached
26.13 "wherever this gospel is preached
Mk 1. 1 The beginning of the gospel
1.14 Jesus came . . preaching the gospel of God
1.15 "repent, and believe in the gospel
8.35 "loses his life for . . the gospel's ⟨sake⟩
10.29 "for my sake and for the gospel
13.10 "g. must first be preached to all nations
14. 9 "wherever the gospel is preached
16.15 "Go into all the world . . preach the g.[k]‡
Acts 15. 7 "Gentiles should hear the word of the g.
20.24 "to testify to the g. of the grace of God
Rom 1. 1 apostle, set apart for the g. of God
1. 9 God . . whom I serve with my spirit in the g.
1.16 For I am not ashamed of the gospel
2.16 when, according to my g., God judges

Rom 10.16 they have not all obeyed the gospel
11.28 As regards the gospel they are enemies
15.16 the priestly service of the gospel of God
15.19 I have fully preached the g. of Christ
[15.29 the blessing *of the gospel* of Christ‡
16.25 to strengthen you according to my g.
1 Cor 4.15 I became your father . . through the gospel
9.12 in the way of the gospel of Christ
9.14 those who proclaim the gospel should get their living by the gospel
9.18 I may make the gospel free of charge, not making full use of my right in the g.
9.23 I do it all for the sake of the gospel
15. 1 in what terms I preached to you the g.
2 Cor 2.12 When I came to Troas to preach the g.
4. 3 even if our gospel is veiled
4. 4 light of the gospel of the glory of Christ
8.18 famous . . for his preaching of the gospel
9.13 acknowledging the gospel of Christ
10.14 to come all the way to you with the g.
11. 4 or if you accept a different gospel
11. 7 I preached God's g. without cost
Gal 1. 6 so quickly . . turning to a different gospel
1. 7 who . . want to pervert the g. of Christ
1.11 the g. . . preached by me is not man's[b]
2. 2 I laid before them . . the g. . . I preach
2. 5 that the truth of the g. . . be preserved
2. 7 entrusted with the g. to the uncircumcised
2.14 not straightforward about the . . gospel
Eph 1.13 word of truth, the g. of your salvation
3. 6 partakers of the promise . . through the g.
6.15 the equipment of the gospel of peace
6.19 to proclaim the mystery of the gospel
Phil 1. 5 thankful for your partnership in the g.
1. 7 defense and confirmation of the gospel
1.12 has really served to advance the gospel
1.16 I am put here for the defense of the g.
1.27 let your manner of life be worthy of the g. . . striving side by side for the faith of the g.
2.22 he has served with me in the gospel
4. 3 they have labored . . with me in the gospel
4.15 in the beginning of the gospel
Col 1. 5 the word of the truth, the gospel
1.23 not shifting from the hope of the gospel
1 Th 1. 5 our gospel came to you not only in word
2. 2 to declare to you the gospel of God
2. 4 to be entrusted with the gospel
2. 8 ready to share with you not only the g.
2. 9 while we preached to you the gospel
3. 2 Timothy, . . God's servant in the gospel
2 Th 1. 8 who do not obey the gospel of our Lord
2.14 To this he called you through our g.
1 Tim 1.11 in accordance with the glorious gospel
2 Tim 1. 8 share in suffering for the gospel
1.10 life and immortality to light through the g.
2. 8 Jesus Christ . . as preached in my gospel
Phm .13 during my imprisonment for the gospel
1 Pet 4.17 those who do not obey the gospel of God
Rev 14. 6 angel . . with an eternal gospel to proclaim
CONTEXTUALLY
Rom 1. 3 the gospel concerning his Son . . from David
Eph 3. 7 Of this g. I was made a minister
2 Tim 1.11 For this gospel I was appointed a preacher
2. 9 the gospel for which I am suffering

GOSPEL BEFOREHAND, PREACH THE

1. *bring good news in advance:* προευαγγελίζομαι PROEUAGGELIZOMAI*
Gal 3. 8 preached the g. beforehand to Abraham

GOSPEL, PREACH A
GOSPEL, PREACH THE

1. *bring good news* (mid.): εὐαγγελίζω EUAGGELIZŌ
Lk 9. 6 preaching the gospel and healing
20. 1 in the temple and preaching the gospel
Acts 8.25 preaching the gospel to many villages
8.40 preached the gospel to all the towns
14. 7 there they preached the gospel
14.21 When they had preached the gospel
16.10 that God had called us to preach the g.
Rom 1.15 eager to preach the gospel to you also
15.20 my ambition to preach the gospel
1 Cor 1.17 not . . to baptize but to preach the g.
9.16 if I preach the g. . . no ground for boasting
9.16 Woe to me if I do not preach the gospel!
2 Cor 10.16 so that we may preach the gospel
Gal 1. 8 if we . . should preach . . a gospel contrary
1. 9 If any one is preaching . . a g. contrary
4.13 that I preached the gospel to you at first
1 Pet 4. 6 why the g. was preached . . to the dead

GOSSIP

1. *silly, foolish:* φλύαρος (subst.) PHLYAROS*
1 Tim 5.13 not only idlers but gossips and busybodies
2. *whispering, gossip:* ψιθυρισμός PSITHYRISMOS*
2 Cor 12.20 slander, gossip, conceit, and disorder
3. *whisperer, slanderer:* ψιθυριστής PSITHYRISTĒS*
Rom 1.29 Full of . . deceit, malignity, they are gossips

GOVERN

1. *tend, herd, govern:* ποιμαίνω POIMAINŌ
Mt 2. 6 " 'a ruler who will govern my people Israel

GOVERNING

1. *be above:* ὑπερέχω (part.) HYPERECHŌ
Rom 13. 1 be subject to the governing authorities

GOVERNOR

1. *ruler of a nation:* ἐθνάρχης ETHNARCHĒS*
2 Cor 11.32 the governor under King Aretas
2. *guide, sovereign:* ἡγεμών HĒGEMŌN
Mt 10.18 "you will be dragged before governors
27. 2 delivered him to Pilate the governor
27.11 Jesus stood before the g.; and the g. asked him, "Are you the King?
27.14 the governor wondered greatly
27.15 at the feast the governor was accustomed
27.21 The g. . . said . . "Which of the two?
27.27 the soldiers of the governor took Jesus
28.14 "if this comes to the governor's ears
Mk 13. 9 "you will stand before governors and kings
Lk 20.20 the authority and jurisdiction of the g.
21.12 "brought before kings and governors
Acts 23.24 "bring him safely to Felix the g.
23.26 "to his Excellency the governor Felix
23.33 delivered the letter to the governor
24. 1 They laid before the governor their case
24.10 when the governor had motioned
26.30 Then the king rose, and the governor
1 Pet 2.14 governors as sent by him to punish
3. *think, lead:* ἡγέομαι (subst. part.) HĒGEOMAI
Acts 7.10 "Pharaoh . . who made him governor

GOVERNOR, BE

1. *rule, be leader:* ἡγεμονεύω HĒGEMONEUŌ*
Lk 2. 2 when Quirinius was governor of Syria
3. 1 Pontius Pilate being governor of Judea

GRACE

1. *grace, favor, gratitude:* χάρις CHARIS
Jn 1.14 dwelt among us, full of grace and truth
1.16 And from his fulness have we all received, grace upon grace
1.17 g. and truth came through Jesus Christ
Acts 4.33 great grace was upon them all
6. 8 Stephen, full of grace and power
11.23 he came and saw the grace of God
13.43 urged them to continue in the g. of God
14. 3 bore witness to the word of his grace
14.26 commended to the grace of God
15.11 "saved through the g. of the Lord Jesus
15.40 commended . . to the grace of the Lord
18.27 those who through grace had believed
20.24 "testify to the gospel of the grace of God
20.32 "I commend you . . to . . word of his grace
Rom 1. 5 we have received grace and apostleship
1. 7 Grace to you and peace from God
3.24 they are justified by his grace as a gift
4.16 that the promise may rest on grace

Rom 5. 2 we have obtained access[g] to this grace
5.15 much more have the g. of God and the free gift in the g... abounded for many
5.17 who receive the abundance of grace
5.20 where sin increased, grace abounded
5.21 that.. grace also might reign
6. 1 to continue in sin that grace may abound?
6.14 you are not under law but under grace
6.15 because we are not under law but under g.
11. 5 there is a remnant, chosen by grace
11. 6 But if it is by grace, it is no longer on the basis of works; otherwise grace would no longer be grace
12. 3 by the grace given to me
12. 6 gifts that differ according to the grace
15.15 because of the grace given me by God
16.20 g. of our Lord Jesus Christ be with you[a]‡
[16.24 *The grace of.. Christ be with you all*‡
1 Cor 1. 3 Grace to you and peace from God
1. 4 because of the grace of God.. given you
3.10 According to the grace of God[0]
15.10 by the grace of God I am what I am, and his grace toward me was not in vain
15.10 it was not I, but the grace of God
16.23 The grace of the Lord Jesus be with you
2 Cor 1. 2 Grace to you and peace from God
1.12 not by earthly wisdom but by the grace
4.15 as grace extends to more and more people
6. 1 not to accept the g. of God in vain
8. 1 to know.. about the grace of God
8. 9 you know the g. of our Lord Jesus
9.14 because of the surpassing grace of God
12. 9 "My grace is sufficient for you
13.14 The grace of the Lord Jesus Christ
Gal 1. 3 Grace to you and peace from God
1. 6 who called you in the grace of Christ
1.15 when he.. had called me through his g.
2. 9 when they perceived the grace
2.21 I do not nullify the grace of God
5. 4 you have fallen away from grace
6.18 The grace of our Lord Jesus Christ
Eph 1. 2 Grace to you and peace from God
1. 6 to the praise of his glorious grace
1. 7 according to the riches of his grace
2. 5 (by grace you have been saved
2. 7 the immeasurable riches of his grace
2. 8 For by grace you have been saved
3. 2 the stewardship of God's grace
3. 7 according to the gift of God's grace
3. 8 this g. was given, to preach to the Gentiles
4. 7 But grace was given to each of us
4.29 may impart grace to those who hear
6.24 G. be with all who love our Lord Jesus
Phil 1. 2 Grace to you and peace from God
1. 7 you are all partakers with me of grace
4.23 The grace of the Lord Jesus Christ
Col 1. 2 Grace to you and peace from God
1. 6 from the day you heard.. the g. of God
4.18 Grace be with you
1 Th 1. 1 Grace to you and peace
5.28 g. of our Lord Jesus Christ be with you
2 Th 1. 2 Grace to you and peace from God
1.12 according to the grace of our God
2.16 who.. gave us.. good hope through grace
3.18 The grace of our Lord Jesus Christ
1 Tim 1. 2 Grace, mercy, and peace from God
1.14 the grace of our Lord overflowed for me
6.21 Grace be with you
2 Tim 1. 2 Grace, mercy, and peace from God
1. 9 grace which he gave us in Christ Jesus
2. 1 be strong in the g. that is in Christ Jesus
4.22 Grace be with you
Tit 1. 4 Grace and peace from God the Father
2.11 For the grace of God has appeared
3. 7 that we might be justified by his grace
3.15 Grace be with you all
Phm . 3 Grace to you and peace from God
Phm .25 The grace of the Lord Jesus Christ
Heb 2. 9 that by.. g. of God he might taste death
4.16 draw near to the throne of grace, that we may.. find grace to help in time of need
10.29 the man who has.. outraged the Spirit of g.
12.15 that no one fail to obtain.. grace of God
13. 9 well that the heart be strengthened by g.
13.25 Grace be with all of you. Amen.
Jas 4. 6 But he gives more grace; therefore it says, "God.. gives grace to the humble
1 Pet 1. 2 May grace and peace be multiplied
1.10 prophets who prophesied of the grace
1.13 hope.. upon the grace that is coming
3. 7 you are joint heirs of the grace of life
4.10 good stewards of God's varied grace
5. 5 "God.. gives grace to the humble
5.10 God of all grace, who has called you
5.12 declaring that this is the true g. of God
2 Pet 1. 2 grace and peace be multiplied to you
3.18 But grow in the grace and knowledge
2 Jn . 3 Grace, mercy, and peace will be with us
Jude . 4 persons who pervert the g. of our God
Rev 1. 4 Grace to you and peace from him
22.21 The grace of the Lord Jesus be with all

GRACIOUS

1. *grace, favor, gratitude:* χάρις CHARIS
[a]gen. [b]B.1.a.1
Lk 4.22 [a]wondered at the gracious words
Col 4. 6 [b]Let your speech always be gracious
2. *fair-sounding, praiseworthy:* εὔφημος EUPHĒMOS*
Phil 4. 8 whatever is lovely, whatever is gracious

GRACIOUS WILL

1. *satisfaction, goodwill:* εὐδοκία EUDOKIA
Mt 11.26 "yea,.. for such was thy gracious will[f]†
Lk 10.21 "yea,.. for such was thy gracious will[h]†

GRACIOUS WORK

1. *grace, favor, gratitude:* χάρις CHARIS
2 Cor 8. 6 he should.. complete.. this gracious work
8. 7 excel in this gracious work also
8.19 to travel with us in this gracious work

GRACIOUSLY, MORE

1. *better, stronger:* κρείσσων (neut.) KREISSŌN
Heb 12.24 more graciously than the blood of Abel

GRAFT

1. *graft:* ἐγκεντρίζω EGKENTRIZŌ*
Rom 11.17 you.. were grafted in their place
11.19 "broken off so that I might be grafted in
11.23 even the others.. will be grafted in, for God has the power to graft them in again
11.24 if you have been.. grafted,.. much more will these.. be grafted back

GRAIN

1. *fruit:* καρπός KARPOS
Mt 13. 8 "Other seeds.. brought forth grain
13.26 "the plants came up and bore grain
Mk 4. 7 "Other seed.. yielded no grain
4. 8 "other seeds.. brought forth grain
4.29 "But when the grain is ripe,.. the sickle
2. *grain, seed:* κόκκος KOKKOS
Mt 13.31 "heaven is like a grain of mustard seed
17.20 "faith as a grain of mustard seed
Mk 4.31 "It is like a grain of mustard seed
Lk 13.19 "It is like a grain of mustard seed
17. 6 "If you had faith as a g. of mustard seed
Jn 12.24 "unless a grain of wheat falls.. and dies
3. *grain, food:* σιτίον (pl.) SITION*
Acts 7.12 "when Jacob heard that there was grain
4. *grain:* σῖτος SITOS
Mk 4.28 "then the full grain in the ear
Lk 12.18 "'there I will store all my grain
CONTEXTUALLY
1 Cor 15.37 perhaps of wheat or of some other grain
Heb 11.12 as many as.. innumerable grains of sand

GRAIN, HEAD OF
1. *ear of grain:* στάχυς STACHYS
Mt 12. 1 they began to pluck heads of grain and to eat[0]
Mk 2.35 disciples began to pluck heads of grain[0]
Lk 6. 1 plucked and ate some heads of grain[0]

GRAIN, TREAD OUT
1. *tread, thresh:* ἀλοάω ALOAŌ
1 Cor 9. 9 "an ox when it is treading out the grain
1 Tim 5.18 "an ox when it is treading out the grain

GRAINFIELD
1. *sown:* σπόριμος (subst.) SPORIMOS*
Mt 12. 1 Jesus went through the grainfields
Mk 2.23 he was going through the grainfields
Lk 6. 1 he was going through the grainfields

GRANARY
1. *storehouse:* ἀποθήκη APOTHĒKĒ
Mt 3.12 "will . . gather his wheat into the granary
Lk 3.17 "to gather the wheat into his granary

GRANDCHILD
1. *born of:* ἔκγονος (subst.) EKGONOS*
1 Tim 5. 4 If a widow has children or grandchildren

GRANDMOTHER
1. *grandmother:* μάμμη MAMMĒ*
2 Tim 1. 5 faith that dwelt . . in your grandmother

GRANT
1. *give graciously:* χαρίζομαι CHARIZOMAI
Acts 3.14 "asked for a murderer to be granted
27.24 " 'God has granted you all those . . with you
Phil 1.29 granted to you that . . you should . . suffer
Phm .22 for I am hoping . . to be granted to you
2. *give:* δίδωμι DIDŌMI
Mt 20.23 "to sit at my right hand . . is not mine to g.
Mk 6.22 "whatever you wish, and I will grant it
10.37 "Grant us to sit, one at your right hand
10.40 "to sit at my right hand . . is not mine to g.
Lk 1.74 "⟨the oath which he swore⟩ to grant us
Jn 5.26 "he has granted the Son also to have life
5.36 "works which the Father has granted me
6.65 "no one can come . . unless it is granted
Acts 4.29 "grant to thy servants[f] to speak thy word
11.18 "to the Gentiles also God has granted
14. 3 granting signs and wonders . . by their hands
Rom 15. 5 God . . grant you to live in such harmony
Eph 3.16 he may grant you to be strengthened
2 Tim 1.16 Lord g. mercy to . . household of Onesiphorus
1.18 the Lord grant him to find mercy
2. 7 the Lord will grant you understanding
2.25 God may . . grant that they will repent
Rev 2. 7 " 'I will grant to eat of the tree of life
3.21 " 'I will grant him to sit with me
11. 3 "I will g. . . witnesses power to prophesy
19. 8 "it was granted her to be clothed
3. *present:* δωρέομαι DŌREOMAI*
Mk 15.45 he granted the body to Joseph
2 Pet 1. 3 His divine power has granted to us
1. 4 he has granted to us his . . promises
4. *confess, acknowledge:* ὁμολογέω HOMOLOGEŌ
Acts 7.17 "the promise . . granted to Abraham
CONTEXTUALLY
Lk 1.43 "why is this granted me?
2 Cor 1.11 blessing granted us in answer to . . prayers
2 Th 1. 7 to g. rest with us to you who are afflicted

GRANTED, BE
1. *come to be, happen, be:* γίνομαι GINOMAI
Lk 23.24 that their demand should be granted

GRAPES
1. *bunch of grapes:* σταφυλή (sg. or pl.) STAPHYLĒ*
Mt 7.16 "Are grapes gathered from thorns?
Lk 6.44 "nor are grapes picked from a bramble bush
Rev 14.18 "gather . . , for its grapes are ripe

GRAPEVINE
1. *grapevine:* ἄμπελος AMPELOS
Jas 3.12 Can . . a grapevine ⟨yield⟩ figs?

GRASP
1. *know, understand:* γινώσκω GINŌSKŌ
Lk 18.34 they did not grasp what was said

GRASPED, A THING TO BE
1. *robbery, rape:* ἁρπαγμός HARPAGMOS*
Phil 2. 6 equality with God a thing to be grasped

GRASS
1. *grass, fodder:* χόρτος CHORTOS
Mt 6.30 "if God so clothes the grass of the field
14.19 the crowds to sit down on the grass
Mk 6.39 commanded them . . to sit . . upon the . . g.
Lk 12.28 "if God so clothes the g. which is alive
Jn 6.10 there was much grass in the place
Jas 1.10 like the flower of the grass he will pass away
1.11 the sun rises . . and withers the grass
1 Pet 1.24 "All flesh is like grass and all its glory like the flower of grass. The grass withers, and the flower falls
Rev 8. 7 all green grass was burnt up
9. 4 they were told not to harm the grass

GRATEFUL
1. *grace, favor, gratitude:* χάρις CHARIS [B.3.a.5]
Heb 12.28 let us be g. for receiving a kingdom that

GRATIFY
1. *finish, fulfill:* τελέω TELEŌ
Gal 5.16 do not gratify the desires of the flesh
CONTEXTUALLY
Rom 13.14 make no provision . . to gratify its desires

GRATITUDE
1. *thankfulness:* εὐχαριστία EUCHARISTIA
Acts 24. 3 "everywhere we accept this with all g.

GRAVE
1. *tomb, memorial:* μνημεῖον MNĒMEION
Lk 11.44 "you are like graves which are not seen
2. *tomb, grave:* τάφος TAPHOS
Rom 3.13 "Their throat is an open grave

GRAVITY
1. *dignity, seriousness:* σεμνότης SEMNOTĒS
Tit 2. 7 in your teaching show integrity, gravity

GREAT (*See also* VALUE, OF GREAT; WAY OFF, A GREAT)
1. *enough:* ἱκανός HIKANOS
Mk 10.46 leaving Jericho with . . a great multitude
Acts 22. 6 "a great light from heaven suddenly shone
2. *strong, powerful:* ἰσχυρός ISCHYROS
Lk 15.14 "a great famine arose in that country
3. *strength, might:* ἰσχύς (gen.) ISCHYS
Eph 1.19 the working of his great might
4. *great:* μέγας MEGAS
Mt 2.10 they rejoiced exceedingly with great joy
4.16 "the people . . have seen a great light
5.19 "shall be called great in the kingdom
5.35 "it is the city of the great King
7.27 "and great was the fall of it
8.24 there arose a great storm on the sea
8.26 there was a great calm
15.28 "O woman, great is your faith!
20.25 "great men exercise authority over them
20.26 "whoever would be g. . . must be . . servant
22.36 "which is the great commandment?
22.38 "the great and first commandment
24.21 "then there will be great tribulation
24.24 "false prophets will . . show great signs
27.60 he rolled a great stone to the door
28. 2 there was a great earthquake
28. 8 they departed . . with fear and great joy
Mk 4.37 a great storm of wind arose
4.39 wind ceased, and there was a great calm
5.11 Now a great herd of swine was feeding
10.42 "their great men exercise authority
10.43 "whoever would be great among you
13. 2 "Do you see these great buildings?
Lk 1.15 "he will be great before the Lord
1.32 "He will be great, and . . called the Son
1.49 "he who is mighty has done great things

Lk 2.10 "I bring you good news of a great joy
4.25 "came a great famine over all the land
5.29 Levi made him a great feast in his house
6.49 "the ruin of that house was great
7.16 "A great prophet has arisen among us!
8.37 for they were seized with great fear
9.48 "he who is least . . is the one who is great
14.16 "A man once gave a great banquet
16.26 " 'between us and you a great chasm
21.11 "there will be great earthquakes
21.11 "there will be . . great signs from heaven
21.23 "great distress shall be upon the earth
24.52 they[b] returned to Jerusalem with g. joy
Jn 7.37 On . . the great day, Jesus stood up
Acts 2.20 " 'the great and manifest day
4.33 with great power . . gave their testimony . . and great grace was upon them all
5. 5 great fear came upon all who heard of it
5.11 great fear came upon the whole church
6. 8 Stephen . . did great wonders and signs
7.11 "a famine . . and great affliction
8. 1 a g. persecution arose against the church
8. 2 buried Stephen, and made g. lamentation
8. 9 saying that he himself was somebody great
8.10 "that power of God which is called Great
8.13 seeing . . great miracles . . , he was amazed
10.11 like a g. sheet, let down by four corners
11. 5 "like a g. sheet, let down from heaven
11.28 that there would be a great famine
15. 3 they gave great joy to all the brethren
16.26 suddenly there was a great earthquake
19.27 "the temple of the great goddess Artemis
19.28 "Great is Artemis of the Ephesians!
19.34 "Great is Artemis of the Ephesians!
19.35 "temple keeper of the great Artemis
23. 9 Then a great clamor arose
26.22 "testifying both to small and great
Rom 9. 2 I have great sorrow . . in my heart
1 Tim 3.16 Great indeed . . is the mystery of our religion
6. 6 There is great gain in godliness
2 Tim 2.20 In a great house there are not only vessels
Tit 2.13 appearing of the glory of our great God
Heb 4.14 Since then we have a great high priest
10.21 we have a great priest over the house
10.35 confidence, which has a great reward
13.20 our Lord Jesus, the great shepherd
Jas 3. 5 the tongue . . boasts of great things
Jude . 6 until the judgment of the great day
Rev 2.22 " 'I will throw into great tribulation
6. 4 he was given a great sword
6.12 there was a great earthquake
6.17 "the great day of their wrath has come
7.14 "have come out of the great tribulation
8. 8 like a great mountain, burning
8.10 a great star fell from heaven
9. 2 like the smoke of a great furnace
9.14 "bound at the great river Euphrates
11. 8 the great city which is . . called Sodom
11.11 great fear fell on those who saw
11.13 there was a great earthquake
11.17 "thou hast taken thy great power
11.18 "who fear thy name, both small and great
12. 1 a great portent appeared in heaven
12. 3 a great red dragon, with seven heads
12. 9 the great dragon was thrown down
12.12 "devil has come down . . in great wrath!
12.14 given the two wings of the great eagle
13. 2 dragon gave his . . great authority
13.13 It works great signs, . . making fire come
13.16 all, both small and great, . . to be marked
14. 8 "Fallen, fallen is Babylon the great
14.19 great wine press of the wrath of God
15. 1 another portent . . great and wonderful
15. 3 "Great and wonderful are thy deeds!
16.12 poured his bowl on the g. river Euphrates
16.14 battle on the great day of God
16.18 a great earthquake such as had never been
Rev 16.19 The great city was split into three parts . . and God remembered great Babylon
16.21 great hailstones, heavy as a hundredweight
17. 1 "the judgment of the great harlot
17. 5 "Babylon the great, mother of harlots
17.18 "the woman . . is the great city
18. 1 another angel . . having great authority
18. 2 "Fallen, fallen is Babylon the great!
18.10 "Alas! alas! thou great city!
18.16 "Alas, alas, for the great city!
18.18 "What city was like the great city?
18.19 "Alas, alas, for the great city!
18.21 a stone like a great millstone
18.21 "So shall . . the great city be thrown
19. 2 "he has judged the great harlot
19. 5 "you who fear him, small and great
19.17 "Come, gather for the great supper of God
19.18 "the flesh of all . . both small and great
20. 1 an angel . . holding . . a great chain
20.11 Then I saw a great white throne
20.12 I saw the dead, great and small
21.10 carried me away to a great, high mountain
21.12 a great, high wall, with twelve gates

5. *for a donkey:* ὀνικός ONIKOS [C.2]
Mt 18. 6 "a g. millstone fastened round his neck
Mk 9.42 "a g. millstone were hung round his neck

6. *all, every, whole:* πᾶς PAS
2 Cor 9.11 enriched in every way for great generosity

7. *many, great:* πολύς POLYS
Mt 4.25 great crowds followed him from Galilee
5.12 "Rejoice and be glad, for your reward is g.
8. 1 When he came down . . great crowds followed
8.18 when Jesus saw great crowds around him
13. 2 great crowds gathered about him
14.14 As he went ashore he saw a great throng
15.30 great crowds came to him
19.22 for he had great possessions
20.29 as they went out . . a great crowd followed
24.30 "coming . . with power and great glory
26.47 a great crowd with swords and clubs
Mk 3. 7 a great multitude from Galilee followed
3. 8 a great multitude, hearing all that he did
5.21 a great crowd gathered about him
5.24 a great crowd followed him
6.34 As he went ashore he saw a great throng
8. 1 when again a great crowd had gathered
9.14 they saw a great crowd about them
10.22 for he had great possessions
12.37 And the great throng heard him gladly
13.26 "Son of man coming . . with great power
Lk 2.36 Anna . . was of a great age
5. 6 they enclosed a great shoal of fish
5.15 great multitudes gathered to hear
6.17 with a great crowd of his disciples and a great multitude of people
6.23 "your reward is great in heaven
6.35 "your reward will be great
7.11 his disciples and a great crowd went
8. 4 when a great crowd came together
9.37 a great crowd met him
14.25 great multitudes accompanied him
21.27 "coming in a cloud with . . great glory
23.27 there followed him a great multitude
Jn 12. 9 the great crowd of the Jews learned
12.12 a great crowd who had come to the feast
Acts 6. 7 great many of the priests were obedient
11.21 a great number . . turned to the Lord
14. 1 so spoke that a great company believed
17. 4 as did a great many of the devout Greeks
21.40 when there was a great hush, he spoke
[24. 7 *"Lysias . . with great violence took him*‡
25.23 Agrippa and Bernice came with g. pomp
26.24 "your great learning is turning you mad
2 Cor 6. 4 through great endurance, in afflictions
7. 4 I have great confidence in you; I have great pride in you
8.22 because of his great confidence in you

Eph 2. 4 out of the great love with which he loved
1 Th 2. 2 in the face of great opposition
2.17 with great desire to see you face to face
1 Tim 3.13 gain . . great confidence in the faith
2 Tim 4.14 Alexander . . did me great harm
Jas 5.16 prayer of a righteous man has g. power
1 Pet 1. 3 By his great mercy we have been born
Rev 7. 9 I looked, and behold, a great multitude
19. 1 the loud voice of a great multitude
19. 6 the voice of a great multitude

IDIOMATICALLY
a. Lk 1.58 that the Lord had shown great mercy to her ὅτι ἐμεγάλυνεν κύριος τὸ ἔλεος αὐτοῦ [MEGALYNŌ]

CONTEXTUALLY
Lk [22.44 *his sweat became like g. drops of blood*‡[o]
Col 1.27 how g. among the Gentiles are the riches

GREAT, HOW

1. *how great, how small:* ἡλίκος HĒLIKOS
Jas 3. 5 How great a forest is set ablaze!
2. *how great:* πηλίκος PĒLIKOS
Heb 7. 4 See how great he is!
3. *how many, how much:* πόσος POSOS
Mt 6.23 "how great is the darkness!
4. *who? what?:* τίς TIS I
Col 1.27

GREAT, MAKE S.

1. *exalt, lift high:* ὑψόω HYPSOŌ
Acts 13.17 "God . . made the people great

GREAT MAN

1. *great man:* μεγιστάν MEGISTAN
Rev 6.15 the great men and the generals
18.23 "thy merchants were the great men

GREAT NUMBERS, IN

1. *more:* πλείων (pl.) PLEIŌN
Acts 28.23 they came to him . . in great numbers

GREAT, SO

1. *so large:* τηλικοῦτος TĒLIKOUTOS
Jas 3. 4 the ships also; though they are so great
Rev 16.18 so great was that earthquake
2. *so large, so many:* τοσοῦτος TOSOUTOS
Mt 15.33 "bread enough . . to feed so great a crowd?
Heb 12. 1 Surrounded by so g. a cloud of witnesses

GREAT, SUCH A

1. *so large:* τηλικοῦτος TĒLIKOUTOS
Heb 2. 3 if we neglect such a great salvation

GREAT, VERY

1. *greatest:* μέγιστος MEGISTOS*
2 Pet 1. 4 his precious and very great promises

GREAT WHILE, A

1. *very much:* λίαν LIAN
Mk 1.35 in the morning, a g. while before day

GREATER

1. *more, rather:* μᾶλλον MALLON
2 Cor 3. 8 Spirit . . attended with greater splendor?
2. *greater:* μείζων MEIZŌN
[a]μειζότερος
Mt 11.11 "there has risen no one greater than John . . ; yet he who is least in the kingdom . . is g. than he
12. 6 "something greater than the temple is here
23.17 "which is greater, the gold or the temple?
23.19 "which is greater, the gift or the altar?
Mk 12.31 "There is no other commandment g.
Lk 7.28 "none is greater than John; yet he who is least in the kingdom of God is greater
22.27 "which is the greater, one who sits?
Jn 1.50 "You shall see greater things than these
4.12 "Are you greater than our father Jacob?
5.20 "greater works than these will he show
5.36 "the testimony which I have is greater
8.53 "Are you g. than our father Abraham?
10.29 "My Father . . is greater than all‡
13.16 "a servant[d] is not g. than his master; nor . . who is sent greater than he who sent him
Jn 14.12 "greater works than these will he do
14.28 "for the Father is greater than I
15.13 "Greater love has no man than this
15.20 " 'servant[i] is not greater than his master
19.11 "he who delivered me . . has the greater sin
1 Cor 14. 5 He who prophesies is greater
Heb 6.13 he had no one greater by whom to swear
6.16 swear by a greater than themselves
9.11 through the greater and more perfect tent[p]
11.26 He considered abuse . . greater wealth
Jas 3. 1 shall be judged with greater strictness
2 Pet 2.11 angels, though greater in might and power
1 Jn 3.20 God is greater than our hearts
4. 4 he who is in you is greater
5. 9 the testimony of God is greater
3 Jn . 4 [a]No greater joy can I have than this
3. *more, greater:* περισσότερος PERISSOTEROS
Mt [23.14 "*you will receive the g. condemnation*‡
Mk 12.40 "will receive the greater condemnation
Lk 20.47 "will receive the greater condemnation
1 Cor 12.23 those . . we invest with the greater honor
12.23 unpresentable parts . . with g. modesty
12.24 the greater honor to the inferior part
4. *more:* πλείων PLEIŌN
Mt 12.41 "something greater than Jonah is here
12.42 "something greater than Solomon is here
Lk 11.31 "something greater than Solomon is here
11.32 "something greater than Jonah is here
Acts 15.28 "to lay upon you no greater burden

GREATER, FAR

1. *still more:* περισσοτέρως PERISSOTERŌS
2 Cor 11.23 far greater labors, far more imprisonments

GREATEST

1. *great:* μέγας MEGAS
Acts 8.10 all gave heed . . from the least to the g.
Heb 8.11 "all shall know . . from the least . . to the g.
2. *greater:* μείζων MEIZŌN
Mt 13.32 "it is the greatest of shrubs
18. 1 "Who is the greatest in the kingdom?
18. 4 "he is the greatest in the kingdom
23.11 "He who is greatest among you
Mk 4.32 "it . . becomes the greatest of all shrubs
9.34 discussed with one another who was the g.
Lk 9.46 argument . . as to which . . was the g.
22.24 which . . was to be regarded as the g.
22.26 "let the g. . . become as the youngest
1 Cor 13.13 but the greatest of these is love

GREATLY (*See also* AMAZED, BE GREATLY; DISTRESSED, BE GREATLY; ENLARGE GREATLY; TROUBLED, BE GREATLY)

1. *very much:* λίαν LIAN
Mt 27.14 the governor wondered greatly
2 Jn . 4 I rejoiced g. to find some . . following . . truth
3 Jn . 3 I greatly rejoiced when some . . arrived
2. *greatly:* μεγάλως MEGALŌS*
Phil 4.10 I rejoice in the Lord greatly
3. *abundance, surplus:* περισσεία PERISSEIA [B.1.a.1]
2 Cor 10.15 that . . our field . . may be greatly enlarged
4. *many, great:* πολύς (neut.) POLYS
Acts 18.27 he greatly helped those who . . had believed
5. *very, very much:* σφόδρα SPHODRA
Mt 17.23 And they were greatly distressed
18.31 "they were greatly distressed
19.25 they were greatly astonished
Acts 6. 7 disciples multiplied greatly in Jerusalem

IDIOMATICALLY
a. Jn 3.29 "the friend . . rejoices greatly ὁ . . φίλος . . χαρᾷ χαίρει [CHARA]
b. Rev 17.6 When I saw her I marveled greatly Καὶ ἐθαύμασα ἰδὼν αὐτὴν θαῦμα μέγα [MEGAS; THAUMA]

CONTEXTUALLY
2 Pet 2. 7 Lot, g. distressed by the licentiousness

GREATLY, HOW

1. *how great, how small:* ἡλίκος HĒLIKOS [A.3.b.1]
Col 2. 1 know how greatly I strive for you

GREATNESS
1. *magnitude, size:* μέγεθος MEGETHOS*
Eph 1.19 the immeasurable greatness of his power

GREECE: Ἑλλάς 'grēs II,D-3
Acts 20. 2 he came to Greece

GREED
1. *greediness:* πλεονεξία PLEONEXIA
1 Th 2. 5 we never used . . a cloak for greed
2 Pet 2. 3 in their greed they will exploit you
2.14 They have hearts trained in greed

GREED, GUILTY OF
1. *one who is greedy:* πλεονέκτης (pred.) PLEONEKTĒS
1 Cor 5.11 if he is guilty of immorality or greed

GREEDY
1. *greediness:* πλεονεξία PLEONEXIA [B.1.a.1]
Eph 4.19 greedy to practice . . uncleanness

GREEDY FOR GAIN
1. *greedy for dishonest gain:* αἰσχροκερδής AISCHROKERDĒS*
1 Tim 3. 8 Deacons likewise . . not greedy for gain
Tit 1. 7 bishop . . must not be . . greedy for gain

GREEDY, THE
1. *one who is greedy:* πλεονέκτης (pl.) PLEONEKTĒS
1 Cor 5.10 the greedy and robbers, or idolaters
6.10 nor thieves, nor the greedy

GREEK
1. *a Greek, a Gentile:* Ἕλλην
Jn 7.35 "Does he intend to go . . among the Greeks and teach the Greeks?
12.20 among those who went . . were some Greeks
Acts 11.20 some . . spoke to the Greeks[i] also‡
14. 1 great company . . of Jews and of Greeks
16. 1 Timothy . . his father was a Greek
16. 3 they all knew that his father was a Greek
17. 4 a great many of the devout Greeks
18. 4 argued . . and persuaded Jews and Greeks
19.10 all . . heard . . , both Jews and Greeks
19.17 known to all . . , both Jews and Greeks
20.21 "testifying both to Jews and to Greeks
21.28 "he also brought Greeks into the temple
Rom 1.14 I am under obligation both to Greeks
1.16 to the Jew first and also to the Greek
2. 9 the Jew first and also the Greek
2.10 the Jew first and also the Greek
3. 9 both Jews and Greeks, are under . . sin
10.12 no distinction between Jew and Greek
1 Cor 1.22 Jews demand signs and Greeks seek wisdom
1.24 who are called, both Jews and Greeks
10.32 Give no offense to Jews or to Greeks
12.13 into one body—Jews or Greeks
Gal 2. 3 even Titus, . . though he was a Greek
3.28 There is neither Jew nor Greek
Col 3.11 Here there cannot be Greek and Jew
2. *Greek:* Ἑλληνικός
Lk [23.38 an inscription over him, *in . . Greek*‡
Rev 9.11 in Greek he is called Apollyon[b]
3. *Greek, Gentile:* Ἑλληνίς
Mk 7.26 Now the woman was a Greek
Acts 17.12 not a few Greek women of high standing
4. *in the Greek language:* Ἑλληνιστί
Jn 19.20 written in Hebrew, in Latin, and in Greek
Acts 21.37 he said, "Do you know Greek?

GREEN
1. *yellowish green, pale:* χλωρός CHLŌROS
Mk 6.39 to sit down . . upon the green grass
Rev 8. 7 and all green grass was burnt up
9. 4 told not to harm . . any green growth
2. *moist, pliant:* ὑγρός HYGROS*
Lk 23.31 "if they do this when the wood is green

GREET
1. *greet:* ἀσπάζομαι ASPAZOMAI
Mk 9.15 ran up to him and greeted him
Lk 1.40 she entered . . and greeted Elizabeth
Acts 18.22 he went up and greeted the church
21. 7 we greeted the brethren and stayed
Acts 21.19 After greeting them, he related . . things
Rom 16. 3 Greet Prisca and Aquila
16. 5 Greet my beloved Epaenetus
16. 6 Greet Mary, who has worked hard
16. 7 Greet Andronicus and Junias
16. 8 Greet Ampliatus, my beloved
16. 9 Greet Urbanus, our fellow worker
16.10 Greet Apelles, who is approved in Christ. Greet . . the family of Aristobulus
16.11 Greet my kinsman Herodion. Greet . . the family of Narcissus
16.12 Greet those workers in the Lord
16.12 Greet the beloved Persis
16.13 Greet Rufus, eminent in the Lord
16.14 Greet Asyncritus, Phlegon, Hermes
16.15 Greet Philologus, Julia, Nereus
16.16 Greet one another with a holy kiss. All the churches of Christ greet you
16.21 Timothy, my fellow worker, greets you
16.22 I Tertius . . greet you in the Lord
16.23 Gaius, who is host to me . . greets you
16.23 Erastus . . and . . Quartus, greet you[b]
1 Cor 16.20 Greet one another with a holy kiss
2 Cor 13.12 Greet one another with a holy kiss
13.13(12) All the saints greet you
Phil 4.21 Greet every saint in Christ Jesus. The brethren who are with me greet you
4.22 All the saints greet you
Col 4.10 Aristarchus my fellow prisoner greets you
4.12 Epaphras . . greets you
4.14 Luke . . and Demas greet you
1 Th 5.26 Greet all the brethren with a holy kiss
2 Tim 4.19 Greet Prisca and Aquila
Tit 3.15 Greet those who love us in the faith
Heb 11.13 having seen it and greeted it from afar
13.24 Greet all your leaders and all the saints
1 Pet 5.14 Greet one another with the kiss of love
2 Jn .13 children of your elect sister greet you
3 Jn .15 The friends greet you. Greet the friends, every one of them
2. *speak a greeting:* λέγειν χαίρειν CHAIRŌ [A.6.a.4]
2 Jn .11 he who greets him shares his wicked work

GREETING
1. *greeting:* ἀσπασμός ASPASMOS
Lk 1.29 what sort of greeting this might be
1.41 when Elizabeth heard the greeting of Mary
1.44 when the voice of your greeting came
1 Cor 16.21 I, Paul, write this greeting
Col 4.18 I, Paul, write this greeting
2 Th 3.17 I, Paul, write this greeting
2. *rejoice:* χαίρω (pres. inf.) CHAIRŌ
Acts 15.23 to the brethren . . . , greeting
23.26 to his Excellency the governor Felix, g.
Jas 1. 1 To the twelve tribes . . : Greeting
2 Jn .10 do not . . give him any greeting

GREETINGS, GIVE ONE'S
GREETINGS, SEND
1. *greet:* ἀσπάζομαι ASPAZOMAI
1 Cor 16.19 The churches of Asia send greetings. Aquila and Prisca . . send you hearty g.
16.20 All the brethren send greetings
Col 4.15 Give my greetings to the brethren
2 Tim 4.21 Eubulus sends greetings to you
Tit 3.15 All who are with me send greetings
Phm .23 Epaphras . . sends greetings to you
Heb 13.24 Those . . from Italy send you greetings
1 Pet 5.13 She who is at Babylon . . sends you g.

GRIEF
1. *grief:* λύπη LYPĒ
2 Cor 7.10 godly grief produces a repentance . . but worldly grief produces death
2. *grieve, cause pain:* λυπέω (aor. pass. inf.) LYPEŌ
2 Cor 7.11 earnestness this godly grief has produced

GRIEF, FEEL
1. *grieve, cause pain:* λυπέω (pass.) LYPEŌ
2 Cor 7. 9 I rejoice . . for you felt a godly grief

GRIEVANCE
1. *thing, deed:* πρᾶγμα PRAGMA
1 Cor 6. 1 When one of you has a grievance

GRIEVE
1. *grieve, cause pain:* λυπέω LYPEŌ
Jn 21.17 Peter was grieved because he said to him
2 Cor 7. 8 for I see that that letter grieved you
7. 9 I rejoice, not because you were grieved, but .. were grieved into repenting
Eph 4.30 do not grieve the Holy Spirit
1 Th 4.13 that you may not grieve as others

GRIEVED
1. *hurt:* συλλυπέω (pass. part.) SYLLYPEŌ*
Mk 3. 5 grieved at their hardness of heart

GRIND
1. *grind:* ἀλήθω ALĒTHŌ*
Mt 24.41 "Two women will be grinding at the mill
Lk 17.35 "There will be two women grinding
2. *grind, gnash:* βρύχω BRYCHŌ*
Acts 7.54 they ground their teeth against him
3. *grind, gnash:* τρίζω TRIZŌ*
Mk 9.18 "he foams and grinds his teeth

GROAN
1. *groan, sigh:* στενάζω STENAZŌ
Rom 8.23 groan inwardly as we wait for adoption
2 Cor 5. 2 Here indeed we groan, and long

GROAN TOGETHER
1. *lament with:* συστενάζω SYSTENAZŌ*
Rom 8.22 creation has been groaning .. together

GROANING
1. *groaning, sighing:* στεναγμός STENAGMOS
Acts 7.34 "'I have surely .. heard their groaning

GROUND
1. *ground, pavement:* ἔδαφος EDAPHOS*
Acts 22. 7 "I fell to the ground and heard a voice
2. *earth, land:* γῆ GĒ
Mt 10.29 "not one of them will fall to the ground
15.35 the crowd to sit down on the ground
25.18 "went and dug in the ground
25.25 "'hid your talent in the ground
Mk 4.26 "if a man should scatter seed upon the g.
4.31 "mustard seed .. sown upon the ground
8. 6 the crowd to sit down on the ground
9.20 he fell on the ground and rolled about
14.35 he fell on the ground
Lk 6.49 "a man who built a house on the ground
13. 7 "'why should it use up the ground?
[22.44 *blood falling down upon the ground*‡
24. 5 bowed their faces to the ground
Jn 8. 6 wrote with his finger on the ground⌜‡
8. 8 wrote with his finger on the ground⌜‡
Acts 7.33 "'for the place .. is holy ground
9. 4 fell to the ground and heard a voice
9. 8 Saul arose from the ground
26.14 "when we had all fallen to the ground
3. *word, reckoning:* λόγος LOGOS
Mt 5.32 "except on the ground of unchastity
4. *found, establish:* θεμελιόω THEMELIOŌ
Eph 3.17 being rooted and grounded in love

GROUND, DASH TO THE
1. *dash to the ground:* ἐδαφίζω EDAPHIZŌ*
Lk 19.44 "⟨enemies will⟩ dash you to the ground

GROUND OF, ON THE
1. *because of:* διά (+acc.) DIA
1 Cor **10.**25, 27
2. *from, out of:* ἐκ (+gen.) EK
Rom **3.**30

GROUND, ON THE
GROUND, TO THE
1. *on the ground:* χαμαί CHAMAI
Jn 9. 6 he spat on the ground and made clay
18. 6 they drew back and fell to the ground

GROUND, ROCKY
1. *rocky, stony:* πετρώδης (subst. sg. or pl.) PETRŌDĒS*
Mt 13. 5 "Other seeds fell on rocky ground
13.20 "As for what was sown on rocky ground
Mk 4. 5 "Other seed fell on rocky ground
4.16 "the ones sown upon rocky ground

GROUND THAT, ON THE
1. *that, because:* ὅτι HOTI
1 Tim **6.**2

GROUP
IDIOMATICALLY
a. Mk 6.40 So they sat down in groups καὶ ἀνέπεσαν πρασιαὶ πρασιαί [PRASIA*]

GROW (*See also, e.g.,* COLD, GROW; DULL, GROW; OLD, GROW)
1. *increase, grow:* αὐξάνω (act. or pass.) AUXANŌ
Mt 6.28 "the lilies of the field, how they grow
13.32 "when it has grown it is the greatest
Lk 1.80 the child grew and became strong
2.40 the child grew and became strong
12.27 "Consider the lilies, how they grow‡
13.19 "mustard seed .. grew and became a tree
Acts 7.17 "the people grew and multiplied
12.24 the word of God grew and multiplied
19.20 So the word of the Lord grew
Eph 2.21 grows into a holy temple in the Lord
4.15 we are to grow up in every way into him
Col 1. 6 it is bearing fruit and growing
2.19 grows with a growth that is from God
1 Pet 2. 2 that .. you may grow up to salvation
2 Pet 3.18 But grow in the grace .. of our Lord
2. *come, go:* ἔρχομαι ERCHOMAI [A.6.a.4, 5]
Mk 5.26 who .. was no better but rather grew worse
3. *lengthen:* μηκύνω (pass.) MĒKYNŌ*
Mk 4.27 "the seed should sprout and grow
4. *bring forth, spring up:* φύω (pass.) PHYŌ
Lk 8. 8 "some fell into good soil and grew
IDIOMATICALLY
a. Mk 6.35 when it grew late ἤδη ὥρας πολλῆς γενομένης [GINOMAI]

GROW ABUNDANTLY
1. *increase exceedingly:* ὑπεραυξάνω HYPERAUXANŌ*
2 Th 1. 3 your faith is growing abundantly

GROW TOGETHER
1. *increase along with:* συναυξάνω (pass.) SYNAUXANŌ*
Mt 13.30 "'Let both grow together until the harvest

GROW UP
1. *go up, come up:* ἀναβαίνω ANABAINŌ
Mt 13. 7 "the thorns grew up and choked them
Mk 4. 7 "the thorns grew up and choked it
4. 8 "growing up and increasing and yielding
4.32 "yet when it is sown it grows up
2. *bring forth, spring up:* φύω (pass.) PHYŌ
Lk 8. 6 "some fell on the rock; and as it grew up

GROW VERY SHORT
1. *draw together, shorten:* συστέλλω (pass.) SYSTELLŌ
1 Cor 7.29 the appointed time has grown very short

GROW WITH
1. *grow together:* συμφύω (pass.) SYMPHYŌ*
Lk 8. 7 "the thorns grew with it and choked it

GROWN UP
1. *great:* μέγας MEGAS
Heb 11.24 "Moses, when he was grown up, refused

GROWTH
1. *growth:* αὔξησις AUXĒSIS*
Eph 4.16 makes bodily growth and upbuilds itself
Col 2.19 grows with a growth that is from God
CONTEXTUALLY
Rev 9. 4 were told not to harm .. any green growth

GROWTH, GIVE
1. *grow, increase:* αὐξάνω AUXANŌ
1 Cor 3. 6 I planted .. but God gave the growth
3. 7 only God who gives the growth

GROWTH, RANK
1. *abundance, surplus:* περισσεία PERISSEIA
Jas 1.21 put away .. rank growth of wickedness

GRUDGE AGAINST, HAVE A
1. *hold within, be hostile:* ἐνέχω ENECHŌ
Mk 6.19 Herodias had a grudge against him

GRUMBLE
1. *grumble, murmur:* γογγύζω GOGGYZŌ
Mt 20.11 "they grumbled at the householder
1 Cor 10.10 nor grumble, as some of them did
2. *groan, sigh:* στενάζω STENAZŌ
Jas 5. 9 Do not grumble, brethren

GRUMBLER
1. *grumbler, murmurer:* γογγυστής GOGGYSTĒS*
Jude .16 These are grumblers, malcontents

GRUMBLING
1. *grumbling, muttering:* γογγυσμός GOGGYSMOS
Phil 2.14 Do all things without grumbling

GUARANTEE
1. *pledge, deposit:* ἀρραβών ARRABŌN*
2 Cor 1.22 his Spirit in our hearts as a guarantee
5. 5 who has given us the Spirit as a guarantee
Eph 1.14 the guarantee of our inheritance

GUARANTEED
1. *firm, steady:* βέβαιος BEBAIOS
Rom 4.16 guaranteed to all his descendants

GUARD
1. *watch closely:* διαφυλάσσω DIAPHYLASSŌ*
Lk 4.10 " 'He will give his angels . . to guard you
2. *servant, helper:* ὑπηρέτης HYPĒRETĒS
Mt 5.25 "lest . . the judge ⟨hand you over⟩ to the g.
26.58 he sat with the guards to see the end
Mk 14.54 Peter . . was sitting with the guards
14.65 the guards received him with blows
3. *guard* (Lat.): κουστωδία KOUSTŌDIA*
Mt 27.65 "You have a guard[o] of soldiers; go
27.66 sealing the stone and setting a guard
28.11 some of the guard went into the city
4. *guard, keep:* φρουρέω PHROUREŌ
2 Cor 11.32 the governor . . guarded . . Damascus
1 Pet 1. 5 by God's power . . guarded through faith
5. *watch, guard, prison:* φυλακή PHYLAKĒ
Acts 12.10 When they had passed the first . . guard
6. *guard, observe:* φυλάσσω PHYLASSŌ
Lk 11.21 "When a strong man . . guards his . . palace
Jn 17.12 "I have guarded them, and none . . is lost
Acts 12. 4 four squads of soldiers to guard him
23.35 he commanded him to be guarded
28.16 by himself, with the soldier that guarded
2 Th 3. 3 he will strengthen you and guard you
1 Tim 6.20 guard what has been entrusted to you
2 Tim 1.12 he is able to guard until that Day
1.14 guard the truth that has been entrusted
7. *keep, observe:* τηρέω TĒREŌ
[a]subst. part.
Mt 28. 4 [a]for fear of him the guards trembled
Acts 12. 6 sentries before the door were guarding

GUARD, KEEP UNDER
1. *guard, observe:* φυλάσσω PHYLASSŌ
Lk 8.29 (he was kept under guard, and bound

GUARD, PRAETORIAN
1. *praetorium, praetorian guard:* πραιτώριον PRAITŌRION
Phil 1.13 known throughout the whole p. guard[c]†

GUARD, SOLDIER OF THE
1. *one of the imperial bodyguard* (Lat.): σπεκουλάτωρ SPEKOULATŌR*
Mk 6.27 the king sent a soldier of the guard

GUARD, UNDER
1. *safely, with certainty:* ἀσφαλῶς ASPHALŌS
Mk 14.44 "seize him and lead him away under guard[o]

GUARDIAN
1. *overseer, guardian:* ἐπίσκοπος EPISKOPOS
1 Pet 2.25 Shepherd and Guardian of your souls
2. *steward, manager:* ἐπίτροπος EPITROPOS
Gal 4. 2 he is under guardians and trustees

GUEST (*See also* WEDDING GUEST)
1. *recline* (at table): ἀνάκειμαι (subst.) ANAKEIMAI
Mt 22.10 "wedding hall was filled with guests
22.11 the king came in to look at the guests
Mk 6.26 because of his oaths and his guests
2. *recline with* (at table): συνανάκειμαι (subst. part.) SYNANAKEIMAI
Mt 14. 9 because of his oaths and his guests
Mk 6.22 she pleased Herod and his guests
IDIOMATICALLY
a. Acts 10.23 So he called them in to be his guests
εἰσκαλεσάμενος οὖν αὐτοὺς ἐξένισεν [XENIZŌ]

GUEST, BE THE
1. *lodge, be the guest:* καταλύω KATALYŌ
Lk 19. 7 "to be the guest of a man who is a sinner
2. *bring together:* συνάγω (pass.) SYNAGŌ
Acts [11.26 they *were guests of* the church†

GUEST ROOM
1. *guest lodging:* κατάλυμα KATALYMA
Mk 14.14 " 'Where is my guest room?
Lk 22.11 " 'Where is the guest room?
2. *hospitality, guest room:* ξενία XENIA
Phm .22 prepare a guest room for me

GUEST, WEDDING
1. *son of the bridal chamber:* υἱὸς τοῦ νυμφῶνος NYMPHŌN [C.5]
Mt 9.15 "Can the wedding guests mourn?
Mk 2.19 "Can the wedding guests fast?
Lk 5.34 "Can you make wedding guests fast?

GUIDE
1. *guide:* ὁδηγέω HODĒGEŌ
Jn 16.13 "he will guide you into all the truth
Acts 8.31 "How can I, unless some one guides me?
Rev 7.17 "he will guide them to springs
2. *guide, leader:* ὁδηγός HODĒGOS*
Mt 15.14 "Let them alone; they are blind guides
23.16 "Woe to you, blind guides
23.24 "You blind guides, straining out a gnat!
Acts 1.16 "Judas who was guide to those who arrested
Rom 2.19 sure that you are a guide to the blind
3. *direct, guide:* κατευθύνω KATEUTHYNŌ
Lk 1.79 "to guide our feet into the way
4. *escort, guide:* μετάγω METAGŌ*
Jas 3. 3 we guide their whole bodies
3. 4 guided by a very small rudder
5. *boy's attendant, leader:* παιδαγωγός PAIDAGŌGOS
1 Cor 4.15 you have countless guides in Christ

GUILE
1. *cunning:* δόλος DOLOS
Jn 1.47 "an Israelite . . in whom is no guile!
2 Cor 12.16 you say ⟨I⟩ got the better of you by guile
1 Th 2. 3 nor is it made with guile
1 Pet 2. 1 So put away all malice and all guile
2.22 no guile was found on his lips
3.10 "keep . . his lips from speaking guile

GUILELESS
1. *pure:* ἀκέραιος AKERAIOS
Rom 16.19 guileless as to what is evil

GUILT
1. *sin, failure, guilt:* ἁμαρτία HAMARTIA
Jn 9.41 "If you were blind, you would have no g.
9.41 "you say, 'We see,' your guilt remains

GUILTLESS
1. *without guilt:* ἀναίτιος ANAITIOS*
Mt 12. 5 "profane the sabbath, and are guiltless
12. 7 "you would not have condemned the g.
2. *blameless:* ἀνέγκλητος ANEGKLĒTOS
1 Cor 1. 8 guiltless in the day of our Lord
3. *pure:* ἁγνός HAGNOS
2 Cor 7.11 you have proved yourselves guiltless

GUILTY (*See also* GREED, GUILTY OF; IMMORALITY, GUILTY OF)
1. *liable, guilty:* ἔνοχος ENOCHOS
Mk 3.29 "but is guilty of an eternal sin
1 Cor 11.27 guilty of profaning the body and blood
Jas 2.10 whoever . . fails . . has become guilty of all

IDIOMATICALLY
a. Lk 23.14 "I did not find this man guilty of any of your charges against him ἐγὼ . . οὐθὲν εὗρον ἐν τῷ ἀνθρώπῳ τούτῳ αἴτιον ὧν κατηγορεῖτε κατ' αὐτοῦ [AITIOS]

GUILTY OF, BE
1. *do, make:* ποιέω POIEŌ
1 Jn 3. 4 who commits sin is guilty of lawlessness

GUSH OUT
1. *pour out:* ἐκχέω (pass.) EKCHEŌ
Acts 1.18 "(all his bowels gushed out

H

HABIT
1. *custom, habit:* ἔθος ETHOS
Heb 10.25 neglecting to meet . . is the habit of some

HABITATION
1. *farm, residence:* ἔπαυλις EPAULIS*
Acts 1.20 " 'Let his habitation become desolate
2. *dwelling place:* κατοικία KATOIKIA*
Acts 17.26 "the boundaries of their habitation
3. *tent, booth:* σκηνή SKĒNĒ
Lk 16. 9 "receive . . into the eternal habitations
4. *tent, habitation:* σκήνωμα SKĒNŌMA
Acts 7.46 "to find a habitation for the God of Jacob

HADES
1. *underworld:* ᾅδης HADĒS
Mt 11.23 "You shall be brought down to Hades
Lk 10.15 "You shall be brought down to Hades
16.23 "in Hades, being in torment
Acts 2.27 " 'thou wilt not abandon my soul to H.
2.31 "Christ . . was not abandoned to Hades
Rev 1.18 "I have the keys of Death and Hades
6. 8 a pale horse . . and Hades followed him
20.13 Death and Hades gave up the dead
20.14 Then Death and Hades were thrown

HAGAR: Ἁγαρ 'hā,gär
Gal 4.24 One . . bearing children for slavery; . . is H.
4.25 Now H. is Mount Sinai in Arabia[i]‡

HAIL
1. *rejoice:* χαίρω (imper.) CHAIRŌ
Mt 26.49 "Hail, Master!"[i] And he kissed him
27.29 "Hail, King of the Jews!
28. 9 Jesus met them and said, "Hail!
Mk 15.18 "Hail, King of the Jews!
Lk 1.28 "Hail, O favored . . , the Lord is with you![c]
Jn 19. 3 "Hail, King of the Jews!
2. *hail:* χάλαζα CHALAZA
Rev 8. 7 there followed hail and fire
11.19 an earthquake, and heavy hail
16.21 till men cursed God for . . the hail

HAILSTONE
1. *hail:* χάλαζα CHALAZA
Rev 16.21 hailstones, heavy as a hundredweight

HAIR (*See also* BRAIDED HAIR)
1 *head:* κεφαλή KEPHALĒ [C.2]
Acts 18.18 he cut his hair, for he had a vow
2. *hair of the head:* κόμη KOMĒ*
1 Cor 11.15 her hair is given to her for a covering
3. *hair:* θρίξ THRIX*
Mt 3. 4 John wore a garment of camel's hair
5.36 "you cannot make one hair white or black
10.30 "the hairs of your head are all numbered
Mk 1. 6 John was clothed with camel's hair
Lk 7.38 wiped them with the hair of her head
7.44 "she has . . wiped them with her hair
12. 7 "the hairs of your head are all numbered
21.18 "But not a hair of your head will perish
Jn 11. 2 Mary . . wiped his feet with her hair
12. 3 Mary . . wiped his feet with her hair
Acts 27.34 "not a hair is to perish from . . any
1 Pet 3. 3 Let not yours be the . . braiding of hair
Rev 1.14 his head and his hair were white
9. 8 their hair like women's hair, and their teeth like lions' teeth

HAIR, CUT OFF ONE'S
1. *cut short, clip:* κείρω (mid.) KEIRŌ
1 Cor 11. 6 then she should cut off her hair

HAIR, HAVE LONG
HAIR, WEAR LONG
1. *let the hair grow long:* κομάω KOMAŌ
1 Cor 11.14 for a man to wear long hair is degrading
11.15 if a woman has long hair, it is her pride

HALF
1 *half:* ἥμισυς HĒMISYS*
Mk 6.23 "I will give . . even half of my kingdom
Lk 19. 8 "the half of my goods I give to the poor
Rev 11. 9 For three days and a half
11.11 after the three and a half days
12.14 a time, and times, and half a time

HALF AN HOUR
1. *half hour:* ἡμίωρον HĒMIŌRON*
Rev 8. 1 silence in heaven for about h. an hour

HALF DEAD
1. *half dead:* ἡμιθανής HĒMITHANĒS*
Lk 10.30 "robbers . . departed, leaving him half dead

HALF-SHEKEL TAX
1. *double drachma:* δίδραχμον DIDRACHMON
Mt 17.24 the collectors of the half-shekel tax

HALL
1. *leisure, school:* σχολή SCHOLĒ*
Acts 19. 9 argued daily in the hall of Tyrannus[r]

HALL, AUDIENCE
1. *audience room:* ἀκροατήριον AKROATĒRION*
Acts 25.23 Agrippa and Bernice . . entered the a. hall

HALL, WEDDING
1. *bridal chamber:* νυμφών NYMPHŌN
Mt 22.10 "wedding hall was filled with guests

HALLELUJAH
1. *praise the Lord* (Heb.): ἀλληλουϊά HALLĒLOUIA*
Rev 19. 1 "H.! Salvation and glory and power
19. 3 Once more they cried, "Hallelujah!
19. 4 twenty-four elders . . saying, "Amen. H.!
19. 6 "Hallelujah! For the Lord . . reigns

HALLOW
1. *make sacred:* ἁγιάζω HAGIAZŌ
Mt 6. 9 "Hallowed be thy name
Lk 11. 2 "Father, hallowed be thy name

HAMOR: Ἑμμώρ 'hāmȯr
Acts 7.16 "from the sons of Hamor in Shechem

HAND (*See also* AT S.'S HANDS; AT THE HANDS OF; STRIKE WITH ONE'S HAND)
1. *hand, arm:* χείρ CHEIR
Mt 3.12 "His winnowing fork is in his hand
4. 6 " 'On their hands they will bear you up
5.30 "if your right hand causes you to sin
8. 3 he stretched out his hand and touched
8.15 he touched her hand, and the fever left
9.18 "come and lay your hand on her
9.25 he went in and took her by the hand
12.10 there was a man with a withered hand
12.13 he said to the man, "Stretch out your h.
12.49 stretching out his h. toward . . disciples
14.31 Jesus immediately reached out his hand
15. 2 "For they do not wash their hands
15.20 "to eat with unwashed hands
17.22 "to be delivered into the hands of men
18. 8 "if your hand or your foot causes you to sin[z]
18. 8 "better . . to enter life . . than . . two hands
19.13 that he might lay his hands on them
19.15 And he laid his hands on them
22.13 " 'Bind him hand and foot, and cast him
26.23 "He who has dipped his hand in the dish
26.45 "betrayed into the hands of sinners
26.50 Then they . . laid hands on Jesus

Mt 26.51 stretched out his hand and drew his sword
27.24 P... washed his hands before the crowd
Mk 1.31 he came and took her by the hand
1.41 he stretched out his hand and touched
3. 1 man.. who had a withered hand
3. 3 the man who had the withered hand
3. 5 "Stretch out your hand." .. and his hand was restored
5.23 "Come and lay your hands on her
5.41 Taking her by the hand
6. 2 "mighty works are wrought by his hands!
6. 5 he laid his hands upon a few sick people
7. 2 his disciples ate with hands defiled
7. 3 (do not eat unless they wash their hands[v]
7. 5 "disciples.. eat with hands defiled
7.32 besought him to lay his hand upon him
8.23 "he took the blind man by the hand
8.23 "when he had.. laid his hands upon him
8.25 again he laid his hands upon his eyes
9.27 But Jesus took him by the hand
9.31 "delivered into the hands of men
9.43 "if your hand causes you to sin[l]
9.43 "better.. to enter life.. than.. two hands
10.16 blessed them, laying his hands upon them
14.41 "betrayed into the hands of sinners
14.46 they laid hands on him and seized him
16.18 "they will lay their hands on the sick[k]‡
Lk 1.66 For the hand of the Lord was with him
1.71 "from the hand of all who hate us
1.74 "delivered from the hand of our enemies
3.17 "His winnowing fork is in his hand
4.11 " 'On their hands they will bear you up
4.40 he laid his hands on every one
5.13 he stretched out his hand, and touched
6. 1 heads of grain, rubbing them in their hands
6. 6 man.. whose right hand was withered
6. 8 the man who had the withered hand
6.10 "Stretch out your hand." And he did so, and his hand was restored
8.54 taking her by the hand he called
9.44 "delivered into the hands of men
9.62 "one who puts his hand to the plow
13.13 he laid his hands upon her
15.22 " 'put a ring on his hand
20.19 chief priests tried to lay hands on him
21.12 "they will lay their hands on you
22.21 "the hand of him who betrays me
22.53 "you did not lay hands on me
23.46 "into thy hands I commit my spirit!
24. 7 "delivered into the hands of sinful men
24.39 "See my hands and my feet
[24.40 *he showed them his hands and his feet*‡
24.50 lifting up his hands he blessed them
Jn 3.35 has given all things into his hand
7.30 no one laid hands on him
7.44 but no one laid hands on him
10.28 "no one shall snatch them out of my h.
10.29 "to snatch them out of the Father's hand
10.39 but he escaped from their hands
11.44 "his hands and feet bound with bandages
13. 3 had given all things into his hands
13. 9 "not my feet only but also my hands!
20.20 he showed them his hands and his side
20.25 "Unless I see in his hands the print.. and place my hand in his side
20.27 "Put your finger here, and see my hands; and put out your hand.. in my side
21.18 "you will stretch out your hands
Acts 2.23 "killed by the hands of lawless men
3. 7 he took him by the right hand
4.28 "whatever thy hand.. predestined
4.30 "thou stretchest out thy hand to heal
5.12 "signs.. done.. by the hands of the apostles
6. 6 prayed and laid their hands upon them
7.25 "giving them deliverance by his hand
7.35 "deliverer by the hand of the angel
7.41 "they.. rejoiced in the works of their hands

Acts 7.50 " 'Did not my hand make all these?
8.17 Then they laid their hands on them
8.18 the laying on of the apostles' hands
8.19 "that any one on whom I lay my hands
9.12 "seen.. Ananias.. lay his hands on him
9.17 laying his hands on him.. "Brother Saul
9.41 he gave her his hand and lifted her up
11.21 the hand of the Lord was with them
11.30 sending.. by the hand of Barnabas and Saul
12. 1 Herod.. laid violent hands upon some
12. 7 And the chains fell off his hands
12.11 "Lord.. rescued me from the h. of Herod
12.17 motioning.. with his hand to be silent
13. 3 laid their hands on them.. sent them off
13.11 "the hand of the Lord is upon you
13.16 Paul stood up, and motioning with his h.
14. 3 wonders to be done by their hands
17.25 "nor is he served by human hands
19. 6 Paul had laid his hands upon them
19.11 God did.. miracles by the hands of Paul
19.26 "that gods made with hands are not gods
19.33 Alexander motioned with his hand
20.34 "these hands ministered to my necessities
21.11 bound his own feet and hands
21.11 " 'deliver.. into the hands of the Gentiles
21.27 Jews from Asia.. laid hands on him
21.40 Paul.. motioned with his hand
23.19 The tribune took him by the hand
[24. 7 *Lysias.. took him out of our hands*‡
26. 1 Paul stretched out his hand
28. 3 a viper.. fastened on his hand
28. 4 saw the creature hanging from his hand
28. 8 Paul.. putting his hands on him healed him
28.17 "delivered.. into the hands of the Romans
Rom 10.21 "All day long I have held out my hands
1 Cor 4.12 working with our own hands
12.15 "Because I am not a hand
12.21 The eye cannot say to the hand
16.21 I, Paul, write.. with my own hand
2 Cor 11.33 I was let down.. and escaped his hands
Gal 6.11 writing to you with my own hand
Eph 4.28 doing honest work with his hands
Col 4.18 I, Paul, write.. with my own hand
1 Th 4.11 to work with your hands
2 Th 3.17 I, Paul, write.. with my own hand
1 Tim 2. 8 lifting holy hands without anger
4.14 the council.. laid their hands upon you
5.22 not.. hasty in the laying on of hands
2 Tim 1. 6 gift.. through the laying on of my hands
Phm .19 I, Paul, write this with my own hand
Heb 1.10 "heavens are the work of thy hands
2. 7 *"didst set him over the works of thy hands*‡
6. 2 ablutions, the laying on of hands
8. 9 "the day when I took them by the hand
10.31 to fall into the hands of the living God
12.12 Therefore lift your drooping hands
Jas 4. 8 Cleanse your hands, you sinners
1 Pet 5. 6 Humble.. under the mighty hand of God
1 Jn 1. 1 looked upon and touched with our hands
Rev 1.16 in his right hand he held seven stars
6. 5 its rider had a balance in his hand
7. 9 with palm branches in their hands
8. 4 from the hand of the angel before God
9.20 not repent of the works of their hands
10. 2 He had a little scroll open in his hand
10. 5 angel.. lifted up his right hand to heaven
10. 8 "scroll.. in the hand of the angel
10.10 little scroll from the hand of the angel
13.16 marked on the right hand or the forehead
14. 9 "receives a mark.. on his hand
14.14 with.. a sharp sickle in his hand
17. 4 holding in her hand a golden cup
20. 1 in his hand the key of the.. pit
20. 4 not received its mark on.. their hands

CONTEXTUALLY
Mt 17.12 "the Son of man will suffer at their hands
1 Cor 14. 3 On the other hand, he.. speaks to men

2 Cor 11.24 I have received at the hands of the Jews
Rev 15. 2 with harps of God in their hands

HAND, AT

1. *near, at hand:* ἐγγύς EGGYS
Mt 26.18 " 'Teacher says, My time is at hand
Jn 2.13 The Passover of the Jews was at hand
6. 4 the feast of the Jews, was at hand
7. 2 feast of Tabernacles was at hand
11.55 the Passover of the Jews was at hand
19.42 as the tomb was close at hand
Phil 4. 5 The Lord is at hand

HAND, BE AT

1. *approach:* ἐγγίζω (perf.) EGGIZŌ
Mt 3. 2 "Repent . . kingdom of heaven is at h.
4.17 "Repent . . kingdom of heaven is at h.
10. 7 " 'The kingdom of heaven is at hand
26.45 "Behold, the hour is at hand
26.46 "see, my betrayer is at hand
Mk 1.15 "the kingdom of God is at hand
14.42 "see, my betrayer is at hand
Lk 21. 8 " 'The time is at hand!
Rom 13.12 night is far gone, the day is at hand
Jas 5. 8 for the coming of the Lord is at hand
1 Pet 4. 7 The end of all things is at hand

HAND, LEAD BY THE

1. *lead by the hand:* χειραγωγέω CHEIRAGŌGEŌ*
Acts 9. 8 so they led him by the hand
22.11 "I was led by the hand . . into Damascus

HAND, LEFT

1. *left:* ἀριστερός ARISTEROS [B.3.b.2]
[a]ἐξ ἀριστερῶν
Mt 6. 3 "do not let your left hand know
Mk 10.37 [a]"Grant us to sit, . . one at your left ⟨hand⟩
2 Cor 6. 7 weapons of righteousness . . for the left ⟨hand⟩
2. *left:* εὐώνυμος EUŌNYMOS [B.3.b.2]
Always ἐξ εὐωνύμων
Mt 20.21 "may sit, . . one at your left ⟨hand⟩
20.23 "to sit . . at my left ⟨hand⟩ is not mine
25.33 "he will place . . the goats at the left ⟨hand⟩
25.41 "he will say to those at his left hand
Mk 10.40 "to sit . . at my left ⟨hand⟩ is not mine

HAND, LIE AT

1. *lie beside:* παράκειμαι PARAKEIMAI
Rom 7.21 a law that . . evil lies close at hand

HAND ON
HAND OVER

1. *give up, allow:* παραδίδωμι PARADIDŌMI
Mt 5.25 "lest your accuser hand you over
Mk 7.13 "your tradition which you hand on
Lk 12.58 "lest . . the judge h. you over to the officer
Jn 18.30 "we would not have handed him over
18.35 "priests have handed you over to me
18.36 "that I might not be handed over
19.16 Then he handed him over to them

HAND, ON THE ONE
HAND, ON THE OTHER

1. (correlative particles): . . μὲν . . δέ MEN
Heb 7.18 On the one h. . . commandment is set aside
7.19 on the other hand . . hope is introduced

HAND, PEOPLE TO LEAD S. BY THE

1. *leader, guide:* χειραγωγός (pl.) CHEIRAGŌGOS*
Acts 13.11 seeking people to lead him by the hand

HAND, RIGHT

1. *right:* δεξιός DEXIOS [B.3.b.2]
[a]ἐκ δεξιῶν
Mt 6. 3 "not . . know what your right hand is doing
20.21 [a]"sons . . may sit, one at your right hand
20.23 [a]"to sit at my right hand and at my left
22.44 [a]" 'Sit at my right hand, till I put
25.33 [a]"he will place the sheep at his r. hand
25.34 [a]"to those at his right hand, 'Come
26.64 [a]"seated at the right hand of Power
27.29 they . . put a reed in his right hand
Mk 10.37 [a]"Grant us to sit, one at your right hand
10.40 [a]"to sit at my right hand or at my left
12.36 [a]" 'The Lord said . . Sit at my right hand
14.62 [a]"sitting at the right hand of Power
16.19 [a]Lord Jesus . . sat . . at the right hand[k]‡
Lk 20.42 [a]" 'The Lord said . . Sit at my right hand
22.69 [a]"seated at the right hand of the power
Acts 2.25 [a]" 'for he is at my right hand
2.33 [a]"exalted at the right hand of God
2.34 [a]" 'The Lord said . . Sit at my right hand
5.31 "God exalted him at his right hand
7.55 [a]Jesus standing at the right hand of God
7.56 [a]"Son of man standing at the right hand
Rom 8.34 who is at the right hand of God
2 Cor 6. 7 for the right hand and for the left
Gal 2. 9 gave to me . . right hand of fellowship
Eph 1.20 made him sit at his right hand
Col 3. 1 where Christ is, seated at the right h.
Heb 1. 3 he sat down at the right hand
1.13 [a]"Sit at my right hand
8. 1 seated at the right hand of the throne
10.12 he sat down at the right hand of God
12. 2 at the right hand of the throne of God
1 Pet 3.22 at the right hand of God, with angels
Rev 1.17 But he laid his right hand upon me
1.20 "stars which you saw in my right hand
2. 1 " 'who holds the seven stars in his right h.
5. 1 in the right hand of him . . on the throne
5. 7 took the scroll from the right hand

HAND, WITH ONE'S OWN

1. *with one's own hand:* αὐτόχειρ AUTOCHEIR*
Acts 27.19 cast out with their own hands the tackle

HANDKERCHIEF

1. *napkin, towel:* σουδάριον SOUDARION
Acts 19.12 handkerchiefs . . were carried away

HANDLE

1. *kindle; touch* (mid.): ἅπτω (mid.) HAPTŌ
Col 2.21 "Do not handle, Do not taste
2. *grope after, feel:* ψηλαφάω PSĒLAPHAŌ
Lk 24.39 "it is I myself; handle me, and see

HANDLE, RIGHTLY

1. *cut in a straight line:* ὀρθοτομέω ORTHOTOMEŌ*
2 Tim 2.15 rightly handling the word of truth

HANDMAID
HANDMAIDEN

1. *bondwoman, female slave:* δούλη DOULĒ
Lk 1.38 "Behold, I am the handmaid of the Lord
1.48 "the low estate of his handmaiden

HANDS, MADE BY
HANDS, MADE WITH

1. *made by hands:* χειροποίητος CHEIROPOIĒTOS
Mk 14.58 " 'this temple that is made with hands
Acts 7.48 "does not dwell in houses made with hands
Eph 2.11 which is made in the flesh by hands
Heb 9.11 perfect tent[p] (not made with hands
9.24 a sanctuary made with hands

HANDS, MADE WITHOUT
HANDS, NOT MADE WITH

1. *not made by hands:* ἀχειροποίητος ACHEIROPOIĒTOS*
Mk 14.58 " 'I will build another, not made with hands
2 Cor 5. 1 a house not made with hands, eternal
Col 2.11 a circumcision made without hands

HANG

1. *hang up:* κρεμάννυμι (act. or mid.) KREMANNYMI
Lk 23.39 One of the criminals who were hanged
Acts 5.30 "Jesus whom you killed by hanging
10.39 "They put him to death by hanging
28. 4 saw the creature hanging from his hand
Gal 3.13 "Cursed be every one who hangs on a tree

HANG ONESELF

1. *strangle, throttle:* ἀπάγχω (mid.) APAGCHŌ*
Mt 27. 5 he went and hanged himself

HANG UPON

1. *hang upon:* ἐκκρεμάννυμι (mid.) EKKREMANNYMI*
Lk 19.48 all the people hung upon his words

HAPPEN
1. *be:* εἰμί EIMI
Mt 16.22 "This shall never happen to you
2. *come to be, happen, be:* γίνομαι GINOMAI
Mk 5.14 to see what it was that had happened
5.16 told what had happened to the demoniac
13.18 "Pray that it may not happen in winter
Lk 2.15 "Let us . . see this thing that has happened
8.34 the herdsmen saw what had happened
8.35 people went out to see what had happened
8.56 to tell no one what had happened
9.18 Now it happened that as he was praying
12.54 " 'A shower is coming'; and so it happens
12.55 " 'There will be . . heat'; and it happens
23.31 "what will happen when it is dry?
[24.12 *he went . . wondering at what had happened*‡
24.18 the things that have happened there
24.21 "it is . . the third day since this happened
Acts 4.21 all . . praised God for what had happened
5. 7 his wife . . not knowing what had happened
10.16 This happened three times
11.10 "This happened three times
28. 8 It happened that the father . . lay sick
3. *happen:* συμβαίνω SYMBAINŌ
Mk 10.32 began to tell them what was to happen
Lk 24.14 about all these things that had happened
Acts 3.10 amazement at what had happened
1 Cor 10.11 Now these things happened to them
1 Pet 4.12 though something strange were happening
2 Pet 2.22 happened . . according to the true proverb
CONTEXTUALLY
Mt 8.33 what had happened to the demoniacs
Lk 24.35 they told what had happened on the road

HAPPIER
1. *blessed, happy:* μακάριος (comp.) MAKARIOS
1 Cor 7.40 she is happier if she remains as she is

HAPPY
1. *blessed, happy:* μακάριος MAKARIOS
Rom 14.22 happy is he who has no reason to judge

HAPPY, CALL
1. *bless, call happy:* μακαρίζω MAKARIZŌ
Jas 5.11 we call those happy who were steadfast

HARAN: Χαρράν 'herən
Acts 7. 2 "Abraham, . . before he lived in Haran
7. 4 "he departed . . and lived in Haran

HARASS
1. *slap, buffet:* κολαφίζω KOLAPHIZŌ
2 Cor 12. 7 a messenger of Satan, to harass me
2. *trouble, annoy:* σκύλλω SKYLLŌ
Mt 9.36 because they were harassed and helpless

HARBOR
1. *harbor, haven:* λιμήν LIMĒN
Acts 27.12 because the harbor was not suitable
27.12 reach Phoenix, a harbor of Crete

HARD
1. *fearfully, terribly:* δεινῶς DEINŌS
Lk 11.53 Pharisees began to press him hard
2. *hard to please, troublesome:* δύσκολος DYSKOLOS*
Mk 10.24 "how hard it is[r] to enter the kingdom!
3. *hardly, with difficulty:* δυσκόλως DYSKOLŌS* [A.4.a]
Mt 19.23 "hard for a rich man to enter the kingdom
Mk 10.23 "How hard . . for those who have riches!
Lk 18.24 "How hard it is for those who have riches!
4. *many, great:* πολύς POLYS
[a]neut. pl. [b]ἔχει πολὺν πόνον
Rom 16. 6 [a]Mary, who has worked hard among you
16.12 [a]Persis, who has worked hard in the Lord
Col 4.13 [b]he has worked hard for you
Heb 10.32 when . . you endured a hard struggle
5. *austere, cruel:* σκληρός SKLĒROS
Mt 25.24 " 'Master, I knew you to be a hard man
Jn 6.60 "a hard saying; who can listen to it?
6. *hardness, austerity:* σκληρότης SKLĒROTĒS* [A.1.b.3]
Rom 2. 5 by your hard and impenitent heart
7. *squeeze, oppress:* θλίβω (perf. pass. part.) THLIBŌ
Mt 7.14 "the way is hard, that leads to life

HARD PRESSED, BE
1. *hold together, impel:* συνέχω (pass.) SYNECHŌ
Phil 1.23 I am hard pressed between the two

HARD TO BEAR
1. *intolerable:* δυσβάστακτος DYSBASTAKTOS*
Mt 23. 4 "They bind heavy burdens, hard to bear[u]‡
Lk 11.46 "you load men with burdens hard to bear

HARD TO EXPLAIN
1. *hard to interpret:* δυσερμήνευτος DYSERMĒNEUTOS*
Heb 5.11 much to say which is hard to explain

HARD TO UNDERSTAND
1. *hard to be understood:* δυσνόητος DYSNOĒTOS*
2 Pet 3.16 some things in them hard to understand

HARDEN
1. *petrify, make callous:* πωρόω PŌROŌ*
Mk 6.52 but their hearts were hardened
8.17 "Are your hearts hardened?
Jn 12.40 "He has . . hardened their heart
Rom 11. 7 but the rest were hardened
2 Cor 3.14 But their minds were hardened
2. *harden:* σκληρύνω SKLĒRYNŌ
Rom 9.18 hardens the heart of whomever he wills
Heb 3. 8 "do not harden your hearts
3.13 that none of you may be hardened
3.15 "do not harden your hearts
4. 7 "do not harden your hearts

HARDENING
1. *dullness, insensibility:* πώρωσις PŌRŌSIS
Rom 11.25 a hardening has come upon part of Israel

HARDER
1. *more, greater:* περισσότερος (neut.) PERISSOTEROS [B.3.b.4]
1 Cor 15.10 I worked harder than any of them

HARDLY
1. *barely, hardly:* μόλις MOLIS
Lk 9.39 "it convulses him . . and will hardly leave
Rom 5. 7 one will hardly die for a righteous man

HARDNESS
1. *dullness, insensibility:* πώρωσις PŌRŌSIS
Mk 3. 5 grieved at their hardness of heart
Eph 4.18 due to their hardness of heart

HARDNESS OF HEART
1. *hardness of heart:* σκληροκαρδία SKLĒROKARDIA*
Mt 19. 8 "For your hardness of heart
Mk 10. 5 "For your hardness of heart he wrote
16.14 their unbelief and hardness of heart[k]‡

HARDSHIP
1. *force, necessity:* ἀνάγκη ANAGKĒ
2 Cor 6. 4 in afflictions, hardships, calamities
12.10 insults, hardships, persecutions
2. *hardship, toil:* μόχθος MOCHTHOS
2 Cor 11.27 in toil and hardship, . . without food

HARD-WORKING
1. *work hard, grow weary:* κοπιάω (part.) KOPIAŌ
2 Tim 2. 6 It is the hard-working farmer

HARK
1. *behold!:* ἰδού IDOU
Acts 5. 9 "Hark, . . those that . . buried your husband

HARLOT
1. *harlot, prostitute:* πόρνη PORNĒ
Mt 21.31 "harlots go into the kingdom of God
21.32 "tax collectors and the harlots believed
Lk 15.30 " 'devoured your living with harlots!
Heb 11.31 By faith Rahab the harlot did not perish
Jas 2.25 Rahab the harlot justified by works
Rev 17. 1 "the judgment of the great harlot
17. 5 "Babylon the great, mother of harlots
17.15 "waters . . , where the harlot is seated
17.16 "they and the beast will hate the harlot
19. 2 "he has judged the great harlot

HARM
1. *do wrong, harm:* ἀδικέω ADIKEŌ
Rev 6. 6 "but do not harm oil and wine!
7. 2 angels who had . . power to harm earth
7. 3 "Do not harm the earth or the sea
9. 4 they were told not to harm the grass
11. 5 if any one would harm them, fire pours
11. 5 if any one would harm . . he is doomed
2. *mistreat:* κακόω KAKOŌ
Acts 18.10 "no man shall attack you to harm you
1 Pet 3.13 who is . . to harm you if you are zealous?
3. *evil, bad:* κακός (subst.) KAKOS
[a]μηδὲν πράσσειν κακόν *do nothing bad* A.6.a.4 [b]pl.
Acts 16.28 [a]"Do not harm yourself, for we are . . here
28. 5 He, however, . . suffered no harm
2 Tim 4.14 [b]A. the coppersmith did me great harm

HARM, DO
1. *harm, injure:* βλάπτω BLAPTŌ
Lk 4.35 "came out . ., having done him no harm
2. *do wrong, do harm:* κακοποιέω KAKOPOIEŌ
Mk 3. 4 "Is it lawful on the sabbath . . to do harm?
Lk 6. 9 "is it lawful on the sabbath . . to do harm?

HARMONY (*See* PERFECT HARMONY)

HARP
1. *lyre:* κιθάρα KITHARA*
1 Cor 14. 7 lifeless instruments, such as . . the harp
Rev 5. 8 elders . . each holding a harp
14. 2 sound of harpers playing on their harps
15. 2 standing . . with harps of God

HARPER
1. *lyre player:* κιθαρῳδός KITHARŌDOS*
Rev 14. 2 sound of harpers playing on their harps
18.22 "sound of harpers and minstrels

HARSH
1. *austere, cruel:* σκληρός SKLĒROS
Jude .15 "harsh things which . . sinners have spoken

HARSH, BE
1. *make sharp, embitter:* πικραίνω (pass.) PIKRAINŌ
Col 3.19 love your wives, and do not be harsh

HARVEST
1. *produce, fruit:* γένημα (pl.) GENĒMA
2 Cor 9.10 the harvest of your righteousness[k]
2. *fruit:* καρπός KARPOS
Rom 1.13 that I may reap some harvest among you
Jas 3.18 the harvest of righteousness is sown
3. *mowing, harvest:* θερισμός THERISMOS*
Mt 9.37 "The harvest is plentiful
9.38 "pray therefore the Lord of the harvest to send out laborers into his harvest
13.30 " 'Let both grow together until the harvest; and at harvest time I will tell the reapers
13.39 "the harvest is the close of the age
Mk 4.29 "ripe, . . because the harvest has come
Lk 10. 2 "The harvest is plentiful . .; pray therefore the Lord of the harvest to send out laborers into his harvest
Jn 4.35 " 'yet four months, then comes the harvest
4.35 "the fields are already white for harvest
Rev 14.15 "the harvest of the earth is fully ripe

HARVESTER
1. *reap:* θερίζω (subst. part.) THERIZŌ
Jas 5. 4 the cries of the harvesters have reached

HASTE
1. *zeal, haste:* σπουδή SPOUDĒ
Mk 6.25 she came in immediately with haste
Lk 1.39 Mary arose and went with haste

HASTE, MAKE
1. *strive for, hasten:* σπεύδω SPEUDŌ
Lk 19. 5 "Zacchaeus, make haste and come down
19. 6 So he made haste and came down
Acts 22.18 " 'Make haste and get . . out of Jerusalem

HASTE, WITH
1. *strive for, hasten:* σπεύδω (part.) SPEUDŌ
Lk 2.16 they went with haste, and found Mary

HASTEN
1. *strive for, hasten:* σπεύδω SPEUDŌ
Acts 20.16 he was hastening to be at Jerusalem
2 Pet 3.12 hastening[i] the coming of the day of God†

HASTY
1. *quickly:* ταχέως TACHEŌS [A.4.a]
1 Tim 5.22 Do not be hasty in the laying on of hands

HATE
1. *hate violently:* ἀποστυγέω APOSTYGEŌ*
Rom 12. 9 hate what is evil, hold fast to . . good
2. *hate:* μισέω MISEŌ
Mt 5.43 "it was said, 'You shall . . hate your enemy
6.24 "he will hate the one and love the other
10.22 "hated by all for my name's sake
24. 9 "you will be hated by all nations
24.10 "many will . . hate one another
Mk 13.13 "you will be hated by all
Lk 1.71 "from the hand of all who hate us
6.22 "Blessed are you when men hate you!
6.27 "do good to those who hate you
14.26 "If any one . . does not hate his . . father
16.13 "he will hate the one and love the other
19.14 "his citizens hated him
21.17 "hated by all for my name's sake
Jn 3.20 every one who does evil hates the light
7. 7 "The world cannot hate you, but it hates me because I testify of it
12.25 "he who hates his life in this world
15.18 "If the world hates you, know that it has hated me before
15.19 "I chose you . . therefore the world hates you
15.23 "He who hates me hates my Father also
15.24 "have seen and hated . . me and my Father
15.25 " 'They hated me without a cause
17.14 "the world has hated them
Rom 7.15 but I do the very thing I hate
9.13 "Jacob I loved, but Esau I hated
Eph 5.29 For no man ever hates his own flesh
Tit 3. 3 hated by men and hating one another
Heb 1. 9 "loved righteousness and hated lawlessness
1 Jn 2. 9 who . . hates his brother is in the darkness
2.11 who hates his brother is in the darkness
3.13 Do not wonder . . that the world hates you
3.15 one who hates his brother is a murderer
4.20 If any one . . hates his brother
Jude .23 hating . . the garment spotted by the flesh[e]
Rev 2. 6 " 'you hate the works of the Nicolaitans, which I also hate
17.16 "they and the beast will hate the harlot

HATED
1. *hated, hateful:* στυγητός STYGĒTOS*
Tit 3. 3 hated by men and hating one another

HATEFUL
1. *hate:* μισέω (perf. mid. part.) MISEŌ
Rev 18. 2 "every foul and hateful bird

HATER OF GOD
1. *hated of God, hating God:* θεοστυγής (subst.) THEOSTYGĒS*
Rom 1.30 slanderers, haters of God, insolent

HATER OF GOOD
1. *not loving the good:* ἀφιλάγαθος (subst.) APHILAGATHOS*
2 Tim 3. 3 profligates, fierce, haters of good

HAUGHTY
1. *arrogant:* ὑπερήφανος HYPERĒPHANOS
Rom 1.30 insolent, haughty, boastful
2. *great:* μέγας MEGAS
Rev 13. 5 a mouth uttering haughty . . words

HAUGHTY, BE
1. *be proud:* ὑψηλοφρονέω HYPSĒLOPHRONEŌ*
1 Tim 6.17 charge them not to be haughty
2. *think proud things:* τὰ ὑψηλὰ φρονεῖν HYPSĒLOS; PHRONEŌ [B.2.d.2]
Rom 12.16 do not be haughty

HAUL

1. *draw, drag:* ἕλκω HELKŌ

Jn 21. 6 now they were not able to haul it in
21.11 Peter went aboard and hauled the net

HAUNT

1. *watch, guard, prison:* φυλακή PHYLAKĒ

Rev 18. 2 "a haunt of every foul spirit, a haunt of every foul and hateful bird

HAVE

1. *one must:* δεῖ DEI

Lk 22. 7 the passover lamb had to be sacrificed
Jn 4. 4 He had to pass through Samaria
Acts 1.16 "the scripture had to be fulfilled
27.26 "we shall have to run on some island
Heb 9.26 he would have had to suffer repeatedly
1 Pet 1. 6 while you may have to suffer various trials

2. *have, hold:* ἔχω ECHŌ

Mt 3. 9 " 'We have Abraham as our father
5.23 "your brother has something against you
5.46 "what reward have you?
6. 1 "for then you will have no reward
7.29 taught them as one who had authority
8.20 "Foxes have holes . . but the Son of man has nowhere to lay his head
9. 6 "the Son of man has authority on earth
9.12 "Those who are well have no need
11.15 "He who has ears to hear,[d] let him hear
11.18 "they say, 'He has a demon
12.11 "What man of you, if he has one sheep
13. 5 "where they had not much soil
13. 5 "since they had no depth of soil
13. 6 "since they had no root they withered
13. 9 "He who has ears,[h] let him hear
13.12 "to him who has will more be given . . but from him who has not, even what he has will be taken away
13.21 "yet he has no root in himself
13.27 " 'How then has it weeds?
13.43 "He who has ears, let him hear
13.44 "sells all that he has and buys that field
13.46 "sold all that he had and bought it
14. 4 "It is not lawful for you to have her
14.17 "We have only five loaves . . and two fish
15.32 "three days, and have nothing to eat
15.34 "How many loaves have you?
16. 8 "the fact that you have no bread
17.20 "if you have faith as a grain of . . seed
18.25 "ordered him . . sold . and all that he had
19.16 "what . . must I do, to have eternal life?
19.21 "you will have treasure in heaven
19.22 sorrowful; for he had great possessions
21. 3 " 'The Lord has need of them
21.21 "if you have faith and never doubt
21.28 "A man had two sons
21.38 " 'let us kill him and have his inheritance
22.24 " 'If a man dies, having no children
22.25 "died . . having no children
22.28 "For they all had her
25.25 " 'Here you have what is yours
25.28 " 'give it to him who has the ten talents
25.29 " 'to every one who has will more be given . . ; but from him who has not, even what he has will be taken away
26.11 "For you always have the poor with you, but you will not always have me
27.16 And they had then a notorious prisoner
27.65 "You have a guard[o] of soldiers; go†

Mk 1.22 taught them as one who had authority
2.10 "know that the Son of man has authority
2.17 "Those who are well have no need
2.19 "As long as they have the bridegroom
3. 1 a man was there who had a withered hand
3. 3 the man who had the withered hand
3.10 all who had diseases pressed upon him
3.15 have authority to cast out demons
3.29 "never has forgiveness, but . . an eternal sin

Mk 3.30 "He has an unclean spirit
4. 5 "on rocky ground, where it had not much soil
4. 5 "sprang up, since it had no depth of soil
4. 6 "since it had no root it withered away
4. 9 "He who has ears to hear, let him hear
4.17 "they have no root in themselves
4.23 "If any . . has ears to hear, let him hear
4.25 "to him who has will more be given; and from him who has not, even what he has will be taken away
4.40 "Why are you afraid? Have you no faith?
5.15 the man who had had the legion
6.18 "not lawful . . to have your brother's wife
6.38 "How many loaves have you?
[7.16 "*if any man has ears to hear*‡
8. 1 had nothing to eat, he called his disciples
8. 2 "because they . . have nothing to eat
8. 5 "How many loaves have you?
8. 7 And they had a few small fish
8.14 they had only one loaf with them
8.16 they discussed it . . "We have no bread
8.17 "Why . . discuss . . that you have no bread?
8.18 "Having eyes do you not see, and having ears do you not hear?
9.17 "my son . . has a dumb spirit
9.50 "Have salt in yourselves, and be at peace
10.21 "sell what you have, and give to the poor, and you will have treasure in heaven
10.22 sorrowful; for he had great possessions
10.23 "How hard . . for those who have riches
11. 3 "say, 'The Lord has need of it
11.22 Jesus answered them, "Have faith in God
11.25 "if you have anything against any one
12. 6 "He had still one other, a beloved son
12.23 "For the seven had her as wife
12.44 "she . . has put in everything she had
14. 7 "For you always have the poor with you . . ; but you will not always have me

Lk 3. 8 " 'We have Abraham as our father
3.11 "He who has two coats, let him share with him who has none; and he who has food, let him do likewise
4.33 who had the spirit of an unclean demon
4.40 all those who had any that were sick
5.24 "Son of man has authority . . to forgive
5.31 "Those . . well have no need of a physician
6. 8 the man who had the withered hand
7.33 "and you say, 'He has a demon
7.40 "Simon, I have something to say to you
8. 6 "withered . . because it had no moisture
8. 8 "He who has ears to hear, let him hear
8.13 "but these have no root
8.18 "to him who has will more be given, and from him who has not, even what he thinks that he has will be taken away
8.27 "a man from the city who had demons
9. 3 "do not have two tunics
9.11 cured those who had need of healing
9.58 "Foxes have holes, and birds . . nests; but the Son of man has nowhere
11. 5 "Which of you who has a friend
11. 6 " 'I have nothing to set before him
11.36 "having no part dark, it will be . . bright
12. 4 "after that have no more . . they can do
12. 5 "who . . has power to cast into hell[m]
12.17 " 'for I have nowhere to store my crops
12.19 " 'Soul, you have ample goods laid up
12.50 "I have a baptism to be baptized with
13. 6 "A man had a fig tree . . in his vineyard
13.11 woman who had had a spirit of infirmity
14.18 " 'I pray you, have me excused
14.19 " 'I pray you, have me excused
14.28 "whether he has enough to complete it
14.35 "He who has ears to hear, let him hear
15. 4 "What man . . having a hundred sheep
15. 8 "what woman, having ten silver coins[t]
15.11 "There was a man who had two sons

Lk 16. 1 "a rich man who had a steward
16.28 " 'for I have five brothers
16.29 " 'They have Moses and the prophets
17. 6 "If you had faith as a .. mustard seed
17. 7 "one of you, who has a servant plowing
18.22 "Sell all that you have and distribute to the poor, and you will have treasure in heaven
18.24 "How hard it is for those who have riches
19.17 " 'you shall have authority over ten cities
19.24 " 'give it to him who has the ten pounds
19.25 "(they said .. 'Lord, he has ten pounds!
19.26 " 'to every one who has will more be given; but from him who has not, even what he has will be taken away
19.31 " 'The Lord has need of it
19.34 they said, "The Lord has need of it
20.24 "Whose likeness and inscription has it?
20.28 "if a man's brother dies, having a wife
20.33 "For the seven had her as wife
21. 4 "she .. put in all the living that she had
22.36 "let him who has a purse take it, and .. let him who has no sword .. buy one
22.37 "what is written about me has its fulfilment
24.39 "a spirit has not flesh and bones as you see that I have[y]
24.41 "Have you anything here to eat?
Jn 2. 3 mother of Jesus said .. "They have no wine
3.15 "whoever believes .. may have eternal life[h]
3.16 should not perish but have eternal life
3.29 "He who has the bride is the bridegroom
3.36 who believes in the Son has eternal life
4.11 "Sir, you have nothing to draw with
4.17 "I have no husband." Jesus said .. "You are right in saying, 'I h. no husband
4.18 "for you have had five husbands, and he whom you now have is not your husband
4.32 "I have food .. of which you do not know
4.44 a prophet has no honor in his own country
5. 2 a pool .. which has five porticoes
5. 7 "I have no man to put me into the pool
5.24 "he who .. believes .. has eternal life
5.26 "as the Father has life in himself, so he has granted the Son also to h. life in himself
5.36 "testimony which I have is greater
5.38 "you do not have his word abiding
5.39 "that in them you have eternal life
5.40 "to come to me that you may have life
5.42 "I know .. you have not the love of God
6. 9 "a lad here who has five barley loaves
6.40 "who .. believes .. should have eternal life
6.47 "he who believes has eternal life
6.53 "unless you eat .. you have no life
6.54 "who eats my flesh .. has eternal life
6.68 "You have the words of eternal life
7.20 "You have a demon!
8. 6 that they might have some charge to bring[r]‡
8.12 "he who follows .. will have the light of life
8.26 "I have much to say about you
8.41 "we have one Father, even God
8.48 "saying that you .. have a demon
8.49 Jesus answered, "I have not a demon
8.52 "Now we know that you have a demon
9.41 "If .. blind, you would have no guilt
10.10 "I came that they may have life, and have it abundantly
10.16 "I have other sheep .. not of this fold
10.18 "I have power to lay it down, and I have power to take it again
10.20 "He has a demon, and he is mad
12. 6 he had the money box
12. 8 "The poor you always have with you, but you do not always have me
12.35 "Walk while you have the light
12.36 "While you have the light, believe
12.48 "He who rejects me .. has a judge
13. 8 "If I do not wash you, you have no part
13.29 because Judas had the money box
Jn 13.35 "if you have love for one another
14.21 "He who has my commandments
14.30 "He has no power over me
15.13 "Greater love has no man than this
15.22 "they would not have sin; but now they have no excuse for their sin
15.24 "If .. not .. they would not have sin
16.12 "I have yet many things to say to you
16.15 "All that the Father has is mine
16.21 "When .. in travail she has sorrow
16.22 "So you have sorrow now
16.33 "that in me you may have peace. In the world you have tribulation
17. 5 "the glory which I had with thee before
17.13 "that they may have my joy fulfilled
18.10 Simon Peter, having a sword, drew it
19. 7 Jews answered him, "We have a law
19.10 "Do you not know that I have power?
19.11 "no power over me unless it had been given
19.11 "who delivered me .. has the greater sin
19.15 "We have no king but Caesar
20.31 believing you may have life in his name
21. 5 "Children, have you any fish?
Acts 2.44 all .. had all things in common
2.45 distributed them .. as any had need
2.47 having favor with all the people
3. 6 "but I give you what I have
4.14 they had nothing to say in opposition
4.35 distribution .. made .. as any had need
9.14 "he has authority from the chief priests
9.31 the church .. had peace and was built up
13. 5 they had John to assist them
14. 9 seeing that he had faith to be made well
15.21 "Moses has had .. those who preach him
16.16 slave girl who had a spirit of divination
18.18 he cut his hair, for he had a vow
19.13 those who had evil spirits
19.38 "If .. the craftsmen .. have a complaint
23.17 "for he has something to tell him
23.18 "he has something to say to you
23.19 "What is it that you have to tell me?
24.15 "having a hope in God which these .. accept
24.16 "to have a clear conscience toward God
24.19 "if they have anything against me
24 23 that he .. should have some liberty
25.19 "they had certain points of dispute
25.26 "I have nothing definite to write
25.26 "that .. I may have something to write
28. 9 the people on the island who had diseases
28.19 "though I had no charge to bring
Rom 2.14 When Gentiles who have not the law
2.14 even though they do not have the law
2.20 having in the law .. knowledge and truth
4. 2 he has something to boast about
5. 1 justified .. we[f] have peace with God‡
8. 9 Any one who does not have the Spirit
8.23 who have the first fruits of the Spirit
9.21 Has the potter no right over the clay?
10 2 witness that they have a zeal for God
12. 4 in one body we have many members, and all .. do not have the same function
12. 6 Having gifts that differ
14.22 The faith that you have, keep
15. 4 written .. that .. we might have hope
15.17 I have reason to be proud of my work
15.23 since I no longer have .. room for work
1 Cor 2.16 But we have the mind of Christ
4. 7 What have you that you did not receive?
4.15 you have countless guides in Christ
6. 1 When one of you has a grievance
6. 4 If then you have such cases
6. 7 To have lawsuits at all .. is defeat
6.19 a temple .. which you have from God
7. 2 each man should have his own wife
7. 7 each has his own special gift from God
7.12 if any brother has a wife .. unbeliever
7.13 If any woman has a husband

1 Cor 7.25 I have no command of the Lord
7.28 who marry will have worldly troubles
7.29 from now on, let those who have wives live as though they had none
7.37 having his desire under control
7.40 I think that I have the Spirit of God
9. 4 Do we not have the right to our food?
9. 5 Do we not have the right . . as the other?
9. 6 is it only . . I who have no right?
9.17 if . . of my own will, I have a reward
11.10 why a woman ought to have a veil[r]
11.22 Do you not have houses to eat . . in? Or do you . . humiliate those who have nothing?
12.12 as the body is one and has many members
12.21 eye cannot say . . "I have no need of you," nor . . the feet, "I have no need of you
13. 1 If I . . have not love
13. 2 if I have prophetic powers, and . . if I have all faith, . . but have not love, I am nothing
13. 3 If I give away all I have, . . but have not love
14.26 each one has a hymn, a lesson
15.31 my pride . . which I have in Christ Jesus
15.34 For some have no knowledge of God
2 Cor 1.15 that you might have a double pleasure[b]
2. 4 the abundant love that I have for you
3. 4 confidence that we have through Christ
3.12 Since we have such a hope, we are . . bold
4. 1 having this ministry by . . mercy of God[e]
4. 7 we have this treasure in earthen vessels
4.13 Since we have the same spirit of faith
5. 1 we have a building from God
6.10 having nothing . . possessing everything
7. 1 Since we have these promises
7. 5 our bodies had no rest . . we were afflicted
8.11 completing it out of what you have
8.12 acceptable according to what a man has, not according to what he has not
9. 8 so that you may always have enough
Gal 2. 4 freedom which we have in Christ Jesus
4.22 Abraham had two sons, one by a slave
6.10 as we have opportunity, let us do good
Eph 1. 7 In him we have redemption
2.12 having no hope and without God
2.18 we both have access in one Spirit
3.12 in whom we have boldness and confidence
5. 5 no . . impure man . . has any inheritance
Phil 2. 2 having the same love, being in . . accord
2.20 I have no one like him
2.27 But God had mercy on him
3. 4 I myself have reason for confidence
3. 9 not having a righteousness of my own
3.17 as you have an example in us
Col 1. 4 the love which you have for all the saints
1.14 in whom we have redemption
2.23 have indeed an appearance of wisdom
3.13 if one has a complaint against another
4. 1 you also have a Master in heaven
1 Th 1. 9 what a welcome we had among you
4. 9 concerning love . . you have no need
4.13 as others do who have no hope
5. 1 as to the times . . you have no need
2 Th 3. 9 not because we have not that right
1 Tim 5. 4 If a widow has children or grandchildren
5.16 If any believing woman[l] has relatives
6. 2 Those who have believing masters
6. 8 if we have food and clothing
6.16 ⟨Lord⟩ who alone has immortality
Tit 2. 8 having nothing evil to say of us
Phm . 5 faith which you have toward the Lord
Heb 2.14 who has the power of death, . . the devil
3. 3 the builder of a house has more honor
4.14 we have a great high priest
4.15 we have not a high priest who is unable
5.14 those who have their faculties trained
6.13 he had no one greater by whom to swear
6.18 we . . have strong encouragement
6.19 We have this as a sure . . anchor
Heb 7. 3 He . . has neither beginning of days
7. 5 who . . have a commandment in the law
7. 6 blessed him who had the promises
7.27 He has no need, like those high priests
8. 1 we have such a high priest
8. 3 necessary . . to have something to offer
9. 1 even the first covenant had regulations
9. 4 having the golden altar of incense
10. 1 law has but a shadow of the good things
10. 2 no longer have any consciousness of sin
10.19 since we have confidence to enter
10.34 you yourselves had a better possession
10.35 confidence, which has a great reward
10.36 you have need of endurance
11.10 the city which has foundations
11.15 they would have had opportunity
12. 9 we have had . . fathers to discipline us
13.10 We have an altar from which those . . have no right to eat
13.14 here we have no lasting city
13.18 sure that we have a clear conscience
Jas 1. 4 let steadfastness have its full effect
2.14 What . . if a man says he has faith but has not works?
2.17 faith . . , if it has no works, is dead
2.18 But some one will say, "You have faith and I have works
3.14 But if you have bitter jealousy
4. 2 You desire and do not have; so you kill. . . You do not have, because you do not ask
2 Pet 1.19 we have the prophetic word
2.14 "They have eyes full of adultery . . They have hearts trained in greed
1 Jn 1. 3 that you may have fellowship with us
1. 6 If we say we have fellowship with him
1. 7 we have fellowship with one another
1. 8 If we say we have no sin, we deceive
2. 1 we have an advocate with the Father
2. 7 an old commandment which you had
2.23 No one who denies the Son has . . Father. He who confesses the Son has the Father
2.27 you have no need that any one . . teach you
2.28 that . . we may have confidence
3.15 no murderer has eternal life
3.17 if any one has the world's goods
3.21 we have confidence before God
4.16 we know . . the love God has for us
4.17 that we may have confidence
4.21 this commandment we have from him
5.10 He . . has the testimony in himself
5.12 He who has the Son has life; he who has not the Son of God has not life
5.13 may know that you have eternal life
5.14 the confidence which we have in him
2 Jn . 5 the one we have had from the beginning
. 9 who goes ahead . . does not have God; he who abides . . has both the Father
.12 I have much to write to you
3 Jn . 4 No greater joy can I have than this
.13 I had much to write to you
Rev 1.18 "I have the keys of Death and Hades
2. 4 " 'I have this against you
2. 6 " 'this you h., you hate . . works . . I also hate
2. 7 " 'He who has an ear, let him hear
2.10 " 'for ten days you will have tribulation
2.11 " 'He who has an ear, let him hear
2.12 " 'who has the sharp two-edged sword
2.14 " 'I h. a few things against you: you have some . . who hold the teaching of Balaam
2.15 " 'h. some who hold . . teaching . . Nicolaitans
2.17 " 'He who has an ear, let him hear
2.18 " 'Son of God, who has eyes like a flame
2.20 " 'I have this against you
2.25 " 'hold fast what you have, until I come
2.29 " 'He who has an ear, let him hear
3. 1 " 'him who has the seven spirits of God
3. 1 " 'you have the name of being alive

Rev 3. 4 " 'you have still a few names in Sardis
3. 6 " 'He who has an ear, let him hear
3. 7 " 'true one, who has the key of David
3. 8 " 'I know that you have but little power
3.11 " 'hold fast what you have
3.13 " 'He who has an ear, let him hear
3.22 " 'He who has an ear, let him hear
6. 2 a white horse, and its rider had a bow
6. 5 its rider had a balance in his hand
8. 6 seven angels who had the seven trumpets
9. 4 those of mankind who have not the seal
9. 9 they had scales like iron breastplates
9.10 They have tails like scorpions
9.11 They have as king over them the angel
9.14 the sixth angel who had the trumpet
10. 2 He had a little scroll open in his hand
11. 6 They have power to shut the sky .. and they have power over the waters
12. 6 she has a place prepared by God
13. 9 If any one has an ear, let him hear
13.11 it had two horns like a lamb
13.17 no one can buy .. unless he has the mark
13.18 let him who has understanding reckon
14. 1 who had his name and his Father's
14.11 "they have no rest, day or night
14.17 another angel .. too had a sharp sickle
14.18 the angel who has power over fire .. called .. to him who had the sharp sickle
16. 9 God who had power over these plagues
17. 1 one of the .. angels who had the seven bowls
17. 3 it had seven heads and ten horns
17.18 the great city which has dominion
18. 1 another angel .. having great authority
18.19 where all who had ships at sea grew rich
19.12 he has a name inscribed
19.16 On his robe .. he has a name inscribed
20. 6 Over such the second death has no power
21. 9 one of the .. angels who had the seven bowls
21.11 ⟨city⟩ having the glory of God
21.12 It had a great, high wall
21.14 wall of the city had twelve foundations
21.15 he who talked to me had a measuring rod
21.23 the city has no need of sun or moon

3. *come to be, happen, be:* γίνομαι GINOMAI
[a]+dat. A.6.c.3 [b]A.6.a.3
Mt 18.12 [a]"If a man has a hundred sheep
Acts 15. 2 [b]Paul and B. had no small dissension
Gal 5.26 [b]Let us have no self-conceit, no provoking

4. *be, exist, belong to:* ὑπάρχω HYPARCHŌ
[a]subst. neut. pl. +gen. [b]+dat. A.6.c.3
Lk 14.33 [a]"whoever .. does not renounce all .. he has
Acts 3. 6 [b]Peter said, "I have no silver and gold
1 Cor 13. 3 [a]If I give away all I have

5. *hold fast, restrain:* κατέχω KATECHŌ
Jn [5. 4 *healed of whatever disease he had*‡

6. *receive, take:* λαμβάνω LAMBANŌ
Acts 25.16 "before the accused .. had opportunity

7. *partake, share:* μεταλαμβάνω METALAMBANŌ
Acts 24.25 "when I have .. opportunity I will summon

8. *know:* οἶδα OIDA [A.6.a.5]
Jn 7.15 "How is it that this man has learning?[p]

9. *ought, owe:* ὀφείλω (+inf.) OPHEILŌ
1 Cor 7.36 if .. it has to be, let him do as he wishes
Heb 2.17 he had to be made like his brethren

10. *be present:* πάρειμι PAREIMI
[a]subst. part. pl. [b]attr. part.
Heb 13. 5 [a]be content with what you have
2 Pet 1.12 [b]established in the truth that you have

11. *do in order that:* ποιεῖν ἵνα (imper.) POIEŌ [A.6.a.4]
Col 4.16 h. it read .. in the church of the Laodiceans

12. *happen, attain:* τυγχάνω TYGCHANŌ
Acts 26.22 "To this day I have had the help

IDIOMATICALLY
a. [EIMI]
Mt **19**.27; **23**.8, 9, 10
Lk **1**.7, 14; **7**.41; **8**.42; **9**.13; **10**.39; **12**.24
Jn **18**.39
Acts **4**.32; **7**.5, 44; **8**.21; **13**.15; **18**.10; **19**.25; **21**.9, 23
Rom **9**.2, 9; **11**.23
1 Cor **15**.19
Phil **3**.7
Rev **22**.14
b. Mk 9.21 "How long has he had this? πόσος χρόνος ἐστὶν ὡς τοῦτο γέγονεν αὐτῷ; [GINOMAI]
c. Lk 1.34 "since I have no husband ἐπεὶ ἄνδρα οὐ γινώσκω [GINŌSKŌ]
d. Jn 1.22 "Let us have an answer for those who sent us ἵνα ἀπόκρισιν δῶμεν τοῖς πέμψασιν ἡμᾶς [DIDŌMI]

HAVE BACK
1. *receive in full:* ἀπέχω APECHŌ
Phm .15 that you might have him back for ever

HAVE GOODS
1. *hold fast, restrain:* κατέχω KATECHŌ
1 Cor 7.30 who buy as though they had no goods

HAVE NOTHING TO DO WITH
1. *ask for, decline:* παραιτέομαι (imper.) PARAITEOMAI
1 Tim 4. 7 Have n. to do with godless and silly myths
2 Tim 2.23 Have n. to do with stupid .. controversies
Tit 3.10 have nothing more to do with him

HAVE OVER
1. *be more, cause to increase:* πλεονάζω PLEONAZŌ
2 Cor 8.15 "who gathered much had nothing over

HAVE TO
IDIOMATICALLY
a. Acts 20.16 so that he might not have to spend time ὅπως μὴ γένηται αὐτῷ χρονοτριβῆσαι [GINOMAI]

HAVE TO DO WITH
1. *have, hold:* ἔχω ECHŌ
1 Jn 4.18 For fear has to do with punishment
2. *mix up together:* συναναμείγνυμι (pass.) SYNANAMEIGNYMI
2 Th 3.14 have nothing to do with him
IDIOMATICALLY
a. Jn 8.44 He .. has nothing to do with the truth ἐκεῖνος .. ἐν τῇ ἀληθείᾳ οὐκ ἔστηκεν [HISTĒMI]

HAVENS, FAIR: II,E-4
1. *good harbor:* Καλοὶ λιμένες KALOS; LIMĒN
Acts 27. 8 we came to a place called Fair Havens

HAVOC OF, MAKE
1. *destroy, plunder:* πορθέω PORTHEŌ
Acts 9.21 "who made havoc in Jerusalem of those

HAY
1. *grass, fodder:* χόρτος CHORTOS
1 Cor 3.12 with gold, .. wood, hay, straw

HE (*For* HEAUTOU *and* IDIOS, *not represented here, see* HIS, HIM)
1. *self; he, she, it:* αὐτός AUTOS
2. *that:* ἐκεῖνος EKEINOS
Jn **1**.8, 18; **2**.21; **3**.28, 30; **4**.25; **5**.19, 35, 38, 43, 46, 47; **6**.29; **7**.11, 45; **8**.42, 44; **9**.9, 11, 12, 25, 28, 36, 37; **13**.25, 26, 27, 30; **14**.21, 26; **15**.26; **16**.8, 13, 14; **18**.17, 25; **19**.35,
Acts **3**.13
2 Cor **8**.9
2 Tim **2**.13, 26
Tit **3**.7
2 Pet **1**.16
1 Jn **2**.6; **3**.3, 5, 7, 16; **4**.17
3. *each:* ἕκαστος HEKASTOS
1 Cor **7**.17
4. *another, different:* ἕτερος HETEROS
1 Cor 10.29 (I mean his conscience, not yours
5. *who, which, what:* ὅς HOS
Mt **3**.12²; **7**.9; **12**.11; **13**.23
Lk **3**.17; **7**.4; **23**.51
Jn **5**.11
Acts **2**.24; **3**.3; **5**.36²; **7**.20, 38, 39; **8**.10; **9**.39; **10**.38; **11**.14, 23; **12**.4; **13**.7, 31; **14**.16; **16**.2, 24; **18**.7, 27; **21**.29, 32; **23**.29; **24**.6², 8; **25**.15, 26; **26**.26; **28**.4, 8
Rom **2**.29; **5**.2

1 Cor **10**.13
2 Cor **1**.10; **13**.3
Eph **1**.7, 13[2]
Phil **3**.8
Col **1**.7, 13, 15, 18, 28; **2**.11; **4**.8
1 Th **5**.24
2 Th **2**.8; **3**.3
1 Tim **3**.16†‡
2 Tim **4**.15, 18
Phm .12, 13
Heb **1**.3; **3**.6; **5**.[7†; **7**.2, 4, 27; **12**.26
1 Pet **1**.8; **2**.4, 22, 23, 24[2]; **5**.9
Rev **20**.11
6. *this:* οὗτος HOUTOS
Mk **6**.2
Lk **9**.26; **12**.5; **19**.19; **20**.13
Jn **5**.6, 38; **6**.27; **9**.31; **10**.3; **13**.24; **21**.21
Acts **4**.10; **5**.31, 37; **10**.40, 43; **13**.27, 39; **21**.9
1 Cor **2**.2; **3**.17
Phil **2**.23
1 Jn **2**.4, 5
7. *such as this:* τοιοῦτος (subst.) TOIOUTOS
Gal **6**.1
IDIOMATICALLY
a. Lk **14**.33 [HEAUTOU]

HE ALSO
HE, AND
1. *and that one:* κἀκεῖνος KAKEINOS
Mk **12**.5
Lk **11**.7; **20**.11; **22**.12
Jn **7**.29
Acts **5**.37
2 Tim **2**.12

HE THAT
HE WHO
1. *who, which, what:* ὅς HOS
[a]+ἐάν [b]+ἄν
Mt **5**.19[a]; **10**.38; **11**.6[a]
Mk **4**.9; **9**.40
Lk **7**.23[a], 47; **8**.18[2b]; **9**.50
Jn **1**.33[b]; **3**.26, 34; **4**.18; **6**.29; **11**.3; **19**.37
Acts **13**.37
Rom **8**.32; **10**.14[2]
1 Jn **4**.6
2. *anyone who, whoever:* ὅστις HOSTIS
Lk 14.15 "Blessed is he who shall eat bread

HEAD
1. *end, extremity:* ἄκρον AKRON
Heb 11.21 bowing in worship over the head of his staff
2. *head:* κεφαλή KEPHALĒ
Mt 5.36 "do not swear by your head
6.17 "anoint your head and wash your face
8.20 "Son of man has nowhere to lay his head
10.30 "hairs of your head are all numbered
14. 8 "Give me the head of John the Baptist
14.11 his head was brought on a platter
21.42 " 'has become the head of the corner
26. 7 she poured it on his head
27.29 "plaiting . . thorns they put it on his head
27.30 took the reed and struck him on the h.
27.37 over his head they put the charge
27.39 derided him, wagging their heads
Mk 6.24 "The head of John the baptizer
6.25 "give me at once the head of John
6.27 the king . . gave orders to bring his head
6.28 brought his head on a platter
12.10 " 'stone . . has become the head of the corner
14. 3 she . . poured it over his head
15.19 they struck his head with a reed
15.29 wagging their heads, and saying, "Aha!
Lk 7.38 wiped them with the hair of her head
7.46 "You did not anoint my head with oil
9.58 "Son of man has nowhere to lay his head
12. 7 "hairs of your head are all numbered
20.17 " 'has become the head of the corner
21.18 "not a hair of your head will perish
Lk 21.28 "look up and raise your heads
Jn 13. 9 "but also my hands and my head!
19. 2 crown of thorns, and put it on his head
19.30 he bowed his head and gave up his spirit
20. 7 napkin, which had been on his head
20.12 one at the head and one at the feet
Acts 4.11 "has become the head of the corner
18. 6 "Your blood be upon your heads!
21.24 "so that they may shave their heads
27.34 "not a hair is to perish from the head
Rom 12.20 "you will heap burning coals upon his head
1 Cor 11. 3 the head of every man is Christ, the head of a woman is her husband, and the head of Christ is God
11. 4 Any man who prays . . with his head covered dishonors his head
11. 5 any woman who prays . . with her head unveiled dishonors her head
11. 7 a man ought not to cover his head
11.10 woman ought to have a veil[r] on her head
12.21 nor . . the head . . "I have no need of you
Eph 1.22 head over all things for the church
4.15 into him who is the head, into Christ
5.23 the husband is the head of the wife as Christ is the head of the church, his body
Col 1.18 He is the head of the body, the church
2.10 the head of all rule and authority
2.19 not holding fast to the Head
1 Pet 2. 7 "become the head of the corner
Rev 1.14 his head and his hair were white
4. 4 with golden crowns upon their heads
9. 7 on their heads . . what looked like crowns
9.17 I saw the horses . . and the heads of the horses were like lions' heads
9.19 their tails are like serpents, with heads
10. 1 with a rainbow over his head
12. 1 on her head a crown of twelve stars
12. 3 a great red dragon, with seven heads . . and seven diadems upon his heads
13. 1 a beast . . with ten horns and seven heads . . and a blasphemous name upon its heads
13. 3 One of its heads seemed to have a . . wound
14.14 man, with a golden crown on his head
17. 3 it had seven heads and ten horns
17. 7 "the beast with seven heads and ten horns
17. 9 "the seven heads are seven mountains
18.19 threw dust on their heads, as they wept
19.12 on his head are many diadems
CONTEXTUALLY
1 Cor 11.13 a woman to pray . . with her h. uncovered?

HEAD OF GRAIN
1. *ear of grain:* στάχυς STACHYS
Mt 12. 1 began to pluck heads of grain and to eat[o]
Mk 2.23 disciples began to pluck heads of grain[o]
Lk 6. 1 plucked and ate some heads of grain[o]

HEAD, WOUND IN THE
1. *strike on the head:* κεφαλιόω KEPHALIOŌ*
Mk 12. 4 "they wounded him in the head

HEADLONG
1. *headfirst:* πρηνής PRĒNĒS*
Acts 1.18 "(falling headlong[b] he burst open†

HEADLONG, THROW DOWN
1. *throw down from a cliff:* κατακρημνίζω KATAKRĒMNIZŌ*
Lk 4.29 that they might throw him down h.

HEADWAY, MAKE
1. *drive:* ἐλαύνω ELAUNŌ
Mk 6.48 they were making headway painfully[o]

HEAL
1. *save, preserve:* διασῴζω DIASŌZŌ
Lk 7. 3 asking him to come and heal his slave
2. *make healthy:* ποιεῖν ὑγιῆ HYGIĒS [B.2.a.1]
Jn 5.11 "The man who healed me said to me
5.15 it was Jesus who had healed him
3. *treat, heal:* ἰάομαι IAOMAI
Mt 8. 8 "say the word, and my servant will be healed

Mt 8.13 servant was healed at that very moment
13.15 " 'lest they . . turn for me to heal them
15.28 her daughter was healed instantly
Mk 5.29 she felt . . that she was healed of her disease
Lk 5.17 power of the Lord was with him to heal[p]
6.17 came to hear him and to be healed
6.19 power came forth . . and healed them
7. 7 "let my servant be healed
8.47 how she had been immediately healed
9. 2 to preach . . kingdom of God and to heal
9.42 rebuked the unclean spirit, and healed
14. 4 Then he took him and healed him
17.15 when he saw that he was healed
22.51 he touched his ear and healed him
Jn 4.47 went and begged him to . . heal his son
5.13 the man who had been healed
12.40 "lest they . . turn for me to heal them
Acts 9.34 "Aeneas, Jesus Christ heals you
10.38 "he went about doing good and healing
28. 8 putting his hands on him healed him
28.27 " 'lest they . . turn for me to heal them
Heb 12.13 that what is lame may . . be healed
Jas 5.16 pray . . that you may be healed
1 Pet 2.24 By his wounds you have been healed

4. *for healing:* εἰς ἴασιν IASIS [B.1.a.2]
Acts 4.30 "thou stretchest out thy hand to heal

5. *save, keep from harm:* σῴζω SŌZŌ
Lk 8.36 he . . possessed with demons was healed
Acts 4. 9 "by what means this man has been healed

6. *serve, treat medically:* θεραπεύω THERAPEUŌ
Mt 4.23 healing every disease and every infirmity
4.24 brought him . . the sick . . and he healed
8. 7 he said to him, "I will come and heal him
8.16 he . . healed all who were sick
9.35 healing every disease and every infirmity
10. 1 to heal every disease and every infirmity
10. 8 "Heal the sick, raise the dead
12.10 "Is it lawful to heal on the sabbath?
12.15 many followed him, and he healed them
12.22 healed him, so that the dumb man spoke
14.14 he had compassion on them, and healed
15.30 put them at his feet, and he healed them
17.16 "your disciples . . could not heal him
19. 2 crowds followed . . and he healed them
21.14 the blind . . came . . and he healed them
Mk 1.34 he healed many who were sick
3. 2 whether he would heal . . on the sabbath
3.10 for he had healed many
6. 5 laid his hands upon a few . . and healed
6.13 anointed with oil many . . and healed them
Lk 4.23 " 'Physician, heal yourself
4.40 laid his hands on . . them and healed them
5.15 multitudes gathered . . to be healed
6. 7 whether he would heal on the sabbath
8. 2 some women who had been healed
8.43 woman who . . could not be healed
9. 6 preaching the gospel and healing
10. 9 "heal the sick in it and say to them
13.14 "because Jesus had healed on the sabbath
13.14 "come on those days and be healed
14. 3 "Is it lawful to heal on the sabbath?
Acts 4.14 seeing the man that had been healed
5.16 those afflicted . . were all healed
8. 7 many who were . . lame were healed
Rev 13. 3 its mortal wound was healed
13.12 beast, whose mortal wound was healed

HEALED

1. *healthy, sound:* ὑγιής HYGIĒS
Mk 5.34 "go in peace, and be healed of your disease
Jn [5. 4 *whoever stepped in first . . was healed*‡
5. 6 "Do you want to be healed?
5. 9 at once the man was healed

HEALER

1. *gifts of healing:* χαρίσματα ἰαμάτων CHARISMA; IAMA [C.2]
1 Cor 12.28 God has appointed in the church . . healers

HEALING

1. *remedy, healing:* ἴαμα IAMA
1 Cor 12. 9 gifts of healing by the one Spirit
12.30 Do all possess gifts of healing?

2. *remedy, healing:* ἴασις IASIS
Acts 4.22 on whom this . . healing was performed

3. *care, healing:* θεραπεία THERAPEIA
Lk 9.11 cured those who had need of healing
Rev 22. 2 leaves . . for the healing of the nations

HEALTH, BE IN

1. *be in good health:* ὑγιαίνω HYGIAINŌ
3 Jn . 2 that you may be in health

HEALTH, PERFECT

1. *wholeness, soundness:* ὁλοκληρία HOLOKLĒRIA*
Acts 3.16 "faith . . has given the man this perfect h.

HEAP

1. *heap up:* σωρεύω SŌREUŌ
Rom 12.20 "you will heap burning coals upon his head

HEAP UP EMPTY PHRASES

1. *babble:* βατταλογέω BATTALOGEŌ*
Mt 6. 7 "in praying do not heap up empty phrases

HEAPED, BE

1. *join, unite:* κολλάω (pass.) KOLLAŌ
Rev 18. 5 "her sins are heaped high as heaven

HEAR

1. *hear:* ἀκούω AKOUŌ
Mt 2. 3 When Herod the king heard this
2. 9 When they had heard the king
2.18 "A voice was heard in Ramah
2.22 when he heard . . Archelaus reigned
4.12 when he heard . . John had been arrested
5.21 "heard that it was said to the men of old
5.27 "You have heard that it was said
5.33 "heard that it was said to the men of old
5.38 "You have heard that it was said
5.43 "You have heard that it was said
7.24 "who hears these words of mine
7.26 "one who hears these words of mine
8.10 When Jesus heard him, he marveled
9.12 But when he heard it, he said
10.27 "what you hear whispered, proclaim
11. 2 when John heard in prison about the deeds
11. 4 "Go and tell John what you hear
11. 5 "lepers are cleansed and the deaf hear
11.15 "He who has ears to hear,[d] let him hear‡
12.19 "nor will any one hear his voice
12.24 when the Pharisees heard it
12.42 "came from the ends of the earth to hear
13. 9 "He who has ears,[h] let him hear
[13. 9 "He who has ears *to hear,* let him hear‡
13.13 "and hearing they do not hear, nor do they understand
13.14 " 'indeed hear but never understand
13.15 " 'their ears are heavy of hearing
13.15 " 'lest they should . . hear with their ears
13.16 "blessed are . . your ears, for they hear
13.17 "many prophets . . longed . . to hear what you hear, and did not hear it
13.18 "Hear then the parable of the sower
13.19 "When . . one hears the word of the kingdom
13.20 "this is he who hears the word
13.22 "this is he who hears the word
13.23 "this is he who hears the word
13.43 "He who has ears, let him hear
[13.43 "He who has ears *to hear,* let him hear‡
14. 1 Herod . . heard about the fame of Jesus
14.13 when Jesus heard this, he withdrew . . But when the crowds heard it, they followed
15.10 "Hear and understand
15.12 "Pharisees were offended when they heard
17. 6 When the disciples heard this, they fell
19.22 When the young man heard this he went
19.25 When the disciples heard this
20.24 the ten heard it, they were indignant
20.30 when they heard that Jesus was passing

Mt 21.16 "Do you hear what these are saying?
21.33 "Hear another parable
21.45 When . . the Pharisees heard his parables
22.22 When they heard it, they marveled
22.33 the crowd heard it, they were astonished
22.34 when the Pharisees heard
24. 6 "you will hear of wars and rumors of wars
26.65 "You have now heard his blasphemy
27.13 "Do you not hear how . . they testify?
27.47 hearing it said, "This man is calling
Mk 2.17 when Jesus heard it, he said to them
3. 8 a . . multitude, hearing all that he did
3.21 when his family heard it
4. 9 And he said, "He who has ears to hear, let him hear
4.12 "that they . . hear but not understand
4.15 "when they hear, Satan . . comes
4.16 "when they hear the word, . . receive it
4.18 "they are those who hear the word
4.20 "ones who hear the word and accept it
4.23 "If any man has ears to hear, let him hear
4.24 "Take heed what you hear
4.33 spoke . . as they were able to hear it
5.27 She had heard the reports about Jesus
[5.36 *hearing* what they said, Jesus said‡
6. 2 many who heard him were astonished
6.11 "if . . they refuse to hear you
6.14 King Herod heard of it
6.16 when Herod heard of it he said, "John
6.20 When he heard him, he was much perplexed; and yet he heard him gladly
6.29 When his disciples heard of it, they came
6.55 to any place where they heard he was
7.14 "Hear me, all of you, and understand
[7.16 *"If any man has ears to hear, let him hear*‡
7.25 immediately a woman . . heard of him
7.37 "he even makes the deaf hear
8.18 "having ears do you not hear?
10.41 the ten heard it, . . began to be indignant
10.47 when he heard . . it was Jesus of Nazareth
11.14 And his disciples heard it
11.18 the chief priests and the scribes heard it
12.28 one of the scribes came up and heard
12.29 "The first is, 'Hear, O Israel
12.37 And the great throng heard him gladly
13. 7 "when you h. of wars and rumors of wars
14.11 when they heard it they were glad
14.58 "We heard him say, 'I will destroy . . temple
14.64 "You have heard his blasphemy
15.35 bystanders hearing it said, "Behold
16.11 But when they heard . . he was alive[k]‡
Lk 1.41 when Elizabeth heard the greeting of Mary
1.58 her neighbors and kinsfolk heard
1.66 all who heard them laid them up
2.18 all who heard it wondered
2.20 praising God for all they had heard
2.47 all who heard him were amazed
4.23 " 'what we have heard you did at Capernaum
4.28 When they heard this, all in the synagogue
5. 1 people pressed . . to hear the word of God
5.15 great multitudes gathered to hear
6.17 who came to hear him and to be healed
6.27 "But I say to you that hear
6.47 "Every one who . . hears my words
6.49 "he who hears and does not do them
7. 3 When he heard of Jesus, he sent . . elders
7. 9 When Jesus heard this he marveled
7.22 "tell John what you have seen and heard: the . . deaf hear, the dead are raised up
7.29 (When they heard this all . . justified God
8. 8 he called out, "He who has ears to hear, let him hear
8.10 "that . . hearing they may not understand
8.12 "along the path are those who have heard
8.13 "who, when they hear the word, receive it
8.14 "among the thorns . . are those who hear
8.15 "they are those who, hearing the word

Lk 8.18 "Take heed then how you hear
8.21 "my brothers are those who hear the word
8.50 Jesus on hearing this answered him
9. 7 Herod . . heard of all that was done
9. 9 "but who is this about whom I hear?
10.16 "He who hears you hears me, and he who rejects you rejects me
10.24 "many prophets and kings desired . . to hear what you hear, and did not hear it
11.28 "Blessed . . are those who hear the word
11.31 "came . . to hear the wisdom of Solomon
12. 3 "whatever you have said . . shall be heard
14.15 When one of those . . heard this
14.35 "He who has ears to hear, let him hear
15. 1 sinners were all drawing near to hear him
15.25 "as he . . drew near . . he heard music
16. 2 " 'What is this that I hear about you?
16.14 "Pharisees . . heard all this, and . . scoffed
16.29 "Abraham said . . 'let them hear them
16.31 " 'If they do not hear Moses and the prophets
18. 6 "Hear what the unrighteous judge says
18.22 when Jesus heard it, he said to him
18.23 But when he heard this he became sad
18.26 Those who heard . . said . . "who can be saved?
18.36 hearing a multitude going by, he inquired
19.11 As they heard . . he proceeded . . a parable
20.16 When they heard . . they said, "God forbid!
20.45 in the hearing of all the people
21. 9 "when you hear of wars and tumults
21.38 all the people came . . to hear him
22.71 "We have heard it ourselves
23. 6 When Pilate heard this, he asked
23. 8 Herod . . had heard about him
Jn 1.37 The two disciples heard him say this
1.40 One of the two who heard John speak
3. 8 "The wind[f] blows . . and you hear
3.29 "who stands and hears him, rejoices greatly
3.32 He bears witness to what he has . . heard
4. 1 Lord knew that the Pharisees had heard
4.42 "for we have heard for ourselves
4.47 When he heard that Jesus had come
5.24 "he who hears my word and believes
5.25 "the dead will hear the voice of the Son of God, and those who hear will live
5.28 "the hour . . when all . . will hear his voice
5.30 "as I hear, I judge
5.37 "His voice you have never heard
6.45 "Every one who has heard and learned
6.60 when they heard it, said, "This is . . hard
7.32 The Pharisees heard the crowd
7.40 When they heard these words
8. 9 when they heard it, they went away[r]‡
8.26 "I declare . . what I have heard
8.38 "what you have heard from your father
8.40 "the truth which I heard from God
8.43 "you cannot bear to hear my word
8.47 "He who is of God hears the words
8.47 "the reason why you do not hear them
9.27 "Why do you want to hear it again?
9.32 "Never . . has it been heard
9.35 Jesus heard that they had cast him out
9.40 the Pharisees near him heard this
10. 3 "the sheep hear his voice, and he calls
10.27 "My sheep hear my voice
11. 4 when Jesus heard . . he said, "This illness
11. 6 when he heard that he was ill, he stayed
11.20 When Martha heard . . she went and met
11.29 when she heard it, she rose quickly
11.41 "I thank thee that thou hast heard me
11.42 "I knew that thou hearest me always
12.12 crowd . . heard that Jesus was coming
12.18 they heard he had done this sign
12.29 The crowd standing by heard it
12.34 "We have heard from the law
12.47 "If any one hears my sayings
14.24 "the word which you hear is not mine
14.28 "You heard me say to you, 'I go away

Jn 15.15 "all that I have heard from my Father
16.13 "whatever he hears he will speak
18.21 "Ask those who have heard me, what I said
18.37 "one who is of the truth hears my voice
19. 8 When Pilate heard . . he was . . afraid
19.13 When Pilate heard . . , he brought Jesus out
21. 7 When . . Peter heard that it was the Lord
Acts 1. 4 he said, "you heard from me
2. 6 each one heard . . in his own language
2. 8 "how is it that we hear, each . . in his own?
2.11 "we hear them telling in our own tongues
2.22 "Men of Israel, hear these words
2.33 "he has poured out this which you . . hear
2.37 when they heard this they were cut
4. 4 many . . who heard the word believed
4.20 "speak of what we have seen and heard
4.24 when they heard it, they lifted their voices
5. 5 Ananias heard . . fell down and died. And . . fear came upon all who heard of it
5.11 great fear came . . upon all who heard
5.21 when they heard this, they entered
5.24 when . . the chief priests heard
5.33 When they heard this they were enraged
6.11 "have heard him speak . . against Moses
6.14 "we have heard him say that this Jesus
7. 2 "Brethren and fathers, hear me
7.12 "when Jacob heard . . grain in Egypt, he sent
7.34 " 'I have . . heard their groaning
7.54 when they heard . . they were enraged
8. 6 when they heard him and saw the signs
8.14 when the apostles at Jerusalem heard
8.30 Philip ran to him, and heard him reading
9. 4 fell to the ground and heard a voice
9. 7 hearing the voice but seeing no one
9.13 "I have heard from many about this man
9.21 all who heard him were amazed
9.38 disciples, hearing that Peter was there
10.22 "directed . . to hear what you have to say
10.33 "we are all here present . . to hear
10.44 Spirit fell on all who heard the word
10.46 they heard them speaking in tongues
11. 1 brethren who were in Judea heard
11. 7 "I heard a voice saying to me, 'Rise
11.18 When they heard this they were silenced
13. 7 who . . sought to hear the word of God
13.44 city gathered together to hear the word
13.48 the Gentiles heard this, they were glad
14.14 the apostles Barnabas and Paul heard
15. 7 "that . . the Gentiles should hear the word
15.24 "we have heard that some . . troubled you
16.14 One who heard us was . . Lydia
16.38 they were afraid when they heard
17. 8 disturbed when they heard this
17.21 except telling or hearing something new
17.32 when they heard of the resurrection . . said, "We will hear you again about this
18. 8 many . . hearing Paul believed
18.26 when Priscilla and Aquila heard him
19. 2 "never . . heard . . there is a Holy Spirit
19. 5 On hearing this, they were baptized
19.10 all the residents of Asia heard the word
19.26 "see and hear that not only at Ephesus
19.28 When they heard . . they were enraged
21.12 When we heard this, we . . begged him
21.20 when they heard it, they glorified God
21.22 "They will . . hear that you have come
22. 1 "Brethren and fathers, hear the defense
22. 2 they heard that he addressed them
22. 7 "I . . heard a voice saying to me, 'Saul
22. 9 "those . . with me . . did not hear the voice
22.14 " 'God . . appointed you . . to hear a voice
22.15 " 'a witness . . of what you have . . heard
22.26 When the centurion heard that, he went
23.16 the son of Paul's sister heard
24. 4 "I beg you . . to hear us briefly
24.24 Felix . . sent for Paul and heard him
Acts 25.22 "I should like to hear the man myself." "To-morrow," said he, "you shall hear
26.14 "I heard a voice saying to me . . 'Saul
26.29 "all who hear me . . might become . . as I am
28.15 they heard . . , came as far as the Forum
28.22 "But we desire to hear from you
28.26 " 'You shall . . hear but never understand
28.27 " 'their ears are heavy of hearing . . ; lest they should . . hear with their ears
Rom 10.14 him of whom they have never heard . . how are they to hear without a preacher?
10.18 But I ask, have they not heard?
11. 8 "spirit of stupor, . . ears that should not hear
15.21 "shall understand who have never heard
1 Cor 2. 9 "What no eye has seen, nor ear heard
11.18 I hear that there are divisions
2 Cor 12. 4 he heard things that cannot be told
12. 6 think more . . than he . . hears from me
Gal 1.13 For you have heard of my former life
1.23 they . . heard . . "He . . is now preaching
4.21 Tell me, . . do you not hear the law?
Eph 1.13 you also, who have heard the word of truth
1.15 because I have heard of your faith
3. 2 that you have heard of the stewardship
4.21 that you have heard about him
4.29 may impart grace to those who hear
Phil 1.27 so that . . I may hear of you
1.30 conflict which you . . now hear to be mine
2.26 because you heard that he was ill
4. 9 What you have . . heard . . in me, do
Col 1. 4 because we have heard of your faith
1. 6 from the day you heard and understood
1. 9 from the day we heard of it
1.23 the hope of the gospel which you heard
2 Th 3.11 we hear . . some . . are living in idleness
2 Tim 1.13 words which you have heard from me
2. 2 what you have heard from me . . entrust
4.17 that all the Gentiles might hear it
Phm . 5 because I hear of your love
Heb 2. 1 attention to what we have heard
2. 3 attested to us by those who heard him
3. 7 "Today, when you hear his voice
3.15 "Today, when you hear his voice
3.16 Who were they that heard?
4. 2 message which they heard did not benefit
4. 7 "Today, when you hear his voice
Jas 1.19 Let every man be quick to hear
5.11 You . . heard of the steadfastness of Job
2 Pet 1.18 we heard this voice borne from heaven
1 Jn 1. 1 which we have heard, which we have seen
1. 3 that which we have seen and heard
1. 5 This is the message we have heard
2. 7 commandment . . which you have heard
2.18 you . . heard that antichrist is coming
2.24 Let what you heard . . abide in you. If what you heard . . abides in you
3.11 this is the message which you have heard
4. 3 antichrist, of which you heard
5.14 that if we ask . . he hears us
5.15 And if we know that he hears us
2 Jn . 6 as you have heard from the beginning
3 Jn . 4 to hear that my children follow the truth
Rev 1. 3 blessed are those who hear, and who keep
1.10 I heard behind me a loud voice
2. 7 " 'He who has an ear, let him hear
2.11 " 'He who has an ear, let him hear
2.17 " 'He who has an ear, let him hear
2.29 " 'He who has an ear, let him hear
3. 3 " 'Remember then what you . . heard
3. 6 " 'He who has an ear, let him hear
3.13 " 'He who has an ear, let him hear
3.20 " 'if any one hears my voice and opens
3.22 " 'He who has an ear, let him hear
4. 1 first voice, which I had heard speaking
5.11 I heard around the throne
5.13 I heard every creature in heaven
6. 1 I heard one of the four living creatures

Rev 6. 3 I heard the second living creature
6. 5 I heard the third living creature say
6. 6 I heard what seemed to be a voice
6. 7 I heard the voice of the fourth living creature
7. 4 I heard the number of the sealed
8.13 I heard an eagle crying with a loud voice
9.13 I heard a voice from the four horns
9.16 I heard their number
9.20 which cannot either see or hear or walk
10. 4 I heard a voice from heaven saying
10. 8 voice which I had heard from heaven
11.12 they heard a loud voice from heaven
12.10 And I heard a loud voice in heaven
13. 9 If any one has an ear, let him hear
14. 2 I heard a voice from heaven
14. 2 voice I heard was like the sound of harpers
14.13 I heard a voice from heaven saying
16. 1 I heard a loud voice from the temple
16. 5 I heard the angel of water say
16. 7 I heard the altar cry, "Yea, Lord God
18. 4 I heard another voice from heaven
18.22 "trumpeters, shall be heard . . no more
18.22 "millstone shall be heard . . no more
18.23 "bride shall be heard in thee no more
19. 1 After this I heard . . a great multitude
19. 6 Then I heard . . a great multitude
21. 3 I heard a loud voice from the throne
22. 8 I John am he who heard and saw . . And when I heard . . them, I fell down to worship
22.17 let him who hears say, "Come
22.18 I warn every one who hears the words

2. *hear to the end:* διακούω DIAKOUŌ*
Acts 23.35 "I will hear you when your accusers arrive

3. *hear, obey:* εἰσακούω EISAKOUŌ
Mt 6. 7 "they think that they will be heard
Lk 1.13 "Zechariah, . . your prayer is heard
Acts 10.31 " 'Cornelius, your prayer has been heard
Heb 5. 7 he was heard for his godly fear

HEAR BEFORE

1. *hear beforehand:* προακούω PROAKOUŌ*
Col 1. 5 Of this you have heard before

HEARD, WHAT IS
HEARS, WHAT ONE

1. *hearing, report:* ἀκοή AKOĒ
[a]gen.
Rom 10.16 "who has believed what he has heard?
10.17 faith comes from what is heard, and what is heard comes by the preaching
1 Th 2.13 [a]word of God which you heard from us
Heb 4. 2 [a]message which they heard did not benefit
2 Pet 2. 8 what that righteous man saw and heard

HEARER

1. *hear:* ἀκούω (subst. part.) AKOUŌ
1 Tim 4.16 save both yourself and your hearers
2 Tim 2.14 disputing about words . . ruins the hearers
Heb 12.19 whose words made the hearers entreat

2. *hearer:* ἀκροατής AKROATĒS*
Rom 2.13 not the hearers . . who are righteous
Jas 1.22 doers of the word, and not hearers only
1.23 For if any one is a hearer of the word
1.25 being no hearer that forgets but a doer

HEARING

1. *hearing, report:* ἀκοή AKOĒ
Lk 7. 1 sayings in the hearing of the people
1 Cor 12.17 where would be the hearing?
Gal 3. 2 by . . the law, or by hearing with faith?
3. 5 by . . the law, or by hearing with faith?
Heb 5.11 since you have become dull of hearing

2. *ear:* οὖς (pl.) OUS
Lk 4.21 "scripture . . fulfilled in your hearing

HEARING, GIVE A

1. *hear:* ἀκούω AKOUŌ
Jn 7.51 "without first giving him a hearing

HEART

1. *heart:* καρδία KARDIA
Mt 5. 8 "Blessed are the pure in heart
5.28 "committed adultery . . in his heart
6.21 "there will your heart be also
9. 4 "Why do you think evil in your hearts?
11.29 "for I am gentle and lowly in heart
12.34 "out of the . . heart the mouth speaks
12.40 "three nights in the heart of the earth
13.15 "this people's heart has grown dull . . lest they . . understand with their heart
13.19 "snatches away what is sown in his heart
15. 8 " 'their heart is far from me
15.18 "what comes . . from the heart . . defiles
15.19 "out of the heart come evil thoughts
18.35 "if you do not forgive . . from your heart
22.37 "love the Lord your God with all your heart
Mk 2. 6 scribes . . questioning in their hearts
2. 8 "Why . . question thus in your hearts?
3. 5 grieved at their hardness of heart
6.52 but their hearts were hardened
7. 6 " 'their heart is far from me
7.19 "it enters, not his heart but his stomach
7.21 "For from within, out of the heart of man
8.17 "Are your hearts hardened?
11.23 "whoever . . does not doubt in his heart
12.30 "you shall love . . with all your heart
12.33 "to love him with all the heart
Lk 1.17 "to turn the hearts of the fathers
1.51 "proud in . . imagination of their hearts
1.66 laid them up in their hearts
2.19 Mary kept . . these things . . in her heart
2.35 "thoughts out of many hearts
2.51 mother kept all these things in her heart
3.15 all men questioned in their hearts
5.22 "Why do you question in your hearts?
6.45 "out of the good treasure of his heart
6.45 "out of the abundance of the heart
8.12 "takes away the word from their hearts
8.15 "hold it fast in an honest and good heart
9.47 perceived the thought of their hearts
10.27 "love the Lord . . with all your heart
12.34 "there will your heart be also
16.15 "but God knows your hearts
21.34 "heed . . lest your hearts be weighed down
24.25 "O foolish men, and slow of heart
24.32 "Did not our hearts burn within us?[c]
24.38 "why do questionings rise in your hearts?
Jn 12.40 "He has . . hardened their heart, lest they . . perceive with their heart
13. 2 devil . . put it into the heart of Judas
14. 1 "Let not your hearts be troubled
14.27 "Let not your hearts be troubled
16. 6 "sorrow has filled your hearts
16.22 "your hearts will rejoice
Acts 2.26 " 'therefore my heart was glad
2.37 when they heard . . they were cut to the h.
2.46 partook . . with glad and generous hearts
4.32 those who believed were of one heart
5. 3 "why has Satan filled your heart to lie?
5. 4 "How . . contrived this deed in your heart?
7.23 "it came into his h. to visit his brethren
7.39 "in their hearts they turned to Egypt
7.51 "uncircumcised in heart and ears
8.21 "your heart is not right before God
8.22 "that . . the intent of your h. . . be forgiven
[8.37 "*If you believe with all your heart*‡
13.22 " 'the son of Jesse a man after my heart
14.17 "satisfying your hearts with . . gladness
15. 9 "but cleansed their hearts by faith
16.14 "The Lord opened her heart to give heed
21.13 "weeping and breaking my heart
28.27 " 'this people's heart has grown dull, . . lest they . . understand with their heart
Rom 1.24 gave them up in the lusts of their hearts
2. 5 by your hard and impenitent heart
2.15 law . . written on their hearts

Rom 2.29 real circumcision is a matter of the heart
5. 5 God's love has been poured into our hearts
6.17 you . . have become obedient from the heart
8.27 he who searches the hearts of men
9. 2 I have . . unceasing anguish in my heart
10. 1 my heart's desire and prayer to God
10. 6 Do not say in your h., "Who will ascend?
10. 8 near you, on your lips and in your heart
10. 9 believe in your heart that God raised
10.10 For man believes with his heart
16.18 deceive the hearts of the simpleminded
1 Cor 2. 9 "nor the heart of man conceived
4. 5 who . . will disclose the purposes of the heart
7.37 is firmly established in his heart . . and has determined this in his heart
14.25 the secrets of his heart are disclosed
2 Cor 1.22 he has . . given us his Spirit in our hearts
2. 4 much affliction and anguish of heart
3. 2 our letter . . written on your[c] hearts
3. 3 but on tablets of human hearts
4. 6 God . . who has shone in our hearts
5.12 pride themselves . . not on his heart
6.11 to you, Corinthians; our heart is wide
7. 3 you are in our hearts, to die together
8.16 earnest care for you into the heart of Titus
Gal 4. 6 God has sent the Spirit . . into our hearts
Eph 1.18 the eyes of your hearts enlightened
3.17 that Christ may dwell in your hearts
4.18 due to their hardness of heart
5.19 making melody . . with all your heart
6. 5 in singleness of heart, as to Christ
6.22 that he may encourage your hearts
Phil 1. 7 because I hold you in my heart
4. 7 peace of God . . will keep your hearts
Col 2. 2 that their hearts may be encouraged
3.15 the peace of Christ rule in your hearts
3.16 with thankfulness in your hearts to God
3.22 in singleness of heart, fearing the Lord
4. 8 that he may encourage your hearts
1 Th 2. 4 to please God who tests our hearts
2.17 bereft of you . . in person not in heart
3.13 so that he may establish your hearts
2 Th 2.17 comfort your hearts and establish them
3. 5 May the Lord direct your hearts
1 Tim 1. 5 love that issues from a pure heart
2 Tim 2.22 call upon the Lord from a pure heart
Heb 3. 8 "do not harden your hearts
3.10 " 'They always go astray in their hearts
3.12 an evil, unbelieving heart
3.15 "do not harden your hearts
4. 7 "do not harden your hearts
4.12 discerning the thoughts . . of the heart
8.10 "I will . . write them on their hearts
10.16 "I will put my laws on their hearts
10.22 let us draw near with a true heart . . , with our hearts sprinkled clean
13. 9 it is well that the heart be strengthened
Jas 1.26 If any one . . deceives his heart
3.14 if . . selfish ambition in your hearts
4. 8 purify your hearts, you men of double mind
5. 5 you have fattened your hearts
5. 8 Establish your hearts, for the coming
1 Pet 1.22 love one another . . from the heart
3. 4 let it be the hidden person of the heart
3.15 in your hearts reverence Christ as Lord
2 Pet 1.19 the morning star rises in your hearts
2.14 They have hearts trained in greed
1 Jn 3.19 we shall . . reassure our hearts before him
3.20 whenever our hearts condemn us; for God is greater than our hearts
3.21 if our hearts do not condemn us
Rev 2.23 " 'I am he who searches mind and heart
17.17 "God has put it into their hearts
18. 7 "in her heart she says, 'A queen I sit

2. *body cavity, belly:* κοιλία KOILIA
Jn 7.38 " 'Out of his heart shall flow rivers

3. *life, soul, self:* ψυχή PSYCHĒ
Eph 6. 6 doing the will of God from the heart

4. *inward parts* (pl.): σπλάγχνον SPLAGCHNON
2 Cor 7.15 his heart goes out all the more to you
Phm . 7 hearts of the saints have been refreshed
.12 I am sending him back . . , my very heart
.20 Refresh my heart in Christ
1 Jn 3.17 if any one . . closes his heart against him

CONTEXTUALLY
Rom 9.18 hardens the heart of whomever he wills
2 Cor 6.13 In return . . widen your hearts also
1 Tim 6.10 pierced their hearts with many pangs

HEART, HARDNESS OF

1. *hardness of heart:* σκληροκαρδία SKLĒROKARDIA*
Mt 19. 8 "For your hardness of heart
Mk 10. 5 "For your hardness of heart he wrote
16.14 their unbelief and hardness of heart[k]‡

HEART, HAVE A TENDER

1. *with healthy bowels, tenderhearted:* εὔσπλαγχνος EUSPLAGCHNOS [A.3.e.2]
1 Pet 3. 8 have . . a tender h. and a humble mind

HEART, LOSE

1. *become weary, despair:* ἐγκακέω EGKAKEŌ
Lk 18. 1 always to pray and not lose heart
2 Cor 4. 1 by the mercy of God,[e] we do not lose h.
4.16 So we do not lose heart
Eph 3.13 So I ask you not to[e] lose heart

2. *relax:* ἐκλύω (pass.) EKLYŌ
Gal 6. 9 we shall reap, if we do not lose heart

HEART, ONE WHO KNOWS THE

1. *knower of hearts:* καρδιογνώστης KARDIOGNŌSTĒS*
Acts 1.24 "Lord, who knowest the hearts of all men
15. 8 "God who knows the heart bore witness

HEART, OPEN ONE'S

1. *make room for, hold, go:* χωρέω CHŌREŌ
2 Cor 7. 2 Open your hearts to us

HEART, TAKE

1. *be of good cheer:* εὐθυμέω EUTHYMEŌ
Acts 27.22 "I now bid you take heart
27.25 "So take heart, men, for I have faith

2. *have confidence:* θαρρέω THARREŌ
Mt 9. 2 he said to the paralytic, "Take heart
9.22 seeing her he said, "Take heart, daughter
14.27 "Take heart, it is I; have no fear
Mk 6.50 "Take heart, it is I; have no fear
10.49 "Take heart; rise, he is calling you

HEARTILY

1. *from the soul:* ἐκ ψυχῆς PSYCHĒ [B.1.a.1]
Col 3.23 work heartily, as serving the Lord

HEARTLESS

1. *without affection:* ἄστοργος ASTORGOS
Rom 1.31 foolish, faithless, heartless, ruthless

HEARTY

1. *many, great:* πολύς POLYS
1 Cor 16.19 Aquila and Prisca . . send . . hearty greetings

HEAT

1. *burning heat:* καῦμα KAUMA
Rev 16. 9 men were scorched by the fierce heat

2. *heat:* θέρμη THERMĒ*
Acts 28. 3 a viper came out because of the heat

HEAT, SCORCHING

1. *burning heat:* καῦμα KAUMA
Rev 7.16 "neither thirst . . nor any scorching heat

2. *burning heat:* καύσων KAUSŌN*
Mt 20.12 " 'who have borne . . the scorching heat
Lk 12.55 " 'There will be scorching heat
Jas 1.11 the sun rises with its scorching heat

HEATHEN

1. *foreign, Gentile:* ἐθνικός ETHNIKOS
3 Jn . 7 they . . accepted nothing from the heathen

2. *nation, people, Gentile:* ἔθνος ETHNOS
1 Cor 12. 2 when you were h., you were led astray
1 Th 4. 5 not in the passion of lust like heathen

HEAVEN

1. *heaven, sky:* οὐρανός (sg. or pl.) OURANOS

Mt 3. 2 "for the kingdom of heaven is at hand
3.16 behold, the heavens were opened[g]
3.17 lo, a voice from heaven
4.17 "for the kingdom of heaven is at hand
5. 3 "for theirs is the kingdom of heaven
5.10 "for theirs is the kingdom of heaven
5.12 "for your reward is great in heaven
5.16 "glory to your Father who is in heaven
5.18 "till heaven and earth pass away
5.19 "called least in the kingdom of heaven
5.19 "called great in the kingdom of heaven
5.20 "you will never enter the kingdom of h.
5.34 "Do not swear at all, either by heaven
5.45 "sons of your Father who is in heaven
6. 1 "from your Father who is in heaven
6. 9 "Our Father who art in heaven
6.10 "Thy will be done, On earth as it is in h.
6.20 "lay up for yourselves treasures in heaven
7.11 "your Father who is in heaven
7.21 "shall enter the kingdom of heaven
7.21 "the will of my Father who is in heaven
8.11 "sit at table . . in the kingdom of heaven
10. 7 " 'The kingdom of heaven is at hand
10.32 "before my Father who is in heaven
10.33 "before my Father who is in heaven
11.11 "who is least in the kingdom of heaven
11.12 "kingdom of h. has suffered violence[c]
11.23 "Capernaum, will you be exalted in heaven?
11.25 "Father, Lord of heaven and earth
12.50 "the will of my Father in heaven
13.11 "the secrets of the kingdom of heaven
13.24 "The kingdom of h. may be compared
13.31 "kingdom of h. is like a grain of mustard
13.33 "The kingdom of heaven is like leaven
13.44 "kingdom of heaven is like treasure
13.45 "the kingdom of heaven is like a merchant
13.47 "the kingdom of heaven is like a net
13.52 "scribe . . trained for the kingdom of h.
14.19 taking the . . fish he looked up to h.
16. 1 asked him to show them a sign from h.
16.17 "my Father who is in heaven
16.19 "keys of the kingdom of heaven, and whatever you bind on earth shall be bound in h.
16.19 "whatever you loose . . shall be loosed in h.
18. 1 "greatest in the kingdom of heaven
18. 3 "you will never enter the kingdom of h.
18. 4 "he is the greatest in the kingdom of h.
18.10 "in heaven their angels always behold the face of my Father who is in heaven[c]
18.14 "not the will of my[d] Father who is in h.
18.18 "whatever you bind . . shall be bound in h.
18.18 "whatever you loose . . shall be loosed in h.
18.19 "done for them by my Father in h.
18.23 "kingdom of heaven may be compared
19.12 "eunuchs for . . the kingdom of h.
19.14 "to such belongs the kingdom of heaven
19.21 "you will have treasure in heaven
19.23 "a rich man to enter the kingdom of h.
20. 1 "kingdom of h. is like a householder
21.25 "From heaven or from men?" . . "If we say, 'From heaven,' he will say to us
22. 2 "kingdom of heaven may be compared
22.30 "they . . are like angels[s] in heaven
23.13 "because you shut the kingdom of heaven
23.22 "he who swears by heaven
24.29 "the stars will fall from heaven, and the powers of the heavens will be shaken
24.30 "the sign of the Son of man in heaven
24.30 "Son of man coming on the clouds of h.
24.31 "from one end of heaven to the other
24.35 "Heaven and earth will pass away
24.36 "not even the angels of heaven
25. 1 "kingdom of heaven shall be compared
26.64 "Son of man . . coming on the clouds of h.
28. 2 angel of the Lord descended from heaven

Mt 28.18 "All authority in heaven and on earth

Mk 1.10 he saw the heavens opened
1.11 from heaven, "Thou . . my beloved Son[d]
6.41 taking . . the two fish he looked up to h.
7.34 looking up to heaven, he sighed
8.11 seeking from him a sign from heaven
10.21 "you will have treasure in heaven
11.25 "your Father also who is in heaven
[11.26 "*neither will your Father who is in heaven*‡
11.30 "Was the baptism of John from heaven?
11.31 "If we say, 'From heaven,' he will say
12.25 "they . . are like angels in heaven
13.25 "stars will be falling from heaven, and the powers in the heavens will be shaken
13.27 "ends of the earth to the ends of heaven
13.31 "Heaven and earth will pass away
13.32 "not even the angels in heaven, nor the Son
14.62 "coming with the clouds of heaven
16.19 taken up into heaven, and sat down[k]‡

Lk 2.15 angels went away from them into h.
3.21 when Jesus . . was praying, the h. was opened
3.22 a voice came from heaven
4.25 "when the heaven was shut up three years
6.23 "your reward is great in heaven
9.16 taking . . the two fish he looked up to h.
9.54 "bid fire come down from heaven
10.15 "will you be exalted to heaven?
10.18 "I saw Satan fall . . from heaven
10.20 "rejoice that your names are written in h.
10.21 "I thank thee, Father, Lord of heaven
11.16 sought from him a sign from heaven
12.33 "treasure in the heavens that does not fail
15. 7 "there will be more joy in heaven
15.18 " 'I will say . . "I have sinned against h.
15.21 " 'Father, I have sinned against heaven
16.17 "easier for heaven and earth to pass away
17.29 "fire and sulphur rained from heaven
18.13 "would not even lift up his eyes to h.
18.22 "you will have treasure in heaven
19.38 "Peace in h. and glory in the highest!
20. 4 "Was the baptism of John from heaven?
20. 5 "If we say, 'From heaven,' he will say
21.11 "there will be . . great signs from h.
21.26 "the powers of the heavens will be shaken
21.33 "Heaven and earth will pass away
[22.43 *angel from heaven, strengthening him*‡
24.51 he . . was carried up into heaven[a]‡

Jn 1.32 "Spirit descend as a dove from heaven
1.51 "you will see heaven opened
3.13 "No one has ascended into heaven but he who descended from heaven
[3.13 "the Son of man *who is in heaven*‡
3.27 "except what is given him from heaven
3.31 he who comes from heaven is above all
6.31 " 'He gave them bread from heaven to eat
6.32 "not Moses who gave . . bread from heaven; my Father gives you the true bread from h.
6.33 "bread . . which comes down from heaven
6.38 "I have come down from heaven
6.41 "bread which came down from heaven
6.42 " 'I have come down from heaven
6.50 "bread which comes down from heaven
6.51 "bread which came down from heaven
6.58 "bread which came down from heaven
12.28 Then a voice came from heaven
17. 1 he lifted up his eyes to heaven

Acts 1.10 while they were gazing into heaven
1.11 "why do you stand looking into heaven?
1.11 "who was taken up from you into h., will come . . as you saw him go into h.
2. 2 suddenly a sound came from heaven
2. 5 men from every nation under heaven
2.19 " 'I will show wonders in the heaven above
2.34 "David did not ascend into the heavens
3.21 "whom heaven must receive until the time
4.12 "there is no other name under heaven
4.24 "Lord, who didst make the heaven

Acts 7.42 "gave them over to worship the host of h.
7.49 " 'H. is my throne, and earth my footstool
7.55 full of the Holy Spirit, gazed into heaven
7.56 "Behold, I see the heavens opened
9. 3 suddenly a light from heaven flashed
10.11 heaven opened, and something descending
10.16 the thing was taken up at once to heaven
11. 5 "let down from heaven by four corners
11. 9 "answered a second time from heaven
11.10 "all was drawn up again into heaven
14.15 "a living God who made the heaven
17.24 "being Lord of heaven and earth
22. 6 "about noon a great light from heaven
Rom 1.18 wrath of God is revealed from heaven
10. 6 "Who will ascend into heaven?
1 Cor 8. 5 so-called gods in heaven or on earth
15.47 the second man is from heaven
2 Cor 5. 1 from God, a house . . eternal in the heavens
12. 2 a man . . caught up to the third heaven
Gal 1. 8 if we, or an angel from heaven
Eph 1.10 all things in him, things in heaven
3.15 from whom every family in heaven
4.10 (ascended far above all the heavens
6. 9 both their Master and yours is in heaven
Phil 3.20 our commonwealth is in heaven
Col 1. 5 the hope laid up for you in heaven
1.16 all things were created, in h. and on earth
1.20 all things, whether on earth or in h.
1.23 preached to every creature under h.
4. 1 you also have a Master in heaven
1 Th 1.10 to wait for his Son from heaven
4.16 Lord himself will descend from heaven
2 Th 1. 7 when . . Lord Jesus is revealed from h.
Heb 1.10 "heavens are the work of thy hands
4.14 high priest . . passed through the heavens
7.26 high priest . . exalted above the heavens
8. 1 at the right hand of the throne . . in h.
9.24 Christ has entered . . into heaven itself
11.12 as many as the stars of heaven
12.23 first-born who are enrolled in heaven
12.25 if we reject him who warns from heaven
12.26 "I will shake . . also the heaven
Jas 5.12 do not swear, either by heaven
5.18 the heaven gave rain
1 Pet 1. 4 inheritance . . unfading, kept in heaven
1.12 the Holy Spirit sent from heaven
3.22 who has gone into heaven
2 Pet 1.18 we heard this voice borne from heaven
3. 5 by the word of God heavens existed
3. 7 the heavens and earth that now exist
3.10 then the heavens will pass away
3.12 the heavens will be kindled!
3.13 we wait for new heavens
Rev 3.12 " 'Jerusalem which comes . . from . . heaven
4. 1 lo, in heaven an open door!
4. 2 lo, a throne stood in heaven!
5. 3 no one in heaven or on earth
5.13 I heard every creature in heaven
8. 1 silence in heaven for about half an hour
8.10 a great star fell from heaven
9. 1 I saw a star fallen from heaven to earth
10. 1 angel coming down from heaven
10. 4 but I heard a voice from heaven
10. 5 angel . . lifted up his right hand to heaven
10. 6 who created heaven and what is in it
10. 8 voice which I had heard from heaven
11.12 a loud voice from heaven . . And . . they went up to heaven in a cloud
11.13 the rest . . gave glory to the God of h.
11.15 there were loud voices in heaven
11.19 God's temple in heaven was opened
12. 1 a great portent appeared in heaven
12. 3 another portent appeared in heaven
12. 4 swept . . a third of the stars of heaven
12. 7 Now war arose in heaven
12. 8 no longer any place for them in heaven
12.10 I heard a loud voice in heaven
Rev 12.12 "Rejoice then, O h. and you . . therein!
13. 6 that is, those who dwell in heaven
13.13 making fire come down from heaven
14. 2 I heard a voice from heaven
14. 7 worship him who made heaven
14.13 I heard a voice from heaven
14.17 angel came out of the temple in heaven
15. 1 I saw another portent in heaven
15. 5 tent of witness in heaven was opened
16.11 cursed the God of heaven for their pain
16.21 hailstones . . , dropped on men from heaven
18. 1 angel coming down from heaven
18. 4 I heard another voice from heaven
18. 5 "her sins are heaped high as heaven
18.20 "Rejoice over her, O heaven
19. 1 voice of a great multitude in heaven
19.11 Then I saw heaven opened
19.14 armies of heaven, arrayed in fine linen
20. 1 an angel coming down from heaven
20. 9 but fire came down from heaven[n]
21. 1 I saw a new heaven and a new earth; for the first heaven . . had passed away
21. 2 new Jerusalem, coming down out of h.
21.10 Jerusalem coming down out of heaven

HEAVEN, FROM
HEAVEN, IN
HEAVEN, OF
HEAVEN, WHO IS IN
HEAVENLY

1. *heavenly:* ἐπουράνιος EPOURANIOS
Jn 3.12 "how can you believe . . heavenly things?
1 Cor 15.48 and as is the man of heaven, so are those who are of heaven
15.49 bear the image of the man of heaven
Eph 1. 3 spiritual blessing in the heavenly places
1.20 at his right hand in the heavenly places
2. 6 sit with him in the heavenly places
3.10 known to . . powers in the heavenly places
6.12 hosts of wickedness in the heavenly places
Phil 2.10 bow, in heaven and on earth
2 Tim 4.18 save me for his heavenly kingdom
Heb 3. 1 brethren, who share in a heavenly call
6. 4 who have tasted the heavenly gift
8. 5 shadow of the heavenly sanctuary
9.23 the heavenly things themselves
11.16 a better country, . . a heavenly one
12.22 you have come to . . the heavenly Jerusalem

2. *heavenly:* οὐράνιος OURANIOS
Mt 5.48 "perfect, as your heavenly Father is perfect
6.14 "your heavenly Father also will forgive you
6.26 "yet your heavenly Father feeds them
6.32 "heavenly Father knows that you need
15.13 "which my heavenly Father has not planted
18.35 "So also my heavenly Father will do
23. 9 "you have one Father, who is in heaven
Lk 2.13 a multitude of the heavenly host
Acts 26.19 "not disobedient to the heavenly vision

3. *heaven:* οὐρανός OURANOS [B.1.a.1]
[a]ἐξ οὐρανοῦ [b]ἐν τοῖς οὐρανοῖς
Lk 11.13 [a]"how much more will the heavenly Father!
2 Cor 5. 2 [a]long to put on our heavenly dwelling
Heb 9.23 [b]copies of the heavenly things to be purified

4. *from heaven:* οὐρανόθεν OURANOTHEN
Acts 14.17 "from heaven rains and fruitful seasons
26.13 "I saw on the way a light from heaven

HEAVY

1. *weigh down:* βαρέω (perf. pass. part.) BAREŌ
Mt 26.43 sleeping, for their eyes were heavy
Lk 9.32 were heavy with sleep

2. *heavily:* βαρέως BAREŌS* [A.4.a]
Mt 13.15 " 'and their ears are heavy of hearing
Acts 28.27 " 'and their ears are heavy of hearing

3. *heavy, severe:* βαρύς BARYS
Mt 23. 4 "They bind heavy burdens, hard to bear[u]

4. *great:* μέγας MEGAS
Rev 11.19 an earthquake, and heavy hail

HEAVY AS A HUNDREDWEIGHT
1. *weighing a talent:* ταλαντιαῖος TALANTIAIOS*
Rev 16.21 hailstones, heavy as a hundredweight

HEAVY, BE
1. *weigh down:* καταβαρύνω (pass.) KATABARYNŌ*
Mk 14.40 sleeping, for their eyes were very heavy

HEAVY LADEN, BE
1. *load:* φορτίζω (perf. pass.) PHORTIZŌ
Mt 11.28 "all who labor and are heavy laden

HEBREW
1. *Hebrew:* Ἑβραϊκός
Lk [23.38 an inscription . . *in letters of . . Hebrew*‡
2. *Jew:* Ἑβραῖος
Acts 6. 1 Hellenists murmured against the Hebrews
2 Cor 11.22 Are they Hebrews? So am I
Phil 3. 5 of the tribe of Benjamin, a Hebrew born of Hebrews; as to the law a Pharisee
3. *Hebrew language:* Ἑβραΐς
Acts 21.40 spoke to them in the Hebrew language
22. 2 addressed them in the Hebrew language
26.14 "I heard a voice . . in the H. language
4. *in Hebrew:* Ἑβραϊστί
Jn 5. 2 a pool, in Hebrew called Bethzatha[j]
19.13 The Pavement, . . in Hebrew, Gabbatha
19.17 which is called in Hebrew Golgotha
19.20 written in H., in Latin, and in Greek
20.16 She . . said to him in H., "Rabboni!
Rev 9.11 his name in Hebrew is Abaddon
16.16 which is called in H. Armageddon

HEDGE
1. *fence:* φραγμός PHRAGMOS*
Mt 21.33 "who planted a vineyard, and set a hedge
Mk 12. 1 "man planted a vineyard, and set a hedge
Lk 14.23 " 'Go out to the highways and hedges

HEED (*See also* APPEAL, HEED AN)
1. *hear:* ἀκούω AKOUŌ
Jn 10. 8 "the sheep did not heed them
10.16 "other sheep . . will heed my voice

HEED, GIVE
1. *hold to, be intent on:* προσέχω PROSECHŌ
Acts 8. 6 with one accord gave heed to . . Philip
8.10 They all gave heed to him
8.11 And they gave heed to him
16.14 opened her heart to give heed to . . Paul
1 Tim 4. 1 by giving heed to deceitful spirits
Tit 1.14 instead of giving heed to Jewish myths

HEED, PAY NO
1. *neglect:* ἀμελέω AMELEŌ
Heb 8. 9 "so I paid no heed to them

HEED, TAKE
1. *see, look:* βλέπω (imper.) BLEPŌ
Mt 24. 4 "Take heed that no one leads you astray
Mk 4.24 "Take heed what you hear
13. 5 "Take heed that no one leads you astray
13. 9 "But take heed to yourselves
13.23 "take heed; I have told you all things
13.33 "Take heed, watch;[a] for you do not know
Lk 8.18 "Take heed then how you hear
21. 8 "Take heed that you are not led astray
1 Cor 10.12 let any one . . take heed lest he fall
Gal 5.15 take heed that you are not consumed
2. *hold upon, aim at:* ἐπέχω EPECHŌ
1 Tim 4.16 Take heed to yourself and to your teaching
3. *beware:* εὐλαβέομαι EULABEOMAI*
Heb 11. 7 Noah . . took heed and constructed an ark
4. *see, perceive:* ὁράω (imper.) HORAŌ
Mt 16. 6 "Take heed and beware of the leaven
Mk 8.15 "Take heed, beware of the leaven
Lk 12.15 "Take heed, and beware of all covetousness
5. *hold to, be intent on:* προσέχω PROSECHŌ
Lk 17. 3 "Take heed to yourselves
21.34 "But take heed to yourselves
Acts 20.28 "Take heed to yourselves and to all

HEEL
1. *heel:* πτέρνα PTERNA*
Jn 13.18 " 'He . . has lifted his heel against me

HEIFER
1. *young cow:* δάμαλις DAMALIS*
Heb 9.13 sprinkling . . with the ashes of a heifer

HEIGHT
1. *height:* ὕψωμα HYPSŌMA
Rom 8.39 height, nor depth, nor anything else
2. *height:* ὕψος HYPSOS
Eph 3.18 breadth and length and height and depth
Rev 21.16 its length and breadth and h. are equal

HEIR
1. *heir:* κληρονόμος KLĒRONOMOS
Mt 21.38 " 'This is the heir; come, let us kill him
Mk 12. 7 " 'This is the heir; come, let us kill him
Lk 20.14 " 'This is the heir; let us kill him
Rom 4.14 If . . adherents of the law . . are . . heirs
8.17 if children, then heirs, heirs of God . . , provided we suffer with him
Gal 3.29 then you are Abraham's offspring, heirs
4. 1 the heir, as long as he is a child
4. 7 if a son then an heir
Tit 3. 7 that we might . . become heirs in hope
Heb 1. 2 a Son, whom he appointed the heir
6.17 to show more convincingly to the heirs
11. 7 became an heir of the righteousness
Jas 2. 5 rich in faith and heirs of the kingdom

HEIR, FELLOW
1. *inheriting with:* συγκληρονόμος (subst.) SYGKLĒRONOMOS
Rom 8.17 and fellow heirs with Christ
Eph 3. 6 how the Gentiles are fellow heirs

HEIR, JOINT
1. *inheriting with:* συγκληρονόμος (subst.) SYGKLĒRONOMOS
1 Pet 3. 7 you are joint heirs of the grace of life

HEIR WITH
1. *joint heir:* συγκληρονόμος (subst.) SYGKLĒRONOMOS
Heb 11. 9 heirs with him of the same promise

HELD, BE
1. *come to be, happen, be:* γίνομαι GINOMAI [A.6.a.5]
Rom 3.19 that . . the . . world may be held accountable

HELI: Ἡλί 'hēlī
Lk 3.23 Joseph, the son of Heli

HELL
1. *valley of Hinnom:* γέεννα GEENNA*
Mt 5.22 " 'fool!' shall be liable to the hell[k] of fire†
5.29 "that your whole body be thrown into hell[k]†
5.30 "that your whole body go into hell[k]†
10.28 "can destroy both soul and body in hell[z]†
18. 9 "than . . be thrown into the hell[b] of fire†
23.15 "make him twice as much a child of hell[w]†
23.33 "are you to escape being sentenced to hell?[w]†
Mk 9.43 "than with two hands to go to hell[m]†
9.45 "than . . to be thrown into hell[m,n]†
9.47 "than . . to be thrown into hell[m]†
Lk 12. 5 "has power to cast into hell[m]†
Jas 3. 6 The tongue is . . set on fire by hell[c]†

HELL, CAST INTO
1. *cast into Tartarus:* ταρταρόω TARTAROŌ*
2 Pet 2. 4 if God . . cast them into hell[f]†

HELLENIST: Ἑλληνιστής
Acts 6. 1 Hellenists murmured against the Hebrews
9.29 disputed against the Hellenists
[11.20 coming to Antioch spoke to the *Hellenists*‡

HELMET
1. *helmet:* περικεφαλαία PERIKEPHALAIA*
Eph 6.17 take the helmet of salvation
1 Th 5. 8 for a helmet the hope of salvation

HELP
1. *hold against:* ἀντέχω (mid.) ANTECHŌ
1 Th 5.14 help the weak, be patient with them all
2. *lay hold of, help* (mid.): ἀντιλαμβάνω ANTILAMBANŌ
Lk 1.54 "He has helped his servant Israel

Acts 20.35 "by so toiling one must help the weak
3. *help, support:* βοήθεια BOĒTHEIA [B.1.a.2]
Heb 4.16 that we may . . find grace to help
4. *come to aid, help:* βοηθέω BOĒTHEŌ
Mt 15.25 knelt before him, saying, "Lord, help me
Mk 9.22 "have pity on us and help us
9.24 "I believe; help my unbelief!
Acts 16. 9 "Come over to Macedonia and help us
21.28 crying out, "Men of Israel, help!
2 Cor 6. 2 "I have . . helped you on the day
Heb 2.18 he is able to help those who are tempted
5. *supply, support:* ἐπιχορηγία EPICHORĒGIA
Phil 1.19 the help of the Spirit of Jesus Christ
6. *aid, help:* ἐπικουρία EPIKOURIA*
Acts 26.22 "the help that comes from God
7. *place beside, stand before:* παρίστημι PARISTĒMI
Rom 16. 2 help her in whatever she may require
8. *gather, seize, conceive:* συλλαμβάνω (mid.) SYLLAMBANŌ
Lk 5. 7 they beckoned . . their partners . . to . . help
Phil 4. 3 true yokefellow, help these women
9. *throw together, compare:* συμβάλλω (mid.) SYMBALLŌ
Acts 18.27 he greatly helped those who . . believed
10. *take part with, help:* συναντιλαμβάνομαι SYNANTILAMBANOMAI*
Lk 10.40 "Lord, . . Tell her then to help me
Rom 8.26 the Spirit helps us in our weakness
11. *join in helping:* συνυπουργέω SYNYPOURGEŌ*
2 Cor 1.11 You also must help us by prayer
IDIOMATICALLY
a. Phil 4.16 you sent me help/†‡ εἰς τὴν χρείαν μοι ἐπέμψατε [CHREIA]
CONTEXTUALLY
Tit 3.14 so as to help cases of urgent need

HELP OF S., COME TO THE
1. *come to aid, help:* βοηθέω BOĒTHEŌ
Rev 12.16 earth came to the help of the woman

HELPER
1. *support, help:* ἀντίλημψις ANTILĒMPSIS* [C.2]
1 Cor 12.28 then healers, helpers, administrators
2. *assisting:* βοηθός (subst.) BOĒTHOS*
Heb 13. 6 "The Lord is my h., I will not be afraid
3. *do a service, minister:* διακονέω (subst. part.) DIAKONEŌ
Acts 19.22 his helpers, Timothy and Erastus
4. *chief, patron:* προστάτις PROSTATIS*
Rom 16. 2 for she has been a helper of many

HELPFUL, BE
1. *bring together, be useful:* συμφέρω SYMPHERŌ
1 Cor 6.12 but not all things are helpful
10.23 but not all things are helpful

HELPLESS, BE
1. *throw, cast out:* ῥίπτω (perf. pass.) RHIPTŌ
Mt 9.36 because they were harassed and helpless

HEM IN
1. *hold together, impel:* συνέχω SYNECHŌ
Lk 19.43 "your enemies will . . hem you in

HEMORRHAGE
1. *fountain of blood:* πηγὴ τοῦ αἵματος HAIMA [A.1.f]
Mk 5.29 immediately the hemorrhage ceased

HEMORRHAGE, SUFFER FROM A
1. *lose blood:* αἱμορροέω HAIMORROEŌ*
Mt 9.20 a woman who had suffered from a h.

HEN
1. *bird, cock, hen:* ὄρνις ORNIS*
Mt 23.37 "as a hen gathers . . under her wings
Lk 13.34 "as a hen gathers . . under her wings

HENCE
1. *for which cause:* δι' ἣν αἰτίαν AITIA [B.1.a.1]
2 Tim 1. 6 Hence I remind you to rekindle the gift
2. *hence:* ἐντεῦθεν ENTEUTHEN
Jn 14.31 "Rise, let us go hence
3. *so that, therefore:* ὥστε HŌSTE
Heb 13. 6 Hence we can confidently say
4. *whence, where:* ὅθεν HOTHEN
Heb 8. 3 hence it is necessary for this priest also
9.18 Hence even the first covenant was not
11.19 hence . . he did receive him back
5. *so, therefore:* οὖν OUN
1 Cor **8.4**

HENCEFORTH
1. *from now:* ἀπ' ἄρτι ARTI [B.1.a.1]
Jn 14. 7 "henceforth you know him
Rev 14.13 "the dead who die in the Lord henceforth
2. *remaining, left:* λοιπός LOIPOS
[a]gen. B.3.b.2 [b]neut.
Gal 6.17 [a]Henceforth let no man trouble me
2 Tim 4. 8 [b]H. there is laid up for me the crown
3. *from now on:* ἀπὸ τοῦ νῦν NYN [B.1.a.1]
Lk 1.48 "h. all generations will call me blessed
5.10 "henceforth you will be catching men
12.52 "h. in one house . . three against two

HER (*See also* SHE)
1. *himself:* ἑαυτοῦ (fem.) HEAUTOU
Lk **13.34**
1 Th **2.7**

HER OWN
1. *himself:* ἑαυτοῦ (fem.) HEAUTOU
Acts 7.21 "brought him up as her own son
2. *one's own:* ἴδιος (fem.) IDIOS
1 Cor 7. 2 each woman ⟨should have⟩ her own husband
7. 4 wife does not rule over her own body

HERALD
1. *public messenger:* κῆρυξ KĒRYX
2 Pet 2. 5 Noah, a herald of righteousness

HERB
1. *garden herb, vegetable:* λάχανον LACHANON
Lk 11.42 "you tithe the mint and rue and every herb

HERD
1. *herd:* ἀγέλη AGELĒ*
Mt 8.30 Now a herd of many swine was feeding
8.31 "send us away into the herd of swine
8.32 the whole herd rushed down the steep bank
Mk 5.11 Now a great herd of swine was feeding
5.13 the herd . . rushed down . . into the sea
Lk 8.32 Now a large herd of swine was feeding
8.33 the herd rushed down the steep bank

HERDSMAN
1. *feed, tend:* βόσκω (subst. part.) BOSKŌ
Mt 8.33 The herdsmen fled, and . . told everything
Mk 5.14 herdsmen fled, and told it in the city
Lk 8.34 When the herdsmen saw . . they fled

HERE
1. *here, there:* αὐτοῦ AUTOU
Mt 26.36 "Sit here, while I go yonder and pray
Lk 9.27 "there are some standing here
2. *hence:* ἐντεῦθεν ENTEUTHEN [A.4.e]
Jn 7. 3 "Leave here and go to Judea
3. *here, hither:* ἐνθάδε ENTHADE
Lk 24.41 "Have you anything here to eat?
Jn 4.15 "that I may not . . come here to draw
4.16 "call your husband, and come here
Acts 16.28 "Do not harm yourself, for we are all h.
17. 6 "These men . . have come here also
25.17 "When therefore they came together here
25.24 "petitioned . ., both at Jerusalem and here
4. *ready, prepared:* ἕτοιμος HETOIMOS
Jn 7. 6 "but your time is always here
5. *here, hither:* ὧδε HŌDE
Mt 8.29 "Have you come here to torment us?
12. 6 "something greater than the temple is here
12.41 "something greater than Jonah is here
12.42 "something greater than Solomon is here
14. 8 "the head of John . . here on a platter
14.17 "We have only five loaves here
14.18 he said, "Bring them here to me
16.28 "some standing here who will not taste d.
17. 4 "Lord, it is well that we are here; if you wish, I will make three booths here
17.17 "Bring him here to me

Mt 20. 6 " 'Why do you stand here idle all day?
22.12 " 'Friend, how did you get in here?
24. 2 "there will not be left here one stone
24.23 "if .. one says .. 'Lo, here is the Christ!
26.38 "remain here, and watch[h] with me
28. 6 "He is not here; for he has risen
Mk 6. 3 "are not his sisters here with us?
8. 4 "can one feed these men with bread here?
9. 1 "some standing h... will not taste death
9. 5 "Master,[j] it is well that we are here
11. 3 " 'The Lord .. will send it back here
13. 2 "There will not be left here one stone
13.21 "if .. one says .. 'Look, here is the Christ!
14.32 "Sit here, while I pray
14.34 "remain here, and watch[d]
16. 6 "He has risen, he is not here
Lk 4.23 " 'do here also in your own country
9.12 "for we are here in a lonely place
9.33 "Master, it is well that we are here
9.41 "Bring your son here
11.31 "something greater than Solomon is here
11.32 "something greater than Jonah is here
15.17 " 'but I perish here with hunger!
16.25 " 'but now he is comforted here
17.21 "nor will they say, 'Lo, here it is!
17.23 "they will say to you .. 'Lo, here!
19.27 " 'bring them here and slay them before me
21. 6 "shall not be left here one stone
22.38 "Look, Lord, here are two swords
[24. 6 "*He is not here, but has risen*‡
Jn 6. 9 "a lad here who has five barley loaves
6.25 "Rabbi, when did you come here?
11.21 "Lord, if you had been here
11.32 "Lord, if you had been here
20.27 "Put your finger here, and see my hands
Acts 9.14 "h. he has authority from the chief priests
9.21 "he has come here for this purpose
Col 4. 9 everything that has taken place here
Heb 7. 8 Here tithes are received by mortal men
13.14 For here we have no lasting city
Jas 2. 3 "Have a seat here, please
Rev 13.10 Here is a call for the endurance
14.12 Here is a call for the endurance

6. *where, wherever:* ὅπου HOPOU
Col 3.11 Here there cannot be Greek and Jew

7. *in this:* ἐν τούτῳ HOUTOS [B.1.a.1]
Jn **4.**37
2 Cor **5.**2

8. *behold! look!:* ἴδε IDE
Mt 25.20 " 'here I have made five talents more
25.22 " 'here I have made two talents more
25.25 "Here you have what is yours
Mk 3.34 "Here are my mother and my brothers!
Jn 3.26 "here he is, baptizing, and all are going
7.26 "And here he is, speaking openly

9. *behold!:* ἰδού IDOU
Mt 12.49 "Here are my mother and my brothers!
Lk 19.20 " 'Lord, here is your pound
Acts 5.28 "yet here you have filled Jerusalem
9.10 And he said, "Here I am, Lord
2 Cor 12.14 Here for the third time I am ready
Heb 2.13 "Here am I, and the children

10. *into the midst:* εἰς τὸ μέσον MESOS [B.1.a.1]
Mk 3. 3 he said to the man .. "Come here
Lk 6. 8 he said to the man .. "Come .. here

CONTEXTUALLY
Lk 19.30 "a colt tied .. ; untie it and bring it here
Acts 19.37 "For you have brought these men here
26.22 "so I stand here testifying .. , saying
28.21 "none .. coming h. has reported or spoken
Phil 1.16 put h. for the defense of the gospel

HERE, BE

1. *be present:* πάρειμι PAREIMI
Mt 26.50 "Friend, why are you here?[j]†
Jn 11.28 "The Teacher is here and is calling
Acts 24.19 "they ought to be here before you

HERE, FROM

1. *hence:* ἐντεῦθεν ENTEUTHEN
Lk 4. 9 "throw yourself down from here
13.31 "Get away from here, for Herod wants

2. *whence, therefore:* ἔνθεν ENTHEN
Mt 17.20 " 'Move from here to there[o]
Lk 16.26 " 'those who would pass from here to you

HERE PRESENT, BE

1. *be present:* πάρειμι PAREIMI
Acts 10.33 "we are all here present in the sight of God

HEREAFTER

1. *from now:* ἀπ' ἄρτι ARTI [B.1.a.1]
Mt 26.64 "hereafter you will see the Son of man

2. *after these things:* μετὰ ταῦτα META [B.1.a.1]
Rev 1.19 "what is to take place hereafter

HERESY

1. *sect, opinion:* αἵρεσις HAIRESIS
2 Pet 2. 1 secretly bring in destructive heresies

HERITAGE, HAVE A

1. *inherit, obtain:* κληρονομέω KLĒRONOMEŌ [B.2.d.1]
Rev 21. 7 "He who conquers shall have this heritage

HERMAS: Ἑρμᾶς 'hərməs
Rom 16.14 Greet .. Hermas, and the brethren

HERMES: Ἑρμῆς 'hər͵mēz
Acts 14.12 Paul .. they called Hermes
Rom 16.14 Greet .. Phlegon, Hermes, Patrobas

HERMOGENES: Ἑρμογένης hər'mäjə͵nēz
2 Tim 1.15 all .. turned away .. , and among them .. H.

HEROD: Ἡρῴδης 'herəd

1. Herod the Great
Mt 2. 1 Jesus was born .. in the days of H. the king
2. 3 When H... heard this, he was troubled
2. 7 Then Herod summoned the wise men
2.12 warned in a dream not to return to H.
2.13 "Herod is about to search for the child
2.15 remained there until the death of Herod
2.16 H., when he saw that he had been tricked
2.19 when H. died, .. an angel .. appeared
2.22 Archelaus .. in place of his father H.
Lk 1. 5 In the days of Herod, king of Judea
Acts 23.35 to be guarded in Herod's praetorium

2. Herod Antipas
Mt 14. 1 H... heard about the fame of Jesus
14. 3 Herod had seized John and bound him
14. 6 when Herod's birthday came, .. daughter of Herodias danced .. and pleased Herod
Mk 6.14 King Herod heard of it
6.16 H... said, "John .. has been raised
6.17 For Herod had sent and seized John
6.18 John said to Herod, "It is not lawful
6.20 for Herod feared John
6.21 H. on his birthday gave a banquet
6.22 she pleased Herod and his guests
8.15 "beware of .. the leaven of Herod[e]‡
Lk 3. 1 Herod being tetrarch of Galilee
3.19 H... had been reproved by him .. for all the evil things that H. had done
8. 3 the wife of Chuza, Herod's steward
9. 7 H... heard of all that was done
9. 9 Herod said, "John I beheaded
13.31 "for Herod wants to kill you
23. 7 when he learned that he belonged to Herod's jurisdiction, he sent him over to H.
23. 8 When H. saw Jesus, he was very glad
23.11 Herod .. treated him with contempt
23.12 Herod and Pilate became friends
23.15 "neither did Herod, for he sent him back
Acts 4.27 "both Herod and Pontius Pilate
13. 1 Manaen a member of the court of Herod

3. Herod Agrippa I
Acts 12. 1 H... laid violent hands upon some
12. 6 when Herod was about to bring him out
12.11 "rescued me from the hand of Herod
12.19 when Herod had sought for him
12.21 H. put on his royal robes, took his seat

CONTEXTUALLY
Acts 12.20 Now H. was angry with the people of Tyre

HERODIANS: Ἡρῳδιανοί
Mt 22.16 sent their disciples.., along with the H.
Mk 3. 6 held counsel with the Herodians
[8.15 "beware of.. the leaven of *the Herodians*‡
12.13 Pharisees and some of the Herodians

HERODIAS: Ἡρῳδιάς hi'rōdēəs
Mt 14. 3 Herodias, his brother Philip's wife[l]
14. 6 the daughter of Herodias danced
Mk 6.17 Herodias, his brother Philip's wife
6.19 Herodias had a grudge against him
6.22 Herodias' daughter came in and danced
Lk 3.19 Herodias, his brother's wife

HERODION: Ἡρῳδίων hi'rōdēən
Rom 16.11 Greet my kinsman Herodion

HERSELF
1. *himself:* ἑαυτοῦ (fem.) HEAUTOU
Mt 9.21 she said to herself, "If I only touch
Lk 1.24 for five months she hid herself
Rev 2.20 " 'Jezebel, who calls herself a prophetess
19. 7 "his Bride has made herself ready

HESITATION
IDIOMATICALLY
a. Acts 10.20 "accompany them without hesitation πορεύου σὺν αὐτοῖς μηδὲν διακρινόμενος [DIAKRINŌ]

HEW
1. *quarry, hew out of the rock:* λατομέω LATOMEŌ*
Mt 27.60 new tomb, which he had hewn in the rock
Mk 15.46 tomb which had been hewn out of the rock

HEZEKIAH: Ἑζεκίας ˌhezə'kīə
Mt 1. 9 Ahaz the father of Hezekiah
1.10 Hezekiah the father of Manasseh

HEZRON: Ἑσρώμ, Ἑσρών 'hezrən
Mt 1. 3 Perez the father of Hezron, and Hezron the father of Ram[a]
Lk 3.33 Arni, the son of H., the son of Perez

HID
HIDDEN
1. *unseen, secret:* ἀφανής APHANĒS*
Heb 4.13 before him no creature is hidden
2. *hidden:* ἀπόκρυφος APOKRYPHOS*
Mk 4.22 "nothing hid, except to be made manifest
Lk 8.17 "nothing.. hid.. shall not be.. manifest
Col 2. 3 in whom are hid all the treasures
3. *conceal:* ἀποκρύπτω (perf. pass. part.) APOKRYPTŌ
1 Cor 2. 7 a secret and hidden wisdom of God
Eph 3. 9 plan of the mystery hidden for ages
Col 1.26 mystery hidden for ages and generations[c]
4. *bury, hide:* κρύπτω (perf. pass. part.) KRYPTŌ
Mt 13.44 "like treasure hidden in a field
Rev 2.17 " 'I will give some of the hidden manna
5. *secret, hidden:* κρυπτός KRYPTOS
Mt 10.26 "nothing.. hidden that will not be known
Lk 12. 2 "Nothing.. hidden that will not be known
1 Cor 4. 5 things now hidden in darkness
1 Pet 3. 4 let it be the hidden person of the heart

HID, BE
HIDDEN, BE
1. *escape notice:* λανθάνω LANTHANŌ
Mk 7.24 yet he could not be hid
Lk 8.47 the woman saw that she was not hidden

HIDE
1. *conceal:* ἀποκρύπτω APOKRYPTŌ
Lk 10.21 "thou hast hidden these.. from the wise
2. *hide:* ἐγκρύπτω EGKRYPTŌ*
Mt 13.33 "like leaven which a woman took and hid
3. *bury, hide:* κρύπτω KRYPTŌ
[a]inf.
Mt 5.14 "A city set on a hill cannot be hid
11.25 "thou hast hidden these.. from the wise
13.35 "I will utter what has been hidden
25.18 "he.. dug.. and hid his master's money
25.25 " 'I.. hid your talent in the ground
Lk 13.21 "like leaven which a woman.. hid
18.34 this saying was hid from them
19.42 "But now they are hid from your eyes
Jn 8.59 they took.. stones..; but Jesus hid himself
12.36 he departed and hid himself
Col 3. 3 you have died, and your life is hid
1 Tim 5.25 [a]good deeds.. cannot remain hidden
Heb 11.23 Moses, when he was born, was hid
Rev 6.15 hid in the caves and among the rocks
6.16 "Fall on us and hide us from.. him
4. *conceal entirely:* περικρύβω PERIKRYBŌ*
Lk 1.24 for five months she hid herself

HIERAPOLIS: Ἱεράπολις ˌhī(ə)'rapələs II,E-3
Col 4.13 those in Laodicea and in Hierapolis

HIGH (*See also* HONOR, HOLD IN HIGH)
1. *high, proud:* ὑψηλός HYPSĒLOS
Mt 4. 8 devil took him to a very high mountain
17. 1 Jesus.. led them up a high mountain
Mk 9. 2 Jesus.. led them up a high mountain
Heb 1. 3 at the right hand of the Majesty on high
Rev 21.10 carried me away to a great, h. mountain
21.12 had a great, high wall, with twelve gates
2. *great:* μέγας MEGAS
Lk 4.38 mother-in-law was ill with a high fever
Jn 19.31 (for that sabbath was a high day

HIGH AS
HIGH AS, AS
1. *until:* ἄχρι ACHRI
Rev 14.20 blood.. as high as a horse's bridle
18. 5 "her sins are heaped high as heaven

HIGH, FROM ON
HIGH, ON
1. *height:* ὕψος HYPSOS [B.1.b]
[a]ἐξ ὕψους [b]εἰς ὕψος
Lk 1.78 [a]"day shall dawn upon[f] us from on high
24.49 [a]"until.. clothed with power from on high
Eph 4. 8 [b]"When he ascended on high he led a host

HIGH, MOST
1. *highest:* ὕψιστος HYPSISTOS
Mk 5. 7 "Jesus, Son of the Most High God
Lk 1.32 "He.. will be called the Son of the Most H.
1.35 "the Most High will overshadow you
1.76 "the prophet of the Most High
6.35 "you will be sons of the Most High
8.28 "Jesus, Son of the Most High God
Acts 7.48 "the Most High does not dwell in houses
16.17 "These men are servants of the Most H. God
Heb 7. 1 Melchizedek,.. priest of the Most H. God

HIGH POSITION
1. *superiority:* ὑπεροχή HYPEROCHĒ
1 Tim 2. 2 kings and all who are in high positions

HIGH PRIEST
1. *chief priest:* ἀρχιερεύς ARCHIEREUS
Mt 26. 3 gathered in the palace of the high priest
26.51 struck the slave of the high priest
26.57 led him to Caiaphas the high priest
26.58 as far as the courtyard of the high priest
26.62 high priest.. said, "Have you no answer?
26.63 high priest said to him, "I adjure you
26.65 the high priest tore his robes
Mk 2.26 "when Abiathar was high priest
14.47 struck the slave of the high priest
14.53 they led Jesus to the high priest
14.54 right into the courtyard of the high priest
14.60 the high priest stood up in the midst
14.61 high priest asked.. "Are you the Christ?
14.63 the high priest tore his garments
14.66 one of the maids of the high priest
Lk 22.50 struck the slave of the high priest
22.54 bringing him into the high priest's house
Jn 11.49 Caiaphas, who was high priest that year
11.51 being high priest that year he prophesied
18.10 Peter.. struck the high priest's slave
18.13 Caiaphas, who was high priest that year

Jn 18.15 As this disciple was known to the h. priest, he entered the court of the h. priest
18.16 disciple . . known to the high priest
18.19 high priest then questioned Jesus
18.22 "Is that how you answer the high priest?
18.24 sent him . . to Caiaphas the high priest
18.26 One of the servants[l] of the h. priest
Acts 4. 6 Annas the high priest and Caiaphas
5.17 h. priest rose up and all . . with him
5.21 Now the high priest came
5.27 the high priest questioned them
7. 1 the high priest said, "Is this so?
9. 1 Saul . . went to the high priest
19.14 sons of a Jewish high priest named Sceva
22. 5 "the high priest and the whole council
23. 2 high priest Ananias commanded
23. 4 "Would you revile God's high priest?
23. 5 "I did not know . . he was the high priest
24. 1 the high priest Ananias came down
Heb 2.17 a merciful and faithful high priest
3. 1 Jesus, . . high priest of our confession
4.14 Since then we have a great high priest
4.15 we have not a h. priest who is unable
5. 1 every high priest chosen from among men
5. 5 did not exalt himself to . . a high priest
5.10 being designated by God a high priest
6.20 having become a high priest for ever
7.26 fitting that we should have such a h. priest
7.27 He has no need, like those high priests
7.28 men in their weakness as high priests
8. 1 we have such a high priest
8. 3 every high priest is appointed to offer
9. 7 into the second only the high priest goes
9.11 when Christ appeared as a high priest
9.25 as the high priest enters the Holy Place
13.11 brought . . by the high priest as a sacrifice

HIGH STANDING, OF
1. *noble, proper:* εὐσχήμων EUSCHĒMŌN
Acts 13.50 the devout women of high standing
17.12 a few Greek women of high standing

HIGHER
1. *higher, above:* ἀνώτερος (neut.) ANŌTEROS
Lk 14.10 " 'Friend, go up higher
2. *greater:* μείζων MEIZŌN
1 Cor 12.31 But earnestly desire the higher gifts

HIGHEST
1. *highest:* ὕψιστος HYPSISTOS
Mt 21. 9 "Hosanna in the highest!
Mk 11.10 "Hosanna in the highest!
Lk 2.14 "Glory to God in the highest!
19.38 "Peace in heaven and glory in the h.!

HIGHLY EXALT
1. *exalt exceedingly:* ὑπερυψόω HYPERYPSOŌ*
Phil 2. 9 Therefore God has highly exalted him

HIGHLY OF ONESELF, THINK MORE
1. *be overproud, be haughty:* ὑπερφρονέω HYPERPHRONEŌ*
Rom 12. 3 not to think of himself more highly

HIGHLY, VERY
1. *superabundantly:* ὑπερεκπερισσῶς HYPEREKPERISSŌS*
1 Th 5.13 to esteem them very highly in love

HIGH-PRIESTHOOD
1. *chief priest:* ἀρχιερεύς ARCHIEREUS [C.2]
Lk 3. 2 in the high-priesthood of Annas

HIGH-PRIESTLY
1. *of the high priest:* ἀρχιερατικός ARCHIERATIKOS*
Acts 4. 6 all . . of the high-priestly family

HIGHWAY
1. *way, road:* ὁδός HODOS
Lk 14.23 " 'Go out to the highways and hedges

HILL
1. *hill:* βουνός BOUNOS*
Lk 3. 5 "every . . hill shall be brought low
23.30 "they will . . say . . to the hills, 'Cover us
2. *mountain, hill:* ὄρος OROS
Mt 5.14 "A city set on a hill cannot be hid
Lk 4.29 led him to the brow of the hill

HILL COUNTRY
1. *hilly:* ὀρεινός OREINOS* [B.3.b.2]
Lk 1.39 Mary . . went with haste into the hill country
1.65 talked about through all the hill country

HILLSIDE
1. *mountain, hill:* ὄρος OROS
Mk 5.11 herd of swine . . feeding . . on the hillside
Lk 8.32 herd of swine . . feeding . . on the hillside

HIM (*See also* HE)
1. *himself:* ἑαυτοῦ HEAUTOU
Mt. **12.45**

HIMSELF
1. *that:* ἐκεῖνος EKEINOS
Jn **5.37**
2. *himself:* ἑαυτοῦ HEAUTOU
Mt 12.26 "he is divided against himself
12.45 "seven other spirits more evil than h.
13.21 "yet he has no root in himself
16.24 "let him deny h. and take up his cross
18. 4 "Whoever humbles himself like this child
23.12 "whoever exalts h. will be humbled, . . whoever humbles h. will be exalted
27.42 "He saved others; he cannot save himself
Mk 3.26 "if Satan has risen up against himself
5. 5 he was . . bruising himself with stones
5.30 "perceiving in h. that power had gone
8.34 "let him deny h. and take up his cross
15.31 "He saved others; he cannot save h.
Lk 7.39 the Pharisee . . said to himself
9.23 "let him deny h. and take up his cross
9.25 "if he gains the . . world and losses . . h.
10.29 he, desiring to justify himself
11.18 "if Satan also is divided against h.
11.26 "seven other spirits more evil than h.
12.17 "he thought to h., 'What shall I do?
14.11 one who exalts h. will be humbled, . . he who humbles h. will be exalted
15.17 "when he came to himself he said
16. 3 "steward said to h., 'What shall I do?
18. 4 "but afterward he said to himself
18.11 "Pharisee stood and prayed thus with h.
18.14 "every one who exalts h. will be humbled, but he who humbles h. will be exalted
23. 2 "saying that he himself is Christ a king
23.35 "He saved others; let him save himself!
24.27 he interpreted . . things concerning h.
Jn 5.18 making himself equal with God
5.26 "as the Father has life in h., so he has granted the Son . . to have life in h.
6.61 "knowing in h. . . his disciples murmured
8.22 Then said the Jews, "Will he kill h.?
9.21 "he is of age, he will speak for himself
13. 4 laid aside his garments, and girded h.
19. 7 "he has made himself the Son of God
19.12 "every one who makes himself a king
21. 1 After this Jesus revealed h. again
Acts 1. 3 To them he presented himself alive
5.36 "Theudas . ., giving h. out to be somebody
8. 9 saying that he h. was somebody great
8.34 "does the prophet say this, about h.?
12.11 Peter came to himself, and said
16.27 drew his sword and was about to kill h.
25. 4 he himself intended to go there shortly
28.16 Paul was allowed to stay by himself
Rom 14. 7 None of us lives to himself, and none of us dies to himself
14.12 each of us shall give account of himself
14.22 happy is he who has no reason to judge h.
15. 3 Christ did not please himself
1 Cor 3.18 Let no one deceive himself
11.28 Let a man examine himself
11.29 eats and drinks judgment upon himself
14. 4 He who speaks in a tongue edifies h.

1 Cor 14.28 let each . . speak to h. and to God
2 Cor 5.18 God . . through Christ reconciled us to h.
5.19 God was . . reconciling[h] the world to h.
10. 7 If any one is confident . . , let him remind h.
10.18 not the man who commends himself
Gal 1. 4 who gave h. for our sins to deliver us
2.12 he drew back and separated himself
2.20 who loved me and gave himself for me
6. 3 when he is nothing, he deceives himself
6. 4 his reason to boast will be in h. alone
Eph 5. 2 as Christ loved us and gave h. . . for us
5.25 as Christ loved the church and gave h.
5.27 that he might present the church to h.
5.28 He who loves his wife loves himself
5.33 let each one of you love his wife as h.
Phil 2. 7 emptied h., taking the form of a servant[d]
2. 8 found in human form he humbled h.
1 Th 4. 4 know how to take a wife for himself[x]†
2 Th 2. 4 who opposes and exalts himself
1 Tim 2. 6 who gave himself as a ransom for all
2 Tim 2.13 for he cannot deny himself
2.21 If any one purifies himself
Tit 2.14 who gave himself for us to redeem us . . and to purify for himself a people
Heb 5. 4 one does not take the honor upon h.
5. 5 So also Christ did not exalt h.
6.13 when God made a promise . . he swore by h.
7.27 once for all when he offered up h.
9. 7 taking blood which he offers for himself
9.14 Christ, who . . offered himself . . to God
9.25 Nor was it to offer himself repeatedly
12. 3 who endured . . such hostility against h.
Jas 1.24 for he observes himself and goes away
1 Jn 3. 3 every one who thus hopes . . purifies h.

IDIOMATICALLY
a. Mt 14.23 he went up on the mountain by himself *ἀνέβη εἰς τὸ ὄρος κατ' ἰδίαν* [IDIOS]
b. Mt 24.48 "if that wicked servant says to himself *ἐὰν . . εἴπῃ ὁ κακὸς δοῦλος ἐκεῖνος ἐν τῇ καρδίᾳ αὐτοῦ* [KARDIA]
c. Lk 12.45 "if that servant says to himself *ἐὰν . . εἴπῃ ὁ δοῦλος ἐκεῖνος ἐν τῇ καρδίᾳ αὐτοῦ* [KARDIA]

HIMSELF, BY
1. *he alone: αὐτὸς μόνος* MONOS [A.3.b.1]
Jn 6.15 Jesus withdrew again . . by himself

HINDER
1. *hinder, oppose: ἐγκόπτω* EGKOPTŌ
Rom 15.22 reason why I have so often been hindered
Gal 5. 7 who hindered you from obeying?
1 Th 2.18 we wanted to come . . but Satan hindered
1 Pet 3. 7 that your prayers may not be hindered
2. *hinder, prevent, withhold: κωλύω* KŌLYŌ
Mt 19.14 "Let the children come . . and do not h.
Mk 10.14 "Let the children come . . do not h.
Lk 11.52 "you hindered those who were entering
18.16 "Let the children come . . and do not h.
1 Th 2.16 hindering us from speaking to the Gentiles

HINDRANCE
1. *stumbling block, trap: σκάνδαλον* SKANDALON
Mt 16.23 "Get behind me, Satan! You are a h.[v]†
Rom 14.13 never . . put a . . h. in the way of a brother

HIRE
1. *let out for hire: μισθόω* (mid.) MISTHOŌ*
Mt 20. 1 "who went out early . . to hire laborers
20. 7 " 'Because no one has hired us
CONTEXTUALLY
Mt 20. 9 "those hired about the eleventh hour came

HIRED DWELLING
1. *contract, rent: μίσθωμα* MISTHŌMA
Acts [28.30 lived there . . *in his own hired dwelling*†

HIRED SERVANT
HIRELING
1. *day laborer, servant: μίσθιος* MISTHIOS*
Lk 15.17 " 'How many of my father's hired servants!
15.19 " ' "treat me as one of your hired servants
[15.21 " *'treat me as one of your hired servants*‡
2. *hired man: μισθωτός* MISTHŌTOS
Mk 1.20 left their father . . with the hired servants
Jn 10.12 "He who is a hireling and not a shepherd
10.13 "He flees because he is a hireling

HIS (*See also* HE)
1. *himself: ἑαυτοῦ* HEAUTOU
Lk 9.47 he took a child and put him by his side
13.19 "seed which a man . . sowed in his garden
15.20 "he arose and came to his father
16. 5 "So, summoning his master's debtors
18.13 "beat his breast, saying, 'God, be merciful
19.13 "Calling ten of his servants
Rom 5. 8 But God shows his love for us
1 Cor 7.37 to keep her as his betrothed[z]
7.38 he who marries his betrothed[z] does well
Eph 5.33 let each one of you love his wife
1 Th 2.11 how, like a father with his children
Heb 12.16 like Esau, who sold his birthright
Jas 1.26 If any one . . does not bridle his tongue but deceives his heart
Rev 10. 7 he announced to his servants the prophets
2. *one's own: ἴδιος* IDIOS
Mt 22. 5 "they . . went off, one to his farm
25.14 "when a man . . called his servants
25.15 "gave . . to each according to his ability
Jn 1.41 He first found his brother Simon
Acts 24.24 Felix came with his wife Drusilla
1 Cor 3. 8 each shall receive . . according to his labor
7.37 having his desire under control, and has determined this in his heart
Eph 4.28 doing honest work with his hands
1 Tim 5. 8 If any . . does not provide for his relatives
Heb 4.10 ceases from . . labors as God did from his

HIS FRIENDS
1. *one's own: ἴδιος* (subst. masc. pl.) IDIOS
Acts 24.23 none of his friends should be prevented

HIS HOME
1. *one's own: ἴδιος* (subst. neut. pl.) IDIOS
Jn 16.32 "will be scattered, every man to his home

HIS OWN
1. *himself: ἑαυτοῦ* HEAUTOU
Lk 2. 3 went to be enrolled, each to his own city
11.21 "When a strong man . . guards his own palace
14.26 "If any one . . does not hate his own father . . and even his own life
14.27 "Whoever does not bear his own cross
Jn 5.19 "Son can do nothing of his own accord
7.18 "He who speaks on his own authority
11.51 He did not say this of his own accord
16.13 "he will not speak on his own authority
19.17 he went out, bearing his own cross
Acts 21.11 coming to us he . . bound his own feet
Rom 4.19 when he considered his own body
8. 3 his own son in . . likeness of sinful flesh
1 Cor 7. 2 each man should have his own wife
10.24 Let no one seek his own good
Gal 6. 4 But let each one test his own work
6. 8 he who sows to his own flesh
Eph 5.29 For no man ever hates his own flesh
Phil 2. 4 each . . look not only to his own interests
1 Th 2.12 who calls you into his own kingdom
[4. 4 know how *to control his own body*†[o]
Heb 5. 3 to offer sacrifice for his own sins as well
2. *one's own: ἴδιος* IDIOS
Mt 9. 1 he crossed over and came to his own city
Mk 4.34 to his own disciples he explained
15.20 they . . put his own clothes on him
Lk 10.34 "then he set him on his own beast
Jn 4.44 prophet has no honor in his own country
5.18 because he . . called God his own Father[o]
5.43 "if another comes in his own name
7.18 "He . . seeks his own glory
10. 3 "he calls his own sheep by name
10. 4 "When he has brought out all his own
13. 1 loved his own who were in the world
Acts 1. 7 "Father has fixed by his own authority

Acts 1.25 "turned aside, to go to his own place
2. 6 heard them speaking in his own language
2. 8 "each of us in his own native language
4.32 no one said that any . . was his own
13.36 "after he . . served . . in his own generation
20.28 "obtained with . . blood of his own Son[w]†[o]
28.30 two whole years at his own expense[h]†
Rom 8.32 He who did not spare his own Son
14. 4 It is before his o. master that he stands
14. 5 Let . . one be . . convinced in his own mind
1 Cor 6.18 the immoral man sins against his own body
7. 4 husband does not rule over his own body
7. 7 each has his own special gift from God
9. 7 Who serves as a soldier at his o. expense?
11.21 each one goes ahead with his own meal
15.23 But each in his own order
Gal 6. 5 each man will have to bear his own load
1 Tim 3. 4 He must manage his own household well
3. 5 know how to manage his own household
2 Tim 1. 9 but in virtue of his own purpose
Heb 7.27 sacrifices daily, first for his own sins
9.12 entered . . , taking[s] . . his own blood
13.12 to sanctify . . through his own blood
Jas 1.14 when . . enticed by his own desire
2 Pet 1. 3 who called us to[b] his own glory
2.16 was rebuked for his own transgression
2.22 The dog turns back to his own vomit

HIS OWN HOME
1. *one's own:* ἴδιος (subst. neut. pl.) IDIOS
Jn 1.11 He came to his own home
19.27 the disciple took her to his own home

HIS OWN, MAKE S.
1. *catch, seize:* καταλαμβάνω KATALAMBANŌ
Phil 3.12 Christ Jesus has made me his own

HIS OWN NATURE
1. *one's own:* ἴδιος (subst. pl.) IDIOS
Jn 8.44 "he speaks according to his own nature

HIS OWN, NOT
1. *foreign:* ἀλλότριος ALLOTRIOS
Heb 9.25 enters . . yearly with blood not his own

HIS OWN, OF
1. *wealthy, special:* περιούσιος PERIOUSIOS
Tit 2.14 to purify for himself a people of his own

HIS OWN PEOPLE
1. *one's own:* ἴδιος (subst. pl.) IDIOS
Jn 1.11 his own people received him not

HIS RELATIVES
1. *one's own:* ἴδιος (subst. masc. pl.) IDIOS
1 Tim 5. 8 If . . one does not provide for his relatives

HITHER
1. *here, hither:* ὧδε HŌDE
Rev 4. 1 "Come up hither, and I will show you
11.12 loud voice . . saying . . "Come up hither!

HITHERTO
1. *until now:* ἕως ἄρτι HEŌS [B.1.a.1]
Jn 16.24 "H. you have asked nothing in my name
1 Cor 8. 7 being hitherto accustomed to idols

HOIST
1. *raise, lift:* ἐπαίρω EPAIRŌ
Acts 27.40 then hoisting the foresail to the wind

HOIST UP
1. *lift, carry away:* αἴρω AIRŌ
Acts 27.17 after hoisting it up, they took measures[c]

HOLD (*See also, e.g.,* HONOR, HELD IN; READY, HOLD)
1. *exchange:* ἀντιβάλλω ANTIBALLŌ*
Lk 24.17 "this conversation which you are holding
2. *make room for, hold, go:* χωρέω CHŌREŌ
Jn 2. 6 each holding twenty or thirty gallons
3. *give:* δίδωμι DIDŌMI [A.6.a.5]
Mk 3. 6 Pharisees . . immediately held counsel
4. *have, hold:* ἔχω ECHŌ
Mt 14. 5 they held him to be a prophet
21.26 "for all hold that John was a prophet
21.46 because they held him to be a prophet
Mk 11.32 "for all held that John was a real prophet
Acts [28.29 *holding much dispute among themselves*‡
Phil 1. 7 because I hold you in my heart
1 Tim 1.19 holding faith and a good conscience
3. 9 they must hold the mystery of the faith
4. 8 godliness . . holds promise for the present
2 Tim 3. 5 holding the form of religion but denying
Heb 7.24 he holds his priesthood permanently
9. 4 a golden urn holding the manna
Jas 2. 1 show no partiality as you hold the faith
1 Pet 4. 8 h. unfailing your love for one another
Rev 1.16 in his right hand he held seven stars
2.24 " 'the rest . . who do not hold this teaching
5. 8 twenty-four elders . . , each holding a harp
17. 4 holding in her hand a golden cup
19.10 "who hold the testimony of Jesus
20. 1 an angel . . holding in his hand the key
5. *be:* εἰμί EIMI [A.6.a.5]
Jn 4.37 "the saying holds true, 'One sows
6. *kindle; touch* (mid.): ἅπτω (mid.) HAPTŌ
Jn 20.17 "Do not h. me, for I have not . . ascended
7. *prepare, get ready:* ἑτοιμάζω HETOIMAZŌ
Variant to: Mk **15.1**
8. *hold fast, restrain:* κατέχω KATECHŌ
Heb 3.14 if only we hold our first confidence firm
9. *seize, hold fast:* κρατέω KRATEŌ
Acts 2.24 "not possible for him to be held by it
Rev 2. 1 " 'words of him who holds the seven stars
2.14 " 'who hold the teaching of Balaam
2.15 " 'who hold the teaching of the Nicolaitans
10. *say, speak:* λέγω LEGŌ
2 Tim 2.18 holding that the resurrection is past already
11. *reckon, count:* λογίζομαι LOGIZOMAI
Rom 3.28 we hold that a man is justified by faith
12. *do, make:* ποιέω POIEŌ
Mk 15. 1 the whole council held a consultation
Var. HETOIMAZŌ
13. *hold together, impel:* συνέχω SYNECHŌ
Lk 22.63 men who were holding Jesus mocked him
14. *keep, observe:* τηρέω TĒREŌ
Acts 25.21 "held until I could send him to Caesar

HOLD S. AGAINST
1. *stand, set:* ἵστημι HISTĒMI
Acts 7.60 "Lord, do not hold this sin against them

HOLD BACK
1. *seize, hold fast:* κρατέω KRATEŌ
Rev 7. 1 angels . . holding back the four winds

HOLD CAPTIVE
1. *hold fast, restrain:* κατέχω KATECHŌ
Rom 7. 6 dead to that which held us captive

HOLD FAST
1. *hold upon, aim at:* ἐπέχω EPECHŌ
Phil 2.16 holding fast the word of life
2. *hold fast, restrain:* κατέχω KATECHŌ
Lk 8.15 "who, hearing the word, hold it fast
1 Cor 15. 2 by which you are saved, if you h. it fast
1 Th 5.21 test everything; hold fast what is good
Heb 3. 6 if we hold fast our confidence and pride
10.23 Let us hold fast the confession of our hope
3. *join, unite:* κολλάω (pass.) KOLLAŌ
Rom 12. 9 hold fast to what is good
4. *seize, hold fast:* κρατέω KRATEŌ
Mk 7. 8 "You . . hold fast the tradition of men
Col 2.19 not holding fast to the Head
Heb 4.14 let us hold fast our confession
Rev 2.13 " 'you hold fast my name
2.25 " 'only hold fast what you have
3.11 " 'hold fast what you have

HOLD FIRM
1. *hold against:* ἀντέχω (mid.) ANTECHŌ
Tit 1. 9 he must hold firm to the sure word

HOLD OF, LAY
1. *seize, hold fast:* κρατέω KRATEŌ
Mt 12.11 "What man . . will not lay hold of it?

HOLD OF, TAKE
1. *take, lay hold of:* ἐπιλαμβάνομαι EPILAMBANOMAI
Lk 20.20 that they might take h. of what he said
Acts 17.19 they took hold of him and brought him
1 Tim 6.12 take hold of the eternal life
6.19 so that they may take hold of the life
2. *seize, hold fast:* κρατέω KRATEŌ
Mt 28. 9 they came up and took hold of his feet

HOLD OUT
1. *spread out:* ἐκπετάννυμι EKPETANNYMI*
Rom 10.21 "All day long I have held out my hands

HOLD TO
1. *continue, remain:* ἐπιμένω EPIMENŌ
1 Tim 4.16 Take heed to yourself . . ; hold to that
2. *seize, hold fast:* κρατέω KRATEŌ
2 Th 2.15 stand firm and hold to the traditions

HOLD S. TO
1. *bring to, present:* προσφέρω PROSPHERŌ
Jn 19.29 a sponge . . and held it to his mouth

HOLD TOGETHER
1. *stand with, commend:* συνίστημι (perf.) SYNISTĒMI
Col 1.17 in him all things hold together

HOLD TRUE
1. *agree with, walk by:* στοιχέω STOICHEŌ
Phil 3.16 hold true to what we have attained

HOLD UP (*See* CONTEMPT, HOLD UP TO)

HOLE
1. *den, lair:* φωλεός PHŌLEOS*
Mt 8.20 "Foxes have holes, and birds . . have nests
Lk 9.58 "Foxes have holes, and birds . . have nests

HOLINESS
1. *sanctification:* ἁγιασμός HAGIASMOS
1 Th 4. 4 take a wife . . in holiness and honor
4. 7 For God . . called us . . in holiness
1 Tim 2.15 if she continues[d] in . . love and holiness
Heb 12.14 Strive for peace . . and for the holiness
2. *holiness:* ἁγιωσύνη HAGIŌSYNĒ*
Rom 1. 4 according to the Spirit of holiness
2 Cor 7. 1 make holiness perfect in the fear of God
1 Th 3.13 establish your hearts unblamable in h.
3. *holiness:* ἁγιότης HAGIOTĒS*
2 Cor 1.12 we have behaved in the world . . with h.
Heb 12.10 that we may share his holiness
4. *piety:* ὁσιότης HOSIOTĒS*
Lk 1.75 "in h. and righteousness before him
Eph 4.24 the new nature, created . . in . . holiness

HOLINESS, OF
1. *sacred, holy:* ἅγιος HAGIOS
2 Pet 3.11 in lives of holiness and godliness

HOLY
1. *sacred, holy:* ἅγιος HAGIOS
[a]superl. (H. S. = Holy Spirit)
Mt 1.18 she was found to be with child of the H. S.
1.20 "that . . conceived in her is of the H. S.
3.11 "he will baptize you with the H. S.
4. 5 the devil took him to the holy city
7. 6 "Do not give dogs what is holy
12.32 "whoever speaks against the H. S.
24.15 "sacrilege . . standing in the holy place
27.53 they went into the holy city
28.19 "baptizing . . in the name of the . . H. S.
Mk 1. 8 "but he will baptize you with the H. S.
1.24 "I know who you are, the Holy One of God
3.29 "whoever blasphemes against the H. S.
6.20 knowing that he was a . . holy man
8.38 "when he comes . . with the holy angels
12.36 "David himself, inspired by[z] the H. S.
13.11 "for it is not you who speak, but the H. S.
Lk 1.15 "he will be filled with the H. S.
1.35 "The H. S. will come upon you . . ; therefore the child to be born[d] will be called holy
1.41 Elizabeth was filled with the H. S.
1.49 "who is mighty . . and holy is his name
1.67 Zechariah was filled with the H. S.
1.70 "spoke by the mouth of his holy prophets
1.72 "to remember his holy covenant
2.23 ("male that opens the womb shall be . . h.
2.25 Simeon . . , the H. S. was upon him
2.26 it had been revealed to him by the H. S.
3.16 "he will baptize you with the H. S.
3.22 the H. S. descended upon him . . as a dove
4. 1 Jesus, full of the H. S., returned
4.34 "I know who you are, the Holy One
9.26 "comes in . . the glory . . of the holy angels
10.21 that same hour he rejoiced in the H. S.
11.13 "will . . give the H. S. to those who ask!
12.10 "he who blasphemes against the H. S.
12.12 "for the H. S. will teach you in that . . hour
Jn 1.33 " 'this is he who baptizes with the H. S.
6.69 "know, that you are the Holy One of God
14.26 "the Counselor, the H. S., . . will teach you
17.11 "Holy Father, keep them in thy name
20.22 he breathed . . and said . . "Receive the H. S.
Acts 1. 2 commandment through the H. S.
1. 5 "you shall be baptized with the H. S.
1. 8 "power when the H. S. has come upon you
1.16 "scripture . . which the H. S. spoke
2. 4 they were all filled with the H. S.
2.33 "having received . . the promise of the H. S.
2.38 "you shall receive the gift of the H. S.
3.14 "you denied the Holy and Righteous One
3.21 "by the mouth of his holy prophets
4. 8 Then Peter, filled with the H. S.
4.25 "who . . didst say by the H. S.
4.27 "against thy holy servant[c] Jesus
4.30 "the name of thy holy servant[c] Jesus
4.31 they were all filled with the H. S.
5. 3 "Satan filled your heart to lie to the H. S.
5.32 "we are witnesses . . and so is the H. S.
6. 5 Stephen, . . full of faith and . . the H. S.
6.13 "to speak words against this holy place
7.33 " 'where you are standing is holy ground
7.51 "you always resist the H. S.
7.55 he, full of the H. S., gazed into heaven
8.15 prayed . . that they might receive the H. S.
8.17 and they received the H. S.
8.19 "that any one . . may receive the H. S.
9.17 "that you may . . be filled with the H. S.
9.31 walking . . in the comfort of the H. S.
10.22 "Cornelius . . was directed by a h. angel
10.38 "how God anointed Jesus . . with the H. S.
10.44 "the H. S. fell on all who heard the word
10.45 the gift of the H. S. had been poured out
10.47 "people who have received the H. S.
11.15 "As I began to speak, the H. S. fell
11.16 " 'you shall be baptized with the H. S.
11.24 good man, full of the H. S. and of faith
13. 2 H. S. said, "Set apart . . Barnabas
13. 4 being sent out by the H. S., they went
13. 9 filled with the H. S., looked intently
13.52 disciples were filled . . with the H. S.
15. 8 "giving them the H. S. just as he did to us
15.28 "it has seemed good to the H. S.
16. 6 having been forbidden by the H. S.
19. 2 "Did you receive the H. S.?
19. 2 "never even heard that there is a H. S.
19. 6 the H. S. came on them; and they spoke
20.23 "the H. S. testifies to me in every city
20.28 "the H. S. has made you overseers
21.11 "Thus says the H. S., 'So shall the Jews
21.28 "he has defiled this holy place
28.25 "The H. S. was right in saying
Rom 1. 2 through . . prophets in the h. scriptures
5. 5 poured into our hearts through the H. S.
7.12 So the law is holy, and the commandment is holy and just and good
9. 1 conscience bears me witness in the H. S.
11.16 If the dough . . is holy, so is the . . lump; and if the root is h., so are the branches

Rom 12. 1 your bodies as a living sacrifice, holy
14.17 peace and joy in the H. S.
15.13 by .. power of the H. S... abound in hope
15.16 acceptable, sanctified by the H. S.
15.19 by the power of the H. S.
16.16 Greet one another with a holy kiss
1 Cor 3.17 God's temple is h., .. that temple you are
6.19 your body is a temple of the H. S.
7.14 would be unclean, but as it is they are h.
7.34 how to be holy in body and spirit
12. 3 "Jesus is Lord" except by the H. S.
16.20 Greet one another with a holy kiss
2 Cor 6. 6 forbearance, kindness, the H. S.
13.12 Greet one another with a holy kiss
13.14(13) fellowship of[n] the H. S. be with you all
Eph 1. 4 that we should be holy and blameless
1.13 you .. were sealed with the promised H. S.
2.21 grows into a holy temple in the Lord
3. 5 revealed to his h. apostles and prophets
4.30 do not grieve the H. S. of God
5.27 that she might be holy and without blemish
Col 1.22 his death, in order to present you holy
3.12 Put on .., holy and beloved, compassion
1 Th 1. 5 not only in word, but also .. in the H. S.
1. 6 in .. affliction, with joy inspired by the H. S.
4. 8 not man but God, who gives his H. S.
5.26 Greet all the brethren with a holy kiss
2 Tim 1. 9 saved us and called us with a holy calling
1.14 truth .. entrusted to you by the H. S.
Tit 3. 5 regeneration and renewal in the H. S.
Heb 2. 4 God .. bore witness .. by gifts of the H. S.
3. 1 Therefore, h. brethren, .. consider Jesus
3. 7 as the H. S. says, "Today, when you hear
6. 4 who .. have become partakers of the H. S.
9. 2 it is called the Holy Place
9. 3 Behind the second curtain stood a tent[p] called the Holy of Holies
9. 8 By this the H. S. indicates
9.12 entered once for all into the Holy Place
9.25 the high priest enters the Holy Place
10.15 the H. S. also bears witness to us
1 Pet 1.12 through the H. S. sent from heaven
1.15 but as he who called you is holy, be holy yourselves in all your conduct
1.16 it is written, "You shall be holy, for I am holy
2. 5 a spiritual house, to be a holy priesthood
2. 9 a royal priesthood, a holy nation
3. 5 the holy women who hoped in God
2 Pet 1.18 we were with him on the holy mountain
1.21 men moved by the H. S. spoke from God[e]
[1.21 *moved by the H. S. holy men of God spoke*‡
2.21 turn back from the h. commandment
3. 2 predictions of the holy prophets
1 Jn 2.20 you have been anointed by the Holy One
Jude .14 "the Lord came with his holy myriads
.20 [a]beloved, build yourselves up on your most holy faith; pray in the H. S.
Rev 3. 7 " 'The words of the holy one
4. 8 they never cease to sing, "Holy, holy, holy, is the Lord God Almighty, who was and is and is to come!
6.10 "O Sovereign Lord, holy and true
11. 2 "they will trample over the holy city
14.10 "in the presence of the holy angels
20. 6 Blessed and holy is he who shares
21. 2 I saw the holy city, new Jerusalem
21.10 he .. showed me the holy city Jerusalem
22.11 "Let .. the holy still be holy
22.19 take away his share in .. the holy city

2. *holy, devout:* ὅσιος HOSIOS*
Acts 2.27 " 'nor let thy Holy One see corruption
13.34 " 'I will give you the h... blessings of David
13.35 " 'not let thy Holy One see corruption
1 Tim 2. 8 that .. men should pray, lifting h. hands
Tit 1. 8 master of himself, .. self-controlled
Heb 7.26 such a high priest, holy, blameless
Rev 15. 4 "For thou alone art holy
16. 5 "thou who art and wast, O Holy One

3. *in a holy manner:* ὁσίως HOSIŌS* [A.4.a]
1 Th 2.10 how holy .. was our behavior to you

CONTEXTUALLY
Jn 11.48 "destroy both our h. place[a] and .. nation†

HOLY, BE

1. *make sacred:* ἁγιάζω (pass.) HAGIAZŌ
Rev 22.11 "Let .. the holy still be holy

HOMAGE

1. *prostrate oneself before:* προσκυνέω PROSKYNEŌ [A.6.c.1]
Mk 15.19 they knelt down in homage to him

HOME (*See also* GO HOME; HIS HOME; HIS OWN HOME; OUR HOME)

1. *abiding, apartment:* μονή MONĒ
Jn 14.23 "we will .. make our home with him

2. *house, household:* οἰκία OIKIA
Mt 8. 6 "my servant is lying paralyzed at home
17.25 "when he came home, Jesus spoke
Mk 13.34 "like a man .. when he leaves home

3. *house, household:* οἶκος OIKOS
Mt 9. 6 "Rise, take up your bed and go home
9. 7 And he rose and went home
Mk 2. 1 it was reported that he was at home
2.11 "rise, take up your pallet and go home
3.19(20) Then he went home
5.19 "Go home to your friends
7.30 she went home, and found the child
8. 3 "if I send them .. hungry to their homes
8.26 he sent him away to his home
Lk 1.23 he went to his home
1.56 Mary .. returned to her home
5.24 "rise, take up your bed and go home
5.25 he rose .. and went home, glorifying God
8.39 "Return to your home, and declare
9.61 "let me first say farewell to those at my h.
15. 6 "when he comes h., he calls .. friends
Acts 2.46 day by day, .. breaking bread in their homes
5.42 every day in the temple and at home
1 Cor 11.34 if any one is hungry, let him eat at home
14.35 let them ask their husbands at home

IDIOMATICALLY
a. Acts 21.6 and they returned home ἐκεῖνοι δὲ ὑπέστρεψαν εἰς τὰ ἴδια [IDIOS]

CONTEXTUALLY
Lk 23.48 returned home beating their breasts
Jn 20.10 the disciples went back to their homes

HOME, BE AT

1. *live at, stay in:* ἐνδημέω ENDĒMEŌ*
2 Cor 5. 6 while we are at home in the body
5. 8 we would rather be .. at h. with the Lord
5. 9 whether we are at home or away

HOME, COME

1. *unloose, return:* ἀναλύω ANALYŌ
Lk 12.36 "waiting for their master to come home

HOMELAND

1. *fatherland:* πατρίς PATRIS
Heb 11.14 clear that they are seeking a homeland

HOMELESS, BE

1. *be unsettled:* ἀστατέω ASTATEŌ*
1 Cor 4.11 we are ill-clad and buffeted and homeless

HONEST

1. *good:* ἀγαθός AGATHOS
Eph 4.28 doing honest work with his hands
Tit 3. 1 to be ready for any honest work

2. *good, beautiful:* καλός KALOS
Lk 8.15 "hold it fast in an honest and good heart

HONEY

1. *honey:* μέλι MELI*
Mt 3. 4 his food was locusts and wild honey
Mk 1. 6 John .. ate locusts and wild honey
Rev 10. 9 "it will be .. sweet as honey in your mouth
10.10 it was sweet as honey in my mouth

HONOR
1. *glory:* δόξα DOXA
[a]A.6.a.3, c.3
Lk 14.10 [a]"honored in . . presence of all . . at table
2 Cor 6. 8 in honor and dishonor, in ill . . and good
2. *extol, honor:* δοξάζω DOXAZŌ
Rom 1.21 they did not honor him as God
1 Cor 12.26 if one member is honored, all rejoice
3. *hold honored:* ἔχειν ἔντιμον ENTIMOS [B.2.a.1]
Phil 2.29 honor such men
4. *make large, extol:* μεγαλύνω MEGALYNŌ
Phil 1.20 Christ will be honored in my body
5. *honor, value:* τιμάω TIMAŌ
Mt 15. 4 "God commanded, 'Honor your father
15. 5 " 'he need not honor his father
15. 8 " 'This people honors me with their lips
19.19 "Honor your father and mother
Mk 7. 6 " 'This people honors me with their lips
7.10 " 'Honor your father and your mother
10.19 " 'Honor your father and mother
Lk 18.20 " 'Honor your father and mother
Jn 5.23 "that all may honor the Son, even as they honor the Father. He who does not honor the Son does not honor the Father who sent him
8.49 "I honor my Father, and you dishonor me
12.26 "the Father will honor him
Acts [28.10 They *honored us with many honors*†
Eph 6. 2 "Honor your father and mother
1 Tim 5. 3 Honor widows who are real widows
1 Pet 2.17 Honor all men. Love the brotherhood. Fear God. Honor the emperor
6. *honor, value:* τιμή TIMĒ
Jn 4.44 a prophet has no honor in his own country
Acts [28.10 They *honored us with many honors*†
Rom 2. 7 those who . . seek for glory and honor
2.10 glory and honor and peace for every one
12.10 outdo one another in showing honor
13. 7 Pay all of them their dues, . . honor to whom honor is due
1 Cor 12.23 those . . we invest with the greater honor
12.24 the greater honor to the inferior part
1 Th 4. 4 know how to take a wife . . in . . honor
1 Tim 1.17 To . . God, be honor and glory
5.17 elders . . worthy of double honor
6. 1 regard their masters as worthy of all h.
6.16 To him be honor and eternal dominion
Heb 2. 7 "crowned him with glory and honor[d]
2. 9 Jesus, . . crowned with glory and honor
3. 3 builder . . has more honor than the house
5. 4 one does not take the h. upon himself
1 Pet 1. 7 redound to praise and glory and honor
3. 7 bestowing honor on the woman
2 Pet 1.17 he received honor and glory from God
Rev 4. 9 whenever the living creatures give . . honor
4.11 "Worthy . . to receive glory and honor
5.12 "Worthy . . to receive power and . . honor
5.13 "to the Lamb be blessing and honor
7.12 "Blessing and . . honor . . be to our God!
21.26 shall bring into it . . the honor of the nations
CONTEXTUALLY
Rom 14. 6 observes it in honor of the Lord
14. 6 He also who eats . . in honor of the Lord
14. 6 he . . abstains in honor of the Lord

HONOR, HELD IN
1. *glorious, honored:* ἔνδοξος ENDOXOS
1 Cor 4.10 You are held in honor, but we in disrepute
2. *held in honor, costly:* τίμιος TIMIOS
Acts 5.34 held in honor by all the people
Heb 13. 4 Let marriage be held in honor among all

HONOR, HOLD IN HIGH
1. *make large, extol:* μεγαλύνω MEGALYNŌ
Acts 5.13 the people held them in high honor

HONOR, PLACE OF
1. *first seat at table:* πρωτοκλισία PRŌTOKLISIA*
Mt 23. 6 "they love the place of honor at feasts
Mk 12.39 "the places of honor at feasts
Lk 14. 7 how they chose the places of honor
14. 8 "do not sit down in a place of honor
20.46 "who . . love . . places of honor at feasts

HONOR, WITHOUT
1. *unhonored, dishonored:* ἄτιμος ATIMOS
Mt 13.57 "A prophet is not without honor except
Mk 6. 4 "A prophet is not without honor, except

HONORABLE
1. *good, beautiful:* καλός KALOS
2 Cor 8.21 for we aim at what is honorable
Tit [3.14 learn to *enter honorable occupations*†
Jas 2. 7 who blaspheme the honorable name
2. *revered, holy:* σεμνός SEMNOS
Phil 4. 8 whatever is honorable, whatever is just

HONORABLE, LESS
1. *unhonored, dishonored:* ἄτιμος (comp.) ATIMOS
1 Cor 12.23 those parts . . we think less honorable

HONORABLY
1. *well, rightly:* καλῶς KALŌS
Heb 13.18 desiring to act honorably in all things

HOOK
1. *fishhook:* ἄγκιστρον AGKISTRON*
Mt 17.27 "go to the sea and cast a hook

HOPE
1. *hope, expectation:* ἐλπίς ELPIS*
[a]B.3.a.5
Acts 2.26 " 'moreover my flesh will dwell in hope
16.19 saw that their hope of gain was gone
23. 6 "with respect to the hope . . of the dead
24.15 "a hope in God which these . . accept
26. 6 "on trial for hope in the promise
26. 7 "for this hope I am accused by Jews!
27.20 hope of our being saved was . . abandoned
28.20 "it is because of the hope of Israel
Rom 4.18 In hope he believed against hope, that he should become the father of . . nations
5. 2 our hope of sharing the glory of God
5. 4 character produces hope
5. 5 hope does not disappoint us
8.20 by the will of him who subjected it in hope
8.24 For in this hope we were saved. Now hope that is seen is not hope
12.12 Rejoice in your hope, be patient
15. 4 that by steadfastness . . we might have h.
15.13 the God of hope fill you with all joy and peace . . that . . you may abound in hope
1 Cor 9.10 the plowman should plow in hope and the thresher thresh in hope
13.13 So faith, hope, love abide, these three
2 Cor 1. 7 Our hope for you is unshaken
3.12 Since we have such a hope, we are . . bold
10.15 our hope is that as your faith increases
Gal 5. 5 we wait for the hope of righteousness
Eph 1.18 what is the hope to which he . . called you
2.12 having no hope and without God
4. 4 just as you were called to the one hope
Phil 1.20 hope that I shall not be at all ashamed
Col 1. 5 the hope laid up for you in heaven
1.23 not shifting from the hope of . . gospel
1.27 Christ in you, the hope of glory
1 Th 1. 3 steadfastness of hope in our Lord Jesus
2.19 For what is our hope or joy?
4.13 not grieve as others do who have no h.
5. 8 for a helmet the hope of salvation
2 Th 2.16 eternal comfort and good hope through grace
1 Tim 1. 1 by command . . of Christ Jesus our hope
Tit 1. 2 in hope of eternal life
2.13 awaiting our blessed hope
3. 7 become heirs in hope of eternal life
Heb 3. 6 if we hold fast our . . pride in our hope[g]
6.11 realizing the full assurance of hope
6.18 encouragement to seize the hope
7.19 a better hope is introduced
10.23 Let us hold fast the confession of our h.
1 Pet 1. 3 we have been born anew to a living h.

1 Pet 1.21 so that your faith and hope are in God[d]
3.15 to account for the hope that is in you
1 Jn 3. 3 [a]one who thus hopes . . purifies himself
2. *hope for, expect:* ἐλπίζω ELPIZŌ
Mt 12.21 "in his name will the Gentiles hope
Lk 6.34 "those from whom you hope to receive
23. 8 hoping to see some sign done by him
24.21 "we . . hoped . . he was the one to redeem
Acts 24.26 he hoped that money would be given
26. 7 "which our twelve tribes hope to attain
Rom 8.24 For who hopes for what he sees?
8.25 if we hope for what we do not see
15.12 "in him shall the Gentiles hope
15.24 I hope to see you in passing
1 Cor 13. 7 Love . . hopes all things, endures
15.19 If for this life only we have hoped
16. 7 I hope to spend some time with you
2 Cor 1.13 I hope you will understand fully
5.11 I hope it is known . . to your conscience
13. 6 I hope you will find . . we have not failed
Phil 2.19 I hope . . to send Timothy to you soon
2.23 I hope therefore to send him just as soon
1 Tim 3.14 I hope to come to you soon
Phm .22 for I am hoping through your prayers
1 Pet 3. 5 the holy women who hoped in God
2 Jn .12 but I hope to come to see you
3 Jn .14 I hope to see you soon
IDIOMATICALLY
a. Acts 17.27 "in the hope that they might feel after him
εἰ ἄρα γε ψηλαφήσειαν αὐτόν [ARA II]
CONTEXTUALLY
Heb 6.19 hope that enters into the inner shrine

HOPE, FIRST
1. *hope before, expect:* προελπίζω PROELPIZŌ*
Eph 1.12 we who first hoped in Christ

HOPE SET, HAVE ONE'S
HOPE, SET ONE'S
1. *hope for, expect:* ἐλπίζω ELPIZŌ
Jn 5.45 "Moses . . , on whom you set your hope
2 Cor 1.10 on him we have set our hope
1 Tim 4.10 we have our hope set on the living God
5. 5 a real widow . . has set her hope on God
6.17 nor . . set their hopes on uncertain riches
1 Pet 1.13 set your hope fully upon the grace

HOPED FOR, S.
1. *hope for, expect:* ἐλπίζω (subst. pass. part.) ELPIZŌ
Heb 11. 1 faith is the assurance of things hoped for

HORN
1. *horn of an animal:* κέρας KERAS*
Lk 1.69 "raised up a horn of salvation for us
Rev 5. 6 I saw a Lamb . . with seven horns
9.13 I heard a voice from the four horns
12. 3 a great red dragon, with . . ten horns
13. 1 I saw a beast rising . . with ten horns . . with ten diadems upon its horns
13.11 it had two horns like a lamb
17. 3 it had seven heads and ten horns
17. 7 "the beast with seven heads and ten horns
17.12 "the ten horns . . are ten kings
17.16 "the ten horns . . will hate the harlot

HORSE
1. *horse:* ἵππος HIPPOS*
Jas 3. 3 we put bits into the mouths of horses
Rev 6. 2 I saw, and behold, a white horse
6. 4 out came another horse, bright red
6. 5 I saw, and behold, a black horse
6. 8 I saw, and behold, a pale horse
9. 7 the locusts were like horses
9. 9 noise of many chariots with horses
9.17 this was how I saw the horses
9.17 heads of the horses were like lions' heads
9.19 power of the horses is in their mouths
14.20 blood . . as high as a horse's bridle
18.13 cattle and sheep, horses and chariots
19.11 heaven opened, and behold, a white horse!
Rev 19.14 armies . . followed him on white horses
19.18 "to eat . . the flesh of horses
19.19 war against him who sits upon the horse
19.21 him who sits upon the horse

HORSEMAN
1. *cavalryman, horseman:* ἱππεύς HIPPEUS*
Acts 23.23 "get ready . . soldiers with seventy horsemen
23.32 leaving the horsemen to go on

HOSANNA
1. *save now* (Heb.): ὡσαννά HŌSANNA*
Mt 21. 9 "Hosanna to the Son of David!
21. 9 "Hosanna in the highest!
21.15 "Hosanna to the Son of David!
Mk 11. 9 those who followed cried out, "Hosanna!
11.10 "Hosanna in the highest!
Jn 12.13 "Hosanna! Blessed is he who comes

HOSEA: Ὡσηέ ˌhōˈzāə, ˌhōˈzēə
Rom 9.25 in H., "Those who were not my people

HOSPITABLE
1. *hospitable:* φιλόξενος PHILOXENOS
1 Tim 3. 2 sensible, dignified, hospitable
Tit 1. 8 hospitable, a lover of goodness

HOSPITABLY
1. *kindly:* φιλοφρόνως PHILOPHRONŌS*
Acts 28. 7 Publius . . entertained us hospitably

HOSPITALITY
1. *hospitality:* φιλοξενία PHILOXENIA*
Rom 12.13 practice hospitality
Heb 13. 2 Do not neglect to show hospitality

HOSPITALITY, PRACTICE
1. *hospitable:* φιλόξενος PHILOXENOS [A.3.e.2]
1 Pet 4. 9 Practice hospitality ungrudgingly

HOSPITALITY, SHOW
1. *entertain strangers:* ξενοδοχέω XENODOCHEŌ*
1 Tim 5.10 brought up children, shown hospitality

HOST
1. *call, name:* καλέω (subst. part.) KALEŌ
Lk 14.10 "so that when your host comes he may say
2. *army:* στρατιά STRATIA*
Lk 2.13 a multitude of the heavenly host
Acts 7.42 "to worship the host of heaven
3. *strange, foreign:* ξένος (subst.) XENOS
Rom 16.23 Gaius, who is host to me . . , greets you

HOST OF CAPTIVES, A
1. *captivity:* αἰχμαλωσία AICHMALŌSIA [C.2]
Eph 4. 8 "When he ascended . . he led a h. of captives

HOSTILE
1. *hostility:* ἔχθρα (pred.) ECHTHRA
Rom 8. 7 mind that is set on the flesh is hostile
2. *hated, hostile:* ἐχθρός ECHTHROS
Col 1.21 you, who once were estranged and h.

HOSTILITY
1. *contradiction, dispute:* ἀντιλογία ANTILOGIA
Heb 12. 3 who endured from sinners such hostility
2. *hostility:* ἔχθρα ECHTHRA
Eph 2.14 has broken down the dividing wall of h.
2.16 thereby bringing the hostility to an end

HOSTS
1. *armies* (Heb.): Σαβαώθ SABAŌTH*
Rom 9.29 "If the Lord of h. had not left us children
Jas 5. 4 the cries . . have reached . . the Lord of hosts
CONTEXTUALLY
Eph 6.12 against the spiritual hosts of wickedness

HOT
1. *hot:* ζεστός ZESTOS*
Rev 3.15 " 'you are neither cold nor hot. Would that you were cold or hot!
3.16 " 'lukewarm, and neither cold nor hot

HOUR (*See also* PRAYER, KEEP THE HOUR OF)
1. *hour, time of day:* ὥρα HŌRA
Mt 10.19 "will be given to you in that hour
20. 3 "going out about the third hour
20. 5 "Going out again about the sixth hour

Mt 20. 9 "those hired about the eleventh hour
20.12 " 'These last worked only one hour
24.36 "But of that day and hour no one knows
24.44 "coming at an hour you do not expect
24.50 "will come . . at an hour he does not know
25.13 "you know neither the day nor the hour
26.40 "could you not watch[h] with me one hour?
26.45 "Behold, the hour is at hand
26.55 At that hour Jesus said to the crowds
27.45 from the sixth hour there was darkness over all the land[m] until the ninth hour
27.46 about the ninth hour Jesus cried . . "Eli
Mk 6.35 "a lonely place, and the hour is now late
13.11 "say whatever is given you in that hour
13.32 "of that day or that hour no one knows
14.35 prayed that . . the hour might pass
14.37 "Could you not watch[d] one hour?
14.41 "It is enough; the hour has come
15.25 the third hour, when they crucified him
15.33 when the sixth hour had come, there was darkness . . until the ninth hour
15.34 at the ninth hour Jesus cried . . "Eloi
Lk 1.10 praying outside at the hour of incense
2.38 coming up at that very hour
7.21 In that hour he cured many
10.21 In that same hour he rejoiced
12.12 "in that very hour what you ought to say
12.39 "at what hour the thief was coming
12.40 "coming at an unexpected hour
12.46 "will come . . at an hour he does not know
13.31 At that very hour some Pharisees came
20.19 tried to lay hands on him at that . . hour
22.14 when the hour came, he sat at table
22.53 "this is your hour, and the power of darkness
22.59 after an interval of about an hour
23.44 It was now about the sixth hour, and there was darkness . . until the ninth hour
24.33 they rose that same hour and returned
Jn 1.39 for it was about the tenth hour
2. 4 "My hour has not yet come
4. 6 It was about the sixth hour
4.21 "Woman, believe me, the hour is coming
4.23 "But the hour is coming, and now is
4.52 asked . . the hour when he began to mend, . . they said . . "Yesterday at the seventh hour
4.53 that was the hour when Jesus had said
5.25 "the hour is coming, and now is
5.28 "the hour is coming when all . . will hear
7.30 because his hour had not yet come
8.20 because his hour had not yet come
11. 9 "Are there not twelve hours in the day?
12.23 "hour has come for the Son of man
12.27 " 'Father, save me from this hour'? No, for this purpose I have come to this h.
13. 1 Jesus knew that his hour had come
16. 2 "the h. is coming when whoever kills you
16. 4 "that when their h. comes you . . remember
16.21 "she has sorrow, because her h. has come
16.25 "h. is coming when I shall . . tell you
16.32 "The h. is coming, indeed it has come
17. 1 "Father, the hour has come
19.14 "it was about the sixth hour
19.27 from that hour the disciple took her
Acts 2.15 "it is only the third hour of the day
3. 1 at the hour of prayer, the ninth hour
5. 7 After an interval of about three hours
10. 3 About the ninth hour of the day
10. 9 went up . . to pray, about the sixth hour
10.30 "Four days ago, about this hour
16.18 And it came out that very hour
16.33 took them the same hour of the night
[19. 9 argued . . *from the fifth hour to the tenth*‡
19.34 for about two hours they . . cried out
22.13 "in that very hour I received my sight
23.23 "At the third hour of the night get ready
Rom 13.11 Besides this you know what hour it is
1 Cor 4.11 To the present hour we hunger
1 Cor 15.30 Why am I in peril every hour?
1 Jn 2.18 Children, it is the last hour
2.18 therefore we know that it is the last hour
Rev 3. 3 " 'not know at what hour I will come
3.10 " 'I will keep you from the hour of trial
9.15 four angels . . held ready for the hour
11.13 at that h. there was a great earthquake
14. 7 "for the hour of his judgment has come
14.15 "for the hour to reap has come
17.12 "to receive authority as kings for one hour
18.10 "In one hour has thy judgment come
18.17 "In one h. all this . . has been laid waste
18.19 "In one hour she has been laid waste

CONTEXTUALLY
Mt 20. 6 "the eleventh h. he went out . . found others

HOUR, HALF AN

1. *half hour:* ἡμίωρον HĒMIŌRON*
Rev 8. 1 silence in heaven for about half an h.

HOUSE

1. *house, household:* οἰκία OIKIA
Mt 2.11 going into the house they saw the child
5.15 "it gives light to all in the house
7.24 "man who built his house upon the rock
7.25 "winds blew and beat upon that house
7.26 "man who built his house upon the sand
7.27 "winds blew and beat against that house
8.14 when Jesus entered Peter's house
9.10 as he sat at table[v] in the house
9.23 when Jesus came to the ruler's house
9.28 When he entered the house
10.12 "As you enter the house, salute it
10.13 "if the h. is worthy, let your peace come
10.14 "shake off the dust . . as you leave that h.
12.25 "no . . h. divided against itself will stand
12.29 "how can one enter a strong man's h.?
12.29 "Then indeed he may plunder his house
13. 1 Jesus went out of the house and sat
13.36 left the crowds and went into the h.
13.57 "not without honor except . . in his own h.
19.29 "every one who has left houses
[23.14 "*for you devour widows' houses*‡
24.17 "not go down to take what is in his h.
24.43 "not have let his house be broken into
26. 6 in the house of Simon the leper
Mk 1.29 entered the house of Simon and Andrew
2.15 as he sat at table in his house
3.25 "And if a house is divided against itself, that house will not be able to stand
3.27 "no one can enter a strong man's house
3.27 "then indeed he may plunder his house
6. 4 "not without honor, except . . in his own h.
6.10 "Where you enter a house, stay
7.24 he entered a h. . . ; yet he could not be hid
9.33 when he was in the house he asked
10.10 in the house the disciples asked him
10.29 "there is no one who has left h.
10.30 "who will not receive . . houses
12.40 "who devour widows' houses
13.15 "let him . . not . . enter his house
13.35 "when the master of the house will come
14. 3 in the house of Simon the leper
Lk 4.38 he arose . . and entered Simon's house
5.29 Levi made him a great feast in his h.
6.48 "he is like a man building a house
6.48 "the stream broke against that house
6.49 "like a man who built a h. on the ground
6.49 "the ruin of that house was great
7. 6 "When he was not far from the house
7.37 he was at table in the Pharisee's house
7.44 "I entered your h., you gave me no water
8.27 lived not in a house but among the tombs
8.51 when he came to the house
9. 4 "whatever house you enter, stay
10. 5 "Whatever h. you enter, first say, 'Peace!
10. 7 "remain in the same house, eating and drinking . . ; do not go from house to house

Lk 10.38 Martha received him into her house
15. 8 "does not light a lamp and sweep the h.?
15.25 "as he . . drew near to the house
17.31 "let him . . , with his goods in the house
18.29 "there is no man who has left house
20.47 "who devour widows' houses
22.10 "follow him into the h. which he enters
22.54 bringing him into the high priest's h.
Jn 8.35 "slave does not continue in the house
11.31 Jews who were with her in the house
12. 3 the h. was filled with the fragrance
14. 2 "In my Father's house are many rooms
Acts 4.34 possessors of lands or houses sold them
9.11 "inquire in the house of Judas
9.17 Ananias departed and entered the h.
10. 6 "Simon, . . whose h. is by the seaside
10.17 having made inquiry for Simon's h.
10.32 " 'he is lodging in the house of Simon
11.11 "three men arrived at the house
12.12 he went to the house of Mary
16.32 they spoke . . to all that were in his house
17. 5 they . . attacked the house of Jason
18. 7 went to the house of a man named Titius[q] . . ; his h. was next door to the synagogue
1 Cor 11.22 Do you not have houses to eat . . in?
2 Cor 5. 1 we have . . a house not made with hands
2 Tim 2.20 In a great house there are . . vessels
2 Jn .10 do not receive him into the house

2. *house, household:* οἶκος OIKOS
Mt 10. 6 "go . . to the lost sheep of the h. of Israel
11. 8 "Behold, those . . are in kings' houses
12. 4 "how he entered the house of God
12.44 "he says, 'I will return to my house
15.24 "I was sent only to . . the house of Israel
21.13 He said to them, "It is written, 'My house shall be called a house of prayer
23.38 "Behold, your house is forsaken
Mk 2.26 "how he entered the house of God
5.38 the house of the ruler of the synagogue
7.17 And when he had entered the house
9.28 when he had entered the house
11.17 "Is it not written, 'My house shall be called a house of prayer for all the nations'?
Lk 1.27 Joseph, of the house of David
1.33 "he will reign over the house of Jacob
1.40 she entered the house of Zechariah
1.69 "in the house of his servant David
2. 4 he was of the h. and lineage of David
6. 4 "how he entered the house of God
7.10 when those . . returned to the house
7.36 he went into the Pharisee's house
8.41 he besought him to come to his house
10. 5 "first say, 'Peace be to this house!
11.24 "he says, 'I will return to my house
12.39 "he . . would not have left his house
12.52 "in one house there will be five divided
13.35 "Behold, your house is forsaken
14. 1 he went to dine at the house of a ruler
14.23 " 'compel people . . that my h. may be filled
16. 4 " 'that people . . receive me into their houses
16.27 " 'send him to my father's house
18.14 "this man went down to his h. justified
19. 5 "I must stay at your house today
19. 9 "Today salvation has come to this house
19.46 " 'My house shall be a house of prayer'; but you have made it a den of robbers
Jn 2.16 "you shall not make my Father's house a house of trade
2.17 "Zeal for thy house will consume me
7.53 They went each to his own house[r]‡
11.20 met him, while Mary sat in the house
Acts 2. 2 a sound . . filled all the house
2.36 "Let all the house of Israel . . know
7.20 "Moses . . was brought up . . in his father's h.
7.42 " 'years in the wilderness, O h. of Israel
7.47 "Solomon who built a house for him
7.49 " 'What house will you build for me?
Acts 10.22 "to send for you to come to his house
10.30 "keeping the ninth hour of prayer in my h.
11.12 "and we entered the man's house
11.13 "he had seen the angel standing in his h.
16.15 "come to my house and stay
16.34 Then he brought them up into his house
19.16 they fled out of that house naked
21. 8 we entered the house of Philip
Rom 16. 5 greet also the church in their house
1 Cor 16.19 together with the church in their house
Col 4.15 Nympha and the church in her house
Phm . 2 ⟨To Philemon⟩ and the church in your house
Heb 3. 2 Moses also was faithful in[e] God's house
3. 3 as the builder . . has more honor than the house
3. 4 (For every house is built by some one
3. 5 Moses was faithful in all God's house
3. 6 Christ was faithful over God's[f] house . . And we are his house if we hold fast
8. 8 "a new covenant with the h. of Israel and with the house of Judah
8.10 "covenant . . I will make with . . h. of Israel
10.21 a great priest over the house of God
1 Pet 2. 5 living stones . . built into a spiritual house

IDIOMATICALLY
a. 1 Tim 5.13 gadding about from house to house περιερχόμεναι τὰς οἰκίας [OIKIA]
b. Acts 8.3 entering house after house κατὰ τοὺς οἴκους εἰσπορευόμενος [OIKOS]
c. Acts 20.20 "teaching you in public and from house to house διδάξαι ὑμᾶς δημοσίᾳ καὶ κατ' οἴκους [OIKOS]

CONTEXTUALLY
Mt 26.18 "I will keep the passover at your house
Mk 5.35 there came from the ruler's house
Lk 2.49 "that I must be in my Father's house
8.49 a man from the ruler's house came
Jn 18.28 they led Jesus from the h. of Caiaphas
Acts 7.48 "Yet the Most High does not dwell in houses
21.16 bringing us to the house of Mnason
2 Tim 2.21 consecrated . . useful to the master of the h.

HOUSE, IN THE
1. *inside:* ἔσω ESŌ
Jn 20.26 his disciples were again in the house

HOUSE, MASTER OF THE
1. *master of the house:* οἰκοδεσπότης OIKODESPOTĒS
Mt 10.25 "called the master of the house Beelzebul

HOUSEHOLD
1. *slaves of a household:* οἰκετεία OIKETEIA*
Mt 24.45 "whom his master has set over his h.

2. *house, household:* οἰκία OIKIA
Jn 4.53 "he himself believed, and all his h.
1 Cor 16.15 the h. of Stephanas were the first converts
Phil 4.22 especially those of Caesar's household
2 Tim 3. 6 who make their way into households

3. *house, household:* οἶκος OIKOS
Acts 7.10 "made him governor . . over all his h.
10. 2 who feared God with all his household
11.14 " 'you will be saved, you and all your h.
16.15 when she was baptized, with her h.
16.31 "you will be saved, you and your h.
18. 8 Crispus . . believed . . with all his h.
1 Cor 1.16 (I did baptize also the h. of Stephanas
1 Tim 3. 4 He must manage his own household
3. 5 how to manage his own household
3.12 Let deacons . . manage . . households well
3.15 how . . to behave in the h. of God
2 Tim 1.16 grant mercy to the h. of Onesiphorus
4.19 Greet Prisca and . . the h. of Onesiphorus
Heb 11. 7 an ark for the saving of his household
1 Pet 4.17 judgment to begin with the h. of God

4. *care, healing:* θεραπεία THERAPEIA
Lk 12.42 "whom his master will set over his h.

IDIOMATICALLY
a. Lk 11.17 "a divided household falls[0] οἶκος ἐπὶ οἶκον πίπτει [OIKOS]

HOUSEHOLD, MEMBER OF THE
HOUSEHOLD, ONE WHO IS OF THE
1. *member of a household:* οἰκεῖος (subst.) OIKEIOS
Gal 6.10 to those who are of the h. of faith
Eph 2.19 you are .. members of the h. of God

HOUSEHOLD, RULE ONE'S
1. *be master of a house:* οἰκοδεσποτέω OIKODESPOTEŌ*
1 Tim 5.14 younger widows .. rule their households

HOUSEHOLD, THOSE OF A
1. *of a house:* οἰκιακός (pl.) OIKIAKOS*
Mt 10.25 "much more will they malign those of his h.
10.36 "a man's foes will be those of his own h.

HOUSEHOLD, WITH ALL ONE'S
1. *with all the household:* πανοικεί PANOIKEI*
Acts 16.34 he rejoiced with all his household

HOUSEHOLDER
1. *master of the house:* οἰκοδεσπότης OIKODESPOTĒS
Mt 13.27 "the servants[j] of the householder came
13.52 "like a h. who brings out of his treasure
20. 1 "the kingdom of heaven is like a h.
20.11 "on receiving it they grumbled at the h.
21.33 "a householder who planted a vineyard
24.43 "if the householder had known
Mk 14.14 "wherever he enters, say to the h.
Lk 12.39 "if the h. had known at what hour
13.25 "once the householder has risen up
14.21 "Then the h. in anger said to his servant
22.11 "tell the h... 'Where is the guest room?

HOUSETOP
1. *housetop:* δῶμα DŌMA
Mt 10.27 "proclaim upon the housetops
24.17 "let him who is on the h. not go down
Mk 13.15 "let him who is on the h. not go down
Lk 12. 3 "shall be proclaimed upon the housetops
17.31 "let him .. on the h... not come down
Acts 10. 9 Peter went up on the housetop to pray

HOW
1. *in order that:* ἵνα HINA
Jn 11.53 they took counsel how to put him to death
1 Cor 7.34 affairs of the Lord, how to be holy
2. *that, in order that:* ὅπως HOPŌS
Mt 12.14 took counsel .. how to destroy him
22.15 took counsel how to entangle him
Lk 24.20 "how our chief priests .. delivered him up
3. *as, so:* ὡς HŌS
Mk **4.27**; **14.72**
Lk **6.4**; **8.47**; **22.61**; **23.55**; **24.6**, 35
Acts **10.28**, 38; **11.16**; **20.20**
Rom **10.15**; **11.2**, 33
Phil **1.8**
1 Th **2.10**, 11
4. *that, because:* ὅτι HOTI
Mt **12.5**; **27.63**
Lk **21.5**
Jn **4.35**
Acts **14.27**; **20.35**
Rom **13.11**
Gal **1.13**
Eph **3.3**
Phil **2.22**
2 Tim **3.15**
Jas **5.11**
Rev **2.2**
5. *as, just as:* καθώς KATHŌS
Acts 15.14 "how God first visited the Gentiles
6. *how:* πῶς PŌS I
Mt 6.28 "the lilies of the field, how they grow
7. 4 "how can you say .. 'Let me take the speck
10.19 "do not be anxious how you are to speak
12. 4 "how he entered the house of God
12.26 "how then will his kingdom stand?
12.29 "how can one enter a strong man's house?
12.34 "vipers! how can you speak good?
16.11 "How is it that you fail to perceive?
21.20 "How did the fig tree wither at once?
Mt 22.12 " 'Friend, how did you get in here?
22.43 "How is it then that D... calls him Lord?
22.45 "If D... calls him Lord, how is he his son?
23.33 "how are you to escape being sentenced?
26.54 "h... should the scriptures be fulfilled?
Mk 2.26 "how he entered the house of God
3.23 "How can Satan cast out Satan?
4.13 "H... will you understand all .. parables?
9.12 "how is it written of the Son of man?
10.23 "How hard .. for those who have riches!
10.24 "how hard it is[r] to enter the kingdom
12.26 "how God said .. 'I am the God of A.
12.35 "How can the scribes say?
14. 1 seeking how to arrest him by stealth
Lk 1.34 "How shall this be, .. I have no husband?
6.42 "how can you say to your brother?
8.18 "Take heed then how you hear
8.36 how he who had .. demons was healed
10.26 "What is written .. ? How do you read?
11.18 "how will his kingdom stand?
12.11 "how or what you are to answer
12.27 "Consider the lilies, how they grow‡
12.50 "I have a baptism .. how I am constrained!
12.56 "why do you not know how to interpret?
14. 7 how they chose the places of honor
18.24 "How hard it is for those who have riches!
20.41 "How can they say .. Christ is D.'s son?
20.44 "D... calls him Lord; so how is he his son?
22. 2 seeking how to put him to death
22. 4 conferred .. how he might betray him
Jn 3. 4 "How can a man be born when he is old?
3. 9 Nicodemus said .. "How can this be?
3.12 "how can you believe .. heavenly things?
4. 9 "How is it that you, a Jew, ask a drink?
5.44 "How can you believe, who receive glory?
5.47 "how will you believe my words?
6.42 "How does he now say, 'I have come down?
6.52 "How can this man give us his flesh?
7.15 "How is it that this man has learning[p]?
8.33 "H. is it that you say .. 'will be .. free'?
9.10 "Then how were your eyes opened?
9.15 asked him how he had received his sight
9.16 "How can .. a sinner do such signs?
9.19 "How then does he now see?
9.21 "how he now sees we do not know
9.26 "How did he open your eyes?
11.36 the Jews said, "See how he loved him!
12.34 "H. can you say .. Son .. must be lifted?
14. 5 "how can we know the way?
14. 9 "h. can you say, 'Show us the Father?
Acts 2. 8 "how is it that we hear, each of us?
8.31 "How can I, unless some one guides me?
9.27 how on the road he had seen the Lord, .. and how at Damascus he had preached
11.13 "he told us how he had seen the angel
12.17 how the Lord had brought him out
15.36 "let us return .. and see how they are
20.18 "You .. know how I lived among you
Rom 3. 6 For then how could God judge the world?
4.10 How then was it reckoned to him?
6. 2 How can we who died to sin still live in it?
10.14 how are men to call upon him .. ? And how are they to believe in him .. ? And how are they to hear?
10.15 how can men preach unless they are sent?
1 Cor 3.10 Let each man take care how he builds
7.32 anxious .. how to please the Lord
7.33 worldly affairs, h. to please his wife
7.34 worldly affairs, how to please her husband
14. 7 how will any one know what is played?
14. 9 how will any one know what is said?
14.16 how can any .. outsider[z] say the "Amen"?
15.12 how can some .. say .. no resurrection?
15.35 one will ask, "How are the dead raised?
Gal 2.14 "how can you compel the Gentiles to live?
4. 9 how can you turn back again?
Eph 5.15 Look carefully then how you walk

Col 4. 6 that you may know how . . to answer
1 Th 1. 9 how you turned to God from idols
4. 1 how you ought to live and to please God
2 Th 3. 7 know how you ought to imitate us
1 Tim 3. 5 if a man does not know how to manage
3.15 you may know how one ought to behave
Heb 2. 3 how shall we escape if we neglect?
1 Jn 3.17 how does God's love abide in him?
[4.20 *how can he* love God whom he has not seen‡

7. *whence, from what:* πόθεν POTHEN
Mt 13.27 " 'How then has it weeds?
Mk 8. 4 "How can one feed these men?
12.37 "D. . . calls him Lord; so how is he his son?
Jn 1.48 Nathanael said . . "How do you know me?
6. 5 Jesus said . . "How are we to buy bread?

8. *who? what?:* τίς TIS I
[a]+ ἐν [b]+ κατά
Mt **5.13**[a]
Mk **9.50**[a]
Lk **1.18**[b]; **14.34**[a]
Jn **14.22**
Rom **8.26**
1 Cor **7.16**[2]; **14.6**

CONTEXTUALLY
Mt **7.11**; **16.3**
Lk **11.13**; **12.56**; **21.14**
Eph **6.22**
Phil **2.23**
Col **4.8**

HOW GREAT

1. *how great, how small:* ἡλίκος HĒLIKOS
Jas 3. 5 How great a forest is set ablaze!

2. *how great:* πηλίκος PĒLIKOS
Heb 7. 4 See how great he is!

3. *how many, how much:* πόσος POSOS
Mt 6.23 "how great is the darkness!

4. *who? what?:* τίς TIS I
Col **1.27**

HOW GREATLY

1. *how great, how small:* ἡλίκος HĒLIKOS [A.3.b.1]
Col 2. 1 know how greatly I strive for you

HOW IS IT?

1. *who? what?:* τίς TIS I
Lk **2.49**
Acts **5.4**, 9

HOW LONG

1. *until when:* ἕως πότε HEŌS; POTE I [B.3.b.4]
Mt 17.17 "how long am I to be with you? How long am I to bear with you?
Mk 9.19 "how long am I to be with you? How long am I to bear with you?
Lk 9.41 "how long am I to be with you?
Jn 10.24 "How long will you keep us in suspense?
Rev 6.10 "how long before thou wilt judge?

2. *how much time:* πόσος χρόνος POSOS; CHRONOS [B.3.b.4]
Mk 9.21 "How long has he had this?

HOW MANY

1. *how many, how much:* πόσος POSOS
Mt 15.34 "How many loaves have you?
16. 9 "and how many baskets you gathered
16.10 "and how many baskets you gathered
27.13 "h. many things they testify against you
Mk 6.38 "How many loaves have you?
8. 5 "How many loaves have you?
8.19 "how many baskets . . did you take up?
8.20 "how many baskets . . did you take up?
15. 4 "h. many charges they bring against you
Lk 15.17 " 'How many of my father's . . servants!
Acts 21.20 "how many thousands . . among the Jews

HOW MUCH

1. *as great as, how great:* ὅσος (neut. pl.) HOSOS
Mk 5.19 "tell them how much the Lord has done
5.20 how much Jesus had done for him
Lk 8.39 "declare how much God has done
8.39 how much Jesus had done for him
Acts 9.13 "how much evil he has done to . . saints
9.16 "I will show him how much he must suffer

2. *how many, how much:* πόσος POSOS
Mt 7.11 "how much more will your Father!
10.25 how much more will they malign those
12.12 "Of how much more value is a man!
Lk 11.13 "h. much more will the heavenly Father!
12.24 "Of how much more value are you!
12.28 "how much more will he clothe you!
16. 5 " 'How much do you owe my master?
16. 7 " 'And how much do you owe?
Rom 11.12 how much more will their full inclusion!
11.24 h. much more will these natural branches
Phm .16 how much more to you, both in the flesh
Heb 9.14 how much more shall the blood of Christ
10.29 H. much worse punishment do you think?

HOW MUCH MORE

1. *let alone, not to mention:* μήτιγε MĒTIGE*
1 Cor 6. 3 H. much more, . . pertaining to this life!

HOW OFTEN

1. *how many times:* ποσάκις POSAKIS*
Mt 18.21 "Lord, how often shall . . I forgive him?
23.37 "How often would I have gathered!
Lk 13.34 "How often would I have gathered!

HOW, THAT IS
HOW, THIS IS

1. *thus, so:* οὕτως HOUTŌS
Jn 18.22 "Is that how you answer the high priest?
1 Cor 4. 1 This is how one should regard us
Rev 9.17 this was how I saw the horses

HOWEVER

1. *but:* ἀλλά ALLA
Jn **6.23**
1 Cor **8.7**

2. *as* (+particle): ὡς ἄν HŌS; AN [B.3.b.4]
1 Cor 12. 2 however you may have been moved

3. *so, therefore:* οὖν OUN
Acts **28.5**

4. *but, however, except:* πλήν PLĒN
Eph 5.33 however, let each one of you love

HOWL

1. *cry aloud:* ὀλολύζω OLOLYZŌ*
Jas 5. 1 Come now, you rich, weep and howl

HUMAN

1. *human:* ἀνθρώπινος ANTHRŌPINOS
Acts 17.25 "nor is he served by human hands
1 Cor 2.13 words not taught by human wisdom
4. 3 judged by you or by any human court
1 Pet 2.13 Be subject . . to every human institution[f]†

2. *man, mankind:* ἄνθρωπος ANTHRŌPOS
[a]gen. [b]κατὰ ἄνθρωπον B.3.b.1
[c]κατὰ ἄνθρωπον λέγειν B.3.b.1
[d]ὡς ἄνθρωπος B.2.a.2
Rom 2. 9 [a]distress for every h. being who does evil
3. 5 [b](I speak in a human way
1 Cor 9. 8 [b]Do I say this on human authority?
Gal 3.15 [c]To give a human example, brethren
Phil 2. 8 [d]found in h. form he humbled himself
Col 2. 8 [a]deceit, according to human tradition
2.22 [a]according to h. precepts and doctrines
1 Pet 4. 2 [a]live . . no longer by human passions
2 Pet 2.16 [a]a dumb ass spoke with human voice
Rev 9. 7 [a]their faces were like human faces
13.18 [a]for it is a human number
18.13 [a]slaves, that is, human souls

3. *fleshly:* σάρκινος SARKINOS
2 Cor 3. 3 not on . . stone but . . tablets of h. hearts

IDIOMATICALLY

a. 2 Cor 5.16 we regard no one from a human point of view; even though we once regarded Christ from a human point of view οὐδένα οἴδαμεν κατὰ σάρκα· εἰ καὶ ἐγνώκαμεν κατὰ σάρκα Χριστόν [SARX]

HUMAN BEING

1. *man, mankind:* ἄνθρωπος ANTHRŌPOS
Jas 3. 8 no human being can tame the tongue

2. *flesh, body:* σάρξ SARX
Mt 24.22 "no human being would be saved
Mk 13.20 "no human being would be saved
Rom 3.20 For no human being will be justified
1 Cor 1.29 so that no human being might boast

HUMAN TERMS, IN
1. *human:* ἀνθρώπινος (neut.) ANTHRŌPINOS
Rom 6.19 I am speaking in human terms

HUMANKIND
1. *human creature:* ἡ φύσις ἡ ἀνθρωπίνη ANTHRŌPINOS [B.3.b.4]
Jas 3. 7 every kind of beast . . has been tamed by h.

HUMANLY
IDIOMATICALLY
a. 1 Cor 15.32 if, humanly speaking, I fought with beasts?
εἰ κατὰ ἄνθρωπον ἐθηριομάχησα; [ANTHRŌPOS]

HUMBLE
1. *gentle, meek:* πραΰς PRAYS
Mt 21. 5 "humble, and mounted on an ass
2. *lower, humble:* ταπεινόω TAPEINOŌ
Mt 18. 4 "Whoever humbles himself like this child
23.12 "whoever exalts himself will be humbled, . . whoever humbles himself will be exalted
Lk 14.11 "who exalts himself will be humbled, . . who humbles himself will be exalted
18.14 "who exalts himself will be humbled, . . who humbles himself will be exalted
2 Cor 12.21 my God may humble me before you
Phil 2. 8 in human form he humbled himself
Jas 4.10 Humble yourselves before the Lord
1 Pet 5. 6 H. yourselves . . under the . . hand of G.
3. *low, poor, humble:* ταπεινός TAPEINOS
2 Cor 10. 1 humble when face to face with you
Jas 4. 6 "God . . gives grace to the humble
1 Pet 5. 5 "God . . gives grace to the humble

HUMBLE MIND, HAVE A
1. *lowly in mind, humble:* ταπεινόφρων TAPEINOPHRŌN* [A.3.e.2]
1 Pet 3. 8 have unity of spirit . . and a humble mind

HUMBLE TASKS
1. *low, poor, humble:* ταπεινός (subst. neut. pl.) TAPEINOS
Rom [12.16 *give yourselves to humble tasks*†

HUMILIATE
1. *put to shame, dishonor:* καταισχύνω KATAISCHYNŌ
1 Cor 11.22 do you . . h. those who have nothing?
2 Cor 9. 4 lest . . we be humiliated

HUMILIATION
1. *humiliation, low estate:* ταπείνωσις TAPEINŌSIS
Acts 8.33 "In his humiliation justice was denied
Jas 1.10 ⟨let⟩ the rich ⟨boast⟩ in his h.

HUMILITY
1. *humility:* ταπεινοφροσύνη TAPEINOPHROSYNĒ
Acts 20.19 "serving the Lord with all humility
Phil 2. 3 but in humility count others better
1 Pet 5. 5 with humility toward one another

HUNDRED, A
1. *two hundred:* διακόσιοι DIAKOSIOI [A.3.c.1]
Jn 21. 8 about a hundred yards[m] off†
2. *hundred:* ἑκατόν HEKATON
[a]κατὰ ἑκατόν
Mt 18.12 "If a man has a hundred sheep
18.28 "one . . who owed him a hundred denarii[g]
Mk 6.40 [a]they sat down . . by hundreds and by fifties
Lk 15. 4 "What man . . , having a hundred sheep
16. 6 "He said, 'A hundred measures of oil
16. 7 "He said, 'A hundred measures of wheat
[24.13 *a h. and sixty stadia* from Jerusalem‡
Jn 19.39 mixture . . , about a h. pounds' weight
21.11 large fish, a hundred and fifty-three
Acts 1.15 (in all about a hundred and twenty
Rev 7. 4 a hundred and forty-four thousand
14. 1 a hundred and forty-four thousand
14. 3 the hundred and forty-four thousand
21.17 wall, a hundred and forty-four cubits

HUNDRED, FIVE
1. *five hundred:* πεντακόσιοι PENTAKOSIOI*
Lk 7.41 "one owed five hundred denarii
1 Cor 15. 6 to more than five hundred brethren

HUNDRED, FOUR
1. *four hundred:* τετρακόσιοι TETRAKOSIOI*
Acts 5.36 "about four hundred, joined him
7. 6 "ill-treat them four hundred years
13.19(20) "for about four hundred and fifty years
Gal 3.17 four hundred and thirty years afterward

HUNDRED, SIX
1. *six hundred:* ἑξακόσιοι HEXAKOSIOI*
Rev 13.18 its number is six hundred and sixty-six[g]
14.20 for one thousand six hundred stadia[i]

HUNDRED, THREE
1. *three hundred:* τριακόσιοι TRIAKOSIOI*
Mk 14. 5 "sold for more than three h. denarii[b]
Jn 12. 5 "Why . . not sold for three hundred denarii[b]?

HUNDRED, TWO
1. *two hundred:* διακόσιοι DIAKOSIOI
Mk 6.37 "two hundred denarii[u] worth of bread
Jn 6. 7 "Two h. denarii[l] would not buy enough
Acts 23.23 "get ready two hundred soldiers . . and two hundred spearmen
27.37 (in all two hundred and seventy-six[d]‡
Rev 11. 3 "one thousand two h. and sixty days
12. 6 one thousand two h. and sixty days

HUNDRED YEARS OLD, A
1. *of a hundred years:* ἑκατονταετής HEKATONTAETĒS*
Rom 4.19 he was about a hundred years old

HUNDREDFOLD, A
1. *hundred:* ἑκατόν HEKATON
Mt 13. 8 "brought forth grain, some a h.
13.23 "yields, in one case a hundredfold
Mk 4. 8 "yielding . . sixtyfold and a hundredfold
4.20 "bear fruit, thirtyfold and . . a h.
2. *a hundredfold:* ἑκατονταπλασίων (neut. pl.) HEKATONTAPLASIŌN*
Mt 19.29 "will receive a h.,[l] and inherit . . life‡
Mk 10.30 "who will not receive a h. now
Lk 8. 8 "some fell into good soil . . and yielded a h.

HUNDREDWEIGHT, HEAVY AS A
1. *weighing a talent:* ταλαντιαῖος TALANTIAIOS*
Rev 16.21 hailstones, heavy as a hundredweight

HUNG ROUND, BE
1. *lie around, wear:* περίκειμαι PERIKEIMAI
[a]+ περί
Mk 9.42 [a]"if a . . millstone were hung round his neck
Lk 17. 2 [a]"if a millstone were hung round his neck

HUNGER
1. *famine, hunger:* λιμός LIMOS
Lk 15.17 " 'but I perish here with hunger!
2 Cor 11.27 in hunger and thirst, often without food
2. *fasting, hunger:* νηστεία NĒSTEIA
2 Cor 6. 5 tumults, labors, watching, hunger
3. *be hungry:* πεινάω PEINAŌ
Mt 5. 6 "who hunger and thirst for righteousness
Lk 6.21 "Blessed are you that hunger now
6.25 "you that are full now . . shall hunger
Jn 6.35 "he who comes to me shall not hunger
1 Cor 4.11 To the present hour we hunger
Rev 7.16 "They shall hunger no more

HUNGER, FACING
1. *be hungry:* πεινάω (inf.) PEINAŌ
Phil 4.12 the secret of facing plenty and hunger

HUNGRY
1. *not eating, fasting:* νῆστις NĒSTIS*
Mt 15.32 "I am unwilling to send them away h.
Mk 8. 3 "if I send them away hungry
2. *be hungry:* πεινάω (part.) PEINAŌ
Mt 25.37 " 'Lord, when did we see thee hungry?
25.44 " 'Lord, when did we see thee hungry?
Lk 1.53 "he has filled the hungry with good things

3. *hungry:* πρόσπεινος PROSPEINOS*
Acts 10.10 became hungry and desired something

HUNGRY, BE
1. *be hungry:* πεινάω PEINAŌ
Mt 4. 2 he fasted . . and afterward he was hungry
12. 1 his disciples were hungry
12. 3 "what David did, when he was hungry
21.18 returning to the city, he was hungry
25.35 " 'for I was hungry and you gave me food
25.42 " 'hungry and you gave me no food
Mk 2.25 "what David did, when he . . was hungry
11.12 when they came . . , he was hungry
Lk 4. 2 when they were ended, he was hungry
6. 3 "what David did when he was hungry
Rom 12.20 "if your enemy is hungry, feed him
1 Cor 11.21 one is hungry and another is drunk
11.34 if any one is hungry, let him eat at home

HURT
1. *do wrong, harm:* ἀδικέω ADIKEŌ
Lk 10.19 "nothing shall hurt you
Rev 2.11 " 'He who conquers shall not be hurt
9.10 power of hurting men . . lies in their tails
2. *harm, injure:* βλάπτω BLAPTŌ
Mk 16.18 "any deadly thing . . will not hurt them[k]‡
3. *austere, cruel:* σκληρός SKLĒROS [A.6.a.3]
Acts 26.14 " 'It hurts you to kick against the goads

HURTFUL
1. *harmful:* βλαβερός BLABEROS*
1 Tim 6. 9 many senseless and hurtful desires

HUSBAND
1. *brother:* ἀδελφός ADELPHOS
1 Cor 7.14 wife is consecrated through her husband
2. *man, husband:* ἀνήρ ANĒR
Mt 1.16 Joseph the husband of Mary
1.19 her husband Joseph, being a just man
Mk 10.12 "if she divorces her husband and marries
Lk 1.34 "How shall this be, since I have no husband?
2.36 Anna . . lived with her h. seven years
16.18 "a woman divorced from her husband
Jn 4.16 "Go, call your h., and come here
4.17 woman answered . . "I have no husband
4.17 "You are right in saying, 'I have no h.
4.18 "for you have had five husbands, and he whom you now have is not your h.
Acts 5. 9 "those that have buried your husband
5.10 they . . buried her beside her husband
Rom 7. 2 woman is bound by law to her husband . . ; but if her husband dies she is discharged from the law concerning the husband
7. 3 adulteress . . while her h. is alive. But if her husband dies she is free
1 Cor 7. 2 each woman ⟨should have⟩ her own h.
7. 3 h. should give to his wife her conjugal rights, and likewise the wife to her h.
7. 4 wife does not . . , but the h. does; likewise the h. does not rule over his own body
7.10 wife should not separate from her h.
7.11 (let her . . be reconciled to her h.
7.11 the husband should not divorce his wife
7.13 a husband who is an unbeliever
7.14 the unbelieving h. is consecrated
7.16 whether you will save your h.? H., how do you know . . you will save your wife?
7.34 anxious . . how to please her husband
7.39 A wife is bound to her husband . . If the husband dies, she is free
11. 3 the head of a woman is her husband
14.35 let them ask their husbands at home
2 Cor 11. 2 as a pure bride to her one husband
Eph 5.22 Wives, be subject to your husbands
5.23 the husband is the head of the wife
5.24 let wives . . be subject . . to . . husbands
5.25 Husbands, love your wives
5.28 husbands should love their wives
5.33 let the wife see that she respects her h.
Col 3.18 Wives, be subject to your husbands
3.19 Husbands, love your wives
1 Tim 3. 2 a bishop must be . . the h. of one wife
3.12 Let deacons be the husband of one wife
5. 9 having been the wife of one husband
Tit 1. 6 blameless, the husband of one wife
2. 5 kind, and submissive to their husbands
1 Pet 3. 1 wives, be submissive to your husbands
3. 5 holy women . . submissive to . . husbands
3. 7 husbands, live considerately with . . wives
Rev 21. 2 as a bride adorned for her husband

HUSBAND, LOVE ONE'S
1. *loving one's husband:* φίλανδρος PHILANDROS* [B.3.a.1]
Tit 2. 4 train . . young women to love their husbands

HUSH
1. *silence:* σιγή SIGĒ
Acts 21.40 when there was a great hush, he spoke

HYMENAEUS: Ὑμέναιος ˌhīmə'nēəs
1 Tim 1.20 H. . . , whom I have delivered to Satan
2 Tim 2.17 Among them are H. and Philetus

HYMN
1. *song of praise:* ὕμνος HYMNOS*
Eph 5.19 psalms and hymns and spiritual songs
Col 3.16 sing psalms and hymns and . . songs
2. *psalm:* ψαλμός PSALMOS
1 Col 14.26 each one has a hymn, a lesson

HYMN, SING A
1. *sing, praise:* ὑμνέω HYMNEŌ
Mt 26.30 when they had sung a hymn, they went
Mk 14.26 when they had sung a hymn, they went
Acts 16.25 Paul . . Silas . . praying and singing hymns

HYPOCRISY
1. *outward show, hypocrisy:* ὑπόκρισις HYPOKRISIS
Mt 23.28 "but within you are full of hypocrisy
Mk 12.15 knowing their hypocrisy, he said
Lk 12. 1 "the leaven of the Pharisees, which is h.

HYPOCRITE
1. *pretender, hypocrite:* ὑποκριτής HYPOKRITĒS*
Mt 6. 2 "as the hypocrites do in the synagogues
6. 5 "you must not be like the hypocrites
6.16 "do not look dismal, like the hypocrites
7. 5 "You hypocrite, first take the log out
15. 7 "You hypocrites! Well did Isaiah prophesy
22.18 "Why put me to the test, you hypocrites?
23.13 "scribes and Pharisees, hypocrites!
Also Mt **23.**[14‡, 15, 23, 25, 27, 29
24.51 "will . . put him with the hypocrites
Mk 7. 6 "Well did Isaiah prophesy of . . hypocrites
Lk 6.42 "You hypocrite, first take the log out
12.56 "hypocrites! You know how to interpret
13.15 Lord answered him, "You hypocrites!

HYSSOP
1. *hyssop:* ὕσσωπος HYSSŌPOS*
Jn 19.29 they put a sponge full of the vinegar on h.
Heb 9.19 he took the blood of calves . . with . . hyssop

I

I (*For entries* 1, 2, *and* 3, *and for Greek words not represented here, see also* ME; MINE; MY)
1. *I:* ἐγώ EGŌ
Mt **3.**11², 14; **5.**22, 28, 32, 34, 39, 44; **8.**7, 9; **10.**16; **11.**10; **12.**27, 28; **14.**27; **16.**15; **20.**15, 22; **21.**27, 30; **22.**32; **23.**34; **24.**5; **25.**27; **26.**15, 22, 25, 32, 33, 35, 39; **28.**20
Mk **1.**2, 7, 8; **6.**16, 50; **8.**27, 29; **9.**25; **10.**38, 39; **11.**33; **12.**26; **13.**6; **14.**19, 28, 29, 31, 36, 58, 62
Lk **1.**18, 19; **2.**48, 49; **3.**16², [22‡; **4.**43; **7.**8; **8.**46; **9.**9, 18, 20; **10.**35²; **11.**18, 19, 20; **13.**33; **15.**17; **16.**9; **19.**5, 22; **20.**8; **21.**8, 15; **22.**15, 27, 32, 53, 70; **23.**14; **24.**39², 49
Jn **1.**20, 23, 26, 27, 30, 31; **3.**28, 30; **4.**14², 26, 32, 38; **5.**7, 30, 31, 34, 36, 43, 45; **6.**20, 35, 40, 41, 48, 51², 63, 70;

7.7, 8, 17, 29, 34, 36; **8.**11‡, 12, 14, 15, 16², 18, 21², 22, 23², 24, 28, 29, 38, 42, 45, 49, 50, 54, 55, 58; **9.**9, 39; **10.**7, 9, 10, 11, 14, 16, 17, 18, 25, 30, 34; **11.**25, 27, 42; **12.**26, 46, 47, 49, 50; **13.**7, 14, 15, 18, 19, 26, 33, 36; **14.**3, 4, 6, 10², 11, 12², 14, 19, 20, 26, 27, 28²; **15.**1, 5, 10, 14, 16, 19, 20, 26; **16.**4, 7², 26, 27, 33; **17.**4, 9, 12, 14², 16, 19, 23, 24, 25; **18.**5, 6, 8, 20, 21, 26, 35, 37, 38; **19.**6
Acts **3.**6; **7.**7, 32; **9.**5, 10, 16; **10.**20, 21, 26; **11.**5, 15, 17; **13.**25², 33, 41; **16.**30; **17.**3, 23; **18.**6, 10², 15; **19.**21²; **20.**22, 25, 29; **21.**13, 37, 39; **22.**1, 3, 6, 8², 17², 19, 21, 28²; **23.**1, 6²; **24.**20, 21; **25.**10, 15, 18, 20, 25; **26.**9, 10, 15², 17, 29; **27.**23, 25; **28.**17
Rom **1.**15; **7.**9², 9(10), 14, 17, 18, 20, 21, 24, 25; **9.**2, 3; **10.**19; **11.**1, 13, 19; **12.**19; **14.**11; **15.**14, 19; **16.**4, 22
1 Cor **1.**12⁴; **3.**4², 6; **4.**15, 18; **5.**3, 12; **6.**12; **7.**10, 12, 28; **9.**6, 15², 26; **10.**30²; **11.**23; **13.**3; **15.**9, 10, 11, 32; **16.**10
2 Cor **1.**19, 23; **2.**2², 10, 13; **7.**4², 7; **10.**1; **11.**23, 29; **12.**11, 13, 15, 16, 21
Gal **1.**12, 15; **2.**19, 20; **4.**12, 18; **5.**2, 10, 11; **6.**17
Eph **3.**1, 13; **4.**1; **5.**32; **6.**20, 21
Phil **1.**7; **2.**16; **3.**4², 7, 13; **4.**11
Col **1.**23, 25; **4.**4
1 Th **2.**18
1 Tim **1.**11, 15; **2.**7
2 Tim **1.**11, [12†; **4.**6
Tit **1.**3, 5
Phm .13, 19², 20
Heb **1.**5²; **2.**13²; **5.**5; **8.**9; **10.**30; **12.**26
1 Pet **1.**16
2 Pet **1.**17
2 Jn .1²
3 Jn .1
Rev **1.**8, 9, 17; **2.**23; **3.**9, 19; **5.**4; **10.**1; **11.**1; **17.**7; **21.**6²; **22.**13, 16², 18

2. *my, mine:* ἐμός EMOS [A.2.b]
Jn **8.**43

3. *we:* ἡμεῖς HĒMEIS
1 Cor **15.**30
3 Jn .12

4. *who, which, what:* ὅς HOS
Acts **22.**4

5. *and I:* κἀγώ KAGŌ
Mt **18.**33
Jn **7.**28; **17.**22
Rom **3.**7
1 Cor **2.**1; **7.**8; **10.**33; **11.**1; **16.**10
Eph **1.**15
Phil **2.**19
1 Th **3.**5
Rev **3.**10; **22.**8

I ALSO; ALSO, I; AND I; BUT I; EVEN SO I; SO I; THEN I; I TOO

1. *and I:* κἀγώ KAGŌ
Mt **2.**8; **10.**32, 33; **11.**28; **16.**18; **21.**24²
Lk **1.**3; **2.**48; **11.**9; **19.**23; **20.**3; **22.**29
Jn **1.**34; **5.**17; **6.**44, 54, 56, 57; **8.**26; **10.**15, 27, 28, 38; **12.**32; **14.**16, 20, 21; **15.**4, 5, 9; **16.**32; **17.**6, 11, 18, 21, 26; **20.**15, 21
Acts **8.**19; **10.**28; **22.**13, 19
Rom **11.**3
1 Cor **2.**3; **3.**1; **7.**40; **15.**8; **16.**4
2 Cor **2.**10; **6.**17; **11.**16, 18, 21, 22³; **12.**20
Gal **4.**12; **6.**14
Phil **2.**28
Heb **8.**9
Jas **2.**18²
Rev **2.**6

I, IF

1. *and I:* κἀγώ KAGŌ
Mt **26.**15

I MYSELF

1. *myself:* ἐμαυτοῦ EMAUTOU
1 Cor 7. 7 I wish that all were as I myself am

2. *and I:* κἀγώ KAGŌ
Jn **1.**31, 33
Rev **2.**27; **3.**21

ICONIUM: Ἰκόνιον ī'kōnēəm II,F-3
Acts 13.51 they shook off the dust . . and went to I.
14. 1 at I. they entered . . the Jewish synagogue
14.19 Jews came there from Antioch and I.
14.21 they returned to Lystra and to I.
16. 2 He was well spoken of . . at . . I.
2 Tim 3.11 my sufferings, what befell me . . at I.

IDLE

1. *idle:* ἀργός ARGOS
Mt 20. 3 "he saw others . . idle in the market place
20. 6 " 'Why do you stand here idle all day?

IDLE, BE

1. *be unemployed:* ἀργέω ARGEŌ*
2 Pet 2. 3 their condemnation has not been idle

2. *be undisciplined:* ἀτακτέω ATAKTEŌ*
2 Th 3. 7 we were not idle when we were with you

IDLE TALE

1. *trash, nonsense:* λῆρος LĒROS*
Lk 24.11 these words seemed to them an idle tale

IDLENESS

1. *in a disorderly manner:* ἀτάκτως ATAKTŌS* [A.3.d.1]
2 Th 3. 6 any brother who is living in idleness
3.11 some of you are living in idleness

IDLER

1. *idle:* ἀργός (subst.) ARGOS
1 Tim 5.13 Besides that, they learn to be idlers, . . and not only idlers but gossips

2. *undisciplined:* ἄτακτος (subst.) ATAKTOS*
1 Th 5.14 admonish the idlers, . . help the weak⁰

IDOL

1. *image, idol:* εἴδωλον EIDŌLON*
Acts 7.41 "they . . offered a sacrifice to the idol
15.20 "to abstain from the pollutions of idols
Rom 2.22 You who abhor idols, do you rob temples?
1 Cor 8. 4 know that "an idol has no real existence
8. 7 being hitherto accustomed to idols
10.19 do I imply . . that an idol is anything?
12. 2 you were led astray to dumb idols
2 Cor 6.16 What agreement has . . God with idols?
1 Th 1. 9 how you turned to God from idols
1 Jn 5.21 Little children, keep yourselves from idols
Rev 9.20 nor give up worshiping demons and idols

IDOL, OFFERED TO AN
IDOL, SACRIFICED TO AN

1. *sacrificed to idols:* εἰδωλόθυτος EIDŌLOTHYTOS*
Acts 15.29 "abstain from what has been s. to idols
21.25 "abstain from what has been s. to idols
1 Cor 8. 1 Now concerning food offered to idols
8. 4 as to the eating of food offered to idols
8. 7 some . . eat food as . . offered to an idol
8.10 encouraged . . to eat food offered to idols
10.19 That food offered to idols is anything?
Rev 2.14 " 'that they might eat food s. to idols
2.20 " 'teaching . . to eat food s. to idols

IDOLATER

1. *idolater:* εἰδωλολάτρης EIDŌLOLATRĒS*
1 Cor 5.10 not at all meaning . . idolaters
5.11 an idolater, reviler, drunkard, or robber
6. 9 neither the immoral, nor idolaters
10. 7 Do not be idolaters as some of them were
Eph 5. 5 one who is covetous (that is, an i.
Rev 21. 8 "sorcerers, idolaters, and all liars
22.15 the dogs and sorcerers . . and idolaters

IDOLATRY

1. *idolatry:* εἰδωλολατρία EIDŌLOLATRIA
Gal 5.20 idolatry, sorcery, enmity, strife
Col 3. 5 Put to death . . covetousness, which is i.
1 Pet 4. 3 carousing, and lawless idolatry

IDOLS, FULL OF

1. *given to idolatry:* κατείδωλος KATEIDŌLOS*
Acts 17.16 he saw that the city was full of idols

IDOL'S TEMPLE

1. *idol's temple:* εἰδωλεῖον EIDŌLEION*
1 Cor 8.10 if any one sees you . . in an idol's temple

IDOLS, WORSHIP OF
1. *idolatry:* εἰδωλολατρία EIDŌLOLATRIA
1 Cor 10.14 my beloved, shun the worship of idols

IDUMEA: Ἰδουμαία ˌidyü'mēə I,B-6
Mk 3. 8 ⟨a great multitude . . followed . . from⟩ I.

IF
1. *if:* ἐάν EAN
[a]ἄν = ἐάν
Mt 4. 9 "if you will fall down and worship me
5.13 "but if salt has lost its taste
5.23 "if you are offering your gift at the altar
5.46 "For if you love those who love you
5.47 "And if you salute only your brethren
6.14 "For if you forgive men their trespasses
6.15 "but if you do not forgive men
6.22 "if your eye is sound, your whole body
6.23 "if your eye is not sound, your whole body
8. 2 "Lord, if you will, you can make me clean
9.21 "If I only touch his garment, I shall be . . well
10.13 "if the house is worthy, let your peace come upon it; but if it is not worthy
12.11 "What man of you, if he has one sheep
15.14 "And if a blind man leads a blind man
16.26 "if he gains the . . world and forfeits his life?
17.20 "if you have faith as a . . mustard seed
18.12 "If a man has a hundred sheep
18.13 "if he finds it . . , he rejoices over it
18.15 "If your brother sins against you
18.15 "If he listens . . , you have gained
18.16 "if he does not listen, take one or two others
18.17 "If he refuses to listen to them, tell it . . ; and if he refuses to listen even to the church
18.19 "if two of you agree on earth
18.35 "if you do not forgive your brother
21. 3 "If any one says anything to you
21.21 "if you have faith and never doubt
21.24 "if you tell me . . , then I also will tell you
21.25 "If we say, 'From heaven,' he will say
21.26 "But if we say, 'From men,' we are afraid
22.24 " 'If a man dies, having no children
24.23 "if any one says to you, 'Lo, here!
24.26 "if they say . . 'Lo, he is in the wilderness
24.48 "if that wicked servant says to himself
28.14 "And if this comes to the governor's ears
Mk 1.40 "If you will, you can make me clean
3.24 "If a kingdom is divided against itself
3.25 "And if a house is divided against itself
5.28 "If I touch even his garments
7.11 " 'If a man tells his father or his mother
8. 3 "if I send them away hungry
9.43 "if your hand causes you to sin[l]
9.45 "if your foot causes you to sin[l]
9.47 "if your eye causes you to sin[l]
9.50 "but if the salt has lost its saltness
10.12 "if she divorces her husband and marries
11. 3 "If any one says to you, 'Why?
11.31 "If we say, 'From heaven,' he will say
12.19 "if a man's brother dies and leaves a wife
13.21 "if any one says to you, 'Look, here!
14.31 "If I must die with you, I will not deny
Lk 4. 7 "If you . . worship me, it shall all be yours
5.12 "Lord, if you will, you can make me clean
6.33 "if you do good to those who do good
6.34 "if you lend to those . . , what credit is that?
10. 6 "And if a son of peace is there
12.45 "But if that servant says to himself
14.34 "Salt is good; but if salt has lost
15. 8 "what woman, . . if she loses one coin
16.30 " 'if some one goes to them from the dead
16.31 " 'If they do not hear Moses and . . prophets
17. 3 "if your brother sins, rebuke him, and if he repents, forgive him
17. 4 "if he sins against you seven times
19.31 "If any one asks you, 'Why are you untying?
19.40 "if these were silent, . . stones would cry
20. 5 "If we say, 'From heaven,' he will say
Lk 20. 6 "if we say, 'From men,' . . people will stone
20.28 "if a man's brother dies, having a wife
22.67 "If I tell you, you will not believe
22.68 "if I ask you, you will not answer
Jn 3.12 "believe if I tell you heavenly things?
5.31 "If I bear witness to myself, my testimony
5.43 "if another comes in his own name
6.51 "if any one eats of this bread, he will live
6.62 "what if you were to see the Son of man?
7.17 "if any man's will is to do his will
7.37 "If any one thirst, let him come to me
8.31 "If you continue in my word
8.36 "if the Son makes you free, you will be free
8.51 "if any one keeps my word
8.52 " 'If any one keeps my word
8.54 "If I glorify myself, my glory is nothing
9.22 if any . . should confess him to be Christ
9.31 "but if any one is a worshiper of God
10. 9 "I am the door; if any one enters
11. 9 "If any one walks in the day
11.10 "if . . one walks in the night, he stumbles
11.40 "that if you would believe you would see
11.48 "If we let him . . , every one will believe
11.57 if any one knew where he was
12.24 "but if it dies, it bears much fruit
12.26 "If any one serves me, he must follow
12.26 "if any . . serves me, the Father will honor
12.47 "If any one hears my sayings
13. 8 "If I do not wash you, you have no part
13.17 "If you know these things, blessed
13.35 "if you have love for one another
14.14 "if you ask[g] anything in my name
14.15 "If you love me, you will keep
14.23 "If a man loves me, . . keep my word
15. 6 "If a man does not abide in me
15. 7 "If you abide in me, and my words abide
15.10 "If you keep my commandments
15.14 "if you do what I command you
16. 7 "if I do not go . . , the Counselor will not come . . ; but if I go, I will send him to you
16.23 [a]"if you ask anything of the Father
19.12 Jews cried out, "If you release this man
20.23 [a]"If you forgive the sins of any
20.23 [a]"if you retain the sins of any
21.22 "If it is my will that he remain until I come
21.23 "If it is my will that he remain until I come
Acts 5.38 "if this plan or this undertaking is of men
9. 2 if he found any belonging to the Way
13.41 " 'you will never believe, if one declares
26. 5 "have known . . , if they are willing to testify
Rom 2.25 Circumcision indeed is of value if you obey the law; but if you break the law
2.26 if a man who is uncircumcised keeps
7. 2 if her husband dies she is discharged
7. 3 adulteress if she lives with another man . . But if her husband dies she is free
10. 9 if you confess . . that Jesus is Lord
11.23 if they do not persist in their unbelief
12.20 "if your enemy is hungry, feed him; if he is thirsty, give him drink
13. 4 But if you do wrong, be afraid
14. 8 If we live, we live to the Lord, and if we die, we die to the Lord
14.23 who has doubts is condemned, if he eats
1 Cor 4.19 I will come . . soon, if the Lord wills
5.11 if he is guilty of immorality or greed
6. 4 If then you have such cases
7.11 (but if she does, let her remain single
7.28 But if you marry, you do not sin, and if a girl marries she does not sin
7.36 if his passions are strong, and it has to be
7.39 If the husband dies, she is free
7.40 she is happier if she remains as she is
8. 8 We are no worse off if we do not eat, and no better off if we do
8.10 if any one sees you, a man of knowledge
9.16 For if I preach the gospel

1 Cor 9.16 Woe to me if I do not preach the gospel!
10.28 (But if some one says to you
11.15 if a woman has long hair, it is her pride
12.15 If the foot should say . . "I do not belong
12.16 if the ear should say . . "I do not belong
13. 1 If I speak in the tongues of men
14. 6 if I come to you speaking in tongues
14. 7 If even lifeless instruments . . do not
14. 8 if the bugle gives an indistinct sound
14. 9 if you in a tongue utter speech
14.11 but if I do not know the meaning
14.14 if I pray in a tongue, my spirit prays
14.16 Otherwise, if you bless[w] with the spirit
14.23 If, therefore, the whole church assembles
14.24 if all prophesy, . . he is convicted by all
14.28 But if there is no one to interpret
14.30 If a revelation is made to another
16. 4 If it seems advisable that I should go also
16. 7 some time with you, if the Lord permits
2 Cor 5. 1 if the earthly tent we live in is destroyed
8.12 if the readiness is there, it is acceptable
9. 4 lest if some Macedonians come with me
10. 8 if I boast a little too much of our authority
12. 6 if I wish to boast, I shall not be a fool
13. 2 if I come again I will not spare them
Gal 5. 2 that if you receive circumcision
6. 1 if a man is overtaken in any trespass
Col 3.13 if one has a complaint against another
4.10 (if he comes to you, receive him
1 Th 3. 8 we live, if you stand fast in the Lord
1 Tim 1. 8 law is good, if any one uses it lawfully
2.15 if she continues[d] in faith and love
3.15 if I am delayed, you may know how
2 Tim 2.21 If any one purifies himself
Heb 3. 6 we are his house if we hold fast
10.38 "if he shrinks . . my soul has no pleasure
13.23 with whom I shall see you if he comes
Jas 2. 2 if a man with gold rings . . comes
2.14 if a man says he has faith but . . not works
2.15 If a brother or sister is ill-clad and in lack
2.17 faith by itself, if it has no works, is dead
4.15 "If the Lord wills, we shall live
5.19 brethren, if any one among you wanders
1 Pet 3.13 who is there to harm you if you are zealous?
1 Jn 1. 6 If we say we have fellowship with him
1. 7 if we walk in the light, as he is in the light
1. 8 If we say we have no sin, we deceive
1. 9 If we confess our sins, he . . will forgive
1.10 If we say we have not sinned
2. 1 if any one does sin, we have an advocate
2. 3 if we keep his commandments
2.15 If any one loves the world
2.24 If what you heard . . abides in you
2.29 If you know that he is righteous
3.21 Beloved, if our hearts do not condemn us
4.12 if we love one another, God abides in us
4.20 If any one says, "I love God," and hates
5.14 if we ask anything according to his will
5.15 if we know that he hears us in whatever
5.16 If any one sees his brother
3 Jn .10 if I come, I will bring up what he is
Rev 3. 3 " 'If you will not awake, I will come
3.20 " 'if any one hears my voice and opens
22.18 if any one adds to them, God will add
22.19 if any one takes away from the words

2. *if indeed:* ἐάνπερ EANPER
Heb 6. 3 And this we will do if God permits[l]

3. *if, since:* εἰ EI
Mt 4. 3 "If you are the Son of God, command
4. 6 "If you are the Son of God, throw yourself
5.29 "If your right eye causes you to sin
5.30 "if your right hand causes you to sin
6.23 "If then the light in you is darkness
6.30 "if God so clothes the grass of the field
7.11 "If you then, who are evil, know how
8.31 "If you cast us out, send us away
10.25 "If they have called the master . . Beelzebul
Mt 11.14 "if you are willing to accept it, he is Elijah
11.21 "if the mighty works . . had been . . in Tyre
11.23 "if the mighty works . . had been . . in Sodom
12. 7 "if you had known what this means
12.26 "if Satan casts out Satan, he is divided
12.27 "if I cast out demons by Beelzebul
12.28 "if it is by the Spirit of God that I cast out
14.28 "Lord, if it is you, bid me come to you
16.24 "If any man would come after me
17. 4 "if you wish, I will make three booths
18. 8 "if your hand or your foot causes you to sin[z]
18. 9 "if your eye causes you to sin[z]
19.10 "If such is the case of a man with his wife
19.17 "If you would enter life, keep
19.21 "If you would be perfect, go, sell
22.45 "If David thus calls him Lord
23.30 " 'If we . . lived in the days of our fathers
24.22 "if those days had not been shortened
24.24 "to lead astray, if possible, even the elect
24.43 "if the householder had known
26.24 "better . . if he had not been born
26.39 "if it be possible, let this cup pass
26.42 "if this cannot pass unless I drink it
26.63 "tell us if you are the Christ
27.40 "If you are the Son of God, come down
27.43 "let God deliver him now, if he desires him
Mk 3.26 "if Satan has risen up against himself
4.23 "If any man has ears to hear, let him hear
8.34 "If any man would come after me
9.22 "if you can do anything, have pity on us
9.23 "If you can! All things are possible to him
9.35 "If any one would be first, he must be last
9.42 "if a great millstone were . . round his neck
11.13 he went to see if he could find anything
11.25 "if you have anything against any one
[11.26 "*But if you do not forgive*‡
13.20 "if the Lord had not shortened the days
13.22 "to lead astray, if possible, the elect
14.21 "better . . if he had not been born
14.35 if it were possible, the hour might pass
15.44 Pilate wondered if he were already dead
Lk 4. 3 "If you are the Son of God, command
4. 9 "If you are the Son of God, throw yourself
6.32 "If you love those who love you
7.39 "If this man were a prophet, he would
9.23 "If any man would come after me
10. 6 "but if not, it shall return to you
10.13 "if the mighty works . . had been . . in Tyre
11.13 "If you then, who are evil, know how
11.18 "if Satan also is divided against himself
11.19 "if I cast out demons by Beelzebul
11.20 "if it is by the finger of God
11.36 "If then your whole body is full of light
12.26 "If then you are not able to do . . that
12.28 "if God so clothes the grass which is alive
12.39 "if the householder had known
13. 9 " 'if it bears fruit next year, . . good
14.26 "If any one . . does not hate his own father
14.32 "if not, . . he sends an embassy
16.11 "If then you have not been faithful
16.12 "if you have not been faithful in that
16.31 "He said . . 'If they do not hear Moses
17. 2 "if a millstone were . . round his neck
17. 6 "If you had faith as a . . mustard seed
19. 8 "if I have defrauded any one of anything
22.42 "if thou art willing, remove this cup
22.67 "If you are the Christ, tell us
23.31 "if they do this when the wood is green
23.35 "let him save himself, if he is the Christ
23.37 "If you are the King . . , save yourself!
Jn 1.25 "if you are neither the Christ, nor Elijah
3.12 "can you believe if I tell you heavenly?
4.10 "If you knew the gift of God
5.46 "If you believed Moses
5.47 "But if you do not believe his writings
7. 4 "If you do these things, show yourself
7.23 "If on the sabbath a man receives

Jn 8.19 "if you knew me, you would know my F.
8.39 "If you were Abraham's children
8.42 "If God were your Father, you would love
8.46 "If I tell the truth, why . . not believe?
9.33 "If this man were not from God
9.41 "If . . blind, you would have no guilt
10.24 "If you are the Christ, tell us plainly
10.35 "If he called them gods to whom the word
10.37 "If I am not doing the works of my father
10.38 "but if I do them, . . believe the works
11.12 "if he has fallen asleep, he will recover
11.21 "Lord, if you had been here
11.32 "Lord, if you had been here
13.14 "If I . . have washed your feet
13.17 "If you know these things, blessed
13.32 "if God is glorified in him, God will also
14. 2 "If it were not so, would I have told you?
14. 7 "If you had known me, . . my Father also
14.28 "If you loved me, you would have rejoiced
15.18 "If the world hates you, know
15.19 "If you were . . , world would love its own
15.20 "If they persecuted me, they will . . you; if they kept my word, they will keep yours
15.22 "If I had not come and spoken to them
15.24 "If I had not done among them the works
18. 8 "if you seek me, let these men go
18.23 "If I have spoken wrongly, bear witness . . ; but if . . rightly, why . . strike?
18.30 "If this man were not an evildoer
18.36 "if my kingship were of this world
20.15 "if you have carried him away, tell me
Acts 4. 9 "if we are being examined today
5.39 "if it is of God, you will not be able
8.22 "that, if possible, the intent . . be forgiven
[8.37 *"If you believe with all your heart*‡
11.17 "If then God gave the same gift
13.15 "if you have any word of exhortation
16.15 "If you have judged me to be faithful
17.11 examining . . to see if these things were so
18.14 "If it were a matter of wrongdoing
19.38 "If . . the craftsmen . . have a complaint
19.39 "But if you seek anything further[t]
20.16 if possible, on the day of Pentecost
23. 9 "What if a spirit or an angel spoke to him?
24.19 "if they have anything against me
25. 5 "if there is anything wrong
25.11 "If then I am a wrongdoer
25.11 "but if there is nothing in their charges
26.32 "set free if he had not appealed to Caesar
27.39 they planned if possible to bring the ship
Rom 2.17 But if you call yourself a Jew
3. 3 What if some were unfaithful?
3. 5 if our wickedness serves to show
3. 7 if through . . falsehood . . truthfulness
4. 2 if Abraham was justified by works
4.14 If it is the adherents of the law
5.10 if while we were enemies we were reconciled
5.15 if many died through one man's trespass
5.17 If, because of one man's trespass, death
6. 5 if we have been united with him
6. 8 if we have died with Christ
7. 7 Yet, if it had not been for the law
7. 7 if the law had not said, "You shall not covet
7.16 Now if I do what I do not want
7.20 Now if I do what I do not want
8.10 But if Christ is in you
8.11 If the Spirit of him who raised Jesus
8.13 if you live according to the flesh you will die, but if . . you put to death the deeds
8.17 if children, then heirs, heirs of God
8.25 But if we hope for what we do not see
8.31 If God is for us, who is against us?
9.22 if God, desiring to show his wrath
9.29 "If the Lord . . had not left us children
11. 6 if it is by grace, it is no longer on . . works
11.12 if their trespass means riches for the world
11.15 if their rejection means the reconciliation

Rom 11.16 If the dough . . is holy, so . . the . . lump; and if the root is holy, so are the branches
11.17 if some of the branches were broken off
11.18 If you do boast, remember
11.21 if God did not spare the natural branches
11.24 if you have been cut from . . a wild olive
12.18 If possible, so far as it depends upon you
14.15 If your brother is being injured
15.27 if the Gentiles have come to share
1 Cor 2. 8 if they had, they would not have crucified
3.12 Now if any one builds on the foundation
3.14 If the work which any man has built
3.15 If any man's work is burned up
3.17 If any one destroys God's temple
3.18 If any one . . thinks that he is wise
4. 7 If then you received it, why do you boast?
6. 2 Do you not know that the saints will judge?
7. 9 But if they cannot exercise self-control
7.12 if any brother has a wife
7.13 If any woman has a husband
7.15 if the . . partner desires to separate
7.21 if you can gain . . freedom, avail yourself
7.36 If any one . . is not behaving properly
8. 2 If any one imagines that he knows
8. 3 if one loves God, one is known by him
8.13 if food is a cause of my brother's falling
9. 2 If to others I am not an apostle
9.11 If we have sown spiritual good . . , is it too much if we reap your . . benefits?
9.12 If others share this rightful claim
9.17 For if I do this of my own will
9.17 but if not of my own will, I am entrusted
10.27 If one of the unbelievers invites you
10.30 If I partake with thankfulness
11. 6 For if a woman will not veil herself
11. 6 but if it is disgraceful . . to be shorn
11.16 If any one is disposed to be contentious
11.31 But if we judged ourselves truly
11.34 if any one is hungry, let him eat at home
12.17 If the whole body were an eye
12.17 If the whole body were an ear
12.19 If all were a single organ
14.35 If there is anything they desire to know
14.37 If any one thinks that he is a prophet
14.38 If any one does not recognize this
15. 2 by which you are saved, if you hold it fast
15.12 Now if Christ is preached as raised
15.13 if there is no resurrection of the dead
15.14 if Christ has not been raised
15.16 For if the dead are not raised
15.17 If Christ has not been raised
15.19 If for this life only we have hoped
15.29 If the dead are not raised at all
15.32 if, humanly speaking, I fought with beasts
15.32 If the dead are not raised, "Let us eat
15.44 If there is a physical . . also a spiritual
16.22 If any one has no love for the Lord
2 Cor 2. 2 For if I cause you pain
2. 5 But if any one has caused pain
2.10 if I have forgiven anything
3. 7 if the dispensation of death . . came
3. 9 if there was splendor in the dispensation
3.11 if what faded away came with splendor
4. 3 even if our gospel is veiled
5.17 Therefore, if any one is in Christ
7. 8 even if I made you sorry with my letter
8.12 if the readiness is there, it is acceptable
10. 7 If any one is confident that he is Christ's
11. 4 if some one comes and preaches another
11. 6 Even if I am unskilled in speaking
11.15 not strange if his servants also disguise
11.20 you bear it if a man makes slaves of you
11.30 If I must boast, I . . boast of . . weakness
12.15 If I love . . , am I to be loved the less?
Gal 1. 9 If any one is preaching . . a gospel contrary
1.10 If I were still pleasing men
2.14 "If you, though a Jew, live like a Gentile

Gal 2.17 if . . we ourselves were found to be sinners
2.18 But if I build up again those things
2.21 for if justification[e] were through the law
3. 4 Did you experience so many things in vain?
3.18 For if the inheritance is by the law
3.21 for if a law . . could make alive
3.29 if you are Christ's, then . . Abraham's
4. 7 you are . . a son, and if a son then an heir
4.15 if possible, you would have plucked out
5.11 if I, brethren, still preach circumcision
5.15 if you bite and devour one another
5.18 But if you are led by the Spirit
5.25 If we live by the Spirit, let us also walk
6. 3 For if any one thinks he is something
Phil 1.22 If it is to be life in the flesh
2.17 Even if I am to be poured as a libation
3. 4 If any other man thinks he has reason
4. 8 if there is any excellence, if there is anything worthy of praise
2 Th 3.10 If any one will not work, let him not eat
3.14 If any one refuses to obey what we say
Col 2.20 If with Christ you died to the . . spirits
3. 1 If then you have been raised with Christ
1 Tim 3. 1 If any one aspires to the office of bishop
3. 5 if a man does not know how to manage
5. 4 If a widow has children
5. 8 If any one does not provide for . . relatives
5.16 If any believing woman[l] has relatives
6. 3 If any one teaches otherwise
2 Tim 2.11 If we have died with him, we shall also live
2.12 if we endure, we shall also reign with him; if we deny him, he also will deny us
2.13 if we are faithless, he remains faithful
Tit 1. 6 if any man is blameless
Phm .17 So if you consider me your partner
.18 If he has wronged you at all
Heb 2. 2 if the message declared by angels was valid
4. 8 if Joshua had given them rest
7.11 Now if perfection had been attainable
8. 4 if . . on earth, he would not be a priest
8. 7 if that first covenant had been faultless
9.13 if the sprinkling of defiled persons
11.15 If they had been thinking of that land
12. 8 If you are left without discipline
12.25 if they did not escape when they refused
Jas 1. 5 If any of you lacks wisdom, let him ask
1.23 if any one is a hearer of the word
1.26 If any one thinks he is religious
2. 8 If you really fulfil the royal law
2. 9 if you show partiality, you . . sin
2.11 If you do not commit adultery
3. 2 if any one makes no mistakes
3. 3 If we put bits into the mouths
3.14 But if you have bitter jealousy
4.11 But if you judge the law
1 Pet 1.17 if you invoke as Father him who judges
2.19 one is approved if . . he endures pain
2.20 if when you do wrong and are beaten
2.20 But if when you do right and suffer for it
3.14 if you do suffer for righteousness' sake
3.17 better to suffer . . if that . . be God's will
4.14 If you are reproached for the name
4.16 yet if one suffers as a Christian
4.17 if it begins with us, what will be the end?
4.18 "If the righteous man is scarcely saved
2 Pet 2. 4 For if God did not spare the angels
2.20 if, after they have escaped the defilements
1 Jn 2.19 for if they had been of us
4.11 if God so loved us, we also ought to love
5. 9 If we receive the testimony of men
2 Jn .10 If any one . . does not bring this doctrine
Rev 2. 5 " 'If not, I will come to you
2.16 " 'If not, I will come to you soon
11. 5 if any one would harm them
11. 5 if any one would harm them
13. 9 If any one has an ear, let him hear
13.10 If any one is to be taken captive
Rev 13.10 if any one slays with the sword
14. 9 "If any one worships the beast
20.15 if any one's name was not found written

4. *if indeed, since:* εἴπερ EIPER
1 Cor 15.15 if it is true that the dead are not raised

5. *whether, or:* εἴτε EITE
Rom 12. 6 if prophecy, in proportion to our faith
12. 7 if service, in our serving
1 Cor 12.26 If one member suffers, all suffer . . ; if one member is honored, all rejoice
14.27 If any speak in a tongue
2 Cor 1. 6 If we are afflicted, it is for your comfort
1. 6 if we are comforted, it is for your comfort
5.13 if we are beside ourselves, it is for God; if we are in our right mind, it is for you

6. *that, because:* ὅτι HOTI
Mk **4.38**

7. *even if:* κἄν KAN
Lk 12.38 "If he comes in the second watch
Jn 8.55 "If I said, I do not know him
1 Cor 13. 3 If I give away all I have

IF, AND

1. *even if:* κἄν KAN
Mk 16.18 "and if they drink any deadly thing[k]‡
Lk 13. 9 " 'And if it bears fruit next year, well
1 Cor 13. 2 And if I have prophetic powers
13. 2 and if I have all faith, so as to remove
13. 3 and if I deliver my body to be burned[v]
Jas 5.15 and if he has committed sins, he will be

IF, EVEN

1. *if:* ἐάν EAN
Jn 8.16 "even if I do judge, my judgment is true
Gal 1. 8 even if we, or an angel from heaven, . . preach

2. *even if:* κἄν KAN
Mt 21.21 "even if you say to this mountain
26.35 "Even if I must die . . , I will not deny you
Jn 8.14 "Even if I do bear witness to myself
2 Cor 11.16 but even if you do, accept me as a fool
Heb 12.20 "If even a beast touches the mountain

IF I

1. *and I:* κἀγώ KAGŌ
Mt 26.15 "What will you give me if I deliver him?

IF ONLY

1. *if indeed:* ἐάνπερ EANPER
Heb 3.14 if only we hold our first confidence firm

IGNOBLE

CONTEXTUALLY
2 Tim 2.21 If any one purifies himself from what is i.

IGNOBLE USE

1. *disgrace, dishonor:* ἀτιμία ATIMIA
2 Tim 2.20 some for noble use, some for ignoble

IGNORANCE

1. *ignorance:* ἄγνοια AGNOIA*
Acts 3.17 "you acted in ignorance, as did . . your rulers
17.30 "The times of ignorance God overlooked
Eph 4.18 because of the ignorance that is in them
1 Pet 1.14 passions of your former ignorance

2. *ignorance:* ἀγνωσία AGNŌSIA
1 Pet 2.15 silence the ignorance of foolish men

IGNORANT

1. *not know:* ἀγνοέω (part.) AGNOEŌ
Heb 5. 2 He can deal gently with the ignorant

2. *ignorant:* ἀμαθής AMATHĒS*
2 Pet 3.16 the ignorant . . twist to their . . destruction

IGNORANT, BE

1. *not know:* ἀγνοέω AGNOEŌ
[a]inf.
Rom 10. 3 being ignorant of the righteousness
2 Cor 1. 8 we do not want you to be ignorant
2.11 we are not ignorant of his designs
1 Th 4.13 [a]we would not have you ignorant
2 Pet 2.12 matters of which they are ignorant

IGNORANTLY
1. *not know:* ἀγνοέω (part.) AGNOEŌ
1 Tim 1.13 I had acted ignorantly in unbelief

IGNORE
1. *escape notice:* λανθάνω LANTHANŌ [A.6.c.3]
2 Pet 3. 5 They deliberately ignore this fact
3. 8 But do not ignore this one fact
2. *overhear, take no heed of:* παρακούω PARAKOUŌ
Mk 5.36 ignoring[q] what they said, Jesus said†‡

ILL
1. *weak, sickly:* ἄρρωστος ARRŌSTOS
1 Cor 11.30 why many of you are weak and ill
2. *be weak, be sickly:* ἀσθενέω (part.) ASTHENEŌ
2 Tim 4.20 Trophimus I left ill at Miletus

ILL, BE
1. *be weak, be sickly:* ἀσθενέω ASTHENEŌ
Jn 4.46 there was an official whose son was ill
11. 1 a certain man was ill, Lazarus
11. 2 Mary . . , whose brother Lazarus was ill
11. 3 "Lord, he whom you love is ill
11. 6 when he heard that he was ill
Phil 2.26 because you heard that he was ill
2.27 Indeed he was ill, near to death
2. *hold together, impel:* συνέχω (pass.) SYNECHŌ
Lk 4.38 Now Simon's mother-in-law was ill
IDIOMATICALLY
a. Jn 5.5 who had been ill for thirty-eight years τριάκοντα καὶ ὀκτὼ ἔτη ἔχων ἐν τῇ ἀσθενείᾳ αὐτοῦ [ASTHENEIA]

ILL REPUTE
1. *slander:* δυσφημία DYSPHĒMIA*
2 Cor 6. 8 ⟨we commend ourselves⟩ in ill repute

ILL-CLAD
1. *naked, bare:* γυμνός GYMNOS
Jas 2.15 If a brother or sister is ill-clad

ILL-CLAD, BE
1. *be naked:* γυμνιτεύω GYMNITEUŌ*
1 Cor 4.11 we are ill-clad and buffeted and homeless

ILLEGITIMATE CHILDREN
1. *illegitimate:* νόθος (subst. pl.) NOTHOS*
Heb 12. 8 then you are illegitimate children

ILLNESS
1. *weakness, sickness:* ἀσθένεια ASTHENEIA
Jn 11. 4 "This illness is not unto death

ILL-TREAT
1. *mistreat:* κακόω KAKOŌ
Acts 7. 6 "ill-treat them four hundred years
2. *wrong, injure:* κακουχέω KAKOUCHEŌ*
Heb 11.37 they went about . . afflicted, ill-treated
13. 3 Remember . . those who are ill-treated

ILL-TREATMENT
1. *oppression:* κάκωσις KAKŌSIS*
Acts 7.34 " 'I have surely seen the ill-treatment

ILL-TREATMENT, SHARE
1. *endure adversity with:* συγκακουχέομαι SYGKAKOUCHEOMAI*
Heb 11.25 choosing rather to share ill-treatment

ILLYRICUM: Ἰλλυρικόν ə'lirikəm II,C-2
Rom 15.19 from Jerusalem and as far round as I.

IMAGE
1. *image, likeness:* εἰκών EIKŌN
Rom 8.29 conformed to the image of his Son
1 Cor 11. 7 since he is the image and glory of God
15.49 we have borne the i. of the man of dust, we shall[a] . . bear the i. of the man of heaven
Col 1.15 He is the image of the invisible God
3.10 renewed . . after the image of its creator
Rev 13.14 bidding them make an i. for the beast
13.15 to give breath to the image of the beast so that the i. of the beast should even speak
13.15 those who would not worship the image
14. 9 "If any one worships the beast and its i.
14.11 "worshipers of the beast and its image
15. 2 who had conquered the beast and its i.
16. 2 men who . . worshiped its image
Rev 19.20 deceived . . those who worshiped its i.
20. 4 not worshiped the beast or its image

IMAGINATION
1. *thought, understanding:* διάνοια DIANOIA
Lk 1.51 "the proud in the i. of their hearts
2. *reflection, idea:* ἐνθύμησις ENTHYMĒSIS
Acts 17.29 "by the art and imagination of man

IMAGINE
1. *think, suppose:* δοκέω DOKEŌ
1 Cor 8. 2 If any one imagines . . he knows something
2. *think about, practice:* μελετάω MELETAŌ
Acts 4.25 " 'Why did . . the peoples i. vain things?
3. *think, believe:* νομίζω NOMIZŌ
1 Tim 6. 5 imagining that godliness is a means of gain

IMITATE
1. *imitate:* μιμέομαι MIMEOMAI*
2 Th 3. 7 know how you ought to imitate us
3. 9 in our conduct an example to imitate
Heb 13. 7 Remember your leaders, . . i. their faith
3 Jn .11 Beloved, do not imitate evil

IMITATING, JOIN IN
1. *joint imitator:* συμμιμητής SYMMIMĒTĒS* [B.2.d.2]
Phil 3.17 Brethren, join in imitating me

IMITATOR
1. *imitator:* μιμητής MIMĒTĒS*
1 Cor 4.16 I urge you, then, be imitators of me
11. 1 Be imitators of me, as I am of Christ
Eph 5. 1 Therefore be imitators of God
1 Th 1. 6 you became imitators of us
2.14 imitators of the churches of God
Heb 6.12 imitators of those who . . inherit the promises

IMMEASURABLE
1. *throw over, exceed:* ὑπερβάλλω (part.) HYPERBALLŌ
Eph 1.19 the immeasurable greatness of his power
2. 7 show the immeasurable riches of his grace

IMMEDIATELY
1. *immediately:* εὐθέως EUTHEŌS
Mt 4.20 I. they left their nets and followed
4.22 I. they left the boat and their father
8. 3 immediately his leprosy was cleansed
13. 5 "Other seeds . . immediately . . sprang up
14.31 Jesus immediately reached out his hand
20.34 immediately they received their sight
24.29 "Immediately after the tribulation
Lk 5.13 And immediately the leprosy left him
14. 5 "Which of you . . will not i. pull him out?
Jn 6.21 immediately the boat was at the land
Acts 9.18 i. something like scales fell from his eyes
9.20 immediately he proclaimed Jesus
9.34 And immediately he rose
12.10 and immediately the angel left him
16.10 i. we sought to go on into Macedonia
17.10 brethren i. sent Paul and Silas away
17.14 brethren immediately sent Paul off
2. *immediately:* εὐθύς EUTHYS II
Mt 3.16 he went up immediately from the water
13.20 "hears the word and i. receives it
13.21 "when tribulation . . arises . . , i. he falls away[i]
14.27 immediately he spoke to them
21. 2 "immediately you will find an ass tied
21. 3 "he will send them immediately
26.74 And immediately the cock crowed
Mk 1.10 immediately he saw the heavens opened
1.12 The Spirit immediately drove him out
1.18 i. they left their nets and followed
1.20 i. he called them; and they left their father
1.21 i. on the sabbath he entered
1.23 i. there was . . a man with an unclean spirit
1.29 immediately he[e] left the synagogue
1.30 immediately they told him of her
1.42 immediately the leprosy left him
2. 8 i. Jesus, perceiving in his spirit
2.12 he rose, and i. took up the pallet
3. 6 Pharisees went out, and i. held counsel

Mk 4. 5 "Other seed . . immediately it sprang up
4.15 "when they hear, Satan immediately comes
4.16 "when they hear the word, i. receive it
4.17 "tribulation . . arises . . , i. they fall away[m]
5.29 immediately the hemorrhage ceased
5.30 Jesus . . i. turned about in the crowd
5.42 immediately the girl got up and walked . . , and they were immediately overcome
6.25 she came in immediately with haste
6.27 i. the king sent a soldier of the guard
6.45 I. he made his disciples get into the boat
6.50 But immediately he spoke to them
6.54 immediately the people recognized him
7.25 immediately a woman . . heard of him
8.10 i. he got into the boat with his disciples
9.15 all the crowd . . were greatly amazed
9.20 immediately it convulsed the boy
9.24 I. the father of the child cried out[i]
10.52 i. he received his sight and followed
11. 2 "i. as you enter it you will find a colt tied
11. 3 " 'The Lord . . will send it back here i.
14.43 i., while he was still speaking, Judas came
14.72 i. the cock crowed a second time
Lk 6.49 "i. it fell, and the ruin . . was great
Jn 13.30 he immediately went out; and it was night

3. *immediately:* παραχρῆμα PARACHRĒMA
Lk 1.64 immediately his mouth was opened
4.39 immediately she rose and served them
5.25 immediately he rose before them
8.44 immediately her flow of blood ceased
8.47 how she had been immediately healed
13.13 immediately she was made straight
18.43 immediately he received his sight
19.11 that the kingdom . . was to appear i.
22.60 immediately . . the cock crowed
Acts 3. 7 i. his feet and ankles were made strong
5.10 I. she fell down at his feet and died
12.23 I. an angel of the Lord smote him
13.11 I. mist and darkness fell upon him
16.26 immediately all the doors were opened

IMMORAL
1. *brothel-keeper, immoral man:* πόρνος (pred.) PORNOS
Heb 12.16 that no one be immoral or irreligious

IMMORAL MAN
1. *fornicate:* πορνεύω (subst. part.) PORNEUŌ
1 Cor 6.18 the i. man sins against his own body
2. *brothel-keeper, immoral man:* πόρνος PORNOS
1 Cor 5. 9 not to associate with immoral men

IMMORAL PERSON
1. *brothel-keeper, immoral man:* πόρνος PORNOS
1 Tim 1.10 immoral persons, sodomites, kidnapers

IMMORAL, THE
1. *brothel-keeper, immoral man:* πόρνος (pl.) PORNOS
1 Cor 5.10 not . . meaning the immoral of this world
6. 9 neither the immoral, nor idolaters
Heb 13. 4 for God will judge the immoral

IMMORALITY
1. *fornication, unchastity:* πορνεία PORNEIA
1 Cor 5. 1 reported that there is i. among you
6.13 The body is not meant for immorality
6.18 Shun immorality
7. 2 because of the temptation to immorality
2 Cor 12.21 impurity, immorality, and licentiousness
Rev 2.21 " 'she refuses to repent of her immorality
9.21 nor did they repent of their . . immorality

IMMORALITY, GUILTY OF
1. *brothel-keeper, immoral man:* πόρνος (pred.) PORNOS
1 Cor 5.11 if he is guilty of immorality or greed

IMMORALITY, INDULGE IN
IMMORALITY, PRACTICE
1. *fornicate:* πορνεύω PORNEUŌ
1 Cor 10. 8 We must not indulge in immorality
Rev 2.14 " 'you have some there who . . practice i.
2.20 " 'beguiling my servants to practice i.

IMMORALLY, ACT
1. *commit fornication:* ἐκπορνεύω EKPORNEUŌ*
Jude . 7 cities, which likewise acted immorally

IMMORTAL
1. *incorruptible, immortal:* ἄφθαρτος APHTHARTOS
Rom 1.23 exchanged the glory of the immortal God
1 Tim 1.17 the King of ages, immortal, invisible

IMMORTALITY
1. *incorruption, immortality:* ἀφθαρσία APHTHARSIA
Rom 2. 7 seek for glory and honor and immortality
2 Tim 1.10 who . . brought life and immortality to light
2. *immortality:* ἀθανασία ATHANASIA*
1 Cor 15.53 this mortal nature must put on i.
15.54 When . . the mortal puts on immortality
1 Tim 6.16 ⟨the Lord⟩ who alone has immortality

IMMOVABLE
1. *immovable:* ἀμετακίνητος AMETAKINĒTOS*
1 Cor 15.58 brethren, be steadfast, immovable
2. *immovable:* ἀσάλευτος ASALEUTOS
Acts 27.41 the bow stuck and remained immovable

IMPART
1. *give:* δίδωμι DIDŌMI
Eph 4.29 that it . . impart grace to those who hear
2. *speak, talk:* λαλέω LALEŌ
1 Cor 2. 6 among the mature we do impart wisdom
2. 7 we impart a secret and hidden wisdom
2.13 we i. this . . not . . by human wisdom
3. *share:* μεταδίδωμι METADIDŌMI
Rom 1.11 that I may i. . . some spiritual gift

IMPARTIALLY
1. *without respect of persons:* ἀπροσωπολήμπτως APROSŌPOLĒMPTŌS*
1 Pet 1.17 who judges each one impartially

IMPEDIMENT IN HIS SPEECH, A MAN WHO HAS AN
1. *speaking with difficulty:* μογιλάλος (subst.) MOGILALOS*
Mk 7.32 a man who had an i. in his speech

IMPENDING
1. *place in, be present:* ἐνίστημι (perf. part.) ENISTĒMI
1 Cor [7.26 in view of the *impending* distress†[0]

IMPENITENT
1. *not to be repented of:* ἀμετανόητος AMETANOĒTOS*
Rom 2. 5 by your hard and impenitent heart

IMPERFECT
1. *part, share:* μέρος MEROS [B.1.a.1]
1 Cor 13. 9 For our knowledge is imperfect and our prophecy is imperfect
13.10 when the perfect comes, the i. will pass

IMPERISHABLE
1. *incorruption, immortality:* ἀφθαρσία APHTHARSIA [B.2.d.2]
1 Cor 15.42 what is raised is imperishable
2. *incorruptible, immortal:* ἄφθαρτος APHTHARTOS
Mk [16.[end] *the sacred and i. proclamation*‡
1 Cor 9.25 do it to receive . . an imperishable ⟨wreath⟩
15.52 the dead will be raised imperishable
1 Pet 1. 4 an inheritance which is imperishable
1.23 born . . , not of perishable seed but of i.
3. 4 i. jewel of a gentle and quiet spirit

IMPERISHABLE, THE
1. *incorruption, immortality:* ἀφθαρσία APHTHARSIA
1 Cor 15.50 nor does the perishable inherit the i.
15.53 this perishable nature must put on the i.
15.54 When the perishable puts on the i.

IMPIOUS
1. *unholy, godless:* ἀσεβής ASEBĒS
1 Pet 4.18 "where will the impious and sinner appear?

IMPLACABLE
1. *implacable, irreconcilable:* ἄσπονδος ASPONDOS*
2 Tim 3. 3 inhuman, implacable, slanderers

IMPLANTED
1. *implanted:* ἔμφυτος EMPHYTOS*
Jas 1.21 receive with meekness the implanted word

IMPLORE
1. *say, speak:* λέγω LEGŌ [A.6.a.5]
Mt 18.26 "servant fell on his knees, imploring him

IMPLY
1. *say, affirm:* φημί PHĒMI
1 Cor 10.19 What do I imply then?
IDIOMATICALLY
a. Gal 3.20 Now an intermediary implies more than one ὁ δὲ μεσίτης ἑνὸς οὐκ ἔστιν [EIMI]
CONTEXTUALLY
1 Cor 10.20 No, I imply that what pagans sacrifice
Gal 3.20 an intermediary implies more than one

IMPORTANCE (*See also* FIRST *b*)
CONTEXTUALLY
1 Cor 15. 3 For I delivered to you as of first i.

IMPORTUNITY
1. *shamelessness, persistence:* ἀναίδεια ANAIDEIA*
Lk 11. 8 "yet because of his importunity he will rise

IMPOSED
1. *lie upon, press upon:* ἐπίκειμαι (part.) EPIKEIMAI
Heb 9.10 imposed until the time of reformation

IMPOSSIBLE
1. *unable, impossible:* ἀδύνατος ADYNATOS
Mt 19.26 "With men this is impossible
Mk 10.27 "With men it is i., but not with God,
Lk 18.27 "What is i. with men is possible with God
Heb 6. 4 impossible to restore again to repentance
6.18 it is i. that God should prove false
10. 4 it is impossible that the blood of bulls
11. 6 without faith it is impossible to please him

IMPOSSIBLE, BE
1. *be unable:* ἀδυνατέω (impers.) ADYNATEŌ*
Mt 17.20 "nothing will be impossible to you[x]
Lk 1.37 "with God nothing will be impossible

IMPOSTOR
1. *sorcerer, cheat:* γόης GOĒS*
2 Tim 3.13 while evil men and impostors will go on
2. *leading astray:* πλάνος (subst.) PLANOS
Mt 27.63 "we remember how that impostor said
2 Cor 6. 8 We are treated as impostors

IMPRISON
1. *throw into prison:* φυλακίζω PHYLAKIZŌ*
Acts 22.19 " 'I imprisoned . . those who believed

IMPRISONED, BE
1. *bind, tie:* δέω (pass.) DEŌ
Acts 21.13 "I am ready not only to be imprisoned

IMPRISONMENT
1. *bond:* δεσμός (pl.) DESMOS
Acts 20.23 "imprisonment and afflictions await me
23.29 "nothing deserving death or imprisonment
26.31 "nothing to deserve death or i.
Phil 1. 7 in my imprisonment and in the defense
1.13 known . . that my i. is for Christ
1.14 confident in the Lord because of my i.
1.17 thinking to afflict me in my i.
Phm .10 whose father I have become in my i.
.13 during my imprisonment for the gospel
2. *watch, guard, prison:* φυλακή PHYLAKĒ
2 Cor 6. 5 beatings, imprisonments, tumults
11.23 greater labors, far more imprisonments
Heb 11.36 Others suffered . . even chains and i.

IMPROPER
IDIOMATICALLY
a. Rom 1.28 God gave them up to a base mind and to improper conduct παρέδωκεν αὐτοὺς ὁ θεὸς εἰς ἀδόκιμον νοῦν, ποιεῖν τὰ μὴ καθήκοντα [KATHĒKŌ]

IMPROVEMENT
1. *restoration, training:* κατάρτισις KATARTISIS*
2 Cor 13. 9 What we pray for is your improvement

IMPULSE
1. *desire, yearning:* ἐπιθυμία EPITHYMIA
2 Tim 3. 6 weak women, . . swayed by various impulses

2. *will, desire:* θέλημα THELĒMA
2 Pet 1.21 no prophecy . . came by the i. of man

IMPURE
1. *unclean:* ἀκάθαρτος AKATHARTOS
Eph 5. 5 no . . impure man . . has any inheritance
2. *fornication, unchastity:* πορνεία (gen.) PORNEIA
Rev 14. 8 "drink the wine of her impure passion
18. 3 "drunk[k] the wine of her impure passion

IMPURITY
1. *uncleanness:* ἀκαθαρσία AKATHARSIA
Rom 1.24 God gave them up . . to impurity
6.19 you once yielded your members to i.
2 Cor 12.21 who . . have not repented of the impurity
Gal 5.19 fornication, impurity, licentiousness
Eph 5. 3 all impurity . . must not even be named
Col 3. 5 fornication, impurity, passion
2. *unclean:* ἀκάθαρτος (subst. neut.) AKATHARTOS
Rev 17. 4 full of the impurities of her fornication

IN
1. *until:* ἄχρι ACHRI
Acts **20**.6
2. *fill up:* ἀναπληρόω (part.) ANAPLĒROŌ
1 Cor **14**.16
3. *from:* ἀπό (+gen.) APO
Mt **13**.44
Lk **19**.39
Acts **12**.14; **15**.7, 38
2 Cor **1**.14; **2**.5
2 Th **2**.2
Rev **22**.19
4. *through:* διά (+gen.) DIA
[a]+acc.
Mt **26**.61
Mk **14**.58
Lk **8**.4
Acts **16**.9; **18**.9
Rom **7**.8, 11; **14**.14
1 Cor **13**.12; **14**.9
2 Cor **6**.8[2]; **9**.12; **11**.33
2 Th **3**.14
Rev **18**.10[a], 15[a]
5. *have, hold:* ἔχω (part.) ECHŌ
Heb **7**.28
Rev **12**.12
6. *into, to, for:* εἰς (+acc.) EIS
Mt **2**.23; **4**.13; **5**.25; **10**.9; **13**.33; **18**.6, 20, 30; **26**.3, 13, 67; **27**.5, 51; **28**.19
Mk **1**.9, 39; **4**.15; **5**.14[2], 34; **6**.8, 56; **9**.42; **10**.10; **13**.9, 16; **14**.9[2], 60; **15**.38
Lk **1**.20; **2**.28; **4**.35, 44; **7**.1, 50; **8**.34[2], 48; **11**.7, 33; **12**.58; **13**.19, 21; **14**.8, 10, 31; **22**.19‡
Jn **1**.12, 18; **2**.11, 23; **3**.16, 18[2], 24, 36; **4**.39; **6**.29, 35, 40; **7**.5, 31, 38, 39, 48; **8**.30; **9**.7, 35, 36; **10**.42; **11**.25, 26, 45, 48; **12**.11, 36, 37, 42, 44[3], 46; **14**.1[2], 12; **16**.9; **17**.20; **20**.7, 25[2], 27
Acts **2**.5; **4**.3; **7**.4, 5, 12; **8**.16, 23; **10**.43; **12**.4; **13**.29; **14**.23; **16**.24; **17**.21; **19**.4, 5, 22; **20**.18, 21; **24**.15, 24; **26**.18; **27**.40
Rom **10**.14
1 Cor **1**.13, 15; **11**.24, 25; **15**.54
2 Cor **1**.21; **2**.9; **6**.1; 8.2, 22; **11**.20
Gal **2**.2, 16; **6**.4[2]
Eph **1**.19; **3**.16
Phil **1**.5, 29; **2**.16[3], 22
Col **2**.5; **3**.10
1 Th **3**.5; **4**.17
2 Th **2**.4
2 Tim **4**.11
Phm .6
Heb **11**.9
1 Pet **1**.21[2]; **3**.5, 20; **4**.4; **5**.12
2 Pet **1**.8
1 Jn **5**.10[2], 13
Rev **1**.11; **6**.15; **11**.9
7. *from, out of:* ἐκ (+gen.) EK
Mt **24**.17

Lk **11**.27
Rom **2**.18
1 Cor **13**.12
2 Cor **13**.4
Rev **16**.10; **18**.4; **22**.19

8. *in, at, by:* ἐν (+dat.) EN

Mt **1**.20; **2**.1^2, 2, 5, 9, 16^2, 18, 19; **3**.1^2, 3, 6, 12; **4**.13, 16^2, 21, 23; **5**.12, 15, 16, 19^2, 28, 45; **6**.1, 2^2, 4^2, 5, 6, 9, 10, 18^2, 20, 23, 29; **7**.3^2, 4, 11, 15, 21; **8**.10, 11, 32; **9**.4, 10, 33, 35; **10**.11, 16, 17, 19, 23, 27^2, 28, 32, 33; **11**.1, 2, 8^2, 11, 16, 21^3, 23^2; **12**.5^2, 19, 32^2, 40^2, 50; **13**.3, 10, 13, 19, 21, 24, 27, 31, 32, 34, 35, 43, 44, 54, 57^2; **14**.2, 3, 10, 13, 33; **15**.33; **16**.17, 19^2, 27, 28; **17**.22; **18**.1, 2, 4, 6, 10^2, 14, 18^2, 19, 20; **19**.21, 28; **20**.3, 21; **21**.9^2, 12, 14, 15, 22, 28, 32, 33, 41, 42^2; **22**.1, 15, 28, 30^2, 36, [43†; **23**.6, 7, 30^2, 34, 39; **24**.15, 16, 18, 19, 26^2, 30, 38, 40; **25**.25, 31, 36, 39, 43, 44; **26**.6, 13, 23, 29, 55, 69; **27**.29, 40, 59, 60^2; **28**.18

Mk **1**.2, 3, 4, 5, 9, 13, 15, 16, 19, 20, 23; **2**.6, 8, 15, 20; **3**.23; **4**.2^2, 11, 17, 28, 36, 38; **5**.13, 20, 21, 27, 30^2; **6**.2, 4^2, 14, 17, 27, 29, 32, 56; **8**.1, 14, 38^2; **9**.33, 36, 38, 50; **10**.21, 30^2, 37; **11**.9, 10, 15, 23, 25, [26‡, 27; **12**.1, 11, 23, 25, 26, 35, [36†, 38^3, 39; **13**.11, 14, 17, 24, 25, 26, 32; **14**.3, 25, 49, 66; **15**.7, 29, 41, 46; **16**.12‡, 17‡

Lk **1**.5, 6, 7, 17, 18, 21, 22, 25, 26, 31, 36, 39, 41, 44, 66, 69, 75, 77, 79, 80; **2**.1, 7^2, 8, 11, 12, 14, 16, 19, 21, 23, 24, 25, [27†, 29, 34, 43, 44, 46, 49, 51, 52 *var. om.*; **3**.1, 2, 4^2, 15, 17, 20; **4**.2(1), 2, 5, 14, 15, 20, 21, 23, 24, 25^2, 27, 28, 33; **5**.7, 12, 22, 29, 35; **6**.12^2, 23^2, 41^2, 42^3; **7**.9, 21, 25^2, 28, 32, 37; **8**.10, 13, 15^2, 27; **9**.12, 26, 31, 36, 49; **10**.3, 7, 9, 13^3, 14, 17, 20^2, 21, 26; **11**.1, 21, 35, 43^2; **12**.1, 3^3, 12, 15, 27, 28, 33, 38^2, 52; **13**.4, 6, 10, 19, 26, 28, 29, 35; **14**.15; **15**.4, 7, 25; **16**.10^4, 11, 12, 23^3, 24, 25; **17**.6, 24‡, 26^2, 28, 31^2, [36‡; **18**.2, 3, 22, 30^2; **19**.17, 20, 38^3, 44, 47; **20**.1, 33, 42, 46^3; **21**.14, 21^2, 23, 25^2, 27, 37, 38; **22**.16, 20‡, 28, 30, 37, [44‡, 53, 55; **23**.4, 7, 19^2, 22, [42‡, 43, 53; **24**.4, 6, 18, 19, 27, 35, 38, 44, 49, 53

Jn **1**.1, 2, 4, 5, 10, 23, 28, 45, 47; **2**.14, 19, 20, 23, 25; **3**.[13‡, 14, 15, 21; **4**.14, 20, 21, 23, 24, 44, 45; **5**.2, 3, 13, 14, 26^2, 28, 35, 38, 39, 43^2; **6**.10, 31, 45, 49, 53, 56^2, 59, 61; **7**.1^2, 4^2, 9, 10, 18, 28; **8**.3‡, 5‡, 12, 17, 20^2, 21, 24^2, 31, 35, 37, 44; **9**.3, 5, 34; **10**.23^2, 25, 34, 38^2; **11**.6, 9, 10^2, 17, 20, 24^2, 30, 31, 56; **12**.13, 25, 35, 46; **13**.1, 31, 32^2; **14**.2, 10^3, 11^2, 13^2, 14, 17, 20^4, 26; **15**.4^3, 5^2, 6, 7^2, 9, 10^2, 11, 16, 25; **16**.23^2, 24, 25^2, 26^2, 33^2; **17**.10, 11^3, 12, 13^2, 17, 19, 21^3, 23^2, 26^2; **18**.20^2, 26, 38; **19**.4, 6, 41^2; **20**.12, 25, 30, 31

Acts **1**.8^2, 10, 15, 20^2; **2**.5, 17, 18, 19, 22, 38; **3**.6, 25, 26; **4**.2, 5, 7, 12, 24, 27, 31; **5**.4, 12, 18, 20, 22, 25^2, 34, 37, 42; **6**.1^2, 7, 15; **7**.2^2, 4, 5, 6, 7, 16^2, 17, 20, 22, 29, 30^2, 34, 35, 36^2, 38^2, 39, 41^2, 42^2, 44, 48; **8**.1, 8, 9, 21, 33; **9**.10, 11, 20, 21, 22, 25, 27, 29(28), 37^2, 43; **10**.3, 12, 30^2, 32, 35, 39, 48; **11**.5^2, 11, 13, 22, 26, 27, 29; **12**.5, 7; **13**.5, 17, 18, 19, 27, 33, 35, 40, 41; **14**.15, 16, 25; **15**.21, 35; **16**.3, 6, 12, 18, 32, 36; **17**.11, 17^2, 22, 24^2, 28; **18**.4, 10, 24, 26; **19**.9, 16, 21, 39; **20**.8, 10, 16, 28; **21**.27, 29, 34; **22**.3, 17; **23**.6, 9, 35; **24**.12^2, 14, 18; **26**.10^2, 21, 26, 28; **27**.31, 37; **28**.7, 11, 18, [30†

Rom **1**.2, 4, 7, 8, 9, 15, 17, 21, 24, 27; **2**.1, 19, 20, 23; **3**.4, 16, 24, 25(26); **5**.2, 3, 11, 13, 15, 17, 21; **6**.2, 4, 11, 12, 23; **7**.5^2, 6, 8, 18, 23^2; **8**.1, 2, 3^2, 4, 8, 9^3, 10, 11^2, 37, 39; **9**.1^2, 17^2, 25, 26, 33; **10**.6, 8, 9; **11**.17, 25; **12**.4, 5, 7^2, 8^2; **13**.9, 13; **14**.5, 14, 17; **15**.13^2, 17, 23, 27, 29, 30, 31; **16**.2^2, 3, 7, 8, 9, 10, 11, 12^2, 13, 22

1 Cor **1**.2^2, 4, 5^2, 7, 8, 10, 21, 30; **2**.3^2, 4^2, 5^2, 11, 13; **3**.1, 16, 18, 19; **4**.10, 15^2, 17^3, 20^2; **5**.4, 5, 9; **6**.11^2, 20; **7**.15, 17, 20, 22, 24, 37^2, 39; **8**.5, 10; **9**.1, 2, 9, 18, 24; **10**.2^2, 5, 25; **11**.11, 21, 22, 25; **12**.6, 18, 25, 28; **14**.10, 19^2, 21, 28, 33, 34, 35; **15**.1, 17, 18, 19, 22^2, 23, 31, 41, 43^4, 52^2, 58^2; **16**.7, 8, 11, 13, 14, 19, 24

2 Cor **1**.1, 4, 8, 12, 19, 20, 22; **2**.10, 12, 14, 17; **3**.7, 10; **4**.4, 6^2, 7, 8, 10^2, 11, 12^2; **5**.1, 4, 6, 17, 19, 21; **6**.3, 4^2, 12, 16; **7**.1, 3, 16; **8**.1, 2, 7^3, 10, 19; **9**.3, 11; **10**.3, 15, 16; **11**.6^2, 9, 10^2, 12, 17, 26^2, 27^2, 33; **12**.2^2, 3, 9, 12, 19; **13**.3^2, 4, 5

Gal **1**.6, 13, 14, [16†; **2**.4, 17, 20^2; **3**.8, 10, 26, 28; **4**.19, 25; **5**.6, 10, 14; **6**.1^2, 12, 13, 14

Eph **1**.3^2, 4, 5(4), 6, 7, 9(8), 9, 10, 11, 12, 13^2, 15, 17, 18, 20^2, 21^2, 23; **2**.2^2, 3, 4, 6^2, 7^3, 10^2, 11^2, 12, 13^2, 15(14), 15, 16, 18, 21^2, 22^2; **3**.6, 9†, 10, 11, 12, 15, 17^2, 21^2; **4**.2, 3, 6, 15, 16, 17^2, 18, 21^2, 24, 30, 32; **5**.2, 5, 8, 9, 20, 24; **6**.1, 4, 5, 9, 10^2, 12, 13, 18, 19, 20, 21

Phil **1**.1, 4, 6, 7^3, [13†, 14, 18, 20, 22, 26^2, 27, 28; **2**.1, 5, 6, 7, 12^2, 13, 15, 19, 24, 29; **3**.1, 3^2, 4^2, 9, 14, 19, 20; **4**.1, 2, 3^2, 4, 6, 7, 9, 10, 11, 12, 13, 15, 16, 19^2, 21

Col **1**.2, 4, 5^2, 6^2, 8, 9, 10, 12, 14, 16^2, 17, 18, 19, 20, 22, 24^2, 27, 28^2; **2**.2, 3, 6, 7^2, 9, 10, 11^2, 12^2, 15, 16, 23; **3**.3, 4, 7^2, 11, 15^2, 16^3, 17^2, 18, 22; **4**.1, 2, 7, 12^2, 13^2, 16, 17

1 Th **1**.1, 5^3, 6, 7^2, 8; **2**.2^2, 13, 14^2; **3**.2, 8, 13; **4**.1, 4, 5, 6, 7, 16, 17; **5**.2, 4, 12, 13, 18^2

2 Th **1**.1, 4^2, 7(8), 10^2, 12^2; **2**.6, 17; **3**.4, 6, 12, 16, 17

1 Tim **1**.2, 4, 13, 14, 16; **2**.2^2, 7, 8, 9, 11, 15; **3**.11, 13^2, 15, 16^4; **4**.1, 12^4; **5**.2, 17; **6**.17, 18

2 Tim **1**.1, 3, 5^2, 9, 13^2, 15, 17; **2**.1^2, 7, 10, 20; **3**.1, 12, 14, 15, 16

Tit **1**.5, 9, 13; **2**.3, 7, 9, 10, 12; **3**.3, 5, 15

Phm .8, 10, 16^2, 20^2, 23

Heb **2**.8, 12; **3**.2, 5, 8^2, 11, 12, 15, 17; **4**.3, 5; **5**.6, 7; **6**.18; **7**.10; **8**.9, 13; **9**.2; **10**.3, 7, 22, 38; **11**.9, 34, 37; **12**.23; **13**.3, 18, 21

Jas **1**.1, 4, 6, 8, 9, 10, 23, 25, 27; **2**.2^2, 5, 10, 16; **3**.2, 13, 14, 18; **4**.1, 5, 16; **5**.5, 10, 14

1 Pet **1**.4, 5, 6, 15; **2**.6^2, 12, 24; **3**.15^2, 16, 19^2, 20; **4**.2, 3, 11; **5**.6, 10

2 Pet **1**.1, 2, 4, 12, 13, 19^2; **2**.3, 12^2, 13^2, 18; **3**.1, 11, 13, 16^2, 18

1 Jn **1**.5, 6, 7^2, 8, 10; **2**.4, 5^2, 6, 8^2, 9^2, 10^2, 11^2, 14, 15^2, 16, 24^4, 27^2, 28; **3**.5, 6, 9, 14, 15, 17, 18, 24^3; **4**.2, 3, 4^2, 9, 10, 12^2, 13^2, 15^2, 16^3, 17^2, 18(17), 18; **5**.10, 11, 19, 20^2

2 Jn .1, 2, 3, 7, 9^2

3 Jn .1

Jude .1, 20, 21

Rev **1**.4, 9, 10, 13, 15, 16^2; **2**.1^2, 7, 8, 12, 13, 18, 24; **3**.1, 4^2, 5, 7, 12, 14; **4**.1, 2^2, 4 *var. om.*; **5**.3, 13; **6**.5, 6; **7**.9, 14; **8**.1, 9, 13; **9**.6, 10, 11, 17, 19; **10**.2, 6^3, 7, 8, 9, 10; **11**.12, 13, 15, 19; **12**.1, 3, 7, 8, 10; **13**.6, 8; **14**.5, 6, 13, 14, 17; **15**.1, 5; **16**.3; **17**.3, 4; **18**.6, 7, 8, 22^3, 23^2, 24; **19**.1, 11, 17^2; **20**.6, 12, 13^2, 15; **21**.8, 10, 22, 27; **22**.[2†, 3, 18, 19

9. *on, at:* ἐπί (+dat.) EPI

except ^{a}+acc. ^{b}+gen.

Mt **18**.5; **24**.5; **27**.42^a, 43^a
Mk **1**.45; **4**.38^a; **7**.30^a; **8**.4^b; **9**.37, 39; **10**.[24‡^{a}; **11**.4^b; **13**.6
Lk **1**.47; **4**.27^b; **9**.48; **11**.22; **12**.54^b; **17**.34^b; **18**.9; **21**.8; **24**.47
Jn **8**.3‡, 4‡
Acts **2**.1^a, 26; **3**.11; **4**.17, 18; **5**.28, 40; **8**.28^b; **9**.42^a; **11**.17^a; **16**.31^a; **20**.9^b; **22**.19^a
Rom **1**.9(10)^b; **4**.24^a; **5**.2; **8**.20; **9**.33; **10**.11; **15**.12
1 Cor **9**.10^2
2 Cor **1**.4; **7**.7; **9**.14
Eph **1**.10, 16^b
Phil **1**.3
1 Th **1**.2^b; **3**.7
1 Tim **1**.16
Tit **1**.2
Phm .4^b
Heb **1**.2^b; **2**.13; **8**.1
1 Pet **2**.6
2 Pet **3**.3^b
1 Jn **3**.3
Jude .18^b
Rev **1**.20^b; **5**.13^b; **11**.8^b; **17**.8^a; **20**.1^a

10. *over, for the sake of:* ὑπέρ (+gen.) HYPER

2 Cor **7**.4, 14
1 Th **3**.2

11. *under:* ὑπό (+acc.) HYPO

Mk **4**.32
Jude .6

12. *in accordance with, for:* κατά (+acc.) KATA

Mt **1**.20; **2**.12, 13, 19, 22; **27**.19
Lk **2**.31; **15**.14
Acts **3**.13, 17, 22; **11**.1; **13**.1; **15**.23, 36; **17**.22; **24**.12; **26**.11
Rom **3**.2; **7**.22; **12**.6; **14**.15; **16**.5
1 Cor **2**.1; **7**.40; **14**.40; **16**.10
Col **3**.20^2; **4**.15
2 Th **2**.3
2 Tim **1**.8

Tit **1**.4; **3**.7
Phm .2
Heb **1**.10; **7**.5, 15; **9**.5; **11**.13
Jas **3**.9
13. *with:* μετά (+gen.) META
Jn **13**.8
Acts **15**.33
2 Th **3**.12
14. *about, concerning:* περί (+gen.) PERI
1 Th **4**.6
15. *to, with, against:* πρός (+acc.) PROS
Lk **22**.56
1 Cor **14**.12
2 Cor **7**.4
Eph **4**.14
Col **2**.23†
1 Th **1**.8
1 Tim **4**.7, 8
Heb **6**.11
1 Jn **5**.14

IN THAT
1. *that, because:* ὅτι HOTI
Rom **5**.8

IN THE HOUSE
1. *inside:* ἔσω ESŌ
Jn 20.26 his disciples were again in the house

IN THE WAY OF
1. *in accordance with, for:* κατά (+acc.) KATA
Eph. **6**.6

INASMUCH AS
1. *inasmuch as:* ἐπειδήπερ EPEIDĒPER*
Lk 1. 1 Inasmuch as many have undertaken
IDIOMATICALLY
a. Rom 11.13 Inasmuch then as I am an apostle to the Gentiles ἐφ' ὅσον μὲν οὖν εἰμι ἐγὼ ἐθνῶν ἀπόστολος [HOSOS]

INCENSE
1. *incense:* θυμίαμα THYMIAMA*
Lk 1.10 praying outside at the hour of incense
1.11 on the right side of the altar of incense
Rev 5. 8 with golden bowls full of incense
8. 3 he was given much incense to mingle
8. 4 the smoke of the incense rose
18.13 cinnamon, spice, incense, myrrh

INCENSE, ALTAR OF
1. *censer, altar of incense:* θυμιατήριον THYMIATĒRION*
Heb 9. 4 the golden altar of incense and the ark

INCENSE, BURN
1. *burn incense:* θυμιάω THYMIAŌ*
Lk 1. 9 to enter the temple of the Lord and burn i.

INCENTIVE
1. *encouragement:* παραμύθιον PARAMYTHION*
Phil 2. 1 if there is .. any incentive of love

INCITE
1. *urge on, incite:* παροτρύνω PAROTRYNŌ*
Acts 13.50 the Jews incited the devout women
2. *trouble, disturb:* ταράσσω TARASSŌ
Acts 17.13 Jews .. came .. inciting the crowds

INCLUDE
IDIOMATICALLY
a. Rom 1. 6 including yourselves ἐν οἷς ἐστε καὶ ὑμεῖς [EN; EIMI]

INCLUSION (*See* FULL INCLUSION)

INCOMPETENT
1. *unworthy, worthless:* ἀνάξιος ANAXIOS*
1 Cor 6. 2 are you incompetent to try trivial cases?

INCREASE (*See also* STRENGTH, INCREASE IN)
1. *increase, grow:* αὐξάνω (act. or pass.) AUXANŌ
Mk 4. 8 "increasing and yielding thirtyfold
Jn 3.30 "He must increase, but I must decrease[i]
Acts 6. 7 And the word of God increased
2 Cor 9.10 will .. i. the harvest of your righteousness[k]
10.15 our hope is that as your faith increases
Col 1.10 increasing in the knowledge of God
2. *collect besides* (pass.): ἐπαθροίζω EPATHROIZŌ*
Lk 11.29 When the crowds were increasing
3. *abound:* περισσεύω PERISSEUŌ
Acts 16. 5 they increased in numbers daily
2 Cor 4.15 as grace extends .. it may i. thanksgiving
4. *be more, cause to increase:* πλεονάζω PLEONAZŌ
Rom 5.20 Law came in, to increase the trespass; but where sin increased, grace abounded
Phil 4.17 the fruit which increases to your credit
1 Th 3.12 may the Lord make you increase
2 Th 1. 3 love .. for one another is increasing
5. *multiply, increase:* πληθύνω PLĒTHYNŌ
Acts 6. 1 disciples were increasing in number
6. *make progress, advance:* προκόπτω PROKOPTŌ
Lk 2.52 Jesus increased in wisdom and in stature[i]
7. *put to, add, continue:* προστίθημι PROSTITHĒMI
Lk 17. 5 The apostles said .. "Increase our faith!

INCREDIBLE
1. *unfaithful, incredible:* ἄπιστος APISTOS
Acts 26. 8 "Why is it thought incredible by any?

INCUR
1. *have, hold:* ἔχω ECHŌ
1 Tim 5.12 and so they incur condemnation
2. *gain:* κερδαίνω KERDAINŌ
Acts 27.21 "you .. should not have .. incurred .. loss
3. *take to oneself:* ἑαυτῷ λαμβάνειν LAMBANŌ [B.2.a.1]
Rom 13. 2 those who resist will incur judgment

INDEBTED, BE
1. *ought, owe:* ὀφείλω OPHEILŌ
Lk 11. 4 "forgive every one who is i. to us

INDEED
1. *true:* ἀληθής ALĒTHĒS [A.3.b.1]
Jn 6.55 "For my flesh is food indeed, and my blood is drink indeed
2. *truly:* ἀληθῶς ALĒTHŌS
Jn 1.47 "Behold, an Israelite indeed!
4.42 "we know that this is indeed the Savior
6.14 "This is indeed the prophet who is to come!
3. *but:* ἀλλά ALLA
Jn **16**.2
4. *so! indeed!:* δή DĒ
Mt 13.23 "he indeed bears fruit, and yields
5. *for:* γάρ GAR
Rom **2**.25; **5**.13; **8**.7
2 Cor **3**.10; **5**.2
Phil **2**.27
1 Th **4**.10
Heb **6**.16; **7**.28
6. *and, even, indeed:* καί KAI
7. *indeed, on the one hand:* μέν MEN
Mt **26**.41
Mk **14**.38
Lk **23**.41
Rom **2**.25; **14**.20
Col **2**.23
8. *rather:* μενοῦνγε MENOUNGE
Rom 10.18 have they not heard? Indeed they have
Phil 3. 8 Indeed I count everything as loss
9. *yes:* ναί NAI
Rev 14.13 "Blessed indeed," says the Spirit
10. *actually, really:* ὄντως ONTŌS
Lk 24.34 "The Lord has risen indeed!
Jn 8.36 "if the Son makes you free, you will be free i.
Gal 3.21 then righteousness would i. be by the law
1 Tim 6.19 take hold of the life which is life indeed
IDIOMATICALLY
a. Mt 13.14; Acts 28.26 " 'You shall indeed hear ἀκοῇ ἀκούσετε [AKOĒ; C.3]
b. Mt 13.14; Acts 28.26 " 'you shall indeed see βλέποντες βλέψετε [BLEPŌ; C.3]
c. Mk 4.12 "so that they may indeed see ἵνα βλέποντες βλέπωσιν [BLEPŌ; C.3]
d. Mk 4.12 "so that they .. may indeed hear ἵνα .. ἀκούοντες ἀκούωσιν [AKOUŌ; C.3]

INDEED, SINCE
1. *if indeed, since:* εἴπερ EIPER
2 Th 1. 6 since indeed God deems it just to repay

INDEPENDENT OF
1. *separately, apart from:* χωρίς CHŌRIS
1 Cor 11.11 (woman is not independent of man

INDESTRUCTIBLE
1. *indestructible:* ἀκατάλυτος AKATALYTOS*
Heb 7.16 by the power of an indestructible life

INDICATE
1. *disclose, show:* δηλόω DĒLOŌ
Heb 9. 8 By this the Holy Spirit indicates
12.27 "Yet once more," indicates the removal
1 Pet 1.11 what person or time was indicated
2. *indicate, report:* σημαίνω SĒMAINŌ
Acts 25.27 "unreasonable . . not to indicate the charges

INDIGNANT, BE
1. *be vexed:* ἀγανακτέω AGANAKTEŌ
Mt 20.24 they were indignant at the two brothers
21.15 chief priests and the scribes . . were i.
26. 8 when the disciples saw it, they were i.
Mk 10.14 when Jesus saw it he was indignant
10.41 they began to be indignant at James
Lk 13.14 the ruler of the synagogue, indignant
2. *set on fire:* πυρόω (pass.) PYROŌ
2 Cor 11.29 Who is made to fall, and I am not i.?

INDIGNANTLY, SAY
1. *be vexed:* ἀγανακτέω AGANAKTEŌ
Mk 14. 4 said to themselves indignantly, "Why?

INDIGNATION
1. *vexation:* ἀγανάκτησις AGANAKTĒSIS*
2 Cor 7.11 this godly grief has produced . . what i.!

INDISPENSABLE
1. *necessary:* ἀναγκαῖος ANAGKAIOS
1 Cor 12.22 parts . . which seem to be weaker are i.

INDISTINCT
1. *unseen, unclear:* ἄδηλος ADĒLOS
1 Cor 14. 8 if the bugle gives an indistinct sound

INDIVIDUALLY
1. *one's own:* ἴδιος IDIOS [A.3.b.1]
1 Cor 12.11 who apportions to each one individually
2. *by part:* ἐκ μέρους MEROS [B.1.a.1]
1 Cor 12.27 Now you are . . individually members of it
IDIOMATICALLY
a. Rom 12.5 and individually members one of another
τὸ δὲ καθ' εἷς ἀλλήλων μέλη [HEIS]

INDULGE (*See also* IMMORALITY, INDULGE IN)
1. *abundance, gratification:* πλησμονή PLĒSMONĒ [B.1.a.2]
Col [2.23 *serving only to indulge the flesh*†
IDIOMATICALLY
a. 2 Pet 2.10 those who indulge in the lust of defiling passion τοὺς ὀπίσω σαρκὸς ἐν ἐπιθυμίᾳ μιασμοῦ πορευομένους [POREUOMAI]
b. Jude .7 which . . indulged in unnatural lust ἀπελθοῦσαι ὀπίσω σαρκὸς ἑτέρας [APERCHOMAI]

INDULGENCE
1. *abundance, gratification:* πλησμονή PLĒSMONĒ*
Col 2.23 checking the indulgence of the flesh[e]†

INEFFECTIVE
1. *idle:* ἀργός ARGOS
2 Pet 1. 8 they keep you from being ineffective

INEXPRESSIBLE
1. *indescribable:* ἀνεκδιήγητος ANEKDIĒGĒTOS*
2 Cor 9.15 Thanks be to God for his i. gift!

INFANT
1. *infant:* βρέφος BREPHOS
Lk 18.15 they were bringing even infants to him
Acts 7.19 "forced our fathers to expose their infants

INFERIOR
1. *smaller, inferior:* ἐλάσσων ELASSŌN
Heb 7. 7 the inferior is blessed by the superior
2. *lack, fail:* ὑστερέω (pass. part.) HYSTEREŌ
1 Cor 12.24 the greater honor to the inferior part

INFERIOR TO, BE
1. *lack, fail:* ὑστερέω HYSTEREŌ
2 Cor 11. 5 I am not in the least inferior to these
12.11 For I was not at all inferior to these

INFIRMITY
1. *weakness, sickness:* ἀσθένεια ASTHENEIA
Mt 8.17 "He took our infirmities . . our diseases
Lk 5.15 gathered . . to be healed of their infirmities
8. 2 healed of evil spirits and infirmities
13.11 woman who had had a spirit of infirmity
13.12 "Woman, you are freed from your infirmity
2. *sickness:* μαλακία MALAKIA*
Mt 4.23 healing every disease and every infirmity
9.35 healing every disease and every infirmity
10. 1 to heal every disease and every infirmity

INFLICT
1. *give:* δίδωμι DIDŌMI
2 Th 1. 8 inflicting vengeance upon those
2. *bring upon, inflict:* ἐπιφέρω EPIPHERŌ
Rom 3. 5 That God is unjust to i. wrath on us?
3. *lay on, add:* ἐπιτίθημι EPITITHĒMI
Acts 16.23 when they had inflicted many blows

INFORM
1. *manifest, make clear:* ἐμφανίζω EMPHANIZŌ
Acts 23.22 "Tell no one that you have informed me
25. 2 principal men . . informed him against Paul
2. *instruct:* κατηχέω KATĒCHEŌ
Lk 1. 4 things of which you have been informed
3. *reveal, inform:* μηνύω MĒNYŌ
1 Cor 10.28 (consideration for the man who informed

INFORMATION, GIVE
1. *manifest:* ἐμφανίζω EMPHANIZŌ
Acts 25.15 "elders . . gave information about him

INFORMED, BE
1. *know:* οἶδα OIDA
Jude . 5 though you were once for all fully i.

INHABITANT
1. *dwell, settle:* κατοικέω (subst. part.) KATOIKEŌ
Acts 1.19 "(known to all the inhabitants of Jerusalem
4.16 "manifest to all the inhabitants of Jerusalem
Rev 13.12 makes . . its inhabitants worship the . . beast

INHERIT
1. *inherit, obtain:* κληρονομέω KLĒRONOMEŌ
Mt 5. 5 "for they shall inherit the earth
19.29 "who has left . . will . . inherit eternal life
25.34 " 'inherit the kingdom prepared for you
Mk 10.17 "what must I do to inherit eternal life?
Lk 10.25 "what shall I do to inherit eternal life?
18.18 "what shall I do to inherit eternal life?
1 Cor 6. 9 the unrighteous will not inherit
6.10 nor robbers will inherit the kingdom of God
15.50 blood cannot i. the kingdom of God, nor does the perishable i. the imperishable
Gal 4.30 "for the son of the slave shall not inherit
5.21 those who do such . . shall not inherit
Heb 6.12 those who . . inherit the promises
12.17 when he desired to inherit the blessing
2. *be an heir:* κληρονόμος εἶναι KLĒRONOMOS [A.6.a.3]
Rom 4.13 that they should inherit the world

INHERITANCE
1. *inheritance:* κληρονομία KLĒRONOMIA*
Mt 21.38 " 'let us kill him and have his inheritance
Mk 12. 7 " 'let us kill him, and the i. will be ours
Lk 12.13 "bid my brother divide the i.
20.14 " 'let us kill him, that the i. may be ours
Acts 7. 5 "yet he gave him no inheritance in it
20.32 "i. among all those who are sanctified
Gal 3.18 if the inheritance is by the law
Eph 1.14 the guarantee of our inheritance
1.18 his glorious inheritance in the saints
5. 5 no . . impure man . . has any inheritance
Col 3.24 from the Lord you will receive the i.
Heb 9.15 may receive the promised eternal i.
11. 8 place which he was to receive as an i.
1 Pet 1. 4 to an inheritance which is imperishable

2. *lot, share:* κλῆρος KLĒROS
Col 1.12 the inheritance of the saints in light

INHERITANCE, GIVE S. AS AN
1. *leave as an inheritance:* κατακληρονομέω KATAKLĒRONOMEŌ*
Acts 13.19 "he gave them their land as an i.

INHERITED FROM ONE'S FATHER
1. *inherited from one's father:* πατροπαράδοτος PATROPARADOTOS*
1 Pet 1.18 futile ways inherited from your fathers

INHUMAN
1. *without affection:* ἄστοργος ASTORGOS
2 Tim 3. 3 inhuman, implacable, slanderers

INIQUITY
1. *wrong, wrong done:* ἀδίκημα ADIKĒMA
Rev. 18. 5 "God has remembered her iniquities
2. *wrongdoing, injustice:* ἀδικία ADIKIA
Lk 13.27 " 'depart from me, all you workers of i.!
Acts 8.23 "you are . . in the bond of iniquity
2 Tim 2.19 "Let . . one . . depart from iniquity
Heb 8.12 "I will be merciful toward . . iniquities
3. *lawlessness:* ἀνομία ANOMIA
Mt 23.28 "you are full of hypocrisy and iniquity
Rom 4. 7 "Blessed are those whose iniquities
6.19 you once yielded . . to greater . . iniquity
2 Cor 6.14 what partnership have righteousness and i.?
Tit 2.14 gave himself . . to redeem us from . . iniquity

INJURE
1. *grieve, cause pain:* λυπέω LYPEŌ
Rom 14.15 If your brother is being injured

INJURY
1. *violence, insolence:* ὕβρις HYBRIS
Acts 27.10 "the voyage will be with injury
27.21 "you . . should not have . . incurred . . injury

INJUSTICE
1. *wrongdoing, injustice:* ἀδικία ADIKIA
Rom 9.14 Is there injustice on God's part?

INK
1. *black:* μέλας (subst. neut.) MELAS
2 Cor 3. 3 written not with ink but with the Spirit
2 Jn .12 I would rather not use paper and ink
3 Jn .13 I would rather not write with pen and ink

INMOST
1. *inside:* ἔσω ESŌ
Rom 7.22 For I delight . . in my inmost self

INN
1. *guest lodging:* κατάλυμα KATALYMA
Lk 2. 7 there was no place for them in the inn
2. *inn:* πανδοχεῖον PANDOCHEION*
Lk 10.34 "then he . . brought him to an inn

INNER
1. *inside:* ἔσω ESŌ
[a]subst.
2 Cor 4.16 [a]our inner nature is being renewed
Eph 3.16 through his Spirit in the inner man
2. *inner:* ἐσώτερος ESŌTEROS*
Acts 16.24 he put them into the inner prison
Heb 6.19 hope that enters into the inner shrine

INNKEEPER
1. *innkeeper:* πανδοχεύς PANDOCHEUS*
Lk 10.35 "two denarii[i] and gave them to the i.

INNOCENT
1. *pure:* ἀκέραιος AKERAIOS
Mt 10.16 "wise as serpents and innocent as doves
Phil 2.15 that you . . be blameless and innocent
2. *guiltless:* ἀθῷος ATHŌOS*
Mt 27. 4 "I have sinned in betraying innocent blood
27.24 "I am innocent of this man's blood[l]
3. *righteous, just:* δίκαιος DIKAIOS
Mt 23.35 "from the blood of innocent Abel
Lk 23.47 "Certainly this man was innocent!
4. *pure:* καθαρός KATHAROS
Acts 18. 6 "Your blood be upon your heads! I am i.
20.26 "I am innocent of the blood of all of you

INNUMERABLE
1. *countless:* ἀναρίθμητος ANARITHMĒTOS*
Heb 11.12 as the innumerable grains of sand
2. *myriad, ten thousand:* μυριάς (pl.+gen.) MYRIAS
Heb 12.22 to innumerable angels in festal gathering

INQUIRE
1. *search, inquire:* ἐραυνάω ERAUNAŌ
1 Pet 1.11 they inquired what person or time
2. *search out, examine:* ἐξεραυνάω EXERAUNAŌ*
1 Pet 1.10 prophets . . inquired about this salvation
3. *inquire about, learn:* πυνθάνομαι PYNTHANOMAI
Mt 2. 4 inquired . . where the Christ was to be born
Lk 18.36 he inquired what this meant
Acts 4. 7 they inquired, "By what power?
21.33 inquired who he was and what . . done
23.20 "as though they were going to inquire
4. *seek, desire:* ζητέω ZĒTEŌ
Acts 9.11 "go to the street called Straight, and i.
CONTEXTUALLY
Lk 1.62 inquiring what he would have him called

INQUIRY FOR, MAKE
1. *cross-question, ask:* διερωτάω DIERŌTAŌ*
Acts 10.17 having made inquiry for Simon's house

INSATIABLE
1. *insatiable* (?): ἀκατάπαστος AKATAPASTOS*
2 Pet 2.14 eyes full of adultery, insatiable for sin
Var. AKATAPAUSTOS
2. *unceasing:* ἀκατάπαυστος AKATAPAUSTOS*
Variant to: 2 Pet **2.14**

INSCRIBE
1. *inscribe:* ἐπιγράφω EPIGRAPHŌ
Rev 21.12 names of the . . tribes . . were inscribed
2. *write:* γράφω GRAPHŌ
Rev 19.12 a name inscribed which no one knows
19.16 a name inscribed, King of kings

INSCRIPTION
1. *inscription, title:* ἐπιγραφή EPIGRAPHĒ*
Mt 22.20 "Whose likeness and inscription is this?
Mk 12.16 "Whose likeness and inscription is this?
15.26 the inscription of the charge against him
Lk 20.24 "Whose likeness and inscription has it?
23.38 There was also an inscription over him[o]
2. *inscribe:* ἐπιγράφω EPIGRAPHŌ [B.2.a.1]
Acts 17.23 "I found also an altar with this inscription

INSCRUTABLE
1. *inscrutable:* ἀνεξιχνίαστος ANEXICHNIASTOS
Rom 11.33 how inscrutable his ways!

INSHORE
CONTEXTUALLY
Acts 27.13 sailed along Crete, close inshore

INSIDE
1. *inside:* ἐντός ENTOS
Mt 23.26 "first cleanse the inside of the cup
2. *inside:* ἔσω ESŌ
Mt 26.58 going inside he sat with the guards
Mk 15.16 the soldiers led him away inside the palace
Acts 5.23 "when we opened it we found no one inside
1 Cor 5.12 Is it not those inside the church?
3. *within, inside:* ἔσωθεν ESŌTHEN
[a]subst. neut.
Mt 23.25 "but inside they are full of extortion
Lk 11.39 [a]"inside you are full of extortion
11.40 [a]"Did not he . . make the inside also?
4. *in the midst of:* ἐν μέσῳ MESOS [B.1.a.1]
Lk 21.21 "let those who are inside the city depart

INSIGHT
1. *intelligence, understanding:* σύνεσις SYNESIS
Eph 3. 4 my insight into the mystery of Christ
2. *practical wisdom:* φρόνησις PHRONĒSIS
Eph 1. 9(8) he has made known to us in all . . insight

INSINCERELY WITH, ACT
1. *pretend to agree with:* συνυποκρίνομαι SYNYPOKRINOMAI*
Gal 2.13 with him the rest . . acted insincerely

INSINCERITY
1. *outward show, hypocrisy:* ὑπόκρισις HYPOKRISIS
Gal 2.13 Barnabas was carried away by their i.
1 Pet 2. 1 So put away all malice and . . i.

INSINCERITY, WITHOUT
1. *without hypocrisy:* ἀνυπόκριτος ANYPOKRITOS
Jas 3.17 wisdom from above is . . without . . i.

INSIST
1. *affirm, be positive:* διαβεβαιόομαι DIABEBAIOOMAI
[a]+περί
Tit 3. 8 [a]I desire you to insist on these things
2. *affirm confidently:* διϊσχυρίζομαι DIISCHYRIZOMAI*
Lk 22.59 after . . about an hour still another insisted
Acts 12.15 But she insisted that it was so
3. *will, wish:* θέλω THELŌ
Col 2.18 Let no one . . insisting on self-abasement
4. *seek, desire:* ζητέω ZĒTEŌ
1 Cor 13. 5 Love does not insist on its own way

INSOLENT
1. *violent man:* ὑβριστής (pred.) HYBRISTĒS
Rom 1.30 haters of God, insolent, haughty

INSPIRE
1. *operate, be effective:* ἐνεργέω ENERGEŌ
1 Cor 12. 6 it is the same God who inspires them all
12.11 inspired by one and the same Spirit
Col 1.29 the energy which he mightily inspires
CONTEXTUALLY
Mt 22.43 "David, inspired by the Spirit[t]†
Mk 12.36 "David himself, inspired by[z] the Spirit†
Lk 2.27 And inspired by the Spirit[h] he came†
1 Th 1. 6 with joy inspired by the Holy Spirit
1 Tim 1.18 inspired by them you may wage . . warfare

INSPIRED BY GOD
1. *inspired by God:* θεόπνευστος THEOPNEUSTOS*
2 Tim 3.16 All scripture is inspired by God[d]†

INSTANTLY
1. *immediately:* εὐθέως EUTHEŌS
Acts 22.29 So those . . withdrew from him instantly
2. *from that moment:* ἀπὸ τῆς ὥρας ἐκείνης HŌRA [B.1.a.1]
Mt 9.22 And instantly the woman was made well
15.28 And her daughter was healed instantly
17.18 and the boy was cured instantly

INSTEAD
INSTEAD OF
1. *opposite, instead of:* ἀντί (+gen.) ANTI
Lk 11.11 "will instead of a fish give him a serpent
Jas 4.15 Instead . . say, "If the Lord wills
2. *more, rather:* μᾶλλον MALLON
Mk 15.11 to . . release for them Barabbas instead
1 Cor [7.21 *make use of your present condition instead*†
Eph 5. 4 but instead let there be thanksgiving
5.11 instead expose ⟨unfruitful works⟩
3. *not:* μή MĒ
Tit 1.14 instead of giving heed to Jewish myths
4. *not, no:* οὐ OU
Heb **10.1**
5. *and not:* καὶ οὐχί OUCHI [B.3.b.4]
1 Cor 6. 1 before the unrighteous instead of the saints
6. *but, however, except:* πλήν PLĒN
Lk 12.31 "Instead, seek his[p] kingdom

INSTIGATE, SECRETLY
1. *throw under, suborn:* ὑποβάλλω HYPOBALLŌ*
Acts 6.11 Then they secretly instigated men

INSTINCT, BY
1. *naturally:* φυσικῶς PHYSIKŌS*
Jude .10 those things that they know by instinct

INSTINCT, CREATURE OF
1. *natural, physical:* φυσικός (subst. neut.) PHYSIKOS
2 Pet 2.12 like irrational animals, creatures of i.

INSTITUTE
1. *appoint, assign:* τάσσω TASSŌ
Rom 13. 1 those . . have been instituted by God

INSTITUTION
1. *founding, creation:* κτίσις KTISIS
1 Pet 2.13 Be subject . . to every human institution[f]

INSTRUCT
1. *negotiate, order:* χρηματίζω CHRĒMATIZŌ
Heb 8. 5 Moses . . was instructed by God
2. *appoint, direct:* διατάσσω DIATASSŌ
Mt 11. 1 finished instructing his twelve disciples
3. *instruct:* κατηχέω KATĒCHEŌ
Acts 18.25 instructed in the way of the Lord
Rom 2.18 because you are instructed in the law
1 Cor 14.19 in order to instruct others
4. *admonish, warn:* νουθετέω NOUTHETEŌ
Rom 15.14 brethren, . . able to instruct one another
5. *discipline, educate:* παιδεύω PAIDEUŌ
Acts 7.22 "Moses was instructed in all the wisdom
6. *make wise, instruct:* σοφίζω SOPHIZŌ
2 Tim 3.15 sacred writings which are able to instruct
7. *bring together, infer, teach:* συμβιβάζω SYMBIBAZŌ
1 Cor 2.16 "who has known . . the Lord so as to i. him?

INSTRUCTION
INSTRUCTIONS
1. *appoint, direct:* διατάσσω (subst. perf. pass. part.) DIATASSŌ
Acts 23.31 soldiers, according to their instructions
2. *teaching:* διδαχή DIDACHĒ
Heb 6. 2 with instruction[k] about ablutions[‡]
3. *teaching:* διδασκαλία DIDASKALIA
Rom 15. 4 written in former days . . for . . instruction
4. *command:* ἐντολή ENTOLĒ
Col 4.10 (you have received instructions
5. *admonition, warning:* νουθεσία NOUTHESIA
1 Cor 10.11 written down for our instruction
Eph 6. 4 bring them up in the . . instruction
6. *command, order:* παραγγελία PARAGGELIA
1 Th 4. 2 you know what instructions we gave
7. *give orders:* παραγγέλλω PARAGGELLŌ [B.2.a.2]
1 Cor 11.17 in the following instructions I do not
CONTEXTUALLY
1 Tim 3.14 I am writing these instructions to you
4. 6 If you put these instructions

INSTRUCTION, GIVE
INSTRUCTIONS, GIVE
1. *command:* διαστέλλω (mid.) DIASTELLŌ
Acts 15.24 "we gave them no instructions
2. *call to, exhort, comfort:* παρακαλέω PARAKALEŌ
Tit 1. 9 that he may be able to give instruction

INSTRUMENT
1. *tool, weapon:* ὅπλον HOPLON
Rom 6.13 Do not yield . . to sin as instruments . . , but yield . . as instruments of righteousness
2. *that which makes a sound:* τὸ φωνὴν διδόν PHŌNĒ [B.2.a.1]
1 Cor 14. 7 instruments, such as the flute or the harp
3. *vessel, tackle:* σκεῦος SKEUOS
Acts 9.15 "Go, for he is a chosen instrument of mine

INSUBORDINATE
1. *not made subject:* ἀνυπότακτος ANYPOTAKTOS
Tit 1. 6 not open to the charge of being . . i.
1.10 there are many insubordinate men

INSULT
1. *violence, insolence:* ὕβρις HYBRIS
2 Cor 12.10 I am content with weaknesses, insults
2. *be insolent:* εἶναι ὑβριστής HYBRISTĒS [B.2.a.1]
1 Tim 1.13 though I formerly . . insulted him
3. *say Raca:* εἰπεῖν ῥακά RHAKA* [B.2.a.1]
Mt 5.22 "whoever insults[j] his brother shall be liable†

INSURRECTION
1. *standing, uprising:* στάσις STASIS
Mk 15. 7 committed murder in the insurrection
Lk 23.19 thrown into prison for an insurrection
23.25 thrown into prison for insurrection

INTEGRITY
1. *incorruption, soundness:* ἀφθορία APHTHORIA*
Tit 2. 7 in your teaching show integrity

INTELLIGENCE, OF
1. *intelligent, wise:* συνετός SYNETOS
Acts 13. 7 Sergius Paulus, a man of intelligence

INTELLIGIBLE
1. *of good signs, clear:* εὔσημος EUSĒMOS*
1 Cor 14. 9 if you . . utter speech that is not intelligible

INTEND
1. *wish, will:* βούλομαι BOULOMAI
Acts 5.28 "i. to bring this man's blood upon us
12. 4 intending . . to bring him out to the people
2. *be about to:* μέλλω (+inf.) MELLŌ
Jn 7.35 "Where does this man intend to go?
7.35 "Does he intend to go to the Dispersion?
Acts 20. 7 intending to depart on the morrow
20.13 Assos, intending to take Paul aboard there
20.13 intending himself to go by land
25. 4 he himself intended to go there shortly
2 Pet 1.12 I intend always to remind you
3. *put forward, propose:* προτίθημι PROTITHĒMI
Rom 1.13 I have often intended to come to you
IDIOMATICALLY
a. 2 Cor 8.20 We intend that no one should blame us
στελλόμενοι τοῦτο, μή τις ἡμᾶς μωμήσηται [STELLŌ]
CONTEXTUALLY
1 Cor 16. 5 for I intend to pass through Macedonia

INTENSELY
1. *very much:* λίαν LIAN
Mk 9. 3 his garments became . . intensely white

INTENT
1. *thought:* ἐπίνοια EPINOIA*
Acts 8.22 "intent of your heart may be forgiven

INTENTION
1. *intent, thought:* ἔννοια ENNOIA
Heb 4.12 discerning the . . intentions of the heart

INTENTLY, LOOK
1. *look intently at:* ἀτενίζω ATENIZŌ
Acts 13. 9 Paul . . looked intently at him
14. 9 Paul, looking intently at him and seeing
23. 1 Paul, looking intently at the council
2. *see clearly, look intently:* διαβλέπω DIABLEPŌ
Mk 8.25 he looked intently and was restored

INTERCEDE
1. *appeal to, plead:* ἐντυγχάνω ENTYGCHANŌ
Rom 8.27 the Spirit intercedes for the saints
8.34 Jesus . . , who indeed intercedes for us[m]
2. *intercede:* ὑπερεντυγχάνω HYPERENTYGCHANŌ*
Rom 8.26 Spirit himself intercedes for us with sighs

INTERCESSION
1. *intercession:* ἔντευξις ENTEUXIS
1 Tim 2. 1 I urge . . prayers, intercessions

INTERCESSION, MAKE
1. *appeal to, plead:* ἐντυγχάνω ENTYGCHANŌ
Heb 7.25 he always lives to make intercession

INTEREST
1. *offspring, interest:* τόκος TOKOS*
Mt 25.27 " 'should have . . what was my own with i.
Lk 19.23 " 'I should have collected it with interest
CONTEXTUALLY
1 Cor 7.34 and his interests are divided
Phil 2. 4 each . . look not only to his own interests, but also to the interests of others
2.21 They all look after their own interests

INTERMEDIARY
1. *mediator, arbitrator:* μεσίτης MESITĒS
Gal 3.19 ordained by angels through an i.
3.20 an intermediary implies more than one

INTERPOSE
1. *mediate:* μεσιτεύω MESITEUŌ*
Heb 6.17 he interposed with an oath

INTERPRET
1. *differentiate, decide:* διακρίνω DIAKRINŌ
Mt 16. 3 "You know how to interpret . . the sky‡
2. *explain:* διερμηνεύω DIERMĒNEUŌ
Lk 24.27 he interpreted to them in all the scriptures
1 Cor 12.30 Do all speak with tongues? Do all i.?
14. 5 unless some one interprets
14.13 he . . should pray for the power to interpret
14.27 If any speak . . , let one interpret
3. *test, approve:* δοκιμάζω DOKIMAZŌ
Lk 12.56 "You know how to interpret the . . earth
12.56 "not . . how to interpret the present time
4. *combine, explain:* συγκρίνω SYGKRINŌ
1 Cor 2.13 the Spirit, interpreting spiritual truths[d]†

INTERPRET, ONE TO
1. *interpreter:* διερμηνευτής DIERMĒNEUTĒS*
1 Cor 14.28 if . . no one to i., let each . . keep silence

INTERPRETATION
1. *explanation:* ἐπίλυσις EPILYSIS*
2 Pet 1.20 a matter of one's own interpretation
2. *explanation, translation:* ἑρμηνεία HERMĒNEIA*
1 Cor 12.10 to another the interpretation of tongues
14.26 a lesson, a revelation, a tongue, or an i.

INTERVAL
1. *interval:* διάστημα DIASTĒMA*
Acts 5. 7 After an interval of about three hours
2. *separate:* διΐστημι DIISTĒMI [B.2.a.2]
Lk 22.59 after an interval of about an hour

INTO
1. *into, to, for:* εἰς (+acc.) EIS
Mt **2.**11; **3.**10, 12; **4.**1, 12, 18; **5.**29, 30; **6.**6, 13, 26, 30; **7.**19; **8.**12, 23, 31, 32², 33; **9.**1, 17², 38; **11.**7; **12.**11; **13.**2, 30², 36, 42, 47, 48, 50; **14.**15, 22, 32; **15.**11, 14, 17², 39; **16.**13; **17.**15², 22; **18.**8, 9; **20.**2, 4, 7; **21.**2, 21, 31; **22.**10, 13; **25.**21, 23, 30, 41, 46²; **26.**18, 41, 45, 52; **27.**6, 27, 53; **28.**11
Mk **1.**12, 14, 21; **2.**22; **4.**1, 8, 37; **5.**13, 18; **6.**36, 45, 51; **7.**15, 18, 33; **8.**10, 13; **9.**22², 31, 42, 45, 47; **11.**2, 11, 23; **12.**41; **14.**13, 20, 38, 41, 54, 68; **16.**12‡, 15‡, 19‡
Lk **1.**39, 79; **2.**15, 27; **3.**3, 9, 17; **4.**14, 37, 42; **5.**3, 4, 19, 37, 38; **6.**38, 39; **7.**24, 36; **8.**8, 22, 29, 31, 33, 37; **9.**12, 44²; **10.**1, 2, 10, 38; **11.**4; **12.**5, 28; **14.**5; **15.**13, 15; **16.**4, 9, 28; **17.**2; **18.**10; **19.**12, 30; **21.**1; **22.**10, 40, 46, 54; **23.**25, 42‡, 46; **24.**7, 26, 51‡
Jn **1.**9, **3.**4, 13, 17, 19, 22; **4.**8, 28, 38; **5.**7, 24; **6.**14, 17, 21, 24; **7.**14; **10.**36; **11.**7, 27, 52; **12.**24, 46; **13.**2, 3, 5, 27; **15.**6; **16.**13, 20, 21, 28; **17.**18²; **18.**11, 37; **19.**27; **20.**6, 11; **21.**3, 7
Acts **1.**10, 11³; **2.**20², 34; **3.**3; **5.**15; **7.**3, 4, 9, 15, 55; **8.**38; **9.**8; **11.**10; **12.**10; **13.**14; **14.**1; **16.**7, 10, 19, 23, 24, 34, 37; **17.**10; **18.**19; **19.**3², 22, 27, 29, 31; **21.**11, 26, 28, 29, 34, 37, 38; **22.**10, 11, 23, 24; **23.**10; **27.**30, 38; **28.**5, 16, 17
Rom **5.**12; **6.**3², 4; **8.**15; **10.**6, 7; **11.**24
1 Cor **1.**9; **10.**2; **12.**13; **14.**9
2 Cor **7.**5, 9; **12.**3(4)
Gal **1.**17, 21; **3.**27; **4.**6
Eph **2.**21; **4.**9, 15
1 Th **2.**12
1 Tim **1.**6, 15; **3.**6, 7; **6.**7, 9²
2 Tim **3.**6
Heb **1.**6; **6.**19; **8.**10; **9.**6, 7, 12, 24²; **10.**5, 31; **13.**11
Jas **1.**25; **2.**2, 6; **3.**3; **4.**13
1 Pet **1.**12; **2.**9; **3.**22
2 Pet **1.**11
1 Jn **3.**14; **4.**1, 9
2 Jn .7, 10
Jude .4
Rev **2.**10, 22; **8.**8; **9.**9; **11.**6; **12.**6, 14; **14.**19; **16.**3, 4, 19; **17.**3, 17; **18.**21; **19.**20; **20.**3, 10, 14, 15; **21.**24, 26
2. *in, at, by:* ἐν (+dat.) EN
Jn **3.**35; [**5.**4‡
Acts **22.**17
Rom **5.**5
2 Cor **8.**16
Eph **3.**4
Rev **14.**10

3. *on, at:* ἐπί (+acc.) EPI
Lk **19.**4, 23
Acts **7.**23
2 Tim **4.**4
Rev **16.**17

INTRODUCE
1. *introduction:* ἐπεισαγωγή EPEISAGŌGĒ* [A.1.a]
Heb 7.19 a better hope is introduced

INTRODUCED, BE
1. *come to be, happen, be:* γίνομαι GINOMAI
Acts 24. 3 "by your provision . . reforms are introduced

INVALID
1. *be weak, be sickly:* ἀσθενέω (subst. part.) ASTHENEŌ
Jn 5. 3 In these lay a multitude of invalids

INVENTOR
1. *contriver, inventor:* ἐφευρετής EPHEURETĒS*
Rom 1.30 inventors of evil, disobedient to parents

INVEST
1. *throw, put:* βάλλω BALLŌ
Mt 25.27 " 'you ought to have invested my money
2. *put around, put on:* περιτίθημι PERITITHĒMI
1 Cor 12.23 we invest with the greater honor

INVISIBLE
1. *unseen:* ἀόρατος AORATOS
Col 1.15 He is the image of the invisible God
1.16 in him all things were created, . . visible and i.
1 Tim 1.17 the King of ages, immortal, invisible
Heb 11.27 he endured as seeing him who is invisible

INVISIBLE NATURE
1. *unseen:* ἀόρατος (subst. neut. pl.) AORATOS
Rom 1.20 invisible nature, namely, his . . power

INVITE
1. *call, name:* καλέω KALEŌ
Mt 22. 3 "those who were invited to the marriage
22. 4 " 'Tell those who are invited, Behold
22. 8 " 'but those invited were not worthy
22. 9 " 'Go . . and invite . . as many as you find
Lk 7.39 the Pharisee who had invited him
14. 7 a parable to those who were invited
14. 8 "When . . invited . . to a marriage feast
14. 8 "lest a more eminent . . be invited
14. 9 "he who invited you both will come
14.10 "when . . invited, . . sit in the lowest place
14.12 said . . to the man who had invited him
14.13 "when you give a feast, invite the poor
14.16 "A man once . . invited many
14.17 "to say to those who had been invited
14.24 " 'none . . who were invited shall taste
Jn 2. 2 Jesus also was invited to the marriage
1 Cor 10.27 If one of the unbelievers invites you
Rev 19. 9 "Blessed are those who are invited
2. *call to, exhort, comfort:* παρακαλέω PARAKALEŌ
Acts 8.31 he invited Philip to come up and sit
28.14 found brethren, and were invited to stay
3. *call, make a sound:* φωνέω PHŌNEŌ
Lk 14.12 "do not invite your friends

INVITE IN RETURN
1. *invite in return:* ἀντικαλέω ANTIKALEŌ*
Lk 14.12 "lest they also invite you in return

INVOKE (*See also* BLESSINGS, INVOKE; CURSE ON ONESELF, INVOKE A)

INVOKE AS
1. *call, surname:* ἐπικαλέω EPIKALEŌ
[a]mid.
Jas 2. 7 the honorable name . . invoked over you[o]
1 Pet 1.17 [a]if you invoke as Father him who judges

INVOLVE
CONTEXTUALLY
Heb 9.16 For where a will[u] is involved

INWARDLY
1. *within, inside:* ἔσωθεν ESŌTHEN
Mt 7.15 "false prophets, who . . i. are ravenous wolves
2. *in himself:* ἐν ἑαυτῷ HEAUTOU [B.1.a.1]
Acts 10.17 while Peter was inwardly perplexed
Rom 8.23 we . . groan inwardly as we wait
3. *in secret:* ἐν τῷ κρυπτῷ KRYPTOS [B.1.a.1]
Rom 2.29 He is a Jew who is one inwardly

IOTA
1. *the letter iota, jot:* ἰῶτα IŌTA*
Mt 5.18 "not an iota . . will pass from the law

IRKSOME
1. *idle, troublesome:* ὀκνηρός OKNĒROS
Phil 3. 1 To write the same things . . is not irksome

IRON
1. *iron:* σίδηρος SIDĒROS*
Rev 18.12 costly wood, bronze, iron and marble
2. *iron, made of iron:* σιδηροῦς SIDĒROUS*
Acts 12.10 they came to the iron gate
Rev 2.27 " 'he shall rule them with a rod of iron
9. 9 they had scales like iron breastplates
12. 5 to rule all the nations with a rod of iron
19.15 he will rule them with a rod of iron

IRRATIONAL
1. *absurd:* ἄλογος ALOGOS
2 Pet 2.12 like i. animals, creatures of instinct
Jude .10 know by instinct as irrational animals do

IRRELIGION
1. *ungodliness, impiety:* ἀσέβεια ASEBEIA
Tit 2.12 training us to renounce irreligion

IRRELIGIOUS
1. *unhallowed, profane:* βέβηλος BEBĒLOS
Heb 12.16 that no one be immoral or irreligious

IRREPROACHABLE
1. *blameless:* ἀνέγκλητος ANEGKLĒTOS
Col 1.22 blameless and irreproachable before him

IRREVOCABLE
1. *not to be regretted:* ἀμεταμέλητος AMETAMELĒTOS
Rom 11.29 gifts and the call of God are irrevocable

IRRITABLE, BE
1. *urge, irritate:* παροξύνω (pass.) PAROXYNŌ
1 Cor 13. 5 Love . . is not irritable or resentful

ISAAC: Ἰσαάκ 'īzik
Mt 1. 2 Abraham was the father of Isaac, and Isaac the father of Jacob
8.11 "many will . . sit at table with Abraham, I.
22.32 " 'I am . . the God of Isaac
Mk 12.26 " 'I am . . the God of Isaac
Lk 3.34 Jacob, the son of Isaac
13.28 "when you see Abraham and Isaac
20.37 "God of Abraham and the God of I.
Acts 3.13 "God of Abraham and of I. and of Jacob
7. 8 "so Abraham became the father of Isaac, . . and Isaac became the father of Jacob
7.32 " 'the God of Abraham and of Isaac
Rom 9. 7 "Through Isaac shall your descendants be
9.10 when Rebecca had conceived . . by . . Isaac
Gal 4.28 we,[j] . . like Isaac, are children of promise
Heb 11. 9 living in tents with Isaac and Jacob
11.17 By faith Abraham . . offered up Isaac
11.18 "Through Isaac shall your descendants be
11.20 By faith Isaac invoked future blessings
Jas 2.21 justified by works, when he offered . . I.

ISAIAH: Ἠσαΐας ī'zāə
Mt 3. 3 who was spoken of by the prophet Isaiah
4.14 what was spoken by the prophet Isaiah
8.17 what was spoken by the prophet Isaiah
12.17 to fulfil what was spoken by the prophet I.
13.14 "With them . . is fulfilled the prophecy of I.
[13.35 what was spoken by the prophet *Isaiah*‡
15. 7 "Well did Isaiah prophesy of you
Mk 1. 2 As it is written in Isaiah the prophet[b]‡
7. 6 "Well did I. prophesy of you hypocrites
Lk 3. 4 As it is written in . . Isaiah the prophet
4.17 given to him the book of the prophet I.
Jn 1.23 " 'Make straight the way . . ,' as . . Isaiah said
12.38 that the word spoken by . . I. . . be fulfilled

Jn 12.39 they could not believe. For Isaiah . . said
12.41 Isaiah said this because he saw his glory
Acts 8.28 in his chariot, he was reading . . Isaiah
8.30 Philip ran to him, and heard him reading I.
28.25 "saying to your fathers through Isaiah
Rom 9.27 Isaiah cries out concerning Israel
9.29 as I. predicted, "If the Lord of hosts
10.16 Isaiah says, "Lord, who has believed?
10.20 I. is so bold as to say, "I have been found
15.12 Isaiah says, "The root of Jesse shall come

ISCARIOT: Ἰσκαριώθ, Ἰσκαριώτης is'kariət
Mt 10. 4 Judas Iscariot, who betrayed him
26.14 Judas Iscariot, went to the chief priests
Mk 3.19 Judas Iscariot, who betrayed him
14.10 Judas Iscariot, who was one of the twelve
Lk 6.16 Judas Iscariot, who became a traitor
22. 3 Satan entered into Judas called Iscariot
Jn 6.71 Judas the son of Simon Iscariot
12. 4 Judas Iscariot, one of his disciples
13. 2 put it into the heart of Judas I.
13.26 gave it to Judas, the son of Simon I.
14.22 Judas (not Iscariot) said to him

ISLAND
1. *island:* νῆσος NĒSOS*
Acts 13. 6 When they had gone through the whole i.
27.26 "But we shall have to run on some island
28. 1 learned that the island was called Malta
28. 7 chief man of the island, named Publius
28. 9 the rest of the people on the island
28.11 a ship which had wintered in the island
Rev 1. 9 I John . . was on the island called Patmos
6.14 every mountain and island was removed
16.20 And every island fled away

ISLAND, SMALL
1. *small island:* νησίον NĒSION*
Acts 27.16 And running under the lee of a small island

ISRAEL: Ἰσραήλ 'izrēəl (*See also* ISRAELITE[a])
[a]ἄνδρες Ἰσραηλῖται *Israelite men!*
Mt 2. 6 " 'a ruler who will govern my people Israel
2.20 "take the child and . . go to the land of I.
2.21 he rose and took the child . . to the land of I.
8.10 "not even[s] in Israel have I found such faith
9.33 "Never was anything like this seen in I.
10. 6 "rather to the lost sheep of the house of I.
10.23 "not . . through all the towns of Israel
15.24 "only to the lost sheep of the house of I.
15.31 they glorified the God of Israel
19.28 "judging the twelve tribes of Israel
27. 9 "price . . set by some of the sons of Israel
27.42 "He is the King of I.; let him come down
Mk 12.29 "The first is, 'Hear, O I.: The Lord our God
15.32 "Let the Christ, the King of I., come down
Lk 1.16 "he will turn many of the sons of Israel
1.54 "He has helped his servant Israel
1.68 "Blessed be the Lord God of Israel
1.80 till the day of his manifestation to I.
2.25 looking for the consolation of Israel
2.32 "for glory to thy people Israel
2.34 "set for the fall and rising of many in I.
4.25 "there were many widows in Israel
4.27 "there were many lepers in Israel
7. 9 "not even in I. have I found such faith
22.30 "sit on thrones judging the . . tribes of I.
24.21 "hoped that he was the one to redeem I.
Jn 1.31 "baptizing . . , that he might be revealed to I.
1.49 "You are the King of Israel!
3.10 "a teacher of I., and . . do not understand?
12.13 "Blessed is he who comes . . , the King of I.!
Acts 1. 6 "at this time restore the kingdom to I.?
2.22 [a]"Men of Israel, hear these words
2.36 "Let all the house of I. . . know assuredly
3.12 [a]"Men of Israel, why do you wonder?
4.10 "be it known . . to all the people of I.
4.27 "the Gentiles and the peoples of Israel
5.21 the council and all the senate of I.
Acts 5.31 "God exalted him . . to give repentance to I.
5.35 [a]"Men of Israel, take care what you do
7.23 "to visit his brethren, the sons of Israel
7.42 " 'Did you offer to me . . beasts . . , Israel?
9.15 "he is . . to carry my name before . . sons of I.
10.36 "You know the word which he sent to I.
13.16 [a]"Men of Israel, and you that fear God
13.17 "The God of this people Israel
13.23 "God has brought to Israel a Savior
13.24 "repentance to all the people of Israel
21.28 [a]"Men of Israel, help! This is the man
28.20 "since it is because of the hope of Israel
Rom 9. 6 For not all who are descended from Israel belong to Israel
9.27 Isaiah cries out concerning Israel: "Though . . Israel be as the sand of the sea
9.31 Israel who pursued the righteousness
10.19 Again I ask, did Israel not understand?
10.21 But of Israel he says, "All day long
11. 2 how he pleads with God against Israel
11. 7 Israel failed to obtain what it sought
11.25 a hardening has come upon part of Israel
11.26 and so all Israel will be saved
1 Cor 10.18 Consider the people of Israel[a]
Gal 6.16 Peace and mercy be . . upon the I. of God
Eph 2.12 alienated from the commonwealth of I.
Phil 3. 5 of the people of I., . . tribe of Benjamin
Heb 8. 8 "a new covenant with the house of I.
8.10 "the covenant . . with the house of Israel
Rev 2.14 " 'a stumbling block before the sons of I.
7. 4 out of every tribe of the sons of Israel
21.12 names of the twelve tribes of the sons of I.
CONTEXTUALLY
Rom 11.11 to the Gentiles, so as to make I. jealous

ISRAELITE: Ἰσραηλίτης (*See also* ISRAEL[a])
[a]ὁ υἱὸς Ἰσραήλ *son of Israel*
Jn 1.47 "an Israelite . . in whom is no guile!
Acts 7.37 [a]"Moses who said to the Israelites
Rom 9. 4 Israelites, . . to them belong the sonship
11. 1 By no means! I myself am an Israelite
2 Cor 3. 7 [a]Israelites could not look at Moses' face
3.13 [a]so that the Israelites might not see
11.22 Are they Israelites? So am I
Heb 11.22 [a]mention of the exodus of the Israelites

ISSACHAR: Ἰσσαχάρ 'isəkər
Rev 7. 7 twelve thousand of the tribe of Issachar

ISSUE
1. *go out:* ἐκπορεύομαι EKPOREUOMAI
Rev 1.16 from his mouth issued a sharp . . sword
4. 5 From the throne issue flashes of lightning
9.17 sulphur issued from their mouths
9.18 sulphur issuing from their mouths
19.15 From his mouth issues a sharp sword
CONTEXTUALLY
1 Tim 1. 5 aim . . is love that issues from a pure heart
Rev 16.13 issuing from the mouth of the dragon

ISSUE FROM
1. *go out:* ἐξέρχομαι EXERCHOMAI
Rev 19.21 the sword that issues from his mouth

IT
1. *self; he, she, it:* αὐτός AUTOS
2. *who, which, what:* ὅς HOS
Mt **13.**32, 48
Acts **7.**45; **10.**12; **11.**6; **27.**17
Phil **3.**20
1 Tim **6.**21
2 Tim **2.**17
Heb **6.**8
1 Pet **5.**12
3. *this:* οὗτος HOUTOS
Mt **12.**11
Mk **5.**32
Jn **14.**13

Heb **11.2**
4. *anyone, any:* τὶς TIS II
Acts **5.2**
Rom **14.14**
1 Cor **11.18**

ITALIAN: Ἰταλικός
Acts 10. 1 what was known as the Italian Cohort

ITALY: Ἰταλία 'itəlē II,B-2
Acts 18. 2 Aquila, . . lately come from Italy
27. 1 it was decided that we should sail for Italy
27. 6 a ship of Alexandria sailing for Italy
Heb 13.24 Those who come from I. send . . greetings

ITCH
1. *scratch:* κνήθω (pass.) KNĒTHŌ*
2 Tim 4. 3 people . . , having itching ears

ITINERANT
1. *go about:* περιέρχομαι (part.) PERIERCHOMAI
Acts 19.13 some of the itinerant Jewish exorcists

ITS OWN
1. *himself:* ἑαυτοῦ HEAUTOU
1 Cor 13. 5 Love does not insist on its own way
2. *one's own:* ἴδιος IDIOS
Lk 6.44 "each tree is known by its own fruit
Jn 15.19 "the world would love its own
1 Cor 15.38 to each kind of seed its own body

ITS OWN ACCORD, OF
1. *acting of one's own will:* αὐτόματος AUTOMATOS
Acts 12.10 It opened to them of its own accord

ITSELF
1. *himself:* ἑαυτοῦ HEAUTOU
Mt 6.34 "for tomorrow will be anxious for itself
12.25 "Every kingdom divided against itself
12.25 "no city or house divided against itself
Mk 3.24 "If a kingdom is divided against itself
3.25 "if a house is divided against itself
Lk 11.17 "Every kingdom divided against itself
Jn 15. 4 "the branch cannot bear fruit by itself
Rom 14.14 nothing is unclean in itself
Eph 4.16 makes bodily growth and upbuilds itself
Jas 2.17 faith by itself, if it has no works, is dead

ITSELF, OF
1. *acting of one's own will:* αὐτόματος AUTOMATOS
Mk 4.28 "The earth produces of itself

ITURAEA: Ἰτουραία ˌityü'rēə I,D-2
Lk 3. 1 Philip tetrarch of the region of Ituraea

IVORY, OF
1. *of ivory:* ἐλεφάντινος ELEPHANTINOS*
Rev 18.12 cargo of gold . . , all articles of ivory

J

JACINTH
1. *hyacinth:* ὑάκινθος HYAKINTHOS*
Rev 21.20 the eleventh jacinth

JACOB: Ἰακώβ 'jākəb
Mt 1. 2 Isaac the father of Jacob, and Jacob the father of Judah
1.15 Matthan the father of Jacob
1.16 J. the father of Joseph the husband of Mary
8.11 "with . . Jacob in the kingdom of heaven
22.32 " 'God of Isaac, and the God of Jacob
Mk 12.26 " 'the God of Isaac, and the God of Jacob
Lk 1.33 "he will reign over the house of Jacob
3.34 ⟨Judah⟩ the son of Jacob, . . son of Isaac
13.28 "when you see Abraham . . Isaac . . Jacob
20.37 "the God of Isaac and the God of Jacob
Jn 4. 5 the field that J. gave to his son Joseph
Jn 4. 6 Jacob's well was there
4.12 "Are you greater than our father Jacob?
Acts 3.13 "God of Abraham and of Isaac and of J.
7. 8 "Isaac became the father of Jacob, and Jacob of the twelve patriarchs
7.12 "Jacob heard that there was grain in Egypt
7.14 "Joseph sent and called to him Jacob
7.15 "Jacob went down into Egypt
7.32 " 'God of Abraham . . of Isaac and of J.
7.46 "to find a habitation for the God of J.
Rom 9.13 As it is written, "Jacob I loved
11.26 "he will banish ungodliness from Jacob
Heb 11. 9 living in tents with Isaac and Jacob
11.20 By faith Isaac invoked . . blessings on J.
11.21 Jacob . . blessed . . the sons of Joseph

JAILER
1. *jailer, torturer:* βασανιστής BASANISTĒS*
Mt 18.34 "lord delivered him to the jailers[h]†
2. *jailer:* δεσμοφύλαξ DESMOPHYLAX*
Acts 16.23 charging the jailer to keep them safely
16.27 When the jailer woke and saw
16.36 the jailer reported the words to Paul

JAIRUS: Ἰάϊρος jā'īrəs, 'jīrəs
Mk 5.22 one of the rulers of the synagogue, J.
Lk 8.41 And there came a man named Jairus

JAMBRES: Ἰαμβρῆς 'jambrēz
2 Tim 3. 8 As Jannes and Jambres opposed Moses

JAMES: Ἰάκωβος 'jāmz
1. son of Zebedee
Mt 4.21 he saw . . J. the son of Zebedee and John
10. 2 J. the son of Zebedee, . . John his brother
17. 1 Jesus took . . Peter and James and John
Mk 1.19 he saw J. the son of Zebedee and John
1.29 he[e] . . entered the house . . with James
3.17 James the son of Zebedee and John the brother of James
5.37 no one . . except Peter and James and John the brother of James
9. 2 Jesus took with him Peter and J. and John
10.35 James and John, the sons of Zebedee
10.41 to be indignant at James and John
13. 3 James and John . . asked him privately
14.33 he took with him Peter and James
Lk 5.10 so also were J. and John, sons of Zebedee
6.14 James and John, and Philip
8.51 no one . . except Peter and John and J.
9.28 he took with him . . John and James
9.54 his disciples James and John saw it
Acts 1.13 John and James and Andrew
12. 2 He killed James the brother of John
2. son of Alphaeus
Mt 10. 3 James the son of Alphaeus
Mk 3.18 Thomas, and James the son of Alphaeus
Lk 6.15 Thomas, and James the son of Alphaeus
Acts 1.13 Matthew, James the son of Alphaeus
3. son of Mary
Mt 27.56 Mary the mother of James and Joseph
Mk 15.40 Mary the mother of James the younger
16. 1 Mary the mother of James
Lk 24.10 Joanna and Mary the mother of James
4. father of Judas
Lk 6.16 Judas the son of James
Acts 1.13 and Judas the son of James
5. brother of Jesus
Mt 13.55 "are not his brothers James and Joseph?
Mk 6. 3 "the son of Mary and brother of James
Acts 12.17 "Tell this to James and to the brethren
15.13 James replied, "Brethren, listen
21.18 Paul went in with us to James
1 Cor 15. 7 Then he appeared to James
Gal 1.19 I saw none . . except J. the Lord's brother
2. 9 J. and Cephas . . , reputed to be pillars
2.12 before certain men came from James
Jas 1. 1 James, a servant of God and of the Lord
Jude . 1 Jude, a . . brother of James

JANNAI: 'Ιανναί 'janī, 'janā,ī
Lk 3.24 Melchi, the son of J., the son of Joseph

JANNES: 'Ιάννης 'janēz
2 Tim 3. 8 Jannes and Jambres opposed Moses

JAR
1. *water jar, vessel:* ὑδρία HYDRIA
Jn 2. 6 Now six stone jars were standing there
2. 7 Jesus said . . "Fill the jars with water
2. *earthenware jar:* κεράμιον KERAMION*
Mk 14.13 "man carrying a j. of water will meet you
Lk 22.10 "man carrying a j. of water will meet you

JAR, WATER
1. *water jar, vessel:* ὑδρία HYDRIA
Jn 4.28 So the woman left her water jar

JARED: 'Ιάρετ 'jerəd
Lk 3.37 Enoch, the son of Jared

JASON: 'Ιάσων 'jāsᵊn
Acts 17. 5 the Jews . . attacked the house of Jason
17. 6 dragged Jason and some of the brethren
17. 7 "Jason has received them
17. 9 when they had taken security from Jason
Rom 16.21 so do Lucius and Jason and Sosipater

JASPER
1. *jasper:* ἴασπις IASPIS*
Rev 4. 3 he who sat there appeared like jasper
21.11 glory of God, its radiance . . like a jasper
21.18 The wall was built of jasper
21.19 the first was jasper, the second sapphire

JEALOUS
1. *strive after, be jealous:* ζηλόω (part.) ZĒLOŌ
Acts 7. 9 "the patriarchs, jealous of Joseph

JEALOUS, BE
1. *strive after, be jealous:* ζηλόω ZĒLOŌ
Acts 17. 5 But the Jews were jealous
1 Cor 13. 4 love is not jealous or boastful

JEALOUS, MAKE
1. *provoke to jealousy:* παραζηλόω PARAZĒLOŌ
Rom 10.19 "I will make you jealous of those
11.11 to the Gentiles, so as to make Israel j.
11.14 in order to make my fellow Jews jealous

JEALOUSLY
1. *envy:* φθόνος PHTHONOS [B.1.a.1]
Jas 4. 5 "He yearns jealously over the spirit

JEALOUSY
1. *zeal, jealousy:* ζῆλος ZĒLOS
Acts 5.17 high priest rose up . . filled with jealousy
13.45 the Jews . . were filled with jealousy
Rom 13.13 let us conduct ourselves . . not in . . j.
1 Cor 3. 3 while there is jealousy and strife among you
2 Cor 11. 2 I feel a divine jealousy for you
12.20 jealousy, anger, selfishness, slander
Gal 5.20 strife, jealousy, anger, selfishness
Jas 3.14 if you have bitter j. . . in your hearts
3.16 where jealousy and selfish ambition exist

JEALOUSY, PROVOKE TO
1. *provoke to jealousy:* παραζηλόω PARAZĒLOŌ
1 Cor 10.22 Shall we provoke the Lord to jealousy?

JECHONIAH: 'Ιεχονίας ,jekə'nīə
Mt 1.11 Josiah the father of Jechoniah
1.12 Jechoniah was the father of Shealtiel[d]

JEHOSHAPHAT: 'Ιωσαφάτ ji'häs(h)ə,fat
Mt 1. 8 Asa[b] the father of Jehoshaphat, and Jehoshaphat the father of Joram

JEPHTHAH: 'Ιεφθάε 'jefthə
Heb 11.32 time would fail me to tell of . . J.

JEREMIAH: 'Ιερεμίας ,jerə'mīə
Mt 2.17 fulfilled what was spoken by . . Jeremiah
16.14 "others say Elijah, and others Jeremiah
27. 9 fulfilled what had been spoken by . . J.

JERICHO: 'Ιεριχώ 'jerə,kō I,C-5
Mt 20.29 as they went out of Jericho, a great crowd
Mk 10.46 they came to Jericho; and as he was leaving Jericho with his disciples
Lk 10.30 "going down from Jerusalem to Jericho
18.35 As he drew near to J., a blind man
19. 1 He entered Jericho and was passing through
Heb 11.30 By faith the walls of Jericho fell down

JERUSALEM: jə'rüs(ə)ləm I,C-5; II,G-4
1. *Jerusalem:* 'Ιεροσόλυμα
Mt 2. 1 wise men from the East came to J.
2. 3 he was troubled, and all J. with him
3. 5 Then went out to him Jerusalem
4.25 great crowds followed him from . . J.
5.35 ⟨"Do not swear at all, either⟩ by Jerusalem
15. 1 Pharisees and scribes came to Jesus from J.
16.21 he must go to J. and suffer many things
20.17 as Jesus was going up to Jerusalem
20.18 "Behold, we are going up to Jerusalem
21. 1 when they drew near to Jerusalem
21.10 when he entered J. . . the city was stirred
Mk 3. 8 ⟨multitude followed from⟩ Jerusalem
3.22 "scribes who came down from J.
7. 1 scribes, who had come from Jerusalem
10.32 they were on the road, going up to J.
10.33 "Behold, we are going up to J.
11. 1 when they drew near to Jerusalem
11.11 he entered J., and went into the temple
11.15 they came to J. And he entered the temple
11.27 they came again to Jerusalem
15.41 women who came up with him to Jerusalem
Lk 2.22 they brought him up to Jerusalem
13.22 He went . . journeying toward Jerusalem
19.28 he went on ahead, going up to J.
23. 7 Herod, who was himself in Jerusalem
Jn 1.19 the Jews sent priests . . from Jerusalem
2.13 Jesus went up to Jerusalem
2.23 he was in Jerusalem at the Passover feast
4.20 "you say that in J. . . men ought to worship
4.21 "neither on this mountain nor in J.
4.45 having seen all that he had done in J.
5. 1 there was a feast . . and Jesus went up to J.
5. 2 in Jerusalem . . a pool, . . Bethzatha[j]
10.22 the feast of the Dedication at J.
11.18 Bethany was near Jerusalem
11.55 many went up from the country to J.
12.12 crowd . . heard that Jesus was coming to J.
Acts 1. 4 he charged them not to depart from J.
8. 1 persecution arose against the church in J.
8.14 when the apostles at Jerusalem heard
8.25 they returned to Jerusalem, preaching
11.27 prophets came down from J. to Antioch
13.13 John left . . and returned to Jerusalem
15. 4 When they came to Jerusalem
16. 4 apostles and elders who were at J.
19.21 Paul resolved . . to . . go to Jerusalem
20.16 for he was hastening to be at Jerusalem
21. 4 they told Paul not to go on to Jerusalem
21.15 we made ready and went up to J.
21.17 When we had come to Jerusalem
25. 1 after three days he went up to J.
25. 7 Jews who had gone down from Jerusalem
25. 9 "Do you wish to go up to Jerusalem?
25.15 "when I was at Jerusalem
25.20 "I asked whether he wished to go to J.
25.24 "Jewish people petitioned me . . at J.
26. 4 "My manner of life . . at Jerusalem
26.10 "And I did so in Jerusalem
26.20 "first to those at Damascus, then at J.
28.17 "yet I was delivered prisoner from J.
Gal 1.17 nor did I go up to Jerusalem to those
1.18 Then after three years I went up to J.
2. 1 after fourteen years I went up again to J.
2. *Jerusalemite:* 'Ιεροσολυμίτης
Mk 1. 5 Judea, and all the people of Jerusalem
Jn 7.25 the people of Jerusalem therefore said

3. *Jerusalem:* Ἰερουσαλήμ

Mt 23.37 "O Jerusalem, Jerusalem, killing the prophets and stoning those who are sent!
Lk 2.25 a man in J., whose name was Simeon
2.38 all . . looking for the redemption of J.
2.41 his parents went to Jerusalem every year
2.43 the boy Jesus stayed behind in Jerusalem
2.45 they returned to Jerusalem, seeking him
4. 9 took him to J., and set him on the pinnacle
5.17 Pharisees . . who had come from . . J.
6.17 people from all Judea and Jerusalem
9.31 departure . . he was to accomplish at J.
9.51 he set his face to go to Jerusalem
9.53 because his face was set toward Jerusalem
10.30 "going down from Jerusalem to Jericho
13. 4 "worse offenders than . . others . . in J.?
13.33 " 'that a prophet should perish away from J.
13.34 "O Jerusalem, Jerusalem, killing the prophets and stoning those who are sent!
17.11 On the way to Jerusalem he was passing
18.31 "Behold, we are going up to Jerusalem
19.11 a parable, because he was near to J.
21.20 "when you see J. surrounded by armies
21.24 "J. will be trodden down by the Gentiles
23.28 "Daughters of J., do not weep for me
24.13 Emmaus, about seven miles[w] from J.
24.18 "Are you the only visitor to J.?
24.33 rose that same hour and returned to J.
24.47 "to all nations,[z] beginning from Jerusalem
24.52 they[b] returned to J. with great joy
Acts 1. 8 "you shall be my witnesses in Jerusalem
1.12 Then they returned to Jerusalem from . . Olivet, which is near Jerusalem
1.19 "(known to all . . inhabitants of Jerusalem
2. 5 there were dwelling in Jerusalem Jews
2.14 "Men of Judea and all who dwell in J.
4. 5 scribes were gathered together in J.
4.16 "manifest to all the inhabitants of J.
5.16 gathered from . . towns around Jerusalem
5.28 "you have filled J. with your teaching
6. 7 the disciples multiplied greatly in J.
8.26 "the road that goes down from J.
8.27 a eunuch . . had come to J. to worship
9. 2 he might bring them bound to J.
9.13 "evil he has done to thy saints at J.
9.21 "this . . man who made havoc in J.
9.26 when he had come to Jerusalem
9.28 he went in and out among them at J.
10.39 "witnesses to all that he did . . in Jerusalem
11. 2 So when Peter went up to Jerusalem
11.22 News of this came to . . the church in J.
12.25 Saul returned from[k] Jerusalem
13.27 "those who live in Jerusalem and their rulers
13.31 "who came up with him from Galilee to J.
15. 2 others were appointed to go up to J.
20.22 "behold, I am going to Jerusalem
21.11 " 'So shall the Jews at Jerusalem bind
21.12 begged him not to go up to Jerusalem
21.13 "I am ready . . even to die at Jerusalem
21.31 word came . . that all J. was in confusion
22. 5 "bring them in bonds to Jerusalem
22.17 "When I had returned to Jerusalem
22.18 " 'Make haste and get quickly out of J.
23.11 "for as you have testified about me at J.
24.11 "since I went up to worship at Jerusalem
25. 3 to have the man sent to Jerusalem
Rom 15.19 from J. and as far round as Illyricum
15.25 I am going to Jerusalem with aid
15.26 some contribution for the poor . . at J.
15.31 that my service for J. may be acceptable
1 Cor 16. 3 I will send those . . to carry your gift to J.
Gal 4.25 Hagar . . corresponds to the present J.
4.26 But the Jerusalem above is free
Heb 12.22 the city of the living God, the heavenly J.
Rev 3.12 " 'the city of my God, the new J.
21. 2 I saw the holy city, new Jerusalem
21.10 he . . showed me the holy city Jerusalem

JESSE: Ἰεσσαί 'jesē

Mt 1. 5 Obed the father of Jesse
1. 6 and Jesse the father of David the king
Lk 3.32 ⟨David⟩ the son of J., the son of Obed
Acts 13.22 " 'I have found in David the son of Jesse
Rom 15.12 Isaiah says, "The root of Jesse shall come

JESUS: Ἰησοῦς 'jēzəs (*See also* JOSHUA)

1. Jesus of Nazareth

(J. C. = Jesus Christ)

Mt 1. 1 book of the genealogy of Jesus Christ
1.16 husband of Mary, of whom J. was born
1.18 birth of J. C.[f] took place in this way‡
1.21 "you shall call his name Jesus
1.25 he called his name Jesus
2. 1 when J. was born in Bethlehem of Judea
3.13 Jesus came from Galilee to the Jordan
3.15 Jesus answered him, "Let it be so now
3.16 when Jesus was baptized, he went up
4. 1 Jesus was led up by the Spirit
4. 7 J. said . . "Again it is written
4.10 Then Jesus said to him, "Begone, Satan!
4.17 From that time Jesus began to preach
7.28 when J. finished . . crowds were astonished
8. 4 J. said . . "See that you say nothing
8.10 When Jesus heard him, he marveled
8.13 And to the centurion Jesus said
8.14 when Jesus entered Peter's house
8.18 when Jesus saw great crowds
8.20 Jesus said to him, "Foxes have holes
8.22 J. said . . "Follow me, and leave the dead
8.34 all the city came out to meet Jesus
9. 2 when Jesus saw their faith he said
9. 4 J., knowing[u] their thoughts, said, "Why?
9. 9 As J. passed on . . , he saw . . Matthew sitting
9.10 sinners came and sat down with J.
9.15 J. said . . "Can . . wedding guests mourn?
9.19 And Jesus rose and followed him
9.22 Jesus turned, and . . said, "Take heart
9.23 when Jesus came to the ruler's house
9.27 as J. passed . . , two blind men followed him
9.28 J. said . . "Do you believe that I am able?
9.30 Jesus sternly charged them, "See
9.35 J. went about all the cities and villages
10. 5 These twelve Jesus sent out
11. 1 when J. had finished instructing
11. 4 Jesus answered them, "Go and tell John
11. 7 Jesus began to speak . . concerning John
11.25 Jesus declared, "I thank thee, Father
12. 1 Jesus went through the grainfields
12.15 Jesus, aware of this, withdrew
13. 1 J. went out . . and sat beside the sea
13.34 All this J. said to the crowds in parables
13.53 when Jesus had finished these parables
13.57 J. said . . "A prophet is not without honor
14. 1 Herod . . heard about the fame of Jesus
14.12 buried it; and they went and told Jesus
14.13 when Jesus heard this, he withdrew
14.16 Jesus said, "They need not go away
14.29 Peter . . walked on the water and came to J.
14.31 Jesus immediately reached out his hand
15. 1 Then Pharisees and scribes came to Jesus
15.21 Jesus went away . . to the district of Tyre
15.28 Jesus answered her . . "great is your faith!
15.29 J. . . passed along the Sea of Galilee
15.32 J. . . said, "I have compassion on the crowd
15.34 J. said . . "How many loaves have you?
16. 6 Jesus said . . "beware of the leaven
16. 8 J. . . said, "O men of little faith
16.13 J. came into the district of Caesarea
16.17 J. answered . . "Blessed are you, Simon!
16.21 Jesus began to show his disciples
16.24 J. told . . "If any . . would come after me
17. 1 J. took with him Peter and James
17. 4 Peter said to J. . . "it is well . . we are here
17. 7 But Jesus came and touched them
17. 8 they saw no one but Jesus only

Mt 17. 9 J. commanded . . "Tell no one the vision
17.17 J. answered, "O faithless . . generation
17.18 J. rebuked him, and the demon came out
17.19 the disciples came to Jesus privately
17.22 J. said . . "The Son of man is to be delivered
17.25 J. spoke . . "What do you think, Simon?
17.26 J. said to him, "Then the sons are free
18. 1 came to J., saying, "Who is the greatest?
18.22 Jesus said . . "seventy times seven[e]
19. 1 Jesus . . entered the region of Judea
19.14 Jesus said, "Let the children come to me
19.18 Jesus said, "You shall not kill
19.21 J. said . . "sell what you possess and give
19.23 J. said . . "it will be hard for a rich man
19.26 J. . . said . . "With men this is impossible
19.28 J. said . . "Truly, . . in the new world
20.17 as Jesus was going up to Jerusalem
20.22 J. answered, "You do not know what
20.25 J. . . said, "You know that the rulers
20.30 two blind men . . heard that J. was passing
20.32 J. . . called them, . . "What do you want?
20.34 Jesus in pity touched their eyes
21. 1 then Jesus sent two disciples
21. 6 disciples . . did as Jesus had directed them
21.11 "This is the prophet J. from Nazareth
21.12 And Jesus entered the temple of God[p]
21.16 Jesus said . . "Yes; have you never read?
21.21 J. answered . . "Truly, . . if you have faith
21.24 J. answered . . "I also will ask you a question
21.27 they answered Jesus, "We do not know
21.31 J. said . . "the harlots go into the kingdom
21.42 J. said . . "Have you never read?
22. 1 again Jesus spoke to them in parables
22.18 Jesus . . said, "Why put me to the test?
22.20 J. said . . "Whose likeness . . is this?
22.29 Jesus answered them, "You are wrong
22.41 the Pharisees were . . together, Jesus asked
23. 1 Then said J. to the crowds and . . disciples
24. 1 J. left the temple and was going away
24. 4 Jesus answered them, "Take heed
26. 1 When Jesus had finished all these sayings
26. 4 took counsel together in order to arrest J.
26. 6 when J. was at . . house of Simon
26.10 J. . . said . . "Why . . trouble the woman?
26.17 disciples came to Jesus, saying, "Where?
26.19 disciples did as Jesus . . directed them
26.26 as they were eating, Jesus took bread
26.31 Jesus said . . "You will all fall away
26.34 J. said . . "Truly, . . this very night
26.36 J. went with them to . . Gethsemane
26.49 he came up to Jesus . . and said, "Hail!
26.50 J. said . . "Friend, why are you here?"[j] Then
they . . laid hands on Jesus
26.51 one . . with Jesus . . drew his sword
26.52 Jesus said to him, "Put your sword back
26.55 At that hour Jesus said to the crowds
26.57 those who had seized J. led . . to Caiaphas
26.59 council sought false testimony against J.
26.63 But Jesus was silent
26.64 Jesus said to him, "You have said so
26.69 "You also were with Jesus the Galilean
26.71 "This man was with Jesus of Nazareth
26.75 Peter remembered the saying of Jesus
27. 1 the people took counsel against Jesus
27.11 Now Jesus stood before the governor
27.11 Jesus said, "You have said so
27.17 "to release for you, Barabbas[k] or Jesus?
27.20 to ask for Barabbas and destroy Jesus
27.22 "Then what shall I do with Jesus?
27.26 having scourged Jesus, delivered him
27.27 soldiers . . took Jesus into the praetorium
27.37 "This is Jesus the King of the Jews
27.46 Jesus cried . . "Eli, Eli, lama sabachthani?
27.50 Jesus cried again with a loud voice
27.54 centurion . . , keeping watch over Jesus
27.55 women . . who had followed J. from Galilee
27.57 Joseph, who also was a disciple of J.

Mt 27.58 He . . asked for the body of Jesus
28. 5 I know that you seek J. who was crucified
28. 9 Jesus met them and said, "Hail!
28.10 Jesus said to them, "Do not be afraid; go
28.16 mountain to which J. had directed them
28.18 Jesus . . said . . "All authority in heaven
Mk 1. 1 beginning of the gospel of Jesus Christ
1. 9 In those days Jesus came from Nazareth
1.14 Jesus came into Galilee, preaching
1.17 Jesus said to them, "Follow me
1.24 "What have you to do with us, Jesus?
1.25 Jesus rebuked him, saying, "Be silent!
2. 5 when Jesus saw their faith, he said
2. 8 J., perceiving . . , said . . "Why . . question?
2.15 many . . sinners were sitting with Jesus
2.17 J. . . said . . "Those . . well have no need
2.19 J. said . . "Can the wedding guests fast?
3. 7 Jesus withdrew with his disciples
5. 6 when he saw Jesus from afar
5. 7 "What have you to do with me, Jesus?
5.15 they came to Jesus, and saw the demoniac
5.20 to proclaim . . how much Jesus had done
5.21 when J. had crossed again in the boat
5.27 She had heard the reports about Jesus
5.30 Jesus, perceiving in himself that power
5.36 J. said . . "Do not fear, only believe
6. 4 J. said . . "A prophet is not without honor
6.30 apostles returned to Jesus, and told him all
8.17 J. said . . "Why do you discuss the fact?
8.27 J. went . . to the villages of Caesarea P.
9. 2 Jesus took with him Peter and James
9. 4 they were talking to Jesus
9. 5 Peter said to Jesus, "Master,[f] it is well
9. 8 no longer saw any one . . but Jesus only
9.23 Jesus said to him, "If you can!
9.25 Jesus saw that a crowd came running
9.27 Jesus took him by the hand and lifted
9.39 Jesus said, "Do not forbid him
10. 5 Jesus said . . "For your hardness of heart
10.14 when Jesus saw it he was indignant
10.18 J. said . . "Why do you call me good?
10.21 Jesus looking upon him loved him
10.23 Jesus . . said . . "How hard it will be for those!
10.24 J. said . . "Children, how hard it is[r] to enter!
10.27 Jesus . . said, "With men it is impossible
10.29 J. said . . "there is no one who has left house
10.32 Jesus was walking ahead of them
10.38 J. said . . "You do not know what
10.39 J. said . . "The cup that I drink you will drink
10.42 J. . . said . . "You know that those who . . rule
10.47 when he heard . . it was J. . . , he began to . .
say, "J., Son of David, have mercy on me!
10.49 Jesus stopped and said, "Call him
10.50 he sprang up and came to Jesus
10.51 J. said . . "What do you want me to do?
10.52 Jesus said to him, "Go your way
11. 6 they told them what Jesus had said
11. 7 they brought the colt to Jesus
11.22 Jesus answered them, "Have faith in God
11.29 Jesus said . . "I will ask you a question
11.33 So they answered Jesus, "We do not know."
And Jesus said . . "Neither will I tell you
12.17 Jesus said to them, "Render to Caesar
12.24 Jesus said . . "Is not this why you are wrong?
12.29 J. answered, "The first is, 'Hear, O Israel
12.34 J. . . said . . "You are not far from the kingdom
12.35 Jesus . . said, "How can the scribes say?
13. 2 J. said . . "Do you see these great buildings?
13. 5 Jesus began to say to them, "Take heed
14. 6 J. said, "Let her alone; why . . trouble her?
14.18 Jesus said . . "one of you will betray me
14.27 Jesus said . . "You will all fall away
14.30 J. said . . "this . . night, before the cock crows
14.48 J. said . . "Have you come . . against a robber?
14.53 they led Jesus to the high priest
14.55 whole council sought testimony against J.
14.60 priest . . asked J., "Have you no answer?

Mk 14.62 J. said, "I am; and you will see the Son
14.67 "You also were with the Nazarene, J.
14.72 Peter remembered how Jesus had said
15. 1 they bound Jesus and led him away
15. 5 But Jesus made no further answer
15.15 having scourged Jesus, he delivered him
15.34 Jesus cried . . "Eloi, Eloi, lama sabachthani?
15.37 And Jesus uttered a loud cry
15.43 Joseph of A. . . asked for the body of J.
16. 6 "Do not be amazed; you seek Jesus of N.
16.19 So then the Lord Jesus . . was taken up[k]‡
[16.end *Jesus . . sent out . . the . . proclamation*‡
Lk 1.31 "you will . . bear a son, and . . call his name J.
2.21 when . . circumcised, he was called Jesus
2.27 when the parents brought in the child J.
2.43 the boy J. stayed behind in Jerusalem
2.52 Jesus increased in wisdom and in stature[i]
3.21 when Jesus also had been baptized
3.23 Jesus . . was about thirty years of age
4. 1 Jesus, full of the Holy Spirit, returned
4. 4 J. answered . . " 'Man shall not live by bread
4. 8 J. answered . . " 'You shall worship the Lord
4.12 J. answered . . " 'You shall not tempt
4.14 J. returned in the power of the Spirit
4.34 "What have you to do with us, J. of N.?
4.35 Jesus rebuked him, saying, "Be silent!
5. 8 when . . Peter saw it, he fell . . at J.'s knees
5.10 Jesus said to Simon, "Do not be afraid
5.12 when he saw J., he fell on his face
5.19 they . . let him down with his bed . . before J.
5.22 When J. perceived their questionings
5.31 Jesus answered . . "Those who are well
5.34 J. said . . "Can you make . . guests fast?
6. 3 Jesus answered, "Have you not read?
6. 9 J. said . . "is it lawful on the sabbath?
6.11 discussed . . what they might do to Jesus
7. 3 When he heard of Jesus, he sent . . elders
7. 4 when they came to J., they besought him
7. 6 And Jesus went with them
7. 9 When Jesus heard this he marveled
7.40 Jesus answering said to him, "Simon
8.28 When he saw Jesus, he cried out and fell
8.28 "What have you to do with me, Jesus?
8.30 J. then asked . . "What is your name?
8.35 they came to Jesus, and found the man . . sitting at the feet of Jesus, clothed
8.39 proclaiming . . how much Jesus had done
8.40 when J. returned, the crowd welcomed him
8.41 falling at Jesus' feet he besought him
8.45 J. said, "Who was it that touched me?
8.46 Jesus said, "Some one touched me
8.50 J. . . answered him, "Do not fear
9.33 Peter said to J., "Master, it is well
9.36 when the voice had spoken, J. was . . alone
9.41 J. answered, "O faithless . . generation
9.42 But Jesus rebuked the unclean spirit
9.47 when Jesus perceived the thought
9.50 Jesus said to him, "Do not forbid him
9.58 Jesus said to him, "Foxes have holes
9.62 J. said . . "No one who puts . . hand to . . plow
10.29 said to J., "And who is my neighbor?
10.30 Jesus replied, "A man was going down
10.37 Jesus said to him, "Go and do likewise
13.12 J. . . said . . "Woman, you are freed
13.14 indignant because J. . . healed on . . sabbath
14. 3 J. spoke . . "lawful to heal on . . sabbath?
17.13 "Jesus, Master, have mercy on us
17.17 Then said J., "Were not ten cleansed?
18.16 J. called . . "Let the children come to me
18.19 J. said . . "Why do you call me good?
18.22 Jesus . . said . . "One thing you still lack
18.24 J. . . said, "How hard it is for those!
18.37 "Jesus of Nazareth is passing by
18.38 "Jesus, Son of David, have mercy on me!
18.40 J. . . commanded him to be brought
18.42 Jesus said to him, "Receive your sight
19. 3 he sought to see who Jesus was
Lk 19. 5 J. . . said . . "Zacchaeus, make haste and come
19. 9 Jesus said . . "Today salvation has come
19.35 they brought it to Jesus, and . . they set Jesus upon it
20. 8 Jesus said . . "Neither will I tell you
20.34 J. said . . "The sons of this age marry
22.47 He drew near to Jesus to kiss him
22.48 J. said to him, "Judas, would you betray?
22.51 But Jesus said, "No more of this!
22.52 Jesus said to the chief priests
23. 8 When Herod saw J., he was very glad
23.20 Pilate . . , desiring to release Jesus
23.25 but Jesus he delivered up to their will
23.26 laid on him the cross, to carry it behind J.
23.28 Jesus turning to them said, "Daughters
23.34 Jesus said, "Father, forgive them‡
23.42 "Jesus, remember me when you come
23.46 Jesus . . said, "Father, into thy hands!
23.52 went to Pilate and asked for the body of J.
[24. 3 did not find the body *of the Lord Jesus*‡
24.15 they were talking . . , Jesus . . drew near
24.19 "Concerning J. of Nazareth, . . a prophet
Jn 1.17 grace and truth came through J. Christ
1.29 he saw Jesus coming toward him
1.36 he looked at Jesus as he walked
1.37 two disciples heard . . and they followed J.
1.38 Jesus . . said . . "What do you seek?
1.42 He brought him to Jesus. J. looked at him, and said, "So you are Simon?
1.43 next day Jesus decided to go to Galilee
1.45 "Jesus of Nazareth, the son of Joseph
1.47 Jesus saw Nathanael coming
1.48 J. answered . . "Before Philip called you
1.50 J. answered . . "Because I said . . I saw you
2. 1 the mother of Jesus was there
2. 2 Jesus also was invited to the marriage
2. 3 mother of J. said . . "They have no wine
2. 4 J. said . . "what have you to do with me?
2. 7 J. said to them, "Fill the jars with water
2.11 first of his signs, Jesus did at Cana
2.13 Jesus went up to Jerusalem
2.19 J. answered . . "Destroy this temple
2.22 believed . . the word which J. had spoken
2.24 Jesus did not trust himself to them
3. 3 J. answered . . "unless one is born anew[e]
3. 5 J. answered . . "unless one is born of water
3.10 J. answered . . "Are you a teacher of Israel?
3.22 After this Jesus . . went into . . Judea
4. 1 that Jesus was . . baptizing more . . than John
4. 2 (although Jesus himself did not baptize
4. 6 Jesus, wearied . . , sat down beside the well
4. 7 Jesus said to her, "Give me a drink
4.10 J. answered . . "If you knew the gift of God
4.13 J. said . . "Every one who drinks of this water
4.16 Jesus said . . "Go, call your husband
4.17 J. said . . "You are right in saying
4.21 J. said to her, "Woman, believe me
4.26 J. said . . "I who speak to you am he
4.34 J. said . . "My food is to do the will of him
4.44 J. . . testified that a prophet has no honor
4.47 he heard that Jesus had come from Judea
4.48 J. . . said . . "Unless you see signs
4.50 J. said to him, "Go; your son will live." The man believed the word that J. spoke
4.53 the hour when J. had said to him
4.54 This was . . the second sign that J. did
5. 1 Jesus went up to Jerusalem
5. 6 J. . . said . . "Do you want to be healed?
5. 8 J. said . . "Rise, take up your pallet
5.13 did not know . . , for Jesus had withdrawn
5.14 Jesus found him in the temple
5.15 that it was Jesus who had healed him
5.16 this was why the Jews persecuted Jesus
5.17 J. answered . . "My Father is working still
5.19 J. said . . "the Son can do nothing of his own
6. 1 Jesus went to the other side of the Sea
6. 3 Jesus went up on the mountain

Jn 6. 5 J. said . . "How are we to buy bread?
6.10 Jesus said, "Make the people sit down
6.11 Jesus then took the loaves
6.15 Jesus withdrew again to the mountain
6.17 dark, and Jesus had not yet come to them
6.19 they saw Jesus walking on the sea
6.22 saw . . that J. had not entered the boat
6.24 when the people saw that J. was not there, . . they . . went to Capernaum, seeking Jesus
6.26 Jesus answered . . "Truly, . . you seek me
6.29 J. answered . . "This is the work of God
6.32 J. said . . "it was not Moses who gave
6.35 Jesus said . . "I am the bread of life
6.42 "Is not this Jesus, the son of Joseph?
6.43 Jesus answered them, "Do not murmur
6.53 J. said . . "unless you eat the flesh
6.61 J. . . said . . "Do you take offense at this?
6.64 Jesus knew from the first who those were
6.67 Jesus said . . "Will you also go away?
6.70 J. answered . . "Did I not choose you?
7. 1 After this Jesus went about in Galilee
7. 6 J. said . . "My time has not yet come
7.14 Jesus went up into the temple and taught
7.16 J. answered . . "My teaching is not mine
7.21 Jesus answered . . "I did one deed
7.28 So Jesus proclaimed . . "You know me
7.33 J. . . said, "I shall be with you a little
7.37 J. . . proclaimed, "If any one thirst
7.39 because Jesus was not yet glorified
8. 1 Jesus went to the Mount of Olives[r]‡
8. 6 J. bent down and wrote with his finger[r]‡
8. 9 Jesus was left alone with the woman[r]‡
8.10 Jesus . . said . . "Woman, where are they?[r]‡
8.11 J. said, "Neither do I condemn you[r]‡
8.12 J. spoke . . "I am the light of the world
8.14 J. answered, "Even if I . . bear witness
8.19 Jesus answered, "You know neither me
8.25 J. said . . "Even what I have told you
8.28 J. said, "When you have lifted up the Son
8.31 Jesus . . said to the Jews who had believed
8.34 J. answered . . "every one who commits sin
8.39 J. said . . "If you were Abraham's children
8.42 J. said . . "If God were your Father
8.49 Jesus answered, "I have not a demon
8.54 Jesus answered, "If I glorify myself
8.58 Jesus said . . "before Abraham was, I am
8.59 Jesus hid . . and went out of the temple
9. 3 J. answered . . "not that this man sinned
9.11 "The man called Jesus made clay
9.14 Jesus made the clay and opened his eyes
9.35 Jesus heard that they had cast him out
9.37 Jesus said to him, "You have seen him
9.39 Jesus said, "For judgment I came
9.41 Jesus said to them, "If you were blind
10. 6 This figure Jesus used with them
10. 7 Jesus . . said . . "I am the door of the sheep
10.23 Jesus was walking in the temple
10.25 Jesus answered them, "I told you
10.32 J. answered . . "I have shown you many
10.34 J. answered . . "Is it not written?
11. 4 J. . . said, "This illness is not unto death
11. 5 Jesus loved Martha and her sister
11. 9 J. answered, "Are there not twelve hours?
11.13 Now Jesus had spoken of his death
11.14 J. told them plainly, "Lazarus is dead
11.17 when J. came, he found that Lazarus[x]
11.20 Martha heard that Jesus was coming
11.21 Martha said to J., . . "if you had been here
11.23 J. said . . "Your brother will rise again
11.25 Jesus said . . "I am the resurrection
11.30 Jesus had not yet come to the village
11.32 she came where Jesus was and saw him
11.33 When Jesus saw her weeping
11.35 Jesus wept
11.38 J., deeply moved . . , came to the tomb
11.39 Jesus said, "Take away the stone
11.40 Jesus said to her, "Did I not tell you?

Jn 11.41 Jesus . . said, "Father, I thank thee
11.44 Jesus said to them, "Unbind him
11.46 some . . told them what Jesus had done
11.51 he prophesied that Jesus should die
11.54 J. therefore no longer went about openly
11.56 They were looking for Jesus
12. 1 before the Passover, J. came to Bethany
12. 1 Lazarus . . , whom J. . . raised from the dead
12. 3 Mary . . anointed the feet of Jesus
12. 7 J. said, "Let her alone, let her keep it
12. 9 Jews . . came, not only on account of J.
12.11 many of the Jews were . . believing in J.
12.12 great crowd . . heard that J. was coming
12.14 J. found a young ass and sat upon it
12.16 when J. was glorified, . . they remembered
12.21 these . . said . . "Sir, we wish to see Jesus
12.22 Andrew went with Philip and they told J.
12.23 J. answered . . "The hour has come
12.30 J. answered, "This voice has come
12.35 J. said . . "The light is with you . . longer
12.36 When Jesus had said this, he departed
12.44 Jesus . . said, "He who believes in me
13. 1 Jesus knew that his hour had come
13. 7 J. answered him, "What I am doing
13. 8 J. answered . . "If I do not wash you
13.10 J. said . . "He who has bathed does not need
13.21 When J. had . . spoken, he was troubled
13.23 One of his disciples, whom Jesus loved, was lying close to the breast of Jesus
13.25 lying thus, close to the breast of Jesus
13.26 J. answered, "It is he to whom I . . give this
13.27 J. said . . "What you are going to do, do
13.29 thought . . Jesus was telling him, "Buy
13.31 J. said, "Now is . . Son of man glorified
13.36 Jesus answered, "Where I am going
13.38 J. answered, "Will you lay down your life?
14. 6 Jesus said to him, "I am the way
14. 9 J. said . . "Have I been with you so long?
14.23 J. answered him, "If a man loves me
16.19 Jesus knew that they wanted to ask him
16.31 Jesus answered . . "Do you now believe?
17. 1 When Jesus had spoken these words
17. 3 "life, that they know thee . . and J. Christ
18. 1 When Jesus had spoken these words
18. 2 Jesus often met there with his disciples
18. 4 Jesus, knowing all that was to befall him
18. 5 They answered him, "Jesus of Nazareth." Jesus said to them, "I am he
18. 7 And they said, "Jesus of Nazareth
18. 8 J. answered, "I told you that I am he
18.11 Jesus said to Peter, "Put your sword
18.12 officers of the Jews seized Jesus
18.15 Simon Peter followed Jesus
18.15 this disciple . . entered . . along with Jesus
18.19 The high priest then questioned J.
18.20 J. answered him, "I have spoken openly
18.22 one of the officers standing by struck J.
18.23 J. answered . . "If I have spoken wrongly
18.28 they led Jesus from the house of Caiaphas
18.32 the word which J. had spoken to show
18.33 called J., and said . . "Are you . . King?
18.34 J. answered, "Do you say this of your own?
18.36 J. answered, "My kingship is not of this
18.37 J. answered, "You say that I am a king
19. 1 Pilate took Jesus and scourged him
19. 5 J. came out, wearing the crown of thorns
19. 9 ⟨Pilate⟩ said to Jesus, "Where are you from?" But Jesus gave no answer
19.11 J. answered . . "You would have no power
19.13 Pilate . . brought J. out and sat down
19.17 So they took Jesus, and he went out
19.18 one on either side, and Jesus between
19.19 "J. of Nazareth, the King of the Jews
19.20 where J. was crucified was near the city
19.23 When the soldiers had crucified Jesus
19.25 by the cross of Jesus were his mother
19.26 Jesus saw his mother, and the disciple

Jn 19.28 Jesus, knowing that all was now finished
19.30 When Jesus had received the vinegar
19.33 they came to J. and saw that he was . . dead
19.38 Joseph of Arimathea, . . a disciple of Jesus, . . asked . . that he might take . . the body of J.
19.40 They took the body of Jesus
19.42 they laid Jesus there
20. 2 the other disciple, the one whom J. loved
20.12 sitting where the body of Jesus had lain
20.14 she turned . . and saw Jesus standing, but she did not know that it was Jesus
20.15 J. said . . "Woman, why are you weeping?
20.16 Jesus said to her, "Mary
20.17 Jesus said to her, "Do not hold me
20.19 Jesus came and stood among them
20.21 Jesus said to them again, "Peace
20.24 Thomas . . was not with them when J. came
20.26 The doors were shut, but Jesus came
20.29 Jesus said to him, "Have you believed?
20.30 Now Jesus did many other signs
20.31 that you may believe that J. is the Christ
21. 1 Jesus revealed himself again
21. 4 day was breaking, J. stood on the beach; . . disciples did not know that it was J.
21. 5 J. said . . "Children, have you any fish?
21. 7 disciple whom Jesus loved said to Peter
21.10 J. said . . "Bring some of the fish
21.12 Jesus said . . "Come and have breakfast
21.13 Jesus came and took the bread
21.14 the third time that Jesus was revealed
21.15 J. said . . "Simon, . . do you love me?
21.17 Jesus said to him, "Feed my sheep
21.20 Peter . . saw . . the disciple whom J. loved
21.21 Peter . . said to J. . . "what about this man?
21.22 J. said . . "If it is my will that he remain
21.23 yet Jesus did not say . . he was not to die
21.25 also many other things which Jesus did
Acts 1. 1 all that Jesus began to do and teach
1.11 "This J., who was taken up from you
1.14 the women and Mary the mother of Jesus
1.16 "Judas . . guide to those who arrested Jesus
1.21 "time that the Lord J. went . . among us
2.22 "Jesus of Nazareth, a man attested
2.32 "This Jesus God raised up
2.36 "Christ, this Jesus whom you crucified
2.38 "be baptized . . in the name of Jesus Christ
3. 6 "in the name of J. Christ of Nazareth, walk
3.13 "God . . glorified his servant[c] Jesus
3.20 "the Christ appointed for you, Jesus
4. 2 proclaiming in Jesus the resurrection
4.10 "by the name of Jesus Christ of Nazareth
4.13 recognized that they had been with J.
4.18 charged . . not to speak . . in the name of J.
4.27 "gathered . . against thy holy servant[c] J.
4.30 "through the name of thy holy servant[c] J.
4.33 testimony to the resurrection of . . J.
5.30 "The God of our fathers raised Jesus
5.40 charged . . not to speak in the name of J.
5.42 teaching and preaching J. as the Christ
6.14 "this Jesus . . will destroy this place
7.55 Jesus standing at the right hand of God
7.59 "Lord Jesus, receive my spirit
8.12 believed . . as he preached . . the name of J.
8.16 baptized in the name of the Lord Jesus
8.35 Philip . . told him the good news of Jesus
[8.37 *"Jesus Christ is the Son of God‡*
9. 5 "I am Jesus, whom you are persecuting
9.17 "Brother Saul, the Lord J., who appeared
9.20 immediately he proclaimed Jesus
9.27 he had preached boldly in the name of J.
9.34 "Aeneas, Jesus Christ heals you
10.36 "preaching good news of peace by J. C.
10.38 "how God anointed Jesus of Nazareth
10.48 to be baptized in the name of Jesus Christ
11.17 "when we believed in the Lord J. Christ
11.20 men of Cyprus . . , preaching the Lord J.
13.23 "God has brought to Israel a Savior, J.
Acts 13.33 "this he has fulfilled . . by raising J.
15.11 "saved through the grace of the Lord J.
15.26 "risked their lives for . . our Lord J. Christ
16. 7 the Spirit of Jesus did not allow them
16.18 "I charge you in . . the name of J. Christ
16.31 "Believe in the Lord J. . . you will be saved
17. 3 "This Jesus, whom I proclaim to you
17. 7 "that there is another king, J.
17.18 he preached J. and the resurrection
18. 5 testifying . . that the Christ was J.
18.25 taught . . the things concerning Jesus
18.28 showing . . that the Christ was Jesus
19. 4 "one who was to come after him, . . J.
19. 5 baptized in the name of the Lord Jesus
19.13 to pronounce the name of the Lord J. . . , saying, "I adjure you by the Jesus
19.15 "Jesus I know, and Paul I know
19.17 the name of the Lord Jesus was extolled
20.21 "testifying . . of faith in our Lord J. Christ
20.24 "ministry . . I received from the Lord J.
20.35 "remembering the words of the Lord J.
21.13 "even to die . . for the name of the Lord J.
22. 8 "'I am J. . . whom you are persecuting
24.24 heard him speak upon faith in Christ J.
25.19 "about their own superstition and . . one J.
26. 9 "opposing the name of Jesus of N.
26.15 "'I am Jesus whom you are persecuting
28.23 trying to convince them about Jesus
28.31 teaching about the Lord Jesus Christ
Rom 1. 1 Paul, a servant[a] of Jesus Christ
1. 4 designated Son of God . . , J. Christ
1. 6 who are called to belong to Jesus Christ
1. 7 from God our Father and the Lord J.
1. 8 I thank my God through Jesus Christ
2.16 God judges the secrets of men by Christ J.
3.22 righteousness of God through faith in J.
3.24 through the redemption . . in Christ J.
3.26 he justifies him who has faith in Jesus
4.24 that raised from the dead J. our Lord
5. 1 peace with God through our Lord J.
5.11 we . . rejoice . . through our Lord J.
5.15 the grace of that one man J. Christ
5.17 life through the one man J. Christ
5.21 eternal life through J. Christ our Lord
6. 3 who have been baptized into Christ J.
6.11 dead to sin and alive to God in Christ J.
6.23 the free gift . . is eternal life in Christ J.
7.25 Thanks be to God through J. Christ!
8. 1 no condemnation for those . . in Christ J.
8. 2 law of the Spirit of life in Christ Jesus
8.11 the Spirit of him who raised Jesus
8.11 he who raised Christ Jesus from the dead
8.34 who is to condemn? Is it Christ Jesus?
8.39 the love of God in Christ Jesus our Lord
10. 9 if you confess . . that Jesus is Lord
13.14 put on the Lord Jesus Christ
14.14 I . . am persuaded in the Lord Jesus
15. 5 to live . . in accord with Christ Jesus
15. 6 God and Father of our Lord J. Christ
15.16 to be a minister of Christ Jesus
15.17 In Christ Jesus, then, I have reason
15.30 I appeal to you . . by our Lord J. Christ
16. 3 Greet . . my fellow workers in Christ J.
16.20 The grace of our Lord Jesus Christ‡
[16.24 *The grace of our Lord Jesus Christ‡*
16.25 according to . . the preaching of J. Christ
16.27 glory for evermore through Jesus Christ!
1 Cor 1. 1 Paul, called . . to be an apostle of Christ J.
1. 2 those sanctified in Christ J., . . who . . call on the name of our Lord Jesus Christ
1. 3 Grace to you . . from . . the Lord J. Christ
1. 4 grace of God . . given you in Christ Jesus
1. 7 the revealing of our Lord Jesus Christ
1. 8 guiltless in the day of our Lord J. Christ
1. 9 fellowship of his Son, J. Christ our Lord
1.10 by the name of our Lord Jesus Christ
1.30 the source of your life in Christ Jesus

1 Cor 2. 2 except Jesus Christ and him crucified
3.11 no other foundation . . than . . Jesus Christ
4.15 I became your father in Christ Jesus
5. 4 ⟨judgment⟩ in . . name of the Lord Jesus
5. 4 assembled . . with the power of our Lord J.
5. 5 saved in the day of the Lord Jesus[h]‡
6.11 justified in . . name of the Lord J. Christ
8. 6 for us there is . . one Lord, Jesus Christ
9. 1 Have I not seen Jesus our Lord?
11.23 Lord J. on the night when he was betrayed
12. 3 no one . . by the Spirit . . says "Jesus be cursed!" and no one . . "J. is Lord" except
15.31 pride . . I have in Christ J. our Lord
15.57 victory through our Lord Jesus Christ
16.23 The grace of the Lord Jesus be with you
16.24 My love be with you all in Christ Jesus
2 Cor 1. 1 Paul, an apostle of Christ Jesus
1. 2 Grace to you . . from . . the Lord J. Christ
1. 3 Blessed be the God . . of our Lord J. Christ
1.14 proud . . on the day of the Lord Jesus
1.19 the Son of God, Jesus Christ
4. 5 we preach . . Jesus Christ as Lord, with ourselves as your servants[f] for Jesus' sake
4.10 carrying . . the death of Jesus, so that the life of J. may also be manifested
4.11 given up to death for Jesus' sake, so that the life of Jesus may be manifested
4.14 he who raised the Lord Jesus will raise us also with Jesus and bring us with you
8. 9 you know the grace of our Lord J. Christ
11. 4 if some one comes and preaches another J.
11.31 The God and Father of the Lord Jesus
13. 5 not realize that J. Christ is in you?
13.14(13) The grace of the Lord Jesus Christ
Gal 1. 1 Paul an apostle . . through Jesus Christ
1. 3 Grace to you . . from . . our Lord Jesus Christ
1.12 it came through a revelation of J. Christ
2. 4 freedom which we have in Christ Jesus
2.16 justified[d] . . through faith in Jesus Christ, even we have believed in Christ Jesus
3. 1 J. C. was publicly portrayed as crucified
3.14 that in Christ J. the blessing of Abraham
3.22 promised to faith in Jesus Christ
3.26 in Christ Jesus you are all sons of God
3.28 for you are all one in Christ Jesus
4.14 received me as an angel . . , as Christ J.
5. 6 in Christ Jesus neither circumcision
5.24 those who belong to Christ Jesus
6.14 except in the cross of our Lord J. Christ
6.17 for I bear on my body the marks of Jesus
6.18 The grace of our Lord Jesus Christ
Eph 1. 1 Paul, an apostle of Christ Jesus . . , To the saints . . faithful[a] in Christ Jesus
1. 2 Grace to you . . from . . the Lord J. Christ
1. 3 Blessed be the God . . of our Lord J. Christ
1. 5 destined . . to be his sons through J. Christ
1.15 I have heard of your faith in the Lord J.
1.17 the God of our Lord Jesus Christ
2. 6 in the heavenly places in Christ Jesus
2. 7 grace in kindness toward us in Christ J.
2.10 created in Christ Jesus for good works
2.13 in Christ J. you . . have been brought near
2.20 Christ Jesus himself . . the cornerstone
3. 1 I, Paul, a prisoner for Christ Jesus
3. 6 partakers of the promise in Christ Jesus
3.11 purpose which he has realized in Christ J.
3.21 glory in the church and in Christ Jesus
4.21 taught in him, as the truth is in Jesus
5.20 thanks in . . name of our Lord Jesus Christ
6.23 God the Father and the Lord Jesus Christ
6.24 all who love our Lord Jesus Christ
Phil 1. 1 Paul and Timothy, servants[a] of Christ J., To all the saints in Christ Jesus
1. 2 God our Father and the Lord Jesus Christ
1. 6 to completion at the day of Jesus Christ
1. 8 I yearn . . with the affection of Christ J.
1.11 fruits . . which come through J. Christ
Phil 1.19 the help of the Spirit of Jesus Christ
1.26 ample cause to glory in Christ Jesus
2. 5 mind . . which is yours in Christ Jesus
2.10 at the name of J. every knee . . bow
2.11 every tongue confess . . J. Christ is Lord
2.19 I hope in the Lord J. to send Timothy
2.21 their . . interests, not those of J. Christ
3. 3 who . . glory in Christ Jesus
3. 8 worth of knowing Christ Jesus my Lord
3.12 Christ Jesus has made me his own
3.14 the upward call of God in Christ Jesus
3.20 we await a Savior, the Lord J. Christ
4. 7 will keep your hearts . . in Christ Jesus
4.19 his riches in glory in Christ Jesus
4.21 Greet every saint in Christ Jesus
4.23 The grace of the Lord Jesus Christ
Col 1. 1 Paul, an apostle of Christ Jesus
1. 3 the Father of our Lord Jesus Christ
1. 4 heard of your faith in Christ Jesus
2. 6 As . . you received Christ Jesus the Lord
3.17 do everything in the name of the Lord J.
4.12 Epaphras, . . a servant[g] of Christ Jesus
1 Th 1. 1 in God . . and the Lord Jesus Christ
1. 3 steadfastness of hope in our Lord J. Christ
1.10 Jesus who delivers us from the wrath
2.14 the churches of God in Christ Jesus
2.15 killed both the Lord J. and the prophets
2.19 boasting before our Lord J. at his coming
3.11 may . . our Lord Jesus, direct our way
3.13 at the coming of our Lord Jesus
4. 1 exhort you in the Lord Jesus
4. 2 instructions we gave . . through the Lord J.
4.14 we believe that Jesus died and rose again
4.14 through Jesus, God will bring with him
5. 9 salvation through our Lord Jesus Christ
5.18 the will of God in Christ Jesus for you
5.23 at the coming of our Lord Jesus Christ
5.28 grace of our Lord J. Christ be with you
2 Th 1. 1 God our Father and the Lord Jesus Christ
1. 2 God the Father and the Lord J. Christ
1. 7 when the Lord Jesus is revealed
1. 8 who do not obey the gospel of our Lord J.
1.12 name of our Lord J. may be glorified
1.12 grace of our God and the Lord J. Christ
2. 1 the coming of our Lord Jesus Christ
2. 8 Lord J. will slay him with the breath
2.14 obtain the glory of our Lord J. Christ
2.16 may our Lord Jesus Christ himself
3. 6 in the name of our Lord Jesus Christ
3.12 we . . exhort in the Lord Jesus Christ
3.18 The grace of our Lord Jesus Christ
1 Tim 1. 1 Paul, an apostle of Christ Jesus
1. 1 God our Savior and of Christ J. our hope
1. 2 mercy, and peace from . . Christ J. our Lord
1.12 I thank him . . , Christ Jesus our Lord
1.14 the faith and love that are in Christ Jesus
1.15 Christ Jesus came . . to save sinners
1.16 that . . J. Christ . . display his . . patience
2. 5 there is one mediator . . , the man Christ Jesus
3.13 the faith which is in Christ Jesus
4. 6 you will be a good minister of Christ J.
5.21 In the presence of God and of Christ J.
6. 3 sound words of our Lord Jesus Christ
6.13 presence of God . . and of Christ Jesus
6.14 until the appearing of our Lord J. Christ
2 Tim 1. 1 Paul, an apostle of Christ Jesus . . according to the promise of the life . . in Christ Jesus
1. 2 mercy, and peace from . . Christ J. our Lord
1. 9 grace which he gave us in Christ Jesus
1.10 the appearing of our Savior Christ J.
1.13 faith and love which are in Christ J.
2. 1 strong in the grace that is in Christ Jesus
2. 3 share . . as a good soldier of Christ Jesus
2. 8 Remember J. Christ, risen from the dead
2.10 may obtain salvation in Christ Jesus
3.12 to live a godly life in Christ Jesus
3.15 salvation through faith in Christ Jesus

2 Tim 4. 1 Christ Jesus who is to judge the living
Tit 1. 1 Paul, . . an apostle of Jesus Christ
1. 4 Grace . . peace from . . Christ J. our Savior
2.13 our great God and Savior[c] Jesus Christ
3. 6 poured out upon us . . through J. Christ
Phm . 1 Paul, a prisoner for Christ Jesus
. 3 Grace . . and peace from . . the Lord J. Christ
. 5 I hear of your love . . toward the Lord J.
. 9 I, Paul, . . a prisoner also for Christ Jesus
.23 my fellow prisoner in Christ Jesus
.25 The grace of the Lord Jesus Christ
Heb 2. 9 J., who for a little while was made lower
3. 1 consider Jesus, the apostle
4.14 we have a great high priest . . , Jesus
6.20 where Jesus has gone as a forerunner
7.22 Jesus the surety of a better covenant
10.10 offering of the body of Jesus Christ
10.19 we have confidence . . by the blood of Jesus
12. 2 J. the pioneer and perfecter of our faith
12.24 Jesus, the mediator of a new covenant
13. 8 Jesus Christ is the same yesterday
13.12 So Jesus also suffered outside the gate
13.20 our Lord Jesus, the great shepherd
13.21 working in you[b] . . through Jesus Christ
Jas 1. 1 James, a servant . . of the Lord Jesus Christ
2. 1 you hold the faith of our Lord J. Christ
1 Pet 1. 1 Peter, an apostle of Jesus Christ
1. 2 sanctified . . for obedience to J. Christ
1. 3 God and Father of our Lord J. Christ!
1. 3 through the resurrection of Jesus Christ
1. 7 honor at the revelation of Jesus Christ
1.13 grace . . at the revelation of Jesus Christ
2. 5 acceptable to God through Jesus Christ
3.21 through the resurrection of J. Christ
4.11 may be glorified through Jesus Christ
2 Pet 1. 1 Peter, a servant . . of Jesus Christ
1. 1 our God and Savior Jesus Christ[a]
1. 2 knowledge of God and of Jesus our Lord
1. 8 knowledge of our Lord Jesus Christ
1.11 kingdom of our . . Savior Jesus Christ
1.14 as our Lord Jesus Christ showed me
1.16 the . . coming of our Lord Jesus Christ
2.20 knowledge of our . . Savior J. Christ
3.18 knowledge of our . . Savior J. Christ
1 Jn 1. 3 our fellowship . . with his Son Jesus Christ
1. 7 the blood of Jesus his Son cleanses us
2. 1 we have an advocate . . , Jesus Christ
2.22 he who denies that J. is the Christ
3.23 we should believe in the name of . . J. C.
4. 2 every spirit which confesses that J. C.
4. 3 every spirit which does not confess Jesus
4.15 confesses that Jesus is the Son of God
5. 1 who believes that Jesus is the Christ
5. 5 who believes that Jesus is the Son of God
5. 6 who came by water and blood, J. Christ
5.20 in him who is true, in his Son J. Christ
2 Jn . 3 peace . . from J. Christ the Father's Son
. 7 will not acknowledge the coming of J. C.
Jude . 1 Jude, a servant of Jesus Christ . . , To those who are . . kept for Jesus Christ
. 4 our only Master and Lord, Jesus Christ[a]
[. 5 *Jesus* who saved a people out of . . Egypt‡
.17 predictions of the apostles of our Lord J. C.
.21 wait for the mercy of our Lord J. C.
.25 through Jesus Christ our Lord, be glory
Rev 1. 1 The revelation of J. C., which God gave
1. 2 witness . . to the testimony of J. Christ
1. 5 from Jesus Christ the faithful witness
1. 9 who share with you in J. the tribulation
1. 9 word of God and the testimony of Jesus
12.17 those who . . bear testimony to Jesus
14.12 those who keep . . the faith of Jesus
17. 6 drunk with . . the blood of the martyrs of J.
19.10 "brethren who hold the testimony of J.
19.10 testimony of J. is the spirit of prophecy
20. 4 beheaded for their testimony to J.
22.16 "I Jesus have sent my angel to you
Rev 22.20 Amen. Come, Lord Jesus!
22.21 grace of the Lord J. be with all the saints[t]

2. Justus
Col 4.11 Jesus who is called Justus ⟨greets you⟩

3. Jesus Barabbas
Mt [27.16 a . . prisoner, called *Jesus* Barabbas‡
[27.17 "Whom do you want . . , *Jesus* Barabbas?‡

CONTEXTUALLY
Mk 1.45 that Jesus[g] could no longer openly enter†
5. 9 J.[o] asked him, "What is your name?†
5.17 And they began to beg Jesus[p] to depart†
6.14 for Jesus'[s] name had become known†
9.21 And J.[h] asked his father, "How long?†
Lk 5.18 to bring him in and lay him before Jesus[q]†
22. 8 So J.[h] sent Peter and John, saying, "Go†
22.63 men who were holding J. mocked him
24.36 J. himself stood among them[x]
Jn 3. 2 This man came to Jesus[d] by night†
13. 3 J., knowing that the Father had given
Acts 2.23 "this J., delivered up according to . . plan
3.16 "and the faith which is through Jesus[d]†
9.22 by proving that Jesus was the Christ
Heb 3. 3 Yet Jesus has been counted worthy
5. 7 J.[j] offered up prayers and supplications†

JEW: Ἰουδαῖος (*See also* FELLOW JEWS; JEWESS; JEWISH; JUDEA 2; JUDEAN)
Mt 2. 2 "he who has been born king of the Jews
27.11 "Are you the King of the Jews?
27.29 "Hail, King of the Jews!
27.37 "This *is* Jesus the King of the Jews
28.15 story has been spread among the Jews
Mk 7. 3 (the Jews, do not eat unless they wash
15. 2 "Are you the King of the Jews?
15. 9 "to release for you the King of the Jews?
15.12 "whom you call the King of the Jews
15.18 "Hail, King of the Jews!
15.26 inscription . . read, "The King of the Jews
Lk 7. 3 he sent to him elders of the Jews
23. 3 "Are you the King of the Jews?
23.37 "If you are the King of the Jews
23.38 inscription . . "This is the King of the Jews
Jn 1.19 when the Jews sent priests and Levites
2.13 The Passover of the Jews was at hand
2.18 The Jews then said to him, "What sign?
2.20 Jews . . said, "It has taken forty-six years
3. 1 Nicodemus, a ruler of the Jews
3.25 between John's disciples and a Jew
4. 9 "How is it that you, a Jew, ask . . ?" . . Jews have no dealings with Samaritans
4.22 "for salvation is from the Jews
5. 1 After this there was a feast of the Jews
5.10 Jews said to the man who was cured
5.15 The man went away and told the Jews
5.16 this was why the Jews persecuted Jesus
5.18 This was why the Jews sought . . to kill
6. 4 the feast of the Jews, was at hand
6.41 The Jews then murmured at him
6.52 Jews then disputed among themselves
7. 1 because the Jews[n] sought to kill him†
7. 2 Jews' feast of Tabernacles was at hand
7.11 Jews were looking for him at the feast
7.13 for fear of the Jews no one spoke openly
7.15 The Jews marveled at it
7.35 The Jews said to one another, "Where?
8.22 Then said the Jews, "Will he kill himself?
8.31 to the Jews who had believed in him
8.48 Jews answered him, "Are we not right?
8.52 Jews said to him, "Now we know
8.57 Jews . . said . . "You are not yet fifty years old
9.18 Jews did not believe . . he had been blind
9.22 because they feared the Jews, for the Jews had already agreed . . one . . was to be put out
10.19 again a division among the Jews
10.24 So the Jews gathered round him
10.31 The Jews took up stones again
10.33 Jews answered . . "It is . . for blasphemy

Jn 11. 8 "Jews were but now seeking to stone you
11.19 many of the Jews had come to Martha
11.31 the Jews who were with her in the house
11.33 Jews who came with her also weeping
11.36 the Jews said, "See how he loved him!
11.45 the Jews . . who had come with Mary
11.54 Jesus . . no longer went . . among the Jews
11.55 Passover of the Jews was at hand
12. 9 When . . the Jews learned . . he was there
12.11 Jews were going away and believing
13.33 "as I said to the Jews so now I say to you
18.12 officers of the Jews seized Jesus
18.14 Caiaphas . . had given counsel to the Jews
18.20 "temple, where all Jews come together
18.31 Jews said . . "It is not lawful for us
18.33 "Are you the King of the Jews?
18.35 Pilate answered, "Am I a Jew?
18.36 "that I . . not be handed . . to the Jews
18.38 "he went out to the Jews again
18.39 "have me release . . the King of the Jews?
19. 3 "Hail, King of the Jews!
19. 7 Jews answered him, "We have a law
19.12 Jews cried out, "If you release this man
19.14 said to the Jews, "Behold your King!
19.19 "Jesus of Nazareth, . . King of the Jews
19.20 Many of the Jews read this title
19.21 chief priests of the Jews then said . . "Do not write, 'The King of the Jews,' but, 'This man said, I am King of the Jews
19.31 Jews asked . . that their legs might be broken
19.38 Joseph of A. . . , for fear of the Jews
19.40 as is the burial custom of the Jews
20.19 doors being shut . . , for fear of the Jews
Acts 2. 5 there were dwelling in Jerusalem Jews
2.10 "from Rome, both Jews and proselytes
9.22 Saul . . confounded the Jews
9.23 the Jews plotted to kill him
10.28 "how unlawful it is for a Jew to associate
10.39 "he did both in the country of the Jews
11.19 speaking the word to none except Jews
12. 3 when he saw that it pleased the Jews
13. 5 proclaimed . . in the synagogues of the Jews
13.43 many Jews and devout converts
13.45 when the Jews saw the multitudes
13.50 the Jews incited the devout women
14. 1 a great company believed, both of Jews
14. 2 unbelieving Jews stirred up the Gentiles
14. 4 some sided with the Jews
14. 5 attempt . . by both Gentiles and Jews
14.19 But Jews came there from Antioch
16. 3 circumcised him because of the Jews
16.20 "These men are Jews and . . are disturbing
17. 1 there was a synagogue of the Jews
17. 5 Jews were jealous, and taking . . rabble
17.13 when the Jews of Thessalonica learned
17.17 argued in the synagogue with the Jews
18. 2 he found a Jew named Aquila
18. 2 Claudius had commanded all the Jews
18. 4 he argued . . and persuaded Jews and Greeks
18. 5 preaching, testifying to the Jews
18.12 Jews made a united attack upon Paul
18.14 Gallio said to the Jews, "If it were a . . crime, I should . . bear with you, O Jews
18.19 he himself . . argued with the Jews
18.24 Jew named Apollos, a native of Alexandria
18.28 he powerfully confuted the Jews
19.10 all the residents of Asia heard . . , both Jews
19.17 known to all . . , both Jews and Greeks
19.33 whom the Jews had put forward
19.34 they recognized that he was a Jew
20. 3 plot was made against him by the Jews
20.19 "befell me through the plots of the Jews
20.21 "testifying both to Jews and to Greeks
21.11 " 'So shall the Jews at Jerusalem bind
21.20 "thousands there are among the Jews
21.21 "that you teach . . Jews . . to forsake Moses
21.27 the Jews from Asia, who had seen him
Acts 21.39 "I am a Jew, from Tarsus in Cilicia
22. 3 "I am a Jew, born at Tarsus in Cilicia
22.12 "Ananias, . . well spoken of by all the Jews
22.30 real reason why the Jews accused him
23.12 Jews made a plot and bound themselves
23.20 "Jews have agreed to ask you to bring Paul
23.27 "This man was seized by the Jews
24. 5 "an agitator among all the Jews
24. 9 The Jews also joined in the charge
24.18 "But some Jews from Asia
24.27 desiring to do the Jews a favor, Felix
25. 2 principal men of the Jews informed him
25. 7 Jews who had gone down from Jerusalem
25. 8 "Neither against the law of the Jews
25. 9 Festus, wishing to do the Jews a favor
25.10 "to the Jews I have done no wrong
25.15 "elders of the Jews gave information
26. 2 "against all the accusations of the Jews
26. 3 "customs and controversies of the Jews
26. 4 "My . . life . . is known by all the Jews
26. 7 "for this hope I am accused by Jews
26.21 "For this reason the Jews seized me
28.17 he called . . the local leaders of the Jews
28.19 "when the Jews objected, I was compelled
[28.29 *the Jews departed, holding . . dispute*‡
Rom 1.16 it is the power of God . . to the Jew first
2. 9 tribulation and distress for . . the Jew first
2.10 glory and honor . . for . . the Jew first
2.17 if you call yourself a Jew
2.28 he is not a real Jew who is one outwardly
2.29 He is a Jew who is one inwardly
3. 1 Then what advantage has the Jew?
3. 9 charged that all men both Jews and Greeks
3.29 Or is God the God of Jews only?
9.24 he has called, not from the Jews only
10.12 no distinction between Jew and Greek
1 Cor 1.22 Jews demand signs and Greeks seek wisdom
1.23 Christ . . , a stumbling block to Jews
1.24 to those who are called, both Jews
9.20 To the Jews I became as a Jew, in order to win Jews
10.32 Give no offense to Jews or to Greeks
12.13 one body—Jews or Greeks, slaves or free
2 Cor 11.24 at the hands of the Jews the forty lashes
Gal 2.13 the rest of the Jews acted insincerely
2.14 "If you, though a Jew, live like a Gentile
2.15 We ourselves, who are Jews by birth
3.28 There is neither Jew nor Greek
Col 3.11 Here there cannot be Greek and Jew
1 Th 2.14 you suffered . . as they did from the Jews
Rev 2. 9 " 'those who say that they are Jews
3. 9 " 'say that they are Jews and are not

CONTEXTUALLY
Acts 17.11 Now these Jews were more noble than those
Rom 3. 2 Jews are entrusted with the oracles of God

JEW, LIKE A: Ἰουδαϊκῶς
Gal 2.14 "If you, though a Jew, live . . not like a Jew

JEW, LIVE LIKE A
1. *live according to Jewish customs:* ἰουδαΐζω IOUDAIZŌ*
Gal 2.14 "compel the Gentiles to live like Jews

JEWEL
1. *precious stone:* λίθος τίμιος LITHOS; TIMIOS [A.1.f]
[a]sg. [b]+τιμιώτατος *most rare jewel*
Rev 17. 4 [a]bedecked with gold and jewels
18.12 [a]cargo of gold, silver, jewels and pearls
18.16 [a]"bedecked with gold, with jewels!
21.11 [b]its radiance like a most rare jewel
21.19 foundations . . were adorned with every j.

JEWESS: Ἰουδαία (*See also* JEW)
Acts 24.24 Drusilla, who was a Jewess

JEWISH
1. *Jewish:* Ἰουδαϊκός
Tit 1.14 instead of giving heed to Jewish myths

2. *Jewish:* Ἰουδαῖος (subst. gen. pl.) (*See also* JEW)
[a]adj.
Lk 23.50(51) Joseph from the Jewish town Arimathea
Jn 2. 6 for the Jewish rites of purification
19.42 because of the Jewish day of Preparation
Acts 10.22 "spoken of by the whole Jewish nation
12.11 "that the Jewish people were expecting
13. 6 [a]a Jewish false prophet, . . Bar-Jesus
14. 1 they entered . . into the Jewish synagogue
16. 1 [a]Timothy, the son of a Jewish woman
17.10 they went into the Jewish synagogue
19.13 some of the itinerant Jewish exorcists
19.14 [a]a Jewish high priest named Sceva
25.24 "the whole Jewish people petitioned me

JEZEBEL: Ἰεζάβελ 'jezə,bel
Rev 2.20 " 'you tolerate the woman Jezebel

JOANAN: Ἰωανάν jō'änən
Lk 3.27 the son of Joanan, the son of Rhesa

JOANNA: Ἰωάννα jō'anə
Lk 8. 3 J., the wife of Chuza, Herod's steward
24.10 it was Mary Magdalene and Joanna

JOB: Ἰώβ 'jōb
Jas 5.11 You have heard of . . steadfastness of Job

JODA: Ἰωδά 'jōdə
Lk 3.26 the son of Josech, the son of Joda

JOEL: Ἰωήλ 'jōəl
Acts 2.16 what was spoken by the prophet Joel

JOHN: Ἰωάννης 'jän
1. the Baptist
Mt 3. 1 In those days came John the Baptist
3. 4 John wore a garment of camel's hair
3.13 Jesus came . . to the Jordan to John
4.12 he heard that John had been arrested
9.14 disciples of John came to him, saying
11. 2 John heard in prison about . . the Christ
11. 4 "Go and tell J. what you hear and see
11. 7 Jesus began to speak . . concerning John
11.11 "there has risen no one greater than J.
11.12 "From the days of J. the Baptist until
11.13 "prophets . . prophesied until John
11.18 "John came neither eating nor drinking
14. 2 "This is J. the Baptist, he has been raised
14. 3 Herod had seized John and bound him
14. 4 John said to him, "It is not lawful
14. 8 "Give me the head of John the Baptist
14.10 he . . had John beheaded in the prison
16.14 "Some say J. the Baptist, others . . Elijah
17.13 he was speaking to them of J. the Baptist
21.25 "The baptism of John, whence was it?
21.26 "for all hold that John was a prophet
21.32 "John came to you in . . righteousness
Mk 1. 4 John the baptizer . . in the wilderness
1. 6 John was clothed with camel's hair
1. 9 Jesus . . was baptized by J. in the Jordan
1.14 after John was arrested, Jesus came
2.18 Now John's disciples . . were fasting
2.18 "Why do John's disciples . . fast?
6.14 "J. the baptizer has been raised
6.16 Herod . . said, "John . . has been raised
6.17 Herod had . . seized John, and bound him
6.18 John said to Herod, "It is not lawful
6.20 for Herod feared John, knowing that
6.24 she said, "The head of John the baptizer
6.25 "the head of John the Baptist on a platter
8.28 "J. the Baptist; and others say, Elijah
11.30 "Was the baptism of John from heaven?
11.32 all held that John was a real prophet
Lk 1.13 "a son, and you shall call his name John
1.60 "Not so; he shall be called John
1.63 he . . wrote, "His name is John
3. 2 the word of God came to John
3.15 all men questioned . . concerning John
3.16 John answered . . "I baptize . . with water
3.20 he shut up John in prison
5.33 "The disciples of John fast often
Lk 7.18 The disciples of John told him of all
7.19 John . . sent them . . , saying, "Are you he?
7.20 "John the Baptist has sent us
7.22 "Go and tell John what you have seen
7.24 When the messengers of J. had gone
7.24 he began to speak . . concerning John
7.28 "among those born . . none is greater than J.
7.29 baptized with the baptism of John
7.33 "J. the Baptist has come eating no bread
9. 7 said by some that J. had been raised
9. 9 "John I beheaded; but who is this?
9.19 "John the Baptist; but others say, Elijah
11. 1 "Lord, teach us to pray, as John taught
16.16 "The law and the prophets were until J.
20. 4 "Was the baptism of J. from heaven?
20. 6 "they are convinced that J. was a prophet
Jn 1. 6 a man sent from God, whose name was John
1.15 (J. bore witness to him, and cried
1.19 And this is the testimony of John
1.26 J. answered them, "I baptize with water
1.28 the Jordan, where John was baptizing
1.32 John bore witness, "I saw the Spirit
1.35 John was standing with two . . disciples
1.40 One of the two who heard John speak
3.23 John also was baptizing at Aenon
3.24 For John had not yet been put in prison
3.25 discussion arose between John's disciples
3.26 they came to John, and said to him
3.27 John answered, "No one can receive
4. 1 Jesus was . . baptizing more . . than John
5.33 "John . . has borne witness to the truth
5.36 "testimony . . is greater than that of J.
10.40 the place where John at first baptized
10.41 "John did no sign, but everything that John said about this man was true
Acts 1. 5 "John baptized with water, but . . you
1.22 "beginning from the baptism of John
10.37 "after the baptism which John preached
11.16 " 'John baptized with water, but you
13.24 "Before his coming John had preached
13.25 "And as John was finishing his course
19. 3 They said, "Into John's baptism
19. 4 "J. baptized with . . baptism of repentance
2. son of Zebedee
Mt 4.21 James the son of Zebedee and John
10. 2 James . . of Zebedee, and J. his brother
17. 1 Jesus took . . James and John his brother
Mk 1.19 James . . of Zebedee and John his brother
1.29 entered the house . . with James and John
3.17 and John the brother of James
5.37 allowed no one to follow . . except . . John
9. 2 Jesus took . . Peter and James and John
9.38 John said to him, "Teacher, we saw a man
10.35 James and John, the sons of Zebedee
10.41 began to be indignant at James and John
13. 3 Peter and James and John and Andrew
14.33 he took . . Peter and James and John
Lk 5.10 James and John, sons of Zebedee
6.14 and James and John, and Philip
8.51 except Peter and John and James
9.28 he took . . Peter and John and James
9.49 John answered, "Master, we saw a man
9.54 his disciples James and John saw it
22. 8 So Jesus[h] sent Peter and John
Acts 1.13 Peter and John and James and Andrew
3. 1 Peter and J. were going up to the temple
3. 3 Seeing Peter and John about to go
3. 4 Peter . . , with John, . . said, "Look at us
3.11 While he clung to Peter and John
4.13 they saw the boldness of Peter and John
4.19 Peter and John answered them
8.14 they sent to them Peter and John
12. 2 He killed James the brother of John
Gal 2. 9 Cephas and John, . . reputed . . pillars
3. others
Jn 1.42 "You are Simon the son of John?
21.15 "Simon, son of John, do you love me?

Jn 21.16 "Simon, son of John, do you love me?
21.17 "Simon, son of John, do you love me?
Acts 4. 6 Annas the high priest . . and John
12.12 John whose other name was Mark
12.25 bringing . . John whose other name was Mark
13. 5 And they had John to assist them
13.13 J. left them and returned to Jerusalem
15.37 Barnabas wanted to take . . J. called Mark
Rev 1. 1 The revelation of Jesus Christ . . to . . J.
1. 4 John to the seven churches . . in Asia
1. 9 I John, your brother, who share with you
22. 8 I John am he who heard and saw these
CONTEXTUALLY
Mt 3.14 John would have prevented him, saying

JOIN
1. *join, unite:* κολλάω KOLLAŌ
[a]pass.
Mt 19. 5 " 'a man shall . . be joined to his wife
Acts 5.13 [a]None of the rest dared join them
8.29 [a]"Go up and join this chariot
9.26 [a]he attempted to join the disciples
17.34 [a]some men joined him and believed
2. *allot, assign:* προσκληρόω (pass.) PROSKLĒROŌ*
Acts 17. 4 some of them . . joined Paul and Silas
3. *turn toward:* προσκλίνω (pass.) PROSKLINŌ*
Acts 5.36 "men, about four hundred, joined him
4. *run together, assemble:* συντρέχω SYNTRECHŌ
1 Pet 4. 4 surprised that you do not . . join them

JOIN IN ATTACKING
IDIOMATICALLY
a. Acts 16.22 The crowd joined in attacking them *καὶ συνεπέστη ὁ ὄχλος κατ' αὐτῶν* [SYNEPHISTĒMI*]

JOIN IN IMITATING
1. *joint imitator:* συμμιμητής SYMMIMĒTĒS* [B.2.d.2]
Phil 3.17 Brethren, join in imitating me

JOIN IN THE CHARGE
1. *join in attacking:* συνεπιτίθεμαι (mid.) SYNEPITITHEMAI*
Acts 24. 9 The Jews also joined in the charge

JOIN ONESELF
1. *join, unite:* κολλάω (pass.) KOLLAŌ
Lk 15.15 "he . . joined himself to one of the citizens
1 Cor 6.16 he who joins himself to a prostitute

JOIN TOGETHER
1. *fit together:* συναρμολογέω SYNARMOLOGEŌ*
Eph 2.21 the whole structure is joined together
4.16 the whole body, joined and knit together
2. *yoke together:* συζεύγνυμι SYZEUGNYMI*
Mt 19. 6 "What therefore God has joined together
Mk 10. 9 "What therefore God has joined together

JOINED, BE
1. *join to:* προσκολλάω (pass.) PROSKOLLAŌ*
Mk 10. 7 " 'a man shall . . be joined to his wife[p]‡
Eph 5.31 "a man shall . . be joined to his wife

JOINT
1. *ligament:* ἁφή HAPHĒ*
Eph 4.16 knit together by every joint
Col 2.19 knit together through its joints
2. *joint:* ἁρμός HARMOS*
Heb 4.12 to the division of . . joints and marrow

JOINT HEIR
1. *inheriting with:* συγκληρονόμος (subst.) SYGKLĒRONOMOS
1 Pet 3. 7 you are joint heirs of the grace of life

JOINT, PUT OUT OF
1. *turn out of course:* ἐκτρέπω (pass.) EKTREPŌ
Heb 12.13 that what is lame may not be put out of j.

JONAH: Ἰωνᾶς 'jōnə
Mt 12.39 "except the sign of the prophet Jonah
12.40 "as J. was three days and three nights
12.41 "Nineveh . . repented at the preaching of J.
12.41 "something greater than Jonah is here
16. 4 "no sign . . except the sign of Jonah
Lk 11.29 "no sign . . except the sign of Jonah
11.30 "Jonah became a sign to . . Nineveh
11.32 "Nineveh . . repented at the preaching of J.
Lk 11.32 "something greater than Jonah is here

JONAM: Ἰωνάμ 'jōnəm
Lk 3.30 the son of Joseph, the son of Jonam

JOPPA: Ἰόππη 'jäpə I,B-4; II,F-4
Acts 9.36 at Joppa a disciple named Tabitha
9.38 Since Lydda was near Joppa
9.42 it became known throughout all Joppa
9.43 he stayed in Joppa for many days
10. 5 "send men to Joppa, and bring one Simon
10. 8 having related . . , he sent them to J.
10.23 some . . brethren from J. accompanied
10.32 " 'Send therefore to J. and ask for Simon
11. 5 "I was in the city of Joppa praying
11.13 " 'Send to Joppa and bring Simon

JORAM: Ἰωράμ 'jȯrəm
Mt 1. 8 Jehoshaphat the father of Joram, and Joram the father of Uzziah

JORDAN: Ἰορδάνης 'jȯrd[ə]n I,D-4
Mt 3. 5 went out . . all the region about the J.
3. 6 they were baptized by him in the river J.
3.13 Jesus came from Galilee to the Jordan
4.15 "toward the sea, across the Jordan
4.25 crowds followed . . from beyond the J.
19. 1 entered the region of Judea beyond the J.
Mk 1. 5 they were baptized by him in the river J.
1. 9 Jesus . . was baptized by John in the J.
3. 8 Idumea and from beyond the Jordan
10. 1 region of Judea and beyond the Jordan
Lk 3. 3 he went into all the region about the J.
4. 1 Jesus . . returned from the Jordan
Jn 1.28 took place in Bethany beyond the J.
3.26 "who was with you beyond the J.
10.40 He went away again across the J.

JORIM: Ἰωρίμ 'jȯrim
Lk 3.29 the son of Jorim, the son of Matthat

JOSECH: Ἰωσήχ 'jōzək
Lk 3.26 Semein, the son of J., the son of Joda

JOSEPH: Ἰωσήφ 'jōzəf
1. son of Jacob
Jn 4. 5 the field that Jacob gave to his son J.
Acts 7. 9 "patriarchs, jealous of J., sold him
7.13 "J. made himself known to his brothers, and J.'s family became known to Pharaoh
7.14 "Joseph sent and called to him Jacob
7.18 "another king who had not known J.
Heb 11.21 Jacob . . blessed each of the sons of J.
11.22 By faith Joseph, at the end of his life
Rev 7. 8 twelve thousand of the tribe of J.
2. in Jesus' genealogy
Lk 3.24 Jannai, the son of Joseph
3.30 Judah, the son of J., the son of Jonam
3. husband of Mary
Mt 1.16 Jacob the father of J. the husband of Mary
1.18 When . . Mary had been betrothed to J.
1.19 her husband Joseph, being a just man
1.20 "J. . . , do not fear to take Mary your wife
1.24 When Joseph woke from sleep, he did
2.13 an angel of the Lord appeared to J.
2.19 an angel . . appeared in a dream to J.
Lk 1.27 betrothed to a man whose name was J.
2. 4 Joseph also went up from Galilee
2.16 found Mary and Joseph, and the babe
3.23 being the son (as was supposed) of J.
4.22 they said, "Is not this Joseph's son?
Jn 1.45 "Jesus of Nazareth, the son of Joseph
6.42 "Is not this Jesus, the son of Joseph?
4. brother of Jesus
Mt 13.55 "are not his brothers James and J.?
5. Joseph of Arimathea
Mt 27.57 a rich man from Arimathea, named J.
27.59 Joseph took the body, and wrapped it
Mk 15.43 J. of A., a respected member of the council
15.45 he granted the body to Joseph
Lk 23.50 a man named J. from . . Arimathea
Jn 19.38 J. of A., who was a disciple of Jesus

6. son of Mary and brother of James
Mt 27.56 Mary the mother of James and J.
7. Joseph called Barsabbas
Acts 1.23 they put forward two, J. called Barsabbas
8. Barnabas
Acts 4.36 J. . . surnamed by the apostles Barnabas

JOSES: Ἰωσῆς 'jōzəz
Mk 6. 3 "the son of Mary and brother of . . Joses
15.40 mother of James the younger and of Joses
15.47 Mary the mother of Joses

JOSHUA: Ἰησοῦς 'jäsh(ə)wə (*See also* JESUS)
Lk 3.29 Joshua, the son of Eliezer
Acts 7.45 "Our fathers in turn brought it in with J.
Heb 4. 8 For if Joshua had given them rest

JOSIAH: Ἰωσίας jō'sīə
Mt 1.10 Amos[c] the father of Josiah
1.11 Josiah the father of Jechoniah

JOTHAM: Ἰωαθάμ 'jōthəm
Mt 1. 9 Uzziah the father of Jotham, and Jotham the father of Ahaz

JOURNEY
1. *travel:* ὁδεύω HODEUŌ*
Lk 10.33 "a Samaritan, as he journeyed, came
2. *walking:* ὁδοιπορία HODOIPORIA*
Jn 4. 6 Jesus, wearied as he was with his journey
2 Cor 11.26 on frequent journeys, in danger
3. *way, road:* ὁδός HODOS
Mt 10.10 "⟨take⟩ no bag for your journey
Mk 6. 8 to take nothing for their journey
10.17 as he was setting out on his journey
Lk 2.44 they went a day's journey
9. 3 "Take nothing for your journey
11. 6 " 'a friend . . has arrived on a journey
Acts 1.12 Olivet, . . a sabbath day's j. away
4. *make a journey:* πορείαν ποιεῖσθαι POREIA [B.2.a.1]
Lk 13.22 teaching, and journeying toward Jerusalem
5. *go, walk:* πορεύομαι POREUOMAI
Acts 9. 3 as he journeyed he approached Damascus
22. 5 "I journeyed to Damascus
26.12 "Thus I journeyed to Damascus
26.13 "round . . those who journeyed with me

JOURNEY, BE ON ONE'S
1. *walk, travel:* ὁδοιπορέω HODOIPOREŌ*
Acts 10. 9 next day, as they were on their journey

JOURNEY, GO ON A
JOURNEY, TAKE ONE'S
1. *be away, go abroad:* ἀποδημέω APODĒMEŌ
Mt 25.14 "as when a man going on a journey
Lk 15.13 "took his journey into a far country

JOURNEY, GO ON ONE'S
JOURNEY, MAKE ONE'S
1. *go, walk:* πορεύομαι POREUOMAI
Acts 21. 5 we departed and went on our journey
22. 6 "I made my j. and drew near to Damascus

JOURNEY, SEND ONE ON HIS
JOURNEY, SPEED ONE ON HIS
1. *send forth, escort:* προπέμπω PROPEMPŌ
Rom 15.24 I hope . . to be sped on my journey
1 Cor 16. 6 that you may speed me on my journey
3 Jn . 6 You will do well to send them on their j.

JOY
1. *great joy:* ἀγαλλίασις AGALLIASIS
Lk 1.44 "the babe in my womb leaped for joy
2. *joy, delight:* χαρά CHARA
Mt 2.10 they rejoiced exceedingly with great joy
13.20 "he who . . immediately receives it with joy
13.44 "in his joy he goes and sells all that he has
25.21 " 'enter into the joy of your master
25.23 " 'enter into the joy of your master
28. 8 departed . . from the tomb with . . great joy
Mk 4.16 "they . . immediately receive it with joy
Lk 1.14 "you will have joy and gladness
2.10 "I bring you good news of a great joy
8.13 "when they hear the word, receive it with j.
Lk 10.17 The seventy[g] returned with joy
15. 7 "there will be more joy in heaven
15.10 "there is joy before the angels of God
24.41 while they still disbelieved for joy
24.52 returned to Jerusalem with great joy
Jn 3.29 "therefore this joy of mine is now full
15.11 "that my joy may be in you, and that your joy may be full
16.20 "but your sorrow will turn into joy
16.21 "for joy that a child[i] is born into the world
16.22 "no one will take your joy from you
16.24 "you will receive, that your j. may be full
17.13 "that they may have my joy fulfilled
Acts 8. 8 So there was much joy in that city
12.14 in her joy she did not open the gate
13.52 the disciples were filled with joy
15. 3 they gave great joy to all the brethren
Rom 14.17 righteousness and peace and joy
15.13 God of hope fill you with all joy
15.32 that . . I may come to you with joy
2 Cor 1.24 we work with you for your joy
2. 3 that my joy would be . . of you all
7.13 we rejoiced still more at the joy of Titus
8. 2 their abundance of joy . . overflowed
Gal 5.22 fruit of the Spirit is love, joy, peace
Phil 1. 4 always . . making my prayer with joy
1.25 for your progress and joy in the faith
2. 2 complete my j. by being of the same mind
2.29 receive him in the Lord with all joy
4. 1 my brethren, . . my joy and crown
Col 1.11 for all endurance and patience with joy
1 Th 1. 6 with joy inspired by the Holy Spirit
2.19 For what is our hope or joy?
2.20 For you are our glory and joy
3. 9 all the joy which we feel for your sake
2 Tim 1. 4 to see you, that I may be filled with joy
Phm . 7 I have derived much joy and comfort
Heb 12. 2 for the joy that was set before him
Jas 1. 2 Count it all joy, my brethren
4. 9 Let . . your joy ⟨be turned⟩ to dejection
1 Pet 1. 8 rejoice with unutterable and exalted joy
1 Jn 1. 4 writing this that our[a] j. may be complete
2 Jn .12 talk with you . . that our j. may be complete
3 Jn . 4 No greater joy can I have than this
CONTEXTUALLY
Lk 6.23 "Rejoice in that day, and leap for joy

JOYFULLY
1. *rejoice:* χαίρω (part.) CHAIRŌ
Lk 19. 6 he made haste . . and received him joyfully
2. *with joy:* μετὰ χαρᾶς CHARA [B.1.a.1]
Heb 10.34 you joyfully accepted the plundering
13.17 Let them do this joyfully

JUDAH: Ἰούδας 'jüdə (*See also* JUDAS)
1. son of Jacob
Mt 1. 2 Jacob the father of Judah
1. 3 Judah the father of Perez and Zerah
Lk 3.30 Simeon, the son of Judah, the son of Joseph
3.33 Perez, the son of Judah
2. tribe
Heb 7.14 our Lord was descended from Judah
8. 8 "I will establish a new covenant with . . J.
Rev 5. 5 "lo, the Lion of the tribe of Judah
7. 5 twelve thousand sealed . . of the tribe of J.
3. territory
Mt 2. 6 " 'you, O Bethlehem, in the land of J., are by no means least among the rulers of J.
Lk 1.39 Mary . . went with haste . . to a city of J.

JUDAISM: Ἰουδαϊσμός
Gal 1.13 you . . heard of my former life in Judaism
1.14 I advanced in Judaism beyond many
CONTEXTUALLY
Acts 13.43 Jews and devout converts to J. followed Paul

JUDAS: Ἰούδας 'jüdəs (*See also* JUDAH; JUDE)
1. Judas Iscariot
Mt 10. 4 Judas Iscariot, who betrayed him
26.14 one of the twelve, . . called Judas Iscariot

Mt 26.25 J., who betrayed him, said, "Is it I?
26.47 Judas came, one of the twelve
27. 3 When J. . . saw that he was condemned
Mk 3.19 Judas Iscariot, who betrayed him
14.10 Then Judas Iscariot, . . one of the twelve
14.43 Judas came, one of the twelve
Lk 6.16 Judas Iscariot, who became a traitor
22. 3 Satan entered into Judas called Iscariot
22.47 the man called Judas, one of the twelve
22.48 "Judas, would you betray the Son of man?
Jn 6.71 He spoke of J. the son of Simon Iscariot
12. 4 Judas Iscariot, one of his disciples
13. 2 put it into the heart of J. Iscariot
13.26 gave it to J., . . son of Simon Iscariot
13.29 because Judas had the money box
18. 2 J., who betrayed him, also knew
18. 3 Judas, procuring a band of soldiers
18. 5 Judas . . was standing with them
Acts 1.16 "the Holy Spirit spoke . . concerning J.
1.25 "to take the place . . from which J. turned
2. the apostle
Lk 6.16 Judas the son of James
Jn 14.22 Judas (not Iscariot) said to him, "Lord
Acts 1.13 Simon the Zealot and J. the son of James
3. brother of Jesus
Mt 13.55 "are not his brothers James and . . J.?
Mk 6. 3 "brother of James and Joses and J.
4. others
Acts 5.37 "After him Judas the Galilean arose
9.11 "inquire in the house of Judas for . . Saul
15.22 They sent Judas called Barsabbas
15.27 "We have therefore sent Judas and Silas
15.32 J. and Silas, who were . . prophets

JUDE: Ἰούδας 'jüd (*See also* JUDAS)
Jude . 1 Jude, a servant of Jesus Christ

JUDEA: jü'dēə I,C-5
1. *Judea:* Ἰουδαία
Mt 2. 1 born in Bethlehem of Judea
2. 5 They told him, "In Bethlehem of J.
2.22 heard that Archelaus reigned over J.
3. 1 John . . , preaching in the wilderness of J.
3. 5 Then went out to him . . all Judea
4.25 great crowds followed him from . . J.
19. 1 he . . entered the region of Judea
24.16 "let those who are in Judea flee
Mk 1. 5 there went out to him all the country of J.
3. 7 multitude from Galilee . . ; also from J.
10. 1 left there and went to the region of J.
13.14 "then let those who are in Judea flee
Lk 1. 5 In the days of Herod, king of Judea
1.65 through all the hill country of J.
2. 4 Joseph also went up . . to Judea
3. 1 Pontius Pilate being governor of Judea
4.44 preaching in the synagogues of Judea[n]‡
5.17 every village of Galilee and Judea
6.17 multitude of people from all Judea
7.17 spread through the whole of Judea
21.21 let those who are in Judea flee
23. 5 teaching throughout all Judea
Jn 4. 3 left J. and departed again to Galilee
4.47 heard that Jesus had come from J.
4.54 when he had come from J. to Galilee
7. 1 he would not go about in Judea
7. 3 "Leave here and go to Judea
11. 7 "Let us go into Judea again
Acts 1. 8 "my witnesses . . in all J. and Samaria
2. 9 "residents of Mesopotamia, Judea
8. 1 scattered throughout the region of J.
9.31 church throughout all J. . . had peace
10.37 "word . . proclaimed throughout all J.
11. 1 brethren who were in Judea heard
11.29 to send relief to the brethren . . in Judea
12.19 Then he went down from Judea
15. 1 some men came down from Judea
21.10 Agabus came down from Judea
26.20 "throughout all the country of Judea
Acts 28.21 "We have received no letters from Judea
Rom 15.31 delivered from the unbelievers in Judea
2 Cor 1.16 to . . have you send me on my way to Judea
Gal 1.22 not known by sight to the churches . . in J.
1 Th 2.14 imitators of the churches . . which are in J.
2. *Jewish:* Ἰουδαῖος (*See also* JEW) [A.3.a.2]
Jn 3.22 Jesus . . went into the land of Judea
Acts 2.14 "Men of Judea and all . . in Jerusalem

JUDEAN: Ἰουδαῖος (*See also* JEW)
Jn [7. 1 because the *Judeans* sought to kill him†

JUDGE
1. *examine closely:* ἀνακρίνω ANAKRINŌ
1 Cor 2.15 The spiritual man judges all things, but is himself to be judged by no one
4. 3 a . . small thing that I should be judged by you . . I do not even judge myself
4. 4 It is the Lord who judges me
2. *differentiate, decide:* διακρίνω DIAKRINŌ
1 Cor 11.31 if we judged ourselves truly
3. *judge:* δικαστής DIKASTĒS*
Acts 7.27 " 'Who made you . . a judge over us?
7.35 " 'Who made you a ruler and a judge?
4. *think, lead:* ἡγέομαι HĒGEOMAI
1 Tim 1.12 he judged me faithful by appointing me
5. *judge, decide:* κρίνω KRINŌ
[a]subst. part.
Mt 7. 1 "Judge not, that you be not judged
7. 2 "you will be judged
19.28 "you . . will also sit . . judging . . Israel
Lk 6.37 "Judge not, and you will not be judged
7.43 "You have judged rightly
12.57 "why do you not judge for yourselves?
22.30 "you may . . sit on thrones judging . . Israel
Jn 5.22 "The Father judges no one
5.30 "as I hear, I judge; . . my judgment is just
7.24 "Do not judge by appearances, but judge with right judgment
7.51 "Does our law judge . . without . . a hearing?
8.15 "You judge according to the flesh, I judge no one
8.16 "even if I do judge, my judgment is true
8.26 "I have much to say . . and much to judge
8.50 [a]"there is One . . and he will be the judge
12.47 "I do not judge him; for I did not come to judge the world
12.48 [a]"He who rejects me . . has a judge
12.48 [a]"word that I have spoken will be his j.
16.11 "the ruler of this world is judged
18.31 "Take him yourselves and judge him
Acts 4.19 "Whether it is right . . , you must judge
7. 7 " 'I will j. the nation which they serve
13.46 "j. yourselves unworthy of eternal life
16.15 "If you have judged me to be faithful
17.31 "a day on which he will judge the world
23. 3 "Are you sitting to judge me?
[24. 6 "*we would have judged him*‡
Rom 2. 1 you have no excuse . . when you judge
2. 1 [a]you, the judge, are doing the very same
2. 3 when you judge those who do such
2.12 all . . under the law . . judged by the law
2.16 when . . God judges the secrets of men
3. 4 "prevail when thou art judged
3. 6 For then how could God judge the world?
14.22 he who has no reason to judge himself
1 Cor 5.12 what have I to do with judging outsiders? Is it not those inside . . you are to judge?
5.13 God judges those outside
6. 2 Do you not know . . the saints will judge?
6. 2 if the world is to be judged by you
6. 3 Do you not know that we are to judge?
10.15 judge for yourselves what I say
11.13 Judge for yourselves; is it proper?
11.31 we should not be judged
11.32 when we are judged by the Lord
2 Tim 4. 1 Christ Jesus who is to judge the living
Heb 10.30 "The Lord will judge his people

Heb 13. 4 for God will judge the immoral
Jas 2.12 act as those who are to be judged
4.11 He that . . judges his brother . . judges the law. But if you judge the law, you are not a doer of the law
4.12 who are you that you j. your neighbor?
5. 9 Do not grumble . . that you . . not be judged
1 Pet 1.17 if you invoke as Father him who judges
2.23 he trusted to him who judges justly
4. 5 who is ready to judge the living
4. 6 though judged in the flesh like men
Rev 6.10 "how long before thou wilt judge?
11.18 "the time for the dead to be judged
18. 8 "mighty is the Lord God who judges
19. 2 "he has judged the great harlot
19.11 he judges and makes war
20.12 dead were judged by what was written
20.13 all were judged by what they had done

6. *judge, umpire:* κριτής KRITĒS*
Mt 5.25 "lest your accuser hand you over to the judge, and the judge to the guard
12.27 "Therefore they shall be your judges
Lk 11.19 "Therefore they shall be your judges
12.14 "Man, who made me a judge?
12.58 "lest he drag you to the judge, and the judge hand you over to the officer
18. 2 "there was a judge who neither feared God
18. 6 "Hear what the unrighteous judge says
Acts 10.42 "he is the one ordained by God to be judge
13.20 "he gave them judges until Samuel
18.15 "I refuse to be a judge of these things
24.10 "for many years you have been judge
2 Tim 4. 8 the Lord, the righteous judge
Heb 12.23 to a judge who is God of all
Jas 2. 4 have you not . . become judges?
4.11 you are not a doer of the law but a judge
4.12 There is one lawgiver and judge
5. 9 the Judge is standing at the doors

JUDGED, BE

1. *think, suppose:* δοκέω DOKEŌ
Heb 4. 1 let us fear lest any of you be judged
2. *receive judgment:* κρίμα λαμβάνειν KRIMA [A.6.a.4]
Jas 3. 1 we who teach shall be judged

JUDGMENT

1. *ordinance, justification:* δικαίωμα DIKAIŌMA
Rev 15. 4 "thy judgments have been revealed
2. *think, suppose:* δοκέω DOKEŌ [A.6.a.2]
Mt 26.66 "What is your judgment?
3. *judgment, opinion, purpose:* γνώμη GNŌMĒ
1 Cor 1.10 united in the same mind and the same j.
7.40 in my judgment she is happier
4. *judgment:* κρίμα KRIMA
Mt 7. 2 "For with the judgment you pronounce
Jn 9.39 "For judgment I came into this world
Acts 24.25 as he argued about . . future judgment
Rom 2. 2 j. of God rightly falls upon those
2. 3 that . . you will escape the j. of God?
5.16 the judgment following one trespass
11.33 How unsearchable are his judgments!
13. 2 those who resist will incur judgment
1 Cor 11.29 eats and drinks judgment upon himself
Gal 5.10 he who is troubling you will bear his j.
Heb 6. 2 resurrection of the dead, and eternal j.
1 Pet 4.17 For the time has come for judgment
Rev 17. 1 "Come, I will show you the judgment
18.20 "God has given j. for you against her!
20. 4 those to whom j. was committed
5. *judge, decide:* κρίνω KRINŌ
[a]A.3.d.1 [b]B.2.a.2
Acts 21.25 [a]"we have sent a letter with our judgment
Rev 16. 5 [b]"Just art thou in these thy judgments
6. *judgment:* κρίσις KRISIS
Mt 5.21 " 'whoever kills shall be liable to judgment
5.22 "every one who is angry . . shall be liable to j.
10.15 "it shall be more tolerable on the day of j.
11.22 "it shall be more tolerable on the day of j.
11.24 "it shall be more tolerable on the day of j.
12.36 "on the day of j. men will render account
12.41 "The men of Nineveh will arise at the j.
12.42 "The queen of the South will arise at the j.
Lk 10.14 "it shall be more tolerable in the j.
11.31 "The queen of the South will arise at the j.
11.32 "The men of Nineveh will arise at the j.
Jn 3.19 this is the j., that the light has come
5.22 "The Father . . has given all j. to the Son
5.24 "he does not come into judgment
5.27 "has given him authority to execute j.
5.29 "those . . to the resurrection of judgment
5.30 "my j. is just, because I seek not my own
7.24 "judge with right judgment
8.16 "my judgment is true
12.31 "Now is the judgment of this world
16. 8 "he will convince[x] . . concerning judgment
16.11 "concerning judgment, because the ruler
2 Th 1. 5 This is evidence of the righteous judgment
1 Tim 5.24 conspicuous, pointing to judgment
Heb 9.27 to die once, and after that comes j.
10.27 a fearful prospect of judgment
Jas 2.13 For judgment is without mercy . . ; yet mercy triumphs over judgment
2 Pet 2. 4 committed them to pits . . until the j.
2. 9 under punishment until the day of j.
2.11 do not pronounce a reviling judgment
3. 7 kept until the day of judgment
1 Jn 4.17 we may have confidence for the day of j.
Jude . 6 kept by him in eternal chains . . until the j.
. 9 not presume to pronounce a reviling j.
.15 "⟨the Lord came⟩ to execute j. on all
Rev 14. 7 "the hour of his judgment has come
16. 7 "true and just are thy judgments!
18.10 "In one hour has thy judgment come
19. 2 "his judgments are true and just

JUDGMENT IS, ONE'S

1. *judge, decide:* κρίνω KRINŌ
Acts 15.19 "my j. is that we should not trouble

JUDGMENT, PASS
JUDGMENT, PRONOUNCE

1. *judge, decide:* κρίνω KRINŌ
Rom 2. 1 passing j. . . you condemn yourself
14. 3 let not him who abstains pass judgment
14. 4 Who are you to pass judgment?
14.10 Why do you pass j. on your brother?
14.13 Then let us no more pass judgment
1 Cor 4. 5 Therefore do not pronounce judgment
5. 3 I have already pronounced judgment
Col 2.16 let no one pass judgment on you

JUDGMENT, RIGHTEOUS

1. *righteous judgment:* δικαιοκρισία DIKAIOKRISIA*
Rom 2. 5 when God's righteous j. will be revealed

JUDGMENT SEAT

1. *step, platform:* βῆμα BĒMA
Mt 27.19 while he was sitting on the j. seat
Jn 19.13 Pilate . . sat down on the j. seat
Rom 14.10 we shall all stand before the judgment seat
2 Cor 5.16 we must all appear before the j. seat

JUDGMENT, SOBER

1. *be of sound mind:* σωφρονέω (inf.) SŌPHRONEŌ
Rom 12. 3 but to think with sober judgment

JULIA: Ἰουλία 'jülyə
Rom 16.15 Greet Philologus, Julia, Nereus

JULIUS: Ἰούλιος 'jülyəs
Acts 27. 1 delivered Paul . . to a centurion . . named J.
27. 3 Julius treated Paul kindly

JUNIAS: Ἰουνιᾶς 'jünyəs
Rom 16. 7 Greet Andronicus and Junias

JURISDICTION

1. *authority, power:* ἐξουσία EXOUSIA
Lk 20.20 deliver him up to the . . j. of the governor
23. 7 learned that he belonged to Herod's j.

JUST
1. *just now:* ἄρτι ARTI
Mt 9.18 "My daughter has just died
2. *righteous, just:* δίκαιος DIKAIOS
Mt 1.19 her husband Joseph, being a just man
5.45 "sends rain on the just and on the unjust
Lk 1.17 "the disobedient to the wisdom of the just
14.14 "repaid at the resurrection of the just
Jn 5.30 "I judge; and my judgment is just
Acts 22.14 " 'God . . appointed you . . to see the Just One
24.15 "a resurrection of both the just
Rom 7.12 commandment is holy and just and good
Phil 4. 8 whatever is just, whatever is pure
2 Th 1. 6 God deems it just to repay with affliction
1 Tim 1. 9 the law is not laid down for the just
Heb 12.23 to the spirits of just men made perfect
1 Jn 1. 9 he is faithful and just, and will forgive
Rev 15. 3 "Just and true are thy ways, O King!
16. 5 "Just art thou in these thy judgments
16. 7 "true and just are thy judgments!
19. 2 "his judgments are true and just
3. *already, now:* ἤδη ĒDĒ
Jn 21. 4 Just as day was breaking, Jesus stood
4. *just, deserved:* ἔνδικος ENDIKOS*
Rom 3. 8 Their condemnation is just
Heb 2. 2 disobedience received a just retribution
5. *at once:* ἐξαυτῆς EXAUTĒS
Phil 2.23 just as soon as I see how it will go
6. *now:* νῦν NYN
Jn 21.10 "the fish that you have just caught
CONTEXTUALLY
Jn 4.27 Just then his disciples came. They marveled
1 Cor 9.18 J. this: that . . I may make the gospel free
16. 7 I do not want to see you now j. in passing
2 Pet 2. 1 j. as there will be false teachers

JUST AS
1. *as, so:* ὡς HŌS
Mk **4.**36
Acts **10.**47
2 Cor **7.**14
Heb **3.**2
Jude .7
2. *just as:* ὥσπερ HŌSPER
Mt 13.40 "Just as the weeds are gathered and burned
Acts 11.15 "the Holy Spirit fell on them just as on us
Rom 6.19 just as you once yielded your members
11.30 Just as you were once disobedient
3. *in accordance with, for:* κατά (+acc.) KATA
Heb 9.27 just as it is appointed for men to die
4. *just as:* καθάπερ KATHAPER
1 Cor 12.12 For just as the body is one and has many
Heb 4. 2 good news came to us just as to them
5. *as, just as:* καθώς KATHŌS
Lk 1. 2 just as they were delivered to us by those
24.24 "found it just as the women had said
Jn 15.10 "just as I have kept my Father's
Acts 15. 8 "giving . . the Holy Spirit just as . . to us
1 Cor 10.33 just as I try to please all men
15.49 Just as we have borne the image of the man
Gal 2. 7 just as Peter had been entrusted
Eph 4. 4 just as you were called to the one hope
Col 2. 7 in the faith, just as you were taught
1 Th 2. 4 just as we have been approved by God
3. 4 just as it has come to pass
4. 1 to please God, just as you are doing
5.11 build one another up, just as you are doing
1 Jn 2.27 just as it has taught you, abide in him
3.23 love . . , just as he has commanded us
2 Jn . 4 just as we have been commanded by the F.
6. *as, just as:* καθώσπερ KATHŌSPER*
Heb 5. 4 called by God, just as Aaron was
7. *in the manner in which:* καθ' ὃν τρόπον TROPOS [B.3.b.1]
Acts 15.11 "we shall be saved . . just as they will
IDIOMATICALLY
a. Heb 9.27 And just as it is appointed for men καὶ καθ' ὅσον ἀπόκειται τοῖς ἀνθρώποις [HOSOS]

JUST AS SOON AS
1. *as, so:* ὡς HŌS
Phil **2.**23

JUST REQUIREMENT
1. *ordinance, justification:* δικαίωμα DIKAIŌMA
Rom 8. 4 that the just r. of the law might be fulfilled

JUST SO
1. *thus, so:* οὕτως HOUTŌS
Lk 15. 7 "Just so, I tell you, there will be . . joy
15.10 "Just so, I tell you there is joy

JUSTICE
1. *righteousness, justice:* δικαιοσύνη DIKAIOSYNĒ
Acts 24.25 he argued about justice and self-control
Rom 3. 5 if our wickedness serves to show the j.
Heb 11.33 conquered kingdoms, enforced justice
2. *right, penalty:* δίκη DIKĒ
Acts 28. 4 "justice has not allowed him to live
3. *judgment:* κρίσις KRISIS
Mt 12.18 "he shall proclaim justice to the Gentiles
12.20 "till he brings justice to victory
23.23 "weightier matters of the law, justice
Lk 11.42 "woe to you Pharisees! . . you . . neglect j.
Acts 8.33 "In his humiliation j. was denied him

JUSTIFICATION
1. *ordinance, justification:* δικαίωμα DIKAIŌMA
Rom 5.16 but the free gift . . brings justification
2. *justification:* δικαίωσις DIKAIŌSIS
Rom 4.25 who was . . raised for our justification
3. *righteousness, justice:* δικαιοσύνη DIKAIOSYNĒ
Gal 2.21 if justification[e] were through the law†

JUSTIFY
1. *justify, vindicate:* δικαιόω DIKAIOŌ
Mt 11.19 "Yet wisdom is justified by her deeds[e]
12.37 "for by your words you will be justified
Lk 7.29 (the tax collectors justified God
7.35 "Yet wisdom is justified by . . her children
10.29 "he, desiring to justify himself, said
16.15 "You are those who justify yourselves
18.14 "man went down to his house justified
Rom 2.13 doers of the law who will be justified
3. 4 "That thou mayest be justified in thy words
3.20 no human . . will be justified in his sight
3.24 they are justified by his grace as a gift
3.26 he justifies him who has faith in Jesus
3.28 we hold that a man is justified by faith
3.30 he will justify the circumcised
4. 2 if Abraham was justified by works
4. 5 who . . trusts him who justifies the ungodly
5. 1 since we are justified by faith
5. 9 we are now justified by his blood
8.30 those whom he called he also justified; . . whom he justified he also glorified
8.33 It is God who justifies
1 Cor 6.11 you were justified in the name of the Lord
Gal 2.16 know that a man is not justified[d] by works†
2.16 we have believed in Christ . . to be justified
2.16 by works . . shall no one be justified
2.17 in our endeavor to be justified in Christ
3. 8 that God would justify . . Gentiles by faith
3.11 no man is justified before God by the law
3.24 that we might be justified by faith
5. 4 you who would be justified by the law
1 Tim [3.16 He[h] was . . *justified* in the Spirit†
Tit 3. 7 that we might be justified by his grace
Jas 2.21 Was not Abraham . . justified by works?
2.24 You see that a man is justified by works
2.25 was not also Rahab . . justified by works?
2. *righteousness, justice:* δικαιοσύνη DIKAIOSYNĒ [B.1.a.2]
Rom 10. 4 that . . one who has faith may be justified
10.10 believes with his heart and so is justified
3. *give reckoning:* ἀποδιδόναι λόγον LOGOS; APODIDŌMI [B.2.a.1]
Acts 19.40 "being no cause . . to justify this commotion

JUSTLY
1. *righteous, just:* δίκαιος (subst. neut.) DIKAIOS [A.1.c.1]
Col 4. 1 Masters, treat your slaves justly
2. *justly, rightly:* δικαίως DIKAIŌS
Lk 23.41 "we indeed justly; . . receiving the due reward
1 Pet 2.23 he trusted to him who judges justly

JUSTUS: Ἰοῦστος ˈjəstəs
Acts 1.23 Barsabbas, who was surnamed J.
18. 7 the house of a man named Titius[q] J.
Col 4.11 Jesus who is called Justus

K

KEEP (*See also, e.g.,* ALERT, KEEP; ALIVE, KEEP)
1. *observe, maintain:* διατηρέω DIATĒREŌ*
Lk 2.51 his mother kept all these . . in her heart
Acts 15.29 "If you keep yourselves from these
2. *have, hold:* ἔχω ECHŌ
Lk 19.20 " 'your pound, which I kept laid away
Rom 14.22 keep between yourself and God
1 Tim 3. 4 keeping his children submissive
1 Pet 3.16 keep your conscience clear
3. *be:* εἰμί EIMI
1 Tim 2.12 she is to keep silent
4. *leave behind:* καταλείπω KATALEIPŌ
Rom 11. 4 "I have kept for myself seven thousand men
5. *hold fast, restrain:* κατέχω KATECHŌ
Lk 4.42 would have kept him from leaving
Phm .13 glad to keep him with me
6. *seize, hold fast:* κρατέω KRATEŌ
Mk 9.10 So they kept the matter to themselves
Lk 24.16 their eyes were kept from recognizing him
7. *cease, stop:* παύω PAUŌ
1 Pet 3.10 "let him keep his tongue from evil
8. *keeping safe, property:* περιποίησις PERIPOIĒSIS [B.1.a.2; B.2.b.1]
Heb 10.39 who have faith and keep their souls
9. *guard, keep:* φρουρέω PHROUREŌ
Phil 4. 7 peace of God . . will keep your hearts
10. *guard, observe:* φυλάσσω PHYLASSŌ
[a]φυλάσσειν φυλακάς
Lk 2. 8 [a]keeping watch over their flock by night
11.28 "who hear the word of God and keep it!
Jn 12.25 "he who hates his life . . will keep it
12.47 "hears my sayings and does not keep them
Acts 7.53 "received the law . . and did not keep it
22.20 " 'keeping the garments of those who killed
Rom 2.26 if a man . . uncircumcised keeps the . . law
Gal 6.13 even those . . do not . . keep the law
1 Tim 5.21 I charge you to keep these rules
1 Jn 5.21 children, keep yourselves from idols
Jude .24 who is able to keep you from falling
11. *do, make:* ποιέω POIEŌ
Mt 26.18 " 'I will keep the passover at your house
28.14 "we will . . keep you out of trouble
Jn 7.19 "Yet none of you keeps the law
Gal 5. 3 he is bound to keep the whole law
Heb 11.28 By faith he kept the Passover
12. *preserve, protect:* συντηρέω SYNTĒREŌ
Lk 2.19 Mary kept all these things, pondering
13. *finish, fulfill:* τελέω TELEŌ
Rom 2.27 those who . . keep the law will condemn you
14. *keep, observe:* τηρέω TĒREŌ
Mt 19.17 "would enter life, k. the commandments
Mk 7. 9 "in order to keep your tradition!
Jn 2.10 "you have kept the good wine until now
8.51 "I say to you, if any one keeps my word
8.52 "you say, 'If any one keeps my word
8.55 "I do know him and I keep his word
9.16 "for he does not keep the sabbath
12. 7 "Let her alone, let her keep it
14.15 "you will keep my commandments
14.21 "has my commandments and keeps them
14.23 "If a man loves me, he will k. my word
Jn 14.24 "does not love me does not k. my words
15.10 "If you keep my commandments, . . as I have kept my Father's commandments
15.20 "if they kept my word, they will keep yours also
17. 6 "and they have kept thy word
17.11 "Holy Father, keep them in thy name
17.12 "I kept them in thy name
17.15 "thou shouldst k. them from the evil one[k]
Acts 12. 5 So Peter was kept in prison
15. 5 "charge them to keep the law of Moses
16.23 charging the jailer to keep them
25. 4 Paul was being kept at Caesarea
1 Cor 7.37 determined . . to keep her as his betrothed[z]
1 Th 5.23 may your . . body be kept sound
1 Tim 5.22 Do not be hasty . . ; keep yourself pure
6.14 keep the commandment unstained
2 Tim 4. 7 I have finished the race, . . kept the faith
Jas 1.27 to keep oneself unstained from the world
2.10 whoever keeps the whole law
1 Pet 1. 4 an inheritance . . kept in heaven for you
2 Pet 2. 4 into hell[f] . . to be kept until the judgment
2. 9 Lord knows how . . to k. the unrighteous
3. 7 kept until the day of judgment
1 Jn 2. 3 if we keep his commandments
2. 5 but whoever keeps his word
3.22 because we keep his commandments
3.24 All who keep his commandments
5. 3 that we keep his commandments
5.18 but He who was born of God keeps him
Jude . 1 To those who are . . kept for Jesus Christ
. 6 angels that did not keep their own position have been kept by him
.21 keep yourselves in the love of God
Rev 1. 3 who keep what is written therein
2.26 " 'who keeps my works until the end
3. 3 " 'keep that, and repent
3. 8 " 'yet you have kept my word
3.10 " 'Because you have kept my word . . , I will keep you from the hour of trial
12.17 "those who keep the commandments
14.12 those who keep the commandments
16.15 ("he who is awake, keeping his garments
22. 7 Blessed is he who keeps the words
22. 9 "those who keep the words of this book
CONTEXTUALLY
Lk 18. 3 "a widow . . who kept coming to him
2 Cor 10.13 will k. to the limits God has apportioned
1 Th 5. 6 but let us keep awake and be sober

KEEP AWAY
1. *depart, withdraw from:* ἀφίστημι APHISTĒMI
Acts 5.38 "I tell you, keep away from these men
2. *stand aloof, avoid* (mid.): στέλλω STELLŌ
2 Th 3. 6 keep away from any brother . . in idleness

KEEP BACK
1. *withhold:* ἀφυστερέω APHYSTEREŌ*
Jas 5. 4 wages . . which you kept back by fraud
2. *put aside for oneself* (mid.): νοσφίζω NOSPHIZŌ
Acts 5. 2 he kept back some of the proceeds
5. 3 "to keep back part of the proceeds

KEEP FROM
1. *hinder, prevent, withhold:* κωλύω KŌLYŌ
Acts 27.43 kept them from carrying out their purpos
IDIOMATICALLY
a. Jn 11.37 "Could not he . . have kept this man from dying? οὐκ ἐδύνατο οὗτος . . ποιῆσαι ἵνα καὶ οὗτος μὴ ἀποθάνῃ; [POIEŌ]
b. 2 Cor 4.4 to keep them from seeing εἰς τὸ μὴ αὐγάσαι [MĒ]
c. Rev 8.12 third . . was kept from shining μὴ φάνῃ τὸ τ. [MĒ]

KEEP FROM BEING
1. *set in order, appoint:* καθίστημι (neg.) KATHISTĒMI
2 Pet 1. 8 they keep you from being ineffective

KEEP FROM, TO
1. *in order that:* ἵνα (neg.) HINA
Jn 16. 1 "said . . this . . to keep you from falling away
2 Cor 2.11 to keep Satan from gaining the advantage

2 Cor 12. 7 to keep me from being too elated
12. 7 to keep me from being too elated
Rev 3.18 " 'to keep . . your nakedness from being seen

KEEP IN CUSTODY
1. *keep, observe:* τηρέω TĒREŌ
Acts 24.23 that he should be kept in custody
25.21 "Paul had appealed to be kept in custody

KEEP IN SUSPENSE
IDIOMATICALLY
a. Jn 10.24 "How long will you keep us in suspense?
ἕως πότε τὴν ψυχὴν ἡμῶν αἴρεις; [AIRŌ; PSYCHĒ]

KEEP SAFE
1. *preserve, protect:* συντηρέω SYNTĒREŌ
Mk 6.20 Herod feared John . . and kept him safe

KEEP SANE
1. *be of sound mind:* σωφρονέω SŌPHRONEŌ
1 Pet 4. 7 keep sane and sober for your prayers

KEEP SHEEP
1. *tend, herd, govern:* ποιμαίνω POIMAINŌ
Lk 17. 7 "one . . who has a servant . . keeping sheep

KEEP UNDER GUARD
1. *guard, observe:* φυλάσσω PHYLASSŌ
Lk 8.29 (he was kept under guard, and bound

KEEP UNDER RESTRAINT
1. *enclose, close:* συγκλείω SYGKLEIŌ
Gal 3.23 under the law, kept under restraint

KEEP WATCH OVER
1. *keep, observe:* τηρέω TĒREŌ
Mt 27.36 they sat down and kept watch over him
27.54 who were . . keeping watch over Jesus

KEEPER, TEMPLE
1. *guardian of a temple:* νεωκόρος NEŌKOROS*
Acts 19.35 "city of the Ephesians is temple keeper

KEEPING
1. *safekeeping:* τήρησις TĒRĒSIS
1 Cor 7.19 keeping the commandments of God

KERNEL
1. *grain, seed:* κόκκος KOKKOS
1 Cor 15.37 what you sow is . . but a bare kernel

KEY
1. *key, bar:* κλείς KLEIS*
Mt 16.19 "I will give you the keys of the kingdom
Lk 11.52 "have taken away the key of knowledge
Rev 1.18 "I have the keys of Death and Hades
3. 7 " 'true one, who has the key of David
9. 1 he was given the key of the shaft
20. 1 angel . . holding in his hand the key

KICK
1. *kick, trample on:* λακτίζω LAKTIZŌ*
Acts 26.14 " 'It hurts you to kick against the goads

KID
1. *kid, goat:* ἔριφος ERIPHOS
Lk 15.29 " 'yet you never gave me a kid

KIDNAPER
1. *kidnaper, slave dealer:* ἀνδραποδιστής ANDRAPODISTĒS*
1 Tim 1.10 sodomites, kidnapers, liars, perjurers

KIDRON: Κεδρών 'kidrən, 'kēdrən
Jn 18. 1 he went forth . . across the Kidron

KILL
1. *take up, kill:* ἀναιρέω ANAIREŌ
Mt 2.16 he sent and killed all the male children
Acts 2.23 "killed by the hands of lawless men
5.33 they were enraged and wanted to kill
7.28 " 'Do you want to kill me as you killed the Egyptian yesterday?
9.23 the Jews plotted to kill him
9.24 They were watching the gates . . to kill him
9.29 but they were seeking to kill him
12. 2 He killed James the brother of John
13.28 "yet they asked Pilate to have him killed
16.27 drew his sword and was about to k. himself
22.20 " 'the garments of those who killed him
23.15 "ready to kill him before he comes near
23.21 "by an oath . . till they have killed him
23.27 "This man . . was about to be killed by them
25. 3 planning an ambush to kill him
2. *kill:* ἀποκτείνω APOKTEINŌ
Mt 10.28 "do not fear those who kill the body but cannot kill the soul
16.21 killed, and on the third day be raised
17.23 "they will kill him, and he will be raised
21.35 "tenants . . beat one, killed another
21.38 " 'This is the heir; come, let us kill him
21.39 " 'they took him . . and killed him
22. 6 "treated them shamefully, and killed them
23.34 "some of whom you will kill and crucify
23.37 "O Jerusalem, . . killing the prophets!
26. 4 to arrest Jesus by stealth and kill him
Mk 3. 4 "Is it lawful . . to save life or to kill?
6.19 Herodias . . wanted to kill him
8.31 the Son of man must . . be killed
9.31 "they will kill him; and when he is killed, after three days he will rise
10.34 "they will mock him . . and kill him
12. 5 "he sent another, and him they killed; . . some they beat and some they killed
12. 7 " 'This is the heir; come, let us kill him
12. 8 "they took him and killed him
14. 1 to arrest him by stealth, and kill him
Lk 9.22 "The Son of man must . . be killed
11.47 "the prophets whom your fathers killed
11.48 "deeds of your fathers; for they killed
11.49 " 'apostles, some of whom they will kill
12. 4 "do not fear those who kill the body
12. 5 "fear him who, after he has killed
13. 4 "the tower in Siloam fell and killed them
13.31 "Get away . . , for Herod wants to kill you
13.34 "O Jerusalem, . . killing the prophets!
18.33 "they will scourge him and kill him
20.14 " 'This is the heir; let us kill him
20.15 "they cast him out . . and killed him
Jn 5.18 the Jews sought all the more to kill him
7. 1 because the Jews[n] sought to kill him
7.19 "Why do you seek to kill me?
7.20 "Who is seeking to kill you?
7.25 "the man whom they seek to kill
8.22 Then said the Jews, "Will he kill himself?
8.37 "yet you seek to kill me
8.40 "but now you seek to kill me
16. 2 "hour is coming when whoever kills you
Acts 3.15 "killed the Author of life, whom God raised
7.52 "killed those who announced beforehand
21.31 as they were trying to kill him, word came
23.12 by an oath . . till they had killed Paul
23.14 "by an oath . . till we have killed Paul
27.42 soldiers' plan was to kill the prisoners
Rom 7.11 deceived me and by it killed me
11. 3 "Lord, they have killed thy prophets
2 Cor 3. 6 for the written code kills
1 Th 2.15 who killed both the Lord Jesus
Rev 2.13 " 'faithful one, who was killed among you
6. 8 to kill with sword and with famine
6.11 until the number . . who were to be killed
9. 5 allowed to torture them . . but not to kill
9.15 released . . to kill a third of mankind
9.18 a third of mankind was killed
9.20 who were not killed by these plagues
11. 5 thus he is doomed to be killed
11. 7 beast . . will . . conquer them and kill them
11.13 seven thousand people were killed
3. *lay hands on, murder* (mid.): διαχειρίζω DIACHEIRIZŌ*
Acts 5.30 "God . . raised Jesus whom you killed
26.21 "Jews seized me . . and tried to kill me
4. *kill, murder:* φονεύω PHONEUŌ
Mt 5.21 "it was said . . of old, 'You shall not kill; and whoever kills shall be liable to judgment
19.18 Jesus said, "You shall not kill
Mk 10.19 "the commandments: 'Do not kill
Lk 18.20 "the commandments: . . 'Do not kill

Rom 13. 9 The commandments, . . "You shall not kill
Jas 2.11 he . . said also, "Do not kill." If you . . kill, you have become a transgressor
4. 2 You desire and do not have; so you kill
5. 6 you have killed the righteous man

5. *destruction:* φθορά PHTHORA [B.1.a.2]
2 Pet 2.12 creatures . . born to be caught and killed

6. *put to death:* θανατόω THANATOŌ
Rom 8.36 "For thy sake we are being killed
2 Cor 6. 9 as punished, and yet not killed

7. *sacrifice, kill:* θύω THYŌ
Mt 22. 4 "'my oxen and my fat calves are killed
Lk 15.23 "'bring the fatted calf and kill it
15.27 "'your father has killed the fatted calf
15.30 "'you killed for him the fatted calf!
Jn 10.10 "thief comes only to steal and kill
Acts 10.13 a voice . . "Rise, Peter; kill and eat
11. 7 "saying . . 'Rise, Peter; kill and eat

KILLED, BE

1. *die by murder:* ἐν φόνῳ ἀποθνήσκειν APOTHNĒSKŌ; PHONOS [B.3.b.4]
Heb 11.37 they were killed with the sword

KIN

1. *congenital, inborn:* συγγενής (subst. pl.) SYGGENĒS
Mk 6. 4 "not without honor, except . . among . . kin

KIND (*See also* ALL KINDS OF; WHAT KIND OF)

1. *good:* ἀγαθός AGATHOS
Tit 2. 5 be sensible, chaste, domestic, kind
1 Pet 2.18 not only to the kind and gentle

2. *good, useful:* χρηστός CHRĒSTOS
Lk 6.35 "for he is kind to the ungrateful
Eph 4.32 be kind to one another, tenderhearted

3. *kind, race, family:* γένος GENOS
Mt 13.47 "gathered fish of every kind
[17.21 "*But this kind . . by prayer and fasting*‡
Mk 9.29 "This kind cannot be driven out

4. *nature, kind:* φύσις PHYSIS
Jas 3. 7 every kind of beast and bird, of reptile

IDIOMATICALLY

a. Acts 10.33 "and you have been kind enough to come
σύ τε καλῶς ἐποίησας παραγενόμενος [KALŌS]

b. Phil 4.14 Yet it was kind of you to share my trouble
πλὴν καλῶς ἐποιήσατε συγκοινωνήσαντές μου τῇ θλίψει [KALŌS]

CONTEXTUALLY
Mt 5.11 "utter all kinds of evil against you
Rom 7. 8 wrought in me all kinds of covetousness
1 Cor 15.39 one kind for men, another for animals
Eph 4.19 greedy to practice every k. of uncleanness
Rev 18.12 cargo . . all kinds of scented wood
22. 2 with its twelve kinds of fruit

KIND, BE

1. *be kind:* χρηστεύομαι CHRĒSTEUOMAI*
1 Cor 13. 4 Love is patient and kind

KIND OF, A

1. *anyone, any:* τὶς TIS II
Jas 1.18

2. *such as this:* τοιοῦτος TOIOUTOS
1 Cor 5. 1 of a kind . . not found even among pagans

KIND OF, EACH

1. *each:* ἕκαστος HEKASTOS
1 Cor 15.38 to each kind of seed its own body

KINDLE

1. *kindle:* ἀνάπτω ANAPTŌ
Lk 12.49 "would that it were already kindled!

2. *kindle; touch* (mid.): ἅπτω HAPTŌ
Acts 28. 2 they kindled a fire and welcomed us

3. *light a fire all around:* περιάπτω PERIAPTŌ*
Lk 22.55 they had kindled a fire in the middle

KINDLED, BE

1. *set on fire:* πυρόω (pass.) PYROŌ
2 Pet 3.12 heavens will be kindled and dissolved!

KINDLY

1. *good:* ἀγαθός AGATHOS [A.3.b.1]
1 Th 3. 6 you always remember us kindly

2. *gentle, kind:* ἤπιος ĒPIOS
2 Tim 2.24 servant must not be quarrelsome but kindly

3. *kindly:* φιλανθρώπως PHILANTHRŌPŌS*
Acts 27. 3 Julius treated Paul kindly

KINDNESS

1. *good, useful:* χρηστός CHRĒSTOS
[a]subst. neut. [b]B.2.a.1
Rom 2. 4 [a]that God's kindness is meant to lead you
1 Pet 2. 3 [b]you have tasted the kindness of the Lord

2. *kindness, uprightness:* χρηστότης CHRĒSTOTĒS
Rom 2. 4 Or do you presume upon . . his kindness?
11.22 the kindness and the severity of God: . . God's kindness to you, provided you continue in his kindness
2 Cor 6. 6 purity, knowledge, forbearance, kindness
Gal 5.22 fruit of the Spirit is love, . . kindness
Eph 2. 7 his grace in kindness toward us
Col 3.12 Put on then . . kindness, lowliness

3. *reasonableness, goodness:* ἐπιείκεια EPIEIKEIA
Acts 24. 4 "I beg you in your kindness to hear us

4. *humanity, benevolence:* φιλανθρωπία PHILANTHRŌPIA
Acts 28. 2 the natives showed us unusual kindness

KINDNESS, LOVING

1. *humanity, benevolence:* φιλανθρωπία PHILANTHRŌPIA
Tit 3. 4 the goodness and loving kindness of God

KINDRED

1. *kinship:* συγγένεια SYGGENEIA*
Lk 1.61 "None of your k. is called by this name
Acts 7. 3 "'Depart from your land and from your k.
7.14 "Jacob his father and all his kindred

KINDS, VARIOUS

1. *kind, race, family:* γένος (pl.) GENOS
1 Cor 12.10 to another various kinds of tongues
12.28 speakers in various kinds of tongues

KING

1. *reign:* βασιλεύω (subst. part.) BASILEUŌ
[a]second use only
1 Tim 6.15 [a]the King of kings and Lord of lords

2. *king:* βασιλεύς BASILEUS
[a]first use only
Mt 1. 6 Jesse the father of David the king
2. 1 J. was born . . in the days of Herod the king
2. 2 "he who has been born king of the Jews
2. 3 When Herod the king heard this
2. 9 When they had heard the king they went
5.35 "for it is the city of the great King
10.18 "you will be dragged before . . kings
11. 8 "Behold, those . . are in kings' houses
14. 9 And the king was sorry
17.25 "From whom do kings . . take toll?
18.23 "a king who wished to settle accounts
21. 5 "Behold, your king is coming to you
22. 2 "a king who gave a marriage feast
22. 7 "king was angry, and he sent his troops
22.11 "the king came in to look at the guests
22.13 "king said to the attendants, 'Bind him
25.34 "King will say to those at his right hand
25.40 "King will answer them, 'Truly, I say
27.11 "Are you the King of the Jews?
27.29 saying, "Hail, King of the Jews!
27.37 "This is Jesus the King of the Jews
27.42 "He is the King of Israel; let him come
Mk 6.14 King Herod heard of it
6.22 king said to the girl, "Ask me
6.25 she came . . with haste to the king
6.26 the king was exceedingly sorry
6.27 the king sent a soldier of the guard
13. 9 "you will stand before . . kings
15. 2 "Are you the King of the Jews?
15. 9 "to release for you the King of the Jews?
15.12 "what shall I do with . . the K. of the Jews?
15.18 "Hail, King of the Jews!

Mk 15.26 the charge . . read, "The King of the Jews
15.32 "the King of Israel, come down now
Lk 1. 5 In the days of Herod, king of Judea
10.24 "many . . kings desired to see what you see
14.31 "what king, going to encounter another king in war, will not . . take counsel?
19.38 "Blessed is the King who comes!
21.12 "you will be brought before kings
22.25 "kings of the Gentiles exercise lordship
23. 2 "saying that he himself is Christ a king
23. 3 "Are you the King of the Jews?
23.37 "If you are the King of the Jews
23.38 "This is the King of the Jews
Jn 1.49 "Rabbi, you are . . the King of Israel!
6.15 take him by force to make him king
12.13 "Blessed is he . . , the King of Israel!
12.15 "Fear not . . ; behold, your king is coming!
18.33 "Are you the King of the Jews?
18.37 Pilate said . . "So you are a king?" Jesus answered, "You say that I am a king
18.39 "release for you the King of the Jews?
19. 3 saying, "Hail, King of the Jews!
19.12 every one who makes himself a king
19.14 said to the Jews, "Behold your King!
19.15 Pilate said . . "Shall I crucify your King?" . . "We have no king but Caesar
19.19 "Jesus of Nazareth, the K. of the Jews
19.21 "Do not write, 'The King of the Jews,' but, 'This man said, I am King of the Jews
Acts 4.26 " 'kings of the earth set themselves in array
7.10 "king of Egypt, who made him governor
7.18 "another k. who had not known Joseph
9.15 "chosen instrument of mine . . before . . kings
12. 1 the king laid violent hands upon some
12.20 Blastus, the king's chamberlain
13.21 "Then they asked for a king
13.22 "he raised up David to be their king
17. 7 "saying that there is another king, Jesus
25.13 Agrippa the king and Bernice arrived
25.14 Festus laid Paul's case before the king
25.24 "King Agrippa and all who are present
25.26 "especially before you, King Agrippa
26. 2 "fortunate that it is before you, King A.
26. 7 "for this hope I am accused by Jews, O k.!
26.13 "At midday, O king, I saw . . a light
26.19 "O King Agrippa, I was not disobedient
26.26 "the king knows about these things
26.27 "King Agrippa, do you believe the prophets?
26.30 the k. rose, and the governor and Bernice
2 Cor 11.32 governor under K. Aretas guarded the city
1 Tim 1.17 To the King of ages, immortal, invisible
2. 2 for kings and all who are in high positions
6.15 [a]the King of kings and Lord of lords
Heb 7. 1 Melchizedek, king of Salem
7. 1 returning from the slaughter of the kings
7. 2 He is first . . king of righteousness, and then he is also king of Salem, that is, king of peace
11.23 they were not afraid of the king's edict
11.27 not being afraid of the anger of the king
Rev 1. 5 Jesus Christ . . , the ruler of kings on earth
6.15 the kings of the earth and the great men
9.11 as king over them the angel . . Abaddon
10.11 "nations and tongues and kings
15. 3 "true are thy ways, O King of the ages![j]
16.12 to prepare . . for the kings from the east
16.14 go abroad to the kings of the . . world
17. 2 "the kings . . have committed fornication
17.10 "they are also seven kings, five . . fallen
17.12 "the ten horns that you saw are ten kings
17.12 "they are to receive authority as kings
17.14 "Lamb will conquer them, for he is Lord of lords and King of kings
17.18 "dominion over the kings of the earth
18. 3 "the kings . . have committed fornication
18. 9 kings . . who committed fornication
19.16 on his thigh he has a name inscribed, King of kings and Lord of lords
Rev 19.18 "⟨Come⟩ to eat the flesh of kings
19.19 I saw the beast and the kings of the earth
21.24 kings . . shall bring their glory into it

KING, BECOME A

1. *reign:* βασιλεύω BASILEUŌ
1 Cor 4. 8 Without us you have become kings!

KINGDOM

1. *kingdom, reign:* βασιλεία BASILEIA
Mt 3. 2 "the kingdom of heaven is at hand
4. 8 showed him all the kingdoms of the world
4.17 "the kingdom of heaven is at hand
4.23 he went . . preaching the gospel of the k.
5. 3 "for theirs is the kingdom of heaven
5.10 "for theirs is the kingdom of heaven
5.19 "shall be called least in the k. of heaven
5.19 "shall be called great in the k. of heaven
5.20 "you will never enter the k. of heaven
6.10 "Thy kingdom come, Thy will be done
[6.13 *For thine is the kingdom and the power*‡
6.33 "seek first his k. and his righteousness
7.21 "Not every one . . shall enter the k. of h.
8.11 "many will . . sit at table . . in the k. of heaven
8.12 "the sons of the kingdom will be thrown
9.35 preaching the gospel of the kingdom
10. 7 " 'The kingdom of heaven is at hand
11.11 "he who is least in the kingdom of heaven
11.12 "the k. of heaven has suffered violence[c]
12.25 "Every kingdom divided against itself
12.26 "how then will his kingdom stand?
12.28 "then the k. of God has come upon you
13.11 "to know the secrets of the k. of heaven
13.19 "When any one hears the word of the k.
13.24 "k. of h. may be compared to a man
13.31 "k. of h. is like a grain of mustard seed
13.33 "The k. of heaven is like leaven
13.38 "good seed means the sons of the kingdom
13.41 "they will gather out of his k. all causes
13.43 "righteous will shine like the sun in the k.
13.44 "k. of heaven is like treasure hidden
13.45 "k. of heaven is like a merchant in search
13.47 "the kingdom of heaven is like a net
13.52 "every scribe . . trained for the k. of h.
16.19 "the keys of the kingdom of heaven
16.28 "the Son of man coming in his kingdom
18. 1 "Who is the greatest in the k. of h.?
18. 3 "you will never enter the k. of heaven
18. 4 "he is the greatest in the k. of heaven
18.23 "kingdom of heaven may be compared
19.12 "eunuchs for . . the k. of heaven
19.14 "for to such belongs the k. of heaven
19.23 "hard for a rich man to enter the k. of h.
19.24 "for a rich man to enter the k. of God
20. 1 "kingdom of heaven is like a householder
20.21 "that these two sons . . may sit . . in your k.
21.31 "harlots go into the k. of God before you
21.43 "k. of God will be taken away from you
22. 2 "kingdom of heaven may be compared
23.13 "you shut the k. of heaven against men
24. 7 "For nation will rise against nation, and kingdom against kingdom
24.14 "this gospel of the k. will be preached
25. 1 "kingdom of heaven shall be compared
25.34 " 'inherit the kingdom prepared for you
26.29 "until . . I drink it . . in my Father's k.
Mk 1.15 "the kingdom of God is at hand; repent
3.24 "If a kingdom is divided against itself, that kingdom cannot stand
4.11 "the secret of the kingdom of God
4.26 "k. of God is as if a man should scatter
4.30 "With what . . compare the k. of God?
6.23 "Whatever you ask . . , even half of my k.
9. 1 "that the k. of God has come with power
9.47 "enter the kingdom of God with one eye
10.14 "for to such belongs the kingdom of God
10.15 "whoever does not receive the k. of God
10.23 "How hard . . to enter the kingdom of God!

Mk 10.24 "how hard it is[r] to enter the k. of God!
10.25 "than for a rich man to enter the k. of God
11.10 "Blessed is the k. of our father David!
12.34 "You are not far from the k. of God
13. 8 "For nation will rise against nation, and kingdom against kingdom
14.25 "until . . I drink it new in the k. of God
15.43 himself looking for the kingdom of God
Lk 1.33 "of his kingdom there will be no end
4. 5 showed him all the kingdoms of the world
4.43 "the good news of the kingdom of God
6.20 "for yours is the kingdom of God
7.28 he who is least in the k. of God is greater
8. 1 the good news of the kingdom of God
8.10 "to know the secrets of the k. of God
9. 2 he sent them . . to preach the k. of God
9.11 spoke to them of the kingdom of God
9.27 "before they see the kingdom of God
9.60 "go and proclaim the kingdom of God
9.62 "No one who . . is fit for the k. of God
10. 9 " 'The k. of God has come near to you
10.11 " 'the kingdom of God has come near
11. 2 "hallowed be thy name. Thy kingdom come
11.17 "Every kingdom divided against itself
11.18 "how will his kingdom stand?
11.20 "then the k. of God has come upon you
12.31 "Instead, seek his[p] kingdom
12.32 "your Father's . . pleasure to give you the k.
13.18 "What is the kingdom of God like?
13.20 "To what shall I compare the k. of God?
13.28 "all the prophets in the kingdom of God
13.29 "sit at table in the kingdom of God
14.15 "who shall eat bread in the k. of God!
16.16 "news of the k. of God is preached
17.20 asked . . when the k. of God was coming
17.20 "The k. of God is not coming with signs
17.21 "the k. of God is in the midst of you[z]
18.16 "for to such belongs the kingdom of God
18.17 "receive the kingdom of God like a child
18.24 "How hard . . to enter the k. of God!
18.25 "for a rich man to enter the k. of God
18.29 "for the sake of the kingdom of God
19.11 supposed . . the k. of God was to appear
19.12 "to receive a kingdom and then return[o]
19.15 "returned, having received the kingdom[o]
21.10 "Nation will rise against nation, and kingdom against kingdom
21.31 "you know that the k. of God is near
22.16 "until it is fulfilled in the k. of God
22.18 "I shall not drink . . until the k. of God
22.29 "and I assign to you . . a kingdom
22.30 "that you may eat . . at my table in my k.
23.42 "when you come into[p] your kingdom‡[o]
23.51 he was looking for the k. of God
Jn 3. 3 "he cannot see the kingdom of God
3. 5 "he cannot enter the kingdom of God
Acts 1. 3 appearing . . and speaking of the k. of God
1. 6 "Lord, will you at this time restore the k.?
8.12 preached good news about the k. of God
14.22 through . . tribulations we . . enter the k.
19. 8 arguing and pleading about the k. of God
20.25 "among whom I have gone . . preaching the k.
28.23 testifying to the kingdom of God
28.31 preaching the kingdom of God
Rom 14.17 the k. of God is not food
1 Cor 4.20 the k. of God does not consist in talk
6. 9 unrighteous will not inherit the k. of God
6.10 nor robbers will inherit the k. of God
15.24 when he delivers the kingdom to God
15.50 flesh . . cannot inherit the k. of God
Gal 5.21 those . . shall not inherit the k. of God
Eph 5. 5 inheritance in the kingdom of Christ
Col 1.13 transferred us to the kingdom of his . . Son
4.11 fellow workers for the kingdom of God
1 Th 2.12 God, who calls you into his own kingdom
2 Th 1. 5 made worthy of the kingdom of God
2 Tim 4. 1 I charge you . . by his appearing and . . k.
2 Tim 4.18 will . . save me for his heavenly kingdom
Heb 1. 8 "the scepter of thy[b] kingdom
11.33 who through faith conquered kingdoms
12.28 let us be grateful for receiving a k.
Jas 2. 5 to be rich in faith and heirs of the k.
2 Pet 1.11 eternal kingdom of our Lord and Savior
Rev 1. 6 made us a kingdom, priests to his God
1. 9 I . . share . . the tribulation and the kingdom
5.10 "hast made them a kingdom and priests
11.15 "The kingdom of the world has become
12.10 "the power and the kingdom of our God
16.10 its kingdom was in darkness

KING'S

1. *royal:* βασιλικός BASILIKOS
Acts 12.20 depended on the king's country for food

KING'S COURT

1. *royal:* βασίλειος (subst.) BASILEIOS
Lk 7.25 "who . . live in luxury are in kings' courts

KINGSHIP

1. *kingdom, reign:* βασιλεία BASILEIA
Jn 18.36 "My kingship is not of this world; if my kingship were of this world
18.36 "but my kingship is not from the world

KINSFOLK

1. *congenital, inborn:* συγγενής (subst. pl.) SYGGENĒS
Lk 1.58 her neighbors and kinsfolk heard
2.44 they sought him among their kinsfolk

KINSMAN

1. *congenital, inborn:* συγγενής (subst.) SYGGENĒS
Lk 14.12 "do not invite your friends or . . kinsmen
21.16 "delivered up even by . . kinsmen
Jn 18.26 One of the servants[l] . . , a kinsman
Acts 10.24 Cornelius . . had called together his kinsmen
Rom 9. 3 my brethren, my kinsmen by race
16. 7 Andronicus and Junias, my kinsmen
16.11 Greet my kinsman Herodion
16.21 Jason and Sosipater, my kinsmen

KINSWOMAN

1. *kinswoman:* συγγενίς SYGGENIS*
Lk 1.36 "your k. Elizabeth . . has also conceived

KISH: Κίς 'kish
Acts 13.21 "God gave them Saul the son of Kish

KISS

1. *kiss, caress:* καταφιλέω KATAPHILEŌ*
Mt 26.49 "Hail, Master!"[i] And he kissed him
Mk 14.45 "Master!"[e] And he kissed him
Lk 7.38 kissed his feet, and anointed them
7.45 "she has not ceased to kiss my feet
15.20 "ran and embraced him and kissed him
Acts 20.37 wept and embraced Paul and kissed him
2. *kiss:* φίλημα PHILĒMA*
Lk 7.45 "You gave me no kiss
22.48 "Judas, would you betray . . with a kiss?
Rom 16.16 Greet one another with a holy kiss
1 Cor 16.20 Greet one another with a holy kiss
2 Cor 13.12 Greet one another with a holy kiss
1 Th 5.26 Greet all the brethren with a holy kiss
1 Pet 5.14 Greet one another with the kiss of love
3. *love, like:* φιλέω PHILEŌ
Mt 26.48 "The one I shall kiss is the man; seize him
Mk 14.44 "The one I shall kiss is the man; seize him
Lk 22.47 He drew near to Jesus to kiss him

KNEE

1. *knee:* γόνυ GONY
Lk 5. 8 Simon Peter . . fell down at Jesus' knees
Rom 11. 4 "men who have not bowed the knee to Baal
14.11 "every knee shall bow to me
Eph 3.14 I bow my knees before the Father
Phil 2.10 at the name . . every knee should bow
Heb 12.12 strengthen your weak knees

IDIOMATICALLY

a. Mt 18.26 "So the servant fell on his knees, imploring him πεσὼν οὖν ὁ δοῦλος προσεκύνει αὐτῷ λέγων [PROSKYNEŌ]

KNEEL

1. *fall on the knee:* γονυπετέω GONYPETEŌ

Mk 1.40 a leper . . kneeling said . . "If you will

KNEEL BEFORE

1. *fall on the knee:* γονυπετέω GONYPETEŌ
[a]+ἔμπροσθεν

Mt 17.14 a man came up . . and kneeling before him
27.29 [a]kneeling before him they mocked him
Mk 10.17 a man ran up and knelt before him

2. *prostrate oneself before:* προσκυνέω PROSKYNEŌ

Mt 8. 2 leper . . knelt before him, saying, "Lord
9.18 ruler came in and knelt before him
15.25 she came and knelt before him
20.20 kneeling before him she asked him

KNEEL DOWN

1. *put down the knees:* τιθέναι τὰ γόνατα GONY [B.2.a.1]

Mk 15.19 they knelt down in homage to him
Lk 22.41 he withdrew . . and knelt down and prayed
Acts 7.60 he knelt down and cried with a loud voice
9.40 Peter put them all outside and knelt down
20.36 he knelt down and prayed with them all
21. 5 kneeling down on the beach we prayed

KNIT TOGETHER

KNIT TOGETHER, BE

1. *bring together, infer, teach:* συμβιβάζω (pass.) SYMBIBAZŌ
[a]part.

Eph 4.16 [a]joined and knit together by every joint
Col 2. 2 as they are knit together in love
2.19 [a]knit together through its joints

KNOCK

1. *strike, knock:* κρούω KROUŌ*

Mt 7. 7 "knock, and it will be opened to you
7. 8 "to him who knocks it will be opened
Lk 11. 9 "knock, and it will be opened to you
11.10 "to him who knocks it will be opened
12.36 "they may open to him . . when he . . knocks
13.25 "begin to stand outside and to knock
Acts 12.13 he knocked at the door of the gateway
12.16 But Peter continued knocking
Rev 3.20 " 'Behold, I stand at the door and knock

KNOW

1. *not know:* ἀγνοέω (double neg.) AGNOEŌ

Rom 1.13 I want you to know, brethren
1 Cor 10. 1 I want you to know, brethren

2. *learn to know, recognize:* ἐπιγινώσκω EPIGINŌSKŌ

Mt 7.16 "You will know them by their fruits
7.20 "Thus you will know them by their fruits
11.27 "no one knows the Son except the Father, and no one knows the Father except the Son
17.12 "Elijah has . . come, and they did not k. him
Mk 6.33 many saw them going, and knew them
Lk 1. 4 that you may know the truth
Acts 9.30 when the brethren knew it
23.28 "desiring to k. the charge . . , I brought him
25.10 "I have done no wrong, as you know
Rom 1.32 Though they know God's decree
1 Tim 4. 3 those who believe and know the truth
2 Pet 2.21 for them never to have known the way . . than after knowing it to turn back

3. *know, understand:* ἐπίσταμαι EPISTAMAI

Acts 10.28 "You yourselves know how unlawful it is
15. 7 "you k. that . . God made choice among you
18.25 he knew only the baptism of John
19.15 "Paul I know; but who are you?
19.25 "you know that from this business
20.18 "You yourselves know how I lived
22.19 " 'they . . know that . . I imprisoned and beat
26.26 "the king knows about these things
1 Tim 6. 4 puffed up with conceit, he knows nothing
Heb 11. 8 not knowing where he was to go
Jas 4.14 you do not know about tomorrow
Jude .10 things that they know by instinct

4. *know, understand:* γινώσκω GINŌSKŌ

Mt 1.25 knew her not until she had borne a son
6. 3 "do not let your left hand know
7.23 " 'I never knew you; depart from me
9.30 "See that no one knows it
10.26 "nothing . . hidden that will not be known
12. 7 "if you had known what this means
12.33 "for the tree is known by its fruit
13.11 "to know the secrets of the kingdom
16. 3 "You know how to interpret . . the sky‡
24.32 "you know that summer is near
24.33 "you know that he is near, at the very gates
24.39 "they did not know until the flood came
24.43 "But know this
24.50 "will come . . at an hour he does not know
25.24 " 'Master, I knew you to be a hard man
Mk 5.43 charged them that no one should know
7.24 he . . would not have any one know it
9.30 he would not have any one know it
13.28 "you know that summer is near
13.29 "know that he is near, at the very gates
Lk 1.18 "How shall I know this? For I am . . old
2.43 His parents did not know it
6.44 "each tree is known by its own fruit
7.39 "If . . a prophet, he would have known
8.10 "To you it has been given to know
8.17 "nothing is . . secret that shall not be known
10.11 " 'know this, . . the kingdom . . has come near
10.22 "no one knows . . the Son . . except the Father
12. 2 "Nothing . . hidden that will not be known
12.39 "But know this, that if the householder
12.46 "will come . . at an hour he does not know
12.47 "that servant who knew his master's will
12.48 "who did not k. . . shall receive
16.15 "but God knows your hearts
19.15 "that he might know what they had gained
19.42 "Would that even today you knew!
19.44 "because you did not know the time
21.20 "know that its desolation has come near
21.30 "know that the summer is already near
21.31 "know that the kingdom of God is near
24.18 "Are you the only visitor . . who does not k.?
24.35 he was known . . in . . breaking . . bread
Jn 1.10 yet the world knew him not
1.48 "How do you know me?
2.25 he knew all men and needed no one . . ; for he himself knew what was in man
4. 1 Lord knew that the Pharisees had heard
4.53 The father knew that was the hour
5. 6 Jesus saw him and knew
5.42 "I know that you have not the love of God
6.69 "we have believed, and have come to know
7.17 "if any man's will is to do his will, he shall k.
7.26 "Can it be that the authorities really know?
7.27 "no one will know where he comes from
7.49 "this crowd, who do not know the law
8.28 "then you will know that I am he
8.32 "you will know the truth
8.52 "Now we know that you have a demon
8.55 "But you have not known him
10.14 "I am the good shepherd; I know my own and my own know me
10.15 "as the Father knows me and I know the Father; and I lay down my life
10.27 "I know them, and they follow me
10.38 "believe the works, that you may know
11.57 if any one knew where he was
13.12 "Do you know what I have done to you?
13.28 no one . . knew why he said this to him
13.35 "men will know that you are my disciples
14. 7 "If you had known me
14. 7 "henceforth you know him and have seen him
14. 9 "yet you do not know me, Philip?
14.17 "it neither sees him nor knows him; you know him, for he dwells with you
14.20 "you will know that I am in my Father
14.31 "that the world may know that I love
15.18 "know that it has hated me before . . you
16. 3 "because they have not known the Father
16.19 Jesus knew that they wanted to ask

Jn 17. 3 "this is eternal life, that they know thee
17. 7 "they know that everything . . is from thee
17. 8 "know in truth that I came from thee
17.23 "so that the world may know
17.25 "O righteous Father, the world has not known thee, but I have known thee; and these know that thou hast sent me
19. 4 "that you may know that I find no crime
21.17 "you know that I love you
Acts 1. 7 "It is not for you to know times
2.36 "Let . . Israel therefore know assuredly
9.24 their plot became known to Saul
17.19 "May we know what this new teaching is?
17.20 "we wish to k. . . what these things mean
19.15 "Jesus I know . . ; but who are you?
19.35 "what man is there who does not know?
20.34 "You . . know that these hands ministered
21.24 "Thus all will know that there is nothing
21.37 And he said, "Do you know Greek?
22.14 " 'God . . appointed you to know his will
22.30 desiring to know the real reason
Rom 1.21 although they knew God they did not honor
2.18 know his will and approve
3.17 "the way of peace they do not know
6. 6 We know that our old self was crucified
7. 1 I am speaking to those who know the law
7. 7 "I should not have known sin
11.34 "who has known the mind of the Lord?
1 Cor 1.21 world did not know God through wisdom
2.16 "who has known the mind of the Lord?
3.20 "Lord knows . . the thoughts of the wise
8. 2 If any one imagines that he knows something, he does not yet know as he ought to know
8. 3 if one loves God, one is known by him
13.12 Now I know in part
14. 7 how will any one know what is played?
14. 9 how will any one know what is said?
2 Cor 2. 4 to let you know the . . love . . I have for you
2. 9 that I . . know whether you are obedient
3. 2 to be known and read by all men
5.21 he made him to be sin who knew no sin
8. 9 you know the grace of our Lord Jesus
Gal 4. 9 now that you have come to know God, or rather to be known by God
Eph 3.19 to know the love of Christ which surpasses
6.22 that you may know how we are
Phil 1.12 I want you to know, brethren
2.22 But Timothy's worth you know
3.10 that I may know him and the power
4. 5 Let all men know your forbearance
Col 4. 8 that you may know how we are
1 Th 3. 5 I sent that I might know your faith
2 Tim 1.18 you . . know all the service he rendered
2.19 "The Lord knows those who are his
Heb 3.10 " 'they have not known my ways
8.11 "shall not teach . . , saying, 'Know the Lord
10.34 you knew . . you . . had a better possession
Jas 1. 3 you know that the testing of your faith
5.20 let him know that whoever brings back
1 Jn 2. 3 by this we may be sure that we know
2. 4 He who says "I know him
2.13 you know him who is from the beginning
2.13 I write to you . . because you know
2.14 I write to you . . because you know
2.18 therefore we know that it is the last hour
3. 1 The reason why the world does not know us is that it did not know him
3. 6 no one who sins has . . known him
3.16 By this we know love
3.19 we shall know that we are of the truth
3.20 for God is greater . . and he knows
3.24 by this we know that he abides
4. 2 By this you know the Spirit of God
4. 6 Whoever knows God listens to us
4. 6 By this we know the spirit of truth
4. 7 he who loves . . knows God
4. 8 who does not love does not know God
1 Jn 4.13 By this we know that we abide in him
4.16 we k. and believe the love God has for us
5. 2 By this we know that we love
5.20 understanding, to know him who is true
2 Jn . 1 but also all who know the truth
Rev 2.23 " 'shall know that I am he who searches mind
3. 3 " 'you will not know at what hour I . . come

5. *known, knowable:* γνωστός GNŌSTOS [A.6.a.3]
Acts 28.22 "we k. that everywhere it is spoken against

6. *learn, understand:* μανθάνω MANTHANŌ
1 Cor 14.35 anything they desire to know

7. *know:* οἶδα OIDA
Mt 6. 8 "for your Father knows what you need
6.32 "Father knows that you need them
7.11 "If you . . know how to give good gifts
9. 4 Jesus, knowing[u] their thoughts, said‡
9. 6 "know that the Son of man has authority
12.25 Knowing their thoughts, he said
15.12 "know that the Pharisees were offended
20.22 "You do not know what you are asking
20.25 "You know that the rulers . . lord it
21.27 they answered Jesus, "We do not know
22.16 "Teacher, we know that you are true
22.29 "you know neither the scriptures
24.36 "of that day and hour no one knows
24.42 "Watch . . , for you do not know on what day
24.43 "if the householder had known
25.12 " 'Truly, . . I do not know you
25.13 "you know neither the day nor the hour
25.26 " 'slothful servant! You knew that I reap
26. 2 "You know that . . Passover is coming
26.70 "I do not know what you mean
26.72 "I do not know the man
26.74 "I do not know the man
27.18 he knew that it was out of envy
28. 5 "for I know that you seek Jesus
Mk 1.24 "I k. who you are, the Holy One of God
1.34 not . . the demons . . , because they knew him
2.10 "know that the Son of man has authority
4.27 "sprout and grow, he knows not how
5.33 knowing what had been done to her
6.20 feared John, knowing . . he was . . righteous
9. 6 For he did not know what to say
10.19 "You know the commandments
10.38 "You do not know what you are asking
10.42 "You know that those who . . rule
11.33 they answered Jesus, "We do not know
12.14 "Teacher, we know that you are true
12.15 knowing their hypocrisy, he said
12.24 "you know neither the scriptures
13.32 "of that day or that hour no one knows
13.33 "you do not know when the time will come
13.35 "you do not k. when the master . . will come
14.40 they did not know what to answer
14.68 "I neither know nor understand
14.71 "I do not k. this man of whom you speak
Lk 2.49 "know that I must be in my Father's house
4.34 "I know who you are, the Holy One
4.41 they knew that he was the Christ
5.24 "know that the Son of man has authority
6. 8 But he knew their thoughts
8.53 laughed at him, knowing that she was dead
9.33 not knowing what he said
[9.55 "*You do not know what manner of spirit*‡
11.13 "If you . . know how to give good gifts
11.17 he, knowing their thoughts, said to them
11.44 "men walk over them without knowing it
12.30 "Father knows that you need them
12.39 "if the householder had known
12.56 "You know how to interpret the . . earth
12.56 "why do you not know . . the present time?
13.25 " 'I do not know where you come from
13.27 " 'I do not know where you come from
18.20 "You know the commandments
19.22 " 'You knew that I was a severe man
20. 7 they did not know whence it was
20.21 "we know that you speak . . rightly

Lk 22.34 "until you three times deny that you k. me
22.57 "Woman, I do not know him
22.60 "I do not know what you are saying
23.34 "for they know not what they do[n]‡
Jn 1.26 "among you . . one whom you do not know
1.31 "I myself did not know him
1.33 "I myself did not know him
2. 9 steward . . did not know where it came from (though the servants . . knew
3. 2 "Rabbi, we know that you are a teacher
3. 8 "you do not know whence it comes
3.11 "we speak of what we know
4.10 "If you knew the gift of God
4.22 "You worship what you do not know; we worship what we know
4.25 "I know that Messiah is coming
4.32 "I have food . . of which you do not know
4.42 "we know that this is indeed the Savior
5.13 man who had been healed did not know
5.32 "I know that the testimony . . is true
6. 6 he himself knew what he would do
6.42 "Jesus . . , whose father and mother we know
6.61 But Jesus, knowing in himself
6.64 Jesus knew from the first who those were
[7.15 "How is it . . this man *knows his letters?*†
7.27 "we know where this man comes from
7.28 "You know me, and you know where I come from? . . he who sent me is true, and him you do not know
7.29 "I know him, for I come from him
8.14 "for I know whence I have come . . , but you do not know whence I come
8.19 Jesus answered, "You know neither me nor my Father; if you knew me, you would know my Father also
8.37 "I k. . . you are descendants of Abraham
8.55 "I know him. If I said, I do not know him, I should be a liar like you; but I do know him and I keep his word
9.12 "Where is he?" He said, "I do not know
9.20 "We know that this is our son
9.21 "but how he now sees we do not know, nor do we know who opened his eyes
9.24 "we know that this man is a sinner
9.25 "Whether he is a sinner, I do not know; one thing I know, that . . now I see
9.29 "We know that God has spoken to Moses, but as for this man, we do not know
9.30 "You do not know where he comes from
9.31 "We k. . . God does not listen to sinners
10. 4 "the sheep . . know his voice
10. 5 "they do not know the voice of strangers
11.22 "I know that whatever you ask from God
11.24 "I know that he will rise again
11.42 "I knew that thou hearest me always
11.49 Caiaphas . . said . . "You know nothing at all
12.35 "he . . does not know where he goes
12.50 "I know that his commandment is . . life
13. 1 Jesus knew that his hour had come
13. 3 knowing that the Father had given all
13. 7 "What I am doing you do not know now
13.11 For he knew who was to betray him
13.17 "If you know these things, blessed
13.18 "I know whom I have chosen
14. 4 "you know the way where I am going[f]
[14. 4 "*where I am going you know, and the way you know*‡
14. 5 "we do not know where you are going; how can we know the way?
14. 7 "you would have known my Father also
15.15 "does not know what his master is doing
15.21 "they do not know him who sent me
16.18 "We do not know what he means
16.30 "Now we know that you know all things, and need none to question you
18. 2 Now Judas . . also knew the place
18. 4 Jesus, knowing all that was to befall him
Jn 18.21 "Ask those who have heard me . . ; they know
19.10 "Do you not know that I have power?
19.28 Jesus, knowing that all was now finished
19.35 he knows that he tells the truth
20. 2 "we do not know where they have laid him
20. 9 as yet they did not know the scripture
20.13 "I do not know where they have laid him
20.14 but she did not know that it was Jesus
21. 4 disciples did not know that it was Jesus
21.12 They knew it was the Lord
21.15 "Yes, Lord; you know that I love you
21.16 "Yes, Lord; you know that I love you
21.17 "Lord, you know everything
21.24 we know that his testimony is true
Acts 2.22 "a man attested . . , as you yourselves know
2.30 "knowing that God had sworn with an oath
3.16 "made this man strong whom you . . know
3.17 "I know that you acted in ignorance
5. 7 wife . . not knowing what had happened
7.18 "king who had not known Joseph
7.40 " 'we do not k. what has become of him
10.36(37) "You k. the word which he sent to Israel
12. 9 he did not know . . what was done . . was real
16. 3 they all knew . . his father was a Greek
19.32 did not know why they had come together
20.22 "not knowing what shall befall me there
20.25 "I know . . you . . will see my face no more
20.29 "I know that . . fierce wolves will come in
23. 5 "I did not know . . he was the high priest
26. 4 "My . . life . . is known by all the Jews
26.27 "King Agrippa, . . I know that you believe
Rom 2. 2 We know that the judgment of God
3.19 we know that whatever the law says
5. 3 knowing that suffering produces endurance
6. 9 we know that Christ . . will never die
6.16 know that if you yield . . , you are slaves
7. 7 I should not have known what it is to covet
7.14 We know that the law is spiritual
7.18 I k. that nothing good dwells within me
8.22 We k. . . the . . creation has been groaning
8.26 we do not k. how to pray as we ought
8.27 he who searches the hearts of men knows
8.28 We know that . . God works for good[k]
11. 2 Do you not know what the scripture says?
13.11 Besides this you know what hour it is
14.14 I k. . . that nothing is unclean in itself
15.29 I know that when I come to you
1 Cor 1.16 (I do not k. whether I baptized any
2. 2 I decided to know nothing among you
2.11 what person knows a man's thoughts?
3.16 Do you not k. . . you are God's temple?
5. 6 Do you not know that a little . . leavens?
6. 2 Do you not k. . . the saints will judge?
6. 3 Do you not k. . . we are to judge angels?
6. 9 not k. . . the unrighteous will not inherit?
6.15 Do you not k. . . your bodies are members?
6.16 not know that he who joins . . becomes?
6.19 not know that your body is a temple?
7.16 do you k. . . you will save your husband? . . do you know . . you will save your wife?
8. 1 we k. . . "all of us possess knowledge
8. 4 we k. . . "an idol has no real existence
9.13 not know that those . . who serve . . share?
9.24 Do you not know that . . all . . compete?
12. 2 You know that when you were heathen
14.11 if I do not k. the meaning of the language
14.16 when he does not k. what you are saying
15.58 knowing that . . your labor is not in vain
16.15 you k. . . the household of Stephanas
2 Cor 1. 7 we k. . . as you share in our sufferings
4.14 knowing that he who raised the Lord Jesus
5. 1 we know that if the earthly tent
5. 6 we k. . . while we are at home in the body
5.11 knowing the fear of the Lord
9. 2 I know your readiness, of which I boast
11.11 God knows I do!
11.31 he who is blessed . . knows that I do not lie

2 Cor 12. 2 I k. a man in Christ who . . was caught up . . whether in the body or out of the body I do not know, God knows
12. 3 I k. . . this man was caught up into Paradise —whether in the body or out of the body I do not know, God knows
Gal 2.16 who k. . . a man is not justified[d] by works
4. 8 when you did not know God
4.13 you know it was because of . . ailment
Eph 1.18 that you may know what is the hope
6. 8 knowing . . he will receive the same again
6. 9 knowing that he . . is in heaven
6.21 that you also may know how I am
Phil 1.16 knowing . . I am put here for the . . gospel
1.19 I k. . . this will turn out for my deliverance
1.25 I know that I shall remain and continue
4.12 I know how to be abased, and I know how to abound; in any and all circumstances
4.15 you Philippians yourselves know
Col 2. 1 I want you to know how greatly I strive
3.24 knowing . . you will receive the inheritance
4. 1 knowing . . you also have a Master in heaven
4. 6 know how you ought to answer every one
1 Th 1. 4 For we know . . that he has chosen you
1. 5 You k. what kind of men we proved to be
2. 1 know . . that our visit . . was not in vain
2. 2 shamefully treated . . ., as you know
2. 5 never . . words of flattery, as you k.
2.11 you k. how . . we exhorted each one of you
3. 3 You . . know that this is to be our lot
3. 4 to suffer affliction; . . as you know
4. 2 you know what instructions we gave
4. 4 each . . of you know how to take a wife
4. 5 like heathen who do not know God
5. 2 you . . k. . . the day . . will come like a thief
2 Th 1. 8 vengeance upon those who do not k. God
2. 6 you know what is restraining him
3. 7 you . . k. how you ought to imitate us
1 Tim 1. 8 Now we know that the law is good
3. 5 if a man does not know how to manage
3.15 may know how one ought to behave
2 Tim 1.12 for I know whom I have believed
2.23 you know that they breed quarrels
3.14 knowing from whom you learned it
Tit 1.16 profess to know God, but they deny him
3.11 knowing that such a person is perverted
Phm .21 knowing that you will do even more
Heb 8.11 "they shall not teach . . ., for all shall know me
10.30 we k. him who said, "Vengeance is mine
12.17 you know that . . he was rejected
Jas 1.19 K. this . . Let every man be quick to hear
3. 1 you k. that we . . shall be judged
4. 4 Do you not k. that friendship with . . world?
4.17 Whoever knows what is right to do
1 Pet [1. 8 Without having *known* him you[c] love him‡
1.18 You know that you were ransomed
5. 9 knowing that the same experience
2 Pet 1.12 you know them and are established
1.14 I know that the putting off of my body[c]
2. 9 the Lord knows how to rescue the godly
1 Jn 2.11 he . . does not know where he is going
2.20 you have been anointed . . and you all k.[d]
2.21 not because you do not know the truth, but because you know it
2.29 If you know that he is righteous
3. 2 we know that . . we shall be like him
3. 5 You k. . . he appeared to take away sins
3.14 We k. . . we have passed out of death
3.15 you k. . . no murderer has eternal life
5.13 that you may k. that you have . . life
5.15 if we k. that he hears us . . ., we know that we have obtained the requests
5.18 We know that any one born of God
5.19 We know that we are of God
5.20 we know that the Son of God has come
3 Jn .12 you know my testimony is true
Rev 2. 2 " 'I know your works
Rev 2. 9 " 'I k. your tribulation and your poverty
2.13 " 'I know where you dwell
2.17 " 'no one knows except him who receives it
2.19 " 'I know your works, your love
3. 1 " 'I know your works
3. 8 " 'I know your works
3.15 " 'I know your works
3.17 " 'not knowing that you are wretched
7.14 I said to him, "Sir, you know
12.12 "because he knows that his time is short!
19.12 a name inscribed which no one knows

8. *foreknow:* προγινώσκω PROGINŌSKŌ
Acts 26. 5 "They have known for a long time

CONTEXTUALLY
Jn 7. 4 "if he seeks to be known openly
3 Jn . 2 I know that it is well with your soul
Rev 2. 3 " 'I know you are enduring patiently

KNOW BEFOREHAND

1. *foreknow:* προγινώσκω PROGINŌSKŌ
2 Pet 3.17 knowing this beforehand, beware

KNOW, COME TO

1. *unto knowledge:* εἰς ἐπίγνωσιν EPIGNŌSIS [B.2.b.1]
2 Tim 2.25 will repent and come to know the truth

KNOW, LET ONE

1. *reveal, inform:* μηνύω MĒNYŌ
Jn 11.57 orders that . . he should let them know

KNOW, NOT

1. *not know:* ἀγνοέω AGNOEŌ
Rom 2. 4 not k. . . God's kindness is . . to lead you?
6. 3 Do you not k. . . all of us . . were baptized?
7. 1 Do you not k. . . that the law is binding?
Gal 1.22 I was still not known by sight

KNOW, WANT S. TO
KNOW, WOULD HAVE S.

1. *make known:* γνωρίζω GNŌRIZŌ
2 Cor 8. 1 We want you to know, brethren
Gal 1.11 For I would have you know, brethren

KNOWING

1. *knowledge:* γνῶσις GNŌSIS
Phil 3. 8 surpassing worth of knowing Christ Jesus

KNOWLEDGE

1. *knowledge, recognition:* ἐπίγνωσις EPIGNŌSIS
Rom 3.20 since through the law comes k. of sin
Eph 1.17 a spirit of . . revelation in the k. of him
4.13 until we . . attain . . the k. of the Son of God
Phil 1. 9 that your love . . abound . . with knowledge
Col 1. 9 that you . . be filled with the k. of his will
1.10 increasing in the knowledge of God
2. 2 the k. of God's mystery, of Christ
3.10 new nature, which is being renewed in k.
1 Tim 2. 4 to come to the knowledge of the truth
2 Tim 3. 7 can never arrive at a k. of the truth
Tit 1. 1 to further . . their knowledge of the truth
Phm . 6 promote the knowledge of all the good
Heb 10.26 if we sin deliberately after receiving the k.
2 Pet 1. 2 grace and peace . . in the k. of God
1. 3 through the k. of him who called us
1. 8 unfruitful in the k. of our Lord Jesus Christ
2.20 escaped . . through the k. of our Lord

2. *know, understand:* γινώσκω GINŌSKŌ [A.6.d]
1 Cor 13. 9 For our knowledge is imperfect

3. *knowledge:* γνῶσις GNŌSIS
Lk 1.77 "to give knowledge of salvation
11.52 "you have taken away the key of k.
Rom 2.20 having in the law the embodiment of k.
11.33 O the depth of the . . knowledge of God!
15.14 filled with all k., and able to instruct
1 Cor 1. 5 enriched in him with all speech and all k.
8. 1 we know that "all of us possess k." "Knowledge" puffs up, but love builds up
8. 7 However, not all possess this k.
8.10 if any one sees you, a man of k.
8.11 by your k. this weak man is destroyed
12. 8 to another the utterance of knowledge
13. 2 if I have . . all k., and if I have all faith

1 Cor 13. 8 as for knowledge, it will pass away
14. 6 shall I benefit you unless I bring . . k.?
2 Cor 2.14 God, who . . spreads the fragrance of the k.
4. 6 light of the k. of the glory of God
6. 6 knowledge, forbearance, kindness
8. 7 as you excel . . in k., in all earnestness
10. 5 every proud obstacle to the k. of God
11. 6 if . . unskilled in speaking, I am not in k.
Eph 3.19 the love of Christ which surpasses k.
Col 2. 3 in whom are hid all the treasures of . . k.
1 Tim 6.20 contradictions of what is falsely called k.
2 Pet 1. 5 supplement . . virtue with knowledge
1. 6 ⟨supplement⟩ knowledge with self-control
3.18 But grow in the grace and k. of our Lord

4. *know as witness, be conscious:* σύνοιδα SYNOIDA [B.2.a.2]
Acts 5. 2 with his wife's k. he kept back some

KNOWLEDGE, HAVE

1. *know:* οἶδα OIDA
Acts 24.22 having a rather accurate k. of the Way

KNOWLEDGE, NO

1. *ignorance:* ἀγνωσία AGNŌSIA
1 Cor 15.34 For some have no knowledge of God

KNOWN (*See also* FULLY KNOWN, MAKE)

1. *known, knowable:* γνωστός GNŌSTOS
Jn 18.15 this disciple was known to the high priest
18.16 disciple, who was k. to the high priest
Acts 1.19 "it became known to all the inhabitants
2.14 "let this be known to you, and give ear
4.10 "be it known to you . . and to all the people
9.42 it became known throughout all Joppa
13.38 "Let it be known to you therefore, brethren
15.18 " 'Lord, who has made these things known
19.17 known to all residents of Ephesus
28.28 "Let it be k. . . that this salvation of God
Rom 1.19 what can be known about God is plain

2. *visible, known:* φανερός PHANEROS
Mt 12.16 ordered them not to make him known
Mk 3.12 he strictly ordered them not to make him k.
6.14 for Jesus'[a] name had become known
Acts 7.13 "Joseph's family became k. to Pharaoh
Phil 1.13 it has become k. throughout the . . guard[c]

KNOWN AS

1. *call, name:* καλέω (pass. part.) KALEŌ
Acts 10. 1 what was known as the Italian Cohort

KNOWN, BE

1. *reach:* ἀφικνέομαι APHIKNEOMAI*
Rom 16.19 while your obedience is known to all
2. *make manifest, make known:* φανερόω (pass.) PHANEROŌ
2 Cor 5.11 but what we are is known to God
5.11 I hope it is known . . to your conscience

KNOWN, MAKE

1. *disclose, show:* δηλόω DĒLOŌ
Col 1. 8 has made known to us your love
2. *interpret, tell:* ἐξηγέομαι EXĒGEOMAI
Jn 1.18 the only Son,[b] . . he has made him known
3. *make known:* γνωρίζω GNŌRIZŌ
Lk 2.15 "which the Lord has made known to us
2.17 when they saw it they made k. the saying
Jn 15.15 "all that I have heard . . I have made k.
17.26 "I made known to them thy name, and I will make it known
Acts 2.28 " 'Thou hast made k. to me the ways of life
Rom 9.22 God, desiring . . to make known his power
9.23 to make known the riches of his glory
16.26 through the prophetic writings is made k.
Eph 1. 9 he has made k. to us . . the mystery
3. 3 the mystery was made known to me
3. 5 not made known to the sons of men
3.10 wisdom of God might now be made k.
Phil 4. 6 let your requests be made k. to God
Col 1.27 To them God chose to make known
2 Pet 1.16 when we made known to you the power
4. *indicate, report:* σημαίνω SĒMAINŌ
Rev 1. 1 he made it known by sending his angel

KNOWN, MAKE ONESELF

1. *make known:* γνωρίζω (pass.) GNŌRIZŌ
Acts 7.13 "Joseph made himself k. to his brothers

KNOWN, WELL

1. *learn to know, recognize:* ἐπιγινώσκω (pass. part.) EPIGINŌSKŌ
2 Cor 6. 9 as unknown, and yet well known

KNOWS THE HEART, ONE WHO

1. *knower of hearts:* καρδιογνώστης KARDIOGNŌSTĒS*
Acts 1.24 "Lord, who knowest the hearts of all men
15. 8 "God who knows the heart bore witness

KORAH: Κόρε 'kòrə
Jude .11 For they . . perish in Korah's rebellion

L

LABOR

1. *work, perform:* ἐργάζομαι ERGAZOMAI
Jn 6.27 "Do not l. for the food which perishes
2. *work, deed:* ἔργον ERGON
Phil 1.22 life in the flesh, that means fruitful labor
Heb 4.10 ceases from his labors as God did
3. *work hard, grow weary:* κοπιάω KOPIAŌ
Mt 11.28 "Come to me, all who labor and are . . laden
Jn 4.38 "that for which you did not labor; others have labored, and you have entered
1 Cor 4.12 we labor, working with our own hands
Gal 4.11 I am afraid I have labored . . in vain
Eph 4.28 rather let him labor, doing honest work
Phil 2.16 I may be proud that I did not . . labor in vain
1 Th 5.12 to respect those who labor among you
1 Tim 5.17 especially those who labor in preaching
4. *work:* κόπος KOPOS
Jn 4.38 "you have entered into their labor
1 Cor 3. 8 receive his wages according to his labor
15.58 in the Lord your labor is not in vain
2 Cor 6. 5 imprisonments, tumults, labors, watching
10.15 We do not boast . . in other men's labors
11.23 far greater labors, far more imprisonments
1 Th 1. 3 your work of faith and labor of love
2. 9 remember our labor and toil, brethren
3. 5 for fear . . that our labor would be in vain
2 Th 3. 8 with . . labor we worked night and day
Rev 14.13 "that they may rest from their labors!

LABOR SIDE BY SIDE WITH

1. *assist, struggle together:* συναθλέω SYNATHLEŌ
Phil 4. 3 they have labored side by side with me

LABORER

1. *workman:* ἐργάτης ERGATĒS
Mt 9.37 "plentiful, but the laborers are few
9.38 "to send out laborers into his harvest
10.10 "for the laborer deserves his food
20. 1 "went out . . to hire laborers for his vineyard
20. 2 "After agreeing with the laborers . . , he sent
20. 8 " 'Call the laborers and pay them
Lk 10. 2 "plentiful, but the laborers are few
10. 2 "to send out laborers into his harvest
10. 7 "for the laborer deserves his wages
1 Tim 5.18 "The laborer deserves his wages
Jas 5. 4 Behold, the wages of the laborers
2. *work hard, grow weary:* κοπιάω (subst. part.) KOPIAŌ
1 Cor 16.16 be subject . . to every fellow worker and l.

LACK

1. *lack, fail:* ὑστερέω HYSTEREŌ
Mt 19.20 "these I have observed; what do I still lack?
Mk 10.21 "You lack one thing; go, sell what you have
Lk 22.35 "When I sent you . . , did you l. anything?
1 Cor 1. 7 so that you are not lacking in any . . gift
2. *leave, be incomplete:* λείπω LEIPŌ
[a]A.6.c.3 [b]pass.
Lk 18.22 [a]"One thing you still lack. Sell all
Tit 3.13 [a]see that they lack nothing

Jas 1. 4 [b]complete, lacking in nothing
1. 5 [b]If any of you lacks wisdom, let him ask
3. *be present:* πάρειμι (neg.) PAREIMI [A.6.c.3]
2 Pet 1. 9 whoever lacks these things is blind

LACK, HAVE
1. *receive less, have less:* ἐλαττονέω ELATTONEŌ*
2 Cor 8.15 "he who gathered little had no lack

LACK, IN
1. *leave, be incomplete:* λείπω (pass. part.) LEIPŌ
Jas 2.15 If a brother . . is . . in lack of daily food

LACKING, WHAT IS
1. *deficiency, need:* ὑστέρημα (pl.) HYSTERĒMA
Col 1.24 in my flesh I complete what is lacking
1 Th 3.10 supply what is lacking in your faith

LAD
1. *young slave, boy:* παιδάριον PAIDARION*
Jn 6. 9 "There is a lad here who has five . . loaves
2. *child, servant:* παῖς PAIS
Acts 20.12 And they took the lad away alive

LADEN, BE HEAVY
1. *load:* φορτίζω (perf. pass.) PHORTIZŌ
Mt 11.28 "all who labor and are heavy laden

LADY
1. *lady* (fem. of *lord*): κυρία KYRIA*
2 Jn . 1 lady . . whom I love in the truth
. 5 I beg you, lady, . . that we love one another

LAID (*See* BARE, BE LAID; CHARGE LAID AGAINST ONE)

LAID AWAY
1. *be laid away:* ἀπόκειμαι (part.) APOKEIMAI
Lk 19.20 " 'your pound, which I kept laid away

LAID, BE
LAID DOWN, BE
1. *lie, be laid:* κεῖμαι KEIMAI
Mt 3.10 "the axe is laid to the root of the trees
Lk 3. 9 "the axe is laid to the root of the trees
23.53 where no one had ever yet been laid
1 Cor 3.11 no . . foundation . . than that which is laid
1 Tim 1. 9 the law is not laid down for the just

LAID DOWN BY
1. *in accordance with, for:* κατά (+acc.) KATA [B.3.b.4]
Acts **24.**14

LAID UP
1. *be laid away:* ἀπόκειμαι (part.) APOKEIMAI
Col 1. 5 because of the hope laid up for you
2. *lie, be laid:* κεῖμαι (part.) KEIMAI
Lk 12.19 " 'Soul, you have ample goods laid up

LAID UP, BE
1. *be laid away:* ἀπόκειμαι APOKEIMAI
2 Tim 4. 8 there is laid up for me the crown

LAID UPON, BE
1. *lie upon, press upon:* ἐπίκειμαι EPIKEIMAI
1 Cor 9.16 For necessity is laid upon me

LAKE
1. *pool of water, lake:* λίμνη LIMNĒ*
Lk 5. 1 he was standing by the lake
5. 2 he saw two boats by the lake
8.22 "Let us go . . to the other side of the lake
8.23 a storm of wind came down on the lake
8.33 herd rushed . . into the lake
Rev 19.20 thrown alive into the lake of fire
20.10 devil . . was thrown into the lake of fire
20.14 Death . . thrown into the lake of fire. This is the second death, the lake of fire
20.15 he was thrown into the lake of fire
21. 8 "their lot shall be in the lake that burns

LAMA: 'lämə
1. *why* (Heb.): λαμά LAMA*
Mk 15.34 Jesus cried . . "Eloi, Eloi, lama sabachthani?
2. *why* (Aram.): λεμά LEMA*
Mt 27.46 Jesus cried . . "Eli, Eli, lama sabachthani?

LAMB
1. *lamb:* ἀμνός AMNOS*
Jn 1.29 "Behold, the Lamb of God!
Jn 1.36 "Behold, the Lamb of God!
Acts 8.32 "As . . a lamb before its shearer is dumb
1 Pet 1.19 like that of a lamb without blemish
2. *lamb:* ἀρήν ARĒN*
Lk 10. 3 "behold, I send you out as lambs
3. *little lamb:* ἀρνίον ARNION*
Jn 21.15 He said to him, "Feed my lambs
Rev 5. 6 I saw a Lamb standing, as though . . slain
5. 8 elders fell down before the Lamb
5.12 "Worthy is the Lamb who was slain
5.13 "to the Lamb be blessing and honor!
6. 1 the Lamb opened one of the seven seals
6.16 "hide us . . from the wrath of the Lamb
7. 9 a great multitude . . before the Lamb
7.10 "Salvation belongs . . to the Lamb!
7.14 "made them white in . . blood of the Lamb
7.17 "the Lamb in the midst of the throne
12.11 "conquered him by . . blood of the Lamb
13. 8 book of life of the Lamb that was slain
13.11 it had two horns like a lamb
14. 1 lo, on Mount Zion stood the Lamb
14. 4 it is these who follow the Lamb
14. 4 as first fruits for God and the Lamb
14.10 "tormented . . in the presence of the L.
15. 3 they sing . . the song of the Lamb
17.14 "they will make war on the Lamb, and the Lamb will conquer them, for he is Lord
19. 7 "for the marriage of the Lamb has come
19. 9 "invited to the marriage supper of the L.
21. 9 "Come, I will show you . . the wife of the L.
21.14 names of the twelve apostles of the L.
21.22 for its temple is the Lord God . . and the L.
21.23 no need of sun . . for . . its lamp is the Lamb
21.27 written in the Lamb's book of life
22. 1 from the throne of God and of the Lamb
22. 3 the throne of God and of the Lamb
CONTEXTUALLY
Rev 8. 1 When the L. opened the seventh seal

LAMB, PASCHAL
1. *Passover, paschal lamb:* πάσχα PASCHA
1 Cor 5. 7 Christ, our paschal l., has been sacrificed

LAME
1. *lame:* χωλός CHŌLOS
Mt 11. 5 "the lame walk, lepers are cleansed
15.30 bringing with them the lame, the maimed
15.31 they saw . . the lame walking
18. 8 "better for you to enter life . . lame
21.14 the blind and the lame came to him
Mk 9.45 "it is better for you to enter life lame
Lk 7.22 "the lame walk, lepers are cleansed
14.13 "invite the poor, the maimed, the lame
14.21 " 'Go out . . and bring in the poor . . and lame
Jn 5. 3 a multitude of invalids, blind, lame
Acts 3. 2 a man lame from birth was being carried
8. 7 many who were . . lame were healed
Heb 12.13 so that what is lame may . . be healed

LAMECH: Λάμεχ 'lāmik
Lk 3.36 Noah, the son of Lamech

LAMENT
1. *sing a dirge, wail:* θρηνέω THRĒNEŌ
Lk 23.27 women who bewailed and lamented him
Jn 16.20 "Truly, . . you will weep and lament

LAMENTATION
1. *noise, mourning:* κοπετός KOPETOS*
Acts 8. 2 buried Stephen, . . made great lamentation
2. *mourning:* ὀδυρμός ODYRMOS
Mt 2.18 "loud lamentation, Rachel weeping

LAMP
1. *lamp, torch:* λαμπάς LAMPAS
Mt 25. 1 "ten maidens who took their lamps
25. 3 "when the foolish took their lamps
25. 4 "the wise took . . oil with their lamps
25. 7 "maidens rose and trimmed their lamps
25. 8 " 'Give us . . oil, for our lamps are going out

2. *lamp:* λύχνος LYCHNOS*
Mt 5.15 "Nor do men light a lamp and put it under
6.22 "The eye is the lamp of the body
Mk 4.21 "Is a lamp . . to be put under a bushel?
Lk 8.16 "No one after lighting a lamp covers it
11.33 "No one . . lighting a l. puts it in a cellar
11.34 "Your eye is the lamp of your body
11.36 "as when a lamp . . gives you light
12.35 "Let your . . lamps ⟨be⟩ burning
15. 8 "if she loses one coin, does not light a lamp?
Jn 5.35 "He was a burning and shining lamp
2 Pet 1.19 as to a lamp shining in a dark place
Rev 18.23 "a lamp shall shine in thee no more
21.23 no need of sun . . , for . . its lamp is the Lamb
22. 5 they need no light of lamp or sun

LAMPSTAND
1. *lampstand:* λυχνία LYCHNIA
Heb 9. 2 outer one, in which were the lampstand
Rev 1.12 I saw seven golden lampstands
1.13 in the midst of the lampstands
1.20 "mystery of . . seven golden lampstands
1.20 "seven lampstands are the seven churches
2. 1 " 'walks among the seven golden lampstands
2. 5 " 'I will come to you and remove your l.
11. 4 lampstands which stand before the Lord

LAND
1. *field:* ἀγρός AGROS
Mt 19.29 "every one who has left houses or . . lands
Mk 10.29 "no one who has left house or . . lands
10.30 "who will not receive . . houses and . . lands
2. *country, place:* χώρα CHŌRA
Lk 12.16 "The l. of a rich man brought forth
Acts 27.27 suspected that they were nearing land
3. *place, district:* χωρίον CHŌRION
Acts 4.34 for as many as were possessors of lands
5. 3 "to keep back . . proceeds of the land
5. 8 "Tell me whether you sold the land
28. 7 lands belonging to the chief man
4. *earth, land:* γῆ GĒ
Mt 2. 6 " 'O Bethlehem, in the land of Judah
2.20 "take the child and . . go to the l. of Israel
2.21 he . . went to the land of Israel
4.15 "The land of Zebulun and the land of Naphtali, toward the sea
10.15 "more tolerable . . for the land of Sodom
11.24 "more tolerable . . for the land of Sodom
14.24 many furlongs distant from the land[m]‡
14.34 they came to land at Gennesaret
27.45 there was darkness over all the land[m]†
Mk 4. 1 crowd was beside the sea on the land
6.47 he was alone on the land
6.53 they came to land at Gennesaret
15.33 there was darkness over the whole land[h]†
Lk 4.25 there came a great famine over all the land
5. 3 asked him to put out a little from the l.
5.11 when they had brought their boats to land
8.27 And as he stepped out on land
14.35 "It is fit neither for the land
23.44 there was darkness over the whole land[q]†
Jn 3.22 his disciples went into the land of Judea
6.21 immediately the boat was at the land
21. 8 for they were not far from the land
21. 9 When they got out on land
Acts 7. 3 " 'Depart from your land and . . go into the land which I will show you
7. 4 "Then he departed from the land
7. 4 "God removed him from there into this land
7. 6 "aliens in a land belonging to others
7.29 "Moses . . became an exile in the land
7.40 " 'Moses who led us out from the land
13.17 "during their stay in the land of Egypt
13.19 "seven nations in the land of Canaan
13.19 "gave them their land as an inheritance
27.39 they did not recognize the land
27.43 who . . could swim to . . make for the land
27.44 And so it was that all escaped to land
Heb 6. 7 For land which has drunk the rain
8. 9 "to lead them out of the land of Egypt
11. 9 he sojourned in the land of promise
11.29 crossed the Red Sea as if on dry land
Jude . 5 saved a people out of the land of Egypt
Rev 10. 2 And he set . . his left foot on the land
10. 5 the angel . . standing on sea and land
10. 8 "angel . . standing on the sea and . . land
5. *go down, come to:* κατέρχομαι KATERCHOMAI
Acts 21. 3 we sailed to Syria, and landed at Tyre
6. *withered, dry:* ξηρός (subst. fem.) XĒROS
Mt 23.15 "traverse sea and land to make . . proselyte
CONTEXTUALLY
Lk 4.26 "to Zarephath, in the land of Sidon
Acts 27.14 the northeaster, struck down from the land
2 Cor 10.16 that we may preach . . in lands beyond

LAND, GO BY
1. *go on foot:* πεζεύω PEZEUŌ*
Acts 20.13 intending himself to go by land

LANE
1. *lane, alley:* ῥύμη RHYMĒ
Lk 14.21 " 'Go out quickly to the streets and lanes

LANGUAGE
1. *discourse, language:* διάλεκτος DIALEKTOS*
Acts 1.19 "called in their language Akeldama
2. 6 each one heard them . . in his own language
2. 8 "each of us in his own native language
21.40 he spoke to them in the Hebrew l.
22. 2 he addressed them in the Hebrew l.
26.14 "a voice saying to me in the Hebrew l.
2. *voice, sound:* φωνή PHŌNĒ
1 Cor 14.10 doubtless many different languages
14.11 but if I do not know the meaning of the l.
CONTEXTUALLY
1 Cor [2.13 *spiritual truths in spiritual language*†

LANTERN
1. *torch:* φανός PHANOS*
Jn 18. 3 soldiers . . went there with lanterns

LAODICEA: Λαοδίκεια lā,ädə'sēə, ,lāədə'sēə II,E-3
Col 2. 1 I strive for you, and for those at L.
4.13 he has worked hard . . for those in L.
4.15 Give my greetings to the brethren at L.
4.16 read also the letter from Laodicea
Rev 1.11 "Write . . and send it . . to Laodicea
3.14 "to the angel of the church in Laodicea write

LAODICEAN: Λαοδικεύς
Col 4.16 read also in the church of the Laodiceans

LAP
1. *bosom, lap:* κόλπος KOLPOS
Lk 6.38 "good measure . . will be put into your lap

LARGE
1. *enough:* ἱκανός HIKANOS
Lk 7.12 a large crowd from the city was with her
8.32 Now a large herd of swine was feeding
Acts 11.24 large company was added to the Lord
11.26 they . . taught a large company of people
2. *great:* μέγας MEGAS
Mk 4.32 "it . . puts forth large branches
14.15 "he will show you a large upper room
16. 4 stone was rolled back—it was very large
Lk 22.12 "he will show you a large upper room
Jn 21.11 hauled the net . . full of large fish
3. *many, great:* πολύς POLYS
Mt 19. 2 large crowds followed him, and he healed
26. 9 "might have been sold for a large sum
Mk 12.41 Many rich people put in large sums
Lk 5.29 there was a l. company of tax collectors
Acts 22.28 "bought this citizenship for a large sum

LARGE, VERY
1. *most:* πλεῖστος PLEISTOS
Mk 4. 1 a very large crowd gathered about him

LARGE, WHAT
1. *how great:* πηλίκος PĒLIKOS
Gal 6.11 See with what large letters I am writing

LARGER
1. *greater:* μείζων MEIZŌN
Lk 12.18 " 'I will pull down my barns, and build l. ones

LASAEA: Λασαία lə'sēə II,D-4
Acts 27. 8 Fair Havens, near which was the city of L.

LASH
CONTEXTUALLY
2 Cor 11.24 at the hands of the Jews the forty lashes

LAST (*See also* BREATHE ONE'S LAST; YEAR, LAST)
1. *last, extreme:* ἔσχατος ESCHATOS
Mt 5.26 "never . . till you have paid the last penny
12.45 "the last state of that man becomes worse
19.30 "But many that are first will be last, and the last first
20. 8 "beginning with the last, up to the first
20.12 " 'These last worked only one hour
20.14 " 'I choose to give to this last as . . to you
20.16 "So the last will be first, and the first last
27.64 "the last fraud will be worse than the first
Mk 9.35 "If any one would be first, he must be last
10.31 "But many that are first will be last, and the last first
12.22 "Last of all the woman also died
Lk 11.26 "last state of that man becomes worse
12.59 "till you have paid the very last copper
13.30 "some are last who will be first, and some are first who will be last
Jn 6.39 "that I should . . raise it up at the last day
6.40 "I will raise him up at the last day
6.44 "I will raise him up at the last day
6.54 "I will raise him up at the last day
7.37 last day of the feast . . Jesus stood up
11.24 "in the resurrection at the last day
12.48 "the word . . will be his judge on the last day
Acts 2.17 " 'in the last days it shall be, God declares
1 Cor 4. 9 God has exhibited us apostles as l. of all
15. 8 Last of all . . he appeared also to me
15.26 last enemy to be destroyed is death
15.45 "last Adam became a life-giving spirit
15.52 in a moment, . . at the last trumpet
2 Tim 3. 1 in the last days there will come . . stress
Heb 1. 2 in these l. days he has spoken . . by a Son
Jas 5. 3 You have laid up treasure[e] for the l. days
1 Pet 1. 5 ready to be revealed in the last time
2 Pet 2.20 the last state has become worse for them
3. 3 scoffers will come in the last days
1 Jn 2.18 Children, it is the last hour
2.18 therefore we know that it is the last hour
Jude .18 "In the last time there will be scoffers
Rev 1.17 "Fear not, I am the first and the last
2. 8 " 'The words of the first and the last
15. 1 seven plagues, which are the last
21. 9 bowls full of the seven last plagues
22.13 "Alpha and the Omega, the first and the l.
IDIOMATICALLY
a. Rom 1.10 asking that somehow . . I may now at last succeed δεόμενος εἴ πως ἤδη ποτὲ εὐοδωθήσομαι [POTE II]
b. 1 Th 2.16 But God's wrath has come upon them at last![b]† ἔφθασεν δὲ ἐπ' αὐτοὺς ἡ ὀργὴ εἰς τέλος [TELOS]

LAST, AT
1. *latter, behind, later:* ὕστερος (neut.) HYSTEROS
Mt 26.60 At last two came forward
2. *remaining, left:* λοιπός (neut.) LOIPOS
Acts 27.20 all hope . . was at last abandoned

LASTING
1. *stay, wait:* μένω (part.) MENŌ
Heb 13.14 For here we have no lasting city

LATE (*See also* AUTUMN, IN LATE)
1. *late in the day:* ὀψέ OPSE
Mk 11.11 as it was already late, he went out
2. *many, great:* πολύς POLYS
Mk 6.35 when it grew late, his disciples came
6.35 "This is a lonely place, and the hour is . . l.

LATE RAIN
1. *late, slow:* ὄψιμος OPSIMOS* [B.3.b.2]
Jas 5. 7 patient . . until it receives . . the late rain

LATELY
1. *recently, lately:* προσφάτως PROSPHATŌS*
Acts 18. 2 lately come from Italy with . . Priscilla

LATER (*See also* APPEAR LATER)

LATER THAN
1. *latter, behind, later:* ὕστερος HYSTEROS
[a]neut.
1 Tim 4. 1 in later times some will depart
Heb 12.11 [a]later it yields . . fruit of righteousness
2. *after:* μετά (+acc.) META [B.3.b.1]
[a]μετὰ ταῦτα
Lk **15.**13
Jn **20.**26
Heb **4.**8[a]; **7.**28
CONTEXTUALLY
Heb 3. 5 testify to the things . . to be spoken later

LATIN
1. *Roman:* Ῥωμαϊκός
Lk [23.38 an inscription . . *in letters of . . Latin*‡
2. *in Latin:* Ῥωμαϊστί
Jn 19.20 written in Hebrew, in L., and in Greek

LATTER
1. *last, extreme:* ἔσχατος ESCHATOS
Rev 2.19 " 'that your latter works exceed the first
CONTEXTUALLY
Phil 1.16 The latter do it out of love

LAUGH
1. *laugh:* γελάω GELAŌ*
Lk 6.21 "Blessed are you that weep . . , you shall l.
6.25 "Woe to you that l. . . , you shall mourn

LAUGH AT
1. *laugh at, mock:* καταγελάω KATAGELAŌ*
Mt 9.24 And they laughed at him
Mk 5.40 And they laughed at him
Lk 8.53 And they laughed at him

LAUGHTER
1. *laughter:* γέλως GELŌS*
Jas 4. 9 Let your l. be turned to mourning

LAVISH
1. *abound:* περισσεύω PERISSEUŌ
Eph 1. 8 ⟨grace⟩ which he lavished upon us

LAW
1. *law, norm:* νόμος NOMOS
Mt 5.17 "not that I have come to abolish the law
5.18 "not a dot, will pass from the law
7.12 "for this is the law and the prophets
11.13 "For . . the law prophesied until John
12. 5 "Or have you not read in the law?
[15. 6 "you have made void the *law* of God‡
22.36 "which is the great commandment in the l.?
22.40 "depend all the law and the prophets
23.23 "the weightier matters of the law
Lk 2.22 purification according to the law of Moses
2.23 (as it is written in the law of the Lord
2.24 according to what is said in the law
2.27 according to the custom of the law
2.39 performed everything according to the law
10.26 "What is written in the law?
16.16 "law and the prophets were until John
16.17 "than for one dot of the law to become void
24.44 "everything written about me in the law
Jn 1.17 For the law was given through Moses
1.45 "him of whom Moses in the law . . wrote
7.19 "Did not Moses give you the law? Yet none of you keeps the law
7.23 "that the l. of Moses may not be broken
7.49 "this crowd, who do not know the law
7.51 "Does our law judge . . without . . a hearing?
8. 5 Now in the law Moses commanded us[r]‡
8.17 "In your law . . the testimony of two men
10.34 "Is it not written in your law?

Jn 12.34 "We have heard from the law
15.25 "It is to fulfil the word . in their law
18.31 "judge him by your own law
19. 7 The Jews answered him, "We have a law, and by that law he ought to die
Acts 6.13 "never ceases to speak . . against . . the law
7.53 "received the law as delivered by angels
13.15 After the reading of the law
13.39 "you could not be freed by the law of M.
15. 5 "to charge them to keep the law of Moses
18.13 "to worship God contrary to the law
18.15 "a matter of questions about . . your own law
21.20 "they are all zealous for the law
21.24 "you yourself live in observance of the law
21.28 "teaching . . against the people and the law
22. 3 "strict manner of the law of our fathers
22.12 "Ananias, a devout man according to the law
23. 3 "sitting to judge me according to the law
23.29 "accused about questions of their law
[24. 6 *"judged him according to our law‡*
24.14 "believing everything laid down by the law
25. 8 "Neither against the law of the Jews
28.23 trying to convince them . . from the law
Rom 2.12 all who have sinned under the law will be judged by the law
2.13 not the hearers of the law . . , but the doers of the law . . will be justified
2.14 When Gentiles who have not the law do by nature what the law requires, they are a law to themselves, even though they do not have the law
2.15 what the l. requires is written on . . hearts
2.17 if you . . rely upon the law and boast
2.18 because you are instructed in the law
2.20 having in the law . . knowledge and truth
2.23 You who boast in the law, do you dishonor God by breaking the law?
2.25 if you obey the law; but if you break the law, . . circumcision becomes uncircumcision
2.26 if a man . . keeps the precepts of the law
2.27 physically uncircumcised but keep the law
2.27 you . . have . . circumcision but break the law
3.19 whatever the law says it speaks to those who are under the law
3.20 no human . . justified . . by works of the l.
3.20 through the law comes knowledge of sin
3.21 righteousness . . manifested apart from law, although . . law . . prophets bear witness
3.28 justified . . apart from works of law
3.31 Do we then overthrow the law . . ? . . On the contrary, we uphold the law
4.13 promise . . did not come through the law
4.14 it is the adherents of the law
4.15 For the law brings wrath, but where there is no law there is no transgression
4.16 not only to the adherents of the law
5.13 sin . . was in the world before the law . . , but sin is not counted where there is no l.
5.20 Law came in, to increase the trespass
6.14 you are not under law but under grace
6.15 Are we to sin because we are not under l.?
7. 1 I am speaking to those who know the l. . . law is binding . . only during his life
7. 2 woman is bound by law to her husband
7. 2 she is discharged from the law
7. 3 husband dies she is free from that law
7. 4 brethren, you have died to the law
7. 5 our sinful passions, aroused by the law
7. 6 now we are discharged from the law
7. 7 What . . shall we say? . . the law is sin?
7. 7 Yet, if it had not been for the law
7. 7 if the law had not said, "You shall not covet
7. 8 Apart from the law sin lies dead
7. 9 I was once alive apart from the law
7.12 law is holy, . . commandment is holy
7.14 We know that the law is spiritual
7.16 I agree that the law is good
Rom 7.21 a law that when I want to do right
7.22 For I delight in the law of God
7.23 I see in my members another law at war with the law of my mind and making me captive to the law of sin
7.25 I . . serve the law of God with my mind, but with my flesh I serve the law of sin
8. 2 the law of the Spirit of life in Christ Jesus has set me free from the law of sin
8. 3 God has done what the law . . could not do
8. 4 that the . . law might be fulfilled in us
8. 7 it does not submit to God's law
9.31 the righteousness which is based on law
9.31 did not succeed in fulfilling that law
10. 4 For Christ is the end of the law
10. 5 righteousness which is based on the law
13. 8 he who loves . . has fulfilled the law
13.10 therefore love is the fulfilling of the law
1 Cor 9. 8 Does not the law say the same?
9. 9 it is written in the law of Moses
9.20 to those under the law I became as one under the law—though not being myself under the law—that I might win those under the law
14.21 In the law it is written
14.34 should be subordinate, as even the law says
15.56 the power of sin is the law
Gal 2.16 a man is not justified[d] by works of the law . . not by works of the law, because by works of the law shall no one be justified
2.19 For I through the law died to the law, that I might live to God
2.21 if justification[e] were through the law
3. 2 Did you receive . . Spirit by works of . . law?
3. 5 Does he . . do so by works of the law?
3.10 For all who rely on works of the law
3.10 "all things written in the book of the law
3.11 no man is justified before God by the law
3.12 but the law does not rest on faith
3.13 Christ redeemed us from the curse of the l.
3.17 the law . . does not annul a covenant
3.18 if the inheritance is by the law
3.19 Why then the law? It was added
3.21 Is the law . . against the promises of God?
3.21 if a law . . could make alive, then righteousness would indeed be by the law
3.23 we were confined under the law
3.24 law was our custodian until Christ came
4. 4 born of woman, born under the law
4. 5 to redeem those who were under the law
4.21 Tell me, you who desire to be under law, do you not hear the law?
5. 3 he is bound to keep the whole law
5. 4 you who would be justified by the law
5.14 the whole law is fulfilled in one word
5.18 if . . led by . . Spirit you are not under . . law
5.23 against such there is no law
6. 2 so fulfil the law of Christ
6.13 those . . do not themselves keep the law
Eph 2.15 abolishing in his flesh the law
Phil 3. 5 a Hebrew . . ; as to the law a Pharisee
3. 6 as to righteousness under the law
3. 9 not . . a righteousness . . based on law
1 Tim 1. 8 Now we know that the law is good
1. 9 the law is not laid down for the just
Heb 7. 5 a commandment in the law to take tithes
7.12 necessarily a change in the law as well
7.19 (for the law made nothing perfect
7.28 the law appoints men in their weakness
7.28 oath, which came later than the law
8. 4 priests who offer gifts according to the l.
8.10 "I will put my laws into their minds
9.19 when . . the law had been declared by Moses
9.22 under the law . . purified with blood
10. 1 law has but a shadow of the good things
10. 8 (these are offered according to the law
10.16 "I will put my laws on their hearts
10.28 A man who has violated the law of Moses

Jas 1.25 he who looks into the perfect law
2. 8 If you really fulfil the royal law
2. 9 convicted by the law as transgressors
2.10 keeps the whole law but fails in one point
2.11 you have become a transgressor of the law
2.12 those who are to be judged under the law
4.11 He that . . judges his brother, speaks evil against the law and judges the law. But if you judge the law, you are not a doer of the law but a judge

LAW, CONTRARY TO THE
1. *transgress the law:* παρανομέω (part.) PARANOMEŌ*
Acts 23. 3 "contrary to the law you order me . . struck?

LAW, GIVING OF THE
1. *legislation:* νομοθεσία NOMOTHESIA*
Rom 9. 4 the covenants, the giving of the law

LAW, GO TO
1. *judge, decide:* κρίνω (pass.) KRINŌ
1 Cor 6. 1 against a brother, does he dare go to law?
6. 6 brother goes to law against brother

LAW, OUTSIDE THE
1. *lawless:* ἄνομος ANOMOS
1 Cor 9.21 To those outside the law I became as one outside the law . . that I might win those outside the law

LAW, OVER THE
1. *relating to laws:* νομικός NOMIKOS [A.3.d.1]
Tit 3. 9 avoid stupid . . quarrels over the law

LAW, RECEIVE THE
1. *frame laws:* νομοθετέω (pass.) NOMOTHETEŌ
Heb 7.11 (for under it the people received the law

LAW, TEACHER OF THE
1. *teacher of the law:* νομοδιδάσκαλος NOMODIDASKALOS*
Lk 5.17 Pharisees and teachers of the law
Acts 5.34 Gamaliel, a teacher of the law
1 Tim 1. 7 desiring to be teachers of the law

LAW, UNDER THE
1. *lawful:* ἔννομος ENNOMOS
1 Cor 9.21 under the law of Christ—that I might win

LAW, WITHOUT
LAW, WITHOUT THE
1. *lawless:* ἄνομος ANOMOS
1 Cor 9.21 not being without law toward God
2. *lawlessly:* ἀνόμως ANOMŌS*
Rom 2.12 All who have sinned without the law will also perish without the law

LAWFUL, BE
1. *it is allowed, it is possible:* ἔξεστι EXESTI
Mt 12. 2 "disciples are doing what is not lawful
12. 4 "which it was not lawful for him to eat
12.10 "Is it lawful to heal on the sabbath?
12.12 "So it is lawful to do good on the sabbath
14. 4 John said to him, "It is not lawful
19. 3 "Is it lawful to divorce one's wife?
22.17 "Is it lawful to pay taxes to Caesar?
27. 6 "It is not l. to put them into the treasury
Mk 2.24 "why are they doing what is not lawful?
2.26 "it is not lawful for any but the priests
3. 4 "Is it lawful on the sabbath to do good?
6.18 John said to Herod, "It is not lawful
10. 2 "Is it lawful for a man to divorce?
12.14 "Is it lawful to pay taxes to Caesar?
Lk 6. 2 "Why are you doing what is not l. to do?
6. 4 "it is not lawful for any but the priests
6. 9 "is it lawful on the sabbath to do good?
14. 3 "Is it lawful to heal on the sabbath?
20.22 "Is it l. for us to give tribute to Caesar?
Jn 5.10 "it is not lawful . . to carry your pallet
18.31 "It is not l. for us to put any . . to death
Acts 16.21 "customs which it is not l. for us Romans
22.25 "Is it lawful . . to scourge . . Roman citizen?
1 Cor 6.12 "All things are lawful for me
6.12 "All things are lawful for me
10.23 "All things are l.," but not . . helpful. "All things are l.," but not all things build up

LAWFULLY
1. *lawfully:* νομίμως NOMIMŌS
1 Tim 1. 8 law is good, if any one uses it lawfully

LAWGIVER
1. *lawgiver:* νομοθέτης NOMOTHETĒS*
Jas 4.12 There is one lawgiver and judge

LAWLESS
1. *lawless:* ἄνομος ANOMOS
Acts 2.23 "killed by the hands of lawless men
2 Th 2. 8 then the lawless one will be revealed
1 Tim 1. 9 the law is . . laid down . . for the lawless
2 Pet 2. 8 (he was vexed . . with their lawless deeds
2. *lawless:* ἀθέμιτος ATHEMITOS
1 Pet 4. 3 revels, carousing, and lawless idolatry
3. *lawless:* ἄθεσμος ATHESMOS
2 Pet 3.17 carried away with . . error of lawless men
CONTEXTUALLY
2 Th 2. 9 The coming of the lawless one by . . Satan

LAWLESSNESS
1. *lawlessness:* ἀνομία ANOMIA
2 Th 2. 3 man of lawlessness[a] is revealed‡
2. 7 mystery of lawlessness is already at work
Heb 1. 9 "Thou hast . . hated lawlessness
1 Jn 3. 4 Every one who commits sin is guilty of lawlessness; sin is lawlessness

LAWSUIT
1. *judgment:* κρίμα KRIMA
1 Cor 6. 7 To have lawsuits . . is defeat for you

LAWYER
1. *relating to laws:* νομικός (subst.) NOMIKOS
Mt 22.35 a lawyer, asked . . a question, to test him
Lk 7.30 (the lawyers rejected the purpose of God
10.25 a lawyer . . put him to the test
11.45 One of the lawyers answered him
11.46 he said, "Woe to you lawyers also!
11.52 "Woe to you lawyers!
14. 3 Jesus spoke to the lawyers . . "Is it lawful?
Tit 3.13 Do your best to speed Zenas the lawyer

LAY (*See also* CASE BEFORE, LAY ONE'S; HOLD OF, LAY; WASTE, LAY)
1. *cause to recline:* ἀνακλίνω ANAKLINŌ
Lk 2. 7 she . . laid him in a manger
2. *throw, put:* βάλλω BALLŌ
Rev 2.24 " 'I do not lay upon you any other burden
Also variant to: Jn **7.**44; *see* LAY ON
3. *stretch out:* ἐκτείνω EKTEINŌ
Lk 22.53 "in the temple, you did not lay hands on me
4. *throw down, strike down:* καταβάλλω (mid.) KATABALLŌ
Heb 6. 1 not laying . . a foundation of repentance
5. *put down:* κατατίθημι KATATITHĒMI
Variant to: Mk **15.46**
6. *incline:* κλίνω KLINŌ
Mt 8.20 "Son of man has nowhere to lay his head
Lk 9.58 "Son of man has nowhere to lay his head
7. *put to, add, continue:* προστίθημι PROSTITHĒMI
Acts 13.36 "David . . was laid with his fathers
8. *lay, put:* τίθημι TITHĒMI
Mt 27.60 laid it in his own new tomb
Mk 6.29 they . . took his body, and laid it in a tomb
6.56 they laid the sick in the market places
10.16 blessed them, laying his hands upon them
15.46 laid him in a tomb which had been hewn *Var.* KATATITHĒMI
15.47 the mother of Joses saw where he was laid
16. 6 "see the place where they laid him
Lk 5.18 bring him in and lay him before Jesus[a]
6.48 "laid the foundation upon rock
14.29 "Otherwise, when he has laid a foundation
23.53 he . . laid him in a rock-hewn tomb
23.55 saw the tomb, and how his body was laid
Jn 10.11 "The good shepherd lays down his life
11.34 "Where have you laid him?
19.41 tomb where no one had ever been laid

Jn 19.42 they laid Jesus there
20. 2 "we do not know where they have laid him
20.13 "I do not know where they have laid him
20.15 "tell me where you have laid him
Acts 3. 2 whom they laid daily at that gate
4.35 laid it at the apostles' feet
4.37 laid it at the apostles' feet
5. 2 laid it at the apostles' feet
5.15 laid them on beds and pallets
7.16 "laid in the tomb.. Abraham had bought
9.37 they laid her in an upper room
13.29 "they took him down.. laid him in a tomb
Rom 9.33 "Behold, I am laying in Zion a stone
1 Cor 3.10 like a.. master builder I laid a foundation
3.11 no other foundation can any one lay
1 Pet 2. 6 "Behold, I am laying in Zion a stone
Rev 1.17 But he laid his right hand upon me
Also variant to: Mk 8.25; *see* LAY UPON

LAY ASIDE
1. *put away:* ἀποτίθημι (mid.) APOTITHĒMI
Heb 12. 1 let us also lay aside every weight
2. *lay, put:* τίθημι TITHĒMI
Jn 13. 4 ⟨Jesus⟩ laid aside his garments

LAY BEFORE
1. *lay upon:* ἀνατίθημι (mid.) ANATITHĒMI*
Acts 25.14 Festus laid Paul's case before the king
Gal 2. 2 I laid before them (but privately
2. *sit down, seat:* καθίζω KATHIZŌ
1 Cor 6. 4 why do you lay them before those?

LAY DOWN
1. *put away:* ἀποτίθημι (mid.) APOTITHĒMI
Acts 7.58 the witnesses laid down their garments
2. *lay, put:* τίθημι TITHĒMI
Lk 19.21 " 'you take up what you did not lay down
19.22 " 'taking up what I did not lay down
Jn 10.15 "I lay down my life for the sheep
10.17 "Father loves me, because I lay down my life
10.18 "but I lay it down of my own accord. I have power to lay it down
13.37 "I will lay down my life for you
13.38 "Will you lay down your life for me?
15.13 "that a man lay down his life for his friends
1 Jn 3.16 he laid down his life for us; and we ought to lay down our lives

LAY ON
LAY UPON
1. *throw upon:* ἐπιβάλλω EPIBALLŌ
[a]+ἐπί [b]B.2.d.1
Mt 26.50 [a]laid hands on Jesus and seized him
Mk 14.46 they laid hands on him and seized him
Lk 20.19 [a]chief priests tried to lay hands on him
21.12 [a]"they will lay their hands on you
Jn 7.30 [a]but no one laid hands on him
7.44 [a]but no one laid hands on him
Var. BALLŌ; *see* LAY
Acts 12. 1 [b]Herod.. laid violent hands upon some
21.27 [a]Jews from Asia.. laid hands on him
1 Cor 7.35 not to lay any restraint upon you
2. *laying on:* ἐπίθεσις EPITHESIS [B.1.a.2]
1 Tim 4.14 council of elders laid their hands upon you
3. *lay on, add:* ἐπιτίθημι EPITITHĒMI
[a]+ἐπί [b]pass.
Mt 9.18 [a]"come and lay your hand on her
19.13 that he might lay his hands on them
19.15 he laid his hands on them
23. 4 [a]"and lay them on men's shoulders
Mk 5.23 "Come and lay your hands on her
6. 5 he laid his hands upon a few sick people
7.32 besought him to lay his hand upon him
8.23 when he.. laid his hands upon him
8.25 he laid his hands upon his eyes
Var. TITHĒMI; *see* LAY
16.18 [a]"they will lay their hands on the sick[k]‡
Lk 4.40 he laid his hands on every one of them
13.13 he laid his hands upon her
15. 5 [a]"he lays it on his shoulders, rejoicing
Lk 23.26 they.. laid on him the cross, to carry
Acts 6. 6 prayed and laid their hands upon them
8.17 [a]Then they laid their hands on them
8.19 "any one on whom I lay my hands
9.12 "come in and lay his hands on him
9.17 [a]laying his hands on him he said
13. 3 laid their hands on them and sent them off
15.28 [b]"to lay upon you no greater burden
19. 6 when Paul had laid his hands upon them
1 Tim 5.22 not be hasty in the laying on of hands

LAY OUT
1. *stretch out:* ἐκτείνω EKTEINŌ
Acts 27.30 under pretense of laying out anchors

LAY UP
1. *store up;* ἀποθησαυρίζω APOTHĒSAURIZŌ*
1 Tim 6.19 thus laying up.. a good foundation
2. *store up:* θησαυρίζω THĒSAURIZŌ
Mt 6.19 "Do not lay up for yourselves treasures
6.20 "lay up for yourselves treasures in heaven
2 Cor 12.14 ought not to lay up for their parents
3. *lay, put:* τίθημι (mid.) TITHĒMI
Lk 1.66 laid them up in their hearts

LAY UP TREASURE
1. *store up:* θησαυρίζω THĒSAURIZŌ
Lk 12.21 "he who lays up treasure for himself
Jas 5. 3 You have laid up treasure[e] for the last days†

LAY UPON (*See* LAY ON)

LAYING ON
1. *laying on:* ἐπίθεσις EPITHESIS
Acts 8.18 the laying on of the apostles' hands
2 Tim 1. 6 through the laying on of my hands
Heb 6. 2 ablutions, the laying on of hands

LAZARUS: Λάζαρος 'laz(ə)rəs
Lk 16.20 "at his gate lay a poor man named L.
16.23 "saw Abraham far off and L. in his bosom
16.24 " 'send L. to dip the end of his finger
16.25 " 'L. in like manner ⟨received⟩ evil things
Jn 11. 1 a certain man was ill, L. of Bethany
11. 2 Mary.., whose brother Lazarus was ill
11. 5 Jesus loved Martha and her sister and L.
11.11 "Our friend Lazarus has fallen asleep
11.14 Jesus told them plainly, "L. is dead
11.43 he cried.. "L., come out
12. 1 Jesus came to Bethany, where L. was
12. 2 L. was one of those at table with him
12. 9 to see L., whom he had raised
12.10 chief priests planned to put L... to death
12.17 when he called L. out of the tomb
CONTEXTUALLY
Jn 11.17 L.[x] had.. been in the tomb four days†

LAZY
1. *idle:* ἀργός ARGOS
Tit 1.12 "Cretans are always liars,.. lazy gluttons

LEAD (*See also* CAPTIVE, LEAD; TRIUMPH, LEAD IN)
1. *lead, bring:* ἄγω AGŌ
Lk 4. 1 Jesus.. was led by the Spirit
4.29 they.. led him to the brow of the hill
22.54 they seized him and led him away
23.32 Two others also.. were led away
Jn 18.13 First they led him to Annas
18.28 they led Jesus from the house of Caiaphas
Acts 8.32 "As a sheep led to the slaughter
Rom 2. 4 God's kindness is meant to lead you
8.14 For all who are led by the Spirit of God
Gal 5.18 if you are led by the Spirit
2. *capture:* αἰχμαλωτεύω AICHMALŌTEUŌ [A.6.a.6]
Eph 4. 8 "he led a host of captives
3. *lead away:* ἀπάγω APAGŌ
Mt 7.13 "the gate is wide.. that leads to destruction
7.14 "the gate is narrow.. that leads to life
26.57 those who had seized Jesus led him
Mk 14.53 And they led Jesus to the high priest
Lk 13.15 "untie his ox.. lead it away to water it
4. *draw through, live:* διάγω DIAGŌ
1 Tim 2. 2 that we may lead a quiet and peaceable life

5. *guide:* ὁδηγέω HODĒGEŌ
Mt 15.14 "And if a blind man leads a blind man
Lk 6.39 "Can a blind man lead a blind man?
6. *bring, bear:* φέρω PHERŌ
Acts 12.10 the iron gate leading into the city
7. *go before, go forward:* προέρχομαι PROERCHOMAI
Lk 22.47 Judas, one of the twelve, was leading them
CONTEXTUALLY
Rom 5.18 one man's trespass led to condemnation
5.18 act of righteousness leads to acquittal
6.16 slaves .. of sin, which leads to death
6.16 obedience, which leads to righteousness
2 Cor 7.10 repentance that leads to salvation
Heb 3.12 unbelieving heart, leading you to fall

LEAD A LIFE
1. *walk, behave:* περιπατέω PERIPATEŌ
1 Cor 7.17 let every one lead the life .. assigned
Eph 4. 1 to lead a life worthy of the calling
Col 1.10 to lead a life worthy of the Lord
1 Th 2.12 lead a life worthy of God, who calls you

LEAD ASTRAY
1. *lead away:* ἀπάγω APAGŌ
1 Cor 12. 2 you were led astray to dumb idols
2. *lead astray:* ἀποπλανάω APOPLANAŌ
Mk 13.22 "False Christs .. will arise .. to lead astray
3. *entice, destroy:* φθείρω PHTHEIRŌ
2 Cor 11. 3 your thoughts will be led astray
4. *cause to wander:* πλανάω PLANAŌ
Mt 24. 4 "Take heed that no one leads you astray
24. 5 "they will lead many astray
24.11 "false prophets will .. lead many astray
24.24 "false Christs .. will arise .. to lead astray
Mk 13. 5 "Take heed that no one leads you astray
13. 6 "saying, 'I am he!' .. they will lead .. astray
Lk 21. 8 " 'Take heed that you are not led astray
Jn 7.12 "No, he is leading the people astray
7.47 "Are you led astray, you also?
Tit 3. 3 we ourselves were once .. led astray

LEAD AWAY
1. *lead away:* ἀπάγω APAGŌ
Mt 27. 2 they bound him and led him away
27.31 led him away to crucify him
Mk 14.44 "seize him and lead him away under guard
15.16 soldiers led him away inside the palace
Lk 22.66 they led him away to their council
23.26 as they led him away, they seized .. Simon
2. *carry away:* ἀποφέρω APOPHERŌ
Mk 15. 1 they bound Jesus and led him away
3. *carry away:* παραφέρω PARAPHERŌ
Heb 13. 9 Do not be led away by diverse .. teachings

LEAD BY THE HAND
1. *lead by the hand:* χειραγωγέω CHEIRAGŌGEŌ*
Acts 9. 8 so they led him by the hand
22.11 "I was led by the hand .. into Damascus

LEAD S. BY THE HAND, PEOPLE TO
1. *leader, guide:* χειραγωγός (pl.) CHEIRAGŌGOS*
Acts 13.11 seeking people to lead him by the hand

LEAD INTO
1. *carry in:* εἰσφέρω EISPHERŌ
Mt 6.13 "And lead us not into temptation
Lk 11. 4 "and lead us not into temptation

LEAD OUT
1. *carry out:* ἐκφέρω EKPHERŌ
Mk 8.23 "he .. led him out of the village
2. *lead out:* ἐξάγω EXAGŌ
Mk 15.20 And they led him out to crucify him
Lk 24.50 he led them out as far as Bethany
Jn 10. 3 "calls his own sheep .. and leads them out
Acts 7.36 "led them out, having performed wonders
7.40 " 'Moses who led us out from .. land of Egypt
13.17 "with uplifted arm he led them out of it
21.38 "led the four thousand men .. out
Heb 8. 9 "to lead them out of the land of Egypt

LEAD PEOPLE
1. *make progress, advance:* προκόπτω PROKOPTŌ
2 Tim 2.16 for it will lead people into more .. ungodliness

LEAD UP
1. *bring back, lead up:* ἀνάγω ANAGŌ
Mt 4. 1 Then Jesus was led up by the Spirit
2. *bring, carry up:* ἀναφέρω ANAPHERŌ
Mt 17. 1 Jesus .. led them up a high mountain apart
Mk 9. 2 Jesus .. led them up a high mountain apart

LEADER
1. *founder, leader:* ἀρχηγός ARCHĒGOS
Acts 5.31 "God exalted him .. as Leader and Savior
2. *think, lead:* ἡγέομαι (subst. part.) HĒGEOMAI
Lk 22.26 let .. leader ⟨become⟩ as one who serves
Heb 13. 7 Remember your leaders
13.17 Obey your leaders and submit to them
13.24 Greet all your leaders and all the saints
3. *first, foremost:* πρῶτος (subst.) PRŌTOS
Acts 28.17 "he called together the local leaders

LEADERSHIP OF, UNDER THE
1. *through:* διά (+gen.) DIA
Heb 3.16 who left Egypt under the l. of Moses

LEADING
1. *think, lead:* ἡγέομαι (part.) HĒGEOMAI
Acts 15.22 and Silas, leading men among the brethren
2. *first, foremost:* πρῶτος PRŌTOS
Mk 6.21 officers and the leading men of Galilee
Acts 13.50 incited .. l. men of the city, and stirred up
16.12 Philippi, .. leading city of the district[x]
17. 4 and not a few of the leading women

LEAF
1. *leaf:* φύλλον PHYLLON*
[a]ἔχων φύλλα
Mt 21.19 he .. found nothing on it but leaves only
24.32 "as soon as its branch .. puts forth its leaves
Mk 11.13 [a]in the distance a fig tree in leaf
11.13 he found nothing but leaves
13.28 "as soon as its branch .. puts forth its leaves
Rev 22. 2 leaves .. for the healing of the nations

LEAF, COME OUT IN
1. *put forward:* προβάλλω PROBALLŌ
Lk 21.30 "as soon as they come out in leaf

LEAFY BRANCH
1. *bed of straw, leaves:* στιβάς STIBAS*
Mk 11. 8 others spread leafy branches

LEAP
1. *spring upon, attack:* ἐφάλλομαι EPHALLOMAI*
Acts 19.16 man in whom .. spirit was leaped on them
2. *spring up:* ἅλλομαι HALLOMAI
Acts 3. 8 leaping up he stood and walked
3. *spring, leap:* σκιρτάω SKIRTAŌ*
Lk 1.41 the babe leaped in her womb
1.44 "the babe in my womb leaped for joy
6.23 "Rejoice in that day, and leap for joy

LEAP UP
1. *leap out of:* ἐξάλλομαι EXALLOMAI*
Acts 3. 8 leaping up he stood and walked

LEARN
1. *learn to know, recognize:* ἐπιγινώσκω EPIGINŌSKŌ
Lk 7.37 when she learned that he was at table
23. 7 learned that he belonged to Herod's
Acts 24. 8 "you will be able to learn from him
28. 1 learned that the island was called Malta
2. *know, understand:* γινώσκω GINŌSKŌ
Mk 15.45 when he learned from the centurion
Lk 9.11 When the crowds learned it, they followed
Jn 7.51 "without first .. learning what he does
12. 9 When the .. Jews learned that he was there
Acts 17.13 when the Jews of Thessalonica learned
21.34 as he could not learn the facts
Rev 2.24 " 'have not learned .. deep things of Satan
3. 9 " 'make them .. learn that I have loved you
3. *learn, understand:* μανθάνω MANTHANŌ
Mt 9.13 "learn what this means, 'I desire mercy

Mt 11.29 "Take my yoke . . and learn from me
24.32 "From the fig tree learn its lesson
Mk 13.28 "From the fig tree learn its lesson
Jn 6.45 "one who has . . learned from the Father
Acts 23.27 "having learned that he was a Roman
1 Cor 4. 6 learn . . not to go beyond what is written
14.31 that all may learn and . . be encouraged
Eph 4.20 You did not so learn Christ!
Phil 4. 9 What you have learned and received
4.11 for I have learned . . to be content
Col 1. 7 as you learned it from Epaphras
1 Tim 2.11 Let a woman learn in silence
5. 4 let them first learn their religious duty
5.13 they learn to be idlers, gadding about
2 Tim 3.14 continue in what you have learned . . , knowing from whom you learned it
Tit 3.14 let our people learn to apply themselves
Heb 5. 8 learned obedience through what he suffered
Rev 14. 3 No one could learn that song execpt

4. *discipline, educate:* παιδεύω (pass.) PAIDEUŌ
1 Tim 1.20 that they may learn not to blaspheme

5. *take, receive:* παραλαμβάνω PARALAMBANŌ
1 Th 4. 1 as you learned from us how . . to live

6. *inquire about, learn:* πυνθάνομαι PYNTHANOMAI
Acts 23.34 he learned that he was from Cilicia

LEARN OF

1. *become aware of:* συνεῖδον SYNEIDON
Acts 14. 6 they learned of it and fled to Lystra

LEARN THE SECRET OF

1. *initiate* (into the mysteries): μυέω (pass.) MYEŌ*
Phil 4.12 have learned the secret of facing plenty

LEARN, TRY TO

1. *test, approve:* δοκιμάζω DOKIMAZŌ
Eph 5.10 try to learn what is pleasing to the Lord

LEARNING

1. *letter, document:* γράμμα (pl.) GRAMMA
Acts 26.24 "your great learning is turning you mad

IDIOMATICALLY
a. Jn 7.15 "How is it that this man has learning?[p]† πῶς οὗτος γράμματα οἶδεν; [GRAMMA]

LEAST (*See also* ESTEEM LEAST)

1. *smallest, least:* ἐλάχιστος ELACHISTOS
Mt 2. 6 " 'by no means l. among . . rulers of Judah
5.19 "relaxes one of the least of . . commandments . . , shall be . . l. in the kingdom of heaven
25.40 " 'as you did it to one of the least of these
25.45 " 'as you did it not to one of the least
1 Cor 15. 9 For I am the least of the apostles
Eph 3. 8 though I am the very least of all the saints

2. *little, small:* μικρός MIKROS
[a]comp.
Mt 11.11 [a]"he who is least in the kingdom of heaven
Lk 7.28 [a]"he who is least in the kingdom of God
9.48 [a]"he who is least among you all is . . great
Acts 8.10 all gave heed to him, from the least
Heb 8.11 "from the least of them to the greatest

LEAST, AT

1. *but:* ἀλλά ALLA
1 Cor 9. 2 If . . I am not an apostle, at l. I am to you

2. *even if:* κἄν KAN
Acts 5.15 at least his shadow might fall on some

LEATHER

1. *of skin, leather:* δερμάτινος DERMATINOS*
Mt 3. 4 a leather girdle around his waist
Mk 1. 6 a leather girdle around his waist

LEAVE (*See also* ASK LEAVE)

1. *raise up, rise:* ἀνίστημι ANISTĒMI [A.6.c]
Mk 10. 1 he left there and went to . . Judea

2. *set free:* ἀπαλλάσσω (pass.) APALLASSŌ
Acts 19.12 diseases left them and the evil spirits

3. *go away:* ἀπέρχομαι (+ἀπό) APERCHOMAI
Mk 1.42 immediately the leprosy left him
Lk 5.13 immediately the leprosy left him
Acts 16.39 they . . asked them to leave the city

4. *let go, leave, forgive:* ἀφίημι APHIĒMI
Mt 4.11 Then the devil left him, and . . angels came
4.20 Immediately they left their nets
4.22 they left the boat and their father
5.24 "leave your gift there before the altar and go
8.15 he touched her hand, and the fever left
8.22 "leave the dead to bury their own dead
13.36 Then he left the crowds and went
18.12 "does he not leave the ninety-nine?
19.27 "we have left everything and followed
19.29 "one who has left houses or brothers
22.22 they left him and went away
22.25 "having no children left . . wife to . . brother
24. 2 "not be left here one stone upon another
24.40 "one is taken and one is left
24.41 "one is taken and one is left
26.44 leaving them again, he went away
Mk 1.18 immediately they left their nets
1.20 they left their father Zebedee in the boat
1.31 the fever left her; and she served them
4.36 leaving the crowd, they took him
7. 8 "You leave the commandment of God
8.13 he left them, and getting into the boat
10.28 "we have left everything and followed
10.29 "there is no one who has left house
12.12 so they left him and went away
12.19 "if a man's brother dies . . but leaves no child
12.20 "and when he died left no children
12.22 "and the seven left no children
13. 2 "will not be left here one stone upon another
13.34 "like a man . . when he leaves home
Lk 4.39 rebuked the fever, and it left her
5.11 they left everything and followed him
9.60 "Leave the dead to bury their own dead
10.30 "departed, leaving him half dead
12.39 "not . . left his house to be broken into
17.34 "one will be taken and the other left
17.35 "one will be taken and the other left[b]
[17.36 *"one will be taken and the other left*‡
18.28 "we have left our homes and followed you
18.29 "no man who has left house or wife
19.44 "they will not leave one stone upon another
21. 6 "not be left here one stone upon another
Jn 4. 3 left Judea and departed again to Galilee
4.28 the woman left her water jar, and went
4.52 "at the seventh hour the fever left him
8.29 "he has not left me alone
10.12 "a hireling . . leaves the sheep and flees
14.18 "I will not leave you desolate
14.27 "Peace I leave with you; my peace
16.28 "again, I am leaving the world
16.32 "when you . . will leave me alone
Acts 14.17 "he did not leave himself without witness
Heb 2. 8 "he left nothing outside his control
6. 1 let us leave the elementary doctrine

5. *depart, withdraw from:* ἀφίστημι APHISTĒMI
Acts 12.10 immediately the angel left him
2 Cor 12. 8 besought the Lord . . that it . . leave me

6. *go from:* ἀποχωρέω APOCHŌREŌ
Lk 9.39 "spirit seizes him . . and will hardly leave
Acts 13.13 John left them and returned to Jerusalem

7. *leave over, abandon:* ἀπολείπω APOLEIPŌ
2 Tim 4.13 bring the cloak that I left with Carpus
4.20 Trophimus I left ill at Miletus
Tit 1. 5 This is why I left you in Crete
Jude . 6 angels that . . left their proper dwelling

8. *separate, divide:* χωρίζω (pass.) CHŌRIZŌ
Acts 18. 1 After this he left Athens
18. 2 commanded all the Jews to leave Rome

9. *give place:* διδόναι τόπον DIDŌMI [B.2.a.1]
Rom 12.19 "leave it[t] to the wrath of God†

10. *permit:* ἐάω EAŌ
Acts 23.32 leaving the horsemen to go on with him
27.40 So they cast off the anchors and left them

11. *leave behind:* ἐγκαταλείπω EGKATALEIPŌ
Rom 9.29 "If the Lord . . had not left us children

12. *go out:* ἐκπορεύομαι EKPOREUOMAI
Mk 6.11 "when you leave, shake off the dust
10.46 he was leaving Jericho with his disciples
13. *go out:* ἐξέρχομαι EXERCHOMAI
[a]+ἔξω [b]+ἀπό [c]+ἐκ
Mt 10.14 [a]"shake off the dust . . as you leave . . house
24. 1 [b]Jesus left the temple and was going away
Mk 1.29 [c]immediately he[e] left the synagogue‡
6.10 "stay there until you leave the place
7.29 [c]"the demon has left your daughter
Lk 9. 5 [b]"when you leave that town shake off . . dust
Phil 4.15 [b]when I left Macedonia
Heb 3.16 [c]Was it not all those who left Egypt?
14. *leave behind:* ὑπολιμπάνω HYPOLIMPANŌ*
Pet 2.21 Christ also suffered . . , leaving . . example
15. *leave behind:* καταλείπω KATALEIPŌ
Mt 4.13 leaving Nazareth he . . dwelt in Capernaum
16. 4 So he left them and departed
19. 5 " 'a man shall leave his father and mother
21.17 leaving them, he went out of the city
Mk 10. 7 " 'a man shall leave his father and mother
12.19 "if a man's brother dies and leaves a wife
12.21 "the second . . died, leaving no children
14.52 he left the linen cloth and ran away naked
Lk 5.28 he left everything, and rose
10.40 "my sister has left me to serve alone
15. 4 "What man . . does not leave the ninety-nine?
20.31 "likewise all seven left no children and died
Jn 8. 9 Jesus was left alone with the woman[r]‡
Acts 18.19 to Ephesus, and he left them there
21. 3 leaving it on the left we sailed to Syria
24.27 Felix left Paul in prison
25.14 "There is a man left prisoner by Felix
Eph 5.31 "a man shall leave his father and mother
Heb 11.27 By faith he left Egypt, not being afraid
16. *pass over:* μεταβαίνω METABAINŌ
Mt 8.34 begged him to leave their neighborhood
Jn 7. 3 "Leave here and go to Judea
Acts 18. 7 he left . . and went to the house of . . Titius[q]
17. *abound:* περισσεύω PERISSEUŌ
Jn 6.13 fragments . . left by those who had eaten
18. *go from:* πορεύομαι ἀπό POREUOMAI [A.6.a.4]
Lk 4.42 would have kept him from leaving them
Acts 5.41 Then they left the presence of the council
CONTEXTUALLY
Mk 7.17 entered the house, and left the people
Lk 4.38 And he arose and left the synagogue
Heb 12. 8 If you are left without discipline

LEAVE BEHIND
1. *leave behind:* καταλείπω KATALEIPŌ
1 Th 3. 1 were willing to be left behind at Athens

LEAVE, GIVE
1. *permit:* ἐπιτρέπω EPITREPŌ
Mk 5.13 So he gave them leave
Lk 8.32 So he gave them leave
Jn 19.38 Pilate gave him leave
Acts 21.40 when he had given him l., Paul . . motioned
27. 3 Julius . . gave him leave to go to his friends

LEAVE OUT
1. *throw out:* ἐκβάλλω EKBALLŌ
Rev 11. 2 "l. that out, . . it is given . . to the nations

LEAVE, TAKE
1. *part from* (mid.): ἀποτάσσω APOTASSŌ
Mk 6.46 after he had taken leave of them
Acts 18.18 Paul . . then took leave of the brethren
18.21 taking leave of them he said, "I will return
2 Cor 2.13 So I took leave of them and went on
2. *greet:* ἀσπάζομαι ASPAZOMAI
Acts 20. 1 Paul . . having exhorted them took leave

LEAVEN
1. *leaven:* ζύμη ZYMĒ*
Mt 13.33 "The kingdom of heaven is like leaven
16. 6 "beware of the leaven of the Pharisees
16.11 "Beware of the leaven of the Pharisees
16.12 not . . beware of the leaven of bread
Mk 8.15 "Take heed, beware of the leaven of the Pharisees and the leaven of Herod[e]
Lk 12. 1 "Beware of the leaven of the Pharisees
13.21 "like leaven which a woman took and hid
1 Cor 5. 6 a little leaven leavens the whole lump
5. 7 Cleanse out the old leaven
5. 8 celebrate the festival, not with the old leaven, the leaven of malice and evil
Gal 5. 9 A little leaven leavens the whole lump
2. *leaven, ferment:* ζυμόω ZYMOŌ*
Mt 13.33 "hid in . . flour, till it was all leavened
Lk 13.21 "hid in . . flour, till it was all leavened
1 Cor 5. 6 that a little . . leavens the whole lump?
Gal 5. 9 A little . . leavens the whole lump

LEBBAEUS: Λεββαῖος le'bēəs
Mt [10. 3 James the son of Alphaeus, and *L.*‡

LEE OF, RUN UNDER THE
1. *run in under:* ὑποτρέχω HYPOTRECHŌ*
Acts 27.16 running under the lee of a small island

LEE OF, SAIL UNDER THE
1. *sail under the lee of:* ὑποπλέω HYPOPLEŌ*
Acts 27. 4 we sailed under the lee of Cyprus
27. 7 we sailed under the lee of Crete

LEFT
1. *left:* ἀριστερός ARISTEROS
[a]ἐξ ἀριστερῶν
Lk 23.33 [a]one on the right and one on the left
2. *left:* εὐώνυμος EUŌNYMOS
[a]ἐξ εὐωνύμων
Mt 27.38 [a]one on the right and one on the left
Mk 15.27 [a]one on his right and one on his left[g]
Acts 21. 3 leaving it on the left we sailed to Syria
Rev 10. 2 he set . . his left foot on the land

LEFT ALL ALONE, BE
1. *make single:* μονόω (pass.) MONOŌ*
1 Tim 5. 5 who is a real widow, and is left all alone

LEFT, BE
1. *leave remaining:* ὑπολείπω (pass.) HYPOLEIPŌ*
Rom 11. 3 "I alone am left, and they seek my life
2. *remain over:* περιλείπομαι PERILEIPOMAI*
1 Th 4.15 who are l. until the coming of the Lord
4.17 we . . who are left, shall be caught up

LEFT HAND
1. *left:* ἀριστερός ARISTEROS [B.3.b.2]
[a]ἐξ ἀριστερῶν
Mt 6. 3 "do not let your left hand know
Mk 10.37 [a]"Grant us to sit, . . one at your left ⟨hand⟩
2 Cor 6. 7 weapons of righteousness . . for the left ⟨hand⟩
2. *left:* εὐώνυμος EUŌNYMOS [B.3.b.2]
Always ἐξ εὐωνύμων
Mt 20.21 "may sit, . . one at your left ⟨hand⟩
20.23 "to sit . . at my left ⟨hand⟩ is not mine
25.33 "he will place . . the goats at the left ⟨hand⟩
25.41 "he will say to those at his left hand
Mk 10.40 "to sit . . at my left ⟨hand⟩ is not mine

LEFT OVER
1. *superfluity:* περίσσευμα PERISSEUMA [A.1.b.5]
Mk 8. 8 they took up the broken pieces left over
2. *abound:* περισσεύω (part.) PERISSEUŌ
[a]subst. neut. [b]A.1.b.2
Mt 14.20 [ab]twelve baskets . . of . . pieces left over
15.37 [ab]seven baskets . . of . . pieces left over
Lk 9.17 [a]what was left over, twelve baskets
Jn 6.12 "Gather up the fragments left over

LEG
1. *leg with the foot, foot:* πούς POUS
Rev 10. 1 angel . . and his legs like pillars of fire
2. *leg:* σκέλος SKELOS*
Jn 19.31 asked . . that their legs might be broken
19.32 the soldiers came and broke the legs
19.33 came to Jesus . . did not break his legs

LEGAL
1. *law, norm:* νόμος NOMOS [A.1.b.5]
Heb 7.16 priest, not according to a legal requirement

LEGAL DEMAND
1. *decree, decision:* δόγμα DOGMA
Col 2.14 canceled the bond . . with its legal demands

LEGION
1. *legion* (Lat.): λεγιών LEGIŌN*
Mt 26.53 "more than twelve legions of angels
Mk 5. 9 He replied, "My name is Legion
5.15 the man who had had the legion
Lk 8.30 he said, "Legion"; for many demons

LEISURE, HAVE
1. *have time, have opportunity:* εὐκαιρέω EUKAIREŌ
Mk 6.31 they had no leisure even to eat

LEND
1. *lend:* δανείζω DANEIZŌ
Lk 6.34 "if you lend to those . . , what credit is that?
6.34 "Even sinners lend to sinners
6.35 "lend, expecting nothing in return[v]
2. *lend:* κίχρημι KICHRĒMI*
Lk 11. 5 " 'Friend, lend me three loaves

LENGTH
1. *step, platform:* βῆμα BĒMA
Acts 7. 5 "no inheritance . . , not even a foot's length
2. *length, height:* μῆκος MEKOS*
Eph 3.18 what is the breadth and length?
Rev 21.16 its length the same as its breadth
21.16 its length and breadth . . are equal
IDIOMATICALLY
a. Lk 23.9 So he questioned him at some length ἐπηρώτα δὲ αὐτὸν ἐν λόγοις ἱκανοῖς [HIKANOS]

LENGTH, AT
1. *at some time, once:* ποτέ POTE II
Phil 4.10 now at length you have revived . . concern

LEOPARD
1. *leopard:* πάρδαλις PARDALIS*
Rev 13. 2 the beast that I saw was like a leopard

LEPER
1. *scaly, leprous:* λεπρός (subst.) LEPROS*
Mt 8. 2 behold, a leper came to him and knelt
10. 8 "raise the dead, cleanse lepers
11. 5 "lepers are cleansed and the deaf hear
26. 6 at Bethany in the house of Simon the leper
Mk 1.40 a leper came to him beseeching him
14. 3 at Bethany in the house of Simon the leper
Lk 4.27 "there were many lepers in Israel
7.22 "the lame walk, lepers are cleansed
17.12 as he entered . . he was met by ten lepers

LEPROSY
1. *leprosy:* λέπρα LEPRA*
Mt 8. 3 immediately his leprosy was cleansed
Mk 1.42 immediately the leprosy left him
Lk 5.12 there came a man full of leprosy
5.13 immediately the leprosy left him

LESS (*See also* ANXIOUS, LESS)
1. *smaller, inferior:* ἐλάσσων ELASSŌN
1 Tim 5. 9 if she is not less than sixty years of age
2. *less, inferior:* ἥσσων HĒSSŌN
2 Cor 12.15 If I love you . . am I to be loved the less?
3. *more than, by:* παρά (+acc.) PARA [B.1.a.5]
2 Cor **11.**24
IDIOMATICALLY
a. Heb 12.25 For if they did not escape . . much less shall we εἰ γὰρ ἐκεῖνοι οὐκ ἐξέφυγον . . πολὺ μᾶλλον ἡμεῖς [MALLON]

LESS, ANY
1. *not, no:* οὐ OU [A.4.c]
1 Cor 12.15 would not make it any l. a part of the body
12.16 would not make it any l. a part of the body

LESS FAVORED IN, BE
1. *be inferior to, be defeated:* ἡττάομαι HĒTTAOMAI
2 Cor 12.13 For in what were you less favored?

LESSON
1. *teaching:* διδαχή DIDACHĒ
1 Cor 14.26 each one has a hymn, a lesson
2. *comparison, parable:* παραβολή PARABOLĒ
Mt 24.32 "From the fig tree learn its lesson
Mk 13.28 "From the fig tree learn its lesson

LEST
1. *in order that:* ἵνα (neg.) HINA
Mt 26. 5 "lest there be a tumult
Mk 3. 9 lest they should crush him
Lk 16.28 " 'lest they also come into this place
Jn 3.20 lest his deeds should be exposed
12.35 "Walk . . lest the darkness overtake you
12.40 "lest they should see with their eyes
12.42 lest they . . be put out of the synagogue
Rom 11.25 Lest you be wise in your own conceits
15.20 lest I build on another man's foundation
1 Cor 1.15 l. any . . say . . you were baptized in my name
1.17 lest the cross of Christ be emptied
7. 5 come together again, lest Satan tempt you
8.13 never . . , lest I cause my brother to fall
11.34 lest you come together to be condemned
Eph 2. 9 not because of works, lest any man . . boast
Phil 2.27 lest I should have sorrow upon sorrow
Col 3.21 lest they become discouraged
2 Pet 3.17 lest you be carried away with the error
Rev 18. 4 "Come out . . lest you take part in her sins, lest you share in her plagues
2. *not:* μή MĒ
[a]μή πως
Mk 13.36 "lest he come suddenly and find you
Lk 11.35 "be careful lest the light in you be darkness
Acts 13.40 "lest there come upon you what is said
27.42 lest any should swim away and escape
1 Cor 8. 9 lest this liberty . . become a stumbling block
9.27 [a]lest after preaching . . I . . be disqualified
10.12 let any one . . take heed lest he fall
2 Cor 9. 4 [a]lest if some Macedonians come with me
Gal 2. 2 lest somehow I should be running . . in vain
6. 1 Look to yourself, lest you too be tempted
3. *perhaps, never:* μήποτε MĒPOTE
Mt 4. 6 " 'lest you strike your foot against a stone
5.25 "l. your accuser hand you . . to the judge
7. 6 "lest they trample them under foot
13.15 " 'lest they should perceive with their eyes
13.29 " 'lest in gathering the weeds you root up
15.32 "unwilling . . lest they faint on the way
27.64 "lest his disciples go and steal him away
Mk 4.12 "l. they should turn again, and be forgiven
14. 2 "lest there be a tumult of the people
Lk 4.11 " 'lest you strike your foot against a stone
12.58 "lest he drag you to the judge
14. 8 "lest a more eminent man . . be invited
14.12 "lest they also invite you in return
21.34 "lest your hearts be weighed down
Acts 28.27 " 'lest they should perceive with their eyes
Heb 2. 1 lest we drift away from it
3.12 lest there be . . an . . unbelieving heart
4. 1 lest any of you be judged to have failed

LET
1. *let go, leave, forgive:* ἀφίημι APHIĒMI
Mt 7. 4 " 'Let me take the speck out of your eye
13.30 " 'Let both grow together until the harvest
19.14 "Let the children come to me
27.49 "Wait, let us see whether Elijah will come
Mk 7.27 "Let the children first be fed
10.14 "Let the children come to me
Lk 6.42 " 'Brother, let me take out the speck
18.16 "Let the children come to me
Jn 11.44 "Unbind him, and let him go
11.48 "If we let him go on . . , every one will believe
18. 8 "so, if you seek me, let these men go
Rev 11. 9 refuse to let them be placed in a tomb
2. *give:* δίδωμι DIDŌMI
Acts 2.27 " 'nor let thy Holy One see corruption
13.35 " 'Thou wilt not l. . . Holy One see corruption
3. *permit:* ἐάω EAŌ
Mt 24.43 "not have let his house be broken into
Acts 19.30 but the disciples would not let him

Acts 27.32 soldiers cut away the ropes .. and let it go
1 Cor 10.13 he will not let you be tempted
4. *permit:* ἐπιτρέπω EPITREPŌ
Mt 8.21 "Lord, let me first go and bury my father
Lk 8.32 they begged him to let them enter these
9.59 "Lord, let me first go and bury my father
9.61 "let me first say farewell to those
Acts 21.39 "I beg you, let me speak to the people
IDIOMATICALLY
a. Gal 3.2 Let me ask you only this τοῦτο μόνον θέλω μαθεῖν ἀφ' ὑμῶν [THELŌ]

LET ALONE
1. *let go, leave, forgive:* ἀφίημι APHIĒMI
Mt 15.14 "Let them alone; they are blind guides
Mk 14. 6 "Let her alone; why do you trouble her?
Lk 13. 8 " 'Let it alone .. this year also, till I dig
Jn 12. 7 "Let her alone, let her keep it
Acts 5.38 "keep away .. and let them alone

LET S. BE SO
1. *let go, leave, forgive:* ἀφίημι APHIĒMI
Mt 3.15 "Let it be so now, for thus it is fitting

LET DEPART
1. *loose from, dismiss:* ἀπολύω APOLYŌ
Lk 2.29 "now lettest thou thy servant depart

LET DOWN
1. *slacken, let down:* χαλάω CHALAŌ
Mk 2. 4 they let down .. pallet on which .. paralytic
Lk 5. 4 "let down your nets for a catch
5. 5 "But at your word I will let down the nets
2 Cor 11.33 but I was let down in a basket
2. *let down, drop:* καθίημι KATHIĒMI*
Lk 5.19 let him down with his bed through the tiles
Acts 9.25 let him down over the wall
10.11 a great sheet, let down by four corners
11. 5 "a great sheet, let down from heaven

LET GO
1. *let go, leave, forgive:* ἀφίημι APHIĒMI
Mk 11. 6 they told them .. and they let them go
2. *loose from, dismiss:* ἀπολύω APOLYŌ
Lk 14. 4 took him and healed him, and let him go
Acts 4.21 let them go, finding no way to punish
5.40 they beat them .. and let them go
16.35 sent .. police, saying, "Let those men go
16.36 "magistrates have sent to let you go
17. 9 they had .. security .., they let them go

LET S. HAVE
1. *let go, leave, forgive:* ἀφίημι APHIĒMI
Mt 5.40 "let him have your cloak as well

LET ONE ALONE
1. *ha!:* ἔα EA
Lk [4.34 "*Let us a.!* What have you to do with us?†

LET OUT
1. *give up:* ἐκδίδωμι (mid.) EKDIDŌMI*
Mt 21.33 "a vineyard .., and let it out to tenants
21.41 "He will .. let out the vineyard to other
Mk 12. 1 "a vineyard, .. and let it out to tenants
Lk 20. 9 "a vineyard, and let it out to tenants
2. *throw, cast out:* ῥίπτω RHIPTŌ
Acts 27.29 they let out four anchors from the stern

LETTER
1. *message, letter:* ἐπιστολή EPISTOLĒ*
Acts 9. 2 letters to the synagogues at Damascus
15.30 to Antioch; and .. they delivered the letter
22. 5 "From them I received letters
23.25 he wrote a letter to this effect
23.33 delivered the letter to the governor
Rom 16.22 I Tertius, the writer of this letter
1 Cor 5. 9 wrote to you in my letter not to associate
16. 3 those whom you accredit by letter
2 Cor 3. 1 do we need .. letters of recommendation?
3. 2 You .. are our letter of recommendation
3. 3 you show that you are a letter from Christ
7. 8 even if I made you sorry with my letter
7. 8 that letter grieved you .. only for a while
2 Cor 10. 9 not .. frightening you with letters
10.10 "His letters are weighty and strong
10.11 what we say by letter when absent
Col 4.16 when this letter has been read among you
1 Th 5.27 that this letter be read to all the brethren
2 Th 2. 2 by letter purporting to be from us
2.15 either by word of mouth or by letter
3.14 to obey what we say in this letter
3.17 This is the mark in every letter of mine
2 Pet 3. 1 second letter that I have written to you
3.16 speaking .. as he does in all his letters
2. *letter, document:* γράμμα GRAMMA
Lk [23.38 inscription over him, ***in letters of Greek***‡
Jn [7.15 "How is it .. this man ***knows his letters?***†
Acts 28.21 "We have received no letters from Judea
2 Cor 3. 7 dispensation of death, carved in letters
Gal 6.11 See with what large letters I am writing
IDIOMATICALLY
a. Acts 15.23 ⟨sent⟩ with the following letter ⟨πέμψαι⟩ γράψαντες διὰ χειρὸς αὐτῶν [GRAPHŌ]
CONTEXTUALLY
Acts 23.34 On reading the letter, he asked

LETTER, SEND A
1. *send a message, write:* ἐπιστέλλω EPISTELLŌ
Acts 21.25 "we have sent a letter with our judgment

LEVEL
1. *flat, level:* πεδινός PEDINOS*
Lk 6.17 he came down .. and stood on a level place

LEVI: Λευί, Λευίς 'lēˌvī
Mk 2.14 he saw Levi the son of Alphaeus
Lk 3.24 Matthat, the son of L., the son of Melchi
3.29 Matthat, the son of Levi
5.27 he .. saw a tax collector, named Levi
5.29 Levi made him a great feast in his house
Heb 7. 5 those descendants of Levi
7. 9 L. himself, who receives tithes, paid tithes
Rev 7. 7 twelve thousand of the tribe of Levi

LEVITE: Λευίτης
Lk 10.32 "likewise a L., when he came to the place
Jn 1.19 when the Jews sent priests and Levites
Acts 4.36 Barnabas .., a Levite, a native of Cyprus

LEVITICAL: Λευιτικός
Heb 7.11 through the Levitical priesthood

LEVITY
1. *ready wit, buffoonery:* εὐτραπελία EUTRAPELIA*
Eph 5. 4 Let there be no filthiness, .. nor levity

LIABLE
1. *liable, guilty:* ἔνοχος ENOCHOS
Mt 5.21 " 'whoever kills shall be liable to judgment
5.22 "who is angry .. shall be liable to judgment; whoever insults[j] .. shall be liable .. and whoever says, 'You fool!' shall be liable

LIAR
1. *false, lying:* ψευδής (subst.) PSEUDĒS
Rev 21. 8 "sorcerers, idolaters, and all liars
2. *lying:* ψευδολόγος (subst.) PSEUDOLOGOS*
1 Tim 4. 2 through the pretensions of liars
3. *liar, cheat:* ψεύστης PSEUSTĒS
Jn 8.44 "for he is a liar and the father of lies
8.55 "I should be a liar like you
1 Tim 1.10 kidnapers, liars, perjurers
Tit 1.12 "Cretans are always liars, evil beasts
1 Jn 1.10 we make him a l., and his word is not in us
2. 4 who .. disobeys his commandments is a l.
2.22 Who is the l. but he who denies that Jesus?
4.20 says, "I love ..," and hates .., he is a l.
5.10 He .. has made him a liar

LIBATION, POUR AS A
1. *make a drink-offering:* σπένδω SPENDŌ
Phil 2.17 if I am to be poured as a libation

LIBERAL
1. *generous:* εὐμετάδοτος EUMETADOTOS*
1 Tim 6.18 rich in good deeds, liberal and generous

LIBERAL GIFT
1. *abundance:* ἁδρότης HADROTĒS*
2 Cor 8.20 this l. gift which we are administering

LIBERALITY
1. *simplicity, liberality:* ἁπλότης HAPLOTĒS
Rom 12. 8 he who contributes, in liberality
2 Cor 8. 2 overflowed in a wealth of liberality

LIBERALLY
1. *many, great:* πολύς POLYS [A.3.b.1]
Acts 10. 2 who . . gave alms liberally to the people

LIBERTY
1. *relief:* ἄνεσις ANESIS
Acts 24.23 orders . . that he . . should have some liberty
2. *freedom:* ἐλευθερία ELEUTHERIA
Rom 8.21 the glorious liberty of the children of God
1 Cor 10.29 For why should my liberty be determined?
Jas 1.25 the perfect law, the law of liberty
2.12 to be judged under the law of liberty
3. *authority, power:* ἐξουσία EXOUSIA
1 Cor 8. 9 lest this liberty . . become a stumbling block
IDIOMATICALLY
a. Lk 4.18 "to set at liberty those who are oppressed
ἀποστεῖλαι τεθραυσμένους ἐν ἀφέσει [APHESIS]

LIBERTY, SET AT
1. *loose from, dismiss:* ἀπολύω APOLYŌ
Acts 28.18 "they wished to set me at liberty

LIBYA: Λιβύη 'libēə II,DE-5
Acts 2.10 "the parts of Libya belonging to Cyrene

LICENTIOUS
1. *licentiousness:* ἀσέλγεια ASELGEIA [A.1.b.2]
2 Pet 2.18 they entice with licentious passions

LICENTIOUSNESS
1. *licentiousness:* ἀσέλγεια ASELGEIA
Mk 7.22 "deceit, licentiousness, envy, slander
Rom 13.13 not in debauchery and licentiousness
2 Cor 12.21 immorality, and licentiousness
Gal 5.19 fornication, impurity, licentiousness
Eph 4.19 given themselves up to licentiousness
1 Pet 4. 3 living in licentiousness, passions
2 Pet 2. 2 many will follow their licentiousness
2. 7 Lot, greatly distressed by the l.
Jude . 4 persons who pervert . . grace . . into l.

LICK
1. *lick over:* ἐπιλείχω EPILEICHŌ*
Lk 16.21 "the dogs came and licked his sores

LIE (*See also* AMBUSH, LIE IN; WAIT, LIE IN)
1. *recline* (at table): ἀνάκειμαι ANAKEIMAI
Jn 13.23 lying close to the breast of Jesus
2. *recline* (at meals): ἀναπίπτω ANAPIPTŌ
Jn 13.25 lying thus, close to the breast of Jesus
21.20 who had lain close to his breast
3. *throw, put:* βάλλω (pass.) BALLŌ
Mt 8. 6 "Lord, my servant is lying paralyzed
8.14 mother-in-law lying sick with a fever
9. 2 a paralytic, lying on his bed
Mk 7.30 found the child lying in bed
Lk 16.20 "at his gate l. a poor man named Lazarus
4. *lie down:* κατάκειμαι KATAKEIMAI
Mk 1.30 Simon's mother-in-law lay sick
2. 4 the pallet on which the paralytic lay
Lk 5.25 took up that on which he lay
Jn 5. 3 In these lay a multitude of invalids
5. 6 he had been lying there a long time
Acts 28. 8 the father of Publius lay sick with fever
5. *lie, be laid:* κεῖμαι KEIMAI
Mt 28. 6 "Come, see the place where he[q] lay
Lk 2.12 "you will find a babe . . lying in a manger
2.16 Joseph, and the babe lying in a manger
Jn 20. 5 he saw the linen cloths lying
20. 6 he saw the linen cloths lying
20. 7 napkin, . . not lying with the linen cloths
20.12 where the body of Jesus had lain
2 Cor 3.15 to this day . . a veil lies over their minds
Rev 21.16 The city lies foursquare
6. *lie, be false:* ψεύδομαι PSEUDOMAI
Acts 5. 3 "why has Satan filled your heart to lie?
5. 4 "You have not lied to men but to God
Rom 9. 1 I am speaking the truth . . , I am not lying
2 Cor 11.31 God . . knows that I do not lie
Gal 1.20 (In what I am writing . . I do not lie!
Col 3. 9 Do not lie to one another
1 Tim 2. 7 (I am telling the truth, I am not lying
1 Jn 1. 6 while we walk in darkness, we lie
Rev 3. 9 " 'who say that they are Jews . . but lie
7. *lie, falsehood:* ψεῦδος PSEUDOS
[a]λαλεῖν τὸ ψεῦδος *speak falsehood* [A.6.a.4]
Jn 8.44 [a]"he lies, he speaks according to . . nature
Rom 1.25 exchanged the truth about God for a lie
1 Jn 2.21 you . . know that no lie is of the truth
2.27 his anointing . . is true, and is no lie
Rev 14. 5 in their mouth no lie was found
CONTEXTUALLY
Rom 7. 8 Apart from the law sin lies dead
Phil 3.13 forgetting what lies behind and straining forward to what lies ahead
Rev 9.10 power of hurting men . . lies in their tails
11. 8 their dead bodies will lie in the street

LIE AT HAND
1. *lie beside:* παράκειμαι PARAKEIMAI
Rom 7.21 a law that . . evil lies close at hand

LIE ON
LIE UPON
1. *lie upon, press upon:* ἐπίκειμαι EPIKEIMAI
[a]+ ἐπί
Jn 11.38 [a]a cave, and a stone lay upon it
21. 9 charcoal fire there, with fish lying on it
Acts 27.20 no small tempest lay on us

LIES, WHO NEVER
1. *without deceit:* ἀψευδής (attr.) APSEUDĒS*
Tit 1. 2 which God, who never lies, promised

LIFE (*See also* AIM IN LIFE; FULNESS OF LIFE, COME TO; NEW LIFE; RISE AGAIN TO LIFE)
1. *behavior:* ἀναστροφή ANASTROPHĒ
Gal 1.13 you have heard of my former l. in Judaism
Heb 13. 7 consider the outcome of their life
Jas 3.13 By his good life let him show his works
2 Pet 3.11 to be in lives of holiness and godliness
2. *everyday life, livelihood:* βίος BIOS
Lk 8.14 "cares and riches and pleasures of life
1 Tim 2. 2 that we . . lead a quiet and peaceable life
1 Jn 2.16 lust of the eyes and the pride of life
3. *life, soul, self:* ψυχή PSYCHĒ
Mt 2.20 "those who sought the child's life are dead
6.25 "do not be anxious about your life . . : Is not life more than food?
10.39 "He who finds his life will lose it, and he who loses his life for my sake will find it
16.25 "whoever would save his life will lose it, and whoever loses his life for my sake
16.26 "gains the whole world and forfeits his life
16.26 "what shall a man give . . for his life?
20.28 "to give his life as a ransom for many
Mk 3. 4 "Is it lawful . . to save life or to kill?
8.35 "whoever would save his life will lose it; and whoever loses his life for my sake
8.36 "gain the whole world and forfeit his life
8.37 "what can a man give . . for his life?
10.45 "to give his life as a ransom for many
Lk 6. 9 "is it lawful . . to save life or to destroy it?
9.24 "whoever would save his life will lose it; and whoever loses his life for my sake
[9.55(56) "*came not to destroy men's lives*‡
12.22 "do not be anxious about your life
12.23 "For life is more than food
14.26 "If any one . . does not hate . . his own life
17.33 "Whoever seeks to gain his life
21.19 "By . . endurance you will gain your lives
Jn 10.11 "The good shepherd lays down his life
10.15 "I lay down my life for the sheep
10.17 "I lay down my life, that I may take it

Jn 12.25 "He who loves his life loses it, and he who hates his life in this world
13.37 "I will lay down my life for you
13.38 "Will you lay down your life for me?
15.13 "that a man lay down his l. for his friends
Acts 15.26 "men who have risked their lives
20.10 "Do not be alarmed, for his life is in him
20.24 "I do not account my life of any value
27.10 "voyage will be with . . loss . . of our lives
27.22 "there will be no loss of life among you
Rom 11. 3 "I alone am left, and they seek my life
16. 4 who risked their necks for my life
Phil 2.30 risking his life to complete your service
1 Jn 3.16 he laid down his life for us; and we ought to lay down our lives
Rev 12.11 "they loved not their lives . . unto death

4. *way, manner:* τρόπος TROPOS
Heb 13. 5 Keep your life free from love of money

5. *live:* ζάω (art. inf.) ZAŌ
2 Cor 1. 8 so . . crushed that we despaired of life itself
Phil 1.22 If it is to be life in the flesh

6. *life:* ζωή ZŌĒ
Mt 7.14 "the way is hard, that leads to life
18. 8 "it is better for you to enter life maimed
18. 9 "better for you to enter life with one eye
19.16 "what . . must I do, to have eternal life?
19.17 "would enter l., keep the commandments
19.29 "will . . inherit eternal life
25.46 "but the righteous into eternal life
Mk 9.43 "it is better for you to enter life maimed
9.45 "it is better for you to enter life lame
10.17 "what must I do to inherit eternal life?
10.30 "and in the age to come eternal life
Lk 1.75 "before him all the days of our life
10.25 "what shall I do to inherit eternal life?
12.15 "man's life does not consist in . . abundance
18.18 "what shall I do to inherit eternal life?
18.30 "and in the age to come eternal life
Jn 1. 4 In him was life,[a] and the life was the light of men
3.15 "whoever believes . . may have eternal life[h]
3.16 should not perish but have eternal life
3.36 He who believes in the Son has eternal life; he who does not obey . . shall not see life
4.14 "a spring . . welling up to eternal life
4.36 "He . . gathers fruit for eternal life
5.24 "believes him who sent me has eternal life
5.24 "but has passed from death to life
5.26 "as the Father has life in himself, . . he has granted the Son . . to have life in himself
5.29 "to the resurrection of life
5.39 "think that in them you have eternal life
5.40 "refuse to come . . that you may have life
6.27 "the food which endures to eternal life
6.33 "bread . . which . . gives life to the world
6.35 "I am the bread of life
6.40 "believes in him should have eternal life
6.47 "he who believes has eternal life
6.48 "I am the bread of life
6.51 "which I shall give for the life of the world
6.53 "unless you eat . . , you have no life in you
6.54 "who . . drinks my blood has eternal life
6.63 "words . . I have spoken to you are . . life
6.68 "You have the words of eternal life
8.12 "he . . will have the light of life
10.10 "I came that they may have life
10.28 "I give them eternal life
11.25 "I am the resurrection and the life[z]‡
12.25 "in this world will keep it for eternal life
12.50 "his commandment is eternal life
14. 6 "I am the way, and the truth, and the life
17. 2 "power over all flesh, to give eternal life
17. 3 "this is eternal life, that they know thee
20.31 that believing you may have life
Acts 2.28 " 'Thou hast made known . . the ways of life
3.15 "killed the Author of life, whom God raised
5.20 "speak . . all the words of this Life
Acts 8.33 "For his life is taken up from the earth
11.18 "God has granted repentance unto life
13.46 "judge yourselves unworthy of eternal life
13.48 as many as were ordained to eternal life
17.25 "since he himself gives to all men life
Rom 2. 7 to those . . he will give eternal life
5.10 much more . . shall we be saved by his l.
5.17 much more will those . . reign in life
5.18 so one man's act . . leads to . . life for all
5.21 grace also might reign . . to eternal life
6. 4 we too might walk in newness of life
6.22 sanctification and its end, eternal life
6.23 the free gift of God is eternal life
7.10 very commandment which promised life
8. 2 the law of the Spirit of life in Christ Jesus
8. 6 to set the mind on the Spirit is life
8.38 I am sure that neither death, nor life
11.15 what will their acceptance mean but life?
1 Cor 3.22 life or death or the present or the future
15.19 If for this life only we have hoped
2 Cor 2.16 to one a fragrance from death to death, to the other a fragrance from life to life
4.10 that the life of Jesus may . . be manifested
4.11 that the life of Jesus may be manifested
4.12 So death is at work in us, but life in you
5. 4 what is mortal may be swallowed up by life
Gal 6. 8 he . . will from the Spirit reap eternal life
Eph 4.18 alienated from the life of God
Phil 1.20 honored . . whether by life or by death
2.16 holding fast the word of life
4. 3 whose names are in the book of life
Col 3. 3 your life is hid with Christ in God
3. 4 When Christ who is our life appears
1 Tim 1.16 who were to believe in him for eternal life
4. 8 as it holds promise for the present life
6.12 the eternal life to which you were called
6.19 so that they may take hold of the life
2 Tim 1. 1 promise of the life which is in Christ J.
1.10 brought life and immortality to light
Tit 1. 2 hope of eternal life which God . . promised
3. 7 become heirs in hope of eternal life
Heb 7. 3 neither beginning of days nor end of life
7.16 by the power of an indestructible life
Jas 1.12 the crown of life which God has promised
4.14 What is your life? For you are a mist
1 Pet 3. 7 you are joint heirs of the grace of life
3.10 "He that would love life and see good days
2 Pet 1. 3 things that pertain to life and godliness
1 Jn 1. 1 concerning the word of life
1. 2 the life was made manifest, and we saw it
1. 2 the eternal life which was with the Father
2.25 what he has promised us,[e] eternal life
3.14 we have passed out of death into life
3.15 no murderer has eternal life abiding
5.11 this is the testimony, that God gave us eternal life, and this life is in his Son
5.12 He who has the Son has life; he who has not the Son of God has not life
5.13 you may know that you have eternal life
5.16 he will ask, and God[i] will give him life
5.20 This is the true God and eternal life
Jude .21 mercy of our Lord . . unto eternal life
Rev 2. 7 " 'I will grant to eat of the tree of life
2.10 " 'and I will give you the crown of life
3. 5 " 'not blot his name out of the book of life
11.11 a breath of life from God entered them
13. 8 has not been written . . in the book of life
17. 8 "have not been written in the book of life
20.12 another book . . which is the book of life
20.15 not found written in the book of life
21. 6 "from the fountain of the water of life
21.27 who are written in the Lamb's book of life
22. 1 the river of the water of life
22. 2 on either side of the river, the tree of life[r]
22.14 may have the right to the tree of life
22.17 take the water of life without price
22.19 will take away his share in the tree of life

IDIOMATICALLY
a. Rom 7.1 only during his life ἐφ' ὅσον χρόνον ζῇ [ZAŌ]
CONTEXTUALLY
Rom 6.10 but the life he lives he lives to God
1 Cor 1.30 He is the source of your l. in Christ Jesus
Gal 2.20 the l. I now live . . I live by faith
3 Jn . 3 and testified to the truth of your life

LIFE, AT THE END OF ONE'S
1. *die, finish:* τελευτάω (part.) TELEUTAŌ
Heb 11.22 By faith Joseph, at the end of his life

LIFE, COME TO
1. *live:* ζάω (aor.) ZAŌ
Rev 2. 8 " 'first and the last, who died and came to l.
20. 4 came to life, and reigned with Christ
20. 5 rest of the dead did not come to life
2. *make alive:* ζῳοποιέω (pass.) ZŌOPOIEŌ
1 Cor 15.36 What you sow does not come to life

LIFE, GIVE
1. *preserve alive:* ζῳογονέω ZŌOGONEŌ
1 Tim 6.13 In the presence of God who gives life
2. *make alive:* ζῳοποιέω ZŌOPOIEŌ
Jn 5.21 "raises the dead and gives them life
5.21 "so also the Son gives life to whom he will
6.63 "It is the spirit that gives life
Rom 4.17 the God . . who gives life to the dead
8.11 he . . will give life to your mortal bodies
2 Cor 3. 6 written code kills, but the Spirit gives life

LIFE, LEAD A
1. *walk, behave:* περιπατέω PERIPATEŌ
1 Cor 7.17 let every one lead the life . . assigned
Eph 4. 1 to lead a life worthy of the calling
Col 1.10 to lead a life worthy of the Lord
1 Th 2.12 lead a life worthy of God, who calls you

LIFE, LIVE A
1. *live:* ζάω ZAŌ
2 Tim 3.12 Indeed all who desire to live a godly l.
Tit 2.12 to live sober, upright, and godly lives

LIFE, MAN WHO HAS BEEN BROUGHT TO
1. *live:* ζάω (subst. part.) ZAŌ
Rom 6.13 men who have been brought from death to l.

LIFE, MANNER OF
LIFE IS, ONE'S MANNER OF
1. *behavior:* ἀναστροφή ANASTROPHĒ
Eph 4.22 which belongs to your former m. of life
2. *way of life:* βίωσις BIŌSIS*
Acts 26. 4 "My manner of l. from my youth . . is known
3. *live as a citizen:* πολιτεύομαι POLITEUOMAI [A.6.a.5]
Phil 1.27 let your manner of life be worthy

LIFE, MATTERS PERTAINING TO THIS
1. *pertaining to life:* βιωτικός (neut. pl.) BIŌTIKOS
1 Cor 6. 3 much more, matters pertaining to this life!

LIFE, OF THIS
1. *pertaining to life:* βιωτικός BIŌTIKOS
Lk 21.34 "drunkenness and cares of this life

LIFE, SPAN OF
1. *age, stature:* ἡλικία HĒLIKIA
Mt 6.27 "can add one cubit to his span of life?[p]†
Lk 12.25 "can add a cubit to his span of life?[n]†

LIFE-GIVING
1. *make alive:* ζῳοποιέω (part.) ZŌOPOIEŌ
1 Cor 15.45 last Adam became a life-giving spirit

LIFELESS
1. *lifeless:* ἄψυχος APSYCHOS*
1 Cor 14. 7 lifeless instruments, such as the flute

LIFELONG
IDIOMATICALLY
a. Heb 2.15 were subject to lifelong bondage διὰ παντὸς τοῦ ζῆν ἔνοχοι ἦσαν δουλείας [ZAŌ]

LIFETIME
1. *life:* ζωή ZŌĒ
Lk 16.25 " 'that you in your lifetime received

LIFT
1. *lift, carry away:* αἴρω AIRŌ
Acts 4.24 they lifted their voices together to God
2. *raise up, rise:* ἀνίστημι ANISTĒMI
Acts 9.41 he gave her his hand and lifted her up
3. *raise, lift:* ἐπαίρω EPAIRŌ
Jn 13.18 ate my bread has lifted his heel against me
1 Tim 2. 8 pray, lifting holy hands without anger

LIFT AND STRENGTHEN
1. *set up again, correct:* ἀνορθόω (+two objects) ANORTHOŌ
Heb 12.12 lift your . . hands and strengthen . . knees

LIFT OUT
1. *raise:* ἐγείρω EGEIRŌ
Mt 12.11 "What man of you . . will not . . lift it out?

LIFT UP
1. *lift, carry away:* αἴρω AIRŌ
Lk 17.13 lifted up their voices and said, "Jesus
Jn 11.41 Jesus lifted up his eyes and said, "Father
Rev 10. 5 angel . . lifted up his right hand to heaven
2. *raise:* ἐγείρω EGEIRŌ
Mk 1.31 took her by the hand and lifted her up
9.27 took him by the hand and lifted him up
Acts 10.26 Peter lifted him up, saying, "Stand up
3. *raise, lift:* ἐπαίρω EPAIRŌ
Mt 17. 8 they lifted up their eyes, they saw no one
Lk 6.20 he lifted up his eyes on his disciples
16.23 "he lifted up his eyes, and saw Abraham
18.13 "not even lift up his eyes to heaven
24.50 lifting up his hands he blessed them
Jn 4.35 "I tell you, lift up your eyes, and see
6. 5 Lifting up his eyes, then, and seeing
17. 1 he lifted up his eyes to heaven
Acts 1. 9 he was lifted up, and a cloud took him
2.14 Peter . . lifted up his voice
14.11 they lifted up their voices
22.22 then they lifted up their voices
4. *exalt, lift high:* ὑψόω HYPSOŌ
Jn 3.14 "as Moses lifted up the serpent . . , so must the Son of man be lifted up
8.28 "When you have lifted up the Son of man
12.32 "I, when I am lifted up from the earth
12.34 "that the Son of man must be lifted up

LIGAMENT
1. *that which binds together:* σύνδεσμος SYNDESMOS
Col 2.19 knit together through its . . ligaments

LIGHT (*See also* SUN'S LIGHT)
1. *light in weight:* ἐλαφρός ELAPHROS
Mt 11.30 "my yoke is easy, and my burden is l.
2. *kindle; touch* (mid.): ἅπτω HAPTŌ
Lk 8.16 "No one after lighting a lamp covers it
11.33 "No one after lighting a lamp puts it
15. 8 "does she not light a lamp and sweep?
3. *kindle, burn:* καίω KAIŌ
Mt 5.15 "Nor do men light a lamp and put it under
4. *lamp, torch:* λαμπάς LAMPAS
Acts 20. 8 many lights in the upper chamber
5. *few, little:* ὀλίγος OLIGOS
Lk 12.48 "he . . shall receive a light beating
6. *visible, known:* φανερός (subst.) PHANEROS
Mk 4.22 "nor . . secret, except to come to light
Lk 8.17 "nor . . secret that shall not . . come to light
7. *light, day:* φέγγος PHEGGOS*
Mt 24.29 "the moon will not give its light
Mk 13.24 "the moon will not give its light
Also variant to: Lk **11.33**
8. *light:* φῶς PHŌS
Mt 4.16 "people . . in darkness have seen a great light, and for those . . light has dawned
5.14 "You are the light of the world
5.16 "Let your light so shine before men
6.23 "If then the light in you is darkness
10.27 "What I tell you in the dark, utter in the l.
17. 2 his garments became white as light
Lk 2.32 "a light for revelation to the Gentiles
8.16 "that those who enter may see the light

Lk 11.33 "that those who enter may see the light
Var. PHEGGOS
11.35 "be careful lest the light in you be darkness
12. 3 "said in the dark shall be heard in the l.
16. 8 "are more shrewd . . than the sons of light
22.56 seeing him as he sat in the light
Jn 1. 4 the life was the light of men
1. 5 The light shines in the darkness
1. 7 to bear witness to the light
1. 8 He was not the light, but came to bear witness to the light
1. 9 true light that enlightens every man
3.19 the light has come into the world, and men loved darkness rather than light
3.20 every one who does evil hates the light, and does not come to the light
3.21 who does what is true comes to the light
5.35 "willing to rejoice for a while in his light
8.12 "I am the light of the world, he who follows . . will have the light of life
9. 5 "I am the light of the world
11. 9 "because he sees the light of this world
11.10 "because the light is not in him
12.35 "The light is with you for a little longer. Walk while you have the light
12.36 "While you have the light, believe in the light, that you may become sons of light
12.46 "I have come as light into the world
Acts 9. 3 suddenly a light from heaven flashed
12. 7 an angel . . appeared, and a light shone
13.47 " 'set you to be a light for the Gentiles
16.29 he called for lights and rushed in
22. 6 "a great light from heaven suddenly shone
22. 9 "those who were with me saw the light
22.11 "I could not see because of . . that light
26.13 "I saw on the way a light from heaven
26.18 " 'that they may turn from darkness to light
26.23 "he would proclaim light both to the people
Rom 2.19 a light to those who are in darkness
13.12 Let us then . . put on the armor of light
2 Cor 4. 6 "Let light shine out of darkness
6.14 what fellowship has light with darkness?
11.14 Satan disguises himself as an angel of light
Eph 5. 8 but now you are light in the Lord; walk as children of light
5. 9 (for the fruit of light is found in all . . good
5.13 when anything is exposed by the light
5.13 anything that becomes visible is light
Col 1.12 the inheritance of the saints in light
1 Th 5. 5 For you are all sons of light
1 Tim 6.16 who . . dwells in unapproachable light
Jas 1.17 coming down from the Father of lights
1 Pet 2. 9 out of darkness into his marvelous light
1 Jn 1. 5 God is light and in him is no darkness
1. 7 if we walk in the light, as he is in the light, we have fellowship with one another
2. 8 the true light is already shining
2. 9 who says he is in the light and hates
2.10 who loves his brother abides in the light
Rev 18.23 "the light . . shall shine in thee no more
21.24 By its light shall the nations walk
22. 5 they need no light of lamp or sun

9. *splendor, radiance:* φωστήρ PHŌSTĒR
Phil 2.15 among whom you shine as lights

10. *light:* φωτισμός PHŌTISMOS*
2 Cor 4. 4 light of the gospel of the glory of Christ
4. 6 to give the light of the knowledge

CONTEXTUALLY
Rev 8.12 so that a third of their l. was darkened

LIGHT, BE
LIGHT, BRING TO

1. *shine, illuminate:* φωτίζω PHŌTIZŌ
1 Cor 4. 5 will bring to light the things now hidden
2 Tim 1.10 brought life and immortality to light
Rev 21.23 for the glory of God is its light
22. 5 for the Lord God will be their light

LIGHT, FULL OF

1. *shining, bright:* φωτεινός PHŌTEINOS
Mt 6.22 "your whole body will be full of light
Lk 11.34 "your whole body is full of light
11.36 "If then your whole body is full of light

LIGHT, GIVE

1. *appear:* ἐπιφαίνω EPIPHAINŌ
Lk 1.79 "to give light to those who sit in darkness
2. *shine out:* ἐπιφαύσκω EPIPHAUSKŌ*
Eph 5.14 "Awake . . and Christ shall give you light
3. *shine, give light:* λάμπω LAMPŌ
Mt 5.15 "it gives light to all in the house
4. *shine, illuminate:* φωτίζω PHŌTIZŌ
Lk 11.36 "as when a lamp . . gives you light

LIGHT OF, MAKE

1. *neglect:* ἀμελέω AMELEŌ
Mt 22. 5 "But they made light of it and went off

LIGHT UP

1. *shine, give light:* λάμπω LAMPŌ
Lk 17.24 "lightning flashes and lights up the sky

LIGHTEN

1. *make light:* κουφίζω KOUPHIZŌ*
Acts 27.38 they lightened the ship

LIGHTLY, REGARD

1. *esteem lightly, neglect:* ὀλιγωρέω OLIGŌREŌ*
Heb 12. 5 "not regard l. . . discipline of the Lord

LIGHTNING
LIGHTNING, FLASH OF

1. *flash of lightning:* ἀστραπή ASTRAPĒ
Mt 24.27 "as the lightning comes from the east
28. 3 His appearance was like lightning
Lk 10.18 "I saw Satan fall like lightning
17.24 "as the lightning flashes and lights up
Rev 4. 5 From the throne issue flashes of lightning
8. 5 flashes of lightning, and an earthquake
11.19 there were flashes of lightning, voices
16.18 there were flashes of lightning, voices

LIKE (*See also* MEASURE OF, A LIKE; WHAT, LIKE)

1. *wish, will:* βούλομαι BOULOMAI
Acts 25.22 "I should like to hear the man myself
2. *in the likeness:* ἐπὶ τῷ ὁμοιώματι (+gen.) HOMOIŌMA [B.1.a.1]
Rom 5.14 whose sins were not like the transgression
3. *like, similar:* ὅμοιος HOMOIOS
Mt 11.16 "like children sitting in the market places
13.31 "heaven is like a grain of mustard seed
13.33 "kingdom of heaven is like leaven
13.44 "The kingdom of heaven is like treasure
13.45 "the kingdom of heaven is like a merchant
13.47 "the kingdom of heaven is like a net
13.52 "every scribe . . is like a householder
20. 1 "kingdom of heaven is like a householder
22.39 "And a second is like it
Lk 6.47 "I will show you what he is like
6.48 "he is like a man building a house
6.49 "he . . is like a man who built a house
7.31 "and what are they like?
7.32 "like children sitting in the market place
12.36 "like men who are waiting for their master
13.18 "What is the kingdom of God like?
13.19 "It is like a grain of mustard seed
13.21 "It is like leaven which a woman took
Jn 8.55 "I should be a liar like you
9. 9 "No, but he is like him
Acts 17.29 "not to think that the Deity is like gold
Gal 5.21 drunkenness, carousing, and the like
1 Jn 3. 2 when he appears we shall be like him
Rev 1.13 in the midst . . one like a son of man
1.15 voice . . like the sound of many waters
2.18 " 'whose feet are like burnished bronze
4. 3 he who sat there appeared like jasper
4. 3 a rainbow that looked like an emerald
4. 6 before the throne . . a sea of glass, like crystal

Rev 4. 7 the first living creature like a lion, the second living creature like an ox, . . the fourth living creature like a flying eagle
9. 7 locusts were like horses arrayed . . ; on their heads . . what looked like crowns
9.10 They have tails like scorpions
9.19 their tails are like serpents, with heads
11. 1 I was given a measuring rod like a staff
13. 2 beast that I saw was like a leopard
13. 4 "Who is like the beast?
13.11 it had two horns like a lamb
14.14 on the cloud one like a son of man
18.18 "What city was like the great city?
21.11 its radiance like a most rare jewel

4. *as, so:* ὡς HŌS
Mt **6.**5, 16, 29; **10.**25[2]; **12.**13; **13.**43; **17.**2; **18.**3, 4; **22.**30; **28.**3, 4
Mk **1.**10; **4.**31; **6.**15, 34; **8.**24; **10.**15; **12.**25; **13.**34
Lk **6.**40; **10.**18; **11.**44; **12.**27; **18.**11, 17; **21.**34(35); **22.**31
Jn **7.**46
Acts **10.**11; **11.**5
Rom **5.**15; 16; **9.**29
1 Cor **3.**10; **4.**9; **13.**11[3]
2 Cor **2.**17
Eph **2.**3
1 Th **2.**7, 11; **5.**2, 4
1 Tim **5.**1, 2[2]
2 Tim **2.**9, 17
Heb **1.**11, 12; **12.**16
Jas **1.**10; **5.**3†
1 Pet **1.**19, 24[2]; **2.**2, 5, 25; **5.**8
2 Pet **2.**12; **3.**10
Rev **1.**10, 14, 15, 16; **2.**18; **3.**3; **4.**1, 6; **6.**12, 14; **8.**8, 10; **9.**2, 3, 5, 7, 8[2], 9[2], 17; **10.**1[2], 7; **12.**15; **13.**2[2], 11; **14.**2[3]; **16.**3, 13, 15; **18.**21; **19.**6[2], 12; **20.**8; **21.**11

5. *as if:* ὡσεί HŌSEI
Mt 3.16 the Spirit of God descending like a dove
9.36 helpless, like sheep without a shepherd
Mk 9.26 the boy was like a corpse
Lk [22.44 *his sweat became like . . drops of blood*‡
Acts 6.15 his face was like the face of an angel
Heb 1.12 "like a mantle thou wilt roll them up

6. *just as:* ὥσπερ HŌSPER
Lk 18.11 " 'I thank thee . . I am not like other men
Acts 2. 2 sound . . like the rush of a mighty wind
Rev 10. 3 a loud voice, like a lion roaring

7. *in accordance with, for:* κατά (+acc.) KATA
Gal 4.28 we,[j] . . like Isaac, are children of promise
Heb 8. 9 "not like the covenant that I made
1 Pet 4. 6 that though judged in the flesh like men, they might live in the spirit like God

8. *just as:* καθάπερ KATHAPER
2 Cor 3.13 not like Moses, who put a veil over his face
1 Th 4. 5 not in the passion of lust like heathen

9. *as, just as:* καθώς KATHŌS
1 Jn 3.12 not be like Cain who was of the evil one

10. *of the same shape as:* σύμμορφος (+dat.) SYMMORPHOS
Phil 3.21 change our lowly body to be like his

11. *will, wish:* θέλω THELŌ
Mk 12.38 "scribes, who like to go about in long robes
Lk 20.46 "scribes, who like to go about in long robes
2 Cor 11.12 those who would like to claim . . they work

IDIOMATICALLY
a. Acts 19.25 with the workmen of like occupation *καὶ τοὺς περὶ τὰ τοιαῦτα ἐργάτας* [TOIOUTOS]
b. Rom 6.5 in a death like his *τῷ ὁμοιώματι τοῦ θανάτου αὐτοῦ* [HOMOIŌMA]
c. Phil 2.20 I have no one like him *οὐδένα γὰρ ἔχω ἰσόψυχον* [ISOPSYCHOS*]

LIKE A MADMAN
1. *be beside oneself:* παραφρονέω (pred. part.) PARAPHRONEŌ*
2 Cor 11.23 I am talking like a madman

LIKE, BE
1. *look like, be like:* ἔοικα EOIKA*
Jas 1. 6 for he who doubts is like a wave of the sea
1.23 is like a man who observes . . in a mirror

2. *make like, compare:* ὁμοιόω (pass.) HOMOIOŌ
Mt 6. 8 "Do not be like them
7.24 "will be like a wise man who built his house
7.26 "like a foolish man who built his house

3. *be like:* παρομοιάζω PAROMOIAZŌ*
Mt 23.27 "for you are like whitewashed tombs

LIKE, BE MADE
1. *make like, compare:* ὁμοιόω (pass.) HOMOIOŌ
[a]+ὡς
Rom 9.29 [a]"would have . . been made l. Gomorrah
Heb 2.17 he had to be made like his brethren

LIKE S., BECOME
1. *be conformed to* (pass.): συμμορφίζω SYMMORPHIZŌ*
Phil 3.10 becoming like him in his death

LIKE MANNER, IN
1. *likewise:* ὁμοίως HOMOIŌS
Mk 4.16 "these in l. manner are the ones sown
Lk 16.25 " 'Lazarus in like manner evil things
Jude . 8 Yet in like manner these men . . defile

LIKE NATURE WITH, OF
1. *having like feelings:* ὁμοιοπαθής HOMOIOPATHĒS*
Acts 14.15 "We also are men, of like nature with you
Jas 5.17 a man of like nature with ourselves

LIKE THIS
1. *thus, so:* οὕτως HOUTŌS
Mt 6. 9 "Pray then like this: Our Father
9.33 "Never was anything like this seen
Mk 2.12 "We never saw anything like this!
Jn 7.46 "No man ever spoke like this man!

LIKE TO PUT ONESELF FIRST
1. *wish to be first:* φιλοπρωτεύω PHILOPRŌTEUŌ
3 Jn . 9 Diotrephes, who likes to put himself first

LIKENESS
1. *image, likeness:* εἰκών EIKŌN
Mt 22.20 "Whose likeness and inscription is this?
Mk 12.16 "Whose likeness and inscription is this?
Lk 20.24 "Whose likeness and inscription has it?
2 Cor 3.18 we . are being changed into his likeness
4. 4 who is the likeness of God

2. *likeness:* ὁμοίωμα HOMOIŌMA
Rom 8. 3 his own Son in the likeness of sinful flesh
Phil 2. 7 being born in the likeness of men

3. *resemblance, likeness:* ὁμοίωσις HOMOIŌSIS*
Jas 3. 9 men . . made in the likeness of God

4. *likeness:* ὁμοιότης HOMOIOTĒS
Heb 7.15 arises in the likeness of Melchizedek

LIKENESS OF, AFTER THE
1. *in accordance with, for:* κατά (+acc.) KATA
Eph 4.24 nature, created after the likeness of God

LIKENESS OF, IN THE
1. *make like, compare:* ὁμοιόω (pass. part.) HOMOIOŌ
Acts 14.11 "gods . . in the likeness of men!

LIKES TO DO, WHAT S.
1. *intention, purpose:* βούλημα (+gen.) BOULĒMA
1 Pet 4. 3 doing what the Gentiles like to do

LIKEWISE
1. *in like manner:* τὸν ὅμοιον τρόπον (acc.) HOMOIOS; TROPOS [A.4.e]
Jude . 7 cities, which likewise acted immorally

2. *likewise:* ὁμοίως HOMOIŌS
Lk 3.11 "he who has food, let him do likewise
10.32 "So likewise a Levite, when he came
10.37 Jesus said to him, "Go and do likewise
13. 3 "you will all likewise perish
17.28 "Likewise as it was in the days of Lot
17.31 "likewise let him who is in the field
22.36 "let him . . take it, and likewise a bag
Jn 5.19 "whatever he does, that the Son does l.
Rom 1.27 men likewise gave up natural relations
1 Cor 7. 3 likewise the wife to her husband
7. 4 likewise the husband does not rule
7.22 Likewise he who was free when called
1 Pet 3. 1 Likewise you wives, be submissive
3. 7 Likewise you husbands, live considerately

1 Pet 5. 5 Likewise you that are younger
Rev 8.12 and likewise a third of the night
3. *in like manner:* ὡσαύτως HŌSAUTŌS
Mk 12.21 "leaving no children; and the third l.
Lk 13. 5 "you will all likewise perish
20.31 "likewise all seven left no children
22.20 And likewise the cup after supper‡
Rom 8.26 L. the Spirit helps us in our weakness
1 Tim 3. 8 Deacons likewise must be serious
3.11 women likewise must be serious
Tit 2. 3 Bid the older women l. to be reverent
2. 6 L. urge the younger men to control
4. *so that, therefore:* ὥστε HŌSTE
Rom 7. 4 Likewise, my brethren, you have died
5. *nearly the same way:* παραπλησίως PARAPLĒSIŌS*
Heb 2.14 he . . likewise partook of the same nature

LIKING
1. *desire, yearning:* ἐπιθυμία EPITHYMIA
2 Tim 4. 3 teachers to suit their own likings

LILY
1. *white lily:* κρίνον KRINON*
Mt 6.28 "Consider the lilies of the field
Lk 12.27 "Consider the lilies, how they grow

LIMIT, BEYOND
IDIOMATICALLY
a. 2 Cor 10.13 But we will not boast beyond limit ἡμεῖς δὲ οὐκ εἰς τὰ ἄμετρα καυχησόμεθα [AMETROS]
b. 2 Cor 10.15 We do not boast beyond limit οὐκ εἰς τὰ ἄμετρα καυχώμενοι [AMETROS]

LIMITATIONS
1. *weakness, sickness:* ἀσθένεια ASTHENEIA
Rom 6.19 because of your natural limitations

LIMITS
1. *the measure of the rule:* τὸ μέτρον τοῦ κανόνος KANŌN; METRON [A.1.f]
2 Cor 10.13 we . . will keep to the limits

LINEAGE
1. *family, lineage:* πατριά PATRIA
Lk 2. 4 he was of the house and l. of David

LINEN
1. *flax, linen:* λίνον LINON
Rev 15. 6 robed in pure bright linen

LINEN CLOTH
1. *linen cloth:* ὀθόνιον OTHONION*
Lk [24.12 *Peter . . saw the linen cloths by themselves*‡
Jn 19.40 took the body . . bound it in linen cloths
20. 5 he saw the linen cloths lying there
20. 6 Then Simon . . saw the linen cloths lying
20. 7 napkin . . not lying with the linen cloths
2. *fine cloth, linen:* σινδών SINDŌN
Mk 14.51 nothing but a linen cloth about his body
14.52 he left the linen cloth and ran away naked

LINEN, FINE
1. *of fine linen:* βύσσινος (subst.) BYSSINOS*
Rev 18.12 fine linen, purple, silk and scarlet
18.16 "great city that was clothed in fine linen
19. 8 "granted her to be clothed with fine linen
19. 8 the fine linen is the righteous deeds
19.14 armies of heaven, arrayed in fine linen
2. *flax, linen:* βύσσος BYSSOS*
Lk 16.19 "who was clothed in purple and fine linen

LINEN SHROUD
1. *fine cloth, linen:* σινδών SINDŌN
Mt 27.59 wrapped it in a clean linen shroud
Mk 15.46 he bought a linen shroud, and taking him down, wrapped him in the linen shroud
Lk 23.53 took it down and wrapped it in a l. shroud

LINUS: Λίνος 'līnəs
2 Tim 4.21 Linus and Claudia and all the brethren

LION
1. *lion:* λέων LEŌN*
2 Tim 4.17 So I was rescued from the lion's mouth
Heb 11.33 stopped the mouths of lions
1 Pet 5. 8 the devil prowls around like a roaring l.
Rev 4. 7 the first living creature like a lion
5. 5 "lo, the Lion of the tribe of Judah
9. 8 and their teeth like lions' teeth
9.17 heads of the horses were like lions' heads
10. 3 with a loud voice, like a lion roaring
13. 2 its mouth was like a lion's mouth

LIP
1. *lip, rim:* χεῖλος CHEILOS
Mt 15. 8 " 'This people honors me with their lips
Mk 7. 6 " 'This people honors me with their lips
Rom 3.13 "The venom of asps is under their lips
1 Cor 14.21 "by the lips of foreigners will I speak
Heb 13.15 fruit of lips that acknowledge his name
1 Pet 3.10 "let him keep . . his lips from speaking guile

LIPS
1. *mouth:* στόμα STOMA
Lk 22.71 "We have heard it . . from his . . lips
Rom 10. 8 The word is near you, on your lips
10. 9 because, if you confess with your lips
10.10 confesses with his lips and so is saved
1 Pet 2.22 no guile was found on his lips

LISTEN
1. *hear:* ἀκούω AKOUŌ
Mt 10.14 "if any one will not receive you or listen
17. 5 "This is my beloved Son[w] . . ; listen to him
18.15 "If he listens to you, you have gained
18.16 "But if he does not listen, take . . others
Mk 4. 3 "Listen! A sower went out to sow
9. 7 "This is my beloved Son;[g] listen to him
Lk 2.46 listening to them and asking . . questions
9.35 "This is my Son, my Chosen;[d] listen!
10.39 Mary, who . . listened to his teaching
Jn 6.60 "This is a hard saying; who can listen to it?
9.27 "I have told you . . and you would not l.
9.31 "God does not listen to sinners, but if any one is a worshiper . . God listens to him
10.20 "he is mad; why listen to him?
Acts 3.22 " 'listen to him in whatever he tells you
3.23 " 'every soul that does not listen
4.19 "to listen to you rather than to God
13.16 "Men of Israel, and you that fear God, l.
14. 9 He listened to Paul speaking
15.12 they listened to Barnabas and Paul
15.13 "Brethren, listen to me
22.22 Up to this word they listened to him
26. 3 "I beg you to listen to me patiently
28.28 "salvation . . to the Gentiles; they will listen[g]
Jas 2. 5 Listen, my beloved brethren
1 Jn 4. 5 the world listens to them
4. 6 Whoever knows God listens to us, and he who is not of God does not listen to us
2. *hear, obey:* εἰσακούω EISAKOUŌ
1 Cor 14.21 "even then they will not listen to me
3. *learn, understand:* μανθάνω MANTHANŌ
2 Tim 3. 7 ⟨weak women⟩ who will listen to anybody
4. *obey one in authority:* πειθαρχέω PEITHARCHEŌ
Acts 27.21 "Men, you should have listened to me

LISTEN, REFUSE TO
1. *overhear, take no heed of:* παρακούω PARAKOUŌ
Mk 18.17 "If he refuses to listen to them
18.17 "if he refuses to listen even to the church

LISTEN TO
1. *hear, overhear:* ἐπακούω EPAKOUŌ*
2 Cor 6. 2 "I have listened to you, and helped you
2. *hear, overhear:* ἐπακροάομαι EPAKROAOMAI*
Acts 16.25 the prisoners were listening to them

LISTENING
1. *hearing, report:* ἀκοή AKOĒ
2 Tim 4. 4 will turn away from listening to the truth

LITERAL
1. *letter:* γράμμα GRAMMA [B.1.a.1]
Rom 2.29 matter of the heart, spiritual and not literal

LITTLE (*See also* CHILD, LITTLE; DAUGHTER, LITTLE; SCROLL, LITTLE)
1. *small:* βραχύς BRACHYS
[a]μετὰ βραχύ [b]βραχύ τι
Lk 22.58 [a]a little later some one else saw him
Jn 6. 7 "bread for each of them to get a little
Acts 27.28 a little farther on they sounded again
Heb 2. 7 [b]"for a little while lower than the angels
2. 9 [b]Jesus, who for a little while was made lower
2. *part, share:* μέρος MEROS [B.2.b]
Rom 15.24 once I have enjoyed your company for a little
3. *little, small:* μικρός MIKROS
Mt 10.42 "whoever gives to one of these little ones
18. 6 "whoever causes one of these little ones
18.10 "do not despise one of these little ones
18.14 "not . . one of these little ones should perish
Mk 9.42 "Whoever causes one of these little ones
Lk 12.32 "Fear not, little flock
17. 2 "than . . cause one of these little ones to sin[v]
Jn 7.33 "I shall be with you a little longer
12.35 "The light is with you for a little longer
1 Cor 5. 6 a little leaven leavens the whole lump
Gal 5. 9 A little leaven leavens the whole lump
Jas 3. 5 So the tongue is a little member
Rev 3. 8 "I know that you have but little power
6.11 told to rest a little longer
20. 3 he must be loosed for a little while
4. *few, little:* ὀλίγος OLIGOS
Mt 25.21 " 'you have been faithful over a little
25.23 " 'you have been faithful over a little
Lk 7.47 "she loved much; but he who is forgiven little, loves little
Acts 14.28 remained no little time with the disciples
19.23 there arose no little stir concerning the Way
19.24 brought no little business to the craftsmen
2 Cor 8.15 "he who gathered little had no lack
1 Tim 5.23 use a little wine for the sake of your stomach
Jas 4.14 a mist that appears for a little time
CONTEXTUALLY
Mk 5.41 "Little girl, I say to you, arise

LITTLE, A
1. *moderately:* μετρίως METRIŌS*
Acts 20.12 they . . were not a little comforted
2. *little, small:* μικρός (neut.) MIKROS
[a]+τι
2 Cor 11. 1 [a]bear with me in a little foolishness
11.16 [a]so that I too may boast a little
3. *few, little:* ὀλίγος (neut.) OLIGOS
Lk 5. 3 to put out a little from the land
4. *anyone, any:* τὶς (neut.) TIS II [A.2.c]
2 Cor **10.8**

LITTLE FAITH
1. *littleness of faith:* ὀλιγοπιστία OLIGOPISTIA*
Mt 17.20 "Because of your little faith

LITTLE FAITH, OF
1. *of little faith:* ὀλιγόπιστος OLIGOPISTOS*
Mt 6.30 "much more clothe you, O men of little faith
8.26 "Why are you afraid, O men of little faith?
14.31 "O man of little faith, why did you doubt?
16. 8 "men of little faith, why do you discuss?
Lk 12.28 "much more . . you, O men of little faith!

LITTLE FARTHER, A
1. *little, small:* μικρός (neut.) MIKROS
Mt 26.39 going a little farther he fell on his face
Mk 14.35 going a little farther, he fell on the ground
2. *few, little:* ὀλίγος (neut.) OLIGOS
Mk 1.19 going on a little farther, he saw James

LITTLE, VERY
1. *smallest, least:* ἐλάχιστος ELACHISTOS
Lk 16.10 "He who is faithful in a very little
16.10 "he who is dishonest in a very little
19.17 " 'you have been faithful in a very little

LITTLE WHILE, A
LITTLE WHILE, FOR A
1. *little, small:* μικρός (neut.) MIKROS
Mt 26.73 After a little while the bystanders came
Mk 14.70 after a little while . . the bystanders said
Jn 13.33 "yet a little while I am with you
14.19 "Yet a little while, . . will see me no more
16.16 "A little while, and . . no more; again a little while, and you will see me
16.17 " 'A little while, and you will not see me, . . again a little while, and you will see me
16.18 "What does he mean by 'a little while'?
16.19 " 'A little while, and you will not see me, and again a little while, and you will
Heb 10.37 "yet a little while, and . . one shall come
2. *few, little:* ὀλίγος (neut.) OLIGOS
1 Pet 1. 6 for a little while you may have to suffer
5.10 after you have suffered a little while
Rev 17.10 "he must remain only a little while

LIVE (*See also* JEW, LIVE LIKE A; LONG, LIVE; PEACE, LIVE IN; PEACEABLY, LIVE; PLEASURE, LIVE IN)
1. *return, behave* (pass.): ἀναστρέφω ANASTREPHŌ
Eph 2. 3 once lived in the passions of our flesh
2 Pet 2.18 escaped from those who live in error
2. *pass one's life:* βιόω BIOŌ*
1 Pet 4. 2 to live for the rest of the time in the flesh
3. *be:* εἰμί EIMI
Mt 23.30 " 'If we had lived in the days of . . fathers
Rom 7. 5 While we were living in the flesh
8. 5 those who live according to the flesh
Eph 1.12 appointed to live for . . praise
4. *stay in, stand by:* ἐμμένω EMMENŌ
Acts 28.30 he lived there two whole years
5. *stay in a place:* ἐπιδημέω EPIDĒMEŌ
Acts 17.21 the foreigners who lived there
6. *come to be, happen, be:* γίνομαι GINOMAI
[a]A.6.a.5
Acts 20.18 "You . . know how I lived among you
Rom 7. 3 [a]an adulteress if she lives with another
7. *be, exist, belong to:* ὑπάρχω HYPARCHŌ
Lk 7.25 "those who . . live in luxury
8. *dwell, settle:* κατοικέω KATOIKEŌ
Acts 1.20 " 'let there be no one to live in it
7. 2 "Abraham . . before he lived in Haran
7. 4 "Then he departed . . and lived in Haran
7. 4 "into this land in which you are now living
9.22 confounded the Jews who lived in Damascus
9.32 to the saints that lived at Lydda
11.29 relief to the brethren who lived in Judea
13.27 "For those who live in Jerusalem
17.24 "God . . does not live in shrines made by man
17.26 "men to live on all the face of the earth
22.12 "well spoken of by all . . who lived there
Heb 11. 9 living in tents with Isaac and Jacob
9. *have residence:* κατοίκησιν ἔχειν KATOIKĒSIS* [B.2.a.1]
Mk 5. 3 who lived among the tombs
10. *stay, wait:* μένω MENŌ
Lk 8.27 lived not in a house but among the tombs
11. *dwell:* οἰκέω OIKEŌ
1 Cor 7.12 if . . she consents to live with him
7.13 If . . he consents to live with her
12. *walk, behave:* περιπατέω PERIPATEŌ
Mk 7. 5 "Why . . not live[v] according to the tradition?†
2 Cor 10. 3 For though we live in the world
Eph 4.17 you must no longer live as the Gentiles do
Phil 3.17 who so live as you have an example
3.18 many . . live as enemies of the cross
Col 2. 6 As . . you received Christ . . , so live in him
1 Th 4. 1 learned from us how you ought to live
2 Th 3. 6 any brother who is living in idleness
3.11 some of you are living in idleness
13. *live as a citizen:* πολιτεύομαι POLITEUOMAI
Acts 23. 1 "lived before God in all good conscience
14. *agree with, walk by:* στοιχέω STOICHEŌ
Acts 21.24 "that you . . live in observance of the law

15. *live:* ζάω ZAŌ
Mt 4. 4 " 'Man shall not live by bread alone
9.18 "lay your hand on her, and she will live
16.16 "the Christ, the Son of the living God
22.32 "not God of the dead, but of the living
26.63 "I adjure you by the living God
Mk 5.23 "that she may be made well, and live
12.27 "not God of the dead, but of the living
Lk 2.36 lived with her husband seven years
4. 4 " 'Man shall not live by bread alone
10.28 "do this, and you will live
15.13 "he squandered his property in loose living
20.38 "Now he is not God of the dead, but of the living; for all live to him
24. 5 "Why . . seek the living among the dead?[u]
Jn 4.10 "he would have given you living water
4.11 "where do you get that living water?
4.50 Jesus said to him, "Go; your son will live
4.51 told him that his son was living
4.53 when Jesus . . said . . "Your son will live
5.25 "those who hear will live
6.51 "I am the living bread which came . . ; if any one eats of this bread, he will live
6.57 "As the living Father sent me, and I live because of the Father, so he who eats me will live because of me
6.58 "who eats this bread will live for ever
7.38 " 'Out of his heart . . rivers of living water
11.25 "though he die, yet shall he live
11.26 "whoever lives and believes in me
14.19 "but you will see me; because I live, you will live also
Acts 7.38 "he received living oracles to give to us
10.42 "to be judge of the living and the dead
14.15 "turn from these vain things to a living God
17.28 " 'In him we live and move
22.22 "For he ought not to live
25.24 "he ought not to live any longer
26. 5 "I have lived as a Pharisee
28. 4 "justice has not allowed him to live
Rom 1.17 "who through faith is righteous shall l.[b]
6. 2 How can we who died to sin still live in it?
6.10 The death he died he died to sin, once for all, but the life he lives he lives to God
7. 2 bound . . to her husband as long as he lives
8.12 not . . to live according to the flesh
8.13 for if you live according to the flesh
8.13 but if . . you put to death . . you will live
9.26 "called 'sons of the living God
10. 5 the man who practices . . shall live by it
12. 1 present your bodies as a living sacrifice
14. 7 None of us lives to himself
14. 8 If we live, we live to the Lord, and if we die, we die to the Lord; so then, whether we live or whether we die, we are the Lord's
14. 9 Christ died and lived again, that he might be Lord both of the dead and of the living
14.11 "As I live . . every knee shall bow to me
1 Cor 7.39 bound to her husband as long as he lives
9.14 those . . get their living by the gospel
15.45 "first man Adam became a living being
2 Cor 3. 3 with the Spirit of the living God
4.11 while we live we are . . being given up
5.15 he died for all, that those who live might live no longer for themselves
6. 9 as dying, and behold, we live
6.16 we are the temple of the living God
13. 4 he . . lives by the power of God . . but in dealing with you we shall live with him
Gal 2.14 "If you, though a Jew, live like a Gentile
2.19 died to the law, that I might live to God
2.20 it is no longer I who live, but Christ who lives in me; and the life I now live in the flesh I live by faith in the Son of God, who loved me and gave himself for me
3.11 " 'who through faith is righteous shall live
3.12 "He who does them shall live by them
Gal 5.25 If we live by the Spirit, let us also walk
Phil 1.21 to live is Christ, and to die is gain
Col 2.20 why do you live as if you still belonged?
3. 7 In these . . , when you lived in them
1 Th 1. 9 to serve a living and true God
3. 8 for now we live, if you stand fast
5.10 so that . . we might live with him
1 Tim 3.15 which is the church of the living God
4.10 we have our hope set on the living God
5. 6 she . . is dead even while she lives
2 Tim 4. 1 Christ Jesus who is to judge the living
Heb 3.12 to fall away from the living God
4.12 the word of God is living and active
7. 8 of whom it is testified that he lives
7.25 he always lives to make intercession
9.14 from dead works to serve the living God
10.20 the new and living way which he opened
10.31 to fall into the hands of the living God
10.38 "my righteous one shall live by faith
12. 9 be subject to the Father . . and live
12.22 to the city of the living God
Jas 4.15 you ought to say, "If the Lord wills
1 Pet 1. 3 born anew to a living hope
1.23 through the living and abiding word of God
2. 4 Come to him, to that living stone
2. 5 like living stones be yourselves built
2.24 that we might die to sin and live
4. 5 ready to judge the living and the dead
4. 6 that . . they might live in the spirit like God
1 Jn 4. 9 God sent his . . Son . . that we might live
Rev 1.18 "⟨first and the last,⟩ and the living one
4. 9 him . . who lives for ever and ever
4.10 worship him who lives for ever
7. 2 angel . . with the seal of the living God
10. 6 swore by him who lives for ever
13.14 beast which was wounded . . yet lived
15. 7 God who lives for ever and ever

IDIOMATICALLY
a. Rom 12.16 Live in harmony with one another τὸ αὐτὸ εἰς ἀλλήλους φρονοῦντες [PHRONEŌ]
b. Rom 15.5 grant you to live in such harmony . . that δῴη ὑμῖν τὸ αὐτὸ φρονεῖν . . , ἵνα [PHRONEŌ]
c. 2 Cor 5.1 if the earthly tent we live in is destroyed ἐὰν ἡ ἐπίγειος ἡμῶν οἰκία τοῦ σκήνους καταλυθῇ [OIKIA]

CONTEXTUALLY
Rom 8. 5 those who live according to the Spirit
1 Pet 2.16 L. as free men, . . without using your freedom
2.16 but live as servants of God

LIVE A LIFE
1. *live:* ζάω ZAŌ
2 Tim 3.12 Indeed all who desire to l. a godly life
Tit 2.12 to live sober, upright, and godly lives

LIVE ACCORDING TO
1. *do, make:* ποιέω POIEŌ
1 Jn 1. 6 we . . do not live according to the truth

LIVE AMONG
1. *dwell among:* ἐγκατοικέω EGKATOIKEŌ*
[a]+ἐν
2 Pet 2. 8 [a](that righteous man . . as he lived among

LIVE IN
1. *dwell in:* ἐνοικέω ENOIKEŌ
[a]+ἐν
2 Cor 6.16 [a]"I will live in . . and move among them

LIVE IN LUXURY
1. *live softly, be licentious:* τρυφάω TRYPHAŌ*
Jas 5. 5 You have lived on the earth in luxury

LIVE ON
1. *participate in, share:* μετέχω METECHŌ
Heb 5.13 every one who lives on milk is unskilled

LIVE QUIETLY
1. *be quiet, be at rest:* ἡσυχάζω HĒSYCHAZŌ
1 Th 4.11 to live quietly, to mind your own affairs

LIVE TOGETHER
LIVE WITH
1. *have, hold:* ἔχω ECHŌ
1 Cor 5. 1 a man is living with his father's wife
2. *dwell together:* συνοικέω SYNOIKEŌ*
1 Pet 3. 7 live considerately with your wives
3. *live with:* συζάω SYZAŌ*
Rom 6. 8 believe that we shall also live with him
2 Cor 7. 3 to die together and to live together
2 Tim 2.11 we shall also live with him

LIVING
1. *everyday life, livelihood:* βίος BIOS
Mk 12.44 "everything she had, her whole living
Lk [8.43 *spent all her living upon physicians*‡
15.12 "he divided his living between them
15.30 " 'this son . . , who has devoured your living
21. 4 "she . . put in all the living that she had
2. *go, walk:* πορεύομαι (perf. part.) POREUOMAI
1 Pet 4. 3 living in licentiousness, passions
3. *having a soul:* ἔχων ψυχήν PSYCHĒ [B.2.a.1]
Rev 8. 9 a third of the living creatures in the sea
4. *life:* ζωή (gen.) ZŌĒ
Rev 7.17 "guide them to springs of living water
16. 3 every living thing died that was in the sea
IDIOMATICALLY
a. 2 Th 3.12 to earn their own living ἵνα . . τὸν ἑαυτῶν ἄρτον ἐσθίωσιν [ARTOS]

LIVING CREATURE
1. *creation, creature:* κτίσμα KTISMA
Rev 8. 9 third of the living creatures in the sea died
2. *living being:* ζῷον ZŌON
Rev 4. 6 round the throne . . four living creatures
4. 7 the first living creature like a lion
4. 7 the second living creature like an ox
4. 7 third l. creature with the face of a man
4. 7 the fourth l. creature like a flying eagle
4. 8 four living creatures . . never cease to sing
4. 9 whenever the living creatures give glory
5. 6 between the throne and the four l. creatures
5. 8 the four living creatures . . fell down
5.11 around the throne and the living creatures
5.14 the four living creatures said, "Amen!
6. 1 I heard one of the four living creatures
6. 3 I heard the second living creature
6. 5 I heard the third living creature
6. 6 in the midst of the four l. creatures
6. 7 I heard the voice of the fourth l. creature
7.11 the elders and the four living creatures
14. 3 they sing . . before the four living creatures
15. 7 one of the . . living creatures gave . . bowls
19. 4 the four living creatures . . worshiped God

LIVING, REFRAIN FROM WORKING FOR A
1. *work, do:* ἐργάζομαι (neg.) ERGAZOMAI
1 Cor 9. 6 right to refrain from working for a living

LO
1. *behold!:* ἰδού IDOU
Mt 2. 9 lo, the star which they had seen in the East
3.17 lo, a voice from heaven, saying
17. 5 lo, a bright cloud overshadowed them
19.27 "Lo, we have left everything
24.23 " 'Lo, here is the Christ!
24.25 "Lo, I have told you beforehand
24.26 " 'Lo, he is in the wilderness
24.26 " 'Lo, he is in the inner rooms
28. 7 "Lo, I have told you
28.20 "lo, I am with you always
Mk 10.28 "Lo, we have left everything
Lk 13. 7 " 'Lo, . . I have come seeking fruit
15.29 " 'Lo, these many years I have served you
17.21 "nor will they say, 'Lo, here it is!
17.23 "And they will say to you, 'Lo, there!' or 'Lo, here!
18.28 "Lo, we have left our homes
Acts 27.24 " 'lo, God has granted you all those
1 Cor 15.51 " 'Lo! I tell you a mystery
Heb 10. 7 " 'Lo, I have come to do thy will, O God
Heb 10. 9 "Lo, I have come to do thy will
Rev 4. 1 lo, in heaven an open door!
4. 2 lo, a throne stood in heaven!
5. 5 "lo, the Lion of the tribe of Judah
14. 1 lo, on Mount Zion stood the Lamb
14.14 Then I looked, and lo, a white cloud
16.15 ("Lo, I am coming like a thief!

LOAD
1. *burden, load:* φορτίον PHORTION
Gal 6. 5 each man will have to bear his own load
2. *load:* φορτίζω PHORTIZŌ
Lk 11.46 "you load men with burdens hard to bear

LOAF
LOAF OF BREAD
1. *loaf of bread, bread:* ἄρτος ARTOS
Mt 4. 3 "these stones to become loaves of bread
14.17 "We have only five loaves . . and two fish
14.19 taking the five loaves and the two fish he . . broke and gave the loaves to the disciples
15.34 "How many loaves have you?
15.36 he took the seven loaves and the fish
16. 9 "Do you not remember the five loaves?
16.10 "the seven loaves of the four thousand
Mk 6.38 "How many loaves have you?
6.41 taking the five loaves and the two fish he . . broke the loaves, and gave them
6.44 those who ate the loaves
6.52 did not understand about the loaves
8. 5 "How many loaves have you?
8. 6 and he took the seven loaves
8.14 they had only one loaf with them
8.19 "When I broke the five loaves
Lk 9.13 "no more than five loaves and two fish
9.16 And taking the five loaves
11. 5 " 'Friend, lend me three loaves
Jn 6. 9 "a lad here who has five barley loaves
6.11 Jesus then took the loaves
6.13 fragments from the five barley loaves
6.26 "because you ate your fill of the loaves

LOCAL
CONTEXTUALLY
Acts 28.17 he called together the local leaders

LOCKED
1. *shut:* κλείω (perf. pass. part.) KLEIŌ
Acts 5.23 "We found the prison securely locked

LOCUST
1. *grasshopper:* ἀκρίς AKRIS*
Mt 3. 4 his food was locusts and wild honey
Mk 1. 6 John . . ate locusts and wild honey
Rev 9. 3 Then from the smoke came locusts
9. 7 the locusts were like horses arrayed

LODGE
1. *lodge:* αὐλίζομαι AULIZOMAI*
Mt 21.17 he went out . . to Bethany and lodged
Lk 21.37 but at night he . . lodged on . . Olivet
2. *lodge, be the guest:* καταλύω KATALYŌ
Lk 9.12 "Send the crowd away . . to lodge
3. *receive as a guest, surprise:* ξενίζω (pass.) XENIZŌ
Acts 10. 6 "he is lodging with Simon, a tanner
10.18 whether Simon . . was lodging there
10.32 " 'he is lodging in the house of Simon
21.16 Mnason . . , with whom we should lodge

LODGING
1. *hospitality, guest room:* ξενία XENIA
Acts 28.23 came to him at his l. in great numbers

LOFTY
1. *superiority:* ὑπεροχή HYPEROCHĒ [A.1.b.5]
1 Cor 2. 1 not . . proclaiming . . in lofty words

LOG
1. *main beam, wooden beam:* δοκός DOKOS*
Mt 7. 3 "not notice the log . . in your own eye?
7. 4 "when there is the log in your own eye
7. 5 "first take the log out of your own eye
Lk 6.41 "not notice the log . . in your own eye?

Lk 6.42 "'you . . do not see the log . . in your own eye
6.42 "first take the log out of your own eye

LOINS
1. *loins:* ὀσφῦς (sg. or pl.) OSPHYS
Lk 12.35 "Let your loins be girded
Eph 6.14 having girded your loins with truth
Heb 7.10 he was still in the loins of his ancestor

LOIS: Λωΐς 'lōəs
2 Tim 1. 5 faith that dwelt . . in your grandmother L.

LONELY
1. *desolate, lonely:* ἔρημος ERĒMOS
Mt 14.13 withdrew . . to a lonely place apart
14.15 "This is a lonely place, and the day is . . over
Mk 1.35 he rose and went out to a lonely place
6.31 "Come away . . to a lonely place, and rest
6.32 went . . to a lonely place by themselves
6.35 "This is a lonely place, and the hour is . . late
Lk 4.42 he . . went into a lonely place
9.12 "for we are here in a lonely place

LONG (*See also* DELAY LONG; HAIR, HAVE LONG; ROBE, LONG; TIME, FOR A LONG)

LONG FOR
1. *eternal:* αἰώνιος AIŌNIOS
Rom 16.25 the mystery . . kept secret for long ages
2. *desire, long for:* ἐπιποθέω EPIPOTHEŌ
Rom 1.11 For I long to see you
2 Cor 5. 2 long to put on our heavenly dwelling
9.14 they long for you and pray for you
Phil 2.26 he has been longing for you all
1 Th 3. 6 you . . long to see us, as we . . to see you
2 Tim 1. 4 I long night and day to see you
1 Pet 2. 2 long for the pure spiritual milk
3. *have a longing:* ἐπιποθίαν ἔχειν EPIPOTHIA* [B.2.a.1]
Rom 15.23 I have longed for . . years to come to you
4. *desire, long for:* ἐπιθυμέω EPITHYMEŌ
Mt 13.17 "righteous men longed to see what you see
1 Pet 1.12 things into which angels long to look
Rev 9. 6 they will long to die, and death will fly
5. *desire, yearning:* ἐπιθυμία EPITHYMIA [A.1.a]
Rev 18.14 "fruit for which thy soul longed has gone
6. *enough:* ἱκανός HIKANOS
[a]ἐξ ἱκανῶν χρόνων *for a long time* B.1.a.1
Lk 8.27 for a long time he had worn no clothes
20. 9 "into another country for a long while
23. 8 [a]for he had long desired to see him
Acts 8.11 for a long time he had amazed them
14. 3 So they remained for a long time
20.11 he conversed with them a long while
7. *far, long:* μακρός MAKROS
Mt [23.14 "*and for a pretense you make long prayers*‡
Mk 12.40 "and for a pretense make long prayers
Lk 20.47 "and for a pretense make long prayers
8. *great:* μέγας MEGAS
Acts 26.29 Paul said, "Whether short or long
9. *many, great:* πολύς POLYS
[a]ἐπὶ πολύ
Mt 25.19 "after a long time the master . . came
Jn 5. 6 knew . . he had been lying there a long time
Acts 27.21 As they had been long without food
28. 6 [a]when they had waited a long time
CONTEXTUALLY
Rom 7. 2 bound . . to her husband as long as he lives
Heb 9. 8 as long as the outer tent[p] is still standing

LONG AGO
1. *for a long time:* ἔκπαλαι EKPALAI
2 Pet 3. 5 heavens existed long ago
2. *long ago:* πάλαι PALAI
Mt 11.21 "they would have repented long ago
Lk 10.13 "they would have repented long ago
Jude . 4 long ago . . designated for . . condemnation

LONG AS, AS
1. *until when:* ἄχρι οὗ ACHRI [B.3.b.4]
Heb 3.13 every day, as long as it is called "today
2. *for as much as:* ἐφ' ὅσον HOSOS [B.3.b.4]
[a]+χρόνον
Mt 9.15 "as long as the bridegroom is with them
1 Cor 7.39 [a]bound to her husband as long as he lives
Gal 4. 1 [a]the heir, as long as he is a child
2 Pet 1.13 I think it right, as long as I am in this body[c]
3. *when, whenever:* ὅταν HOTAN
Jn 9. 5 "As long as I am in the world
4. *when:* ὅτε HOTE
Heb 9.17 as long as the one who made it is alive

LONG FOR (*See* LONG)

LONG, HOW
1. *how much time:* πόσος χρόνος CHRONOS; POSOS [B.3.b.4]
Mk 9.21 "How long has he had this?
2. *until when:* ἕως πότε POTE I; HEŌS [B.3.b.4]
Mt 17.17 "how long am I to be with you? How long am I to bear with you?
Mk 9.19 "how long am I to be with you? How long am I to bear with you?
Lk 9.41 "how long am I to be with you?
Jn 10.24 "How long will you keep us in suspense?
Rev 6.10 "how long before thou wilt judge?

LONG, LIVE
1. *be long-lived:* εἶναι μακροχρόνιος MAKROCHRONIOS [A.6.a.3]
Eph 6. 3 "that you may live long on the earth

LONG, MAKE
1. *make large, extol:* μεγαλύνω MEGALYNŌ
Mt 23. 5 "they make . . their fringes long

LONG, SO
1. *so large, so many:* τοσοῦτος TOSOUTOS
[a]+χρόνος
Jn 14. 9 [a]"Have I been with you so long . . , Philip?
Heb 4. 7 saying through David so long afterward

LONG WAY, A
1. *from far off:* ἀπὸ μακρόθεν MAKROTHEN [B.3.b.4]
Mk 8. 3 "some of them have come a long way

LONGER
1. *still, yet:* ἔτι ETI
[a]ἔτι χρόνον μικρόν
Mt 5.13 "It is no longer good for anything
Lk 16. 2 " 'for you can no longer be steward
Jn 7.33 [a]"I shall be with you a little longer
12.35 [a]"The light is with you for a little longer
Acts 18.18 After this Paul stayed many days longer
Heb 10. 2 no longer have any consciousness of sin
Rev 6.11 [a]Then they . . told to rest a little longer
12. 8 no longer any place for them in heaven
2. *more:* πλείων PLEIŌN
Acts 18.20 asked him to stay for a longer period
CONTEXTUALLY
Jn 11. 6 he stayed two days longer in the place

LONGER, ANY
1. *no longer, no more:* μηκέτι (+neg.) MĒKETI
Acts 25.24 "that he ought not to live any longer

LONGER, NO
1. *no longer, no more:* μηκέτι MĒKETI
Mk 1.45 Jesus[g] could no longer . . enter a town
2. 2 there was no longer room for them
Rom 6. 6 we might no longer be enslaved to sin
15.23 I no longer have any room for work
2 Cor 5.15 might live no longer for themselves
Eph 4.14 so that we may no longer be children
4.17 you must no longer live as the Gentiles do
4.28 Let the thief no longer steal
1 Th 3. 1 when we could bear it no longer
3. 5 when I could bear it no longer
1 Tim 5.23 No longer drink only water
1 Pet 4. 2 to live . . no longer by human passions
2. *no longer, no more:* οὐκέτι OUKETI
Mt 19. 6 "So they are no longer two but one flesh
Mk 7.12 "you no longer permit him to do anything
9. 8 they no longer saw any one with them
10. 8 "they are no longer two but one flesh
Lk 15.19 " ' "no longer worthy to be called your son

Lk 15.21 " 'no longer worthy to be called your son[v]
20.40 they no longer dared to ask him
Jn 4.42 "It is no longer because of your words
6.66 no longer went about with him
11.54 Jesus . . no longer went about openly
14.30 "I will no longer talk much with you
15.15 "No longer do I call you servants[h]
16.21 "she no longer remembers the anguish
16.25 "when I shall no longer speak to you
Rom 6. 9 death no longer has dominion over him
7.17 So then it is no longer I that do it
7.20 it is no longer I that do it, but sin
11. 6 it is no longer on the basis of works; otherwise grace would no longer be grace
14.15 you are no longer walking in love
2 Cor 5.16 we regard him thus no longer
Gal 2.20 it is no longer I who live
3.18 it is no longer by promise
3.25 we are no longer under a custodian
4. 7 through God you are no longer a slave
Eph 2.19 So then you are no longer strangers
Phm .16 no longer as a slave but more than a slave
Heb 10.18 there is no longer any offering for sin
10.26 there no longer remains a sacrifice for sins

LONGER, STILL
IDIOMATICALLY
a. Acts 20.9 as Paul talked still longer διαλεγομένου τοῦ Παύλου ἐπὶ πλεῖον [PLEIŌN]

LONGING
1. *longing for:* ἐπιπόθησις EPIPOTHĒSIS*
2 Cor 7. 7 as he told us of your longing
7.11 what alarm, what longing, what zeal!

LONGING, EAGER
1. *earnest expectation:* ἀποκαραδοκία APOKARADOKIA
Rom 8.19 the creation waits with eager longing

LONGS FOR, WHOM ONE
1. *longed for, desired:* ἐπιπόθητος (subst. appos.) EPIPOTHĒTOS*
Phil 4. 1 brethren, whom I love and long for

LOOK (*See also* DISMAL, LOOK)
1. *look away:* ἀφοράω APHORAŌ
Heb 12. 2 looking to Jesus the pioneer . . of our faith
2. *see, look:* βλέπω BLEPŌ
Lk 9.62 "No one who . . looks back is fit
Jn 13.22 The disciples looked at one another
Acts 1. 9 as they were looking on, he was lifted up
1.11 "why do you stand looking into heaven?
3. 4 Peter . . , with John, . . said, "Look at us
27.12 looking northeast and southeast[a]
Eph 5.15 Look carefully then how you walk
3. *see, perceive:* εἶδον EIDON
Rev 4. 1 I looked, and lo, in heaven an open door!
5.11 Then I looked, and I heard
6.12 When he opened the sixth seal, I looked
7. 9 After this I looked, and behold
8.13 Then I looked, and I heard an eagle
14. 1 Then I looked, and lo, on Mount Zion
14.14 Then I looked, and lo, a white cloud
15. 5 I looked, and the temple . . was opened
4. *see, perceive:* ὁράω HORAŌ
Jn 19.37 scripture says, "They shall look on him
5. *behold! look!:* ἴδε IDE
Mk 2.24 "L., why are they doing what is not lawful?
11.21 Peter . . said . . "Master,[v] look!
13. 1 "Look, Teacher, what wonderful stones!
13.21 "then if any one says to you, 'Look, here is the Christ!' or 'Look, there he is!
Jn 12.19 "look, the world has gone after him
6. *behold:* ἰδού IDOU
Mt 12. 2 they said to him, "Look, your disciples
Lk 22.38 "Look, Lord, here are two swords
Jas 3. 4 Look at the ships also
7. *consider, perceive:* κατανοέω KATANOEŌ
Acts 7.31 "as he drew near to look, the voice . . came
7.32 "Moses . . did not dare to look
8. *stoop to look:* παρακύπτω PARAKYPTŌ
Jas 1.25 he who looks into the perfect law
1 Pet 1.12 things into which angels long to look
IDIOMATICALLY
a. Mk 8.24 "but they look like trees ὅτι ὡς δένδρα ὁρῶ [HORAŌ]
b. Rev 4. 3 a rainbow that looked like an emerald ἶρις . . ὅμοιος ὁράσει σμαραγδίνῳ [HORASIS]
CONTEXTUALLY
Rev 9. 7 on their heads were what looked like crowns

LOOK AFTER
1. *tend, herd, govern:* ποιμαίνω POIMAINŌ
Jude .12 looking after themselves
2. *seek, desire:* ζητέω ZĒTEŌ
Phil 2.21 They all look after their own interests

LOOK AROUND
LOOK AROUND AT
LOOK AROUND ON
LOOK ROUND AT
1. *look around:* περιβλέπω (mid.) PERIBLEPŌ*
Mk 3. 5 he looked around at them with anger
3.34 looking around on those . . about him
5.32 he looked around to see who had done it
9. 8 looking around they no longer saw any
10.23 looked around and said to his disciples
11.11 when he had looked round at everything
Lk 6.10 he looked around on them all, and said

LOOK AT
1. *look intently at:* ἀτενίζω ATENIZŌ
2 Cor 3. 7 Israelites could not look at Moses' face
2. *see, look:* βλέπω BLEPŌ
Mt 5.28 "every one who looks at a woman lustfully
2 Cor 10. 7 Look at what is before your eyes
3. *see, perceive:* εἶδον EIDON
Mk 12.15 "Bring me a coin,[z] and let me look at it
Lk 18.24 Jesus looking at him said, "How hard it is!
21.29 "Look at the fig tree, and all the trees
4. *look at:* ἐμβλέπω EMBLEPŌ
Mt 6.26 "Look at the birds of the air
19.26 Jesus looked at them and said
Mk 10.27 Jesus looked at them and said
14.67 she looked at him, and said, "You also
Lk 20.17 he looked at them and said
22.61 the Lord turned and looked at Peter
Jn 1.36 he looked at Jesus as he walked
1.42 Looked at him, . . said, "So you are Simon
5. *behold:* θεάομαι THEAOMAI
Mt 22.11 "the king came in to look at the guests

LOOK CLOSELY AT
1. *look intently at:* ἀτενίζω ATENIZŌ
Acts 11. 6 "Looking at it closely I observed animals

LOOK FOR
1. *seek:* ἀναζητέω ANAZĒTEŌ
Acts 11.25 Barnabas went to Tarsus to look for Saul
2. *accept, expect:* προσδέχομαι PROSDECHOMAI
Mk 15.43 also himself looking for the kingdom
Lk 2.25 looking for the consolation of Israel
2.38 looking for the redemption of Jerusalem
23.51 was looking for the kingdom of God
3. *wait for, expect:* προσδοκάω PROSDOKAŌ
Mt 11. 3 "Are you he . . or shall we look for another?
Lk 7.19 "Are you he . . or shall we look for another?
7.20 " 'Are you he . . or shall we look for another?
4. *seek, desire:* ζητέω ZĒTEŌ
Lk 2.48 "father and I have been looking for you
Jn 7.11 Jews were looking for him at the feast
11.56 They were looking for Jesus
Acts 10.19 "Behold, three men are looking for you
10.21 "I am the one you are looking for

LOOK FORWARD TO
1. *wait for:* ἐκδέχομαι EKDECHOMAI
Heb 11.10 For he looked forward to the city

LOOK IN, STOOP AND
LOOK, STOOP TO
1. *stoop to look:* παρακύπτω PARAKYPTŌ
Lk [24.12 *stooping and looking in, he saw the linen*‡
Jn 20.11 she stooped to look into the tomb

LOOK INTENTLY
1. *look intently at:* ἀτενίζω ATENIZŌ
Acts 13. 9 Paul . . looked intently at him
14. 9 Paul, looking intently at him and seeing
23. 1 Paul, looking intently at the council
2. *see clearly, look intently:* διαβλέπω DIABLEPŌ
Mk 8.25 he looked intently and was restored

LOOK INTO
1. *see, look:* βλέπω BLEPŌ
Rev 5. 3 able to open the scroll or to look into it
5. 4 to open the scroll or to look into it

LOOK ON
1. *see, look upon:* ἐπεῖδον EPEIDON
Lk 1.25 "looked on me, to take away my reproach
2. *think, lead:* ἡγέομαι HĒGEOMAI
2 Th 3.15 Do not look on him as an enemy
3. *look at, observe:* θεωρέω THEŌREŌ
Mt 27.55 women there, looking on from afar
Mk 15.40 also women looking on from afar

LOOK OUT FOR
1. *see, look:* βλέπω BLEPŌ
Phil 3. 2 Look out for the dogs, look out for the evil-workers, look out for those who mutilate the flesh

LOOK ROUND AT (*See* LOOK AROUND)

LOOK TO
1. *pay attention:* ἀποβλέπω APOBLEPŌ*
Heb 11.26 for he looked to the reward
2. *see, look:* βλέπω (imper.) BLEPŌ
2 Jn . 8 Look to yourselves, that you may not lose
3. *consider, look out for:* σκοπέω SKOPEŌ
2 Cor 4.18 we look not to the things that are seen
Gal 6. 1 Look to yourself, lest you too be tempted
Phil 2. 4 each . . look not only to his own interests

LOOK UP
1. *look up, receive sight:* ἀναβλέπω ANABLEPŌ
Mt 14.19 he looked up to heaven, and blessed
Mk 6.41 he looked up to heaven, and blessed
7.34 looking up to heaven, he sighed
8.24 he looked up and said, "I see men
16. 4 looking up, they saw . . stone was rolled
Lk 9.16 he looked up to heaven, and blessed
19. 5 looked up and said to him, "Zacchaeus
21. 1 He looked up and saw the rich
2. *lift up the head:* ἀνακύπτω ANAKYPTŌ
Lk 21.28 "look up and raise your heads
Jn 8.10 Jesus looked up and said to her[r]‡

LOOK UPON
1. *look at:* ἐμβλέπω EMBLEPŌ
Mk 10.21 Jesus looking upon him loved him
2. *see, look upon:* ἐπεῖδον EPEIDON
Acts 4.29 "now, Lord, look upon their threats
3. *look at, consider:* ἐπιβλέπω EPIBLEPŌ
Lk 9.38 "I beg you to look upon my son
4. *behold:* θεάομαι THEAOMAI
1 Jn 1. 1 which we have looked upon

LOOKING (*See* SAD, LOOKING)

LOOKS LIKE, WHAT
1. *as, so:* ὡς HŌS [B.3.b.4]
Rev **9.7**

LOOSE
1. *dissolutely, loosely:* ἀσώτως ASŌTŌS* [A.4.a]
Lk 15.13 "he squandered his property in loose living
2. *break up, unbind:* λύω LYŌ
Mt 16.19 "and whatever you loose on earth shall be loosed in heaven
18.18 "and whatever you loose on earth shall be loosed in heaven
Lk 13.16 "ought not this woman . . be loosed?
Acts 2.24 "having loosed the pangs of death
Rev 20. 3 he must be loosed for a little while
20. 7 Satan will be loosed from his prison
CONTEXTUALLY
Lk 1.64 his mouth was opened and his tongue loosed

LOOSEN
1. *let go:* ἀνίημι ANIĒMI
Acts 27.40 loosening the ropes that tied the rudders

LORD
1. *master, lord:* δεσπότης DESPOTĒS
Lk 2.29 "Lord, . . lettest thou thy servant depart
2. *be lord, rule:* κυριεύω (subst. part.) KYRIEUŌ
1 Tim 6.15 the King of kings and . . of lords
3. *lord, master:* κύριος KYRIOS
Mt 1.20 an angel of the Lord appeared to him
1.22 to fulfil what the Lord had spoken
1.24 did as the angel of the Lord commanded
2.13 an angel of the Lord appeared to Joseph
2.15 what the L. had spoken by the prophet
2.19 an angel of the L. appeared in a dream
3. 3 "Prepare the way of the Lord
4. 7 " 'You shall not tempt the Lord
4.10 " 'You shall worship the Lord your God
5.33 " 'perform to the L. what you have sworn
7.21 "Not every one who says to me, 'Lord, Lord,' shall enter the kingdom
7.22 " 'Lord, Lord, did we not prophesy in your name, and cast out demons?
8. 2 "Lord, if you will, you can make me clean
8. 6 "L., my servant is lying paralyzed at home
8. 8 "Lord, I am not worthy to have you
8.21 "Lord, let me first go and bury my father
8.25 "Save, Lord; we are perishing
9.28 They said to him, "Yes, Lord
9.38 "pray therefore the Lord of the harvest
11.25 "Father, Lord of heaven and earth
12. 8 "the Son of man is lord of the sabbath
14.28 "Lord, if it is you, bid me come to you
14.30 he cried out, "Lord, save me
15.22 "Have mercy on me, O Lord, Son of David
15.25 she . . knelt . . saying, "Lord, help me
15.27 "Yes, Lord, yet even the dogs eat
16.22 began to rebuke him, . . "God forbid, L.!
17. 4 "Lord, it is well that we are here
17.15 "Lord, have mercy on my son
18.21 "Lord, how often shall . . I forgive him?
18.25 "his lord ordered him to be sold
18.26 " 'Lord, have patience with me
18.27 "the lord of that servant released him
18.31 "they went and reported to their lord
18.32 "Then his lord summoned him
18.34 "his lord delivered him to the jailers[h]
[20.30 cried out, "*Lord*, have mercy on us‡
20.31 "Lord, have mercy on us, Son of David!
20.33 "Lord, let our eyes be opened
21. 3 " 'The Lord has need of them
21. 9 "he who comes in the name of the Lord!
21.42 " 'the Lord's doing, and it is marvelous
22.37 "You shall love the Lord your God
22.43 "How is it . . that David . . calls him Lord?
22.44 " 'The Lord said to my Lord, Sit at my right hand, till I put thy enemies under
22.45 "If David thus calls him Lord
23.39 " 'he who comes in the name of the Lord
24.42 "on what day your Lord is coming
25.11 "the other maidens came also, saying, 'Lord, lord, open to us
25.37 " 'Lord, when did we see thee hungry?
25.44 " 'Lord, when did we see thee hungry?
26.22 they . . began to say . . "Is it I, Lord?
27.10 "as the Lord directed me
28. 2 for an angel of the Lord descended
[28. 6 "see the place where *the Lord* lay‡
Mk 1. 3 "Prepare the way of the Lord
2.28 "Son of man is lord even of the sabbath
5.19 "tell them how much the Lord has done

Mk 7.28 "Yes, Lord; yet even the dogs . . eat
11. 3 "say, 'The Lord has need of it
11. 9 "he who comes in the name of the Lord!
12.11 " 'the Lord's doing, and it is marvelous
12.29 "The first is, 'Hear, O Israel: The Lord our God, the Lord is one
12.30 " 'you shall love the Lord your God
12.36 " 'The Lord said to my Lord, Sit at my right hand, till I put thy enemies under
12.37 "David himself calls him Lord
13.20 "if the Lord had not shortened the days
16.19 the Lord Jesus . . was taken up into heaven[k]‡
16.20 while the Lord worked with them[k]‡
Lk 1. 6 walking in all the . . ordinances of the L.
1. 9 it fell to him . . to enter the temple of the L.
1.11 an angel of the Lord standing on the right
1.15 "for he will be great before the Lord
1.16 "he will turn many . . to the Lord their God
1.17 "to make ready for the Lord a people
1.25 "Thus the Lord has done to me
1.28 "O favored one, the Lord is with you![c]
1.32 "the Lord God will give to him the throne
1.38 "I am the handmaid of the Lord
1.43 "why . . the mother of my Lord should come?
1.45 "what was spoken to her from the Lord
1.46 Mary said, "My soul magnifies the Lord
1.58 the Lord had shown great mercy to her
1.66 For the hand of the Lord was with him
1.68 "Blessed be the Lord God of Israel
1.76 "for you will go before the Lord
2. 9 an angel of the Lord appeared to them, and the glory of the Lord shone
2.11 "a Savior, who is Christ the Lord
2.15 "which the Lord has made known to us
2.22 brought him . . to present him to the L.
2.23 (as it is written in the law of the Lord, "Every male . . shall be called holy to the L.
2.24 what is said in the law of the Lord
2.26 before he had seen the Lord's Christ
2.39 according to the law of the Lord
3. 4 "Prepare the way of the Lord
4. 8 " 'You shall worship the Lord your God
4.12 " 'You shall not tempt the Lord your God
4.18 "The Spirit of the Lord is upon me
4.19 "to proclaim the acceptable year of the L.
5. 8 "Depart . . for I am a sinful man, O Lord
5.12 "Lord, . . you can make me clean
5.17 power of the Lord was with him to heal[p]
6. 5 "The Son of man is lord of the sabbath
6.46 "Why do you call me 'Lord, Lord,' and not do what I tell you?
7. 6 "Lord, do not trouble yourself
7.13 the Lord . . had compassion on her
7.19 John . . sent them to the Lord
9.54 "Lord, do you want us to bid fire come?
9.59 "Lord, let me first go and bury my father
9.61 Another said, "I will follow you, Lord
10. 1 After this the Lord appointed seventy[q]
10. 2 "pray therefore the Lord of the harvest
10.17 "Lord, even the demons are subject to us!
10.21 "Father, Lord of heaven and earth
10.27 "You shall love the Lord your God
10.39 Mary, who sat at the Lord's feet
10.40 Martha . . said, "Lord, do you not care?
10.41 the Lord answered her, "Martha, Martha
11. 1 "Lord, teach us to pray, as John taught
11.39 the Lord said . . "you Pharisees cleanse
12.41 "L., are you telling this parable for us?
12.42 Lord said, "Who . . is the . . wise steward?
13.15 Lord answered him, "You hypocrites!
13.23 "Lord, will those who are saved be few?
13.25 "you will . . knock . . saying, 'Lord, open
13.35 " 'he who comes in the name of the Lord
17. 5 said to the Lord, "Increase our faith!
17. 6 the Lord said, "If you had faith
17.37 they said to him, "Where, Lord?
18. 6 Lord said, "Hear what the . . judge says
Lk 18.41 He said, "Lord, let me receive my sight
19. 8 Zacchaeus . . said to the Lord . . "Lord, . . the half of my goods I give to the poor
19.16 " 'Lord, your pound has made ten pounds
19.18 " 'L., your pound has made five pounds
19.20 " 'L., here is your pound, which I kept
19.25 "(they said . . 'Lord, he has ten pounds!
19.31 "say this, 'The Lord has need of it
19.34 they said, "The Lord has need of it
19.38 "who comes in the name of the Lord
20.37 "he calls the Lord the God of Abraham
20.42 "David himself says . . 'The Lord said to my Lord, Sit at my right hand
20.44 "David thus calls him Lord
22.33 "Lord, I am ready to go with you
22.38 "Look, Lord, here are two swords
22.49 "Lord, shall we strike with the sword?
22.61 Lord turned and looked at Peter. And Peter remembered the word of the Lord
[24. 3 they did not find the body *of the Lord Jesus*‡
24.34 "The Lord has risen indeed!
Jn 1.23 " 'Make straight the way of the Lord
4. 1 Lord knew that the Pharisees had heard
[5. 4 *for an angel of the Lord went down*‡
6.23 they ate . . after the Lord had given thanks
6.34 "Lord give us this bread always
6.68 "Lord, to whom shall we go?
8.11 She said, "No one, Lord[r]‡
9.38 He said, "Lord, I believe
11. 2 It was Mary who anointed the Lord
11. 3 "Lord, he whom you love is ill
11.12 "Lord, if he has fallen asleep
11.21 "Lord, if you had been here
11.27 She said to him, "Yes, Lord; I believe
11.32 "Lord, if you had been here
11.34 They said to him, "Lord, come and see
11.39 "Lord, by this time there will be an odor
12.13 "he who comes in the name of the Lord
12.38 "Lord, who has believed our report?
12.38 "to whom . . arm of the Lord . . revealed?
13. 6 "Lord, do you wash my feet?
13. 9 "L., not my feet only but also my hands!
13.13 "You call me Teacher and Lord
13.14 "If I then, your Lord and Teacher
13.25 he said to him, "Lord, who is it?
13.36 "Lord, where are you going?
13.37 "Lord, why cannot I follow you now?
14. 5 "Lord, we do not know where you are going
14. 8 Philip said . . "Lord, show us the Father
14.22 "Lord, how is it that you will manifest?
20. 2 "They have taken the L. out of the tomb
20.13 "they have taken away my Lord
20.18 said to the disciples, "I have seen the L.
20.20 glad when they saw the Lord
20.25 told him, "We have seen the Lord
20.28 "My Lord and my God!
21. 7 said to Peter, "It is the Lord!
21. 7 When . . Peter heard that it was the Lord
21.12 They knew it was the Lord
21.15 "Yes, Lord; you know that I love you
21.16 "Yes, Lord; you know that I love you
21.17 "Lord, you know everything
21.20 "L., who is it that is going to betray you?
21.21 "Lord, what about this man?
Acts 1. 6 "L., will you at this time restore the kingdom?
1.21 "all the time that the Lord Jesus went in
1.24 "Lord, who knowest the hearts of all men
2.20 " 'before the day of the Lord comes
2.21 " 'whoever calls on the name of the L.
2.25 " 'I saw the Lord always before me
2.34 "but he himself says, 'The Lord said to my Lord, Sit at my right hand
2.36 "God has made him both Lord and Christ
2.39 "whom the Lord our God calls to him
2.47 And the Lord added to their number
3.19 "refreshing . . from the presence of the Lord
3.22 " 'The L. . . will raise up for you a prophet

Acts 4.26 " 'rulers were gathered . . against the Lord
4.29 "now, Lord, look upon their threats
4.33 testimony to the resurrection of the Lord
5. 9 "to tempt the Spirit of the Lord
5.14 believers were added to the Lord
5.19 an angel of the Lord opened the prison
7.31 "the voice of the Lord came
7.33 "Lord said to him, 'Take off the shoes
7.49 " 'What house will you build . ., says the L.
7.59 "Lord Jesus, receive my spirit
7.60 "Lord, do not hold this sin against them
8.16 baptized in the name of the L. Jesus
8.22 "pray to the Lord that, if possible
8.24 "Pray for me to the Lord
8.25 when they had . . spoken the word of the L.
8.26 But an angel of the Lord said to Philip
8.39 the Spirit of the Lord caught up Philip
9. 1 threats . . against the disciples of the Lord
9. 5 he said, "Who are you, Lord?
9.10 The Lord said to him . . "Ananias." And he said, "Here I am, Lord
9.11 the Lord said to him, "Rise and go
9.13 "Lord, I have heard . . about this man
9.15 But the Lord said to him, "Go
9.17 "the Lord Jesus, who appeared to you
9.27 how on the road he had seen the Lord
9.29(28) preaching boldly in the name of the Lord
9.31 walking in the fear of the Lord
9.35 and they turned to the Lord
9.42 and many believed in the Lord
10. 4 in terror . . said, "What is it, Lord?
10.14 Peter said, "No, Lord; for I have never
10.33 "you have been commanded by the Lord
10.36 "peace by Jesus Christ (he is Lord of all
11. 8 " 'No, L.; for nothing common or unclean
11.16 "I remembered the word of the Lord
11.17 "when we believed in the Lord Jesus Christ
11.20 men of Cyprus . . preaching the Lord Jesus
11.21 the hand of the Lord was with them, and a . . number . . turned to the Lord
11.23 exhorted them . . to remain faithful to the L.
11.24 a large company was added to the L.
12. 7 behold, an angel of the Lord appeared
12.11 "I am sure that the L. has sent his angel
12.17 how the L. had brought him out of . . prison
12.23 an angel of the Lord smote him
13. 2 While they were worshiping the Lord
13.10 "making crooked the . . paths of the L.?
13.11 "behold, the hand of the Lord is upon you
13.12 he was astonished at the teaching of the L.
13.47 "For so the Lord has commanded us
13.49 And the word of the Lord spread
14. 3 speaking boldly for the Lord
14.23 they committed them to the Lord
15.11 "saved through the grace of the L. Jesus
15.17 " 'that the rest of men may seek the L.
15.18(17) " 'L., who has made these things known
15.26 "risked their lives for . . our L. Jesus C.
15.35 teaching and preaching the word of the L.
15.36 "where we proclaimed the word of the L.
15.40 commended . . to the grace of the L.
16.14 The L. opened her heart to give heed
16.15 "If you have judged me . . faithful to the L.
16.31 "Believe in the L. J., and you will be saved
16.32 they spoke the word of the Lord to him
17.24 "God . ., being Lord of heaven and earth
18. 8 Crispus . . believed in the Lord
18. 9 the Lord said to Paul . . "Do not be afraid
18.25 instructed in the way of the Lord
19. 5 baptized in the name of the Lord Jesus
19.10 all . . of Asia heard the word of the Lord
19.13 to pronounce the name of the Lord Jesus
19.17 the name of the Lord Jesus was extolled
19.20 the word of the Lord grew and prevailed
20.19 "serving the Lord with all humility
20.21 "faith in our Lord Jesus Christ
20.24 "ministry which I received from the L. J.

Acts [20.28 overseers, to care for the church *of the L.*‡[o]
20.35 "remembering the words of the L. Jesus
21.13 "even to die . . for the name of the L. Jesus
21.14 "The will of the Lord be done
22. 8 "And I answered, 'Who are you, Lord?
22.10 "And I said, 'What shall I do, Lord?' And the Lord said to me, 'Rise, and go
22.19 " 'Lord, they . . know that . . I . . beat those
23.11 following night the Lord stood by him
25.26 "I have nothing definite to write to my lord
26.15 "I said, 'Who are you, Lord?' And the L. said, 'I am Jesus whom you are persecuting
28.31 teaching about the Lord Jesus Christ

Rom 1. 4 designated Son of God . ., Jesus Christ our L.
1. 7 Grace to you . . from . . the L. Jesus Christ
4. 8 "against whom the L. will not reckon his sin
4.24 that raised from the dead Jesus our L.
5. 1 peace with God through our L. Jesus C.
5.11 we . . rejoice . . through our L. Jesus Christ
5.21 eternal life through Jesus Christ our L.
6.23 free gift . . is eternal life in C. Jesus our L.
7.25 Thanks . . through Jesus Christ our Lord!
8.39 the love of God in Christ Jesus our Lord
9.28 "the Lord will execute his sentence
9.29 "If the L. of hosts had not left us
10. 9 if you confess . . that Jesus is Lord
10.12 no distinction . . ; the same . . is Lord of all
10.13 "who calls upon the name of the Lord
10.16 "L., who has believed what he has heard?
11. 3 "L., they have killed thy prophets
11.34 "who has known the mind of the Lord?
12.11 be aglow with the Spirit, serve the Lord
12.19 "Vengeance is mine, I will repay, says the L.
13.14 But put on the Lord Jesus Christ
14. 6 He . . observes it in honor of the Lord. He also who eats, eats in honor of the Lord
14. 6 who abstains, abstains in honor of the L.
14. 8 If we live, we live to the Lord, and if we die, we die to the Lord; so then, whether we live or . . die, we are the Lord's
14.11 "says the L., every knee shall bow
14.14 I know and am persuaded in the L. Jesus
15. 6 God and Father of our L. Jesus Christ
15.11 "Praise the Lord, all Gentiles
15.30 I appeal . . by our Lord Jesus Christ
16. 2 that you may receive her in the Lord
16. 8 Greet Ampliatus, my beloved in the L.
16.11 Greet those in the Lord who belong to
16.12 Greet those workers in the Lord
16.12 Persis, who has worked hard in the Lord
16.13 Greet Rufus, eminent in the Lord
16.18 For such persons do not serve our Lord
16.20 grace of our L. Jesus Christ be with you[a]‡
16.22 I Tertius . . greet you in the Lord
[16.24 *grace of our L. Jesus Christ be with you*‡

1 Cor 1. 2 who . . call on the name of our L. Jesus C.
1. 3 Grace to you . . from . . the L. Jesus Christ
1. 7 the revealing of our Lord Jesus Christ
1. 8 in the day of our Lord Jesus Christ
1. 9 fellowship of his Son, Jesus Christ our L.
1.10 by the name of our Lord Jesus Christ
1.31 "Let him who boasts, boast of the Lord
2. 8 would not have crucified the L. of glory
2.16 "who has known the mind of the Lord?
3. 5 you believed, as the Lord assigned
3.20 "L. knows that the thoughts of the wise
4. 4 It is the Lord who judges me
4. 5 before the time, before the Lord comes
4.17 Timothy, my . . faithful child in the Lord
4.19 I will come to you soon, if the L. wills
5. 4 in the name of the Lord Jesus
5. 4 assembled . . with the power of our L. Jesus
5. 5 saved in the day of the Lord Jesus[h]
6.11 justified in the name of the L. Jesus C.
6.13 "The body is not meant for immorality, but for the L., and the L. for the body
6.14 God raised the Lord and will also raise us

1 Cor 6.17 who is united to the Lord becomes one
7.10 I give charge, not I but the Lord
7.12 To the rest I say, not the Lord
7.17 lead the life which the Lord has assigned
7.22 For he who was called in the Lord as a slave is a freedman of the Lord
7.25 I have no command of the Lord
7.25 who by the Lord's mercy is trustworthy
7.32 The unmarried man is anxious about the affairs of the Lord, how to please the Lord
7.34 anxious about the affairs of the Lord
7.35 your undivided devotion to the Lord
7.39 free to be married . . , only in the L.
8. 5 there are many "gods" and many "lords"
8. 6 for us there is . . one Lord, Jesus Christ
9. 1 Have I not seen Jesus our Lord? Are not you my workmanship in the Lord?
9. 2 you are the seal of my apostleship in the L.
9. 5 the brothers of the Lord and Cephas
9.14 Lord commanded that those who proclaim
10. 9 We must not put the Lord[p] to the test‡
10.21 You cannot drink the cup of the Lord
10.21 table of the L. and the table of demons
10.22 Shall we provoke the Lord to jealousy?
10.26 "earth is the Lord's, and everything in it
11.11 (in the Lord woman is not independent
11.23 I received from the Lord what I . . delivered . . , that the Lord Jesus . . took bread
11.26 you proclaim the Lord's death
11.27 Whoever . . drinks the cup of the Lord
11.27 profaning the body and blood of the Lord
11.32 But when we are judged by the Lord
12. 3 no one can say "Jesus is Lord" except
12. 5 varieties of service, but the same Lord
14.21 "they will not listen to me, says the Lord
14.37 I am writing . . a command of the Lord
15.31 which I have in Christ Jesus our Lord
15.57 victory through our Lord Jesus Christ
15.58 abounding in the work of the L., knowing that in the L. your labor is not in vain
16. 7 some time with you, if the Lord permits
16.10 for he is doing the work of the Lord
16.19 send you hearty greetings in the Lord
16.22 If any one has no love for the Lord
16.23 The grace of the Lord Jesus be with you

2 Cor 1. 2 Grace to you . . from . . the Lord Jesus Christ
1. 3 God and Father of our Lord Jesus Christ
1.14 proud . . on the day of the Lord Jesus
2.12 a door was opened for me in the Lord
3.16 when a man turns to the Lord
3.17 Now the Lord is the Spirit, and where the Spirit of the Lord is, there is freedom
3.18 beholding[d] the glory of the Lord
3.18 comes from the Lord who is the Spirit
4. 5 we preach . . Jesus Christ as Lord
4.14 knowing that he who raised the Lord Jesus
5. 6 in the body we are away from the Lord
5. 8 we would rather be . . at home with the L.
5.11 knowing the fear of the L., we persuade
6.17 "be separate from them, says the Lord
6.18 "I will be a father . . says the Lord Almighty
8. 5 first they gave themselves to the Lord
8. 9 the grace of our Lord Jesus Christ
8.19 carrying on, for the glory of the Lord
8.21 honorable not only in the Lord's sight
10. 8 our authority, which the Lord gave
10.17 "Let him who boasts, boast of the Lord
10.18 the man whom the Lord commends
11.17 (I say not with the Lord's authority
11.31 The God and Father of the Lord Jesus
12. 1 visions and revelations of the Lord
12. 8 Three times I besought the Lord
13.10 authority which the Lord has given me
13.14(13) The grace of the Lord Jesus Christ

Gal 1. 3 Grace to you . . from . . our Lord Jesus Christ
1.19 none . . except James the Lord's brother
5.10 I have confidence in the Lord
6.14 the cross of our Lord Jesus Christ
6.18 The grace of our Lord Jesus Christ

Eph 1. 2 Grace to you . . from . . the Lord Jesus Christ
1. 3 God and Father of our Lord Jesus Christ
1.15 I have heard of your faith in the L. Jesus
1.17 the God of our Lord Jesus Christ
2.21 grows into a holy temple in the Lord
3.11 eternal purpose . . in Christ Jesus our Lord
4. 1 I . . , a prisoner for the Lord, beg you
4. 5 one Lord, one faith, one baptism
4.17 Now this I affirm and testify in the Lord
5. 8 but now you are light in the Lord
5.10 try to learn what is pleasing to the Lord
5.17 understand what the will of the Lord is
5.19 singing and making melody to the Lord
5.20 in the name of our Lord Jesus Christ
5.22 subject to your husbands, as to the Lord
6. 1 Children, obey your parents in the Lord
6. 4 discipline and instruction of the Lord
6. 7 service with a good will as to the Lord
6. 8 he will receive the same again from the L.
6.10 Finally, be strong in the Lord
6.21 Tychicus the . . faithful minister in the Lord
6.23 from God the Father and the L. Jesus Christ
6.24 all who love our Lord Jesus Christ

Phil 1. 2 Grace to you . . from . . the Lord Jesus Christ
1.14 brethren . . made confident in the Lord
2.11 confess that Jesus Christ is Lord
2.19 I hope in the Lord Jesus to send
2.24 I trust in the Lord that . . I . . shall come
2.29 receive him in the Lord with all joy
3. 1 Finally, my brethren, rejoice in the Lord
3. 8 worth of knowing Christ Jesus my Lord
3.20 a Savior, the Lord Jesus Christ
4. 1 stand firm thus in the Lord, my beloved
4. 2 I entreat Syntyche to agree in the Lord
4. 4 Rejoice in the Lord always
4. 5 The Lord is at hand
4.10 I rejoice in the Lord greatly
4.23 The grace of the Lord Jesus Christ

Col 1. 3 the Father of our Lord Jesus Christ
1.10 to lead a life worthy of the Lord
2. 6 As . . you received Christ Jesus the Lord
3.13 as the Lord has forgiven you
3.17 do everything in the name of the L. Jesus
3.18 be subject . . , as is fitting in the Lord
3.20 obey your parents . . , for this pleases the L.
3.22 in singleness of heart, fearing the Lord
3.23 work heartily, as serving the Lord
3.24 from the L. you will receive the inheritance
3.24 you are serving the Lord Christ
4. 7 minister and fellow servant in the Lord
4.17 "ministry which you . . received in the Lord

1 Th 1. 1 God the Father and the Lord Jesus Christ
1. 3 hope in our Lord Jesus Christ
1. 6 became imitators of us and of the Lord
1. 8 has the word of the Lord sounded forth
2.15 killed both the L. Jesus and the prophets
2.19 crown of boasting before our Lord Jesus
3. 8 now we live, if you stand fast in the Lord
3.11 may . . our Lord Jesus, direct our way
3.12 may the Lord make you increase
3.13 at the coming of our Lord Jesus
4. 1 we . . exhort you in the Lord Jesus
4. 2 instructions we gave . . through the L. J.
4. 6 the Lord is an avenger in all these things
4.15 declare to you by the word of the Lord
4.15 left until the coming of the Lord
4.16 Lord himself will descend from heaven
4.17 in the clouds to meet the Lord in the air; and so we shall always be with the Lord
5. 2 day of the Lord will come like a thief
5. 9 salvation through our Lord Jesus Christ
5.12 those who . . are over you in the Lord
5.23 at the coming of our Lord Jesus Christ
5.27 I adjure you by the Lord
5.28 grace of our L. Jesus Christ be with you

2 Th 1. 1 God our Father and the Lord Jesus Christ
1. 2 Grace to you . . from . . the L. Jesus Christ
1. 7 when the Lord Jesus is revealed
1. 8 who do not obey the gospel of our L. J.
1. 9 exclusion from the presence of the Lord
1.12 that . . our L. Jesus may be glorified
1.12 the grace of . . the Lord Jesus Christ
2. 1 the coming of our Lord Jesus Christ
2. 2 that the day of the Lord has come
2. 8 the Lord Jesus will slay him
2.13 brethren beloved by the Lord
2.14 obtain the glory of our Lord Jesus Christ
2.16 may our Lord Jesus Christ himself
3. 1 that the word of the Lord may speed on
3. 3 But the Lord is faithful; he will strengthen
3. 4 we have confidence in the Lord about you
3. 5 May the Lord direct your hearts
3. 6 in the name of our Lord Jesus Christ
3.12 we . . exhort in the Lord Jesus Christ
3.16 the Lord of peace himself give you peace . . The Lord be with you all
3.18 grace of our L. Jesus Christ be with you
1 Tim 1. 2 peace from . . Christ Jesus our Lord
1.12 I thank him . . , Christ Jesus our Lord
1.14 the grace of our Lord overflowed
6. 3 the sound words of our Lord Jesus Christ
6.14 the appearing of our Lord Jesus Christ
6.15 Sovereign, the King of kings and Lord
2 Tim 1. 2 peace from . . Christ Jesus our Lord
1. 8 not . . ashamed . . of testifying to our Lord
1.16 May the L. grant mercy to the household
1.18 may the Lord grant him to find mercy from the Lord on that Day
2. 7 the Lord will grant you understanding
2.14 charge them before the Lord[b] to avoid‡
2.19 "The Lord knows those who are his," and "Let every one who names the . . Lord
2.22 those who call upon the Lord
2.24 the Lord's servant must not be quarrelsome
3.11 yet from them all the Lord rescued me
4. 8 the Lord, the righteous judge, will award
4.14 the Lord will requite him for his deeds
4.17 Lord stood by me and gave me strength
4.18 Lord will rescue me from every evil
4.22 The Lord be with your spirit
Phm . 3 Grace to you . . from . . the Lord Jesus C.
. 5 faith . . you have toward the Lord Jesus
.16 brother . . , both in the flesh and in the Lord
.20 I want some benefit from you in the Lord
.25 The grace of the Lord Jesus Christ
Heb 1.10 "Thou, Lord, didst found the earth
2. 3 It was declared at first by the Lord
7.14 our Lord was descended from Judah
7.21 "The Lord has sworn and will not change
8. 2 set up not by man but by the Lord
8. 8 "The days will come, says the Lord
8. 9 "so I paid no heed to them, says the Lord
8.10 "This is the covenant . . , says the Lord
8.11 "shall not teach . . saying, 'Know the L.
10.16 "This is the covenant . . says the Lord
10.30 "The Lord will judge his people
12. 5 "not regard lightly the discipline of the L.
12. 6 Lord disciplines him whom he loves
12.14 without which no one will see the Lord
13. 6 "The Lord is my helper, I will not be afraid
13.20 brought again from the dead our L. Jesus
Jas 1. 1 James, a servant . . of the Lord Jesus Christ
1. 7 will ⟨not⟩ receive anything from the Lord
2. 1 the faith of our Lord Jesus Christ
3. 9 With it we bless the Lord and Father
4.10 Humble yourselves before the Lord
4.15 "If the Lord wills, we shall live
5. 4 reached the ears of the Lord of hosts
5. 7 Be patient . . until the coming of the Lord
5. 8 the coming of the Lord is at hand
5.10 prophets who spoke in the name of the L.
Jas 5.11 you have seen the purpose of the Lord, how the Lord is compassionate
5.14 anointing him . . in the name of the Lord
5.15 the Lord will raise him up
1 Pet 1. 3 "Blessed be the God . . of our Lord Jesus C.!
1.25 "the word of the Lord abides for ever
2. 3 you have tasted the kindness of the Lord
2.13 Be subject for the Lord's sake
3. 6 Sarah obeyed Abraham, calling him lord
3.12 "eyes of the Lord are upon the righteous
3.12 "face of the L. is against those that do evil
3.15 in your hearts reverence Christ as Lord
2 Pet 1. 2 knowledge of God and of Jesus our Lord
1. 8 knowledge of our Lord Jesus Christ
1.11 kingdom of our Lord and Savior Jesus C.
1.14 as our Lord Jesus Christ showed me
1.16 power and coming of our Lord Jesus C.
2. 9 Lord knows how to rescue the godly
2.11 judgment upon them before the Lord
2.20 knowledge of our L. and Savior J. C.
3. 2 commandment of the Lord and Savior
3. 8 with the L. one day is as a thousand years
3. 9 Lord is not slow about his promise
3.10 day of the Lord will come like a thief
3.15 forbearance of our Lord as salvation
3.18 knowledge of our Lord and Savior J. C.
Jude . 4 who . . deny our only Master and L., J. C.[a]
[. 5 *the Lord* who saved a people out of . . Egypt‡
. 9 Michael . . said, "The Lord rebuke you
.14 "Behold, the L. came with his holy myriads
.17 predictions of the apostles of our L. J. C.
.21 wait for the mercy of our Lord J. C.
.25 through Jesus Christ our Lord, be glory
Rev 1. 8 the Lord God, who is and who was
4. 8 "Holy, holy, holy, is the L. God Almighty!
4.11 "Worthy art thou, our Lord and God
11. 4 lampstands . . before the Lord of the earth
11. 8 Egypt, where their Lord was crucified
11.15 "has become the kingdom of our Lord
11.17 "We give thanks to thee, L. God Almighty
14.13 "Blessed are the dead who die in the L.
15. 3 "Great . . are thy deeds, O Lord God!
15. 4 "Who shall not fear . . thy name, O Lord?
16. 7 I heard the altar cry, "Yea, Lord God
17.14 "the Lamb will conquer them, for he is Lord of lords and King of kings
18. 8 "for mighty is the Lord God who judges
19. 6 "For the L. our God the Almighty reigns
19.16 on his thigh he has a name inscribed, King of kings and Lord of lords
21.22 no temple . . , for its temple is the Lord God
22. 5 for the Lord God will be their light
22. 6 "the Lord, the God of the spirits
22.20 Come, Lord Jesus!
22.21 grace of the L. Jesus be with all the saints[t]

LORD, BE
1. *be lord, rule:* κυριεύω KYRIEUŌ
Rom 14. 9 might be Lord both of . . dead and of . . living

LORD COME, OUR
1. *our Lord, come!* (Aram.): μαράνα θᾶ MARANATHA*
1 Cor 16.22 let him be accursed. Our Lord, come![c]†

LORD IT OVER
1. *domineer completely:* κατακυριεύω KATAKYRIEUŌ
Mt 20.25 "rulers of the Gentiles lord it over them
Mk 10.42 "who . . rule . . the Gentiles lord it over them
2. *be lord, rule:* κυριεύω KYRIEUŌ
2 Cor 1.24 Not that we lord it over your faith

LORD, SOVEREIGN
1. *master, lord:* δεσπότης DESPOTĒS
Acts 4.24 "Sovereign L., who didst make the heaven
Rev 6.10 "O Sovereign Lord, holy and true

LORD'S
1. *belonging to the lord:* κυριακός KYRIAKOS*
1 Cor 11.20 it is not the Lord's supper that you eat
Rev 1.10 I was in the Spirit on the Lord's day

LORDSHIP OVER, EXERCISE
1. *be lord, rule:* κυριεύω KYRIEUŌ
Lk 22.25 "kings of the Gentiles exercise l. over them

LOSE (*See also* COURAGE, LOSE)
1. *destroy utterly:* ἀπόλλυμι APOLLYMI
Mt 5.29 "better that you lose one of your members
5.30 "better that you lose one of your members
10. 6 "to the lost sheep of the house of Israel
10.39 "He who finds his life will lose it, and he who loses his life for my sake will find it
10.42 "I say to you, he shall not lose his reward
15.24 "to the lost sheep of the house of Israel
16.25 "whoever would save his life will lose it, and whoever loses his life for my sake will find
[18.11 "*For the Son of man came to save the lost*‡
Mk 2.22 "the wine is lost, and so are the skins
8.35 "whoever would save his life will lose it; and whoever loses his life for my sake
9.41 "will by no means lose his reward
Lk 9.24 "whoever would save his life will lose it; and whoever loses his life for my sake
9.25 "if he gains the . . world and loses . . himself
15. 4 "What man . . , if he has lost one of them, does not . . go after the one which is lost?
15. 6 " 'I have found my sheep which was lost
15. 8 "what woman, . . if she loses one coin
15. 9 " 'I have found the coin which I had lost
15.24 " 'this my son . . was lost, and is found
15.32 " 'this your brother . . was lost, and is found
17.33 "Whoever seeks to gain his life will lose it, but whoever loses his life will preserve
19.10 "Son of man came to . . save the lost
Jn 6.12 "Gather up . . , that nothing may be lost
6.39 "lose nothing of all that he has given me
12.25 "He who loves his life loses it
17.12 "none . . is lost but the son of perdition
18. 9 "Of those . . thou gavest me I lost not one
2 Jn . 8 may not lose what you[a] have worked for
Rev 18.14 "thy dainties and thy splendor are lost!
2. *go through, elapse:* διαγίνομαι DIAGINOMAI
Acts 27. 9 As much time had been lost
3. *fall out:* ἐκπίπτω EKPIPTŌ
2 Pet 3.17 beware lest you . . lose your own stability

LOSE HEART
1. *become weary, despair:* ἐγκακέω EGKAKEŌ
Lk 18. 1 always to pray and not lose heart
2 Cor 4. 1 by the mercy of God,[e] we do not l. heart
4.16 So we do not lose heart
Eph 3.13 So I ask you not to[e] lose heart†

LOSE SALTNESS
1. *become saltless:* ἄναλος γίνεσθαι GINOMAI; ANALOS* [B.3.a.2]
Mk 9.50 "but if the salt has lost its saltness

LOSES ITS TASTE, S.
1. *make foolish:* μωραίνω (pass.) MŌRAINŌ
Mt 5.13 "but if salt has lost its taste
Lk 14.34 "but if salt has lost its taste

LOSS
1. *throwing away, loss:* ἀποβολή APOBOLĒ
Acts 27.22 "there will be no loss of life among you
2. *damage, loss:* ζημία ZĒMIA*
Acts 27.10 "the voyage will be with . . much loss
27.21 "should not have . . incurred this . . loss
Phil 3. 7 I counted as loss for the sake of Christ
3. 8 Indeed I count everything as loss

LOSS, BE AT A
1. *be in doubt:* ἀπορέω (mid.) APOREŌ
Acts 25.20 "Being at a loss how to investigate

LOSS, SUFFER
1. *cause loss:* ζημιόω (pass.) ZĒMIOŌ
1 Cor 3.15 he will suffer l., though he . . will be saved
2 Cor 7. 9 so that you suffered no loss through us
Phil 3. 8 For his sake I have suffered the loss of all

LOT
LOTS
1. *lot, share:* κλῆρος KLĒROS
Mt 27.35 divided his garments . . by casting lots
Mk 15.24 divided his garments . . , casting lots
Lk 23.34 they cast lots to divide his garments
Jn 19.24 "for my clothing they cast lots
Acts 1.26 And they cast lots for them, and the lot fell on Matthias
8.21 "You have neither part nor lot in this
2. *part, share:* μέρος MEROS
Rev 21. 8 "their lot shall be in the lake that burns
IDIOMATICALLY
a. 1 Th 3.3 that this is to be our lot ὅτι εἰς τοῦτο κείμεθα [KEIMAI]

LOT: Λώτ 'lät
Lk 17.28 "Likewise as it was in the days of Lot
17.29 "the day when Lot went out from Sodom
17.32 Remember Lot's wife
2 Pet 2. 7 if he rescued righteous Lot

LOT, FALL TO ONE BY
LOTS, CAST
1. *obtain by lot:* λαγχάνω LAGCHANŌ
Lk 1. 9 it fell to him by lot to enter the temple
Jn 19.24 "Let us not tear it, but cast lots for it

LOUD
1. *strong, powerful:* ἰσχυρός ISCHYROS
Heb 5. 7 Jesus[j] offered up prayers . . with loud cries
2. *great:* μέγας MEGAS
Mt 24.31 "send . . his angels with a loud trumpet call
27.46 Jesus cried with a loud voice
27.50 Jesus cried again with a loud voice
Mk 1.26 unclean spirit, . . crying with a loud voice
5. 7 with a loud voice . . "What have you to do?
15.34 Jesus cried with a loud voice
15.37 Jesus uttered a loud cry
Lk 1.42 she exclaimed with a loud cry, "Blessed!
4.33 he cried out with a loud voice
8.28 with a loud voice, "What have you to do?
17.15 praising God with a loud voice
19.37 began to . . praise God with a loud voice
23.23 urgent, demanding with loud cries
23.46 Then Jesus, crying with a loud voice
Jn 11.43 he cried with a loud voice, "Lazarus
Acts 7.57 they cried out with a loud voice
7.60 knelt down and cried with a loud voice
8. 7 unclean spirits . . crying with a loud voice
14.10 in a loud voice, "Stand upright
16.28 Paul cried with a loud voice, "Do not harm
26.24 Festus said with a loud voice, "Paul
Rev 1.10 I heard . . a loud voice like a trumpet
5. 2 angel proclaiming with a loud voice
5.12 with a loud voice, "Worthy is the Lamb
6.10 with a loud voice, "O Sovereign Lord
7. 2 with a loud voice to the four angels
7.10 crying out with a loud voice, "Salvation
8.13 I heard an eagle crying with a loud voice
10. 3 with a loud voice, like a lion roaring
11.12 they heard a loud voice from heaven
11.15 there were loud voices in heaven
12.10 And I heard a loud voice in heaven
14. 2 a voice . . like the sound of loud thunder
14. 7 he said with a loud voice, "Fear God
14. 9 angel . . , saying with a loud voice
14.15 calling with a loud voice to him
14.18 he called with a loud voice to him
16. 1 I heard a loud voice from the temple
16.17 a loud voice came out of the temple[0]
19. 1 what seemed to be the loud voice[0]
19.17 with a loud voice he called to all the birds
21. 3 I heard a loud voice from the throne[0]
3. *many, great:* πολύς POLYS
Mt 2.18 "A voice was heard . . , and loud lamentation

LOUD NOISE, WITH A
1. *with a rushing sound:* ῥοιζηδόν RHOIZĒDON*
2 Pet 3.10 heavens will pass away with a loud noise

LOUDLY
1. *many, great:* πολύς (neut. pl.) POLYS
Mk 5.38 saw . . people weeping and wailing loudly

LOUD-MOUTHED
IDIOMATICALLY
a. Jude .16 loud-mouthed boasters καὶ τὸ στόμα αὐτῶν λαλεῖ ὑπέρογκα [STOMA; HYPEROGKOS]

LOVE
1. *love:* ἀγαπάω AGAPAŌ
Mt 5.43 "it was said, 'You shall love your neighbor
5.44 "But I say to you, Love your enemies
5.46 "For if you love those who love you, what reward have you?
6.24 "he will hate the one and love the other
19.19 "You shall love your neighbor as yourself
22.37 "You shall love the Lord your God
22.39 "You shall love your neighbor as yourself
Mk 10.21 Jesus looking upon him loved him
12.30 " 'you shall love the Lord your God
12.31 " 'You shall love your neighbor as yourself
12.33 "to love him with all the heart . . , and to love one's neighbor as oneself
Lk 6.27 "Love your enemies, do good to those
6.32 "If you love those who love you, what credit is that to you? For even sinners love those who love them
6.35 "But love your enemies, and do good
7. 5 "he loves our nation, . . built . . our synagogue
7.42 "Now which of them will love him more?
7.47 "forgiven, for she loved much; but he who is forgiven little, loves little
10.27 "You shall love the Lord your God
11.43 "you love the best seat in the synagogues
16.13 "he will hate the one and love the other
Jn 3.16 God so loved the world that he gave
3.19 men loved darkness rather than light
3.35 the Father loves the Son
8.42 "If God were your Father, you would l. me
10.17 "For this reason the Father loves me
11. 5 Jesus loved Martha and her sister
12.43 they loved the praise of men
13. 1 having loved his own who were in the world, he loved them to the end
13.23 One of his disciples, whom Jesus loved
13.34 "commandment . . that you love one another; even as I have loved you, that you also love one another
14.15 "If you love me, . . keep my commandments
14.21 "he it is who loves me; and he who loves me will be loved by my Father, and I will love him and manifest myself to him
14.23 "If a man loves me, he will keep my word, and my Father will love him
14.24 "He who does not love me does not keep
14.28 "If you loved me, you would have rejoiced
14.31 "world may know that I love the Father
15. 9 "As the Father has loved me, so have I loved you; abide in my love
15.12 "This is my commandment, that you love one another as I have loved you
15.17 "This I command you, to love one another
17.23 "thou hast sent me and hast loved them even as thou hast loved me
17.24 "which thou hast given me in thy love
17.26 "with which thou hast loved me
19.26 disciple whom he loved standing near
21. 7 That disciple whom Jesus loved
21.15 "Simon, son of John, do you love me?
21.16 "Simon, son of John, do you love me?
21.20 saw . . the disciple whom Jesus loved
Rom 8.28 God works for good[k] with those who l. him[l]
8.37 conquerors through him who loved us
9.13 "Jacob I loved, but Esau I hated
13. 8 Owe no one . . , except to love one another
13. 8 he who loves . . has fulfilled the law
13. 9 "You shall love your neighbor as yourself
1 Cor 2. 9 "God has prepared for those who love him
8. 3 if one loves God, one is known by him
2 Cor 9. 7 for God loves a cheerful giver
11.11 And why? Because I do not love you?
12.15 If I love you the more, am I to be loved the less?
Gal 2.20 faith in the Son of God, who loved me
5.14 "You shall love your neighbor as yourself
Eph 2. 4 the great love with which he loved us
5. 2 as Christ loved us and gave himself up
5.25 Husbands, love your wives, as Christ loved the church and gave himself up for her
5.28 Even so husbands should love their wives as their own bodies. He who loves his wife loves himself
5.33 let each . . love his wife as himself
6.24 Grace be with all who love our Lord J. C.
Col 3.19 Husbands, love your wives
1 Th 4. 9 taught by God to love one another
2 Th 2.16 God our Father, who loved us
2 Tim 4. 8 to all who have loved his appearing
4.10 Demas, in love with this present world
Heb 1. 9 "Thou hast loved righteousness
12. 6 "Lord disciplines him whom he loves
Jas 1.12 God has promised to those who love him
2. 5 he has promised to those who love him
2. 8 "You shall love your neighbor as yourself
1 Pet 1. 8 Without having seen[b] him you[c] love him†
1.22 love one another earnestly from the heart
2.17 Love the brotherhood. Fear God
3.10 "He that would love life and see good days
2 Pet 2.15 Balaam, . . who loved gain from wrongdoing
1 Jn 2.10 who loves his brother abides in the light
2.15 Do not love the world or the things in the world. If any one loves the world
3.10 nor he who does not love his brother
3.11 that we should love one another
3.14 into life, because we love the brethren. He who does not love abides in death
3.18 let us not love in word or speech
3.23 commandment, that we . . love one another
4. 7 Beloved, let us love one another; . . he who loves is born of God
4. 8 who does not love does not know God
4.10 not that we loved God but that he loved us and sent his Son to be the expiation
4.11 Beloved, if God so loved us, we also ought to love one another
4.12 if we love one another, God abides in us
4.19 We love, because he first loved us
4.20 If any one says, "I love God," and hates
4.20 for he who does not love his brother whom he has seen, cannot[h] love God
4.21 commandment . . that he who loves God should love his brother also
5. 1 every one who loves the parent loves the child
5. 2 we know that we love the children of God, when we love God and obey
2 Jn . 1 the elect lady . . whom I love in the truth
. 5 commandment, . . that we love one another
3 Jn . 1 Gaius, whom I love in the truth
Rev 1. 5 To him who loves us and has freed us
3. 9 " 'and learn that I have loved you
12.11 "they loved not their lives even unto death

2. *love:* ἀγάπη AGAPĒ
Mt 24.12 "most men's love will grow cold
Lk 11.42 "you . . neglect justice and the love of God
Jn 5.42 "I know that you have not the love of God
13.35 "if you have love for one another
15. 9 "abide in my love
15.10 "you will abide in my love, just as I . . abide in his love
15.13 "Greater love has no man than this
17.26 "that the love . . may be in them
Rom 5. 5 God's love has been poured into our hearts
5. 8 But God shows his love for us
8.35 Who shall separate us from the love of C.?

Rom 8.39 to separate us from the love of God
12. 9 Let love be genuine; hate what is evil
13.10 Love does no wrong to a neighbor; therefore love is the fulfilling of the law
14.15 you are no longer walking in love
15.30 I appeal to you .. by the love of the Spirit
1 Cor 4.21 Shall I come .. with love in .. gentleness?
8. 1 "Knowledge" puffs up, but l. builds up
13. 1 If I speak in .. tongues .., but have not l.
13. 2 if I have all faith .., but have not love
13. 3 if I deliver my body .., but have not love
13. 4 Love is patient and kind; love is not jealous or boastful
13. 8 Love never ends; as for prophecies
13.13 So faith, hope, love abide, these three; but the greatest of these is love
14. 1 Make l. your aim, and .. desire .. gifts
16.14 Let all that you do be done in love
16.24 My love be with you all in Christ Jesus
2 Cor 2. 4 the abundant love that I have for you
2. 8 I beg you to reaffirm your love for him
5.14 For the love of Christ controls us
6. 6 kindness, the Holy Spirit, genuine love
8. 7 as you excel .. in your love for us
8. 8 to prove .. that your love also is genuine
8.24 give proof .. of your love and .. our boasting
13.11 God of love and peace will be with you
13.14(13) grace of the Lord .. and the love of God
Gal 5. 6 but faith working[z] through love
5.13 through love be servants of one another
5.22 fruit of the Spirit is love, joy, peace
Eph 1. 5(4) He destined us in love[b] to be his sons
1.15 your faith in the Lord Jesus and your love[c]‡
2. 4 rich in mercy, out of the great love
3.17 you, being rooted and grounded in love
3.19 to know the love of Christ
4. 2 patience, forbearing one another in love
4.15 Rather, speaking the truth in love
4.16 the whole body .. upbuilds itself in love
5. 2 walk in love, as Christ loved us
6.23 love with faith, from God the Father
Phil 1. 9 that your love may abound more
1.16 The latter do it out of love
2. 1 So if there is .. any incentive of love
2. 2 having the same love, being in full accord
Col 1. 4 the love which you have for all the saints
1. 8 made known to us your love in the Spirit
2. 2 as they are knit together in love
3.14 above all these put on love
1 Th 1. 3 remembering .. your .. labor of love
3. 6 the good news of your faith and love
3.12 abound in love to one another
5. 8 put on the breastplate of faith and love
5.13 to esteem them very highly in love
2 Th 1. 3 love of every one of you for one another
2.10 they refused to love the truth
3. 5 direct your hearts to the love of God
1 Tim 1. 5 whereas the aim of our charge is love
1.14 grace of our Lord overflowed .. with .. love
2.15 continues[d] in faith and love and holiness
4.12 set the believers an example .. in love
6.11 aim at righteousness, godliness, faith, love
2 Tim 1. 7 spirit of power and love and self-control
1.13 faith and l. which are in Christ Jesus
2.22 aim at righteousness, faith, love
3.10 you have observed .. my patience, my love
Tit 2. 2 Bid the older men be .. sound in faith, in l.
Phm . 5 because I hear of your love
. 7 I have .. much .. comfort from your love
. 9 yet for love's sake I prefer to appeal
Heb 6.10 the love which you showed for his sake
10.24 how to stir up one another to love
1 Pet 4. 8 Above all hold unfailing your love .., since love covers a multitude of sins
5.14 Greet one another with the kiss of love
2 Pet 1. 7 ⟨supplement⟩ brotherly affection with love
1 Jn 2. 5 in him truly love for God is perfected
1 Jn 2.15 love for the Father is not in him
3. 1 See what love the Father has given us
3.16 we know love, that he laid down his life
3.17 how does God's love abide in him?
4. 7 for love is of God
4. 8 does not know God; for God is love
4. 9 the love of God was made manifest
4.10 In this is love, .. God .. sent his Son
4.12 God abides in us and his love is perfected
4.16 we know and believe the love God has for us. God is love, and he who abides in love abides in God
4.17 In this is love perfected with us
4.18 There is no fear in love, but perfect love casts out fear .. and he who fears is not perfected in love
5. 3 For this is the love of God
2 Jn . 3 peace will be with us .. in truth and love
. 6 this is love, .. follow his commandments
3 Jn . 6 testified to your love before the church
Jude . 2 mercy, peace, and love be multiplied
.21 keep yourselves in the love of God
Rev 2. 4 " 'you have abandoned the love you had
2.19 " 'I know your works, your love

3. *love, like:* φιλέω PHILEŌ
Mt 6. 5 "hypocrites .. love to stand and pray
10.37 "who loves father or mother more than me
10.37 "who loves son or daughter more than me
23. 6 "they love the place of honor at feasts
Lk 20.46 "the scribes, who .. love salutations
Jn 5.20 "For the Father loves the Son
11. 3 "Lord, he whom you love is ill
11.36 the Jews said, "See how he loved him!
12.25 "He who loves his life loses it
15.19 "the world would love its own
16.27 "the Father himself loves you, because you have loved me and have believed
20. 2 other disciple, the one whom Jesus loved
21.15 "Yes, Lord; you know that I love you
21.16 "Yes, Lord; you know that I love you
21.17 "Simon, son of John, do you love me?
21.17 the third time, "Do you love me?
21.17 "you know that I love you
1 Cor 16.22 If any one has no love for the Lord
Tit 3.15 Greet those who love us in the faith
Rev 3.19 " 'Those whom I love, I reprove
22.15 one who loves and practices falsehood

4. *dearly loving toward:* φιλόστοργος εἰς PHILOSTORGOS [A.3.e.2]
Rom 12.10 love one another with brotherly affection

CONTEXTUALLY
1 Cor 13. 5 Love does not insist on its own way
13. 7 Love bears all things, believes all things
1 Th 4.10 indeed you do love all the brethren

LOVE, BROTHERLY

1. *brotherly love:* φιλαδελφία PHILADELPHIA
Heb 13. 1 Let brotherly love continue

LOVE FEAST

1. *love:* ἀγάπη AGAPĒ
2 Pet [2.13 reveling in their *love feasts*‡
Jude .12 These are blemishes[d] on your l. feasts

LOVE OF MONEY

1. *love of money:* φιλαργυρία PHILARGYRIA*
1 Tim 6.10 love of money is the root of all evils

LOVE OF MONEY, FREE FROM

1. *not loving money:* ἀφιλάργυρος APHILARGYROS
Heb 13. 5 Keep your life free from love of money

LOVE OF THE BRETHREN

1. *brotherly love:* φιλαδελφία PHILADELPHIA
1 Th 4. 9 concerning love of the brethren
1 Pet 1.22 for a sincere love of the brethren

LOVE OF THE BRETHREN, HAVE

1. *loving one's brother:* φιλάδελφος PHILADELPHOS* [A.3.e.2]
1 Pet 3. 8 have .. sympathy, love of the brethren

LOVE ONE'S CHILDREN
1. *loving one's children:* φιλότεκνος PHILOTEKNOS* [B.3.a.1]
Tit 2. 4 train . . young women to love their . . children

LOVE ONE'S HUSBAND
1. *loving one's husband:* φίλανδρος PHILANDROS* [B.3.a.1]
Tit 2. 4 train . . young women to love their husbands

LOVELY
1. *pleasing:* προσφιλής PROSPHILĒS*
Phil 4. 8 whatever is lovely, whatever is gracious

LOVER OF GOD
1. *loving God, pious:* φιλόθεος (subst.) PHILOTHEOS*
2 Tim 3. 4 lovers of pleasure rather than lovers of God

LOVER OF GOODNESS
1. *loving goodness:* φιλάγαθος (subst.) PHILAGATHOS*
Tit 1. 8 a lover of goodness, master of himself

LOVER OF MONEY
1. *fond of money:* φιλάργυρος (subst.) PHILARGYROS*
Lk 16.14 "Pharisees, who were lovers of money
2 Tim 3. 2 men will be lovers of self, lovers of money

LOVER OF MONEY, NO
1. *not loving money:* ἀφιλάργυρος (subst.) APHILARGYROS
1 Tim 3. 3 not quarrelsome, and no lover of money

LOVER OF PLEASURE
1. *fond of pleasure:* φιλήδονος (subst.) PHILĒDONOS*
2 Tim 3. 4 lovers of pleasure rather than lovers of God

LOVER OF SELF
1. *loving oneself, selfish:* φίλαυτος (subst.) PHILAUTOS*
2 Tim 3. 2 men will be lovers of self, lovers of money

LOVES, WHOM ONE
1. *beloved:* ἀγαπητός (attr.) AGAPĒTOS
Phil 4. 1 my brethren, whom I love and long for

LOVING KINDNESS
1. *humanity, benevolence:* φιλανθρωπία PHILANTHRŌPIA
Tit 3. 4 the goodness and loving kindness of God

LOW
1. *unborn, ignoble:* ἀγενής AGENĒS*
1 Cor 1.28 God chose what is low and despised

LOW, BRING
1. *lower, humble:* ταπεινόω TAPEINOŌ
Lk 3. 5 "every mountain . . shall be brought low

LOW DEGREE, OF
1. *low, poor, humble:* ταπεινός TAPEINOS
Lk 1.52 "he has . . exalted those of low degree

LOW ESTATE
1. *humiliation, low estate:* ταπείνωσις TAPEINŌSIS
Lk 1.48 "regarded the low estate of his handmaiden

LOWER
1. *slacken, let down:* χαλάω CHALAŌ
Acts 9.25 let him down . . , lowering him in a basket
27.17 they lowered the gear, and so were driven
27.30 sailors . . lowered the boat into the sea
2. *lower:* κατώτερος KATŌTEROS*
Eph 4. 9 ("had also descended into the lower parts

LOWER, MAKE
1. *make less:* ἐλαττόω ELATTOŌ
Heb 2. 7 "didst make him . . lower than the angels
2. 9 Jesus . . was made lower than the angels

LOWEST
1. *last, extreme:* ἔσχατος ESCHATOS
Lk 14. 9 "you will begin . . to take the lowest place
14.10 "go and sit in the lowest place

LOWLINESS
1. *humility:* ταπεινοφροσύνη TAPEINOPHROSYNĒ
Eph 4. 2 with all lowliness and meekness
Col 3.12 kindness, lowliness, meekness

LOWLY
1. *low, poor, humble:* ταπεινός TAPEINOS
Mt 11.29 "for I am gentle and lowly in heart
Rom 12.16 associate with the lowly[a]†
Jas 1. 9 Let the l. brother boast in his exaltation
2. *humiliation, low estate:* ταπείνωσις (gen.) TAPEINŌSIS
Phil 3.21 who will change our lowly body

LOYAL
1. *faithful, trustworthy:* πιστός PISTOS
3 Jn . 5 Beloved, it is a loyal thing you do

LUCIUS: Λούκιος 'lüshəs
Acts 13. 1 Lucius of Cyrene, Manaen
Rom 16.21 so do Lucius and Jason and Sosipater

LUKE: Λουκᾶς 'lük
Col 4.14 Luke the beloved physician and Demas
2 Tim 4.11 Luke alone is with me
Phm .24 Demas, and Luke, my fellow workers

LUKEWARM
1. *warm, lukewarm:* χλιαρός CHLIAROS*
Rev 3.16 " 'lukewarm, and neither cold nor hot

LUMP
1. *what is mixed, dough:* φύραμα PHYRAMA*
Rom 9.21 clay, to make out of the same lump
11.16 If the dough . . is holy, so is the . . lump
1 Cor 5. 6 a little leaven leavens the whole lump
5. 7 Cleanse . . that you may be a new lump
Gal 5. 9 A little leaven leavens the whole lump

LURE
1. *draw, drag out:* ἐξέλκω EXELKŌ*
Jas 1.14 when . . lured and enticed by his own desire

LUST
1. *desire, yearning:* ἐπιθυμία EPITHYMIA
Rom 1.24 God gave them up in the lusts
Eph 4.22 nature . . corrupt through deceitful lusts
1 Th 4. 5 not in the passion of lust like heathen
1 Jn 2.16 all that is in the world, the lust of the flesh and the lust of the eyes
2.17 the world passes away, and the lust of it

IDIOMATICALLY
a. 2 Pet 2.10 those who indulge in the lust of defiling passion *τοὺς ὀπίσω σαρκὸς ἐν ἐπιθυμίᾳ μιασμοῦ πορευομένους* [SARX]
b. Jude .7 and indulged in unnatural lust *καὶ ἀπελθοῦσαι ὀπίσω σαρκὸς ἑτέρας* [SARX]

LUSTFULLY
1. *desire, long for:* ἐπιθυμέω EPITHYMEŌ [B.2.a.1]
Mt 5.28 "every one who looks at a woman lustfully

LUXURY
1. *softness, indulgence:* τρυφή TRYPHĒ
Lk 7.25 those who . . live in l. are in kings' courts

LUXURY, LIVE IN
1. *live softly, be licentious:* τρυφάω TRYPHAŌ*
Jas 5. 5 You have lived on the earth in luxury

LYCAONIA: Λυκαονία ˌlikā'ōnēə II,F-3
Acts 14. 6 Lystra and Derbe, cities of Lycaonia

LYCAONIAN: Λυκαονιστί
Acts 14.11 they lifted up their voices, saying in L.

LYCIA: Λυκία 'lish(ē)ə II,E-3
Acts 27. 5 we came to Myra in Lycia

LYDDA: Λύδδα 'lidə I,B-5
Acts 9.32 to the saints that lived at Lydda
9.35 all the residents of Lydda and Sharon
9.38 Since Lydda was near Joppa

LYDIA: Λυδία 'lidēə
Acts 16.14 One who heard us was a woman named L.
16.40 So they went out . . and visited Lydia

LYSANIAS: Λυσανίας lī'sānēəs
Lk 3. 1 Lysanias tetrarch of Abilene

LYSIAS
LYSIAS, CLAUDIUS: Κλαύδιος Λυσίας 'klôdēəs 'lisēəs
Acts 23.26 "Claudius Lysias to his Excellency
[24. 7 "*chief captain Lysias came and . . took him*‡
24.22 "When Lysias the tribune comes down

LYSTRA: Λύστρα 'listrə II,F-3
[a]pl.
Acts 14. 6 they . . fled to Lystra and Derbe
14. 8 [a]Now at Lystra there was a man
14.21 they returned to Lystra and to Iconium

Acts 16. 1 he came also to Derbe and to Lystra
16. 2 [a]well spoken of . . at Lystra and Iconium
2 Tim 3.11 [a]what befell me . . at Lystra

M

MAATH: Μάαθ 'māəth
Lk 3.26 Maath, the son of Mattathias

MACEDONIA: Μακεδονία ˌmasə'dōnēə II,D-2
Acts 16. 9 saying, "Come over to M. and help us
16.10 immediately we sought to go on into M.
16.12 Philippi, which is the leading city . . of M.
18. 5 When Silas and Timothy arrived from M.
19.21 Paul resolved . . to pass through M.
19.22 having sent into M. two of his helpers
20. 1 Paul . . took leave . . and departed for M.
20. 3 he determined to return through M.
Rom 15.26 For M. and Achaia have been pleased
1 Cor 16. 5 I will visit you after passing through M., for I intend to pass through M.
2 Cor 1.16 I wanted to visit you on my way to M., and to come back to you from M.
2.13 I took leave of them and went on to M.
7. 5 For even when we came into M.
8. 1 grace of God . . shown in the churches of M.
11. 9 needs were supplied by . . brethren . . from M.
Phil 4.15 in the beginning . . , when I left M.
1 Th 1. 7 an example to all the believers in M.
1. 8 word . . sounded forth from you in M.
4.10 you . . love all the brethren throughout M.
1 Tim 1. 3 As I urged you when I was going to M.

MACEDONIA, OF
MACEDONIAN
1. *Macedonian:* Μακεδών
Acts 16. 9 a man of M. was standing beseeching
19.29 Gaius and Aristarchus, Macedonians
27. 2 accompanied by Aristarchus, a M.
2 Cor 9. 2 I boast about you to the people of M.
9. 4 lest if some Macedonians come with me

MAD
IDIOMATICALLY
a. Acts 26.24 "your great learning is turning you mad τὰ πολλά σε γράμματα εἰς μανίαν περιτρέπει [MANIA*]

MAD, BE
1. *rage, be mad:* μαίνομαι MAINOMAI*
Jn 10.20 "He has a demon, and he is mad
Acts 12.15 They said to her, "You are mad
26.24 Festus said . . "Paul, you are mad
26.25 Paul said, "I am not mad
1 Cor 14.23 will they not say that you are mad?

MADE
MADE, BE
1. *be:* εἰμί EIMI
1 Cor 11. 8 (For man was not made from woman
2. *come to be, happen, be:* γίνομαι GINOMAI
[a]part.
Mt 9.16 "and a worse tear is made
Mk 2.21 "and a worse tear is made
2.27 "The sabbath was made for man
Lk 8.17 "nothing . . that shall not be made manifest
Jn 1. 3 all things were made through him, and without him was not anything made that was made†
1.10 the world was made through him
8.33 "How is it . . 'You will be made free'?
Acts 12. 5 earnest prayer for him was made to God
14. 5 attempt was made by . . Gentiles and Jews
19.26 [a]gods made with hands are not gods
20. 3 plot was made against him by the Jews
26. 6 [a]"for hope in the promise made by God
1 Cor 16. 2 so that contributions need not be made
Eph 3. 7 Of this gospel I was made a minister
Heb 5. 5 not exalt himself to be made a high priest
11. 3 what is seen was made out of things
Jas 3. 9 who are made in the likeness of God

MADE BY HANDS
MADE BY MAN
MADE WITH HANDS
1. *made by hands:* χειροποίητος CHEIROPOIĒTOS*
Mk 14.58 " 'this temple that is made with hands
Acts 7.48 "does not dwell in houses made with hands
17.24 "God . . does not live in shrines made by man
Eph 2.11 circumcision, which is made . . by hands
Heb 9.11 more perfect tent[p] (not made with hands
9.24 not into a sanctuary made with hands

MADE, THINGS THAT HAVE BEEN
1. *anything made, creation:* ποίημα (pl.) POIĒMA
Rom 1.20 perceived in the things that have been m.

MADE WITH HANDS, NOT
MADE WITHOUT HANDS
1. *not made by hands:* ἀχειροποίητος ACHEIROPOIĒTOS*
Mk 14.58 " 'I will build another, not made with hands
2 Cor 5. 1 a house not made with hands, eternal
Col 2.11 a circumcision made without hands

MADMAN, LIKE A
1. *be beside oneself:* παραφρονέω (pred. part.) PARAPHRONEŌ*
2 Cor 11.23 I am talking like a madman

MADNESS
1. *wandering of mind:* παραφρονία PARAPHRONIA*
2 Pet 2.16 ass . . restrained the prophet's madness

MAGADAN: Μαγαδάν 'magəˌdan
[a]Μαγεδᾶ(ν)
Mt 15.39 he . . went to the region of Magadan
Mk [8.10 [a]he . . went to the district of *Magadan*‡

MAGDALA: Μαγδαλά 'magdələ I,D-3
Mk [8.10 he . . went to the district of *Magdala*‡

MAGDALENE: Μαγδαληνή 'magdəˌlēn
Mt 27.56 among whom were Mary M., and Mary
27.61 Mary M. and the other Mary were there
28. 1 Mary M. and the other Mary went to see
Mk 15.40 Mary M., and Mary the mother of James
15.47 Mary M. and Mary the mother of Joses
16. 1 Mary M., Mary the mother of James
16. 9 when he rose . . he appeared first to Mary M.[k]‡
Lk 8. 2 Mary, called M., from whom seven demons
24.10 Now it was Mary M. and Joanna
Jn 19.25 Mary the wife of Clopas, and Mary M.
20. 1 on the first day of the week Mary M.
20.18 Mary M. went and said to the disciples

MAGIC
1. *magic:* μαγεία MAGEIA*
Acts 8.11 he had amazed them with his magic

MAGIC ARTS
1. *meddlesome, curious:* περίεργος (subst. pl.) PERIERGOS
Acts 19.19 those who practiced magic arts

MAGIC, PRACTICE
1. *use magic arts:* μαγεύω MAGEUŌ*
Acts 8. 9 Simon who . . previously practiced magic

MAGICIAN
1. *Magus, magician:* μάγος MAGOS
Acts 13. 6 they came upon a certain magician
13. 8 Elymas the magician . . withstood them

MAGISTRATE
1. *ruler:* ἄρχων ARCHŌN
Lk 12.58 "As you go with your accuser before the m.
2. *leader, magistrate:* στρατηγός STRATĒGOS
Acts 16.20 brought them to the magistrates
16.22 magistrates tore the garments off them
16.35 the magistrates sent the police
16.36 "magistrates have sent to let you go
16.38 reported these words to the magistrates

MAGNIFICENCE
1. *majesty, greatness:* μεγαλειότης MEGALEIOTĒS
Acts 19.27 "she may even be deposed from her m.

MAGNIFY
1. *extol, honor:* δοξάζω DOXAZŌ
Rom 11.13 as . . apostle . . , I magnify my ministry
2. *make large, extol:* μεγαλύνω MEGALYNŌ
Lk 1.46 Mary said, "My soul magnifies the Lord

MAGOG: Μαγώγ 'mā,gäg
Rev 20. 8 Gog and Magog, to gather them for battle

MAHALALEEL: Μαλελεήλ mə'halə,lēl
Lk 3.37 Jared, the son of M., the son of Cainan

MAID
1. *female slave:* παιδίσκη PAIDISKĒ
Mt 26.69 maid . . said, "You also were with Jesus
Mk 14.66 one of the maids of the high priest
14.69 maid . . began . . to say . . "This man is one
Lk 22.56 maid . . said, "This man also was with him
Jn 18.17 maid . . said . . "Are not you also one?
Acts 12.13 a maid named Rhoda came to answer
CONTEXTUALLY
Mt 26.71 when he went . . another maid saw him

MAID WHO KEEPS THE DOOR
1. *doorkeeper:* θυρωρός (fem.) THYRŌROS
Jn 18.16 spoke to the maid who kept the door

MAIDEN
1. *maiden, girl:* παρθένος PARTHENOS
Mt 25. 1 "ten maidens who took their lamps
25. 7 "maidens rose and trimmed their lamps
25.11 "maidens came also, saying, 'Lord, lord

MAIDSERVANT
1. *bondwoman, female slave:* δούλη DOULĒ
Acts 2.18 " 'my maidservants in those days
2. *female slave:* παιδίσκη PAIDISKĒ
Lk 12.45 "begins to beat . . the maidservants

MAIMED
1. *mutilated:* ἀνάπηρος ANAPĒROS*
Lk 14.13 "invite the poor, the maimed
14.21 " 'bring in the poor and maimed
2. *deformed:* κυλλός KYLLOS*
Mt 15.30 the lame, the maimed, the blind
15.31 they saw . . the maimed whole
18. 8 "it is better for you to enter life maimed
Mk 9.43 "it is better for you to enter life maimed

MAINTAIN
1. *have, hold:* ἔχω ECHŌ
1 Pet 2.12 M. good conduct among the Gentiles
2. *hold fast, restrain:* κατέχω KATECHŌ
1 Cor 11. 2 maintain the traditions even as I have
3. *keep, observe:* τηρέω TĒREŌ
Eph 4. 3 eager to maintain the unity of the Spirit

MAJESTIC
1. *magnificent:* μεγαλοπρεπής MEGALOPREPĒS*
2 Pet 1.17 voice . . borne to him by the M. Glory

MAJESTY
1. *majesty, greatness:* μεγαλειότης MEGALEIOTĒS
Lk 9.43 all were astonished at the majesty of God
2 Pet 1.16 we were eyewitnesses of his majesty
2. *majesty, greatness:* μεγαλωσύνη MEGALŌSYNĒ*
Heb 1. 3 at the right hand of the M. on high
8. 1 at the right hand of . . the M. in heaven
Jude .25 to the only God . . be glory, majesty

MAJORITY
1. *more:* πλείων (subst. pl.) PLEIŌN
Acts 27.12 the m. advised to put to sea from there
2 Cor 2. 6 this punishment by the majority is enough

MAKE (*See also, e.g.,* ANSWER, MAKE; CLEAN, MAKE)
1. *compel:* ἀναγκάζω ANAGKAZŌ
[a]imperf.
Mt 14.22 he made the disciples get into the boat
Mk 6.45 he made his disciples get into the boat
Acts 26.11 [a]"I . . tried to make them blaspheme
2. *arrange:* διατίθημι (mid.) DIATITHEMI
Heb 8.10 "covenant that I will make with . . Israel
9.16 the death of the one who made it
9.17 as long as the one who made it is alive
10.16 "the covenant that I will make with them
3. *give:* δίδωμι DIDŌMI
Lk 12.58 "make an effort to settle with him
Eph 1.22 he . . has made him the head over all things
Rev 3. 9 " 'I will m. those of the synagogue . . come
4. *be:* εἰμί EIMI [A.6.a.5]
Mk 12.42 two copper coins, which make a penny
1 Cor 12.15 that would not make it any less a part
12.16 that would not make it any less a part
5. *say, speak:* εἶπον EIPON [A.6.a.6]
Acts 28.25 after Paul had made one statement
6. *say, speak:* ἐρῶ ERŌ [A.6.a.6]
Gal 3.16 promises were made to Abraham
7. *go out:* ἔξειμι EXEIMI
Acts 27.43 ordered those . . to . . make for the land
8. *come to be, happen, be:* γίνομαι GINOMAI [A.6.e]
1 Cor 1.30 Christ Jesus, whom God made our wisdom
Heb 7.22 This makes Jesus the surety of a better
9. *put in order, make:* καταρτίζω KATARTIZŌ
Rom 9.22 vessels of wrath made for destruction
10. *set in order, appoint:* καθίστημι KATHISTĒMI
Lk 12.14 "Man, who made me a judge or divider?
Acts 7.10 "Pharaoh . . , who made him governor
7.27 " 'Who made you a ruler . . over us?
7.35 " 'Who made you a ruler and a judge?
Rom 5.19 as by one . . many were made sinners, so by one . . many will be made righteous
Jas 4. 4 makes himself an enemy of God
11. *gain:* κερδαίνω KERDAINŌ
Mt 25.16 "and he made five talents more
25.17 "So also, he . . made two talents more
25.20 " 'here I have made five talents more
25.22 " 'here I have made two talents more
12. *do, make:* ποιέω (act. or mid.) POIEŌ
Mt 3. 3 "Prepare the way . . , make his paths straight
4.19 "I will make you fishers of men
5.32 "who divorces . . makes her an adulteress
5.36 "you cannot make one hair white or black
12.16 ordered them not to make him known
12.33 "make the tree good, and its fruit good; or make the tree bad, and its fruit bad
17. 4 "if you wish, I will make three booths
19. 4 "he who made them from the beginning made them male and female
[19. 9 "*makes her commit adultery*‡
20.12 " 'you have made them equal to us
21.13 "but you make it a den of robbers
23.15 "to make a single proselyte, and . . you make him twice as much a child of hell[w]
Mk 1. 3 "Prepare the way . . , make his paths straight
1.17 "I will make you become fishers of men
2.23 One sabbath . . as they made their way
3.12 he . . ordered them not to make him known
7.37 "he even makes the deaf hear
9. 5 "let us make three booths, one for you
10. 6 " 'God made them male and female
11.17 "you have made it a den of robbers
Lk 3. 4 "Prepare the way . . , make his paths straight
5.29 Levi made him a great feast
5.34 "Can you make wedding guests fast?
9.15 And they . . made them all sit down
9.33 "let us make three booths, one for you
11.40 "You fools! Did not he who made the outside make the inside also?
16. 9 "I tell you, make friends for yourselves
19.18 " 'your pound has made five pounds
19.46 " you have made it a den of robbers
Jn 2.15 making a whip of cords, he drove them
2.16 "you shall not make my Father's house
4. 1 Jesus was making . . more disciples than John
4.46 where he had made the water wine
5.18 making himself equal with God
6.10 Jesus said, "Make the people sit down
6.15 to . . take him by force to make him king
7.23 "I made a man's whole body well
9. 6 he spat on the ground and made clay
9.11 "Jesus made clay and anointed my eyes
9.14 a sabbath . . when Jesus made the clay

Jn 10.33 "you, being a man, make yourself God
12. 2 There they made him a supper
14.23 "come to him and make our home with him
18.18 officers had made a charcoal fire
19. 7 "he has made himself the Son of God
19.12 "every one who makes himself a king
19.23 took his garments and made four parts
Acts 2.36 "God has made him both Lord and Christ
3.12 "as though . . we had made him walk
4.24 "Lord, who didst make the heaven
7.40 " 'Make for us gods to go before us
7.43 " 'the figures which you made to worship
7.44 "even as he . . directed him to make it
7.50 " 'Did not my hand make all these things?
8. 2 Devout men . . made great lamentation
9.39 other garments which Dorcas made
14.15 "a living God who made the heaven
15.18(17) " 'who has made these things known
17.24 "The God who made the world
17.26 "he made from one every nation of men
19.24 Demetrius . . made silver shrines of Artemis
23.12 Jews made a plot and bound themselves
23.13 more than forty who made this conspiracy
25.17 "I made no delay, but on the next day
26.28 "you think to make me a Christian!
Rom 9.20 "Why have you made me thus?
9.21 right . . to make out of the same lump
13.14 make no provision for the flesh
15.26 pleased to make some contribution
1 Cor 6.15 and make them members of a prostitute
2 Cor 5.21 For our sake he made him to be sin
Eph 2.14 our peace, who has made us both one
2.15 create . . one new man . . , so making peace
4.16 the whole body . . makes bodily growth
Phil 1. 4 making my prayer with joy
1 Tim 2. 1 I urge that . . thanksgivings be made for all
Heb 1. 3 When he had made purification for sins
1. 7 "Who makes his angels winds
8. 5 "make everything according to the pattern
8. 9 "covenant that I made with their fathers
12.13 make straight paths for your feet
12.27 what is shaken, as of what has been made
Jas 3.18 sown in peace by those who make peace
1 Jn 1.10 If we say we have not . . , we make him a liar
5.10 He who does not . . has made him a liar
Rev 1. 6 made us a kingdom, priests to his God
3. 9 " 'I will m. ⟨those of . . synagogue⟩ come
3.12 " 'I will make him a pillar in the temple
5.10 "⟨thou⟩ hast made them a kingdom
11. 7 the beast . . will make war upon them
12.17 the dragon . . went off to make war
13. 7 it was allowed to make war on the saints‡
13.12 It . . makes the earth . . worship the first beast
13.13 great signs, even making fire come down
13.14 bidding them make an image for the beast
14. 7 "worship him who made heaven
17.16 "they will make her desolate and naked
19.19 armies gathered to make war against
21. 5 "Behold, I make all things new

13. *spread:* στρωννύω STRŌNNYŌ
Acts 9.34 "rise and make your bed

14. *lay, put:* τίθημι (act. or mid.) TITHĒMI
Lk 20.43 " 'till I make thy enemies a stool
Acts 2.35 " 'till I make thy enemies a stool
20.28 "the Holy Spirit has made you overseers
Rom 4.17 "I have made you . . father of many nations
1 Cor 9.18 that . . I may make the gospel free
Heb 1.13 "till I make thy enemies a stool for thy feet
10.13 until his enemies should be made a stool
2 Pet 2. 6 he . . made them an example to those

IDIOMATICALLY
a. Acts 10.40 "and made him manifest καὶ ἔδωκεν αὐτὸν ἐμφανῆ γενέσθαι [DIDŌMI; GINOMAI]
b. 1 Tim 5.4 and make some return to their parents καὶ ἀμοιβὰς ἀποδιδόναι τοῖς προγόνοις [APODIDŌMI]
c. 1 Jn 5.15 we . . obtained the requests made of him ἔχομεν τὰ αἰτήματα ἃ ᾐτήκαμεν ἀπ' αὐτοῦ [AITEŌ]

MAKE FOR
1. *hold fast, restrain:* κατέχω KATECHŌ
Acts 27.40 then . . they made for the beach

MAKE MORE
1. *earn in addition:* προσεργάζομαι PROSERGAZOMAI*
Lk 19.16 " 'your pound has made ten pounds more

MAKE PEACE
1. *make peace:* εἰρηνοποιέω EIRĒNOPOIEŌ*
Col 1.20 making peace by the blood of his cross

MAKE READY
1. *make preparations:* ἐπισκευάζομαι EPISKEUAZOMAI*
Acts 21.15 After these days we made ready

MAKE SIGNS
1. *nod, beckon:* διανεύω DIANEUŌ*
Lk 1.22 he made signs . . and remained dumb
2. *nod, make signs:* ἐννεύω ENNEUŌ*
Lk 1.62 they made signs to his father

MAKE STRAIGHT
1. *set up again, correct:* ἀνορθόω ANORTHOŌ
Lk 13.13 immediately she was made straight
2. *make straight, direct:* εὐθύνω EUTHYNŌ
Jn 1.23 " 'Make straight the way of the Lord

MAKE UP
1. *fill up:* ἀναπληρόω ANAPLĒROŌ
1 Cor 16.17 they have made up for your absence
IDIOMATICALLY
a. 2 Cor 9.7 Each one must do as he has made up his mind ἕκαστος καθὼς προῄρηται τῇ καρδίᾳ [PROAIREŌ*]

MAKE WELL
1. *save, preserve:* διασῴζω DIASŌZŌ
Mt 14.36 as many as touched it were made well
2. *save, keep from harm:* σῴζω SŌZŌ
Mt 9.21 "If I only touch . . , I shall be made well
9.22 "your faith has made you well." And instantly the woman was made well
Mk 5.23 "Come . . , so that she may be made well
5.28 "If I touch . . , I shall be made well
5.34 "your faith has made you well
6.56 as many as touched it were made w.
10.52 "Go . . ; your faith has made you well
Lk 8.48 "your faith has made you well; go
17.19 "Rise and go . . ; your faith has made you w.
18.42 "your faith has made you well
Acts 14. 9 he had faith to be made well

MAKER
1. *maker, creator:* δημιουργός DĒMIOURGOS*
Heb 11.10 city . . whose builder and maker is God

MALCHUS: Μάλχος 'malkəs
Jn 18.10 The slave's name was Malchus

MALCONTENT
1. *faultfinding:* μεμψίμοιρος MEMPSIMOIROS*
Jude .16 These are grumblers, malcontents

MALE
1. *male:* ἄρσην ARSĒN
Mt 19. 4 "from the beginning . . male and female
Mk 10. 6 " 'God made them male and female
Lk 2.23 "Every male that opens the womb
Gal 3.28 there is neither male nor female
Rev 12. 5 she brought forth a male child
12.13 the woman who had borne the male child

MALE CHILD
1. *child, servant:* παῖς PAIS
Mt 2.16 he sent and killed all the male children

MALICE
1. *badness:* κακία KAKIA
Rom 1.29 filled with all manner of . . malice
1 Cor 5. 8 the leaven of malice and evil
Eph 4.31 put away from you, with all malice
Col 3. 8 wrath, malice, slander, and foul talk
Tit 3. 3 passing our days in malice and envy
1 Pet 2. 1 put away all malice and all guile
2. *wickedness:* πονηρία PONĒRIA
Mt 22.18 But Jesus, aware of their malice

MALIGN
CONTEXTUALLY
Mt 10.25 "how much more will they malign those

MALIGNITY
1. *bad disposition, malignity:* κακοήθεια KAKOĒTHEIA*
Rom 1.29 strife, deceit, malignity, they are gossips

MALTA: Μελίτη 'mȯltə II,B-3
Acts 28 1 we . . learned that the island was called M.

MAMMON
1. *wealth* (Aram.): μαμωνᾶς MAMŌNAS*
Mt 6.24 "You cannot serve God and mammon[x]
Lk 16. 9 "by means of unrighteous mammon[a]
16.11 " 'not . . faithful in the unrighteous mammon[a]
16.13 "You cannot serve God and mammon[a]

MAN (*See also, e.g.,* EACH MAN; GREAT MAN; YOUNG MAN)
1. *man, husband:* ἀνήρ ANĒR
Mt 7.24 "like a wise man who built his house
7.26 "like a foolish man who built his house
12.41 "men of Nineveh will arise at the judgment
14.21 about five thousand men, besides women
14.35 when the men of that place recognized
15.38 Those who ate were four thousand men
Mk 6.20 he was a righteous and holy man
6.44 those who ate . . were five thousand men
10. 2 "Is it lawful for a man to divorce?
Lk 1.27 betrothed to a man whose name was Joseph
5. 8 "Depart from me, for I am a sinful man
5.12 there came a man full of leprosy
5.18 behold, men were bringing on a bed
6. 8 the man who had the withered hand
7.20 when the men had come to him
8.27 there met him a man from the city
8.38 man from whom the demons had gone
8.41 there came a man named Jairus
9.14 there were about five thousand men
9.30 behold, two men talked with him
9.32 the two men who stood with him
9.38 behold, a man from the crowd cried
11.31 "will arise . . with the men of this generation
11.32 "men of Nineveh will arise at the judgment
14.24 " 'none of those men who were invited
19. 2 there was a man named Zacchaeus
19. 7 "He has gone in to be the guest of a man
22.63 men who were holding Jesus mocked him
23.50 there was a man named Joseph . . , a good and righteous man
24. 4 behold, two men stood by them
Jn 1.13 nor of the will of man, but of God
1.30 " 'After me . . a man who ranks before me
6.10 the men sat down, . . about five thousand
Acts 1.10 two men stood by them in white robes
1.11 "Men of Galilee, why do you stand?
1.21 "one of the men who have accompanied
2. 5 devout men from every nation
2.14 "Men of Judea and all . . in Jerusalem
2.22 "Men of Israel, hear these words: Jesus of Nazareth, a man attested
3. 2 man lame from birth was being carried
3.12 "Men of Israel, why do you wonder at this?
4. 4 the men came to about five thousand
5. 1 a man named Ananias with his wife
5.14 multitudes both of men and women
5.25 "The men whom you put in prison
5.35 "Men of Israel, take care what you do
5.36 "a number of men, about four hundred
6. 3 "pick out from among you seven men
6. 5 they chose Stephen, a man full of faith
6.11 they secretly instigated men
7.26 " 'Men, . . why do you wrong each other?
8. 2 Devout men buried Stephen
8. 3 he dragged off men and women
8. 9 there was a man named Simon
8.12 baptized, both men and women
9. 2 any belonging to the Way, men or women
Acts 9. 7 men who were traveling with him
9.12 "he has seen a man named Ananias
9.13 "Lord, I have heard . . about this man
9.38 disciples . . sent two men . . entreating
10. 1 there was a man named Cornelius
10. 5 "send men to Joppa, and bring one Simon
10.17 men that were sent by Cornelius
10.19 "Behold, three men are looking for you
10.21 Peter went down to the men
10.22 "an upright and God-fearing man
10.30 "behold, a man stood before me
11. 3 "Why did you go to uncircumcised men?
11.11 "At that very moment three men arrived
11.12 "we entered the man's house
11.20 some of them, men of Cyprus
11.24 a good man, full of the Holy Spirit
13. 7 Sergius Paulus, a man of intelligence
13.16 "Men of Israel, and you that fear God
13.21 "Saul . . , a man of the tribe of Benjamin
13.22 " 'David . . a man after my heart
14. 8 at Lystra there was a man sitting
14.15 "Men, why are you doing this?
15.22 to choose men from among them
15.22 Barsabbas, and Silas, leading men
15.25 "it has seemed good to us . . to choose men
16. 9 a man of Macedonia was standing
17.12 women of high standing as well as men
17.22 "Men of Athens, . . you are very religious
17.31 "he will judge the world . . by a man
17.34 some men joined him and believed
18.24 Apollos . . was an eloquent man
19.25 "Men, you know that from this business
19.35 "Men of Ephesus, . . who does not know?
19.37 "For you have brought these men here
20.30 "from among your own selves will arise men
21.11 " 'So shall the Jews . . bind the man
21.23 "We have four men who are under a vow
21.26 Then Paul took the men
21.28 crying out, "Men of Israel, help!
21.38 "the four thousand men of the Assassins
22. 4 "delivering to prison both men and women
22.12 "a devout man according to the law
23.21 "more than forty of their men . . in ambush
23.27 "This man was seized by the Jews
23.30 "there would be a plot against the man
24. 5 "we have found this man a pestilent fellow
25. 5 "if there is anything wrong about the man
25.14 "There is a man left prisoner by Felix
25.17 "I . . ordered the man to be brought in
25.23 the prominent men of the city
27.21 "Men, you should have listened to me
27.25 "take heart, men, for I have faith in God
Rom 4. 8 "man against whom the Lord will not reckon
7. 3 an adulteress if she lives with another man
7. 3 if she marries another man she is not
1 Cor 11. 3 that the head of every man is Christ
11. 4 Any man who prays or prophesies
11. 7 For a man ought not to cover his head
11. 7 but woman is the glory of man
11. 8 (For man was not made from woman, but woman from man
11. 9 (Neither was man created for woman, but woman for man
11.11 (Nevertheless, in the Lord woman is not independent of man nor man of woman
11.12 (for as woman was made from man, so man is now born of woman
11.14 for a man to wear long hair is degrading
13.11 I became a man, I gave up childish ways
1 Tim 2. 8 in every place the men should pray
2.12 no woman . . to have authority over men
Jas 1. 7, 8 a double-minded man, unstable
1.12 Blessed is the man who endures trial
1.20 anger of man does not work . . righteousness
1.23 like a man who observes his natural face
2. 2 if a man with gold rings . . comes
3. 2 perfect man, able to bridle the . . body

2. *man, mankind:* ἄνθρωπος ANTHRŌPOS
[a]κατὰ ἄνθρωπον

Mt 4. 4 " 'Man shall not live by bread alone
4.19 "I will make you fishers of men
5.13 "except to be . . trodden under foot by men
5.16 "Let your light so shine before men
5.19 "Whoever . . teaches men so, shall be . . least
6. 1 "practicing your piety before men
6. 2 "that they may be praised by men
6. 5 "that they may be seen by men
6.14 "For if you forgive men their trespasses
6.15 "if you do not forgive men their trespasses
6.16 "that their fasting may be seen by men
6.18 "that your fasting may not be seen by men
7. 9 "what man of you, if his son asks him?
7.12 "whatever you wish that men would do
8. 9 "For I am a man under authority
8.20 "Son of man has nowhere to lay his head
8.27 the men marveled, saying, "What sort?
9. 6 "know that the Son of man has authority
9. 8 who had given such authority to men
9. 9 m. called Matthew sitting at the tax office
10.17 "Beware of men; for they will deliver you
10.23 "not . . gone . . before the Son of man comes
10.32 "one who acknowledges me before men
10.33 "whoever denies me before men
10.35 "come to set a man against his father
10.36 "a man's foes will be . . his own household
11. 8 "To see a man[a] clothed in soft raiment?
11.19 "Son of man came eating and drinking
12. 8 "the Son of man is lord of the sabbath
12.10 "there was a man with a withered hand
12.11 "What man of you, if he has one sheep
12.12 "Of . . much more value is a man than a sheep!
12.13 said to the man, "Stretch out your hand
12.31 "every sin . . will be forgiven men
12.32 "whoever says a word against the Son of m.
12.35 "The good man out of his good treasure
12.35 "the evil man out of his evil treasure
12.36 "men will render account for every . . word
12.40 "so will the Son of man be three days
12.43 "When . . unclean spirit has gone out of a m.
12.45 "the last state of that man becomes worse
13.24 "a man who sowed good seed in his field
13.25 "while men were sleeping, his enemy came
13.31 "which a man took and sowed in his field
13.37 "He who sows the good seed is the Son of m.
13.41 "The Son of man will send his angels
13.44 "which a man found and covered up
15. 9 " 'teaching . . the precepts of men
15.11 "not what goes into the mouth defiles a man, but what comes out . . defiles a man
15.18 "what comes out of the mouth . . defiles a m.
15.20 "These are what defile a m.; but to eat with unwashed hands does not defile a m.
16.13 "Who do men say that the Son of man is?
16.23 "not on the side of God, but of men
16.26 "will it profit a man, if he gains the whole . . ? Or what shall a m. give . . for his life?
16.27 "Son of man is to come with his angels
16.28 "before they see the Son of man coming
17. 9 "until the Son of man is raised from the dead
17.12 "Son of man will suffer at their hands
17.14 a man came up to him and kneeling
17.22 "The Son of man is to be delivered into the hands of men
18. 7 "man by whom the temptation comes
[18.11 "*the Son of man came to save the lost*‡
18.12 "If a man has a hundred sheep
19. 5 " 'a man shall leave his father and mother
19. 6 "let not man put asunder
19.10 "the case of a man with his wife
19.12 "who have been made eunuchs by men
19.26 "With men this is impossible
19.28 "Son of man . . on his glorious throne
20.18 "the Son of man will be delivered
20.28 "Son of man came not to be served

Mt 21.25 "From heaven or from men?
21.26 "if we say, 'From men,' we are afraid
21.28 "A man had two sons
22.11 "a man who had no wedding garment
22.16 "you do not regard the position of men
23. 4 They . . lay them on men's shoulders
23. 5 "do all their deeds to be seen by men
23. 7 "⟨they love⟩ being called rabbi by men
23.13 "shut the kingdom of heaven against men
23.28 "outwardly appear righteous to men
24.27 "so will be the coming of the Son of man
24.30 "sign of the Son of man in heaven
24.30 "Son of man coming on the clouds
24.37 "so will be the coming of the Son of man
24.39 "so will be the coming of the Son of man
24.44 "for the Son of man is coming
25.14 "as when a man going on a journey
25.24 " 'Master, I knew you to be a hard man
25.31 "When the Son of m. comes in his glory
26. 2 "Son of man will be delivered up
26.24 "The Son of m. goes as it is written of him, but woe to that m. by whom the Son of m. is betrayed! It would have been better for that m. if he had not been born
26.45 "Behold, . . the Son of m. is betrayed
26.64 "hereafter you will see the Son of m.
26.72 "I do not know the man
26.74 "I do not know the man
27.32 they came upon a man of Cyrene . . ; this man they compelled to carry his cross
27.57 there came a rich man from Arimathea

Mk 1.17 "I will make you . . fishers of men
1.23 there was . . a man with an unclean spirit
2.10 "know that the Son of m. has authority
2.27 "The sabbath was made for man, not man for the sabbath
2.28 "Son of m. is lord . . of the sabbath
3. 1 a man was there who had a withered hand
3. 3 the man who had the withered hand
3. 5 said to the man, "Stretch out your hand
3.28 "all sins will be forgiven the sons of men
4.26 "as if a man should scatter seed
5. 2 there met him out of the tombs a man
5. 8 "Come out of the man, you unclean spirit!
7. 7 " 'as doctrines the precepts of men
7. 8 "You . . hold fast the tradition of men
7.11 " 'If a man tells his father or his mother
7.15 "nothing outside a man . . can defile him; but the things which come out of a man
7.18 "whatever goes into a man from outside
7.20 "What comes out of a man is what defiles a man
7.21 "from within, out of the heart of man
7.23 "evil things . . from within, . . they defile a m.
8.24 he looked up and said, "I see men
8.27 "Who do men say that I am?
8.31 that the Son of man must suffer
8.33 "not on the side of God, but of men
8.36 "For what does it profit a man?
8.37 "what can a man give in return for his life?
8.38 "will the Son of man also be ashamed
9. 9 until the Son of man should have risen
9.12 "how is it written of the Son of m.?
9.31 "The Son of man will be delivered into the hands of men
10. 7 " 'a man shall leave his father and mother
10. 9 "let not man put asunder
10.27 "With men it is impossible, but not with God
10.33 "the Son of man will be delivered
10.45 "Son of m. also came not to be served
11.30 "baptism of John from heaven or . . men?
11.32 "But shall we say, 'From men'?
12. 1 "A man planted a vineyard
12.14 "you do not regard the position of men
13.26 "they will see the Son of man coming
13.34 "It is like a man going on a journey
14.13 "a m. carrying a jar of water will meet you

Mk 14.21 "Son of m. goes as it is written of him, but woe to that m. by whom the Son of m. is betrayed! . . better for that m. if he had not been born
14.41 "It is enough; . . the Son of man is betrayed
14.62 "Son of man seated at the right hand
14.71 "I do not know this m. of whom you speak
15.39 "Truly this man was the Son[x] of God!
Lk 1.25 "to take away my reproach among men
2.14 "and on earth peace among men
2.25 there was a man in Jerusalem, . . Simeon, and this man was righteous
2.52 Jesus increased . . in favor with God and m.
4. 4 " 'Man shall not live by bread alone
4.33 there was a man who had the spirit
5.10 "henceforth you will be catching men
5.18 on a bed a man who was paralyzed
5.20 "Man, your sins are forgiven you
5.24 "Son of man has authority on earth
6. 5 "Son of man is lord of the sabbath
6. 6 a man . . whose right hand was withered
6.22 "Blessed are you when men hate you
6.22 "cast out . . on account of the Son of man!
6.31 "as you wish that men would do to you
6.45 "good m. out of . . good treasure of his heart
6.48 "he is like a man building a house
6.49 "like a m. who built a house on the ground
7. 8 " 'I am a man set under authority
7.25 "A man clothed in soft raiment?
7.31 "To what then shall I compare the men?
7.34 "The Son of man has come eating
8.29 the unclean spirit to come out of the man
8.33 the demons came out of the man
8.35 man from whom the demons had gone
9.22 "Son of man must suffer many things
9.25 "what does it profit a man if he gains?
9.26 "the Son of man be ashamed
9.44 "Son of man is to be delivered into the hands of men
[9.56 *"for the Son of man came not to destroy men's lives but to save them‡*
9.58 "Son of m. has nowhere to lay his head
10.30 "A man was going down from Jerusalem
11.24 "unclean spirit has gone out of a man
11.26 "last state of that man becomes worse
11.30 "so will the Son of man be
11.44 "men walk over them without knowing it
11.46 "you load men with burdens hard to bear
12. 8 "who acknowledges me before men, the Son of man also will acknowledge
12. 9 "he who denies me before men
12.10 "who speaks a word against the Son of m.
12.14 "Man, who made me a judge or divider?
12.16 "The land of a rich man brought forth
12.36 "like men who are waiting for their master
12.40 "be ready; for the Son of man is coming
13.19 "seed which a man took and sowed
14. 2 there was a man . . who had dropsy
14.16 "A man once gave a great banquet
14.30 " 'This man began to build
15. 4 "What man . . , having a hundred sheep?
15.11 "There was a man who had two sons
16. 1 "There was a rich man who had a steward
16.15 "You . . who justify yourselves before men
16.15 "what is exalted among men is . . abomination
16.19 "a rich man, who was clothed in purple
17.22 "one of the days of the Son of man
17.24 "so will the Son of m. be in his day[a]
17.26 "so will it be in the days of the Son of m.
17.30 "when the Son of man is revealed
18. 2 "neither feared God nor regarded man
18. 4 " 'I neither fear God nor regard man
18. 8 "when the Son of m. comes, will he find faith?
18.10 "Two men went up into the temple
18.11 " 'I thank thee . . I am not like other men
18.27 "What is impossible with men
18.31 "everything that is written of the Son of m.
Lk 19.10 "Son of man came to seek and to save
19.21 " 'because you are a severe man
19.22 " 'You knew that I was a severe man
20. 4 "Was the baptism of John . . from men?
20. 6 "if we say, 'From men,' all . . will stone us
20. 9 "A man planted a vineyard
21.26 "⟨will be signs,⟩ men fainting with fear
21.27 "Son of man coming in a cloud
21.36 "strength . . to stand before the Son of m.
22.10 "a man carrying a jar of water
22.22 "Son of m. goes as it has been determined; . . woe to that m. by whom he is betrayed!
22.48 "Judas, would you betray the Son of m.?
22.58 But Peter said, "Man, I am not
22.60 Peter said, "Man, I do not know
22.69 "Son of m. shall be seated at the right
23. 4 "I find no crime in this man
23. 6 asked whether the man was a Galilean
23.14 "You brought me this man
23.14 "behold, I did not find this man guilty
23.47 "Certainly this man was innocent!
24. 7 "the Son of man must be delivered into the hands of sinful men
Jn 1. 4 the life was the light of men
1. 6 There was a man sent from God
1. 9 The true light that enlightens every man
1.51 "angels . . descending upon the Son of m.
2.10 "Every man serves the good wine first
2.25 he . . needed no one to bear witness of man; for he himself knew what was in man
3. 1 a man of the Pharisees, named Nicodemus
3. 4 "How can a man be born when he is old?
3.13 "he who descended . . , the Son of man[g]
3.14 "so must the Son of man be lifted up
3.19 men loved darkness rather than light
4.29 "a man who told me all that I ever did
4.50 man believed the word that Jesus spoke
5. 5 One man was there, who had been ill
5. 7 "I have no man to put me into the pool
5. 9 "at once the man was healed
5.12 "Who is the man who said to you?
5.15 The man went away and told the Jews
5.27 "because he is the Son of man
5.34 "Not that the testimony . . is from man
5.41 "I do not receive glory from men
6.27 "which the Son of man will give to you
6.53 "eat the flesh of the Son of man
6.62 "Son of man ascending where he was
7.22 "you circumcise a man upon the sabbath
7.23 "If on the sabbath a man receives
7.23 "I made a man's whole body well
7.46 The officers answered, "No man ever spoke like this man!
7.51 "Does our law judge a m. without . . hearing?
8.17 "the testimony of two men is true
8.28 "When you have lifted up the Son of man
8.40 "a man who has told you the truth
9. 1 he saw a man blind from his birth
9.11 "The man called Jesus made clay
9.16 Pharisees said, "This man is not from God
9.16 "How can a man . . do such signs?
9.24 the second time they called the man
9.24 "we know that this man is a sinner
9.30 man answered, "Why, this is a marvel!
9.35 "Do you believe in the Son of man?[v]‡
10.33 "you, being a man, make yourself God
11.47 "For this man performs many signs
11.50 "one man should die for the people
12.23 "The hour has come for the Son of m.
12.34 "that the Son of man must be lifted up? Who is this Son of man?
12.43 they loved the praise of men
13.31 "Now is the Son of man glorified
17. 6 "I have manifested thy name to the men
18.14 that one man should die for the people
18.17 "Are not you . . one of this man's disciples?
18.29 "What accusation . . against this man?

Jn 19. 5 Pilate said to them, "Behold the man!
Acts 4.12 "there is no other name . . given among men
4.13 they were uneducated, common men
4.14 seeing the man that had been healed
4.16 "What shall we do with these men?
4.22 man on whom this . . healing was performed
5. 4 "You have not lied to men but to God
5.28 "to bring this man's blood upon us
5.29 "We must obey God rather than men
5.34 ordered the men to be put outside
5.35 "take care what you do with these men
5.38 "I tell you, keep away from these men
5.38 "if this plan or this undertaking is of men
6.13 "This man never ceases to speak
7.56 "Son of m. standing at the right hand
9.33 There he found a man named Aeneas
10.26 "Stand up; I too am a man
10.28 "that I should not call any man common
12.22 "The voice of a god, and not of man!
14.11 "gods . . in the likeness of men!
14.15 "We also are men, of like nature with you
15.17 " 'that the rest of men may seek the Lord
15.26 "men who have risked their lives
16.17 "These men are servants of . . God
16.20 "These men are Jews and . . are disturbing
16.35 saying, "Let those men go
16.37 "uncondemned, men who are Roman
17.26 "he made from one every nation of men
17.29 "a representation by the art . . of man
17.30 "commands all men everywhere to repent
18.13 "persuading men to worship God
19.16 "the man in whom the evil spirit was leaped
19.35 "what man is there who does not know?
21.28 "This is the man who is teaching
22.15 " 'a witness for him to all men
22.25 "Is it lawful for you to scourge a man?
22.26 "For this man is a Roman citizen
23. 9 "We find nothing wrong in this man
24.16 "to have a clear conscience . . toward men
25.22 "I should like to hear the man myself
26.31 "This man is doing nothing to deserve
26.32 "This man could have been set free
28. 4 "No doubt this man is a murderer
Rom 1.18 wickedness of men who . . suppress the truth
1.23 images resembling mortal man
2. 1 you have no excuse, O m., whoever you are
2. 3 Do you suppose, O man, . . you will escape?
2.16 when . . God judges the secrets of men
2.29 His praise is not from men but from God
3. 4 Let God be true though every m. be false
3.28 that a man is justified by faith
4. 6 man to whom God reckons righteousness
5.12 as sin came into the world through one man . . so death spread to all men
5.15 in the grace of that one man Jesus C.
5.18 trespass led to condemnation for all men, . . righteousness leads to . . life for all men
5.19 by one man's disobedience many . . sinners
7.24 Wretched man that I am!
9.20 who are you, a man, to answer back?
10. 5 the man who practices the righteousness
14.18 acceptable to God and approved by men
1 Cor 1.25 foolishness of God is wiser than men, . . the weakness of God is stronger than men
2. 5 faith might not rest in the wisdom of men
2. 9 "nor the heart of man conceived
2.11 what person knows a man's thoughts except the spirit of the man . . in him?
2.14 unspiritual[e] m. does not receive the . . Spirit
3. 3 are you not . . behaving like ordinary men?
3. 4 are you not merely men?
3.21 So let no one boast of men
4. 9 we have become a spectacle . . to men
6.18 Every other sin which a man commits
7. 1 well for a man not to touch a woman
7.23 do not become slaves of men
11.28 Let a man examine himself
1 Cor 13. 1 If I speak in the tongues of men
14. 2 who speaks in a tongue speaks not to men
14. 3 he who prophesies speaks to men
15.19 we are of all men most to be pitied
15.21 For as by a man came death, by a man has come also the resurrection
15.39 there is one kind for men
15.45 "first man Adam became a living being
15.47 The first man was from the earth . . ; the second man is from heaven
2 Cor 3. 2 to be known and read by all men
4. 2 commend . . to every man's conscience
5.11 knowing . . fear of the Lord, we persuade men
8.21 honorable . . also in the sight of men
12. 2 I know a man in Christ
12. 3 I know that this man was caught up
12. 4 he heard things . . which m. may not utter
Gal 1. 1 Paul an apostle—not from men nor through man, but through Jesus Christ and God
1.10 Am I now seeking the favor of men, or of God? Or am I trying to please men? If I were still pleasing men
1.11 [a]gospel . . preached by me is not man's[b]†
1.12 For I did not receive it from man
2.16 know that a man is not justified[d] by works
3.15 no one annuls even a man's will[g]
5. 3 I testify again to every man
6. 1 if a man is overtaken in any trespass
6. 7 whatever a man sows, . . he will also reap
Eph 2.15 one new man in place of the two
3. 5 not made known to the sons of men
3.16 through his Spirit in the inner man
4. 8 "When he ascended . . he gave gifts to men
4.14 carried about . . by the cunning of men
5.31 "a man shall leave his father and mother
6. 7 as to the Lord and not to men
Phil 2. 7 being born in the likeness of men
4. 5 Let all men know your forbearance
Col 1.28 warning every man and teaching every man in all wisdom, that we may present every man mature in Christ
3.23 heartily, as serving the Lord and not men
1 Th 2. 4 so we speak, not to please men
2. 6 nor did we seek glory from men
2.13 you accepted it not as the word of men
2.15 displease God and oppose all men
4. 8 disregards not man but God
2 Th 2. 3 the man of lawlessness[a] is revealed
3. 2 delivered from wicked and evil men
1 Tim 2. 1 that . . thanksgivings be made for all men
2. 4 who desires all men to be saved
2. 5 there is one mediator between God and men, the man Christ Jesus
4.10 God, who is the Savior of all men
5.24 The sins of some men are conspicuous
6. 5 wrangling among men who are depraved
6. 9 desires that plunge men into ruin
6.11 as for you, man of God, shun all this
6.16 whom no man has ever seen or can see
2 Tim 2. 2 entrust to faithful men who will be able
3. 2 For men will be lovers of self
3. 8 men of corrupt mind and counterfeit faith
3.13 evil men and impostors will go on
3.17 that the man of God may be complete
Tit 1.14 commands of men who reject the truth
2.11 appeared for the salvation of all men
3. 2 to show perfect courtesy toward all men
3. 8 these are excellent and profitable to men
3.10 As for a man who is factious
Heb 2. 6 "What is man that thou art mindful of him, or the son of man?
5. 1 every high priest chosen from among men is appointed to act on behalf of men
6.16 Men indeed swear by a greater
7. 8 Here tithes are received by mortal men
7.28 the law appoints men in their weakness
8. 2 set up not by man but by the Lord

Heb 9.27 appointed for men to die once
13. 6 "I will not be afraid; what can m. do to me?
Jas 1.19 Let every man be quick to hear
2.20 Do you want to be shown, you shallow man?[o]
2.24 see that a man is justified by works
3. 9 with it we curse men
5.17 Elijah was a man of like nature
1 Pet 2. 4 that living stone, rejected by men
2.15 silence the ignorance of foolish men
4. 6 though judged in the flesh like men
2 Pet 1.21 no prophecy . . by the impulse of man, but men moved by the Holy Spirit spoke
3. 7 day of judgment . . of ungodly men
1 Jn 5. 9 If we receive the testimony of men
Rev 1.13 in the midst . . one like a son of man
4. 7 living creature with the face of a man
8.11 many men died of the water
9. 5 like . . a scorpion, when it stings a man
9. 6 in those days men will seek death
9.10 power of hurting men for five months
13.13 making fire come down . . in the sight of men
14.14 on the cloud one like a son of man
16. 2 evil sores came upon the men
16. 8 it was allowed to scorch men with fire
16. 9 men were scorched by the fierce heat
16.18 never . . since men were on the earth
16.21 hailstones . . dropped on men from heaven, till men cursed God for the plague
21. 3 "Behold, the dwelling of God is with men
21.17 forty-four cubits by a man's measure

3. *race, generation:* γενεά GENEA
Col [1.26 mystery hidden *from angels and men*†

CONTEXTUALLY (including instances of "man" in substantive constructions)
Mt **1.**19; **2.**1, 7, 16²; **5.**11, 12, 15, 21, 33; **6.**30; **8.**26, 27; **9.**27, 28, 33; **10.**41³; **12.**13, 22, 29³, 48; **13.**17, 48, 54, 56; **14.**31; **15.**14²; **19.**11, 20, 22, 23, 24; **20.**25, 30; **23.**9, 19, 27, 34; **24.**40; **26.**48, 62; **27.**19, 24, 32; **28.**4
Mk **2.**3; **3.**27²; **5.**15, 18, 20; **6.**2, 12, 21; **7.**32; **8.**4, 22, 23; **10.**4, 25, 42, 49, 51; **12.**19†; **14.**44, 51, 60; **15.**7, 12; **16.**5
Lk **3.**15; **5.**24; **6.**39²; **7.**12, 14, 15; **9.**33; **10.**36; **11.**14, 21, 30; **12.**15, 28, 48; **13.**29; **14.**8, 9, 12, 35; **16.**20, 21, 22²; **17.**[36‡; **18.**25, 35; **19.**14, 47; **20.**28†; **22.**47; **23.**2, [17‡, 18, 25; **24.**5, 25
Jn **2.**10; **4.**20; **5.**10, 11, 13; **7.**12, 25, 27; **9.**6, 8, 9, 13, 17, 18, 29, 32; **10.**41; **11.**39, 44; **12.**32; **13.**35; **18.**8, 26, 40; **19.**12
Acts **1.**22, 24; **2.**15, 17², 23; **3.**16²; **4.**21; **5.**6, 10; **7.**24, 27, 58; **9.**11, 21; **10.**2; **13.**23, 38, 50; **17.**6, 25, 31; **20.**9; **21.**24; **23.**17, 18, 22; **24.**20; **25.**2, 3, 5, 24; **27.**31; **28.**7
Rom **2.**6, 26; **3.**9; **5.**7²; **6.**13; **8.**27; **9.**16, 33; **10.**10, 14, 15; **11.**32; **14.**1, 2, 5²; **15.**20; **16.**7
1 Cor **1.**20; **2.**15; **3.**1², 10; **4.**5, 9; **5.**4(3), 5, 9; **6.**18; **7.**2, 32, 33; **8.**10, 11; **9.**19, 22; **10.**15, 28, 33; **14.**17; **15.**36, 48², 49²; **16.**16, 18
2 Cor **1.**17; **2.**17; **3.**16; **5.**12; **8.**12, 24; **10.**15, 18²; **11.**13; **12.**5
Gal **3.**7, 9; **6.**10
Eph **3.**9; **5.**5, 15
Phil **2.**29
Col **3.**11; **4.**11
1 Th **3.**12; **4.**6
2 Th **3.**14
1 Tim **5.**1², 22
2 Tim **3.**8, 9
Tit **1.**10; **2.**2, 6; **3.**3
Heb **7.**6; **10.**29; **11.**2, 19; **12.**14, 23; **13.**17
Jas **1.**5, 11, 26; **2.**2, 3, 6; **4.**8; **5.**6, 15, 16
1 Pet **2.**8, 16, 17; **4.**18
2 Pet **2.**8, 18; **3.**17
1 Jn **2.**13, 14
2 Jn .7
3 Jn .8
Jude .8, 10
Rev **2.**2; **5.**9; **6.**4, 15; **11.**9; **13.**4; **16.**3, 6, 10; **18.**17, 23; **19.**18²

MAN, A
MAN, ONE
1. *one:* εἷς HEIS
Mk 10.17 "a man ran up and knelt before him
Lk [23.17 *Now he was obliged to release one man*‡
Jn 18.39 "custom that I should release one man
Rom 5.15 if many died through one man's trespass
5.16 not like the effect of that one man's sin
5.17 because of one man's trespass, death reigned through that one man
5.17 righteousness . . through the one m. Jesus
5.18 as one man's trespass led to condemnation . . , so one man's . . righteousness leads to . . life
5.19 by one man's obedience many . . righteous
9.10 conceived children by one man
Heb 11.12 from one man, and him as good as dead
2. *who, which, what:* ὅς HOS
Rom 14. 5 One man esteems one day as better
3. *anyone, any:* τὶς TIS II
Mt **22.**24
Mk **9.**38; **12.**19
Lk **8.**49; **9.**49, 57; **13.**6; **20.**28
Jn **6.**50; **14.**23; **15.**6, 13
Acts **18.**7; **19.**24
1 Cor **5.**1
2 Cor **11.**20
1 Tim **3.**5
Heb **10.**28
Jas **2.**14
2 Pet **2.**19

MAN, EACH
MAN, EVERY
1. *each:* ἕκαστος (subst.) HEKASTOS
Mt 16.27 "will repay every man for what he has done
Jn 16.32 "scattered, every man to his home
Rom 2. 6 to every man according to his works
1 Cor 3.10 Let each man take care how he builds
3.13 each man's work will become manifest
4. 5 every man will receive his commendation
7. 2 each man should have his own wife
Gal 6. 5 each man will have to bear his own load

MAN, MADE BY
1. *made by hands:* χειροποίητος CHEIROPOIĒTOS
Acts 17.24 "God . . does not live in shrines made by m.

MAN, ONE (*See* MAN, A)

MAN, THAT IS COMMON TO
1. *human:* ἀνθρώπινος ANTHRŌPINOS
1 Cor 10.13 No temptation . . that is not common to m.

MANAEN: Μαναήν 'manēən
Acts 13. 1 M. a member of the court of Herod

MANAGE
1. *be strong, prevail:* ἰσχύω ISCHYŌ
Acts 27.16 we managed . . to secure the boat
2. *set over, direct:* προΐστημι (act. or mid.) PROISTĒMI
1 Tim 3. 4 He must manage his own household
3. 5 if a man does not know how to manage
3.12 let them manage their children . . well

MANASSEH: Μανασσῆς mə'nasə
Mt 1.10 Hezekiah the father of Manasseh, and Manasseh the father of Amos[c]
Rev 7. 6 twelve thousand of the tribe of M.

MANGER
1. *crib, manger:* φάτνη PHATNĒ*
Lk 2. 7 she gave birth . . and laid him in a manger
2.12 "you will find a babe . . lying in a m.
2.16 found . . the babe lying in a manger
13.15 "Does not each . . untie . . ox . . from the m.?

MANHOOD
1. *man, husband:* ἀνήρ ANĒR
Eph 4.13 until we all attain . . to mature manhood

MANIFEST
1. *show, make known:* δείκνυμι DEIKNYMI
1 Tim 6.15 will be made m. at the proper time

2. *manifest, visible:* ἐμφανής EMPHANĒS
Acts 10.40 "God raised him .. and made him m.
3. *manifest, make clear:* ἐμφανίζω EMPHANIZŌ
Jn 14.21 "I will love him and manifest myself
14.22 "how is it that you will manifest yourself?
4. *coming to light:* ἐπιφανής EPIPHANĒS*
Acts 2.20 " 'day of the Lord .., the great and m. day
5. *make manifest, make known:* φανερόω PHANEROŌ
Jn 2.11 first of his signs .. manifested his glory
17. 6 "I have manifested thy name to the men
Rom 3.21 righteousness .. has been manifested
2 Cor 4.10 that the life of Jesus may .. be manifested
4.11 that the life of Jesus may be manifested
1 Tim 3.16 He[h] was manifested in the flesh
2 Tim 1.10 manifested through .. our Savior Christ J.
Tit 1. 3 at the proper time manifested in his word
1 Pet 5. 4 when the chief Shepherd is manifested
6. *visible, known:* φανερός PHANEROS
Lk 8.17 "nothing is hid that shall not be made m.
Acts 4.16 "that a .. sign has been performed .. is m.
1 Cor 3.13 each man's work will become manifest

MANIFEST, MAKE
1. *make manifest, make known:* φανερόω PHANEROŌ
Mk 4.22 "nothing hid, except to be made manifest
Jn 9. 3 "that the works of God might be made m.
Col 1.26 mystery .. now made manifest to his saints
1 Pet 1.20 made manifest at the end of the times
1 Jn 1. 2 the life was made manifest, and we saw it
1. 2 eternal life which .. was made m. to us
4. 9 In this the love of God was made m.

MANIFESTATION
1. *manifestation:* ἀνάδειξις ANADEIXIS*
Lk 1.80 the day of his manifestation to Israel
2. *manifestation, disclosure:* φανέρωσις PHANERŌSIS
1 Cor 12. 7 To each is given the manifestation
CONTEXTUALLY
1 Cor 14.12 eager for manifestations of the Spirit

MANIFOLD
MANIFOLD MORE
1. *many times as much:* πολλαπλασίων POLLAPLASIŌN*
Mt [19.29 "will receive *manifold more*‡
Lk 18.30 "who will not receive manifold more
2. *much variegated:* πολυποίκιλος POLYPOIKILOS*
Eph 3.10 through the church the manifold wisdom

MANKIND
1. *man, mankind:* ἄνθρωπος (pl.) ANTHRŌPOS
Rev 9. 4 those of mankind who have not the seal
9.15 angels .. held ready .. to kill a third of m.
9.18 By these three .. a third of m. was killed
9.20 The rest of mankind, who were not killed
14. 4 these have been redeemed from mankind

MANKIND, REST OF
1. *remaining, left:* λοιπός (subst. pl.) LOIPOS
Eph 2. 3 children of wrath, like the rest of m.

MANNA
1. *manna:* μάννα MANNA*
Jn 6.31 "Our fathers ate the m. in the wilderness
6.49 "fathers ate the manna in the wilderness
Heb 9. 4 urn holding the manna, and Aaron's rod
Rev 2.17 " 'To him .. I will give some of the hidden m.

MANNER (*See* ALL MANNER OF; LIFE IS, ONE'S MANNER OF; LIFE, MANNER OF; STRICT MANNER; UNWORTHY MANNER, IN AN; WHAT MANNER OF)

MANNER, IN LIKE
1. *likewise:* ὁμοίως HOMOIŌS
Mk 4.16 "these in like m. are the ones sown
Lk 16.25 " 'Lazarus in like manner evil things
Jude . 8 Yet in like manner these men .. defile

MANSERVANT
1. *slave:* δοῦλος DOULOS
Acts 2.18 " 'on my menservants and my maidservants
2. *child, servant:* παῖς PAIS
Lk 12.45 "servant .. begins to beat the menservants

MANSLAYER
1. *murderer:* ἀνδροφόνος ANDROPHONOS*
1 Tim 1. 9 the law is .. laid down .. for manslayers

MANTLE
1. *outer garment:* ἱμάτιον HIMATION
Mt 24.18 "let him .. not turn back to take his m.
Mk 10.50 throwing off his mantle he sprang up
13.16 "let him .. not turn back to take his m.
Lk 22.36 "let him who has no sword sell his m.
Acts 12. 8 "Wrap your m. around you and follow
2. *what is thrown around, covering:* περιβόλαιον PERIBOLAION
Heb 1.12 "like a mantle thou wilt roll them up

MANURE
1. *manure, filth:* κόπριον KOPRION*
Lk 13. 8 " 'Let it alone .. till I .. put on manure

MANY
1. *enough:* ἱκανός HIKANOS
Acts 9.23 When many days had passed
9.43 he stayed in Joppa for many days
12.12 where many were gathered together
14.21 When they .. had made many disciples
18.18 After this Paul stayed many days longer
20. 8 There were m. lights in the upper chamber
Rom 15.23 I have longed for many years to come
2. *crowd, populace:* ὄχλος OCHLOS
Acts 6. 7 a great many of the priests were obedient
3. *more:* πλείων PLEIŌN
Acts 2.40 he testified with many other words
13.31 "for many days he appeared to those
25.14 as they stayed there many days
27.20 neither sun nor stars appeared for m. a day
4. *multitude, mass:* πλῆθος PLĒTHOS
Acts 17. 4 joined .. ; as did a great many .. Greeks
5. *often, many times:* πολλάκις POLLAKIS [A.4.a]
2 Cor 11.27 through many a sleepless night
6. *many, great:* πολύς POLYS
Mt 3. 7 when he saw many of the Pharisees
7.13 "those who enter by it are many
7.22 "On that day many will say to me, 'Lord, .. did we not .. do many mighty works?
8.11 "many will come from east and west
8.16 That evening they brought to him many
8.30 a herd of many swine was feeding
9.10 behold, many tax collectors .. came
10.31 "you are of more value than many sparrows
12.15 many followed him, and he healed
13. 3 "he told them many things in parables
13.17 "many prophets and righteous men longed
13.58 he did not do m. mighty works there
14.24 boat by this time was many furlongs‡
15.30 crowds came .., bringing with them .. many
16.21 suffer many things from the elders
19.30 "many that are first will be last
20.28 "to give his life as a ransom for many
22.14 "many are called, but few are chosen
24. 5 "For many will come in my name .. and they will lead many astray
24.10 "And then many will fall away[y]
24.11 "And many false prophets will arise and lead many astray
26.28 "this is my blood .. poured out for many
26.60 many false witnesses came forward
27.52 many bodies of the saints .. were raised
27.53 went into the holy city and appeared to m.
27.55 There were also many women there
Mk 1.34 he healed many who were sick .. and cast out many demons
2. 2 And many were gathered together
2.15 m. tax collectors .. were sitting with Jesus .. ; for there were many who followed him
3.10 for he had healed many
4. 2 he taught them many things in parables
4.33 With many such parables he spoke
5. 9 "My name is Legion; for we are m.
5.26 who had suffered much under m. physicians
6. 2 many who heard him were astonished

Mk 6.13 anointed with oil many that were sick
6.31 For many were coming and going
6.33 many saw them going, and knew them
6.34 he began to teach them many things
7. 4 (many other traditions which they observe
7.13 "And many such things you do
8.31 Son of man must suffer many things
9.12 "written . . that he should suffer m. things
10.31 "But many that are first will be last
10.45 "to give his life as a ransom for many
10.48 m. rebuked him, telling him to be silent
11. 8 many spread their garments on the road
12. 5 "so with many others, some they beat
12.41 Many rich people put in large sums
13. 6 "Many will come . . saying, 'I am he!' and
they will lead many astray
14.24 "blood . . which is poured out for many
14.56 many bore false witness against him
15. 3 chief priests accused him of many things
15.41 many other women who came up with him
Lk 1. 1 as many have undertaken . . a narrative
1.14 "many will rejoice at his birth
1.16 "he will turn many of the sons of Israel
2.34 "the fall and rising of many in Israel
2.35 "thoughts out of m. hearts may be revealed
3.18 with m. other exhortations, he preached
4.25 "there were many widows in Israel
4.27 "there were many lepers in Israel
4.41 demons also came out of many
7.21 In that hour he cured many of diseases . . ,
and on many . . he bestowed sight
7.47 "her sins, which are many, are forgiven
8. 3 Susanna, and many others, who provided
8.29 (For many a time it had seized him
8.30 for many demons had entered him
9.22 "Son of man must suffer many things
10.24 "m. prophets . . desired to see what you see
10.41 "Martha, you are anxious . . about m. things
12. 7 "you are of more value than m. sparrows
12.19 " 'you have ample goods . . for many years
13.24 "for many, I tell you, will seek to enter
14.16 "gave a great banquet, and invited m.
15.13 "Not many days later, the younger son
17.25 "first he must suffer many things
21. 8 "for many will come in my name
22.65 spoke many other words against him
Jn 2.23 at the Passover feast, many believed
4.39 Many Samaritans from that city
4.41 many more believed because of his word
6.60 M. of his disciples, when they heard
6.66 After this m. of his disciples drew back
7.31 Yet many of the people believed in him
8.30 As he spoke thus, many believed in him
10.20 Many of them said, "He has a demon
10.32 "I have shown you many good works
10.41 And many came to him
10.42 And many believed in him there
11.19 many of the Jews had come to Martha
11.45 Many of the Jews . . believed in him
11.47 "For this man performs many signs
11.55 many went up from the country
12.11 m. of the Jews were . . believing in Jesus
12.42 many even of the authorities believed
14. 2 "In my Father's house are many rooms
16.12 "I have yet many things to say to you
19.20 Many of the Jews read this title
20.30 Now Jesus did many other signs
21.25 many other things which Jesus did
Acts 1. 3 he presented himself alive . . by m. proofs
1. 5 "before many days you shall be baptized
2.43 many wonders and signs were done
4. 4 m. of those who heard the word believed
5.12 many signs and wonders were done
8. 7 unclean spirits came out of many . . ; and
many who were . . lame were healed
8.25 preaching the gospel to many villages
9.13 "I have heard from m. about this man

Acts 9.42 many believed in the Lord
10.27 he went in and found many . . gathered
13.43 many Jews . . followed Paul and Barnabas
14.22 through m. tribulations we must enter
15.32 exhorted the brethren with many words
15.35 remained in Antioch . . with m. others also
16.18 this she did for many days
16.23 when they had inflicted many blows
17.12 Many of them therefore believed
18. 8 many of the Corinthians . . believed
18.10 "for I have many people in this city
19.18 Many also of those who were . . believers
24.10 "for many years you have been judge
25. 7 bringing against him m. serious charges
26. 9 "many things . . opposing the name of Jesus
26.10 "I not only shut up many of the saints
28.10 They presented many gifts to us[f]
Rom 4.17 "I . . made you the father of many nations
4.18 become the father of many nations
5.15 if m. died through one man's trespass . .
grace of that one man J. C. abounded for m.
5.16 the free gift following many trespasses
5.19 as by one man's disobedience m. were made
sinners, so . . m. will be made righteous
8.29 the first-born among many brethren
12. 4 as in one body we have many members
12. 5 we, though m., are one body in Christ
16. 2 she has been a helper of many
1 Cor 1.26 consider your call . . ; not many of you were
wise . . , not many were powerful, not many
were of noble birth
4.15 you do not have many fathers
8. 5 as indeed there are many "gods" and many
"lords
10.17 we who are many are one body
10.33 not . . my own advantage, but that of m.
11.30 That is why many of you are weak
12.12 as the body is one and has many members, . .
the members . . , though many, are one body
12.14 not . . of one member but of many
12.20 there are many parts, yet one body
16. 9 there are many adversaries
2 Cor 1.11 that m. will give thanks . . for the blessing
granted us in answer to many prayers
2. 4 I wrote you . . with many tears
2.17 we are not, like so many, peddlers
6.10 as poor, yet making many rich
8.22 our brother . . found earnest in m. matters
9.12 overflows in many thanksgivings to God
11.18 (since many boast of worldly things
12.21 I may have to mourn over many
Gal 1.14 I advanced . . beyond m. of my own age
3.16 not . . "And to offsprings," referring to m.
4.27 "children of the desolate one are many more[o]
Phil 3.18 many . . live as enemies of the cross
1 Tim 6. 9 those . . fall . . into many senseless . . desires
6.10 pierced their hearts with many pangs
6.12 confession in the presence of m. witnesses
2 Tim 2. 2 what you have heard . . before m. witnesses
Tit 1.10 there are many insubordinate men
Heb 2.10 he, . . in bringing many sons to glory
9.28 offered once to bear the sins of many
12.15 by it the many become defiled
Jas 3. 1 Let not many of you become teachers
3. 2 we all make many mistakes
2 Pet 2. 2 many will follow their licentiousness
1 Jn 2.18 so now many antichrists have come
4. 1 for many false prophets have gone out
2 Jn . 7 For many deceivers have gone out
Rev 1.15 voice . . like the sound of many waters
5.11 I heard . . the voice of many angels
8.11 many men died of the water
9. 9 like the noise of many chariots
10.11 "again prophesy about many peoples
14. 2 voice . . like the sound of many waters
17. 1 "harlot who is seated upon m. waters
19. 6 voice . . like the sound of many waters

Rev 19.12 on his head are many diadems
7. *so large, so many:* τοσοῦτος (pl.) TOSOUTOS
1 Cor 14.10 doubtless many different languages
CONTEXTUALLY
Lk 12. 1 when so m. thousands . . gathered together

MANY AS, AS
1. *until:* ἕως HEŌS
Mt 18.21 "As many as seven times?
2. *as great as, how great:* ὅσος (pl.) HOSOS
[a]+ἐάν [b]+ἄν
Mt 14.36 as many as touched it were made well
22. 9 [a]" 'invite . . as many as you find
Mk 6.56 [b]as many as touched it were made well
Acts 4.34 as many as were possessors of lands
13.48 as m. as were ordained to . . life believed
Gal 3.27 as many of you as were baptized
IDIOMATICALLY
a. Heb 11.12 as many as the stars of heaven καθὼς τὰ ἄστρα τοῦ οὐρανοῦ τῷ πλήθει [PLĒTHOS]

MANY, HOW
1. *how many, how much:* πόσος POSOS
Mt 15.34 "How many loaves have you?
16. 9 "how many baskets you gathered
16.10 "how many baskets you gathered
27.13 "how m. things they testify against you
Mk 6.38 "How many loaves have you?
8. 5 "How many loaves have you?
8.19 "how many baskets full . . did you take up?
8.20 "how many baskets . . did you take up?
15. 4 "how m. charges they bring against you
Lk 15.17 " 'How many of my father's . . servants!
Acts 21.20 "see . . how many . . there are among the Jews

MANY IN NUMBER
1. *more:* πλείων (pl.) PLEIŌN
Heb 7.23 former priests were many in number

MANY, SO
MANY, THESE
1. *so large, so many:* τοσοῦτος (pl.) TOSOUTOS
Lk 15.29 " 'Lo, these many years I have served you
Jn 6. 9 "but what are they among so many?
12.37 Though he had done so many signs
21.11 although . . so many, the net was not torn
Gal 3. 4 Did you experience so m. things in vain?

MANY THINGS
1. *more:* πλείων (neut. pl.) PLEIŌN
Lk 11.53 to provoke him to speak of many things

MANY WAYS, IN
1. *in many ways:* πολυμερῶς POLYMERŌS*
Heb 1. 1 In many and various ways God spoke

MANY WORDS
1. *much speaking, wordiness:* πολυλογία POLYLOGIA*
Mt 6. 7 "think . . they will be heard for their m. words

MARBLE
1. *marble:* μάρμαρος MARMAROS*
Rev 18.12 cargo of . . bronze, iron and marble

MARCH UP
1 *go up, come up:* ἀναβαίνω ANABAINŌ
Rev 20. 9 they marched up over the broad earth

MARK (*See also* MISS THE MARK)
1. *mark, inscription:* χάραγμα CHARAGMA
[a]διδόναι χάραγμα A.6.a.4
Rev 13.16 [a]all . . to be marked on the right hand
13.17 no one can buy or sell unless he has the m.
14. 9 "If any one . . receives a mark on his forehead
14.11 "whoever receives the mark of its name
16. 2 men who bore the mark of the beast
19.20 who had received the mark of the beast
20. 4 souls . . who . . had not received its mark
2. *hold upon, aim at:* ἐπέχω EPECHŌ
Lk 14. 7 he marked how they chose the places
3. *sign, portent:* σημεῖον SĒMEION
2 Th 3.17 This is the mark in every letter of mine
4. *consider, look out for:* σκοπέω SKOPEŌ
Phil 3.17 mark those who so live
5. *mark, spot:* στίγμα STIGMA*
Gal 6.17 for I bear on my body the marks of Jesus
6. *place:* τόπος TOPOS
Jn 20.25 "my finger in the mark of the nails

MARK: Μᾶρκος 'märk
Acts 12.12 John whose other name was Mark
12.25 bringing . . John whose other name was M.
15.37 Barnabas wanted to take . . John called M.
15.39 Barnabas took Mark with him and sailed
Col 4.10 Mark the cousin of Barnabas
2 Tim 4.11 Get Mark and bring him with you
Phm .24 so do Mark, Aristarchus, Demas
1 Pet 5.13 sends . . greetings; and so does my son M.

MARKET
1. *marketplace:* ἀγορά AGORA
Mk [7. 4 (*and they do not eat anything from the m.*‡[0]

MARKET, MEAT
1. *enclosure, market:* μάκελλον MAKELLON*
1 Cor 10.25 Eat whatever is sold in the meat market

MARKET PLACE
1. *marketplace:* ἀγορά AGORA*
Mt 11.16 "like children sitting in the market places
20. 3 "others standing idle in the m. place
23. 7 "salutations in the market places
Mk 6.56 they laid the sick in the market places
7. 4 (when they come from the market place†
12.38 "have salutations in the market places
Lk 7.32 "like children sitting in the market place
11.43 "love . . salutations in the market places
20.46 "love salutations in the market places
Acts 16.19 dragged them into the market place
17.17 argued . . in the market place every day

MARKS OF CIRCUMCISION, REMOVE THE
1. *draw the prepuce forward:* ἐπισπάομαι EPISPAOMAI*
1 Cor 7.18 not seek to remove the m. of circumcision

MARRIAGE
1. *marry:* γαμέω (inf.) GAMEŌ
1 Tim 4. 3 forbid marriage and enjoin abstinence
2. *wedding, wedding celebration:* γάμος GAMOS
Jn 2. 1 there was a marriage at Cana in Galilee
2. 2 Jesus also was invited to the marriage
Heb 13. 4 Let marriage be held in honor among all
Rev 19. 7 "the marriage of the Lamb has come
19. 9 "those who are invited to the m. supper
3. *woman, wife:* γυνή GYNĒ [C.2]
1 Cor 7.27 Do not seek marriage

MARRIAGE BED
1. *marriage bed:* κοίτη KOITĒ
Heb 13. 4 let the marriage bed be undefiled

MARRIAGE FEAST
1. *wedding, wedding celebration:* γάμος GAMOS
Mt 22. 2 "a king who gave a marriage feast
22. 3 "who were invited to the marriage feast
22. 4 " 'come to the marriage feast
22. 9 " 'invite to the marriage feast as many
25.10 "went in with him to the marriage feast
Lk 12.36 "to come home from the marriage feast
14. 8 "When . . invited . . to a marriage feast

MARRIAGE, GIVE IN
1. *give in marriage:* γαμίσκω GAMISKŌ*
Lk 20.34 "sons of this age marry and are given in m.
2. *give in marriage:* γαμίζω GAMIZŌ
Mt 22.30 "neither marry nor are given in marriage
24.38 "marrying and giving in marriage
Mk 12.25 "neither marry nor are given in marriage
Lk 17.27 "they married, they were given in marriage
20.35 "neither marry nor are given in marriage

MARRIAGE, REFRAIN FROM
1. *give in marriage:* γαμίζω (neg.) GAMIZŌ
1 Cor 7.38 who refrains from m. will do better

MARRIED
MARRIED MAN
MARRIED WOMAN

1. *marry:* γαμέω (subst. part.) GAMEŌ
1 Cor 7.10 To the married I give charge
7.33 but the married man is anxious
7.34 but the married woman is anxious
2. *subject to a man:* ὕπανδρος HYPANDROS*
Rom 7. 2 Thus a married woman is bound by law

MARRIED, BE

1. *have a husband:* ἔχειν ἄνδρα ANĒR [B.3.a.4]
Gal 4.27 "more than the children of her that is m.[0]

MARROW

1. *marrow, fat:* μυελός MYELOS*
Heb 4.12 piercing to the division . . of joints and m.

MARRY

1. *marry as next of kin:* ἐπιγαμβρεύω EPIGAMBREUŌ*
Mt 22.24 " 'his brother must marry the widow
2. *marry:* γαμέω GAMEŌ
Mt 5.32 "whoever marries a divorced woman
19. 9 "whoever divorces . . and marries another‡
[19. 9 "*he who marries a divorced woman*‡
19.10 "it is not expedient to marry
22.25 "the first married, and died
22.30 "in the resurrection they neither marry
24.38 "marrying and giving in marriage
Mk 6.17 because he had married her
10.11 "Whoever divorces . . and marries another
10.12 "if she divorces . . and marries another
12.25 "when they rise . . they neither marry
Lk 14.20 " 'I have married a wife, and . . I cannot come
16.18 "who divorces his wife and marries another
16.18 "he who marries a woman divorced
17.27 "They ate, they drank, they married
20.34 "The sons of this age marry
20.35 "neither marry nor are given in marriage
1 Cor 7. 9 they should marry. For it is better to marry than to be aflame with passion
7.28 But if you marry, you do not sin, and if a girl[z] marries she does not sin
7.36 let them marry—it is no sin
7.39 free to be married to whom she wishes
1 Tim 5.11 when they grow wanton . . they desire to m.
5.14 I would have younger widows marry
3. *give in marriage:* γαμίζω GAMIZŌ
1 Cor 7.38 he who marries his betrothed[z] does well

IDIOMATICALLY
a. Rom 7.3 and if she marries another man γενομένην ἀνδρὶ ἑτέρῳ [GINOMAI]

MARTHA: Μάρθα 'märthə
Lk 10.38 a woman named Martha received him
10.40 M. was distracted with much serving
10.41 "Martha, Martha, you are anxious and troubled about many things
Jn 11. 1 Bethany, the village of Mary and . . M.
11. 5 Jesus loved M. and her sister and Lazarus
11.19 many of the Jews had come to Martha
11.20 When M. heard that Jesus was coming
11.21 M. said . . "Lord, if you had been here
11.24 M. said . . "I know that he will rise again
11.30 Jesus . . was still . . where M. had met him
11.39 M. . . said . . "Lord, . . there will be an odor
12. 2 M. served, and Lazarus was . . at table

MARTYR

1. *witness, martyr:* μάρτυς MARTYS
Rev 17. 6 drunk with . . the blood of the martyrs

MARVEL

1. *wonderful:* θαυμαστός (subst.) THAUMASTOS
Jn 9.30 The man answered, "Why, this is a m.!
2. *marvel, admire:* θαυμάζω (act.; fut. pass.) THAUMAZŌ
Mt 8.10 When Jesus heard him, he marveled
8.27 marveled, saying, "What sort of man?
9.33 dumb man spoke; . . the crowds marveled
21.20 When the disciples saw it they marveled
22.22 When they heard it, they marveled
Mk 5.20 and all men marveled
6. 6 he marveled because of their unbelief
Lk 1.63 And they all marveled
2.33 his father and his mother marveled
7. 9 When Jesus heard this he marveled at him
8.25 they marveled, saying to one another
9.43 all marveling at everything he did
11.14 dumb man spoke, and the people marveled
20.26 marveling at his answer they were silent
Jn 3. 7 "Do not marvel that I said to you
4.27 marveled that he was talking with a woman
5.20 "greater works . . , that you may marvel
5.28 "Do not marvel at this
7.15 The Jews marveled at it
7.21 "I did one deed, and you all marvel
2 Th 1.10 to be marveled at in all who have believed
Rev 17. 6 When I saw her I marveled greatly
17. 7 the angel said to me, "Why marvel?
17. 8 "dwellers . . will marvel to behold the beast

MARVELOUS

1. *wonderful:* θαυμαστός THAUMASTOS
Mt 21.42 " 'this was the Lord's doing, and it is m.
Mk 12.11 " 'this was the Lord's doing, and it is m.
1 Pet 2. 9 who called you . . into his marvelous light

MARY: Μαρία, Μαριάμ 'merē
1. mother of Jesus
Mt 1.16 Joseph the husband of Mary
1.18 When his mother M. had been betrothed
1.20 "do not fear to take Mary your wife
2.11 they saw the child with Mary his mother
13.55 "Is not his mother called Mary?
Mk 6. 3 "Is not this the carpenter, the son of Mary?
Lk 1.27 and the virgin's name was Mary
1.30 angel said to her, "Do not be afraid, Mary
1.34 M. said to the angel, "How shall this be?
1.38 Mary said, "Behold, I am the handmaid
1.39 Mary arose and went with haste
1.41 when Elizabeth heard the greeting of Mary
1.46 Mary said, "My soul magnifies the Lord
1.56 M. remained with her about three months
2. 5 M., his betrothed, who was with child
2.16 they . . found Mary and Joseph, and the babe
2.19 But Mary kept all these things
2.34 Simeon . . said to M. his mother, "Behold
Acts 1.14 the women and Mary the mother of Jesus
2. Mary Magdalene
[1]and Mary the mother of James [2]and the other Mary [3]and Mary the mother of Joses [4]and Mary the wife of Clopas
Mt 27.56 [1]M. M., and Mary the mother of James
27.61 [2]M. M. and the other Mary were there
28. 1 [2]M. M. and the other Mary went to see
Mk 15.40 [1]M. M., and Mary the mother of James
15.47 [3]M. M. and Mary the mother of Joses
16. 1 [1]M. M., Mary the mother of James
16. 9 M. M., from whom he . . cast out . . demons[k]‡
Lk 8. 2 M., called Magdalene, from whom seven
24.10 [1]M. M. . . and Mary the mother of James
Jn 19.25 [4]Mary the wife of Clopas, and M. M.
20. 1 M. M. came to the tomb early
20.11 Mary stood weeping outside the tomb
20.16 Jesus said to her, "Mary
20.18 M. M. . . said . . "I have seen the Lord
3. sister of Martha and Lazarus
Lk 10.39 And she had a sister called Mary
10.42 "Mary has chosen the good portion
Jn 11. 1 Bethany, the village of M. and . . Martha
11. 2 It was Mary who anointed the Lord
11.19 Jews had come to Martha and Mary
11.20 Martha . . went . . , while M. sat in the house
11.28 she went and called her sister Mary
11.31 Jews . . saw M. rise quickly and go out
11.32 Mary, when she came where Jesus was
11.45 Jews . . who had come with Mary

Jn 12. 3 Mary took a pound of costly ointment
4. others (*See also above*, 2[1, 2, 3, 4])
Acts 12.12 the house of Mary, the mother of John
Rom 16. 6 Greet Mary, who has worked hard among you

MASTER
1. *master, lord:* δεσπότης DESPOTĒS
1 Tim 6. 1 their masters as worthy of all honor
6. 2 Those who have believing masters
Tit 2. 9 Bid slaves . . be submissive to . . masters
1 Pet 2.18 Servants, be submissive to your masters
2 Pet 2. 1 denying the Master who bought them
Jude . 4 who . . deny our only Master and Lord†
2. *one who is set over, governor:* ἐπιστάτης EPISTATĒS*
Lk 5. 5 "Master, we toiled all night
8.24 they went and woke him, saying, "Master, Master, we are perishing!
8.45 "Master, the multitudes surround you
9.33 "Master, it is well that we are here
9.49 "M., we saw a man casting out demons
17.13 "Jesus, Master, have mercy on us
3. *domineer completely:* κατακυριεύω KATAKYRIEUŌ
Acts 19.16 the man . . mastered all of them
4. *teacher:* καθηγητής KATHĒGĒTĒS*
Mt 23.10 "Neither be called masters, for you have one master, the Christ
5. *lord, master:* κύριος KYRIOS
Mt 6.24 "No one can serve two masters
10.24 "nor a servant[y] above his master
10.25 "and the servant[y] like his master
15.27 "the crumbs . . from their master's table
24.45 "whom his m. has set over his household
24.46 "that servant whom his master . . will find
24.48 " 'My master is delayed
24.50 "the master of that servant will come
25.18 "he . . hid his master's money
25.19 "after a long time the master . . came
25.20 " 'M., you delivered to me five talents
25.21 "His master said to him, 'Well done . . ; enter into the joy of your master
25.22 " 'M., you delivered to me two talents
25.23 "His master said to him, 'Well done . . ; enter into the joy of your master
25.24 " 'Master, I knew you to be a hard man
25.26 "his m. answered . . 'You wicked . . servant!
Mk 13.35 "when the master of the house will come
Lk 12.36 "men who are waiting for their master
12.37 "servants whom the master finds awake
12.42 "whom his m. will set over his household
12.43 "that servant whom his master . . will find
12.45 " 'My master is delayed in coming
12.46 "the master of that servant will come
12.47 "that servant who knew his master's will
14.21 "servant came and reported this to his m.
14.23 "the master said to the servant
16. 3 " 'my master is taking the stewardship
16. 5 "summoning his master's debtors . . he said . . 'How much do you owe my master?
16. 8 "m. commended the dishonest steward
16.13 "No servant can serve two masters
Jn 13.16 "a servant[d] is not greater than his master
15.15 "does not know what his master is doing
15.20 " 'A servant[i] is not greater than his master
Rom 14. 4 It is before his own master that he stands
14. 4 for the Master is able to make him stand
Eph 6. 5 those who are your earthly masters
6. 9 Masters, do the same to them
6. 9 he who is both their Master and yours
Col 3.22 those who are your earthly masters
4. 1 Masters, treat your slaves justly
4. 1 you also have a Master in heaven
6. *my master* (Heb.): ῥαββί RHABBI
Mt 26.25 Judas, who betrayed him, said, "Is it I, M.?[f]†
26.49 he came up . . and said, "Hail, M.![i]†
Mk 9. 5 "Master,[f] it is well that we are here†
11.21 "Master,[v] look! The fig tree . . withered†
14.45 he went up . . and said, "Master![e]†
7. *my master* (Heb.): ῥαββουνί RHABBOUNI
Mk 10.51 "Master,[t] let me receive my sight†

MASTER BUILDER
1. *master builder:* ἀρχιτέκτων ARCHITEKTŌN*
1 Cor 3.10 like a . . master builder I laid a foundation

MASTER OF ONESELF
1. *of sound mind, prudent:* σώφρων SŌPHRŌN [A.3.a.3]
Tit 1. 8 a lover of goodness, master of himself

MASTER OF THE HOUSE
1. *master, lord:* δεσπότης DESPOTĒS
2 Tim 2.21 useful to the master of the house
2. *master of the house:* οἰκοδεσπότης OIKODESPOTĒS
Mt 10.25 "called the master of the house Beelzebul

MATCH
1. *sound together, harmonize with:* συμφωνέω (+dat.) SYMPHŌNEŌ
Lk 5.36 "the piece from the new will not match
IDIOMATICALLY
a. 2 Cor 8.11 so that your readiness in desiring it may be matched by your completing it ὅπως καθάπερ ἡ προθυμία τοῦ θέλειν, οὕτως καὶ τὸ ἐπιτελέσαι [KATHAPER; HOUTŌS]

MATERIAL
1. *fleshly:* σαρκικός SARKIKOS
Rom 15.27 service to them in material blessings
1 Cor 9.11 too much if we reap your m. benefits?

MATTATHA: Ματταθά 'matəthə
Lk 3.31 Menna, the son of M., the son of Nathan

MATTATHIAS: Ματταθίας ˌmatə'thīəs
Lk 3.25 Mattathias, the son of Amos
3.26 Maath, the son of M., the son of Semein

MATTER (*See also* LIFE, MATTERS PERTAINING TO THIS)
1. *word, reckoning:* λόγος LOGOS
Mk 9.10 So they kept the matter to themselves
Acts 8.21 "You have neither part nor lot in this m.
15. 6 elders were gathered . . to consider this m.
2. *thing, deed:* πρᾶγμα PRAGMA
2 Cor 7.11 proved yourselves guiltless in the m.
1 Th 4. 6 that no man . . wrong his brother in this m.[c]†
CONTEXTUALLY
Mt 23.23 "have neglected the weightier matters
Mk 10.10 disciples asked him again about this m.
Acts 18.15 "it is a m. of questions about words
28.23 And he expounded the matter to them
Rom 2.29 real circumcision is a m. of the heart
1 Cor 7. 1 the matters about which you wrote
2 Cor 8.10 And in this matter I give my advice
8.22 tested and found earnest in many matters
2 Pet 1.20 a matter of one's own interpretation
2.12 in matters of which they are ignorant

MATTER OF, A
1. *anyone, any:* τὶς TIS II
Acts **18.14**

MATTER OF, AS A
1. *from, out of:* ἐκ (+gen.) EK
2 Cor **8.14**(13)

MATTHAN: Ματθάν, Μαθθάν 'mathən
Mt 1.15 Eleazar the father of Matthan, and Matthan the father of Jacob

MATTHAT: [a]Ματθάτ [b]Μαθθάτ 'mathət
Lk 3.24 [a]the son of Matthat, the son of Levi
3.29 [b]the son of Matthat, the son of Levi

MATTHEW: Ματθαῖος, Μαθθαῖος 'math,yü
Mt 9. 9 a man called M. sitting at the tax office
10. 3 Thomas and Matthew the tax collector
Mk 3.18 Matthew, and Thomas, and James
Lk 6.15 Matthew, and Thomas, and James
Acts 1.13 Thomas, Bartholomew and Matthew

MATTHIAS: Ματθίας, Μαθθίας mə'thīəs
Acts 1.23 they put forward two, . . Barsabbas, . . and M.
1.26 the lot fell on M.; and he was enrolled

MATURE
1. *perfect, complete:* τέλειος TELEIOS
1 Cor 2. 6 among the mature we do impart wisdom

1 Cor 14.20 be babes in evil, but in thinking be mature
Eph 4.13 until we all attain . . to mature manhood
Phil 3.15 Let . . us who are mature be thus minded
Col 1.28 that we may present every man mature
4.12 that you may stand mature
Heb 5.14 But solid food is for the mature

MATURES, ONE'S FRUIT
1. *bring fruit to maturity:* τελεσφορέω TELESPHOREŌ*
Lk 8.14 "their fruit does not mature

MATURITY
1. *perfection, completeness:* τελειότης TELEIOTĒS
Heb 6. 1 let us . . go on to maturity

MAY
1. *be able:* δύναμαι (+inf.) DYNAMAI
Acts 17.19 "May we know what this new teaching is?
24.11 "As you may ascertain, it is not
2. *it is allowed, it is possible:* ἔξεστι EXESTI [A.6.c.3]
Acts 2.29 "Brethren, I may say to you confidently
[8.37 "*If you believe with all your heart, you may*‡
21.37 'May I say something to you?
2 Cor 12. 4 things . . which man may not utter

MAY BE, IT
1. *equally, perhaps:* ἴσως ISŌS*
Lk 20.13 " 'it may be they will respect him

ME
1. *I:* ἐγώ EGŌ
Mt **2**.8; **3**.11, 14; **4**.9, 19; **7**.21, 22, 23; **8**.2, 21, 22; **9**.9; **10**.32, 33, 37^{4}, 38^{2}, 40^{3}; **11**.6, 27, 29, 38; **12**.30^{3}; **14**.8, 18, 28, 30; **15**.5, 8^{2}, 9, 22, 25, 32; **16**.23^{2}, 24^{2}; **17**.17, 27; **18**.5, 6, 21, 26, 29, 32; **19**.14, 17, 21, 28; **20**.13; **21**.2, 24; **22**.18, 19; **23**.39; **25**.20, 22, 35^{2}, 36^{2}, 40, 41, 42^{2}, 43^{3}, 45; **26**.10, 11, 12, 15, 21, 23^{2}, 31, 34, 38, 39, 40, 53, 55^{2}, 75; **27**.10, 46; **28**.10, 18
Mk **1**.7, 17, 40; **2**.14; **5**.7^{2}, 31; **6**.22, 23, 25; **7**.6^{2}, 7, 11, 14; **8**.2, 33, 34^{2}, 38; **9**.19, 37^{4}, 39, 42; **10**.14, 18, 21, 36, 47, 48; **11**.29, 30; **12**.15; **14**.6, 7, 18, 20, 36
Lk **1**.25, 38, 43^{2}, 48, 49; **2**.49; **4**.6, 7, 18^{3}, 23; **5**.8, 12, 27; **6**.46, 47; **7**.23, 44, 45; **8**.28^{2}, 45, 46^{2}; **9**.23^{2}, 26, 48^{3}, 59^{2}, 61; **10**.16^{4}, 22, 40^{2}; **11**.5, 7^{2}, 23^{3}; **12**.8, 9, 13, 14; **13**.27, 35; **14**.18, 19, 26, 27; **15**.6, 9, 12, 19, [21‡, 29, 31; **16**.3, 4, 24; **17**.8; **18**.3, 5^{2}, 13, 16, 19, 22, 38, 39; **19**.27^{2}; **20**.3, 24; **22**.21^{2}, 28, 29, 34, 37^{2}, 42, 53, 61; **23**.14, 28, 42, 43; **24**.39, 44
Jn **1**.15^{3}, 27, 30^{3}, 33^{2}, 43, 48; **2**.4, 17; **3**.28; **4**.7, 9, 10, 15, 21, 29, 34, 39; **5**.7^{2}, 11^{2}, 24, 30, 32^{2}, 36^{3}, 37^{2}, 39, 40, 43, 46^{2}; **6**.26, 35, 36, 37^{3}, 38, 39^{2}, 44^{2}, 45, 56, 57^{3}, 65; **7**.7, 16, 19, 23, 28, 29, 33, 34^{2}, 36^{2}, 37, 38; **8**.12, 16, 18^{2}, 19^{2}, 21, 26, 28, 29^{3}, 37, 40, 42^{2}, 45, 46^{2}, 49, 54; **9**.4, 11; **10**.8, 9, 14, 15, 17, 18, 25, 27, 29, 32, 37, 38; **11**.25, 26, 41, 42^{2}; **12**.8, 26^{3}, 27, 44^{3}, 45^{2}, 46, 48, 49; **13**.8, 13, 18, 20^{3}, 21, 33, 36, 38^{2}; **14**.1, 6, 7, 9^{2}, 10, 11^{3}, [14‡, 15, 19^{2}, 20, 21^{2}, 23, 24^{2}, 28, 30, 31; **15**.4^{2}, 5^{2}, 6, 7, 9, 16, 18, 20, 21, 23, 24, 25, 26, 27; **16**.3, 5^{2}, 9, 10, 14, 16^{2}, 17^{2}, 19^{2}, 23, 27, 32, 33; **17**.4, 5, 6, 7, 8^{2}, 9, 11, 12, 18, 20, 21^{2}, 22, 23^{3}, 24^{4}, 25, 26; **18**.8, 9, 11, 21, 23, 34, 35; **19**.10, 11^{2}; **20**.15, 17, 21, 29; **21**.15, 16, 17^{2}, 19, 22
Acts **1**.4; **2**.28^{2}; **3**.22; **5**.8; **7**.7, 28, 37, 42, 49; **8**.24^{2}, 31; **9**.4, 17; **10**.29; **11**.5, 7, 8, 11, 12^{2}; **12**.8, 11; **13**.2, 25; **15**.13; **16**.15; **20**.19, 22, 23^{2}, 34; **21**.39; **22**.5, 6, 7^{2}, 8, 9^{2}, 10, 11, 13^{2}, 18^{2}, 21, 27; **23**.3^{2}, 11, 18, 19, 22, 30; **24**.12, 13, 18, 19; **25**.9, 11^{2}, 24, 27; **26**.3, 13^{2}, 14^{2}, 16, 18, 21, 28, 29; **27**.21, 23; **28**.18
Rom **7**.8, 10, 11, 13^{2}, 17, 18^{2}, 20, 23, 24; **8**.2; **9**.1, 19, 20; **10**.20^{2}; **12**.3; **14**.11; **15**.3, 15, 18, 30; **16**.7, 23
1 Cor **1**.11, 17; **3**.10; **4**.3, 4, 16; **6**.12^{2}; **9**.3, 16^{3}; **11**.1, 2; **14**.11, 21; **15**.10^{2}; **16**.4, 6, 9, 11
2 Cor **2**.2, 3, 5, 12; **7**.7; **9**.1, 4; **11**.1^{2}, 10, 16^{2}, 28, 32; **12**.6^{3}, 7^{2}, 8, 9^{2}, 11, 13, 21; **13**.3, 10
Gal **1**.2, 11, 15, 16, 17, 24; **2**.3, 6^{2}, 8, 9^{2}, 20^{3}; **4**.12, 14, 15, 21; **6**.14^{2}, 17
Eph **3**.2, 3, 7, 8; **6**.19^{2}
Phil **1**.7^{2}, 12, 19, 21, 22, 26; **2**.18, 22, 23, 27, 30; **3**.1, 17; **4**.3, 9, 10, 13, 15, 16‡, 21
Col **1**.25, 29; **4**.11
1 Tim **1**.12^{2}, 16
2 Tim **1**.8, 12†, 13, 15, 16, 17; **2**.2; **3**.11^{2}; **4**.8^{3}, 9, 10, 11^{2}, 14, 16, 17^{2}, 18
Tit **3**.12, 15
Phm .11, 13, 16, 17^{2}, 19, 22
Heb **2**.13; **8**.11; **10**.5, 7; **11**.32; **13**.6
Jas **2**.18
2 Pet **1**.14
Rev **1**.10, 12, 17; **3**.4, 18, 20, 21; **4**.1; **5**.5; **7**.13, 14; **10**.8, 9^{2}; **17**.1, 3, 7, 15; **19**.9^{2}, 10; **21**.6, 9, 10^{2}, 15; **22**.1, 6, 8, 9, 10
2. *myself:* ἐμαυτοῦ EMAUTOU
Mt 8. 9 "under authority, with soldiers under me
Lk 7. 8 "under authority, with soldiers under me
Phm .13 glad to keep him with me
3. *we:* ἡμεῖς HĒMEIS
3 Jn .10
IDIOMATICALLY
a. 2 Cor 1.23 But I call God to witness against me Ἐγὼ δὲ μάρτυρα τὸν θεὸν ἐπικαλοῦμαι ἐπὶ τὴν ἐμὴν ψυχήν [EMOS]

ME, OF
ME, WHAT BELONGS TO
1. *my, mine:* ἐμός EMOS
^{a}subst. neut. pl.
Mt 20.15 ^{a}" 'what I choose with what belongs to me
Lk 22.19 "Do this in remembrance of me‡
1 Cor 11.24 "Do this in remembrance of me
11.25 "Do this . . in remembrance of me

MEAL
1. *eating, food:* βρῶσις BRŌSIS
Heb 12.16 Esau, who sold his birthright for a . . meal
2. *meal, dinner:* δεῖπνον DEIPNON
1 Cor 11.21 each one goes ahead with his own m.

MEAN
1. *obscure, insignificant:* ἄσημος ASĒMOS*
Acts 21.39 "I am . . a citizen of no mean city
2. *explained says:* διερμηνευόμενος λέγεται DIERMĒNEUŌ [A.6.a.4]
Acts 9.36 named Tabitha, which means Dorcas^{x}
3. *be:* εἰμί EIMI
Mt 9.13 "Go and learn what this means
12. 7 "And if you had known what this means
13.38 "good seed means the sons of the kingdom
Mk 9.10 what the rising from the dead meant
Lk 8. 9 disciples asked him what this parable meant
15.26 called one . . and asked what this meant
18.36 hearing . . he inquired what this meant
Acts 10.17 perplexed . . what the vision . . might mean
Rom 9. 8 This means that it is not the children
Eph 4. 9 ("He ascended," what does it mean?
4. *interpret:* ἑρμηνεύω (pass.) HERMĒNEUŌ
Jn 1.42 "called Cephas" (which means Peter^{c}
9. 7 "pool of Siloam" (which means Sent
5. *speak, talk:* λαλέω LALEŌ
Jn 16.18 "We do not know what he means
6. *say, tell:* λέγω LEGŌ
^{a}mid. ^{b}λέγεται μεθερμηνευόμενον *interpreted says* A.6.a.4
^{c}διερμηνευομένη λέγεται *explained says* A.6.a.4
Mt 26.70 "I do not know what you mean
27.33 ^{a}(which means the place of a skull
Mk 14.68 "nor understand what you mean
Jn 1.38 ^{b}"Rabbi" (which means Teacher
11.13 that he meant taking rest in sleep
16.18 "What does he mean by 'a little while'?
20.16 ^{a}"Rabboni!" (which means Teacher
Acts 9.36 ^{c}named Tabitha, which means Dorcas^{x}
1 Cor 1.12 I mean . . each one of you says
10.29 (I mean his conscience, not yours
Gal 3.17 This is what I mean
4. 1 I mean that the heir . . is no better
7. *translate:* μεθερμηνεύω METHERMĒNEUŌ
^{a}pass. periphr. A.6.c.3
^{b}λέγεται μεθερμηνευόμενον *interpreted says* A.6.a.4
Mt 1.23 ^{a}"Emmanuel" (which means, God with us
Mk 5.41 ^{a}"Talitha cumi"; which means
15.22 ^{a}(which means the place of a skull
15.34 ^{a}"lama sabachthani?" which means
Jn 1.38 ^{b}"Rabbi" (which means Teacher

Jn 1.41 [a]"the Messiah" (which means Christ
Acts 4.36 [a](which means, Son of encouragement
8. *say, affirm:* φημί PHĒMI
1 Cor 7.29 I mean . . the . . time has grown very short
9. *will, wish:* θέλω THELŌ
Mk 6.48 He meant to pass by them
Acts 2.12 "What does this mean?
17.20 "to know . . what these things mean
IDIOMATICALLY
a. Jn 7.36 "What does he mean by saying? τίς ἐστιν ὁ λόγος οὗτος ὃν εἶπεν; [LOGOS]
b. 1 Cor 15.29 what do people mean by being baptized? τί ποιήσουσιν οἱ βαπτιζόμενοι; [POIEŌ]
CONTEXTUALLY
Jn 16.19 "asking yourselves, what I meant by saying
Rom 2. 4 God's kindness is meant to lead you
11.12 if their trespass means riches for the world
11.12 failure means riches for the Gentiles
11.12 how much more will their full inclusion m.!
11.15 if their rejection means . . reconciliation
11.15 what will their acceptance m. but life?
1 Cor 5.10 not at all meaning the immoral of this world
6.13 "Food is meant for the stomach
6.13 The body is not meant for immorality
2 Cor 8.13 I do not mean that others should be eased
Phil 1.22 that means fruitful labor for me

MEANING
1. *power, ability:* δύναμις DYNAMIS
1 Cor 14.11 but if I do not know the meaning

MEANING OF, BE THE
1. *translate:* μεθερμηνεύω (pass.) METHERMĒNEUŌ
Acts 13. 8 (for that is the meaning of his name

MEANING, WITHOUT
1. *voiceless:* ἄφωνος APHŌNOS
1 Cor 14.10 languages . . , and none is without m.

MEANS (*See also* GAIN, MEANS OF)
1. *power, ability:* δύναμις DYNAMIS
2 Cor 8. 3 gave according to their means, . . and beyond their means, of their own free will
2. *be, exist, belong to:* ὑπάρχω (subst. neut. pl.) HYPARCHŌ
Lk 8. 3 provided for them[z] out of their means
CONTEXTUALLY
Acts 4. 9 "by what means this man has been healed

MEANS, BY ALL
1. *in all ways, assuredly:* πάντως PANTŌS
1 Cor 9.22 that I might by all means save some

MEANS, BY NO
1. *come to be, happen, be:* γίνομαι (neg. opt.) GINOMAI [B.3.b.8]
Rom 3. 4 By no means! Let God be true
3. 6 By no means! . . how could God judge?
3.31 Do we . . overthrow the law . . ? By no m.!
6. 2 ⟨Are we to continue in sin?⟩ By no means!
6.15 Are we to sin . . ? By no means!
7. 7 That the law is sin? By no means!
7.13 Did that . . bring death . . ? By no means!
9.14 Is there injustice . . ? By no means!
11. 1 has God rejected his people? By no m.!
11.11 stumbled so as to fall? By no means!
2. *not* (emph.): οὐ μή OU MĒ
Mk 9.41 "whoever gives . . will by no m. lose . . reward
3. *by no means:* οὐδαμῶς OUDAMŌS*
Mt 2. 6 " 'by no means least among the rulers

MEANS OF, BY
1. *through:* διά (+gen.) DIA
Mk **16.**[end]‡
2 Pet **3.5**
2. *from, out of:* ἐκ (+gen.) EK
Lk **16.9**
3. *in, at, by:* ἐν (+dat.) EN
Rev **9.19**[2]

MEANTIME
CONTEXTUALLY
Lk 12. 1 In the m., when so many . . had gathered

MEANWHILE
1. *in the between* (time): ἐν τῷ μεταξύ METAXY [B.1.a.1; B.3.b.2]
Jn 4.31 Meanwhile the disciples besought him

MEASURE
1. *bath* (Heb., a liquid measure): βάτος BATOS II*
Lk 16. 6 "He said, 'A hundred measures of oil
2. *kor* (Heb., a dry measure): κόρος KOROS*
Lk 16. 7 "He said, 'A hundred measures of wheat
3. *count, measure:* μετρέω METREŌ
2 Cor 10.12 But when they measure themselves
Rev 11. 1 "Rise and measure the temple of God
11. 2 "do not measure the court outside
21.15 to measure the city and its gates
21.16 he measured the city with his rod
21.17 He also measured its wall
4. *measure:* μέτρον METRON
Mt 7. 2 "and the measure you give . . you get
23.32 "Fill up, then, the measure of your fathers
Mk 4.24 "the measure you give . . you get
Lk 6.38 "good m., pressed down, shaken together . . For the measure you give . . you get back
Jn 3.34 not by measure that he gives the Spirit
Rom 12. 3 each according to the measure of faith
Eph 4. 7 according to the m. of Christ's gift
4.13 m. of the stature of the fulness of Christ
Rev 21.17 forty-four cubits by a man's measure
5. *seah* (Heb., a dry measure): σάτον SATON*
Mt 13.33 "hid in three measures of flour
Lk 13.21 "hid in three measures of flour

MEASURE, BEYOND
1. *to excess:* καθ' ὑπερβολήν HYPERBOLĒ [B.1.b]
Rom 7.13 that sin . . might become sinful b. measure
2. *beyond all measure:* ὑπερπερισσῶς HYPERPERISSŌS*
Mk 7.37 they were astonished beyond measure

MEASURE, GET
MEASURE, GIVE
IDIOMATICALLY
a. Mt 7.2 *and* Mk 4.24 "the measure you give will be the measure you get ἐν ᾧ μέτρῳ μετρεῖτε μετρηθήσεται ὑμῖν [METREŌ]
b. Lk 6.38 "For the measure you give will be the measure you get back ᾧ γὰρ μέτρῳ μετρεῖτε ἀντιμετρηθήσεται ὑμῖν [METREŌ]

MEASURE, GET BACK A
1. *measure in return:* ἀντιμετρέω (pass.) ANTIMETREŌ*
Lk 6.38 "will be the measure you get back

MEASURE OF, A LIKE
1. *so large, so many:* τοσοῦτος TOSOUTOS
Rev 18. 7 " 'give her a like measure of torment

MEASURE OF, FILL UP THE
1. *fill up:* ἀναπληρόω ANAPLĒROŌ
1 Th 2.16 to fill up the measure of their sins

MEASURES, TAKE
IDIOMATICALLY
a. Acts 27.17 they took measures[c] to undergird the ship† βοηθείαις ἐχρῶντο, ὑποζωννύντες τὸ πλοῖον [BOĒTHEIA; CHRAOMAI]

MEASURING
1. *measure:* μέτρον METRON [A.1.b.2]
Rev 21.15 he who talked to me had a m. rod

MEASURING ROD
1. *reed, staff:* κάλαμος KALAMOS
Rev 11. 1 Then I was given a measuring rod

MEAT
1. *meat, flesh:* κρέας KREAS*
Rom 14.21 it is right not to eat meat or drink wine
1 Cor 8.13 I will never eat m., lest . . my brother . . fall

MEAT MARKET
1. *enclosure, market:* μάκελλον MAKELLON*
1 Cor 10.25 Eat whatever is sold in the meat market

MEDE: Μῆδος
Acts 2. 9 "Parthians and Medes and Elamites

MEDIATE
1. *mediator, arbitrator:* μεσίτης MESITĒS [A.1.a]
Heb 8. 6 as the covenant he mediates is better

MEDIATOR
1. *mediator, arbitrator:* μεσίτης MESITĒS
1 Tim 2. 5 one mediator between God and men
Heb 9.15 he is the mediator of a new covenant
12.24 Jesus, the mediator of a new covenant

MEDITATE BEFOREHAND
1. *practice beforehand:* προμελετάω PROMELETAŌ*
Lk 21.14 "not to m. beforehand how to answer

MEEK
1. *gentle, meek:* πραΰς PRAYS
Mt 5. 5 "Blessed are the m., for they shall inherit

MEEKNESS
1. *gentleness:* πραΰτης PRAYTĒS
2 Cor 10. 1 I . . entreat you, by the m. . . of Christ
Eph 4. 2 with all lowliness and meekness
Col 3.12 lowliness, meekness, and patience
Jas 1.21 receive with meekness the implanted word
3.13 show his works in the m. of wisdom

MEET (*See also* FAIL TO MEET THE TEST; TEST, TO HAVE MET THE)
1. *meet:* ἀπαντάω APANTAŌ*
Mk 14.13 "man carrying a jar of water will m. you
Lk 17.12 as he entered . . he was met by ten lepers
2. *meeting:* ἀπάντησις APANTĒSIS* [B.1.a.2]
Mt 25. 6 " 'the bridegroom! Come out to meet him
Acts 28.15 the brethren . . came . . to meet us
1 Th 4.17 then we . . shall . . meet the Lord in the air
3. *have, hold:* ἔχω ECHŌ
Acts 25.16 "before the accused met the accusers
4. *gathering together:* ἐπισυναγωγή EPISYNAGŌGĒ [A.1.d]
Heb 10.25 not neglecting to meet together
5. *go to meet:* ὑπαντάω HYPANTAŌ
Mt 8.28 when he came . . two demoniacs met him
28. 9 Jesus met them and said, "Hail!
Mk 5. 2 there met him out of the tombs a man
Lk 8.27 there met him a man from the city
14.31 "whether he is able . . to meet him
Jn 4.51 his servants met him and told him
11.20 she went and met him, while Mary sat
11.30 the place where Martha had met him
Acts 16.16 we were met by a slave girl
6. *coming to meet:* ὑπάντησις HYPANTĒSIS* [B.1.a.2]
Mt 8.34 all the city came out to meet Jesus
25. 1 "maidens . . went to meet the bridegroom[c]
Jn 12.13 they . . went out to meet him
7. *fall in with, encounter:* περιπίπτω (+dat.) PERIPIPTŌ
Jas 1. 2 when you meet various trials
8. *throw together, compare:* συμβάλλω SYMBALLŌ
Acts 17.18 Epicurean and Stoic philosophers met him
20.14 when he met us at Assos
9. *bring together:* συνάγω (pass.) SYNAGŌ
Jn 18. 2 Jesus often met there with his disciples
Acts 11.26 they met with[j] the church, and taught†
10. *meet together, happen:* συναντάω SYNANTAŌ
Lk 9.37 a great crowd met him
22.10 "man carrying a jar of water will m. you
Acts 10.25 Cornelius met him and fell . . at his feet
Heb 7. 1 Melchizedek . . met Abraham returning
7.10 when Melchizedek met him
11. *come together:* συνέρχομαι SYNERCHOMAI
Acts 22.30 commanded . . all the council to meet
1 Cor 11.20 When you meet together
CONTEXTUALLY
2 Th 2. 1 and our assembling to meet him

MEET, GO TO
1. *go to meet:* ὑπαντάω HYPANTAŌ
Jn 12.18 why the crowd went to meet him

MEET WITH
1. *mix, compose:* συγκεράννυμι SYGKERANNYMI
Heb 4. 2 it did not m. with faith in the hearers[h]‡

MEETING
CONTEXTUALLY
Acts 13.43 when the m. of the synagogue broke up

MELCHI: Μελχί 'melkī
Lk 3.24 Levi, the son of M., the son of Jannai
3.28 Melchi, the son of Addi

MELCHIZEDEK: Μελχισέδεκ mel'kizə,dek
Heb 5. 6 "Thou art a priest . . after the order of M.
5.10 a high priest after the order of M.
6.20 a high priest for ever after the order of M.
7. 1 this Melchizedek, king of Salem
7.10 when Melchizedek met him
7.11 another priest . . after the order of M.
7.15 another priest . . in the likeness of M.
7.17 "a priest for ever, after the order of M.

MELEA: Μελεά 'mēlēə
Lk 3.31 Melea, the son of Menna

MELODY, MAKE
1. *pluck, sing to a harp:* ψάλλω PSALLŌ
Eph 5.19 singing and making melody to the Lord

MELT
1. *melt, dissolve:* τήκω (pass.) TĒKŌ*
2 Pet 3.12 the elements will melt with fire!

MEMBER (*See also* HOUSEHOLD, MEMBER OF THE)
1. *part, limb:* μέλος MELOS
Mt 5.29 "better that you lose one of your members
5.30 "better that you lose one of your members
Rom 6.13 Do not yield your members to sin . . , but yield . . your members to God
6.19 you . . yielded your members to impurity
6.19 yield your members to righteousness
7. 5 at work in our members to bear fruit
7.23 I see in my members another law
7.23 captive to the law . . in my members
12. 4 as in one body we have many members
12. 4 members do not have the same function
12. 5 individually members one of another
1 Cor 6.15 know that your bodies are members of Christ? Shall I . . take the members of Christ and make them members of a prostitute?
12.12 as the body . . has many members, and all the members . . are one body
12.14 the body does not consist of one member
12.25 that . . members may have the same care
12.26 If one member suffers, all suffer . . ; if one member is honored, all rejoice
12.27 you are . . individually members of it
Eph 4.25 for we are members one of another
5.30 because we are members of his body
Jas 3. 5 the tongue is a little member and boasts
3. 6 an unrighteous world among our members
4. 1 passions that are at war in your members
CONTEXTUALLY
Rom 11. 1 a member of the tribe of Benjamin
1 Cor 6. 5 decide between members of the brotherhood

MEMBER OF THE COUNCIL
1. *councillor:* βουλευτής BOULEUTĒS*
Mk 15.43 Joseph of A., a . . member of the council
Lk 23.50 Joseph . . was a member of the council

MEMBER OF THE COURT
1. *brought up together with:* σύντροφος (subst.) SYNTROPHOS*
Acts 13. 1 Manaen a member of the court of Herod

MEMBER OF THE SAME BODY
1. *united in one body:* σύσσωμος (subst.) SYSSŌMOS*
Eph 3. 6 Gentiles are . . members of the same body

MEMORIAL
1. *remembrance:* μνημόσυνον MNĒMOSYNON
Acts 10. 4 "your alms . . as a memorial before God

MEMORY
1. *remembrance:* μνημόσυνον MNĒMOSYNON
Mt 26.13 "what she has done will be told in memory
Mk 14. 9 "what she has done will be told in memory

MEN
1. *male:* ἄρσην (subst. pl.) ARSĒN
Rom 1.27 men . . gave up natural relations with women . . , men committing shameless acts with men and receiving . . the due penalty
2. *lord, master:* κύριος (voc. pl.) KYRIOS
Acts 16.30 "Men, what must I do to be saved?
3. *all, every, whole:* πᾶς (subst. pl.) PAS
Acts 21.28 "Men of Israel, help!

MEN, ORDAINED FOR
1. *human:* ἀνθρώπινος ANTHRŌPINOS
1 Pet [2.13 to every *institution ordained for men*†

MEND
1. *put in order, make:* καταρτίζω KATARTIZŌ
Mt 4.21 brothers . . in the boat . . mending their nets
Mk 1.19 who were in their boat mending the nets
IDIOMATICALLY
a. Jn 4.52 So he asked them the hour when he began to mend ἐπύθετο οὖν τὴν ὥραν παρ' αὐτῶν ἐν ᾗ κομψότερον ἔσχεν [KOMPSOTERON*]

MEND ONE'S WAYS
1. *put in order, make:* καταρτίζω (pass.) KATARTIZŌ
2 Cor 13.11 Mend your ways, heed my appeal

MENIAL USE
1. *dishonor, disgrace:* ἀτιμία ATIMIA
Rom 9.21 one . . for beauty and another for menial use

MENNA: Μεννά 'menə
Lk 3.31 Melea, the son of M., the son of Mattatha

MEN-PLEASER
1. *pleaser of men:* ἀνθρωπάρεσκος ANTHROPARESKOS*
Eph 6. 6 not . . as men-pleasers, but as servants[f]
Col 3.22 not with eyeservice, as men-pleasers

MENTION
1. *make mention:* μνείαν ποιεῖν MNEIA [B.3.a.3]
Rom 1. 9 I mention you always in my prayers
1 Th 1. 2 constantly mentioning you in our prayers

MENTION, MAKE
1. *remember, mention:* μνημονεύω MNĒMONEUŌ
Heb 11.22 made m. of the exodus of the Israelites

MERCHANT
1. *traveler, trader:* ἔμπορος EMPOROS*
Mt 13.45 "like a merchant in search of fine pearls
Rev 18. 3 "merchants of the earth have grown rich
18.11 merchants of the earth weep and mourn
18.15 merchants . . will stand far off, in fear
18.23 "for thy merchants were the great men

MERCIFUL
1. *merciful:* ἐλεήμων ELEĒMŌN*
Mt 5. 7 "Blessed are the merciful
Heb 2.17 that he might become a m. . . high priest
2. *gracious:* ἵλεως HILEŌS
Heb 8.12 "I will be merciful toward their iniquities
3. *merciful:* οἰκτίρμων OIKTIRMŌN*
Lk 6.36 "Be merciful, even as your Father is merciful
Jas 5.11 the Lord is compassionate and merciful

MERCIFUL, BE
1. *conciliate, expiate:* ἱλάσκομαι HILASKOMAI
Lk 18.13 " 'God, be merciful to me a sinner!

MERCY
1. *mercy:* ἔλεος ELEOS
Mt 9.13 " 'I desire mercy, and not sacrifice
12. 7 " 'I desire mercy, and not sacrifice
23.23 "weightier matters . . , justice and mercy
Lk 1.50 "his mercy is on those who fear him
1.54 "He has helped . . in remembrance of his m.
1.58 the Lord had shown great mercy to her
1.72 "the mercy promised to our fathers
1.78 "through the tender mercy of our God
10.37 "The one who showed mercy on him
Rom 9.23 his glory for the vessels of mercy
11.31 in order that by the mercy shown to you
15. 9 that the Gentiles . . glorify God for his m.
Gal 6.16 Peace and mercy be upon all
Eph 2. 4 But God, who is rich in mercy
1 Tim 1. 2 Grace, mercy, and peace from God
2 Tim 1. 2 Grace, mercy, and peace from God
1.16 Lord grant m. to . . household of Onesiphorus
1.18 the Lord grant him to find mercy
Tit 3. 5 he saved us . . in virtue of his own mercy
Heb 4.16 that we may receive mercy and find grace
Jas 2.13 to one who has shown no mercy; yet mercy triumphs over judgment
3.17 full of mercy and good fruits
1 Pet 1. 3 By his great m. we have been born
2 Jn . 3 Grace, mercy, and peace will be with us
Jude . 2 May mercy, peace, and love be multiplied
.21 wait for the m. of our Lord Jesus Christ
2. *compassion:* οἰκτιρμός OIKTIRMOS
Rom 12. 1 I appeal to you . . by the mercies of God
2 Cor 1. 3 Father of mercies and God of all comfort
Heb 10.28 dies without m. at the testimony of two
IDIOMATICALLY
a. Rom 9.16 So it depends . . upon God's mercy ἄρα οὖν . . τοῦ ἐλεῶντος θεοῦ [ELEEŌ]
b. 1 Cor 7.25 as one who by the Lord's mercy is trustworthy ὡς ἠλεημένος ὑπὸ κυρίου πιστὸς εἶναι [ELEEŌ]
c. 2 Cor 4.1 having this ministry by the mercy of God[e]† ἔχοντες τὴν διακονίαν ταύτην, καθὼς ἠλεήθημεν [ELEEŌ]

MERCY, DO ACTS OF
1. *show mercy:* ἐλεέω ELEEŌ
Rom 12. 8 he who does acts of m., with cheerfulness

MERCY, OBTAIN
MERCY, RECEIVE
1. *show mercy:* ἐλεέω (pass.) ELEEŌ
Mt 5. 7 "the merciful, for they shall obtain mercy
Rom 11.30 you . . now have received mercy
11.31 that . . they also may[p] receive mercy
1 Tim 1.13 received m. because I had acted ignorantly
1.16 I received mercy for this reason
1 Pet 2.10 once you had not received mercy but now you have received mercy

MERCY ON, HAVE
MERCY UPON, HAVE
1. *show mercy:* ἐλεέω ELEEŌ
Mt 9.27 "Have mercy on us, Son of David
15.22 "Have m. on me, O Lord, Son of David
17.15 "Lord, have mercy on my son
18.33 " 'should not you have had mercy . . , as I had mercy on you?
20.30 "Have mercy on us, Son of David!
20.31 "Lord, have m. on us, Son of David!
Mk 5.19 "tell . . how he has had mercy on you
10.47 "Jesus, Son of David, have mercy on me!
10.48 "Son of David, have mercy on me!
Lk 16.24 " 'Father Abraham, have mercy upon me
17.13 "Jesus, Master, have mercy on us
18.38 "Jesus, Son of David, have mercy on me!
18.39 "Son of David, have mercy on me!
Rom 9.15 For he says to Moses, "I will have mercy on whom I have mercy
9.18 he has mercy upon whomever he wills
11.32 that he may have mercy upon all
Phil 2.27 But God had mercy on him
Jude .23 on some have mercy with fear

MERCY SEAT
1. *means of expiation:* ἱλαστήριον HILASTĒRION
Heb 9. 5 cherubim . . overshadowing the m. seat

MERCY, WITHOUT
1. *unmerciful:* ἀνέλεος ANELEOS*
Jas 2.13 For judgment is without mercy

MERE
1. *but:* ἀλλά ALLA [A.5.b]
2 Th **3.11**

MERELY
1. *only, alone:* μόνος (neut.) MONOS
Rom 4.12 who are not merely circumcised
CONTEXTUALLY
1 Cor 3. 4 are you not merely men?

MERRY, BE
MERRY, MAKE
1. *gladden:* εὐφραίνω (pass.) EUPHRAINŌ
Lk 12.19 " 'take your ease, eat, drink, be merry
15.23 " 'let us eat and make merry
15.24 "And they began to make merry
15.29 " 'that I might make m. with my friends
15.32 " 'fitting to make merry and be glad
Rev 11.10 make merry and exchange presents

MESOPOTAMIA: Μεσοποταμία ˌmes(ə)pəˈtāmēə
Acts 2. 9 "Elamites and residents of Mesopotamia
7. 2 "Abraham, when he was in Mesopotamia

MESSAGE
1. *message:* ἀγγελία AGGELIA*
1 Jn 1. 5 the message we have heard from him
3.11 this is the message which you have heard
2. *proclamation:* κήρυγμα KĒRYGMA
1 Cor 2. 4 my message . . not in plausible words
2 Tim 4.17 strength to proclaim the message fully[o]
3. *word, reckoning:* λόγος LOGOS
Mk 16.20 they . . confirmed the message by the signs[k]‡
Acts 13.26 "to us has been sent the message
2 Cor 5.19 entrusting to us the m. of reconciliation
2 Tim 4.15 for he strongly opposed our message
Heb 2. 2 if the message declared by angels was valid
4. 2 the m. which they heard did not benefit
4. *word, saying:* ῥῆμα (pl.) RHĒMA
Acts 11.14 " 'he will declare to you a message

MESSAGE, SPEAK A
IDIOMATICALLY
a. Heb 12.19 that no further messages be spoken to them
μὴ προστεθῆναι αὐτοῖς λόγον [LOGOS]

MESSENGER
1. *messenger, angel:* ἄγγελος AGGELOS
Mt 11.10 " 'Behold, I send my m. before thy face
Mk 1. 2 "Behold, I send my m. before thy face
Lk 7.24 When the messengers of John had gone
7.27 " 'Behold, I send my m. before thy face
9.52 And he sent messengers ahead of him
2 Cor 12. 7 a messenger of Satan, to harass me
Jas 2.25 when she received the messengers
2. *ambassador, messenger:* ἀπόστολος APOSTOLOS
2 Cor 8.23 as for our brethren, they are messengers[j]†
Phil 2.25 your messenger and minister to my need

MESSIAH
1. *Messiah* (Aram.): Μεσσίας MESSIAS*
Jn 1.41 "We have found the Messiah
4.25 "I know that Messiah is coming

METHUSELAH: Μαθουσάλα məˈth(y)üz(ə)lə
Lk 3.37 Methuselah, the son of Enoch

MICHAEL: Μιχαήλ ˈmīkəl
Jude . 9 archangel M., contending with the devil
Rev 12. 7 M. and his angels fighting . . the dragon

MIDDAY, AT
1. *in the middle of the day:* ἡμέρας μέσης (gen.) HĒMERA; MESOS [A.1.f]
Acts 26.13 "At m., O king, I saw on the way a light

MIDDLE
1. *be in the middle:* μεσόω MESOŌ* [B.2.a.2]
Jn 7.14 About the middle of the feast
2. *middle, in the middle:* μέσος MESOS
[a]subst.
Lk 22.55 [a]a fire in the middle of the courtyard
Acts 17.22 [a]Paul, standing in the m. of the Areopagus
Rev 22. 2 [a]through the m. of the street of the city†

MIDDLE, IN THE
1. *middle, in the middle:* μέσος MESOS
Acts 1.18 "(he burst open in the middle

MIDHEAVEN
1. *zenith, midheaven:* μεσουράνημα MESOURANĒMA*
Rev 8.13 I heard an eagle crying . . as it flew in m.
14. 6 I saw another angel flying in midheaven
19.17 he called to all the birds that fly in m.

MIDIAN: Μαδιάμ ˈmidēən
Acts 7.29 "Moses . . became an exile in the land of M.

MIDNIGHT
1. *midnight:* μεσονύκτιον MESONYKTION*
Mk 13.35 "master . . will come, in the evening, or at m.
Lk 11. 5 "Which of you . . will go to him at m.
Acts 16.25 about m. Paul and Silas were praying
20. 7 he prolonged his speech until midnight
2. *midnight:* μέση νύξ MESOS; NYX [A.1.f]
[a]κατὰ μέσον τῆς νυκτός
Mt 25. 6 "But at midnight there was a cry
Acts 27.27 [a]about midnight the sailors suspected

MIDST
1. *middle, in the middle:* μέσος (subst.) MESOS
[a]prep. [b]ἀνὰ μέσον
Mt 10.16 "I send you . . in the midst of wolves
18. 2 calling . . a child he put him in the midst
18.20 "there am I in the midst of them
Mk 9.36 he took a child, and put him in the midst
14.60 the high priest stood up in the midst
Lk 4.30 passing through the midst of them
4.35 demon had thrown him down in the m.
5.19 let him down with his bed . . into the m.
10. 3 "as lambs in the midst of wolves
Jn 8. 3 brought a woman . . placing her in the m.[r]‡
Acts 2.22 "signs . . God did through him in your m.
4. 7 when they had set them in the midst
Phil 2.15 [a]in the m. of a crooked . . generation
Heb 2.12 "in the m. of the congregation I will praise
Rev 1.13 in the m. of the lampstands . . a son of man
6. 6 a voice in the m. of the four living creatures
7.17 [b]"For the Lamb in the midst of the throne
[22. 2 *In the midst of the street of the city*†

MIDST OF, IN THE
1. *in, at, by:* ἐν (+dat.) EN
Jas 1.11 fade away in the midst of his pursuits
2. *inside:* ἐντός ENTOS
Lk 17.21 "the kingdom of God is in the m. of you[z]†

MIGHT
1. *be able:* δύναμαι (+inf.) DYNAMAI
Mt 26. 9 "this ointment might have been sold
Mk 14. 5 "this ointment might have been sold
1 Th 2. 6(7) we might have made demands as apostles
2. *power, ability:* δύναμις DYNAMIS
Eph 3.16 strengthened with might through his Spirit
3. *strength, might:* ἰσχύς ISCHYS
Eph 6.10 be strong . . in the strength of his might
2 Th 1. 9 exclusion . . from the glory of his might
2 Pet 2.11 angels, though greater in might and power
Rev 5.12 "Worthy is the Lamb . . to receive . . might!
7.12 "power and might be to our God!
4. *strength, sovereignty:* κράτος KRATOS
Eph 1.19 according to the working of his great m.
Col 1.11 all power, according to his glorious m.
Rev 5.13 "To him . . be . . glory and might for ever!

MIGHTIER
1. *strong, powerful:* ἰσχυρός (comp.) ISCHYROS
Mt 3.11 "but he who is coming after me is m.
Mk 1. 7 "After me comes he who is m. than I
Lk 3.16 "but he who is mightier than I is coming

MIGHTILY
1. *in power:* ἐν δυνάμει DYNAMIS [B.1.a.1]
Col 1.29 energy which he mightily inspires
2. *by might:* κατὰ κράτος KRATOS [B.1.a.1]
Acts 19.20 the word of the Lord grew and prevailed m.

MIGHTY
1. *violent:* βίαιος BIAIOS*
Acts 2. 2 a sound . . like the rush of a mighty wind
2. *power, ability:* δύναμις (gen.) DYNAMIS
2 Th 1. 7 revealed from heaven with his mighty angels
3. *possible, strong:* δυνατός DYNATOS
Lk 1.49 "he who is mighty has done great things
24.19 "Jesus . . who was a prophet mighty in deed
Acts 7.22 "he was mighty in his words and deeds

4. *strong, powerful:* ἰσχυρός ISCHYROS
Heb 11.34 became mighty in war
Rev 10. 1 Then I saw another mighty angel
18. 2 he called out with a mighty voice
18. 8 "mighty is the Lord God who judges
18.10 "Alas! alas! . . thou mighty city, Babylon!
18.21 Then a mighty angel took up a stone
19. 6 like the sound of mighty thunderpeals
19.18 "to eat . . the flesh of mighty men
5. *strong, mighty:* κραταιός KRATAIOS*
1 Pet 5. 6 under the mighty hand of God

MIGHTY, THE
1. *ruler:* δυνάστης (pl.) DYNASTĒS
Lk 1.52 "he has put down the m. from . . thrones

MIGHTY WORK
1. *power, ability:* δύναμις DYNAMIS
Mt 7.22 " 'did we not . . do . . m. works in your name?
11.20 where . . his m. works had been done
11.21 "if the mighty works done in you
11.23 "if the mighty works done in you
13.54 "Where did this man get . . these m. works?
13.58 he did not do many m. works there
Mk 6. 2 "What m. works are wrought by his hands!
6. 5 And he could do no mighty work there
9.39 "no one who does a mighty work
Lk 10.13 if the mighty works done in you
19.37 the mighty works that they had seen
Acts 2.22 "a man attested . . by God with m. works
2 Cor 12.12 signs of a true apostle . . with . . m. works
2. *splendid, magnificent:* μεγαλεῖος (subst. neut.) MEGALEIOS*
Acts 2.11 "we hear them telling . . the m. works of God

MILE
1. *Roman mile:* μίλιον MILION*
Mt 5.41 "if any one forces you to go one mile
2. *stade* (200+ yards): στάδιον STADION [A.1.f]
Lk 24.13 Emmaus, . . seven miles[w] from Jerusalem†‡
Jn 6.19 they had rowed about three or four miles[m]†
11.18 near Jerusalem, about two miles[v] off†

MILETUS: Μίλητος mī'lētəs II,E-3
Acts 20.15 the day after that we came to Miletus
20.17 from Miletus he sent to Ephesus
2 Tim 4.20 Trophimus I left ill at Miletus

MILITARY
CONTEXTUALLY
Acts 25.23 with the m. tribunes and the prominent men

MILK
1. *milk:* γάλα GALA*
1 Cor 3. 2 I fed you with milk, not solid food
9. 7 Who tends a flock without getting . . milk?
Heb 5.12 You need milk, not solid food
5.13 every one who lives on milk is unskilled
1 Pet 2. 2 long for the pure spiritual milk

MILL
1. *grinder, mill:* μύλος MYLOS
Mt 24.41 "Two women will be grinding at the mill

MILLSTONE
1. *stone for a mill:* λίθος μυλικός MYLIKOS* [A.1.f]
Lk 17. 2 "if a millstone were hung round his neck
2. *made of millstone:* μύλινος (subst.) MYLINOS*
Rev 18.21 angel took up a stone like a great m.
3. *grinder, mill:* μύλος MYLOS
Mt 18. 6 "great millstone fastened round his neck
Mk 9.42 "if a great m. were hung round his neck
Rev 18.22 "sound of the m. shall be heard . . no more

MIND (*See also* ANXIOUS MIND, BE OF; CONSIDER IN ONE'S MIND; HUMBLE MIND, HAVE A)
1. *thought, understanding:* διάνοια DIANOIA
Mt 22.37 "You shall love the Lord . . with all your m.
Mk 12.30 " 'you shall love the Lord . . with all your m.
Lk 10.27 "You shall love the Lord . . with all your m.
Eph 2. 3 following the desires of body and mind
Col 1.21 you, who once were . . hostile in mind
Heb 8.10 "I will put my laws into their minds
10.16 "I will . . write them on their minds
1 Pet 1.13 Therefore gird up your minds, be sober
2 Pet 3. 1 I have aroused your sincere mind
2. *judgment, opinion, purpose:* γνώμη GNŌMĒ
Rev 17.13 "These are of one mind
17.17 "carry out his purpose by being of one m.
3. *heart:* καρδία KARDIA
Lk 21.14 "Settle it therefore in your minds
Rom 1.21 their senseless minds were darkened
2 Cor 3.15 to this day . . a veil lies over their minds
9. 7 one must do as he has made up his mind
4. *care:* μέλει (imper.) MELEI [A.6.e]
1 Cor 7.21 Were you a slave when called? Never mind
5. *kidney:* νεφρός NEPHROS*
Rev 2.23 " 'I am he who searches mind and heart
6. *mind, thought:* νόημα NOĒMA
2 Cor 3.14 But their minds were hardened
4. 4 god of this world has blinded the minds
Phil 4. 7 peace of God . . will keep . . minds in C. J.
7. *mind, understanding:* νοῦς NOUS
Lk 24.45 he opened their minds to . . the scriptures
Rom 1.28 God gave them up to a base mind
7.23 another law at war with the law of my m.
7.25 I . . serve the law of God with my mind
11.34 "who has known the mind of the Lord?
12. 2 be transformed by the renewal of your m.
14. 5 Let every one be . . convinced in his . . m.
1 Cor 1.10 that you be united in the same mind
2.16 "For who has known the mind of the Lord . . ?" But we have the mind of Christ
14.14 my spirit prays but my m. is unfruitful
14.15 I will pray with the mind also; . . I will sing with the mind also
14.19 rather speak five words with my mind
Eph 4.17 as . . Gentiles . . , in the futility of their minds
4.23 be renewed in the spirit of your minds
Col 2.18 puffed up . . by his sensuous mind
2 Th 2. 2 not to be quickly shaken in mind
1 Tim 6. 5 men who are depraved in mind
2 Tim 3. 8 men of corrupt m. and counterfeit faith
Tit 1.15 their very minds . . are corrupted
Rev 17. 9 "This calls for a mind with wisdom
8. *thought, purpose:* φρόνημα PHRONĒMA
Rom 8.27 he . . knows what is the m. of the Spirit
9. *wind, breath, spirit:* πνεῦμα PNEUMA
2 Cor 2.13 but my mind could not rest
7.13 because his mind has been set at rest
10. *do, practice:* πράσσω PRASSŌ
1 Th 4.11 to live quietly, to mind your own affairs
11. *life, soul, self:* ψυχή PSYCHĒ
Acts 14. 2 unbelieving Jews . . poisoned their minds
15.24 "troubled you . . , unsettling your minds
Phil 1.27 with one mind striving side by side
IDIOMATICALLY
a. 1 Cor 15.34 Come to your right mind ἐκνήψατε δικαίως [EKNĒPHŌ*]
b. 2 Cor 2.1 For I made up my mind ἔκρινα δὲ ἐμαυτῷ τοῦτο [KRINŌ]
CONTEXTUALLY
Lk 1.29 considered in her m. what sort of greeting

MIND, BE IN ONE'S RIGHT
MIND, IN ONE'S RIGHT
1. *be of sound mind:* σωφρονέω SŌPHRONEŌ
[a]pass. part.
Mk 5.15 [a]demoniac . . clothed and in his right m.
Lk 8.35 [a]found the man . . clothed and in his right m.
2 Cor 5.13 if we are in our right mind, it is for you

MIND, BE OF A
MIND, HAVE A
MIND ON, SET ONE'S
MINDED, BE
1. *think, set one's mind on:* φρονέω PHRONEŌ
Rom 8. 5 set their minds on the things of the flesh
Phil 2. 2 complete my joy by being of the same mind, . . being . . of one mind
2. 5 Have this mind among yourselves
3.15 Let those . . who are mature be thus minded

Phil 3.15 if in anything you are otherwise minded
3.19 shame, with minds set on earthly things
Col 3. 2 Set your minds on things that are above

MIND, CHANGE ONE'S
1. *change, alter:* μεταβάλλω (mid.) METABALLŌ*
Acts 28. 6 they .. waited .. and .. changed their minds
2. *regret, repent:* μεταμέλομαι METAMELOMAI
Heb 7.21 "The Lord .. will not change his mind

MIND, HAVE A HUMBLE
1. *lowly in mind, humble:* ταπεινόφρων TAPEINOPHRŌN* [A.3.e.2]
1 Pet 3. 8 have unity of spirit .. and a humble mind

MIND, MAN OF DOUBLE
1. *double-minded:* δίψυχος (subst.) DIPSYCHOS
Jas 4. 8 purify your hearts, you men of double mind

MIND ON, TO SET THE
1. *thought, purpose:* φρόνημα (+gen.) PHRONĒMA
Rom 8. 6 To set the mind on the flesh is death, but to set the mind on the Spirit is life

MIND THAT IS SET ON
1. *thought, purpose:* φρόνημα (+gen.) PHRONĒMA
Rom 8. 7 mind that is set on the flesh is hostile

MINDED, BE (*See* MIND, BE OF A)

MINDFUL
1. *in consciousness:* διὰ συνείδησιν SYNEIDĒSIS [B.1.a.1]
1 Pet 2.19 one is approved if, mindful of God

MINDFUL, BE
1. *remind oneself, remember:* μιμνῄσκομαι MIMNĒSKOMAI
Heb 2. 6 "What is man that thou art m. of him?

MINE

MINE, OF
1. *I:* ἐγώ EGŌ
Mt **7.**24, 26; **20.**21
Lk **2.**30; **11.**6; **19.**27
Jn **12.**30; **15.**2
Acts **9.**15
Rom **1.**12; **12.**19; **16.**13
2 Cor **11.**10
Phil **1.**4, 30²
Heb **10.**30
2. *my, mine:* ἐμός EMOS
Mt 20.23 "to sit at my right hand .. is not m. to grant
Mk 10.40 "to sit at my right hand .. is not m. to grant
Jn 3.29 "therefore this joy of mine is now full
7.16 "My teaching is not mine, but his
14.24 "the word which you hear is not mine
16.15 "All that the Father has is mine
17.10 "all mine are thine, and thine are mine, and I am glorified in them

MINE, WHAT IS
1. *my, mine:* ἐμός (subst. neut. sg. or pl.) EMOS
Lk 15.31 " 'Son, .. all that is mine is yours
Jn 16.14 "he will take what is mine and declare it
16.15 "he will take what is mine and declare it

MINGLE (*See also* MYRRH, MINGLED WITH)
1. *give:* δίδωμι DIDŌMI
Rev 8. 3 incense to mingle with the prayers
2. *mix, join:* μείγνυμι MEIGNYMI
Mt 27.34 offered him wine .. mingled with gall
Lk 13. 1 whose blood .. mingled with their sacrifices
Rev 15. 2 a sea of glass mingled with fire

MINISTER
1. *do a service, minister:* διακονέω DIAKONEŌ
Mt 4.11 angels came and ministered to him
25.44 " 'when did we .. not minister to thee?
27.55 women .. who had followed J. .. ministering
Mk 1.13 the angels ministered to him
15.41 ⟨women⟩ who .. ministered to him
2. *servant:* διάκονος DIAKONOS
2 Cor 3. 6 competent to be ministers of a new covenant
Eph 3. 7 Of this gospel I was made a minister
6.21 Tychicus .. faithful minister in the Lord
Col 1. 7 He is a faithful minister of Christ
1.23 gospel .. of which I, Paul, became a m.
1.25 ⟨church⟩ of which I became a minister
4. 7 Tychicus .. is a .. faithful minister
1 Tim 4. 6 you will be a good minister of Christ J.
3. *ruler:* δυνάστης DYNASTĒS
Acts 8.27 a eunuch, a minister of the Candace
4. *serve:* ὑπηρετέω HYPĒRETEŌ
Acts 20.34 "these hands ministered to my necessities
5. *servant, helper:* ὑπηρέτης HYPĒRETĒS
Lk 1. 2 eyewitnesses and ministers of the word
6. *minister, servant:* λειτουργός LEITOURGOS
Rom 13. 6 for the authorities are ministers of God
15.16 to be a minister of Christ Jesus
Phil 2.25 your messenger and minister to my need
Heb 8. 2 a minister in the sanctuary

MINISTERING
1. *ministering:* λειτουργικός LEITOURGIKOS*
Heb 1.14 Are they not all ministering spirits?

MINISTRY
1. *service:* διακονία DIAKONIA
Acts 1.17 "allotted his share in this ministry
1.25 "place in this ministry and apostleship
6. 4 "to prayer and to the m. of the word
20.24 "if only I may accomplish .. the ministry
21.19 things that God had done .. through his m.
Rom 11.13 I magnify my ministry
2 Cor 4. 1 having this ministry by the mercy of God[e]
5.18 who .. gave us the ministry of reconciliation
6. 3 that no fault may be found with our m.
Eph 4.12 to equip the saints for the work of m.
Col 4.17 "See that you fulfil the ministry
2 Tim 4. 5 As for you, .. fulfil your ministry
2. *service, ministry:* λειτουργία LEITOURGIA
Heb 8. 6 Christ[o] has obtained a ministry
CONTEXTUALLY
Lk 3.23 when he began his m., was about thirty

MINSTREL
1. *musical:* μουσικός (subst.) MOUSIKOS*
Rev 18.22 "the sound of harpers and minstrels

MINT
1. *green mint:* ἡδύοσμον HĒDYOSMON*
Mt 23.23 "you tithe mint and dill and cummin
Lk 11.42 "you tithe mint and rue and every herb

MIRACLE
1. *power, ability:* δύναμις DYNAMIS
Acts 8.13 seeing .. great miracles .., he was amazed
19.11 extraordinary miracles by the hands of Paul
1 Cor 12.10 to another the working of miracles
12.29 Are all teachers? Do all work miracles?
Gal 3. 5 he who .. works miracles among you
Heb 2. 4 God .. bore witness by .. various miracles

MIRACLES, WORKER OF
1. *power, ability:* δύναμις DYNAMIS [C.2]
1 Cor 12.28 then workers of miracles, then healers

MIRE
1. *mire, filth:* βόρβορος BORBOROS*
2 Pet 2.22 the sow is washed only to wallow in the m.

MIRROR
1. *mirror:* ἔσοπτρον ESOPTRON*
1 Cor 13.12 For now we see in a mirror dimly
Jas 1.23 man who observes his natural face in a m.

MISCHIEF-MAKER
1. *busybody:* ἀλλοτριεπίσκοπος ALLOTRIEPISKOPOS*
1 Pet 4.15 let none .. suffer as a .. mischief-maker

MISDEED
1. *lawlessness:* ἀνομία ANOMIA
Heb 10.17 "I will remember .. their misdeeds no more

MISERABLE
1. *badly, ill:* κακῶς KAKŌS [A.4.a]
Mt 21.41 "He will put .. to a miserable death

MISERY
1. *distress:* ταλαιπωρία TALAIPŌRIA*
Rom 3.16 "in their paths are ruin and misery
Jas 5. 1 weep and howl for the miseries

MISFORTUNE
1. *out of place, wrong:* ἄτοπος (subst.) ATOPOS
Acts 28. 6 they . . saw no misfortune come to him

MISMATED
1. *draw unequally:* ἑτεροζυγέω (part.) HETEROZYGEŌ*
2 Cor 6.14 Do not be mismated with unbelievers

MISREPRESENT
1. *false witness:* ψευδόμαρτυς PSEUDOMARTYS [A.1.a]
1 Cor 15.15 found to be misrepresenting God

MISS THE MARK
1. *miss the mark:* ἀστοχέω ASTOCHEŌ
1 Tim 6.21 missed the mark as regards the faith

MISSION
1. *mission, office of apostle:* ἀποστολή APOSTOLĒ
Gal 2. 8 (through Peter for the m. to the circumcised
2. *service:* διακονία DIAKONIA
Acts 12.25 when they had fulfilled their mission
CONTEXTUALLY
2 Cor 11.12 that in their boasted mission they work

MIST
1. *mist:* ἀχλύς ACHLYS*
Acts 13.11 mist and darkness fell upon him
2. *moist vapor:* ἀτμίς ATMIS
Jas 4.14 For you are a mist that appears
3. *fog, mist:* ὁμίχλη HOMICHLĒ*
2 Pet 2.17 These are waterless springs and mists

MISTAKE, MAKE A
1. *stumble, fall:* πταίω PTAIŌ
Jas 3. 2 For we all make many mistakes, and if any one makes no mistakes

MITYLENE: Μιτυλήνη ˌmitəˈlēnē II,E-3
Acts 20.14 we took him on board and came to M.

MIX
1. *mix, blend:* κεράννυμι KERANNYMI
Rev 18. 6 "mix a double draught for her in the cup she mixed
2. *mix, join:* μείγνυμι MEIGNYMI
Rev 8. 7 hail and fire, mixed with blood

MIXTURE
1. *mixture, compound:* μίγμα MIGMA*
Jn 19.39 bringing a mixture of myrrh and aloes

MNASON: Μνάσων ˈnāsən
Acts 21.16 bringing us to the house of M. of Cyprus

MOB
1. *multitude, mass:* πλῆθος PLĒTHOS
Acts 21.36 the mob of the people followed

MOCK
1. *scoff:* χλευάζω CHLEUAZŌ*
Acts 17.32 when they heard . . , some mocked
2. *deceive:* διαχλευάζω DIACHLEUAZŌ*
Acts 2.13 others mocking said, "They are filled
3. *mock:* ἐμπαίζω EMPAIZŌ
Mt 20.19 "deliver him . . to be mocked
27.29 they mocked him, saying, "Hail, King!
27.31 And when they had mocked him
27.41 chief priests, with the . . elders, mocked him
Mk 10.34 "they will mock him, and spit upon him
15.20 And when they had mocked him
15.31 So also the chief priests mocked him
Lk 14.29 "all who see it begin to mock him
18.32 "will be mocked and shamefully treated
22.63 men who were holding Jesus mocked him
23.11 Herod with his soldiers . . mocked him
23.36 The soldiers also mocked him
4. *sneer at:* μυκτηρίζω MYKTĒRIZŌ*
Gal 6. 7 Do not be deceived; God is not mocked

MOCKING
1. *mockery:* ἐμπαιγμός EMPAIGMOS*
Heb 11.36 Others suffered mocking and scourging

MODEL
1. *pattern, image:* τύπος TYPOS
Tit 2. 7 Show yourself . . a model of good deeds

MODESTLY
1. *with modesty:* μετὰ αἰδοῦς AIDŌS* [B.1.a.1]
1 Tim 2. 9 women should adorn themselves modestly

MODESTY
1. *gracefulness, propriety:* εὐσχημοσύνη EUSCHĒMOSYNĒ*
1 Col 12.23 our unpresentable parts . . with greater m.
2. *soundness of mind, prudence:* σωφροσύνη SŌPHROSYNĒ
1 Tim 2.15 in faith and love and holiness, with m.

MOISTURE
1. *moisture:* ἰκμάς IKMAS*
Lk 8. 6 "it withered away, because it had no m.

MOLDED, WHAT IS
1. *what is molded, image:* πλάσμα PLASMA*
Rom 9.20 Will what is molded say to its molder?

MOLDER
1. *form, mold:* πλάσσω (subst. part.) PLASSŌ
Rom 9.20 Will what is molded say to its molder?

MOLEST
1. *insult, treat arrogantly:* ὑβρίζω HYBRIZŌ
Acts 14. 5 an attempt was made . . to molest them

MOLOCH: Μολόχ ˈmōˌläk
Acts 7.43 " 'And you took up the tent of Moloch

MOMENT
1. *uncut, indivisible:* ἄτομος (subst.) ATOMOS*
1 Cor 15.52 in a moment, in the twinkling of an eye
2. *hour, time of day:* ὥρα HŌRA
Mt 8.13 the servant was healed at that very m.
Gal 2. 5 we did not yield . . even for a moment
3. *be present:* πάρειμι (subst. part. neut.) PAREIMI
Heb 12.11 For the m. all discipline seems painful
4. *spot, moment:* στιγμή STIGMĒ*
Lk 4. 5 showed him all the kingdoms . . in a m.

MOMENT, AT THAT VERY
1. *at once:* ἐξαυτῆς EXAUTĒS
Acts 11.11 "At that very moment three men arrived

MOMENT, THAT
1. *then, formerly:* τότε TOTE
Mt 26.16 from that moment he sought an opportunity

MOMENTARY
1. *immediately, for the present:* παραυτίκα PARAUTIKA [A.4.a]
2 Cor 4.17 For this slight momentary affliction

MONEY
1. *silver, money:* ἀργύριον ARGYRION
Mt 25.18 "he . . dug . . and hid his master's money
25.27 " 'you ought to have invested my money
28.12 they gave a sum of money to the soldiers
28.15 they took the m. and did as . . directed
Mk 14.11 they . . promised to give him money
Lk 9. 3 "Take . . no staff, nor bag, . . nor money
19.15 "servants, to whom he had given the m.
19.23 " 'Why then did you not put my money?
22. 5 they were glad, and engaged to give him m.
2. *copper, brass, bronze:* χαλκός CHALKOS
Mk 6. 8 take nothing . . ; no bread, no bag, no money
12.41 multitude putting m. into the treasury
3. *property, money* (pl.): χρῆμα CHRĒMA
[a]sg.
Acts 4.37 [a]sold a field . . and brought the money
8.18 when Simon saw . . , he offered them money
8.20 "obtain the gift of God with money
24.26 he hoped that m. would be given him
4. *custom, current coin:* νόμισμα NOMISMA*
Mt 22.19 "Show me the money for the tax
5. *honor, value:* τιμή TIMĒ
Mt 27. 6 "not lawful . . , since they are blood money
CONTEXTUALLY
Phil [4.16 you sent me *money for my needs*‡

MONEY BOX
1. *money box:* γλωσσόκομον GLŌSSOKOMON*
Jn 12. 6 as he had the m. box he used to take
13.29 because Judas had the money box

MONEY, FREE FROM LOVE OF
1. *not loving money:* ἀφιλάργυρος APHILARGYROS
Heb 13. 5 Keep your life free from love of money

MONEY, LOVE OF
1. *love of money:* φιλαργυρία PHILARGYRIA*
1 Tim 6.10 love of money is the root of all evils

MONEY, LOVER OF
1. *fond of money:* φιλάργυρος (subst.) PHILARGYROS*
Lk 16.14 Pharisees, who were lovers of money
2 Tim 3. 2 men will be lovers of self, lovers of money

MONEY, NO LOVER OF
1. *not loving money:* ἀφιλάργυρος (subst.) APHILARGYROS
1 Tim 3. 3 not quarrelsome, and no lover of money

MONEY-CHANGER
1. *money-changer:* κερματιστής KERMATISTĒS*
Jn 2.14 the money-changers at their business
2. *small money-changer:* κολλυβιστής KOLLYBISTĒS*
Mt 21.12 overturned . . tables of . . money-changers
Mk 11.15 overturned . . tables of . . money-changers
Jn 2.15 poured out . . coins of . . money-changers

MONTH
1. *month:* μήν MĒN II*
Lk 1.24 for five months she hid herself
1.26 In the sixth m. the angel Gabriel was sent
1.36 "this is the sixth month with her
1.56 Mary remained . . about three months
4.25 heaven was shut up . . years and six months
Acts 7.20 "he was brought up for three months
18.11 he stayed a year and six months
19. 8 he . . for three months spoke boldly
20. 3 There he spent three months
28.11 After three months we set sail in a ship
Gal 4.10 You observe days, and months!
Jas 5.17 three years and six months it did not rain
Rev 9. 5 to torture them for five months
9.10 power of hurting men for five months
9.15 held ready for the hour, . . the month
11. 2 "trample over . . city for forty-two months
13. 5 exercise authority . . forty-two . . months
22. 2 yielding its fruit each month

MONTHS, FOUR
1. *of four months:* τετράμηνος (subst. fem.) TETRAMĒNOS*
Jn 4.35 " 'There are yet four months

MONTHS, THREE
1. *of three months:* τρίμηνος (subst. fem.) TRIMĒNOS*
Heb 11.23 hid for three months by his parents

MONUMENT
1. *tomb, memorial:* μνημεῖον MNĒMEION
Mt 23.29 "adorn . . monuments of the righteous

MOON
1. *moon:* σελήνη SELĒNĒ*
Mt 24.29 "the moon will not give its light
Mk 13.24 "the moon will not give its light
Lk 21.25 "there will be signs in sun and moon
Acts 2.20 " 'moon ⟨shall be turned⟩ into blood
1 Cor 15.41 There is . . another glory of the moon
Rev 6.12 the full moon became like blood
8.12 a third of the moon ⟨was struck⟩
12. 1 woman . . with the moon under her feet
21.23 the city has no need of sun or moon

MOON, NEW
1. *new moon, first of the month:* νεομηνία NEOMĒNIA*
Col 2.16 a festival or a new moon or a sabbath

MOOR TO THE SHORE
1. *bring to anchor at:* προσορμίζω (pass.) PROSORMIZŌ*
Mk 6.53 came to land . . and moored to the shore

MORALS
1. *custom, usage:* ἦθος (pl.) ĒTHOS*
1 Cor 15.33 "Bad company ruins good morals

MORBID CRAVING, HAVE A
1. *be sick, suffer:* νοσέω NOSEŌ*
1 Tim 6. 4 he has a morbid craving for controversy

MORE (*See also* ABOUND ALL THE MORE; ABUNDANTLY, FAR MORE; ACCURATELY 1[a]; CLOSELY 1[a]; CONQUEROR, BE MORE THAN; EARNESTLY, THE MORE; EMINENT 2[a]; EVIL 6[a]; EXACTLY, MORE; GIVE STILL MORE; HOW MUCH MORE; MAKE MORE; MANIFOLD MORE; NECESSARY 1[a]; NO MORE; NOBLE 1[a]; ONCE MORE; PRECIOUS 2[a]; PRESENTABLE, MORE; SPEND MORE; TOLERABLE, MORE; VALUE, BE OF MORE; ZEALOUSLY, MORE)
1. *other, another:* ἄλλος (pl.) ALLOS
Mt 25.16 "and he made five talents more
25.17 "So also, he . . made two talents more
25.20 "he . . came . . bringing five talents more
25.20 " 'here I have made five talents more
25.22 " 'here I have made two talents more
2. *still, yet:* ἔτι ETI
Heb 8.12 "I will remember their sins no more
10.17 "I will remember their sins . . no more
11.32 And what more shall I say?
Rev 7.16 "They shall hunger no more
18.21 "Babylon . . shall be found no more
18.22 "harpers . . shall be heard . . no more; . . a craftsman . . shall be found . . no more; . . the millstone shall be heard in thee no more
18.23 "a lamp shall shine in thee no more; . . bride shall be heard in thee no more
20. 3 he should deceive the nations no more
21. 1 Then I saw . . and the sea was no more
21. 4 "and death shall be no more
22. 3 There shall no m. be anything accursed
22. 5 And night shall be no more
3. *more, rather:* μᾶλλον MALLON
Mt 6.30 "will he not much more clothe you?
7.11 "how much m. will your Father . . give!
10.25 "how much more will they malign
18.13 "more than over the ninety-nine
Lk 11.13 "how much m. will the heavenly Father!
12.28 "how much more will he clothe you!
Jn 12.43 praise of men m. than the praise of God
Acts 20.35 " 'more blessed to give than to receive
27.11 centurion paid m. attention to the captain
Rom 5. 9 much more shall we be saved by him
5.10 much more, now that we are reconciled
5.15 much more have . . grace . . and the free gift
5.17 much more will those who receive . . grace
11.12 how much m. will their full inclusion mean!
11.24 how much m. will these natural branches
1 Cor 9.12 If others share . . , do not we still more?
14. 5 I want you all . . even more to prophesy
14.18 I speak in tongues more than you all
2 Cor 3.11 what is permanent must have much more
Gal 4.27 "children of the desolate one are many more[0]
Phil 1. 9 it is my prayer that your love may abound more and more
2.12 so now, . . much more in my absence, work
3. 4 If any . . has reason for confidence . . , I have m.
Phm .16 to me but how much more to you
Heb 9.14 how much more shall the blood of Christ
12. 9 Shall we not much more be subject?
2 Pet 1.10 be the m. zealous to confirm your call
4. *greater:* μείζων MEIZŌN
Jas 4. 6 But he gives more grace
5. *superfluous, extraordinary:* περισσός (neut.) PERISSOS
Mt 5.47 "what more are you doing than others?
6. *more, greater:* περισσότερος (neut.) PERISSOTEROS
Lk 12. 4 "after that . . no more that they can do
12.48 "of him . . they will demand the more
Heb 7.15 This becomes even more evident
7. *more:* πλείων PLEIŌN
[a]neut. [b]neut. subst.
Mt 20.10 [a]"they thought they would receive more
Lk 7.42 [a]"Now which of them will love him more?
7.43 [b]"The one . . to whom he forgave more
9.13 [a]"We have no more than five loaves
Jn 4. 1 Jesus was making . . more disciples than John
4.41 many more believed because of his word
7.31 "will he do more signs than this man?
15. 2 "he prunes, that it may bear more fruit

Heb 3. 3 as the builder . . has m. honor than the house
11. 4 a more acceptable sacrifice than Cain

IDIOMATICALLY

a. Lk 22.51 "No more of this! ἐᾶτε ἕως τούτου [HEŌS]
b. Rom 5.3 More than that, we[h] rejoice οὐ μόνον δέ, ἀλλὰ καὶ καυχώμεθα [MONOS]
c. Phil 4.18 I have received full payment, and more ἀπέχω δὲ πάντα καὶ περισσεύω [PERISSEUŌ]

CONTEXTUALLY

Mt 13.12 "For to him who has will more be given
25.29 " 'to every one who has will m. be given
Mk 4.25 "For to him who has will more be given
Lk 8.18 "to him who has will more be given
15. 7 "will be m. joy in heaven over one sinner
19.26 " 'to every one who has will more be given
1 Cor 15.34 Come to your right mind, and sin no more
Tit 3.10 have nothing more to do with him

MORE, ALL THE

1. *more, rather:* μᾶλλον MALLON
[a]πολλῷ μᾶλλον
Mk 10.48 [a]but he cried out all the more
Lk 18.39 [a]but he cried out all the more
Jn 5.18 why the Jews sought all the m. to kill him
Acts 9.22 Saul increased all the more in strength
2 Cor 12. 9 all the m. gladly boast of my weaknesses
2. *even more:* περισσῶς PERISSŌS
Mt 27.23 shouted all the more, "Let him be crucified
Mk 15.14 they shouted all the more, "Crucify him
3. *still more:* περισσοτέρως PERISSOTERŌS
2 Cor 7.15 his heart goes out all the more to you

IDIOMATICALLY

a. Heb 10.25 and all the more as you see καὶ τοσούτῳ μᾶλλον ὅσῳ βλέπετε [MALLON]

MORE AND MORE

MORE AND MORE, DO SO

1. *more:* πλείων PLEIŌN
2 Cor 4.15 as grace extends to more and more people
2 Tim 2.16 lead . . into more and more ungodliness

IDIOMATICALLY

a. 1 Th 4.1 just as you are doing, you do so more and more καθὼς καὶ περιπατεῖτε, ἵνα περισσεύητε μᾶλλον [PERISSEUŌ; MALLON]
b. 1 Th 4.10 But we exhort you, brethren, to do so more and more Παρακαλοῦμεν δὲ ὑμᾶς, ἀδελφοί, περισσεύειν μᾶλλον [PERISSEUŌ; MALLON]

MORE, ANY

1. *still, yet:* ἔτι (+neg.) ETI
Lk 20.36 "for they cannot die any more
Rev 7.16 "They shall . . neither thirst any more
21. 4 "neither shall there be . . pain any more
2. *no longer, no more:* μηκέτι (+neg.) MĒKETI
Lk 8.49 "do not trouble the Teacher any more
3. *no longer, no more:* οὐκέτι (+neg.) OUKETI
Mt 22.46 nor . . did any one . . ask . . more questions
Mk 5. 3 "no one could bind him any more
Rev 18.11 no one buys their cargo any more

MORE, ANYTHING

1. *superfluous, extraordinary:* περισσός (subst. neut.) PERISSOS
Mt 5.37 "anything more than this comes from evil[l]

MORE, AS MUCH

1. *more:* πλείων PLEIŌN
Heb 3. 3 worthy of as much m. glory than Moses

MORE CONVINCINGLY

1. *more, greater:* περισσότερος (neut.) PERISSOTEROS
Heb 6.17 God desired to show more convincingly

MORE EXCELLENT

1. *different, excellent:* διάφορος (comp.) DIAPHOROS
Heb 1. 4 name he has obtained is more excellent
8. 6 a ministry which is as much more excellent
2. *to excess:* καθ' ὑπερβολήν HYPERBOLĒ [B.1.a.1]
1 Cor 12.31 I will show you a . . more excellent way

MORE, FAR

1. *still more:* περισσοτέρως PERISSOTERŌS
2 Cor 11.23 greater labors, far more imprisonments

MORE GRACIOUSLY

1. *better, stronger:* κρείσσων (neut.) KREISSŌN
Heb 12.24 blood that speaks more graciously

MORE, MUCH

1. *still more:* περισσοτέρως PERISSOTERŌS
Phil 1.14 brethren . . are much more bold to speak

MORE, NO (*See also* NO 3[a], 8[a])

1. *no longer, no more:* μηκέτι MĒKETI
Jn 5.14 "See, you are well! Sin no more
Acts 4.17 "let us warn them to speak no more
13.34 "no more to return to corruption
Rom 14.13 no more pass judgment on one another
2. *not, no:* οὐ OU
Mt **2.18**
3. *no longer, no more:* οὐκέτι OUKETI
Jn 14.19 "the world will see me no more
16.10 "you will see me no more
16.16 "you will see me no more
17.11 "And now I am no more in the world
Acts 8.39 the eunuch saw him no more
20.25 "all you . . will see my face no more
20.38 that they should see his face no more
Rev 10. 6 that there should be no more delay
4. *and not:* οὔτε OUTE
Jas 3.12 No more can salt water yield fresh

MORE, ONCE

1. *from above, anew:* ἄνωθεν ANŌTHEN
[a]+πάλιν
Gal 4. 9 [a]whose slaves you want to be once more
2. *second:* δεύτερος (neut.) DEUTEROS
Rev 19. 3 Once more they cried, "Hallelujah!
3. *again, back:* πάλιν PALIN
Lk 23.20 Pilate addressed them once more
Jn 8. 8 once more he bent down and wrote[r]‡

IDIOMATICALLY

a. Heb 12.26 "Yet once more I will shake not only the earth ἔτι ἅπαξ ἐγὼ σείσω οὐ μόνον τὴν γῆν [HAPAX]
b. Heb 12.27 This phrase, "Yet once more," indicates τὸ δὲ ἔτι ἅπαξ δηλοῖ [HAPAX]

MORE, SO MUCH THE

1. *more, rather:* μᾶλλον MALLON
Lk 5.15 so much the more the report went abroad

MORE, STILL

1. *more, rather:* μᾶλλον MALLON
[a]+περισσοτέρως
2 Cor 7. 7 so that I rejoiced still more
7.13 [a]we rejoiced still more at the joy of Titus
2. *still more:* περισσοτέρως PERISSOTERŌS
2 Cor 1.12 we have behaved . . still more toward you

MORE THAN

1. *above:* ἐπάνω EPANŌ
Mk 14. 5 sold for more than three hundred denarii[b]
1 Cor 15. 6 he appeared to m. than five hundred
2. *over, more than:* ὑπέρ (+acc.) HYPER
Mt 10.37 "who loves father or mother more than me
10.37 "who loves son or daughter more than me
2 Cor 12. 6 may think m. of me than he sees in me
Phm .16 no longer as a slave but more than a slave
.21 you will do even more than I say
3. *more, greater:* περισσότερος (neut.) PERISSOTEROS
Mt 11. 9 "Yes, I tell you, and more than a prophet
Lk 7.26 "Yes, I tell you, and more than a prophet
4. *more:* πλείων PLEIŌN
[a]neut.
Mt 6.25 [a]"Is not life more than food?
21.36 "he sent other servants, more than the first
26.53 "more than twelve legions of angels
Mk 12.43 [a]"widow has put in more than all those
Lk 3.13 "Collect no more than is appointed you
12.23 [a]"For life is more than food
21. 3 [a]"widow has put in m. than all of them
Jn 21.15 [a]"Simon, . . do you love me m. than these?
Acts 4.22 the man . . was more than forty years old
23.13 m. than forty who made this conspiracy
23.21 "m. than forty of their men lie in ambush

Acts 24.11 "it is not more than twelve days
25. 6 stayed . . not more than eight or ten days

MORE THAN EVER

1. *more, rather:* μᾶλλον MALLON
Acts 5.14 more than ever believers were added

MORE THAN, MUCH

1. *more, greater:* περισσότερος (neut.) PERISSOTEROS
Mk 12.33 "much m. than all whole burnt offerings

MORE, THE

1. *as great as, how great:* ὅσος (neut.) HOSOS
Mk 7.36 but the more he charged them
2. *more, rather:* μᾶλλον MALLON
Jn 19. 8 When Pilate heard . . , he was the m. afraid
Acts 22. 2 when they heard . . , they were the m. quiet
3. *greater:* μείζων (neut.) MEIZŌN
Mt 20.31 cried out the m., "Lord, have mercy on us!
4. *still more:* περισσοτέρως PERISSOTERŌS
2 Cor 12.15 If I love you the m., am I to be loved . . less?
1 Th 2.17 we endeavored the more eagerly
5. *more:* πλείων (subst.) PLEIŌN
1 Cor 9.19 a slave to all, that I might win the more

MOREOVER

1. *but even:* ἀλλὰ καί ALLA [B.3.b.4]
[a]δὲ καί
Lk 16.21 "m. the dogs came and licked his sores
24.22 "M., some women of our company amazed us
1 Tim 3. 7 [a]m. he must be well thought of by outsiders
2. *and yet:* ἔτι δέ/ἔτι τε ETI [A.4.e]
Acts 2.26 " 'moreover my flesh will dwell in hope
21.28 "moreover he also brought Greeks
3. *remaining, left:* λοιπός (neut.) LOIPOS
1 Cor 4. 2 Moreover it is required of stewards

MORNING

1. *early, early in the day:* πρωΐ PRŌI
Acts 28.23 he expounded . . from m. till evening
2. *early morning:* πρωΐα PRŌIA
Mt 27. 1 When m. came, . . elders . . took counsel
3. *early, early in the morning:* πρωϊνός PRŌINOS*
Rev 2.28 " 'and I will give him the morning star
22.16 "I Jesus . . am . . the bright morning star

IDIOMATICALLY

a. Mk 15.1 as soon as it was morning Καὶ εὐθὺς πρωΐ [PRŌI]

MORNING, EARLY IN THE

1. *at daybreak:* ὀρθρινός ORTHRINOS* [A.3.b.1]
Lk 24.22 "at the tomb early in the morning
2. *dawn, about daybreak:* ὄρθρος (gen.) ORTHROS
Jn 8. 2 Early in the morning he came again[r]‡

IDIOMATICALLY

a. Mt 20.1 "who went out early in the morning ὅστις ἐξῆλθεν ἅμα πρωΐ [PRŌI]
b. Lk 21.38 early in the morning all the people came to him πᾶς ὁ λαὸς ὤρθριζεν πρὸς αὐτόν [ORTHRIZŌ*]

MORNING, IN THE

1. *early, early in the day:* πρωΐ PRŌI
Mt 16. 3 "in the morning, 'It will be stormy today‡
21.18 In the morning, as he was returning
Mk 1.35 in the morning, a great while before day
11.20 in the morning, they saw the fig tree
13.35 "at midnight, or at cockcrow, or in the m.

MORNING STAR

1. *bringing light:* φωσφόρος (subst.) PHŌSPHOROS*
2 Pet 1.19 until . . morning star rises in your hearts

MORROW

1. *tomorrow:* αὔριον AURION [B.3.b.2]
Acts 4. 3 put them in custody until the morrow
4. 5 On the morrow their rulers and elders

MORROW, FOR THE

1. *for the day, for the morrow:* ἐπιούσιος EPIOUSIOS
Mt [6.11 "Give us this day *our bread for the m.*†
Lk [11. 3 "Give us each day *our bread for the m.*†

MORROW, ON THE

1. *tomorrow:* ἐπαύριον EPAURION [B.3.b.2]
Acts 20. 7 intending to depart on the morrow
21. 8 On the morrow we departed
Acts 22.30 on the m., desiring to know the real reason
23.32 on the m. they returned to the barracks
25.23 on the morrow Agrippa and Bernice came

MORSEL

1. *bit of bread:* ψωμίον PSŌMION*
Jn 13.26 "It is he to whom I shall give this m. . ." So when he had dipped the morsel
13.27 after the morsel, Satan entered into him
13.30 after receiving the m., he . . went out

MORTAL

1. *die:* ἀποθνῄσκω (part.) APOTHNĒSKŌ
Heb 7. 8 Here tithes are received by mortal men
2. *perishable:* φθαρτός PHTHARTOS
Rom 1.23 images resembling mortal man
3. *death:* θάνατος THANATOS
[a]B.1.a.1 [b]gen.
1 Jn 5.16 [a]brother committing what is not a mortal sin
5.16 [a]life for those whose sin is not mortal. There is sin which is mortal
5.17 [a]but there is sin which is not mortal
Rev 13. 3 [ab]One of its heads seemed to have a mortal wound, but its mortal wound was healed
13.12 [b]beast, whose mortal wound was healed
4. *mortal:* θνητός THNĒTOS*
Rom 6.12 Let not sin . . reign in your mortal bodies
8.11 he . . will give life to your mortal bodies
1 Cor 15.53 mortal nature must put on immortality
15.54 When . . the mortal puts on immortality
2 Cor 4.11 life of Jesus . . manifested in our m. flesh
5. 4 what is m. may be swallowed up by life

MOSES: Μωϋσῆς 'mōzəz
Mt 8. 4 "offer the gift that Moses commanded
17. 3 there appeared to them M. and Elijah
17. 4 "booths . . , one for you and one for M.
19. 7 "Why . . did M. command . . a certificate?
19. 8 "Moses allowed you to divorce your wives
22.24 "Teacher, Moses said, 'If a man dies
23. 2 "the Pharisees sit on Moses' seat
Mk 1.44 "offer . . what Moses commanded
7.10 "M. said, 'Honor your father
9. 4 there appeared to them Elijah with Moses
9. 5 "booths, one for you and one for M.
10. 3 "What did Moses command you?
10. 4 "M. allowed a man to write a certificate
12.19 "M. wrote . . that if a man's brother dies
12.26 "have you not read in the book of Moses?
Lk 2.22 purification according to the law of M.
5.14 "make an offering . . as M. commanded
9.30 two men talked with him, M. and Elijah
9.33 "booths, one for you and one for M.
16.29 " 'They have Moses and the prophets
16.31 " 'If they do not hear M. and the prophets
20.28 "M. wrote . . that if a man's brother dies
20.37 "that the dead are raised, even M. showed
24.27 beginning with M. and all the prophets
24.44 "everything . . about me in the law of M.
Jn 1.17 For the law was given through Moses
1.45 "We have found him of whom M. . . wrote
3.14 "as Moses lifted up the serpent
5.45 "it is Moses who accuses you
5.46 "If you believed M., you would believe
6.32 "it was not M. who gave you the bread
7.19 "Did not Moses give you the law?
7.22 "Moses gave you circumcision (not that it is from M., but from the fathers
7.23 "that the law of M. may not be broken
8. 5 "in the law M. commanded us to stone[r]‡
9.28 "but we are disciples of Moses
9.29 "We know that God has spoken to Moses
Acts 3.22 "M. said, . . 'God will raise up . . a prophet
6.11 "We . . heard him speak . . words against M.
6.14 "the customs which M. delivered to us
7.20 "At this time Moses was born
7.22 "Moses was instructed in all the wisdom
7.29 "At this retort Moses fled
7.31 "When Moses saw it he wondered

Acts 7.32 “M. trembled and did not dare to look
7.35 “This Moses whom they refused
7.37 “This is the M. who said to the Israelites
7.40 “ ‘as for . . M. who led us out from . . Egypt
7.44 “as he who spoke to Moses directed him
13.39 “you could not be freed by the law of M.
15. 1 “circumcised according to . . custom of M.
15. 5 “charge them to keep the law of Moses
15.21 “Moses has had . . those who preach him
21.21 “that you teach all the Jews . . to forsake M.
26.22 “what . . Moses said would come to pass
28.23 to convince them . . from the law of M.
Rom 5.14 death reigned from Adam to Moses
9.15 he says to Moses, “I will have mercy
10. 5 Moses writes that the man who practices
10.19 First Moses says, “I will make you jealous
1 Cor 9. 9 For it is written in the law of Moses
10. 2 all were baptized into M. in the cloud
2 Cor 3. 7 Israelites could not look at Moses' face
3.13 Moses, who put a veil over his face
3.15 to this day whenever Moses is read
2 Tim 3. 8 As Jannes and Jambres opposed Moses
Heb 3. 2 as M. . . was faithful in[e] God's house
3. 3 worthy of as much more glory than M.
3. 5 Moses was faithful in all God's house
3.16 left Egypt under the leadership of M.
7.14 with that . . M. said nothing about priests
8. 5 when Moses was about to erect the tent[n]
9.19 declared by Moses to all the people
10.28 A man who has violated the law of M.
11.23 By faith M., . . was hid for three months
11.24 By faith M., when he was grown up
12.21 Moses said, “I tremble with fear
Jude . 9 Michael . . disputed about the body of M.
Rev 15. 3 And they sing the song of Moses

MOST (*See also* EXCELLENT, MOST; GLADLY 2[a]; HIGH, MOST; HOLY 1[a]; RARE, MOST)
1. *more:* πλείων (pl.) PLEIŌN
1 Cor 10. 5 with most of them God was not pleased
15. 6 brethren . ., most of whom are still alive
Phil 1.14 most . . brethren have been made confident
2. *most:* πλεῖστος PLEISTOS
Mt 11.20 cities where most of his mighty works
21. 8 M. of the crowd spread their garments

MOST, AT
1. *most:* πλεῖστος (subst. neut.) PLEISTOS
1 Cor 14.27 in a tongue, let there be . . at most three

MOST MEN
1. *many, great:* πολύς (subst. pl.) POLYS
Mt 24.12 “most men's love will grow cold

MOST OF ALL
1. *especially:* μάλιστα MALISTA
Acts 20.38 sorrowing m. of all because of the word

MOST OF, MAKE THE
1. *buy from, redeem:* ἐξαγοράζω (mid.) EXAGORAZŌ
Eph 5.16 making the most of the time
Col 4. 5 wisely . ., making the most of the time

MOST OF THEM
1. *more:* πλείων (subst. pl.) PLEIŌN
Acts 19.32 most of them did not know why
2 Cor 9. 2 your zeal has stirred up most of them
2. *many, great:* πολύς (subst. pl.) POLYS
Mk 9.26 most of them said, “He is dead

MOTH
1. *moth:* σής SĒS*
Mt 6.19 “on earth, where moth and rust[o] consume
6.20 “heaven, where neither moth nor rust[o]
Lk 12.33 “treasure . . where . . no moth destroys

MOTH-EATEN
1. *eaten by moths:* σητόβρωτος SĒTOBRŌTOS*
Jas 5. 2 your garments are moth-eaten

MOTHER
1. *mother:* μήτηρ MĒTĒR
Mt 1.18 When his m. Mary had been betrothed
2.11 they saw the child with Mary his mother
2.13 “Rise, take the child and his mother
2.14 he . . took the child and his m. by night
2.20 “Rise, take the child and his mother
2.21 he rose and took the child and his m.
10.35 “to set . . a daughter against her m.
10.37 “He who loves father or m. more than me
12.46 his mother and his brothers stood outside
[12.47 “*Your m. and your brothers are . . outside*‡
12.48 “Who is my m., and who are my brothers?
12.49 “Here are my mother and my brothers!
12.50 “whoever does the will . . is my . . mother
13.55 “Is not his mother called Mary?
14. 8 Prompted by her m., she said, “Give me
14.11 she brought it to her mother
15. 4 “ ‘Honor your father and your mother
15. 4 “ ‘He who speaks evil of father or mother
15. 5 “ ‘If any one tells his father or his m.
19. 5 “ ‘a man shall leave his father and mother
19.19 “Honor your father and mother
19.29 “every one who has left . . father or mother
20.20 the m. of the sons of Zebedee came up
27.56 Mary the mother of James and Joseph, and the mother of the sons of Zebedee
Mk 3.31 And his mother and his brothers came
3.32 “Your m. and your brothers[l] are outside
3.33 “Who are my mother and my brothers?
3.34 “Here are my mother and my brothers!
3.35 “Whoever does the will . . is my . . m.
5.40 they . . took the child's father and m.
6.24 said to her mother, “What shall I ask?
6.28 the girl gave it to her mother
7.10 “ ‘Honor your father and your mother
7.10 “ ‘He who speaks evil of father or mother
7.11 “ ‘If a man tells his father or his mother
7.12 “to do anything for his father or mother
10. 7 “ ‘a man shall leave his father and mother
10.19 “ ‘Honor your father and mother
10.29 “no one who has left . . mother or father
10.30 “who will not receive . . mothers
15.40 Mary the mother of James the younger
Lk 1.15 “even from his mother's womb
1.43 “that the mother of my Lord should come
1.60 but his mother said, “Not so
2.33 And his father and his mother marveled
2.34 Simeon . . said to Mary his mother
2.48 his m. said . . “why have you treated us so?
2.51 his m. kept all these things in her heart
7.12 man who had died . ., the only son of his m.
7.15 And he gave him to his mother
8.19 his m. and his brothers came to him
8.20 “m. and your brothers are . . outside
8.21 “My mother and my brothers are those
8.51 the father and mother of the child
12.53 “they will be divided, . . mother against daughter and daughter against her mother
14.26 “If any one . . does not hate his own . . m.
18.20 “ ‘Honor your father and mother
Jn 2. 1 Cana . ., and the m. of Jesus was there
2. 3 m. of Jesus said . . “They have no wine
2. 5 His mother said to the servants
2.12 he went . . to Capernaum, with his m.
3. 4 “Can he enter . . into his mother's womb?
6.42 “Jesus, . . whose father and m. we know
19.25 standing by the cross of Jesus were his mother, and his mother's sister
19.26 When Jesus saw his m. . . he said to his m., “Woman, behold, your son!
19.27 he said to the disciple, “Behold, your m.!
Acts 1.14 together with . . Mary the m. of Jesus
12.12 the house of Mary, the mother of John
Rom 16.13 Greet Rufus . ., also his m. and mine
Gal 4.26 Jerusalem above is free, and she is our m.
Eph 5.31 “a man shall leave his father and m.
6. 2 “Honor your father and mother
1 Tim 5. 2 ⟨treat⟩ older women like mothers
2 Tim 1. 5 faith that dwelt first in . . your m. Eunice

Rev 17. 5 "Babylon the great, mother of harlots
CONTEXTUALLY
Mk 15.47 Mary the m. of Joses saw where he was laid
16. 1 Mary Magdalene, and Mary the m. of James
Lk 24.10 Mary the m. of James and the other women

MOTHER, MURDERER OF

1. *one who slays his mother, matricide:* μητρολῴας MĒTROLŌAS*
1 Tim 1. 9 the law is . . for . . murderers of mothers

MOTHER, WITHOUT

1. *motherless:* ἀμήτωρ AMĒTŌR*
Heb 7. 3 He is without father or mother

MOTHER-IN-LAW

1. *mother-in-law:* πενθερά PENTHERA*
Mt 8.14 he saw his mother-in-law lying sick
10.35 "to set . . against her mother-in-law
Mk 1.30 Simon's mother-in-law lay sick
Lk 4.38 Simon's mother-in-law was ill
12.53 "divided, . . m. against her daughter-in-law and daughter-in-law against her m.

MOTION

1. *shake down, wave:* κατασείω KATASEIŌ*
Acts 12.17 motioning to them . . to be silent
13.16 Paul stood up, and motioning with his hand
19.33 Alexander motioned with his hand
21.40 Paul, standing on the steps, motioned
2. *nod, beckon:* νεύω NEUŌ
Acts 24.10 when the governor had motioned

MOUNT

1. *go upon, mount, board:* ἐπιβαίνω EPIBAINŌ
Mt 21. 5 "Behold, your king . . mounted on an ass
2. *beast:* κτῆνος KTĒNOS
Acts 23.24 "Also provide mounts for Paul to ride
3. *mountain, hill:* ὄρος OROS
[1]Mount of Olives
Mt 21. 1 [1]they drew near . . to the Mount of Olives
24. 3 [1]As he sat on the Mount of Olives
26.30 [1]they went out to the Mount of Olives
Mk 11. 1 [1]at the Mount of Olives, he sent two
13. 3 [1]as he sat on the Mount of Olives
14.26 [1]they went out to the Mount of Olives
Lk 19.29 at the mount that is called Olivet
19.37 [1]at the descent of the Mount of Olives
21.37 he . . lodged on the mount called Olivet
22.39 [1]he . . went . . to the Mount of Olives
Jn 8. 1 [1]but Jesus went to the Mount of Olives[r]‡
Acts 1.12 they returned . . from the m. called Olivet
7.30 "an angel . . in the wilderness of M. Sinai
7.38 "the angel who spoke to him at Mount Sinai
Gal 4.24 One is from Mount Sinai, . . Hagar†‡
4.25 Now Hagar is Mount Sinai in Arabia[i]
Heb 12.22 But you have come to Mount Zion
Rev 14. 1 lo, on Mount Zion stood the Lamb

MOUNTAIN

1. *mountain, hill:* ὄρος OROS
Mt 4. 8 devil took him to a very high mountain
5. 1 Seeing the crowds, he went up on the m.
8. 1 When he came down from the mountain
14.23 he went up on the m. by himself to pray[0]
15.29 he went up on the m., and sat down there[0]
17. 1 Jesus . . led them up a high mountain apart
17. 9 as they were coming down the mountain
17.20 "you will say to this mountain, 'Move
18.12 "leave the ninety-nine on the mountains[0]
21.21 "if you say to this mountain, 'Be taken up
24.16 "let those . . flee to the mountains
28.16 eleven disciples went to Galilee, to the m.
Mk 3.13 he went up on the m., and called to him[0]
5. 5 among the tombs and on the mountains
6.46 he went up on the mountain to pray[0]
9. 2 Jesus . . led them up a high mountain
9. 9 as they were coming down the mountain
11.23 "whoever says to this m., 'Be taken up
13.14 "let those . . in Judea flee to the mountains
Lk 3. 5 "every m. and hill shall be brought low
6.12 he went out to the mountain to pray[0]
Lk 9.28 he . . went up on the mountain to pray
9.37 when they had come down from the m.
21.21 "let those . . in Judea flee to the mountains
23.30 "to say to the mountains, 'Fall on us
Jn 4.20 "Our fathers worshiped on this mountain
4.21 "neither on this m. nor in Jerusalem
6. 3 Jesus went up on the m., and there sat[0]
6.15 Jesus withdrew again to the mountain[0]
1 Cor 13. 2 if I have . . faith . . to remove mountains
Gal [4.25 *For Sinai is a mountain* in Arabia†‡
Heb 8. 5 "pattern which was shown you on the m.
11.38 wandering over deserts and mountains
12.20 "If even a beast touches the mountain
2 Pet 1.18 we were with him on the holy mountain
Rev 6.14 every mountain and island was removed
6.15 hid . . among the rocks of the mountains
6.16 calling to the mountains . . "Fall on us
8. 8 something like a great m. . . was thrown
16.20 no mountains were to be found
17. 9 "the seven heads are seven mountains[0]
21.10 he carried me away to a great high m.

MOURN

1. *weep, cry:* κλαίω KLAIŌ
1 Cor 7.30 those who mourn as though they were not mourning
2. *cut, strike:* κόπτω (mid.) KOPTŌ
Mt 11.17 " 'we wailed, and you did not mourn
24.30 all the tribes of the earth will mourn
3. *mourn, bewail:* πενθέω PENTHEŌ*
Mt 5. 4 "Blessed are those who mourn
9.15 "Can the wedding guests mourn?
Mk 16.10 She . . told those . . as they mourned[k]‡
Lk 6.25 "Woe to you . . , for you shall mourn
1 Cor 5. 2 Ought you not rather to mourn?
2 Cor 12.21 I may have to mourn over many
Jas 4. 9 Be wretched and mourn and weep
Rev 18.11 merchants of the earth . . mourn for her
18.15 merchants . . will stand . . mourning aloud
18.19 they wept and mourned, crying out

MOURNING

1. *mourning:* ὀδυρμός ODYRMOS
2 Cor 7. 7 longing, your mourning, your zeal for me
2. *mourning, grief:* πένθος PENTHOS*
Jas 4. 9 Let your laughter be turned to m.
Rev 18. 7 "so give her a like measure of . . m.
18. 7 " 'A queen I sit, I am no widow, m.
18. 8 "pestilence and mourning and famine
21. 4 "neither shall there be mourning

MOUTH

1. *mouth:* στόμα STOMA
Mt 4. 4 " 'by every word . . from the mouth of God
5. 2 he opened his mouth and taught them
12.34 "For out of . . the heart the mouth speaks
13.35 "I will open my mouth in parables
15.11 "not what goes into the mouth defiles a man, but what comes out of the mouth
15.17 "whatever goes into the mouth passes
15.18 "what comes out of the m. . . defiles a man
17.27 "when you open its m. you will find a shekel
21.16 " 'Out of the mouth of babes and sucklings
Lk 1.64 immediately his mouth was opened
1.70 "he spoke by the m. of his holy prophets
4.22 words which proceeded out of his m.
6.45 "out of . . the heart his mouth speaks
19.22 " 'I will condemn you out of your own m.!
21.15 "for I will give you a mouth and wisdom
Jn 19.29 they put a sponge . . and held it to his m.
Acts 1.16 "the H. Spirit spoke . . by the m. of David
3.18 "foretold by the m. of all the prophets
3.21 "that God spoke by the m. of his . . prophets
4.25 "who by the mouth of our father David
8.32 "As a sheep . . so he opens not his mouth
8.35 Then Philip opened his mouth
10.34 Peter opened his m. and said: "Truly
11. 8 " 'nothing . . unclean has ever entered my m.
15. 7 "that by my m. the Gentiles should hear

Acts 18.14 when Paul was about to open his m.
22.14 " 'appointed you . . to hear . . from his m.
23. 2 commanded those . . to strike him on the m.
Rom 3.14 "Their mouth is full of curses
3.19 so that every mouth may be stopped
2 Cor 6.11 Our m. is open to you, Corinthians
Eph 4.29 Let no evil talk come out of your mouths
6.19 in opening my m. boldly to proclaim
Col 3. 8 put . . away . . foul talk from your mouth
2 Th 2. 8 will slay him with the breath of his m.
2 Tim 4.17 So I was rescued from the lion's mouth
Heb 11.33 through faith . . stopped the mouths of lions
Jas 3. 3 bits into the mouths of horses
3.10 From the same m. . . blessing and cursing
Rev 1.16 from his mouth issued a sharp . . sword
2.16 " 'war against them with the sword of my m.
3.16 " 'I will spew you out of my mouth
9.17 sulphur issued from their mouths
9.18 sulphur issuing from their mouths
9.19 power of the horses is in their mouths
10. 9 "it will be . . sweet as honey in your mouth
10.10 it was sweet as honey in my mouth
11. 5 fire pours from their mouth
12.15 water like a river out of his mouth
12.16 earth opened its m. and swallowed the river which the dragon had poured from his m.
13. 2 the beast . . was like a leopard, . . its mouth was like a lion's mouth
13. 5 the beast was given a mouth
13. 6 opened its mouth to utter blasphemies
14. 5 in their mouth no lie was found
16.13 issuing from the mouth of the dragon and from the mouth of the beast and from the mouth of the false prophet
19.15 From his mouth issues a sharp sword
19.21 the sword that issues from his mouth

CONTEXTUALLY
Mk 9.20 and rolled about, foaming at the mouth
Acts 15.27 "will tell you the same things by word of m.
2 Th 2.15 either by word of mouth or by letter

MOVE (*See also* PITY, MOVED WITH)
1. *bring, lead:* ἄγω AGŌ
1 Cor 12. 2 however you may have been moved
2. *move, remove:* κινέω KINEŌ
Mt 23. 4 "they themselves will not move them
Acts 17.28 " 'In him we live and move
3. *pass over:* μεταβαίνω METABAINŌ
Mt 17.20 "you will say to this mountain, 'Move from here to there,' and it will move
4. *bring, bear:* φέρω PHERŌ
2 Pet 1.21 men moved by the Holy Spirit spoke

MOVE AMONG
1. *walk about in:* ἐμπεριπατέω EMPERIPATEŌ*
2 Cor 6.16 "I will live in them and m. among them

MOVED, BE
1. *wag the tail, fawn upon:* σαίνω (pass.) SAINŌ*
1 Th 3. 3 that no one be moved by . . afflictions

MOVED, BE DEEPLY
MOVED, DEEPLY
1. *admonish, be deeply moved:* ἐμβριμάομαι EMBRIMAOMAI
[a]part.
Jn 11.33 he was deeply moved in spirit
11.38 [a]Then Jesus, deeply moved again

MOVING
1. *motion, change:* κίνησις KINĒSIS
Jn [5. 3 invalids . . *waiting for the m. of the water*‡

MOW
1. *reap, cut:* ἀμάω AMAŌ*
Jas 5. 4 the laborers who mowed your fields

MUCH (*See also, e.g.,* HOW MUCH; MORE, MUCH; MORE THAN, MUCH; PERPLEXED, BE MUCH)
1. *enough:* ἱκανός HIKANOS
Acts 27. 9 much time had been lost
2. *many, great:* πολύς POLYS
[a]πολλῷ [b]πολύ
Mt 6.30 [a]"will he not much more clothe you?
[9.14 "Why do we and the Pharisees fast *much*?‡
13. 5 "ground, where they had not much soil
25.21 " 'I will set you over much
25.23 " 'I will set you over much
27.19 "I have suffered much over him today
Mk 4. 5 "rocky ground, where it had not much soil
5.26 suffered much under many physicians
6.20 When he heard . . he was much perplexed
Lk 7.47 "her sins . . are forgiven, for she loved m.
10.40 Martha was distracted with much serving
12.48 "Every one to whom much is given, of him will much be required; and of him to whom men commit much
16.10 "who is faithful in . . little is faithful also in much; . . who is dishonest in . . little is . . also in much
Jn 3.23 because there was much water there
6.10 there was much grass in the place
7.12 there was much muttering about him
8.26 "I have much to say about you
12.24 "if it dies, it bears much fruit
14.30 "I will no longer talk much with you
15. 5 "he it is that bears much fruit
15. 8 "glorified, that you bear much fruit
Acts 8. 8 So there was much joy in that city
15. 7 after there had been much debate
16.16 brought her owners much gain
20. 2 he . . had given them m. encouragement
24. 2 "Since through you we enjoy much peace
27.10 "the voyage will be with . . much loss
[28.29 *the Jews departed, holding much dispute*‡
Rom 3. 2 Much in every way
5. 9 [a]much more shall we be saved by him
5.10 [a]much more, now that we are reconciled
5.15 [a]much more have the grace of God
5.17 [a]much more will those who receive
9.22 if God . . has endured with much patience
1 Cor 2. 3 I was with you . . in much fear
2 Cor 2. 4 I wrote you out of much affliction
3.11 [a]permanent must have m. more splendor
8.15 "He who gathered m. had nothing over
Phil 2.12 [a]but much more in my absence, work
1 Th 1. 6 you received the word in much affliction
1 Tim 3. 8 not addicted to much wine
Phm . 7 I have derived much joy and comfort
Heb 5.11 About this we have much to say
12. 9 [b]Shall we not much more be subject?
12.25 [b]m. less shall we escape if we reject him
2 Jn .12 Though I have much to write to you
3 Jn .13 I had much to write to you
Rev 5. 4 I wept m. that no one was found worthy
8. 3 he was given much incense to mingle

MUCH, AS
1. *equal, same:* ἴσος (neut. pl.) ISOS
Lk 6.34 "Even sinners lend . . to receive as m. again
2. *so large, so many:* τοσοῦτος TOSOUTOS
Heb 1. 4 having become as m. superior to angels

MUCH AS, AS
1. *as great as, how great:* ὅσος HOSOS
Jn 6.11 so also the fish, as much as they wanted

MUCH OF, MAKE
1. *strive after, be jealous:* ζηλόω ZĒLOŌ
Gal 4.17 They make m. of you, . . for no good purpose; . . that you may make much of them
4.18 it is always good to be made much of

MUCH, SO
1. *so large, so many:* τοσοῦτος TOSOUTOS
Acts 5. 8 "Tell me whether you sold the land for so m." And she said, "Yes, for so much

MUCH, TOO
1. *great:* μέγας (interrog.) MEGAS
1 Cor 9.11 is it too m. if we reap your . . benefits?

IDIOMATICALLY
a. 2 Cor 10.8 For even if I boast a little too much ἐάν τε γὰρ περισσότερόν τι καυχήσωμαι [PERISSOTEROS]

MULTIPLY
1. *multiply, increase:* πληθύνω (act. or pass.) PLĒTHYNŌ
Mt 24.12 "because wickedness is multiplied
Acts 6. 7 the number of the disciples multiplied
7.17 "the people grew and multiplied in Egypt
9.31 the church . . was multiplied
12.24 the word of God grew and multiplied
2 Cor 9.10 He . . will supply and m. your resources[l]
Heb 6.14 "Surely I will bless you and multiply you
1 Pet 1. 2 May grace . . be multiplied to you
2 Pet 1. 2 May grace . . be multiplied to you
Jude . 2 May . . peace, and love be multiplied to you

MULTITUDE
1. *crowd, populace:* ὄχλος OCHLOS
[a]+πολύς
Mt 21.26 "we are afraid of the multitude
21.46 they feared the multitudes
Mk 7.33 taking him aside from the multitude
8.34 he called to him the multitude
10.46 he was leaving Jericho with . . a great m.
11.18 they feared him, because all the m.
12.12 they tried to arrest him, but feared the m.
12.41 he . . watched the m. putting money
Lk 3. 7 He said therefore to the multitudes
3.10 multitudes asked . . "What . . shall we do?
5.15 great multitudes gathered to hear
7. 9 Jesus . . turned and said to the m.
8.45 "Master, the multitudes surround you!
12. 1 when . . the multitude had gathered
12.13 One of the m. said to him, "Teacher
12.54 He also said to the multitudes
14.25 great multitudes accompanied him
18.36 hearing a multitude going by
19.39 Pharisees in the multitude said to him
22. 6 to betray him . . in the absence of the m.
23. 4 Pilate said to . . the multitudes
23.48 all the multitudes who assembled
Jn 6. 2 [a]m. followed . . , because they saw the signs
6. 5 [a]a multitude was coming to him
Acts 8. 6 multitudes . . gave heed to . . Philip
13.45 when the Jews saw the multitudes
14.14 rushed out among the multitude, crying
Rev 7. 9 multitude which no man could number
17.15 "The waters . . are peoples and multitudes
19. 1 "loud voice of a great m. in heaven
19. 6 seemed to be the voice of a great m.
2. *multitude, mass:* πλῆθος PLĒTHOS
Mk 3. 7 a great multitude from Galilee followed
3. 8 great m., hearing all that he did
Lk 1.10 the whole m. . . were praying outside
2.13 with the angel a m. of the heavenly host
6.17 a great m. . . who came to hear him
19.37 whole m. of the disciples began to rejoice
23.27 there followed him a great multitude
Jn 5. 3 In these lay a multitude of invalids
Acts 2. 6 at this sound the m. came together
5.14 were added to the Lord, multitudes
6. 5 what they said pleased the whole m.
Jas 5.20 save his soul . . and . . cover a m. of sins
1 Pet 4. 8 love covers a multitude of sins

MURDER
1. *kill, murder:* φονεύω PHONEUŌ
Mt 23.31 "sons of those who murdered the prophets
23.35 "Zechariah . . , whom you murdered
2. *murderer, slayer:* φονεύς PHONEUS [B.3.a.2]
Acts 7.52 "the Righteous One, whom you . . murdered
3. *murder, slaughter:* φόνος PHONOS
Mt 15.19 "evil thoughts, murder, adultery
Mk 7.21 "evil thoughts, fornication, theft, murder
15. 7 who had committed m. . . called Barabbas
Lk 23.19 a man . . thrown into prison . . for murder
23.25 who had been thrown into prison for . . m.
Acts 9. 1 Saul, still breathing threats and murder
Rom 1.29 Full of envy, murder, strife, deceit
Gal [5.21 *murder*, drunkenness, carousing, and the like‡
Rev 9.21 nor did they repent of their murders
4. *slaughter, kill:* σφάζω SPHAZŌ
1 Jn 3.12 not . . like Cain who . . murdered his brother. And why did he murder him?

MURDERER
1. *murderer:* ἀνθρωποκτόνος ANTHRŌPOKTONOS*
Jn 8.44 "He was a murderer from the beginning
1 Jn 3.15 one who hates his brother is a murderer, and . . no murderer has eternal life
2. *murderer, slayer:* φονεύς PHONEUS
Mt 22. 7 "king was angry . . and destroyed . . murderers
Acts 3.14 "asked for a m. to be granted to you
28. 4 "No doubt this man is a murderer
1 Pet 4.15 let none of you suffer as a murderer
Rev 21. 8 "as for murderers, fornicators, sorcerers
22.15 Outside are the dogs . . and murderers

MURDERER OF FATHER
1. *one who slays his father, parricide:* πατρολῴας PATROLŌAS*
1 Tim 1. 9 the law is . . for murderers of fathers

MURDERER OF MOTHER
1. *one who slays his mother, matricide:* μητρολῴας MĒTROLŌAS*
1 Tim 1. 9 the law is . . for . . murderers of mothers

MURMUR
1. *mutter, complain:* διαγογγύζω DIAGOGGYZŌ*
Lk 15. 2 Pharisees and the scribes murmured
19. 7 when they saw it they all murmured
2. *grumbling, muttering:* γογγυσμός GOGGYSMOS* [B.3.a.2]
Acts 6. 1 Hellenists murmured against the Hebrews
3. *grumble, murmur:* γογγύζω GOGGYZŌ
Lk 5.30 Pharisees and their scribes murmured
Jn 6.41 The Jews then murmured at him
6.43 "Do not murmur among yourselves
6.61 knowing . . his disciples murmured at it

MUSIC
1. *harmony, orchestra:* συμφωνία SYMPHŌNIA*
Lk 15.25 "as he came and drew near . . he heard music

MUST
1. *necessity, force:* ἀνάγκη (+inf.) ANAGKĒ
[a]B.3.a.5 [b]B.3.b.2, 3
Lk 14.18 [a]" 'I have bought a field, and I must go
Rom 13. 5 [b]one must be subject . . to avoid . . wrath
Heb 9.16 [b]the death . . must be established
2. *one must:* δεῖ DEI
Mt 16.21 Jesus began to show . . that he must go
17.10 "scribes say that first Elijah must come
24. 6 "this m. take place, but the end is not yet
26.35 "if I must die with you, I will not deny
26.54 "how then . . fulfilled, that it must be so?
Mk 8.31 Son of man must suffer many things
9.11 "scribes say that first Elijah must come
13. 7 "this m. take place, but the end is not yet
13.10 "the gospel must first be preached
14.31 "If I must die . . , I will not deny you
Lk 2.49 "that I must be in my Father's house
4.43 "I must preach the good news
9.22 "The Son of man must suffer many things
13.33 " 'I m. go on my way today and tomorrow
17.25 "first he must suffer many things
19. 5 "Zacchaeus, . . I m. stay at your house today
21. 9 "for this must first take place
22.37 "this scripture must be fulfilled in me
24. 7 "the Son of man must be delivered
24.44 "everything written . . must be fulfilled
Jn 3. 7 " 'You must be born anew[e]
3.14 "so must the Son of man be lifted up
3.30 "He must increase, but I . . decrease[i]
4.24 "those who worship . . m. worship in spirit
9. 4 "We must work the works of him
10.16 "other sheep . . ; I must bring them also
12.34 "that the Son of man must be lifted up

Jn 20. 9 that he must rise from the dead
Acts 1.22(21) "one of these . . must become . . witness
3.21 "whom heaven m. receive until the time
4.12 "no other name . . by which we m. be saved
5.29 "We must obey God rather than men
9.16 "how much he m. suffer for . . my name
14.22 through . . tribulations we m. enter . . kingdom
16.30 "Men, what must I do to be saved?
19.21 "After . . there, I must also see Rome
20.35 " 'by so toiling one m. help the weak
23.11 "so you must bear witness also at Rome
27.24 " 'you must stand before Caesar
1 Cor 11.19 for there must be factions among you
15.25 he m. reign until he has put all his enemies
15.53 perishable nature m. put on . . imperishable
2 Cor 5.10 we m. . . appear before the judgment seat
11.30 If I m. boast, I will boast of . . weakness
12. 1 I m. boast; there is nothing to be gained
1 Tim 3. 2 a bishop must be above reproach
3. 7 moreover he must be well thought of
2 Tim 2.24 Lord's servant must not be quarrelsome
Tit 1. 7 a bishop . . must be blameless
1.11 they must be silenced
Heb 2. 1 we must pay the closer attention
11. 6 whoever would draw near . . must believe
Rev 1. 1 to show . . what must soon take place
4. 1 "I will show you what must take place
10.11 I was told, "You m. again prophesy
13.10 with the sword must he be slain
17.10 "when he comes he must remain
20. 3 After that he must be loosed for a little
22. 6 "to show . . what must soon take place

3. *in order that:* ἵνα (as imper.) HINA
Mk 12.19 "the man[y] must take the wife
Lk 20.28 "the man[g] must take the wife

4. *see, perceive:* ὁράω (imper.) HORAŌ
Rev 19.10 he said to me, "You must not do that!
22. 9 he said to me, "You must not do that!

CONTEXTUALLY
Mt 19.16 "Teacher, what good deed must I do?
22.24 " 'his brother must marry the widow
24.44 "Therefore you also must be ready
Mk 10.17 "what must I do to inherit eternal life?
Lk 12.40 "You also m. be ready; for the Son of man
17. 4 "and says, 'I repent,' you must forgive him
Jn 6.28 "What m. we do, to be doing . . works of God?
12.26 "If any one serves me, he m. follow me
Acts 4.19 "Whether it is right . . , you must judge
10.15 "God . . cleansed, you m. not call common
11. 9 " 'God . . cleansed, you m. not call common
26.23 "that the Christ must suffer
Rom 2.22 who say that one m. not commit adultery
6.11 you also m. consider yourselves dead to sin
1 Cor 10. 8 We must not indulge in immorality
10. 9 We must not put the Lord[p] to the test
2 Cor 1.11 You also must help us by prayer
3. 9 righteousness must . . exceed it in splendor
3.11 what is permanent must have much more
9. 7 Each one m. do as he has made up his mind
11.21 I must say, we were too weak for that!
13. 1 Any charge m. be sustained by the evidence
Eph 4.17 you m. no longer live as the Gentiles do
5. 3 covetousness must not even be named
Col 3.13 as the Lord has forgiven you, so you . . must
1 Tim 3. 4 He must manage his own household well
3. 6 He must not be a recent convert
3. 8 Deacons likewise must be serious
3. 9 they must hold the mystery of the faith
3.11 women likewise m. be serious, no slanderers
5.10 she m. be well attested for her good deeds
6. 2 Those . . must not be disrespectful
6. 2 rather they must serve all the better
Tit 1. 9 he m. hold firm to the sure word as taught
Jas 1. 7 m. not suppose that a double-minded man
2 Pet 1.20 First of all you must understand this
3. 3 First of all you must understand this
Jude .17 But you must remember, . . predictions

MUST BE

1. *be:* εἰμί (fut.) EIMI
Mt 5.48 "You, therefore, must be perfect
6. 5 "you must not be like the hypocrites
20.26 "great among you must be your servant
20.27 "first among you must be your slave
Mk 9.35 "one would be first, he must be last
10.43 "great among you must be your servant
10.44 "first among you must be slave of all

MUSTARD

1. *mustard:* σίναπι SINAPI*
Mt 13.31 "heaven is like a grain of mustard seed
17.20 "if you have faith as a grain of m. seed
Mk 4.31 "It is like a grain of mustard seed
Lk 13.19 "It is like a grain of mustard seed
17. 6 "If you had faith as a grain of m. seed

MUTILATE

1. *cut off:* ἀποκόπτω (mid.) APOKOPTŌ
Gal 5.12 I wish those . . would m. themselves!

MUTILATE THE FLESH, THOSE WHO

1. *incision, mutilation:* κατατομή KATATOMĒ* [C.2]
Phil 3. 2 look out for those who mutilate the flesh

MUTTER

1. *grumble, murmur:* γογγύζω GOGGYZŌ
Jn 7.32 Pharisees heard the crowd . . muttering

MUTTERING

1. *grumbling, muttering:* γογγυσμός GOGGYSMOS
Jn 7.12 there was much muttering about him

MUTUAL

1. *one another:* ἀλλήλων ALLĒLŌN [B.1.a.1]
Rom 14.19 pursue what makes for . . mutual upbuilding

MUTUALLY ENCOURAGED, BE

1. *appeal together:* συμπαρακαλέω (pass.) SYMPARAKALEŌ*
Rom 1.12 that we may be mutually encouraged

MUZZLE

1. *muzzle:* κημόω KĒMOŌ*
1 Cor 9. 9 "shall not m. an ox when it is treading
2. *muzzle, put to silence:* φιμόω PHIMOŌ
1 Tim 5.18 "shall not m. an ox when it is treading

MY
MY OWN
MY OWN, OF
MY OWN, WHAT IS

1. *I:* ἐγώ EGŌ
Mt **2**.6, 15; **3**.17; **5**.11; **7**.21; **8**.6, 8[2], 9, 21; **9**.18; **10**.18, 22, 32, 33, 39; **11**.10, 27, 29, 30[2]; **12**.18[4], 44, 48[2], 49[2], 50[2]; **13**.30, 35; **15**.13, 22; **16**.17, 18, 25; **17**.5, 15; **18**.5, 10, 14‡, 19, 21, 35; **20**.23[3]; **21**.13, 37; **22**.4[2], 44[2]; **24**.5, 9, 35, 48; **25**.27, 34, 40; **26**.12, 18[2], 26, 28, 29, 37, 38, 42, 53; **27**.46[2]; **28**.10
Mk **1**.2, 11; **3**.33, 34[2], 35; **5**.9, 23, 30; **6**.23; **8**.35; **9**.7, 17, 24, 37, 39; **10**.20, 29, 40; **11**.17; **12**.6, 36[2]; **13**.6, 9, 13, 31; **14**.8, 14[2], 22, 24, 34, 42; **15**.34[2]; **16**.17‡
Lk **1**.18, 20, 25, 43, 44[2], 46, 47[2]; **2**.49; **3**.22; **6**.47; **7**.6, 7, 8, 27, 44, 45, 46[2]; **8**.21[2]; **9**.24, 35, 38[2], 48, 59, 61; **10**.22, 29, 40; **11**.7, 24; **12**.4, 13, 17, 18[2], 19, 45; **14**.23, 24, 26, 27, 33; **15**.6, 17, 18, 24[2]; **16**.3, 5, 24, 27; **18**.3; **19**.8, 23, 46; **20**.13, 42[2]; **21**.8, 12, 17, 33; **22**.11, 19, 20‡, 28, 29, 30[2], 42; **23**.46; **24**.39[2], 44, 49
Jn **2**.4, 16; **4**.49; **5**.17, 24, 31, 43; **6**.32, 40, 51, 54[2], 55[2], 56[2]; **8**.14, 19[3], 31, 49, 50, 52, 54[2]; **9**.11, 15, 30; **10**.15, 16, 17, 18, 25, 27, 28, 29, 37; **11**.21, 32; **12**.7, 27, 47, 48; **13**.6, 8, 9, 18, 37; **14**.2, 7, 13, 14, 20, 21[2], 23[2], 24, 26; **15**.1, 7, 8[2], 10[3], 14, 15, 16, 20, 21, 23, 24; **16**.23, 24, 26; **18**.37; **19**.24[2]; **20**.13, 17[3], 25[2], 27[2], 28[2]; **21**.15, 16, 17
Acts **1**.8; **2**.14, 17, 18[3], 25[2], 26[2], 27, 34[2]; **7**.34, 49[3], 50, 59; **8**.36; **9**.15, 16; **10**.30[2]; **13**.22[2], 33; **15**.7, 17; **16**.15; **20**.24, 25, 29, 34; **21**.13; **24**.17; **26**.4[3]; **28**.18, 19
Rom **1**.8, 9[2], 10(9); **2**.16; **7**.4, 23[3]; **9**.1, 2, 3[2], 17[2], 25[2], 26; **10**.21; **11**.3, 13, 14, 27; **15**.14, 30, 31; **16**.3, 4, 5, 7[2], 8, 9, 11, 21[2], 25
1 Cor **1**.11; **2**.4[2]; **4**.14, 17[2]; **8**.13[2]; **9**.1, 2, 15, 18[2], 27; **10**.14, 29; **11**.24, 33; **13**.3; **14**.14[2], 19, 39; **15**.58; **16**.24
2 Cor **2**.12, 13[2]; **6**.16; **11**.9, 30; **12**.5, 9, 21

Gal **1**.14[2]; **4**.14, 19, 20; **6**.17
Eph **1**.16; **3**.4, 14; **6**.19
Phil **1**.3, 7, 8, 13, 14, 17, 20[2]; **2**.2, 12[3], 25[2]; **3**.1, 8; **4**.1[2], 3, 14, [16‡, 19
Col **1**.24; **2**.1; **4**.7, 10, 18
2 Tim **1**.3, 6, 16; **2**.1, 8; **3**.10; **4**.6, 16[2]
Phm .4[2], 18, 20, 23, 24
Heb **1**.5[2], 13; **2**.12; **3**.9, 10, 11[2]; **4**.3[2], 5; **5**.5; **8**.9, 10[2]; **10**.16, 38[2]; **12**.5; **13**.6
Jas **1**.2, 16, 19; **2**.1, 3, 5, 14, 18; **3**.1, 10, 12; **5**.12, 19
1 Pet **5**.13
2 Pet **1**.14, 17
1 Jn **2**.1
Rev **1**.20; **2**.3, 13[4], 16, 26, 27; **3**.2, 5, 8[2], 10, 12[5], 16, 20, 21[2]; **10**.10[2]; **11**.3; **18**.4; **21**.7; **22**.12, 16

2. *myself:* ἐμαυτοῦ EMAUTOU [B.3.b.1]
Note that "behalf," "accord," and "authority" are contextual.
[a]*περὶ ἐμαυτοῦ* B.1.a.1 [b]B.3.b.4

Jn 5.30 "I can do nothing on my own authority
7.17 "whether . . speaking on my own authority
7.28 "I have not come of my own accord
8.28 "I do nothing on my own authority
8.42 "I came not of my own accord
10.18 "I lay it down of my own accord
12.49 "have not spoken on my own authority
14.10 "I do not speak on my own authority
Acts 24.10 [a]"I cheerfully make my defense
1 Cor 10.33 not seeking my own advantage
2 Cor 2. 1 [b]I made up my mind not to . . visit
12. 5 on my own behalf I will not boast

3. *my, mine:* ἐμός EMOS
[a]subst. neut.

Mt 18.20 "two or three are gathered in my name
19.29 "who has left . . for my name's sake
25.27 [a]"I should have received what was my own
Mk 8.38 "whoever is ashamed . . of my words
Lk 9.26 "whoever is ashamed of . . my words
Jn 4.34 "My food is to do the will of him
5.30 "my judgment is just, because I seek not my own will but the will of him
5.47 "how will you believe my words?
6.38 "I have come . . , not to do my own will
7. 6 "My time has not yet come
7. 8 "for my time has not yet fully come
7.16 "My teaching is not mine, but his
8.16 "even if I do judge, my judgment is true
8.31 "If you continue in my word
8.37 "because my word finds no place in you
8.43 "because you cannot bear to hear my word
8.51 "I say to you, if any one keeps my word
8.56 "Abraham rejoiced that he was to see my day
10.14 "I am the good shepherd; I know my own and my own know me
10.26 "because you do not belong to my sheep
10.27 "My sheep hear my voice, and I know
12.26 "where I am, there shall my servant be
13.35 "men will know that you are my disciples
14.15 "If you love me, . . keep my commandments
14.27 "my peace I give to you; not as the world
15. 9 "so have I loved you; abide in my love
15.11 "that my joy may be in you
15.12 "This is my commandment, that you love
17.13 "that they may have my joy fulfilled
17.24 "to behold my glory which thou hast given
18.36 "My kingship is not of this world; if my kingship were of this world, my servants would fight . . ; but my kingship is not from the world
Rom 3. 7 if through my falsehood God's truthfulness
10. 1 my heart's desire and prayer to God
1 Cor 1.15 say that you were baptized in my name
5. 4 When . . assembled, and my spirit is present
7.40 in my judgment she is happier
9. 3 This is my defense to those
11.25 "This . . is the new covenant in my blood
16.18 they refreshed my spirit as well as yours
1 Cor 16.21 I . . write this greeting with my own hand
2 Cor 2. 3 that my joy would be the joy of you all
8.23 As for Titus, he is my partner
Gal 1.13 you have heard of my former life
6.11 writing to you with my own hand
Phil 1.26 because of my coming to you again
3. 9 not having a righteousness of my own
Col 4.18 I . . write this greeting with my own hand
2 Th 3.17 I . . write this greeting with my own hand
Phm .10 I appeal to you for my child, Onesimus
.12 sending him back . . , sending my very heart
.19 I . . write this with my own hand
2 Pet 1.15 that after my departure you may be able
3 Jn . 4 hear that my children follow the truth
Rev 2.20 " 'teaching and beguiling my servants

4. *we:* ἡμεῖς HĒMEIS
3 Jn .9, 12

MY OWN, MAKE S.
1. *catch, seize:* καταλαμβάνω KATALAMBANŌ
Phil 3.12 but I press on to make it my own
3.13 not . . that I have made it my own

MYRA: Μύρα 'mīrə II,F-3
Acts [21. 1 from there to Patara *and Myra*‡
27. 5 across the sea . . we came to M. in Lycia

MYRIAD
1. *myriad, ten thousand:* μυριάς MYRIAS
Jude .14 "Behold, the Lord came with his . . myriads
Rev 5.11 many angels, numbering myriads of myriads and thousands of thousands

MYRRH
1. *sweet oil, perfume:* μύρον MYRON
Rev 18.13 cinnamon, spice, incense, myrrh
2. *myrrh:* σμύρνα SMYRNA*
Mt 2.11 gifts, gold and frankincense and myrrh
Jn 19.39 bringing a mixture of myrrh and aloes

MYRRH, MINGLED WITH
1. *flavor with myrrh:* σμυρνίζω (perf. pass. part.) SMYRNIZŌ*
Mk 15.23 they offered him wine mingled with m.

MYSELF
1. *I:* ἐγώ EGŌ
Rom **16**.2
2. *myself:* ἐμαυτοῦ EMAUTOU
Jn 5.31 "If I bear witness to myself
8.14 "Even if I do bear witness to myself
8.18 "I bear witness to myself
8.54 "If I glorify m., my glory is nothing
12.32 "I . . will draw all men to myself
14. 3 "I . . will take you to myself
14.21 "I will . . manifest myself to him
17.19 "for their sake I consecrate myself
Acts 20.24 "I do not account my life . . as precious to m.
26. 2 "I think myself fortunate . . , King Agrippa
26. 9 "I myself was convinced that I ought
Rom 11. 4 "I have kept for myself seven thousand
1 Cor 4. 3 I do not even judge myself
4. 4 I am not aware of anything against m.
4. 6 I have applied all this to m. and Apollos
9.19 I have made myself a slave to all
2 Cor 11. 7 Did I commit a sin in abasing myself?
Gal 2.18 then I prove myself a transgressor

MYSELF, I
1. *myself:* ἐμαυτοῦ EMAUTOU
1 Cor 7. 7 I wish that all were as I myself am
2. *and I:* κἀγώ KAGŌ
Jn 1.31 "I myself did not know him
1.33 "I myself did not know him
Rev 2.27 " 'even as I myself have received
3.21 " 'as I myself conquered and sat down

MYSIA: Μυσία 'mish(ē)ə II,E-3
Acts 16. 7 when they had come opposite Mysia
16. 8 passing by M., they went down to Troas

MYSTERY
1. *mystery, religious truth:* μυστήριον MYSTĒRION
Rom 11.25 I want you to understand this mystery

Rom 16.25 according to the revelation of the m.
1 Cor [2. 1 not . . proclaiming . . the *m.* . . . in lofty words‡
4. 1 stewards of the mysteries of God
13. 2 And if I . . understand all mysteries
14. 2 but he utters mysteries in the Spirit
15.51 Lo! I tell you a mystery
Eph 1. 9 he has made known . . the m. of his will
3. 3 the mystery was made known to me
3. 4 my insight into the mystery of Christ
3. 9 the plan of the mystery hidden for ages
5.32 This mystery is a profound one
6.19 boldly to proclaim the m. of the gospel
Col 1.26 mystery hidden for ages and generations[c]
1.27 this mystery, which is Christ in you
2. 2 the knowledge of God's m., of Christ
4. 3 to declare the mystery of Christ
2 Th 2. 7 the m. of lawlessness is already at work
1 Tim 3. 9 they must hold the mystery of the faith
3.16 Great . . is the mystery of our religion
Rev 1.20 "As for the mystery of the seven stars
10. 7 the m. of God . . should be fulfilled
17. 5 on her forehead was written a name of m.
17. 7 "I will tell you the m. of the woman

MYTH
1. *myth:* μῦθος MYTHOS*
1 Tim 1. 4 nor to occupy themselves with myths
4. 7 Have nothing to do with . . silly myths
2 Tim 4. 4 turn . . from . . truth and wander into myths
Tit 1.14 instead of giving heed to Jewish myths
2 Pet 1.16 we did not follow cleverly devised myths

N

NAAMAN: Ναιμάν 'nāəmən
Lk 4.27 "none of them was cleansed, but only N.

NAGGAI: Ναγγαί 'nagī, 'nagā,ī
Lk 3.25 the son of Esli, the son of Naggai

NAHOR: Ναχώρ 'nāhȯr
Lk 3.34 Terah, the son of Nahor

NAHSHON: Ναασσών 'nāshȯn
Mt 1. 4 and Amminadab the father of Nahshon, and Nahshon the father of Salmon
Lk 3.32 the son of Sala, the son of Nahshon

NAHUM: Ναούμ 'nā(h)əm
Lk 3.25 Amos, the son of N., the son of Esli

NAIL
1. *nail:* ἧλος HĒLOS*
Jn 20.25 "Unless I see . . the print of the nails, and place my finger in the mark of the nails
2. *nail, fix to:* προσηλόω PROSĒLOŌ*
Col 2.14 this he set aside, nailing it to the cross

NAIN: Ναΐν 'nān, 'nā,in I,C-3
Lk 7.11 afterward[y] he went to a city called N.

NAKED
1. *naked, bare:* γυμνός GYMNOS
Mt 25.36 " 'I was naked and you clothed me
25.38 " 'when did we see thee . . naked?
25.43 " 'I was . . naked and you did not clothe me
25.44 " 'Lord, when did we see thee . . naked?
Mk 14.52 left the linen cloth and ran away naked
Acts 19.16 they fled out of that house naked
2 Cor 5. 3 putting it on we may not be found naked
Rev 3.17 " 'not knowing that you are . . naked
16.15 ("that he may not go naked!
17.16 "they will make her desolate and naked

NAKEDNESS
1. *nakedness:* γυμνότης GYMNOTĒS
Rom 8.35 famine, or nakedness, or peril, or sword
Rev 3.18 " 'keep the shame of your nakedness

NAME
1. *call, name:* καλέω KALEŌ
Rom 9. 7 "Through Isaac shall . . be named
Heb 11.18 "Through Isaac shall . . be named
2. *name:* ὄνομα ONOMA
Mt 1.21 "you shall call his name Jesus
1.23 "his name shall be called Emmanuel
1.25 and he called his name Jesus
6. 9 "Our Father . . , Hallowed be thy name
7.22 " 'did we not prophesy in your name, and cast out demons in your name, and do many mighty works in your name?
10. 2 The names of the twelve apostles are these
10.22 "you will be hated . . for my name's sake
12.21 "in his name will the Gentiles hope
18. 5 "Whoever receives one such child in my n.
18.20 "two or three . . gathered in my name
19.29 "left houses . . for my name's sake
21. 9 "who comes in the name of the Lord!
23.39 " 'who comes in the name of the Lord
24. 5 "For many will come in my name
24. 9 "you will be hated . . for my name's sake
27.32 a man of Cyrene, Simon by name
28.19 "baptizing them in the name of the Father
Mk 5. 9 Jesus[o] asked him, "What is your name?" He replied, "My name is Legion
5.22 one of the rulers . . , Jairus by name
6.14 Jesus's[s] name had become known
9.37 "Whoever receives one such child in my n.
9.38 "casting out demons in your name[k]
9.39 "who does a mighty work in my name
9.41 "because you bear the name of Christ
11. 9 "who comes in the name of the Lord!
13. 6 "Many will come in my name
13.13 "you will be hated . . for my name's sake
16.17 "in my name they will cast out demons[k]
Lk 1. 5 he had a wife . . her name was Elizabeth
1.13 "you shall call his name John
1.27 betrothed to a man whose name was Joseph . . ; and the virgin's name was Mary
1.31 "and you shall call his name Jesus
1.49 "has done great things . . , and holy is his n.
1.61 "None of your kindred is called by this n.
1.63 he . . wrote, "His name is John
2.21 Jesus, the name given by the angel
2.25 a man . . whose name was Simeon
6.22 "when men . . cast out your name as evil!
8.30 Jesus . . asked . . "What is your name?
9.48 "Whoever receives this child in my n.
9.49 "a man casting out demons in your name
10.17 "demons are subject to us in your name!
10.20 "rejoice . . your names are written in heaven
11. 2 "Father, hallowed be thy name
13.35 " 'who comes in the name of the Lord!
19.38 "who comes in the name of the Lord!
21. 8 "for many will come in my name
21.12 "brought before kings . . for my name's sake
21.17 "you will be hated . . for my name's sake
24.47 "repentance . . should be preached in his n.
Jn 1. 6 man sent from God, whose name was John
1.12 to all . . who believed in his name
2.23 many believed in his name when they saw
3.18 because he has not believed in the n.
5.43 "I have come in my Father's name
5.43 "if another comes in his own name
10. 3 "he calls his own sheep by name
10.25 "works that I do in my Father's name
12.13 "he who comes in the name of the Lord!
12.28 "Father, glorify thy name
14.13 "Whatever you ask in my name
14.14 "if you ask[g] anything in my name
14.26 "whom the Father will send in my name
15.16 "whatever you ask the Father in my name
16.23 "he will give it to you in my name
16.24 "you have asked nothing in my name
16.26 "In that day you will ask in my name
17. 6 "I have manifested thy name

Jn 17.11 "Holy Father, keep them in thy name
17.12 "I kept them in thy name
17.26 "I made known to them thy name
18.10 The slave's name was Malchus
20.31 that believing you may have life in his n.
Acts 2.21 " 'whoever calls on the name of the Lord
2.38 "be baptized . . in the name of Jesus Christ
3. 6 "in the name of Jesus Christ of Nazareth
3.16 "his name, by faith in his name, has made this man strong whom you see
4. 7 "by what name did you do this?
4.10 "by the name of Jesus Christ of Nazareth
4.12 "there is no other name under heaven
4.17 "to speak no more to any one in this name
4.18 not to speak . . in the name of Jesus
4.30 "wonders are performed through the name
5.28 "not to teach in this name
5.40 not to speak in the name of Jesus
5.41 worthy to suffer dishonor for the name
8.12 preached good news about . . the n. of Jesus
8.16 baptized in the name of the Lord Jesus
9.14 "authority . . to bind all who call upon thy n.
9.15 "to carry my name before the Gentiles
9.16 "must suffer for the sake of my name
9.21 "havoc . . who called on this n.?
9.27 he . . preached boldly in the name of Jesus
9.29(28) preaching boldly in the name of the Lord
10.43 "forgiveness of sins through his name
10.48 to be baptized in the name of Jesus Christ
13. 8 (for that is the meaning of his name
15.14 "to take out of them a people for his name
15.17 " 'Gentiles who are called by my name
16.18 "charge you in the n. of Jesus Christ
18.15 "questions about words and names
19. 5 baptized in the name of the Lord Jesus
19.13 to pronounce the name of the Lord Jesus
19.17 the name of the Lord Jesus was extolled
21.13 "even to die . . for the n. of the Lord Jesus
22.16 " 'wash away your sins, calling on his name
26. 9 "opposing the name of Jesus of Nazareth
Rom 1. 5 obedience of faith for the sake of his name
2.24 "The name of God is blasphemed
9.17 "that my name may be proclaimed
10.13 "who calls upon the name of the Lord
15. 9 "I will praise thee . . and sing to thy name
1 Cor 1. 2 those who . . call on the name of our Lord
1.10 by the name of our Lord Jesus Christ
1.13 were you baptized in the name of Paul?
1.15 lest . . one . . say . . you were baptized in my n.
5. 4 in the name of the Lord Jesus
6.11 justified in . . n. of the Lord Jesus Christ
Eph 1.21 above every name that is named
5.20 thanks in the n. of our Lord Jesus Christ
Phil 2. 9 God has . . bestowed on him the name which is above every name
2.10 at the n. of Jesus every knee . . bow
4. 3 whose names are in the book of life
Col 3.17 do everything in . . n. of the Lord Jesus
2 Th 1.12 that the n. of our Lord J. . . be glorified
3. 6 in the name of our Lord Jesus Christ
1 Tim 6. 1 that the n. of God . . may not be defamed
2 Tim 2.19 "who names the name of the Lord
Heb 1. 4 become as much superior . . as the name
2.12 "I will proclaim thy n. to my brethren
13.15 fruit of lips that acknowledge his name
Jas 2. 7 the honorable n. which was invoked over you
5.10 prophets who spoke in the n. of the Lord
5.14 anointing him . . in the name of the Lord
1 Pet 4.14 If . . reproached for the name of Christ
4.16 under that name let him glorify God
1 Jn 3.23 believe in the name of his Son Jesus Christ
5.13 who believe in the name of the Son of God
Rev 2. 3 " 'bearing up for my name's sake
2.13 " 'you hold fast my n. and . . did not deny
2.17 " 'with a new name written on the stone
3. 1 " 'you have the name of being alive
3. 4 " 'you have still a few names in Sardis

Rev 3. 5 " 'I will not blot his name out of the book of life; I will confess his name
3. 8 " 'you . . have not denied my n.
3.12 " 'I will write on him the name of my God, and the name of the city of my God, . . and my own new name
6. 8 a pale horse, and its rider's n. was Death
8.11 The name of the star is Wormwood
9.11 his name in Hebrew is Abaddon
11.18 "for rewarding . . those who fear thy name
13. 1 a blasphemous name upon its heads
13. 6 blaspheming his name and his dwelling
13. 8 every one whose n. has not been written
13.17 unless he has the mark, that is, the n. of the beast or the number of its n.
14. 1 who had his name and his Father's name written on their foreheads
14.11 "whoever receives the mark of its name
15. 2 its image and the number of its name
15. 4 "Who shall not fear and glorify thy name?
16. 9 they cursed the name of God
17. 3 beast . . full of blasphemous names
17. 5 on her forehead . . a name of mystery
17. 8 "whose names have not been written
19.12 he has a name inscribed
19.13 name by which he is called is The Word
19.16 on his thigh he has a name inscribed
21.12 on the gates the names of . . twelve tribes
21.14 twelve names of the . . apostles of the Lamb
22. 4 his name shall be on their foreheads

3. *name, specify:* ὀνομάζω ONOMAZŌ
Mk [3.14 twelve, ***whom also he named apostles***‡
Lk 6.13 twelve, whom he named apostles
6.14 Simon, whom he named Peter
Rom 15.20 not where Christ has already been named
Eph 1.21 above every name that is named
3.15 from whom every family . . is named
5. 3 must not even be named among you
2 Tim 2.19 "one who names the name of the Lord

CONTEXTUALLY
Acts 19.14 sons of a Jewish high priest named Sceva
Heb 7. 2 He is first, by translation of his name
Rev 20.15 if any one's n. was not found written

NAME S. AFTER

IDIOMATICALLY
a. Lk 1.59 named him Zechariah after his father ἐκάλουν αὐτὸ ἐπὶ τῷ ὀνόματι τοῦ πατρὸς αὐτοῦ Z. [ONOMA]

NAME OF, BEAR THE

1. *name, specify:* ὀνομάζω (pass.) ONOMAZŌ
1 Cor 5.11 one who bears the name of brother

NAME WAS, WHOSE OTHER

1. *call, surname:* ἐπικαλέω (pass. part. attr.) EPIKALEŌ
Acts 12.12 John whose other name was Mark
12.25 John whose other name was Mark

NAMED

1. *call, name:* καλέω (pass. part.) KALEŌ
[a]+ὀνόματι
Lk 19. 2 [a]And there was a man named Zacchaeus
Acts 7.58 at the feet of a young man named Saul

2. *say, declare:* λέγω (pass. inf.) LEGŌ [A.6.b]
Heb 7.11 one named after the order of Aaron

3. *name:* ὄνομα (dat.) ONOMA
[a]ᾧ/ᾗ ὄνομα B.3.b.2 [b]ὄνομα αὐτῷ B.3.b.2
Lk 1. 5 there was a priest named Zechariah[b]
1.26 [a]to a city of Galilee named Nazareth
5.27 saw a tax collector, named Levi
8.41 [a]And there came a man named Jairus
10.38 a woman named Martha received him
16.20 "poor man named Lazarus, full of sores
23.50 Now there was a man named Joseph
24.13 [a]were going to a village named Emmaus
24.18 one of them, named Cleopas, answered
Jn 3. 1 [b]a man of the Pharisees, named Nicodemus
Acts 5. 1 a man named Ananias with his wife
5.34 Pharisee in the council named Gamaliel
8. 9 there was a man named Simon

Acts 9.10 a disciple at Damascus named Ananias
9.11 "inquire . . for a man of Tarsus n. Saul
9.12 "he has seen a man named Ananias
9.33 There he found a man named Aeneas
9.36 at Joppa a disciple named Tabitha
10. 1 At Caesarea . . a man named Cornelius
11.28 one of them named Agabus stood up
12.13 a maid named Rhoda came to answer
13. 6 [a]a Jewish false prophet, named Bar-Jesus
16. 1 A disciple was there, named Timothy
16.14 a woman named Lydia, from . . Thyatira
17.34 a woman named Damaris
18. 2 he found a Jew named Aquila
18. 7 to the house of a man named Titius[q]
18.24 Jew n. Apollos, a native of Alexandria
19.24 man named Demetrius, a silversmith
20. 9 a young man named Eutychus
21.10 a prophet named Agabus came down
27. 1 centurion of . . Augustan Cohort, n. Julius
28. 7 chief man of the island, named Publius

4. *by name* (+acc.): τοὔνομα TOUNOMA*
Mt 27.57 rich man from Arimathea, n. Joseph

NAPHTALI: Νεφθαλίμ 'naftəlī
Mt 4.13 he . . dwelt . . in the territory of . . Naphtali
4.15 "The land of Zebulun and the land of N.
Rev 7. 6 twelve thousand of the tribe of N.

NAPKIN
1. *napkin, towel:* σουδάριον SOUDARION
Lk 19.20 " 'here is your pound, which I kept . . in a n.
Jn 20. 7 napkin, which had been on his head

NARCISSUS: Νάρκισσος när'sisəs
Rom 16.11 Greet those . . who belong to the family of N.

NARD
1. *oil of spikenard:* νάρδος NARDOS*
Mk 14. 3 ointment of pure nard, very costly
Jn 12. 3 Mary took . . costly ointment of pure n.

NARRATIVE
1. *narrative:* διήγησις DIĒGĒSIS*
Lk 1. 1 many have undertaken to compile a n.

NARROW
1. *narrow:* στενός STENOS*
Mt 7.13 "Enter by the narrow gate
7.14 "the gate is narrow and the way is hard
Lk 13.24 "Strive to enter by the narrow door

NATHAN: Ναθάμ 'nāthən
Lk 3.31 Mattatha, . . son of N., the son of David

NATHANAEL: Ναθαναήλ nə'thanyəl
Jn 1.45 Philip found N., and said . . "We have found
1.46 N. said . . "Can anything good come?
1.47 Jesus saw N. . . and said . . "Behold!
1.48 N. said . . "How do you know me?
1.49 "N. answered . . "you are the Son of God!
21. 2 N. of Cana in Galilee, the sons of Zebedee

NATION
1. *nation, people, Gentile:* ἔθνος ETHNOS
Mt 21.43 "kingdom of God will be . . given to a nation
24. 7 "For nation will rise against nation, and kingdom against kingdom
24. 9 "you will be hated by all nations
24.14 "preached . . as a testimony to all nations
25.32 "Before him . . gathered all the nations
28.19 "Go . . and make disciples of all nations
Mk 11.17 " 'a house of prayer for all the nations
13. 8 "For nation will rise against nation, and kingdom against kingdom
13.10 "gospel must . . be preached to all nations
Lk 7. 5 "he loves our nation, and he built
12.30 "nations of the world seek these things
21.10 "Nation will rise against nation, and kingdom against kingdom
21.24 "they will . . be led captive among all nations
21.25 "upon the earth distress of nations
Lk 23. 2 "We found this man perverting our nation
24.47 "preached in his name to all nations[z]
Jn 11.48 "destroy both our holy place[a] and our n.
11.50 "that the whole n. should not perish
11.51 that Jesus should die for the nation
11.52 ⟨Jesus should die⟩ not for the n. only
18.35 "Your own n. . . handed you over to me
Acts 2. 5 devout men from every n. under heaven
7 .7 " 'I will judge the n. which they serve
7.45 "when they dispossessed the nations
8. 9 amazed the nation of Samaria
10.22 "well spoken of by the whole Jewish n.
10.35 "in every nation any one who fears him
13.19 "when he had destroyed seven nations
14.16 he allowed all the nations to walk
17.26 "he made from one every nation of men
24. 2 "reforms . . on behalf of this nation
24.10 "you have been judge over this nation
24.17 "I came to bring to my nation alms
26. 4 "from the beginning among my own n.
28.19 "no charge to bring against my nation
Rom 1. 5 for . . his name among all the nations
4.17 "I have made you . . father of many nations
4.18 "become the father of many nations
10.19 "jealous of those who are not a nation; with a foolish nation I will make you angry
16.26 ⟨mystery⟩ made known to all nations
Gal 3. 8 "In you shall all the nations be blessed
1 Tim 3.16 He[h] was . . preached among the nations
1 Pet 2. 9 you are a chosen race, . . a holy nation
Rev 2.26 " 'I will give him power over the nations
5. 9 "thou . . didst ransom men . . from every . . n.
7. 9 from every nation, from all tribes
10.11 "again prophesy about many . . nations
11. 2 "for it is given over to the nations
11. 9 men from the peoples and . . nations
11.18 "The nations raged, but thy wrath came
12. 5 one who is to rule all the nations
13. 7 authority . . over every tribe and . . nation
14. 6 gospel to proclaim . . to every nation
14. 8 "she who made all nations drink
[15. 3 "O King of *the nations*!‡
15. 4 "All nations shall come and worship thee
16.19 the cities of the nations fell
17.15 "The waters . . are peoples . . and nations
18. 3 "all nations have drunk[k] the wine
18.23 "all nations were deceived by thy sorcery
19.15 sword with which to smite the nations
20. 3 should deceive the nations no more
20. 8 will come out to deceive the nations
21.24 By its light shall the nations walk
21.26 the glory and the honor of the nations
22. 2 leaves . . for the healing of the nations

NATION, ONE OF ANOTHER
1. *of another tribe:* ἀλλόφυλος (subst.) ALLOPHYLOS*
Acts 10.28 "unlawful . . to visit any one of another n.

NATIVE
1. *non-Greek, foreign:* βάρβαρος (subst.) BARBAROS
Acts 28. 2 the natives showed us unusual kindness
28. 4 When the natives saw the creature
2. *kind, race, family:* γένος GENOS [B.3.b.4]
Acts 4.36 Barnabas . . , a Levite, a native of Cyprus
18. 2 a Jew named Aquila, a native of Pontus
18.24 a Jew named Apollos, a n. of Alexandria

IDIOMATICALLY
a. Acts 2.8 "each of us in his own native language ἕκαστος τῇ ἰδίᾳ διαλέκτῳ ἡμῶν ἐν ᾗ ἐγεννήθημεν [GENNAŌ]

NATURAL
1. *origin, birth:* γένεσις (gen.) GENESIS
Jas 1.23 like a man who observes his n. face
2. *natural, physical:* φυσικός PHYSIKOS
Rom 1.26 Their women exchanged n. relations
1.27 men likewise gave up natural relations
3. *nature, origin:* φύσις PHYSIS [B.1.a.1]
Rom 11.21 God did not spare the n. branches
11.24 how much more will these n. branches

4. *physical, of the soul:* ψυχικός PSYCHIKOS
1 Cor [2.14 the *n.* man does not receive the gifts†
5. *flesh, body:* σάρξ (gen.) SARX
Rom 6.19 because of your natural limitations

NATURE (*See also* HIS OWN NATURE; INVISIBLE NATURE)
1. *man, mankind:* ἄνθρωπος ANTHRŌPOS [C.2]
2 Cor 4.16 our outer nature is wasting away
Eph 4.22 your old nature which . . is corrupt
4.24 new n., created after the likeness of God
Col 3. 9 you have put off the old nature
2. *origin, birth:* γένεσις GENESIS
Jas 3. 6 setting on fire the cycle of nature[b]†
3. *foundation, reality, confidence:* ὑπόστασις HYPOSTASIS
Heb 1. 3 bears the very stamp of his nature
4. *nature, kind:* φύσις PHYSIS
Rom 2.14 When Gentiles . . do by nature . . the law
11.24 cut from what is by n. a wild olive tree, and grafted, contrary to nature
1 Cor 11.14 Does not nature itself teach you
Gal 4. 8 beings that by nature are no gods
Eph 2. 3 we were by nature children of wrath
2 Pet 1. 4 become partakers of the divine nature
5. *seed, offspring:* σπέρμα SPERMA
1 Jn 3. 9 for God's[f] nature abides in him†
CONTEXTUALLY
1 Cor 15.53 perishable n. must put on the imperishable
15.53 this mortal n. must put on immortality
Col 3.10 and have put on the new nature
Heb 2.14 he himself likewise partook of the same n.

NATURE, HIS OWN
1. *one's own:* ἴδιος (subst. pl.) IDIOS
Jn 8.44 "he speaks according to his own nature

NATURE WITH, OF LIKE
1. *having like feelings:* ὁμοιοπαθής HOMOIOPATHĒS*
Acts 14.15 "We also are men, of like nature with you
Jas 5.17 Elijah was . . of like n. with ourselves

NAZARENE (*See also* NAZARETH)
1. *Nazareth:* Ναζαρά, Ναζαρέτ, Ναζαρέθ
Mt 2.23 "He shall be called a Nazarene
2. *from Nazareth:* Ναζαρηνός
Mk 14.67 "You also were with the Nazarene, Jesus
3. *Nazarene:* Ναζωραῖος
Acts 24. 5 "a ringleader of the sect of the Nazarenes

NAZARETH: 'naz(ə)rəth I,C-3 (*See also* NAZARENE 1)
1. *Nazareth:* Ναζαρά, Ναζαρέτ, Ναζαρέθ
Mt 4.13 and leaving Nazareth he went
21.11 "This is the prophet Jesus from Nazareth
Mk 1. 9 Jesus came from Nazareth of Galilee
Lk 1.26 Gabriel was sent from God to . . Nazareth
2. 4 Joseph also went . . from the City of N.
2.39 they returned into Galilee, to . . Nazareth
2.51 he went down . . and came to Nazareth
4.16 Nazareth, where he had been brought up
Jn 1.45 "Jesus of Nazareth, the son of Joseph
1.46 "Can anything good come out of Nazareth?
Acts 10.38 "how God anointed Jesus of Nazareth
2. *from Nazareth:* Ναζαρηνός
Mk 1.24 "What have you to do with us, Jesus of N.?
10.47 he heard that it was Jesus of Nazareth
16. 6 "Jesus of Nazareth, who was crucified
Lk 4.34 "What have you to do with us, Jesus of N.?
24.19 "Jesus of Nazareth, who was a prophet
3. *Nazarene:* Ναζωραῖος
Mt 2.23 he . . dwelt in a city called Nazareth
26.71 "This man was with Jesus of Nazareth
Lk 18.37 "Jesus of Nazareth is passing by
Jn 18. 5 They answered him, "Jesus of Nazareth
18. 7 And they said, "Jesus of Nazareth
19.19 "Jesus of Nazareth, the King of the Jews
Acts 2.22 "Jesus of Nazareth, . . attested . . by God
3. 6 "in the name of Jesus Christ of N., walk
4.10 "the name of Jesus Christ of Nazareth
6.14 "Jesus of N. will destroy this place
Acts 22. 8 "he said to me, 'I am Jesus of Nazareth
26. 9 "opposing the name of Jesus of Nazareth

NEAPOLIS: Νέα πόλις nē'apələs II,D-2
Acts 16.11 voyage . . the following day to Neapolis

NEAR (*See also* DRAW NEAR; STAND NEAR)
1. *near, at hand:* ἐγγύς EGGYS
Mt 24.32 "you know that summer is near
24.33 "you know that he is near
Mk 13.28 "you know that summer is near
13.29 "you know that he is near
Lk 19.11 because he was near to Jerusalem
21.30 "know that the summer is already near
21.31 "know that the kingdom of God is near
Jn 3.23 baptizing at Aenon near Salim
6.19 they saw Jesus . . drawing near to the boat
6.23 boats from Tiberias came near
11.18 Bethany was near Jerusalem
11.54 Jesus . . went . . to the country near
19.20 where Jesus was crucified was n. the city
Acts 1.12 Olivet, which is near Jerusalem
9.38 Since Lydda was near Joppa
27. 8 near which was the city of Lasea
Rom 10. 8 The word is near you, on your lips
Eph 2.13 you . . have been brought near in the blood
2.17 preached . . peace to those who were near
Heb 6. 8 worthless and near to being cursed
Rev 1. 3 blessed are those . . ; for the time is near
22.10 "Do not seal up . . , for the time is n.
2. *with:* μετά (+gen.) META
Jn 9.40 "Some of the Pharisees near him heard
3. *coming near:* παραπλήσιος (neut.) PARAPLĒSIOS*
Phil 2.27 Indeed he was ill, near to death
4. *near:* πλησίον (prep.) PLĒSION
Jn 4. 5 Sychar, near the field that Jacob gave
5. *bring to, come near:* προσάγω PROSAGŌ
Acts 27.27 suspected that they were nearing land
CONTEXTUALLY
2 Cor 11.23 with countless beatings, and often n. death

NEAR, COME
NEAR, DRAW
NEAR TO, DRAW
1. *bring near, approach:* ἐγγίζω EGGIZŌ
Mt 21. 1 when they drew near to Jerusalem
21.34 "When the season of fruit drew near
Mk 11. 1 when they drew near to Jerusalem
Lk 7.12 he drew near to the gate of the city
10. 9 " 'kingdom of God has come near to you
10.11 " 'the kingdom of God has come near
15. 1 sinners were all drawing near to hear him
15.25 "as he came and drew near to the house
18.35 As he drew near to Jericho
18.40 when he came near, he asked him
19.29 When he drew near to Bethphage
19.37 As he was now drawing near
19.41 when he drew near and saw the city
21.20 "know that its desolation has come near
21.28 "because your redemption is drawing near
22. 1 feast of Unleavened Bread drew near
22.47 He drew near to Jesus to kiss him
24.15 Jesus himself drew near
24.28 So they drew near to the village
Acts 7.17 "as the time of the promise drew near
10. 9 as they were . . coming near the city
22. 6 "As I . . drew near to Damascus
23.15 "ready to kill him before he comes near
Heb 7.19 through which we draw near to God
10.25 more as you see the Day drawing near
Jas 4. 8 Draw near to God and he will draw near to you
2. *come to, approach:* προσέρχομαι PROSERCHOMAI
Acts 7.31 "as he drew near to look, the voice . . came
Heb 4.16 Let us then with confidence draw near
7.25 to save those who draw near to God
10. 1 never . . make perfect those who draw n.
10.22 let us draw near with a true heart
11. 6 whoever would draw near to God

NEAR, GET
1. *bring near, approach:* προσεγγίζω PROSEGGIZŌ*
Mk 2. 4 when they could not get near him

NEARER
1. *near, at hand:* ἐγγύς (comp.) EGGYS
Rom 13.11 For salvation is nearer to us now

NEARLY
IDIOMATICALLY
a. Phil 2.30 he nearly died for the work of Christ διὰ τὸ ἔργον Χριστοῦ μέχρι θανάτου ἤγγισεν [EGGIZŌ]

NECESSARILY
1. *out of necessity:* ἐξ ἀνάγκης ANAGKĒ [B.1.a.1]
Heb 7.12 there is necessarily a change in the law

NECESSARY
1. *necessary:* ἀναγκαῖος ANAGKAIOS
[a]comp.
Acts 13.46 "It was n. that the word . . be spoken
2 Cor 9. 5 I thought it n. to urge the brethren
Phil 1.24 [a]to remain in the flesh is more necessary
2.25 I have thought it n. to send
Heb 8. 3 it is necessary for this priest also

NECESSARY, BE
NECESSARY, FIND
1. *necessity, force:* ἀνάγκη (+inf.) ANAGKĒ
[a]A.3.e.2 [b]B.3.a.5
Mt 18. 7 [a]"it is necessary that temptations come
Heb 9.23 [a]it was n. for the copies . . to be purified
Jude . 3 [b]I found it necessary to write appealing
2. *one must:* δεῖ DEI
Lk 24.26 "Was it not n. that . . Christ . . suffer?
Acts 15. 5 "It is necessary to circumcise them
17. 3 it was n. for the Christ to suffer

NECESSARY THINGS
1. *compulsory, necessary:* ἐπάναγκες (subst. neut. pl.) EPANAGKES*
Acts 15.28 "no greater burden than these n. things

NECESSITY
1. *necessity, force:* ἀνάγκη ANAGKĒ
1 Cor 7.37 being under no necessity
9.16 For necessity is laid upon me
2. *need, want:* χρεία CHREIA
Acts 20.34 "these hands ministered to my necessities

NECK
1. *neck, throat:* τράχηλος TRACHĒLOS
Mt 18. 6 "millstone fastened round his neck
Mk 9.42 "if a . . millstone were hung round his n.
Lk 17. 2 "if a millstone were hung round his neck
Acts 15.10 "a yoke upon the neck of the disciples
Rom 16. 4 who risked their necks for my life

NEED (*See also* ASHAMED, HAVING NO NEED TO BE; TIME OF NEED, IN)
1. *necessity, force:* ἀνάγκη ANAGKĒ
Heb 7.27 He has no need, like those high priests
2. *need, want:* χρεία CHREIA
[a]χρείαν ἔχειν [b]γίνεσθαι χρείαν ἔχων
Mt 3.14 [a]"I need to be baptized by you
6. 8 [a]"your Father knows what you need
9.12 "Those who are well have no need
14.16 [a]Jesus said, "They need not go away
21. 3 " 'The Lord has need of them
26.65 [a]"Why do we still need witnesses?
Mk 2.17 "Those who are well have no need
2.25 [a]"what David did, when he was in need
11. 3 "say, 'The Lord has need of it
14.63 [a]"Why do we still need witnesses?
Lk 5.31 "Those who are well have no need
9.11 he . . cured those who had need of healing
15. 7 [a]"righteous . . who need no repentance
19.31 "say this, 'The Lord has need of it
19.34 they said, "The Lord has need of it
22.71 [a]"What further testimony do we need?
Jn 2.25 [a]needed no one to bear witness of man
13.10 [a]"who has bathed does not n. to wash
13.29 [a]"Buy what we need for the feast
Jn 16.30 [a]"you . . need none to question you
Acts 2.45 they . . distributed them . . , as any had n.
4.35 distribution was made . . as any had need
Rom 12.13 Contribute to the needs of the saints
1 Cor 12.21 to the hand, "I have no need of you
12.21 to the feet, "I have no need of you
Eph 4.28 [a]able to give to those in need
Phil 2.25 your messenger and minister to my need
[4.16 you sent me *money for my needs*†‡
4.19 God will supply every need of yours
1 Th 1. 8 [a]so that we need not say anything
4. 9 no need to have any one write to you
5. 1 no n. to have anything written to you
Tit 3.14 so as to help cases of urgent need
Heb 5.12 [a]you need some one to teach you again
5.12 [b]You need milk, not solid food
7.11 what further need would there have been?
10.36 For you have need of endurance
1 Jn 2.27 no need that any one should teach you
3.17 [a]if any one . . sees his brother in need
Rev 3.17 [a]" 'I have prospered, . . I need nothing
21.23 the city has no need of sun or moon
22. 5 [a]they need no light of lamp or sun
3. *want, lack, desire:* χρῄζω CHRĒZŌ
Mt 6.32 "heavenly Father knows that you need
Lk 11. 8 "he will . . give him whatever he needs
12.30 "your Father knows that you n. them
2 Cor 3. 1 do we need . . letters of recommendation?
4. *deficiency, need:* ὑστέρημα HYSTERĒMA
2 Cor 11. 9 my needs were supplied by the brethren
5. *ought, owe:* ὀφείλω OPHEILŌ
1 Cor 5.10 you would need to go out of the world
6. *need besides:* προσδέομαι PROSDEOMAI*
Acts 17.25 "as though he needed anything
IDIOMATICALLY
a. Acts 28.10 they put on board whatever we needed ἐπέθεντο τὰ πρὸς τὰς χρείας [CHREIA]
CONTEXTUALLY
Mt 15. 5 " 'he need not honor his father
1 Cor 16. 2 that contributions n. not be made

NEEDED
1. *made for a purpose, necessary:* ἐπιτήδειος EPITĒDEIOS*
Jas 2.16 without giving them the things needed

NEEDFUL
1. *need, want:* χρεία CHREIA [A.1.b.4]
Lk 10.42 "one thing is needful[j]

NEEDLE
1. *needle:* βελόνη BELONĒ*
Lk 18.25 "a camel . . through the eye of a needle
2. *needle:* ῥαφίς RHAPHIS*
Mt 19.24 "a camel . . through the eye of a needle
Mk 10.25 "a camel . . through the eye of a needle

NEEDS, ATTEND TO
1. *serve:* ὑπηρετέω HYPĒRETEŌ
Acts 24.23 prevented from attending to his needs

NEEDY
1. *deficient, poor:* ἐνδεής ENDEĒS*
Acts 4.34 not a needy person among them

NEGLECT
1. *neglect:* ἀμελέω AMELEŌ
1 Tim 4.14 Do not neglect the gift you have
Heb 2. 3 if we neglect such a great salvation
2. *let go, leave, forgive:* ἀφίημι APHIĒMI
Mt 23.23 "neglected the weightier matters
23.23 "these . . done, without neglecting . . others
3. *leave behind:* ἐγκαταλείπω EGKATALEIPŌ
Heb 10.25 not neglecting to meet together
4. *forget, neglect:* ἐπιλανθάνομαι EPILANTHANOMAI
Heb 13. 2 Do not neglect to show hospitality
13.16 Do not neglect to do good
5. *overlook:* παραθεωρέω PARATHEŌREŌ*
Acts 6. 1 because their widows were neglected
6. *pass by, transgress:* παρέρχομαι PARERCHOMAI
Lk 11.42 "you . . neglect justice and the love of God

7. *disregard, slacken:* παρίημι PARIĒMI
Lk 11.42 "ought to have done, without neglecting

NEIGHBOR

1. *neighbor:* γείτων GEITŌN*
Lk 14.12 "do not invite your . . rich neighbors
15. 6 "calls together his friends and . . neighbors
15. 9 "calls together her friends and neighbors
Jn 9. 8 neighbors . . who had seen him . . as a beggar
2. *dwell around:* περιοικέω (subst. part.) PERIOIKEŌ*
Lk 1.65 fear came on all their neighbors
3. *dwelling around:* περίοικος (subst.) PERIOIKOS*
Lk 1.58 her neighbors and kinsfolk heard
4. *near:* πλησίον (subst.) PLĒSION
Mt 5.43 " 'love your n. and hate your enemy
19.19 "You shall love your n. as yourself
22.39 "You shall love your n. as yourself
Mk 12.31 " 'You shall love your n. as yourself
12.33 "to love one's neighbor as oneself
Lk 10.27 "You shall love . . your n. as yourself
10.29 "And who is my neighbor?
10.36 "Which of these three . . proved neighbor?
Acts 7.27 "the man who was wronging his neighbor
Rom 13. 9 "You shall love your neighbor as yourself
13.10 Love does no wrong to a neighbor
15. 2 let each of us please his n. for his good
Gal 5.14 "You shall love your neighbor as yourself
Eph 4.25 let every one speak the truth with his n.
Jas 2. 8 "You shall love your n. as yourself
4.12 who are you that you judge your n.?

NEIGHBOR, ONE'S

1. *another, different:* ἕτερος (subst.) HETEROS
Rom 13. 8 he who loves his n. has fulfilled the law
1 Cor 10.24 Let . . one seek . . the good of his n.
Gal 6. 4 his reason to boast will be . . not in his n.

NEIGHBORHOOD

1. *country, place:* χώρα CHŌRA
Mk 6.55 ⟨people⟩ ran about the whole n.
2. *boundary:* ὅριον (pl.) HORION
Mt 8.34 they begged him to leave their n.
Mk 5.17 to beg Jesus[p] to depart from their n.
CONTEXTUALLY
Acts 28. 7 Now in the n. of that place were lands

NEITHER

1. *not:* μή MĒ [A.4.c]
Mt 22.29 "you know n. the scriptures nor . . God
Mk 12.24 "you know n. the scriptures nor . . God
Lk 18. 2 "judge who n. feared God nor . . man
2. *and not, nor:* μηδέ MĒDE
Mt 23.10 "Neither be called masters
Jn 14.27 "neither let them be afraid
3. *and not:* μήτε MĒTE
Mt 11.18 "John came neither eating nor drinking
Acts 23.12 by an oath neither to eat nor drink
23.21 "by an oath neither to eat nor drink
27.20 n. sun nor stars appeared for many a day
Heb 7. 3 n. beginning of days nor end of life
4. *not, no:* οὐ OU [A.4.c]
Mt **6.26**, 28; **23.13**; **25.13**
Lk **12.24**[2], 27; **18.4**
Jn **1.25**; **14.17**
Acts **8.21**; **9.9**
1 Cor **11.9**
Gal **3.28**[3]
Heb **10.8**
5. *nor, and not:* οὐδέ OUDE
Mt 6.15 "n. will . . Father forgive your trespasses
9.17 "N. is new wine put into old wineskins
21.27 "N. will I tell you by what authority
Mk [11.26 *"neither will your Father . . forgive‡*
11.33 "N. will I tell you by what authority
Lk 16.31 " 'n. will they be convinced if some one
20. 8 "N. will I tell you by what authority
23.15 "n. did Herod, for he sent him back
Jn 8.11 Jesus said, "N. do I condemn you[r]‡
15. 4 "n. can you, unless you abide in me
Acts 24.13 "Neither can they prove to you
Rom 11.21 neither will he spare you
Rev 7.16 "They shall . . neither thirst any more
6. *and not:* οὔτε OUTE
Mt 6.20 "where neither moth nor rust[o] consumes
22.30 "they n. marry nor are given in marriage
Mk 12.25 "they n. marry nor are given in marriage
14.68 "I neither know nor understand
Lk [12.27 *"they neither spin nor weave‡*
14.35 "fit n. for the land nor for the dunghill
20.35 "neither marry nor are given in marriage
Jn 4.21 "n. on this mountain nor in Jerusalem
8.19 "You know neither me nor my Father
Acts 15.10 "n. our fathers nor we have been able
19.37 "who are n. sacrilegious nor blasphemers
25. 8 "N. against the law . . nor against Caesar
Rom 8.38 n. death, nor life, nor angels
1 Cor 3. 7 n. he who plants nor he who waters
6. 9 neither the immoral, nor idolaters
Gal 5. 6 neither circumcision nor uncircumcision
6.15 n. circumcision counts . . nor uncircumcision
Rev 3.15 " 'you are neither cold nor hot
3.16 " 'lukewarm, and neither cold nor hot
21. 4 "n. . . mourning nor crying nor pain

NEITHER . . . ANYTHING

1. *no one, nothing:* οὐδείς OUDEIS
1 Cor 7.19 neither circumcision counts for anything

NEREUS: Νηρεύς 'nērüs, 'nirēəs
Rom 16.15 Greet Philologus, Julia, Nereus

NERI: Νηρί 'nērī
Lk 3.27 Shealtiel,[l] the son of Neri

NEST

1. *camp, nest:* κατασκήνωσις KATASKĒNŌSIS*
Mt 8.20 "Foxes have holes, and birds . . have nests
Lk 9.58 "Foxes have holes, and birds . . have nests

NESTS, MAKE

1. *encamp, rest:* κατασκηνόω KATASKĒNOŌ
Mt 13.32 "birds . . come and m. nests in its branches
Mk 4.32 "birds . . can make nests in its shade
Lk 13.19 "birds . . made nests in its branches

NET

1. *casting net:* ἀμφίβληστρον AMPHIBLĒSTRON*
Mt 4.18 he saw two brothers . . casting a net
2. *net:* δίκτυον DIKTYON*
Mt 4.20 they left their nets and followed him
4.21 James . . and John . . mending their nets
Mk 1.18 they left their nets and followed him
1.19 who were in their boat mending the nets
Lk 5. 2 fishermen . . were washing their nets
5. 4 "let down your nets for a catch
5. 5 "at your word I will let down the nets
5. 6 as their nets were breaking
Jn 21. 6 "Cast the n. on the right side of . . boat
21. 8 dragging the net full of fish
21.11 Simon Peter . . hauled the net ashore . . ; and . . the net was not torn
3. *large dragnet:* σαγήνη SAGĒNĒ*
Mt 13.47 "the kingdom of heaven is like a net

NET, CAST A

1. *throw around:* ἀμφιβάλλω AMPHIBALLŌ*
Mk 1.16 he saw Simon . . casting a net in the sea

NETHER GLOOM

1. *darkness:* ζόφος ZOPHOS
2 Pet 2. 4 committed them to pits of nether gloom
2.17 for them the nether gloom of darkness
Jude . 6 in eternal chains in the nether gloom
.13 for whom the nether gloom of darkness

NEVER

1. *unto eternity:* εἰς τὸν αἰῶνα (neg., sg. or pl.) AIŌN
Mk 3.29 "never has forgiveness, but is guilty
Jn 4.14 "whoever drinks . . will never thirst
8.51 "he will never see death
8.52 " 'he will never taste death

Jn 10.28 "they shall never perish
11.26 "whoever . . believes in me shall never die
13. 8 "You shall never wash my feet
1 Cor 8.13 I will never eat meat, lest
2. *if, since:* εἰ (in an oath) EI [C.3]
Heb 3.11 " 'They shall never enter my rest
4. 3 " 'They shall never enter my rest
4. 5 "They shall never enter my rest
3. *not:* μή MĒ
[a]μὴ γένοιτο
Mt 18.13 "the ninety-nine that n. went astray
21.21 "if you have faith and never doubt
Jn 7.15 "How . ., when he has never studied?
Rom 12.11 N. flag in zeal, be aglow with the Spirit
12.16 never be conceited
12.19 Beloved, never avenge yourselves
14.13 decide never to put a stumbling block
1 Cor 6.15 [a]make them members of a prostitute? N.!
7.21 Were you a slave . .? Never mind
1 Tim 5.19 N. admit any charge against an elder
Heb 3.18 swear that they should n. enter his rest
2 Pet 2.21 better . . never to have known the way
4. *never:* μηδέποτε MĒDEPOTE*
2 Tim 3. 7 n. arrive at a knowledge of the truth
5. *not, no:* οὐ OU
Mt [**17.21**‡
Mk **3.29**; **13**.19
Lk **23.29**[2]
Jn **9.32**
Acts **6.13**
Rom **10.14**; **15.21**[2]
Heb **1.12**
Rev **4.8**; **16.18**; **21.25**
6. *not* (emph.): οὐ μή OU MĒ
[a]οὐ μή . . εἰς τὸν αἰῶνα [b]+πώποτε [c]οὐ μή . . ἔτι
Mt 5.20 "you will never enter the kingdom
5.26 "you will never get out till you have paid
13.14 " 'You shall . . hear but never understand, and you shall . . see but never perceive
16.22 "This shall never happen to you
18. 3 "you will never enter the kingdom
24.21 "great tribulation, such as . . never will be
Mk 13.19 "such tribulation as . . never will be
Lk 12.59 "you will never get out till you have paid
[22.16 "I shall *never* eat it *again* until†‡
Jn 4.14 [a]"whoever drinks of the water . . will n. thirst
6.35 [b]"he who believes in me shall never thirst
8.51 [a]"he will never see death
8.52 [a]" 'he will never taste death
10.28 [a]"they shall never perish
11.26 [a]"whoever . . believes in me shall never die
13. 8 [a]"You shall never wash my feet
Acts 13.41 " 'I do a deed . . you will never believe
28.26 " 'You shall . . hear but never understand, and you shall . . see but never perceive
1 Cor 8.13 [a]if food is a cause . ., I will n. eat meat
Heb 13. 5 "I will never fail you nor forsake you
2 Pet 1.10 for if you do this you will never fall
Rev 3.12 [c]" 'never shall he go out of it
18. 7 " 'I am no widow, mourning I shall n. see
18.14 "lost to thee, never to be found again!
21.25 its gates shall never be shut by day
7. *never:* οὐδέποτε OUDEPOTE
Mt 7.23 " 'I never knew you; depart from me
9.33 "N. was anything like this seen in Israel
21.16 "Yes; have you never read?
21.42 "Have you never read in the scriptures?
26.33 "I will never fall away
Mk 2.12 "We never saw anything like this!
2.25 "Have you never read what David did?
Lk 15.29 " 'I never disobeyed your command; yet you never gave me a kid
Acts 10.14 "I have n. eaten anything . . common
14. 8 a cripple from birth, who had never walked
1 Cor 13. 8 Love never ends
Heb 10. 1 it can never, by the same sacrifices
10.11 sacrifices, which can never take away sins

8. *ever yet:* πώποτε (+neg.) PŌPOTE
[a]οὔτε [b]οὐ μή [c]οὐδείς
Jn 5.37 [a]"His voice you have never heard
6.35 [b]"he who believes in me shall never thirst
8.33 [c]"We . . have n. been in bondage to any
9. *at some time, once:* ποτέ (neg.) POTE II
1 Th 2. 5 we never used either words of flattery
2 Pet 1.10 if you do this you will never fall
IDIOMATICALLY
a. Jn 5.37 "His voice you have never heard, his form you have never seen οὔτε φωνὴν αὐτοῦ πώποτε ἀκηκόατε οὔτε εἶδος αὐτοῦ ἑωράκατε [OUTE]

NEVER AGAIN
1. *no longer, no more:* μηκέτι MĒKETI
Mk 9.25 "come out . ., and never enter him again
2. *no longer, no more:* οὐκέτι OUKETI
Rom 6. 9 Christ being raised . . will never die again

NEVER EVEN
1. *nor, and not:* οὐδέ OUDE
Acts 19. 2 "we have n. even heard that there is

NEVERTHELESS
1. *but:* ἀλλά ALLA
Jn **16.7**
1 Cor **9.12**; **10.5**; **14.19**
2. *yet, nevertheless:* ὅμως μέντοι MENTOI [B.3.b.6]
Jn 12.42 N. many even of the authorities believed
3. *but, however, except:* πλήν PLĒN
Mt 26.39 "n., not as I will, but as thou wilt
Lk 10.11 " 'n. know . . the kingdom . . has come near
10.20 "N. do not rejoice in this
13.33 " 'N. I must go on my way today
18. 8 "N., when the Son of man comes
22.42 "n. not my will, but thine, be done[l]
1 Cor 11.11 (N., in the Lord woman is not independent

NEW (*See also* WINE, NEW)
1. *new, fresh:* καινός KAINOS
Mt 13.52 "brings out of his treasure what is new
[26.28 "this is my blood of the *new* covenant‡
26.29 "until that day when I drink it new
27.60 laid it in his own new tomb
Mk 1.27 "What is this? A new teaching!
2.21 "the patch tears . ., the new from the old
[14.24 "This is my blood of the *new* covenant‡
14.25 "until that day when I drink it new
16.17 "they will speak in new tongues[k]‡
Lk 5.36 "No one tears a piece from a n. garment . . if he does, he will tear the new, and the piece from the new will not match the old
22.20 "cup . . is the new covenant in my blood[j]‡
Jn 13.34 "A new commandment I give to you
19.41 and in the garden a new tomb
Acts 17.19 "May we know what this n. teaching is?
17.21 except telling or hearing something new
1 Cor 11.25 "This cup is the new covenant
2 Cor 3. 6 to be ministers of a new covenant
5.17 if any one is in Christ, he is a n. creation[g] . . behold, the new has come
Gal 6.15 nor uncircumcision, but a new creation
Eph 2.15 might create in himself one new man
4.24 put on the new nature
Heb 8. 8 "when I will establish a new covenant
8.13 In speaking of a new covenant
9.15 he is the mediator of a new covenant
2 Pet 3.13 we wait for new heavens and a new earth in which righteousness dwells
1 Jn 2. 7 no new commandment, but an old
2. 8 I am writing you a new commandment
2 Jn . 5 writing you a new commandment
Rev 2.17 " 'a new name written on the stone
3.12 " 'I will write on him . . the name of . . the new Jerusalem . . and my own new name
5. 9 and they sang a new song
14. 3 they sing a new song before the throne
21. 1 Then I saw a new heaven and a new earth; for the first . . had passed away
21. 2 I saw the holy city, new Jerusalem

Rev 21. 5 "Behold, I make all things new
2. *new, young:* νέος NEOS
Mt 9.17 "Neither is n. wine put into old wineskins; .. but new wine is put into fresh wineskins
Mk 2.22 "no one puts n. wine into old wineskins; .. but new wine is for fresh skins[j]‡
Lk 5.37 no one puts n. wine into old wineskins; .. the new wine will burst the skins
5.38 n. wine must be put into fresh wineskins
5.39 "no one after drinking old wine desires n.
1 Cor 5. 7 that you may be a new lump
Col 3.10 the new nature, which is being renewed
Heb 12.24 Jesus, the mediator of a new covenant
3. *new, fresh:* πρόσφατος PROSPHATOS*
Heb 10.20 by the new and living way

NEW LIFE
1. *newness:* καινότης KAINOTĒS
Rom 7. 6 we serve .. in the new life of the Spirit

NEW MOON
1. *new moon, first of the month:* νεομηνία NEOMĒNIA*
Col 2.16 a festival or a new moon or a sabbath

NEW WORLD
1. *rebirth, regeneration:* παλιγγενεσία PALIGGENESIA
Mt 19.28 "in the new world, when .. Son .. shall sit

NEWBORN
1. *just born:* ἀρτιγέννητος ARTIGENNĒTOS*
1 Pet 2. 2 Like n. babes, long for the pure .. milk

NEWNESS
1. *newness:* καινότης KAINOTĒS
Rom 6. 4 we too might walk in newness of life

NEWS
1. *word, reckoning:* λόγος LOGOS
Mk 1.45 went out and began .. to spread the n.
Acts 11.22 N. of this came to the ears of the church
IDIOMATICALLY
a. Phil 2.19 so that I may be cheered by news of you ἵνα κἀγὼ εὐψυχῶ γνοὺς τὰ περὶ ὑμῶν [GINŌSKŌ]

NEWS, BRING GOOD
NEWS, PREACH GOOD
NEWS, PREACH THE GOOD
NEWS, TELL GOOD
1. *bring good news* (mid.): εὐαγγελίζω EUAGGELIZŌ
Mt 11. 5 "the poor have good n. preached to them
Lk 1.19 "I was sent .. to bring you this good news
2.10 "I bring you good news of a great joy
3.18 he preached good news to the people
4.18 "he has anointed me to preach good news
4.43 "I must preach the good news
7.22 "poor have good n. preached to them
8. 1 bringing the good news of the kingdom
16.16 "good n. of the kingdom of God is preached
Acts 8.12 they believed .. as he preached good n.
8.35 he told him the good news of Jesus
10.36 "sent .., preaching good news of peace
13.32 "And we bring you the good news
14.15 "We also are men .. and bring you good n.
Rom 10.15 "feet of those who preach good news!
1 Th 3. 6 Timothy .. has brought us the good news
1 Pet 1.12 who preached the good news to you

NEWS COMES TO ONE, GOOD
NEWS, RECEIVE THE GOOD
1. *bring good news* (mid.): εὐαγγελίζω (pass.) EUAGGELIZŌ
Heb 4. 2 For good news came to us just as to them
4. 6 those who formerly received the good n.

NEWS, GOOD
IDIOMATICALLY
a. 1 Pet 1.25 That word is the good news which was preached to you τοῦτο δέ ἐστιν τὸ ῥῆμα τὸ εὐαγγελισθὲν εἰς ὑμᾶς [EUAGGELIZŌ]

NEXT
1. *have, hold:* ἔχω (part.) ECHŌ
Mk 1.38 "Let us go on to the next towns
Acts 21.26 the next day he purified himself
2. *come:* ἔρχομαι (pres. part.) ERCHOMAI
Acts 13.44 The next sabbath almost the whole city
3. *another, different:* ἕτερος HETEROS
Mt 10.23 "persecute you in one town, flee to the next
4. *next to:* ἑξῆς HEXĒS
Lk 9.37 On the next day, when they had come
5. *between:* μεταξύ (attr.) METAXY
Acts 13.42 might be told them the next sabbath
IDIOMATICALLY
a. Lk 13.9 "And if it bears fruit next year κἂν μὲν ποιήσῃ καρπὸν εἰς τὸ μέλλον [MELLŌ]

NEXT DAY
NEXT DAY, ON THE
1. *tomorrow:* αὔριον AURION
Lk 10.35 "the next day he took out two denarii[i]
2. *tomorrow:* ἐπαύριον EPAURION [B.3.b.2]
Mt 27.62 Next day, that is, after .. Preparation
Jn 1.29 The next day he saw Jesus coming
1.35 The next day again John was standing
1.43 The next day Jesus decided to go
6.22 On the next day the people .. saw
12.12 The next day a great crowd .. heard
Acts 10. 9 The n. day, as they were on their journey
10.23 The next day he rose and went off
14.20 on the next day he went on with Barnabas
25. 6 n. day he took his seat on the tribunal
3. *another, different:* ἕτερος HETEROS [B.3.b.2]
Acts 20.15 the next day we touched at Samos
27. 3 The next day we put in at Sidon
4. *next:* ἑξῆς HEXĒS [B.3.b.2]
Lk [7.11 *Next day* he went to a city‡
Acts 21. 1 we came .. the next day to Rhodes
25.17 "on the next day took my seat
27.18 they began next day to throw the cargo

NEXT DOOR TO, BE
1. *border on:* συνομορέω SYNOMOREŌ*
Acts 18. 7 his house was n. door to the synagogue

NICANOR: Νικάνωρ nī'kānər
Acts 6. 5 Philip, and Prochorus, and Nicanor

NICODEMUS: Νικόδημος ˌnikə'dēməs
Jn 3. 1 a man of the Pharisees, named N.
3. 4 N. said .. "How can a man be born?
3. 9 N. said to him, "How can this be?
7.50 N., who had gone to him before
19.39 N. .. who had .. come to him by night

NICOLAITAN: Νικολαΐτης ˌnikə'lāətən
Rev 2. 6 "you hate the works of the Nicolaitans
2.15 " 'who hold the teaching of the Nicolaitans

NICOLAUS: Νικόλαος ˌnikə'lāəs
Acts 6. 5 Nicolaus, a proselyte of Antioch

NICOPOLIS: Νικόπολις ni'käpələs II,D-3
Tit 3.12 do your best to come to me at N.

NIGER: Νίγερ 'nījər
Acts 13. 1 Simeon who was called Niger

NIGHT (*See also* PART OF THE NIGHT)
1. *night:* νύξ NYX
Mt 2.14 took the child and his mother by night
4. 2 fasted forty days and forty nights
12.40 "Jonah was three days and three nights
12.40 "Son of man be three days and three nights
14.25 in the fourth watch of the n. he came
26.31 "You will all fall away .. this night
26.34 "this very night, before the cock crows
28.13 " 'disciples came by night and stole him
Mk 4.27 "should sleep and rise night and day
5. 5 Night and day among the tombs
6.48 about the fourth watch of the night
14.30 "Truly, I say to you, this very night
Lk 2. 8 keeping watch over their flock by night
2.37 with fasting and prayer night and day
5. 5 "we toiled all night and took nothing!
12.20 " 'This night your soul is required of you
17.34 "in that n. there will be two in one bed
18. 7 "his elect, who cry to him day and night
21.37 at night he .. lodged on the mount

Jn 3. 2 This man came to Jesus[d] by night
9. 4 "night comes, when no one can work
11.10 "if any one walks in the night
13.30 he immediately went out; and it was n.
19.39 who had at first come to him by n.
21. 3 but that night they caught nothing
Acts 5.19 at night an angel . . opened the prison
9.24 watching the gates day and night
9.25 his disciples took him by night
12. 6 The very night when Herod was about
16. 9 a vision appeared to Paul in the night
16.33 took them the same hour of the night
17.10 sent Paul and Silas away by night
18. 9 the Lord said to Paul one night
20.31 "I did not cease n. or day to admonish
23.11 The following n. the Lord stood by him
23.23 "At the third hour of the night get ready
23.31 took Paul and brought him by night
26. 7 "as they earnestly worship n. and day
27.23 "this very n. there stood by me an angel
27.27 When the fourteenth night had come
Rom 13.12 the night is far gone, the day is at hand
1 Cor 11.23 Jesus on the n. when he was betrayed
1 Th 2. 9 we worked n. and d . . while we preached
3.10 praying earnestly night and day
5. 2 the Lord will come like a thief in the n.
5. 5 we are not of the night or of darkness
5. 7 those who sleep sleep at night, and those who get drunk are drunk at night
2 Th 3. 8 we worked night and day
1 Tim 5. 5 supplications and prayers n. and day
2 Tim 1. 4(3) I long night and day to see you
Rev 4. 8 day and n. they never cease to sing
7.15 "serve him day and n. within his temple
8.12 kept from shining . . a third of the night
12.10 "who accuses them day and night
14.11 "they have no rest, day or night
20.10 they will be tormented day and night
21.25 and there shall be no night there
22. 5 And night shall be no more

CONTEXTUALLY
Mt 24.43 "in what part of the n. the thief was coming

NIGHT, A SLEEPLESS

1. *sleeplessness, watching:* ἀγρυπνία AGRYPNIA
2 Cor 11.27 through many a sleepless night

NIGHT AND A DAY, A

1. *a night and a day:* νυχθήμερον NYCHTHĒMERON*
2 Cor 11.25 a night and a day I have been adrift

NIGHT, CONTINUE ALL

1. *pass the night:* διανυκτερεύω DIANYKTEREUŌ*
Lk 6.12 all night he continued in prayer

NINE

1. *nine:* ἐννέα ENNEA
Lk 17.17 "Were not ten cleansed? Where are the n.?

NINETY-NINE

1. *ninety-nine:* ἐνενήκοντα ἐννέα ENENĒKONTA*; ENNEA [A.3.c]
Mt 18.12 "does he not leave the ninety-nine?
18.13 "rejoices over it more than over the n.
Lk 15. 4 "What man of you . . does not leave the n.
15. 7 "more joy in heaven . . than over n. righteous

NINEVEH: Νινευίτης 'ninəvə
Mt 12.41 "The men of N. will arise at the judgment
Lk 11.30 "Jonah became a sign to the men of N.
11.32 "men of N. will arise at the judgment

NINTH

1. *ninth:* ἔνατος ENATOS*
Mt 20. 5 "about . . the n. hour, he did the same
27.45 darkness over . . land[m] until the n. hour
27.46 about the ninth hour Jesus cried
Mk 15.33 there was darkness . . until the n. hour
15.34 at the ninth hour Jesus cried
Lk 23.44 there was darkness . . until the ninth hour
Acts 3. 1 at the hour of prayer, the ninth hour
10. 3 About the n. hour . . he saw . . an angel
Acts 10.30 "I was keeping the ninth hour of prayer
Rev 21.20 the eighth beryl, the ninth topaz

NO

1. *but:* ἀλλά ALLA
Jn **12.**27
Rom **8.**37; **12.**20
1 Cor **10.**20
2. *if, since:* εἰ (in an oath) EI [C.3]
Mk 8.12 "I say to you, no sign shall be given
3. *not:* μή MĒ
[a]pres. imper. *no more*
Mt 6. 2 "when you give alms, sound no trumpet
8.28 so fierce that no one could pass that way
10. 5 "enter no town of the Samaritans
10. 9 "Take no gold, nor silver, nor copper
10.10 "⟨take⟩ no bag for your journey
10.26 "So have no fear of them
11. 6 "blessed is he who takes no offense
13. 6 since they had no root they withered
14.27 "Take heart, it is I; have no fear
17. 7 "Rise, and have no fear
22.23 who say that there is no resurrection
22.24 " 'If a man dies, having no children
22.25 "having no children left his wife
23. 9 "And call no man your father
24. 4 "Take heed that no one leads you astray
Mk 4. 6 "since it had no root it withered
6. 8 He charged them to take nothing for their journey except a staff; no bread, no bag, no money in their belts
6.50 "Take heart, it is I; have no fear
12.18 who say that there is no resurrection
12.19 "dies and leaves a wife, but leaves no child
12.21 "took her, and died, leaving no children
13. 5 "Take heed that no one leads you astray
Lk 5.19 finding no way to bring him in
7.33 "John . . has come eating no bread
8. 6 "withered . . because it had no moisture
10. 4 "Carry no purse, no bag, no sandals
11.36 "full of light, having no part dark
12. 4 "have no more that they can do
20.27 who say that there is no resurrection
Jn 15. 2 "Every branch . . that bears no fruit
Acts 1.20 " 'let there be no one to live in it
23. 8 say that there is no resurrection
Rom 5.13 not counted where there is no law
13. 3 Would you have no fear of him?
13.14 make no provision for the flesh
14.22 happy is he who has no reason to judge
1 Cor 1.29 so that no human being might boast
7.30 who buy as though they had no goods
7.31 as though they had no dealings
7.37 being under no necessity
14.28 But if there is no one to interpret
15.34 [a]Come to your right mind, and sin no more
16.11 So let no one despise him
2 Cor 5.21 made him to be sin who knew no sin
11.16 I repeat, let no one think me foolish
12. 6 so that no one may think more of me
Gal 4. 8 to beings that by nature are no gods
5.26 Let us have no self-conceit
Eph 2.12 no hope and without God in the world
4.29 Let no evil talk come out of your mouths
5.11 Take no part in the . . works of darkness
Col 2. 8 that no one makes a prey of you
2.16 let no one pass judgment on you
1 Th 4. 6 that no man . . wrong his brother
4.13 as others do who have no hope
2 Th 2. 3 Let no one deceive you in any way
1 Tim 3. 3 no drunkard, not violent but gentle
3.11 The women likewise . . , no slanderers
Tit 1.11 what they have no right to teach
Heb 12.15 that no one fail to obtain the grace of God; that no "root of bitterness" spring up
12.16 that no one be immoral or irreligious
12.19 that no further messages be spoken

Jas 2. 1 show no partiality as you hold the faith
2.13 to one who has shown no mercy
2.17 faith by itself, if it has no works, is dead
1 Pet 3.14 Have no fear of them, nor be troubled
Also Acts **4**.14; **24**.4; 1 Cor **1**.10; 2 Cor **6**.3; **8**.20; Heb **4**.11; Rev. **11**.6; **13**.17; **20**.3

4. *by no means:* *μηδαμῶς* MĒDAMŌS*
Acts 10.14 "No, Lord; . . I have never eaten anything
11. 8 " 'No, Lord; for nothing common or unclean

5. *no one:* *μηδείς* MĒDEIS
[a]B.2.d.1
Mk 5.26 [a]she . . was no better but . . grew worse
Lk 3.13 [a]"Collect no more than is appointed
4.35 he came out . . , having done him no harm
Acts 4.21 [a]finding no way to punish them
11.12 "Spirit told me . . , making no distinction
15.28 [a]"to lay upon you no greater burden
19.40 "there being no cause that we can give
23.14 "to taste no food till we have killed Paul
25.17 "When . . they came . . I made no delay
28. 6 they . . saw no misfortune come to him
28.18 no reason for the death penalty
2 Cor 6. 3 We put no obstacle in any one's way
7. 9 [a]so that you suffered no loss through us
1 Tim 5.14 give the enemy no occasion to revile us
Heb 10. 2 [a]no longer have any consciousness of sin
Jas 1. 6 [a]let him ask in faith, with no doubting

6. *and not:* *μήτε* MĒTE
Lk 9. 3 "Take nothing for your journey, no staff

7. *not, no:* *οὐ* OU
Mt **5**.37[2], **6**.1; **9**.12; **11**.11; **12**.25, 39; **13**.21, 29; **16**.4, 7, 8; **20**.13; **21**.19; **22**.11; **25**.3, 42[2]; **27**.14
Mk **2**.17; **4**.7, 17, 40; **8**.16, 17; **9**.3; **12**.20, 22, 31, 32; **13**.20
Lk **1**.7, 33, 34; **2**.7; **5**.31; **6**.43; **7**.44, 45; **8**.13, 27, 51; **9**.13; **11**.29; **12**.33; **15**.7; **16**.2; **17**.18; **20**.21, 31
Jn **1**.21, 47; **2**.3, 25; **3**.27; **4**.9, 17[2], 44; **5**.7; **6**.53, 63; **7**.12, 18, 52; **8**.37, 44; **9**.41; **10**.28; **13**.8; **15**.22; **19**.6, 9, 15; **21**.5
Acts **3**.6; **7**.5[2], 11; **10**.34; **12**.18; **13**.37; **14**.28; **15**.2, 24; **16**.37; **19**.23, 24; **21**.39; **27**.20; **28**.19
Rom **2**.11; **3**.18, 20, 22; **4**.15, 20; **6**.14; **9**.21; **10**.12; **13**.1, 10
1 Cor **2**.9; **7**.25, 36; **9**.6, 15, 16; **11**.16; **12**.21[2]; **15**.12, 13; **16**.22
2 Cor **1**.17[2], 18, 19; **3**.10; **8**.15; **11**.14
Gal **2**.6; **4**.17; **5**.23
Eph **5**.5; **6**.9
Phil **3**.3
Col **2**.23; **3**.25
1 Th **4**.9; **5**.1
1 Tim **2**.12
Heb **4**.13; **7**.27; **8**.7; **9**.22; **10**.6, 38; **12**.17; **13**.10, 14
Jas **1**.17, 25; **3**.2; **5**.12[2]
1 Pet **2**.10, 22
2 Pet **1**.21
1 Jn **1**.5, 8; **2**.7, 10, 27[2]; **3**.5; **4**.18(17)
3 Jn .4
Rev **7**.16; **14**.5, 11; **16**.20; **18**.7; **20**.6, 11; **21**.1, 4, 22, 23, 25; **22**.3, 5[2]
Also Rom **10**.11; Gal **2**.16; 1 Jn **3**.6[2], 9

8. *not* (emph.): *οὐ μή* OU MĒ
[a]+*ἔτι no more*
Lk 1.15 "he shall drink no wine nor strong drink
Heb 8.12 [a]"I will remember their sins no more
10.17 [a]"I will remember their sins . . no more
Rev 18.21 [a]"So . . Babylon . . shall be found no more
18.22 [a]"the sound of harpers . . shall be heard in thee no more; and a craftsman . . found . . no more; . . the millstone . . heard . . no more
18.23 [a]"a lamp shall shine in thee no more; and the voice . . shall be heard in thee no more

9. *not, no* (emph.): *οὐχί* OUCHI
Lk **12**.51; **13**.3, 5; **16**.30
Jn **9**.9
Rom **3**.27

10. *nor, and not:* *οὐδέ* OUDE
[a]A.4.c
Mt 11.27 [a]"no one knows the Father except the Son
Acts 4.12 "no other name . . by which we must be saved
Acts 4.32 no one said that any . . was his own
Rom 4.15 where . . no law there is no transgression
1 Pet 2.22 no guile was found on his lips
1 Jn 2.23 [a]No one who denies the Son has the Father
Rev 12. 8 [a]no longer any place for them in heaven

11. *no one, nothing:* *οὐδείς* OUDEIS
[a]attr. [b]obj. of verb [c]+gen. pl. noun [d]A.4.c [e]*οὐθέν*
Mt 26.62 [b]"Have you no answer to make?
27.12 [b]when . . accused . . he made no answer
Mk 6. 5 [a]he could do no mighty work there
14.60 [b]"Have you no answer to make?
14.61 [b]But he was silent and made no answer
15. 4 [b]"Have you no answer to make?
15. 5 [b]But Jesus made no further answer
Lk 4.24 [a]"no prophet is acceptable in his own
16.13 [a]"No servant can serve two masters
23. 4 [a]"I find no crime in this man
23. 9 [b]but he made no answer
23.22 [a]"I have found in him no crime
Jn 6.63 [b]"the spirit . . gives life, the flesh is of no avail
10.41 [a]they said, "John did no sign
14.30 [d]"He has no power over me
18.38 [a]"I find no crime in him
19. 4 [a]"know that I find no crime in him
19.11 [a]"You would have no power over me
Acts 15. 9 [e]"no distinction between us and them
18.17 [d]But Gallio paid no attention to this
25.10 [b]"to the Jews I have done no wrong
25.18 [a]"they brought no charge in his case
27.22 [a]"there will be no loss of life among you
28. 5 [a]He, however, . . suffered no harm
Rom 8. 1 [a]no condemnation for those . . in Christ Jesus
1 Cor 8. 4 [d]know that "an idol has no real existence
8. 4 [a]"there is no God but one
2 Cor 7. 5 [a]when we came . . our bodies had no rest
Gal 2. 6 [b](what they were makes no difference
4. 1 [b]a child, is no better than a slave
4.12 [b]You did me no wrong
5. 2 [b]Christ will be of no advantage to you
5.10 [b]you will take no other view than mine
Phil 4.15 [a]no church entered into partnership
1 Tim 6.16 [c]whom no man has ever seen
2 Tim 2. 4 [a]No soldier on service gets entangled
2.14 [a]avoid disputing . . , which does no good
Jas 3. 8 [c]no human being can tame the tongue
1 Jn 1. 5 [a]in him is no darkness at all

12. *and not:* *οὔτε* OUTE [A.4.c]
Acts 28.21 "We have received no letters from Judea
1 Cor 8. 8 We are no worse off if we do not eat

13. *all, every, whole:* *πᾶς* (+neg.) PAS
Mt 12.25 "no city or house divided against itself
24.22 "no human being would be saved
Mk 13.20 "no human being would be saved
Rom 3.20 no human being will be justified
1 Cor 1.29 that no human being might boast
Eph 4.29 Let no evil talk come out of your mouths
5. 5 no fornicator . . has any inheritance
2 Pet 1.20 no prophecy . . is a matter of one's own
1 Jn 2.21 know that no lie is of the truth
2.23 No one who denies the Son
3.15 that no murderer has eternal life

NO, AND

1. *and not, nor:* *μηδέ* MĒDE
Eph 4.27 and give no opportunity to the devil

2. *and not:* *μήτε* MĒTE
Lk 7.33 " 'eating no bread and drinking no wine

3. *nor, and not:* *οὐδέ* OUDE
Mt 24.21 "not . . until now, no, and never will be
Lk 12.33 "no thief approaches and no moth destroys

4. *and not:* *οὔτε* OUTE
1 Cor 8. 8 and no better off if we do

NO . . . ANY ONE
NO . . . ANYTHING

1. *no one:* *μηδείς* (neut.) MĒDEIS [A.4.c]
Phil 4. 6 Have no anxiety about anything

2. *no one, nothing:* οὐδείς OUDEIS
Mt 5.13 "It is no longer good for anything
1 Cor 3.11 no other foundation can any one lay

NO . . . EVER

1. *never:* οὐδέποτε OUDEPOTE
Jn 7.46 "No man ever spoke like this man!

NO LONGER

1. *no longer, no more:* μηκέτι MĒKETI
Mk 1.45 Jesus[g] could no longer . . enter a town
2. 2 there was no longer room for them
Rom 6. 6 we might no longer be enslaved to sin
15.23 I no longer have any room for work
2 Cor 5.15 might live no longer for themselves
Eph 4.14 so that we may no longer be children
4.17 you must no longer live as the Gentiles do
4.28 Let the thief no longer steal
1 Th 3. 1 when we could bear it no longer
3. 5 when I could bear it no longer
1 Tim 5.23 No longer drink only water
1 Pet 4. 2 to live . . no longer by human passions

2. *no longer, no more:* οὐκέτι OUKETI
Mt 19. 6 "So they are no longer two but one flesh
Mk 7.12 "you no longer permit him to do anything
9. 8 they no longer saw any one with them
10. 8 "they are no longer two but one flesh
Lk 15.19 " ' "no longer worthy to be called your son
15.21 " 'no longer worthy to be called your son[v]
20.40 they no longer dared to ask him
Jn 4.42 "no longer because of your words
6.66 no longer went about with him
11.54 Jesus . . no longer went about openly
14.30 "I will no longer talk much with you
15.15 "No longer do I call you servants[h]
16.21 "she no longer remembers the anguish
16.25 "when I shall no longer speak to you
Rom 6. 9 death no longer has dominion over him
7.17 So then it is no longer I that do it
7.20 it is no longer I that do it, but sin
11. 6 it is no longer on the basis of works; otherwise grace would no longer be grace
14.15 you are no longer walking in love
2 Cor 5.16 we regard him thus no longer
Gal 2.20 it is no longer I who live, but Christ
3.18 it is no longer by promise
3.25 we are no longer under a custodian
4. 7 through God you are no longer a slave
Eph 2.19 So then you are no longer strangers
Phm .16 no longer as a slave but more than a slave
Heb 10.18 there is no longer any offering for sin
10.26 there no longer remains a sacrifice for sins

NO MAN

1. *no one:* μηδείς MĒDEIS
Lk [6.35 "lend, *despairing of no man*‡
Gal 6.17 Henceforth let no man trouble me

2. *no one, nothing:* οὐδείς OUDEIS
Mt 22.16 "we know that you . . care for no man
Mk 12.14 "we know that you . . care for no man
Lk 18.29 "there is no man who has left house
Jn 7. 4 "no man works in secret . . to be known
15.13 "Greater love has no man than this
Acts 18.10 "no man shall attack you to harm you
1 Cor 6. 5 is no man among you wise enough?
Gal 3.11 it is evident that no man is justified
Eph 5.29 For no man ever hates his own flesh
1 Jn 4.12 No man has ever seen God
Rev 7. 9 multitude which no man could number

NO MEANS, BY

1. *come to be, happen, be:* γίνομαι (neg. opt.) GINOMAI [B.3.b.8]
Rom 3. 4 By no means! Let God be true
3. 6 By no means! . . how could God judge?
3.31 Do we . . overthrow the law . . ? By no m.!
6. 2 ⟨Are we to continue in sin?⟩ By no means!
6.15 Are we to sin . . ? By no means!
7. 7 the law is sin? By no means!
7.13 Did that . . bring death . . ? By no means!
Rom 9.14 Is there injustice . . ? By no means!
11. 1 has God rejected his people ? By no m.!
11.11 stumbled so as to fall ? By no means!

2. *not* (emph.): οὐ μή OU MĒ
Mk 9.41 "whoever gives . . will by no m. lose . . reward

3. *by no means:* οὐδαμῶς OUDAMŌS*
Mt 2. 6 " 'by no means least among the rulers

NO MORE (*See also* NO 3[a], 8[a])

1. *no longer, no more:* μηκέτι MĒKETI
Jn 5.14 "See, you are well! Sin no more
Acts 4.17 "let us warn them to speak no more
13.34 "no more to return to corruption
Rom 14.13 no more pass judgment on one another

2. *not, no:* οὐ OU
Mt **2.18**

3. *no longer, no more:* οὐκέτι OUKETI
Jn 14.19 "the world will see me no more
16.10 "you will see me no more
16.16 "you will see me no more
17.11 "And now I am no more in the world
Acts 8.39 the eunuch saw him no more
20.25 "all you . . will see my face no more
20.38 that they should see his face no more
Rev 10. 6 that there should be no more delay

4. *and not:* οὔτε OUTE
Jas 3.12 No more can salt water yield fresh

NO, NOT

1. *nor, and not:* οὐδέ OUDE
Rom 3.10 "None is righteous, no, not one

NO ONE

1. *no one:* μηδείς MĒDEIS
Mt 9.30 "See that no one knows it
16.20 to tell no one that he was the Christ
17. 9 commanded them, "Tell no one the vision
Mk 5.43 charged them that no one should know
7.36 he charged them to tell no one
8.30 he charged them to tell no one
9. 9 he charged them to tell no one
11.14 "May no one . . eat fruit from you again
Lk 3.14 "Rob no one by violence
5.14 he charged him to tell no one
8.56 he charged them to tell no one
9.21 commanded them to tell this to no one
10. 4 "salute no one on the road
Acts 9. 7 hearing the voice but seeing no one
23.22 "Tell no one that you have informed me
Rom 12.17 Repay no one evil for evil
13. 8 Owe no one anything, except to love
1 Cor 3.18 Let no one deceive himself
3.21 So let no one boast of men
10.24 Let no one seek his own good
Eph 5. 6 Let no one deceive you
Col 2. 4 in order that no one may delude you
2.18 Let no one disqualify you
1 Th 3. 3 no one be moved by these afflictions
1 Tim 4.12 Let no one despise your youth
Tit 2.15 Let no one disregard you
3. 2 to speak evil of no one
Jas 1.13 Let no one say when he is tempted
1 Jn 3. 7 children, let no one deceive you
Rev 3.11 " 'that no one may seize your crown

2. *not, no:* οὐ OU [A.4.c]
Lk **17.18**
Rom **3.11**[2], 12

3. *no one, nothing:* οὐδείς OUDEIS
Mt 6.24 "No one can serve two masters
[8.10 "*with no one* in Israel have I found such faith‡
9.16 "no one puts a piece of unshrunk cloth
11.27 "no one knows the Son except the Father
17. 8 they saw no one but Jesus only
20. 7 " 'Because no one has hired us
22.46 no one was able to answer him a word
24.36 "of that day and hour no one knows
Mk 2.21 "No one sews a piece of unshrunk cloth
2.22 "no one puts new wine into old wineskins
3.27 "no one can enter a strong man's house

Mk 5. 3 no one could bind him any more
5. 4 no one had the strength to subdue him
5.37 he allowed no one to follow him
9.39 "for no one who does a mighty work
10.18 "No one is good but God alone
10.29 "there is no one who has left house
11. 2 "a colt . . on which no one has ever sat
12.34 no one dared to ask him any question
13.32 "of that day or that hour no one knows
Lk 5.36 "No one tears a piece from a new garment
5.37 no one puts new wine into old wineskins
5.39 "no one after drinking old wine
8.16 "No one after lighting a lamp covers it
9.36 they kept silence and told no one
9.62 "No one who puts his hand to the plow
10.22 "no one knows who the Son is except
11.33 "No one after lighting a lamp puts it
15.16 "no one gave him anything
18.19 "No one is good but God alone
19.30 "a colt . . on which no one has . . sat
23.53 where no one had ever yet been laid
Jn 1.18 No one has ever seen God
3. 2 "no one can do these signs that you do
3.13 "No one has ascended into heaven
3.32 yet no one receives his testimony
5.22 "The Father judges no one
6.44 "No one can come to me unless
6.65 "I told you that no one can come to me
7.13 for fear of the Jews no one spoke openly
7.27 "no one will know where he comes from
7.30 but no one laid hands on him
7.44 but no one laid hands on him
8.10 "Has no one condemned you?[r]‡
8.11 She said, "No one, Lord[r]‡
8.15 "I judge no one
8.20 "but no one arrested him
9. 4 "night comes, when no one can work
10.18 "No one takes it from me
10.29 "no one is able to snatch them
13.28 no one at the table knew why he said this
14. 6 "no one comes to the Father, but by me
15.24 "the works which no one else did
16.22 "no one will take your joy from you
19.41 tomb where no one had ever been laid
Acts 4.12 "there is salvation in no one else
5.23 "when we opened it we found no one
20.33 "I coveted no one's silver or gold
25.11 "no one can give me up to them. I appeal
1 Cor 2.11 "no one comprehends the thoughts of God
2.15 spiritual man . . is . . to be judged by no one
12. 3 no one speaking by the Spirit of God
12. 3 no one can say "Jesus is Lord" except
14. 2 for no one understands him
2 Cor 5.16 we regard no one from a human . . view
7. 2 Open your hearts to us; we have wronged no one, we have corrupted no one, we have taken advantage of no one
Gal 3.15 no one annuls even a man's will[g]
Phil 2.20 I have no one like him
2 Tim 4.16 no one took my part; all deserted me
Heb 6.13 he had no one greater by whom to swear
7.13 tribe, from which no one has ever served
12.14 without which no one will see the Lord
Jas 1.13 he himself tempts no one
Rev 2.17 " 'name . . which no one knows except him
3. 7 " 'the holy one, . . who opens and no one shall shut, who shuts and no one opens
3. 8 " 'open door, which no one is able to shut
5. 3 no one . . was able to open the scroll
5. 4 I wept . . that no one was found worthy
14. 3 No one could learn that song except
15. 8 no one could enter the temple until
18.11 no one buys their cargo any more
19.12 name . . which no one knows but himself

4. *all, every, whole:* πᾶς (+neg.) PAS
Rom 10.11 "No one who believes in him
Gal 2.16 by . . the law shall no one be justified
1 Jn 3. 6 No one who abides in him sins; no one who sins has either seen him or known him
3. 9 No one born of God commits sin

5. *anyone, any:* τὶς (+neg.) TIS II
Mt **8.**28; **11.**27; **24.**4
Mk **13.**5
Lk **8.**51
Jn **2.**25; **10.**28
1 Cor **16.**11
2 Cor **8.**20; **11.**16; **12.**6
Col **2.**8, 16
2 Th **2.**3
Heb **4.**11; **12.**15, 16
Rev **13.**17

NO, WITH

1. *without, apart from:* ἄτερ ATER
Lk 22.35 "When I sent you out with no purse

NOAH: Νῶε ˈnōə
Mt 24.37 "As were the days of N., so will be
24.38 "until the day when N. entered the ark
Lk 3.36 Shem, the son of N., the son of Lamech
17.26 "As it was in the days of N., so will it be
17.27 "until the day when N. entered the ark
Heb 11. 7 By faith N., being warned by God
1 Pet 3.20 God's patience waited in the days of N.
2 Pet 2. 5 preserved N., a herald of righteousness

NOBLE

1. *wellborn, noble:* εὐγενής EUGENĒS
[a]comp.
Acts 17.11 [a]these Jews were more noble than those
2. *good, beautiful:* καλός KALOS
Lk 21. 5 it was adorned with noble stones
Rom 12.17 take thought for what is noble
1 Tim 3. 1 the office of bishop, . . a noble task

NOBLE BIRTH, OF

1. *wellborn, noble:* εὐγενής EUGENĒS
1 Cor 1.26 not many were of noble birth

NOBLE USE

1. *honor, value:* τιμή TIMĒ
2 Tim 2.20 some for noble use, some for ignoble
2.21 then he will be a vessel for noble use

NOBLEMAN

1. *a noble man:* ἄνθρωπος εὐγενής EUGENĒS [A.1.f]
Lk 19.12 "A nobleman went into a far country

NOBODY

1. *no one:* μηδείς MĒDEIS
1 Th 4.12 that you may . . be dependent on nobody

NOISE

1. *voice, sound:* φωνή PHŌNĒ
Rev 9. 9 the noise of their wings was like the noise of many chariots with horses

NOISE, WITH A LOUD

1. *with a rushing sound:* ῥοιζηδόν RHOIZĒDON*
2 Pet 3.10 heavens will pass away with a loud noise

NOISY

1. *ring, sound:* ἠχέω (part.) ĒCHEŌ*
1 Cor 13. 1 I am a noisy gong or a clanging cymbal

NONE

1. *quite all:* ἅπας (neg.) HAPAS
Lk 21.15 "wisdom, which none . . will . . withstand
2. *one:* εἷς (neg.) HEIS
1 Cor 4. 6 that none of you may be puffed up
3. *not:* μή MĒ [A.4.c]
[a]μή τις
Lk 3.11 "let him share with him who has n.
11.24 "finding none he says, 'I will return
1 Cor 7.29 who have wives live as though they had n.
1 Th 5.15 [a]See that none of you repays evil
1 Pet 4.15 [a]let none of you suffer as a murderer
4. *no one:* μηδείς MĒDEIS
Acts 11.19 speaking the word to none except Jews
24.23 none of his friends should be prevented
5. *not, no:* οὐ OU [A.4.c]
Mt **12.**43; **26.**60

Mk **14.55**
Lk **13.6**, 7
Rom **3.10**
Gal **1.19**
6. *no one, nothing:* οὐδείς OUDEIS
[a]οὐθείς
Lk 1.61 "N. of your kindred is called by this name
4.26 "Elijah was sent to none of them
4.27 "none of them was cleansed
7.28 I tell you, .. none is greater than John
14.24 " 'none of those men who were invited
18.34 they understood none of these things
Jn 4.27 none said, "What do you wish?
7.19 "Yet none of you keeps the law
16. 5 "none .. asks me, 'Where are you going?
17.12 "none .. is lost but the son of perdition
21.12 none of the disciples dared ask him
Acts 5.13 None of the rest dared join them
26.26 [a]"n. of these things has escaped his notice
Rom 14. 7 None of us lives to himself, and none of us dies to himself
1 Cor 1.14 I baptized none of you except Crispus
2. 8 N. of the rulers of this age understood
14.10 many .. languages .. n. is without meaning
7. *anyone, any:* τὶς (+neg.) TIS II
Jn **16.30**
Acts **28.21**
1 Th **5.15**
Heb **3.13**
1 Pet **4.15**
CONTEXTUALLY
Jn 16.30 "know all things, and need n. to question

NONE, AND

1. *and not, nor:* μηδέ MĒDE
Lk 16.26 " 'and none may cross from there to us
2. *and not:* οὔτε OUTE [A.4.c]
Acts 28.21 "and none of the brethren .. has reported

NOON

1. *midday, the south:* μεσημβρία MESĒMBRIA
Acts [8.26 "Rise and go *at noon* to the road†
22. 6 "about noon a great light from heaven

NOR

1. *or, than:* ἤ (+neg.) Ē
Jn **9.21**
1 Cor **12.21**
Eph **5.4**
2. *in order that:* ἵνα (neg.) HINA
Rev **9.20**
3. *and not:* καὶ μή MĒ [A.4.c]
[a]om. καί B.3.b.5
Lk **12.29**; **18.2**
Tit **2.10**[a]
4. *and not, nor:* μηδέ MĒDE
Mt **6.25**; **10.9**[2], 10[3]; **22.29**
Mk **12.24**; **13.15**
Lk **12.22**
Jn **4.15**
1 Cor **10.10**
1 Tim **1.4**; **5.22**; **6.17**
2 Tim **1.8**
Heb **12.5**
1 Pet **3.14**
5. *and not:* μήτε MĒTE
Mt **11.18**
Lk **9.3**[3]
Acts **23.8**[2], 12, 21; **27.20**
Heb **7.3**
6. *and not:* καὶ οὐ OU [A.4.c]
[a]om. καί B.3.b.5
1 Cor **2.9**[2]; **6.10**[3a]; **9.15**
Rev **9.21**
7. *nor, and not:* οὐδέ OUDE
Mt **5.15**; **6.26**[2], 28; **7.18**; **10.24**; **12.4**, 19; **13.13**; **22.46**; **23.13**; **24.36**‡; **25.13**
Mk **4.22**; **13.32**
Lk **6.43**, 44; **8.17**; **12.24**[2], 27; **17.21**; **18.4**
Jn **1.13**[2], 25[2]; **6.24**; **13.16**; **14.17**; **16.3**
Acts **2.27**; 8.21; **9.9**; **17.25**
Rom **2.28**
1 Cor **11.16**; **15.50**
2 Cor **7.12**
Gal **1.1**, 17; **3.28**[2]
1 Th **2.3**
Heb **9.25**; **10.8**; **13.5**
Rev **7.16**
8. *and not:* οὔτε OUTE
[a] + οὐδέ
Mt **6.20**; **22.30**
Mk **12.25**; **14.68**
Lk **12**.[27‡; **14.35**; **20.35**
Jn **4.21**; **8.19**
Acts **2.31**; **15.10**; **19.37**; **25.8**[2]
Rom **8.38-39**[9]
1 Cor **3.7**; **6.9-10**[8]; **11.11**
Gal **1.12**[a]; **5.6**; **6.15**
1 Th **2.6**
Rev **3.15**, 16; **21.4**
CONTEXTUALLY
Lk **1.15**; Acts **13.27**; **20.24**

NORTH

1. *north, north wind:* βορρᾶς BORRAS*
Lk 13.29 "men will come from .. north and south
Rev 21.13 on the north three gates

NORTHEAST

1. *southwest* (wind): λίψ LIPS*
Acts 27.12 Phoenix, .. looking northeast and southeast[a]†

NORTHEASTER

1. *the northeast wind:* εὐρακύλων EURAKYLŌN*
Acts 27.14 soon a tempestuous wind, called the n.

NORTHWEST

1. *northwest* (Lat.): χῶρος CHŌROS
Acts [27.12 harbor .. looking *southwest and northwest*†

NOT

1. *not:* μή MĒ
Mt **1.20**; **2.12**; **3.9**, 10; **5.17**, 34, 39, 42; **6.3**, 7, 8, 13, 15, 16, 18, 19, 25, 31, 34; **7.1**[2], 6, 19, 26; **10.13**, 14, 19, 28, 31, 34; **12.30**[2]; **13.5**, 19; **18.10**, 16, 25, 35; **19.14**; **23.3**, 8; **24.6**, 17, 18, 22, 23, 26[2]; **25.29**; **26.5**; **28.5**, 10
Mk **2.4**; **3.20**; **4.5**; **5.7**, 36; **6.9**, 11; **8.26**; **9.39**; **10.9**, 14, 15, 19[5]; **11.23**; **12.14**; **13.7**, 11, 15, 16, 20, 21; **14.2**; **16.6**
Lk **1.13**, 30; **2.10**, 26, 45; **3.8**, 9; **5.10**; **6.29**, 30, 37[2], 49; **7.6**, 13, 30, 42; **8.18**, 28, 49, 50, 52; **9.5**, 33, 50; **10.6**, 7, 10, 20; **11.4**, 7, 23[2]; **12.4**, 7, 11, 21, 22, 29, 32, 33, 47, 48; **13.9**, 11, 14; **14.8**, 12, 29, 32; **16.26**; **17.23**, 31[2]; **18.1**, 16, 17, 20[4]; **19.26**, 27; **20.7**; **21.8**[2], 9, 14, 21; **22.36**, 40, 42; **23.28**; **24.23**
Jn **2.16**; **3.7**, 18[2]; **5.23**, 28, 45; **6.20**, 27, 43, 64; **7.24**, 49; **9.33**, 39; **10.1**, 37, 38; **12.15**, 47, 48; **13.8**, 9; **14.1**, 2, 24, 27; **15.6**, 22, 24; **16.7**; **18.17**, 25, 30, 40; **19.21**, 24; **20.17**, 27, 29
Acts **1.4**; **3.23**; **5.7**, 28, 40; **7.19**, 60; **9.26**; **10.15**; **11.9**; **12.19**; **15.19**, 38[2]; **17.6**; **18.9**[2]; **19.31**; **20.10**, 16, 20, 22, 29; **21.4**, 12, 14, 21, 34; **23.21**; **25.24**, 27; **26.32**; **27.7**, 15, 21, 24
Rom **2.14**[2], 22; **3.8**; **4.5**, 17, 19; **5.14**; **6.12**; **7.3**, 7[2]; **8.4**; **9.29**, 30; **10.6**, 20[2]; **11.8**[2], 18, 20, 23; **12.2**, 3, 14, 16, 21; **13.13**; **14.1**, 15, 16, 20, 21; **15.1**
1 Cor **1.7**, 28; **4.5**, 7, 18; **5.9**, 11; **6.9**; **7.1**, 5, 10, 11, 12, 13, 18[2], 23, 27[2], 30[2]; **8.8**; **9.16**, 18, 20, 21; **10.6**, 29(28), 33; **11.22**; **13.1**, 2, 3; **14.7**, 9, 11, 20, 39; **15.33**
2 Cor **2.1**, 13; **3.7**, 13; **4.7**, 18; **5.12**, 19; **6.1**, 9, 14; **9.5**, 7; **10.2**, 14; **12.21**; **13.7**
Gal **4.18**; **5.1**, 13, 15; **6.7**, 9[2]
Eph **3.13**; **4.26**[2], 30; **5.7**, 15, 17, 18; **6.4**, 6
Phil **1.28**; **2.4**, 12; **3.9**
Col **1.23**; **2.21**; **3.2**, 9, 19, 21, 22
1 Th **1.8**; **2.9**; **4.5**[2]; **5.6**, 19, 20
2 Th **1.8**[2]; **2.2**, 12; **3.6**, 8, 13, 15
1 Tim **1.3**, 20; **2.9**; **3.3**, 6, 8[3]; **4.14**; **5.1**, 9, 13, 16; **6.2**, 3, 17

2 Tim **1**.8; **4**.16
Tit **1**.6, 7; **2**.3, 9
Heb **3**.8, 15; **4**.2, 7; **6**.1; **7**.6; **9**.17; **10**.25, 35; **11**.3, 5, 8, 13, 27; **12**.5, 25; **13**.2, 9, 16, 17
Jas **1**.7, 16, 22, 26; **2**.11^{2}, 14; **3**.1, 14; **4**.2, 11; **5**.9, 12, 17
1 Pet **1**.8, 14; **3**.7, 9; **4**.4, 12, 16; **5**.2
2 Pet **3**.8, 9
1 Jn **2**.15; **3**.10^{2}, 13, 14, 18, 21; **4**.1, 3, 8, 20; **5**.10, 12, 16^{2}
2 Jn .7, 9, 10
3 Jn .10, 11
Jude .5, 6
Rev **1**.17; **2**.5, 10, 16; **3**.3; **5**.5; **6**.6; **7**.3, 16; **10**.4; **11**.2; **13**.15; **19**.10; **22**.9, 10
Also Mt **12**.16; **17**.27; **24**.20; **26**.41; Mk **3**.12; **4**.12^{2}; **5**.10; **13**.18; **14**.38; Lk **8**.10^{2}, 12, 31; **9**.45; **22**.32, 46; Jn **3**.16; **4**.15; **6**.50; **7**.23; **11**.50; **12**.46; **18**.28, 36; Acts **2**.25; 1 Cor **2**.5; **11**.32; **12**.24; **16**.2; 2 Cor **1**.9; **2**.3, 5; **9**.3; **10**.9; **13**.10; Gal **6**.12; 1 Th **4**.13; 1 Tim **6**.1; Tit **2**.5; **3**.14; Phm .14; Heb **6**.12; **11**.28, 40; **12**.3, 13; Jas **5**.9, 12; 1 Jn **2**.1, 28; 2 Jn .8; Rev **7**.1; **9**.4, 5; **16**.15

2. *and not, nor:* μηδέ MĒDE
Mt **7**.6; Lk **17**.23; Rom **6**.13; 1 Cor **10**.7, 8, 9; Col **2**.21^{2}; 1 Th **3**.10; 1 Pet **5**.2, 3

3. *no one:* μηδείς MĒDEIS [A.4.c]
Acts **16**.28; 1 Tim **5**.22

4. *perhaps, never:* μήποτε MĒPOTE
Heb 9.17 not in force as long as . . one . . is alive

5. *and not:* μήτε MĒTE
Mt **5**.36

6. *not, no:* οὐ OU
Mt **1**.25; **3**.11; **4**.4, 7; **5**.17, 21, 27, 33; **6**.5, 20, 26, 30; **7**.3, 21, 22, 25, 29; **8**.8; **9**.13^{2}, 14, 24; **10**.20, 24, 26^{2}, 29, 34, 37^{2}, 38^{2}; **11**.17^{2}, 20; **12**.2, 3, 4, 5, 7^{2}, 19, 20, 31, 32; **13**.5, 11, 12, 13^{2}, 17^{2}, 55^{2}, 57, 58; **14**.4, 16; **15**.2, 11, 13, 17, 20, 23, 26; **16**.11, 12, 17, 18, 23; **17**.12, 16, 19, 24; **18**.14, 22, 33; **19**.4, 8, 10, 11, 18^{4}; **20**.15, 22, 23, 26, 28; **21**.21, 25, 27, 29, 30, 32; **22**.3, 8, 16, 17, 31, 32; **23**.3, 4, 30, 37; **24**.2^{3}, 21, 29, 39, 42, 43, 44, 50^{2}; **25**.9, 12, 24^{2}, 26^{2}, 43^{3}, 44, 45; **26**.11, 24, 39, 40, 55, 70, 72, 74; **27**.6, 13, 34; **28**.6
Mk **1**.7, 22, 34; **2**.17, 18, 24, 26, 27; **3**.25; **4**.5, 13, 21, 25, 27, 34, 38; **5**.39; **6**.3^{2}, 4, 18, 19, 26, 52; **7**.3, 4, 5, 18, 19, 24, 27; **8**.18^{3}, 33; **9**.6, 18, 28, 30, 37, [38‡, 38, 40, 48^{2}; **10**.27, 38, 40, 43, 45; **11**.13, 16, 17, [26‡, 31, 33; **12**.14^{2}, 24, 26, 27, 34; **13**.11, 14, 19, 24, 33, 35; **14**.7, 21, 29, 36, 37, 40, 49, 56, 71; **15**.23; **16**.6, 14‡
Lk **1**.20, 22; **2**.37, 43, 49, 50; **3**.16; **4**.4, 12, 41; **5**.32, 36; **6**.2, 4, 40, 41, 42, 44, 46, 48; **7**.6^{2}, 32^{2}, 45, 46; **8**.14, 17^{2}, 19, 27, 43, 47, 52; **9**.40, 49, 50, 53, [55‡, [55(56)‡; **10**.24^{2}, 40, 42; **11**.8, 38, 40, 44, 46, 52; **12**.2^{2}, 6, 10, 15, 39, 46^{2}, 56, 57; **13**.15, 16, 24, 25, 27, 34; **14**.3, 5, 6, 26, 27, 30, 33; **15**.4, 13; **16**.3, 11, 12, 31; **17**.17, 20, 22; **18**.11, 13, 34; **19**.3, 14, 21^{2}, 22^{2}, 23, 44^{2}, 48; **20**.5, 22, 26, 38; **21**.6^{2}, 9; **22**.26, 34, 53, 57, 58, 60; **23**.34‡, 51; **24**.3, [5(6)‡, 18, 24, 39
Jn **1**.5, 8, 10, 11, 13, 20^{2}, 21, 26, 27, 31, 33; **2**.9, 24; **3**.8, 10, 11, 12, 17, 18, 20, 28, 34, 36; **4**.2, 18, 22, 32, 35, 38; **5**.10, 13, 18, 23, 24, 30, 31, 34, 38^{2}, 41, 42, 43, 44, 47; **6**.7, 22, 24, 26, 32, 35^{2}, 36, 37, 38, 46, 58, 64, 70; **7**.1, 8‡, 10, 16, 19, 22, 25, 28^{2}, 34, 35, 36, 42, 45; **8**.13, 14, 16, 23, 27, 29, 35, 40, 41, 43, 45, 46, 47^{2}, 48, 49, 50, 55^{2}; **9**.8, 12, 16^{2}, 18, 21, 25, 27, 29, 30, 31; **10**.5^{2}, 6, 8, 12^{2}, 16, 21, 25, 26^{2}, 33, 34, 37; **11**.4, 9, 10, 15, 21, 32, 37, 40, 51, 52; **12**.5, 6, 8, 9, 16, 30, 35, 37, 39, 42, 44, 47^{2}, 49; **13**.7, 10, 16, 18; **14**.5, 9, 10^{2}, 18, 22, 24^{2}, 27; **15**.15, 16, 19, 20, 21, 22, 24; **16**.3, 4, 7, 9, 13, 17, 18, 19, 26, 32; **17**.9, 14^{2}, 15, 16^{2}, 20, 25; **18**.17, 25, 26, 28, 30, 31, 36^{2}; **19**.10^{2}, 11, 12, 33, 36; **20**.2, 5, 7, 13, 14, 24, 30; **21**.4, 8, 11, 18, 23^{3}
Acts **1**.7; **2**.15, 24, 27, 34; **5**.4, 22, 39, 42; **6**.2, 10; **7**.18, 25, 32, 40, 48, 52, 53; **8**.21, 32; **9**.21; **10**.41; **12**.9, 14, 22, 23; **13**.10, 25^{2}, 35, 39(38); **14**.17; **16**.7, 21; **17**.4, 12, 24, 27, 29; **19**.26^{2}, 27, 30, 32, 35; **20**.12, 27, 31; **21**.13, 38; **22**.9, 11, 18, 22; **23**.5^{2}; **24**.11; **25**.6, 7, 11, 16; **26**.19, 26, 29; **27**.10, 39; **28**.4
Rom **1**.16, 21, 28, 32; **2**.13, 21, 26, 28, 29^{2}; **3**.9, 12, 17; **4**.2, 4, 10, 12, 13, 16, 23; **5**.5, 11, 13, 15, 16; **6**.14, 15, 16; **7**.6, 7^{3}, 15^{2}, 16, 19^{2}, 20; **8**.7, 9^{3}, 12, 15, 18, 20, 23, 24, 25, 26, 32; **9**.1, 6^{2}, 8, 10, 11(12), 16, 24, 25^{2}, 26, 31, 32, 33; **10**.2, 3, 14, 16, 18, 19^{2}; **11**.2^{2}, 4, 18, 21; **12**.4; **13**.3, 4, 5, 9^{4}; **14**.17, 23^{2}; **15**.3, 18, 20; **16**.4, 18
1 Cor **1**.16, 17^{2}, 21, 26^{3}; **2**.1, 4, 6, 8, 12, 13, 14^{2}; **3**.1, 2, 4, 16; **4**.4, 7, 14, 15, 19, 20; **5**.6^{2}, 10; **6**.2, 3, 9^{2}, 12^{2}, 13, 15, 16, 19^{2}; **7**.4^{2}, 6, 10, 12, 15, 28^{2}, 35; **8**.7, 8; **9**.1^{3}, 2, 8, 9, 12^{2}, 13, 24, 26^{2}; **10**.5, 13^{2}, 18, 20^{2}, 23^{2}; **11**.6, 7, 8, 17^{2}, 20, 22^{2}, 31; **12**.1, 14, 15^{3}, 16^{3}, 24; **13**.4, 5^{3}, 6; **14**.2, 16, 17, 22^{2}, 23, 33, 34; **15**.10^{2}, 14, 15^{2}, 16, 17, 29, 32, 36, 37, 39, 46, 51, 58; **16**.7, 12
2 Cor **1**.8, 12, 18, 19, 24; **2**.4, 5, 11, 13, 17; **3**.3^{2}, 5, 6, 13; **4**.1, 5, 8^{2}, 9^{2}, 16; **5**.3, 4, 7, 12; **6**.12; **7**.3, 7, 8, 9, 12, 14; **8**.5, 8, 10, 12^{2}, 13, 19, 21; **9**.12; **10**.3, 4, 8^{2}, 12, 13, 14, 15, 18; **11**.6, 9, 10, 11, 15, 17, 29^{2}, 31; **12**.2, 3, 4, 5, 6, 13, 14^{3}, 16, 18^{2}, 20^{2}; **13**.2, 3, 5, 6, 7, 10
Gal **1**.1, 7, 10, 11, 16, 20; **2**.14^{2}, 15, 16^{2}, 21; **3**.10, 12, 16, 17; **4**.8, 14, 21, 27^{2}, 31; **5**.8, 18, 21; **6**.4, 7
Eph **1**.16, 21; **2**.8, 9; **3**.5; **4**.20; **5**.4; **6**.7, 12
Phil **1**.17, 29; **2**.6, 16, 21, 27; **3**.1, 12, 13; **4**.11, 17
Col **1**.9; **2**.1, 8, 19; **3**.23
1 Th **1**.5, 8; **2**.1, 3, 4, 8, 13, 17; **4**.7, 8, 13; **5**.4, 5, 9
2 Th **2**.5; **3**.2, 7, 9, 10
1 Tim **1**.9; **2**.7, 14; **3**.5; **5**.8, 13, 18
2 Tim **1**.7, 9, 12, 16; **2**.5, 9, 20, 24; **3**.9; **4**.3, 8
Tit **3**.5
Heb **2**.5, 11, 16; **3**.10, 16; **4**.2, 8, 15; **5**.4, 5, 12; **6**.10; **7**.16, 20, 21; **8**.2, 9^{2}; **9**.7, 11^{2}, 24; **10**.2, 5, 37, 39; **11**.1, 5, 16, 23, 31, 38, 39; **12**.7, 8, 9, 18, 20, 25, 26; **13**.6, 9^{2}
Jas **1**.20, 23; **2**.4, 5, 6, 7, 11, 21, 24, 25; **3**.10, 15; **4**.1, 2^{2}, 3, 4, 11, 14; **5**.6, 17
1 Pet **1**.12, 18, 23; **2**.10, 18, 23^{2}; **3**.3, 21
2 Pet **1**.16; **2**.3^{2}, 4, 5, 10, 11; **3**.9
1 Jn **1**.6, 8, 10^{2}; **2**.2, 4, 11, 15, 16, 19^{2}, 21^{2}; **3**.1^{2}, 10, 12; **4**.3, 6^{2}, 8, 10, 18, 20; **5**.3, 6, 10, 12, 16, 17, 18^{2}
2 Jn .1, 5, 9, 10, 12
3 Jn .9, 11, 13
Jude .9, 10
Rev **2**.2, 3, 9, 13, 24^{3}; **3**.2, 4, 8, 9, 17; **9**.4, 6, 20; **12**.11; **13**.8; **14**.4; **16**.9, 11; **17**.8^{3}, 11; **20**.4^{2}, 5, 15

7. *not* (emph.): οὐ μή OU MĒ
^{a}+οὐχί ^{b}+οὐδέ
Mt **5**.18; **10**.23, 42; **15**.5; **16**.28; **23**.39; **24**.2, 34, 35; **25**.9; **26**.29, 35
Mk **9**.1; **10**.15; **13**.2, 30, 31; **14**.25, 31; **16**.18‡
Lk **6**.37^{2}; **8**.17; **9**.27; **13**.35; **18**.7, 17^{a}, 30; **21**.18, 32, 33; **22**.16†‡, 18, 67, 68
Jn **4**.48; **6**.35, 37; **8**.12; **10**.5; **11**.56; **13**.38; **16**.7; **18**.11; **20**.25
Rom **4**.8
Gal **4**.30; **5**.16
1 Th **4**.15; **5**.3
Heb **8**.11
1 Pet **2**.6
Rev **2**.11; **3**.3, 5; **7**.16^{b}; **9**.6; **15**.4

8. *not, no* (emph.): οὐχί OUCHI
^{a}οὐχὶ μή
Mt **5**.46, 47; **6**.25; **10**.29; **12**.11; **13**.27, 56; **18**.12; **20**.13
Lk **4**.22; **6**.39; **12**.6; **14**.28, 31; **15**.8; **17**.8; **18**.30^{a}; **22**.27; **23**.39; **24**.26, 32
Jn **6**.42; **11**.9; **13**.10, 11; **14**.22
Acts **2**.7; **5**.4; **7**.50
Rom **3**.2; **8**.32
1 Cor **1**.20; **3**.3; **5**.2, 12; **6**.7^{2}; **8**.10; **9**.1; **10**.16^{2}, 29
2 Cor **3**.8
1 Th **2**.19
Heb **1**.14; **3**.17

9. *nor, and not:* οὐδέ OUDE
Mt **16**.9; **25**.45
Mk **12**.10
Lk **6**.3; **7**.7; **12**.26; **23**.40
Jn **1**.3; **8**.42; **11**.50; **21**.25
Acts **4**.34
1 Cor **3**.2; **11**.14
Gal **1**.12
2 Th **3**.8
Heb **8**.4; **9**.12
Rev **9**.20

10. *no one, nothing:* οὐδείς (attr.) OUDEIS
Jn **16**.29
11. *not yet:* οὔπω OUPŌ
1 Cor 3. 2 for you were not ready for it
12. *and not:* οὔτε OUTE
Jn **9**.3
Acts **2**.31
1 Cor **11**.11
IDIOMATICALLY
a. 1 Tim 5.25 and even when they are not καὶ τὰ ἄλλως ἔχοντα [ALLŌS]

NOT AGAIN
1. *no longer, no more:* μηκέτι MĒKETI
Jn 8.11 "go, and do not sin again[r]‡

NOT, AND
1. *and not:* μήτε MĒTE
Lk 9. 3 "and do not have two tunics
2. *nor, and not:* οὐδέ OUDE
Rom **9**.7

NOT ANY
1. *no one:* μηδείς MĒDEIS
2 Th 3.11 some of you are . . not doing any work
2. *no one, nothing:* οὐδείς OUDEIS [A.4.c]
[a]οὐθείς
Lk 23.14 [a]"I did not find . . guilty of any . . charges
Acts 27.34 "not a hair is to perish from . . any of you

NOT ANY ONE
1. *no one, nothing:* οὐδείς OUDEIS
Mk **7**.24

NOT ANYTHING
1. *no one, nothing:* οὐδείς OUDEIS
1 Cor 4. 4 I am not aware of a. against myself

NOT, AS YET
1. *not yet:* οὐδέπω OUDEPŌ
Jn 20. 9 as yet they did not know the scripture
2. *not yet:* οὔπω OUPŌ
Jn 7.39 as yet the Spirit had not been given

NOT AT ALL
1. *no one, nothing:* οὐδείς OUDEIS [A.4.c]
2 Cor 12.11 For I was not at all inferior to these
Phil 1.20 I shall not be at all ashamed

NOT, BUT
1. *nor, and not:* οὐδέ OUDE
Mk **16**.13[k]‡

NOT, CERTAINLY
1. *may it not be:* μὴ γένοιτο MĒ; GINOMAI [B.3.b.8]
Gal 2.17 is Christ . . an agent of sin? Certainly not!
3.21 against the promises of God? Certainly not!

NOT EVEN
1. *and not, nor:* μηδέ MĒDE
Mk **2**.2; **8**.26
1 Cor **5**.11
Eph **5**.3
2. *nor, and not:* οὐδέ OUDE
Mt **6**.29; **8**.10‡; **21**.32; **24**.36; **27**.14
Mk **13**.32; **14**.59
Lk **7**.9; **12**.27
Jn **7**.5
Acts **7**.5
1 Cor **4**.3; **5**.1; **14**.21
Gal **2**.3, 5; **6**.13
Heb **9**.18

NOT IN THE LEAST
1. *no one:* μηδείς (neut.) MĒDEIS
2 Cor 11. 5 I am not in the least inferior to these

NOT, NO
1. *nor, and not:* οὐδέ OUDE
Rom 3.10 "None is righteous, no, not one

NOT, NOW . . .
1. *no longer, no more:* οὐκέτι OUKETI
Jn 21. 6 now they were not able to haul it in

NOT ONE
1. *no one, nothing:* οὐδείς OUDEIS
Jn **18**.9

NOT ONLY
1. *indeed, on one hand:* μέν MEN
2 Cor 8.17 For he not only accepted our appeal
2. *and, both . . . and:* τέ TE [B.3.b.5]
Acts **26**.10

NOT SO
1. *not, no* (emph.): οὐχί OUCHI
Lk 1.60 "Not so; he shall be called John

NOT, THEN . . .
1. *nor, and not:* οὐδέ OUDE
1 Cor 15.13 then Christ has not been raised
15.16 then Christ has not been raised

NOT YET
1. *not yet:* μήπω MĒPŌ*
Rom 9.11 though they were not yet born
Heb 9. 8 way into the sanctuary is not yet opened
2. *not yet:* οὐδέπω OUDEPŌ
Jn 7.39 because Jesus was not yet glorified
Acts 8.16 it had not yet fallen on any of them
3. *not yet:* οὔπω OUPŌ
Mt 16. 9 "Do you not yet perceive?
24. 6 "must take place, but the end is **not yet**
Mk 8.17 "Do you not yet perceive or understand?
8.21 "Do you not yet understand?
13. 7 "must take place, but the end is not yet
Jn 2. 4 "My hour has not yet come
3.24 John had not yet been put in prison
6.17 Jesus had not yet come to them
7. 6 "My time has not yet come
[7. 8 "I am not *yet* going up to this feast‡
7. 8 "for my time has not yet fully come
7.30 because his hour had not yet come
8.20 because his hour had not yet come
8.57 "You are not yet fifty years old
11.30 Jesus had not yet come to the village
20.17 "I have not yet ascended to the father
1 Cor 8. 2 he does not yet know as he ought
Heb 2. 8 not yet see everything in subjection
12. 4 you have not yet resisted to the point
1 Jn 3. 2 it does not yet appear what we shall be
Rev 17.10 "the other has not yet come
17.12 "have not yet received royal power

NOTABLE
1. *known, knowable:* γνωστός GNŌSTOS
Acts 4.16 "a notable sign has been performed

NOTE
1. *see, perceive:* εἶδον EIDON
Rom 11.22 Note then the kindness and the severity
2. *sound, voice:* φθόγγος PHTHOGGOS
1 Cor 14. 7 If . . instruments . . do not give distinct notes
3. *seal, make known:* σημειόω (mid.) SĒMEIOŌ*
2 Th 3.14 note that man, and have nothing to do

NOTE, MAN OF
1. *prominent, outstanding:* ἐπίσημος (subst.) EPISĒMOS
Rom 16. 7 they are men of n. among the apostles

NOTE, TAKE
1. *consider, look out for:* σκοπέω SKOPEŌ
Rom 16.17 take n. of those who create dissensions

NOTHING
1. *other, another:* ἄλλος (subst. neut. neg.) ALLOS
2 Cor 1.13 we write you n. but what you can read
2. *who, which, what:* ὅς (+neg.) HOS
Lk **11**.6
3. *not:* μή MĒ [A.4.c]
Jn 6.39 "I should lose n. . . he has given me
1 Cor 11.22 do you . . humiliate those who have n.?
2 Cor 6.17 "Therefore . . touch nothing unclean
9. 4 lest . . we be humiliated—to say n. of you
2 Th 3.14 note . . and have nothing to do with him
Phm .19 to say nothing of your owing me

4. *no one:* μηδείς (neut.) MĒDEIS
[a]A.4.c; not neut. [b]μηθείς
Mt 8. 4 "See that you say nothing to any one
27.19 "Have nothing to do with that . . man
Mk 6. 8 charged them to take n. for their journey
Lk 6.35 "lend, expecting nothing in return[v]‡
9. 3 "Take nothing for your journey
Acts 8.24 "Pray . . that n. . . may come upon me
13.28 [a]"charge him with n. deserving death
19.36 "be quiet and do nothing rash
23.29 "charged with nothing deserving death
25.25 "he had done nothing deserving death
27.33 [b]"you have continued . . , having taken n.
2 Cor 6.10 having n., and yet possessing everything
Gal 6. 3 thinks he is something, when he is n.
Phil 2. 3 Do n. from selfishness or conceit
1 Tim 5.21 keep these rules . . , doing n. from partiality
6. 4 puffed up with conceit, he knows n.
Tit 2. 8 having nothing evil to say of us
3.13 see that they lack nothing
Jas 1. 4 perfect and complete, lacking in nothing
1 Pet 3. 6 if you do right and let n. terrify you
3 Jn . 7 they . . have accepted n. from the heathen
5. *not, no:* οὐ OU [A.4.c]
Mk **4.22** (*Var.* TIS II)
Lk **8.17**
Jn **8.44**; **10.13**
Rom **7.18**
2 Cor **8.15**; **12.1**
6. *no one, nothing:* οὐδείς OUDEIS
[a]οὐθείς
Mt 10.26 "n. is covered that will not be revealed
13.34 he said n. to them without a parable
17.20 "nothing will be impossible to you[x]
21.19 he . . found nothing on it but leaves only
23.16 " 'If any one swears by the temple, it is n.
23.18 " 'If any one swears by the altar, it is n.
27.24 Pilate saw that he was gaining nothing
Mk 7.15 "nothing outside a man . . can defile him
11.13 When he came . . , he found n. but leaves
16. 8 they said nothing to any one
Lk 4. 2 And he ate nothing in those days
5. 5 "we toiled all night and took nothing!
10.19 "nothing shall hurt you
12. 2 "N. is covered up that will not be revealed
22.35 [a]"did you lack anything?" They said, "N.
23.15 "n. deserving death has been done by him
23.41 "this man has done nothing wrong
Jn 5.19 "the Son can do n. of his own accord
5.30 "I can do nothing on my own authority
7.26 "here he is, . . and they say nothing to him!
8.28 "that I do n. on my own authority
8.54 "If I glorify myself, my glory is n.
9.33 "If . . not from God, he could do n.
12.19 "You see that you can do nothing
15. 5 "apart from me you can do nothing
16.23 "In that day you will ask nothing of me
16.24 "you have asked nothing in my name
18.20 "I have said nothing secretly
21. 3 but that night they caught nothing
Acts 4.14 they had nothing to say in opposition
5.36 "all . . were dispersed and came to n.
9. 8 when his eyes were opened, he could see n.
17.21 Athenians . . spent their time in n. except
19.27 [a]"the temple of . . Artemis may count for n.
21.24 "there is n. in what they have been told
23. 9 "We find nothing wrong in this man
25.11 if there is n. in their charges against me
26.22 "n. but what . . Moses said would come
26.31 "This man is doing n. to deserve death
28.17 "though I had done n. against the people
Rom 14.14 persuaded . . that n. is unclean in itself
1 Cor 13. 2 [a]if I . . have not love, I am nothing
13. 3 if I . . have not love, I gain nothing
2 Cor 12.11 I was not at all inferior . . though I am n.
Gal 2. 6 those . . who were of repute added n. to me
1 Tim 4. 4 n. . . rejected if . . received with thanksgiving
1 Tim 6. 7 for we brought nothing into the world
Tit 1.15 to the corrupt . . nothing is pure
Phm .14 I preferred to do n. without your consent
Heb 2. 8 he left nothing outside his control
7.14 in connection with that . . Moses said n.
7.19 (for the law made nothing perfect
Rev 3.17 " 'For you say, . . I need nothing
7. *and not:* οὔτε OUTE [A.4.c]
Jn 4.11 "Sir, you have nothing to draw with
8. *all, every, whole:* πᾶς (neut.+neg.) PAS
[a]+ῥῆμα [b]οὐ μή
Lk 1.37 [a]"with God nothing will be impossible
Rev 21.27 [b]But nothing unclean shall enter it
9. *who? what?:* τίς (+neg.) TIS I
Mt **15.32**
Mk **8.1**, 2
10. *anyone, any:* τὶς (+neg.) TIS II
Jn **5.14**; **6.12**
Acts **25.26**
Rom **9.11**
1 Cor **2.2**
Also variant to: Mk **4.22**
CONTEXTUALLY
Mk **14.51**
Jn **8.44**; **10.13**

NOTHING, AND
1. *and not anything:* μηδέ τι MĒDE [A.4.c]
Rom **9.11**

NOTHING AT ALL
1. *no one, nothing:* οὐδείς (neut.+neg.) OUDEIS
Jn 11.49 Caiaphas . . said . . "You know n. at all

NOTHING, BRING TO
1. *make ineffective, hinder:* καταργέω KATARGEŌ
1 Cor 1.28 to bring to nothing things that are

NOTHING . . . EVER
1. *never:* οὐδέποτε OUDEPOTE
Acts 11. 8 " 'n. . . unclean has ever entered my mouth

NOTHING TO DO WITH, HAVE
1. *ask for, decline:* παραιτέομαι (imper.) PARAITEOMAI
1 Tim 4. 7 Have n. to do with godless and silly myths
2 Tim 2.23 Have n. to do with stupid . . controversies
Tit 3.10 have nothing more to do with him

NOTICE
1. *consider, perceive:* κατανοέω KATANOEŌ
Mt 7. 3 "Why . . not n. the log . . in your own eye?
Lk 6.41 "Why . . not n. the log . . in your own eye?
Acts 27.39 they noticed a bay with a beach

NOTICE, ESCAPE ONE'S
1. *escape notice:* λανθάνω LANTHANŌ
Acts 26.26 "none of these things has escaped his n.

NOTICE, GIVE
1. *proclaim:* διαγγέλλω DIAGGELLŌ
Acts 21.26 went into the temple, to give notice
2. *manifest, make clear:* ἐμφανίζω EMPHANIZŌ
Acts 23.15 "give n. . . to the tribune to bring him down

NOTORIOUS
1. *prominent, outstanding:* ἐπίσημος EPISĒMOS
Mt 27.16 they had then a notorious prisoner

NOURISH
1. *nourish, rear:* ἐκτρέφω EKTREPHŌ
Eph 5.29 For . . man . . nourishes ⟨his own flesh⟩
2. *bring up, rear:* ἐντρέφω ENTREPHŌ*
1 Tim 4. 6 nourished on the words of the faith
3. *supply, furnish:* ἐπιχορηγέω EPICHORĒGEŌ
Col 2.19 body, nourished and knit together
4. *feed, nourish:* τρέφω TREPHŌ
Rev 12. 6 she has a place . . in which to be nourished
12.14 the place where she is to be nourished

NOW
1. *but:* ἀλλά ALLA
2 Cor **8.7**
2. *just now:* ἄρτι ARTI
[a]ἀπ' ἄρτι [b]ἕως ἄρτι *until now*
Mt 3.15 "Let it be so now, for thus it is fitting

Mt 11.12 "From the days of John the Baptist until n.
Jn 2.10 "you have kept the good wine until now
9.19 "How then does he now see?
9.25 "though I was blind, now I see
13. 7 "What I am doing you do not know now
13.19 [a]"I tell you this now, before it takes place
13.33 " 'as I said to the Jews so now I say to you
13.37 "why cannot I follow you now?
16.12 "but you cannot bear them now
16.31 "Do you now believe?
1 Cor 4.13 [b]we have become, and are n., as . . refuse
13.12 For now we see in a mirror dimly . . Now I know in part; then I shall understand
16. 7 I do not want to see you n. just in passing
Gal 1. 9 As we have said before, so now . . again
1.10 Am I now seeking the favor of men?
4.20 I could wish to be present with you now
1 Th 3. 6 now that Timothy has come to us
2 Th 2. 7 only he who now restrains it will do so
1 Pet 1. 6 n. for a little while you may have to suffer
1. 8 though you do not n. see him you[c] believe
Rev 12.10 "Now the salvation and the power

3. *already, now:* ἤδη ĒDĒ
Mt 3.10 "Even now the axe is laid to the root
14.15 "a lonely place, and the day is now over
15.32 "they have been with me now three days
Mk 6.35 "a lonely place, and the hour is now late
8. 2 "they have been with me now three days
Lk 3. 9 "Even now the axe is laid to the root
11. 7 " 'Do not bother me; the door is n. shut
14.17 " 'Come; for all is now ready
19.37 As he was now drawing near
23.44 It was now about the sixth hour
24.29 "Stay with us, . . the day is now far spent
Jn 6.17 It was n. dark, and Jesus had not yet come
19.28 Jesus, knowing that all was now finished
21.14 This was n. the third time . . Jesus . . revealed
Rom 1.10 asking that . . I may now at last succeed
13.11 how it is full time now for you to wake
Phil 4.10 I rejoice . . that n. . . you have revived
2 Pet 3. 1 now the second letter that I have written

4. *for:* γάρ GAR
Heb **2**.8; **11**.5

5. *behold! look!:* ἴδε IDE
Gal 5. 2 Now I, Paul, say to you

6. *behold!:* ἰδού IDOU
Lk 2.25 Now there was a man in Jerusalem
23.50 Now there was a man named Joseph

7. *now:* νῦν NYN
[a]subst.
Mt 24.21 [a]"from the beginning of the world until n.
26.65 "You have now heard his blasphemy
27.42 "let him come down now from the cross
27.43 "let God deliver him n., if he desires him
Mk 10.30 "will . . receive a hundredfold n. in this time
13.19 [a]"from the beginning of the creation until n.
15.32 "Let the Christ . . come down now
Lk 2.29 "Lord, now lettest thou thy servant depart
6.21 "Blessed are you that hunger now
6.21 "Blessed are you that weep now
6.25 "Woe to you that are full now
6.25 "Woe to you that laugh now
11.39 "Now you Pharisees cleanse the outside
16.25 " 'now he is comforted here
19.42 "But now they are hid from your eyes
22.36 "But n., let him who has a purse take it
Jn 2. 8 "N. draw . . and take it to the steward
4.18 "whom you now have is not your husband
4.23 "the hour is coming, and now is
5.25 "the hour is coming, and now is
6.42 "How does he n. say, 'I have come down
8.40 "but now you seek to kill me
8.52 "Now we know that you have a demon
9.21 "how he now sees we do not know
9.41 "but now that you say, 'We see
11. 8 "Jews were but now seeking to stone you
11.22 "n. I know that whatever you ask
Jn 12.27 "Now is my soul troubled
12.31 "N. is the judgment of this world, now shall the ruler of this world be cast out
13.31 "Now is the Son of man glorified
13.36 "Where I am going you cannot follow . . n.
14.29 "n. I have told you before it takes place
15.22 "n. they have no excuse for their sin
15.24 "n. they have seen . . me and my Father
16. 5 "now I am going to him who sent me
16.22 "you have sorrow n., but I will see you
16.29 "Ah, now you are speaking plainly!
16.30 "N. we know that you know all things
17. 5 "now, Father, glorify thou me
17. 7 "N. they know that everything . . is from thee
17.13 "But now I am coming to thee
Acts 3.17 "n. . . I know that you acted in ignorance
4.29 "now, Lord, look upon their threats
7. 4 "this land in which you are now living
7.34 "now come, I will send you to Egypt
7.52 "whom you have now betrayed
10. 5 "n. send men to Joppa, and bring . . Simon
10.33 "Now therefore we are all here present
12.11 "Now . . the Lord has sent his angel
13.11 "now, behold, the hand of the Lord
13.31 "who are n. his witnesses to the people
15.10 "N. . . why do you make trial of God
16.36 "now . . come out and go in peace
16.37 "do they now cast us out secretly?
17.30 "now he commands all men everywhere
20.22 "now, behold, I am going to Jerusalem
20.25 "now, behold, I know that all you
20.32 "And now I commend you to God
22.16 " 'And now why do you wait?
23.15 "give notice now to the tribune
23.21 "n. they are ready, waiting for the promise
26. 6 "n. I stand . . trial for hope in the promise
27.22 "I now bid you take heart
Rom 5. 9 we are now justified by his blood
5.11 we have now received our reconciliation
6.19 now yield your members to righteousness
6.21 things of which you are now ashamed
8. 1 There is . . now no condemnation
8.22 [a]creation has been groaning . . until now
11.30 you . . now have received mercy
11.31 so they have now been disobedient
[11.31 that . . they . . may *now* receive mercy‡
13.11 full time now for you to wake from sleep
16.26 ⟨the mystery which⟩ is now disclosed
1 Cor [5.11 But *now I write* to you†
14. 6 N. . . if I come to you speaking in tongues
16.12 it was not at all his will[b] to come now
2 Cor 6. 2 Behold, now is the acceptable time; behold, now is the day of salvation
13. 2 I warn them now while absent
Gal 1.23 "He who . . persecuted us is n. preaching
2.20 life I n. live in the flesh I live by faith
3. 3 are you now ending with the flesh?
4. 9 now that you have come to know God
4.29 as at that time he . . persecuted . . , so it is n.
Eph 2. 2 n. at work in the sons of disobedience
3. 5 has n. been revealed to his holy apostles
3.10 wisdom of God might n. be made known
5. 8 you were darkness, but n. you are light
Phil 1. 5 [a]partnership . . from the first day until now
1.20 that with full courage now as always
1.30 conflict which you . . now hear to be mine
2.12 so now, not only as in my presence
3.18 For many, of whom I . . now tell you
Col 1.24 N. I rejoice in my sufferings for your sake
1.26 but now made manifest to his saints
1 Th 3. 8 now we live, if you stand fast in the Lord
2 Th 2. 6 restraining him n. . . that he may be revealed
2 Tim 1.10 n. has manifested through the appearing
Heb 9. 5 Of these . . we cannot now speak in detail
9.24 now to appear in the presence of God
12.26 now he has promised, "Yet once more
Jas 4.13 Come now, you who say, "Today

Jas 5. 1 Come now, you rich, weep and howl
1 Pet 1.12 things which have now been announced
2.10 but now you are God's people; . . now you have received mercy
2.25 you . . have n. returned to the Shepherd
3.21 Baptism . . now saves you . . as an appeal
2 Pet 3. 7 the heavens and earth that now exist
3.18 To him be the glory both n. and to the day
1 Jn 2.18 so now many antichrists have come
2.28 And now, little children, abide in him
3. 2 Beloved, we are God's children now
4. 3 now it is in the world already
2 Jn . 5 n. I beg you . . that we love one another
Jude .25 before all time and now and for ever

8. *now:* νυνί NYNI
Acts 22. 1 "the defense which I now make before you
24.13 "what they now bring up against me
Rom 3.21 n. . . righteousness . . has been manifested
6.22 now that you have been set free
7. 6 now we are discharged from the law
15.23 now, since I no longer have any room
2 Cor 8.10(11) best . . now to complete what . . you began
8.22 who is now more earnest than ever
Eph 2.13 n. in Christ J. you . . have been brought near
Col 1.21 you, who once were estranged
3. 8 now put them all away: anger, wrath
Phm . 9 I, . . now a prisoner also for Christ Jesus
.11 (n. he is indeed useful[b] to you and to me

9. *so, therefore:* οὖν OUN
Lk **7**.42; **20**.29
Jn **3**.25; **4**.1; **11**.17; **20**.30
Acts **1**.18; **8**.4, 25; **11**.19; **19**.32; **25**.1
Eph **4**.17
1 Tim **3**.2
Heb **7**.11; **8**.4; **9**.1
Rev **1**.19

NOW . . . NOT

1. *no longer, no more:* οὐκέτι OUKETI
Jn 21. 6 now they were not able to haul it in

NOW ON, FROM

1. *remaining, left:* λοιπός (neut.) LOIPOS
1 Cor 7.29 from now on, let those who have wives
2. *from the present:* ἀπὸ τοῦ νῦν NYN [B.1.b]
Lk 22.18 "from n. on I shall not drink of the fruit
22.69 "from now on the Son of man shall be
Acts 18. 6 "From n. on I will go to the Gentiles
2 Cor 5.16 From now on . . we regard no one

NOWHERE

1. *not:* μή MĒ [A.4.c]
Mt 10. 5 "Go nowhere among the Gentiles
2. *where, how:* ποῦ (neg.) POU I
Mt 8.20 "the Son of man has n. to lay his head
Lk 9.58 "Son of man has n. to lay his head
12.17 " 'for I have nowhere to store my crops

NULL, BE

1. *empty, make void:* κενόω (perf. pass.) KENOŌ
Rom 4.14 faith is null and the promise is void

NULLIFY

1. *deny, nullify:* ἀθετέω ATHETEŌ
Gal 2.21 I do not nullify the grace of God
2. *make ineffective, hinder:* καταργέω KATARGEŌ
Rom 3. 3 Does . . faithlessness n. the faithfulness of God?

NUMBER (*See also* FULL NUMBER)

1. *number, count:* ἀριθμέω ARITHMEŌ*
Mt 10.30 "the hairs of your head are all numbered
Lk 12. 7 "the hairs of your head are all numbered
Rev 7. 9 multitude which no man could number
2. *number, total:* ἀριθμός ARITHMOS*
Lk 22. 3 Judas . . , who was of the n. of the twelve
Jn 6.10 men sat down, in n. about five thousand
Acts 4. 4 n. of the men came to about five thousand
5.36 "Theudas arose . . , and a n. of men . . joined
6. 7 the number of the disciples multiplied
11.21 great n. that believed turned to the Lord
Acts 16. 5 they increased in numbers daily
Rom 9.27 "Though the n. . . of Israel be as the sand
Rev 7. 4 I heard the number of the sealed
9.16 The number of the troops of cavalry
9.16 I heard their number
13.17 name of the beast or the n. of its name
13.18 let him . . reckon the n. of the beast, for it is a human number, its number is six hundred and sixty-six[a]
15. 2 its image and the number of its name
20. 8 their number is like the sand of the sea
3. *enough:* ἱκανός (subst.) HIKANOS
Acts 19.19 a n. of those who practiced magic arts
4. *count:* καταριθμέω KATARITHMEŌ*
Acts 1.17 "For he was numbered among us
CONTEXTUALLY
Mk 5.13 herd, numbering about two thousand, rushed
Acts 2.47 the Lord added to their n. day by day
6. 1 when the disciples were increasing in n.
Rev 6.11 until the n. of their fellow servants

NUMBER, MANY IN

1. *more:* πλείων (pl.) PLEIŌN
Heb 7.23 former priests were many in number

NUMBER OF, A

1. *enough:* ἱκανός HIKANOS
Acts 27. 7 We sailed slowly for a n. of days

NUMBERING

1. *number, total:* ἀριθμός ARITHMOS [B.2.a.1]
Rev 5.11 angels, numbering myriads of myriads

NUMBERS, IN GREAT

1. *more:* πλείων (pl.) PLEIŌN
Acts 28.23 they came to him . . in great numbers

NURSE

1. *feeder, nurse:* τροφός TROPHOS*
1 Th 2. 7 like a nurse taking care of her children

NYMPHA: Νύμφα 'nimfə
Col 4.15 greetings . . to N. and . . church in her house

O

O

1. *O:* ὦ Ō II
Mt 15.28 "O woman, great is your faith!
17.17 "O faithless and perverse generation!
Mk 9.19 "O faithless generation, how long?
Lk 9.41 "O faithless . . generation, how long?
24.25 "O foolish men, and slow of heart!
Acts 1. 1 In the first book, O Theophilus
18.14 "reason to bear with you, O Jews
Rom 2. 1 Therefore you have no excuse, O man
2. 3 Do you suppose, O man, . . you will escape?
11.33 O the depth of the . . knowledge of God!
Gal 3. 1 O foolish Galatians! Who has bewitched?
1 Tim 6.20 O Timothy, guard what has been entrusted

OATH

1. *something dedicated, curse:* ἀνάθεμα ANATHEMA
Acts 23.14 "We have . . bound ourselves by an oath
2. *taking an oath:* ὁρκωμοσία HORKŌMOSIA*
Heb 7.20 it was not without an oath
7.21(20–21) formerly . . priests took . . office without an oath, but this one was . . with an o.
7.28 the word of the o. . . appoints a Son
3. *oath:* ὅρκος HORKOS
Mt 14. 7 promised with an o. to give her whatever
14. 9 because of his oaths . . he commanded it
26.72 again he denied it with an oath
Mk 6.26 because of his oaths . . he did not . . break
Lk 1.73 "the oath which he swore to . . Abraham
Acts 2.30 "God had sworn with an oath to him
Heb 6.16 in all their disputes an oath is final
6.17 he interposed with an oath

Jas 5.12 do not swear . . with any other oath
CONTEXTUALLY
Mt 23.16 " 'he is bound by his oath
23.18 " 'he is bound by his oath

OATH, BIND BY AN
OATH, BIND STRICTLY BY AN
1. *bind by a curse:* ἀναθεματίζω ANATHEMATIZŌ
[a]+ἀναθέματι C.3
Acts 23.12 bound themselves by an oath neither to eat
23.14 [a]"have strictly bound ourselves by an o.
23.21 "bound themselves by an oath neither to eat

OBED: Ἰωβήδ 'ōbed
Mt 1. 5 Boaz the father of Obed by Ruth, and Obed the father of Jesse
Lk 3.32 Jesse, the son of Obed, the son of Boaz

OBEDIENCE
1. *obedience:* ὑπακοή HYPAKOĒ
Rom 1. 5 to bring about the obedience of faith
5.19 by one man's o. many will be made righteous
6.16 obedience, which leads to righteousness
15.18 to win obedience from the Gentiles
16.19 while your obedience is known to all
16.26 to bring about the obedience of faith
2 Cor 7.15 he remembers the obedience of you all
10. 6 when your obedience is complete
Phm .21 Confident of your obedience, I write
Heb 5. 8 he learned o. through what he suffered
1 Pet 1. 2 sanctified by the Spirit for obedience
1.22 purified your souls by your obedience
2. *subordination:* ὑποταγή HYPOTAGĒ
2 Cor 9.13 you[m] will glorify God by your obedience

OBEDIENT
1. *obedience:* ὑπακοή HYPAKOĒ
[a]B.1.a.1 [b]gen.
Rom 6.16 [a]if you yield . . to any one as o. slaves
1 Pet 1.14 [b]As o. children, do not be conformed
2. *obedient, subject:* ὑπήκοος HYPĒKOOS
2 Cor 2. 9 that I might . . know whether you are o.
Phil 2. 8 he humbled himself and became o.

OBEDIENT, BE
OBEDIENT, BECOME
1. *listen, obey:* ὑπακούω HYPAKOUŌ
Acts 6. 7 many of the priests were o. to the faith
Rom 6.17 you . . once slaves of sin have become o.
Eph 6. 5 Slaves, be o. to . . your earthly masters
2. *subject, place under:* ὑποτάσσω (pass.) HYPOTASSŌ
Lk 2.51 he went down . . and was o. to them
3. *obey one in authority:* πειθαρχέω PEITHARCHEŌ
Tit 3. 1 Remind them . . to be o., to be ready

OBEY
1. *obedience:* ὑπακοή HYPAKOĒ [B.1.a.2]
2 Cor 10. 5 take every thought captive to o. Christ
2. *listen, obey:* ὑπακούω HYPAKOUŌ
Mt 8.27 "even winds and sea obey him
Mk 1.27 "even the unclean spirits . . obey him
4.41 "even wind and sea obey him
Lk 8.25 "commands . . wind and water, and they o.
17. 6 "If you had faith . . it would obey you
Rom 6.12 Let not sin . . make you obey . . passions
6.16 you are slaves of the one whom you obey
10.16 they have not all obeyed the gospel[o]
Eph 6. 1 Children, obey your parents
Phil 2.12 my beloved, as you have always obeyed
Col 3.20 Children, obey your parents
3.22 Slaves, obey . . your earthly masters
2 Th 1. 8 vengeance . . upon those who do not obey
3.14 If any one refuses to o. what we say
Heb 5. 9 eternal salvation to all who obey him
11. 8 Abraham obeyed when he was called
1 Pet 3. 6 Sarah obeyed Abraham, calling him lord
3. *obedient, subject:* ὑπήκοος HYPĒKOOS [B.3.a.2]
Acts 7.39 "Our fathers refused to obey him
4. *obey one in authority:* πειθαρχέω PEITHARCHEŌ
Acts 5.29 "We must obey God rather than men
5.32 "whom God has given to those who obey
5. *persuade:* πείθω (pass.) PEITHŌ
Rom 2. 8 those who are factious and . . o. wickedness
Gal 5. 7 who hindered you from obeying the truth?
Heb 13.17 Obey your leaders and submit to them
Jas 3. 3 bits into the mouths . . that they may obey
6. *do, make:* ποιέω POIEŌ
1 Jn 5. 2 when we . . obey his commandments
7. *do, practice:* πράσσω PRASSŌ
Rom 2.25 Circumcision . . is of value if you o. the law

OBEY, NOT
1. *disobey:* ἀπειθέω APEITHEŌ
Jn 3.36 he who does not obey . . shall not see life
Rom 2. 8 those who are factious and do not o.
1 Pet 3. 1 some, though they do not o. . . may be won
3.20 ⟨spirits⟩ who formerly did not obey
4.17 what . . of those who do not obey?

OBJECT (*See also* WORSHIP, OBJECT OF)
1. *speak against:* ἀντιλέγω ANTILEGŌ
Acts 28.19 "when the Jews objected, I was compelled

OBJECTION, WITHOUT
1. *without opposition:* ἀναντιρρήτως ANANTIRRĒTŌS*
Acts 10.29 "when I was sent for, I came without o.

OBLIGATION, UNDER
1. *debtor:* ὀφειλέτης (pred.) OPHEILETĒS
Rom 1.14 I am under obligation both to Greeks

OBLIGED, BE
1. *have necessity:* ἀνάγκην ἔχειν ANAGKĒ [B.3.a.5]
Lk [23.17 *he was obliged to release one man*‡

OBSERVANCE, FOR
1. *guard, observe:* φυλάσσω (inf.) PHYLASSŌ
Acts 16. 4 they delivered to them for observance

OBSERVANCE, IN
1. *guard, observe:* φυλάσσω (part.) PHYLASSŌ
Acts 21.24 "you yourself live in observance of the law

OBSERVE
1. *examine carefully:* ἀναθεωρέω ANATHEŌREŌ
Acts 17.23 "I . . observed the objects of your worship
2. *consider, perceive:* κατανοέω KATANOEŌ
Acts 11. 6 "Looking at it closely I observed animals
Jas 1.23 who observes his natural face in a mirror
1.24 he observes himself and . . at once forgets
3. *seize, hold fast:* κρατέω KRATEŌ
Mk 7. 3 (Jews . . wash . . , observing the tradition
7. 4 (many other traditions which they observe
4. *follow closely, understand:* παρακολουθέω PARAKOLOUTHEŌ
2 Tim 3.10 Now you have observed my teaching
5. *watch closely, observe:* παρατηρέω (mid.) PARATĒREŌ
Gal 4.10 You observe days, and months!
6. *walk, behave:* περιπατέω (+dat.) PERIPATEŌ
Acts 21.21 "telling them not to . . o. the customs
7. *think, set one's mind on:* φρονέω PHRONEŌ
Rom 14. 6 He who observes the day, observes it in honor of the Lord
8. *guard, observe:* φυλάσσω (act. or mid.) PHYLASSŌ
Mt 19.20 "All these I have observed
Mk 10.20 "all these I have observed from my youth
Lk 18.21 "All these I have observed from my youth
9. *keep, observe:* τηρέω TĒREŌ
Mt 23. 3 "practice and o. whatever they tell you
28.20 "to observe all that I have commanded

OBSERVED, SIGNS TO BE
1. *observation:* παρατήρησις PARATĒRĒSIS*
Lk 17.20 "not coming with signs to be observed

OBSOLETE, BECOME
1. *make old:* παλαιόω (pass.) PALAIOŌ
Heb 8.13 what is becoming o. . . is ready to vanish

OBSOLETE, TREAT AS
1. *make old:* παλαιόω PALAIOŌ
Heb 8.13 he treats the first ⟨covenant⟩ as o.

OBSTACLE
1. *hindrance:* ἐγκοπή EGKOPĒ*
1 Cor 9.12 rather than . . an o. in the way of the gospel
2. *raise, lift:* ἐπαίρω (pass. part.) EPAIRŌ [A.3.a.4]
2 Cor 10. 5 every proud o. to the knowledge of God

3. *cause for offense:* προσκοπή PROSKOPĒ*
 2 Cor 6. 3 We put no obstacle in any one's way

OBTAIN (*See also* FAIL TO OBTAIN; MERCY, OBTAIN)
1. *have, hold:* ἔχω ECHŌ
 [a]pres.
 Rom 5. 2 Through him we have obtained access[g]
 1 Jn 5.15 [a]we know that we have obtained the requests
2. *find, attain:* ἐπιτυγχάνω EPITYGCHANŌ
 Rom 11. 7 Israel failed to obtain what it sought. The elect obtained it
 Heb 6.15 Abraham[m] . . obtained the promise
 Jas 4. 2 you covet[d] and cannot obtain
3. *catch:* καταλαμβάνω KATALAMBANŌ
 1 Cor 9.24 So run that you may obtain it
4. *inherit, obtain:* κληρονομέω KLĒRONOMEŌ
 Heb 1. 4 name he has obtained is more excellent
 1.14 those who are to obtain salvation
 1 Pet 3. 9 called, that you may obtain a blessing
5. *bring, carry off:* κομίζω (mid.) KOMIZŌ
 1 Pet 1. 9 As . . outcome of . . faith you o. . . salvation
 5. 4 you will o. the unfading crown of glory
6. *seize, hold fast:* κρατέω KRATEŌ
 Acts 27.13 supposing . . they had obtained . . purpose
7. *acquire, get:* κτάομαι KTAOMAI
 Acts 8.20 "you thought you could obtain the gift!
8. *obtain by lot:* λαγχάνω LAGCHANŌ
 2 Pet 1. 1 have obtained a faith of equal standing
9. *receive, take:* λαμβάνω LAMBANŌ
 Phil 3.12 Not that I have already obtained
10. *acquire, save* (mid.): περιποιέω PERIPOIEŌ
 Acts 20.28 "he obtained with the blood of his own Son[w]
11. *keeping safe, property:* περιποίησις PERIPOIĒSIS [B.1.a.2]
 1 Th 5. 9 God has . . destined us . . to obtain salvation
 2 Th 2.14 so that you may obtain the glory
12. *happen, attain:* τυγχάνω TYGCHANŌ
 2 Tim 2.10 that they also may obtain salvation
 Heb 8. 6 Christ[o] . . obtained a ministry . . more excellent
CONTEXTUALLY
 Rom 8.21 o. . . glorious liberty of . . children of God

OCCASION
1. *origin, occasion:* ἀφορμή APHORMĒ
 1 Tim 5.14 give the enemy no occasion to revile us
IDIOMATICALLY
 a. Heb 8.7 there would have been no occasion for a second
 οὐκ ἂν δευτέρας ἐζητεῖτο τόπος [TOPOS]

OCCASION, AS FITS THE
1. *need, want:* χρεία (gen.) CHREIA
 Eph 4.29 no evil talk . . only such . . as fits the o.

OCCUPATION
1. *work, deed:* ἔργον ERGON
 Tit [3.14 learn to *enter honorable occupations*†
CONTEXTUALLY
 Acts 19.25 with the workmen of like occupation

OCCUPIED WITH, BE
1. *hold together, impel:* συνέχω (pass.) SYNECHŌ
 Acts 18. 5 Paul was occupied with preaching

OCCUPY ONESELF WITH
1. *hold to, be intent on:* προσέχω PROSECHŌ
 1 Tim 1. 4 nor to occupy themselves with myths

OCCUR
1. *come to be, happen, be:* γίνομαι GINOMAI
 Acts 13.12 believed, when he saw what had occurred
 Heb 9.15 a death has occurred which redeems

ODOR, BE AN
1. *smell, stink:* ὄζω OZŌ*
 Jn 11.39 "by this time there will be an odor

OF
1. *from:* ἀπό (+gen.) APO
 Mt **3**.4; **7**.15; **10**.17; **12**.43; **14**.29; **16**.6, 11, 12[2]; **17**.18; **20**.29; **27**.21, 24
 Mk **5**.29, 34; **6**.43; **8**.15; **12**.2; **15**.43
 Lk **4**.35, 41; **5**.15; **6**.17(18), 30; **7**.21; **8**.2, 29[2], 33; **11**.24, 51; **12**.1, 15, 20; **20**.20, 46; **22**.18
 Jn **1**.45; **5**.19; **7**.28; **8**.42; **10**.18; **11**.1, 51; **18**.34; **19**.38; **21**.2, 20
 Acts **3**.21; **5**.2, 3; **8**.22; **10**.38; **13**.23; **15**.19; **16**.18, 40; **17**.13; **20**.26; **27**.44
 2 Cor **3**.5
 1 Th **2**.17
 Heb **7**.2
 1 Jn **5**.15
2. *through:* διά (+gen.) DIA
 1 Cor **11**.12
3. *into, to, for:* εἰς (+acc.) EIS
 1 Pet **1**.11
4. *from, out of:* ἐκ (+gen.) EK
 Mt **1**.16, 18, 20; **6**.27; **7**.9; **10**.29; **12**.11; **13**.47; **18**.12, 19; **21**.31; **22**.35; **23**.25, 34; **25**.2, 8; **26**.21, 27, 29, 73; **27**.29, 48
 Mk **9**.17; **14**.18, 23, 25, 69, 70; **16**.12‡
 Lk **1**.5[2], 27, [35‡, 61; **2**.4, 36; **10**.11; **11**.5, 15, 49; **12**.6, 13, 15, 25; **14**.28, 33; **15**.4[2]; **17**.7, 15; **21**.16, 18; **22**.3, 23, 50, 58; **24**.13, 22
 Jn **1**.13[4], 35, 40; **2**.15; **3**.1, 5, 6[2], 8, 31[2]; **4**.7, 13, 14; **6**.8, 26, 39, 50, 51, 60, 64, 66, 70, 71; **7**.19, 25, 31, 40, 44, 48[2], 50; **8**.23[2], 41, 44[2], 47[2]; **9**.6, 16, 40; **10**.16, 20; **11**.19, 37, 45, 46, 49; **12**.2, 9, 42; **13**.21, 23; **15**.19[2]; **16**.5, 17; **17**.12, 14[2], 16[2]; **18**.9, 17, 25, 26, 36[2], 37; **19**.2; **20**.24; **21**.2
 Acts **1**.24; **2**.30; **4**.6; **5**.38, 39; **10**.1; **11**.20, 28; **13**.21; **15**.23; **17**.4, 12; **19**.33; **21**.8; **23**.21
 Rom **4**.14, 26; **9**.5; **11**.14
 1 Cor **9**.7; **10**.17; **11**.28[2]; **12**.15, 16; **15**.6
 2 Cor **2**.17
 Gal **3**.7, 9; **4**.4, 23[2]
 Phil **3**.5; **4**.22
 Col **4**.9, 11, 12
 Tit **1**.12
 Heb **3**.13; **4**.1; **7**.4
 Jas **2**.16
 1 Pet **1**.23
 1 Jn **2**.16[2], 19[3], 21, 29; **3**.8, 9[2], 10, 12, 19; **4**.1, 2, 3, 4, 5[2], 6[2], 7[2], 13; **5**.4, 18[2], 19
 2 Jn .4
 3 Jn .11
 Rev **2**.7, 9, 10, 21, 22; **3**.9; **5**.5[2]; **6**.1[2]; **7**.5[2], 6[3], 7[3], 8[2], 13; **8**.11; **9**.20, 21; **13**.3; **15**.7; **16**.11; **17**.1; **18**.12; **21**.9; 21
5. *in, at, by:* ἐν (+dat.) EN
 Rom **11**.2
 Acts **11**.[26†
 1 Cor **1**.31; **3**.21; **4**.2; **11**.30; **15**.12
 2 Cor **10**.17; **12**.5, 9
 Gal **1**.22
 2 Th **1**.4; **3**.11
 2 Pet **2**.10
6. *on, at:* ἐπί (+acc.) EPI
 except [a]+dat.
 Mk **9**.12, 13
 Jn **12**.16[a]
 Rom **10**.19[a]
 2 Cor **2**.3; **12**.21[a]
 Heb **7**.13
7. *over, for the sake of:* ὑπέρ (+gen.) HYPER
 Jn **1**.30
 2 Cor **1**.8; **5**.12
8. *by:* ὑπό (+gen.) HYPO
 2 Pet **3**.2
 Jude .17
9. *in accordance with, for:* κατά (+acc.) KATA
 except [a]+gen.
 Rom **9**.11
 1 Cor **15**.15[a]
 2 Cor **11**.18
 Phil **4**.11
 Heb **9**.19
10. *from:* παρά (+gen.) PARA
 Mt **2**.4
 Lk **12**.48
 Jn **4**.9
 Acts **3**.2

11. *about, concerning:* περί (+gen.) PERI
except [a]+acc.
Mt **4.6**; **11.10**; **15.7**; **17.13**; **22.42**; **24.36**; **26.24**
Mk **1.30**; **7.6**, 25; **13.32**; **14.21**
Lk **1.1**; **2.38**; **4.10**, 37; **7.3**, 18, 27; **9.11**; **11.53**; **13.1**; **21.5**
Jn **1.47**; **2.21**, 25; **5.46**; **7.7**, 13; **8.46**; **11.13**; **12.41**; **13.18**, 22, 24; **16.8**[3], 9, 10, 11, 25
Acts **1.3**; **2.29**, 31; **11.22**; **13.29**; **24.22**; **28.15**
Rom **14.12**; **15.21**
2 Cor **10.8**
Phil **1.27**
1 Tim **1.19**[a]
Tit **2.8**
Heb **2.5**; **4.4**, 8; **9.5**; **10.7**; **11.22**, 32
1 Pet **1.10**
2 Pet **1.12**; **3.16**
Jude .3, 15[2]
12. *to, with, against:* πρός (+acc.) PROS
Rom **10.21**
Heb **1.7**, 8; **11.18**

OFF
1. *from:* ἀπό (+gen.) APO [B.1.a.1]
Jn **11.18**; **21.8**
2. *from, out of:* ἐκ (+gen.) EK
Acts **12.7**
3. *in accordance with, for:* κατά (+acc.) KATA
Acts 27. 5 across the sea which is off Cilicia
27. 7 arrived with difficulty off Cnidus, .. sailed under the lee of Crete off Salmone

OFFEND
1. *sin, miss the mark:* ἁμαρτάνω HAMARTANŌ
Acts 25. 8 "nor against Caesar have I offended at all
2. *cause to stumble, offend:* σκανδαλίζω SKANDALIZŌ
Mt 15.12 "know that the Pharisees were offended?

OFFENDER
1. *debtor:* ὀφειλέτης OPHEILETĒS
Lk 13. 4 "think that they were worse offenders?

OFFENSE, GIVE
OFFENSE, GIVE NO
1. *giving no offense:* ἀπρόσκοπος APROSKOPOS [A.6.a.3]
1 Cor 10.32 Give no offense to Jews or to Greeks
2. *cause to stumble, offend:* σκανδαλίζω SKANDALIZŌ
Mt 17.27 "not to give o. to them, go to the sea

OFFENSE, TAKE
1. *cause to stumble, offend:* σκανδαλίζω SKANDALIZŌ
[a]pass. [b]A.6.c.3
Mt 11. 6 [a]"blessed is he who takes no offense at me
13.57 [a]"And they took offense at him
Mk 6. 3 [a]"And they took offense[r] at him†
Lk 7.23 [a]"blessed is he who takes no offense at me
Jn 6.61 [b]"Do you take offense at this?

OFFER (*See also* SACRIFICE, OFFER; WORSHIP, OFFER)
1. *lead up, bring back:* ἀνάγω ANAGŌ
Acts 7.41 "they .. offered a sacrifice to the idol
2. *bring, carry up:* ἀναφέρω ANAPHERŌ
Heb 7.27 no need .. to offer sacrifices daily
Jas 2.21 he offered his son Isaac upon the altar
1 Pet 2. 5 to offer spiritual sacrifices acceptable
3. *give:* δίδωμι DIDŌMI
Mt 27.34 they offered him wine to drink
Mk 15.23 they offered him wine mingled with myrrh
Lk 2.24 to offer a sacrifice according to .. law
4. *show, offer, cause:* παρέχω PARECHŌ
Lk 6.29 "To him who strikes you .. offer the other
5. *do, make:* ποιέω (mid.) POIEŌ
Lk 5.33 "The disciples of John .. offer prayers
6. *bring to, present:* προσφέρω PROSPHERŌ
Mt 2.11 offered him gifts, gold and frankincense
5.23 "if you are offering your gift at the altar
5.24 "then come and offer your gift
8. 4 "offer the gift that Moses commanded
Mk 1.44 "offer .. what Moses commanded
Lk 23.36 soldiers .. mocked him, .. offering .. vinegar
Jn 16. 2 "will think he is offering service to God
Acts 7.42 " 'Did you offer to me slain beasts?
8.18 when Simon saw .. he offered them money
Heb 5. 1 every high priest .. is appointed .. to offer
5. 3 Because of this he is bound to offer sacrifice
8. 3 every high priest is appointed to offer
8. 3 necessary .. to have something to offer
8. 4 there are priests who offer gifts
9. 7 taking blood which he offers for himself
9. 9 gifts and sacrifices are offered
9.14 Christ .. offered himself without blemish
9.25 Nor was it to offer himself repeatedly
9.28 so Christ, having been offered once
10. 1 sacrifices which are continually offered
10. 2 would .. have ceased to be offered
10. 8 (these are offered according to the law
10.11 offering repeatedly the same sacrifices
10.12 when Christ[w] had offered for all time
11. 4 By faith Abel offered to God
CONTEXTUALLY
Rom 11.16 If the dough offered as first fruits

OFFER UP
1. *bring, carry up:* ἀναφέρω ANAPHERŌ
Heb 7.27 once for all when he offered up himself
13.15 let us continually offer up a sacrifice
2. *bring to, present:* προσφέρω PROSPHERŌ
Heb 5. 7 Jesus[j] offered up prayers .. with loud cries
11.17 Abraham, when he was tested, offered up Isaac, and .. was ready to o. up his only son

OFFERED IN SACRIFICE
1. *offered to a god:* ἱερόθυτος HIEROTHYTOS*
1 Cor 10.28 ("This has been offered in sacrifice

OFFERED TO AN IDOL
1. *sacrificed to idols:* εἰδωλόθυτος EIDŌLOTHYTOS
1 Cor 8. 1 Now concerning food offered to idols
8. 4 as to the eating of food offered to idols
8. 7 some .. eat food as .. offered to an idol
8.10 encouraged .. to eat food offered to idols
10.19 That food offered to idols is anything?

OFFERING
1. *votive offering:* ἀνάθημα ANATHĒMA*
Lk 21. 5 adorned with noble stones and offerings
2. *service:* διακονία DIAKONIA
2 Cor 9. 1 to write to you about the o. for the saints
3. *gift:* δῶρον DŌRON
Mt [15. 5 " 'What you would have gained .. is *an o.*†
Mk [7.11 " 'Corban' (that is, *an offering*†
4. *service, ministry:* λειτουργία LEITOURGIA
Phil 2.17 a libation upon the sacrificial offering
5. *smell, scent:* ὀσμή OSMĒ [C.4]
Phil 4.18 the gifts you sent, a fragrant offering
6. *present, offering:* προσφορά PROSPHORA*
Acts 21.26 offering presented for every one of them
24.17 "I came to bring to my nation .. offerings
Rom 15.16 so that the offering .. may be acceptable
Eph 5. 2 a fragrant offering and sacrifice to God
Heb 10. 5 "offerings thou hast not desired
10. 8 "nor taken pleasure in .. offerings
10.10 we have been sanctified through the o.
10.14 by a single o. he has perfected for all time
10.18 there is no longer any offering for sin
CONTEXTUALLY
Rom [8. 3 and *as a sin offering*†
Heb 10. 6 "in .. sin offerings .. hast taken no pleasure
10. 8 "Nor taken pleasure in .. sin offerings

OFFERING, BURNT
1. *whole burnt offering:* ὁλοκαύτωμα HOLOKAUTŌMA
Heb 10. 6 "in burnt offerings .. thou hast .. no pleasure
10. 8 "nor taken pleasure in .. burnt offerings

OFFERING, MAKE AN
1. *bring to, present:* προσφέρω PROSPHERŌ
Lk 5.14 "make an offering for your cleansing

OFFERING, WHOLE BURNT
1. *whole burnt offering:* ὁλοκαύτωμα HOLOKAUTŌMA
Mk 12.33 "more than all whole burnt offerings

OFFERINGS, SACRIFICIAL
1. *altar:* θυσιαστήριον THYSIASTĒRION [C.2]
1 Cor 9.13 those who serve . . share in the sacrificial o.

OFFICE (*See also* PRIESTLY OFFICE)
1. *visitation, office of bishop:* ἐπισκοπή EPISKOPĒ
Acts 1.20 " 'His office let another take
2. *stewardship, management:* οἰκονομία OIKONOMIA
Col 1.25 the divine office which was given to me
CONTEXTUALLY
Heb 7.21 took their office without an oath
7.23 prevented by death from continuing in o.

OFFICE OF BISHOP
1. *visitation, office of bishop:* ἐπισκοπή EPISKOPĒ
1 Tim 3. 1 If any one aspires to the o. of bishop

OFFICE, TAX
1. *customhouse:* τελώνιον TELŌNION*
Mt 9. 9 he saw . . Matthew sitting at the tax office
Mk 2.14 he saw Levi . . sitting at the tax office
Lk 5.27 he . . saw . . Levi, sitting at the tax office

OFFICER
1. *captain over a thousand:* χιλίαρχος CHILIARCHOS
Mk 6.21 Herod . . gave a banquet for his . . officers
2. *servant, helper:* ὑπηρέτης HYPĒRETĒS
Jn 7.32 Pharisees sent officers to arrest him
7.45 officers then went back to the . . Pharisees
7.46 officers answered, "No man ever spoke!
18. 3 some officers from the chief priests
18.12 the officers of the Jews seized Jesus
18.18 officers had made a charcoal fire
18.22 one of the officers . . struck Jesus
19. 6 the officers . . cried out, "Crucify him
Acts 5.22 officers . . did not find them in the prison
5.26 officers . . brought them . . without violence
3. *one who does, bailiff:* πράκτωρ PRAKTŌR*
Lk 12.58 "lest . . the judge hand you over to the officer, and the officer put you in prison
4. *leader, magistrate:* στρατηγός STRATĒGOS
Lk 22. 4 he . . conferred with the . . officers[0]
22.52 Jesus said to the chief priests and officers[0]

OFFICIAL
1. *royal:* βασιλικός (subst.) BASILIKOS
Jn 4.46 there was an official whose son was ill
4.49 official said to him, "Sir, come down

OFFSCOURING
1. *anything wiped off:* περίψημα PERIPSĒMA*
1 Cor 4.13 we have become . . the o. of all things

OFFSPRING
1. *kind, race, family:* γένος GENOS
Acts 17.28 " 'For we are indeed his offspring
17.29 "Being then God's offspring, we ought
Rev 22.16 "I am the root and the offspring of David
2. *seed, offspring:* σπέρμα SPERMA
Gal 3.16 promises were made to Abraham and to his o. It does not say, "And to offsprings," . . but, referring to one, "And to your o.
3.19 law . . was added . . till the o. should come
3.29 then you are Abraham's offspring
1 Jn [3. 9 for *the offspring of God abide* in him†
Rev 12.17 to make war on the rest of her o.

OFTEN
1. *often, many times:* πολλάκις POLLAKIS
Mt 17.15 "for often he falls into the fire, and often into the water
Mk 5. 4 he had often been bound with fetters
9.22 "it has often cast him into the fire
Jn 18. 2 Jesus often met there with his disciples
Acts 26.11 "I punished them o. in all the synagogues
Rom 1.13 I have often intended to come to you
2 Cor 8.22 our brother whom we have often tested
11.23 with . . beatings, and often near death
11.27 in hunger and thirst, often without food
Phil 3.18 of whom I have often told you
2 Tim 1.16 Onesiphorus . . often refreshed me
Heb 6. 7 drunk the rain that often falls upon it

2. *close, frequent:* πυκνός PYKNOS
[a]neut. pl. [b]comp.
Mt [9.14 [a]"Why do we and the Pharisees fast *often?*‡
Lk 5.33 [a]"The disciples of John fast often
Acts 24.26 [b]So he sent for him often and conversed

OFTEN AS, AS
1. *as many times as:* ὁσάκις HOSAKIS*
[a]+ἐάν
1 Cor 11.25 [a]"Do this, as often as you drink it
11.26 [a]For as often as you eat this bread
Rev 11. 6 [a]power . . to smite . . as o. as they desire

OFTEN, HOW
1. *how many times:* ποσάκις POSAKIS*
Mt 18.21 "Lord, how often shall . . I forgive him?
23.37 "How often would I have gathered!
Lk 13.34 "How often would I have gathered!

OFTEN, SO
1. *many, great:* πολύς (subst. neut. pl.) POLYS
Rom 15.22 why I have so often been hindered

OIL
1. *olive oil:* ἔλαιον ELAION*
Mt 25. 3 "the foolish . . took no oil with them
25. 4 "but the wise took flasks of oil
25. 8 " 'Give us some of your oil
Mk 6.13 anointed with oil many that were sick
Lk 7.46 "You did not anoint my head with oil
10.34 "bound up his wounds, pouring on oil
16. 6 "He said, 'A hundred measures of oil
Heb 1. 9 "God . . has anointed thee with the oil
Jas 5.14 pray over him, anointing him with oil
Rev 6. 6 "but do not harm oil and wine!
18.13 incense, myrrh, frankincense, wine, oil

OINTMENT
1. *sweet oil, perfume:* μύρον MYRON
Mt 26. 7 flask of very expensive ointment
26.12 "In pouring this ointment on my body
Mk 14. 3 flask of ointment of pure nard
14. 4 "Why was the ointment thus wasted?
14. 5 "this ointment might have been sold
Lk 7.37 brought an alabaster flask of ointment
7.38 she . . anointed them with the ointment
7.46 "she has anointed my feet with ointment
23.56 they returned, and prepared . . ointments
Jn 11. 2 Mary who anointed the Lord with o.
12. 3 Mary took a pound of costly ointment
12. 3 filled with the fragrance of the o.
12. 5 "Why was this ointment not sold?
CONTEXTUALLY
Mt 26. 9 "o. might have been sold for a large sum

OLD (*See also* TWO YEARS OLD)
1. *from the beginning, old:* ἀρχαῖος ARCHAIOS
Lk 9. 8 one of the old prophets had risen
9.19 "one of the old prophets has risen
2 Cor 5.17 the old has passed away, behold, the new
2. *old man:* γέρων (pred.) GERŌN*
Jn 3. 4 "How can a man be born when he is old?
3. *long ago:* πάλαι PALAI
2 Pet 1. 9 he was cleansed from his old sins
4. *old, aged:* παλαιός PALAIOS*
Mt 9.16 "unshrunk cloth on an old garment
9.17 "Neither . . new wine . . into old wineskins
13.52 "brings out . . what is new and what is old
Mk 2.21 "unshrunk cloth on an old garment
2.21 "patch tears away . . , the new from the old
2.22 "no one puts new wine into o. wineskins
Lk 5.36 "No one . . puts it upon an old garment
5.36 "piece from the new will not match the old
5.37 "no one puts new wine into o. wineskins
5.39 "no one after drinking old wine desires new; for he says, 'The old is good[s]
Rom 6. 6 We know that our old self was crucified
1 Cor 5. 7 Cleanse out the old leaven
5. 8 celebrate . . , not with the old leaven
2 Cor 3.14 when they read the old covenant
Eph 4.22 Put off your o. nature which . . is corrupt

Col 3. 9 you have put off the old nature
1 Jn 2. 7 an old commandment which you had . . ; the old commandment is the word

IDIOMATICALLY
a. Acts 7.23 "When he was forty years old Ὡς δὲ ἐπληροῦτο αὐτῷ τεσσερακονταέτης χρόνος [CHRONOS; PLĒROŌ]

CONTEXTUALLY
Mk 6.15 "like one of the prophets of old
Lk 2.42 when he was twelve years o., they went up
Jn 8.57 "You are not yet fifty years old
Acts 4.22 man . . was more than forty years old
Heb 8. 6 which is as much more excellent than the o.

OLD, A HUNDRED YEARS
1. *of a hundred years:* ἑκατονταετής HEKATONTAETĒS*
Rom 4.19 he was about a hundred years old

OLD AGE
1. *old age:* γῆρας GĒRAS*
Lk 1.36 "Elizabeth in . . old age has also conceived

OLD, BE
1. *grow old:* γηράσκω GĒRASKŌ
Jn 21.18 "when you are old, you will stretch out

OLD CODE
1. *age, obsoleteness:* παλαιότης PALAIOTĒS*
Rom 7. 6 we serve not under the old written code

OLD, FROM OF
OLD, OF
1. *from eternity:* ἀπ' αἰῶνος AIŌN [B.1.b]
Lk 1.70 "spoke by . . his holy prophets from of old
Acts 3.21 "spoke by . . his holy prophets from of old
15.18 "has made these things known from of old
2. *for a long time:* ἔκπαλαι EKPALAI
2 Pet 2. 3 from of o. . . condemnation has not been idle
3. *long ago:* πάλαι PALAI
Heb 1. 1 God spoke of old to our fathers

OLD, GROW
1. *grow old:* γηράσκω GĒRASKŌ
Heb 8.13 what is . . growing old is ready to vanish
2. *make old:* παλαιόω (pass.) PALAIOŌ
Lk 12.33 "provide . . purses that do not grow old
Heb 1.11 "they will all grow old like a garment

OLD MAN
OLD, MAN OF
1. *from the beginning, old:* ἀρχαῖος (subst.) ARCHAIOS
Mt 5.21 "heard that it was said to the men of old
5.33 "heard that it was said to the men of old
2. *elder, older:* πρεσβύτερος (subst.) PRESBYTEROS
Acts 2.17 " 'your old men shall dream dreams
Heb 11. 2 by it the men of old received . . approval
3. *old man:* πρεσβύτης PRESBYTĒS
Lk 1.18 "I am an old man, and my wife is advanced
Phm [. 9 I, Paul, an *old man* and . . prisoner†

OLD, OF (*See* OLD, FROM OF)

OLDER MAN
1. *elder, older:* πρεσβύτερος (subst.) PRESBYTEROS
1 Tim 5. 1 Do not rebuke an older man
2. *old man:* πρεσβύτης PRESBYTĒS
Tit 2. 2 Bid the older men be temperate

OLDER WOMAN
1. *elder, older:* πρεσβύτερος (subst.) PRESBYTEROS
1 Tim 5. 2 ⟨treat⟩ older women like mothers
2. *old woman:* πρεσβῦτις PRESBYTIS*
Tit 2. 3 Bid the o. women likewise to be reverent

OLIVE
1. *olive tree, olive:* ἐλαία ELAIA
Mt 21. 1 when they . . came . . to the Mount of Olives
24. 3 As he sat on the Mount of Olives
26.30 they went out to the Mount of Olives
Mk 11. 1 at the Mount of Olives, he sent two
13. 3 as he sat on the Mount of Olives
14.26 they went out to the Mount of Olives
Lk 19.37 at the descent of the Mount of Olives
22.39 as was . . custom, to the Mount of Olives
Jn 8. 1 Jesus went to the Mount of Olives[r]‡
Jas 3.12 Can a fig tree, my brethren, yield olives?

OLIVE SHOOT, WILD
1. *wild olive tree:* ἀγριέλαιος AGRIELAIOS
Rom 11.17 you, a wild olive shoot, were grafted

OLIVE TREE
1. *olive tree, olive:* ἐλαία ELAIA
Rom 11.17 to share the richness[o] of the olive tree
11.24 grafted back into their own olive tree
Rev 11. 4 These are the two olive trees

OLIVE TREE, CULTIVATED
1. *garden olive tree:* καλλιέλαιος KALLIELAIOS*
Rom 11.24 grafted . . into a cultivated olive tree

OLIVE TREE, WILD
1. *wild olive tree:* ἀγριέλαιος AGRIELAIOS
Rom 11.24 what is by nature a wild olive tree

OLIVET
1. *olive grove:* ἐλαιών ELAIŌN*
Lk 19.29 at the mount that is called Olivet
21.37 he . . lodged on the mount called Olivet
Acts 1.12 the mount called O., which is near Jerusalem

OLYMPAS: Ὀλυμπᾶς ō'limpəs
Rom 16.15 Greet . . Olympas, and all the saints

OMEGA
1. *omega, last:* Ω ō ı*
Rev 1. 8 "I am the Alpha and the Omega
21. 6 "I am the Alpha and the Omega
22.13 "I am the Alpha and the Omega

OMEN, CLEAR
1. *sign, proof:* ἔνδειξις ENDEIXIS
Phil 1.28 a clear o. to them of their destruction

ON
1. *elsewhere:* ἀλλαχοῦ ALLACHOU*
Mk 1.38 "Let us go on to the next towns
2. *from:* ἀπό (+gen.) APO [B.1.b]
Jn **5.30**; **7.17**, 18; **8.28**; **14.10**; **16.13**
Rev **21.13**[4]
3. *through:* διά (+gen.) DIA
[a]+acc.
Acts **23.28**[a]
Heb **11.29**
4. *into, to, for:* εἰς (+acc.) EIS
Mt **5.1**, 39; **14.23**; **15.29**; **27.30**
Mk **3.13**; **6.46**; **8.23**; **10.17**; **11.8**; **13.3**
Lk **6.20**; **8.23**; **9.28**; **15.22**[2]; **17.31**; **21.37**
Jn **5.45**; **6.3**; **8.6**‡, 8‡; **19.37**; **21.4**, 6, 9
Acts **27.17**, 26, 39
2 Cor **1.10**
Eph **4.8**
Rev **2.22**; **8.5**, 7; **9.3**; **14.19**; **16.1**, 2
5. *from, out of:* ἐκ (+gen.) EK
Mt **27.38**[2]
Mk **15.27**[2]
Lk **1.11**; **11.6**; **15.16**; **23.33**[2]
Jn **12.49**
Rev **6.10**
6. *in, at, by:* ἐν (+dat.) EN
Mt **7.22**; **8.24**; **10.15**; **11.22**, 24; **12.2**, 36; **15.32**; **20.17**; **21.8**[2], 19; **22.40**; **24.50**
Mk **4.1**, 35; **5.5**; **8.3**, 27; **9.33**, 34; **10.32**, 52; **11.13**; **16.5**
Lk **1.59**; **4.16**, 31; **5.17**; **6.1**, 6, 7; **8.32**; **10.12**; **12.46**, 51, 58; **13.6**, 7, 10, 14[2]; **14.5**; **17.31**; **19.36**; **24.32**, 35
Jn **4.20**, 21; **5.16**; **7.23**[2], 37; **12.48**; **19.31**
Acts **8.1**; **9.17**, 27; **10.40**(*Var. om.*); **17.31**; **20.7**; **28.9**
Rom **2.5**, 15, 16; **10.8**
1 Cor **11.23**
2 Cor **1.14**; **3.2**, 3[2]; **5.12**[2]; **6.2**
Gal **6.17**
Col **2.18**
2 Th **1.10**
2 Tim **1.18**; **4.8**
Heb **1.3**; **4.4**; **8.5**, 9
Jas **4.3**
1 Pet **2.22**
2 Pet **1.18**
Jude .12
Rev **1.9**, 10; **3.21**[2]; **14.2**

7. *above:* ἐπάνω EPANŌ
Mt 5.14 "A city set on a hill cannot be hid
23.18 " 'swears by the gift that is on the altar
23.20 " 'swears by it and by everything on it
8. *on, at:* ἐπί (+gen.) EPI
except [a]+dat. [b]+acc.
Mt **3.16**[b]; **4.5**[b], 6; **5.15**[b], 45[b2]; **6.10**, 19; **7.25**[b]; **9.2**, 6, 16[a], 18[b]; **10.34**[b]; **13.2**[b], 5[b], 8[b], 20[b], 23[b]; **14.8**[a], 11[a], 14[a], 19, 25[b], 26, 28[b], 29[b]; **15.32**[b], 35[b]; **16.18**[a], 19[2]; **17.6**[b]; **18.12**[b], 18[2], 19; **19.28**, 28[b]; **21.5**[b2], [44‡[b2]; **23.2**, 4[b], 9, 35; **24.3**, 17, 30; **25.31**; **26.7**, 12, 39[b], 64; **27.19**, 25[b2], 29; **28.18**
Mk **2.10**, 21[b]; **4.1**, 5[b], 21[b], 31; **6.25**[a], 28[a], 34[b], 47, 48, 49, 55[a]; **8.2**[b], 6; **9.3**, 20, 22[b]; **11.2**[b]; **13.15**; **14.35**; **16.18**‡[b]
Lk **1.65**[b]; **2.14**; **4.9**[b], 11, 29; **5.12**[b], 18, 19[b], 24, 25[b], 36[b]; **6.17**, 29[b], 49[b]; **7.13**[a], 13[b]; **8.6**[b], 13, 16, 27[b]; **10.34**[b]; **11.33**[b]; **15.5**[b]; **17.16**[b], 31; **18.8**; **19.30**[b], 35[b]; **20.18**[b2], 19[b]; **21.12**[b]; **22.21**, 30, 53[b]; **23.30**[b]
Jn **1.32**[b], 33[b]; **6.2**, 19; **7.30**[b], 44[b]; **9.15**[b]; **12.15**[b]; **17.4**; **19.13**, 19, 31; **20.7**
Acts **1.26**[b]; **2.3**[b], 18[b], 19; **4.5**[b], 22[b]; **5.15**, 30; **8.16**[a], 17[b]; **9.17**[b]; **10.9**[b], 39, 44[b], 45[b]; **11.15**[b]; **14.10**[b]; **17.26**; **19.6**[b], 16[b]; **21.5**[b], 27[b], 40; **25.6**, 17; **27.44**, 44[a]; **28.3**[b]
Rom **15.3**[b], 20[b]
1 Cor **3.12**[b]; **8.5**; **11.10**; **14.25**[b]
2 Cor **1.9**[a]
Gal **3.13**
Eph **1.10**; **3.15**; **4.26**[a]; **6.3**
Col **1.16**, 20; **3.2**
1 Tim **4.10**[a]; **5.5**[b], 19; **6.17**[a]
Heb **8.4**, 6[a], 10, 10[b]; **10.16**[b2]; **11.13**; **12.25**
Jas **5.5**, 17
1 Pet **2.24**†[b]; **5.7**[b]
Rev **2.17**[b]; **3.10**, 12[b]; **4.2**[b], 4[b], 9, 10; **5.1**, 1[b], 3, 7, 10, 13[2]; **6.16**[a], 16[b]; **7.1**, 11[b]; **8.10**[b], 13; **9.7**[b]; **10.2**[2], 5, 8[2]; **11.10**[2], 11[b2], 16[b2]; **12.1**, 17[b]; **13.8**, 14, 16; **14.1**, 1[b], 6, 6[b], 9, 9[b], 14, 14[b], 16[b]; **16.8**[b], 10[b], 12[b], 18, 21[b]; **17.3**[b], 5[b], 8, 9; **18.19**[b], 24; **19.4**[a], 12[b], 14[a], 16[b2]; **20.4**[b2]; **21.14**; **22.4**
9. *below, under:* ὑποκάτω HYPOKATŌ
Mk **6.11**
10. *in accordance with, for:* κατά (+acc.) KATA
except [a]+gen.
Lk **10.4**
Acts **25.3**; **26.13**; **27.29**
Rom **4.16**
1 Cor **16.2**
Heb **3.8**
Jude .**15**[a]
11. *with:* μετά (+gen.) META
Lk **10.37**
Rev **12.17**; **13.7**‡; **17.14**
12. *about, concerning:* περί (+gen.) PERI
Acts **25.9**
Tit **3.8**
13. *at, near:* πρός (+dat.) PROS
Mk **5.11**

ON EACH SIDE
1. *in a circle, round about:* κύκλῳ KYKLŌ
Rev 4. 6 on each side of the throne, . . creatures

ON S.'S PART
1. *beside, with:* παρά (+dat.) PARA
Rom **9.14**

ON THE FOLLOWING DAY
ON THE MORROW
1. *tomorrow:* ἐπαύριον EPAURION [B.3.b.2]
[a]τῇ ἐπαύριον
Mk 11.12 [a]On the following day, when they came
Acts 10.24 [a]on the following day they entered Caesarea
20. 7 [a]intending to depart on the morrow
21. 8 [a]On the morrow we departed
22.30 [a]But on the morrow . . he unbound him
23.32 [a]on the morrow they returned to . . barracks
25.23 [a]on the morrow Agrippa and Bernice came

ON THE ONE HAND
ON THE OTHER HAND
1. (correlative particles): . . μέν . . δέ MEN
Heb **7.18** On the one h. . . commandment is set aside
Heb 7.19 on the other hand . . hope is introduced

ONCE (*See also* WHEN ONCE)
1. (particle): ἄν AN
Lk 13.25 "When once the householder has risen up
2. *once for all:* ἅπαξ HAPAX
2 Cor 11.25 once I was stoned
Phil 4.16 you sent me help[f] once and again
Heb 6. 4 those who have once been enlightened
9. 7 the high priest goes . . but once a year
9.27 it is appointed for men to die once
9.28 Christ, having been offered once
10. 2 if the worshipers had once been cleansed
3. *one:* εἷς HEIS [A.3.b.1]
Tit 3.10 after admonishing him once or twice
4. *at some time, once:* ποτέ POTE II
Rom 7. 9 I was once alive apart from the law
11.30 Just as you were once disobedient
Gal 1.23 "He who once persecuted us is now preaching the faith he once tried to destroy
Eph 2. 2 ⟨through sins⟩ in which you once walked
2. 3 Among these we all once lived
2.13 in Christ J. you who once were far off
5. 8 once you were darkness, but now . . light
Col 1.21 you, who once were estranged
3. 7 In these you once walked
Tit 3. 3 For we ourselves were once foolish
1 Pet 2.10 Once you were no people but now
3. 5 So o. the holy women . . used to adorn
5. *when first:* ἐὰν πρῶτον PRŌTOS [B.3.b.4]
Rom 15.24 once I have enjoyed your company
CONTEXTUALLY
Lk **14.16**
Rom **6.17**, 19
2 Cor **3.10**; **5.16**
Gal **3.15**

ONCE, AT
1. *just now:* ἄρτι ARTI
Mt 26.53 "he will at once send me more
2. *immediately:* εὐθέως EUTHEŌS
Mt 25.16 "He . . went at once and traded with them
26.49 came up to Jesus at once and said, "Hail!
27.48 one . . at once ran and took a sponge
Lk 12.36 "so that they may open to him at once
12.54 "you say at once, 'A shower is coming
17. 7 " 'Come at once and sit down at table
21. 9 "but the end will not be at once
Jn 5. 9 And at once the man was healed
18.27 and at once the cock crowed
Acts 21.30 and at once the gates were shut
Jas 1.24 at once forgets what he was like
Rev 4. 2 At once I was in the Spirit
3. *immediately:* εὐθύς EUTHYS II
Mk 1.28 at once his fame spread everywhere
1.43 he . . sent him away at once
4.29 "when . . ripe, at once he puts in the sickle
14.45 when he came, he went up to him at once
Jn 13.32 "God will also glorify him . . and . . at once
19.34 at once there came out blood and water
Acts 10.16 the thing was taken up at once to heaven
4. *at once:* ἐξαυτῆς EXAUTĒS
Mk 6.25 "give me at once the head of John
Acts 10.33 "So I sent to you at once
21.32 He at once took soldiers and centurions
23.30 "I sent him to you at once
5. *immediately:* παραχρῆμα PARACHRĒMA
Mt 21.19 And the fig tree withered at once
21.20 "How did the fig tree wither at once?
Lk 8.55 spirit returned, and she got up at once
Acts 16.33 baptized at once, with all his family
CONTEXTUALLY
2 Cor 1.17 man, ready to say Yes and No at once

ONCE FOR ALL
1. *at once, once for all:* ἐφάπαξ EPHAPAX
Rom 6.10 he died to sin, once for all
Heb 7.27 o. for all when he offered up himself
9.12 entered once for all into the Holy Place

Heb 10.10 offering of the body of Jesus C. once for all
2. *once for all:* ἅπαξ HAPAX
Heb 9.26 as it is, he has appeared once for all
1 Pet 3.18 Christ also died[h] for sins once for all
Jude . 3 the faith which was once for all delivered
. 5 you were once for all fully informed

ONCE MORE
1. *from above, anew:* ἄνωθεν ANŌTHEN
[a]+πάλιν
Gal 4. 9 [a]whose slaves you want to be once more
2. *second:* δεύτερος (neut.) DEUTEROS
Rev 19. 3 Once more they cried, "Hallelujah!
3. *again, back:* πάλιν PALIN
Lk 23.20 Pilate addressed them once more
Jn 8. 8 once more he bent down and wrote[r]‡
IDIOMATICALLY
a. Heb 12.26 "Yet once more I will shake not only the earth ἔτι ἅπαξ ἐγὼ σείσω οὐ μόνον τὴν γῆν [HAPAX]
b. Heb 12.27 This phrase, "Yet once more," indicates τὸ δὲ ἔτι ἅπαξ δηλοῖ [HAPAX]

ONE (*See also* ACCORD, WITH ONE)
1. *other, another:* ἄλλος ALLOS
Jn 4.37 " 'One sows and another reaps
1 Cor 15.39 but there is one kind for men
15.41 There is one glory of the sun
2. *man, mankind:* ἄνθρωπος ANTHRŌPOS
Jn 3.27 "No one can receive . . except what is given
Acts 25.16 "not . . give up any o. before the accused met
1 Cor 4. 1 This is how one should regard us
3. *that:* ἐκεῖνος EKEINOS
Rom 14.15 the ruin of one for whom Christ died
4. *one:* εἷς HEIS
Mt 5.19 "Whoever then relaxes one of the least
5.29 "better that you lose one of . . members
5.30 "better that you lose one of . . members
5.36 "you cannot make one hair white or black
5.41 "if any one forces you to go one mile
6.24 "he will hate the one and love the other, or he will be devoted to . . one and despise . . other
6.27 "can add one cubit to his span of life?[p]
6.29 "Solomon . . was not arrayed like one of these
10.29 "not one of them will fall to the ground
10.42 "whoever gives to one of these . . water
12.11 "What man of you, if he has one sheep
13.46 "on finding one pearl of great value
16.14 "others say . . one of the prophets
17. 4 "if you wish, I will make three booths here, one for you and one for Moses and one for Elijah
18. 5 "Whoever receives one such child
18. 6 "one of these little ones who believe
18.10 "do not despise one of these little ones
18.12 "If . . one of them has gone astray
18.14 "not . . that one of these . . should perish
18.16 "take one or two others along with you
18.24 "one was brought to him who owed him
18.28 "one of his fellow servants who owed him
19. 5 " 'the two shall become one flesh
19. 6 "they are no longer two but one flesh
19.16 one came up to him, saying, "Teacher
19.17 "One there is who is good
20.12 " 'These last worked only one hour
20.13 "he replied to one of them, 'Friend
20.21 "that these two sons of mine may sit, one at your right hand and one at your left
22.35 one of them, a lawyer, asked him
23. 8 "for you have one teacher
23. 9 "you have one Father, who is in heaven
23.10 "for you have one master, the Christ
24.40 "Then two men will be in the field; one is taken and one is left
24.41 "Two women will be grinding at the mill; one is taken and one is left
25.15 "he gave . . to another two, to another one
25.18 "he who had received the one talent
25.24 "He . . who had received the one talent
Mt 25.40 "you did it to one of the least of these
25.45 " 'you did it not to one of the least of these
26.14 one of the twelve, . . called Judas Iscariot
26.21 "I say to you, one of you will betray me
26.22 began to say to him one after another
26.40 "could you not watch[h] with me one hour?
26.47 Judas came, one of the twelve
26.51 behold, one of those who were with Jesus
27.15 any one prisoner whom they wanted
27.38 two robbers were crucified with him, one on the right and one on the left
27.48 one of them . . ran and took a sponge
Mk 5.22 one of the rulers of the synagogue
6.15 "prophet, like one of the prophets of old
8.14 had only one loaf with them in the boat
8.28 "others ⟨say⟩ one of the prophets
9. 5 "Master,[f] it is well that we are here; let us make three booths, one for you and one for Moses and one for Elijah
9.17 one of the crowd answered him
9.37 "Whoever receives one such child
9.42 "Whoever causes one of these little ones
10. 8 " 'the two shall become one flesh.' So they are no longer two but one flesh
10.37 "Grant us to sit, one at your right hand and one at your left, in your glory
12. 6 "He had still one other, a beloved son
12.28 one of the scribes came up and heard
12.29 " 'The Lord our God, the Lord is one
12.32 "you have truly said that he is one
13. 1 one of his disciples said to him, "Look!
14.10 Judas Iscariot, who was one of the twelve
14.18 "I say to you, one of you will betray me
14.19 say to him one after another, "Is it I?
14.20 He said . . "It is one of the twelve
14.37 "Could you not watch[d] one hour?
14.43 Judas came, one of the twelve
14.47 one of those who stood by drew his sword
14.66 one of the maids of the high priest
15. 6 he used to release for them one prisoner
15.27 with him they crucified two robbers, one on his right and one on his left[g]
Lk 4.40 he laid his hands on every one of them
5. 3 Getting into one of the boats
5.12 While he was in one of the cities
5.17 one of those days, as he was teaching
7.41 "one owed five hundred denarii
8.22 One day he got into a boat with his disciples
9.33 "it is well that we are here; let us make three booths, one for you and one for Moses and one for Elijah
[10.42 *"few things are needful, or only one*‡
11.46 "you . . do not touch . . with o. of your fingers
12. 6 "not o. of them is forgotten before God
12.27 "Solomon . . not arrayed like one of these
12.52 "in one house there will be five divided
13.10 teaching in one of the synagogues
15. 4 "hundred sheep, if he has lost one of them
15. 7 "more joy in heaven over one sinner
15. 8 "having ten silver coins,[t] if she loses one coin
15.10 "joy . . over one sinner who repents
15.15 "joined himself to one of the citizens
15.19 " ' "treat me as one of your . . servants
[15.21 *"treat me as one of your hired servants*‡
15.26 "he called one of the servants
16.13 "he will hate the one and love the other, or he will be devoted to the one
16.17 "than for o. dot of the law to become void
17. 2 "than . . cause one of these little ones to sin[y]
17.15 Then one . . turned back, praising God
17.22 "you will desire to see one of the days
17.34 "there will be two in one bed; one will be taken and the other left
17.35 "one will be taken and the other left[b]
[17.36 *"one will be taken and the other left*‡
18.10 "one a Pharisee . . other a tax collector
20. 1 One day, as he was teaching the people

Lk 22.47 man called Judas, one of the twelve
22.50 one . . struck the slave of the high priest
23.39 One of the criminals who were hanged
24.18 one of them, named Cleopas, answered
Jn 1.40 One of the two who heard John speak
6. 8 One of his disciples, Andrew
6.22 that there had been only one boat there
6.70 "the twelve, and one of you is a devil
6.71 he, one of the twelve, was to betray him
7.21 "I did one deed, and you all marvel
7.50 Nicodemus, . . who was one of them
8. 9 they went away, one by one, beginning with the eldest[r]‡
8.41 "we have one Father, even God
10.16 "they will heed my voice. So there shall be one flock, one shepherd
10.30 "I and the Father are one
11.49 o. of them, Caiaphas, . . was high priest
11.50 "one man should die for the people
11.52 to gather into one the children of God
12. 2 Lazarus was one of those at table
12. 4 Judas Iscariot, one of his disciples
13.21 "I say to you, one of you will betray me
13.23 One of his disciples, whom Jesus loved
17.11 "that they may be one, even as we are
17.21 "that they may all be one
17.22 "I have given to them, that they may be one even as we are one
17.23 "that they may become perfectly one
18.14 expedient that one man should die
18.22 "one of . . officers standing by struck Jesus
18.26 One of the servants[l] of the high priest
19.34 one of the soldiers pierced his side
20.12 she saw two angels in white, sitting . . , one at the head and one at the feet
20.24 Thomas, one of the twelve
21.25 were every one of them to be written
Acts 1.22 "one . . must become with us a witness
1.24 "which o. of these two thou hast chosen
2. 3 tongues as of fire . . resting on each one
2. 6 each one heard . . in his own language
4.32 the company . . were of one heart . . and no one said that any . . was his own
11.28 one of them named Agabus stood up
12.10 they . . passed on through one street
17.26 "he made from one every nation of men
17.27 "Yet he is not far from each one of us
19.34 they all with one voice cried out
20.31 "I did not cease . . to admonish every one
21. 7 we . . stayed with them for one day
21.26 offering presented for every one of them
23. 6 perceived that one part were Sadducees
23.17 Paul called one of the centurions
24.21 "this one thing which I cried out
28.13 after one day a south wind sprang up
28.25 after Paul had made one statement
Rom 3.10 "None is righteous, no, not one
3.12 "no one does good, not even one
3.30 since God is one; and he will justify
5.12 sin came into the world through one man
5.15 the grace of that one man Jesus C.
5.16 the judgment following one trespass
5.19 by one man's disobedience many . . sinners
12. 4 in one body we have many members
12. 5 we, though many, are one body in Christ
15. 6 with one voice glorify the God
1 Cor 4. 6 puffed up in favor of one against another
6.16 who joins . . a prostitute becomes one body
6.16 "The two shall become one flesh
6.17 united to the Lord becomes one spirit
8. 4 "there is no God but one
8. 6 yet for us there is one God, . . and one Lord, Jesus Christ
9.24 all . . compete, but . . one receives the prize
10.17 Because there is one bread, we who are many are one body, for we all partake of the one bread
1 Cor 12. 9 gifts of healing by the one Spirit
12.11 All these are inspired by one . . Spirit
12.12 as the body is one . . and all the members of the body, though many, are one body
12.13 by one Spirit we were all baptized into one body . . and all were made to drink of one Spirit
12.14 the body does not consist of one member
12.18 God arranged the organs . . , each one
12.20 there are many parts, yet one body
12.26 If one member suffers, all suffer
14.27 each in turn; and let one interpret
2 Cor 5.14 convinced that one has died for all
11. 2 a pure bride to her one husband
11.24 I have received . . the forty lashes less one
Gal 3.16 referring to one, "And to your offspring
3.20 Now an intermediary implies more than one; but God is one
3.28 for you are all one in Christ Jesus
4.22 Abraham had two sons, one by a slave and one by a free woman
4.24 two covenants. O. is from Mount Sinai
5.14 the whole law is fulfilled in one word
Eph 2.14 he is our peace, who has made us both one
2.15 that he might create . . one new man
2.16 reconcile us both to God in one body
2.18 through him we . . have access in one Spirit
4. 4 There is one body and one Spirit, just as you were called to the one hope that belongs to your call
4. 5 one Lord, one faith, one baptism
4. 6 one God and Father of us all
5.31 "and the two shall become one flesh
Phil 1.27 stand firm in one spirit, with one mind striving side by side for the faith
2. 2 being in full accord and of one mind
Col 3.15 you were called in the one body
4. 6 how you ought to answer every one
1 Th 2.11 we exhorted each one of you
2 Th 1. 3 love of every one of you . . is increasing
1 Tim 2. 5 there is one God, and there is one mediator between God and men
3. 2 a bishop must be . . the husband of o. wife
3.12 Let deacons be the husband of one wife
5. 9 a widow . . the wife of one husband
Tit 1. 6 if any man is . . the husband of one wife
Heb 2.11 he . . and those . . sanctified have . . one origin
Jas 2.19 You believe that God is one; you do well
4.12 There is one lawgiver and judge
2 Pet 3. 8 with the Lord one day is as a thousand years, and a thousand years as one day
Rev 5. 5 Then one of the elders said to me
6. 1 Lamb opened one of the seven seals, and I heard one of the four living creatures
7.13 one of the elders addressed me
13. 3 One of its heads seemed to have a . . wound
15. 7 one of . . creatures gave the . . angels . . bowls
17. 1 one of the . . angels who had the seven bowls
17.10 "kings, five of whom have fallen, one is
17.12 "to receive authority as kings for one hour
17.13 "These are of one mind and give . . authority
17.17 "carry out his purpose by being of o. mind
18.10 "In one hour has thy judgment come
18.17 "In one hour all this wealth . . laid waste
18.19 "In one hour she has been laid waste
21. 9 "Then came one of the seven angels

5. *another, different:* ἕτερος HETEROS [B.3.b.5]
1 Cor 15.40 the glory of the celestial is one

6. *who on the one hand:* ὃς μέν HOS
[a]+ὃς δέ *who on the other hand*
Mt 21.35 "tenants . . beat one, killed another
22. 5 "one to his farm, another to his business
25.15 "to one he gave five talents,[d] to another
Lk 23.33 [a]crucified . . criminals, one on the right and one on the left
Rom 9.21 of the same lump one vessel for beauty
14. 2 One believes he may eat anything

1 Cor 11.21 one is hungry and another is drunk
12. 8 To one is given through the Spirit
2 Cor 2.16 to one a fragrance from death to death
7. *this:* *οὗτος* HOUTOS
Mt **8.9**; **10.**23
Lk **7.8**
Acts **15.**38
1 Cor **6.**13
8. *anyone, any:* *τὶς* TIS II
Mt **12.**29
Mk **8.4**; **15.**36
Lk **7.**36; **9.**8, 19; **11.**1, 45; **12.**13; **14.**15; **16.**31; **23.**26
Jn **3.**3, 5; **5.**5
Acts **7.**24; **9.**43; **10.**5; **13.**41; **16.**14; **22.**12; **25.**19
Rom **5.**7[2]
1 Cor **3.**4; **6.**1; **8.**3; **10.**27
Col **3.**13
Tit **1.**12
Heb **5.**4
Jas **2.**16
1 Pet **2.**19
IDIOMATICALLY
a. Lk 16.5 "So, summoning his master's debtors one by one *καὶ προσκαλεσάμενος ἕνα ἕκαστον τῶν χρεοφειλετῶν τοῦ κυρίου ἑαυτοῦ* [HEIS; HEKASTOS]
b. Acts 21.19 he related one by one the things that God had done *ἐξηγεῖτο καθ' ἓν ἕκαστον ὧν ἐποίησεν ὁ θεός* [HEIS; HEKASTOS]
c. 1 Cor 7.7 each has his own special gift from God, one of one kind and one of another *ἕκαστος ἴδιον ἔχει χάρισμα ἐκ θεοῦ, ὁ μὲν οὕτως, ὁ δὲ οὕτως* [HOUTŌS]
d. 1 Cor 14.31 For you can all prophesy one by one *δύνασθε γὰρ καθ' ἕνα πάντες προφητεύειν* [HEIS]
e. Gal 2.16 because by works of the law shall no one be justified *ὅτι ἐξ ἔργων νόμου οὐ δικαιωθήσεται πᾶσα σάρξ* [SARX]

ONE ANOTHER

1. *one another:* *ἀλλήλων* ALLĒLŌN
Mt 24.10 "then many will . . betray one another, and hate one another
25.32 "he will separate them one from another
Mk 4.41 said to one another, "Who then is this?
8.16 they discussed it with one another
9.34 they had discussed with one another
9.50 "be at peace with one another
15.31 chief priests mocked him to one another
Lk 2.15 the shepherds said to one another
4.36 said to one another, "What is this word?
6.11 they . . discussed with one another
7.32 "like children . . calling to one another
8.25 they marveled, saying to one another
12. 1 so many . . that they trod upon one another
Jn 4.33 So the disciples said to one another
5.44 "you . . who receive glory from one another
11.56 saying to one another . . in the temple
13.14 "you . . ought to wash one another's feet
13.22 disciples looked at one another, uncertain
13.34 "A new commandment . . love one another
13.34 "that you also love one another
13.35 "if you have love for one another
15.12 "commandment, that you love one another
15.17 "This I command you, to love one another
16.17 his disciples said to one another
19.24 said to one another, "Let us not tear it
Acts 4.15 they conferred with one another
19.38 "let them bring charges against one another
21. 5(6) we prayed and bade one another farewell
26.31 withdrawn, they said to one another
28. 4 to one another . . "No doubt . . a murderer
Rom 1.27 consumed with passion for one another
12. 5 individually members one of another
12.10 love one another with brotherly affection; outdo one another in showing honor
12.16 Live in harmony with one another
13. 8 except to love one another
14.13 no more pass judgment on one another
Rom 15. 5 to live in such harmony with one another
15. 7 Welcome one another, therefore
15.14 you . . are . . able to instruct one another
16.16 Greet one another with a holy kiss
1 Cor 7. 5 Do not refuse one another except
11.33 wait for one another
12.25 have the same care for one another
16.20 Greet one another with a holy kiss
2 Cor 13.12 Greet one another with a holy kiss
Gal 5.13 through love be servants of one another
5.15 if you . . devour one another take heed that you are not consumed by one another
5.26 Let us have no . . provoking of one another, no envy of one another
6. 2 Bear one another's burdens
Eph 4. 2 with patience, forbearing one another
4.25 for we are members one of another
4.32 be kind to one another, tenderhearted
5.21 Be subject to one another out of reverence
Col 3. 9 Do not lie to one another
3.13 forbearing one another and . . forgiving
1 Th 3.12 abound in love to one another
4. 9 taught by God to love one another
4.18 comfort one another with these words
5.11 Therefore encourage one another
5.15 always seek to do good to one another
2 Th 1. 3 love of every one of you for one another
Tit 3. 3 hated by men and hating one another
Heb 10.24 how to stir up one another to love
Jas 4.11 Do not speak evil against one another
5. 9 Do not grumble . . against one another
5.16 confess your sins to one another, and pray for one another
1 Pet 1.22 love one another earnestly from the heart
4. 9 Practice hospitality . . to one another
5. 5 with humility toward one another
5.14 Greet one another with the kiss of love
1 Jn 1. 7 we have fellowship with one another
3.11 that we should love one another
3.23 that we should . . love one another
4. 7 Beloved, let us love one another
4.11 we also ought to love one another
4.12 if we love one another, God abides in us
2 Jn . 5 commandment . . that we love one another
Rev 6. 4 so that men should slay one another
2. *himself:* *ἑαυτοῦ* HEAUTOU
Mt 21.25 they argued with one another
Mk [10.26 they said *to one another*‡
11.31 And they argued with one another
12. 7 "those tenants said to one another
16. 3 to one another, "Who will roll . . the stone?
Lk 20. 5 they discussed it with one another
22.23 they began to question one another
Jn 7.35 The Jews said to one another
12.19 Pharisees then said to one another
1 Cor 6. 7 To have lawsuits at all with one another
2 Cor 10.12 measure themselves by one another, and compare themselves with one another
Eph 4.32 forgiving one another, as God . . forgave
5.19 addressing one another in psalms
Col 3.16 teach and admonish one another
Heb 3.13 exhort one another every day
1 Pet 4. 8 hold unfailing your love for one another
4.10 a gift, employ it for one another
IDIOMATICALLY
a. Acts 2.12 saying to one another *ἄλλος πρὸς ἄλλον λέγοντες* [ALLOS]
b. 1 Th 5.11 build one another up *οἰκοδομεῖτε εἷς τὸν ἕνα* [HEIS]

ONE, ANY (*See* ANY ONE)

ONE EYE, WITH

1. *one-eyed:* *μονόφθαλμος* MONOPHTHALMOS*
Mt 18. 9 "better for you to enter life with one eye
Mk 9.47 "better for you to enter . . with one eye

ONE FACT
1. *one:* εἷς (neut.) HEIS
2 Pet 3. 8 do not ignore this one fact, beloved

ONE HAND (*See* ON THE ONE HAND)

ONE MAN
1. *one:* εἷς HEIS
Lk [23.17 *Now he was obliged to release one man*‡
Jn 18.39 "custom that I should release one man
Rom 5.15 if many died through one man's trespass
5.16 not like the effect of that one man's sin
5.17 because of one man's trespass, death reigned through that one man
5.17 righteousness . . through the one man Jesus
5.18 as o. man's trespass led to condemnation . . , so o. man's . . righteousness leads to . . life
5.19 by one man's obedience many . . righteous
9.10 Rebecca . . conceived children by one man
Heb 11.12 from one man, and him as good as dead
2. *who, which, what:* ὅς HOS
Rom 14. 5 One man esteems one day as better

ONE, NO
1. *no one:* μηδείς MĒDEIS
Mt 9.30 "See that no one knows it
16.20 charged the disciples to tell no one
17. 9 "Tell no one . . until . . Son of man is raised
Mk 5.43 charged them that no one should know
7.36 he charged them to tell no one
8.30 he charged them to tell no one
9. 9 he charged them to tell no one
11.14 "May no o. ever eat fruit from you again
Lk 3.14 "Rob no one by violence
5.14 he charged him to tell no one
8.56 he charged them to tell no one
9.21 he charged . . them to tell this to no one
10. 4 "salute no one on the road
Acts 9. 7 hearing the voice but seeing no one
23.22 "Tell no one that you have informed me
Rom 12.17 Repay no one evil for evil
13. 8 Owe no one anything, except to love
1 Cor 3.18 Let no one deceive himself
3.21 So let no one boast of men
10.24 Let no one seek his own good
Eph 5. 6 Let no one deceive you with . . words
Col 2. 4 that no one may delude you with . . speech
2.18 Let no one disqualify you
1 Th 3. 3 that no one be moved by these afflictions
1 Tim 4.12 Let no one despise your youth
Tit 2.15 Let no one disregard you
3. 2 to speak evil of no one, . . to be gentle
Jas 1.13 Let no one say when he is tempted
1 Jn 3. 7 Little children, let no one deceive you
Rev 3.11 " 'hold fast . . so . . no one may seize . . crown
2. *not, no:* οὐ OU [A.4.c]
Lk **17.**18
Rom **3.**11[2], 12
3. *no one, nothing:* οὐδείς OUDEIS
Mt 6.24 "No one can serve two masters
[8.10 "*with no one* in Israel have I found such faith‡
9.16 "no one puts a piece of unshrunk cloth
11.27 "no one knows the Son except the Father
17. 8 they saw no one but Jesus only
20. 7 " 'Because no one has hired us
22.46 no one was able to answer him a word
24.36 "of that day and hour no one knows
Mk 2.21 "No one sews a piece of unshrunk cloth
2.22 "no one puts new wine into old wineskins
3.27 "no one can enter a strong man's house
5. 3 no one could bind him any more
5. 4 no one had the strength to subdue him
5.37 he allowed no one to follow him
9.39 "no one who does a mighty work
10.18 "No one is good but God alone
10.29 "there is no one who has left house
11. 2 "a colt . . , on which no one has ever sat
12.34 after that no one dared to ask him any
13.32 "of that day or that hour no one knows
Lk 5.36 "No o. tears a piece from a new garment
5.37 no one puts new wine into old wineskins
5.39 "no o. after drinking old wine desires new
8.16 "No one after lighting a lamp covers it
9.36 they kept silence and told no one
9.62 "No one who puts his hand to the plow
10.22 "no one knows who . . Son is except . . Father
11.33 "No o. . . lighting a lamp puts it in a cellar
15.16 "no one gave him anything
18.19 "No one is good but God alone
19.30 "a colt . . on which no one has ever yet sat
23.53 tomb, where no one had . . been laid
Jn 1.18 No one has ever seen God
3. 2 "no one can do these signs that you do
3.13 "No one has ascended into heaven but he
3.32 yet no one receives his testimony
5.22 "The Father judges no one
6.44 "No o. can come . . unless the Father
6.65 "no o. can come . . unless it is granted
7.13 no one spoke openly of him
7.27 "no one will know where he comes from
7.30 but no one laid hands on him
7.44 no one laid hands on him
8.10 "Has no one condemned you?[r]‡
8.11 She said, "No one, Lord[r]‡
8.15 "I judge no one
8.20 but no one arrested him
9. 4 "night comes, when no one can work
10.18 "No one takes it from me
10.29 "no one is able to snatch them
13.28 no one . . knew why he said this to him
14. 6 "no o. comes to the Father, but by me
15.24 "the works which no one else did
16.22 "no one will take your joy from you
19.41 tomb where no one had . . been laid
Acts 4.12 "there is salvation in no one else
5.23 "when we opened it we found no one
20.33 "I coveted no one's silver or gold
25.11 "no one can give me up to them
1 Cor 2.11 no one comprehends the thoughts of God
2.15 spiritual man . . is . . to be judged by no one
12. 3 no one speaking by the Spirit of God
12. 3 no one can say "Jesus is Lord" except
14. 2 no o. understands . . , but he utters mysteries
2 Cor 5.16 we regard no o. from a human . . view
7. 2 Open your hearts . . ; we have wronged no one, we have corrupted no one, we have taken advantage of no one
Gal 3.15 no one annuls even a man's will[g]
Phil 2.20 I have no one like him
2 Tim 4.16 no one took my part; all deserted me
Heb 6.13 he had no one greater by whom to swear
7.13 no one has ever served at the altar
12.14 without which no one will see the Lord
Jas 1.13 God . . himself tempts no one
Rev 2.17 " 'new name . . which no o. knows except him
3. 7 " 'holy one . . , who opens and no one shall shut, who shuts and no one opens
3. 8 " 'open door, which no one is able to shut
5. 3 no one . . was able to open the scroll
5. 4 no o. was found worthy to open the scroll
14. 3 No one could learn that song except
15. 8 no one could enter the temple until
18.11 no one buys their cargo any more
19.12 a name inscribed which no one knows
4. *all, every, whole:* πᾶς (+neg.) PAS
Rom 10.11 "No one who believes in him
Gal 2.16 by . . the law shall no one be justified
1 Jn 3. 6 No one who abides in him sins; no one who sins has either seen him or known him
3. 9 No one born of God commits sin
5. *anyone, any:* τὶς (+neg.) TIS II
Mt **8.**28; **11.**27; **24.**4
Mk **13.**5
Lk **8.**51
Jn **2.**25; **10.**28
1 Cor **16.**11

2 Cor **8**.20; **11**.16; **12**.6
Col **2**.8, 16
2 Th **2**.3
Heb **4**.11; **12**.15, 16
Rev **13**.17

ONE POINT
ONE THING
ONE THING I DO
1. *one:* εἷς (neut.) HEIS
Mk 10.21 "You lack one thing; go, sell . . and give
Lk 10.42 "⟨Martha,⟩ one thing is needful[j]‡
18.22 "One thing you still lack
Jn 9.25 "one thing I know, that . . now I see
Phil 3.13 one t. I do, forgetting what lies behind
Jas 2.10 keeps the whole law but fails in o. point
2. *anyone, any:* τὶς (neut.) TIS II
Acts **19**.32; **21**.34

ONE, THE
ONE WHO
ONE WHO, THE
1. *who, which, what:* ὅς HOS
[a]+ἄν B.3.b.4
Mt 26.48 [a]"The one I shall kiss is the man
Mk 14.44 [a]"The one I shall kiss is the man
Lk 7.43 "The one . . to whom he forgave more
Jn 1.26 "among you . . one whom you do not know
Rom 6.16 you are slaves of the o. whom you obey
Heb 7.13 the o. of whom these things are spoken
8. 1 one who is seated at the right hand
2 Jn . 5 the one we have had from the beginning
Rev 12. 5 one who is to rule all the nations

ONE TIME, AT
1. *at once, once for all:* ἐφάπαξ EPHAPAX
1 Cor 15. 6 five hundred brethren at one time

ONE WHO (*See* ONE, THE)

ONE'S OWN (*See* AGE, S. OF ONE'S OWN; OWN, ONE'S)

ONESELF (*See also* MASTER OF ONESELF)
1. *himself:* ἑαυτοῦ HEAUTOU
Mk 12.33 "to love one's neighbor as oneself
Jas 1.27 keep oneself unstained from the world

ONESIMUS: Ὀνήσιμος ō'nesəməs
Col 4. 9 O., the faithful and beloved brother
Phm .10 I appeal to you for my child, O.

ONESIPHORUS: Ὀνησίφορος ˌänə'sifərəs
2 Tim 1.16 Lord grant mercy to the household of O.
4.19 Greet . . the household of Onesiphorus

ONLY (*See also, e.g.,* NOT ONLY)
1. *if, since:* εἰ EI [B.3.b.4]
Eph 4.29 but only such as is good for edifying
2. *if not, except:* εἰ μή EI MĒ
[a]+neg.
Mt 12.24 [a]"It is only by Beelzebul, the prince
14.17 [a]"We have only five loaves here
15.24 [a]"I was sent only to the lost sheep
Mk 8.14 [a]they had only one loaf with them
Jn 10.10 [a]"The thief comes only to steal and kill
1 Cor 7.17 Only, let every one lead the life which
3. *thus, so:* οὕτως HOUTŌS
1 Cor 3.15 he . . will be saved, but only as through fire
4. *only, unique:* μονογενής MONOGENĒS*
Lk 7.12 a man . . , the only son of his mother
8.42 he had an only daughter, about twelve
9.38 "my son, for he is my only child
Jn 1.14 glory as of the o. Son from the Father
1.18 the only Son[b] . . has made him known
3.16 he gave his o. Son, that whoever believes
3.18 in the name of the only Son of God
Heb 11.17 Abraham . . was ready to offer up his o. son
1 Jn 4. 9 God sent his only Son into the world
5. *only, alone:* μόνος MONOS
[a]neut.
Mt 4.10 "it is written . . 'him only shall you serve
5.47 [a]"if you salute only your brethren
Mt 8. 8 [a]"only say the word, and my servant will
9.21 [a]"If I only touch his garment, I shall be . . well
12. 4 "not lawful for him . . but only for the priests
14.36 [a]that they might only touch the fringe
17. 8 they saw no one but Jesus only
21.19 [a]found nothing on it but leaves only
21.21 [a]"you will not only do what has been done
24.36 "not even the angels . . , but the Father only
Mk 5.36 [a]"Do not fear, only believe
9. 8 they no longer saw any . . but Jesus only
Lk 4. 8 "It is written . . 'him only shall you serve
5.21 "Who can forgive sins but God only?
8.50 [a]"only believe, and she shall be well
24.18 "Are you the o. visitor . . who does not know?
Jn 5.18 [a]because he not only broke the sabbath
5.44 "the glory that comes from the only God
11.52 [a]⟨should die⟩ not for the nation only
12. 9 [a]they came, not only on account of Jesus
13. 9 [a]"not my feet only but also my hands!
17. 3 "that they know thee the only true God
17.20 [a]"I do not pray for these only
Acts 8.16 [a]but they had only been baptized
18.25 [a]he knew only the baptism of John
19.26 [a]"hear that not only at Ephesus
19.27 [a]"danger not o. that this trade of ours
21.13 [a]"I am ready not only to be imprisoned
26.29 [a]"not o. you but also all who hear me
27.10 [a]"loss, not o. of the cargo and the ship
Rom 1.32 [a]they not o. do them but approve those
3.29 [a]Or is God the God of Jews only?
4.16 [a]not only to the adherents of the law
5.11 [a]Not o. so, but we also rejoice in God
8.23 [a]not o. the creation, but we ourselves
9.10 [a]not o. so, but also when Rebecca
9.24 [a]not . . Jews o. but also from the Gentiles
13. 5 [a]subject, not o. to avoid God's wrath
16. 4 not only I but also all the churches
16.27 to the only wise God be glory!
1 Cor 7.39 [a]free to be married . . o. in the Lord
9. 6 is it only Barnabas and I who have no right?
14.36 are you the only ones it has reached?
15.19 [a]If for this life only we have hoped
2 Cor 7. 7 [a]not o. by his coming but . . by the comfort
8.10 [a]began not only to do but to desire
8.19 [a]not o. that, but he has been appointed
8.21 [a]honorable not only in the Lord's sight
9.12 [a]this service not only supplies the wants
Gal 1.23 [a]they o. heard . . "He . . is now preaching
2.10 [a]only they would have us remember
3. 2 [a]Let me ask you o. this: Did you receive?
4.18 [a]not only when I am present with you
5.13 [a]o. do not use . . freedom as an opportunity
6.12 [a]o. . . that they may not be persecuted
Eph 1.21 [a]not o. in this age but . . in that . . to come
Phil 1.27 [a]O. let your manner of life be worthy
1.29 [a]you should not only believe in him
2.12 [a]so now, not only as in my presence
2.27 [a]mercy . . not o. on him but on me also
4.15 no church . . with me . . except you only
Col 4.11 These are the o. men of the circumcision
1 Th 1. 5 [a]gospel came to you not only in word
1. 8 [a]not o. has the word . . sounded forth
2. 8 [a]to share with you not only the gospel
2 Th 2. 7 [a]only he who now restrains it will do so
1 Tim 1.17 To . . the only God, be honor and glory
5.13 [a]not o. idlers but gossips and busybodies
6.15 the blessed and only Sovereign
2 Tim 2.20 [a]there are not only vessels of gold
4. 8 [a]not only to me but also to all who
Heb 9. 7 into the second only the high priest
9.10 [a]deal only with food and drink
12.26 [a]"I will shake not only the earth
Jas 1.22 [a]be doers of the word, and not hearers o.
1 Pet 2.18 [a]not only to the kind and gentle
1 Jn 2. 2 [a]the expiation for our sins, and not for ours o.
5. 6 [a]Jesus Christ, not with the water only
2 Jn . 1 whom I love in the truth, and not o. I

Jude . 4 ungodly persons who . . deny our o. Master
.25 to the only God, our Saviour

6. *but, however, except:* πλήν PLĒN
Phil 1.18 Only that . . Christ is proclaimed
3.16 Only let us hold true to what we have
Rev 2.25 " 'only hold fast what you have

IDIOMATICALLY

a. Jn 6.22 that there had been only one boat there ὅτι πλοιάριον ἄλλο οὐκ ἦν ἐκεῖ εἰ μὴ ἕν [EI MĒ; ALLOS]

CONTEXTUALLY

Mt **19**.11; **20**.12
Lk **17**.10
Jn **4**.2
Acts **2**.15; **5**.2; **20**.24
Rom **4**.9; **9**.27; **11**.20; **14**.2
1 Cor **3**.7; **8**.9; **9**.24; **14**.27
2 Cor **3**.14; **4**.3; **13**.8
Phil **2**.4
Col **2**.17
1 Tim **5**.23
Heb **9**.17
2 Pet **2**.22
Rev **17**.10; **21**.27

ONLY, BUT

1. *but:* ἀλλά ALLA
Mt **19**.11
Jn **4**.2
1 Cor **3**.7
2 Cor **13**.8

2. *if not, except:* ἂν (=ἐὰν) μή AN [B.3.b.4]
Jn 5.19 "but only what he sees the father doing

3. *if not, except:* εἰ μή EI MĒ
Mk 13.32 "not even the angels . . but only the Father
Lk 4.26 "to none of them but only to Zarephath
4.27 "none of them was cleansed, but o. Naaman
Rev 9. 4 but only those . . who have not the seal
21.27 but only those . . in the Lamb's book of life

4. *but, however, except:* πλήν PLĒN
Acts 27.22 "no loss of life . . but only of the ship

ONLY, IF

1. *if indeed:* ἐάνπερ EANPER
Heb 3.14 if only we hold our first confidence firm

ONYX

1. *sardonyx:* σαρδόνυξ SARDONYX*
Rev 21.20 the fifth onyx, the sixth carnelian

OPEN (*See also* REASON, OPEN TO)

1. *open:* ἀνοίγω ANOIGŌ*
Mt 2.11 opening their treasures, they offered . . gifts
3.16 behold, the heavens were opened[g]
5. 2 he opened his mouth and taught
7. 7 "knock, and it will be opened to you
7. 8 "to him who knocks it will be opened
9.30 And their eyes were opened
13.35 "I will open my mouth in parables
17.27 "when you open its mouth you will find
20.33 "Lord, let our eyes be opened
25.11 "maidens . . saying, 'Lord, . . open to us
27.52 the tombs also were opened
Mk 7.35 And his ears were opened
Lk 1.64 immediately his mouth was opened
3.21 Jesus . . was praying, the heaven was opened
4.17 He opened the book and found the place
11. 9 "knock, and it will be opened to you
11.10 "to him who knocks it will be opened
12.36 "so that they may open to him at once
13.25 "knock . . , saying, 'Lord, open to us
Jn 1.51 "I say to you, you will see heaven opened
9.10 "Then how were your eyes opened?
9.14 a sabbath . . when Jesus . . opened his eyes
9.17 "since he has opened your eyes
9.21 "nor do we know who opened his eyes
9.26 "How did he open your eyes?
9.30 "You do not know . . yet he opened my eyes
9.32 "opened the eyes of a man born blind
Jn 10. 3 "To him the gatekeeper opens
10.21 "Can a demon open the eyes of the blind?
11.37 "he who opened the eyes of the blind man
Acts 5.19 an angel of the Lord opened the prison
5.23 "when we opened it we found no one
8.32 "As a sheep . . so he opens not his mouth
8.35 Philip opened his mouth, and . . told him
9. 8 when his eyes were opened, . . they led him
9.40 she opened her eyes, and . . sat up
10.11 heaven opened, and something descending
10.34 Peter opened his mouth and said
12.10 It opened to them of its own accord
12.14 in her joy she did not open the gate
12.16 when they opened, they saw him
14.27 how he had opened a door of faith
16.26 immediately all the doors were opened
16.27 saw that the prison doors were open
18.14 Paul was about to open his mouth
26.18 " '⟨I send you⟩ to open their eyes
Rom 3.13 "Their throat is an open grave
1 Cor 16. 9 a wide door . . has opened to me
2 Cor 2.12 door was opened for me in the Lord
6.11 Our mouth is open to you, Corinthians
Col 4. 3 that God may open to us a door
Rev 3. 7 " 'holy one, . . who opens and no one shall shut, who shuts and no one opens
3. 8 " 'I have set before you an open door
3.20 " 'if any one hears my voice and opens
4. 1 I looked, and lo, in heaven an open door!
5. 2 "Who is worthy to open the scroll?
5. 3 no one . . was able to open the scroll
5. 4 no one was found worthy to o. the scroll
5. 5 "he can open the scroll and its . . seals
5. 9 "Worthy art thou . . to open its seals
6. 1 I saw when the Lamb opened one
6. 3 When he opened the second seal
6. 5 When he opened the third seal
6. 7 When he opened the fourth seal
6. 9 When he opened the fifth seal
6.12 When he opened the sixth seal
8. 1 When the Lamb opened the seventh seal
9. 2 he opened the shaft of the bottomless pit
10. 2 He had a little scroll open in his hand
10. 8 "Go, take the scroll which is open
11.19 God's temple in heaven was opened
12.16 earth opened its mouth and swallowed
13. 6 opened its mouth to utter blasphemies
15. 5 tent of witness in heaven was opened
19.11 Then I saw heaven opened
20.12 books were opened. Also another book was opened, which is the book of life

2 *lay open, explain:* διανοίγω DIANOIGŌ
Mk 7.34 "Ephphatha," that is, "Be opened
Lk 2.23 ("Every male that opens the womb
24.31 eyes were opened and they recognized
24.32 "while he opened to us the scriptures
24.45 he opened their minds to . . scriptures
Acts 7.56 "Behold, I see the heavens opened
16.14 The Lord opened her heart to give heed

3. *inaugurate:* ἐγκαινίζω EGKAINIZŌ
Heb 10.20 living way which he opened for us

4. *naked, bare:* γυμνός GYMNOS
Heb 4.13 no creature is hidden, but all are open

5. *make manifest, make known:* φανερόω PHANEROŌ
Heb 9. 8 way into the sanctuary is not . . opened

6. *divide, split:* σχίζω SCHIZŌ
Mk 1.10 he saw the heavens opened

CONTEXTUALLY

Tit 1. 6 not o. to . . charge of being profligate
1 Pet 3.12 "and his ears are open to their prayer

OPEN, BE

1. *lead, bring:* ἄγω (pass.) AGŌ
Acts 19.38 "courts are open, . . there are proconsuls

OPEN ONE'S HEART

1. *make room for, hold, go:* χωρέω CHŌREŌ
2 Cor 7. 2 Open your hearts to us

OPEN STATEMENT
1. *manifestation, disclosure:* φανέρωσις PHANERŌSIS
2 Cor 4. 2 by the open statement of the truth

OPEN STREET
1. *street, quarter of town:* ἄμφοδον AMPHODON*
Mk 11. 4 a colt tied . . out in the open street

OPENING
1. *opening:* ἄνοιξις ANOIXIS*
Eph 6.19 in opening my mouth . . to proclaim
2. *hole, opening:* ὀπή OPĒ
Jas 3.11 from the same opening fresh . . and brackish?

OPENING, MAKE AN
1. *dig out:* ἐξορύσσω EXORYSSŌ
Mk 2. 4 when they had made an o., they let down

OPENLY
1. *outspokenness:* παρρησία PARRĒSIA
[a]B.1.a.1 [b]dat.
Jn 7. 4 [a]"no man works in secret . . to be known o.
7.13 [b]for fear . . no one spoke openly of him
7.26 [b]"here he is, speaking openly
11.54 [b]Jesus . . no longer went about o.
18.20 [b]"I have spoken openly to the world
Acts 28.31 [a]teaching . . quite openly and unhindered
2. *openly:* φανερῶς PHANERŌS
Mk 1.45 Jesus[g] could no longer o. enter a town

OPINION
1. *calculation, argument:* διαλογισμός DIALOGISMOS
Rom 14. 1 but not for disputes over opinions
2. *judgment, opinion, purpose:* γνώμη GNŌMĒ
1 Cor 7.25 I give my o. as one who . . is trustworthy

OPPONENT
1. *retaliate upon:* ἀντιδιατίθημι (subst. mid. part.) ANTIDIATITHĒMI*
2 Tim 2.25 correcting . . opponents with gentleness
2. *be opposed:* ἀντίκειμαι (subst. part.) ANTIKEIMAI
Phil 1.28 not frightened . . by your opponents
IDIOMATICALLY
a. Tit 2.8 so that an opponent may be put to shame
ἵνα ὁ ἐξ ἐναντίας ἐντραπῇ [ENANTIOS]

OPPORTUNE (*See* TIME, OPPORTUNE)

OPPORTUNITY (*See also* AVAIL ONESELF OF THE OPPORTUNITY)
1. *occasion, origin:* ἀφορμή APHORMĒ
Rom 7. 8 sin, finding o. in the commandment
7.11 sin, finding o. in the commandment
Gal 5.13 do not use . . freedom as . . o. for the flesh
2. *good season, opportunity:* εὐκαιρία EUKAIRIA*
Mt 26.16 from that moment he sought an o.
Lk 22. 6 sought an o. to betray him to them
3. *a suitable day:* ἡμέρα εὔκαιρος EUKAIROS; HĒMERA [A.1.f]
Mk 6.21 an opportunity came . . on his birthday
4. *time, opportunity:* καιρός KAIROS
Acts 24.25 "when I have an o. I will summon you
Gal 6.10 as we have o., let us do good to all men
Heb 11.15 they would have had o. to return
5. *place:* τόπος TOPOS
Acts 25.16 "before . . accused . . had o. to make . . defense
Eph 4.27 give no opportunity to the devil
IDIOMATICALLY
a. Mk 14.11 And he sought an opportunity to betray him
καὶ ἐζήτει πῶς αὐτὸν εὐκαίρως παραδοῖ [EUKAIRŌS]

OPPORTUNITY, HAVE
1. *have time, have opportunity:* εὐκαιρέω EUKAIREŌ
1 Cor 16.12 He will come when he has opportunity

OPPORTUNITY, HAVE NO
1. *be without opportunity:* ἀκαιρέομαι AKAIREOMAI*
Phil 4.10 you were . . concerned . . , but you had no o.

OPPOSE
1. *withstand:* ἀνθίστημι ANTHISTĒMI
Gal 2.11 when Cephas came to Antioch I opposed
2 Tim 3. 8 As Jannes and Jambres opposed Moses, so these men also oppose the truth
4.15 for he strongly opposed our message
2. *be opposed:* ἀντίκειμαι ANTIKEIMAI
2 Th 2. 4 who opposes . . every so-called god
3. *set opposite to:* ἀντιτάσσω (mid.) ANTITASSŌ
Acts 18. 6 "when they opposed and reviled him
Jas 4. 6 "God opposes the proud, but gives grace
1 Pet 5. 5 "God opposes the proud, but gives grace

OPPOSED, BE
1. *be opposed:* ἀντίκειμαι ANTIKEIMAI
Gal 5.17 for these are opposed to each other

OPPOSES, WHO
1. *opposite, contrary:* ἐναντίος (attr. + dat.) ENANTIOS
1 Th 2.15 who . . displease God and oppose all men

OPPOSING GOD
1. *fighting against God:* θεομάχος THEOMACHOS*
Acts 5.39 "You might even be found opposing God!

OPPOSING, IN
1. *opposite, contrary:* ἐναντίος ENANTIOS [A.3.b.1]
Acts 26. 9 "do . . things in opposing the name of Jesus

OPPOSITE
1. *opposite:* ἄντικρυς ANTIKRYS*
Acts 20.15 we came the following day o. Chios
2. *over against:* ἀντιπέρα ANTIPERA*
Lk 8.26 country of the Gerasenes,[a] which is o. Galilee
3. *opposite:* ἀπέναντι APENANTI
Mt 27.61 Mary . . sitting opposite the sepulchre
4. *in accordance with, for:* κατά (+acc.) KATA
Acts 16. 7 when they had come opposite Mysia
5. *opposite:* κατέναντι KATENANTI
Mt 21. 2 "Go into the village opposite you
Mk 11. 2 "Go into the village opposite you
12.41 he sat down opposite the treasury
13. 3 sat on the Mount of Olives o. the temple
Lk 19.30 "Go into the village opposite

OPPOSITION
1. *struggle:* ἀγών AGŌN
1 Th 2.2 declare . . the gospel . . in . . face of great o.

OPPOSITION, SAY IN
1. *speak against:* ἀντεῖπον ANTEIPON
Acts 4.14 they had nothing to say in opposition

OPPOSITION TO, IN
1. *more than, by:* παρά (+acc.) PARA
Rom 16.17 those who create dissensions . . in o. to

OPPRESS
1. *oppress:* καταδυναστεύω KATADYNASTEUŌ*
Acts 10.38 "healing all that were oppressed
Jas 2. 6 Is it not the rich who oppress you?

OPPRESSED
1. *break in pieces:* θραύω (perf. pass. part.) THRAUŌ*
Lk 4.18 "to set at liberty those who are oppressed
2. *subdue, oppress:* καταπονέω (part.) KATAPONEŌ
Acts 7.24 "he defended the oppressed man

OR
1. *or, than:* ἤ Ē
Mt **5.**36; **6.**24, 25, 31[2]; **7.**4, 9, 10, 16; **9.**5; **10.**11, 14, 19, 37[2]; **11.**3; **12.**5, 25, 29, 33; **13.**21; **15.**4, 5; **16.**14, 26; **17.**25[2]; **18.**8[3], 16[2], 20; **19.**29[6]; **20.**15[2]; **21.**25; **22.**17; **23.**17, 19; **24.**23; **25.**37, 38, 39, 44[5]; **27.**17
Mk **2.**9; **3.**4[2]; **4.**17, 21, 30; **6.**56; **7.**10, 11, 12; **10.**29[6], 38, 40; **11.**28, 30; **12.**14, 15(14); **13.**21, 32, 35[3]
Lk **2.**24; **5.**23; **6.**9[2], 42; **7.**19, 20; **8.**16; **9.**25; **10.**[42‡; **11.**[11‡, 12; **12.**11[2], 14, 41, 47; **13.**4, 15; **14.**3, 5, 12, 31; **15.**8; **16.**13; **17.**7, 21, 23; **18.**11, 29[4]; **20.**2, 4, 22; **21.**15; **22.**27
Jn **2.**6; **4.**27; **6.**19; **7.**17, 48; **8.**14; **9.**2; **13.**29; **18.**34
Acts **1.**7; **3.**12[2]; **4.**7, 34; **5.**38; **7.**49; **8.**34; **10.**28[2]; **11.**8; **17.**21, 29[2]; **18.**14; **19.**12; **20.**33[2]; **23.**9, 29; **24.**12, 20; **25.**6; **26.**31; **28.**6, 17, 21
Rom **1.**21; **2.**4, 15; **3.**1, 29; **4.**9, 10; **6.**16; **8.**35[6]; **9.**11; **10.**7; **11.**34, 35; **14.**4, 10, 13, [21[2]‡
1 Cor **1.**13; **2.**1; **4.**3, 21; **5.**10[2], 11[3]; **7.**11, 15; **9.**6; **10.**19; **11.**4, 5, 6, 22, 27; **13.**1; **14.**6[3], 23, 24, 27, 29, 36, 37; **15.**37; **16.**6
2 Cor **3.**1[2]; **6.**14, 15; **9.**7; **10.**12; **11.**4[2]; **12.**6
Gal **1.**8, 10[2]; **2.**2; **3.**2, 5, 15

Eph **3**.20; **5**.3, 5², 27²
Phil **3**.12
Col **2**.16³; **3**.17
1 Th **2**.19²
2 Th **2**.4
1 Tim **2**.9³; **5**.4, [16‡, 19
Tit **1**.6; **3**.12
Phm .18
Heb **2**.6, **10**.28; **12**.16
Jas **1**.17‡; **2**.3, 15; **3**.12; **4**.5, 11, 13, 15
1 Pet **1**.11, 18; **3**.9; **4**.15³
Rev **3**.15; **13**.16, 17²; **14**.9

2. *whether, or:* εἴτε EITE
1 Cor **3**.22⁷; 8.5; **10**.31²; **12**.13²; **14**.7; **15**.11
2 Cor **5**.9, 10; **12**.2, 3
Eph **6**.8
Phil **1**.18, 20, 27
Col **1**.16³, 20
1 Th **5**.10
2 Th **2**.15
1 Pet **2**.14

3. *in order that:* ἵνα (neg.) HINA
Lk **18**.5
1 Tim **3**.6, 7

4. *even if:* κἄν KAN [B.3.b.5]
Lk **12**.38

5. *not:* μή MĒ
[a]μή πως [b]καὶ . . μή
2 Cor **2**.7[a]
Tit **1**.7⁴
2 Jn .10[b]

6. *and not, nor:* μηδέ MĒDE
Mt **10**.14; **24**.20
Lk **3**.14; **14**.12³
Acts **4**.18; **21**.21
Rom **14**.21²
2 Cor **4**.2
Phil **2**.3
2 Th **2**.2
Tit **2**.3
1 Jn **2**.15; **3**.18

7. *and not:* μήτε MĒTE
Mt **5**.35²
2 Th **2**.2²
1 Tim **1**.7
Jas **5**.12²
Rev **7**.1², 3²

8. *and not:* καὶ οὐ OU [A.4.c]
Mt **12**.20

9. *nor, and not:* οὐδέ OUDE
Mt **12**.19; **16**.10
Mk **8**.17
Lk **11**.33
Acts **16**.21; **24**.18
Rom **9**.16
1 Cor **2**.6
Gal **4**.14
Phil **2**.16
1 Th **2**.3; **5**.5
1 Tim **2**.12; **6**.16
2 Pet **1**.8
1 Jn **3**.6
Rev **5**.3²; **9**.4²; **20**.4; **21**.23

10. *and not:* οὔτε OUTE
Mt **12**.32
Jn **9**.3
Acts **24**.12²
1 Th **2**.5, 6
Rev **5**.3, 4; **9**.20², 21³

11. *and, both . . . and:* τέ TE
Rom **14**.8

ORACLE
1. *oracle:* λόγιον LOGION
Acts 7.38 "he received living oracles to give to us
Rom 3. 2 Jews are entrusted with the oracles of God
1 Pet 4.11 whoever speaks, as one who utters oracles

ORATION, MAKE AN
1. *make public speeches:* δημηγορέω DĒMĒGOREŌ*
Acts 12.21 Herod . . took his seat . . , made an oration

ORDAIN
1. *appoint, direct:* διατάσσω DIATASSŌ
Gal 3.19 and it was ordained by angels
2. *determine, appoint:* ὁρίζω HORIZŌ
Acts 10.42 he is the one ordained by God to be judge
3. *appoint, assign:* τάσσω TASSŌ
Acts 13.48 as many as were ordained to eternal life

ORDAINED (*See* MEN, ORDAINED FOR)

ORDEAL, FIERY
1. *burning, proving by fire:* πύρωσις PYRŌSIS
1 Pet 4.12 do not be surprised at the fiery ordeal

ORDER
1. *say, speak:* εἶπον EIPON
Acts 22.24 tribune . . ordered him to be examined
2. *command:* ἐντολή ENTOLĒ
Jn 11.57 orders that if any one knew where he was
3. *rebuke:* ἐπιτιμάω EPITIMAŌ
Mt 12.16 ordered them not to make him known
Mk 3.12 ordered them not to make him known
4. *order, command:* κελεύω KELEUŌ
Mt 14.19 he ordered the crowds to sit down
18.25 "his lord ordered him to be sold
27.58 Pilate ordered it to be given to him
27.64 "order the sepulchre to be made secure
Acts 5.34 Gamaliel . . stood up and ordered the men
12.19 ordered that they should be put to death
21.33 tribune . . ordered him to be bound
21.34 ordered him . . brought into the barracks
23. 3 "yet contrary . . you o. me to be struck
25. 6 he . . ordered Paul to be brought
25.17 "I . . ordered the man to be brought in
27.43 He ordered . . who could swim . . overboard
5. *stewardship, management:* οἰκονομία OIKONOMIA
1 Tim [1. 4 speculations rather than the divine *order*†
6. *give orders:* παραγγέλλω PARAGGELLŌ
Acts 23.30 "ordering his accusers . . to state before you
7. *order, class:* τάγμα TAGMA*
1 Cor 15.23 But each in his own order
8. *order, rank:* τάξις TAXIS
1 Cor 14.40 but all things . . decently and in order
Heb 5. 6 "a priest . . after the o. of Melchizedek
5.10 a high priest after the o. of Melchizedek
6.20 a high priest . . after the o. of Melchizedek
7.11 priest . . after the o. of Melchizedek, rather than one . . after the o. of Aaron
7.17 "a priest . . after the o. of Melchizedek

CONTEXTUALLY
Mk 10. 2 in o. to test him asked, "Is it lawful?
Rom 15. 9 in o. that the Gentiles might glorify God
2 Cor 11.32 guarded the city . . in o. to seize me
Col 1.22 in o. to present you holy and blameless

ORDER GIVEN
1. *command:* διαστέλλω (subst. pass. part. neut.) DIASTELLŌ
Heb 12.20 could not endure the o. that was given

ORDER, GOOD
1. *noble, proper:* εὐσχήμων (subst. neut.) EUSCHĒMŌN
1 Cor 7.35 I say this . . to promote good order
2. *order, rank:* τάξις TAXIS
Col 2. 5 rejoicing to see your good order

ORDER, IN
1. *into, to, for:* εἰς (+acc.) EIS
Rom **8**.29; **15**.8
1 Pet **3**.7
2. *in a row, in order:* καθεξῆς KATHEXĒS
Acts 11. 4 Peter began and explained to them in o.
3. *to, with, against:* πρός (+acc.) PROS
Mt **6**.1

ORDER, PUT IN
1. *prepare, adorn:* κοσμέω KOSMEŌ
Mt 12.44 "finds it empty, swept, and put in o.
Lk 11.25 "he finds it swept and put in order

ORDER THAT, IN
ORDER TO, IN

1. *that somehow:* εἴ πως EI; PŌS II [A.5.b]
Rom 11.14 in order to make my fellow Jews jealous
2. *for the sake of:* ἕνεκα HENEKA
2 Cor 7.12 in order that your zeal . . be revealed
3. *in order that:* ἵνα HINA
Mt 26. 4 took counsel together in o. to arrest Jesus
Mk 7. 9 "rejecting . ., in o. to keep your tradition!
14.10 went to the chief priests in o. to betray
Acts 4.17 "in order that it may spread no further
Rom 1.13 in order that I may reap some harvest
4.16 in o. that . . promise may rest on grace
7. 4 in order that we may bear fruit for God
7.13 in o. that sin might be shown to be sin
8. 4 in o. that . . the law might be fulfilled in us
8.17 in order that we may also be glorified
9.11 in o. that God's purpose . . continue
9.23 in o. to make known the riches
11.31 in o. that . . they . . may[p] receive mercy
1 Cor 9.20 I became as a Jew, in order to win Jews
11.19 in o. that those . . genuine . . be recognized
14.19 I would rather speak . . in o. to instruct
2 Cor 11.12 in o. to undermine the claim of those
13.10 I write this . . in o. that when I come
Gal 1.16 to reveal . . in o. that I might preach
2.16 in o. to be justified by faith in Christ
6.12 in o. that they may not be persecuted
Phil 3. 8 in order that I may gain Christ
Col 2. 4 in order that no one may delude you
Phm .13 in order that he might serve me
.14 in o. that . . goodness . . be . . of . . free will
Heb 10. 9 abolishes . . in o. to establish the second
12.27 in o. that what cannot be shaken . . remain
13.12 in o. to sanctify the people
13.19 in order that I may be restored to you
1 Pet 4.11 in o. that in everything God . . be glorified
4. *that, in order that:* ὅπως HOPŌS
Lk 16.26 " 'in o. that those who would pass . . may not

ORDER TO PREVENT FROM, IN

1. *in order that:* ἵνα (neg.) HINA
Jn 19.31 in o. to prevent . . bodies from remaining

ORDERLY

1. *in a row, in order:* καθεξῆς KATHEXĒS
Lk 1. 3 to write an orderly account for you

ORDERS, GIVE

1. *appoint, direct:* διατάσσω DIATASSŌ
Acts 24.23 Then he gave orders to the centurion
2. *enjoin, order:* ἐπιτάσσω EPITASSŌ
Mk 6.27 the king . . gave orders to bring his head
3. *order, command:* κελεύω KELEUŌ
Mt 8.18 he gave orders to go over to the other side
Acts 16.22 magistrates . . gave orders to beat them

ORDINANCE

1. *ordinance, justification:* δικαίωμα DIKAIŌMA
Lk 1. 6 walking in all . . ordinances . . blameless
2. *decree, decision:* δόγμα DOGMA
Eph 2.15 abolishing . . the law of . . ordinances

ORDINARY

CONTEXTUALLY
1 Cor 3. 3 of the flesh, and behaving like o. men

ORGAN

1. *part, limb:* μέλος MELOS
1 Cor 12.18 God arranged the organs in the body
12.19 If . . a single o., where would the body be?

ORIGINATE

1. *go out:* ἐξέρχομαι EXERCHOMAI
1 Cor 14.36 Did the word of God originate with you?

ORPHAN

1. *without parents, neglected:* ὀρφανός (subst.) ORPHANOS
Jas 1.27 to visit orphans and widows in . . affliction

OTHER (*See also* NAME WAS, WHOSE OTHER; PASS BY ON THE OTHER SIDE)

1. *other, another:* ἄλλος ALLOS
Mt 4.21 from there he saw two other brothers
5.39 "if . . the right cheek, turn . . the other
12.13 it was restored, whole like the other
13. 5 "Other seeds fell on rocky ground
13. 7 "Other seeds fell upon thorns
13. 8 "Other seeds fell on good soil
16.14 "Some say John the B., others say Elijah
20. 3 "he saw others . . idle in the market place
20. 6 "he went out and found others standing
21. 8 others cut branches from the trees
21.36 "he sent o. servants, more than the first
21.41 "let out the vineyard to other tenants
22. 4 "he sent o. servants, saying, 'Tell those
27.42 "He saved others; he cannot save himself
27.61 the o. Mary . . opposite the sepulchre
28. 1 the o. Mary went to see the sepulchre
Mk 4. 5 "Other seed fell on rocky ground
4. 7 "Other seed fell among thorns
4. 8 "other seeds fell into good soil
4.18 "others are the ones sown among thorns
4.36 And other boats were with him
6.15 But others said, "It is Elijah." And others said, "It is a prophet
7. 4 (many o. traditions which they observe
8.28 they told him . . "others say, Elijah; and others one of the prophets
11. 8 others spread leafy branches
12. 5 "so with many others, some they beat
12. 9 "He will . . give the vineyard to others
12.31 "There is no o. commandment greater
12.32 "You are right, . . there is no o. but he
15.31 "He saved others; he cannot save himself
15.41 many o. women who came up with him
Lk 5.29 tax collectors and others . . at table[r]
6.29 "To him who strikes . . cheek, offer the o.
9. 8 ⟨said⟩ by others that one . . had risen
9.19 "but others say, Elijah; and others, that one of the old prophets has risen
20.16 "He will . . give the vineyard to others
23.35 "He saved others; let him save himself!
Jn 4.38 "others have labored, and you . . entered
7.12 others said . . "he is leading . . astray
7.41 Others said, "This is the Christ
9. 9 others said, "No, but he is like him
9.16 others said, "How can a . . sinner do such?
10.16 "I have other sheep, . . not of this fold
10.21 Others said, "These are not the sayings
12.29 Others said, "An angel has spoken
18.16 the o. disciple, . . known to the high priest
18.34 "did others say it to you about me?
19.18 crucified him, and with him two others
19.32 broke the legs of the first, and of the o.
20. 2 the other disciple, . . whom Jesus loved
20. 3 Peter then came out with the o. disciple
20. 4 the other disciple outran Peter
20. 8 the other disciple . . reached the tomb first
20.25 o. disciples told . . "We have seen the Lord
20.30 Now Jesus did many other signs
21. 2 two others of his disciples were together
21. 8 the other disciples came in the boat
21.25 But there are also many other things
Acts 15. 2 some of the others were appointed
1 Cor 3.11 no other foundation can any one lay
9. 2 If to others I am not an apostle
9.12 If others share this rightful claim
9.27 lest after preaching to others I . . should be
14.19 I would rather speak . . to instruct others
14.29 let the others weigh what is said
2 Cor 8.13 I do not mean that others should be eased
11. 8 I robbed o. churches by accepting support
Gal 5.10 confidence . . that you will take no o. view
Phil 3. 4 If any other man thinks he has reason
1 Th 2. 6 whether from you or from others
Jas 5.12 do not swear . . with any other oath

Rev 2.24 " 'I do not lay upon you any o. burden
17.10 "seven kings, . . the o. has not yet come
2. *foreign:* ἀλλότριος ALLOTRIOS
Mt 17.25 "From their sons or from others?
17.26 And when he said, "From others
2 Cor 10.15 We do not boast . . in other men's labors
3. *man, mankind:* ἄνθρωπος ANTHRŌPOS [B.2.d.1]
Lk 13. 4 "worse offenders than all the others
4. *another, different:* ἕτερος HETEROS
Mt 6.24 "he will hate the one and love the o., or . . be devoted to the one and despise the o.
12.45 "brings with him seven other spirits
15.30 the blind, the dumb, and many others
16.14 "Some say John . . , and others Jeremiah
Lk 3.18 with . . other exhortations, he preached
4.43 "I must preach . . . to the other cities also
5. 7 beckoned to . . partners in the other boat
7.41 "two debtors; . . the other ⟨owed⟩ fifty
8. 3 many others, who provided for them[z]
10. 1 the Lord appointed seventy[g] others
11.16 others, to test him, sought . . a sign
11.26 "he goes and brings seven o. spirits
16.13 "he will hate the one and love the o., or . . be devoted to the one and despise the o.
17.34 "one will be taken and the other left
17.35 "one will be taken and the other left[b]
[17.36 "*one will be taken and the other left*‡
18.10 "one a Pharisee and the o. a tax collector
22.65 spoke many other words against him
23.32 Two others also, who were criminals
23.40 But the other rebuked him
Acts 2. 4 they . . began to speak in other tongues
2.13 others . . said . . "filled with new wine
2.40 he testified with many other words
4.12 "no o. name . . by which we must be saved
15.35 preaching the word . . , with many others also
17.34 a woman named Damaris and others
[19.39 "if you seek *about other matters*‡
23. 6 "one part . . Sadducees and the o. Pharisees
27. 1 delivered Paul and some other prisoners
Rom 2.21 you then who teach others
13. 9 The commandments, . . and any other
1 Cor 14.17 but the other man is not edified
2 Cor 8. 8 to prove by the earnestness of others
Gal 1.19 I saw none of the other apostles
Eph 3. 5 the sons of men in other generations
Phil 2. 4 look . . also to the interests of others
2 Tim 2. 2 men who will be able to teach others
Heb 11.36 Others suffered mocking and scourging
5. *who, which, what:* ὅς HOS [B.3.b.5]
[a]+δέ
2 Cor **2.16**[a]
6. *remaining, left:* λοιπός LOIPOS
Mt 25.11 "Afterward the other maidens came
27.49 the others said, "Wait, let us see
Mk 4.19 "the desire for other things
Lk 8.10 "for others they are in parables
18. 9 trusted in themselves . . and despised others
18.11 " 'I thank thee . . I am not like other men
24.10 and . . other women with them who told
1 Cor 9. 5 to be accompanied . . , as the o. apostles
11.34 About the o. things I will give directions
15.37 a bare kernel . . of some other grain
2 Cor 13. 2 warned . . all the others, and I warn them
1 Th 4.13 that you may not grieve as others do
5. 6 So then let us not sleep, as others do
2 Pet 3.16 twist . . as they do the other scriptures
Rev 8.13 "at the blasts of the other trumpets
7. *anyone, any:* τὶς TIS II
Phil **1.15**
1 Tim **5.24**
IDIOMATICALLY
a. Mt 18.16 "take one or two others along with you παράλαβε μετὰ σοῦ ἔτι ἕνα ἢ δύο [ETI]
b. Mt 24.31 "from one end of heaven to the other ἀπ' ἄκρων οὐρανῶν ἕως [τῶν] ἄκρων αὐτῶν [AKRON]
c. Lk 17.24 "lights up the sky from one side to the other ἐκ τῆς ὑπὸ τὸν οὐρανὸν εἰς τὴν ὑπ' οὐρανὸν λάμπει [OURANOS; B.3.b.2]

OTHER, EACH
1. *one another:* ἀλλήλων ALLĒLŌN
[a]B.1.a.1
Lk 23.12 friends with each other that very day
24.14 talking with each other about all these
24.17 conversation . . with each o. as you walk
24.32 to each other, "Did not our hearts burn?
Acts 7.26 " 'why do you wrong each other?
15.39 they separated from each other
Rom 1.12 [a]encouraged by each other's faith
Gal 5.17 these are opposed to each other
2. *himself:* ἑαυτοῦ HEAUTOU
[a]αὐτοῦ
Lk 23.12 [a]they had been at enmity with each other
Col 3.13 forgiving each other; as the Lord has

OTHER, EVEN THE
OTHER, THE
1. *that:* ἐκεῖνος EKEINOS
Lk 18.14 "this man . . justified rather than the o.
2. *and that one:* κἀκεῖνος KAKEINOS
Mt 23.23 "ought . . , without neglecting the others
Lk 11.42 "ought . . , without neglecting the others
Rom 11.23 even the others, if they do not persist

OTHER, NO
1. *such as this:* τοιοῦτος (neg.) TOIOUTOS
1 Cor 11.16 we recognize no other practice

OTHER SIDE OF, ON THE
OTHER SIDE OF, TO THE
OTHER SIDE, THE
1. *on the other side, beyond:* πέραν PERAN
[a]subst. neut. [b]prep.
Mt 8.18 [a]he gave orders to go over to the other side
8.28 [a]when he came to the other side
14.22 [a]he made the disciples . . go . . to the o. side
16. 5 [a]When the disciples reached the o. side
Mk 4.35 [a]"Let us go across to the other side
5. 1 [a]They came to the other side of the sea
5.21 [a]when Jesus had crossed . . to the other side
6.45 [a]he made his disciples . . go . . to the o. side
8.13 [a]he departed to the other side
Lk 8.22 [a]"Let us go across to the other side
Jn 6. 1 [b]Jesus went to the o. side of the Sea of G.
6.22 [b]who remained on the o. side of the sea
6.25 [b]they found him on the o. side of the sea

OTHER THINGS
1. *besides, except for:* παρεκτός PAREKTOS [B.3.b.2]
2 Cor 11.28 apart from o. things, . . the daily pressure

OTHERS
1. *one another:* ἀλλήλων ALLĒLŌN
Phil 2. 3 in humility count others better

OTHERS, BELONGING TO
1. *foreign:* ἀλλότριος ALLOTRIOS
Acts 7. 6 "aliens in a land belonging to others

OTHERWISE
1. *since, otherwise:* ἐπεί EPEI
Rom 11. 6 o. grace would no longer be grace
11.22 otherwise you too will be cut off
1 Cor 7.14 O., your children would be unclean
14.16 Otherwise, if you bless[w] with the spirit
15.29 O., what do people mean . . being baptized?
Heb 10. 2 Otherwise, would they not have ceased?
2. *differently:* ἑτέρως HETERŌS* [A.4.a]
Phil 3.15 if in anything you are otherwise minded
3. *in order that:* ἵνα (neg.) HINA
Lk 14.29 "Otherwise, when he has laid a foundation

OTHERWISE, TEACH
1. *teach false doctrine:* ἑτεροδιδασκαλέω HETERODIDASKALEŌ
1 Tim 6. 3 If any one teaches otherwise

OUGHT
1. *it is necessary:* χρή (impers.) CHRĒ*
Jas 3.10 My brethren, this ought not to be so
2. *one must:* δεῖ DEI
Mt 23.23 "these you ought to have done

Mt 25.27 " 'you o. to have invested my money
Mk 13.14 "sacrilege set up where it o. not to be
Lk 11.42 "these you ought to have done
12.12 "that very hour what you ought to say
13.14 "six days on which work o. to be done
13.16 "ought not this woman . . be loosed?
18. 1 a parable . . that they o. always to pray
Jn 4.20 "Jerusalem . . where men o. to worship
Acts 19.36 "you o. to be quiet and do nothing rash
24.19 "they ought to be here before you
25.10 "Caesar's tribunal, where I o. to be tried
25.24 "that he ought not to live any longer
26. 9 "convinced that I o. to do many things
Rom 8.26 we do not know how to pray as we o.
12. 3 not . . more highly than he o. to think
1 Cor 8. 2 he does not yet know as he ought
Eph 6.20 I may declare it boldly, as I o. to speak
Col 4. 4 I may make it clear, as I o. to speak
4. 6 know how you ought to answer
1 Th 4. 1 learned from us how you ought to live
2 Th 3. 7 you . . know how you o. to imitate us
1 Tim 3.15 you may know how one o. to behave
2 Tim 2. 6 farmer . . ought to have the first share
2 Pet 3.11 what sort of persons ought you to be

3. *be proper:* καθήκω KATHĒKŌ [A.6.c.3]
Acts 22.22 "For he ought not to live

4. *ought, owe:* ὀφείλω OPHEILŌ
Jn 13.14 "you . . ought to wash one another's feet
19. 7 "by that law he ought to die
Acts 17.29 "o. not to think . . the Deity is like gold
Rom 15. 1 We . . o. to bear with the failings of the weak
15.27 they o. . . to be of service to them
1 Cor 11. 7 a man ought not to cover his head
11.10 That is why a woman o. to have a veil[r]
2 Cor 12.11 I ought to have been commended by you
12.14 children o. not . . lay up for their parents
Heb 5.12 by this time you ought to be teachers
1 Jn 2. 6 he who says he abides in him ought
3.16 and we ought to lay down our lives
4.11 we also ought to love one another
3 Jn . 8 So we ought to support such men

CONTEXTUALLY
1 Cor 5. 2 Ought you not rather to mourn?
Jas 4.15 Instead you o. to say, "If the Lord wills

OUR

1. *himself:* ἑαυτοῦ HEAUTOU
2 Th **3.**9

2. *we:* ἡμεῖς HĒMEIS
Mt **6.**9, 11, 12²; **8.**17; **15.**23; **20.**33; **21.**42; **23.**30; **25.**8; **27.**25
Mk **11.**10; **12.**7, 11, 29
Lk **1.**55, 71, 72, 73, 75, 78, 79; **7.**5; **10.**11; **11.**3, 4; **13.**26; **17.**5; **20.**14; **23.**2; **24.**20, 22, 32
Jn **3.**11; **4.**12, 20; **6.**31; **7.**51; **8.**39, 53; **9.**20; **11.**11, 48; **12.**38
Acts **2.**39; **3.**13; **4.**25; **5.**30; **7.**2, 11, 12, 15, 19, 38, 39, 44, 45²; **13.**17; **15.**10, 25, 26; **16.**20; **17.**20; **19.**27, 37; **20.**21; **21.**5; **22.**14; **24.**[7‡; **26.**6, 7; **27.**10, 20
Rom **1.**4, 7; **3.**5; **4.**1, 12, 24², 25²; **5.**1, 5, 11, 21; **6.**6, 23; **7.**5, 25; **8.**16, 23, 26, 39; **9.**10; **15.**6, 30; **16.**1, 9, 18, 20‡, [24‡
1 Cor **1.**2², 3, 7, 8, 9, 10, 30; **2.**7; **5.**4, 7; **6.**11; **9.**1, 10²; **10.**1, 11; **12.**23, 24; **15.**3, 14, 31, 57
2 Cor **1.**2, 3, 4, 7, 12², 18, 22; **3.**2, [2‡, 5; **4.**3, 6, 10, 11, 16²; **5.**2, 21; **6.**11²; **7.**3, 4, 5, 13, 14; **8.**9, 19, 22, 23, 24; **9.**3; **10.**4, 8, 15
Gal **1.**3, 4²; **2.**4; **3.**24; **4.**6, 26; **6.**14, 18
Eph **1.**2, 3, 14, 17; **2.**3, 14; **3.**11; **5.**20; **6.**24
Phil **1.**2; **3.**20, 21; **4.**20
Col **1.**2, 3, 7, 7‡; **3.**4
1 Th **1.**2, 3², 5; **2.**1, 2, 3, 4, 9, 19², 20; **3.**2, 5, 7, 9, 11², 13²; **5.**9, 23, 28
2 Th **1.**1, 8, 10, 11, 12²; **2.**1², 14², 16²; **3.**6, 18
1 Tim **1.**1², 2, 12, 14; **2.**3; **6.**3, 14
2 Tim **1.**2, 8, 9, 10
Tit **1.**3, 4; **2.**10, 13‡; **3.**4
Phm .1, 2, 3, 6
Heb **3.**1; **4.**15; **6.**20; **7.**14; **9.**[14‡, 24; **12.**29; **13.**20, 23
Jas **2.**1, 21; **3.**6
1 Pet **1.**3; **2.**24
2 Pet **1.**1², 2, 8, 11, 14, 16; **2.**20; **3.**15², 18
1 Jn **1.**1², 4‡, 9²; **2.**2; **3.**19, 20², 21; **4.**10; **5.**4
2 Jn .12
Jude .3, 4², 17, 21, 25²
Rev **1.**5; **4.**11; **5.**10; **6.**10; **7.**3, 10, 12; **11.**15; **12.**10³; **19.**1, 5, 6

3. *our:* ἡμέτερος HĒMETEROS
[a]subst.
Acts [24. 6 "*judged him according to our law*‡
26. 5 "the strictest party of our religion
Rom 15. 4 was written for our instruction
2 Tim 4.15 he strongly opposed our message
Tit 3.14 [a]let our people learn to apply themselves
1 Jn 1. 3 our fellowship is with the Father

OUR HOME

1. *one's own:* ἴδιος (subst. neut. pl.) IDIOS
Lk 18.28 Peter said, "Lo, we have left our homes

OUR OWN

1. *himself:* ἑαυτοῦ HEAUTOU
1 Th 2. 8 ready to share with you . . our own selves
2. *our:* ἡμέτερος HĒMETEROS
Acts 2.11 "we hear them . . in our own tongues
3. *one's own:* ἴδιος IDIOS
Acts 3.12 "as though by our own power or piety
1 Cor 4.12 labor, working with our own hands

OURS

1. *our:* ἡμέτερος (subst.) HĒMETEROS
1 Jn 2. 2 expiation for our sins, and not . . ours only

OURSELVES

1. *himself:* ἑαυτοῦ HEAUTOU
Acts 23.14 "We have strictly bound ourselves
Rom 15. 1 We . . ought to bear . . not to please o.
1 Cor 11.31 But if we judged ourselves truly
2 Cor 1. 9 to make us rely not on ourselves
3. 1 Are we beginning to commend o.?
3. 5 Not that we are competent of ourselves
4. 2 commend ourselves to every . . conscience
4. 5 For what we preach is not ourselves, but . . ourselves as your servants[f]
5.12 We are not commending ourselves
6. 4 we commend ourselves in every way
7. 1 let us cleanse o. from every defilement
10.12 Not that we venture to . . compare o.
10.14 we are not overextending ourselves
1 Jn 1. 8 If we say we have no sin, we deceive o.
2. *we:* ἡμεῖς HĒMEIS
Jas **5.**17

OUT
OUT FROM
OUT OF

1. *from:* ἀπό (+gen.) APO
Lk **5.**2
Acts **1.**9; **13.**50
Heb **11.**34
2. *separately, apart from:* χωρίς CHŌRIS
2 Cor 12. 3 whether in the body or out of the body
3. *because of:* διά (+acc.) DIA
Mt **27.**18
Mk **15.**10
Eph **2.**4
4. *from, out of:* ἐκ (+gen.) EK
Mt **2.**15; **7.**4, 5²; **8.**28; **12.**34, 35²; **13.**41, 52; **15.**11, 18, 19; **21.**16; **27.**53
Mk **1.**10, 25, 26; **5.**2², 8; **6.**54; **7.**15, 20, 21, 26; **9.**7, 25; **12.**44²; **13.**1; **15.**46
Lk **2.**35; **4.**22; **6.**42, 45³; **8.**3; **9.**35; **16.**4; **19.**22; **21.**4²
Jn **1.**46; **2.**15; **4.**30; **7.**38; **8.**59; **10.**28, 29; **12.**17; **13.**1; **15.**19; **17.**6, 15; **20.**2
Acts **7.**10, 40; **8.**39; **12.**17; **13.**17; **15.**14; **19.**16; **22.**18; [**24.**7‡
Rom **9.**21
1 Cor **5.**10
2 Cor **2.**4; **4.**6; **8.**11

Eph **4.**29
Phil **1.**16, 17
2 Th **2.**7
Heb **8.**9; **11.**3
1 Pet **2.**9
2 Pet **3.**5
1 Jn **3.**14
3 Jn .10
Jude .5, 23
Rev **3.**5, 12, 16; **7.**4, 5, 8, 14; **12.**15; **13.**1, 11; **14.**15, 17, 18; **15.**6; **16.**17; **18.**4; **20.**[9†[‡]; **21.**2, 10

5. *except, outside:* ἐκτός (prep.) EKTOS
2 Cor 12. 2 whether in the body or out of the body

6. *in, at, by:* ἐν (+dat.) EN
Eph **5.**21

7. *outside:* ἔξω EXŌ
Mt 5.13 "except to be thrown out and trodden
Mk 1.45 Jesus[g] . . was out in the country
5.10 he begged him . . not to send them out
11. 4 a colt tied at the door out in the open
Jn 11.43 he cried . . , "Lazarus, come out
19. 4 "See, I am bringing him out to you
19.13 he brought Jesus out and sat down
Acts 4.15 commanded them to go . . out of the council
14.19 stoned . . and dragged him out of the city
16.30 brought them out and said, "Men
21.30 they seized Paul and dragged him out
1 Jn 4.18 but perfect love casts out fear
Rev 3.12 " 'never shall he go out of it

8. *outside:* ἔξωθεν EXŌTHEN
Rev 11. 2 "leave that o., for it is given . . to the nations

OUT, GO (*See* GO OUT)

OUT ON

1. *middle, in the middle:* μέσος MESOS [B.1.a.5]
[a]neut. [b]ἐν μέσῳ
Mt [14.24 [a]the boat . . was *out on the sea*‡
Mk 6.47 [b]the boat was out on the sea

OUTCOME

1. *way out:* ἔκβασις EKBASIS
Heb 13. 7 consider the outcome of their life

2. *end, goal:* τέλος TELOS
1 Pet 1. 9 As the o. of your faith you obtain

OUTDO

1. *guide, go before:* προηγέομαι PROĒGEOMAI*
Rom 12.10 outdo one another in showing honor

OUTER

1. *outside:* ἔξω EXŌ
2 Cor 4.16 our outer nature is wasting away

2. *outer:* ἐξώτερος EXŌTEROS*
Mt 8.12 "will be thrown into the outer darkness
22.13 " 'cast him into the outer darkness
25.30 " 'cast the . . servant into the outer darkness

3. *first, foremost:* πρῶτος PRŌTOS
Heb 9. 2 a tent[p] was prepared, the outer one
9. 6 priests go continually into the outer tent[p]
9. 8 as long as the outer tent[p] is still standing

OUTRAGE

1. *insult:* ἐνυβρίζω ENYBRIZŌ*
Heb 10.29 the man who . . outraged the Spirit of grace

OUTRUN

1. *run in advance, outrun:* προτρέχω PROTRECHŌ
[a]+τάχιον A.6.a.4
Jn 20. 4 [a]the other disciple outran Peter

OUTSIDE (*See also* CONTROL, OUTSIDE S.'S; PUT OUTSIDE)

1. *except, outside:* ἐκτός EKTOS
Mt 23.26 "that the outside also may be clean
1 Cor 6.18 Every other sin . . is outside the body

2. *outside:* ἔξω EXŌ
[a]πρὸς τῷ μνημείῳ ἔξω
Mt 12.46 his mother and his brothers stood o.
[12.47 *"your brothers are standing outside*‡
26.69 Peter was sitting outside in the courtyard
Mk 3.31 standing outside they sent to him
3.32 "Your mother and your brothers[l] are o.
4.11 "for those o. everything is in parables
Lk 1.10 praying outside at the hour of incense
8.20 "your brothers are standing outside
13.25 "you will begin to stand outside
Jn 18.16 while Peter stood outside at the door
20.11 [a]Mary stood weeping outside the tomb
Acts 5.34 ordered the men to be put outside
16.13 we went o. the gate to the riverside
21. 5 till we were outside the city
1 Cor 5.13 God judges those outside
Heb 13.11 those animals . . are burned o. the camp
13.12 Jesus also suffered outside the gate
13.13 let us go forth to him o. the camp
Rev 22.15 Outside are the dogs and sorcerers

3. *outside:* ἔξωθεν EXŌTHEN
Mt 23.25 "you cleanse the outside of the cup
Mk 7.15 "there is nothing outside a man
Lk 11.39 "you Pharisees cleanse the outside
11.40 "Did not he who made the o.?
Rev 11. 2 "do not measure the court outside
14.20 wine press was trodden outside the city

OUTSIDE, FROM

1. *outside:* ἔξωθεν EXŌTHEN
Mk 7.18 "whatever goes into a man from outside

OUTSIDE THE LAW

1. *lawless:* ἄνομος ANOMOS
1 Cor 9.21 To those outside the law I became as one outside the law . . that I might win those outside the law

OUTSIDER

1. *outside:* ἔξω (subst.) EXŌ
1 Cor 5.12 what have I to do with judging outsiders?
Col 4. 5 Conduct yourselves . . toward outsiders
1 Th 4.12 command the respect of outsiders

2. *outside:* ἔξωθεν (subst.) EXŌTHEN
1 Tim 3. 7 he must be well thought of by outsiders

3. *private individual, layman:* ἰδιώτης IDIŌTĒS
1 Cor 14.16 how can . . an outsider[x] say the "Amen"?†
14.23 If . . outsiders or unbelievers enter
14.24 if . . an unbeliever or outsider enters

OUTWARD

1. *outside:* ἔξωθεν (attr.) EXŌTHEN
1 Pet 3. 3 Let not yours be the outward adorning

OUTWARDLY

1. *outside:* ἔξωθεν EXŌTHEN
Mt 23.27 "tombs, which o. appear beautiful
23.28 "you also o. appear righteous to men

2. *visible, known:* φανερός (subst.) PHANEROS [B.1.a.1]
Rom 2.28 he is not a real Jew who is one outwardly

OVEN

1. *potter's oven:* κλίβανος KLIBANOS*
Mt 6.30 "grass . . which . . is thrown into the oven
Lk 12.28 "grass which . . is thrown into the oven

OVER

1. *because of:* διά (+acc.) DIA
[a]+gen.
Mt **27.**19
Jn **7.**43
Acts **9.**25[a]

2. *into, to, for:* εἰς (+acc.) EIS
Gal **4.**11

3. *in, at, by:* ἐν (+dat.) EN
Jn **14.**30
Eph **3.**13

4. *above:* ἐπάνω EPANŌ
Mt 2. 9 the star . . came to rest over the place
27.37 over his head they put the charge
Lk 4.39 he stood over her and rebuked the fever
11.44 "men walk over them without knowing it
19.17 " 'you shall have authority over ten cities
19.19 " 'And you are to be over five cities
Rev 20. 3 shut it and sealed it over him

5. *on, at:* ἐπί (+dat.) EPI
[a]+gen. [b]+acc.
Mt 18.13 "I say to you, he rejoices over it more than over the ninety-nine

Mt 24.45 [a]"his master has set over his household
24.47 "he will set him over . . his possessions
25.21 [ba]" 'you have been faithful over a little, I will set you over much
25.23 [ba]" 'you have been faithful over a little, I will set you over much
27.45 [b]there was darkness over all the land[m]
Mk 15.33 [b]there was darkness over the whole land[h]
Lk 1.33 [b]"he will reign over the house of Jacob
2. 8 [b]keeping watch over their flock
4.25 [b]"there came a great famine over all
9. 1 [b]authority over all demons and to cure
10.19 [b]"authority . . over . . power of the enemy
12.14 [b]"who made me a judge . . over you?
12.42 [a]"his master will set over his household
12.44 "he will set him over . . his possessions
15. 7 "more joy in heaven over one sinner who repents than over ninety-nine righteous
15.10 "joy . . over one sinner who repents
18. 7 "Will he delay long over them?
19.14 [b]" 'We do not want this man . . over us
19.27 [b]" 'did not want me to reign over them
19.41 [b]when he . . saw the city he wept over it
23.38 There was also an inscription over him[o]
23.44 [b]there was darkness over the whole land[q]
Acts 7.10 "⟨God⟩ made him governor over Egypt
7.18 [b]"there arose over Egypt another king
7.27 [a]" 'Who made you a ruler . . over us?
8. 2 made great lamentation over him
11.19 persecution that arose over Stephen
11.28 [b]a great famine over all the world
19.13 [b]pronounce . . o. those who had evil spirits
Rom 5.14 [b]death reigned . . even over those
9. 5 [a]God who is over all be blessed
16.19 so that I rejoice over you
2 Cor 3.13 [b]Moses, who put a veil over his face
3.15 [b]to this day . . a veil lies over their minds
Heb [2. 7 [b]"*set him over the works of thy hands*‡
3. 6 [b]Christ was faithful over God's[f] house
10.21 [b]we have a great priest over the house
11.21 [b]bowing . . over the head of his staff
11.38 wandering over deserts and mountains
Jas 5. 7 farmer . . being patient o. it until . . rain
5.14 [b]let them pray over him, anointing
Rev 2.26 [a]" 'I will give him power o. the nations
6. 8 [b]power over a fourth of the earth
9.11 [a]They have as king over them the angel
10. 1 [b]with a rainbow over his head
11. 6 [a]they have power over the waters
11.10 rejoice over them and make merry
13. 7 [b]authority was given it over every tribe
14.18 [a]the angel who has power over fire
16. 9 [b]God who had power over these plagues
17.18 [a]"city which has dominion over the kings
18.20 "Rejoice over her, O heaven!
20. 6 [a]O. such the second death has no power
20. 9 [b]they marched up over the broad earth

6. *over:* ὑπέρ (+gen.) HYPER
[a]+acc.
Eph **1.22**[a]
Heb **13.17**

7. *down from, against:* κατά (+gen.) KATA
Jn 19.11 "You would have no power over me unless

8. *about, concerning:* περί (+gen.) PERI
Jn 3.25 Now a discussion arose . . over purifying

OVER, BE

1. *pass by, transgress:* παρέρχομαι (aor.) PARERCHOMAI
Mt 14.15 "the day is now o.; send the crowds away

2. *set over, direct:* προΐστημι (mid.) PROISTĒMI
1 Th 5.12 those who . . are over you in the Lord

OVER, HAVE

1. *be more, cause to increase:* πλεονάζω PLEONAZŌ
2 Cor 8.15 "who gathered much had nothing over

OVERBEARING

1. *crooked, unjust:* σκολιός SKOLIOS
1 Pet 2.18 be submissive . . also to the overbearing

OVERBOARD (*See* THROW CARGO OVERBOARD)

OVERBOARD, THROW ONESELF

1. *throw oneself down:* ἀπορίπτω APORIPTŌ*
Acts 27.43 ordered . . to throw themselves o. first

OVERCOME

1. *be inferior to, be defeated:* ἡττάομαι HĒTTAOMAI [A.6.c.3]
2 Pet 2.19 whatever overcomes a man

2. *catch:* καταλαμβάνω KATALAMBANŌ
Jn 1. 5 the darkness has not overcome it

3. *conquer, prevail:* νικάω NIKAŌ
Lk 11.22 "when one stronger than he . . overcomes him
Jn 16.33 "be of good cheer, I have o. the world
Rom 12.21 Do not be overcome by evil, but overcome evil with good
1 Jn 2.13 you have overcome the evil one
2.14 you have overcome the evil one
4. 4 Little children, you . . have o. them
5. 4 whatever is born of God overcomes the world; and this . . overcomes the world
5. 5 Who is it that overcomes the world?

OVERCOME, BE

1. *displace, amaze:* ἐξίστημι EXISTĒMI [A.6.a.6]
Mk 5.42 they were . . overcome with amazement

2. *bring down, sink:* καταφέρω (pass.) KATAPHERŌ
Acts 20. 9 being overcome by sleep, he fell down

OVEREXTEND

1. *stretch out beyond:* ὑπερεκτείνω HYPEREKTEINŌ*
2 Cor 10.14 we are not overextending ourselves

OVERFLOW

1. *abound exceedingly:* ὑπερπλεονάζω HYPERPLEONAZŌ*
1 Tim 1.14 grace of our Lord overflowed for me

2. *abound:* περισσεύω PERISSEUŌ
2 Cor 8. 2 their . . joy and . . poverty have overflowed
9.12 this service . . overflows in . . thanksgivings

OVERHEAR

1. *overhear, take no heed of:* παρακούω PARAKOUŌ
Mk [5.36 *overhearing* what they said, Jesus said†

OVERJOYED, BE

1. *be overcome by joy:* ὑπερπερισσεύεσθαι τῇ χαρᾷ CHARA [A.6.a.4]
2 Cor 7. 4 With all our affliction, I am overjoyed

OVERLOOK

1. *forget, neglect:* ἐπιλανθάνομαι EPILANTHANOMAI
Heb 6.10 not so unjust as to overlook your work

2. *look over, disregard:* ὑπερεῖδον HYPEREIDON*
Acts 17.30 "The times of ignorance God overlooked

OVERPOWER

1. *prevail against:* ἰσχύω κατά ISCHYŌ [A.6.a.4]
Acts 19.16 the man . . overpowered them

OVERPOWERED, BE

1. *be inferior to, be defeated:* ἡττάομαι HĒTTAOMAI
2 Pet 2.20 For if . . they are . . overpowered

OVERSEER

1. *overseer, guardian:* ἐπίσκοπος EPISKOPOS
Acts 20.28 "the Holy Spirit has made you overseers[0]
Phil [1. 1 the saints . . at Philippi, with the *overseers*†

OVERSHADOW

1. *overshadow, darken:* ἐπισκιάζω EPISKIAZŌ
Mt 17. 5 a bright cloud overshadowed them
Mk 9. 7 And a cloud overshadowed them
Lk 1.35 "power of the Most High will o. you
9.34 cloud came and overshadowed them

2. *overshadow:* κατασκιάζω KATASKIAZŌ*
Heb 9. 5 cherubim . . overshadowing the mercy seat

OVERSIGHT, EXERCISE

1. *look upon, consider:* ἐπισκοπέω EPISKOPEŌ
1 Pet [5. 2 *exercising the o.*, not by constraint‡

OVERTAKE

1. *catch:* καταλαμβάνω KATALAMBANŌ
Jn 12.35 "lest the darkness overtake you

2. *receive, take:* λαμβάνω LAMBANŌ
1 Cor 10.13 No temptation has overtaken you

3. *take before, go before:* προλαμβάνω PROLAMBANŌ
Gal 6. 1 if a man is overtaken in any trespass

OVERTHROW
1. *put down, destroy:* καταλύω KATALYŌ
Acts 5.39 "you will not be able to overthrow them
2. *make ineffective, hinder:* καταργέω KATARGEŌ
Rom 3.31 Do we . . overthrow the law by this faith?
3. *lay low, kill:* καταστρώννυμι KATASTRŌNNYMI*
1 Cor 10. 5 they were overthrown in the wilderness

OVERTURN
1. *upset:* ἀνατρέπω ANATREPŌ
Jn 2.15 he drove them . . overturned their tables
2. *upset, turn down:* καταστρέφω KATASTREPHŌ
Mt 21.12 drove out all . . and . . overturned the tables
Mk 11.15 and he overturned the tables

OVERWHELM
1. *swallow:* καταπίνω KATAPINŌ
2 Cor 2. 7 he may be overwhelmed by . . sorrow

OWE
1. *ought, owe:* ὀφείλω OPHEILŌ
Mt 18.28 "came upon one . . who owed him a hundred denarii[g] and . . said, 'Pay what you owe
Lk 7.41 "one owed five hundred denarii
16. 5 " 'How much do you owe my master?
16. 7 " 'And how much do you owe?
Rom 13. 8 Owe no one anything, except to love
Phm .18 If he . . owes you anything, charge that
2. *owe besides:* προσοφείλω PROSOPHEILŌ*
Phm .19 your owing me even your own self

OWES, ONE WHO
1. *debtor:* ὀφειλέτης OPHEILETĒS
Mt 18.24 "one . . who owed him ten thousand talents[f]

OWN (*See also, e.g.,* MY OWN; OUR OWN; YOUR OWN)
1. *be:* εἰμί EIMI [A.6.a.5]
Acts 21.11 " 'shall . . bind the man who owns this girdle
IDIOMATICALLY
a. 1 Pet 2.9 But you are . . God's own people[e]† ὑμεῖς δὲ . . λαὸς εἰς περιποίησιν [PERIPOIĒSIS]

OWN ACCORD, OF ITS
1. *acting of one's own will:* αὐτόματος AUTOMATOS
Acts 12.10 It opened to them of its own accord

OWN, ITS

OWN, ONE'S (*See also* MY OWN; OUR OWN; WILL, NOT OF ONE'S OWN; YOUR OWN)
1. *himself:* ἑαυτοῦ HEAUTOU
Mt 8.22 "leave the dead to bury their own dead
Lk 2. 3 And all went . . , each to his own city
2.39 they returned . . to their own city
9.60 "Leave the dead to bury their own dead
11.21 "When a strong man . . guards his own palace
14.26 "If any . . does not hate his own father and mother . . and even his own life
14.27 "Whoever does not bear his own cross
16. 8 "shrewd in dealing with their o. generation
Jn 5.19 "Son can do nothing of his own accord
7.18 "He who speaks on his own authority
11.51 He did not say this of his own accord
16.13 "he will not speak on his own authority
19.17 he went out, bearing his own cross
Acts 7.21 "brought him up as her own son
21.11 he . . bound his own feet and hands
Rom 1.27 receiving in their own persons . . penalty
4.19 when he considered his own body
8. 3 his own Son in . . likeness of sinful flesh
11.25 Lest you be wise in your own conceits
16.18 such . . serve . . their own appetites[z]
1 Cor 6.19 You are not your own
7. 2 each man should have his own wife
10.24 Let no one seek his own good
13. 5 Love does not insist on its own way
Gal 6. 4 But let each one test his own work
6. 8 For he who sows to his own flesh
Eph 5.28 love their wives as their own bodies
5.29 For no man ever hates his own flesh
Phil 2. 4 each . . look not only to his own interests
2.12 work out your own salvation with fear
2.21 They all look after their own interests
1 Th 2. 8 to share with you . . our own selves
2.12 who calls you into his own kingdom
[4. 4 know how *to control his own body*†[o]
2 Th 3.12 we command . . to earn their own living
Heb 5. 3 bound to offer sacrifice for his own sins
6. 6 crucify the Son . . on their own account
Jude . 6 angels . . did not keep their own position
.13 casting up the foam of their own shame
.18 "following their own ungodly passions
2. *one's own:* ἴδιος IDIOS
Mt 9. 1 crossed over and came to his own city
Mk 4.34 to his own disciples he explained
15.20 they . . put his own clothes on him
Lk 6.41 "not notice the log . . in your own eye?
6.44 "each tree is known by its own fruit
10.34 "then he set him on his own beast
Jn 4.44 prophet has no honor in his own country
5.18 he . . also called God his own Father[o]
5.43 "if another comes in his own name
7.18 "He . . seeks his own glory
10. 3 "he calls his own sheep by name
10. 4 "he has brought out all his own
10.12 "hireling . . , whose own the sheep are not
13. 1 loved his own who were in the world
15.19 "the world would love its own
Acts 1. 7 "Father has fixed by his own authority
1.25 "Judas turned . . , to go to his own place
2. 6 each one heard them . . in his own language
2. 8 "each of us in his own native language
3.12 "as though by our own power or piety
4.32 no one said that any . . was his own
13.36 "David . . served . . in his own generation
20.28 "obtained with the blood of his own Son[w]†
25.19 "dispute . . about their own superstition
28.30 two whole years at his own expense[h]
Rom 8.32 He who did not spare his own Son
10. 3 to establish their own . . righteousness
11.24 grafted back into their own olive tree
14. 4 before his own master . . he stands or falls
14. 5 fully convinced in his own mind
1 Cor 4.12 labor, working with our own hands
6.18 the immoral . . sins against his own body
7. 2 woman ⟨should have⟩ her own husband
7. 4 wife does not rule over her own body
7. 4 husband does not rule over his own body
7. 7 each has his own special gift from God
9. 7 serves as a soldier at his o. expense
11.21 each one goes ahead with his own meal
15.23 But each in his own order
15.38 to each kind of seed its own body
Gal 6. 5 each man will have to bear his own load
1 Th 2.14 you suffered . . from your own countrymen
1 Tim 3. 4 He must manage his own household
3. 5 how to manage his own household
5. 4 religious duty to their own family
2 Tim 1. 9 in virtue of his own purpose
4. 3 teachers to suit their own likings
Tit 1.12 One of themselves, a prophet of their own
Heb 7.27 sacrifices daily, first for his own sins
9.12 he entered . . , taking[s] . . his own blood
13.12 to sanctify the people through his o. blood
Jas 1.14 when . . lured and enticed by his o. desire
2 Pet 1. 3 who called us to[b] his own glory
1.20 a matter of one's own interpretation
2.16 rebuked for his own transgression
2.22 The dog turns back to his own vomit
3. 3 scoffing, following their own passions
3.16 the ignorant . . to their o. destruction
3.17 beware lest you . . lose your own stability

OWN, MAKE S. ONE'S
1. *catch:* καταλαμβάνω KATALAMBANŌ
Phil 3.12 but I press on to make it my own because Christ Jesus has made me his own
3.13 not . . that I have made it my own

OWN NATURE, ONE'S
1. *one's own:* ἴδιος (subst. pl.) IDIOS
Jn 8.44 "he speaks according to his own nature

OWN, NOT ONE'S
1. *foreign:* ἀλλότριος ALLOTRIOS
Heb 9.25 enters .. yearly with blood not his own

OWN, OF ONE'S
1. *wealthy, special:* περιούσιος PERIOUSIOS*
Tit 2.14 to purify for himself a people of his own

OWN, ONE'S (*See* OWN, ITS)

OWN PEOPLE, ONE'S
1. *one's own:* ἴδιος (subst. pl.) IDIOS
Jn 1.11 his own people received him not

OWN, WHAT IS ONE'S
1. *my, mine:* ἐμός (subst. neut.) EMOS
Mt 25.27 "received what was my own with interest

OWNER
1. *lord, master:* κύριος KYRIOS
Mt 20. 8 "o. of the vineyard said to his steward
21.40 "When .. owner of the vineyard comes
Mk 12. 9 "What will the o. of the vineyard do?
Lk 19.33 its owners said .. "Why are you untying?
20.13 "o. of the vineyard said, 'What shall I do?
20.15 "What .. will the o. of the vineyard do?
Acts 16.16 slave girl .. brought her owners .. gain
16.19 owners saw .. their hope of gain was gone
Gal 4. 1 no better than a slave, though .. owner

OWNER OF A SHIP
1. *ship owner, captain:* ναύκληρος NAUKLĒROS*
Acts 27.11 paid more attention .. to the o. of the ship

OX
1. *bull, ox, cow:* βοῦς BOUS*
Lk 13.15 "Does not each .. on .. sabbath untie his ox?
14. 5 "an ox that has fallen into a well
14.19 " 'I have bought five yoke of oxen
Jn 2.14 he found those who were selling oxen
2.15 he drove them all, with the .. oxen, out
1 Cor 9. 9 "You shall not muzzle an ox .. treading
9. 9 Is it for oxen that God is concerned?
1 Tim 5.18 "You shall not muzzle an ox .. treading
2. *calf, young bull:* μόσχος MOSCHOS
Rev 4. 7 the second living creature like an ox
3. *bull:* ταῦρος TAUROS
Mt 22. 4 " 'my oxen and my fat calves are killed
Acts 14.13 the priest of Zeus .. brought oxen

P

PAGAN
1. *nation, people, Gentile:* ἔθνος ETHNOS
1 Cor 5. 1 a kind .. not found even among pagans
10.20 what pagans sacrifice they offer to demons

PAID BACK, BE
1. *bring, carry off:* κομίζω (mid.) KOMIZŌ
Col 3.25 the wrongdoer will be paid back

PAIN
1. *touchstone, test, torture:* βάσανος BASANOS
Mt 4.24 those afflicted with various .. pains
2. *grief:* λύπη (sg. or pl.) LYPĒ
2 Cor 2. 3 so that .. I might not suffer pain⁰
1 Pet 2.19 if .. he endures pain .. suffering unjustly
3. *grieve, cause pain:* λυπέω LYPEŌ
2 Cor 2. 2 who .. but the one whom I have pained
4. *work, stress, pain:* πόνος PONOS
Rev 16.11 cursed .. God .. for their pain and sores
21. 4 "neither shall there be .. pain any more

PAIN, CAUSE
1. *grieve, cause pain:* λυπέω LYPEŌ
2 Cor 2. 2 For if I cause you pain
2. 4 I wrote you .., not to cause you pain
2. 5 But if any one has caused pain

PAINFUL
1. *grief:* λύπη LYPĒ
[a]B.1.a.1 [b]gen.
2 Cor 2. 1 [a]not to make you another painful visit
Heb 12.11 [b]For the moment all discipline seems p.

PAINFULLY
1. *question by torture, torment:* βασανίζω (pass. part.) BASANIZŌ
Mk 6.48 they were making headway painfully⁰

PAINS, TAKE
1. *practice, train:* ἀσκέω ASKEŌ*
Acts 24.16 "I .. take pains to have a clear conscience

PAIR
1. *yoke, pair:* ζεῦγος ZEUGOS
Lk 2.24 "a p. of turtledoves, or two .. pigeons

PALACE
1. *court, courtyard:* αὐλή AULĒ
Mt 26. 3 gathered in the palace of the high priest
Mk 15.16 soldiers led him away inside the palace
Lk 11.21 "When a strong man .. guards his own palace

PALE
1. *yellowish green, pale:* χλωρός CHLŌROS
Rev 6. 8 a p. horse, and its rider's name was Death

PALLET
1. *mattress:* κράβαττος KRABATTOS
Mk 2. 4 made an opening, they let down the p.
2. 9 " 'Rise, take up your pallet and walk
2.11 "rise, take up your pallet and go home
2.12 he rose, and .. took up the pallet
6.55 to bring sick people on their pallets
Jn 5. 8 "Rise, take up your pallet, and walk
5. 9 he took up his pallet and walked
5.10 "it is not lawful .. to carry your pallet
5.11 " 'Take up your pallet, and walk
Acts 5.15 they .. laid them on beds and pallets
CONTEXTUALLY
Jn 5.12 "who said to you, 'Take up your pallet'?

PALM BRANCH
1. *date palm tree, palm frond:* φοῖνιξ PHOINIX
Rev 7. 9 in white robes, with palm branches

PALM TREE
1. *date palm tree, palm frond:* φοῖνιξ PHOINIX
Jn 12.13 So they took branches of palm trees

PAMPHYLIA: Παμφυλία pam'fileə II,F-3
Acts 2.10 "Phrygia and Pamphylia, Egypt
13.13 Paul .. came to Perga in Pamphylia
14.24 Then they .. came to Pamphylia
15.38 one who had withdrawn from them in P.
27. 5 the sea which is off Cilicia and P.

PANG
1. *birth pangs, suffering:* ὠδίν ŌDIN
Acts 2.24 "having loosed the pangs of death
2. *pain, distress:* ὀδύνη ODYNĒ
1 Tim 6.10 pierced their hearts with many pangs

PANGS OF BIRTH, IN ONE'S
1. *suffer birth pangs:* ὠδίνω (part. fem.) ŌDINŌ
Rev 12. 2 she cried out in her pangs of birth

PAPER
1. *papyrus:* χάρτης CHARTĒS*
2 Jn .12 I would rather not use paper and ink

PAPHOS: Πάφος 'pā,fäs II,F-4
Acts 13. 6 When they had gone .. as far as Paphos
13.13 Paul and his company set sail from P.

PARABLE
1. *comparison, parable:* παραβολή PARABOLĒ
Mt 13. 3 he told them many things in parables
13.10 "Why do you speak to them in parables?
13.13 "This is why I speak to them in parables
13.18 "Hear then the parable of the sower
13.24 Another parable he put before them
13.31 Another parable he put before them
13.33 He told them another parable

Mt 13.34 All this Jesus said to the crowds in parables; .. he said nothing to them without a p.
13.35 "I will open my mouth in parables
13.36 "Explain to us the parable of the weeds
13.53 when Jesus had finished these parables
15.15 Peter said .. "Explain the p. to us
21.33 "Hear another parable
21.45 When the .. Pharisees heard his parables
22. 1 again Jesus spoke to them in parables
Mk 3.23 "he .. said to them in parables
4. 2 he taught .. many things in parables
4.10 those .. asked .. concerning the parables
4.11 "for those .. everything is in parables
4.13 "Do you not understand this p.? How .. will you understand all the parables?
4.30 "what parable shall we use for it?
4.33 With many such parables he spoke
4.34 he did not speak to them without a p.
7.17 his disciples asked him about the p.
12. 1 he began to speak to them in parables
12.12 he had told the parable against them
Lk 5.36 He told them a parable also
6.39 He also told them a parable
8. 4 he said in a parable
8. 9 disciples asked .. what this parable meant
8.10 "for others they are in parables
8.11 "the parable is this: The seed is the word
12.16 he told them a parable, saying
12.41 "are you telling this parable for us?
13. 6 this parable: "A man had a fig tree
14. 7 he told a p. to those who were invited
15. 3 So he told them this parable
18. 1 he told them a parable, to the effect
18. 9 He also told this parable to some
19.11 he proceeded to tell a parable
20. 9 he began to tell the people this parable
20.19 he had told this parable against them
21.29 he told them a p.: "Look at the fig tree

PARADISE

1. *garden, paradise:* παράδεισος PARADEISOS*
Lk 23.43 "today you will be with me in Paradise
2 Cor 12. 3(4) this man was caught up into Paradise
Rev 2. 7 " 'which is in the paradise of God

PARALYTIC

1. *lame:* παραλυτικός (subst.) PARALYTIKOS
Mt 4.24 they brought him all the sick, .. paralytics
9. 2 behold, they brought to him a paralytic
9. 2 he said to the paralytic, "Take heart
9. 6 he then said to the paralytic—"Rise
Mk 2. 3 they came, bringing to him a paralytic
2. 4 the pallet on which the paralytic lay
2. 5 he said to the paralytic, "My son
2. 9 "Which is easier, to say to the paralytic?
2.10 he said to the paralytic

PARALYZE

1. *undo, disable:* παραλύω PARALYŌ
Lk 5.18 on a bed a man who was paralyzed
5.24 he said to the man who was paralyzed
Acts 8. 7 many who were paralyzed or lame
9.33 man named Aeneas, who .. was paralyzed

PARALYZED

1. *lame:* παραλυτικός PARALYTIKOS
Mt 8. 6 "Lord, my servant is lying paralyzed
2. *withered, dry:* ξηρός XĒROS
Jn 5. 3 invalids, blind, lame, paralyzed[k]

PARCHMENT

1. *parchment:* μεμβράνα MEMBRANA*
2 Tim 4.13 bring .. above all the parchments

PARENT

1. *beget, bear:* γεννάω (subst. part.) GENNAŌ
1 Jn 5. 1 one who loves the p. loves the child
2. *begetter, parent:* γονεύς GONEUS*
Always plural
Mt 10.21 "children will rise against parents
Mk 13.12 "children will rise against parents
Lk 2.27 parents brought in the child Jesus
2.41 his parents went to Jerusalem every year
2.43 His parents did not know it
8.56 And her parents were amazed
18.29 "no man who has left .. brothers or parents
21.16 "You will be delivered up .. by parents
Jn 9. 2 "who sinned, this man or his parents?
9. 3 "not that this man sinned, or his parents
9.18 until they called the parents of the man
9.20 His parents answered, "We know
9.22 parents said this because they feared
9.23 parents said, "He is of age, ask him
Rom 1.30 insolent, haughty, .. disobedient to parents
2 Cor 12.14 for children ought not to lay up for their parents, but parents for their children
Eph 6. 1 obey your parents in the Lord
Col 3.20 Children, obey your parents
2 Tim 3. 2 disobedient to their parents, ungrateful
3. *father:* πατήρ PATĒR
Heb 11.23 hid for three months by his parents
4. *ancestor, parent* (subst.): πρόγονος PROGONOS
1 Tim 5. 4 let them .. make some return to .. parents

PARMENAS: Παρμενᾶς 'pärmənəs
Acts 6. 5 they chose Stephen, .. and Parmenas

PART (*See also* UTTERMOST PARTS)

1. *draw away:* ἀποσπάω (pass.) APOSPAŌ
Acts 21. 1 when we had parted from them
2. *separate, divide:* χωρίζω CHŌRIZŌ
Phm .15 Perhaps this is why he was parted
3. *separate:* διαχωρίζω (pass.) DIACHŌRIZŌ*
Lk 9.33 And as the men were parting from him
4. *divide:* διαμερίζω DIAMERIZŌ
Jn 19.24 "They parted my garments among them
5. *separate:* διΐστημι DIISTĒMI
Lk 24.51 While he blessed them, he parted
6. *part, limb:* μέλος MELOS
1 Cor 12.20 there are many parts, yet one body
12.22 parts of the body which seem .. weaker
7. *part, portion:* μερίς MERIS
Acts 8.21 "You have neither part nor lot
8. *part, share:* μέρος MEROS
Lk 11.36 "having no part dark, it will be .. bright
Jn 13. 8 "If I do not wash you, you have no p.
19.23 took his garments and made four parts
Acts 2.10 "Egypt and the parts of Libya
5. 2 he kept back some .. and brought only a p.
20. 2 When he had gone through these parts
23. 6 one p. .. Sadducees .. the other Pharisees
Rom 11.25 hardening has come upon part of Israel
1 Cor 13.12 I know in p.; then I shall understand
2 Cor 1.14 as you have understood in part
Eph 4. 9 (he had also descended into the lower parts
4.16 when each part is working properly
Rev 16.19 The great city was split into three parts
CONTEXTUALLY
Acts 5. 3 "to keep back part of the proceeds
1 Cor 12.15 would not make it .. less a p. of the body
12.16 would not make it .. less a p. of the body
12.23 those parts .. we think less honorable
12.23 unpresentable parts .. with greater modesty
12.24 more presentable parts do not require
12.24 giving .. greater honor to the inferior p.
2 Cor 8. 2 in a wealth of liberality on their part
Heb 7. 2 to him Abraham apportioned a tenth part

PART OF THE NIGHT

1. *watch, guard, prison:* φυλακή PHYLAKĒ
Mt 24.43 "what p. of the night the thief was coming

PART, TAKE

1. *companion, partner:* κοινωνός KOINŌNOS [A.3.e.1]
Mt 23.30 " 'we would not have taken part with them
2. *take part in, share:* συγκοινωνέω SYGKOINŌNEŌ
Eph 5.11 Take no part in the unfruitful works
Rev 18. 4 "Come out .., lest you take part in .. sins

PART, TAKE S.'S

1. *arrive, stand by:* παραγίνομαι (+dat.) PARAGINOMAI
2 Tim 4.16 no one took my part; all deserted me

PART, TAKING
1. *fellowship, sharing:* κοινωνία KOINŌNIA
2 Cor 8. 4 begging us . . for the favor of taking part
PARTAKE
1. *partake, share:* μεταλαμβάνω METALAMBANŌ
Acts 2.46 they partook of food with glad . . hearts
2. *participate in, share:* μετέχω METECHŌ
1 Cor 10.17 for we all partake of the one bread
10.21 You cannot p. of the table of the Lord
10.30 If I partake with thankfulness
Heb 2.14 he himself . . partook of the same nature
PARTAKER
PARTAKER WITH
1. *companion, partner:* κοινωνός KOINŌNOS
1 Pet 5. 1 witness . . as well as a partaker in the glory
2 Pet 1. 4 become partakers of the divine nature
2. *sharing in:* μέτοχος (subst.) METOCHOS
Heb 6. 4 once . . partakers of the Holy Spirit
3. *partner:* συγκοινωνός SYGKOINŌNOS
Phil 1. 7 for you are all partakers with me
4. *partaking with:* συμμέτοχος (subst.) SYMMETOCHOS
Eph 3. 6 partakers of the promise in Christ Jesus
PARTHIAN: Πάρθος
Acts 2. 9 "Parthians and Medes and Elamites
PARTIALITY
1. *inclination:* πρόσκλισις PROSKLISIS*
1 Tim 5.21 keep these rules . . , doing nothing from p.
2. *respect of persons, partiality:* προσωπολημψία PROSŌPOLĒMPSIA*
[a]pl.
Rom 2.11 For God shows no partiality
Eph 6. 9 there is no partiality with him
Col 3.25 will be paid back . . , and there is no p.
Jas 2. 1 [a]show no partiality as you hold the faith
PARTIALITY, SHOW
1. *show partiality:* προσωπολημπτέω PROSŌPOLĒMPTEŌ*
Jas 2. 9 if you show partiality, you commit sin
2. *respecter of persons:* προσωπολήμπτης PROSŌPOLĒMPTĒS* [B.3.a.1]
Acts 10.34 "I perceive that God shows no partiality
IDIOMATICALLY
a. Lk 20.21 "we know that you . . show no partiality
οἴδαμεν ὅτι . . οὐ λαμβάνεις πρόσωπον [PROSŌPON]
b. Gal 2.6 (God shows no partiality πρόσωπον [ὁ] θεὸς ἀνθρώπου οὐ λαμβάνει [PROSŌPON]
PARTICIPATE
PARTICIPATE IN
1. *share in:* κοινωνέω KOINŌNEŌ
1 Tim 5.22 nor participate in another man's sins
2. *be sharing in:* γίνεσθαι μέτοχος METOCHOS [B.2.d.2]
Heb 12. 8 discipline, in which all have participated
PARTICIPATION
1. *fellowship, sharing:* κοινωνία KOINŌNIA
1 Cor 10.16 participation[q] in the blood of Christ?†
10.16 is it not a participation[q] in the body?†
2 Cor [13.14(13) and *participation in* the Holy Spirit†
Phil 2. 1 So if there is . . any p. in the Spirit
PARTISANSHIP
1. *selfish ambition:* ἐριθεία ERITHEIA
Phil 1.17 proclaim Christ out of p., not sincerely
PARTLY
1. *part, share:* μέρος (acc.) MEROS
[a]+τι
1 Cor 11.18 [a]I hear . . and I partly believe it
PARTNER
1. *companion, partner:* κοινωνός KOINŌNOS
Lk 5.10 sons of Zebedee, . . partners with Simon
1 Cor 10.18 are not those . . partners in the altar?
10.20 not want you to be partners with demons
2 Cor 8.23 Titus, he is my p. and fellow worker
Phm .17 So if you consider me your partner
Heb 10.33 being partners with those so treated
2. *sharing in:* μέτοχος (subst.) METOCHOS
Lk 5. 7 beckoned to their partners . . to come

CONTEXTUALLY
1 Cor 7.15 if the unbelieving p. desires to separate
PARTNERSHIP
1. *fellowship, sharing:* κοινωνία KOINŌNIA
Phil 1. 5 thankful for your partnership
2. *sharing, participation:* μετοχή METOCHĒ*
2 Cor 6.14 what p. have righteousness and iniquity?
PARTNERSHIP WITH, ENTER INTO
1. *share in:* κοινωνέω KOINŌNEŌ
Phil 4.15 no church entered into p. with me
PARTY
1. *sect, opinion:* αἵρεσις HAIRESIS
Acts 5.17 that is, the party of the Sadducees
15. 5 belonged to the p. of the Pharisees
26. 5 "according to . . strictest p. . . a Pharisee
Gal 5.20 selfishness, dissension, party spirit
2. *part, share:* μέρος MEROS
Acts 23. 9 some of the scribes of the Pharisees' p.
CONTEXTUALLY
Acts 11. 2 the circumcision p. criticized him
Gal 2.12 separated . . , fearing the circumcision p.
Tit 1.10 especially the circumcision party
PASCHAL LAMB
1. *Passover, paschal lamb:* πάσχα PASCHA
1 Cor 5. 7 Christ, our p. lamb, has been sacrificed
PASS (*See also* COME TO PASS; JUDGMENT, PASS)
1. *go away:* ἀπέρχομαι APERCHOMAI
Rev 9.12 The first woe has passed
11.14 The second woe has passed
2. *make room for, hold, go:* χωρέω CHŌREŌ
Mt 15.17 "whatever goes into the mouth passes
3. *stride, go through:* διαβαίνω DIABAINŌ
Lk 16.26 " 'that those who would pass from here
4. *go through, elapse:* διαγίνομαι DIAGINOMAI
Mk 16. 1 when the sabbath was past
Acts 25.13 Now when some days had passed
5. *go through:* διαπορεύομαι DIAPOREUOMAI
Rom 15.24 I hope to see you in passing
6. *pass through:* διέρχομαι DIERCHOMAI
Lk 19. 4 ran . . to see him, for he was to p. that way
Acts 12.10 When they had passed the first . . guard
7. *come, go:* ἔρχομαι ERCHOMAI
Mt 15.29 Jesus . . passed along the Sea of Galilee
8. *be above:* ὑπερέχω HYPERECHŌ
Phil 4. 7 peace of God . . passes all understanding
9. *pass over:* μεταβαίνω METABAINŌ
Jn 5.24 "he . . has passed from death to life
1 Jn 3.14 we have passed out of death into life
10. *pass by:* παραπορεύομαι PARAPOREUOMAI
Mk 9.30 from there and passed through Galilee
11. *pass by, transgress:* παρέρχομαι PARERCHOMAI
Mt 5.18 "not an iota . . will pass from the law
8.28 so fierce that no one could pass that way
26.39 "let this cup pass from me
26.42 "if this cannot pass unless I drink it
Mk 14.35 that . . the hour might pass from him
12. *fill full, complete:* πληρόω (pass.) PLĒROŌ
Acts 7.30 "Now when forty years had passed
9.23 When many days had passed
PASS ALONG
1. *pass through:* διέρχομαι DIERCHOMAI
Lk 17.11 passing along between Samaria and Galilee
Acts 17.23 "For as I passed along, and observed
2. *pass by:* παράγω PARAGŌ
Mk 1.16 And passing along by the Sea of Galilee
PASS AWAY
1. *go away:* ἀπέρχομαι APERCHOMAI
Rev 21. 1 for the first heaven . . had passed away
21. 4 "the former things have passed away
2. *make ineffective, hinder:* καταργέω (pass.) KATARGEŌ
1 Cor 13. 8 as for prophecies, they will pass away; . . as for knowledge, it will pass away
13.10 the imperfect will pass away
3. *pass by:* παράγω (act. or pass.) PARAGŌ
1 Cor 7.31 the form of this world is passing away

1 Jn 2. 8 because[b] the darkness is passing away
2.17 the world passes away, and the lust of it
4. *pass by, transgress:* παρέρχομαι PARERCHOMAI
Mt 5.18 "till heaven and earth pass away
24.34 "this generation will not pass away till
24.35 "Heaven and earth will pass away, but my words will not pass away
Mk 13.30 "this generation will not p. away before
13.31 "Heaven and earth will pass away, but my words will not pass away
Lk 16.17 "easier for heaven and earth to pass away
21.32 "this generation will not pass away till
21.33 "Heaven and earth will pass away, but my words will not pass away
2 Cor 5.17 the old has passed away, behold, the new
Jas 1.10 like . . flower of . . grass he will pass away
2 Pet 3.10 then the heavens will pass away

PASS AWAY, BE DOOMED TO
1. *make ineffective, hinder:* καταργέω (pass.) KATARGEŌ
1 Cor 2. 6 rulers . . who are doomed to pass away

PASS BY
1. *pass by:* παράγω PARAGŌ
Mt 20.30 they heard that Jesus was passing by
Jn 9. 1 As he passed by, he saw a man blind
2. *pass by:* παραπορεύομαι PARAPOREUOMAI
Mt 27.39 those who passed by derided him
Mk 11.20 As they passed by in the morning
15.29 those who passed by derided him
3. *pass by, transgress:* παρέρχομαι PARERCHOMAI
Mk 6.48 He meant to pass by them
Lk 18.37 "Jesus of Nazareth is passing by
Acts 16. 8 passing by Mysia, they went . . to Troas

PASS BY ON THE OTHER SIDE
1. *pass by on the opposite side:* ἀντιπαρέρχομαι ANTIPARERCHOMAI*
Lk 10.31 "a priest . . passed by on the other side
10.32 "a Levite . . passed by on the other side

PASS ON
1. *pass through:* διέρχομαι DIERCHOMAI
Acts 8.40 passing on he preached the gospel to all
13.14 they passed on from Perga . . to Antioch
2. *throw out:* ἐκβάλλω EKBALLŌ
Mt 15.17 "into the stomach, and so passes on[q]†
3. *go out:* ἐκπορεύομαι EKPOREUOMAI
Mk 7.19 "enters . . his stomach, and so passes on[b]†
4. *pass by:* παράγω PARAGŌ
Mt 9. 9 As Jesus passed on from there
9.27 as Jesus passed on from there
Mk 2.14 as he passed on, he saw Levi

PASS ON THROUGH
1. *go before, go forward:* προέρχομαι PROERCHOMAI
Acts 12.10 they . . passed on through one street

PASS ONE'S DAYS
1. *draw through, live:* διάγω DIAGŌ
Tit 3. 3 passing our days in malice and envy

PASS OVER
1. *letting go, passing over:* πάρεσις PARESIS* [B.1.a.2]
Rom 3.25 he had passed over former sins

PASS THROUGH
1. *pass through:* διέρχομαι DIERCHOMAI
Mt 12.43 "he passes through waterless places
Lk 4.30 passing through the midst of them
11.24 "he passes through waterless places
19. 1 He entered . . and was passing through
Jn 4. 4 He had to pass through Samaria
Acts 14.24 Then they passed through Pisidia
15. 3 they passed through . . Phoenicia
19. 1 Paul passed through the upper country
19.21 resolved . . to pass through Macedonia
1 Cor 10. 1 our fathers . . all passed through the sea
16. 5 I will visit you after passing through Macedonia, for I intend to pass through
Heb 4.14 who has passed through the heavens
2. *travel through:* διοδεύω DIODEUŌ
Acts 17. 1 when they had passed through Amphipolis

PASSAGE
1. *content:* περιοχή PERIOCHĒ*
Acts 8.32 the p. of the scripture . . he was reading
CONTEXTUALLY
Mk 12.26 "book of Moses, in the p. about the bush

PASSER-BY
1. *pass by:* παράγω (subst. part.) PARAGŌ
Mk 15.21 they compelled a p., Simon of Cyrene

PASSING
1. *passage, passing by:* πάροδος PARODOS*
1 Cor 16. 7 I do not want to see you . . in passing

PASSION
1. *desire, yearning:* ἐπιθυμία EPITHYMIA
Rom 6.12 Let not sin . . make you obey . . passions
Eph 2. 3 we all once lived in the passions
2 Tim 2.22 shun youthful passions . . aim at . . faith
Tit 2.12 training us to renounce . . passions
3. 3 led astray, slaves to various passions
1 Pet 1.14 do not be conformed to the passions
2.11 abstain from the passions of the flesh
4. 2 live . . no longer by human passions
4. 3 living in licentiousness, passions
2 Pet 1. 4 corruption . . in the world because of p.
2.10 who indulge in . . defiling passion
2.18 they entice with licentious passions
3. 3 scoffing, following their own passions
Jude .16 malcontents, following their own passions
.18 "following their own ungodly passions
2. *pleasure, enjoyment:* ἡδονή HĒDONĒ
Jas 4. 1 Is it not your passions that are at war?
4. 3 You ask . . to spend it on your passions
3. *desire:* ὄρεξις OREXIS*
Rom 1.27 consumed with passion for one another
4. *suffer, experience:* πάσχω (art. inf.) PASCHŌ
Acts 1. 3 he presented himself alive after his p.
5. *experience, passion:* πάθος PATHOS*
Rom 1.26 gave them up to dishonorable passions
Col 3. 5 Put to death therefore . . impurity, p.
1 Th 4. 5 not in the passion of lust like heathen
6. *strong feeling, wrath:* θυμός THYMOS
Rev 14. 8 "made . . nations drink . . of her impure p.
18. 3 "nations have drunk[k] . . of her impure p.
IDIOMATICALLY
a. 1 Cor 7.36 if his passions are strong ἐὰν ᾖ ὑπέρακμος [HYPERAKMOS*]

PASSIONS
1. *suffering, misfortune:* πάθημα (pl.) PATHĒMA
Rom 7. 5 sinful passions, aroused by the law
Gal 5.24 have crucified the flesh with its passions

PASSOVER
1. *Passover, paschal lamb:* πάσχα PASCHA
Mt 26. 2 "after two days the P. is coming
26.17 "Where . . have us prepare for . . the p.?
26.18 " 'I will keep the passover at your house
26.19 disciples . . prepared the passover
Mk 14. 1 It was now two days before the P.
14.12 when they sacrificed the passover lamb
14.12 "Where will you have us . . prepare . . the p.?
14.14 " 'room, where I am to eat the passover
14.16 the disciples . . prepared the passover
Lk 2.41 every year at the feast of the Passover
22. 1 the feast . . which is called the Passover
22. 7 on which . . p. lamb had to be sacrificed
22. 8 "Go and prepare the passover for us
22.11 " 'where I am to eat the p. with . . disciples
22.13 and they prepared the passover
22.15 "I have . . desired to eat this p. with you
Jn 2.13 The Passover of the Jews was at hand
2.23 when he was in Jerusalem at the P. feast
6. 4 P., the feast of the Jews, was at hand
11.55 Now the P. of the Jews was at hand, and many went . . before the P., to purify
12. 1 before the P., Jesus came to Bethany
13. 1 Now before the feast of the Passover
18.28 not be defiled, but might eat the passover

Jn 18.39 "custom that I . . release one man . . at the P.
19.14 it was the day of Preparation of the P.
Acts 12. 4 intending after the P. to bring him out
Heb 11.28 By faith he kept the Passover

PAST (*See also* TIME PAST, FOR SOME)
1. *more than, by:* παρά (+acc.) PARA
Heb 11.11 Sarah . . when she was past the age
2. *pass by, transgress:* παρέρχομαι (perf. part. attr.) PARERCHOMAI
1 Pet 4. 3 Let the time that is past suffice
3. *be gone:* παροίχομαι (perf. pass. part.) PAROICHOMAI*
Acts 14.16 In past generations he allowed all

PAST, BE
1. *come to be, happen, be:* γίνομαι (perf.) GINOMAI
2 Tim 2.18 holding that the resurrection is past

PASTOR
1. *shepherd:* ποιμήν POIMĒN
Eph 4.11 his gifts were that some . . be . . pastors

PASTURE
1. *pasturage:* νομή NOMĒ
Jn 10. 9 "he will . . go in and out and find pasture

PATARA: Πάταρα 'patərə II,E-3
Acts 21. 1 next day to Rhodes, and from there to P.[x]

PATCH
1. *fullness:* πλήρωμα PLĒRŌMA
Mt 9.16 "patch tears away from the garment
Mk 2.21 "if he does, the patch tears away

PATH
1. *way, road:* ὁδός HODOS
Mt 13. 4 "as he sowed, some seeds fell along the p.
13.19 "this is what was sown along the path
Mk 4. 4 "as he sowed, some seed fell along the p.
4.15 "these are the ones along the path
Lk 8. 5 "as he sowed, some fell along the path
8.12 "ones along the p. are those who . . heard
Acts 13.10 "stop making crooked the straight paths
Rom 3.16 "in their paths are ruin and misery
2. *worn track, path:* τρίβος TRIBOS*
Mt 3. 3 "Prepare . . way . . , make his paths straight
Mk 1. 3 "Prepare . . way . . , make his paths straight
Lk 3. 4 "Prepare . . way . . , make his paths straight
3. *wheel track, path:* τροχιά TROCHIA*
Heb 12.13 make straight paths for your feet

PATIENCE
1. *endurance:* ὑπομονή HYPOMONĒ
Lk 8.15 "bring forth fruit with patience
Rom 2. 7 who by p. in well-doing seek for glory
8.25 if we hope . . , we wait . . with patience
2 Cor 12.12 signs . . were performed . . in all patience
2. *patience, forbearance:* μακροθυμία MAKROTHYMIA
Rom 2. 4 his kindness and forbearance and p.
9.22 What if God . . has endured with much p.?
Gal 5.22 fruit of the Spirit is love, joy, peace, p.
Eph 4. 2 with all lowliness and meekness, with p.
Col 1.11 for all endurance and p. with joy
3.12 Put on then, . . kindness, lowliness, . . and p.
1 Tim 1.16 Jesus Christ might display his perfect p.
2 Tim 3.10 you . . observed . . my faith, my patience
4. 2 exhort, be unfailing in patience
Heb 6.12 imitators of those who through . . patience
Jas 5.10 an example of suffering and patience
1 Pet 3.20 did not obey, when God's patience waited

PATIENCE, HAVE
1. *be patient, persevere:* μακροθυμέω MAKROTHYMEŌ
Mt 18.26 "imploring him, 'Lord, have patience
18.29 " 'Have patience with me, and I will pay

PATIENT (*See* ENDURANCE, PATIENT)

PATIENT, BE
1. *be patient under, stand firm:* ὑπομένω HYPOMENŌ
Rom 12.12 Rejoice in your hope, be p. in tribulation
2. *be patient, persevere:* μακροθυμέω MAKROTHYMEŌ
1 Cor 13. 4 Love is patient and kind
1 Th 5.14 we exhort you, . . be p. with them all
Jas 5. 7 Be patient . . until the coming of the Lord. Behold, the farmer waits . . , being patient
5. 8 You also be patient

PATIENTLY
1. *patiently:* μακροθύμως MAKROTHYMŌS*
Acts 26. 3 "therefore I beg you to listen to me p.

PATIENTLY ENDURE
1. *endurance:* ὑπομονή HYPOMONĒ
[a]B.1.a.2 [b]B.3.a.5
2 Cor 1. 6 [a]when you patiently e. the same sufferings
Rev 2. 3 [b]" 'I know you are enduring patiently
2. *be patient, persevere:* μακροθυμέω MAKROTHYMEŌ
Heb 6.15 Abraham,[m] having patiently endured

PATIENTLY, TAKE S.
1. *be patient under, stand firm:* ὑπομένω HYPOMENŌ
1 Pet 2.20 when . . beaten for it you take it p.
2.20 when you do right . . you take it p.

PATMOS: Πάτμος 'patməs II,E-3
Rev 1. 9 I John . . was on the island called P.

PATRIARCH
1. *father:* πατήρ PATĒR
Rom 9. 5 to them belong the patriarchs
15. 8 the promises given to the patriarchs
2. *father of a nation:* πατριάρχης PATRIARCHĒS*
Acts 2.29 "say to you confidently of the p. David
7. 8 "Jacob ⟨father⟩ of the twelve patriarchs
7. 9 "And the patriarchs, jealous of Joseph
Heb 7. 4 Abraham the patriarch gave him a tithe

PATROBAS: Πατροβᾶς 'patrəbəs
Rom 16.14 Greet . . Phlegon, Hermes, Patrobas

PATTERN
1. *model, pattern:* ὑποτύπωσις HYPOTYPŌSIS
2 Tim 1.13 Follow the pattern of the sound words
2. *pattern, image:* τύπος TYPOS
Acts 7.44 "to make it, according to the pattern
Heb 8. 5 "make everything according to the p.

PAUL: Παῦλος 'pôl (*See also* SERGIUS PAULUS)
Acts 13. 9 Saul, who is also called Paul
13.13 Now Paul . . set sail from Paphos
13.16 Paul stood up, . . said: "Men of Israel
13.43 converts to Judaism followed Paul
13.45 contradicted what was spoken by P.
13.46 Paul and Barnabas spoke out boldly
13.50 Jews . . stirred up persecution against P.
14. 9 He listened to Paul speaking
14.11 when the crowds saw what P. had done
14.12 P. . . they called Hermes
14.14 Barnabas and Paul . . tore their garments
14.19 stoned P. and dragged him out of the city
15. 2 when P. and Barnabas had . . debate with them, P. and Barnabas . . were appointed
15.12 to Barnabas and P. as they related
15.22 send them to Antioch with Paul
15.25 "send . . with our beloved Barnabas and P.
15.35 P. and Barnabas remained in Antioch
15.36 P. said to Barnabas . . "let us return
15.38 P. thought best not to take with them
15.40 Paul chose Silas and departed
16. 3 P. wanted Timothy to accompany him
16. 9 a vision appeared to Paul in the night
16.14 to give heed to what was said by Paul
16.17 She followed Paul and us, crying
16.18 P. was annoyed, and . . said . . "come out
16.19 seized P. and Silas and dragged them
16.25 midnight Paul and Silas were praying
16.28 But Paul cried . . "Do not harm yourself
16.29 with fear he fell down before P. and Silas
16.36 the jailer reported the words to Paul
16.37 P. said . . , "They have beaten us publicly
17. 2 Paul went in, as was his custom
17. 4 some . . were persuaded, and joined P.
17.10 The brethren . . sent P. and Silas away
17.13 word . . was proclaimed by P. at Beroea

Acts 17.14 brethren immediately sent Paul off
17.15 Those who conducted P. brought him
17.16 while P. was waiting for them at Athens
17.22 P., standing in . . the Areopagus
17.33 So Paul went out from among them
18. 5 Paul was occupied with preaching
18. 9 Lord said to Paul . . "Do not be afraid
18.12 Jews made a united attack upon Paul
18.14 when P. was about to open his mouth
18.18 After this P. stayed many days longer
19. 1 Paul passed through the upper country
19. 4 P. said, "John baptized with . . baptism
19. 6 when P. had laid his hands upon them
19.11 God did extraordinary miracles by . . P.
19.13 "I adjure you by the Jesus . . P. preaches
19.15 "Jesus I know, and Paul I know
19.21 P. resolved . . to pass through Macedonia
19.26 "P. . . persuaded . . a considerable company
19.29 Macedonians . . were Paul's companions
19.30 Paul wished to go in among the crowd
20. 1 P. sent for . . disciples and . . took leave
20. 7 P. talked with them, intending to depart
20. 9 sank into . . sleep as P. talked still longer
20.10 Paul went down and bent over him
20.13 intending to take Paul aboard there
20.16 Paul had decided to sail past Ephesus
20.37 they all wept and embraced Paul
21. 4 Through . . Spirit they told P. not to go
21.11 coming to us he took Paul's girdle
21.13 Paul answered, "What are you doing?
21.18 Paul went in with us to James
21.26 P. took the men, and . . purified himself
21.29 supposed that Paul had brought him
21.30 they seized Paul and dragged him out
21.32 when they saw . . , they stopped beating P.
21.37 As P. was about to be brought
21.39 Paul replied, "I am a Jew
21.40 Paul, standing on the steps, motioned
22.25 P. said . . "Is it lawful for you to scourge?
22.28 Paul said, "But I was born a citizen
22.30 brought P. . . and set him before them
23. 1 P., looking intently at the council
23. 3 Paul said to him, "God shall strike you!
23. 5 Paul said, "I did not know, brethren
23. 6 P. perceived that . . part were Sadducees
23.10 afraid that P. would be torn in pieces
23.12 by an oath . . till they had killed P.
23.14 "by an oath . . till we have killed P.
23.16 son of Paul's sister heard of their ambush; so he . . entered the barracks and told P.
23.17 Paul called one of the centurions
23.18 "P. the prisoner . . asked me to bring this
23.20 "Jews . . agreed to ask you to bring P. down
23.24 "Also provide mounts for Paul to ride
23.31 soldiers . . took P. . . by night to Antipatris
23.33 they presented Paul also before him
24. 1 laid before the governor . . case against P.
24.10 when the governor . . motioned . . , P. replied
24.24 he sent for P. and heard him speak
24.26 hoped that money would be given . . by P.
24.27 to do . . a favor, Felix left Paul in prison
25. 2 chief priests . . informed him against P.
25. 4 Paul was being kept at Caesarea
25. 6 he . . ordered Paul to be brought
25. 8 Paul said in his defense
25. 9 Festus, . . to do the Jews a favor, said to P.
25.10 P. said . . "before Caesar's tribunal
25.14 Festus laid Paul's case before the king
25.19 "Jesus, . . whom P. asserted to be alive
25.21 "P. . . appealed to be kept in custody
25.23 by command of Festus P. was brought in
26. 1 Agrippa said to P., "You have permission to speak . ." Then Paul . . made his defense
26.24 Festus said . . "Paul, you are mad
26.25 P. said, "I am not mad, most excellent F.
26.28 Agrippa said to Paul, "In a short time
26.29 P. said, "Whether short or long, I would

Acts 27. 1 delivered Paul . . to a centurion . . Julius
27. 3 Julius treated P. . . kindly, and gave . . leave
27. 9 As . . voyage was . . dangerous . . , P. advised
27.11 more attention to . . the owner . . than to . . P.
27.21 Paul then came forward among them
27.24 "he said, 'Do not be afraid, Paul
27.31 P. said to the centurion and . . soldiers
27.33 P. urged them all to take some food
27.43 the centurion, wishing to save Paul
28. 3 Paul had gathered a bundle of sticks
28. 8 Paul visited him and prayed
28.15 On seeing them Paul thanked God
28.16 Paul was allowed to stay by himself
28.25 departed, after P. . . made one statement
Rom 1. 1 Paul, a servant[a] of Jesus Christ
1 Cor 1. 1 Paul, called by the will of God
1.12 one of you says, "I belong to Paul
1.13 Was Paul crucified for you? Or were you baptized in the name of Paul?
3. 4 when one says, "I belong to Paul
3. 5 What then is Apollos? What is Paul?
3.22 whether Paul or Apollos or Cephas
16.21 I, P., write this greeting with my own hand
2 Cor 1. 1 Paul, an apostle of Christ Jesus
10. 1 I, Paul, myself entreat you
Gal 1. 1 P. an apostle—not from men nor through man
5. 2 I, P., say . . that if you receive circumcision
Eph 1. 1 Paul, an apostle of Christ Jesus
3. 1 For this reason I, Paul, a prisoner
Phil 1. 1 P. and Timothy, servants[a] of Christ
Col 1. 1 Paul, an apostle of Christ Jesus
1.23 of which I, Paul, became a minister
4.18 I, P., write this greeting with my own hand
1 Th 1. 1 P., Silvanus, and Timothy, To the church
2.18 we wanted to come . . I, Paul, again
2 Th 1. 1 P., Silvanus, and Timothy, To the church
3.17 I, P., write this greeting with my own hand
1 Tim 1. 1 Paul, an apostle of Christ Jesus
2 Tim 1. 1 Paul, an apostle of Christ Jesus
Tit 1. 1 Paul, a servant[a] of God and an apostle
Phm . 1 Paul, a prisoner for Christ Jesus
. 9 I, P., an ambassador[a] and now a prisoner
.19 I, Paul, write this with my own hand
2 Pet 3.15 So . . our beloved brother P. wrote to you
CONTEXTUALLY
Acts 18. 8 many . . Corinthians hearing P. believed
20.11 when P. had gone up and had broken bread
22.29 realized that P. was a Roman citizen

PAULUS (*See* SERGIUS PAULUS)

PAVEMENT
1. *paved with stones:* λιθόστρωτος (subst.) LITHOSTRŌTOS*
Jn 19.13 sat down . . at a place called The Pavement

PAY (*See also* ATTENTION, PAY; ATTENTION TO, PAY; HEED, PAY NO; TITHES, PAY)
1. *give up, return:* ἀποδίδωμι APODIDŌMI
Mt 5.26 "never . . till you have paid the last penny
18.25 "as he could not pay, his lord ordered
18.26 " 'Lord, have patience . . , and I will pay
18.28 "same servant . . said, 'Pay what you owe
18.29 " 'Have patience . . and I will pay you
18.30 "He . . put him in prison till he should pay
18.34 "to the jailers,[h] till he should pay
20. 8 " 'Call the laborers and pay them
Lk 7.42 "When they could not pay, he forgave
12.59 "you will never get out till you have paid
Rom 13. 7 Pay all of them their dues, taxes
2. *give, offer:* δίδωμι DIDŌMI
Mt 22.17 "Is it lawful to pay taxes to Caesar?
Mk 12.14 "Is it lawful to pay taxes to Caesar?
12.15 Should we pay them, or should we not?
3. *stand, set:* ἵστημι HISTĒMI
Mt 26.15 they paid him thirty pieces of silver
4. *finish, fulfill:* τελέω TELEŌ
Mt 17.24 "Does not your teacher pay the tax?
Rom 13. 6 For the same reason you also pay taxes

PAY EXPENSES
IDIOMATICALLY
a. Acts 21.24 "pay their expenses δαπάνησον ἐπ' αὐτοῖς [DAPANAŌ]

PAY, WITHOUT
1. *freely, as a gift:* δωρεάν DŌREAN
Mt 10. 8 "raise the dead, . . give without pay

PAYING, WITHOUT
PAYMENT, WITHOUT
1. *freely, as a gift:* δωρεάν DŌREAN
Mt 10. 8 "You received without paying, give[0]
2 Th 3. 8 did not eat . . bread without paying
Rev 21. 6 "I will give . . water . . without payment[0]

PAYMENT (*See* RECEIVE PAYMENT)

PAYMENT, MAKE
1. *give up, return:* ἀποδίδωμι APODIDŌMI
Mt 18.25 "his lord ordered . . payment to be made

PEACE
1. *peace:* εἰρήνη EIRĒNĒ
Mt 10.13 "if . . worthy, let your p. come upon it; but if it is not . . , let your p. return to you
10.34 "not . . come to bring peace on earth; I have not come to bring p., but a sword
Mk 5.34 "go in p., and be healed of your disease
Lk 1.79 "guide our feet into the way of peace
2.14 "p. among men with whom he is pleased![g]
2.29 "now lettest thou thy servant depart in p.
7.50 he said to the woman . . "go in peace
8.48 he said to her, "Daughter, . . go in peace
10. 5 "first say, 'Peace be to this house!
10. 6 "if a son of peace is there, your peace shall rest upon him
11.21 "a . . man . . guards . . , his goods are in p.
12.51 "Do you think that I have come to give p.?
14.32 "he sends an embassy and asks terms of p.
19.38 "P. in heaven and glory in the highest!
19.42 "the things that make for peace!
[24.36 Jesus . . *said to them, "Peace to you!*‡
Jn 14.27 "Peace I leave with you; my peace I give to you; not as the world gives
16.33 "I have said this . . that . . you may have p.
20.19 Jesus . . said . . "Peace be with you
20.21 Jesus said . . again, "Peace be with you
20.26 Jesus came . . and said, "Peace be with you
Acts 9.31 church throughout all Judea . . had peace
10.36 "good news of peace by Jesus Christ
12.20 people of Tyre and Sidon . . asked for peace
15.33 sent off in peace by the brethren
16.36 "therefore come out and go in peace
24. 2 "Since through you we enjoy much peace
Rom 1. 7 Grace to you and peace from God
2.10 peace for every one who does good
3.17 "the way of peace they do not know
5. 1 justified by faith, we[f] have peace
8. 6 to set the mind on the Spirit is . . peace
14.17 the kingdom of God is . . peace and joy
14.19 Let us then pursue what makes for p.
15.13 God of hope fill you with all joy and p.
15.33 The God of peace be with you all
16.20 the God of p. will soon crush Satan
1 Cor 1. 3 Grace to you and peace from God
7.15 For God has called us[l] to peace
14.33 God is not a God of confusion but of p.
16.11 Speed him on his way in peace
2 Cor 1. 2 Grace to you and peace from God
13.11 God of love and peace will be with you
Gal 1. 3 Grace to you and peace from God
5.22 fruit of the Spirit is love, joy, peace
6.16 Peace . . be upon all who walk by this rule
Eph 1. 2 Grace to you and peace from God
2.14 he is our peace, who has made us both one
2.15 one new man in place of . . two, . . making p.
2.17 he came and preached peace to you . . far off and peace to those who were near
4. 3 unity of the Spirit in the bond of peace
Eph 6.15 the equipment of the gospel of peace
6.23 Peace be to the brethren, and love
Phil 1. 2 Grace to you and peace from God
4. 7 p. of God, which passes . . understanding
4. 9 the God of peace will be with you
Col 1. 2 Grace to you and peace from God
3.15 the peace of Christ rule in your hearts
1 Th 1. 1 Grace to you and peace
5. 3 When people say, "There is peace
5.23 the God of p. . . sanctify you wholly
2 Th 1. 2 Grace to you and peace from God
3.16 Now may the Lord of peace himself give you peace at all times
1 Tim 1. 2 Grace, mercy, and peace from God
2 Tim 1. 2 Grace, mercy, and peace from God
2.22 aim at righteousness, faith, love, and p.
Tit 1. 4 Grace and peace from God the Father
Phm . 3 Grace to you and peace from God
Heb 7. 2 also king of Salem, that is, king of p.
12.14 Strive for peace with all men
13.20 God of p. who brought again . . our Lord
Jas 2.16 "Go in peace, be warmed and filled
3.18 the harvest of righteousness is sown in peace by those who make peace
1 Pet 1. 2 grace and peace be multiplied to you
3.11 "let him seek peace and pursue it
5.14 Peace to all of you that are in Christ
2 Pet 1. 2 grace and peace be multiplied to you
3.14 be zealous to be found by him . . at peace
2 Jn . 3 Grace, mercy, and peace will be with us
3 Jn .15 Peace be to you. The friends greet you
Jude . 2 mercy, p., and love be multiplied to you
Rev 1. 4 Grace to you and peace from him
6. 4 its rider was permitted to take peace
2. *be still:* σιωπάω (imper.) SIŌPAŌ
Mk 4.39 he . . said to the sea, "Peace! Be still!

PEACE, BE AT
PEACE, LIVE IN
1. *keep peace:* εἰρηνεύω EIRĒNEUŌ
Mk 9.50 "be at peace with one another
2 Cor 13.11 agree with one another, live in peace
1 Th 5.13 Be at peace among yourselves

PEACE, MAKE
1. *make peace:* εἰρηνοποιέω EIRĒNOPOIEŌ*
Col 1.20 making peace by the blood of his cross

PEACEABLE
1. *peaceful:* εἰρηνικός EIRĒNIKOS
Jas 3.17 wisdom from above is first pure, then p.
2. *quiet:* ἡσύχιος HĒSYCHIOS
1 Tim 2. 2 that we may lead a quiet and p. life

PEACEABLY, LIVE
1. *keep peace:* εἰρηνεύω EIRĒNEUŌ
Rom 12.18 so far as it depends upon you, live p.

PEACEFUL
1. *peaceful:* εἰρηνικός EIRĒNIKOS
Heb 12.11 discipline . . later . . yields the peaceful fruit

PEACEMAKER
1. *making peace:* εἰρηνοποιός (subst.) EIRĒNOPOIOS*
Mt 5. 9 "Blessed are the peacemakers

PEAL OF THUNDER
1. *thunder:* βροντή BRONTĒ
Rev 4. 5 From the throne issue . . peals of thunder
8. 5 there were peals of thunder, voices
11.19 peals of thunder, an earthquake
16.18 peals of thunder, and a great earthquake

PEARL
1. *pearl:* μαργαρίτης MARGARITĒS*
Mt 7. 6 "do not throw your pearls before swine
13.45 "like a merchant in search of fine pearls
13.46 "on finding one pearl of great value
1 Tim 2. 9 not with braided hair or gold or pearls
Rev 17. 4 arrayed in purple and scarlet, and . . pearls
18.12 cargo of gold, silver, jewels and pearls
18.16 "bedecked with gold . . and with pearls!

Rev 21.21 the twelve gates were twelve pearls, each of the gates made of a single p.

PEDDLER

1. *peddle, trade in:* καπηλεύω (subst. part.) KAPĒLEUŌ*
2 Cor 2.17 not, like so many, peddlers of God's word

PELEG: Φάλεκ 'pēleg
Lk 3.35 Reu, the son of Peleg, the son of Eber

PEN

1. *reed, staff:* κάλαμος KALAMOS
3 Jn .13 I would rather not write with p. and ink

PENALTY

CONTEXTUALLY
Acts 28.18 "there was no reason for the death penalty

PENALTY, DUE

1. *recompense:* ἀντιμισθία ANTIMISTHIA
Rom 1.27 receiving in their own persons the due p.

PENNY

1. *assarius* (Roman coin): ἀσσάριον ASSARION*
Mt 10.29 "Are not two sparrows sold for a penny?
Lk 12. 6 "five sparrows sold for two pennies
2. *quadrans* (Roman coin): κοδράντης KODRANTĒS*
Mt 5.26 "never .. till you have paid the last penny
Mk 12.42 two copper coins, which make a penny

PENTECOST

1. *fiftieth part, Pentecost:* πεντηκοστή PENTĒKOSTĒ*
Acts 2. 1 When the day of Pentecost had come
20.16 at Jerusalem, if possible, on the day of P.
1 Cor 16. 8 I will stay in Ephesus until Pentecost

PEOPLE (*See also* COMPANY OF PEOPLE; HIS OWN PEOPLE; LEAD S. BY THE HAND, PEOPLE TO; LEAD PEOPLE; SOME PEOPLE; WORLDLY PEOPLE)

1. *man, mankind:* ἄνθρωπος (pl.) ANTHRŌPOS
[a]ὀνόματα ἀνθρώπων
Jn 4.28 woman .. went .. and said to the people
6.10 Jesus said, "Make the people sit down
6.14 When the people saw the sign
Rev 11.13 [a]seven thousand people were killed
2. *people, popular assembly:* δῆμος DĒMOS
Acts 12.22 the p. shouted, "The voice of a god!
17. 5 seeking to bring them out to the people
19.33 wishing to make a defense to the p.
3. *kind, race, family:* γένος GENOS
2 Cor 11.26 danger from my own people
Gal 1.14 I advanced in Judaism .. among my people
Phil 3. 5 circumcised .., of the people of Israel
4. *people:* λαός LAOS*
Mt 1.21 he will save his p. from their sins
2. 4 assembling .. scribes of the people
2. 6 " 'who will govern my people Israel
4.16 "p. who sat in darkness have seen .. light
4.23 healing .. infirmity among the people
13.15 " 'For this people's heart has grown dull
15. 8 " 'This people honors me with their lips
21.23 elders of the people came up to him
26. 3 elders of the p. gathered in the palace
26. 5 "lest there be a tumult among the p.
26.47 crowd .. from .. elders of the people
27. 1 elders of the people took counsel
27.25 people answered, "His blood be on us
27.64 "lest his disciples .. tell the p.
Mk 7. 6 " 'This people honors me with their lips
14. 2 "lest there be a tumult of the people
Lk 1.10 whole multitude of the p. were praying
1.17 "make ready for the Lord a p. prepared
1.21 the people were waiting for Zechariah
1.68 "he has visited and redeemed his people
1.77 "knowledge of salvation to his people
2.10 "a great joy which will come to all the p.
2.31 "prepared in the presence of all peoples
2.32 "for glory to thy people Israel
3.15 As the people were in expectation
3.18 he preached good news to the people
3.21 Now when all the people were baptized
6.17 place, with .. a great multitude of p.
7. 1 all his sayings in the hearing of the p.
Lk 7.16 "God has visited his people!
7.29 (the p. and .. tax collectors justified God
8.47 she .. declared in the presence of .. the p.
9.13 "unless we are to .. buy food for all these p.
18.43 p., when they saw it, gave praise to God
19.47 principal men of the p. sought to destroy
19.48 for all the people hung upon his words
20. 1 One day, as he was teaching the people
20. 6 "if we say, 'From men,' .. p. will stone us
20. 9 he began to tell the people this parable
20.19 but they feared the people
20.26 not able in the presence of the people
20.45 in the hearing of all the people he said
21.23 "in those days .. wrath upon this people
21.38 all the p. came to him in the temple
22. 2 for they feared the people
22.66 elders of the people gathered together
23. 5 "He stirs up the people, teaching
23.13 Pilate then called .. rulers and the people
23.14 "as one who was perverting the people
23.27 there followed .. multitude of the p.
23.35 the people stood by, watching
24.19 "prophet mighty in .. word before .. all the p.
Jn 8. 2 all the p. came to him, and he .. taught[r]‡
11.50 "that one man .. die for the people
18.14 that one man should die for the p.
Acts 2.47 having favor with all the people
3. 9 p. saw him walking and praising God
3.11 all the p. ran together .. in the portico
3.12 when Peter saw it he addressed the p.
3.23 " 'prophet shall be destroyed from the p.
4. 1 And as they were speaking to the people
4. 2 because they were teaching the people
4. 8 "Rulers of the people and elders
4.10 "be it known .. to all the people of Israel
4.17 "that it may spread no further among the p.
4.21 no way to punish them, because of the p.
4.25 " 'Why did .. peoples imagine vain things?
4.27 "with the Gentiles and the peoples of Israel
5.12 many signs .. done among the people
5.13 but the people held them in high honor
5.20 "speak to the people .. words of this Life
5.25 "The men .. are .. teaching the people
5.26 afraid of being stoned by the people
5.34 Gamaliel, .. held in honor by all the p.
5.37 "Judas the Galilean .. drew away .. p.
6. 8 Stephen .. did great .. signs among the p.
6.12 they stirred up the people and the elders
7.17 "the p. grew and multiplied in Egypt
7.34 " 'I have .. seen the ill-treatment of my p.
10. 2 who .. gave alms liberally to the people
10.41 "⟨manifest⟩ not to all the p. but to us
10.42 "he commanded us to preach to the p.
12. 4 intending .. to bring him out to the p.
12.11 "from all that the Jewish p. were expecting
13.15 "if you have any word .. for the people
13.17 "God of this p. Israel chose our fathers and made the people great
13.24 "John had preached .. to all the p. of Israel
13.31 "who are now his witnesses to the p.
15.14 "to take out of them a people for his name
18.10 "for I have many people in this city
19. 4 "John baptized .., telling the p. to believe
21.28 "teaching men everywhere against the p.
21.30 the p. ran together; they seized Paul
21.36 p. followed, crying, "Away with him!
21.39 "I beg you, let me speak to the people
21.40 Paul .. motioned with his hand to the p.
23. 5 " 'shall not speak evil of a ruler of your p.
26.17 " 'delivering you from the people
26.23 "he would proclaim light both to the p.
28.17 "though I had done nothing against the p.
28.26 " 'Go to this p., and say, You shall .. hear
28.27 " 'For this people's heart has grown dull
Rom 9.25 he says in Hosea, "Those who were not my people I will call 'my people
9.26 "where it was said .. 'You are not my p.

Rom 10.21 "I have held out my hands to a . . contrary p.
11. 1 I ask, then, has God rejected his p.?
11. 2 God has not rejected his people
15.10 "Rejoice, O Gentiles, with his people
15.11 "let all the peoples praise him
1 Cor 10. 7 "The people sat down to eat and drink
14.21 "by . . foreigners will I speak to this people
2 Cor 6.16 "I will be their God, and they shall be my p.
Tit 2.14 gave himself . . to purify for himself a people
Heb 2.17 to make expiation for the sins of the p.
4. 9 there remains a sabbath rest for the p.
5. 3 for his own sins as well as . . those of the p.
7. 5 commandment . . to take tithes from the p.
7.11 (for under it the people received the law
7.27 for his own sins and . . those of the p.
8.10 "I will be their God, and they shall be my p.
9. 7 for himself and for the errors of the p.
9.19 law had been declared . . to all the p.
9.19 sprinkled . . book itself and all the p.
10.30 "The Lord will judge his people
11.25 choosing . . to share ill-treatment with the p.
13.12 to sanctify the p. through his own blood
1 Pet 2. 9 you are a chosen race, . . God's own people[e]
2.10 Once you were no people but now you are God's people
2 Pet 2. 1 false prophets also arose among the people
Jude . 5 who saved a p. out of the land of Egypt
Rev 5. 9 "didst ransom men . . from every . . people
7. 9 a great multitude . . from all . . peoples
10.11 "again prophesy about many peoples
11. 9 three days and a half men from the peoples
13. 7 authority was given it over every . . people
14. 6 an eternal gospel to proclaim . . to every . . p.
17.15 "The waters . . are peoples and multitudes
18. 4 "Come out of her, my people
21. 3 "and they shall be his people[o]‡

5. *crowd, populace:* ὄχλος OCHLOS
Mt 12.23 all the people were amazed
12.46 he was still speaking to the people
14. 5 he feared the people
15.10 he called the people to him
27.20 elders persuaded the p. to ask for Barabbas
Mk 7.14 he called the people to him again
7.17 when he had . . left the p., his disciples asked
11.32 they were afraid of the people
Lk 4.42 the people sought him and came to him
5. 1 people pressed upon him to hear the word
5. 3 he . . taught the people from the boat
8.42 As he went, the p. pressed round him
9.18 "Who do the people say that I am?
11.14 dumb man spoke, and the p. marveled
13.14 the ruler of the synagogue . . said to the p.
13.17 the p. rejoiced at all the glorious things
Jn 6.22 the p. who remained on the other side
6.24 when the p. saw that Jesus was not there
7.12 muttering about him among the people
7.12 "No, he is leading the people astray
7.20 p. answered, "You have a demon!
7.31 Yet many of the people believed in him
7.40 some . . p. said, "This is really the prophet
7.43 So there was a division among the people
11.42 "I have said this on account of the p.
Acts 14.13 priest . . wanted to offer sacrifice with the p.
14.18 they scarcely restrained the people
14.19 having persuaded the p., they stoned Paul
17. 8 the p. and . . authorities were disturbed

6. *multitude, mass:* πλῆθος PLĒTHOS
Lk 8.37 all the p. of the surrounding country
Acts 5.16 The p. also gathered from the towns
14. 4 But the people of the city were divided
25.24 "about whom the . . Jewish p. petitioned

IDIOMATICALLY
a. 1 Cor 10.18 Consider the people of Israel[a]†[o] βλέπετε τὸν Ἰσραὴλ κατὰ σάρκα [SARX]

CONTEXTUALLY
Mt 8. 4 "offer the gift . . for a proof to the p.[r]†
19.13 The disciples rebuked the people
28.13 "Tell people . . 'disciples came by night
Mk 1. 5 went out . . all the people of Jerusalem
1.44 "offer . . for a proof to the people[f]†
1.45 people came to him from every quarter
2.18 people came and said to him, "Why?
5.14 people came to see what . . happened
5.38 he saw . . people weeping . . loudly
6. 5 he laid his hands upon a few sick p.
6.41 gave them . . to set before the people
6.54 immediately the people recognized him
6.55 began to bring sick p. on their pallets
8. 6 gave them . . to set before the people
8. 9 there were about four thousand p.
8.22 some p. brought to him a blind man
12.41 Many rich people put in large sums
Lk 5.14 "an offering . . for a proof to the p.[o]†
8. 4 p. from town after town came to him
8.35 p. went out to see what had happened
9.53 but the people would not receive him
14.23 " 'compel people to come in
16. 4 that p. may receive me into their houses
Jn 3.23 people came and were baptized
6. 5 "bread, so that these p. may eat
7.25 Some of the p. of Jerusalem . . said
Acts 7.51 "You stiff-necked people . . resist
10.47 "water for baptizing these people
12.20 Herod was angry with the p. of Tyre
13.42 p. begged that these things . . be told
1 Cor 1.11 it has been reported . . by Chloe's p.
4.19 find out not the talk of these . . p.
15.29 what do people mean by being baptized?
15.29 why are p. baptized on their behalf?
2 Cor 4.15 as grace extends to more and more p.
9. 2 which I boast about you to the p.
10.11 Let such p. understand that . . we do
1 Th 5. 3 When p. say, "There is peace
2 Tim 3. 5 Avoid such people
4. 3 when p. will not endure sound teaching
Tit 3.14 let our p. learn to apply themselves
Heb 11.29 By faith the p. crossed the Red Sea
Rev 3. 4 p. who have not soiled their garments

PEOPLE, REST OF THE
1. *remaining, left:* λοιπός (subst. pl.) LOIPOS
Acts 28. 9 the rest of the people on the island

PEOPLE THERE
1. *local:* ἐντόπιος (subst. pl.) ENTOPIOS*
Acts 21.12 the people there begged him not to go

PERCEIVE
1. *understand:* αἰσθάνομαι AISTHANOMAI*
Lk 9.45 concealed . . , that they should not perceive
2. *see, perceive:* εἶδον EIDON
Mt 13.14 " 'you shall indeed see but never perceive
13.15 " 'lest they should perceive with their eyes
Mk 4.12 "they may indeed see but not perceive
Lk 9.47 Jesus perceived the thought of their hearts
Acts 28.26 " 'you shall indeed see but never perceive
28.27 " 'lest they should perceive with their eyes
3. *learn to know, recognize:* ἐπιγινώσκω EPIGINŌSKŌ
Mk 2. 8 Jesus, perceiving . . that they . . questioned
5.30 perceiving . . that power had gone forth
Lk 1.22 they perceived that he had seen a vision
5.22 When Jesus perceived their questionings
4. *know, understand:* γινώσκω GINŌSKŌ
Mt 21.45 perceived that he was speaking about them
Mk 12.12 perceived that he had told . . against them
15.10 he perceived that it was out of envy
Lk 8.46 "I p. that power has gone forth from me
20.19 perceived that he had told . . against them
Jn 6.15 Perceiving . . that they were about to come
Acts 23. 6 Paul perceived . . part were Sadducees
Gal 2. 9 they perceived the grace . . given to me
5. *catch:* καταλαμβάνω (mid.) KATALAMBANŌ
Acts 4.13 perceived that they were uneducated
10.34 "I p. that God shows no partiality
6. *consider, perceive:* κατανοέω KATANOEŌ
Lk 20.23 But he perceived their craftiness

7. *behold, perceive:* καθοράω KATHORAŌ*
Rom 1.20 his . . deity, has been . . perceived
8. *think, consider, perceive:* νοέω NOEŌ
Mt 16. 9 "Do you not yet perceive?
16.11 "How is it that you fail to perceive?
Mk 8.17 "Do you not yet perceive or understand?
Jn 12.40 "lest they should . . p. with their heart
Eph 3. 4 you can p. my insight into the mystery
9. *know:* οἶδα OIDA
Lk 9.47 Jesus perceived the thought of their hearts
10. *look at, observe:* θεωρέω THEŌREŌ
Jn 4.19 "Sir, I perceive that you are a prophet
Acts 17.22 "I perceive that . . you are very religious
27.10 "I p. that the voyage will be with injury

PERDITION
1. *destruction:* ἀπώλεια APŌLEIA
Jn 17.12 "none of them is lost but the son of p.
2 Th 2. 3 the man of lawlessness[a] . . , the son of p.
Rev 17. 8 "The beast that . . is to . . go to perdition
17.11 "it belongs to the seven, and it goes to p.

PEREZ: Φαρές 'pērez
Mt 1. 3 Judah the father of Perez . . by Tamar, and Perez the father of Hezron
Lk 3.33 Hezron, the son of P., the son of Judah

PERFECT
1. *quite all:* ἅπας (attr.) HAPAS
1 Tim 1.16 Christ might display his p. patience
2. *all, every, whole:* πᾶς PAS
[a]ἐν παντί B.1.a.1
2 Cor 7.16 [a]because I have p. confidence in you
Tit 3. 2 to show perfect courtesy toward all men
3. *fill full, complete:* πληρόω (perf. pass. part.) PLĒROŌ
Rev 3. 2 " 'I have not found your works perfect
4. *make perfect, complete:* τελειόω TELEIOŌ
Heb 9. 9 sacrifices are offered which cannot perfect
10.14 by a single offering he has perfected
1 Jn 2. 5 in him truly love for God is perfected
4.12 if we love . . , his love is perfected in us
4.17 In this is love perfected with us
4.18 he who fears is not perfected in love
5. *perfect, complete:* τέλειος TELEIOS
Mt 5.48 "You, therefore, must be perfect, as your heavenly Father is perfect
19.21 "If you would be perfect, go, sell
Rom 12. 2 what is good and acceptable and perfect[r]
1 Cor 13.10 when the p. comes, the imperfect will pass
Jas 1. 4 that you may be perfect and complete
1.17 every perfect gift is from above
1.25 he who looks into the perfect law
3. 2 makes no mistakes . . he is a p. man
1 Jn 4.18 perfect love casts out fear
CONTEXTUALLY
Mt 21.16 " 'thou hast brought perfect praise

PERFECT, BE
1. *make perfect, complete:* τελειόω (perf. pass.) TELEIOŌ
Phil 3.12 Not that I . . am already perfect

PERFECT HARMONY
1. *perfection, completeness:* τελειότης TELEIOTĒS
Col 3.14 love . . binds everything . . in p. harmony

PERFECT HEALTH
1. *wholeness, soundness:* ὁλοκληρία HOLOKLĒRIA*
Acts 3.16 "faith . . has given the man this p. health

PERFECT, MAKE
1. *finish, complete:* ἐπιτελέω EPITELEŌ
2 Cor 7. 1 make holiness perfect in the fear of God
2. *make perfect, complete:* τελειόω TELEIOŌ
Heb 2.10 make the pioneer . . p. through suffering
5. 9 being made p. he became the source
7.19 (for the law made nothing perfect
7.28 a Son who has been made perfect for ever
10. 1 the law . . can never . . make perfect
11.40 apart from us they should not be made p.
12.23 to the spirits of just men made perfect
3. *finish, fulfill:* τελέω TELEŌ
2 Cor 12. 9 "for my power is made p. in weakness

PERFECT, MORE
1. *perfect, complete:* τέλειος (comp.) TELEIOS
Heb 9.11 through the greater and more p. tent[p]

PERFECTER
1. *accomplisher:* τελειωτής TELEIŌTĒS*
Heb 12. 2 Jesus the pioneer and p. of our faith

PERFECTION
1. *fulfillment:* τελείωσις TELEIŌSIS
Heb 7.11 if p. . . attainable through . . priesthood

PERFECTLY
1. *make perfect, complete:* τελειόω (perf. pass. part.) TELEIOŌ [A.3.b]
Jn 17.23 "that they may become perfectly one

PERFORM (*See also* WORK, PERFORM)
1. *give up, return:* ἀποδίδωμι APODIDŌMI
Mt 5.33 " 'You . . shall p. . . what you have sworn
2. *bring to an end:* ἀποτελέω APOTELEŌ
Lk 13.32 " 'I cast out demons and p. cures
3. *finish, complete:* ἐπιτελέω EPITELEŌ
Heb 9. 6 priests . . performing their ritual duties
4. *achieve:* κατεργάζομαι KATERGAZOMAI
2 Cor 12.12 signs . . were performed among you
5. *do, make:* ποιέω POIEŌ
Lk 1.72 "to p. the mercy promised to our fathers
Jn 11.47 "For this man performs many signs
Acts 7.36 "led them out, having performed wonders
Rev 16.14 they are demonic spirits, performing signs
6. *do, practice:* πράσσω PRASSŌ
Acts 26.20 "should . . p. deeds worthy of . . repentance
7. *finish, fulfill:* τελέω TELEŌ
Lk 2.39 when they had performed everything

PERFORMED
1. *come to be, happen, be:* γίνομαι (part.) GINOMAI
Acts 8.13 seeing signs and great miracles performed

PERFORMED, BE
1. *come to be, happen, be:* γίνομαι GINOMAI
Acts 4.16 "a notable sign has been performed
4.22 man on whom this sign . . was performed
4.30 "signs and wonders are performed

PERGA: Πέργη 'pərgə II,F-3
Acts 13.13 set sail from Paphos, and came to P.
13.14 they passed on from Perga . . to Antioch
14.25 when they had spoken the word in Perga

PERGAMUM: Πέργαμον 'pərgəməm II,E-3
Rev 1.11 send it to the seven churches, to . . P.
2.12 "to the angel of the church in P. write

PERHAPS (*See also* EXCEPT PERHAPS)
1. *perhaps, never:* μήποτε MĒPOTE
Mt 25. 9 " 'P. there will not be enough for us
2 Tim 2.25 God may p. grant that they will repent
2. *in some way, perhaps:* πώς PŌS II
2 Cor 12.20 I fear that p. I may come and find
12.20 that perhaps there may be quarreling
3. *presently, perhaps:* τάχα TACHA*
Rom 5. 7 p. for a good man one will dare . . to die
Phm .15 P. this is why he was parted from you
4. *happen, attain:* τυγχάνω TYGCHANŌ
[a]εἰ τύχοι B.3.b.8 [b]neut. part.
1 Cor 15.37 [a]p. of wheat or of some other grain
16. 6 [b]perhaps I will stay with you

PERHAPS, WHETHER
1. *perhaps, never:* μήποτε MĒPOTE
Lk 3.15 whether perhaps he were the Christ

PERIL
1. *hazard, risk:* κίνδυνος KINDYNOS
Rom 8.35 Who shall separate us . . ? Shall . . peril?
IDIOMATICALLY
a. 2 Cor 1.10 he delivered us from so deadly a peril ὃς ἐκ τηλικούτου θανάτου ἐρρύσατο ἡμᾶς [TĒLIKOUTOS]

PERIL, BE IN
1. *be daring, run a risk:* κινδυνεύω KINDYNEUŌ
1 Cor 15.30 Why am I in peril every hour?

PERIOD
1. *time, period:* χρόνος CHRONOS
Acts 18.20 asked him to stay for a longer period

2. *time, opportunity:* καιρός KAIROS
Acts 17.26 "having determined allotted periods

PERISH

1. *make unseen, destroy:* ἀφανίζω (pass.) APHANIZŌ
Acts 13.41 " 'Behold, you scoffers, .. and perish
2. *destruction:* ἀπώλεια APŌLEIA [A.6.a.3]
Acts 8.20 "Your silver perish with you!
3. *destroy utterly:* ἀπόλλυμι (mid.) APOLLYMI
Mt 8.25 "Save, Lord; we are perishing
18.14 "that one of these little ones should p.
26.52 "who take the sword will p. by the sword
Mk 4.38 "Teacher, do you not care if we p.?
Lk 8.24 "Master, Master, we are perishing!
11.51 "the blood of Zechariah, who perished
13. 3 "unless you repent you will all likewise p.
13. 5 "unless you repent you will all likewise p.
13.33 " 'prophet .. perish away from Jerusalem
15.17 " 'but I perish here with hunger!
21.18 "But not a hair of your head will perish
Jn 3.16 whoever believes in him should not p.
6.27 "not labor for the food which perishes
10.28 "and they shall never perish
11.50 "the whole nation should not perish
Acts 5.37 "Judas the Galilean arose .. also perished
27.34 "not a hair is to perish from the head
Rom 2.12 will also perish without the law
1 Cor 1.18 the cross is folly to those who are perishing
15.18 who have fallen asleep .. have perished
2 Cor 2.15 aroma .. among those who are perishing
4. 3 veiled only to those who are perishing
2 Th 2.10 deception for those who are to perish
Heb 1.11 "they will perish, but thou remainest
Jas 1.11 its flower falls, and its beauty perishes
2 Pet 3. 6 was deluged with water and perished
3. 9 not wishing that any should perish
Jude .11 they .. perish in Korah's rebellion
4. *die:* ἀποθνήσκω APOTHNĒSKŌ
Mt 8.32 the whole herd .. perished in the waters
5. *destruction:* φθορά PHTHORA [A.6.a.3]
Col 2.22 (things which all p. as they are used

PERISH WITH

1. *destroy together:* συναπόλλυμι (mid.) SYNAPOLLYMI*
Heb 11.31 By faith Rahab the harlot did not p. with

PERISHABLE

PERISHABLE, THE

1. *destroy utterly:* ἀπόλλυμι (mid. part.) APOLLYMI
1 Pet 1. 7 more precious than gold which though p.
2. *perishable:* φθαρτός PHTHARTOS
1 Cor 9.25 They do it to receive a p. wreath
15.53 p. nature must put on the imperishable
15.54 When the p. puts on the imperishable
1 Pet 1.18 you were ransomed .., not with p. things
1.23 You have been born anew, not of p. seed
3. *destruction:* φθορά PHTHORA
[a]B.2.d.1
1 Cor 15.42 [a]What is sown is perishable
15.50 nor does the p. inherit the imperishable

PERJURER

1. *perjured:* ἐπίορκος (subst.) EPIORKOS*
1 Tim 1.10 sodomites, kidnapers, liars, perjurers

PERMANENT

1. *stay, wait:* μένω (part.) MENŌ
2 Cor 3.11 what is p. must have much more splendor

PERMANENTLY

1. *permanent:* ἀπαράβατος APARABATOS* [A.3.b.4]
Heb 7.24 he holds his priesthood permanently

PERMISSION, HAVE

1. *permit:* ἐπιτρέπω EPITREPŌ [A.6.c.3]
Acts 26. 1 "You have p. to speak for yourself

PERMIT

1. *let go, leave, forgive:* ἀφίημι APHIĒMI
Mk 1.34 he would not p. the demons to speak
7.12 "then you no longer p. him to do anything
Lk 8.51 he permitted no one to enter with him
2. *give:* δίδωμι DIDŌMI
Rev 6. 4 its rider was permitted to take peace
3. *permit:* ἐπιτρέπω EPITREPŌ
[a]A.6.c.3
1 Cor 14.34 [a]women .. are not permitted to speak
16. 7 some time with you, if the Lord permits
1 Tim 2.12 I permit no woman to teach
Heb 6. 3 this we will do if God permits[l]

PERPLEXED, BE

1. *be in doubt:* ἀπορέω (act. or mid.) APOREŌ
Mk 6.20 When he heard him, he was much p.
Lk 24. 4 While they were perplexed about this
2 Cor 4. 8 We are .. perplexed, but not .. to despair
Gal 4.20 for I am perplexed about you
2. *be quite at a loss:* διαπορέω DIAPOREŌ
Lk 9. 7 Herod the tetrarch .. was perplexed
Acts 2.12 all were amazed and perplexed
10.17 while Peter was inwardly perplexed

PERPLEXED, BE MUCH

1. *be quite at a loss:* διαπορέω DIAPOREŌ
Acts 5.24 the chief priests .. were much perplexed

PERPLEXITY

1. *distress, anxiety:* ἀπορία APORIA*
Lk 21.25 "there will be .. distress of nations in p.

PERSECUTE

1. *pursue:* διώκω DIŌKŌ
Mt 5.10 "Blessed are those who are persecuted
5.11 "Blessed are you when men .. p. you
5.12 "for so men persecuted the prophets
5.44 "pray for those who persecute you
10.23 "When they persecute you in one town
23.34 "some you will .. p. from town to town
Lk 11.49 " 'some of whom they will kill and p.
21.12 "they will lay their hands on you and p.
Jn 5.16 this was why the Jews persecuted Jesus
15.20 "If they persecuted me, they will p. you; if they kept my word, they will keep yours
Acts 7.52 "Which .. prophets did not your fathers p.?
9. 4 "Saul, Saul, why do you persecute me?
9. 5 "I am Jesus, whom you are persecuting
22. 4 "I persecuted this Way to the death
22. 7 " 'Saul, Saul, why do you persecute me?
22. 8 " 'I am Jesus .. whom you are persecuting
26.11 "I persecuted them even to foreign cities
26.14 " 'Saul, Saul, why do you persecute me?
26.15 " 'I am Jesus whom you are persecuting
Rom 12.14 Bless those who persecute you
1 Cor 4.12 when persecuted, we endure
15. 9 because I persecuted the church of God
2 Cor 4. 9 persecuted, but not forsaken
Gal 1.13 how I persecuted the church of God
1.23 "who once persecuted us is now preaching
4.29 as at that time he .. persecuted him
5.11 brethren, .. why am I still persecuted?
6.12 that they may not be persecuted
2 Tim 3.12 all .. in Christ Jesus will be persecuted
2. *pursuer, persecutor:* διώκτης DIŌKTĒS* [A.6.a.3]
1 Tim 1.13 I formerly blasphemed and persecuted

PERSECUTION

1. *pursuit, persecution:* διωγμός DIŌGMOS*
Mt 13.21 "when .. p. arises on account of the word
Mk 4.17 "when .. p. arises on account of the word
10.30 "now in this time, houses and .. persecutions
Acts 8. 1 on that day a great persecution arose
13.50 the Jews .. stirred up p. against Paul
Rom 8.35 Who shall separate us .. ? Shall .. p.?
2 Cor 12.10 then, I am content with .. persecutions
2 Th 1. 4 your .. faith in all your persecutions
2 Tim 3.11 my persecutions, my sufferings, .. at Lystra, what persecutions I endured
2. *affliction, oppression:* θλῖψις THLIPSIS
Acts 11.19 those who were scattered because of the p.

PERSECUTOR

1. *pursue:* διώκω (subst. part.) DIŌKŌ
Phil 3. 6 as to zeal a persecutor of the church

PERSEVERANCE
1. *endurance:* ὑπομονή HYPOMONĒ
Heb 12. 1 run with p. the race that is set before us
2. *patience, perseverance:* προσκαρτέρησις PROSKARTERĒSIS*
Eph 6.18 To that end keep alert with all p.

PERSEVERE
1. *stay beside, endure:* παραμένω PARAMENŌ
Jas 1.25 he who . . perseveres . . shall be blessed

PERSIS: Περσίς 'pərsəs
Rom 16.12 Greet the beloved P., who has worked

PERSIST
1. *continue, remain:* ἐπιμένω EPIMENŌ
Rom 11.23 if they do not persist in their unbelief
CONTEXTUALLY
1 Tim 5.20 As for those who p. in sin, rebuke them

PERSON (*See also* CERTAIN PERSON; IMMORAL PERSON; WHAT PERSON)
1. *man, mankind:* ἄνθρωπος ANTHRŌPOS
Rom 7. 1 law is binding on a p. only during . . life
1 Cor 7.26 it is well for a p. to remain as he is
Jas 1.7, 8 For that person must not suppose
1 Pet 3. 4 let it be the hidden person of the heart
2. *name:* ὄνομα ONOMA
Acts 1.15 (persons . . about a hundred and twenty
3. *face, person:* πρόσωπον PROSŌPON
[a]dat.
1 Th 2.17 [a]we were bereft of you . . in p. not in heart
4. *life, soul, self:* ψυχή PSYCHĒ
Acts 27.37 (two hundred and seventy-six[d] persons
Rom 13. 1 Let every p. be subject to the . . authorities
1 Pet 3.20 a few, that is, eight persons
CONTEXTUALLY
Acts 10.27 he . . found many persons gathered
17.17 with the Jews and the devout persons
Rom 1.27 receiving in their own persons . . penalty
16.18 such persons do not serve our Lord Christ
1 Cor 5.13 "Drive out the wicked p. from among you
[12. 1 concerning *spiritual persons,* brethren†[o]
2 Th 3.12 such persons we command and exhort
1 Tim 1.10 immoral persons, sodomites, kidnapers
Tit 3.11 knowing that such a p. is perverted
Heb 9.13 For if the sprinkling of defiled persons
Jas 1.14 each p. is tempted when he is lured
2 Pet 3.11 what sort of persons ought you to be
Jude . 4 ungodly persons who pervert . . grace

PERSON, A
1. *anyone, any:* τὶς TIS II
Acts **4.34**

PERSON, EACH
1. *each:* ἕκαστος (subst.) HEKASTOS
Jas 1.14 each person is tempted when he is lured

PERSUADE
1. *persuade:* ἀναπείθω ANAPEITHŌ*
Acts 18.13 "persuading men . . contrary to the law
2. *persuade:* πείθω PEITHŌ
Mt 27.20 elders persuaded the people to ask
Acts 12.20 persuaded Blastus, the king's chamberlain
14.19 having persuaded . . people, they stoned
17. 4 And some of them were persuaded
18. 4 he argued . . and persuaded Jews and Greeks
19.26 "Paul has persuaded and turned away
21.14 when he would not be persuaded
26.26 "I am persuaded that none . . escaped . . notice
Rom 14.14 I . . am persuaded . . that nothing is unclean
2 Cor 5.11 knowing the fear of the Lord, we p. men

PERSUASION
1. *persuasion:* πεισμονή PEISMONĒ*
Gal 5. 8 This persuasion is not from him

PERTAIN
CONTEXTUALLY
2 Pet 1. 3 granted to us all things that p. to life

PERTAINING (*See* LIFE, MATTERS PERTAINING TO THIS)

PERVERSE
1. *twist about:* διαστρέφω (perf. pass. part.) DIASTREPHŌ
Mt 17.17 "O faithless and perverse generation
Lk 9.41 "O faithless and perverse generation
Acts 20.30 "will arise men speaking perverse things
Phil 2.15 a crooked and perverse generation

PERVERT
1. *turn away, turn back:* ἀποστρέφω APOSTREPHŌ
Lk 23.14 "one who was perverting the people
2. *twist about:* διαστρέφω DIASTREPHŌ
Lk 23. 2 "We found this man perverting our nation
3. *change entirely:* ἐκστρέφω EKSTREPHŌ*
Tit 3.11 such a person is perverted and sinful
4. *turn about, change:* μεταστρέφω METASTREPHŌ
Gal 1. 7 some . . want to p. the gospel of Christ
5. *transpose, change:* μετατίθημι METATITHĒMI
Jude . 4 persons who p. the grace of our God

PERVERTS, SEXUAL
1. *effeminate men and homosexuals:* μαλακοὶ καὶ ἀρσενοκοῖται MALAKOS; ARSENOKOITĒS [A.1.f]
1 Cor 6. 9 nor sexual p. ⟨will inherit the kingdom⟩[o]

PESTILENCE
1. *plague, pest:* λοιμός LOIMOS
Lk 21.11 "will be . . in various places . . pestilences
2. *death:* θάνατος THANATOS
Rev 6. 8 power over a fourth . . to kill . . with p.
18. 8 "her plagues . . in a single day, pestilence

PESTILENT FELLOW
1. *plague, pest:* λοιμός LOIMOS
Acts 24. 5 "we have found this man a p. fellow

PETER: Πέτρος 'pētər
Mt 4.18 two brothers, Simon . . called P. and Andrew
8.14 when Jesus entered Peter's house
10. 2 first, Simon, who is called Peter
14.28 P. answered . . "Lord, if it is you, bid me
14.29 So Peter got out of the boat and walked
15.15 P. said . . "Explain the parable to us
16.16 Simon P. replied, "You are the Christ
16.18 "I tell you, you are P.,[s] and on this rock[t]†
16.22 P. took him and began to rebuke him
16.23 he . . said to P., "Get behind me, Satan!
17. 1 Jesus took with him Peter and James
17. 4 P. said . . "Lord, it is well that we are here
17.24 collectors of the . . tax went up to Peter
18.21 P. . . said . . "how often shall . . I forgive?
19.27 P. said . . "Lo, we have left everything
26.33 Peter declared . . "I will never fall away
26.35 P. said . . "Even if I must die with you
26.37 taking . . P. . . he began to be sorrowful
26.40 he said to P., "So, could you not watch[h]?
26.58 But Peter followed him at a distance
26.69 Peter was sitting outside in the courtyard
26.73 said to P., "Certainly you are also one
26.75 P. remembered . . "Before the cock crows
Mk 3.16 Simon[x] whom he surnamed Peter
5.37 allowed no one to follow him except P.
8.29 P. answered him, "You are the Christ
8.32 Peter took him, and began to rebuke him
8.33 he rebuked P. . . "Get behind me, Satan!
9. 2 Jesus took with him Peter and James
9. 5 P. said . . "Master,[f] it is well that we are here
10.28 P. began . . "Lo, we have left everything
11.21 P. remembered . . "Master,[v] look! The fig
13. 3 Peter and . . Andrew asked him privately
14.29 P. said . . "Even though they all fall away
14.33 he took . . P. . . and began to be . . distressed
14.37 said to P., "Simon, are you asleep?
14.54 Peter had followed him at a distance
14.66 as Peter was below in the courtyard
14.67 seeing Peter warming himself, she . . said
14.70 again the bystanders said to Peter
14.72 P. remembered . . "Before the cock crows
16. 7 "go, tell his disciples and Peter
[16.[end] *they reported briefly to Peter*‡
Lk 5. 8 when Simon P. saw it, he fell down

Lk 6.14 Simon, whom he named Peter
8.45 P.[c] said, "Master, the multitudes surround!
8.51 he permitted no one . . except P. and John
9.20 Peter answered, "The Christ of God
9.28 he took with him Peter and John
9.32 Peter and those . . were heavy with sleep
9.33 P. said . . "it is well that we are here
12.41 P. said, "Lord, are you telling this . . for us?
18.28 Peter said, "Lo, we have left our homes
22. 8 Jesus[h] sent P. . . saying, "Go and prepare
22.34 "I tell you, P., the cock will not crow
22.54 Peter followed at a distance
22.55 when they had . . a fire . . , P. sat among them
22.58 But Peter said, "Man, I am not
22.60 Peter said, "Man, I do not know what
22.61 Lord . . looked at P. And P. remembered the word . . "Before the cock crows today
[24.12 *Peter rose and ran to the tomb*‡
Jn 1.40 One . . was Andrew, Simon Peter's brother
1.42 "You shall be . . Cephas" (which means P.[c]
1.44 Bethsaida, the city of Andrew and P.
6. 8 Andrew, Simon Peter's brother
6.68 "Simon P. answered . . "to whom shall we go?
13. 6 He came to Simon Peter
13. 8 P. said . . "You shall never wash my feet
13. 9 Simon P. said . . "Lord, not my feet only!
13.24 Simon P. . . said, "Tell us who it is
13.36 Simon P. said . . "Lord, where are you going?
13.37 P. said . . "Lord, why cannot I follow you?
18.10 Simon Peter, having a sword, drew it
18.11 Jesus said to Peter, "Put your sword
18.15 Simon Peter followed Jesus
18.16 Peter stood outside at the door. So the other disciple . . brought Peter in
18.17 The maid . . said to P., "Are not you also one?
18.18 Peter also was with them, standing
18.25 Simon P. was standing and warming
18.26 the man whose ear Peter had cut off
18.27 P. again denied it; and . . the cock crowed
20. 2 So she ran, and went to Simon P.
20. 3 P. then came out with the other disciple
20. 4 but the other disciple outran Peter
20. 6 Simon Peter came, following him
21. 2 Simon P., Thomas . . , the sons of Zebedee
21. 3 Simon P. said . . "I am going fishing
21. 7 disciple . . said to P., "It is the Lord!" When Simon P. heard . . , he put on his clothes
21.11 Simon P. went aboard and hauled the net
21.15 Jesus said to Simon P. . . "do you love me?
21.17 P. was grieved because . . the third time
21.20 P. . . saw following them the disciple
21.21 When Peter saw him, he said to Jesus
Acts 1.13 where they were staying, P. and John
1.15 Peter stood up among the brethren
2.14 Peter, standing with the eleven
2.37 Peter and the rest of the apostles
2.38 P. said . . "Repent, and be baptized
3. 1 P. and John were going up to the temple
3. 3 Seeing Peter and John . . , he asked for alms
3. 4 Peter directed his gaze at him
3. 6 Peter said, "I have no silver and gold
3.11 he clung to Peter and John
3.12 when P. saw it he addressed the people
4. 8 Peter, filled with the Holy Spirit
4.13 they saw the boldness of P. and John
4.19 Peter and John answered them
5. 3 P. said . . "why has Satan filled your heart?
5. 8 P. said . . "Tell me whether you sold
5. 9 P. said . . "How is it that you have agreed?
5.15 carried out the sick . . , that as P. came by
5.29 Peter . . answered, "We must obey God
8.14 they sent to them Peter and John
8.20 Peter said . . "Your silver perish with you
9.32 Now as Peter went here and there
9.34 P. said . . "Aeneas, Jesus Christ heals you
9.38 disciples, hearing that P. was there
9.39 So Peter rose and went with them
Acts 9.40 But Peter put them all outside
9.40 when she saw Peter she sat up
10. 5 "bring one Simon who is called Peter
10. 9 Peter went up on the housetop to pray
10.13 there came a voice . . "Rise, P.; kill and eat
10.14 Peter said, "No, Lord; for I have never
10.17 while Peter was inwardly perplexed
10.18 Simon . . called Peter was lodging there
10.19 while Peter was pondering the vision
10.21 Peter went down to the men
10.25 When Peter entered, Cornelius met him
10.26 Peter lifted him up, saying, "Stand up
10.32 " 'ask for Simon who is called Peter
10.34 P. . . said: "Truly . . God shows no partiality
10.44 While Peter was still saying this
10.45 believers . . who came with P. were amazed
10.46 P. declared, ⟨"Can any . . forbid water?⟩
11. 2 when Peter went up to Jerusalem
11. 4 P. began and explained to them in order
11. 7 "a voice . . 'Rise, Peter; kill and eat
11.13 " 'Send to Joppa and bring Simon . . P.
12. 3 he proceeded to arrest Peter
12. 5 So Peter was kept in prison
12. 6 Peter was sleeping between two soldiers
12. 7 struck Peter on the side and woke him
12.11 Peter came to himself, and said
12.14 Recognizing Peter's voice, in her joy she . . told that Peter was standing at the gate
12.16 But Peter continued knocking
12.18 no small stir . . over what had become of P.
15. 7 Peter rose and said to them, "Brethren
Gal 2. 7 as P. had been entrusted with the gospel
2. 8 (who worked through Peter for the mission
1 Pet 1. 1 Peter, an apostle of Jesus Christ
2 Pet 1. 1 Simeon[x] Peter, a servant and apostle

PETITION

1. *appeal to, plead:* ἐντυγχάνω ENTYGCHANŌ
Acts 25.24 "the whole Jewish people petitioned me

PHANUEL: Φανουήλ 'fanyüəl, fə'nyüəl
Lk 2.36 a prophetess, Anna, the daughter of P.

PHARAOH: Φαραώ 'ferō, 'fārō
Acts 7.10 "favor and wisdom before Pharaoh
7.13 "Joseph's family became known to P.
7.21 "Pharaoh's daughter adopted him
Rom 9.17 scripture says to P., "I have raised you
Heb 11.24 refused to be . . son of Pharaoh's daughter

PHARISEE: Φαρισαῖος
Mt 3. 7 he saw many of the Pharisees . . coming
5.20 "righteousness exceeds that of the . . Pharisees
9.11 Pharisees . . said . . "Why does your teacher?
9.14 "Why do we and the Pharisees fast[w]?
9.34 Pharisees said, "He casts out demons‡
12. 2 when the Pharisees saw it, they said to nim
12.14 the Pharisees went out and took counsel
12.24 when the Pharisees heard it they said
12.38 some . . Pharisees said . . "we wish . . a sign
15. 1 Pharisees . . came to Jesus from Jerusalem
15.12 "Pharisees were offended when they heard
16. 1 Pharisees . . asked him to show them a sign
16. 6 "beware of the leaven of the Pharisees
16.11 "Beware of the leaven of the Pharisees
16.12 teaching of the Pharisees and Sadducees
19. 3 Pharisees came up . . asking, "Is it lawful?
21.45 When the . . Pharisees heard his parables
22.15 the Pharisees went and took counsel
22.34 when the Pharisees heard . . , they came
22.41 while the Pharisees were gathered together
23. 2 "the Pharisees sit on Moses' seat
23.13 "Woe to you, scribes and Pharisees!
Also Mt **23.**[14‡, 15, 23, 25, 27, 29
23.26 "You blind P.! first cleanse the inside
27.62 the Pharisees gathered before Pilate
Mk 2.16 "scribes of[h] the Pharisees, when they saw‡
2.18 Pharisees were fasting; and people . . said . . "Why do . . disciples of the Pharisees fast?
2.24 Pharisees said . . "Look, why are they doing?

Mk 3. 6 Pharisees went out, and . . held counsel
7. 1 when . . Pharisees gathered together to him
7. 3 (Pharisees . . do not eat unless they wash
7. 5 Pharisees and the scribes asked him
8.11 Pharisees came and began to argue
8.15 "beware of the leaven of the Pharisees
10. 2 Pharisees . . asked, "Is it lawful?
12.13 they sent to him some of the Pharisees
Lk 5.17 there were Pharisees . . sitting by
5.21 Pharisees began to question . . "Who is this?
5.30 Pharisees . . murmured against . . disciples
5.33 "so do the disciples of the Pharisees
6. 2 some of the Pharisees said, "Why?
6. 7 Pharisees watched him, to see whether
7.30 (Pharisees . . rejected the purpose of God
7.36 One of the Pharisees asked him to eat . . and he went into the Pharisee's house
7.37 he was at table in the Pharisee's house
7.39 the P. who had invited him saw it
11.37 a Pharisee asked him to dine with him
11.38 P. was astonished . . that he did not . . wash
11.39 "Pharisees cleanse . . outside of the cup
11.42 "woe to you Pharisees! for you tithe
11.43 "Woe to . . Pharisees! . . you love the best
11.53 Pharisees began to press him hard
12. 1 "Beware of the leaven of the Pharisees
13.31 Pharisees . . said . . "Get away from here
14. 1 a ruler who belonged to the Pharisees
14. 3 Jesus spoke to . . Pharisees . . "Is it lawful?
15. 2 Pharisees and the scribes murmured
16.14 Pharisees, who were lovers of money
17.20 asked by the Pharisees when the kingdom
18.10 "one a P. and the other a tax collector
18.11 "The Pharisee stood and prayed thus
19.39 Pharisees . . said . . "rebuke . . disciples
Jn 1.24 they had been sent from the Pharisees
3. 1 man of the Pharisees, named Nicodemus
4. 1 Pharisees . . heard . . Jesus was making
7.32 Pharisees heard . . crowd thus muttering
7.32 Pharisees sent officers to arrest him
7.45 officers . . went back to the . . Pharisees
7.47 Pharisees answered . . "Are you led astray?
7.48 "Have any . . Pharisees believed?
8. 3 Pharisees brought a woman . . caught[r]‡
8.13 Pharisees . . said . . "You are bearing
9.13 They brought to the Pharisees the man
9.15 Pharisees . . asked . . how he . . received . . sight
9.16 Pharisees said, "This man is not from God
9.40 Pharisees . . said . . "Are we also blind?
11.46 some of them went to the Pharisees
11.47 the Pharisees gathered the council
11.57 Pharisees had given orders that if any
12.19 Pharisees . . said . . "you can do nothing
12.42 for fear of the Pharisees they did not
18. 3 procuring . . officers from . . the Pharisees
Acts 5.34 Pharisee in the council named Gamaliel
15. 5 believers who belonged to . . Pharisees
23. 6 Paul perceived . . one part were . . Pharisees, he cried out in the council, "Brethren, I am a Pharisee, a son of Pharisees
23. 7 between the Pharisees and . . Sadducees
23. 8 the Pharisees acknowledge them all
23. 9 some . . scribes of the Pharisees' party
26. 5 "known . . that . . I have lived as a Pharisee
Phil 3. 5 a Hebrew . . ; as to the law a Pharisee

PHILADELPHIA: Φιλαδέλφεια ˌfilə'delfyə I,D-5; II,E-3
Rev 1.11 "send it to the seven churches, . . to P.
3. 7 "to the angel of the church in P. write

PHILEMON: Φιλήμων fī'lēmən, fə'lēmən
Phm . 1 To Philemon our beloved fellow worker

PHILETUS: Φίλητος fī'lētəs, fi'lētəs
2 Tim 2.17 Among them are Hymenaeus and P.

PHILIP: Φίλιππος 'filəp
1. the tetrarch
Mt 14. 3 Herodias, his brother Philip's wife[l]‡
Mk 6.17 Herodias, his brother Philip's wife
Lk 3. 1 Philip tetrarch of the region of Ituraea
2. the apostle
Mt 10. 3 Philip and Bartholomew; Thomas
Mk 3.18 Andrew, and Philip, and Bartholomew
Lk 6.14 James and John, and Philip
Jn 1.43 he found Philip and said . . "Follow me
1.44 P. was from Bethsaida, the city of Andrew
1.45 Philip found Nathanael, and said
1.46 Philip said to him, "Come and see
1.48 "Before Philip called you . . I saw you
6. 5 said to P., "How are we to buy bread?
6. 7 P. answered . . "Two hundred denarii[l]
12.21 P., who was from Bethsaida in Galilee
12.22 Philip went and told Andrew; Andrew went with Philip
14. 8 P. said . . "Lord, show us the Father
14. 9 "yet you do not know me, Philip?
Acts 1.13 John and James and Andrew, Philip
3. the evangelist
Acts 6. 5 they chose Stephen, . . P., and Prochorus
8. 5 P. went down to a city of Samaria
8. 6 gave heed to what was said by P.
8.12 when they believed P. . . they were baptized
8.13 Simon . . believed, and . . continued with Philip
8.26 an angel of the Lord said to Philip
8.29 Spirit said to P., "Go . . join this chariot
8.30 P. ran to him, . . heard him reading Isaiah
8.31 he invited Philip to come up and sit
8.34 eunuch said to P., "About whom, pray?
8.35 P. . . told him the good news of Jesus
[8.37 *Philip said, "If you believe . . , you may*‡
8.38 into the water, P. and the eunuch
8.39 the Spirit of the Lord caught up P.
8.40 Philip was found at Azotus
21. 8 the house of Philip the evangelist

PHILIPPI: Φίλιπποι fə'lipī, 'filəˌpī II,D-2 (*See also* CAESAREA PHILIPPI)
Acts 16.12 P. . . the leading city of . . Macedonia
20. 6 but we sailed away from Philippi
Phil 1. 1 To all the saints in Christ Jesus . . at P.
1 Th 2. 2 we had . . been shamefully treated at P.

PHILIPPIAN: Φιλιππήσιος
Phil 4.15 you Philippians . . know that . . when I left

PHILOLOGUS: Φιλόλογος fi'läləgəs
Rom 16.15 Greet P., Julia, Nereus and his sister

PHILOSOPHER
1. *lover of wisdom, philosopher:* φιλόσοφος PHILOSOPHOS*
Acts 17.18 Epicurean and Stoic philosophers met him

PHILOSOPHY
1. *love of knowledge, philosophy:* φιλοσοφία PHILOSOPHIA*
Col 2. 8 that no one makes a prey of you by p.

PHLEGON: Φλέγων 'flēgən
Rom 16.14 Greet Asyncritus, Phlegon, Hermes

PHOEBE: Φοίβη 'fēbē
Rom 16. 1 I commend . . our sister P., a deaconess

PHOENICIA: Φοινίκη fə'nish(ē)ə I,C-2
Acts 11.19 Stephen traveled as far as Phoenicia
15. 3 they passed through both Phoenicia
21. 2 having found a ship crossing to Phoenicia

PHOENIX: Φοῖνιξ 'fēniks II,D-4
Acts 27.12 chance that . . they could reach Phoenix

PHRASE
CONTEXTUALLY
Heb 12.27 This phrase, "Yet once more," indicates

PHRASES, HEAP UP EMPTY
1. *babble:* βατταλογέω BATTALOGEŌ*
Mt 6. 7 "not heap up empty p. as the Gentiles do

PHRYGIA: Φρυγία 'frij(ē)ə II,F-3
Acts 2.10 Phrygia and Pamphylia, Egypt
16. 6 they went through the region of P.
18.23 went from place to place through . . P.

PHYGELUS: Φύγελος 'fīgələs, fi'geləs
2 Tim 1.15 all . . in Asia . . among them Phygelus

PHYLACTERY
1. *safeguard, amulet:* φυλακτήριον PHYLAKTĒRION*
Mt 23. 5 "they make their phylacteries broad

PHYSICAL
1. *physical, of the soul:* ψυχικός PSYCHIKOS
1 Cor 15.44 sown a p. body, it is raised a spiritual . . If there is a p. body, there is also a spiritual
15.46 not the spiritual which is first but the p.
2. *in the flesh:* ἐν σαρκί SARX [B.1.a.1]
Rom 2.28 nor is true circumcision something . . p.

PHYSICALLY
1. *by nature:* ἐκ φύσεως PHYSIS [B.1.a.1]
Rom 2.27 those who are physically uncircumcised

PHYSICIAN
1. *physician:* ἰατρός IATROS*
Mt 9.12 "Those who are well have no need of a p.
Mk 2.17 "Those who are well have no need of a p.
5.26 suffered much under many physicians
Lk 4.23 "this proverb, 'Physician, heal yourself
5.31 "Those who are well have no need of a p.
[8.43 *spent all her living upon physicians*‡
Col 4.14 Luke the beloved physician

PICK
1. *gather in:* τρυγάω TRYGAŌ
Lk 6.44 "nor are grapes picked from a bramble

PICK OUT
1. *look upon, visit:* ἐπισκέπτομαι EPISKEPTOMAI
Acts 6. 3 "pick out from among you seven men

PICK UP
1. *lift, carry away:* αἴρω AIRŌ
Mk 16.18 "they will pick up serpents[k]‡

PIECE (*See also* CUT IN PIECES; PROPERTY, PIECE OF; SILVER, PIECE OF; TEAR IN PIECES)
1. *piece, covering:* ἐπίβλημα EPIBLĒMA*
Mt 9.16 "no one puts a piece of unshrunk cloth
Mk 2.21 "No one sews a piece of unshrunk cloth
Lk 5.36 "No one tears a p. from a new garment
5.36 "the piece from the new will not match
2. *part, share:* μέρος MEROS
Lk 24.42 They gave him a piece of broiled fish
3. *anyone, any:* τὶς TIS II [B.3.b.2]
Acts **27**.44
CONTEXTUALLY
Acts 19.19 it came to fifty thousand pieces of silver

PIECE, BROKEN
1. *fragment, piece:* κλάσμα KLASMA
Mt 14.20 twelve baskets full of the broken pieces
15.37 seven baskets full of the broken pieces
Mk 6.43 twelve baskets full of broken pieces
8. 8 took up the broken pieces left over
8.19 "how many baskets . . of broken pieces?
8.20 "how many baskets full of broken pieces?
Lk 9.17 twelve baskets of broken pieces

PIECES, BREAK IN
1. *shatter, grind:* συντρίβω SYNTRIBŌ
Mk 5. 4 the fetters he broke in pieces
Rev 2.27 " 'as when earthen pots are broken in pieces

PIECES, BREAK TO
1. *crush together:* συνθλάω SYNTHLAŌ*
Mt [21.44 "*he . . will be broken to pieces*‡
Lk 20.18 "one who falls . . will be broken to pieces

PIERCE
1. *penetrate:* διϊκνέομαι DIIKNEOMAI*
Heb 4.12 piercing to . . division of soul and spirit
2. *pierce:* ἐκκεντέω EKKENTEŌ*
Jn 19.37 "look on him whom they have pierced
Rev 1. 7 every one who pierced him
3. *stab, pierce:* νύσσω NYSSŌ*
Mt [27.49 *another took a spear and pierced his side*‡
Jn 19.34 one of the soldiers pierced his side
4. *pierce through:* περιπείρω PERIPEIRŌ*
1 Tim 6.10 pierced their hearts with many pangs

PIERCE THROUGH
1. *pass through:* διέρχομαι DIERCHOMAI
Lk 2.35 "(a sword will pierce through your own

PIETY
1. *righteousness, justice:* δικαιοσύνη DIKAIOSYNĒ
Mt 6. 1 "Beware of practicing your p. before men
2. *reverence, piety:* εὐσέβεια EUSEBEIA
Acts 3.12 "as though by our own power or p.

PIGEON
1. *dove:* περιστερά PERISTERA
Mt 21.12 the seats of those who sold pigeons
Mk 11.15 the seats of those who sold pigeons
Lk 2.24 "turtledoves, or two young pigeons
Jn 2.14 In the temple . . selling oxen and . . pigeons
2.16 he told those who sold the pigeons

PILATE: Πιλᾶτος 'pīlət
Mt 27. 2 they . . delivered him to P. the governor
27.13 Pilate said to him, "Do you not hear?
27.17 Pilate said to them, "Whom do you want?
27.22 P. said . . "what shall I do with Jesus?
27.24 when P. saw that he was gaining nothing
27.58 He went to P. and asked for the body . . Then Pilate ordered it to be given to him
27.62 the Pharisees gathered before Pilate
27.65 Pilate said to them, "You have a guard[o]
Mk 15. 1 they bound Jesus and led him . . to P.
15. 2 P. asked . . "Are you the King of the Jews?
15. 4 P. . . asked . . "Have you no answer to make?
15. 5 no further answer, so that P. wondered
15. 8(9) the crowd came up and began to ask P.
15.12 P. . . said . . "what shall I do with the man?
15.14 P. said . . "Why, what evil has he done?
15.15 Pilate, wishing to satisfy the crowd
15.43 Joseph of A. . . went to P., and asked
15.44 Pilate wondered if he were already dead
Lk 3. 1 Pontius Pilate being governor of Judea
13. 1 Galileans whose blood P. had mingled
23. 1 arose, and brought him before Pilate
23. 3 P. asked . . "Are you the King of the Jews?
23. 4 P. said . . "I find no crime in this man
23. 6 P. . . asked whether the man was a Galilean
23.11 Herod . . sent him back to Pilate
23.12 And Herod and Pilate became friends
23.13 P. then called together the chief priests
23.20 Pilate addressed them once more
23.24 P. gave sentence that . . demand . . be granted
23.52 went to Pilate and asked for the body
Jn 18.29 P. . . said, "What accusation do you bring?
18.31 P. said . . "Take him yourselves and judge
18.33 Pilate entered the praetorium again
18.35 Pilate answered, "Am I a Jew?
18.37 P. said to him, "So you are a king?
18.38 Pilate said to him, "What is truth?
19. 1 Pilate took Jesus and scourged him
19. 4 P. went out again, and said
19. 6 P. said . . "Take him yourselves . . crucify
19. 8 When P. heard . . he was the more afraid
19.10 P. . . said . . "You will not speak to me?
19.12 Upon this Pilate sought to release him
19.13 When P. heard . . he brought Jesus out
19.15 P. said . . "Shall I crucify your King?
19.19 P. also wrote a title and put it
19.21 chief priests . . said to P., "Do not write
19.22 Pilate answered, "What I have written
19.31 Jews asked P. that their legs . . be broken
19.38 Joseph of A. . . asked P. that he might take away the body . . and Pilate gave him leave
Acts 3.13 "whom you . . denied in the presence of P.
4.27 "were gathered together . . Pontius P.
13.28 "they asked Pilate to have him killed
1 Tim 6.13 in his testimony before Pontius P.
CONTEXTUALLY
Jn 19. 5 Pilate said to them, "Behold the man!

PILFER
1. *put aside for oneself* (mid.): νοσφίζω NOSPHIZŌ
Tit 2.10 nor to pilfer, but to show . . true fidelity

PILLAR
1. *pillar, pole:* στῦλος STYLOS*
Gal 2. 9 James and Cephas . . reputed to be pillars
1 Tim 3.15 the church . . the pillar . . of the truth
Rev 3.12 " 'I will make him a pillar in the temple
10. 1 mighty angel . . his legs like pillars

PILOT
1. *make straight, direct:* εὐθύνω (subst. part.) EUTHYNŌ
Jas 3. 4 wherever the will of the pilot directs

PINNACLE
1. *end, edge:* πτερύγιον PTERYGION*
Mt 4. 5 devil . . set him on . . pinnacle of the temple
Lk 4. 9 set him on the pinnacle of the temple

PIONEER
1. *founder, leader:* ἀρχηγός ARCHĒGOS
Heb 2.10 make the p. of their salvation perfect
12. 2 Jesus the p. and perfecter of our faith

PIPE
1. *play the flute:* αὐλέω AULEŌ
Mt 11.17 " 'We piped to you, and you did not dance
Lk 7.32 " 'We piped to you, and you did not dance

PISIDIA: pə'sidēə II,F-3
1. *Pisidia:* Πισιδία
Acts 14.24 Then they passed through Pisidia
2. *Pisidian:* Πισίδιος
Acts 13.14 they . . came to Antioch of Pisidia

PIT
1. *abyss, underworld:* ἄβυσσος ABYSSOS
Rev 20. 3 threw him into the pit, and shut it
2. *hole, trench:* βόθυνος BOTHYNOS*
Mt 12.11 "if . . it falls into a pit on the sabbath
15.14 "if a blind man . . , both will fall into a p.
Lk 6.39 "Will they not both fall into a pit?
3. *vat:* ὑπολήνιον HYPOLĒNION*
Mk 12. 1 "A man . . dug a pit for the wine press
4. *pit:* σιρός SIROS*
2 Pet 2. 4 committed them to pits of nether gloom

PIT, BOTTOMLESS
1. *abyss, underworld:* ἄβυσσος ABYSSOS
Rev 9. 1 key of the shaft of the bottomless pit
9. 2 opened the shaft of the bottomless pit
9.11 as king . . angel of the bottomless pit
11. 7 beast . . ascends from . . bottomless pit
17. 8 "beast . . to ascend from the bottomless pit
20. 1 in his hand the key of the bottomless pit

PITFALL
1. *stumbling block, trap:* σκάνδαλον SKANDALON
Rom 11. 9 "Let their table become a snare and . . a p.

PITIABLE
1. *pitied, miserable:* ἐλεεινός ELEEINOS
Rev 3.17 " 'not knowing that you are . . pitiable

PITIED, MOST TO BE
1. *pitied, miserable:* ἐλεεινός (comp.) ELEEINOS
1 Cor 15.19 we are of all men most to be pitied

PITY, HAVE
PITY, IN
PITY, MOVED WITH
PITY, OUT OF
1. *feel pity:* σπλαγχνίζομαι SPLAGCHNIZOMAI
[a]part.
Mt 18.27 [a]"out of p. for him the lord . . released
20.34 [a]Jesus in pity touched their eyes
Mk 1.41 [a]"Moved with p., he stretched out . . hand
9.22 "have pity on us and help us

PLACE (*See also* DWELLING PLACE; TAKE PLACE; THIS PLACE)
1. *throw, put:* βάλλω BALLŌ
Jn 20.25 "Unless I . . place my finger in the mark of the nails, and p. my hand in his side
20.27 "put out your hand, . . place it in my side
2. *place, district:* χωρίον CHŌRION
Mt 26.36 Jesus went . . to a p. called Gethsemane
Mk 14.32 they went to a p. . . called Gethsemane
3. *from that place:* ἐκεῖθεν EKEITHEN [A.4.d]
Mk 6.10 "stay there until you leave the place
4. *stand, set:* ἵστημι HISTĒMI
Mt 25.33 "he will place the sheep at his right
Jn 8. 3 brought a woman . . placing her in the midst[r]‡
5. *lot, share:* κλῆρος KLĒROS
Acts 26.18 " 'a place among those who are sanctified
6. *lay, put:* τίθημι TITHĒMI
Rev 11. 9 refuse to let them be placed in a tomb
7. *place:* τόπος TOPOS
Mt 12.43 "he passes through waterless places
14.13 Jesus . . withdrew . . to a lonely p. apart
14.15 "This is a lonely p., and . . day is . . over
14.35 the men of that place recognized him
24. 7 "will be famines . . in various places
24.15 "Daniel, standing in the holy place
26.52 "Put your sword back into its place
27.33 they came to a place called Golgotha (which means the place of a skull
28. 6 "Come, see the place where he[q] lay
Mk 1.35 he rose and went out to a lonely place
6.11 "if any place will not receive you
6.31 "Come away . . to a lonely place, and rest
6.32 they went away in the boat to a lonely p.
6.35 "This is a lonely p., . . the hour is . . late
13. 8 "will be earthquakes in various places
15.22 brought him to the place called Golgotha (which means the place of a skull
16. 6 "see the place where they laid him
Lk 2. 7 there was no place for them in the inn
4.17 found the place where it was written
4.37 reports of him went out into every place
4.42 he . . went into a lonely place
6.17 he came down . . and stood on a level p.
9.12 "for we are here in a lonely place
10. 1 sent them . . into every town and place
10.32 "when he came to the place and saw him
11. 1 He was praying in a certain place
11.24 "he passes through waterless places
14. 9 " 'Give p. to this man,' . . then you will begin with shame to take the lowest p.
14.10 "go and sit in the lowest place
16.28 " 'lest they also come into this place
19. 5 when Jesus came to the place
21.11 "there will be . . in various places famines
22.40 when he came to the place
23.33 when they came to the place
Jn 4.20 "the place where men ought to worship
5.13 as there was a crowd in the place
6.10 there was much grass in the place
6.23 boats from Tiberias came near the p.
10.40 the place where John at first baptized
11. 6 stayed two days longer in the place
11.30 still in the place where Martha . . met him
11.48 "Romans will come and destroy . . our holy p.[a]
14. 2 "that I go to prepare a place for you
14. 3 "when I go and prepare a place for you
18. 2 Now Judas . . also knew the place
19.13 sat . . at a place called The Pavement
19.17 took Jesus . . to . . the place of a skull
19.20 the place where Jesus was crucified
19.41 the place where he was crucified
20. 7 napkin . . rolled up in a place by itself
Acts 1.25 "to take the p. in this ministry . . from which Judas turned aside, to go to his own p.
4.31 p. in which they . . gathered . . was shaken
6.13 "to speak words against this holy place
6.14 "that this Jesus . . will destroy this p.
7. 7 " 'they shall . . worship me in this place
7.33 " 'p. where you are standing is holy ground
7.49 " 'what is the place of my rest?
12.17 he departed and went to another place
16. 3 the Jews that were in those places
21.28 "the man who is teaching . . against . . this place; . . he has defiled this holy place
27. 8 we came to a p. called Fair Havens
28. 7 in the neighborhood of that place
Rom 9.26 "in the very place where it was said
1 Cor 1. 2 who in every place call on the name

1 Tim 2. 8 that in every place the men should pray
Heb 11. 8 he was called to go out to a place
2 Pet 1.19 a lamp shining in a dark place
Rev 2. 5 " 'I will . . remove your lampstand from its p.
6.14 every . . island was removed from its p.
12. 6 she has a place prepared by God
12. 8 no longer any place for them in heaven
12.14 the place where she is to be nourished
16.16 at the p. . . called . Armageddon
20.11 and no place was found for them
IDIOMATICALLY
a. Jn 13.12 When he had . . resumed his place Ὅτε οὖν . . ἀνέπεσεν πάλιν [ANAPIPTŌ]
CONTEXTUALLY
Mt 2. 9 till it came to rest over the place
Mk 6.55 to any place where they heard he was
Acts 2. 1 they were all together in one place
16.13 where we supposed there was a p. of prayer
16.16 As we were going to the place of prayer
Rom 11.17 grafted in their p. to share the richness°
1 Cor 11.18 in the first p., when you assemble
Eph 1. 3 spiritual blessing in the heavenly places
1.20 at his right hand in the heavenly places
2. 6 sit with him in the heavenly places
2.15 one new man in place of the two
3.10 and powers in the heavenly places
6.12 of wickedness in the heavenly places
Col 4. 9 tell you of everything that has taken p.
Heb 4. 5 And again in this place he said
5. 6 as he says also in another place
9. 2 it is called the Holy Place
9.12 he entered once for all into the Holy P.
9.25 high priest enters the Holy Place yearly

PLACE AT TABLE, TAKE ONE'S
1. *cause to lie down:* κατακλίνω (pass.) KATAKLINŌ
Lk 7.36 he went . . and took his place at table°

PLACE, FIND A
1. *make room for, hold, go:* χωρέω CHŌREŌ
Jn 8.37 "because my word finds no place in you

PLACE, MARKET
1. *marketplace:* ἀγορά AGORA*
Mt 11.16 "like children sitting in the market places
20. 3 "others standing idle in the market p.
23. 7 "salutations in the market places
Mk 6.56 they laid the sick in the market places
7. 4 (when they come from the market place†
12.38 "have salutations in the market places
Lk 7.32 "like children sitting in the market p.
11.43 "love . . salutations in the market places
20.46 "love salutations in the market places
Acts 16.19 dragged them into the market place
17.17 argued . . in the market p. every day

PLACE OF HONOR
1. *first seat at table:* πρωτοκλισία PRŌTOKLISIA*
Mt 23. 6 "they love the place of honor at feasts
Mk 12.39 "the places of honor at feasts
Lk 14. 7 how they chose the places of honor
14. 8 "do not sit down in a place of honor
20.46 "who . . love . . places of honor at feasts

PLACE OF, IN
1. *opposite, instead of:* ἀντί (+gen.) ANTI
Mt 2.22 Archelaus reigned . . in p. of his father

PLACE TO PLACE, FROM
1. *in a row, in order:* καθεξῆς KATHEXĒS
Acts 18.23 departed and went from place to place

PLAGUE
1. *whip, plague:* μάστιξ MASTIX
Lk 7.21 he cured many of diseases and plagues
2. *blow, stroke:* πληγή PLĒGĒ
Rev 9.18 By . . three plagues a third of mankind
9.20 who were not killed by these plagues
11. 6 to smite the earth with every plague
15. 1 seven angels with seven plagues
15. 6 seven angels with the seven plagues
15. 8 until the seven plagues . . were ended
Rev 16. 9 God who had power over these plagues
16.21 men cursed God for the p. of the hail, so fearful was that plague
18. 4 "Come out . . lest you share in her plagues
18. 8 "so shall her plagues come in a . . day
21. 9 bowls full of the seven last plagues
22.18 God will add to him the plagues described

PLAIN
1. *clear:* δῆλος DĒLOS
1 Cor 15.27 it is p. that he is excepted who put all
2. *quite evident:* ἔκδηλος EKDĒLOS*
2 Tim 3. 9 for their folly will be plain to all
3. *visible, known:* φανερός PHANEROS
Rom 1.19 what can be known about God is plain
Gal 5.19 Now the works of the flesh are plain

PLAIN, BE
1. *make manifest, make known:* φανερόω (pass.) PHANEROŌ
1 Jn 2.19 they went out, that it might be plain

PLAIN, MAKE
1. *make manifest, make known:* φανερόω PHANEROŌ
2 Cor 11. 6 in every way we have made this plain

PLAINLY
1. *rightly:* ὀρθῶς ORTHŌS
Mk 7.35 tongue was released, and he spoke p.
2. *outspokenness:* παρρησία (dat.) PARRĒSIA
Mk 8.32 he said this plainly. And Peter took him
Jn 10.24 "If you are the Christ, tell us plainly
11.14 Jesus told them p., "Lazarus is dead
16.25 "I shall . . tell you plainly of the Father
16.29 "Ah, now you are speaking plainly!

PLAIT
1. *twine, plait:* πλέκω PLEKŌ*
Mt 27.29 plaiting a crown of thorns they put it
Mk 15.17 plaiting a crown of thorns they put it
Jn 19. 2 soldiers plaited a crown of thorns

PLAN
1. *will, purpose:* βουλή BOULĒ
Acts 2.23 "delivered up according to the definite p.
4.28 "to do whatever . . thy plan . . predestined
5.38 "for if this plan . . is of men, it will fail
27.42 soldiers' plan was to kill the prisoners
2. *deliberate, plan* (mid.): βουλεύω BOULEUŌ
Jn 12.10 planned to put Lazarus also to death
Acts 27.39 they planned . . to bring the ship ashore
3. *stewardship, management:* οἰκονομία OIKONOMIA
Eph 1.10 as a plan for the fulness of time
3. 9 what is the plan of the mystery
4. *do, make:* ποιέω POIEŌ
Acts 25. 3 planning an ambush to kill him

PLANK
1. *board, plank:* σανίς SANIS*
Acts 27.44 the rest on planks or . . pieces of the ship

PLANS, MAKE
1. *deliberate, plan* (mid.): βουλεύω BOULEUŌ
2 Cor 1.17 Do I make . . plans like a worldly man?

PLANT
1. *plant, planting:* φυτεία PHYTEIA*
Mt 15.13 "Every plant . . will be rooted up
2. *plant, engender:* φυτεύω PHYTEUŌ*
Mt 15.13 "which my . . Father has not planted
21.33 "a householder who planted a vineyard
Mk 12. 1 "A man planted a vineyard
Lk 13. 6 "A man had a fig tree planted
17. 6 " 'Be rooted up, . . be planted in the sea
17.28 "they sold, they planted, they built
20. 9 "A man planted a vineyard
1 Cor 3. 6 I planted, Apollos watered
3. 7 neither . . who plants nor . . who waters
3. 8 He who plants and he who waters
9. 7 Who plants a vineyard without eating?

PLANTS
1. *grass, fodder:* χόρτος CHORTOS
Mt 13.26 "the plants came up and bore grain

PLATE
1. *dish:* παροψίς PAROPSIS*
Mt 23.25 "you cleanse the outside . . of the plate
23.26 "first cleanse the inside . . of the plate

PLATTER
1. *platter:* πίναξ PINAX
Mt 14. 8 "the head of John the Baptist . . on a p.
14.11 his head was brought on a platter
Mk 6.25 "the head of John the Baptist on a p.
6.28 brought his head on a platter . . to the girl

PLAUSIBLE
1. *persuasive:* πειθός PEITHOS*
1 Cor 2. 4 not in plausible words of wisdom

PLAY (*See also* WANTON, PLAY THE)
1. *play the cithara or lyre:* κιθαρίζω KITHARIZŌ
Rev 14. 2 sound of harpers playing on their harps
IDIOMATICALLY
a. 1 Cor 14.7 how will any one know what is played?
πῶς γνωσθήσεται τὸ αὐλούμενον ἢ τὸ κιθαριζόμενον;
[AULEŌ; KITHARIZŌ]

PLAYER, FLUTE
1. *flute player:* αὐλητής AULĒTĒS*
Mt 9.23 when Jesus . . saw the flute players
Rev 18.22 "the sound of . . flute players

PLAYMATE
1. *comrade:* ἑταῖρος HETAIROS
Mt 11.16 "like children . . calling to . . playmates

PLEAD
1. *appeal to, plead:* ἐντυγχάνω ENTYGCHANŌ
Rom 11. 2 Elijah, how he pleads with God
2. *persuade:* πείθω PEITHŌ
Acts 19. 8 pleading about the kingdom of God

PLEASANT
1. *joy, delight:* χαρά (gen.) CHARA
Heb 12.11 discipline seems painful rather than p.

PLEASE
1. *please:* ἀρέσκω ARESKŌ
Mt 14. 6 Herodias danced . . and pleased Herod
Mk 6.22 "Herodias' daughter . . pleased Herod
Acts 6. 5 what they said pleased the . . multitude
Rom 8. 8 those . . in the flesh cannot please God
15. 1 We . . ought . . not to please ourselves
15. 2 let each of us please his neighbor
15. 3 "For Christ did not please himself
1 Cor 7.32 unmarried man is anxious . . to p. the Lord
7.33 married man is anxious . . to p. his wife
7.34 married woman is anxious . . to p. . . husband
10.33 I try to please all men in everything I do
Gal 1.10 am I trying to p. men? If I were still pleasing men, I should not be a servant[a]
1 Th 2. 4 to please God who tests our hearts
4. 1 how you ought to live and to p. God
2. *be pleasing:* ἀρεστὸς εἶναι ARESTOS [A.6.a.3]
Acts 12. 3 when he saw that it pleased the Jews
3. *be pleasing:* εὐαρεστέω EUARESTEŌ
Heb 11. 5 he was attested as having pleased God
11. 6 without faith it is impossible to p. him
4. *be pleasing:* εὐάρεστος εἶναι EUARESTOS [A.6.a.3]
2 Cor 5. 9 we make it our aim to please him
Col 3.20 obey . . parents . . , for this pleases the Lord
5. *well, rightly:* καλῶς KALŌS
Jas 2. 3 you . . say, "Have a seat here, please
6. *will, wish:* θέλω THELŌ
Mt 17.12 "did to him whatever they pleased
Mk 9.13 "did to him whatever they pleased
CONTEXTUALLY
Acts 9.38 "Please come to us without delay

PLEASED, BE
PLEASED, BE WELL
1. *be well pleased:* εὐδοκέω EUDOKEŌ
Mt 3.17 "Son,[h] with whom I am well pleased
12.18 "with whom my soul is well pleased
17. 5 "Son,[w] with whom I am well pleased
Mk 1.11 "Son;[d] with thee I am well pleased
Lk 3.22 "Son;[j] with thee I am well pleased[k]‡
Rom 15.26 have been p. to make . . contribution
15.27 they were pleased to do it
1 Cor 10. 5 with most of them God was not p.
Gal 1.16(15) ⟨he⟩ was p. to reveal his Son to[c] me
Col 1.19 all the fulness of God was p. to dwell
2 Pet 1.17 "Son,[d] with whom I am well pleased

PLEASED, WITH WHOM ONE IS
1. *satisfaction, goodwill:* εὐδοκία (gen.) EUDOKIA
Lk 2.14 "peace among men with whom he is p.![g]‡

PLEASES ONE, IT
1. *be well pleased:* εὐδοκέω EUDOKEŌ [A.6.e]
1 Cor 1.21 it pleased God through . . what we preach

PLEASES, WHAT
1. *pleasing:* ἀρεστός (neut. pl.) ARESTOS
1 Jn 3.22 because we . . do what pleases him

PLEASING
1. *to satisfaction:* εἰς ἀρεσκείαν ARESKEIA* [B.1.a.1]
Col 1.10 a life worthy of the Lord, fully pleasing
2. *pleasing:* εὐάρεστος EUARESTOS
Eph 5.10 try to learn what is pleasing to the Lord
Phil 4.18 a sacrifice acceptable and p. to God
Heb 13.21 working . . that which is p. in his sight

PLEASING TO S., BE
1. *be pleasing:* εὐαρεστέω EUARESTEŌ [A.6.c.3]
Heb 13.16 for such sacrifices are pleasing to God

PLEASING, WHAT IS
1. *pleasing:* ἀρεστός (neut. pl.) ARESTOS
Jn 8.29 "I always do what is pleasing to him

PLEASURE
1. *pleasure:* ἀπόλαυσις APOLAUSIS
[a]sg.
Heb 11.25 [a]than to enjoy the fleeting pleasures of sin
2. *joy, delight:* χαρά CHARA
2 Cor 1.15 that you might have a double pleasure[b]‡
3. *think, suppose:* δοκέω (subst. neut. part.) DOKEŌ
Heb 12.10 they disciplined us . . at their pleasure
4. *pleasure, enjoyment:* ἡδονή HĒDONĒ
Lk 8.14 "the cares and riches and pleasures of life
Tit 3. 3 slaves to various passions and pleasures
2 Pet 2.13 They count it pleasure to revel

PLEASURE, GOOD
1. *satisfaction, goodwill:* εὐδοκία EUDOKIA
Phil 2.13 to will and to work for his good pleasure

PLEASURE, HAVE
PLEASURE IN, TAKE
1. *be well pleased:* εὐδοκέω EUDOKEŌ
2 Th 2.12 who . . had pleasure in unrighteousness
Heb 10. 6 "in burnt offerings . . thou hast taken no p.
10. 8 "Thou hast neither desired nor taken p.
10.38 "my soul has no pleasure in him

PLEASURE, IT IS ONE'S GOOD
1. *be well pleased:* εὐδοκέω EUDOKEŌ [A.6.e]
Lk 12.32 "it is your Father's good pleasure

PLEASURE, LIVE IN
1. *live softly, live indulgently:* σπαταλάω SPATALAŌ
Jas 5. 5 You have lived on the earth . . in pleasure

PLEASURE, LOVER OF
1. *fond of pleasure:* φιλήδονος (subst.) PHILĒDONOS*
2 Tim 3. 4 lovers of p. rather than lovers of God

PLEDGE
1. *trust, faith:* πίστις PISTIS
1 Tim 5.12 condemnation . . having violated . . first p.

PLENTIFUL
1. *many, great:* πολύς POLYS
Mt 9.37 "The harvest is p., but the laborers . . few
Lk 10. 2 "The harvest is p., but the laborers . . few

PLENTIFULLY, BRING FORTH
1. *bear well, be fruitful:* εὐφορέω EUPHOREŌ*
Lk 12.16 "land of a rich man brought forth p.

PLENTY, FACING
1. *feed, fatten:* χορτάζω (inf.) CHORTAZŌ
Phil 4.12 the secret of facing plenty and hunger

PLOT
1. *plot, plan against s.:* ἐπιβουλή EPIBOULĒ*
Acts 9.24 their plot became known to Saul
20. 3 when a plot was made against him
20.19 "trials which befell me through the plots
23.30 "there would be a plot against the man
2. *advise, recommend:* συμβουλεύω (mid.) SYMBOULEUŌ
Acts 9.23 the Jews plotted to kill him
3. *seditious meeting:* συστροφή SYSTROPHĒ
Acts 23.12 When it was day, the Jews made a plot

PLOW
1. *plow:* ἀροτριάω AROTRIAŌ*
Lk 17. 7 "Will any . . who has a servant plowing
1 Cor 9.10 the plowman should plow in hope
2. *plow:* ἄροτρον AROTRON*
Lk 9.62 "No one who puts his hand to the plow

PLUCK
1. *pluck:* τίλλω TILLŌ*
Mt 12. 1 began to pluck heads of grain and to eat
Mk 2.23 disciples began to pluck heads of grain
Lk 6. 1 plucked and ate some heads of grain

PLUCK OUT
1. *throw out:* ἐκβάλλω EKBALLŌ
Mk 9.47 "if your eye causes you to sin,[l] p. it out
2. *take out:* ἐξαιρέω EXAIREŌ
Mt 5.29 "If your . . eye causes you to sin, p. it out
18. 9 "if your eye causes you to sin,[z] p. it out
3. *dig out:* ἐξορύσσω EXORYSSŌ
Gal 4.15 you would have plucked out your eyes

PLUNDER
1. *plunder thoroughly:* διαρπάζω DIARPAZŌ*
Mt 12.29 "Then indeed he may plunder his house
Mk 3.27 "no one can . . plunder his goods
3.27 "then indeed he may plunder his house
2. *seize, snatch up:* ἁρπάζω HARPAZŌ
Mt 12.29 "how can one . . plunder his goods?

PLUNDERING
1. *robbery, plunder:* ἁρπαγή HARPAGĒ
Heb 10.34 you joyfully accepted the plundering

PLUNGE
1. *sink, plunge:* βυθίζω BYTHIZŌ
1 Tim 6. 9 that plunge men into ruin and destruction

POD
1. *carob pod:* κεράτιον KERATION*
Lk 15.16 "he would gladly have fed on[u] the pods

POET
1. *maker, poet:* ποιητής POIĒTĒS
Acts 17.28 "as even some of your poets have said

POINT (*See also* DISPUTE, POINT OF; SACRIFICED, BE ON THE POINT OF BEING)
1. *sum total, main point:* κεφάλαιον KEPHALAION
Heb 8. 1 the point in what we are saying is this
2. *lead forward:* προάγω PROAGŌ
1 Tim 1.18 utterances which pointed to you
5.24 conspicuous, pointing to judgment
IDIOMATICALLY
a. Mk 5.23 "My little daughter is at the point of death
τὸ θυγάτριόν μου ἐσχάτως ἔχει [ESCHATŌS]
CONTEXTUALLY
2 Cor 5.16 regard no one from a human point of view
5.16 regarded Christ from a human p. of view
7.11 At every p. you have proved yourselves
9. 6 The p. is this: he who sows sparingly

POINT, BE AT THE
1. *be about to* (+inf.): μέλλω MELLŌ
Lk 7. 2 who was sick at the point of death
Jn 4.47 for he was at the point of death
Rev 3. 2 " 'what remains and is on the p. of death

POINT OF, TO THE
1. *as far as:* μέχρι MECHRI
Heb 12. 4 not yet . . to the p. of shedding your blood

POINT, ONE
1. *one:* εἷς (neut.) HEIS
Jas 2.10 keeps the whole law but fails in one p.

POINT OUT
1. *show, point out:* ἐπιδείκνυμι EPIDEIKNYMI
Mt 24. 1 disciples came to point out to him

POISON
1. *venom, poison:* ἰός IOS
Jas 3. 8 tongue—a restless evil, full of deadly p.
2. *mistreat:* κακόω KAKOŌ
Acts 14. 2 poisoned their minds against the brethren

POLICE
1. *one who carries a staff:* ῥαβδοῦχος (pl.) RHABDOUCHOS*
Acts 16.35 "the magistrates sent the police
16.38 p. reported these words to . . magistrates

POLLUTED
1. *loathe, be sick:* βδελύσσομαι (perf. pass. part.) BDELYSSOMAI
Rev 21. 8 "But as for the cowardly, . . the polluted

POLLUTION
1. *pollution:* ἀλίσγημα ALISGĒMA*
Acts 15.20 "to abstain from the pollutions of idols

POMMEL
1. *strike under the eye, wear out:* ὑπωπιάζω HYPŌPIAZŌ
1 Cor 9.27 I pommel my body and subdue it

POMP
1. *appearance, ostentation:* φαντασία PHANTASIA*
Acts 25.23 Agrippa and Bernice came with great p.

PONDER
1. *consider, reflect:* διενθυμέομαι DIENTHYMEOMAI*
[a] + περί
Acts 10.19 [a]while Peter was pondering the vision
2. *throw together, compare:* συμβάλλω SYMBALLŌ
Lk 2.19 Mary kept all these things, pondering them

PONTIUS: Πόντιος 'pänchəs
Lk 3. 1 Pontius Pilate being governor of Judea
Acts 4.27 "gathered . . both Herod and P. Pilate
1 Tim 6.13 in his testimony before P. Pilate

PONTUS: 'päntəs II,F-2
1. *from Pontus:* Ποντικός
Acts 18. 2 a Jew named Aquila, a native of Pontus
2. *Pontus:* Πόντος
Acts 2. 9 "residents of Mesopotamia, . . P. and Asia
1 Pet 1. 1 To the exiles of the Dispersion in Pontus

POOL
1. *swimming pool:* κολυμβήθρα KOLYMBĒTHRA*
Jn 5. 2 in Jerusalem by the Sheep Gate a pool
[5. 4 *an angel . . went down . . into the pool*‡
5. 7 "I have no man to put me into the pool
9. 7 "Go, wash in the pool of Siloam

POOR
1. *smaller, inferior:* ἐλάσσων ELASSŌN
Jn 2.10 "when men have drunk . . , then the poor wine
2. *day laborer, poor man:* πένης (pl.) PENĒS*
2 Cor 9. 9 "He scatters abroad, he gives to the poor
3. *poor, needy:* πενιχρός PENICHROS*
Lk 21. 2 he saw a poor widow put in two . . coins
4. *poor, beggarly:* πτωχός PTŌCHOS
Mt 5. 3 "Blessed are the poor in spirit
11. 5 "the poor have good news preached to them
19.21 "sell what you possess and give to the poor
26. 9 "might have been sold . . given to the p.
26.11 "For you always have the poor with you
Mk 10.21 "sell what you have, and give to the p.
12.42 a poor widow . . put in two copper coins
12.43 "this poor widow has put in more
14. 5 "might have been sold . . given to the p.
14. 7 "For you always have the poor with you
Lk 4.18 "to preach good news to the poor
6.20 "Blessed are you p., for yours is the kingdom
7.22 "poor have good news preached to them
14.13 "when you give a feast, invite the p.
14.21 " 'bring in the poor and maimed and blind
16.20 "a p. man named Lazarus, full of sores
16.22 "p. man died . . was carried by the angels
18.22 "Sell all . . and distribute to the poor
19. 8 "the half of my goods I give to the poor
21. 3 "this p. widow has put in more than all

Jn 12. 5 "Why was this . . not sold . . given to the p.?
12. 6 he said, not that he cared for the poor
12. 8 "The poor you always have with you
13.29 that he should give something to the poor
Rom 15.26 to make some contribution for the poor
2 Cor 6.10 as poor, yet making many rich
Gal 2.10 they would have us remember the poor
Jas 2. 2 if . . a p. man in shabby clothing . . comes
2. 3 you say to the p. man, "Stand there
2. 5 Has not God chosen those who are poor?
2. 6 you have dishonored the poor man
Rev 3.17 " 'not knowing that you are . . poor, blind
13.16 causes all, both . . rich and p., . . to be marked

POOR, BECOME

1. *be a beggar:* πτωχεύω PTŌCHEUŌ*
2 Cor 8. 9 yet for your sake he became poor

PORCH

1. *gateway:* πυλών PYLŌN
Mt 26.71 when he went out to the porch

PORCIUS (*See* FESTUS, PORCIUS)

PORT

1. *place:* τόπος TOPOS
Acts 27. 2 to sail to . . ports along the coast of Asia

PORTENT

1. *sign, portent:* σημεῖον SĒMEION
Rev 12. 1 a great portent appeared in heaven
12. 3 another portent appeared in heaven
15. 1 I saw another portent in heaven

PORTICO

1. *roofed colonnade:* στοά STOA*
Jn 5. 2 a pool . . which has five porticoes
10.23 Jesus was walking . . in the p. of Solomon
Acts 3.11 people ran . . to . . the p. called Solomon's
5.12 were all together in Solomon's Portico

PORTION

1. *part, portion:* μερίς MERIS
Lk 10.42 "Mary has chosen the good portion

PORTION OF FOOD

1. *ration of grain:* σιτομέτριον SITOMETRION*
Lk 12.42 "to give them their portion of food

PORTRAY, PUBLICLY

1. *write before:* προγράφω (pass.) PROGRAPHŌ
Gal 3. 1 was publicly portrayed as crucified

POSITION

1. *origin, rule:* ἀρχή ARCHĒ
Jude . 6 the angels that did not keep their own p.
2. *face, person:* πρόσωπον PROSŌPON [C.2]
Mt 22.16 "for you do not regard the position of men
Mk 12.14 "for you do not regard the position of men
2 Cor 5.12 those who pride themselves on a man's p.
3. *place:* τόπος TOPOS
1 Cor 14.16 how can any one in the p. of an outsider[z]?

POSITION, HIGH

1. *superiority:* ὑπεροχή HYPEROCHĒ
1 Tim 2. 2 kings and all who are in high positions

POSSESS (*See also* SPIRIT, THOSE WHO POSSESS THE)

1. *have, hold:* ἔχω ECHŌ
1 Cor 8. 1 we know that "all of us p. knowledge
12.30 Do all possess gifts of healing?
2. *be, exist, belong to:* ὑπάρχω (+dat.) HYPARCHŌ
Mt 19.21 "go, sell what you possess and give
Acts 4.32 no one said that . . things . . he possessed
3. *hold fast, restrain:* κατέχω KATECHŌ
2 Cor 6.10 having nothing, . . possessing everything

CONTEXTUALLY
1 Cor 8. 7 However, not all p. this knowledge

POSSESSED, BE
POSSESSED BY, BE

1. *have, hold:* ἔχω ECHŌ
Mk 3.22 "He is possessed by Beelzebul
7.25 daughter was p. by an unclean spirit
Acts 8. 7 spirits came out of many who were p.

POSSESSED BY A DEMON, BE

1. *be possessed by a demon:* δαιμονίζομαι DAIMONIZOMAI
Mt 15.22 "my daughter is severely p. by a demon

POSSESSED WITH DEMONS, ONE WHO IS

1. *be possessed by a demon:* δαιμονίζομαι (subst. part.) DAIMONIZOMAI
Mt 8.16 many who were possessed with demons
Mk 1.32 all who were . . possessed with demons
5.18 who had been possessed with demons
Lk 8.36 who had been possessed with demons

POSSESSION

1. *be, exist, belong to:* ὑπάρχω (subst. neut. pl.) HYPARCHŌ
Mt 24.47 "he will set him over all his possessions
Lk 12.15 "man's life does not consist in . . possessions
12.33 "Sell your possessions, and give alms
12.44 "he will set him over all his possessions
2. *property:* ὕπαρξις HYPARXIS
Heb 10.34 you yourselves had a better possession
3. *holding back, possession:* κατάσχεσις KATASCHESIS
Acts 7. 5 "promised to give it to him in possession
4. *anything gotten, property:* κτῆμα KTĒMA
Mt 19.22 sorrowful; for he had great possessions
Mk 10.22 sorrowful; for he had great possessions
Acts 2.45 they sold their possessions and goods

IDIOMATICALLY
a. Eph 1.14 guarantee of our inheritance until we acquire possession of it ἀρραβὼν τῆς κληρονομίας ἡμῶν, εἰς ἀπολύτρωσιν τῆς περιποιήσεως [PERIPOIĒSIS]

POSSESSOR

1. *owner:* κτήτωρ KTĒTŌR*
Acts 4.34 as many as were possessors of lands

POSSIBLE (*See also* SOON AS POSSIBLE)

1. *then:* ἄρα ARA II [A.5.b]
Acts 8.22 "that, if p., the intent . . be forgiven
2. *be able:* δύναμαι DYNAMAI [A.6.e]
Acts 27.39 planned if p. to bring the ship ashore
3. *possible, strong:* δυνατός DYNATOS
Mt 19.26 "but with God all things are possible
24.24 "to lead astray, if possible, even the elect
26.39 "My Father, if it be p., let this cup pass
Mk 9.23 "All things are p. to him who believes
10.27 "for all things are possible with God
13.22 "to lead astray, if possible, the elect
14.35 that, if it were p., the hour might pass
14.36 "Father, all things are possible to thee
Lk 18.27 "What is impossible . . is p. with God
Acts 2.24 "it was not p. for him to be held by it
20.16 to be at J., if p., on . . Pentecost
Rom 12.18 If p., so far as it depends upon you
Gal 4.15 if p., . . have plucked out your eyes

POSSIBLE, IF

1. *in some way, perhaps:* πώς PŌS II
Phil 3.11 that if p. I may attain the resurrection

POSTERITY

1. *seed, offspring:* σπέρμα SPERMA
Lk 1.55 "spoke . . to Abraham and to his p. for ever
Acts 3.25 " 'in your posterity shall all . . be blessed
7. 5 "promised to give it to him . . and to his p.
7. 6 "that his p. would be aliens in a land
13.23 "Of this man's p. God has brought

POT

1. *vessel, tackle:* σκεῦος SKEUOS
Rev 2.27 " 'as when earthen pots are broken
2. *pitcher:* ξέστης XESTĒS*
Mk 7. 4 (washing of cups and pots and vessels

POTTER

1. *potter:* κεραμεύς KERAMEUS*
Mt 27. 7 bought with them the potter's field
27.10 "they gave them for the potter's field
Rom 9.21 Has the potter no right over the clay?

POUND

1. *pound* (12 ounces; a silver coin): λίτρα LITRA*
Jn 12. 3 Mary took a pound of costly ointment
19.39 myrrh and aloes, . . a hundred pounds'

2. *mina* (a weight, a sum of money): μνᾶ MNA*
Lk 19.13 "his servants, he gave them ten pounds[e]
19.16 "The first came before him, saying, 'Lord, your p. has made ten pounds more
19.18 "the second came, saying, 'Lord, your pound has made five pounds
19.20 " 'Lord, here is your pound, which I kept
19.24 " 'Take the pound from him, and give it to him who has the ten pounds
19.25 "(they said . . 'Lord, he has ten pounds!

POUR
1. *throw, put:* βάλλω BALLŌ
Mt 26.12 "In pouring this ointment on my body
Jn 13. 5 Then he poured water into a basin
Rev 12.15 The serpent poured water like a river
12.16 the river which the dragon had poured
2. *pour out:* ἐκχέω EKCHEŌ
Rom 5. 5 God's love . . poured into our hearts
Rev 16. 2 first angel . . poured . . bowl on the earth
16. 3 second angel poured . . bowl into the sea
16. 4 third angel poured . . bowl into the rivers
16. 8 fourth angel poured . . bowl on the sun
16.10 fifth angel poured . . bowl on the throne
16.12 sixth angel poured . . bowl on the . . river
16.17 seventh angel poured . . bowl into the air
3. *pour over:* καταχέω KATACHEŌ
Mt 26. 7 she poured it on his head, as he sat
4. *mix, blend:* κεράννυμι KERANNYMI
Rev 14.10 "wine of God's wrath, poured unmixed

POUR AS A LIBATION
1. *make a drink offering:* σπένδω SPENDŌ
Phil 2.17 if I am to be poured as a libation

POUR FORTH
1. *burst forth, gush:* βρύω BRYŌ*
Jas 3.11 Does a spring p. forth . . brackish ⟨water⟩?

POUR FROM
1. *go out:* ἐκπορεύομαι EKPOREUOMAI
Rev 11. 5 fire pours from their mouth

POUR ON
1. *pour over:* ἐπιχέω EPICHEŌ*
Lk 10.34 "bound up his wounds, pouring on oil

POUR OUT
1. *pour out:* ἐκχέω EKCHEŌ
Mt 26.28 "blood of the[g] covenant, . . poured out
Mk 14.24 "blood of the[c] covenant, . . poured out
Lk 22.20 "This cup which is poured out for you‡
Jn 2.15 poured out . . coins of the money-changers
Acts 2.17 " 'I will p. out my Spirit upon all flesh
2.18 " 'in those days I will p. out my Spirit
2.33 "he has poured out this which you see
10.45 the Holy Spirit had been poured out
Tit 3. 6 which he poured out upon us richly
Rev 16. 1 "pour out on the earth the seven bowls

POUR OVER
1. *pour over:* καταχέω KATACHEŌ
Mk 14. 3 she . . poured it over his head

POVERTY
1. *deficiency, need:* ὑστέρημα HYSTERĒMA
Lk 21. 4 "but she out of her p. put in all the living
2. *shortcoming, need:* ὑστέρησις HYSTERĒSIS
Mk 12.44 "she out of her p. has put in everything
3. *extreme poverty:* πτωχεία PTŌCHEIA*
2 Cor 8. 2 their . . joy and . . p. have overflowed
8. 9 so that by his p. you might become rich
Rev 2. 9 " 'I know your tribulation and your p.

POWER (*See also* ROYAL POWER)
1. *power, ability:* δύναμις DYNAMIS
Mt [6.13 *"thine is . . the power and the glory*‡
14. 2 " 'that is why these powers are at work
22.29 "know neither the scriptures nor the p.
24.29 "powers of the heavens will be shaken
24.30 "Son of man coming . . with power
26.64 "Son of man seated at the right hand of P.
Mk 5.30 Jesus, perceiving in himself that p.
6.14 "why these powers are at work in him
9. 1 "the kingdom of God has come with power
12.24 "know neither the scriptures nor the p.
13.25 "powers in the heavens will be shaken
13.26 "see the Son of man coming . . with great p.
14.62 "seated at the right hand of Power
Lk 1.17 "he will go . . in . . spirit and p. of Elijah
1.35 "p. of the Most High will overshadow
4.14 Jesus returned in the p. of the Spirit
4.36 "with . . p. he commands . . unclean spirits
5.17 the p. of the Lord was with him to heal[p]
6.19 power came forth from him and healed
8.46 "I perceive that p. has gone . . from me
9. 1 he . . gave them power . . over all demons
10.19 "authority . . over all the p. of the enemy
21.26 "the powers of the heavens will be shaken
21.27 "Son of man coming in a cloud with p.
22.69 "seated at the right hand of the power
24.49 "stay . . until you are clothed with p.
Acts 1. 8 "shall receive p. when the Holy Spirit
3.12 "as though by our own power or piety
4. 7 "By what power . . did you do this?
4.33 with great p. the apostles gave . . testimony
6. 8 And Stephen, full of grace and power
8.10 "This man is . . p. of God . . called Great
10.38 "anointed . . with the Holy Spirit and . . p.
Rom 1. 4 designated Son of God in power
1.16 it is the power of God for salvation
1.20 namely, his eternal power and deity
8.38 neither death, nor life, . . nor powers
9.17 "for the very purpose of showing my p.
15.13 that by the power of the Holy Spirit
15.19 by the power of signs and wonders, by the power of the Holy Spirit
1 Cor 1.18 word of the cross . . to us . . the p. of God
1.24 Christ the p. of God and the wisdom
2. 4 in demonstration of the Spirit and power
2. 5 that your faith . . rest . . in the p. of God
4.19 I will find out not the talk . . but their p.
4.20 kingdom of God does . . consist . . in power
5. 4 assembled . . with the p. of our Lord Jesus
6.14 God . . will also raise us up by his p.
15.24 destroying every rule and . . power
15.43 It is sown in weakness, it is raised in p.
15.56 the power of sin is the law
2 Cor 4. 7 the transcendent power belongs to God
6. 7 truthful speech, and the p. of God
12. 9 "my p. is made perfect in weakness
12. 9 "that the p. of Christ may rest upon me
13. 4 was crucified . . but lives by the p. of God
13. 4 we shall live with him by the p. of God
Eph 1.19 immeasurable greatness of his p. in us
1.21 above all rule and authority and p.
3. 7 according to the gift . . given me by . . his p.
3.20 to him who by the p. at work within us
Phil 3.10 know him and the p. of his resurrection
Col 1.11 May you be strengthened with all power
1 Th 1. 5 gospel came . . not only in word, but also in p.
2 Th 1.11 that . . God may . . fulfil . . work . . by his p.
2. 9 coming of the lawless one . . will be with all p.
2 Tim 1. 7 God did . . give us . . a spirit of p. and love
1. 8 suffering for the gospel in the p. of God
3. 5 holding the form . . but denying the power
Heb 1. 3 upholding the universe by his word of p.
6. 5 tasted . . the powers of the age to come
7.16 by the power of an indestructible life
11.11 By faith Sarah herself received power
1 Pet 1. 5 who by God's power are guarded
3.22 authorities, and powers subject to him
[4.14 the spirit of glory *and of power*‡
2 Pet 1. 3 His divine power has granted to us all things
1.16 when we made known to you the power
2.11 angels, though greater in might and p.
Rev 3. 8 " 'I know that you have but little power
4.11 "Worthy . . to receive glory and . . power
5.12 "Worthy is the Lamb . . to receive power!

Rev 7.12 "Blessing and . . power . . be to our God!
11.17 "that thou hast taken thy great p.
12.10 "the salvation and the p. . . have come
13. 2 And to it the dragon gave his power
15. 8 temple was filled with smoke from . . his p.
17.13 "These . . give over their p. . . to the beast
19. 1 "Salvation and . . p. belong to our God
2. *possible, strong:* δυνατός (subst.) DYNATOS
Rom 9.22 God, desiring . . to make known his power
3. *operation, activity:* ἐνέργεια ENERGEIA
Phil 3.21 will change our lowly body . . by the power
4. *authority, power:* ἐξουσία EXOUSIA
Lk 12. 5 "fear him who . . has p. to cast into hell[m]
22.53 "this is your hour, and the p. of darkness
Jn 1.12 he gave p. to become children of God
10.18 "I have power to lay it down, and I have power to take it again
17. 2 "thou hast given him p. over all flesh
19.10 "Do you not know that I have power to release you, and power to crucify you?
19.11 "You would have no p. . . unless . . given you
Acts 8.19 "Give me also this power
26.18 " 'that they may turn . . from the p. of Satan
Eph 2. 2 following the prince of the p. of the air
3.10 known to the principalities and powers
6.12 we are . . contending against . . the powers
Col 2.15 He disarmed the principalities and powers
Rev 2.26 " 'I will give him power over the nations
6. 8 power over a fourth of the earth
9. 3 they were given power like the power of scorpions of the earth
9.10 power of hurting men for five months
9.19 the p. of the horses is in their mouths
11. 6 They have power to shut the sky . . and they have power over the waters
14.18 the angel who has power over fire
16. 9 God who had power over these plagues
20. 6 Over such the second death has no power
5. *strength, sovereignty:* κράτος KRATOS
Heb 2.14 might destroy him who has the p. of death
6. *gate:* πύλη PYLĒ [C.2]
Mt 16.18 "the powers of death[u] shall not prevail†
CONTEXTUALLY
Jn 14.30 "He has no power over me
Rom 3. 9 both Jews and Greeks, are under the p.
1 Cor 1.17 cross of Christ be emptied of its power
14.13 should pray for the p. to interpret
Rev 2.27(28) " 'as I myself have received power
7. 2 who had been given p. to harm earth
11. 3 "I will grant my two witnesses power

POWER, HAVE
1. *possible, strong:* δυνατός DYNATOS [B.2.d.2; B.3.b.2]
Rom 11.23 God has the power to graft them in
2 Cor 10. 4 have divine power to destroy strongholds
2. *be strong enough:* ἐξισχύω EXISCHYŌ*
Eph 3.18 have p. to comprehend with all the saints
3. *be strong, prevail:* ἰσχύω ISCHYŌ
Jas 5.16 prayer of a righteous man has great p.

POWER OF, BE IN THE
1. *lie in:* κεῖμαι ἐν KEIMAI [B.2.d.1]
1 Jn 5.19 world is in the power of the evil one

POWERFUL
1. *possible, strong:* δυνατός DYNATOS
1 Cor 1.26 consider your call, . . not many were p.

POWERFUL, BE
1. *be strong:* δυνατέω DYNATEŌ
2 Cor 13. 3 He is not weak . . but is powerful in you

POWERFULLY
1. *vigorously:* εὐτόνως EUTONŌS
Acts 18.28 he p. confuted the Jews in public

POWERS, PROPHETIC
1. *prophecy:* προφητεία PROPHĒTEIA
1 Cor 13. 2 if I have prophetic p., and understand

PRACTICE (*See also* IMMORALITY, PRACTICE)
1. *pursue:* διώκω DIŌKŌ
Rom 12.13 practice hospitality
2. *function, business:* ἐργασία ERGASIA [B.1.a.2]
Eph 4.19 greedy to p. every kind of uncleanness
3. *habit, skill:* ἕξις HEXIS*
Heb 5.14 trained by p. to distinguish good
4. *think about, practice:* μελετάω MELETAŌ
1 Tim 4.15 P. these duties, devote yourself to them
5. *walk in:* περιπατέω ἐν PERIPATEŌ [A.6.a.4]
2 Cor 4. 2 we refuse to p. cunning or to tamper
6. *do, make:* ποιέω POIEŌ
Mt 6. 1 "Beware of practicing . . piety before men
23. 3 "p. and observe whatever they tell you . .; for they preach, but do not practice
Acts 16.21 "customs . . not lawful for us Romans to . . p.
Rom 10. 5 who practices . . the law shall live by it
Rev 21.27 nor any one who practices abomination
22.15 every one who . . practices falsehood
7. *thing, deed:* πρᾶγμα PRAGMA
Jas 3.16 there will be disorder and every vile p.
8. *do, practice:* πράσσω PRASSŌ
Acts 19.19 those who practiced magic arts
Rom 1.32 they . . approve those who p. them
2 Cor 12.21 licentiousness which they have practiced
9. *practice, act:* πρᾶξις PRAXIS
Acts 19.18 confessing and divulging their practices
Col 3. 9 put off the old nature with its practices
10. *custom, practice:* συνήθεια SYNĒTHEIA
1 Cor 11.16 we recognize no other practice

PRACTICE HOSPITALITY
1. *hospitable:* φιλόξενος PHILOXENOS [A.3.e.2]
1 Pet 4. 9 Practice hospitality ungrudgingly

PRACTICE MAGIC
1. *use magic arts:* μαγεύω MAGEUŌ*
Acts 8. 9 Simon . . had previously practiced magic

PRAETORIAN GUARD
1. *praetorium, praetorian guard:* πραιτώριον PRAITŌRION
Phil 1.13 known throughout the whole p. guard[c]†

PRAETORIUM
1. *praetorium, praetorian guard:* πραιτώριον PRAITŌRION
Mt 27.27 the governor took Jesus into the p.
Mk 15.16 led him . . inside the palace (that is, the p.
Jn 18.28 they led Jesus from . . Caiaphas to the p. . . They . . did not enter the praetorium
18.33 Pilate entered the praetorium again
19. 9 he entered the praetorium again
Acts 23.35 commanded him to be guarded in Herod's p.

PRAISE
1. *approve, glorify:* αἰνέω AINEŌ*
Lk 2.13 the heavenly host praising God
2.20 shepherds returned, . . praising God
19.37 disciples began to rejoice and praise God
Acts 2.47 praising God and having favor with all
3. 8 walking and leaping and praising God
3. 9 people saw him walking . . praising God
Rom 15.11 "Praise the Lord, all Gentiles
Rev 19. 5 "Praise our God, all you his servants
2. *praise:* αἴνεσις AINESIS*
Heb 13.15 continually offer up a sacrifice of praise
3. *praise:* αἶνος AINOS
Mt 21.16 " 'thou hast brought perfect praise
Lk 18.43 when they saw it, gave praise to God
4. *glory:* δόξα DOXA
Lk 17.18 "Was no one found to return and give p.?
Jn 9.24 "Give God the praise; . . this man is a sinner
12.43 for they loved the praise of men more than the praise of God
5. *extol, honor:* δοξάζω DOXAZŌ
Mt 6. 2 "that they may be praised by men
Lk 13.13 she was made straight, and . . praised God
17.15 one of them . . turned back, praising God
23.47 when the centurion saw . . , he praised God
Acts 4.21 men praised God for what had happened

6. *approve, praise:* ἐπαινέω EPAINEŌ
Rom 15.11 "let all the peoples praise him
7. *praise, approval:* ἔπαινος EPAINOS
Rom 2.29 His praise is not from men but from God
Eph 1. 6 to the praise of his glorious grace
1.12 to live for the praise of his glory
1.14 possession of it, to the praise of his glory
Phil 1.11 to the glory and praise of God
4. 8 if there is anything worthy of praise
1 Pet 1. 7 that . . faith . . may redound to praise
2.14 sent by him . . to praise those who do right
8. *agree:* ἐξομολογέω (mid.) EXOMOLOGEŌ
Rom 15. 9 "I will praise thee among the Gentiles
9. *sing, praise:* ὑμνέω HYMNEŌ
Heb 2.12 "in . . the congregation I will praise thee

PRAISE, GIVE
1. *agree:* ἐξομολογέω (mid.) EXOMOLOGEŌ
Rom 14.11 "every tongue shall give praise[u] to God†

PRAISE, SING
1. *pluck, sing to a harp:* ψάλλω PSALLŌ
Jas 5.13 Is any cheerful? Let him sing praise

PRATE
1. *talk nonsense:* φλυαρέω PHLYAREŌ*
3 Jn .10 prating against me with evil words

PRAY
1. *entreaty, prayer:* δέησις DEĒSIS [B.2.b.1]
2 Cor 9.14 they long for you and pray for you
2. *pray, beg:* δέομαι DEOMAI
Mt 9.38 "pray therefore the Lord of the harvest
Lk 10. 2 "pray therefore the Lord of the harvest
21.36 "But watch at all times, praying
22.32 "I have prayed . . that your faith . . not fail
Acts 4.31 when they . . prayed, the place . . was shaken
8.22 "pray . . that . . the intent . . be forgiven you
8.24 "Pray for me to the Lord
8.34 "About whom, pray, does the prophet say?
10. 2 a devout man who . . prayed constantly
1 Th 3.10 praying . . we may . . supply what is lacking
3. *call, surname:* ἐπικαλέω (mid.) EPIKALEŌ
Acts 7.59 he prayed, "Lord Jesus, receive my spirit
4. *ask, question, beg:* ἐρωτάω ERŌTAŌ
Lk 14.18 " 'I pray you, have me excused
14.19 " 'I pray you, have me excused
Jn 14.16 "I will p. the Father, and he will give
17. 9 "I am praying for them; I am not praying for the world
17.15 "I do not p. that thou shouldst take them
17.20 "I do not pray for these only
1 Jn 5.16 I do not say that one is to p. for that
5. *pray, wish:* εὔχομαι EUCHOMAI
Acts 27.29 let out four anchors . . and prayed for day
2 Cor 13. 7 we pray . . that you may not do wrong
13. 9 What we pray for is your improvement
3 Jn . 2 I pray that all may go well with you
6. *pray:* προσεύχομαι PROSEUCHOMAI
Mt 5.44 "pray for those who persecute you
6. 5 "when you pray, you must not be . . hypocrites; . . they . . p. . . that they may be seen
6. 6 "when you pray, go into your room . . and pray to your Father who is in secret
6. 7 "in praying do not heap up empty phrases
6. 9 "Pray then like this: Our Father
14.23 he went up on the mountain . . to pray
19.13 might lay his hands on them and pray
24.20 "P. that your flight may not be in winter
26.36 "Sit here, while I go yonder and pray
26.39 he fell on his face and prayed
26.41 "pray that you . . not enter into temptation
26.42 he went away and prayed, "My Father
26.44 he . . prayed for the third time
Mk 1.35 he . . went . . to a lonely place, and . . prayed
6.46 he went up on the mountain to pray
11.25 "whenever you stand praying, forgive
13.18 "Pray that it may not happen in winter
[13.33 "Take heed, watch *and pray*‡
Mk 14.32 "Sit here, while I pray
14.35 he fell on the ground and prayed
14.38 "pray that you . . not enter into temptation
14.39 again he went away and prayed
Lk 1.10 praying outside at the hour of incense
3.21 when Jesus . . was praying
5.16 he withdrew to the wilderness and prayed
6.12 he went out to the mountain to pray
6.28 "pray for those who abuse you
9.18 "it happened . . as he was praying alone
9.28 he . . went up on the mountain to pray
9.29 praying, . . his countenance was altered
11. 1 He was praying in a certain place, and . . his disciples said . . "Lord, teach us to pray
11. 2 "When you p., say: "Father, hallowed be
18. 1 a parable . . that they ought always to p.
18.10 "Two men went up into the temple to p.
18.11 "The Pharisee stood and prayed thus
22.40 "Pray that you . . not enter into temptation
22.41 he withdrew . . and knelt down and prayed
[22.44 *in an agony he prayed more earnestly*‡
22.46 pray that you . . not enter into temptation
Acts 1.24 they prayed and said, "Lord
6. 6 they prayed and laid their hands upon them
8.15 who came down and prayed for them
9.11 "inquire . . for . . Saul; for . . he is praying
9.40 Peter . . knelt down and prayed
10. 9 Peter went up on the housetop to pray
11. 5 "I was in the city of Joppa praying
12.12 many were gathered together . . praying
13. 3 after . . praying they laid their hands on
16.25 Paul and Silas were praying and singing
20.36 he knelt down and prayed with them
21. 5 kneeling down on the beach we prayed
22.17 "When I . . was praying . . I fell into a trance
28. 8 Paul visited him and prayed
Rom 8.26 we do not know how to pray
1 Cor 11. 4 Any man who prays or prophesies
11. 5 any woman who prays . . unveiled
11.13 proper for a woman to pray . . uncovered?
14.13 he who speaks in a tongue should pray
14.14 if I pray in a tongue, my spirit prays but my mind is unfruitful
14.15 I will pray with the spirit and I will pray with the mind also
Eph 6.18 Pray at all times in the Spirit
Col 1. 3 We . . thank God . . when we pray for you
1. 9 we have not ceased to pray for you
4. 3 pray . . that God may open to us a door
1 Th 5.17 pray constantly
5.25 Brethren, pray for us
2 Th 1.11 To this end we always pray for you
3. 1 Finally, brethren, pray for us
1 Tim 2. 8 I desire then that . . the men should pray
Heb 13.18 Pray for us, for we are sure
Jas 5.13 Is any one . . suffering? Let him pray
5.14 let them pray over him, anointing him
5.16 p. for one another, that you . . be healed
5.17 Elijah . . prayed fervently that it . . not rain
5.18 he prayed again and . . heaven gave rain
Jude .20 pray in the Holy Spirit
CONTEXTUALLY
Phm . 6 I pray that the sharing of your faith

PRAYER
1. *entreaty, prayer:* δέησις DEĒSIS
Lk 1.13 "Zechariah, . . your prayer is heard
2.37 worshiping with fasting and prayer
5.33 "The disciples of John . . offer prayers
Rom 10. 1 my . . prayer . . is that they . . be saved
2 Cor 1.11 You also must help us by prayer
Phil 1. 4 in every prayer of mine for you all making my prayer with joy
1.19 through your prayers . . this will turn out
1 Tim 2. 1 I urge that supplications, prayers
2 Tim 1. 3 I remember you constantly in my prayers
Heb 5. 7 Jesus[j] offered up prayers and supplications

Jas 5.16 p. of a righteous man has great power
1 Pet 3.12 "his ears are open to their prayer
2. *intercession:* ἔντευξις ENTEUXIS
1 Tim 4. 5 consecrated by the word of God and p.
3. *vow, prayer:* εὐχή EUCHĒ
Jas 5.15 prayer of faith will save the sick man
4. *prayer, chapel:* προσευχή PROSEUCHĒ
Mt [17.21 *"never . . except by prayer and fasting*‡
21.13 " 'My house shall be called a house of p.
21.22 "whatever you ask in p., you will receive
Mk 9.29 "cannot be driven out by anything but p.[j]
11.17 " 'My house shall be called a house of p.
Lk 6.12 all night he continued in p. to God
19.46 " 'My house shall be a house of prayer
22.45 And when he rose from prayer
Acts 1.14 devoted themselves to prayer
2.42 the breaking of bread and the prayers
3. 1 going up to the temple at the hour of p.
6. 4 "But we will devote ourselves to prayer
10. 4 "Your prayers . . have ascended . . before God
10.31 " 'Cornelius, your prayer has been heard
12. 5 prayer for him was made to God
16.13 we supposed there was a place of prayer
16.16 As we were going to the place of prayer
Rom 1. 9(10) I mention you always in my prayers
12.12 be patient in tribulation, be constant in p.
15.30 strive together with me in your prayers
1 Cor 7. 5 that you may devote yourselves to p.
Eph 1.16 remembering you in my prayers
6.18 Pray . . with all prayer and supplication
Phil 4. 6 in everything by p. and supplication
Col 4. 2 Continue steadfastly in prayer
4.12 remembering you . . in his prayers
1 Th 1. 2 constantly mentioning you in our prayers
2. 1 I urge that . . prayers . . be made for all men
5. 5 continues in . . prayers night and day
Phm . 4 when I remember you in my prayers
.22 I am hoping through your prayers
1 Pet 3. 7 that your prayers may not be hindered
4. 7 keep sane and sober for your prayers
Rev 5. 8 which are the prayers of the saints
8. 3 incense to mingle with the prayers
8. 4 the incense rose with the prayers
5. *pray:* προσεύχομαι PROSEUCHOMAI
[a]A.6.c.2 [b]part. [c]A.6.c.3
Mk 11.24 [a]"whatever you ask in prayer, believe
Acts 14.23 [b]appointed elders . . with p. and fasting
Phil 1. 9 [c]it is my p. that your love . . abound

PRAYER, KEEP THE HOUR OF
PRAYERS, MAKE

1. *pray:* προσεύχομαι PROSEUCHOMAI
[a]B.3.b.4
Mt [23.14 *"for a pretense you make long prayers*‡
Mk 12.40 "who . . for a pretense make long prayers
Lk 20.47 "who . . for a pretense make long prayers
Acts 10.30 [a]"I was keeping the ninth hour of prayer

PREACH

1. *bring good news* (mid.): εὐαγγελίζω EUAGGELIZŌ
Acts 5.42 did not cease . . preaching Jesus
8. 4 those . . went about preaching the word
11.20 men of Cyprus . . , preaching the Lord Jesus
15.35 Paul and Barnabas . . preaching the word
17.18 he preached Jesus and the resurrection
1 Cor 9.18 in . . preaching I . . make the gospel free
15. 1 in what terms I preached to you
2 Cor 11. 7 because I preached God's gospel
Gal 1. 8 contrary to that which we preached
1.11 the gospel which was preached by me
1.16 that I might p. him among the Gentiles
1.23 "who . . persecuted us is now preaching
Eph 2.17 he came and preached peace to you
3. 8 grace was given, to p. to the Gentiles
2. *proclaim:* κηρύσσω KĒRYSSŌ
Mt 3. 1 preaching in the wilderness of Judea
4.17 From that time Jesus began to preach
4.23 preaching the gospel of the kingdom
Mt 9.35 preaching the gospel of the kingdom
10. 7 "preach as you go, saying, 'The kingdom
11. 1 he went on . . to . . preach in their cities
24.14 "gospel of the kingdom will be preached
26.13 "wherever this gospel is preached
Mk 1. 4 preaching a baptism of repentance
1. 7 preached, saying, "After me comes he
1.14 Jesus came into Galilee, preaching
1.38 "Let us go on . . , that I may p. there also
1.39 he went . . preaching in their synagogues
3.14 he appointed twelve[k] . . to be sent out to p.
6.12 So they went out and preached
13.10 "gospel must first be preached to all
14. 9 "wherever the gospel is preached
16.15 "Go into all the world and preach[k]‡
16.20 they went forth and preached everywhere[k]‡
Lk 3. 3 preaching a baptism of repentance
4.44 he was preaching in the synagogues
8. 1 he went . . preaching . . the good news
9. 2 he sent them out to preach the kingdom
24.47 "forgiveness . . should be preached
Acts 10.37 "after the baptism which John preached
10.42 "commanded us to preach to the people
15.21 "Moses has had . . those who preach him
19.13 "I adjure . . by the Jesus . . Paul preaches
20.25 "among whom I have gone preaching
28.31 preaching the kingdom of God
Rom 2.21 you preach against stealing, do you steal?
10. 8 (that is, the word of faith which we preach
10.15 how can men preach unless they are sent?
1 Cor 1.23 but we preach Christ crucified
9.27 lest after preaching . . I . . be disqualified
15.11 so we preach and so you believed
15.12 Now if Christ is preached as raised
2 Cor 1.19 Jesus Christ, whom we preached
4. 5 what we preach is not ourselves
11. 4 if some one . . preaches another Jesus than the one we preached
Gal 2. 2 I laid before them . . the gospel . . I preach
5.11 if I, brethren, still preach circumcision
Phil 1.15 Some indeed preach Christ from envy
Col 1.23 the gospel . . preached to every creature
1 Th 2. 9 we preached to you the gospel of God
1 Tim 3.16 He[h] was . . preached among the nations
2 Tim 4. 2 preach the word, be urgent in season
1 Pet 3.19 he . . preached to the spirits in prison
3. *speak, talk:* λαλέω LALEŌ
Mk 2. 2 he was preaching the word to them
4. *say, speak:* λέγω LEGŌ
Mt 23. 3 "for they preach, but do not practice
CONTEXTUALLY
Rom 15.19 I . . fully preached the gospel of Christ
2 Cor 2.12 When I came to Troas to p. the gospel

PREACH BEFORE

1. *proclaim beforehand:* προκηρύσσω PROKĒRYSSŌ*
Acts 13.24 "Before his coming John had preached

PREACH BOLDLY

1. *speak freely:* παρρησιάζομαι PARRĒSIAZOMAI
Acts 9.27 at Damascus he had preached boldly
9.29(28) preaching boldly in . . name of the Lord

PREACH GOOD NEWS
PREACH THE GOOD NEWS
PREACH A GOSPEL
PREACH THE GOSPEL

1. *bring good news* (mid.): εὐαγγελίζω EUAGGELIZŌ
[a]pass.
Mt 11. 5 [a]"poor have good news preached to them
Lk 3.18 he preached good news to the people
4.18 "he has anointed me to preach good news
4.43 "I must p. the good news of the kingdom
7.22 [a]"poor have good news preached to them
9. 6 went . . preaching the gospel . . everywhere
16.16 [a]"since then the good news . . is preached
20. 1 as he was . . preaching the gospel
Acts 8.12 Philip . . preached good news
8.25 they returned . . , preaching the gospel

Acts 8.40 he preached the gospel to all the towns
10.36 "preaching good news of peace by Jesus C.
14. 7 there they preached the gospel
14.21 they had preached the gospel to that city
16.10 God had called us to p. the gospel to them
Rom 1.15 I am eager to p. the gospel to you also
10.15 "feet of those who preach good news!
15.20 my ambition to preach the gospel
1 Cor 1.17 not send me to baptize but to p. the gospel
9.16 If I p. the gospel, that gives .. no ground
9.16 Woe to me if I do not p. the gospel!
2 Cor 10.16 that we may preach the gospel in lands
Gal 1. 8 if we .. should preach to you a gospel
1. 9 If .. one is preaching .. a gospel contrary
4.13 I preached the gospel to you at first
1 Pet 1.12 who preached the good news to you
4. 6 this is why the gospel was preached

PREACH THE GOSPEL BEFOREHAND
1. *bring good news in advance:* προευαγγελίζομαι PROEUAGGELIZOMAI*
Gal 3. 8 scripture .. preached the gospel beforehand

PREACHER
1. *one who proclaims:* καταγγελεύς KATAGGELEUS*
Acts 17.18 "He seems to be a p. of foreign divinities
2. *proclaim:* κηρύσσω (subst. part.) KĒRYSSŌ
Rom 10.14 how are they to hear without a p.?
3. *public messenger:* κῆρυξ KĒRYX
1 Tim 2. 7 For this I was appointed a p. and apostle
2 Tim 1.11 For this gospel I was appointed a p.

PREACHES, WHAT ONE
PREACHING
1. *proclamation:* κήρυγμα KĒRYGMA
Mt 12.41 "they repented at the preaching of Jonah
Lk 11.32 "they repented at the p. of Jonah
Rom 16.25 my gospel and the preaching of Jesus
1 Cor 1.21 it pleased God through .. what we preach
15.14 then our preaching is in vain
Tit 1. 3 manifested in his word through the p.
2. *word, message:* λόγος LOGOS
Acts 18. 5 Paul was occupied with preaching
1 Tim 5.17 those who labor in p. and teaching
3. *exhortation, comfort:* παράκλησις PARAKLĒSIS
1 Tim 4.13 attend .. to preaching, to teaching
4. *word, saying:* ῥῆμα RHĒMA
Rom 10.17 what is heard comes by the p. of Christ
CONTEXTUALLY
Acts 6. 2 "It is not right that we should give up p.
2 Cor 8.18 famous among all the churches for his p.

PRECEDE
1. *come first, arrive:* φθάνω (pass.) PHTHANŌ
1 Th 4.15 shall not p. those who have fallen asleep

PRECEPT
1. *ordinance, justification:* δικαίωμα DIKAIŌMA
Rom 2.26 if a man .. keeps the precepts of the law
2. *commandment:* ἔνταλμα ENTALMA*
Mt 15. 9 " 'teaching as doctrines .. precepts of men
Mk 7. 7 " 'teaching as doctrines .. precepts of men
Col 2.22 ⟨regulations⟩ according to human precepts

PRECIOUS
1. *honored, valuable:* ἔντιμος ENTIMOS
1 Pet 2. 4 that living stone, .. chosen and precious
2. 6 "a cornerstone chosen and precious
2. *very valuable:* πολύτιμος POLYTIMOS
[a]comp.
1 Pet 1. 7 [a]your faith, more precious than gold
3. *honor, value:* τιμή (pred.) TIMĒ
1 Pet 2. 7 To you .. who believe, he is precious
4. *held in honor, costly:* τίμιος TIMIOS
Acts 20.24 "I do not account my life .. p. to myself
1 Cor 3.12 if any one builds .. with .. precious stones
Jas 5. 7 the farmer waits for the precious fruit
1 Pet 1.19 with the precious blood of Christ
2 Pet 1. 4 he has granted to us his p. promises

PRECIOUS, VERY
1. *very expensive:* πολυτελής POLYTELĒS
1 Pet 3. 4 quiet spirit .. in God's sight is very p.

PREDESTINE
1. *determine beforehand:* προορίζω PROORIZŌ
Acts 4.28 "whatever .. thy plan had predestined
Rom 8.29 whom he foreknew he also predestined
8.30 whom he predestined he also called

PREDICT
1. *foretell, say before:* προεῖπον PROEIPON
Rom 9.29 Isaiah predicted, "If the Lord of hosts
2. *witness to beforehand:* προμαρτύρομαι PROMARTYROMAI*
1 Pet 1.11 when predicting the sufferings of Christ

PREDICTION
1. *word spoken beforehand:* τὸ προειρημένον ῥῆμα PROEIPON [A.1.f]
2 Pet 3. 2 predictions of the holy prophets
Jude .17 remember .. predictions of the apostles

PRE-EMINENT
1. *be the first, excel:* πρωτεύω (part.) PRŌTEUŌ*
Col 1.18 that in everything he might be p.

PREFER
1. *wish:* θέλω THELŌ
Phm .14 but I preferred to do nothing
CONTEXTUALLY
Phm . 9 for love's sake I p. to appeal to

PREPARATION, DAY OF
1. *preparation:* παρασκευή PARASKEUĒ*
Mt 27.62 Next day, that is, after the day of P.
Mk 15.42 since it was the day of Preparation
Lk 23.54 It was the day of Preparation
Jn 19.14 Now it was the day of Preparation
19.31 Since it was the day of Preparation
19.42 So because of the Jewish day of P.

PREPARATIONS, MAKE
1. *prepare, construct:* κατασκευάζω KATASKEUAZŌ
Heb 9. 6 preparations having thus been made

PREPARE (*See also* BURIAL, PREPARE FOR)
1. *prepare, get ready:* ἑτοιμάζω HETOIMAZŌ
Mt 3. 3 "Prepare the way of the Lord
20.23 "it has been prepared by my Father
25.34 " 'inherit the kingdom prepared for you
25.41 " 'eternal fire prepared for the devil
26.17 "Where will you have us p. .. passover?
26.19 they prepared the passover
Mk 1. 3 "Prepare the way of the Lord
10.40 "those for whom it has been prepared
14.12 "Where will you have us .. p. .. passover?
14.15 "a large upper room .. ; there prepare for us
14.16 they prepared the passover
Lk 1.76 "you will go before .. to prepare his ways
2.31 "hast prepared in the presence of all
3. 4 "Prepare the way of the Lord
12.20 " 'things .. prepared, .. whose will they be?
17. 8 " 'Prepare supper for me, .. gird yourself
22. 8 "Go and prepare the passover for us
22. 9 "Where will you have us prepare it?
22.13 they prepared the passover
23.56 then they returned, and prepared spices
24. 1 taking .. spices .. they had prepared
Jn 14. 2 "that I go to prepare a place for you
14. 3 "when I go and prepare a place
1 Cor 2. 9 "what God has prepared for those who love
Phm .22 At the same time, prepare a guest room
Heb 11.16 for he has prepared for them a city
Rev 12. 6 she has a place prepared by God
16.12 to prepare the way for the kings
21. 2 prepared as a bride .. for her husband
2. *put in order, make:* καταρτίζω (mid.) KATARTIZŌ
Heb 10. 5 "but a body hast thou prepared for me
3. *prepare, construct:* κατασκευάζω KATASKEUAZŌ
Mt 11.10 " 'who shall p. thy way before thee
Mk 1. 2 "my messenger .. shall prepare thy way
Lk 1.17 "ready for the Lord a people prepared
7.27 " 'who shall prepare thy way before thee

Heb 9. 2 For a tent[p] was prepared, the outer one
4. *achieve:* κατεργάζομαι KATERGAZOMAI
2 Cor 4.17 affliction is preparing for us . . glory
5. 5 He who has prepared us for this
5. *prepare:* παρασκευάζω PARASKEUAZŌ
Acts 10.10 while they were preparing it, he fell

PREPARE BEFOREHAND
1. *get ready beforehand:* προετοιμάζω PROETOIMAZŌ*
Rom 9.23 he has prepared beforehand for glory
Eph 2.10 works, which God prepared beforehand

PREPARED
1. *ready, prepared:* ἕτοιμος HETOIMOS
1 Pet 3.15 Always be prepared to make a defense

PRESENCE (*See also* THY *a*)
1. *presence, arrival:* παρουσία PAROUSIA
2 Cor 10.10 "but his bodily presence is weak
Phil 2.12 you . . obeyed, . . not only as in my presence
2. *face, person:* πρόσωπον PROSŌPON
Lk 2.31 "thou hast prepared in the presence of all
Acts 2.28 " 'full of gladness with thy presence
3.13 "whom you . . denied in the p. of Pilate
3.19 "refreshing . . from the p. of the Lord
5.41 they left the presence of the council
2 Cor 2.10 for your sake in the presence of Christ
2 Th 1. 9 exclusion from the presence of the Lord
Heb 9.24 to appear in the presence of God
Rev 20.11 from his p. earth and sky fled away
3. *presentation, purpose:* πρόθεσις PROTHESIS
Mt 12. 4 "he . . ate the bread of the Presence
Mk 2.26 "he . . ate the bread of the Presence
Lk 6. 4 "he . . ate the bread of the Presence
Heb 9. 2 in which were . . bread of the Presence[q]†
CONTEXTUALLY
Jn 17. 5 "Father, glorify thou me in thy own p.
2 Cor 4.14 and bring us with you into his presence
Rev 7.15 "will shelter them with his presence

PRESENCE, IN S.'S
PRESENCE OF, IN THE
1. *opposite:* ἀπέναντι APENANTI
Acts 3.16 perfect health in the presence of you all
2. *opposite, facing:* ἐναντίον ENANTION
Lk 20.26 not able in the presence of the people
3. *face to face, before:* ἐνώπιον ENŌPION
Lk 1.19 "I am Gabriel, who stand in the p. of God
8.47 declared in the presence of all the people
13.26 " 'We ate and drank in your presence
14.10 "you will be honored in the p. of all
Jn 20.30 many other signs in the p. of the disciples
Acts 27.35 giving thanks to God in the p. of all
1 Cor 1.29 that no human . . boast in the p. of God
1 Tim 5.20 rebuke them in the presence of all
5.21 In the p. of God and of Christ Jesus
6.12 confession in the p. of many witnesses
6.13 In the presence of God who gives life
2 Tim 4. 1 I charge you in the presence of God
Rev 13.12 exercises . . authority of the first beast in its p.
13.14 allowed to work in the p. of the beast
14.10 "tormented . . in the p. of the holy angels and in the presence of the Lamb
19.20 prophet who in its p. had worked
4. *opposite:* κατέναντι KATENANTI
Rom 4.17 in the p. of the God in whom he believed

PRESENCE OF, BEFORE THE
1. *opposite, before:* κατενώπιον KATENŌPION
Jude .24 before the presence of his glory

PRESENT
1. *just now:* ἄρτι (attr.) ARTI
1 Cor 4.11 To the present hour we hunger
2. *gift:* δῶρον DŌRON
Rev 11.10 make merry and exchange presents
3. *place in, be present:* ἐνίστημι (perf. part.) ENISTĒMI
Rom 8.38 neither death, nor life, nor . . things p.
1 Cor 3.22 life or death or the p. or the future
7.26 in view of the present[m] distress†[0]
Gal 1. 4 to deliver us from the present evil age
Heb 9. 9 (which is symbolic for the present age
4. *stand, set:* ἵστημι HISTĒMI
Jude .24 who is able . . to p. you without blemish
5. *this:* οὗτος HOUTOS
Lk **12.56**
6. *speak, talk:* λαλέω LALEŌ
Acts 17.19 "what this new teaching is which you p.
7. *now:* νῦν (attr.) NYN
Rom 3.26 it was to prove at the present time
8.18 sufferings of this p. time are not worth
11. 5 at the present time there is a remnant
2 Cor 8.14 your abundance at the present time
Gal 4.25 she corresponds to the p. Jerusalem
1 Tim 4. 8 as it holds promise for the present life
2 Tim 4.10 Demas, in love with this present world
8. *be present:* πάρειμι (part.) PAREIMI
1 Cor 5. 3 as if p., I have . . pronounced judgment
9. *place beside, stand before:* παρίστημι PARISTĒMI
Lk 2.22 they brought him . . to p. him to the Lord
Acts 1. 3 To them he presented himself alive
9.41 he . . lifted her up . . presented her alive
23.33 they presented Paul also before him
Rom 12. 1 present your bodies as a living sacrifice
2 Cor 11. 2 to present you as a pure bride
Eph 5.27 that he might p. the church to himself
Col 1.22 in order to p. you holy and blameless
1.28 that we may present every man mature
2 Tim 2.15 present yourself to God as one approved
10. *bring to, present:* προσφέρω PROSPHERŌ
Acts 21.26 offering presented for every one of them
11. *honor, value:* τιμάω TIMAŌ [A.6.a.6]
Acts 28.10 They presented many gifts to us[f]†
IDIOMATICALLY
a. Acts 5.38 "So in the present case I tell you *καὶ τὰ νῦν λέγω ὑμῖν* [NYN]
b. Acts 24.25 "Go away for the present *τὸ νῦν ἔχον πορεύου* [NYN]
CONTEXTUALLY
1 Cor 5. 4 When you are assembled, and my spirit is p.
[7.21 *make use of your present condition instead*†
Eph 6.12 against . . world rulers of this p. darkness

PRESENT, AT
1. *now:* νυνί NYNI
Rom 15.25 At present . . I am going to Jerusalem

PRESENT, BE
PRESENT, BE HERE
1. *arrive, stand by:* παραγίνομαι PARAGINOMAI
Acts 21.18 and all the elders were present
2. *be present:* πάρειμι PAREIMI
Lk 13. 1 There were some p. at that very time
Acts 10.33 "we are all here p. in the sight of God
1 Cor 5. 3 though absent in body I am p. in spirit
2 Cor 10. 2 I beg of you that when I am present
10.11 what we say by letter . . , we do when p.
13. 2 I warn them now . . as I did when present
Gal 4.18 not only when I am present with you
4.20 I could wish to be present with you now

PRESENT WITH, BE
1. *be present together:* συμπάρειμι SYMPAREIMI*
Acts 25.24 "King Agrippa and all who are p. with us

PRESENTABLE, MORE
1. *noble, proper:* εὐσχήμων EUSCHĒMŌN
1 Cor 12.24 which our more p. parts do not require

PRESERVE
1. *guard, observe:* φυλάσσω PHYLASSŌ
2 Pet 2. 5 preserved Noah . . herald of righteousness
2. *preserve, protect:* συντηρέω SYNTĒREŌ
Mt 9.17 "into fresh wineskins, and so . . preserved
3. *preserve alive:* ζῳογονέω ZŌOGONEŌ
Lk 17.33 "whoever loses his life will preserve it

PRESERVED, BE
1. *persist, persevere:* διαμένω DIAMENŌ
Gal 2. 5 truth of the gospel might be p. for you

PRESS
1. *hold within, be hostile:* ἐνέχω ENECHŌ
Lk 11.53 Pharisees began to press him hard
CONTEXTUALLY
Mk 12. 1 "and dug a pit for the wine press

PRESS AROUND
1. *press together:* συνθλίβω SYNTHLIBŌ
Mk 5.31 "You see the crowd pressing around you

PRESS DOWN
1. *press tight, press down:* πιέζω PIEZŌ*
Lk 6.38 "good measure, pressed down, shaken

PRESS ON
1. *pursue:* διώκω DIŌKŌ
Phil 3.12 but I press on to make it my own
3.14 I press on toward the goal for the prize

PRESS ROUND
1. *press closely, choke:* συμπνίγω SYMPNIGŌ
Lk 8.42 As he went, .. people pressed round him

PRESS UPON
1. *press tightly:* ἀποθλίβω APOTHLIBŌ*
Lk 8.45 "Master, the multitudes .. press upon you!
2. *lie upon, press upon:* ἐπίκειμαι EPIKEIMAI
Lk 5. 1 While the people pressed upon him
3. *fall upon:* ἐπιπίπτω EPIPIPTŌ
Mk 3.10 all who had diseases pressed upon him

PRESS, WINE
1. *tub, wine vat:* ληνός LĒNOS*
Mt 21.33 "a householder .. dug a wine press
Rev 14.19 threw it into the great wine press
14.20 wine press was trodden outside .. city
14.20 blood flowed from the wine press
19.15 he will tread the wine press of the fury

PRESSED, BE HARD
1. *hold together, impel:* συνέχω (pass.) SYNECHŌ
Phil 1.23 I am hard pressed between the two

PRESSURE
1. *care, pressure, attack:* ἐπίστασις EPISTASIS
2 Cor 11.28 there is the daily pressure upon me

PRESUME
1. *consider oneself worthy:* ἀξιοῦν ἑαυτόν AXIOŌ [A.6.a.4]
Lk 7. 7 "I did not presume to come to you
2. *think, suppose:* δοκέω DOKEŌ
Mt 3. 9 "do not presume to say to yourselves
3. *dare:* τολμάω TOLMAŌ
Jude . 9 did not p. to pronounce a .. judgment

PRESUME UPON
1. *look down upon, despise:* καταφρονέω KATAPHRONEŌ
Rom 2. 4 Or do you presume upon .. his kindness?

PRETEND
1. *reply, deceive:* ὑποκρίνομαι HYPOKRINOMAI*
Lk 20.20 spies, who pretended to be sincere

PRETENDED
1. *lie, falsehood:* ψεῦδος (gen.) PSEUDOS
2 Th 2. 9 coming of the lawless one .. with p. signs

PRETENSE
1. *pretense, excuse:* πρόφασις PROPHASIS
Mt [23.14 *"for a pretense you make long prayers*‡
Mk 12.40 "for a pretense make long prayers
Lk 20.47 "for a pretense make long prayers
Acts 27.30 under pretense of laying out anchors
Phil 1.18 in every way, whether in p. or in truth

PRETENSIONS
1. *outward show, hypocrisy:* ὑπόκρισις HYPOKRISIS
1 Tim 4. 2 p. of liars whose consciences are seared

PRETEXT
1. *veil:* ἐπικάλυμμα EPIKALYMMA*
1 Pet 2.16 without using .. freedom as a p. for evil

PREVAIL
PREVAIL AGAINST
1. *be strong, prevail:* ἰσχύω ISCHYŌ
Acts 19.20 the word of the Lord grew and prevailed
2. *overpower, prevail against:* κατισχύω KATISCHYŌ
Mt 16.18 "powers of death[u] shall not p. against it
Lk 23.23 And their voices prevailed
3. *conquer, prevail:* νικάω NIKAŌ
Rom 3. 4 "That thou mayest .. p. when .. judged

PREVAIL UPON
1. *do by force, compel:* παραβιάζομαι PARABIAZOMAI
Acts 16.15 And she prevailed upon us

PREVENT
PREVENT FROM, IN ORDER TO
PREVENT FROM, TO
1. *prevent, hinder:* διακωλύω DIAKŌLYŌ*
Mt 3.14 John would have prevented him
2. *in order that:* ἵνα (neg.) HINA
Jn 19.31 in order to p. the bodies from remaining
Gal 5.17 to p. you from doing what you would
3. *hinder, prevent, withhold:* κωλύω KŌLYŌ
Acts 8.36 "What is to prevent my being baptized?[h]
24.23 none of his friends should be prevented
Rom 1.13 (but thus far have been prevented
Heb 7.23 prevented by death from continuing

PREVIOUSLY (*See also* RATIFY PREVIOUSLY)
1. *exist before:* προϋπάρχω PROYPARCHŌ [A.6.c.1]
Acts 8. 9 who had previously practiced magic

PREVIOUSLY, SEE
1. *see before one, foresee:* προοράω PROORAŌ
Acts 21.29 they had previously seen Trophimus

PREY (*See* BEAST OF PREY)

PREY OF, MAKE A
1. *carry away captive, rob:* συλαγωγέω SYLAGŌGEŌ*
Col 2. 8 that no one makes a prey of you

PREY UPON
1. *devour, eat up:* κατεσθίω KATESTHIŌ
2 Cor 11.20 you bear it if a man .. preys upon you

PRICE
1. *honor, value:* τιμή TIMĒ
Mt 27. 9 "the thirty pieces of silver, the price
1 Cor 6.20 you were bought with a price
7.23 You were bought with a price
IDIOMATICALLY
a. Mt 27.9 "of him on whom a price had been set τοῦ τετιμημένου ὃν ἐτιμήσαντο [TIMAŌ]

PRICE, WITHOUT
1. *freely, as a gift:* δωρεάν DŌREAN
Rev 22.17 let him .. take the water of life without p.

PRIDE
1. *false pretension:* ἀλαζονεία ALAZONEIA
1 Jn 2.16 the lust of the eyes and the pride of life
2. *glory:* δόξα DOXA
1 Cor 11.15 if a woman has long hair, it is her pride
3. *arrogance:* ὑπερηφανία HYPERĒPHANIA*
Mk 7.22 "envy, slander, pride, foolishness
4. *object of boasting, boast:* καύχημα KAUCHĒMA
Heb 3. 6 if we hold fast our .. pride in our hope[g]
5. *boasting:* καύχησις KAUCHĒSIS
1 Cor 15.31 "I protest, brethren, by my pride in you
2 Cor 7. 4 I have great pride in you

PRIDE, EXPRESS
PRIDE ONESELF
1. *boast:* καυχάομαι KAUCHAOMAI
2 Cor 5.12 able to answer those who p. themselves
7.14 I have expressed to him some p. in you

PRIEST
1. *priest:* ἱερεύς HIEREUS*
Mt 8. 4 "go, show yourself to the priest
12. 4 "not lawful .., but only for the priests
12. 5 "priests in the temple profane the sabbath
Mk 1.44 "go, show yourself to the priest
2.26 "not lawful for any but the priests to eat
Lk 1. 5 there was a priest named Zechariah[b]
5.14 "go and show yourself to the priest
6. 4 "it is not lawful for any but the priests
10.31 "a priest was going down that road
17.14 "Go and show yourselves to the priests
Jn 1.19 "when the Jews sent priests and Levites
Acts 4. 1 as they were speaking .., the priests .. came

Acts 6. 7 many . . priests were obedient to the faith
14.13 the priest of Zeus . . brought oxen
Heb 5. 6 "art a p. for ever, after . . Melchizedek
7. 1 Melchizedek, . . p. of the Most High God
7. 3 resembling the Son . . he continues a p.
7.11 another p. to arise after . . Melchizedek
7.14 with that . . Moses said nothing about priests
7.15 another p. . . in . . likeness of Melchizedek
7.17 "art a p. for ever, after . . Melchizedek
7.21(20) Those who formerly became priests
7.21 " 'Thou art a priest for ever
7.23 The former priests were many
8. 4 if . . on earth, he would not be a priest
9. 6 priests go continually into the outer tent[p]
10.11 every priest stands daily at his service
10.21 we have a great p. over the house of God
Rev 1. 6 made us a kingdom, priests to his God
5.10 "hast made them . . priests to our God
20. 6 but they shall be priests of God
CONTEXTUALLY
Heb 7.16 who has become a priest
8. 3 hence it is necessary for this priest also

PRIEST, CHIEF
1. *chief priest:* ἀρχιερεύς ARCHIEREUS
Always plural
Mt 2. 4 assembling all the chief priests and scribes
16.21 suffer many things from . . chief priests
20.18 "will be delivered to the chief priests
21.15 chief priests . . saw the wonderful things
21.23 chief priests . . said, "By what authority?
21.45 the chief priests . . heard his parables
26. 3 the chief priests . . gathered in the palace
26.14 Judas Iscariot, went to the chief priests
26.47 a great crowd . . from the chief priests
26.59 chief priests . . sought false testimony
27. 1 chief priests . . took counsel against Jesus
27. 3 brought back . . silver to the chief priests
27. 6 chief priests, taking the pieces of silver
27.12 when he was accused by the chief priests
27.20 chief priests . . persuaded the people
27.41 also the chief priests . . mocked him
27.62 chief priests . . gathered before Pilate
28.11 some of the guard . . told . . chief priests
Mk 8.31 must . . be rejected by . . chief priests
10.33 "Son of man . . delivered to . . chief priests
11.18 chief priests . . sought . . to destroy him
11.27 chief priests . . and . . elders came to him
14. 1 chief priests . . seeking how to . . kill him
14.10 Judas Iscariot . . went to the chief priests
14.43 with swords . . , from the chief priests
14.53 chief priests and . . scribes were assembled
14.55 chief priests . . sought testimony against
15. 1 chief priests . . held a consultation
15. 3 the chief priests accused him of many things
15.10 chief priests had delivered him up
15.11 the chief priests stirred up the crowd
15.31 also the chief priests mocked him
Lk 9.22 "rejected by the elders and chief priests
19.47 chief priests . . sought to destroy him
20. 1 chief priests and the scribes . . came up
20.19 chief priests tried to lay hands on him
22. 2 chief priests and . . scribes were seeking how
22. 4 conferred with the chief priests and captains
22.52 chief priests and officers of the temple
22.66 assembly . . , both chief priests and scribes
23. 4 Pilate said to the chief priests
23.10 chief priests and the scribes stood by
23.13 Pilate . . called together the chief priests
24.20 "chief priests and rulers delivered him up
Jn 7.32 chief priests and Pharisees sent officers
7.45 officers . . went back to the chief priests
11.47 the chief priests . . gathered the council
11.57 the chief priests . . had given orders
12.10 chief priests planned to put Lazarus
18. 3 officers from the chief priests . . went
18.35 "chief priests have handed you over to me
Jn 19. 6 chief priests . . cried out, "Crucify him
19.15 chief priests answered, "We have no king
19.21 chief priests of the Jews . . said to Pilate
Acts 4.23 reported what the chief priests . . said
5.24 when . . chief priests heard these words
9.14 "he has authority from the chief priests
9.21 "to bring them . . before the chief priests
22.30 commanded the chief priests . . to meet
23.14 they went to the chief priests and elders
25. 2 chief priests . . informed him against Paul
25.15 "chief priests . . gave information
26.10 "by authority from the chief priests
26.12 "with the authority . . of the chief priests

PRIEST, HIGH
1. *chief priest:* ἀρχιερεύς ARCHIEREUS
Mt 26. 3 gathered in the palace of the high priest
26.51 struck the slave of the high priest
26.57 led him to Caiaphas the high priest
26.58 as far as the courtyard of the high priest
26.62 high priest . . said, "Have you no answer?
26.63 high priest said to him, "I adjure you
26.65 Then the high priest tore his robes
Mk 2.26 "when Abiathar was high priest
14.47 struck the slave of the high priest
14.53 they led Jesus to the high priest
14.54 right into the courtyard of the high priest
14.60 the high priest stood up in the midst
14.61 high priest asked . . "Are you the Christ?
14.63 the high priest tore his garments
14.66 one of the maids of the high priest
Lk 22.50 struck the slave of the high priest
22.54 bringing him into the high priest's house
Jn 11.49 Caiaphas, who was high priest that year
11.51 being high priest that year he prophesied
18.10 Peter . . struck the high priest's slave
18.13 Caiaphas, who was high priest that year
18.15 As this disciple was known to the high p., he entered the court of the high p.
18.16 disciple . . known to the high priest
18.19 The high priest then questioned Jesus
18.22 "Is that how you answer the high priest?
18.24 sent him . . to Caiaphas the high priest
18.26 One of the servants[l] of the high p.
Acts 4. 6 Annas the high priest and Caiaphas
5.17 high priest rose up and all . . with him
5.21 Now the high priest came
5.27 the high priest questioned them
7. 1 the high priest said, "Is this so?
9. 1 Saul . . went to the high priest
19.14 Seven sons of a Jewish high priest
22. 5 "the high priest and the whole council
23. 2 the high priest Ananias commanded
23. 4 "Would you revile God's high priest?
23. 5 "I did not know . . he was the high priest
24. 1 the high priest Ananias came down
Heb 2.17 a merciful and faithful high priest
3. 1 Jesus, . . high priest of our confession
4.14 Since then we have a great high priest
4.15 we have not a high p. who is unable
5. 1 every high priest chosen from among men
5. 5 did not exalt himself to . . a high priest
5.10 being designated by God a high priest
6.20 having become a high priest for ever
7.26 fitting that we should have such a high p.
7.27 He has no need, like those high priests
7.28 men in their weakness as high priests
8. 1 we have such a high priest
8. 3 every high priest is appointed to offer
9. 7 into the second only the high priest goes
9.11 when Christ appeared as a high priest
9.25 as the high priest enters the Holy Place
13.11 brought . . by the high priest as a sacrifice

PRIEST, SERVE AS
1. *be a priest:* ἱερατεύω HIERATEUŌ*
Lk 1. 8 Now while he was serving as priest

PRIESTHOOD
1. *priesthood:* ἱερατεία HIERATEIA
Lk 1. 9 according to the custom of the p.
2. *priesthood:* ἱεράτευμα HIERATEUMA*
1 Pet 2. 5 a spiritual house, . . a holy priesthood
2. 9 you are a chosen race, a royal p.
3. *priesthood:* ἱερωσύνη HIERŌSYNĒ*
Heb 7.11 if . . attainable through the Levitical p.
7.12 when there is a change in the priesthood
7.24 he holds his priesthood permanently

PRIESTLY OFFICE
1. *priesthood:* ἱερατεία HIERATEIA
Heb 7. 5 those . . who receive the p. office

PRIESTLY SERVICE, IN
1. *act as a priest:* ἱερουργέω (part.+acc.) HIEROURGEŌ*
Rom 15.16 Gentiles in the p. service of the gospel

PRINCE
1. *ruler:* ἄρχων ARCHŌN
Mt 9.34 "He casts out demons by the p. of demons[a]‡
12.24 "by Beelzebul, the prince of demons
Mk 3.22 "by the p. of demons he casts out . . demons
Lk 11.15 "casts out demons by . . the p. of demons
Eph 2. 2 the prince of the power of the air

PRINCIPAL
1. *first, foremost:* πρῶτος PRŌTOS
Lk 19.47 the p. men . . sought to destroy him
Acts 25. 2 the p. men . . informed him against Paul

PRINCIPALITIES
1. *origin, rule:* ἀρχή (pl.) ARCHĒ
Rom 8.38 neither death, nor life, . . nor p.
Eph 3.10 might now be made known to the p.
6.12 we are . . contending against . . the p.
Col 1.16 in him all things were created, . . whether . . p.
2.15 He disarmed the principalities and powers

PRINCIPLE
1. *law, norm:* νόμος NOMOS
Rom 3.27 It is excluded. On what principle? . . on the principle of faith
2. *element:* στοιχεῖον STOICHEION
Heb 5.12 to teach you again the first principles

PRINT
1. *pattern, image:* τύπος TYPOS
Jn 20.25 "Unless I see . . the print of the nails

PRISCA, PRISCILLA: Πρίσκα, Πρίσκιλλα 'priskə, pri'silə
Acts 18. 2 Jew named Aquila . . with his wife Priscilla
18.18 sailed . . with him Priscilla and Aquila
18.26 when Priscilla and Aquila heard him
Rom 16. 3 Greet Prisca and Aquila
1 Cor 16.19 Aquila and Prisca . . send you . . greetings
2 Tim 4.19 Greet Prisca and Aquila

PRISON
1. *prison:* δεσμωτήριον DESMŌTĒRION*
Mt 11. 2 John heard in prison about the deeds
Acts 5.21 sent to the prison to have them brought
5.23 "We found the prison securely locked
16.26 foundations of the prison were shaken
2. *watch, guard, prison:* φυλακή PHYLAKĒ
Mt 5.25 "quickly . . ., lest . . you be put in prison
14. 3 Herod had . . put him in prison
14.10 he . . had John beheaded in the prison
18.30 "He . . put him in prison till he should pay
25.36 " 'I was in prison and you came to me
25.39 " 'when did we see thee sick or in p.?
25.43 " 'in prison and you did not visit me
25.44 " 'Lord, when did we see thee . . in prison?
Mk 6.17 Herod . . bound him in prison
6.27 He went and beheaded him in the p.
Lk 3.20 he shut up John in prison
12.58 "lest . . the officer put you in prison
21.12 "delivering you up to . . prisons
22.33 "Lord, I am ready to go with you to p.
23.19 a man who had been thrown into p.
23.25 the man who had been thrown into p.
Jn 3.24 John had not yet been put in prison
Acts 5.19 an angel of the Lord opened the prison
5.22 they did not find them in the prison
5.25 "The men whom you put in prison
8. 3 Saul . . committed them to prison
12. 4 when he had seized him, he put him in p.
12. 5 So Peter was kept in prison
12. 6 sentries . . were guarding the prison
12.17 the Lord had brought him out of the p.
16.23 they threw them into prison
16.24 he put them into the inner prison
16.27 saw that the prison doors were open
16.37 "They . . have thrown us into prison
16.40 So they went out of the prison
22. 4 delivering to p. both men and women
26.10 "shut up many of the saints in prison
1 Pet 3.19 he . . preached to the spirits in prison
Rev 2.10 " 'about to throw some of you into p.
20. 7 Satan will be loosed from his prison
3. *safekeeping:* τήρησις TĒRĒSIS
Acts 5.18 they . . put them in the common p.

PRISON, BE IN
1. *bind, tie:* δέω (perf. pass.) DEŌ
Col 4. 3 on account of which I am in prison

PRISON, IN
1. *bind, tie:* δέω (perf. pass. part.) DEŌ
Mk 15. 7 among the rebels in p. . . was . . Barabbas
Acts 24.27 Felix left Paul in prison

PRISON, ONE WHO IS IN
1. *prisoner:* δέσμιος DESMIOS
Heb 13. 3 Remember those who are in prison

PRISON WITH, IN
1. *bind together:* συνδέω (pass. part.) SYNDEŌ*
Heb 13. 3 Remember . . as though in p. with them

PRISONER
1. *prisoner:* δέσμιος DESMIOS
Mt 27.15 to release for the crowd any one p.
27.16 they had . . a notorious p., called Barabbas[k]
Mk 15. 6 he used to release for them one p.
Acts 16.25 the prisoners were listening to them
16.27 supposing . . the prisoners had escaped
23.18 "Paul the p. . . asked me to bring this . . man
25.14 "There is a man left prisoner by Felix
25.27 "unreasonable, in sending a prisoner
28.17 "I was delivered p. from Jerusalem
Eph 3. 1 I, Paul, a prisoner for Christ Jesus
4. 1 I therefore, a prisoner for the Lord
2 Tim 1. 8 Do not be ashamed . . of me his prisoner
Phm . 1 Paul, a prisoner for Christ Jesus
. 9 now a prisoner also for Christ Jesus
Heb 10.34 you had compassion on the prisoners
2. *prisoner:* δεσμώτης DESMŌTĒS*
Acts 27. 1 delivered Paul and some other prisoners
27.42 soldiers' plan was to kill the prisoners

PRISONER, FELLOW
1. *fellow prisoner:* συναιχμάλωτος SYNAICHMALŌTOS*
Rom 16. 7 my kinsmen and my fellow prisoners
Col 4.10 Aristarchus my fellow p. greets you
Phm .23 Epaphras, my fellow p. in Christ Jesus

PRIVATE
1. *secret, hidden:* κρυπτός KRYPTOS
Jn 7.10 he also went up, not publicly but in p.

PRIVATELY
1. *by oneself:* κατ' ἰδίαν IDIOS [B.1.a.1]
Mt 17.19 the disciples came to Jesus privately
24. 3 the disciples came to him privately
Mk 4.34 p. to his own disciples he explained
7.33 taking him aside from the multitude p.
9.28 his disciples asked him privately
13. 3 John and Andrew asked him privately
Lk 10.23 turning to the disciples he said p.
Acts 23.19 The tribune . . asked him privately
Gal 2. 2 I laid before them (but privately

PRIZE
1. *prize:* βραβεῖον BRABEION*
1 Cor 9.24 all . . compete, but only one receives the p.
Phil 3.14 I press on toward the goal for the prize

PROCEED
1. *put to, add, continue:* προστίθημι PROSTITHĒMI
Lk 19.11 he proceeded to tell a parable
Acts 12. 3 he proceeded to arrest Peter also
CONTEXTUALLY
Rom 14.23 whatever does not p. from faith is sin[w]

PROCEED FROM
PROCEED OUT OF
1. *go out:* ἐκπορεύομαι EKPOREUOMAI
Mt 4. 4 " 'by every word that proceeds from . . God
Lk 4.22 which proceeded out of his mouth
Jn 15.26 "Spirit . . who proceeds from the Father
2. *go out:* ἐξέρχομαι EXERCHOMAI
Mt 15.18 "what comes out of the mouth proceeds
Jn 8.42 "I proceeded and came forth from God

PROCEEDS
1. *honor, value:* τιμή (sg. or pl.) TIMĒ
Acts 4.34 many . . brought the p. of what was sold
5. 2 he kept back some of the proceeds
5. 3 "to keep back part of the proceeds

PROCHORUS: Πρόχορος 'präkərəs
Acts 6. 5 they chose Stephen, . . Philip, and Prochorus

PROCLAIM
1. *report:* ἀναγγέλλω ANAGGELLŌ
1 Jn 1. 5 This is the message we . . proclaim to you
2. *bring tidings:* ἀπαγγέλλω APAGGELLŌ
Mt 12.18 "he shall p. justice to the Gentiles
Heb 2.12 "I will p. thy name to my brethren
1 Jn 1. 2 we . . proclaim to you the eternal life
1. 3 that which we have seen . . we proclaim
3. *point out:* ἀποδείκνυμι APODEIKNYMI
2 Th 2. 4 proclaiming himself to be God
4. *proclaim:* διαγγέλλω DIAGGELLŌ
Lk 9.60 "as for you, go and proclaim the kingdom
Rom 9.17 "that my name may be proclaimed
5. *bring good news* (mid.): εὐαγγελίζω (act.) EUAGGELIZŌ [A.6.a.6]
Rev 14. 6 with an eternal gospel to proclaim
6. *come to be, happen, be:* γίνομαι GINOMAI [A.6.a.5]
Acts 10.37 "the word which was proclaimed
7. *make known:* γνωρίζω GNŌRIZŌ
Eph 6.19 to proclaim the mystery of the gospel
8. *proclaim, announce:* καταγγέλλω KATAGGELLŌ
Acts 3.24 "prophets . . also proclaimed these days
4. 2 proclaiming in Jesus the resurrection
13. 5 at Salamis, they proclaimed the word
13.38 "forgiveness of sins is proclaimed
15.36 "we proclaimed the word of the Lord
16.17 "who p. to you the way of salvation
17. 3 "This Jesus, whom I proclaim to you
17.13 word of God was proclaimed . . at Beroea
17.23 "What . . you worship as unknown, this I p.
26.23 "he would proclaim light . . to the people
Rom 1. 8 your faith is proclaimed in all the world
1 Cor 2. 1 proclaiming . . the testimony[c] of God
9.14 those who proclaim the gospel
11.26 proclaim the Lord's death until he comes
Phil 1.17 proclaim Christ out of partisanship
1.18 Christ is proclaimed; . . in that I rejoice
Col 1.28 Him we proclaim, warning every man
9. *proclaim:* κηρύσσω KĒRYSSŌ
Mt 10.27 "what you hear whispered, proclaim
Mk 5.20 he went away and began to proclaim
7.36 the more zealously they proclaimed it
Lk 4.18 "He has sent me to proclaim release
4.19 "to p. the acceptable year of the Lord
8.39 proclaiming . . how much Jesus had done
12. 3 "what you . . whispered . . shall be proclaimed
Acts 8. 5 Philip . . proclaimed to them the Christ
9.20 in the synagogues . . he proclaimed Jesus
Rev 5. 2 I saw a strong angel proclaiming
10. *cry out, shout:* κράζω KRAZŌ
Jn 7.28 So Jesus proclaimed . . "You know me?
7.37 Jesus . . proclaimed, "If any one thirst
CONTEXTUALLY
2 Tim 4.17 gave me strength to p. the message

PROCLAMATION
1. *proclamation:* κήρυγμα KĒRYGMA
Mk [16.[end] *the sacred and imperishable proclamation*‡

PROCONSUL
1. *proconsul:* ἀνθύπατος ANTHYPATOS*
Acts 13. 7 He was with the p., Sergius Paulus
13. 8 seeking to turn . . the p. from the faith
13.12 Then the proconsul believed
18.12 when Gallio was proconsul of Achaia
19.38 "courts are open, . . there are proconsuls

PROCURE
1. *receive, take:* λαμβάνω LAMBANŌ
Jn 18. 3 Judas, procuring a band of soldiers

PRODUCE
1. *work, do:* ἐργάζομαι ERGAZOMAI
2 Cor 7.10 For godly grief produces a repentance
2. *come to be, happen, be:* γίνομαι GINOMAI [A.6.a.5]
1 Tim 6. 4 disputes about words, which produce envy
3. *bear fruit:* καρποφορέω KARPOPHOREŌ
Mk 4.28 "The earth produces of itself
4. *achieve:* κατεργάζομαι KATERGAZOMAI
Rom 5. 3 suffering produces endurance
2 Cor 7.10 worldly grief produces death
7.11 see what . . this godly grief has produced!
9.11 generosity . . will produce thanksgiving
Jas 1. 3 testing of . . faith produces steadfastness
5. *do, make:* ποιέω POIEŌ
Mt 21.43 "given to a nation producing the fruits
6. *present, bring forth:* προφέρω PROPHERŌ*
Lk 6.45 "good man out of . . his heart produces good, and the evil man . . produces evil
CONTEXTUALLY
Rom 5. 4 and endurance produces character
5. 4 and character produces hope

PROFANE
1. *desecrate:* βεβηλόω BEBĒLOŌ*
Mt 12. 5 "priests in the temple profane the sabbath
Acts 24. 6 "He even tried to profane the temple
2. *unhallowed, profane:* βέβηλος BEBĒLOS
1 Tim 1. 9 the law is . . laid down for the . . profane
3. *consider common:* κοινὸν ἡγοῦσθαι KOINOS [A.6.a.4]
Heb 10.29 has . . profaned the blood of the covenant
CONTEXTUALLY
1 Cor 11.27 will be guilty of profaning the body

PROFESS
1. *promise, profess:* ἐπαγγέλλομαι EPAGGELLOMAI
1 Tim 2.10 as befits women who profess religion
6.21 by professing it some have missed
2. *confess, acknowledge:* ὁμολογέω HOMOLOGEŌ
Tit 1.16 They profess to know God

PROFIT
1. *help, aid:* ὠφελέω ŌPHELEŌ
[a]A.6.c.3
Mt 16.26 [a]"what will it p. . . if he gains the . . world?
Mk 8.36 "what does it p. . . to gain the . . world?
Lk 9.25 [a]"what does it p. . . if he gains the . . world?
2. *advantage, benefit:* ὄφελος OPHELOS
Jas 2.14 What does it profit, my brethren?
2.16 without . . things needed . . , what does it p.?

PROFITABLE
PROFITABLE, WHAT IS
1. *useful, beneficial:* ὠφέλιμος ŌPHELIMOS
2 Tim 3.16 All scripture is . . profitable for teaching
Tit 3. 8 these are excellent and profitable to men
2. *bring together, be useful:* συμφέρω (subst. part. neut.) SYMPHERŌ
Acts 20.20 "declaring to you anything that was p.

PROFLIGACY
1. *profligacy, dissipation:* ἀσωτία ASŌTIA
1 Pet 4. 4 you do not now join . . in the same wild p.

PROFLIGATE
1. *powerless, intemperate:* ἀκρατής AKRATĒS*
2 Tim 3. 3 profligates, fierce, haters of good
2. *profligacy, dissipation:* ἀσωτία (gen.) ASŌTIA
Tit 1. 6 open to the charge of being profligate

PROFOUND
1. *great:* μέγας MEGAS
Eph 5.32 This mystery is a profound one[0]

PROGRESS
1. *progress:* προκοπή PROKOPĒ
Phil 1.25 for your progress and joy in the faith
1 Tim 4.15 that all may see your progress

PROLONG
1. *extend:* παρατείνω PARATEINŌ*
Acts 20. 7 he prolonged his speech until midnight

PROMINENT
1. *prominence:* ἐξοχή EXOCHĒ* [B.1.a.1]
Acts 25.23 Agrippa . . with the . . p. men of the city

PROMISE
1. *promise:* ἐπαγγελία EPAGGELIA
[a]B.1.a.2 [b]A.6.a.3
Lk 24.49 "I send the promise of my Father
Acts 1. 4 to wait for the promise of the Father
2.33 "from the Father the p. of the . . Spirit
2.39 "the p. is to you and to your children
7.17 "as the time of the promise drew near
13.23 [a]"a Savior, Jesus, as he promised
13.32 [b]"what God promised to the fathers
23.21 "waiting for the promise from you
26. 6 "I stand here on trial for hope in the p.
Rom 4.13 The p. . . that they should inherit . . world
4.14 faith is null and the promise is void
4.16 that the promise may rest on grace
4.20 No distrust . . concerning the p. of God
9. 4 to them belong . . the law . . and the promises
9. 8 children of the promise are reckoned
9. 9 For this is what the promise said
15. 8 to confirm the promises given
2 Cor 1.20 promises of God find their Yes in him
7. 1 Since we have these promises, beloved
Gal 3.14 that we might receive the promise
3.16 the promises were made to Abraham
3.17 not . . so as to make the promise void
3.18 it is no longer by promise; but God gave it to Abraham by a promise
3.21 Is the law then against the promises?
3.29 Abraham's offspring, heirs according to p.
4.23 son of the free woman through p.
4.28 we,[j] . . like Isaac, are children of promise
Eph 2.12 strangers to the covenants of promise
3. 6 partakers of the p. in Christ Jesus
6. 2 "(the first commandment with a p.
1 Tim 4. 8 as it holds promise for the present life
2 Tim 1. 1 apostle . . according to the p. of the life
Heb 4. 1 while the p. of entering his rest remains
6.12 who through faith . . inherit the promises
6.15 Abraham[m] . . obtained the promise
6.17 to show . . to the heirs of the promise
7. 6 blessed him who had the promises
8. 6 since it is enacted on better promises
11. 9 he sojourned in the land of promise
11. 9 heirs with him of the same promise
11.17 who had received the promises was ready
11.33 who through faith . . received promises
2 Pet 3. 4 "Where is the promise of his coming?
3. 9 The Lord is not slow about his p.
2. *promise, profess:* ἐπαγγέλλομαι EPAGGELLOMAI
Mk 14.11 they . . promised to give him money
Acts 7. 5 "promised to give it to him in possession
Rom 4.21 God was able to do what he had promised
Tit 1. 2 hope of eternal life which God . . promised
Heb 10.23 for he who promised is faithful
11.11 considered him faithful who had promised
12.26 but now he has promised, "Yet once
Jas 1.12 the crown of life which God has promised
2. 5 the kingdom which he has promised
2 Pet 2.19 They promise them freedom
1 Jn 2.25 this is what he has promised us,[e] . . life
3. *promise:* ἐπάγγελμα EPAGGELMA*
2 Pet 1. 4 his precious and very great promises
3.13 But according to his promise we wait
4. *confess, acknowledge:* ὁμολογέω HOMOLOGEŌ
Mt 14. 7 so that he promised with an oath
5. *announce before:* προεπαγγέλλω (mid.) PROEPAGGELLŌ
2 Cor 9. 5 arrange . . for this gift you . . promised
CONTEXTUALLY
Rom 7.10 very commandment which promised life

PROMISE BEFOREHAND
1. *announce before:* προεπαγγέλλω (mid.) PROEPAGGELLŌ
Rom 1. 2 promised beforehand through . . prophets

PROMISE, MAKE A
1. *promise, profess:* ἐπαγγέλλομαι EPAGGELLOMAI
Gal 3.19 offspring . . to whom the p. had been made
Heb 6.13 when God made a promise to Abraham

PROMISED
1. *promise:* ἐπαγγελία EPAGGELIA
[a]gen. [b]A.1.b.5
Eph 1.13 [a]were sealed with the p. Holy Spirit
Heb 9.15 [b]receive the promised eternal inheritance
CONTEXTUALLY
Lk 1.72 the mercy promised to our fathers

PROMISED, WHAT IS
1. *promise:* ἐπαγγελία EPAGGELIA
Gal 3.22 that what was p. to faith . . be given
Heb 10.36 endurance . . that you . . receive what is p.
11.13 died . . , not having received what was p.
11.39 these . . did not receive what was p.

PROMOTE
1. *become active in:* ἐνεργὴς γίνεσθαι ἐν ENERGĒS [B.3.a.2]
Phm . 6 that . . your faith may p. the knowledge
2. *show, offer, cause:* παρέχω PARECHŌ
1 Tim 1. 4 genealogies which promote speculations
CONTEXTUALLY
Col 2.23 These have . . wisdom in promoting rigor

PROMPT
1. *cause to come forward:* προβιβάζω PROBIBAZŌ*
Mt 14. 8 Prompted by her mother, she said, "Give
2. *bring together, infer, teach:* συμβιβάζω SYMBIBAZŌ
Acts 19.33 Some of the crowd prompted Alexander

PRONOUNCE (*See also* JUDGMENT, PRONOUNCE)
1. *bring upon, inflict:* ἐπιφέρω EPIPHERŌ
Jude . 9 he did not presume to p. a . . judgment
2. *judge, decide:* κρίνω KRINŌ [A.6.a.6]
Mt 7. 2 "with the judgment you pronounce
3. *say, speak:* λέγω LEGŌ
Rom 4. 6 So also David pronounces a blessing
4. *name, specify:* ὀνομάζω ONOMAZŌ
Acts 19.13 undertook to p. the name of the Lord Jesus
5. *bring, bear:* φέρω PHERŌ
2 Pet 2.11 angels . . do not p. a reviling judgment
CONTEXTUALLY
Rom 4. 9 pronounced only upon the circumcised?

PROOF
1. *test, proof:* δοκιμή DOKIMĒ
2 Cor 13. 3 you desire proof that Christ is speaking
2. *sign, proof:* ἔνδειξις ENDEIXIS
2 Cor 8.24 So give proof, before the churches
3. *testimony, proof:* μαρτύριον MARTYRION
Mt 8. 4 "gift that Moses commanded, for a p.
Mk 1.44 "what Moses commanded, for a p.
Lk 5.14 "as Moses commanded, for a proof
4. *sign, proof:* τεκμήριον TEKMĒRION*
Acts 1. 3 many proofs, appearing to them

PROPER (*See also* TIME, PROPER)
1. *one's own:* ἴδιος IDIOS
1 Tim 2. 6 testimony . . was borne at the p. time

1 Tim 6.15 made manifest at the proper time
Tit 1. 3 at the p. time manifested in his word

PROPER, BE
1. *be fitting:* πρέπω PREPŌ
1 Cor 11.13 is it p. . . to pray . . with her head uncovered?

PROPER, ONE'S
1. *one's own:* ἴδιος IDIOS
Jude . 6 angels that . . left their proper dwelling

PROPERLY
1. *in measure:* ἐν μέτρῳ METRON [B.1.a.1]
Eph 4.16 when each part is working properly

PROPERLY, NOT BEHAVE
1. *behave disgracefully:* ἀσχημονέω ASCHĒMONEŌ
1 Cor 7.36 thinks that he is not behaving properly

PROPERTY
1. *be, exist, belong to:* ὑπάρχω (subst. neut. pl.) HYPARCHŌ
Mt 25.14 "when a man . . entrusted to them his p.
Heb 10.34 accepted the plundering of your p.
2. *what is one's own, property:* οὐσία OUSIA*
Lk 15.12 " 'Father, give me the share of property
15.13 "there he squandered his property

PROPERTY, PIECE OF
1. *anything gotten, property:* κτῆμα KTĒMA
Acts 5. 1 man named Ananias . . sold a piece of p.

PROPHECY
1. *prophecy:* προφητεία PROPHĒTEIA
Mt 13.14 "indeed is fulfilled the p. of Isaiah
Rom 12. 6 if prophecy, in proportion to our faith
1 Cor 12.10 ⟨To one is given . . faith⟩, to another p.
13. 8 as for prophecies, they will pass away
14. 6 how shall I benefit you unless I bring . . p.?
14.22 while prophecy is not for unbelievers
2 Pet 1.20 no p. . . of one's own interpretation
1.21 no p. ever came by the impulse of man
Rev 1. 3 Blessed is he who reads . . the prophecy
19.10 the testimony of Jesus is the spirit of p.
22. 7 Blessed is he who keeps the words of the p.
22.10 "Do not seal up the words of the prophecy
22.18 I warn every one who hears . . the p.
22.19 if any . . takes away from the words of . . p.
2. *be a prophet, prophesy:* προφητεύω PROPHĒTEUŌ [A.6.a.2]
1 Cor 13. 9 our knowledge . . and our p. is imperfect

PROPHESY
1. *be a prophet, prophesy:* προφητεύω PROPHĒTEUŌ
Mt 7.22 " 'Lord, did we not p. in your name?
11.13 "the prophets . . prophesied until John
15. 7 "Well did Isaiah prophesy of you
26.68 "Prophesy to us, you Christ!
Mk 7. 6 "Well did Isaiah prophesy of you
14.65 some began . . to strike him, saying . . "P.!
Lk 1.67 his father Zechariah . . prophesied
22.64 "Prophesy! Who is it that struck you?
Jn 11.51 but being high priest . . he prophesied
Acts 2.17 " 'your sons and . . daughters shall p.
2.18 " 'I will pour . . my Spirit; . . they shall p.
19. 6 they spoke with tongues and prophesied
21. 9 four . . daughters, who prophesied
1 Cor 11. 4 who . . prophesies with his head covered
11. 5 who . . prophesies with her head unveiled
14. 1 desire . . that you may prophesy
14. 3 who prophesies speaks . . for . . upbuilding
14. 4 he who prophesies edifies the church
14. 5 I want you . . even more to prophesy. He who prophesies is greater
14.24 if all p. . . an unbeliever . . is convicted
14.31 For you can all prophesy one by one
14.39 brethren, earnestly desire to prophesy
1 Pet 1.10 prophets who prophesied of the grace
Jude .14 It was of these . . that Enoch . . prophesied
Rev 10.11 "You must . . p. about many peoples
11. 3 "I will grant my two witnesses power to p.

PROPHESYING
1. *prophecy:* προφητεία PROPHĒTEIA
1 Th 5.20 do not despise prophesying

Rev 11. 6 that no rain may fall during . . their p.

PROPHET
1. *herald, interpreter, prophet:* προφήτης PROPHĒTĒS*
Mt 1.22 what the Lord had spoken by the p.
2. 5 "for so it is written by the prophet
2.15 what the Lord had spoken by the p.
2.17 what was spoken by the p. Jeremiah
2.23 what was spoken by the prophets
3. 3 who was spoken of by the p. Isaiah
4.14 what was spoken by the prophet Isaiah
5.12 "for so men persecuted the prophets
5.17 "not . . to abolish . . law and the prophets
7.12 "for this is the law and the prophets
8.17 to fulfil what was spoken by the p. Isaiah
10.41 "He who receives a prophet because he is a prophet shall receive a prophet's reward
11. 9 "Why then did you go out? To see a prophet?[b] Yes, I tell you, and more than a p.
11.13 "the prophets . . prophesied until John
12.17 what was spoken by the prophet Isaiah
12.39 "except the sign of the prophet Jonah
13.17 "many prophets . . longed to see
13.35 to fulfil what was spoken by the prophet[k]
13.57 "A prophet is not without honor
14. 5 because they held him to be a prophet
16.14 they said . . "Jeremiah or one of the prophets
21. 4 to fulfil what was spoken by the p.
21.11 "This is the p. Jesus from Nazareth
21.26 "for all hold that John was a prophet
21.46 because they held him to be a prophet
22.40 "On these . . depend all . . the prophets
23.29 "for you build the tombs of the prophets
23.30 " 'shedding the blood of the prophets
23.31 "sons of those who murdered the prophets
23.34 "I send you prophets and wise men
23.37 "O Jerusalem, . . killing the prophets!
24.15 "sacrilege spoken of by the p. Daniel
26.56 "that the . . prophets might be fulfilled
27. 9 fulfilled what had been spoken by the p.
Mk 1. 2 As it is written in Isaiah the prophet[b]‡
6. 4 "A prophet is not without honor
6.15 And others said, "It is a prophet, like one of the prophets of old
8.28 they told him . . "one of the prophets
11.32 "for all held that John was a real prophet
Lk 1.70 "spoke by the mouth of his holy prophets
1.76 "you, child, will be called the prophet
3. 4 in the book of the words of Isaiah the p.
4.17 given to him the book of the p. Isaiah
4.24 "no p. is acceptable in his own country
4.27 "in the time of the prophet Elisha
6.23 "for so their fathers did to the prophets
7.16 "A great prophet has arisen among us!
7.26 "What . . did you go out to see? A p.? Yes, I tell you, and more than a prophet
7.39 "If this man were a prophet
9. 8 that one of the old prophets had risen
9.19 "that one of the old prophets has risen
10.24 "many prophets and kings desired to see
11.47 "you build the tombs of the prophets
11.49 " 'I will send . . prophets and apostles
11.50 "the blood of all the prophets, shed
13.28 "all the prophets in the kingdom of God
13.33 " 'that a p. . . perish away from Jerusalem
13.34 "O Jerusalem, . . killing the prophets!
16.16 "law and the prophets were until John
16.29 " 'They have Moses and the prophets
16.31 " 'If they do not hear . . the prophets
18.31 "everything . . written . . by the prophets
20. 6 "they are convinced that John was a p.
24.19 "Jesus . . a p. mighty in deed and word
24.25 "all that the prophets have spoken!
24.27 beginning with Moses and . . the prophets
24.44 "everything written . . in . . the prophets
Jn 1.21 "Are you the p.?" And he answered, "No
1.23 "I am the voice . . , as the p. Isaiah said

Jn 1.25 "if.. neither the Christ.. nor the prophet
1.45 "of whom.. the prophets wrote, Jesus
4.19 "Sir, I perceive that you are a prophet
4.44 a p. has no honor in his own country
6.14 "This is indeed the p. who is to come!
6.45 "It is written in the prophets
7.40 the people said, "This is really the p.
7.52 "no prophet is to rise from Galilee
8.52 "Abraham died, as did the prophets
8.53 "And the prophets died!
9.17 He said, "He is a prophet
12.38 the word spoken by the prophet Isaiah
Acts 2.16 "what was spoken by the prophet Joel
2.36 "Being.. a p., and knowing.. God had sworn
3.18 "foretold by the mouth of.. the prophets
3.21 "that God spoke by.. his holy prophets
3.22 " 'The Lord God will raise up for you a p.
3.23 " 'every soul that does not listen to that p.
3.24 "all the prophets who have spoken
3.25 "You are the sons of the prophets
7.37 " 'God will raise up for you a prophet
7.42 "written in the book of the prophets
7.48 "does not dwell in houses.. as the p. says
7.52 "prophets.. your fathers ⟨did⟩ persecute
8.28 he was reading the prophet Isaiah
8.30 heard him reading Isaiah the prophet
8.34 "About whom.. does the p. say this?
10.43 "To him all the prophets bear witness
11.27 in these days prophets came down
13. 1 at Antioch there were prophets
13.15 reading of the law and the prophets
13.20 "judges until Samuel the prophet
13.27 "prophets which are read every sabbath
13.40 "lest.. what is said in the prophets
15.15 "the words of the prophets agree
15.32 who were themselves prophets, exhorted
21.10 a prophet named Agabus came down
24.14 "everything.. written in the prophets
26.22 "what the prophets.. said would come
26.27 "Agrippa, do you believe the prophets?
28.23 to convince them.. from the prophets
28.25 "The Holy Spirit.. through Isaiah the p.
Rom 1. 2 promised.. through his prophets
3.21 the law and the prophets bear witness
11. 3 "Lord, they have killed thy prophets
1 Cor 12.28 God has appointed.. second prophets
12.29 Are all apostles? Are all prophets?
14.29 Let two or three prophets speak
14.32 and the spirits of prophets are subject to prophets
14.37 If any one thinks that he is a prophet
Eph 2.20 built upon the foundation of.. prophets
3. 5 has now been revealed to his.. prophets
4.11 some should be apostles, some prophets
1 Th 2.15 killed both.. Jesus and the prophets
Tit 1.12 One of themselves, a prophet.., said
Heb 1. 1 God spoke of old.. by the prophets
11.32 David and Samuel and the prophets
Jas 5.10 As an example.. take the prophets
1 Pet 1.10 prophets who prophesied of the grace
2 Pet 2.16 restrained the prophet's madness
3. 2 the predictions of the holy prophets
Rev 10. 7 announced to his servants the prophets
11.10 these two prophets had been a torment
11.18 "rewarding thy servants, the prophets
16. 6 "For men have shed the blood of.. prophets
18.20 "O saints and apostles and prophets
18.24 "in her was found the blood of prophets
22. 6 "the God of the spirits of the prophets
22. 9 "I am a fellow servant with.. the prophets

PROPHET, FALSE
1. *false prophet:* ψευδοπροφήτης PSEUDOPROPHĒTĒS*
Mt 7.15 "Beware of false prophets
24.11 "many false prophets will arise
24.24 "false prophets will arise
Mk 13.22 "false prophets will arise
Lk 6.26 "so their fathers did to the false prophets
Acts 13. 6 magician, a Jewish false prophet
2 Pet 2. 1 false prophets.. arose among the people
1 Jn 4. 1 many false prophets have gone out
Rev 16.13 from the mouth of the false prophet
19.20 the beast was captured, and.. the false p.
20.10 where the beast and the false p. were

PROPHETESS
1. *prophetess:* προφῆτις PROPHĒTIS*
Lk 2.36 there was a prophetess, Anna
Rev 2.20 " 'Jezebel, who calls herself a prophetess

PROPHETIC
1. *prophetic:* προφητικός PROPHĒTIKOS*
Rom 16.26 through the p. writings is made known
2 Pet 1.19 we have the p. word made more sure

PROPHETIC POWERS
PROPHETIC UTTERANCE
1. *prophecy:* προφητεία PROPHĒTEIA
1 Cor 13. 2 if I have p. powers, and understand
1 Tim 1.18 the prophetic utterances which pointed
4.14 the gift.. given you by p. utterance

PROPORTION
1. *proportion:* ἀναλογία ANALOGIA*
Rom 12. 6 if prophecy, in proportion to our faith

PROSELYTE
1. *proselyte, convert:* προσήλυτος PROSĒLYTOS
Mt 23.15 "you traverse sea and land to make a.. p.
Acts 2.10 "from Rome, both Jews and proselytes
6. 5 Nicolaus, a proselyte of Antioch

PROSPECT
1. *receiving, expectation:* ἐκδοχή EKDOCHĒ*
Heb 10.27 but a fearful prospect of judgment

PROSPER
1. *help on the way, gain:* εὐοδόω (pass.) EUODOŌ
1 Cor 16. 2 put something aside.. as he may prosper
2. *be rich, become rich:* πλουτέω PLOUTEŌ
Rev 3.17 " 'For you say,.. I have prospered

PROSTITUTE
1. *harlot, prostitute:* πόρνη PORNĒ
1 Cor 6.15 Shall I.. make them members of a p.?
6.16 he who joins himself to a p. becomes one

PROTEST
CONTEXTUALLY
1 Cor 15.31 I p., brethren, by my pride in you

PROUD
1. *boaster:* ἀλαζών (pred.) ALAZŌN
2 Tim 3. 2 For men will be lovers of self,.. proud
2. *arrogant:* ὑπερήφανος HYPERĒPHANOS
Lk 1.51 "he has scattered the proud
Jas 4. 6 "God opposes the p., but gives grace
1 Pet 5. 5 "God opposes the p., but gives grace
3. *height:* ὕψωμα HYPSŌMA [A.1.b.5]
2 Cor 10. 5 every p. obstacle to the knowledge of God

PROUD, BE
1. *object of boasting, boast:* καύχημα KAUCHĒMA
[a]B.2.d.2 [b]A.1.d [c]B.1.a.2
2 Cor 1.14 [a]that you can be p. of us as we.. of you
5.12 [b]giving you cause to be proud of us
Phil 2.16 [c]that in the day of Christ I may be proud

PROUD, BECOME
1. *think proud things:* ὑψηλὰ φρονεῖν HYPSĒLOS; PHRONEŌ [B.2.d.2]
Rom 11.20 So do not become proud

PROUD, REASON TO BE
1. *boasting:* καύχησις KAUCHĒSIS
Rom 15.17 I have reason to be proud of my work

PROVE (*See also* FALSE, PROVE; VAIN, PROVE)
PROVE TO BE
1. *point out:* ἀποδείκνυμι APODEIKNYMI
Acts 25. 7 serious charges which they could not p.
2. *test, approve:* δοκιμάζω DOKIMAZŌ
Rom 12. 2 that you may p. what is the will of God
2 Cor 8. 8 I say this.. to p... your love.. is genuine

3. *be:* εἰμί EIMI
1 Tim 3.10 if they prove themselves blameless
4. *sign, proof:* ἔνδειξις ENDEIXIS [B.1.a.2]
Rom 3.26 to prove . . that he himself is righteous
5. *come to be, happen, be:* γίνομαι GINOMAI
Mt 13.22 "choke the word, and it proves unfruitful
Mk 4.19 "choke the word, and it proves unfruitful
Lk 10.36 "Which . . proved neighbor to the man?
Jn 15. 8 "bear . . fruit, and . . prove to be my disciples
2 Cor 7.14 our boasting before Titus has proved true
1 Th 1. 5 what kind of men we proved to be among you
6. *find:* εὑρίσκω (pass.) HEURISKŌ
Rom 7.10 commandment . . proved to be death to me
7. *place before:* παρατίθημι (mid.) PARATITHĒMI
Acts 17.3 proving . . it . . necessary for the Christ
8. *place beside, stand before:* παρίστημι PARISTĒMI
Acts 24.13 "Neither can they prove to you
9. *temptation, trial:* πειρασμός PEIRASMOS [B.1.a.2]
1 Pet 4.12 the fiery ordeal which comes . . to prove you
10. *bring together, infer, teach:* συμβιβάζω SYMBIBAZŌ
Acts 9.22 Saul . . confounded . . by proving that Jesus
11. *stand with, commend:* συνίστημι SYNISTĒMI
2 Cor 7.11 you have proved yourselves guiltless
Gal 2.18 then I prove myself a transgressor

PROVERB
1. *comparison, parable:* παραβολή PARABOLĒ
Lk 4.23 "Doubtless you will quote to me this p.
2. *figure, proverb:* παροιμία PAROIMIA
2 Pet 2.22 It . . happened . . according to the true p.

PROVIDE
1. *do a service, minister:* διακονέω DIAKONEŌ
Lk 8. 3 provided for them[z] out of their means
2. *supply, furnish:* ἐπιχορηγέω EPICHORĒGEŌ
2 Pet 1.11 there will be richly provided for you
3. *place beside, stand before:* παρίστημι PARISTĒMI
Acts 23.24 "Also provide mounts for Paul to ride
4. *do, make:* ποιέω POIEŌ
Lk 12.33 "provide yourselves with purses
1 Cor 10.13 God . . will also p. the way of escape
5. *foresee, provide:* προνοέω PRONOEŌ
1 Tim 5. 8 If any one does not p. for his relatives
CONTEXTUALLY
Lk 10. 7 "eating and drinking what they provide

PROVIDE IN ABUNDANCE
1. *abound:* περισσεύω PERISSEUŌ
2 Cor 9. 8 God is able to provide . . in abundance, so that you . . may provide in abundance

PROVIDED
PROVIDED THAT
1. *if:* ἐάν EAN
Rom 11.22 provided you continue in his kindness
2. *if indeed:* εἴ γε EI [A.5.a]
Col 1.23 provided that you continue in the faith
3. *if indeed, since:* εἴπερ EIPER
Rom 8.17 fellow heirs with Christ, p. we suffer

PROVINCE
1. *province:* ἐπαρχεία EPARCHEIA*
Acts 23.34 he asked to what province he belonged
25. 1 when Festus had come into his province
Var. EPARCHEIOS
2. *of an eparch:* ἐπάρχειος EPARCHEIOS* [B.3.b.2]
Variant to: Acts **25.1**

PROVISION
1. *foresight:* πρόνοια PRONOIA*
Acts 24. 2 "by your provision, most excellent Felix
Rom 13.14 make no provision for the flesh
CONTEXTUALLY
1 Cor 9.15 nor am I writing . . to secure any such p.

PROVISIONS
1. *stock of provisions:* ἐπισιτισμός EPISITISMOS*
Lk 9.12 "Send the crowd away, to . . get provisions

PROVOKE
1. *rouse to anger, excite:* ἐρεθίζω ERETHIZŌ
Col 3.21 Fathers, do not provoke your children
2. *urge, irritate:* παροξύνω PAROXYNŌ
Acts 17.16 at Athens, his spirit was provoked
3. *call forth:* προκαλέω (mid.) PROKALEŌ*
Gal 5.26 nor provoking of one another, no envy

PROVOKE TO ANGER
1. *make angry:* παροργίζω PARORGIZŌ
Eph 6. 4 do not provoke your children to anger

PROVOKE TO JEALOUSY
1. *provoke to jealousy:* παραζηλόω PARAZĒLOŌ
1 Cor 10.22 Shall we provoke the Lord to jealousy?

PROVOKE TO SPEAK
1. *interrogate:* ἀποστοματίζω APOSTOMATIZŌ*
Lk 11.53 to p. him to speak of many things

PROVOKED, BE
1. *be angry, be offended:* προσοχθίζω PROSOCHTHIZŌ*
Heb 3.10 " 'Therefore I was p. with that generation
3.17 with whom was he provoked forty years?

PROWL AROUND
1. *walk, behave:* περιπατέω PERIPATEŌ
1 Pet 5. 8 Your adversary the devil prowls around

PRUNE
1. *cleanse, refine, prune:* καθαίρω KATHAIRŌ*
Jn 15. 2 "branch that does bear . . he prunes

PSALM
1. *psalm:* ψαλμός PSALMOS
Lk 20.42 "David . . says in the Book of Psalms
24.44 "the psalms must be fulfilled
Acts 1.20 "For it is written in the book of Psalms
13.33 "as also it is written in the second psalm
Eph 5.19 addressing one another in psalms
Col 3.16 teach . . and sing psalms and hymns
CONTEXTUALLY
Acts 13.35 "Therefore he says also in another p.

PTOLEMAIS: Πτολεμαΐς ˌtälə'māəs II,F-4
Acts 21. 7 from Tyre, we arrived at Ptolemais

PUBLIC
1. *outspokenness:* παρρησία PARRĒSIA [B.1.a.1]
Col 2.15 He . . made a public example of them
CONTEXTUALLY
1 Tim 4.13 attend to the p. reading of scripture

PUBLIC, IN
PUBLICLY
1. *common, public:* δημόσιος (fem. dat.) DĒMOSIOS
Acts 16.37 "They have beaten us publicly
18.28 he powerfully confuted the Jews in p.
20.20 "I did not shrink from . . teaching you in p.
2. *openly:* φανερῶς PHANERŌS
Jn 7.10 then he also went up, not publicly

PUBLICLY EXPOSE
1. *be on the stage, put to shame:* θεατρίζω THEATRIZŌ*
Heb 10.33 being publicly exposed to abuse

PUBLICLY PORTRAY
1. *write before:* προγράφω PROGRAPHŌ
Gal 3. 1 Jesus . . was p. portrayed as crucified

PUBLIUS: Πόπλιος 'pəblēəs
Acts 28. 7 the chief man of the island, named P.
28. 8 the father of P. lay sick with fever

PUDENS: Πούδης 'pyüdᵊnz
2 Tim 4.21 Eubulus sends greetings to you, as do P.

PUFF UP
1. *puff up:* φυσιόω PHYSIOŌ
1 Cor 4. 6 that none of you may be puffed up
8. 1 "Knowledge" puffs up, but love builds
Col 2.18 Let no one . . , puffed up without reason

PUFFED UP WITH CONCEIT, BE
1. *be crazy, be conceited:* τυφόομαι TYPHOOMAI
1 Tim 3. 6 he may be puffed up with conceit
6. 4 he is puffed up with conceit

PULL DOWN
1. *take down, destroy:* καθαιρέω KATHAIREŌ
Lk 12.18 " 'I will p. down my barns, and build larger

PULL OUT
1. *pull up:* ἀνασπάω ANASPAŌ
Lk 14. 5 "Which of you . . will not . . pull him out?

PUNISH
1. *cut in two:* διχοτομέω DICHOTOMEŌ*
Mt 24.51 "⟨master of that servant⟩ will p.[b] him†
Lk 12.46 "the master of that servant . . will p.[r] him†
2. *avenge, punish:* ἐκδικέω EKDIKEŌ
2 Cor 10. 6 ready to punish every disobedience
3. *vengeance, punishment:* ἐκδίκησις EKDIKĒSIS [B.1.a.2]
1 Pet 2.14 governors as sent by him to punish
4. *expose, test, refute:* ἐλέγχω ELEGCHŌ
Heb 12. 5 "do not . . lose courage when . . punished
5. *punish:* κολάζω KOLAZŌ
Acts 4.21 let them go, finding no way to p. them
6. *discipline, educate:* παιδεύω PAIDEUŌ
2 Cor 6. 9 as punished, and yet not killed
7. *be an avenger:* τιμωρέω TIMŌREŌ*
Acts 22. 5 "bring them . . to Jerusalem to be punished
26.11 "I punished them . . in all the synagogues

PUNISHMENT
1. *right, penalty:* δίκη DIKĒ
2 Th 1. 9 shall suffer the p. of eternal destruction
Jude . 7 example by undergoing a p. of eternal fire
2. *vengeance, punishment:* ἐκδίκησις EKDIKĒSIS
2 Cor 7.11 what zeal, what punishment!
3. *penalty:* ἐπιτιμία EPITIMIA*
2 Cor 2. 6 punishment by the majority is enough
4. *correction:* κόλασις KOLASIS*
Mt 25.46 "they will go away into eternal p.
1 Jn 4.18 For fear has to do with punishment
5. *retribution:* τιμωρία TIMŌRIA*
Heb 10.29 How much worse p. do you think?

PUNISHMENT, UNDER
1. *punish:* κολάζω (pres. pass. part.) KOLAZŌ
2 Pet 2. 9 to keep the unrighteous under p.

PURE
1. *unadulterated:* ἄδολος ADOLOS*
1 Pet 2. 2 long for the pure spiritual milk
2. *pure, sincere:* εἰλικρινής EILIKRINĒS
Phil 1.10 p. and blameless for the day of Christ
3. *pure:* ἁγνός HAGNOS
2 Cor 11. 2 as a pure bride to her one husband
Phil 4. 8 whatever is just, whatever is pure
1 Tim 5.22 keep yourself pure
Jas 3.17 the wisdom from above is first pure
1 Jn 3. 3 every one . . purifies himself as he is pure
4. *pure:* καθαρός KATHAROS
Mt 5. 8 "Blessed are the pure in heart
1 Tim 1. 5 love that issues from a pure heart
2 Tim 2.22 who call upon the Lord from a p. heart
Tit 1.15 To the pure all things are pure, but to the corrupt and unbelieving nothing is pure; their . . consciences are corrupted
Heb 10.22 our bodies washed with pure water
Jas 1.27 Religion that is pure and undefiled
Rev 15. 6 seven angels . . in pure bright linen
19. 8 "clothed with fine linen, bright and p.
19.14 armies . . , in fine linen, white and p.
21.18 the city was pure gold, clear as glass
21.21 the street of the city was pure gold
5. *genuine:* πιστικός PISTIKOS*
Mk 14. 3 flask of ointment of pure nard
Jn 12. 3 pound of costly ointment of pure nard

PURE DEVOTION
1. *purity:* ἁγνότης HAGNOTĒS
2 Cor 11. 3 a sincere and pure devotion to Christ

PURIFICATION
1. *purification:* ἁγνισμός HAGNISMOS*
Acts 21.26 to give notice when the days of p.
2. *purification:* καθαρισμός KATHARISMOS
Lk 2.22 when the time came for their purification
Jn 2. 6 six stone jars . . for the Jewish rites of p.
Heb 1. 3 When he had made purification for sins
3. *purity:* καθαρότης KATHAROTĒS*
Heb 9.13 sprinkling . . sanctifies for the p. of the flesh

PURIFIED
1. *cleanse:* ἁγνίζω (perf. pass. part.) HAGNIZŌ
Acts 24.18 "they found me purified in the temple

PURIFY
1. *clean out:* ἐκκαθαίρω EKKATHAIRŌ
2 Tim 2.21 one purifies himself from what is ignoble
2. *cleanse:* ἁγνίζω HAGNIZŌ*
Jn 11.55 many went up . . to purify themselves
Acts 21.24 "take these men and purify yourself
21.26 the next day he purified himself
Jas 4. 8 p. your hearts, you men of double mind
1 Pet 1.22 Having purified your souls by . . obedience
1 Jn 3. 3 every one who thus hopes . . purifies himself
3. *cleanse:* καθαρίζω KATHARIZŌ
Tit 2.14 to purify for himself a people
Heb 9.14 purify your[t] conscience from dead works
9.22 almost everything is purified with blood
9.23 necessary for the copies . . to be purified
4. *sprinkle, purify:* ῥαντίζω (mid.) RHANTIZŌ
Mk 7. 4 (do not eat unless they p.[w] themselves[a]‡

PURIFYING
1. *purification:* καθαρισμός KATHARISMOS
Jn 3.25 Now a discussion arose . . over purifying

PURITY
1. *purity, chastity:* ἁγνεία HAGNEIA*
1 Tim 4.12 set the believers an example . . in purity
5. 2 ⟨treat⟩ . . younger women . . in all purity
2. *purity:* ἁγνότης HAGNOTĒS
2 Cor 6. 6 by purity, knowledge, forbearance

PURPLE
1. *purple dye, purple cloth:* πορφύρα PORPHYRA
Lk 16.19 "a rich man, who was clothed in purple
Rev 18.12 pearls, fine linen, purple, silk
2. *purple:* πορφυροῦς PORPHYROUS*
Jn 19. 2 soldiers . . arrayed him in a purple robe
19. 5 Jesus came out, wearing . . the p. robe
Rev 17. 4 The woman was arrayed in purple
18.16 "alas, for the great city . . clothed . . in p.

PURPLE CLOAK
1. *purple dye, purple cloth:* πορφύρα PORPHYRA
Mk 15.17 they clothed him in a purple cloak
15.20 they stripped him of the purple cloak

PURPLE, SELLER OF
1. *woman dealer in purple:* πορφυρόπωλις PORPHYROPŌLIS*
Acts 16.14 woman named Lydia, . . a seller of p. goods

PURPORTING TO BE
1. *as, so:* ὡς HŌS
2 Th **2.2**

PURPOSE
1. *will, purpose:* βουλή BOULĒ
Lk 7.30 (lawyers rejected the purpose of God
23.51 who had not consented to their purpose
1 Cor 4. 5 will disclose the purposes of the heart
Heb 6.17 unchangeable character of his purpose
2. *intention, purpose:* βούλημα BOULĒMA
Acts 27.43 kept them from carrying out their p.
3. *satisfaction, goodwill:* εὐδοκία EUDOKIA
Eph 1. 5 destined . . according to the p. of his will
1. 9 he has made known . . according to his p.
4. *judgment, opinion, purpose:* γνώμη GNŌMĒ
Rev 17.17 "into their hearts to carry out his p.
5. *presentation, purpose:* πρόθεσις PROTHESIS
Acts 11.23 to remain faithful . . with steadfast p.
27.13 supposing . . they had obtained their p.
Rom 8.28 who are called according to his purpose
9.11 that God's p. of election might continue
Eph 1.11 according to the purpose of him
3.11 This was according to the eternal p.
2 Tim 1. 9 but in virtue of his own purpose
6. *end, goal:* τέλος TELOS
Jas 5.11 you have seen the purpose of the Lord

CONTEXTUALLY
Lk 4.43 "for I was sent for this purpose
Jn 12.27 "No, for this p. I have come to this hour
Acts 9.21 "he has come here for this purpose
26.16 " 'I have appeared to you for this purpose
Rom 4.11 p. was to make him the father of all
Gal 4.18 For a good p. it is always good
Eph 6.22 I have sent him to you for this very p.
Col 4. 8 I have sent him to you for this very p.

PURPOSE, TO NO
1. *freely, as a gift:* δωρεάν DŌREAN
Gal 2.21 then Christ died to no purpose

PURSE
1. *bag, purse:* βαλλάντιον BALLANTION*
Lk 10. 4 "Carry no purse, no bag, no sandals
12.33 "provide yourselves with purses
22.35 "When I sent you out with no purse
22.36 "now, let him who has a purse take it

PURSUE
1. *pursue:* διώκω DIŌKŌ
Rom 9.30 Gentiles who did not p. righteousness
9.31 Israel who pursued the righteousness
14.19 Let us then pursue what makes for peace
1 Pet 3.11 "let him seek peace and pursue it
Rev 12.13 the dragon.. pursued the woman
2. *pursue closely:* καταδιώκω KATADIŌKŌ*
Mk 1.36 those who were with him pursued him[0]

PURSUIT
1. *journey, course:* πορεία POREIA
Jas 1.11 will.. fade away in the midst of his pursuits
2. *occupation, undertaking:* πραγματεία PRAGMATEIA*
2 Tim 2. 4 No soldier.. entangled in civilian pursuits

PUT (*See also, e.g.,* DEATH, PUT TO; SEA, PUT TO; SHAME, PUT TO)
1. *put away:* ἀποτίθημι (mid.) APOTITHĒMI
Mt 14. 3 Herod.. bound him and p. him in prison
2. *throw, put:* βάλλω BALLŌ
Mt 5.25 "Make friends.. lest.. you be put in prison
9.17 "Neither is new wine put into old wineskins;.. new wine is put into fresh wineskins
18.30 "put him in prison till he should pay
27. 6 "not lawful to p. them into the treasury
Mk 2.22 "no one puts new wine into old wineskins
7.33 he put his fingers into his ears
12.41 multitude putting money into the treasury. Many rich people put in large sums
Lk 5.37 "no one puts new wine into old wineskins
12.58 "lest.. the officer put you in prison
21. 1 the rich putting.. gifts into the treasury
Jn 3.24 John had not yet been put in prison
5. 7 "I have no man to put me into the pool
13. 2 devil had.. put it into the heart of Judas
18.11 "Put your sword into its sheath
Acts 16.24 he put them into the inner prison
Jas 3. 3 we put bits into the mouths of horses
Rev 2.14 " 'taught Balak to put a stumbling block
3. *give:* δίδωμι DIDŌMI
[a]B.2.d.1
Mk 13.34 [a]"he.. puts his servants in charge
Lk 6.38 "good measure.. will be put into your lap
15.22 " 'Bring.. the best robe, and put it on him
19.23 " 'Why.. not put my money into the bank?
2 Cor 6. 3 We put no obstacle in any one's way
8.16 who puts the same earnest care for you
Heb 8.10 "I will put my laws into their minds
10.16 "I will put my laws on their hearts
Rev 17.17 "for God has put it into their hearts
4. *stand, set:* ἵστημι HISTĒMI
Mt 18. 2 calling.. a child he put him in the midst
Mk 9.36 he took a child, and put him in the midst
Lk 9.47 he took a child and put him by his side
5. *bring, bear:* φέρω PHERŌ
Jn 20.27 "Put your finger here, and see my hands; and put out your hand, and place it
6. *do, make:* ποιέω POIEŌ
Acts 5.34 ordered the men to be put outside
7. *throw, cast out:* ῥίπτω RHIPTŌ
Mt 15.30 they put them at his feet, and he healed
8. *lay, put:* τίθημι (act. or mid.) TITHĒMI
Mt 5.15 "Nor do men.. put it under a bushel
12.18 "I will put my Spirit upon him
22.44 " 'till I put thy enemies under thy feet
24.51 "⟨master⟩ will.. put him with.. hypocrites
Mk 4.21 "Is a lamp.. to be put under a bushel?
12.36 " 'till I put thy enemies under thy feet
Lk 8.16 "No one after lighting a lamp.. puts it under a bed, but puts it on a stand
11.33 "after lighting a lamp puts it in a cellar
12.46 "master.. will.. put him with the unfaithful
Jn 19.19 wrote a title and put it on the cross
Acts 4. 3 put them in custody until the morrow
5.18 put them in the common prison
5.25 "The men whom you put in prison
12. 4 when he.. seized him, he p. him in prison
Rom 14.13 decide never to put a stumbling block
1 Cor 15.25 until he has put all his enemies under
16. 2 each of you is to put something aside
2 Cor 3.13 Moses, who put a veil over his face
IDIOMATICALLY
a. Jn 16.2 They will put you out of the synagogues
ἀποσυναγώγους ποιήσουσιν ὑμᾶς [POIEŌ]

PUT AWAY
1. *lift, carry away:* αἴρω AIRŌ
Eph 4.31 Let all.. slander be put away from you
2. *loose from, dismiss:* ἀπολύω APOLYŌ
Mt 19. 7 "Why.. command one.. to put her away?
Mk 10. 4 "Moses allowed a man.. to put her away
3. *put away:* ἀποτίθημι (mid.) APOTITHĒMI
Eph 4.25 Therefore, putting away falsehood
Col 3. 8 put them all away: anger, wrath
Jas 1.21 put away all filthiness and.. wickedness
1 Pet 2. 1 put away all malice and all guile
4. *abolition, rejection:* ἀθέτησις ATHETĒSIS* [B.1.a.2]
Heb 9.26 he has appeared.. to put away sin

PUT BACK
1. *turn back, turn away:* ἀποστρέφω APOSTREPHŌ
Mt 26.52 "Put your sword back into its place

PUT, BE
1. *lie, be laid:* κεῖμαι KEIMAI
Phil 1.16 I am put here for.. defense of the gospel

PUT BEFORE
1. *lay down:* ὑποτίθημι (mid.) HYPOTITHĒMI
1 Tim 4. 6 put these instructions before the brethren
2. *place before:* παρατίθημι PARATITHĒMI
Mt 13.24 Another parable he put before them
13.31 Another parable he put before them

PUT DOWN
1. *take down, destroy:* καθαιρέω KATHAIREŌ
Lk 1.52 "put down the mighty from their thrones

PUT FORTH
1. *produce:* ἐκφύω EKPHYŌ*
Mt 24.32 "as its branch.. puts forth its leaves
Mk 13.28 "as its branch.. puts forth its leaves
2. *do, make:* ποιέω POIEŌ
Mk 4.32 "grows up.. and puts forth large branches

PUT FORWARD
1. *stand, set:* ἵστημι HISTĒMI
Acts 1.23 they put forward.. Joseph.. and Matthias
2. *put forward:* προβάλλω PROBALLŌ
Acts 19.33 Alexander, whom the Jews had p. forward
3. *put forward, propose:* προτίθημι PROTITHĒMI
Rom 3.25 God put forward as an expiation

PUT IN
PUT INTO
1. *send away:* ἀποστέλλω APOSTELLŌ
Mk 4.29 "when the grain is ripe,.. he puts in the sickle
2. *throw, put:* βάλλω BALLŌ
Mk 12.42 a poor widow.. put in two copper coins
12.43 "this poor widow has put in more

Mk 12.44 "she .. has put in everything she had
Lk 21. 2 saw a poor widow put in two copper coins
21. 3 "this poor widow has put in more than all
21. 4 "she .. put in all the living that she had
Jn 12. 6 he used to take what was put into it
3. *lead down, bring home:* κατάγω (pass.) KATAGŌ
Acts 27. 3 The next day we put in at Sidon
28.12 Putting in at Syracuse, we stayed there
4. *send:* πέμπω PEMPŌ
Rev 14.15 "Put in your sickle, and reap
14.18 "Put in your sickle, and gather

PUT IN SUBJECTION
1. *subject, place under:* ὑποτάσσω HYPOTASSŌ
1 Cor 15.27 "put all .. in subjection under his feet
15.27 says, "All things are put in subjection
Heb 2. 8 "putting everything in subjection under
2. 8 now in putting everything in subjection

PUT IN THE WAY
1. *give:* δίδωμι DIDŌMI [A.6.a.5]
1 Cor 9.12 rather than put an obstacle in the way

PUT, MUST BE
1. *one must put:* βλητέος BLĒTEOS*
Lk 5.38 "new wine must be p. into fresh wineskins

PUT OFF
1. *postpone* (mid.): ἀναβάλλω ANABALLŌ*
Acts 24.22 Felix .. put them off .. "When Lysias
2. *strip off:* ἀπεκδύομαι APEKDYOMAI
Col 3. 9 you have put off the old nature
3. *put away:* ἀποτίθημι (mid.) APOTITHĒMI
Eph 4.22 P. off your old nature which .. is corrupt

PUT ON
PUT TO
PUT UPON
1. *throw, put:* βάλλω BALLŌ
Lk 13. 8 " 'Let it alone .. till I .. put on manure
2. *tie around, put on:* διαζώννυμι DIAZŌNNYMI
Jn 21. 7 he put on his clothes, for he was stripped
3. *put on, clothe:* ἐνδύω (act. or mid.) ENDYŌ
Mt 6.25 "not .. anxious about .. what you shall p. on
27.31 they .. put his own clothes on him
Mk 6. 9 to wear sandals and not put on two tunics
15.20 they .. put his own clothes on him
Lk 12.22 "not .. anxious about .. what you shall p. on
15.22 " 'Bring .. the best robe, and p. it on him
Acts 12.21 Herod put on his royal robes
Rom 13.12 Let us .. put on the armor of light
13.14 But put on the Lord Jesus Christ
1 Cor 15.53 perishable nature must p. on .. imperishable, and this mortal .. put on immortality
15.54 When .. perishable puts on the imperishable, and the mortal puts on immortality
2 Cor 5. 3 by putting it on we .. not be found naked
Gal 3.27 For as many .. have put on Christ
Eph 4.24 put on the new nature .. in .. righteousness
6.11 Put on the whole armor of God
6.14 put on the breastplate of righteousness
Col 3.10 have put on the new nature
3.12 Put on then .. compassion, kindness
1 Th 5. 8 put on the breastplate of faith
4. *put on over:* ἐπενδύομαι EPENDYOMAI
2 Cor 5. 2 long to put on our heavenly dwelling
5. *throw upon:* ἐπιβάλλω EPIBALLŌ
Mt 9.16 "no one puts a piece of unshrunk cloth on
Lk 5.36 "No one .. puts it upon an old garment
9.62 "No one who puts his hand to the plow
6. *lay on, add:* ἐπιτίθημι EPITITHĒMI
Mt 21. 7 they .. put their garments on them
27.29 plaiting a crown .. they put it on his head
Jn 9.15 "He put clay on my eyes, and I washed
19. 2 plaited a crown .. and put it on his head
Acts 15.10 "by putting a yoke upon the neck
28. 3 gathered .. sticks and put them on the fire
28. 8 putting his hands on him healed him
7. *fasten underneath:* ὑποδέω (mid.) HYPODEŌ
Acts 12. 8 "Dress yourself and put on your sandals
8. *put around, put on:* περιτίθημι PERITITHĒMI
Mt 27.28 stripped him and put a .. robe upon him
27.48 took a sponge .. and put it on a reed
Mk 15.17 plaiting a crown .. they put it on him
15.36 filling a sponge .., put it on a reed
Jn 19.29 put a sponge full of the vinegar on hyssop

PUT ON BOARD
1. *take into, put on board:* ἐμβιβάζω EMBIBAZŌ*
Acts 27. 6 found a ship .. and put us on board
2. *lay on, add:* ἐπιτίθημι (mid.) EPITITHĒMI
Acts 28.10 they put on board whatever we needed

PUT OUT (*See also* SYNAGOGUE, PUT OUT OF THE)
PUT OUTSIDE
[a]+ἔξω [b]+ἐκ
1. *throw out:* ἐκβάλλω EKBALLŌ
Mt 9.25 when the crowd had been put outside
Mk 5.40 But he put them all outside
Lk 4.29 [a]they rose up and put him out of the city
Acts 9.40 [a]But Peter put them all outside
3 Jn .10 [b]he .. puts them out of the church
2. *bring up, turn back, put out to sea:* ἐπανάγω EPANAGŌ
Lk 5. 3 asked him to put out a little from .. land
5. 4 said to Simon, "Put out into the deep
3. *change, remove:* μεθίστημι METHISTĒMI
Lk 16. 4 " 'when I am put out of the stewardship

PUT TO (*See* PUT ON)

PUT TO SEA
1. *lead up, bring back:* ἀνάγω (mid. or pass.) ANAGŌ
Acts 27. 2 we p. to sea, accompanied by Aristarchus
27. 4 putting to sea from there we sailed
27.12 the majority advised to put to sea

PUT UNDER
1. *subject, place under:* ὑποτάσσω HYPOTASSŌ
1 Cor 15.27 who put all things under him
15.28 to him who put all things under him
Eph 1.22 he has put all things under his feet

PUT UPON (*See* PUT ON)

PUTEOLI: Ποτίολοι pyü'tēəlī II,B-2
Acts 28.13 on the second day we came to Puteoli

PUTTING OFF
1. *putting off:* ἀπέκδυσις APEKDYSIS*
Col 2.11 by putting off the body of flesh
2. *getting rid of:* ἀπόθεσις APOTHESIS
2 Pet 1.14 putting off of my body[c] will be soon

PYRRHUS: Πύρρος 'pirəs
Acts 20. 4 Sopater .., the son of P., accompanied him

Q

QUALIFY
1. *make sufficient, qualify:* ἱκανόω HIKANOŌ
Col 1.12 thanks to the Father, who has qualified us[b]

QUANTITY
1. *multitude, mass:* πλῆθος PLĒTHOS
Jn 21. 6 not able to haul it in, for the q. of fish

QUARREL
1. *battle, fighting:* μάχη MACHĒ
2 Tim 2.23 you know that they breed quarrels
Tit 3. 9 But avoid .. quarrels over the law
2. *quarrel, fight:* μάχομαι MACHOMAI
Acts 7.26 "he appeared .. as they were quarreling

QUARRELING
1. *calculation, argument:* διαλογισμός DIALOGISMOS
1 Tim 2. 8 lifting holy hands without .. quarreling
2. *strife, rivalry:* ἔρις (sg. or pl.) ERIS
Rom 13.13 becomingly .., not in q. and jealousy
1 Cor 1.11 reported to me .. that there is quarreling
2 Cor 12.20 perhaps there may be quarreling
IDIOMATICALLY
a. Tit 3.2 to avoid quarreling ἀμάχους εἶναι [AMACHOS]

QUARRELSOME, BE
1. *quarrel, fight:* μάχομαι MACHOMAI
2 Tim 2.24 the Lord's servant must not be q.

QUARRELSOME, NOT
1. *without battle:* ἄμαχος AMACHOS
1 Tim 3. 3 not quarrelsome, and no lover of money

QUART
1. *choenix* (a dry measure): χοῖνιξ CHOINIX*
Rev 6. 6 "A quart of wheat for a denarius,[a] and three quarts of barley for a denarius[a]!

QUARTER, FROM EVERY
1. *from every side:* πάντοθεν PANTOTHEN
Mk 1.45 people came to him from every quarter

QUARTUS: Κούαρτος 'kwôrtəs
Rom 16.23 Erastus . . and our brother Q., greet you[b]

QUEEN
1. *queen:* βασίλισσα BASILISSA*
Mt 12.42 "The queen of the South will arise
Lk 11.31 "The queen of the South will arise
Acts 8.27 the Candace, queen of the Ethiopians
Rev 18. 7 "in her heart she says, 'A queen I sit

QUENCH
1. *quench, put out:* σβέννυμι SBENNYMI
Mt 12.20 "he will not . . quench a smoldering wick
Mk 9.48 "where . . the fire is not quenched
Also Mk **9.** [44‡, [46‡
Eph 6.16 you can quench all the flaming darts
1 Th 5.19 Do not quench the Spirit
Heb 11.34 quenched raging fire, escaped . . the sword

QUESTION
1. *calculate, argue:* διαλογίζομαι DIALOGIZOMAI
Mk 2. 6 scribes were . . questioning in their hearts
2. 8 they thus questioned within themselves
2. 8 "Why do you q. thus in your hearts?
Lk 3.15 all men questioned in their hearts
5.21 scribes and the Pharisees began to q.
5.22 "Why do you question in your hearts?
2. *consult, ask a question:* ἐπερωτάω EPERŌTAŌ
Lk 23. 9 So he questioned him at some length
Acts 5.27 And the high priest questioned them
3. *ask, beg:* ἐρωτάω ERŌTAŌ
Jn 16.30 "we know . . and need none to question you
18.19 high priest then questioned Jesus
4. *word, reason:* λόγος LOGOS [B.2.d.1]
Mt 21.24 "I also will ask you a question
Mk 11.29 "I will ask you a question; answer me
Lk 20. 3 "I also will ask you a q.; now tell me
5. *examine together with, dispute:* συζητέω SYZĒTEŌ
Mk 1.27 they questioned among themselves
9.10 questioning what the rising . . meant
Lk 22.23 they began to question one another
6. *what is sought, question:* ζήτημα ZĒTĒMA
Acts 15. 2 to go up to Jerusalem . . about this q.
18.15 "a matter of questions about words
23.29 "accused about questions of their law
7. *seeking, controversy:* ζήτησις ZĒTĒSIS
Acts 25.20 "how to investigate these questions
CONTEXTUALLY
Col 2.16 in questions of food and drink

QUESTION, ASK A
1. *consult, ask a question:* ἐπερωτάω EPERŌTAŌ
Mt 22.23 Sadducees . . asked him a question
22.35 lawyer . . asked him a question, to test him
22.41 Jesus asked them a question
22.46 nor . . dare to ask him any more questions
Mk 11.29 "I will ask you a question; answer me
12.18 Sadducees . . asked him a question
12.34 no one dared to ask him any question
Lk 2.46 among the teachers, . . asking . . questions
20.28(27) they asked him a question, . . "Teacher
20.40 no longer dared to ask him any question

QUESTION, RAISE A
1. *examine closely:* ἀνακρίνω ANAKRINŌ
1 Cor 10.25 Eat . . without raising any question
1 Cor 10.27 eat . . without raising any question

QUESTIONING
1. *calculation, argument:* διαλογισμός DIALOGISMOS
Lk 5.22 Jesus perceived their questionings
24.38 "why do questionings rise in your hearts?
Phil 2.14 Do all things without . . questioning

QUICK
1. *quick:* ταχύς TACHYS
Jas 1.19 Let every man be quick to hear

QUICKLY
1. *quickly:* ταχέως TACHEŌS
Lk 14.21 " 'Go out q. to the streets and lanes
16. 6 " 'sit down quickly and write fifty
Jn 11.31 Jews . . saw Mary rise quickly and go out
Gal 1. 6 astonished that you are so q. deserting
2 Th 2. 2 not to be quickly shaken in mind
2. *sooner, faster:* τάχιον TACHION
Jn 13.27 "What you are going to do, do quickly
3. *with speed:* ἐν τάχει TACHOS [B.1.a.1]
Acts 12. 7 woke him, saying, "Get up quickly
22.18 " 'get quickly out of Jerusalem
4. *quick:* ταχύς (neut.) TACHYS
Mt 5.25 "Make friends quickly with your accuser
28. 7 "Then go quickly and tell his disciples
Mt 28. 8 they departed quickly from the tomb
Lk 15.22 " 'Bring quickly the best robe
Jn 11.29 she rose quickly and went to him

QUICK-TEMPERED
1. *inclined to anger:* ὀργίλος ORGILOS*
Tit 1. 7 bishop . . must not be arrogant or q.

QUIET
QUIET, BE
1. *quiet:* ἤρεμος ĒREMOS*
1 Tim 2. 2 that we may lead a quiet . . life
2. *cause silence:* παρέχειν ἡσυχίαν HĒSYCHIA [B.2.d.1]
Acts 22. 2 when they heard . . , they were the more q.
3. *restrain:* καταστέλλω KATASTELLŌ*
[a]pass. part.
Acts 19.35 the town clerk had quieted the crowd
19.36 [a]"you ought to be q. and do nothing rash
4. *gentle, meek:* πραΰς PRAYS
1 Pet 3. 4 jewel of a gentle and quiet spirit

QUIETLY
1. *secretly:* λάθρᾳ LATHRA
Mt 1.19 Joseph . . resolved to divorce her quietly
Jn 11.28 called . . , saying q., "The Teacher is here

QUIETLY, LIVE
1. *be quiet, be at rest:* ἡσυχάζω HĒSYCHAZŌ
1 Th 4.11 to live quietly, to mind your own affairs

QUIETNESS
1. *silence, rest:* ἡσυχία HĒSYCHIA
2 Th 3.12 to do their work in quietness

QUIRINIUS: Κυρήνιος kwi'rinēəs
Lk 2. 2 first enrollment, when Q. was governor

QUITE
1. *all, every, whole:* πᾶς PAS [A.3.b.1]
Acts 28.31 teaching . . quite openly and unhindered
2. *many, great:* πολύς (neut.) POLYS
Mk 12.27 "God . . of the living; you are quite wrong

QUOTE
1. *say, speak:* ἐρῶ ERŌ
Lk 4.23 "Doubtless you will quote . . this proverb
IDIOMATICALLY
a. Heb 4.7 in the words already quoted καθὼς προείρηται [PROEIPON]

R

RABBI
1. *my master* (Heb.): ῥαββί RHABBI
Mt 23. 7 "⟨they love⟩ being called rabbi by men

Mt 23. 8 "But you are not to be called rabbi
[26.25 Judas . . said, "Is it I, *Rabbi*?†
[26.49 he . . said, "Hail, *Rabbi!*†
Mk [9. 5 Peter said to Jesus, "*Rabbi*, it is well†
[11.21 Peter . . said . . "*Rabbi*, look!†
[14.45 he went up to him . . and said, "*Rabbi!*†
Jn 1.38 said . . "Rabbi" (which means Teacher
1.49 "Rabbi, you are the Son of God!
3. 2 "R., we know that you are a teacher
3.26 came to John, and said to him, "Rabbi
4.31 disciples besought him, saying, "R., eat
6.25 "Rabbi, when did you come here?
9. 2 "R., who sinned, this man or his parents?
11. 8 "R., the Jews were . . seeking to stone you
2. *my master* (Heb.): ῥαββουνί RHABBOUNI
Mk [10.51 the blind man said to him, "*Rabbi*†

RABBLE
1. *pertaining to the market:* ἀγοραῖος (subst. pl.) AGORAIOS
Acts 17. 5 taking some wicked fellows of the rabble

RABBONI: ra'bōnī
1. *my master* (Heb.): ῥαββουνί RHABBOUNI
Jn 20.16 "Rabboni!" (which means Teacher

RACE
1. *struggle:* ἀγών AGŌN
Heb 12. 1 let us run with perseverance the race
2. *course, race:* δρόμος DROMOS
2 Tim 4. 7 I have finished the race
3. *kind, race, family:* γένος GENOS
Acts 7.19 "He dealt craftily with our race
1 Pet 2. 9 you are a chosen race, . . a holy nation
4. *flesh, body:* σάρξ SARX [C.2]
Rom 9. 3 my brethren, my kinsmen by race
5. *stade* (200+ yards): στάδιον STADION
1 Cor 9.24 in a race all the runners compete
CONTEXTUALLY
Rom 9. 5 and of their race . . is the Christ

RACHEL: Ῥαχήλ 'rāchəl
Mt 2.18 "Rachel weeping for her children

RADIANCE
1. *splendor, radiance:* φωστήρ PHŌSTĒR
Rev 21.11 its radiance like a most rare jewel

RAGE
1. *make angry:* ὀργίζω (pass.) ORGIZŌ
Rev 11.18 "The nations raged, but thy wrath came
2. *be haughty:* φρυάσσω PHRYASSŌ*
Acts 4.25 " 'Why did the Gentiles rage?

RAGE, BE IN A
1. *make angry:* θυμόω (pass.) THYMOŌ*
Mt 2.16 Then Herod . . was in a furious rage

RAGING
1. *power, ability:* δύναμις (gen.) DYNAMIS
Heb 11.34 quenched r. fire, escaped . . the sword
2. *even more:* περισσῶς PERISSŌS [A.4.a]
Acts 26.11 "in raging fury . . I persecuted them
IDIOMATICALLY
a. Lk 8.24 he . . rebuked . . the raging waves ἐπετίμησεν . . τῷ κλύδωνι τοῦ ὕδατος [KLYDŌN]

RAHAB: [a]Ῥαχάβ [b]Ῥαάβ 'rāhab
Mt 1. 5 [a]Salmon the father of Boaz by Rahab
Heb 11.31 [b]By faith Rahab the harlot did not perish
Jas 2.25 [b]was not also Rahab the harlot justified?

RAIL AT
1. *slander, blaspheme:* βλασφημέω BLASPHĒMEŌ
Lk 23.39 One of the criminals . . railed at him

RAIMENT
1. *garment:* ἔνδυμα ENDYMA
Mt 28. 3 his raiment white as snow
2. *clothing:* ἱματισμός HIMATISMOS
Lk 9.29 his raiment became dazzling white

RAIMENT, SOFT
1. *soft, gentle:* μαλακός (subst. pl.) MALAKOS
Mt 11. 8 "To see a man[a] clothed in soft raiment? Behold, those who wear soft raiment

RAIN
1. *wet, rain:* βρέχω BRECHŌ*
Lk 17.29 "fire and sulphur rained from heaven
Jas 5.17 Elijah . . prayed . . that it might not rain, and . . it did not rain on the earth
2. *rain:* βροχή BROCHĒ*
Mt 7.25 "the rain fell, and the floods came
7.27 "the rain fell, and the floods came
3. *rain, heavy shower:* ὑετός HYETOS*
Acts 14.17 "he . . gave you from heaven rains
28. 2 welcomed us all, because it had begun to r.
Heb 6. 7 land which has drunk the rain
Jas 5.18 prayed again and the heaven gave rain
Rev 11. 6 They have power . . that no rain may fall

RAIN, EARLY
1. *early:* πρόϊμος PROIMOS* [B.3.b.2]
Jas 5. 7 patient . . until it receives the early . . rain

RAIN, LATE
1. *late, slow:* ὄψιμος OPSIMOS* [B.3.b.2]
Jas 5. 7 patient . . until it receives . . the late rain

RAIN, SEND
1. *wet, rain:* βρέχω BRECHŌ
Mt 5.45 "sends rain on the just and on the unjust

RAINBOW
1. *halo, rainbow:* ἶρις IRIS*
Rev 4. 3 rainbow that looked like an emerald
10. 1 wrapped . . with a rainbow over his head

RAISE (*See also* QUESTION, RAISE A)
1. *raise up, rise:* ἀνίστημι ANISTĒMI
Acts 13.33 "this he has fulfilled . . by raising Jesus
13.34 "the fact that he raised him from the dead
17.31 "given assurance to all . . by raising him
2. *raise:* ἐγείρω EGEIRŌ
Mt 10. 8 "Heal the sick, raise the dead
14. 2 " 'John the Baptist . . has been raised
16.21 that he must . . on the third day be raised
17. 9 "Tell no one . . until the Son of man is raised
17.23 "they will kill him, and he will be raised
20.19 "he will be raised on the third day
27.52 saints who had fallen asleep were raised
Mk 6.14 "John the baptizer has been raised
6.16 "John, whom I beheaded, has been raised
12.26 "And as for the dead being raised
Lk 9. 7 John had been raised from the dead
9.22 "killed, and on the third day be raised
20.37 "the dead are raised, even Moses showed
Jn 2.22 When . . he was raised from the dead
5.21 "For as the Father raises the dead
12. 1 Lazarus . . , whom Jesus had raised
12. 9 to see Lazarus, whom he had raised
12.17 he called Lazarus out . . and raised him
21.14 after he was raised from the dead
Acts 3.15 "whom God raised from the dead
4.10 "whom God raised from the dead
5.30 "The God of our fathers raised Jesus
10.40 "God raised him on the third day
13.30 "But God raised him from the dead
26. 8 "Why . . incredible . . that God raises . . dead?
Rom 4.24 raised from the dead Jesus our Lord
4.25 who was . . raised for our justification
6. 4 as Christ was raised from the dead
6. 9 Christ being raised from the dead
7. 4 him who has been raised from the dead
8.11 the Spirit of him who raised Jesus
8.11 he who raised Christ Jesus from the dead
8.34 yes, who was raised from the dead
10. 9 believe in your heart that God raised him
1 Cor 6.14 And God raised the Lord
15. 4 that he was raised on the third day
15.12 if Christ is preached as raised
15.13 then Christ has not been raised
15.14 if Christ has not been raised
15.15 we testified of God that he raised Christ, whom he did not raise if it is true that the dead are not raised

1 Cor 15.16 For if the dead are not raised, then Christ has not been raised
15.17 If Christ has not been raised
15.20 But in fact Christ has been raised
15.29 If the dead are not raised at all
15.32 If the dead are not raised, "Let us eat
15.35 one will ask, "How are the dead raised?
15.42 what is raised is imperishable
15.43 sown in dishonor, it is raised in glory
15.43 sown in weakness, it is raised in power
15.44 it is raised a spiritual body
15.52 the dead will be raised imperishable
2 Cor 1. 9 rely . . on God who raises the dead
4.14 knowing that he who raised the Lord Jesus will raise us also with Jesus
5.15 might live . . for him who . . was raised
Gal 1. 1 the Father, who raised him from the dead
Eph 1.20 when he raised him from the dead
Col 2.12 God, who raised him from the dead
1 Th 1.10 whom he raised from the dead, Jesus
Heb 11.19 that God was able to raise men
1 Pet 1.21 confidence in God, who raised him
3. *raise, lift:* ἐπαίρω EPAIRŌ
Lk 11.27 a woman in the crowd raised her voice
21.28 "look up and raise your heads

RAISE UP
1. *raise up, rise:* ἀνίστημι ANISTĒMI
Mt 22.24 " 'brother must marry . . and r. up children
Jn 6.39 "I should . . raise it up at the last day
6.40 "I will raise him up at the last day
6.44 "I will raise him up at the last day
6.54 "I will raise him up at the last day
Acts 2.24 "But God raised him up, having loosed
2.32 "This Jesus God raised up
3.22 " 'God will raise up for you a prophet
3.26 "God, having raised up his servant[c]
7.37 " 'God will raise up for you a prophet
2. *raise:* ἐγείρω EGEIRŌ
Mt 3. 9 " 'able from these stones to raise up children
11. 5 "the deaf hear, and the dead are raised up
26.32 "after I am raised up, I will go before
Mk 14.28 "after I am raised up, I will go before
Lk 1.69 "has raised up a horn of salvation for us
3. 8 "from these stones to raise up children
7.22 "deaf hear, the dead are raised up
Jn 2.19 "in three days I will raise it up
2.20 "will you raise it up in three days?
Acts 3. 7 took . . by the right hand and raised him up
13.22 "he raised up David to be their king
13.37 "he whom God raised up saw no corruption
Jas 5.15 the Lord will raise him up
3. *raise up, rise:* ἐξανίστημι EXANISTĒMI
Mk 12.19 "must . . raise up children for his brother
Lk 20.28 "must . . raise up children for his brother
4. *raise* (from the dead), *awaken:* ἐξεγείρω EXEGEIRŌ*
Rom 9.17 "I have raised you up for the . . purpose
1 Cor 6.14 raised the Lord and will also raise us up

RAISE UP WITH
RAISE WITH
1. *help in raising:* συνεγείρω SYNEGEIRŌ*
Eph 2. 6 ⟨God⟩ raised us up with him
Col 2.12 you were . . raised with him through faith
3. 1 If . . you have been raised with Christ

RAISED, WHAT HAS BEEN
1. *fruit:* καρπός KARPOS [C.2]
Rom 15.28 delivered to them what has been raised[x]†

RAM: Ἀράμ 'ram
Mt 1. 3 Hezron the father of Ram[a]†
1. 4 Ram[a] the father of Amminadab†

RAMAH: Ῥαμά 'rāmə
Mt 2.18 "A voice was heard in Ramah, wailing

RANK
1. *come to be, happen, be:* γίνομαι GINOMAI [A.6.a.5]
Jn 1.15 " 'He who comes after me ranks before me
Jn 1.30 " 'After me . . a man who ranks before me

RANK GROWTH
1. *abundance, surplus:* περισσεία PERISSEIA
Jas 1.21 put away . . rank growth of wickedness

RANSOM
1. *buy in the market:* ἀγοράζω AGORAZŌ
Rev 5. 9 "and by thy blood didst ransom men
2. *ransom:* ἀντίλυτρον ANTILYTRON*
1 Tim 2. 6 who gave himself as a ransom for all
3. *price of release, ransom:* λύτρον LYTRON*
Mt 20.28 "to give his life as a ransom for many
Mk 10.45 "to give his life as a ransom for many

RANSOMED, BE
1. *redeem:* λυτρόω (pass.) LYTROŌ
1 Pet 1.18 you were ransomed from the futile ways

RAPACITY
1. *lack of self-control:* ἀκρασία AKRASIA
Mt 23.25 "but inside they are full of . . rapacity

RARE, MOST
1. *held in honor, costly:* τίμιος (superl.) TIMIOS
Rev 21.11 its radiance like a most rare jewel

RASH
1. *rash, reckless:* προπετής PROPETĒS
Acts 19.36 "ought to be quiet and do nothing rash

RATHER (*See also* ACCURATE, RATHER)
1. *but:* ἀλλά ALLA
Lk **17.8**; **22.26**
1 Tim **6.2**
2. *more, rather:* μᾶλλον MALLON
Mt 10. 6 "but go rather to the lost sheep . . of Israel
10.28 "rather fear him who can destroy both soul
25. 9 " 'go rather to the dealers and buy
27.24 "but rather that a riot was beginning
Mk 5.26 she . . was no better but rather grew worse
Jn 3.19 men loved darkness rather than light
Acts 4.19 "to listen to you rather than to God
5.29 "We must obey God rather than men
Rom 14.13 rather . . never to put a stumbling block
1 Cor 5. 2 Ought you not rather to mourn?
6. 7 Why not rather suffer wrong? Why not rather be defrauded?
9.15 rather die than have any one deprive me
2 Cor 2. 7 so you should rather turn to forgive
5. 8 we would rather be away from the body
Gal 4. 9 or rather to be known by God
Eph 4.28 no longer steal but rather let him labor
1 Tim 1. 4 speculations r. than the divine training[a]
2 Tim 3. 4 lovers of pleasure r. than lovers of God
Heb 11.25 choosing rather to share ill-treatment
12.13 not be put out of joint but r. be healed
3. *so then, on the contrary:* μενοῦν MENOUN*
Lk 11.28 "Blessed rather are those who hear!
4. *now:* νῦν NYN
1 Cor 5.11 rather I wrote[i] to you not to associate†
CONTEXTUALLY
1 Cor 14.19 r. speak five words with my mind
Eph 4.15 Rather, speaking the truth in love
Heb 7.11 r. than one named after the order of Aaron
2 Jn .12 I would rather not use paper and ink
3 Jn .13 I would r. not write with pen and ink

RATHER THAN
1. *but:* ἀλλά (+neg.) ALLA
Heb **12.11**
2. *in order that:* ἵνα (+neg.) HINA
1 Cor 9.12 anything rather than put an obstacle
3. *not, no:* οὐ OU [B.3.b.4]
[a]καὶ οὐ [b]+ἀλλά
Heb **7.11**[a]; **12.11**[b]
4. *more than, by:* παρά (+acc.) PARA
Lk 18.14 "this man . . justified rather than the other
Rom 1.25 served the creature r. than the Creator!

RATIFY
1. *inaugurate:* ἐγκαινίζω EGKAINIZŌ
Heb 9.18 covenant was not ratified without blood

2. *confirm, ratify:* κυρόω KYROŌ
Gal 3.15 no one annuls . . once it has been ratified

RATIFY PREVIOUSLY
1. *ratify before:* προκυρόω PROKYROŌ*
Gal 3.17 not annul a covenant previously ratified

RAVAGE
1. *harm, damage:* λυμαίνω (mid.) LYMAINŌ*
Acts 8. 3 But Saul was ravaging the church[0]

RAVEN
1. *raven, crow:* κόραξ KORAX*
Lk 12.24 "Consider the ravens: they neither sow

RAVENOUS
1. *robbing:* ἅρπαξ HARPAX
Mt 7.15 "false prophets, who . . are ravenous wolves

RAY
1. *flash of lightning:* ἀστραπή ASTRAPĒ
Lk 11.36 "when a lamp with its rays gives you light

REACH
1. *make room for, hold, go:* χωρέω CHŌREŌ
2 Pet 3. 9 but that all should reach repentance
2. *enter, go in:* εἰσέρχομαι EISERCHOMAI
Jas 5. 4 cries of the harvesters have reached
3. *aim at, reach:* ἐφικνέομαι EPHIKNEOMAI*
2 Cor 10.13 will keep to the limits . ., to r. even to you
10.14 as though we did not reach you
4. *go to, enter:* ἔρχομαι εἰς ERCHOMAI [A.6.a.4]
Mt 16. 5 When the disciples reached . . other side
Jn 20. 4 the other disciple . . reached . . tomb first
20. 8 other disciple, who reached . . tomb first
5. *come down to, arrive:* καταντάω KATANTAŌ
Acts 27.12 the chance . . they could reach Phoenix
1 Cor 14.36 are you the only ones it has reached?
6. *judge, decide:* κρίνω KRINŌ [A.6.a.5]
Acts 16. 4 the decisions which had been reached
7. *come together with, happen to:* συντυγχάνω SYNTYGCHANŌ*
Lk 8.19 they could not reach him for the crowd
CONTEXTUALLY
Heb 4. 1 lest . . you be judged to have failed to r. it

REACH OUT
1. *stretch out:* ἐκτείνω EKTEINŌ
Mt 14.31 Jesus . . reached out his hand and caught

READ
1. *read:* ἀναγινώσκω ANAGINŌSKŌ
Mt 12. 3 "Have you not read what David did?
12. 5 "have you not read in the law how . . priests?
19. 4 "Have you not read that he who made them?
21.16 "have you never r., 'Out of the mouth . .'?
21.42 "Have you never read in the scriptures?
22.31 "have you not read what was said to you?
Mk 2.25 "Have you never read what David did?
12.10 "Have you not read this scripture?
12.26 "have you not r. in the book of Moses
Lk 4.16 And he stood up to read
6. 3 "Have you not read what David did?
10.26 "What is written . . ? How do you read?
Jn 19.20 Many of the Jews read this title
Acts 8.28 he was reading the prophet Isaiah
8.30 heard him reading Isaiah . . and asked, "Do you understand what you are reading?
8.32 the scripture which he was reading
13.27 "prophets which are read every sabbath
15.21 "Moses . . is read every sabbath
15.31 when they read it, they rejoiced
23.34 On reading the letter, he asked
2 Cor 1.13 write you nothing but what you can read
3. 2 to be known and read by all men
3.15 whenever Moses is read a veil lies
Eph 3. 4 When you read this you can perceive
Col 4.16 when this . . has been read among you, have it read . . in the church of the Laodiceans; and . . read . . the letter from Laodicea
1 Th 5.27 that this letter be read to all the brethren
Rev 1. 3 Blessed is he who reads . . the prophecy
2. *reading:* ἀνάγνωσις ANAGNŌSIS [B.1.a.2]
2 Cor 3.14 when they read the old covenant
3. *inscribe:* ἐπιγράφω (pluperf. pass. periphr.) EPIGRAPHŌ [B.3.b.4]
Mk 15.26 inscription of the charge . . read, "The King
4. *write, inscribe:* γραφω (pluperf. pass. periphr.) GRAPHŌ [B.3.b.4]
Jn 19.19 it read, "Jesus of Nazareth, the King

READ, WHICH
1. *write:* γράφω (perf. pass. part.) GRAPHŌ
Mt 27.37 over his head . . the charge . ., which read

READER
1. *read:* ἀναγινώσκω (subst. part.) ANAGINŌSKŌ
Mt 24.15 "(let the reader understand
Mk 13.14 "(let the reader understand

READILY
1. *well, rightly:* καλῶς KALŌS
2 Cor 11. 4 you submit to it readily enough

READINESS
1. *willingness, goodwill:* προθυμία PROTHYMIA
2 Cor 8.11 that your r. in desiring it . . be matched
8.12 if the r. is there, it is acceptable
9. 2 I know your readiness, of which I boast

READING
1. *reading:* ἀνάγνωσις ANAGNŌSIS
Acts 13.15 After the r. of the law and the prophets
1 Tim 4.13 attend to the public r. of scripture

READY (*See also* MAKE READY)
1. *near, at hand:* ἐγγύς EGGYS
Heb 8.13 what is . . obsolete and . . r. to vanish away
2. *prepare, get ready:* ἑτοιμάζω (perf. pass. part.) HETOIMAZŌ
2 Tim 2.21 then he will be . . r. for any good work
3. *ready, prepared:* ἕτοιμος HETOIMOS
Mt 22. 4 " 'everything is r.; come to the . . feast
22. 8 "he said to his servants, 'The wedding is r.
24.44 "Therefore you also must be ready
25.10 "those who were ready went in
Mk 14.15 "large upper room furnished and r.
Lk 12.40 "be ready; for the Son of man is coming
14.17 " 'Come; for all is now ready
22.33 "Lord, I am ready to go with you
Acts 23.15 "we are ready to kill him before he comes
23.21 "now they are ready, waiting
2 Cor 9. 5 that it may be ready not as an exaction
10. 6 ready to punish every disobedience
Tit 3. 1 to be ready for any honest work
1 Pet 1. 5 ready to be revealed in the last time
4. *readily:* ἑτοίμως HETOIMŌS* [A.4.a]
1 Pet 4. 5 they will give account to him who is ready
CONTEXTUALLY
2 Cor 1.17 ready to say Yes and No at once
Heb 11.17 he . . was ready to offer up his only son

READY, BE
1. *be able:* δύναμαι DYNAMAI
1 Cor 3. 2 for you were not ready for it; and even yet you are not ready
2. *be well pleased:* εὐδοκέω EUDOKEŌ
1 Th 2. 8 we were ready to share with you
3. *readily:* ἑτοίμως HETOIMŌS [B.3.a.5]
Acts 21.13 "I am ready not only to be imprisoned
2 Cor 12.14 Here for the third time I am ready
4. *prepare:* παρασκευάζω (perf. mid.) PARASKEUAZŌ
2 Cor 9. 2 Achaia has been ready since last year
9. 3 that you may be r., as I said you would

READY, GET
1. *prepare, get ready:* ἑτοιμάζω HETOIMAZŌ
Acts 23.23 "get ready two hundred soldiers
2. *prepare:* παρασκευάζω (mid.) PARASKEUAZŌ
1 Cor 14. 8 who will get ready for battle?

READY, HAVE
1. *persist in:* προσκαρτερέω PROSKARTEREŌ
Mk 3. 9 told . . disciples to have a boat r. for him

READY, HOLD
READY, MAKE
1. *make preparations:* ἐπισκευάζομαι EPISKEUAZOMAI*
Acts 21.15 After these days we made ready
2. *prepare, get ready:* ἑτοιμάζω HETOIMAZŌ
Mt 22. 4 " 'I have made ready my dinner
Lk 1.17 "to make ready for the Lord a people
9.52 sent messengers . . to make ready for him
12.47 "that servant who . . did not make ready
22.12 "he will show you a . . room . . ; there make r.
Rev 8. 6 seven angels . . made ready to blow them
9.15 angels . . had been held r. for the hour
19. 7 "his Bride has made herself ready

READY, NOT
1. *unprepared:* ἀπαρασκεύαστος APARASKEUASTOS*
2 Cor 9. 4 lest if some . . find that you are not ready

REAFFIRM
1. *confirm, ratify:* κυρόω KYROŌ
2 Cor 2. 8 I beg you to reaffirm your love for him

REAL
1. *true:* ἀληθής ALĒTHĒS
Acts 12. 9 what was done by the angel was real
2. *actually, really:* ὄντως (attr.) ONTŌS
[a]A.4.a
Mk 11.32 [a]all held that John was a real prophet
1 Tim 5. 3 Honor widows who are real widows
5. 5 who is a real widow, and is left all alone
5.16 assist those who are real widows
CONTEXTUALLY
Rom 2.28 he is not a r. Jew who is one outwardly
2.29 r. circumcision is a matter of the heart

REAL REASON, THE
1. *certain, safe:* ἀσφαλής (subst. neut.) ASPHALĒS
Acts 22.30 desiring to know the real reason why

REALITIES
1. *thing, deed:* πρᾶγμα (pl.) PRAGMA
Heb 10. 1 instead of the true form of these realities

REALIZE
1. *learn to know, recognize:* ἐπιγινώσκω EPIGINŌSKŌ
[a]+ἑαυτούς
Acts 22.29 he realized that Paul was a Roman citizen
2 Cor 13. 5 [a]Do you not r. that . . Christ is in you?
2. *know, understand:* ἐπίσταμαι EPISTAMAI
Acts 24.10 "Realizing that . . you have been judge
3. *do, make:* ποιέω POIEŌ
Eph 3.11 the eternal purpose which he has realized
4. *become aware of:* συνεῖδον SYNEIDON
Acts 12.12 When he realized this, he went
CONTEXTUALLY
Heb 6.11 realizing the full assurance of hope

REALLY
1. *truly:* ἀληθῶς ALĒTHŌS
Jn 7.26 "Can it be that the authorities really know?
7.40 "This is really the prophet
1 Th 2.13 as what it really is, the word of God
2. *more, rather:* μᾶλλον MALLON
Phil 1.12 has really served to advance the gospel
3. *yet, nevertheless:* μέντοι MENTOI
Jas 2. 8 If you really fulfil the royal law
4. *actually, really:* ὄντως ONTŌS
1 Cor 14.25 declare that God is really among you
CONTEXTUALLY
1 Cor 5. 7 as you really are unleavened
8. 7 some . . eat food as r. offered to an idol
Gal 3. 4 many things in vain?—if it r. is in vain

REAP
1. *have, hold:* ἔχω ECHŌ [A.6.a.5]
Rom 1.13 that I may r. some harvest among you
2. *reap:* θερίζω THERIZŌ
Mt 6.26 "birds of the air . . neither sow nor reap
25.24 " 'reaping where you did not sow
25.26 " 'that I reap where I have not sowed
Lk 12.24 "the ravens . . neither sow nor reap
19.21 " 'you . . reap what you did not sow
19.22 " 'reaping what I did not sow
Jn 4.36 "He who reaps receives wages
4.37 " 'One sows and another reaps
4.38 "to r. that for which you did not labor
1 Cor 9.11 is it too much if we r. your . . benefits?
2 Cor 9. 6 who sows sparingly will . . r. sparingly
9. 6 who sows bountifully will . . r. bountifully
Gal 6. 7 whatever a man sows, that he will also r.
6. 8 will from the flesh reap corruption
6. 8 will from the Spirit reap eternal life
6. 9 for in due season we shall reap
Rev 14.15 "Put in your sickle, and reap, for the hour to reap has come
14.16 swung his sickle . . the earth was reaped

REAPER
1. *reaper:* θεριστής THERISTĒS*
Mt 13.30 " 'at harvest time I will tell the reapers
13.39 "enemy . . is the devil; . . reapers are angels
2. *reap:* θερίζω (subst. part.) THERIZŌ
Jn 4.36 "sower and reaper may rejoice together

REASON (*See also* BOAST, ONE'S REASON TO; CONFIDENCE, REASON FOR; PROUD, REASON TO BE)
1. *charge, cause:* αἰτία AITIA
Acts 10.21 "what is the reason for your coming?
28.18 "there was no r. for the death penalty
28.20 "For this reason . . I have asked to see you
2. *reckon, count:* λογίζομαι LOGIZOMAI
1 Cor 13.11 I was a child, . . I reasoned like a child
IDIOMATICALLY
a. Acts 18.14 "I should have reason to bear with you κατὰ λόγον ἂν ἀνεσχόμην ὑμῶν [LOGOS]
CONTEXTUALLY
Jn 10.17 "For this reason the Father loves me
Rom 1.26 For this reason God gave them up
13. 6 For the same reason you also pay taxes
14.22 who has no reason to judge himself
Eph 1.15 For this r., because I have heard
1 Th 3. 5 For this r. . . I sent that I might know
3. 7 for this r. . . , in all our distress
1 Tim 1.16 but I received mercy for this reason
2 Pet 1. 5 For this very r. make every effort
1 Jn 3. 8 r. the Son . . appeared was to destroy

REASON, FOR A
1. *opposite, instead of:* ἀντί (+gen.) ANTI
Eph 5.31 "For this r. a man shall leave his father
2. *for the sake of:* χάριν CHARIN [B.1.b]
Eph 3. 1 For this r. I, Paul, a prisoner
3.14 For this reason I bow my knees
3. *for the sake of:* ἕνεκα HENEKA [B.1.b]
Mt 19. 5 " 'For this r. a man shall leave his father
Mk 10. 7 " 'For this r. a man shall leave his father
Acts 26.21 "For this reason the Jews seized me

REASON, OPEN TO
1. *obedient, compliant:* εὐπειθής EUPEITHĒS*
Jas 3.17 gentle, open to reason, full of mercy

REASON, THE REAL
1. *certain, safe:* ἀσφαλής (subst. neut.) ASPHALĒS
Acts 22.30 desiring to know the real reason why

REASON WHY, THE
1. *because of this:* διὰ τοῦτο HOUTOS [B.1.a.2]
Jn **8.47**; **12.18**
1 Jn **3.1**

REASON WHY, THIS IS THE
1. *therefore:* διό DIO
Rom 15.22 This is the r. why I have . . been hindered

REASON, WITHOUT
1. *without purpose:* εἰκῇ EIKĒ
Col 2.18 puffed up without r. by his . . mind

REASSURE
1. *persuade:* πείθω PEITHŌ
1 Jn 3.19 By this we shall . . reassure our hearts

REBECCA: Ῥεβέκκα riʹbekə
Rom 9.10 when Rebecca had conceived children

REBEL

1. *revolutionary:* στασιαστής STASIASTĒS*
Mk 15. 7 among the rebels . . there was . . Barabbas

REBELLION

1. *contradiction, dispute:* ἀντιλογία ANTILOGIA
Jude .11 For they . . perish in Korah's rebellion
2. *rebellion:* ἀποστασία APOSTASIA
2 Th 2. 3 unless the rebellion comes first
3. *provocation, revolt:* παραπικρασμός PARAPIKRASMOS*
Heb 3. 8 "do not harden your hearts as in the r.
3.15 "do not harden your hearts as in the r.

REBELLIOUS, BE

1. *provoke, rebel against:* παραπικραίνω PARAPIKRAINŌ*
Heb 3.16 Who were they that . . were rebellious?

REBUILD

1. *build up again:* ἀνοικοδομέω ANOIKODOMEŌ*
Acts 15.16 " 'I will rebuild the dwelling of David . . ; I will rebuild its ruins, and I will set it up

REBUKE

1. *expose, test, refute:* ἐλέγχω ELEGCHŌ
1 Tim 5.20 rebuke them in the presence of all
Tit 1.13 Therefore rebuke them sharply
2. *have a rebuke:* ἔλεγξιν ἔχειν ELEGXIS* [B.3.a.5]
2 Pet 2.16 rebuked for his own transgression
3. *strike, rebuke:* ἐπιπλήσσω EPIPLĒSSŌ*
1 Tim 5. 1 Do not rebuke an older man
4. *rebuke:* ἐπιτιμάω EPITIMAŌ
Mt 8.26 Then he rose and rebuked the winds
16.22 Peter took him and began to r. him
17.18 Jesus rebuked him, . . the boy was cured
19.13 The disciples rebuked the people
20.31 crowd rebuked them . . ; but they cried out
Mk 1.25 Jesus rebuked him, saying, "Be silent!
4.39 he awoke and rebuked the wind
8.32 Peter took him, and began to rebuke him
8.33 seeing his disciples, he rebuked Peter
9.25 Jesus . . rebuked the unclean spirit
10.13 the disciples rebuked them
10.48 rebuked him, telling him to be silent
Lk 4.35 Jesus rebuked him, saying, "Be silent!
4.39 he stood over her and rebuked the fever
4.41 rebuked . . , and would not allow them
8.24 And he awoke and rebuked the wind
9.42 But Jesus rebuked the unclean spirit
9.55 But he turned and rebuked them[f]
17. 3 "if your brother sins, rebuke him
18.15 when the disciples saw it, they rebuked
18.39 those who were in front rebuked him
19.39 "Teacher, rebuke your disciples
23.40 But the other rebuked him
2 Tim 4. 2 preach the word, . . convince, rebuke
Jude . 9 "The Lord rebuke you

RECALL

1. *remind:* ἀναμιμνήσκω (pass.) ANAMIMNĒSKŌ
Heb 10.32 But recall the former days when
2. *make remembrance:* τὴν μνήμην ποιεῖσθαι MNĒMĒ* [A.6.a.4]
2 Pet 1.15 be able at any time to recall these

RECEIVE (*See also* APPROVAL, RECEIVE; BEATING, RECEIVE A; CIRCUMCISION, RECEIVE; MERCY, RECEIVE; TITHES, RECEIVE)

1. *take up, receive:* ἀναδέχομαι ANADECHOMAI*
Acts 28. 7 Publius . . received us and entertained
Heb 11.17 he who had received the promises
2. *receive in full:* ἀπέχω APECHŌ
Mt 6. 2 "Truly, . . they have received their reward[o]
6. 5 "Truly, . . they have received their reward[o]
6.16 "Truly, . . they have received their reward[o]
Lk 6.24 "you have received your consolation
3. *receive favorably:* ἀποδέχομαι APODECHOMAI
Acts 2.41 those who received his word were baptized
18.27 wrote to the disciples to receive him
21.17 the brethren received us gladly
4. *take from, get back:* ἀπολαμβάνω APOLAMBANŌ
Lk 15.27 " 'he has received him safe and sound
16.25 " 'you . . received your good things
23.41 "for we are receiving the due reward
Rom 1.27 receiving . . due penalty for their error
Gal 4. 5 that we might receive adoption as sons
Col 3.24 you will receive the inheritance
5. *make room for, hold, go:* χωρέω CHŌREŌ
Mt 19.11 "Not all men can receive this saying
19.12 "He who is able to receive this, let him receive it
6. *receive, accept:* δέχομαι DECHOMAI
Mt 10.14 "if any one will not receive you
10.40 "He who receives you receives me, and he who receives me receives him who sent me
10.41 "He who receives a prophet
10.41 "he who receives a righteous man
18. 5 "Whoever receives one such child in my name receives me
Mk 6.11 "if any place will not receive you
9.37 "Whoever receives one such child in my name receives me; and whoever receives me, receives not me but him who sent me
10.15 "whoever does not receive the kingdom
Lk 8.13 "who . . hear the word, receive it with joy
9. 5 "wherever they do not receive you
9.48 "Whoever receives this child in my name receives me, and whoever receives me receives him who sent me
9.53 but the people would not receive him
10. 8 "Whenever you enter . . and they receive you
10.10 "whenever you enter . . and they do not r.
16. 4 " 'what to do, so that people may r. me
16. 9 "that when it fails they may receive you
18.17 "whoever does not receive the kingdom
Acts 3.21 "whom heaven must r. until the time
7.38 "he received living oracles to give to us
7.59 "Lord Jesus, receive my spirit
8.14 Samaria had received the word of God
11. 1 Gentiles . . received the word of God
17.11 they received the word with . . eagerness
22. 5 "From them I received letters
28.21 "We have received no letters from Judea
1 Cor 2.14 unspiritual[e] man does not r. the gifts
2 Cor 7.15 trembling with which you received him
Gal 4.14 but received me as an angel of God
Phil 4.18 having received from Epaphroditus
Col 4.10 (if he comes to you, receive him
1 Th 1. 6 you received the word in much affliction
Jas 1.21 r. with meekness the implanted word
7. *have, hold:* ἔχω ECHŌ
Rom 13. 3 you will receive his approval
2 Cor 1. 9 felt . . we . . received the sentence of death
8. *find, attain:* ἐπιτυγχάνω EPITYGCHANŌ
Heb 11.33 enforced justice, received promises
9. *come to be, happen, be:* γίνομαι GINOMAI [A.6.c.3]
1 Cor 4. 5 every man will receive his commendation
10. *welcome, entertain as guest:* ὑποδέχομαι HYPODECHOMAI*
Lk 10.38 a woman named Martha received him
19. 6 he made haste . . and received him joyfully
Acts 17. 7 "Jason has received them
Jas 2.25 when she received the messengers
11. *bring, carry off:* κομίζω (mid.) KOMIZŌ
Mt 25.27 "received . . my own with interest
2 Cor 5.10 so that each one may receive good
Eph 6. 8 he will receive the same again
Heb 10.36 so that you may . . r. what is promised
11.13 not having received what was promised
11.39 did not receive what was promised
12. *receive, take:* λαμβάνω LAMBANŌ
Mt 7. 8 "For every one who asks receives
10. 8 "You received without paying
10.41 "shall receive a prophet's reward
10.41 "shall r. a righteous man's reward
13.20 "immediately receives it with joy
19.29 "every one . . will receive a hundredfold[l]
20. 9 "each of them received a denarius
20.10 "they thought they would receive more; but each of them also received a denarius
20.11 "on receiving it they grumbled

Mt 21.22 "you will receive, if you have faith
[23.14 *"you will receive . . greater condemnation*‡
25.16 "He who had received the five talents
25.18 "he who had received the one talent
25.20 "he who had received the five talents
25.24 "He . . who had received the one talent
Mk 4.16 "who, when they hear the word, . . r. it
10.30 "who will not receive a hundredfold
11.24 "believe that you have received[a] it‡o
12.40 "will receive the greater condemnation
14.65 the guards received him with blows
Lk 6.34 "those from whom you hope to receive
11.10 "For every one who asks receives
18.30 "who will not receive manifold more
19.12 "A nobleman went . . to receive a kingdom
19.15 "returned, having received the kingdom
20.47 "will receive the greater condemnation
Jn 1.12 to all who received him, who believed
1.16 we all received, grace upon grace
3.11 "but you do not receive our testimony
3.27 "No one can receive anything except
3.32 yet no one receives his testimony
3.33 who receives his testimony sets his seal
4.36 "He who reaps receives wages
5.34 "Not that the testimony which I receive
5.41 "I do not receive glory from men
5.43 "I have come . . and you do not receive me; if another comes . . , him you will r.
5.44 "who receive glory from one another
7.23 "on the sabbath . . receives circumcision
7.39 the Spirit, which those . . were to receive
10.18 "this charge I . . received from my Father
12.48 "He who . . does not receive my sayings
13.20 "Truly, truly, I say to you, he who receives any one whom I send receives me; and he who receives me receives him who sent me
13.30 after receiving the morsel, he . . went out
14.17 "whom the world cannot receive
16.24 "receive, that your joy may be full
17. 8 "they have received them and know
19.30 When Jesus had received the vinegar
20.22 "Receive the Holy Spirit
Acts 1. 8 "you shall r. power when the Holy Spirit
2.33 "having received . . promise of the . . Spirit
2.38 "you shall receive the gift of the . . Spirit
3. 5 expecting to receive something
7.53 "who received the law . . did not keep it
8.15 that they might receive the Holy Spirit
8.17 and they received the Holy Spirit
8.19 "that any . . on whom I lay . . hands may r.
10.43 "one who believes . . receives forgiveness
10.47 "who have received the Holy Spirit
16.24 Having received . . charge, he put them
17.15 receiving a command for Silas
19. 2 "Did you receive the Holy Spirit?
20.24 "ministry which I received from the Lord
20.35 " 'more blessed to give than to receive
26.18 " 'that they may r. forgiveness of sins
Rom 1. 5 through whom we have received grace
4.11 He received circumcision as a sign
5.11 we have now received our reconciliation
5.17 those who r. the abundance of grace
8.15 you did not receive the spirit of slavery . . but you . . received the spirit of sonship
1 Cor 2.12 we . . received not the spirit of the world
3. 8 and each shall receive his wages
3.14 If the work . . survives, he will r. a reward
4. 7 What have you that you did not receive? If then you received it, why do you boast?
9.24 all . . compete, but . . one receives the prize
9.25 They do it to r. a perishable wreath
2 Cor 11. 4 or if you receive a different spirit from the one you received
11.24 Five times I have received . . forty lashes
Gal 3. 2 Did you receive the Spirit by works?
3.14 that we might receive the promise
Col 4.10 (you have received instructions
1 Tim 4. 4 if it is received with thanksgiving
Heb 2. 2 disobedience received a just retribution
4.16 that we may r. mercy and find grace
7. 5 descendants . . who r. the priestly office
7. 8 Here tithes are received by mortal men
7. 9 Levi himself, who receives tithes
9.15 that those . . may r. the . . inheritance
10.26 after receiving . . knowledge of the truth
11. 8 which he was to r. as an inheritance
11.11 Sarah . . received power to conceive
11.35 Women received their dead
Jas 1. 7, 8 man, unstable . . , will ⟨not⟩ receive
1.12 he will receive the crown of life
4. 3 You ask and do not receive
5. 7 patient . . until it receives . . the late rain
1 Pet 4.10 As each has received a gift, employ it
2 Pet 1.17 when he received honor and glory
1 Jn 2.27 the anointing which you received
3.22 we receive from him whatever we ask
5. 9 If we receive the testimony of men
2 Jn .10 do not receive him into the house
Rev 2.17 " 'no one knows except him who receives it
2.27 " 'even as I myself have received power
3. 3 " 'Remember then what you received
4.11 "Worthy art thou . . to receive glory
5.12 "Worthy is the Lamb . . to receive power
14. 9 "If any . . receives a mark on his forehead
14.11 "whoever receives the mark of its name
17.12 "kings who have not yet received royal power, but they are to r. authority
19.20 had received the mark of the beast
20. 4 not received its mark on their foreheads

13. *partake, share:* μεταλαμβάνω METALAMBANŌ
Heb 6. 7 land . . receives a blessing from God

14. *participation, receiving:* μετάλημψις METALĒMPSIS* [B.1.a.2]
1 Tim 4. 3 foods which God created to be received

15. *accept, receive:* παραδέχομαι PARADECHOMAI
Heb 12. 6 "chastises every son whom he receives

16. *take, receive:* παραλαμβάνω PARALAMBANŌ
Jn 1.11 his own people received him not
1 Cor 11.23 I received . . what I also delivered
15. 1 I preached . . gospel, which you received
15. 3 of first importance what I also received
Gal 1. 9 contrary to that which you received
1.12 For I did not receive it from man
Phil 4. 9 What you have learned and received
Col 2. 6 As therefore you received Christ Jesus
4.17 "the ministry which you have received
1 Th 2.13 when you received the word of God
2 Th 3. 6 the tradition that you received from us
Heb 12.28 be grateful for receiving a kingdom

17. *accept, expect:* προσδέχομαι PROSDECHOMAI
Lk 15. 2 "receives sinners and eats with them
Rom 16. 2 that you may receive her in the Lord
Phil 2.29 receive him in the Lord with all joy

18. *receive in addition:* προσλαμβάνω (mid.) PROSLAMBANŌ
Phm .17 receive him as you would . . me

CONTEXTUALLY
Rom 3.25 to be received by faith

RECEIVE AGAIN

1. *take from, get back:* ἀπολαμβάνω APOLAMBANŌ
Lk 6.34 "sinners lend . . to receive as much again

RECEIVE BACK

1. *bring, carry off:* κομίζω (mid.) KOMIZŌ
Heb 11.19 he did receive him back

RECEIVE ONE'S SIGHT

1. *look up, receive sight:* ἀναβλέπω ANABLEPŌ
Mt 11. 5 "blind r. their sight and the lame walk
20.34 they received their sight and followed
Mk 10.51 "Master,[t] let me receive my sight
10.52 he received his sight and followed
Lk 7.22 blind r. their sight, the lame walk
18.41 "Lord, let me receive my sight
18.42 Jesus said . . "Receive your sight
18.43 he received his sight and followed

Jn 9.11 "I . . washed and received my sight
9.15 asked him how he had received his sight
9.18 blind and had received his sight
9.18 the man who had received his sight
Acts 22.13 " 'Brother Saul, r. your sight.' And in that very hour I received my sight

RECEIVE PAYMENT
1. *receive in full:* ἀπέχω APECHŌ
Phil 4.18 I have received full payment

RECEIVE THE GOOD NEWS
1. *bring good news* (mid.): εὐαγγελίζω (pass.) EUAGGELIZŌ
Heb 4. 6 those who formerly received the good news

RECEIVE THE LAW
1. *frame laws:* νομοθετέω (pass.) NOMOTHETEŌ
Heb 7.11 (under it the people received the law

RECEIVE UP
1. *taking up:* ἀνάλημψις ANALĒMPSIS* [A.1.d]
Lk 9.51 days drew near for him to be received up

RECEIVING
1. *taking hold, accepting:* λῆμψις LĒMPSIS*
Phil 4.15 no church entered into partnership . . in r.

RECENT CONVERT
1. *newly planted:* νεόφυτος (subst.) NEOPHYTOS*
1 Tim 3. 6 He must not be a recent convert

RECENTLY
1. *before these days:* πρὸ τούτων τῶν ἡμερῶν HĒMERA [B.1.a.1]
Acts 21.38 "Egyptian . . who r. stirred up a revolt

RECKLESS
1. *rash, reckless:* προπετής PROPETĒS
2 Tim 3. 4 treacherous, reckless, swollen with conceit

RECKON (*See also* RIGHTEOUS, RECKON)
1. *reckon, count:* λογίζομαι LOGIZOMAI
Mk [15.28 "*He was reckoned with the transgressors*‡
Lk 22.37 " 'he was reckoned with transgressors
Rom 4. 3 "it was reckoned to him as righteousness
4. 4 his wages are not reckoned as a gift
4. 5 his faith is reckoned as righteousness
4. 6 to whom God reckons righteousness
4. 8 "against whom the Lord will not r. . . sin
4. 9 faith was reckoned to Abraham
4.10 How then was it reckoned to him?
4.11 who thus have righteousness reckoned
4.22 why his faith was "reckoned to him
4.23 the words, "it was reckoned to him
4.24 It will be reckoned to us who believe
9. 8 children of the promise are reckoned
Gal 3. 6 "reckoned to him as righteousness
Jas 2.23 "reckoned to him as righteousness
2. *count, reckon:* ψηφίζω PSĒPHIZŌ
Rev 13.18 let him who has understanding reckon
3. *take up together, reckon:* συναίρω SYNAIRŌ
Mt 18.24 "When he began the reckoning

RECOGNITION TO, GIVE
1. *learn to know, recognize:* ἐπιγινώσκω EPIGINŌSKŌ
1 Cor 16.18 Give recognition to such men

RECOGNIZE
1. *have, hold:* ἔχω ECHŌ
1 Cor 11.16 we r. no other practice, nor do . . churches
2. *learn to know, recognize:* ἐπιγινώσκω EPIGINŌSKŌ
Mt 14.35 the men of that place recognized him
Mk 6.54 immediately the people recognized him
Lk 24.16 eyes were kept from recognizing him
24.31 they recognized him; and he vanished
Acts 3.10 recognized him as . . one who sat for alms
4.13 recognized that they had been with J.
12.14 Recognizing Peter's voice, . . she . . told
19.34 they recognized that he was a Jew
27.39 they did not recognize the land

RECOGNIZE, NOT
1. *not know:* ἀγνοέω AGNOEŌ
Acts 13.27 "because they did not recognize him
1 Cor 14.38 If any one does not recognize this, he is not recognized

RECOGNIZED
1. *visible, known:* φανερός PHANEROS
1 Cor 11.19 that those who are genuine . . be recognized

RECOMMENDATION
CONTEXTUALLY
2 Cor 3. 2 You yourselves are our letter of r.

RECOMMENDATION, OF
1. *introducing, commending:* συστατικός SYSTATIKOS*
2 Cor 3. 1 letters of recommendation to you

RECOMPENSE
1. *reward, wages:* μισθός MISTHOS
Rev 22.12 "I am coming soon, bringing my r.

RECONCILE
1. *reconcile again:* ἀποκαταλλάσσω APOKATALLASSŌ*
Eph 2.16 might r. us both to God in one body
Col 1.20 through him to r. to himself all things
1.22 he has now reconciled in his body
2. *change, reconcile:* διαλλάσσω DIALLASSŌ*
Mt 5.24 "first be reconciled to your brother
3. *change, reconcile:* καταλλάσσω KATALLASSŌ*
Rom 5.10 if while we were enemies we were reconciled . . , now . . reconciled, shall we be saved
1 Cor 7.11 (or else be reconciled to her husband
2 Cor 5.18 God, who through Christ reconciled us
5.19 in Christ God was reconciling[h] the world
5.20 We beseech you . . , be reconciled to God
4. *reconcile:* συναλλάσσω SYNALLASSŌ*
Acts 7.26 "he appeared . . and would have reconciled

RECONCILIATION
1. *exchange, reconciliation:* καταλλαγή KATALLAGĒ*
Rom 5.11 through whom we have . . received our r.
11.15 For if their rejection means . . r.
2 Cor 5.18 gave us the ministry of reconciliation
5.19 entrusting to us the message of r.

RECOVER
1. *save, keep from harm:* σῴζω (pass.) SŌZŌ
Jn 11.12 "if he has fallen asleep, he will recover
IDIOMATICALLY
a. Mk 16.18 "they will recover[k]‡ καλῶς ἕξουσιν [KALŌS]

RECOVERING OF SIGHT
1. *recovery of sight:* ἀνάβλεψις ANABLEPSIS*
Lk 4.18 "to proclaim . . recovering of sight

RED
1. *red:* ἐρυθρός ERYTHROS*
Acts 7.36 "signs in Egypt and at the Red Sea
Heb 11.29 By faith the people crossed the Red Sea
2. *flame-colored, red:* πυρρός PYRROS
Rev 12. 3 a great red dragon, with seven heads

RED, BE
1. *be fiery red:* πυρράζω PYRRAZŌ*
Mt 16. 2 " 'fair weather; for the sky is red‡
16. 3 " 'stormy today, for the sky is red‡

RED, BRIGHT
1. *flame-colored, red:* πυρρός PYRROS
Rev 6. 4 out came another horse, bright red

REDEEM
1. *buy in the market:* ἀγοράζω AGORAZŌ
Rev 14. 3 who had been redeemed from the earth
14. 4 these have been redeemed from mankind
2. *ransoming, deliverance:* ἀπολύτρωσις APOLYTRŌSIS [B.1.a.2]
Heb 9.15 a death has occurred which redeems
3. *buy from, redeem:* ἐξαγοράζω EXAGORAZŌ
Gal 3.13 "Christ redeemed us from the curse
4. 5 to redeem those who were under the law
4. *redeem:* λυτρόω (mid.) LYTROŌ
Lk 24.21 "had hoped . . he was the one to r. Israel
Tit 2.14 who gave himself for us to redeem us
5. *make redemption:* ποιεῖν λύτρωσιν LYTRŌSIS [B.3.a.3]
Lk 1.68 "he has visited and redeemed his people

REDEMPTION
1. *ransoming, deliverance:* ἀπολύτρωσις APOLYTRŌSIS
Lk 21.28 "because your r. is drawing near

Rom 3.24 the redemption which is in Christ Jesus
8.23 we wait for . . the r. of our bodies
1 Cor 1.30 Christ Jesus, whom God made our . . r.
Eph 1. 7 we have redemption through his blood
4.30 you were sealed for the day of r.
Col 1.14 in whom we have redemption
2. *redemption, ransoming:* λύτρωσις LYTRŌSIS
Lk 2.38 looking for the redemption of Jerusalem
Heb 9.12 thus securing an eternal redemption

REDOUND
1. *find:* εὑρίσκω (pass.) HEURISKŌ
1 Pet 1. 7 that . . your faith . . may redound to praise

REED
1. *reed, staff:* κάλαμος KALAMOS
Mt 11. 7 "A reed shaken by the wind?
12.20 "he will not break a bruised reed
27.29 they . . put a reed in his right hand
27.30 they . . took the reed and struck him
27.48 took a sponge . . and put it on a reed
Mk 15.19 they struck his head with a reed
15.36 put it on a reed and gave it to him
Lk 7.24 "A reed shaken by the wind?

REEF
1. *spot, reef:* σπιλάς SPILAS
Jude [.12 These are *reefs* on your love feasts†

REFER
CONTEXTUALLY
Col 2.22 (referring to things which all perish

REFER TO
IDIOMATICALLY
a. Eph 5.32 I am saying that it refers to⁰ ἐγὼ . . λέγω εἰς [EIS]

REFERRING
1. *as, so:* ὡς HŌS
Gal **3.16**[2]

REFINED
1. *set on fire:* πυρόω (perf. pass. part.) PYROŌ
Rev 1.15 burnished bronze, r. as in a furnace
3.18 " 'buy from me gold refined by fire

REFLECT
1. *radiance:* ἀπαύγασμα APAUGASMA* [A.6.a.3]
Heb 1. 3 He reflects the glory of God
2. *show as in a mirror:* κατοπτρίζω (mid.) KATOPTRIZŌ
2 Cor [3.18 *reflecting* the glory of the Lord†

REFORM
1. *making straight, reform:* διόρθωμα DIORTHŌMA*
Acts 24. 2 "by your provision . . reforms are introduced

REFORMATION
1. *making straight, correction:* διόρθωσις DIORTHŌSIS*
Heb 9.10 imposed until the time of reformation

REFRACTORY, BE
1. *speak against:* ἀντιλέγω ANTILEGŌ
Tit 2. 9 they are not to be refractory

REFRAIN
REFRAIN FROM (*See also* BURDENING *a;* MARRIAGE, REFRAIN FROM; WORKING FOR A LIVING, REFRAIN FROM)
1. *not:* μή MĒ [A.4.c]
1 Cor 7.38 who refrains from marriage will do better
9. 6 have no right to refrain from working
2. *refrain from, spare:* φείδομαι PHEIDOMAI
2 Cor 12. 6 if I wish to boast . . But I r. from it
IDIOMATICALLY
a. 2 Cor 1.23 it was to spare you that I refrained from coming ὅτι φειδόμενος ὑμῶν οὐκέτι ἦλθον [OUKETI]
b. 2 Cor 11.9 I refrained and will refrain from burdening you ἀβαρῆ ἐμαυτὸν ὑμῖν ἐτήρησα καὶ τηρήσω [TĒREŌ; EMAUTOU]

REFRESH
1. *make to cease, cause to rest:* ἀναπαύω ANAPAUŌ
1 Cor 16.18 they refreshed my spirit as well as yours
Phm . 7 hearts of the saints have been refreshed
.20 Refresh my heart in Christ
2. *cool, refresh:* ἀναψύχω ANAPSYCHŌ*
2 Tim 1.16 Onesiphorus, for he often refreshed me

REFRESHED IN S.'S COMPANY, BE
1. *rest with:* συναναπαύομαι (+dat.) SYNANAPAUOMAI*
Rom 15.32 that . . I may . . be r. in your company

REFRESHING
1. *relief:* ἀνάψυξις ANAPSYXIS*
Acts 3.19 "that times of refreshing may come

REFUSE
1. *let go, leave, forgive:* ἀφίημι (neg.) APHIĒMI
Mk 5.19 he refused, and said to him, "Go home
2. *defraud:* ἀποστερέω APOSTEREŌ
1 Cor 7. 5 Do not refuse one another except
3. *turn back, turn away:* ἀποστρέφω (aor. pass.) APOSTREPHŌ
Mt 5.42 "do not refuse him who would borrow
4. *deny:* ἀρνέομαι ARNEOMAI
Acts 7.35 "This Moses whom they refused
Heb 11.24 Moses . . refused to be called
5. *wish, will:* βούλομαι (neg.) BOULOMAI
Acts 18.15 "I refuse to be a judge of these things
6. *receive, accept:* δέχομαι (neg.) DECHOMAI
2 Th 2.10 they refused to love the truth
7. *not:* μή MĒ [A.4.c]
2 Cor 4. 2 we refuse to practice cunning
8. *not, no:* οὐ OU [A.4.c]
2 Th 3.14 If any one refuses to obey what we say
Heb 11.35 tortured, refusing to accept release
Rev 11. 9 refuse to let them be placed in a tomb
9. *and not:* οὔτε OUTE [A.4.c]
3 Jn .10 he refuses . . to welcome the brethren
10. *ask for, decline:* παραιτέομαι PARAITEOMAI
1 Tim 5.11 But refuse to enrol younger widows
Heb 12.25 do not r. him who is speaking. For if they did not escape when they refused
11. *what is thrown away in cleansing:* περικάθαρμα (pl.) PERIKATHARMA*
1 Cor 4.13 we . . are now, as the refuse of the world
12. *dung:* σκύβαλον SKYBALON*
Phil 3. 8 For his sake I . . count them as refuse
13. *will, wish:* θέλω (neg.) THELŌ
Mt 2.18 "Rachel . . refused to be consoled
18.30 "He refused and . . put him in prison
Lk 15.28 "he was angry and refused to go in
18. 4 "For a while he refused
Jn 5.40 "yet you refuse to come to me
Acts 7.39 "Our fathers refused to obey him
Rev 2.21 " 'she refuses to repent of her immorality

REFUSE, AND
1. *and not, nor:* μηδέ MĒDE [A.4.c]
Mk 6.11 "and they refuse to hear you . . , shake off

REFUSE TO LISTEN
1. *overhear, take no heed of:* παρακούω PARAKOUŌ
Mt 18.17 "If he refuses to listen to them
18.17 "if he refuses to listen even to the church

REGAIN ONE'S SIGHT
1. *look up, receive sight:* ἀναβλέπω ANABLEPŌ
Acts 9.12 "so that he might regain his sight
9.17 "sent me that you may r. your sight
9.18 he regained his sight. Then he rose

REGARD
1. *see, look:* βλέπω BLEPŌ
Mt 22.16 "you do not regard the position of men
Mk 12.14 "you do not regard the position of men
2. *put to shame:* ἐντρέπω (pass.) ENTREPŌ
Lk 18. 2 "neither feared God nor regarded man
18. 4 " 'Though I neither fear God nor r. man
3. *look at, consider:* ἐπιβλέπω EPIBLEPŌ
Lk 1.48 "regarded the . . estate of his handmaiden
4. *know, understand:* γινώσκω GINŌSKŌ
2 Cor 5.16 though we once regarded Christ . . , we regard him thus no longer
5. *think, lead:* ἡγέομαι HĒGEOMAI
1 Tim 6. 1 Let all . . regard their masters as worthy
6. *reckon, count:* λογίζομαι LOGIZOMAI
Rom 2.26 will not his uncircumcision be regarded?
8.36 "regarded as sheep to be slaughtered

1 Cor 4. 1 This is how one should regard us
1 Pet 5.12 a faithful brother as I regard him
7. *know:* οἶδα OIDA
2 Cor 5.16 we r. no one from a human point of view
CONTEXTUALLY
Rom 6.20 you were free in r. to righteousness

REGARD LIGHTLY
1. *esteem lightly, neglect:* ὀλιγωρέω OLIGŌREŌ*
Heb 12. 5 "not r. lightly . . discipline of the Lord

REGARD TO, WITH
REGARDING
1. *in the matter of:* ἐν μέρει MEROS [B.1.b]
Col 2.16 with regard to a festival or a new moon
2. *about, concerning:* περί (+gen.) PERI
Acts 25.20 "and be tried there regarding them
28.22 "with regard to this sect we know

REGARDED, BE
1. *think, suppose:* δοκέω DOKEŌ
Lk 22.24 which . . was to be regarded as the greatest

REGARDS, AS
1. *in accordance with, for:* κατά (+acc.) KATA
Rom 11.28 As regards the gospel they are enemies . . ; but as regards election they are beloved
2. *about, around:* περί (+acc.) PERI
1 Tim 6.21 some have missed the mark as r. the faith

REGENERATION
1. *rebirth, regeneration:* παλιγγενεσία PALIGGENESIA
Tit 3. 5 by the washing of regeneration

REGION
1. *country, place:* χώρα CHŌRA
Mt 4.16 "those . . in the r. and shadow of death
Lk 2. 8 in that region there were shepherds
3. 1 tetrarch of the region of Ituraea
Acts 8. 1 scattered throughout the r. of Judea
13.49 word . . spread throughout all the region
16. 6 went through the region of Phrygia
18.23 through the region of Galatia
2. *boundary:* ὅριον (pl.) HORION
Mt 2.16 killed all the male children . . in all that r.
15.22 a Canaanite woman from that region
15.39 he . . went to the region of Magadan
19. 1 he . . entered the region of Judea
Mk 7.24 he . . went away to the region of Tyre
7.31 he returned from the r. of Tyre, and went . . through the r. of the Decapolis
10. 1 he . . went to the region of Judea
3. *latitude, region:* κλίμα KLIMA*
Rom 15.23 no . . room for work in these regions
2 Cor 11.10 not . . silenced in the regions of Achaia
Gal 1.21 into the regions of Syria and Cilicia
4. *around a place:* περίχωρος PERICHŌROS [B.3.b.2]
Mt 14.35 they sent round to all that region

REGION ABOUT
REGION, SURROUNDING
1. *around a place:* περίχωρος PERICHŌROS [B.3.b.2]
Mt 3. 5 Judea and all the r. about the Jordan
Mk 1.28 all the surrounding region of Galilee
Lk 3. 3 into all the region about the Jordan
4.37 reports . . went out into . . surrounding r.

REGRET
1. *regret, repent:* μεταμέλομαι METAMELOMAI
2 Cor 7. 8 even if I made you sorry with my letter, I do not regret it (though I did regret it

REGRET, THAT BRINGS NO
1. *not to be regretted:* ἀμεταμέλητος AMETAMELĒTOS
2 Cor 7.10 godly grief . . that . . brings no regret

REGULAR
1. *lawful:* ἔννομος ENNOMOS
Acts 19.39 "it shall be settled in the r. assembly

REGULATION
1. *ordinance, justification:* δικαίωμα DIKAIŌMA
Heb 9. 1 even the first covenant had regulations
9.10 regulations . . until . . time of reformation

REGULATIONS, SUBMIT TO
1. *lay down as an opinion:* δογματίζω (pass.) DOGMATIZŌ*
Col 2.20 Why do you submit to regulations?

REHOBOAM: Ῥοβοάμ ˌrē(h)əˈbōəm
Mt 1. 7 Solomon the father of Rehoboam, and Rehoboam the father of Abijah

REIGN
1. *reign:* βασιλεύω BASILEUŌ
Mt 2.22 heard that Archelaus reigned over Judea
Lk 1.33 "will r. over the house of Jacob for ever
19.14 " 'We do not want this man to reign
19.27 " 'who did not want me to r. over them
Rom 5.14 death reigned from Adam to Moses
5.17 If . . death reigned through that one man, much more will those . . reign in life
5.21 as sin reigned in death, grace also might reign through righteousness
6.12 Let not sin . . r. in your mortal bodies
1 Cor 4. 8 And would that you did reign!
15.25 must r. until he has put all his enemies
Rev 5.10 "made them a kingdom . . and they shall r.
11.15 "he shall reign for ever and ever
11.17 "thou hast taken . . power and begun to r.
19. 6 "Hallelujah! For the Lord . . reigns
20. 4 They came to life, and reigned
20. 6 they shall r. with him a thousand years
22. 5 they shall reign for ever and ever
2. *authority, leadership:* ἡγεμονία HĒGEMONIA*
Lk 3. 1 In . . fifteenth year of the r. of Tiberius

REIGN WITH
1. *rule together with:* συμβασιλεύω SYMBASILEUŌ
2 Tim 2.12 if we endure, we shall also r. with him

REJECT
1. *reject on scrutiny:* ἀποδοκιμάζω APODOKIMAZŌ
Mt 21.42 " 'The very stone . . the builders rejected
Mk 8.31 Son of man must . . be rejected by . . elders
12.10 " 'The very stone . . the builders rejected
Lk 9.22 "Son of man must . . be rejected by . . elders
17.25 "he must . . be rejected by this generation
20.17 " 'The very stone . . the builders rejected
Heb 12.17 he desired to inherit . . , he was rejected
1 Pet 2. 7 "The very stone . . the builders rejected
2. *turn back, turn away:* ἀποστρέφω (mid.) APOSTREPHŌ
Tit 1.14 commands of men who reject the truth
Heb 12.25 much less shall we escape if we reject him
3. *thrust away:* ἀπωθέω (mid.) APŌTHEŌ
Rom 11. 1 I ask, . . has God rejected his people?
11. 2 God has not rejected his people
1 Tim 1.19 rejecting conscience . . have made shipwreck
4. *deny, nullify:* ἀθετέω ATHETEŌ
Lk 7.30 the lawyers rejected the purpose of God
10.16 "He who hears you hears me, and he who rejects you rejects me, and he who rejects me rejects him who sent me
Jn 12.48 "He who rejects me . . has a judge; the word
Jude . 8 these men . . reject authority, and revile
5. *treat with contempt:* ἐξουθενέω EXOUTHENEŌ
Acts 4.11 "This is the stone which was rejected

REJECTED
1. *to be thrown away:* ἀπόβλητος APOBLĒTOS*
1 Tim 4. 4 everything . . is good, and nothing . . to be r.
2. *reject on scrutiny:* ἀποδοκιμάζω (perf. pass. part.) APODOKIMAZŌ
1 Pet 2. 4 that living stone, rejected by men

REJECTING, HAVE A WAY OF
1. *deny, nullify:* ἀθετέω ATHETEŌ [A.6.a.5]
Mk 7. 9 "You have a fine way of rejecting

REJECTION
1. *throwing away, loss:* ἀποβολή APOBOLĒ
Rom 11.15 if their r. means the reconciliation

REJOICE
1. *rejoice greatly:* ἀγαλλιάω (act. or dep.) AGALLIAŌ
Mt 5.12 "Rejoice and be glad, for your reward
Lk 1.47 "my spirit rejoices in God my Savior

Lk 10.21 he rejoiced in the Holy Spirit
Jn 5.35 "willing to rejoice for a while in his light
8.56 "Abraham rejoiced . . to see my day
Acts 2.26 " 'my heart was glad, . . my tongue rejoiced
16.34 he rejoiced with all his household
1 Pet 1. 6 you r.,[a] though now . . you may . . suffer†
1. 8 you[c] believe in him and rejoice

2. *rejoice:* χαίρω CHAIRŌ
Mt 2.10 they rejoiced exceedingly with great joy
18.13 "I say to you, he rejoices over it more
Lk 1.14 "and many will rejoice at his birth
6.23 "Rejoice in that day, and leap for joy
10.20 "do not rejoice in this, . . but r. that your names are written in heaven
13.17 people rejoiced at . . the glorious things
15. 5 "he lays it on his shoulders, rejoicing
19.37 multitude of the disciples began to r.
Jn 3.29 "rejoices greatly at . . bridegroom's voice
4.36 "sower and reaper may rejoice together
14.28 "you would have rejoiced, because I go
16.20 "you will weep . . , but the world will r.
16.22 "sorrow now, but . . your hearts will r.
Acts 5.41 rejoicing that they were counted worthy
8.39 the eunuch . . went on his way rejoicing
15.31 they rejoiced at the exhortation
Rom 12.12 Rejoice in your hope, be patient
12.15 Rejoice with those who rejoice, weep with those who weep
16.19 your obedience is known . . , so that I r.
1 Cor 7.30 those who rejoice as though they were not rejoicing
13. 6 it does not rejoice at wrong
16.17 I rejoice at the coming of Stephanas
2 Cor 2. 3 those who should have made me r.
6.10 as sorrowful, yet always rejoicing
7. 7 so that I rejoiced still more
7. 9 I rejoice, not because you were grieved
7.13 we rejoiced still more at the joy of Titus
7.16 I r., because I have . . confidence
Phil 1.18 Christ is proclaimed; and in that I r.
1.19(18) Yes, and I shall rejoice
2.28 that you may rejoice at seeing him again
3. 1 my brethren, rejoice in the Lord
4. 4 Rejoice in the Lord always; again I will say, Rejoice
4.10 I rejoice in the Lord greatly
Col 1.24 I rejoice in my sufferings for your sake
2. 5 yet I am with you in spirit, rejoicing
1 Th 5.16 Rejoice always
1 Pet 4.13 r. . . as you share Christ's sufferings, that you may also r. . . when his glory
2 Jn . 4 I rejoiced . . to find some . . following
3 Jn . 3 I . . rejoiced when some . . arrived
Rev 11.10 those who dwell on the earth will r.
19. 7 "Let us rejoice . . and give him the glory

3. *gladden:* εὐφραίνω (pass.) EUPHRAINŌ
Acts 7.41 "they . . offered a sacrifice . . and rejoiced
Rom 15.10 "Rejoice, O Gentiles, with his people
Gal 4.27 "Rejoice, O barren one who does not bear
Rev 12.12 "Rejoice . . , O heaven and you . . therein!
18.20 "Rejoice over her, O heaven, O saints!

4. *boast:* καυχάομαι KAUCHAOMAI
Rom 5. 2 we[h] r. in . . hope of sharing . . glory of God†
5. 3 we[h] rejoice in our sufferings†
5.11 we also rejoice in God through our Lord

5. *rejoice with:* συγχαίρω SYGCHAIRŌ
1 Cor 13. 6 but rejoices in the right

REJOICE TOGETHER
REJOICE WITH

1. *rejoice with:* συγχαίρω SYGCHAIRŌ
Lk 1.58 kinsfolk heard . . and they rejoiced with her
15. 6 " 'R. with me, for I have found my sheep
15. 9 " 'R. with me, for I have found the coin
1 Cor 12.26 if one . . is honored, all rejoice together
Phil 2.17 I am glad and rejoice with you all
2.18 Likewise you also should . . rejoice with me

REJOICING

1. *great joy:* ἀγαλλίασις AGALLIASIS
Jude .24 who is able . . to present you . . with r.

REKINDLE

1. *rekindle:* ἀναζωπυρέω ANAZŌPYREŌ*
2 Tim 1. 6 rekindle the gift of God . . within you

RELATE

1. *interpret, tell:* ἐξηγέομαι EXĒGEOMAI
Acts 10. 8 having related everything to them
15.12 as they related what signs . . God had done
15.14 "related how God . . visited the Gentiles
21.19 related . . the things that God had done

RELATION

CONTEXTUALLY
Rom 2.17 and boast of your relation to God
Heb 5. 1 to act on behalf of men in r. to God

RELATIONS

1. *use, function:* χρῆσις CHRĒSIS*
Rom 1.26 Their women exchanged natural r.
1.27 men likewise gave up natural relations

RELATIVE (*See also* HIS RELATIVES)

CONTEXTUALLY
1 Tim 5. 8 If any one does not provide for . . relatives
5.16 If any believing woman[l] has relatives

RELAX

1. *break up, unbind:* λύω LYŌ
Mt 5.19 "Whoever . . relaxes one of the least

RELEASE

1. *release, forgiveness:* ἄφεσις APHESIS
Lk 4.18 "sent me to proclaim r. to the captives

2. *ransoming, deliverance:* ἀπολύτρωσις APOLYTRŌSIS
Heb 11.35 Some were tortured, refusing to accept r.

3. *loose from, dismiss:* ἀπολύω APOLYŌ
Mt 18.27 "the lord of that servant released him
27.15 to release for the crowd any one prisoner
27.17 "Whom do you want me to release?
27.21 "Which . . do you want me to release?
27.26 Then he released for them Barabbas
Mk 15. 6 he used to r. for them one prisoner
15. 9 "Do you want me to r. . . King of the Jews?
15.11 to . . r. for them Barabbas instead
15.15 Pilate . . released for them Barabbas
Lk 23.16 "I will . . chastise him and release him[m]
[23.17 *he was obliged to release one man*‡
23.18 "release to us Barabbas
23.20 Pilate . . , desiring to release Jesus
23.22 "I will . . chastise him and release him
23.25 He released the man . . thrown into prison
Jn 18.39 "a custom that I should release one man . . ; will you have me r. . . the King of the Jews?
19.10 "Do you not know . . I have power to r.?
19.12 Upon this Pilate sought to release him
19.12 "If you r. . . you are not Caesar's friend
Acts 3.13 "when he had decided to release him
4.23 When they were released they went
Heb 13.23 our brother Timothy has been released

4. *break up, unbind:* λύω LYŌ
Mk 7.35 his tongue was released, and he spoke
Rev 9.14 "R. the four angels who are bound
9.15 So the four angels were released

RELIEF

1. *service:* διακονία DIAKONIA
[a]B.1.a.1
Acts 11.29 [a]determined . . to send relief to the brethren
2 Cor 8. 4 taking part in the relief of the saints

RELIEVE

1. *help:* ἐπαρκέω EPARKEŌ
1 Tim 5.10 as one who has . . relieved the afflicted

RELIGION

1. *reverence, piety:* εὐσέβεια EUSEBEIA
1 Tim 3.16 Great . . is the mystery of our religion
2 Tim 3. 5 holding the form of religion but denying

2. *reverence for God, piety:* θεοσέβεια THEOSEBEIA*
1 Tim 2.10 as befits women who profess religion

3. *religion, worship:* θρησκεία THRĒSKEIA
Acts 26. 5 "the strictest party of our religion
Jas 1.26 this man's religion is vain
1.27 Religion that is pure and undefiled

RELIGIOUS
1. *superstitious, religious:* θρησκός THRĒSKOS*
Jas 1.26 If any one thinks he is religious

RELIGIOUS DUTY
1. *show piety toward:* εὐσεβέω (inf.) EUSEBEŌ
1 Tim 5. 4 first learn their r. duty to their . . family

RELIGIOUS, VERY
1. *religious:* δεισιδαίμων (comp.) DEISIDAIMŌN*
Acts 17.22 "I perceive that in every way you are very r.

RELUCTANTLY
1. *with sorrow:* ἐκ λύπης LYPĒ [B.1.a.1]
2 Cor 9. 7 he has made up his mind, not reluctantly

RELY
1. *be:* εἰμί EIMI [B.2.d.1]
Gal 3.10 For all who rely on works of the law
2. *persuade:* πείθω (perf. periphr.) PEITHŌ
2 Cor 1. 9 that was to make us r. not on ourselves

RELY UPON
1. *rest upon, rely upon:* ἐπαναπαύομαι EPANAPAUOMAI
Rom 2.17 call yourself a Jew and r. upon the law

REMAIN
1. *leave over, abandon:* ἀπολείπω (pass.) APOLEIPŌ
Heb 4. 6 it remains for some to enter it
4. 9 there remains a . . rest for the people
10.26 there no longer remains a sacrifice for sins
2. *persist, persevere:* διαμένω DIAMENŌ
Lk 1.22 he made signs . . and remained dumb
Heb 1.11 " 'they will perish, but thou remainest
3. *spend time:* διατρίβω DIATRIBŌ
Jn 3.22 he remained with them and baptized
Acts 12.19 went . . to Caesarea, and remained there
14. 3 remained for a long time, speaking
14.28 remained no little time with the disciples
15.35 Paul and Barnabas remained in Antioch
16.12 We remained in this city some days
4. *be:* εἰμί EIMI
Mt 2.13 "and remain there till I tell you
2.15 remained there until the death of Herod
1 Cor 7.26 it is well for a person to r. as he is
5. *continue, remain:* ἐπιμένω EPIMENŌ
Acts 10.48 they asked him to remain for some days
[15.34 *But it seemed good to Silas to remain*‡
Gal 1.18 to visit Cephas, and remained with him
Phil 1.24 to remain in the flesh is more necessary
6. *stand, set:* ἵστημι (perf.) HISTĒMI
Jn 6.22 people who remained on the other side
7. *be patient under, stand firm:* ὑπομένω HYPOMENŌ
Acts 17.14 but Silas and Timothy remained there
8. *leave behind:* καταλείπω (mid.) KATALEIPŌ
Heb 4. 1 the promise of entering his rest remains
9. *stay, wait:* μένω MENŌ
Mt 11.23 "it would have remained until this day
26.38 "remain here, and watch[h] with me
Mk 14.34 "remain here, and watch[d]
Lk 1.56 Mary remained with her . . three months
10. 7 "remain in the same house, eating
Jn 1.32 "I saw the Spirit descend . . it remained
1.33 " 'on whom you see the Spirit . . remain
7. 9 So saying, he remained in Galilee
9.41 "you say, 'We see,' your guilt remains
10.40 went . . across the Jordan . . and . . remained
12.24 "unless a grain . . dies, it remains alone
12.34 "heard . . that the Christ remains for ever
12.46 "whoever believes . . may not r. in darkness
19.31 to prevent the bodies from remaining
21.22 "If it is my will that he r. until I come
21.23 "If it is my will that he r. until I come
Acts 5. 4 "While it remained unsold, did it not remain your own?
[20.15 *after remaining at Trogyllium*‡
27.41 striking a shoal[e] . . remained immovable
1 Cor 7. 8 it is well for them to remain single
7.11 (let her r. single or else be reconciled
7.20 should r. in the state in which . . called
7.24 there let him remain with God
7.40 she is happier if she remains as she is
2 Cor 3.14 that same veil remains unlifted
Phil 1.25 I shall remain and continue with you
2 Tim 2.13 if we are faithless, he remains faithful
4.20 Erastus remained at Corinth
Heb 12.27 "that what cannot be shaken may r.
Rev 17.10 "when he comes he must r. only a little
10. *wait for, stay with:* προσμένω PROSMENŌ
1 Tim 1. 3 As I urged you . . , remain at Ephesus
CONTEXTUALLY
1 Tim 5.25 they cannot remain hidden

REMAIN FAITHFUL
1. *wait for, stay with:* προσμένω PROSMENŌ
Acts 11.23 he exhorted them all to remain faithful

REMAINS, WHAT
1. *remaining, left:* λοιπός (subst. neut. pl.) LOIPOS
Rev 3. 2 " 'Awake, and strengthen what remains

REMEMBER (*See also* EARNESTLY, REMEMBER)
1. *remind:* ἀναμιμνῄσκω (pass.) ANAMIMNĒSKŌ
Mk 11.21 Peter remembered and said . . "Master,"[v] look!
14.72 Peter remembered how Jesus had said
2 Cor 7.15 he remembers the obedience of you all
2. *remind:* ὑπομιμνῄσκω (pass.) HYPOMIMNĒSKŌ
Lk 22.61 Peter remembered the word of the Lord
3. *remind oneself, remember:* μιμνῄσκομαι MIMNĒSKOMAI
Mt 5.23 "offering your gift . . , and there remember
26.75 Peter remembered the saying of Jesus
27.63 "Sir, we remember how that impostor
Lk 1.72 "to remember his holy covenant
16.25 " 'Son, remember that . . in your lifetime
23.42 "Jesus, remember me when you come
24. 6 "Remember how he told you . . in Galilee
24. 8 And they remembered his words
Jn 2.17 disciples remembered . . it was written
2.22 disciples remembered that he had said
12.16 remembered that this had been written
Acts 10.31 " 'your alms have been remembered
11.16 "I remembered the word of the Lord
1 Cor 11. 2 because you remember me in everything
2 Tim 1. 4 As I r. your tears, I long night and day
Heb 8.12 "I will remember their sins no more
10.17 "I will remember their sins . . no more
13. 3 Remember those who are in prison
2 Pet 3. 2 you should remember the predictions
Jude .17 remember, beloved, the predictions
Rev 16.19 God remembered great Babylon
4. *mention, remembrance:* μνεία MNEIA
[a]B.3.a.3 [b]B.3.a.5
Eph 1.16 [a]remembering you in my prayers
1 Th 3. 6 [b]you always remember us kindly
2 Tim 1. 3 [b]when I r. you constantly in my prayers
Phm . 4 [a]I thank my God always when I r. you
5. *remember, mention:* μνημονεύω MNĒMONEUŌ
Mt 16. 9 "Do you not remember the five loaves?
Mk 8.18 "And do you not remember?
Lk 17.32 "Remember Lot's wife
Jn 15.20 "Remember the word that I said to you
16. 4 "that . . you may r. that I told you
16.21 "she no longer remembers the anguish
Acts 20.31 "alert, remembering that . . I did not cease
20.35 "remembering the words of the Lord Jesus
Gal 2.10 they would have us remember the poor
Eph 2.11 r. that at one time you Gentiles
Col 4.18 R. my fetters. Grace be with you
1 Th 1. 3 remembering . . your work of faith
2. 9 For you remember our labor and toil
2 Th 2. 5 Do you not r. . . when I was still with you?
2 Tim 2. 8 R. Jesus Christ, risen from the dead
Heb 13. 7 R. your leaders . . and imitate their faith
Rev 2. 5 " 'R. then from what you have fallen
3. 3 " 'Remember then what you received
18. 5 "God has remembered her iniquities

CONTEXTUALLY
Rom 11.18 r. it is not you that support the root
Eph 2.12 r. that you were at that time separated

REMEMBRANCE
1. *calling to mind:* ἀνάμνησις ANAMNĒSIS
Lk 22.19 "Do this in remembrance of me‡
1 Cor 11.24 "Do this in remembrance of me
11.25 "Do this . . in remembrance of me
2. *mention, remembrance:* μνεία MNEIA
Phil 1. 3 I thank my God in all my r. of you

REMEMBRANCE, BRING TO
1. *remind:* ὑπομιμνῄσκω HYPOMIMNĒSKŌ
Jn 14.26 "Spirit . . will . . bring to your r.

REMEMBRANCE, IN
1. *remind oneself, remember:* μιμνῄσκομαι (pass. inf.) MIMNĒSKOMAI
Lk 1.54 "helped his servant Israel, in r. of his mercy

REMIND
1. *remind:* ἀναμιμνῄσκω ANAMIMNĒSKŌ
1 Cor 4.17 to remind you of my ways in Christ
2 Tim 1. 6 I remind you to rekindle the gift of God
2. *remind:* ὑπομιμνῄσκω HYPOMIMNĒSKŌ
2 Tim 2.14 Remind them of this, and charge them
Tit 3. 1 R. them to be submissive to rulers
2 Pet 1.12 I intend always to remind you of these
Jude . 5 Now I desire to remind you
IDIOMATICALLY
a. 2 Cor 10.7 let him remind himself that as he is Christ's, so are we τοῦτο λογιζέσθω πάλιν ἐφ' ἑαυτοῦ, ὅτι καθὼς αὐτὸς Χριστοῦ, οὕτως καὶ ἡμεῖς [LOGIZOMAI]

REMIND, WOULD
1. *make known:* γνωρίζω GNŌRIZŌ
1 Cor 15. 1 Now I would remind you, brethren

REMINDED, BE
1. *take a reminder:* ὑπόμνησιν λαμβάνειν HYPOMNĒSIS [B.3]
2 Tim 1. 5 I am reminded of your sincere faith

REMINDER
1. *calling to mind:* ἀνάμνησις ANAMNĒSIS
Heb 10. 3 in these sacrifices there is a reminder of sin
2. *remind:* ἐπαναμιμνῄσκω EPANAMIMNĒSKŌ* [B.2.a.2]
Rom 15.15 I have written . . by way of reminder
3. *reminder:* ὑπόμνησις HYPOMNĒSIS
2 Pet 1.13 to arouse you by way of reminder
3. 1 aroused your sincere mind by way of r.

REMNANT
1. *remainder, remnant:* ὑπόλειμμα HYPOLEIMMA*
Rom 9.27 "only a remnant of them will be saved
2. *residue, remnant:* λεῖμμα LEIMMA*
Rom 11. 5 there is a remnant, chosen by grace

REMOVAL
1. *getting rid of:* ἀπόθεσις APOTHESIS
1 Pet 3.21 Baptism . . saves you, not as a r. of dirt
2. *change of position:* μετάθεσις METATHESIS
Heb 12.27 indicates the r. of what is shaken

REMOVE
1. *lift, carry away:* αἴρω AIRŌ
1 Cor 5. 2 Let him who has done this be removed
2. *unroof:* ἀποστεγάζω APOSTEGAZŌ* [A.6.a.6]
Mk 2. 4 they removed the roof above him
3. *make ineffective, hinder:* καταργέω KATARGEŌ
Gal 5.11 the stumbling block . . has been removed
4. *move, remove:* κινέω KINEŌ
Rev 2. 5 " 'If not, I will . . remove your lampstand
6.14 every . . island was removed from its place
5. *change, remove:* μεθίστημι METHISTĒMI
Acts 13.22 " 'he . . removed him, he raised up David
1 Cor 13. 2 all faith, so as to remove mountains
6. *emigrate, remove:* μετοικίζω METOIKIZŌ*
Acts 7. 4 "God removed him from there into this land
7.43 " 'I will remove you beyond Babylon
7. *carry away:* παραφέρω PARAPHERŌ
Mk 14.36 "Father, . . remove this cup from me
Lk 22.42 "Father, . . remove this cup from me
8. *take away, strip off:* περιαιρέω PERIAIREŌ
2 Cor 3.16 when a man turns . . the veil is removed

REMOVE THE MARKS OF CIRCUMCISION
1. *draw the prepuce forward:* ἐπισπάομαι EPISPAOMAI*
1 Cor 7.18 not seek to r. the marks of circumcision

RENDER
1. *give back, repay:* ἀνταποδίδωμι ANTAPODIDŌMI
1 Th 3. 9 what thanksgiving can we r. to God
2. *give up, return:* ἀποδίδωμι APODIDŌMI
[a]ἀποδιδόναι λόγον
Mt 12.36 [a]"the day of judgment men will r. account
22.21 "R. . . to Caesar . . things that are Caesar's
Mk 12.17 "R. to Caesar . . things that are Caesar's
Lk 20.25 "r. to Caesar . . things that are Caesar's
Rom 2. 6 For he will render to every man
Rev 18. 6 "Render to her as she herself has rendered, and repay her double

RENDER SERVICE
1. *do a service, minister:* διακονέω DIAKONEŌ
2 Tim 1.18 the service he rendered at Ephesus
1 Pet 4.11 whoever renders service
2. *serve, be a slave:* δουλεύω DOULEUŌ
Eph 6. 7 rendering service with a good will
3. *work, do:* ἐργάζομαι ERGAZOMAI
3 Jn . 5 a loyal thing . . when you r. any service

RENDERING
1. *service:* διακονία DIAKONIA
2 Cor 9.12 the r. of this service not only supplies

RENEW
1. *renew:* ἀνακαινόω ANAKAINOŌ*
2 Cor 4.16 our inner nature is being renewed
Col 3.10 the new nature, which is being renewed

RENEWAL
1. *renewal:* ἀνακαίνωσις ANAKAINŌSIS*
Rom 12. 2 transformed by the r. of your mind
Tit 3. 5 saved us . . by . . r. in the Holy Spirit

RENEWED, BE
1. *renew, revive:* ἀνανεόω (pass.) ANANEOŌ*
Eph 4.23 be renewed in the spirit of your minds

RENOUNCE
1. *speak out, forbid:* ἀπεῖπον (mid.) APEIPON*
2 Cor 4. 2 We have renounced disgraceful . . ways
2. *part from* (mid.): ἀποτάσσω APOTASSŌ
Lk 14.33 "whoever . . does not r. all that he has
3. *deny:* ἀρνέομαι ARNEOMAI
Tit 2.12 training us to renounce irreligion

REPAID, BE
1. *there is repayment:* γίνεται ἀνταπόδομα ANTAPODOMA [A.6.e]
Lk 14.12 "lest . . in return . . you be repaid

REPAY
1. *give back, repay:* ἀνταποδίδωμι ANTAPODIDŌMI
Lk 14.14 "they cannot repay you. You will be repaid at the resurrection
Rom 11.35 "who has given . . that he might be repaid?
12.19 "Vengeance is mine, I will repay
2 Th 1. 6 God deems it just to repay with affliction
Heb 10.30 "Vengeance is mine, I will repay
2. *give up, return:* ἀποδίδωμι APODIDŌMI
Mt 16.27 "then he will repay every man
Lk 10.35 " 'I will repay you when I come back
Rom 12.17 Repay no one evil for evil
1 Th 5.15 See that none of you repays evil for evil
Rev 22.12 "recompense, to repay every one
3. *repay, compensate:* ἀποτίνω APOTINŌ*
Phm .19 I, Paul, write this . . , I will repay it
4. *repeat, double:* διπλόω DIPLOŌ*
Rev 18. 6 "repay her double for her deeds

REPEAT
1. *say again:* πάλιν λέγειν PALIN [B.3.b.4]
2 Cor 11.16 I repeat, let no one think me foolish

REPEATEDLY
1. *often, many times:* πολλάκις POLLAKIS
Heb 9.25 Nor was it to offer himself repeatedly

Heb 9.26 he would have had to suffer repeatedly
10.11 offering repeatedly the same sacrifices

REPENT

1. *regret, repent:* μεταμέλομαι METAMELOMAI
Mt 21.29 "'I will not'; but afterward he repented
21.32 "you did not afterward r. and believe
27. 3 repented and brought back the . . silver

2. *perceive afterward, repent:* μετανοέω METANOEŌ*
Mt 3. 2 "Repent, for the kingdom . . is at hand
4.17 "Repent, for the kingdom . . is at hand
11.20 to upbraid . . because they did not r.
11.21 "they would have repented long ago
12.41 "repented at the preaching of Jonah
Mk 1.15 "repent, and believe in the gospel
6.12 they . . preached that men should r.
Lk 10.13 "they would have repented long ago
11.32 "repented at the preaching of Jonah
13. 3 "unless you repent you will all . . perish
13. 5 "unless you repent you will all . . perish
15. 7 "more joy . . over one sinner who repents
15.10 "there is joy . . over one sinner who repents
16.30 "'if . . one goes . . from the dead, they will r.
17. 3 "if he repents, forgive him
17. 4 "if he . . says, 'I r.,' you must forgive him
Acts 2.38 said to them, "Repent, and be baptized
3.19 "Repent therefore, and turn again
8.22 "Repent therefore of this wickedness
17.30 "commands all men everywhere to r.
26.20 "they should repent and turn to God
2 Cor 12.21 those who sinned . . and have not repented
Rev 2. 5 "'r. and do the works you did at first . . I will . . remove . . lampstand . . unless you r.
2.16 "'Repent then. If not, I will come
2.21 "'I gave her time to repent, but she refuses to repent of her immorality
2.22 "'great tribulation, unless they repent
3. 3 "'Remember . . what you . . heard . . and r.
3.19 "'so be zealous and repent
9.20 mankind . . did not repent of the works
9.21 nor did they repent of their murders
16. 9 they did not repent and give him glory
16.11 ⟨men⟩ did not repent of their deeds

3. *change of mind, repentance:* μετάνοια METANOIA
[a]A.1.e [b]gen.
2 Tim 2.25 [a]God may . . grant that they will repent
Heb 12.17 [b]for he found no chance to repent

REPENTANCE

1. *change of mind, repentance:* μετάνοια METANOIA
Mt 3. 8 "Bear fruit that befits repentance
3.11 "I baptize you with water for repentance
Mk 1. 4 preaching a baptism of repentance
Lk 3. 3 preaching a baptism of repentance
3. 8 "Bear fruits that befit repentance
5.32 "I have . . come to call . . sinners to r.
15. 7 "righteous persons who need no r.
24.47 "r. and forgiveness of sins . . be preached
Acts 5.31 "to give repentance to Israel
11.18 "God has granted repentance unto life
13.24 "John had preached a baptism of r.
19. 4 "John baptized with the baptism of r.
20.21 "testifying . . of repentance to God
26.20 "perform deeds worthy of their r.
Rom 2. 4 God's kindness is meant to lead you to r.
2 Cor 7.10 For godly grief produces a repentance
Heb 6. 1 not laying again a foundation of r.
6. 4(6) it is impossible to restore again to r.
2 Pet 3. 9 wishing . . that all should reach r.

REPENTING

1. *change of mind, repentance:* μετάνοια METANOIA
2 Cor 7. 9 you were grieved into repenting

REPHAN: Ῥομφά 'rēfən
Acts 7.43 "'you took up . . the star of the god R.

REPLY

1. *answer again:* ἀνταποκρίνομαι ANTAPOKRINOMAI
Lk 14. 6 And they could not reply to this

2. *reply:* ἀποκρίνομαι APOKRINOMAI
[a]A.6.b
Mt 12.48 he replied . . "Who is my mother?
16.16 Peter replied, "You are the Christ
17.11 He replied, "Elijah does come
19.27 [a]Peter said in reply, "Lo, we have left
20.13 "replied . . 'Friend, I am doing you no wrong
25. 9 "replied . . 'there will not be enough
25.12 "he replied, 'Truly, I say to you
Mk 3.33 replied, "Who are my mother . . my brothers?
Jn 7.52 They replied, "Are you from Galilee too?
Acts [8.37 *And he replied, "I believe*‡
15.13 James replied, "Brethren, listen
24.10 the governor . . motioned . . , Paul replied
25. 4 Festus replied that Paul was being kept

3. *say, speak:* εἶπον EIPON
Acts 21.39 Paul replied, "I am a Jew, from Tarsus

4. *take up, assume:* ὑπολαμβάνω HYPOLAMBANŌ
Lk 10.30 replied, "A man was going . . to Jericho

5. *say, speak:* λέγω LEGŌ
Mk 5. 9 He replied, "My name is Legion

REPLY, GOD'S

1. *divine statement:* χρηματισμός CHRĒMATISMOS
Rom 11. 4 But what is God's reply to him?

REPORT

1. *hearing, report:* ἀκοή AKOĒ
Jn 12.38 "Lord, who has believed our report?

2. *bring tidings:* ἀπαγγέλλω APAGGELLŌ
Lk 14.21 "servant . . reported this to his master
Acts 4.23 reported what the chief priests . . had said
5.22 they did not find . . and they . . reported
16.36 the jailer reported the words to Paul
16.38 The police reported these words
28.21 "none . . has reported . . any evil about you
1 Th 1. 9 they themselves report concerning us

3. *disclose, show:* δηλόω DĒLOŌ
1 Cor 1.11 reported to me by Chloe's people

4. *show plainly:* διασαφέω DIASAPHEŌ
Mt 18.31 "they went and reported to their lord

5. *tell in detail:* ἐκδιηγέομαι EKDIĒGEOMAI
Acts 15. 3 reporting the conversion of the Gentiles

6. *make known, proclaim:* ἐξαγγέλλω EXAGGELLŌ
Mk [16.end *But they reported briefly to Peter*‡

7. *word, reckoning:* λόγος LOGOS
Lk 5.15 so much the more the report went abroad
7.17 this report concerning him spread

8. *report, rumor:* φήμη PHĒMĒ*
Mt 9.26 the r. . . went through all that district
Lk 4.14 a report concerning him went out

CONTEXTUALLY
Mk 5.27 She had heard the reports about Jesus
1 Th 3. 6 reported that you always remember us

REPORTED, BE

1. *hear:* ἀκούω (pass.) AKOUŌ
Mk 2. 1 it was reported that he was at home
1 Cor 5. 1 It is actually r. . . there is immorality

REPORTS

1. *sound, noise:* ἦχος ĒCHOS I
Lk 4.37 reports of him went out into every place

REPRESENTATION

1. *mark, inscription:* χάραγμα CHARAGMA
Acts 17.29 "a representation by the art . . of man

REPROACH

1. *admonish, be deeply moved:* ἐμβριμάομαι EMBRIMAOMAI
Mk 14. 5 And they reproached her

2. *insult, treat arrogantly:* ὑβρίζω HYBRIZŌ
Lk 11.45 "Teacher, in saying this you reproach us

3. *reproach:* ὀνειδισμός ONEIDISMOS
Rom 15. 3 "The reproaches of those . . fell on me
1 Tim 3. 7 he may fall into reproach and the snare

4. *reproach:* ὀνειδίζω ONEIDIZŌ
Rom 15. 3 it is written . . "those who reproached thee
Jas 1. 5 God . . gives to all . . without reproaching
1 Pet 4.14 reproached for the name of Christ

5. *reproach, disgrace:* ὄνειδος ONEIDOS*
Lk 1.25 "to take away my reproach among men

REPROACH, ABOVE
REPROACH, FREE FROM
REPROACH, WITHOUT
1. *blameless:* ἀνεπίλημπτος ANEPILĒMPTOS*
1 Tim 3. 2 a bishop must be above reproach
5. 7 so that they may be without reproach
6.14 free from reproach until the appearing

REPROACH, SUFFER
1. *reproach:* ὀνειδίζω (pass.) ONEIDIZŌ
1 Tim [4.10 to this end we toil and *suffer reproach*‡

REPROOF
1. *reproof, rebuke:* ἐλεγμός ELEGMOS*
2 Tim 3.16 All scripture is . . profitable . . for reproof

REPROVE
1. *expose, test, refute:* ἐλέγχω ELEGCHŌ
Lk 3.19 Herod . . had been reproved by him
Tit 2.15 exhort and reprove with all authority
Rev 3.19 " 'whom I love, I reprove and chasten

REPTILE
1. *creeping thing, reptile:* ἑρπετόν HERPETON*
Acts 10.12 In it were all kinds of . . reptiles and birds
11. 6 "Looking at it closely I observed . . reptiles
Rom 1.23 images resembling . . animals or reptiles
Jas 3. 7 every kind of beast and bird, of reptile

REPUTE, GOOD
1. *good repute, good report:* εὐφημία EUPHĒMIA*
2 Cor 6. 8 ⟨we commend ourselves⟩ in . . good repute

REPUTE, ILL
1. *slander:* δυσφημία DYSPHĒMIA*
2 Cor 6. 8 ⟨we commend ourselves⟩ in ill repute

REPUTE, OF GOOD
1. *bear witness, testify:* μαρτυρέω (pass. part.) MARTYREŌ
Acts 6. 3 "pick out . . seven men of good repute

REPUTE, ONE WHO IS OF
REPUTED, ONE WHO IS
1. *think, suppose:* δοκέω (subst. part.) DOKEŌ
Gal 2. 2 I laid before them . . (who were of repute
2. 6 those who were reputed to be something
2. 6 those . . who were of repute added nothing
2. 9 who were reputed to be pillars

REQUEST
1. *request:* αἴτημα AITĒMA
Phil 4. 6 let your requests be made known
1 Jn 5.15 we have obtained the requests made of him

REQUIRE
REQUIRE OF
1. *ask, request:* αἰτέω AITEŌ
Variant to: Lk **12.20**
2. *demand back:* ἀπαιτέω APAITEŌ
Lk 12.20 " 'This night your soul is required of you
Var. AITEŌ
3. *have need:* χρείαν ἔχειν CHREIA [A.6.a.4]
1 Cor 12.24 which . . presentable parts do not require
4. *want, lack, desire:* χρῄζω CHRĒZŌ
Rom 16. 2 whatever she may require from you
5. *seek out:* ἐκζητέω EKZĒTEŌ
Lk 11.50 "blood . . required of this generation
11.51 "it shall be required of this generation
6. *finish, complete:* ἐπιτελέω EPITELEŌ
1 Pet 5. 9 suffering is required of your brotherhood
7. *work, deed:* ἔργον ERGON [A.1.a]
Rom 2.15 They show that what the law requires
8. *seek, desire:* ζητέω ZĒTEŌ
Lk 12.48 "of him will much be required
1 Cor 4. 2 Moreover it is required of stewards
CONTEXTUALLY
Rom 2.14 do by nature what the law requires

REQUIRED, WHAT IS
1. *be proper:* ἀνήκω (subst. part. neut.) ANĒKŌ
Phm . 8 to command you to do what is required

REQUIREMENT
1. *command:* ἐντολή ENTOLĒ
Heb 7.16 not according to a legal requirement

REQUIREMENT, JUST
1. *ordinance, justification:* δικαίωμα DIKAIŌMA
Rom 8. 4 that the just requirement of the law

REQUITE
1. *give up, return:* ἀποδίδωμι APODIDŌMI
2 Tim 4.14 the Lord will requite him for his deeds

RESCUE
1. *take out:* ἐξαιρέω (mid.) EXAIREŌ
Acts 7.10 "rescued him out of all his afflictions
12.11 "Lord has sent his angel and rescued me
23.27 "I came . . with . . soldiers and rescued him
2. *save, rescue:* ῥύομαι RHYOMAI
2 Tim 3.11 yet from them all the Lord rescued me
4.17 I was rescued from the lion's mouth
4.18 Lord will rescue me from every evil
2 Pet 2. 7 if he rescued righteous Lot
2. 9 Lord knows how to rescue the godly

RESEMBLE
1. *make like:* ἀφομοιόω (perf. pass.) APHOMOIOŌ*
Heb 7. 3 resembling the Son of God he continues

RESEMBLING
1. *likeness* ὁμοίωμα HOMOIŌMA [A.1.b.5]
Rom 1.23 images resembling mortal man

RESENTFUL, BE
1. *consider evil:* λογίζεσθαι τὸ κακόν KAKOS; LOGIZOMAI [A.6.a.4]
1 Cor 13. 5 Love . . is not irritable or resentful

RESERVE
1. *keep, observe:* τηρέω TĒREŌ
2 Pet 2.17 for them . . gloom . . has been reserved
Jude .13 for whom . . gloom . . has been reserved

RESIDENT
1. *dwell, settle:* κατοικέω (subst. part.) KATOIKEŌ
Acts 2. 9 "residents of Mesopotamia, Judea
9.35 all the residents of Lydda . . saw him
19.10 all the residents of Asia heard the word
19.17 known to all residents of Ephesus

RESIST
1. *withstand:* ἀνθίστημι ANTHISTĒMI
Mt 5.39 "I say to you, Do not resist one who is evil
Rom 9.19 "For who can resist his will?
13. 2 he . . resists what God has appointed
13. 2 those who resist will incur judgment
Jas 4. 7 R. the devil and he will flee from you
1 Pet 5. 9 Resist him, firm in your faith
2. *set against, oppose:* ἀντικαθίστημι ANTIKATHISTĒMI*
Heb 12. 4 you have not yet resisted to the point
3. *collide, be adverse:* ἀντιπίπτω ANTIPIPTŌ*
Acts 7.51 "you always resist the Holy Spirit
4. *set opposite to:* ἀντιτάσσω (mid.) ANTITASSŌ
Rom 13. 2 Therefore he who resists the authorities
Jas 5. 6 he does not resist you

RESOLVE
1. *wish, will:* βούλομαι BOULOMAI
Mt 1.19 husband . . resolved to divorce her quietly
2. *satisfaction, goodwill:* εὐδοκία EUDOKIA
2 Th 1.11 that our God may . . fulfil every good r.
3. *lay, put:* τίθημι (mid.) TITHĒMI
Acts 19.21 Paul resolved in the Spirit to . . go

RESOURCES
1. *seed, sowing:* σπόρος SPOROS
2 Cor 9.10 will supply and multiply your resources[l]†

RESPECT
1. *put to shame:* ἐντρέπω (pass.) ENTREPŌ
Mt 21.37 "saying, 'They will respect my son
Mk 12. 6 "saying, 'They will respect my son
Lk 20.13 " 'it may be they will respect ⟨my . . son⟩
Heb 12. 9 earthly fathers . . we respected them
2. *know:* οἶδα OIDA
1 Th 5.12 respect those who labor among you

3. *terrify:* φοβέω (pass.) PHOBEŌ
Eph 5.33 let . . wife see that she respects . . husband
4. *fear:* φόβος PHOBOS
Rom 13. 7 Pay all of them their dues, . . respect to whom respect is due
1 Pet 2.18 Servants, be submissive . . with all respect
IDIOMATICALLY
a. 1 Th 4.12 so that you may command the respect of outsiders ἵνα περιπατῆτε εὐσχημόνως πρὸς τοὺς ἔξω [EUSCHĒMONŌS]
CONTEXTUALLY
Tit 2. 7 in all respects a model of good deeds
2. 9 to give satisfaction in every respect
Heb 2.17 made like his brethren in every respect
4.15 who in every respect has been tempted

RESPECT TO, WITH
1. *about, concerning:* περί (+gen.) PERI
Acts 23. 6 "with r. to . . resurrection . . I am on trial
24.21 " 'With r. to the resurrection . . I am on trial

RESPECTED
1. *noble, proper:* εὐσχήμων EUSCHĒMŌN
Mk 15.43 Joseph of A., a r. member of the council

RESPECTFUL
1. *dignity, seriousness:* σεμνότης SEMNOTĒS [B.1.a.1]
1 Tim 2. 2 godly and respectful in every way
3. 4 keeping his children . . r. in every way

REST
1. *make to cease, cause to rest:* ἀναπαύω (mid.) ANAPAUŌ
Mk 6.31 "Come away . . and rest a while
1 Pet 4.14 the spirit . . of God rests upon you
Rev 6.11 they were . . told to rest a little longer
14.13 "that they may rest from their labors!
2. *rest:* ἀνάπαυσις ANAPAUSIS
Mt 11.29 "you will find rest for your souls
12.43 "he passes through . . places seeking rest
Lk 11.24 "he passes through . . places seeking rest
Rev 14.11 "they have no rest, day or night
3. *relief:* ἄνεσις ANESIS
[a]B.3.a.5
2 Cor 2.13 [a]but my mind could not rest
7. 5 bodies had no rest but we were afflicted
2 Th 1. 7 to grant rest . . to you who are afflicted
4. *be:* εἰμί EIMI [B.2.d.1]
1 Cor 2. 5 that your faith . . not rest in the wisdom
Gal 3.12 but the law does not rest on faith
5. *left, remaining:* ἐπίλοιπος EPILOIPOS* [A.3.a.4]
1 Pet 4. 2 so as to live for the rest of the time
6. *be quiet, be at rest:* ἡσυχάζω HĒSYCHAZŌ
Lk 23.56 On the sabbath they rested
7. *stand, set:* ἵστημι (pass.) HISTĒMI
Mt 2. 9 the star . . came to rest . . where the child was
8. *left, remaining:* κατάλοιπος (subst.) KATALOIPOS*
Acts 15.17 " 'that the rest of men may seek the Lord
9. *stop, rest:* καταπαύω KATAPAUŌ
Heb 4. 4 "And God rested on the seventh day
10. *rest, place of rest:* κατάπαυσις KATAPAUSIS*
Acts 7.49 " 'what is the place of my rest?
Heb 3.11 " 'They shall never enter my rest
3.18 that they should never enter his rest
4. 1 the promise of entering his rest remains
4. 3 we who have believed enter that rest
4. 3 " 'They shall never enter my rest
4. 5 "They shall never enter my rest
4.10 whoever enters God's rest . . ceases . . labors
4.11 Let us therefore strive to enter that rest
11. *sit down, seat:* καθίζω KATHIZŌ
Acts 2. 3 tongues as of fire, . . resting on each
12. *remaining, left:* λοιπός LOIPOS
[a]subst. [b]A.3.a.4
Mt 22. 6 [a]"while the rest seized his servants
Mk 16.13 [a]they went back and told the rest[k]‡
Lk 12.26 [a]"why are you anxious about the rest?
24. 9 [a]told all this to the eleven and to all the rest
Acts 2.37 [b]said to Peter and the rest of . . apostles
5.13 [a]None of the rest dared join them
17. 9 [a]security from Jason and the rest
27.44 [a]the r. on planks or . . pieces of the ship
Rom 1.13 [b]as well as among the rest of the Gentiles
11. 7 [a]but the rest were hardened
1 Cor 7.12 [a]To the rest I say, not the Lord
2 Cor 12.13 [b]less favored than the r. of the churches?
Gal 2.13 [b]the rest of the Jews acted insincerely
Phil 1.13 [a]it has become known . . to all the rest
4. 3 [b]and the rest of my fellow workers
1 Tim 5.20 [a]so that the rest may stand in fear
Rev 2.24 [a]" 'But to the rest of you in Thyatira
9.20 [a]The rest of mankind . . did not repent
11.13 [a]the rest were terrified and gave glory
12.17 [a]to make war on the rest of her offspring
19.21 [a]the rest were slain by the sword
20. 5 [a]The rest of . . dead did not come to life
13. *stay, wait:* μένω MENŌ
Jn 3.36 but the wrath of God rests upon him
CONTEXTUALLY
Rom 4.16 that the promise may rest on grace

REST, GIVE
1. *make to cease, cause to rest:* ἀναπαύω ANAPAUŌ
Mt 11.28 "Come to me . . and I will give you rest
2. *stop, rest:* καταπαύω KATAPAUŌ
Heb 4. 8 For if Joshua had given them rest

REST OF MANKIND
REST OF THE PEOPLE
1. *remaining, left:* λοιπός (subst. pl.) LOIPOS
Acts 28. 9 the rest of the people on the island . . came
Eph 2. 3 children of wrath, like the rest of mankind

REST, SABBATH
1. *Sabbath observance:* σαββατισμός SABBATISMOS*
Heb 4. 9 there remains a sabbath r. for the people

REST, SET AT
REST, TAKE
1. *make to cease, cause to rest:* ἀναπαύω ANAPAUŌ
[a]mid.
Mt 26.45 [a]"Are you still sleeping and taking your r.?
Mk 14.41 [a]"Are you still sleeping and taking your r.?
2 Cor 7.13 his mind has been set at rest

REST, TAKING
1. *lying down to sleep:* κοίμησις KOIMĒSIS*
Jn 11.13 thought . . he meant taking rest in sleep

REST UPON
1. *rest upon, rely upon:* ἐπαναπαύομαι EPANAPAUOMAI
Lk 10. 6 "your peace shall rest upon him
2. *dwell upon:* ἐπισκηνόω EPISKĒNOŌ*
2 Cor 12. 9 the power of Christ may rest upon me

RESTLESS
1. *unstable:* ἀκατάστατος AKATASTATOS
Jas 3. 8 the tongue—a r. evil, full of . . poison

RESTORE (*See also* SALTNESS, RESTORE)
1. *renew:* ἀνακαινίζω ANAKAINIZŌ*
Heb 6. 4(6) impossible to r. again to repentance
2. *give up, return:* ἀποδίδωμι APODIDŌMI
Lk 19. 8 "if I have defrauded any . . , I restore it
3. *reestablish, restore:* ἀποκαθίστημι APOKATHISTĒMI*
Mt 12.13 it was restored, whole like the other
17.11 "Elijah does come, . . he is to r. all things
Mk 3. 5 stretched it . . , and his hand was restored
8.25 he looked intently and was restored
9.12 "Elijah does come first to r. all things
Lk 6.10 he did so, and his hand was restored
Acts 1. 6 "will you at this time restore the kingdom?
Heb 13.19 that I may be restored to you . . sooner
4. *put in order, make:* καταρτίζω KATARTIZŌ
Gal 6. 1 restore him in a spirit of gentleness
1 Pet 5.10 God . . will himself restore . . you

RESTRAIN
1. *stop, rest:* καταπαύω KATAPAUŌ
Acts 14.18 they scarcely restrained the people
2. *hold fast, restrain:* κατέχω KATECHŌ
2 Th 2. 6 you know what is restraining him
2. 7 only he who now restrains it will do so
3. *hinder, prevent, withhold:* κωλύω KŌLYŌ
2 Pet 2.16 dumb ass . . restrained . . prophet's madness

RESTRAINT
1. *noose, halter:* βρόχος BROCHOS*
1 Cor 7.35 for your . . benefit, not to lay any r.

RESTRAINT, KEEP UNDER
1. *enclose, close:* συγκλείω SYGKLEIŌ
Gal 3.23 under the law, kept under restraint

RESTRICT
1. *crowd, cramp:* στενοχωρέω STENOCHŌREŌ
2 Cor 6.12 You are not restricted by us, but you are restricted in your own affections

RESUME
IDIOMATICALLY
a. Jn 13.12 When he had . . resumed his place Ὅτε οὖν . . ἀνέπεσεν πάλιν [PALIN]

RESURRECTION
1. *resurrection, rising:* ἀνάστασις ANASTASIS
Mt 22.23 Sadducees . . , who say . . there is no r.
22.28 "In the r. . . to which . . will she be wife?
22.30 "in the resurrection they neither marry
22.31 "as for the r. . . have you not read?
Mk 12.18 Sadducees . . , who say . . there is no r.
12.23 "In the r. whose wife will she be?
Lk 14.14 "You will be repaid at the r. of the just
20.27 Sadducees, . . who say . . there is no r.
20.33 "In the r. . . whose wife will the woman be?
20.35 "accounted worthy to attain . . to the r.
20.36 "sons of God, being sons of the r.
Jn 5.29 "who have done good, to the r. of life
5.29 "who have done evil, to the r. of judgment
11.24 "I know that he will rise again in the r.
11.25 "I am the resurrection and the life[z]
Acts 1.22 "one . . must become . . a witness to his r.
2.31 "he foresaw and spoke of the r.
4. 2 proclaiming in Jesus the r. from the dead
4.33 apostles gave their testimony to the r.
17.18 because he preached Jesus and the r.
17.32 Now when they heard of the r.
23. 6 "with respect to . . the r. . . I am on trial
23. 8 the Sadducees say that there is no r.
24.15 "will be a r. of . . the just and the unjust
24.21 " 'With respect to the r. . . I am on trial
Rom 1. 4 designated Son of God . . by his r.
6. 5 shall . . be united with him in a r. like his
1 Cor 15.12 how can some . . say that there is no r.?
15.13 if there is no resurrection of the dead
15.21 by a man has come also the resurrection
15.42 So is it with the r. of the dead
Phil 3.10 that I may know . . the power of his r.
2 Tim 2.18 holding that the r. is past already
Heb 6. 2 with instruction[k] about . . the resurrection
11.35 Women received their dead by r.
1 Pet 1. 3 born anew to a living hope through the r.
3.21 Baptism . . as an appeal . . through the r.
Rev 20. 5 This is the first resurrection
20. 6 Blessed . . he who shares in the first r.!
2. *awaking:* ἔγερσις EGERSIS*
Mt 27.53 coming out of the tombs after his r.
3. *removal, resurrection:* ἐξανάστασις EXANASTASIS*
Phil 3.11 that if possible I may attain the r.

RETAIN
1. *seize, hold fast:* κρατέω KRATEŌ
Jn 20.23 "if you retain the sins of any, they are retained

RETORT
1. *word, reckoning:* λόγος LOGOS
Acts 7.29 "At this r. Moses fled, and became an exile

RETRIBUTION
1. *repayment:* ἀνταπόδομα ANTAPODOMA
Rom 11. 9 "Let their table become a snare . . and a r.
2. *payment of wages, recompense:* μισθαποδοσία MISTHAPODOSIA
Heb 2. 2 disobedience received a just retribution

RETURN (*See also* EXPECT IN RETURN; INVITE IN RETURN; REVILE IN RETURN)
1. *bend back, return:* ἀνακάμπτω ANAKAMPTŌ*
Mt 2.12 warned in a dream not to r. to Herod
Lk 10. 6 "but if not, it shall return to you
Acts 18.21 "I will return to you if God wills
Heb 11.15 they would have had opportunity to r.
2. *return; behave* (pass.): ἀναστρέφω ANASTREPHŌ
Acts 5.22 the officers . . returned and reported
15.16 " 'After this I will r., and I will rebuild
3. *give up, return:* ἀποδίδωμι APODIDŌMI
1 Pet 3. 9 Do not return evil for evil or reviling
4. *bring up, turn back, put out to sea:* ἐπανάγω EPANAGŌ
Mt 21.18 returning to the city, he was hungry
5. *go back, return:* ἐπανέρχομαι EPANERCHOMAI
Lk 19.15 "he returned, having received the kingdom
6. *turn around, return:* ἐπιστρέφω (act. or aor. pass.) EPISTREPHŌ
Mt 10.13 "if it is not worthy, let your peace return
12.44 "Then he says, 'I will r. to my house
Lk 2.39 returned into Galilee, to . . Nazareth
8.55 her spirit returned, and she got up
Acts 15.36 "let us return and visit the brethren
1 Pet 2.25 you . . have now returned to the Shepherd
7. *come, go:* ἔρχομαι ERCHOMAI
Rom 9. 9 "I will return and Sarah shall have a son
1 Cor 16.11 Speed him . . that he may return to me
8. *turn away, return:* ὑποστρέφω HYPOSTREPHŌ
Lk 1.56 And Mary . . returned to her home
2.20 the shepherds returned, . . praising God
2.43 as they were returning, . . Jesus stayed
2.45 they returned to Jerusalem, seeking him
4. 1 Jesus, full of the . . Spirit, returned
4.14 Jesus returned in . . power of the Spirit
7.10 those who had been sent returned
8.37 so he got into the boat and returned
8.39 "Return to your home, and declare
8.40 when Jesus returned, the crowd welcomed
9.10 On their return the apostles told him
10.17 The seventy[g] returned with joy
11.24 "finding none he says, 'I will return
17.18 "Was no one found to r. and give praise?
19.12 "went . . to receive a kingdom and then r.
23.48 all the multitudes . . returned home
23.56 then they returned, and prepared spices
24. 9 returning from the tomb they told
24.33 they rose that same hour and returned
24.52 returned to Jerusalem with great joy
Acts 1.12 Then they returned to Jerusalem
8.25 when they had testified . . they returned
8.28 ⟨an Ethiopian, a eunuch⟩ was returning
12.25 Barnabas and Saul returned
13.13 John left . . and returned to Jerusalem
13.34 "raised him from the dead, no more to r.
14.21 they returned to Lystra and to I.
20. 3 he determined to r. through Macedonia
21. 6 we went on board . . and they returned
22.17 "When I had returned to Jerusalem
23.32 they returned to the barracks
Gal 1.17 and again I returned to Damascus
Heb 7. 1 Abraham returning from the slaughter
9. *fruit, profit:* καρπός KARPOS
Rom 6.21 what return did you get from the things?
6.22 the return you get is sanctification
10. *enter again:* εἰσέρχομαι πάλιν EISERCHOMAI; PALIN [A.6.a.4]
Mk 2. 1 when he returned to Capernaum
11. *go out again:* πάλιν ἐξέρχομαι EXERCHOMAI; PALIN [A.6.a.4]
Mk 7.31 Then he returned from . . Tyre
12. *bring together:* συνάγω (pass.) SYNAGŌ
Mk 6.30 apostles returned to Jesus, and told him
IDIOMATICALLY
a. 2 Cor 6.13 In return—I speak as to children τὴν δὲ αὐτὴν ἀντιμισθίαν, ὡς τέκνοις λέγω [ANTIMISTHIA]

RETURN FOR, S. IN
1. *what is given in exchange for:* ἀντάλλαγμα (+gen.) ANTALLAGMA*
Mt 16.26 "what shall a man give in return for his life?

Mk 8.37 "what can a man give in return for his life?

RETURN, SOME
1. *recompense:* ἀμοιβή (pl.) AMOIBĒ*
1 Tim 5. 4 let them . . make some r. to their parents

REU: Ῥαγαύ 'rē,ü, 'rü
Lk 3.35 Serug, the son of R., the son of Peleg

REUBEN: Ῥουβήν 'rübən
Rev 7. 5 twelve thousand of the tribe of R.

REVEAL
1. *revelation, uncovering:* ἀποκάλυψις APOKALYPSIS [A.1.a]
Rom 2. 5 God's . . judgment will be revealed
2 Th 1. 7 when the Lord Jesus is revealed
1 Pet 4.13 be glad when his glory is revealed
2. *uncover, reveal:* ἀποκαλύπτω APOKALYPTŌ
Mt 10.26 "nothing . . that will not be revealed
11.25 "that thou hast . . revealed them to babes
11.27 "to whom the Son chooses to reveal him
16.17 "flesh and blood has not revealed this
Lk 2.35 "thoughts . . of many hearts may be revealed
10.21 "that thou hast . . revealed them to babes
10.22 "to whom the Son chooses to r. him
12. 2 "Nothing . . that will not be revealed
17.30 "when the Son of man is revealed
Jn 12.38 "to whom has . . arm . . been revealed?
Rom 1.17 "the righteousness of God is revealed
1.18 wrath of God is revealed from heaven
8.18 the glory that is to be revealed to us
1 Cor 2.10 God has revealed . . through the Spirit
3.13 because it will be revealed with fire
Gal 1.16 was pleased to reveal his Son to[c] me
3.23 under restraint until faith . . be revealed
Eph 3. 5 now . . revealed to his holy apostles
Phil 3.15 God will reveal that also to you
2 Th 2. 3 man of lawlessness[a] is revealed
2. 6 so that he may be revealed in his time
2. 8 then the lawless one will be revealed
1 Pet 1. 5 a salvation ready to be revealed
1.12 revealed . . that they were serving . . you
5. 1 a partaker in the glory . . to be revealed
3. *negotiate, order:* χρηματίζω CHRĒMATIZŌ
Lk 2.26 revealed to him by the Holy Spirit
4. *make manifest, make known:* φανερόω PHANEROŌ
Jn 1.31 "that he might be revealed to Israel
21. 1 After this Jesus revealed himself again . . ; and he revealed himself in this way
21.14 the third time that Jesus was revealed
2 Cor 7.12 that your zeal for us might be revealed
Rev 15. 4 "for thy judgments have been revealed

REVEALING
1. *revelation, uncovering:* ἀποκάλυψις APOKALYPSIS
Rom 8.19 waits . . for the r. of the sons of God
1 Cor 1. 7 not lacking . . as you wait for the revealing

REVEL
1. *delight in:* ἐντρυφάω ENTRYPHAŌ*
2 Pet 2.13 reveling in their dissipation[g]
2. *softness, indulgence:* τρυφή TRYPHĒ [A.1.d]
2 Pet 2.13 They count it pleasure to revel

REVELATION
1. *revelation, uncovering:* ἀποκάλυψις APOKALYPSIS
Lk 2.32 "a light for revelation to the Gentiles
Rom 16.25 according to the r. of the mystery
1 Cor 14. 6 unless I bring you some revelation
14.26 each one has a hymn, a lesson, a r.
2 Cor 12. 1 I will go on to visions and revelations
12. 7 elated by . . abundance of revelations
Gal 1.12 it came through a r. of Jesus Christ
2. 2 I went up by r.; and I laid before them
Eph 1.17 a spirit of wisdom and of revelation
3. 3 the mystery . . made known to me by r.
1 Pet 1. 7 honor at the revelation of Jesus Christ
1.13 grace . . coming . . at the r. of Jesus Christ
Rev 1. 1 The r. of Jesus Christ, which God gave him

REVELATION, MAKE A
1. *uncover, reveal:* ἀποκαλύπτω APOKALYPTŌ
1 Cor 14.30 If a revelation is made to another

REVELING
REVELS
1. *revelry:* κῶμος (pl.) KŌMOS
Rom 13.13 let us conduct ourselves . . not in reveling
1 Pet 4. 3 Let the time . . past suffice for . . revels

REVENUE
1. *end, goal:* τέλος TELOS
Rom 13. 7 Pay all of them their dues, . . revenue to whom revenue is due

REVERENCE
1. *discretion, reverence:* εὐλάβεια EULABEIA
Heb 12.28 offer . . acceptable worship, with r.
2. *make sacred:* ἁγιάζω HAGIAZŌ
1 Pet 3.15 but in your hearts reverence Christ
3. *fear:* φόβος PHOBOS
Eph 5.21 Be subject to one another out of r.
1 Pet 3.15(16) yet do it with gentleness and r.

REVERENT
1. *holy, reverent:* ἱεροπρεπής HIEROPREPĒS*
Tit 2. 3 Bid the older women likewise to be r.
2. *fear:* φόβος PHOBOS [B.1.a.1]
1 Pet 3. 2 when they see your reverent . . behavior

REVILE
1. *slander, blaspheme:* βλασφημέω BLASPHĒMEŌ
Lk 22.65 they spoke many other words . . , reviling him
Acts 13.45 Jews . . filled with jealousy . . reviled him
18. 6 when they opposed and reviled him
2 Pet 2. 2 the way of truth will be reviled
2.10 not afraid to revile the glorious ones
2.12 reviling in matters . . they are ignorant
Jude . 8 these men . . revile the glorious ones[c]
.10 r. whatever they do not understand
2. *threaten, disparage, mistreat:* ἐπηρεάζω EPĒREAZŌ
1 Pet 3.16 those who revile your good behavior
3. *abuse, revile:* λοιδορέω LOIDOREŌ*
Jn 9.28 reviled him, saying, "You are his disciple
Acts 23. 4 "Would you revile God's high priest?
1 Cor 4.12 When reviled, we bless
1 Pet 2.23 When . . reviled, he did not . . in return
4. *abuse, reproach:* λοιδορία LOIDORIA [B.1.a.2]
1 Tim 5.14 give the enemy no occasion to revile us
5. *reproach:* ὀνειδίζω ONEIDIZŌ
Mt 5.11 "Blessed are you when men revile you
27.44 robbers . . reviled him in the same way
Mk 15.32 Those . . crucified with him . . reviled him
Lk 6.22 "when they exclude you and revile you

REVILE IN RETURN
1. *abuse in return:* ἀντιλοιδορέω ANTILOIDOREŌ*
1 Pet 2.23 he did not revile in return

REVILER
1. *abusive person:* λοίδορος LOIDOROS*
1 Cor 5.11 an idolater, reviler, drunkard
6.10 nor drunkards, nor revilers, nor robbers

REVILING
1. *slander, profane speech:* βλασφημία (gen.) BLASPHĒMIA
Jude . 9 did not . . pronounce a reviling judgment
2. *blasphemous, slanderous:* βλάσφημος BLASPHĒMOS
2 Pet 2.11 angels . . do not pronounce a r. judgment
3. *abuse, reproach:* λοιδορία LOIDORIA
1 Pet 3. 9 Do not return evil for evil or reviling for reviling but on the contrary bless

REVIVE
1. *grow up again, revive:* ἀναθάλλω ANATHALLŌ*
Phil 4.10 you have revived your concern for me
2. *come to life again:* ἀναζάω ANAZAŌ
Rom 7. 9 the commandment came, sin revived

REVOLT, STIR UP A
1. *upset, disturb:* ἀναστατόω ANASTATOŌ
Acts 21.38 "Egyptian . . recently stirred up a revolt

REWARD
1. *retribution:* ἀνταπόδοσις ANTAPODOSIS*
Col 3.24 will receive the inheritance as your r.
2. *give up, return:* ἀποδίδωμι APODIDŌMI
Mt 6. 4 "Father who sees in secret will r. you

Mt 6. 6 "Father who sees in secret will r. you
6.18 "Father who sees in secret will r. you
3. *payment of wages, recompense:* μισθαποδοσία MISTHAPODOSIA
Heb 10.35 confidence, which has a great reward
11.26 for he looked to the reward
4. *be a rewarder:* μισθαποδότης γίνεσθαι MISTHAPODOTĒS* [A.6.a.3]
Heb 11. 6 he rewards those who seek him
5. *reward, wages:* μισθός MISTHOS
[a]διδόναι τὸν μισθὸν
Mt 5.12 "be glad, for your r. is great in heaven
5.46 "if you love those . . , what r. have you?
6. 1 "for then you will have no reward
6. 2 "Truly, . . they have received their reward
6. 5 "Truly, . . they have received their reward
6.16 "Truly, . . they have received their reward
10.41 he . . shall receive a prophet's reward
10.41 "he . . shall receive a righteous man's r.
10.42 "I say to you, he shall not lose his reward
Mk 9.41 "whoever gives . . will by no means lose . . r.
Lk 6.23 "behold, your r. is great in heaven
6.35 "lend, . . and your reward will be great
Acts 1.18 "(this man bought a field with the r.
1 Cor 3.14 If the work . . survives, he will receive a r.
9.17 if . . of my own will, I have a reward
9.18 What then is my reward? Just this
2 Jn . 8 Look . . that you . . may win a full reward
Rev 11.18 [a]"the time . . for rewarding thy servants

REWARD, DUE
1. *worthy:* ἄξιος (subst. pl.) AXIOS
Lk 23.41 "receiving the due reward of our deeds

RHEGIUM: Ῥήγιον 'rējəm II,C-3
Acts 28.13 we made a circuit and arrived at R.

RHESA: Ῥησά 'rēsə
Lk 3.27 Rhesa, the son of Zerubbabel

RHODA: Ῥόδη 'rōdə
Acts 12.13 a maid named Rhoda came to answer

RHODES: Ῥόδος 'rōdz II,E-3
Acts 21. 1 we came . . the next day to Rhodes

RICH
1. *fatness, wealth:* πιότης (gen.) PIOTĒS
Rom [11.17 grafted in . . to share the *rich root*†‡
2. *wealthy:* πλούσιος PLOUSIOS*
Mt 19.23 "hard for a r. man to enter the kingdom
19.24 "than for a r. man to enter the kingdom
27.57 there came a r. man from Arimathea
Mk 10.25 "than for a r. man to enter the kingdom
12.41 Many rich people put in large sums
Lk 6.24 "But woe to you that are rich
12.16 "The land of a rich man brought forth
14.12 "do not invite your . . rich neighbors
16. 1 "There was a r. man who had a steward
16.19 "a rich man, . . clothed in purple
16.21 "what fell from the rich man's table
16.22 "The rich man also died and was buried
18.23 he became sad, for he was very rich
18.25 "than for a r. man to enter the kingdom
19. 2 he was a chief tax collector, and rich
21. 1 He . . saw the rich putting their gifts
2 Cor 8. 9 though he was rich, yet for your sake
Eph 2. 4 But God, who is rich in mercy
1 Tim 6.17 As for the rich in this world
Jas 1.10 the r. in his humiliation . . will pass away
1.11 So will the rich man fade away
2. 5 chosen those who are poor . . to be rich
2. 6 Is it not the rich who oppress you?
5. 1 Come now, you rich, weep and howl
Rev 2. 9 "I know . . your poverty (but you are r.
3.17 " 'you say, I am rich, I have prospered
6.15 Then . . the rich . . hid in the caves
13.16 it causes . . both rich and poor . . to be marked
3. *be rich, become rich:* πλουτέω (part.) PLOUTEŌ
Lk 1.53 "the rich he has sent empty away
12.21 "So is he who . . is not rich toward God

RICH, BE
RICH, BECOME
RICH, GROW
RICHES, BESTOW ONE'S
1. *be rich, become rich:* πλουτέω PLOUTEŌ
Rom 10.12 same Lord . . bestows his riches upon all
1 Cor 4. 8 Already you have become rich!
2 Cor 8. 9 that by his poverty you might become rich
1 Tim 6. 9 who desire to be r. fall into temptation
6.18 They are . . to be rich in good deeds
Rev 3.18 " 'buy from me gold . . that you may be rich
18. 3 "merchants of the earth have grown rich
18.19 "all who had ships at sea grew rich!

RICH, MAKE
1. *make wealthy:* πλουτίζω PLOUTIZŌ
2 Cor 6.10 as poor, yet making many rich

RICHES
1. *property, money* (pl.): χρῆμα CHRĒMA
Mk 10.23 "How hard . . for those who have riches!
[10.24 "how hard . . *for those who trust in riches*‡
Lk 18.24 "How hard . . for those who have riches!
2. *riches, wealth:* πλοῦτος PLOUTOS
Mt 13.22 "the delight in riches choke the word
Mk 4.19 "the delight in riches . . choke the word
Lk 8.14 "they are choked by the cares and riches
Rom 2. 4 do you presume upon the riches?
9.23 in order to make known the riches
11.12 if their trespass means r. for . . world
11.12 if their failure means r. for . . Gentiles
11.33 O the depth of the riches and wisdom!
Eph 1. 7 according to the riches of his grace
1.18 what are the r. of his . . inheritance
2. 7 that . . he might show the . . r. of his grace
3. 8 grace was given, to preach . . r. of Christ
3.16 that according to the r. of his glory
Phil 4.19 according to his r. in glory in Christ
Col 1.27 how great . . are the riches of the glory
2. 2 all the r. of assured understanding
1 Tim 6.17 not . . to set their hopes on uncertain r.
Jas 5. 2 Your riches have rotted

RICHLY
1. *abundantly:* πλουσίως PLOUSIŌS*
Col 3.16 Let the word of Christ dwell in you r.
1 Tim 6.17 God who r. furnishes us . . everything
Tit 3. 6 which he poured out upon us richly
2 Pet 1.11 there will be richly provided for you

RICHNESS
1. *fatness, wealth:* πιότης PIOTĒS*
Rom 11.17 grafted . . to share the r.[o] of . . olive tree†‡

RIDE
1. *go, walk:* πορεύομαι POREUOMAI [A.6.a.5]
Lk 19.36 as he rode . . , they spread their garments
IDIOMATICALLY
a. Acts 23.24 "Also provide mounts for Paul to ride, and bring him safely to Felix κτήνη τε παραστῆσαι, ἵνα ἐπιβιβάσαντες τὸν Παῦλον διασώσωσι πρὸς Φ. [EPIBIBAZŌ]

RIDER
1. *sit down:* κάθημαι (subst. part.) KATHĒMAI [A.6.a.4]
[a]+ἐπί [b]+ἐπάνω
Rev 6. 2 [a]a white horse, and its rider had a bow
6. 4 [a]its rider was permitted to take peace
6. 5 [a]its rider had a balance in his hand
6. 8 [b]horse, . . its rider's name was Death
9.17 [a]the riders wore breastplates
19.18 [a]"to eat . . flesh of horses and their riders

RIGHT (*See also* TIME, RIGHT)
1. *good:* ἀγαθός AGATHOS
1 Pet 3.11 "let him turn away from evil and do r.
3.13 if you are zealous for what is right
2. *truth:* ἀλήθεια ALĒTHEIA
1 Cor 13. 6 ⟨Love⟩ rejoices in the right
3. *pleasing:* ἀρεστός ARESTOS
Acts 6. 2 "It is not r. that we . . give up preaching

4. *right:* δεξιός DEXIOS
ªἐκ δεξιῶν
Mt 5.29 "If your right eye causes you to sin
5.30 "if your right hand causes you to sin
5.39 "if any . . strikes you on the right cheek
27.38 ªone on the right and one on the left
Mk 15.27 ªone on his right and one on his left[g]
Lk 6. 6 man . . whose right hand was withered
22.50 struck the slave . . and cut off his r. ear
23.33 ªone on the right and one on the left
Jn 18.10 struck the . . slave and cut off his r. ear
21. 6 "Cast the net on the right side
Acts 3. 7 took him by the r. hand and raised him
Rev 1.16 in his right hand he held seven stars
10. 2 And he set his right foot on the sea
10. 5 angel . . lifted up his r. hand to heaven
13.16 marked on the r. hand or the forehead
5. *righteous, just:* δίκαιος DIKAIOS
Mt 20. 4 " 'whatever is right I will give you
Lk 12.57 "judge for yourselves what is right
Jn 7.24 "judge with right judgment
Acts 4.19 "Whether it is right in the sight of God
Eph 6. 1 obey your parents . . for this is right
Phil 1. 7 It is right for me to feel thus
2 Pet 1.13 right, as long as I am in this body[c]
6. *righteousness, justice:* δικαιοσύνη DIKAIOSYNĒ
1 Jn 2.29 every one who does right is born of him
3. 7 He who does right is righteous
3.10 whoever does not do right is not of God
Rev 22.11 "Let . . the righteous still do right
7. *straight:* εὐθύς EUTHYS I
Acts 8.21 "your heart is not right before God
2 Pet 2.15 Forsaking . . r. way they have gone astray
8. *authority, power:* ἐξουσία EXOUSIA
Rom 9.21 Has the potter no right over the clay?
1 Cor 9. 4 Do we not have the right to our food?
9. 5 the right to be accompanied by a wife[n]
9. 6 is it only . . I who have no r. to refrain?
9.12 we have not made use of this right
9.18 not making full use of my right
2 Th 3. 9 not because we have not that right
Heb 13.10 from which those . . have no r. to eat
Rev 22.14 that they may have the r. to the tree
9. *good, beautiful:* καλός KALOS
Mk 7.27 "it is not r. to take the children's bread
Rom 7.18 I can will what is r., but I cannot do it
7.21 when I want to do r., evil lies close
14.21 it is right not to eat meat or drink wine
2 Cor 13. 7 we pray . . that you may do what is right
Jas 4.17 knows what is right . . and fails to do it
10. *well, rightly:* καλῶς KALŌS [A.4.a]
Jn 4.17 "You are r. in saying . . 'no husband
8.48 Jews answered him, "Are we not right?
Acts 28.25 "The Holy Spirit was right in saying
11. *rightly:* ὀρθῶς ORTHŌS
Lk 10.28 "You have answered right; do this
IDIOMATICALLY
a. 1 Cor 15.34 Come to your right mind ἐκνήψατε δικαίως [DIKAIŌS]
CONTEXTUALLY
1 Cor 9.15 have made no use of any of these rights

RIGHT, BE
1. *say rightly:* καλῶς λέγειν KALŌS [B.2.d.1]
Jn 13.13 "and you are right, for so I am

RIGHT, DO
1. *do good:* ἀγαθοποιέω AGATHOPOIEŌ
1 Pet 2.15 by doing right you . . silence . . foolish men
2.20 when you do right and suffer for it
3. 6 if you do right and let nothing terrify you
3.17 it is better to suffer for doing right
2. *doing good:* ἀγαθοποιΐα AGATHOPOIIA* [B.1.a.3]
1 Pet 4.19 let those who suffer . . do right and entrust

RIGHT HAND
1. *right:* δεξιός DEXIOS [B.3.b.2]
ªἐκ δεξιῶν
Mt 6. 3 "not . . know what your right hand is doing
20.21 ª"sons . . may sit, one at your right hand
20.23 ª"to sit at my right hand and at my left
22.44 ª" 'Sit at my right hand, till I put
25.33 ª"he will place the sheep at his r. hand
25.34 ª"to those at his right hand, 'Come
26.64 ª"Son of man seated at the right hand
27.29 they . . put a reed in his right hand
Mk 10.37 ª"Grant us to sit, one at your right hand
10.40 ª"to sit at my right hand or at my left
12.36 ª" 'The Lord said . . Sit at my right hand
14.62 ª"sitting at the right hand of Power
16.19 ªLord Jesus . . sat . . at the right hand[k]‡
Lk 20.42 ª" 'The Lord said . . Sit at my right hand
22.69 ª"seated at the right hand of the power
Acts 2.25 ª" 'for he is at my right hand
2.33 ª"exalted at the right hand of God
2.34 ª" 'The Lord said . . Sit at my right hand
5.31 "God exalted him at his right hand
7.55 ªJesus standing at the right hand of God
7.56 ª"Son of man standing at the right hand
Rom 8.34 who is at the right hand of God
2 Cor 6. 7 for the right hand and for the left
Gal 2. 9 gave to me . . right hand of fellowship
Eph 1.20 made him sit at his right hand
Col 3. 1 where Christ is, seated at the r. hand
Heb 1. 3 he sat down at the right hand
1.13 ª"Sit at my right hand
8. 1 seated at the right hand of the throne
10.12 he sat down at the right hand of God
12. 2 at the right hand of the throne of God
1 Pet 3.22 at the right hand of God, with angels
Rev 1.17 But he laid his right hand upon me
1.20 "stars which you saw in my right hand
2. 1 " 'holds the seven stars in his right hand
5. 1 in the right hand of him . . on the throne
5. 7 took the scroll from the right hand

RIGHT, HAVE A
1. *one must:* δεῖ DEI
Tit 1.11 what they have no right to teach

RIGHT INTO
IDIOMATICALLY
a. Mk 14.54 followed him . . right into the courtyard
ἠκολούθησεν αὐτῷ ἕως ἔσω εἰς τὴν αὐλὴν [ESŌ; HEŌS]

RIGHT MIND, BE IN ONE'S
RIGHT MIND, IN ONE'S
1. *be of sound mind:* σωφρονέω SŌPHRONEŌ
ªpass. part.
Mk 5.15 ªdemoniac . . clothed and in his r. mind
Lk 8.35 ªfound the man . . clothed and in his r. mind
2 Cor 5.13 if we are in our right mind, it is for you

RIGHT, ONE WHO DOES
1. *doing good:* ἀγαθοποιός (subst.) AGATHOPOIOS*
1 Pet 2.14 sent . . to praise those who do right

RIGHT SIDE
1. *right:* δεξιός DEXIOS [B.3.b.2]
ªἐκ δεξιῶν
Mk 16. 5 a young man sitting on the right side
Lk 1.11 ªthe Lord standing on the right side

RIGHT, WHAT IS
1. *righteousness, justice:* δικαιοσύνη DIKAIOSYNĒ
Acts 10.35 "any one who . . does what is r. is acceptable
Eph 5. 9 (light is found in all that is good and r.

RIGHT, YOU ARE
1. *well, rightly:* καλῶς KALŌS
Mk 12.32 "You are right, Teacher

RIGHTEOUS
1. *righteous, just:* δίκαιος DIKAIOS
Mt 9.13 "I came not to call the righteous
10.41 "he who receives a righteous man because he is a righteous man shall receive a righteous man's reward
13.17 "r. men longed to see what you see
13.43 "the righteous will shine like the sun
13.49 "angels will . . separate the evil from the r.
23.28 "So you also outwardly appear righteous

Mt 23.29 "you . . adorn the monuments of the r.
23.35 "upon you . . all the r. blood shed on earth
25.37 "the r. will answer . . 'when did we see thee?
25.46 "but the righteous into eternal life
27.19 "Have nothing to do with that r. man
[27.24 "innocent of this *righteous* blood‡
[27.24 "innocent of this *righteous* man's blood‡
Mk 2.17 "I came not to call the r., but sinners
6.20 knowing that he was a righteous . . man
Lk 1. 6 they were both righteous before God
2.25 Simeon . . was righteous and devout
5.32 "I have not come to call the righteous
15. 7 "r. persons who need no repentance
18. 9 they were righteous and despised others
23.50 Joseph . . of Arimathea . . , a . . r. man
Jn 17.25 "r. Father, the world has not known thee
Acts 3.14 "you denied the Holy and R. One
7.52 "announced . . the coming of the R. One
Rom 1.17 "He who through faith is righteous†
2.13 it is not the hearers . . who are r.
3.10 "None is righteous, no, not one
3.26 to prove . . that he himself is righteous
5. 7 one will hardly die for a righteous man
5.19 by one . . many will be made righteous
Gal 3.11 "He who through faith is r. shall live[f]†
2 Th 1. 5 evidence of the r. judgment of God
2 Tim 4. 8 the Lord, the righteous judge, will award
Heb 10.38 "my righteous one shall live by faith
11. 4 Abel . . received approval as righteous
Jas 5. 6 you have killed the righteous man
5.16 prayer of a r. man has great power
1 Pet 3.12 "eyes of the Lord are upon the r.
3.18 Christ . . died[h] . . , the r. for . . unrighteous
4.18 "If the righteous man is scarcely saved
2 Pet 2. 7 if he rescued righteous Lot
2. 8 (by what that righteous man saw and heard . . , he was vexed in his r. soul
1 Jn 2. 1 we have an advocate . . , Jesus Christ the r.
2.29 If you know that he is righteous
3. 7 let no one deceive you. He who does right is righteous, as he is righteous
3.12 his . . deeds were evil and his brother's r.
Rev 22.11 "the righteous still do right

2. *justly, rightly:* δικαίως DIKAIŌS [A.4.a]
1 Th 2.10 how holy and r. . . was our behavior to you

3. *straightness, righteousness:* εὐθύτης (gen.) EUTHYTĒS*
Heb 1. 8 "the righteous scepter is . . of thy[b] kingdom

RIGHTEOUS DEED

1. *ordinance, justification:* δικαίωμα DIKAIŌMA
Rev 19. 8 "the fine linen is the r. deeds of the saints

RIGHTEOUS JUDGMENT

1. *righteous judgment:* δικαιοκρισία DIKAIOKRISIA*
Rom 2. 5 when God's r. judgment will be revealed

RIGHTEOUS, RECKON

1. *justify, vindicate:* δικαιόω DIKAIOŌ
Gal [2.16 know . . a man is not *reckoned righteous*†

RIGHTEOUSNESS

1. *righteousness, justice:* δικαιοσύνη DIKAIOSYNĒ
Mt 3.15 "thus it is fitting for us to fulfil all r.
5. 6 "Blessed are those who hunger . . for r.
5.10 "persecuted for righteousness' sake
5.20 "unless your r. exceeds that of . . scribes
6.33 "But seek first his kingdom and his r.
21.32 "John came to you in the way of r.
Lk 1.75 "in . . r. before him all . . our life
Jn 16. 8 "convince[x] the world concerning . . r.
16.10 "r., because I go to the Father
Acts 13.10 "you enemy of all righteousness
17.31 "he will judge the world in r.
Rom 1.17 in it the r. of God is revealed
3.21 now the r. of God has been manifested
3.22 the righteousness of God through faith
3.25 This was to show God's righteousness
4. 3 "it was reckoned to him as righteousness
4. 5 his faith is reckoned as righteousness
4. 6 the man to whom God reckons r.
Rom 4. 9 faith was reckoned to Abraham as r.
4.11 circumcision as a . . seal of the r.
4.11 who thus have r. reckoned to them
4.13 The promise . . through the r. of faith
4.22 his faith was "reckoned to him as r.
5.17 who receive . . the free gift of r.
5.21 that . . grace also might reign through r.
6.13 yield yourselves . . as instruments of r.
6.16 obedience, which leads to righteousness
6.18 free from sin, have become slaves of r.
6.19 so now yield your members to r.
6.20 slaves of sin, you were free in regard to r.
8.10 your spirits are alive because of r.
9.30 Gentiles who did not pursue r. have attained it, that is, r. through faith
9.31 the righteousness which is based on law
10. 3 ignorant of the r. that comes from God, . . they did not submit to God's r.
10. 5 the man who practices the righteousness
10. 6 the righteousness based on faith says
14.17 the kingdom of God is not food . . but r.
1 Cor 1.30 Christ Jesus, whom God made our . . r.
2 Cor 3. 9 the dispensation of r. must far exceed
5.21 that . . we might become the r. of God
6. 7 weapons of r. for the right hand
6.14 what partnership have r. and iniquity?
9. 9 "his righteousness[k] endures for ever†
9.10 He . . will . . increase the harvest of your r.[k]†
11.15 disguise themselves as servants of r.
Gal [2.21 for if *righteousness* were through the law†
3. 6 "it was reckoned to him as r.
3.21 then r. would indeed be by the law
5. 5 we wait for the hope of righteousness
Eph 4.24 created after the likeness of God in . . r.
6.14 put on the breastplate of righteousness
Phil 1.11 filled with the fruits of righteousness
3. 6 as to r. under the law blameless
3. 9 not having a righteousness of my own, . . but . . the r. from God that depends on faith
1 Tim 6.11 aim at righteousness, godliness, faith
2 Tim 2.22 shun youthful passions and aim at r.
3.16 All scripture is . . profitable . . for training in r.
4. 8 there is laid up for me the crown of r.
Tit 3. 5 not because of deeds done by us in r.
Heb 1. 9 "Thou hast loved righteousness
5.13 one who lives on milk is unskilled in . . r.
7. 2 He is first, by translation . . , king of r.
11. 7 Noah . . became an heir of . . r.
12.11 later it yields the peaceful fruit of r.
Jas 1.20 anger of man does not work the r. of God
2.23 "it was reckoned to him as righteousness
3.18 the harvest of r. is sown in peace
1 Pet 2.24 that we might die to sin and live to r.
3.14 if you do suffer for righteousness' sake
2 Pet 1. 1 faith of equal standing with ours in . . r.
2. 5 Noah, a herald of righteousness
2.21 better for them never to have known . . r.
3.13 a new earth in which r. dwells
Rev 19.11 "in r. he judges and makes war

RIGHTEOUSNESS, ACT OF

1. *ordinance, justification:* δικαίωμα DIKAIŌMA
Rom 5.18 one man's act of r. leads to acquittal

RIGHTFUL CLAIM

1. *authority, power:* ἐξουσία EXOUSIA
1 Cor 9.12 If others share this r. claim upon you

RIGHTLY

1. *truth:* ἀλήθεια ALĒTHEIA [B.1.a.1]
Rom 2. 2 judgment of God r. falls upon those

2. *well, rightly:* καλῶς KALŌS
Jn 18.23 "if I have spoken r., why do you strike?

3. *rightly:* ὀρθῶς ORTHŌS
Lk 7.43 he said to him, "You have judged r.
20.21 "we know that you speak and teach r.

RIGHTLY HANDLE

1. *cut in a straight line:* ὀρθοτομέω ORTHOTOMEŌ*
2 Tim 2.15 rightly handling the word of truth

RIGHTS, CONJUGAL
1. *debt, one's due:* ὀφειλή OPHEILĒ
1 Cor 7. 3 should give to his wife her conjugal r.

RIGID, BECOME
1. *dry up:* ξηραίνω (pass.) XĒRAINŌ
Mk 9.18 "wherever it seizes him, . . he . . becomes rigid

RIGOR OF DEVOTION
1. *self-chosen religion:* ἐθελοθρησκία ETHELOTHRĒSKIA*
Col 2.23 wisdom in promoting rigor of devotion

RIGOR, WITH
1. *bring to an end:* συντελέω (part.) SYNTELEŌ
Rom 9.28 "Lord will execute his sentence . . with r.

RING
1. *ring:* δακτύλιος DAKTYLIOS*
Lk 15.22 "the father said . . 'put a ring on his hand

RINGLEADER
1. *chief, leader:* πρωτοστάτης PRŌTOSTATĒS*
Acts 24. 5 "a r. of the sect of the Nazarenes

RINGS, WITH GOLD
1. *with a gold ring:* χρυσοδακτύλιος CHRYSODAKTYLIOS*
Jas 2. 2 man with gold rings and in fine clothing

RIOT
1. *noise, uproar:* θόρυβος THORYBOS
Mt 27.24 Pilate saw . . that a riot was beginning

RIOTING
1. *standing, uprising:* στάσις STASIS
Acts 19.40 "in danger of being charged with rioting

RIPE, BE
1. *be ripe:* ἀκμάζω AKMAZŌ*
Rev 14.18 gather the clusters . . , for . . grapes are r.
2. *give up, allow:* παραδίδωμι PARADIDŌMI
Mk 4.29 "the grain is ripe, . . he puts in the sickle

RIPE, BE FULLY
1. *dry up:* ξηραίνω (pass.) XĒRAINŌ
Rev 14.15 "the harvest of the earth is fully ripe

RISE
1. *go up, come up:* ἀναβαίνω ANABAINŌ
Lk 24.38 "why do questionings r. in your hearts?
Rev 8. 4 the incense rose with the prayers
9. 2 from the shaft rose smoke
13. 1 I saw a beast rising out of the sea
13.11 beast which rose out of the earth
2. *first of the resurrection:* πρῶτος ἐξ ἀναστάσεως ANASTASIS [B.1.a.2]
Acts 26.23 "by being the first to rise from the dead
3. *make to rise:* ἀνατέλλω ANATELLŌ
Mt 13. 6 "when the sun rose they were scorched
Mk 4. 6 "when the sun rose it was scorched
16. 2 went to the tomb when the sun had risen
Lk 12.54 "When you see a cloud rising in the west
Jas 1.11 the sun rises with its scorching heat
2 Pet 1.19 the morning star rises in your hearts
4. *raise up, rise:* ἀνίστημι ANISTĒMI
Mt 9. 9 And he rose and followed him
Mk 1.35 he rose and went out to a lonely place
2.14 And he rose and followed him
8.31 be killed, and after three days rise again
9. 9 until the Son of man should have risen
9.10 what the rising from the dead meant
9.31 "when . . killed, after three days he will rise
10.34 "and after three days he will rise
12.25 "For when they rise from the dead
16. 9 when he rose early on the first day[k]‡
Lk 4.39 immediately she rose and served them
5.25 immediately he rose before them
5.28 left everything, and rose and followed
6. 8 "Come . ." And he rose and stood there
9. 8 that one of the old prophets had risen
9.19 "that one of the old prophets has risen
16.31 " 'if some one should rise from the dead
17.19 he said to him, "Rise and go your way
Lk 18.33 "and on the third day he will rise
22.45 when he rose from prayer, he came
22.46 "Why do you sleep? Rise and pray
24. 7 "be crucified, and on the third day rise
[24.12 *But Peter rose and ran to the tomb*‡
24.33 they rose that same hour and returned
24.46 "on the third day rise from the dead
Jn 11.31 saw Mary rise quickly and go out
20. 9 they did not know . . that he must rise
Acts 5. 6 young men rose and wrapped him up
8.26 Lord said to Philip, "Rise and go . . south[g]
8.27 And he rose and went
9. 6 "rise and enter the city
9.11 "R. and go to the street called Straight
9.18 Then he rose and was baptized
9.34 "Jesus Christ heals you; rise and make your bed." And immediately he rose
9.39 So Peter rose and went with them
9.40 he said, "Tabitha, rise." And . . she sat up
10.13 a voice . . "Rise, Peter; kill and eat
10.20 "R. and go down, and accompany them
10.23 The next day he rose and went off
10.41 "ate and drank with him after he rose
11. 7 "a voice . . 'Rise, Peter; kill and eat
15. 7 after . . much debate, Peter rose
17. 3 to suffer and to rise from the dead
22.10 "Lord said . . 'R., and go into Damascus
22.16 " 'why do you wait? Rise and be baptized
26.16 " 'But rise and stand upon your feet
26.30 Then the king rose, and the governor
Rom 15.12 "he who rises to rule the Gentiles
1 Th 4.16 the dead in Christ will rise first
5. *stir up, arouse:* διεγείρω DIEGEIRŌ
Jn 6.18 The sea rose because a strong wind
6. *raise:* ἐγείρω (pass.) EGEIRŌ
[a]act. imper.
Mt 2.13 "Rise, take the child and his mother
2.14 he rose . . took the child and his mother
2.20 "Rise, take the child and his mother
2.21 he rose . . took the child and his mother
8.15 the fever left her, and she rose
8.26 Then he rose and rebuked the winds
9. 5 [a]"which is easier, to say . . 'Rise and walk'?
9. 6 [a]"Rise, take up your bed and go home
9. 7 And he rose and went home
9.19 And Jesus rose and followed him
11.11 "there has risen no one greater than John
17. 7 saying, "Rise, and have no fear
24. 7 "For nation will rise against nation
25. 7 "maidens rose and trimmed their lamps
26.46 "Rise . . ; see, my betrayer is at hand
27.63 " 'After three days I will rise again
27.64 "lest . . disciples . . tell . . people, 'He has risen
28. 6 "He is not here; for he has risen
28. 7 "tell his disciples that he has risen
Mk 2. 9 "Which is easier, to say . . 'Rise . . walk'?
2.11 [a]"I say to you, rise, take up your pallet
2.12 he rose, . . took up the pallet and went
4.27 "should sleep and rise night and day
10.49 [a]"Take heart; rise, he is calling you
13. 8 "For nation will rise against nation
14.42 "Rise . . ; see, my betrayer is at hand
16. 6 "He has risen, he is not here
16.14 those who saw him after he had risen[k]‡
Lk 5.23 [a]"Which is easier, to say . . 'Rise and walk'?
5.24 [a]"I say to you, rise, take up your bed
11. 8 "because of his importunity he will rise
21.10 "Nation will rise against nation
[24. 5(6) *"He is not here, but has risen*‡
24.34 "The Lord has risen indeed!
Jn 5. 8 [a]"Rise, take up your pallet, and walk
7.52 "no prophet is to rise from Galilee[r]
11.29 when she heard it, she rose quickly
13. 4 rose from supper, laid aside . . garments
14.31 "Rise, let us go hence
2 Tim 2. 8 Jesus Christ, risen from the dead
Rev 11. 1 [a]"Rise and measure the temple of God

RISE AGAIN
1. *raise up, rise:* ἀνίστημι ANISTĒMI
Jn 11.23 "Your brother will rise again
11.24 "I know that he will rise again
1 Th 4.14 we believe . . Jesus died and rose again

RISE AGAIN TO LIFE
1. *experience a resurrection:* ἀναστάσεως τυγχάνειν ANASTASIS [B.3.b.4]
Heb 11.35 that they . . rise again to a better life

RISE AGAINST
1. *set up again:* ἐπανίστημι (mid.) EPANISTĒMI*
Mt 10.21 "children will rise against parents
Mk 13.12 "children will rise against parents

RISE, MAKE
1. *make to rise:* ἀνατέλλω ANATELLŌ
Mt 5.45 "makes his sun rise on the evil and . . good

RISE UP
1. *raise up, rise:* ἀνίστημι ANISTĒMI
Mk 3.26 "if Satan has risen up against himself
Lk 4.29 they rose up and put him out of the city
Acts 5.17 high priest rose up . . filled with jealousy
14.20 he rose up and entered the city
1 Cor 10. 7 "The people . . rose up to dance
2. *raise:* ἐγείρω (pass.) EGEIRŌ
Lk 13.25 "once the householder has risen up
3. *raise up, rise:* ἐξανίστημι EXANISTĒMI
Acts 15. 5 believers . . of the Pharisees rose up

RISING
1. *resurrection, rising:* ἀνάστασις ANASTASIS
Lk 2.34 "this child is set for the . . rising of many
2. *rising, east:* ἀνατολή ANATOLĒ
Rev 7. 2 angel ascend from the rising of the sun

RISK
1. *lay down:* ὑποτίθημι HYPOTITHĒMI
Rom 16. 4 who risked their necks for my life
2. *venture, expose oneself:* παραβολεύομαι PARABOLEUOMAI*
Phil 2.30 risking his life to complete your service
3. *give up, allow:* παραδίδωμι PARADIDŌMI
Acts 15.26 "men who have risked their lives

RITE
CONTEXTUALLY
Heb 9.23 copies . . to be purified with these rites

RITUAL DUTY
1. *worship, service, duty:* λατρεία LATREIA
Heb 9. 6 priests . . performing their ritual duties

RIVALRY
1. *strife, rivalry:* ἔρις ERIS
Phil 1.15 Some indeed preach Christ from . . rivalry

RIVER
1. *river, stream:* ποταμός POTAMOS
Mt 3. 6 baptized by him in the river Jordan
Mk 1. 5 baptized by him in the river Jordan
Jn 7.38 " 'Out of his heart shall flow rivers
2 Cor 11.26 on . . journeys, in danger from rivers
Rev 8.10 it fell on a third of the rivers
9.14 "angels . . bound at the . . river Euphrates
12.15 The serpent poured water like a river
12.16 and the earth . . swallowed the river
16. 4 third angel poured . . bowl into the rivers
16.12 poured . . on the great river Euphrates
22. 1 showed me the river of the water of life
22. 2 on either side of the river, . . tree of life[r]

RIVERSIDE
1. *beside the river:* παρὰ ποταμόν POTAMOS [B.1.a.1]
Acts 16.13 we went outside the gate to the r.

ROAD
1. *way, road:* ὁδός HODOS
Mt 21. 8 Most . . spread their garments on the road, . . others . . spread ⟨branches⟩ on the road
Mk 10.32 on the road, going up to Jerusalem
11. 8 many spread their garments on the road
Lk 9.57 As they were going along the road
10. 4 "salute no one on the road
10.31 "a priest was going down that road
Lk 19.36 they spread their garments on the road
24.32 "while he talked to us on the road
24.35 they told what had happened on the road
Acts 8.26 "to the r. that goes down from Jerusalem
8.36 along the road they came to some water
9.17 "Jesus, who appeared to you on the road
9.27 how on the road he had seen the Lord

ROADSIDE
1. *beside the road:* παρὰ τὴν ὁδόν HODOS [B.1.a.1]
Mt 20.30 two blind men sitting by the roadside
Mk 10.46 Bartimaeus . . sitting by the roadside
Lk 18.35 blind man was sitting by the roadside

ROAR
1. *low, bellow:* μυκάομαι MYKAOMAI*
Rev 10. 3 with a loud voice, like a lion roaring
2. *roar, howl:* ὠρύομαι ŌRYOMAI*
1 Pet 5. 8 devil prowls around like a roaring lion

ROARING
1. *sound, noise:* ἦχος ĒCHOS II*
Lk 21.25 "in perplexity at the roaring of the sea

ROB
1. *strip, plunder:* συλάω SYLAŌ*
2 Cor 11. 8 I robbed . . churches by accepting support

ROB BY FALSE ACCUSATION
1. *oppress, defraud:* συκοφαντέω SYKOPHANTEŌ
Lk 3.14 "Rob no one . . by false accusation

ROB BY VIOLENCE
1. *shake violently, extort money by violence:* διασείω DIASEIŌ*
Lk 3.14 he said . . "Rob no one by violence

ROB TEMPLES
1. *rob a temple:* ἱεροσυλέω HIEROSYLEŌ*
Rom 2.22 You who abhor idols, do you r. temples?

ROBBER
1. *robbing:* ἅρπαξ (subst.) HARPAX
1 Cor 5.10 not . . meaning . . the greedy and robbers
5.11 not to associate with any . . if . . robber
6.10 nor robbers will inherit the kingdom
2. *robber:* λῃστής LĒSTĒS*
Mt 21.13 "but you make it a den of robbers
26.55 "Have you come . . as against a robber?
27.38 two robbers were crucified with him
27.44 the robbers who were crucified with him
Mk 11.17 "But you have made it a den of robbers
14.48 "Have you come . . as against a robber?
15.27 And with him they crucified two robbers
Lk 10.30 "he fell among robbers, who stripped him
10.36 "the man who fell among the robbers
19.46 "you have made it a den of robbers
22.52 "Have you come . . as against a robber?
Jn 10. 1 "that man is a thief and a robber
10. 8 "All who came before me are . . robbers
18.40 Now Barabbas was a robber
2 Cor 11.26 danger from rivers, . . from robbers

ROBE
1. *short mantle, cloak:* χλαμύς CHLAMYS*
Mt 27.28 stripped him and put a scarlet robe
27.31 they stripped him of the robe
2. *clothing:* ἐσθής ESTHĒS
[a]sg.
Acts 1.10 two men stood by them in white robes
12.21 [a]Herod put on . . royal robes, took his seat
3. *outer garment:* ἱμάτιον HIMATION
Mt 26.65 Then the high priest tore his robes
Jn 19. 2 soldiers . . arrayed him in a purple robe
19. 5 Jesus came out, wearing . . the purple robe
Rev 19.13 He is clad in a robe dipped in[m] blood
19.16 On his robe . . he has a name inscribed
4. *robe, garment:* στολή STOLĒ
Mk 16. 5 a young man . . dressed in a white robe
Lk 15.22 " 'Bring quickly the best robe
Rev 6.11 they were each given a white robe
7. 9 before the throne . . in white robes
7.13 "Who are these, clothed in white robes?

Rev 7.14 "washed their robes . . made them white
22.14 Blessed are those who wash their robes[s]‡

ROBE, LONG

1. *reaching to the feet:* ποδήρης (subst.) PODĒRĒS*
Rev 1.13 a son of man, clothed with a long robe
2. *robe, garment:* στολή STOLĒ
Mk 12.38 "who like to go about in long robes
Lk 20.46 "who like to go about in long robes

ROBED

1. *put on, clothe:* ἐνδύω (mid. part.) ENDYŌ
Rev 15. 6 angels . . robed in pure bright linen

ROCK

1. *rock:* πέτρα PETRA
Mt 7.24 "wise man who built . . upon the rock
7.25 "it had been founded on the rock
16.18 "on this rock[t] I will build my church†
27.51 earth shook, and the rocks were split
27.60 new tomb, which he had hewn in the rock
Mk 15.46 tomb . . hewn out of the rock
Lk 6.48 laid the foundation upon rock
[6.48 "it had been *founded upon the rock*‡
8. 6 some fell on the rock; and as it grew up
8.13 "ones on the r. are those who . . receive it
Rom 9.33 "a rock that will make them fall
1 Cor 10. 4 drank from the supernatural[o] Rock which followed . . , and the Rock was Christ
1 Pet 2. 8 "a rock that will make them fall
Rev 6.15 hid in the caves and among the rocks
6.16 calling to the . . rocks, "Fall on us
2. *rough places* (pl.): τραχεῖς τόποι TRACHYS [A.1.f]
Acts 27.29 fearing that we might run on the rocks

ROCK-HEWN

1. *hewn out of the rock:* λαξευτός LAXEUTOS*
Lk 23.53 laid him in a rock-hewn tomb

ROCKY GROUND

1. *rocky, stony:* πετρώδης (subst. sg. or pl.) PETRŌDĒS*
Mt 13. 5 "Other seeds fell on rocky ground
13.20 "As for what was sown on rocky ground
Mk 4. 5 "Other seed fell on rocky ground
4.16 "the ones sown upon rocky ground

ROD

1. *reed, staff:* κάλαμος KALAMOS
Rev 21.15 a measuring rod of gold to measure
21.16 he measured the city with his rod
2. *rod, staff of office:* ῥάβδος RHABDOS
1 Cor 4.21 Shall I come to you with a rod?
Heb 9. 4 the ark . . , which contained . . Aaron's rod
Rev 2.27 " 'he shall rule them with a rod of iron
12. 5 to rule all the nations with a rod of iron
19.15 he will rule them with a rod of iron

ROD, MEASURING

1. *reed, staff:* κάλαμος KALAMOS
Rev 11. 1 Then I was given a measuring rod

RODS, BEAT WITH

1. *beat with a rod:* ῥαβδίζω RHABDIZŌ*
Acts 16.22 gave orders to beat them with rods
2 Cor 11.25 Three times I have been beaten with r.

ROLL

1. *roll:* κεφαλίς KEPHALIS*
Heb 10. 7 "written of me in the roll of the book
2. *roll up to:* προσκυλίω PROSKYLIŌ*
Mt 27.60 he rolled a great stone to the door
Mk 15.46 rolled a stone against . . door of the tomb

ROLL ABOUT

1. *roll:* κυλίω (pass.) KYLIŌ*
Mk 9.20 he . . rolled about, foaming at the mouth

ROLL AWAY

1. *roll away:* ἀποκυλίω APOKYLIŌ
Mk 16. 3 "Who will roll away the stone for us?
Lk 24. 2 they found the stone rolled away

ROLL BACK

1. *roll away:* ἀνακυλίω ANAKYLIŌ*
Mk 16. 4 they saw that the stone was rolled back
2. *roll away:* ἀποκυλίω APOKYLIŌ
Mt 28. 2 angel . . came and rolled back the stone

ROLL UP

1. *wrap up, fold up:* ἐντυλίσσω ENTYLISSŌ
Jn 20. 7 napkin . . rolled up in a place by itself
2. *revolve, roll:* ἑλίσσω HELISSŌ*
Heb 1.12 "like a mantle thou wilt roll them up
Rev 6.14 vanished like a scroll that is rolled up

ROMAN (*See also* ROME, FROM)

ROMAN CITIZEN

1. *Roman:* Ῥωμαῖος
Jn 11.48 "Romans will come and destroy both
Acts 16.21 "customs . . not lawful for us Romans
16.37 "They have beaten us . . who are R. citizens
16.38 they heard that they were R. citizens
22.25 "Is it lawful . . to scourge . . a R. citizen?
22.26 "For this man is a Roman citizen
22.27 "Tell me, are you a Roman citizen?
22.29 realized that Paul was a Roman citizen
23.27 "having learned that he was a R. citizen
25.16 "it was not the custom of the Romans
28.17 "prisoner . . into the hands of the Romans
CONTEXTUALLY
Acts 16.12 the leading city . . and a Roman colony

ROME: Ῥώμη 'rōm II,B-2
Acts 18. 2 Claudius . . commanded . . Jews to leave R.
19.21 "After I have been there, I must . . see R.
23.11 "so you must bear witness also at Rome
28.14 And so we came to Rome
28.16 when we came into R., Paul was allowed
Rom 1. 7 To all God's beloved in Rome
1.15 I am eager to preach . . to you . . in Rome
2 Tim 1.17 in Rome he searched for me eagerly

ROME, FROM: Ῥωμαῖος
Acts 2.10 "visitors from R., . . Jews and proselytes

ROOF

1. *housetop:* δῶμα DŌMA
Lk 5.19 they went up on the r. and let him down
2. *shelter, roof:* στέγη STEGĒ*
Mt 8. 8 "I am not worthy to have you . . under my r.
Mk 2. 4 they removed the roof above him
Lk 7. 6 "I am not worthy to have you . . under my r.

ROOM

ROOM, INNER

ROOM, PRIVATE

1. *abiding, apartment:* μονή MONĒ
Jn 14. 2 "In my Father's house are many rooms
2. *storeroom:* ταμεῖον TAMEION
Mt 6. 6 "when you pray, go into your room
24.26 "if they say . . 'Lo, he is in the inner rooms
Lk 12. 3 "what you . . whispered in private rooms
3. *place:* τόπος TOPOS
Lk 14.22 "the servant said . . 'still there is room
Rom 15.23 I no longer have any room for work

ROOM, BE

1. *make room for, hold, go:* χωρέω CHŌREŌ
Mk 2. 2 there was no longer room for them

ROOM, GUEST

1. *guest lodging:* κατάλυμα KATALYMA
Mk 14.14 " 'Where is my guest room?
Lk 22.11 " 'Where is the guest room?
2. *hospitality, guest room:* ξενία XENIA
Phm .22 prepare a guest room for me

ROOM, UPPER

1. *room upstairs:* ἀνάγαιον ANAGAION*
Mk 14.15 "he will show you a large upper room
Lk 22.12 "he will show you a large upper room
2. *upper story, spare room:* ὑπερῷον HYPERŌON
Acts 1.13 they went up to the upper room
9.37 they laid her in an upper room
9.39 they took him to the upper room

ROOT

1. *root:* ῥίζα RHIZA*
Mt 3.10 "the axe is laid to the root of the trees

Mt 13. 6 "since they had no r. they withered away
13.21 "yet he has no root in himself
Mk 4. 6 "since it had no root it withered away
4.17 "they have no root in themselves
11.20 saw .. fig tree withered away to its roots
Lk 3. 9 "the axe is laid to the root of the trees
8.13 "they .. receive it with joy; but .. have no root
Rom 11.16 if the root is holy, so are the branches
[11.17 to share the *rich root* of the olive tree‡
11.18 it is not you that support the root, but the root that supports you
15.12 Isaiah .. "The root of Jesse shall come
1 Tim 6.10 love of money is the root of all evils
Heb 12.15 that no "root of bitterness" spring up
Rev 5. 5 "the Root of David, has conquered
22.16 "I am the root and the offspring of David

ROOT UP
1. *root out:* ἐκριζόω EKRIZOŌ
Mt 13.29 " 'No; lest .. you root up the wheat
15.13 "Every plant .. will be rooted up
Lk 17. 6 " 'Be rooted up, and be planted in the sea

ROOTED
ROOTED, BEING
1. *cause to take root:* ῥιζόω (perf. pass. part.) RHIZOŌ*
Eph 3.17 you, being rooted and grounded in love
Col 2. 7 ⟨so live in him,⟩ r. and built up in him

ROPE
1. *small rope, cord:* σχοινίον SCHOINION
Acts 27.32 soldiers cut away the ropes of the boat
2. *bands, ropes:* ζευκτηρία ZEUKTĒRIA*
Acts 27.40 loosening .. ropes that tied the rudders

ROT
1. *make rotten, corrupt:* σήπω SĒPŌ*
Jas 5. 2 Your riches have rotted

ROUGH
1. *rough, jagged:* τραχύς TRACHYS
Lk 3. 5 "the rough ways shall be made smooth

ROUND (*See also* HUNG ROUND, BE; LOOK ROUND AT; PRESS ROUND; SEND ROUND; SHINE ROUND)
1. *in a circle, round about:* κύκλῳ KYKLŌ
[a]κύκλῳ μέχρι
Rom 15.19 [a]from Jerusalem and as far r. as Illyricum
Rev 7.11 all the angels stood round the throne
2. *from all around:* κυκλόθεν KYKLOTHEN
Rev 4. 3 round the throne was a rainbow
4. 4 R. the throne were twenty-four thrones
3. *in the midst of:* ἐν μέσῳ MESOS [B.1.a.1; D.2]
Rev 4. 6 And round the throne, on each side
4. *to what is behind:* εἰς τὰ ὀπίσω OPISŌ [B.1.a.1]
Jn 20.14 she turned round and saw Jesus
5. *about, around:* περί (+acc.) PERI
Mt 18. 6 "great millstone fastened round his neck
Mk 9.42 "a great millstone .. hung round his neck
Lk 17. 2 "if a millstone were hung round his neck
6. *at, near:* πρός (+dat.) PROS
Rev 1.13 with a golden girdle round his breast

ROUND ABOUT
1. *in a circle, round about:* κύκλῳ KYKLŌ
Mk 6.36 "send them .. into the country .. round about
Lk 9.12 "to go into the .. country round about

ROUND, ALL
1. *from all around:* κυκλόθεν KYKLOTHEN
Rev 4. 8 creatures, .. full of eyes all r. and within

ROUND, GATHER
1. *surround, encircle:* κυκλόω KYKLOŌ
Jn 10.24 the Jews gathered round him

ROW
1. *drive:* ἐλαύνω ELAUNŌ
Jn 6.19 When they had rowed .. three or four miles[m]

ROYAL
1. *royal:* βασίλειος BASILEIOS
1 Pet 2. 9 you are a chosen race, a r. priesthood
2. *royal:* βασιλικός BASILIKOS
Acts 12.21 Herod put on his royal robes
Jas 2. 8 If you really fulfil the royal law

ROYAL POWER
1. *kingdom, reign:* βασιλεία BASILEIA
Rev 17.12 "kings who have not yet .. r. power
17.17 "giving over their r. power to the beast

RUB
1. *rub:* ψώχω PSŌCHŌ*
Lk 6. 1 ate some heads of grain, rubbing them

RUDDER
1. *rudder:* πηδάλιον PĒDALION*
Acts 27.40 loosening .. ropes that tied the rudders
Jas 3. 4 are guided by a very small rudder

RUDE, BE
1. *behave disgracefully:* ἀσχημονέω ASCHĒMONEŌ
1 Cor 13. 5 ⟨love⟩ is not arrogant or rude

RUE
1. *rue:* πήγανον PĒGANON*
Lk 11.42 "woe to you .. for you tithe mint and rue

RUFUS: Ῥοῦφος 'rüfəs
Mk 15.21 Simon of Cyrene .., the father of .. Rufus
Rom 16.13 Greet Rufus, eminent in the Lord

RUIN
1. *upset, turn down:* καταστρέφω (subst. perf. pass. part.) KATASTREPHŌ
Acts 15.16 " 'I will rebuild its ruins, and I will set it up
2. *destruction, ruin:* καταστροφή KATASTROPHĒ [B.1.a.4]
2 Tim 2.14 disputing about words .. ruins the hearers
3. *destruction, death:* ὄλεθρος OLETHROS
1 Tim 6. 9 desires that plunge men into ruin
4. *entice, destroy:* φθείρω PHTHEIRŌ
1 Cor 15.33 "Bad company ruins good morals
5. *breakage:* ῥῆγμα RHĒGMA*
Lk 6.49 "the ruin of that house was great
6. *fracture, affliction:* σύντριμμα SYNTRIMMA*
Rom 3.16 "in their paths are ruin and misery

RUIN OF, CAUSE THE
1. *destroy utterly:* ἀπόλλυμι APOLLYMI
Rom 14.15 Do not let what you eat cause .. r. of one

RULE
1. *origin, rule:* ἀρχή ARCHĒ
1 Cor 15.24 destroying every rule and .. authority
Eph 1.21 far above all rule and authority
Col 2.10 who is .. head of all rule and authority
2. *rule; begin* (mid.): ἄρχω ARCHŌ
Mk 10.42 "who are supposed to rule .. Gentiles
Rom 15.12 "he who rises to rule the Gentiles
3. *act as judge, direct:* βραβεύω BRABEUŌ*
Col 3.15 let .. peace of Christ rule in your hearts
4. *appoint, direct:* διατάσσω DIATASSŌ [A.6.a.2]
1 Cor 7.17 This is my rule in all the churches
5. *exercise authority over:* ἐξουσιάζω EXOUSIAZŌ
1 Cor 7. 4 wife does not rule over her own body
7. 4 husband does not rule over his own body
6. *province, rule:* κανών KANŌN
Gal 6.16 mercy be upon all who walk by this rule
7. *tend, herd, govern:* ποιμαίνω POIMAINŌ
Rev 2.27 " 'he shall rule them with a rod of iron
12. 5 who is to rule all the nations with a rod
19.15 he will rule them with a rod of iron
8. *set over, direct:* προΐστημι PROISTĒMI
1 Tim 5.17 Let .. elders who rule well be considered
CONTEXTUALLY
1 Tim 5.21 I charge you to keep these rules

RULE ONE'S HOUSEHOLD
1. *be master of a house:* οἰκοδεσποτέω OIKODESPOTEŌ*
1 Tim 5.14 younger widows .. rule their households

RULE WITH, SHARE THE
1. *rule together with:* συμβασιλεύω SYMBASILEUŌ
1 Cor 4. 8 that we might share the rule with you!

RULER
1. *origin, rule:* ἀρχή ARCHĒ
Lk 12.11 "when they bring you before .. the rulers

Tit 3. 1 submissive to rulers and authorities
2. *ruler of the synagogue:* ἀρχισυνάγωγος ARCHISYNAGŌGOS
Mk 5.35 there came from the ruler's house some
Lk 8.49 a man from the ruler's house came
3. *ruler:* ἄρχων ARCHŌN
Mt 9.18 a ruler came in and knelt before him
9.23 when Jesus came to the ruler's house
20.25 "rulers of the Gentiles lord it over them
Lk 8.41 Jairus, . . a ruler of the synagogue
14. 1 a ruler who belonged to the Pharisees
18.18 a ruler asked him, "Good Teacher
23.13 Pilate then called together . . the rulers
23.35 people stood by, . . but the rulers scoffed
24.20 "chief priests and rulers delivered him up
Jn 3. 1 Nicodemus, a ruler of the Jews
12.31 "now shall the r. of this world be cast out
14.30 "for the ruler of this world is coming
16.11 "the ruler of this world is judged
Acts 3.17 "acted in ignorance, as did . . your rulers
4. 5 their rulers . . were gathered together
4. 8 "Rulers of the people and elders
4.26 " 'the rulers were gathered together
7.27 " 'Who made you a ruler . . over us?
7.35 " 'Who made you a ruler and a judge?
7.35 "This Moses . . God sent as both ruler
13.27 "those . . in Jerusalem and their rulers
14. 5 both Gentiles and Jews, with their rulers
16.19 owners . . dragged them . . before the rulers
23. 5 " 'You shall not speak evil of a ruler
Rom 13. 3 rulers are not a terror to good conduct
1 Cor 2. 6 not a wisdom of this age or of the rulers
2. 8 None of the rulers of this age understood
Rev 1. 5 Jesus Christ . . the ruler of kings on earth
4. *guide, sovereign:* ἡγεμών HĒGEMŌN
Mt 2. 6 " 'by no means least among the rulers of J.
5. *think, lead:* ἡγέομαι (subst. part.) HĒGEOMAI
Mt 2. 6 " 'for from you shall come a ruler

RULER OF THE SYNAGOGUE
1. *ruler of the synagogue:* ἀρχισυνάγωγος ARCHISYNAGŌGOS
Mk 5.22 one of the rulers of the synagogue
5.36 Jesus said to the ruler of the synagogue
5.38 to the house of the r. of the synagogue
Lk 13.14 the ruler of the synagogue, indignant
Acts 13.15 the rulers of the synagogue sent to them
18. 8 Crispus, the ruler of the synagogue
18.17 seized Sosthenes, the r. of the synagogue

RULER, WORLD
1. *lord of the world:* κοσμοκράτωρ KOSMOKRATŌR*
Eph 6.12 contending . . against the world rulers

RULES, ACCORDING TO THE
1. *lawfully:* νομίμως NOMIMŌS
2 Tim 2. 5 unless he competes according to the r.

RUMOR
1. *hearing, report:* ἀκοή AKOĒ
Mt 24. 6 "you will hear of wars and rumors of wars
Mk 13. 7 "you hear of wars and rumors of wars

RUN
1. *run in:* εἰστρέχω EISTRECHŌ*
Acts 12.14 she did not open the gate but ran in
2. *run together, assemble:* συντρέχω SYNTRECHŌ
Mk 6.33 they ran there . . from all the towns
3. *run, move quickly:* τρέχω TRECHŌ
Mt 27.48 one . . at once ran and took a sponge
28. 8 they . . ran to tell his disciples
Mk 5. 6 when he saw Jesus from afar, he ran
15.36 one ran and, filling a sponge full
Lk 15.20 "his father . . ran and embraced him
[24.12 *But Peter rose and ran to the tomb*‡
Jn 20. 2 she ran, and went to Simon Peter
20. 4 both ran, but the other disciple outran
1 Cor 9.24 So run that you may obtain it
9.26 Well, I do not run aimlessly
Gal 2. 2 lest somehow I should be running or had run in vain
5. 7 You were running well; who hindered?
Phil 2.16 proud that I did not run in vain
Heb 12. 1 let us run with perseverance the race

RUN ABOUT
1. *run about:* περιτρέχω PERITRECHŌ*
Mk 6.55 ⟨people⟩ ran about the . . neighborhood

RUN AGROUND
1. *bring* (ships) *to shore:* ἐπικέλλω EPIKELLŌ*
Acts 27.41 striking a shoal[e] they ran the vessel a.

RUN AWAY
1. *flee, avoid:* φεύγω PHEUGŌ
Mk 14.52 left the linen cloth and ran away naked

RUN DOWN
1. *run down:* κατατρέχω KATATRECHŌ*
Acts 21.32 He at once took soldiers . . and ran down

RUN ON
1. *fall out:* ἐκπίπτω EKPIPTŌ
Acts 27.17 fearing . . they should run on the Syrtis
27.26 "we shall have to run on some island
27.29 fearing that we might run on the rocks

RUN ON AHEAD
1. *run in advance, outrun:* προτρέχω PROTRECHŌ
[a]+εἰς τὸ ἔμπροσθεν
Lk 19. 4 [a]So he ran on ahead and climbed up

RUN OVER
1. *pour out over:* ὑπερεκχύννω (pass.) HYPEREKCHYNNŌ*
Lk 6.38 "good measure . . running over, will be put

RUN TO
RUN UP
1. *run up to:* προστρέχω PROSTRECHŌ*
Mk 9.15 crowd . . ran up to him and greeted him
10.17 a man ran up and knelt before him
Acts 8.30 Philip ran to him, and heard him reading

RUN TOGETHER
1. *running together:* συνδρομή SYNDROMĒ* [A.6.a.3]
Acts 21.30 all the city was aroused, . . ran together
2. *run together, assemble:* συντρέχω SYNTRECHŌ
Acts 3.11 all the people ran together to them

RUN UNDER THE LEE OF
1. *run in under:* ὑποτρέχω HYPOTRECHŌ*
Acts 27.16 running under the lee of a small island

RUNNER
1. *run, move quickly:* τρέχω (subst. part.) TRECHŌ
1 Cor 9.24 in a race all the runners compete

RUNNING TOGETHER, COME
1. *run together:* ἐπισυντρέχω EPISYNTRECHŌ*
Mk 9.25 a crowd came running together

RUSH
1. *start, rush:* ὁρμάω HORMAŌ*
Mt 8.32 whole herd rushed down the steep bank
Mk 5.13 the herd . . rushed down the steep bank
Lk 8.33 the herd rushed down the steep bank
Acts 7.57 they . . rushed together upon him
19.29 they rushed together into the theater
2. *bring, bear:* φέρω PHERŌ [B.2.d.1]
Acts 2. 2 a sound . . like the rush of a mighty wind
3. *run, move quickly:* τρέχω TRECHŌ
Rev 9. 9 noise of many chariots with horses rushing

RUSH IN
1. *leap in:* εἰσπηδάω EISPĒDAŌ*
Acts 16.29 he called for lights and rushed in

RUSH OUT
1. *leap out, start:* ἐκπηδάω EKPĒDAŌ*
Acts 14.14 they tore their garments and rushed out

RUST
1. *eating, food:* βρῶσις BRŌSIS
Mt 6.19 "on earth, where moth and rust[o] consume
6.20 "where neither moth nor rust[o] consumes†
2. *rust:* ἰός IOS
Jas 5. 3 their rust will be evidence against you
3. *become rusty:* κατιόω (pass.) KATIOŌ*
Jas 5. 3 Your gold and silver have rusted

RUTH: Ῥούθ 'rüth
Mt 1. 5 Boaz the father of Obed by Ruth

RUTHLESS
1. *merciless:* ἀνελεήμων ANELEĒMŌN*
Rom 1.31 foolish, faithless, heartless, ruthless

S

SABACHTHANI: sə'bäkthə,nī, səbäk'thä,nē
1. *thou hast forsaken me* (Aram.): σαβαχθάνι SABACHTHANI*
Mt 27.46 Jesus cried . . "Eli, Eli, lama sabachthani?
Mk 15.34 Jesus cried . . "Eloi, Eloi, lama sabachthani?

SABBATH
1. *Sabbath* (Heb.), *week:* σάββατον SABBATON
Mt 12. 1 Jesus went through the grainfields on the s.
12. 2 "doing what is not lawful to do on the s.
12. 5 "have you not read in the law how on the s. the priests in the temple profane the s.?
12. 8 "the Son of man is lord of the sabbath
12.10 "Is it lawful to heal on the sabbath?
12.11 "if . . it falls into a pit on the sabbath
12.12 "So it is lawful to do good on the sabbath
24.20 "Pray that your flight may not be . . on a s.
28. 1 after the sabbath, toward the dawn
Mk 1.21 on the s. he entered the synagogue
2.23 One s. he was going through . . grainfields
2.24 "doing what is not lawful on the sabbath
2.27 he said to them, "The sabbath was made for man, not man for the sabbath
2.28 "Son of man is lord even of the s.
3. 2 he would heal him on the sabbath
3. 4 "Is it lawful on the sabbath to do good?
6. 2 on the sabbath he began to teach
16. 1 when the s. was past, Mary Magdalene
Lk 4.16 as his custom was, on the sabbath day
4.31 he was teaching them on the sabbath
6. 1 On a s.,[t] . . going through the grainfields
6. 2 "what is not lawful to do on the sabbath
6. 5 "Son of man is lord of the sabbath
6. 6 On another sabbath, when he entered
6. 7 to see whether he would heal on the s.
6. 9 "is it lawful on the sabbath to do good?
13.10 he was teaching . . on the sabbath
13.14 indignant because Jesus . . healed on the s.
13.14 "be healed . . not on the sabbath day
13.15 "Does not each . . on the s. untie his ox?
13.16 "loosed from this bond on the s. day?
14. 1 One sabbath when he went to dine
14. 3 "Is it lawful to heal on the sabbath?
14. 5 "Which . . will not . . pull him out on a s.?
23.54 the sabbath was beginning[s]
23.56 On the sabbath they rested
Jn 5. 9 Now that day was the sabbath
5.10 "It is the s., it is not lawful . . to carry
5.16 because he did this on the sabbath
5.18 because he not only broke the sabbath
7.22 "you circumcise a man upon the sabbath
7.23 "If on the s. a man receives circumcision
7.23 "because on the s. I made a . . body well
9.14 it was a s. day when Jesus made the clay
9.16 "not from God, for he does not keep the s.
19.31 to prevent . . from remaining on the cross on the s. (for that s. was a high day
Acts 1.12 mount called Olivet, . . a s. day's journey
13.14 on the s. . . they went into the synagogue
13.27 "the prophets which are read every s.
13.42 that these things . . be told them the next s.
13.44 next s. almost the whole city gathered
15.21 "Moses . . is read every s. in . . synagogues
16.13 on the s. day we went outside the gate
[17. 2 for three *sabbaths* he argued with them†
18. 4 he argued in the synagogue every s.
Col 2.16 judgment . . with regard to . . a sabbath

SABBATH REST
1. *Sabbath observance:* σαββατισμός SABBATISMOS*
Heb 4. 9 there remains a s. rest for the people

SABBATH, THE DAY BEFORE THE
1. *eve of the Sabbath:* προσάββατον PROSABBATON*
Mk 15.42 Preparation, . . the day before the s.

SACKCLOTH
1. *coarse cloth of hair, sack:* σάκκος SAKKOS*
[a]σάκκος τρίχινος
Mt 11.21 "they would have repented . . in sackcloth
Lk 10.13 "they would have repented . . in sackcloth
Rev 6.12 [a]the sun became black as sackcloth
11. 3 "I will grant . . witnesses . . to prophesy . . in s.

SACRED
1. *holy:* ἱερός HIEROS
Mk [16.[end] *the sacred . . proclamation of . . salvation*‡
2 Tim 3.15 acquainted with the sacred writings

SACRED, MAKE
1. *make sacred:* ἁγιάζω HAGIAZŌ
Mt 23.17 "temple that has made the gold sacred
23.19 "the altar that makes the gift sacred

SACRED STONE THAT FELL FROM THE SKY
1. *fallen from heaven:* διοπετής (subst. neut.) DIOPETĒS* [D.1]
Acts 19.35 "the sacred stone that fell from the sky[s]

SACRIFICE
SACRIFICE, OFFER
1. *sacrifice, kill:* θύω THYŌ
Mk 14.12 when they sacrificed the passover lamb
Lk 22. 7 the passover lamb had to be sacrificed
Acts 14.13 priest of Zeus . . wanted to offer sacrifice
14.18 restrained the people from offering s.
1 Cor 5. 7 Christ, our . . lamb, has been sacrificed
10.20 what pagans s. they offer to demons
2. *offering, sacrifice:* θυσία THYSIA
Mt 9.13 " 'I desire mercy, and not sacrifice
12. 7 " 'I desire mercy, and not sacrifice
Mk [9.49 "*every sacrifice will be salted with salt*‡
12.33 "to love . . is . . more than all . . sacrifices
Lk 2.24 to offer a sacrifice according to . . the law
13. 1 blood Pilate . . mingled with . . sacrifices
Acts 7.41 "they . . offered a sacrifice to the idol
7.42 " 'Did you offer . . slain beasts and sacrifices?
Rom 12. 1 present your bodies as a living sacrifice
1 Cor 10.18 are not those who eat the sacrifices?
Eph 5. 2 a fragrant offering and sacrifice to God
Phil 4.18 gifts you sent, . . a sacrifice acceptable
Heb 5. 1 high priest . . is appointed . . to offer . . sacrifices
7.27 He has no need . . to offer sacrifices daily
8. 3 high priest is appointed to offer . . sacrifices
9. 9 sacrifices are offered which cannot perfect
9.23 heavenly things . . with better sacrifices
9.26 to put away sin by the s. of himself
10. 1 it can never, by the same sacrifices
10. 5 "Sacrifices . . thou hast not desired
10. 8 "Thou hast neither desired . . sacrifices
10.11 offering repeatedly the same sacrifices
10.12 when Christ[w] had offered . . a single s.
10.26 there no longer remains a sacrifice for sins
11. 4 Abel offered . . a more acceptable sacrifice
13.15 let us . . offer up a sacrifice of praise
13.16 for such sacrifices are pleasing to God
1 Pet 2. 5 priesthood, to offer spiritual sacrifices
CONTEXTUALLY
Heb 5. 3 bound to offer s. for his own sins
10. 3 in these sacrifices there is a reminder
13.11 bodies . . brought . . as a sacrifice for sin

SACRIFICE, OFFERED IN
1. *offered to a god:* ἱερόθυτος HIEROTHYTOS*
1 Cor 10.28 ("This has been offered in sacrifice

SACRIFICED, BE ON THE POINT OF BEING
1. *make a drink offering:* σπένδω (pass.) SPENDŌ
2 Tim 4. 6 I am already on the point of being s.

SACRIFICED TO AN IDOL
1. *sacrificed to idols:* εἰδωλόθυτος EIDŌLOTHYTOS
Acts 15.29 "abstain from what has been s. to idols
21.25 "abstain from what has been s. to idols
Rev 2.14 " 'that they might eat food s. to idols
2.20 " 'teaching . . to eat food s. to idols

SACRIFICIAL
1. *offering, sacrifice:* θυσία THYSIA [A.1.b.3]
Phil 2.17 as a libation upon the sacrificial offering

SACRIFICIAL OFFERINGS
1. *altar:* θυσιαστήριον THYSIASTĒRION [C.2]
1 Cor 9.13 those who serve . . share in the s. offerings

SACRILEGE
1. *loathsome thing:* βδέλυγμα BDELYGMA
Mt 24.15 "when you see the desolating sacrilege
Mk 13.14 "when you see the desolating sacrilege

SACRILEGIOUS
1. *temple robber, sacrilegious person:* ἱερόσυλος (pred.) HIEROSYLOS*
Acts 19.37 "these men . . who are neither sacrilegious

SAD
1. *very sad, deeply grieved:* περίλυπος PERILYPOS
Lk 18.23 he became sad, for he was very rich

SAD, LOOKING
1. *with a sad look, sullen:* σκυθρωπός SKYTHRŌPOS
Lk 24.17 And they stood still, looking sad

SADDUCEE: Σαδδουκαῖος
Mt 3. 7 he saw many of the . . Sadducees coming
16. 1 Sadducees came, and to test him
16. 6 beware of the leaven of the . . Sadducees
16.11 Beware of the leaven of the . . Sadducees
16.12 beware . . the teaching of the . . Sadducees
22.23 The same day Sadducees came to him
22.34 heard . . he had silenced the Sadducees
Mk 12.18 Sadducees came to him . . and . . asked
Lk 20.27 There came to him some Sadducees
Acts 4. 1 the Sadducees came upon them
5.17 high priest rose up and . . the Sadducees
23. 6 Paul perceived . . part were Sadducees
23. 7 a dissension arose between . . Sadducees
23. 8 Sadducees say . . there is no resurrection

SADLY
1. *groan, sigh:* στενάζω (part.) STENAZŌ
Heb 13.17 Let them do this joyfully, and not sadly

SAFE
1. *certain, safe:* ἀσφαλής ASPHALĒS
Phil 3. 1 To write the same things . . is safe for you

SAFE AND SOUND
1. *be in good health:* ὑγιαίνω (part.) HYGIAINŌ
Lk 15.27 " 'he has received him safe and sound

SAFE, KEEP
1. *preserve, protect:* συντηρέω SYNTĒREŌ
Mk 6.20 Herod feared John . . and kept him safe

SAFELY
1. *safely, with certainty:* ἀσφαλῶς ASPHALŌS
Acts 16.23 charging the jailer to keep them safely

SAFELY, BRING ONE
1. *save, preserve:* διασῴζω DIASŌZŌ
Acts 23.24 "bring him safely to Felix the governor

SAIL
1. *lead up, bring back:* ἀνάγω (mid. or pass.) ANAGŌ
Acts 28.10 when we sailed, they put on board
2. *sail away:* ἀποπλέω APOPLEŌ*
Acts 13. 4 from there they sailed to Cyprus
14.26 from there they sailed to Antioch
20.15 sailing from there we came . . following day
27. 1 it was decided . . we should sail for Italy
3. *sail away:* ἐκπλέω EKPLEŌ
Acts 18.18 After this Paul . . sailed for Syria
4. *sail, go by sea:* πλέω PLEŌ
Lk 8.23 and as they sailed he fell asleep
Acts 21. 3 leaving it on the left we sailed to Syria
27. 2 embarking in a ship . . about to sail to . . Asia
Acts 27. 6 a ship of Alexandria sailing for Italy
27.24 " 'granted you all those who sail with you

SAIL ACROSS
1. *sail through:* διαπλέω DIAPLEŌ*
Acts 27. 5 when we had sailed across the sea

SAIL ALONG
1. *sail along:* παραλέγομαι PARALEGOMAI
Acts 27.13 weighed anchor and sailed along Crete

SAIL AWAY
1. *sail away:* ἐκπλέω EKPLEŌ
Acts 15.39 Barnabas took Mark . . and sailed away
20. 6 but we sailed away from Philippi

SAIL PAST
1. *sail past:* παραπλέω PARAPLEŌ*
Acts 20.16 Paul had decided to sail past Ephesus

SAIL, SET
1. *lead up, bring back:* ἀνάγω (mid. or pass.) ANAGŌ
Acts 13.13 Paul . . set sail from Paphos
16.11 Setting sail therefore from Troas
18.21 and he set sail from Ephesus
20. 3 as he was about to set sail for Syria
20.13 going ahead . ., we set sail for Assos
21. 1 when we . . parted from them and set sail
21. 2 having found a ship . ., we . . set sail
27.21 "you . . should not have set sail from Crete
28.11 After three months we set sail in a ship

SAIL SLOWLY
1. *sail slowly:* βραδυπλοέω BRADYPLOEŌ*
Acts 27. 7 We sailed slowly for a number of days

SAIL UNDER THE LEE OF
1. *sail under the lee of:* ὑποπλέω HYPOPLEŌ*
Acts 27. 4 we sailed under the lee of Cyprus
27. 7 we sailed under the lee of Crete

SAILOR
1. *seaman:* ναύτης NAUTĒS*
Acts 27.27 about midnight the sailors suspected
27.30 sailors were seeking to escape . . the ship
Rev 18.17 "sailors and all whose trade is on the sea

SAINT
1. *sacred, holy:* ἅγιος (subst.) HAGIOS
Mt 27.52 many bodies of the saints . . were raised
Acts 9.13 "much evil he has done to thy saints
9.32 he came down . . to the saints . . at Lydda
9.41 Then calling the saints and widows
26.10 "I not only shut up many of the saints
Rom 1. 7 To . . God's beloved . . called to be saints
8.27 the Spirit intercedes for the saints
12.13 Contribute to the needs of the saints
15.25 to Jerusalem with aid for the saints
15.26 contribution for the poor among the saints
15.31 service . . acceptable to the saints
16. 2 receive her in the Lord as befits . . saints
16.15 Greet Philologus . . and all the saints
1 Cor 1. 2 to those sanctified . ., called to be saints
6. 1 the unrighteous instead of the saints
6. 2 the saints will judge the world
14.33 As in all the churches of the saints
16. 1 concerning . . contribution for the saints
16.15 they . . devoted themselves to . . the saints
2 Cor 1. 1 To the church . . at Corinth, with all the saints
8. 4 taking part in the relief of the saints
9. 1 Now . . about the offering for the saints
9.12 not only supplies the wants of the saints
13.13(12) All the saints greet you
Eph 1. 1 To the saints who are also faithful[a]
1.15 heard of . . your love[c] toward all . . saints
1.18 his glorious inheritance in the saints
2.19 you are fellow citizens with the saints
3. 8 I am the very least of all the saints
3.18 power to comprehend with . . the saints
4.12 to equip the saints for . . ministry
5. 3 not . . named . ., as is fitting among saints
6.18 making supplication for all the saints

Phil 1. 1 To all the saints in Christ Jesus
4.21 Greet every saint in Christ Jesus
4.22 All the saints greet you
Col 1. 2 To the saints . . in Christ at Colossae
1. 4 love which you have for all the saints
1.12 to share in the inheritance of the saints
1.26 the mystery . . now . . manifest to his saints
1 Th 3.13 the coming of our Lord . . with all his saints
2 Th 1.10 he comes . . to be glorified in his saints
1 Tim 5.10 who has . . washed the feet of the saints
Phm . 5 I hear of your love . . toward . . the saints
. 7 hearts of the saints have been refreshed
Heb 6.10 the love . . you showed . . in serving the saints
13.24 Greet all your leaders and all the saints
Jude . 3 faith . . once for all delivered to . . saints
Rev 5. 8 bowls . . of incense, . . prayers of . . saints
8. 3 to mingle with the prayers of . . the saints
8. 4 smoke . . rose with . . prayers of the saints
11.18 "the time . . for rewarding . . the . . saints
13. 7 it was allowed to make war on the saints‡
13.10 a call for the endurance . . of the saints
14.12 a call for the endurance of the saints
16. 6 "For men have shed the blood of saints
17. 6 drunk with the blood of the saints
18.20 "O saints and apostles and prophets!
18.24 "in her was found the blood . . of saints
19. 8 "linen is . . righteous deeds of the saints
20. 9 surrounded the camp of the saints
22.21 grace of the Lord Jesus be with . . the saints'‡

SAKE, FOR S.'S
SAKE OF, FOR THE
1. *because of:* διά (+acc.) DIA
Mt **10.**22; **14.**3; **15.**3, 6; **19.**12; **24.**9, 22
Mk **6.**17; **13.**13, 20
Lk **21.**17
Jn **11.**15; **12.**30; **14.**11
Rom **4.**23; **11.**28[2]; **13.**5
1 Cor **4.**10; **9.**10[2], 23
2 Cor **2.**10; **4.**5, 11, 15; **8.**9
Phil **3.**7, 8
1 Th **1.**5; **3.**9
1 Tim **5.**23
2 Tim **2.**10
Phm .9
Heb **1.**14; **6.**7
1 Pet **1.**20; **2.**13; **3.**14
1 Jn **2.**12
Rev **2.**3
2. *for the sake of:* ἕνεκα HENEKA
Mt 5.10 "who are persecuted for righteousness' s.
10.18 "you will be dragged before . . kings for my s.
10.39 "who loses his life for my sake will find it
16.25 "whoever loses his life for my sake
19.29 "who has left houses . . for my name's sake
Mk 8.35 "whoever loses his life for my sake
10.29 "no one who has left house . . for my sake
13. 9 "you will stand before . . kings for my s.
Lk 9.24 "whoever loses his life for my sake
18.29 "for the sake of the kingdom of God
21.12 "brought before kings . . for my name's s.
Rom 8.36 "For thy sake we are being killed
14.20 Do not, for the sake of food, destroy
3. *over, for the sake of:* ὑπέρ (+gen.) HYPER
Jn 17.19 "for their sake I consecrate myself
Acts 9.16 "he must suffer for the sake of my name
15.26 "risked . . for the sake of . . Jesus Christ
Rom 1. 5 obedience . . for the sake of his name
9. 3 cut off . . for the sake of my brethren
2 Cor 5.15 for him who for their sake died
5.21 For our sake he made him to be sin
12.10 For the sake of Christ . . I am content
Phil 1.29 for the sake of Christ . . not only believe in him but also suffer for his sake
Col 1.24 I rejoice in my sufferings for your sake
1.24 for the sake of his body, . . the church
3 Jn . 7 For they have set out for his sake

IDIOMATICALLY
a. Heb 6.10 the love which you showed for his sake *τῆς ἀγάπης ἧς ἐνεδείξασθε εἰς τὸ ὄνομα αὐτοῦ* [ONOMA]
b. 1 Jn 2.12 because your sins are forgiven for his sake *ὅτι ἀφέωνται ὑμῖν αἱ ἁμαρτίαι διὰ τὸ ὄνομα αὐτοῦ* [ONOMA]
CONTEXTUALLY
1 Cor 10.28 (out of consideration . . for conscience' s.
Jude .11 abandon themselves for the sake of gain

SALA: Σαλά 'sālə (*See also* SHELAH)
Lk 3.32 Boaz, the son of Sala, . . son of Nahshon

SALAMIS: Σαλαμίς 'saləməs II,F-4
Acts 13. 5 When they arrived at Salamis

SALEM: Σαλήμ 'sāləm
Heb 7. 1 this Melchizedek, king of Salem
7. 2 then he is also king of Salem

SALIM: Σαλίμ 'sā,lim I,C-4; D-4
Jn 3.23 John . . was baptizing at Aenon near S.

SALMON: Σαλμών 'salmən
Mt 1. 4 Nahshon the father of Salmon
1. 5 Salmon the father of Boaz by Rahab

SALMONE: Σαλμώνη sal'mōnē II,E-4
Acts 27. 7 under the lee of Crete off Salmone

SALOME: Σαλώμη sə'lōmē
Mk 15.40 Mary the mother of James . . , and S.
16. 1 Mary the mother of James, and S.

SALT
1. *salt:* ἅλας HALAS*
Mt 5.13 "You are the salt of the earth; but if salt has lost its taste
Mk 9.50 "Salt is good; but if the salt has lost its saltness, how will you season it? Have salt in yourselves, and be at peace
Lk 14.34 "Salt is good; but if salt has lost its taste, how shall its saltness be restored?
Col 4. 6 Let your speech . . be . . seasoned with salt
2. *salt:* ἁλίζω HALIZŌ
Mk 9.49 "For every one will be salted with fire°
[9.49 "*every sacrifice will be salted with salt*‡
3. *salt:* ἅλς HALS
Mk [9.49 "*every sacrifice will be salted with salt*‡
4. *salty:* ἁλυκός HALYKOS*
Jas 3.12 No more can salt water yield fresh

SALTNESS, LOSE
1. *become saltless:* ἄναλος γίνεσθαι ANALOS*; GINOMAI [B.3.a.2]
Mk 9.50 "but if the salt has lost its saltness

SALTNESS, RESTORE
1. *season:* ἀρτύω ARTYŌ
Lk 14.34 "how shall its saltness be restored?
2. *salt:* ἁλίζω HALIZŌ [A.6.a.5]
Mt 5.13 "how shall its saltness be restored?

SALUTATION
1. *greeting:* ἀσπασμός ASPASMOS
Mt 23. 7 "salutations in the market places
Mk 12.38 "like . . salutations in the market places
Lk 11.43 "love . . salutations in the market places
20.46 "love salutations in the market places

SALUTE
1. *greet:* ἀσπάζομαι ASPAZOMAI
Mt 5.47 "if you salute only your brethren
10.12 "As you enter the house, salute it
Mk 15.18 "they began to salute him, "Hail, King!
Lk 10. 4 "salute no one on the road

SALVATION
1. *salvation, preservation:* σωτηρία SŌTĒRIA
Mk [16.end *sacred . . proclamation of eternal salvation*‡
Lk 1.69 "raised up a horn of salvation for us
1.77 "to give knowledge of s. to his people
19. 9 "Today salvation has come to this house
Jn 4.22 "for salvation is from the Jews
Acts 4.12 "there is salvation in no one else

Acts 13.26 "to us has been sent the message of this s.
13.47 " 'that you may bring s. to . . the earth
16.17 "who proclaim to you the way of s.
Rom 1.16 it is the power of God for salvation
11.11 through their trespass s. has come
13.11 For salvation is nearer to us now
2 Cor 1. 6 If we are afflicted, it is for your . . s.
6. 2 I . . helped you on the day of salvation
6. 2 behold, now is the day of salvation
7.10 a repentance that leads to salvation
Eph 1.13 who have heard . . the gospel of your s.
Phil 1.28 This is a clear omen . . of your salvation
2.12 work out your own salvation with fear
1 Th 5. 8 put on . . for a helmet the hope of s.
5. 9 God has . . destined us . . to obtain salvation
2 Tim 2.10 that they also may obtain salvation
3.15 sacred writings . . able to instruct you for s.
Heb 1.14 for . . those who are to obtain salvation
2. 3 if we neglect such a great salvation
2.10 should make the pioneer of their s. perfect
5. 9 he became the source of eternal salvation
6. 9 sure of better things that belong to s.
1 Pet 1. 5 guarded through faith for a s.
1. 9 As . . outcome of your faith you obtain . . s.
1.10 The prophets . . inquired about this s.
2. 2 that by it you may grow up to s.
2 Pet 3.15 count the forbearance of our Lord as s.
Jude . 3 eager to write to you of our common s.
Rev 7.10 "Salvation belongs to our God!
12.10 "Now the s. and the power . . have come
19. 1 "Salvation and glory . . belong to our God

2. *saving, delivering:* σωτήριος SŌTĒRIOS*
[a]subst. neut. [b]pred. A.3.b.3
Lk 2.30 [a]"for mine eyes have seen thy salvation
3. 6 [a]"all flesh shall see the s. of God
Acts 28.28 [a]"this s. . . has been sent to the Gentiles
Eph 6.17 [a]take the helmet of salvation
Tit 2.11 [b]grace of God has appeared for the s.

SALVE
1. *salve, eye salve:* κολλούριον KOLLOURION*
Rev 3.18 " 'buy . . salve to anoint your eyes

SAMARIA: sə'merēə I,C-4
1. *Samaria:* Σαμάρεια
Lk 17.11 passing along between S. and Galilee
Jn 4. 4 He had to pass through Samaria
4. 5 came to a city of Samaria, called Sychar
4. 7 There came a woman of S. to draw water
Acts 1. 8 "you shall be my witnesses in . . Samaria
8. 1 all scattered throughout the region of . . S.
8. 5 Philip went down to a city of S.
8. 9 Simon . . amazed the nation of Samaria
8.14 Samaria had received the word of God
9.31 the church throughout . . S. had peace
15. 3 passed through both Phoenicia and S.

2. *Samaritan:* Σαμαρῖτις [A.3.a.2]
Jn 4. 9 "you, a Jew, ask . . a woman of S.

SAMARITAN (*See also* SAMARIA 2)
1. *Samaritan:* Σαμαρίτης
Mt 10. 5 "enter no town of the Samaritans
Lk 9.52 entered a village of the Samaritans
10.33 "a Samaritan . . came to where he was
17.16 Now he was a Samaritan
Jn 4. 9 The S. woman said to him, "How is it?
4. 9 Jews have no dealings with Samaritans
4.39 Many Samaritans . . believed in him
4.40 So when the Samaritans came
8.48 "saying that you are a Samaritan
Acts 8.25 preaching the gospel to . . the Samaritans

SAME (*See also* MEMBER OF THE SAME BODY; WAY IN WHICH, IN THE SAME)
1. *that:* ἐκεῖνος EKEINOS
Mt 22.23 The same day Sadducees came
Acts 16.33 And he took them the same hour
2. *equal, same:* ἴσος ISOS
Acts 11.17 "God gave the same gift to them

SAME AS, THE
1. *as great as, how great:* ὅσος HOSOS
Rev 21.16 its length the same as its breadth

SAME, THAT
1. *that:* ἐκεῖνος EKEINOS
Mt 13. 1 That same day Jesus went out of the house
18.28 "that same servant, as he went out

SAME, THE
1. *in like manner:* ὡσαύτως HŌSAUTŌS
Mt 20. 5 "Going out again . . , he did the same
21.30 "he went to the second and said the same
21.36 "he sent other servants . . and they did the s.
Mk 14.31 And they all said the same
2. *this:* οὗτος HOUTOS
Rom **13.6**
1 Cor **9.8**
Eph **6.8**

SAME TIME, AT THE
1. *at the same time:* ἅμα HAMA
[a]*ἅμα καί* [b]*ἅμα δὲ καί*
Acts 24.26 [a]At the s. time he hoped that money
27.40 at the same time loosening the ropes
Phm .22 [b]At the same time, prepare a guest room

SAME TRADE, OF THE
1. *practicing the same skill:* ὁμότεχνος HOMOTECHNOS*
Acts 18. 3 because he was of the same trade

SAME WAY, IN THE
1. *in like manner:* ὁμοίως HOMIŌS
Heb 9.21 in the s. way he sprinkled with the blood
Jas 2.25 in the s. way was not . . Rahab . . justified?
2. *in like manner:* ὡσαύτως HŌSAUTŌS
1 Cor 11.25 In the s. way also the cup, after supper

SAMOS: Σάμος 'sā,mäs II,E-3
Acts 20.15 the next day we touched at Samos

SAMOTHRACE: Σαμοθρᾴκη 'samə,thrās II,E-3
Acts 16.11 we made a direct voyage to Samothrace

SAMSON: Σαμψών 'samsən
Heb 11.32 For time would fail me to tell of . . S.

SAMUEL: Σαμουήλ 'samyə(wə)l
Acts 3.24 "all the prophets who have spoken, from S.
13.20 "he gave them judges until Samuel
Heb 11.32 For time would fail me to tell of . . S.

SANCTIFICATION
1. *sanctification:* ἁγιασμός HAGIASMOS
Rom 6.19 so now yield your members . . for s.
6.22 the return you get is sanctification
1 Cor 1.30 Christ Jesus, whom God made our . . s.
1 Th 4. 3 For this is the will of God, your s.
2 Th 2.13 to be saved, through s. by the Spirit[c]

SANCTIFIED BY
1. *sanctification:* ἁγιασμός (+gen.) HAGIASMOS
Pet 1. 2 destined by God . . and s. by the Spirit

SANCTIFY
1. *make sacred:* ἁγιάζω HAGIAZŌ
Jn 17.17 "Sanctify them in the truth
Acts 20.32 "inheritance among all . . who are sanctified
26.18 " 'a place among those who are sanctified
Rom 15.16 offering of the Gentiles may be . . sanctified
1 Cor 1. 2 to those sanctified in Christ Jesus
6.11 you were sanctified, you were justified
Eph 5.26 ⟨loved the church⟩ that he might sanctify
1 Th 5.23 May the God of peace . . sanctify you
Heb 2.11 For he who sanctifies and those who are sanctified have all one origin
9.13 sanctifies for . . purification of the flesh
10.10 by that will we have been sanctified
10.14 he has perfected . . those who are sanctified
10.29 the blood . . by which he was sanctified
13.12 Jesus also suffered . . to s. the people

SANCTUARY
1. *sacred, holy:* ἅγιος (subst. neut. sg. or pl.) HAGIOS
Heb 8. 2 a minister in the s. and the true tent[n]
9. 1 regulations for worship and an earthly s.

Heb 9. 8 the way into the s. is not yet opened
9.24 entered, not into a s. made with hands
10.19 since we have confidence to enter the s.
13.11 whose blood is brought into the s.
2. *temple, shrine:* ναός NAOS
Mt 23.35 "murdered between the s. and the altar
3. *house, household:* οἶκος OIKOS
Lk 11.51 "perished between the altar and the s.
CONTEXTUALLY
Heb 8. 5 and shadow of the heavenly sanctuary

SAND
1. *sand:* ἄμμος AMMOS*
Mt 7.26 "man who built his house upon the sand
Rom 9.27 "Though .. Israel be as the s. of the sea
Heb 11.12 descendants as many as .. grains of s.
Rev 12.17(18) And he stood[e] on the sand of the sea
20. 8 their number is like the sand of the sea

SANDAL
1. *sandal:* ὑπόδημα HYPODĒMA
Mt 3.11 "whose sandals I am not worthy to carry
10.10 "no bag for your journey, .. nor sandals
Mk 1. 7 "whose sandals I am not worthy to .. untie
Lk 3.16 "whose sandals I am not worthy to untie
10. 4 "Carry no purse, no bag, no sandals
22.35 "When I sent you out with no .. sandals
Jn 1.27 "whose sandal I am not worthy to untie
Acts 13.25 " 'the sandals .. I am not worthy to untie
2. *sandal:* σανδάλιον SANDALION*
Mk 6. 9 to wear sandals and not put on two tunics
Acts 12. 8 "Dress .. and put on your sandals

SANE, KEEP
1. *be of sound mind:* σωφρονέω SŌPHRONEŌ
1 Pet 4. 7 keep sane and sober for your prayers

SAPPHIRA: Σάπφιρα sə'fīrə
Acts 5. 1 Ananias with his wife S. sold .. property

SAPPHIRE
1. *hyacinthine, blue:* ὑακίνθινος HYAKINTHINOS*
Rev 9.17 the color of fire and of sapphire[c]†
2. *lapis lazuli, sapphire:* σάπφιρος SAPPHIROS*
Rev 21.19 the first was jasper, the second sapphire

SARAH: Σάρρα 'serə
Rom 4.19 the barrenness of Sarah's womb
9. 9 "I will return and S. shall have a son
Heb 11.11 By faith S. .. received power to conceive
1 Pet 3. 6 Sarah obeyed Abraham, calling him lord

SARDIS: Σάρδεις 'särdəs II,E-3
Rev 1.11 "Write .. to the seven churches, .. to S.
3. 1 "to the angel of the church in S. write
3. 4 " 'you have still a few names in Sardis

SATAN
1. *satan, adversary:* σατανᾶς SATANAS*
Mt 4.10 Jesus said to him, "Begone, Satan!
12.26 "if Satan casts out Satan, he is divided against himself
16.23 said to Peter, "Get behind me, Satan!
Mk 1.13 in .. wilderness forty days, tempted by S.
3.23 he called them to him, and said .. "How can Satan cast out Satan?
3.26 "if Satan has risen up against himself
4.15 "Satan .. comes and takes away the word
8.33 rebuked Peter, .. "Get behind me, Satan!
Lk 10.18 "I saw S. fall like lightning from heaven
11.18 "if Satan .. is divided against himself
13.16 "a daughter of Abraham whom S. bound
22. 3 Then Satan entered into Judas
22.31 "Simon, behold, S. demanded to have you[k]
Jn 13.27 after the morsel, S. entered into him
Acts 5. 3 "Ananias, why has S. filled your heart?
26.18 " 'that they .. turn .. from the power of S.
Rom 16.20 the God of peace will soon crush Satan
1 Cor 5. 5 you are to deliver this man to Satan
7. 5 come together again, lest S. tempt you
2 Cor 2.11 to keep S. from gaining the advantage
11.14 even Satan disguises himself as an angel
12. 7 in the flesh, a messenger of Satan
1 Th 2.18 we wanted to come .. but S. hindered us
2 Th 2. 9 coming of .. lawless one by .. activity of S.
1 Tim 1.20 Alexander, whom I have delivered to S.
5.15 some have already strayed after Satan
Rev 2. 9 " 'slander of .. a synagogue of Satan
2.13 " 'where you dwell, where Satan's throne
2.13 " 'among you, where Satan dwells
2.24 " 'what some call the deep things of S.
3. 9 " 'those of the synagogue of Satan
12. 9 ancient serpent, .. called the Devil and S.
20. 2 ancient serpent, who is the Devil and S.
20. 7 Satan will be loosed from his prison

SATISFACTION, GIVE
1. *be pleasing:* εὐάρεστος εἶναι EUARESTOS [B.3.b.4]
Tit 2. 9 Bid slaves .. to give satisfaction

SATISFACTION ONE FEELS
1. *blessing:* μακαρισμός MAKARISMOS
Gal 4.15 What has become of the s. you felt?

SATISFIED, BE
1. *persuade:* πείθω (perf. pass.) PEITHŌ
Rom 15.14 I myself am satisfied about you

SATISFY
1. *please:* ἀρέσκω ARESKŌ
2 Tim 2. 4 to satisfy the one who enlisted him
2. *suffice, satisfy:* ἀρκέω ARKEŌ
Jn 14. 8 "show us .. and we shall be satisfied
3. *feed, fatten:* χορτάζω CHORTAZŌ
Mt 5. 6 "those who hunger .. shall be satisfied
14.20 they all ate and were satisfied
15.37 they all ate and were satisfied
Mk 6.42 they all ate and were satisfied
8. 8 they ate, and were satisfied
Lk 6.21 "you that hunger .. shall be satisfied
9.17 all ate and were satisfied
4. *fill quite full:* ἐμπίμπλημι EMPIMPLĒMI
Acts 14.17 "satisfying your hearts with food
5. *make satisfactory:* τὸ ἱκανὸν ποιεῖν HIKANOS [A.6.a.4]
Mk 15.15 So Pilate, wishing to satisfy the crowd
6. *persuade:* πείθω PEITHŌ
Mt 28.14 "s. him and keep you out of trouble

SAUL: 'sȯl
1. king of Israel: Σαούλ
Acts 13.21 "God gave them Saul the son of Kish
2. the apostle Paul: Σαῦλος
[a]Σαούλ
Acts 7.58 laid down .. garments at the feet of .. S.
8. 1 Saul was consenting to his death
8. 3 But Saul was ravaging the church
9. 1 Saul, still breathing threats and murder
9. 4 [a]heard a voice saying to him, "Saul, Saul, why do you persecute me?
9. 8 Saul arose from the ground
9.11 "inquire .. for a man of Tarsus named S.
9.17 [a]"Brother S., the Lord Jesus .. sent me
9.22 Saul increased all the more in strength
9.24 their plot became known to Saul
11.25 Barnabas went to Tarsus to look for Saul
11.30 sending .. by the hand of Barnabas and S.
12.25 Barnabas and S. returned from[k] Jerusalem
13. 1 at Antioch there were prophets .., and S.
13. 2 "Set apart for me Barnabas and Saul
13. 7 Sergius Paulus .. summoned Barnabas and S.
13. 9 Saul, who is also called Paul
22. 7 [a]"heard a voice saying to me, 'Saul, Saul, why do you persecute me?
22.13 [a]" 'Brother Saul, receive your sight
26.14 [a]"I heard a voice saying to me .. 'Saul, Saul, why do you persecute me?

SAVE
1. *save, preserve:* διασῴζω DIASŌZŌ
Acts 27.43 the centurion, wishing to save Paul
1 Pet 3.20 eight persons, .. saved through water
2. *salvation, preservation:* σωτηρία SŌTĒRIA [B.1.a.2]
Rom 10. 1 my heart's desire .. is that they .. be saved
10.10 he confesses with his lips and so is saved

2 Th 2.13 because God chose you . . to be saved
Heb 9.28 Christ . . will appear a second time . . to s.
3. *save, keep from harm:* σῴζω SŌZŌ
Mt 1.21 "he will save his people from their sins
8.25 "Save, Lord; we are perishing
10.22 "he who endures to the end will be saved
14.30 he cried out, "Lord, save me
16.25 "whoever would save his life will lose it
[18.11 *"the Son of man came to save the lost*‡
19.25 "Who then can be saved?
24.13 "he who endures to the end will be saved
24.22 "no human being would be saved
27.40 "save yourself! . . come down from the cross
27.42 "He saved others; he cannot save himself. He is the King of Israel
27.49 "see whether Elijah will come to save him[n]
Mk 3. 4 "Is it lawful on the sabbath . . to s. life?
8.35 "whoever would save his life will lose it; . . whoever loses his life . . will save it
10.26 "Then who can be saved?
13.13 "he who endures to the end will be saved
13.20 "no human being would be saved
15.30 "save yourself, . . come down from the cross!
15.31 the chief priests mocked him . . , saying, "He saved others; he cannot save himself
16.16 "He who believes . . will be saved[k]‡
Lk 6. 9 "is it lawful on the sabbath . . to save life?
7.50 "Your faith has saved you; go in peace
8.12 "that they may not believe and be saved
9.24 "whoever would save his life will lose it; and whoever loses his life . . will save it
[9.55(56) *"the Son of man came . . to save them*‡
13.23 "Lord, will those who are saved be few?
18.26 "Then who can be saved?
19.10 "the Son of man came . . to save the lost
23.35 the rulers scoffed at him, saying, "He saved others; let him save himself!
23.37 "If . . King of the Jews, save yourself!
23.39 "Are you not the Christ? Save yourself!
Jn 3.17 that the world might be saved
5.34 "but I say this that you may be saved
10. 9 "he will be saved, and will go in
12.27 "shall I say . . 'save me from this hour'?
12.47 "not come to judge the world but to s.
Acts 2.21 " 'whoever calls on the . . Lord shall be saved
2.40 "Save yourselves from this . . generation
2.47 Lord added . . those who were being saved
4.12 "no other . . by which we must be saved
11.14 " 'a message by which you will be saved
15. 1 "Unless . . circumcised . . you cannot be saved
15.11 "But we believe that we shall be saved
16.30 "Men, what must I do to be saved?
16.31 "Believe . . , and you will be saved
27.20 all hope of . . being saved was . . abandoned
27.31 "Unless these . . stay . . you cannot be saved
Rom 5. 9 much more shall we be saved by him
5.10 much more . . shall we be saved by his life
8.24 For in this hope we were saved
9.27 "only a remnant of them will be saved
10. 9 if you . . believe . . , you will be saved
10.13 "who calls upon . . the Lord will be saved
11.14 to make . . Jews jealous, and thus s. some
11.26 and so all Israel will be saved
1 Cor 1.18 to us who are being saved it is . . power
1.21 it pleased God . . to save those who believe
3.15 loss, though he himself will be saved
5. 5 that his spirit may be saved in the day
7.16 whether you will save your husband
7.16 whether you will save your wife
9.22 that I might by all means save some
10.33 advantage . . of many, that they . . be saved
15. 2 you are saved, if you hold it fast
2 Cor 2.15 among those who are being saved
Eph 2. 5 (by grace you have been saved
2. 8 For by grace you have been saved
1 Th 2.16 to the Gentiles that they may be saved
2 Th 2.10 refused to love the truth and so be saved
1 Tim 1.15 Christ Jesus came into the world to s.
2. 4 who desires all men to be saved
2.15 woman will be saved through bearing
4.16 will save both yourself and your hearers
2 Tim 1. 9 ⟨God,⟩ who saved us and called us
4.18 The Lord will . . save me for his . . kingdom
Tit 3. 5 he saved us, not because of deeds done
Heb 5. 7 who was able to save him from death
7.25 he is able for all time to save those
Jas 1.21 word, which is able to save your souls
2.14 Can his faith save him?
4.12 There is one . . judge . . who is able to save
5.15 the prayer of faith will save the sick man
5.20 whoever brings back a sinner . . will s. his soul
1 Pet 3.21 Baptism . . now saves you . . as an appeal
4.18 "If the righteous man is scarcely saved
Jude . 5 he[b] who saved a people out of . . Egypt
.23 save some, by snatching them out
IDIOMATICALLY
a. Lk 1.71 "that we should be saved from our enemies
σωτηρίαν ἐξ ἐχθρῶν ἡμῶν [SŌTĒRIA]

SAVING
1. *salvation, preservation:* σωτηρία SŌTĒRIA
Heb 11. 7 an ark for the saving of his household

SAVIOR
1. *deliverer, savior:* σωτήρ SŌTĒR*
Lk 1.47 "my spirit rejoices in God my Savior
2.11 "for to you is born this day . . a Savior
Jn 4.42 "we know that this is indeed the Savior
Acts 5.31 "God exalted him at his right hand as . . S.
13.23 "God has brought to Israel a Savior
Eph 5.23 Christ is . . himself its Savior
Phil 3.20 from it we await a S., the Lord Jesus
1 Tim 1. 1 an apostle . . by command of God our S.
2. 3 it is acceptable in the sight of God our S.
4.10 the living God, who is the S. of all men
2 Tim 1.10 our S. Christ Jesus, who abolished death
Tit 1. 3 preaching . . by command of God our S.
1. 4 God the Father and Christ Jesus our S.
2.10 may adorn the doctrine of God our S.
2.13 our great God and Savior[c] Jesus Christ
3. 4 the . . loving kindness of God our Savior
3. 6 poured out . . through Jesus Christ our S.
2 Pet 1. 1 righteousness of our God and Savior
1.11 kingdom of our Lord and S. Jesus Christ
2.20 knowledge of . . Lord and S. Jesus Christ
3. 2 the commandment of the Lord and Savior
3.18 knowledge of our Lord and S. Jesus Christ
1 Jn 4.14 the Father has sent his Son as the Savior
Jude .25 to the only God, our S. through Jesus

SAW IN TWO
1. *saw, file:* πρίζω PRIZŌ*
Heb 11.37 they were sawn in two,[y] . . were killed

SAY (*See also* DEFENSE, SAY IN ONE'S; FAREWELL, SAY; INDIGNANTLY, SAY)
1. *bear a message:* ἀγγέλλω AGGELLŌ*
Jn 20.18 Mary Magdalene . . said to the disciples
2. *bring tidings:* ἀπαγγέλλω APAGGELLŌ
Acts 22.26 When the centurion heard that, he . . said
3. *reply:* ἀποκρίνομαι APOKRINOMAI
Mt 12.38 some . . Pharisees said to him, "Teacher
Mk 9. 6 For he did not know what to say
Acts 5. 8 Peter said to her, "Tell me
24.25 Felix was alarmed and said, "Go away
4. *calculate, argue:* διαλογίζομαι DIALOGIZOMAI
Lk 20.14 "said to themselves, 'This is the heir
5. *say, speak:* εἶπον EIPON
Mt **2.**8; **3.**7; **4.**3, 9; **5.**[22†, 22; **8.**4, 8, 10, 13, 19, 21, 32; **9.**2, 3, 4, 5², 12, 15, 22; **11.**3; **12.**2, 3, 11, 24, 25, 32, 49; **13.**10, 27, 52, 57; **14.**2, 16, 18, 29; **15.**10, 15, 16, 27, 32, 34; **16.**6, 8, 14, 23; **17.**4, 7, 19, 22, 24, 26; **18.**3, 21; **19.**5, 11, 14, 16, 17, 23, 26, 27, 28; **20.**4, 17, 21, 25, 32; **21.**3, 16, 21, 25, 26, 27, 28, 30, 38; **22.**13, 18, 24, 44; **23.**39; **24.**23, 26, 48; **25.**8, 22, 24; **26.**1, 10, 15, 18², 21, 25², 26, 35, 44, 49, 50, 55, 61, 62, 63, 64, 73; **27.**4, 6, 17, 21², 43, 49, 63; **28.**5, 6

Mk **1**.17, 44; **2**.9[2], 19; **4**.39, 40; **5**.34; **6**.22, 24[2]; **7**.6, 10, 29; **8**.5, 34; **9**.21, 23, 29, 36, 39; **10**.4, 5, 14, 18, 21, 36, 37, 38, 39[2], 49, 51[2], 52; **11**.3[2], 6, 14, 23, 29, 31, 32; **12**.7, 15, 16, 17, 26, 32[2], 34, 36, 43; **13**.2, 21; **14**.6, 14, 18, 20, 22, 24, 39, 48, 62, 72; **15**.39; **16**.8, 15‡

Lk **1**.13, 18, 28, 30, 34, 35, 38, 46, 60, 61; **2**.10, 28, 34, 48, 49; **3**.12, 13, 14; **4**.3, 6, 9, 23, 24, 43; **5**.4, 10, 13, 20, 23[2], 24, 27, 33, 34; **6**.2, 8, 9, 10; **7**.7, 9, 13, 14, 20, 39, 40[2], 43, 48, 50; **8**.4, 10, 21, 22, 25, 28, 30, 45[2], 46, 48, 52; **9**.3, 9, 12, 13[2], 14, 20, 22, 33, 43, 48, 50, 54, [55‡, 57, 58, 59[2], 60, 61, 62; **10**.10, 18, 21, 23, 26, 28, 29, 35, 37[2], 40; **11**.1, 2, 5[2], 15, 17, 27, 28, 39, 46, 49; **12**.3, 11, 12, 13, 14, 15, 18, 20, 22, 41, 42, 45; **13**.7, 12, 20, 23[2], 32, 35; **14**.5, 15, 16, 17, 18, 19, 20, 21, 22, 23, 25; **15**.11, 12, 21, 22, 27, 31; **16**.2, 3, 6[2], 7[2], 15, 25, 27, 30, 31; **17**.1, 5, 6, 14, 17, 19, 22, 37; **18**.4, 6, 19, 21, 22, 24, 26, 27, 28, 29, 31, 41, 42; **19**.5, 8, 9, 12, 13, 17, 19, 24, 25, 28, 30, 33, 34, 39; **20**.2, 5, 6, 8, 13, 16, 17, 23, 24, 25, 34, 41, 42, 45; **21**.3, 5, 8; **22**.8, 9, 10, 15, 17, 25, 33, 34, 35[2], 36, 38[2], 40, 46, 48, 49, 52, 56, 60, 61, 70, 71; **23**.4, 14, 22, 28, 43, 46[2]; **24**.5, 17, 19, 24, 25, 32, 38, [40‡, 41, 44, 46

Jn **1**.15, 22, 23, 30, 33, 38, 42, 46, 50; **2**.18, 20, 22; **3**.2, 7, 9, 26, 28; **4**.13, 17, 27, 32, 48, 52, 53; **5**.11, 12, 14; **6**.10, 25, 28, 30, 32, 34, 35, 36, 41, 53, 59, 60, 61, 67; **7**.3, 9, 33, 35, 36, 38, 39, 42, 45; **8**.7‡, 10‡, 11‡, 21, 25, 28, 41, 42, 52, 55, 57, 58; **9**.6, 7, 11, 12, 15, 17, 22, 23, 24, 26, 28, 35, 37, 39, 40, 41; **10**.7, 34, 36, 41; **11**.4, 12, 16, 21, 25, 28[2], 34, 37, 41, 42, 43, 49, 51; **12**.6, 7, 19, 27, 35, 39, 41, 44, 49; **13**.11, 12, 28, 33; **14**.26, 28; **15**.20; **16**.4, 15, 17, 19[2]; **17**.1; **18**.6, 7, 11, 21, 22[2], 25[2], 31[2], 33, 34, 37, 38; **19**.21, 24, 30; **20**.14, 17, 18, 20, 21, 22, 25, 26; **21**.6, 17[2], 19, 20, 23

Acts **1**.7, 9, 11, 15, 24; **2**.29, 34, 37; **3**.4, 6, 22; **4**.8, 23, 24, 25; **5**.3, 8, 19, 35; **6**.2; **7**.1, 3, 7, 26, 27, 33, 35, 37, 40, 56, 60; **8**.20, 29, 31, 34, [37‡; **9**.5, 10[2], 15, 17, 34, 40; **10**.3, 4[2], 14, 19, 21, 22, 34; **11**.8, 13; **12**.8, 11, 15, 17; **13**.2, 10, 16, 22, 46; **14**.10; **15**.7, 36; **16**.18, 20, 31; **17**.32; **18**.6, 9, 14, 21; **19**.2, 3[2], 4, 21, 25, 41; **20**.10, 18, 35; **21**.11, 14, 20, 37; **22**.8, 10[2], 13, 14, 19, 21, 25, 27; **23**.1, 3, 4, 11, 14, 20, 23; **24**.20, 22; **25**.9, 10; **26**.15[2]; **27**.21, 31, 35; **28**.21, 26, [29‡

Rom **10**.6

1 Cor **1**.15; **10**.28; **11**.22, 24; **12**.3, 15, 16, 21; **15**.27

2 Cor **4**.6; **6**.16

Gal **2**.14

Col **4**.17

Tit **1**.12

Heb **1**.5; **3**.10; **7**.9; **10**.7, 30; **12**.21

Jas **2**.3[2], 11[2], 16

1 Jn **1**.6, 8, 10; **4**.20

Jude .9

Rev **7**.14; **17**.7; **21**.5, 6; **22**.6, 17

6. *say, speak:* ἐρῶ ERŌ

Mt 5.21 "heard that it was said to the men of old
5.27 "it was said, 'You shall not commit adultery
5.31 "It was also said, 'Whoever divorces
5.33 "it was said to the men of old
5.38 "it was said, 'An eye for an eye
5.43 "it was said, 'You shall love . . neighbor
7. 4 "how can you say to your brother?
7.22 "many will say to me, 'Lord, Lord
17.20 "you will say to this mountain, 'Move
21. 3 "you shall say, 'The Lord has need
21.25 "he will say . . 'Why . . did you not believe?
22.31 "have you not read what was said to you?
25.34 "King will say to those at his right hand
25.41 "he will say to those at his left hand
Mk 11.31 "he will say, 'Why . . did you not believe?
Lk 2.24 according to what is said in the law
4.12 "It is said, 'You shall not tempt the Lord
12.19 " 'I will say to my soul, . . take your ease
13.27 "he will say, 'I tell you, I do not know
14. 9 "he . . will . . say . . 'Give place to this man
14.10 "may say to you, 'Friend, go up higher
15.18 " 'I will say . . "Father, I have sinned
17. 7 "Will any . . who has a servant . . say to him?
17. 8 "Will he not rather say to him, 'Prepare . . '?
Lk 17.21 "nor will they say, 'Lo, here it is!
17.23 "they will say to you, 'Lo, there!
19.31 "you shall say . . 'The Lord has need of it
20. 5 "he will say, 'Why did you not believe?
23.29 "they will say, 'Blessed are the barren!
Jn 4.18 "not your husband; this you said truly
Acts 8.24 "that nothing . . you have said may come
13.40 "lest . . what is said in the prophets
17.28 "as even some of your poets have said
Rom 3. 5 if . . wickedness serves . . , what shall we s.?
6. 1 What shall we say . . ? Are we to continue?
7. 7 What . . shall we say? That the law is sin?
8.31 What then shall we say to this?
9.14 What shall we say . . ? Is there injustice?
9.19 You will say . . "Why does he . . find fault?
9.20 Will what is molded say to its molder?
9.26 "in the very place where it was said
9.30 What shall we say, then? That Gentiles
11.19 You will say, "Branches were broken off
1 Cor 14.16 how can . . an outsider[x] say the "Amen"?
14.23 will they not say that you are mad?
2 Cor 12. 9 he said . . "My grace is sufficient for you
Phil 4. 4 again I will say, Rejoice
Heb 1.13 to what angel has he . . said, "Sit"?
4. 3 as he has said, "As I swore in my wrath
10.15 Spirit also bears witness . . after saying
13. 5 he has said, "I will never fail you
Jas 2.18 some one will say, "You have faith
Rev 7.14 I said to him, "Sir, you know

7. *speak, talk:* λαλέω LALEŌ

Mt 10.19 "what you are to say will be given . . you
13.34 All this Jesus said . . in parables; . . he said nothing to them without a parable
23. 1 Then said Jesus to the crowds
28.18 Jesus . . said . . "All authority in heaven
Mk 5.36 But ignoring[q] what they said, Jesus
8.32 he said this plainly. And Peter took him
11.23 "what he says will come to pass
13.11 "do not be anxious . . what you are to say; but say whatever is given you
14.31 But he said vehemently, "If I must die
Lk 2.15 the shepherds said to one another
2.33 marveled at what was said about him
12. 3 "whatever you have said in the dark
24.36 As they were saying this, Jesus . . stood
Jn 1.37 The two disciples heard him say this
8.26 "I have much to say about you
10. 6 did not understand what he was saying
12.36 When Jesus had said this, he departed
12.50 "What I say, therefore, I say as the Father has bidden me
16. 1 "I . . said . . this . . to keep you from falling away
16. 4 "But I have said these things to you
16. 6 "because I have said these things to you
16.25 "I have said this to you in figures
16.33 "I . . said this . . that . . you may have peace
18.20 "I have said nothing secretly
18.21 "Ask those . . what I said to them
Acts 8.26 an angel of the Lord said to Philip
10.44 While Peter was still saying this
16.14 to give heed to what was said by Paul
23. 7 when he had said this, a dissension arose
23.18 "as he has something to say to you
26.22 "saying nothing but what the prophets
26.31 they said . . "This man is doing nothing
28.25 "The Holy Spirit was right in saying
1 Cor 9. 8 Do I say this on human authority?
14. 9 how will any one know what is said?
15.34 I say this to your shame
2 Cor 7.14 as everything we said to you was true
11.17 (What I am saying I say not with the Lord's authority but as a fool
1 Th 1. 8 so that we need not say anything
1 Tim 5.13 busybodies, saying what they should not
Heb 5. 5 who said to him, "Thou art my Son
7.14 with that . . Moses said nothing about priests
11.18 of whom it was said, "Through Isaac

1 Jn 4. 5 therefore what they say is of the world
Rev 10. 4 "Seal up what the seven thunders . . said
17. 1 one of the seven angels . . said to me, "Come

8. *speech, dialect:* λαλιά LALIA [A.1.a]
Jn 8.43 "Why do you not understand what I say?

9. *say, speak:* λέγω LEGŌ
Mt **1**.20; **2**.1(2), 13, 20; **3**.3, 9, 14, 17; **4**.6, 10, 17, 19; **5**.2, 18, 22, 26, 28, 32, 34, 39, 44; **6**.2, 5, 16, 31; **7**.21; **8**.2, 3, 4, 6, 7, 9, 10, 20, 22, 25, 26, 27; **9**.6, 9, 11, 14, 18, 21, 24, 28[2], 29, 33, 34‡, 37; **10**.7, 15, 23, 42; **11**.11, 18, 19; **12**.13, 23, 38, 44; **13**.3, 14, 17, 24, 28, 31, 36, 51, 54; **14**.4, 15, 17, 26, 27, 31, 33; **15**.1, 5, 7, 12, 23, 25, 33, 34; **16**.2‡, 7, 13, 15, 22, 28; **17**.5, 10, 15, 20[2], 25[2]; **18**.1, 3, 13, 18, 19, 22[2], 28, 32; **19**.7, 8, 9, 10, 18, 20, 23, 25, 28; **20**.6, 7[2], 8, 12, 21, 22, 23, 33; **21**.2, 4, 10, 11, 13, 16[2], 19, 20, 21, 23, 31[2], 37, 41, 42; **22**.1, 4, 8, 12, 16, 20, 21[2], 23, 24, 42[2], 43[2]; **23**.16, 30, 36; **24**.2, 3, 5, 34, 47; **25**.11, 12, 20, 40; **26**.5, 8, 13, 17, 18, 21, 22, 25, 27, 31, 34, 35, 36, 38, 40, 45, 48, 52, 64, 65, 68, 69, 70, 71; **27**.4, 9, 11, 13, 22[2], 24, 29, 40, 41, 47, 49, 54, 63; **28**.9, 10, 13
Mk **1**.7, 15, 25, 27, 37, 38, 40, 41, 44; **2**.5, 8, 10, 11, 12, 14, 16, 17, 18, 24, 25, 27; **3**.3, 4, 5, 21, 22, 23, 28, 30, 32, 34; **4**.2, 9, 11, 13, 21, 24, 26, 30, 35, 38, 41; **5**.7, 8, 19, 23, 28, 30, 31[2], 35, 36, 39, 41[2]; **6**.2, 4, 10, 14‡, 15[2], 16, 18, 25, 31, 35, 37, 38[2], 50; **7**.9, 11, 14, 18, 20, 27, 34, 37; **8**.1, 12[2], 15, 17, 19, 20, 21, 24, 26, 27, 29, 33; **9**.1[2], 5, 11, 24, 25, 26, 31, 35, 41; **10**.11, 15, 23, 24, 26, 27, 28, 29, 35, 42, 47, 49; **11**.2, 5, 17, 21, 23, 28, 33; **12**.6, 14, 16, 18[2], 26, 35[2], 38, 43; **13**.1, 5, 6, 30, 37[2]; **14**.2, 9, 12, 13, 14, 18, 19, 25, 27, 30[2], 31, 32, 34, 36, 37, 41, 44, 45, 57, 58, 63, 65, 67, 68, 69, 70; **15**.2, 12, 14, [28‡, 29, 31, 35, 36; **16**.3, 6
Lk **1**.24, 66, 67; **2**.13; **3**.7, 8; **4**.21, 22, 24, 35; **5**.8, 13, 21, 24, 26, 30, 39; **6**.5, 20, 27, 42; **7**.4, 6, 8, 14, 16, 19, 20, 33, 34, 49; **8**.8, 24, 25, 38, 49, 54; **9**.7, 20, 23, 33, 34, 35; **10**.2, 5, 9, 17, 25; **11**.2, 18, 24, 27, 29, 45; **12**.1, 16, 37, 44[o], 54[2], 55; **13**.14, 17, 18, 25, 26, 31; **14**.3, 7, 12, 30; **15**.2, 6, 9; **16**.1, 5, 7, 29; **17**.4, 6, 10, 13, 37; **18**.1, 3, 6, 13, 16, 17, 29, 34; **19**.14, 16, 18, 20, 22, 30, 38, 42, 46; **20**.27, 28, 41, 42; **21**.8, 10, 32; **22**.11, 19, 20‡, 57, 59, 60, 67, 70; **23**.2[2], 3, 5, 30, 34‡, 35, 37, 39, 42, 43, 47; **24**.23[2], 29, 34, [36‡
Jn **1**.21, 22, 29, 36, 38, 39, 41, 43, 45, 46, 47, 48, 51[2]; **2**.3, 4, 5, 7, 8, 10, 22; **3**.3, 4, 5, 11; **4**.7, 9, 10, 11, 15, 16, 17, 19, 20, 21, 25, 26, 28, 31, 33, 34, 35, 42, 49, 50; **5**.6, 8, 10, 19[2], 24, 25, 34; **6**.5, 6, 8, 14, 20, 26, 32, 42[2], 47, 52, 53, 65; **7**.6, 11, 12[2], 15, 25, 26, 31, 40, 41[2], 50; **8**.4‡, 5‡, 6‡, 12, 19, 22[2], 23, 25, 31, 33, 34, 39, 48, 51, 52, 54, 58; **9**.8, 9[3], 10, 12, 16[2], 17[2], 19, 41; **10**.1, 7, 20, 21, 24, 36, 41; **11**.3, 7, 8, 11, 23, 24, 27, 32, 34, 36, 39[2], 40, 44, 47, 56; **12**.4, 21, 24, 29[2], 33, 34; **13**.6, 8, 9, 10, 16, 20, 21, 24, 25, 27, 31, 33, 36, 37, 38; **14**.5, 6, 8, 9[2], 10, 12, 22; **16**.12, 17, 18, 20, 23, 26, 29; **18**.4, 5, 17[2], 34, 37, 38; **19**.3, 4, 5, 6, 9, 10, 14, 15, 21, 26, 27, 28, 37; **20**.2, 13[2], 15[2], 16[2], 17, 19, 22, 27, 29; **21**.3[2], 5, 7, 10, 12, 15[3], 16[3], 17[3], 18, 21, 22
Acts **2**.7, 12, 13, 25, 34, 40; **3**.25; **4**.16, 32; **5**.28; **6**.11, 13, 14; **7**.48, 49; **8**.6, 9, 10, 19, 34; **9**.4, 21; **10**.26; **11**.3, 7, 16, 18; **12**.7, 8, 15; **13**.15[2], 25, 35; **14**.11; **15**.5, 18(17); **16**.9, 15, 35; **17**.7, 18[2], 19; **18**.13; **19**.13, 26; **21**.11, 37, 40; **22**.7, 18, 22; **23**.8; **24**.2; **25**.14; **26**.14, 22; **27**.10, 11, 24, 33; **28**.4, 6, 17, 24
Rom **2**.22; **3**.8, 19; **4**.3, 9; **7**.7; **9**.15, 17, 25; **10**.6, 8, 11, 16, 19, 20, 21; **11**.2, 9; **12**.19; **14**.11; **15**.10, 12
1 Cor **1**.12; **3**.4; **6**.5; **7**.6, 8, 12, 35; **9**.8; **11**.25; **12**.3; **14**.16, 21, 34; **15**.12
2 Cor **6**.2, 17, 18; **7**.3; **8**.8; **9**.3, 4; **11**.21
Gal **1**.9; **3**.16; **4**.30; **5**.2, 16
Eph **4**.8; **5**.14, 32[o]
Col **2**.4
1 Th **5**.3
1 Tim **1**.7; **4**.1; **5**.18
2 Tim **2**.7
Tit **2**.8
Phm .19, 21
Heb **1**.6, 7; **2**.12; **3**.7, 15; **4**.7; **5**.6, 11; **6**.14; **8**.1, 8[2], 9, 10, 11; **9**.20; **10**.5, 8, 16; **11**.32; **13**.6
Jas **1**.13; **2**.14, 23; **4**.5, 6, 13, 15
2 Pet **3**.4
1 Jn **2**.4, 6, 9; **5**.16
Jude .14, 18
Rev **1**.8, 11, 17; **2**.7, 9, 11, 17, 24, 29; **3**.6, 9, 13, 17, 22; **4**.1; **5**.4, 9, 12, 13, 14; **6**.1, 3, 5, 6, 7; **7**.3, 12, 13; **9**.14; **10**.4, 8, 9; **11**.12, 15, 17; **12**.10; **13**.4; **14**.7, 8, 9, 13[2]; **15**.3; **16**.5, 17; **17**.15; **18**.4, 7, 10, 21; **19**.4, 9[2], 10; **21**.3, 5, 9; **22**.9, 10, 17, 20

10. *word, reckoning:* λόγος LOGOS
[a]B.2.a.1 [b]A.1.a [c]B.3.a.1
2 Cor 10.11 [a]what we say by letter when absent
2 Th 3.14 [b]If any one refuses to obey what we say
Heb 5.11 [c]About this we have much to say

11. *say, affirm:* φημί PHĒMI
Mt 4. 7 Jesus said to him, "Again it is written
13.28 "He said to them, 'An enemy has done this
13.29 "he said, 'No; lest in gathering the weeds
14. 8 she said, "Give me the head of John
17.26 Jesus said . . "Then the sons are free
19.18 And Jesus said, "You shall not kill
19.21 Jesus said . . "If you would be perfect
21.27 he said to them, "Neither will I tell you
22.37 he said to him, "You shall love the Lord
25.21 "His master said to him, 'Well done
25.23 "His master said to him, 'Well done
26.34 Jesus said . . "this very night . . you will deny
26.61 "This fellow said, 'I am able to destroy
27.11 "King of the Jews?" Jesus said, "You
27.23 he said, "Why, what evil has he done?
27.65 Pilate said . . "You have a guard[o]
Mk 9.12 he said to them, "Elijah does come first
9.38 John said . . "Teacher, we saw a man casting
10.20 he said . . "Teacher, . . these I have observed
10.29 Jesus said . . "no one who has left house
12.24 Jesus said . . "Is not this why you are wrong?
14.29 Peter said . . "Even though . . all fall away
Lk 7.44 he said . . "Do you see this woman?
15.17 "when he came to himself he said
22.58 some one else . . said, "You also are one . ."
But Peter said, "Man, I am not
22.70 "Are you the Son of God . . ?" And he said
23.40 rebuked him, saying, "Do you not fear God?
Jn 1.23 He said, "I am the voice of one crying
9.38 He said, "Lord, I believe
18.29 So Pilate went out to them and said
Acts 7. 2 Stephen said: "Brethren and fathers, hear
8.36 the eunuch said, "See, here is water!
10.28 he said to them, "You yourselves know
10.30 Cornelius said, "Four days ago
10.31 "⟨stood before me⟩, saying, 'Cornelius
16.30 said, "Men, what must I do to be saved?
16.37 Paul said . . "They have beaten us publicly
17.22 Paul, . . in . . middle of the Areopagus, said
19.35 town clerk . . said, "Men of Ephesus
21.37 And he said, "Do you know Greek?
22. 2 in the Hebrew language . . he said
22.27 "are you a Roman . . ?" And he said, "Yes
22.28 Paul said, "But I was born a citizen
23. 5 Paul said, "I did not know, brethren
23.17 Paul . . said, "Take this young man
23.18 brought him to the tribune and said
23.35 he said, "I will hear you when
25. 5 "So," said he, "let the men of authority
25.22 "Tomorrow," said he, "you shall hear
25.24 Festus said, "King Agrippa and all
26. 1 Agrippa said to Paul, "You have permission
26.24 Festus said . . "Paul, you are mad
26.25 But Paul said, "I am not mad
26.32 Agrippa said to Festus, "This man
1 Cor 10.15 judge for yourselves what I say
2 Cor 10.10 they say, "His letters are weighty
Heb 8. 5 Moses . . was instructed by God, saying

12. *word, saying:* ῥῆμα RHĒMA [A.1.a]
Lk 20.26 not able . . to catch him by what he said
Acts 10.22 "to send . . to hear what you have to say

13. *talk with:* συλλαλέω SYLLALEŌ
Lk 4.36 were all amazed and said to one another

IDIOMATICALLY
a. Lk 11.54 to catch at something he might say θηρεῦσαί τι ἐκ τοῦ στόματος αὐτοῦ [STOMA]

SAY ABOUT
1. *say, speak:* ἐρῶ ERŌ
Rom 4. 1 What then shall we say about[e] Abraham?

SAY BEFORE
1. *foretell, say before:* προεῖπον PROEIPON
2 Cor 7. 3 I said before that you are in our hearts
Gal 1. 9 As we . . said before, so now I say again

SAY IN OPPOSITION
1. *speak against:* ἀντεῖπον ANTEIPON
Acts 4.14 they had nothing to say in opposition

SAY INDIGNANTLY
1. *be vexed:* ἀγανακτέω AGANAKTEŌ
Mk 14. 4 said to themselves indignantly, "Why?

SAYING
1. *word, reckoning:* λόγος LOGOS
Mt 7.28 when Jesus finished these sayings
15.12 "offended when they heard this saying?
19. 1 when Jesus had finished these sayings
19.11 "Not all men can receive this saying[0]
26. 1 When Jesus had finished all these sayings
Mk 7.29 "For this saying you may go your way
10.22 At that saying his countenance fell
Lk 1.29 she was greatly troubled at the saying
9.28 about eight days after these sayings
Jn 4.37 "For here the saying holds true
6.60 "This is a hard s.; who can listen to it?
21.23 The s. spread abroad among the brethren
1 Cor 15.54 then shall come to pass the saying
1 Tim 1.15 The s. is sure and worthy of . . acceptance
3. 1 The s. is sure: If any . . aspires to . . bishop
4. 9 The s. is sure and worthy of . . acceptance
2 Tim 2.11 The s. is sure: If we have died with him
Tit 3. 8 ⟨that we . . become heirs⟩ The s. is sure
2. *word, saying:* ῥῆμα RHĒMA
Mt 26.75 Peter remembered the saying of Jesus
Mk 9.32 But they did not understand the saying
Lk 2.17 they made known the saying
2.50 they did not understand the saying
7. 1 After he had ended all his sayings
9.45 they did not understand this saying
9.45 they were afraid to ask him about this s.
18.34 this saying was hid from them
Jn 10.21 "These are not the sayings of one
12.47 "If any one hears my sayings
12.48 "He who . . does not receive my sayings

SAYS, WHAT ONE
1. *word, reckoning:* λόγος LOGOS
Mt 5.37 "Let what you s. be simply 'Yes' or 'No
Lk 20.20 that they might take . . what he said
Acts 6. 5 what they said pleased the . . multitude
Jas 3. 2 if . . one makes no mistakes in what he says

SCALE
1. *coat, plate, scale:* λεπίς LEPIS*
Acts 9.18 something like scales fell from his eyes
2. *coat of mail, chest:* θώραξ THŌRAX
Rev 9. 9 they had scales like iron breastplates

SCARCELY
1. *barely, hardly:* μόλις MOLIS
Acts 14.18 they scarcely restrained the people
1 Pet 4.18 "If the righteous man is scarcely saved

SCARLET
1. *scarlet:* κόκκινος KOKKINOS*
Mt 27.28 they . . put a scarlet robe upon him
Heb 9.19 he took the blood . . with . . scarlet wool
Rev 17. 3 a woman sitting on a scarlet beast
17. 4 The woman was arrayed in . . scarlet
18.12 cargo of gold, silver, jewels . . and scarlet
18.16 "the great city . . clothed in . . scarlet

SCATTER
SCATTER ABROAD
1. *throw, put:* βάλλω BALLŌ
Mk 4.26 "if a man should s. seed upon the ground
2. *scatter abroad, squander:* διασκορπίζω DIASKORPIZŌ
Mt 26.31 " 'the sheep of the flock will be scattered
Mk 14.27 "it is written . . 'the sheep will be scattered
Lk 1.51 "he has scattered the proud
Jn 11.52 the children of God . . scattered abroad
Acts 5.37 "all who followed him were scattered
3. *scatter:* διασπείρω DIASPEIRŌ*
Acts 8. 1 were all scattered throughout the region
8. 4 who were scattered went about preaching
11.19 were scattered because of the persecution
4. *disperse, scatter:* σκορπίζω SKORPIZŌ*
Mt 12.30 "he who does not gather with me scatters
Lk 11.23 "he who does not gather with me scatters
Jn 10.12 "wolf snatches them and scatters them
16.32 "when you will be scattered, every man
2 Cor 9. 9 "He scatters abroad, he gives to the poor

SCENTED
1. *from the citron tree:* θύϊνος THYINOS*
Rev 18.12 cargo of . . all kinds of scented wood

SCEPTER
1. *rod, staff of office:* ῥάβδος RHABDOS
Heb 1. 8 "the righteous scepter is the scepter of thy[b] kingdom

SCEVA: Σκευᾶς 'sēvə
Acts 19.14 sons of a Jewish high priest named Sceva

SCOFF AT
1. *ridicule:* ἐκμυκτηρίζω EKMYKTĒRIZŌ*
Lk 16.14 Pharisees . . heard . . and . . scoffed at him
23.35 the rulers scoffed . . "He saved others

SCOFFER
1. *mocker:* ἐμπαίκτης EMPAIKTĒS*
2 Pet 3. 3 scoffers will come in the last days
Jude .18 "In the last time there will be scoffers
2. *despiser:* καταφρονητής KATAPHRONĒTĒS*
Acts 13.41 " 'Behold, you scoffers, and wonder

SCOFFING
1. *mockery:* ἐμπαιγμονή EMPAIGMONĒ*
2 Pet 3. 3 scoffers will come in the last days with s.

SCORCH
1. *burn:* καυματίζω KAUMATIZŌ*
Mt 13. 6 "when the sun rose they were scorched
Mk 4. 6 "when the sun rose it was scorched
Rev 16. 8 it was allowed to scorch men with fire
16. 9 men were scorched by the fierce heat

SCORCHING HEAT
1. *burning heat:* καῦμα KAUMA
Rev 7.16 "the sun shall not strike . . , nor any s. heat
2. *burning heat:* καύσων KAUSŌN*
Mt 20.12 " 'who have borne . . the scorching heat
Lk 12.55 "you say, 'There will be scorching heat
Jas 1.11 the sun rises with its scorching heat

SCORN
1. *treat with contempt:* ἐξουθενέω EXOUTHENEŌ
Gal 4.14 you did not scorn or despise me

SCORPION
1. *scorpion:* σκορπίος SKORPIOS*
Lk 10.19 "authority to tread upon . . scorpions
11.12 "if he asks for an egg, will give him a s.?
Rev 9. 3 locusts . . were given power like . . scorpions
9. 5 their torture was like the torture of a s.
9.10 They have tails like scorpions, and stings

SCOURGE
1. *whip, flog:* μαστιγόω MASTIGOŌ
Mt 20.19 "to be . . scourged and crucified
23.34 "some you will s. in your synagogues
Mk 10.34 "they will mock him . . and scourge him
Lk 18.33 "they will scourge him and kill him
Jn 19. 1 Then Pilate took Jesus and scourged him
2. *whip, flog:* μαστίζω MASTIZŌ*
Acts 22.25 "Is it lawful for you to s. . . a Roman?

3. *flog:* φραγελλόω PHRAGELLOŌ*
Mt 27.26 having scourged Jesus, delivered him
Mk 15.15 having scourged Jesus, .. delivered him

SCOURGING
1. *whip, plague:* μάστιξ MASTIX
[a]acc.
Acts 22.24 [a]ordered him to be examined by scourging
Heb 11.36 Others suffered mocking and scourging

SCRIBE
1. *secretary, registrar:* γραμματεύς GRAMMATEUS
Mt 2. 4 assembling .. the chief priests and scribes
5.20 "righteousness .. of .. scribes and Pharisees
7.29 had authority, and not as their scribes
8.19 a scribe came up and said to him
9. 3 scribes said .. "This man is blaspheming
12.38 scribes .. said .. "Teacher, we wish .. a sign
13.52 "every scribe .. trained for the kingdom
15. 1 Pharisees and scribes came to Jesus
16.21 must .. suffer many things from .. scribes
17.10 "why do the scribes say that first Elijah?
20.18 "Son of man will be delivered to .. scribes
21.15 when .. chief priests and the scribes saw
23. 2 "scribes and .. Pharisees sit on Moses' seat
23.13 "woe to you, scribes and Pharisees!
Also Mt **23.**[14‡, 15, 23, 25, 27, 29
23.34 "I send you prophets and .. scribes
26.57 the scribes and the elders had gathered
27.41 the scribes and elders, mocked him
Mk 1.22 who had authority, and not as the scribes
2. 6 some of the scribes were sitting there
2.16 the scribes of[h] the Pharisees
3.22 scribes who came down from Jerusalem
7. 1 scribes, who had come from Jerusalem
7. 5 Pharisees and the scribes asked him
8.31 rejected by .. chief priests and .. scribes
9.11 "Why do the scribes say that first Elijah?
9.14 saw a great crowd .. and scribes arguing
10.33 "Son of man will be delivered to .. scribes
11.18 the chief priests and the scribes heard it
11.27 the scribes and the elders came to him
12.28 one of the scribes came up and heard
12.32 scribe said .. "You are right, Teacher
12.35 "How can the scribes say that the Christ?
12.38 "Beware of the scribes, who like .. robes
14. 1 scribes were seeking how to arrest him
14.43 a crowd with swords .. from .. the scribes
14.53 elders and the scribes were assembled
15. 1 elders and scribes .. held a consultation
15.31 "chief priests mocked him .. with the scribes
Lk 5.21 scribes and .. Pharisees began to question
5.30 Pharisees and their scribes murmured
6. 7 scribes and the Pharisees watched him
9.22 "Son of man must .. be rejected by .. scribes
11.53 the scribes .. began to press him hard
15. 2 Pharisees and the scribes murmured
19.47 the scribes .. sought to destroy him
20. 1 as he was teaching .. the scribes .. came up
20.19 The scribes .. tried to lay hands on him
20.39 some of the scribes answered, "Teacher
20.46 "Beware of the scribes, who like .. robes
22. 2 scribes were seeking .. to put him to death
22.66 assembly .., both chief priests and scribes
23.10 scribes stood by, .. accusing him
Jn 8. 3 The scribes .. brought a woman[r]‡
Acts 4. 5 scribes were gathered .. in Jerusalem
6.12 they stirred up the people and .. the scribes
23. 9 scribes of the Pharisees' party stood up
1 Cor 1.20 Where is the wise man? Where is the s.?

SCRIPTURE
1. *writing:* γραφή GRAPHĒ
Mt 21.42 "Have you never read in the scriptures?
22.29 "you know neither the scriptures
26.54 "how .. should the scriptures be fulfilled?
26.56 "that the scriptures .. might be fulfilled
Mk 12.10 "Have you not read this scripture?
12.24 "you know neither the scriptures
Mk 14.49 "But let the scriptures be fulfilled
[15.28 *the scripture was fulfilled*‡
Lk 4.21 "Today this scripture has been fulfilled
24.27 interpreted to them in .. the scriptures
24.32 "while he opened to us the scriptures
24.45 opened their minds to .. the scriptures
Jn 2.22 they believed the scripture and the word
5.39 "You search the scriptures, because
7.38 "as[q] the s. has said, 'Out of his heart
7.42 "s. said that the Christ is descended
10.35 "(and scripture cannot be broken
13.18 "it is that the scripture may be fulfilled
17.12 "that the scripture might be fulfilled
19.24 This was to fulfil the scripture
19.28 Jesus .. said (to fulfil the s.), "I thirst
19.36 took place that the s. might be fulfilled
19.37 another s. says, "They shall look on him
20. 9 as yet they did not know the scripture
Acts 1.16 "Brethren, the scripture had to be fulfilled
8.32 the s. which he was reading was this
8.35 beginning with this s. he told him
17. 2 argued with them from the scriptures
17.11 examining the scriptures daily to see
18.24 eloquent .., well versed in the scriptures
18.28 showing by the scriptures that .. Christ
Rom 1. 2 which he promised .. in the holy scriptures
4. 3 For what does the scripture say?
9.17 s. says to Pharaoh, "I have raised you up
10.11 s. says, "No one who believes in him
11. 2 Do you not know what the s. says?
15. 4 by the encouragement of the scriptures
1 Cor 15. 3 died .. in accordance with the scriptures
15. 4 raised .. in accordance with .. scriptures
Gal 3. 8 s., foreseeing that God would justify
3.22 the scripture consigned all things to sin
4.30 But what does the scripture say?
1 Tim 5.18 the s. says, "You shall not muzzle an ox
2 Tim 3.16 All s. is inspired by God and[d] profitable
Jas 2. 8 according to the s., "You shall love
2.23 s. was fulfilled which says, "Abraham
4. 5 scripture says, "He yearns jealously
1 Pet 2. 6 it stands in s. .. "I am laying in Zion
2 Pet 1.20 no .. s. is .. of one's own interpretation
3.16 twist .., as they do the other scriptures
2. *write:* γράφω (subst. perf. pass. part.) GRAPHŌ
Lk 22.37 "this scripture must be fulfilled in me
CONTEXTUALLY
1 Tim 4.13 attend to the public reading of scripture

SCROLL
1. *book, document:* βιβλίον BIBLION
Rev 5. 1 in the .. hand of him .. on the throne a s.
5. 2 "Who is worthy to open the scroll?
5. 3 no one .. was able to open the scroll
5. 4 no one was found worthy to open the s.
5. 5 "he can open the scroll and its .. seals
5. 8 And when he had taken the scroll
5. 9 "Worthy art thou to take the scroll
6.14 the sky vanished like a scroll
10. 8 take the s. which is open in the hand
CONTEXTUALLY
Rev 5. 7 took the s. from the right hand of him

SCROLL, LITTLE
1. *small roll, little book:* βιβλαρίδιον BIBLARIDION*
Rev 10. 2 He had a little scroll open in his hand
10. 9 I .. told him to give me the little scroll
10.10 I took the little scroll from the hand

SCRUPLES
1. *conscience, consciousness:* συνείδησις SYNEIDĒSIS
1 Cor 10.29 determined by another man's scruples

SCYTHIAN: Σκύθης
Col 3.11 Here there cannot be .. barbarian, S., slave

SEA
1. *high sea:* πέλαγος PELAGOS
Acts 27. 5 when we had sailed across the sea

2. *sea:* θάλασσα THALASSA
Mt 4.15 "Naphtali, toward the s., across . . Jordan
4.18 As he walked by the Sea of Galilee
4.18 Peter . . casting a net into the sea
8.24 there arose a great storm on the sea
8.26 Then he rose and rebuked . . the sea
8.27 "even winds and sea obey him
8.32 "rushed down the steep bank into the sea
13. 1 Jesus went out . . and sat beside the sea
13.47 "like a net which was thrown into the sea
[14.24 the boat . . was *out on the sea*‡
14.25 he came to them, walking on the sea
14.26 disciples saw him walking on the sea
15.29 Jesus . . passed along the Sea of Galilee
17.27 "go to the sea and cast a hook
18. 6 "better for him . . to be drowned in . . the sea
21.21 " 'Be taken up and cast into the sea
23.15 "you traverse sea . . to make a . . proselyte
Mk 1.16 passing along by the Sea of Galilee, he saw Simon and Andrew . . casting a net in the s.
2.13 He went out again beside the sea
3. 7 Jesus withdrew with . . disciples to the s.
4. 1 Again he began to teach beside the sea
4. 1 he got into a boat and sat in it on the sea; . . the whole crowd was beside the sea
4.39 he awoke . . and said to the sea, "Peace!
4.41 "Who . . , that . . wind and sea obey him?
5. 1 They came to the other side of the sea
5.13 rushed down the steep bank into the sea, and were drowned in the sea
5.21 crowd gathered . . and he was beside the sea
6.47 the boat was out on the sea
6.48 he came to them, walking on the sea
6.49 when they saw him walking on the sea
7.31 went through Sidon to the Sea of Galilee
9.42 "better . . if . . he were thrown into the sea
11.23 " 'Be taken up and cast into the sea
Lk 17. 2 "better . . if . . he were cast into the sea
17. 6 " 'Be rooted up, and be planted in the sea
21.25 "in perplexity at the roaring of the sea
Jn 6. 1 to the other side of the S. of Galilee
6.16 his disciples went down to the sea
6.17 started across the sea to Capernaum
6.18 The sea rose because a strong wind
6.19 they saw Jesus walking on the sea
6.22 remained on the other side of the sea
6.25 found him on the other side of the sea
21. 1 Jesus revealed . . by the S. of Tiberias
21. 7 Simon Peter . . sprang into the sea
Acts 4.24 "Lord, who didst make . . the sea
7.36 "signs in Egypt and at the Red Sea
14.15 "turn . . to a living God who made . . the sea
17.14 sent Paul off on his way to the sea
27.30 sailors . . had lowered . . boat into the sea
27.38 throwing out the wheat into the sea
27.40 cast off . . anchors and left them in the sea
28. 4 "Though he has escaped from the sea
Rom 9.27 "Though . . sons . . be as the sand of the sea
1 Cor 10. 1 our fathers . . all passed through the sea
10. 2 all were baptized into Moses . . in the sea
2 Cor 11.26 danger in the wilderness, danger at sea
Heb 11.29 By faith the people crossed the Red Sea
Jas 1. 6 he who doubts is like a wave of the sea
Jude .13 wild waves of the sea, casting up . . foam
Rev 4. 6 before the throne there is . . a sea of glass
5.13 I heard every creature . . in the sea
7. 1 that no wind might blow on earth or sea
7. 2 angels . . given power to harm earth and s.
7. 3 "Do not harm the earth or the sea
8. 8 a great mountain . . was thrown into the s.
8. 9(8) a third of the sea became blood
8. 9 a third of the . . creatures in the sea died
10. 2 he set his right foot on the sea
10. 5 the angel whom I saw standing on sea
10. 6 who created . . the sea and what is in it
10. 8 "the angel who is standing on the sea
12.12 "But woe to you, O earth and sea!
Rev 12.17(18) And he stood[e] on the sand of the sea
13. 1 I saw a beast rising out of the sea
14. 7 worship him who made . . the sea
15. 2 I saw what appeared to be a sea of glass
15. 2 standing beside the sea of glass
16. 3 angel poured his bowl into the sea, and . . every living thing died that was in the sea
18.17 sailors and all whose trade is on the sea
18.19 "where all who had ships at sea grew rich
18.21 took . . a stone . . and threw it into the sea
20. 8 their number is like the sand of the sea
20.13 the sea gave up the dead in it
21. 1 and the sea was no more

IDIOMATICALLY
a. 2 Cor 11.25 a night and a day I have been adrift at sea
νυχθήμερον ἐν τῷ βυθῷ πεποίηκα [BYTHOS*]

CONTEXTUALLY
Acts 27.27 as we were drifting across the sea

SEA, BY THE

1. *beside the sea:* παραθαλάσσιος PARATHALASSIOS*
Mt 4.13 he . . dwelt in Capernaum by the sea

SEA CREATURE

1. *of the sea:* ἐνάλιος (subst.) ENALIOS*
Jas 3. 7 every . . sea creature, can be tamed

SEA, PUT TO

1. *lead up, bring back:* ἀνάγω (mid. or pass.) ANAGŌ
Acts 27. 2 we put to s., accompanied by Aristarchus
27. 4 putting to sea from there we sailed
27.12 the majority advised to put to sea

SEACOAST

1. *by the sea:* παράλιος (subst.) PARALIOS*
Lk 6.17 people from . . the s. of Tyre and Sidon

SEAFARING MAN

1. *sail, go by sea:* πλέω (subst. part.) PLEŌ
Rev 18.17 And all shipmasters and seafaring men

SEAL
SEAL, SET ONE'S
SEAL UP
SEAL UPON, PUT ONE'S

1. *signet, warrant:* σφραγίς SPHRAGIS*
Rom 4.11 circumcision as a . . seal of . . righteousness
1 Cor 9. 2 for you are the seal of my apostleship
2 Tim 2.19 God's . . foundation stands, bearing this s.
Rev 5. 1 I saw . . a scroll . . sealed with seven seals
5. 2 "Who is worthy to . . break its seals?
5. 5 "he can open the scroll and its seven seals
5. 9 "Worthy art thou . . to open its seals
6. 1 the Lamb opened one of the seven seals
6. 3 When he opened the second seal, I heard
6. 5 When he opened the third seal, I heard
6. 7 When he opened the fourth seal, I heard
6. 9 When he opened the fifth seal, I saw
6.12 When he opened the sixth seal, I looked
7. 2 another angel . . with the seal of . . God
8. 1 When the Lamb opened the seventh seal
9. 4 those of mankind who have not the seal

2. *close with a seal, certify:* σφραγίζω SPHRAGIZŌ
Mt 27.66 made the sepulchre secure by sealing
Jn 3.33 he . . sets his seal to this, that God is true
6.27 "on him has God the Father set his seal
2 Cor 1.22 he has put his seal upon us
Eph 1.13 you . . were sealed with the . . Holy Spirit
4.30 in whom you were sealed for the day
Rev 7. 3 "till we have sealed the servants of . . God
7. 4 I heard the number of the sealed, a hundred and forty-four thousand sealed
7. 5 twelve thousand sealed out of . . Judah
7. 8 twelve thousand sealed out of . . Benjamin
10. 4 "Seal up what the . . thunders have said
20. 3 threw him into the pit . . and sealed it
22.10 "Do not seal up the words of the prophecy

SEALED

1. *seal, seal up:* κατασφραγίζω (perf. pass. part.) KATASPHRAGIZŌ
Rev 5. 1 a scroll . . , sealed with seven seals

SEAM, WITHOUT
1. *seamless:* ἄραφος ARAPHOS*
Jn 19.23 But the tunic was without seam

SEAR
1. *brand:* καυστηριάζω KAUSTĒRIAZŌ*
1 Tim 4. 2 liars whose consciences are seared

SEARCH
SEARCH FOR
SEARCH OF, IN
1. *seek out:* ἐκζητέω EKZĒTEŌ
1 Pet 1.10 searched and inquired about this salvation
2. *search, inquire:* ἐραυνάω ERAUNAŌ
Jn 5.39 "You search the scriptures, because
7.52 "Search and you will see that no prophet
Rom 8.27 he who searches the hearts of men
1 Cor 2.10 For the Spirit searches everything
Rev 2.23 " 'I am he who searches mind and heart
3. *examine well:* ἐξετάζω EXETAZŌ
Mt 2. 8 "Go and search diligently for the child
4. *seek, desire:* ζητέω ZĒTEŌ
[a]part. [b]A.6.c.1
Mt 2.13 "Herod is about to search for the child
13.45 [a]"like a merchant in search of fine pearls
18.12 [b]"go in search of the one that went astray
Mk 1.37 "Every one is searching for you
2 Tim 1.17 he searched for me eagerly and found me

SEASHORE
1. *the edge of the sea:* τὸ χεῖλος τῆς θαλάσσης THALASSA; CHEILOS [A.1.f]
Heb 11.12 as . . innumerable grains of sand by the s.

SEASIDE
1. *sea:* θάλασσα THALASSA [A.1.f]
Acts 10. 6 "Simon, a tanner, whose house is by the s.
10.32 " 'the house of Simon, a tanner, by the s.

SEASON
1. *season:* ἀρτύω ARTYŌ
Mk 9.50 "lost its saltness, how will you season it?
Col 4. 6 Let your speech . . be . . seasoned with salt
2. *time, opportunity:* καιρός KAIROS
Mt 21.34 "When the season of fruit drew near
21.41 "will give him the fruits in their seasons
Mk 11.13 for it was not the season for figs
Acts 1. 7 "It is not for you to know . . seasons
14.17 "he did good and gave . . fruitful seasons
1 Cor 7. 5 except perhaps by agreement for a s.
Gal 4.10 You observe days, . . months, and seasons!
6. 9 for in due season we shall reap
1 Th 5. 1 But as to the times and the seasons

SEASON, CERTAIN
1. *time, opportunity:* καιρός KAIROS
Jn [5. 4 *an angel . . went down at certain seasons*‡

SEASON, IN
1. *seasonably:* εὐκαίρως EUKAIRŌS
2 Tim 4. 2 preach the word, be urgent in season

SEASON, OUT OF
1. *unseasonably:* ἀκαίρως AKAIRŌS*
2 Tim 4. 2 preach the word, be urgent . . out of s.

SEAT (*See also* JUDGMENT SEAT)
1. *chair:* καθέδρα KATHEDRA*
Mt 21.12 overturned . . the seats of those who sold
23. 2 "the Pharisees sit on Moses' seat
Mk 11.15 overturned . . the seats of those who sold

SEAT, BEST
1. *first seat:* πρωτοκαθεδρία PRŌTOKATHEDRIA*
Mt 23. 6 "love . . the best seats in the synagogues
Mk 12.39 "⟨like⟩ the best seats in the synagogues
Lk 11.43 "Pharisees . . love the best seat
20.46 "scribes . . love . . the best seats

SEAT, HAVE A
1. *sit down:* κάθημαι (imper.) KATHĒMAI
Jas 2. 3 you . . say, "Have a seat here, please

SEAT, MERCY
1. *means of expiation:* ἱλαστήριον HILASTĒRION
Heb 9. 5 cherubim . . overshadowing the mercy seat

SEAT, TAKE ONE'S
1. *sit down, seat:* καθίζω KATHIZŌ
Acts 12.21 Herod . . took his seat upon the throne
25. 6 he took his seat on the tribunal
25.17 "next day took my seat on the tribunal
2 Th 2. 4 he takes his seat in the temple of God

SEATED
1. *sit down:* κάθημαι (part.) KATHĒMAI
Mt 26.64 "you will see the Son of man seated
Mk 14.62 "you will see the Son of man seated[o]
Acts 8.28 seated in his chariot, he was reading
Col 3. 1 where Christ is, seated at . . right hand
Rev 4. 2 with one seated on the throne!
4. 4 seated on the thrones were . . elders
14.14 s. on the cloud one like a son of man

SEATED, BE
1. *recline* (at table): ἀνάκειμαι ANAKEIMAI
Jn 6.11 distributed . . to those who were seated
2. *sit down:* κάθημαι KATHĒMAI
[a]periphr. [b]subst.
Lk 22.69 [a]"Son of man shall be seated at the right
Rev 4. 9 [b]thanks to him who is s. on the throne
4.10 [b]before him who is seated on the throne
5. 1 [b]of him who was seated on the throne
5. 7 [b]of him who was seated on the throne
6.16 [b]"face of him who is seated on the throne
17. 1 [b]"harlot who is seated upon many waters
17. 9 "seven mountains on which the woman is s.
17.15 "The waters . . where the harlot is seated
19. 4 God who is seated on the throne
3. *sit down, seat:* καθίζω (aor. or perf.) KATHIZŌ
Heb 8. 1 one who is seated at the right hand
12. 2 seated at the right hand of the throne
Rev 20. 4 I saw thrones, and seated on them were

SECOND
1. *second:* δεύτερος DEUTEROS
Mt 21.30 "he went to the second and said the same
22.26 "So too the second and third
22.39 "a s. is like it, . . love your neighbor
26.42 the s. time, he went away and prayed
Mk 12.21 "the second took her, and died
12.31 "The s. is this, . . 'love your neighbor
14.72 immediately the cock crowed a s. time
Lk 12.38 "If he comes in the second watch
19.18 "the second came, saying, 'Lord
20.30 "and the second ⟨took her⟩
Jn 3. 4 "Can he enter a s. time into . . womb?
4.54 now the second sign that Jesus did
9.24 the second time they called the man
21.16 A s. time he said to him, "Simon
Acts 7.13 "at . . s. visit Joseph made himself known
10.15 the voice came to him . . a second time
11. 9 "voice answered a s. time from heaven
12.10 When they had passed . . the second guard
13.33 "as . . it is written in the second psalm
1 Cor 12.28 in the church first apostles, s. prophets
15.47 the second man is from heaven
2 Cor 13. 2 I warn them now . . as . . on my second visit
Heb 8. 7 there would have been no occasion for a s.
9. 3 Behind the second curtain stood a tent[p]
9. 7 into the second only the high priest goes
9.28 so Christ . . will appear a second time
10. 9 He abolishes the first . . to establish the s.
2 Pet 3. 1 This is . . the s. letter . . I have written
Rev 2.11 " 'He . . shall not be hurt by the s. death
4. 7 the second living creature like an ox
6. 3 When he opened the second seal, I heard the second living creature say, "Come!
8. 8 The second angel blew his trumpet
11.14 The second woe has passed
14. 8 Another angel, a second, followed
16. 3 The s. angel poured his bowl into the sea
20. 6 Over such the s. death has no power
20.14 This is the second death, the lake of fire
21. 8 "lake that burns . . , which is the s. death
21.19 the first was jasper, the second sapphire

SECOND DAY, ON THE
1. *on the second day:* δευτεραῖος (pl.) DEUTERAIOS*
Acts 28.13 on the second day we came to Puteoli

SECOND FIRST
1. *second s. after the first:* δευτερόπρωτος DEUTEROPRŌTOS*
Lk [6. 1 On *the second first* sabbath‡

SECRET
1. *hidden, secret:* κρυφαῖος KRYPHAIOS*
Mt 6.18 "fasting . . seen . . by your Father who is in s.; . . Father who sees in s. will reward
2. *secret, hidden:* κρυπτός KRYPTOS
Mt 6. 4 "that your alms may be in secret; and your Father who sees in s. will reward you
6. 6 "pray to your Father who is in secret; and your Father who sees in secret
Mk 4.22 "nor is anything s., except to come to light
Lk 8.17 "nor anything s. that shall not be known
Jn 7. 4 "no man works in s. if he seeks to be known
Rom 2.16 God judges the secrets of men by Christ
1 Cor 14.25 the secrets of his heart are disclosed
3. *mystery, religious truth:* μυστήριον MYSTĒRION
[a]B.3.b.4
Mt 13.11 "it has been given to know the secrets
Mk 4.11 "To you has been given the secret
Lk 8.10 "it has been given to know the secrets
1 Cor [2. 1 not . . proclaiming . . the *s.* . . in lofty words‡
2. 7 [a]we impart a secret . . wisdom of God

SECRET, IN
1. *secretly, in secret:* κρυφῇ KRYPHĒ*
Eph 5.12 to speak of the things that they do in s.

SECRET, KEEP
1. *be silent, keep secret:* σιγάω SIGAŌ
Rom 16.25 mystery which was kept s. for long ages

SECRET OF, LEARN THE
1. *initiate* (into the mysteries): μυέω (pass.) MYEŌ*
Phil 4.12 have learned the secret of facing plenty

SECRETLY
1. *bury, hide:* κρύπτω (perf. pass. part.) KRYPTŌ
Jn 19.38 Joseph . . , who was a disciple . . , but s.
2. *in secret:* ἐν κρυπτῷ KRYPTOS [B.1.a.1]
Jn 18.20 "I have said nothing secretly
3. *secretly:* λάθρᾳ LATHRA
Mt 2. 7 Herod summoned the wise men secretly
Acts 16.37 "do they now cast us out secretly?

SECRETLY BRING IN
1. *admit secretly:* παρεισάγω PAREISAGŌ*
2 Pet 2. 1 false teachers . . will s. bring in . . heresies

SECRETLY BROUGHT IN
1. *introduced secretly, smuggled in:* παρείσακτος PAREISAKTOS*
Gal 2. 4 false brethren secretly brought in

SECRETLY GAIN ADMISSION
1. *slip in, penetrate:* παρεισδύνω PAREISDYNŌ*
Jude . 4 admission has been secretly gained

SECRETLY INSTIGATE
1. *throw under, suborn:* ὑποβάλλω HYPOBALLŌ*
Acts 6.11 Then they secretly instigated men

SECT
1. *sect, opinion:* αἵρεσις HAIRESIS
Acts 24. 5 "ringleader of the sect of the Nazarenes
24.14 "the Way, which they call a sect
28.22 "for with regard to this sect we know

SECUNDUS: Σεκοῦνδος si'kəndəs
Acts 20. 4 the Thessalonians, Aristarchus and S.

SECURE
1. *be in control:* περικρατὴς γίνεσθαι PERIKRATĒS [A.6.a.3]
Acts 27.16 we managed . . to secure the boat
2. *find:* εὑρίσκω (mid.) HEURISKŌ
Heb 9.12 thus securing an eternal redemption
IDIOMATICALLY
a. 1 Cor 9.15 to secure any such provision ἵνα οὕτως γένηται ἐν ἐμοί [GINOMAI]

SECURE, MAKE
1. *fortify:* ἀσφαλίζω (mid.) ASPHALIZŌ
Mt 27.64 "order the sepulchre to be made secure
27.65 "make it as secure as you can[p]
27.66 made the sepulchre secure by sealing

SECURELY
1. *certainty, security:* ἀσφάλεια ASPHALEIA [B.1.a.1]
Acts 5.23 "We found the prison securely locked

SECURITY
1. *certainty, security:* ἀσφάλεια ASPHALEIA
1 Th 5. 3 When people say, "There is peace and s.
2. *enough:* ἱκανός (subst. neut.) HIKANOS
Acts 17. 9 when they had taken s. from Jason

SEE (*See also* DIFFERENT IN, SEE S.)
1. *look away:* ἀφοράω APHORAŌ
Phil 2.23 as soon as I see how it will go with me
2. *look intently at:* ἀτενίζω ATENIZŌ
2 Cor 3.13 so that the Israelites might not see
3. *see distinctly:* αὐγάζω AUGAZŌ*
2 Cor 4. 4 to keep them from seeing the light
4. *see, look:* βλέπω BLEPŌ
Mt 6. 4 "Father who sees in secret will reward you
6. 6 "Father who sees in secret will reward you
6.18 "Father who sees in secret will reward you
7. 3 "you see the speck . . in your brother's eye
11. 4 "Go and tell John what you hear and see
12.22 so that the dumb man spoke and saw
13.13 "because seeing they do not see, and hearing they do not hear
13.14 " 'you shall indeed see but never perceive
13.16 "blessed are your eyes, for they see
13.17 "what you see, and . . what you hear
14.30 when he saw the wind,[n] he was afraid
15.31 "when they saw the dumb speaking, . . the lame walking, and the blind seeing
24. 2 "You see all these, do you not?
Mk 4.12 "so that they may indeed see
5.31 "You see the crowd pressing around you
8.18 "Having eyes do you not see?
8.23 he asked him, "Do you see anything?
8.24 "I see men; but they look like trees
13. 2 "Do you see these great buildings?
Lk 6.41 "you see the speck . . in your brother's eye?
6.42 "you . . do not see the log . . in your own eye?
7.44 "Do you see this woman?
8.10 "so that seeing they may not see, and hearing they may not understand
8.16 "that those who enter may see the light
10.23 to the disciples he said privately, "Blessed . . the eyes which see what you see!
10.24 "many prophets . . desired . . what you see
11.33 "that those who enter may see the light
21.30 "you see for yourselves and know
[24.12 *he saw the linen cloths by themselves*‡
Jn 1.29 he saw Jesus coming toward him
5.19 "only what he sees the Father doing
9. 7 "went and washed and came back seeing
9.15 "He put clay on my eyes, . . and I see
9.19 "How then does he now see?
9.21 "but how he now sees we do not know
9.25 "though I was blind, now I see
9.39 "For judgment I came into this world, that those who do not see may see, and that those who see may become blind
9.41 "you say, 'We see,' your guilt remains
11. 9 "he does not stumble, because he sees
20. 1 Mary Magdalene . . saw that the stone
20. 5 he saw the linen cloths lying there
21. 9 they saw a charcoal fire there, with fish
21.20 Peter turned and saw . . the disciple
Acts 2.33 "he has poured out this which you see
4.14 seeing the man . . , they had nothing to say
8. 6 when they heard him and saw the signs
12. 9 he . . thought he was seeing a vision
13.11 "you shall be blind and unable to see
28.26 " 'you shall indeed s. but never perceive

Rom 7.23 I see in my members another law at war
8.24 Now hope that is seen is not hope. For who hopes for what he sees?
8.25 But if we hope for what we do not see
11. 8 "God gave them . . eyes that should not see
11.10 let . . eyes be darkened so . . they cannot see
1 Cor 13.12 For now we see in a mirror dimly
16.10 see that you put him at ease among you
2 Cor 4.18 we look not to the things that are seen . . ; for . . things that are seen are transient
7. 8 for I see that that letter grieved you
Col 2. 5 rejoicing to see your good order and . . faith
4.17 "See that you fulfil the ministry
Heb 2. 9 But we see Jesus, . . lower than the angels
3.19 So we see that they were unable to enter
10.25 as you see the Day drawing near
11. 1 the conviction of things not seen
11. 3 what is seen was made out of things
12.25 See that you do not refuse him
Jas 2.22 You see that faith was active . . with . . works
Rev 1.11 "Write what you s. in a book and send it
1.12 Then I turned to see the voice
3.18 " 'to anoint your eyes, that you may see
9.20 idols . . which cannot either see or hear
16.15 ("that he may not . . be seen exposed!
18. 9 when they see the smoke of her burning
18.18 as they saw the smoke of her burning
22. 8 I John am he who heard and saw these things. And when I heard and saw them

5. *see, perceive:* εἶδον EIDON

Mt 2. 2 "For we have seen his star in the East
2. 9 the star which they had seen in the East
2.10 When they saw the star, they rejoiced
2.11 saw the child with Mary his mother
2.16 when he saw that he had been tricked
3. 7 when he saw many of the Pharisees
3.16 he saw the Spirit of God descending
4.16 "the people . . have seen a great light
4.18 he saw two brothers, Simon . . and Andrew
4.21 from there he saw two other brothers
5. 1 Seeing the crowds, he went up
5.16 "that they may see your good works
8.14 he saw his mother-in-law lying sick
8.18 Now when Jesus saw great crowds
8.34 they saw him, they begged him to leave
9. 2 when Jesus saw their faith he said
[9. 4 Jesus, *seeing* their thoughts, said, "Why?‡
9. 8 When the crowds saw it, they were afraid
9. 9 he saw . . Matthew sitting at the tax office
9.11 when the Pharisees saw this, they said
9.22 seeing her he said, "Take heart, daughter
9.23 Jesus came . . and saw the flute players
9.36 When he saw the crowds, he had compassion
11. 8 "To see a man[a] clothed in soft raiment?
11. 9 "To see a prophet?[b] Yes, I tell you
12. 2 when the Pharisees saw it, they said to him
12.38 "Teacher, we wish to see a sign from you
13.17 "prophets and righteous men longed to see . . , and did not see it
14.14 As he went ashore he saw a great throng
14.26 the disciples saw him walking on the sea
16.28 "who will not taste death before they see
17. 8 they saw no one but Jesus only
18.31 "fellow servants saw what had taken place
20. 3 "saw others standing idle in the market
21.15 scribes saw the wonderful things . . he did
21.19 seeing a fig tree by the wayside
21.20 When the disciples saw it they marveled
21.32 "when you saw it, you did not . . repent
21.38 "But when the tenants saw the son
22.11 "saw . . a man who had no wedding garment
23.39 "I tell you, you will not see me again
24.15 "when you see the desolating sacrilege
24.33 "So also, when you see all these things
25.37 " 'Lord, when did we see thee hungry?
25.38 " 'when did we see thee a stranger?
25.39 " 'when did we see thee sick or in prison?

Mt 25.44 " 'Lord, when did we see thee hungry?
26. 8 "the disciples saw . . , they were indignant
26.58 he sat with the guards to see the end
26.71 another maid saw him
27. 3 When Judas . . saw . . he was condemned
27.24 when Pilate saw . . he was gaining nothing
27.49 "Wait, let us see whether Elijah will come
27.54 the centurion . . saw the earthquake
28. 6 Come, see the place where he[q] lay
28.17 when they saw him they worshiped him
Mk 1.10 immediately he saw the heavens opened
1.16 by . . Galilee, he saw Simon and Andrew
1.19 he saw James the son of Zebedee
2. 5 when Jesus saw their faith, he said
2.12 "We never saw anything like this!
2.14 he saw Levi . . sitting at the tax office
2.16 they saw that he was eating with sinners
5. 6 when he saw Jesus from afar, he ran
5.14 people came to see what . . had happened
5.16 who had seen it told what had happened
5.22 and seeing him, he fell at his feet
5.32 looked around to see who had done it
6.33 many saw them going, and knew them
6.34 As he went ashore he saw a great throng
6.38 "How many loaves have you? Go and see
6.48 he saw that they were making headway
6.49 when they saw him walking on the sea
6.50 for they all saw him, and were terrified
7. 2 they saw that some . . ate with hands defiled
8.33 But turning and seeing his disciples
9. 1 "before they see the kingdom of God
9. 8 they no longer saw any one with them
9. 9 to tell no one what they had seen
9.14 they saw a great crowd about them
9.15 all the crowd, when they saw him
9.20 when the spirit saw him, . . it convulsed
9.25 when Jesus saw that a crowd came running
9.38 "we saw a man casting out demons
10.14 when Jesus saw it he was indignant
11.13 he went to see if he could find anything
11.20 they saw the fig tree withered away
12.28 seeing that he answered them well
12.34 Jesus saw that he answered wisely
13.14 "when you see the desolating sacrilege
13.29 "when you see these things taking place
14.67 seeing Peter warming himself, she . . said
14.69 the maid saw him, and began . . to say
15.32 "Let . . Christ . . come down . . that we may see
15.36 "Wait, let us see whether Elijah will come
15.39 when the centurion . . saw . . , he said
16. 5 they saw a young man sitting on the right
Lk 1.12 Zechariah was troubled when he saw
2.15 "Let us go . . to Bethlehem and see this
2.17 when they saw it they made known
2.20 praising God for all they had . . seen
2.26 revealed to him . . that he should not see death before he had seen the . . Christ
2.30 "for mine eyes have seen thy salvation
2.48 when they saw him they were astonished
5. 2 And he saw two boats by the lake
5. 8 when Simon Peter saw it, he fell down
5.12 when he saw Jesus, he fell on his face
5.20 when he saw their faith he said
5.26 "We have seen strange things today
7.13 the Lord saw her, he had compassion
7.22 "Go and tell John what you have seen
7.25 "What then did you go out to see?
7.26 "What then did you go out to see?
7.39 when the Pharisee . . saw it, he said
8.20 "standing outside, desiring to see you
8.28 When he saw Jesus, he cried out
8.34 When the herdsmen saw what . . happened
8.35 people went out to see what . . happened
8.36 those who had seen it told them
8.47 when the woman saw . . she was not hidden
9. 9 And he sought to see him
9.27 "before they see the kingdom of God

Lk 9.32 they saw his glory and the two men
9.49 "we saw a man casting out demons
9.54 his disciples James and John saw it
10.24 "many prophets and kings desired to see . . and did not see it, and to hear
10.31 "when he saw him he passed by
10.32 "a Levite, when he . . saw him, passed by
10.33 "when he saw him, he had compassion
11.38 The Pharisee was astonished to see
12.54 "When you see a cloud rising in the west
13.12 when Jesus saw her, he called her
13.35 "you will not see me until you say
14.18 " 'I have bought a field, and I must . . see it
15.20 "his father saw him and had compassion
17.14 When he saw them he said . . "Go
17.15 when he saw . . he was healed, turned back
17.22 "to see one of the days of . . Son of man
18.15 when . . disciples saw it, they rebuked them
18.43 people, when they saw it, gave praise
19. 3 he sought to see who Jesus was
19. 4 climbed . . a sycamore tree to see him
19. 7 when they saw it they all murmured
19.37 for all the mighty works . . they had seen
19.41 when he . . saw the city he wept over it
20.14 "when the tenants saw him, they said
21. 1 He . . saw the rich putting their gifts
21. 2 he saw a poor widow put in two . . coins
21.20 "when you see Jerusalem surrounded
21.31 "when you see these things taking place
22.49 when those who were about him saw
22.56 a maid, seeing him as he sat
22.58 "a little later some one else saw him
23. 8 When Herod saw Jesus, he was very glad, for he had long desired to see him . . , and he was hoping to see some sign
23.47 centurion saw what had taken place
24.24 "but him they did not see
24.39 "See my hands and my feet, that it is I myself; handle me, and see
Jn 1.33 " 'on whom you see the Spirit descend
1.39 He said to them, "Come and see
1.46 Philip said to him, "Come and see
1.47 Jesus saw Nathanael coming to him
1.48 "when you were under the fig tree, I saw
1.50 "Because I said to you, I saw you
3. 3 "he cannot see the kingdom of God
4.29 "Come, see a man who told me all
4.48 "Unless you see signs and wonders
5. 6 When Jesus saw him and knew
6.14 When the people saw the sign
6.22 people . . on the other side of the sea saw
6.24 the people saw that Jesus was not there
6.26 "you seek me, not because you saw signs
6.30 "what sign do you do, that we may see?
7.52 "you will see . . no prophet . . from Galilee
8.56 "Abraham rejoiced that he was to see my day; he saw it and was glad
9. 1 he saw a man blind from his birth
11.31 When the Jews . . saw Mary rise quickly
11.32 Mary, when she . . saw him, fell at his feet
11.33 When Jesus saw her weeping
11.34 They said to him, "Lord, come and see
12. 9 great crowd . . came . . also to see Lazarus
12.21 "Sir, we wish to see Jesus
12.40 "He has blinded their eyes . . lest they . . see
12.41 Isaiah said this because he saw his glory
18.26 "Did I not see you in the garden?
19. 6 When the . . officers saw him, they cried out
19.26 When Jesus saw his mother
19.33 they . . saw that he was already dead
20. 8 the other disciple . . saw and believed
20.20 disciples . . glad when they saw the Lord
20.25 "Unless I see in his hands the print
20.27 "Put your finger here, and see my hands
20.29 Blessed are those who have not seen
21.21 When Peter saw him, he said to Jesus
Acts 2.27 " 'not . . let thy Holy One see corruption
Acts 2.31 "nor did his flesh see corruption
3. 3 Seeing Peter . . about to go into . . temple
3. 9 And all the people saw him walking
3.12 when Peter saw it he addressed . . people
4.20 "cannot but speak of what we have seen
6.15 all . . saw that his face was like . . an angel
7.24 "seeing one of them being wronged
7.31 "When Moses saw it he wondered
7.55 gazed into heaven and saw the glory
8.18 Simon saw that the Spirit was given
8.39 the eunuch saw him no more
9.12 "he has seen a man named Ananias
9.27 how on the road he had seen the Lord
9.35 residents of Lydda and Sharon saw him
9.40 when she saw Peter she sat up
10. 3 he saw clearly in a vision an angel
10.17 perplexed as to . . the vision . . he had seen
11. 5 "I saw a vision, something descending
11.13 "he told us how he had seen the angel
11.23 he came and saw the grace of God
12. 3 when he saw that it pleased the Jews
12.16 they saw him and were amazed
13.12 when he saw what had occurred
13.35 " 'not let thy Holy One see corruption
13.36 "David . . fell asleep . . and saw corruption
13.37 "he whom God raised . . saw no corruption
13.45 when the Jews saw the multitudes
14. 9 seeing that he had faith to be made well
14.11 the crowds saw what Paul had done
16.10 when he had seen the vision
16.19 her owners saw that their hope . . was gone
16.27 saw that the prison doors were open
16.40 when they had seen the brethren
19.21 "After . . there, I must also see Rome
21.32 when they saw . . tribune and . . soldiers
22.14 " 'God . . appointed you . . to see the Just
22.18 "⟨I fell into a trance⟩ and saw him
26.13 "I saw on the way a light from heaven
26.16 " 'the things in which you have seen me
28. 4 saw the creature hanging from his hand
28.15 On seeing them Paul thanked God
28.20 "therefore I have asked to see you
Rom 1.11 For I long to see you, that I may impart
1 Cor 2. 9 "What no eye has seen, nor ear heard
8.10 if any . . sees you . . in an idol's temple
16. 7 I do not want to see you . . in passing
Gal 1.19 I saw none of the other apostles except
2. 7 when they saw that I had been entrusted
2.14 I saw that they were not straightforward
6.11 See with what large letters I am writing
Phil 1.27 whether I come and see you or am absent
1.30 in the same conflict which you saw
2.28 that you may rejoice at seeing him again
4. 9 What you have . . heard and seen in me, do
1 Th 2.17 we endeavored . . to see you face to face
3. 6 reported that you . . long to see us
3.10 that we may see you face to face
1 Tim 6.16 who alone has immortality . . , whom no man has ever seen or can see
2 Tim 1. 4 I long night and day to see you
Heb 3. 9 "fathers . . saw my works for forty years
11. 5 taken up so . . he should not see death
11.13 having seen . . and greeted it from afar
11.23 they saw that the child was beautiful
Jas 5.11 you have seen the purpose of the Lord
1 Pet 1. 8 Without having seen[b] him you[c] love him‡
3.10 "He that would love life . . see good days
1 Jn 3. 1 See what love the Father has given us
5.16 If any . . sees his brother committing . . sin
3 Jn .14 I hope to see you soon, and we will talk
Rev 1. 2 who bore witness . . to all that he saw
1.12 to see the voice that was speaking to me
1.17 When I saw him, I fell at his feet
1.19 "Now write what you see, what is
1.20 "seven stars . . you saw in my right hand,
5. 1 And I saw in the right hand of him
5. 2 "and I saw a strong angel proclaiming

Rev 5. 6 I saw a Lamb standing, as though . . slain
6. 1 I saw when the Lamb opened one
6. 2 And I saw, and behold, a white horse
6. 5 And I saw, and behold, a black horse
6. 8 And I saw, and behold, a pale horse
6. 9 I saw under the altar the souls of those
7. 1 After this I saw four angels standing
7. 2 Then I saw another angel ascend
8. 2 Then I saw the seven angels who stand
9. 1 I saw a star fallen from heaven to earth
9.17 this was how I saw the horses
10. 1 I saw another mighty angel coming down
10. 5 the angel whom I saw standing on sea
12.13 dragon saw that he had been thrown down
13. 1 And I saw a beast rising out of the sea
13. 2 the beast that I saw was like a leopard
13.11 I saw another beast . . out of the earth
14. 6 I saw another angel flying in midheaven
15. 1 Then I saw another portent in heaven
15. 2 I saw what appeared to be a sea of glass
16.13 I saw, . . from the mouth of the dragon
17. 3 I saw a woman sitting on a . . beast
17. 6 I saw the woman, drunk with . . blood
17. 6 When I saw her I marveled greatly
17. 8 "The beast that you saw was, and is not
17.12 "the ten horns that you saw are . . kings
17.15 "The waters that you saw . . are peoples
17.16 "horns that you saw . . will hate the harlot
17.18 "woman that you saw is the great city
18. 1 After this I saw another angel coming
18. 7 "she says . . 'mourning I shall never see
19.11 I saw heaven opened, and behold!
19.17 I saw an angel standing in the sun
19.19 I saw the beast and the kings of . . earth
20. 1 Then I saw an angel coming down
20. 4 I saw thrones, and seated on them
20.11 Then I saw a great white throne
20.12 And I saw the dead, great and small
21. 1 I saw a new heaven and a new earth
21. 2 I saw the holy city, new Jerusalem
21.22 And I saw no temple in the city

6. *look at:* ἐμβλέπω EMBLEPŌ
Mk 8.25 he . . was restored, and saw everything clearly
Acts 22.11 "I could not see because of the brightness

7. *watch, observe:* ἐποπτεύω EPOPTEUŌ*
1 Pet 2.12 so that . . they may see your good deeds
3. 2 when they see your reverent . . behavior

8. *know, understand:* γινώσκω GINŌSKŌ
Gal 3. 7 So you see that it is men of faith

9. *see, perceive:* ὁράω HORAŌ
Mt 5. 8 "the pure in heart, for they shall see God
8. 4 "See that you say nothing to any one
9.30 "See that no one knows it
18.10 "See that you do not despise one of these
24. 6 "see that you are not alarmed
24.30 "they will see the Son of man coming
26.64 "you will see the Son of man seated
28. 7 "to Galilee; there you will see him
28.10 "to Galilee, and there they will see me
Mk 1.44 "See that you say nothing to any one
13.26 "they will see the Son of man coming
14.62 "you will see the Son of man seated
16. 7 "to Galilee; there you will see him
Lk 1.22 perceived that he had seen a vision
3. 6 "all flesh shall see the salvation of God
9.36 told no one . . anything . . they had seen
13.28 "you will weep . . when you see Abraham
16.23 "he . . saw Abraham far off and Lazarus
17.22 "you will desire to see one of the days
21.27 "they will see the Son of man coming
23.49 stood at a distance . . saw these things
24.23 "they had even seen a vision of angels
Jn 1.18 No one has ever seen God
1.34 "I have seen and have borne witness
1.39 He said to them, "Come and see
1.50 "You shall see greater . . than these
1.51 "you will see heaven opened
Jn 3.11 "we . . bear witness to what we have seen
3.32 He bears witness to what he has seen
3.36 who does not obey . . Son shall not see life
4.45 Galileans . . , having seen all . . he had done
5.37 "his form you have never seen
6. 2 because they saw the signs which he did
6.36 "you have seen me and yet do not believe
6.46 "Not that any one has seen the Father except him . . ; he has seen the Father
8.38 "I speak of what I have seen
8.57 Jews . . said . . "have you seen Abraham?[u]‡
9.37 Jesus said to him, "You have seen him
11.40 "if you would believe you would see
14. 7 "henceforth you know . . and have seen him
14. 9 "He who has seen me has seen the Father; how can you say, 'Show us?
15.24 "they have seen . . both me and my Father
16.16 "again a little while, and you will see me
16.17 " 'again a little while, and you will see me
16.19 " 'again a little while, and you will see me
16.22 "sorrow now, but I will see you again
19.35 He who saw it has borne witness
20.18 Mary M. said . . "I have seen the Lord
20.25 told him, "We have seen the Lord
20.29 "Have you believed because you have seen?
Acts 2.17 " 'your young men shall see visions
7.44 "according to the pattern . . he had seen
8.23 "I see . . you are in the gall of bitterness
20.25 "all you . . will see my face no more
22.15 " 'a witness . . of what you have seen
Rom 15.21 "They shall see who have never been told
1 Cor 9. 1 Have I not seen Jesus our Lord?
Col 2. 1 for all who have not seen my face
1 Th 5.15 See that none of you repays evil
1 Tim 3.16 He[h] was manifested . . , seen by angels
Heb 2. 8 "we do not . . see everything in subjection
8. 5 "See that you make everything according
11.27 endured as seeing him who is invisible
12.14 without which no one will see the Lord
13.23 with whom I shall see you if he comes
Jas 2.24 You see that a man is justified by works
1 Pet 1. 8 though you do not . . see . . you[c] believe
1 Jn 1. 1 which we have seen with our eyes
1. 2 the life was made manifest, . . we saw it
1. 3 that which we have seen and heard
3. 2 for we shall see him as he is
3. 6 no one who sins has either seen him
4.20 who does not love . . whom he has seen, cannot[h] love God whom he has not seen
3 Jn .11 he who does evil has not seen God
Rev 1. 7 he is coming . . and every eye will see him
11.19 the ark of his covenant was seen
22. 4 they shall see his face

Also variant to: Jn **6.2**

10. *behold! look!:* ἴδε IDE
Mk 15. 4 "See how many charges they bring
16. 6 "see the place where they laid him
Jn 5.14 "See, you are well! Sin no more
11.36 the Jews said, "See how he loved him!
19. 4 "See, I am bringing him out to you[0]

11. *behold!:* ἰδού IDOU
Mt 26.46 "see, my betrayer is at hand
Mk 14.42 "see, my betrayer is at hand
2 Cor 7.11 "see what . . this godly grief has produced

12. *think, consider, perceive:* νοέω NOEŌ
Mt 15.17 "Do you not see that whatever goes into?
Mk 7.18 "Do you not see that whatever goes into?

13. *know:* οἶδα OIDA
Mk 12.28 seeing that he answered them well

14. *visible, known:* φανερός PHANEROS [B.3.a.1]
1 Tim 4.15 so that all may see your progress

15. *behold:* θεάομαι THEAOMAI
Mt 6. 1 "Beware of practicing . . piety . . to be seen
23. 5 "They do . . their deeds to be seen by men
Mk 16.11 when they heard . . he . . had been seen[k]‡
16.14 they had not believed those who saw[k]‡
Lk 5.27 "he . . saw a tax collector, named Levi

Lk 23.55 The women who . . followed . . saw the tomb
Jn 1.32 "I saw the Spirit descend as a dove
1.38 Jesus turned, and saw them following
4.35 "you . . say . . 'There are yet four months
6. 5 seeing that a multitude was coming
11.45 Many . . , who . . had seen what he did
Acts 1.11 "This Jesus . . will come . . as you saw him go
21.27 the Jews from Asia, who had seen him
22. 9 "those who were with me saw the light
Rom 15.24 I hope to see you in passing as I go
1 Jn 4.12 No man has ever seen God
4.14 we have seen . . that the Father . . sent . . Son
16. *look at, observe:* θεωρέω THEŌREŌ
Mt 28. 1 the other Mary went to see . . sepulchre
Mk 5.15 they came to Jesus, and saw the demoniac
5.38 he saw a tumult, and people weeping
15.47 mother of Joses saw where he was laid
16. 4 they saw that the stone was rolled back
Lk 10.18 "I saw Satan fall like lightning
14.29 "all who see it begin to mock him
21. 6 "As for these things which you see
23.48 when they saw what had taken place
24.37 they . . supposed that they saw a spirit
24.39 "flesh and bones as you see that I have[y]
Jn 2.23 many believed . . when they saw the signs
6. 2 because they saw the signs which he did
Var. HORAŌ
6.19 they saw Jesus walking on the sea
6.40 "every one who sees the Son and believes
6.62 "to see the Son of man ascending
7. 3 "that your disciples may see the works
8.51 "truly, I say . . , he will never see death
9. 8 who had seen him before as a beggar
10.12 "a hireling . . sees the wolf coming and leaves
12.19 "You see that you can do nothing
12.45 "And he who sees me sees him who sent me
14.17 "it neither sees him nor knows him
14.19 "the world will see me no more, but you will see me; because I live, you will live
16.10 "I go . . and you will see me no more
16.16 "A . . while, and you will see me no more
16.17 " 'A . . while, and you will not see me
16.19 " 'A . . while, and you will not see me
20. 6 he saw the linen cloths lying
20.12 she saw two angels in white, sitting
20.14 Saying this, she turned . . and saw Jesus
Acts 3.16 "has made this man strong whom you see
4.13 when they saw the boldness of Peter
7.56 "Behold, I see the heavens opened
8.13 seeing signs . . performed, he was amazed
9. 7 hearing the voice but seeing no one
10.11 saw the heaven opened, and something
17.16 as he saw that the city was full of idols
19.26 "you see . . that not only at Ephesus
20.38 that they should see his face no more
21.20 "You see, brother, how many thousands
25.24 "King Agrippa . . , you see this man
28. 6 they . . saw no misfortune come to him
Heb 7. 4 See how great he is!
1 Jn 3.17 if any one . . sees his brother in need
Rev 11.11 great fear fell on those who saw them
IDIOMATICALLY
a. Mk 11.13 he went to see if he could find anything on it
ἦλθεν εἰ ἄρα τι εὑρήσει ἐν αὐτῇ [ARA II]

SEE BEFORE
1. *see before one, foresee:* προοράω (mid.) PROORAŌ
[a]+ἐνώπιον
Acts 2.25 [a]" 'I saw the Lord always before me

SEE, CAN
1. *see, look:* βλέπω BLEPŌ [A.6.a.5]
Acts 9. 8 eyes were opened, he could see nothing

SEE CLEARLY
1. *see clearly, look intently:* διαβλέπω DIABLEPŌ
Mt 7. 5 "then you will s. clearly to take the speck
Lk 6.42 " 'then you will s. clearly to take . . speck

SEE, GO TO
1. *come to, approach:* προσέρχομαι PROSERCHOMAI
Acts 18. 2 And he went to see them

SEE HERE IS
1. *behold!:* ἰδού IDOU
Acts 8.36 the eunuch said, "See, here is water!

SEE IN
1. *see, look:* βλέπω BLEPŌ
2 Cor 12. 6 think more of me than he sees in me

SEE, MAKE
1. *shine, illuminate:* φωτίζω PHŌTIZŌ
Eph 3. 9 to make all men see what is the plan

SEE PREVIOUSLY
1. *see before one, foresee:* προοράω PROORAŌ
Acts 21.29 they had previously seen Trophimus

SEE THAT
1. *in order that:* ἵνα (as imper.) HINA
2 Cor 8. 7 see that you excel in this gracious work
Col 4.16 see that you read . . letter from Laodicea
Tit 3.13 see that they lack nothing

SEE TO IT
1. *see, look:* βλέπω (imper.) BLEPŌ
Col 2. 8 See to it that no one makes a prey
2. *look upon, consider:* ἐπισκοπέω EPISKOPEŌ
Heb 12.15 See to it that no one fail to obtain
3. *see, perceive:* ὁράω (imper.) HORAŌ
Mt 27. 4 "What is that to us? See to it yourself
27.24 "I am innocent . . ; see to it yourselves
Acts 18.15 "see to it yourselves; I refuse
4. *be eager:* σπουδάζω SPOUDAZŌ
2 Pet 1.15 I will see to it that after my departure

SEED
1. *seed, offspring:* σπέρμα SPERMA
Mt 13.24 "a man who sowed good seed
13.27 " 'did you not sow good seed in . . field?
13.32 "it is the smallest of all seeds
13.37 "who sows the good seed is the Son of man
13.38 "good seed means . . sons of the kingdom
Mk 4.31 "the smallest of all the seeds on earth
1 Cor 15.38 to each kind of seed its own body
2 Cor 9.10 He who supplies seed to the sower
2. *seed, sowing:* σπορά SPORA*
1 Pet 1.23 born anew, not of perishable seed
3. *seed, sowing:* σπόρος SPOROS
Mk 4.26 "is as if a man should scatter seed
4.27 "and the seed should sprout and grow
Lk 8. 5 "A sower went out to sow his seed
8.11 "The seed is the word of God
CONTEXTUALLY
Mt 13. 4 "some seeds fell along the path
13. 5 "Other seeds fell on rocky ground
13. 7 "Other seeds fell upon thorns
13. 8 "Other seeds fell on good soil
13.31 "kingdom . . is like a grain of mustard seed
17.20 "if you have faith as . . mustard s.
Mk 4. 4 "some seed fell along the path
4. 5 "Other seed fell on rocky ground
4. 7 "Other seed fell among thorns
4. 8 "other seeds fell into good soil
4.31 "It is like a grain of mustard seed
Lk 13.19 "It is like a grain of mustard seed
17. 6 "If you had faith as a grain of mustard s.

SEEK (*See also* CIRCUMCISION, SEEK; ESCAPE, SEEK TO; FAVOR OF, SEEK THE)

SEEK FOR
1. *seek:* ἀναζητέω ANAZĒTEŌ
Lk 2.44 they sought him among their kinsfolk
2.45 they returned to Jerusalem, seeking him
2. *pursue:* διώκω DIŌKŌ
1 Th 5.15 always seek to do good to one another
3. *seek out:* ἐκζητέω EKZĒTEŌ
Acts 15.17 " 'that the rest of men may seek the Lord
Rom 3.11 "no one understands, no one seeks for God
Heb 11. 6 that he rewards those who seek him
12.17 no chance to repent, though he sought it

4. *put one's hand to, attempt:* ἐπιχειρέω EPICHEIREŌ
Acts 9.29 but they were seeking to kill him
5. *seek after, demand:* ἐπιζητέω EPIZĒTEŌ*
Mt 6.32 "For the Gentiles seek all these things
12.39 "An evil . . generation seeks for a sign
16. 4 "An evil . . generation seeks for a sign
Lk 4.42 the people sought him and came
12.30 "For all the nations . . seek these things
Acts 12.19 when Herod had sought for him
13. 7 Sergius Paulus . . sought to hear the word
19.39 "But if you seek anything further[t]
Rom 11. 7 Israel failed to obtain what it sought
Phil 4.17 Not that I seek the gift; but I seek the fruit which increases to your credit
Heb 11.14 clear that they are seeking a homeland
13.14 but we seek the city which is to come
6. *seek, desire:* ζητέω ZĒTEŌ
Mt 2.20 "those who sought the child's life
6.33 "seek first his kingdom and his righteousness
7. 7 "seek, and you will find; knock
7. 8 "he who seeks finds, and to him who knocks
12.43 "unclean spirit . . passes . . seeking rest
26.16 he sought an opportunity to betray
26.59 the whole council sought false testimony
28. 5 "for I know that you seek Jesus
Mk 8.11 seeking from him a sign from heaven
8.12 "Why does this generation seek a sign?
11.18 scribes . . sought a way to destroy him
14. 1 scribes were seeking how to arrest him
14.11 he sought an opportunity to betray him
14.55 council sought testimony against Jesus
16. 6 "you seek Jesus of N., who was crucified
Lk 2.49 "How is it that you sought me?
5.18 they sought to . . lay him before Jesus[q]
6.19 all the crowd sought to touch him
9. 9 And he sought to see him
11. 9 "seek, and you will find; knock
11.10 "he who seeks finds, and to him who knocks
11.16 to test him, sought from him a sign
11.24 "unclean spirit . . passes . . seeking rest
11.29 "it seeks a sign, but no sign shall be given
12.29 "And do not seek what you are to eat
12.31 "Instead, seek his[p] kingdom
13. 6 "came seeking fruit on it and found none
13. 7 " 'three years I have come seeking fruit
13.24 "for many, I tell you, will seek to enter
15. 8 "what woman . . does not . . seek diligently?
17.33 "Whoever seeks to gain his life will lose
19. 3 he sought to see who Jesus was
19.10 "the Son of man came to seek and to save
19.47 the principal men . . sought to destroy him
22. 2 scribes were seeking . . to put him to death
22. 6 he . . sought an opportunity to betray
24. 5 "Why . . seek the living among the dead?[u]
Jn 1.38 Jesus . . said . . "What do you seek?
4.23 "such the Father seeks to worship him
5.18 the Jews sought all the more to kill him
5.30 "because I seek not my own will
5.44 "who . . do not seek the glory . . from . . God
6.24 they . . went to Capernaum, seeking Jesus
6.26 "you seek me, not because you saw signs
7. 1 because the Jews[n] sought to kill him
7. 4 "no man . . if he seeks to be known openly
7.18 "who speaks on his own . . seeks his own glory; but he who seeks the glory of him
7.19 "Why do you seek to kill me?
7.20 "Who is seeking to kill you?
7.25 "Is not this . . whom they seek to kill?
7.30 So they sought to arrest him
7.34 "you will seek me and you will not find
7.36 " 'You will seek me and you will not find
8.21 "you will seek me and die in your sin
8.37 "yet you seek to kill me, because my word
8.40 "but now you seek to kill me
8.50 "Yet I do not seek my own glory; there is One who seeks it
11. 8 "Jews were . . seeking to stone you
Jn 13.33 "You will seek me
18. 4 Jesus . . said . . "Whom do you seek?
18. 7 Again he asked . . "Whom do you seek?
18. 8 "so, if you seek me, let these men go
19.12 Upon this Pilate sought to release him
20.15 "why are you weeping? Whom do you seek?
Acts 13. 8 seeking to turn away the proconsul
13.11 went about seeking people to lead him
16.10 we sought to go on into Macedonia
17. 5 seeking to bring them out to the people
17.27 "that they should seek God, in the hope
27.30 as the sailors were seeking to escape
Rom 2. 7 who by . . well-doing seek for glory
10. 3 seeking to establish . . own . . righteousness
10.20 "found by those who did not seek me
11. 3 "I alone am left, and they seek my life
1 Cor 1.22 Jews demand signs . . Greeks seek wisdom
7.27 Do not seek to be free. Are you free from a wife? Do not seek marriage
10.24 Let no one seek his own good
10.33 not seeking my own advantage
2 Cor 12.14 for I seek not what is yours but you
Col 3. 1 seek the things that are above
1 Th 2. 6 nor did we seek glory from men
1 Pet 3.11 "let him seek peace and pursue it
5. 8 roaring lion, seeking some one to devour
Rev 9. 6 men will seek death and will not find it
CONTEXTUALLY
1 Cor 7.18 Let him not seek to remove the marks
7.18 Let him not seek circumcision

SEEK OUT
1. *find out:* ἀνευρίσκω ANEURISKŌ
Acts 21. 4 having sought out the disciples

SEEM
1. *think, suppose:* δοκέω DOKEŌ
Acts 17.18 "seems to be a preacher of foreign divinities
25.27 "For it seems to me unreasonable
1 Cor 12.22 parts of the body which seem . . weaker
2 Cor 10. 9 I would not seem to be frightening you
Heb 12.11 all discipline seems painful rather than
2. *as, so:* ὡς HŌS [B.3.b.4]
Rev **13.3**
3. *appear to be like:* φαίνειν ὡσεί (pass.) PHAINŌ [A.6.a.4]
Lk 24.11 these words seemed to them an idle tale

SEEM GOOD
1. *think, suppose:* δοκέω DOKEŌ
Lk 1. 3 it seemed good to me . . to write an . . account
Acts 15.22 Then it seemed good to the apostles
15.25 "it has seemed good to us . . to choose men
15.28 "it has seemed good to the Holy Spirit
[15.34 *it seemed good to Silas to remain there*‡

SEEMLY
1. *well ordered, modest:* κόσμιος KOSMIOS
1 Tim 2. 9 should adorn themselves . . in s. apparel

SEEMS TO BE, WHAT
1. *as, so:* ὡς HŌS [B.3.b.4]
Rev 6. 6 I heard what seemed to be a voice
19. 1 heard what seemed to be the loud voice
19. 6 Then I heard what seemed to be the voice

SEEN
1. *visible, known:* φανερός PHANEROS
1 Jn 3.10 By this it may be seen who are the children

SEEN, BE
SEEN, BE CLEARLY
1. *bring to light, shine:* φαίνω (pass.) PHAINŌ
Mt 6. 5 "that they may be seen by men
6.16 "that their fasting may be seen by men
6.18 "that your fasting . . not be seen by men
9.33 "Never was anything like this seen
2. *make manifest, make known:* φανερόω (pass.) PHANEROŌ
Jn 3.21 it may be clearly seen that his deeds
Rev 3.18 "to keep . . nakedness from being seen

SEEN, NOT
1. *unseen:* ἄδηλος ADĒLOS
Lk 11.44 "you are like graves which are not seen

SEES, WHAT ONE
1. *look, glance:* βλέμμα BLEMMA* [A.1.e]
2 Pet 2. 8 (what that righteous man saw and heard

SEIZE
1. *take, lay hold of:* ἐπιλαμβάνομαι EPILAMBANOMAI
Lk 23.26 they seized one Simon of Cyrene
Acts 16.19 seized Paul and Silas and dragged them
18.17 seized Sosthenes, . . ruler of the synagogue
21.30 they seized Paul and dragged him out
2. *catch:* καταλαμβάνω KATALAMBANŌ
Mk 9.18 "wherever it seizes him, it dashes him
3. *seize, hold fast:* κρατέω KRATEŌ
Mt 14. 3 Herod had seized John and bound him
18.28 "seizing him by the throat he said, 'Pay
22. 6 "seized his servants . . and killed them
26.48 "The one I shall kiss is the man; seize him
26.50 laid hands on Jesus and seized him
26.55 "in the temple . . you did not seize me
26.57 those who had seized Jesus led him
Mk 3.21 his family . . went out to seize him
6.17 For Herod had sent and seized John
14.44 "The one I shall kiss is the man; seize him
14.46 they laid hands on him and seized him
14.49 "in the temple . . you did not seize me
14.51 young man followed . . and they seized him
Acts 24. 6 "to profane the temple, but we seized him[z]
Heb 6.18 to seize the hope set before us
Rev 20. 2 seized the dragon, that ancient serpent
4. *receive, take:* λαμβάνω LAMBANŌ
Lk 5.26 "And amazement seized them all
7.16 Fear seized them all
9.39 "a spirit seizes him, and he . . cries out
Rev 3.11 " 'so that no one may seize your crown
5. *take hold of:* πιάζω PIAZŌ
Acts 12. 4 when he . . seized him, he put him in prison
2 Cor 11.32 Aretas guarded . . Damascus . . to seize me
6. *gather, seize, conceive:* συλλαμβάνω (act. or mid.) SYLLAMBANŌ
Lk 22.54 they seized him and led him away
Jn 18.12 the officers of the Jews seized Jesus
Acts 23.27 "This man was seized by the Jews
26.21 "For this reason the Jews seized me
7. *snatch and carry away with:* συναρπάζω SYNARPAZŌ
Lk 8.29 (For many a time it had seized him
Acts 6.12 they came upon him and seized him
8. *hold together, impel:* συνέχω SYNECHŌ
Lk 8.37 for they were seized with great fear

SELEUCIA: Σελεύκεια sə'lüsh(ē)ə II,G-3
Acts 13. 4 by the Holy Spirit, they went down to S.

SELF
1. *man, mankind:* ἄνθρωπος ANTHRŌPOS
Rom 6. 6 We know that our old self was crucified
7.22 I delight in the law . . , in my inmost self
2. *self; he, she, it:* αὐτός AUTOS
3. *life, soul, self:* ψυχή PSYCHĒ
1 Th 2. 8 ready to share with you . . our own selves

SELF, LOVER OF
1. *loving oneself, selfish:* φίλαυτος (subst.) PHILAUTOS*
2 Tim 3. 2 men will be lovers of self, lovers of money

SELF, YOUR OWN
1. *yourself:* σεαυτοῦ SEAUTOU
Phm .19 your owing me even your own self

SELF-ABASEMENT
1. *humility:* ταπεινοφροσύνη TAPEINOPHROSYNĒ
Col 2.18 Let no one . . , insisting on self-abasement
2.23 promoting rigor of devotion and s.

SELF-CONCEIT
IDIOMATICALLY
a. Gal 5.26 Let us have no self-conceit μὴ γινώμεθα κενόδοξοι [KENODOXOS*]

SELF-CONDEMNED
1. *self-condemned:* αὐτοκατάκριτος AUTOKATAKRITOS*
Tit 3.11 person is perverted and sinful; he is s.

SELF-CONTROL
1. *self-control:* ἐγκράτεια EGKRATEIA*
Acts 24.25 he argued about justice and self-control
Gal 5.23 self-control; against such there is no law
2 Pet 1. 6 ⟨supplement⟩ knowledge with self-control, and self-control with steadfastness
2. *moderation, self-discipline:* σωφρονισμός SŌPHRONISMOS*
2 Tim 1. 7 a spirit of power and love and s.

SELF-CONTROL, EXERCISE
1. *exercise self-control:* ἐγκρατεύομαι EGKRATEUOMAI*
1 Cor 7. 9 But if they cannot exercise self-control
9.25 Every athlete exercises self-control

SELF-CONTROL, LACK OF
1. *lack of self-control:* ἀκρασία AKRASIA
1 Cor 7. 5 lest Satan tempt you through lack of s.

SELF-CONTROLLED
1. *self-controlled, disciplined:* ἐγκρατής EGKRATĒS*
Tit 1. 8 upright, holy, and self-controlled

SELF-INDULGENT, BE
1. *live softly, live indulgently:* σπαταλάω SPATALAŌ
1 Tim 5. 6 whereas she who is self-indulgent is dead

SELFISH
1. *sick, base, evil:* πονηρός PONĒROS
Lk 6.35 "he is kind to the ungrateful and . . selfish

SELFISH AMBITION
SELFISHNESS
1. *selfish ambition:* ἐριθεία ERITHEIA
[a]pl.
2 Cor 12.20 [a]perhaps there may be . . selfishness
Gal 5.20 [a]anger, selfishness, dissension
Phil 2. 3 Do nothing from selfishness or conceit
Jas 3.14 if you have . . selfish ambition in . . hearts
3.16 where jealousy and selfish ambition exist

SELL
1. *give up, return:* ἀποδίδωμι (mid.) APODIDŌMI
Acts 5. 8 "Tell me whether you sold the land
7. 9 "patriarchs, jealous of Joseph, sold him
Heb 12.16 like Esau, who sold his birthright
2. *sell:* πιπράσκω PIPRASKŌ*
Mt 13.46 "finding one pearl of great value, . . sold all
18.25 "lord ordered him to be sold, with his wife
26. 9 "this ointment might have been sold
Mk 14. 5 "this ointment might have been sold
Jn 12. 5 "Why was this ointment not sold
Acts 2.45 they sold their possessions and goods
4.34 possessors of lands or houses sold them
5. 4 "sold, was it not at your disposal?
Rom 7.14 but I am carnal, sold under sin
3. *sell:* πωλέω PŌLEŌ
Mt 10.29 "Are not two sparrows sold for a penny?
13.44 "in his joy he . . sells all that he has
19.21 "sell what you possess and give to the poor
21.12 drove out all who sold and . . overturned . . seats of those who sold pigeons
Mk 10.21 "sell what you have, and give to the poor
11.15 began to drive out those who sold and . . overturned . . seats of those who sold
Lk 12. 6 "five sparrows sold for two pennies
12.33 "Sell your possessions, and give alms
17.28 "they bought, they sold, they planted
18.22 "Sell all that you have and distribute
19.45 he . . began to drive out those who sold
22.36 "let him who has no sword sell his mantle
Jn 2.14 who were selling oxen and sheep
2.16 he told those who sold the pigeons
Acts 4.34 possessors of lands or houses sold them
4.37 sold a field which belonged to him
5. 1 Sapphira sold a piece of property
1 Cor 10.25 Eat whatever is sold in the meat market
Rev 13.17 no one can . . sell unless he has the mark

SELLER OF PURPLE
1. *woman dealer in purple:* πορφυρόπωλις PORPHYROPŌLIS*
Acts 16.14 Lydia, . . a seller of purple goods

SEMEIN: Σεμεΐν se'mēən
Lk 3.26 Mattathias, . . son of S., . . son of Josech

SENATE
1. *senate, Sanhedrin* (of the Jews): γερουσία GEROUSIA*
Acts 5.21 the council and all the senate of Israel

SEND (*See also* GREETINGS, SEND; RAIN, SEND)
1. *send up, send back:* ἀναπέμπω ANAPEMPŌ
Acts 25.21 "held until I could send him to Caesar
2. *send away:* ἀποστέλλω APOSTELLŌ
Mt 2.16 he sent and killed all the male children
10.40 "who receives me receives him who sent me
11.10 " 'Behold, I send my messenger
13.41 "The Son of man will send his angels
15.24 "I was sent only to . . lost sheep of . . Israel
20. 2 "agreeing . . , he sent them into his vineyard
21. 1 then Jesus sent two disciples
21. 3 "he will send them immediately
21.34 "he sent his servants to the tenants
21.36 "he sent other servants, more than the first
21.37 "Afterward he sent his son to them
22. 3 "sent his servants to call those . . invited
22. 4 "Again he sent other servants
22.16 And they sent their disciples to him
23.34 "I send you prophets and wise men
23.37 "killing the prophets . . who are sent to you!
24.31 "he will send out his angels
27.19 while he was sitting . . , his wife sent word
Mk 1. 2 "Behold, I send my messenger
3.31 standing outside they sent to him
5.10 begged . . not to s. them out of the country
6. 7 began to send them out two by two
6.17 For Herod had sent and seized John
6.27 immediately the king sent a soldier
8.26 he sent him away to his home
9.37 "receives not me but him who sent me
11. 1 he sent two of his disciples
11. 3 " 'The Lord . . will send it back
12. 2 "he sent a servant to the tenants
12. 3 "they . . sent him away empty-handed
12. 4 "Again he sent to them another servant
12. 5 "he sent another, and him they killed
12. 6 "still . . a beloved son; finally he sent him
12.13 they sent to him some of the Pharisees
14.13 he sent two of his disciples
Lk 1.19 "I am Gabriel . . ; and I was sent . . to you
1.26 the angel Gabriel was sent from God
4.18 "He has sent me to proclaim release
4.43 "for I was sent for this purpose
7. 3 When he heard of Jesus, he sent to him
7.20 "John the Baptist has sent us to you
7.27 " 'Behold, I send my messenger
9.48 "receives him who sent me
9.52 And he sent messengers ahead of him
10. 1 Lord appointed seventy[g] others, and sent
10.16 "who rejects me rejects him who sent me
11.49 " 'I will send them prophets and apostles
13.34 "stoning those who are sent to you!
14.17 "at the time for the banquet he sent
14.32 "he sends an embassy and asks terms
19.14 "citizens hated him and sent an embassy
19.29 at . . Olivet, he sent two of the disciples
19.32 So those who were sent went away
20.10 "When the time came, he sent a servant
20.20 So they watched him, and sent spies
22. 8 Jesus[h] sent Peter and John, saying, "Go
Jn 1. 6 There was a man sent from God
1.19 when the Jews sent priests . . to ask him
1.24 they had been sent from the Pharisees
3.17 For God sent the Son into the world
3.28 "but I have been sent before him
3.34 he whom God has sent utters the words
4.38 "I sent you to reap . . ; others have labored
5.33 "You sent to John, . . he has borne witness
5.36 "witness that the Father has sent me
5.38 "you do not believe . . whom he has sent
6.29 "that you believe in him whom he has sent
Jn 6.57 "the living Father sent me, and I live
7.29 "I come from him, and he sent me
7.32 Pharisees sent officers to arrest him
8.42 "not of my own accord, but he sent me
9. 7 "the pool of Siloam" (which means Sent
10.36 "whom the Father . . sent into the world
11. 3 the sisters sent to him, saying, "Lord
11.42 "that they . . believe that thou didst send me
17. 3 "know . . Christ whom thou hast sent
17. 8 "believed that thou didst send me
17.18 "As thou didst send me into the world, so I have sent them into the world
17.21 "that . . world may believe . . thou hast sent
17.23 "may know that thou hast sent me
17.25 "these know that thou hast sent me
18.24 Annas . . sent him bound to Caiaphas
20.21 "As the Father has sent me, even so
Acts 3.20 "that he may send the Christ appointed
3.26 "God . . sent him to you first, to bless
5.21 the high priest . . sent to the prison
7.14 "Joseph sent and called to him Jacob
7.34 " 'now come, I will send you to Egypt
7.35 "This Moses . . God sent as both ruler
8.14 they sent to them Peter and John
9.17 "Jesus, who appeared . . , has sent me
9.38 "disciples . . sent two men . . entreating him
10. 8 he sent them to Joppa
10.17 men that were sent by Cornelius
10.20 "accompany them . . ; for I have sent them
10.36 "You know the word which he sent
11.11 "three men . . , sent to me from Caesarea
11.13 " 'Send to Joppa and bring Simon
11.30 sending it to the elders by . . Barnabas
13.15 rulers of the synagogue sent to them
15.27 "We have therefore sent Judas and Silas
16.35 the magistrates sent the police
16.36 "magistrates have sent to let you go
19.22 having sent into Macedonia two . . helpers
26.17 "the Gentiles—to whom I send you
28.28 "this salvation of God has been sent
Rom 10.15 how can men preach unless they are sent?
1 Cor 1.17 For Christ did not send me to baptize
2 Cor 12.17 through any of those whom I sent to you
2 Tim 4.12 Tychicus I have sent to Ephesus
1 Pet 1.12 the Holy Spirit sent from heaven
1 Jn 4. 9 God sent his only Son into the world
4.10 he loved us and sent his Son
4.14 the Father has sent his Son as the Savior
Rev 1. 1 made it known by sending his angel
22. 6 "has sent his angel to show his servants
3. *send out:* ἐξαποστέλλω EXAPOSTELLŌ
Lk 24.49 "behold, I send the promise of my Father
Acts 11.22 they sent Barnabas to Antioch
12.11 "I am sure . . the Lord has sent his angel
13.26 "to us has been sent the message of this
Gal 4. 6 God has sent the Spirit of his Son
4. *place beside, stand before:* παρίστημι PARISTĒMI
Mt 26.53 "he will . . send me . . legions of angels
5. *send:* πέμπω PEMPŌ
Mt 2. 8 he sent them to Bethlehem, saying, "Go
11. 2 when John heard in prison . . he sent word
14.10 he sent and had John beheaded
22. 7 "king was angry, and he sent his troops
Mk 5.12 they begged . . , "Send us to the swine
Lk 4.26 "Elijah was sent to none of them
7. 6 the centurion sent friends to him
7.10 those who had been sent returned
7.19 John . . sent them to the Lord
15.15 "who sent him into his fields to feed swine
16.24 " 'have mercy upon me, and send Lazarus
16.27 " 'Then I beg you, father, to send him
20.11 "And he sent another servant
20.12 "And he sent yet a third
20.13 " 'I will send my beloved son
Jn 1.22 "an answer for those who sent us
1.33 "he who sent me to baptize with water
4.34 "to do the will of him who sent me

Jn 5.23 "does not honor the Father who sent
5.24 "he who .. believes him who sent me
5.30 "I seek .. the will of him who sent me
5.37 "Father who sent me has .. borne witness
6.38 "to do .. the will of him who sent me
6.39 "this is the will of him who sent me
6.44 "unless .. Father who sent me draws him
7.16 "My teaching is .. his who sent me
7.18 "who seeks the glory of him who sent him
7.28 "he who sent me is true
7.33 "then I go to him who sent me
8.16 "not I alone .. but I and he[s] who sent me
8.18 "the Father who sent me bears witness
8.26 "he who sent me is true, and I declare
8.29 "he who sent me is with me
9. 4 "must work the works of him who sent me
12.44 "He .. believes .. in him who sent me
12.45 "he who sees me sees him who sent me
12.49 "who sent me has .. given .. commandment
13.16 "nor is he .. greater than he who sent him
13.20 "who receives .. whom I send receives me
13.20 "who receives me receives him who sent
14.24 "the word .. is .. the Father's who sent me
14.26 "Holy Spirit, whom the Father will send
15.21 "they do not know him who sent me
15.26 "Counselor .., whom I shall send to you
16. 5 "I am going to him who sent me
16. 7 "but if I go, I will send him to you
20.21 "As the Father .., even so I send you
Acts 10. 5 "send men to Joppa, and bring one Simon
10.32 " 'Send therefore to Joppa and ask for Simon
10.33 "So I sent to you at once
11.29 the disciples determined .. to send relief
15.22 to choose men .. and send them to Antioch
15.25 "to choose men and send them to you
19.31 Asiarchs .. sent to him and begged him
20.17 from Miletus he sent to Ephesus
23.30 "I sent him to you at once
25.25 "as he .. appealed .., I decided to send him
25.27 "in sending a prisoner, not to indicate
Rom 8. 3 sending his .. Son in the likeness of .. flesh
1 Cor 4.17 Therefore I sent[g] to you Timothy†
16. 3 I will send those whom you accredit
2 Cor 9. 3 But I am sending the brethren
Eph 6.22 I .. sent him to you for this very purpose
Phil 2.19 I hope in the Lord Jesus to send Timothy
2.23 I hope therefore to send him just as soon
2.25 thought it necessary to s. .. Epaphroditus
2.28 I am the more eager to send him
4.16 even in Thessalonica you sent me help[f]
Col 4. 8 I .. sent him to you for this .. purpose
1 Th 3. 2 we sent Timothy .. to establish you
3. 5 I sent that I might know your faith
2 Th 2.11 God sends upon them a .. delusion
Tit 3.12 When I send Artemas .., do your best
1 Pet 2.14 ⟨Be subject⟩ to governors as sent by him
Rev 1.11 "Write what you see in a book and send
22.16 "I Jesus have sent my angel to you

6. *send along with:* συμπέμπω SYMPEMPŌ
2 Cor 8.18 With him we are sending the brother

CONTEXTUALLY
Phil 4.18 having received .. the gifts you sent

SEND A LETTER

1. *send a message, write:* ἐπιστέλλω EPISTELLŌ
Acts 21.25 "we have sent a letter with our judgment

SEND AWAY

1. *loose from, dismiss:* ἀπολύω APOLYŌ
Mt 14.15 "send the crowds away .. into the villages
15.23 "Send her away, for she is crying after us
15.32 "I am unwilling to s. them away hungry
15.39 sending away .. crowds, he got into .. boat
Mk 6.36 "send them away, to go into the country
8. 3 "if I s. them away hungry .., they will faint
8.10(9) And he sent them away
Lk 8.38 The man .. begged .. ; but he sent him away
9.12 "Send the crowd away .. into the villages

2. *send away:* ἀποστέλλω APOSTELLŌ
Mt 8.31 "send us away into the herd of swine

3. *throw out:* ἐκβάλλω EKBALLŌ
Mk 1.43 charged him, and sent him away at once

4. *send out:* ἐκπέμπω EKPEMPŌ
Acts 17.10 sent Paul and Silas away by night

5. *send out:* ἐξαποστέλλω EXAPOSTELLŌ
Lk 1.53 "the rich he has sent empty away
20.10 "tenants .. sent him away empty-handed
20.11 "they .. sent him away empty-handed
Acts 22.21 " 'I will send you far away to the Gentiles

SEND BACK

1. *send up, send back:* ἀναπέμπω ANAPEMPŌ
Lk 23.11 Herod .. sent him back to Pilate
23.15 "neither did Herod, for he sent him back
Phm .12 I am sending him back to you

SEND FOR

1. *send for:* μεταπέμπω (mid.) METAPEMPŌ
Acts 10.22 "Cornelius .. was directed .. to send for you
10.29 "So when I was sent for, I came. .. I ask then why you sent for me
20. 1 Paul sent for the disciples and .. took leave
24.24 he sent for Paul and heard him speak
24.26 So he sent for him often and conversed

SEND FORTH

SEND OFF

1. *loose from, dismiss:* ἀπολύω APOLYŌ
Acts 13. 3 laid their hands on them and sent them off
15.30 when they were sent off, they went down
15.33 were sent off in peace by the brethren

2. *send away:* ἀποστέλλω APOSTELLŌ
Acts 15.33 were sent off in peace by the brethren
Heb 1.14 ministering spirits sent forth to serve

3. *send out:* ἐξαποστέλλω EXAPOSTELLŌ
Acts 7.12 "he sent forth our fathers the first time
9.30 the brethren .. sent him off to Tarsus
17.14 the brethren immediately sent Paul off
Gal 4. 4 God sent forth his Son, born of woman

SEND ONE ON HIS JOURNEY

SEND ONE ON HIS WAY

1. *send forth, escort:* προπέμπω PROPEMPŌ
Acts 15. 3 being sent on their way by the church
2 Cor 1.16 have you send me on my way to Judea
3 Jn . 6 send them on their journey as befits

SEND OUT

SEND ROUND

1. *send away:* ἀποστέλλω APOSTELLŌ
Mt 10. 5 twelve Jesus sent out, charging them
10.16 "Behold, I send you out as sheep
14.35 they sent round to all that region
Mk 3.14 he appointed twelve[k] .. to be sent out
13.27 "then he will send out the angels
Lk 9. 2 he sent them out to preach the kingdom
10. 3 "behold, I send you out as lambs
22.35 "When I sent you out with no purse
Rev 5. 6 spirits .. sent out into all the earth

2. *throw out:* ἐκβάλλω EKBALLŌ
Mt 9.38 "Lord of the harvest to send out laborers
Lk 10. 2 "pray .. the Lord .. to send out laborers
Jas 2.25 received .. messengers and sent them out

3. *send out:* ἐκπέμπω EKPEMPŌ
Acts 13. 4 So, being sent out by the Holy Spirit

4. *send out:* ἐξαποστέλλω EXAPOSTELLŌ
Mk [16.end *Jesus himself sent out by means of them*‡

SEND OVER

1. *send up, send back:* ἀναπέμπω ANAPEMPŌ
Lk 23. 7 he sent him over to Herod

SEND WITH

1. *send along with:* συμπέμπω SYMPEMPŌ
2 Cor 8.22 with them we are sending our brother

2. *send together with:* συναποστέλλω SYNAPOSTELLŌ*
2 Cor 12.18 I .. sent the brother with him

SENSE OF SMELL

1. *sense of smell:* ὄσφρησις OSPHRĒSIS*
1 Cor 12.17 where would be the sense of smell?

SENSELESS
1. *unintelligent:* ἀνόητος ANOĒTOS
1 Tim 6. 9 many senseless and hurtful desires
2. *uneducated, boorish:* ἀπαίδευτος APAIDEUTOS*
2 Tim 2.23 Have nothing to do with s. controversies
3. *unintelligible, senseless:* ἀσύνετος ASYNETOS
Rom 1.21 their senseless minds were darkened

SENSIBLE
1. *sensible, prudent:* φρόνιμος PHRONIMOS
1 Cor 10.15 I speak as to sensible men
2. *of sound mind, prudent:* σώφρων SŌPHRŌN
1 Tim 3. 2 a bishop must be . . sensible, dignified
Tit 2. 2 Bid the older men be . . serious, sensible
2. 5 ⟨train the young women⟩ to be sensible

SENSIBLY
1. *soundness of mind, prudence:* σωφροσύνη SŌPHROSYNĒ [B.1.a.1]
1 Tim 2. 9 that women . . adorn themselves . . sensibly

SENSUOUS
1. *flesh, body:* σάρξ (gen.) SARX
Col 2.18 puffed up . . by his sensuous mind

SENT, HAVE S.
1. *send for:* μεταπέμπω (mid.) METAPEMPŌ
Acts 25. 3 to have the man sent to Jerusalem

SENT, ONE WHO IS
1. *ambassador, messenger:* ἀπόστολος APOSTOLOS
Jn 13.16 "nor is he who is sent greater than he

SENTENCE
1. *judicial sentence:* ἀπόκριμα APOKRIMA*
2 Cor 1. 9 we felt . . we had received the s. of death
2. *judgment of condemnation:* καταδίκη KATADIKĒ*
Acts 25.15 "elders . . asking for sentence against him
3. *word, reckoning:* λόγος LOGOS
Rom 9.28 "the Lord will execute his sentence
13. 9 commandments . . are summed up in this s.
IDIOMATICALLY
a. Mt 23.33 "how are you to escape being sentenced to hell?[w] πῶς φύγητε ἀπὸ τῆς κρίσεως τῆς γεέννης; [KRISIS]
CONTEXTUALLY
Lk 23.40 "since you are under the same sentence

SENTENCE, GIVE
1. *decide, adjudge:* ἐπικρίνω EPIKRINŌ*
Lk 23.24 Pilate gave s. that . . demand . . be granted

SENTENCED TO DEATH
1. *condemned to death:* ἐπιθανάτιος EPITHANATIOS*
1 Cor 4. 9 apostles . . , like men sentenced to death

SENTRY
1. *guard, sentinel:* φύλαξ PHYLAX*
Acts 5.23 "prison . . locked and the sentries standing
12. 6 sentries before the door were guarding
12.19 he examined the sentries and ordered

SEPARATE
1. *separate, appoint:* ἀφορίζω APHORIZŌ
Mt 13.49 "angels will come out and separate . . evil
25.32 "he will separate them one from another as a shepherd separates the sheep
2 Cor 6.17 "be separate from them, says the Lord
Gal 2.12 he drew back and separated himself
2. *separate from:* ἀποχωρίζω (pass.) APOCHŌRIZŌ
Acts 15.39 so that they separated from each other
3. *separate, divide:* χωρίζω CHŌRIZŌ
Rom 8.35 Who shall s. us from . . love of Christ?
8.39 nor anything else . . will be able to s. us
1 Cor 7.10 wife should not s. from her husband
7.15 if the unbelieving partner desires to s.
Heb 7.26 such a high priest, . . separated from sinners

SEPARATED FROM
1. *separately, apart from:* χωρίς CHŌRIS
Eph 2.12 were . . separated from Christ, alienated

SEPULCHRE
1. *tomb, grave:* τάφος TAPHOS
Mt 27.61 were . . sitting opposite the sepulchre
27.64 "order the sepulchre to be made secure
Mt 27.66 they . . made the s. secure by sealing
28. 1 the other Mary went to see the sepulchre

SERGIUS PAULUS: Σέργιος Παῦλος 'sərj(i)əs 'pȯləs
Acts 13. 7 He was with . . proconsul, Sergius Paulus

SERIOUS
1. *heavy, severe:* βαρύς BARYS
Acts 25. 7 bringing against him many s. charges
2. *revered, holy:* σεμνός SEMNOS
1 Tim 3. 8 Deacons likewise must be serious
3.11 The women likewise must be serious
Tit 2. 2 Bid the older men be temperate, serious

SERPENT
1. *serpent:* ὄφις OPHIS*
Mt 7.10 "if he asks for a fish, will give him a s.?
10.16 "wise as serpents and innocent as doves
23.33 "You serpents, you brood of vipers
Mk 16.18 "they will pick up serpents[k]‡
Lk 10.19 "authority to tread upon serpents
11.11 "What father . . will . . give him a serpent?
Jn 3.14 "as Moses lifted up the s. in the wilderness
1 Cor 10. 9 some . . were destroyed by serpents
2 Cor 11. 3 as the s. deceived Eve by his cunning
Rev 9.19 their tails are like serpents, with heads
12. 9 that ancient s., who is called the Devil
12.14 that she might fly from the serpent
12.15 The serpent poured water like a river
20. 2 that ancient serpent, who is the Devil

SERUG: Σερούχ 'sirəg
Lk 3.35 ⟨Nahor,⟩ the son of S., the son of Reu

SERVANT
1. *servant:* διάκονος DIAKONOS
Mt 20.26 "whoever would be great . . must be your s.
23.11 "greatest among you shall be your s.
Mk 9.35 "he must be last of all and servant
10.43 "whoever would be great . . must be your s.
Jn 2. 5 His mother said to the servants, "Do
2. 9 (servants who had drawn the water knew
12.26 "where I am, there shall my s. be also
Rom 13. 4 for he is God's servant for your good . . ; he is the s. of God to execute his wrath
15. 8 Christ became a s. to the circumcised
1 Cor 3. 5 Servants through whom you believed
2 Cor 6. 4 as servants of God we commend ourselves
11.15 not strange if his servants also disguise themselves as servants of righteousness
11.23 Are they servants of Christ?
1 Th 3. 2 Timothy, our brother and God's servant
2. *slave:* δοῦλος DOULOS II
Mt 10.24 "nor a servant[y] above his master†
10.25 "for . . servant[y] ⟨to be⟩ like his master†
13.27 "servants[j] of the householder came†
13.28 "servants[j] said . . 'do you want us to go?†
18.23 "to settle accounts with his servants
18.26 "servant fell on his knees, imploring him
18.27 "the lord of that servant released him
18.28 "that same servant, as he went out
18.32 " 'You wicked servant! I forgave you
21.34 "he sent his servants to the tenants
21.35 "tenants took his servants and beat one
21.36 "sent other servants, more than the first
22. 3 "sent his servants to call those . . invited
22. 4 "Again he sent other servants, saying
22. 6 "while the rest seized his servants
22. 8 "said to . . servants, 'The wedding is ready
22.10 "those servants went out into the streets
24.45 "Who then is the faithful and wise s.?
24.46 "Blessed is that servant whom his master
24.48 "if that wicked servant says to himself
24.50 "master of that s. will come on a day
25.14 "going on a journey called his servants
25.19 "the master of those servants came
25.21 " 'Well done, good and faithful servant
25.23 " 'Well done, good and faithful servant
25.26 " 'You wicked and slothful servant!
25.30 " 'cast the worthless s. into . . darkness

Mk 12. 2 “he sent a servant to the tenants
12. 4 “Again he sent to them another servant
13.34 “he leaves . . and puts his servants in charge
Lk 2.29 “now lettest thou thy servant depart
12.37 “Blessed are . . servants whom the master
12.43 “Blessed is that servant whom his master
12.45 “But if that servant says to himself
12.46 “master of that s. will come on a day
12.47 “that servant who knew his master’s will
14.17 “he sent his servant . . to those . . invited
14.21 “So the servant came and reported
14.21 “householder in anger said to his servant
14.22 “servant said, ‘Sir, what you commanded
14.23 “the master said to the servant, ‘Go out
15.22 “the father said to his servants, ‘Bring
17. 7 “Will any one of you, who has a s.?
17. 9 “Does he thank the s. because he did?
17.10 “ say,‘We are unworthy servants
19.13 “Calling ten of his servants, he gave them
19.15 “he commanded these servants
19.17 “ ‘Well done, good servant!
19.22 “ ‘I will condemn you . . , you wicked s.!
20.10 “he sent a servant to the tenants
20.11 “And he sent another servant
Jn 4.51 he was going down, his servants met him
13.16 “servant[d] is not greater than his master†
15.15 “No longer . . call you servants,[h] for the s.[i] does not know what his master is doing†
15.20 “ ‘A s.[i] is not greater than his master†
18.18 servants[l] and officers . . made a . . fire†
18.26 One of the servants[l] of the high priest†
Acts 4.29 “grant to thy servants[f] to speak . . word†
16.17 “These men . . servants of the Most High
Rom 1. 1 Paul, a servant[a] of Jesus Christ†
2 Cor 4. 5 ourselves . . servants[f] for Jesus’ sake†
Gal 1.10 I should not be a servant[a] of Christ†
Eph 6. 6 not . . men-pleasers, but . . servants[f] of Christ†
Phil 1. 1 Paul and Timothy, servants[a] of Christ†
2. 7 emptied himself, taking the form of a s.[d]†
Col 4.12 Epaphras, . . a servant[g] of Christ Jesus†
2 Tim 2.24 the Lord’s s. must not be quarrelsome
Tit 1. 1 Paul, a servant[a] of God and . . apostle†
Jas 1. 1 James, a s. of God and of the Lord Jesus
1 Pet 2.16 but live as servants of God
2 Pet 1. 1 Simeon[x] Peter, a servant and apostle
Jude . 1 Jude, a servant of Jesus . . and brother
Rev 1. 1 which God gave . . to show to his servants
1. 1 sending his angel to his servant John
2.20 “ ‘Jezebel . . is teaching . . my servants
7. 3 “till we have sealed the servants of . . God
10. 7 announced to his servants the prophets
11.18 “the time . . for rewarding thy servants
15. 3 the song of Moses, the servant of God
19. 2 “avenged . . the blood of his servants
19. 5 “Praise our God, all you his servants
22. 3 his servants shall worship him
22. 6 “has sent his angel to show his servants

3. *servant, helper:* ὑπηρέτης HYPĒRETĒS
Jn 18.36 “if . . of this world, my servants would fight
1 Cor 4. 1 should regard us, as servants of Christ

4. *minister, servant:* λειτουργός LEITOURGOS
Heb 1. 7 “Who makes . . his servants flames of fire

5. *household slave:* οἰκέτης OIKETĒS*
Lk 16.13 No servant can serve two masters
Acts 10. 7 he called two of his servants
Rom 14. 4 Who are you to pass judgment on the s.?
1 Pet 2.18 Servants, be submissive to . . masters

6. *child, servant:* παῖς PAIS
Mt 8. 6 “Lord, my servant is lying paralyzed
8. 8 “only say the word, . . my s. will be healed
8.13 “the s. was healed at that very moment
12.18 “Behold, my s. whom I have chosen
14. 2 “he said to his servants, ‘This is John
Lk 1.54 “He has helped his servant Israel
1.69 “salvation . . in the house of his s. David
7. 7 “say the word, and let my s. be healed
15.26 “he called one of the servants and asked
Acts 3.13 “God . . glorified his servant[c] Jesus†
3.26 “God, having raised up his s.,[c] sent him†
4.25 “who by . . our father David, thy servant[c]†
4.27 “gathered . . against thy holy servant[c] Jesus†
4.30 “the name of thy holy servant[c] Jesus†

7. *servant, attendant:* θεράπων THERAPŌN*
Heb 3. 5 Now Moses was faithful . . as a servant

CONTEXTUALLY
Lk 12.38 “blessed are those servants!

SERVANT, BE A

1. *serve, be a slave:* δουλεύω DOULEUŌ
Gal 5.13 through love be servants of one another

SERVANT, FELLOW

1. *fellow slave:* σύνδουλος SYNDOULOS*
Mt 18.28 “came upon one of his fellow servants
18.29 “So his fellow servant fell down
18.31 “When his fellow servants saw
18.33 “ ‘should . . have had mercy on your fellow s.
24.49 “begins to beat his fellow servants
Col 1. 7 Epaphras our beloved fellow servant
4. 7 faithful minister and fellow servant
Rev 6.11 the number of their fellow servants
19.10 “I am a fellow servant with you
22. 9 “I am a fellow servant with you

SERVANT, HIRED

1. *day laborer, servant:* μίσθιος MISTHIOS*
Lk 15.17 “ ‘How many of my father’s hired servants!
15.19 “ ‘ “treat me as one of your hired servants
[15.21 “ ‘*treat me as one of your hired servants*‡

2. *hired man:* μισθωτός MISTHŌTOS
Mk 1.20 left their father . . with the hired servants

SERVE (*See also* SOLDIER, SERVE AS A)

1. *do a service, minister:* διακονέω DIAKONEŌ
Mt 8.15 fever left . . and she rose and served him
20.28 “the Son of man came not to be served but to serve, and to give his life as a ransom
Mk 1.31 the fever left her; and she served them
10.45 “the Son of man also came not to be served but to serve, and to give his life
Lk 4.39 immediately she rose and served them
10.40 “my sister has left me to serve alone
12.37 “he will gird himself . . and serve them
17. 8 “ ‘gird yourself and serve me, till I eat
22.26 “the leader as one who serves
22.27 “one who sits at table, or one who serves
22.27 “But I am among you as one who serves
Jn 12. 2 they made him a supper; Martha served
12.26 “If any one serves me, he must follow
12.26 “if . . one serves me, the Father will honor
Acts 6. 2 “not right that we should . . serve tables
Phm .13 glad to keep him . . that he might serve me
Heb 6.10 love . . you showed . . in serving the saints
1 Pet 1.12 serving not themselves but you

2. *service, ministry:* διακονία DIAKONIA [B.1.a.2]
2 Cor 11. 8 support from them in order to serve you
Heb 1.14 ministering spirits sent forth to serve

3. *serve, be a slave:* δουλεύω DOULEUŌ
Mt 6.24 “No one can serve two masters; . . You cannot serve God and mammon[x]
Lk 15.29 “ ‘Lo, these many years I have served you
16.13 “No servant can serve two masters; . . You cannot serve God and mammon[a]
Acts 7. 7 “ ‘I will judge the nation which they serve
20.19 “serving the Lord with all humility
Rom 7. 6 we serve not under the old written code
7.25 I of myself serve the law of God
9.12 “The elder will serve the younger
12.11 be aglow with the Spirit, serve the Lord
14.18 he who thus serves Christ is acceptable
16.18 such persons do not serve our Lord
Phil 2.22 he has served with me in the gospel
Col 3.24 you are serving the Lord Christ
1 Th 1. 9 how you turned . . to serve a living . . God
1 Tim 6. 2 rather they must serve all the better

4. *come, go:* ἔρχομαι ERCHOMAI
Phil 1.12 has really served to advance the gospel

5. *serve:* ὑπηρετέω HYPĒRETEŌ
Acts 13.36 "after he had served the counsel of God
6. *servant, helper:* ὑπηρέτης HYPĒRETĒS [A.1.d]
Acts 26.16 " 'to serve and bear witness to the things
7. *serve, worship:* λατρεύω LATREUŌ
Mt 4.10 " 'him only shall you serve
Lk 1.74 "that we . . might serve him without fear
4. 8 " 'him only shall you serve
Rom 1. 9 God is my witness, whom I serve
1.25 worshiped and served the creature
2 Tim 1. 3 God whom I serve with a clear conscience
Heb 8. 5 They serve a copy and shadow
9.14 purify your[t] conscience . . to serve . . God
13.10 an altar from which those who serve
Rev 7.15 "before the throne of God, and serve him
8. *wait upon, serve:* παρεδρεύω PAREDREUŌ*
1 Cor 9.13 those who serve at the altar share
9. *hold to, be intent on:* προσέχω PROSECHŌ
Heb 7.13 from which no one . . served at the altar
10. *serve, treat medically:* θεραπεύω THERAPEUŌ
Acts 17.25 "nor is he served by human hands
11. *lay, put:* τίθημι TITHĒMI
Jn 2.10 "Every man serves the good wine first
CONTEXTUALLY
Col [2.23 *serving only to indulge the flesh*†
3.23 as serving the Lord and not men

SERVE AS
1. *be set before, be exposed:* πρόκειμαι PROKEIMAI
Jude . 7 Sodom and Gomorrah . . s. as an example

SERVE AS DEACON
1. *do a service, minister:* διακονέω DIAKONEŌ
1 Tim 3.10 if . . blameless let them serve as deacons
3.13 those who serve well as deacons gain

SERVE AS PRIEST
1. *be a priest:* ἱερατεύω HIERATEUŌ*
Lk 1. 8 Now while he was serving as priest

SERVE TO SHOW
1. *stand with, commend:* συνίστημι SYNISTĒMI
Rom 3. 5 if our wickedness serves to show . . justice

SERVICE (*See also* SOLDIER ON SERVICE)
1. *service, ministry:* διακονία DIAKONIA
Rom 12. 7 if service, in our serving
15.31 that my service . . be acceptable
1 Cor 12. 5 varieties of service, but the same Lord
16.15 devoted themselves to . . s. of the saints
2 Cor 9.13 Under . . test of this s., you[m] will glorify
1 Tim 1.12 by appointing me to his service
Rev 2.19 " 'I know your works, your . . service
2. *good deed:* εὐεργεσία EUERGESIA
1 Tim 6. 2 who benefit by their s. are believers
3. *worship, service, duty:* λατρεία LATREIA
Jn 16. 2 "will think he is offering service to God
4. *service, ministry:* λειτουργία LEITOURGIA
Lk 1.23 when his time of service was ended
2 Cor 9.12 this service not only supplies the wants
Phil 2.30 risking his life to complete your s.
CONTEXTUALLY
2 Cor 8.23 my partner and fellow worker in your s.
Heb 2.17 faithful high priest in the service of God
3 Jn . 6 send . . on their journey as befits God's s.

SERVICE, AT ONE'S
1. *serve, minister:* λειτουργέω (part.) LEITOURGEŌ
Heb 10.11 every priest stands daily at his service

SERVICE, BE OF
1. *serve, minister:* λειτουργέω LEITOURGEŌ
Rom 15.27 they ought also to be of service to them

SERVICE, IN PRIESTLY
1. *act as a priest:* ἱερουργέω (part.+acc.) HIEROURGEŌ*
Rom 15.16 minister . . in the priestly s. of the gospel

SERVICE, RENDER
1. *do a service, minister:* διακονέω DIAKONEŌ
2 Tim 1.18 the service he rendered at Ephesus
1 Pet 4.11 whoever renders service

2. *serve, be a slave:* δουλεύω DOULEUŌ
Eph 6. 7 rendering service with a good will
3. *work, do:* ἐργάζομαι ERGAZOMAI
3 Jn . 5 a loyal thing . . when you render any s.

SERVICE, TEMPLE
1. *holy:* ἱερός (subst. neut. pl.) HIEROS
1 Cor 9.13 those who are employed in the temple s.

SERVING
1. *service, ministry:* διακονία DIAKONIA
Lk 10.40 Martha was distracted with much s.
Rom 12. 7 if service, in our serving
2 Tim 4.11 for he is very useful in serving me
IDIOMATICALLY
a. Col [2.23 these . . are of no value, *serving only to indulge the flesh*† ἅτινά ἐστιν . . οὐκ ἐν τιμῇ τινι πρὸς πλησμονὴν τῆς σαρκός [PROS]

SET (*See also, e.g.,* FREE, SET; HOPE, SET ONE'S)
1. *lift, carry away:* αἴρω AIRŌ
Col 2.14 this he set aside, nailing it to the cross
2. *divide in two:* διχάζω DICHAZŌ* [A.6.a.5]
Mt 10.35 "I . . come to s. a man against his father
3. *give:* δίδωμι DIDŌMI
Rev 3. 8 " 'I have set before you an open door
4. *sink into, set:* δύνω DYNŌ
Lk 4.40 Now when the sun was setting
5. *come to be, happen, be:* γίνομαι GINOMAI [A.6.a.5]
1 Tim 4.12 set the believers an example in speech
6. *stand, set:* ἵστημι HISTĒMI
Mt 4. 5 Then the devil . . set him on the pinnacle
Lk 4. 9 he . . set him on the pinnacle of the temple
Acts 4. 7 when they had set them in the midst
5.27 they set them before the council
6. 6 These they set before the apostles
22.30 brought Paul . . and set him before them
7. *determine, appoint:* ὁρίζω HORIZŌ
Heb 4. 7 again he sets a certain day, "Today
8. *set in order, appoint:* καθίστημι KATHISTĒMI
Mt 24.45 "his master has set over his household
24.47 "he will set him over all his possessions
25.21 " 'Well done, . . I will set you over much
25.23 " 'Well done, . . I will set you over much
Lk 12.42 "his master will set over his household
12.44 "he will set him over all his possessions
Heb [2. 7 "Thou . . *didst set him over the works*‡
9. *sit down, seat:* καθίζω KATHIZŌ
Acts 2.30 "set one of his descendants upon . . throne
10. *lie, be laid:* κεῖμαι (part.) KEIMAI
Mt 5.14 "A city set on a hill cannot be hid
11. *go, walk:* πορεύομαι (part.) POREUOMAI
Lk 9.53 his face was set toward Jerusalem
12. *support, fix:* στηρίζω STĒRIZŌ
Lk 9.51 he set his face to go to Jerusalem
13. *appoint, assign:* τάσσω TASSŌ
Lk 7. 8 "I am a man set under authority
14. *lay, put:* τίθημι TITHĒMI
Acts 13.47 " 'I . . set you to be a light for . . Gentiles
Rev 10. 2 And he set his right foot on the sea
IDIOMATICALLY
a. Mt 27.9 "the price of him on whom a price had been set by some of the sons of Israel τὴν τιμὴν τοῦ τετιμημένου ὃν ἐτιμήσαντο ἀπὸ υἱῶν Ἰσραήλ [TIMAŌ]
b. Mt 27.66 they . . made the sepulchre secure by sealing the stone and setting a guard ἠσφαλίσαντο τὸν τάφον σφραγίσαντες τὸν λίθον μετὰ τῆς κουστωδίας [META]
c. Lk 4.18 "He has sent me . . to set at liberty those who are oppressed ἀπέσταλκέν με . . ἀποστεῖλαι τεθραυσμένους ἐν ἀφέσει [APOSTELLŌ]

SET ABLAZE
1. *kindle:* ἀνάπτω ANAPTŌ
Jas 3. 5 a forest is set ablaze by a small fire!

SET APART
1. *separate, appoint:* ἀφορίζω APHORIZŌ
Acts 13. 2 "Set apart for me Barnabas and Saul
Rom 1. 1 apostle, set apart for the gospel of God
Gal 1.15 who had set me apart before I was born

SET AROUND
1. *put around, put on:* περιτίθημι PERITITHĒMI
Mt 21.33 "planted a vineyard, and set a hedge
Mk 12. 1 "planted a vineyard, and set a hedge

SET ASIDE
1. *abolition, rejection:* ἀθέτησις ATHETĒSIS [B.3.a.2]
Heb 7.18 a former commandment is set aside

SET, BE
1. *lie, be laid:* κεῖμαι KEIMAI
Lk 2.34 "this child is set for the fall and rising

SET BEFORE
1. *place before:* παρατίθημι PARATITHĒMI
Mk 6.41 the loaves . . to set before the people
8. 6 seven loaves . . to set before the people; and they set them before the crowd
8. 7 that these . . should be set before them
Lk 9.16 loaves and . . fish . . to set before the crowd
10. 8 "eat what is set before you
11. 6 " 'I have nothing to set before him
Acts 16.34 into his house, and set food before them
1 Cor 10.27 eat whatever is set before you
2. *be set before, be exposed:* πρόκειμαι PROKEIMAI
Heb 6.18 to seize the hope set before us
12. 1 let us run . . race that is set before us
12. 2 who for the joy that was set before him

SET FOOT
1. *go upon, mount, board:* ἐπιβαίνω EPIBAINŌ
Acts 20.18 "from the . . day that I set foot in Asia

SET FORTH
1. *put forward, propose:* προτίθημι PROTITHĒMI
Eph 1. 9 his purpose which he set forth in Christ

SET ON
SET UPON
1. *put upon:* ἐπιβιβάζω EPIBIBAZŌ
Lk 10.34 "then he set him on his own beast
19.35 brought it . . and . . they set Jesus upon it

SET ON FIRE
1. *set on fire, burn:* φλογίζω PHLOGIZŌ*
Jas 3. 6 the tongue is a fire . . , setting on fire the cycle of nature,[b] and set on fire by hell[c]

SET ON, MIND THAT IS
1. *thought, purpose:* φρόνημα (+gen.) PHRONĒMA
Rom 8. 7 mind that is set on the flesh is hostile

SET ONESELF AGAINST
1. *speak against:* ἀντιλέγω ANTILEGŌ
Jn 19.12 "one . . sets himself against Caesar

SET ONESELF IN ARRAY
1. *place beside, stand before:* παρίστημι PARISTĒMI
Acts 4.26 " 'kings of the earth set themselves in array

SET OUT
1. *lead up, bring back:* ἀνάγω (mid. or pass.) ANAGŌ
Lk 8.22 "Let us go across . . " So they set out
2. *go out:* ἐκπορεύομαι EKPOREUOMAI
Mk 10.17 as he was setting out on his journey
3. *go out:* ἐξέρχομαι EXERCHOMAI
Mk 14.16 the disciples set out and went to the city
3 Jn . 7 For they have set out for his sake

SET SAIL
1. *lead up, bring back:* ἀνάγω (mid. or pass.) ANAGŌ
Acts 13.13 Paul and . . company set sail from Paphos
16.11 Setting sail therefore from Troas
18.21 and he set sail from Ephesus
20. 3 as he was about to set sail for Syria
20.13 going ahead . . , we set sail for Assos
21. 1 when we . . parted from them and set sail
21. 2 having found a ship . . , we . . set sail
27.21 "you . . should not have set sail from Crete
28.11 After three months we set sail in a ship

SET, THE DATE
1. *a fixed time:* προθεσμία PROTHESMIA*
Gal 4. 2 he is under guardians . . until the date set

SET UP
1. *set up again, correct:* ἀνορθόω ANORTHOŌ
Acts 15.16 " 'I will rebuild its ruins, and I will set it up
2. *stand, set:* ἵστημι HISTĒMI
Acts 6.13 ⟨they⟩ set up false witnesses who said
3. *build, set up:* πήγνυμι PĒGNYMI*
Heb 8. 2 sanctuary . . which is set up not by man

SET UP, BE
1. *stand, set:* ἵστημι (perf.) HISTĒMI
Mk 13.14 "sacrilege s. up where it ought not to be

SET UP DIVISIONS
1. *mark off by dividing:* ἀποδιορίζω APODIORIZŌ*
Jude .19 who set up divisions, worldly people

SET UPON (*See* SET ON)

SETH: Σήθ 'seth
Lk 3.38 Enos, the son of Seth, the son of Adam

SETTLE
1. *set free:* ἀπαλλάσσω (pass.) APALLASSŌ
Lk 12.58 "make an effort to settle with him
2. *loose, explain, solve:* ἐπιλύω EPILYŌ
Acts 19.39 "it shall be settled in the regular assembly
3. *take up together, reckon:* συναίρω SYNAIRŌ [A.6.a.5]
Mt 18.23 "a king who wished to settle accounts
25.19 "the master . . came and settled accounts
4. *found, establish:* θεμελιόω THEMELIOŌ
1 Pet [5.10 will . . *establish, strengthen and settle*‡
5. *lay, put:* τίθημι TITHĒMI
Lk 21.14 "Settle it therefore in your minds

SEVEN
1. *seven:* ἑπτά HEPTA
Mt 12.45 "s. other spirits more evil than himself
15.34 They said, "Seven, and a few small fish
15.36 he took the seven loaves and the fish
15.37 they took up s. baskets full of . . pieces
16.10 "the seven loaves of the four thousand
18.22 "I . . say to you . . seventy times seven[e]†
22.25 "there were seven brothers among us
22.28 "to which of the seven will she be wife?
Mk 8. 5 "How many loaves have you?" . . "Seven
8. 6 he took the seven loaves, and . . broke them
8. 8 they took up . . seven baskets full
8.20 "And the seven for the four thousand, how many baskets full . . ?" . . "Seven
12.20 "There were seven brothers
12.22 "the seven left no children
12.23 "For the seven had her as wife
16. 9 from whom he had cast out seven demons[k]‡
Lk 2.36 she . . lived with her husband seven years
8. 2 from whom seven demons had gone out
11.26 "he goes and brings seven other spirits
20.29 "Now there were seven brothers
20.31 "likewise all seven left no children and died
20.33 "For the seven had her as wife
Acts 6. 3 "pick out from among you seven men
13.19 "when he had destroyed seven nations
19.14 Seven sons of a Jewish high priest
20. 6 Troas, where we stayed for seven days
21. 4 we stayed there for seven days
21. 8 Philip . . , who was one of the seven
21.27 When the s. days were almost completed
28.14 invited to stay with them for seven days
Heb 11.30 after they had been encircled for s. days
Rev 1. 4 John to the s. churches that are in Asia
1. 4 the s. spirits who are before his throne
1.11 "Write . . and send it to the seven churches
1.12 I saw seven golden lampstands
1.16 in his right hand he held seven stars
1.20 "As for the mystery of the seven stars which you saw in my right hand, and the seven golden lampstands, the seven stars are the angels of the seven churches and the seven lampstands are the seven churches
2. 1 " 'words of him who holds the seven stars . . , who walks among the s. golden lampstands

Rev 3. 1 " 'The words of him who has the seven spirits of God and the seven stars
4. 5 before the throne burn s. torches of fire, which are the seven spirits of God
5. 1 I saw . . a scroll . . sealed with seven seals
5. 5 "he can open the scroll and its seven seals
5. 6 I saw a Lamb standing . . , with seven horns and with seven eyes, which are the seven spirits of God sent out into all the earth
6. 1 the Lamb opened one of the seven seals
8. 2 the seven angels who stand before God, and seven trumpets were given . . them
8. 6 Now the seven angels who had the seven trumpets made ready to blow them
10. 3 he called out, the s. thunders sounded
10. 4 when the seven thunders had sounded
10. 4 "Seal up what the s. thunders have said
11.13 seven thousand people were killed
12. 3 a great red dragon, with s. heads and ten horns, and s. diadems upon his heads
13. 1 a beast . . with ten horns and s. heads
15. 1 I saw another portent in heaven, . . s. angels with s. plagues, which are the last
15. 6 out of the temple came the seven angels with the seven plagues
15. 7 gave the seven angels seven golden bowls full of the wrath of God
15. 8 no one could enter . . until the seven plagues of the seven angels were ended
16. 1 I heard a loud voice . . telling the s. angels, "Go and pour out . . the seven bowls
17. 1 Then one of the seven angels who had the seven bowls came and said to me, "Come
17. 3 a scarlet beast which . . had seven heads
17. 7 "the beast with seven heads and ten horns
17. 9 "the seven heads are seven mountains on which the woman is seated
17.10 "they are also seven kings, five . . fallen
17.11 "it is an eighth but it belongs to the seven
21. 9 Then came one of the seven angels who had the seven bowls full of the seven last plagues, and spoke to me

2. *sixty:* ἑξήκοντα HEXĒKONTA [A.3.c.1]
Lk 24.13 about seven miles[w] from Jerusalem†‡

SEVEN OTHER

IDIOMATICALLY
a. 2 Pet 2.5 but preserved Noah, a herald of righteousness, with seven other persons *ἀλλὰ ὄγδοον Νῶε δικαιοσύνης κήρυκα ἐφύλαξεν* [OGDOOS]

SEVEN THOUSAND

1. *seven thousand:* ἑπτακισχίλιοι HEPTAKISCHILIOI*
Rom 11. 4 "I have kept for myself s. thousand men

SEVEN TIMES

1. *seven times:* ἑπτάκις HEPTAKIS*
Mt 18.21 "shall . . I forgive . . ? As many as s. times?
18.22 "I do not say to you seven times
Lk 17. 4 "if he sins against you seven times in the day, and turns to you seven times

SEVENTH

1. *seventh:* ἕβδομος HEBDOMOS*
Jn 4.52 "at the seventh hour the fever left him
Heb 4. 4 he has somewhere spoken of the s. day . . , "And God rested on the seventh day
Jude .14 Enoch in the s. generation from Adam
Rev 8. 1 When the Lamb opened the seventh seal
10. 7 trumpet . . sounded by the seventh angel
11.15 the seventh angel blew his trumpet
16.17 The s. angel poured . . bowl into the air
21.20 the seventh chrysolite, the eighth beryl

IDIOMATICALLY
a. Mt 22.26 "So too the second . . down to the seventh *ὁμοίως καὶ ὁ δεύτερος . . ἕως τῶν ἑπτά* [HEPTA]

SEVENTY

1. *seventy:* ἑβδομήκοντα HEBDOMĒKONTA
Lk 10. 1 After this the Lord appointed s.[g] others‡
Lk 10.17 The seventy[g] returned with joy‡
Acts 23.23 "two hundred soldiers with s. horsemen

SEVENTY TIMES

1. *seventy times:* ἑβδομηκοντάκις HEBDOMĒKONTAKIS
Mt 18.22 "not . . seven times, but s. times seven[e]†

SEVENTY-FIVE

1. *seventy-five:* ἑβδομήκοντα πέντε HEBDOMĒKONTA; PENTE [A.3.c]
Acts 7.14 "Joseph . . called to him . . seventy-five souls

SEVENTY-SEVEN

1. *seventy times* (*and*) *seven:* ἑβδομηκοντάκις ἑπτά HEBDOMĒKONTAKIS; HEPTA [A.3.c]
Mt [18.22 "not . . seven times, but *seventy-seven times*†

SEVENTY-SIX

1. *seventy-six:* ἑβδομήκοντα ἕξ HEBDOMĒKONTA; HEX [A.3.c]
Acts 27.37 (We were . . seventy-six[d] persons in the ship

SEVENTY-TWO

1. *seventy-two:* ἑβδομήκοντα δύο HEBDOMĒKONTA; DYO [A.3.c]
Lk [10. 1 the Lord appointed *seventy-two* others‡
[10.17 The *seventy-two* returned with joy‡

SEVERAL

1. *anyone, any:* τὶς (pl.) TIS II
Acts **9.**19

SEVERE

1. *severely:* ἀποτόμως APOTOMŌS [A.4.a]
2 Cor 13.10 that . . I may not have to be severe
2. *harsh, strict:* αὐστηρός AUSTĒROS*
Lk 19.21 " 'I was afraid . . because you are a s. man
19.22 " 'You knew that I was a severe man
3. *many, great:* πολύς POLYS
[a]A.1.c
Lk 12.47 [a]"that servant . . shall receive a s. beating
2 Cor 8. 2 in a s. test of affliction, their abundance

SEVERED, BE

1. *make ineffective, hinder:* καταργέω (pass.) KATARGEŌ
Gal 5. 4 You are severed from Christ

SEVERELY

1. *badly, ill:* κακῶς KAKŌS
Mt 15.22 "my daughter is s. possessed by a demon

SEVERELY, PUT IT TOO

1. *weigh down:* ἐπιβαρέω EPIBAREŌ
2 Cor 2. 5 in some measure—not to put it too s.

SEVERITY

1. *unsparing treatment:* ἀφειδία APHEIDIA*
Col 2.23 promoting rigor of . . severity to the body
2. *severity:* ἀποτομία APOTOMIA*
Rom 11.22 Note then . . the s. of God: s. toward those who have fallen, but . . kindness to you

SEW

1. *sew on:* ἐπιράπτω EPIRAPTŌ*
Mk 2.21 "No one sews a piece of unshrunk cloth

SEX

1. *vessel, tackle:* σκεῦος SKEUOS [C.2]
1 Pet 3. 7 honor . . the woman as the weaker sex

SEXUAL PERVERTS

1. *effeminate men and homosexuals:* μαλακοὶ καὶ ἀρσενοκοῖται MALAKOS; ARSENOKOITĒS [A.1.f]
1 Cor 6. 9 nor s. perverts ⟨will inherit . . kingdom⟩[o]

SHABBY

1. *dirty:* ῥυπαρός RHYPAROS
Jas 2. 2 a poor man in s. clothing also comes in

SHADE

1. *shadow, shade:* σκιά SKIA
Mk 4.32 "so that the birds . . can make nests in its s.

SHADOW

1. *shadow:* ἀποσκίασμα APOSKIASMA*
Jas 1.17 there is no variation or s. due to change[a]‡
2. *shadow, shade:* σκιά SKIA
Mt 4.16 "those who sat in the . . shadow of death
Lk 1.79 "those who sit . . in the shadow of death
Acts 5.15 that . . at least his s. might fall on some
Col 2.17 These are only a s. of what is to come

Heb 8. 5 a .. shadow of the heavenly sanctuary
10. 1 the law has but a s. of the good things

SHAFT
1. *artificial well, shaft:* φρέαρ PHREAR
Rev 9. 1 the key of the s. of the bottomless pit
9. 2 he opened the shaft of the bottomless pit, and from the shaft rose smoke
9. 2 darkened with the smoke from the shaft

SHAKE
1. *shake:* σαλεύω SALEUŌ
Mt 11. 7 "A reed shaken by the wind?
24.29 "powers of the heavens will be shaken
Mk 13.25 "powers in the heavens will be shaken
Lk 6.38 "good measure, .. shaken together
6.48 "the stream broke .. and could not shake it
7.24 "A reed shaken by the wind?
21.26 "powers of the heavens will be shaken
Acts 2.25 " 'at my right .. that I may not be shaken
4.31 when they .. prayed, the place .. was shaken
16.26 foundations of the prison were shaken
2 Th 2. 2 not to be quickly shaken in mind
Heb 12.26 His voice then shook the earth
12.27 indicates the removal of what is shaken, .. that what cannot be shaken may remain
2. *shake, agitate:* σείω SEIŌ
Mt 27.51 earth shook, and the rocks were split
Heb 12.26 "I will shake not only the earth
Rev 6.13 as .. fig tree sheds its .. fruit when shaken

SHAKE OFF
1. *shake off:* ἀποτινάσσω APOTINASSŌ*
Lk 9. 5 "when you leave that town s. off .. dust
Acts 28. 5 He, however, shook off the creature
2. *shake off, shake out:* ἐκτινάσσω EKTINASSŌ
Mt 10.14 "shake off the dust from your feet
Mk 6.11 "when you leave, shake off the dust
Acts 13.51 they shook off the dust from their feet

SHAKE OUT
1. *shake off, shake out:* ἐκτινάσσω EKTINASSŌ
Acts 18. 6 reviled .., he shook out his garments

SHAKEN, THAT CANNOT BE
1. *immovable:* ἀσάλευτος ASALEUTOS
Heb 12.28 a kingdom that cannot be shaken

SHALLOW
1. *empty, vain:* κενός KENOS
Jas 2.20 Do you want to be shown, you s. man?[o]

SHAME
1. *shameful:* αἰσχρός (neut.) AISCHROS
Eph 5.12 a shame even to speak of the things
2. *shame:* αἰσχύνη AISCHYNĒ
Lk 14. 9 "with shame .. take the lowest place
Phil 3.19 they glory in their shame
Heb 12. 2 endured the cross, despising the shame
Jude .13 casting up the foam of their own shame
Rev 3.18 " 'to keep the shame of your nakedness
3. *disgrace, dishonor:* ἀτιμία ATIMIA
2 Cor 11.21 To my shame .., we were too weak for that!
4. *humiliation:* ἐντροπή ENTROPĒ*
1 Cor 6. 5 I say this to your shame
15.34 I say this to your shame
5. *put to shame, dishonor:* καταισχύνω KATAISCHYNŌ
1 Cor 1.27 God chose what is foolish .. to s. the wise
1.27 God chose what is weak .. to s. the strong

SHAME, PUT TO
1. *be ashamed:* αἰσχύνομαι AISCHYNOMAI
2 Cor 10. 8 I shall not be put to shame
2. *make an example:* δειγματίζω DEIGMATIZŌ
Mt 1.19 Joseph, .. unwilling to put her to s.
3. *put to shame:* ἐντρέπω ENTREPŌ
Tit 2. 8 an opponent may be put to shame
4. *put to shame, dishonor:* καταισχύνω KATAISCHYNŌ
Lk 13.17 all his adversaries were put to shame
Rom 9.33 "he who believes .. will not be put to s.
10.11 "No one who believes .. will be put to s.
2 Cor 7.14 I was not put to shame
1 Pet 2. 6 "who believes in him will not be put to s.
3.16 that .. those who revile .. may be put to s.

SHAME, SHRINK FROM S. IN
1. *be ashamed:* αἰσχύνομαι AISCHYNOMAI
1 Jn 2.28 we may .. not shrink from him in shame

SHAMEFUL
1. *shameful:* αἰσχρός AISCHROS
1 Cor 14.35 it is s. for a woman to speak in church

SHAMEFUL GAIN, FOR
1. *in greed for dishonest gain:* αἰσχροκερδῶς AISCHROKERDŌS*
1 Pet 5. 2 willingly,[l] not for s. gain but eagerly

SHAMEFULLY, TREAT
1. *hold in no honor, insult:* ἀτιμάζω ATIMAZŌ
Mk 12. 4 "they wounded him .. and treated him s.
Lk 20.11 "him also they beat and treated s.
2. *insult, treat arrogantly:* ὑβρίζω HYBRIZŌ
Mt 22. 6 "seized his servants, treated them s.
Lk 18.32 "he will be .. s. treated and spit upon
1 Th 2. 2 we had .. been s. treated at Philippi

SHAMELESS ACTS
1. *obscene conduct:* ἀσχημοσύνη ASCHĒMOSYNĒ
Rom 1.27 men committing s. acts with men

SHARE (*See also* ABUNDANTLY, SHARE)

SHARE, HAVE A
1. *lot, share:* κλῆρος KLĒROS
Acts 1.17 "he .. was allotted his s. in this ministry
2. *share in:* κοινωνέω KOINŌNEŌ
Rom 15.27 Gentiles .. share in their .. blessings
Gal 6. 6 Let him .. share all good things with him
Heb 2.14 Since .. the children s. in flesh and blood
1 Pet 4.13 rejoice .. as you share Christ's sufferings
2 Jn .11 he who greets him shares his wicked work
3. *companion, partner:* κοινωνός KOINŌNOS [A.3.e.1]
2 Cor 1. 7 know that as you s. in our sufferings
4. *receive, take:* λαμβάνω LAMBANŌ
Rev 18. 4 "Come out .. lest you share in her plagues
5. *part, portion:* μερίς MERIS [B.1.a.2]
Col 1.12 qualified us[b] to share in the inheritance
6. *part, share:* μέρος MEROS
[a]ἔχειν μέρος B.3.a.5
Lk 15.12 " 'Father, give me the share of property
Rev 20. 6 [a]he who shares in the first resurrection!
22.19 God will take away his s. in .. tree of life
7. *share:* μεταδίδωμι METADIDŌMI
Lk 3.11 "He who has two coats, let him share
1 Th 2. 8 we were ready to share .. the gospel
8. *partake, share:* μεταλαμβάνω METALAMBANŌ
2 Tim 2. 6 ought to have the first s. of the crops
Heb 12.10 disciplines us .. that we may s. .. holiness
9. *participate in, share:* μετέχω METECHŌ
[a]A.6.b
1 Cor 9.10 [a]thresh in hope of a share in the crop
9.12 If others s. this rightful claim upon you
10. *be sharing in:* μέτοχος γίνεσθαι METOCHOS [A.6.a.3]
Heb 3.14 we s. in Christ, if .. we hold .. confidence
11. *take part in, share:* συγκοινωνέω SYGKOINŌNEŌ
Phil 4.14 Yet it was kind of you to share my trouble
12. *partner:* συγκοινωνός SYGKOINŌNOS
[a]συγκοινωνὸς γίνεσθαι A.6.a.3 [b]B.2.c
Rom 11.17 [a]wild olive shoot, .. grafted in .. to share
1 Cor 9.23 [a]I do it all .. that I may s. in its blessings
Rev 1. 9 [b]I John, your brother, who s. with you
13. *take a share in:* συμμερίζομαι SYMMERIZOMAI*
1 Cor 9.13 those who serve at the altar share
IDIOMATICALLY
a. Phil 3.10 that I may know him .. and may share his sufferings τοῦ γνῶναι αὐτὸν .. καὶ κοινωνίαν παθημάτων αὐτοῦ [KOINŌNIA]
CONTEXTUALLY
Rom 4.16 to those who share the faith of Abraham
5. 2 rejoice in our hope of sharing the glory

SHARE ILL-TREATMENT
1. *endure adversity with:* συγκακουχέομαι SYGKAKOUCHEOMAI*
Heb 11.25 choosing rather to share ill-treatment

SHARE IN SUFFERING
1. *suffer together with:* συγκακοπαθέω SYGKAKOPATHEŌ*
2 Tim 1. 8 share in suffering for the gospel[0]
2. 3 Share in suffering as a good soldier[0]

SHARE THE RULE WITH
1. *rule together with:* συμβασιλεύω SYMBASILEUŌ
1 Cor 4. 8 that we might share the rule with you!

SHARE WHAT ONE HAS, TO
1. *fellowship, sharing:* κοινωνία KOINŌNIA [A.1.d]
Heb 13.16 Do not neglect . . to share what you have

SHARES, WHO
1. *sharing in:* μέτοχος METOCHOS [A.3.d.3]
Heb 3. 1 brethren, who share in a heavenly call

SHARING
1. *fellowship, sharing:* κοινωνία KOINŌNIA
Phm . 6 that the sharing of your faith . . promote

SHARON: Σαρων 'sherən
Acts 9.35 residents of Lydda and Sharon saw him

SHARP (*See also* CONTENTION, SHARP)
1. *sharp, quick:* ὀξύς OXYS
Rev 1.16 from his mouth . . a sharp two-edged sword
2.12 " 'who has the sharp two-edged sword
14.14 like a son of man, with . . a sharp sickle
14.17 another angel . . , and he too had a s. sickle
14.18 called . . to him who had the s. sickle
19.15 From his mouth issues a sharp sword

SHARPER
1. *cutting, sharp:* τομός (comp.) TOMOS*
Heb 4.12 sharper than any two-edged sword

SHARPLY
1. *severely:* ἀποτόμως APOTOMŌS
Tit 1.13 rebuke them s., that they may be sound

SHATTER
1. *shatter, grind:* συντρίβω SYNTRIBŌ
Lk 9.39 "it convulses him . . and shatters him

SHAVE
1. *shave:* ξυράω XYRAŌ*
[a]mid. [b]pass.
Acts 21.24 [a]"so that they may shave their heads
1 Cor 11. 5 [b]it is the same as if her head were shaven
11. 6 [a]disgraceful for a woman to be . . shaven

SHE (*For* HEAUTOU, *not represented here, see* HER)

SHE WHO
1. *self; he, she, it:* αὐτός AUTOS
2. *that:* ἐκεῖνος (fem.) EKEINOS
Mk 16.10 She . . told those who had been with him[k]‡
Jn 11.29 when she heard it, . . rose quickly and went
20.15 Supposing him to be . . gardener, she said
20.16 She turned and said to him in Hebrew
3. *who, which, what:* ὅς HOS
Lk **2.37**
Acts **16.14**
Rev **14.8**

SHE, AND
1. *anyone who, whoever:* ὅστις HOSTIS
Gal 4.26 Jerusalem . . . , and she is our mother

SHEALTIEL: Σαλαθιήλ shē'altēəl
Mt 1.12 Jechoniah was the father of Shealtiel,[d] and Shealtiel[d] the father of Zerubbabel†
Lk 3.27 Zerubbabel, the son of S.,[l] the son of Neri†

SHEAR
1. *cut short, clip:* κείρω KEIRŌ
1 Cor 11. 6 disgraceful for a woman to be shorn

SHEARER
1. *cut short, clip:* κείρω (subst. part.) KEIRŌ
Acts 8.32 "As . . a lamb before its shearer is dumb

SHEATH
1. *case, sheath:* θήκη THĒKĒ*
Jn 18.11 "Put your sword into its sheath

SHECHEM: Συχέμ 'shekəm
Acts 7.16 "they were carried back to S. and laid in the tomb that Abraham . . bought . . in S.

SHED
1. *throw, put:* βάλλω BALLŌ
Rev 6.13 as the fig tree sheds its winter fruit
2. *pour out:* ἐκχέω EKCHEŌ
Mt 23.35 "all the righteous blood shed on earth
Lk 11.50 "shed from the foundation of the world
Acts 22.20 " 'when the blood of Stephen . . was shed
Rom 3.15 "Their feet are swift to shed blood
Rev 16. 6 "For men have shed the blood of saints
CONTEXTUALLY
Mt 23.30 " 'not have taken part . . in shedding
Heb 12. 4 resisted to the point of shedding . . blood

SHEDDING OF BLOOD, THE
1. *the shedding of blood:* αἱματεκχυσία HAIMATEKCHYSIA*
Heb 9.22 without . . shedding of blood . . no forgiveness

SHEEP
1. *little sheep:* προβάτιον PROBATION*
Jn 21.16 He said to him, "Tend my sheep
21.17 Jesus said to him, "Feed my sheep
2. *sheep, flocks:* πρόβατον PROBATON
Mt 7.15 "who come to you in sheep's clothing
9.36 helpless, like sheep without a shepherd
10. 6 "to the lost sheep of the house of Israel
10.16 "as sheep in the midst of wolves
12.11 "if he has one s. and it falls into a pit
12.12 "Of how much more value is a man than a s.!
15.24 "I was sent only to the lost s. of . . Israel
18.12 If a man has a hundred sheep
25.32 "shepherd separates the s. from . . goats
25.33 "he will place the sheep at his right hand
26.31 " 'I will strike . . , and the s. will be scattered
Mk 6.34 they were like sheep without a shepherd
14.27 " 'I will strike . . and the s. will be scattered
Lk 15. 4 "What man of you, having a hundred s.
15. 6 " 'I have found my s. which was lost
Jn 2.14 he found those who were selling . . sheep
2.15 he drove them all, with the sheep
10. 2 "but he . . is the shepherd of the sheep
10. 3 "the sheep hear his voice, and he calls his own sheep by name and leads them
10. 4 "he goes before . . , and the sheep follow him
10. 7 "I say to you, I am the door of the sheep
10. 8 "but the sheep did not heed them
10.11 "shepherd lays down his life for the s.
10.12 "a hireling . . , whose own the sheep are not, . . leaves the sheep and flees
10.13 "a hireling and cares nothing for the s.
10.15 "and I lay down my life for the sheep
10.16 "other sheep, that are not of this fold
10.26 "because you do not belong to my sheep
10.27 "My s. hear my voice, and I know them
Acts 8.32 "As a s. led to the slaughter . . is dumb
Rom 8.36 "we are regarded as s. to be slaughtered
Heb 13.20 Lord Jesus, the great shepherd of the s.
1 Pet 2.25 For you were straying like sheep
Rev 18.13 cattle and sheep, horses and chariots

SHEEP GATE
1. *of sheep:* προβατικός PROBATIKOS* [B.3.b.2]
Jn 5. 2 in Jerusalem by the Sheep Gate a pool

SHEEP, KEEP
1. *tend, herd, govern:* ποιμαίνω POIMAINŌ
Lk 17. 7 "one . . who has a servant . . keeping sheep

SHEEP, SKIN OF
1. *sheepskin:* μηλωτή MĒLŌTĒ*
Heb 11.37 they went about in skins of sheep

SHEEPFOLD
1. *fold for the sheep:* αὐλὴ τῶν προβάτων AULĒ; PROBATON [A.1.f]
Jn 10. 1 "he who does not enter the sheepfold

SHEET
1. *fine linen, a cloth:* ὀθόνη OTHONĒ*
Acts 10.11 something descending, like a great s.
11. 5 "something descending, like a great s.

SHEKEL
1. *stater* (coin): *στατήρ* STATĒR*
Mt 17.27 "when you open its mouth . . find a s.

SHELAH: Σαλά 'shēlə
Lk 3.35 Eber, the son of Shelah

SHELTER
1. *encamp, settle:* *σκηνόω* SKĒNOŌ
Rev 7.15 "who sits upon the throne will s. them

SHEM: Σήμ 'shem
Lk 3.36 Arphaxad, . . son of S., the son of Noah

SHEPHERD
1. *shepherd:* *ποιμήν* POIMĒN
Mt 9.36 helpless, like sheep without a shepherd
25.32 "as a shepherd separates the sheep
26.31 " 'I will strike the shepherd
Mk 6.34 they were like sheep without a shepherd
14.27 " 'I will strike the shepherd
Lk 2. 8 shepherds . . in the field, keeping watch
2.15 shepherds said to one another, "Let us go
2.18 wondered at what the shepherds told
2.20 shepherds returned, . . praising God
Jn 10. 2 "he who enters by the door is the shepherd
10.11 "I am the good shepherd. The good shepherd lays down his life for the sheep
10.12 "He who is a hireling and not a shepherd
10.14 "I am the good shepherd
10.16 "there shall be one flock, one shepherd
Heb 13.20 Jesus, the great shepherd of the sheep
1 Pet 2.25 you . . have now returned to the Shepherd

SHEPHERD, BE A
1. *tend, herd, govern:* *ποιμαίνω* POIMAINŌ
Rev 7.17 "For the Lamb . . will be their shepherd

SHEPHERD, CHIEF
1. *chief shepherd:* *ἀρχιποίμην* ARCHIPOIMĒN*
1 Pet 5. 4 when the chief Shepherd is manifested

SHIELD
1. *oblong shield:* *θυρεός* THYREOS*
Eph 6.16 besides . . these, taking the s. of faith

SHIFT
1. *shift, remove:* *μετακινέω* (mid.) METAKINEŌ*
Col 1.23 provided that you continue . . , not shifting

SHINE
1. *shine out:* *ἐκλάμπω* EKLAMPŌ*
Mt 13.43 "Then the righteous will shine like the sun
2. *shine, give light:* *λάμπω* LAMPŌ
Mt 5.16 "Let your light so shine before men
17. 2 his face shone like the sun
Acts 12. 7 a light shone in the cell
2 Cor 4. 6 the God who said, "Let light shine out of darkness," who has shone in our hearts
3. *flash around:* *περιαστράπτω* PERIASTRAPTŌ
Acts 22. 6 "light from heaven suddenly shone
4. *bring to light, shine:* *φαίνω* PHAINŌ
[a]pass.
Mt 24.27 [a]"as . . lightning . . shines as far as the west
Jn 1. 5 The light shines in the darkness
5.35 "He was a burning and shining lamp
Phil 2.15 [a]among whom you shine as lights
2 Pet 1.19 pay attention . . as to a lamp shining
1 Jn 2. 8 the true light is already shining
Rev 1.16 his face was like the sun shining
8.12 a third of the day . . kept from shining
18.23 "a lamp shall shine in thee no more
21.23 city has no need of sun . . to shine upon it

SHINE AROUND
SHINE ROUND
1. *shine around, light up:* *περιλάμπω* PERILAMPŌ*
Lk 2. 9 the glory of the Lord shone around them
Acts 26.13 "brighter than the sun, shining round me

SHIP
1. *boat, ship:* *πλοῖον* PLOION
Acts 20.13 going ahead to the ship, we set sail
20.38 And they brought him to the ship
21. 2 having found a ship crossing to Phoenicia
21. 3 for there the ship was to unload its cargo
21. 6 Then we went on board the ship
27. 2 embarking in a ship of Adramyttium
27. 6 centurion found a ship of Alexandria
27.10 "loss, not only of the cargo and the ship
27.15 when the s. was caught . . , we . . were driven
27.17 took measures[c] to undergird the ship
27.19 they cast out . . the tackle of the ship
27.22 "no loss of life . . , but only of the ship
27.30 sailors . . seeking to escape from the ship
27.31 "Unless these men stay in the ship
27.37 (two hundred and seventy-six[d] . . in the s.
27.38 lightened the s., throwing out . . wheat
27.39 planned if possible to bring . . s. ashore
27.44 the rest on planks or on pieces of the s.
28.11 After three months we set sail in a ship
Jas 3. 4 Look at the ships also
Rev 8. 9 a third of the ships were destroyed
18.19 "where all who had ships at sea grew rich!

SHIP, OWNER OF A
1. *shipowner, captain:* *ναύκληρος* NAUKLĒROS*
Acts 27.11 paid . . attention . . to the owner of the ship

SHIPMASTER
1. *steersman, pilot:* *κυβερνήτης* KYBERNĒTĒS
Rev 18.17 And all shipmasters and seafaring men

SHIPWRECK, MAKE
SHIPWRECKED, BE
1. *suffer shipwreck:* *ναυαγέω* NAUAGEŌ*
2 Cor 11.25 Three times I have been shipwrecked
1 Tim 1.19 certain persons have made s. of . . faith

SHIRT
1. *tunic, undergarment:* *χιτών* CHITŌN
Lk 6.29 "and from him . . not withhold even your s.[0]

SHOAL
1. *a place between two seas:* *τόπος διθάλασσος* DITHALASSOS* [A.1.f]
Acts 27.41 striking a s.[e] they ran the vessel aground†
2. *multitude, mass:* *πλῆθος* PLĒTHOS
Lk 5. 6 they enclosed a great shoal of fish

SHOE
1. *sandal:* *ὑπόδημα* HYPODĒMA
Lk 15.22 " 'put a ring on . . , and shoes on his feet
Acts 7.33 " 'Take off the shoes from your feet
2. *fasten underneath:* *ὑποδέω* (mid.) HYPODEŌ
Eph 6.15 having shod . . feet with the equipment

SHOOT, WILD OLIVE
1. *wild olive tree:* *ἀγριέλαιος* AGRIELAIOS
Rom 11.17 you, a wild olive s., were grafted in

SHORE, MOOR TO THE
1. *bring to anchor at:* *προσορμίζω* (pass.) PROSORMIZŌ*
Mk 6.53 came to land . . and moored to the shore

SHORT
1. *few, little:* *ὀλίγος* OLIGOS
Acts 26.28 "In a s. time . . to make me a Christian!
26.29 "Whether short or long, I would to God
Heb 12.10 they disciplined us for a short time
Rev 12.12 "he knows that his time is short!
IDIOMATICALLY
a. 1 Th 2.17 since we were bereft . . for a short time Ἡμεῖς . . ἀπορφανισθέντες . . πρὸς καιρὸν ὥρας [HŌRA]

SHORT, GROW VERY
1. *draw together, shorten:* *συστέλλω* (pass.) SYSTELLŌ
1 Cor 7.29 the appointed time has grown very short

SHORT OF, FALL
1. *lack, fail:* *ὑστερέω* (pass.) HYSTEREŌ
Rom 3.23 all . . fall short of the glory of God

SHORTEN
1. *curtail, shorten:* *κολοβόω* KOLOBOŌ*
Mt 24.22 "if those days had not been shortened
24.22 "those days will be shortened
Mk 13.20 "if the Lord had not shortened the days
13.20 "for . . the elect . . he shortened the days

SHORTLY
1. *quickly:* ταχέως TACHEŌS
Phil 2.24 shortly I myself shall come also
2. *with speed:* ἐν τάχει TACHOS [B.1.a.1]
Acts 25. 4 he himself intended to go there shortly

SHORTSIGHTED, BE
1. *be shortsighted, blink:* μυωπάζω MYŌPAZŌ*
2 Pet 1. 9 whoever lacks these . . is blind and s.

SHOULD
1. (particle): ἄν AN
Mt 25.27 " 'I should have received what was my own
Lk 19.23 " 'I should have collected it with interest
Acts 18.14 "I should have reason to bear with you
1 Cor 11.31 we should not be judged
Gal 1.10 I should not be a servant[a] of Christ
2. *one must:* δεῖ DEI
Mt 18.33 " 'should not you have had mercy?
Acts 27.21 "Men, you should have listened to me
2 Cor 2. 3 those who should have made me rejoice
1 Tim 5.13 busybodies, saying what they should not
3. *be about to:* μέλλω (+inf.) MELLŌ
Jn 11.51 he prophesied that Jesus should die
Acts 20.38 that they should see his face no more
Gal 3.23 under restraint until faith s. be revealed
4. *ought, owe:* ὀφείλω (+inf.) OPHEILŌ
1 Cor 9.10 the plowman should plow in hope
Eph 5.28 so husbands should love their wives

SHOULDER
1. *shoulder:* ὦμος ŌMOS
Mt 23. 4 "heavy burdens . . on men's shoulders
Lk 15. 5 "he lays it on his shoulders, rejoicing

SHOUT
SHOUT OUT
1. *cry aloud, shout:* βοάω BOAŌ
Acts 25.24 "shouting that he ought not to live
Gal 4.27 "O barren one . . ; break forth and shout
2. *call out:* ἐπιφωνέω EPIPHŌNEŌ*
Lk 23.21 they shouted out, "Crucify, crucify him!
Acts 12.22 people shouted, "The voice of a god!
21.34 Some in the crowd shouted one thing
22.24 to find out why they shouted thus
3. *cry out, shout:* κράζω KRAZŌ
Mt 21. 9 crowds . . shouted, "Hosanna to the Son!
27.23 they shouted . . "Let him be crucified
Mk 15.14 they shouted all the more, "Crucify him

SHOW (*See also* BOLDNESS, SHOW)
1. *report:* ἀναγγέλλω ANAGGELLŌ
Jn 4.25 "when he comes, he will show us all
2. *lift up and show:* ἀναδείκνυμι ANADEIKNYMI
Acts 1.24 "show which . . of these . . thou hast chosen
3. *show, make known:* δείκνυμι DEIKNYMI
Mt 4. 8 the devil . . showed him all the kingdoms
8. 4 "but go, show yourself to the priest
16.21 began to show his disciples that he must go
Mk 1.44 "but go, show yourself to the priest
14.15 "he will show you a large upper room
Lk 4. 5 the devil . . showed him all the kingdoms
5.14 but "go and show yourself to the priest
20.24 "Show me a coin.[f] Whose likeness . . has it?
22.12 "he will show you a large upper room
[24.40 *he showed them his hands and his feet*‡
Jn 2.18 "What sign have you to show us for . . this?
5.20 "Father loves the Son, and shows him all
5.20 "greater works than these will he s. him
10.32 "I have shown you many good works
14. 8 Philip said . . "Lord, show us the Father
14. 9 "how can you say, 'Show us the Father'?
20.20 he showed them his hands and his side
Acts 7. 3 " 'go into the land which I will show you
10.28 "God has shown me . . I should not call
1 Cor 12.31 I will show you a . . more excellent way
Heb 8. 5 "according to the pattern . . shown you
Jas 2.18 Show me your faith apart from your works, and I by my works will s. you my faith
3.13 By his good life let him show his works
Rev 1. 1 revelation . . God gave . . to s. . . his servants
4. 1 "I will show you what must take place
17. 1 "Come, I will show you the judgment
21. 9 "Come, I will show you the Bride
21.10 he . . showed me the holy city Jerusalem
22. 1 he showed me the river of the water
22. 6 "sent his angel to show his servants
22. 8 the angel who showed them to me
4. *disclose, show:* δηλόω DĒLOŌ
2 Pet 1.14 as our Lord Jesus Christ showed me
5. *give:* δίδωμι DIDŌMI
Mt 24.24 "false prophets will . . show great signs
Mk 13.22 "false prophets will . . show signs
Var. POIEŌ
Acts 2.19 " 'I will show wonders in . . heaven above
2 Cor 8. 1 grace of God which has been shown
6. *manifest, visible:* ἐμφανής EMPHANĒS [A.6.a.3]
Rom 10.20 "shown myself to those who did not ask
7. *show, display:* ἐνδείκνυμι (mid.) ENDEIKNYMI
Rom 2.15 They show that what the law requires
9.17 "the very purpose of showing my power
9.22 if God, desiring to show his wrath
Eph 2. 7 he might show the immeasurable riches
Tit 2.10 to show entire and true fidelity
3. 2 to show perfect courtesy toward all men
Heb 6.10 the love which you showed for his sake
6.11 each . . of you to show . . same earnestness
8. *sign, proof:* ἔνδειξις ENDEIXIS [B.1.a.2]
Rom 3.25 This was to show God's righteousness
9. *show, point out:* ἐπιδείκνυμι EPIDEIKNYMI
Mt 16. 1 asked him to s. . . a sign from heaven
22.19 "Show me the money for the tax
Lk 17.14 "Go and show yourselves to the priests
Acts 9.39 showing . . garments which Dorcas made
18.28 he . . confuted . . , showing by the scriptures
Heb 6.17 God desired to show more convincingly
10. *indicate, show:* ὑποδείκνυμι HYPODEIKNYMI
Lk 6.47 "I will show you what he is like
Acts 9.16 "I will show him how . . he must suffer
20.35 "I have shown you that by so toiling
11. *reveal, inform:* μηνύω MĒNYŌ
Lk 20.37 "that the dead are raised . . Moses showed
12. *show, offer, cause:* παρέχω PARECHŌ
Acts 28. 2 the natives showed us unusual kindness
Tit 2. 7 Show yourself in all respects a model
13. *make manifest, make known:* φανερόω PHANEROŌ
Jn 7. 4 "If you do . . , show yourself to the world
Rom 1.19 plain . . , because God has shown it to them
2 Cor 3. 3 you s. that you are a letter from Christ
14. *do, make:* ποιέω POIEŌ
Lk 1.51 "He has shown strength with his arm
10.37 "The one who showed mercy on him
Jas 2.13 to one who has shown no mercy
Also variant to: Mk **13.**22
15. *indicate, report:* σημαίνω SĒMAINŌ
Jn 12.33 said this to s. by what death he was to die
18.32 spoken to s. by what death he was to die
21.19 (This he said to show by what death
16. *stand with, commend:* συνίστημι SYNISTĒMI
Rom 5. 8 But God shows his love for us in that
17. *dare:* τολμάω TOLMAŌ [A.6.a.5]
2 Cor 10. 2 such confidence as I count on showing

IDIOMATICALLY
a. Lk 20.21 "we know that you . . show no partiality οἴδαμεν ὅτι . . οὐ λαμβάνεις πρόσωπον [LAMBANŌ]
b. Rom 15.8 to show God's truthfulness ὑπὲρ ἀληθείας θεοῦ [HYPER]
c. Gal 2.6 (God shows no partiality πρόσωπον [ὁ] θεὸς ἀνθρώπου οὐ λαμβάνει [LAMBANŌ]

CONTEXTUALLY
Rom 2.11 For God shows no partiality
11.31 in order that by the mercy shown to you
12.10 outdo one another in showing honor
2 Cor 8.19 appointed . . to show our good will
11.30 boast of the things that s. my weakness
Heb 13. 2 Do not neglect to show hospitality
Jas 2. 1 s. no partiality as you hold the faith

SHOW HOSPITALITY
1. *entertain strangers:* ξενοδοχέω XENODOCHEŌ*
1 Tim 5.10 brought up children, shown hospitality

SHOW PARTIALITY
1. *show partiality:* προσωπολημπτέω PROSŌPOLĒMPTEŌ*
Jas 2. 9 if you show partiality, you commit sin
2. *respecter of persons:* προσωπολήμπτης PROSŌPOLĒMPTĒS* [B.3.a.1]
Acts 10.34 "I perceive that God shows no partiality

SHOW, SERVE TO
1. *stand with, commend:* συνίστημι SYNISTĒMI
Rom 3. 5 if our wickedness serves to show . . justice

SHOWER
1. *rainstorm, shower:* ὄμβρος OMBROS*
Lk 12.54 " 'A shower is coming'; and so it happens

SHOWING, MAKE A GOOD
1. *make a good showing:* εὐπροσωπέω EUPROSŌPEŌ*
Gal 6.12 who want to make a good s. in the flesh

SHOWN, BE
1. *know, understand:* γινώσκω GINŌSKŌ
Jas 2.20 Do you want to be s., you shallow man?
2. *bring to light, shine:* φαίνω (pass.) PHAINŌ
Rom 7.13 that sin might be shown to be sin

SHREWD, MORE
1. *sensible, prudent:* φρόνιμος (comp.) PHRONIMOS
Lk 16. 8 "more shrewd in dealing with their own[0]

SHREWDNESS
1. *wisely, shrewdly:* φρονίμως PHRONIMŌS* [B.2.a.2]
Lk 16. 8 "commended the . . steward for his s.[0]

SHRINE
1. *temple, shrine:* ναός NAOS
Acts 17.24 "does not live in shrines made by man
19.24 a silversmith, who made silver shrines
CONTEXTUALLY
Heb 6.19 a hope that enters into the inner shrine

SHRINK (*See* SHAME, SHRINK FROM S. IN)

SHRINK BACK
SHRINK FROM
1. *draw back:* ὑποστέλλω (mid.) HYPOSTELLŌ
Acts 20.20 "I did not shrink from declaring to you
20.27 "I did not shrink from declaring to you
Heb 10.38 "if he shrinks back, my soul has no pleasure

SHRINK BACK, THOSE WHO
1. *shrinking, timidity:* ὑποστολή HYPOSTOLĒ* [C.2]
Heb 10.39 we are not of those who shrink back

SHROUD, LINEN
1. *fine cloth, linen:* σινδών SINDŌN
Mt 27.59 wrapped it in a clean linen shroud
Mk 15.46 he bought a linen shroud, and taking him down, wrapped him in the linen shroud
Lk 23.53 took it down and wrapped it in a linen s.

SHRUB
1. *garden herb, vegetable:* λάχανον LACHANON
Mt 13.32 "when . . grown it is the greatest of shrubs
Mk 4.32 "it . . becomes the greatest of all shrubs

SHUDDER
1. *bristle, shiver:* φρίσσω PHRISSŌ*
Jas 2.19 Even the demons believe—and shudder

SHUN
1. *flee, avoid:* φεύγω PHEUGŌ
1 Cor 6.18 Shun immorality
10.14 my beloved, shun the worship of idols
1 Tim 6.11 as for you, man of God, shun all this
2 Tim 2.22 s. youthful passions and aim at . . peace

SHUT
1. *shut up:* ἀποκλείω APOKLEIŌ*
Lk 13.25 "once the householder has . . shut the door
2. *shut:* κλείω KLEIŌ
Mt 6. 6 "shut the door and pray to your Father
23.13 "because you shut . . kingdom of heaven
25.10 "to the . . feast; and the door was shut
Lk 11. 7 " 'Do not bother me; the door is now shut
Jn 20.19 doors being s. where the disciples were
Jn 20.26 "The doors were shut, but Jesus came
Acts 21.30 dragged him out . . and . . gates were shut
Rev 3. 7 " 'the true one, . . who opens and no one shall shut, who shuts and no one opens
3. 8 " 'an open door, which no one is able to s.
11. 6 They have power to shut the sky
20. 3 threw him into the pit, and shut it
21.25 its gates shall never be shut by day

SHUT OUT
1. *shut out:* ἐκκλείω EKKLEIŌ
Gal 4.17 they want to shut you out

SHUT UP
1. *shut up, confine:* κατακλείω KATAKLEIŌ*
Lk 3.20 he shut up John in prison
Acts 26.10 "I not only shut up many of the saints
2. *shut:* κλείω KLEIŌ
Lk 4.25 "in . . days of Elijah, . . heaven was shut up

SICK
1. *weak, sickly:* ἄρρωστος ARRŌSTOS
Mt 14.14 he had compassion . . and healed their sick
Mk 6. 5 laid his hands upon a few sick people
6.13 anointed with oil many that were sick
16.18 "they will lay their hands on the sick[k]‡
2. *be weak, be sickly:* ἀσθενέω (part.) ASTHENEŌ
Mt 10. 8 "Heal the sick, raise the dead
25.39 " 'when did we see thee sick . . and visit thee?
Mk 6.56 they laid the sick in the market places
Jn 5. 7 sick man answered . . "Sir, I have no man
Acts 19.12 handkerchiefs . . were carried . . to the s.
3. *weak, sickly:* ἀσθενής ASTHENĒS
Mt 25.43 " 'I was . . sick . . and you did not visit me
25.44 " 'Lord, when did we see thee . . sick?
Lk 10. 9 "heal the sick in it and say to them
Acts 5.15 they . . carried out the sick into the streets
5.16 people also gathered . . , bringing the sick
4. *being ill:* ἔχων κακῶς KAKŌS [B.3.b.4]
Mt 4.24 they brought him all the sick
Mk 6.55 began to bring sick people on . . pallets
5. *be weary, be ill:* κάμνω (part.) KAMNŌ
Jas 5.15 prayer of faith will save the sick man
6. *hold together, impel:* συνέχω (pass. part.) SYNECHŌ
Acts 28. 8 the father of Publius lay sick with fever
CONTEXTUALLY
Mt 8.14 mother-in-law lying sick with a fever
Mk 1.30 Simon's mother-in-law lay sick

SICK, BE
SICK, FALL
1. *be weak, be sickly:* ἀσθενέω ASTHENEŌ
Mt 25.36 " 'I was sick and you visited me
Lk 4.40 any that were sick with various diseases
Acts 9.37 In those days she fell sick and died
Jas 5.14 Is any among you sick?
2. *be ill:* ἔχειν κακῶς KAKŌS [B.3.a.5]
Mt 8.16 he . . healed all who were sick
9.12 "well have no need . . , but those who are s.
14.35 they . . brought to him all that were sick
Mk 1.32 brought to him all who were sick
1.34 he healed many who were sick
2.17 "well have no need . . , but those who are s.
Lk 5.31 "well have no need . . , but those who are s.
7. 2 a centurion had a slave . . who was sick

SICKBED
1. *bed, couch:* κλίνη KLINĒ
Rev 2.22 " 'Behold, I will throw her on a sickbed

SICKLE
1. *sickle, scythe:* δρέπανον DREPANON*
Mk 4.29 "puts in the s., because . . harvest has come
Rev 14.14 son of man, with . . a sharp s. in his hand
14.15 "Put in your sickle, and reap
14.16 he who sat upon the cloud swung his s.
14.17 another angel . . had a sharp sickle
14.18 called . . to him who had the sharp sickle, "Put in your s., and gather the clusters
14.19 the angel swung his sickle on the earth

SIDE (*See also* PASS BY ON THE OTHER SIDE; RIGHT SIDE)
1. *be:* εἰμί EIMI
Acts 14. 4 some sided with the Jews
2. *part, share:* μέρος (pl.) MEROS
Jn 21. 6 "Cast the net on the right side
3. *side:* πλευρά PLEURA*
Mt [27.49 *And another . . pierced his side*‡
Jn 19.34 one of the soldiers pierced his side
20.20 he showed them his hands and his side
20.25 "Unless I . . place my hand in his side
20.27 "put out your hand, . . place it in my s.
Acts 12. 7 he struck Peter on the side and woke him
IDIOMATICALLY
a. Mt 16.23; Mk 8.33 "for you are not on the side of God ὅτι οὐ φρονεῖς τὰ τοῦ θεοῦ [PHRONEŌ]
CONTEXTUALLY
Lk 17.24 "lights up . . sky from one s. to the other

SIDE BY SIDE WITH, LABOR
SIDE BY SIDE WITH, STRIVE
1. *assist, struggle together:* συναθλέω SYNATHLEŌ
Phil 1.27 firm . . , with one mind striving s. by side
4. 3 they have labored side by side with me

SIDE, ON EACH
SIDE, ON EITHER
SIDE, ON EVERY
SIDES, ON ALL
1. *in a circle, round about:* κύκλῳ KYKLŌ
Rev 4. 6 on each s. of the throne, . . creatures
2. *from every side:* πάντοθεν PANTOTHEN
Lk 19.43 "enemies will . . hem you in on every side
Heb 9. 4 the ark . . covered on all sides with gold
IDIOMATICALLY
a. Jn 19.18 with him two others, one on either side μετ' αὐτοῦ ἄλλους δύο ἐντεῦθεν καὶ ἐντεῦθεν [ENTEUTHEN]
b. Rev. 22.2 on either side of the river τοῦ ποταμοῦ ἐντεῦθεν καὶ ἐκεῖθεν [EKEITHEN; ENTEUTHEN]

SIDE, THE OTHER
SIDE OF, THE OTHER
1. *on the other side, beyond:* πέραν PERAN
[a]subst. neut. [b]prep.
Mt 8.18 [a]he gave orders to go over to the other side
8.28 [a]when he came to the other side
14.22 [a]made . . disciples . . go . . to the other side
16. 5 [a]When . . disciples reached the other side
Mk 4.35 [a]"Let us go across to the other side
5. 1 [a]They came to the other side of the sea
5.21 [a]Jesus . . crossed . . to the other side
6.45 [a]made . . disciples . . go . . to the other side
8.13 [a]he departed to the other side
Lk 8.22 [a]"Let us go . . to the other s. of the lake
Jn 6. 1 [b]Jesus went to the other side of the Sea
6.22 [b]remained on the other side of the sea
6.25 [b]found him on the other side of the sea

SIDES, ON ALL (*See* SIDE, ON EACH)

SIDON: 'sīdᵊn I,C-1; II,G-4
1. *Sidon:* Σιδών
Mt 11.21 "if the . . works . . had been done in . . S.
11.22 "on the day of judgment for Tyre and S.
15.21 withdrew to the district of Tyre and S.
Mk 3. 8 from . . Tyre and S. a great multitude
7.24 went away to the region of Tyre and S.[c]‡
7.31 he . . went through S. to the Sea of Galilee
Lk 6.17 multitude . . from . . seacoast of Tyre and S.
10.13 "if the . . works . . had been done in . . S.
10.14 "more tolerable in the judgment for . . S.
Acts 27. 3 The next day we put in at Sidon
2. *of Sidon, Sidonian:* Σιδώνιος
Lk 4.26 Elijah was sent . . to Zarephath, in . . S.
Acts 12.20 Herod was angry with . . Tyre and Sidon

SIFT
1. *sift, winnow:* σινιάζω SINIAZŌ*
Lk 22.31 "that he might sift you[k] like wheat

SIGH
1. *groaning, sighing:* στεναγμός STENAGMOS
Rom 8.26 Spirit himself intercedes . . with sighs
2. *groan, sigh:* στενάζω STENAZŌ
Mk 7.34 looking up to heaven, he sighed, and said
2 Cor 5. 4 in this tent, we sigh with anxiety

SIGH DEEPLY
1. *groan for:* ἀναστενάζω ANASTENAZŌ*
Mk 8.12 he sighed deeply in his spirit, and said

SIGHT
1. *see, look:* βλέπω (inf.) BLEPŌ
Lk 7.21 on many that were blind he bestowed s.
2. *form, appearance:* εἶδος EIDOS
2 Cor 5. 7 for we walk by faith, not by sight
3. *vision, sight:* ὅραμα HORAMA
Acts 7.31 "Moses . . wondered at the sight
4. *eye:* ὀφθαλμός (pl.) OPHTHALMOS
Acts 1. 9 a cloud took him out of their sight
5. *make visible:* φαντάζω (subst. pass. part. neut.) PHANTAZŌ*
Heb 12.21 so terrifying was the s. that Moses said
6. *look at, observe:* θεωρέω THEŌREŌ [B.2.c]
Rev 11.12 in the sight of their foes they went up
7. *spectacle, sight:* θεωρία THEŌRIA*
Lk 23.48 multitudes who assembled to see the s.
IDIOMATICALLY
a. Gal 1.22 And I was still not known by sight ἤμην δὲ ἀγνοούμενος τῷ προσώπῳ [PROSŌPON]
CONTEXTUALLY
Lk 24.31 and he vanished out of their sight
1 Pet 2. 4 but in God's sight chosen and precious

SIGHT, BE WITHOUT
1. *see, look:* βλέπω (neg. periphr.) BLEPŌ
Acts 9. 9 for three days he was without sight

SIGHT, IN S.'S
SIGHT OF, IN THE
1. *face to face, before:* ἐνώπιον ENŌPION
Lk 16.15 "an abomination in the sight of God
Acts 4.19 "Whether it is right in the sight of God
7.46 "who found favor in the sight of God
10.33 "we are all here present in the s. of God
19.19 burned them in the sight of all
Rom 3.20 justified in his sight by works of the law
12.17 thought for what is noble in the s. of all
2 Cor 4. 2 every man's conscience in the s. of God
7.12 that . . zeal . . be revealed . . in the s. of God
8.21 what is honorable not only in the Lord's sight but also in the sight of men
1 Tim 2. 3 it is acceptable in the sight of God
5. 4 for this is acceptable in the sight of God
Heb 13.21 that which is pleasing in his sight
1 Pet 3. 4 quiet spirit . . in God's sight is . . precious
Rev 3. 2 "'not found . . perfect in the s. of . . God
13.13 making fire come down . . in the s. of men
2. *opposite:* κατέναντι KATENANTI
2 Cor 2.17 in the sight of God we speak in Christ
12.19 in the s. of God . . we have been speaking

SIGHT OF, COME IN
1. *cause to appear:* ἀναφαίνω ANAPHAINŌ
Acts 21. 3 When we had come in sight of Cyprus

SIGHT, RECEIVE ONE'S
SIGHT, REGAIN ONE'S
1. *look up, receive sight:* ἀναβλέπω ANABLEPŌ
Mt 11. 5 "blind receive their s. and the lame walk
20.34 they received their sight and followed
Mk 10.51 "Master,[l] let me receive my sight
10.52 he received his sight and followed
Lk 7.22 "blind receive their s., the lame walk
18.41 "Lord, let me receive my sight
18.42 Jesus said . . "Receive your sight
18.43 he received his sight and followed
Jn 9.11 "I . . washed and received my sight
9.15 asked him how he had received his sight
9.18 blind and had received his sight
9.18 the man who had received his sight
Acts 9.12 "so that he might regain his sight
9.17 "sent me that you may regain your s.
9.18 he regained his sight. Then he rose

Acts 22.13 " 'Brother Saul, receive your s.' And in that very hour I received my sight

SIGHT, RECOVERING OF

1. *recovery of sight:* ἀνάβλεψις ANABLEPSIS*
Lk 4.18 "to proclaim .. recovering of sight

SIGN

1. *sign, portent:* σημεῖον SĒMEION
Mt 12.38 "Teacher, we wish to see a sign from you
12.39 "An evil and adulterous generation seeks for a sign; but no sign shall be given to it except the sign of the prophet Jonah
16. 1 they asked him to show them a sign
16. 3 "you cannot interpret the signs of the times‡
16. 4 "An evil and adulterous generation seeks for a sign, but no sign shall be given to it except the sign of Jonah
24. 3 "what will be the sign of your coming?
24.24 "false prophets will .. show great signs
24.30 "the sign of the Son of man in heaven
26.48 the betrayer had given them a sign
Mk 8.11 seeking from him a sign from heaven
8.12 "Why does this generation seek a sign? .. no sign shall be given to this generation
13. 4 "when will this be, and what will be the s.?
13.22 "false prophets will arise and show signs
16.17 "And these signs will accompany those[k]‡
16.20 confirmed the message by the signs[k]‡
Lk 2.12 "this will be a sign for you
2.34 "child is set .. for a s. .. spoken against
11.16 others .. sought from him a s. from heaven
11.29 "This generation is an evil generation; it seeks a sign, but no sign shall be given to it except the sign of Jonah
11.30 "Jonah became a sign to the men of Nineveh
21. 7 "when will this be, .. what will be the s.?
21.11 "there will be terrors and great signs
21.25 "there will be signs in sun and moon
23. 8 he was hoping to see some s. done by him
Jn 2.11 the first of his signs, Jesus did at Cana
2.18 "What sign have you to show us?
2.23 many believed .. when they saw the signs
3. 2 "no one can do these signs that you do
4.48 "Unless you see signs .. you will not believe
4.54 This was .. the second sign that Jesus did
6. 2 followed him, because they saw .. signs
6.14 When the people saw the s. .. they said
6.26 "you seek me, not because you saw signs
6.30 "what s. do you do, that we may .. believe?
7.31 "will he do more signs than this man?
9.16 "How can .. a sinner do such signs?
10.41 they said, "John did no sign
11.47 "For this man performs many signs
12.18 they heard he had done this sign
12.37 Though he had done so many signs
20.30 other signs in the presence of .. disciples
Acts 2.19 " 'I will show .. signs on the earth beneath
2.22 "with .. signs which God did through him
2.43 signs were done through the apostles
4.16 "that a notable sign has been performed
4.22 on whom this s. of healing was performed
4.30 "signs .. performed through the name
5.12 many signs .. done among the people
6. 8 Stephen .. did .. signs among the people
7.36 "led them out, having performed .. signs
8. 6 they heard him and saw the signs
8.13 seeing signs .. performed, he was amazed
14. 3 granting signs .. to be done by their hands
15.12 as they related what signs .. God had done
Rom 4.11 He received circumcision as a sign
15.19 by the power of signs and wonders
1 Cor 1.22 Jews demand signs and Greeks seek wisdom
14.22 tongues are a sign not for believers
2 Cor 12.12 signs of a true apostle were performed .. with signs and wonders and mighty works
2 Th 2. 9 coming of .. lawless one .. will be with .. signs
Heb 2. 4 while God also bore witness by signs
Rev 13.13 It works great signs, .. making fire come
13.14 the signs which it is allowed to work
16.14 they are demonic spirits, performing signs
19.20 the false prophet who .. had worked .. signs

2. *signal:* σύσσημον SYSSĒMON*
Mk 14.44 Now the betrayer had given them a sign

SIGNS, MAKE

1. *nod, beckon:* διανεύω DIANEUŌ*
Lk 1.22 he made signs .. and remained dumb

2. *nod, make signs:* ἐννεύω ENNEUŌ*
Lk 1.62 they made signs to his father

SIGNS TO BE OBSERVED

1. *observation:* παρατήρησις PARATĒRĒSIS*
Lk 17.20 "not coming with signs to be observed

SILAS: Σίλας 'sīləs
Acts 15.22 They sent Judas called Barsabbas, and S.
15.27 "We have therefore sent Judas and Silas
15.32 Judas and Silas, who were .. prophets
[15.34 *it seemed good to Silas to remain there*‡
15.40 Paul chose Silas and departed
16.19 they seized Paul and S. and dragged
16.25 Paul and Silas were praying and singing
16.29 with fear he fell down before Paul and S.
17. 4 some .. were persuaded, .. joined Paul and S.
17.10 brethren .. sent Paul and S. away by night
17.14 but Silas and Timothy remained there
17.15 a command for S. and Timothy to come
18. 5 S. and Timothy arrived from Macedonia

SILENCE

1. *stop the mouth of:* ἐπιστομίζω EPISTOMIZŌ*
Tit 1.11 must be silenced, since they are upsetting

2. *silence, rest:* ἡσυχία HĒSYCHIA
1 Tim 2.11 Let a woman learn in silence

3. *muzzle, put to silence:* φιμόω PHIMOŌ
Mt 22.34 the Pharisees heard that he had silenced

4. *fence in, stop up:* φράσσω PHRASSŌ
2 Cor 11.10 this boast of mine shall not be silenced

5. *silence:* σιγή SIGĒ
Rev 8. 1 Lamb opened .. seventh seal, there was s.

SILENCE, KEEP

1. *be silent, keep secret:* σιγάω SIGAŌ
Lk 9.36 they kept silence and told no one
Acts 15.12 And all the assembly kept silence
1 Cor 14.28 let each of them keep silence in church
14.34 women should keep s. in the churches

SILENCE, PUT TO

1. *muzzle, put to silence:* φιμόω PHIMOŌ
1 Pet 2.15 by doing right you should put to s.

SILENCED, BE

1. *be quiet, be at rest:* ἡσυχάζω HĒSYCHAZŌ
Acts 11.18 "When they heard this they were s.

SILENT, BE

SILENT, KEEP

1. *be quiet, be at rest:* ἡσυχάζω HĒSYCHAZŌ
Lk 14. 4 But they were silent

2. *be in silence:* εἶναι ἐν ἡσυχίᾳ HĒSYCHIA [B.2.d.2]
1 Tim 2.12 she is to keep silent

3. *muzzle, put to silence:* φιμόω (pass.) PHIMOŌ
Mk 1.25 "Be silent, and come out of him!
Lk 4.35 "Be silent, and come out of him!

4. *be silent, keep secret:* σιγάω SIGAŌ
Lk 18.39 rebuked him, telling him to be silent
20.26 marveling at his answer they were silent
Acts 12.17 motioning to them with his hand to be s.
1 Cor 14.30 let the first be silent

5. *be still:* σιωπάω SIŌPAŌ
Mt 20.31 rebuked them, telling them to be silent
26.63 But Jesus was silent
Mk 3. 4 But they were silent
9.34 But they were silent
10.48 many rebuked him, telling him to be s.
14.61 he was silent and made no answer
Lk 1.20 "you will be silent and unable to speak
19.40 "if these were s., .. stones would cry out
Acts 18. 9 "speak and do not be silent

SILK
1. *silken:* σιρικός (subst. neut.) SIRIKOS*
Rev 18.12 fine linen, purple, silk and scarlet

SILLY
1. *characteristic of old women:* γραώδης GRAŌDĒS*
1 Tim 4. 7 Have nothing to do with . . silly myths

SILLY TALK
1. *silly talk:* μωρολογία MŌROLOGIA*
Eph 5. 4 Let there be no filthiness, nor silly talk

SILOAM: Σιλωάμ sī'lōəm
Lk 13. 4 "eighteen upon whom the tower in S. fell
Jn 9. 7 "Go, wash in the pool of Siloam
9.11 " 'Go to Siloam and wash'; so I went

SILVANUS: Σιλουανός sil'vānəs
2 Cor 1.19 we preached . . , S. and Timothy and I
1 Th 1. 1 Paul, S., and Timothy, To the church
2 Th 1. 1 Paul, S., and Timothy, To the church
1 Pet 5.12 By S., a faithful brother as I regard him

SILVER
SILVER, OF
SILVER, PIECE OF
1. *silver, money:* ἀργύριον ARGYRION
Mt 26.15 they paid him thirty pieces of silver
27. 3 brought back the thirty pieces of silver
27. 5 throwing down . . pieces of s. in the temple
27. 6 chief priests, taking the pieces of silver
27. 9 "they took the thirty pieces of silver
Acts 3. 6 "I have no s. and gold, but I give you
7.16 "Abraham had bought for a sum of s.
8.20 Peter said . . "Your s. perish with you!
19.19 it came to fifty thousand pieces of s.
20.33 "I coveted no one's silver or gold
1 Cor 3.12 if . . one builds on the foundation with . . s.
1 Pet 1.18 you were ransomed . . , not with . . silver
2. *silver, money:* ἄργυρος ARGYROS*
Mt 10. 9 "Take no gold, nor silver, nor copper
Acts 17.29 "not to think that the Deity is like . . s.
Jas 5. 3 Your gold and silver have rusted
Rev 18.12 cargo of gold, silver, jewels and pearls
3. *of silver:* ἀργυροῦς ARGYROUS*
Acts 19.24 Demetrius . . made silver shrines of Artemis
2 Tim 2.20 there are not only vessels of gold and s.
Rev 9.20 worshiping . . idols of gold and silver

SILVER COIN
1. *drachma:* δραχμή DRACHMĒ
Lk 15. 8 "what woman, having ten silver coins[t]?

SILVERSMITH
1. *silversmith:* ἀργυροκόπος ARGYROKOPOS*
Acts 19.24 a man named Demetrius, a s.

SIMEON: Συμεών 'simēən
1. tribe of Israel
Rev 7. 7 twelve thousand of the tribe of Simeon
2. ancestor of Jesus
Lk 3.30 Simeon, the son of Judah
3. devout man in Jerusalem
Lk 2.25 a man in Jerusalem, whose name was S.
2.34 Simeon blessed them and said to Mary
4. Simon Peter
Acts 15.14 "Simeon . . related how God first visited‡[0]
2 Pet 1. 1 Simeon[x] Peter, a servant and apostle‡[0]
5. Simeon called Niger
Acts 13. 1 at Antioch . . Simeon who was called Niger[0]

SIMON: Σίμων 'sīmən
1. Simon Peter
Mt 4.18 brothers, S. . . called Peter and Andrew
10. 2 apostles . . : first, S., . . called Peter
16.16 S. Peter replied, "You are the Christ
16.17 "Blessed are you, Simon Bar-Jona!
17.25 Jesus spoke . . "What do you think, S.?
Mk 1.16 passing along by the Sea of Galilee, he saw S. and Andrew the brother of S. casting
1.29 he[e] . . entered the house of S. and Andrew
1.30 Simon's mother-in-law lay sick
1.36 Simon and those . . with him pursued him
3.16 Simon[x] whom he surnamed Peter
14.37 he said to Peter, "S., are you asleep?
Lk 4.38 he arose and left . . and entered Simon's house. Now Simon's mother-in-law was ill
5. 3 one of the boats, which was Simon's
5. 4 he said to S., "Put out into the deep
5. 5 Simon answered, "Master, we toiled
5. 8 when S. Peter saw it, he fell down
5.10 sons of Zebedee, . . partners with Simon. And Jesus said to S., "Do not be afraid
6.14 S., whom he named Peter, and Andrew
22.31 "Simon, Simon, behold, Satan demanded to have you,[k] that he might sift you[k]
24.34 "Lord has risen . . , and . . appeared to S.!
Jn 1.40 One . . was Andrew, Simon Peter's brother
1.41 He first found his brother Simon
1.42 "So you are Simon the son of John?
6. 8 Andrew, Simon Peter's brother, said
6.68 S. Peter answered . . "to whom shall we go?
13. 6 He came to S. Peter; and Peter said
13. 9 S. Peter said . . "Lord, not my feet only!
13.24 S. Peter beckoned . . "Tell us who it is
13.36 S. Peter said . . "where are you going?
18.10 Simon Peter, having a sword, drew it
18.15 S. Peter followed . . , and so did another
18.25 S. Peter was standing . . warming himself
20. 2 she ran, and went to Simon Peter
20. 6 Then Simon Peter came, following him
21. 2 Simon Peter, Thomas called the Twin
21. 3 S. Peter said . . "I am going fishing
21. 7 When S. Peter heard that it was the Lord
21.11 S. Peter went aboard and hauled the net
22.15 Jesus said to S. Peter, "S., son of John, do you love me more than these?
21.16 "Simon, son of John, do you love me?
21.17 "Simon, son of John, do you love me?
Acts 10. 5 "bring one Simon who is called Peter
10.18 to ask whether S. . . was lodging there
10.32 "Send therefore to Joppa and ask for S.
11.13 " 'Send to Joppa . . bring S. called Peter
2 Pet [1. 1 *Simon* Peter, a servant and apostle‡[0]
2. brother of Jesus
Mt 13.55 "are not his brothers . . Joseph and S.?
Mk 6. 3 "Is not this the . . brother of . . Simon?
3. father of Judas Iscariot
Jn 6.71 Judas the son of Simon Iscariot
13. 2 Judas Iscariot, Simon's son, to betray
13.26 he gave it to Judas, . . son of S. Iscariot
4. Simon the Zealot or Cananaean
Mt 10. 4 S. the Cananaean, and Judas Iscariot
Mk 3.18 Thaddaeus, and S. the Cananaean
Lk 6.15 Simon who was called the Zealot
Acts 1.13 S. the Zealot and Judas . . son of James
5. Pharisee
Lk 7.40 "Simon, I have something to say to you
7.43 S. answered . . "to whom he forgave more
7.44 turning toward the woman he said to S.
6. leper
Mt 26. 6 at Bethany in the house of S. the leper
Mk 14. 3 at Bethany in the house of S. the leper
7. Simon of Cyrene
Mt 27.32 they came upon a man of Cyrene, S.
Mk 15.21 compelled a passer-by, S. of Cyrene
Lk 23.26 they seized one S. of Cyrene
8. tanner of Joppa
Acts 9.43 he stayed in Joppa . . with one S., a tanner
10. 6 "he is lodging with Simon, a tanner
10.17 made inquiry for Simon's house
10.32 " 'lodging in the house of S., a tanner
9. Simon the magician
Acts 8. 9 But there was a man named Simon
8.13 Even Simon himself believed
8.18 when S. saw that the Spirit was given
8.24 S. answered, "Pray for me to the Lord

SIMPLE-MINDED
1. *innocent:* ἄκακος AKAKOS
Rom 16.18 they deceive the hearts of the s.

SIMPLY
CONTEXTUALLY
Mt 5.37 "Let what you say be simply 'Yes' or 'No

SIN
1. *sin, miss the mark:* ἁμαρτάνω HAMARTANŌ
[a]part. A.3.d.3 [b]A.6.e
Mt 18.15 "If your brother sins against you, go
18.21 "how often shall my brother s. against me?
27. 4 saying, "I have sinned in betraying
Lk 15.18 " ' "Father, I have sinned against heaven
15.21 " 'Father, I have sinned against heaven
17. 3 "if your brother sins, rebuke him
17. 4 "if he sins against you seven times
Jn 5.14 "Sin no more, that nothing worse befall
8.11 "go, and do not sin again[r]‡
9. 2 "who sinned, this man or his parents?
9. 3 "It was not that this man sinned
Rom 2.12 All who have sinned without the law . . and all who have sinned under the law
3.23 since all have sinned and fall short
5.12 so death spread . . because all men sinned
5.14 [a]over those whose sins were not like
5.16 [a]not like the effect of that one man's sin
6.15 Are we to sin because . . not under law?
1 Cor 6.18 immoral man sins against . . own body
7.28 But if you marry, you do not sin, and if a girl[z] marries she does not sin
7.36 [b]let them marry—it is no sin
8.12 Thus, sinning against your brethren . . , you sin against Christ
15.34 Come to your right mind, and s. no more
Eph 4.26 Be angry but do not sin
1 Tim 5.20 [a]As for those who persist in sin, rebuke
Heb 3.17 Was it not with those who sinned?
10.26 if we sin deliberately after receiving
2 Pet 2. 4 God did not spare . . angels when they sinned
1 Jn 1.10 If we say we have not sinned
2. 1 I am writing . . so that you may not sin; . . if any one does sin, we have an advocate
3. 6 No one who abides in him sins; no one who sins has either seen . . or known him
3. 8 the devil has sinned from the beginning
3. 9 cannot sin because he is[g] born of God
5.16 [a]for those whose sin is not mortal
5.18 that any one born of God does not sin
2. *failure, fault, sinful act:* ἁμάρτημα HAMARTĒMA*
Mk 3.28 "all sins will be forgiven the sons of men
3.29 "is guilty of an eternal sin
Rom 3.25 he had passed over former sins
1 Cor 6.18 Every other sin which a man commits
3. *sin, failure, guilt:* ἁμαρτία HAMARTIA
Mt 1.21 "he will save his people from their sins
3. 6 were baptized . . , confessing their sins
9. 2 "my son; your sins are forgiven
9. 5 "easier, to say, 'Your sins are forgiven'?
9. 6 Son of man has authority . . to forgive sins
12.31 "sin and blasphemy will be forgiven
26.28 "poured out . . for the forgiveness of sins
Mk 1. 4 repentance for the forgiveness of sins
1. 5 baptized by him . . , confessing their sins
2. 5 "My son, your sins are forgiven
2. 7 "Who can forgive sins but God alone?
2. 9 "easier, to say . . 'Your sins are forgiven'?
2.10 "Son of man has authority . . to forgive sins
Lk 1.77 "knowledge . . in the forgiveness of . . sins
3. 3 repentance for the forgiveness of sins
5.20 "Man, your sins are forgiven you
5.21 "Who can forgive sins but God only?
5.23 "easier, to say, 'Your sins are forgiven . .'?
5.24 "Son . . has authority . . to forgive sins
7.47 "her sins, which are many, are forgiven
7.48 said to her, "Your sins are forgiven
7.49 "Who is this, who even forgives sins?
Lk 11. 4 "forgive us our sins, for we . . forgive
24.47 that . . forgiveness of sins . . be preached
Jn 1.29 "who takes away the sin of the world!
8.21 "you will seek me and die in your sin
8.24 "I told you that you would die in your sins, for you will die in your sins unless
8.34 "Truly, truly, I say to you, every one who commits sin is a slave to sin
8.46 "Which of you convicts me of sin?
9.34 "You were born in utter sin
15.22 "If I had not come . . they would not have s.; but now they have no excuse for their s.
15.24 "If I had not . . , they would not have sin
16. 8 "will convince[x] the world concerning s.
16. 9 "concerning s., because they do not believe
19.11 "he who delivered me . . has the greater sin
20.23 "If you forgive the sins of any
Acts 2.38 "for the forgiveness of your sins
3.19 "that your sins may be blotted out
5.31 "exalted . . , to give . . forgiveness of sins
7.60 "Lord, do not hold this s. against them
10.43 "believes . . receives forgiveness of sins
13.38 "through this man forgiveness of sins
22.16 " 'be baptized, and wash away your sins
26.18 " 'that they . . receive forgiveness of sins
Rom 3. 9 Jews and Greeks, . . under the power of s.
3.20 through the law comes knowledge of sin
4. 7 "Blessed . . those . . whose sins are covered
4. 8 "the Lord will not reckon his sin
5.12 as sin came into the world through one man and death through sin
5.13 sin . . was in the world before the law . . , but sin is not counted where there is no law
5.20 where sin increased, grace abounded
5.21 so that, as sin reigned in death
6. 1 to continue in sin that grace . . abound?
6. 2 How can we who died to sin still live in it?
6. 6 that . . we . . no longer be enslaved to sin
6. 7 For he who has died is freed from sin
6.10 death he died he died to sin, once for all
6.11 consider yourselves dead to sin
6.12 Let not s. . . reign in your mortal bodies
6.13 Do not yield your members to sin
6.14 For sin will have no dominion over you
6.16 you are slaves . . either of s. . . or of obedience
6.17 that you who were once slaves of sin
6.18 having been set free from sin
6.20 When you were slaves of sin
6.22 now that you have been set free from s.
6.23 For the wages of sin is death
7. 7 What . . shall we say? That the law is sin?
7. 7 Yet . . I should not have known sin
7. 8 sin, finding opportunity . . , wrought
7. 8 Apart from the law sin lies dead
7. 9 when the commandment came, sin revived
7.11 sin, finding opportunity . . , deceived
7.13 It was sin, working death in me through what is good, in order that sin might be shown to be sin
7.14 but I am carnal, sold under sin
7.17 it is no longer I that do it, but sin
7.20 no longer I . . , but s. which dwells within
7.23 making me captive to the law of sin
7.25 but with my flesh I serve the law of sin
8. 2 free from the law of sin and death
8. 3 sending his own Son . . for sin,[i] he condemned sin in the flesh†
8.10 your bodies are dead because of sin
11.27 "covenant . . when I take away their sins
14.23 whatever . . not . . from faith is sin[w]
1 Cor 15. 3 Christ died for our sins in accordance
15.17 faith is futile and you are still in . . sins
15.56 The sting of death is sin, and the power of sin is the law
2 Cor 5.21 he made him to be s. who knew no s., so . . we might become . . righteousness
11. 7 Did I commit a sin in abasing myself?

Gal 1. 4 gave himself for our sins to deliver us
2.17 is Christ then an agent of sin?
3.22 the scripture consigned all things to sin
Eph 2. 1 when you were dead through the . . sins
Col 1.14 redemption, the forgiveness of sins
1 Th 2.16 to fill up the measure of their sins
2 Th [2. 3 unless . . the man of *sin* is revealed‡
1 Tim 5.22 nor participate in another man's sins
5.24 The sins of some men are conspicuous
2 Tim 3. 6 weak women, burdened with sins
Heb 1. 3 When he had made purification for sins
2.17 expiation for the sins of the people
3.13 none . . hardened by the deceitfulness of s.
4.15 tempted as we are, yet without sin[o]
5. 1 to offer gifts and sacrifices for sins
5. 3 bound to offer sacrifice for his own sins
7.27 sacrifices daily, first for his own sins
8.12 "I will remember their sins no more
9.26 to put away s. by the sacrifice of himself
9.28 offered once to bear the sins of many
9.28 not to deal with sin but to save those
10. 2 no longer have any consciousness of sin
10. 3 in these sacrifices there is a reminder of s.
10. 4 impossible that . . goats . . take away sins
10. 6 "in burnt offerings and sin offerings
10. 8 "nor taken pleasure in . . sin offerings
10.11 sacrifices . . can never take away sins
10.12 offered . . a single sacrifice for sins
10.17 "I will remember their sins . . no more
10.18 there is no longer any offering for sin
10.26 no longer remains a sacrifice for sins
11.25 than . . enjoy the fleeting pleasures of sin
12. 1 let us . . lay aside every weight, and sin
12. 4 In your struggle against sin
13.11 animals whose blood is . . sacrifice for s.
Jas 1.15 desire when it has conceived gives birth to sin; . . sin . . brings forth death
2. 9 if you show partiality, you commit sin
4.17 knows . . and fails . . , for him it is sin
5.15 if . . committed sins, he will be forgiven
5.16 confess your sins to one another
5.20 will cover a multitude of sins
1 Pet 2.22 He committed no sin
2.24 He himself bore our sins in his body on the tree,[g] that we might die to sin
3.18 For Christ also died[h] for sins once for all
4. 1 whoever has suffered . . has ceased from s.
4. 8 since love covers a multitude of sins
2 Pet 1. 9 he was cleansed from his old sins
2.14 eyes full of adultery, insatiable for sin
1 Jn 1. 7 blood of . . Son cleanses us from all sin
1. 8 If we say . . no sin, we deceive ourselves
1. 9 If we confess our sins, he . . will forgive our sins and cleanse us
2. 2 he is the expiation for our sins
2.12 your sins are forgiven for his sake
3. 4 Every one who commits sin is guilty of lawlessness; sin is lawlessness
3. 5 You know that he appeared to take away sins, and in him there is no sin
3. 8 He who commits sin is of the devil
3. 9 No one born of God commits sin
4.10 his Son to be the expiation for our sins
5.16 committing what is not a mortal sin
5.16 There is sin which is mortal
5.17 All wrongdoing is sin, but there is sin which is not mortal
Rev 1. 5 loves us and . . freed us from our sins
18. 4 "Come . . , lest you take part in her sins
18. 5 "for her sins are heaped high as heaven

CONTEXTUALLY
Heb 9.22 without . . blood . . no forgiveness of sins

SIN BEFORE
1. *sin beforehand:* προαμαρτάνω PROAMARTANŌ*
2 Cor 12.21 to mourn over many . . who sinned before
13. 2 I warned those who sinned before

SIN, CAUSE OF
1. *stumbling block, trap:* σκάνδαλον SKANDALON
Mt 13.41 "angels . . will gather . . all causes of s.

SIN, CAUSE S. TO
1. *cause to stumble, offend:* σκανδαλίζω SKANDALIZŌ
Mt 5.29 "If your right eye causes you to sin
5.30 "if your right hand causes you to sin
18. 6 "whoever causes one of these . . to sin[z]†
18. 8 "if . . hand . . causes you to sin,[z] cut it off†
18. 9 "if . . eye causes you to sin,[z] pluck it out†
Mk 9.42 "Whoever causes one of these . . to sin[l]†
9.43 "if . . hand causes you to sin,[l] cut it off†
9.45 "if . . foot causes you to sin,[l] cut it off†
9.47 if . . eye causes you to sin,[l] pluck it out†
Lk 17. 2 "than . . cause one of these . . to sin[y]†

SIN OFFERING
IDIOMATICALLY
a. [Rom 8.3 *as a sin offering*† περὶ ἁμαρτίας [HAMARTIA]

SIN, TEMPTATION TO
1. *stumbling block, trap:* σκάνδαλον SKANDALON
Mt 18. 7 "Woe . . for temptations to sin![a]†
Lk 17. 1 "Temptations to sin[x] are sure to come†

SIN, WITHOUT
1. *unerring, sinless:* ἀναμάρτητος ANAMARTĒTOS
Jn 8. 7 "Let him who is without sin . . be . . first[r]‡

SINAI: Σινά 'sī͵nī
Acts 7.30 "an angel . . in the wilderness of Mount S.
7.38 "angel who spoke to him at Mount Sinai
Gal 4.24 two covenants. One is from Mount S.
4.25 Now Hagar is Mount Sinai in Arabia[i]

SINCE
1. *from:* ἀπό (+gen.) APO
Mt **13.**35
Lk **16.**16
Heb **9.**26
2. *because of:* διά (+acc.) DIA
Mt **13.**5, 6
Mk **4.**5, 6
3. *because, since:* διότι DIOTI
1 Pet 1.16 since it is written, "You shall be holy
4. *if, since:* εἰ EI
Acts 18.15 "since it is a matter of . . your own law
1 Th 4.14 since we believe that Jesus died
5. *since, otherwise:* ἐπεί EPEI
Mt 27. 6 "not lawful . . , since they are blood money
Mk 15.42 since it was the day of Preparation
Lk 1.34 "How shall this be, s. I have no husband?
Jn 19.31 Since it was the day of Preparation
1 Cor 5.10 s. . . you would need to go out of . . world
14.12 since you are eager for . . the Spirit
2 Cor 11.18 (since many boast of worldly things
13. 3 since you desire proof that Christ
Heb 2.14 S. . . children share in flesh and blood
4. 6 Since . . it remains for some to enter it
5. 2 since he himself is beset with weakness
5.11 since you have become dull of hearing
6.13 s. . . no one greater by whom to swear
9.17 only at death, since it is not in force
9.26 since the foundation of the world
11.11 since she considered him faithful
6. *since:* ἐπειδή EPEIDĒ
Acts 13.46 "Since you thrust it from you
15.24 "S. we have heard that some persons
1 Cor 1.21 since, in the wisdom of God, the world
7. *since indeed:* ἐπείπερ EPEIPER*
Rom 3.30 since God is one; and he will justify
8. *for:* γάρ GAR
Acts **2.**15; **27.**34; **28.**20
Rom **3.**20, 23; **6.**14; **14.**6
9. *who, which, what:* ὅς HOS [B.1.a.1]
[a]+ἀφ' οὗ/ἧς [b]+ἐν
Lk **1.**[78[b]†‡; **24.**21[a]
Acts **24.**11[a]
Rev **16.**18[a]

10. *as, so:* ὡς HŌS
Heb **13.**3
Jas **5.**[3†
1 Pet **3.**7
11. *anyone who, whoever:* ὅστις HOSTIS [B.3.b.4]
Heb 8. 6 since it is enacted on better promises
12. *that, because:* ὅτι HOTI
Mk **7.**19
Lk **16.**3; **23.**40
Jn **8.**22; **9.**17
1 Tim **6.**2
1 Pet **4.**8
Rev **18.**7, 11
13. *as, just as:* καθώς KATHŌS
Jn 17. 2 "since thou hast given him power
Rom 1.28 since they did not . . acknowledge God
14. *so far as, as:* καθότι KATHOTI
Lk 19. 9 "since he also is a son of Abraham
CONTEXTUALLY
Jn 9.32 "Never s. . . world began has it been heard
Acts 17.25 "since he himself gives to all men life
24. 2 "S. through you we enjoy much peace, and since by your provision
Rom 5. 1 since we are justified by faith
5. 9 S. . . we are now justified by his blood
15.23 s. I no longer have any room for work
15.23 s. I have longed for many years to come
1 Cor 11. 7 since he is the image and glory of God
2 Cor 3.12 S. we have such a hope, we are very bold
4.13 Since we have the same spirit of faith
7. 1 Since we have these promises, beloved
1 Th 2.17 But s. we were bereft of you, brethren
Tit 1.11 since they are upsetting whole families
Heb 4.14 Since then we have a great high priest
6. 6 s. they crucify . . Son of God on their own
7.25 s. he always lives to make intercession
9.15 s. a death has occurred which redeems
10. 1 For s. the law has but a shadow
10.19 s. we have confidence to enter . . sanctuary
10.21 s. we have a great priest over the house
10.34 since you knew that you yourselves
11.40 s. God had foreseen something better
12. 1 Therefore, since we are surrounded
1 Pet 4. 1 S. therefore Christ suffered in . . flesh[i]
2 Pet 1.14 s. I know that the putting off of . . body[c]
3.11 S. all these things are . . to be dissolved
3.14 beloved, since you wait for these

SINCE, EVER
1. *from:* ἀπό (+gen.) APO
[a]ἀφ' ἧς B.3.b.2
Rom **1.**20
2 Pet **3.**4[a]

SINCE HIS AIM IS
1. *in order that:* ἵνα HINA
2 Tim 2. 4 since his aim is to satisfy the one

SINCE INDEED
1. *if indeed, since:* εἴπερ EIPER
2 Th 1. 6 since indeed God deems it just to repay

SINCERE
1. *without hypocrisy:* ἀνυπόκριτος ANYPOKRITOS
1 Tim 1. 5 a good conscience and sincere faith
2 Tim 1. 5 I am reminded of your sincere faith
1 Pet 1.22 for a sincere love of the brethren
2. *righteous, just:* δίκαιος DIKAIOS
Lk 20.20 spies, who pretended to be sincere
3. *pure, sincere:* εἰλικρινής EILIKRINĒS
2 Pet 3. 1 I have aroused your sincere mind

SINCERE DEVOTION
1. *simplicity, liberality:* ἁπλότης HAPLOTĒS
2 Cor 11. 3 a sincere and pure devotion to Christ

SINCERELY
1. *purely:* ἁγνῶς HAGNŌS*
Phil 1.17 the former proclaim Christ . . , not sincerely

SINCERITY
1. *purity:* εἰλικρίνεια EILIKRINEIA*
1 Cor 5. 8 with the unleavened bread of sincerity
2 Cor 1.12 we have behaved . . with . . godly sincerity
2.17 as men of s., as commissioned by God

SINFUL
1. *failure, guilt, sin:* ἁμαρτία (gen.) HAMARTIA
Rom 6. 6 that the s. body might be destroyed
7. 5 our s. passions, aroused by the law
8. 3 his own Son in the likeness of s. flesh
2. *sinful:* ἁμαρτωλός HAMARTŌLOS
Mk 8.38 "this adulterous and sinful generation
Lk 5. 8 "Depart from me, for I am a sinful man
24. 7 "delivered into the hands of sinful men
Rom 7.13 that sin . . might become s. beyond measure

SINFUL, BE
1. *sin, miss the mark:* ἁμαρτάνω HAMARTANŌ
Tit 3.11 such a person is perverted and sinful

SING
1. *sing:* ᾄδω ADŌ*
Eph 5.19 singing and making melody to the Lord
Col 3.16 s. psalms and hymns and spiritual songs[o]
Rev 5. 9 they sang a new song, saying, "Worthy
14. 3 they sing a new song before the throne
15. 3 they sing the song of Moses
2. *say, speak:* λέγω LEGŌ
Rev 4. 8 four living creatures . . never cease to s.
4.10 cast . . crowns before the throne, singing
3. *pluck, sing to a harp:* ψάλλω PSALLŌ
Rom 15. 9 "Therefore I will . . sing to thy name
1 Cor 14.15 I will sing with the spirit and I will sing with the mind also

SING A HYMN
1. *sing, praise:* ὑμνέω HYMNEŌ
Mt 26.30 when they had sung a hymn, they went
Mk 14.26 when they had sung a hymn, they went
Acts 16.25 Paul and Silas were . . singing hymns

SING PRAISE
1. *pluck, sing to a harp:* ψάλλω PSALLŌ
Jas 5.13 Is any cheerful? Let him sing praise

SINGLE
1. *unmarried:* ἄγαμος AGAMOS
1 Cor 7.11 (but if she does, let her remain single
2. *one:* εἷς HEIS
Mt 23.15 "you traverse sea . . to make a s. proselyte
27.14 no answer, not even to a s. charge
1 Cor 10. 8 twenty-three thousand fell in a s. day
12.19 If all were a single organ
Heb 10.12 offered for all time a single sacrifice
10.14 by a single offering he has perfected
12.16 sold his birthright for a single meal
Rev 18. 8 "so shall her plagues come in a s. day
21.21 each of the gates made of a s. pearl
CONTEXTUALLY
1 Cor 7. 8 I say that it is well for them to remain s.

SINGLENESS
1. *simplicity, liberality:* ἁπλότης HAPLOTĒS
Eph 6. 5 in singleness of heart, as to Christ
Col 3.22 in singleness of heart, fearing the Lord

SINK
1. *plunge, sink:* βυθίζω (pass.) BYTHIZŌ
Lk 5. 7 filled both . . , so that they began to s.
2. *bring down, sink:* καταφέρω (pass.) KATAPHERŌ
Acts 20. 9 He sank into a deep sleep as Paul talked
3. *throw into the sea, drown:* καταποντίζω (pass.) KATAPONTIZŌ
Mt 14.30 beginning to s. he cried out, "Lord

SINK, LET S.
1. *lay, put:* τίθημι (mid. imper.) TITHĒMI
Lk 9.44 "Let these words sink into your ears

SINNER
1. *sinful:* ἁμαρτωλός (subst.) HAMARTŌLOS
Mt 9.10 sinners came and sat down with Jesus
9.11 "Why does . . teacher eat with . . sinners?

Mt 9.13 "not to call the righteous, but sinners
11.19 " 'a friend of tax collectors and sinners!
26.45 "betrayed into the hands of sinners
Mk 2.15 many . . sinners were sitting with Jesus
2.16 they saw . . he was eating with sinners
2.16 "Why does he eat[i] with . . sinners?
2.17 "not to call the righteous, but sinners
14.41 "betrayed into the hands of sinners
Lk 5.30 "Why do you eat and drink with . . sinners?
5.32 "to call . . sinners to repentance
6.32 "even sinners love those who love them
6.33 "For even sinners do the same
6.34 "Even sinners lend to sinners, to receive as much again
7.34 " 'friend of tax collectors and sinners!
7.37 a woman of the city, who was a sinner
7.39 "he would have known who . . , for she is a s.
13. 2 "that these Galileans were worse sinners?
15. 1 sinners were all drawing near to hear him
15. 2 "This man receives sinners and eats
15. 7 "more joy in heaven over one sinner
15.10 "joy before the angels . . over one s.
18.13 " 'God, be merciful to me a sinner!
19. 7 "the guest of a man who is a sinner
Jn 9.16 "How can . . a sinner do such signs?
9.24 "we know that this man is a sinner
9.25 "Whether he is a sinner, I do not know
9.31 "God does not listen to sinners
Rom 3. 7 why am I still being condemned as a s.?
5. 8 while we were . . sinners Christ died for us
5.19 as by one . . many were made sinners
Gal 2.15 Jews by birth and not Gentile sinners
2.17 if . . we ourselves were found to be sinners
1 Tim 1. 9 the law is . . for the ungodly and sinners
1.15 Christ Jesus came . . to save sinners
Heb 7.26 unstained, separated from sinners
12. 3 who endured from sinners such hostility
Jas 4. 8 Cleanse your hands, you sinners
5.20 whoever brings back a s. from the error
1 Pet 4.18 "where will the impious and s. appear?
Jude .15 "things . . ungodly sinners have spoken

SIR

1. *man, husband:* ἀνήρ (voc.) ANĒR
Acts 27.10 "Sirs, I perceive that the voyage
2. *lord, master:* κύριος (voc.) KYRIOS
Mt 13.27 " 'Sir, did you not sow good seed?
21.30 "he answered, 'I go, sir,' but did not go
27.63 "Sir, we remember how that impostor
Lk 13. 8 " 'Let it alone, sir, this year also
14.22 " 'Sir, what you commanded has been done
Jn 4.11 "Sir, you have nothing to draw with
4.15 woman said . . "Sir, give me this water
4.19 "Sir, I perceive that you are a prophet
4.49 "Sir, come down before my child dies
5. 7 "Sir, I have no man to put me into
9.36 "who is he, sir, that I may believe?
12.21 "Sir, we wish to see Jesus
20.15 "Sir, if you have carried him away
Rev 7.14 I said to him, "Sir, you know

SISTER

1. *sister:* ἀδελφή ADELPHĒ*
Mt 12.50 "does the will of my Father . . is my . . s.
13.56 "And are not all his sisters with us?
19.29 "who has left houses or . . sisters
Mk [3.32 "your brothers *and . . sisters* are outside‡
3.35 "Whoever does the will of God is my . . s.
6. 3 "are not his sisters here with us?
10.29 "no one who has left house or . . sisters
10.30 "will . . receive . . brothers and sisters
Lk 10.39 she had a sister called Mary
10.40 "do you not care that my s. has left me?
14.26 "If any one . . does not hate his own . . sisters
Jn 11. 1 Bethany, the village of Mary and her s.
11. 3 So the sisters sent to him
11. 5 Jesus loved Martha and her sister
Jn 11.28 she went and called her sister Mary
11.39 Martha, the sister of the dead man
19.25 by the cross of Jesus were . . his mother's s.
Acts 23.16 son of Paul's s. heard of their ambush
Rom 16. 1 I commend . . our s. Phoebe, a deaconess
16.15 Greet Philologus, . . Nereus and his s.
1 Cor 7.15 the brother or sister is not bound
1 Tim 5. 2 ⟨treat⟩ younger women like sisters
Phm . 2 ⟨To⟩ Apphia our sister and Archippus
Jas 2.15 If a brother or sister is ill-clad
2 Jn .13 The children of your elect sister

SIT

1. *recline* (at meals): ἀναπίπτω ANAPIPTŌ
Lk 14.10 "go and sit in the lowest place
2. *sit upon:* ἐπικαθίζω EPIKATHIZŌ*
Mt 21. 7 put . . garments on them, and he sat thereon
3. *sit down:* κάθημαι KATHĒMAI
Mt 4.16 "who sat in darkness have seen a great light, and for those who sat in the region
9. 9 saw . . Matthew sitting at the tax office
11.16 "like children sitting in the market places
13. 1 Jesus went out . . and sat beside the sea
13. 2 he got into a boat and sat there
19.28 "who . . followed me will . . sit on . . thrones
20.30 two blind men sitting by the roadside
22.44 " 'Lord said to my Lord, Sit at my right
23.22 "throne of God and . . him who sits upon it
24. 3 As he sat on the Mount of Olives
26.58 going inside he sat with the guards
26.69 Peter was sitting outside in . . courtyard
27.19 he was sitting on the judgment seat
27.61 there, sitting opposite the sepulchre
28. 2 angel . . rolled back the stone, and sat
Mk 2. 6 some of the scribes were sitting there
2.14 he saw Levi . . sitting at the tax office
3.32 a crowd was sitting about him
3.34 looking around on those who sat about
4. 1 he got into a boat and sat in it
5.15 they . . saw the demoniac sitting there
10.46 Bartimaeus . . was sitting by the roadside
12.36 " 'Lord said to my Lord, Sit at my right
13. 3 as he sat on the Mount of Olives
16. 5 they saw a young man sitting on . . right
Lk 1.79 "light to those who sit in darkness
5.27 he . . saw . . Levi, sitting at the tax office
7.32 "like children sitting in the market place
8.35 found the man . . sitting at . . feet of J.
10.13 "repented . . , sitting in sackcloth
18.35 blind man was sitting by the roadside
20.42 " 'Lord said to my Lord, Sit at my right
22.30 "that you may . . sit on thrones judging
22.55 kindled a fire . . and . . Peter sat among
22.56 seeing him as he sat in the light
Jn 9. 8 "the man who used to sit and beg
12.15 "your king is coming, sitting on . . colt!
Acts 2. 2 filled . . house where they were sitting
2.34 " 'Lord said to my Lord, Sit at my right
3.10 recognized him as . . one who sat for alms
14. 8 Now at Lystra there was a man sitting
23. 3 "sitting to judge me according to the law
Heb 1.13 "Sit at my right . . till I make thy enemies
Jas 2. 3 "Stand there," or, "Sit at my feet
Rev 4. 3 he who sat there appeared like jasper
5.13 "To him who sits upon the throne
7.10 "our God who sits upon the throne
7.15 "who sits upon the throne will shelter
11.16 twenty-four elders who sit on . . thrones
14.15 calling . . to him who sat upon the cloud
14.16 who sat upon the cloud swung his sickle
17. 3 I saw a woman sitting on a . . beast
18. 7 " 'A queen I sit, I am no widow
19.11 He who sat upon it is called Faithful
19.19 war against him who sits upon the horse
19.21 sword of him who sits upon the horse
20.11 white throne and him who sat upon it
21. 5 he who sat upon the throne said

4. *sit down:* καθέζομαι KATHEZOMAI
Mt 26.55 "Day after day I sat in the temple
Lk 2.46 in the temple, sitting among the teachers
Jn 11.20 met him, while Mary sat in the house
20.12 she saw two angels in white, sitting
Acts 6.15 all who sat in the council saw . . his face
20. 9 Eutychus was sitting in the window
5. *sit down, seat:* καθίζω KATHIZŌ
Mt 19.28 "Son of man shall sit on his . . throne
20.21 "that these two sons of mine may sit
20.23 "to sit at my right hand and at my left
23. 2 "the Pharisees sit on Moses' seat
25.31 "then he will sit on his glorious throne
26.36 "Sit here, while I go yonder and pray
Mk 10.37 "Grant us to sit, one at your right hand
10.40 "to sit at my right hand or at my left
11. 2 "colt tied, on which no one has ever sat
11. 7 they brought the colt . . and he sat upon it
14.32 "Sit here, while I pray
Lk 19.30 "colt tied, on which no one has ever yet sat
Jn 12.14 Jesus found a young ass and sat upon it
Acts 8.31 he invited Philip to . . sit with him
Rev 3.21 " 'I will grant him to sit with me
6. *sit down beside:* παρακαθέζομαι PARAKATHEZOMAI*
Lk 10.39 Mary, who sat at the Lord's feet

SIT AT TABLE
SIT AT TABLE, HAVE S.
SIT DOWN AT TABLE
1. *recline* (at table): ἀνάκειμαι ANAKEIMAI
Mt 9.10 as he sat at table[v] in the house†
26. 7 poured it on his head, as he sat at table
26.20 he sat at table with the twelve
Mk 16.14 he appeared . . as they sat at table[k]‡
Lk 22.27 "which is . . greater, one who sits at table . .? Is it not the one who sits at table?
2. *cause to recline:* ἀνακλίνω ANAKLINŌ
[a]pass.
Mt 8.11 [a]"many will . . sit at table with Abraham
Lk 12.37 "he will . . have them sit at table
13.29 [a]"will . . sit at table in the kingdom
3. *recline with* (at table): ἀναπίπτω ANAPIPTŌ
Lk 11.37 so he went in and sat at table
17. 7 " 'Come at once and sit down at table
22.14 when the hour came, he sat at table
4. *lie down:* κατάκειμαι KATAKEIMAI
Mk 2.15 as he sat at table in his house
14. 3 as he sat at table, a woman came
Lk 5.29 tax collectors . . sitting at table[r]†

SIT AT TABLE WITH
1. *recline* (at meals): συνανάκειμαι SYNANAKEIMAI
Lk 14.10 "presence of all who s. at table with you
14.15 one of those who sat at table with him

SIT BY
1. *sit down:* κάθημαι KATHĒMAI
Lk 5.17 teachers of the law ⟨were⟩ sitting by
1 Cor 14.30 If a revelation . . to another sitting by

SIT DOWN (*See also* SIT AT TABLE)
1. *cause to recline:* ἀνακλίνω (pass.) ANAKLINŌ
Mt 14.19 he ordered the crowds to sit down
Mk 6.39 he commanded them all to sit down
2. *recline* (at meals): ἀναπίπτω ANAPIPTŌ
Mt 15.35 commanding the crowd to sit down
Mk 6.40 So they sat down in groups, by hundreds
8. 6 he commanded the crowd to sit down
Jn 6.10 Jesus said, "Make the people sit down" . . so the men sat down, . . five thousand
3. *cause to lie down:* κατακλίνω KATAKLINŌ
Lk 14. 8 "do not sit down in a place of honor
4. *sit down:* κάθημαι KATHĒMAI
Mt 15.29 went up on the mountain, and sat down
27.36 they sat down and kept watch over him
Jn 6. 3 went up on the mountain, and . . sat down
5. *sit down:* καθέζομαι KATHEZOMAI
Jn 4. 6 Jesus . . sat down beside the well
6. *sit down, seat:* καθίζω KATHIZŌ
Mt 5. 1 when he sat down his disciples came
Mt 13.48 "men drew it ashore and sat down
Mk 9.35 he sat down and called the twelve
12.41 he sat down opposite the treasury
16.19 sat down at the right hand of God[k]‡
Lk 4.20 closed the book, . . and sat down
5. 3 he sat down and taught the people
14.28 "which of you . . does not first sit down?
14.31 "king . . will . . s. down . . and take counsel
16. 6 " 'sit down quickly and write fifty
Jn 8. 2 he sat down and taught them[r]‡
19.13 Pilate . . brought Jesus out and sat down
Acts 13.14 went into the synagogue and sat down
16.13 we sat down and spoke to the women
1 Cor 10. 7 "The people sat down to eat and drink
Heb 1. 3 he sat down at the right hand
10.12 he sat down at the right hand of God
Rev 3.21 " 'I . . sat down with my Father

SIT DOWN, MAKE S.
1. *cause to lie down:* κατακλίνω KATAKLINŌ
Lk 9.14 "Make them sit down in companies
9.15 they . . made them all sit down

SIT DOWN TOGETHER
1. *cause to sit down with:* συγκαθίζω SYGKATHIZŌ
Lk 22.55 sat down together, Peter . . among them

SIT DOWN WITH
1. *recline with* (at table): συνανάκειμαι SYNANAKEIMAI
Mt 9.10 sinners came and sat down with Jesus

SIT, MAKE S.
1. *sit down, seat:* καθίζω KATHIZŌ
Eph 1.20 when he . . made him s. at his right hand

SIT UP
1. *sit up:* ἀνακαθίζω ANAKATHIZŌ*
Lk 7.15 dead man sat up, and began to speak
Acts 9.40 when she saw Peter she sat up

SIT WITH
1. *sit together:* συγκάθημαι SYGKATHĒMAI*
Mk 14.54 Peter . . was sitting with the guards
Acts 26.30 king rose, . . and those . . sitting with them
2. *cause to sit down with:* συγκαθίζω SYGKATHIZŌ
Eph 2. 6 raised us up . . and made us sit with him
3. *recline with* (at table): συνανάκειμαι SYNANAKEIMAI
Mk 2.15 sinners were sitting with Jesus

SIX
1. *six:* ἕξ HEX
Mt 17. 1 after s. days Jesus took with him Peter
Mk 9. 2 after s. days Jesus took with him Peter
Lk 4.25 "heaven was shut . . three years . . s. months
13.14 "s. days on which work ought to be done
Jn 2. 6 six stone jars were standing there
12. 1 Six days before . . Passover, Jesus came
Acts 11.12 "These six brethren . . accompanied me
18.11 he stayed a year and six months
Jas 5.17 for three years and six months it did not
Rev 4. 8 creatures, each of them with six wings

SIX HUNDRED
1. *six hundred:* ἑξακόσιοι HEXAKOSIOI*
Rev 13.18 its number is six hundred and sixty-six[g]
14.20 for one thousand six hundred stadia[i]

SIXTEEN
1. *ten (and) six:* δέκα ἕξ HEX; DEKA [A.3.c]
Rev [13.18 its number is six hundred and *sixteen*‡

SIXTH
1. *sixth:* ἕκτος HEKTOS*
Mt 20. 5 "Going out again about the sixth hour
27.45 from the sixth hour there was darkness
Mk 15.33 when the s. hour had come, . . darkness
Lk 1.26 In the sixth month the angel Gabriel
1.36 "this is the sixth month with her
23.44 It was now about the sixth hour
Jn 4. 6 It was about the sixth hour
19.14 it was about the sixth hour
Acts 10. 9 Peter went up . . to pray, about the s. hour
Rev 6.12 When he opened the sixth seal
9.13 Then the sixth angel blew his trumpet

Rev 9.14 the sixth angel who had the trumpet
16.12 The sixth angel poured his bowl
21.20 the fifth onyx, the sixth carnelian

SIXTY
1. *sixty:* ἑξήκοντα HEXĒKONTA
Mt 13. 8 "some a hundredfold, some sixty
13.23 "in one case a hundredfold, in another s.
Lk [24.13 about *a hundred and sixty stadia*‡
1 Tim 5. 9 if she is not less than sixty years of age
Rev 11. 3 "one thousand two hundred and s. days
12. 6 one thousand two hundred and s. days

SIXTYFOLD
1. *at the rate of sixty:* ἐν ἑξήκοντα HEXĒKONTA [B.1.a.1]
Mk 4. 8 "grain, . . yielding . . s. and a hundredfold
4.20 "bear fruit, thirtyfold and sixtyfold

SIXTY-SIX
1. *sixty-six:* ἑξήκοντα ἕξ HEXĒKONTA; HEX [A.3.c]
Rev 13.18 its number is six hundred and sixty-six[g]‡

SKILLED
1. *wise, learned:* σοφός SOPHOS
1 Cor 3.10 like a s. . . builder I laid a foundation

SKIN
1. *wineskin:* ἀσκός ASKOS
Mt 9.17 "the skins burst, and the wine is spilled, and the skins are destroyed
Mk 2.22 "if he does, the wine will burst the skins, and the wine is lost, and so are the skins; but new wine is for fresh skins[j]‡
Lk 5.37 "will burst the skins and it will be spilled, and the skins will be destroyed
2. *skin:* δέρμα DERMA*
Heb 11.37 they went about in skins of . . goats

SKIN OF SHEEP
1. *sheepskin:* μηλωτή MĒLŌTĒ*
Heb 11.37 they went about in skins of sheep

SKULL
1. *upper part of head, skull:* κρανίον KRANION*
Mt 27.33 Golgotha (which means the place of a s.
Mk 15.22 Golgotha (which means the place of a s.
Lk 23.33 came to the place which is called The S.
Jn 19.17 the place called the place of a skull

SKY
1. *heaven, sky:* οὐρανός OURANOS
Mt 16. 2 " 'fair weather; for the sky is red‡
16. 3 " 'stormy . . , for the s. is red and threatening.' You know how to interpret . . the sky‡
Lk 12.56 "You know how to interpret the . . sky
17.24 "lights up the s. from one side to . . other
Rev 6.13 the stars of the sky fell to the earth
6.14 sky vanished like a scroll . . rolled up
11. 6 They have power to shut the sky
20.11 from his presence . . sky fled away

SKY, SACRED STONE THAT FELL FROM THE
1. *fallen from heaven:* διοπετής (subst. neut.) DIOPETĒS* [D.1]
Acts 19.35 "the sacred stone that fell from the sky[s]

SLAIN BEAST
1. *victim, sacrifice:* σφάγιον SPHAGION*
Acts 7.42 " 'Did you offer to me slain beasts?

SLANDER
1. *slander, profane speech:* βλασφημία BLASPHĒMIA
[a]indef. pl.
Mt 15.19 [a]"out of the heart come evil thoughts, . . s.
Mk 7.22 "envy, slander, pride, foolishness
Eph 4.31 Let all . . slander be put away from you
Col 3. 8 put them all away: . . malice, slander
1 Tim 6. 4 dissension, slander, base suspicions
Rev 2. 9 " 'I know . . the slander of those who say
2. *speak ill of:* δυσφημέω DYSPHĒMEŌ*
1 Cor 4.13 when slandered, we try to conciliate
3. *evil report, slander:* καταλαλία KATALALIA*
2 Cor 12.20 there may be quarreling, . . slander
1 Pet 2. 1 So put away all malice and . . all slander

SLANDERER
1. *slanderous:* διάβολος (subst.) DIABOLOS
1 Tim [3. 6 fall into the condemnation of the *s.*†
[3. 7 fall into . . the snare of the *slanderer*†
3.11 women likewise must be . . no slanderers
2 Tim 3. 3 inhuman, implacable, slanderers
Tit 2. 3 not to be slanderers or slaves to drink
2. *slanderer* (subst.): κατάλαλος KATALALOS*
Rom 1.30 slanderers, haters of God, insolent

SLANDEROUSLY
1. *blaspheme, slander:* βλασφημέω BLASPHĒMEŌ [B.2.c]
Rom 3. 8 as some people slanderously charge us

SLAP
1. *strike with a stick, slap:* ῥαπίζω RHAPIZŌ
Mt 26.67 and some slapped him

SLAUGHTER
1. *cutting:* κοπή KOPĒ*
Heb 7. 1 met Abraham returning from the s.
2. *slaughter:* σφαγή SPHAGĒ
Acts 8.32 "As a sheep led to the slaughter
Jas 5. 5 fattened your hearts in a day of s.

SLAUGHTERED, TO BE
1. *slaughter:* σφαγή (gen.) SPHAGĒ
Rom 8.36 "we are regarded as sheep to be s.

SLAVE
1. *slave:* δοῦλος DOULOS II
Mt 8. 9 "I say . . to my s., 'Do this,' and he does
[10.24 "nor a *slave* above his master†
[10.25 "for . . the *slave* ⟨to be⟩ like his master†
[13.27 "the *slaves* of the householder came†
[13.28 "The *slaves* said . . 'do you want us to go?†
20.27 "whoever would be first . . must be . . slave
26.51 struck the slave of the high priest
Mk 10.44 "whoever would be first . . must be s. of all
14.47 struck the slave of the high priest
Lk 7. 2 centurion had a s. who was dear[x] to him
7. 3 asking him to come and heal his slave
7. 8 "I say . . to my s., 'Do this,' and he does
7.10 they found the slave well
22.50 struck the slave of the high priest
Jn 8.34 "every one who commits sin is a s. to sin
8.35 "The slave does not continue in the house
[13.16 "a *slave* is not greater than his master†
[15.15 "No longer do I call you *slaves*, for the *slave* does not know†
[15.20 " 'A *slave* is not greater than his master†
18.10 Peter . . struck the high priest's slave . . The slave's name was Malchus
[18.18 the *slaves* and officers had . . a . . fire†
[18.26 One of the *slaves* of the high priest†
Acts [4.29 "grant to thy *slaves* to speak thy word†
Rom [1. 1 Paul, a *slave* of Jesus Christ†
6.16 if you yield . . to any . . as obedient slaves, you are slaves of the one whom you obey
6.17 you who were once slaves of sin
6.20 When you were slaves of sin
1 Cor 7.21 Were you a slave when called?
7.22 he who was called in the Lord as a s.
7.22 he who was free when called is a slave
7.23 do not become slaves of men
12.13 Jews or Greeks, slaves or free
2 Cor [4. 5 with ourselves as your *slaves*†
Gal [1.10 I should not be a *slave* of Christ†
3.28 there is neither slave nor free
4. 1 heir, as . . a child, is no better than a s.
4. 7 through God you are no longer a slave
Eph 6. 5 Slaves, be obedient to . . earthly masters
[6. 6 as *slaves* of Christ, doing the will of God†
6. 8 same . . , whether he is a slave or free
Phil [1. 1 Paul and Timothy, *slaves* of Christ Jesus†
[2. 7 emptied himself, taking the form of a *slave*†
Col 3.11 cannot be Greek and Jew, . . s., free man
3.22 Slaves, obey . . your earthly masters
4. 1 Masters, treat your slaves justly
[4.12 a *slave* of Christ Jesus, greets you†

Tit [1. 1 Paul, a *slave* of God and an apostle†
2. 9 Bid slaves to be submissive
Phm .16 no longer as a slave but more than a slave, as a beloved brother
2 Pet 2.19 they themselves are slaves of corruption
Rev 6.15 every one, s. and free, hid in the caves
13.16 both free and slave, to be marked
19.18 "to eat . . the flesh of all . . , both free and s.

2. *female slave:* παιδίσκη PAIDISKĒ
Gal 4.22 one by a slave and one by a free woman
4.23 son of . . s. was born according to . . flesh
4.30 "Cast out the slave and her son; for the son of the slave shall not inherit
4.31 brethren, we are not children of the s.

3. *body:* σῶμα SŌMA
Rev 18.13 chariots, and slaves, that is, human souls

SLAVE, BE A

1. *serve, be a slave:* δουλεύω DOULEUŌ
Gal 4. 9 whose slaves you want to be once more
Tit 3. 3 led astray, slaves to various passions

SLAVE, BECOME A

1. *enslave:* δουλόω (pass.) DOULOŌ
Rom 6.18 have become slaves of righteousness
6.22 you . . have become slaves of God
Gal 4. 3 we were slaves to the elemental spirits
Tit 2. 3 not to be slanderers or slaves to drink

SLAVE GIRL

1. *female slave:* παιδίσκη PAIDISKĒ
Acts 16.16 we were met by a slave girl

SLAVE, MAKE A

1. *enslave:* δουλόω DOULOŌ
1 Cor 9.19 I have made myself a slave to all

SLAVERY

1. *bondage, slavery:* δουλεία DOULEIA
Rom 8.15 you did not receive the spirit of slavery
Gal 4.24 Mount Sinai, bearing children for s.
5. 1 do not submit again to a yoke of slavery

2. *slave:* δοῦλος DOULOS II [B.3.b.4]
1 Tim 6. 1 all . . under the yoke of slavery

SLAVERY, BE IN

1. *serve, be a slave:* δουλεύω DOULEUŌ
Gal 4.25 for she is in slavery with her children

SLAVES OF, MAKE

1. *enslave:* καταδουλόω KATADOULOŌ
2 Cor 11.20 you bear it if a man makes slaves of you

SLAY

1. *take up, kill:* ἀναιρέω ANAIREŌ
Acts 5.36 "he was slain and all . . were dispersed
2 Th 2. 8 will slay him with . . breath of his mouth

2. *kill:* ἀποκτείνω APOKTEINŌ
Rev 13.10 if any one slays with the sword, with the sword must he be slain
13.15 those who . . worship the image . . to be slain
19.21 the rest were slain by the sword

3. *slaughter, strike down:* κατασφάζω KATASPHAZŌ*
Lk 19.27 " 'bring them here and s. them before me

4. *slaughter, kill:* σφάζω SPHAZŌ
Rev 5. 6 a Lamb . . , as though it had been slain
5. 9 "Worthy art thou . . , for thou wast slain
5.12 "Worthy is the Lamb who was slain
6. 4 so that men should slay one another
6. 9 souls of those who had been slain
13. 8 book of life of the Lamb that was slain
18.24 "of all who have been slain on earth

SLEEP

1. *sleep:* ὕπνος HYPNOS*
Mt 1.24 When Joseph woke from sleep, he did
Lk 9.32 those . . with him were heavy with sleep
Jn 11.13 thought . . he meant taking rest in sleep
Acts 20. 9 He sank into a deep sleep as Paul talked . . ; and being overcome by sleep, he fell down
Rom 13.11 time now for you to wake from sleep

2. *sleep, be asleep:* καθεύδω KATHEUDŌ
Mt 9.24 "the girl is not dead but sleeping
13.25 "while men were sleeping, . . enemy came
25. 5 "they all slumbered and slept
26.40 he came . . and found them sleeping
26.43 again he came and found them sleeping
26.45 "Are you still sleeping and taking . . rest?
Mk 4.27 "⟨as if a man⟩ should sleep and rise
5.39 "The child is not dead but sleeping
14.37 he came and found them sleeping
14.40 again he came and found them sleeping
14.41 "Are you still sleeping and taking . . rest?
Lk 8.52 "for she is not dead but sleeping
22.46 "Why do you sleep? Rise and pray
1 Th 5. 6 let us not sleep, as others do
5. 7 For those who sleep sleep at night, and those who get drunk are drunk at night
5.10 so that whether we wake or sleep

3. *put to sleep:* κοιμάω (pass.) KOIMAŌ
Lk 22.46 "Why do you sleep? Rise and pray
Acts 12. 6 Peter was sleeping between two soldiers
1 Cor 15.51 a mystery. We shall not all sleep

SLEEP, AWAKE OUT OF

1. *awaken from sleep:* ἐξυπνίζω EXYPNIZŌ*
Jn 11.11 "but I go to awake him out of sleep

SLEEPER

1. *sleep, be asleep:* καθεύδω (subst. part.) KATHEUDŌ
Eph 5.14 "Awake, O sleeper, . . arise from the dead

SLEEPLESS NIGHT, A

1. *sleeplessness, watching:* ἀγρυπνία AGRYPNIA
2 Cor 11.27 through many a sleepless night

SLIGHT

1. *light in weight:* ἐλαφρός ELAPHROS
2 Cor 4.17 For this slight momentary affliction

SLIP IN

1. *come in:* παρεισέρχομαι PAREISERCHOMAI
Gal 2. 4 who slipped in to spy out our freedom

SLOTHFUL

1. *idle, troublesome:* ὀκνηρός OKNĒROS
Mt 25.26 " 'You wicked and slothful servant!

SLOW

1. *slow:* βραδύς BRADYS*
Lk 24.25 "O foolish men, and slow of heart!
Jas 1.19 Let every man be quick to hear, slow to speak, slow to anger

SLOW ABOUT S., BE

1. *delay, loiter:* βραδύνω BRADYNŌ
2 Pet 3. 9 The Lord is not s. about his promise

SLOWLY, SAIL

1. *sail slowly:* βραδυπλοέω BRADYPLOEŌ*
Acts 27. 7 We sailed slowly for a number of days

SLOWNESS

1. *slowness, sluggishness:* βραδύτης BRADYTĒS*
2 Pet 3. 9 not slow . . as some count slowness

SLUGGISH

1. *dull, slothful:* νωθρός NŌTHROS
Heb 6.12 so that you may not be sluggish

SLUMBER

1. *doze, be half asleep:* νυστάζω NYSTAZŌ
Mt 25. 5 "they all slumbered and slept

SMALL (*See also* FISH, SMALL; ISLAND, SMALL)

1. *how great, how small:* ἡλίκος HĒLIKOS
Jas 3. 5 a forest is set ablaze by a small fire

2. *little, small:* μικρός MIKROS
Lk 19. 3 could not . . because he was s. of stature
Acts 26.22 "testifying both to small and great
Rev 11.18 "who fear thy name, both small and great
13.16 it causes all, both small and great
19. 5 "you who fear him, small and great
19.18 "to eat . . flesh of . . both small and great
20.12 And I saw the dead, great and small

3. *few, little:* ὀλίγος OLIGOS
Acts 12.18 there was no s. stir among the soldiers
15. 2 Paul and Barnabas had no s. dissension
27.20 no small tempest lay on us

SMALL A THING AS THAT, AS
1. *smallest, least:* ἐλάχιστος (subst. neut.) ELACHISTOS
Lk 12.26 "not able to do as small a thing as that

SMALL, VERY
1. *smallest, least:* ἐλάχιστος ELACHISTOS
1 Cor 4. 3 But with me it is a very small thing
Jas 3. 4 they are guided by a very small rudder

SMALLEST
1. *little, small:* μικρός (comp.) MIKROS
Mt 13.32 "it is the smallest of all seeds
Mk 4.31 "when sown . . is the s. of all the seeds

SMELL, SENSE OF
1. *sense of smell:* ὄσφρησις OSPHRĒSIS*
1 Cor 12.17 where would be the sense of smell?

SMITE
1. *strike, beat:* πατάσσω PATASSŌ
Acts 12.23 an angel of the Lord smote him
Rev 11. 6 to smite the earth with every plague
19.15 sword with which to s. the nations

SMOKE
1. *smoke:* καπνός KAPNOS*
Acts 2.19 " 'signs on the earth . . , blood . . and . . smoke
Rev 8. 4 the smoke of the incense rose
9. 2 from the shaft rose smoke like the smoke of a great furnace, and the sun and the air were darkened with the smoke
9. 3 Then from the smoke came locusts
9.17 fire and smoke and sulphur issued
9.18 killed, by the fire and s. and sulphur
14.11 "smoke of their torment goes up for ever
15. 8 temple was filled with s. from the glory
18. 9 when they see the smoke of her burning
18.18 as they saw the smoke of her burning
19. 3 "The smoke from her goes up for ever

SMOLDER
1. *smoke:* τύφω (pass.) TYPHŌ*
Mt 12.20 "he will not . . quench a smoldering wick

SMOOTH
1. *plain, soft:* λεῖος LEIOS*
Lk 3. 5 "the rough ways shall be made smooth

SMYRNA: Σμύρνα 'smərnə II,E-3
Rev 1.11 "Write what you see . . and send it . . to S.
2. 8 "to the angel of the church in Smyrna

SNARE
1. *snare, trap:* παγίς PAGIS*
Lk 21.34(35) "lest . . day . . come upon you . . like a s.
Rom 11. 9 "Let their table become a s. and a trap
1 Tim 3. 7 he may fall into . . the snare of the devil[f]
6. 9 fall into temptation, into a snare
2 Tim 2.26 they may escape from the s. of the devil

SNATCH
SNATCH AWAY
1. *seize, snatch up:* ἁρπάζω HARPAZŌ
Mt 13.19 "evil one . . snatches away what is sown
Jn 10.12 "the wolf snatches them and scatters
10.28 "no one shall snatch them out of my hand
10.29 "no one is able to snatch them
Jude .23 some, by snatching them out of the fire

SNOW
1. *snow:* χιών CHIŌN*
Mt 28. 3 his raiment white as snow
Rev 1.14 his head and . . hair were . . white as snow

SO
1. *but:* ἀλλά ALLA
2 Cor **2.13**
2. *then:* ἄρα ARA II
[a]ἄρα οὖν
Lk 11.48 "So you are witnesses and consent
Rom 7.21 So I find it to be a law
9.16 [a]So it depends not upon man's will
10.17 So faith comes from what is heard
14.12 [a]So each of us shall give account
2 Cor 7.12 So although I wrote to you
Gal 3. 7 So you see that it is men of faith
3. *so! indeed!:* δή DĒ
1 Cor 6.20 So glorify God in your body
4. *therefore:* διό DIO
[a]and so
Acts 10.29 "So when I was sent for, I came
24.26 So he sent for him often
27.25 "So take heart, men, for I have faith
2 Cor 2. 8 So I beg you to reaffirm your love
4.13 [a]who wrote, "I believed, and so I spoke
4.13 [a]we too believe, and so we speak
4.16 So we do not lose heart
5. 9 So whether we are at home or away
Gal 4.31 So, brethren, we are not children
Eph 3.13 So I ask you not to[e] lose heart
Heb 13.12 So Jesus also suffered outside the gate
5. *likewise:* ὁμοίως HOMOIŌS
Mt 22.26 "So too the second and third
26.35 And so said all the disciples
27.41 So also the chief priests, with . . scribes
Mk 15.31 So also the chief priests mocked him
Lk 5.10 so also were James and John
5.33 "so do the disciples of the Pharisees
6.31 "as you wish . . men would . . , do so to them
Jn 6.11 so also the fish, as much as they wanted
21.13 took the bread . . , and so with the fish
Rev 2.15 " 'So you also have some who hold
6. *in like manner:* ὡσαύτως HŌSAUTŌS
Mt 25.17 So also, he who had the two talents
1 Tim 5.25 So also good deeds are conspicuous
7. *so that, therefore:* ὥστε HŌSTE
Mt 12.12 So it is lawful to do good on the sabbath
19. 6 "So they are no longer two but one flesh
Mk 2.28 "so the Son of man is lord . . of the sabbath
10. 8 "So they are no longer two but one flesh
Rom 7.12 So the law is holy
1 Cor 3. 7 So neither he who plants
3.21 So let no one boast of men
14.39 So, my brethren, . . desire to prophesy
2 Cor 2. 7 so you should rather turn to forgive
4.12 So death is at work in us, but life in you
Gal 4. 7 So . . you are no longer a slave but a son
8. *this:* οὗτος HOUTOS [A.2.c]
[a]ἐν τούτῳ [b]διὰ τοῦτο [B.1.a.1]
Jn **7.9**
Acts **24.16**[a]
Rom **12.20**
Col **1.9**[b]
1 Tim **4.16**
3 Jn **.10**[b]
Rev **18.8**[b]
9. *thus, so:* οὕτως HOUTŌS
[a]οὕτως ἔχειν
[b]+ὡς, ὥσπερ, καθώς
[c]οὕτως οὖν
[d]οὕτως . . οὕτως
Mt 2. 5 "for so it is written by the prophet
5.12 "for so men persecuted the prophets
5.16 "Let your light so shine before men
5.19 "Whoever . . teaches men so, shall be called
6.30 "if God so clothes the grass of the field
7.12 "So whatever you wish that men would
7.17 "So, every sound tree bears good fruit
12.40 [b]"so will the Son of man be three days
12.45 "So shall it be . . with this evil generation
13.40 [b]"so will it be at the close of the age
13.49 "So it will be at the close of the age
17.12 "So also the Son of man will suffer
18.14 "So it is not the will of my[d] Father
18.35 "So also my heavenly Father will do
19. 8 "but from the beginning it was not so
19.12 "eunuchs who have been so from birth
20.16 "So the last will be first, and the first last
20.26 "It shall not be so among you
23.28 "So you also outwardly appear righteous
24.27 [b]"so will be the coming of the Son of man
24.33 "So also, when you see all these things
24.37 [b]"so will be the coming of the Son of man

Mt 24.39 [b]"so will be the coming of the Son of man
24.46 "whom his master . . will find so doing
26.40 "So, could you not watch[h] with me?
26.54 "But how then . . , that it must be so?
Mk 10.43 "But it shall not be so among you
13.29 "So also, when you see these things
14.59 not even so did their testimony agree
Lk 2.48 "Son, why have you treated us so?
9.15 they did so, and made them all sit
11.30 [b]"as Jonah . . , so will the Son of man be
12.21 "So is he who lays up . . for himself
12.28 "But if God so clothes the grass
12.38 "If he comes . . and finds them so, blessed!
12.43 "whom his master . . will find so doing
12.54 " 'A shower is coming'; and so it happens
14.33 "So therefore, whoever of you does not
17.10 "So you also, when you have done all
17.24 [b]"so will the Son of man be in his day[a]
17.26 [b]"so will it be in . . days of the Son of man
21.31 "So also, when you see these things
22.26 "But not so with you
Jn 3. 8 "so it is with every one . . born of . . Spirit
3.14 [b]"so must the Son of man be lifted up
3.16 For God so loved the world
5.21 [b]"as . . Father . . gives . . life, so . . the Son
5.26 [b]"as . . Father has life . . , so he . . granted
Acts 7. 1 [a]And the high priest said, "Is this so?
7. 8 "so Abraham became the father of Isaac
8.32 [b]"As a sheep . . , so he opens not his mouth
12. 8 "put on your sandals." And he did so
12.15 [a]But she insisted that it was so
13.47 "For so the Lord has commanded us
14. 1 so spoke that a great company believed
17.11 [a]examining . . to see if these . . were so
17.33 So Paul went out from among them
19.20 So the word of the Lord . . prevailed
20.11 conversed . . until daybreak, and so departed
20.13 for so he had arranged
20.35 "by so toiling one must help the weak
21.11 " 'So shall the Jews at Jerusalem bind
23.11 [b]"so you must bear witness also at Rome
24. 9 [a]Jews also . . affirming that . . this was so
27.17 lowered the gear, and so were driven
27.44 And so it was that all escaped to land
28.14 And so we came to Rome
Rom 1.15 so I am eager to preach the gospel
4.18 "So shall your descendants be
5.12 [b]so death spread to all men
5.18 [b]so one man's act . . leads to acquittal
5.19 [b]so by one man's obedience many
6.11 So you . . must consider yourselves dead
6.19 [b]so . . yield your members to righteousness
11. 5 [c]So too at the present time . . a remnant
11.26 so all Israel will be saved
11.31 [b]so they have now been disobedient
12. 5 so we, though many, are one body
1 Cor 2.11 So also no one comprehends . . God
9.24 So run that you may obtain it
11.12 [b](so man is now born of woman
11.28 so eat of the bread and drink of the cup
12.12 as the body is one . . , so it is with Christ
14. 9 So with yourselves; if you . . utter
14.12 So with yourselves; since you are eager
14.25 so, falling on his face, he will worship God
15.11 [d]Whether then it was I or they, so we preach and so you believed
15.22 [b]as in Adam all die, so also in Christ
15.42 So is it with the resurrection
16. 1 [b]as I directed the churches . . , so you also
2 Cor 1. 5 [b]so through Christ we share abundantly
7.14 [b]so our boasting . . has proved true
10. 7 [b]as he is Christ's, so are we
Gal 1. 6 that you are so quickly deserting him
3. 3 Are you so foolish?
4. 3 So with us; when we were children
4.29 [b]But as at that time . . , so it is now
6. 2 Bear . . another's burdens, and so fulfil
Eph 4.20 You did not so learn Christ!
5.24 [b]so let wives . . be subject in everything
Phil 3.17 [b]who so live as you have an example in us
Col 3.13 [b]as the Lord . . , so you also must forgive
1 Th 2. 4 [b]so we speak, not to please men
2. 8 So, being affectionately desirous of you
4.17 so we shall always be with the Lord
2 Tim 3. 8 so these men also oppose the truth
Heb 5. 5 So also Christ did not exalt himself
9.28 so Christ, having been offered once
10.33 being partners with those so treated
12.21 so terrifying was the sight that Moses
Jas 1.11 So will the rich man fade away
2.12 [db]So speak and so act as those who are to be judged under the law of liberty
2.17 So faith by itself . . is dead
2.26 so faith apart from works is dead
3. 5 So the tongue is a little member
3.10 My brethren, this ought not to be so
1 Pet 3. 5 So once the holy women who hoped
2 Pet 1.11 so there will be richly provided for you
1 Jn 4.11 if God so loved us, we also ought to love
Rev 2.15 So you also have some who hold
3.16 So, because you are lukewarm
18.21 "So shall Babylon the great city be thrown

10. *just as:* καθάπερ KATHAPER
Rom 4. 6 So also David pronounces a blessing

11. *as, just as:* καθώς KATHŌS
Col 1. 6 so among yourselves, from the day
2 Pet 3.15 So also our beloved brother Paul

12. *very much:* λίαν LIAN
Mt 8.28 so fierce that no one could pass that way

13. *and now:* νυνὶ δέ NYNI [B.3.b.4]
1 Cor 13.13 So faith, hope, love abide, these three

14. *certainly not:* οὐκοῦν (interrog.) OUKOUN*
Jn 18.37 Pilate said to him, "So you are a king?

15. *so, therefore:* οὖν OUN
Mt **1**.17; **5**.23; **6**.22; **7**.12; **10**.16, 26, 32; **18**.26, 29; **23**.3, 20; **24**.15, 26; **25**.28; **27**.17; **28**.19
Mk **16**.19‡
Lk **3**.18
Jn **4**.5, 6, 28, 33, 40, 45, 46, 52; **5**.10; **6**.10, 13, 24, 30, 53; **7**.3, 16, 28, 30, 43; **8**.28, 36, 59; **9**.7, 11, 17, 24; **10**.7, 24; **11**.3, 6, 36, 41, 47, 53; **12**.21; **13**.24, 25, 30; **16**.22; **18**.3, 8, 12, 16, 29; **19**.5, 17(16), 24, 25(24), 29, 32, 38, 42; **20**.2, 25; **21**.6, 11
Acts **1**.6, 21; **2**.41; **9**.31; **10**.23, 33; **12**.5; **13**.4; **14**.3; **15**.3, 30; **16**.5; **17**.17; **22**.29; **23**.18, 22, 31; **25**.5, 23; **26**.22
Rom **2**.26; **7**.25; **8**.12; **9**.16, 18; **11**.11; **14**.12, 16; **16**.19
1 Cor **10**.31; **16**.11
2 Cor **5**.6, 20; **8**.24; **9**.5; **11**.15
Gal **6**.10
Eph **2**.19
Phil **2**.1, 29
1 Th **5**.6
2 Th **2**.15
1 Tim **5**.14
Phm .17
1 Pet **2**.1; **5**.1
3 Jn .8

16. *very, very much:* σφόδρα SPHODRA
Rev 16.21 cursed God . . , so fearful was that plague

17. *such as this:* τοιοῦτος TOIOUTOS
1 Cor 15.48 so are those who are of the dust
15.48 so are those who are of heaven

SO, AND

1. *in order that:* ἵνα HINA
Tit 2. 4 and so train the young women to love

SO AS

1. *into, to, for:* εἰς (+acc.) EIS
1 Th 2.16 so as . . to fill up the measure of . . sins

2. *so that, therefore:* ὥστε HŌSTE
Mt 24.24 "so as to lead astray, if possible
Lk 20.20 so as to deliver him up to the authority
1 Cor 13. 2 all faith, so as to remove mountains

SO, EVEN
SO, JUST
1. *thus, so:* οὕτως HOUTŌS
Lk 15. 7 "Just so, I tell you, there will be .. joy
15.10 "Just so, I tell you, there is joy
Eph 5.28 Even so husbands should love their wives
1 Th 4.14 even so .. God will bring .. those
2. *yes:* ναί NAI
Rev 1. 7 the earth will wail .. Even so. Amen

SO I
1. *and I:* κἀγώ KAGŌ
Jn 15. 9 "As the Father .., so have I loved you
17.18 "so I have sent them into the world
2 Cor 11.22 Are they Hebrews? So am I. Are they Israelites? So am I. Are they descendants of Abraham? So am I

SO THAT
1. *since indeed:* εἴ γε EI [B.3.b.4]
2 Cor 5. 3 so that .. we may not be found naked
2. *in order that:* ἵνα HINA
Mt **12.**10
Mk **3.**2, 10; **4.**12[2]; **5.**23; **11.**25; **16.**1
Lk **6.**7; **8.**10; **12.**36; **14.**10; **16.**4, 9
Jn **4.**36; **6.**5; **7.**23; **11.**4, 15; **14.**29, 31; **15.**16; **17.**21, 23; **18.**28[2]
Acts **21.**24
Rom **3.**19; **5.**21; **6.**4, 6; **11.**19; **15.**16, 32
1 Cor **4.**8; **11.**32; **14.**5, 31; **16.**2, 6
2 Cor **1.**11, 15; **2.**3; **4.**10, 11, 15; **5.**4, 10, 12, 21; **6.**3; **7.**9; **8.**9, 14; **9.**3[2], 8; **11.**7, 16
Gal **4.**5
Eph **4.**14, 28
Phil **1.**26, 27; **2.**19
1 Th **4.**12; **5.**10
2 Th **2.**12
1 Tim **3.**15; **4.**15; **5.**7, 16, 20; **6.**1, 19
Tit **1.**9; **2.**8, 10; **3.**7, 8
Heb **2.**17; **6.**12, 18; **10.**36; **11.**28; **12.**3, 13
1 Pet **1.**7; **2.**12; **3.**1, 16
1 Jn **1.**3; **2.**28[2]; **4.**9
2 Jn .12
Rev **3.**11; **6.**4; **8.**12[2]; **13.**15, 17
3. *that, in order that:* ὅπως HOPŌS
Mt 5.45 "so that you may be sons of your Father
6. 4 "so that your alms may be in secret
Lk 16.28 " ⟨send him⟩ so that he may warn them
Jn 11.57 so that they might arrest him
Acts 9. 2 so that if .. any belonging to the Way
9.12 "so that he might regain his sight
20.16 so that he might not have to spend time
Rom 9.17 "so that my name may be proclaimed
1 Cor 1.29 so that no human being might boast
2 Cor 8.11 so that your readiness in desiring it
2 Th 1.12 so that the name of our Lord Jesus
Heb 2. 9 so that .. he might taste death
9.15 so that those who are called may receive
4. *so that, therefore:* ὥστε HŌSTE
Mt 8.24 so that the boat was being swamped
8.28 so fierce that no one could pass that way
12.22 so that the dumb man spoke and saw
13. 2 so that he got into a boat and sat there
13.32 "so that the birds of the air come
13.54 he taught .., so that they were astonished
15.31 so that the throng wondered
27.14 so that the governor wondered greatly
Mk 1.27 were all amazed, so that they questioned
1.45 so that Jesus[g] could no longer openly
2. 2 so that there was no longer room
2.12 so that they were all amazed
3.10 so that all who had diseases pressed
3.20 so that they could not even eat
4. 1 so that he got into a boat and sat in it
4.32 "so that .. birds .. make nests in its shade
4.37 so that the boat was already filling
9.26 so that most of them said, "He is dead
15. 5 no .. answer, so that Pilate wondered
Lk 5. 7 so that they began to sink
Acts 1.19 "(so that the field was called .. Akeldama
5.15 so that they even carried out the sick
15.39 so that they separated from each other
16.26 so that the foundations .. were shaken
19.10 so that all the residents of Asia heard
19.12 so that handkerchiefs .. were carried away
19.16 so that they fled out of that house
Rom 7. 6 so that we serve not under the old .. code
15.19 so that from Jerusalem .. I have .. preached
1 Cor 1. 7 so that you are not lacking in any .. gift
7.38 So that he who marries .. does well
2 Cor 7. 7 he told us .., so that I rejoiced still more
Gal 2.13 so that even Barnabas was carried away
3.24 So that the law was our custodian
Phil 1.13 so that it has become known
1 Th 1. 7 so that you became an example to all
1. 8 so that we need not say anything
2 Th 2. 4 so that he takes his seat in the temple
1 Pet 1.21 so that your faith and hope are in God[d]
5. *whence, for which reason:* ὅθεν HOTHEN
Mt 14. 7 so that he promised with an oath

SO THEN
1. *therefore then:* ἄρα οὖν OUN ; ARA II
[a]ἄρα
Rom 7.25 So then, I of myself serve the law
8.12 So then, brethren, we are debtors
9.18 So then he has mercy upon whomever
Gal 6.10 So then, as we have opportunity
Eph 2.19 So then you are no longer strangers
1 Th 5. 6 So then let us not sleep, as others do
2 Th 2.15 So then, brethren, stand firm and hold
Heb 4. 9 [a]So then, there remains a sabbath rest
2. *so that, therefore:* ὥστε HŌSTE
1 Cor 11.33 So then .., when you come together to eat
Gal 3. 9 So then, those who are men of faith
3. *and now:* νυνὶ δέ NYNI [B.3.b.4]
Rom 7.17 So then it is no longer I that do it
4. *so, therefore:* οὖν OUN [B.3.b.4]
[a]+μέν
Mk 16.19 [a]So then the Lord Jesus .. was taken up[k]‡
Rom 14. 8 so then, whether we live or .. die

SOBER
1. *cautiously, soberly:* σωφρόνως SŌPHRONŌS* [A.4.a]
Tit 2.12 training us .. to live s. .. and godly lives
2. *soundness of mind, prudence:* σωφροσύνη SŌPHROSYNĒ [A.1.b.3]
Acts 26.25 "but I am speaking the sober truth

SOBER, BE
SOBER, KEEP
1. *be self-controlled:* νήφω NĒPHŌ
1 Th 5. 6 let us keep awake and be sober
5. 8 since we belong to the day, let us be s.
1 Pet 1.13 Therefore gird up your minds, be sober
4. 7 keep sane and sober for your prayers
5. 8 Be sober, be watchful

SOBER JUDGMENT
1. *be of sound mind:* σωφρονέω (inf.) SŌPHRONEŌ
Rom 12. 3 but to think with sober judgment

SO-CALLED
1. *say, speak:* λέγω (pass. part.) LEGŌ
1 Cor 8. 5 although there may be so-called gods
2 Th 2. 4 exalts himself against every so-called god

SODOM: Σόδομα 'sädəm
Mt 10.15 "more tolerable .. for the land of S.
11.23 "if the .. works .. had been done in S.
11.24 "more tolerable .. for the land of S.
Lk 10.12 "it shall be more tolerable .. for Sodom
17.29 "on the day when Lot went out from S.
Rom 9.29 "we would have fared like Sodom
2 Pet 2. 6 by turning the cities of S. .. to ashes
Jude . 7 as S. and Gomorrah .. serve as an example
Rev 11. 8 the great city .. allegorically[d] called S.

SODOMITE
1. *homosexual:* ἀρσενοκοίτης ARSENOKOITĒS
1 Tim 1.10 immoral persons, sodomites, kidnapers

SOFT
1. *soft, gentle:* μαλακός MALAKOS
Lk 7.25 "A man clothed in soft clothing?

SOFT RAIMENT
1. *soft, gentle:* μαλακός (subst. pl.) MALAKOS
Mt 11. 8 "To see a man[a] clothed in soft raiment? Behold, those who wear soft raiment

SOIL
1. *earth, land:* γῆ GĒ
Mt 13. 5 "where they had not much s., and . . they sprang up, since they had no depth of s.
13. 8 "Other seeds fell on good soil
13.23 "As for what was sown on good soil
Mk 4. 5 "where it had not much soil, and . . it sprang up, since it had no depth of soil
4. 8 "other seeds fell into good soil
4.20 "those that were sown upon the good soil
Lk 8. 8 "some fell into good soil and grew
8.15 "And as for that in the good soil
2. *stain, defile:* μολύνω MOLYNŌ
Rev 3. 4 " 'who have not soiled their garments

SOJOURN
1. *live near, inhabit:* παροικέω PAROIKEŌ
Heb 11. 9 By faith he sojourned in the land

SOJOURNER
1. *foreign:* πάροικος (subst.) PAROIKOS
Eph 2.19 So then you are no longer . . sojourners

SOLDIER
1. *wage war:* στρατεύομαι (subst. part.) STRATEUOMAI
Lk 3.14 Soldiers . . asked . . "what shall we do?
2. *soldier:* στρατιώτης STRATIŌTĒS*
Mt 8. 9 "For I am a man . . with soldiers under me
27.27 soldiers of the governor took Jesus
28.12 they gave . . money to the soldiers
Mk 15.16 soldiers led him away inside the palace
Lk 7. 8 "For I am a man . . with soldiers under me
23.36 The soldiers also mocked him
Jn 19. 2 the soldiers plaited a crown of thorns
19.23 When the soldiers had crucified Jesus they took his garments . . , one for each s.
19.25 So the soldiers did this
19.32 soldiers came and broke the legs
19.34 one of the soldiers pierced his side
Acts 10. 7 he called two . . servants and a devout s.
12. 4 delivered him to four squads of soldiers
12. 6 Peter was sleeping between two soldiers
12.18 no small stir among the soldiers
21.32 He at once took soldiers and centurions, . . when they saw . . the soldiers, they stopped
21.35 he was actually carried by the soldiers
23.23 "get ready two hundred soldiers
23.31 soldiers . . took Paul and brought him
27.31 Paul said to the centurion and . . soldiers
27.32 Then the soldiers cut away the ropes
27.42 soldiers' plan was to kill the prisoners
28.16 allowed to stay by himself, with the s.
2 Tim 2. 3 Share in suffering as a good soldier
CONTEXTUALLY
Mt 27.65 "You have a guard[o] of soldiers

SOLDIER, FELLOW
1. *fellow soldier:* συστρατιώτης SYSTRATIŌTĒS*
Phil 2.25 fellow worker and fellow soldier
Phm . 2 Archippus our fellow soldier

SOLDIER OF THE GUARD
1. *one of the imperial bodyguard* (Lat.): σπεκουλάτωρ SPEKOULATŌR*
Mk 6.27 the king sent a soldier of the guard

SOLDIER ON SERVICE
1. *wage war:* στρατεύομαι (subst. part.) STRATEUOMAI
2 Tim 2. 4 No soldier on service gets entangled

SOLDIER, SERVE AS A
1. *wage war:* στρατεύομαι STRATEUOMAI
1 Cor 9. 7 Who serves as a s. at his own expense?

SOLDIERS
1. *army:* στράτευμα (sg. or pl.) STRATEUMA
Lk 23.11 Herod with his soldiers . . mocked him
Acts 23.10 commanded the soldiers to go down
23.27 "I came upon them with the soldiers

SOLDIERS, BAND OF
1. *cohort, tactical unit:* σπεῖρα SPEIRA
Jn 18. 3 Judas, procuring a band of soldiers
18.12 the band of soldiers . . seized Jesus

SOLEMNLY FOREWARN
IDIOMATICALLY
a. 1 Th 4.6 as we solemnly forewarned you καθὼς καὶ προείπαμεν ὑμῖν καὶ διεμαρτυράμεθα
[DIAMARTYROMAI; PROEIPON]

SOLID
1. *strong, firm:* στερεός STEREOS
Heb 5.12 You need milk, not solid food
5.14 But solid food is for the mature
CONTEXTUALLY
1 Cor 3. 2 I fed you with milk, not solid food

SOLOMON: Σολομών 'säləmən
Mt 1. 6 David was the father of Solomon
1. 7 Solomon the father of Rehoboam
6.29 "yet I tell you, even S. in all his glory
12.42 "she came . . to hear the wisdom of S.
12.42 "something greater than S. is here
Lk 11.31 "she came . . to hear the wisdom of S.
11.31 "something greater than S. is here
12.27 "yet I tell you, even S. in all his glory
Jn 10.23 Jesus was walking . . in the portico of S.
Acts 3.11 people ran . . to . . portico called Solomon's
5.12 together in Solomon's Portico
7.47 "it was S. who built a house for him

SOME
SOME WHO
1. *other, another:* ἄλλος (pl.) ALLOS
Jn 9. 9 Some said, "It is he
Heb 11.35 Some were tortured, refusing . . release
2. *another, different:* ἕτερος HETEROS
Lk 8. 6 "some fell on the rock; and . . it withered
8. 7 "some fell among thorns; and . . choked
8. 8 "And some fell into good soil and grew
3. *enough:* ἱκανός HIKANOS
1 Cor 11.30 many of you are weak . . , and s. have died[t]
4. *who, which, what:* ὅς HOS
[a]+μέν [b]+δέ
Mt **13.4**[a], 8[3ab]
Mk **4.4**[a]; **12.5**[2ab]
Lk **8.5**[a]; **13.30**[2]
2 Tim **2.20**[2ab]
Jude .22[a], 23[b]
5. *to a little* (extent): πρὸς ὀλίγον OLIGOS [B.1.a.1]
1 Tim 4. 8 while bodily training is of some value
6. *more:* πλείων PLEIŌN
Acts 21.10 While we were staying for some days
24.17 "Now after some years I came to bring
7. *anyone, any:* τὶς (sg. or pl.) TIS II
Mt **9.3**; **12.38**; **16.28**; **27.47**; **28.11**
Mk **2.6**; **7.1**, 2; **8.3**; **9.1**; **12.13**; **14.4**, 57, 65; **15.35**
Lk **6.2**; **8.2**; **9.7**, 8, 27; **11.15**; **13.1**, 31; **18.9**; **19.39**; **20.27**, 39; **21.5**; **23.8**; **24.22**, 24
Jn **6.64**; **7.25**, 44; **9.16**; **11.37**, 46; **12.20**; **13.29**
Acts **5.15**; **6.9**; **8.36**; **10.23**, 48; **11.20**; **12.1**; **15.2**, 5, 36; **16.12**; **17.4**, 5, 6, 18[2], 20, 28, 34; **18.23**; **19.1**, 9, 13, 31; **23.9**; **24.1**, 18, 24; **25.13**; **27.1**, 26
Rom **1.11**, 13; **3.3**; **11.14**, 17; **15.26**
1 Cor **4.18**; **6.11**; **8.7**; **9.22**; **10.7**, 8, 9, 10; **15.6**, 12, 34, 35, 37; **16.7**
2 Cor **3.1**; **7.14**; **10.2**, 12
Gal **1.7**
Phil **1.15**
2 Th **3.11**

1 Tim **4.**1; **5.**15, 24; **6.**10, 21
2 Tim **2.**18
Heb **4.**6; **10.**25; **13.**2
1 Pet **3.**1
2 Pet **3.**9
Jude .4
IDIOMATICALLY
a. Acts 19.32 Now some cried one thing, some another ἄλλοι μὲν οὖν ἄλλο τι ἔκραζον [ALLOS]
b. Acts 21.34 Some in the crowd shouted one thing, some another ἄλλοι δὲ ἄλλο τι ἐπεφώνουν ἐν τῷ ὄχλῳ [ALLOS]
c. Rom 15.15 on some points I have written to you ἔγραψα ὑμῖν ἀπὸ μέρους [MEROS]
d. 2 Cor 2.5 but in some measure ἀλλὰ ἀπὸ μέρους [MEROS]
CONTEXTUALLY
Mt **23.**34[2]; **25.**8; **27.**9
Mk **2.**1; **5.**35; **6.**14‡; **8.**22; **12.**2
Lk **6.**1; **11.**49; **16.**31; **20.**10, 20; **21.**16
Jn **2.**8; **7.**40; **9.**40; **16.**17; **18.**3; **21.**6, 10, 20
Acts **5.**2, 37; **15.**33; **19.**33; **21.**16; **24.**23; **27.**33, 34, 36
1 Cor **9.**7; **14.**5, 6
2 Cor **2.**5; **9.**4; **11.**4
2 Jn .4
3 Jn .3
Rev **2.**10, 14, 15, 17, 24

SOME MEN
1. *anyone, any:* τὶς (pl.) TIS II
Acts **15.**1

SOME ONE (*See also* ELSE, SOME ONE)
1. *anyone, any:* τὶς TIS II
Mt **12.**[47‡
Lk **8.**46; **13.**23; **16.**30, 31
Acts **5.**25; **8.**31, 34
1 Cor **10.**28
Heb **3.**4; **5.**12
Jas **2.**18; **5.**19
1 Pet **5.**8

SOME PEOPLE
1. *anyone, any:* τὶς (pl.) TIS II
Rom **3.**8

SOME PERSONS
1. *anyone, any:* τὶς (pl.) TIS II
Acts **15.**24

SOME TIME
1. *long ago:* πάλαι PALAI
Mk [15.44 asked . . whether he *had been some time* dead‡

SOME WHO (*See* SOME)

SOMEBODY
1. *anyone, any:* τὶς TIS II
Acts **5.**36; **8.**9

SOMEHOW
1. *in some way, perhaps:* πώς PŌS II
Acts 27.12 that s. they could reach Phoenix
Rom 1.10 that s. by God's will I may . . succeed
1 Cor 8. 9 lest . . liberty . . s. become a . . stumbling block
Gal 2. 2 lest s. I should be running . . in vain
1 Th 3. 5 fear that s. the tempter had tempted

SOMETHING
SOME THINGS
1. *some object:* σκεῦός τι SKEUOS [A.1.f]
Acts 10.11 saw . . heaven opened, and s. descending
11. 5 "I saw a vision, something descending
2. *who? what?:* τίς TIS I
Mk **6.**36
Acts **25.**26
3. *anyone, any:* τὶς TIS II
Mt **5.**23; **20.**20
Lk **7.**40; **11.**54
Jn **13.**29
Acts **3.**5; **17.**21; **21.**37; **23.**17, 18
1 Cor **8.**2
Gal **2.**6; **6.**3
Heb **8.**3; **11.**40
2 Pet **3.**16
3 Jn .9
CONTEXTUALLY
Mt 12. 6 "s. greater than the temple is here
14.16 "you give them something to eat
Mk 5.43 told them to give her something to eat
6.37 "You give them something to eat
Lk 8.55 that s. should be given her to eat
9.13 "You give them something to eat
Acts 9.18 s. like scales fell from his eyes
10.10 became hungry and desired s. to eat
Rom 2.28 nor is true circumcision s. external
4. 2 s. to boast about, but not before God
1 Cor 16. 2 put something aside and store it up
1 Pet 4.12 as though s. strange were happening
Rev 8. 8 s. like a great mountain . . was thrown

SOMETHING LIKE
1. *as, so:* ὡς HŌS
Acts **9.**18

SOMETIMES
1. *indeed, on the one hand:* μέν MEN
Heb **10.**33

SOMEWHAT
1. *anyone, any:* τὶς TIS II
Acts **23.**20

SOMEWHERE
1. *somewhere, about:* πού POU II
Heb 2. 6 It has been testified s., "What is man?
4. 4 he has s. spoken of the seventh day

SON
1. *son:* υἱός HUIOS
Mt 1. 1 genealogy of Jesus Christ, . . s. of David
1.20 "Joseph, son of David, do not fear
1.21 "she will bear a son, and you shall call
1.23 "a virgin shall conceive and bear a son
1.25 knew her not until she had borne a son
2.15 "Out of Egypt have I called my son
3.17 "This is my beloved Son,[h] with whom
4. 3 "If you are the Son of God, command
4. 6 "If you are the Son of God, throw
5. 9 "for they shall be called sons of God
5.45 "that you may be sons of your Father
7. 9 "if his son asks him for bread
8.12 "sons of the kingdom will be thrown
8.20 "Son of man has nowhere to lay his head
8.29 "What . . to do with us, O Son of God?
9. 6 "know that the Son of man has authority
9.27 "Have mercy on us, Son of David
10.23 "not . . before the Son of man comes
10.37 "who loves son or daughter more than me
11.19 "Son of man came eating and drinking
11.27 "no one knows the Son except the Father, and no one knows the Father except the S. and any one to whom the S. chooses to reveal
12. 8 "the Son of man is lord of the sabbath
12.23 "Can this be the Son of David?
12.27 "by whom do your sons cast them out?
12.32 "word against . . S. of man will be forgiven
12.40 "so will the Son of man be three days
13.37 "He who sows . . is the Son of man
13.38 "good seed means the sons of the kingdom; the weeds are the sons of the evil one
13.41 "The Son of man will send his angels
13.55 "Is not this the carpenter's son?
14.33 "Truly you are the Son of God
15.22 "Have mercy on me, . . Son of David
16.13 "Who do men say . . the Son of man is?
16.16 "the Christ, the Son of the living God
16.27 "For the Son of man is to come
16.28 "not . . before they see . . S. of man coming
17. 5 "This is my beloved Son,[w] with whom
17. 9 "until the Son of man is raised
17.12 "So also the Son of man will suffer
17.15 "Lord, have mercy on my son
17.22 "The Son of man is to be delivered
17.25 "From their sons or from others?

Mt 17.26 Jesus said . . "Then the sons are free
[18.11 *"the Son of man came to save the lost*‡
19.28 "Son of man shall sit on his . . throne
20.18 "the Son of man will be delivered
20.20 the mother of the sons of Zebedee came up to him, with her sons
20.21 "that these two sons of mine may sit
20.28 "the Son of man came not to be served
20.30 "Have mercy on us, Son of David!
20.31 "Lord, have mercy on us, S. of David!
21. 9 "Hosanna to the Son of David!
21.15 "Hosanna to the Son of David!
21.37 "Afterward he sent his son to them, saying, 'They will respect my son
21.38 "But when the tenants saw the son
22. 2 "king who gave a marriage feast for his s.
22.42 "What . . of the Christ? Whose son is he?
22.45 "If . . Lord, how is he his son?
23.31 "you are sons of those who murdered
23.35 "Zechariah the son of Barachiah
24.27 "so . . the coming of the Son of man
24.30 "the sign of the Son of man in heaven
24.30 "they will see the Son of man coming
24.36 "no one knows, not even . . the Son[a]‡
24.37 "so . . the coming of the Son of man
24.39 "so . . the coming of the Son of man
24.44 "the Son of man is coming at an hour
25.31 "When the Son of man comes
26. 2 "the Son of man will be delivered
26.24 "The Son of man goes as it is written
26.24 "by whom the Son of man is betrayed
26.37 taking . . the two sons of Zebedee
26.45 "the Son of man is betrayed
26.63 "if you are the Christ, the S. of God
26.64 "hereafter you will see the Son of man
27. 9 "price . . set by some of the sons of Israel
27.40 "If you are the Son of God
27.43 "for he said, 'I am the Son of God
27.54 "Truly this was the Son[x] of God!†
27.56 the mother of the sons of Zebedee
28.19 "baptizing them in the name of . . the Son
Mk 1. 1 gospel of Jesus Christ, the Son of God[a]‡
1.11 "Thou art my beloved Son;[d] with thee
2.10 "that the Son of man has authority
2.28 "Son of man is lord even of the sabbath
3.11 "You are the Son of God
3.17 Boanerges, that is, sons of thunder
3.28 "sins will be forgiven the sons of men
5. 7 "Jesus, Son of the Most High God
6. 3 "the carpenter, the son of Mary
8.31 to teach . . that the S. of man must suffer
8.38 "of him will the S. of man . . be ashamed
9. 7 "This is my beloved Son;[g] listen to him
9. 9 until the S. of man should have risen
9.12 "how is it written of the Son of man?
9.17 "Teacher, I brought my son to you
9.31 "The Son of man will be delivered
10.33 "the Son of man will be delivered
10.35 James and John, the sons of Zebedee
10.45 "Son of man . . came not to be served
10.46 a blind beggar, the son of Timaeus
10.47 "Jesus, S. of David, have mercy on me!
10.48 "Son of David, have mercy on me!
12. 6 "He had still one other, a beloved son
12. 6 "saying, 'They will respect my son
12.35 "that the Christ is the son of David
12.37 "calls him Lord; so how is he his son?
13.26 "they will see the Son of man coming
13.32 "no one knows, not even . . the Son
14.21 "Son of man goes as it is written of him
14.21 "by whom the Son of man is betrayed
14.41 "It is enough; . . the S. of man is betrayed
14.61 "Are you the Christ, the S. of the Blessed?
14.62 "you will see the Son of man seated
15.39 "Truly this man was the Son[x] of God!†
Lk 1.13 "your wife Elizabeth will bear you a son
1.16 "he will turn many of the sons of Israel
Lk 1.31 "you will conceive . . and bear a son
1.32 "will be called the S. of the Most High
1.35 "child . . will be called . . the Son of God
1.36 "Elizabeth . . has also conceived a son
1.57 Elizabeth . . gave birth to a son
2. 7 she gave birth to her first-born son
3. 2 word . . came to John the son of Zechariah
3.22 "Thou art my beloved Son;[j] with thee
3.23 the son (as was supposed) of Joseph
4. 3 "If you are the Son of God, command
4. 9 "If you are the Son of God, throw
4.22 "Is not this Joseph's son?
4.41 "You are the Son of God!
5.10 James and John, sons of Zebedee
5.24 "know that the S. of man has authority
6. 5 "The Son of man is lord of the sabbath
6.22 "revile you . . on account of the Son of man!
6.35 "you will be sons of the Most High
7.12 the only son of his mother, . . a widow
7.34 "The Son of man has come eating
8.28 "Jesus, Son of the Most High God
9.22 "Son of man must suffer many things
9.26 "of him will the S. of man be ashamed
9.35 "This is my Son, my Chosen;[d] listen!
9.38 "I beg you to look upon my son
9.41 "Bring your son here
9.44 "for the Son of man is to be delivered
[9.55(56) *"the Son of man came . . to save them*‡
9.58 "S. of man has nowhere to lay his head
10. 6 "if a son of peace is there
10.22 "no one knows who . . Son is except . . Father, or who . . Father is except . . Son and any . . to whom the Son chooses to reveal
11.11 "What father . . , if his son asks for[l] a fish?
11.19 "by whom do your sons cast them out?
11.30 "so will . . S. of man be to this generation
12. 8 "the Son of man . . will acknowledge
12.10 "a word against the Son of man
12.40 "for the Son of man is coming
12.53 "they will be divided, father against son and son against father
14. 5 "Which of you, having a son[s] or an ox‡[o]
15.11 "There was a man who had two sons
15.13 "the younger son gathered all he had
15.19 " ' "no longer worthy to be called your s.
15.21 "son said . . 'Father, I have sinned . . ; I am no longer worthy to be called your son[v]
15.24 " 'this my s. was dead, and is alive again
15.25 "his elder son was in the field
15.30 " 'when this son of yours came
16. 8 "the sons of this world[w] are more shrewd . . than the sons of light
17.22 "one of the days of the Son of man
17.24 "so will the Son of man be in his day[a]
17.26 "so . . in the days of the Son of man
17.30 "so . . when the Son of man is revealed
18. 8 "when the Son of man comes
18.31 "everything . . written of the Son of man
18.38 "Jesus, Son of David, have mercy on me!
18.39 "Son of David, have mercy on me!
19. 9 "since he also is a son of Abraham
19.10 "Son of man came to seek and to save
20.13 " 'I will send my beloved son
20.34 "The sons of this age marry
20.36 "equal to angels and are sons of God, being sons of the resurrection
20.41 "say that the Christ is David's son
20.44 "calls him Lord; so how is he his son?
21.27 "then they will see the Son of man
21.36 "to stand before the Son of man
22.22 "S. of man goes as it has been determined
22.48 "betray the Son of man with a kiss?
22.69 "S. of man shall be seated at the right
22.70 "Are you the Son of God, then?
24. 7 "the Son of man must be delivered
Jn 1.18 the only Son[b] . . , he has made him known‡
1.34 "witness that this is the Son of God

Jn 1.42 "So you are Simon the son of John?
1.45 "Jesus of Nazareth, the son of Joseph
1.49 "Rabbi, you are the Son of God!
1.51 "angels . . descending upon the S. of man
3.13 "he who descended . . , the Son of man[g]
3.14 "so must the Son of man be lifted up
3.16 God so loved . . that he gave his only Son
3.17 For God sent the Son into the world
3.18 the name of the only Son of God
3.35 the Father loves the Son
3.36 who believes in the S. has . . life; . . who does not obey the S. shall not see life
4. 5 field that Jacob gave to his son Joseph
4.12 "Jacob . . drank from it . . , and his sons
4.46 there was an official whose son was ill
4.47 he went and begged him to . . heal his son
4.50 "Go; your son will live
4.53 when Jesus . . said . . "Your son will live
5.19 "Son can do nothing of his own accord
5.19 "whatever he does, that the Son does
5.20 "For the Father loves the Son
5.21 "so also the S. gives life to whom he will
5.22 "Father . . has given all judgment to the S.
5.23 "that all may honor the Son
5.23 "He who does not honor the Son
5.25 "the dead will hear . . the S. of God
5.26 "granted the Son also to have life
5.27 "because he is the Son of man
6.27 "which the Son of man will give to you
6.40 "that every one who sees the Son
6.42 "Is not this Jesus, the son of Joseph?
6.53 "eat the flesh of the Son of man
6.62 "what if you were to see the S. of man?
8.28 "When you have lifted up the S. of man
8.35 "the son continues for ever
8.36 "So if the Son makes you free
9.19 "Is this your son, who . . was born blind?
9.20 "We know that this is our son
9.35 "Do you believe in the Son of man?[v]
10.36 "I said, 'I am the Son of God
11. 4 "that the S. of God may be glorified
11.27 "that you are the Christ, the S. of God
12.23 "hour has come for the S. of man
12.34 "How . . say that the Son of man must be lifted up? Who is this Son of man?
12.36 "that you may become sons of light
13.31 "Now is the Son of man glorified
14.13 "that the Father . . be glorified in the S.
17. 1 "Father, the hour has come; glorify thy Son that the Son may glorify thee
17.12 "none . . is lost but the son of perdition
19. 7 "he has made himself the Son of God
19.26 "Woman, behold, your son!
20.31 that Jesus is the Christ, the S. of God

Acts 2.17 " 'your sons and . . daughters shall prophesy
3.25 "You are the sons of the prophets
4.36 (which means, Son of encouragement
7.16 "Abraham . . bought . . from . . sons of Hamor
7.21 "brought him up as her own son
7.23 "to visit his brethren, the sons of Israel
7.29 "where he became the father of two sons
7.56 "the Son of man standing at the right
[8.37 *"I believe . . Jesus Christ is the Son of God*‡
9.15 "to carry my name before . . sons of Israel
9.20 "He is the Son of God
13.10 "You son of the devil, you enemy
13.21 "God gave them Saul the son of Kish
13.26 "Brethren, sons of . . family of Abraham
13.33 " 'Thou art my Son, today I have begotten
16. 1 Timothy, the son of a Jewish woman
19.14 Seven sons of a Jewish high priest
23. 6 "I am a Pharisee, a son of Pharisees
23.16 son of Paul's sister heard of their ambush

Rom 1. 3 the gospel concerning his Son
1. 4 designated Son of God in power
1. 9 whom I serve . . in the gospel of his Son
5.10 reconciled to God by the death of his S.
8. 3 sending his own Son in the likeness
8.14 all . . led by the Spirit of G. are sons of God
8.19 longing for . . revealing of the sons of God
8.29 be conformed to the image of his Son
8.32 He who did not spare his own Son
9. 9 "I will return and Sarah shall have a son
9.26 "will be called 'sons of the living God
9.27 "Though . . sons of Israel be as the sand

1 Cor 1. 9 called into the fellowship of his Son
15.28 the Son himself will also be subjected

2 Cor 1.19 Son of God, . . in him it is always Yes
6.18 "you shall be my sons and daughters

Gal 1.16 to reveal his Son . . that I might preach
2.20 I live by faith in the Son of God
3. 7 men of faith . . are the sons of Abraham
3.26 in Christ Jesus you are all sons of God
4. 4 God sent forth his Son, born of woman
4. 6 because you are sons, God has sent the Spirit of his Son into our hearts
4. 7 you are no longer a slave but a son, and if a son then an heir
4.22 it is written that Abraham had two sons
4.30 "Cast out the slave and her son; for the son of the slave shall not inherit with the son of the free woman

Eph 2. 2 spirit . . at work in . . sons of disobedience
3. 5 not made known to the sons of men
4.13 the knowledge of the Son of God
5. 6 wrath . . upon the sons of disobedience

Col 1.13 transferred us to the kingdom of his . . S.
[3. 6 wrath . . *upon the sons of disobedience*‡

1 Th 1.10 to wait for his Son from heaven
5. 5 you are all sons of light and sons of the day; . . not of the night or of darkness

2 Th 2. 3 man of lawlessness[a] . . , the son of perdition

Heb 1. 2 he has spoken to us by a Son
1. 5 "Thou art my Son today I have begotten
1. 5 "I will be to him a father, and he . . a son
1. 8 of the Son he says, "Thy throne, O God[a]
2. 6 "What is man . . , or the son of man?
2.10 he, . . in bringing many sons to glory
3. 6 faithful over God's[f] house as a son
4.14 a great high priest . . , Jesus, the Son of God
5. 5 "Thou art my Son, today I have begotten
5. 8 Although . . a Son, he learned obedience
6. 6 since they crucify the Son of God
7. 3 resembling the Son of God he continues
7.28 a Son who has been made perfect
10.29 the man who has spurned the Son of God
11.21 Jacob . . blessed . . the sons of Joseph
11.24 Moses . . refused to be called the son
12. 5 exhortation which addresses you as sons
12. 5 "My son, do not regard lightly . . discipline
12. 6 "Lord . . chastises every son . . he receives
12. 7 God is treating you as sons; for what son is there whom his father does not discipline?
12. 8 illegitimate children and not sons

Jas 2.21 offered his son Isaac upon the altar

1 Pet 5.13 sends . . greetings; and so does my s. Mark

2 Pet 1.17 "This is my beloved Son,[d] with whom

1 Jn 1. 3 our fellowship . . with his S. Jesus Christ
1. 7 the blood of Jesus his S. cleanses us
2.22 he who denies the Father and the Son
2.23 No one who denies . . Son has the Father
2.23 who confesses the Son has the Father
2.24 then you will abide in the Son
3. 8 The reason the Son of God appeared
3.23 we should believe in the name of his Son
4. 9 God sent his only Son into the world
4.10 he loved us and sent his Son
4.14 the Father has sent his Son as the Savior
4.15 confesses that Jesus is the Son of God
5. 5 believes that Jesus is the Son of God
5. 9 he has borne witness to his Son
5.10 He who believes in the Son of God
5.10 testimony that God has borne to his S.
5.11 God gave us eternal life . . in his Son

1 Jn 5.12 He who has the Son has life; he who has not the Son of God has not life
5.13 who believe in . . name of the Son of God
5.20 we know that the S. of God has come
5.20 we are in him . . , in his Son Jesus Christ
2 Jn . 3 from Jesus Christ the Father's Son
. 9 he . . has both the Father and the Son
Rev 1.13 in the midst . . one like a son of man
2.14 " 'stumbling block before . . sons of Israel
2.18 " 'The words of the Son of God
7. 4 of every tribe of the sons of Israel
14.14 on the cloud one like a son of man
21. 7 "I will be his God and he shall be my s.
21.12 twelve tribes of the sons of Israel

2. *adoption as a son:* υἱοθεσία HUIOTHESIA [B.1.a.1]
Eph 1. 5 He destined us in love[b] to be his sons

3. *child, servant:* παῖς PAIS
Jn 4.51 servants . . told him . . his son was living

4. *child:* τέκνον TEKNON
[a]voc. *my son*
Mt 9. 2 [a]"my son; your sins are forgiven
21.28 "What do you think? A man had two sons
21.28 " 'Son, go and work in the vineyard
Mk 2. 5 [a]"My son, your sins are forgiven
Lk 2.48 "Son, why have you treated us so?
15.31 " 'Son, you are always with me
16.25 " 'S., remember that you in your lifetime
Phil 2.22 how as a son with a father he has served
1 Tim 1.18 [a]I commit to you, Timothy, my son
2 Tim 2. 1 my son, be strong in the grace

CONTEXTUALLY
Mt 4.21 brothers, James the son of Zebedee
10. 2 James the son of Zebedee, and John
10. 3 James the s. of Alphaeus, and Thaddaeus[x]
22.42 They said to him, "The son of David
Mk 1.19 he saw James the son of Zebedee and John
2.14 he saw Levi the son of Alphaeus
3.17 James the son of Zebedee and John
3.18 James the s. of Alphaeus, and Thaddaeus
Lk 3.23, 24[5], 25[5], 26[5], 27[5], 28[5], 29[5], 30[5], 31[5], 32[5], 33[6], 34[5], 35[5], 36[5], 37[5], 38[4]
6.15 James the son of Alphaeus, and Simon
6.16 Judas . . s. of James, and Judas Iscariot
Jn 1.14 glory as of the only S. from the Father
6.71 spoke of Judas the s. of Simon Iscariot
13. 2 Judas Iscariot, Simon's s., to betray him
13.26 gave . . to Judas, the s. of Simon Iscariot
21. 2 the sons of Zebedee, and two others
21.15 "Simon, s. of John, do you love me more?
21.16 "Simon, son of John, do you love me?
21.17 "Simon, son of John, do you love me?
Acts 1.13 James the s. of Alphaeus and Simon the Zealot and Judas the son of James
13.22 " 'I have found in David the son of Jesse
20. 4 Sopater of Beroea, the son of Pyrrhus
20.28 "obtained with the blood of his own Son[w†0]
Gal 4.23 son of the slave . . according to the flesh
4.23 son of the free woman through promise
Heb 11.17 he . . was ready to offer up his only son
2 Pet 2.15 Balaam, the s. of Beor, who loved gain

SONG
1. *ode, song:* ᾠδή ŌDĒ*
Eph 5.19 addressing one another in . . spiritual songs
Col 3.16 sing psalms and . . spiritual songs
Rev 5. 9 and they sang a new song
14. 3 they sing a new song before the throne . . No one could learn that song
15. 3 they sing the song of Moses

SONS, ADOPTION AS
1. *adoption as a son:* υἱοθεσία HUIOTHESIA
Rom 8.23 we wait for adoption as sons
Gal 4. 5 that we might receive adoption as sons

SONSHIP
1. *adoption as a son:* υἱοθεσία HUIOTHESIA
Rom 8.15 you have received the spirit of sonship
9. 4 to them belong the sonship, the glory

SOON (*See also* AFTERWARD, SOON)
1. *immediately:* εὐθέως EUTHEŌS
3 Jn .14 I hope to see you soon, and we will talk

2. *after not long:* μετὰ οὐ πολύ META [B.1.a.1]
Acts **27.**14

3. *many, great:* πολύς (neg.) POLYS [B.1.a.1]
Acts 27.14 soon a tempestuous wind . . struck down

4. *quickly:* ταχέως TACHEŌS
1 Cor 4.19 I will come to you s., if the Lord wills
Phil 2.19 I hope . . to send Timothy to you soon
2 Tim 4. 9 Do your best to come to me soon

5. *swift, sudden:* ταχινός (pred.) TACHINOS
2 Pet 1.14 the putting off of my body[c] will be soon

6. *sooner, faster:* τάχιον TACHION
Heb 13.23 with whom I shall see you if he comes s.
Also variant to: 1 Tim **3.**14

7. *with speed:* ἐν τάχει TACHOS [B.1.a.1]
Rom 16.20 the God of peace will soon crush Satan
1 Tim 3.14 I hope to come to you soon
Var. TACHION
Rev 1. 1 to show . . what must soon take place
22. 6 "to show . . what must soon take place

8. *quick:* ταχύς (neut.) TACHYS
Rev 2.16 " 'If not, I will come to you soon and war
3.11 " 'I am coming soon; hold fast
11.14 behold, the third woe is soon to come
22. 7 "And behold, I am coming soon
22.12 "Behold, I am coming soon
22.20 "Surely I am coming soon." Amen

SOON AFTER
1. *quick:* ταχύς (neut.) TACHYS
Mk 9.39 "no one . . able soon after to speak evil

SOON AS, AS
1. *when, as soon as:* ὡς ἄν HŌS [A.4.e]
Phil 2.23 just as soon as I see how it will go

IDIOMATICALLY
a. Mt 24.32; Mk 13.28 "as soon as its branch becomes tender ὅταν ἤδη ὁ κλάδος αὐτῆς γένηται ἁπαλός [ĒDĒ; HOTAN]
b. Mk 15.1 as soon as it was morning εὐθὺς πρωΐ [EUTHYS II]
c. Lk 21.30 "as soon as they come out in leaf ὅταν προβάλωσιν ἤδη [ĒDĒ; HOTAN]

SOON AS POSSIBLE
1. *quickly:* ταχέως (superl.) TACHEŌS
Acts 17.15 Timothy to come . . as soon as possible

SOONER, THE
1. *sooner, faster:* τάχιον TACHION
Heb 13.19 that I may be restored to you the s.

SOOTHSAYING, BY
1. *give an oracle, prophesy:* μαντεύομαι (part.) MANTEUOMAI*
Acts 16.16 brought her owners much gain by s.

SOPATER: Σώπατρος 'sōpətər
Acts 20. 4 Sopater of Beroea, the son of Pyrrhus

SORCERER
1. *magician, sorcerer:* φάρμακος PHARMAKOS*
Rev 21. 8 "as for murderers, fornicators, sorcerers
22.15 Outside are the dogs and sorcerers

SORCERY
1. *use of drugs, magic:* φαρμακεία PHARMAKEIA*
Gal 5.20 idolatry, sorcery, enmity, strife
Rev 9.21 nor did they repent of . . their sorceries
18.23 "all nations were deceived by thy sorcery

SORE
1. *sore, ulcer:* ἕλκος HELKOS*
Lk 16.21 "the dogs came and licked his sores
Rev 16. 2 foul and evil sores came upon the men
16.11 cursed the God of heaven for their . . sores

SORES, BE FULL OF
1. *wound, ulcerate:* ἑλκόω (pass.) HELKOŌ*
Lk 16.20 "poor man named Lazarus, full of s.

SORROW
1. *grief:* λύπη LYPĒ
Lk 22.45 he came . . and found them sleeping for s.
Jn 16. 6 "sorrow has filled your hearts
16.20 "but your sorrow will turn into joy

Jn 16.21 "When a woman is in travail she has s.
16.22 "So you have sorrow now
Rom 9. 2 I have great s. and unceasing anguish
2 Cor 2. 7 he may be overwhelmed by excessive s.
Phil 2.27 But God had mercy on him . . lest I should have sorrow upon sorrow
2. *cause pain:* ὀδυνάω (pass.) ODYNAŌ
Acts 20.38 sorrowing . . that they should see . . no more

SORROWFUL
1. *grieve, cause pain:* λυπέω (pass. part.) LYPEŌ
Mt 19.22 the young man . . went away sorrowful
Mk 10.22 countenance fell, and he went away s.
2 Cor 6.10 as sorrowful, yet always rejoicing

SORROWFUL, BE
1. *grieve, cause pain:* λυπέω (pass.) LYPEŌ
Mt 26.22 they were very s., and began to say
26.37 he began to be sorrowful and troubled
Mk 14.19 They began to be s., and to say to him
Jn 16.20 "the world will rejoice; you will be s.

SORROWFUL, VERY
1. *very sad, deeply grieved:* περίλυπος PERILYPOS
Mt 26.38 "My soul is very s., even to death
Mk 14.34 "My soul is very s., even to death

SORRY, BE
1. *grieve, cause pain:* λυπέω (pass.) LYPEŌ
Mt 14. 9 king was s.; but because of his oaths

SORRY, EXCEEDINGLY
1. *very sad, deeply grieved:* περίλυπος PERILYPOS
Mk 6.26 the king was exceedingly sorry

SORRY, MAKE
1. *grieve, cause pain:* λυπέω LYPEŌ
2 Cor 7. 8 even if I made you sorry with my letter

SORT
1. *example, pattern:* ὑπόδειγμα HYPODEIGMA
Heb 4.11 fall by the same sort of disobedience
2. *gather, collect:* συλλέγω SYLLEGŌ
Mt 13.48 "drew it ashore . . and sorted the good

SORT OF, WHAT
1. *of what sort:* ὁποῖος HOPOIOS
1 Cor 3.13 fire will test what sort of work
2. *of what sort:* ποταπός POTAPOS
Mt 8.27 "What sort of man is this?
Lk 1.29 what sort of greeting this might be
7.39 "he would have known . . what s. of woman
2 Pet 3.11 what sort of persons ought you to be!

SOSIPATER: Σωσίπατρος sō'sipətər
Rom 16.21 Timothy . . greets you; so do . . Jason and S.

SOSTHENES: Σωσθένης 'sästhənēz
Acts 18.17 all seized S., . . ruler of the synagogue
1 Cor 1. 1 Paul, . . an apostle . . , and our brother S.

SOUL
1. *life, soul, self:* ψυχή PSYCHĒ
Mt 10.28 "do not fear those who . . cannot kill the soul; rather fear him who can destroy both soul
11.29 "you will find rest for your souls
12.18 "beloved with whom my s. is well pleased
22.37 "You shall love the Lord . . with all your . . s.
Mk 12.30 " 'you shall love the Lord . . with all your . . s.
14.34 "My s. is very sorrowful, even to death
Lk 1.46 Mary said, "My s. magnifies the Lord
2.35 "(a sword will pierce through your own s.
10.27 "You shall love the Lord . . with all your . . s.
12.19 " 'I will say to my soul, Soul, you have ample goods laid up for many years
12.20 " 'This night your soul is required of you
Jn 12.27 "Now is my soul troubled
Acts 2.27 " 'thou wilt not abandon my s. to Hades
2.41 were added . . about three thousand souls
2.43 And fear came upon every soul
3.23 " 'that every soul that does not listen
4.32 the company . . were of one heart and s.
7.14 "all his kindred, seventy-five souls
14.22 strengthening the souls of the disciples
2 Cor 12.15 gladly spend and be spent for your souls
1 Th 5.23 may your . . soul and body be kept sound
Heb 4.12 piercing to the division of s. and spirit
6.19 sure and steadfast anchor of the soul
10.38 "my soul has no pleasure in him
10.39 who have faith and keep their souls
13.17 they are keeping watch over your souls
Jas 1.21 which is able to save your souls
5.20 will save his soul from death
1 Pet 1. 9 you obtain the salvation of your souls
1.22 purified your souls by your obedience
2.11 passions . . that wage war against your s.
2.25 Shepherd and Guardian of your souls
4.19 entrust their souls to . . Creator
2 Pet 2. 8 (he was vexed in his righteous soul
2.14 They entice unsteady souls
3 Jn . 2 I know that it is well with your soul
Rev 6. 9 I saw under the altar the souls
18.13 slaves, that is, human souls
18.14 "fruit for which thy s. longed has gone
20. 4 Also I saw the souls of those

SOUND (*See also* TRUMPET, SOUND OF THE)
1. *good:* ἀγαθός AGATHOS
Mt 7.17 "So, every sound tree bears good fruit
2. *take soundings:* βολίζω BOLIZŌ*
Acts 27.28 they sounded and found twenty fathoms; . . they sounded again and found fifteen
3. *sound, noise:* ἦχος ĒCHOS I
Acts 2. 2 suddenly a sound came from heaven
Heb 12.19 the sound of a trumpet, and a voice
4. *single, pure:* ἁπλοῦς HAPLOUS*
Mt 6.22 "if . . eye is sound, . . body will be . . light
Lk 11.34 "when . . eye is s., . . body is full of light
5. *complete, whole:* ὁλόκληρος HOLOKLĒROS
1 Th 5.23 may your . . soul and body be kept sound
6. *be in good health:* ὑγιαίνω (part.) HYGIAINŌ
1 Tim 1.10 whatever else is contrary to s. doctrine
6. 3 does not agree with sound words
2 Tim 1.13 Follow the pattern of sound words
4. 3 when people will not endure s. teaching
Tit 1. 9 able to give instruction in s. doctrine
2. 1 teach what befits sound doctrine
2. 2 Bid the older men be . . sound in faith
7. *healthy, sound:* ὑγιής HYGIĒS
Tit 2. 8 sound speech that cannot be censured
8. *speak, talk:* λαλέω LALEŌ
Rev 10. 3 when he called . . , the . . thunders sounded
10. 4 when the seven thunders had sounded
9. *voice, sound:* φωνή PHŌNĒ
Jn 3. 8 "wind[f] blows . . , and you hear the s. of it
Acts 2. 6 at this s. the multitude came together
1 Cor 14. 8 if the bugle gives an indistinct sound
Rev 1.15 his voice was like the s. of many waters
14. 2 heard a voice . . like the s. of many waters and like the sound of loud thunder
18.22 "the sound of harpers and minstrels . . and the s. of the millstone . . heard . . no more
19. 6 multitude, like the s. of many waters and like the s. of mighty thunderpeals

SOUND A TRUMPET
1. *sound a trumpet:* σαλπίζω SALPIZŌ
[a]B.3.b.4
Mt 6. 2 "when you give alms, sound no trumpet
1 Cor 15.52 trumpet will s., and . . dead will be raised
Rev 10. 7 [a]the trumpet call to be sounded

SOUND, BE
1. *be in good health:* ὑγιαίνω HYGIAINŌ
Tit 1.13 that they may be sound in the faith

SOUND FORTH
1. *utter sounds:* ἐξηχέω (pass.) EXĒCHEŌ*
1 Th 1. 8 the word of the Lord sounded forth

SOUND, NOT
1. *sick, base, evil:* πονηρός PONĒROS
Mt 6.23 "if your eye is not s., your whole body
Lk 11.34 "when it is not sound, your body is full

SOUND, SAFE AND
1. *be in good health:* ὑγιαίνω (part.) HYGIAINŌ
Lk 15.27 " 'he has received him safe and sound

SOURCE
1. *responsible:* αἴτιος (subst. masc.) AITIOS
Heb 5. 9 he became . . source of eternal salvation
CONTEXTUALLY
1 Cor 1.30 He is . . s. of your life in Christ Jesus

SOUTH
1. *midday, the south:* μεσημβρία MESĒMBRIA
Acts 8.26 "Rise and go toward the south[g]†
2. *south, south wind:* νότος NOTOS*
Mt 12.42 "queen of . . S. will arise at the judgment
Lk 11.31 "queen of . . S. will arise at the judgment
12.55 "when you see the s. wind blowing
13.29 "men will come . . from north and south
Acts 27.13 when the south wind blew gently
28.13 after one day a south wind sprang up
Rev 21.13 on the s. three gates, and on the west

SOUTHEAST
1. *northwest* (Lat.): χῶρος CHŌROS*
[a]κατὰ χῶρον
Acts 27.12 [a]harbor . . looking northeast and southeast[a]†

SOUTHWEST
1. *southwest* (wind): λίψ LIPS
Acts [27.12 harbor . . looking *southwest and northwest*†

SOVEREIGN
1. *ruler:* δυνάστης DYNASTĒS
1 Tim 6.15 the blessed and only Sovereign

SOVEREIGN LORD
1. *master, lord:* δεσπότης DESPOTĒS
Acts 4.24 "S. Lord, who didst make the heaven
Rev 6.10 "O Sovereign Lord, holy and true

SOW
1. *throw, put:* βάλλω BALLŌ
Lk 13.19 "seed which a man . . sowed in his garden
2. *sow with seed:* ἐπισπείρω EPISPEIRŌ*
Mt 13.25 "his enemy came and sowed weeds
3. *sow, female of the swine:* ὗς HYS*
2 Pet 2.22 s. is washed only to wallow in the mire
4. *sow:* σπείρω SPEIRŌ
Mt 6.26 "they neither sow nor reap nor gather
13. 3 saying: "A sower went out to sow
13. 4 "as he sowed, . . seeds fell along the path
13.19 "evil one . . snatches away what is sown . . ; this is what was sown along the path
13.20 "As for what was sown on rocky ground
13.22 "As for what was sown among thorns
13.23 "As for what was sown on good soil
13.24 "a man who sowed good seed
13.27 " 'Sir, did you not sow good seed?
13.31 "like . . mustard seed which a man . . sowed
13.37 "who sows the good seed is the Son of man
13.39 "the enemy who sowed them is the devil
25.24 " 'reaping where you did not sow
25.26 " 'that I reap where I have not sowed
Mk 4. 3 "Listen! A sower went out to sow
4. 4 "as he sowed, some seed fell along
4.14 "The sower sows the word
4.15 "along the path, where the word is sown
4.15 "Satan . . takes away . . word which is sown
4.16 "the ones sown upon rocky ground
4.18 "the ones sown among thorns
4.20 "those . . sown upon the good soil
4.31 "like a grain of mustard seed, . . when sown
4.32 "yet when it is sown it grows up
Lk 8. 5 "A sower went out to sow his seed; and as he sowed, some fell along the path
12.24 "the ravens: they neither sow nor reap
19.21 " 'you . . reap what you did not sow
19.22 " 'severe man, . . reaping what I did not s.
Jn 4.37 "the saying . . 'One sows and another reaps
1 Cor 9.11 we have sown spiritual good among you
15.36 What you sow does not come to life
15.37 what you sow is not the body . . to be
1 Cor 15.42 What is sown is perishable
15.43 It is sown in dishonor, . . raised in glory. It is sown in weakness, . . raised in power
15.44 It is sown a physical body, it is raised
2 Cor 9. 6 who sows sparingly will . . reap sparingly, . . who sows bountifully will . . reap bountifully
Gal 6. 7 whatever a man sows, that he will . . reap
6. 8 who sows to his . . flesh will . . reap corruption; . . who sows to the Spirit will . . reap . . life
Jas 3.18 harvest of righteousness is sown

SOWER
1. *sow:* σπείρω (subst. part.) SPEIRŌ
Mt 13. 3 "A sower went out to sow
13.18 "Hear then the parable of the sower
Mk 4. 3 "Listen! A sower went out to sow
4.14 "The sower sows the word
Lk 8. 5 "A sower went out to sow his seed
Jn 4.36 "that s. and reaper may rejoice together
2 Cor 9.10 He who supplies seed to the sower

SPAIN: Σπανία 'spān
Rom 15.24 to see you in passing as I go to Spain
15.28 I shall go on by way of you to Spain

SPAN OF LIFE
1. *age, stature:* ἡλικία HĒLIKIA
Mt 6.27 "can add one cubit to his s. of life?[p]†
Lk 12.25 "can add a cubit to his s. of life?[n]†

SPARE
1. *refrain from, spare:* φείδομαι PHEIDOMAI
Acts 20.29 "wolves will come . . , not sparing the flock
Rom 8.32 He who did not spare his own Son
11.21 For if God did not spare the natural branches, neither will he spare you
1 Cor 7.28 worldly troubles, and I would s. you that
2 Cor 1.23 it was to spare you that I refrained
13. 2 if I come again I will not spare them
2 Pet 2. 4 if God did not spare the angels
2. 5 if he did not spare the ancient world

SPARE, HAVE ENOUGH AND TO
1. *abound:* περισσεύω PERISSEUŌ
Lk 15. 17 " 'servants have bread enough and to spare

SPARINGLY
1. *sparingly, thriftily:* φειδομένως PHEIDOMENŌS*
2 Cor 9. 6 he who sows sparingly will also reap sparingly

SPARROW
1. *sparrow:* στρουθίον STROUTHION*
Mt 10.29 "Are not two sparrows sold for a penny?
10.31 "you are of more value than . . sparrows
Lk 12. 6 "five sparrows sold for two pennies
12. 7 "you are of more value than . . sparrows

SPEAK (*See also* MESSAGE, SPEAK A; TRUTH, SPEAK THE)
1. *speak out:* ἀποφθέγγομαι APOPHTHEGGOMAI
Acts 26.25 "but I am speaking the sober truth
2. *say, speak:* εἶπον EIPON
Mt 12.32 "whoever speaks against the Holy Spirit
16.11 "I did not speak about bread
17.13 he was speaking to them of John
22. 1 again Jesus spoke to them in parables
Lk 6.26 "Woe to you, when all speak well of you
14. 3 Jesus spoke to . . lawyers . . "Is it lawful?
20.39 "Teacher, you have spoken well
Jn 2.22 believed . . the word . . Jesus had spoken
4.50 man believed the word that Jesus spoke
11.11 Thus he spoke, and then he said to them
12.38 the word spoken by the prophet Isaiah
13.21 When Jesus had . . spoken, he was troubled
18. 1 When Jesus had spoken . . , he went forth
18. 9 to fulfil the word which he had spoken
18.16 disciple . . went out and spoke to the maid
18.32 to fulfil the word . . Jesus had spoken
Acts 20.36 when he had spoken thus, he knelt down
3. *say, speak:* ἐρῶ ERŌ
Mt 1.22 to fulfil what the Lord had spoken
2.15 to fulfil what the Lord had spoken
2.17 Then was fulfilled what was spoken
2.23 that what was spoken by the prophets

Mt 3. 3 who was spoken of by the prophet Isaiah
4.14 that what was spoken . . might be fulfilled
8.17 to fulfil what was spoken by the prophet
12.17 to fulfil what was spoken by the prophet
13.35 to fulfil what was spoken by the prophet[k]
21. 4 to fulfil what was spoken by the prophet
24.15 "sacrilege spoken of by the prophet
27. 9 what had been spoken by the prophet
Lk 12.10 "who speaks a word against the Son of man
Jn 11.13 Now Jesus had spoken of his death
Acts 2.16 "what was spoken by the prophet Joel
13.34 "he spoke in this way, 'I will give you
20.38 because of the word he had spoken
23. 5 " 'You shall not speak evil of a ruler
2 Cor 12. 6 for I shall be speaking the truth
Heb 4. 4 he has . . spoken of the seventh day

4. *come to be, happen, be:* γίνομαι GINOMAI [A.6.a.5]
Lk 9.36 when the voice had spoken

5. *speak, talk:* λαλέω LALEŌ
Mt 9.18 While he was thus speaking to them
9.33 dumb man spoke; . . the crowds marveled
10.19 "do not be anxious how you are to speak
10.20 "it is not you who speak, but the Spirit of your Father speaking through you
12.22 so that the dumb man spoke and saw
12.34 "how can you s. good, when you are evil? For out of . . the heart the mouth speaks
12.46 While he was . . speaking to the people . . his mother . . stood outside, asking to s.
[12.47 *"your brothers are . . asking to s. to you*‡
13.10 "Why do you s. to them in parables?
13.13 "This is why I s. to them in parables
14.27 he spoke to them, saying, "Take heart
15.31 when they saw the dumb speaking
17. 5 still speaking, when lo, a bright cloud
26.47 he was still speaking, Judas came
Mk 1.34 would not permit the demons to speak
2. 7 "Why does this man speak thus?
4.33 With many such parables he spoke
4.34 did not s. to them without a parable
5.35 While he was still speaking
6.50 he spoke to them . . "Take heart, it is I
7.35 his tongue was released, and he spoke
7.37 "makes the deaf hear and the dumb speak
12. 1 he began to speak to them in parables
13.11 "it is not you who s., but the . . Spirit
14.43 while he was still speaking, Judas came
16.17 "they will speak in new tongues[k]‡
16.19 Lord Jesus, after he had spoken to them[k]‡
Lk 1.19 "I am Gabriel . . ; and I was sent to s.
1.20 "you will be silent and unable to speak
1.22 when he came out, he could not speak
1.45 "fulfilment of what was spoken to her
1.55 "as he spoke to our fathers, to Abraham
1.64 his tongue ⟨was⟩ loosed, and he spoke
1.70 "as he spoke by the mouth of . . prophets
2.38 she gave thanks to God, . . spoke of him
2.50 the saying which he spoke to them
4.41 But he . . would not allow them to speak
5. 4 when he had ceased speaking
5.21 "Who is this that speaks blasphemies?
6.45 "for out of . . the heart his mouth speaks
7.15 dead man sat up, and began to speak
8.49 While he was . . speaking, a man . . came
9.11 spoke to them of the kingdom of God
11.14 dumb man spoke, and . . people marveled
11.37 While he was speaking, a Pharisee asked
22.47 While he was still speaking, there came
22.60 while he was . . speaking, the cock crowed
24.25 "all that the prophets have spoken!
24.44 "These are my words which I spoke to you
Jn 3.11 "we speak of what we know
3.31 and of the earth he speaks
4.26 Jesus said . . "I who speak to you am he
6.63 "words . . I have spoken to you are spirit
7.13 Yet for fear . . no one spoke openly of him
7.17 "whether I am speaking on my own
Jn 7.18 "He who speaks on his own authority
7.26 "here he is, speaking openly
7.46 "No man ever spoke like this man!
8.12 Again Jesus spoke to them
8.20 These words he spoke in the treasury
8.28 "I . . speak . . as the Father taught me
8.30 As he spoke thus, many believed
8.38 "I speak of what I have seen
8.44 "he speaks according to his own nature
9.21 "he is of age, he will speak for himself
9.29 "We know that God has spoken to Moses
9.37 Jesus said . . "it is he who speaks to you
12.29 Others said, "An angel has spoken to him
12.41 he saw his glory and spoke of him
12.48 "word . . I have spoken will be his judge
12.49 "I have not spoken on my own authority
12.49 "given me commandment . . what to speak
14.10 "I do not speak on my own authority
14.25 "These things I have spoken to you
15. 3 "clean by the word which I have spoken
15.11 "These things I have spoken to you
15.22 "If I had not come and spoken to them
16.13 "he will not speak on his own authority, but whatever he hears he will speak
16.25 "I shall no longer speak . . in figures
16.29 "Ah, now you are speaking plainly!
17. 1 When Jesus had spoken these words
17.13 "these things I speak in the world
18.20 "I have spoken openly to the world
18.23 "If I have spoken wrongly, bear witness
19.10 Pilate . . said . . "You will not speak to me?
Acts 2. 4 they . . began to speak in other tongues
2. 6 heard them speaking in his own language
2. 7 "Are not all . . who are speaking Galileans?
2.31 "spoke of the resurrection of the Christ
3.21 "all that God spoke by . . his . . prophets
3.24 "And all the prophets who have spoken
4. 1 as they were speaking to the people
4.17 "let us warn them to speak no more
4.20 "we cannot but s. of what we have seen
4.29 "grant . . thy servants[f] to speak thy word
4.31 spoke the word of God with boldness
5.20 "s. to the people . . the words of this Life
5.40 not to speak in the name of Jesus
6.10 could not withstand the wisdom . . he spoke
6.11 "We have heard him s. . . against Moses
6.13 "never ceases to s. . . against this . . place
7. 6 "God spoke to this effect
7.38 "angel who spoke to him at Mount Sinai
7.44 "as he who spoke to Moses directed him
8.25 they had . . spoken the word of the Lord
9.27 he had seen the Lord, who spoke to him
9.29 And he spoke . . against the Hellenists
10. 7 angel who spoke to him had departed
10.46 they heard them speaking in tongues
11.15 "As I began to s., the . . Spirit fell
11.19 speaking the word to none except Jews
11.20 coming to Antioch spoke to the Greeks[i]
13.45 contradicted what was spoken by Paul
13.46 "that the word . . be spoken first to you
14. 1 so spoke that a great company believed
14. 9 He listened to Paul speaking
14.25 when they had spoken the word in Perga
16. 6 forbidden . . to speak the word in Asia
16.13 we sat down and spoke to the women
16.32 they spoke the word of the Lord to him
18. 9 "Do not be afraid, but speak
18.25 fervent in spirit, he spoke and taught
19. 6 they spoke with tongues and prophesied
20.30 "will arise men speaking perverse things
21.39 "I beg you, let me speak to the people
22. 9 "did not hear . . the one who was speaking
23. 9 "What if . . an angel spoke to him?
26.26 "the king knows . . , to him I speak freely
28.21 "none . . has . . spoken any evil about you
Rom 3.19 it speaks to those who are under the law
7. 1 speaking to those who know the law

Rom 15.18 I will not venture to s. of anything
1 Cor 12. 3 no one speaking by the Spirit of God
12.30 Do all speak with tongues?
13. 1 If I s. in . . tongues of men and of angels
13.11 When I was a child, I spoke like a child
14. 2 For one who speaks in a tongue speaks not to men but to God
14. 3 he who prophesies speaks to men
14. 4 who speaks in a tongue edifies himself
14. 5 Now I want you all to speak in tongues
14. 5 greater than he who speaks in tongues
14. 6 if I come to you speaking in tongues
14. 9 For you will be speaking into the air
14.13 he who speaks in a tongue should pray
14.18 I thank God that I speak in tongues
14.19 I would rather speak five words
14.21 "by . . foreigners will I s. to this people
14.23 If, therefore, . . all speak in tongues
14.27 If any s. in a tongue, . . let one interpret
14.28 let each . . speak to himself and to God
14.29 Let two or three prophets speak
14.34 For they are not permitted to speak
14.35 shameful for a woman to s. in church
14.39 do not forbid speaking in tongues
2 Cor 2.17 in the sight of God we speak in Christ
4.13 as he . . wrote, "I believed, and so I spoke," we too believe, and so we s.
12.19 we have been speaking in Christ
13. 3 proof that Christ is speaking in me
Eph 4.25 let every one speak the truth
6.20 may declare it boldly, as I ought to s.
Phil 1.14 much more bold to s. the word of God
Col 4. 4 may make it clear, as I ought to speak
1 Th 2. 4 so we speak, not to please men
2.16 hindering us from speaking to . . Gentiles
Heb 1. 1 God spoke of old to our fathers
1. 2 he has spoken to us by a Son
2. 5 world to come, of which we are speaking
3. 5 the things that were to be spoken later
4. 8 God[i] would not s. later of another day
6. 9 Though we speak thus, . . we feel sure
11. 4 through his faith he is still speaking
12.24 blood that speaks more graciously
12.25 do not refuse him who is speaking
13. 7 those who spoke to you the word of God
Jas 1.19 Let every man be . . slow to speak
2.12 So s. and so act as those . . to be judged
5.10 prophets who spoke in . . name of the Lord
1 Pet 3.10 "let him keep . . lips from speaking guile
4.11 whoever speaks, as one who utters oracles
2 Pet 1.21 men moved by the Holy Spirit spoke
3.16 speaking . . as he does in all his letters
Jude .15 things . . ungodly sinners have spoken
Rev 1.12 to see the voice that was speaking to me
4. 1 first voice, which I had heard speaking
10. 8 the voice . . from heaven spoke to me
13.11 like a lamb and it spoke like a dragon
13.15 that the image of the beast should even s.
21. 9 one of the seven angels . . spoke to me

6. *say, speak:* λέγω LEGŌ
Mt 11. 7 Jesus began to speak to the crowds
21.45 perceived that he was speaking about them
Mk 14.71 "I do not know this man of whom you s.
Lk 7.24 he began to speak . . concerning John
9.31 who appeared in glory and spoke
20.21 "Teacher, we know that you s. . . rightly
21. 5 spoke of the temple, how it was adorned
22.65 spoke many other words against him
Jn 2.21 he spoke of the temple of his body
6.71 He spoke of Judas the son of Simon
8.27 that he spoke to them of the Father
13.18 "I am not speaking of you all
13.22 disciples . . , uncertain of whom he spoke
13.24 "Tell us who it is of whom he speaks
Acts 1. 3 speaking of the kingdom of God
24.10 the governor had motioned to him to s.
26. 1 "You have permission to s. for yourself
Rom 3. 5 (I speak in a human way
6.19 I am speaking in human terms
9. 1 I am speaking the truth in Christ
11.13 Now I am speaking to you Gentiles
1 Cor 9.10 Does he not s. entirely for our sake?
10.15 I speak as to sensible men
2 Cor 6.13 I speak as to children—widen your hearts
11.21 I am speaking as a fool
Eph 5.12 it is a shame even to s. of the things
Heb 7.13 one of whom these things are spoken
8.13 In speaking of a new covenant
9. 5 Of these . . we cannot now s. in detail
11.14 people who speak thus make it clear

7. *utter, speak:* φθέγγομαι PHTHEGGOMAI
Acts 4.18 charged them not to s. or teach at all
2 Pet 2.16 a dumb ass spoke with human voice

CONTEXTUALLY
Jn 1.40 One . . who heard John speak . . was Andrew
Acts 24.24 heard him s. upon faith in Christ Jesus

SPEAK AGAINST

1. *speak against:* ἀντιλέγω ANTILEGŌ
Lk 2.34 "for a sign that is spoken against
Acts 28.22 "everywhere it is spoken against

2. *speak against:* καταλαλέω KATALALEŌ
1 Pet 2.12 in case they speak against you

SPEAK BEFOREHAND

1. *foretell, say before:* προεῖπον PROEIPON
Acts 1.16 "which the Holy Spirit spoke beforehand

SPEAK BOLDLY
SPEAK OUT BOLDLY

1. *speak freely:* παρρησιάζομαι PARRĒSIAZOMAI
Acts 13.46 Paul and Barnabas spoke out boldly
14. 3 remained . . a long time, speaking boldly
18.26 He began to s. boldly in the synagogue
19. 8 entered the synagogue and . . spoke boldly

SPEAK EVIL AGAINST
SPEAK EVIL OF
SPEAK OF S. AS EVIL

1. *blaspheme, slander:* βλασφημέω BLASPHĒMEŌ
Rom 14.16 do not let your good be spoken of as evil
Tit 3. 2 to s. evil of no one, to avoid quarreling

2. *revile, abuse:* κακολογέω KAKOLOGEŌ*
Mt 15. 4 " 'He who speaks evil of father or mother
Mk 7.10 " 'He who speaks evil of father or mother
9.39 "be able soon after to speak evil of me
Acts 19. 9 disbelieved, speaking evil of the Way

3. *speak against:* καταλαλέω KATALALEŌ
Jas 4.11 Do not speak evil against one another . . He that speaks evil against a brother . . , speaks evil against the law

SPEAK FIRST

1. *anticipate, be beforehand:* προφθάνω PROPHTHANŌ* [A.6.a.5]
Mt 17.25 when he came . . , Jesus spoke to him first

SPEAK OUT BOLDLY (*See* SPEAK BOLDLY)

SPEAK, PROVOKE TO

1. *interrogate:* ἀποστοματίζω APOSTOMATIZŌ*
Lk 11.53 to provoke him to s. of many things

SPEAK TO
SPEAK WITH

1. *talk to:* προσλαλέω PROSLALEŌ*
Acts 13.43 Paul and Barnabas, who spoke to them
28.20 "I have asked to see you and s. with you

2. *call to, address:* προσφωνέω PROSPHŌNEŌ
Acts 21.40 spoke to them in the Hebrew language

SPEAK WELL OF

1. *bear witness, testify:* μαρτυρέω MARTYREŌ
Lk 4.22 all spoke well of him, and wondered
Acts 10.22 God-fearing man, who is well spoken of
16. 2 He was well spoken of by the brethren
22.12 well spoken of by all the Jews . . there

SPEAKER
1. *speak, talk:* λαλέω (subst. part.) LALEŌ
1 Cor 14.11 I shall be a foreigner to the speaker and the speaker a foreigner to me
IDIOMATICALLY
a. Acts 14.12 because he was the chief speaker ἐπειδὴ αὐτὸς ἦν ὁ ἡγούμενος τοῦ λόγου [LOGOS]
CONTEXTUALLY
1 Cor 12.28 speakers in various kinds of tongues

SPEAKING (*See also* FIGURATIVELY SPEAKING; FINISH SPEAKING)
1. *word, reckoning:* λόγος LOGOS
2 Cor 11. 6 Even if I am unskilled in speaking

SPEAR
1. *spear, lance:* λόγχη LOGCHĒ*
Mt [27.49 *another took a spear and pierced his side*‡
Jn 19.34 soldiers pierced his side with a spear

SPEARMAN
1. *spearman:* δεξιολάβος DEXIOLABOS*
Acts 23.23 "get ready . . two hundred spearmen to go

SPECIAL GIFT
1. *gift, favor bestowed:* χάρισμα CHARISMA
1 Cor 7. 7 each has his own special gift from God

SPECK
1. *chip:* κάρφος KARPHOS*
Mt 7. 3 "the speck that is in your brother's eye
7. 4 " 'Let me take the s. out of your eye
7. 5 "you will see clearly to take the s. out
Lk 6.41 "the speck that is in your brother's eye
6.42 " 'Brother, let me take out the speck
6.42 "you will see clearly to take out the s.

SPECTACLE
1. *theater, spectacle:* θέατρον THEATRON
1 Cor 4. 9 we have become a spectacle to the world

SPECULATION
1. *research, speculation:* ἐκζήτησις EKZĒTĒSIS*
1 Tim 1. 4 genealogies which promote speculations

SPEECH
1. *tongue, speech:* γλῶσσα GLŌSSA
1 Jn 3.18 let us not love in word or speech
2. *word, reckoning:* λόγος LOGOS
Acts 20. 7 he prolonged his speech until midnight
1 Cor 1. 5 you were enriched in him with all s.
2. 4 s. and . . message . . not in plausible words
14. 9 if you in a tongue utter speech
2 Cor 6. 7 truthful speech, and the power of God
10.10 "but . . his speech of no account
Col 4. 6 Let your speech always be gracious
1 Tim 4.12 set the believers an example in speech
Tit 2. 8 sound speech that cannot be censured

SPEECH, A MAN WHO HAS AN IMPEDIMENT IN HIS
1. *speaking with difficulty:* μογιλάλος (subst.) MOGILALOS*
Mk 7.32 a man who . . had an impediment in his s.

SPEECH, BEGUILING
1. *persuasive argument:* πιθανολογία PITHANOLOGIA*
Col 2. 4 that no one . . delude you with b. speech

SPEECHLESS
1. *dumb, senseless:* ἐνεός ENEOS*
Acts 9. 7 men . . traveling with him stood speechless

SPEECHLESS, BE
1. *muzzle, put to silence:* φιμόω (pass.) PHIMOŌ
Mt 22.12 "And he was speechless

SPEED ON
1. *run, move quickly:* τρέχω TRECHŌ
2 Th 3. 1 that the word of the Lord may speed on

SPEED ONE ON HIS JOURNEY
SPEED ONE ON HIS WAY
1. *send forth, escort:* προπέμπω PROPEMPŌ
Rom 15.24 I hope . . to be sped on my journey
1 Cor 16. 6 that you may speed me on my journey
16.11 Speed him on his way in peace
Tit 3.13 speed Zenas . . and Apollos on their way

SPEEDILY
1. *with speed:* ἐν τάχει TACHOS [B.1.a.1]
Lk 18. 8 "I tell you, he will vindicate them s.

SPEND (*See also* WINTER, SPEND THE)
1. *spend, consume:* δαπανάω DAPANAŌ
Mk 5.26 who had suffered much . . and had spent all
Lk 15.14 "when he had spent everything, a . . famine
2 Cor 12.15 I will most gladly s. . . for your souls
Jas 4. 3 you ask wrongly, to s. it on . . passions
2. *spend completely, exhaust:* ἐκδαπανάω EKDAPANAŌ*
2 Cor 12.15 I will . . gladly . . be spent for your souls
3. *continue, remain:* ἐπιμένω EPIMENŌ
1 Cor 16. 7 I hope to spend some time with you
4. *do, make:* ποιέω POIEŌ
Acts 15.33 after they had spent some time
18.23 After spending some time . . he departed
20. 3 There he spent three months
Jas 4.13 "we will . . s. a year there and trade
5. *spend lavishly:* προσαναλίσκω PROSANALISKŌ
Lk [8.43 *spent all her living upon physicians*‡

SPEND MORE
1. *spend in addition:* προσδαπανάω PROSDAPANAŌ*
Lk 10.35 " 'whatever more you s., I will repay you

SPEND ONE'S TIME
SPEND TIME
1. *waste time:* χρονοτριβέω CHRONOTRIBEŌ*
Acts 20.16 might not have to spend time in Asia
2. *have time, have opportunity:* εὐκαιρέω EUKAIREŌ
Acts 17.21 spent their time . . hearing something new

SPENT
1. *come to be, happen, be:* γίνομαι (part.) GINOMAI
Acts 26. 4 "spent from the beginning among my own

SPENT, BE FAR
1. *incline:* κλίνω (perf.) KLINŌ
Lk 24.29 "Stay with us, for . . the day is . . far s.

SPEW
1. *vomit, spit out:* ἐμέω EMEŌ*
Rev 3.16 " 'I will spew you out of my mouth

SPICE
1. *amomum* (an Indian spice plant): ἄμωμον AMŌMON*
Rev 18.13 cinnamon, spice, incense, myrrh
2. *aromatic herb or spice:* ἄρωμα ARŌMA*
Mk 16. 1 bought spices . . that they might . . anoint him
Lk 23.56 they returned, and prepared spices
24. 1 went to the tomb, taking the spices
Jn 19.40 bound it in linen cloths with the spices

SPILL
1. *pour out:* ἐκχέω EKCHEŌ
Mt 9.17 "wine is spilled, . . the skins are destroyed
Lk 5.37 "it will be spilled, . . the skins . . destroyed

SPIN
1. *spin:* νήθω NĒTHŌ*
Mt 6.28 "the lilies . . neither toil nor spin
Lk 12.27 "the lilies . . neither toil nor spin[o]

SPIRIT (*See also* DIVINATION, SPIRIT OF)
1. *wind, breath, spirit:* πνεῦμα PNEUMA
[a]B.3.b.6 (H. S. = Holy Spirit)
Mt 1.18 she was found to be with child of the H. S.
1.20 "that . . conceived in her is of the H. S.
3.11 "he will baptize you with the H. S.
3.16 the S. of God descending like a dove
4. 1 Jesus was led . . by the S. . . to be tempted
5. 3 "Blessed are the poor in spirit
8.16 he cast out the spirits with a word
10. 1 gave them authority over unclean spirits
10.20 "it is . . the S. of your Father speaking
12.18 "I will put my Spirit upon him
12.28 "if . . by the S. of God . . I cast out demons
12.31 "blasphemy against . . S. will not be forgiven
12.32 "whoever speaks against the H. S.
12.43 "When the unclean spirit has gone out
12.45 "brings with him seven . . spirits more evil
22.43 "David, inspired by the S.,[t] calls him Lord
26.41 "the s. . . is willing, but the flesh is weak

Mt 27.50 Jesus cried again . . and yielded up his s.
28.19 "baptizing . . in the name of the . . H. S.
Mk 1. 8 "he will baptize you with the H. S.
1.10 he saw . . the S. descending . . like a dove
1.12 The S. . . drove him . . into the wilderness
1.23 there was . . a man with an unclean s.
1.26 the unclean spirit, convulsing him
1.27 "he commands even the unclean spirits
2. 8 "Jesus, perceiving in his spirit
3.11 whenever the unclean spirits beheld him
3.29 "whoever blasphemes against the H. S.
3.30 they had said, "He has an unclean s.
5. 2 there met him . . a man with an unclean s.
5. 8 "Come out of the man, you unclean s.!
5.13 the unclean spirits came out
6. 7 gave . . authority over the unclean spirits
7.25 daughter was possessed by an unclean s.
8.12 And he sighed deeply in his spirit
9.17 "I brought my son . . , for he has a dumb s.
9.20 when the s. saw him . . , it convulsed the boy
9.25 he rebuked the unclean spirit . . "You dumb and deaf spirit, . . come out of him
12.36 "David himself, inspired by[z] the H. S.
13.11 "for it is not you who speak, but the H. S.
14.38 "the s. . . is willing, but the flesh is weak
Lk 1.15 "he will be filled with the H. S.
1.17 "will go before him in the s. . . of Elijah
1.35 "The Holy Spirit will come upon you
1.41 Elizabeth was filled with the H. S.
1.47 "my spirit rejoices in God my Savior
1.67 Zechariah was filled with the H. S.
1.80 the child grew and became strong in s.
2.25 Simeon, . . the H. S. was upon him
2.26 revealed to him by the Holy Spirit
2.27 by the S.[h] he came into the temple
3.16 "he will baptize you with the H. S.
3.22 the Holy Spirit descended upon him
4. 1 Jesus, full of the Holy Spirit, returned . . and was led by the Spirit
4.14 Jesus returned in the power of the S.
4.18 "The Spirit of the Lord is upon me
4.33 man who had the s. of an unclean demon
4.36 "he commands the unclean spirits
6.18 those . . troubled with unclean spirits
7.21 he cured many of . . evil spirits
8. 2 some women . . healed of evil spirits
8.29 he had commanded the unclean spirit
8.55 her spirit returned, and she got up
9.39 "a spirit seizes him, and he . . cries out
9.42 But Jesus rebuked the unclean spirit
[9.55 "*what manner of spirit you are of*‡
10.20 "do not rejoice . . that . . spirits are subject
10.21 that same hour he rejoiced in the H. S.
11.13 "will . . give the H. S. to those who ask!
11.24 "When the unclean s. has gone out
11.26 "he goes and brings seven other spirits
12.10 "he who blasphemes against the H. S.
12.12 "for the H. S. will teach you in that . . hour
13.11 woman who had had a spirit of infirmity
23.46 "Father, into thy hands I commit my s.!
24.37 they . . supposed that they saw a spirit
24.39 "for a spirit has not flesh and bones
Jn 1.32 "I saw the Spirit descend as a dove
1.33 " 'He on whom you see the S. descend . . is he who baptizes with the H. S.
3. 5 "unless one is born of water and the S.
3. 6 "That which is born of the flesh is flesh, and that . . born of the Spirit is spirit[f]
3. 8 "with every one who is born of the S.
3.34 not by measure that he gives the S.
4.23 "worship the Father in s. and truth
4.24 "God is spirit, and those who worship him must worship in spirit and truth
6.63 "It is the s. that gives life . . ; the words that I have spoken to you are s. and life
7.39 Now this he said about the Spirit . . ; for as yet the S. had not been given
Jn 11.33 he was deeply moved in spirit
13.21 "he was troubled in spirit, and testified
14.17 "⟨another Counselor,⟩ even the S. of truth
14.26 "But the Counselor, the Holy Spirit
15.26 "the Counselor . . , even the S. of truth
16.13 "When the Spirit of truth comes
19.30 he bowed his head and gave up his s.
20.22 "Receive the Holy Spirit
Acts 1. 2 commandment through the Holy Spirit
1. 5 "you shall be baptized with the H. S.
1. 8 "power when the H. S. has come upon you
1.16 "scripture . . which the H. S. spoke
2. 4 they were all filled with the H. S. and began to speak . . , as the S. gave them
2.17 " 'I will pour out my S. upon all flesh
2.18 " 'in those days I will pour out my S.
2.33 "having received . . the promise of the H. S.
2.38 "you shall receive the gift of the H. S.
4. 8 Then Peter, filled with the H. S., said
4.25 "who . . didst say by the H. S.
4.31 they were all filled with the H. S.
5. 3 "Satan filled your heart to lie to the H. S.
5. 9 "agreed . . to tempt the S. of the Lord
5.16 those afflicted with unclean spirits
5.32 "we are witnesses . . and so is the H. S.
6. 3 seven men of good repute, full of the S.
6. 5 Stephen, . . full of faith and of the H. S.
6.10 they could not withstand . . the Spirit
7.51 "you always resist the Holy Spirit
7.55 full of the H. S., gazed into heaven
7.59 prayed, "Lord Jesus, receive my s.
8. 7 unclean spirits came out of many
8.15 prayed . . that they might receive the H. S.
8.17 they received the Holy Spirit
8.18 Simon saw that the S. was given
8.19 "that any one . . may receive the H. S.
8.29 the Spirit said to Philip, "Go up
8.39 the S. of the Lord caught up Philip
9.17 "that you may . . be filled with the H. S.
9.31 walking . . in the comfort of the H. S.
10.19 while Peter was pondering . . , the S. said
10.38 "how God anointed Jesus . . with the H. S.
10.44 the H. S. fell on all who heard the word
10.45 the gift of the H. S. had been poured out
10.47 "people who have received the H. S.
11.12 "the S. told me to go with them
11.15 "As I began to speak, the H. S. fell
11.16 " 'you shall be baptized with the H. S.
11.24 a good man, full of the H. S. and of faith
11.28 Agabus stood up and foretold by the S.
13. 2 H. S. said, "Set apart for me Barnabas
13. 4 being sent out by the H. S., they went
13. 9 Paul, filled with the H. S., looked intently
13.52 the disciples were filled . . with the H. S.
15. 8 "giving them the H. S. just as he did to us
15.28 "it has seemed good to the H. S. and to us
16. 6 having been forbidden by the H. S.
16. 7 the Spirit of Jesus did not allow them
16.16 [a]slave girl who had a s. of divination
16.18 Paul . . said to the spirit . . "come out of her
17.16 at Athens, his s. was provoked within
18.25 being fervent in spirit, he spoke
19. 2 "Did you receive the Holy S. . . ?" . . "No, we . . never . . heard that there is a Holy S.
19. 6 the H. S. came on them; and they spoke
19.12 the evil spirits came out of them
19.13 over those who had evil spirits, saying
19.15 evil s. answered them, "Jesus I know
19.16 the man in whom the evil spirit was
19.21 Paul resolved in the S. to pass through
20.22 "going to Jerusalem, bound in the S.
20.23 "the H. S. testifies to me in every city
20.28 "the H. S. has made you overseers
21. 4 Through the S. they told Paul not to go
21.11 "Thus says the H. S., 'So shall the Jews
23. 8 Sadducees say . . there is no . . angel, nor s.
23. 9 "What if a s. or an angel spoke to him?

Acts 28.25 "The H. S. was right in saying
Rom 1. 4 in power according to the S. of holiness
1. 9 God . . , whom I serve with my spirit
5. 5 poured into our hearts through the H. S.
7. 6 we serve . . in the new life of the Spirit
8. 2 law of the Spirit of life in Christ Jesus
8. 4 in us, who walk . . according to the S.
8. 5 those who live according to the S. set their minds on the things of the Spirit
8. 6 to set the mind on the Spirit is life
8. 9 you are in the S., if in fact the S. of God dwells in you. Any . . who does not have the S. of Christ
8.10 if Christ is in you, . . spirits are alive
8.11 If the Spirit of him who raised Jesus
8.11 through his Spirit which dwells in you
8.13 if by the S. you put to death the deeds
8.14 all who are led by the Spirit of God
8.15 you did not receive the s. of slavery
8.15 you have received the s. of sonship
8.16 it is the S. himself bearing witness with our s. that we are children of God
8.23 who have the first fruits of the S.
8.26 the Spirit helps us in our weakness; . . the Spirit himself intercedes for us
8.27 knows what is the mind of the S.
9. 1 conscience bears me witness in the H. S.
11. 8 "God gave them a spirit of stupor
12.11 be aglow with the Spirit, serve the Lord
14.17 peace and joy in the Holy Spirit
15.13 by . . power of the H. S. . . abound in hope
15.16 acceptable, sanctified by the H. S.
15.19 by the power of the Holy Spirit
15.30 I appeal to you . . by the love of the S.
1 Cor 2. 4 in demonstration of the S. and power
2.10 God has revealed to us through the Spirit. For the Spirit searches everything
2.11 the spirit of the man which is in him
2.11 no one comprehends . . except . . S. of God
2.12 we have received not the spirit of the world, but the Spirit which is from God
2.13 impart this in words . . taught by the S.
2.14 gifts of the S. of God . . are folly to him
3.16 know . . that God's Spirit dwells in you
4.21 Shall I come . . in a s. of gentleness?
5. 3 though absent in body I am present in s.
5. 4 you are assembled, and my s. is present
5. 5 that his spirit may be saved in the day
6.11 you were justified . . in the S. of our God
6.17 united to the Lord becomes one spirit
6.19 your body is a temple of the H. S.
7.34 how to be holy in body and spirit
7.40 I think that I have the Spirit of God
12. 3 no one speaking by the Spirit of God
12. 3 no one can say . . except by the H. S.
12. 4 varieties of gifts, but the same Spirit
12. 7 each is given the manifestation of the S.
12. 8 through the S. the utterance of wisdom, . . knowledge according to the same S.
12. 9 to another faith by the same Spirit, . . gifts of healing by the one Spirit
12.10 ability to distinguish between spirits
12.11 inspired by one and the same Spirit
12.13 by one Spirit we were all baptized . . and all were made to drink of one Spirit
14. 2 but he utters mysteries in the Spirit
14.12 eager for manifestations of the Spirit
14.14 my spirit prays but my mind is unfruitful
14.15 What am I to do? I will pray with the s. . . I will sing with the spirit
14.16 Otherwise, if you bless[w] with the spirit
14.32 spirits of prophets . . subject to prophets
15.45 last Adam became a life-giving s.
16.18 refreshed my spirit as well as yours
2 Cor 1.22 he has . . given us his S. in our hearts
3. 3 written not with ink but with the S.
2 Cor 3. 6 not in a written code but in the S.; . . the written code kills, but the S. gives life
3. 8 will not the dispensation of the S.?
3.17 Now the Lord is the S., and where the S. of the Lord is, there is freedom
3.18 comes from the Lord who is the S.
4.13 Since we have the same spirit of faith
5. 5 God . . has given us the S. as a guarantee
6. 6 forbearance, kindness, the Holy Spirit
7. 1 every defilement of body and spirit
11. 4 if you receive a different spirit
12.18 Did we not act in the same spirit?
13.14(13) the fellowship of[n] the Holy Spirit
Gal 3. 2 Did you receive the Spirit by works?
3. 3 Having begun with the Spirit
3. 5 he who supplies the Spirit to you
3.14 that we . . receive the promise of the S.
4. 6 God has sent the Spirit of his Son
4.29 him who was born according to the S.
5. 5 through the Spirit, by faith, we wait
5.16 But I say, walk by the Spirit
5.17 desires of the flesh are against the S., and the desires of the S. are against the flesh
5.18 if you are led by the Spirit
5.22 fruit of the Spirit is love, joy, peace
5.25 If we live by the Spirit, let us also walk by the Spirit
6. 1 restore him in a spirit of gentleness
6. 8 but he who sows to the Spirit will from the Spirit reap eternal life
6.18 Lord Jesus Christ be with your spirit
Eph 1.13 you . . were sealed with the promised H. S.
1.17 that . . God . . give you a spirit of wisdom
2. 2 the s. . . at work in . . sons of disobedience
2.18 we both have access in one Spirit
2.22 a dwelling place of God in the Spirit
3. 5 as it has now been revealed . . by the S.
3.16 strengthened with might through his S.
4. 3 eager to maintain the unity of the S.
4. 4 There is one body and one Spirit
4.23 be renewed in the spirit of your minds
4.30 do not grieve the Holy Spirit of God
5.18 but be filled with the Spirit
6.17 sword of the S., which is . . word of God
6.18 Pray at all times in the Spirit
Phil 1.19 the help of the Spirit of Jesus Christ
1.27 that you stand firm in one spirit
2. 1 if there is . . any participation in the S.
3. 3 true circumcision, who worship . . in s.[e†‡]
4.23 the Lord Jesus Christ be with your s.
Col 1. 8 made known to us your love in the S.
2. 5 yet I am with you in spirit
1 Th 1. 5 not only in word, but also . . in the H. S.
1. 6 with joy inspired by the Holy Spirit
4. 8 not man but God, who gives his H. S.
5.19 Do not quench the Spirit
5.23 may your s. and soul . . be kept sound
2 Th 2. 2 not to be quickly shaken . . by spirit
2.13 through sanctification by the Spirit[c†]
1 Tim 3.16 He[h] was . . vindicated[i] in the Spirit
4. 1 the S. expressly says that in later times
4. 1 by giving heed to deceitful spirits
2 Tim 1. 7 a s. of power and love and self-control
1.14 truth . . entrusted to you by the H. S.
4.22 The Lord be with your spirit
Tit 3. 5 regeneration and renewal in the H. S.
Phm .25 the Lord Jesus Christ be with your s.
Heb 1.14 Are they not all ministering spirits?
2. 4 God . . bore witness . . by gifts of the H. S.
3. 7 the H. S. says, "Today, when you hear
4.12 piercing to the division of soul and s.
6. 4 have become partakers of the H. S.
9. 8 By this the Holy Spirit indicates
9.14 through the eternal S. offered himself
10.15 the H. S. also bears witness to us
10.29 the man who has . . outraged the S. of grace
12. 9 be subject to the Father of spirits

Heb 12.23 to the spirits of just men made perfect
Jas 2.26 body apart from the spirit is dead
4. 5 "He yearns jealously over the spirit
1 Pet 1. 2 destined by God . . sanctified by the S.
1.11 what . . was indicated by the S. of Christ
1.12 through the H. S. sent from heaven
3. 4 jewel of a gentle and quiet spirit
3.18 to God, being . . made alive in the spirit
3.19 he went and preached to the spirits
4. 6 they might live in the spirit like God
4.14 s. of glory[j] and of God rests upon you
2 Pet 1.21 men moved by the H. S. spoke from God[e]
1 Jn 3.24 by the Spirit which he has given us
4. 1 do not believe every spirit, but test the spirits to see whether
4. 2 By this you know the Spirit of God: every spirit which confesses that Jesus Christ
4. 3 every s. which does not confess Jesus
4. 6 By this we know the spirit of truth and the spirit of error
4.13 because he has given us of his own S.
5. 7(6) the Spirit is the witness, because the Spirit is the truth
5. 8 There are three witnesses, the Spirit
Jude .19 worldly people, devoid of the Spirit
.20 pray in the Holy Spirit
Rev 1. 4 Grace to you . . from the seven spirits
1.10 I was in the Spirit on the Lord's day
2. 7 " 'let him hear what the Spirit says to the churches
Also Rev **2**.11, 17, 29; **3**.6, 13, 22
3. 1 " 'him who has the seven spirits of God
4. 2 At once I was in the Spirit
4. 5 torches . . are the seven spirits of God
5. 6 eyes, which are the seven spirits of God
14.13 "Blessed indeed," says the Spirit
16.13 I saw . . three foul spirits like frogs
16.14 they are demonic spirits, performing signs
17. 3 he carried me away in the Spirit
18. 2 "It has become . . a haunt of every foul s.
19.10 testimony of Jesus is the s. of prophecy
21.10 in the S. he carried me . . to a . . mountain
22. 6 "the God of the spirits of the prophets
22.17 The Spirit and the Bride say, "Come

CONTEXTUALLY
Rom 8.27 knows what is the mind of the Spirit
Gal 5.20 selfishness, dissension, party spirit
1 Jn 4. 3 every s. which does not confess Jesus

SPIRIT, ELEMENTAL
1. *element:* στοιχεῖον STOICHEION
Gal 4. 3 we were slaves to the elemental spirits
4. 9 turn back again to the . . elemental spirits
Col 2. 8 prey . . according to the elemental spirits
2.20 If . . you died to the elemental spirits

SPIRIT, HAVE UNITY OF
1. *agreeing, like-minded:* ὁμόφρων HOMOPHRŌN* [A.3.e.2]
1 Pet 3. 8 have unity of spirit, sympathy, love

SPIRIT, THOSE WHO POSSESS THE
1. *spiritual, of wind:* πνευματικός (subst. pl.) PNEUMATIKOS
1 Cor 2.13 interpreting . . to those who possess the S.[d]†

SPIRITUAL
1. *of speech, possessed of reason:* λογικός LOGIKOS*
Rom 12. 1 sacrifice . . , which is your s. worship
1 Pet 2. 2 Like . . babes, long for the pure s. milk
2. *wind, breath, spirit:* πνεῦμα PNEUMA [B.1.a.1]
Rom 2.29 of the heart, spiritual and not literal
3. *spiritual, of wind:* πνευματικός PNEUMATIKOS
Rom 1.11 that I may impart . . some spiritual gift
7.14 We know that the law is spiritual
15.27 to share in their spiritual blessings
1 Cor 2.13 interpreting spiritual truths
[2.13 interpreting . . *in spiritual language*†
[2.13 taught by the Spirit, *comparing spiritual things with spiritual*†
2.15 The spiritual man judges all things
3. 1 I . . could not address you as s. men
1 Cor 9.11 If we have sown spiritual good
12. 1 concerning spiritual gifts,[z] brethren†[o]
[12. 1 concerning *spiritual persons*,[z] brethren†[o]
14. 1 earnestly desire the spiritual gifts
14.37 If any one thinks that he is . . spiritual
15.44 it is raised a s. body. If there is a physical body, there is also a s. body
15.46 it is not the spiritual which is first but the physical, and then the s.
Gal 6. 1 you who are s. should restore him
Eph 1. 3 who has blessed us . . with every s. blessing
5.19 addressing one another in . . s. songs
6.12 against the spiritual hosts of wickedness
Col 1. 9 in all s. wisdom and understanding
3.16 sing . . s. songs with thankfulness
1 Pet 2. 5 be yourselves built into a spiritual house
2. 5 to offer s. sacrifices acceptable to God

SPIRITUAL GIFT
1. *gift, favor bestowed:* χάρισμα CHARISMA
1 Cor 1. 7 you are not lacking in any spiritual gift

SPIRITUALLY
1. *spiritually:* πνευματικῶς PNEUMATIKŌS
1 Cor 2.14 because they are spiritually discerned

SPIT
1. *spit into, spit upon:* ἐμπτύω EMPTYŌ*
Mt 26.67 they spat in his face, and struck him
27.30 they spat upon him, and . . struck him
Mk 10.34 "they will mock him, and spit upon him
14.65 some began to spit on him
15.19 struck his head . . and spat upon him
Lk 18.32 "he will be . . mocked . . and s. upon
2. *spit out:* πτύω PTYŌ*
Mk 7.33 he spat and touched his tongue
8.23 when he had spit on his eyes
Jn 9. 6 he spat on the ground and made clay

SPITTLE
1. *spittle, saliva:* πτύσμα PTYSMA*
Jn 9. 6 he spat . . and made clay of the spittle

SPLENDOR
1. *glory:* δόξα DOXA
2 Cor 3. 7 dispensation of death . . came with such s.
3. 8 dispensation of the Spirit . . with greater s.
3. 9 if . . s. in the dispensation of condemnation, . . righteousness must far exceed it in s.
3.10 because of the s. that surpasses it
3.11 if what faded away came with s., what is permanent must have . . more s.
Rev 18. 1 earth was made bright with his s.
2. *bright, radiant:* λαμπρός (subst. pl.) LAMPROS
Rev 18.14 "all thy dainties and thy s. are lost!

CONTEXTUALLY
2 Cor 3.13 might not see the end of the fading s.

SPLENDOR, HAVE
1. *extol, honor:* δοξάζω (pass.) DOXAZŌ
2 Cor 3.10 in this case, what once had splendor has come to have no splendor at all

SPLENDOR, IN
1. *glorious, honored:* ἔνδοξος ENDOXOS
Eph 5.27 that he might present the church . . in s.

SPLIT
1. *divide, split:* σχίζω SCHIZŌ
Mt 27.51 earth shook, and the rocks were split

SPLIT, BE
1. *come to be, happen, be:* γίνομαι GINOMAI [A.6.a.5]
Rev 16.19 The great city was split into three parts

SPOIL
SPOILS
1. *best of a heap, booty* (pl.): ἀκροθίνιον AKROTHINION*
Heb 7. 4 Abraham . . gave . . a tithe of the spoils
2. *spoils, booty* (pl.): σκῦλον SKYLON*
Lk 11.22 "takes away his armor . . divides his spoil

SPOKESMAN
1. *advocate, public speaker:* ῥήτωρ RHĒTŌR*
Acts 24. 1 Ananias came . . with some elders and a s.

SPONGE
1. *sponge:* σπόγγος SPOGGOS*
Mt 27.48 took a sponge, filled it with vinegar
Mk 15.36 filling a sponge full of vinegar
Jn 19.29 they put a sponge full of the vinegar

SPOT
1. *stain, soil:* σπιλόω SPILOŌ
Jude .23 hating .. garment spotted by the flesh[e]
2. *stain, blemish:* σπίλος SPILOS
Eph 5.27 might present the church .. without s.

SPOT, WITHOUT
1. *without blemish:* ἄσπιλος ASPILOS
1 Pet 1.19 like that of a lamb without .. spot
2 Pet 3.14 found by him without spot or blemish

SPOTLESS
1. *unblemished:* ἄμωμος AMŌMOS
Rev 14. 5 no lie was found, for they are spotless

SPREAD
1. *go away:* ἀπέρχομαι APERCHOMAI
Mt 4.24 So his fame spread throughout all Syria
2. *distribute:* διανέμω (pass.) DIANEMŌ*
Acts 4.17 that it .. s. no further among the people
3. *spread widely, make known:* διαφημίζω DIAPHĒMIZŌ
Mt 28.15 this story has been s. among the Jews
Mk 1.45 he went .. and began .. to s. the news
4. *carry through, differ:* διαφέρω (pass.) DIAPHERŌ
Acts 13.49 word of the Lord s. throughout .. region
5. *pass through:* διέρχομαι DIERCHOMAI
Rom 5.12 death s. to all men because all .. sinned
6. *go out:* ἐξέρχομαι EXERCHOMAI
Mk 1.28 at once his fame spread everywhere
Lk 7.17 this report concerning him spread
7. *lay, spread out:* ὑποστρωννύω HYPOSTRŌNNYŌ*
Lk 19.36 they spread their garments on the road
8. *make manifest, make known:* φανερόω PHANEROŌ
2 Cor 2.14 through us spreads the fragrance .. of him
9. *spread:* στρωννύω STRŌNNYŌ
Mt 21. 8 crowd s. their garments on the road, and others cut branches .. and s. them
Mk 11. 8 many s. their garments on the road

SPREAD ABROAD
1. *go out:* ἐξέρχομαι EXERCHOMAI
Jn 21.23 saying s. abroad among the brethren

SPREAD S.'S FAME
1. *spread widely, make known:* διαφημίζω DIAPHĒMIZŌ
Mt 9.31 they went away and spread his fame

SPRING
1. *throw oneself:* βάλλειν ἑαυτόν BALLŌ [A.6.a.4]
Jn 21. 7 Simon Peter .. sprang into the sea
2. *running water, spring:* πηγή PĒGĒ
Jn 4.14 "a spring of water welling up to .. life
Jas 3.11 Does a s. pour .. fresh .. and brackish?
2 Pet 2.17 These are waterless springs and mists
Rev 7.17 "guide them to springs of living water
3. *bring forth, spring up:* φύω PHYŌ
Heb 12.15 That no "root of bitterness" spring up
CONTEXTUALLY
1 Th 2. 3 our appeal does not spring from error

SPRING UP
1. *jump up:* ἀναπηδάω ANAPĒDAŌ*
Mk 10.50 throwing off his mantle he sprang up
2. *come up:* ἐπιγίνομαι EPIGINOMAI*
Acts 28.13 after one day a south wind sprang up
3. *spring up:* ἐξανατέλλω EXANATELLŌ*
Mt 13. 5 "sprang up, since they had no depth
Mk 4. 5 "it sprang up, since it had no depth
4. *spring up:* ἅλλομαι HALLOMAI
Acts 14.10 And he sprang up and walked

SPRINKLE
SPRINKLE CLEAN
1. *make the sprinkling:* ποιεῖν τὴν πρόσχυσιν PROSCHYSIS* [A.6.a.4]
Heb 11.28 kept .. Passover and sprinkled the blood
2. *sprinkle, purify:* ῥαντίζω RHANTIZŌ
[a]mid.
Heb 9.19 sprinkled both .. book .. and .. people
9.21 sprinkled with .. blood both the tent[p]
10.22 [a]with our hearts sprinkled clean
Rev [19.13 clad in a robe *sprinkled with* blood‡

SPRINKLED
1. *sprinkling:* ῥαντισμός (gen.) RHANTISMOS
Heb 12.24 s. blood that speaks more graciously

SPRINKLING
1. *sprinkling:* ῥαντισμός RHANTISMOS
1 Pet 1. 2 chosen .. for sprinkling with his blood
2. *sprinkle, purify:* ῥαντίζω RHANTIZŌ [B.2.d.1]
Heb 9.13 if the s. of defiled persons .. sanctifies

SPROUT
1. *produce, sprout:* βλαστάνω BLASTANŌ
Mk 4.27 "the seed should sprout and grow

SPURN
1. *tread underfoot:* καταπατέω KATAPATEŌ
Heb 10.29 the man who has spurned the Son of God

SPY
1. *put in secretly:* ἐγκάθετος (subst.) EGKATHETOS*
Lk 20.20 So they watched him, and sent spies
2. *inspector, spy:* κατάσκοπος KATASKOPOS*
Heb 11.31 had given friendly welcome to the spies

SPY OUT
1. *keep a lookout, view closely:* κατασκοπέω KATASKOPEŌ*
Gal 2. 4 who slipped in to spy out our freedom

SQUAD
1. *guard of four soldiers:* τετράδιον TETRADION*
Acts 12. 4 four squads of soldiers to guard him

SQUANDER
1. *scatter abroad, squander:* διασκορπίζω DIASKORPIZŌ
Lk 15.13 "there he squandered his property

STABILITY
1. *firmness:* στηριγμός STĒRIGMOS*
2 Pet 3.17 beware lest you .. lose your own stability

STABLE
1. *found, establish:* θεμελιόω (perf. pass. part.) THEMELIOŌ
Col 1.23 that you continue in the faith, stable

STACHYS: Στάχυς 'stākis
Rom 16. 9 Greet Urbanus .. and my beloved S.

STADIUM
1. *stade* (200+ yards): στάδιον STADION
Lk [24.13 about *a hundred and sixty stadia*‡
Rev 14.20 for one thousand six hundred stadia[i]
21.16 measured .. city .. , twelve thousand stadia[q]

STAFF
1. *rod, staff of office:* ῥάβδος RHABDOS
Mt 10.10 "nor two tunics, nor sandals, nor a s.
Mk 6. 8 take nothing for their journey except a s.
Lk 9. 3 "Take nothing for your journey, no s.
Heb 11.21 Joseph, bowing .. over the head of his s.
Rev 11. 1 I was given a measuring rod like a s.

STAIN
1. *stain soil:* σπιλόω SPILOŌ
Jas 3. 6 tongue is a fire .. , staining the whole body

STAMP, VERY
1. *die, stamp, character:* χαρακτήρ CHARAKTĒR*
Heb 1.3 bears the very stamp of his nature

STAND (*See also* AWE, STAND IN; CONDEMNED, STAND; TEST, STAND THE)
1. *raise up, rise:* ἀνίστημι ANISTĒMI
Acts 14.10 "Stand upright on your feet
2. *be:* εἰμί EIMI
Jn 8. 9 with the woman standing before him[r]‡
Col 2.14 the bond which stood against us
3. *stand by:* ἐφίστημι EPHISTĒMI
Lk 4.39 stood over her and rebuked the fever
Acts 10.17 men that were sent .. stood before .. gate
4. *stand, set:* ἵστημι HISTĒMI
Mt 6. 5 "hypocrites .. love to stand and pray
12.25 "no city .. divided against itself will s.

Mt 12.26 “how then will his kingdom stand?
12.46 his mother and his brothers stood outside
[12.47 “*your brothers are standing outside*‡
13. 2 the whole crowd stood on the beach
16.28 “some standing . . who will not taste death
20. 3 “others standing idle in . . market place
20. 6 “he went out and found others standing
20. 6 “ ‘Why do you stand here idle all day?
24.15 “the desolating sacrilege . . ., standing
27.11 Now Jesus stood before the governor
Mk 3.24 “If . . divided . . ., that kingdom cannot stand
3.25 “that house will not be able to stand
3.26 “if Satan . . is divided, he cannot s.
9. 1 “some standing . . who will not taste death
11. 5 those who stood there said to them
13. 9 “you will s. before governors and kings
Lk 1.11 an angel . . standing on the right side
5. 1 he was standing by . . lake of Gennesaret
6. 8 he said to the man . . “Come and stand here.” And he rose and stood there
6.17 came down . . and stood on a level place
7.38 standing behind . . at his feet, weeping
8.20 “your brothers are standing outside
9.27 “some standing . . who will not taste death
11.18 “if . . divided . . ., how will his kingdom s.?
13.25 “you will begin to stand outside
17.12 ten lepers, who stood at a distance
18.11 “The Pharisee stood and prayed thus
18.13 “the tax collector, standing far off
19. 8 Zacchaeus stood and said to the Lord
21.36 “strength . . to s. before the Son of man
23.10 scribes stood by, . . accusing him
23.35 the people stood by, watching
23.49 the women . . stood at a distance and saw
24.36 Jesus himself stood among them[x]
Jn 1.35 again John was standing with two
3.29 “the friend . . who stands and hears him
11.56 looking . . as they stood in the temple
12.29 The crowd standing by heard it
18. 5 Judas . . was standing with them
18.16 while Peter stood outside at the door
18.18 standing and warming themselves; Peter also was with them, standing
18.25 Simon Peter was standing and warming
19.25 standing by the cross of Jesus
20.11 Mary stood weeping outside the tomb
20.14 turned round and saw Jesus standing
20.19 Jesus came and stood among them
20.26 Jesus came and stood among them
21. 4 Jesus stood on the beach
Acts 1.11 “why do you stand looking into heaven?
2.14 But Peter, standing with the eleven
3. 8 leaping up he stood and walked
4.14 seeing the man . . standing beside them
5.20 “Go and stand in the temple and speak
5.23 “the sentries standing at the doors
5.25 “The men . . are standing in the temple
7.33 “ ‘place where you are standing is holy
7.55 Jesus standing at . . right hand of God
7.56 “Son of man standing at the right hand
9. 7 men . . traveling with him stood speechless
10.30 “a man stood before me in bright apparel
11.13 “had seen . . angel standing in his house
12.14 told that Peter was standing at the gate
16. 9 a man of Macedonia was standing
17.22 standing in . . middle of the Areopagus
21.40 Paul, standing on . . steps, motioned
22.25 to the centurion who was standing by
24.20 “when I stood before the council
24.21 “I cried out while standing among them
25.10 “I am standing before Caesar’s tribunal
26. 6 “now I stand here on trial for hope
26.16 “ ‘But rise and stand upon your feet
26.22 “so I stand here testifying both to small
Rom 5. 2 access[g] to this grace in which we stand
11.20 but you stand fast only through faith
14. 4 the Master is able to make him stand
1 Cor 10.12 let any one who thinks that he stands
15. 1 which you received, in which you s.
Eph 6.11 able to s. against the wiles of the devil
6.13 and having done all, to stand
6.14 Stand therefore, having girded . . loins
Col 4.12 you may s. mature and fully assured
2 Tim 2.19 But God’s firm foundation stands
Heb 10.11 every priest stands daily at his service
Jas 2. 3 you say to the poor man, “Stand
5. 9 the Judge is standing at the doors
Rev 3.20 “ ‘Behold, I stand at the door and knock
5. 6 a Lamb standing, as though . . slain
6.17 “who can stand before it?
7. 1 After this I saw four angels standing
7. 9 multitude . . standing before the throne
7.11 all the angels stood round the throne
8. 2 the seven angels who stand before God
8. 3 another angel came and stood at . . altar
10. 5 the angel whom I saw standing on sea
10. 8 “the angel who is standing on the sea
11. 4 lampstands which stand before the Lord
12. 4 the dragon stood before the woman
12.17(18) And he stood[e] on the sand of the sea‡
14. 1 on Mount Zion stood the Lamb
15. 2 standing beside the sea of glass
18.10 they will stand far off, in fear
18.15 merchants . . will stand far off, in fear
18.17 whose trade is on the sea, stood far off
19.17 I saw an angel standing in the sun
20.12 great and small, standing before . . throne

5. *lie, be laid:* κεῖμαι KEIMAI
Jn 2. 6 Now six stone jars were standing there
19.29 A bowl full of vinegar stood there
Rev 4. 2 lo, a throne stood in heaven!

6. *lampstand:* λυχνία LYCHNIA
Mt 5.15 “men light a lamp and put it . . on a stand
Mk 4.21 “put under a bushel, or . . on a stand?
Lk 8.16 “after lighting a lamp . . puts it on a s.
11.33 “after lighting a lamp puts it . . on a s.

7. *place beside, stand before:* παρίστημι PARISTĒMI
Mk 15.39 the centurion, who stood facing him
Lk 1.19 “I . . Gabriel, who s. in . . presence of God
Acts 4.10 “by him this man is standing before you

8. *contain, hold fast:* περιέχω PERIECHŌ
1 Pet 2. 6 For it stands in scripture: “Behold

9. *have a position:* ἔχειν στάσιν STASIS [B.3.a.5]
Heb 9. 8 as long as . . outer tent[p] is still standing

10. *stand:* στήκω STĒKŌ
Mk 3.31 standing outside they sent to him
11.25 “whenever you stand praying, forgive
Jn 1.26 “stands one whom you do not know
Rom 14. 4 before his . . master . . he stands or falls

CONTEXTUALLY
Heb 9. 3 stood a tent[p] called the Holy of Holies

STAND ABOUT

1. *stand around:* περιίστημι PERIISTĒMI
Acts 25. 7 Jews. . . stood about . . ., bringing . . charges

STAND BEFORE
STAND BESIDE
STAND BY
STAND NEAR

1. *stand by:* ἐφίστημι EPHISTĒMI
Lk 24. 4 two men stood by them in dazzling apparel
Acts 22.13 “standing by me said . . ‘Brother Saul
22.20 “ ‘I also was standing by and approving
23.11 The following night the Lord stood by

2. *place beside, stand before:* παρίστημι PARISTĒMI
[a]mid.
Mk 14.47 one of those who stood by drew . . sword
Lk 19.24 “he said to those who stood by
Jn 18.22 one of . . officers standing by struck Jesus
19.26 disciple whom he loved standing near
Acts 1.10 two men stood by them in white robes
9.39 the widows stood beside him weeping
23. 2 commanded those who stood by him
23. 4 who stood by said, “Would you revile?

Acts 27.23 "this . . night there stood by me an angel
27.24 " 'you must stand before Caesar
Rom 14.10 [a]we shall all stand before . . judgment seat
2 Tim 4.17 But the Lord stood by me and gave
3. *stand around:* περιίστημι (perf.) PERIISTĒMI
Jn 11.42 "on account of the people standing by

STAND FAST
STAND FIRM
1. *stand, set:* ἵστημι HISTĒMI
[a]perf. [b]2 aor.
2 Cor 1.24 [a]for you stand firm in your faith
1 Pet 5.12 [b]the true grace of God; stand fast in it
2. *stand:* στήκω STĒKŌ
1 Cor 16.13 Be watchful, stand firm in your faith
Gal 5. 1 stand fast therefore, and do not submit
Phil 1.27 that you stand firm in one spirit
4. 1 s. firm thus in the Lord, my beloved
1 Th 3. 8 we live, if you stand fast in the Lord
2 Th 2.15 stand firm and hold to the traditions

STAND IN
1. *have, hold:* ἔχω ECHŌ [A.6.a.5]
1 Tim 5.20 so that the rest may stand in fear

STAND NEAR (*See* STAND BEFORE)

STAND ON, TAKE ONE'S
1. *set foot upon, enter:* ἐμβατεύω EMBATEUŌ*
Col 2.18 Let no one . . taking his stand on visions

STAND STILL
1. *stand, set:* ἵστημι HISTĒMI
[a]aor. pass.
Lk 7.14 touched the bier, and the bearers stood s.
24.17 [a]And they stood still, looking sad

STAND UP
1. *lift up the head:* ἀνακύπτω ANAKYPTŌ
Jn 8. 7 he stood up and said to them[r]‡
2. *raise up, rise:* ἀνίστημι ANISTĒMI
Mt 26.62 the high priest stood up and said
Mk 14.57 some stood up and bore false witness
14.60 high priest stood up in the midst
Lk 4.16 And he stood up to read
10.25 lawyer stood up to put him to the test
Acts 1.15 Peter stood up among the brethren
5.34 Gamaliel, a teacher of the law, . . stood up
10.26 Peter lifted him up, saying, "Stand up
11.28 one of them named Agabus stood up
13.16 So Paul stood up, and motioning
23. 9 Pharisees' party stood up and contended
3. *stand, set:* ἵστημι (act., pluperf., aor. pass.) HISTĒMI
Jn 7.37 On the last day . . Jesus stood up
Acts 25.18 "When the accusers stood up
Rev 11.11 they stood up on their feet

STAND WITH
1. *stand with, commend:* συνίστημι SYNISTĒMI
Lk 9.32 they saw . . two men who stood with him

STANDARD (*See also* WORLDLY STANDARDS, ACCORDING TO)
1. *pattern, image:* τύπος TYPOS
Rom 6.17 obedient . . to the standard of teaching

STANDING
1. *step, degree:* βαθμός BATHMOS*
1 Tim 3.13 gain a good standing for themselves

STANDING, OF EQUAL
1. *equal in honor or value:* ἰσότιμος ISOTIMOS*
2 Pet 1. 1 a faith of equal standing with ours

STANDING, OF HIGH
1. *noble, proper:* εὐσχήμων EUSCHĒMŌN
Acts 13.50 Jews incited . . devout women of high s.
17.12 a few Greek women of high standing

STAR
1. *star:* ἀστήρ ASTĒR*
Mt 2. 2 "For we have seen his star in the East
2. 7 ascertained . . what time the s. appeared
2. 9 the s. which they had seen in the East
2.10 When they saw the star, they rejoiced
Mt 24.29 "the stars will fall from heaven
Mk 13.25 "the stars will be falling from heaven
1 Cor 15.41 There is one glory of the sun, . . another glory of the moon, and another glory of the stars; for star differs from star in glory
Jude .13 wandering stars for whom . . darkness
Rev 1.16 in his right hand he held seven stars
1.20 "As for the mystery of the seven stars
1.20 "stars are the angels of the . . churches
2. 1 " 'words of him who holds the seven stars
2.28 " 'and I will give him the morning star
3. 1 " 'seven spirits of God and the seven stars
6.13 the stars of the sky fell to the earth
8.10 and a great star fell from heaven
8.11 The name of the star is Wormwood
8.12 struck . . a third of the stars
9. 1 I saw a s. fallen from heaven to earth
12. 1 on her head a crown of twelve stars
12. 4 His tail swept down a third of the stars
22.16 "I Jesus . . am . . the bright morning s.
2. *star:* ἄστρον ASTRON*
Lk 21.25 "signs in sun and moon and stars
Acts 7.43 " 'you took up . . the s. of the god Rephan
27.20 when neither sun nor stars appeared
Heb 11.12 descendants as many as the stars

STAR, MORNING
1. *bringing light:* φωσφόρος (subst.) PHŌSPHOROS*
2 Pet 1.19 until . . morning star rises in your hearts

STARE AT
1. *look intently at:* ἀτενίζω ATENIZŌ
Acts 3.12 "Men of Israel, . . why do you stare at us?
10. 4 And he stared at him in terror

START
1. *come, go:* ἔρχομαι ERCHOMAI
Jn 6.17 started across the sea to Capernaum

STARTED
1. *come to be, happen, be:* γίνομαι (part.) GINOMAI
Lk 23.19 for an insurrection started in the city

STARTLE
1. *scare, excite:* πτοέω PTOEŌ
Lk 24.37 they were startled and frightened

STATE
1. *call, position:* κλῆσις KLĒSIS
1 Cor 7.20 remain in the s. in which he was called
2. *say, speak:* λέγω LEGŌ
Acts 23.30 "ordering . . accusers also to s. before you
CONTEXTUALLY
Mt 12.45 "the last s. of that man becomes worse
Lk 11.26 "the last s. of that man becomes worse
1 Cor 7.24 in whatever s. each was called . . remain
Phil 4.11 in whatever state I am, to be content
2 Pet 2.20 the last s. has become worse for them

STATEMENT
1. *word, saying:* ῥῆμα RHĒMA
Acts 28.25 after Paul had made one statement

STATEMENT, OPEN
1. *manifestation, disclosure:* φανέρωσις PHANERŌSIS
2 Cor 4. 2 by the open statement of the truth

STATURE
1. *age, stature:* ἡλικία HĒLIKIA
Mt [6.27 "which . . can add one cubit to his *stature?*†
Lk 2.52 Jesus increased in wisdom and in stature[i]†
[12.25 "which . . can add a cubit to his *stature?*†
19. 3 could not, . . because he was small of s.
Eph 4.13 measure of the s. of . . fulness of Christ

STAY
1. *spend time:* διατρίβω DIATRIBŌ
Acts 20. 6 Troas, where we stayed for seven days
25. 6 When he had stayed among them
25.14 as they stayed there many days, Festus
2. *hold upon, aim at:* ἐπέχω EPECHŌ
Acts 19.22 he himself stayed in Asia for a while

3. *continue, remain:* ἐπιμένω EPIMENŌ
Acts 21. 4 having sought out . . disciples, we stayed
21.10 While we were staying for some days
28.12 Putting in at Syracuse, we stayed there
28.14 invited to s. with them for seven days
1 Cor 16. 8 I will stay in Ephesus until Pentecost
4. *stay, reside:* καταμένω KATAMENŌ*
Acts 1.13 upper room, where they were staying
1 Cor 16. 6 perhaps I will stay with you
5. *sit down, seat:* καθίζω KATHIZŌ
Lk 24.49 "stay in . . city, until . . clothed with power
Acts 18.11 And he stayed a year and six months
6. *stay, wait:* μένω MENŌ
Mt 10.11 "stay with him until you depart
Mk 6.10 "stay there until you leave the place
Lk 9. 4 "stay there, and from there depart
19. 5 "I must stay at your house today
24.29 "Stay with us, for it is toward evening . ." So he went in to stay with them
Jn 1.38 "Rabbi . ., where are you staying?
1.39 They came and saw where he was staying; and they stayed with him that day
2.12 there they stayed for a few days
4.40 they asked him to stay with them; and he stayed there two days
11. 6 he stayed two days longer in the place
11.54 went . . to . . Ephraim; and there he stayed
Acts 9.43 he stayed in Joppa for many days
16.15 "come to my house and stay
18. 3 he stayed with them and they worked
18.20 asked him to stay for a longer period
21. 7 greeted the brethren . . stayed with them
21. 8 house of Philip . . and stayed with him
27.31 "Unless these men stay in the ship
28.16 Paul was allowed to stay by himself
7. *sojourn:* παροικία PAROIKIA
Acts 13.17 "during their stay in the land of Egypt
8. *wait for, stay with:* προσμένω PROSMENŌ
Acts 18.18 Paul stayed many days longer

STAY BEHIND
1. *be patient under, stand firm:* ὑπομένω HYPOMENŌ
Lk 2.43 boy Jesus stayed behind in Jerusalem

STAY WITH
1. *eat salt with, bring together:* συναλίζω (pass.) SYNALIZŌ*
Acts 1. 4 staying[a] with them he charged them†

STEADFAST
1. *steady, firm:* βέβαιος BEBAIOS
Heb 6.19 We have . . a sure and steadfast anchor
2. *steadfast, firm:* ἑδραῖος HEDRAIOS
1 Cor 15.58 be s., immovable, always abounding
Col 1.23 steadfast, not shifting from the hope
3. *heart:* καρδία (gen.) KARDIA
Acts 11.23 faithful to the Lord with s. purpose

STEADFAST, BE
1. *be patient under, stand firm:* ὑπομένω HYPOMENŌ
Jas 5.11 we call those happy who were steadfast

STEADFASTLY, CONTINUE
1. *persist in:* προσκαρτερέω PROSKARTEREŌ
Col 4. 2 Continue steadfastly in prayer

STEADFASTNESS
1. *endurance:* ὑπομονή HYPOMONĒ
Rom 15. 4 s. and . . encouragement of the scriptures
15. 5 God of steadfastness and encouragement
1 Th 1. 3 s. of hope in our Lord Jesus Christ
2 Th 1. 4 s. and faith in all your persecutions
3. 5 direct your hearts . . to the s. of Christ
1 Tim 6.11 aim at righteousness, . . love, steadfastness
2 Tim 3.10 you have observed . . my love, my s.
Tit 2. 2 sound in faith, in love, and in s.
Jas 1. 3 the testing of your faith produces s.
1. 4 let steadfastness have its full effect
5.11 You have heard of the s. of Job
2 Pet 1. 6 ⟨supplement⟩ self-control with s., and steadfastness with godliness

STEADY, BE
1. *be self-controlled:* νήφω NĒPHŌ
2 Tim 4. 5 always be steady, endure suffering

STEAL
STEAL AWAY
1. *steal:* κλέπτω KLEPTŌ
[a]inf.
Mt 6.19 "earth, . . where thieves break in and steal
6.20 "heaven, . . where thieves do not . . steal
19.18 "You shall not kill, . . You shall not s.
27.64 "lest his disciples go and steal him away
28.13 "Tell people . . 'disciples . . stole him away
Mk 10.19 "'Do not s., Do not bear false witness
Lk 18.20 "'Do not s., Do not bear false witness
Jn 10.10 "The thief comes only to steal and kill
Rom 2.21 [a]you then who teach others, . . While you preach against stealing, do you steal?
13. 9 "You shall not s., You shall not covet
Eph 4.28 Let the thief no longer steal

STEALTH
1. *cunning:* δόλος DOLOS
Mt 26. 4 to arrest Jesus by stealth and kill him
Mk 14. 1 seeking how to arrest him by stealth

STEEP BANK
1. *cliff, crag:* κρημνός KRĒMNOS*
Mt 8.32 whole herd rushed down the steep bank
Mk 5.13 swine . . rushed down the steep bank
Lk 8.33 the herd rushed down the steep bank

STEP
1. *step:* ἀναβαθμός ANABATHMOS*
Acts 21.35 And when he came to the steps
21.40 Paul, standing on the steps
2. *footstep:* ἴχνος ICHNOS
2 Cor 12.18 Did we not take the same steps?
1 Pet 2.21 that you should follow in his steps

STEP DOWN
1. *come down, go down:* καταβαίνω KATABAINŌ
Jn 5. 7 "while I am going another steps down

STEP IN
1. *step in, embark:* ἐμβαίνω EMBAINŌ
Jn [5. 4 *whoever stepped in first . . was healed*‡

STEP OUT
1. *go out:* ἐξέρχομαι EXERCHOMAI
Lk 8.27 And as he stepped out on land

STEPHANAS: Στεφανᾶς 'stefənəs
1 Cor 1.16 (I did baptize also the household of S.
16.15 household of S. were the first converts
16.17 I rejoice at the coming of Stephanas

STEPHEN: Στέφανος 'stēvən
Acts 6. 5 they chose Stephen, a man full of faith
6. 8 Stephen, full of grace and power
6. 9 some . . arose and disputed with Stephen
7.59 as they were stoning S., he prayed
8. 2 Devout men buried Stephen
11.19 the persecution that arose over S.
22.20 "'when the blood of S. . . was shed
CONTEXTUALLY
Acts 7. 2 S. said: "Brethren and fathers, hear me

STERN
1. *stern of a ship:* πρύμνα PRYMNA*
Mk 4.38 he was in the s., asleep on the cushion
Acts 27.29 they let out four anchors from the s.
27.41 the stern was broken up by the surf

STERNLY CHARGE
1. *admonish, be deeply moved:* ἐμβριμάομαι EMBRIMAOMAI
Mt 9.30 And Jesus sternly charged them
Mk 1.43 he s. charged him, and sent him away

STEWARD
1. *steward, manager:* ἐπίτροπος EPITROPOS
Mt 20. 8 "the owner of the vineyard said to his s.
Lk 8. 3 Joanna, the wife of Chuza, Herod's s.
2. *steward, administrator:* οἰκονόμος OIKONOMOS
Lk 12.42 "Who then is the faithful and wise s.?
16. 1 "There was a rich man who had a s.

Lk 16. 3 "the s. said to himself, 'What shall I do?
16. 8 "The master commended the dishonest s.
1 Cor 4. 1 stewards of the mysteries of God
4. 2 Moreover it is required of stewards
Tit 1. 7 a bishop, as God's s., must be blameless
1 Pet 4.10 as good stewards of God's varied grace

STEWARD, BE
1. *manage as a house steward:* οἰκονομέω OIKONOMEŌ*
Lk 16. 2 "'for you can no longer be steward

STEWARD OF THE FEAST
1. *headwaiter:* ἀρχιτρίκλινος ARCHITRIKLINOS*
Jn 2. 8 "take it to the steward of the feast
2. 9 the steward of the feast tasted the water
2. 9 s. of the feast called the bridegroom

STEWARDSHIP
1. *stewardship, management:* οἰκονομία OIKONOMIA
Lk 16. 2 "'Turn in the account of your stewardship
16. 3 "'my master is taking the s. away from me
16. 4 "'when I am put out of the stewardship
Eph 3. 2 you have heard of the s. of God's grace
1 Tim [1. 4 speculations rather than the divine *s.*†

STICK
1. *prop, press down, jam fast:* ἐρείδω EREIDŌ*
Acts 27.41 the bow stuck and remained immovable
2. *dry stick:* φρύγανον PHRYGANON*
Acts 28. 3 Paul had gathered a bundle of sticks

STIFF-NECKED
1. *stiff-necked:* σκληροτράχηλος SKLĒROTRACHĒLOS*
Acts 7.51 "stiff-necked people, uncircumcised

STILL (*See also* GIVE STILL MORE; LONGER, STILL *a*; MORE, STILL)
1. *as yet:* ἀκμήν AKMĒN*
Mt 15.16 "Are you also s. without understanding?
2. *until now:* ἕως ἄρτι ARTI [A.4.e]
Jn 5.17 "My Father is working still, and I am
1 Cor 15. 6 most of whom are still alive
1 Jn 2. 9 who . . hates his brother is in . . darkness s.
3. *still, yet:* ἔτι ETI
Mt 12.46 While he was s. speaking to the people
17. 5 He was still speaking, when lo
19.20 "these I have observed; what do I s. lack?
26.47 While he was s. speaking, Judas
26.65 "Why do we still need witnesses?
27.63 "imposter said, while he was still alive
Mk 5.35 While he was s. speaking, there came
12. 6 "He had still one other, a beloved son
14.43 while he was still speaking, Judas came
14.63 "Why do we still need witnesses?
Lk 8.49 While he was s. speaking, a man . . came
14.22 "servant said, 'Sir, . . still there is room
18.22 "One thing you still lack. Sell all
22.47 While he was s. speaking, there came
22.60 while he was s. speaking, the cock crowed
24. 6 "he told you, while he was still in Galilee
24.41 while they still disbelieved for joy
24.44 "I spoke . . while I was s. with you
Jn 11.30 Now Jesus . . was still in the place
20. 1 came to the tomb . . while it was s. dark
Acts 9. 1 Saul, s. breathing threats and murder
10.44 While Peter was still saying this
Rom 3. 7 why am I still being condemned?
5. 6 While we were still weak, . . Christ died[0]
6. 2 How can we who died to sin s. live in it?
9.19 You will say . . "Why does he s. find fault?
1 Cor 3. 3 for you are still of the flesh
12.31 I will show you a still more excellent way
15.17 faith is futile. . you are s. in your sins
Gal 1.10 If I were still pleasing men
5.11 But if I, brethren, still preach circumcision, why am I still persecuted?
2 Th 2. 5 when I was s. with you I told you this
Heb 7.10 he was still in the loins of his ancestor
9. 8 as long as the outer tent[p] is still standing
11. 4 through his faith he is still speaking
Rev 9.12 behold, two woes are still to come
Rev 22.11 "Let the evildoer still do evil, and the filthy still be filthy, and the righteous still do right, and the holy still be holy
4. *remaining, left:* λοιπός (neut.) LOIPOS
[a]subst.
Mt 26.45 "Are you still sleeping and taking . . rest?
Mk 14.41 [a]"Are you still sleeping and taking . . rest?
5. *anyone, any:* τὶς TIS II [A.2.c]
Lk 22.59 after . . an hour still another insisted
CONTEXTUALLY
Rom **4.**11
2 Cor **5.**4
Gal **1.**22
Col **2.**20
Heb **6.**10
Rev **3.**4

STILL, BE
1. *stay, wait:* μένω MENŌ
Jn 14.25 "I have spoken . . while I am s. with you
2. *muzzle, put to silence:* φιμόω (pass.) PHIMOŌ
Mk 4.39 he . . said to the sea, "Peace! Be still!

STILL, STAND
1. *stand, set:* ἵστημι HISTĒMI
[a]aor. pass.
Lk 7.14 touched the bier, and . . bearers stood s.
24.17 [a]And they stood still, looking sad

STING
1. *sharp point, sting:* κέντρον KENTRON
1 Cor 15.55 "O death, where is thy sting?
15.56 The sting of death is sin
Rev 9.10 They have tails like scorpions, . . stings
2. *strike:* παίω PAIŌ
Rev 9. 5 like . . a scorpion, when it stings a man

STIR
1. *shake, agitate:* σείω SEIŌ
Mt 21.10 city was stirred, saying, "Who is this?
2. *disturbance, disorder:* τάραχος TARACHOS*
Acts 12.18 there was no small stir among . . soldiers
19.23 there arose . . stir concerning the Way

STIR UP
1. *shake up:* ἀνασείω ANASEIŌ*
Mk 15.11 the chief priests stirred up the crowd
Lk 23. 5 "He stirs up the people, teaching
2. *rouse up:* ἐπεγείρω EPEGEIRŌ*
Acts 13.50 stirred up persecution against Paul
14. 2 unbelieving Jews stirred up . . Gentiles
3. *make pressure:* ἐπίστασιν ποιεῖν EPISTASIS [B.3.a.3]
Acts 24.12 "did not find me . . stirring up a crowd
4. *rouse to anger, excite:* ἐρεθίζω ERETHIZŌ
2 Cor 9. 2 your zeal has stirred up most of them
5. *irritation, provoking:* παροξυσμός PAROXYSMOS [B.1.a.2]
Heb 10.24 consider how to stir up one another
6. *shake:* σαλεύω SALEUŌ
Acts 17.13 Jews . . came there . . , stirring up . . crowds
7. *confuse:* συγχέω SYGCHEŌ
Acts 21.27 [a]Jews from Asia . . stirred up . . the crowd
8. *excite, stir up:* συγκινέω SYGKINEŌ*
Acts 6.12 stirred up the people and the elders

STIR UP A REVOLT
1. *upset, disturb:* ἀναστατόω ANASTATOŌ
Acts 21.38 "Egyptian . . who . . stirred up a revolt

STOCKS
1. *tree, wood:* ξύλον XYLON
Acts 16.24 he . . fastened their feet in the stocks

STOIC: Στοϊκός
Acts 17.18 Some . . Stoic philosophers met him

STOMACH
1. *body cavity, belly:* κοιλία KOILIA
Mt 15.17 "goes into the mouth passes into the s.
Mk 7.19 "it enters, not his heart but his stomach
1 Cor 6.13 "Food is meant for the s. and the s. for food"—and God will destroy both
Rev 10. 9 "it will be bitter to your stomach
10.10 when I had eaten it my s. was . . bitter

2. *stomach:* στόμαχος STOMACHOS*
1 Tim 5.23 use a little wine for the sake of your s.

STONE

1. *stone to death:* καταλιθάζω KATALITHAZŌ*
Lk 20. 6 "if we say, 'From men,' .. people will s. us
2. *throw stones:* λιθάζω LITHAZŌ*
Jn 8. 5 "Moses commanded us to stone such[r]‡
10.31 Jews took up stones again to stone him
10.32 "for which of these do you stone me?
10.33 "not for a good work that we stone you
11. 8 "Jews were but now seeking to s. you
Acts 5.26 for they were afraid of being stoned
14.19 they stoned Paul and dragged him out
2 Cor 11.25 once I was stoned
Heb 11.37 They were stoned, .. sawn in two[y]
3. *made of stone:* λίθινος LITHINOS*
Jn 2. 6 six stone jars were standing there
2 Cor 3. 3 you are a letter .. , not on tablets of s.
Rev 9.20 idols of gold and silver .. bronze and s.
4. *pelt with stones:* λιθοβολέω LITHOBOLEŌ*
Mt 21.35 "tenants .. killed another, .. stoned another
23.37 "stoning those who are sent to you!
Lk 13.34 "stoning those who are sent to you!
Acts 7.58 cast him out of the city and stoned him
7.59 they were stoning Stephen, he prayed
14. 5 an attempt was made .. to s. them
Heb 12.20 "If .. a beast touches .. , it shall be stoned
5. *stone:* λίθος LITHOS
Mt 3. 9 "'able from these stones to raise up children
4. 3 "command these stones to become loaves
4. 6 "'lest you strike your foot against a s.
7. 9 "what man of you .. will give him a s.?
21.42 "'The very s. which the builders rejected
[21.44 *"And he who falls on this stone*‡
24. 2 "not be left here one stone upon another
27.60 he rolled a great stone to the door
27.66 by sealing the stone and setting a guard
28. 2 an angel .. came and rolled back the s.
Mk 5. 5 he was .. bruising himself with stones
12.10 "'The very s. which the builders rejected
13. 1 "Look, .. what wonderful stones!
13. 2 "not be left here one stone upon another
15.46 rolled a s. against the door of the tomb
16. 3 "Who will roll away the stone for us?
16. 4 they saw that the stone was rolled back
Lk 3. 8 "able from .. stones to raise up children
4. 3 "command this stone to become bread
4.11 "'lest you strike your foot against a s.
[11.11 "What father .. *will give him a stone?*‡
19.40 "the very stones would cry out
19.44 "they will not leave one s. upon another
20.17 "'The very s. which the builders rejected
20.18 "Every one who falls on that stone
21. 5 how it was adorned with noble stones
21. 6 "not be left here one s. upon another
22.41 he withdrew .. about a stone's throw
24. 2 they found the stone rolled away
Jn 8. 7 "Let him .. be the first to throw a stone[r]‡
8.59 they took up stones to throw at him
10.31 The Jews took up stones again
11.38 a cave, and a stone lay upon it
11.39 Jesus said, "Take away the stone
11.41 So they took away the stone
20. 1 saw that the s. had been taken away
Acts 4.11 "This is the stone which was rejected
17.29 "that the Deity is like gold, or silver, or s.
Rom 9.32 They .. stumbled over the stumbling s.
9.33 "Behold, I am laying in Zion a stone
1 Cor 3.12 if any .. builds .. with .. precious stones
2 Cor 3. 7 dispensation .. carved in letters on s.
1 Pet 2. 4 Come to him, to that living stone
2. 5 like living stones be yourselves built
2. 6 "Behold, I am laying in Zion a s.
2. 7 "The very stone .. the builders rejected
2. 8 "A stone that will make men stumble
Rev 18.21 Then a mighty angel took up a stone
6. *pebble, vote:* ψῆφος PSĒPHOS
Rev 2.17 "'I will give him a white stone, with a new name written on the stone

STONE THAT FELL FROM THE SKY, SACRED

1. *fallen from heaven:* διοπετής (subst. neut.) DIOPETĒS* [D.1]
Acts 19.35 "the sacred stone that fell from the sky[s]

STOOL

1. *footstool:* ὑποπόδιον HYPOPODION
Lk 20.43 "'till I make thy enemies a stool
Acts 2.35 "'till I make thy enemies a stool
Heb 1.13 "till I make thy enemies a stool
10.13 until his enemies should be made a s.

STOOP AND LOOK
STOOP TO LOOK

1. *stoop to look:* παρακύπτω PARAKYPTŌ
Lk [24.12 *stooping and looking in, he saw .. linen*‡
Jn 20. 5 stooping to look in, he saw the linen
20.11 she stooped to look into the tomb

STOOP DOWN

1. *bend forward, stoop:* κύπτω KYPTŌ
Mk 1. 7 "I am not worthy to s. down and untie

STOP

1. *stand, set:* ἵστημι (2 aor., aor. pass.) HISTĒMI
Mt 20.32 And Jesus stopped and called them
Mk 10.49 Jesus stopped and said, "Call him
Lk 18.40 Jesus stopped, and commanded him
Acts 8.38 he commanded the chariot to stop
2. *hinder, prevent, withhold:* κωλύω KŌLYŌ
3 Jn .10 stops those who want to welcome them
3. *cease, stop:* παύω (mid.) PAUŌ
Acts 13.10 "will you not s. making crooked .. paths?
21.32 they saw .. , they stopped beating Paul
4. *fence in, stop up:* φράσσω PHRASSŌ
Rom 3.19 so that every mouth may be stopped
Heb 11.33 who .. stopped the mouths of lions
5. *hold together, impel:* συνέχω SYNECHŌ
Acts 7.57 they cried out .. and stopped their ears

STORE

1. *bring together:* συνάγω SYNAGŌ
Lk 12.17 "'for I have nowhere to store my crops
12.18 "'there I will store all my grain

STORE UP

1. *store up:* θησαυρίζω THĒSAURIZŌ
Rom 2. 5 you are storing up wrath for yourself
1 Cor 16. 2 put something aside and store it up
Jas [5. 3 *since you have stored up fire*†
2 Pet 3. 7 heavens .. have been stored up for fire

STOREHOUSE

1. *storeroom:* ταμεῖον TAMEION
Lk 12.24 "they have neither storehouse nor barn

STORM

1. *strong storm, hurricane:* λαῖλαψ LAILAPS*
Mk 4.37 And a great storm of wind arose
Lk 8.23 a storm of wind came down on the lake
2 Pet 2.17 waterless springs and mists driven by a s.
2. *shaking, earthquake:* σεισμός SEISMOS
Mt 8.24 there arose a great storm on the sea

STORM-TOSSED, BE

1. *pass the winter, raise a storm:* χειμάζω (pass.) CHEIMAZŌ*
Acts 27.18 As we were violently storm-tossed

STORMY

1. *winter, stormy weather:* χειμών CHEIMŌN [A.1.b.4]
Mt 16. 3 "'It will be s. today, for the sky is red‡

STORY

1. *word, reckoning:* λόγος LOGOS
Mt 28.15 this s. has been spread among the Jews

STORY, THIRD

1. *third story:* τρίστεγον TRISTEGON*
Acts 20. 9 he fell down from the third story

STRAIGHT

1. *straight:* εὐθύς EUTHYS I
Mt 3. 3 "Prepare the way .. , make his paths s.

Mk 1. 3 "Prepare the way . . , make his paths s.
Lk 3. 4 "Prepare the way . . , make his paths s.
3. 5 "the crooked shall be made straight
Acts 9.11 "Rise and go to the street called S.
13.10 "making crooked the s. paths of the Lord
2. *straight, upright:* ὀρθός ORTHOS
Heb 12.13 make straight paths for your feet

STRAIGHT COURSE, BY A
1. *run a straight course:* εὐθυδρομέω (part.) EUTHYDROMEŌ
Acts 21. 1 we came by a straight course to Cos

STRAIGHT, MAKE
1. *set up again, correct:* ἀνορθόω ANORTHOŌ
Lk 13.13 immediately she was made straight
2. *make straight, direct:* εὐθύνω EUTHYNŌ
Jn 1.23 " 'Make straight the way of the Lord

STRAIGHTEN ONESELF
1. *lift up the head:* ἀνακύπτω ANAKYPTŌ
Lk 13.11 she . . could not fully straighten herself

STRAIGHTFORWARD, BE
1. *walk straight:* ὀρθοποδέω ORTHOPODEŌ*
Gal 2.14 when I saw that they were not s.

STRAIN
1. *filter thoroughly:* διϋλίζω DIYLIZŌ*
Mt 23.24 "You blind guides, straining out a gnat!

STRAIN FORWARD
1. *stretch:* ἐπεκτείνομαι EPEKTEINOMAI*
Phil 3.13 straining forward to what lies ahead

STRANGE
1. *great:* μέγας MEGAS
2 Cor 11.15 it is not s. if his servants . . disguise
2. *receive as a guest, surprise:* ξενίζω (pass. part.) XENIZŌ
Acts 17.20 "you bring some s. things to our ears
3. *strange, foreign:* ξένος XENOS
Heb 13. 9 Do not be led away by . . s. teachings
1 Pet 4.12 as though something s. were happening

STRANGE THINGS
1. *contrary to expectation:* παράδοξος (subst. neut. pl.) PARADOXOS*
Lk 5.26 "We have seen strange things today

STRANGE TONGUES, MEN OF
1. *of another tongue:* ἑτερόγλωσσος (subst. pl.) HETEROGLŌSSOS*
1 Cor 14.21 "By men of s. tongues . . will I speak

STRANGER
1. *foreign:* ἀλλότριος (subst.) ALLOTRIOS
Jn 10. 5 "A s. they will not follow, . . for they do not know the voice of strangers
2. *strange, foreign:* ξένος (subst.) XENOS
Mt 25.35 " 'I was a stranger and you welcomed me
25.38 " 'when did we see thee a stranger?
25.43 " 'I was a s. and you did not welcome me
25.44 " 'Lord, when did we see thee . . a s.?
27. 7 the potter's field, to bury strangers in
Eph 2.12 you were . . strangers to the covenants
2.19 So then you are no longer strangers
Heb 11.13 they were strangers . . on the earth
3 Jn . 5 when you render any service . . to strangers
CONTEXTUALLY
Heb 13. 2 show hospitality to strangers

STRANGLED
1. *strangled:* πνικτός PNIKTOS*
Acts 15.20 "write . . them to abstain . . from what is s.[n]‡
15.29 "that you abstain . . from what is strangled[n]‡
21.25 "that they . . abstain . . from what is s.[v]‡

STRAW
1. *stubble, stalk, straw:* καλάμη KALAMĒ*
1 Cor 3.12 Now if any one builds . . with . . straw[0]

STRAY
1. *turn out of course:* ἐκτρέπω (pass.) EKTREPŌ
1 Tim 5.15 some have already strayed after Satan
2. *cause to wander:* πλανάω (pass.) PLANAŌ
1 Pet 2.25 For you were straying like sheep

STREAM
1. *river, stream:* ποταμός POTAMOS
Lk 6.48 "when a flood arose, the stream broke
6.49 "a house . . against which the stream broke

STREET
1. *way, road:* ὁδός HODOS
Mt 22.10 "those servants went out into the streets
2. *street:* πλατεῖα PLATEIA*
Mt 6. 5 "they love to . . pray . . at the s. corners
12.19 "nor will any . . hear his voice in . . streets
Lk 10.10 "go into its streets and say
13.26 "will . . say . . 'you taught in our streets
14.21 " 'Go out quickly to the streets
Acts 5.15 even carried out the sick into . . streets
Rev 11. 8 their dead bodies will lie in the street
21.21 the street of the city was pure gold
22. 2 through the middle of the s. of the city
3. *lane, alley:* ῥύμη RHYMĒ
Mt 6. 2 "as the hypocrites do . . in the streets
Acts 9.11 "go to the street called Straight
12.10 went out and passed on through one s.

STREET, OPEN
1. *street, quarter of town:* ἄμφοδον AMPHODON*
Mk 11. 4 a colt tied . . out in the open street

STRENGTH
1. *strength, might:* ἰσχύς ISCHYS
Mk 12.30 " 'love the Lord . . with all your s.
12.33 "to love him . . with all the strength
Lk 10.27 "love the Lord . . with all your strength
1 Pet 4.11 by the strength which God supplies
2. *strength, sovereignty:* κράτος KRATOS
Lk 1.51 He has shown strength with his arm
Eph 6.10 be strong . . in the s. of his might
3. *salvation, preservation:* σωτηρία SŌTĒRIA
Acts 27.34 take some food; it will give you strength
IDIOMATICALLY
a. 1 Cor 10.13 tempted beyond your strength πειρασθῆναι ὑπὲρ ὃ δύνασθε [DYNAMAI]

STRENGTH, FULL
1. *power, ability:* δύναμις DYNAMIS
Rev 1.16 like the sun shining in full strength

STRENGTH, GIVE
1. *strengthen, confirm:* ἐνδυναμόω ENDYNAMOŌ
1 Tim 1.12 I thank him who has given me strength
2 Tim 4.17 Lord . . gave me s. to proclaim the message

STRENGTH, HAVE
1. *overpower, prevail against:* κατισχύω KATISCHYŌ
Lk 21.36 praying that you may have s. to escape

STRENGTH, INCREASE IN
1. *strengthen, confirm:* ἐνδυναμόω (pass.) ENDYNAMOŌ
Acts 9.22 Saul increased all the more in strength

STRENGTH TO, HAVE THE
1. *be strong, prevail:* ἰσχύω ISCHYŌ
Mk 5. 4 no one had the strength to subdue him

STRENGTH, WIN
1. *strengthen:* δυναμόω (pass.) DYNAMOŌ
Heb 11.34 ⟨who⟩ won strength out of weakness

STRENGTHEN (*See also* LIFT AND STRENGTHEN)
1. *confirm, establish:* βεβαιόω BEBAIOŌ
Heb 13. 9 that the heart be strengthened by grace
2. *strengthen:* δυναμόω DYNAMOŌ
Col 1.11 May you be strengthened with . . power
3. *strengthen, confirm:* ἐνδυναμόω ENDYNAMOŌ
Phil 4.13 all things in him who strengthens me
4. *strengthen:* ἐνισχύω ENISCHYŌ*
Lk [22.43 *angel from heaven, strengthening him*‡
Acts 9.19 took food and was strengthened
5. *make fast, support:* ἐπιστηρίζω EPISTĒRIZŌ*
Acts 14.22 strengthening the souls of the disciples
15.32 exhorted the brethren . . strengthened
15.41 through Syria . . , strengthening . . churches
6. *make firm:* στερεόω STEREOŌ
Acts 16. 5 So the churches were strengthened

7. *support, fix:* στηρίζω STĒRIZŌ
Lk 22.32 "when you have turned again, strengthen
Acts 18.23 went.., strengthening all the disciples
Rom 1.11 impart.. some spiritual gift to s. you
16.25 to him who is able to strengthen you
2 Th 3. 3 Lord is faithful; he will strengthen you
Rev 3. 2 " 'Awake, and strengthen what remains
8. *strengthen:* σθενόω STHENOŌ*
1 Pet 5.10 restore, establish, and strengthen[m] you

STRENGTHENED, BE
1. *strengthen:* κραταιόω (pass.) KRATAIOŌ
Eph 3.16 he may grant you to be strengthened

STRESS, OF
1. *difficult, dangerous:* χαλεπός CHALEPOS
2 Tim 3. 1 in the last days.. will come times of s.

STRETCH OUT
1. *stretch out:* ἐκτείνω EKTEINŌ
Mt 8. 3 stretched out his hand and touched
12.13 said to the man, "Stretch out your hand." And the man stretched it out
12.49 stretching out.. hand toward.. disciples
26.51 stretched out his hand and drew.. sword
Mk 1.41 stretched out his hand and touched
3. 5 "Stretch out your hand." He stretched it out, and.. was restored
Lk 5.13 stretched out his hand, and touched
6.10 said to him, "Stretch out your hand
Jn 21.18 "you will stretch out your hands
Acts 4.30 "thou stretchest out thy hand to heal
26. 1 Then Paul stretched out his hand

STRICT MANNER
1. *exactness:* ἀκρίβεια AKRIBEIA*
Acts 22. 3 "educated according to the s. manner

STRICTEST
1. *precise:* ἀκριβής (superl.) AKRIBĒS*
Acts 26. 5 "the strictest party of our religion

STRICTLY (*See also* BIND STRICTLY BY AN OATH; CHARGE, STRICTLY)
1. *many, great:* πολύς (neut. pl.) POLYS
Mk 3.12 he s. ordered them not to make.. known
5.43 he s. charged.. that no one should know
IDIOMATICALLY
a. Acts 5.28 "We strictly charged you not to teach παραγγελίᾳ παρηγγείλαμεν ὑμῖν μὴ διδάσκειν [PARAGGELIA]

STRICTNESS
CONTEXTUALLY
Jas 3. 1 who teach shall be judged with greater s.

STRIFE
1. *strife, rivalry:* ἔρις ERIS
Rom 1.29 Full of envy, murder, strife, deceit
1 Cor 3. 3 there is jealousy and strife among you
Gal 5.20 idolatry, sorcery, enmity, strife

STRIKE
1. *throw, put:* βάλλω BALLŌ
Acts 27.14 northeaster, struck down from the land
2. *skin, flay:* δέρω DERŌ
Jn 18.23 "why do you strike me?
2 Cor 11.20 if a man.. strikes you in the face
3. *slap, buffet:* κολαφίζω KOLAPHIZŌ
Mt 26.67 they spat in his face, and struck him
Mk 14.65 some began to spit.. and to s. him
4. *strike:* παίω PAIŌ
Mt 26.68 "Prophesy..! Who is it that struck you?
Mk 14.47 drew his sword, and struck the slave
Lk 22.64 "Prophesy! Who is it that struck you?
Jn 18.10 drew it and struck.. high priest's slave
5. *strike, beat:* πατάσσω PATASSŌ
Mt 26.31 "it is written, 'I will strike the shepherd
26.51 struck the slave of the high priest
Mk 14.27 "it is written, 'I will strike the shepherd
Lk 22.49 "Lord, shall we strike with the sword?
22.50 struck the slave of the high priest
Acts 7.24 "avenged him by striking the Egyptian
12. 7 struck Peter on the side and woke him
6. *fall upon:* περιπίπτω εἰς PERIPIPTŌ [A.6.a.4]
Acts 27.41 striking a shoal[e] they ran.. aground
7. *fall upon:* πίπτω ἐπί PIPTŌ [A.6.a.4]
Rev 7.16 "the sun shall not strike them
8. *strike:* πλήσσω PLĒSSŌ*
Rev 8.12 a third of the sun was struck
9. *strike against:* προσκόπτω PROSKOPTŌ
Mt 4. 6 " 'lest you s. your foot against a stone
Lk 4.11 " 'lest you s. your foot against a stone
10. *strike with a stick, slap:* ῥαπίζω RHAPIZŌ
Mt 5.39 "if any.. strikes you on the right cheek
11. *strike, beat:* τύπτω TYPTŌ
Mt 27.30 they.. took the reed and struck him
Mk 15.19 they struck his head with a reed
Lk 6.29 "To him who strikes you on the cheek
Acts 23. 2 commanded those.. to s. him on the mouth
23. 3 Paul said to him, "God shall strike you!
23. 3 "yet.. you order me to be struck?

STRIKE DEAD
IDIOMATICALLY
a. Rev 2.23 " 'I will strike her children dead τὰ τέκνα αὐτῆς ἀποκτενῶ ἐν θανάτῳ [APOKTEINŌ]

STRIKE DOWN
1. *throw down, strike down:* καταβάλλω KATABALLŌ
2 Cor 4. 9 struck down, but not destroyed

STRIKE WITH ONE'S HAND
1. *give a blow:* διδόναι ῥάπισμα RHAPISMA [B.2.d.1]
Jn 18.22 one.. struck Jesus with his hand
19. 3 they.. struck him with their hands

STRIP
1. *take off:* ἐκδύω EKDYŌ
Mt 27.28 they stripped him and put.. robe upon him
27.31 they stripped him of the robe
Mk 15.20 they stripped him of the purple cloak
Lk 10.30 "robbers, who stripped.. and beat him

STRIPPED
1. *naked, bare:* γυμνός GYMNOS
Jn 21. 7 he put on his clothes, for he was s. for work

STRIVE
1. *have a struggle:* ἀγῶνα ἔχειν AGŌN [B.3.a.5]
Col 2. 1 I want you to know how greatly I s.
2. *fight, contend:* ἀγωνίζομαι AGŌNIZOMAI
Lk 13.24 "Strive to enter by the narrow door
Col 1.29 I toil, striving with all the energy
1 Tim 4.10 For to this end we toil and strive[j]‡
3. *be eager:* σπουδάζω SPOUDAZŌ
Heb 4.11 Let us therefore strive to enter that rest
4. *seek, search for:* ζητέω ZĒTEŌ
1 Cor 14.12 strive to excel in building up the church

STRIVE FOR
1. *pursue:* διώκω DIŌKŌ
Heb 12.14 Strive for peace with all men

STRIVE SIDE BY SIDE WITH
1. *assist, struggle together:* συναθλέω SYNATHLEŌ
Phil 1.27 with one mind striving side by side

STRIVE TOGETHER WITH
1. *contend along with, assist:* συναγωνίζομαι SYNAGŌNIZOMAI*
Rom 15.30 strive together with me in your prayers

STRONG
1. *possible, strong:* δυνατός DYNATOS
Rom 15. 1 We.. strong ought to bear with.. failings
2 Cor 12.10 for when I am weak, then I am strong
13. 9 glad when we are weak and you are s.
2. *operation, activity:* ἐνέργεια ENERGEIA [A.1.b.1]
2 Th 2.11 God sends upon them a s. delusion
3. *strong, powerful:* ἰσχυρός ISCHYROS
Mt 12.29 "how can one enter a strong man's house.. unless he first binds the strong man?
[14.30 he saw the *strong* wind, he was afraid‡
Mk 3.27 "no one can enter a strong man's house.. unless he first binds the strong man
Lk 11.21 "When a strong man, fully armed
1 Cor 1.27 God chose what is weak.. to shame the s.

1 Cor 4.10 We are weak, but you are strong
2 Cor 10.10 "His letters are weighty and strong
Heb 6.18 we .. might have s. encouragement
1 Jn 2.14 you, young men, because you are strong
Rev 5. 2 I saw a strong angel proclaiming
6.15 the rich and the strong, and every one
4. *great:* μέγας MEGAS
Jn 6.18 The sea rose because a strong wind
5 *austere, cruel:* σκληρός SKLĒROS
Jas 3. 4 the ships .. are driven by strong winds
IDIOMATICALLY
a. 1 Cor 7.36 if his passions are strong ἐὰν ᾖ ὑπέρακμος [HYPERAKMOS*]

STRONG, BE
STRONG, BECOME
STRONG, GROW
1. *strengthen, confirm:* ἐνδυναμόω (pass.) ENDYNAMOŌ
Rom 4.20 he grew s. in his faith as he gave glory
Eph 6.10 Finally, be strong in the Lord
2 Tim 2. 1 be s. in the grace that is in Christ
2. *strengthen:* κραταιόω (pass.) KRATAIOŌ
Lk 1.80 child grew and became strong in spirit
2.40 the child grew and became strong
1 Cor 16.13 firm in your faith, be courageous, be s.

STRONG DRINK
1. *fermented liquor:* σίκερα SIKERA*
Lk 1.15 "he shall drink no wine nor s. drink

STRONG ENOUGH, BE
1. *be strong, prevail:* ἰσχύω ISCHYŌ
Lk 16. 3 " 'I am not strong enough to dig

STRONG, MAKE
1. *make firm:* στερεόω STEREOŌ
Acts 3. 7 his feet and ankles were made strong
3.16 "faith in his name, has made this man s.

STRONGER
1. *strong, powerful:* ἰσχυρός (comp.) ISCHYROS
Lk 11.22 "when one stronger than he assails him
1 Cor 1.25 the weakness of God is stronger than men
10.22 Are we stronger than he?

STRONGHOLD
1. *fortress, prison:* ὀχύρωμα OCHYRŌMA*
2 Cor 10. 4 divine power to destroy strongholds

STRONGLY
1. *very much:* λίαν LIAN
2 Tim 4.15 for he strongly opposed our message
2. *many, great:* πολύς (neut. pl.) POLYS
1 Cor 16.12 I strongly urged him to visit you

STRUCTURE
1. *building, edification:* οἰκοδομή OIKODOMĒ
Eph 2.21 in whom the whole structure is joined

STRUGGLE
1. *struggle against:* ἀνταγωνίζομαι ANTAGŌNIZOMAI*
Heb 12. 4 In your struggle against sin
2. *contest, struggle:* ἄθλησις ATHLĒSIS*
Heb 10.32 you endured a hard s. with sufferings

STUBBORN, BE
1. *harden:* σκληρύνω (pass.) SKLĒRYNŌ
Acts 19. 9 when some were s. and disbelieved

STUDY
1. *learn, understand:* μανθάνω MANTHANŌ
Jn 7.15 "How .., when he has never studied?

STUMBLE
1. *strike against:* προσκόπτω PROSKOPTŌ
Jn 11. 9 "If .. one walks in the day, he does not s.
11.10 "if .. one walks in the night, he stumbles
Rom 9.32 stumbled over the stumbling stone
14.21 anything that makes your brother s.[v]
1 Pet 2. 8 they stumble because they disobey
2. *stumble, fall:* πταίω PTAIŌ
Rom 11.11 have they stumbled so as to fall?
3. *cause to stumble, offend:* σκανδαλίζω SKANDALIZŌ
Mt [13.21 "immediately he *stumbles*†
[24.10 "And then many will *stumble,* and betray†
Mk [4.17 "immediately they *stumble*†
[6. 3 And they *stumbled* at him†

STUMBLE, THAT WILL MAKE MEN
STUMBLING BLOCK
STUMBLING, CAUSE FOR
1. *offense, obstacle:* πρόσκομμα PROSKOMMA
[a]gen.
Rom 9.33 [a]"a stone that will make men stumble
14.13 never to put a stumbling block .. in the way
1 Cor 8. 9 lest this liberty .. become a stumbling block
1 Pet 2. 8 [a]"A stone that will make men stumble
2. *stumbling block, trap:* σκάνδαλον SKANDALON
1 Cor 1.23 Christ crucified, a stumbling block
Gal 5.11 the stumbling block of the cross
1 Jn 2.10 in it[c] there is no cause for stumbling
Rev 2.14 " 'to put a stumbling block before .. Israel

STUMBLING
1. *offense, obstacle:* πρόσκομμα (gen.) PROSKOMMA
Rom 9.32 They .. stumbled over the stumbling stone

STUPID
1. *dull, stupid:* μωρός MŌROS
2 Tim 2.23 nothing to do with s. .. controversies
Tit 3. 9 avoid s. controversies, genealogies

STUPOR
1. *stupefaction:* κατάνυξις KATANYXIS*
Rom 11. 8 "God gave them a spirit of stupor

SUBDUE
1. *tame, subdue:* δαμάζω DAMAZŌ
Mk 5. 4 no one had the strength to s. him
2. *bring into subjection:* δουλαγωγέω DOULAGŌGEŌ*
1 Cor 9.27 but I pommel my body and subdue it

SUBJECT
SUBJECTION, PUT IN
1. *subject, place under:* ὑποτάσσω HYPOTASSŌ
Lk 10.17 "even the demons are subject to us!
10.20 "that the spirits are subject to you
Rom 8.20 the creation was subjected to futility .. by .. him who subjected it in hope
13. 1 Let every person be s. to the .. authorities
13. 5 one must be s. .. for the sake of conscience
1 Cor 14.32 spirits of prophets .. subject to prophets
15.27 "God[z] has put all things in subjection
15.27 "All things are put in subjection
15.28 When all things are subjected to him, .. the Son .. will also be subjected to him
16.16 I urge you to be subject to such men
Eph 5.21 subject to one another out of reverence
5.24 As the church is subject to Christ
Phil 3.21 enables him even to subject all things
Col 3.18 Wives, be subject to your husbands
Heb 2. 5 it was not to angels that God subjected
2. 8 "putting everything in subjection
2. 8 putting everything in subjection to him
2. 8 we do not yet see everything in subjection
12. 9 much more be subject to the Father
1 Pet 2.13 Be subject .. to every human institution[f]
3.22 authorities, and powers subject to him
5. 5 you .. younger be subject to the elders

SUBJECT TO
1. *liable, guilty:* ἔνοχος (+gen.) ENOCHOS
Heb 2.15 through fear .. s. to lifelong bondage

SUBMISSION
1. *subordination:* ὑποταγή HYPOTAGĒ
Gal 2. 5 to them we did not yield submission

SUBMISSIVE
1. *subordination:* ὑποταγή HYPOTAGĒ [B.1.a.1]
1 Tim 3. 4 keeping his children submissive

SUBMISSIVE, BE
1. *subject, place under:* ὑποτάσσω (pass.) HYPOTASSŌ
Tit 2. 5 to be sensible, .. s. to their husbands
2. 9 Bid slaves to be s. to their masters
3. 1 Remind them to be submissive to rulers
1 Pet 2.18 Servants, be s. to your masters

1 Pet 3. 1 you wives, be s. to your husbands
3. 5 holy women . . were s. to their husbands

SUBMISSIVENESS
1. *subordination:* ὑποταγή HYPOTAGĒ
1 Tim 2.11 Let a woman learn in silence with all s.

SUBMIT (*See also* REGULATIONS, SUBMIT TO)
SUBMIT ONESELF
1. *bear up, endure* (mid.): ἀνέχω ANECHŌ
2 Cor 11. 4 if . . one . . preaches another Jesus . . , you s.
2. *hold within, be hostile:* ἐνέχω (pass.) ENECHŌ
Gal 5. 1 do not submit again to a yoke of slavery
3. *yield, give way:* ὑπείκω HYPEIKŌ*
Heb 13.17 Obey your leaders and submit to them
4. *subject, place under:* ὑποτάσσω (pass.) HYPOTASSŌ
Rom 8. 7 it does not submit to God's law
10. 3 did not s. to God's righteousness
Jas 4. 7 Submit yourselves therefore to God

SUBORDINATE, BE
1. *subject, place under:* ὑποτάσσω (pass.) HYPOTASSŌ
1 Cor 14.34 women . . should be s., as . . the law says

SUBSEQUENT
1. *after these things:* μετὰ ταῦτα (attr.) META [B.1.a.1]
1 Pet 1.11 when predicting . . the subsequent glory

SUBSTANCE
1. *body:* σῶμα SŌMA
Col 2.17 but the substance belongs to Christ

SUCCEED
SUCCEED IN
1. *successor:* διάδοχος DIADOCHOS [B.3.a.6]
Acts 24.27 Felix was succeeded by . . Festus
2. *help on the way, gain:* εὐοδόω (pass.) EUODOŌ
Rom 1.10 I may now at last s. in coming to you

SUCCEED IN FULFILLING
1. *attain unto:* φθάνω εἰς PHTHANŌ [A.6.a.4]
Rom 9.31 Israel . . did not s. in fulfilling that law

SUCH
SUCH AS
1. *whether, or:* εἴτε EITE
1 Cor 14. 7 lifeless instruments, such as the flute
2. *what, such as:* οἷος HOIOS
ᵃ+τοιοῦτος
Mt 24.21 "great tribulation, such as has not been
Mk 13.19 ᵃ"such tribulation as has not been
Rev 16.18 great earthquake s. as had never been
3. *who, which, what:* ὅς HOS
Acts **25**.18
2 Cor **10**.2
4. *this:* οὗτος HOUTOS
1 Cor **6**.11
2 Tim **3**.5
2 Jn .7
Rev **20**.6
5. *thus, so:* οὕτως HOUTŌS [A.4.a]
Mt 11.26 "yea, . . for such was thy gracious will[f]†
19.10 "If s. is the case of a man with . . wife
Lk 10.21 "yea, . . for such was thy gracious will[h]†
1 Cor 5. 4(3) the man who has done such a thing
9.15 writing . . to secure any such provision
6. *as, just as:* καθώς KATHŌS
Jn 6.58 not such as the fathers ate and died
7. *closely resembling:* παρόμοιος PAROMOIOS*
Mk 7.13 "And many such things you do
8. *anyone, any:* τις TIS II [B.3.b.4]
Eph 4.29 but only such as is good for edifying
9. *such as this:* τοιοῦτος TOIOUTOS
Mt 9. 8 God, who had given s. authority to men
18. 5 "Whoever receives one such child
19.14 "to s. belongs the kingdom of heaven
Mk 4.33 With many such parables he spoke
7.13 "And many such things you do
9.37 "Whoever receives one such child
10.14 "for to s. belongs the kingdom of God
Lk 9. 9 "who . . about whom I hear such things?
18.16 "for to such belongs the kingdom of God
Jn 4.23 "for s. the Father seeks to worship him
Jn 8. 5 "Moses commanded us to stone such[r]‡
9.16 "How can . . a sinner do such signs?
Acts 22.22 "Away with such a fellow from the earth!
26.29 "I would . . that . . all . . become such as I
Rom 1.32 those who do such things deserve to die
2. 2 judgment . . upon those who do s. things
2. 3 when you judge those who do s. things
16.18 such persons do not serve our Lord
1 Cor 5.11 not even to eat with such a one
7.15 in such a case the brother . . is not bound
16.16 I urge you to be subject to such men
16.18 Give recognition to such men
2 Cor 2. 6 For s. a one this punishment . . is enough
3. 4 Such is the confidence that we have
3.12 Since we have s. a hope, we are very bold
10.11 Let such people understand that . . we do
11.13 For such men are false apostles
Gal 5.21 who do such things shall not inherit
5.23 self-control; against s. there is no law
Eph 5.27 without spot or wrinkle or any s. thing
Phil 2.29 So receive him . . ; and honor s. men
2 Th 3.12 s. persons we command and exhort
Tit 3.11 such a person is perverted and sinful
Heb 7.26 fitting that we . . have such a high priest
8. 1 we have such a high priest
12. 3 who endured from sinners s. hostility
13.16 for such sacrifices are pleasing to God
Jas 4.16 All such boasting is evil
3 Jn . 8 So we ought to support such men
10. *so large, so many:* τοσοῦτος TOSOUTOS
Mt 8.10 "not . . in Israel have I found such faith
Lk 7. 9 "not . . in Israel have I found such faith
CONTEXTUALLY
Rom **15**.5
2 Cor **3**.7
2 Tim **2**.16
Jas **3**.15
1 Pet **1**.18
Jude .15

SUCH AND SUCH
1. *this:* ὅδε (attr.) HODE
Jas 4.13 "we will go into such and such a town

SUCK
SUCK, GIVE
1. *give suck, suck:* θηλάζω THĒLAZŌ
Mt 24.19 "alas . . those who give s. in those days!
Mk 13.17 "alas . . those who give s. in those days!
Lk 11.27 "Blessed . . the breasts that you sucked!
21.23 "Alas . . those who give s. in those days!
2. *feed, nourish:* τρέφω TREPHŌ
Lk 23.29 "'Blessed . . the breasts that never gave s.!

SUCKLING
1. *give suck, suck:* θηλάζω (subst. part.) THĒLAZŌ
Mt 21.16 "'Out of . . mouth of babes and sucklings

SUDDEN
1. *sudden:* αἰφνίδιος AIPHNIDIOS
1 Th 5. 3 then sudden destruction will come

SUDDENLY
1. *sudden:* αἰφνίδιος AIPHNIDIOS [A.3.b.3]
Lk 21.34 "that day come upon you s. like a snare
2. *unawares, suddenly:* ἄφνω APHNŌ*
Acts 2. 2 suddenly a sound came from heaven
16.26 suddenly there was a great earthquake
28. 6 expecting him to . . s. fall down dead
3. *unexpectedly:* ἐξαίφνης EXAIPHNĒS*
Mk 13.36 "lest he come s. and find you asleep
Lk 2.13 s. there was with the angel a multitude
9.39 "a spirit seizes him, and he s. cries out
Acts 9. 3 s. a light from heaven flashed about him
22. 6 "light from heaven s. shone about me
4. *suddenly:* ἐξάπινα EXAPINA*
Mk 9. 8 s. looking around they no longer saw

SUE
1. *judge, decide:* κρίνω (pass.) KRINŌ
Mt 5.40 "if any one would sue you

SUFFER (*See also, e.g.,* AFFLICTION, SUFFER; DISHONOR, SUFFER)
1. *have, hold:* ἔχω ECHŌ
 2 Cor 2. 3 that when I came I might not s. pain[o]
2. *suffer misfortune:* κακοπαθέω KAKOPATHEŌ
 2 Tim 2. 9 the gospel for which I am suffering
 Jas 5.13 Is any one among you suffering?
3. *grieve, cause pain:* λυπέω (pass.) LYPEŌ
 1 Pet 1. 6 you may have to suffer various trials
4. *suffer, experience:* πάσχω PASCHŌ
 Mt 16.21 to show his disciples that he must . . s.
 17.12 "also the Son of man will suffer
 17.15 "have mercy on my son, for he . . suffers
 27.19 "I have suffered much over him today
 Mk 5.26 had suffered much under many physicians
 8.31 to teach . . that the Son of man must s.
 9.12 "that he should suffer many things
 Lk 9.22 "The Son of man must s. many things
 13. 2 "worse sinners . . because they suffered?
 17.25 "But first he must suffer many things
 22.15 "to eat this passover . . before I suffer
 24.26 "necessary that the Christ should s.
 24.46 "it is written, that the Christ should s.
 Acts 3.18 "foretold . . that his Christ should s.
 9.16 "I will show him how much he must s.
 17. 3 "it was necessary for the Christ to s.
 28. 5 He, however, . . suffered no harm
 1 Cor 12.26 If one member suffers
 2 Cor 1. 6 endure the same sufferings that we s.
 Phil 1.29 not only believe in him but also suffer
 1 Th 2.14 for you suffered the same things
 2 Th 1. 5 kingdom . . , for which you are suffering
 2 Tim 1.12 and therefore I suffer as I do
 Heb 2.18 For because he himself has suffered
 5. 8 obedience through what he suffered
 9.26 then he would have had to suffer
 13.12 So Jesus also suffered outside the gate
 1 Pet 2.19 endures pain while suffering unjustly
 2.20 when you do right and suffer for it
 2.21 because Christ also suffered for you
 2.23 when he suffered, he did not threaten
 3.14 if you do s. for righteousness' sake
 3.17 it is better to suffer for doing right
 [3.18 Christ also *suffered* for sins once for all‡
 4. 1 Since . . Christ suffered in the flesh[i]
 4. 1 whoever has suffered in the flesh
 4.15 let none of you suffer as a murderer
 4.19 those who s. according to God's will
 5.10 after you have suffered a little while
 Rev 2.10 " 'Do not fear what you are about to s.
5. *undergo trial:* πεῖραν λαμβάνειν PEIRA [A.6.a.4]
 Heb 11.36 Others suffered mocking and scourging
6. *affliction, oppression:* θλῖψις THLIPSIS [A.1.a]
 Eph 3.13 not . . lose heart over what I am suffering
7. *pay, make atonement for:* τίνω TINŌ*
 2 Th 1. 9 They shall suffer the punishment
CONTEXTUALLY
 Heb 11.26 considered abuse suffered for Christ
 1 Pet 4.16 yet if one suffers as a Christian

SUFFER, ALREADY
1. *suffer beforehand:* προπάσχω PROPASCHŌ*
 1 Th 2. 2 though we had already suffered

SUFFER, MUST
1. *subject to suffering:* παθητός PATHĒTOS* [A.6.a.3]
 Acts 26.23 "⟨testifying⟩ that the Christ must suffer

SUFFER TOGETHER
SUFFER WITH
1. *experience the same as another:* συμπάσχω SYMPASCHŌ*
 Rom 8.17 fellow heirs . . , provided we s. with him
 1 Cor 12.26 If one member . . , all suffer together

SUFFER WRONG
1. *do wrong, harm:* ἀδικέω (pass.) ADIKEŌ
 1 Cor 6. 7 Why not rather suffer wrong?
 2 Cor 7.12 the one who suffered the wrong
 2 Pet 2.13 suffering wrong for their wrongdoing

SUFFERING
1. *suffering, distress:* κακοπάθεια KAKOPATHEIA*
 Jas 5.10 an example of suffering and patience
2. *suffering, misfortune:* πάθημα PATHĒMA
 Rom 8.18 the sufferings of this present time
 2 Cor 1. 5 as we share . . in Christ's sufferings
 1. 6 when you . . endure the same sufferings
 1. 7 that as you share in our sufferings
 Phil 3.10 that I may . . share his sufferings
 Col 1.24 Now I rejoice in my sufferings
 2 Tim 3.11 my persecutions, my sufferings
 Heb 2. 9 crowned . . because of the s. of death
 2.10 make the pioneer . . perfect through s.
 10.32 endured a hard struggle with sufferings
 1 Pet 1.11 predicting the sufferings of Christ
 4.13 so far as you share Christ's sufferings
 5. 1 a witness of the sufferings of Christ
 5. 9 the same experience of s. is required
3. *affliction, oppression:* θλῖψις THLIPSIS
 Rom 5. 3 we[h] rejoice in our sufferings, knowing that suffering produces endurance

SUFFERING, ENDURE
1. *suffer misfortune:* κακοπαθέω KAKOPATHEŌ
 2 Tim 4. 5 always be steady, endure suffering

SUFFERING, SHARE IN
1. *suffer together with:* συγκακοπαθέω SYGKAKOPATHEŌ*
 2 Tim 1. 8 but share in suffering for the gospel[o]
 2. 3 Share in suffering as a good soldier[o]

SUFFICE
1. *sufficient:* ἀρκετός ARKETOS [A.6.a.3]
 1 Pet 4. 3 Let the time that is past s. for doing

SUFFICIENT
1. *sufficient:* ἀρκετός ARKETOS
 Mt 6.34 "Let the day's own trouble be sufficient
2. *enough:* ἱκανός HIKANOS
 2 Cor 2.16 Who is sufficient for these things?

SUFFICIENT, BE
1. *suffice, satisfy:* ἀρκέω ARKEŌ
 2 Cor 12. 9 "My grace is sufficient for you

SUIT, TO
1. *in accordance with, for:* κατά (+acc.) KATA [B.3.b.4]
 2 Tim 4. 3 teachers to suit their own likings

SUITABLE, NOT
1. *inconvenient:* ἀνεύθετος ANEUTHETOS*
 Acts 27.12 the harbor was not suitable to winter in

SULPHUR
1. *sulphur:* θεῖον THEION
 Lk 17.29 "fire and sulphur rained from heaven[o]
 Rev 9.17 sulphur issued from their mouths
 9.18 sulphur issuing from their mouths
 14.10 "he shall be tormented with fire and s.[o]
 19.20 the lake of fire that burns with s.[o]
 20.10 thrown into the lake of fire and sulphur[o]
 21. 8 "the lake that burns with fire and s.[o]

SULPHUR, THE COLOR OF
1. *sulphurous, yellow:* θειώδης THEIŌDĒS*
 Rev 9.17 riders wore breastplates the color of . . s.

SUM
1. *sum total, main point:* κεφάλαιον KEPHALAION
 Acts 22.28 "I bought this citizenship for a large sum
2. *honor, value:* τιμή TIMĒ
 Acts 7.16 "tomb that Abraham had bought for a s.
CONTEXTUALLY
 Mt 26. 9 "might have been sold for a large sum
 28.12 they gave a s. of money to the soldiers
 Mk 12.41 Many rich people put in large sums

SUM UP
1. *sum up, recapitulate:* ἀνακεφαλαιόω ANAKEPHALAIOŌ
 Rom 13. 9 and any other commandment, . . summed up

SUMMER
1. *summer, summer fruits:* θέρος THEROS*
 Mt 24.32 "you know that summer is near
 Mk 13.28 "you know that summer is near
 Lk 21.30 "know that the summer is already near

SUMMON
1. *call, name:* καλέω KALEŌ
Mt 2. 7 Herod summoned the wise men secretly
2. *recall, summon:* μετακαλέω (mid.) METAKALEŌ
Acts 24.25 "when I have an opportunity I will s. you
3. *call on, summon:* προσκαλέω (mid.) PROSKALEŌ
Mt 18.32 "his lord summoned him and said
Mk 15.44 summoning the centurion, he asked
Lk 16. 5 " 'summoning his master's debtors
Acts 6. 2 summoned the body of the disciples
13. 7 Sergius Paulus . . summoned Barnabas

SUMPTUOUSLY
1. *utterly, splendidly:* λαμπρῶς LAMPRŌS*
Lk 16.19 "who feasted sumptuously every day

SUN
1. *sun, sunshine:* ἥλιος HĒLIOS
Mt 5.45 "he makes his sun rise on . . evil and . . good
13. 6 "when the sun rose they were scorched
13.43 "the righteous will shine like the sun
17. 2 his face shone like the sun
24.29 "the sun will be darkened
Mk 4. 6 "when the sun rose it was scorched
13.24 "the sun will be darkened, and the moon
16. 2 went to the tomb when the s. had risen
Lk 4.40 Now when the sun was setting
21.25 "there will be signs in sun and moon
[23.45 while *the sun was eclipsed*†
Acts 2.20 "'sun shall be turned into darkness
13.11 "shall be blind and unable to see the s.
26.13 "light from heaven, brighter than the s.
27.20 when neither sun nor stars appeared
1 Cor 15.41 There is one glory of the sun
Eph 4.26 do not let the s. go down on your anger
Jas 1.11 the sun rises with its scorching heat
Rev 1.16 his face was like the sun shining
6.12 the sun became black as sackcloth
7. 2 angel ascend from the rising of the sun
7.16 "the sun shall not strike them
8.12 a third of the sun was struck
9. 2 the sun and the air were darkened
10. 1 his face was like the sun
12. 1 a woman clothed with the sun
16. 8 fourth angel poured his bowl on the sun
19.17 I saw an angel standing in the sun
21.23 the city has no need of sun or moon
22. 5 they need no light of lamp or sun

SUNDOWN, AT
1. *when the sun set:* ὅτε ἔδυσεν ὁ ἥλιος DYNŌ; HĒLIOS [B.2.a.2]
Mk 1.32 at s., they brought . . all who were sick

SUN'S LIGHT
1. *sun, sunshine:* ἥλιος HĒLIOS [C.2]
Lk 23.45 while the sun's light failed[r]†

SUPERFLUOUS
1. *superfluous, extraordinary:* περισσός PERISSOS
2 Cor 9. 1 it is superfluous for me to write

SUPERIOR
1. *better, stronger:* κρείσσων KREISSŌN
Heb 1. 4 as much superior to angels as the name
7. 7 the inferior is blessed by the superior

SUPERLATIVE
1. *exceedingly:* ὑπερλίαν (attr.) HYPERLIAN*
2 Cor 11. 5 I am not . . inferior to these s. apostles
12.11 I am not . . inferior to these s. apostles

SUPERNATURAL
1. *spiritual, of wind:* πνευματικός PNEUMATIKOS
1 Cor 10. 3 all ate the same supernatural[o] food†
10. 4 all drank the same s.[o] drink. For they drank from the s.[o] Rock

SUPERSTITION
1. *religion, religious feeling:* δεισιδαιμονία DEISIDAIMONIA*
Acts 25.19 "points of dispute . . about their own s.

SUPPER
1. *dine:* δειπνέω DEIPNEŌ
[a]B.2.a.1 [b]inf.
Lk 17. 8 [a]"'Prepare supper for me . . and serve me
22.20 [b]And likewise the cup after supper‡
1 Cor 11.25 [b]In the same way also the cup, after s.
2. *meal, dinner:* δεῖπνον DEIPNON
Jn 12. 2 There they made him a supper
13. 2 during s., when the devil had already
13. 4 rose from s., laid aside his garments
21.20 had lain close to his breast at the s.
1 Cor 11.20 it is not the Lord's s. that you eat
Rev 19. 9 "invited to . . marriage s. of the Lamb
19.17 "Come, gather for the great s. of God

SUPPLEMENT
1. *supply, furnish:* ἐπιχορηγέω EPICHORĒGEŌ
2 Pet 1. 5 every effort to supplement your faith

SUPPLICATION
1. *entreaty, prayer:* δέησις DEĒSIS
Eph 6.18 Pray . . with all prayer and supplication
6.18 making supplication for all the saints
Phil 4. 6 by prayer and s. with thanksgiving
1 Tim 2. 1 I urge that supplications . . be made
5. 5 continues in supplications and prayers
2. *supplication, prayer:* ἱκετηρία HIKETĒRIA*
Heb 5. 7 Jesus[j] offered up . . supplications

SUPPLIED, WITH WHICH IT IS
1. *supply, support:* ἐπιχορηγία (gen.) EPICHORĒGIA
Eph 4.16 by every joint with which it is supplied

SUPPLY
1. *lead a chorus, supply:* χορηγέω CHORĒGEŌ*
2 Cor 9.10 He . . will s. and multiply your resources[l]
1 Pet 4.11 by the strength which God supplies
2. *supply, furnish:* ἐπιχορηγέω EPICHORĒGEŌ
2 Cor 9.10 He who supplies seed to the sower
Gal 3. 5 he who supplies the Spirit to you
3. *be for:* γίνομαι εἰς GINOMAI [A.6.a.5]
2 Cor 8.14 their abundance may supply your want
4. *put in order, make:* καταρτίζω KATARTIZŌ
1 Th 3.10 supply what is lacking in your faith
5. *fill full, complete:* πληρόω PLĒROŌ
Phil 4.19 my God will supply every need
6. *fill up:* προσαναπληρόω PROSANAPLĒROŌ*
2 Cor 9.12 this service not only supplies the wants
11. 9 my needs were supplied by the brethren

SUPPORT
1. *lift up, carry:* βαστάζω BASTAZŌ
Rom 11.18 it is not you that support the root
2. *take up, assume:* ὑπολαμβάνω HYPOLAMBANŌ
3 Jn . 8 So we ought to support such men
3. *salary, pay:* ὀψώνιον OPSŌNION
2 Cor 11. 8 I robbed other churches by accepting s.

SUPPOSE
1. *think, suppose:* δοκέω DOKEŌ
Lk 19.11 they supposed that the kingdom
24.37 they . . supposed that they saw a spirit
Jn 11.31 supposing that she was going
20.15 Supposing him to be the gardener
Acts 27.13 supposing that they had obtained
Jas 4. 5 Or do you suppose it is in vain?
2. *take up, assume:* ὑπολαμβάνω HYPOLAMBANŌ
Lk 7.43 "I suppose, to whom he forgave more
Acts 2.15 "these men are not drunk, as you s.
3. *suppose, suspect:* ὑπονοέω HYPONOEŌ
Acts 13.25 "'What do you suppose that I am?
25.18 "no charge . . of such evils as I supposed
4. *reckon, count:* λογίζομαι LOGIZOMAI
Rom 2. 3 Do you s., O man, that when you judge?
5. *think, believe:* νομίζω NOMIZŌ
Lk 2.44 supposing him to be in the company
3.23 the son (as was supposed) of Joseph
Acts 7.25 "supposed that his brethren understood
14.19 supposing that he was dead
16.13 where we supposed there was a place
16.27 supposing . . the prisoners had escaped

Acts 21.29 they supposed that Paul had brought him
6. *expect, think:* οἴομαι OIOMAI
Jn 21.25 I suppose that the world itself could not
Jas 1. 7, 8 For that person must not suppose

SUPPOSED TO, BE
1. *think, suppose:* δοκέω DOKEŌ
Mk 10.42 "who are supposed to rule . . the Gentiles

SUPPRESS
1. *hold fast, restrain:* κατέχω KATECHŌ
Rom 1.18 who by their wickedness s. the truth

SUPREME
1. *be above:* ὑπερέχω (part.) HYPERECHŌ
1 Pet 2.13 whether it be to the emperor as s.

SURE
1 *impossible:* ἀνένδεκτος (neg.) ANENDEKTOS*
Lk 17. 1 "Temptations to sin[x] are sure to come
2. *certain, safe:* ἀσφαλής ASPHALĒS
Heb 6.19 as a sure and steadfast anchor
3. *faithful, trustworthy:* πιστός PISTOS
1 Tim 1.15 saying is s. and worthy of . . acceptance
3. 1 The saying is sure: If any one aspires
4. 9 saying is s. and worthy of . . acceptance
2 Tim 2.11 The saying is sure: If we . . died with him
Tit 1. 9 must hold firm to the s. word as taught
3. 8 ⟨he saved us⟩ The saying is s.

SURE, BE
SURE, FEEL
1. *know truly:* εἰδέναι ἀληθῶς ALĒTHŌS; OIDA [B.3.b.4]
Acts 12.11 "I am sure that the Lord has sent
2. *persuade:* πείθω PEITHŌ
[a] + σεαυτόν
Rom 2.19 [a]if you are sure that you are a guide
8.38 For I am sure that neither death
2 Cor 2. 3 for I felt sure of all of you
Phil 1. 6 I am s. that he who began a good work
2 Tim 1. 5 faith that . . , I am sure, dwells in you
1.12 I am sure that he is able to guard
Heb 6. 9 we feel sure of better things that belong
13.18 we are sure . . we have a clear conscience
3. *trust, boldness:* πεποίθησις PEPOITHĒSIS [A.1.e]
2 Cor 1.15 Because I was sure of this, I wanted
IDIOMATICALLY
a. Eph 5.5 Be sure of this τοῦτο γὰρ ἴστε γινώσκοντες [GINŌSKŌ; OIDA]

SURE BLESSINGS
1. *faithful, trustworthy:* πιστός (subst. neut. pl.) PISTOS
Acts 13.34 "'will give . . the s. blessings of David

SURE, MADE MORE
1. *firm, steady:* βέβαιος (comp.) BEBAIOS
2 Pet 1.19 the prophetic word made more sure

SURE, MAY BE
1. *know, understand:* γινώσκω GINŌSKŌ
1 Jn 2. 3 we may be sure that we know him
2. 5 we may be sure that we are in him
2.29 may be sure that . . one who does right

SURELY
1. *surely, doubtless:* δήπου DĒPOU*
Heb 2.16 For surely it is not with angels
2. *yes:* ναί NAI
Rev 22.20 "Surely I am coming soon." Amen
IDIOMATICALLY
a. Mt 15.4; Mk 7.10 "'He who speaks evil . . , let him surely die ὁ κακολογῶν . . θανάτῳ τελευτάτω [THANATOS; C.3]
b. Acts 7.34 "'I have surely seen the ill-treatment of my people ἰδὼν εἶδον τὴν κάκωσιν τοῦ λαοῦ μου [EIDON; C.3]
c. Heb 6.14 "Surely I will bless you εἰ μὴν εὐλογῶν εὐλογήσω σε [EULOGEŌ; EI MĒN*; C.3]
CONTEXTUALLY
2 Cor 1.18 As surely as God is faithful

SURETY
1. *secured, reliable:* ἔγγυος (subst.) EGGYOS*
Heb 7.22 makes Jesus the s. of a better covenant

SURF
1. *force:* βία BIA
Acts 27.41 the stern was broken up by the surf

SURNAME
1. *call, surname:* ἐπικαλέω EPIKALEŌ
Acts 1.23 Barsabbas, who was surnamed Justus
4.36 Joseph who was surnamed . . Barnabas
2. *add a name:* ἐπιτιθέναι ὄνομα (+dat.) EPITITHĒMI; ONOMA [A.6.a.4]
Mk 3.16 Simon[x] whom he surnamed Peter
3.17 James . . and John . . he surnamed Boanerges

SURPASS
1. *throw over, exceed:* ὑπερβάλλω HYPERBALLŌ
2 Cor 3.10 the splendor that surpasses it
9.14 the surpassing grace of God in you
Eph 3.19 love of Christ . . surpasses knowledge

SURPASSING WORTH
1. *be above:* ὑπερέχω (subst. part. neut.) HYPERECHŌ
Phil 3. 8 the s. worth of knowing Christ Jesus

SURPRISE
1. *catch:* καταλαμβάνω KATALAMBANŌ
1 Th 5. 4 for that day to s. you like a thief

SURPRISED, BE
1. *receive as a guest, surprise:* ξενίζω (mid.) XENIZŌ
1 Pet 4. 4 They are s. that you do not . . join them
4.12 do not be surprised at the fiery ordeal

SURROUND
1. *wind around, surround:* κυκλεύω KYKLEUŌ*
Rev 20. 9 they . . surrounded . . camp of the saints
2. *surround, encircle:* κυκλόω KYKLOŌ
Lk 21.20 "when you see Jerusalem surrounded
3. *lie around, wear:* περίκειμαι PERIKEIMAI
Heb 12. 1 Therefore, since we are surrounded
4. *encircle, surround:* περικυκλόω PERIKYKLOŌ*
Lk 19.43 days . . when your enemies will . . s. you
5. *hold together, impel:* συνέχω SYNECHŌ
Lk 8.45 "Master, the multitudes surround you!

SURROUNDING
1. *about, around:* περί (+acc.) PERI [B.3.b.4]
Jude .7

SURROUNDING COUNTRY
SURROUNDING REGION
1. *around a place:* περίχωρος PERICHŌROS [B.3.b.2]
Mk 1.28 throughout all the s. region of Galilee
Lk 4.14 report . . went . . through all the s. country
4.37 reports . . into every place in . . s. region
7.17 report . . spread through . . all the s. country
8.37 people of the s. country of . . Gerasenes[a]
Acts 14. 6 fled to Lystra and . . the s. country

SURVIVE
1. *stay, wait:* μένω MENŌ
1 Cor 3.14 If the work . . survives, . . a reward

SUSANNA: Σουσάννα sü'zanə
Lk 8. 3 S., and . . others, who provided for them[z]

SUSPECT
1. *suppose, suspect:* ὑπονοέω HYPONOEŌ
Acts 27.27 sailors suspected . . they were nearing land
2. *reckon, count:* λογίζομαι LOGIZOMAI
2 Cor 10. 2 who s. us of acting in worldly fashion

SUSPENSE, IN
1. *wait for, expect:* προσδοκάω (part.) PROSDOKAŌ
Acts 27.33 "continued in suspense and without food

SUSPENSE, KEEP IN
IDIOMATICALLY
a. Jn 10.24 "How long will you keep us in suspense? ἕως πότε τὴν ψυχὴν ἡμῶν αἴρεις; [AIRŌ; PSYCHĒ]

SUSPICION
1. *conjecture, suspicion:* ὑπόνοια HYPONOIA*
1 Tim 6. 4 disputes . . which produce . . base suspicions

SUSTAIN
1. *confirm, establish:* βεβαιόω BEBAIOŌ
1 Cor 1. 8 will sustain you to the end, guiltless

2. *stand, set:* ἵστημι HISTĒMI
2 Cor 13. 1 charge must be sustained by the evidence

SWADDLING CLOTHS, WRAP IN
1. *swathe:* σπαργανόω SPARGANOŌ*
Lk 2. 7 she .. wrapped him in swaddling cloths
2.12 "a babe wrapped in swaddling cloths

SWALLOW
SWALLOW UP
1. *swallow:* καταπίνω KATAPINŌ
Mt 23.24 "straining .. a gnat .. swallowing a camel!
1 Cor 15.54 "Death is swallowed up in victory
2 Cor 5. 4 mortal may be swallowed up by life
Rev 12.16 earth .. opened .. and swallowed the river

SWAMP
1. *cover, hide:* καλύπτω KALYPTŌ
Mt 8.24 boat was being swamped by the waves

SWAY
1. *lead, bring:* ἄγω AGŌ
2 Tim 3. 6 weak women, .. swayed by various impulses

SWEAR
1. *swear:* ὀμνύω OMNYŌ
Mt 5.34 "But I say to you, Do not swear at all
5.36 "And do not swear by your head
23.16 " 'If any one swears by the temple
23.16 " 'if any one swears by the gold of the temple
23.18 " 'If any one swears by the altar
23.18 " 'if .. one swears by .. gift .. on the altar
23.20 "So he who swears by the altar, swears by it and by everything on it
23.21 "he who swears by the temple, swears by it and by him who dwells in it
23.22 "he who swears by heaven, swears by the throne of God and by him .. upon it
26.74 he began to invoke a curse .. and to swear
Mk 14.71 he began to invoke a curse .. and to swear
Lk 1.73 "oath which he swore to our father Abraham
Acts 2.30 "God had sworn with an oath to him
Heb 3.11 "As I swore .. 'They shall never enter
3.18 to whom did he s. that they should never?
4. 3 "As I swore .., 'They shall never enter
6.13 since he had no one greater by whom to swear, he swore by himself
6.16 Men .. s. by a greater than themselves
7.21 "The Lord has sworn and will not change
Jas 5.12 above all, my brethren, do not swear
Rev 10. 6 swore by him who lives for ever

SWEAR FALSELY
1. *swear falsely:* ἐπιορκέω EPIORKEŌ*
Mt 5.33 " 'You shall not swear falsely

SWEAT
1. *sweat:* ἱδρώς HIDRŌS*
Lk [22.44 *his s. became like great drops of blood*‡

SWEEP
1. *sweep clean:* σαρόω SAROŌ*
Mt 12.44 "when he comes he finds it empty, swept
Lk 11.25 "when he comes he finds it swept
15. 8 "does not light a lamp and sweep the house?

2. *draw, sweep:* σύρω SYRŌ
Rev 12. 4 His tail swept down a third of the stars

SWEEP AWAY
1. *lift, carry away:* αἴρω AIRŌ
Mt 24.39 "the flood came and swept them all away

IDIOMATICALLY
a. Rev 12.15 to sweep her away with the flood ἵνα αὐτὴν ποταμοφόρητον ποιήσῃ [POIEŌ]

SWEET
1. *sweet, fresh:* γλυκύς GLYKYS
Rev 10. 9 "it will be .. s. as honey in your mouth
10.10 it was sweet as honey in my mouth

SWELL UP
1. *blow up, distend:* πίμπρημι PIMPRĒMI*
Acts 28. 6 They waited, expecting him to swell up

2. *become prostrate, become swollen:* πρηνὴς γίνεσθαι PRĒNĒS [A.6.a.3]
Acts [1.18 (*swelling up* he burst open in the middle†

SWERVE
1. *miss the mark:* ἀστοχέω ASTOCHEŌ
1 Tim 1. 6 Certain persons by swerving from these
2 Tim 2.18 who have swerved from the truth

SWIFT
1. *sharp, quick:* ὀξύς OXYS
Rom 3.15 "Their feet are swift to shed blood
2. *swift, sudden:* ταχινός TACHINOS
2 Pet 2. 1 bringing upon themselves s. destruction

SWIM
1. *swim, plunge headlong:* κολυμβάω KOLYMBAŌ*
Acts 27.43 He ordered those who could swim

SWIM AWAY
1. *plunge into the sea, swim away:* ἐκκολυμβάω EKKOLYMBAŌ*
Acts 27.42 lest any should swim away and escape

SWINE
1. *swine, young pig:* χοῖρος CHOIROS*
Mt 7. 6 "do not throw your pearls before swine
8.30 Now a herd of many swine was feeding
8.31 "send us away into the herd of swine
8.32 they came out and went into the swine
Mk 5.11 Now a great herd of swine was feeding
5.12 "Send us to the s., let us enter them
5.13 the unclean spirits .. entered the swine
5.16 told what had happened .. to the swine
Lk 8.32 a large herd of swine was feeding there
8.33 Then the demons .. entered the swine
15.15 "sent him into his fields to feed swine
15.16 "fed on[u] the pods that the swine ate

SWING
1. *throw, put:* βάλλω BALLŌ
Rev 14.16 So he .. swung his sickle on the earth
14.19 the angel swung his sickle on the earth

SWOLLEN WITH CONCEIT, BE
1. *be crazy, be conceited:* τυφόομαι TYPHOOMAI
2 Tim 3. 4 swollen with conceit, lovers of pleasure

SWORD
1. *dagger, saber:* μάχαιρα MACHAIRA*
Mt 10.34 "I have not come to bring peace, but a s.
26.47 a great crowd with swords and clubs
26.51 stretched out his hand and drew his s.
26.52 Then Jesus said to him, "Put your sword back into its place; for all who take the sword will perish by the sword
26.55 "as against a robber, with swords
Mk 14.43 a crowd with swords and clubs
14.47 one of those who stood by drew his s.
14.48 "as against a robber, with swords
Lk 21.24 "they will fall by the edge of the sword
22.36 "let him who has no sword .. buy one
22.38 "Look, Lord, here are two swords
22.49 "Lord, shall we strike with the sword?
22.52 "as against a robber, with swords
Jn 18.10 Simon Peter, having a sword, drew it
18.11 "Put your sword into its sheath
Acts 12. 2 He killed James .. with the sword
16.27 drew his s. and was about to kill himself
Rom 8.35 Shall .. nakedness, or peril, or sword?
13. 4 he does not bear the sword in vain
Eph 6.17 s. of the Spirit, which is the word of God
Heb 4.12 sharper than any two-edged sword
11.34 escaped the edge of the sword
11.37 they were killed with the sword
Rev 6. 4 and he was given a great sword
13.10 if any one slays with the sword, with the sword must he be slain
13.14 beast which was wounded by the sword
2. *large sword:* ῥομφαία RHOMPHAIA*
Lk 2.35 "(a sword will pierce .. your own soul also
Rev 1.16 from his mouth .. a sharp two-edged s.
2.12 " 'who has the sharp two-edged sword
2.16 " 'I will come .. with the s. of my mouth

Rev 6. 8 they were given power.. to kill with s.
19.15 From his mouth issues a sharp sword
19.21 the rest were slain by the sword

SWORN, WHAT ONE HAS
1. *oath:* ὅρκος (pl.) HORKOS
Mt 5.33 " 'perform.. what you have sworn

SYCAMINE TREE
1. *mulberry tree:* συκάμινος SYKAMINOS*
Lk 17. 6 "you could say to this sycamine tree

SYCAMORE TREE
1. *sycamore-fig tree:* συκομορέα SYKOMOREA*
Lk 19. 4 climbed up into a sycamore tree to see

SYCHAR: Συχάρ 'sīkär I,C-4
Jn 4. 5 a city of Samaria, called Sychar

SYMBOLIC
1. *comparison, parable:* παραβολή PARABOLĒ [A.1.b.4]
Heb 9. 9 (which is symbolic for the present age

SYMPATHIZE
1. *sympathize with:* συμπαθέω SYMPATHEŌ
Heb 4.15 we have not a high priest.. unable to s.

SYMPATHY
1. *compassion:* οἰκτιρμός OIKTIRMOS
Phil 2. 1 if there is.. any affection and sympathy

SYMPATHY, HAVE
1. *sympathetic:* συμπαθής SYMPATHĒS* [A.3.e.2]
1 Pet 3. 8 all of you, have unity of spirit, s.

SYNAGOGUE
1. *meeting, meeting place:* συναγωγή SYNAGŌGĒ
Mt 4.23 he went about.., teaching in.. synagogues
6. 2 "as the hypocrites do in the synagogues
6. 5 "stand and pray in the synagogues
9.35 teaching in.. synagogues and preaching
10.17 "they will.. flog you in their synagogues
12. 9 he.. entered their synagogue
13.54 "he taught them in their synagogue
23. 6 "love.. the best seats in the synagogues
23.34 "you will scourge in your synagogues
Mk 1.21 he entered the synagogue and taught
1.23 in their s. a man with an unclean spirit
1.29 immediately he[e] left the synagogue
1.39 he went.., preaching in their synagogues
3. 1 Again he entered the synagogue
6. 2 he began to teach in the synagogue
12.39 "⟨like⟩ the best seats in the synagogues
13. 9 "you will be beaten in synagogues
Lk 4.15 he taught in their synagogues
4.16 went to the s., as his custom was
4.20 eyes of all in the synagogue were fixed
4.28 all in the s. were filled with wrath
4.33 in the synagogue there was a man
4.38 he arose and left the synagogue
4.44 he was preaching in the synagogues
6. 6 he entered the synagogue and taught
7. 5 "loves our nation, and he built us our s.
8.41 Jairus, who was a ruler of the s.
11.43 "you love.. best seat in the synagogues
12.11 "they bring you before the synagogues
13.10 teaching in one of the synagogues
20.46 "love.. the best seats in the synagogues
21.12 "delivering you up to the synagogues
Jn 6.59 This he said in the synagogue
18.20 "I have always taught in synagogues
Acts 6. 9 some of those who belonged to the s.
9. 2 letters to the synagogues at Damascus
9.20 in the synagogues.. he proclaimed
13. 5 proclaimed the word.. in the synagogues
13.14 on the sabbath day they went into the s.
13.43 when the meeting of the s. broke up
14. 1 they entered together into the Jewish s.
15.21 "read every sabbath in the synagogues
17. 1 to Thessalonica, where there was a s.
17.10 they went into the Jewish synagogue
17.17 So he argued in the synagogue
18. 4 he argued in the s. every sabbath
Acts 18. 7 his house was next door to the s.
18.19 he himself went into the synagogue
18.26 He began to speak boldly in the s.
19. 8 he entered the s. and.. spoke boldly
22.19 in every s. I imprisoned and beat
24.12 either in.. temple or in the synagogues
26.11 I punished them.. in all the synagogues
Rev 2. 9 those who.. are a synagogue of Satan
3. 9 " 'I will make those of.. s. of Satan.. bow

SYNAGOGUE, PUT OUT OF THE
1. *expelled from the synagogue:* ἀποσυνάγωγος APOSYNAGŌGOS*
Jn 9.22 he was to be put out of the synagogue
12.42 lest they should be put out of the s.
16. 2 will put you out of the synagogues

SYNAGOGUE, RULER OF THE
1. *ruler of the synagogue:* ἀρχισυνάγωγος ARCHISYNAGŌGOS
Mk 5.22 one of the rulers of the synagogue
5.36 Jesus said to the ruler of the synagogue
5.38 to the house of the ruler of the s.
Lk 13.14 the ruler of the synagogue, indignant
Acts 13.15 rulers of the synagogue sent to them
18. 8 Crispus, the ruler of the synagogue
18.17 seized Sosthenes, the ruler of the s.

SYNTYCHE: Συντύχη 'sintikē
Phil 4. 2 I entreat Euodia and.. S. to agree

SYRACUSE: Συράκουσαι 'sirə,kyüs II,C-3
Acts 28.12 Putting in at S., we stayed.. three days

SYRIA: Συρία 'sirēə II,G-3
Mt 4.24 his fame spread throughout all Syria
Lk 2. 2 when Quirinius was governor of Syria
Acts 15:23 "to the brethren.. of the Gentiles in.. S.
15.41 he went through Syria and Cilicia
18.18 then took leave.. and sailed for Syria
20. 3 as he was about to set sail for Syria
21. 3 leaving it on the left we sailed to Syria
Gal 1.21 Then I went into the regions of Syria

SYRIAN: Σύρος
Lk 4.27 "none.., but only Naaman the Syrian

SYROPHOENICIAN: Συροφοινίκισσα
Mk 7.26 the woman was a Greek, a S. by birth

SYRTIS: Σύρτις 'sərtəs II,B-4, C-5
Acts 27.17 fearing that they should run on the S.

T

TABERNACLE
1. *tent, booth:* σκηνή SKĒNĒ
Heb [8. 2 a minister in.. the true *tabernacle*†
[8. 5 Moses was about to erect the *tabernacle*†
[9. 2 For a *tabernacle* was prepared†
[9. 3 Behind.. second curtain stood a *tabernacle*†
[9. 6 priests go.. into the outer *tabernacle*†
[9. 8 as long as.. outer *tabernacle* is.. standing†
[9.11 through the.. more perfect *tabernacle*†
[9.21 in.. same way he sprinkled.. the *tabernacle*†
[13.10 those who serve the *tabernacle*†

TABERNACLES, FEAST OF
1. *setting up of tents:* σκηνοπηγία SKĒNOPĒGIA*
Jn 7. 2 Jews' feast of Tabernacles was at hand

TABITHA: Ταβιθά 'tabəthə
Acts 9.36 there was at Joppa a disciple named T.
9.40 turning to the body he said, "T., rise

TABLE
1. *tablet, table:* πλάξ PLAX
Heb 9. 4 contained.. the tables of the covenant
2. *table:* τράπεζα TRAPEZA
Mt 15.27 "eat.. crumbs.. from their masters' table
21.12 the tables of the money-changers
Mk 7.28 "dogs under the table eat the.. crumbs
11.15 the tables of the money-changers
Lk 16.21 "what fell from the rich man's table

Lk 22.21 "the hand of him . . is with me on the table
22.30 "you may eat and drink at my table
Jn 2.15 drove them . . and overturned their tables
Acts 6. 2 "not . . give up preaching . . to serve tables
Rom 11. 9 "Let their table become a snare[0]
1 Cor 10.21 You cannot partake of the table of the Lord and the table of demons
Heb 9. 2 the table and the bread of the Presence[q]

TABLE, AT
1. *recline* (at table): ἀνάκειμαι (part.) ANAKEIMAI
Jn 12. 2 Lazarus was one of those at table
13.28 no one at the table knew why
2. *lie down:* κατάκειμαι (pass. part.) KATAKEIMAI
1 Cor 8.10 sees you . . at table in an idol's temple

TABLE, BE AT
TABLE, SIT AT
TABLE, SIT DOWN AT
TABLE, TAKE ONE'S PLACE AT
1. *recline* (at table): ἀνάκειμαι ANAKEIMAI
Mt 9.10 as he sat at table[v] in the house†
26. 7 poured it on his head, as he sat at table
26.20 he sat at table with the twelve disciples[e]
Mk 14.18 as they were at table eating
16.14 he appeared . . as they sat at table[k]‡
Lk 22.27 "which is the greater, one who sits at t. . . ? Is it not the one who sits at table?
2. *cause to recline:* ἀνακλίνω (pass.) ANAKLINŌ
Mt 8.11 "many will . . sit at table with Abraham
Lk 13.29 "will . . sit at table in the kingdom
3. *recline* (at meals): ἀναπίπτω ANAPIPTŌ
Lk 11.37 so he went in and sat at table
17. 7 "'Come at once and sit down at table
22.14 when the hour came, he sat at table
4. *lie down:* κατάκειμαι KATAKEIMAI
Mk 2.15 as he sat at table in his house
14. 3 as he sat at table, a woman came
Lk 5.29 tax collectors and others sitting at table[r]†
7.37 when she learned that he was at table
5. *cause to lie down:* κατακλίνω (pass.) KATAKLINŌ
Lk 7.36 he went . . and took his place at table
24.30 When he was at t. . . , he took the bread

TABLE, HAVE S. SIT AT
1. *cause to recline:* ἀνακλίνω ANAKLINŌ
Lk 12.37 "he will . . have them sit at table

TABLE WITH, BE AT
TABLE WITH, SIT AT
1. *recline with* (at table): συνανάκειμαι SYNANAKEIMAI
Lk 7.49 who were at table with him began to say
14.10 "presence of all who sit at table with you
14.15 one . . who sat at table with him heard

TABLET
1. *tablet, table:* πλάξ PLAX
2 Cor 3. 3 you are a letter . . , not on tablets of stone but on tablets of human hearts

TABLET, WRITING
1. *writing tablet:* πινακίδιον PINAKIDION*
Lk 1.63 he asked for a writing tablet, and wrote

TACKLE
1. *equipment, tackle:* σκευή SKEUĒ*
Acts 27.19 they cast out . . the tackle of the ship

TAIL
1. *tail:* οὐρά OURA*
Rev 9.10 They have tails like scorpions, and stings, and their power . . lies in their tails
9.19 power of the horses is . . in their tails; their tails are like serpents
12. 4 His tail swept down a third of the stars

TAKE (*See also, e.g.,* CAPTIVE, TAKE; HEED, TAKE; PLEASURE IN, TAKE)
1. *lead, bring:* ἄγω AGŌ
Lk 4. 9 he took him to Jerusalem, and set him
2. *lift, carry away:* αἴρω AIRŌ
Mt 11.29 "Take my yoke upon you, and learn
14.12 his disciples came and took the body
17.27 "take the first fish that comes up
20.14 "'Take what belongs to you, and go
24.17 "not go down to t. what is in his house
24.18 "not turn back to take his mantle
25.28 "'take the talent from him, and give it
Mk 6. 8 He charged them to take nothing . . except
6.29 they came and took his body
13.16 "not turn back to take his mantle
15.24 casting lots . . to decide what each should t.
Lk 9. 3 "Take nothing for your journey
19.24 "'Take the pound from him, and give it
22.36 "now, let him who has a purse take it
Jn 2.16 "Take these things away
10.18 "No one takes it from me
16.22 "no one will take your joy from you
17.15 "thou shouldst t. them out of the world
20. 2 "have taken the Lord out of the tomb
Acts 21.11 coming to us he took Paul's girdle
1 Cor 6.15 Shall I . . take the members of Christ?
3. *lead up, bring back:* ἀνάγω ANAGŌ
Acts 9.39 they took him to the upper room
4. *take up:* ἀναλαμβάνω ANALAMBANŌ
Acts 23.31 soldiers . . took Paul and brought him
Eph 6.13 Therefore take the whole armor of God
6.16 besides all these, taking . . shield of faith
5. *lead away:* ἀπάγω APAGŌ
Acts 23.17 "Take this young man to the tribune[0]
[24. 7 "*with . . violence took him out of our hands*‡
6. *lift up, carry:* βαστάζω BASTAZŌ
Jn 12. 6 he used to take what was put into it
7. *receive, accept:* δέχομαι DECHOMAI
Lk 16. 6 "'Take your bill, and . . write fifty
16. 7 "'Take your bill, and write eighty
22.17 he took a cup, and when he had given
Eph 6.17 take the helmet of salvation
8. *have, hold:* ἔχω (imper.) ECHŌ
Mt [27.65 "*Take a guard* of soldiers; go†
9. *take, seize:* ἐπιλαμβάνομαι EPILAMBANOMAI
Mk 8.23 he took the blind man by the hand
Lk 9.47 took a child and put him by his side
14. 4 Then he took him and healed him
Acts 9.27 Barnabas took him, and brought him
23.19 The tribune took him by the hand
Heb 8. 9 "the day when I took them by the hand
10. *take up, assume:* ὑπολαμβάνω HYPOLAMBANŌ
Acts 1. 9 a cloud took him out of their sight
11. *hold fast, restrain:* κατέχω KATECHŌ
Lk 14. 9 "you will begin . . to take the lowest place
12. *seize, hold fast:* κρατέω KRATEŌ
Mt 9.25 he went in and took her by the hand
Mk 1.31 he came and took her by the hand
5.41 Taking her by the hand he said
9.27 But Jesus took him by the hand
Lk 8.54 taking her by the hand he called
13. *acquire, get:* κτάομαι KTAOMAI
Mt 10. 9 "Take no gold, nor silver, nor copper
1 Th 4. 4 know how to take a wife for himself[x]†
14. *receive, take:* λαμβάνω LAMBANŌ
Mt 5.40 "if any one would . . take your coat
8.17 "took our infirmities and bore our diseases
10.38 "he who does not take his cross
12.14 the Pharisees . . took counsel against him
13.31 "grain of mustard seed which a man took
13.33 "like leaven which a woman took
14.19 taking the five loaves and the two fish
15.26 "not fair to take the children's bread
15.36 he took the seven loaves and the fish
17.25 "From whom do kings of . . earth take toll?
17.27 "take that and give it to them for me
21.35 "tenants took his servants and beat one
21.39 "'they took him and cast him out
22.15 the Pharisees went and took counsel
25. 1 "ten maidens who took their lamps
25. 3 "For when the foolish took their lamps, they took no oil with them
25. 4 "but the wise took flasks of oil

Mt 26.26 as they were eating, Jesus took bread . . and said, "Take, eat; this is my body
26.27 took a cup, and when he had given thanks
26.52 "for all who take the sword will perish
27. 1 the elders of the people took counsel
27. 6 "chief priests, taking the pieces of silver
27. 7 So they took counsel, and bought
27. 9 "they took the thirty pieces of silver
27.24 he took water and washed his hands
27.30 they . . took the reed and struck him
27.48 one of them . . ran and took a sponge
[27.49 *another took a spear and pierced his side*‡
27.59 Joseph took the body, and wrapped it
28.12 when they had . . taken counsel, they gave
28.15 they took the money and did as . . directed
Mk 6.41 taking the five loaves and the two fish
7.27 "it is not right to take the children's bread
8. 6 he took the seven loaves, . . broke them
9.36 he took a child, . . put him in the midst
12. 3 "they took him and beat him, . . sent him
12. 8 "they took him and killed him
12.19 "the man[y] must take the wife
12.20 "the first took a wife, and when he died
12.21 "the second took her, and died
14.22 as they were eating, he took bread . . and said, "Take; this is my body
14.23 he took a cup, and when he had given
15.23 offered him wine . . ; but he did not take it
Lk 5. 5 "we toiled all night and took nothing!
6. 4 "took and ate the bread of the Presence
9.16 taking the five loaves and the two fish
13.19 "grain of mustard seed which a man took
13.21 "It is like leaven which a woman took
20.28 "the man[g] must take the wife
20.29 "the first took a wife, and died
20.31 "the third took her, and likewise all seven
22.17 "T. this, and divide it among yourselves
22.19 he took bread, and . . broke it and gave it
24.30 he took . . bread and blessed, and broke it
24.43 he took it and ate before them
Jn 6.11 Jesus then took the loaves
6.21 they were glad to t. him into the boat
10.17 "I lay down my life, that I may take it
10.18 "I have power to take it again
12. 3 Mary took a pound of costly ointment
12.13 they took branches of palm trees
13.12 When he had . . taken his garments
16.14 "he will take what is mine and declare it
16.15 "I said that he will take what is mine
18.31 "Take him yourselves and judge him
19. 1 Pilate took Jesus and scourged him
19. 6 "Take him yourselves and crucify him
19.23 the soldiers . . took his garments
19.27 the disciple took her to his own home
19.40 They took the body of Jesus
21.13 Jesus came and took the bread
Acts 1.20 "'His office let another take
1.25 "to take the place in this ministry
9.19 took food and was strengthened
9.25 his disciples took him by night
15.14 "to take out of them a people for his name
16. 3 he took him and circumcised him
17. 9 when they had taken security from Jason
27.35 he took bread, and giving thanks to God
28.15 Paul thanked God and took courage
1 Cor 11.23 when he was betrayed took bread
Phil 2. 7 taking . . form of a servant,[d] being born
Heb 5. 4 one does not t. the honor upon himself
9.19 he took the blood of calves and goats
Jas 5.10 As . . example . . , brethren, take the prophets
Rev 5. 7 he went and took the scroll
5. 8 when he had taken the scroll
5. 9 "Worthy art thou to take the scroll
6. 4 its rider was permitted to take peace
8. 5 angel took the censer and filled it
10. 8 "Go, take the scroll which is open
10. 9 "Take it and eat; it will be bitter
Rev 10.10 I took the little scroll from the hand
11.17 "thou hast taken thy great power
22.17 let him who desires t. the water of life

15. *partake, share:* μεταλαμβάνω METALAMBANŌ
Acts 27.33 "without food, having taken nothing
27.34 "I urge you to take some food

16. *transpose, change:* μετατιθημι METATITHĒMI
Heb 11. 5 not found, because God had taken him

17. *take, receive:* παραλαμβάνω PARALAMBANŌ
Mt 1.20 "do not fear to take Mary your wife
1.24 he did as . . commanded . . ; he took his wife
2.13 "Rise, take the child and his mother
2.14 he rose and took . . child and his mother
2.20 "Rise, take the child and his mother
2.21 he rose and took . . child and his mother
4. 5 the devil took him to the holy city
4. 8 devil took him to a . . high mountain
18.16 "if he does not listen, take . . others along
20.17 he took the twelve disciples aside
24.40 "two men will be in the field; one is taken
24.41 "Two . . will be grinding . . ; one is taken
27.27 soldiers . . took Jesus into . . praetorium
Mk 5.40 took the child's father and mother
10.32 taking the twelve again, he began to tell
Lk 9.10 he took them and withdrew apart
17.34 "one will be taken and the other left
17.35 "one will be taken and the other left[b]
[17.36 "*one will be taken and the other left*‡
18.31 taking the twelve, he said to them
Jn 14. 3 "I will come again and will take you
19.17(16) they took Jesus, and he went out
Acts 16.33 he took them the same hour
21.24 "take these men and purify yourself
21.26 Paul took the men, . . purified himself
21.32 He at once took soldiers and centurions
23.18 So he took him and brought him

18. *bring, bear:* φέρω PHERŌ
Lk 24. 1 went to the tomb, taking the spices
Jn 2. 8 "Now draw some out, and take it to the steward of the feast." So they took it

19. *take hold of:* πιάζω PIAZŌ
Acts 3. 7 he took him by the right hand

20. *receive in addition:* προσλαμβάνω (mid.) PROSLAMBANŌ
Mt 16.22 Peter took him and began to rebuke
Mk 8.32 Peter took him, and began to rebuke
Acts 17. 5 taking some wicked fellows of . . rabble
18.26 they took him and expounded to him
27.33 "without food, having taken nothing

21. *gather, seize, conceive:* συλλαμβάνω SYLLAMBANŌ
Lk 5. 9 the catch of fish which they had taken

IDIOMATICALLY
a. Heb 11.5 before he was taken πρὸ . . τῆς μεταθέσεως [METATHESIS]

CONTEXTUALLY
Jn 2.20 "It has taken forty-six years to build
Acts 22. 5 "to take those also who were there
Col 4. 9 tell . . of everything that has taken place
Heb 7.21 priests took their office without . . oath
9. 7 taking blood which he offers for himself

TAKE ABOARD
TAKE ON BOARD

1. *take up:* ἀναλαμβάνω ANALAMBANŌ
Acts 20.13 intending to take Paul aboard there
20.14 at Assos, we took him on board

TAKE ALONG WITH ONE

1. *take along with one:* συμπαραλαμβάνω SYMPARALAMBANŌ
Gal 2. 1 I went . . , taking Titus along with me

TAKE ASIDE

1. *take from, get back:* ἀπολαμβάνω (mid.) APOLAMBANŌ
Mk 7.33 taking him aside from the multitude

TAKE AWAY

1. *lead, bring:* ἄγω AGŌ
Acts 20.12 And they took the lad away alive

2. *lift, carry away:* αἴρω AIRŌ
Mt 13.12 "even what he has will be taken away
21.43 "the kingdom of God will be taken away

Mt 25.29 "'even what he has will be taken away
Mk 4.15 "Satan .. comes and takes away the word
4.25 "even what he has will be taken away
13.15 "not go down .. to take anything away
Lk 6.29 "from him who takes away your coat
6.30 "of him who takes away your goods
8.12 "devil comes and takes away the word
8.18 "what he thinks .. he has will be taken away
11.22 "one stronger .. takes away his armor
11.52 "you have taken away .. key of knowledge
17.31 "let him .. not come .. to t. them away
19.26 "'even what he has will be taken away
Jn 1.29 "who takes away the sin of the world!
11.39 Jesus said, "Take away the stone
11.41 So they took away the stone
15. 2 "that bears no fruit, he takes away
19.31 Jews asked .. that they .. be taken away
19.38 that he might t. away the body of Jesus
19.38 So he came and took away his body
20. 1 stone had been taken away from .. tomb
20.13 "they have taken away my Lord
20.15 "tell me .. and I will take him away
1 Jn 3. 5 he appeared to take away sins

3. *carry off:* ἀπαίρω APAIRŌ*
Mt 9.15 "when the bridegroom is taken away
Mk 2.20 "when the bridegroom is taken away
Lk 5.35 "when the bridegroom is taken away

4. *take away:* ἀφαιρέω APHAIREŌ
Lk 1.25 "to take away my reproach among men
10.42 "which shall not be taken away from her
16. 3 "'master is taking the stewardship away
Rom 11.27 "my covenant .. when I t. away their sins
Heb 10. 4 that .. blood of .. goats should t. away sins
Rev 22.19 if any one takes away from the words .., God will take away his share in the tree

5. *make ineffective, hinder:* καταργέω KATARGEŌ
2 Cor 3.14 only through Christ is it taken away

6. *take away, strip off:* περιαιρέω PERIAIREŌ
Heb 10.11 sacrifices, which can never t. away sins

TAKE BY FORCE

1. *seize, snatch up:* ἁρπάζω HARPAZŌ
Mt 11.12 "men of violence take it by force
Jn 6.15 take him by force to make him king
Acts 23.10 take him by force from among them

TAKE DOWN

1. *take down, destroy:* καθαιρέω KATHAIREŌ
Mk 15.36 "Elijah will come to take him down
15.46 taking him down, wrapped him in .. linen
Lk 23.53 took it down .. wrapped it in a .. shroud
Acts 13.29 "they took him down from the tree

TAKE HOLD OF

1. *take, lay hold of:* ἐπιλαμβάνομαι EPILAMBANOMAI
Lk 20.20 that they might t. hold of what he said
Acts 17.19 they took hold of him and brought him
1 Tim 6.12 take hold of the eternal life
6.19 so that they may take hold of the life

TAKE IN ONE'S ARMS

1. *take in one's arms:* ἐναγκαλίζομαι ENAGKALIZOMAI*
Mk 9.36 he took a child .. in his arms
10.16 he took them in his arms and blessed them

TAKE MEASURES

IDIOMATICALLY

a. Acts 27.17 they took measures[c] to undergird the ship†
βοηθείαις ἐχρῶντο, ὑποζωννύντες τὸ πλοῖον
[BOĒTHEIA; CHRAOMAI]

TAKE OFF

1. *break up, unbind:* λύω LYŌ
Acts 7.33 "'Take off the shoes from your feet

TAKE ONE'S PLACE AT TABLE

1. *cause to lie down:* κατακλίνω (pass.) KATAKLINŌ
Lk 7.36 he went .. and took his place at table

TAKE OUT

1. *throw out:* ἐκβάλλω EKBALLŌ
Mt 7. 4 "'Let me take the speck out of your eye
7. 5 "take the log out of your own eye, .. then .. take .. speck out of your brother's eye
Lk 6.42 "'Brother, let me take out the speck
6.42 "take the log out of your own eye, .. then .. take out .. speck .. in your brother's
10.35 "the next day he took out two denarii[i]

2. *carry out:* ἐκφέρω EKPHERŌ
1 Tim 6. 7 cannot take anything out of the world

3. *lead out:* ἐξάγω EXAGŌ
Acts 16.37 "No! let them come .. and take us out
16.39 they took them out and asked them

TAKE PART

1. *companion, partner:* κοινωνός KOINŌNOS [A.6.a.3]
Mt 23.30 "'we would not have taken part with them

2. *take part in, share:* συγκοινωνέω SYGKOINŌNEŌ
Eph 5.11 Take no part in the unfruitful works
Rev 18. 4 "Come out .., lest you take part in her sins

TAKE S.'S PART

1. *arrive, stand by:* παραγίνομαι (+dat.) PARAGINOMAI
2 Tim 4.16 no one took my part; all deserted me

TAKE PLACE

1. *be:* εἰμί EIMI
Mt 1.18 the birth .. took place in this way

2. *come to be, happen, be:* γίνομαι GINOMAI
Mt 1.22 All this took place to fulfil .. the prophet
18.31 "servants saw what had taken place .. and .. reported .. all that had taken place
21. 4 This took place to fulfil .. the prophet
24. 6 "for this must take place
24.34 "not .. till all these things take place
26.56 "But all this has taken place
27.54 the centurion .. saw .. what took place
28.11 the guard .. told .. all that had taken place
Mk 13. 7 "this must take place, but .. not yet
13.29 "when you see these things taking place
13.30 "not .. before all these things take place
Lk 21. 7 "the sign when this is about to take place
21. 9 "for this must first take place
21.28 "when these things begin to take place
21.31 "when you see these things taking place
21.32 "not .. till all has taken place
21.36 "strength to escape all .. that will take p.
23.47 the centurion saw what had taken place
23.48 when they saw what had taken place
Jn 1.28 This took place in Bethany
13.19 "I tell you this now, before it takes place, that when it does take place
14.29 "I have told you before it takes place, so that when it does take place
19.36 took p. that .. scripture might be fulfilled
Acts 4.28 "thy plan had predestined to take place
11.28 this took place in the days of Claudius
28. 9 And when this had taken place
Rev 1. 1 to show .. what must soon take place
1.19 "write .. what is to take place hereafter
4. 1 "I will show you what must take place
22. 6 "to show .. what must soon take place

TAKE UP

1. *lift, carry away:* αἴρω AIRŌ
Mt 9. 6 "Rise, take up your bed and go home
14.20 they took up twelve baskets full
15.37 took up seven baskets full of the pieces
16.24 "let him .. take up his cross and follow
21.21 "'Be taken up and cast into the sea
Mk 2. 9 "'Rise, take up your pallet and walk
2.11 "I say to you, rise, take up your pallet
2.12 he rose, .. took up the pallet and went
6.43 they took up twelve baskets full
8. 8 they took up the broken pieces left over
8.19 "how many baskets full .. did you take up?
8.20 "how many baskets full .. did you take up?
8.34 "let him deny himself and t. up his cross
11.23 "'Be taken up and cast into the sea
Lk 5.24 "rise, take up your bed and go home
5.25 he .. took up that on which he lay
9.17 they took up what was left over
9.23 "let him deny himself and t. up his cross

Lk 19.21 "'you t. up what you did not lay down
19.22 " 'taking up what I did not lay down
Jn 5. 8 "Rise, take up your pallet, and walk
5. 9 and he took up his pallet and walked
5.11 " 'Take up your pallet, and walk
5.12 " 'Take up your pallet, and walk
8.59 they took up stones to throw at him
Acts 8.33 "For his life is taken up from the earth
20. 9 he fell down.. and was taken up dead
Rev 18.21 Then a mighty angel took up a stone
2. *lead up, bring back:* ἀνάγω ANAGŌ
Lk 4. 5 the devil took him up, and showed him
3. *take up:* ἀναλαμβάνω ANALAMBANŌ
Mk 16.19 the Lord Jesus.. was taken up into heaven[k]‡
Acts 1. 2 until the day when he was taken up
1.11 "Jesus, who was taken up from you
1.22 "until the day when he was taken up
7.43 "'you took up the tent of Moloch
10.16 thing was taken up at once to heaven
1 Tim 3.16 believed on in.. world, taken up in glory
4. *lift up, carry:* βαστάζω BASTAZŌ
Jn 10.31 Jews took up stones again to stone him
5. *receive, accept:* δέχομαι DECHOMAI
Lk 2.28 took him up in his arms and blessed God
6. *transpose, change:* μετατίθημι METATITHĒMI
Heb 11. 5 By faith Enoch was taken up

TAKE WITH ONE
1. *separate, appoint:* ἀφορίζω APHORIZŌ
Acts 19. 9 taking the disciples with him
2. *take, receive:* παραλαμβάνω PARALAMBANŌ
Mt 17. 1 Jesus took with him Peter and James
26.37 taking with him Peter and the two sons
Mk 4.36 they took him with them in the boat
9. 2 Jesus took with him Peter and James
14.33 he took with him Peter and James
Lk 9.28 he took with him Peter and John
Acts 15.39 Barnabas took Mark with him and sailed
3. *take along with one:* συμπαραλαμβάνω SYMPARALAMBANŌ
Acts 15.37 Barnabas wanted to take with them.. Mark
15.38 Paul thought best not to take with them

TAKING
1. *through:* διά (+gen.) DIA [B.1.a.2]
Heb 9.12 taking[s] not the blood of goats and calves†

TAKING PART
1. *fellowship, sharing:* κοινωνία KOINŌNIA
2 Cor 8. 4 begging us.. for the favor of taking part

TALE, IDLE
1. *trash, nonsense:* λῆρος LĒROS*
Lk 24.11 these words seemed to them an idle tale

TALENT
1. *talent* (a weight, a sum of money): τάλαντον TALANTON*
Mt 18.24 "who owed him ten thousand talents[f]
25.15 "to one he gave five talents[d]
25.16 "He who had received the five talents went.. and he made five talents more
25.20 "he who had received the five talents came forward, bringing five talents more, saying.. 'you delivered to me five talents; here I have made five talents more
25.22 "he.. who had the two talents came forward, saying.. you delivered to me two talents; here I have made two talents more
25.24 "He also who had received the one talent
25.25 "'I.. hid your talent in the ground
25.28 " 'take the talent from him, and give it to him who has the ten talents
CONTEXTUALLY
Mt 25.17 "So also, he who had the two talents made two talents more
25.18 "But he who had received the one talent

TALITHA: 'taləthə
1. *little girl* (Aram.): ταλιθά TALITHA*
Mk 5.41 he said to her, "Talitha, cumi

TALK
1. *discuss:* διαλέγομαι DIALEGOMAI
Acts 20. 7 Paul talked with them,.. and he prolonged
20. 9 He sank into a deep sleep as Paul talked
2. *speak to:* ὁμιλέω HOMILEŌ
Lk 24.14 talking with each other about all.. things
24.15 While they were talking and discussing
3. *proclaim:* κηρύσσω KĒRYSSŌ
Mk 1.45 he went out and began to talk freely
4. *speak, talk:* λαλέω LALEŌ
Lk 24.32 "while he talked to us on the road
Jn 4.27 marveled.. he was talking with a woman
4.27 "Why are you talking with her?
[8.25 Jesus said.. "*Why do I talk to you at all?*†
14.30 "I will no longer talk much with you
2 Cor 11.23 I am talking like a madman
2 Jn .12 I hope to.. talk with you face to face
3 Jn .14 we will talk together face to face
Rev 21.15 he who talked to me had a measuring rod
5. *word, reckoning:* λόγος LOGOS
Mt 22.15 counsel how to entangle him in his talk
Mk 12.13 they sent.. to entrap him in his talk
1 Cor 4.19 not the talk of these arrogant people
4.20 kingdom of God does not consist in talk
Eph 4.29 Let no evil t. come out of your mouths
2 Tim 2.17 their talk will eat its way like gangrene
6. *talk with:* συλλαλέω SYLLALEŌ
Mt 17. 3 Moses and Elijah, talking with him
Mk 9. 4 Elijah with Moses;.. they were talking
Lk 9.30 two.. talked with him, Moses and Elijah

TALK ABOUT
1. *talk with:* διαλαλέω DIALALEŌ
Lk 1.65 all these things were talked about

TALK, FOUL
1. *obscenity:* αἰσχρολογία AISCHROLOGIA*
Col 3. 8 malice, slander, and foul talk

TALK, SILLY
1. *silly talk:* μωρολογία MŌROLOGIA*
Eph 5. 4 Let there be no filthiness, nor silly talk

TALK WITH
1. *converse with:* συνομιλέω SYNOMILEŌ*
Acts 10.27 as he talked with him, he went in

TALKER (*See* EMPTY TALKER)

TAMAR: Θαμάρ 'tāmər
Mt 1. 3 Judah the father of Perez.. by T.

TAME
1. *tame, subdue:* δαμάζω DAMAZŌ
Jas 3. 7 every kind of beast.. can be tamed and has been tamed by humankind
3. 8 no human being can tame the tongue

TAMPER WITH
1. *disguise, ensnare:* δολόω DOLOŌ*
2 Cor 4. 2 we refuse to.. tamper with God's word

TANNER
1. *tanner:* βυρσεύς BYRSEUS*
Acts 9.43 stayed in Joppa.. with one Simon, a t.
10. 6 "he is lodging with Simon, a tanner
10.32 "'lodging in the house of Simon, a tanner

TARRY
1. *spend time, linger:* χρονίζω CHRONIZŌ
Heb 10.37 "coming one shall come and shall not t.

TARSUS: Ταρσός 'tärsəs II,F-3
Acts 9.30 brethren knew it,.. sent him off to T.
11.25 Barnabas went to T. to look for Saul
22. 3 "I am a Jew, born at Tarsus in Cilicia

TARSUS, A MAN OF
TARSUS, FROM
1. *of Tarsus:* Ταρσεύς
Acts 9.11 "inquire.. for a man of Tarsus named Saul
21.39 "I am a Jew, from Tarsus in Cilicia

TASK (*See also* HUMBLE TASKS)
1. *work, deed:* ἔργον ERGON
1 Tim 3. 1 aspires to.. bishop, he desires a noble t.

2. *do, make:* ποιέω POIEŌ [A.6.d]
Col 3.23 Whatever your task, work heartily

TASTE
1. *taste:* γεύομαι GEUOMAI
Mt 16.28 "some . . here who will not taste death
27.34 when he tasted it, he would not drink it
Mk 9. 1 "some . . here who will not taste death
Lk 9.27 "some . . here who will not taste death
14.24 "'none of those . . shall taste my banquet
Jn 2. 9 tasted the water now become wine
8.52 "'he will never taste death
Acts 23.14 "to taste no food till we have killed Paul
Col 2.21 "Do not handle, Do not t., Do not touch
Heb 2. 9 that . . he might t. death for every one
6. 4 who have tasted the heavenly gift
6. 5 have tasted the goodness of the word
1 Pet 2. 3 you have tasted the kindness of the Lord

TASTE, S. LOSES ITS
1. *make foolish:* μωραίνω (pass.) MŌRAINŌ
Mt 5.13 "but if salt has lost its taste
Lk 14.34 "but if salt has lost its taste

TAUGHT
1. *teaching:* διδαχή DIDACHĒ [B.1.a.2]
Tit 1. 9 hold firm to the sure word as taught
2. *taught:* διδακτός DIDAKTOS*
Jn 6.45 "'they shall all be taught by God
1 Cor 2.13 words not taught by human wisdom but taught by the Spirit

TAUGHT, BE
1. *learn, understand:* μανθάνω MANTHANŌ
Rom 16.17 doctrine which you have been taught

TAUGHT BY GOD
1. *taught by God:* θεοδίδακτος THEODIDAKTOS*
1 Th 4. 9 taught by God to love one another

TAVERNS, THREE: II,B-2
1. *three taverns:* Τρεῖς ταβέρναι TREIS; TABERNĒ*
Acts 28.15 came as far as . . Three Taverns to meet us

TAX
TAXES
1. *double drachma:* δίδραχμον DIDRACHMON
Mt 17.24 "Does not your teacher pay the tax?
2. *poll tax, census* (Lat.): κῆνσος KĒNSOS
Mt 22.17 "Is it lawful to pay taxes to Caesar?
22.19 "Show me the money for the tax
Mk 12.14 "Is it lawful to pay taxes to Caesar?
3. *tribute, tax:* φόρος (sg. or pl.) PHOROS
Rom 13. 6 For the same reason you also pay taxes
13. 7 Pay all of them their dues, taxes to whom taxes are due

TAX COLLECTOR
1. *farmer or collector of taxes:* τελώνης TELŌNĒS*
Mt 5.46 "Do not even . . tax collectors do the same?
9.10 many tax collectors and sinners came
9.11 "Why . . eat with tax collectors?
10. 3 Matthew the tax collector
11.19 "'a friend of tax collectors and sinners!
18.17 "let him be to you as . . a tax collector
21.31 "tax collectors . . go into the kingdom
21.32 "tax collectors and . . harlots believed him
Mk 2.15 many tax collectors . . sitting with Jesus
2.16 he was eating with . . tax collectors
2.16 "Why does he eat[i] with tax collectors?
Lk 3.12 Tax collectors also came to be baptized
5.27 saw a tax collector, named Levi
5.29 tax collectors and others sitting at table[r]
5.30 "Why do you eat . . with tax collectors?
7.29 (the tax collectors justified God
7.34 "'a friend of tax collectors and sinners!
15. 1 tax collectors . . were all drawing near
18.10 "one a Pharisee . . the other a tax collector
18.11 "'that I am not like . . this tax collector
18.13 "the tax collector, standing far off

TAX COLLECTOR, CHIEF
1. *chief tax collector:* ἀρχιτελώνης ARCHITELŌNĒS*
Lk 19. 2 Zacchaeus . . a chief tax collector, and rich

TAX, HALF-SHEKEL
1. *double drachma:* δίδραχμον DIDRACHMON
Mt 17.24 the collectors of the half-shekel tax

TAX OFFICE
1. *customhouse:* τελώνιον TELŌNION*
Mt 9. 9 he saw . . Matthew sitting at the tax office
Mk 2.14 he saw Levi . . sitting at the tax office
Lk 5.27 he . . saw . . Levi, sitting at the tax office

TEACH
1. *teach:* διδάσκω DIDASKŌ
Mt 4.23 he went about all Galilee, teaching
5. 2 he opened his mouth and taught them
5.19 "Whoever . . teaches men so, shall be . . least . . ; but he who does them and teaches
7.29 he taught them as one who had authority
9.35 Jesus went . . , teaching in their synagogues
11. 1 he went on from there to teach
13.54 he taught them in their synagogue
15. 9 "'teaching as doctrines . . precepts of men
21.23 came up to him as he was teaching
22.16 "you . . teach the way of God truthfully
26.55 "I sat in the temple teaching
28.20 "teaching them . . all . . I have commanded
Mk 1.21 he entered the synagogue and taught
1.22 he taught them as one who had authority
2.13 crowd gathered . . , and he taught them
4. 1 he began to teach beside the sea
4. 2 he taught them many things in parables
6. 2 he began to teach in the synagogue
6. 6 he went about . . the villages teaching
6.30 told him all that they had . . taught
6.34 he began to teach them many things
7. 7 "'teaching as doctrines . . precepts of men
8.31 to teach . . that . . Son of man must suffer
9.31 for he was teaching his disciples
10. 1 as his custom was, he taught them
11.17 he taught, and said to them
12.14 "you . . truly teach the way of God
12.35 as Jesus taught in the temple
14.49 "I was with you in the temple teaching
Lk 4.15 And he taught in their synagogues
4.31 he was teaching them on the sabbath
5. 3 he sat down and taught the people
5.17 one of those days, as he was teaching
6. 6 he entered the synagogue and taught
11. 1 disciples said to him, "Lord, teach us to pray, as John taught his disciples
12.12 "for the Holy Spirit will teach you
13.10 he was teaching in one of the synagogues
13.22 He went on his way . . , teaching
13.26 "'you taught in our streets
19.47 he was teaching daily in the temple
20. 1 as he was teaching . . people in the temple
20.21 "we know that you speak and teach rightly, and . . truly teach the way of God
21.37 every day he was teaching in the temple
23. 5 "He stirs up the people, teaching
Jn 6.59 This he said . . as he taught at Capernaum
7.14 Jesus went up into the temple and taught
7.28 Jesus proclaimed, as he taught
7.35 "Does he intend to . . teach the Greeks?
8. 2 and he sat down and taught them[r]‡
8.20 he spoke in the treasury, as he taught
8.28 "I . . speak thus as the Father taught me
9.34 They answered . . "would you teach us?
14.26 "he will teach you all things
18.20 "I have always taught in synagogues
Acts 1. 1 all that Jesus began to do and teach
4. 2 because they were teaching the people
4.18 charged them not to speak or t. at all
5.21 entered . . temple at daybreak and taught
5.25 "standing in the temple and teaching
5.28 "We strictly charged you not to teach

Acts 5.42 did not cease teaching and preaching
11.26 taught a large company of people
15. 1 some men . . from Judea . . were teaching
15.35 Paul and Barnabas . . remained . . , teaching
18.11 teaching the word of God among them
18.25 he spoke and taught accurately
20.20 "I did not shrink from . . teaching you
21.21 "teach . . Jews who are among the Gentiles
21.28 "This is the man who is teaching men
28.31 teaching about the Lord Jesus Christ
Rom 2.21 you then who teach others, will you not teach yourself?
12. 7 he who teaches, in his teaching
1 Cor 4.17 as I teach . . everywhere in every church
11.14 Does not nature itself teach you?
Gal 1.12 I did not receive . . , nor was I taught it
Eph 4.21 assuming that you . . were taught in him
Col 1.28 teaching every man in all wisdom
2. 7 in the faith, just as you were taught
3.16 teach and admonish . . in all wisdom[0]
2 Th 2.15 traditions which you were taught by us
1 Tim 2.12 I permit no woman to teach
4.11 Command and teach these things
6. 2 Teach and urge these duties
2 Tim 2. 2 faithful men who will be able to teach
Tit 1.11 upsetting . . families by teaching for . . gain
Heb 5.12 you need some one to teach you again
8.11 " 'they shall not teach every one his fellow
1 Jn 2.27 no need that any . . should teach you; as his anointing teaches you . . everything, . . just as it has taught you, abide
Rev 2.14 " 'Balaam, who taught Balak
2.20 " 'Jezebel, who . . is teaching . . my servants

2. *put in order, make:* καταρτίζω KATARTIZŌ
Lk 6.40 "every one when he is fully taught

3. *instruct:* κατηχέω KATĒCHEŌ
Gal 6. 6 Let him who is taught the word share all good things with him who teaches

4. *speak, talk:* λαλέω LALEŌ
Tit 2. 1 teach what befits sound doctrine

CONTEXTUALLY
Jas 3. 1 you know that we who t. shall be judged

TEACH A DIFFERENT DOCTRINE
TEACH OTHERWISE

1. *teach false doctrine:* ἑτεροδιδασκαλέω HETERODIDASKALEŌ*
1 Tim 1. 3 charge . . not to teach any different doctrine
6. 3 If any one teaches otherwise

TEACH WHAT IS GOOD

1. *teaching what is good:* καλοδιδάσκαλος KALODIDASKALOS* [A.3.e.1]
Tit 2. 3 they are to teach what is good

TEACHER

1. *teacher:* διδάσκαλος DIDASKALOS*
Mt 8.19 "T., I will follow you wherever you go
9.11 "Why does your t. eat with . . sinners?
10.24 "A disciple is not above his teacher
10.25 "enough for the disciple to be like his t.
12.38 "Teacher, we wish to see a sign from you
17.24 "Does not your teacher pay the tax?
19.16 "Teacher, what good deed must I do?
22.16 "Teacher, we know that you are true
22.24 "Teacher, Moses said, 'If a man dies
22.36 "T., which is the great commandment?
23. 8 "you have one t., and you are . . brethren
26.18 " 'The T. says, My time is at hand
Mk 4.38 "T., do you not care if we perish?
5.35 "Why trouble the Teacher any further?
9.17 "Teacher, I brought my son to you
9.38 "T., we saw a man casting out demons
10.17 "Good T., what must I do to inherit?
10.20 "T., . . these I have observed from . . youth
10.35 "T., we want you to do for us whatever
12.14 "Teacher, we know that you are true
12.19 "T., Moses wrote . . that if a . . brother dies
12.32 "T.; you have truly said that he is one
13. 1 "Look, Teacher, what wonderful stones!
14.14 " 'The T. says, Where is my guest room?
Lk 2.46 in the temple, sitting among the teachers
3.12 said to him, "Teacher, what shall we do?
6.40 "A disciple is not above his t., but every one when he is fully taught will be like his t.
7.40 he answered, "What is it, Teacher?
8.49 "do not trouble the Teacher any more
9.38 "T., I beg you to look upon my son
10.25 "T., what shall I do to inherit eternal life?
11.45 "T., in saying this you reproach us also
12.13 "T., bid my brother divide . . with me
18.18 "Good T., what shall I do to inherit?
19.39 "Teacher, rebuke your disciples
20.21 "T., we know that you . . teach rightly
20.28 "T., Moses wrote . . that if a . . brother dies
20.39 "Teacher, you have spoken well
21. 7 asked him, "Teacher, when will this be?
22.11 " 'The T. says . . Where is the guest room?
Jn 1.38 they said . . "Rabbi" (which means T.
3. 2 "we know . . you are a teacher come from God
3.10 "Are you a teacher of Israel?
8. 4 "Teacher, this woman has been caught[r‡]
11.28 "The T. is here and is calling for you
13.13 "You call me Teacher and Lord
13.14 "If I . . , your . . T., have washed your feet
20.16 She . . said . . "Rabboni!" (which means T.
Acts 13. 1 at Antioch there were . . teachers
Rom 2.20 corrector of the foolish, a t. of children
1 Cor 12.28 appointed in the church . . teachers
12.29 Are all teachers? Do all work miracles?
Eph 4.11 gifts were that some should be . . teachers
1 Tim 2. 7 I was appointed . . a t. of the Gentiles
2 Tim 1.11 For this gospel I was appointed a . . t.
4. 3 teachers to suit their own likings
Heb 5.12 by this time you ought to be teachers
Jas 3. 1 Let not many of you become teachers

TEACHER, APT

1. *skillful in teaching:* διδακτικός (subst.) DIDAKTIKOS*
1 Tim 3. 2 a bishop must be . . an apt teacher
2 Tim 2.24 Lord's servant must . . be . . an apt teacher

TEACHER, FALSE

1. *false teacher:* ψευδοδιδάσκαλος PSEUDODIDASKALOS*
2 Pet 2. 1 there will be false teachers among you

TEACHER OF THE LAW

1. *teacher of the law:* νομοδιδάσκαλος NOMODIDASKALOS*
Lk 5.17 Pharisees and teachers of the law
Acts 5.34 Gamaliel, a teacher of the law
1 Tim 1. 7 desiring to be teachers of the law

TEACHING

1. *teaching:* διδαχή DIDACHĒ
Mt 7.28 the crowds were astonished at his t.
16.12 the t. of the Pharisees and Sadducees
22.33 they were astonished at his teaching
Mk 1.22 they were astonished at his teaching
1.27 "What is this? A new teaching!
4. 2 in his teaching he said to them
11.18 the multitude was astonished at his t.
12.38 in his t. he said, "Beware of the scribes
Lk 4.32 they were astonished at his teaching
Jn 7.16 "My t. is not mine, but his who sent me
7.17 "he shall know whether the t. is from God
18.19 high priest . . questioned Jesus about his . . t.
Acts 2.42 devoted themselves to the apostles' t.
5.28 "you have filled Jerusalem with your t.
13.12 for he was astonished at the teaching
17.19 "May we know what this new teaching is?
Rom 6.17 obedient . . to the standard of teaching
1 Cor 14. 6 unless I bring you some revelation or . . t.
2 Tim 4. 2 be unfailing in patience and in t.
Heb 13. 9 not . . led away by diverse . . teachings
Rev 2.14 " 'some there who hold the t. of Balaam
2.15 " 'some who hold the t. of . . Nicolaitans
2.24 " 'you in Thyatira, who do not hold this t.

2. *teaching:* διδασκαλία DIDASKALIA
Rom 12. 7 he who teaches, in his teaching
1 Tim 4.13 attend . . to preaching, to teaching

1 Tim 4.16 Take heed to yourself and to your t.
5.17 those who labor in preaching and t.
6. 1 so that . . the t. may not be defamed
6. 3 teaching which accords with godliness
2 Tim 3.10 Now you have observed my teaching
3.16 All scripture is . . profitable for teaching
4. 3 people will not endure sound teaching
Tit 2. 7 in your teaching show integrity
3. *word, reckoning:* λόγος LOGOS
Lk 10.39 Mary, who . . listened to his teaching

TEAR
1. *tear:* δάκρυον DAKRYON*
Mk [9.24 father of the child cried out *with tears*‡
Lk 7.38 she began to wet his feet with her tears
7.44 "but she has wet my feet with her tears
Acts 20.19 "serving the Lord . . with tears and . . trials
20.31 "to admonish every one with tears
2 Cor 2. 4 I wrote you . . with many tears
2 Tim 1. 4 I remember your tears, I long . . to see you
Heb 5. 7 supplications, with loud cries and tears
12.17 no chance . . , though he sought it with tears
Rev 7.17 "God will wipe away every tear
21. 4 "will wipe away every t. from their eyes
2. *break through:* διαρήγνυμι DIARĒGNYMI
Mt 26.65 Then the high priest tore his robes
Mk 14.63 the high priest tore his garments
Acts 14.14 they tore their garments and rushed out
3. *break:* ῥήγνυμι RHĒGNYMI
Lk 9.42 the demon tore him and convulsed him
4. *division, split:* σχίσμα SCHISMA
Mt 9.16 "for . . a worse tear is made
Mk 2.21 "if he does, . . a worse tear is made
5. *divide, split:* σχίζω SCHIZŌ
Mt 27.51 curtain of the temple was torn in two
Mk 15.38 curtain of the temple was torn in two
Lk 5.36 "No one tears a piece from a new garment . . ; if he does, he will tear the new
23.45 curtain of the temple was torn in two
Jn 19.24 "Let us not tear it, but cast lots for it
21.11 although . . so many, the net was not torn

TEAR AWAY
1. *lift, carry away:* αἴρω AIRŌ
Mt 9.16 "the patch tears away from the garment
Mk 2.21 "if he does, the patch tears away from it

TEAR DOWN
1. *put down, destroy:* καταλύω KATALYŌ
Gal 2.18 if I build up . . things which I tore down

TEAR IN PIECES
1. *tear apart:* διασπάω DIASPAŌ
Acts 23.10 afraid . . Paul would be torn in pieces

TEAR OFF
1. *break off all around, strip:* περιρήγνυμι PERIRĒGNYMI*
Acts 16.22 magistrates tore the garments off them

TEARING DOWN
1. *pulling down:* καθαίρεσις KATHAIRESIS
2 Cor 13.10 for building up and not for t. down

TEARS, WITH
1. *weep, cry:* κλαίω (part.) KLAIŌ
Phil 3.18 I . . now tell you even with tears

TELL (*See also* TRUTH, TELL THE)
1. *report:* ἀναγγέλλω ANAGGELLŌ
Rom 15.21 "They shall see who have never been told
2 Cor 7. 7 as he told us of your longing
2. *bring tidings:* ἀπαγγέλλω APAGGELLŌ
Mt 8.33 going into the city they told everything
11. 4 "Go and t. John what you hear and see
14.12 and they went and told Jesus
28. 8 departed . . and ran to tell his disciples
28.10 "go and tell my brethren to go to Galilee
28.11 the guard went into the city and told
Mk 5.14 herdsmen fled, and told it in the city
5.19 "tell them how much the Lord has done
6.30 apostles . . told him all . . they had done
16.10 She . . told those who had been with him[k]‡
16.13 And they went back and told the rest[k]‡
Lk 7.18 disciples of John told him of all these
7.22 "Go and tell John what you have seen
8.20 he was told, "Your mother and . . brothers
8.34 they fled, and told it in the city
8.36 those who had seen it told them how
9.36 they kept silence and told no one
13. 1 some . . told him of the Galileans
18.37 They told him, "Jesus . . is passing by
24. 9 they told all this to the eleven
Jn 16.25 "I shall . . tell you plainly of the Father
Acts 5.25 "some one came and told them
11.13 " 'he told us how he had seen the angel
12.14 ran in and told that Peter was . . at . . gate
12.17 "Tell this to James and to the brethren
15.27 "Judas and Silas, who . . will tell you
23.16 entered the barracks and told Paul
23.17 "for he has something to tell him
23.19 "What is it that you have to tell me?
3. *set out in detail:* διηγέομαι DIĒGEOMAI
Mk 5.16 told what had happened to the demoniac
9. 9 he charged them to tell no one
Lk 9.10 the apostles told him what they had done
Heb 11.32 time would fail me to tell of Gideon
4. *say, speak:* εἶπον EIPON
Mt 2.13 "flee to Egypt, and remain . . till I tell you
2. 5 They told him, "In Bethlehem of Judea
[12.47 *Some one told him, "Your mother*‡
15. 5 " 'If any one tells his father or . . mother
16.12 they understood . . he did not tell them
16.20 charged the disciples to tell no one
16.24 Then Jesus told his disciples
17. 9 Jesus commanded . . "Tell no one the vision
18.17 "If he refuses . . , tell it to the church
21. 5 "Tell the daughter of Zion, Behold
22. 4 " 'Tell those who are invited, Behold
22.17 "Tell us, then, what you think
23. 3 "observe whatever they tell you
24. 3 "Tell us, when will this be?
26.63 "tell us if you are the Christ
27.64 " 'lest his disciples . . tell the people
28. 7 "Then go quickly and tell his disciples
28. 7 "Lo, I have told you
Mk 3. 9 he told his disciples to have a boat
5.33 fell down before him, and told him
5.43 told them to give her something to eat
7.11 " 'If a man tells his father or his mother
8.28 they told him, "John the Baptist
11. 6 they told them what Jesus had said
12.12 he had told the parable against them
13. 4 "Tell us, when will this be
14.16 disciples . . found it as he had told them
16. 7 "tell his disciples and Peter that he is going . . ; there you will see him, as he told you
Lk 5.14 he charged him to tell no one
6.39 He also told them a parable
8.56 he charged them to tell no one
10.40 "Tell her then to help me
12.16 he told them a parable
13.32 "Go and tell that fox, 'Behold
15. 3 So he told them this parable
18. 9 He also told this parable to some
19.11 he proceeded to tell a parable
19.32 So those . . found it as he had told them
20. 2 "T. us by what authority you do these
20. 3 "I . . will ask you a question; now tell me
20.19 he had told this parable against them
21.29 he told them a parable
22.67 "If you are the Christ, tell us." . . "If I tell you, you will not believe
Jn 2.16 he told those who sold the pigeons
3.12 "If I have told you earthly things
3.12 "how . . if I tell you heavenly things?
4.29 "see a man who told me all that I ever did
4.39 "He told me all that I ever did
5.15 The man . . told the Jews that it was Jesus
8.24 "I told you . . you would die in your sins
9.27 "I have told you already

Jn 10.24 "If you are the Christ, tell us plainly
10.25 Jesus answered them, "I told you
11.14 Jesus told them . . "Lazarus is dead
11.40 Jesus said . . "Did I not tell you?
11.46 some . . told them what Jesus had done
13.24 "Tell us who it is of whom he speaks
14. 2 "if it were not so, would I have told you?
16. 4 "remember that I told you of them
18. 8 "I told you that I am he
20.15 "tell me where you have laid him
Acts 5. 8 "Tell me whether you sold the land
11.12 "the Spirit told me to go with them

5. *blurt out:* ἐκλαλέω EKLALEŌ*
Acts 23.22 "Tell no one . . you have informed me

6. *say, speak:* ἐρῶ ERŌ
Mt 13.30 " 'at harvest time I will tell the reapers
21.24 "if you tell me the answer, then I also
Mk 11.29 "and I will tell you by what authority
Lk 22.11 "tell the householder, 'The Teacher says
22.13 went, and found it as he had told them
Jn 6.65 "I told you that no one can come to me
14.29 "I have told you before it takes place
Rom 4.18 he had been told, "So shall . . descendants
9.12 she was told, "The elder will serve
Rev 6.11 they were . . told to rest a little longer
9. 4 they were told not to harm the grass
17. 7 "I will tell you the mystery of the woman

7. *interpret, tell:* ἐξηγέομαι EXĒGEOMAI
Lk 24.35 they told what had happened on the road

8. *make known:* γνωρίζω GNŌRIZŌ
Eph 6.21 Tychicus . . will tell you everything
Col 4. 7 Tychicus will tell you . . about my affairs
4. 9 They will tell you of everything

9. *instruct:* κατηχέω KATĒCHEŌ
Acts 21.21 "they have been told about you
21.24 "what they have been told about you

10. *speak, talk:* λαλέω LALEŌ
Mt 13. 3 he told them many things in parables
13.33 He told them another parable
26.13 "what she has done will be told in memory
Mk 14. 9 "what she has done will be told in memory
Lk 2.17 the saying which had been told them
2.18 wondered at what the shepherds told
2.20 heard and seen, as it had been told them
24. 6 "how he told you, while . . still in Galilee
Jn 8.25 "what I have told you from . . beginning[t]†
8.40 "a man who has told you the truth
Acts 2.11 "telling in our . . tongues the . . works of God
3.22 " 'listen to him in whatever he tells you
9. 6 "you will be told what you are to do
13.42 begged that these things might be told
22.10 " 'you will be told all that is appointed
27.25 "it will be exactly as I have been told

11. *say, speak:* λέγω LEGŌ
Mt 3. 9 " 'I t. you, God is able from these stones
5.20 "I tell you, unless your righteousness
6.25 "Therefore I tell you, do not be anxious
6.29 "I tell you, even Solomon in . . his glory
8.11 "I tell you, many will come
10.27 "What I tell you in the dark, utter
11. 9 "Yes, I tell you, and more than a prophet
11.22 "But I tell you, it shall be more tolerable
11.24 "I tell you that it shall be more tolerable
12. 6 "I tell you, something greater than . . temple
12.31 "I tell you, every sin . . will be forgiven
12.36 "I tell you, . . men will render account
12.48 he replied to the man who told him
16.18 "I tell you, you are Peter[s]
17.12 "I tell you that Elijah has already come
18.10 "for I tell you that in heaven their angels
19.24 "Again I tell you, it is easier for a camel
21.27 "Neither will I t. you by what authority
21.43 "I tell you, . . kingdom . . will be taken away
23.39 "I tell you, you will not see me again
26.29 "I tell you I shall not drink again of this
26.64 "I tell you, . . you will see the Son of man
Mk 1.30 immediately they told him of her
7.36 he charged them to tell no one
8.30 he charged them to tell no one
9.13 "But I tell you that Elijah has come
10.32 began to tell them what was to happen
11.24 "I tell you, whatever you ask in prayer
11.33 "Neither will I t. you by what authority
Lk 3. 8 "I tell you, God is able from these stones
4.25 "I tell you, there were many widows
5.36 He told them a parable also
6.46 "Why do you . . not do what I tell you?
7. 9 "I tell you, not . . in Israel have I found
7.26 "Yes, I tell you, and more than a prophet
7.28 "I tell you, among those born of women
7.47 "I tell you, her sins, which are many
9.21 commanded them to tell this to no one
9.27 "I tell you truly, there are some standing
10.12 "I tell you, it shall be more tolerable
10.24 "I tell you . . many prophets . . desired
11. 8 "I tell you, though he will not get up
11. 9 "I tell you, Ask, and it will be given
11.51 "Yes, I tell you, it shall be required
12. 4 "I tell you, my friends, do not fear
12. 5 "yes, I tell you, fear him!
12. 8 "I tell you, every one who acknowledges
12.22 "Therefore I tell you, do not be anxious
12.27 "I tell you, even Solomon in all his glory
12.41 "are you telling this parable for us?
12.51 "No, I tell you, but rather division
12.59 "I tell you, you will never get out till
13. 3 "I tell you, No; but unless you repent
13. 5 "I tell you, No; but unless you repent
13. 6 And he told this parable
13.24 "for many, I tell you, will seek to enter
13.27 " 'I tell you, I do not know where
13.35 "I tell you, you will not see me until
14. 7 Now he told a parable to those
14.24 " 'For I tell you,[a] none of those . . invited
15. 7 "I tell you, there will be more joy
15.10 "Just so, I tell you there is joy
16. 9 "I t. you, make friends for yourselves
17.34 "I tell you, in that night there will be
18. 1 he told them a parable, to the effect
18. 8 "I tell you, he will vindicate them speedily
18.14 "I tell you, this man went down
19.26 " 'I tell you, that to every one who has
19.40 "I tell you, if these were silent
20. 8 "Neither will I t. you by what authority
20. 9 he began to tell the people this parable
21. 3 "Truly I tell you, this poor widow
22.16 "for I tell you I shall not eat it[i]
22.18 "I t. you . . from now on I shall not drink
22.34 "I tell you, Peter, the cock will not crow
22.37 "I tell you that this . . must be fulfilled
24.10 the other women with them who told this
Jn 2. 5 "Do whatever he tells you
4.35 "I tell you, lift up your eyes, and see
4.51 his servants met him and told him
6.12 he told his disciples, "Gather up
8.45 "because I tell the truth, you do not believe
8.46 "If I t. the truth, why do you not believe?
12.22 Philip went and told Andrew; Andrew went with Philip and they told Jesus
13.19 "I tell you this now, before it takes place
13.29 thought . . Jesus was telling him, "Buy
16. 7 "Nevertheless I tell you the truth
18.38 told them, "I find no crime in him
19.35 he knows that he tells the truth
20.25 So the other disciples told him
Acts 5.38 "in the present case I tell you, keep away
17.21 telling or hearing something new
19. 4 "telling the people to believe in the one
21. 4 Through the Spirit they told Paul
21.21 "they have been told about you
21.23 "Do therefore what we tell you
22.27 "Tell me, are you a Roman citizen?
Rom 15. 8 I tell you that Christ became a servant
1 Cor 15.51 Lo! I tell you a mystery

Gal 4.21 Tell me, you who desire to be under law
Phil 3.18 many, of whom I have often told you and now tell you even with tears
2 Th 2. 5 when I was still with you I told you this
1 Tim 2. 7 (I am telling the truth, I am not lying
Rev 10. 9 told him to give me the little scroll
10.11 I was told, "You must again prophesy
11. 1 I was told: "Rise and measure
16. 1 a loud voice . . telling the seven angels
12. *give orders:* παραγγέλλω PARAGGELLŌ
Mk [16.end *they reported . . all . . they had been told*‡
13. *say, affirm:* φημί PHĒMI
1 Cor 15.50 I tell you . . : flesh . . cannot inherit
IDIOMATICALLY
a. Mt 21.24 "and if you tell me the answer ὃν ἐὰν εἴπητέ μοι [EIPON]
CONTEXTUALLY
Mt 20.31 rebuked them, telling them to be silent
Mk 10.48 rebuked him, telling him to be silent
Lk 18.39 rebuked him, telling him to be silent
Jn 20.18 she told them . . he had said these things

TELL BEFOREHAND
1. *foretell, say before:* προεῖπον PROEIPON
Mt 24.25 "Lo, I have told you beforehand
Mk 13.23 "I have told you all things beforehand
2. *foretell, proclaim:* προλέγω PROLEGŌ
1 Th 3. 4 told you beforehand . . we were to suffer

TELL, CAN
1. *make known:* γνωρίζω GNŌRIZŌ
Phil 1.22 which I shall choose I cannot tell

TELL GOOD NEWS
1. *bring good news* (mid.): εὐαγγελίζω EUAGGELIZŌ
Acts 8.35 he told him the good news of Jesus

TELL S. HIS FAULT
1. *expose, test, refute:* ἐλέγχω ELEGCHŌ
Mt 18.15 "go and tell him his fault

TELL PEOPLE
1. *say, speak:* εἶπον (imper.) EIPON
Mt 28.13 "Tell people, . . 'disciples came by night

TEMPERATE
1. *sober:* νηφάλιος NĒPHALIOS*
1 Tim 3. 2 the husband of one wife, temperate
3.11 but temperate, faithful in all things
Tit 2. 2 Bid the older men be temperate, serious

TEMPEST
1. *winter, stormy weather:* χειμών CHEIMŌN
Acts 27.20 no small tempest lay on us
2. *hurricane, thunderstorm:* θύελλα THYELLA*
Heb 12.18 darkness, and gloom, and a tempest

TEMPESTUOUS
1. *like a whirlwind:* τυφωνικός TYPHŌNIKOS*
Acts 27.14 a t. wind . . struck down from the land

TEMPLE
1. *holy place, temple:* ἱερόν HIERON*
Mt 4. 5 set him on the pinnacle of the temple
12. 5 "how on the sabbath the priests in the t.
12. 6 "something greater than the t. is here
21.12 Jesus entered the temple of God[p] and drove out all who sold . . in the t.
21.14 the lame came to him in the temple
21.15 crying out in the temple, "Hosanna!
21.23 when he entered the temple
24. 1 Jesus left the t. and was going away
24. 1 to point out . . the buildings of the temple
26.55 "Day after day I sat in the t. teaching
Mk 11.11 entered Jerusalem, and went into the t.
11.15 he entered the t. and began to drive out those who sold . . in the temple
11.16 to carry anything through the temple
11.27 as he was walking in the temple
12.35 as Jesus taught in the temple
13. 1 as he came out of the temple
13. 3 sat on the Mount of Olives opposite the t.
14.49 "I was with you in the temple teaching
Lk 2.27 inspired by the Spirit[h] he came into . . t.
2.37 She did not depart from the temple
2.46 After three days they found him in the t.
4. 9 he . . set him on the pinnacle of the temple
18.10 "Two men went up into the t. to pray
19.45 he entered the t. and began to drive out
19.47 he was teaching daily in the temple
20. 1 as he was teaching the people in the t.
21. 5 some spoke of the t., how it was adorned
21.37 every day he was teaching in the temple
21.38 all the people came to him in the t.
22.52 Jesus said to the . . officers of the temple
22.53 "I was with you day after day in the t.
24.53 continually in the temple blessing God
Jn 2.14 In the t. he found those who were selling
2.15 he drove them all . . out of the temple
5.14 Afterward, Jesus found him in the t.
7.14 Jesus went up into the temple
7.28 Jesus proclaimed, as he taught in the t.
8. 2 he came again to the temple[r]‡
8.20 These words . . as he taught in the temple
8.59 Jesus hid . . , and went out of the temple
10.23 Jesus was walking in the temple
11.56 They were . . saying . . as they stood in the t.
18.20 "I have always taught . . in the temple
Acts 2.46 day by day, attending the t. together
3. 1 going up to the t. at the hour of prayer
3. 2 whom they laid daily at that gate of the t. . . to ask alms of those who entered the t.
3. 3 Seeing Peter . . about to go into the t.
3. 8 he stood and . . entered the t. with them
3.10 sat for alms at . . Beautiful Gate of the t.
4. 1 the captain of the t. . . came upon them
5.20 "Go and stand in the temple and speak
5.21 they entered the temple at daybreak
5.24 captain of the t. . . heard these words
5.25 "standing in the temple and teaching
5.42 every day in the t. . . they did not cease
19.27 "the temple of the great goddess Artemis
21.26 went into the temple, to give notice
21.27 Jews . . who had seen him in the temple
21.28 "he also brought Greeks into the temple
21.29 that Paul had brought him into the t.
21.30 seized Paul and dragged him out of . . t.
22.17 "I had returned . . and was praying in the t.
24. 6 "He even tried to profane the temple
24.12 "they did not find me disputing . . in the t.
24.18 "they found me purified in the temple
25. 8 "Neither against the law . . nor . . the t.
26.21 "For this reason . . Jews seized me in the t.
1 Cor 9.13 those . . get their food from the temple
2. *temple, shrine:* ναός NAOS
Mt 23.16 " 'If any one swears by the temple
23.16 "if any one swears by the gold of the t.
23.17 "For which is greater, the gold or the t.?
23.21 "he who swears by the temple
26.61 " 'I am able to destroy the temple of God
27. 5 throwing down the pieces of silver in . . t.
27.40 "You who would destroy the temple
27.51 curtain of the temple was torn in two
Mk 14.58 "heard him say, 'I will destroy this t.
15.29 "Aha! You who would destroy the t.
15.38 curtain of the temple was torn in two
Lk 1. 9 it fell to him by lot to enter the temple
1.21 wondered at his delay in the temple
1.22 he had seen a vision in the temple
23.45 curtain of the temple was torn in two
Jn 2.19 "Destroy this t., and . . I will raise it up
2.20 "taken forty-six years to build this t.
2.21 he spoke of the temple of his body
1 Cor 3.16 Do you not know that you are God's t.?
3.17 If any one destroys God's temple, God will destroy him. For God's t. is holy
6.19 know that your body is a temple
2 Cor 6.16 What agreement has the t. . . with idols? For we are the t. of the living God
Eph 2.21 the whole structure . . grows into a holy t.

2 Th 2. 4 he takes his seat in the temple of God
Rev 3.12 " 'I will make him a pillar in the temple
7.15 serve him day and night within his t.
11. 1 "Rise and measure the temple of God
11. 2 "measure the court outside the temple
11.19 Then God's t. in heaven was opened, and the ark . . was seen within his temple
14.15 another angel came out of the temple
14.17 another angel came out of the temple
15. 5 the t. of the tent of witness . . was opened
15. 6 out of the temple came the seven angels
15. 8 the temple was filled with smoke . . and no one could enter the temple
16. 1 I heard a loud voice from the temple
16.17 a loud voice came out of the temple
21.22 I saw no temple in the city, for its temple is the Lord God the Almighty

CONTEXTUALLY
Acts 14.13 whose temple was in front of the city

TEMPLE, IDOL'S
1. *idol's temple:* εἰδωλεῖον EIDŌLEION*
1 Cor 8.10 if any one sees you . . in an idol's temple

TEMPLE KEEPER
1. *guardian of a temple:* νεωκόρος NEŌKOROS*
Acts 19.35 "city of the Ephesians is temple keeper

TEMPLE SERVICE
1. *holy:* ἱερός (subst. neut. pl.) HIEROS
1 Cor 9.13 those . . employed in the temple service

TEMPLES, ROB
1. *rob a temple:* ἱεροσυλέω HIEROSYLEŌ*
Rom 2.22 You who abhor idols, do you rob temples?

TEMPT
1. *tempt:* ἐκπειράζω EKPEIRAZŌ
Mt 4. 7 " 'You shall not tempt the Lord your God
Lk 4.12 " 'You shall not tempt the Lord your God
2. *tempt, try:* πειράζω PEIRAZŌ
Mt 4. 1 Jesus was led . . to be tempted by the devil
Mk 1.13 he was . . forty days, tempted by Satan
Lk 4. 2 for forty days . . , tempted by the devil
Acts 5. 9 "agreed together to tempt the Spirit
1 Cor 7. 5 come together again, lest Satan t. you
10.13 not . . be tempted beyond your strength
Gal 6. 1 Look to yourself, lest you . . be tempted
1 Th 3. 5 fear that . . the tempter had tempted you
Heb 2.18 because he himself has . . been tempted, he is able to help those who are tempted
4.15 one who . . has been tempted as we are
[11.37 they were sawn in two, . . *were tempted*‡
Jas 1.13 Let no one say when he is tempted, "I am tempted by God"; for God . . himself tempts no one
1.14 each person is tempted when he is lured

TEMPTATION
1. *temptation, trial:* πειρασμός PEIRASMOS
Mt 6.13 "lead us not into temptation
26.41 "pray that you may not enter into t.
Mk 14.38 "pray that you may not enter into t.
Lk 4.13 when the devil had ended every t.
8.13 "they believe . . and in time of t. fall away
11. 4 "lead us not into temptation
22.40 "Pray that you may not enter into t.
22.46 "pray that you may not enter into t.
1 Cor 10.13 No temptation has overtaken you
10.13 with the t. . . provide the way of escape
1 Tim 6. 9 those who desire to be rich fall into t.
2. *stumbling block, trap:* σκάνδαλον SKANDALON
Mt 18. 7 "necessary that temptations come, but woe to the man by whom the t. comes

CONTEXTUALLY
1 Cor 7. 2 because of the temptation to immorality

TEMPTATION TO SIN
1. *stumbling block, trap:* σκάνδαλον SKANDALON
Mt 18. 7 "Woe . . for temptations to sin![a]†
Lk 17. 1 "Temptations to sin[x] are sure to come!†

TEMPTED, NOT TO BE
1. *incapable of being tempted:* ἀπείραστος APEIRASTOS*
Jas 1.13 for God cannot be tempted with evil

TEMPTER
1. tempt, try: πειράζω (subst. part.) PEIRAZŌ
Mt 4. 3 the tempter came and said to him
1 Th 3. 5 fear that . . the tempter had tempted you

TEN
1. *ten:* δέκα DEKA
Mt 20.24 the ten heard it, they were indignant
25. 1 "ten maidens who took their lamps
25.28 " 'give it to him who has the ten talents
Mk 10.41 the ten heard it, . . began to be indignant
Lk 14.31 "able with ten thousand to meet him
15. 8 "what woman, having ten silver coins[t]
17.12 he was met by ten lepers . . at a distance
17.17 said Jesus, "Were not ten cleansed?
19.13 "Calling ten of his servants, he gave them ten pounds[e]
19.16 " 'your pound has made ten pounds more
19.17 " 'you shall have authority over ten cities
19.24 " 'give it to him who has the t. pounds
19.25 "(they said . . 'Lord, he has ten pounds!
Acts 25. 6 stayed . . not more than eight or ten days
Rev 2.10 " 'for ten days you will have tribulation
12. 3 dragon, with seven heads and ten horns
13. 1 beast . . with ten horns and seven heads, with ten diadems upon its horns
17. 3 a scarlet beast which . . had . . ten horns
17. 7 "the beast with seven heads and ten horns
17.12 "the ten horns . . are ten kings who have not yet received royal power
17.16 "the ten horns . . will hate the harlot

TEN THOUSAND
1. *myriad, ten thousand:* μυριάς MYRIAS
Rev 9.16 ten thousand; I heard their number
2. *ten thousand:* μύριοι MYRIOI*
Mt 18.24 "who owed him ten thousand talents[f]
1 Cor 14.19 rather . . than t. thousand words in a tongue

TEN THOUSAND, TWICE
1. *twenty thousand:* δισμυριάς DISMYRIAS*
Rev 9.16 cavalry was twice ten thousand times

TENANT
1. *farmer, tenant:* γεωργός GEŌRGOS
Mt 21.33 "built a tower, and let it out to tenants
21.34 "he sent his servants to the tenants
21.35 "tenants took his servants and beat one
21.38 "But when the tenants saw the son
21.40 "what will he do to those tenants?
21.41 "let out the vineyard to other tenants
Mk 12. 1 "built a tower, and let it out to tenants
12. 2 "he sent a servant to the tenants
12. 7 "those tenants said to one another
12. 9 "He will come and destroy the tenants
Lk 20. 9 "planted a vineyard, . . let it . . to tenants
20.10 "he sent a servant to the tenants . . ; but the tenants beat him
20.14 "when the tenants saw him, they said
20.16 "He will come and destroy those tenants

TEND
1. *tend, herd, govern:* ποιμαίνω POIMAINŌ
Jn 21.16 He said to him, "Tend my sheep
1 Cor 9. 7 Who tends a flock without getting . . milk?
1 Pet 5. 2 Tend the flock . . that is your charge[k]

TENDER
1. *tender, soft to the touch:* ἁπαλός HAPALOS*
Mt 24.32 "as soon as its branch becomes tender
Mk 13.28 as soon as its branch becomes tender
2. *inward parts:* σπλάγχνον SPLAGCHNON [A.1.b.5]
Lk 1.78 "through the tender mercy of our God

TENDER HEART, HAVE A
TENDERHEARTED
1. *with healthy bowels, tenderhearted:* εὔσπλαγχνος EUSPLAGCHNOS*
[a]A.3.e.2

Eph 4.32 be kind to one another, tenderhearted
1 Pet 3. 8 [a]have . . a t. heart and a humble mind

TENT
1. *tent, booth:* σκηνή SKĒNĒ
Acts 7.43 " 'you took up the tent of Moloch
7.44 "Our fathers had the tent of witness
Heb 8. 2 minister in the sanctuary and the true t.[n]†
8. 5 "when Moses was about to erect the tent[n]†
9. 2 For a tent[p] was prepared, the outer one†
9. 3 a tent[p] called the Holy of Holies†
9. 6 priests go continually into the outer tent[p]†
9. 8 as long as the outer tent[p] is still standing†
9.11 through the greater and more perfect t.[p]
9.21 sprinkled with the blood both the tent[p]†
11. 9 as in a foreign land, living in tents
13.10 those who serve the tent[a] have no right†
Rev 15. 5 the temple of the tent of witness
2. *tent, hut:* σκῆνος SKĒNOS*
2 Cor 5. 1 if the earthly t. we live in is destroyed
5. 4 while we are still in this tent, we sigh

TENTH
1. *tenth:* δέκατος DEKATOS
[a]subst. fem. [b]subst. neut.
Jn 1.39 for it was about the tenth hour
Acts [19. 9 argued . . *from the fifth hour to the t.*‡
Heb 7. 2 [a]to him Abraham apportioned a tenth
Rev 11.13 [b]earthquake, and a t. of the city fell
21.20 the ninth topaz, the tenth chrysoprase

TENTMAKER
1. *tentmaker:* σκηνοποιός SKĒNOPOIOS*
Acts 18. 3 for by trade they were tentmakers

TERAH: Θάρα ˌtirə
Lk 3.34 Abraham, . . son of T., the son of Nahor

TERM
CONTEXTUALLY
Lk 14.32 "sends an embassy and asks terms of peace

TERMS (*See also* HUMAN TERMS, IN)
1. *word, reckoning:* λόγος LOGOS
1 Cor 15. 1(2) in what t. I preached to you the gospel

TERMS, WORK ON THE SAME
1. *find:* εὑρίσκω (pass.) HEURISKŌ
2 Cor 11.12 they work on the same t. as we

TERRESTRIAL
1. *of the earth:* ἐπίγειος EPIGEIOS
1 Cor 15.40 There are celestial bodies and . . t. bodies; but . . the glory of the t. is another

TERRIBLE
1. *terribly:* δεινῶς DEINŌS [A.4.a]
Mt 8. 6 "paralyzed at home, in terrible distress

TERRIBLY
1. *badly, ill:* κακῶς KAKŌS
Mt 17.15 "an epileptic and he suffers terribly
2. *many, great:* πολύς (neut. pl.) POLYS
Mk 9.26 crying out and convulsing him t.

TERRIFIED
1. *terrible, afraid:* ἔμφοβος EMPHOBOS
Rev 11.13 were t. and gave glory to the God

TERRIFY
1. *terrify:* φοβέω PHOBEŌ
[a]+πτόησιν A.6.a.6
1 Pet 3. 6 [a]if you . . let nothing terrify you
2. *scare, excite:* πτοέω PTOEŌ
Lk 21. 9 "when you hear . . , do not be terrified
3. *trouble, disturb:* ταράσσω TARASSŌ
Mt 14.26 were terrified, saying, "It is a ghost!
Mk 6.50 for they all saw him, and were terrified

TERRIFYING
1. *fearful, terrible:* φοβερός PHOBEROS
Heb 12.21 so t. . . that Moses said, "I tremble

TERRITORY
1. *boundary:* ὅριον (pl.) HORION
Mt 4.13 in the t. of Zebulun and Naphtali

TERROR
1. *terror, terrible sight:* φόβητρον PHOBĒTRON*
Lk 21.11 "there will be terrors and great signs
2. *fear:* φόβος PHOBOS
Rom 13. 3 rulers are not a t. to good conduct

TERROR, IN
1. *terrified:* ἔμφοβος EMPHOBOS
Acts 10. 4 And he stared at him in terror

TERTIUS: Τέρτιος 'tərsh(ē)əs
Rom 16.22 I Tertius, the writer of this letter

TERTULLUS: Τέρτυλλος tər'tələs
Acts 24. 1 some elders and a spokesman, one T.
24. 2 Tertullus began to accuse him

TEST
1. *examination:* δοκιμασία DOKIMASIA*
Heb 3. 9 "where your fathers put me to the test
2. *test, approve:* δοκιμάζω DOKIMAZŌ
1 Cor 3.13 the fire will test what sort of work
2 Cor 8.22 our brother whom we have often tested
13. 5 Test yourselves. Do you not realize?
Gal 6. 4 let each one test his own work
1 Th 2. 4 to please God who tests our hearts
5.21 test everything; hold fast what is good
1 Tim 3.10 And let them also be tested first
1 Pet 1. 7 though perishable is tested by fire
1 Jn 4. 1 test the spirits to see whether . . of God
3. *test, proof:* δοκιμή DOKIMĒ
[a]B.2.b.1; B.3.b.4
2 Cor 2. 9 [a]I wrote, that I might t. you and know
8. 2 in a severe test of affliction, their . . joy
9.13 Under the test of this service
4. *tempt, try:* πειράζω PEIRAZŌ
Mt 16. 1 to test him . . asked him to show . . a sign
19. 3 Pharisees came up . . and tested him
22.18 "Why put me to the t. you hypocrites?
22.35 lawyer, asked . . a question, to t. him
Mk 8.11 seeking . . a sign from heaven, to t. him
10. 2 Pharisees came up . . in order to test him
12.15 "Why put me to the test?
Lk 11.16 others, to test him, sought . . a sign
Jn 6. 6 This he said to test him
8. 6 This they said to test him[r]‡
Heb 11.17 By faith Abraham, when he was tested
Rev 2. 2 " 'cannot bear evil men but have tested
2.10 " 'into prison, that you may be tested

TEST, FAIL TO MEET THE
1. *be worthless:* ἀδόκιμος εἶναι ADOKIMOS [A.6.a.3]
2 Cor 13. 5 unless indeed you fail to meet the test!

TEST, PUT TO THE
1. *tempt:* ἐκπειράζω EKPEIRAZŌ
Lk 10.25 a lawyer stood up to put him to the t.
1 Cor 10. 9 We must not put the Lord[p] to the test
2. *tempt, try:* πειράζω PEIRAZŌ
Heb 3. 9 "where your fathers put me to the test

TEST, STAND THE
TEST, TO HAVE MET THE
1. *approved:* δόκιμος DOKIMOS
[a]B.2.d.2
2 Cor 13. 7 not that we . . appear to have met the t.
Jas 1.12 [a]Blessed, . . for when he has stood the t.

TESTIFY
1. *bear witness to:* διαμαρτύρομαι DIAMARTYROMAI
Acts 2.40 he testified with many other words
8.25 when they had testified . . , they returned
10.42 "to testify that he is the one ordained
18. 5 Paul was . . testifying to the Jews
20.21 "testifying both to Jews and to Greeks
20.23 "the Holy Spirit testifies to me
20.24 "to t. to the gospel of the grace of God
23.11 "have testified about me at Jerusalem
28.23 testifying to the kingdom of God
Heb 2. 6 It has been testified . . "What is man?
2. *bear witness, testify:* μαρτυρέω MARTYREŌ
Jn 4.44 Jesus himself testified that a prophet
7. 7 "I testify of it that its works are evil

Jn 13.21 he was troubled in spirit, and testified
Acts 13.22 "raised up David . . ; of whom he testified
26. 5 "if they are willing to testify
1 Cor 15.15 we testified of God that he raised Christ
2 Cor 8. 3 according to their means, as I can t.
Heb 7. 8 of whom it is testified that he lives
1 Jn 1. 2 we saw it, . . testify to it, and proclaim
4.14 we have seen and t. that the Father
3 Jn . 3 brethren . . testified to . . truth of your life
. 6 testified to your love before the church
.12 Demetrius has testimony . . ; I t. to him too
Rev 22.20 He who testifies to these things says
3. *testimony, proof:* μαρτύριον MARTYRION [B.1.a.2]
Heb 3. 5 Moses was faithful . . , to testify
4. *call to witness:* μαρτύρομαι MARTYROMAI
Acts 20.26 "Therefore I testify to you this day
26.22 "testifying both to small and great
Gal 5. 3 I testify again to every man
Eph 4.17 this I affirm and testify in the Lord

TESTIFY AGAINST
1. *bear witness against:* καταμαρτυρέω KATAMARTYREŌ*
Mt 26.62 "What is it . . these men t. against you?
27.13 "how many things they t. against you
Mk 14.60 "What is it . . these men t. against you?

TESTIFYING
1. *testimony, proof:* μαρτύριον MARTYRION
2 Tim 1. 8 Do not be ashamed then of testifying

TESTIMONY
TESTIMONY, BEAR
1. *bear witness, testify:* μαρτυρέω MARTYREŌ [A.6.b]
Rev 22.16 "I . . sent my angel to you with this t.
2. *testimony, evidence:* μαρτυρία MARTYRIA
Mk 14.55 council sought testimony against Jesus
14.59 Yet not even so did their t. agree
Lk 22.71 "What further testimony do we need?
Jn 1. 7 He came for testimony, to bear witness
1.19 this is the testimony of John
3.11 "but you do not receive our testimony
3.32 yet no one receives his testimony
3.33 who receives his t. sets his seal to this
5.31 "If . . to myself, my testimony is not true
5.32 "I know . . the t. . . he bears to me is true
5.34 "Not that the t. . . I receive is from man
5.36 "the t. . . I have is greater than that of John
8.13 "witness to yourself; your t. is not true
8.14 "if I . . witness to myself, my t. is true
8.17 "the testimony of two men is true
19.35 his testimony is true, and he knows
21.24 we know that his testimony is true
Acts 22.18 "'they will not accept your t. about me
Tit 1.13 This testimony is true
1 Jn 5. 9 If we receive the testimony of men, the testimony of God is greater; for this is the testimony of God
5.10 He who believes . . has the t. in himself
5.10 the t. that God has borne to his Son
5.11 this is the t., that God gave us . . life
3 Jn .12 you know my testimony is true
Rev 1. 2 bore witness . . to the t. of Jesus Christ
1. 9 on . . Patmos on account of the . . t. of Jesus
11. 7 when they have finished their t.
12.11 "conquered him . . by the word of their t.
12.17 war on . . those who . . bear t. to Jesus
19.10 "brethren who hold the testimony of Jesus
19.10 the t. of Jesus is the spirit of prophecy
20. 4 who had been beheaded for their t.
3. *testimony, proof:* μαρτύριον MARTYRION
[a]εἰς μαρτύριον *to bear testimony* B.1.a.2
Mt 10.18 [a]"dragged before . . kings . . , to bear t.
24.14 "this gospel . . will be preached . . as a t.
Mk 6.11 "shake off the dust . . for a testimony
13. 9 [a]"stand before . . kings . . to bear testimony
Lk 9. 5 "shake off the dust from . . feet as a t.
21.13 [a]"a time for you to bear testimony
Acts 4.33 with great power the apostles gave their t.
1 Cor 1. 6 as the t. to Christ was confirmed
1 Cor 2. 1 not . . proclaiming . . t.[c] . . in lofty words‡
2 Cor 1.12 our boast is . . the t. of our conscience
2 Th 1.10 our testimony to you was believed
1 Tim 2. 6 t. to which was borne at the proper time
IDIOMATICALLY
a. Jn 4.39 because of the woman's testimony διὰ τὸν λόγον τῆς γυναικὸς μαρτυρούσης [MARTYREŌ]
CONTEXTUALLY
Heb 10.28 at the t. of two or three witnesses

TESTIMONY, FALSE
1. *false witness, perjury:* ψευδομαρτυρία PSEUDOMARTYRIA
Mt 26.59 the whole council sought false testimony

TESTIMONY, HAVE
1. *bear witness, testify:* μαρτυρέω (pass.) MARTYREŌ
3 Jn .12 Demetrius has t. from every one

TESTIMONY, IN ONE'S
1. *bear witness, testify:* μαρτυρέω (part.) MARTYREŌ
1 Tim 6.13 in his t. before Pontius Pilate

TESTING
1. *test, proof:* δοκίμιον DOKIMION
Jas 1. 3 t. of your faith produces steadfastness
2. *temptation, trial:* πειρασμός PEIRASMOS
Heb 3. 8 "on the day of t. in the wilderness

TETRARCH
1. *tetrarch:* τετράρχης TETRARCHĒS*
Mt 14. 1 At that time Herod the tetrarch heard
Lk 3.19 Herod the t., who had been reproved
9. 7 Herod the t. heard of all that was done
Acts 13. 1 the court of Herod the tetrarch

TETRARCH, BE
1. *be tetrarch:* τετραρχέω TETRARCHEŌ*
Lk 3. 1 Herod being t. of Galilee, and his brother Philip t. of the region of Ituraea . . , and Lysanias t. of Abilene

THADDAEUS: Θαδδαῖος 'thadēəs, tha'dēəs
Mt 10. 3 James the son of Alphaeus, and T.[x]‡
Mk 3.18 James the son of Alphaeus, and T.

THAN
1. *or, than:* ἤ Ē
Mt **10**.15; **11**.22, 24; **18**.8, 9, 13; **19**.24
Mk **9**.43, 45, 47; **10**.25
Lk **9**.13; **10**.12, 14; **15**.7; **16**.17; **17**.2; **18**.25
Jn **3**.19; **4**.1
Acts **4**.19; **5**.29; **20**.35; **27**.11
Rom **13**.11
1 Cor **7**.9; **9**.15; **14**.5, 19
Gal **4**.27
1 Tim **1**.4
2 Tim **3**.4
Heb **11**.25
1 Pet **3**.17
2 Pet **2**.21
1 Jn **4**.4
2. *than even:* ἤπερ ĒPER*
Jn 12.43 praise of men more than . . praise of God
3. *over, more than:* ὑπέρ (after comp.+acc.) HYPER
Lk **16**.8
2 Cor **12**.13
Eph **3**.20
Heb **4**.12
4. *not, no:* οὐ OU [A.4.c]
2 Cor **11**.4
5. *more than, by:* παρά (+acc.) PARA [B.1.a.5]
Lk 3.13 "Collect no more than is appointed you
Rom 12. 3 not to think . . more highly than he ought
1 Cor 3.11 no . . foundation can any one lay than that
Heb 1. 4 the name . . is more excellent than theirs
2. 7 "for a little while lower t. the angels
2. 9 who . . was made lower than the angels
3. 3 counted worthy of . . more glory t. Moses
9.23 purified . . with better sacrifices t. these
11. 4 Abel . . more acceptable sacrifice t. Cain
12.24 Jesus . . more . . than the blood of Abel
6. *but, however, except:* πλήν (+neg. and comp.) PLĒN
Acts 15.28 "no greater burden t. . . necessary things

THAN EVER
1. *many, great:* πολύς (+comp.) POLYS
2 Cor 8.22 who is now more earnest than ever

THANK
1. *have thankfulness:* ἔχειν χάριν CHARIS [B.3.a.5]
Lk 17. 9 "Does he thank the servant?
1 Tim 1.12 I thank him who has given me strength
2 Tim 1. 3 I thank God whom I serve
2. *be thankful, return thanks:* εὐχαριστέω EUCHARISTEŌ
Lk 18.11 "I thank thee . . I am not like other men
Jn 11.41 "I thank thee that thou hast heard me
Acts 28.15 On seeing them Paul thanked God
Rom 1. 8 I thank my God through Jesus Christ
1 Cor [1.14 *I thank God* that I baptized none of you†‡
14.18 I thank God that I speak in tongues
Phil 1. 3 I thank my God in all my remembrance
Col 1. 3 We always thank God, the Father
1 Th 2.13 we also thank God constantly
Phm . 4 I t. my God always when I remember
3. *agree:* ἐξομολογέω (mid.) EXOMOLOGEŌ
Mt 11.25 "I thank thee, Father, Lord of heaven
Lk 10.21 "I thank thee, Father, Lord of heaven

THANKFUL
1. *thankful:* εὐχάριστος EUCHARISTOS*
Col 3.15 And be thankful
CONTEXTUALLY
Phil 1. 5 t. for your partnership in the gospel

THANKFUL, BE
1. *be thankful, return thanks:* εὐχαριστέω EUCHARISTEŌ
1 Cor 1.14 I am thankful[b] that I baptized none†‡

THANKFULNESS
1. *grace, favor, gratitude:* χάρις CHARIS
1 Cor 10.30 If I partake with thankfulness
Col 3.16 sing psalms and hymns . . with thankfulness

THANKS
1. *grace, favor, gratitude:* χάρις CHARIS
Rom 6.17 t. be to God, that you who were . . slaves
7.25 Thanks . . to God through Jesus Christ!
1 Cor 15.57 t. be to God, who gives us the victory
2 Cor 2.14 t. be to God, who . . leads us in triumph
8.16 t . . to God who puts . . care . . into the heart
9.15 T. be to God for his inexpressible gift!
2. *thankfulness:* εὐχαριστία EUCHARISTIA
Rev 4. 9 whenever the living creatures give . . t.

THANKS, GIVE
1. *make a covenant, return thanks to God:* ἀνθομολογέομαι ANTHOMOLOGEOMAI*
Lk 2.38 that very hour she gave thanks to God
2. *be thankful, return thanks:* εὐχαριστέω EUCHARISTEŌ
Mt 15.36 having given thanks he broke them
26.27 took a cup, and when he had given thanks
Mk 8. 6 having given thanks he broke them
14.23 took a cup, and when he had given thanks
Lk 17.16 fell on his face . . , giving him thanks
22.17 took a cup, and when he had given thanks
22.19 when he had given thanks he broke it
Jn 6.11 when he had given t., he distributed
6.23 they ate . . after the Lord had given t.
Acts 27.35 he took bread, and giving thanks to God
Rom 1.21 did not honor him as God or give thanks
14. 6 eats in honor of the Lord, since he gives t.
14. 6 abstains in honor of the Lord and gives t.
16. 4 the churches of the Gentiles give thanks
1 Cor 1. 4 I give thanks to God[a] always for you
10.30 because of that for which I give thanks
11.24 when he had given thanks, he broke it
14.17 For you may give thanks well enough
2 Cor 1.11 many will give thanks on our behalf
Eph 1.16 I do not cease to give thanks for you
5.20 giving t. in the name of our Lord Jesus
Col 1.12 giving thanks to the Father
3.17 giving thanks to God the Father
1 Th 1. 2 We give t. to God always for you all
5.18 give thanks in all circumstances
2 Th 1. 3 We are bound to give thanks to God
2.13 bound to give t. to God always for you
Rev 11.17 "We give t. to thee, . . God Almighty

THANKSGIVING
1. *thankfulness:* εὐχαριστία EUCHARISTIA
1 Cor 14.16 how can . . one . . say the "Amen" to your t.
2 Cor 4.15 as grace extends . . it may increase t.
9.11 generosity . . through us will produce t.
9.12 overflows in many thanksgivings to God
Eph 5. 4 but instead let there be thanksgiving
Phil 4. 6 with t. let your requests be made known
Col 2. 7 as you were taught, abounding in t.
4. 2 being watchful in it with t.
1 Th 3. 9 what t. can we render to God?
1 Tim 2. 1 I urge that . . thanksgivings be made
4. 3 foods . . to be received with thanksgiving
4. 4 nothing . . rejected if it is received with t.
Rev 7.12 "Blessing and glory and wisdom and t.!

THAT
THAT WHICH
1. *if:* ἐάν EAN
1 Cor **7.8**
2. *if, since:* εἰ EI
Acts **19.2**; **26.8**, 23[2]
Rom **1.10**
Phil **3.11**
1 Jn **3.13**
3. *that:* ἐκεῖνος EKEINOS
[a]A.2.b
Mt **3.1**; **7.22**, 25, 27; **8.13**, 28; **9.26**, 31; **10.14**, 15, 19; **11.25**; **12.1**, 45; **13.44**; **14.1**, 35[2]; **15.22**; **17.27**; **18.1**, 27, 32; **21.40**; **22.7**, 10, 46; **24.19**, 22[2], 29, 36, 38, 46, 48, 50; **25.7**, 19; **26.24**[2], 29, 55; **27.8**, 19, 63
Mk **1.9**; **2.20**; **3.24**, 35; **4.11**, 20, 35; **8.1**; **12.7**; **13.11**, 17, 19, 24[2], 32; **14.21**[2], 25
Lk **2.1**; **4.2**; **5.35**; **6.23**, 48, 49; **7.21**; **9.5**, 36; **10.12**[2], 31; **11.26**; **12.37**, 38, 43, 45, 46, 47; **13.4**; **14.24**; **15.14**, 15; **17.31**; **18.3**; **20.18**, 35; **21.23**, 34; **22.22**
Jn **1.39**; **4.39**, 53; **5.9**; **10.1**; **11.49**, 51, 53; **14.20**; **16.23**, 26; **18.13**; **19.27**, 31; **20.19**; **21.3**, 7
Acts **2.18**, 41; **3.23**; **7.41**; **8.1**, 8; **9.37**; **12.1**; **14.21**; **16.3**, 35; **19.16**, 23; **22.11**; **28.7**
Rom **6.21**
2 Cor **7.8**; **10.18**[a]
Eph **2.12**
2 Th **1.10**
2 Tim **1.12**, 18; **3.9**; **4.8**
Heb **4.11**; **6.7**; **8.7**, 10; **10.16**; **11.15**
Jas **1.7–8**; **4.15**
1 Jn **5.16**
Rev **9.6**; **11.13**
4. *in order that:* ἵνα HINA
Mt **4.14**; **5.29**, 30; **7.1**, 12; **9.6**; **14.36**; **18.14**, 16; **19.13**; **20.21**; **23.26**; **24.20**; **26.41**, 56
Mk **1.38**; **2.10**; **5.18**, 43; **6.12**, 56; **9.12**; **10.13**; **13.18**; **14.35**, 38; **15.32**
Lk **1.4**, 43; **5.24**; **6.31**; **8.12**, 16; **9.45**; **11.33**, 50; **14.23**; **15.29**; **17.2**; **18.15**; **19.15**; **20.10**, 14, 20; **21.36**; **22.8**, 30, 32, 46
Jn **1.31**; **3.15**, 16[2], 17, 21; **4.15**; **5.14**, 20, 23, 34; **6.12**, 29, 30, 39, 40, 50, 57; **7.3**; **8.6**‡, 56; **9.2**, 3, 22, 36, 39; **10.10**, 17, 38; **11.16**, 42, 50, 57; **12.36**, 38, 46; **13.15**, 18, 19, 29, 34[2]; **14.3**, 13; **15.2**, 8, 11, 12, 13, 16; **16.4**, 7, 24, 33; **17.1**, 3, 11, 12, 13, 15[2], 19, 21[2], 22, 23, 24, 26; **18.36**, 39; **19.4**, 31, 35, 36, 38; **20.31**[2]
Acts **2.25**; **5.15**; **8.19**
Rom **1.11**; **3.8**; **6.1**; **11.32**; **14.9**; **15.4**, 6, 31; **16.2**
1 Cor **1.10**; **2.5**, 12; **3.18**; **4.2**, 3, 6[2]; **5.5**, 7; **7.5**; **9.18**, 19, 20, 21, 22[2], 23, 24; **10.33**; **12.25**; **13.**[3†‡; **14.1**; **15.28**; **16.10**, 11
2 Cor **2.9**; **4.7**; **5.15**; **8.6**, 13; **11.12**; **12.8**, 9; **13.7**[2]
Gal **2.4**, 5, 9, 19; **3.14**[2], 22, 24; **4.17**; **6.13**
Eph **1.17**; **2.7**, 10, 15; **3.10**, 16, 17(18), 19; **4.10**, 29; **5.26**, 27[2]; **6.3**, 13, 19, 20, 21, 22
Phil **1.9**; **2.10**, 15, 28
Col **1.9**, 18, 28; **2.2**; **4.3**, 4, 8, 12, 17
1 Th **2.16**; **4.1**, 13

2 Th **1**.11; **3**.1, 2, 14
1 Tim **1**.3, 16, 18, 20; **2**.2
2 Tim **1**.4; **2**.10; **3**.17
Tit **1**.5, 13
Phm .15
Heb **2**.14; **3**.13; **4**.11, 16; **11**.35, 40
Jas **1**.4; **5**.9, 12
1 Pet **2**.2, 21, 24; **3**.9, 18; **4**.6, 13; **5**.6
2 Pet **1**.4
1 Jn **1**.4; **2**.1, 19, 27; **3**.1, 11, 23; **4**.17, 21; **5**.3, 13, 16
2 Jn .5, 6[2], 8
3 Jn .8
Rev **2**.10; **3**.18[2]; **7**.1; **11**.6; **12**.4, 14; **14**.13; **16**.15; **20**.3; **22**.14

5. *that, in order that:* ὅπως HOPŌS
Mt **2**.8, 23; **5**.16; **6**.2, 5, 16, 18; **23**.35; **26**.59
Lk **2**.35
Acts **3**.19; **8**.15, 24; **9**.17; **15**.17; **25**.26
Rom **3**.4
2 Cor **8**.14
Phm .6
Jas **5**.16
1 Pet **2**.9

6. *who, which, what:* ὅς HOS
Mt **10**.26[2]; **15**.16; **20**.22
Mk **3**.17; **7**.11, 34; **10**.38, 39; **15**.42
Lk **1**.20; **5**.21; **8**.17[2]; **11**.27; **12**.2[2]; **15**.16; **19**.37; **21**.4; **23**.29[2]; **24**.25
Jn **1**.3†, [4†, 9; **3**.2; **4**.5, 14, 29, 38, 39, 50; **5**.20; **6**.37, 39, 63, 64; **10**.16, 25; **12**.48; **14**.12, 26; **15**.20; **16**.17; **21**.10
Acts **1**.1; **2**.32; **3**.21; **7**.16, 44; **10**.39[2]; **19**.40; **20**.18; **21**.19; **22**.10; **23**.19
Rom **2**.16; **7**.6; **14**.21, 22
1 Cor **4**.7; **10**.30
2 Cor **1**.6; **2**.4
Gal **1**.8, 9
Eph **3**.20; **5**.5
Col **1**.24[2]
2 Th **3**.6
2 Tim **4**.13
Heb **7**.2, 14; **8**.9, 10; **10**.10, 16
1 Jn **1**.1, 3; **5**.10
Rev **13**.2; **17**.8, 11, 12, 15, 16, 18; **21**.17

7. *as, so:* ὡς HŌS
Lk **16**.1
Acts **17**.22
Rom **1**.9

8. *as great as, how great:* ὅσος HOSOS
Mt **13**.46; **18**.25; **28**.20
Mk **6**.30
Lk **18**.12, 22
Jn **4**.45; **10**.41; **16**.15; **17**.7
Jude .10

9. *so that, therefore:* ὥστε HŌSTE
Lk **4**.29; **12**.1
Jn **3**.16
Acts **14**.1
2 Cor **1**.8; **3**.7

10. *anyone who, whoever:* ὅστις HOSTIS
[a]+ ἄν
Mt **27**.62
Acts **3**.23[a]
1 Cor **5**.1
1 Tim **6**.9
2 Tim **1**.5
1 Pet **2**.11
Rev **1**.12

11. *that, because:* ὅτι HOTI
Mt **2**.16, 22; **4**.12; **5**.17, 21, 22, 23, 27, 28, 32, 33, 38, 43; **6**.32; **8**.27; **9**.6, 28; **10**.34; **11**.24, 25; **15**.12, 17; **16**.11, 12, 20, 21; **17**.10, 12, 13; **18**.10; **19**.4; **20**.25, 30; **21**.45; **22**.16, 34; **23**.31; **24**.32, 33, 43; **25**.26; **26**.2, 53, 54; **27**.3, 18, 24; **28**.5, 7
Mk **2**.8, 10, 16; **4**.41; **5**.29; **7**.2, 18; **8**.31; **9**.13, 25; **10**.42, 47; **11**.23, 24, 32; **12**.12, 14, 19, 28, 32, 34, 35; **13**.28, 29; **15**.10, 39; **16**.4, 7, 11‡
Lk **1**.22, 45†, 58; **2**.49[2]; **5**.24; **7**.37; **8**.25, 47, 53; **9**.7, 8[2], 19; **10**.11, 20[2], 21, 24, 40; **11**.38; **12**.30, 39, 51; **13**.2, 4; **16**.25; **17**.15; **18**.9, 11; **19**.11, 22, 26; **20**.19, 21, 37; **21**.20, 31(30), 31; **22**.18, 37, 70; **23**.7; **24**.7, 21, 39, 44
Jn **1**.34; **2**.17, 22; **3**.2, 7, 19, 21, 28, 33; **4**.1[2], 19, 20, 25, 27, 42, 44, 47, 51, 53; **5**.6, 15, 32, 36, 42, 45; **6**.5, 15, 22[2], 24, 36, 46, 61, 65, 69; **7**.22, 26, 35, 42, 52; **8**.17, 24[2], 27, 28, 37, 47, 48, 52, 54; **9**.18, 20[2], 24, 25, 29, 31, 32, 35; **10**.38; **11**.6, 13, 15, 20, 22, 24, 27, 31, 40, 41, 42[2], 50, 51, 56; **12**.6, 9, 12, 16, 18, 19, 34[2], 50; **13**.1, 3[2], 19, 29, 35; **14**.2, 10, 11, 20, 22, 31; **15**.18; **16**.4, 15, 19, 21, 26, 27, 30[2]; **17**.7, 8[2], 21, 23, 25; **18**.8, 14, 37; **19**.4, 10, 28, 35; **20**.9, 14, 31; **21**.4, 7, 15, 16, 17, 23[2], 24
Acts **2**.29, 30, 31, 36; **3**.17; **4**.10, 13[2], 16; **5**.4, 9, 41; **6**.14; **7**.6, 25; **8**.14, 18; **9**.22, 26, 38; **10**.34, 42; **11**.1; **12**.3, 9, 11; **13**.32(33), 38; **14**.9, 22; **15**.7, 24; **16**.3, 10, 19, 38; **17**.3, 13; **19**.25, 26[2], 34; **20**.23[2], 25, 26, 29, 31, 34, 35, 38; **21**.21, 22, 24, 29, 31; **22**.2, 19; **23**.6, 22, 27, 34; **24**.14, 26; **25**.16; **26**.5, 27; **27**.10, 25; **28**.1, 22, 28
Rom **1**.13, 32; **2**.2, 3, 4; **3**.19; **4**.21; **5**.3; **6**.3, 6, 8, 9, 16, 17; **7**.1, 14, 16, 18, 21; **8**.16, 18, 22, [27†, 28, 38; **9**.2, 30; **10**.2, 5, 9; **14**.14; **15**.14, 29
1 Cor **1**.5, 11, 12, 14, 15; **3**.16, 20; **5**.6; **6**.2, 3, 9, 15, 16, 19; **7**.26; **8**.1, 4; **9**.13, 24; **10**.1, 19[2], 20; **11**.3, 14, 23; **12**.2, 3; **14**.23, 25, 37; **15**.3, 4[2], 5, 12, 15, 27, 58; **16**.15
2 Cor **1**.10, 12, 14, 24; **2**.3; **3**.3, 5; **4**.14; **5**.1, 6, 14; **7**.3, 8; **8**.9; **10**.7, 11; **11**.31; **12**.3(4), 13, 19; **13**.2, 5, 6
Gal **1**.6, 11; **2**.7, 14, 16; **3**.7, 8[2], 11; **4**.13, 15; **5**.2, 3, 10, 21
Eph **2**.11, 12; **4**.9; **5**.5; **6**.8, 9
Phil **1**.6, 12, 16, 18, 19, 20, 25, 27; **2**.11, 16, 24, 26; **3**.12; **4**.10, 11, 15, 17
Col **3**.24; **4**.1, 13
1 Th **2**.1, 13; **3**.3, 4, 6; **4**.14, 15; **5**.2
2 Th **2**.2, 5; **3**.4
1 Tim **1**.8, 9, 15; **4**.1; **6**.[7‡
2 Tim **1**.12, 15; **2**.23; **3**.1
Tit **3**.11
Phm .21
Heb **2**.6; **3**.19; **7**.8, 14; **11**.6, 13, 14, 19; **12**.17; **13**.18
Jas **1**.3, 7; **2**.19, 20, 22, 24; **4**.4, 5; **5**.20
1 Pet **1**.12, 18
2 Pet **1**.14, 20; **3**.3, 5, 8
1 Jn **1**.5; **2**.3, 5, [8†, 18[2], 19, 21, 22, 29[2]; **3**.1, 2, 5, 14, 15, 16, 19, 24; **4**.3, 9, 10[2], 13, 14, 15; **5**.1, 2, 5, 9, 11, 13, 14, 15[2], 18, 19, 20
Jude .5
Rev **2**.4, 20, 23; **3**.8, 9; **5**.4; **10**.6; **11**.17; **12**.12, 13

12. *this:* οὗτος HOUTOS
Mt **27**.46
Mk **7**.2
Lk **1**.39; **8**.21; **12**.4; **13**.32; **17**.34; **20**.16
Jn **5**.19
Acts **1**.15, 19; **7**.7; **13**.20; **19**.4
Rom **1**.12; **7**.18; **10**.6, 7, 8
1 Cor **6**.4, 6, 8; **12**.23; **16**.3
Gal **2**.18; **6**.7, 12
Phil **1**.18, 22; **3**.15
2 Th **3**.14
Phm .18
Heb **2**.14, 15; **3**.10; **7**.5; **9**.11, 27; **10**.20; **11**.16; **13**.11, 15, 17
1 Pet **1**.25; **3**.20; **4**.16
2 Pet **2**.19
3 Jn .10
Jude .10
Rev **20**.3

13. *thus, so:* οὕτως HOUTŌS [A.4.a]
Acts **13**.8

14. *lest perhaps:* μή πως MĒ [A.4.e]
2 Cor **11**.3; **12**.20[2]

15. *lest perhaps:* μή που POU II [A.5.a, b]
Acts **27**.29

16. *such as this:* τοιοῦτος TOIOUTOS
1 Cor **7**.28

THAT, AND

1. *anyone who, whoever:* ὅστις HOSTIS
1 Cor **3**.17

THAT, AS FOR THE FACT
THAT, THE FACT
1. *that, because:* ὅτι HOTI [B.3.b.2]
Mt **16.**8
Mk **8.**17
Acts **13.**34

THAT, CAN IT BE
THAT HOW, IS
1. *thus, so:* οὕτως HOUTŌS
[a]interrog.
Jn 18.22 [a]"Is that how you answer the high priest?
1 Cor 6. 5 [a]Can it be that there is no man . . wise?

THAT, IN ORDER
1. *for the sake of:* ἕνεκα HENEKA
2 Cor 7.12 in order that your zeal . . be revealed
2. *in order that:* ἵνα HINA
Acts **4.**17
Rom **1.**13; **4.**16; **7.**4, 13; **8.**4, 17; **9.**11; **11.**31
1 Cor **11.**19
2 Cor **13.**10
Gal **1.**16; **6.**12
Phil **3.**8
Col **2.**4
Phm .13, 14
Heb **12.**27; **13.**19
1 Pet **4.**11
3. *that, in order that:* ὅπως HOPŌS
Lk 16.26 " 'in order that . . who would pass . . may not

THAT SAME
1. *that one:* ἐκεῖνος EKEINOS
Mt 13. 1 That same day Jesus went out of the house
18.28 "that same servant, as he went out

THAT, SEE
1. *in order that:* ἵνα (as imper.) HINA
2 Cor **8.**7
Col **4.**16
Tit **3.**13

THAT, SO (*See* SO THAT)

THAT WAY
1. *that, that one:* ἐκεῖνος (gen.) EKEINOS
Lk 19. 4 for he was to pass that way

THAT WHICH (*See* THAT)

THE
1. *the:* ὁ HO

THEATER
1. *theater, spectacle:* θέατρον THEATRON
Acts 19.29 they rushed together into the theater
19.31 begged him not to venture into the t.

THEE
1. *you, thou:* σύ SY
Mt **11.**25, [26†; **25.**37, 38, 39², 44²
Mk **1.**11; **14.**36
Lk **3.**22‡; **10.**21, [21†; **18.**11
Jn **11.**41; **17.**1, 3, 4, 5, 7, 8, 11, 13, 21, 25²
Acts **13.**33; **22.**19
Rom **15.**3, 9
Heb **1.**5, 9; **2.**12; **5.**5
Rev **11.**17; **15.**4; **18.**14², 22³, 23²

THEFT
1. *thing stolen, fraud:* κλέμμα KLEMMA*
Rev 9.21 nor did they repent of . . their thefts
2. *theft:* κλοπή KLOPĒ*
Mt 15.19 "out of the heart come evil thoughts, . . t.
Mk 7.21 "out of the heart . . come evil thoughts, . . t.

THEIR (*See also* THEY)
1. *himself:* ἑαυτοῦ (pl.) HEAUTOU
Mt 21. 8 Most of the crowd spread t. garments
25. 1 "ten maidens who took their lamps
25. 4 "the wise took . . oil with their lamps
25. 7 "maidens rose and trimmed their lamps
Lk 12.36 "like men who are waiting for t. master
16. 4 " 'that people . . receive me into t. houses
19.36 they spread their garments on the road
Acts 14.14 they tore their garments and rushed
16. 4 who risked their necks for my life
Eph 5.28 Even so husbands should love t. wives
1 Tim 6.10 some have . . pierced t. hearts with . . pangs
2. *one's own:* ἴδιος IDIOS
1 Cor 14.35 let them ask their husbands at home
1 Tim 3.12 let them manage . . their households well
6. 1 Let all . . regard their masters as worthy
Tit 2. 5 kind, and submissive to their husbands
2. 9 slaves to be submissive to their masters
1 Pet 3. 5 women . . were submissive to their husbands

THEIR FRIENDS
1. *one's own:* ἴδιος (subst. pl.) IDIOS
Acts 4.23 they went to their friends

THEIR OWN
1. *himself:* ἑαυτοῦ HEAUTOU
Mt 8.22 "leave the dead to bury their own dead
Lk 2.39 they returned . . to their own city, Nazareth
9.60 "Leave the dead to bury their own dead
16. 8 "dealing with their own generation
Rom 1.27 receiving in t. own persons the . . penalty
16.18 such persons . . serve . . their own appetites[z]
Eph 5.28 love their wives as their own bodies
Phil 2.21 They all look after their own interests
2 Th 3.12 exhort . . to earn their own living
Heb 6. 6 crucify the Son . . on their own account
Jude . 6 angels that did not keep t. own position
.13 casting up the foam of their own shame
.18 "following their own ungodly passions
2. *one's own:* ἴδιος IDIOS
Acts 25.19 "dispute . . about their own superstition
Rom 10. 3 seeking to establish t. own . . righteousness
11.24 grafted back into their own olive tree
1 Tim 5. 4 religious duty to their own family
2 Tim 4. 3 teachers to suit their own likings
Tit 1.12 One of themselves, a prophet of their own
2 Pet 3. 3 scoffing, following their own passions
3.16 the ignorant . . twist to t. own destruction

THEIR PROPER
1. *one's own:* ἴδιος IDIOS
Jude . 6 the angels that . . left their proper dwelling

THEM (*See also* THEY)
1. *himself:* ἑαυτοῦ HEAUTOU
Mt 15.30 crowds . . bringing with them the lame
25. 3 "the foolish . . took no oil with them
Mk 8.14 they had only one loaf with them
9. 8 they no longer saw any one with them
Jn 19.24 "They parted my garments among them
Acts 20.30 "to draw away the disciples after them

THEMSELVES
1. *one another:* ἀλλήλων ALLĒLŌN
Lk 20.14 "said to themselves, 'This is the heir
Jn 6.52 Jews then disputed among themselves
Acts 28.25 as they disagreed among themselves
2. *himself:* ἑαυτοῦ (pl.) HEAUTOU
Mt 9. 3 some of the scribes said to themselves
14.15 "send the crowds . . to . . buy food for t.
16. 7 "they discussed it among themselves
19.12 "who have made themselves eunuchs
21.38 "said to themselves, 'This is the heir
Mk 1.27 they questioned among themselves
2. 8 they thus questioned within themselves
4.17 "they have no root in themselves
6.36 "send them away, to . . buy t. something
9.10 So they kept the matter to themselves
14. 4 some . . said to themselves indignantly
Lk 7.30 (rejected the purpose of God for t.
7.49 began to say among themselves
18. 9 trusted in t. that they were righteous
Jn 11.55 went up . . to Jerusalem . . to purify t.
17.13 "that they . . have my joy fulfilled in t.
Acts 23.12 bound t. . . neither to eat nor drink
23.21 "bound t. . . neither to eat nor drink
[28.29 *holding much dispute among themselves*‡
Rom 2.14 they are a law to themselves
1 Cor 16.15 devoted t. to the service of the saints

2 Cor 5.15 that those who live . . live no longer for t.
8. 5 first they gave t. to the Lord
10.12 some of those who commend themselves
10.12 when they measure themselves by one another, and compare t.
Eph 4.19 they . . have given t. up to licentiousness
1 Tim 2. 9 women should adorn t. modestly
3.13 those . . gain a good standing for t.
6.19 laying up for t. a good foundation
2 Tim 4. 3 they will accumulate for t. teachers
1 Pet 1.12 they were serving not t. but you
3. 5 So . . the holy women . . used to adorn t.
2 Pet 2. 1 bringing upon t. swift destruction
Jude .12 carouse together, looking after t.
Rev 2. 2 " 'those who call t. apostles but are not

THEMSELVES, BY

1. *only, alone:* *μόνος* MONOS [A.3.b.1]
Mk 9. 2 Jesus . . led them . . apart by themselves
Lk [24.12 *he saw the linen cloths by themselves*‡

IDIOMATICALLY
a. Mk 6.32 And they went away . . by themselves *καὶ ἀπῆλθον . . κατ' ἰδίαν* [IDIOS]

THEN

1. *but:* ἀλλά ALLA
Mt **11.**8, 9
Lk **7.**25, 26
2. *then:* ἄρα ARA II
[a]*ἄρα γε* [b]*ἄρα οὖν*
Mt 12.28 "then the kingdom of God has come
17.26 [a]Jesus said . . , "Then the sons are free
19.25 "Who then can be saved?"
19.27 "What then shall we have?
24.45 "Who t. is the faithful and wise servant?
Mk 4.41 "Who then is this, that . . wind and sea obey?
Lk 1.66 "What then will this child be?
8.25 "Who then is this, that he commands?
11.20 "then the kingdom of God has come
12.42 "Who t. is the faithful and wise steward?
Acts 11.18 "T. to the Gentiles also God has granted
21.38 "Are you not the Egyptian, then?
Rom 5.18 [b]Then as one man's trespass led
14.19 [b]Let us then pursue what makes for peace
1 Cor 5.10 t. you would need to go out of the world
15.14 then our preaching is in vain
15.18 T. those . . asleep in Christ have perished
Gal 2.21 then Christ died to no purpose
3.29 then you are Abraham's offspring
Heb 12. 8 then you are illegitimate children
3. (interrog. particle): ἆρα ARA III
Gal 2.17 is Christ then an agent of sin?
4. *therefore:* *διό* DIO
2 Cor 12.10 For the sake of Christ, t., I am content
5. *if not, except:* *εἰ μή* EI MĒ
Mt 6. 1 "for then you will have no reward
6. *then, next:* *εἶτα* EITA
[a]*εἶτεν*
Mk 4.17 "t., when tribulation or persecution arises
4.28 [a]"first the blade, then the ear, then the full grain in the ear
8.25 T. again he laid his hands upon his eyes
Lk 8.12 "then the devil comes and takes away
Jn 13. 5 Then he poured water into a basin
19.27 Then he said to the disciple, "Behold!
20.27 T. he said to Thomas, "Put your finger
1 Cor 15. 5 he appeared to Cephas, then to the twelve
15. 7 he appeared to James, then to all
15.24 T. comes the end, when he delivers
1 Tim 2.13 For Adam was formed first, then Eve
3.10 then if they prove themselves blameless
Jas 1.15 Then desire when it has conceived
7. *thereupon:* *ἔπειτα* EPEITA*
Lk 16. 7 "T. he said to another, 'And how much?
Jn 11. 7 Then after this he said to the disciples
1 Cor 12.28 then workers of miracles, then healers
15. 6 T. he appeared to more than five hundred
15. 7 Then he appeared to James
15.23 then at his coming those who belong
15.46 first . . the physical, and then the spiritual
Gal 1.18 T. after three years I went . . to Jerusalem
1.21 Then I went into the regions of Syria
2. 1 Then after fourteen years I went up
1 Th 4.17 then we who are alive, who are left
Heb 7. 2 and then he is also king of Salem
7.27 first for his own sins and t. for those
Jas 3.17 then peaceable, gentle, open to reason
4.14 a mist that appears . . and then vanishes
8. *for:* *γάρ* GAR
Phil **1.**18
9. *this:* *οὗτος* HOUTOS [B.1.a.1]
[a]*ἐπὶ τούτῳ at this* [b]*μετὰ τοῦτο after this*
[c]*διὰ τοῦτο because of this*
Jn **4.**27[a]; **11.**11[b]
Rev **12.**12[c]
10. *thus, so:* *οὕτως* HOUTŌS
[a]*οὐδ' οὕτως*
Mk 7.18 "T. are you also without understanding?
1 Cor 14.21 [a]"even then they will not listen to me
11. *and from there:* *κἀκεῖθεν* KAKEITHEN
Acts 13.21 "Then they asked for a king
12. *remaining, left:* *λοιπός* (neut.) LOIPOS
Heb 10.13 ⟨sat down⟩ then to wait until his enemies
13. *after this:* *μετὰ τοῦτο* META [B.1.a.1]
Jn 11.11 Thus he spoke, and then he said to them
14. *so, therefore:* *οὖν* OUN
Mt **5.**19; **6.**9, 23; **7.**11, 24; **12.**26; **13.**18, 27, 28, 56; **17.**10; **19.**7; **21.**25; **22.**17, 43; **25.**27; **26.**54; **27.**22
Mk **11.**31; **15.**12
Lk **3.**10; **4.**7; **7.**31; **8.**18; **10.**40; **11.**13, 36; **12.**26; **16.**11, 27; **20.**15, 17; **22.**70
Jn **1.**21, 22, 25; **2.**18, 20; **6.**5, 11, 15, 21, 28, 30, 32, 41, 52, 62; **7.**33, 45; **8.**13, 22, 31, 57; **9.**10, 19; **11.**32, 38; **12.**19, 28; **13.**14; **18.**4, 10, 19, 24, 28; **19.**16, 21; **20.**3, 6, 10, 20
Acts **5.**41; **10.**29; **11.**17; **17.**29; **19.**3, 36; **21.**22; **25.**11; **28.**28
Rom **2.**21; **3.**1, 9, 27, 31; **4.**1, 10; **5.**18; **6.**1, 15; **7.**7, 13; **8.**31; **9.**14, 19, 30; **11.**1, 7, 13, 22; **13.**12; **14.**13, 19; **15.**17
1 Cor **3.**5; **4.**16; **6.**4; **9.**18; **10.**19; **14.**26; **15.**11
Gal **3.**19, 21
Eph **5.**15
Col **3.**1, 12
1 Tim **2.**1, 8
2 Tim **1.**8; **2.**1, 21
Heb **4.**14, 16; **13.**15
Rev **2.**5, 16; **3.**3
15. *and, both . . . and:* *τέ* TE
Acts **16.**34; **21.**30; **26.**30; **27.**17
Rom **14.**8
16. *therefore:* *τοίνυν* TOINYN
Lk 20.25 "T. render to Caesar the things that are
17. *then, formerly:* *τότε* TOTE
Mt 2. 7 T. Herod summoned . . wise men secretly
2.16 T. Herod, when . . he had been tricked
2.17 Then was fulfilled what was spoken
3. 5 Then went out to him Jerusalem
3.13 T. Jesus came from Galilee to the Jordan
3.15 "Let it be so now . ." Then he consented
4. 1 Then Jesus was led up by the Spirit
4. 5 T. the devil took him to the holy city
4.10 Then Jesus said to him, "Begone
4.11 Then the devil left him, and behold
5.24 "then come and offer your gift
7. 5 "t. you will see clearly to take the speck out
7.23 "t. will I declare to them, 'I never knew
8.26 Then he rose and rebuked the winds
9. 6 he then said to the paralytic—"Rise
9.14 Then the disciples of John came to him
9.15 "bridegroom is taken . . , t. they will fast
9.29 Then he touched their eyes, saying
9.37 Then he said . . "The harvest is plentiful
11.20 Then he began to upbraid the cities
12.13 Then he said . . "Stretch out your hand
12.22 Then a blind and dumb demoniac
12.29 "Then indeed he may plunder his house
12.38 Then some . . said . . "we wish to see a sign

Mt 12.44 “T. he says, ‘I will return to my house
12.45 “Then he . . brings . . seven other spirits
13.26 “plants came up . . , t. the weeds appeared
13.36 Then he left the crowds and went
13.43 “T. the righteous will shine like the sun
15. 1 T. . . scribes came to Jesus from Jerusalem
15.12 Then the disciples came and said to him
15.28 Then Jesus answered her, “O woman
16.12 T. they understood that he did not tell
16.20 Then he strictly charged the disciples
16.24 T. Jesus told . . “If any man would come
16.27 “then he will repay every man
17.13 Then the disciples understood
17.19 T. the disciples came to Jesus privately
18.21 Then Peter came up and said to him
18.32 “Then his lord summoned him and said
19.13 Then children were brought to him
19.27 Then Peter said . . “we have left everything
20.20 Then the mother of the sons of Zebedee
21. 1 then Jesus sent two disciples
22. 8 “Then he said . . ‘The wedding is ready
22.13 “Then the king said to the attendants
22.15 T. the Pharisees went and took counsel
22.21 Then he said . . “Render . . to Caesar
23. 1 Then said Jesus to the crowds
24. 9 “T. they will deliver you up to tribulation
24.10 “And then many will fall away[y]
24.14 “and then the end will come
24.16 “then let those who are in Judea flee
24.21 “then there will be great tribulation
24.23 “Then if any one says to you
24.30 “t. will appear the sign of the Son of man in heaven, and t. all . . will mourn
24.40 “Then two men will be in the field
25. 1 “Then the kingdom . . shall be compared
25. 7 “T. all those maidens rose and trimmed
25.31 “then he will sit on his glorious throne
25.34 “T. the King will say to those at his right
25.37 “T. the righteous will answer him, ‘Lord
25.41 “Then he will say to those at his left
25.44 “Then they also will answer, ‘Lord
25.45 “Then he will answer them, ‘Truly
26. 3 Then the chief priests and the elders
26.14 Then one of the twelve, . . Judas Iscariot
26.31 Then Jesus said . . “You will all fall away
26.36 Then Jesus went with them to a place
26.38 T. he said . . “My soul is very sorrowful
26.45 Then he came to the disciples
26.50 Then they came . . and laid hands on Jesus
26.52 Then Jesus said . . “Put your sword back
26.56 T. all the disciples forsook him and fled
26.65 Then the high priest tore his robes
26.67 T. they spat in his face, and struck him
26.74 T. he began to invoke a curse on himself
27. 9 Then was fulfilled what had been spoken
27.13 Then Pilate said . . “Do you not hear?
27.16 they had then a notorious prisoner
27.26 Then he released for them Barabbas
27.27 T. the soldiers of the governor took Jesus
27.38 T. two robbers were crucified with him
27.58 T. Pilate ordered it to be given to him
28.10 T. Jesus said to them, “Do not be afraid
Mk 2.20 “then they will fast in that day
3.27 “then indeed he may plunder his house
13.14 “then let those who are in Judea flee
13.21 “then if any one says to you, ‘Look!
13.26 “then they will see the Son of man
13.27 “then he will send out the angels
Lk 5.35 “then they will fast in those days
6.42 “take the log out . . , and then you will see
11.26 “T. he goes and brings seven other spirits
13.26 “Then you will begin to say, ‘We ate
14. 9 “then you will . . take the lowest place
14.10 “then you will be honored
14.21 “Then the householder in anger said
16.16 “since then the good news . . is preached
21.10 Then he said to them, “Nation will rise
Lk 21.20 “t. know . . its desolation has come near
21.21 “Then let those who are in Judea flee
21.27 “then they will see the Son of man
23.30 “T. they will . . say to . . mountains, ‘Fall
24.45 T. he opened their minds to understand
Jn 7.10 then he also went up, not publicly
8.28 “then you will know that I am he
11.14 T. Jesus told them . . “Lazarus is dead
12.16 Jesus was glorified, t. they remembered
13.27 Then after the morsel, Satan entered
19. 1 Then Pilate took Jesus and scourged him
19.16 Then he handed him over to them
20. 8 Then the other disciple . . also went in
Acts 1.12 Then they returned to Jerusalem
4. 8 T. Peter, filled with the Holy Spirit
5.26 Then the captain with the officers went
6.11 Then they secretly instigated men
7. 4 “Then he departed from the land
8.17 Then they laid their hands on them
10.46 T. Peter declared, ⟨“Can any . . forbid?⟩
10.48 Then they asked him to remain
13. 3 Then . . they laid their hands on them
13.12 Then the proconsul believed
15.22 Then it seemed good to the apostles
17.14 T. the brethren . . sent Paul off on his way
21.13 T. Paul answered, “What are you doing?
21.26 T. Paul took the men, . . purified himself
21.33 T. the tribune came up and arrested him
23. 3 Then Paul said . . “God shall strike you!
25.12 T. Festus . . answered, “You have appealed
26. 1 Then Paul stretched out his hand
27.21 Paul then came forward among them
27.32 Then the soldiers cut away the ropes
28. 1 we then learned . . the island was . . Malta
Rom 6.21 But then what return did you get?
1 Cor 4. 5 T. every man will receive . . commendation
13.12 now we see in a mirror . . , but t. face to face
15.28 t. the Son himself will also be subjected
15.54 then shall come to pass the saying
2 Cor 12.10 then, I am content with weaknesses
12.10 for when I am weak, then I am strong
Gal 6. 4 t. his reason to boast will be in himself
Col 3. 4 then you . . will appear with him in glory
1 Th 5. 3 then sudden destruction will come
2 Th 2. 8 then the lawless one will be revealed
Heb 10. 7 “Then I said, ‘Lo, I have come
10. 9 then he added, “Lo, I have come
12.26 His voice then shook the earth
2 Pet 3. 6 the world that then existed was deluged

THEN, AND

1. *in which:* ἐν ᾗ HOS [B.1.a.2]
2 Pet **3.10**

THEN, FOR

1. *since, otherwise:* ἐπεί EPEI
Rom 3. 6 For then how could God judge the world?

THEN I

1. *and I:* κἀγώ KAGŌ
2 Cor 6.17 “come out . . ; then I will welcome you

THEN . . . NOT

1. *nor, and not:* οὐδέ OUDE
1 Cor 15.13 then Christ has not been raised
15.16 then Christ has not been raised

THEN, SO

1. *therefore then:* ἄρα οὖν OUN; ARA II
[a]ἄρα
Rom 7.25 So then, I of myself serve the law
8.12 So then, brethren, we are debtors
9.18 So then he has mercy upon whomever
Gal 6.10 So then, as we have opportunity
Eph 2.19 So then you are no longer strangers
1 Th 5. 6 So then let us not sleep, as others do
2 Th 2.15 So then, brethren, stand firm and hold
Heb 4. 9 [a]So then, there remains a sabbath rest

2. *so that, therefore:* ὥστε HŌSTE
1 Cor 11.33 So then . . when you come together to eat
Gal 3. 9 So then, those who are men of faith
3. *and now:* νυνὶ δέ NYNI [B.3.b.4]
Rom 7.17 So then it is no longer I that do it
4. *so, therefore:* οὖν OUN [B.3.b.4]
[a]+μέν
Mk 16.19 [a]So then the Lord Jesus . . was taken up[k]‡
Rom 14. 8 so then, whether we live or . . die

THEOPHILUS: Θεόφιλος thē'äfələs
Lk 1. 3 an orderly account . . , most excellent T.
Acts 1. 1 In the first book, O Theophilus

THERE
1. *here, there:* αὐτοῦ AUTOU
Acts 18.19 came to Ephesus, and he left them there
21. 4 we stayed there for seven days
2. *there:* ἐκεῖ EKEI
Mt 2.13 "flee to Egypt, and remain there
2.15 remained there until the death of Herod
2.22 afraid to go there, and being warned
5.24 "leave your gift there before the altar
6.21 "there will your heart be also
8.12 "t. men will weep and gnash their teeth
12.45 "seven other spirits . . enter and dwell there
13.42 "t. men will weep and gnash their teeth
13.50 "t. men will weep and gnash their teeth
13.58 he did not do many mighty works t.
14.23 When evening came he was t. alone
15.29 went up on the mountain, and sat down t.
17.20 "you will say . . 'Move from here to t.[0]
18.20 "there am I in the midst of them
19. 2 he healed them there
21.17 he went . . to Bethany and lodged there
22.11 "t. a man who had no wedding garment
22.13 " 't. men will weep and gnash their teeth
24.28 "t. the eagles[z] will be gathered together
24.51 "t. men will weep and gnash their teeth
25.30 "t. men will weep and gnash their teeth
27.36 sat down and kept watch over him there
27.55 There were also many women there
27.61 were there, sitting opposite the sepulchre
28. 7 "to Galilee; there you will see him
Mk 1.38 "Let us go on . . , that I may preach t.
2. 6 some of the scribes were sitting there
3. 1 man was there who had a withered hand
5.11 a great herd of swine was feeding there
6. 5 he could do no mighty work there
6.10 "stay there until you leave the place
6.33 ran there on foot from all the towns
11. 5 those who stood there said to them
13.21 "if any one says . . 'Look, there he is!
14.15 "upper room . . ; there prepare for us
16. 7 "to Galilee; there you will see him
Lk 2. 6 while they were t., the time came for her
6. 6 man was t. whose right hand was withered
8.32 a large herd of swine was feeding t.
9. 4 "whatever house you enter, stay there
10. 6 "if a son of peace is there
11.26 "seven other spirits . . enter and dwell t.
12.18 " 'there I will store all my grain
12.34 "there will your heart be also
13.28 "T. you will weep and gnash your teeth
15.13 "there he squandered his property
17.21 " 'Lo, here it is!' or 'There!
17.23 "And they will say to you, 'Lo, there!
17.37 "there the eagles[c] will be gathered
22.12 "upper room . . ; there make ready
23.33 there they crucified him
Jn 2. 1 Cana . . , and the mother of Jesus was t.
2. 6 six stone jars were standing there
2.12 there they stayed for a few days
3.22 there he remained with them
3.23 because . . much water there
4. 6 Jacob's well was there
4.40 he stayed there two days
5. 5 One man was there, who had been ill
Jn 6. 3 Jesus . . there sat down with his disciples
6.22 had been only one boat there
6.24 people saw that Jesus was not there
10.40 there he remained
10.42 And many believed in him there
11. 8 "you are going there again?
11.15 "for your sake I am glad that I was not t.
11.31 that she was going . . to weep there
12. 2 There they made him a supper
12. 9 the Jews learned that he was there
12.26 "there shall my servant be also
18. 2 Jesus often met there with his disciples
18. 3 Judas, procuring a band . . , went there
19.42 the tomb was close . . , they laid Jesus t.
Acts 9.33 There he found a man named Aeneas
16. 1 A disciple was there, named Timothy
17.14 but Silas and Timothy remained there
19.21 "After I have been t., I must . . see Rome
25. 9 "to go up to Jerusalem, and t. be tried
25.14 And as they stayed there many days
Rom 15.24 to be sped on my journey there by you
Tit 3.12 I have decided to spend the winter t.
Heb 7. 8 there, by one of whom it is testified
Jas 2. 3 "Stand there," or, "Sit at my feet
3.16 t. will be disorder and every vile practice
4.13 "we will go . . and spend a year there
Rev 2.14 " 'some there who hold the teaching
21.25 shall be no night there
3. *there, thither:* ἐκεῖσε EKEISE*
Acts 21. 3 for there the ship was to unload its cargo
22. 5 "to take those also who were there
4. *from that place:* ἐκεῖθεν EKEITHEN
Acts 18. 7 he left t. and went to the house of . . Titius[q]
20.13 intending to take Paul aboard there
Mk 10. 1 he left t. and went to . . region of Judea
5. *here, hither:* ἐνθάδε ENTHADE
Acts 10.18 to ask whether Simon . . was lodging there
6. *where, wherever:* ὅπου HOPOU
Jn 19.18 There they crucified him
7. *where:* οὗ HOU
Acts 28.14 T. we found brethren, and were invited
8. *in this:* ἐν τούτῳ HOUTOS [B.1.a.1]
1 Cor 7.24
9. *and there:* κἀκεῖ KAKEI
Acts 27. 6 There the centurion found a ship
10. *lie, be laid:* κεῖμαι (part.) KEIMAI
Jn 21. 9 they saw a charcoal fire there, with fish

THERE, AND
THERE TOO
1. *and there:* κἀκεῖ KAKEI
Mt 5.23 "and there remember that your brother
28.10 "and there they will see me
Mk 1.35 to a lonely place, and there he prayed
Jn 11.54 and there he stayed with the disciples
Acts 14. 7 and there they preached the gospel
17.13 they came there too, stirring up
22.10 " 'and there you will be told all . . to do
25.20 "and be tried there regarding them
2. *and from there:* κἀκεῖθεν KAKEITHEN
Acts 28.15 And the brethren t., when they heard

THERE, BE
1. *be set before, be exposed:* πρόκειμαι PROKEIMAI
2 Cor 8.12 if the readiness is there, it is acceptable

THERE, FROM
1. *from that place:* ἐκεῖθεν EKEITHEN
Mt 4.21 going on from there he saw two . . brothers
9. 9 As Jesus passed on from t., he saw a man
9.27 as Jesus passed on from t., two blind men
11. 1 he went on from there to teach
12. 9 he went on from there, and entered
12.15 Jesus, aware of this, withdrew from t.
13.53 he went away from there
14.13 he withdrew from there in a boat
15.21 Jesus went away from there and withdrew
15.29 Jesus went on from there . . along the Sea
Mk 6. 1 He went away from t. . . to his own country

Mk 7.24 from there he arose and went away
Lk 9. 4 "stay . . , and from there depart
16.26 " 'none may cross from there to us
Jn 11.54 Jesus . . went from there to the country
Acts 13. 4 from there they sailed to Cyprus
27.12 majority advised to put to sea from t.
2. *whence, where:* ὅθεν HOTHEN
Acts 28.13 And from there we made a circuit
3. *and from there:* κἀκεῖθεν KAKEITHEN
Mk 9.30 They went on from there and passed
Lk 11.53 As he went away from t., the scribes
Acts 7. 4 "God removed him from t. into this land
14.26 and from there they sailed to Antioch
16.12 and from there to Philippi
20.15 And sailing from there we came
21. 1 we came . . from there to Patara[x]
27. 4 putting to sea from there we sailed

THERE, PEOPLE
1. *local:* ἐντόπιος (subst. pl.) ENTOPIOS*
Acts 21.12 the people there begged him not to go

THERE TOO (*See* THERE, AND)

THEREBY
1. *this:* οὗτος HOUTOS [B.1.a.1]
[a]ἐν τούτῳ [b]διὰ ταύτης
1 Cor **4.4**[a]
Heb **13.2**[b]

THEREFORE
1. *for which reason:* διὰ ἣν αἰτίαν AITIA [B.1.a.1]
2 Tim 1.12 therefore I suffer as I do
Tit 1.13 Therefore rebuke them sharply
2. *for which* (reason): ἀνθ' ὧν ANTI [B.1.a.1]
Lk 12. 3 "Therefore whatever you have said[0]
3. *then:* ἄρα ARA II
Rom 8. 1 There is t. now no condemnation
2 Cor 5.14 one has died for all; t. all have died
4. *because of which:* οὗ χάριν CHARIN [B.1.a.1]
Lk 7.47 "T. I tell you, her sins, which are many
5. *so! indeed!:* δή DĒ
Acts 6. 3 "T. . . pick out from among you seven
6. *therefore:* διό DIO
Mt 27. 8 T. . . called the Field of Blood to this day
Lk 1.35 "t. . . child to be born[d] will be called holy
7. 7 "t. I did not presume to come
Acts 15.19 "Therefore . . we should not trouble
20.31 "Therefore be alert, remembering
25.26 "T. I have brought him before you
26. 3 "therefore I beg you to listen to me
27.34 "T. I urge you to take some food
Rom 1.24 T. God gave them up in the lusts
2. 1 Therefore you have no excuse, O man
13. 5 Therefore one must be subject
15. 7 therefore, as Christ has welcomed you
1 Cor 12. 3 Therefore I want you to understand
14.13 T., he who speaks in a tongue should pray
2 Cor 6.17 "T. come out from them, . . be separate
Eph 2.11 Therefore remember that . . you Gentiles
4. 8 Therefore it is said, "When he ascended
4.25 Therefore, putting away falsehood
5.14 Therefore it is said, "Awake, O sleeper
Phil 2. 9 Therefore God has highly exalted him
1 Th 3. 1 T. when we could bear it no longer
5.11 Therefore encourage one another
Heb 3. 7 T., as the Holy Spirit says, "Today
3.10 "T. I was provoked with that generation
6. 1 T. let us leave the elementary doctrine
11.12 T. from one man, . . him as good as dead
11.16 T. God is not ashamed to be . . their God
12.12 Therefore lift your drooping hands
12.28 T. let us be grateful for . . a kingdom
Jas 1.21 Therefore put away all filthiness
4. 6 t. it says, "God opposes the proud
1 Pet 1.13 Therefore gird up your minds, be sober
2 Pet 1.10 T., brethren, be the more zealous
1.12 T. I intend always to remind you
3.14 T., beloved, since you wait for these
7. *therefore:* διόπερ DIOPER*
1 Cor 8.13 T., if food is a cause of . . falling
10.14 T., my beloved, shun . . worship of idols
8. *because, since:* διότι DIOTI
Acts 13.35 "Therefore he says also in another psalm
20.26 "Therefore I testify to you this day
9. *so that, therefore:* ὥστε HŌSTE
Rom 13. 2 Therefore he who resists the authorities
1 Cor 4. 5 Therefore do not pronounce judgment
5. 8 Let us, therefore, celebrate the festival
10.12 T. let any one who thinks that he stands
11.27 Whoever, therefore, eats the bread
15.58 T., my beloved brethren, be steadfast
2 Cor 5.16 From now on, t., we regard no one
5.17 Therefore, if any one is in Christ
Phil 2.12 T., . . beloved, as you have always obeyed
4. 1 T., my brethren, whom I love and long for
1 Th 4.18 T. comfort one another with these words
2 Th 1. 4 T. we . . boast of you in . . churches of God
1 Pet 4.19 T. let those who suffer . . do right
10. *whence, where:* ὅθεν HOTHEN
Heb 2.17 T. he had to be made like his brethren
3. 1 T., holy brethren, . . consider Jesus
1 Jn 2.18 therefore we know that it is the last hour
11. *because of this:* διὰ τοῦτο HOUTOS [B.1.a.1]
Mt **6**.25; **12**.27, 31; **13**.52; **18**.23; **21**.43; **23**.[14‡, 34; **24**.44
Mk **11**.24
Lk **11**.19, 49; **12**.22; **14**.20
Jn **9**.23; **12**.39; **15**.19; **16**.15; **19**.11
Acts **2**.26
Rom **5**.12; **15**.9
1 Cor **4**.17
2 Cor **4**.1; **7**.13
Eph **5**.17; **6**.13
2 Th **2**.11
2 Tim **2**.10
Heb **1**.9; **2**.1; **9**.15
1 Jn **4**.5
Rev **7**.15
12. *so, therefore:* οὖν OUN
Mt **3**.10; **5**.48; **6**.31, 34; **9**.38; **10**.31; **19**.6; **21**.40; **22**.9, 21, 28; **24**.42; **25**.13; **27**.64; **28**.19
Mk **10**.9; **13**.35
Lk **3**.7, 9; **10**.2; **11**.35; **14**.33; **19**.12; **20**.33; **21**.14; **23**.16, 22
Jn **2**.22; **3**.29; **4**.48; **7**.25; **8**.19; **11**.45, 54; **12**.50; **19**.10
Acts **2**.30; 33, 36; **3**.19; **8**.22; **10**.32, 33; **13**.38, 40; **15**.10, 27; **16**.11, 36; **17**.12, 20, 23; **19**.38; **21**.23; **23**.15; **25**.17; **28**.20
Rom **5**.1, 9; **6**.4, 12; **12**.1; **13**.10; **15**.28
1 Cor **6**.15; **14**.23
2 Cor **5**.11
Gal **5**.1
Eph **4**.1; **5**.1, 7; **6**.14
Phil **2**.23, 28
Col **2**.6, 16; **3**.5
Heb **2**.14; **4**.1, 6, 11; **10**.19, 35
Jas **4**.4, 7; **5**.7, 16
1 Pet **2**.7; **4**.1, 7; **5**.6
2 Pet **3**.17
13. *for that very reason:* τοιγαροῦν TOIGAROUN*
1 Th 4. 8 Therefore whoever disregards this
Heb 12. 1 T., since we are surrounded by so great
14. *therefore:* τοίνυν TOINYN
Heb 13.13 Therefore let us go forth to him
CONTEXTUALLY
1 Cor **1**.31
Rev **3**.18

THEREON
1. *on them:* ἐπάνω αὐτῶν EPANŌ
Mt 21. 7 brought the ass and the colt . . and he sat t.

THESSALONIAN: Θεσσαλονικεύς (*See also* THESSALONICA 2)
Acts 20. 4 of the Thessalonians, Aristarchus
1 Th 1. 1 To the church of the Thessalonians
2 Th 1. 1 To the church of the Thessalonians

THESSALONICA: ˌthesələˈnīkə II,D-3
1. *Thessalonica:* Θεσσαλονίκη
Acts 17. 1 they came to Thessalonica

Acts 17.11 Jews were more noble than those in T.
17.13 when the Jews of Thessalonica learned
Phil 4.16 even in Thessalonica you sent me help[f]
2 Tim 4.10 Demas . . has deserted me and gone to T.
2. *Thessalonian:* Θεσσαλονικεύς [A.3.a.2]
Acts 27. 2 Aristarchus . . from Thessalonica

THEUDAS: Θευδᾶς 'th(y)üdəs
Acts 5.36 "For before these days Theudas arose

THEY (*For entry* 2, *and for* IDIOS, *not represented here, see also* THEIR; THEM)
1. *self; he, she, it:* αὐτός AUTOS
2. *that:* ἐκεῖνος EKEINOS
Mt **13**.11; **20**.4
Mk **16**.13‡, 20‡
Jn **5**.39; **10**.6, 35; **11**.13; **19**.15; **20**.13
Acts **10**.9; **21**.6
1 Cor **9**.25; **10**.11; **15**.11
2 Cor **8**.14[2]
Heb **4**.2; **12**.25
3. *himself:* ἑαυτοῦ HEAUTOU
Rev 2. 9 " 'who say that they are Jews and are not
3. 9 " 'who say that they are Jews and are not
4. *who, which, what:* ὅς HOS
Acts **1**.3; **17**.34; **22**.5; **24**.19; **25**.16; **28**.10, 15, 23
Rom **3**.8
2 Cor **11**.15
Gal **2**.5
Phil **3**.19[2]
Col **1**.27
1 Tim **1**.20
2 Tim **3**.15
Tit **1**.11
Heb **13**.7
1 Pet **1**.12; **2**.8; **4**.5
2 Pet **2**.2, 3, 17; **3**.16
3 Jn .6
5. *this:* οὗτος HOUTOS
Mt **11**.7; Mk **11**.28; Jn **6**.9; **10**.25; Acts **25**.20; Rom **11**.30; Col **3**.7; 1 Tim **4**.15; 2 Tim **3**.6; 2 Pet **2**.20; Rev **22**.8
6. *and that one:* κἀκεῖνος KAKEINOS
Acts 15.11 "we shall be saved . . , just as they will
1 Cor 10. 6 warnings . . not to desire evil as they did
Heb 4. 2 good news came to us just as to them

THEY ALSO
THEY, AND
THEY, BUT
1. *anyone who, whoever:* ὅστις HOSTIS
Col 4.11 and they have been a comfort to me
2. *and that one:* κἀκεῖνος KAKEINOS
Mk **12**.4; **16**.11‡, 13‡; Jn **10**.16; **17**.24; Acts **18**.19

THEY, FOR
1. *anyone who, whoever:* ὅστις HOSTIS
Acts 17.11 for they received the word with . . eagerness
Phil 4. 3 for they have labored side by side with me

THIEF
1. *thief, cheat:* κλέπτης KLEPTĒS*
Mt 6.19 "earth, . . where thieves break in and steal
6.20 "heaven, . . where thieves do not break in
24.43 "what part of the night the t. was coming
Lk 12.33 "the heavens . . , where no thief approaches
12.39 "at what hour the thief was coming
Jn 10. 1 "that man is a thief and a robber
10. 8 "All who came before me are thieves
10.10 "The thief comes only to steal and kill
12. 6 This he said . . because he was a thief
1 Cor 6.10 nor thieves . . will inherit the kingdom
1 Th 5. 2 day of the Lord will come like a thief
5. 4 for that day to surprise you like a thief
1 Pet 4.15 But let none of you suffer as . . a thief
2 Pet 3.10 day of the Lord will come like a thief
Rev 3. 3 " 'I will come like a thief
16.15 ("Lo, I am coming like a thief!
2. *steal:* κλέπτω (subst. part.) KLEPTŌ
Eph 4.28 Let the thief no longer steal

THIGH
1. *thigh:* μηρός MĒROS*
Rev 19.16 on his thigh he has a name inscribed

THINE
1. *your, thy:* σός SOS
[a]subst. neut. [b]pred.
Lk 22.42 [a]"nevertheless not my will, but thine
Jn 17. 6 [b]"t. they were, and thou gavest them to me
17. 9 [b]"I am praying for them; . . for they are t.
17.10 [ba]"all mine are thine, and thine are mine, and I am glorified in them
2. *you, thou:* σύ SY
Mt **6**.[13‡

THING
1. *work, deed:* ἔργον ERGON
Mt 26.10 "For she has done a beautiful thing to me
Mk 14. 6 "She has done a beautiful thing to me
2. *thing, deed:* πρᾶγμα PRAGMA
Lk 1. 1 to compile a narrative of the things
Heb 6.18 through two unchangeable things
11. 1 faith is . . assurance of things hoped for
3. *word, saying:* ῥῆμα RHĒMA
Lk 1.65 all these things were talked about
2.15 "Let us . . see this t. that has happened
2.19 Mary kept all these things, pondering
2.51 mother kept . . these things in her heart
Acts 5.32 "And we are witnesses to these things
13.42 that these things might be told them
2 Cor 12. 4 he heard things that cannot be told
4. *vessel, tackle:* σκεῦος SKEUOS
Acts 10.16 the thing was taken up at once to heaven
IDIOMATICALLY
a. Rev 16.3 and every living thing died *καὶ πᾶσα ψυχὴ ζωῆς ἀπέθανεν* [PSYCHĒ]

THING I DO, ONE
THING, ONE
1. *one:* εἷς (neut.) HEIS
Mk 10.21 "You lack one t.; go, sell what you have
Lk 10.42 "⟨Martha,⟩ one thing is needful[j]‡
18.22 "One thing you still lack. Sell all
Jn 9.25 "one thing I know, that . . now I see
Phil 3.13 one t. I do, forgetting what lies behind
2. *anyone, any:* τὶς (neut.) TIS II
Acts **19**.32; **21**.34

THINK (*See also* BEST, THINK)
THINK ABOUT
THINK OF
THINK OVER
1. *calculate, argue:* διαλογίζομαι DIALOGIZOMAI
Lk 12.17 "he thought to himself, 'What shall I do?
2. *think, suppose:* δοκέω DOKEŌ
Mt 6. 7 "for they think that they will be heard
17.25 Jesus spoke . . "What do you think, Simon?
18.12 "What do you think? If a man has . . sheep
21.28 "What do you t.? A man had two sons
22.17 "Tell us . . Is it lawful to pay taxes?
22.42 "What do you think of the Christ?
26.53 "Do you think that I cannot appeal?
Mk 6.49 when they saw . . they thought it was a ghost
Lk 8.18 "what he thinks that he has will be taken
10.36 "Which of these three, do you think?
12.51 "Do you t. that I have come to give peace?
13. 2 "Do you t. . . these Galileans were worse?
13. 4 "do you t. . . they were worse offenders?
Jn 5.39 "you t. . . in them you have eternal life
5.45 "Do not think that I shall accuse you
11.13 they thought that he meant taking rest
11.56 "What do you t.? That he will not come?
13.29 Some thought . . Jesus was telling him
16. 2 "whoever kills you will t. he is offering
Acts 12. 9 but thought he was seeing a vision
1 Cor 3.18 If any one among you thinks . . he is wise
4. 9 I think that God has exhibited us
7.40 I think that I have the Spirit of God
10.12 let any one who thinks that he stands
12.23 those parts . . which we t. less honorable

1 Cor 14.37 If any one thinks that he is a prophet
2 Cor 11.16 I repeat, let no one think me foolish
12.19 Have you been thinking all along?
Gal 6. 3 if any one thinks he is something
Phil 3. 4 If any other man thinks he has reason
Heb 10.29 How much worse punishment do you t.?
Jas 1.26 If any one thinks he is religious

3. *ponder, consider:* ἐνθυμέομαι ENTHYMEOMAI
Mt 9. 4 "Why do you think evil in your hearts?

4. *think, lead:* ἡγέομαι HĒGEOMAI
Acts 26. 2 "I t. myself fortunate that . . before you
2 Cor 9. 5 I thought it necessary to urge . . brethren
Phil 2.25 I have thought it necessary to send
2 Pet 1.13 I think it right, as long as I am

5. *judge, decide:* κρίνω KRINŌ
Acts 26. 8 "Why is it thought incredible by any?

6. *reckon, count:* λογίζομαι LOGIZOMAI
Rom 14.14 for any one who thinks it unclean
2 Cor 11. 5 I think that I am not in the least inferior
12. 6 so that no one may think more of me
Phil 4. 8 think about these things

7. *remember, mention:* μνημονεύω MNĒMONEUŌ
Heb 11.15 If they had been thinking of that land

8. *think, consider, perceive:* νοέω NOEŌ
Eph 3.20 more abundantly than all that we . . t.
2 Tim 2. 7 Think over what I say

9. *think, believe:* νομίζω NOMIZŌ
Mt 5.17 "Think not that I have come to abolish
10.34 "Do not t. . . I have come to bring peace
20.10 "they thought they would receive more
Acts 8.20 "you thought you could obtain the gift!
17.29 "ought not to t. . . the Deity is like gold
1 Cor 7.26 I t. . . in view of the present[m] distress
7.36 If . . one thinks that he is not behaving

10. *expect, think:* οἴομαι OIOMAI
Phil 1.17 thinking to afflict me in my imprisonment

11. *persuade:* πείθω PEITHŌ
Acts 26.28 "you think to make me a Christian!

12. *think, set one's mind on:* φρονέω PHRONEŌ
Rom 12. 3 not . . more highly than he ought to think, but to think with sober judgment
1 Cor 13.11 When . . a child, . . I thought like a child

THINK MORE HIGHLY OF ONESELF

1. *be overproud, be haughty:* ὑπερφρονέω HYPERPHRONEŌ*
Rom 12. 3 not to think of himself more highly

THINKING

1. *calculation, argument:* διαλογισμός (pl.) DIALOGISMOS
Rom 1.21 they became futile in their thinking

2. *heart, mind:* φρήν (pl.) PHRĒN*
1 Cor 14.20 do not be children in your thinking; be babes in evil, but in t. be mature

THIRD

1. *third:* τρίτος TRITOS
[a]neut.
Mt 16.21 he must . . on the third day be raised
17.23 "he will be raised on the third day
20. 3 "about the third hour he saw others
20.19 "he will be raised on the third day
22.26 "So too the second and third
26.44 he went away and prayed for the t. time
27.64 "to be made secure until the third day
Mk 12.21 "the second . . died . . ; and the third likewise
15.25 the third hour, when they crucified him
Lk 9.22 "must . . on the third day be raised
12.38 "in the second watch, or in the third
13.32 "'the third day I finish my course
18.33 "on the third day he will rise
20.12 "And he sent yet a third
20.31 "the third took her, . . likewise all seven
24. 7 "must . . on the third day rise
24.21 "besides all this, it is now the third day
24.46 "on the third day rise from the dead
Jn 2. 1 On . . third day there was a marriage
Acts 2.15 "it is only the third hour of the day
10.40 "but God raised him on the third day
23.23 "At the third hour of the night get ready
27.19 the third day they cast out . . the tackle
1 Cor 12.28 [a]second prophets, third teachers
15. 4 that he was raised on the third day
2 Cor 12. 2 was caught up to the third heaven
Rev 4. 7 t. living creature with . . face of a man
6. 5 When he opened the third seal, I heard the third living creature say, "Come!
8. 7 a third of the earth was burnt up, and a third of the trees were burnt up
8. 9(8) a third of the sea became blood
8. 9 a third of the living creatures in the sea died, and a third of the ships
8.10 The third angel blew his trumpet, and a great star . . fell on a third of the rivers
8.11 A third of the waters became wormwood
8.12 a third of the sun was struck, and a third of the moon, and a third of the stars, so that a third of their light was darkened; a third of the day was kept from shining, and likewise a third of the night
9.15 four angels . . to kill a third of mankind
9.18 a third of mankind was killed
11.14 behold, the third woe is soon to come
12. 4 His tail swept down a third of the stars
14. 9 another angel, a third, followed them
16. 4 third angel poured . . bowl into the rivers
21.19 adorned with every jewel; . . the t. agate

THIRD STORY

1. *third story:* τρίστεγον TRISTEGON*
Acts 20. 9 he fell down from the third story

THIRD TIME, THE

1. *third:* τρίτος (neut.) TRITOS
Mk 14.41 he came the third time, and said to them
Lk 23.22 A third time he said to them, "Why?
Jn 21.14 the third time that Jesus was revealed
21.17 said to him the third time, "Simon
21.17 because he said to him the third time
2 Cor 12.14 for the third time I am ready to come
13. 1 This is the third time I am coming

THIRST

1. *thirst, be thirsty:* διψάω DIPSAŌ
Mt 5. 6 "Blessed are those who hunger and t.
Jn 4.13 "who drinks of this water will thirst again
4.14 whoever drinks of the water . . will never t.
4.15 "give me this water, that I may not t.
6.35 "he who believes in me shall never thirst
7.37 "If any one thirst, let him come to me
19.28 After this Jesus . . said . . "I thirst
1 Cor 4.11 To the present . . we hunger and thirst
Rev 7.16 "shall hunger no more, neither thirst

2. *thirst:* δίψος DIPSOS*
2 Cor 11.27 in hunger and thirst, often without food

THIRSTY

1. *thirst, be thirsty:* διψάω (part.) DIPSAŌ
Mt 25.37 "'Lord, when did we see thee . . thirsty?
25.44 "'Lord, when did we see thee . . thirsty?
Rev 21. 6 "To the t. I will give from the fountain

THIRSTY, BE

1. *thirst, be thirsty:* διψάω DIPSAŌ
Mt 25.35 "'I was thirsty and you gave me drink
25.42 "'I was thirsty and you gave me no drink
Rom 12.20 "if he is thirsty, give him drink
Rev 22.17 And let him who is thirsty come

THIRTY

1. *three:* τρεῖς TREIS [A.3.c.1]
Jn 2. 6 each holding twenty or thirty gallons

2. *thirty:* τριάκοντα TRIAKONTA
Mt 13. 8 "brought forth . . a hundredfold, . . some t.
13.23 "bears fruit, . . a hundredfold, . . in another t.
26.15 they paid him thirty pieces of silver
27. 3 brought back the thirty pieces of silver
27. 9 "they took the thirty pieces of silver
Lk 3.23 Jesus . . was about thirty years of age
Gal 3.17 four hundred and thirty years afterward

THIRTY-EIGHT

1. *thirty and eight:* τριάκοντα καὶ ὀκτώ TRIAKONTA; OKTŌ [A.3.c]

Jn 5. 5 man . . who had been ill for t. years

THIRTYFOLD

1. *thirty:* τριάκοντα TRIAKONTA [B.1.a.1]

Mk 4. 8 "brought forth grain, . . yielding thirtyfold
4.20 "the ones who . . bear fruit, thirtyfold

THIS (*See also* ALL THIS)

1. *that:* ἐκεῖνος EKEINOS

Mt 24.43 "know this, that if the householder
Lk 8.32 they begged him to let them enter these
Jn 18.15 this disciple was known to the high priest
19.21 "'This man said, I am King of the Jews
21.23 that this disciple was not to die
Acts 20. 2 When he had gone through these parts

2. *who, which, what:* ὅς HOS

Acts **3.**15; **6.**6; **7.**20; **15.**29; **19.**25; **26.**7
Eph **2.**3
Col **1.**5, 29; **2.**17; **3.**6, 7
2 Th **1.**11; **2.**14; **3.**17
1 Tim **1.**6; **2.**7; **6.**10
Heb **5.**11; **6.**19; **9.**5; **11.**7
1 Pet **1.**6, 10
2 Pet **1.**19

3. *anyone who, whoever:* ὅστις HOSTIS

Gal 4.24 Now this is an allegory
Eph 6. 2 (this is the first commandment
Phil 1.28 This is a clear omen to them

4. *this:* οὗτος HOUTOS

Mt **1.**20, 22; **3.**3, 9, 17; **4.**3, 9; **5.**19, 37; **6.**29, 32^2, 33; **7.**12, 24, 26, 28; **8.**9, 27; **9.**3, 26, 28; **10.**2, 5, 42; **11.**10, 16, 25; **12.**23, 24, 32, 41, 42, 45; **13.**15, 19, 20, 22, 23, 28, 34, 51, 53, 54^2, 55, 56^2; **14.**2; **15.**8, 11, 20; **16.**18, 22; **17.**5, 20, [21‡; **18.**4, 6, 10, 14; **19.**1, 5, 11, 20, 22, 26; **20.**12, 14, 21; **21.**4, 10, 11, 16, 21, 23^2, 24, 27, 38, 42, [44‡; **22.**20, 38, 40; **23.**23, 36^2; **24.**2, 3, 8, 14, 33, 34^2; **25.**40, 45; **26.**1, 8, 9, 12, 13, 26, 28, 29, 31, 34, 39, 42, 56, 61, 62, 71; **27.**24, 32, 37, 47, 54; **28.**14, 15

Mk **1.**27; **2.**7; **4.**13, 15, 16, 41; **5.**43; **6.**2^2, 3; **7.**6, 23, 29; **8.**4, 7, 12^2, 38; **9.**7, 21, 29, 42; **10.**5, 7, 10, 20, 30; **11.**3, 23, 28^2, 29, 33; **12.**7, 10, 11, 16, 31^2, 43; **13.**2, 4, 8, 29, 30^2; **14.**5, 22, 24, 30, 36, 58, 60, 69, 71; **15.**39; **16.**12‡, 17‡, [end‡

Lk **1.**18, 19, 20, 24, 29, 34, 36, 43, 61, 65, 66; **2.**2, 12, 15, 17, 19, 25, 34; **3.**8, 20; **4.**3, 6, 21, 22, 23, 28, 36, 43; **5.**6, 21, 27; **6.**12; **7.**4, 8, 9, 17, 18, 27, 31, 39, 44, 49; **8.**8, 9, 11, 13, 25; **9.**9, 13, 21, 28, 34, 35, 44, 45^2, 48; **10.**1, 5, 11, 20, 21, 28, 36; **11.**27, 29, 30, 31, 32, 42, 45, 50, 51; **12.**18, 20, 27, 30^2, 31, 39, 41; **13.**2, 6, 7, 8, 16^2, 17; **14.**6, 9, 15, 21, 30; **15.**2, 3, 24, 26, 30, 32; **16.**1, 2, 8, 14, 24, 26, 28; **17.**2, 6, 18, 25; **18.**5, 9, 11, 14, 21, 23, 30, 34^2, 36; **19.**9, 11, 14, 15, 27, 28, 40; **20.**2^2, 8, 9, 12, 14, 17, 19, 34; **21.**3, 6, 7^2, 9, 12, 22, 23, 28, 31, 32, 36; **22.**15, 17, 19, 19‡, 20‡, 23, 37, 42, 51, 53, 56, 59; **23.**2, 4, 14^2, 18, 31, 38, 41, 46, 47, 49, 52; **24.**4, 9, 10, 11, 14, 17, 18, 21^2, 26, 36, [40‡, 44, 48

Jn **1.**15, 19, 28, 30, 31, 33, 34, 50; **2.**11, 12, 16, 18, 19, 20, 22; **3.**2^2, 9, 10, 19, 22, 29; **4.**13, 15, 18, 20, 21, 29, 42, 54; **5.**1, 3, 16, 20, 28, 34; **6.**1, 5, 6, 14, 29, 34, 39, 40, 42, 50, 51, 52, 58^2, 59, 60, 61^2, 66; **7.**1, 4, 8, 15, 25, 26, 27, 31, 35, 39, 40^2, 41, 46, 49; **8.**4‡, 6‡, 20, 23^2, 40; **9.**2, 3, 6, 8, 16, 19; 20, 22, 24, 29, 30, 33, 39, 40; **10.**6, 16, 17, 18, 19, 21, 41; **11.**4, 7, 9, 26, 28, 37, 43, 47, 51; **12.**5, 6, 16^2, 18, 21, 25, 27^3, 30, 31^2, 33, 34, 36, 41; **13.**1, 17, 28, 35; **14.**12, 25; **15.**8, 11, 12, 13, 17, 21; **16.**1, 3, 4^2, 6, 11, 17, 19, 25, 30, 33; **17.**1, 3, 13, 20, 25; **18.**1, 8, 17, 22, 29, 30, 34, 36^2, 37^2, 38, 40; **19.**8, 12^2, 13, 20, 25(24), 28, 36, 38; **20.**14, 18, 20, 22, 30, 31, 34; **21.**1, 14, 15, 19^2, 21, 24^3

Acts **1.**6, 9, 11, 14, 17, 18, 22, 24, 25; **2.**6, 7, 12, 14, 15, 16, 22, 23, 29, 32, 33, 36, 40; **3.**12, 16^2, 24; **4.**7, 9, 10, 11, 16, 17, 22, 27; **5.**4, 5, 11, 20, 24^2, 28^2, 32, 35, 36, 38^3; **6.**1, 3, 13^2, 14^2; **7.**1, 4, 7, 29, 35, 37, 38, 40, 50, 54, 60^2; **8.**10, 19, 21, 22, 26, 29, 32, 34, 35; **9.**13, 21^3; **10.**16, 30, 44, 47; **11.**10, 12, 18, 27; **12.**17; **13.**17, 23, 26, 33, 38, 42; **14.**15^2, 18; **15.**2, 6, 15, 16, 18(17), 28; **16.**12, 17, 18, 20, 38; **17.**3, 6, 7, 8, 11^2, 18, 19, 20, 23, 32; **18.**1, 10, 13, 15, 17; **19.**10, 14, 17, 21, 25, 26, 27, 36, 37, 40, 41(40); **20.**5, 34; **21.**11, 12, 15, 24, 28^3; **22.**3, 4, 22, 26, 28; **23.**1, 7, 9, 13, 17, 18, 22, 25, 27; **24.**2, 5, 9, 10, 14, 15, 20, 21; **25.**9, 20, 24; **26.**16, 21, 22, 26^3, 29, 31, 32; **27.**21, 23, 31, 35; **28.**4, 9, 20^2, 22, 26, 27, 28, [29‡

Rom **1.**26; **4.**9; **5.**2; **7.**24; **8.**31, 37; **9.**8, 9^2; **11.**24, 25, 27; **12.**2; **13.**9, 11; **14.**9; **15.**23, 28^2

1 Cor **1.**20; **2.**6^2, 8; **3.**18, 19; **4.**6, 14; **5.**2, 10; **7.**6, 31^2, 35, 37; **8.**9; **9.**3, 8, 12, 15^2, 17; **10.**6, 11, 28; **11.**22, 24^2, 25^2, 26; **12.**11; **13.**13^2; **14.**21; **15.**19, 50, 53^2

2 Cor **1.**12, 15, 17; **2.**6, 16; **3.**10^2; **4.**1, 4, 7; **5.**5; **7.**1; **8.**6, 7, 10^2, 19, 20; **9.**3, 5, 6, 12, 13; **11.**10, 17; **12.**8, 13; **13.**1, 10

Gal **3.**2, 17; **4.**24; **5.**17; **6.**16

Eph **1.**15, 21; **2.**2, 8; **3.**1, 8, 14; **4.**17; **5.**5, 6, 31, 32; **6.**1, 12, 22

Phil **1.**19, 25, 28; **2.**5; **4.**8

Col **1.**27; **2.**4; **3.**14, 20; **4.**8, 11

1 Th **2.**13; **3.**3^2, 5, 7; **4.**3, 6, 15, 18; **5.**18

2 Th **2.**5; **3.**10

1 Tim **1.**9, 16, 18; **2.**3; **3.**14; **4.**6, 10, 11, 15; **5.**4, 7, 21; **6.**2, 8, 11

2 Tim **2.**14, 19; **3.**1, 8

Tit **1.**5, 13; **2.**15; **3.**8^2

Heb **1.**1; **4.**5; **6.**3; **7.**1, 13, 27; **8.**3, 10; **9.**6, 8, 11, 20, 23; **10.**16, 18; **11.**13, 39; **13.**17, 19

Jas **1.**26, 27; **3.**10, 15; **4.**15

1 Pet **2.**21; **3.**9; **5.**12

2 Pet **1.**4, 5, 8, 9, 10, 12, 13, 15, 17, 18, 20; **2.**12, 17; **3.**1, 3, 5, 8, 11, 14, 16

1 Jn **1.**4, 5; **2.**1, 3, 5, 22, 25, 26; **3.**10, 11, 16, 19, 23, 24; **4.**2, 3, 6, 9, 10, 13, 17^2, 21; **5.**2, 3, 4, 6, 9, 11^2, 13, 14, 20

2 Jn .6^2, 10

3 Jn .4

Jude .4, 8, 10, 12, 14, 16, 19

Rev **2.**6, 24; **4.**1^2; **7.**1, 9, 13, 14; **9.**18, 20; **11.**4, 10; **14.**4^3; **15.**5; **16.**5, 9; **18.**1, 15; **19.**1, 9; **20.**5, 14; **21.**5, 7; **22.**6, 7, 8, 9, 10, 16, 18^2, 19^2, 20

5. *thus, so:* οὕτως HOUTŌS [A.4.a]

Lk 19.31 "you shall say this, 'The Lord has need
1 Cor 7.17 This is my rule in all the churches

6. *now:* νῦν (attr.) NYN

1 Tim 6.17 As for the rich in this world
Tit 2.12 to live . . godly lives in this world

7. *such as this:* τοιοῦτος TOIOUTOS

Acts 16.24 Having received this charge
1 Cor 5. 5 you are to deliver this man to Satan
2 Cor 12. 3 this man was caught up into Paradise
12. 5 On behalf of this man I will boast

IDIOMATICALLY

a. Rev 13.18 This calls for wisdom Ὧδε ἡ σοφία ἐστίν [HŌDE]
b. Rev 17. 9 "This calls for a mind with wisdom ὧδε ὁ νοῦς ὁ ἔχων σοφίαν [HŌDE]

THIS, AND

1. *anyone who, whoever:* ὅστις HOSTIS

Acts 11.28 and this took place in . . days of Claudius

2. *and that one:* κἀκεῖνος KAKEINOS

Mt 15.18 "and this defiles a man

THIS IS HOW
THIS WAY, IN

1. *thus, so:* οὕτως HOUTŌS

Mt 1.18 birth of Jesus . . *f* took place in this way
Jn 21. 1 Jesus . . revealed himself in this way
Acts 13.34 "he spoke in this way
1 Cor 4. 1 This is how one should regard us
Heb 4. 4 spoken of the seventh day in this way
Rev 9.17 this was how I saw the horses

THIS PLACE

1. *here, hither:* ὧδε HŌDE

Lk 23. 5 "all Judea, from Galilee even to this p.

THISTLE

1. *prickly plant:* τρίβολος TRIBOLOS*

Mt 7.16 "Are . . figs ⟨gathered⟩ from thistles?
Heb 6. 8 if it bears thorns and thistles

THOMAS: Θωμᾶς 'täməs

Mt 10. 3 Thomas and Matthew the tax collector

Mk 3.18 Matthew, and Thomas, and James
Lk 6.15 Matthew, and Thomas, and James
Jn 11.16 T. called the Twin, said . . "Let us also go
14. 5 T. said to him, "Lord, we do not know
20.24 T., one of the twelve, called the Twin
20.26 Eight days later . . T. was with them
20.27 he said to T., "Put your finger here
20.28 T. answered . . "My Lord and my God!
21. 2 Simon Peter, T. called the Twin
Acts 1.13 James and Andrew, Philip and T.

THONG
1. *leather strap:* ἱμάς HIMAS*
Mk 1. 7 "the t. of whose sandals I am not worthy
Lk 3.16 "the t. of whose sandals I am not worthy
Jn 1.27 "the t. of whose sandal I am not worthy
Acts 22.25 they had tied him up with the thongs

THORN
1. *thorn, thorn plant:* ἄκανθα AKANTHA*
Mt 7.16 "Are grapes gathered from thorns?
13. 7 "Other seeds fell upon thorns, and the thorns grew up and choked them
13.22 "As for what was sown among thorns
27.29 plaiting a crown of thorns they put it
Mk 4. 7 "Other seed fell among thorns and the thorns grew up and choked it
4.18 "others are the ones sown among thorns
Lk 6.44 "For figs are not gathered from thorns
8. 7 "And some fell among thorns; and the thorns grew with it and choked it
8.14 "And as for what fell among the thorns
Jn 19. 2 the soldiers plaited a crown of thorns
Heb 6. 8 But if it bears thorns . . , it is worthless
2. *thorn, stake:* σκόλοψ SKOLOPS*
2 Cor 12. 7 a thorn was given me in the flesh

THORNS, OF
1. *made of thorns:* ἀκάνθινος AKANTHINOS*
Mk 15.17 plaiting a crown of thorns they put it
Jn 19. 5 Jesus . . , wearing the crown of thorns

THOROUGHFARE
IDIOMATICALLY
a. Mt 22.9 " 'Go . . to the thoroughfares πορεύεσθε . . ἐπὶ τὰς διεξόδους τῶν ὁδῶν [DIEXODOS*; HODOS]

THOSE (*See* THAT)

THOSE WHICH
THOSE WHO
1. *who, which, what:* ὅς HOS
Mt **19.**11; **20.**23
Mk **3.**13; **10.**40
Lk **8.**13
Jn **17.**9
Acts **26.**16
Rom **4.**7; **8.**29
2 Cor **2.**3; **12.**17
2. *as great as, how great:* ὅσος HOSOS
Lk 4.40 all those who had any that were sick
Gal 6.12 It is those who want to make a . . showing
Phil 3.15 Let those of us who are mature be thus
Rev 3.19 " 'Those whom I love, I reprove
13.15 those who would not worship the image
3. *anyone who, whoever:* ὅστις HOSTIS
Lk 8.15 "those who, hearing the word, hold it fast

THOU (*For entry* 1, *and for* SOS, *not represented here, see also* YOUR; YOURS)
1. *you, thou:* σύ SY
Mt **26.**39
Mk **1.**11; **14.**36
Lk **3.**22
Jn **11.**42; **17.**5, 8, 21[2], 23[2], 25
Acts **4.**30; **13.**33
Rom **3.**4
Heb **1.**5, 10, 11, 12; **5.**5, 6; **7.**17, 21
Rev **4.**11

THOUGH
THOUGH, EVEN
1. *if:* ἐάν EAN
Rom 9.27 "Though . . sons of Israel be as the sand
1 Cor 4.15 t. you have countless guides in Christ
2. *if, since:* εἰ EI
[a]εἰ καί [b]καὶ εἰ
Mt 26.33 "Though they . . fall away because of you
Mk 14.29 [a]"Even though they . . fall away, I will not
Lk 11. 8 [a]"t. he will not get up and give him
18. 4 [a]" 'T. I neither fear God nor regard man
2 Cor 4.16 [a]T. our outer nature is wasting away
5.16 [a]even though we once regarded Christ
7. 8 [a]I do not regret it (though I did regret it
7. 8 [a]letter grieved you, t. only for a while
12.11 [a]not . . inferior . . , even though I am nothing
Col 2. 5 [a]For though I am absent in body
Heb 6. 9 [a]T. we speak thus, yet in your case
1 Pet 1. 6 though now . . you may have to suffer
3. 1 [b]though they do not obey the word
3. *for:* γάρ GAR
Rom **5.**7; **9.**11
2 Cor **12.**6
4. *as, so:* ὡς HŌS
Acts **28.**19
5. *although:* καίπερ KAIPER
Phil 3. 4 T. I myself have reason for confidence
Heb 7. 5 t. these . . are descended from Abraham
12.17 no chance to repent, t. he sought it
2 Pet 1.12 though you know them and are established
6. *even if:* κἄν KAN
Jn 10.38 "even though you do not believe me
11.25 "he who believes in me, though he die

THOUGHT
1. *calculation, argument:* διαλογισμός DIALOGISMOS
Mt 15.19 "For out of the heart come evil thoughts
Mk 7.21 "out of the heart . . come evil thoughts
Lk 2.35 "that thoughts . . of many . . may be revealed
6. 8 But he knew their thoughts
9.47 Jesus perceived the t. of their hearts
1 Cor 3.20 "the thoughts of the wise are futile
Jas 2. 4 have . . become judges with evil thoughts
2. *thought, notion:* διανόημα DIANOĒMA*
Lk 11.17 knowing their thoughts, said to them
3. *intent, thought:* ἔννοια ENNOIA
1 Pet 4. 1 arm yourselves with the same thought
4. *reflection, idea:* ἐνθύμησις ENTHYMĒSIS
Mt 9. 4 But Jesus, knowing[u] their thoughts
12.25 Knowing their thoughts, he said
Heb 4.12 discerning the thoughts . . of the heart
5. *reasoning:* λογισμός LOGISMOS
Rom 2.15 their conflicting thoughts accuse
6. *mind, thought:* νόημα NOĒMA
2 Cor 10. 5 We . . take every t. captive to obey Christ
11. 3 your thoughts will be led astray
IDIOMATICALLY
a. 1 Tim 3.7 he must be well thought of by outsiders δεῖ δὲ καὶ μαρτυρίαν καλὴν ἔχειν ἀπὸ τῶν ἔξωθεν [MARTYRIA]
CONTEXTUALLY
1 Cor 2.11 what person knows a man's thoughts?
2.11 no one comprehends the thoughts of God

THOUGHT FOR, TAKE
1. *foresee, provide:* προνοέω (mid.) PRONOEŌ
Rom 12.17 take thought for what is noble

THOUSAND
THOUSANDS
1. *thousand:* χιλιάς CHILIAS*
Lk 14.31 "whether . . able with ten t. to meet him who comes against him with twenty t.
Acts 4. 4 number of the men came to about five t.
1 Cor 10. 8 twenty-three t. fell in a single day
Rev 5.11 the voice of many angels, numbering . . thousands of thousands
7. 4 hundred and forty-four thousand sealed
7. 5 twelve t. sealed out of the tribe of Judah,

twelve t. of the tribe of Reuben, twelve t. of the tribe of Gad
Rev 7. 6 twelve t. of the tribe of Asher, twelve t. of the tribe of Naphtali, twelve t. of the tribe of Manasseh
7. 7 twelve t. of the tribe of Simeon, twelve t. of the tribe of Levi, twelve t. of the tribe of Issachar
7. 8 twelve t. of the tribe of Zebulun, twelve t. of the tribe of Joseph, twelve t. . . of the tribe of Benjamin
11.13 seven t. . . were killed in the earthquake
14. 1 with him a hundred and forty-four t.
14. 3 except the hundred and forty-four t.
21.16 he measured the city . . , twelve t. stadia[q]

2. *thousand:* χίλιοι CHILIOI*
2 Pet 3. 8 with the Lord one day is as a thousand years, and a thousand years as one day
Rev 11. 3 "to prophesy for one t. two hundred
12. 6 nourished for one t. two hundred
14.20 for one thousand six hundred stadia[i]
20. 2 bound him for a thousand years
20. 3 till the thousand years were ended
20. 4 reigned with Christ a t. years
20. 5 until the thousand years were ended
20. 6 they shall reign with him a t. years
20. 7 when the thousand years are ended

3. *myriad, ten thousand:* μυριάς MYRIAS
[a]μυριάδας πέντε *five ten thousands*
Lk 12. 1 thousands of the multitude . . gathered
Acts 19.19 [a]it came to fifty thousand pieces of silver
21.20 "thousands there are among the Jews

THOUSAND, FIVE
1. *five thousand:* πεντακισχίλιοι PENTAKISCHILIOI*
Mt 14.21 five t. men, besides women and children
16. 9 "remember the five loaves of the five t.?
Mk 6.44 those who ate . . were five thousand men
8.19 "I broke the five loaves for the five t.
Lk 9.14 there were about five thousand men
Jn 6.10 men sat down, in number about five t.

THOUSAND, FOUR
1. *four thousand:* τετρακισχίλιοι TETRAKISCHILIOI*
Mt 15.38 Those who ate were four thousand men
16.10 "the seven loaves of the four thousand
Mk 8. 9 there were about four t. people
8.20 "the seven for the four thousand
Acts 21.38 "the four thousand men of the Assassins

THOUSAND, SEVEN
1. *seven thousand:* ἑπτακισχίλιοι HEPTAKISCHILIOI*
Rom 11. 4 "I have kept for myself s. thousand men

THOUSAND, TEN
1. *myriad, ten thousand:* μυριάς MYRIAS
Rev 9.16 ten thousand; I heard their number
2. *ten thousand:* μύριοι MYRIOI*
Mt 18.24 "who owed him ten thousand talents[f]
1 Cor 14.19 than ten t. words in a tongue

THOUSAND, THREE
1. *three thousand:* τρισχίλιοι TRISCHILIOI*
Acts 2.41 added . . about three thousand souls

THOUSAND, TWICE TEN
1. *twenty thousand:* δισμυριάς DISMYRIAS*
Rev 9.16 cavalry was twice ten thousand times

THOUSAND, TWO
1. *two thousand:* δισχίλιοι DISCHILIOI*
Mk 5.13 herd, numbering about two thousand

THREAT
1. *threat:* ἀπειλή APEILĒ
Acts 4.29 "now, Lord, look upon their threats
9. 1 Saul, still breathing threats and murder

THREATEN
1. *hold out promise or threat:* ἀπειλέω APEILEŌ
1 Pet 2.23 when he suffered, he did not threaten
2. *have a gloomy look:* στυγνάζω STYGNAZŌ
Mt 16. 3 " 'for the sky is red and threatening‡

THREATEN, FURTHER
1. *threaten besides:* προσαπειλέω PROSAPEILEŌ*
Acts 4.21 when they had further threatened them

THREATENING
1. *threat:* ἀπειλή APEILĒ
Eph 6. 9 do the same to them, and forbear t.

THREE
1. *twenty-five:* εἴκοσι πέντε EIKOSI; PENTE [A.3.c.1]
Jn 6.19 they had rowed about t. or four miles[m]†
2. *three:* τρεῖς TREIS
Mt 12.40 "as Jonah was three days and three nights in the belly of the whale, so will the Son of man be three days and three nights in the heart of the earth
13.33 "took and hid in three measures of flour
15.32 "they have been with me now three days
17. 4 "I will make three booths here
18.16 "the evidence of two or three witnesses
18.20 "where two or t. are gathered in my name
26.61 " 'I am able . . to build it in three days
27.40 "You who would . . build it in t. days
27.63 " 'After three days I will rise again
Mk 8. 2 "they have been with me now three days
8.31 must suffer . . , and after three days rise
9. 5 "let us make three booths, one for you
9.31 "when . . killed, after t. days he will rise
10.34 "and after three days he will rise
14.58 " 'in three days I will build another
15.29 "You who would . . build it in three days
Lk 1.56 Mary remained with her about t. months
2.46 After t. days they found him in . . temple
4.25 heaven was shut up t. years . . six months
9.33 "let us make three booths, one for you
10.36 "Which of these three . . proved neighbor?
11. 5 " 'Friend, lend me three loaves
12.52 "in one house there will be five divided, three against two and two against three
13. 7 " 'three years I have come seeking fruit
13.21 "took and hid in t. measures of flour
Jn 2.19 "in three days I will raise it up
2.20 "will you raise it up in three days?
Acts 5. 7 After an interval of about three hours
7.20 "he was brought up for three months
9. 9 for three days he was without sight
10.19 "Behold, three men are looking for you
11.11 "At that very moment t. men arrived
17. 2 for three weeks[p] he argued with them
19. 8 for three months spoke boldly, arguing
20. 3 There he spent three months
25. 1 after t. days he went up to Jerusalem
28. 7 entertained us hospitably for t. days
28.11 After t. months we set sail in a ship
28.12 at Syracuse, we stayed . . for three days
28.17 After t. days he called . . local leaders
1 Cor 13.13 So faith, hope, love abide, these three
14.27 let there be only two or at most three
14.29 Let two or three prophets speak
2 Cor 13. 1 This is the t. time I am coming to you
Gal 1.18 after three years I went up to Jerusalem
1 Tim 5.19 except on the evidence of . . t. witnesses
Heb 10.28 dies . . at the testimony of . . t. witnesses
Jas 5.17 t. years and six months it did not rain
1 Jn 5. 8(7) t. witnesses, the Spirit, the water, and the blood; and these three agree
Rev 6. 6 "three quarts of barley for a denarius[a]!
8.13 "which the t. angels are about to blow!
9.18 By these t. plagues a third . . was killed
11. 9 For three days and a half men . . gaze
11.11 after . . t. and a half days a breath of life
16.13 I saw . . three foul spirits like frogs
16.19 The great city was split into three parts
21.13 on the east three gates, on the north three gates, on the south three gates, and on the west three gates

THREE HUNDRED
1. *three hundred:* τριακόσιοι TRIAKOSIOI*
Mk 14. 5 "sold for more than three hundred denarii[b]
Jn 12. 5 "Why . . not sold for t. hundred denarii[b]?

THREE MONTHS
1. *of three months:* τρίμηνος (subst. fem.) TRIMĒNOS*
Heb 11.23 was hid for three months by his parents

THREE TAVERNS: II,B-2
1. *three taverns:* Τρεῖς ταβέρναι TREIS; TABERNĒ*
Acts 28.15 came as far as . . Three Taverns to meet us

THREE THOUSAND
1. *three thousand:* τρισχίλιοι TRISCHILIOI*
Acts 2.41 added . . about three thousand souls

THREE TIMES
1. *three times:* τρίς TRIS*
Mt 26.34 "this . . night, . . you will deny me t. times
26.75 remembered . . "you will deny me t. times
Mk 14.30 "this . . night, . . you will deny me t. times
14.72 remembered . . "you will deny me t. times
Lk 22.34 "until you t. times deny . . you know me
22.61 remembered . . "you will deny me t. times
Jn 13.38 "not . . till you have denied me t. times
Acts 10.16 This happened three times
11.10 "This happened three times
2 Cor 11.25 T. times I have been beaten with rods
11.25 Three times I have been shipwrecked
12. 8 T. times I besought the Lord about this

THREE YEARS
1. *period of three years:* τριετία TRIETIA*
Acts 20.31 "for three years I did not cease

THRESH
1. *tread, thresh:* ἀλοάω ALOAŌ
1 Cor 9.10 should . . thresh in hope of a share

THRESHING FLOOR
1. *threshing floor:* ἅλων HALŌN*
Mt 3.12 "he will clear his threshing floor
Lk 3.17 "to clear his threshing floor

THROAT
1. *larynx, throat:* λάρυγξ LARYGX*
Rom 3.13 "Their throat is an open grave

IDIOMATICALLY
a. Mt 18.28 "and seizing him by the throat καὶ κρατήσας αὐτὸν ἔπνιγεν [PNIGŌ]

THRONE
1. *step, platform:* βῆμα BĒMA
Acts 12.21 Herod . . took his seat upon the throne
2. *seat, throne:* θρόνος THRONOS*
Mt 5.34 "not . . by heaven, for it is the t. of God
19.28 "when the Son of man shall sit on his . . t., you . . will also sit on twelve thrones
23.22 "he . . swears by the throne of God
25.31 "then he will sit on his glorious throne
Lk 1.32 "the Lord God will give to him the throne
1.52 "put down the mighty from their thrones
22.30 "that you may . . sit on thrones judging
Acts 2.30 "set one of his descendants upon his t.
7.49 " 'Heaven is my t., and earth my footstool
Col 1.16 thrones or dominions or principalities
Heb 1. 8 "Thy throne, O God,[a] is for ever
4.16 Let us . . draw near to the t. of grace
8. 1 seated at the right hand of the throne
12. 2 seated at the right hand of the throne
Rev 1. 4 seven spirits who are before his t.
2.13 " 'where you dwell, where Satan's t. is
3.21 " 'I will grant him to sit . . on my t., as I . . sat down with my Father on his t.
4. 2 and lo, a throne stood in heaven, with one seated on the throne!
4. 3 round the throne was a rainbow
4. 4 Round the throne were twenty-four thrones, and seated on the thrones were twenty-four elders
4. 5 From the t. issue flashes of lightning, . . and before the t. burn seven torches
Rev 4. 6 before the throne there is . . a sea of glass
4. 6 round the throne, on each side of the throne, are four living creatures
4. 9 thanks to him who is seated on the t.
4.10 before him who is seated on the throne
4.10 they cast their crowns before the throne
5. 1 hand of him who was seated on the t.
5. 6 between the t. and . . four living creatures
5. 7 hand of him who was seated on the t.
5.11 I heard around the throne . . the voice
5.13 "To him who sits upon the throne
6.16 "the face of him who is seated on the t.
7. 9 before the t. and before the Lamb
7.10 "our God who sits upon the throne
7.11 all the angels stood round the throne . . and they fell on their faces before the t.
7.15 "Therefore are they before the throne . .; and he who sits upon the t. will shelter
7.17 "the Lamb in the midst of the throne
8. 3 upon the golden altar before the t.
11.16 elders who sit on their thrones
12. 5 child was caught up to God and to his t.
13. 2 to it the dragon gave . . his throne
14. 3 they sing a new song before the throne
16.10 fifth angel poured his bowl on the t.
16.17 voice . . from the t. saying, "It is done!
19. 4 God who is seated on the throne
19. 5 from the throne came a voice crying
20. 4 I saw thrones, and seated on them
20.11 Then I saw a great white throne
20.12 I saw the dead . . standing before the t.
21. 3 I heard a loud voice from the throne
21. 5 he who sat upon the t. said, "Behold
22. 1 water of life . . flowing from the throne
22. 3 the throne of God and of the Lamb

THRONG
1. *crowd, populace:* ὄχλος OCHLOS
Mt 14.14 As he went ashore he saw a great t.
15.31 the throng wondered, when they saw
Mk 6.34 As he went ashore he saw a great t.
12.37 And the great throng heard him gladly

THRONG ABOUT
1. *press together:* συνθλίβω SYNTHLIBŌ
Mk 5.24 a great crowd . . thronged about him

THROUGH
1. *from:* ἀπό (+gen.) APO
Heb **5.**8
2. *through:* διά (+gen.) DIA
[a]+acc.
Mt **12.**1; **19.**24
Mk **7.**31; **9.**30
Lk **1.**78[a]; **5.**19; **18.**25
Jn **1.**3, 7, 10, 17[2]; **3.**17; **17.**20
Acts **1.**2; **2.**22, 43; **3.**16; **4.**16, 30; **8.**18; **10.**43; **13.**38; **14.**22; **15.**11, 12; **18.**27; **20.**3; **21.**4, 19; **24.**2; **28.**25
Rom **1.**2, 5, 8; **3.**20, 22, 24, 30; **4.**13[2]; **5.**1, 2, 5, 11[2], 12[2], 17[2], 21[2]; **7.**4, 13[2], 25; **8.**11, 37; **11.**36; **15.**18; **16.**26, 27
1 Cor **1.**21[2]; **2.**10; **3.**5, 15; **4.**15; **7.**5[a]; **8.**6[2]; **12.**8; **15.**57
2 Cor **1.**5, 20; **2.**14; **3.**4; **5.**18, 20; **9.**11; **11.**33; **12.**17
Gal **1.**1[2], 12, 15; **2.**16, 19, 21; **3.**14, 26; **4.**7, 23; **5.**6, 13; **6.**[14†
Eph **1.**5, 7; **2.**8, 16, 18; **3.**6, 10, 12, 16, 17; **4.**6
Phil **1.**11, 19; **3.**9
Col **1.**16, 20; **2.**12, 19, **3.**17
1 Th **3.**7; **4.**2, 14; **5.**9
2 Th **2.**14
1 Tim **2.**15†
2 Tim **1.**6, 10[2]; **3.**15
Tit **3.**6
Phm .7, 22
Heb **1.**2; **2.**10, 14; **6.**12, 18; **7.**9, 11, 19, 25; **9.**11, 14; **10.**10, 20; **11.**4[2], 33; **13.**12, 15, 21
1 Pet **1.**3, 5, 21, 23; **2.**5; **3.**20, 21; **4.**11
2 Pet **1.**3, 4; **3.**6
1 Jn **4.**9
Jude .25

3. *from, out of:* ἐκ (+gen.) EK
Rom **1**.17, 17†; **9**.30, 32
2 Cor **7**.9
Gal **3**.11†
4. *in, at, by:* ἐν (+dat.) EN
Mt **9**.31; **10**.20
Lk **1**.65; **7**.17
Acts **20**.19
Rom **3**.7; **9**.7
1 Cor **7**.14[2]
2 Cor **3**.14; **6**.4; **11**.27
2 Th **2**.13, 16
1 Tim **4**.2
Tit **1**.3
Heb **4**.7; **11**.18
1 Pet **1**.12
2 Pet **2**.20
Rev **22**.2†
5. *down from, against:* κατά (+gen.) KATA
[a]+acc.
Lk 4.14 report . . went out t. all the . . country
Eph 4.22 [a]old nature which . . is corrupt t. . . lusts
6. *in the midst of:* ἀνὰ μέσον MESOS [B.1.a.1]
Mk 7.31 went . . through . . region of the Decapolis

THROUGHOUT
1. *into, to, for:* εἰς (+acc.) EIS
Mt **4**.24
Mk **1**.28, 39
2. *in, at, by:* ἐν (+dat.) EN
Mt **24**.14
Phil **1**.13†
1 Pet **5**.9
3. *on, at:* ἐπί (+acc.) EPI
Acts 7.11 "there came a famine t. all Egypt
4. *whole, entire:* ὅλος HOLOS [B.1.a.1]
1 Th 4.10 you . . love all the brethren t. Macedonia
5. *down from, against:* κατά (+gen.) KATA
[a]+acc.
Lk 8.39 [a]proclaiming t. the whole city how much
23. 5 "teaching throughout all Judea
Acts 8. 1 [a]they were all scattered t. . . Judea
9.31 church throughout . . Judea and Galilee
9.42 it became known throughout all Joppa
10.37 "word which was proclaimed t. all Judea
24. 5 [a]"an agitator among . . Jews t. the world
CONTEXTUALLY
Acts **19**.26; **26**.20
1 Pet **1**.17

THROW
1. *throw, put:* βάλλω BALLŌ
Mt 3.10 "cut down and thrown into the fire
4. 6 "If . . the Son of God, t. yourself down
5.13 "no longer good . . except to be thrown out
5.29 "pluck it out and t. it away; it is better . . than that . . body be thrown into hell[k]
5.30 "cut it off and throw it away
6.30 "tomorrow is thrown into the oven
7. 6 "do not throw your pearls before swine
7.19 "cut down and thrown into the fire
13.42 "throw them into the furnace of fire
13.47 "like a net which was thrown into the sea
13.48 "sorted the good . . but threw away the bad
13.50 "throw them into the furnace of fire
15.26 "to take the children's bread and throw it
18. 8 "cut it off and throw it away; it is better . . than . . to be thrown into the . . fire
18. 9 "pluck it out and throw it away; it is better . . than . . to be thrown into . . fire
Mk 7.27 "to take the children's bread and throw it
9.42 "better . . if . . he were thrown into . . sea
9.45 "better . . than . . to be thrown into hell[mn]
9.47 "better . . than . . to be thrown into hell[m]
Lk 3. 9 "cut down and thrown into the fire
4. 9 "If you are the Son . ., t. yourself down
12.28 "tomorrow is thrown into the oven
14.35 "men throw it away
Lk 23.19 who had been thrown into prison
23.25 man who had been thrown into prison
Jn 8. 7 "Let him . . be the first to throw a stone[r]‡
8.59 they took up stones to throw at him
15. 6 "branches are gathered, thrown into . . fire
Acts 16.23 they threw them into prison
16.37 "They have . . thrown us into prison
22.23 cried out and . . threw dust into the air
Rev 2.10 "devil is about to t. some . . into prison
2.22 "Behold, I will throw her on a sickbed
8. 5 angel took the censer . . and threw it
8. 8 something . . was thrown into the sea
14.19 threw it into the great wine press
18.19 they threw dust on their heads
18.21 angel took up a stone . . and threw it
19.20 thrown alive into the lake of fire
20. 3 threw him into the pit, and shut it
20.10 devil . . was thrown into the lake of fire
20.14 Death and Hades were thrown into . . fire
20.15 he was thrown into the lake of fire
2. *throw:* βολή BOLĒ*
Lk 22.41 he withdrew . . about a stone's throw
3. *throw out:* ἐκβάλλω EKBALLŌ
Mt 8.12 "will be thrown into the outer darkness

THROW AWAY
THROW OFF
1. *throw away, throw off:* ἀποβάλλω APOBALLŌ
Mk 10.50 throwing off his mantle he sprang up
Heb 10.35 do not throw away your confidence

THROW CARGO OVERBOARD
IDIOMATICALLY
a. Acts 27.18 they began . . to throw the cargo overboard
ἐκβολὴν ἐποιοῦντο [EKBOLĒ*]

THROW DOWN
1. *throw, put:* βάλλω BALLŌ
Rev 12. 9 the great dragon was thrown down . .—he was thrown down to the earth, and his angels were thrown down with him
12.10 "the accuser . . has been thrown down
12.13 saw that he had been thrown down
18.21 "So shall Babylon . . be thrown down
2. *put down, destroy:* καταλύω KATALYŌ
Mt 24. 2 "not . . one stone . . will not be thrown down
Mk 13. 2 "not . . one stone . . will not be thrown down
Lk 21. 6 "not . . one stone . . will not be thrown down
3. *throw, cast out:* ῥίπτω RHIPTŌ
Mt 27. 5 throwing down the pieces of silver
Lk 4.35 when the demon had thrown him down

THROW DOWN HEADLONG
1. *throw down from a cliff:* κατακρημνίζω KATAKRĒMNIZŌ*
Lk 4.29 that they might t. him down headlong

THROW OFF (*See* THROW AWAY)

THROW ON
1. *throw upon:* ἐπιβάλλω EPIBALLŌ
Mk 11. 7 they . . threw their garments on it
2. *throw upon:* ἐπιρίπτω EPIRIPTŌ
Lk 19.35 throwing their garments on the colt

THROW ONESELF OVERBOARD
1. *throw oneself down:* ἀπορίπτω APORIPTŌ*
Acts 27.43 to throw themselves overboard first

THROW OUT
1. *throw out:* ἐκβάλλω EKBALLŌ
Acts 27.38 throwing out the wheat into the sea

THRUST ASIDE
THRUST FROM ONE
1. *thrust away:* ἀπωθέω (mid.) APŌTHEŌ
Acts 7.27 "man who was wronging . . thrust him aside
7.39 "Our fathers . . thrust him aside
13.46 "Since you thrust it from you

THRUST OUT
1. *throw out:* ἐκβάλλω EKBALLŌ
Lk 13.28 "the prophets in . . and . . yourselves t. out
2. *expel, drive on shore:* ἐξωθέω EXŌTHEŌ
Acts 7.45 "the nations which God thrust out

THUNDER
THUNDER, PEAL OF
THUNDERPEAL

1. *thunder:* βροντή BRONTĒ*
[a]βροντὴν γεγονέναι A.6.a.3
Mk 3.17 Boanerges, that is, sons of thunder
Jn 12.29 [a]The crowd . . said that it had thundered
Rev 4. 5 From the throne issue . . peals of thunder
6. 1 as with a voice of thunder, "Come!
8. 5 there were peals of thunder, voices
10. 3 he called out, . . seven thunders sounded
10. 4 when the seven thunders had sounded
10. 4 "Seal up what the seven thunders . . said
11.19 peals of thunder, an earthquake
14. 2 voice . . like the sound of loud thunder
16.18 peals of thunder, and a great earthquake
19. 6 like the sound of mighty thunderpeals

THUS

1. *then indeed:* ἄρα γε ARA II [B.3.b.8]
Mt 7.20 "Thus you will know them by their fruits
2. *for:* γάρ GAR
Rom **7**.2
3. *this:* ὅδε (neut. pl.) HODE
Acts 22.11 "T. says the Holy Spirit, 'So shall the Jews
4. *who, which, what:* ὅς HOS [B.1.a.1]
[a]+ἐν [b]+διά
Acts **26**.12[a]
Heb **12**.28[b]
5. *so that, therefore:* ὥστε HŌSTE
Mt 23.31 Thus you witness against yourselves
1 Cor 14.22 T., tongues are a sign not for believers
6. *this:* οὗτος (neut.) HOUTOS
[a]ἐν τούτῳ B.1.a.1
Mt **9**.18
Mk **2**.8
Lk **13**.2; **18**.11
Jn **7**.32; **8**.28, 30; **11**.11; **13**.21
Acts **20**.36; **26**.24
Rom **14**.18[a]
Phil **1**.7; **3**.15
1 Jn **3**.3
7. *thus, so:* οὕτως HOUTŌS
Mt 3.15 "Let it be so now, for thus it is fitting
Mk 2. 7 "Why does this man speak thus?
2. 8 perceiving . . that they t. questioned
15.39 saw that he thus[i] breathed his last
Lk 1.25 "T. the Lord has done to me in the days
24.46 "T. it is written, . . Christ should suffer
Jn 11.48 "If we let him go on thus
13.25 lying thus, close to . . breast of Jesus
Acts 3.18 "what God foretold . . he thus fulfilled
22.24 why they shouted thus against him
Rom 9.20 "Why have you made me thus?
15.20 t. making it my ambition to preach
1 Cor 8.12 Thus, sinning against your brethren
15.45 T. it is written, "The first man Adam
Phil 4. 1 stand firm t. in the Lord, my beloved
Heb 6. 9 Though we speak t., yet in your case
6.15 t. Abraham,[m] having patiently endured
9. 6 preparations having thus been made
2 Pet 3.11 all these things are thus to be dissolved
Rev 3. 5 " 'He who conquers shall be clad thus
11. 5 thus he is doomed to be killed
8. *as, just as:* καθώς KATHŌS
Gal 3. 6 Thus Abraham "believed God
9. *so, therefore:* οὖν OUN
Mt **6**.2; **22**.45
Lk **20**.44
Heb **9**.23
10. *such as this:* τοιοῦτος TOIOUTOS [A.3.b.1]
Heb 11.14 people who speak thus make it clear

IDIOMATICALLY
a. Rom 1.13 (but thus far have been prevented καὶ ἐκωλύθην ἄχρι τοῦ δεῦρο [ACHRI]

CONTEXTUALLY
Mk **7**.13, 19; **14**.4
Rom **4**.11
2 Cor **5**.16
1 Tim **6**.19
Heb **9**.12

THWART

1. *deny, nullify:* ἀθετέω ATHETEŌ
1 Cor 1.19 "the cleverness of the clever I will t.

THY

1. *your, thy:* σός SOS
Jn 17.17 "thy word is truth
2. *you, thou:* σύ SY
Mt **6**.9, 10²; **11**.10², 26†; **22**.44²; **26**.42
Mk **1**.2²; **12**.36²
Lk **2**.29², 30, 32; **7**.27²; **10**.21†; **11**.2²; **20**.43²; **23**.46
Jn **2**.17; **12**.28; **17**.1, 6², 11, 12, 14, 26
Acts **2**.27, 28, 35²; **4**.25, 27, 28, 29², 30; **9**.13, 14; **13**.35; **22**.20
Rom **3**.4; **8**.36; **11**.3²; **15**.9
1 Cor **15**.55²
Heb **1**.8, 8‡, 9², 10, 12, 13²; **2**.[7‡, 12; **10**.7, 9
Rev **4**.11; **5**.9; **11**.17, 18³; **15**.3², 4²; **16**.7; **18**.10, 14, 23²

IDIOMATICALLY
a. Jn 17.5 "glorify thou me in thy own presence δόξασόν με σύ . . παρὰ σεαυτῷ [SEAUTOU]

THYATIRA: Θυάτιρα ˌthīə'tīrə II,E-3
Acts 16.14 Lydia, from the city of Thyatira
Rev 1.11 "to the seven churches, . . to T.
2.18 "to the angel of the church in T. write
2.24 " 'But to the rest of you in Thyatira

TIBERIAS: Τιβεριάς tī'birēəs I,D-3
Jn 6. 1 Sea of Galilee, which is the Sea of T.
6.23 boats from T. came near the place
21. 1 revealed himself again . . by the Sea of T.

TIBERIUS: Τιβέριος tī'birēəs
Lk 3. 1 fifteenth year of the reign of T. Caesar

TIE

1. *bind, tie:* δέω DEŌ
Mt 21. 2 "you will find an ass tied, and a colt
Mk 11. 2 "as you enter it you will find a colt tied
11. 4 "a colt tied at the door out in the open
Lk 19.30 "on entering you will find a colt tied

TIE UP

1. *stretch out:* προτείνω PROTEINŌ*
Acts 22.25 when they . . tied him up with the thongs

TILE

1. *earthen vessel, tile:* κέραμος KERAMOS*
Lk 5.19 let . . down . . his bed through the tiles

TILL

1. *until:* ἄχρι ACHRI
[a]ἄχρι οὗ [b]ἄχρις ἄν
Acts 7.18 [a]"till there arose over Egypt another king
Gal 3.19 [b]added . . till the offspring should come
Rev 7. 3 "t. we have sealed the servants of our God
20. 3 till the thousand years were ended
2. *until, while:* ἕως HEŌS
[a]ἕως ἄν [b]ἕως οὗ [c]ἕως ὅτου
Mt 2. 9 the star . . went before . . till it came to rest
2.13 [a]"remain there till I tell you
5.18 [a]"till heaven and earth pass away
5.26 [a]"you will never get out till you have paid
12.20 [a]"till he brings justice to victory
13.33 [b]"hid in . . flour, till it was all leavened
18.30 "in prison till he should pay the debt
18.34 [b]"to the jailers,[h] t. he should pay . . his debt
22.44 [a]"till I put thy enemies under thy feet
24.34 [a]"not . . till all these things take place
Mk 12.36 [a]" 'till I put thy enemies under thy feet
Lk 1.80 he was in the wilderness till the day
2.37 as a widow till she was eighty-four
12.59 "will never get out till you have paid
13. 8 [c]" 'Let it alone, sir, . . till I dig about it
13.21 [b]"hid in . . flour, till it was all leavened
17. 8 " 'serve me, till I eat and drink
20.43 [a]" 't. I make . . enemies a stool for thy feet

Lk 21.32 [a]"not pass away till all has taken place
Jn 13.38 [b]"till you have denied me three times
Acts 2.35 [a]" 't. I make . . enemies a stool for thy feet
8.40 to all the towns till he came to Caesarea
21. 5 till we were outside the city
23.12 [b]an oath . . till they had killed Paul
23.14 [b]"taste no food till we have killed Paul
23.21 [b]"an oath . . till they have killed him
28.23 expounded . . from morning till evening
1 Tim 4.13 Till I come, attend to the public reading
Heb 1.13 [a]"t. I make . . enemies a stool for thy feet
3. *who, which, what:* ὅς HOS [B.1.a.1]
[a]ἕως οὗ [b]ἐν ᾧ [c]ἄχρι οὗ
Mt **13.33**[a]; **18.34**[a]
Lk **13.21**[a]; **19.13**[b]
Jn **13.38**[a]
Acts **7.18**[c]; **23.12**[a], 14[a], 21[a]
IDIOMATICALLY
a. Lk 9.39 "convulses him till he foams σπαράσσει αὐτὸν μετὰ ἀφροῦ [META]
CONTEXTUALLY
Rev 16.21 till men cursed God for the plague

TIMAEUS: Τιμαῖος tī'mēəs
Mk 10.46 Bartimaeus, a blind beggar, . . son of T.

TIME (*See also* FIRST TIME, FOR THE; SOME TIME; THIRD TIME, THE)
1. *age:* αἰών AIŌN
Jude .25 before all time and now and for ever
2. *time, period:* χρόνος CHRONOS
Mt 2. 7 ascertained . . what t. the star appeared
2.16 according to the time . . ascertained
25.19 "after a long time the master . . came
Lk 1.57 t. came for Elizabeth to be delivered
4. 5 all the kingdoms . . in a moment of t.
8.27 for a long t. he had worn no clothes
8.29 (For many a time it had seized him
Jn 5. 6 he had been lying there a long time
Acts 1. 6 "will you at this t. restore the kingdom?
1. 7 "It is not for you to know times
1.21 "during all the time that . . Jesus went
3.21 "whom heaven must receive until the t.
7.17 "as the time of the promise drew near
8.11 for a long time he had amazed them
14. 3 So they remained for a long time
14.28 remained no little t. with the disciples
15.33 after they had spent some time
17.30 "The times of ignorance God overlooked
18.23 After spending some time there
20.18 "all the time from the first day
27. 9 As much time had been lost
1 Cor 16. 7 I hope to spend some time with you
Gal 4. 4 when the time had fully come
1 Th 5. 1 But as to the times and the seasons
Heb 5.12 by this time you ought to be teachers
11.32 time would fail me to tell of Gideon
1 Pet 1.17 throughout the time of your exile
1.20 manifest at the end of the times
4. 2 to live for the rest of the t. in the flesh
4. 3 Let the time that is past suffice
Jude .18 "In the last time there will be scoffers
Rev 2.21 " 'I gave her time to repent
3. *day, tribunal:* ἡμέρα (pl.) HĒMERA
Lk 1.23 when his time of service was ended
2. 6 the time came for her to be delivered
2.22 when the t. came for their purification
23. 7 Herod . . was . . in Jerusalem at that time
Heb 12.10 they disciplined us for a short time
4. *hour, time of day:* ὥρα HŌRA
Mt 18. 1 At that t. the disciples came to Jesus
Lk 14.17 "at the time for the banquet he sent
5. *time, opportunity:* καιρός KAIROS
Mt 8.29 "Have you come here . . before the time?
11.25 At that t. Jesus declared, "I thank thee
12. 1 At that t. Jesus went . . on the sabbath
13.30 " 'at harvest time I will tell the reapers
14. 1 At that time Herod the tetrarch heard
Mt 16. 3 "you cannot interpret . . signs of the times‡
26.18 " 'The Teacher says, My t. is at hand
Mk 1.15 "The time is fulfilled, and the kingdom
10.30 "will . . receive a hundredfold now in this t.
12. 2 "When the time came, he sent a servant
13.33 "you do not know when the t. will come
Lk 1.20 "words, which will be fulfilled in their t.
8.13 "in time of temptation fall away
12.56 "not . . how to interpret the present time
13. 1 There were some present at that very time
18.30 "will . . receive manifold more in this time
19.44 "not know the time of your visitation
20.10 "When the time came, he sent a servant
21. 8 " 'I am he!' and, 'The time is at hand!
21.24 "until the times of . . Gentiles are fulfilled
21.36 "But watch at all times, praying
Jn 7. 6 Jesus said . . "My time has not yet come, but your time is always here
7. 8 "for my time has not yet fully come
Acts 3.19 "that times of refreshing may come
7.20 "At this time Moses was born
12. 1 About that time Herod . . laid violent hands
13.11 "blind and unable to see the sun for a t.
19.23 About that t. there arose no little stir
Rom 3.26 it was to prove at the present time
8.18 the sufferings of this present time
9. 9 "About this time I will return
11. 5 at the present time there is a remnant
1 Cor 4. 5 do not pronounce judgment before the t.
2 Cor 6. 2 "At the acceptable t. I have listened
6. 2 Behold, now is the acceptable time
8.14 your abundance at the present time
Eph 1.10 as a plan for the fulness of time
2.12 at that time separated from Christ
5.16 making the most of the time
6.18 Pray at all times in the Spirit
Col 4. 5 making the most of the time
1 Th 2.17 we were bereft of you . . for a short time
2 Th 2. 6 so that he may be revealed in his time
1 Tim 2. 6 testimony . . was borne at the proper t.
4. 1 in later times some will depart
6.15 manifest at the proper time
2 Tim 3. 1 there will come times of stress
4. 3 t. . . when people will not endure . . teaching
4. 6 the time of my departure has come
Tit 1. 3 at the proper t. manifested in his word
Heb 9.10 imposed until the t. of reformation
1 Pet 1. 5 ready to be revealed in the last time
1.11 what person or time was indicated
4.17 the time has come for judgment
Rev 1. 3 keep what is written . . ; for the t. is near
11.18 "the time for the dead to be judged
12.12 "he knows that his time is short!
12.14 that she might fly . . to the place where she is to be nourished for a time, and times, and half a time
22.10 "Do not . . , for the time is near
IDIOMATICALLY
a. Lk 21.13 "This will be a time for you to bear testimony ἀποβήσεται ὑμῖν εἰς μαρτύριον [APOBAINŌ]
b. Heb 7.25 he is able for all time to save σῴζειν εἰς τὸ παντελὲς δύναται [PANTELĒS]
c. Heb 10.12, 14 for all time εἰς τὸ διηνεκές [DIĒNEKĒS]
CONTEXTUALLY
Mt 1.11 at the t. of the deportation to Babylon
26.44 went away and prayed for the third time
Mk 14.72 the cock crowed a second time
Lk 4.27 "in the time of the prophet Elisha
7.45 "from the t. I came in she has not ceased
Jn 3. 4 "Can he enter a second time?
9.24 for the second time they called the man
21.16 A second t. he said to him, "Simon
Acts 7.12 "he sent forth our fathers the first t.
10.15 the voice came to him again a second t.
11. 9 "voice answered a second t. from heaven
26.28 "In a short t. . . to make me a Christian!
1 Cor 7.18 at the t. of his call already circumcised

1 Cor 7.18 at the t. of his call uncircumcised
2 Th 3.16 give you peace at all times in all ways
Heb 9.28 appear a second t., not to deal with sin
Rev 9.16 twice ten thousand times ten thousand

TIME, APPOINTED
TIME, DUE
TIME, FULL
TIME, OPPORTUNE
TIME, PROPER
TIME, RIGHT
1. *time, opportunity:* καιρός KAIROS
Mt 24.45 "to give them . . food at the proper time
Lk 4.13 departed from him until an opportune t.
12.42 "to give them . . food at the proper time
Rom 5. 6 at the right time Christ died
13.11 how it is full time now for you to wake
1 Cor 7.29 the appointed time has grown very short
1 Pet 5. 6 that in due time he may exalt you

TIME, AT ANY
1. *each time, always:* ἑκάστοτε HEKASTOTE*
2 Pet 1.15 able at any time to recall these things

TIME, AT ONE
1. *at some time, once:* ποτέ POTE II
Eph 2.11 at one time you Gentiles in the flesh

TIME, AT THAT
1. *then, formerly:* τότε TOTE
Gal 4.29 as at that time he who was born

TIME, AT THE SAME
1. *at the same time:* ἅμα HAMA
[a]ἅμα καί [b]ἅμα δὲ καί
Acts 24.26 [a]At the same time he hoped
27.40 at the same time loosening the ropes
Phm .22 [b]At the same time, prepare a guest room

TIME, BY THIS
1. *already, now:* ἤδη ĒDĒ
Mt 14.24 the boat by this time was . . distant
Jn 11.39 "Lord, by this t. there will be an odor

TIME, FOR A LONG
TIME PAST, FOR SOME
1. *from above, anew:* ἄνωθεν ANŌTHEN
Lk 1. 3 followed . . closely[a] for some time past
Acts 26. 5 "They have known for a long time

TIME OF NEED, IN
1. *well-timed:* εὔκαιρος EUKAIROS [A.3.b.1, d.1]
Heb 4.16 may . . find grace to help in time of need

TIME, SPEND
TIME, SPEND ONE'S
1. *waste time:* χρονοτριβέω CHRONOTRIBEŌ*
Acts 20.16 that he might not . . spend time in Asia
2. *have time, have opportunity:* εὐκαιρέω EUKAIREŌ
Acts 17.21 spent their time . . hearing something new

TIME, THAT
1. *then, formerly:* τότε TOTE
Mt 4.17 From that time Jesus began to preach
16.21 From that time Jesus began to show

TIMES (*See, e.g.,* FIVE TIMES; SEVEN TIMES; SEVENTY TIMES; TIME)

TIMIDITY
1. *timidity, cowardice:* δειλία DEILIA*
2 Tim 1. 7 God did not give us a spirit of timidity

TIMON: Τίμων 'tīmən
Acts 6. 5 Prochorus, and Nicanor, and Timon

TIMOTHY: Τιμόθεος 'timəthē
Acts 16. 1 Timothy, the son of a Jewish woman
17.14 brethren . . sent Paul . . , but T. remained
17.15 T. to come to him as soon as possible
18. 5 When . . T. arrived from Macedonia
19.22 having sent . . T. . . , he . . stayed in Asia
20. 4 Gaius of Derbe, and Timothy
Rom 16.21 Timothy, my fellow worker, greets you
1 Cor 4.17 I sent[g] to you Timothy, my beloved
16.10 When T. comes, . . put him at ease among you
2 Cor 1. 1 Paul, an apostle of Christ Jesus . . , and T.
1.19 whom we preached . . , T. and I
Phil 1. 1 Paul and T., servants[a] of Christ Jesus
2.19 I hope . . to send Timothy to you soon
Col 1. 1 Paul, an apostle of Christ Jesus . . , and T.
1 Th 1. 1 Paul, Silvanus, and T., To the church
3. 2 we sent T., our brother . . , to establish you
3. 6 now that T. has come to us from you
2 Th 1. 1 Paul, Silvanus, and T., To the church
1 Tim 1. 2 To T., my true child in the faith
1.18 This charge I commit to you, T.
6.20 T., guard what has been entrusted to you
2 Tim 1. 2 To Timothy, my beloved child
Phm . 1 Paul, a prisoner for Christ Jesus, and T.
Heb 13.23 our brother T. has been released
CONTEXTUALLY
Acts 16. 3 Paul wanted T. to accompany him
Phil 2.22 But Timothy's worth you know

TITHE
1. *tithe:* ἀποδεκατόω APODEKATOŌ
Mt 23.23 "you tithe mint and dill and cummin
Lk 11.42 "you tithe mint and rue and every herb
2. *tenth:* δέκατος (subst. fem.) DEKATOS
Heb 7. 4 Abraham the patriarch gave him a tithe
7. 8 Here tithes are received by mortal men
7. 9 Levi himself, who receives tithes

TITHES FROM, TAKE
1. *tithe:* ἀποδεκατόω APODEKATOŌ
Heb 7. 5 to take tithes from the people

TITHES OF, GIVE
1. *pay a tithe:* ἀποδεκατεύω APODEKATEUŌ*
Lk 18.12 " 'I fast . . , I give tithes of all that I get

TITHES, PAY
1. *take tithes:* δεκατόω (pass.) DEKATOŌ
Heb 7. 9 Levi himself . . paid t. through Abraham

TITHES, RECEIVE
1. *take tithes:* δεκατόω DEKATOŌ
Heb 7. 6 this man . . received tithes from Abraham

TITIUS: Τίτιος 'tishəs
Acts 18. 7 went to the house of a man named T.[q]‡

TITLE
1. *inscription, title* (Lat.): τίτλος TITLOS*
Jn 19.19 wrote a title and put it on the cross
19.20 Many of the Jews read this title

TITUS: Τίτος 'tītəs
Acts [18. 7 went to the house of a man named *T.*‡
2 Cor 2.13 I did not find my brother Titus there
7. 6 comforted us by the coming of Titus
7.13 we rejoiced still more at the joy of Titus
7.14 our boasting before T. has proved true
8. 6 Accordingly we have urged Titus
8.16 God . . puts . . care for you into . . heart of T.
8.23 As for Titus, he is my partner
12.18 I urged Titus to go . . Did Titus take advantage of you?
Gal 2. 1 went up again . . with Barnabas, taking T.
2. 3 T. . . was not compelled to be circumcised
2 Tim 4.10 Titus ⟨has gone⟩ to Dalmatia
Tit 1. 4 T., my true child in a common faith

TO
1. *until:* ἄχρι ACHRI
Mk **16.**[end]‡
Acts **2.**29; **11.**5; **22.**4; **26.**22
1 Cor **4.**11
2 Cor **3.**14; **10.**13
Heb **4.**12
2. *from:* ἀπό (+gen.) APO
Col **2.**20
Rev **18.**14
3. *into, to, for:* εἰς (+acc.) EIS
Mt **2.**1, 8, 12, 13, 14, 20, 21, 22; **4.**5, 8; **5.**22; **7.**13, 14; **8.**18, 28²; **9.**1, 23; **10.**17, 21, 22, 23; **12.**20, 44; **13.**54; **14.**13, 19, 22, 35; **15.**21, 24, 39; **16.**21; **17.**24, 27; **20.**17, 18²; **21.**1³, 17, 18; **22.**3, 4, 5, 9; **23.**34; **24.**9, 13, 16; **25.**10; **26.**10, 30, 32, 36, 71; **27.**33; **28.**7, 10, 16

Mk **1**.35, 38; **2**.1; **4**.22, 35; **5**.1^{2}, 12, 21, 38; **6**.1, 31, 32, 41, 45; **7**.24, 31, 34; **8**.3, 10, 22, 26, 27; **9**.33, 43^{2}; **10**.1, 32, 33, 46; **11**.1^{2}, 11, 15, 27; **12**.43; **13**.9, 10, 12, 13, 14; **14**.16, 26, 28, 32; **15**.41; **16**.7
Lk **1**.23, 26, 44, 56; **2**.3, 4^{2}, 22, 39^{2}, 41, 45, 51; **4**.9, 16^{2}, 26, 31; **5**.32; **6**.12; **7**.10, 11; **8**.17, 22, 39, 41, 51; **9**.10, 16, 51, 56; **10**.7, 11, 30, 34; **11**.24; **14**.8, 21, 23; **15**.17; **16**.22, 27; **17**.11, 24; **18**.13, 14, 31, 35; **19**.28, 29; **21**.12, 21; **22**.33^{2}, 39, 66; **24**.5, 13, 28, 33, 47, 52
Jn **1**.11, 43; **2**.2, 12, 13; **4**.3, 5, 14, 43, 45^{2}, 46, 47, 54; **5**.1, 24, 29^{2}; **6**.15, 17, 21, 24, 27; **7**.3, 8^{2}, 10, 35, 53‡; **8**.1‡, 2‡, 26; **9**.11; **10**.40; **11**.30, 31, 38, 54^{2}, 55, 56; **12**.1, 12^{2}, 27; **13**.1; **15**.21; **16**.32; **17**.1; **18**.28; **19**.17; **20**.1
Acts **1**.12, 13, 25; **2**.22, 27, 31; **3**.1; **5**.21, 36; **7**.16, 34, 39; **8**.3, 5, 25, 26, 27, 40; **9**.2, 26, 30^{2}, 39; **10**.5, 8, 16, 22, 32; **11**.2, 13, 20, 22, 25, 26, 27; **12**.17, 19, [25‡; **13**.4^{2}, 13^{2}, 14, 31, 34, 46, 48, 51; **14**.6, 20, 21^{3}, 24, 25, 26; **15**.2, 4, 22, 30, 38, 39; **16**.1^{2}, 8, 9, 11^{2}, 12, 15, 16; **17**.1, 5, 10, 20; **18**.1, 6, 7, 19, 22, 24, 27; **19**.1, 21; **20**.2, 14, 15, 17, 21, 22, 38; **21**.1^{3}, 2, 3, 4, 8, 12, 15, 17; **22**.4, 5^{2}, 7, 17, 21; **23**.15, 20, 28, 31, 32, 33; **24**.17; **25**.1, 3, 6, 9, 20; **26**.6, 7, 11, 12, 14, 17, 18; **27**.2, 5, 8; **28**.6, 13, 14
Rom **1**.24, 26, 28; **2**.4; **3**.7; **5**.2, 12, 21; **6**.17; **8**.7, 18; **10**.18^{2}; **11**.32, 36; **13**.6; **14**.9; **15**.16, 24, 25, 28; **16**.19, 26
1 Cor **4**.6; **10**.31; **16**.3, 15
2 Cor **1**.16^{2}, 23; **2**.12, 13, 16^{2}; **3**.18; **4**.11, 15; **7**.15; **8**.24; **9**.5; **10**.1; **11**.3, 6; **12**.1
Gal **1**.6, 17^{2}, 18; **2**.1, 9^{2}, 11; **6**.8^{2}
Eph **1**.6, 14; **3**.21; **4**.13^{3}, 32; **5**.32
Phil **1**.11; **2**.11; **3**.16; **4**.17
Col **1**.6, 13, 20; **3**.9; **3**.15
1 Th **1**.5; **2**.9; **3**.12^{3}; **4**.8; **5**.15^{2}
2 Th **2**.14; **3**.5^{2}
1 Tim **1**.3, 12; **2**.4; **5**.24; **6**.12
2 Tim **4**.10^{3}, 12
Heb **2**.3, 10; **6**.4(6); **11**.8, 26; **12**.2
Jas **1**.19; **4**.9^{2}
1 Pet **1**.3, 4, 7, 25; **2**.2, 21; **3**.9, 12, 21; **4**.9; **5**.10
2 Pet **3**.18
3 Jn .5
Rev **1**.11^{7}; **6**.13; **9**.1; **10**.5; **11**.12; **12**.4, 9, 13, 14; **13**.10, 13; **17**.8, 11; **19**.9

4. *from, out of:* ἐκ (+gen.) EK
Mk **11**.20
Gal **3**.22

5. *in, at, by:* ἐν (+dat.) EN
Mt **3**.9; **9**.3, 21: **17**.12; **21**.38
Mk **14**.6
Lk **1**.17; **3**.8; **5**.16; **7**.39; **12**.17; **16**.3; **18**.4
Acts **11**.23 *var. om.;* **12**.11
Rom **1**.19; **7**.6, 23
1 Cor **7**.15; **14**.11; **15**.28
2 Cor **4**.3; **5**.11, 19
Gal **1**.16†
Eph **4**.4
Col **1**.23; **2**.20
1 Tim **4**.15

6. *face to face, before:* ἐνώπιον ENŌPION
Lk 24.11 these words seemed to them an idle tale

7. *on, at:* ἐπί (+acc.) EPI
except ^{a}+dat. ^{b}+gen.
Mt **3**.13; **6**.27; **10**.13, 29; **14**.34; **21**.19; **22**.5, 9; **24**.16
Mk **6**.53; **11**.13; **15**.22; **16**.2
Lk **1**.16, 17; **3**.2, 20^{a}; **5**.11; **6**.35; **9**.62; **10**.6, 9; **12**.25; **19**.5; **22**.40^{b}; **23**.33; **24**.1, [12‡, 24
Jn **6**.16; **19**.33
Acts **2**.47; **6**.3^{b}; **8**.26, 32, 36; **9**.4, 11, 35; **11**.21; **12**.10, 12; **14**.13, 15; **15**.19; **17**.14, 19; **19**.12; **21**.32, 35; **25**.12; **26**.18, 20; **27**.44
Rom **11**.22; **12**.20
1 Cor **14**.16^{a}
Gal **3**.16^{b2}; **4**.9; **5**.13^{a}
2 Th **1**.10
1 Tim **1**.18
2 Tim **3**.13
Heb **6**.1
Jas **2**.3
1 Pet **2**.[24†, 25
2 Pet **2**.22
Rev **7**.17; **14**.6^{2}; **16**.14; **21**.10; **22**.14, 18^{2}

8. *until:* ἕως HEŌS
^{a}+ἐπί
Mt **1**.17^{3}; **11**.23^{2}; **23**.35; **24**.31; **27**.8, 51; **28**.20
Mk **13**.27; **15**.38
Lk **2**.15; **4**.29, 42; **10**.15^{2}; **11**.51
Acts **1**.8; **8**.10; **9**.38; **11**.22; **13**.47; **17**.14^{a}; **19**.[9‡
1 Cor **1**.8
2 Cor **3**.15; **12**.2
Heb **8**.11

9. *under:* ὑπό (+acc.) HYPO
Gal **3**.22; **4**.3

10. *in accordance with, for:* κατά (+acc.) KATA
except ^{a}+gen.
Lk **10**.32, 33
2 Cor **10**.5^{a}; **11**.21
Gal **2**.11
Jas **3**.14^{a}

11. *as far as:* μέχρι MECHRI
Mt 28.15 story has been spread . . to this day
Rom 5.14 death reigned from Adam to Moses
Heb [3. 6 if we hold fast . . *firm to the end*‡
3.14 if only we hold . . firm to the end

12. *with:* μετά (+gen.) META
Mk **6**.50
Lk **1**.72
Jn **9**.37; **11**.56
Rev **1**.12; **4**.1; **10**.8; **17**.1; **21**.9, 15

13. *about, concerning:* περί (+gen.) PERI
Jn **1**.7, 8, 15; **5**.31, 32^{2}, 37, 39; **8**.13, 14, 18^{2}; **10**.25; **15**.26; **18**.23; **21**.24
1 Jn **5**.9, 10

14. *to, with, against:* πρός (+acc.) PROS
Mt **2**.12; **3**.5, 10, 13, 14; **7**.15; **10**.6, 13; **11**.28; **14**.25, 28, 29; **17**.14; **19**.14; **21**.32, 34, 37; **23**.37; **25**.9, 36; **26**.14, 18, 40, 45, 57; **27**.4, 14, 19
Mk **1**.5, 32, 40, 45; **2**.3; **3**.7, 8, 13, 31; **4**.41; **5**.15, 19; **6**.25, 30, 45, 48; **7**.1; **9**.10, 14, 17, 20; **10**.1, 7‡, 14, 26, 50; **11**.7, 27; **12**.2, 4, 6, 7, 13, 18; **14**.4, 10, 53; **15**.31, 43; **16**.3
Lk **1**.13, 18, 19, 27, 28, 34, 43, 55, 61, 73, 80; **2**.15, 34, 48, 49; **3**.9, 12, 13; **4**.21, 23, 26^{2}, 36, 40, 43; **5**.4, 10, 33, 34; **6**.9, 47; **7**.3, 4, 6, 7, 19, 20^{2}, 24, 40, 50; **8**.4, 19, 21, 22, 25, 35; **9**.3, 13, 14, 23, 33, 43, 50, 57, 59, 62; **10**.2, 23, 26, 29; **11**.1, 5^{2}, 39; **12**.1, 15, 22, 58; **13**.7, 23, 34; **14**.3, 5, 6, 7^{2}, 23, 25, 26; **15**.18, 20, 22; **16**.1, 26^{2}, 30; **17**.1, 4, 22; **18**.3, 9, 16, 31, 40; **19**.5, 8, 9, 13, 33, 35, 39; **20**.2, 10, 14, 23, 25, 41; **21**.38; **22**.15, 45, 52, 70; **23**.4, 7, 14, 15, 22, 28; **24**.5, 10, 17, 25, 32, 44
Jn **1**.42, 47; **2**.3; **3**.2, 4, 20, 21, 26^{2}; **4**.15, 30, 33, 40, 48, 49; **5**.33, 40, 45; **6**.5^{2}, 17, 28, 34, 35, 37^{2}, 44, 45, 65, 68; **7**.3, 33, 35, 37, 45, 50^{2}; **8**.2‡, 31, 33, 57; **9**.13; **10**.35, 41; **11**.3, 15, 19, 21, 29, 46; **12**.19, 32; **13**.1, 3, 6; **14**.3, 6, 12, 18, 23, 28^{2}; **16**.5, 7^{2}, 10, 17^{2}, 28; **17**.11, 13; **18**.13, 24, 29, 38; **19**.3, 24, 39; **20**.2^{2}, 10, 17^{3}; **21**.22, 23
Acts **1**.7; **2**.12, 29, 37, 38; **3**.11, 25^{2}; **4**.1, 8, 23^{2}, 24; **5**.8, 9, 35; **7**.3; **8**.14, 20, 24, 26; **9**.2, 10, 11, 15, 27, 32, 38, 40; **10**.3, 13, 15, 21, 28, 33; **11**.3, 11, 14, 20, 30; **12**.5, 8, 15, 20, 21; **13**.15, 31, 32; **14**.11; **15**.2, 7, 25, 33, 36; **16**.36, 37; **17**.15; **18**.6, 14, 21; **19**.2, 31; **20**.6, 18; **21**.11, 18, 37, 39; **22**.5, 8, 10, 13, 15, 21, 25; **23**.3, 17, 18^{2}, 24, 30; **25**.21, 22; **26**.1, 14, 26, 28, 31; **27**.3; **28**.4, 17, 21, 23, 25, 26, 30
Rom **1**.10, 13; **8**.31; **10**.1, 21; **15**.22, 23, 29, 30, 32
1 Cor **2**.1; **4**.18, 19, 21; **6**.5; **12**.2; **13**.12; **14**.6; **15**.34; **16**.11
2 Cor **1**.15, 18, 20; **3**.1, 16; **4**.2; **6**.11; **7**.12; **8**.17; **12**.14, 17; **13**.1
Gal **1**.17; **6**.10^{2}
Eph **2**.18; **5**.31; **6**.9, 22
Phil **1**.26; **2**.25, 30; **4**.6
Col **4**.8, 10
1 Th **1**.9; **2**.1, 2, 18; **3**.6, 11
1 Tim **3**.14
2 Tim **2**.24; **4**.9
Tit **3**.12^{2}
Heb **1**.13; **5**.5, 7; **13**.13
1 Pet **2**.4

2 Pet **3**.16
2 Jn .10, 12
3 Jn .14
Rev **3**.20; **10**.9; **12**.5[2], 12

TO, AS
1. *in accordance with, for:* κατά (+acc.) KATA
Phil **3**.5, 6[2]
2. *about, concerning:* περί (+gen.) PERI
1 Cor **8**.4
1 Th **5**.1

TO, DOWN
1. *until:* ἕως HEŌS
Mt 22.26 "second and third, d. to the seventh
Rom 11. 8 "should not hear, down to this very day

TO, EVEN
1. *until:* ἕως HEŌS
[a]ἕως καὶ εἰς
Mt 26.38 "My soul is very sorrowful, even to death
Mk 14.34 "My soul is very sorrowful, even to death
Lk 23. 5 "from Galilee even to this place
Acts 26.11 [a]"I persecuted them even to foreign cities

TO, UP
1. *until:* ἄχρι ACHRI
Acts 22.22 Up to this word they listened
23. 1 "in all good conscience up to this day
2. *until:* ἕως HEŌS
Mt 20. 8 " 'beginning with the last, up to the first

TODAY
1. *today:* σήμερον SĒMERON
Mt 6.30 "grass of the field, which today is alive
16. 3 "in the morning, 'It will be stormy t.‡
21.28 " 'Son, go and work in the vineyard t.
27.19 "I have suffered much over him today
Lk [3.22 *"today I have begotten thee*‡
4.21 "Today this scripture has been fulfilled
5.26 "We have seen strange things today
12.28 "grass which is alive in the field today
13.32 " 'I . . perform cures today and tomorrow
13.33 " 'Nevertheless I must go on my way t.
19. 5 "I must stay at your house today
19. 9 "Today salvation has come to this house
22.61 "Before the cock crows today
23.43 "today you will be with me in Paradise
Acts 4. 9 "if we are being examined today
13.33 " 'my Son, today I have begotten thee
19.40 "danger of being charged with rioting t.
26. 2 "I am to make my defense today
27.33 "T. is the fourteenth day . . without food
Heb 1. 5 "my Son, today I have begotten thee
3. 7 "Today, when you hear his voice
3.13 every day, as long as it is called "today
3.15 "Today, when you hear his voice
4. 7 again he sets a certain day, "Today," saying . . "Today, when you hear his voice
5. 5 "my Son, today I have begotten thee
13. 8 the same yesterday and today
Jas 4.13 you who say, "Today or tomorrow

IDIOMATICALLY
a. Lk 19.42 "Would that even today you knew εἰ ἔγνως ἐν τῇ ἡμέρᾳ ταύτῃ καὶ σύ [HĒMERA]

TOGETHER
1. *at the same time:* ἅμα HAMA
Rom 3.12 "together they have gone wrong
1 Th 4.17 then we . . shall be caught up together
2. *together with one mind:* ὁμοθυμαδόν HOMOTHYMADON
Acts 2.46 attending the temple together
4.24 they lifted their voices together to God
5.12 all together in Solomon's Portico
7.57 they . . rushed together upon him
19.29 they rushed together into the theater
Rom 15. 6 that together you may . . glorify the God
3. *at the same place:* ὁμοῦ HOMOU
Jn 4.36 "so that sower and reaper may rejoice t.
21. 2 two others of his disciples were together
Acts 2. 1 they were all together in one place
4. *with the whole multitude:* παμπληθεί PAMPLĒTHEI*
Lk 23.18 all cried out t., "Away with this man

TOGETHER WITH
1. *with:* σύν (+dat.) SYN
Acts **1**.14; **18**.8
1 Cor **1**.2; **16**.19

TOIL
1. *work hard, grow weary:* κοπιάω KOPIAŌ
Mt 6.28 "lilies of the field . . neither t. nor spin
Lk 5. 5 "we toiled all night and took nothing!
12.27 "the lilies . . neither toil nor spin[o]‡
Acts 20.35 " 'by so toiling one must help the weak
Col 1.29 For this I t., striving with all . . energy
1 Tim 4.10 For to this end we toil and strive[j]
2. *work:* κόπος KOPOS
2 Cor 11.27 in t. and hardship, . . in hunger and thirst
Rev 2. 2 " 'I know your works, your toil
3. *hardship, toil:* μόχθος MOCHTHOS
1 Th 2. 9 For you remember our labor and toil
2 Th 3. 8 but with toil and labor we worked

TOLD, THAT CANNOT BE
1. *not to be spoken:* ἄρρητος (attr.) ARRĒTOS*
2 Cor 12. 4 he heard things that cannot be told

TOLERABLE, MORE
1. *bearable:* ἀνεκτός (comp.) ANEKTOS*
Mt 10.15 "shall be more t. . . for the land of Sodom
11.22 "shall be more t. . . for Tyre and Sidon
11.24 "shall be more t. . . for the land of Sodom
Lk 10.12 "shall be more tolerable . . for Sodom
10.14 "shall be more t. . . for Tyre and Sidon

TOLERATE
1. *let go, leave, forgive:* ἀφίημι APHIĒMI
Rev 2.20 " 'you tolerate the woman Jezebel

TOLL
1. *end, goal:* τέλος TELOS
Mt 17.25 "From whom do kings . . take toll or tribute?

TOMB
1. *tomb, memorial:* μνῆμα MNĒMA*
Mk 5. 3 who lived among the tombs
5. 5 Night and day among the tombs
15.46 laid him in a t. which had been hewn out
Lk 8.27 lived not in a house but among . . tombs
23.53 laid him in a rock-hewn tomb
24. 1 at early dawn, they went to the tomb
Acts 2.29 "his tomb is with us to this day
7.16 "in the tomb that Abraham had bought
Rev 11. 9 refuse to let them be placed in a tomb
Also variant to: Mk **16**.2
2. *tomb, memorial:* μνημεῖον MNĒMEION
Mt 8.28 demoniacs . . , coming out of the tombs
27.52 the tombs also were opened
27.53 out of the tombs after his resurrection
27.60 laid it in his own new tomb
27.60 he rolled a . . stone to the door of the t.
28. 8 they departed quickly from the t.
Mk 5. 2 there met him out of the tombs a man
6.29 took his body, and laid it in a tomb
15.46 rolled a stone against the door of the t.
16. 2 went to the t. when the sun had risen
Var. MNĒMA
16. 3 "Who will roll away . . stone . . from . . the t.?
16. 5 entering the t., they saw a young man
16. 8 they went out and fled from the tomb
Lk 11.47 "you build the tombs of the prophets
11.48 "they killed them, and you build their tombs
23.55 women . . followed, and saw the tomb
24. 2 found the stone . . away from the tomb
24. 9 returning from the tomb they told all
[24.12 *Peter rose and ran to the tomb*‡
24.22 "They were at the tomb early
24.24 "Some . . who were with us went to the t.
Jn 5.28 "all . . in the tombs will hear his voice
11.17 Lazarus[z] had . . been in the t. four days
11.31 supposing . . she was going to the t.
11.38 Jesus, deeply moved . . , came to the tomb

Jn 12.17 he called Lazarus out of the tomb
19.41 there was .. in the garden a new tomb
19.42 as the tomb was close at hand
20. 1 Mary Magdalene came to the tomb early .. and saw .. the stone .. away from the tomb
20. 2 "They have taken the Lord out of the t.
20. 3 they went toward the tomb
20. 4 the other disciple .. reached the tomb first
20. 6 Simon Peter .. went into the tomb
20. 8 other disciple, who reached the t. first
20.11 Mary stood .. outside the t., and as she wept she stooped to look into the tomb
Acts 13.29 "took him down .. and laid him in a tomb
3. *tomb, grave:* τάφος TAPHOS
Mt 23.27 "for you are like whitewashed tombs
23.29 "for you build the tombs of the prophets

TOMORROW

1. *tomorrow:* αὔριον AURION
[a]ἡ αὔριον B.3.b.2
Mt 6.30 "which .. t. is thrown into the oven
6.34 [a]"do not be anxious about tomorrow
6.34 [a]"for t. will be anxious for itself
Lk 12.28 "which .. t. is thrown into the oven
13.32 " 'I .. perform cures today and t.
13.33 " 'I must go on my way today and t.
Acts 23.20 "to bring Paul down to the council t.
25.22 "Tomorrow .. you shall hear him
1 Cor 15.32 "Let us eat and drink, for t. we die
Jas 4.13 "tomorrow we will go into .. such a town
4.14 [a]whereas you do not know about t.

TONE

1. *voice, sound:* φωνή PHŌNĒ
Gal 4.20 I could wish .. to change my tone

TONGUE

1. *tongue, speech:* γλῶσσα GLŌSSA
Mk 7.33 he spat and touched his tongue
7.35 his tongue was released, and he spoke
16.17 "they will speak in new tongues[k]‡
Lk 1.64 his tongue loosed, and he spoke
16.24 " 'send Lazarus to .. cool my tongue
Acts 2. 3 there appeared .. tongues as of fire
2. 4 they .. began to speak in other tongues
2.11 "we hear them telling in our own tongues
2.26 " 'my heart was glad, and my t. rejoiced
10.46 they heard them speaking in tongues
19. 6 they spoke with tongues and prophesied
Rom 3.13 "they use their tongues to deceive
14.11 "every tongue shall give praise[u] to God
1 Cor 12.10 to another various kinds of tongues, to another the interpretation of tongues
12.28 speakers in various kinds of tongues
12.30 Do all speak with tongues?
13. 1 If I speak in the tongues of men
13. 8 as for tongues, they will cease
14. 2 For one who speaks in a tongue
14. 4 He who speaks in a tongue edifies himself
14. 5 Now I want you all to speak in tongues
14. 5 greater than he who speaks in tongues
14. 6 if I come to you speaking in tongues
14. 9 if you in a tongue utter speech
14.13 he who speaks in a tongue should pray
14.14 if I pray in a tongue, my spirit prays
14.18 I thank God that I speak in tongues
14.19 rather .. than ten thousand words in a t.
14.22 tongues are a sign not for believers
14.23 If, therefore, .. all speak in tongues
14.26 a revelation, a t., or an interpretation
14.27 If any speak in a t., .. let one interpret
14.39 do not forbid speaking in tongues
Phil 2.11 every t. confess that Jesus Christ is Lord
Jas 1.26 If any one .. does not bridle his tongue
3. 5 the t. is a little member and boasts
3. 6 And the tongue is a fire. The tongue is an unrighteous world
3. 8 no human being can tame the tongue
1 Pet 3.10 "let him keep his tongue from evil
Rev 5. 9 "thou .. didst ransom .. from every .. t.
7. 9 a great multitude .. from all .. tongues
10.11 "prophesy about .. nations and tongues
11. 9 men from the peoples .. and tongues
13. 7 authority was given it over every .. t.
14. 6 to proclaim .. to every nation and .. t.
16.10 men gnawed their tongues in anguish
17.15 "The waters .. are peoples and .. tongues

TONGUES, MEN OF STRANGE

1. *of another tongue:* ἑτερόγλωσσος (subst. pl.)
HETEROGLŌSSOS*
1 Cor 14.21 "By men of strange t. will I speak

TOOTH

1. *tooth:* ὀδούς ODOUS*
Mt 5.38 "You have heard that it was said, 'An eye for an eye and a tooth for a tooth
8.12 "there men will weep and gnash their teeth
Also Mt **13.**42, 50; **22.**13; **24.**51; **25.**30
Mk 9.18 "and he foams and grinds his teeth
Lk 13.28 "you will weep and gnash your teeth
Acts 7.54 they ground their teeth against him
Rev 9. 8 ⟨locusts⟩ and their teeth like lions'

TOP

IDIOMATICALLY
a. Mt 27.51; Mk 15.38 the curtain .. was torn .. from top to bottom τὸ καταπέτασμα .. ἐσχίσθη ἀπ' ἄνωθεν ἕως κάτω [ANŌTHEN]
b. Jn 19.23 woven from top to bottom ἐκ τῶν ἄνωθεν ὑφαντὸς δι' ὅλου [ANŌTHEN]

TOPAZ

1. *topaz:* τοπάζιον TOPAZION*
Rev 21.20 the ninth topaz, the tenth chrysoprase

TORCH

1. *lamp, torch:* λαμπάς LAMPAS
Jn 18. 3 went there with lanterns and torches
Rev 4. 5 before the throne burn seven torches
8.10 a great star fell .., blazing like a torch

TORMENT

1. *torture:* βασανισμός BASANISMOS
Rev 14.11 "the smoke of their torment goes up
18. 7 " 'give her a like measure of torment
18.10 they will stand far off, in fear of her t.
18.15 will stand far off, in fear of her torment
2. *question by torture, torment:* βασανίζω BASANIZŌ
Mt 8.29 "Have you come here to torment us?
Mk 5. 7 "I adjure you .., do not torment me
Lk 8.28 "I beseech you, do not torment me
Rev 11.10 these two prophets had been a torment
14.10 "he shall be tormented with fire
20.10 they will be tormented day and night
3. *touchstone, test, torture:* βάσανος (pl.) BASANOS
Lk 16.23 "being in torment, he lifted up his eyes
16.28 " 'lest they also come into this place of t.

TORTURE

1. *torture:* βασανισμός BASANISMOS
Rev 9. 5 their torture was like the torture of a scorpion, when it stings a man
2. *question by torture, torment:* βασανίζω BASANIZŌ
Rev 9. 5 they were allowed to torture them
3. *beat a drum:* τυμπανίζω TYMPANIZŌ*
Heb 11.35 tortured, refusing to accept release

TOSS

1. *blow about, hurl:* ῥιπίζω RHIPIZŌ*
Jas 1. 6 like a wave .. that is .. tossed by the wind

TOSSED TO AND FRO

1. *be buffeted by heavy seas:* κλυδωνίζομαι (part.)
KLYDŌNIZOMAI*
Eph 4.14 tossed to and fro and carried about

TOUCH

1. *kindle; touch* (mid.): ἅπτω (mid.) HAPTŌ
Mt 8. 3 stretched out his hand and touched him
8.15 he touched her hand, and the fever left
9.20 touched the fringe of his garment
9.21 she said .. "If I only touch his garment

Mt 9.29 Then he touched their eyes
14.36 might . . t. the fringe of his garment; and as many as touched it were made well
17. 7 Jesus came and touched them
20.34 Jesus in pity touched their eyes
Mk 1.41 he . . touched him, and said . . "be clean
3.10 pressed upon him to touch him
5.27 She . . came up . . and touched his garment
5.28 she said, "If I t. even his garments
5.30 "Who touched my garments?
5.31 "yet you say, 'Who touched me?
6.56 might t. . . the fringe of his garment; and as many as touched it were made well
7.33 he spat and touched his tongue
8.22 some people . . begged him to touch him
10.13 bringing children . . , that he might t. them
Lk 5.13 touched him, saying, "I will; be clean
6.19 all the crowd sought to touch him
7.14 he came and touched the bier
7.39 "what sort of woman . . is touching him
8.44 touched the fringe of his garment
8.45 "Who was it that touched me?
8.46 Jesus said, "Some one touched me
8.47 declared . . why she had touched him
18.15 bringing . . infants . . that he might t. them
22.51 he touched his ear and healed him
1 Cor 7. 1 well for a man not to touch a woman
2 Cor 6.17 come out from them, . . t. nothing unclean
1 Jn 5.18 the evil one does not touch him

2. *throw beside, approach:* παραβάλλω PARABALLŌ*
Acts 20.15 the next day we touched at Samos

3. *touch upon:* προσψαύω PROSPSAUŌ*
Lk 11.46 "you yourselves do not touch the burdens

4. *grope after, feel:* ψηλαφάω PSĒLAPHAŌ
Heb 12.18 have not come to what may be touched
1 Jn 1. 1 which we have . . touched with our hands

5. *handle, touch:* θιγγάνω THIGGANŌ*
Col 2.21 "Do not handle, Do not taste, Do not t.
Heb 11.28 that the Destroyer . . might not t. them
12.20 "If even a beast touches the mountain

TOWARD

1. *into, to, for:* εἰς (+acc.) EIS
Lk **9.53**; **12.21**; **13.22**
Jn **20.3**
1 Cor **15.10**
Eph **1.15**
2 Pet **3.9**‡

2. *on, at:* ἐπί (+acc.) EPI
Mt 12.49 stretching out his hand t. his disciples
Rom 11.22 severity toward those who have fallen
1 Cor 7.36 not behaving properly t. his betrothed[z]
Eph 2. 7 his grace in kindness toward us
Heb 6. 1 foundation of repentance . . faith t. God

3. *way, road:* ὁδός (acc. as prep.) HODOS
Mt 4.15 "The land of Zebulun . . toward the sea

4. *in accordance with, for:* κατά (+acc.) KATA
Acts 8.26 "Rise and go toward the south[o]†
Phil 3.14 I press on t. the goal for the prize

5. *to, with, against:* πρός (+acc.) PROS
Lk 7.44 turning t. the woman he said to Simon
24.29 "Stay with us, for it is toward evening
Jn 1.29 next day he saw Jesus coming t. him
Acts 24.16 "to have a clear conscience toward God
2 Cor 1.12 we have behaved . . t. you, with holiness
3. 4 the confidence that we have . . t. God
Col 4. 5 Conduct yourselves wisely t. outsiders
Tit 3. 2 show perfect courtesy toward all men
Phm . 5 faith which you have t. the Lord Jesus

TOWEL

1. *cloth, napkin, towel:* λέντιον LENTION*
Jn 13. 4 rose . . and girded himself with a towel
13. 5 began . . to wipe them with the towel

TOWER

1. *tower:* πύργος PYRGOS*
Mt 21.33 "dug a wine press in it, and built a tower
Mk 12. 1 "dug a . . wine press, and built a tower
Lk 13. 4 "those eighteen upon whom the t. . . fell
14.28 "which of you, desiring to build a t.?

TOWN (*See also* CLERK, TOWN)

1. *market town:* κωμόπολις KŌMOPOLIS*
Mk 1.38 "Let us go on to the next towns

2. *city, city-state:* πόλις POLIS
Mt 10. 5 "enter no town of the Samaritans
10.11 "whatever town or village you enter
10.14 "shake off the dust . . as you leave that . . t.
10.15 "more tolerable . . for . . S. . . than . . that t.
10.23 "When they persecute you in one town, flee
10.23 "not . . through all the towns of Israel
14.13 followed him on foot from the towns
23.34 "some you will scourge in your synagogues and persecute from town to town
Mk 1.45 Jesus[g] could no longer openly enter a t.
6.33 they ran there . . from all the towns
Lk 9. 5 "when you leave that t. shake off . . dust
10. 1 two by two, into every town and place
10. 8 "Whenever you enter a town
10.10 "But whenever you enter a town
10.11 " 'Even the dust of your town that clings
10.12 "more tolerable . . for Sodom than for that t.
13.22 He went on his way through towns
23.50(51) Joseph from the . . t. of Arimathea
Jn 11.54 Jesus . . went . . to a t. called Ephraim
Acts 5.16 people also gathered from the towns
8.40 he preached the gospel to all the towns
Tit 1. 5 appoint elders in every town
Jas 4.13 we will go into such and such a town

IDIOMATICALLY
a. Lk 8.4 people from town after town came to him τῶν κατὰ πόλιν ἐπιπορευομένων πρὸς αὐτόν [POLIS]

TRACHONITIS: Τραχωνῖτις ˌtrakəˈnītəs I,E-2
Lk 3. 1 Philip tetrarch . . of Ituraea and T.

TRADE

1. *travel, be a merchant:* ἐμπορεύομαι EMPOREUOMAI
Jas 4.13 "spend a year there and t. and get gain

2. *market center:* ἐμπόριον EMPORION*
Jn 2.16 "not make my Father's house a house of t.

3. *work, do:* ἐργάζομαι ERGAZOMAI
Mt 25.16 "went at once and traded with them

4. *part, share:* μέρος MEROS
Acts 19.27 "that this t. . . come into disrepute

5. *be engaged in business:* πραγματεύομαι PRAGMATEUOMAI*
Lk 19.13 " 'Trade with these till I come

6. *art, skill:* τέχνη TECHNĒ
Acts 18. 3 for by trade they were tentmakers

IDIOMATICALLY
a. Rev 18.17 and all whose trade is on the sea καὶ ὅσοι τὴν θάλασσαν ἐργάζονται [ERGAZOMAI]

TRADE, OF THE SAME

1. *practicing the same skill:* ὁμότεχνος HOMOTECHNOS*
Acts 18. 3 because he was of the same trade

TRADING, GAIN BY

1. *gain by trading:* διαπραγματεύομαι DIAPRAGMATEUOMAI*
Lk 19.15 "what they had gained by trading

TRADITION

1. *handing down, transmission:* παράδοσις PARADOSIS*
Mt 15. 2 "Why do your disciples transgress the t.?
15. 3 "why . . transgress . . for the sake of your t.?
15. 6 "So, for the sake of your tradition
Mk 7. 3 (observing the tradition of the elders
7. 5 "not live[y] according to the tradition
7. 8 "You . . hold fast the tradition of men
7. 9 "in order to keep your tradition!
7.13 "making void the word . . through your t.
1 Cor 11. 2 because you . . maintain the traditions
Gal 1.14 so extremely zealous was I for . . traditions
Col 2. 8 prey . . , according to human tradition
2 Th 2.15 stand firm and hold to the traditions
3. 6 the tradition that you received from us

2. *what one receives:* ὃ παραλαμβάνει PARALAMBANŌ [B.2.a.1]
Mk 7. 4 (many other traditions which they observe

TRAIN
1. *train gymnastically:* γυμνάζω GYMNAZŌ*
1 Tim 4. 7 Train yourself in godliness
Heb 5.14 have their faculties trained by practice
12.11 to those who have been trained by it
2 Pet 2.14 They have hearts trained in greed
2. *discipline, educate:* παιδεύω PAIDEUŌ
Tit 2.12 training us to renounce irreligion
3. *train the mind:* σωφρονίζω SŌPHRONIZŌ*
Tit 2. 4 so train the young women to love

TRAINED, BE
1. *be a pupil, make disciples:* μαθητεύω (pass.) MATHĒTEUŌ
Mt 13.52 "every scribe who has been t. for .. kingdom

TRAINING
1. *exercise, training:* γυμνασία GYMNASIA*
1 Tim 4. 8 while bodily training is of some value
2. *stewardship, management:* οἰκονομία ŌIKONOMIA
1 Tim 1. 4 speculations rather than the divine t.[a]†
3. *teaching, training:* παιδεία PAIDEIA
2 Tim 3.16 All scripture is .. profitable .. for t.

TRAITOR
1. *betrayer, traitor:* προδότης PRODOTĒS
Lk 6.16 Judas Iscariot, who became a traitor

TRAMPLE
1. *tread underfoot:* καταπατέω KATAPATEŌ
Mt 7. 6 "lest they trample them under foot
2. *tread, trample:* πατέω PATEŌ
Rev 11. 2 "they will trample over the holy city

TRANCE
1. *displacement, ecstasy:* ἔκστασις EKSTASIS
Acts 10.10 he became hungry and .. fell into a trance
11. 5 "in a trance I saw a vision
22.17 "praying in the temple, I fell into a t.

TRANSCENDENT
1. *excess:* ὑπερβολή HYPERBOLĒ [A.1.b.5]
2 Cor 4. 7 the transcendent power belongs to God

TRANSFER
1. *change, remove:* μεθίστημι METHISTĒMI
Col 1.13 He has .. transferred us to the kingdom

TRANSFIGURED, BE
1. *transform:* μεταμορφόω (pass.) METAMORPHOŌ
Mt 17. 2 he was transfigured before them
Mk 9. 2 he was transfigured before them

TRANSFORMED, BE
1. *transform:* μεταμορφόω (pass.) METAMORPHOŌ
Rom 12. 2 but be t. by the renewal of your mind

TRANSGRESS
1. *go beyond:* ὑπερβαίνω HYPERBAINŌ*
1 Th 4. 6 that no man t., and wrong his brother
2. *go by the side of:* παραβαίνω PARABAINŌ
Mt 15. 2 "Why do your disciples t. the tradition?
15. 3 "And why do you t. the commandment?

TRANSGRESSION
1. *digression, transgression:* παράβασις PARABASIS
Rom 4.15 where there is no law there is no t.
5.14 whose sins were not like the t. of Adam
Gal 3.19 It was added because of transgressions
Heb 2. 2 if .. every t. .. received a just retribution
9.15 redeems them from the transgressions
2. *transgression of law:* παρανομία PARANOMIA*
2 Pet 2.16 but was rebuked for his own t.

TRANSGRESSOR
1. *lawless:* ἄνομος (subst.) ANOMOS
Mk [15.28 "*He was reckoned with the transgressors*‡
Lk 22.37 "'he was reckoned with transgressors
2. *digression, transgression:* παράβασις PARABASIS [B.1.a.1]
1 Tim 2.14 the woman .. became a transgressor
3. *transgressor:* παραβάτης PARABATĒS
Gal 2.18 then I prove myself a transgressor
Jas 2. 9 convicted by the law as transgressors
2.11 you have become a t. of the law

TRANSIENT
1. *temporary:* πρόσκαιρος PROSKAIROS
2 Cor 4.18 things that are seen are transient

TRANSLATION, BY
1. *interpret:* ἑρμηνεύω (pass. part.) HERMĒNEUŌ
Heb 7. 2 He is first, by t. of his name, king

TRANSPARENT
1. *translucent:* διαυγής DIAUGĒS*
Rev 21.21 the street .. was pure gold, t. as glass

TRAP
1. *hunting of wild beasts:* θήρα THĒRA*
Rom 11. 9 "Let their table become a snare and a t.

TRAVAIL
1. *birth pangs, suffering:* ὠδίν ŌDIN
1 Th 5. 3 destruction will come upon them as t.

TRAVAIL, BE IN
TRAVAIL WITH, BE IN
1. *suffer birth pangs:* ὠδίνω ŌDINŌ
Gal 4.19 children, with whom I am again in t.!
4.27 "shout, you who are not in travail
2. *bear, bring forth:* τίκτω TIKTŌ
Jn 16.21 "When a woman is in t. she has sorrow

TRAVAIL TOGETHER
1. *be in travail together:* συνωδίνω SYNŌDINŌ [B.2.c]
Rom 8.22 creation has been .. in travail together

TRAVEL
1. *pass through:* διέρχομαι DIERCHOMAI
Acts 11.19 Stephen traveled as far as Phoenicia
2. *traveling companion:* συνέκδημος SYNEKDĒMOS [A.1.d]
2 Cor 8.19 appointed by the churches to travel

TRAVEL, COMPANION IN
1. *traveling companion:* συνέκδημος SYNEKDĒMOS
Acts 19.29 who were Paul's companions in travel

TRAVEL WITH
1. *travel in company:* συνοδεύω SYNODEUŌ*
Acts 9. 7 The men who were traveling with him

TRAVERSE
1. *lead around, go about:* περιάγω PERIAGŌ
Mt 23.15 "hypocrites! for you t. sea and land

TREACHEROUS
1. *betrayer, traitor:* προδότης (pred.) PRODOTĒS
2 Tim 3. 4 treacherous, reckless, swollen with conceit

TREAD
TREAD DOWN
1. *tread, trample:* πατέω PATEŌ
Lk 10.19 "authority to tread upon serpents
21.24 "Jerusalem will be trodden down
Rev 14.20 wine press was trodden outside the city
19.15 he will tread the wine press of the fury

TREAD OUT GRAIN
1. *tread, thresh:* ἀλοάω ALOAŌ
1 Cor 9. 9 "an ox when it is treading out the grain
1 Tim 5.18 "an ox when it is treading out the grain

TREAD UNDER FOOT
TREAD UPON
1. *tread underfoot:* καταπατέω KATAPATEŌ
Mt 5.13 "except to be .. trodden under foot
Lk 8. 5 "some .. was trodden under foot
12. 1 so many .. that they trod upon one another

TREASURE
1. *treasure:* γάζα GAZA*
Acts 8.27 eunuch .. in charge of all her treasure
2. *store, treasure:* θησαυρός THĒSAUROS*
Mt 2.11 opening their treasures, they offered him
6.19 "Do not lay up for yourselves treasures
6.20 "lay up for yourselves treasures in heaven
6.21 "where your t. is, there will your heart be
12.35 "out of his good treasure brings forth good, and .. out of his evil t. brings forth evil
13.44 "The kingdom of heaven is like t.
13.52 "brings out of his treasure what is new
19.21 "you will have treasure in heaven
Mk 10.21 "you will have treasure in heaven

Lk 6.45 "The good man out of the good treasure
12.33 "with a treasure in the heavens
12.34 "where your t. is, there will your heart be
18.22 "you will have treasure in heaven
2 Cor 4. 7 But we have this t. in earthen vessels
Col 2. 3 in whom are hid all the treasures
Heb 11.26 greater . . than the treasures of Egypt

TREASURE, LAY UP

1. *store up:* θησαυρίζω THESAURIZŌ
Lk 12.21 "he who lays up treasure for himself
Jas 5. 3 You have laid up t.[e] for the last days†

TREASURER

1. *steward, administrator:* οἰκονόμος OIKONOMOS
Rom 16.23 Erastus, the city t., and . . greet you[b]

TREASURY

1. *treasury:* γαζοφυλακεῖον GAZOPHYLAKEION*
Mk 12.41 he sat down opposite the t., and watched the multitude putting money into the t.
12.43 "those who are contributing to the t.
Lk 21. 1 putting their gifts into the treasury
Jn 8.20 These words he spoke in the treasury
2. *temple treasury:* κορβανᾶς KORBANAS*
Mt 27. 6 "not lawful to put them into the t.

TREAT (*See also* CONTEMPT, TREAT WITH; OBSOLETE, TREAT AS)

1. *make use of, act:* χράομαι CHRAOMAI
Acts 27. 3 Julius treated Paul kindly
2. *show, offer, cause:* παρέχω (mid.) PARECHŌ [A.6.a.5]
Col 4. 1 Masters, treat your slaves justly
3. *do, make:* ποιέω POIEŌ
Lk 2.48 "Son, why have you treated us so?
15.19 " ' "t. me as one of your hired servants
[15.21 " '*t. me as one of your hired servants*‡
4. *bring to, present:* προσφέρω (pass.+dat.) PROSPHERŌ
Heb 12. 7 God is treating you as sons
CONTEXTUALLY
2 Cor 6. 8 are treated as impostors, . . yet are true

TREAT SHAMEFULLY

1. *hold in no honor, insult:* ἀτιμάζω ATIMAZŌ
Mk 12. 4 "they wounded him . . and treated him s.
Lk 20.11 "him also they beat and treated s.
2. *insult, treat arrogantly:* ὑβρίζω HYBRIZŌ
Mt 22. 6 "seized . . , treated them shamefully
Lk 18.32 "shamefully treated and spit upon
1 Th 2. 2 shamefully treated at Philippi

TREATED

1. *return; behave* (pass.): ἀναστρέφω (pass. part.) ANASTREPHŌ
Heb 10.33 being partners with those so treated

TREE

1. *tree:* δένδρον DENDRON*
Mt 3.10 "the axe is laid to the root of the trees; every tree . . that does not bear good fruit
7.17 "So, every sound tree bears good fruit, but the bad tree bears evil fruit
7.18 "A sound tree cannot bear evil fruit, nor can a bad tree bear good fruit
7.19 "Every tree that does not bear good fruit
12.33 "Either make the tree good, and its fruit good; or make the tree bad, and its fruit bad; for the tree is known by its fruit
13.32 "the smallest of all seeds . . becomes a tree
21. 8 others cut branches from the trees
8.24 "I see men; but they look like trees
Lk 3. 9 "axe is laid to the root of the trees; every tree . . that does not bear good fruit
6.43 "For no good tree bears bad fruit, nor again does a bad tree bear good fruit
6.44 "for each tree is known by its own fruit
13.19 "mustard seed . . grew and became a tree
21.29 "Look at the fig . . , and all the trees
Jude .12 fruitless trees in late autumn, twice dead
Rev 7. 1 that no wind might blow . . against any t.
7. 3 "Do not harm the earth or . . the trees
8. 7 a third of the trees were burnt up
9. 4 they were told not to harm . . any tree
2. *tree, wood:* ξύλον XYLON
Acts 5.30 "you killed by hanging him on a tree
10.39 "put him to death by hanging him on a t.
13.29 "they took him down from the tree
Gal 3.13 "Cursed be every one who hangs on a tree
1 Pet 2.24 bore our sins in his body on the tree[g]
Rev 2. 7 " 'I will grant to eat of the tree of life
22. 2 on either side of the river, the tree of life[r]
22. 2 leaves of the t. . . for . . healing of . . nations
22.14 have the right to the tree of life
22.19 will take away his share in the t. of life

TREE, CULTIVATED OLIVE

1. *garden olive tree:* καλλιέλαιος KALLIELAIOS*
Rom 11.24 grafted . . into a cultivated olive tree

TREE, FIG

1. *fig tree:* συκῆ SYKĒ*
Mt 21.19 seeing a fig tree by the wayside
21.19 And the fig tree withered at once
21.20 "How did the fig tree wither at once?
21.21 "do what has been done to the fig tree
24.32 "From the fig tree learn its lesson
Mk 11.13 seeing in the distance a fig tree in leaf
11.20 they saw the fig tree withered away
11.21 "The fig tree which you cursed has withered
13.28 "From the fig tree learn its lesson
Lk 13. 6 "A man had a fig tree planted
13. 7 " 'I have come seeking fruit on this fig t.
21.29 "Look at the fig tree, and all the trees
Jn 1.48 "when you were under the fig tree
1.50 "I said . . , I saw you under the fig tree
Jas 3.12 Can a fig tree, my brethren, yield olives?
Rev 6.13 as the fig tree sheds its winter fruit

TREE, OLIVE

1. *olive tree, olive:* ἐλαία ELAIA
Rom 11.17 to share the richness[o] of the olive tree
11.24 grafted back into their own olive tree
Rev 11. 4 These are the two olive trees

TREE, PALM

1. *date palm tree, palm frond:* φοῖνιξ PHOINIX
Jn 12.13 So they took branches of palm trees

TREE, SYCAMINE

1. *mulberry tree:* συκάμινος SYKAMINOS*
Lk 17. 6 "you could say to this sycamine tree

TREE, SYCAMORE

1. *sycamore-fig tree:* συκομορέα SYKOMOREA*
Lk 19. 4 climbed up into a sycamore tree to see

TREE, WILD OLIVE

1. *wild olive tree:* ἀγριέλαιος AGRIELAIOS
Rom 11.24 what is by nature a wild olive tree

TREMBLE

1. *trembling:* ἔντρομος ENTROMOS [A.6.a.3]
Acts 7.32 "Moses trembled and did not dare to look
Heb 12.21 Moses said, "I tremble with fear
2. *shake, agitate:* σείω (pass.) SEIŌ
Mt 28. 4 for fear of him the guards trembled
3. *tremble, be afraid:* τρέμω TREMŌ
Mk 5.33 came in fear and trembling and fell
Lk 8.47 she came trembling, and falling down

TREMBLING

1. *trembling:* ἔντρομος ENTROMOS [B.3.a.2]
Acts 16.29 trembling with fear he fell down
2. *trembling, unsteady:* τρόμος TROMOS*
Mk 16. 8 for trembling . . had come upon them
1 Cor 2. 3 I was with you in . . much fear and t.
2 Cor 7.15 fear and t. with which you received him
Eph 6. 5 Slaves, be obedient . . , with fear and t.
Phil 2.12 work out your . . salvation with fear and t.

TRESPASS

1. *false step, transgression:* παράπτωμα PARAPTŌMA*
Mt 6.14 "For if you forgive men their trespasses
6.15 "if . . not forgive men their trespasses, neither will . . Father forgive your trespasses
Mk 11.25 "that . . Father . . forgive . . your trespasses[w]
[11.26 "*neither . . forgive your trespasses*‡

Rom 4.25 who was put to death for our trespasses
5.15 the free gift is not like the trespass. For if many died through one man's t.
5.16 the free gift following many trespasses
5.17 If, because of one man's trespass, death
5.18 as one man's t. led to condemnation
5.20 Law came in, to increase the trespass
11.11 through their t. salvation has come
11.12 if their t. means riches for the world
2 Cor 5.19 God was . . not counting their trespasses
Gal 6. 1 if a man is overtaken in any trespass
Eph 1. 7 we have . . the forgiveness of our trespasses
2. 1 you were dead through the trespasses
2. 5 we were dead through our trespasses
Col 2.13 you, who were dead in trespasses
2.13 having forgiven us all our trespasses

TRIAL

1. *temptation, trial:* πειρασμός PEIRASMOS
Lk 22.28 "who . . continued with me in my trials
Acts 20.19 "trials which befell me through the plots
Gal 4.14 though my condition was a trial to you
Jas 1. 2 Count it all joy . . when you meet . . trials
1.12 Blessed is the man who endures trial
1 Pet 1. 6 you may have to suffer various trials
2 Pet 2. 9 how to rescue the godly from trial
Rev 3.10 "'I will keep you from the hour of trial

IDIOMATICALLY

a. Acts 26.6 "And now I stand here on trial καὶ νῦν . . ἕστηκα κρινόμενος [KRINŌ]

CONTEXTUALLY

Mk 13.11 "when they bring you to t. and deliver you

TRIAL, BE ON

1. *judge, decide:* κρίνω (pass.) KRINŌ
Acts 23. 6 "with respect to . . resurrection . . I am on t.
24.21 "'With respect to . . resurrection . . I am on t.

TRIAL OF, MAKE

1. *tempt, try:* πειράζω PEIRAZŌ
Acts 15.10 "therefore why do you make trial of God?

TRIAL, ON

1. *judge, decide:* κρίνω (pass. part.) KRINŌ
Acts 26. 6 "now I stand here on trial for hope

TRIBE

1. *race, nation, tribe:* φυλή PHYLĒ*
Mt 19.28 "will also sit . . judging the twelve tribes
24.30 "the tribes of the earth will mourn
Lk 2.36 prophetess, Anna, . . of the tribe of Asher
22.30 "sit . . judging the twelve tribes of Israel
Acts 13.21 "Saul . . , a man of the t. of Benjamin
Rom 11. 1 a member of the tribe of Benjamin
Phil 3. 5 of the tribe of Benjamin, a Hebrew
Heb 7.13 the one . . belonged to another tribe
7.14 in connection with that t. Moses said
Jas 1. 1 To the twelve tribes in the Dispersion
Rev 1. 7 all tribes of the earth will wail
5. 5 "lo, the Lion of the tribe of Judah
5. 9 "thou . . didst ransom men . . from every t.
7. 4 out of every t. of the sons of Israel
7. 5 twelve thousand . . out of the t. of Judah, twelve thousand of the tribe of Reuben, twelve thousand of the t. of Gad
7. 6 twelve thousand of the t. of Asher, twelve thousand of the t. of Naphtali, twelve thousand of the t. of Manasseh
7. 7 twelve thousand of the t. of Simeon, twelve thousand of the t. of Levi, twelve thousand of the t. of Issachar
7. 8 twelve thousand of the t. of Zebulun, twelve thousand of the t. of Joseph, twelve thousand . . of the t. of Benjamin
7. 9 from every nation, from all tribes
11. 9 men from the peoples and tribes . . gaze
13. 7 authority was given it over every tribe
14. 6 an eternal gospel . . to every . . tribe
21.12 names of the twelve tribes of . . Israel

TRIBES, TWELVE

1. *twelve tribes:* δωδεκάφυλον DŌDEKAPHYLON*
Acts 26. 7 "to which our twelve tribes hope to attain

TRIBULATION

1. *affliction, oppression:* θλῖψις THLIPSIS
Mt 13.21 "when tribulation or persecution arises
24. 9 "they will deliver you up to tribulation
24.21 "For then there will be great tribulation
24.29 "after the tribulation of those days
Mk 4.17 "when tribulation or persecution arises
13.19 "such tribulation as has not been
13.24 "after that t., the sun will be darkened
Jn 16.33 "In the world you have tribulation
Acts 14.22 through . . tribulations we must enter
Rom 2. 9 There will be tribulation and distress
8.35 Shall t., or distress, or persecution?
12.12 Rejoice in your hope, be patient in t.
Rev 1. 9 who share . . the t. and the kingdom
2. 9 " 'I know your t. and your poverty
2.10 " 'for ten days you will have tribulation
2.22 " 'those . . I will throw into great t.
7.14 "who have come out of the great t.

TRIBUNAL

1. *step, platform:* βῆμα BĒMA
Acts 18.12 brought him before the tribunal
18.16 he drove them from the tribunal
18.17 they . . beat him in front of the tribunal
25. 6 the next day he took his seat on the t.
25.10 "I am standing before Caesar's tribunal
25.17 "the next day took my seat on the t.

TRIBUNE

1. *captain over a thousand:* χιλίαρχος CHILIARCHOS
Acts 21.31 word came to the t. of the cohort
21.32 when they saw the t. and the soldiers
21.33 the tribune came up and arrested him
21.37 he said to the tribune, "May I say?
22.24 the t. commanded him to be brought
22.26 he went to the tribune and said to him
22.27 the t. . . said . . "are you a Roman citizen?
22.28 t. answered, "I bought this citizenship
22.29 the t. also was afraid, for he realized
23.10 the t., afraid that Paul would be torn
23.15 "give notice . . to the t. to bring him
23.17 "Take this young man to the tribune
23.18 So he . . brought him to the tribune
23.19 The tribune took him by the hand
23.22 the tribune dismissed the young man
24.22 "When Lysias the tribune comes down
25.23 they entered . . with the military tribunes

TRIBUTE

1. *poll tax, census* (Lat.): κῆνσος KĒNSOS
Mt 17.25 "From whom do kings . . take . . tribute?
2. *tribute, tax:* φόρος PHOROS
Lk 20.22 "Is it lawful for us to give t. to Caesar?
23. 2 "forbidding us to give t. to Caesar

TRICK

1. *mock:* ἐμπαίζω EMPAIZŌ
Mt 2.16 Herod . . saw that he had been tricked

TRIM

1. *prepare, adorn:* κοσμέω KOSMEŌ
Mt 25. 7 "all those maidens . . trimmed their lamps

TRIUMPH

1. *extol, honor:* δοξάζω (pass.) DOXAZŌ
2 Th 3. 1 that the word of the Lord may . . triumph

TRIUMPH, LEAD IN
TRIUMPH OVER

1. *exult over:* κατακαυχάομαι KATAKAUCHAOMAI
Jas 2.13 yet mercy triumphs over judgment
2. *lead in triumph, triumph over:* θριαμβεύω THRIAMBEUŌ*
2 Cor 2.14 God, who . . always leads us in triumph
Col 2.15 triumphing over them in him[d]

TRIVIAL

1. *smallest, least:* ἐλάχιστος ELACHISTOS
1 Cor 6. 2 are you incompetent to try trivial cases?

TROAS: Τρῳάς 'trō‚as II, E-3
Acts 16. 8 passing by Mysia, they went down to T.
16.11 Setting sail therefore from Troas
20. 5 These . . were waiting for us at Troas
20. 6 in five days we came to them at Troas
2 Cor 2.12 When I came to Troas to preach
2 Tim 4.13 the cloak that I left with Carpus at T.

TROGYLLIUM: Τρωγύλλιον trō'jilēəm II,E-3
Acts [20.15 *after remaining at Trogyllium*‡

TROOPS
1. *army:* στράτευμα (pl.) STRATEUMA
Mt 22. 7 "he sent his troops and destroyed those
Rev 9.16 The number of the troops of cavalry

TROPHIMUS: Τρόφιμος 'trōfəməs
Acts 20. 4 the Asians, Tychicus and Trophimus
21.29 For they had previously seen T.
2 Tim 4.20 Trophimus I left ill at Miletus

TROUBLE
TROUBLES
1. *trouble, annoy:* ἐνοχλέω ENOCHLEŌ
Lk 6.18 who were troubled with unclean spirits
2. *badness:* κακία KAKIA
Mt 6.34 "Let the day's own trouble be sufficient
3. *cause difficulty:* κόπους παρέχειν KOPOS [B.3.b.4]
Mt 26.10 "Why do you trouble the woman?
Mk 14. 6 "Let her alone; why do you t. her?
Gal 6.17 Henceforth let no man trouble me
4. *annoy:* παρενοχλέω PARENOCHLEŌ*
Acts 15.19 "we should not t. those of the Gentiles
5. *trouble, annoy:* σκύλλω SKYLLŌ
Mk 5.35 "Why trouble the Teacher any further?
Lk 8.49 "do not trouble the Teacher any more
6. *trouble, disturb:* ταράσσω TARASSŌ
Mt 2. 3 When Herod . . heard . . , he was troubled
Lk 1.12 Zechariah was troubled when he saw
24.38 he said to them, "Why are you troubled?
Jn [5. 4 *an angel . . troubled the water*‡
5. 7 "into the pool when the water is troubled
11.33 he was deeply moved . . and troubled
12.27 "Now is my soul troubled
13.21 When Jesus had . . spoken, he was troubled
14. 1 "Let not your hearts be troubled
14.27 "Let not your hearts be troubled
Acts 15.24 "some persons from us have troubled you
Gal 1. 7 but there are some who trouble you
5.10 who is troubling you will bear . . judgment
1 Pet 3.14 Have no fear of them, nor be troubled
7. *affliction, oppression:* θλῖψις THLIPSIS
1 Cor 7.28 who marry will have worldly troubles
Phil 4.14 it was kind of you to share my trouble

TROUBLE, CAUSE
1. *trouble, annoy:* ἐνοχλέω ENOCHLEŌ
Heb 12.15 that no "root of bitterness" . . cause t.

TROUBLE ONESELF
1. *trouble, annoy:* σκύλλω (pass.) SKYLLŌ
Lk 7. 6 "Lord, do not trouble yourself

TROUBLE, OUT OF
1. *free from care:* ἀμέριμνος AMERIMNOS
Mt 28.14 "satisfy him and keep you out of t.

TROUBLED, BE
1. *be dismayed, be anxious:* ἀδημονέω ADĒMONEŌ
Mt 26.37 he began to be sorrowful and troubled
Mk 14.33 he . . began to be . . troubled
2. *cause trouble:* θορυβάζω (pass.) THORYBAZŌ*
Lk 10.41 "Martha, Martha, you are . . troubled

TROUBLED, BE GREATLY
1. *confuse, perplex:* διαταράσσω (pass.) DIATARASSŌ*
Lk 1.29 she was greatly troubled at the saying

TROUBLING
1. *disturbance:* ταραχή TARACHĒ
Jn [5. 4 *after the troubling of the water*‡

TRUE
1. *good:* ἀγαθός AGATHOS
Tit 2.10 to show entire and true fidelity
2. *truth:* ἀλήθεια ALĒTHEIA
[a]B.1.a.1 [b]A.1.b.4 [c]gen.
2 Cor 7.14 [a]as everything we said to you was true
7.14 [b]so our boasting before Titus . . proved t.
Eph 4.24 [c]in true righteousness and holiness
3. *true:* ἀληθής ALĒTHĒS
Mt 22.16 "Teacher, we know that you are true
Mk 12.14 "Teacher, we know that you are true
Jn 3.33 his testimony sets his seal . . that God is t.
5.31 "If . . to myself, my testimony is not true
5.32 "the testimony which he bears to me is t.
7.18 "he . . is t., and in him . . is no falsehood
8.13 "your testimony is not true
8.14 "Even if . . to myself, my testimony is t.
8.17 "the testimony of two men is true
8.26 "but he who sent me is true
10.41 "everything . . said about this man was t.
21.24 we know that his testimony is true
Rom 3. 4 By no means! Let God be true
2 Cor 6. 8 treated as impostors, and yet are true
Phil 4. 8 whatever is true, whatever is honorable
Tit 1.13 This testimony is true
1 Pet 5.12 that this is the true grace of God
2 Pet 2.22 happened . . according to the t. proverb
1 Jn 2. 8 which is true in him and in you
2.27 his anointing teaches you . . and is true
3 Jn .12 you know my testimony is true
4. *true:* ἀληθινός ALĒTHINOS*
Lk 16.11 who will entrust to you the true riches?
Jn 1. 9 true light that enlightens every man
4.23 when the true worshipers will worship
4.37 For here the saying holds true
6.32 my Father gives you the true bread
7.28 he who sent me is true
8.16 even if I do judge, my judgment is t.
15. 1 "I am the true vine
17. 3 that they know thee the only t. God
19.35 his testimony is true, and he knows
1 Th 1. 9 to serve a living and true God
Heb 8. 2 the sanctuary and the true tent[n]
9.24 not into . . a copy of the t. one, but . . heaven
10.22 let us draw near with a true heart
1 Jn 2. 8 the true light is already shining
5.20 understanding, to know . . who is true; and we are in him who is true, . . Jesus Christ. This is the true God and eternal life
Rev 3. 7 " 'words of the holy one, the true one
3.14 " 'the Amen, the faithful and true witness
6.10 "O Sovereign Lord, holy and true
15. 3 "Just and true are thy ways, O King!
16. 7 "true and just are thy judgments!
19. 2 "his judgments are true and just
19. 9 "These are true words of God
19.11 "He . . is called Faithful and True
21. 5 "these words are trustworthy and true
22. 6 "These words are trustworthy and true
5. *true, genuine:* γνήσιος GNĒSIOS
Phil 4. 3 true yokefellow, help these women
1 Tim 1. 2 To Timothy, my true child in the faith
Tit 1. 4 To Titus, my t. child in a common faith

IDIOMATICALLY
a. 1 Cor 15.15 if it is true that the dead are not raised εἴπερ ἄρα νεκροὶ οὐκ ἐγείρονται [ARA II]

CONTEXTUALLY
Rom 2.28 nor is t. circumcision something external
2 Cor 12.12 The signs of a t. apostle were performed
Phil 3. 3 For we are the true circumcision
Heb 10. 1 instead of the true form of these realities

TRUE, HOLD
1. *agree with, walk by:* στοιχέω STOICHEŌ
Phil 3.16 let us hold true to what we have attained

TRUE, THAT IS
1. *well, rightly:* καλῶς KALŌS [B.3.b.4]
Rom 11.20 That is true

TRUE, WHAT IS

1. *truth:* ἀλήθεια ALĒTHEIA
Jn 3.21 who does what is t. comes to the light
Eph 5. 9 (all that is good and right and true

TRULY

1. *truth:* ἀλήθεια ALĒTHEIA [B.1.a.1]
Mk 12.14 "you . . truly teach the way of God
12.32 "you have truly said that he is one
Lk 20.21 "but truly teach the way of God
Acts 4.27 "truly . . there were gathered together
10.34 "Truly . . God shows no partiality
2. *true:* ἀληθής (neut.) ALĒTHĒS
Jn 4.18 "this you said truly
3. *truly:* ἀληθῶς ALĒTHŌS
Mt 14.33 "Truly you are the Son of God
27.54 "Truly this was the Son[x] of God!
Mk 15.39 "Truly this man was the Son[x] of God!
Lk 9.27 "truly, there are some standing here
12.44 "Truly, I say to you, he will set him
21. 3 "Truly I tell you, this poor widow
Jn 8.31 "you are truly my disciples
1 Jn 2. 5 in him truly love for God is perfected
4. *truly* (Heb.): ἀμήν AMĒN
[a]ἀμὴν, ἀμήν
Mt 5.18 "truly, I say to you, till heaven . . pass
5.26 "truly, I say to you, you will never get out
6. 2 "T., I say to you, they have received
6. 5 "Truly, I say to you, they have received
6.16 "T., I say to you, they have received
8.10 "T., I say to you, not even[s] in Israel
10.15 "T., I say to you, it shall be more tolerable
10.23 "t., I say to you, you will not have gone
10.42 "t., I say to you, he shall not lose
11.11 "T., I say to you, . . no . . greater than John
13.17 "T., I say to you, many . . longed
16.28 "T., I say to you, there are some . . here
17.20 "t., I say to you, if you have faith
18. 3 "Truly, I say to you, unless you turn
18.13 "truly, I say to you, he rejoices over it
18.18 "T., I say to you, whatever you bind
19.23 "Truly, I say to you, it will be hard
19.28 "T., I say to you, in the new world
21.21 "Truly, I say to you, if you have faith
21.31 "Truly, I say to you, the tax collectors
23.36 "Truly, I say to you, all this will come
24. 2 "T., I say to you, there will not be left
24.34 "T., I say to you, this generation will not
24.47 "T., I say to you, he will set him over all
25.12 " 'T., I say to you, I do not know you
25.40 " 'T., I say to you, as you did it to one
25.45 " 'T., I say to you, as you did it not to one
26.13 "T., I say to you, wherever this gospel
26.21 "T., I say to you, one of you will betray
26.34 "Truly, I say to you, this very night
Mk 3.28 "T., I say to you, all sins will be forgiven
8.12 "T., I say to you, no sign shall be given
9. 1 "T., I say to you, there are some . . here
9.41 "t., I say to you, whoever gives you a cup
10.15 "T., I say to you, whoever does not receive
10.29 "T., I say to you, . . no one . . has left house
11.23 "T., I say to you, whoever says
12.43 "T., I say to you, this poor widow
13.30 "Truly, I say to you, this generation
14. 9 "t., I say to you, wherever the gospel
14.18 "T., I say to you, one of you will betray
14.25 "T., I say to you, I shall not drink again
14.30 "Truly, I say to you, this very night
Lk 4.24 "T., I say to you, no prophet is acceptable
12.37 "t., I say to you, he will gird himself
18.17 "T., I say to you, whoever does not receive
18.29 "Truly, I say to you, there is no man
21.32 "T., I say to you, this generation will not
23.43 "T., I say to you, today you will be with me
Jn 1.51 [a]"Truly, truly, I say to you [you *pl.*]
Also [a]Jn **5.**19, 24, 25; **6.**26, 32, 47, 53; **8.**34, 51, 58; **10.**1, 7; **12.**24; **13.**16, 20, 21; **14.**12; **16.**20, 23
Jn 3. 3 [a]"Truly, truly, I say to you [you *sg.*]
Also [a]Jn **3.**5, 11; **13.**38; **21.**18
CONTEXTUALLY
1 Cor 11.31 But if we judged ourselves truly

TRULY, DEAL

1. *speak truth:* ἀληθεύω ALĒTHEUŌ
Gal [4.16 become your enemy *by dealing t. with you?*†

TRUMPET
TRUMPET CALL
TRUMPET, SOUND OF THE

1. *war trumpet, trumpet call:* σάλπιγξ SALPIGX
Mt 24.31 "his angels with a loud trumpet call
1 Cor 15.52 in the twinkling of an eye, at the last t.
1 Th 4.16 the Lord himself . . with . . sound of the t.
Heb 12.19 the sound of a trumpet, and a voice
Rev 1.10 I heard behind me a loud voice like a t.
4. 1 I had heard speaking to me like a t.
8. 2 seven trumpets were given to them
8. 6 angels who had the seven trumpets
8.13 "at the blasts of the other trumpets
9.14 the sixth angel who had the trumpet

TRUMPET, BLOW ONE'S
TRUMPET, SOUND A

1. *sound a trumpet:* σαλπίζω SALPIZŌ
[a]B.3.b.4
Mt 6. 2 "when you give alms, sound no trumpet
1 Cor 15.52 t. will sound, and . . dead will be raised
Rev 8. 7 The first angel blew his trumpet
8. 8 The second angel blew his trumpet
8.10 The third angel blew his trumpet
8.12 The fourth angel blew his trumpet
9. 1 the fifth angel blew his trumpet
9.13 the sixth angel blew his trumpet
10. 7 [a]"the t. call to be sounded by . . angel
11.15 the seventh angel blew his trumpet

TRUMPETER

1. *trumpeter:* σαλπιστής SALPISTĒS*
Rev 18.22 "sound of harpers and . . trumpeters

TRUST

1. *give up, allow:* παραδίδωμι PARADIDŌMI
1 Pet 2.23 he trusted to him who judges justly
2. *persuade:* πείθω (perf. or pluperf.) PEITHŌ
Mt 27.43 "He trusts in God; let God deliver him
Mk [10.24 "how hard . . *for those who trust in riches*‡
Lk 11.22 "his armor in which he trusted
18. 9 to some who trusted in themselves
Phil 2.24 I trust in the Lord that shortly I myself
3. *believe, trust:* πιστεύω PISTEUŌ
Jn 2.24 Jesus did not trust himself to them
Rom 4. 5 one who does not work but trusts him

TRUST, PUT ONE'S

1. *persuade:* πείθω (fut. perf. periphr.) PEITHŌ
Heb 2.13 "I will put my trust in him

TRUSTEE

1. *steward, administrator:* οἰκονόμος OIKONOMOS
Gal 4. 2 he is under guardians and trustees

TRUSTWORTHY

1. *faithful, trustworthy:* πιστός PISTOS
1 Cor 4. 2 required of stewards that they be . . t.
7.25 one who by the Lord's mercy is t.
Rev 21. 5 "these words are trustworthy and true
22. 6 "These words are trustworthy and true

TRUTH

1. *truth:* ἀλήθεια ALĒTHEIA
Mk 5.33 the woman . . told him the whole truth
Lk 4.25 in t., I tell you, there were many widows
Jn 1.14 dwelt among us, full of grace and t.
1.17 truth came through Jesus Christ
4.23 "will worship the Father in spirit and t.
4.24 "must worship in spirit and truth
5.33 "he has borne witness to the truth
8.32 "and you will know the truth, and the truth will make you free
8.40 "a man who has told you the truth

Jn 8.44 "He . . has nothing to do with the truth, because there is no truth in him
8.45 "because I tell the t., you do not believe me
8.46 "If I tell the t., why do you not believe?
14. 6 "I am the way, and the truth, and the life
14.17 "Spirit of t., whom the world cannot receive
15.26 "the Counselor . . , even the Spirit of t.
16. 7 "Nevertheless I tell you the truth
16.13 "When the Spirit of truth comes, he will guide you into all the truth
17.17 "Sanctify them in the truth; thy word is truth
17.19 "that they also may be consecrated in t.
18.37 "I have come . . to bear witness to the t. Every one who is of the truth hears
18.38 Pilate said to him, "What is truth?
Acts 26.25 "I am speaking the sober truth
Rom 1.18 by their wickedness suppress the truth
1.25 they exchanged the truth about God
2. 8 factious and do not obey the truth
2.20 in the law the embodiment of . . truth
9. 1 I am speaking the truth in Christ
1 Cor 5. 8 the unleavened bread of sincerity and t.
2 Cor 4. 2 by the open statement of the truth
11.10 As the truth of Christ is in me
12. 6 for I shall be speaking the truth
13. 8 we cannot do anything against the truth, but only for the truth
Gal 2. 5 that the t. of the gospel . . be preserved
2.14 not straightforward about the truth
5. 7 who hindered you from obeying the t.?
Eph 1.13 who have heard the word of truth
4.21 taught in him, as the truth is in Jesus
4.25 every one speak the t. with his neighbor
6.14 having girded your loins with truth
Phil 1.18 in every way, whether in pretense or in t.
Col 1. 5 in the word of the truth, the gospel
1. 6 you . . understood the grace of God in t.
2 Th 2.10 because they refused to love the truth
2.12 all . . who did not believe the truth
2.13 saved . . by . . Spirit[c] and belief in the t.
1 Tim 2. 4 to come to the knowledge of the truth
2. 7 (I am telling the t., I am not lying), a teacher of the Gentiles in faith and t.
3.15 the pillar and bulwark of the truth
4. 3 those who believe and know the truth
6. 5 depraved in mind and bereft of the truth
2 Tim 2.15 rightly handling the word of truth
2.18 who have swerved from the truth
2.25 repent and come to know the truth
3. 7 can never arrive at a knowledge of the t.
3. 8 so these men also oppose the truth
4. 4 will turn away from listening to the truth
Tit 1. 1 to further . . their knowledge of the t.
1.14 commands of men who reject the truth
Heb 10.26 after receiving the knowledge of the truth
Jas 1.18 brought us forth by the word of truth
3.14 do not boast and be false to the t.
5.19 if any one . . wanders from the truth
1 Pet 1.22 purified . . by your obedience to the t.
2 Pet 1.12 established in the t. that you have
2. 2 the way of truth will be reviled
1 Jn 1. 6 we . . do not live according to the truth
1. 8 deceive ourselves, and the t. is not in us
2. 4 a liar, and the truth is not in him
2.21 not because you do not know the truth
2.21 you . . know that no lie is of the truth
3.18 let us . . love . . in deed and in truth
3.19 we shall know that we are of the truth
4. 6 By this we know the spirit of truth
5. 7(6) because the Spirit is the truth
2 Jn . 1 elect lady . . whom I love in the truth, . . not only I but also all who know the t.
. 2 because of the truth which abides in us
. 3 Grace, mercy, and peace . . in truth and love
. 4 some of your children following the t.
3 Jn . 1 beloved Gaius, whom I love in the truth
3 Jn . 3 brethren . . testified to the truth of your life, as indeed you do follow the t.
. 4 hear that my children follow the truth
. 8 that we may be fellow workers in the t.
.12 Demetrius has testimony from . . the t.

2. *true:* ἀληθής ALĒTHĒS [B.3.b.4]
Jn 19.35 he knows that he tells the truth

3. *security, certainty:* ἀσφάλεια ASPHALEIA
Lk 1. 4 that you may know the truth

4. *good, beautiful:* καλός KALOS [A.3.a.4]
2 Tim 1.14 guard the truth that has been entrusted

CONTEXTUALLY
1 Cor 2.13 interpreting spiritual truths to those†

TRUTH, IN

1. *truly:* ἀληθῶς ALĒTHŌS
Jn 17. 8 "they . . know in t. that I came from thee

TRUTH, SPEAK THE
TRUTH, TELL THE

1. *speak truth:* ἀληθεύω ALĒTHEUŌ*
Gal 4.16 become your enemy by telling you the t.?[h]†
Eph 4.15 Rather, speaking the truth in love

TRUTHFUL
TRUTHFULLY

1. *truth:* ἀλήθεια ALĒTHEIA
[a]B.1.a.1 [b]gen.
Mt 22.16 [a]"you . . teach the way of God truthfully
2 Cor 6. 7 [b]t. speech, and the power of God

TRUTHFULNESS

1. *truth:* ἀλήθεια ALĒTHEIA
Rom 3. 7 if . . God's t. abounds to his glory
15. 8 Christ became a servant . . to show God's t.

TRY (*See also* CONCILIATE, TRY TO; LEARN, TRY TO)

1. *judge, decide:* κρίνω KRINŌ
Acts 25. 9 "Do you wish to . . be tried . . before me?
25.10 "before Caesar's tribunal . . to be tried
25.20 "to go to Jerusalem and be tried there

2. *attempt, try:* πειράω (mid.) PEIRAŌ*
Acts 26.21 "the Jews seized me . . and tried to kill me

3. *tempt, try:* πειράζω PEIRAZŌ
Acts 24. 6 "He even tried to profane the temple
Rev 3.10 "'to try those who dwell upon the earth

4. *seek, desire:* ζητέω ZĒTEŌ
Mt 21.46 But when they tried to arrest him
Mk 12.12 they tried to arrest him, but feared
Lk 20.19 chief priests tried to lay hands on him
Jn 10.39 they tried to arrest him, but he escaped
Acts 21.31 as they were trying to kill him, word came
Gal 1.10 Or am I trying to please men?

CONTEXTUALLY
Acts 26.11 "I . . tried to make them blaspheme
28.23 and trying to convince them about Jesus
1 Cor 6. 2 are you incompetent to t. trivial cases?
10.33 I t. to please all men in everything I do
Gal 1.13 persecuted . . and tried to destroy it
1.23 "preaching . . faith he once tried to destroy

TRYPHAENA: Τρύφαινα trī'fēnə
Rom 16.12 workers in the Lord, T. and Tryphosa

TRYPHOSA: Τρυφῶσα trī'fōsə
Rom 16.12 workers in the Lord, Tryphaena and T.

TUMULT

1. *instability:* ἀκαταστασία AKATASTASIA
Lk 21. 9 "when you hear of wars and tumults
2 Cor 6. 5 beatings, imprisonments, tumults

2. *noise, uproar:* θόρυβος THORYBOS
Mt 26. 5 "lest there be a t. among the people
Mk 5.38 he saw a tumult, and people weeping
14. 2 "lest there be a tumult of the people
Acts 24.18 "in the temple, without any crowd or t.

TUMULT, MAKE A

1. *make a disturbance:* θορυβέω (pass.) THORYBEŌ
Mt 9.23 saw . . the crowd making a tumult
Mk 5.39 "Why do you make a tumult and weep?

TUNIC

1. *tunic, undergarment:* χιτών CHITŌN
Mt 10.10 "no bag for your journey, nor two tunics
Mk 6. 9 to wear sandals and not put on two tunics
Lk 9. 3 "Take nothing . . do not have two tunics
Jn 19.23 soldiers . . took his garments and . . his tunic. But the tunic was without seam
Acts 9.39 showing tunics . . which Dorcas made[0]

TURN

1. *turn about, return:* ἐπιστρέφω (act. or aor. pass.) EPISTREPHŌ
Mt 13.15 " 'lest they . . t. for me to heal them
24.18 "let him who is in the field not turn back
Mk 8.33 But turning and seeing his disciples
13.16 "let him who is in the field not turn back
Lk 1.16 "he will turn many of the sons of Israel
1.17 "he will go . . to t. the hearts of the fathers
17. 4 "if he sins . . and turns to you seven times
17.31 let him who is in the field not turn back
Jn 21.20 Peter turned and saw following them
Acts 9.35 saw him, and they turned to the Lord
9.40 turning to the body he said, "Tabitha
11.21 a great number . . turned to the Lord
14.15 "you should t. from these vain things
15.19 "not trouble those . . who turn to God
16.18 Paul . . turned and said to the spirit
26.18 " 'that they may turn from darkness
26.20 "that they should repent and turn to God
28.27 " 'lest they . . turn for me to heal them
2 Cor 3.16 when a man turns to the Lord
1 Th 1. 9 how you turned to God from idols
Rev 1.12 Then I turned to see the voice
1.12 on turning I saw seven . . lampstands

2. *come to be, happen, be:* γίνομαι GINOMAI
Jn 16.20 "but your sorrow will turn into joy

3. *turn about, change:* μεταστρέφω METASTREPHŌ
Acts 2.20 " 'the sun shall be turned into darkness

4. *overthrow, turn back:* μετατρέπω METATREPŌ*
Jas 4. 9 Let . . laughter be turned to mourning

5. *divert:* περιτρέπω PERITREPŌ*
Acts 26.24 "your great learning is turning you mad

6. *turn, return:* στρέφω (act. or aor. pass.) STREPHŌ
Mt 5.39 "if . . on the right cheek, t. . . the other
7. 6 "lest they . . turn to attack you
9.22 Jesus turned, and . . said, "Take heart
16.23 he turned . . to Peter, "Get behind me!
18. 3 "unless you turn and become like children
Lk 7. 9 Jesus . . turned and said to the multitude
7.44 turning toward the woman he said
9.55 But he turned and rebuked them[f]
10.23 turning to the disciples he said privately
14.25 he turned and said to them
22.61 the Lord turned and looked at Peter
23.28 Jesus turning to them said, "Daughters
Jn 1.38 Jesus turned, and saw them following
12.40 lest they . . turn for me to heal them
20.14 she turned round and saw Jesus
20.16 She turned and said to him in Hebrew
Acts 7.39 in their hearts they turned to Egypt
7.42 "God turned and gave them over
13.46 "behold, we turn to the Gentiles
Rev 11. 6 they have power . . to turn them into blood

CONTEXTUALLY
2 Cor 2. 7 you should rather t. to forgive . . him
7. 5 but we were afflicted at every turn
Gal 1. 6 and turning to a different gospel

TURN ABOUT
TURN AGAIN

1. *turn about, return:* ἐπιστρέφω EPISTREPHŌ
[a]pass.
Mk 4.12 "lest they . . turn again, and be forgiven
5.30 [a]Jesus . . turned about in the crowd
Lk 22.32 "when you have turned again, strengthen
Acts 3.19 "Repent therefore, and turn again

TURN ASIDE

1. *turn away:* ἐκκλίνω EKKLINŌ
Rom 3.12 "All have turned aside

2. *go by the side of:* παραβαίνω PARABAINŌ
Acts 1.25 "Judas turned aside, to go to his own place

TURN AWAY

1. *turn back, turn away:* ἀποστρέφω APOSTREPHŌ
2 Tim 1.15 all who are in Asia turned away from me
4. 4 will turn away from listening to the truth

2. *twist about:* διαστρέφω DIASTREPHŌ
Acts 13. 8 seeking to t. away . . proconsul from . . faith

3. *turn away:* ἐκκλίνω EKKLINŌ
1 Pet 3.11 "let him t. away from evil and do right

4. *change, remove:* μεθίστημι METHISTĒMI
Acts 19.26 "Paul has . . turned a. . . people

TURN BACK

1. *turn about, return:* ἐπιστρέφω EPISTREPHŌ
Gal 4. 9 how can you t. back again to . . spirits?
2 Pet 2.22 The dog turns back to his own vomit

2. *turn away, return:* ὑποστρέφω HYPOSTREPHŌ
Lk 17.15 one of them . . turned back, praising God
2 Pet 2.21 after knowing it to turn back

TURN FROM

1. *turn back, turn away:* ἀποστρέφω APOSTREPHŌ
Acts 3.26 "in turning . . you from your wickedness

TURN IN

1. *give up, return:* ἀποδίδωμι APODIDŌMI
Lk 16. 2 " 'Turn in the account of your stewardship

TURN, IN

1. *receive one from another:* διαδέχομαι (part.) DIADECHOMAI
Acts 7.45 "fathers in t. brought it in with Joshua

IDIOMATICALLY
a. 1 Cor 14.27 or at most three, and each in turn ἢ τὸ πλεῖστον τρεῖς, καὶ ἀνὰ μέρος [MEROS]

TURN OUT

1. *step off from, go away:* ἀποβαίνω APOBAINŌ
Phil 1.19 this will turn out for my deliverance

TURN TO ASHES

1. *burn to ashes:* τεφρόω TEPHROŌ*
2 Pet 2. 6 turning . . Sodom and Gomorrah to ashes

TURN UPSIDE DOWN

1. *upset, disturb:* ἀναστατόω ANASTATOŌ
Acts 17. 6 "who have turned the world upside down

TURNING

1. *turn, change:* τροπή TROPĒ
Jas [1.17 no variation *due to a shadow of turning*†‡

TURTLEDOVE

1. *turtledove:* τρυγών TRYGŌN*
Lk 2.24 to offer a sacrifice . . "a pair of turtledoves

TWELFTH

1. *twelfth:* δωδέκατος DŌDEKATOS*
Rev 21.20 eleventh jacinth, the twelfth amethyst

TWELVE

1. *twelve:* δώδεκα DŌDEKA*
Mt 9.20 suffered from a hemorrhage for t. years
10. 1 he called to him his twelve disciples
10. 2 The names of the t. apostles are these
10. 5 These twelve Jesus sent out
11. 1 Jesus . . finished instructing his t. disciples
14.20 they took up twelve baskets full
19.28 "you . . will also sit on twelve thrones, judging the twelve tribes of Israel
20.17 he took the twelve disciples aside
26.14 one of the twelve, . . called Judas Iscariot
26.20 he sat at table with the t. disciples[e]
26.47 Judas came, one of the twelve
26.53 "more than twelve legions of angels
Mk 3.14 he appointed twelve,[k] to be with him
[3.16 *So he appointed the twelve*‡[0]
4.10 those who were about him with the t.
5.25 had a flow of blood for twelve years
5.42 (she was twelve years of age

Mk 6. 7 he called . . the t., and began to send them
6.43 they took up twelve baskets full
8.19 "how many baskets full . . ?" They said . . "T.
9.35 he sat down and called the twelve
10.32 taking the t. again, he began to tell
11.11 he went out to Bethany with the twelve
14.10 Judas Iscariot, who was one of the t.
14.17 when it was evening he came with the t.
14.20 "It is one of the twelve
14.43 Judas came, one of the twelve
Lk 2.42 when he was t. years old, they went up
6.13 called his disciples, . . chose from them t.
8. 1 went . . preaching . . And the t. were with him
8.42 he had an only daughter, about twelve
8.43 had a flow of blood for twelve years[b]
9. 1 he called the twelve together
9.12 the twelve . . said . . "Send the crowd away
9.17 left over, t. baskets of broken pieces
18.31 taking the twelve, he said to them
22. 3 Judas . ., who was of the number of the t.
22.30 "sit on thrones judging the twelve tribes
22.47 Judas, one of the t., was leading them
Jn 6.13 So they . . filled t. baskets with fragments
6.67 Jesus said to the t., "Do you . . wish to go?
6.70 "Did I not choose you, the twelve?
6.71 He spoke of Judas . ., one of the t.
11. 9 "Are there not twelve hours in the day?
20.24 Thomas, one of the t., called the Twin
Acts 6. 2 the t. summoned the body of the disciples
7. 8 "Jacob ⟨father⟩ of the t. patriarchs
19. 7 There were about twelve of them in all
24.11 "it is not more than twelve days since
1 Cor 15. 5 he appeared to Cephas, then to the twelve
Jas 1. 1 To the t. tribes in the Dispersion
Rev 7. 5 t. thousand sealed out of the tribe of Judah, twelve thousand of the tribe of Reuben, twelve thousand of the tribe of Gad
7. 6 t. thousand of the tribe of Asher, t. thousand of the tribe of Naphtali, t. thousand of the tribe of Manasseh
7. 7 t. thousand of the tribe of Simeon, twelve thousand of the tribe of Levi, t. thousand of the tribe of Issachar
7. 8 t. thousand of the tribe of Zebulun, t. thousand of the tribe of Joseph, t. thousand . . out of the tribe of Benjamin
12. 1 and on her head a crown of twelve stars
21.12 a great, high wall, with t. gates, and at the gates t. angels, and on the gates the names of the t. tribes of the sons of Israel
21.14 the wall of the city had t. foundations, and on them the twelve names of the twelve apostles of the Lamb
21.16 he measured the city . ., t. thousand stadia[q]
21.21 the t. gates were twelve pearls, each . . made of a single pearl
22. 2 the tree of life[r] with its t. kinds of fruit

TWELVE TRIBES

1. *twelve tribes:* δωδεκάφυλον DŌDEKAPHYLON*
Acts 26. 7 "to which our t. tribes hope to attain

TWENTY

1. *two:* δύο DYO [A.3.c.1]
Jn 2. 6 each holding twenty or thirty gallons
2. *twenty:* εἴκοσι EIKOSI
Lk 14.31 "able . . to meet him . . with t. thousand
Acts 1.15 (in all about a hundred and twenty
27.28 they sounded and found twenty fathoms

TWENTY-FOUR

1. *twenty-four:* εἴκοσι τέσσαρες EIKOSI; TESSARES [A.3.c]
Rev 4. 4 Round the throne were t. thrones, and . . on the thrones were t. elders
4.10 the twenty-four elders fall down
5. 8 the t. elders fell down before the Lamb
11.16 the t. elders who sit on their thrones
19. 4 the t. elders and the four living creatures

TWENTY-THREE

1. *twenty-three:* εἴκοσι τρεῖς EIKOSI; TREIS [A.3.c]
1 Cor 10. 8 twenty-three thousand fell in a single day

TWICE

1. *second:* δεύτερος DEUTEROS [B.1.a.2]
Tit 3.10 after admonishing him once or twice
2. *twice:* δίς DIS
Mk 14.30 "before the cock crows t., you will deny
14.72 "Before the cock crows t., you will deny
Lk 18.12 "'I fast twice a week, I give tithes
Jude .12 fruitless trees in late autumn, t. dead

TWICE AS MUCH

1. *double:* διπλοῦς (comp.) DIPLOUS
Mt 23.15 "you make him t. as much a child of hell[w]

TWICE TEN THOUSAND

1. *twenty thousand:* δισμυριάς DISMYRIAS*
Rev 9.16 cavalry was twice ten thousand times

TWIN

1. *double:* δίδυμος DIDYMOS*
Jn 11.16 Thomas, called the T., said . . "Let us also go
20.24 Thomas . ., called the T., was not with them
21. 2 Simon Peter, Thomas called the Twin

TWIN BROTHERS (The Dioscuri): Διόσκουροι
Acts 28.11 ship . . with the Twin Brothers as figurehead

TWINKLING

1. *twinkling, rapid movement:* ῥιπή RHIPĒ*
1 Cor 15.52 in a moment, in the twinkling of an eye

TWIST

1. *twist:* στρεβλόω STREBLOŌ*
2 Pet 3.16 the . . unstable t. to their own destruction

TWO (*See also* SAW IN TWO)

1. *fifteen:* δεκαπέντε DEKAPENTE [A.3.c.1]
Jn 11.18 near Jerusalem, about two miles[y] off†
2. *two:* δύο DYO
[a]δύο δύο
Mt 4.18 by . . Sea of Galilee, he saw t. brothers
4.21 going on . . he saw two other brothers
5.41 "go with him two miles
6.24 "No one can serve two masters
8.28 when he came . ., two demoniacs met him
9.27 Jesus passed on . ., t. blind men followed
10.10 "nor two tunics, nor sandals, nor a staff
10.29 "Are not two sparrows sold for a penny?
14.17 "We have only five loaves here and t. fish
14.19 taking the five loaves and the two fish
18. 8 "better . . than with two hands or two feet to be thrown into the eternal fire
18. 9 "with two eyes to be thrown into . . hell[b]
18.16 "take one or two others along with you
18.16 "by the evidence of two or three witnesses
18.19 "if two of you agree on earth
18.20 "where two or three are gathered
19. 5 "'and the two shall become one flesh
19. 6 "they are no longer two but one flesh
20.21 "that these two sons of mine may sit
20.24 they were indignant at the t. brothers
20.30 two blind men sitting by the roadside
21. 1 then Jesus sent two disciples
21.28 "A man had two sons
21.31 "Which of the two did the will of his father?
22.40 "On these two commandments depend all
24.40 "Then two men will be in the field
24.41 "Two women will be grinding at the mill
25.15 "he gave five talents,[d] to another two
25.17 "So also, he who had the two talents made two talents more
25.22 "he . . who had the two talents came . ., saying . . 'you delivered to me two talents; here I have made two talents more
26. 2 "after two days the Passover is coming
26.37 taking with him . . the two sons of Zebedee
26.60 At last two came forward
27.21 "Which of . . t. do you want me to release?

Mt 27.38 two robbers were crucified with him
27.51 the curtain of the temple was torn in two
Mk 6. 7 [a]he called to him the twelve, and began to send them out two by two
6. 9 to wear sandals and not put on two tunics
6.38 they said, "Five, and two fish
6.41 taking the five loaves and the two fish
6.41 he divided the two fish among them all
9.43 "better . . than with two hands to go to hell[m]
9.45 "with two feet to be thrown into hell[m, n]
9.47 "with two eyes to be thrown into hell[m]
10. 8 " 'and the two shall become one flesh.' So they are no longer two but one flesh
11. 1 he sent two of his disciples
12.42 a poor widow . . put in two copper coins
14. 1 It was now two days before the Passover
14.13 he sent two of his disciples
15.27 with him they crucified two robbers
15.38 curtain of the temple was torn in two
16.12 he appeared in another form to two of them[k]‡
Lk 2.24 to offer a sacrifice . . "two young pigeons
3.11 "who has two coats, let him share
5. 2 he saw two boats by the lake
7.19 John, calling to him two of his disciples
7.41 "A certain creditor had two debtors
9. 3 "Take nothing . . ; and do not have two tunics
9.13 "no more than five loaves and two fish
9.16 taking the five loaves and the two fish
9.30 two . . talked with him, Moses and Elijah
9.32 they saw . . the t. men who stood with him
10.35 "the next day he took out two denarii[i]
12. 6 "five sparrows sold for two pennies
12.52 "there will be five divided, three against two and two against three
15.11 "There was a man who had two sons
16.13 "No servant can serve two masters
17.34 "there will be two in one bed[o]
17.35 "There will be two women grinding
[17.36 "*Two men will be in the field*‡
18.10 "Two men went . . into the temple to pray
19.29 he sent two of the disciples
21. 2 a poor widow put in two copper coins
22.38 "Look, Lord, here are two swords
23.32 Two others also, who were criminals
24. 4 t. men stood by them in dazzling apparel
24.13 two of them were going to a village
Jn 1.35 John . . standing with t. of his disciples
1.37 The two disciples heard him say this
1.40 One of the two who heard John speak
4.40 he stayed there two days
4.43 After the two days he departed
6. 9 "who has five barley loaves and two fish
8.17 "the testimony of two men is true
11. 6 he stayed two days longer in the place
19.18 crucified him, and with him two others
20.12 she saw two angels in white
21. 2 two others of his disciples were together
Acts 1.10 two men stood by them in white robes
1.23 put forward two, Joseph . . and Matthias
1.24 "which one of these two thou hast chosen
7.29 "he became the father of two sons
9.38 sent two men to him entreating him
10. 7 "he called two of his servants
12. 6 Peter was sleeping between two soldiers, bound with two chains
19.10 This continued for two years
19.22 sent into Macedonia two of his helpers
19.34 for . . two hours they all with one voice
21.33 ordered him to be bound with two chains
23.23 Then he called two of the centurions
1 Cor 6.16 "The two shall become one flesh
14.27 let there be only two or at most three
14.29 Let two or three prophets speak
2 Cor 13. 1 sustained by . . evidence of two . . witnesses
Gal 4.22 written that Abraham had two sons
4.24 these women are two covenants
Eph 2.15 one new man in place of the two
Eph 5.31 "the two shall become one flesh
Phil 1.23 I am hard pressed between the two
1 Tim 5.19 the evidence of two or three witnesses
Heb 6.18 through two unchangeable things
10.28 the testimony of two or three witnesses
Rev 9.12 behold, two woes are still to come
11. 3 "I will grant my two witnesses power
11. 4 the two olive trees and the two lampstands which stand before the Lord
11.10 these two prophets had been a torment
12.14 the woman was given the two wings
13.11 it had two horns like a lamb
19.20 two were thrown alive into the lake

CONTEXTUALLY
2 Tim 3. 9 as was that of those two men

TWO BY TWO
1. *at the rate of two:* ἀνὰ δύο δύο DYO; ANA [B.3.b.8]
Lk 10. 1 sent them on ahead of him two by two

TWO HUNDRED
1. *two hundred:* διακόσιοι DIAKOSIOI
Mk 6.37 "two hundred denarii[u] worth of bread
Jn 6. 7 "Two h. denarii[l] would not buy enough
Acts 23.23 "get ready two hundred soldiers . . and two hundred spearmen
27.37 (in all two hundred and seventy-six[d]‡
Rev 11. 3 "one thousand two h. and sixty days
12. 6 one thousand two h. and sixty days

TWO, IN
1. *middle, in the middle:* μέσος (neut.) MESOS
Lk 23.45 curtain of the temple was torn in two

TWO THOUSAND
1. *two thousand:* δισχίλιοι DISCHILIOI*
Mk 5.13 herd, numbering about two thousand

TWO YEARS
1. *period of two years:* διετία DIETIA*
Acts 24.27 when two years had elapsed
28.30 he lived there two whole years

TWO YEARS OLD
1. *of two years, two years old:* διετής DIETĒS*
Mt 2.16 male children . . two years old or under

TWO-EDGED
1. *double-mouthed, two-edged:* δίστομος DISTOMOS*
Heb 4.12 sharper than any two-edged sword
Rev 1.16 from his mouth issued a sharp t. sword
2.12 " 'who has the sharp two-edged sword

TYCHICUS: Τυχικός 'tikəkəs
Acts 20. 4 the Asians, Tychicus and Trophimus
Eph 6.21 T. . . beloved brother and faithful minister
Col 4. 7 T. will tell you all about my affairs
2 Tim 4.12 Tychicus I have sent to Ephesus
Tit 3.12 When I send Artemas or T.

TYPE
1. *pattern, image:* τύπος TYPOS
Rom 5.14 Adam, who was a t. of the one . . to come

TYRANNUS: Τύραννος tī'ranəs
Acts 19. 9 argued daily in the hall of T.[r]

TYRE: 'tī(ə)r I,C-2; II,G-4
1. *Tyre:* Τύρος
Mt 11.21 "if the . . works . . had been done in Tyre
11.22 "on . . day of judgment for Tyre and Sidon
15.21 withdrew to . . district of Tyre and Sidon
Mk 3. 8 from about T. and Sidon a . . multitude
7.24 went away to . . region of T. and Sidon[c]
7.31 he returned from the region of Tyre
Lk 6.17 from . . the seacoast of Tyre and Sidon
10.13 "if the . . works . . had been done in Tyre
10.14 "more tolerable in the judgment for Tyre
Acts 21. 3 we sailed to Syria, and landed at Tyre
21. 7 we had finished the voyage from Tyre
2. *of Tyre, Tyrian:* Τύριος
Acts 12.20 Herod was angry with the people of T.

U

UNABLE
1. *not:* μή MĒ [B.3.b.4]
Acts 13.11 “you shall be blind and unable to see

UNABLE, BE
1. *be able:* δύναμαι (neg.) DYNAMAI
[a]μή [b]οὐ
Lk 1.20 [a]“you will be silent and unable to speak
Heb 3.19 [b]were u. to enter because of unbelief
4.15 [a]not a high priest who is u. to sympathize

UNAPPROACHABLE
1. *inaccessible:* ἀπρόσιτος APROSITOS*
1 Tim 6.16 who . . dwells in unapproachable light

UNAWARES
1. *escape notice:* λανθάνω LANTHANŌ [A.6.c.1]
Heb 13. 2 some have entertained angels unawares

UNBEARABLY
1. *beyond ability:* ὑπὲρ δύναμιν DYNAMIS [B.1.a.1]
2 Cor 1. 8 we were so utterly, unbearably crushed

UNBELIEF
1. *distrust, faithlessness:* ἀπιστία APISTIA
Mt 13.58 not . . many . . works . . , because of their u.
Mk 6. 6 he marveled because of their unbelief
9.24 “I believe; help my unbelief!
16.14 he upbraided them for their unbelief[k]‡
Rom 11.20 They were broken off because of their u.
11.23 if they do not persist in their unbelief
1 Tim 1.13 I had acted ignorantly in unbelief
Heb 3.19 unable to enter because of unbelief

UNBELIEVER
1. *disobey:* ἀπειθέω (subst. part.) APEITHEŌ
Rom 15.31 delivered from the unbelievers in Judea
2. *unfaithful, incredible:* ἄπιστος (subst.) APISTOS
1 Cor 6. 6 brother goes to law . . before unbelievers
7.12 if any brother has a wife who is an u.
7.13 If any . . has a husband who is an u.
10.27 If one of the unbelievers invites you
14.22 Thus, tongues are a sign . . for unbelievers, while prophecy is not for unbelievers
14.23 If . . outsiders or unbelievers enter
14.24 if . . an unbeliever or outsider enters
2 Cor 4. 4 blinded the minds of the unbelievers
6.14 Do not be mismated with unbelievers
6.15 what has a believer in common with an u.?
1 Tim 5. 8 he . . is worse than an unbeliever

UNBELIEVING
1. *disobey:* ἀπειθέω (part.) APEITHEŌ
Acts 14. 2 the u. Jews stirred up the Gentiles
2. *distrust, faithlessness:* ἀπιστία APISTIA
Heb 3.12 lest . . an evil, unbelieving heart
3. *unfaithful, incredible:* ἄπιστος APISTOS
1 Cor 7.14 the u. husband is consecrated through his wife, and the u. wife . . through her husband
7.15 if the u. partner desires to separate
Tit 1.15 to the corrupt and u. nothing is pure

UNBIND
1. *break up, unbind:* λύω LYŌ
Jn 11.44 “Unbind him, and let him go
Acts 22.30 But on the morrow . . he unbound him

UNBLAMABLE
1. *blameless:* ἄμεμπτος AMEMPTOS
1 Th 3.13 that he may establish your hearts u.

UNCEASING
1. *unceasing:* ἀδιάλειπτος ADIALEIPTOS
Rom 9. 2 I have . . unceasing anguish in my heart

UNCERTAIN
1. *uncertainty:* ἀδηλότης (+gen.) ADĒLOTĒS*
1 Tim 6.17 nor to set their hopes on u. riches

UNCERTAIN, BE
1. *be in doubt:* ἀπορέω (mid.) APOREŌ
Jn 13.22 disciples . . , uncertain of whom he spoke

UNCERTAINTY, WITHOUT
1. *undecided, unwavering:* ἀδιάκριτος ADIAKRITOS*
Jas 3.17 good fruits, without u. or insincerity

UNCHANGEABLE
1. *unalterable:* ἀμετάθετος AMETATHETOS
Heb 6.18 through two unchangeable things

UNCHANGEABLE CHARACTER, THE
1. *unalterable:* ἀμετάθετος (subst. neut.) AMETATHETOS
Heb 6.17 the u. character of his purpose

UNCHASTITY
1. *fornication, unchastity:* πορνεία PORNEIA
Mt 5.32 “who divorces . . , except on . . ground of u.
19. 9 “whoever divorces his wife, except for u.[j]
Acts 15.20 “write to them to abstain from . . unchastity
15.29 “that you abstain . . from unchastity
21.25 “that they should abstain from . . u.
1 Th 4. 3 that you abstain from unchastity[o]

UNCIRCUMCISED
1. *foreskin, uncircumcision:* ἀκροβυστία AKROBYSTIA
[a]B.3.a.5 [b]B.1.a.2 [c]B.1.a.1 [d]C.2
Acts 11. 3 [a]“Why did you go to uncircumcised men?
Rom 4.11 [b]he had by faith while he was still u.
1 Cor 7.18 [c]Was any one at the time of his call u.?
Col 3.11 [d]Greek and Jew, circumcised and u.
2. *uncircumcised:* ἀπερίτμητος APERITMĒTOS*
Acts 7.51 “stiff-necked people, u. in heart and ears

UNCIRCUMCISED, A MAN WHO IS
UNCIRCUMCISED, THE
UNCIRCUMCISED, THOSE WHO ARE
1. *foreskin, uncircumcision:* ἀκροβυστία AKROBYSTIA [C.2]
Rom 2.26 if a man who is u. keeps the precepts
2.27 those who are . . u. but keep the law
3.30 will justify . . the u. through their faith
4. 9 Is this blessing . . also upon the u.?
Gal 2. 7 entrusted with the gospel to the u.

UNCIRCUMCISION
1. *foreskin, uncircumcision:* ἀκροβυστία AKROBYSTIA
Rom 2.25 your circumcision becomes uncircumcision
2.26 will not his u. be regarded as circumcision?
1 Cor 7.19 neither circumcision counts . . nor u.
Gal 5. 6 in Christ Jesus neither circumcision nor u.
6.15 neither circumcision counts . . , nor u.
Eph 2.11 you Gentiles in the flesh, called the u.
Col 2.13 dead in . . the u. of your flesh

UNCLEAN
1. *unclean:* ἀκάθαρτος AKATHARTOS
Mt 10. 1 gave them authority over u. spirits
12.43 “When the u. spirit has gone out of a man
Mk 1.23 in . . synagogue a man with an u. spirit
1.26 the unclean spirit, convulsing him
1.27 “he commands even the unclean spirits
3.11 whenever the unclean spirits beheld him
3.30 they had said, “He has an unclean spirit
5. 2 out of . . tombs a man with an u. spirit
5. 8 “Come out of the man, you u. spirit!
5.13 the unclean spirits came out
6. 7 gave them authority over the u. spirits
7.25 daughter was possessed by an u. spirit
9.25 he rebuked the unclean spirit
Lk 4.33 man who had the spirit of an u. demon
4.36 “he commands the unclean spirits
6.18 those who were troubled with u. spirits
8.29 commanded the u. spirit to come out
9.42 But Jesus rebuked the unclean spirit
11.24 “When the u. spirit has gone out of a man
Acts 5.16 those afflicted with unclean spirits
8. 7 For unclean spirits came out of many
10.14 “I have never eaten anything . . unclean
10.28 “that I should not call any man . . u.
11. 8 “ ‘nothing . . u. has ever entered my mouth
1 Cor 7.14 Otherwise, your children would be u.
2 Cor 6.17 “come out from them . . and touch nothing u.

2. *common, profane:* κοινός KOINOS
Rom 14.14 I . . am persuaded . . that nothing is unclean in itself; but it is unclean for any one who thinks it unclean
Rev 21.27 But nothing unclean shall enter it

UNCLEANNESS
1. *uncleanness:* ἀκαθαρσία AKATHARSIA
Mt 23.27 "like whitewashed tombs, . . full of . . all u.
Eph 4.19 greedy to practice every kind of u.
1 Th 2. 3 our appeal does not spring from . . u.
4. 7 For God has not called us for u.

UNCLOTHED, BE
1. *take off:* ἐκδύω (pass.) EKDYŌ
2 Cor 5. 4 not that we would be unclothed

UNCONDEMNED
1. *uncondemned:* ἀκατάκριτος AKATAKRITOS*
Acts 16.37 "They have beaten us publicly, u.
22.25 "Is it lawful . . to scourge . . a Roman . . u.?

UNCOVERED
1. *uncovered:* ἀκατακάλυπτος AKATAKALYPTOS
1 Cor 11.13 to pray to God with her head u.

UNDEFILED
1. *undefiled:* ἀμίαντος AMIANTOS
Heb 13. 4 let the marriage bed be undefiled
Jas 1.27 Religion that is pure and undefiled
1 Pet 1. 4 an inheritance which is imperishable, u.

UNDER
1. *through:* διά (+gen.) DIA
2 Cor **9**.13
2. *from, out of:* ἐκ (+gen.) EK
2 Cor **9.7**
3. *in, at, by:* ἐν (+dat.) EN
Mt **7.6**
Lk **23**.40
Rom **2**.12; **3**.19
Phil **3**.6
1 Pet **4**.16
4. *on, at:* ἐπί (+gen.) EPI
except [a]+dat.
Heb 7.11 (for under it the people received the law
9.15 [a]transgressions under the first covenant[u]
5. *under:* ὑπό (+acc.) HYPO
except [a]+gen.
Mt **5**.15; **8**.8, 9[2]; **23**.37
Mk **4**.21[2]; **5**.26[a]
Lk **7**.6, 8[2]; **11**.33; **13**.34
Jn **1**.48
Acts **2**.5; **4**.12
Rom **3**.9, 13; **6**.14[2], 15[2]; **7**.14; **16**.20
1 Cor **9**.20[4]; **10**.1; **15**.25, 27
Gal **3**.10, 23, 25; **4**.2, 4, 5, 21; **5**.18
Eph **1**.22
Col **1**.23
1 Tim **6**.1
Jas **5**.12
1 Pet **5**.6
6. *below, under:* ὑποκάτω HYPOKATŌ
Mt 22.44 " 'till I put thy enemies under thy feet
Mk 7.28 "even the dogs u. the table eat . . crumbs
12.36 " 'till I put thy enemies under thy feet
Lk 8.16 "No one . . puts it under a bed
Jn 1.50 "I said to you, I saw you u. the fig tree
Heb 2. 8 "everything in subjection under his feet
Rev 5. 3 no one . . u. the earth was able to open
5.13 I heard every creature . . under the earth
6. 9 I saw under the altar the souls of those
12. 1 a woman . . with the moon under her feet
7. *in accordance with, for:* κατά (+acc.) KATA
Heb 9.22 u. the law almost everything is purified
8. *below, lower:* κατωτέρω KATŌTERŌ*
Mt 2.16 male children . . two years old or under

UNDER, BE
1. *have, hold:* ἔχω ECHŌ [A.6.a.2]
1 Cor 7.37 in his heart, being under no necessity

IDIOMATICALLY
a. Acts 21.23 "We have four men who are under a vow εἰσὶν ἡμῖν ἄνδρες τέσσαρες εὐχὴν ἔχοντες ἀφ' ἑαυτῶν [HEAUTOU]

UNDER THE LEADERSHIP OF
1. *through:* διά (+gen.) DIA
Heb 3.16 left Egypt u. the leadership of Moses

UNDERGIRD
1. *brace:* ὑποζώννυμι HYPOZŌNNYMI*
Acts 27.17 they took measures[c] to undergird the ship

UNDERGO
1. *hold under, undergo:* ὑπέχω HYPECHŌ*
Jude . 7 an example by undergoing a punishment

UNDERHANDED
1. *secret, hidden:* κρυπτός KRYPTOS
2 Cor 4. 2 We have renounced . . underhanded ways

UNDERMINE
1. *cut out, cut off:* ἐκκόπτω EKKOPTŌ
2 Cor 11.12 in order to undermine the claim

UNDERSTAND
1. *not know:* ἀγνοέω (double neg.) AGNOEŌ
Rom 11.25 I want you to understand this mystery
2. *hear:* ἀκούω AKOUŌ
1 Cor 14. 2 for no one understands him
3. *learn to know, recognize:* ἐπιγινώσκω EPIGINŌSKŌ
2 Cor 1.13 nothing but what you can read and u.; I hope you will understand fully
1.14 as you have understood in part
Col 1. 6 understood the grace of God in truth
4. *know, understand:* ἐπίσταμαι EPISTAMAI
Mk 14.68 "I neither know nor u. what you mean
5. *know, understand:* γινώσκω GINŌSKŌ
Mk 4.13 "How then will you u. all the parables?
Jn 3.10 "yet you do not understand this
8.27 did not u. that he spoke . . of the Father
8.43 "Why do you not understand what I say?
10. 6 they did not u. what he was saying
10.38 "that you may know and understand
12.16 His disciples did not understand this
13. 7 "but afterward you will understand
Acts 8.30 "Do you u. what you are reading?
Rom 7.15 I do not understand my own actions
10.19 Again I ask, did Israel not understand?
1 Cor 2. 8 None of the rulers of this age understood
2.14 he is not able to understand them
2 Tim 3. 1 understand this, that in the last days
Heb 13.23 u. that . . Timothy has been released
2 Pet 1.20 First of all you must understand this
3. 3 First of all you must understand this
6. *reckon, count:* λογίζομαι LOGIZOMAI
Jn 11.50 "you do not u. that it is expedient
2 Cor 10.11 Let such people understand
7. *think, consider, perceive:* νοέω NOEŌ
Mt 24.15 "(let the reader understand
Mk 13.14 "(let the reader understand
1 Tim 1. 7 teachers . . without understanding . . things
Heb 11. 3 we u. that the world was created
8. *know:* οἶδα OIDA
Mk 4.13 "Do you not understand this parable?
1 Cor 2.12 that we might u. the gifts bestowed on us
11. 3 But I want you to understand
13. 2 if I . . u. all mysteries and all knowledge
1 Tim 1. 9 understanding . . that . . law is . . for . . lawless
Jude .10 these . . revile whatever they do not u.
9. *understand, perceive:* συνίημι SYNIĒMI
Mt 13.13 "they do not hear, nor do they understand
13.14 " 'You shall . . hear but never understand
13.15 " 'lest they . . understand with their heart
13.19 "When any one hears . . and does not u.
13.23 "he who hears the word and understands it
13.51 "Have you understood all this?
15.10 "Hear and understand
16.12 they understood that he did not tell
17.13 understood that he was speaking . . of John
Mk 4.12 "may indeed hear but not understand
6.52 they did not understand about the loaves

Mk 7.14 "Hear me, all of you, and understand
8.17 "Do you not yet perceive or understand?
8.21 "Do you not yet understand?
Lk 2.50 they did not understand the saying
8.10 "that . . hearing they may not understand
18.34 they understood none of these things
24.45 he opened their minds to understand
Acts 7.25 "supposed that his brethren understood . . , but they did not understand
28.26 " 'You shall indeed hear but never u.
28.27 " 'lest they . . understand with their heart
Rom 3.11 "no one understands, no one seeks for God
15.21 "they shall u. who have never heard
Eph 5.17 do not be foolish, but understand

UNDERSTAND FULLY

1. *learn to know, recognize:* ἐπιγινώσκω EPIGINŌSKŌ
1 Cor 13.12 then I shall understand fully, even as I have been fully understood

UNDERSTAND, HARD TO

1. *hard to be understood:* δυσνόητος DYSNOĒTOS*
2 Pet 3.16 some things in them hard to understand

UNDERSTAND, NOT

1. *not know:* ἀγνοέω AGNOEŌ
Mk 9.32 they did not understand the saying
Lk 9.45 they did not understand this saying
Acts 13.27 "they did not . . u. the utterances

UNDERSTAND, WANT S. TO

1. *make known:* γνωρίζω GNŌRIZŌ
1 Cor 12. 3 Therefore I want you to understand

UNDERSTANDING

1. *thought, understanding:* διάνοια DIANOIA
Eph 4.18 they are darkened in their understanding
1 Jn 5.20 the Son of God . . has given us u.
2. *knowing, expert:* ἐπιστήμων EPISTĒMŌN*
Jas 3.13 Who is wise and u. among you?
3. *mind, reason:* νοῦς NOUS
Phil 4. 7 the peace of God, which passes all u.
Rev 13.18 let him who has understanding reckon
4. *intelligence, understanding:* σύνεσις SYNESIS
Mk 12.33 "to love him with all the heart, and . . u.
Lk 2.47 all who heard him were amazed at his u.
Col 1. 9 knowledge of his will in all spiritual . . u.
2. 2 to have all the riches of assured u.
2 Tim 2. 7 for the Lord will grant you u.
5. *intelligent, wise:* συνετός SYNETOS
Mt 11.25 "hast hidden these things from the . . u.
Lk 10.21 "hast hidden these things from the . . u.

UNDERSTANDING, BE WITHOUT

1. *understand, perceive:* συνίημι (neg.) SYNIĒMI
2 Cor 10.12 they are without understanding

UNDERSTANDING, WITHOUT

1. *unintelligible, senseless:* ἀσύνετος ASYNETOS
Mt 15.16 "Are you also . . without understanding?
Mk 7.18 "are you also without understanding?

UNDERTAKE

1. *put one's hand to, attempt:* ἐπιχειρέω EPICHEIREŌ
Lk 1. 1 many have undertaken to compile
Acts 19.13 Jewish exorcists undertook to pronounce

UNDERTAKING

1. *work, deed:* ἔργον ERGON
Acts 5.38 "if this plan or this undertaking is of men

UNDIVIDED

1. *uninterrupted:* ἀπερισπάστως APERISPASTŌS*
1 Cor 7.35 to secure your u. devotion to the Lord

UNDYING

1. *incorruption, immortality:* ἀφθαρσία APHTHARSIA [B.1.a.1]
Eph 6.24 who love our Lord Jesus Christ with love u.

UNEDUCATED

1. *illiterate:* ἀγράμματος AGRAMMATOS*
Acts 4.13 perceived that they were uneducated

UNEXPECTED

1. *think, suppose:* δοκέω (neg.) DOKEŌ [B.2.a.1]
Lk 12.40 "Son of man is coming at an u. hour

UNFADING

1. *unfading:* ἀμαράντινος AMARANTINOS*
1 Pet 5. 4 you will obtain the u. crown of glory
2. *unfading:* ἀμάραντος AMARANTOS*
1 Pet 1. 4 inheritance which is imperishable, . . and u.

UNFAILING

1. *friendly, extended, constant:* ἐκτενής (acc.) EKTENĒS*
1 Pet 4. 8 hold u. your love for one another
2. *all, every, whole:* πᾶς PAS [B.2.d.2]
2 Tim 4. 2 be u. in patience and in teaching

UNFAITHFUL

1. *unfaithful, incredible:* ἄπιστος APISTOS
Lk 12.46 "will punish[r] him, and put him with the u.

UNFAITHFUL, BE

1. *disbelieve, be faithless:* ἀπιστέω APISTEŌ
Rom 3. 3 What if some were unfaithful?

UNFAITHFUL CREATURE

1. *adulteress:* μοιχαλίς MOICHALIS
Jas 4. 4 Unfaithful creatures! Do you not know?

UNFASTEN

1. *let go:* ἀνίημι ANIĒMI
Acts 16.26 every one's fetters were unfastened

UNFIT

1. *counterfeit, worthless:* ἀδόκιμος ADOKIMOS
Tit 1.16 disobedient, unfit for any good deed
2. *enough:* ἱκανός (neg.) HIKANOS
1 Cor 15. 9 I am . . least . . , u. to be called . . apostle

UNFRUITFUL

1. *without fruit:* ἄκαρπος AKARPOS
Mt 13.22 "choke the word, and it proves unfruitful
Mk 4.19 "choke the word, and it proves unfruitful
1 Cor 14.14 my spirit prays but my mind is unfruitful
Eph 5.11 Take no part in the unfruitful works
Tit 3.14 so as to help . . and not to be unfruitful
2 Pet 1. 8 keep you from being ineffective or u.

UNGODLINESS

1. *impiety, ungodliness:* ἀσέβεια ASEBEIA
Rom 1.18 wrath of God is revealed . . against all u.
11.26 "he will banish ungodliness from Jacob
2 Tim 2.16 it will lead people into more and more u.
Jude .15 "to convict all the ungodly of all their . . u.

UNGODLY

1. *impiety, ungodliness:* ἀσέβεια (gen.) ASEBEIA
Jude .18 "scoffers, following their own u. passions
2. *unholy, godless:* ἀσεβής ASEBĒS
Rom 4. 5 one who . . trusts him who justifies the u.
5. 6 at the right time Christ died for the u.
1 Tim 1. 9 the law is . . laid down . . for the ungodly
2 Pet 2. 5 a flood upon the world of the ungodly
3. 7 until the day of . . destruction of u. men
Jude . 4 ungodly persons who pervert the grace
.15 "to convict all the u. of all their deeds
.15 "harsh things which u. sinners have spoken

UNGODLY, BE

1. *be impious:* ἀσεβέω ASEBEŌ
2 Pet 2. 6 an example to those who were to be u.

UNGODLY WAY, COMMIT IN SUCH AN

1. *be impious:* ἀσεβέω ASEBEŌ
Jude .15 "deeds . . they . . committed in such an u. way

UNGRATEFUL

1. *ungracious, ungrateful:* ἀχάριστος ACHARISTOS*
Lk 6.35 "for he is kind to the u. and the selfish
2 Tim 3. 2 disobedient to their parents, ungrateful

UNGRUDGINGLY

1. *without muttering:* ἄνευ γογγυσμοῦ GOGGYSMOS [B.1.a.1]
1 Pet 4. 9 Practice hospitality ungrudgingly

UNHINDERED

1. *without hindrance:* ἀκωλύτως (adv.) AKŌLYTŌS*
Acts 28.31 teaching . . quite openly and unhindered

UNHOLY
1. *unholy, profane:* ἀνόσιος ANOSIOS*
1 Tim 1. 9 the law is . . laid down . . for the unholy
2 Tim 3. 2 disobedient to their parents, . . unholy

UNINFORMED, BE
1. *not know:* ἀγνοέω AGNOEŌ
1 Cor 12. 1 I do not want you to be uninformed

UNITE
1. *sum up, recapitulate:* ἀνακεφαλαιόω (mid.) ANAKEPHALAIOŌ
Eph 1.10 as a plan . . to unite all things in him
2. *put in order, make:* καταρτίζω KATARTIZŌ
1 Cor 1.10 that you be united in the same mind
3. *mix, compose:* συγκεράννυμι SYGKERANNYMI
Heb [4. 2 because *they were not united in faith*‡

UNITED
1. *together, with one mind:* ὁμοθυμαδόν HOMOTHYMADON [A.4.a]
Acts 18.12 Jews made a united attack upon Paul
2. *grown together:* σύμφυτος SYMPHYTOS*
Rom 6. 5 if we have been u. with him in a death

UNITED, BE
1. *join, unite:* κολλάω (pass.) KOLLAŌ
1 Cor 6.17 But he who is united to the Lord

UNITY
1. *unity, union:* ἑνότης HENOTĒS*
Eph 4. 3 unity of the Spirit in the bond of peace
4.13 until we all attain to the u. of the faith

UNITY OF SPIRIT, HAVE
1. *agreeing, like-minded:* ὁμόφρων HOMOPHRŌN* [A.3.e.2]
1 Pet 3. 8 have unity of spirit, sympathy, love

UNIVERSE
1. *world, world order:* κόσμος KOSMOS
Gal 4. 3 slaves to the elemental spirits of the u.
Col 2. 8 according to . . elemental spirits of the u.
2.20 died to the elemental spirits of the u.
2. *all things:* τὰ πάντα PAS [B.3.b.8]
Heb 1. 3 upholding the u. by his word of power

UNJUST
1. *unjust, unrighteous:* ἄδικος ADIKOS
Mt 5.45 "sends rain on the just and on the u.
Lk 18.11 " 'I am not like other men . . u., adulterers
Acts 24.15 "resurrection of both the just and the u.
Rom 3. 5 That God is u. to inflict wrath on us?
Heb 6.10 God is not so unjust as to overlook

UNJUSTLY
1. *unjustly:* ἀδίκως ADIKŌS*
1 Pet 2.19 he endures pain while suffering u.

UNKNOWN
UNKNOWN, AS
1. *not know:* ἀγνοέω (part.) AGNOEŌ
[a]+ὡς
Acts 17.23 "What therefore you worship as unknown
2 Cor 6. 9 [a]as unknown, and yet well known
2. *unknown:* ἄγνωστος AGNŌSTOS*
Acts 17.23 "altar with this inscription, 'To an u. god

UNLAWFUL
1. *lawless:* ἀθέμιτος ATHEMITOS
Acts 10.28 "You yourselves know how unlawful it is

UNLEAVENED
1. *unleavened:* ἄζυμος AZYMOS
1 Cor 5. 7 as you really are unleavened

UNLEAVENED BREAD
1. *unleavened:* ἄζυμος (subst.) AZYMOS
Mt 26.17 on the first day of Unleavened Bread
Mk 14. 1 two days before . . the feast of U. Bread
14.12 "on the first day of Unleavened Bread
Lk 22. 1 feast of Unleavened Bread drew near
22. 7 Then came the day of Unleavened Bread
Acts 12. 3 during the days of Unleavened Bread
20. 6 after the days of Unleavened Bread
1 Cor 5. 8 celebrate . . with the u. bread of sincerity

UNLESS
1. *if not, except:* ἐὰν μή EAN MĒ
Mt 5.20 "unless your righteousness exceeds that
12.29 "unless he first binds the strong man
18. 3 "unless you turn and become like children
26.42 "if this cannot pass unless I drink it
Mk 3.27 "unless he first binds the strong man
7. 3 (do not eat unless they wash their hands[v]
7. 4 (do not eat unless they purify[w] themselves[a]
Lk 13. 3 "unless you repent you will all . . perish
13. 5 "unless you repent you will all . . perish
Jn 3. 2 "no one can . . unless God is with him
3. 3 "unless one is born anew,[e] he cannot
3. 5 "u. one is born of water and the Spirit
4.48 "Unless you see signs and wonders
6.44 "unless the Father who sent me draws him
6.53 "u. you eat the flesh of the Son of man
6.65 "unless it is granted him by the Father
8.24 "unless you believe that I am he
12.24 "unless a grain of wheat . . dies
15. 4 "branch cannot . . u. it abides in the vine. neither can you, u. you abide in me
20.25 "Unless I see in his hands the print
Acts 8.31 "How can I, unless some one guides me?
15. 1 "Unless you are circumcised
27.31 "Unless these men stay in the ship
Rom 10.15 how can men preach unless they are sent?
1 Cor 14. 6 how . . unless I bring you some revelation?
15.36 does not come to life unless it dies
2 Th 2. 3 unless the rebellion comes first
2 Tim 2. 5 unless he competes according to the rules
Rev 2. 5 " 'I will . . remove . . , unless you repent
2.22 " 'unless they repent of her doings
2. *if not, except:* εἰ μή EI MĒ
[a]ἐκτὸς εἰ μή
Jn 19.11 "u. it had been given you from above
1 Cor 14. 5 [a]greater than he . . u. some one interprets
15. 2 [a]you are saved . . —u. you believed in vain
Rev 13.17 no one can buy . . unless he has the mark
3. *unless indeed:* εἰ μήτι MĒTI [B.3.b.8]
[a]unless indeed
Lk 9.13 "unless we are to go and buy food
2 Cor 13. 5 [a]unless indeed you fail to meet the test!

UNLIFTED
1. *uncover:* ἀνακαλύπτω (pass. part., neg.) ANAKALYPTŌ
2 Cor 3.14 that same veil remains unlifted

UNLOAD
1. *discharge one's cargo:* ἀποφορτίζομαι APOPHORTIZOMAI*
Acts 21. 3 there the ship was to unload its cargo

UNMARRIED
1. *unmarried:* ἄγαμος AGAMOS
1 Cor 7. 8 To the unmarried . . I say that it is well
7.32 The u. man is anxious about the . . Lord
7.34 the u. . . girl[z] is anxious about . . the Lord
2. *maiden, girl, virgin:* παρθένος PARTHENOS
[a]A.1.b.2 [b]pl.
Acts 21. 9 [a]he had four unmarried daughters
1 Cor 7.25 [b]concerning the u.,[y] I have no command†

UNMIXED
1. *unmixed:* ἄκρατος AKRATOS*
Rev 14.10 "poured u. into the cup of his anger

UNNATURAL
1. *another, different:* ἕτερος HETEROS
Jude . 7 cities, which . . indulged in u. lust
2. *contrary to nature:* παρὰ φύσιν PHYSIS [B.1.a.1]
Rom 1.26 exchanged natural relations for u.

UNPRESENTABLE
1. *shameful, ugly:* ἀσχήμων ASCHĒMŌN*
1 Cor 12.23 our u. parts are treated with . . modesty

UNPROFITABLE
1. *useless, harmful:* ἀνωφελής ANŌPHELĒS
Tit 3. 9 for they are unprofitable and futile

UNQUENCHABLE
1. *unquenchable:* ἄσβεστος ASBESTOS*
Mt 3.12 "the chaff he will burn with u. fire

Mk 9.43 "to go to hell,[m] to the unquenchable fire[n]
Lk 3.17 "he will burn with unquenchable fire

UNREASONABLE
1. *absurd:* ἄλογος ALOGOS
Acts 25.27 "For it seems to me unreasonable

UNRIGHTEOUS
1. *wrongdoing, injustice:* ἀδικία (gen.) ADIKIA
Lk 16. 9 "make friends . . by means of u. mammon[a]
18. 6 "Hear what the unrighteous judge says
Jas 3. 6 The tongue is an unrighteous world
2. *unjust, unrighteous:* ἄδικος ADIKOS
Lk 16.11 "If . . not . . faithful in the u. mammon[a]
1 Cor 6. 1 does he dare go to law before the u.?
6. 9 the u. will not inherit the kingdom
1 Pet 3.18 Christ . . died[h] . . , the righteous for the u.
2 Pet 2. 9 to keep the u. under punishment

UNRIGHTEOUSNESS
1. *wrongdoing, injustice:* ἀδικία ADIKIA
2 Th 2.12 all . . who . . had pleasure in u.
1 Jn 1. 9 he . . will . . cleanse us from all u.

UNSEARCHABLE
1. *not to be searched out:* ἀνεξεραύνητος ANEXERAUNĒTOS*
Rom 11.33 How unsearchable are his judgments!
2. *inscrutable:* ἀνεξιχνίαστος ANEXICHNIASTOS
Eph 3. 8 to preach . . the u. riches of Christ

UNSEEN
1. *see, look:* βλέπω (pass. part., neg.) BLEPŌ
2 Cor 4.18 we look . . to the things that are u.; . . the things that are unseen are eternal
Heb 11. 7 concerning events as yet unseen

UNSETTLE
1. *dismantle, upset:* ἀνασκευάζω ANASKEUAZŌ*
Acts 15.24 "some persons . . unsettling your minds
2. *upset, disturb:* ἀναστατόω ANASTATOŌ
Gal 5.12 I wish those who unsettle you

UNSHAKEN
1. *firm, steady:* βέβαιος BEBAIOS
2 Cor 1.17 Our hope for you is unshaken

UNSHRUNK
1. *unwashed, unbleached:* ἄγναφος AGNAPHOS*
Mt 9.16 "no one puts a piece of unshrunk cloth
Mk 2.21 "No one sews a piece of unshrunk cloth

UNSKILLED
1. *inexperienced:* ἄπειρος APEIROS*
Heb 5.13 unskilled in the word of righteousness
2. *private individual, layman:* ἰδιώτης (pred.) IDIŌTĒS
2 Cor 11. 6 Even if I am unskilled in speaking

UNSOLD
CONTEXTUALLY
Acts 5. 4 "unsold, did it not remain your own?

UNSPIRITUAL
1. *physical, of the soul:* ψυχικός PSYCHIKOS
1 Cor 2.14 The u.[e] man does not receive the gifts†
Jas 3.15 This wisdom . . is earthly, unspiritual

UNSTABLE
1. *unstable:* ἀκατάστατος AKATASTATOS
Jas 1. 8 double-minded man, u. in all his ways
2. *not supported by a staff:* ἀστήρικτος ASTĒRIKTOS
2 Pet 3.16 some things . . which the . . unstable twist

UNSTAINED
1. *undefiled:* ἀμίαντος AMIANTOS
Heb 7.26 unstained, separated from sinners
2. *without blemish:* ἄσπιλος ASPILOS
1 Tim 6.14 keep the commandment unstained
Jas 1.27 keep oneself unstained from the world

UNSTEADY
1. *not supported by a staff:* ἀστήρικτος ASTĒRIKTOS
2 Pet 2.14 They entice unsteady souls

UNTIE
1. *break up, unbind:* λύω LYŌ
Mt 21. 2 "untie them and bring them to me
Mk 1. 7 "I am not worthy to stoop down and u.
11. 2 "you will find a colt tied . . ; untie it
Mk 11. 4 found a colt tied . . ; and they untied it
11. 5 "What are you doing, untying the colt?
Lk 3.16 "whose sandals I am not worthy to u.
13.15 "Does not each . . untie his ox or his ass?
19.30 "untie it and bring it here
19.31 " 'Why are you untying it?
19.33 as they were untying the colt, its owners said . . "Why are you untying the colt?
Jn 1.27 "whose sandal I am not worthy to untie
Acts 13.25 " 'sandals . . I am not worthy to untie

UNTIL
1. *until:* ἄχρι ACHRI
[a]ἄχρι οὗ/ἧς [b]ἄχρι οὗ ἄν
Mt 24.38 "until the day . . Noah entered the ark
Lk 1.20 "unable to speak u. . . these . . come to pass
4.13 he departed . . until an opportune time
17.27 "until the day . . Noah entered the ark
21.24 [a]"u. the times of the Gentiles are fulfilled
Acts 1. 2 [a]until the day when he was taken up
3.21 "whom heaven must receive u. the time
20.11 he conversed with them . . until daybreak
Rom 8.22 groaning in travail together until now
11.25 [a]u. the full number of the Gentiles come
1 Cor 11.26 [a]proclaim the Lord's death u. he comes
15.25 [a]must reign u. he has put all his enemies
Gal 4. 2 under guardians . . until the date set
Phil 1. 5 your partnership . . from . . first day u. now
Heb 6.11 full assurance of hope until the end
Rev 2.25 [b]" 'hold . . what you have, u. I come
2.26 " 'who keeps my works until the end
15. 8 until the seven plagues . . were ended
17.17 "until the words of God shall be fulfilled
20. 5 until the thousand years were ended
2. *into, to, for:* εἰς (+acc.) EIS
Acts **4**.3
Gal **3**.23, 24
Eph **1**.14
1 Th **4**.15
2 Tim **1**.12
2 Pet **2**.4, 9; **3**.7
Jude .6
3. *until, while:* ἕως HEŌS
[a]ἕως οὗ/ἧς [b]ἕως ἄν [c]ἕως ὅτου
Mt 1.25 [a]knew her not until she had borne a son
2.15 remained there until the death of Herod
5.18 [b]"will ⟨not⟩ pass . . u. all is accomplished
10.11 [b]"stay with him until you depart
11.12 "From . . John the Baptist until now
11.13 "all the prophets . . prophesied until John
13.30 " 'Let both grow together until . . harvest
17. 9 [a]"u. the Son of man is raised from the dead
23.39 [b]"u. you say, 'Blessed is he who comes
24.21 "from the beginning of the world u. now
24.39 "they did not know until the flood came
26.29 "until that day when I drink it new
27.45 darkness . . until the ninth hour
27.64 "to be made secure until the third day
Mk 6.10 [b]"stay there until you leave the place
13.19 "from the beginning . . until now
14.25 "until that day when I drink it new
15.33 darkness . . until the ninth hour
Lk 12.50 [c]"constrained until it is accomplished!
13.35 "u. you say, 'Blessed is he who comes!
15. 4 "and go after the one . . until he finds it
15. 8 [a]"and seek diligently until she finds it
22.16 [c]"I shall not eat it[i] until it is fulfilled
22.18 [a]"until the kingdom of God comes
22.34 "u. you three times deny that you know me
23.44 darkness . . until the ninth hour
24.49 [a]"until you are clothed with power
Jn 2.10 "you have kept the good wine until now
9.18 [c]until they called the parents of the man
21.22 "If it is my will that he remain u. I come
21.23 "If it is my will that he remain u. I come
Acts 1.22 [a]"until the day when he was taken up
7.45 "So it was until the days of David

Acts 13.20 "judges until Samuel the prophet
25.21 [a]"held until I could send him to Caesar
1 Cor 16. 8 I will stay in Ephesus until Pentecost
2 Th 2. 7 restrains . . until he is out of the way
Heb 10.13 u. his enemies should be made a stool
Jas 5. 7 patient . . until the coming of the Lord
5. 7 u. it receives the early and the late rain
2 Pet 1.19 [a]pay attention . . until the day dawns
Rev 6.11 until the number of their fellow servants
4. *except when:* εἰ μὴ ὅταν (+neg.) HOTAN [B.3.b.4]
Mk 9. 9 until the Son of man should have risen
5. *as far as:* μέχρι MECHRI
[a]μέχρις οὗ
Mt 11.23 "it would have remained until this day
Lk 16.16 "the prophets were until John
Acts 20. 7 he prolonged his speech until midnight
Gal 4.19 [a]in travail until Christ be formed in you!
Eph 4.13 until we all attain to the unity
1 Tim 6.14 until the appearing of our Lord Jesus C.
Heb 9.10 imposed until the time of reformation

UNTIMELY BORN, ONE
1. *miscarriage:* ἔκτρωμα EKTRŌMA*
1 Cor 15. 8 Last of all, as to one untimely born

UNTO
1. *until:* ἄχρι ACHRI
Rev 2.10 " 'Be faithful unto death
2. *into, to, for:* εἰς (+acc.) EIS
Acts **11.**18
Jude .21
3. *as far as:* μέχρι MECHRI
Phil 2. 8 he . . became obedient unto death
4. *to, with, against:* πρός (+acc.) PROS
Jn 11. 4 "This illness is not unto death

UNTO, EVEN
1. *until:* ἄχρι ACHRI
Rev 12.11 "they loved not their lives even unto death

UNUSUAL
1. *happen, attain:* τυγχάνω (part. neg.) TYGCHANŌ
Acts 28. 2 the natives showed us unusual kindness

UNUTTERABLE
1. *unutterable:* ἀνεκλάλητος ANEKLALĒTOS*
1 Pet 1. 8 rejoice with unutterable and exalted joy

UNVEIL
1. *uncover:* ἀνακαλύπτω ANAKALYPTŌ
2 Cor 3.18 we all, with unveiled face, beholding[d]

UNVEILED
1. *uncovered:* ἀκατακάλυπτος AKATAKALYPTOS
1 Cor 11. 5 prays or prophesies with her head u.

UNWASHED
1. *unwashed:* ἄνιπτος ANIPTOS*
Mt 15.20 "to eat with u. hands does not defile
Mk 7. 2 with hands defiled, that is, unwashed

UNWILLING, BE
1. *will, wish:* θέλω (neg.) THELŌ
[a]μή [b]οὐ
Mt 1.19 [a]being . . unwilling to put her to shame
15.32 [b]"I am unwilling to send them away

UNWISE
1. *foolish, unwise:* ἄσοφος ASOPHOS*
Eph 5.15 walk, not as unwise men but as wise

UNWORTHY
1. *useless:* ἀχρεῖος ACHREIOS
Lk 17.10 "you, say, 'We are unworthy servants
2. *worthy:* ἄξιος (neg.) AXIOS
Acts 13.46 "judge yourselves u. of eternal life

UNWORTHY MANNER, IN AN
1. *unworthily:* ἀναξίως ANAXIŌS*
1 Cor 11.27 Whoever . . eats . . in an unworthy manner

UP
1. *above, upward:* ἄνω ANŌ
Heb 12.15 that no "root of bitterness" spring up

UP TO
1. *until:* ἄχρι ACHRI
Acts 22.22 Up to this word they listened
23. 1 "in all good conscience up to this day
2. *until:* ἕως HEŌS
Mt 20. 8 " 'beginning with the last, up to the first

UPBRAID
1. *reproach:* ὀνειδίζω ONEIDIZŌ
Mt 11.20 Then he began to upbraid the cities
Mk 16.14 he upbraided them for their unbelief[k]‡

UPBUILD
1. *building, edification:* οἰκοδομή OIKODOMĒ [B.2.b.1]
Eph 4.16 makes bodily growth and upbuilds itself

UPBUILDING
1. *building, edification:* οἰκοδομή OIKODOMĒ
Rom 14.19 what makes for peace and for mutual u.
1 Cor 14. 3 speaks to men for their upbuilding
2 Cor 12.19 all for your upbuilding, beloved

UPHOLD
1. *stand, set:* ἵστημι HISTĒMI
Rom 3.31 On the contrary, we uphold the law
14. 4 he will be upheld, for the Master is able
2. *bring, bear:* φέρω PHERŌ
Heb 1. 3 upholding the universe by his word

UPLIFTED
1. *high, proud:* ὑψηλός HYPSĒLOS
Acts 13.17 "with uplifted arm he led them out of it

UPON
1. *opposite, instead of:* ἀντί (+gen.) ANTI
Jn 1.16 we ⟨have⟩ all received, grace u. grace
2. *into, to, for:* εἰς (+acc.) EIS
Mt **27.**30
Mk **1.**10
Rom **10.**12
1 Cor **10.**11
Gal **3.**14
Eph **1.**8
3. *from, out of:* ἐκ (+gen.) EK
Jn **19.**12
4. *in, at, by:* ἐν (+dat.) EN
Jn **7.**22
1 Pet **4.**12
2 Pet **3.**10
5. *above:* ἐπάνω EPANŌ
Mt 23.22 swears . . by him who sits upon it
28. 2 rolled back the stone, and sat upon it
Lk 10.19 authority to tread upon serpents
6. *on, at:* ἐπί (+gen., dat., or acc.) EPI
Mt **7.**24, 26; **10.**13, 27, 29; **11.**29; **12.**18, 28; **13.**7; **23.**35, 36; **24.**2
Mk **4.**16, 20, 26, 31; **6.**39; **8.**25; **10.**16; **11.**7; **13.**2
Lk **1.**12, 35; **2.**25, 40; **3.**22; **4.**18; **6.**48, [48‡; **9.**38; **10.**6; **11.**17, 20; **12.**3, 49; **13.**4; **19.**43, 44; **21.**6, 23, 25, 34, 35²; **22.** [44‡; **24.**49
Jn **1.**51; **3.**36; **11.**38; **12.**24
Acts **1.**8; **2.**17, 30; **4.**29, 33; **5.**5, 11², 28; **7.**57; **8.**24; **10.**11, 21; **13.**11²; **15.**10; **18.**6; **19.**17; **26.**16
Rom **2.**2; **4.**9²; **9.**28
2 Cor **12.**9
Gal **6.**16²
Eph **2.**20; **5.**6
Phil **2.**17, 27
Col **3.**[6‡
1 Th **2.**16
Tit **3.**6
Heb **6.**7
Jas **2.**21
1 Pet **1.**13; **3.**12; **4.**14
Rev **1.**17; **2.**24; **3.**3, 10; **4.**4; **6.**10; **7.**3, 10, 15²; **8.**3; **9.**4; **12.**3; **13.**1²; **14.**15, 16; **16.**2; **17.**1; **19.**11, 19, 21; **20.**11; **21.**5
7. *down from, against:* κατά (+gen.) KATA
2 Pet 2.11 judgment upon them before the Lord
8. *with:* μετά (+gen.) META
Rev 11. 7 beast . . will make war upon them

9. *about, concerning:* περί (+gen.) PERI
Acts 24.24 heard him speak upon faith in Christ Jesus

UPPER
1. *upper, inland:* ἀνωτερικός ANŌTERIKOS*
Acts 19. 1 Paul passed through the upper country

UPPER CHAMBER
UPPER ROOM
1. *room upstairs:* ἀνάγαιον ANAGAION*
Mk 14.15 "he will show you a large upper room
Lk 22.12 "he will show you a large upper room
2. *upper story, spare room:* ὑπερῷον HYPERŌON*
Acts 1.13 they went up to the upper room
9.37 they laid her in an upper room
9.39 they took him to the upper room
20. 8 lights in the u. chamber where we were

UPRIGHT
1. *righteous, just:* δίκαιος DIKAIOS
Acts 10.22 "Cornelius, . . an u. and God-fearing man
Tit 1. 8 master of himself, upright, holy
2. *justly, rightly:* δικαίως DIKAIŌS [A.4.a]
Tit 2.12 to live sober, upright, and godly lives
3. *straight, upright:* ὀρθός ORTHOS
Acts 14.10 "Stand upright on your feet

UPROAR
1. *noise, uproar:* θόρυβος THORYBOS
Acts 20. 1 After the uproar ceased, Paul sent
21.34 he could not learn . . because of the u.

UPROAR, SET IN AN
1. *make a disturbance:* θορυβέω THORYBEŌ
Acts 17. 5 they . . set the city in an uproar

UPROOT
1. *root out:* ἐκριζόω EKRIZOŌ
Jude .12 fruitless trees . . , twice dead, uprooted

UPSET
1. *upset:* ἀνατρέπω ANATREPŌ
2 Tim 2.18 They are upsetting the faith of some
Tit 1.11 since they are upsetting whole families

UPSET, BE
1. *cause to stumble, offend:* σκανδαλίζω (pass.) SKANDALIZŌ
Rom [14.21 makes your brother stumble *or be upset*‡

UPSIDE DOWN, TURN
1. *upset, disturb:* ἀναστατόω ANASTATOŌ
Acts 17. 6 "who have turned the world upside down

UPWARD
1. *above, upward:* ἄνω ANŌ
Phil 3.14 the upward call of God in Christ Jesus

URBANUS: Οὐρβανός ˌərˈbānəs
Rom 16. 9 Greet U., our fellow worker in Christ

URGE
1. *call to, exhort, comfort:* παρακαλέω PARAKALEŌ
Acts 25. 2 principal men of the Jews . . urged him
27.33 Paul urged them all to take some food
27.34 "I urge you to take some food
1 Cor 4.16 I urge you, then, be imitators of me
16.12 I strongly urged him to visit you
2 Cor 8. 6 Accordingly we have urged Titus
9. 5 thought it necessary to u. the brethren
12.18 I urged Titus to go
1 Tim 1. 3 As I urged you . . , remain at Ephesus
2. 1 I urge that supplications . . be made
6. 2 Teach and urge these duties
Tit 2. 6 urge the younger men to control
Heb 13.19 I urge you the more earnestly to do
2. *persuade:* πείθω PEITHŌ
Acts 13.43 urged them to continue in the grace
CONTEXTUALLY
1 Cor 16.16 I u. you to be subject to such men

URGENT
1. *necessary:* ἀναγκαῖος ANAGKAIOS
Tit 3.14 so as to help cases of urgent need

URGENT, BE
1. *stand by:* ἐφίστημι EPHISTĒMI
2 Tim 4. 2 be urgent in season and out of season

2. *lie upon, press upon:* ἐπίκειμαι EPIKEIMAI
Lk 23.23 they were u., demanding with loud cries
3. *make strong, prevail:* ἐπισχύω EPISCHYŌ*
Lk 23. 5 were u., saying, "He stirs up the people

URIAH: Οὐρίας yüˈrīə
Mt 1. 6 father of Solomon by the wife of U.

URN
1. *earthen jar:* στάμνος STAMNOS*
Heb 9. 4 a golden urn holding the manna

US
1. *himself:* ἑαυτοῦ (pl.) HEAUTOU
2 Cor 3. 5 to claim anything as coming from us
2. *we:* ἡμεῖς HĒMEIS
Mt **1**.23; **3**.15; **6**.11, 12, 13^{2}; **8**.29^{2}, 31^{2}; **9**.27; **13**.36, 56; **15**.15; **20**.7, 12, 30, 31; **21**.25; **22**.17, 25; **24**.3; **25**.8, 9, 11; **26**.63, 68; **27**.4. 25
Mk **1**.24^{2}; **5**.12; **6**.3; **9**.22^{2}, 38, 40^{2}; **10**.35, 37; **12**.19; **13**.4; **14**.15; **16**.3
Lk **1**.1, 2, 69, 71, 74(73), 78; **2**.15, 48; **4**.34^{2}; **7**.5, 16, 20; **9**.49; **10**.17; **11**.1, 3, 4^{3}, 45; **12**.41; **13**.25; **16**.26^{2}; **17**.13; **19**.14; **20**.2, 6, 22, 28; **22**.8, 67; **23**.15, 18, 24, 30^{2}, 32‡, 32^{2}, 39; **24**.22
Jn **1**.14, 22; **2**.18; **4**.12, 25; **6**.34, 52; **8**.5‡; **9**.34; **10**.24^{2}; **14**. 8, 9, 22; **16**.17; **17**.21; **18**.31
Acts **1**.7, 21^{2}, 22^{2}; **2**.8, 29; **3**.4, 12; **5**.28; **6**.14; **7**.27, 38, 40^{3}; **9**.38; **10**.41, 42; **11**.13, 15, 17; **13**.26, 47; **14**.11; **15**.8, 9, 24, 25, 28; **16**.9, 10, 15, 17, 21, 37^{3}; **17**.27; **20**.5, 14; **21**.5, 11, 16, 17, 18; **24**.4; **25**.24; **27**.6, 7; **28**.2^{2}, 7, 10, 15^{2}
Rom **3**.8; **4**.16; **5**.5, 8^{2}; **8**.4, 18, 31^{2}, 32^{2}, 34, 35, 37, 39; **9**.24, 29; **10**.16; **12**.6; **13**.11; **14**.7, 12; **15**.2
1 Cor **1**.18; **2**.10, 12; **4**.1, 6, 8, 9; **6**.14; **7**.15‡; **8**.6, 8; **10**.6; **15**.57
2 Cor **1**.4, 10, 11^{3}, 14, 21, 22; **2**.14^{2}; **3**.3, 6; **4**.7, 12, 14, 17; **5**.5^{2}, 12, 14, 18^{2}, 19, 20; **6**.12; **7**.2, 6, 7, 9, 12; **8**.4, 5, 7,19, 20; **9**.11; **10**.2, 13
Gal **1**.4, 23; **2**.4; **3**.13^{2}; **4**.3; **5**.1
Eph **1**.3, 4, 5, 6, 8, 9, 19; **2**.4, 5, 7; **3**.20; **4**.7; **5**.2
Phil **3**.17
Col **1**.8, 12‡, 13; **2**.13, 14; **4**.3^{2}
1 Th **1**.6, 9, 10; **2**.8, 13, 15, 16, 18; **3**.6^{4}; **4**.1, 7; **5**.9, 10, 25
2 Th **1**.7; **2**.2, 15, 16; **3**.1, 6, 7
1 Tim **6**.17
2 Tim **1**.7, 9^{2}, 12, 14
Tit **2**.8, 12, 14^{2}; **3**.5^{2}, 6^{2}, 15
Heb **2**.3; **10**.15, 20; **11**.40^{2}; **12**.1; **13**.18
Jas **1**.18; **3**.3; **4**.5
1 Pet **3**.18; **4**.[1‡, 17
2 Pet **1**.3^{2}, 4
1 Jn **1**.2, 3, 7, 8, 9, 10; **2**.19^{5}, 25‡; **3**.1^{2}, 16, 21, 23, 24^{2}; **4**.6^{2}, 9, 10, 11, 12^{2}, 13^{2}, 16, 17, 19; **5**.11, 14, 15, 20
2 Jn .2^{2}
Rev **1**.5^{2}, 6; **6**.16^{2}

USE (*See also* IGNOBLE USE; MENIAL USE; NOBLE USE; WORSHIP, USED IN)
1. *consumption, using up:* ἀπόχρησις APOCHRĒSIS* [A.1.e]
Col 2.22 (things which all perish as they are used
2. *make use of, act:* χράομαι CHRAOMAI
1 Tim 1. 8 law is good, if . . one uses it lawfully
5.23 use a little wine for . . your stomach
3. *have, hold:* ἔχω ECHŌ
1 Pet 2.16 without using your freedom as a pretext
4. *say, speak:* εἶπον EIPON [A.6.a.5]
Jn 10. 6 This figure Jesus used with them
IDIOMATICALLY
a. Mk 4.30 "or what parable shall we use for it? *ἢ ἐν τίνι αὐτὴν παραβολῇ θῶμεν;* [TITHĒMI]
b. 1 Th 2.5 For we never used either words of flattery *οὔτε γάρ ποτε ἐν λόγῳ κολακείας ἐγενήθημεν* [GINOMAI]
CONTEXTUALLY
Mk 15. 6 he used to release for them one prisoner
Jn 9. 8 "Is . . this the man who used to sit and beg?
12. 6 he used to take what was put into it
Rom 3.13 "they use their tongues to deceive
12. 6 Having gifts that differ . . , let us use them
Gal 5.13 do not u. your freedom as an opportunity

1 Pet 3. 5 holy women . . used to adorn themselves
2 Jn .12 I would rather not use paper and ink

USE OF, MAKE
1. *make use of, act:* χράομαι CHRAOMAI
1 Cor [7.21 *make use of your present condition instead*†
9.12 we have not made use of this right
9.15 I have made no use of any

USE OF, MAKE FULL
1. *make full use of:* καταχράομαι KATACHRAOMAI
1 Cor 9.18 not making full use of my right

USE UP
1. *make ineffective, hinder:* καταργέω KATARGEŌ
Lk 13. 7 " 'why should it use up the ground?

USEFUL
1. *useful:* εὔχρηστος EUCHRĒSTOS*
2 Tim 2.21 useful to the master of the house
4.11 for he is very useful in serving me
Phm .11 (but now he is indeed useful[b] to you
2. *suitable:* εὔθετος EUTHETOS
Heb 6. 7 brings forth vegetation useful to those

USELESS
1. *useless:* ἄχρηστος ACHRĒSTOS*
Phm .11 (Formerly he was useless to you

USELESSNESS
1. *useless, harmful:* ἀνωφελής (subst. neut.) ANŌPHELĒS
Heb 7.18 commandment . . set aside because of its . . u.

UTTER
1. *let go, leave, forgive:* ἀφίημι APHIĒMI [A.6.a.5]
Mk 15.37 And Jesus uttered a loud cry
2. *give:* δίδωμι DIDŌMI [A.6.a.5]
1 Cor 14. 9 if you . . u. speech that is not intelligible
3. *say, speak:* εἶπον EIPON
Mt 5.11 "u. all kinds of evil against you falsely
10.27 "What I tell you . . utter in the light
4. *blurt out:* ἐρεύγομαι EREUGOMAI*
Mt 13.35 "I will utter what has been hidden
5. *whole, entire:* ὅλος HOLOS [B.3.b.4]
Jn 9.34 "You were born in utter sin
6. *speak, talk:* λαλέω LALEŌ
Mt 12.36 "account for every careless word they u.
Jn 3.34 For he . . utters the words of God
1 Cor 14. 2 but he utters mysteries in the Spirit
2 Cor 12. 4 heard things . . which man may not utter
Rev 13. 5 given a mouth uttering haughty . . words
7. *utter, speak:* φθέγγομαι PHTHEGGOMAI
2 Pet 2.18 uttering loud boasts of folly, they entice
CONTEXTUALLY
Mk 3.28 "and whatever blasphemies they utter
2 Cor 1.20 That is why we u. the Amen through him
1 Pet 4.11 whoever speaks, as one who utters oracles
Rev 13. 6 it opened its mouth to u. blasphemies

UTTER BLASPHEMY
1. *blaspheme, slander:* βλασφημέω BLASPHĒMEŌ
[a]+βλασφημία A.6.a.6
Mt 26.65 "He has uttered blasphemy
Mk 3.28 [a]"whatever blasphemies they utter

UTTERANCE
1. *speak out:* ἀποφθέγγομαι (inf.) APOPHTHEGGOMAI
Acts 2. 4 other tongues, as the Spirit gave them u.
2. *word, reckoning:* λόγος LOGOS
1 Cor 12. 8 To one is given . . the u. of wisdom, and to another the u. of knowledge
2 Cor 8. 7 Now as you excel in everything— . . in u.
Eph 6.19 that utterance may be given me
3. *voice, sound:* φωνή PHŌNĒ
Acts 13.27 "they did not . . understand the utterances

UTTERANCE, PROPHETIC
1. *prophecy:* προφητεία PROPHĒTEIA
1 Tim 1.18 the prophetic utterances which pointed
4.14 gift . . given you by prophetic u.

UTTERLY
1. *to excess:* καθ' ὑπερβολήν HYPERBOLĒ [B.1.a.1]
2 Cor 1. 8 we were so utterly . . crushed
2. *very much:* λίαν LIAN
[a]+ἐκ περισσοῦ B.3.b.6
Mk 6.51 [a]And they were utterly astounded

UTTERMOST PARTS
1. *last, extreme:* ἔσχατος (subst.) ESCHATOS
Acts 13.47 " 'salvation to the u. parts of the earth

UZZIAH: Ὀζίας ə'zīə
Mt 1. 8 Joram the father of Uzziah
1. 9 Uzziah the father of Jotham

V

VACILLATE
1. *act with vacillation:* τῇ ἐλαφρίᾳ χρᾶσθαι ELAPHRIA; CHRAOMAI [B.2.a.1]
2 Cor 1.17 Was I vacillating when I wanted to?

VAIN
1. *empty, vain:* κενός KENOS
Acts 4.25 " 'Why did . . the peoples imagine v. things?
2. *empty, idle, foolish:* μάταιος MATAIOS
Acts 14.15 "that you should turn from these v. things
Jas 1.26 this man's religion is vain

VAIN DISCUSSION
1. *idle talk:* ματαιολογία MATAIOLOGIA*
1 Tim 1. 6 wandered away into vain discussion

VAIN, IN
1. *without purpose:* εἰκῇ EIKĒ
Rom 13. 4 for he does not bear the sword in vain
1 Cor 15. 2 unless you believed in vain
Gal 3. 4 Did you experience so many things in vain?—if it really is in vain
4.11 I am afraid I have labored over you in v.
2. *empty, vain:* κενός (pred.) KENOS
[a]εἰς κενόν
1 Cor 15.10 his grace toward me was not in vain
15.14 then our preaching is in vain and your faith is in vain
15.58 in the Lord your labor is not in vain
2 Cor 6. 1 [a]not to accept the grace of God in v.
Gal 2. 2 [a]lest somehow I . . had run in vain
Phil 2.16 [a]that in the day of Christ I may be proud that I did not run in vain or labor in vain
1 Th 2. 1 that our visit to you was not in vain
3. 5 [a]for fear . . that our labor would be in vain
3. *in vain:* κενῶς KENŌS*
Jas 4. 5 Or do you suppose it is in vain?
4. *in vain, falsely:* μάτην MATĒN*
Mt 15. 9 " 'in vain do they worship me
Mk 7. 7 " 'in vain do they worship me

VAIN, PROVE
1. *empty, make void:* κενόω (pass.) KENOŌ
2 Cor 9. 3 so that our boasting . . may not prove vain

VALID
1. *firm, steady:* βέβαιος BEBAIOS
Heb 2. 2 if the message declared by angels was v.

VALLEY
1. *torrent, valley:* χείμαρρος CHEIMARROS*
Jn 18. 1 he went forth . . across the Kidron valley
2. *ravine:* φάραγξ PHARAGX*
Lk 3. 5 "Every valley shall be filled

VALUABLE
1. *honored, valuable:* ἔντιμος ENTIMOS
Lk [7. 2 had a slave who was *valuable* to him†

VALUE
1. *help, profit:* ὠφέλεια ŌPHELEIA
Rom 3. 1 Or what is the value of circumcision?
2. *honor, value:* τιμή TIMĒ
Acts 19.19 they counted the value of them
Col 2.23 they are of no value in checking
IDIOMATICALLY
a. Acts 20.24 "I do not account my life of any value nor as

precious to myself οὐδενὸς λόγου ποιοῦμαι τὴν ψυχὴν τιμίαν ἐμαυτῷ [LOGOS]

VALUE, BE OF
1. *help, aid:* ὠφελέω ŌPHELEŌ
Rom 2.25 Circumcision indeed is of value

VALUE, BE OF MORE
1. *carry through, differ:* διαφέρω DIAPHERŌ
Mt 6.26 "Are you not of more value than they?
10.31 "you are of more v. than many sparrows
12.12 "Of how much more value is a man!
Lk 12. 7 "you are of more v. than many sparrows
12.24 "Of how much more value are you!

VALUE, OF
1. *useful, beneficial:* ὠφέλιμος ŌPHELIMOS
1 Tim 4. 8 while bodily training is of some value, godliness is of value in every way

VALUE, OF GREAT
1. *very valuable:* πολύτιμος POLYTIMOS
Mt 13.46 "on finding one pearl of great value

VANISH
1. *make unseen, destroy:* ἀφανίζω (pass.) APHANIZŌ
Jas 4.14 a mist that appears . . and then vanishes
2. *become invisible:* ἄφαντος γίνεσθαι APHANTOS* [A.6.a.3]
Lk 24.31 he vanished out of their sight
3. *separate from:* ἀποχωρίζω (pass.) APOCHŌRIZŌ
Rev 6.14 sky vanished like a scroll that is rolled

VANISH AWAY
1. *destruction:* ἀφανισμός APHANISMOS* [B.1.a.2]
Heb 8.13 what is . . old is ready to vanish away

VAPOR
1. *moist vapor:* ἀτμίς ATMIS
Acts 2.19 " 'I will show . . fire, and vapor of smoke

VARIATION
1. *movement, variety:* παραλλαγή PARALLAGĒ*
Jas 1.17 Father of lights with whom there is no v.

VARIED
1. *diversified:* ποικίλος POIKILOS
1 Pet 4.10 good stewards of God's varied grace

VARIETY
1. *divisibility, difference:* διαίρεσις DIAIRESIS*
1 Cor 12. 4 Now there are varieties of gifts
12. 5 there are varieties of service
12. 6 varieties of working, but it is the same God

VARIOUS (*See also* KINDS, VARIOUS)
1. *different, excellent:* διάφορος (pl.) DIAPHOROS
Heb 9.10 food and drink and various ablutions
2. *diversified:* ποικίλος POIKILOS
Mt 4.24 those afflicted with various diseases
Mk 1.34 many who were sick with v. diseases
Lk 4.40 any that were sick with various diseases
2 Tim 3. 6 weak women, . . swayed by v. impulses
Tit 3. 3 slaves to various passions and pleasures
Heb 2. 4 signs and wonders and various miracles
Jas 1. 2 Count it all joy . . when you meet v. trials
1 Pet 1. 6 you may have to suffer various trials
CONTEXTUALLY
Mt 24. 7 "famines and earthquakes in v. places
Mk 13. 8 "there will be earthquakes in v. places
Lk 21.11 "in v. places famines and pestilences

VARIOUS WAYS, IN
1. *in many ways:* πολυτρόπως POLYTROPŌS*
Heb 1. 1 In many and v. ways God spoke of old

VEGETABLE
1. *garden herb, vegetable:* λάχανον LACHANON
Rom 14. 2 the weak man eats only vegetables

VEGETATION
1. *pasture, fodder:* βοτάνη BOTANĒ*
Heb 6. 7 the rain . . brings forth vegetation

VEHEMENTLY
1. *more exceedingly:* ἐκπερισσῶς EKPERISSŌS*
Mk 14.31 he said v., "If I must die with you
2. *vigorously:* εὐτόνως EUTONŌS
Lk 23.10 chief priests . . stood by, v. accusing

VEIL
1. *authority, power:* ἐξουσία EXOUSIA [D.1]
1 Cor 11.10 why a woman ought to have a veil[r]†
2. *head covering, covering:* κάλυμμα KALYMMA*
2 Cor 3.13 Moses, who put a veil over his face
3.14 that same veil remains unlifted
3.15 to this day . . a veil lies over their minds
3.16 the veil is removed
3. *cover, hide:* καλύπτω KALYPTŌ
2 Cor 4. 3 even if our gospel is veiled, it is veiled only to those who are perishing

VEIL ONESELF
VEIL, WEAR A
1. *cover up:* κατακαλύπτω (mid.) KATAKALYPTŌ
1 Cor 11. 6 if a woman will not veil herself
11. 6 if it is disgraceful . . , let her wear a v.

VENGEANCE
1. *vengeance, punishment:* ἐκδίκησις EKDIKĒSIS
Lk 21.22 "for these are days of vengeance
Rom 12.19 "Vengeance is mine, I will repay
2 Th 1. 8 inflicting v. upon those who do not know
Heb 10.30 "Vengeance is mine, I will repay

VENOM
1. *venom, poison:* ἰός IOS
Rom 3.13 "The venom of asps is under their lips

VENTURE
1. *give oneself:* διδόναι ἑαυτόν DIDŌMI [B.2.a.1]
Acts 19.31 begged him not to v. into the theater
2. *dare:* τολμάω TOLMAŌ
Rom 15.18 I will not v. to speak of anything
2 Cor 10.12 Not that we venture to class or compare

VERSED, WELL
1. *possible, strong:* δυνατός DYNATOS
Acts 18.24 He was . . well versed in the scriptures

VERY
1. *that:* ἐκεῖνος (adj.) EKEINOS
Acts 12. 6 The very night when Herod was about to
2. *very much:* λίαν LIAN
Mt 4. 8 devil took him to a v. high mountain
Mk 16. 2 very early on the first day of the week
Lk 23. 8 When Herod saw Jesus, he was v. glad
3. *all, every, whole:* πᾶς PAS [A.3.b.1]
Jude . 3 Beloved, being very eager to write
4. *many, great:* πολύς POLYS [A.3.b.1]
2 Cor 3.12 Since we have such a hope, we are v. bold
5. *very, very much:* σφόδρα SPHODRA
Mt 26.22 And they were very sorrowful
Mk 16. 4 stone was rolled back—it was v. large
Lk 18.23 he became sad, for he was very rich
IDIOMATICALLY
a. Mk 14.30 "this very night σήμερον ταύτῃ τῇ νυκτί [SĒMERON]
b. Rom 11.8 "down to this very day ἕως τῆς σήμερον ἡμέρας [SĒMERON]
CONTEXTUALLY
Rom 7.15 but I do the very thing I hate
Phm .12 I am sending . . back . . my very heart

VERY FAR
1. *to a greater* (extent): ἐπὶ πλεῖον PLEIŌN [B.1.a.1]
2 Tim 3. 9 but they will not get very far

VESSEL
1. *vessel:* ἄγγος AGGOS*
Mt 13.48 "sorted the good into vessels
2. *vessel, ship:* ναῦς NAUS*
Acts 27.41 they ran the vessel aground
3. *vessel, tackle:* σκεῦος SKEUOS
Lk 8.16 "No one . . covers it with a vessel
Rom 9.21 to make out of the same lump one vessel
9.22 endured . . the vessels . . made for destruction
9.23 his glory for the vessels of mercy
2 Cor 4. 7 we have this treasure in earthen vessels
2 Tim 2.20 not only vessels of gold and silver
2.21 then he will be a vessel for noble use
Heb 9.21 all the vessels used in worship

VESSEL OF BRONZE
1. *copper vessel, kettle:* χαλκίον CHALKION*
Mk 7. 4 (the washing of . . vessels of bronze[x]

VEX
1. *question by torture, torment:* βασανίζω BASANIZŌ
2 Pet 2. 8 (he was vexed in his righteous soul

VICIOUS
1. *sick, base, evil:* πονηρός PONĒROS
Acts 18.14 "a matter of wrongdoing or vicious crime

VICTORY
1. *victory, mastery:* νίκη NIKĒ*
1 Jn 5. 4 the victory that overcomes the world
2. *victory:* νῖκος NIKOS*
Mt 12.20 "till he brings justice to victory
1 Cor 15.54 "Death is swallowed up in victory
15.55 "O death, where is thy victory?
15.57 God, who gives us the victory

VIEW
1. *think, set one's mind on:* φρονέω PHRONEŌ [B.2.d.2]
Acts 28.22 "to hear from you what your views are
CONTEXTUALLY
2 Cor 5.16 regard no one from a human point of view
5.16 regarded Christ from a human point of v.

VIEW OF, IN
1. *because of:* διά (+acc.) DIA
1 Cor 7.26

VIEW, TAKE A
1. *think, set one's mind on:* φρονέω PHRONEŌ [A.6.a.5]
Gal 5.10 you will take no other view than mine

VILE
1. *cheap, mean, bad:* φαῦλος PHAULOS
Jas 3.16 disorder and every vile practice

VILLAGE
1. *unwalled village, quarter of a city:* κώμη KŌMĒ*
Mt 9.35 Jesus went about all the . . villages
10.11 "whatever town or village you enter
14.15 "send the crowds . . to go into the villages
21. 2 "Go into the village opposite you
Mk 6. 6 he went about among the villages
6.36 "send them . . into the country and villages
6.56 wherever he came, in villages
8.23 "he . . led him out of the village
8.26 "Do not even enter the village
8.27 went . . to the villages of Caesarea
11. 2 "Go into the village opposite you
Lk 5.17 who had come from every v. of Galilee
8. 1 he went on through cities and villages
9. 6 they . . went through the villages
9.12 "Send the crowd . . into the villages
9.52 who went and entered a village
9.56 they went on to another village
10.38 as they went . . , he entered a village
13.22 He went on his way through . . villages
17.12 as he entered a village, he was met
19.30 "Go into the village opposite
24.13 two of them were going to a village
24.28 So they drew near to the village
Jn 7.42 "Bethlehem, the v. where David was
11. 1 Lazarus of Bethany, the v. of Mary
11.30 Jesus had not yet come to the village
Acts 8.25 preaching the gospel to many villages

VILLAINY
1. *laziness, knavery:* ῥᾳδιουργία RHADIOURGIA*
Acts 13.10 "full of all deceit and villainy

VINDICATE
1. *justify, vindicate:* δικαιόω DIKAIOŌ
1 Tim 3.16 vindicated[i] in the Spirit, seen by angels†
2. *avenge, punish:* ἐκδικέω EKDIKEŌ
Lk 18. 3 " 'Vindicate me against my adversary
18. 5 " 'this widow bothers me, I will v. her
3. *make vengeance:* ποιεῖν τὴν ἐκδίκησιν EKDIKĒSIS [A.6.a.4]
Lk 18. 7 "And will not God vindicate his elect?
18. 8 "I tell you, he will vindicate them speedily

VINE
1. *grapevine:* ἄμπελος AMPELOS
Mt 26.29 "shall not drink again of this fruit of the v.
Mk 14.25 "shall not drink again of the fruit of the v.
Lk 22.18 "I shall not drink of the fruit of the vine
Jn 15. 1 "I am the true vine
15. 4 "branch cannot . . unless it abides in the v.
15. 5 "I am the vine, you are the branches
Rev 14.18 "gather the clusters of the vine

VINEDRESSER
1. *vinedresser:* ἀμπελουργός AMPELOURGOS*
Lk 13. 7 "he said to the vinedresser, 'Lo
2. *farmer, tenant:* γεωργός GEŌRGOS
Jn 15. 1 "my Father is the vinedresser

VINEGAR
1. *poor wine, vinegar:* ὄξος OXOS*
Mt 27.48 took a sponge, filled it with vinegar
Mk 15.36 filling a sponge full of vinegar
Lk 23.36 coming up and offering him vinegar
Jn 19.29 A bowl full of vinegar stood there; so they put a sponge full of the v. on hyssop
19.30 When Jesus had received the vinegar

VINEYARD
1. *vineyard:* ἀμπελών AMPELŌN*
Mt 20. 1 "went . . to hire laborers for his vineyard
20. 2 "he sent them into his vineyard
20. 4 " 'You go into the vineyard too
20. 7 " 'You go into the vineyard too
20. 8 "owner of the v. said to his steward
21.28 " 'Son, go and work in the vineyard today
21.33 "a householder who planted a vineyard
21.39 "they took him and cast him out of the v.
21.40 "When . . the owner of the vineyard comes
21.41 "He will . . let out the v. to other tenants
Mk 12. 1 "planted a vineyard, and set a hedge
12. 2 "to get . . some of the fruit of the v.
12. 8 "they . . cast him out of the vineyard
12. 9 "What will the owner of the vineyard do?
12. 9 "He will . . give the vineyard to others
Lk 13. 6 "A man had a fig tree planted in his v.
20. 9 "A man planted a v., and let it out
20.10 "should give him some . . fruit of the v.
20.13 "Then the owner of the vineyard said
20.15 "they cast him out of the vineyard
20.15 "What . . will the owner of the v. do?
20.16 "He will . . give the v. to others
1 Cor 9. 7 Who plants a v. without eating . . fruit?

VINTAGE
1. *grapevine:* ἄμπελος AMPELOS
Rev 14.19 the angel . . gathered the v. of the earth

VIOLATE
1. *deny, nullify:* ἀθετέω ATHETEŌ
1 Tim 5.12 having violated their first pledge
Heb 10.28 A man who has violated the law

VIOLENCE
1. *force:* βία BIA
Acts 5.26 brought them, but without violence
21.35 because of the violence of the crowd
[24. 7 "*Lysias . . with great violence took him*‡
2. *sudden rush, impulse:* ὅρμημα HORMĒMA*
Rev 18.21 "shall . . be thrown down with violence

VIOLENCE, MAN OF
1. *mighty man, violent man:* βιαστής BIASTĒS*
Mt 11.12 "men of violence take it by force

VIOLENCE, ROB BY
1. *shake violently, extort money by violence:* διασείω DIASEIŌ*
Lk 3.14 "Rob no one by violence

VIOLENCE, SUFFER
1. *constrain:* βιάζω (pass.) BIAZŌ
Mt 11.12 "the kingdom of heaven has suffered v.[c]†

VIOLENT
1. *mistreat:* κακόω KAKOŌ [A.6.b]
Acts 12. 1 the king laid violent hands upon some

2. *striker, brawler:* πλήκτης (pred.) PLĒKTĒS*
1 Tim 3. 3 no drunkard, not violent but gentle
Tit 1. 7 he must not be arrogant . . or violent
3. *many, great:* πολύς POLYS
Acts 23.10 when the dissension became violent

VIOLENTLY
1. *to excess:* καθ' ὑπερβολήν HYPERBOLĒ [B.1.a.1]
Gal 1.13 I persecuted the church of God violently
2. *violently, vehemently:* σφοδρῶς SPHODRŌS*
Acts 27.18 As we were violently storm-tossed

VIOLENTLY, COME
VIOLENTLY, ENTER
1. *constrain:* βιάζω (mid.) BIAZŌ
[a]+εἰς A.6.a.4, 5
Mt [11.12 "kingdom . . *has been coming violently*†
Lk 16.16 [a]"every one enters it violently

VIPER
1. *viper:* ἔχιδνα ECHIDNA*
Mt 3. 7 "You brood of vipers! Who warned you?
12.34 "You brood of vipers!
23.33 "You serpents, you brood of vipers
Lk 3. 7 "You brood of vipers! Who warned you?
Acts 28. 3 a viper came out because of the heat

VIRGIN
1. *maiden, girl:* παρθένος PARTHENOS
Mt 1.23 "Behold, a virgin shall conceive
Lk 1.27 v. betrothed to a man whose name was Joseph, . . and the virgin's name was Mary

VIRGINITY
1. *virginity:* παρθενία PARTHENIA*
Lk 2.36 with her husband seven years from her v.

VIRTUE
1. *goodness, excellence:* ἀρετή ARETĒ
2 Pet 1. 5 supplement your faith with virtue, and virtue with knowledge

VIRTUE OF, IN
1. *in accordance with, for:* κατά (+acc.) KATA
2 Tim 1. 9 called us . . not in virtue of our works but in virtue of his own purpose
Tit 3. 5 he saved us . . in virtue of his own mercy

VISIBLE
1. *visible, to be seen:* ὁρατός HORATOS*
Col 1.16 in heaven and on earth, v. and invisible

VISIBLE, BECOME
1. *make manifest, make known:* φανερόω (pass.) PHANEROŌ
Eph 5.13 exposed by the light it becomes v., for anything that becomes v. is light

VISION
1. *vision, sight:* ὅραμα HORAMA
Mt 17. 9 Jesus commanded . . , "Tell no one the v.
Acts 9.10 Lord said to him in a vision, "Ananias
10. 3 he saw clearly in a vision an angel
10.17 perplexed as to what the v. . . might mean
10.19 while Peter was pondering the vision
11. 5 "in a trance I saw a vision
12. 9 but thought he was seeing a vision
16. 9 a vision appeared to Paul in the night
16.10 when he had seen the vision
18. 9 the Lord said to Paul one night in a v.
2. *what one sees:* ὃ ὁρᾷ HORAŌ [B.2.a.1]
Col 2.18 taking his stand on visions, puffed up
3. *vision, appearance:* ὅρασις HORASIS
Acts 2.17 " 'your young men shall see visions
Rev 9.17 how I saw the horses in my vision
4. *vision:* ὀπτασία OPTASIA*
Lk 1.22 perceived that he had seen a vision
24.23 "that they had even seen a vision
Acts 26.19 "I was not disobedient to the heavenly v.
2 Cor 12. 1 I will go on to visions and revelations

VISIT
1. *enter, go into:* εἰσέρχομαι πρός EISERCHOMAI [A.6.a.4]
Acts 16.40 went out of the prison, and visited Lydia
28. 8 Paul visited him and prayed
2. *entrance:* εἴσοδος EISODOS
1 Th 2. 1 our visit to you was not in vain
3. *look upon, visit:* ἐπισκέπτομαι EPISKEPTOMAI
Mt 25.36 " 'I was sick and you visited me
25.43 " 'in prison and you did not visit me
Lk 1.68 "he has visited and redeemed his people
[1.78 "*whereby the dayspring will visit us*†
[1.78 "*since the dayspring has visited us*‡
7.16 "God has visited his people!
Acts 7.23 "it came into his heart to v. his brethren
15.14 "how God first visited the Gentiles
15.36 "let us return and visit the brethren
Jas 1.27 to visit orphans . . in their affliction
4. *come to:* ἔρχομαι πρός ERCHOMAI [A.6.a.4]
Mt 25.39 " 'when did we see thee . . and visit thee?
1 Cor 16. 5 I will visit you after . . Macedonia
16.12 As for . . Apollos, I . . urged him to visit you
5. *inquire into, observe:* ἱστορέω HISTOREŌ*
Gal 1.18 I went up to Jerusalem to visit Cephas
6. *come to, approach:* προσέρχομαι PROSERCHOMAI
Acts 10.28 "to visit any one of another nation
IDIOMATICALLY
a. 2 Cor 1.16 I wanted to visit you on my way to Macedonia ⟨ἐβουλόμην⟩ δι' ὑμῶν διελθεῖν εἰς M. [DIERCHOMAI]
CONTEXTUALLY
Acts 7.13 "at the second v. Joseph made himself known
2 Cor 13. 2 as I did when present on my second visit

VISIT, MAKE A
1. *come to:* ἔρχομαι πρός ERCHOMAI [A.6.a.4]
2 Cor 2. 1 not to make you another painful visit

VISITATION
1. *visitation, office of bishop:* ἐπισκοπή EPISKOPĒ
Lk 19.44 "did not know the time of your v.
1 Pet 2.12 they may . . glorify God on the day of v.

VISITOR
1. *stay in a place:* ἐπιδημέω (subst. part.) EPIDĒMEŌ
Acts 2.10 "visitors from Rome
2. *live near, inhabit:* παροικέω (subst. part.) PAROIKEŌ
Lk 24.18 "Are you the only visitor to Jerusalem?

VOICE
1. *voice, sound:* φωνή PHŌNĒ
Mt 2.18 "A voice was heard in Ramah
3. 3 "The v. of one crying in the wilderness
3.17 lo, a voice from heaven
12.19 "nor will any one hear his voice
17. 5 a voice . . said, "This is my beloved Son[w]
27.46 Jesus cried with a loud voice, "Eli, Eli
27.50 Jesus cried again with a loud voice
Mk 1. 3 "the v. of one crying in the wilderness
1.11 a voice came from heaven
1.26 unclean spirit, . . crying with a loud v.
5. 7 crying out with a loud voice
9. 7 a voice came out of the cloud
15.34 Jesus cried with a loud v., "Eloi, Eloi
Lk 1.44 "when the voice of your greeting came
3. 4 "The v. of one crying in the wilderness
3.22 a voice came from heaven
4.33 he cried out with a loud voice
8.28 he cried out . . and said with a loud voice
9.35 a voice came out of the cloud
9.36 when the voice had spoken
11.27 a woman in the crowd raised her voice
17.13 ⟨ten lepers⟩ lifted up their voices
17.15 praising God with a loud voice
19.37 began to . . praise God with a loud v.
23.23 And their voices prevailed
23.46 Jesus, crying with a loud voice
Jn 1.23 "the v. of one crying in the wilderness
3.29 "rejoices greatly at . . bridegroom's voice
5.25 "the dead will hear the v. of the Son
5.28 "all . . in the tombs will hear his v.
5.37 "His voice you have never heard
10. 3 "the sheep hear his voice, and he calls
10. 4 "sheep follow . . , for they know his voice
10. 5 "they do not know the v. of strangers
10.16 "they will heed my voice

Jn 10.27 "My sheep hear my voice
11.43 he cried with a loud voice, "Lazarus
12.28 Then a voice came from heaven
12.30 "This voice has come for your sake
18.37 "one who is of the truth hears my v.
Acts 2.14 lifted up his v. and addressed them
4.24 they lifted their voices together to God
7.31 "the voice of the Lord came
7.57 they cried out with a loud voice
7.60 he knelt down and cried with a loud voice
8. 7 unclean spirits . . , crying with a loud v.
9. 4 heard a voice saying to him, "Saul
9. 7 hearing the voice but seeing no one
10.13 there came a voice to him, "Rise, Peter
10.15 voice came to him again a second time
11. 7 "I heard a v. saying to me, 'Rise, Peter
11. 9 "the voice answered a second time
12.14 Recognizing Peter's v. . . , she did not open
12.22 "The voice of a god, and not of man!
14.10 said in a loud voice, "Stand upright
14.11 the crowds . . lifted up their voices
16.28 But Paul cried with a loud voice
19.34 they all with one voice cried out
22. 7 "I . . heard a voice saying to me, 'Saul
22 9 "saw the light but did not hear the voice
22.14 " 'to hear a voice from his mouth
22.22 then they lifted up their voices
26.14 "I heard a v. saying to me in . . Hebrew
26.24 Festus said with a loud voice
Heb 3. 7 "Today, when you hear his voice
3.15 "Today, when you hear his voice
4. 7 "Today, when you hear his voice
12.19 the sound of a trumpet, and a voice
12.26 His voice then shook the earth
2 Pet 1.17 v. . . borne to him by the Majestic Glory
1.18 we heard this voice borne from heaven
2.16 a dumb ass spoke with human voice
Rev 1.10 I heard behind me a loud voice
1.12 Then I turned to see the voice
1.15 voice . . like the sound of many waters
3.20 " 'if any . . hears my v. and opens the door
4. 1 the first voice, which I had heard
4. 5 From the throne . . voices and . . thunder
5. 2 strong angel proclaiming with a loud v.
5.11 I heard . . the voice of many angels
5.12 with a loud voice, "Worthy is the Lamb!
6. 1 with a voice of thunder, "Come!
6. 6 a voice in the midst of the . . creatures
6. 7 I heard the v. of the fourth . . creature
6.10 they cried out with a loud voice
7. 2 he called with a loud voice
7.10 crying out with a loud voice, "Salvation
8. 5 there were peals of thunder, voices[o]
8.13 I heard an eagle crying with a loud voice
9.13 I heard a voice from the four horns
10. 3 called out with a loud voice, like a lion
10. 4 I heard a voice from heaven
10. 8 the v. which I had heard from heaven
11.12 they heard a loud voice from heaven
11.15 there were loud voices in heaven
11.19 there were flashes of lightning, voices[o]
12.10 I heard a loud voice in heaven
14. 2 I heard a voice from heaven . . ; the v. . . was like the sound of harpers
14. 7 he said with a loud voice, "Fear God
14. 9 another angel, . . saying with a loud v.
14.13 I heard a voice from heaven
14.15 calling with a loud voice to him
14.18 he called with a loud voice to him
16. 1 I heard a loud voice from the temple
16.17 a loud voice came out of the temple
16.18 there were flashes of lightning, voices[o]
18. 2 he called out with a mighty voice
18. 4 I heard another voice from heaven
18.23 "the voice of bridegroom and bride
19. 1 the loud voice of a great multitude
19. 5 from the throne came a voice crying
Rev 19. 6 I heard . . the voice of a great multitude
19.17 with a loud v. he called to all the birds
21. 3 I heard a loud voice from the throne

2. *sound, voice:* φθόγγος PHTHOGGOS
Rom 10.18 "Their v. has gone out to all the earth

3. *mouth:* στόμα STOMA [C.2]
Rom 15. 6 that together you may with one voice glorify

VOID, BE

1. *make ineffective:* καταργέω (pass.) KATARGEŌ
Rom 4.14 faith is null and the promise is void

VOID, BECOME

1. *fall, fail:* πίπτω PIPTŌ
Lk 16.17 "for one dot of the law to become void

VOID, MAKE

1. *cancel:* ἀκυρόω AKYROŌ
Mt 15. 6 "you have made void the word[p] of God
Mk 7.13 "making void the word of God

2. *make ineffective, hinder:* καταργέω KATARGEŌ
Gal 3.17 so as to make the promise void

VOMIT

1. *vomit:* ἐξέραμα EXERAMA*
2 Pet 2.22 The dog turns back to his own vomit

VOTE

1. *pebble, vote:* ψῆφος PSĒPHOS
Acts 26.10 "I cast my vote against them

VOW

1. *vow, prayer:* εὐχή EUCHĒ
Acts 18.18 he cut his hair, for he had a vow
21.23 "We have four men who are under a vow

2. *swear:* ὀμνύω OMNYŌ
Mk 6.23 he vowed to her, "Whatever you ask me

VOYAGE

1. *sailing, voyage:* πλόος PLOOS*
Acts 21. 7 When we had finished the voyage
27. 9 the voyage was already dangerous
27.10 "the voyage will be with injury

VOYAGE, MAKE A DIRECT

1. *run a straight course:* εὐθυδρομέω EUTHYDROMEŌ
Acts 16.11 we made a direct voyage to Samothrace

VULTURE

1. *eagle:* ἀετός AETOS
Mt [24.28 "there the *vultures* will be gathered†
Lk [17.37 "there the *vultures* will be gathered†

W

WAG

1. *move, remove:* κινέω KINEŌ
Mt 27.39 derided him, wagging their heads
Mk 15.29 derided him, wagging their heads

WAGE (*See also* WAR, WAGE)

1. *wage war:* στρατεύομαι STRATEUOMAI [A.6.a.6]
1 Tim 1.18 that . . you may wage the good warfare

WAGES

1. *reward, wages:* μισθός MISTHOS
Mt 20. 8 "owner . . said . . , 'pay them their wages
Lk 10. 7 "for the laborer deserves his wages
Jn 4.36 "He who reaps receives wages
Rom 4. 4 his wages are not reckoned as a gift
1 Cor 3. 8 shall receive his w. according to his labor
1 Tim 5.18 "The laborer deserves his wages
Jas 5. 4 Behold, the wages of the laborers

2. *salary, pay:* ὀψώνιον (pl.) OPSŌNION
Lk 3.14 "Rob no one . . , and be content with your w.
Rom 6.23 For the wages of sin is death

WAIL

1. *wail loudly:* ἀλαλάζω ALALAZŌ
Mk 5.38 a tumult, and people . . wailing loudly

2. *cut, strike:* κόπτω (mid.) KOPTŌ
Rev 1. 7 all tribes of the earth will wail
18. 9 kings of the earth . . will weep and wail

3. *sing a dirge, wail:* θρηνέω THRĒNEŌ
Mt 11.17 " 'we wailed, and you did not mourn
Lk 7.32 " 'we wailed, and you did not weep

WAILING
1. *weeping, crying:* κλαυθμός KLAUTHMOS
Mt 2.18 "A voice was heard in Ramah, wailing

WAIST
1. *loins:* ὀσφῦς OSPHYS
Mt 3. 4 John wore . . a leather girdle around his w.
Mk 1. 6 John . . had a leather girdle around his w.

WAIT
1. *let go, leave, forgive:* ἀφίημι (imper.) APHIĒMI
Mk 15.36 "Wait, let us see whether Elijah will come
2. *wait for:* ἐκδέχομαι EKDECHOMAI
Heb 10.13 ⟨sat . . at . . right hand of God⟩ to wait
3. *be about to:* μέλλω MELLŌ
Acts 22.16 " 'And now why do you wait?
4. *stay, wait:* μένω MENŌ
Acts 20. 5 These went on and were waiting for us
5. *wait for, expect:* προσδοκάω PROSDOKAŌ
Acts 28. 6 They waited, expecting him to swell up
28. 6 when they had waited a long time

WAIT, EAGERLY
1. *expect eagerly:* ἀπεκδέχομαι APEKDECHOMAI
Heb 9.28 to save those who are eagerly waiting

WAIT FOR
1. *wait for:* ἀναμένω ANAMENŌ*
1 Th 1.10 to wait for his Son from heaven
2. *expect eagerly:* ἀπεκδέχομαι APEKDECHOMAI
Rom 8.19 creation waits . . for . . the sons of God
8.23 groan inwardly as we wait for adoption
8.25 if we hope . . we w. for it with patience
1 Cor 1. 7 as you wait for . . our Lord Jesus Christ
Gal 5. 5 we wait for the hope of righteousness
1 Pet 3.20 God's patience waited in . . days of Noah
3. *wait for:* ἐκδέχομαι EKDECHOMAI
Jn [5. 3 *waiting for the moving of the water*‡
Acts 17.16 Paul was waiting for them at Athens
1 Cor 11.33 when you come . . to eat, w. for one another
Jas 5. 7 the farmer waits for the precious fruit
4. *wait for, endure:* περιμένω PERIMENŌ*
Acts 1. 4 to wait for the promise of the Father
5. *accept, expect:* προσδέχομαι PROSDECHOMAI
Lk 12.36 "like men who are waiting for their master
Acts 23.21 "waiting for the promise from you
Jude .21 w. for . . mercy of our Lord Jesus Christ
6. *wait for, expect:* προσδοκάω PROSDOKAŌ
Lk 1.21 the people were waiting for Zechariah
8.40 for they were all waiting for him
2 Pet 3.12 waiting for . . coming of the day of God
3.13 we wait for new heavens
3.14 since you wait for these, be zealous

WAIT, LIE IN
1. *lie in wait:* ἐνεδρεύω ENEDREUŌ
Lk 11.54 lying in w. for him, to catch . . something

WAIT ON
1. *persist in:* προσκαρτερέω PROSKARTEREŌ
Acts 10. 7 among those that waited on him

WAKE
1. *raise:* ἐγείρω EGEIRŌ
[a]pass.
Mt 1.24 [a]When Joseph woke from sleep
8.25 they went and woke him
Mk 4.38 they woke him and said . . "Teacher
Acts 12. 7 struck Peter on the side and woke him
Rom 13.11 [a]how it is full time now for you to wake
2. *become awakened:* ἔξυπνος γίνεσθαι EXYPNOS* [A.6.a.3]
Acts 16.27 When the jailer woke and saw
3. *be awake, watch:* γρηγορέω GRĒGOREŌ
1 Th 5.10 whether we w. or sleep we might live

WAKEN
1. *awake fully:* διαγρηγορέω DIAGRĒGOREŌ
Lk 9.32 when they wakened they saw his glory[o]

2. *stir up, arouse:* διεγείρω DIEGEIRŌ
Lk 8.24 they . . woke him, saying, "Master

WALK
1. *walk, behave:* περιπατέω PERIPATEŌ
Mt 4.18 As he walked by the Sea of Galilee
9. 5 "which is easier, . . to say, 'Rise and w.'?
11. 5 "blind receive their sight and the lame w.
14.25 he came to them, walking on the sea
14.26 disciples saw him walking on the sea
14.29 Peter . . walked on the water
15.31 when they saw . . the lame walking
Mk 2. 9 " 'Rise, take up your pallet and walk
5.42 immediately the girl got up and walked
6.48 he came to them, walking on the sea
6.49 when they saw him walking on the sea
8.24 "they look like trees, walking
11.27 as he was walking in the temple
16.12 as they were walking into the country[k]‡
Lk 5.23 "Which is easier, . . to say, 'Rise and w.'?
7.22 "the lame walk, lepers are cleansed
11.44 "men walk over them without knowing it
24.17 "What is this conversation . . as you walk?
Jn 1.36 he looked at Jesus as he walked
5. 8 "Rise, take up your pallet, and walk
5. 9 he took up his pallet and walked
5.11 " 'Take up your pallet, and walk
5.12 " 'Take up your pallet, and walk
6.19 they saw Jesus walking on the sea
8.12 "he . . will not walk in darkness
10.23 Jesus was walking in the temple
11. 9 "If any one walks in the day
11.10 "But if any one walks in the night
12.35 "Walk while you have the light
12.35 "who walks in the darkness does not know
21.18 "you . . walked where you would
Acts 3. 6 "in the name of Jesus Christ . . , walk
3. 8 leaping up he stood and walked
3. 8 walking and leaping and praising God
3. 9 all the people saw him walking
3.12 "as though . . we had made him walk
14. 8 cripple from birth, who had never walked
14.10 he sprang up and walked
Rom 6. 4 we too might walk in newness of life
8. 4 who walk not according to the flesh
14.15 you are no longer walking in love
2 Cor 5. 7 for we walk by faith, not by sight
Gal 5.16 But I say, walk by the Spirit
Eph 2. 2 ⟨sins⟩ in which you once walked
2.10 good works . . that we should w. in them
5. 2 walk in love, as Christ loved us
5. 8 walk as children of light
5.15 Look carefully then how you walk
Col 3. 7 In these you once walked
1 Jn 1. 6 while we walk in darkness
1. 7 if we w. in the light, as he is in the light
2. 6 he who says he abides in him ought to walk in the same way in which he walked
2.11 he who hates . . walks in the darkness
Rev 2. 1 " 'walks among the seven . . lampstands
3. 4 " 'they shall walk with me in white
9.20 idols . . which cannot . . hear or walk
21.24 By its light shall the nations walk
2. *go, walk:* πορεύομαι POREUOMAI
Lk 1. 6 walking in all the commandments
Acts 9.31 walking in the fear of the Lord
14.16 "he allowed all . . to w. in their own ways
Jude .11 For they walk in the way of Cain
3. *agree with, walk by:* στοιχέω STOICHEŌ
Gal 5.25 let us also walk by the Spirit
6.16 Peace . . upon all who w. by this rule

WALK AHEAD
1. *lead forward:* προάγω PROAGŌ
Mk 10.32 Jesus was walking ahead of them

WALL
1. *city wall:* τεῖχος TEICHOS*
Acts 9.25 disciples . . let him down over the wall

2 Cor 11.33 let down . . through a window in the wall
Heb 11.30 By faith the walls of Jericho fell down
Rev 21.12 It had a great, high wall
21.14 wall of the city had twelve foundations
21.15 to measure the city and its . . walls
21.17 He also measured its wall
21.18 The wall was built of jasper
21.19 foundations of the wall of the city
2. *wall of a house:* τοῖχος TOICHOS*
Acts 23. 3 Paul said . . "you whitewashed wall!

WALL, DIVIDING
1. *dividing wall:* μεσότοιχον MESOTOICHON*
Eph 2.14 he . . has broken down the dividing wall

WALLOW
1. *rolling:* κυλισμός KYLISMOS* [B.1.a.2]
2 Pet 2.22 the sow is washed only to wallow

WANDER
WANDER AWAY
1. *lead astray:* ἀποπλανάω (pass.) APOPLANAŌ
1 Tim 6.10 through this craving . . some . . wandered a.
2. *turn out of course:* ἐκτρέπω (pass.) EKTREPŌ
1 Tim 1. 6 wandered away into vain discussion
2 Tim 4. 4 will turn away . . and wander into myths
3. *cause to wander:* πλανάω (pass.) PLANAŌ
Heb 11.38 wandering over deserts and mountains
Jas 5.19 if any one . . wanders from the truth

WANDERING
1. *wanderer, planet:* πλανήτης PLANĒTĒS* [A.1.b.2]
Jude .13 ⟨these are⟩ wandering stars

WANT (*See also* BENEFIT, WANT SOME; KNOW, WANT S. TO; UNDERSTAND, WANT S. TO)
1. *wish, will:* βούλομαι BOULOMAI
Acts 5.33 enraged and wanted to kill them
15.37 Barnabas wanted to take . . Mark
2 Cor 1.15 I wanted to come to you first
1.17 Was I vacillating when I wanted . . this?
Phil 1.12 I w. you to know . . what has happened
3 Jn .10 those who want to welcome them
2. *deficiency, need:* ὑστέρημα HYSTERĒMA
2 Cor 8.14 your abundance . . should supply their w., so that their abundance may supply your w.
9.12 not only supplies the wants of the saints
3. *lack, fail:* ὑστερέω (inf.) HYSTEREŌ
Phil 4.12 the secret of facing plenty and . . want
4. *shortcoming, need:* ὑστέρησις HYSTERĒSIS
Phil 4.11 Not that I complain of want
5. *will, wish:* θέλω THELŌ
Mt 13.28 " 'do you want us to go and gather them?
14. 5 though he wanted to put him to death
20.21 he said to her, "What do you want?
20.32 "What do you want me to do for you?
27.15 to release . . prisoner whom they wanted
27.17 "Whom do you want me to release?
27.21 "Which . . do you want me to release?
Mk 6.19 Herodias . . wanted to kill him
6.25 "I want . . the head of John the Baptist
6.26 he did not want to break his word
10.35 "we want you to do . . whatever we ask
10.36 "What do you want me to do for you?
10.51 "What do you want me to do for you?
15. 9 "want me to release . . King of the Jews?
Lk 9.54 "do you want us to bid fire come down?
13.31 "Get away . . ., for Herod wants to kill you
18.41 "What do you want me to do for you?
19.14 " 'We do not want this man to reign
19.27 " 'who did not want me to reign over them
Jn 5. 6 "Do you want to be healed?
6.11 also the fish, as much as they wanted
7.44 Some of them wanted to arrest him
9.27 "Why do you want to hear it again? Do you too want to become his disciples?
16.19 Jesus knew that they wanted to ask him
Acts 7.28 " 'Do you want to kill me?
14.13 wanted to offer sacrifice with the people
16. 3 Paul wanted Timothy to accompany him
Rom 1.13 I want you to know, brethren
7.15 For I do not do what I want
7.16 Now if I do what I do not want
7.19 For I do not do the good I want, but the evil I do not want is what I do
7.20 if I do what I do not want
7.21 when I want to do right, evil lies close
11.25 I want you to understand this mystery
1 Cor 7.32 I want you to be free from anxieties
10. 1 I want you to know, brethren
10.20 not want you to be partners with demons
11. 3 But I want you to understand
12. 1 I do not want you to be uninformed
14. 5 Now I want you all to speak in tongues
16. 7 I do not want to see you . . in passing
2 Cor 1. 8 we do not want you to be ignorant
Gal 1. 7 who . . w. to pervert the gospel of Christ
4. 9 whose slaves you want to be once more
4.17 they want to shut you out
6.12 who want to make a good showing
Col 2. 1 I want you to know how . . I strive
1 Th 2.18 because we wanted to come to you
Jas 2.20 Do you want to be shown?
CONTEXTUALLY
2 Cor 1.16 I wanted to visit you on my way

WANT, BE IN
1. *lack, fail:* ὑστερέω (pass.) HYSTEREŌ
Lk 15.14 "he began to be in want
2 Cor 11. 9 I was with you and was in want

WANTON AGAINST, GROW
1. *behave wantonly toward:* καταστρηνιάω KATASTRĒNIAŌ*
1 Tim 5.11 for when they grow wanton against Christ

WANTON, BE
WANTON, PLAY THE
1. *run riot, live in luxury:* στρηνιάω STRĒNIAŌ*
Rev 18. 7 " 'she glorified herself and played the w.
18. 9 kings of the earth, who . . were w. with her

WANTONNESS
1. *insolence, sensuality:* στρῆνος STRĒNOS*
Rev 18. 3 "rich with the wealth of her w.

WAR
1. *fight, make war:* πολεμέω POLEMEŌ
Rev 2.16 " 'I will come to you soon and war
2. *fight, war:* πόλεμος POLEMOS
Mt 24. 6 "you will hear of wars and rumors of wars; see that you are not alarmed
Mk 13. 7 "when you hear of wars and rumors of wars, do not be alarmed
Lk 14.31 "going to encounter another king in war
21. 9 "when you hear of wars and tumults
Heb 11.34 ⟨who⟩ became mighty in war
Jas 4. 1 What causes wars . . among you?
Rev 11. 7 the beast . . will make war upon them
12. 7 Now war arose in heaven
12.17 dragon . . went off to make war
13. 7 it was allowed to make war on the saints‡
19.19 gathered to make war against him

WAR, BE AT
WAR, CARRY ON A
WAR, MAKE
WAR, WAGE
WAR WITH, AT
1. *make war against:* ἀντιστρατεύομαι (part.) ANTISTRATEUOMAI*
Rom 7.23 another law at w. with . . law of my mind
2. *fight, make war:* πολεμέω POLEMEŌ
Jas 4. 2 so you fight and wage war
Rev 17.14 "they will make war on the Lamb
19.11 in righteousness he judges and makes war
3. *wage war:* στρατεύομαι STRATEUOMAI
2 Cor 10. 3 we are not carrying on a worldly war
Jas 4. 1 Is it not your passions that are at war?
1 Pet 2.11 passions of the flesh that wage war

WARE
CONTEXTUALLY
Rev 18.15 The merchants of these wares . . will stand

WARFARE
1. *campaign, fight:* στρατεία STRATEIA*
2 Cor 10. 4 the weapons of our warfare are not worldly
1 Tim 1.18 you may wage the good warfare

WARM ONESELF
WARMED, BE
1. *warm, heat:* θερμαίνω (mid.) THERMAINŌ*
Mk 14.54 he was . . warming himself at the fire
14.67 seeing Peter warming himself
Jn 18.18 they were . . warming themselves. Peter also was . . warming himself
18.25 Peter was standing and warming himself
Jas 2.16 "Go in peace, be warmed and filled

WARN
1. *hold out promise or threat:* ἀπειλέω APEILEŌ
Acts 4.17 "let us warn them to speak no more
2. *negotiate, order:* χρηματίζω CHRĒMATIZŌ
Mt 2.12 being warned in a dream not to return
2.22 being warned in a dream he withdrew
Heb 11. 7 By faith Noah, being warned by God
12.25 they refused him who warned them
3. *bear witness to:* διαμαρτύρομαι DIAMARTYROMAI
Lk 16.28 " 'w. them, lest they also come into this place
4. *indicate, show:* ὑποδείκνυμι HYPODEIKNYMI
Mt 3. 7 "Who warned you to flee from the wrath?
Lk 3. 7 "Who warned you to flee from the wrath?
12. 5 "But I will warn you whom to fear
5. *bear witness, testify:* μαρτυρέω MARTYREŌ
Rev 22.18 I warn every one who hears . . prophecy
6. *admonish, warn:* νουθετέω NOUTHETEŌ
Col 1.28 warning every man and teaching
2 Th 3.15 but warn him as a brother
7. *foretell, say before:* προεῖπον PROEIPON
2 Cor 13. 2 I warned those who sinned before
8. *foretell, proclaim:* προλέγω PROLEGŌ
2 Cor 13. 2 I warn them now while absent
Gal 5.21 I warn you . . that those who do such

WARN BEFORE
1. *foretell, say before:* προεῖπον PROEIPON
Gal 5.21 as I warned you b. . . , those who do such

WARNING
1. *pattern, image:* τύπος TYPOS
1 Cor 10. 6 Now these things are warnings

WARNING, AS A
1. *as an example:* τυπικῶς TYPIKŌS*
1 Cor 10.11 these things happened to them as a w.

WASH
1. *wash off, wash clean:* ἀπονίπτω APONIPTŌ*
Mt 27.24 he took water and washed his hands
2. *dip, plunge, baptize:* βαπτίζω (pass.) BAPTIZŌ
Lk 11.38 he did not first wash before dinner
3. *wash:* λούω LOUŌ
Acts 9.37 when they had washed her
16.33 washed their wounds, and . . was baptized
Heb 10.22 with . . our bodies washed with pure water
2 Pet 2.22 the sow is washed only to wallow
4. *wash, cleanse:* νίπτω (act. or mid.) NIPTŌ*
Mt 6.17 "when you fast, . . wash your face
15. 2 "For they do not wash their hands
Mk 7. 3 (do not eat unless they w. their hands[v]
Jn 9. 7 "Go, wash in the pool of Siloam" . . So he went and washed
9.11 " 'Go to Siloam and wash'; so I went and washed and received my sight
9.15 "He put clay on my eyes, and I washed
13. 5 he . . began to wash the disciples' feet
13. 6 Peter said . . "Lord, do you wash my feet?
13. 8 "You shall never wash my feet
13. 8 "If I do not wash you, you have no part
13.10 "He who has bathed does not need to w.
13.12 When he had washed their feet
Jn 13.14 "If I then . . have washed your feet, you also ought to w. one another's feet
1 Tim 5.10 she . . washed the feet of the saints
5. *wash, clean:* πλύνω PLYNŌ*
Lk 5. 2 fishermen . . were washing their nets
Rev 7.14 "they have washed their robes
22.14 Blessed are those who w. their robes[s]‡

WASH AWAY
WASHED, BE
1. *wash off, wash clean:* ἀπολούω (mid.) APOLOUŌ
Acts 22.16 " 'be baptized, and wash away your sins
1 Cor 6.11 you were washed, you were sanctified

WASHING
1. *dipping in water, baptism:* βαπτισμός BAPTISMOS
Mk 7. 4 (washing of cups and pots and vessels
2. *bath, washing:* λουτρόν LOUTRON*
Eph 5.26 by the washing of water with the word
Tit 3. 5 by the washing of regeneration

WASTE
1. *destruction:* ἀπώλεια APŌLEIA
[a]A.6.a.3
Mt 26. 8 indignant, saying, "Why this waste?
Mk 14. 4 [a]"Why was the ointment thus wasted?
2. *scatter abroad, squander:* διασκορπίζω DIASKORPIZŌ
Lk 16. 1 "that this man was wasting his goods

WASTE AWAY
1. *destroy utterly:* διαφθείρω (pass.) DIAPHTHEIRŌ
2 Cor 4.16 our outer nature is wasting away

WASTE, LAY
1. *strip bare, lay waste:* ἐρημόω ERĒMOŌ
Mt 12.25 "Every kingdom divided . . is laid waste
Lk 11.17 "Every kingdom divided . . is laid waste
Rev 18.17 "all this wealth has been laid waste
18.19 "In one hour she has been laid waste

WATCH (*See also* KEEP WATCH OVER)
1. *keep watch:* ἀγρυπνέω AGRYPNEŌ
Mk 13.33 "Take heed, watch;[a] for you do not know
Lk 21.36 "But watch at all times, praying
Heb 13.17 they are keeping watch over your souls
2. *be awake, watch:* γρηγορέω GRĒGOREŌ
Mt 24.42 "W. . . , for you do not know on what day
24.43 "the householder . . would have watched
25.13 "W. . . , for you know neither the day
26.38 "remain here, and watch[h] with me†
26.40 "could you not w.[h] with me one hour?†
26.41 "W.[h] and pray that you may not enter†
Mk 13.34 "commands . . doorkeeper to be on the w.
13.35 "Watch . . —for you do not know when
13.37 "what I say to you I say to all: Watch
14.34 "remain here, and watch[d]†
14.37 "Could you not watch[d] one hour?†
14.38 "W.[d] and pray that you may not enter†
Lk [12.39 "he *would have watched and* . . not . . left‡[o]
3. *watch closely, observe:* παρατηρέω (act. or mid.) PARATĒREŌ
Mk 3. 2 watched him . . so that they might accuse
Lk 6. 7 watched him . . so that they might find
14. 1 when he went . . , they were watching him
20.20 So they watched him, and sent spies
Acts 9.24 were watching the gates . . , to kill him
4. *watch, guard, prison:* φυλακή PHYLAKĒ
[a]φυλάσσειν φυλακάς
Mt 14.25 in the fourth w. of the night he came
Mk 6.48 the fourth w. of the night he came
Lk 2. 8 [a]keeping w. over their flock by night
12.38 "If he comes in the second watch
5. *look at, observe:* θεωρέω THEŌREŌ
Mk 12.41 he sat down . . and watched the multitude
Lk 23.35 And the people stood by, watching

WATCHFUL, BE
1. *be awake, watch:* γρηγορέω GRĒGOREŌ
1 Cor 16.13 Be watchful, stand firm in your faith
Col 4. 2 Continue . . in prayer, being w. in it
1 Pet 5. 8 Be sober, be watchful

WATCHING
1. *sleeplessness, watching:* ἀγρυπνία (pl.) AGRYPNIA
2 Cor 6. 5 tumults, labors, watching, hunger

WATER (*See also* FILL WITH WATER)
1. *water:* ὕδωρ HYDŌR
Mt 3.11 "I baptize you with water for repentance
3.16 he went up immediately from the w.
8.32 the whole herd . . perished in the waters
14.28 "bid me come to you on the water
14.29 So Peter . . walked on the water
17.15 "he falls . . often into the water
27.24 he took water and washed his hands
[27.49 *out came water and blood*‡
Mk 1. 8 "I have baptized you with water
1.10 when he came up out of the water
9.22 "it has often cast him . . into the water
9.41 "whoever gives you a cup of water
14.13 "man carrying a jar of w. will meet you
Lk 3.16 "I baptize you with water
7.44 "you gave me no water for my feet
8.25 "he commands even wind and water
16.24 " 'send Lazarus to dip . . his finger in w.
22.10 "man carrying a jar of w. will meet you
Jn 1.26 "I baptize with water
1.31 "for this I came baptizing with water
1.33 "he who sent me to baptize with water
2. 7 "Fill the jars with water
2. 9 steward of the feast tasted the water
2. 9 (servants who had drawn the w. knew
3. 5 "unless one is born of w. and the Spirit
3.23 because there was much water there
4. 7 a woman of Samaria to draw water
4.10 "he would have given you living water
4.11 "where do you get that living water?
4.13 "who drinks of this w. will thirst again
4.14 "the water that I shall give him
4.14 "the water that I shall give him
4.14 "a spring of water welling up
4.15 "Sir, give me this water
4.46 where he had made the water wine
[5. 3 *waiting for the moving of the water*‡
[5. 4 *an angel . . troubled the water*‡
[5. 4 *after the troubling of the water*‡
5. 7 "into the pool when the w. is troubled
7.38 " 'Out of his heart shall flow . . living w.
13. 5 Then he poured water into a basin
19.34 at once there came out blood and water
Acts 1. 5 "for John baptized with water
8.36 they came to some water, and the eunuch said, "See, here is water!
8.38 they both went down into the water
8.39 when they came up out of the water
10.47 "Can any one forbid water for baptizing?
11.16 " 'John baptized with water
Eph 5.26 cleansed her by the washing of water
Heb 9.19 he took the blood of calves . . , with water
10.22 our bodies washed with pure water
Jas 3.12 No more can salt water yield fresh
1 Pet 3.20 eight persons, were saved through water
2 Pet 3. 5 an earth formed out of water and by means of water
3. 6 world . . was deluged with water
1 Jn 5. 6 This is he who came by water and blood, Jesus Christ, not with the water only but with the water and the blood
5. 8 the Spirit, the water, and the blood
Rev 1.15 voice . . like the sound of many waters
7.17 "guide them to springs of living water
8.10 great star fell . . on the fountains of w.
8.11 A third of the waters became wormwood, and many men died of the water
11. 6 they have power over the waters
12.15 The serpent poured water like a river
14. 2 voice . . like the sound of many waters
14. 7 "who made . . the sea and the fountains of w.
16. 4 poured his bowl into . . the fountains of w.
Rev 16. 5 I heard the angel of water say
16.12 and its water was dried up
17. 1 "harlot who is seated upon many waters
17.15 "waters . . where the harlot is seated
19. 6 like the sound of many waters
21. 6 "from the fountain of the water of life
22. 1 showed me the river of the w. of life
22.17 let him . . take the water of life
2. *water, give to drink:* ποτίζω POTIZŌ
Lk 13.15 "Does not each . . untie his ox . . to w. it?
1 Cor 3. 6 I planted, Apollos watered
3. 7 nor he who waters is anything
3. 8 who plants and he who waters are equal

WATER, COLD
1. *cold:* ψυχρός PSYCHROS [B.3.b.2]
Mt 10.42 "whoever gives . . even a cup of cold water

WATER, DRINK
1. *drink water:* ὑδροποτέω HYDROPOTEŌ*
1 Tim 5.23 No longer drink only water

WATER, FILL WITH
1. *fill completely:* συμπληρόω (pass.) SYMPLĒROŌ
Lk 8.23 they were filling with water

WATER JAR
1. *water jar, vessel:* ὑδρία HYDRIA
Jn 4.28 So the woman left her water jar

WATERLESS
1. *waterless:* ἄνυδρος ANYDROS*
Mt 12.43 "he passes through waterless places
Lk 11.24 "he passes through waterless places
2 Pet 2.17 These are waterless springs and mists
Jude .12 w. clouds, carried along by winds

WAVE
WAVES
1. *water:* ὕδωρ HYDŌR
Lk 8.24 rebuked the wind and the raging waves
2. *wave, waves, surf:* κλύδων KLYDŌN
Jas 1. 6 he who doubts is like a wave of the sea
3. *wave:* κῦμα KYMA*
Mt 8.24 boat was being swamped by the waves
14.24 the boat . . was . . beaten by the waves
Mk 4.37 the waves beat into the boat
Jude .13 wild waves of the sea, casting up . . foam
4. *throw, cast out:* ῥίπτω RHIPTŌ
Acts 22.23 they cried out and waved . . garments
5. *tossing motion:* σάλος SALOS*
Lk 21.25 "the roaring of the sea and the waves

WAVER, MAKE ONE
1. *differentiate, decide:* διακρίνω (pass.) DIAKRINŌ
Rom 4.20 No distrust made him waver

WAVERING, WITHOUT
1. *unswerving:* ἀκλινής (acc.) AKLINĒS*
Heb 10.23 confession of our hope without wavering

WAY (*See also* ALL THE WAY TO; ANOTHER WAY, BY; BY WAY OF; ESCAPE, WAY OF; GIVE WAY; GO ON ONE'S WAY; GO ONE'S WAY; IN THE WAY OF; LONG WAY, A; PUT IN THE WAY; REJECTING, HAVE A WAY OF; SAME WAY, IN THE; UNGODLY WAY, COMMIT IN SUCH AN)
1. *way, road:* ὁδός HODOS
Mt 2.12 they departed . . by another way
3. 3 "Prepare the way of the Lord
7.13 "the gate is wide and the way is easy[q]
7.14 "the way is hard, that leads to life
8.28 so fierce that no one could pass that way
11.10 " 'who shall prepare thy way before thee
15.32 "lest they faint on the way
20.17 took the twelve . . and on the w. he said
21.32 "John came . . in the way of righteousness
22.16 "you . . teach the w. of God truthfully
Mk 1. 2 "my messenger . . , who shall prepare thy way
1. 3 "Prepare the way of the Lord
2.23 as they made their way
8. 3 "some of them have come a long way
8.27 on the w. he asked . . "Who do men say?
9.33 "What were you discussing on the way?

Mk 9.34 for on the way they had discussed
10.52 he . . followed him on the way
12.14 "you . . truly teach the way of God
Lk 1.76 "go before the Lord to prepare his ways
1.79 "to guide our feet into the w. of peace
3. 4 "Prepare the way of the Lord
3. 5 "the rough ways shall be made smooth
7.27 " 'who shall prepare thy way before thee
12.58 "an effort to settle with him on the way
20.21 "you . . truly teach the way of God
Jn 1.23 " 'Make straight the way of the Lord
14. 4 "you know the way where I am going[f]
14. 5 "how can we know the way?
14. 6 "I am the w., and the truth, and the life
Acts 2.28 " 'Thou hast made known . . the ways of life
8.39 eunuch . . went on his way rejoicing
9. 2 if he found any belonging to the Way
14.16 allowed all . . to walk in their own ways
16.17 "proclaim to you the way of salvation
18.25 instructed in the way of the Lord
18.26 expounded to him the way of God
19. 9 disbelieved, speaking evil of the Way
19.23 there arose . . stir concerning the W.
22. 4 "I persecuted this Way to the death
24.14 "the Way, which they call a sect
24.22 Felix, having . . knowledge of the Way
25. 3 an ambush to kill him on the way
26.13 "I saw on the way a light from heaven
Rom 3.17 "the way of peace they do not know
11.33 how inscrutable his ways!
1 Cor 4.17 to remind you of my ways in Christ
12.31 I will show you a still more excellent way
1 Th 3.11 may our God . . direct our way to you
Heb 3.10 " 'they have not known my ways
9. 8 way into the sanctuary is not yet opened
10.20 by the new and living way
Jas 1. 7, 8 double-minded . . , unstable in all his ways
2.25 in the same way was . . Rahab . . justified
5.20 brings . . a sinner from the error of his w.
2 Pet 2. 2 the way of truth will be reviled
2.15 Forsaking the right way . . they have followed the way of Balaam
2.21 better . . never to have known the w.
Jude .11 For they walk in the way of Cain
Rev 15. 3 "Just and true are thy ways!
16.12 to prepare the way for the kings

2. *middle, in the middle:* μέσος MESOS [B.2.d.1]
2 Th 2. 7 it will do so until he is out of the way

3. *what sort? what:* ποῖος POIOS [B.3.b.2]
Lk 5.19 but finding no way to bring him in

4. *way, manner:* τρόπος TROPOS
Rom 3. 2 Much in every way
Phil 1.18 in every way, . . in pretense or in truth
2 Th 2. 3 Let no one deceive you in any way
3.16 the Lord . . give you peace . . in all ways

IDIOMATICALLY
a. Lk 17.11 On the way to Jerusalem ἐν τῷ πορεύεσθαι εἰς Ἰερουσαλήμ [POREUOMAI]
b. Acts 4.21 finding no way to punish them μηδὲν εὑρίσκοντες τὸ πῶς κολάσωνται αὐτούς [PŌS I]

CONTEXTUALLY
Mt 27.44 robbers . . reviled him in the same way
Acts 17.22 "in every way you are very religious
Rom 14.13 hindrance in the way of a brother
1 Cor 1. 5 in every way you were enriched in him
13. 5 Love does not insist on its own way
13.11 when . . a man, I gave up childish ways
2 Cor 1.16 to visit you on my way to Macedonia
4. 8 We were afflicted in every way
6. 4 we commend ourselves in every way
9.11 You will be enriched in every way
11. 6 in every way we have made this plain
11. 9 refrain from burdening you in any way
Eph 4.15 we are to grow up in every way into him
1 Tim 2. 2 a quiet . . life, godly . . in every way
3. 4 children . . respectful in every way
4. 8 godliness is of value in every way
1 Tim 5.10 devoted herself to doing good in every w.

WAY AS, IN THE SAME
1. *in the manner in which:* ὃν τρόπον (acc.) TROPOS
Acts 1.11 "in the same way as you saw him go

WAY, BRING ON ONE'S
WAY, SEND ONE ON HIS
WAY, SPEED ONE ON HIS
1. *send forth, escort:* προπέμπω PROPEMPŌ
Acts 15. 3 sent on their way by the church
21. 5 they all . . brought us on our way
1 Cor 16.11 Speed him on his way in peace
2 Cor 1.16 have you send me on my way to Judea
Tit 3.13 speed Zenas . . and Apollos on their way

WAY, IN EVERY
1. *in every way:* πάντῃ PANTĒ*
Acts 24. 3 "In every way . . we accept this

WAY, IN THE
WAY, IN THIS
WAY, IT IS THE
1. *thus, so:* οὕτως HOUTŌS
Mt 1.18 Now the birth . . took place in this way
Jn 21. 1 Jesus . . revealed himself in this way
Acts 13.34 "he spoke in this way
1 Cor 9.14 In the same way, the Lord commanded
2 Th 3.17 This is the mark . . ; it is the w. I write
Heb 4. 4 spoken of the seventh day in this way

WAY IN WHICH, IN THE SAME
1. *as, just as:* καθώς KATHŌS
1 Jn 2. 6 in the same way in which he walked

WAY INTO, MAKE ONE'S
1. *go into, creep in:* ἐνδύνω ENDYNŌ*
2 Tim 3. 6 who make their way into households

WAY OFF, A GREAT
1. *far off, at a distance:* πόρρω PORRŌ
Lk 14.32 "while the other is yet a great way off

WAY, ON ONE'S
1. *go, walk:* πορεύομαι POREUOMAI [A.6.b]
Acts 17.14 sent Paul off on his way to the sea

WAY, SEND ONE ON HIS
WAY, SPEED ONE ON HIS (*See* WAY, BRING ON ONE'S)

WAY TO, A
1. *how:* πῶς (+subj.) PŌS I
Mk 11.18 scribes . . sought a way to destroy him

WAYS (*See also* MANY WAYS, IN; MEND ONE'S WAYS; VARIOUS WAYS, IN)
1. *behavior:* ἀναστροφή ANASTROPHĒ
1 Pet 1.18 you were ransomed from . . futile ways

WAYSIDE
1. *way, road:* ὁδός HODOS
Mt 21.19 seeing a fig tree by the wayside

WAYWARD
1. *cause to wander:* πλανάω (pass. part.) PLANAŌ
Heb 5. 2 He can deal gently with the . . wayward

WE (*For entry* 1, *and for Greek words not represented here, see also* OUR; OURS; US)
1. *we:* ἡμεῖς HĒMEIS
Mt **6.12**; **9.14**; **15.33**; **17.4**, 19; **19.27**[2]; **28.13**, 14
Mk **9.5**, 28; **10.28**; **14.58**
Lk **3.14**; **9.13**[2], 33; **18.28**; **23.41**; **24.21**
Jn **1.16**; **4.22**; **6.42**, 69; **7.35**; **8.41**, 48; **9.4**, 21, 24, 28, 29, 40; **11.16**; **12.34**; **14.8**; **17.11**, 22; **19.7**; **21.3**
Acts **2.8**, 32; **3.15**; **4.9**, 12, 20; **5.32**; **6.2**, 4; **10.33**, 39, 47; **13.32**; **14.15**, 22; **15.10**; **16.16**[2]; **19.25**; **20.6**, 7, 13; **21.1**, 7, 12, 17, 23, 25; **24.8**; **26.14**; **27.1**, 18, 26, 27; **28.21**, 22
Rom **5.6**, 8; **6.4**, 6; **7.6**; **8.23**; **15.1**
1 Cor **1.23**; **2.12**, 16; **4.8**, 10[3]; **8.6**[2]; **9.11**[2], 12, 25; **11.16**; **12.13**; **15.52**
2 Cor **1.4**, 5[2], 6, 8[2], 19, 20; **3.18**; **4.11**, 13, 18; **5.1**, 10, 16, 21; **6.16**; **7.5**; **8.6**, 19, 20; **9.4**; **10.7**, 13; **11.12**, 21; **13.4**, 6, 7[2], 9
Gal **1.8**; **2.9**, 15, 16; **4.28**; **5.5**
Eph **1.4**, 12; **2.3**; **6.12**, 22
Phil **3.3**
Col **1.9**, 28; **4.8**

1 Th **1**.8; **2**.13, 17; **3**.6, 12; **4**.15, 17; **5**.8
2 Th **1**.4; **2**.13; **3**.14
Heb **2**.1, 3; **3**.6; **4**.13; **5**.11; **7**.26; **10**.26, 39; **12**.1, 25; **13**.6
Jas **1**.18
1 Pet **1**.3
2 Pet **1**.18
1 Jn **1**.4; **3**.14, 16; **4**.6, 10, 11, 14, 16, 17, 19
3 Jn .8
2. *who, which, what:* ὅς HOS
Rom **4**.24

WEAK
1. *unable, impossible:* ἀδύνατος ADYNATOS
Rom 15. 1 ought to bear with the failings of the weak
2. *be weak, be sickly:* ἀσθενέω (part.) ASTHENEŌ
Acts 20.35 "by so toiling one must help the weak
Rom 14. 1 for the man who is weak in faith
14. 2 the weak man eats only vegetables
1 Cor 8.11 this weak man is destroyed
3. *weak, sickly:* ἀσθενής ASTHENĒS
Mt 26.41 "the spirit . . is willing, but the flesh is w.
Mk 14.38 "the spirit . . is willing, but the flesh is w.
Rom 5. 6 While we were still weak, . . Christ died[0]
1 Cor 4.10 We are weak, but you are strong
8. 7 their conscience, being weak, is defiled
8. 9 lest . . a stumbling block to the weak
8.10 encouraged, if his conscience is weak
9.22 To the weak I become weak, that I might win the weak. I have become all things to all men
11.30 That is why many of you are weak
2 Cor 10.10 "but his bodily presence is weak
Gal 4. 9 the weak and beggarly elemental spirits
1 Th 5.14 help the weak, be patient with . . all
4. *undo, disable:* παραλύω (perf. pass. part.) PARALYŌ
Heb 12.12 strengthen your weak knees

WEAK, BE
1. *be weak, be sickly:* ἀσθενέω ASTHENEŌ
1 Cor 8.12 their conscience when it is weak
2 Cor 11.21 I must say, we were too weak for that!
11.29 Who is weak, and I am not w.? Who is made to fall, and I am not indignant?
12.10 when I am weak, then I am strong
13. 3 He is not weak in dealing with you
13. 4 For we are weak in him
13. 9 For we are glad when we are weak

WEAK, WHAT IS
1. *weak, sickly:* ἀσθενής (subst. neut.) ASTHENĒS
1 Cor 1.27 God chose what is weak in the world

WEAK WOMAN
1. *silly woman:* γυναικάριον GYNAIKARION*
2 Tim 3. 6 weak women, burdened with sins

WEAKEN
WEAKENED, BE
1. *be weak, be sickly:* ἀσθενέω ASTHENEŌ
[a]B.2.a.1
Rom 4.19 He did not weaken in faith
8. 3 [a]the law, weakened by the flesh
[14.21 makes your brother stumble *or be weakened*‡

WEAKER
1. *weak, sickly:* ἀσθενής (comp.) ASTHENĒS
1 Cor 12.22 parts of the body which seem to be w.
1 Pet 3. 7 the woman as the weaker sex

WEAKNESS
1. *weakness, sickness:* ἀσθένεια ASTHENEIA
Rom 8.26 the Spirit helps us in our weakness
1 Cor 2. 3 I was with you in weakness
15.43 sown in weakness, it is raised in power
2 Cor 11.30 I will boast of the things that show my w.
12. 5 I will not boast, except of my weaknesses
12. 9 "my power is made perfect in weakness
12. 9 "more gladly boast of my weaknesses
12.10 then, I am content with weaknesses
13. 4 For he was crucified in weakness
Heb 4.15 to sympathize with our weaknesses
5. 2 since he himself is beset with weakness
7.28 the law appoints men in their weakness
Heb 11.34 won strength out of weakness
2. *weak, sickly:* ἀσθενής (subst. neut.) ASTHENĒS
1 Cor 1.25 the weakness of God is stronger than men
Heb 7.18 because of its weakness and uselessness

WEALTH
1. *power, ability:* δύναμις DYNAMIS
Rev 18. 3 "rich with the w. of her wantonness
2. *ease, plenty:* εὐπορία EUPORIA*
Acts 19.25 "from this business we have our wealth
3. *riches, wealth:* πλοῦτος PLOUTOS
2 Cor 8. 2 overflowed in a wealth of liberality
Heb 11.26 greater w. than the treasures of Egypt
Rev 5.12 "Worthy . . to receive power and w.!
18.17 "all this wealth has been laid waste
4. *costliness:* τιμιότης TIMIOTĒS*
Rev 18.19 "all who had ships . . grew rich by her w.!

WEALTH, GAIN
1. *be rich, become rich:* πλουτέω PLOUTEŌ
Rev 18.15 merchants . . who gained wealth from her

WEAPON
1. *tool, weapon:* ὅπλον HOPLON
Jn 18. 3 with lanterns and torches and weapons
2 Cor 6. 7 with the weapons of righteousness
10. 4 the weapons of our warfare

WEAR (*See also* HAIR, WEAR LONG; VEIL, WEAR A)
1. *have, hold:* ἔχω ECHŌ
Mt 3. 4 John wore a garment of camel's hair
Rev 9.17 the riders wore breastplates
2. *put on, clothe:* ἐνδύω (mid.) ENDYŌ
Lk 8.27 for a long time he had worn no clothes
3. *fasten underneath:* ὑποδέω (mid.) HYPODEŌ
Mk 6. 9 wear sandals and not put on two tunics
4. *throw around, put on:* περιβάλλω (pass.) PERIBALLŌ
Mt 6.31 "anxious, saying . . 'What shall we wear?
5. *bear, wear:* φορέω PHOREŌ
Mt 11. 8 "Behold, those who wear soft raiment
Jn 19. 5 Jesus came out, wearing the crown
Jas 2. 3 the one who wears the fine clothing
IDIOMATICALLY
a. 2 Tim 2.9 for which I am suffering and wearing fetters
ἐν ᾧ κακοπαθῶ μέχρι δεσμῶν [MECHRI]

WEAR AWAY
1. *incline:* κλίνω KLINŌ
Lk 9.12 Now the day began to wear away

WEAR OUT
1. *strike under the eye, wear out:* ὑπωπιάζω HYPŌPIAZŌ
Lk 18. 5 " 'she will wear me out by her . . coming

WEARIED AS ONE IS
1. *work hard, grow weary:* κοπιάω (perf. part.) KOPIAŌ
Jn 4. 6 Jesus, wearied as he was with his journey

WEARING
1. *putting on:* ἔνδυσις ENDYSIS*
1 Pet 3. 3 not . . the . . wearing of fine clothing

WEARY, BE
WEARY, GROW
1. *become weary, despair:* ἐγκακέω EGKAKEŌ
Gal 6. 9 let us not grow weary in well-doing
2 Th 3.13 do not be weary in well-doing
2. *be weary, be ill:* κάμνω KAMNŌ
Heb 12. 3 so that you may not grow weary
3. *work hard, grow weary:* κοπιάω KOPIAŌ
Rev 2. 3 " 'you have not grown weary

WEATHER, FAIR
1. *fair weather:* εὐδία EUDIA*
Mt 16. 2 "you say, 'It will be fair weather‡

WEAVE
1. *create, weave:* ὑφαίνω HYPHAINŌ
Lk [12.27 the lilies; *they neither spin nor weave*‡

WEDDING
1. *wedding, wedding celebration:* γάμος GAMOS
[a]gen.
Mt 22. 8 "he said to his servants, 'The w. is ready
22.11 [a]"a man who had no wedding garment
22.12 [a]" 'how did you . . without a w. garment?

WEDDING GUEST
1. *son of the bridal chamber:* υἱὸς τοῦ νυμφῶνος NYMPHŌN [C.5]
Mt 9.15 "Can the wedding guests mourn?
Mk 2.19 "Can the wedding guests fast?
Lk 5.34 "Can you make wedding guests fast?

WEDDING HALL
1. *bridal chamber:* νυμφών NYMPHŌN
Mt 22.10 "wedding hall was filled with guests

WEED
1. *darnel:* ζιζάνιον ZIZANION*
Mt 13.25 "his enemy came and sowed weeds
13.26 "then the weeds appeared also
13.27 " 'How then has it weeds?
13.29 " 'lest in gathering the weeds you root up
13.30 " 'Gather the weeds first and bind them
13.36 "Explain to us the parable of the weeds
13.38 "the weeds are the sons of the evil one
13.40 "as the weeds are gathered and burned

WEEK
1. *Sabbath, week* (Heb.): σάββατον SABBATON
Mt 28. 1 the dawn of the first day of the week
Mk 16. 2 very early on the first day of the week
16. 9 early on the first day of the week[k]‡
Lk 18.12 " 'I fast twice a week, I give tithes
24. 1 on the first day of the week, at . . dawn
Jn 20. 1 Now on the first day of the week
20.19 the evening of . . the first day of the week
Acts 17. 2 for three weeks[p] he argued with them†
20. 7 On the first day of the week
1 Cor 16. 2 On the first day of every week

WEEP
1. *shed tears:* δακρύω DAKRYŌ*
Jn 11.35 Jesus wept
2. *weep, cry:* κλαίω KLAIŌ
Mt 2.18 "Rachel weeping for her children
26.75 And he went out and wept bitterly
Mk 5.38 people weeping and wailing loudly
5.39 "Why do you make a tumult and weep?
14.72 And he broke down and wept
16.10 She . . told . . , as they mourned and wept[k]‡
Lk 6.21 "Blessed are you that weep now
6.25 "Woe . . , for you shall mourn and weep
7.13 he . . said to her, "Do not weep
7.32 " 'we wailed, and you did not weep
7.38 weeping, she began to wet his feet
8.52 all were weeping and bewailing her; but he said, "Do not weep
19.41 when he . . saw the city he wept over it
22.62 And he went out and wept bitterly
23.28 "do not weep for me, but weep for yourselves and for your children
Jn 11.31 that she was going to the tomb to w.
11.33 When Jesus saw her weeping, and the Jews . . also weeping
16.20 "I say to you, you will w. and lament
20.11 Mary stood weeping outside the tomb, and as she wept she stooped
20.13 "Woman, why are you weeping?
20.15 "Woman, why are you weeping?
Acts 9.39 widows stood beside him weeping
21.13 "What are you doing, weeping?
Rom 12.15 Rejoice with those who rejoice, weep with those who weep
Jas 4. 9 Be wretched and mourn and weep
5. 1 Come now, you rich, weep and howl
Rev 5. 4 I wept much that no one was . . worthy
5. 5 "Weep not; lo, the Lion of . . Judah
18. 9 kings of the earth . . will weep . . over her
18.11 merchants of the earth weep and mourn
18.15 merchants . . , weeping and mourning aloud
18.19 as they wept and mourned, crying out
3. *weeping, crying:* κλαυθμός KLAUTHMOS [A.6.a.3]
[a]+εἰμί [b]+γίνομαι
Mt 8.12 [a]"there men will w. and gnash their teeth
Also **13.**42, 50; **22.**13; **24.**51; **25.**30
Lk 13.28 [a]"There you will w. and gnash your teeth
Acts 20.37 [b]they all wept and embraced Paul

WEIGH
1. *differentiate, decide:* διακρίνω DIAKRINŌ
1 Cor 14.29 let the others weigh what is said

WEIGH ANCHOR
1. *lift, carry away:* αἴρω AIRŌ
Acts 27.13 weighed anchor and sailed along Crete

WEIGH DOWN
1. *weigh down:* βαρέω BAREŌ
Lk 21.34 "lest your hearts be weighed down

WEIGHT
1. *weight:* βάρος BAROS
2 Cor 4.17 preparing . . an eternal weight of glory
2. *weight:* ὄγκος OGKOS*
Heb 12. 1 let us also lay aside every weight
CONTEXTUALLY
Jn 19.39 myrrh and aloes about a hundred pounds' w.

WEIGHTIER
1. *heavy, severe:* βαρύς (comp.) BARYS
Mt 23.23 "the weightier matters of the law

WEIGHTY
1. *heavy, severe:* βαρύς BARYS
2 Cor 10.10 "His letters are weighty and strong

WELCOME
WELCOME, GIVE
1. *receive favorably:* ἀποδέχομαι APODECHOMAI
Lk 8.40 Jesus returned, the crowd welcomed him
9.11 he welcomed them and spoke
Acts 28.30 he . . welcomed all who came to him
2. *greet:* ἀσπάζομαι ASPAZOMAI
Acts 25.13 arrived at Caesarea to w. Festus
3. *receive, accept:* δέχομαι DECHOMAI
Jn 4.45 the Galileans welcomed him
Heb 11.31 she had given friendly w. to the spies
4. *take in:* εἰσδέχομαι EISDECHOMAI*
2 Cor 6.17 "then I will welcome you
5. *entrance:* εἴσοδος EISODOS
1 Th 1. 9 what a welcome we had among you
6. *receive, recognize:* ἐπιδέχομαι EPIDECHOMAI
3 Jn .10 he refuses himself to w. the brethren
7. *admit, receive:* παραδέχομαι PARADECHOMAI
Acts 15. 4 they were welcomed by the church
8. *receive in addition:* προσλαμβάνω (mid.) PROSLAMBANŌ
Acts 28. 2 natives . . kindled a fire and welcomed us
Rom 14. 1 welcome him, but not for disputes
14. 3 for God has welcomed him
15. 7 Welcome one another, therefore, as Christ has welcomed you
9. *bring together:* συνάγω SYNAGŌ
Mt 25.35 " 'I was a stranger and you welcomed me
25.38 " 'when did we see thee a stranger and w.?
25.43 " 'I was a stranger and you did not w. me

WELFARE
CONTEXTUALLY
Phil 2.20 who will be genuinely anxious for your w.

WELL (*See also* AS WELL AS; ATTESTED, BE WELL; ATTESTED, WELL; KNOWN, WELL; PLEASED, BE WELL; SPEAK WELL OF; VERSED, WELL)
1. *precisely:* ἀκριβῶς AKRIBŌS
1 Th 5. 2 you . . know w. that the day of the Lord
2. *better:* βελτίων (neut.) BELTIŌN*
2 Tim 1.18 you w. know . . the service he rendered
3. *well, well done:* εὖ EU
Acts 15.29 "you will do well. Farewell
Eph 6. 3 "that it may be well with you
4. *healthy, sound:* ὑγιής HYGIĒS
Jn 5.14 "See, you are well! Sin no more
7.23 "I made a man's whole body well
Acts 4.10 "this man is standing before you w.
5. *good, beautiful:* καλός (pred.) KALOS
[a]A.3.b.1
Mt 17. 4 "Lord, it is well that we are here
Mk 9. 5 "Master,[f] it is well that we are here

Lk 9.33 "Master, it is well that we are here
1 Cor 7. 1 It is well . . not to touch a woman
7. 8 it is well for them to remain single
7.26 it is well for a person to remain
Heb 13. 9 it is well that the heart be strengthened
1 Tim 3. 7 [a]he must be w. thought of by outsiders

6. *well, rightly:* καλῶς KALŌS
[a]comp. *very well*
Mt 15. 7 "Well did Isaiah prophesy of you
Mk 7. 6 "Well did Isaiah prophesy of you
7.37 "He has done all things well
12.28 seeing that he answered them well
Lk 6.26 "Woe to you, when all speak well of you
6.48 "because it had been well built[w]‡
20.39 "Teacher, you have spoken well
Acts 25.10 [a]"done no wrong, as you know very well
1 Cor 7.37 to keep her as his betrothed,[z] he will do w.
7.38 he who marries his betrothed[z] does w.
14.17 For you may give thanks well enough
Gal 5. 7 You were running well
1 Tim 3. 4 must manage his own household well
3.12 let them manage their children . . well
3.13 those who serve well as deacons gain
5.17 Let the elders who rule well
Jas 2. 8 If you . . fulfil the royal law . . you do well
2.19 You believe that God is one; you do w.
2 Pet 1.19 You will do well to pay attention
3 Jn . 6 You will do well to send them

7. *running water, spring:* πηγή PĒGĒ
Jn 4. 6 Jacob's well was there, and so Jesus . . sat down beside the well

8. *artificial well, shaft:* φρέαρ PHREAR
Lk 14. 5 "an ox that has fallen into a well
Jn 4.11 The woman said . . "Sir, . . the well is deep
4.12 "our father Jacob, who gave us the well

9. *therefore:* τοίνυν TOINYN
1 Cor 9.26 Well, I do not run aimlessly

CONTEXTUALLY
Lk **13.9**
Heb **11.39**

WELL, BE

1. *be in good health:* ὑγιαίνω HYGIAINŌ
Lk 5.31 "Those who are well have no need
7.10 they found the slave well

2. *be strong, prevail:* ἰσχύω ISCHYŌ
Mt 9.12 "Those who are well have no need
Mk 2.17 "Those who are well have no need

3. *save, keep from harm:* σῴζω (pass.) SŌZŌ
Lk 8.50 "only believe, and she shall be well

WELL, BE S. AS

1. *put to, add, continue:* προστίθημι (pass.+dat.) PROSTITHĒMI
Mt 6.33 "all these things shall be yours as well
Lk 12.31 "these things shall be yours as well

WELL DONE

1. *well, well done:* εὖ EU
[a]εὖ γε
Mt 25.21 " 'Well done, good and faithful servant
25.23 " 'Well done, good and faithful servant
Lk 19.17 [a]" 'Well done, good servant!

WELL, MAKE

1. *save, preserve:* διασῴζω DIASŌZŌ
Mt 14.36 as many as touched it were made well

2. *save, keep from harm:* σῴζω SŌZŌ
Mt 9.21 "If I only touch . . , I shall be made well
9.22 "your faith has made you well." And instantly the woman was made well
Mk 5.23 "Come . . , so that she may be made well
5.28 "If I touch . . , I shall be made well
5.34 "your faith has made you well
6.56 as many as touched it were made w.
10.52 "Go . . ; your faith has made you well
Lk 8.48 "your faith has made you well; go
17.19 "go your way; your faith has made you w.
18.42 "your faith has made you well
Acts 14. 9 he had faith to be made well

WELL PLEASED, BE

1. *be well pleased:* εὐδοκέω EUDOKEŌ
Mt 3.17 "Son,[h] with whom I am well pleased
12.18 "with whom my soul is well pleased
17. 5 "Son,[w] with whom I am well pleased
Mk 1.11 "Son;[d] with thee I am well pleased
Lk 3.22 "Son;[j] with thee I am well pleased[k]‡
2 Pet 1.17 "Son,[d] with whom I am well pleased

WELL UP

1. *spring up:* ἅλλομαι HALLOMAI
Jn 4.14 "water welling up to eternal life

WELL WITH ONE, GO
WELL WITH ONE, IT IS

1. *help on the way, gain:* εὐοδόω (pass.) EUODOŌ
3 Jn . 2 I pray that all may go well with you
. 2 I know that it is well with your soul

WELL-DOING

1. *good work:* ἔργον ἀγαθόν AGATHOS; ERGON [A.1.f]
Rom 2. 7 by patience in well-doing seek for glory

2. *do good:* καλοποιέω (part.) KALOPOIEŌ*
2 Th 3.13 do not be weary in well-doing

3. *doing what is good:* τὸ καλὸν ποιῶν KALOS; POIEŌ [B.2.a.2]
Gal 6. 9 let us not grow weary in well-doing

WELL-PLEASING

1. *satisfaction, goodwill:* εὐδοκία (pred.) EUDOKIA
Mt [11.26 *"it was well-pleasing before thee*†
Lk [10.21 *"it was well-pleasing before thee*†

WEST

1. *setting, west:* δύσις DYSIS*
Mk [16.[end] *Jesus himself sent out . . from east to west*‡

2. *setting:* δυσμή (pl.) DYSMĒ*
Mt 8.11 "many will come from east and west
24.27 "lightning . . shines as far as the west
Lk 12.54 "When you see a cloud rising in the west
13.29 "men will come from east and west
Rev 21.13 on the west three gates

WET

1. *wet, rain:* βρέχω BRECHŌ
Lk 7.38 began to wet his feet with her tears
7.44 "she has wet my feet with her tears

WHALE

1. (any) *sea monster:* κῆτος KĒTOS*
Mt 12.40 "three nights in the belly of the whale

WHAT (*See also* LARGE, WHAT)

1. *but:* ἀλλά ALLA
2 Cor **7.11**[6]

2. *or, than:* ἤ Ē
1 Cor **14.36**

3. *that:* ἐκεῖνος (neut. sg.) EKEINOS
Mk 7.20 "out of a man is what defiles a man

4. *what, such as:* οἷος HOIOS
2 Cor 10.11 what we say by letter when absent
12.20 I may . . find you not what I wish, and . . you may find me not what you wish
2 Tim 3.11 sufferings, what befell me at Antioch, . . at Lystra, what persecutions I endured

5. *of what sort:* ὁποῖος HOPOIOS
Gal 2. 6 (what they were makes no difference
1 Th 1. 9 what a welcome we had among you

6. *who, which, what:* ὅς HOS
Mt **6.8**; **10.27**[2]; **11.4**; **12.2**; **13.**12, 17[2]; **15.5**; **19.6**; **20.15**; **25.**29; **26.**13
Mk **1.44**; **2.24**; **4.25**; **5.33**; **7.11**; **9.9**; **10.9**; **11.23**; **13.37**; **14.**8, 9
Lk **6.**2, 3, 46; **7.22**; **8.18**; **9.**33, 36; **10.**23, 24[2]; **12.**3, 12; **14.22**; **17.**10; **19.**21, 22[2], 26, 60
Jn **3.**11[2], 32; **4.22**[2]; **8.**26, 38[2]; **10.**[29‡; **11.**45, 46; **12.50**; **13.**7, 27, 29; **15.**14; **18.**21; **19.**22
Acts **3.**6, 18; **4.20**; **8.**24, 30; **10.15**; **11.9**; **14.11**; **17.23**; **21.**23, 24; **22.15**[2]; **24.**13; **26.22**; **28.22**
Rom **4.21**; **7.**15, 16, 20; **8.**24, 25; **11.7**; **14.22**; **15.18**
1 Cor **2.9**[2]; **4.6**; **10.**15, 20; **11.23**; **14.37**; **15.**3, 10, 36, 37
2 Cor **1.13**; **2.10**; **5.10**; **11.**12, 17
Gal **1.20**

Phil **3.16**; **4.9**
1 Tim **1.7**
2 Tim **2.2**, 7; **3.14**
Tit **1.11**; **2.1**
Heb **5.8**
1 Jn **2.24**², 25
2 Jn .8
3 Jn .10
Rev **1.1**², 11, 19³; **2.10**, 25; **3.11**; **4.1**; **10.4**; **22.6**
7. *as great as, how great:* ὅσος (neut. pl.) HOSOS
Mk 10.21 "go, sell what you have
Lk 4.23 " 'what we have heard you did . ., do here
9.10 apostles told him what they had done
Acts 4.23 reported what the chief priests . . had said
15.12 they related what signs . . God had done
1 Cor 2. 9 "what God has prepared for those
8. *anyone who, whoever:* ὅστις (neut.) HOSTIS
Jn 8.25 "w. I have told you from the beginning'†
Acts 9. 6 "you will be told what you are to do
9. *this:* οὗτος HOUTOS [B.3.b.4]
Rom **7.19**
1 Cor **1.12**
2 Cor **13.9**
10. *as, just as:* καθώς KATHŌS [A.4.d]
Mk 11. 6 they told them what Jesus had said
11. *what sort? what:* ποῖος POIOS
Mt 21.23 "By what authority are you doing these?
21.24 "then I also will tell you by w. authority
21.27 "Neither will I tell you by w. authority
22.42 "What do you think of the Christ?
24.43 "w. part of the night the thief was coming
Mk 11.28 "By what authority are you doing these?
11.29 "by what authority I do these things
11.33 "by what authority I do these things
Lk 6.32 "what credit is that to you?
6.33 "what credit is that to you?
6.34 "what credit is that to you?
12.39 "at what hour the thief was coming
20. 2 "by what authority you do these things
20. 8 "by what authority I do these things
24.19 And he said to them, "What things?
Jn 12.33 to show by what death he was to die
18.32 to show by what death he was to die
21.19 (by what death he was to glorify God
Acts 4. 7 "By what power . . did you do this?
7.49 " 'What house will you build for me?
23.34 he asked to what province he belonged
Rom 3.27 It is excluded. On what principle?
Jas 4.14 What is your life?
1 Pet 2.20 For what credit is it, if . . you do wrong?
Rev 3. 3 at what hour I will come upon you
12. *how:* πῶς PŌS I
Mk 5.16 those who had seen it told w. . . happened
Rev 3. 3 " 'Remember . . what you received
13. *how many, how much:* πόσος POSOS
2 Cor 7.11 see what earnestness this godly grief
14. *of what sort:* ποταπός POTAPOS
1 Jn 3. 1 See what love the Father has given us
15. *who? what?:* τίς TIS I
Mt **5.46**, 47; **6.3**, 25³, 31³; **7.9**; **8.29**; **9.13**; **10.19**²; **11.7**, [8†, [9†‡, 16; **12.3**, 7, 11; **16.26**²; **17.25**; **18.12**; **19.16**, 20, 27; **20.21**, 22, 32; **21.16**, 28, 40; **22.17**, 42; **24.3**; **26.15**, 62, 66, 70; **27.4**, 22, 23
Mk **1.24**, 27; **2.25**; **4.24**, 30; **5.7**, 9, 14; **6.2**, 24; **8.36**, 37; **9.6**, 10, 16, 33; **10.3**, 17, 36, 38, 51; **11.5**; **12.9**; **13.4**, 11; **14.36**², 40, 60, 64, 68; **15.12**, 14, 24
Lk **1.62**, 66; **3.10**, 12, 14; **4.34**, 36 ; **6.11**, 47; **7.24**, 25, 26, 31²; **8.9**, 28, 30; **9.25**; **10.25**, 26; **11.11**; **12.11**², 17, 22², 29²; **13.18**², 20; **14.31**; **15.4**, 8, 26; **16.2**, 3, 4; **18.6**, 18, 36, 41; **19.15**; **20.13**, 15, 17; **21.7**; **22.71**; **23.22**, 31, 34‡; **24.17**
Jn **1.21**, 22, 38; **2.4**, 18, 25; **4.27**; **6.6**, 9, 28, 30²; **7.36**, 51; **8.5**‡; **9.26**; **10.6**; **11.47**, 56; **12.27**, 49²; **13.12**; **15.15**; **16.17**, 18²; **18.21**, 29, 35, 38; **21.22**, 23
Acts **2.12**, 37; **4.9**, 16; **5.24**, 35; **7.40**, 49; **8.36**; **10.4**, 17, 21; **12.18**; **13.25**; **16.30**; **17.18**, 19, 20; **19.3**, 35; **21.13**, 22, 33; **22.10**, 26; **23.19**; **24.20**
Rom **3.1**², 3, 5, 9; **4.1**, 3; **6.1**, 15, 21; **7.7**; **8.27**, 31; **9.14**, 30, **10.8**; **11.2**, 4, 7, 15; **12.2**
1 Cor **3.5**²; **4.7**, 21; **5.12**; **9.18**; **10.19**; **11.22**; **14.15**, 16, 26; **15.29**, 32
2 Cor **6.14**², 15², 16; **12.13**
Gal **4.30**
Eph **1.18**², 19; **3.9**, 18; **4.9**; **5.10**, 17; **6.21**
Phil **1.18**
1 Th **2.19**; **3.9**; **4.2**
Heb **1.5**, 13; **2.6**; **7.11**; **11.32**; **12.7**; **13.6**
Jas **2.14**, 16
1 Pet **4.17**
1 Jn **3.2**
Rev **2.7**, 11, 17, 29; **3.6**, 13, 22; **18.18**
16. *anyone, any:* τὶς TIS II
[a]εἴ τις
Mt **18.28**[a]
Jn **5.19**
17. *such as this:* τοιοῦτος TOIOUTOS
Mk 6. 2 "What mighty works are wrought!

WHAT ABOUT
1. *who? what?:* τίς TIS I
Jn **21.21**

WHAT BECOMES OF
1. *where, how:* ποῦ POU I
Rom 3.27 Then what becomes of our boasting?

WHAT CAUSES
WHAT, FROM
1. *whence, from what:* πόθεν POTHEN
Jas 4. 1 What causes wars, and what causes fightings among you?
Rev 2. 5 " 'Remember . . from w. you have fallen

WHAT HAS BECOME OF
1. *where, how:* ποῦ POU I
Gal 4.15 What has become of the satisfaction?

WHAT IS IT
1. *say, speak:* εἶπον (imper.) EIPON
Lk 7.40 he answered, "What is it, Teacher?

WHAT KIND OF
WHAT MANNER OF
1. *what sort? what:* ποῖος POIOS
Lk [9.55 *"You do not know what manner of spirit*‡
1 Cor 15.35 "With what kind of body do they come?

WHAT KIND OF MAN
1. *what, such as:* οἷος HOIOS
1 Th 1. 5 You know what kind of men we proved

WHAT, LIKE
1. *of what sort:* ὁποῖος HOPOIOS
Jas 1.24 at once forgets what he was like

WHAT PERSON
1. *who? what?:* τίς TIS I
1 Cor **2.11**
1 Pet **1.11**

WHAT SORT OF
1. *of what sort:* ὁποῖος HOPOIOS
1 Cor 3.13 fire will test what sort of work
2. *of what sort:* ποταπός POTAPOS
Mt 8.27 "What sort of man is this?
Lk 1.29 what sort of greeting this might be
7.39 "he would have known . . w. sort of woman
2 Pet 3.11 what sort of persons ought you to be!

WHAT, WITH
1. *how:* πῶς PŌS I
Mk 4.30 "What w. can we compare the kingdom?

WHAT WONDERFUL
1. *of what sort:* ποταπός POTAPOS
Mk 13. 1 "Look, Teacher, what wonderful stones and what wonderful buildings!

WHATEVER
1. *of whatever kind:* οἱοσδηποτοῦν HOIOSDĒPOTOUN*
Jn [5. 4 *was healed of whatever disease he had*‡

2. *who, which, what:* ὅς HOS
[a]+ἄν [b]+ἐάν [c]πᾶν ὅ
Mt **10.11**[a]; **14.7**[b]; **16.19**[2b]; **20.4**[b]
Mk **6.22**[b]; **10.35**[b]; **13.11**[b]
Lk **9.4**[a]; **10.5**[a]
Jn **5.**[4‡, 19[a]; **15.7**[b]
Rom **14.23**[c]; **16.2**[a]
1 Cor **7.24**
2 Cor **11.21**[a]
Gal **6.7**[b]
Phil **4.11**
Col **3.23**[b]
2 Pet **2.19**
1 Jn **3.22**[b]; **5.15**[b]
Also variant to: Mk **6.23**[b]

3. *as great as, how great:* ὅσος (neut. pl.) HOSOS
[a]πάντα ὅσα ἐάν [b]ὅσα ἐάν [c]πάντα ὅσα ἄν
[d]πάντα ὅσα [e]ὅσα ἄν
Mt 7.12 [a]"whatever you wish that men would do
17.12 "did to him whatever they pleased
18.18 [b]"w. you bind on earth shall be bound
18.18 [b]"w. you loose on earth shall be loosed
21.22 [c]"w. you ask in prayer, you will receive
23. 3 [a]"observe whatever they tell you
Mk 3.28 [b]"whatever blasphemies they utter
9.13 "they did to him w. they pleased
11.24 [d]"whatever you ask in prayer, believe
Lk 11. 8 "he will . . give him whatever he needs
12. 3 "whatever you have said in the dark[0]
Jn 11.22 [e]"I know that w. you ask from God
16.13 "whatever he hears he will speak
Acts 3.22 [c]" 'listen to him in w. he tells you
4.28 "w. thy hand . . had predestined
Rom 3.19 whatever the law says it speaks to those
15. 4 whatever was written in former days
Phil 4. 8 Finally, brethren, whatever is true, whatever is honorable, whatever is just, whatever is pure, whatever is lovely, whatever is gracious, if there is any excellence, if there is anything worthy of praise, think about these things
Jude .10 revile whatever they do not understand

4. *anyone who, whoever:* ὅστις (neut.) HOSTIS
[a]ὅ τι ἐάν [b]ὅ τι ἄν [c]πᾶν ὅ τι ἐάν
Mk 6.23 [a]"W. you ask me, I will give you
Var. HOS
Lk 10.35 [b]" 'w. more you spend, I will repay
Jn 2. 5 [b]"Do whatever he tells you
14.13 [b]"W. you ask in my name, I will do it
15.16 [b]"whatever you ask the Father in my name
Phil 3. 7 w. gain I had, I counted as loss
Col 3.17 [c]whatever you do, in word or deed

5. *all, every, whole:* πᾶς (+subst. part. neut.) PAS
Mt 15.17 "whatever goes into the mouth passes
Mk 7.18 "whatever goes into a man from outside
Rom 14.23 whatever does not proceed from faith
1 Cor 10.25 Eat whatever is sold in the meat market
10.27 eat whatever is set before you
1 Jn 5. 4 w. is born of God overcomes the world

6. *anyone, any:* τὶς TIS II
[a]+ἐάν
1 Cor **10.31**
Eph **6.8**[a]

CONTEXTUALLY
Acts 28.10 they put on board whatever we needed

WHEAT

1. *grain:* σῖτος SITOS
Mt 3.12 "he will . . gather his w. into the granary
13.25 "enemy . . sowed weeds among the wheat
13.29 " 'No; lest . . you root up the wheat
13.30 " 'but gather the wheat into my barn
Lk 3.17 "to gather the wheat into his granary
16. 7 " 'A hundred measures of wheat
22.31 "that he might sift you[k] like wheat
Jn 12.24 "unless a grain of w. falls into the earth
Acts 27.38 throwing out the wheat into the sea
1 Cor 15.37 of wheat or of some other grain
Rev 6. 6 "A quart of wheat for a denarius[a]
18.13 fine flour and wheat, cattle and sheep

WHEEL

1. *wheel:* τροχός TROCHOS
Jas [3. 6 setting on fire the *wheel of birth*†

WHEN
WHEN ONCE

1. *if:* ἐάν EAN
Jn 12.32 "I, when I am lifted up from the earth
14. 3 "when I go and prepare a place for you
1 Cor 16.10 When Timothy comes, . . put him at ease
Heb 3. 7 "Today, when you hear his voice
3.15 "Today, when you hear his voice
4. 7 "Today, when you hear his voice
1 Jn 2.28 abide in him, so that when he appears
3. 2 we know that when he appears

2. *if, since:* εἰ EI
Heb 7.15 more evident when another priest arises

3. *in, at, by:* ἐν (+dat.) EN [B.1.a.2]
Mt **27.12**
Lk **1.78**††[‡]; **3.21**; **8.40**; **9.36**, 51; **10.35**; **14.1**; **19.15**; **23.31**[2], **24.30**
Acts **2.1**; **7.45**; **8.6**
Rom **3.4**
Gal **4.18**
2 Th **1.7**

4. *when, as soon as:* ἐπάν EPAN*
Mt 2. 8 "w. you have found him bring me word
Lk 11.22 "when one stronger than he assails him
11.34 "w. it is not sound, . . full of darkness

5. *since:* ἐπειδή EPEIDĒ
1 Cor 14.16 when he does not know what

6. *on, at:* ἐπί (+dat.) EPI
[a]+gen.
Mk **2.26**[a]
2 Cor **3.14**

7. *at the time when:* ἡνίκα HĒNIKA
2 Cor 3.16 when a man turns . . the veil is removed

8. *until:* ἕως οὗ HEŌS [B.3.b.8]
Acts 21.26 notice w. the days . . would be fulfilled

9. *in order that:* ἵνα HINA
Jn 16. 2 "hour is coming when whoever kills you
16.32 "The hour . . when you will be scattered

10. *who, which, what:* ὅς HOS [B.1.a.1]
[a]+dat. [b]+ἐν [c]ἀφ' οὗ ἄν
[d]ἄχρι ἧς [e]ἕως οὗ/ἧς [f]ὃ ἐάν
Mt **24.50**[a]
Lk **1.78**[b]††[‡]; **12.46**[a]; **13.25**[c]; **17.29**[a], 30[a]; **21.6**[b]; **23.29**[b]
Jn **4.52**[b], 53[b]; **5.28**[b]; **9.14**[b]
Acts **1.2**[d], 22[e]; **21.26**[e]
Rom **8.15**[b]
Heb **10.32**[b]
1 Pet **3.16**[b]
3 Jn .5[f]

11. *as, so:* ὡς HŌS
Lk **1.23**, 41, 44; **2.15**, 39; **4.25**; **5.4**; **6.4**; **11.1**; **19.5**, 29, 41; **22.66**
Jn **2.9**, 23; **4.1**, 40, 45; **6.12**, 16; **11.6**, 20, 29, 32, 33; **18.6**; **19.33**; **21.9**
Acts **5.24**; **7.23**; **9.23**; **10.7**, 25; **13.29**; **14.5**; **16.10**, 15; **17.13**; **18.5**; **19.9**; **20.14**, 18; **21.1**, 12, 27; **22.11**, 25; **27.1**, 27; **28.4**
1 Cor **11.34**
2 Tim **1.3**

12. *when, whenever:* ὅταν HOTAN
Mt 5.11 "Blessed are you when men revile you
6. 2 "when you give alms, sound no trumpet
6. 5 "w. you pray, . . not be like the hypocrites
6. 6 "when you pray, go into your room
6.16 "when you fast, do not look dismal
9.15 "when the bridegroom is taken away
10.19 "W. they deliver you up, do not be anxious
10.23 "When they persecute you in one town
12.43 "When the unclean spirit has gone out
13.32 "but when it has grown it is the greatest

Mt 15. 2 "do not wash their hands when they eat
19.28 "when the Son of man shall sit
21.40 "When . . the owner of the vineyard comes
23.15 "when he becomes a proselyte
24.15 "when you see the desolating sacrilege
24.33 "when you see all these things
25.31 "When the Son of man comes in his glory
26.29 "that day when I drink it new with you
Mk 2.20 "when the bridegroom is taken away
4.15 "w. they hear, Satan immediately comes
4.16 "when they hear the word, . . receive it
4.29 "w. the grain is ripe, . . he puts in the sickle
4.31 "when sown upon the ground
4.32 "when it is sown it grows up
8.38 "w. he comes in the glory of his Father
11.19 when evening came they[u] went out
12.25 "For when they rise from the dead
13. 4 "Tell us, when will this be
13. 7 "w. you hear of wars and rumors of wars
13.11 "w. they bring you to trial and deliver you
13.14 "when you see the desolating sacrilege
13.29 "when you see these things taking place
14.25 "until that day when I drink it new
Lk 5.35 "when the bridegroom is taken away
6.22 "Blessed are you w. men hate you, and w. they exclude you and revile you
6.26 "Woe to you, when all speak well of you
8.13 "who, when they hear the word, receive it
9.26 "ashamed when he comes in his glory
11. 2 "When you pray, say: Father, hallowed
11.21 "When a strong man, fully armed
11.24 "When the unclean spirit has gone
11.34 "when your eye is sound
11.36 "as when a lamp . . gives you light
12.11 "w. they bring you before the synagogues
12.54 "When you see a cloud rising in the west
12.55 "w. you see the south wind blowing
13.28 "when you see Abraham and Isaac
14. 8 "When you are invited by any one
14.10 "when you are invited, go and sit . . so that w. your host comes he may say
14.12 "When you give a dinner or a banquet
14.13 "when you give a feast, invite the poor
16. 4 " 'when I am put out of the stewardship
16. 9 "when it fails they may receive you
17.10 "w. you have done all that is commanded
21. 7 "sign w. this is about to take place
21. 9 "when you hear of wars and tumults
21.20 "when you see Jerusalem surrounded
21.31 "w. you see these things taking place
23.42 "when you come into[p] your kingdom
Jn 2.10 "when men have drunk freely
4.25 "when he comes, he will show us all
5. 7 "into the pool when the water is troubled
7.27 "w. the Christ appears, no one will know
7.31 "W. the Christ appears, will he do more?
8.28 "W. you have lifted up the Son of man
8.44 "W. he lies, he speaks according to his own
10. 4 "When he has brought out all his own
13.19 "that when it does take place
14.29 "so that when it does take place
15.26 "But when the Counselor comes
16. 4 "that when their hour comes
16.13 "When the Spirit of truth comes
16.21 "W. a woman is in travail she has sorrow . . , but when she is delivered of the child
21.18 "w. you are old, you will stretch out
Acts 23.35 "I will hear you w. your accusers arrive
24.22 "When Lysias the tribune comes down
Rom 2.14 When Gentiles who have not the law
11.27 "when I take away their sins
1 Cor 3. 4 when one says, "I belong to Paul
13.10 when the perfect comes
14.26 When you come together
15.24 when he delivers the kingdom to God
15.27 w. it says, "All things are . . in subjection
15.28 When all things are subjected to him
1 Cor 15.54 W. the perishable puts on . . imperishable
16. 2 need not be made when I come
16. 3 when I arrive, I will send those
16.12 He will come when he has opportunity
2 Cor 10. 6 when your obedience is complete
12.10 when I am weak, then I am strong
13. 9 For we are glad when we are weak
Col 3. 4 When Christ who is our life appears
4.16 when this letter has been read among you
1 Th 5. 3 When people say, "There is peace
2 Th 1.10 w. he comes on that day to be glorified
1 Tim 5.11 when they grow wanton against Christ
Tit 3.12 When I send Artemas or Tychicus
Heb 1. 6 w. he brings the first-born into the world
Jas 1. 2 Count it all joy . . when you meet . . trials
1 Jn 5. 2 when we love God and obey
Rev 8. 1 W. the Lamb opened the seventh seal
9. 5 like . . a scorpion, when it stings a man
11. 7 when they have finished their testimony
12. 4 her child when she brought it forth
17.10 "when he comes he must remain . . a little
18. 9 when they see the smoke of her burning
20. 7 when the thousand years are ended

13. *when:* ὅτε HOTE

Mt 7.28 when Jesus finished these sayings
9.25 when the crowd had been put outside
11. 1 when Jesus had finished instructing
12. 3 "what David did, when he was hungry
13.26 "w. the plants came up and bore grain
13.48 "when it was full, men drew it ashore
13.53 when Jesus had finished these parables
19. 1 when Jesus had finished these sayings
21. 1 when they drew near to Jerusalem
21.34 "When the season of fruit drew near
26. 1 When Jesus had finished all these sayings
27.31 when they had mocked him
Mk 2.25 "what David did, when he was in need
4. 6 "when the sun rose it was scorched
4.10 w. he was alone, those who were about him
6.21 w. Herod on his birthday gave a banquet
7.17 when he had entered the house
8.19 "When I broke the five loaves
11. 1 when they drew near to Jerusalem
14.12 when they sacrificed the passover lamb
15.20 when they had mocked him
15.41 who, when he was in Galilee, followed
Lk 2.22 w. the time came for their purification
2.42 when he was twelve years old
4.25 "when the heaven was shut up three years
6. 3 "what David did when he was hungry
6.13 w. it was day, he called his disciples
15.30 " 'when this son of yours came
17.22 "days are coming w. you will desire to see
22.14 when the hour came, he sat at table
22.35 "When I sent you out with no purse
23.33 w. they came to the place . . called The Skull
Jn 1.19 when the Jews sent priests and Levites
2.22 When . . he was raised from the dead
4.21 "hour . . when neither on this mountain
4.23 "when the true worshipers will worship
4.45 So when he came to Galilee
5.25 "when the dead will hear the voice
6.24 when . . people saw that Jesus was not there
9. 4 "night comes, when no one can work
12.16 w. Jesus was glorified, . . they remembered
12.17 w. he called Lazarus out of the tomb
13.12 When he had washed their feet
13.31 W. he had gone out, Jesus said, "Now
16.25 "w. I shall no longer speak . . in figures
19. 6 W. . . officers saw him, they cried out
19. 8 When Pilate heard these words
19.23 When the soldiers had crucified Jesus
19.30 When Jesus had received the vinegar
20.24 Thomas . . was not with them w. Jesus came
21.15 When they had finished breakfast
21.18 "w. you were young, you girded yourself
Acts 1.13 when they had entered, they went up

Acts 8.12 w. they believed Philip as he preached
8.39 when they came up out of the water
11. 2 when Peter went up to Jerusalem
12. 6 when Herod was about to bring him out
21. 5 when our days there were ended
21.35 when he came to the steps
22.20 " 'when the blood of Stephen . . was shed
27.39 when it was day, they did not recognize
28.16 w. we came into Rome, Paul was allowed
Rom 6.20 When you were slaves of sin
13.11 nearer . . now than when we first believed
1 Cor 12. 2 You know that when you were heathen
13.11 When I was a child, I spoke like a child . . ; when . . a man, I gave up childish ways
Gal 1.15 when he who had set me apart
2.11 when Cephas came to Antioch
2.12 when they came he drew back
2.14 when I saw that they were not
4. 3 when we were children, we were slaves
4. 4 when the time had fully come
Phil 4.15 in the beginning . . , w. I left Macedonia
Col 3. 7 once . . , when you lived in them
1 Th 3. 4 when we were with you, we told you
2 Th 3.10 even when we were with you
2 Tim 4. 3 w. people will not endure sound teaching
Tit 3. 4 when the goodness . . of God . . appeared
Heb 7.10 when Melchizedek met him
1 Pet 3.20 did not obey, w. God's patience waited
Jude . 9 when the archangel Michael . . disputed
Rev 1.17 When I saw him, I fell at his feet
5. 8 when he had taken the scroll
6. 1 when the Lamb opened one of the . . seals
6. 3 When he opened the second seal
6. 5 When he opened the third seal
6. 7 When he opened the fourth seal
6. 9 When he opened the fifth seal
6.12 When he opened the sixth seal
10. 3 w. he called out, the . . thunders sounded
10. 4 when the seven thunders had sounded
10.10 I . . ate it; . . but when I had eaten it
12.13 w. the dragon saw . . he had been thrown
22. 8 when I heard and saw them, I fell down

14. *when:* πότε POTE I
Mt 24. 3 "Tell us, when will this be?
25.37 " 'Lord, when did we see thee hungry?
25.38 " 'when did we see thee a stranger?
25.39 " 'when did we see thee sick or in prison?
25.44 " 'when did we see thee hungry or thirsty?
Mk 13.14 "when you see the desolating sacrilege
13.33 "you do not know w. the time will come
13.35 "you do not know w. the master . . will come
Lk 17.20 when the kingdom of God was coming
21. 7 "Teacher, when will this be?
Jn 6.25 When they found him on the other side

15. *at some time, once:* ποτέ POTE II
Lk 14.29 "Otherwise, when he has laid a foundation

CONTEXTUALLY
1 Tim 4.14 w. the . . elders laid their hands upon you

WHENCE

1. *whence, from what:* πόθεν POTHEN
Mt 21.25 "The baptism of John, whence was it?
Lk 20. 7 they did not know whence it was
Jn 3. 8 "you do not know whence it comes
8.14 "I know whence I have come . . , but you do not know whence I come
Rev 7.13 "whence have they come?

WHENEVER

1. *whenever:* ἡνίκα ἄν HĒNIKA [A.4.e]
2 Cor 3.15 to this day whenever Moses is read
2. *whoever:* ὃς ἄν HOS [B.3.b.4]
Lk 10. 8 "W. you enter a town and they receive you
10.10 "w. you enter . . and they do not receive you
3. *whatever:* ὅστις ἐάν (neut.) HOSTIS
1 Jn 3.20 whenever our hearts condemn us
4. *when, whenever:* ὅταν HOTAN
Mk 3.11 whenever the unclean spirits beheld him
11.25 "whenever you stand praying, forgive
14. 7 "whenever you will, you can do good
Rev 4. 9 whenever the living creatures give glory

WHERE

1. *where, wherever:* ὅπου HOPOU
Mt 6.19 "earth, where moth and rust[o] consume and where thieves break in
6.20 "where neither moth nor rust[o] consumes and where thieves do not break in
6.21 "w. your treasure is, there will your heart be
13. 5 "where they had not much soil
25.24 " 'reaping where you did not sow
25.26 " 'that I reap where I have not sowed
26.57 where the scribes . . had gathered
28. 6 "Come, see the place where he[q] lay
Mk 4. 5 "rocky ground, w. it had not much soil
4.15 these are the ones . . w. the word is sown
5.40 he . . went in where the child was
6.10 "Where you enter a house, stay there
6.55 to any place where they heard he was
9.48 "where their worm does not die
Also **9.**[44‡, [46‡
13.14 "set up where it ought not to be
14.14 " 'room, where I am to eat the passover
16. 6 "see the place where they laid him
Lk 12.33 "the heavens . . , w. no thief approaches
12.34 "w. your treasure is, there will your heart
17.37 "Where the body is, there the eagles[c]
22.11 " 'room, where I am to eat the passover
Jn 1.28 Bethany . . , where John was baptizing
3. 8 "The wind[f] blows where it wills
4.20 "place where men ought to worship
4.46 where he had made the water wine
6.23 the place where they ate the bread
6.62 "Son of man ascending w. he was before
7.34 "where I am you cannot come
7.36 " 'Where I am you cannot come
7.42 "Bethlehem, the village where David was
8.21 "where I am going, you cannot come
8.22 " 'Where I am going, you cannot come
10.40 the place where John at first baptized
11.30 the place where Martha had met him
11.32 she came where Jesus was and saw him
12. 1 Jesus came to Bethany, w. Lazarus was
12.26 "where I am, there shall my servant be
13.33 " 'Where I am going you cannot come
13.36 "Where I am going you cannot follow me
14. 3 "that where I am you may be also
14. 4 "you know the way where I am going[f]
17.24 "that they . . may be with me w. I am
18. 1 valley, where there was a garden
18.20 "temple, where all Jews come together
19.20 the place where Jesus was crucified
19.41 in the place where he was crucified
20.12 where the body of Jesus had lain
20.19 doors being shut where the disciples were
21.18 "you . . walked where you would
21.18 "will . . carry you where you do not wish
Acts 17. 1 Thessalonica, w. there was a synagogue
20. 6 Troas, where we stayed for seven days
Rom 15.20 not where Christ has already been named
Heb 6.20 where Jesus has gone as a forerunner
9.16 For where a will[u] is involved
10.18 Where there is forgiveness of these
Jas 3.16 w. jealousy and selfish ambition exist
Rev 2.13 " 'you dwell, w. Satan's throne is; . . where Satan dwells
11. 8 Egypt, where their Lord was crucified
12. 6 where she has a place prepared
12.14 to the place where she is to be nourished
20.10 w. the beast and the false prophet were

2. *in which:* ἐν ᾧ/ᾗ HOS [B.2.a.1]
Mt **11.**20
Lk **19.**30
Jn **11.**6; **19.**41
Acts **7.**33; **15.**36

Rev **18.**19
3. *as, so:* ὡς HŌS
Lk **20.**37
4. *whence, where:* ὅθεν HOTHEN
Mt 25.24 " 'gathering where you did not winnow
25.26 " 'I . . gather w. I have not winnowed
Acts 14.26 where they had been commended
5. *where:* οὗ HOU
Mt 2. 9 the place where the child was
18.20 "w. two . . are gathered in my name
Lk 4.16 Nazareth, where he had been brought up
4.17 found the place where it was written
10. 1 where he himself was about to come
23.53 where no one had ever yet been laid
Acts 1.13 upper room, where they were staying
2. 2 filled all the house w. they were sitting
7.29 "w. he became the father of two sons
12.12 where many were gathered together
16.13 where we supposed there was a place
20. 8 upper chamber where we were gathered
25.10 "tribunal, where I ought to be tried
Rom 4.15 w. there is no law there is no transgression
5.20 where sin increased, grace abounded
9.26 "in the very place where it was said
2 Cor 3.17 where the Spirit of the Lord is
Col 3. 1 things that are above, w. Christ is
Heb 3. 9 "where your fathers put me to the test
Rev 17.15 "where the harlot is seated
6. *whence, from what:* πόθεν POTHEN
Mt 13.54 "Where did this man get this wisdom?
13.56 "Where then did this man get all this?
15.33 "Where are we to get bread enough?
Mk 6. 2 "Where did this man get all this?
Jn 4.11 "where do you get that living water?
7. *where, how:* ποῦ POU I
Mt 2. 2 "Where is he who has been born king?
2. 4 where the Christ was to be born
26.17 "Where will you have us prepare?
Mk 14.12 "Where will you have us go and prepare?
14.14 " 'Teacher says, Where is my guest room?
15.47 mother of Joses saw where he was laid
Lk 8.25 He said to them, "Where is your faith?
17.17 "Where are the nine?
17.37 they said to him, "Where, Lord?
22. 9 "Where will you have us prepare it?
22.11 " 'Teacher says . . W. is the guest room?
Jn 1.38 "Rabbi . . , where are you staying?
1.39 They . . saw where he was staying
7.11 The Jews were . . saying, "Where is he?
7.35 "Where does this man intend to go?
8.10 "Woman, where are they?"[r]‡
8.19 "Where is your Father?
9.12 They said to him, "Where is he?
11.34 he said, "Where have you laid him?
11.57 if any one knew where he was
12.35 "he . . does not know where he goes
13.36 "Lord, where are you going?
14. 5 "we do not know where you are going
16. 5 "none . . asks me, 'Where are you going?
20. 2 "we do not know w. they have laid him
20.13 "I do not know w. they have laid him
20.15 "tell me where you have laid him
1 Cor 1.20 Where is the wise man? Where is the scribe? Where is the debater of this age?
12.17 where would be the hearing?
12.17 where would be the sense of smell?
12.19 where would the body be?
15.55 "O death, where is thy victory? O death, where is thy sting?
Heb 11. 8 not knowing where he was to go
1 Pet 4.18 "w. will the impious and sinner appear?
2 Pet 3. 4 "Where is the promise of his coming?
1 Jn 2.11 does not know where he is going
Rev 2.13 " 'I know where you dwell
IDIOMATICALLY
a. Lk **10.**33 [KATA]

WHERE, FROM
1. *whence, from what:* πόθεν POTHEN
Lk 13.25 " 'I do not know where you come from
13.27 " 'I do not know where you come from
Jn 2. 9 did not know where it came from
7.27 "we know where this man comes from
7.27 "no one will know where he comes from
7.28 "you know where I come from?
9.29 "we do not know where he comes from
9.30 "You do not know where he comes from
19. 9 "Where are you from?

WHEREAS
1. *where, wherever:* ὅπου HOPOU
2 Pet 2.11 w. angels . . do not pronounce . . judgment

WHEREBY
1. *who, which, what:* ὅς (+ἐν) HOS [B.1.a.1]
Lk **1.**[78†

WHEREFORE
1. *whence, where:* ὅθεν HOTHEN
Acts 26.19 "W., O . . Agrippa, I was not disobedient

WHEREVER
1. *where, wherever:* ὅπου HOPOU
[a]+ἐάν [b]+ἄν
Mt 8.19 [a]"Teacher, I will follow you w. you go
24.28 [a]"W. the body is, there the eagles[z]
26.13 [a]"wherever this gospel is preached
Mk 6.56 [b]wherever he came, in villages, cities
9.18 [a]"w. it seizes him, it dashes him down
14. 9 [a]"wherever the gospel is preached
14.14 [a]"w. he enters, say to the householder
Lk 9.57 [b]"I will follow you wherever you go
Jas 3. 4 wherever the will of the pilot directs
Rev 14. 4 [b]who follow the Lamb wherever he goes
2. *as much as ever:* ὅσος ἄν HOSOS [B.3.b.4]
Lk 9. 5 "wherever they do not receive you
3. *wherever:* οὗ ἐάν HOU [A.5.a]
1 Cor 16. 6 that you may speed me on my journey, w.

WHETHER (*See also* PERHAPS, WHETHER)
WHETHER, TO SEE
1. *if:* ἐάν EAN
[a]ἐάν τε . . ἐάν τε
Rom 14. 8 [a]so then, whether we live or whether we die, we are the Lord's
2. *if, since:* εἰ EI
Mt 27.49 "let us see whether Elijah will come
Mk 3. 2 to see whether he would heal him
15.36 "let us see whether Elijah will come
15.44 asked . . whether he was already dead[j]
Lk 6. 7 to see whether he would heal
14.28 "whether he has enough to complete it
14.31 "and take counsel whether he is able
23. 6 asked whether the man was a Galilean
Jn 9.25 "Whether he is a sinner, I do not know
Acts 4.19 "Whether it is right in the sight of God
5. 8 "Tell me whether you sold the land
10.18 to ask whether Simon . . was lodging there
25.20 "whether he wished to go to Jerusalem
1 Cor 1.16 (do not know w. I baptized any one else
7.16 know w. you will save your husband?
7.16 know w. you will save your wife?
2 Cor 2. 9 that I might . . know w. you are obedient
13. 5 to see w. you are holding to your faith
1 Jn 4. 1 to see whether they are of God
3. *whether, or:* εἴτε EITE
1 Cor 3.22 whether Paul or Apollos or Cephas
10.31 So, whether you eat or drink
15.11 Whether then it was I or they
2 Cor 5. 9 So whether we are at home or away
12. 2 w. in the body or out of the body
12. 3 w. in the body or out of the body
Eph 6. 8 whether he is a slave or free
Phil 1.18 in every way, w. in pretense or in truth
1.20 honored . . , whether by life or by death
1.27 w. I come and see you or am absent
Col 1.16 w. thrones or dominions or principalities

Col 1.20 all things, w. on earth or in heaven
1 Th 5.10 so that whether we wake or sleep
1 Pet 2.13 w. it be to the emperor as supreme
4. *and not:* οὔτε OUTE
1 Th 2. 6 whether from you or from others
5. *whether:* πότερον POTERON*
Jn 7.17 "know whether the teaching is from God

WHICH
1. *what, such as:* οἷος HOIOS
Phil 1.30 same conflict w. you saw and now hear
2. *who, which, what:* ὅς HOS
Mt **1**.23; **2**.16; **12**.4; **13**.31, 44; **15**.13; **21**.42; **26**[50†; **27**.33, 60
Mk **2**.26; **4**.31; **5**.41; **7**.4, 13, 15; **10**.38, 39; **11**.2, 21; **12**.10, 42; **13**.19; **14**.32; **15**.22, 34, 46
Lk **1**.4, 73; **2**.15, 31; **3**.19; **4**.29; **5**.3, 9, 25; **6**.4, 49; **9**.31; **11**.22; **13**.14, 19, 21; **19**.20, 30; **20**.17; **21**.6, 15; **22**.7, 10; **24**.1, 17, 44
Jn **1**.38, 41, 42; **2**.22; **4**.32; **5**.36[2]; **6**.2, 14, 21, 27, 51; **7**.39; **8**.40; **9**.7; **13**.5; **14**.24; **15**.24; **17**.4, 5, 8, 11, 12, 22, 24, 26; **18**.1, 9, 11, 32; **19**.17; **20**.7, 16, 30; **21**.25
Acts **1**.4, 7, 12, 24, 25; **2**.22, 33; **3**.25; **4**.12, 31, 36; **6**.10; **7**.3, 4, 7, 17, 43, 45; **8**.6; **9**.17, 36; **10**.36, 37; **11**.11, 14; **13**.2, 39; **15**.10; **16**.21; **17**.31; **20**.24, 28, 38; **23**.28; **24**.8, 14, 15, 21; **25**.7; **26**.7, 16; **27**.8, 39
Rom **1**.2; **5**.2; **6**.17, 21; **10**.8; **16**.17
1 Cor **3**.11; **6**.18, 19; **7**.1; **10**.16[2]; **12**.23; **15**.1[2], 2, 31
2 Cor **1**.4; **9**.2; **10**.8; **12**.21; **13**.10
Gal **2**.2, 4, 10, 18; **3**.16; **6**.14†
Eph **1**.6, 8, 9, 14, 20; **2**.2, 4, 10; **3**.5, 11; **4**.1; **5**.4; **6**.16, 17, 20
Phil **2**.5
Col **1**.4, 23, 25, 27; **2**.12, 14, 22; **3**.14, 15; **4**.3, 17
1 Th **2**.13; **3**.9
2 Th **1**.4, 5; **2**.15; **3**.4
1 Tim **1**.11; **3**.[16‡; **4**.3, 6, 14; **6**.4, 12
2 Tim **1**.13; **2**.9; **4**.8
Tit **1**.2, 3; **3**.6
Phm .5
Heb **6**.10, 18; **7**.13, 19; **8**.2; **9**.2, 4, 7, 20; **10**.1, 20, 29; **11**.4, 8, 15; **12**.8, 14; **13**.9, 10
Jas **1**.12; **2**.5; **4**.5
1 Pet **1**.12[2]; **2**.7; **3**.4, 19, 20, 21; **4**.11[2]
2 Pet **1**.4; **2**.12[2]; **3**.6, 12, 13, 16
1 Jn **1**.1[3]; **2**.7[2], 8, 27; **3**.11, 24; **4**.2, 3[2]; **5**.14
Jude .15[2]
Rev **1**.1, 20; **2**.6, 7, 17; **3**.8; **4**.1, 5; **5**.6, 8[2]; **7**.9[2]; **9**.20; **10**.8; **12**.16; **13**.14[2]; **19**.12, 20; **20**.12; **21**.8
3. *as great as, how great:* ὅσος HOSOS
Acts 9.39 showing tunics . . which Dorcas made
4. *anyone who, whoever:* ὅστις HOSTIS
Mt 23.27 "tombs, w. outwardly appear beautiful
Lk 1.20 "words, w. will be fulfilled in their time
2. 4 city of David, w. is called Bethlehem
2.10 "joy which will come to all the people
8.26 country of . . Gerasenes,[a] w. is opposite
10.42 "portion, which shall not be taken away
12. 1 "leaven of the Pharisees, w. is hypocrisy
Acts 16.12 Philippi, which is the leading city
2 Cor 9.11 generosity, w. . . will produce thanksgiving
Eph 1.23 ⟨the church,⟩ which is his body
3.13 suffering for you, which is your glory
Col 3. 5 covetousness, which is idolatry
1 Tim 1. 4 genealogies which promote speculations
3.15 household of God, which is the church
Heb 9. 9 sacrifices are offered w. cannot perfect
10.11 sacrifices, w. can never take away sins
10.35 confidence, which has a great reward
12. 5 the exhortation which addresses
1 Jn 1. 2 eternal life which was with the Father
Rev 11. 8 city which is allegorically[d] called Sodom
5. *what sort? what:* ποῖος POIOS
Mt 19.18 He said to him, "Which?
22.36 "which is the great commandment?
Mk 12.28 "Which commandment is the first of all?
Jn 10.32 "for which of these do you stone me?
6. *who? what?:* τίς TIS I
Mt **6**.27; **9**.5; **21**.31; **22**.28; **23**.17, 19; **27**.21
Mk **2**.9
Lk **5**.23; **7**.42; **9**.46; **10**.36; **11**.5; **12**.25; **14**.5, 28; **22**.23, 24, 27
Jn **8**.46
Acts **7**.52
Phil **1**.22
1 Tim **1**.7

WHICH, IN
1. *there:* ἐκεῖ EKEI
Rev 12. 6 she has a place . . in w. to be nourished

WHICH, ON
1. *where, wherever:* ὅπου HOPOU
Mk 2. 4 the pallet on which the paralytic lay
Rev 17. 9 "mountains on which the woman is seated

WHICH, TO
1. *where:* οὗ HOU
Mt 28.16 mountain to which Jesus had directed
Lk 24.28 the village to which they were going

WHILE (*See also* GREAT WHILE, A)
1. *as much time as:* ὅσον χρόνον CHRONOS; HOSOS [A.4.e]
Mk 2.19 "while the bridegroom is with them
2. *since indeed:* εἴ γε EI [B.3.b.8]
Rom 5. 6 While we were still weak, . . Christ died
3. *in, at, by:* ἐν (+dat.) EN [B.1.a.2]
Mt **13**.25
Lk **1**.8; **2**.6; **5**.1, 12; **11**.37; **24**.4, 15, 51
Acts **4**.30; **19**.1
Rom **4**.11
Heb **3**.15
4. *until, while:* ἕως HEŌS
[a]ἕως ὅτου [b]ἕως οὗ
Mt 5.25 [a]"while you are going with him to court
14.22 [b]while he dismissed the crowds
26.36 [b]"Sit here, while I go yonder and pray
Mk 6.45 while he dismissed the crowd
14.32 "Sit here, while I pray
Jn 9. 4 "We must work . . while it is day
5. *where, wherever:* ὅπου HOPOU
1 Cor 3. 3 For while there is jealousy . . among you
6. *hour, time of day:* ὥρα HŌRA
Jn 5.35 "you were willing to rejoice for a while
2 Cor 7. 8 grieved you, though only for a while
Phm .15 he was parted from you for a while
7. *who, which, what:* ὅς HOS [B.1.a.1]
[a]+ἕως οὗ [b]+ἐν ᾧ
Mt **14**.22[a]; **26**.36[a]
Mk **2**.19[b]
Lk **5**.34[b]
Jn **5**.7[b]
8. *as, so:* ὡς HŌS
Lk **24**.32[2]
Jn **9**.4; **12**.35, 36
Acts **1**.10; **10**.17
9. *when:* ὅτε (+imperf.) HOTE
Jn 17.12 "While I was with them, I kept them
Rom 7. 5 While we were living in the flesh
10. *time, opportunity:* καιρός KAIROS
Lk 8.13 "believe for a while and . . fall away
IDIOMATICALLY
a. Heb 10.37 "For yet a little while ἔτι γὰρ μικρὸν ὅσον ὅσον [HOSOS]

WHILE, A
1. *few, little:* ὀλίγος (neut.) OLIGOS
Mk 6.31 "Come away . . , and rest a while

WHILE, FOR A
1. *small:* βραχύς (neut.) BRACHYS
Acts 5.34 the men to be put outside for a while
2. *time, period:* χρόνος (acc.) CHRONOS
[a]+ἐπί [b]pl.
Lk 18. 4 [a]"For a while he refused
20. 9 [b]"into another country for a long while
Acts 19.22 he himself stayed in Asia for a while
Rev 20. 3 he must be loosed for a little while

WHIP
1. *whip* (Lat. *flagellum*): φραγέλλιον PHRAGELLION*
Jn 2.15 making a w. of cords, he drove them

WHISPER
IDIOMATICALLY
a. Mt 10.27 "what you hear whispered ὃ εἰς τὸ οὖς ἀκούετε [OUS]
b. Lk 12.3 "what you have whispered ὃ πρὸς τὸ οὖς ἐλαλήσατε [OUS]

WHITE
1. *bright, white:* λευκός LEUKOS*
Mt 5.36 "you cannot make one hair white
17. 2 his garments became white as light
28. 3 his raiment white as snow
Mk 9. 3 his garments became . . intensely white
16. 5 a young man . . , dressed in a white robe
Lk 9.29 his raiment became dazzling white
Jn 4.35 "fields are already white for harvest
20.12 she saw two angels in white, sitting
Acts 1.10 two men stood by them in white robes
Rev 1.14 his head and his hair were white as white wool
2.17 " 'I will give him a white stone
3. 4 " 'they shall walk with me in white
3. 5 " 'shall be clad thus in white garments
3.18 " 'buy . . white garments to clothe you
4. 4 elders, clad in white garments
6. 2 I saw, and behold, a white horse
6.11 they were each given a white robe
7. 9 multitude . . clothed in white robes
7.13 "Who are these, clothed in white robes?
14.14 Then I looked, and lo, a white cloud
19.11 heaven opened, and behold, a w. horse!
19.14 armies . . arrayed in fine linen, white . . , followed him on white horses
20.11 Then I saw a great white throne

WHITE, MAKE
1. *make white:* λευκαίνω LEUKAINŌ
Rev 7.14 "made them w. in the blood of the Lamb

WHITEWASHED
1. *plaster with lime, daub over:* κονιάω (perf. pass. part.) KONIAŌ*
Mt 23.27 "you are like whitewashed tombs
Acts 23. 3 "God shall strike you, you w. wall!

WHITHER
1. *where, how:* ποῦ POU I
Jn 3. 8 "whence it comes or whither it goes
8.14 "I know . . whither I am going, but you do not know . . whither I am going

WHO (*See also* HE WHO; THOSE WHO; WHOSE; WHOSE OWN)
1. *who, which, what:* ὅς HOS
Mt **1**.16; **3**.11; **11**.10^{2}; **12**.18^{2}; **17**.5; **18**.7, 23, 28; **22**.10; **23**.35; **24**.45, 46; **26**.24; **27**.9, 15, 56, 57
Mk **1**.2, 7; **3**.[14‡; **4**.16, 25^{2}; **5**.3; **6**.16; **7**.25; **9**.[38‡, 39; **10**.29; **13**.20; **14**.21; **15**.6, 12, 41, 43; **16**.9‡
Lk **1**.27; **2**.11, 25; **3**.16; **4**.6; **5**.10, 17, 18; **6**.13, 14, 16, 17, 34, 48; **7**.2, 27^{2}; **8**.2^{2}, 35, 38; **9**.27, 31; **10**.30, 39; **12**.8, 10, 37, 42, 43, 48^{2}; **13**.1, 4, 16; **16**.1; **17**.1, 7, 12, 31; **18**.29, 30; **19**.15; **20**.47; **22**.22; **23**.27; **24**.19, 23
Jn **1**.13, 15, 27, 30^{2}, 45, 47; **3**.26; **4**.29, 46; **5**.21, 38, 45; **6**.9, 42; **7**.25; '**8**.40, 54; **9**.19, 24; **10**.12, 29‡, 35, 36; **11**.2; **12**.1, 9; **13**.23, 24; **14**.17, 26; **15**.26^{2}; **17**.2, 3, 24^{2}; **18**.9, 13; **20**.2; **21**.7, 20^{2}
Acts **1**.2, 23; **3**.2, 13, 15, 21; **4**.10^{2}, 22, 27; **5**.30, 32; **6**.3; **7**.18, 35, 40, 46, 52; **9**.5, 33; **10**.5, 6, 45; **13**.22^{2}, 25; **14**.8, 15; **15**.17; **17**.3, 31; **19**.13, 16, 27, 35; **20**.25; **21**.11, 16; **22**.8; **25**.19, 24; **26**.15, 17; **27**.23^{2}; **28**.7
Rom **1**.5, 9, 25; **3**.25; **4**.6, 7, 8, 17, 25; **5**.11, 14; **8**.30^{3}, 34^{2}; **9**.15^{2}, 24^{2}; **10**.13; **14**.15; **15**.21^{2}; **16**.4, 5
1 Cor **1**.8, 9, 30; **3**.5; **4**.5; **7**.39; **8**.6^{2}, 11; **10**.11; **15**.6, 15; **16**.3
2 Cor **3**.6; **4**.4, 6; **8**.18, 22; **10**.1
Gal **1**.5; **3**.1, 10, 19; **4**.9, 19; **6**.[14†
Eph **2**.21, 22; **3**.12, 15; **4**.15, 16, 30
Phil **2**.6, 15; **3**.18, 21; **4**.3
Col **1**.14; **2**.3, 10, 19; **4**.9, 10
1 Th **1**.10
1 Tim **1**.20; **2**.4; **4**.10; **6**.16^{2}
2 Tim **1**.3, 12
Tit **2**.14
Phm .10^{2}
Heb **1**.2^{2}; **2**.10^{2}; **3**.17; **4**.13; **6**.7; **7**.16; **9**.14; **11**.10, 18, 33, 38; **12**.2, 6^{3}, 7, 16, 19; **13**.11, 21, 23
Jas **1**.12, 17; **5**.10
1 Pet **1**.8^{2}; **3**.22
2 Pet **1**.17; **2**.15
1 Jn **4**.20^{2}
2 Jn .1
3 Jn .1, 6
Jude .13
Rev **1**.2, 4; **2**.8, 13, 14; **3**.4; **7**.2; **8**.2; **9**.20; **10**.5, 6; **13**.8, 12; **14**.4; **16**.14; **17**.2, 8; **20**.2
2. *as great as, how great:* ὅσος HOSOS
Jn 10. 8 "All who came before me are thieves
Acts 3.24 "all the prophets who have spoken
5.36 "he was slain and all who followed him
5.37 "all who followed him were scattered
10.45 believers . . who came with Peter
Rev 2.24 " 'you . . who do not hold this teaching
3. *anyone who, whoever:* ὅστις HOSTIS
Mt 2. 6 " 'ruler who will govern my people Israel
7.15 "who come to you in sheep's clothing
7.24 "Every one then who hears these words
10.32 "So every one who acknowledges me
13.12 "to him who has will more be given . . ; but from him who has not
13.52 "like a householder who brings out
16.28 "some . . who will not taste death
19.12 "eunuchs who have been so from birth
19.12 "eunuchs w. have been made eunuchs
19.12 "who have made themselves eunuchs
19.29 "And every one who has left houses
20. 1 "a householder who went out early
21.33 "householder who planted a vineyard
21.41 "tenants who will give him the fruits
22. 2 "a king who gave a marriage feast
25. 1 "ten maidens who took their lamps
27.55 many women . . who had followed Jesus
Mk 4.20 "ones who hear the word and accept it
9. 1 "some . . who will not taste death
12.18 who say that there is no resurrection
15. 7 rebels . . who had committed murder
Lk 7.37 a woman of the city, who was a sinner
7.39 "sort of woman . . who is touching him
8. 3 many others, who provided for them[z]
8.43 woman who had had a flow of blood
15. 7 "persons who need no repentance
23.55 women who had come with him
Jn 8.53 "our father Abraham, who died
Acts 7.53 "you who received the law
8.15 who came down and prayed for them
10.41 "to us . . who ate and drank with him
10.47 "who have received the Holy Spirit
11.20 "who on coming to Antioch spoke
13.31 "who are now his witnesses
13.43 Paul and Barnabas, who spoke to them
16.17 "servants . . who proclaim to you the way
Rom 6. 2 can we who died to sin still live in it?
11. 4 "men who have not bowed the knee
16. 4 who risked their necks for my life
16. 6 Mary, who has worked hard among you
16.12 Persis, who has worked hard in the Lord
Gal 2. 4 who slipped in to spy out our freedom
5. 4 you who would be justified by the law
Phil 2.20 who will be . . anxious for your welfare
2 Tim 2. 2 men who will be able to teach
2.18 who have swerved from the truth
Heb 13. 7 those who spoke to you the word of God
2 Pet 2. 1 who will secretly bring in . . heresies
Rev 2.24 " 'w. have not learned . . deep things of Satan
9. 4 those . . who have not the seal of God
12.13 woman who had borne the male child
17.12 "kings who have not yet . . power

Rev 19. 2 "great harlot who corrupted the earth
20. 4 who had not worshiped the beast

4. *this:* οὗτος HOUTOS
Rom 9.8

5. *who? what?:* τίς TIS I
Mt 3.7; 10.11; 12.27, 48[2]; 16.13, 15; 17.25; 18.1; 19.25; 21.10, 23; 22.20, 42; 24.45; 26.68; 27.17
Mk 1.24; 2.7; 3.33; 4.41; 5.30, 31; 8.27, 29; 9.34; 10.26; 11.28; 12.16, 23; 16.3
Lk 3.7; 4.34; 5.21[2]; 7.39, 49; 8.25, 45; 9.9, 18, 20; 10.22[2], 29; 11.19; 12.5, 14, 20, 42; 16.11, 12; 18.26; 19.3; 20.2, 24, 33; 22.64
Jn 1.19, 22; 4.10; 5.12, 13; 6.60, 64[2], 68; 7.20; 8.25, 53; 9.2, 17, 21, 36; 12.34, 38[2]; 13.18, 22, 24, 25; 18.4, 7; 19.24; 20.15; 21.12[2], 20
Acts 7.27, 35; 8.33, 34; 9.5; 11.17; 19.15; 21.33; 22.8; 26.15
Rom 7.24; 8.24, 31, 33, 34, 35; 9.19, 20; 10.6, 7, 16; 11.34[2], 35; 14.4
1 Cor 2.16; 4.7; 9.7[3]; 14.8
2 Cor 2.2, 16; 11.29[2]
Gal 3.1; 5.7
2 Tim 3.14
Heb 3.16, 17, 18
Jas 3.13; 4.12
1 Pet 3.13
1 Jn 2.22; 5.5
Rev 5.2; 6.17; 7.13; 13.4[2]; 15.4

WHO, A MAN

1. *anyone who, whoever:* ὅστις HOSTIS
Lk 23.19 a man who had been thrown into prison

WHO, THE MAN

1. *who, which, what:* ὅς HOS
Jn 18.26 kinsman of the man whose ear Peter . . cut

WHOEVER

1. *who, which, what:* ὅς HOS
[a]+ἄν [b]+ἐάν [c]πᾶς ὅς [d]πᾶς ὅς ἐάν
Mt 5.19[b], 21[a], 22[2a], 31[a], 32[b]; 10.42[b]; 12.32[2ba]; 16.25[2ba]; 18.5[b], 6[a]; 19.9[a]; 20.26[b], 27[a]
Mk 3.29[a], 35[a]; 8.35[2ba], 38[b]; 9.37[2a], 41[a], 42[a]; 10.11[a], 15[a], 43[a], 44[a]; 11.23[a]
Lk 9.24[2ba], 26[a], 48[2ba]; 14.33[c]; 17.33[2ba]; 18.17[a]
Jn 4.14[a]
Acts 2.21[d]
Rom 9.18[2]
1 Cor 7.37; 11.27[a]
Jas 4.4[b]
2 Pet 1.9
1 Jn 2.5[a]; 4.15[b]

2. *anyone who, whoever:* ὅστις HOSTIS
[a]+ἄν [b]+ἐάν
Mt 10.33 [a]"whoever denies me before men
12.50 [a]"whoever does the will of my Father
18. 4 "Whoever humbles himself like this child
23.12 "w. exalts himself will be humbled, and w. humbles himself will be exalted
Lk 14.27 "Whoever does not bear his own cross
Gal 5.10 [b]he . . will bear his judgment, w. he is
Jas 2.10 w. keeps the whole law but fails in one

3. *all, every, whole:* πᾶς PAS [B.3.b.4]
[a]+ὅς [b]+subst. part.
Lk 14.33 [a]"w. of you does not renounce all
Jn 3.15 [b]"w. believes in him may have eternal life[h]
3.16 [b]w. believes in him should not perish
11.26 [b]"w. lives and believes in me shall never die
12.46 [b]"w. believes in me may not remain
16. 2 [b]"hour is coming when w. kills you
1 Jn 3.10 [b]whoever does not do what is right

4. *if anyone:* εἴ τις TIS II
1 Pet 4.11[2]
Rev 14.11

IDIOMATICALLY
a. Rom 2.1 O man, whoever you are, when you judge ὦ ἄνθρωπε πᾶς ὁ κρίνων [PAS]

WHOLE

1. *quite all:* ἅπας HAPAS
Lk 19.37 the w. multitude . . began to rejoice
23. 1 Then the whole company of them arose
Acts 25.24 "the whole Jewish people petitioned me

2. *whole, entire:* ὅλος HOLOS
Mt 5.29 "your w. body be thrown into hell[k]
5.30 "that your whole body go into hell[k]
6.22 "your w. body will be full of light
6.23 "your w. body will be full of darkness
16.26 "if he gains the whole world and forfeits
24.14 "preached throughout the whole world
26.13 "wherever . . preached in the w. world
26.59 the whole council sought false testimony
27.27 they gathered the whole battalion
Mk 1.33 the whole city was gathered together
6.55 ran about the whole neighborhood
8.36 "to gain the whole world and forfeit
12.44 "she . . has put in . . her whole living
14. 9 "wherever . . preached in the whole world
14.55 the whole council sought testimony
15. 1 the whole council held a consultation
15.16 they called together the w. battalion
15.33 there was darkness over the whole land[h]
Lk 7.17 spread through the whole of Judea
8 39 proclaiming throughout the whole city
9.25 "if he gains the whole world and loses
11.34 "your whole body is full of light
11.36 "If then your whole body is full of light
23.44 there was darkness over the whole land[q]
Jn 7.23 "I made a man's whole body well
11.50 "that the w. nation should not perish
Acts 5.11 great fear came upon the whole church
10.22 "well spoken of by the w. Jewish nation
11.26 For a whole year they met
13. 6 they had gone through the whole island
15.22 the elders, with the whole church
28.30 he lived there two whole years
Rom 16.23 host to me and to the whole church
1 Cor 5. 6 a little leaven leavens the whole lump
12.17 If the whole body were an eye
12.17 If the whole body were an ear
14.23 If, therefore, the w. church assembles
2 Cor 1. 1 saints who are in the whole of Achaia
Gal 5. 3 he is bound to keep the whole law
5. 9 A little leaven leavens the whole lump
Phil 1.13 throughout the w. praetorian guard[c]
Tit 1.11 they are upsetting whole families
Jas 2.10 whoever keeps the whole law but fails
3. 2 able to bridle the whole body also
3. 3 we guide their whole bodies
3. 6 tongue is . . staining the whole body
1 Jn 2. 2 expiation . . for the sins of the w. world
5.19 w. world is in the power of the evil one
Rev 3.10 " 'trial which is coming on the w. world
12. 9 Satan the deceiver of the w. world
13. 3 the whole earth followed the beast
16.14 go abroad to the kings of the w. world

3. *healthy, sound:* ὑγιής HYGIĒS
Mt 12.13 it was restored, whole like the other
15.31 when they saw . . the maimed whole

4. *all, every, whole:* πᾶς PAS
Mt 8.32 w. herd rushed down the steep bank
13. 2 the whole crowd stood on the beach
Mk 4. 1 the whole crowd was beside the sea
5.33 the woman . . told him the whole truth
16.15 "preach the gospel to the whole creation[k]‡
Lk 1.10 the whole multitude . . were praying
21.35 "all who dwell upon . . the whole earth
Acts 6. 5 what they said pleased the w. multitude
13.44 almost the w. city gathered together
20.27 "declaring to you the w. counsel of God
22. 5 "whole council of elders bear me witness
Rom 3.19 the w. world may be held accountable
8.22 the w. creation has been groaning
Gal 5.14 the whole law is fulfilled in one word
Eph 2.21 in whom the w. structure is joined
4.16 from whom the whole body, joined
Col 1. 6 in the whole world it is bearing fruit
2. 9 in him the w. fulness of deity dwells

Col 2.19 the whole body, nourished
CONTEXTUALLY
Rom 11.16 If.. dough.. is holy, so is the whole lump

WHOLE ARMOR
1. *full armor:* πανοπλία PANOPLIA
Eph 6.11 Put on the whole armor of God
6.13 take the whole armor of God

WHOLE BURNT OFFERING
1. *whole burnt offering:* ὁλοκαύτωμα HOLOKAUTŌMA
Mk 12.33 "more than all whole burnt offerings

WHOLLY
1. *whole, entire:* ὅλος HOLOS [A.3.b.2]
Lk 11.36 "no part dark, it will be wholly bright
2. *complete:* ὁλοτελής HOLOTELĒS* [A.3.b.1]
1 Th 5.23 May the God of peace.. sanctify you w.

WHOSE (*See also* WHO)
WHOSE OWN
1. *one's own:* ἴδιος IDIOS
[a]+οὗ
Jn 10.12 [a]"shepherd, whose own the sheep are not
1 Tim 4. 2 liars whose consciences are seared

WHY (*See also* REASON WHY, THE)
1. *for which cause:* διὰ ἣν αἰτίαν AITIA [B.1.a.1]
Lk 8.47 declared.. why she had touched him
Acts 22.24 to find out why they shouted
2. *but:* ἀλλά ALLA
Lk **12.7**
2 Cor **1.9**
3. *on account of:* χάριν CHARIN [B.1.a.1]
[a]τούτου χάριν [b]χάριν τίνος
Tit 1. 5 [a]This is why I left you in Crete
1 Jn 3.12 [b]And why did he murder him?
4. *for:* γάρ GAR
Mt **27.23**
Mk **15.14**
Lk **23.22**
Jn **9.30**; **11.39**
Rom **5.7**
5. *because of what:* τίνος ἕνεκα HENEKA [B.1.a.1]
Acts 19.32 did not know why they had come
6. *why:* ἱνατί HINATI*
Mt 9. 4 "Why do you think evil in your hearts?
27.46 "my God, why hast thou forsaken me?
Lk 13. 7 " 'why should it use up the ground?
Acts 4.25 " 'Why did the Gentiles rage?
7.26 " 'why do you wrong each other?
1 Cor 10.29 why should my liberty be determined?
7. *for what:* ἐφ' ὅ HOS [B.1.a.1]
Mt **26.50**†
8. *anyone who, whoever:* ὅστις (neut.) HOSTIS
Jn [8.25 *Why do I talk to you at all?*†
9. *because of this:* διὰ τοῦτο HOUTOS [B.1.a.1]
Mk **12.24**
10. *for what reason:* τίνι λόγῳ LOGOS [B.3.b.4]
Acts 10.29 "I ask then why you sent for me
11. *whence, from what:* πόθεν POTHEN
Lk 1.43 "why is this granted me?
12. *who? what?:* τίς TIS I
[a]διὰ τί
Mt **6.28**; **7.3**; **8.26**; **9.11**[a], 14[a]; **11.8**†, 9†‡; **13.10**[a]; **14.31**; **15.2**[a], 3[a]; **16.8**; **17.10**, 19[a]; **19.7**, 17; **20.6**; **21.25**[a]; **22.18**; **26.8**, 10, 65
Mk **2.7**, 8, 18[a], 24; **4.40**; **5.35**, 39; **7.5**[a]; **8.12**, 17; **10.18**; **11.3**, 31[a]; **12.15**; **14.4**, 6, 63; **15.34**
Lk **2.48**; **5.22**, 30[a]; **6.2**, 41, 46; **12.26**, 57; **18.19**; **19.23**[a], 31[a], 33; **20.5**[a]; **22.46**; **24.5**, 38, 38[a]
Jn **1.25**; **4.27**; **7.19**, 45[a]; **8.43**[a], 46[a]; **9.27**; **10.20**; **12.5**[a]; **13.28**, 37[a]; **18.21**, 23; **20.13**, 15
Acts **1.11**; **3.12**[2]; **5.3**[a]; **9.4**; **10.29**; **14.15**; **15.10**; **19.32**; **22.7**, 16, 30; **26.8**, 14
Rom **3.7**; **9.19**, 20, 32[a]; **14.10**[2]
1 Cor **4.7**; **6.7**[2a]; **10.30**; **15.29**, 30
2 Cor **11.11**[a]
Gal **3.19**; **5.11**
Col **2.20**
1 Jn **3.12**
Rev **17.7**[a]

WHY, THAT IS
1. *for which cause:* διὰ ἣν αἰτίαν AITIA [B.1.a.2]
Heb 2.11 That is why he is not ashamed
2. *therefore:* διό DIO
Rom 4.22 That is why.. faith was "reckoned to him
2 Cor 1.20 That is why we utter the Amen
3. *this:* οὗτος HOUTOS [B.1.a 2]
[a]διὰ τοῦτο [b]εἰς τοῦτο
Mt **14.2**[a]
Mk **1.38**[b]; **6.14**[a]
Jn **13.11**[a]
Rom **4.16**[a]
1 Cor **11.10**[a], 30[a]

WHY, THIS IS
1. *this:* οὗτος HOUTOS [B.1.a.2]
[a]διὰ τοῦτο [b]εἰς τοῦτο
Mt **13.13**[a]
Jn **5.16**[a], 18[a]; **6.65**[a]
2 Cor **2.9**[b]
Phm .15[a]
1 Pet **4.6**[b]

WICK
1. *flax, linen:* λίνον LINON
Mt 12.20 "he will not.. quench a smoldering wick

WICKED
1. *wrongdoing, injustice:* ἀδικία (gen.) ADIKIA
2 Th 2.10 with all wicked deception for those
2. *lawless:* ἄθεσμος ATHESMOS
2 Pet 2. 7 distressed by the licentiousness of the w.
3. *out of place, wrong:* ἄτοπος ATOPOS
2 Th 3. 2 that we may be delivered from wicked
4. *evil, bad:* κακός KAKOS
Mt 24.48 "if that wicked servant says to himself
5. *sick, base, evil:* πονηρός PONĒROS
Mt 18.32 " 'You wicked servant! I forgave you
25.26 " 'You wicked and slothful servant!
Lk 19.22 " 'I will condemn you.., you w. servant!
Acts 17. 5 taking some w. fellows of the rabble
1 Cor 5.13 "Drive out the wicked person
2 Jn .11 he who greets him shares his w. work

WICKEDNESS
1. *wrongdoing, injustice:* ἀδικία ADIKIA
Acts 1.18 "(bought a field with the reward of his w.
Rom 1.18 wrath.. is revealed.. against all.. w. of men who by.. w. suppress the truth
1.29 They were filled with all manner of w.
2. 8 for those who.. obey wickedness,.. wrath
3. 5 w. serves to show the justice of God
6.13 your members.. as instruments of w.
2. *lawlessness:* ἀνομία ANOMIA
Mt 24.12 "because wickedness is multiplied
3. *badness:* κακία KAKIA
Acts 8.22 "Repent therefore of this wickedness
Jas 1.21 put away.. rank growth of wickedness
4. *wickedness:* πονηρία PONĒRIA
Mk 7.22 "coveting, wickedness, deceit
Lk 11.39 "inside you are full of extortion and w.
Acts 3.26 "turning.. you from your wickedness
Eph 6.12 against the spiritual hosts of wickedness

WIDE
1. *long:* μέγας MEGAS
1 Cor 16. 9 wide door for effective work has opened
2. *broad, wide:* πλατύς PLATYS*
Mt 7.13 "the gate is wide and the way is easy[q]

WIDE, BE
WIDEN
1. *widen, make broad:* πλατύνω (pass.) PLATYNŌ
[a]perf.
2 Cor 6.11 [a]our heart is wide
6.13 widen your hearts also

WIDOW
1. *widow:* χήρα CHĒRA*
Mt [23.14 *"for you devour widows' houses*‡
Mk 12.40 "who devour widows' houses
12.42 poor widow came, and put in two . . coins
12.43 "this poor widow has put in more
Lk 2.37 a widow till she was eighty-four
4.25 "there were many widows in Israel
4.26 "sent . . to a woman who was a widow
7.12 only son of his mother, and she was a widow
18. 3 " 'widow . . who kept coming to him
18. 5 " 'because this widow bothers me
20.47 "⟨scribes,⟩ who devour widows' houses
21. 2 saw a poor widow put in two . . coins
21. 3 "this poor widow has put in more
Acts 6. 1 because their widows were neglected
9.39 widows stood beside him weeping
9.41 Then calling the saints and widows
1 Cor 7. 8 To . . the widows I say . . remain single
1 Tim 5. 3 Honor widows who are real widows
5. 4 If a w. has children . . , let them . . learn
5. 5 a real widow, and is left all alone
5. 9 Let a widow be enrolled if she is . . sixty
5.11 But refuse to enrol younger widows
5.16 If any . . has relatives who are widows
5.16 assist those who are real widows
Jas 1.27 Religion . . is this: to visit . . widows
Rev 18. 7 " 'I am no w., mourning I shall never see
2. *woman, wife:* γυνή GYNĒ
Mt 22.24 " 'his brother must marry the widow
CONTEXTUALLY
1 Tim 5.14 So I would have younger widows marry

WIFE
1. *woman, wife:* γυνή GYNĒ
Mt 1.20 "do not fear to take Mary your wife
1.24 Joseph woke from sleep . . ; he took his wife
5.31 " 'Whoever divorces his wife
5.32 "every one who divorces his wife
14. 3 Herodias, his brother Philip's wife[l]
18.25 "to be sold, with his wife and children
19. 3 "Is it lawful to divorce one's wife?
19. 5 " 'a man shall . . be joined to his wife
19. 8 "Moses allowed you to divorce your wives
19. 9 "whoever divorces his wife
19.10 "If such is the case of a man with his w.
22.25 "died, and . . left his wife to his brother
22.28 "to which of the seven will she be wife?
27.19 his wife sent word to him
Mk 6.17 Herodias, his brother Philip's wife
6.18 "not lawful . . to have your brother's w.
10. 2 "Is it lawful . . to divorce his wife?
10. 7 " 'a man shall . . be joined to his wife[p]‡
10.11 "Whoever divorces his wife
12.19 "if a man's brother dies and leaves a wife, . . the man[y] must take the wife
12.20 "the first took a wife, and when he died
12.23 "In the resurrection whose wife will she be? For the seven had her as wife
Lk 1. 5 he had a wife of the daughters of Aaron
1.13 "your wife Elizabeth will bear . . a son
1.18 "my wife is advanced in years
1.24 his wife Elizabeth conceived
3.19 reproved . . for Herodias, his brother's wife
8. 3 the wife of Chuza, Herod's steward
14.20 " 'I have married a w., and . . cannot come
14.26 "If any one . . does not hate his own . . wife
16.18 "Every one who divorces his wife
17.32 "Remember Lot's wife
18.29 "no man who has left house or wife
20.28 " 'if a man's brother dies, having a wife . . , the man[g] must take the wife
20.29 "the first took a wife, and died
20.33 "whose wife will the woman be? For the seven had her as wife
Acts 5. 1 man named Ananias with his wife S.
5. 2 with his wife's knowledge he kept . . some
Acts 5. 7 After an interval . . his wife came in
18. 2 Jew named Aquila, . . with his wife Priscilla
21. 5 they all, with wives and children
24.24 Felix came with his wife Drusilla
1 Cor 5. 1 a man is living with his father's wife
7. 2 each man should have his own wife
7. 3 husband should give to his wife her conjugal rights, and likewise the wife
7. 4 w. does not rule over her own body
7. 4 husband does not rule . . , but the w. does
7.10 w. should not separate from her husband
7.11 the husband should not divorce his wife
7.12 if any . . has a wife who is an unbeliever
7.14 husband is consecrated through his w., and the . . wife . . through her husband
7.16 W., how do you know whether you will?
7.16 whether you will save your wife
7.27 Are you bound to a wife?
7.27 Are you free from a wife?
7.29 from now on, let those who have wives
7.33 man is anxious . . how to please his w.
7.39 A wife is bound to her husband
9. 5 right to be accompanied by a wife[n]†
Eph 5.22 Wives, be subject to your husbands
5.23 husband is the head of the wife
5.24 let wives . . be subject in everything
5.25 Husbands, love your wives
5.28 so husbands should love their wives . . He who loves his wife loves himself
5.31 "a man shall . . be joined to his wife
5.33 let each one of you love his wife . . , and let the wife see that she respects
Col 3.18 Wives, be subject to your husbands
3.19 Husbands, love your wives
1 Tim 3. 2 bishop must be . . the husband of one w.
3.12 Let deacons be the husband of one wife
5. 9 having been the wife of one husband
Tit 1. 6 if any man is . . the husband of one w.
1 Pet 3. 1 Likewise you wives, be submissive
3. 1 won . . by the behavior of their wives
Rev 21. 9 "the Bride, the wife of the Lamb
2. *vessel, tackle:* σκεῦος SKEUOS
1 Th 4. 4 how to take a wife for himself[x]†
CONTEXTUALLY
Mt 1. 6 father of Solomon by the w. of Uriah
Jn 19.25 Mary the wife of Clopas

WILD
1. *wild:* ἄγριος AGRIOS*
Mt 3. 4 his food was locusts and wild honey
Mk 1. 6 John . . ate locusts and wild honey
Jude .13 w. waves of the sea, casting up the foam
2. *flood, excess:* ἀνάχυσις ANACHYSIS [A.1.b.5]
1 Pet 4. 4 you do not . . join . . in . . wild profligacy

WILD OLIVE SHOOT
WILD OLIVE TREE
1. *wild olive tree:* ἀγριέλαιος AGRIELAIOS*
Rom 11.17 you, a wild olive shoot, were grafted
11.24 what is by nature a wild olive tree

WILDERNESS
1. *desert, solitude:* ἐρημία ERĒMIA
2 Cor 11.26 danger in the city, danger in the w.
2. *desolate, lonely:* ἔρημος (subst. fem.) ERĒMOS
Mt 3. 1 John the Baptist, preaching in the w.
3. 3 "The voice of one crying in the w.
4. 1 Jesus was led up by the Spirit into the w.
11. 7 "out into the wilderness to behold
24.26 " 'Lo, he is in the wilderness
Mk 1. 3 "the voice of one crying in the w.
1. 4 John the baptizer appeared[c] in the w.
1.12 The Spirit . . drove him out into the w.
1.13 he was in the wilderness forty days
Lk 1.80 in the w. till . . his manifestation
3. 2 John the son of Zechariah in the w.
3. 4 "The voice of one crying in the w.
4. 2(1) for forty days in the wilderness
5.16 he withdrew to the w. and prayed

Lk 7.24 "What did you go .. into .. w. to behold?
15. 4 "leave the ninety-nine in the w.
Jn 1.23 "I am the voice of one crying in the w.
3.14 "Moses lifted up the serpent in the w.
6.31 "Our fathers ate the manna in the w.
6.49 "Your fathers ate the manna in the w.
11.54 to the country near the wilderness
Acts 7.30 "an angel appeared to him in the w.
7.36 "in the wilderness for forty years
7.38 "in the congregation in the wilderness
7.42 " 'forty years in the w., O .. Israel
7.44 "the tent of witness in the wilderness
13.18 "he bore with[m] them in the wilderness
21.38 "led .. the Assassins out into the w.
1 Cor 10. 5 they were overthrown in the w.
Heb 3. 8 "on the day of testing in the w.
3.17 whose bodies fell in the wilderness
Rev 12. 6 the woman fled into the wilderness
12.14 she might fly from the serpent into the w.
17. 3 carried me away in the Spirit into a w.

WILES
1. *craftiness: μεθοδεία* (sg. or pl.) METHODEIA*
Eph 4.14 by their craftiness in deceitful wiles
6.11 stand against the wiles of the devil

WILFUL
1. *self-willed, surly: αὐθάδης* AUTHADĒS
2 Pet 2.10 Bold and wilful, they are not afraid

WILL (*See also* WOULD)
1. *intention, purpose: βούλημα* BOULĒMA
Rom 9.19 "For who can resist his will?
2. *wish, will: βούλομαι* BOULOMAI
1 Cor 12.11 to each one individually as he wills
2 Jn .12 I would rather not use paper and ink
3. *covenant: διαθήκη* DIATHĒKĒ
Gal 3.15 no one annuls even a man's will[g]†
Heb 9.16 For where a will[u] is involved†
9.17 For a will[u] takes effect only at death†
4. *impulse, effort: ὁρμή* HORMĒ
Jas 3. 4 wherever the will of the pilot directs
5. *will, desire: θέλημα* THELĒMA
Mt 6.10 "Thy kingdom come, Thy will be done
7.21 "he who does the will of my Father
12.50 "whoever does the will of my Father
18.14 "it is not the will of my[d] Father
21.31 "Which .. did the will of his father?
26.42 "if this cannot pass .., thy will be done
Mk 3.35 "Whoever does the will of God
Lk 12.47 "servant who knew his master's will, but did not .. act according to his will
22.42 "not my will, but thine, be done[l]
23.25 Jesus he delivered up to their will
Jn 1.13 born, not of blood nor of the will of the flesh nor of the will of man
4.34 "My food is to do the will of him
5.30 "I seek not my own will but the will of him who sent me
6.38 "I have come .. not to do my own will, but the will of him who sent me
6.39 "this is the will of him who sent me
6.40 "For this is the will of my Father
7.17 "if any .. will .. to do his will, he shall know
9.31 "if any one .. does his will, God listens
Acts 13.22 " 'a man .. who will do all my will
21.14 "The will of the Lord be done
22.14 " 'God .. appointed you to know his will
Rom 1.10 that .. by God's will I may .. succeed
2.18 ⟨if you⟩ know his will and approve
12. 2 that you may prove what is the w. of God
15.32 that by God's w. I may come to you
1 Cor 1. 1 Paul, called by the will of God
16.12 it was not at all his will[b] to come now
2 Cor 1. 1 Paul, an apostle .. by the will of God
8. 5 gave themselves .. by the will of God
Gal 1. 4 according to the will of our God
Eph 1. 1 Paul, an apostle .. by the will of God
Eph 1. 5 according to the purpose of his will
1. 9 made known .. the mystery of his will
1.11 according to the counsel of his will
5.17 understand what the will of the Lord is
6. 6 doing the will of God from the heart
Col 1. 1 Paul, an apostle .. by the will of God
1. 9 filled with the knowledge of his will
4.12 fully assured in all the will of God
1 Th 4. 3 the will of God, your sanctification
5.18 this is the will of God in Christ
2 Tim 1. 1 Paul, an apostle .. by the will of God
2.26 being captured by him to do his will[c]
Heb 10. 7 " 'Lo, I have come to do thy will
10. 9 "Lo, I have come to do thy will
10.10 by that will we have been sanctified
10.36 so that you may do the will of God
13.21 equip you .. that you may do his will
1 Pet 2.15 it is God's will that by doing right
3.17 it is better .. if that should be God's w.
4. 2 so as to live .. by the will of God
4.19 who suffer according to God's will
1 Jn 2.17 who does the will of God abides for ever
5.14 if we ask anything according to his w.
Rev 4.11 "by thy will they existed
6. *will, a willing: θέλησις* THELĒSIS*
Heb 2. 4 distributed according to his own will
7. *will, wish: θέλω* THELŌ
[a]subst. part.
Mt 5.40 "if any one would sue you
5.42 "do not refuse him who would borrow
8. 2 "if you will, you can make me clean
8. 3 touched him, saying, "I will; be clean
16.24 "If any man would come after me
16.25 "whoever would save his life will lose it
19.17 "If you would enter life
19.21 "If you would be perfect, go, sell
20.26 "whoever would be great among you
20.27 "whoever would be first among you
21.29 "he answered, 'I will not
22. 3 "but they would not come
23. 4 "they .. will not move them with their finger
23.37 "How often would I have gathered your children together .., and you would not!
26.15 "What will you give me if I deliver him?
26.39 "nevertheless, not as I will, but as thou
27.34 he tasted it, he would not drink it
Mk 1.40 "If you will, you can make me clean
1.41 "I will; be clean
7.24 he .. would not have any one know
8.34 "If any man would come after me
8.35 "whoever would save his life will lose it
9.30 he would not have any one know it
9.35 "If any .. would be first, he must be last
10.43 "whoever would be great among you
10.44 "whoever would be first among you
14. 7 "whenever you will, you can do good
14.36 "remove this cup .. ; yet not what I will
Lk 1.62 inquiring what he would have him called
4. 6 "I give it to whom I will
5.12 "if you w., you can make me clean
5.13 touched him, saying, "I will; be clean
9.23 "If any man would come after me
9.24 "whoever would save his life will lose it
13.34 "How often would I have gathered your children .., and you would not!
16.26 " 'that those who would pass from here
18.13 "would not even lift up his eyes
Jn 3. 8 "The wind[f] blows where it wills
5.21 "the Son gives life to whom he will
7. 1 he would not go about in Judea
15. 7 "ask whatever you will
21.18 "you .. walked where you would
Acts 17.18 "What would this babbler say?
18.21 "I will return to you if God wills
[24. 6 "*we would have judged him*‡
Rom 7.18 I can w. what is right, but I cannot do it
9.16 [a]it depends not upon man's will

Rom 9.18 he has mercy upon whomever he wills, and he hardens . . whomever he wills
13. 3 Would you have no fear of him?
16.19 I would have you wise as to what is good
1 Cor 4.19 I will come . . soon, if the Lord wills
14.19 I would rather speak five words
2 Cor 5. 4 not that we would be unclothed
Gal 5.17 to prevent you from doing what you would
Phil 2.13 God is at work . . , both to will and to work
1 Th 4.13 we would not have you ignorant
2 Th 3.10 If any . . will not work, let him not eat
Jas 4.15 "If the Lord wills, we shall live
1 Pet 3.10 "He that would love life and see good days
3 Jn . 3 I would rather not write with pen
Rev 11. 5 if any one would harm them
11. 5 if any one would harm them

WILL, BE ONE'S
1. *will, wish:* θέλω THELŌ
Jn 7.17 "if any man's will is to do
8.44 "your will is to do your father's desires
21.22 "If it is my will that he remain
21.23 "If it is my will that he remain

WILL, FREE
1. *voluntary, willing:* ἑκούσιος (subst.) HEKOUSIOS*
Phm .14 but of your own free will

WILL, GOOD
WILL, GRACIOUS
1. *goodwill, satisfaction:* εὐδοκία EUDOKIA
Mt 11.26 "yea, . . for such was thy gracious will[f]†
Lk [2.14 "peace, *good will among men*‡
10.21 "yea, . . for such was thy gracious will[h]†
Phil 1.15 Some . . preach Christ . . from good will
2. *goodwill, favor:* εὔνοια EUNOIA*
Eph 6. 7 rendering service with a good will

WILL HAVE
1. *wish, will:* βούλομαι BOULOMAI
Jn 18.39 "will you h. me release . . King of . . Jews?
1 Tim 5.14 I would have younger widows marry
2. *will, wish:* θέλω THELŌ
Mt 26.17 "Where will you have us prepare?
Mk 14.12 "Where will you have us go and prepare?
Lk 22. 9 "Where will you have us prepare it?

WILL, NOT OF ONE'S OWN
1. *involuntary:* ἄκων AKŌN*
1 Cor 9.17 if not of my own will, I am entrusted

WILL, OF ONE'S OWN
1. *wish, will:* βούλομαι (pred. part.) BOULOMAI
Jas 1.18 Of his own will he brought us forth
2. *willingly:* ἑκών HEKŌN*
Rom 8.20 subjected to futility, not of its own w.
1 Cor 9.17 For if I do this of my own will

WILL, OF ONE'S OWN FREE
1. *by free choice:* αὐθαίρετος AUTHAIRETOS
2 Cor 8. 3 beyond their means, of their own free w.

WILLING (*See also* GIFT, WILLING)
1. *ready, eager:* πρόθυμος PROTHYMOS
Mt 26.41 "the spirit indeed is willing
Mk 14.38 "the spirit indeed is willing

WILLING, BE
1. *wish, will:* βούλομαι BOULOMAI
Lk 22.42 "if thou art willing, remove this cup
2. *be well pleased:* εὐδοκέω EUDOKEŌ
1 Th 3. 1 we were w. to be left behind at Athens
3. *will, wish:* θέλω THELŌ
Mt 11.14 "if you are w. to accept it, he is Elijah
Jn 5.35 "you were willing to rejoice for a while
Acts 26. 5 "if they are willing to testify

WILLINGLY
1. *willingly, deliberately:* ἑκουσίως HEKOUSIŌS
1 Pet 5. 2 Tend the flock . . , not by constraint but w.[l]

WIN (*See also* STRENGTH, WIN)
1. *take from, get back:* ἀπολαμβάνω APOLAMBANŌ
2 Jn . 8 Look . . that you . . may win a full reward
2. *gain:* κερδαίνω KERDAINŌ
1 Cor 9.19 myself a slave . . that I might win the more
9.20 I became as a Jew, in order to win Jews
9.20 that I might win those under the law
9.21 that I might w. those outside the law
9.22 weak, that I might win the weak
1 Pet 3. 1 husbands . . may be won without a word
CONTEXTUALLY
Rom 15.18 wrought through me to win obedience

WIND
1. *wind:* ἄνεμος ANEMOS
Mt 7.25 "winds blew and beat upon that house
7.27 "winds blew and beat against that house
8.26 he rose and rebuked the winds
8.27 "even winds and sea obey him
11. 7 "A reed shaken by the wind
14.24 for the wind was against them
14.30 when he saw the wind,[n] he was afraid
14.32 they got into the boat, the w. ceased
24.31 "will gather . . elect from the four winds
Mk 4.37 a great storm of wind arose
4.39 he awoke and rebuked the wind . . And the wind ceased
4.41 "even wind and sea obey him
6.48 for the wind was against them
6.51 he got into the boat . . and the w. ceased
13.27 "gather his elect from the four winds
Lk 7.24 "A reed shaken by the wind
8.23 a storm of wind came down on the lake
8.24 he awoke and rebuked the wind
8.25 "he commands even wind and water
Jn 6.18 because a strong wind was blowing
Acts 27. 4 because the winds were against us
27. 7 the wind did not allow us to go on
27.24 tempestuous w., called the northeaster
27.15 the ship . . could not face the wind
Eph 4.14 carried about with every w. of doctrine
Jas 3. 4 ships . . are driven by strong winds
Jude .12 clouds, carried along by winds
Rev 7. 1 angels . . holding back the four winds . . , that no wind might blow on earth
2. *blow, breathe:* πνέω (subst. part.) PNEŌ
Acts 27.40 hoisting the foresail to the wind
3. *wind, breath, spirit:* πνεῦμα PNEUMA
Jn 3. 8 "The wind[f] blows where it wills
Heb 1. 7 "Who makes his angels winds
4. *wind, breath:* πνοή PNOĒ
Acts 2. 2 like the rush of a mighty wind
CONTEXTUALLY
Lk 12.55 "And when you see the south wind blowing
Acts 27.13 And when the south wind blew gently
28.13 and after one day a south w. sprang up

WIND, BE DRIVEN BY THE
1. *be driven by the wind* (pass.): ἀνεμίζω ANEMIZŌ*
Jas 1. 6 sea that is driven and tossed by the w.

WINDOW
1. *opening, window:* θυρίς THYRIS*
Acts 20. 9 Eutychus was sitting in the window
2 Cor 11.33 I was let down in a basket through a w.

WINE
1. *wine:* οἶνος OINOS
Mt 9.17 "Neither is new w. put into old wineskins; if it is, . . the w. is spilled . . ; but new w. is put into fresh wineskins
27.34 they offered him wine to drink
Mk 2.22 "no one puts new w. into old wineskins; if he does, the w. will burst the skins, and the wine is lost . . ; but new wine is for fresh skins[j]‡
15.23 they offered him w. mingled with myrrh
Lk 1.15 "he shall drink no w. nor strong drink
5.37 "no one puts new w. into old wineskins; if he does, the . . w. will burst the skins
5.38 "new w. must be put into fresh wineskins
7.33 "John . . has come . . drinking no w.
10.34 "bound up his wounds, pouring on . . w.

Jn 2. 3 When the w. gave out, the mother of Jesus said to him, "They have no w.
2. 9 the water now become wine
2.10 "Every man serves the good w. first . . ; but you have kept the good w. until now
4.46 where he had made the water wine
Rom 14.21 it is right not to eat meat or drink w.
Eph 5.18 do not get drunk with wine
1 Tim 3. 8 not addicted to much wine, not greedy
5.23 use a little w. for . . your stomach
Rev 6. 6 "but do not harm oil and wine!
14. 8 "the wine of her impure passion
14.10 "the wine of God's wrath
17. 2 "the wine of whose fornication
18. 3 "the wine of her impure passion
18.13 myrrh, frankincense, wine, oil
CONTEXTUALLY
Mk 12. 1 "and dug a pit for the wine press
Lk 5.39 "no one after drinking old w. desires new

WINE, NEW
1. *sweet new wine:* γλεῦκος GLEUKOS*
Acts 2.13 "They are filled with new wine

WINE PRESS
1. *tub, wine vat:* ληνός LĒNOS*
Mt 21.33 "a householder . . dug a wine press
Rev 14.19 threw it into the great wine press
14.20 wine press was trodden outside . . city
14.20 blood flowed from the wine press
19.15 he will tread the wine press of the fury

WINESKIN
1. *wineskin:* ἀσκός ASKOS
Mt 9.17 "Neither . . new w. . . into old wineskins; . . but new wine . . into fresh wineskins
Mk 2.22 "puts new wine into old wineskins
Lk 5.37 "puts new wine into old wineskins
5.38 "wine must be put into fresh wineskins

WING
1. *wing, bird:* πτέρυξ PTERYX*
Mt 23.37 "hen gathers her brood under her wings
Lk 13.34 "hen gathers her brood under her wings
Rev 4. 8 creatures, each of them with six wings
9. 9 noise of their wings . . like . . chariots
12.14 the two wings of the great eagle

WINNOW
1. *scatter abroad, squander:* διασκορπίζω DIASKORPIZŌ
Mt 25.24 " 'gathering where you did not winnow
25.26 " 'I . . gather where I have not winnowed

WINNOWING FORK
1. *winnowing shovel:* πτύον PTYON*
Mt 3.12 "His winnowing fork is in his hand
Lk 3.17 "His winnowing fork is in his hand

WINTER
WINTER IN
1. *winter, stormy weather:* χειμών CHEIMŌN
Mt 24.20 "Pray that your flight may not be in w.
Mk 13.18 "Pray that it may not happen in winter
Jn 10.23(22) it was w., and Jesus was . . in the temple
2 Tim 4.21 Do your best to come before winter
2. *wintering in:* παραχειμασία PARACHEIMASIA* [B.1.a.2]
Acts 27.12 harbor was not suitable to winter in
3. *winter at:* παραχειμάζω PARACHEIMAZŌ
Acts 27.12 reach Phoenix . . and winter there
28.11 a ship which had wintered in the island

WINTER FRUIT
1. *late fig:* ὄλυνθος OLYNTHOS*
Rev 6.13 as the fig tree sheds its winter fruit

WINTER, SPEND THE
1. *winter at:* παραχειμάζω PARACHEIMAZŌ
1 Cor 16. 6 perhaps I will . . even spend the w.
Tit 3.12 I have decided to spend the w. there

WIPE
1. *wipe off:* ἐκμάσσω EKMASSŌ*
Lk 7.38 wiped them with the hair of her head
7.44 "she . . wiped them with her hair
Jn 11. 2 who . . wiped his feet with her hair
12. 3 Mary . . wiped his feet with her hair
13. 5 he . . began . . to wipe them with the towel

WIPE AWAY
1. *wipe out:* ἐξαλείφω EXALEIPHŌ
Rev 7.17 "God will wipe away every tear
21. 4 "he will wipe away every tear

WIPE OFF AGAINST
1. *wipe off:* ἀπομάσσω (mid.) APOMASSŌ*
Lk 10.11 " 'dust of . . our feet, we wipe off against you

WISDOM
1. *practical wisdom:* φρόνησις PHRONĒSIS
Lk 1.17 "disobedient to the wisdom of the just
2. *wisdom, cleverness:* σοφία SOPHIA
Mt 11.19 "wisdom is justified by her deeds[e]
12.42 "she came . . to hear the w. of Solomon
13.54 "Where did this man get this wisdom?
Mk 6. 2 "What is the wisdom given to him?
Lk 2.40 the child . . became strong, filled with w.
2.52 Jesus increased in wisdom and in stature[i]
7.35 "wisdom is justified by all her children
11.31 "she came . . to hear the w. of Solomon
11.49 "the W. of God said, 'I will send
21.15 "I will give you a mouth and wisdom
Acts 6. 3 "pick out . . men . . full of . . wisdom
6.10 they could not withstand the wisdom
7.10 "gave him favor and w. before Pharaoh
7.22 "Moses was instructed in all the wisdom
Rom 11.33 the riches and w. and knowledge of God!
1 Cor 1.17 send me . . to preach . . not with eloquent w.
1.19 "I will destroy the w. of the wise
1.20 God made foolish the w. of the world
1.21 in the wisdom of God, the world did not know God through wisdom
1.22 Jews demand signs and Greeks seek w.
1.24 Christ the power . . and the w. of God
1.30 Christ Jesus, whom God made our w.
2. 1 I did not come proclaiming . . in . . w.
2. 4 not in plausible words of wisdom
2. 5 that your faith . . not rest in the w. of men
2. 6 among the mature we do impart w., although it is not a wisdom of this age
2. 7 we impart a secret . . wisdom of God
2.13 words not taught by human wisdom
3.19 the w. of this world is folly with God
12. 8 To one is given . . the utterance of w.
2 Cor 1.12 we have behaved . . not by earthly w.
Eph 1. 9(8) he has made known to us in all wisdom
1.17 that . . God . . may give you a spirit of w.
3.10 that . . the manifold wisdom of God
Col 1. 9 in all spiritual w. and understanding
1.28 teaching every man in all wisdom
2. 3 in whom are hid all the treasures of w.
2.23 These have . . an appearance of w.
3.16 admonish one another in all wisdom
Jas 1. 5 If any . . lacks w., let him ask God
3.13 show his works in the meekness of w.
3.15 This wisdom is not such as comes down
3.17 the wisdom from above is first pure
2 Pet 3.15 Paul wrote . . according to the w. given
Rev 5.12 "Worthy is the Lamb . . to receive . . w.!
7.12 "Blessing and glory and wisdom!
13.18 This calls for wisdom
17. 9 "This calls for a mind with wisdom

WISE
1. *sensible, prudent:* φρόνιμος PHRONIMOS
Mt 7.24 "like a wise man who built his house
10.16 "so be wise as serpents
24.45 "Who then is the faithful and w. servant?
25. 2 "Five . . were foolish, and five were w.
25. 4 "but the wise took flasks of oil
25. 8 "the foolish said to the wise
25. 9 "the w. replied . . 'there will not be enough
Lk 12.42 "Who then is the faithful and w. steward?
Rom 11.25 Lest you be wise in your own conceits
1 Cor 4.10 but you are wise in Christ

2 Cor 11.19 you . . bear with fools, being w. yourselves!
2. *wise, learned:* σοφός SOPHOS
Mt 11.25 "thou hast hidden these . . from the w.
23.34 "I send you prophets and wise men
Lk 10.21 "thou hast hidden these . . from the w.
Rom 1.14 both to the wise and to the foolish
1.22 Claiming to be wise, they became fools
16.19 I would have you w. as to what is good
16.27 to the only wise God be glory!
1 Cor 1.19 "I will destroy the wisdom of the wise
1.20 Where is the wise man?
1.26 not many of you were wise
1.27 chose what is foolish . . to shame the w.
3.18 If any one . . thinks that he is w. . . , let him become a fool that he may become w.
3.19 "He catches the wise in their craftiness
3.20 "the thoughts of the wise are futile
6. 5 no man among you wise enough
Eph 5.15 walk, not as unwise men but as wise
Jas 3.13 Who is w. and understanding among you?

WISE MAN
1. *Magus, magician:* μάγος MAGOS
Mt 2. 1 behold, wise men from the East came
2. 7 Herod summoned the wise men secretly
2.16 he had been tricked by the wise men
2.16 time . . ascertained from the wise men

WISELY
1. *wisely, thoughtfully:* νουνεχῶς NOUNECHŌS*
Mk 12.34 Jesus saw that he answered wisely
2. *wisdom, cleverness:* σοφία SOPHIA [B.1.a.1]
Col 4. 5 Conduct yourselves w. toward outsiders

WISER
1. *wise, learned:* σοφός (comp.) SOPHOS
1 Cor 1.25 the foolishness of God is wiser than men

WISH
1. *wish, will:* βούλομαι BOULOMAI
Mk 15.15 Pilate, wishing to satisfy the crowd
Acts 17.20 "we w. to know . . what these things mean
18.27 when he wished to cross to Achaia
19.30 Paul wished to go in among the crowd
25.20 "whether he wished to go to Jerusalem
27.43 the centurion, wishing to save Paul
28.18 "they wished to set me at liberty
Jas 4. 4 whoever wishes to be a friend of the world
2 Pet 3. 9 not wishing that any should perish
2. *pray, wish:* εὔχομαι EUCHOMAI
Rom 9. 3 I could wish that I myself were accursed
3. *would that:* ὄφελον OPHELON
2 Cor 11. 1 I wish you would bear with me
Gal 5.12 I wish those . . would mutilate themselves!
4. *will, wish:* θέλω THELŌ
Mt 7.12 "whatever you wish that men would do
12.38 "Teacher, we wish to see a sign from you
17. 4 "if you wish, I will make three booths
18.23 "a king who wished to settle accounts
Mk 6.22 "Ask me for whatever you wish
Lk 6.31 "as you wish that men would do to you
Jn 6.67 "Do you also wish to go away?[o]
12.21 "Sir, we wish to see Jesus
21.18 "where you do not wish to go
Acts 19.33 wishing to make a defense to the people
25. 9 Festus, wishing to do the Jews a favor
25. 9 "Do you wish to go up to Jerusalem?
1 Cor 4.21 What do you wish?
7. 7 I wish that all were as I myself am
7.36 let him do as he wishes: let them marry
7.39 free to be married to whom she wishes
2 Cor 12. 6 if I wish to boast, I shall not be a fool
12.20 I may . . find you not what I wish, and . . you may find me not what you wish
Gal 4.20 I could wish to be present with you now
5. *seek, desire:* ζητέω ZĒTEŌ
Jn 4.27 none said, "What do you wish?

WITH
1. *from:* ἀπό (+gen.) APO
Mt **20.**8
Lk **6.**18; **12.**58; **16.**21; **21.**26; **24.**27
Jn **8.**9‡
Acts **8.**35
1 Cor **14.**36
1 Pet **4.**17[2]
2. *through:* διά (+gen.) DIA
Acts **8.**20; **15.**32; **19.**26; **20.**28
Rom **8.**25
2 Cor **1.**4; **2.**4; **3.**11; **6.**7; **10.**9
Eph **6.**18
Heb **12.**1
3 Jn .13
3. *have, hold:* ἔχω (part.) ECHŌ
Mt 8. 9 "I am a man under authority, w. soldiers
12.10 there was a man with a withered hand
18. 8 "than w. two hands . . thrown into . . fire
18. 9 "better for you to enter life w. one eye
26. 7 came up to him with an alabaster flask
Mk 9.43 "than with two hands to go to hell[m]
9.45 "than w. two feet to be thrown into hell[m]
9.47 "than w. two eyes to be thrown into hell[m]
14. 3 a woman came with an alabaster flask
Lk 7. 8 "a man set under authority, with soldiers
Acts 27.39 they noticed a bay with a beach
1 Cor 11. 4 Any man who prays . . with his head covered
Rev 4. 7 third living creature with . . face of a man
4. 8 creatures, each of them with six wings
5. 6 a Lamb standing, . . with seven horns
7. 2 angel . . with the seal of the living God
8. 3 stood at the altar with a golden censer
9.19 their tails are like serpents, with heads
12. 3 a great red dragon, with seven heads
13. 1 beast . . with ten horns and seven heads
14. 6 another angel . . , with an eternal gospel
14.14 one like a son of man, w. a golden crown
15. 1 seven angels with seven plagues
15. 2 with harps of God in their hands
15. 6 seven angels with the seven plagues
17. 7 "the beast with seven heads and ten horns
17. 9 "This calls for a mind with wisdom
21.12 a great, high wall, with twelve gates
4. *into, to, for:* εἰς (+acc.) EIS
Rom **12.**16
Eph **3.**19
2 Pet **1.**17
5. *from, out of:* ἐκ (+gen.) EK
Mt **27.**7
Mk **12.**30[4], 33[3]
Lk **10.**27
Jn **4.**6; **12.**3
Acts **1.**18; **8.**[37‡
Rev **8.**5; **9.**2; **17.**2, 6; **18.**1, 3; **19.**21
6. *in, at, by:* ἐν (+dat.) EN
[a]B.1.b
Mt **3.**11[2], 17; **7.**2; **17.**5; **20.**15; **21.**25; **22.**37[3]; **25.**16
Mk **1.**11, 23; **5.**2; **9.**1, 50
Lk **1.**51; **3.**16, 22‡; **4.**32, 36; **8.**15; **10.**27[3]; **14.**31; **21.**34; **22.**49
Jn **1.**26, 31, 33[2]; **8.**44; **12.**35
Acts **1.**5; **2.**29, 46; **11.**16, 26†
Rom **1.**9, 27[2]; **9.**22; **10.**9; **12.**8[2], 21; **15.**5, 6, 32; **16.**16
1 Cor **1.**5, 17; **3.**13; **4.**21[2]; **5.**8[2]; **10.**5; **14.**16; **16.**20
2 Cor **1.**12; **3.**7, 8; **7.**8; **10.**1, 14; **11.**23[2]; **12.**10; **13.**12
Eph **1.**3; **5.**18, 26; **6.**2, 14, 15, 16, 18, 24[a]
Phil **1.**8, 9, 20
Col **1.**11; **2.**4; **3.**16, 22; **4.**2
1 Th **1.**5; **2.**3, 17; **4.**16[3], 18; **5.**26
2 Th **2.**9, 10; **3.**7, 8
1 Tim **2.**9, 11; **3.**9
2 Tim **1.**3; **2.**25
Heb **9.**22, 25; **11.**37; **13.**21
Jas **1.**21; **3.**9[2]
1 Pet **1.**17; **2.**18; **3.**4; **5.**14[2]
2 Pet **2.**16, 18; **3.**3

1 Jn **5.6**^{2}
Jude .14, 23, 24
Rev **2.16**, 27; **5.2**; **6.8**^{3}; **8.7**; **11.6**; **12.5**; **13.10**^{2}; **14.7**, 9, 10, 15; **15.1**; **16.8**; **17.16**; **18.2**, 8, 16; **19.2**, 15^{2}, 17, 20

7. *on, at:* ἐπί (+dat.) EPI
except ^{a}+acc.
Mt **18.26**, 29
Acts **5.35**
Rom **10.19**
2 Cor **7.4**
Heb **8.8**^{2a}; **9.10**
3 Jn .10
Rev **12.17**; **18.9**^{a}

8. *by:* ὑπό (+gen.) HYPO
Acts **5.16**

9. *in accordance with, for:* κατά (+acc.) KATA
Mk **1.27**
Col **1.29**

10. *with:* μετά (+gen.) META
Mt **1.23**; **2.3**, 11; **4.21**; **5.25**, 41; **8.11**; **9.11**, 15; **12.3**, 4, 30^{2}, 41, 42, 45; **13.20**; **14.7**; **15.30**; **16.27**; **17.3**, 17; **18.16**, 23; **19.10**; **20.2**, 20; **21.2**; **24.30**, 31, 49, 51; **25.3**, 4, 10, 19, 31; **26.11**, 18, 20, 23, 29, 36, 38, 40, 47^{2}, 51, 55, 58, 69, 71, 72; **27.34**, 41, 54; **28.8**, 12, 20
Mk **1.13**, 20, 29, 36; **2.16**^{2}, 19^{2}, 25; **3.5**, 6, 7, 14; **4.16**, 36; **5.18**, 24, 40; **6.25**; **8.10**, 14, 38; **9.8**, [24‡; **10.30**; **11.11**; **13.26**; **14.7**, 14, 17, 18, 20, 33, 43^{2}, 48, 54, 62, 67; **15.1** [28‡, 31; **16.10**‡
Lk **1.28**, 39, 58, 66; **2.36**, 51; **5.29**, 30, 34; **6.3**, 4, 17; **7.36**; **8.13**; **9.49**; **10.17**; **11.7**, 23^{2}, 31, 32; **12.13**, 46, 58; **13.1**; **14.9**, 31; **15.29**, 30, 31; **17.15**, 20; **21.27**; **22.11**, 15, 21, 28, 33, 37, 52, 53, 59; **23.12**, 43; **24.29**, 30, 52
Jn **3.2**, 22, 26; **4.27**^{2}; **6.3**, 66; **7.33**; **8.29**; **11.16**, 31, 54; **12.8**, 17; **13.33**; **14.9**, 16, 30; **15.27**; **16.4**, 32; **17.12**, 24; **18.2**, 3, 5, 18, 26; **19.18**, 40; **20.7**, 24, 26
Acts **1.26**; **2.28**; **4.29**, 31; **7.9**, 38, 45; **9.19**, 28, 39; **10.38**; **11.21**; **13.17**; **14.23**, 27; **15.4**, 35; **17.11**; **18.10**; **20.19**, 31, 34; **24.1**, 3, [7‡; **25.12**, 23; **26.12**; **27.10**, 24
Rom **12.15**^{2}, 18; **15.10**, 33; **16.20**‡, [24‡
1 Cor **6.7**; **7.12**, 13; **16.11**, 12, 23, 24
2 Cor **6.15**, 16; **7.15**; **8.18**; **13.11**, 14(13)
Gal **2.1**, 12; **4.25**, 30; **6.18**
Eph **4.2**^{2}, 25; **6.5**, 7, 23, 24
Phil **1.4**; **2.12**, 29; **4.3**, 6, 9, 23
Col **1.11**; **4.18**
1 Th **1.6**; **3.13**; **5.28**
2 Th **1.7**^{2}; **3.16**, 18
1 Tim **1.14**; **2.15**; **4.3**, 4; **6.6**, 21
2 Tim **2.10**; **4.11**^{2}, 22^{2}
Tit **2.15**; **3.15**^{2}
Phm .25
Heb **4.16**; **5.7**; **7.21**; **9.19**; **10.22**; **11.9**; **12.14**, 17, 28; **13.23**, 25
1 Pet **3.15**
1 Jn **1.3**^{3}, 6, 7; **2.19**; **4.17**
2 Jn .2, 3
Rev **1.7**; **2.22**; **3.4**, 20^{2}, 21^{2}; **12.9**; **14.1**, 4; **17.2**, 12, 14; **18.3**, 9; **19.20**; **20.4**, 6; **21.3**^{3}; **22.21**

11. *beside, with:* παρά (+dat.) PARA
^{a}+gen.
Mt **8.**[10‡; **19.26**^{2}
Mk **10.27**^{2}
Lk **1.30**, 37^{a}; **2.52**; **11.37**; **18.27**
Jn **1.40**; **4.40**; **8.38**; **14.17**, 23, 25; **17.5**
Acts **9.43**; **10.6**; **18.3**; **21.7**, 8, 16; **28.14**
1 Cor **3.19**; **7.24**
Eph **6.9**
2 Tim **4.13**
Jas **1.17**
2 Pet **3.8**

12. *about, around:* περί (+acc.) PERI
^{a}+gen.
Mk **16.**[^{end}‡
Lk **10.40**
Acts **1.1**^{a}

13. *throw around, put on:* περιβάλλω (perf. pass. part.) PERIBALLŌ
Mk 14.51 man . . with nothing but a linen cloth

14. *gird about:* περιζώννυμι (perf. pass. part.) PERIZŌNNYMI [A.6.a.6]
Rev 1.13 son of man . . with a golden girdle

15. *do, make:* ποιέω (part.) POIEŌ
Rev 22. 2 tree of life^{r} with its twelve kinds of fruit

16. *to, with, against:* πρός (+acc.) PROS
Mt **13.56**
Mk **6.3**, 51; **8.16**; **9.14**, 16, 19^{2}, 34; **11.31**; **14.49**
Lk **6.11**; **9.41**; **18.11**; **20.5**; **23.12**; **24.14**, 17
Jn **1.1**, 2; **11.45**
Acts **2.47**; **4.15**; **13.36**; **15.2**; **17.17**; **24.12**; **25.19**
Rom **5.1**; **8.18**
1 Cor **2.3**; **16.6**, 7
2 Cor **5.8**; **6.14**, 15; **11.9**
Gal **1.18**; **4.18**, 20
Col **3.19**
1 Th **3.4**; **5.14**
2 Th **2.5**; **3.10**
Phm .13
Heb **4.13**; **10.16**
1 Jn **1.2**; **2.1**

17. *with:* σύν (+dat.) SYN
Mt **25.27**; **26.35**; **27.38**, 44
Mk **2.26**; **4.10**; **8.34**; **9.4**; **15.27**, 32
Lk **1.56**; **2.5**, 13; **5.9**, 19; **7.6**, 12; **8.1**, 38, [45‡, 51; **9.32**; **19.23**; **20.1**; **22.14**, 56; **23.11**, 32; **24.10**, 24, 29, 33, 44
Jn **12.2**; **18.1**; **21.3**
Acts **1.14**, 22; **2.14**; **3.4**, 8; **4.13**, 27; **5.1**, 17, 21, 26; **8.20**, 31; **10.2**, 23; **13.7**; **14.4**^{2}, 5, 13, 20, 28; **15.22**^{2}, 25; **17.34**; **18.18**; **19.38**; **20.36**; **21.5**, 16, 18, 26, 29; **22.9**; **23.27**, 32; **24.24**; **25.23**; **26.13**; **28.16**
Rom **6.8**; **8.32**; **16.14**, 15
1 Cor **5.4**; **10.13**; **15.10**
2 Cor **1.1**, 21; **4.14**^{2}; **9.4**; **13.4**
Gal **1.2**; **2.3**; **3.9**; **5.24**
Eph **3.18**; **4.31**
Phil **1.1**, 23; **2.22**; **4.21**
Col **2.5**, 13, 20; **3.3**, 4, 9; **4.9**
1 Th **4.14**, 17^{2}; **5.10**
Jas **1.11**
2 Pet **1.18**

18. *and, both . . . and:* τέ TE
Jn **2.15**

WITH, ALONG

1. *at the same time:* ἅμα (prep.) HAMA
Mt 13.29 " 'root up the wheat along with them

2. *with:* μετά (+gen.) META
Mt **22.16**
2 Tim **2.22**

3. *with:* σύν (+dat.) SYN
Acts **21.24**; **23.15**
1 Cor **11.32**

WITH S., AND

1. *and there:* κἀκεῖ KAKEI
Mt 10.11 "and stay with him until you depart

WITHDRAW

1. *withdraw:* ἀναχωρέω ANACHŌREŌ
Mt 2.22 he withdrew to the district of Galilee
4.12 he withdrew into Galilee
12.15 Jesus, aware of this, withdrew from there
14.13 when Jesus heard this, he withdrew
15.21 Jesus . . withdrew to the district of Tyre
Mk 3. 7 Jesus withdrew with his disciples
Jn 6.15 Jesus withdrew again to the mountain
Acts 26.31 when they had withdrawn, they said

2. *depart, withdraw from:* ἀφίστημι APHISTĒMI
Acts 15.38 one who had withdrawn . . in Pamphylia
19. 9 he withdrew . . , taking the disciples
22.29 those . . withdrew from him instantly

3. *draw away:* ἀποσπάω (pass.) APOSPAŌ
Lk 22.41 he withdrew . . about a stone's throw

4. *shun, avoid, turn aside:* ἐκνεύω EKNEUŌ*
Jn 5.13 did not know . . , for Jesus had withdrawn

5. *go back, avoid:* ὑποχωρέω HYPOCHŌREŌ*
Lk 5.16 But he withdrew to the wilderness
9.10 he took them and withdrew apart

WITHER
WITHER AWAY

1. *dry up:* ξηραίνω (pass.) XĒRAINŌ
[a]act.
Mt 13. 6 "since they had no root they withered away
21.19 And the fig tree withered at once
21.20 "How did the fig tree wither at once?
Mk 4. 6 "since it had no root it withered away
11.21 "fig tree which you cursed has withered
Lk 8. 6 "as it grew up, it withered away
Jn 15. 6 "he is cast forth as a branch and withers
Jas 1.11 [a]the sun rises . . and withers the grass
1 Pet 1.24 "grass withers, and the flower falls

WITHERED
WITHERED AWAY

1. *dry up:* ξηραίνω (perf. pass. part.) XĒRAINŌ
Mk 3. 1 a man was there who had a w. hand
11.20 fig tree withered away to its roots
2. *withered, dry:* ξηρός XĒROS
Mt 12.10 there was a man with a w. hand
Mk 3. 3 said to the man who had the w. hand
Lk 6. 6 man . . whose right hand was withered
6. 8 the man who had the withered hand

WITHHOLD

1. *hinder, prevent, withhold:* κωλύω KŌLYŌ
Lk 6.29 "do not withhold even your shirt

WITHIN
WITHIN, FROM

1. *in, at, by:* ἐν (+dat.) EN
Mk **2.**8
Lk **19.**44; **24.**32‡
Jn **5.**42
Acts **17.**16
Rom **7.**17, 18, 20
1 Cor **6.**19
Eph **3.**20
Col **1.**29
2 Tim **1.**6, 14
Rev **7.**15; **11.**19
2. *inside:* ἐντός ENTOS
Lk [17.21 "the kingdom of God is *within you*†
3. *within, inside:* ἔσωθεν ESŌTHEN
Mt 23.27 "within they are full of dead men's bones
23.28 "within you are full of hypocrisy
Mk 7.21 "For from within . . come evil thoughts
7.23 "All these evil things come from within
Lk 11. 7 "he will answer from w., 'Do not bother
2 Cor 7. 5 fighting without and fear within
Rev 4. 8 full of eyes all round and within
5. 1 a scroll written within and on the back

WITHOUT
WITHOUT ANY

1. *without:* ἄνευ ANEU
Mt 10.29 "not one . . will fall . . w. your Father's will
1 Pet 3. 1 they . . may be won without a word
2. *separately, apart from:* χωρίς CHŌRIS
Mt 13.34 he said nothing to them w. a parable
Mk 4.34 did not speak to them w. a parable
Lk 6.49 "built a house . . without a foundation
Jn 1. 3 without him was not anything made
Rom 10.14 how are they to hear w. a preacher?
1 Cor 4. 8 Without us you have become kings!
Phil 2.14 Do all things without grumbling
1 Tim 2. 8 lifting holy hands without anger
5.21 keep these rules without favor
Phm .14 to do nothing without your consent
Heb 4.15 tempted as we are, yet without sin
7.20 And it was not without an oath
7.21(20) priests took their office without an oath
9. 7 once a year, and not w. taking blood
9.18 covenant was not ratified w. blood
9.22 without the shedding of blood
Heb 10.28 w. mercy at the testimony of . . witnesses
11. 6 w. faith it is impossible to please him
12. 8 If you are left without discipline
12.14 w. which no one will see the Lord
3. *if not, unless:* ἐὰν μή EAN MĒ
Jn 7.51 "Does our law judge . . w. . . a hearing?
4. *outside:* ἔξωθεν EXŌTHEN
2 Cor 7. 5 fighting without and fear within
5. *not:* μή MĒ [A.4.c]
[a]μὴ ἔχων *not having*
Mt 9.36 [a]like sheep without a shepherd
22.12 [a]" 'how did you get in . . w. a . . garment?
23.23 "these . . , without neglecting the others
Mk 6.34 [a]like sheep without a shepherd
Lk 11.42 "these . . , without neglecting the others
Acts 9. 9 for three days he was without sight
9.38 "Please come to us without delay
1 Cor 11.29 who eats . . w. discerning the body
Eph 5.27 [a]might present the church . . , w. spot
1 Tim 1. 7 teachers of the law, w. understanding
Jas 1. 5 God, who gives to all . . w. reproaching
2.16 without giving them the things needed
1 Pet 2.16 w. using your freedom as a pretext
6. *no one:* μηδείς (neut.) MĒDEIS [A.4.c]
Acts **10.**20
1 Cor **10.**25, 27
7. *with:* μετά (neg.+gen.) META
Acts **5.**26; **24.**18
8. *not, no:* οὐ OU [A.4.c]
1 Cor **9.**7[2]
2 Cor **10.**16
1 Pet **1.**8

WITHOUT GIFTS, HE THAT IS

1. *private individual, layman:* ἰδιώτης IDIŌTĒS
1 Cor [14.16 in the position of *him that is w. gifts*†

WITHOUT LAW
WITHOUT THE LAW

1. *lawless:* ἄνομος ANOMOS
1 Cor 9.21 not being without law toward God
2. *lawlessly:* ἀνόμως ANOMŌS*
Rom 2.12 All who have sinned without the law will also perish without the law

WITHSTAND

1. *withstand:* ἀνθίστημι ANTHISTĒMI
Lk 21.15 "none . . will be able to w. or contradict
Acts 6.10 they could not withstand the wisdom
13. 8 But Elymas . . withstood them
Eph 6.13 that you may be able to withstand
2. *hinder, prevent, withhold:* κωλύω KŌLYŌ
Acts 11.17 "who was I that I could withstand God?

WITNESS
WITNESS, BE A
WITNESS, BEAR

1. *bear witness, testify:* μαρτυρέω MARTYREŌ
[a]subst. part.
Mt 23.31 "Thus you witness against yourselves
Jn 1. 7 He came . . to bear w. to the light
1. 8 He . . came to bear witness to the light
1.15 (John bore witness . . "This was he
1.32 John bore witness, "I saw the Spirit
1.34 "I have seen and have borne witness
2.25 he . . needed no one to bear w. of man
3.11 "we . . bear witness to what we have seen
3.26 "he . . to whom you bore w., here he is
3.28 "You yourselves bear me witness
3.32 He bears witness to what he has seen
5.31 "If I bear witness to myself
5.32 "another who bears witness to me
5.33 "he has borne witness to the truth
5.36 "the works . . bear me witness
5.37 "the Father . . has himself borne witness
5.39 "it is they that bear witness to me
8.13 "You are bearing witness to yourself
8.14 "Even if I do bear witness to myself
8.18 "I bear witness to myself, and the Father . . bears witness to me

Jn 10.25 "The works . . bear witness to me
12.17 The crowd . . bore witness
15.26 "Spirit of truth . . will bear w. to me
15.27 "you also are witnesses
18.23 "If I have spoken wrongly, bear w.
18.37 "I have come . . to bear w. to the truth
19.35 He who saw it has borne witness
21.24 This is the disciple who is bearing w.
Acts 10.43 "To him all the prophets bear witness
14. 3 bore witness to the word of his grace
15. 8 "God . . bore witness to them
22. 5 "the whole council of elders bear me w.
23.11 "so you must bear witness also at Rome
Rom 3.21 law and the prophets bear w.
10. 2 I bear them w. that they have a zeal
Gal 4.15 For I bear you witness that, if possible
Col 4.13 I bear him w. that he has worked hard
Heb 7.17 it is witnessed of him, "Thou art a priest
10.15 the Holy Spirit also bears witness to us
11. 4 God bearing w. by accepting his gifts
1 Jn 5. 7(6) [a]And the Spirit is the witness
5. 8(7) [a]There are three witnesses
5. 9 he has borne witness to his Son
Rev 1. 2 who bore witness to the word of God

2. *testimony, evidence:* μαρτυρία MARTYRIA
Mk 14.56 For many bore false witness against him
Rev 6. 9 slain . . for the witness they had borne

3. *testimony, proof:* μαρτύριον MARTYRION
Acts 7.44 "the tent of witness in the wilderness
Rev 15. 5 the temple of the tent of w. in heaven

4. *witness, martyr:* μάρτυς MARTYS
[a]A.1.d
Mt 18.16 "evidence of two or three witnesses
26.65 "Why do we still need witnesses?
Mk 14.63 "Why do we still need witnesses?
Lk 11.48 "So you are witnesses and consent
24.48 "You are witnesses of these things
Acts 1. 8 "you shall be my witnesses in Jerusalem
1.22 "one . . must become with us a witness
2.32 "of that we all are witnesses
3.15 "To this we are witnesses
5.32 "we are witnesses to these things
6.13 ⟨they⟩ set up false witnesses
7.58 the witnesses laid down their garments
10.39 "we are witnesses to all that he did
10.41 "who were chosen by God as witnesses
13.31 "now his witnesses to the people
22.15 " 'for you will be a witness for him
22.20 " 'the blood of Stephen thy witness
26.16 [a]" 'appoint you to serve and bear witness
Rom 1. 9 For God is my witness
2 Cor 1.23 [a]I call God to witness against me
13. 1 evidence of two or three witnesses
Phil 1. 8 God is my witness, how I yearn
1 Th 2. 5 we never used . . flattery, . . as God is w.
2.10 You are witnesses, and God also
1 Tim 5.19 the evidence of two or three witnesses
6.12 confession in the presence of . . witnesses
2 Tim 2. 2 what you have heard . . before . . witnesses
Heb 10.28 the testimony of two or three witnesses
12. 1 so great a cloud of witnesses
1 Pet 5. 1 a witness of the sufferings of Christ
Rev 1. 5 Jesus Christ the faithful witness
2.13 " 'Antipas my witness, my faithful one
3.14 " 'the Amen, the faithful and true witness
11. 3 "I will grant my two witnesses power

5. *confirm, bear testimony with:* συμμαρτυρέω SYMMARTYREŌ
Rom 9. 1 my conscience bears me witness

WITNESS, ALSO BEAR

1. *confirm, bear testimony with:* συμμαρτυρέω SYMMARTYREŌ
Rom 2.15 their conscience also bears witness

2. *join in attesting:* συνεπιμαρτυρέω SYNEPIMARTYREŌ*
Heb 2. 4 God also bore witness by signs

WITNESS, BEAR FALSE

1. *be a false witness:* ψευδομαρτυρέω PSEUDOMARTYREŌ*
Mt 19.18 "You shall not bear false witness
Mk 10.19 " 'Do not bear false witness
14.56 many bore false witness against him
14.57 some . . bore false witness against him
Lk 18.20 " 'Do not bear false witness

WITNESS, FALSE

1. *false witness, perjury:* ψευδομαρτυρία PSEUDOMARTYRIA
Mt 15.19 "fornication, theft, false witness, slander

2. *false witness:* ψευδόμαρτυς PSEUDOMARTYS
Mt 26.60 many false witnesses came forward

WITNESS WITH, BEAR

1. *confirm, bear testimony with:* συμμαρτυρέω SYMMARTYREŌ
Rom 8.16 Spirit . . bearing witness with our spirit

WITNESS, WITHOUT

1. *without witness:* ἀμάρτυρος AMARTYROS*
Acts 14.17 "he did not leave himself without w.

WOE

1. *woe, alas:* οὐαί OUAI
Mt 11.21 "Woe to you Chorazin! woe to you, Bethsaida!
18. 7 "W. to the world for temptations to sin![a]
18. 7 "w. to the man by whom the temptation!
23.13 "woe to you, scribes and Pharisees!
Also Mt **23.**[14‡, 15, 23, 25, 27, 29
23.16 "Woe to you, blind guides
26.24 "woe to that man by whom the Son!
Mk 14.21 "woe to that man by whom the Son!
Lk 6.24 "But woe to you that are rich
6.25 "Woe to you that are full now
6.25 "Woe to you that laugh now
6.26 "Woe to you, when all speak well of you
10.13 "Woe to you, Chorazin! woe to you, Bethsaida!
11.42 "But woe to you Pharisees!
11.43 "Woe to you Pharisees!
11.44 "W. to you! for you are like graves
11.46 "Woe to you lawyers also!
11.47 "Woe to you! for you build the tombs
11.52 "Woe to you lawyers!
17. 1 "but woe to him by whom they come!
22.22 "w. to that man by whom he is betrayed!
1 Cor 9.16 "Woe to me if I do not preach the gospel!
Jude .11 Woe to them!
Rev 8.13 I heard an eagle crying with a loud voice . . "Woe, woe, woe to those who dwell on the earth!
9.12 The first woe has passed; behold, two woes are still to come
11.14 The second woe has passed; behold, the third woe is soon to come
12.12 "But woe to you, O earth and sea!

WOLF

1. *wolf:* λύκος LYKOS*
Mt 7.15 "who . . inwardly are ravenous wolves
10.16 "as sheep in the midst of wolves
Lk 10. 3 "as lambs in the midst of wolves
Jn 10.12 "a hireling . . sees the wolf . . and flees; and the wolf snatches them
Acts 20.29 "after my departure . . wolves will come

WOMAN (*See also* DIVORCED WOMAN)

1. *feminine:* γυναικεῖος (subst.) GYNAIKEIOS*
1 Pet 3. 7 bestowing honor on the woman

2. *woman, wife:* γυνή GYNĒ
Mt 5.28 "every one who looks at a woman lustfully
9.20 w. who had suffered from a hemorrhage
9.22 instantly the woman was made well
11.11 "among those born of women
13.33 "like leaven which a w. took and hid
14.21 five thousand men, besides women
15.22 Canaanite woman . . came out and cried
15.28 "O woman, great is your faith!
15.38 four thousand men, besides women
22.27 "After them all, the woman died
26. 7 a woman came up to him
26.10 "Why do you trouble the woman?
27.55 There were also many women there

Mt 28. 5 But the angel said to the women
Mk 5.25 a woman who had had a flow of blood
5.33 the w... came in fear and trembling
7.25 w., whose little daughter was possessed
7.26 Now the woman was a Greek
12.22 "Last of all the woman also died
14. 3 A woman came with an alabaster flask
15.40 also women looking on from afar
Lk [1.28 *"Blessed are you among women!*‡
1.42 "Blessed are you among women!
4.26 "sent.. to a woman who was a widow
7.28 among those born of women
7.37 a woman of the city, who was a sinner
7.39 "who and what sort of woman this is
7.44 turning toward the woman he said to Simon, "Do you see this woman?
7.50 to the w., "Your faith has saved you
8. 2 also some women who had been healed
8.43 a woman who had had a flow of blood
8.47 the woman saw that she was not hidden
10.38 a woman named Martha received him
11.27 a woman in the crowd raised her voice
13.11 a w. who had had a spirit of infirmity
13.12 "W., you are freed from your infirmity
13.21 "leaven which a woman took and hid
15. 8 "what woman, having ten silver coins[t]
20.32 "Afterward the woman also died
20.33 "whose wife will the woman be?
22.57 "Woman, I do not know him
23.27 multitude.. of women who bewailed
23.49 the women who had followed him
23.55 The women who had come with him
24.22 "women of our company amazed us
24.24 "found it just as the women had said
Jn 2. 4 "O woman, what have you to do with me?
4. 7 There came a woman of Samaria
4. 9 The Samaritan woman said to him, "How is it that you.. ask.. me, a woman?
4.11 The woman said to him, "Sir
4.15 The woman said to him, "Sir
4.17 The w. answered.. "I have no husband
4.19 The woman said to him, "Sir
4.21 "W., believe me, the hour is coming
4.25 The woman said to him, "I know
4.27 marveled that he was talking with a w.
4.28 So the woman left her water jar
4.39 because of the woman's testimony
4.42 They said to the woman
8. 3 a woman who had been caught in adultery[r]‡
8. 4 "Teacher, this woman has been caught[r]‡
8. 9 Jesus was left alone with the woman[r]‡
8.10 "Woman, where are they?[r]‡
16.21 "When a w. is in travail she has sorrow
19.26 "Woman, behold, your son!
20.13 "Woman, why are you weeping?
20.15 "Woman, why are you weeping?
Acts 1.14 prayer.. with the women and Mary
5.14 multitudes both of men and women
8. 3 he dragged off men and women
8.12 baptized, both men and women
9. 2 so that if he found any.., men or women
13.50 the Jews incited the devout women
16. 1 a Jewish woman who was a believer
16.13 we sat down and spoke to the women
16.14 One who heard us was a woman
17. 4 not a few of the leading women
17.12 not a few Greek women of high standing
17.34 a woman named Damaris
22. 4 "delivering to prison.. men and women
Rom 7. 2 a married woman is bound by law
1 Cor 7. 1 It is well for a man not to touch a w.
7.13 If any woman has a husband
7.34 the unmarried woman or girl[z] is anxious
11. 3 the head of a woman is her husband
11. 5 any woman who prays or prophesies
11. 6 if a woman will not veil herself
11. 6 disgraceful for a woman to be shorn
1 Cor 11. 7 but woman is the glory of man
11. 8 (For man was not made from woman, but woman from man
11. 9 (Neither was man created for woman, but woman for man
11.10 why a woman ought to have a veil[r]
11.11 (in the Lord woman is not independent of man nor man of woman
11.12 (for as woman was made from man, so man is now born of woman
11.13 is it proper for a woman to pray?
11.15 if a w. has long hair, it is her pride
14.34 women should keep silence in the churches
14.35 shameful for a woman to speak in church
Gal 4. 4 God sent forth his Son, born of woman
1 Tim 2. 9 women should adorn themselves modestly
2.10 by good deeds, as befits women
2.11 Let a woman learn in silence
2.12 I permit no woman to teach
2.14 Adam was not deceived, but the woman
3.11 The women likewise must be serious
Heb 11.35 Women received their dead
1 Pet 3. 5 the holy women who hoped in God
Rev 2.20 " 'that you tolerate the woman Jezebel
9. 8 their hair like women's hair
12. 1 a woman clothed with the sun
12. 4 the dragon stood before the woman
12. 6 the woman fled into the wilderness
12.13 the dragon.. pursued the woman
12.14 the woman was given the two wings
12.15 The serpent poured water.. after the w.
12.16 earth came to the help of the woman
12.17 the dragon was angry with the woman
14. 4 have not defiled themselves with women
17. 3 a woman sitting on a scarlet beast
17. 4 The woman was arrayed in purple
17. 6 w., drunk with the blood of the saints
17. 7 "I will tell you the mystery of the w.
17. 9 "mountains on which the w. is seated
17.18 "the w. that you saw is the great city
3. *female:* θῆλυς (subst. fem.) THĒLYS
Rom 1.26 women exchanged natural relations
1.27 gave up natural relations with women
CONTEXTUALLY
Mt **5.**32; **19.**[9‡; **24.**41
Mk **15.**41
Lk **13.**16; **16.**18; **17.**35; **24.**10
1 Cor **7.**2
Gal **4.**22, 23, 24, 30, 31
Phil **4.**3
1 Th **5.**3
1 Tim **2.**15; **5.**2[2], 16
Tit **2.**4

WOMAN, EACH
1. *each:* ἕκαστος (subst. fem.) HEKASTOS
1 Cor 7. 2 each woman her own husband

WOMAN, WEAK
1. *silly woman:* γυναικάριον GYNAIKARION*
2 Tim 3. 6 weak women, burdened with sins

WOMB
1. *belly:* γαστήρ GASTĒR
Lk 1.31 "behold, you will conceive in your w.
2. *body cavity, belly:* κοιλία KOILIA
Lk 1.15 "filled.., even from his mother's w.
1.41 the babe leaped in her womb
1.42 "blessed is the fruit of your womb!
1.44 "the babe in my womb leaped for joy
2.21 before he was conceived in the womb
11.27 "Blessed is the womb that bore you
23.29 " 'Blessed.. the wombs that never bore!
Jn 3. 4 "enter a second time into his mother's w.
3. *womb:* μήτρα MĒTRA*
Lk 2.23 ("Every male that opens the womb
Rom 4.19 the barrenness of Sarah's womb

WONDER
WONDER AT
1. *wonder, portent:* τέρας TERAS*
Mt 24.24 "will . . show . . wonders, so as to lead astray
Mk 13.22 "show signs and wonders, to lead astray
Jn 4.48 "Unless you see signs and wonders
Acts 2.19 " 'I will show wonders in the heaven
2.22 "attested . . with mighty works and wonders
2.43 many wonders and signs were done
4.30 "signs and wonders are performed
5.12 many signs and wonders were done
6. 8 Stephen . . did great wonders and signs
7.36 "having performed wonders and signs
14. 3 granting signs and wonders to be done
15.12 they related what signs and wonders
Rom 15.19 the power of signs and wonders
2 Cor 12.12 signs and wonders and mighty works
2 Th 2. 9 with pretended signs and wonders
Heb 2. 4 bore witness by signs and wonders
2. *wonder, amazement:* θάμβος THAMBOS
Acts 3.10 they were filled with wonder
3. *wonder, marvel:* θαῦμα THAUMA
2 Cor 11.14 no w., for even Satan disguises himself
4. *marvel, admire:* θαυμάζω THAUMAZŌ
Mt 15.31 so that the throng wondered
27.14 so that the governor wondered greatly
Mk 15. 5 no . . answer, so that Pilate wondered
15.44 Pilate wondered if he were already dead
Lk 1.21 wondered at his delay in the temple
2.18 all who heard it wondered
4.22 all . . wondered at the gracious words
[24.12 *he went . . wondering at what had happened*‡
24.41 disbelieved for joy, and wondered
Acts 2. 7 they were amazed and wondered
3.12 "Men of Israel, why do you w. at this?
4.13 when they saw . ., they wondered
7.31 "When Moses saw it he wondered
13.41 " 'Behold, you scoffers, and wonder
1 Jn 3.13 Do not w. . . that the world hates you
IDIOMATICALLY
a. Rev 13.3 the whole earth followed the beast with wonder
ἐθαυμάσθη ὅλη ἡ γῆ ὀπίσω τοῦ θηρίου [THAUMAZŌ]
CONTEXTUALLY
Acts 5.24 wondering what this would come to

WONDERFUL (*See also* WHAT WONDERFUL)
1. *wonderful:* θαυμάσιος THAUMASIOS*
Mt 21.15 the scribes saw the w. things that he did
2. *wonderful:* θαυμαστός THAUMASTOS
Rev 15. 1 another portent . ., great and wonderful
15. 3 "Great and wonderful are thy deeds!

WONDERFUL DEEDS
1. *excellence, goodness:* ἀρετή (pl.) ARETĒ
1 Pet 2. 9 that you may declare the w. deeds

WONT
CONTEXTUALLY
Mk 15. 8 to do as he was wont to do for them

WOOD
1. *tree, wood:* ξύλον XYLON
Lk 23.31 "if they do this when the wood is green
1 Cor 3.12 if any . . builds on the foundation with . . w.
Rev 18.12 cargo of . . all kinds of scented w. . ., all articles of costly wood, bronze

WOOD, OF
1. *wooden:* ξύλινος XYLINOS*
2 Tim 2.20 vessels . . of wood and earthenware
Rev 9.20 idols of gold . . and stone and wood

WOOL
1. *wool:* ἔριον ERION*
Heb 9.19 he took the blood of calves . ., with . . wool
Rev 1.14 white as white wool, white as snow

WORD (*See also* FLATTERING WORDS)
1. *oracle:* λόγιον (pl.) LOGION
Heb 5.12 the first principles of God's word
2. *word, reckoning:* λόγος LOGOS
Mt 7.24 "Every one then who hears these words
7.26 "every one who hears these words
8. 8 "say the w., and my servant will be healed
8.16 he cast out the spirits with a word
10.14 "if any one will not . . listen to your words
12.32 "whoever says a word against the Son
12.37 "by your words you will be justified, and by your words you will be condemned
13.19 "When any one hears the word
13.20 "who hears the word and . . receives it
13.21 "persecution arises on account of the w.
13.22 "this is he who hears the word, but . . the delight in riches choke the word
13.23 "who hears the word and understands it
15. 6 "you have made void the word[p] of God‡
15.23 But he did not answer her a word
22.46 no one was able to answer him a word
24.35 "but my words will not pass away
26.44 he . . prayed . ., saying the same words
Mk 2. 2 he was preaching the word to them
4.14 "The sower sows the word
4.15 "along the path, where the word is sown
4.15 "Satan . . comes and takes away the w.
4.16 "who, when they hear the word
4.17 "persecution arises on account of the w.
4.18 "they are those who hear the word
4.19 "cares . . and . . delight in riches . . choke the w.
4.20 "who hear the word and accept it
4.33 With . . parables he spoke the w. to them
7.13 "making void the word of God
8.38 "whoever is ashamed . . of my words
10.24 disciples were amazed at his words
13.31 "but my words will not pass away
14.39 he . . prayed, saying the same words
Lk 1. 2 eyewitnesses and ministers of the word
1.20 "because you did not believe my words
3. 4 in the book of the words of Isaiah
4.22 all . . wondered at the gracious words
4.32 for his word was with authority
4.36 "What is this word?
5. 1 pressed upon him to hear the w. of God
6.47 "Every one who . . hears my words
7. 7 "say the w., and let my servant be healed
8.11 "The seed is the word of God
8.12 "devil comes and takes away the word
8.13 "when they hear the word, receive it
8.15 "who, hearing the word, hold it fast
8.21 "those who hear the word of God
9.26 "whoever is ashamed . . of my words
9.44 "Let these words sink into your ears
11.28 "Blessed rather are those who hear the w.!
12.10 "who speaks a w. against the Son of man
21.33 "but my words will not pass away
24.19 "a prophet mighty in deed and word
24.44 "my words which I spoke to you
Jn 1. 1 In the beginning was the Word, and the Word was with God, and the Word was God
1.14 W. became flesh and dwelt among us
2.22 the word which Jesus had spoken
4.41 many more believed because of his w.
4.50 believed the word that Jesus spoke
5.24 "he who hears my word and believes
5.38 "you do not have his w. abiding in you
7.40 When they heard these words
8.31 "If you continue in my word
8.37 "because my word finds no place in you
8.43 "because you cannot bear to hear my word
8.51 "if any one keeps my word
8.52 " 'If any one keeps my word
8.55 "I do know him and I keep his word
10.19 a division . . because of these words
10.35 "called them gods to whom the w. . . came
12.38 the word spoken by the prophet Isaiah
12.48 "w. that I have spoken will be his judge
14.23 "If a man loves me, he will keep my w.
14.24 "He . . does not keep my words

Jn 14.24 "the word which you hear is not mine
15. 3 "You are already made clean by the w.
15.20 "Remember the word that I said to you
15.20 "if they kept my w., they will keep yours
15.25 "It is to fulfil the word that is written
17. 6 "they have kept thy word
17.14 "I have given them thy word
17.17 "thy word is truth
17.20 "who believe in me through their word
18. 9 This was to fulfil the word
18.32 This was to fulfil the word
19. 8 When Pilate heard these words
19.13 When Pilate heard these words
Acts 2.22 "Men of Israel, hear these words
2.40 he testified with many other words
2.41 those who received his w. were baptized
4. 4 many . . who heard the word believed
4.29 "to speak thy word with all boldness
4.31 spoke the word of God with boldness
5. 5 When Ananias heard these words
5.24 the chief priests heard these words
6. 2 "give up preaching the word of God
6. 4 "devote ourselves . . to the ministry of the w.
6. 7 And the word of God increased
7.22 "he was mighty in his words and deeds
8. 4 those . . went about preaching the word
8.14 Samaria had received the word of God
8.25 when they had . . spoken the word
10.36 "You know the word which he sent
10.44 Holy Spirit fell on all who heard the w.
11. 1 the Gentiles also had received the w.
11.19 speaking the word to none except Jews
12.24 the word of God grew and multiplied
13. 5 they proclaimed the word of God
13. 7 who . . sought to hear the word of God
13.15 "if you have any word of exhortation
13.44 gathered together to hear the w. of God
13.46 "that the word of God should be spoken
13.48 they . . glorified the word of God
13.49 the word of the Lord spread
14. 3 bore witness to the word of his grace
14.25 when they had spoken the w. in Perga
15. 7 "Gentiles should hear . . w. of the gospel
15.15 "with this the words of . . prophets agree
15.24 "some . . have troubled you with words
15.27 "who . . will tell you . . by word of mouth
15.32 exhorted the brethren with many words
15.35 preaching the word of the Lord
15.36 "we proclaimed the word of the Lord
16. 6 forbidden . . to speak the word in Asia
16.32 they spoke the word of the Lord to him
16.36 the jailer reported the words to Paul
17.11 they received the w. with all eagerness
17.13 the word of God was proclaimed by Paul
18.11 teaching the w. of God among them
18.15 "it is a matter of questions about words
19.10 all the residents of Asia heard the word
19.20 So the word of the Lord grew
20.32 "I commend you . . to the word of his grace
20.35 "remembering . . words of the Lord Jesus
20.38 because of the word he had spoken
22.22 Up to this word they listened to him
Rom 3. 4 "That thou . . be justified in thy words
9. 6 not as though the w. of God had failed
15.18 to win obedience . . by word and deed
1 Cor 1.18 For the word of the cross is folly
2. 1 not . . proclaiming . . in lofty words
2. 4 not in plausible words of wisdom
2.13 we impart this in words not taught
14.19 rather . . five words with my mind . . than ten thousand words in a tongue
14.36 Did the word of God originate with you?
2 Cor 1.18 our w. to you has not been Yes and No
2.17 we are not . . peddlers of God's word
4. 2 we refuse . . to tamper with God's word
Gal 5.14 the whole law is fulfilled in one word
6. 6 Let him who is taught the word share
Eph 1.13 who have heard the word of truth
5. 6 Let no one deceive . . with empty words
Phil 1.14 more bold to speak the word of God
2.16 holding fast the word of life
Col 1. 5 heard before in the word of the truth
1.25 to make the word of God fully known
3.16 Let the word of Christ dwell in you
3.17 whatever you do, in word or deed
4. 3 that God may open . . a door for the w.
1 Th 1. 5 our gospel came to you not only in word
1. 6 you received the word in much affliction
1. 8 the word of the Lord sounded forth
2. 5 we never used either words of flattery
2.13 when you received the word of God
2.13 accepted it not as the word of men
2.13 word of God, which is at work in you
4.15 we declare . . by the word of the Lord
4.18 comfort one another with these words
2 Th 2. 2 not . . excited, either by spirit or by w.
2.15 taught by us, either by word of mouth
2.17 establish them in every good . . word
3. 1 that the word of the Lord may speed
1 Tim 4. 5 it is consecrated by the word of God
4. 6 nourished on the words of the faith
6. 3 sound words of our Lord Jesus Christ
2 Tim 1.13 Follow the pattern of the sound words
2. 9 But the word of God is not fettered
2.15 rightly handling the word of truth
4. 2 preach the word, be urgent in season
Tit 1. 3 at the proper time manifested in his w.
1. 9 he must hold firm to the sure word
2. 5 that the w. of God . . not be discredited
Heb 4.12 the word of God is living and active
5.13 unskilled in the word of righteousness
7.28 word of the oath, which came later
13. 7 those who spoke to you the w. of God
13.22 bear with my word of exhortation
Jas 1.18 he brought us forth by the word of truth
1.21 receive with meekness the implanted w.
1.22 be doers of the word, and not hearers
1.23 a hearer of the word and not a doer
1 Pet 1.23 the living and abiding word of God
2. 8 stumble because they disobey the w.
3. 1 some, though they do not obey the word, may be won without a word
2 Pet 1.19 the prophetic word made more sure
2. 3 they will exploit you with false words
3. 5 by the word of God heavens existed
3. 7 by the same word the heavens
1 Jn 1. 1 concerning the word of life
1.10 his word is not in us
2. 5 whoever keeps his word
2. 7 the old commandment is the word
2.14 the word of God abides in you
3.18 let us not love in word or speech
3 Jn .10 prating against me with evil words
Rev 1. 2 bore witness to the word of God
1. 3 Blessed is he who reads . . the words
1. 9 on . . Patmos on account of the w. of God
3. 8 " 'yet you have kept my word
3.10 " 'Because you have kept my word
6. 9 who had been slain for the w. of God
12.11 "conquered . . by the w. of their testimony
17.17 "until the words of God shall be fulfilled
19. 9 "These are true words of God
19.13 the name . . is The Word of God
20. 4 souls . . beheaded . . for the word of God
21. 5 "these words are trustworthy and true
22. 6 "These words are trustworthy and true
22. 7 Blessed is he who keeps the words
22. 9 "those who keep the words of this book
22.10 "Do not seal up the words of the prophecy
22.18 I warn every one who hears the words
22.19 if any one takes away from the words

Also variant to: Lk **22.61**

3. *word, report:* φάσις PHASIS*
Acts 21.31 word came to the tribune of the cohort

4. *word, saying:* ῥῆμα RHĒMA
Mt 4. 4 “ ‘by every word that proceeds from . . God
12.36 “for every careless word they utter
18.16 “that every word may be confirmed
Lk 1.38 “let it be to me according to your word
2.29 “depart in peace, according to thy word
3. 2 the word of God came to John
5. 5 “at your word I will let down the nets
22.61 Peter remembered the w. of the Lord
Var. LOGOS
24. 8 they remembered his words
24.11 these words seemed to them an idle tale
Jn 3.34 he . . utters the words of God
5.47 “how will you believe my words?
6.63 “the words that I have spoken to you
6.68 “You have the words of eternal life
8.20 These words he spoke in the treasury
8.47 “who is of God hears the words of God
14.10 “The words that I say to you
15. 7 “If . . my words abide in you, ask
17. 8 “I have given them the words
Acts 2.14 “Men of Judea . . , give ear to my words
5.20 “speak . . all the words of this Life
6.11 “blasphemous words against Moses
6.13 “to speak words against this holy place
10.37 “w. . . proclaimed throughout all Judea
11.16 “I remembered the word of the Lord
16.38 reported these words to the magistrates
Rom 10. 8 The word is near you, on your lips . . (that is, the word of faith which we preach
10.18 “their words to the ends of the world
Eph 5.26 by the washing of water with the word
6.17 sword of the spirit, . . the word of God
Heb 1. 3 upholding the universe by his w. of power
6. 5 tasted the goodness of the word of God
11. 3 world was created by the word of God
12.19 whose words made the hearers entreat
1 Pet 1.25 “word of the Lord abides for ever.” That word is the good news

IDIOMATICALLY
a. Mt 27.19 his wife sent word to him ἀπέστειλεν πρὸς αὐτὸν ἡ γυνὴ αὐτοῦ λέγουσα [LEGŌ]
b. Acts 14.18 With these words καὶ ταῦτα λέγοντες [LEGŌ]

CONTEXTUALLY
Mt 11. 2 he sent word by his disciples
Lk 22.65 they spoke many other words against him
Jn 17. 1 When Jesus had spoken these words
18. 1 When Jesus had spoken these words
Acts [28.29 *And when he had said these words*‡
Rom 4.23 words . . written not for his sake alone
Rev 13. 5 uttering haughty and blasphemous words

WORD, BRING
1. *bring tidings:* ἀπαγγέλλω APAGGELLŌ
Mt 2. 8 “when you have found him bring me w.

WORD TO, BREAK ONE’S
1. *deny, nullify:* ἀθετέω ATHETEŌ
Mk 6.26 king . . did not want to break his word to her

WORDS
1. *speech, dialect:* λαλιά LALIA
Jn 4.42 “It is no longer because of your words

IDIOMATICALLY
a. Lk 19.48 for all the people hung upon his words ὁ λαὸς γὰρ ἅπας ἐξεκρέματο αὐτοῦ ἀκούων [AKOUŌ]
b. Rev 2.1 “ ‘The words of Τάδε λέγει [LEGŌ]
Also Rev **2.**8, 12, 18; **3.**1, 7, 14

WORDS, DISPUTE ABOUT
1. *fight about words:* λογομαχέω LOGOMACHEŌ*
2 Tim 2.14 to avoid disputing about words
2. *war about words:* λογομαχία LOGOMACHIA*
1 Tim 6. 4 craving . . for disputes about words

WORDS, FAIR
1. *fair speaking:* χρηστολογία CHRĒSTOLOGIA*
Rom 16.18 by fair and flattering words they deceive

WORDS, MANY
1. *much speaking, wordiness:* πολυλογία POLYLOGIA*
Mt 6. 7 “think . . they will be heard for their many w.

WORDS, TOO DEEP FOR
1. *inexpressible:* ἀλάλητος ALALĒTOS*
Rom 8.26 intercedes . . with sighs too deep for words

WORK (*See also* ALREADY DONE, WORK; MIGHTY WORK)
WORK, DO
WORK FOR
WORK IN, BE AT
WORK, PERFORM
WORK WITHIN, BE AT
WROUGHT, BE
1. *operation, activity:* ἐνέργεια ENERGEIA [B.1.a.2]
Eph 4.16 when each part is working properly
2. *operate, be effective:* ἐνεργέω ENERGEŌ
[a]+ ἐν
Mt 14. 2 “why these powers are at work in him
Mk 6.14 [a]“why these powers are at work in him
Rom 7. 5 [a]passions . . were at work in our members
2 Cor 4.12 [a]So death is at work in us, but life in you
Gal 2. 8 (for he who worked through Peter . . worked through me also for the Gentiles
3. 5 Does he who . . works miracles among you?
5. 6 but faith working[x] through love†
Eph 2. 2 [a]following . . the spirit that is now at w.
3.20 [a]who by the power at work within us
Phil 2.13 [a]God is at work in you, both to will and to work for his good pleasure
1 Th 2.13 [a]word . . , which is at work in you believers
2 Th 2. 7 mystery of lawlessness is already at w.
3. *work, do:* ἐργάζομαι ERGAZOMAI
Mt 21.28 “ ‘Son, go and work in the vineyard today
Lk 13.14 “six days on which work ought to be done
Jn 3.21 his deeds have been wrought in God
5.17 Jesus answered them, “My Father is working still, and I am working
6.30 “What work do you perform?
9. 4 “We must work the works of him who sent me . . ; night comes, when no one can w.
Acts 18. 3 he stayed with them, and they worked
Rom 4. 4 to one who works, his wages are . . his due
4. 5 to one who does not work but trusts
1 Cor 4.12 we labor, working with our own hands
Eph 4.28 doing honest work with his hands
Col 3.23 Whatever your task, work heartily
1 Th 2. 9 we worked night and day
4.11 to work with your hands
2 Th 3. 8 with toil . . we worked night and day
3.10 If any one will not work, let him not eat
3.11 busybodies, not doing any work
3.12 exhort . . to do their w. in quietness
Jas 1.20 the anger of man does not work
2 Jn . 8 not lose what you[a] have worked for‡
4. *work, deed:* ἔργον ERGON
Mt 5.16 “that they may see your good works
Mk 13.34 “servants in charge, each with his work
Jn 4.34 “My food is . . to accomplish his work
5.20 “greater works than these will he show
5.36 “works which the Father has granted me . . , these very works which I am doing
6.28 “to be doing the works of God
6.29 “This is the w. of God, that you believe
7. 3 “that your disciples may see the works
7. 7 “I testify of it that its works are evil
9. 3 “that . . works of God might be . . manifest
9. 4 “the works of him who sent me
10.25 “works that I do in my Father’s name
10.32 “I have shown you many good works
10.33 “not for a good work that we stone you
10.37 “If I am not doing . . works of my Father
10.38 “believe the works, that you may know
14.10 “but the Father . . does his works
14.11 “believe me for the sake of the works
14.12 “who believes in me will also do the works
15.24 “If I had not done among them the works

Jn 17. 4 "the work which thou gavest me to do
Acts 7.41 "rejoiced in the works of their hands
9.36 full of good works and . . charity
13. 2 "Set apart for me . . Saul for the work
14.26 they had been commended . . for the w.
15.38 who . . had not gone with them to the w.
Rom 2. 6 to every man according to his works
3.20 no . . being will be justified . . by works
3.27 It is excluded. . . On the principle of works?
3.28 justified by faith apart from works
4. 2 if Abraham was justified by works
4. 6 reckons righteousness apart from works
9.11 not because of works but . . his call
9.32 as if it were based on works
11. 6 it is no longer on the basis of works
13.12 then cast off the works of darkness
14.20 Do not . . destroy the work of God
1 Cor 3.13 each man's work will become manifest
3.13 fire will test what sort of work
3.14 the work which any man has built
3.15 If any man's work is burned up
15.58 always abounding in . . w. of the Lord
16.10 he is doing the work of the Lord
2 Cor 9. 8 provide in abundance for every good w.
Gal 2.16 a man is not justified[d] by works of the law
2.16 not by works of the law, because by works of the law shall no one be justified
3. 2 Did you receive the Spirit by works?
3. 5 Does he . . do so by works of the law?
3.10 all who rely on works of the law
5.19 Now the works of the flesh are plain
6. 4 let each one test his own work
Eph 2. 9 not because of works, lest any . . boast
2.10 created in Christ Jesus for good works
4.12 to equip the saints for the w. of ministry
5.11 the unfruitful works of darkness
Phil 1. 6 he who began a good work in you
2.30 he nearly died for the work of Christ
Col 1.10 bearing fruit in every good work
1 Th 1. 3 your work of faith and labor of love
5.13 to esteem them . . because of their work
2 Th 1.11 fulfil every . . w. of faith by his power
2.17 establish them in every good work
2 Tim 1. 9 called us . . not in virtue of our works
2.21 a vessel . . ready for any good work
3.17 complete, equipped for every good w.
4. 5 do the work of an evangelist
Tit 3. 1 to be ready for any honest work
Heb 1.10 "heavens are the work of thy hands
[2. 7 "*set him over the works of thy hands*‡
3. 9 "fathers . . saw my works for forty years
4. 3 although his works were finished
4. 4 "God rested . . from all his works
6. 1 foundation of repentance from . . works
6.10 not so unjust as to overlook your work
9.14 purify your[t] conscience from . . works
10.24 stir up one another to . . good works
Jas 2.14 if . . he has faith but has not works
2.17 So faith . . , if it has no works, is dead
2.18 "You have faith and I have works." Show me your faith apart from . . works, and I by my works will show you my faith
2.20 that faith apart from works is barren
2.21 Was not Abraham . . justified by works?
2.22 faith was active along with his works, and faith was completed by works
2.24 a man is justified by works
2.25 was not . . Rahab . . justified by works?
2.26 so faith apart from works is dead
3.13 let him show his works in the meekness
2 Pet 3.10 the works that are upon it will be burned up
1 Jn 3. 8 to destroy the works of the devil
2 Jn .11 who greets him shares his wicked work
Rev 2. 2 " 'I know your works, your toil
2. 5 " 'repent and do the works you did at first
2. 6 " 'you hate the works of the Nicolaitans
Rev 2.19 " 'I know your works, . . and that your latter works exceed the first
2.23 " 'to each of you as your works deserve
2.26 " 'who keeps my works until the end
3. 1 " 'I know your works
3. 2 " 'I have not found your works perfect
3. 8 " 'I know your works
3.15 " 'I know your works
9.20 The rest . . did not repent of the works

5. *come to be, happen, be:* γίνομαι GINOMAI
Mk 6. 2 "mighty works are wrought by his hands!

6. *achieve:* κατεργάζομαι KATERGAZOMAI
Rom 7. 8 sin . . wrought . . all kinds of covetousness
7.13 It was sin, working death in me
15.18 what Christ has wrought through me

7. *work hard, grow weary:* κοπιάω KOPIAŌ
Rom 16. 6 Mary, who has worked hard among you
16.12 Persis, who has worked hard in the Lord
1 Cor 15.10 I worked harder than any of them

8. *do, make:* ποιέω POIEŌ
Mt 20.12 " 'These last worked only one hour
Jn 7. 4 "For no man works in secret
Heb 13.21 working in you[b] that which is pleasing
Rev 13.13 It works great signs, . . making fire
13.14 signs which it is allowed to work
19.20 in its presence had worked the signs

9. *have work:* ἔχειν πόνον PONOS [B.3.a.5]
Col 4.13 he has worked hard for you

CONTEXTUALLY
Jn 21. 7 for he was stripped for work
Rom 15.17 reason to be proud of my w. for God
15.23 since I no longer have any room for work
1 Cor 12.29 Are all teachers? Do all work miracles?

WORK, FOR EFFECTIVE

1. *effective, active:* ἐνεργής ENERGĒS
1 Cor 16. 9 a wide door for effective work has opened

WORK, GRACIOUS

1. *grace, favor, gratitude:* χάρις CHARIS
2 Cor 8. 6 he should . . complete . . this gracious work
8. 7 excel in this gracious work also
8.19 to travel with us in this gracious work

WORK ON THE SAME TERMS

1. *find:* εὑρίσκω (pass.) HEURISKŌ
2 Cor 11.12 they work on the same terms as we do

WORK OUT

1. *achieve:* κατεργάζομαι KATERGAZOMAI
Phil 2.12 work out your own salvation with fear

WORK WITH

1. *work together with:* συνεργέω SYNERGEŌ
Mk 16.20 while the Lord worked with them[k]‡
Rom 8.28 God works for good[k] with those who love
2 Cor 6. 1 Working together with him, . . we entreat

2. *helper, fellow worker:* συνεργός SYNERGOS [B.3.a.1]
2 Cor 1.24 we work with you for your joy

WORKER (*See also* MIRACLES, WORKER OF)

1. *workman:* ἐργάτης ERGATĒS
Lk 13.27 " 'depart . . , all you workers of iniquity!

2. *work hard, grow weary:* κοπιάω (subst. part.) KOPIAŌ
Rom 16.12 Greet those workers in the Lord

CONTEXTUALLY
1 Cor 12.28 third teachers, then workers of miracles

WORKER, FELLOW

1. *work together with:* συνεργέω (subst. part.) SYNERGEŌ
1 Cor 16.16 be subject . . to every fellow worker

2. *helper, fellow worker:* συνεργός SYNERGOS
Rom 16. 3 Prisca and Aquila, my fellow workers
16. 9 Urbanus, our fellow worker in Christ
16.21 Timothy, my fellow worker
1 Cor 3. 9 For we are God's fellow workers
2 Cor 8.23 Titus . . is my . . fellow worker
Phil 2.25 Epaphroditus my . . fellow worker
4. 3 Clement and the rest of my fellow workers
Col 4.11 my fellow workers for the kingdom
Phm . 1 To Philemon our beloved fellow worker
.24 Demas, and Luke, my fellow workers

3 Jn . 8 fellow workers in the truth

WORKING

1. *operation, activity:* ἐνέργεια ENERGEIA
   Eph 1.19 the working of his great might
   3. 7 given me by the working of his power
   Col 2.12 through faith in the working of God
2. *activity:* ἐνέργημα (pl.) ENERGĒMA*
   1 Cor 12. 6 there are varieties of working
   12.10 to another the working of miracles

WORKING FOR A LIVING, REFRAIN FROM

1. *work, do:* ἐργάζομαι (neg.) ERGAZOMAI
   1 Cor 9. 6 right to refrain from working for a living

WORKMAN

1. *workman:* ἐργάτης ERGATĒS
   Acts 19.25 "with the workmen of like occupation
   2 Cor 11.13 false apostles, deceitful workmen
   2 Tim 2.15 w. who has no need to be ashamed

WORKMANSHIP

1. *work, deed:* ἔργον ERGON
   1 Cor 9. 1 Are not you my w. in the Lord?
2. *anything made, creation:* ποίημα POIĒMA
   Eph 2.10 For we are his workmanship

WORLD

1. *age:* αἰών AIŌN
   [a]ἐκ τοῦ αἰῶνος
   Mt 13.22 "cares of the world . . choke the word
   Mk 4.19 "cares of the world . . choke the word
   Lk 16. 8 "the sons of this w.[w] are more shrewd†
   Jn 9.32 [a]"Never since the world began
   Rom 12. 2 Do not be conformed to this world[q]†
   2 Cor 4. 4 god of this world has blinded the minds
   1 Tim 6.17 As for the rich in this world
   2 Tim 4.10 Demas, in love with this present world
   Tit 2.12 upright, and godly lives in this world
   Heb 1. 2 through whom also he created the world
   11. 3 the world was created by the word
2. *world, world order:* κόσμος KOSMOS
   Mt 4. 8 showed him all the kingdoms of the w.
   5.14 "You are the light of the world
   13.35 "hidden since the foundation of the w.
   13.38 "the field is the world
   16.26 "what . . profit . . if he gains the whole w.
   18. 7 "Woe to the w. for temptations to sin![a]
   24.21 "from the beginning of the world
   25.34 " 'from the foundation of the world
   26.13 "wherever . . preached in the whole world
   Mk 8.36 "what . . profit . . , to gain the whole world?
   14. 9 "wherever . . preached in the whole world
   16.15 "Go into all the world and preach[k]‡
   Lk 9.25 "what . . profit . . if he gains the whole world?
   11.50 "shed from the foundation of the world
   12.30 "nations of the world seek these things
   Jn 1. 9 true light . . was coming into the w.
   1.10 He was in the world, and the world was made through him, yet the world knew him not
   1.29 "who takes away the sin of the world!
   3.16 For God so loved the world
   3.17 For God sent the Son into the world, not to condemn the world, but that the world might be saved
   3.19 the light has come into the world
   4.42 "this is indeed the Savior of the world
   6.14 "the prophet who is to come into the w.!
   6.33 "the bread . . which . . gives life to the world
   6.51 "bread . . for the life of the world
   7. 4 "show yourself to the world
   7. 7 "The world cannot hate you
   8.12 "I am the light of the world
   8.23 "you are of this world, I am not of this world
   8.26 "I declare to the w. what I have heard
   9. 5 "As long as I am in the world, I am the light of the world
   9.39 "For judgment I came into this world
   10.36 "whom the Father . . sent into the world
   11. 9 "because he sees the light of this world
   Jn 11.27 "he who is coming into the world
   12.19 "look, the world has gone after him
   12.25 "who hates his life in this world
   12.31 "Now is the judgment of this w., now shall the ruler of this w. be cast out
   12.46 "I have come as light into the world
   12.47 "for I did not come to judge the world but to save the world
   13. 1 hour . . to depart out of this world
   13. 1 having loved his own . . in the world
   14.17 "Spirit . . , whom the w. cannot receive
   14.19 "the world will see me no more
   14.22 "you will manifest yourself . . not to the w.
   14.27 "not as the world gives do I give to you
   14.30 "for the ruler of this world is coming
   14.31 "so that the world may know
   15.18 "If the world hates you
   15.19 "If you were of the world, the world would love its own; but because you are not of the world, but I chose you out of the world, therefore the world hates you
   16. 8 "he will convince[x] the w. concerning sin
   16.11 "the ruler of this world is judged
   16.20 "you will weep . . but the w. will rejoice
   16.21 "for joy that a child[j] is born into the w.
   16.28 "I . . have come into the world; again, I am leaving the world
   16.33 "In the w. you have tribulation; but be of good cheer, I have overcome the w.
   17. 5 "glory . . before the world was made
   17. 6 "whom thou gavest me out of the w.
   17. 9 "I am not praying for the world
   17.11 "now I am no more in the world, but they are in the world
   17.13 "these things I speak in the world
   17.14 "the world has hated them because they are not of the world, even as I am not of the world
   17.15 "not . . take them out of the world
   17.16 "They are not of the world, even as I am not of the world
   17.18 "thou didst send me into the world, so I have sent them into the world
   17.21 "so that the world may believe
   17.23 "so that the world may know
   17.24 "love . . before the foundation of the w.
   17.25 "Father, the world has not known thee
   18.20 "I have spoken openly to the world
   18.36 "My kingship is not of this world; if my kingship were of this world
   18.37 "for this I have come into the world
   21.25 the w. . . could not contain the books
   Acts 17.24 "The God who made the world
   Rom 1. 8 your faith is proclaimed in all the w.
   1.20 Ever since the creation of the world
   3. 6 For then how could God judge the world?
   3.19 the whole w. may be held accountable
   4.13 that they should inherit the world
   5.12 as sin came into the world
   5.13 sin . . was in the w. before the law
   11.12 if their trespass means riches for the w.
   11.15 means the reconciliation of the world
   1 Cor 1.20 God made foolish the wisdom of the w.
   1.21 w. did not know God through wisdom
   1.27 God chose what is foolish in the world
   1.27 God chose what is weak in the world
   1.28 what is low and despised in the world
   2.12 received not the spirit of the world
   3.19 wisdom of this world is folly with God
   3.22 whether Paul . . or the world or life
   4. 9 we have become a spectacle to the w.
   4.13 we . . are now, as the refuse of the w.
   5.10 not . . meaning the immoral of this w.
   5.10 you would need to go out of the w.
   6. 2 the saints will judge the world? And if the world is to be judged by you
   7.31 those who deal with the world
   7.31 the form of this world is passing away

1 Cor 11.32 not . . condemned along with the world
14.10 many different languages in the world
2 Cor 1.12 we have behaved in the world
5.19 in Christ God was reconciling[h] the w.
Gal 6.14 by which[l] the world has been crucified to me, and I to the world
Eph 1. 4 before the foundation of the world
2. 2 following the course of this world
2.12 having no hope and without God in the w.
Phil 2.15 among whom you shine as lights in the w.
Col 1. 6 in the whole world it is bearing fruit
2.20 if you still belonged to the world
1 Tim 1.15 Christ Jesus came into the world
3.16 He[h] was . . believed on in the world
6. 7 we brought nothing into the world
Heb 4. 3 finished from the foundation of the w.
9.26 since the foundation of the world
10. 5 when Christ[v] came into the world
11. 7 by this he condemned the world
11.38 of whom the world was not worthy
Jas 1.27 keep oneself unstained from the world
2. 5 those who are poor in the world
3. 6 The tongue is an unrighteous world
4. 4 friendship with the world is enmity
4. 4 friend of the w. makes himself an enemy
1 Pet 1.20 before the foundation of the world
5. 9 your brotherhood throughout the w.
2 Pet 1. 4 the corruption that is in the world
2. 5 if he did not spare the ancient world
2. 5 a flood upon the world of the ungodly
2.20 escaped the defilements of the world
3. 6 the world that then existed was deluged
1 Jn 2. 2 for the sins of the whole world
2.15 Do not love the world or the things in the world. If any one loves the world, love for the Father is not in him
2.16 For all that is in the world . . is not of the Father but is of the world
2.17 world passes away, and the lust of it
3. 1 why the world does not know us
3.13 Do not wonder . . that the w. hates you
3.17 if any one has the world's goods
4. 1 false prophets have gone out into the w.
4. 3 spirit of antichrist . . is in the world
4. 4 greater than he who is in the world
4. 5 They are of the world, therefore what they say is of the world, and the world listens to them
4. 9 God sent his only Son into the world
4.14 sent his Son as the Savior of the world
4.17 as he is so are we in this world
5. 4 whatever is born of God overcomes the w.
5. 4 the victory that overcomes the world
5. 5 Who is it that overcomes the world?
5.19 whole w. is in the power of the evil one
2 Jn . 7 deceivers have gone out into the w.
Rev 11.15 "The kingdom of the world
13. 8 before the foundation of the world
17. 8 "from the foundation of the world

3. *inhabited region, Roman world:* οἰκουμένη OIKOUMENĒ*
Mt 24.14 "preached throughout the whole world
Lk 2. 1 all the world should be enrolled
4. 5 showed him all the kingdoms of the w.
21.26 "foreboding of what is coming on the w.
Acts 11.28 a great famine over all the world
17. 6 "have turned the world upside down
17.31 "day on which he will judge the world
19.27 "whom all Asia and the w. worship
24. 5 "among all the Jews throughout the w.
Rom 10.18 "their words to the ends of the world
Heb 1. 6 he brings the first-born into the world
2. 5 not to angels that God subjected the w.
Rev 3.10 " 'trial which is coming on the whole w.
12. 9 the deceiver of the whole world
16.14 who go abroad to the kings of the . . w.

4. *flesh, body:* σάρξ SARX
2 Cor 10. 3 For though we live in the world

WORLD, FROM THE
1. *hence:* ἐντεῦθεν ENTEUTHEN
Jn 18.36 "my kingship is not from the world

WORLD, NEW
1. *rebirth, regeneration:* παλιγγενεσία PALIGGENESIA
Mt 19.28 "in the new world, when . . Son . . shall sit

WORLD RULER
1. *lord of the world:* κοσμοκράτωρ KOSMOKRATŌR*
Eph 6.12 contending . . against the world rulers

WORLDLY
1. *of the world:* κοσμικός KOSMIKOS
Tit 2.12 renounce irreligion and worldly passions
2. *world, world order:* κόσμος (gen.) KOSMOS
1 Cor 7.33 married man is anxious about w. affairs
7.34 woman is anxious about w. affairs
2 Cor 7.10 but worldly grief produces death
3. *fleshly:* σαρκικός SARKIKOS
2 Cor 10. 4 weapons of our warfare are not w.
4. *flesh, body:* σάρξ SARX
[a]B.3.b.4 [b]B.1.a.1
1 Cor 7.28 [a]who marry will have w. troubles
2 Cor 10. 3 [b]we are not carrying on a worldly war

WORLDLY FASHION, IN A
WORLDLY MAN, LIKE A
WORLDLY STANDARDS, ACCORDING TO
WORLDLY THINGS, OF
1. *according to the flesh:* κατὰ σάρκα SARX [B.1.b]
1 Cor 1.26 wise according to worldly standards
2 Cor 1.17 Do I make my plans like a w. man?
10. 2 suspect us of acting in worldly fashion
11.18 (since many boast of worldly things

WORLDLY PEOPLE
1. *physical, of the soul:* ψυχικός (subst. pl.) PSYCHIKOS
Jude .19 worldly people, devoid of the Spirit

WORM
1. *eating, food:* βρῶσις BRŌSIS
Mt [6.20 "neither moth nor *worm* consumes†
2. *worm, earthworm:* σκώληξ SKŌLĒX*
Mk 9.48 "where their worm does not die
Also Mk **9.**[44‡, [46‡

WORMS, EATEN BY
1. *eaten by worms:* σκωληκόβρωτος SKŌLĒKOBRŌTOS*
Acts 12.23 he was eaten by worms and died

WORMWOOD
1. *wormwood:* ἄψινθος APSINTHOS*
Rev 8.11 The name of the star is Wormwood. A third of the waters became w.

WORSE
1. *inferior, more severe:* χείρων CHEIRŌN*
Mt 9.16 "a worse tear is made
12.45 "last state of that man becomes w.
27.64 "last fraud will be worse than the first
Mk 2.21 "a worse tear is made
5.26 she . . was no better but rather grew w.
Lk 11.26 "last state of that man becomes w.
Jn 5.14 "Sin no more, that nothing w. befall
1 Tim 5. 8 he . . is worse than an unbeliever
2 Tim 3.13 impostors will go on from bad to w.
Heb 10.29 How much worse punishment?
2 Pet 2.20 the last state has become worse
2. *less, inferior:* ἥσσων HĒSSŌN
1 Cor 11.17 not for the better but for the worse

WORSE OFF, BE
1. *lack, fail:* ὑστερέω (pass.) HYSTEREŌ
1 Cor 8. 8 We are no worse off if we do not eat

WORSE THAN
1. *more than, by:* παρά (+acc.) PARA [B.1.a.5]
Lk 13. 2 "that these . . were w. sinners than . . others?
13. 4 "that they were w. offenders than . . others?

WORSHIP
1. *show piety toward:* εὐσεβέω EUSEBEŌ
Acts 17.23 "What therefore you worship as unknown

2. *worship, service, duty:* λατρεία LATREIA
Rom 9. 4 to them belong . . the w., and the promises
12. 1 to present . . bodies . . is your spiritual w.
Heb 9. 1 the first covenant had regulations for w.
3. *serve, worship:* λατρεύω LATREUŌ
Lk 2.37 not depart from the temple, worshiping
Acts 7. 7 " 'they shall . . worship me in this place
7.42 "to worship the host of heaven
24.14 "I worship the God of our fathers
26. 7 "they earnestly worship night and day
27.23 "God to whom I belong and whom I w.
Phil 3. 3 who worship God in spirit[e]
Rev 22. 3 his servants shall worship him
4. *serve, minister:* λειτουργέω LEITOURGEŌ
Acts 13. 2 they were worshiping . . and fasting
5. *prostrate oneself before:* προσκυνέω PROSKYNEŌ
Mt 2. 2 "we . . have come to worship him
2. 8 "I too may come and worship him
2.11 they fell down and worshiped him
4. 9 "if you will fall down and worship me
4.10 " 'You shall worship the Lord your God
14.33 those in the boat worshiped him
28. 9 took hold of his feet and worshiped
28.17 when they saw him they worshiped
Mk 5. 6 he ran and worshiped him
Lk 4. 7 "If you, then, will worship me
4. 8 " 'You shall worship the Lord your God
[24.52 ⟨he parted . .⟩ And they *worshiped him*‡
Jn 4.20 "fathers worshiped on this mountain
4.20 "the place where men ought to w.
4.21 "nor in Jerusalem will you worship
4.22 "You worship what you do not know; we worship what we know
4.23 "will worship the Father in spirit . . , for such the Father seeks to worship him
4.24 "God is spirit, and those who worship him must worship in spirit and truth
9.38 He said, ". . I believe"; and he worshiped
12.20 those who went up to w. at the feast
Acts 7.43 " 'the figures which you made to w.
8.27 Ethiopian . . had come to Jerusalem to w.
10.25 fell down at his feet and worshiped
24.11 "I went up to worship at Jerusalem
1 Cor 14.25 falling on his face, he will worship God
Heb 1. 6 "Let all God's angels worship him
Rev 4.10 twenty-four elders fall down . . and w.
5.14 the elders fell down and worshiped
7.11 they fell on their faces . . and worshiped
9.20 did not . . give up worshiping demons
11. 1 "measure . . those who worship there
11.16 the twenty-four elders . . worshiped God
13. 4 Men worshiped the dragon . . and they worshiped the beast
13. 8 all who dwell on earth will worship it
13.12 its inhabitants w. the first beast
13.15 those who would not w. the image
14. 7 "w. him who made heaven and earth
14. 9 "If any one worships the beast
15. 4 "All nations shall come and worship
16. 2 the men who . . worshiped its image
19. 4 the twenty-four elders . . worshiped God
19.10 Then I fell down at his feet to w. . . , but he said to me, . . "Worship God
19.20 those who worshiped its image
20. 4 who had not worshiped the beast
22. 8 I fell down to worship at the feet
22. 9 "You must not do that! . . W. God
6. *be afraid, worship:* σεβάζομαι SEBAZOMAI*
Rom 1.25 they . . worshiped and served the creature
7. *worship, honor:* σέβω (mid.) SEBŌ
Mt 15. 9 " 'in vain do they worship me
Mk 7. 7 " 'in vain do they worship me
Acts 18.13 "to worship God contrary to the law
19.27 "whom all Asia and the world worship
8. *religion, worship:* θρησκεία THRĒSKEIA
Col 2.18 insisting on . . worship of angels

WORSHIP, BOW IN
1. *prostrate oneself before:* προσκυνέω PROSKYNEŌ
Heb 11.21 Jacob . . blessed each . . , bowing in worship

WORSHIP, OBJECT OF
1. *object of worship:* σέβασμα SEBASMA*
Acts 17.23 "observed the objects of your worship
2 Th 2. 4 every so-called god or object of worship

WORSHIP OF IDOLS
1. *idolatry:* εἰδωλολατρία EIDŌLOLATRIA
1 Cor 10.14 my beloved, shun the worship of idols

WORSHIP, OFFER
1. *serve, worship:* λατρεύω LATREUŌ
Heb 12.28 let us offer to God acceptable worship

WORSHIP, USED IN
1. *service, ministry:* λειτουργία (gen.) LEITOURGIA
Heb 9.21 sprinkled . . the vessels used in w.

WORSHIPER
1. *serve, worship:* λατρεύω (subst. part.) LATREUŌ
Heb 9. 9 cannot perfect the conscience of the w.
10. 2 If the worshipers had once been cleansed
2. *prostrate oneself before:* προσκυνέω (subst.) PROSKYNEŌ
Rev 14.11 "these worshipers of the beast
3. *worshiper:* προσκυνητής PROSKYNĒTĒS*
Jn 4.23 "when the true worshipers will worship
4. *worship, honor:* σέβω (subst. mid. part.) SEBŌ
Acts 16.14 Lydia, . . who was a worshiper of God
18. 7 Titius[q] Justus, a worshiper of God

WORSHIPER OF GOD
1. *fearing God, devout:* θεοσεβής (subst.) THEOSEBĒS*
Jn 9.31 "but if any one is a worshiper of God

WORTH
1. *test, proof:* δοκιμή DOKIMĒ
Phil 2.22 Timothy's worth you know
CONTEXTUALLY
Mk 6.37 "buy two hundred denarii[u] w. of bread

WORTH COMPARING
1. *worthy:* ἄξιος AXIOS
Rom 8.18 not worth comparing with the glory

WORTH, SURPASSING
1. *be above:* ὑπερέχω (subst. part. neut.) HYPERECHŌ
Phil 3. 8 surpassing worth of knowing Christ

WORTHLESS
1. *useless:* ἀχρεῖος ACHREIOS
Mt 25.30 " 'cast the w. servant into the . . darkness
2. *counterfeit, worthless:* ἀδόκιμος ADOKIMOS
Heb 6. 8 it is w. and near to being cursed

WORTHY
1. *worthy:* ἄξιος AXIOS
Mt 10.11 "find out who is worthy in it
10.13 "if the house is w., let your peace come upon it; but if it is not worthy
10.37 "who loves father . . more than me is not w.
10.37 "who loves son . . more than me is not w.
10.38 "who does not take his cross . . is not w.
22. 8 " 'but those invited were not worthy
Lk 7. 4 "He is worthy to have you do this
15.19 " ' "no longer w. to be called your son
15.21 " 'no longer w. to be called your son[v]
Jn 1.27 "whose sandal I am not w. to untie
Acts 13.25 " 'sandals . . I am not w. to untie
26.20 "perform deeds w. of their repentance
1 Tim 1.15 The saying is . . w. of full acceptance
4. 9 The saying is . . w. of full acceptance
6. 1 regard their masters as w. of all honor
Heb 11.38 of whom the world was not worthy
Rev 3. 4 " 'shall walk with me . . , for they are w.
4.11 "Worthy art thou, our Lord and God
5. 2 "Who is worthy to open the scroll?
5. 4 no one was found w. to open the scroll
5. 9 "Worthy art thou to take the scroll
5.12 "Worthy is the Lamb who was slain
2. *worthily:* ἀξίως (+gen.) AXIŌS
Eph 4. 1 to lead a life worthy of the calling
Phil 1.27 let your manner of life be worthy

Col 1.10 to lead a life worthy of the Lord
1 Th 2.12 to lead a life worthy of God
3. *enough:* ἱκανός HIKANOS
Mt 3.11 "whose sandals I am not w. to carry
8. 8 "Lord, I am not w. to have you come
Mk 1. 7 "whose sandals I am not w. to .. untie
Lk 3.16 "whose sandals I am not w. to untie
7. 6 "I am not w. to have you come
CONTEXTUALLY
Phil 4. 8 if there is anything worthy of praise

WORTHY, BE ACCOUNTED
WORTHY, BE COUNTED
WORTHY, BE MADE
1. *consider worthy:* καταξιόω (pass.) KATAXIOŌ*
Lk 20.35 "those who are accounted w. to attain
Acts 5.41 were counted worthy to suffer dishonor
2 Th 1. 5 that you .. be made w. of the kingdom

WORTHY, CONSIDER
WORTHY, COUNT
WORTHY, MAKE
1. *consider worthy:* ἀξιόω AXIOŌ
2 Th 1.11 that our God may make you worthy
1 Tim 5.17 considered worthy of double honor
Heb 3. 3 counted w. of as much more glory

WOULD (*See also* WILL; GLADLY, WOULD)
1. (particle): ἄν AN
Mt 11.21 "they would have repented long ago
11.23 "it would have remained until this day
12. 7 "you w. not have condemned the guiltless
23.30 " 'we w. not have taken part with them
24.22 "no human being would be saved
24.43 "he w. have watched and w. not have let his house be broken into
Mk 13.20 "no human being would be saved
Lk 7.39 "he w. have known .. what sort of woman
10.13 "they would have repented long ago
12.39 "he[q] w. not have left his house
17. 6 "If you had faith .. it would obey you
Jn 4.10 "you would have asked him, and he would have given you living water
5.46 "you would believe me
8.19 "you would know my Father also
8.42 "If God were your Father, you w. love
9.41 "If .. blind, you w. have no guilt
11.21 "my brother would not have died
11.32 "my brother would not have died
14. 2 "if it were not so, w. I have told you?
14. 7 "you would have known my Father
14.28 "If you loved me, you w. have rejoiced
15.19 "the world would love its own
18.30 "we would not have handed him over
18.36 "my servants would fight
Rom 9.29 "we would have fared like Sodom
1 Cor 2. 8 they would not have crucified the Lord
Gal 3.21 righteousness w. indeed be by the law
Heb 4. 8 God[i] w. not speak later of another day
8. 4 he would not be a priest at all
8. 7 there would have been no .. second
10. 2 w. they not have ceased to be offered?
11.15 w. have had opportunity to return
1 Jn 2.19 they would have continued with us
2. *pray, wish:* εὔχομαι (aor. opt.) EUCHOMAI
[a]+ἄν
Acts 26.29 [a]And Paul said, ".. I would to God
3. *be well pleased:* εὐδοκέω (+inf.) EUDOKEŌ
2 Cor 5. 8 we would rather be away from the body
4. *be about to:* μέλλω (+inf.) MELLŌ
Acts 26.22 "what .. Moses said would come to pass
IDIOMATICALLY
a. Lk 12.49 "would that it were already kindled! τί θέλω εἰ ἤδη ἀνήφθη [THELŌ]
b. Lk 19.42 "Would that even today you knew! εἰ ἔγνως ἐν τῇ ἡμέρᾳ ταύτῃ καὶ σύ [EI]
c. 2 Cor 10.9 I would not seem to be frightening you ἵνα μὴ δόξω ὡσὰν ἐκφοβεῖν ὑμᾶς [HINA]

WOULD THAT
1. *would that:* ὄφελον OPHELON
1 Cor 4. 8 And would that you did reign!
Rev 3.15 " 'Would that you were cold or hot!

WOUND
1. *do wrong, harm:* ἀδικέω ADIKEŌ
Rev 9.19 by means of them they wound
2. *mark of a stripe, bruise:* μώλωψ MŌLŌPS*
1 Pet 2.24 By his wounds you have been healed
3. *blow, stroke:* πληγή PLĒGĒ
Acts 16.33 he took them .. and washed their wounds
Rev 13. 3 but its mortal wound was healed
13.12 beast, whose mortal w. was healed
4. *hurt, wound:* τραῦμα TRAUMA*
Lk 10.34 "went .. and bound up his wounds
5. *wound:* τραυματίζω TRAUMATIZŌ*
Lk 20.12 "this one they wounded and cast out
Acts 19.16 they fled out of that house .. wounded
6. *strike, beat:* τύπτω TYPTŌ
1 Cor 8.12 wounding their conscience .., you sin
IDIOMATICALLY
a. Rev 13.3 One of its heads seemed to have a mortal wound μίαν ἐκ τῶν κεφαλῶν αὐτοῦ ὡς ἐσφαγμένην εἰς θάνατον [SPHAZŌ]

WOUND IN THE HEAD
1. *strike on the head:* κεφαλιόω KEPHALIOŌ*
Mk 12. 4 "they wounded him in the head

WOUNDED, BE
1. *have a blow:* ἔχειν τὴν πληγήν PLĒGĒ [B.3.a.5]
Rev 13.14 beast which was wounded by the sword

WOVEN
1. *woven:* ὑφαντός HYPHANTOS*
Jn 19.23 without seam, w. from top to bottom

WRANGLE
1. *quarrel, wrangle:* ἐρίζω ERIZŌ*
Mt 12.19 "He will not wrangle or cry aloud

WRANGLING
1. *constant wrangling:* διαπαρατριβή (pl.) DIAPARATRIBĒ*
1 Tim 6. 5 wrangling among men who are depraved

WRAP
1. *wrap up in:* ἐνειλέω ENEILEŌ*
Mk 15.46 he .. wrapped him in the linen shroud
2. *wrap up, fold up:* ἐντυλίσσω ENTYLISSŌ
Mt 27.59 wrapped it in a clean linen shroud
Lk 23.53 wrapped it in a linen shroud
3. *bind, wrap around:* περιδέω PERIDEŌ*
Jn 11.44 his face wrapped with a cloth

WRAP S. AROUND
WRAP S. IN
1. *throw around, put on:* περιβάλλω PERIBALLŌ
[a]pass.
Acts 12. 8 "W. your mantle around you and follow
Rev 10. 1 [a]another mighty angel .., wrapped in a cloud

WRAP IN SWADDLING CLOTHS
1. *swathe:* σπαργανόω SPARGANOŌ*
Lk 2. 7 she .. wrapped him in swaddling cloths
2.12 "a babe wrapped in swaddling cloths

WRAP UP
1. *draw together, shorten:* συστέλλω SYSTELLŌ
Acts 5. 6 young men rose and wrapped him up

WRATH
1. *wrath, anger:* ὀργή ORGĒ
Mt 3. 7 "Who warned you to flee from the w.?
Lk 3. 7 "Who warned you to flee from the w.?
21.23 "shall be .. wrath upon this people
Jn 3.36 the wrath of God rests upon him
Rom 1.18 For the wrath of God is revealed
2. 5 you are storing up wrath for yourself on the day of wrath
2. 8 for those .. there will be wrath and fury
3. 5 That God is unjust to inflict w. on us?
4.15 For the law brings wrath
5. 9 saved by him from the w. of God

Rom 9.22 if God, desiring to show his wrath.., has endured.. the vessels of w.
12.19 leave it[t] to the wrath of God
13. 4 servant of God to execute his w.
13. 5 not only to avoid God's wrath
Eph 2. 3 we were by nature children of wrath
5. 6 that the wrath of God comes
Col 3. 6 the wrath of God is coming[f]
1 Th 1.10 who delivers us from the w. to come
2.16 God's w. has come upon them at last![b]
5. 9 God has not destined us for wrath
Heb 3.11 "As I swore in my wrath
4. 3 "As I swore in my wrath
Rev 6.16 "hide us.. from the wrath of the Lamb
6.17 "the great day of their w. has come
11.18 "nations raged, but thy wrath came
16.19 drain the cup of the fury of his wrath
19.15 fury of the w. of God the Almighty

2. *strong feeling, wrath:* θυμός THYMOS
Lk 4.28 all in the synagogue were filled with w.
Eph 4.31 Let all.. wrath.. be put away from you
Col 3. 8 put them all away: anger, wrath
Rev 12.12 "devil has come down to you in great w.
14.10 "he.. shall drink the wine of God's w.
14.19 the great wine press of the w. of God
15. 1 with them the wrath of God is ended
15. 7 golden bowls full of the wrath of God
16. 1 "the seven bowls of the wrath of God

WREATH

1. *crown, prize:* στέφανος STEPHANOS
1 Cor 9.25 They do it to receive a perishable w.

WRENCH APART

1. *tear apart:* διασπάω DIASPAŌ
Mk 5. 4 but the chains he wrenched apart

WRETCH

1. *evil, bad:* κακός (subst.) KAKOS
Mt 21.41 "He will put those wretches to.. death

WRETCHED

1. *miserable:* ταλαίπωρος TALAIPŌROS*
Rom 7.24 "Wretched man that I am!
Rev 3.17 " 'you are wretched, pitiable, poor

WRETCHED, BE

1. *endure hardship:* ταλαιπωρέω TALAIPŌREŌ*
Jas 4. 9 Be wretched and mourn and weep

WRINKLE

1. *wrinkle, pucker:* ῥυτίς RHYTIS*
Eph 5.27 without spot or w. or any such thing

WRITE

WRITE DOWN

1. *inscribe:* ἐγγράφω EGGRAPHŌ
2 Cor 3. 3 you are a letter.., written not with ink

2. *send a message, write:* ἐπιστέλλω EPISTELLŌ
Acts 15.20 "write to them to abstain from.. idols
Heb 13.22 for I have written to you briefly

3. *write:* γράφω GRAPHŌ
Mt 2. 5 "for so it is written by the prophet
4. 4 "It is written, 'Man shall not live
4. 6 "it is written, 'He will give his angels
4. 7 "it is written, 'You shall not tempt
4.10 "for it is written, 'You shall worship
11.10 "of whom it is written, 'Behold, I send
21.13 "It is written, 'My house shall be
26.24 "Son of man goes as it is written of him
26.31 "it is written, 'I will strike the shepherd
Mk 1. 2 As it is written in Isaiah the prophet[b]
7. 6 "as it is written, 'This people honors
9.12 "how is it written of the Son of man?
9.13 "they did.. as it is written of him
10. 4 "to write a certificate of divorce
10. 5 "he wrote you this commandment
11.17 "Is it not written, 'My house shall be..'?
12.19 "Teacher, Moses wrote for us
14.21 "Son of man goes as it is written of him
14.27 "You will all fall away; for it is written
Lk 1. 3 to write an orderly account for you
Lk 1.63 he asked for a writing tablet, and wrote
2.23 (as it is written in the law of the Lord
3. 4 As it is written.. "The voice of one
4. 4 Jesus answered him, "It is written
4. 8 "It is written, 'You shall worship
4.10 "it is written, 'He will give his angels
4.17 found the place where it was written
7.27 "of whom it is written, 'Behold, I send
10.26 "What is written in the law?
16. 6 " 'sit down quickly and write fifty
16. 7 " 'Take your bill, and write eighty
18.31 "everything that is written of the Son
19.46 "It is written, 'My house shall be
20.17 "What then is this that is written?
20.28 "Teacher, Moses wrote for us
21.22 "vengeance, to fulfil all that is written
24.44 "everything written about me in the law
24.46 "it is written, that.. Christ should suffer
Jn 1.45 "of whom Moses.. and.. the prophets wrote
2.17 that it was written, "Zeal for thy house
5.46 "for he wrote of me
6.31 "as it is written, 'He gave them bread
6.45 "It is written in the prophets
8. 8 he bent down and wrote with his finger[r]‡
8.17 "In your law it is written
10.34 "Is it not written in your law?
12.14 Jesus.. sat upon it; as it is written
12.16 this had been written of him
15.25 "the word that is written in their law
19.19 Pilate also wrote a title
19.20 it was written in Hebrew, in Latin
19.21 "Do not write, 'The King of the Jews
19.22 Pilate answered, "What I have written I have written
20.30 signs.. not written in this book
20.31 these are written that you may believe
21.24 disciple.. who has written these things
21.25 were every one of them to be written
21.25 the books that would be written
Acts 1.20 "For it is written in the book of Psalms
7.42 "as it is written in.. the prophets
13.29 "they had fulfilled all that was written
13.33 "also it is written in the second psalm
15.15 "the prophets agree, as it is written
18.27 the brethren.. wrote to the disciples
23. 5 "it is written, 'You shall not speak evil
23.25 he wrote a letter to this effect
24.14 "everything laid down by the law or written
25.26 "But I have nothing definite to write
25.26 "that.. I may have something to write
Rom 1.17 as it is written, "He who through faith
2.24 as it is written, "name.. is blasphemed
3. 4 as it is written, "That thou.. be justified
3.10 as it is written: "None is righteous
4.17 as it is written, "I have made you.. father
4.23 were written not for his sake alone
8.36 As it is written, "For thy sake
9.13 As it is written, "Jacob I loved
9.33 As it is written, "Behold, I am laying
10. 5 Moses writes that the man who practices
10.15 as it is written, "How beautiful!
11. 8 as it is written, "God gave them a spirit
11.26 as it is written, ".. Deliverer will come
12.19 for it is written, "Vengeance is mine
14.11 for it is written.. "every knee shall bow
15. 3 as it is written.. "reproaches.. fell on me
15. 4 was written for our instruction
15. 9 As it is written.. "I will praise
15.15 I have written to you very boldly
15.21 as it is written, "They shall see
1 Cor 1.19 For it is written, "I will destroy
1.31 as it is written, "Let him who boasts
2. 9 as it is written, "What no eye has seen
3.19 For it is written, "He catches the wise
4. 6 not to go beyond what is written[o]
4.14 I do not write this to make you ashamed
5. 9 I wrote to you in my letter

1 Cor 5.11 rather I wrote[i] to you not to associate†
7. 1 the matters about which you wrote
9. 9 it is written in the law of Moses
9.10 It was written for our sake
9.15 nor am I writing this to secure . . provision
10. 7 as it is written, "The people sat down
10.11 were written down for our instruction
14.21 In the law it is written
14.37 what I am writing to you is a command
15.45 Thus it is written, "The first man Adam
15.54 come to pass the saying that is written
2 Cor 1.13 we w. . . nothing but what you can read
2. 3 I wrote as I did, so that when I came
2. 4 I wrote you out of much affliction
2. 9 I wrote, that I might test you
4.13 the same spirit . . as he had who wrote
7.12 So although I wrote to you
8.15 As it is written, "He who gathered
9. 1 superfluous for me to write to you
9. 9 As it is written, "He scatters abroad
13.10 I write this while I am away from you
Gal 1.20 (In what I am writing . . , I do not lie!
3.10 for it is written, "Cursed be
3.10 "all things written in the book of the law
3.13 for it is written, "Cursed be
4.22 it is written that Abraham had two sons
4.27 For it is written, "Rejoice, O barren
6.11 See with what large letters I am writing
Phil 3. 1 To write the same things . . is not irksome
1 Th 4. 9 you have no need to have any one write
5. 1 no need to have anything written
2 Th 3.17 it is the way I write
1 Tim 3.14 I am writing these instructions
Phm .19 I, Paul, write this with my own hand
.21 Confident of your obedience I write
Heb 10. 7 "as it is written of me in the roll
1 Pet 1.16 since it is written, "You shall be holy
5.12 I have written briefly to you
2 Pet 3. 1 second letter that I have written to you
3.15 our beloved brother Paul wrote to you
1 Jn 1. 4 we are writing this
2. 1 I am writing this to you
2. 7 I am writing . . no new commandment
2. 8 I am writing you a new commandment
2.12 I am writing to you, little children
2.13 I am writing to you, fathers
2.13 I am writing to you, young men
2.13 I write to you, children
2.14 I write to you, fathers
2.14 I write to you, young men
2.21 I write to you . . because you know it
2.26 I write . . about those who would deceive
5.13 I write this to you who believe
2 Jn . 5 not as . . writing . . a new commandment
.12 Though I have much to write to you
3 Jn . 9 I have written something to the church
.13 I had much to w. to you, but I would rather not w. with pen and ink
Jude . 3 being very eager to write to you . . , I found it necessary to write appealing
Rev 1. 3 blessed . . who keep what is written
1.11 "Write what you see in a book
1.19 "Now write what you see, what is
2. 1 "To . . angel of . . church in Ephesus write
2. 8 "to . . angel of . . church in Smyrna write
2.12 "to . . angel of . . church in Pergamum w.
2.17 " 'a new name written on the stone
2.18 "to . . angel of . . church in Thyatira w.
3. 1 "to . . angel of the church in Sardis write
3. 7 "to . . angel of . . Philadelphia write
3.12 " 'I will write on him the name of my God
3.14 "to . . angel of . . Laodicea write
5. 1 a scroll written within and on the back
10. 4 I was about to write, but I heard a voice . . "do not write it down
13. 8 one whose name has not been written
14. 1 name written on their foreheads
Rev 14.13 "Write this: Blessed are the dead
17. 5 on her forehead was written a name
17. 8 "whose names have not been written
19. 9 the angel said[l] to me, "Write this
20.12 judged by what was written in the books
20.15 if any one's name was not found written
21. 5 "Write this, for these words are . . true
21.27 only those who are written in the . . book

4. *engrave, record:* *καταγράφω* KATAGRAPHŌ*
Jn 8. 6 Jesus . . wrote with his finger[r]‡

5. *write before:* *προγράφω* PROGRAPHŌ
Eph 3. 3 as I have written briefly

CONTEXTUALLY
Lk 22.37 "what is written about me has . . fulfilment
1 Cor 16.21 I, Paul, w. this greeting with my own hand
Col 4.18 I, Paul, w. this greeting with my own hand
2 Th 3.17 I, Paul, w. this greeting with my own hand

WRITE IN
WRITE ON

1. *inscribe:* *ἐγγράφω* EGGRAPHŌ
Lk 10.20 "your names are written in heaven
2 Cor 3. 2 our letter . . , written on your[c] hearts

2. *inscribe:* *ἐπιγράφω* EPIGRAPHŌ
Heb 8.10 "I will . . write them on their hearts
10.16 "I will . . write them on their minds

WRITE IN FORMER DAYS

1. *write before:* *προγράφω* PROGRAPHŌ
Rom 15. 4 whatever was written in former days

WRITER

1. *write:* *γράφω* (subst. aor. part.) GRAPHŌ
Rom 16.22 I Tertius, the writer of this letter

WRITING

1. *letter, document:* *γράμμα* GRAMMA
Jn 5.47 "if you do not believe his writings
2 Tim 3.15 acquainted with the sacred writings

2. *writing:* *γραφή* GRAPHĒ
Rom 16.26 through . . prophetic writings . . made known

WRITING TABLET

1. *writing tablet:* *πινακίδιον* PINAKIDION*
Lk 1.63 he asked for a writing tablet, and wrote

WRITTEN

1. *written:* *γραπτός* GRAPTOS*
Rom 2.15 the law . . is written on their hearts

WRITTEN, AS IT IS

1. *say, affirm:* *φημί* (indef.) PHĒMI
1 Cor 6.16 For, as it is written

WRITTEN CODE

1. *letter, document:* *γράμμα* GRAMMA
Rom 2.27 you who have the written code
7. 6 we serve not under the old written code
2 Cor 3. 6 not in a written code but in the Spirit; for the written code kills

WRONG

1. *do wrong, harm:* *ἀδικέω* ADIKEŌ
Acts 7.24 "seeing one of them being wronged
7.26 " 'why do you wrong each other?
7.27 "man who was wronging his neighbor
1 Cor 6. 8 you yourselves wrong and defraud
2 Cor 7. 2 we have wronged no one
Phm .18 If he has wronged you at all

2. *wrongdoing, injustice:* *ἀδικία* ADIKIA
1 Cor 13. 6 it does not rejoice at wrong
2 Cor 12.13 Forgive me this wrong!

3. *out of place, wrong:* *ἄτοπος* ATOPOS
Lk 23.41 "this man has done nothing wrong
Acts 25. 5 "if there is anything w. about the man

4. *evil, bad:* *κακός* KAKOS
Jn 18.23 "bear witness to the wrong
Acts 23. 9 "We find nothing wrong in this man
Rom 13. 4 if you do wrong, be afraid
13.10 Love does no wrong to a neighbor
14.20 it is wrong . . to make others fall
2 Cor 13. 7 pray . . that you may not do wrong

5. *defraud:* πλεονεκτέω PLEONEKTEŌ
1 Th 4. 6 that no man . . wrong his brother†

WRONG, BE

1. *cause to wander:* πλανάω (pass.) PLANAŌ
Mt 22.29 "You are w., because you know neither
Mk 12.24 "Is not this why you are wrong?
12.27 "you are quite wrong

WRONG, DO

1. *do wrong, harm:* ἀδικέω ADIKEŌ
Mt 20.13 " 'Friend, I am doing you no wrong
Acts 25.10 "to the Jews I have done no wrong
2 Cor 7.12 not on account of the one who did the w.
Gal 4.12 You did me no wrong
Col 3.25 paid back for the wrong he has done
2. *miss the mark, sin:* ἁμαρτάνω HAMARTANŌ
1 Pet 2.20 if when you do wrong and are beaten
3. *do wrong, do harm:* κακοποιέω KAKOPOIEŌ
1 Pet 3.17 for doing right . . than for doing wrong

WRONG, GO

1. *render useless:* ἀχρειόω (pass.) ACHREIOŌ*
Rom 3.12 "together they have gone wrong

WRONG, ONE WHO DOES

1. *doing evil:* κακοποιός (subst.) KAKOPOIOS
1 Pet 2.14 sent . . to punish those who do wrong

WRONG, SUFFER

1. *do wrong, harm:* ἀδικέω (pass.) ADIKEŌ
1 Cor 6. 7 Why not rather suffer wrong?
2 Cor 7.12 the one who suffered the wrong
2 Pet 2.13 suffering wrong for their wrongdoing

WRONGDOER

WRONGDOER, BE A

1. *do wrong, harm:* ἀδικέω ADIKEŌ
[a]subst. part.
Acts 25.11 "If then I am a wrongdoer
Col 3.25 [a]For the wrongdoer will be paid back
2. *doing evil:* κακοποιός (subst.) KAKOPOIOS
1 Pet 2.12 they speak against you as wrongdoers
4.15 let none of you suffer as . . a wrongdoer
3. *one who does what is wrong:* ὁ τὸ κακὸν πράσσων KAKOS; PRASSŌ [B.2.a.1]
Rom 13. 4 to execute his wrath on the w.

WRONGDOING

1. *wrong, wrong done:* ἀδίκημα ADIKĒMA
Acts 18.14 "If it were a matter of wrongdoing
24.20 "let these men . . say what wrongdoing
2. *wrongdoing, injustice:* ἀδικία ADIKIA
2 Pet 2.13 suffering wrong for their wrongdoing
2.15 Balaam . . , who loved gain from w.
1 Jn 5.17 All wrongdoing is sin

WRONGLY

1. *badly, ill:* κακῶς KAKŌS
Jn 18.23 "If I have spoken w., bear witness
Jas 4. 3 You . . do not receive, because you ask w.

WROUGHT (*See* WORK)

Y

YARD

1. *forearm, cubit:* πῆχυς PĒCHYS [B.3.b.4]
Jn 21. 8 about a hundred yards[m] off†

YEA

1. (particle): γέ GE
Acts 2.18
2. *yes:* ναί NAI
Mt 11.26 "yea, Father, for such was thy . . will[f]
Lk 10.21 "yea, Father, for such was thy . . will[h]
Rev 16. 7 "Yea, Lord God the Almighty

YEAR

1. *year, anniversary:* ἐνιαυτός ENIAUTOS
Lk 4.19 "to proclaim the acceptable y. of the Lord
Jn 11.49 "Caiaphas, who was high priest that year
11.51 being high priest that y. he prophesied
Jn 18.13 Caiaphas, who was high priest that year
Acts 11.26 For a whole y. they met with[j] the church
18.11 he stayed a year and six months
Gal 4.10 You observe days, . . seasons, and years!
Heb 9. 7 only the high priest goes, . . once a year
Jas 4.13 "spend a year there and trade
5.17 three years and six months it did not rain
Rev 9.15 held ready for the hour . . and the year
2. *year:* ἔτος ETOS
Mt 9.20 had . . a hemorrhage for twelve years
Mk 5.25 had a flow of blood for twelve years
5.42 girl . . walked (she was twelve years of age
Lk 2.36 lived with her husband seven years
2.41 parents went to Jerusalem every year
2.42 when he was twelve years old
3. 1 the fifteenth y. of the reign of Tiberius
3.23 Jesus . . was about thirty years of age
4.25 "shut up three years and six months
8.42 daughter, about twelve years of age
8.43 a flow of blood for twelve years[b]
12.19 " 'ample goods laid up for many years
13. 7 " 'three years I have come seeking fruit
13. 8 " 'Let it alone, sir, this year also
13.11 a spirit of infirmity for eighteen years
13.16 "whom Satan bound for eighteen years
15.29 " 'Lo, these many years I have served you
Jn 2.20 "forty-six years to build this temple
5. 5 who had been ill for thirty-eight years
8.57 "You are not yet fifty years old
Acts 4.22 man . . was more than forty years old
7. 6 "ill-treat them four hundred years
7.30 "Now when forty years had passed
7.36 "in the wilderness for forty years
7.42 " 'forty years in the wilderness, O . . Israel
9.33 who had been bedridden for eight years
13.19(20) "about four hundred and fifty years
13.21 "God gave them Saul . . for forty years
19.10 This continued for two years
24.10 "for many years you have been judge
24.17 "after some years . . to bring . . alms
Rom 15.23 longed for many years to come to you
2 Cor 12. 2 a man in Christ who fourteen years ago
Gal 1.18 after three years I went up to Jerusalem
2. 1 after fourteen years I went up again
3.17 four hundred and thirty years afterward
1 Tim 5. 9 if she is not less than sixty years of age
Heb 1.12 "thy years will never end
3. 9 "fathers . . saw my works for forty years
3.17 with whom was he provoked forty years?
2 Pet 3. 8 one day is as a thousand years, and a thousand years as one day
Rev 20. 2 he . . bound him for a thousand years
20. 3 till the thousand years were ended
20. 4 reigned with Christ a thousand years
20. 5 until the thousand years were ended
20. 6 they shall reign with him a thousand years
20. 7 when the thousand years are ended
3. *day, tribunal:* ἡμέρα HĒMERA
Lk 1. 7 both were advanced in years
1.18 "my wife is advanced in years

IDIOMATICALLY

a. Heb 10.1 by the same sacrifices which are . . offered year after year κατ' ἐνιαυτὸν ταῖς αὐταῖς θυσίαις ἃς προσφέρουσιν [ENIAUTOS]
b. Heb 10.3 there is a reminder of sin year after year ἀνάμνησις ἁμαρτιῶν κατ' ἐνιαυτόν [ENIAUTOS]

YEAR AGO, A

YEAR, LAST

1. *last year:* πέρυσι PERYSI
[a]B.1.a.1
2 Cor 8.10 [a]what a year ago you began . . to desire
9. 2 Achaia has been ready since last year

YEARLY

1. *year, anniversary:* ἐνιαυτός ENIAUTOS [B.1.a.1]
Heb 9.25 high priest enters the Holy Place y.

YEARN FOR
YEARN OVER
1. *desire, long for:* ἐπιποθέω EPIPOTHEŌ
Phil 1. 8 God is my witness, how I yearn for you
Jas 4. 5 "He yearns jealously over the spirit

YEARS
1. *age, stature:* ἡλικία HĒLIKIA
Lk [2.52 And Jesus increased . . in *years*†

YEARS, FORTY
1. *forty years:* τεσσαρακονταετής TESSARAKONTAETĒS*
Acts 7.23 "When he was forty years old
13.18 "about forty years he bore with[m] them

YEARS OLD, A HUNDRED
1. *of a hundred years:* ἑκατονταετής HEKATONTAETĒS*
Rom 4.19 he was about a hundred years old

YEARS OLD, TWO
1. *of two years, two years old:* διετής DIETĒS*
Mt 2.16 male children . . two years old or under

YEARS, THREE
1. *period of three years:* τριετία TRIETIA*
Acts 20.31 "for three years I did not cease

YEARS, TWO
1. *period of two years:* διετία DIETIA*
Acts 24.27 when two years had elapsed
28.30 he lived there two whole years

YES
1. *but:* ἀλλά ALLA
[a]+γε
Lk **24.21**[a]
2 Cor **3.15**
Phil **1.19**(18)
2. *still, yet:* ἔτι ETI
Lk 14.26 "does not hate . . , yes, . . even his own life
3. *more, rather:* μᾶλλον MALLON
Rom 8.34 Jesus, who died, yes, who was raised
4. *yes:* ναί NAI
[a](τὸ) ναὶ ναί
Mt 5.37 [a]"Let what you say be simply 'Yes'
9.28 They said to him, "Yes, Lord
11. 9 "Yes, I tell you, . . more than a prophet
13.51 They said to him, "Yes
15.27 "Yes, Lord, yet even the dogs eat
17.25 He said, "Yes
21.16 "Do you hear . . ?" And Jesus said . . "Yes
Mk 7.28 "Yes, Lord; yet even the dogs . . eat
Lk 7.26 "Yes, I tell you, and more than a prophet
11.51 "Yes, I tell you, it shall be required
12. 5 "yes, I tell you, fear him!
Jn 11.27 She said to him, "Yes, Lord
21.15 He said to him, "Yes, Lord; you know
21.16 "Yes, Lord; you know that I love you
Acts 5. 8 And she said, "Yes, for so much
22.27 "are you a Roman citizen?" . . "Yes
Rom 3.29 Yes, of Gentiles also
2 Cor 1.17 [a]ready to say Yes and No at once
1.18 our word to you has not been Yes and No
1.19 the Son of God . . was not Yes and No; but in him it is always Yes
1.20 promises of God find their Yes in him
Phm .20 Yes, brother, I want some benefit
Jas 5.12 [a]But above all, . . let your yes be yes and your no be no

YESTERDAY
1. *yesterday:* ἐχθές ECHTHES*
Jn 4.52 "Y. at the seventh hour the fever left him
Acts 7.28 " 'as you killed the Egyptian yesterday
Heb 13. 8 Jesus Christ is the same yesterday

YET
1. *but:* ἀλλά ALLA
Mk **14.36**
Jn **7.27**; **8.37**
Acts **7.48**
Rom **5.14**; **7.7**
1 Cor **8.6**
Col **2.5**
1 Pet **3.15**
Rev **2.6**; **3.4**
2. *still, yet:* ἔτι ETI
Lk 14.32 "while the other is yet a great way off
15.20 "But while he was yet at a distance
Jn 4.35 " 'There are yet four months
13.33 "yet a little while I am with you
14.19 "Yet a little while, and . . you will see
16.12 "I have yet many things to say
Rom 5. 8 while we were y. sinners Christ died
Heb 10.37 "For y. a little while, . . the coming one
12.26 "Yet once more I will shake . . the earth
12.27 This phrase, "Yet once more
3. *for:* γάρ GAR
Mt **15.27**
Heb **3.3**
4. (particle): γέ GE
Lk **11.8**; **18.5**; **19.17**
Acts **17.27**
5. *and yet:* καίτοι KAITOI
Acts 14.17 "yet he did not leave himself
6. *more, rather:* μᾶλλον MALLON
Phm . 9 yet for love's sake I prefer to appeal
7. *yet, nevertheless:* μέντοι MENTOI
Jn 7.13 Yet for fear of the Jews no one spoke
21. 4 yet the disciples did not know
Jude . 8 Yet in like manner these men . . defile
8. *now:* νῦν NYN
1 Cor 3. 2 and even yet you are not ready
9. *again, back:* πάλιν PALIN
1 Jn 2. 8 Yet I am writing . . a new commandment
10. *but, however, except:* πλήν PLĒN
Phil 4.14 Yet it was kind of you to share
CONTEXTUALLY
Lk **19.30**; **20.12**
Jn **11.25**; **12.37**
Acts **28.17**
2 Cor **8.9**
Heb **3.16**; **4.15**

YET, AS
1. *not yet:* μηδέπω MĒDEPŌ* [A.4.c]
Heb 11. 7 concerning events as yet unseen

YET, EVER
1. *not yet:* οὔπω (+neg.) OUPŌ
Lk 23.53 where no one had ever yet been laid

YET, NOT
YET NOT, AS
1. *not yet:* μήπω MĒPŌ*
Rom 9.11 though they were not yet born
Heb 9. 8 way into the sanctuary is not yet opened
2. *not yet:* οὐδέπω OUDEPŌ
Jn 7.39 because Jesus was not yet glorified
20. 9 as yet they did not know the scripture
Acts 8.16 it had not yet fallen on any of them
3. *not yet:* οὔπω OUPŌ
Mt 16. 9 "Do you not yet perceive?
24. 6 "must take place, but the end is not yet
Mk 8.17 "Do you not yet perceive or understand?
8.21 "Do you not yet understand?
13. 7 "must take place, but the end is not yet
Jn 2. 4 "My hour has not yet come
3.24 John had not yet been put in prison
6.17 Jesus had not yet come to them
7. 6 "My time has not yet come
[7. 8 "I am not *yet* going up to this feast‡
7. 8 "for my time has not yet fully come
7.30 because his hour had not yet come
7.39 as yet the Spirit had not been given
8.20 because his hour had not yet come
8.57 "You are not yet fifty years old
11.30 Jesus had not yet come to the village
20.17 "I have not yet ascended to the Father
1 Cor 8. 2 he does not yet know as he ought
Heb 2. 8 not yet see everything in subjection
12. 4 you have not yet resisted to the point

1 Jn 3. 2 it does not yet appear what we shall be
Rev 17.10 "the other has not yet come
17.12 "have not yet received royal power

YIELD

1. *let go, leave, forgive:* ἀφίημι APHIĒMI
Mt 27.50 Jesus . . yielded up his spirit
2. *give up, return:* ἀποδίδωμι APODIDŌMI
Heb 12.11 later it yields the peaceful fruit
Rev 22. 2 yielding its fruit each month
3. *give:* δίδωμι DIDŌMI
Mk 4. 7 "choked it, and it yielded no grain
4. *give way:* εἴκω EIKŌ*
Gal 2. 5 to them we did not yield submission
5. *place beside, stand before:* παρίστημι PARISTĒMI
Rom 6.13 Do not yield your members to sin . . but yield yourselves to God as men
6.16 if you yield yourselves to any one
6.19 just as you once yielded to impurity . . now yield your members to righteousness
6. *persuade:* πείθω (pass.) PEITHŌ
Acts 23.21 "But do not yield to them
7. *bring, bear:* φέρω PHERŌ
Mk 4. 8 "fell into good soil . . yielding thirtyfold
8. *do, make:* ποιέω POIEŌ
[a]+καρπόν B.3.a.3
Mt 13.23 "yields, in one case a hundredfold
Lk 8. 8 [a]"some yielded a hundredfold
Jas 3.12 Can a fig tree . . yield olives . . ? No more can salt water yield fresh

YOKE

1. *yoke, pair:* ζεῦγος ZEUGOS
Lk 14.19 " 'I have bought five yoke of oxen
2. *yoke, crossbar:* ζυγός ZYGOS
Mt 11.29 "Take my yoke upon you, and learn
11.30 "For my yoke is easy
Acts 15.10 "by putting a yoke upon the neck
Gal 5. 1 do not submit again to a y. of slavery
1 Tim 6. 1 who are under the yoke of slavery

YOKEFELLOW

1. *one yoked with another, comrade:* σύζυγος SYZYGOS*
Phil 4. 3 I ask you also, true yokefellow

YONDER

1. *there:* ἐκεῖ EKEI
Mt 26.36 "Sit here, while I go yonder and pray

YOU (*For entries* 1, 3, *and* 5, *and for Greek words not represented here, see also* YOUR; YOURS)

1. *himself:* ἑαυτοῦ HEAUTOU
Mt **26**.11
Mk **14**.7
Jn **5**.42; **6**.53; **12**.8
2. *you, ye:* ὑμεῖς HYMEIS
Mt **3**.7, 9, 11^2; **4**.19; **5**.11^2, 12, 13, 14, 18, 20, 22, 28, 32, 34, 37, 39, 44^2, 46, 48; **6**.2, 5, 8, 14, 16, 25, 26, 27, 29, 30; **7**.2, 6, 7^2, 9, 11, 12, 15, 23; **8**.10, 11; **9**.29; **10**.13, 14, 15, 16, 17^2, 19^2, 20^2, 23^2, 27, 31, 40, 42; **11**.9, 11, 17, 21, 22^2, 24, 28, 29; **12**.6, 11, 28, 31, 36; **13**.11, 17; **14**.16; **15**.3, 5, 7, 16; **16**.15, 28; **17**.12, 17^2, 20^2; **18**.3, 10, 12, 13, 18, 19^2, 35; **19**.8, 9, 23, 24, 28^2; **20**.4^2, 7, 26^2, 27, 32; **21**.2, 3, 13, 21, 24^2, 27, 28, 31^2, 32^2, 43^2; **22**.31, 42; **23**.3, 8^3, 9, 10, 11, 13^2, [14‡, 15, 16, 23, 25, 27, 28, 29, 34, 35, 36, 39; **24**.2, 4, 9^2, 23, 25, 26, 33, 34, 44, 47; **25**.9, 12^2, 34, 40, 45; **26**.13, 15, 21^2, 29^2, 31, 32, 64; **27**.17, 21; **28**.7^2, 14, 20^2
Mk **1**.8^2, 17; **3**.28; **4**.11, 24^2; **6**.11^2, 37; **7**.6, 11, 18; **8**.12, 29; **9**.1, 13, 19^2, 41^2; **10**.3, 5, 15, 29, 36, 43^2, 44; **11**.2, 3, 17, 23, 24, 25, [26†, 29^2, 33; **12**.43; **13**.5, 9, 11^3, 21, 23, 29, 30, 36, 37; **14**.9, 13, 15, 18^2, 25, 28, 49; **15**.9; **16**.7^2
Lk **2**.10, 11, 12; **3**.7, 8, 13, 16^2; **4**.24, 25; **6**.9, 22^2, 24, 25, 26, 27^2, 28^2, 31, 32^2, 33^2, 34, 38^2, 47; **7**.9, 26, 28, 32; **8**.10; **9**.5, 13, 20, 27, 41^2, 48, 50^2; **10**.3, 6, 8^2, 9, 10, 11, 12, 13, 14, 16^2, 19^2, 20, 24^2; **11**.5, 8, 9^3, 11, 13, 20, 39^2, 41, 42, 43, 44, 46, 47, 48, 51, 52; **12**.4, 5^2, 8, 11, 12, 14, 22, 24, 25, 27, 28, 32, 37, 40, 44, 51; **13**.3, 5, 15, 24, 25^2, 27, 35; **14**.5, 24, 28, 33; **15**.4, 7, 10; **16**.9^2, 11, 12, 15, 26^2; **17**.6, 7, 10^2, 21, 23, 34; **18**.8, 14, 17, 29; **19**.26, 31, 40, 46; **20**.3, 8; **21**.3, 12, 13, 15, 16, 31, 32, 34; **22**.10^2, 12, 15, 16, 18, 19‡, 20‡, 26^2, 27, 28, 29, 31, 35, 37, 53, 67, 70; **23**.14; **24**.6, [36‡, 44^2, 48, 49
Jn **1**.26^2, 51; **2**.5; **3**.7, 12^2, 28; **4**.20, 22, 32, 35^2, 38^3; **5**.19, 20, 24, 25, 33, 34, 35, 38^2, 39, 44, 45^3; **6**.26, 27, 32^3, 36, 47, 53, 61, 63, 64, 65, 67, 70^2; **7**.7, 19^2, 22, 28, 33, 34, 36, 47; **8**.7‡, 14, 15, 21, 22, 23^2, 24, 25, 26, 31, 32, 34, 36, 37, 38, 40, 41, 44, 46^2, 47, 49, 51, 54, 55, 58; **9**.19, 27^2, 30; **10**.1, 7, 25, 26, 32, 36; **11**.49, 50, 56; **12**.24, 35^2; **13**.10, 12, 13, 14, 15^3, 16, 18, 19, 20, 21^2, 33^3, 34^3; **14**.2^2, 3^3, 9, 10, 12, 16^2, 17^3, 18^2, 19^2, 20^3, 25^2, 26^2, 27^3, 28^2, 29, 30; **15**.3^2, 4^2, 5, 7^2, 9, 11^2, 12, 14^2, 15^3, 16^5, 17, 18^2, 19^2, 20^2, 21, 26, 27; **16**.1, 2^2, 4^4, 5, 6, 7^4, 13^2, 14, 15, 20^3, 22^3, 23^2, 25^3, 26^2, 27^2, 33; **18**.8, 39^3; **19**.4, 35; **20**.19, 21^2, 26
Acts **1**.5, 7, 8, 11; **2**.14, 15, 22, 29, 33, 36, 38, 39; **3**.13, 14^2, 16, 20, 22^2, 25, 26^3; **4**.7, 10^3, 11, 19; **5**.9, 28, 30, 38; **6**.3; **7**.4, 37, 43, 51^2, 52; **10**.36(37); **11**.16; **13**.15, 26, 32, 34, 38^2, 41, 46; **14**.15^2, 17; **15**.7^2, 24, 25, 28; **16**.17; **17**.3, 22, 23; **18**.14, 21; **19**.13, 15, 36; **20**.18, 20^2, 25, 26, 27, 28, 29, 32, 35; **22**.1, 3, 25; **23**.15^2; **24**.21; **25**.5, 26; **26**.8; **27**.22^2, 31, 34^2; **28**.20, 28
Rom **1**.7, 8, 9, 10, 11^3, 13^3, 15; **2**.24; **6**.11, 14, 22; **7**.4^2; **8**.9^2, 10, 11^2; **9**.26; **10**.19^2; **11**.13, 25, 30; **12**.1, 2, 3, 14, 18; **13**.11; **15**.5, 7, 13^2, 14, 15, 22, 23, 24^3, 29, 30, 32, 33; **16**.1, 2, 6, 16, 17^2, 19^2, 20‡, 21, 22, 23^2, [24‡, 25
1 Cor **1**.3, 4^2, 6, 7, 8, 10^2, 11, 12, 13, 14; **2**.1^2, 2, 3; **3**.1, 2, 3, 16, 17, 18, 23; **4**.3, 8, 10^3, 16, 17^2, 18, 19, 21; **5**.1, 2^2, 4, 9, 11, 12, 13; **6**.1, 2, 5, 7, 8, 19; **7**.5, 28, 32, 35; **9**.1, 2^2, 11, 12; **10**.1, 13^2, 20, 27^2, 28; **11**.2^2, 3, 14, 18^2, 19^2, 20, 22^2, 23, 24, 30; **12**.1, 3, 21, 27, 31; **14**.5, 6^3, 18, 25, 36^2, 37; **15**.1^2, 3, 12, 51; **16**.1, 2, 5, 6^2, 7^2, 10, 12, 14, 16(15), 16, 19, 23, 24
2 Cor **1**.2, 7, 8, 11, 12, 13, 14^2, 15, 16^3, 18, 19, 21, 23; **2**.1, 2, 3^2, 4^2, 5, 7, 8, 9; **3**.1^2; **4**.12, 14; **5**.12^2, 13; **6**.1, 11, 17, 18^2; **7**.4^2, 7, 8^2, 11, 12^2, 13, 14^2, 15^2, 16; **8**.1, 6, 9, 10, 13, 16, 17, 22, 24; **9**.1, 2, 3, 4^2, 5^2, 8, 14^3; **10**.1^3, 8, 9, 13, 14^2, 15, 16; **11**.2^2, 6, 7^2, 8, 9^2, 11, 20^2; **12**.11^2, 12, 13, 14^2, 15, 16^2, 17^2, 18, 19, 20^2, 21; **13**.1, 3^2, 4, 5, 7^2, 9, 11, 13(12), 13(14)
Gal **1**.3, 6, 7, 8^2, 9, 11, 20; **2**.5; **3**.1, 2, 5^2, 28, 29; **4**.11, 12^2, 13, 14, 15^2, 16, 17^2, 18, 19, 20^2, [28‡; **5**.2^2, 7, 8, 10, 12, 13, 21; **6**.1, 11, 12, 13
Eph **1**.2, 13, 16, 17, 18; **2**.1, 11, 13, 17, 22; **3**.1, 2, 13, 16; **4**.1, 17, 20, 31, 32; **5**.3, 6, 33; **6**.11, 21^2, 22
Phil **1**.2, 3, 4, 6, 7^3, 8, 10, 12, 25, 26^2, 27^2, 29; **2**.13, 17, 18, 19^2, 25, 26; **3**.1^2, 15, 18; **4**.9, 15^2, 18, 21, 22
Col **1**.2, 3, 5, 6, 9, 21, 22, 25, 27; **2**.1^2, 4, 5, 8, 13, 16, 18, **3**.4, 7, 13^2, 16; **4**.1, 6, 7, 8, 9, 10^2, 12^2, 13, 14, 16, 18
1 Th **1**.1, 2, 4, 5^2, 6, 7, 8, 9; **2**.1, 2, 6, 7, 8^2, 9^2, 10^2, 11, 11(12)^2, 12, 13, 14^2, 17^2, 18, 19, 20; **3**.2, 4^2, 5, 6^2, 7, 8, 9, 10, 11, 12^2; **4**.1^2, 2, 3, 4, 6, 8, 9, 10, 11, 13, 15; **5**.1, 4^2, 5, 12^4, 14, 18, 23, 24, 27, 28
2 Th **1**.2, 3^2, 4, 5, 6, 7, 10, 11^2, 12^2; **2**.1, 3, 5^2, 13^2, 14; **3**.1, 3, 4, 6^2, 7, 8, 9, 10^2, 11, 16^2, 18
1 Tim **6**.21
2 Tim **4**.22
Tit **3**.15
Phm .3, 22
Heb **3**.12, 13; **4**.1; **5**.12; **6**.11; **9**.20; **12**.5, 7; **13**.7, 17, 19, 21, 21‡, 22^2, 23, 24, 25
Jas **1**.5; **2**.6^3, 7, 16; **3**.13; **4**.1, 2, 7, 8, 10, 15; **5**.1, 3, 4, 6, 8, 13, 14, 19
1 Pet **1**.2, 4, 12^3, 13, 15, 25; **2**.7, 9^2, 12, 21^2; **3**.13, 15^2, 21; **4**.[1‡, 4, 12^3, 14, 15; **5**.1, 6, 7, 10, 12, 13, 14
2 Pet **1**.2, 11, 12, 13, 15, 16; **2**.1, 3, 13; **3**.1, 9‡, 11, 15, 17
1 Jn **1**.2, 3^2, 5; **2**.1, 7, 8^2, 12, 13–14^6, 20, 21, 24^4, 26^2, 27^5; **3**.7, 13; **4**.4^2; **5**.13
2 Jn .10, 12^2
Jude .2, 3^2, 5, 17, 18, 20, 24
Rev **1**.4; **2**.10, 13, 23, 24^2; **12**.12; **18**.20; **22**.16
3. *yourself:* σεαυτοῦ SEAUTOU
2 Tim 4.11 Get Mark and bring him with you
4. *you, thou:* σύ SY
Mt **2**.6^2, 13; **3**.14^2; **4**.6^2, 9; **5**.23, 25, 26, 29^2, 30^2, 33, 39, 40, 41, 42^2; **6**.2, 3, 4, 6^2, 17, 18, 23; **8**.13, 19, 29; **9**.22; **11**.3, 21^2, 23^2, 24; **12**.38, [47‡; **14**.4, 28^2; **15**.28; **16**.16, 17, 18^2, 19, 22; **17**.4, 25; **18**.8^2, 9^2, 15^3, 16, 17, 22, 26, 29, 32, 33^2; **19**.21, 27; **20**.13, 14; **21**.5, 19, 23; **22**.17; **25**.21, 23,

24, 27; **26**.17, 25, 33, 34, 35[2], 62, 63[2], 64, 68, 69, 73[2]; **27**.11[2], 13
Mk **1**.24, 37; **2**.11; **3**.11, 32; **4**.38; **5**.7[2], 19[2], 31, 34, 41; **6**.18, 23; **8**.29; **9**.5, 17, 25, 43[2], 45[2], 47[2]; **10**.21, 28, 35, 49, 51, 52; **11**.14, 28; **14**.30[2], 31[2], 60, 61, 67, 68; **15**.2[2], 4
Lk **1**.3, 13, 14, 19[2], 28, [28‡, 35[2], [35‡, 42, 76; **2**.48; **4**.6, 7, 10[2], 11, 34, 41; **5**.20, 23, 24; **6**.29, 30; **7**.7, 14, 19, 20[2], 40, 47, 50; **8**.20, 28[2], 39, 45, 48; **9**.33, 38, 57, 60, 61; **10**.13[2], 15, 35, 36, 40; **11**.7, 27, 35, 36; **12**.20, 58[3], 59; **13**.31; **14**.8, 9[2], 10[2], 12[2], 14[2], 18, 19; **15**.18, 21, 29, 31; **16**.2, 7, 25, 27; **17**.4[2], 8, 19; **18**.22, 28, 41, 42; **19**.19, 21, 22, 42, 43[4], 44[3]; **20**.2; **22**.11, 32[2], 33, 34, 58, 64, 67, 70; **23**.3[2], 37, 39, 40, 43; **24**.18
Jn **1**.19, 21[2], 25, 42[2], 48[2], 49[2], 50[2]; **2**.4, 10, 20; **3**.2, 3, 5, 7, 10, 11, 26[2]; **4**.9, 10[3], 12, 19, 26; **5**.10, 12, 14; **6**.30[2], 69; **7**.3, 20, 52; **8**.5‡, 10‡, 11‡, 13, 25, 33, 48, 52, 53, [57‡; **9**.17, 26, 28, 34[2], 35, 37; **10**.24, 33[2]; **11**.8, 22, 27, 28, 40; **12**.34; **13**.6, 7, 8, 37[2], 38; **14**.9; **16**.30; **18**.17, 25, 26, 33, 34[2], 35, 37[2]; **19**.9, 10[2], 11[2]; **20**.15; **21**.3, 12, 15[2], 16[2], 17[3], 18[2], 20, 22, 23
Acts **3**.6; **5**.9; **7**.3, 27, 28, 34, 35; **8**.20, 21, 22, 23; **9**.5, 6[2], 17, 34; **10**.15, 19, 22[2], 33[3]; **11**.9, 14[2]; **13**.11, 47[2]; **16**.18, 31; **17**.19, 32; **18**.10[3]; **21**.21, 23, 24, 37, 38, 39; **22**.8, 10[2], 14, 21, 27; **23**.3[2], 11, 18[2], 20, 21, 30[2], 35; **24**.2, 4[2], [8‡, 10, 11, 13, 14, 19, 25; **25**.10, 26; **26**.1, 2, 3, 14, 15, 16[3], 17[2], 24, 29; **27**.24[3]; **28**.21[2], 22
Rom **2**.3, 4, 17, 27; **4**.17; **9**.17[2], 20; **10**.8; **11**.17, 18[2], 20, 21, 22[2], 24; **14**.4, 10[2], 15, 22
1 Cor **4**.7; **8**.10; **12**.21; **14**.17; **15**.36
2 Cor **6**.2[2]; **12**.9
Gal **2**.14; **3**.8; **6**.1
Eph **5**.14; **6**.3
Phil **4**.3
1 Tim **1**.3, 18[2]; **3**.14[2]; **4**.14[2]; **6**.11, 14
2 Tim **1**.3, 4, 5, 6[2], 18; **2**.1, 7; **3**.10, 15; **4**.21
Tit **1**.5[2]; **2**.15; **3**.8, 12, 15
Phm .4, 7, 8, 10, 11[2], 12, 16, 18, 20, 21, 23
Heb **6**.14[2]; **8**.5; **13**.5[2]
Jas **2**.18[2], 19; **4**.12
2 Jn .5[2], 13
3 Jn .2, 3, 13, 14, 15[2]
Jude .9
Rev **2**.4[2], 5, 10, 14, 15, 16, 20; **3**.3, 8, 9, 10, 16, 17, 18; **4**.1; **7**.14; **10**.11; **17**.1, 7; **19**.10; **21**.9; **22**.9

IDIOMATICALLY
a. Jn **8**.53; Rom **2**.19 [SEAUTOU]
b. Acts **27**.34; Rom **11**.31; 1 Cor **15**.31 [HYMETEROS]

YOU, WHAT BELONGS TO

1. *your, thy:* σός (subst. neut.) SOS
Mt 20.14 " 'Take what belongs to you, and go

YOU YOURSELVES

1. *you, ye:* ὑμεῖς HYMEIS
Lk **13**.28

YOUNG (*See also* ASS, YOUNG)

1. *new, young:* νέος NEOS
[a]comp.
Jn 21.18 [a]"when . . y., you girded yourself
Acts 5. 6 [a]young men rose and wrapped him up
Tit 2. 4 so train the young women to love
2. *young bird, young animal:* νοσσός NOSSOS* [A.1.b.1]
Lk 2.24 "a pair of turtledoves, or two y. pigeons

YOUNG MAN

1. *young man:* νεανίας NEANIAS*
Acts 7.58 at the feet of a young man named Saul
20. 9 a young man named Eutychus
23.17 "Take this young man to the tribune
2. *youth, servant:* νεανίσκος NEANISKOS*
Mt 19.20 The young man said to him
19.22 When the y. man heard . . he went away
Mk 14.51 a young man followed him
16. 5 entering the tomb, they saw a y. man
Lk 7.14 "Young man, I say to you, arise
Acts 2.17 " 'your young men shall see visions
5.10 When the y. men came in they found her
23.18 "to bring this young man to you
23.22 tribune dismissed the young man
1 Jn 2.13 I am writing to you, young men
2.14 I write to you, young men

YOUNGER

1. *smaller, inferior:* ἐλάσσων ELASSŌN
Rom 9.12 "The elder will serve the younger
2. *little, small:* μικρός MIKROS
Mk 15.40 Mary the mother of James the younger
3. *new, young:* νέος (comp.) NEOS
Lk 15.12 "the younger of them said to his father
15.13 "the younger son gathered all he had
1 Tim 5. 1 treat younger men like brothers
5. 2 ⟨treat⟩ younger women like sisters
5.11 But refuse to enrol younger widows
5.14 I would have younger widows marry
Tit 2. 6 urge the y. men to control themselves
1 Pet 5. 5 you that are younger be subject

YOUNGEST

1. *new, young:* νέος (comp.) NEOS
Lk 22.26 "let the greatest . . become as the y.

YOUR

1. *you, ye:* ὑμεῖς HYMEIS
Mt **5**.12, 16[3], 20, 44, 45, 47, 48; **6**.1[2], 8, 14, 15[2], 25[2], 26, 32; **7**.6, 11[2]; **9**.4, 11, 29; **10**.9, 13[2], 14[2], 20, 29, 30; **11**.29; **12**.27[2]; **13**.16[2]; **15**.3, 6; **17**.20, 24; **18**.[14‡, 35; **19**.8[2]; **20**.26, 27; **23**.9, 11, 32, 34, 38; **24**.20, 42; **25**.8; **26**.66
Mk **2**.8; **6**.11; **7**.9, 13; **8**.17; **10**.5, 43; **11**.25[2], [26[2]‡; **14**.64
Lk **3**.14; **4**.21; **5**.4, 22; **6**.22, 23, 24, 27, 35[2], 36, 38; **8**.25; **9**.5, 44; **10**.6, 11, 20; **11**.13, 19[2], 46, 47, 48; **12**.7, 22, 30, 32, 33, 34[2], 35; **13**.35; **16**.15; **21**.14, 15, 18, 19[2], 28[2], 34; **22**.53; **23**.28; **24**.38
Jn **4**.35; **6**.49; **8**.21, 24[2], 41, 42, 44, 54, 56; **9**.19, 41; **10**.34; **11**.15; **12**.30; **13**.14; **14**.1, 26, 27; **15**.11, 16; **16**.6, 12, 20, 22[2], 24; **19**.14, 15; **20**.17[2]
Acts **2**.17[4], 22, 38, 39; **3**.17, 19, 22, 25; **5**.28; **7**.37, 51, 52; **13**.41; **14**.17; **15**.24; **17**.23, 28; **18**.6; **24**.22; **28**.25
Rom **1**.8; **6**.12, 13[2], 19[3]; **8**.11; **11**.28; **12**.1[2]; **14**.16; **15**.28, 32; **16**.19, 20
1 Cor **1**.26; **2**.5; **4**.6, 14, 15; **5**.6; **6**.5, 15, 19, 20; **7**.14, 35; **9**.11; **15**.14, 17[2], 34, 58; **16**.3
2 Cor **1**.6[2], 24[2]; **2**.10; **3**.2‡; **4**.5, 15; **5**.11; **7**.7[3], 12; **8**.7 *var.*, 9, 14[2], 23, 24; **9**.2[2], 10[2], 13; **10**.6, 15; **11**.3; **12**.15, 19; **13**.9
Gal **4**.15, 16; **6**.18
Eph **1**.13, 15, 18; **3**.13, 17; **4**.4, 23, 26, 29; **5**.19; **6**.1, 4, 14, 22
Phil **1**.5, 9, 19, 24, 25, 28; **2**.17, 20, 25, 30; **4**.5, 6, 7[2], 17, 23
Col **1**.4, 8, 24; **2**.5[2], 13; **3**.3, 8, 15, 16, 21; **4**.6, 8
1 Th **1**.3, 5, 8; **3**.2, 5, 6, 7, 9, 10, 13; **4**.3, 11; **5**.23
2 Th **1**.3, 4[2]; **2**.17; **3**.5
Phm .22, 25
Heb **3**.8, 9, 15; **4**.7; **6**.9, 10; **9**.14‡; **10**.34, 35; **12**.13; **13**.7, 17[2], 24
Jas **1**.3, 21; **2**.2; **3**.14; **4**.1[2], 3, 9, 14, 16; **5**.2[2], 3[2], 4, 5, 8, 12
1 Pet **1**.7, 9, 13, 14, 17, 20, 21, 22; **2**.25; **3**.2, 7, 15, 16; **5**.2, 7, 8, 9
2 Pet **1**.5, 10, 19; **3**.1, 2, [9‡
Jude .12, 20
Rev **1**.9; **2**.23
2. *your:* ὑμέτερος HYMETEROS
Jn 7. 6 "but your time is always here
8.17 "In your law it is written
1 Cor 16.17 they have made up for your absence
2 Cor 8. 8 to prove . . that y. love also is genuine
Gal 6.13 that they may glory in your flesh
3. *one's own:* ἴδιος IDIOS
Eph 5.25 love your wives, as Christ loved
1 Pet 3. 1 wives, be submissive to your husbands
4. *your, thy:* σός SOS
Mt 7.22 " 'did we not prophesy in your name, and cast out demons in your name, and do . . works in your name?
13.27 " 'did you not sow good seed in y. field?
24. 3 "what will be the sign of your coming?
Mk 2.18 "but your disciples do not fast
5.19 "Go home to your friends, and tell
Jn 4.42 "no longer because of your words
Acts 5. 4 "was it not at your disposal?
24. 2 "by your provision, most excellent Felix

Acts 24. 4 "I beg you in your kindness to hear us
1 Cor 8.11 by your knowledge this weak man
14.16 say the "Amen" to your thanksgiving
Phm .14 to do nothing without your consent

5. *you, thou:* σύ SY
Mt **1.**20; **4.**6, 7, 10; **5.**23^{2}, 24^{3}, 25, 29^{3}, 30^{3}, 36, 40, 43^{2}; **6.**3^{2}, 4^{2}, 6^{3}, 17^{2}, 18^{2}, 21^{2}, 22^{2}, 23^{2}; **7.**3, 4^{2}, 5; **9.**2, 5, 6, 14, 18, 22; **12.**2, 13, 37^{2}, [47^{2}‡; **15.**2, 28; **17.**16; **18.**8^{2}, 9, 15^{2}, 33; **19.**19; **20.**[15†, 21^{2}; **21.**5; **22.**37^{4}, 39; **23.**37; **25.**21, 23, 25; **26.**52, 73
Mk **1.**44; **2.**5, 9^{2}, 11; **3.**5, 32^{2}, [32‡; **5.**9, 34^{2}, 35; **6.**18; **7.**5, 10^{2}, 29; **9.**18, 38, 43, 45, 47; **10.**19, 37^{2}, 52; **12.**30^{5}, 31
Lk **1.**13^{2}, 36, 38, 42, 44, 61; **2.**35, 48; **4.**8, 11, 12; **5.**5, 14, 20, 23, 24; **6.**10, 29, 41, 42^{3}; **7.**44, 48, 50; **8.**20^{2}, 30, 39, 48, 49; **9.**40, 41, 49; **10.**17, 27^{6}; **11.**34^{4}, 36; **12.**20, 58; **13.**12, 26, 34; **14.**10, 12^{3}; **15.**19^{2}, 21, [21‡, 27^{2}, 29, 30, 32; **16.**2, 6, 7, 25^{2}; **17.**3, 19; **18.**20, 42; **19.**5, 16, 18, 20, 39, 42, 43, 44^{2}; **22.**32^{2}; **23.**42
Jn **4.**16, 18, 50, 53; **5.**8, 11; **7.**3; **8.**13, 19; **9.**10, 17, 26; **11.**23; **12.**15; **13.**38; **19.**26, 27; **20.**27^{2}; **21.**18
Acts **3.**25; **5.**3, 4, 9; **7.**3^{2}, 32, 33; **8.**20, 21, 22, [37‡; **10.**4^{2}, 31^{2}; **11.**14; **12.**8^{2}; **14.**10; **16.**31; **22.**16, 18; **23.**5, 35; **26.**16
Rom **2.**5, 25; **4.**18; **9.**7; **10.**6, 8^{2}, 9^{2}; **12.**20; **13.**4, 9; **14.**10^{2}, 15, 21
Gal **3.**16; **5.**14
Eph **6.**2
1 Tim **4.**12, 15, 16; **5.**23
2 Tim **1.**4, 5^{3}; **4.**5, 22
Phm .2, 5, 6, 7, 13, 14, 21
Heb **11.**18
Jas **2.**8, 18
2 Jn .4, 13
3 Jn .2, 3, 6
Rev **2.**2^{2}, 5, 9, 19^{3}; **3.**1, 2, 8, 9, 11, 15, 18^{2}; **10.**9^{2}; **14.**15, 18; **19.**10; **22.**9

IDIOMATICALLY
a. Jn 18.34 "of your own accord ἀπὸ σεαυτοῦ [SEAUTOU]
b. Acts 9.34 "rise and make your bed ἀνάστηθι καὶ στρῶσον σεαυτῷ [SEAUTOU]

YOUR GOODS

1. *your, thy:* σός (subst. neut. pl.) SOS
Lk 6.30 "of him who takes away your goods

YOUR OWN

1. *himself:* ἑαυτοῦ HEAUTOU
Rom 11.25 Lest you be wise in your own conceits
1 Cor 6.19 You are not your own
Phil 2.12 work out your own salvation
2. *you, ye:* ὑμεῖς HYMEIS
Jn **18.**31
Acts **18.**15; **20.**30
2 Cor **6.**12
Eph **2.**8
3. *your:* ὑμέτερος (subst. neut.) HYMETEROS
Lk 16.12 "who will give you that which is your own?
4. *one's own:* ἴδιος IDIOS
Lk 6.41 "not notice . . log that is in your own eye
1 Th 2.14 you suffered . . from your own countrymen
2 Pet 3.17 lest you . . lose your own stability
5. *your, thy:* σός SOS
Mt 7. 3 "not notice . . log that is in your own eye
Jn 18.35 "Your own nation . . have handed you over
6. *you, thou:* σύ SY
Mt **7.**4, 5
Lk **4.**23; **6.**42^{2}; **19.**22
Acts **5.**4

YOUR OWN AFFAIRS

1. *one's own:* ἴδιος (subst. neut. pl.) IDIOS
1 Th 4.11 to mind your own affairs, and to work

YOURS
YOURS, OF
YOURS, WHAT IS

1. *himself:* ἑαυτοῦ (gen.) HEAUTOU
1 Cor 10.29 (I mean his conscience, not yours
2. *who, which, what:* ὅς HOS
1 Pet **3.**3
3. *you, ye:* ὑμεῖς HYMEIS
Mt **6.**33
Mk **11.**24
Lk **12.**31
Rom **1.**12
1 Cor **3.**21, 22; **8.**9; **16.**18
2 Cor **12.**14
Eph **6.**9
Phil **4.**19
1 Pet **1.**10
2 Pet **1.**8
4. *your:* ὑμέτερος HYMETEROS
^{a}pred. ^{b}subst.
Lk 6.20 ^{a}for yours is the kingdom of God
Jn 15.20 ^{b}"if they kept my word, they will keep y.
5. *your, thy:* σός (pred.) SOS
^{a}subst. neut. ^{b}subst. ^{c}pred.
Mt 25.25 ^{a}"'Here you have what is y.
Lk 5.33 ^{b}"but yours eat and drink
15.31 ^{c}"'all that is mine is yours
6. *you, thou:* σύ SY
Lk **4.**7; **15.**30
Acts **8.**22

YOURSELF

1. *yourself:* σεαυτοῦ SEAUTOU
Mt 4. 6 "If you are . . , throw yourself down
8. 4 "go, show yourself to the priest
19.19 "love your neighbor as yourself
22.39 "You shall love your neighbor as yourself
27.40 "You who would . . build it . . , save y.!
Mk 1.44 "go, show yourself to the priest
12.31 "'love your neighbor as yourself
15.30 "save yourself, and come down!
Lk 4. 9 "throw yourself down from here
4.23 "'Physician, heal yourself
5.14 "go and show yourself to the priest
10.27 "love . . your neighbor as yourself
23.37 "If you are the King . . , save yourself!
23.39 "Save yourself and us!
Jn 1.22 "What do you say about yourself?
7. 4 "show yourself to the world
8.13 "You are bearing witness to yourself
10.33 "you, being a man, make yourself God
14.22 "how is it that you will manifest yourself?
21.18 "you girded yourself and walked
Acts 16.28 "Do not harm y., for we are all here
26. 1 "You have permission to speak for y.
Rom 2. 1 in passing judgment . . you condemn y.
2. 5 you are storing up wrath for yourself
2.21 will you not teach yourself?
13. 9 "You shall love your neighbor as y.
14.22 keep between yourself and God
Gal 5.14 "You shall love your neighbor as yourself
6. 1 Look to y., lest you too be tempted
1 Tim 4. 7 Train yourself in godliness
4.16 Take heed to y. and to your teaching; . . by so doing you will save both y.
5.22 keep yourself pure
2 Tim 2.15 to present y. to God as one approved
Tit 2. 7 Show yourself in all respects a model
Jas 2. 8 "love your neighbor as yourself
2. *you, thou:* σύ SY
Mt **17.**27; **27.**4
2 Tim **4.**15

YOURSELVES

1. *one another:* ἀλλήλων ALLĒLŌN
^{a}B.3.b.4
Jn 6.43 "Do not murmur among yourselves
16.19 ^{a}"Is this what you are asking y.?
2. *himself:* ἑαυτοῦ HEAUTOU
Mt 3. 9 "do not presume to say to yourselves
16. 8 "why do you discuss among yourselves?
23.31 "Thus you witness against yourselves
25. 9 "go rather . . and buy for yourselves
Mk 9.50 "Have salt in yourselves, and be at peace
13. 9 "But take heed to yourselves

Lk 3. 8 "do not begin to say to yourselves
12.33 "provide yourselves with purses
12.57 "why do you not judge for yourselves?
16. 9 "I tell you, make friends for y.
16.15 "You are those who justify yourselves
17. 3 "Take heed to yourselves
17.14 "Go and show yourselves to the priests
21.30 "you see for yourselves and know
21.34 "But take heed to yourselves
22.17 "Take this, and divide it among y.
23.28 "do not weep for me, but weep for y.
Acts 13.46 "you . . judge y. unworthy of eternal life
15.29 "If you keep yourselves from these
20.28 "Take heed to yourselves
Rom 6.11 consider yourselves dead to sin
6.13 but yield yourselves to God
6.16 if you yield y. to any one as . . slaves
12.19 Beloved, never avenge yourselves
2 Cor 7.11 what eagerness to clear yourselves!
13. 5 Examine yourselves, to see . . Test yourselves
Phil 2. 3 count others better than yourselves
1 Th 5.13 Be at peace among yourselves
Heb 10.34 you yourselves had a better possession
Jas 1.22 be . . not hearers only, deceiving y.
2. 4 have you not made distinctions among y.?
1 Jn 5.21 Little children, keep y. from idols
2 Jn . 8 Look to y., that you may not lose
Jude .20 build y. up on your most holy faith
.21 keep yourselves in the love of God

3. *you, ye:* ὑμεῖς HYMEIS
Mt **6**.19, 20; **23**.15; **27**.24
Jn **7**.8; **18**.31; **19**.6
Acts **10**.28; **20**.18
1 Cor **10**.15; **11**.13; **14**.9, 12
2 Cor **3**.2
Phil **2**.5
Col **1**.6; **4**.9, 12
1 Th **4**.9

IDIOMATICALLY
a. Mk 6.31 "Come away by yourselves δεῦτε ὑμεῖς αὐτοὶ κατ' ἰδίαν [IDIOS]

YOUTH
1. *youth:* νεότης NEOTĒS*
Mk 10.20 "all these I have observed from my y.
Lk 18.21 "All these I have observed from my y.
Acts 26. 4 "My manner of life from my youth
1 Tim 4.12 Let no one despise your youth

YOUTHFUL
1. *youthful:* νεωτερικός NEŌTERIKOS*
2 Tim 2.22 So shun youthful passions

Z

ZACCHAEUS: Ζακχαῖος za'kēəs
Lk 19. 2 there was a man named Zacchaeus
19. 5 "Zacchaeus, make haste and come down
19. 8 Zacchaeus stood and said to the Lord

ZADOK: Σαδώκ 'zādôk
Mt 1.14 Azor the father of Zadok, and Zadok the father of Achim

ZAREPHATH: Σάρεπτα 'zarə,fath I,C-2
Lk 4.26 "Elijah was sent . . only to Zarephath

ZEAL
1. *zeal, haste:* σπουδή SPOUDĒ
Rom 12. 8 he who gives aid, with zeal
12.11 Never flag in z., be aglow with the Spirit
2 Cor 7.12 that your zeal . . might be revealed
2. *zeal, jealousy:* ζῆλος ZĒLOS
Jn 2.17 "Zeal for thy house will consume me
Rom 10. 2 they have a zeal for God
2 Cor 7. 7 he told us of . . your zeal
7.11 see . . what longing, what zeal!
9. 2 your zeal has stirred up most of them
Phil 3. 6 as to zeal a persecutor of the church

ZEALOT
1. *zealous admirer:* ζηλωτής ZĒLŌTĒS
Lk 6.15 Simon who was called the Zealot
Acts 1.13 Simon the Zealot

ZEALOUS
1. *zealous admirer:* ζηλωτής (pred.) ZĒLŌTĒS
Acts 21.20 "they are all zealous for the law
22. 3 "being zealous for God as you all are
Gal 1.14 so extremely z. was I for the traditions
Tit 2.14 a people of his own who are zealous
1 Pet 3.13 if you are zealous for what is right

ZEALOUS, BE
1. *be eager:* σπουδάζω SPOUDAZŌ
2 Pet 1.10 brethren, be the more zealous
3.14 be zealous to be found . . without spot
2. *be jealous of, strive after:* ζηλεύω ZĒLEUŌ*
Rev 3.19 " 'so be zealous and repent

ZEALOUSLY, MORE
1. *more, greater:* περισσότερος (neut.) PERISSOTEROS
[a]+μᾶλλον B.3.b.6
Mk 7.36 [a]the more zealously they proclaimed it

ZEBEDEE: Ζεβεδαῖος 'zebə,dē
Mt 4.21 James the son of Z. and John his brother in the boat with Z. their father
10. 2 James the son of Zebedee
20.20 the mother of the sons of Zebedee
26.37 Peter and the two sons of Zebedee
27.56 the mother of the sons of Zebedee
Mk 1.19 James the son of Zebedee
1.20 they left their father Z. in the boat
3.17 James the son of Zebedee
10.35 James and John, the sons of Zebedee
Lk 5.10 James and John, sons of Zebedee
Jn 21. 2 the sons of Zebedee, and two others

ZEBULUN: Ζαβουλών 'zebyələn
Mt 4.13 Capernaum . . , in the territory of Z.
4.15 "The land of Z. . . , toward the sea
Rev 7. 8 twelve thousand of the tribe of Z.

ZECHARIAH: Ζαχαρίας ,zekə'rīə
1. Old Testament martyr
Mt 23.35 "Zechariah the son of Barachiah
Lk 11.51 "Z., who perished between the altar
2. father of John the Baptist
Lk 1. 5 there was a priest named Zechariah[b]†
1.12 Z. was troubled when he saw him
1.13 "Do not be afraid, Zechariah
1.18 Z. said to the angel, "How shall I know?
1.21 the people were waiting for Zechariah
1.40 she entered the house of Z.
1.59 they would have named him Z.
1.67 Z. was filled with the Holy Spirit
3. 2 word of God came to John the son of Z.

ZENAS: Ζηνᾶς 'zēnəs
Tit 3.13 Do your best to speed Zenas the lawyer

ZERAH: Ζάρα 'zirə
Mt 1. 3 father of Perez and Z. by Tamar

ZERUBBABEL: Ζοροβαβέλ zi'rəbəbəl
Mt 1.12 Shealtiel[d] the father of Zerubbabel
1.13 Zerubbabel the father of Abiud
Lk 3.27 Zerubbabel, the son of Shealtiel[l]

ZEUS: Ζεύς 'züs
Acts 14.12 Barnabas they called Zeus
14.13 the priest of Zeus . . brought oxen

ZION: Σιών 'zīən
Mt 21. 5 "Tell the daughter of Zion
Jn 12.15 "Fear not, daughter of Zion
Rom 9.33 "Behold, I am laying in Z. a stone
11.26 "The Deliverer will come from Zion
Heb 12.22 you have come to Mount Zion
1 Pet 2. 6 "Behold, I am laying in Z. a stone
Rev 14. 1 lo, on Mount Zion stood the Lamb

INDEX–LEXICON

AN INDEX TO THE ANALYTICAL CONCORDANCE AND A LEXICON OF NEW TESTAMENT GREEK

Under each transliterated Greek word is the English used by the Revised Standard Version to translate it, together with the frequency of occurrence in parentheses. An English translation followed by a grammatical note or prefaced by the symbol § should not be taken as a simple definition of the related Greek word. Supplementary definition and a bracketed reference to Appendix I may be found on the respective subtitle line in the text of the Concordance. For further description of the Index-Lexicon, see Explanatory Notes, p. xiv. See also Abbreviations; Signs and Symbols.

A

ABARĒS ἀβαρής
[*without weight, light*]
IDIOMATICALLY
burdening *a*

ABBA ἀββά
abba (3)

ABYSSOS ἄβυσσος
abyss (2)
bottomless pit (6)
pit

ACHARISTOS ἀχάριστος
ungrateful (2)

ACHEIROPOIĒTOS ἀχειροποίητος
made with hands, not (2)
made without hands

ACHLYS ἀχλύς
mist

ACHREIOŌ ἀχρειόω
wrong, go (*pass.*)

ACHREIOS ἀχρεῖος
unworthy
worthless

ACHRĒSTOS ἄχρηστος
useless

ACHRI ἄχρι (ἄχρις)
§all the way to
§*as*
at
before
far as, as (2)
for
high as
high as, as
in
§long as, as
till (4)
to (8)+
until (20)
unto
unto, even
up to (2)
IDIOMATICALLY
thus *a*

ACHYRON ἄχυρον
chaff (2)

ADAPANOS ἀδάπανος
charge, free of

ADĒLOS ἄδηλος
indistinct
seen, not

ADĒLŌS ἀδήλως
aimlessly

ADĒLOTĒS ἀδηλότης
uncertain (+*gen.*)

ADELPHĒ ἀδελφή
sister (24)+
NOT TRANSLATED
1 Cor **9.5**

ADELPHOS ἀδελφός
brother (338)+
husband
IDIOMATICALLY
brotherhood *a*
NOT TRANSLATED
Mk **12.19**
Lk **20.28**

ADELPHOTĒS ἀδελφότης
brotherhood (2)

ADĒMONEŌ ἀδημονέω
distressed, be
troubled, be (2)

ADIAKRITOS ἀδιάκριτος
uncertainty, without

ADIALEIPTOS ἀδιάλειπτος
constantly (*neut.*)
unceasing

ADIALEIPTŌS ἀδιαλείπτως
ceasing, without
constantly (3)

ADIKĒMA ἀδίκημα
iniquity
wrongdoing (2)

ADIKEŌ ἀδικέω
evildoer (*subst. part.*)
harm (6)
hurt (3)
wound
wrong (6)
wrong, do (5)
wrong, suffer (*pass.*) (3)
wrongdoer (*subst. part.*)
wrongdoer, be a

ADIKIA ἀδικία
dishonest (*gen.*)
falsehood
iniquity (4)
injustice
unrighteous (*gen.*) (3)
unrighteousness (2)
wicked (*gen.*)
wickedness (7)
wrong (2)
wrongdoing (3)

ADIKOS ἄδικος
dishonest (2)
unjust (5)
unrighteous (5)

ADIKŌS ἀδίκως
unjustly

ADŌ ᾄδω
sing (5)

ADOKIMOS ἀδόκιμος
base
counterfeit
disqualified
§fail to meet the test
§failed, have (2)
unfit
worthless

ADOLOS ἄδολος
pure

ADYNATEŌ ἀδυνατέω
impossible, be (*impers.*) (2)

ADYNATOS ἀδύνατος
§cannot
impossible (7)
weak
IDIOMATICALLY
cannot *a*

AEI ἀεί
always (7)

AĒR ἀήρ
air (7)

AETOS ἀετός
eagle (5)
(vulture †)

AGALLIAŌ ἀγαλλιάω
exult
glad, be (*dep.*)
rejoice (*act. or dep.*) (9)

AGALLIASIS ἀγαλλίασις
§glad
gladness (2)
joy
rejoicing

AGAMOS ἄγαμος
single
unmarried (3)

AGANAKTEŌ ἀγανακτέω
indignant, be (6)
indignantly, say

AGANAKTĒSIS ἀγανάκτησις
indignation

AGAPAŌ ἀγαπάω
beloved (*perf. pass. part.*) (8)
love (134)

AGAPĒ ἀγάπη
beloved (*gen.*)
love (113)
love feast +
NOT TRANSLATED
1 Cor **13**.4

AGAPĒTOS ἀγαπητός
beloved (59) +
dear, very
loves, whom one (*attr.*)

AGATHOERGEŌ ἀγαθοεργέω
good, do (2)

AGATHOPOIEŌ ἀγαθοποιέω
good, do (5)
right, do (4)

AGATHOPOIIA ἀγαθοποιΐα
§right, do

AGATHOPOIOS ἀγαθοποιός
right, one who does (*subst.*)

AGATHOS ἀγαθός
clear (2)
good (86)†
goodness (*subst. neut.*)
goods (*subst. neut. pl.*) (2)
honest (2)
kind (2)
§kindly
right (2)
sound
true
§well-doing
IDIOMATICALLY
generosity *a*

AGATHŌSYNĒ ἀγαθωσύνη
good (*gen.*)
good, what is
goodness (2)

AGE ἄγε
come (2)

AGELĒ ἀγέλη
herd (7)

AGENEALOGĒTOS ἀγενεαλόγητος
genealogy, without

AGENĒS ἀγενής
low

AGGAREUŌ ἀγγαρεύω
compel (2)
force to go

AGGEION ἀγγεῖον
flask

AGGELIA ἀγγελία
message (2)

AGGELLŌ ἀγγέλλω
say

AGGELOS ἄγγελος
angel (167) +
messenger (7)

AGGOS ἄγγος
vessel

AGKALĒ ἀγκάλη
arm

AGKISTRON ἄγκιστρον
hook

AGKYRA ἄγκυρα
anchor (4)

AGNAPHOS ἄγναφος
unshrunk (2)

AGNOĒMA ἀγνόημα
error

AGNOEŌ ἀγνοέω
ignorant (*part.*)
ignorant, be (5)
ignorantly (*part.*)
know (*double neg.*) (2)
know, not (4)
recognize, not
understand (*double neg.*)
understand, not (3)
uninformed, be
unknown (*part.*)
unknown, as (*part.*)
(*Note:* AGNOEŌ *is translated twice in* Acts **13**.27.)

AGNOIA ἄγνοια
ignorance (4)

AGNŌSIA ἀγνωσία
ignorance
knowledge, no

AGNŌSTOS ἄγνωστος
unknown

AGŌ ἄγω
bring (43)
drag
go (7)
lead (10)
move
open, be (*pass.*)
sway
take
take away
IDIOMATICALLY
be *a*

AGŌGĒ ἀγωγή
conduct

AGŌN ἀγών
conflict
fight (2)
opposition
race
§strive

AGŌNIA ἀγωνία
(agony)

AGŌNIZOMAI ἀγωνίζομαι
athlete (*subst. part.*)
§earnestly, remember
fight (3)
strive (3)

AGORA ἀγορά
(market)
market place (11)

AGORAIOS ἀγοραῖος
court (*subst.*)
rabble (*subst. pl.*)

AGORAZŌ ἀγοράζω
buy (27)
ransom
redeem (2)

AGRA ἄγρα
catch (2)

AGRAMMATOS ἀγράμματος
uneducated

AGRAULEŌ ἀγραυλέω
field, be out in the

AGREUŌ ἀγρεύω
entrap

AGRIELAIOS ἀγριέλαιος
wild olive shoot
wild olive tree

AGRIOS ἄγριος
wild (3)

AGROS ἀγρός
country (8)
farm
field (23) +
land (3)

AGRYPNEŌ ἀγρυπνέω
alert, keep
watch (3)

AGRYPNIA ἀγρυπνία
sleepless night, a
watching (*pl.*)

AICHMALŌSIA αἰχμαλωσία
§captive, take
§captives, a host of
captivity

AICHMALŌTEUŌ αἰχμαλωτεύω
§lead

AICHMALŌTIZŌ αἰχμαλωτίζω
captive, lead
captive, make
captive, take
capture

AICHMALŌTOS αἰχμάλωτος
captive

AIDIOS ἀΐδιος
eternal (2)

AIDŌS αἰδώς
[*modesty, respect*]
§modestly

AIGEIOS αἴγειος
goat, of a
AIGIALOS αἰγιαλός
§ashore
beach (5)
AINEŌ αἰνέω
praise (8)
AINESIS αἴνεσις
praise
AINIGMA αἴνιγμα
[*dark saying, riddle*]
§dimly
AINOS αἶνος
praise (2)
AIŌN αἰών
age (26)
(angel†)
course
eternal (*gen. pl.*)
eternity
never (*neg., sg. or pl.*) (8)
§old, from of
old, of (2)
time
world (11)
IDIOMATICALLY
ever *a, b;* ever, for *a* (17), *b* (6)+, *c;* ever, for ever and *d, e* (18; Gr. 36), *f* (1; Gr. 2), *g* (1; Gr. 2), *h* (1; Gr. 2); evermore, for *a* (2; Gr. 4)
AIŌNIOS αἰώνιος
eternal (66)+
ever, for (*neut.*)
long
NOT TRANSLATED
2 Tim **1**.9
Tit **1**.2
AIPHNIDIOS αἰφνίδιος
sudden
§suddenly
AIRŌ αἴρω
away with (*imper.*) (5)
bear up (2)
carry (4)
deny
destroy
hoist up
lift
lift up (3)
pick up
put away
remove
set
sweep away
take (21)
take away (25)
take up (28)
tear away (2)
weigh anchor
IDIOMATICALLY
keep in suspense *a*
AISCHROKERDĒS αἰσχροκερδής
greedy for gain (2)
AISCHROKERDŌS αἰσχροκερδῶς
shameful gain, for
AISCHROLOGIA αἰσχρολογία
foul talk
AISCHROS αἰσχρός
base
disgraceful
shame (*neut.*)
shameful
AISCHROTĒS αἰσχρότης
filthiness
AISCHYNĒ αἰσχύνη
disgraceful (*gen.*)
shame (5)
AISCHYNOMAI αἰσχύνομαι
ashamed, be (3)
shame, put to
shame, shrink from s. in
AISTHANOMAI αἰσθάνομαι
perceive
AISTHĒSIS αἴσθησις
discernment
AISTHĒTĒRION αἰσθητήριον
faculty
AITĒMA αἴτημα
demand
request (2)
AITEŌ αἰτέω
ask (*act. or mid.*) (61)
ask leave (*mid.*)
beg from (2)
call for
demand (*act. or mid.*) (3)
(require)
IDIOMATICALLY
call *a;* make *c*
AITIA αἰτία
case
cause
charge (5)
crime (3)
§hence
reason (3)
§therefore (2)
§why (2)
§why, that is
IDIOMATICALLY
charge *b*
AITIŌMA αἰτίωμα
charge
AITIOS αἴτιος
cause (*subst. neut.*)
crime (*subst. neut.*) (2)
source (*subst. masc.*)
IDIOMATICALLY
guilty *a*
AKAIREOMAI ἀκαιρέομαι
opportunity, have no
AKAIRŌS ἀκαίρως
season, out of
AKAKOS ἄκακος
blameless
simple-minded
AKANTHA ἄκανθα
thorn (14)
AKANTHINOS ἀκάνθινος
thorns, of (2)
AKARPOS ἄκαρπος
fruitless
unfruitful (6)
AKATAGNŌSTOS ἀκατάγνωστος
censured, that cannot be
AKATAKALYPTOS ἀκατακάλυπτος
uncovered
unveiled
AKATAKRITOS ἀκατάκριτος
uncondemned (2)
AKATALYTOS ἀκατάλυτος
indestructible
AKATAPASTOS ἀκατάπαστος
insatiable
AKATAPAUSTOS ἀκατάπαυστος
(insatiable)
AKATASTASIA ἀκαταστασία
confusion
disorder (2)
tumult (2)
AKATASTATOS ἀκατάστατος
restless
unstable
AKATHARSIA ἀκαθαρσία
impurity (6)
uncleanness (4)
AKATHARTOS ἀκάθαρτος
foul (3)
impure
impurity (*subst. neut.*)
unclean (26)
AKERAIOS ἀκέραιος
guileless
innocent (2)
AKLINĒS ἀκλινής
wavering, without (*acc.*)
AKMAZŌ ἀκμάζω
ripe, be
AKMĒN ἀκμήν
still
AKOĒ ἀκοή
ear (4)
fame (3)
heard, what is (2)
hearing (5)
hears, what one (4)
listening
report
rumor (2)
IDIOMATICALLY
indeed *a* (2)
AKOLOUTHEŌ ἀκολουθέω
follow (89)
AKŌLYTŌS ἀκωλύτως
unhindered (*adv.*)
AKŌN ἄκων
will, not of one's own
AKOUŌ ἀκούω
ears, come to the (*pass.*) (2)
hear (388)+
hearer (*subst. part.*) (3)
hearing, give a
heed (2)
listen (28)
reported, be (*pass.*) (2)
understand
IDIOMATICALLY
indeed *d;* words *a*
AKRASIA ἀκρασία
rapacity
self-control, lack of
AKRATĒS ἀκρατής
profligate
AKRATOS ἄκρατος
unmixed
AKRIBEIA ἀκρίβεια
strict manner
AKRIBĒS ἀκριβής
strictest (*superl.*)
AKRIBOŌ ἀκριβόω
ascertain (2)
AKRIBŌS ἀκριβῶς
§accurate, rather
accurately (2)†
carefully
closely (2)
diligently
exactly, more (*comp.*)
well

AKRIS ἀκρίς
locust (4)

AKROATĒRION ἀκροατήριον
audience hall

AKROATĒS ἀκροατής
hearer (4)

AKROBYSTIA ἀκροβυστία
§circumcised (4)
§uncircumcised (4)
§uncircumcised, a man who is
§uncircumcised, the (3)
§uncircumcised, those who are
uncircumcision (7)

AKROGŌNIAIOS ἀκρογωνιαῖος
cornerstone (*subst.*) (2)

AKRON ἄκρον
end (4)
head
IDIOMATICALLY
other *b*

AKROTHINION ἀκροθίνιον
spoils (*pl.*)

AKYROŌ ἀκυρόω
annul
void, make (2)

ALABASTROS ἀλάβαστρος
alabaster flask (3)
flask

ALALAZŌ ἀλαλάζω
clang
wail

ALALĒTOS ἀλάλητος
words, too deep for

ALALOS ἄλαλος
dumb (3)

ALAZŌN ἀλαζών
boastful (*pred.*)
proud (*pred.*)

ALAZONEIA ἀλαζονεία
arrogance (*pl.*)
pride

ALEIPHŌ ἀλείφω
anoint (9)

ALEKTŌR ἀλέκτωρ
cock (11)+

ALEKTOROPHŌNIA ἀλεκτοροφωνία
cockcrow

ALĒTHEIA ἀλήθεια
§certainly
right
§rightly
§true (3)
true, what is (2)
§truly (5)
truth (92)
truthful (*gen.*)
§truthfully
truthfulness (2)

ALĒTHĒS ἀληθής
§indeed (2)
real
true (21)
truly (*neut.*)
§truth

ALĒTHEUŌ ἀληθεύω
(truly, deal †)
truth, speak the
truth, tell the

ALĒTHINOS ἀληθινός
true (28)

ALĒTHŌ ἀλήθω
grind (2)

ALĒTHŌS ἀληθῶς
certainly (2)
indeed (3)
really (3)
§sure, be
truly (8)
truth, in

ALEURON ἄλευρον
flour (2)

ALISGĒMA ἀλίσγημα
pollution

ALLA ἀλλά
again
but (529)+
but only (4)
certainly
contrary, on the (2)
except
for
however (2)
indeed
least, at
§*mere*
§moreover (2)
nevertheless (4)
no (4)
now
rather (3)
rather than (+*neg.*)
so
then (4)
what (6)
why (2)
yes (3)
yet (11)
IDIOMATICALLY
OR NOT TRANSLATED
Mt **18**.30
Mk **14**.29
Lk **1**.60; **23**.15
Jn **4**.14; **6**.32; **7**.12, 28; **11**.4; **12**.30, 49; **13**.18; **15**.25
Acts **10**.20; **16**.37; **19**.2
Rom **2**.29; **5**.3; **7**.13; **8**.9
1 Cor **3**.2; **4**.3, 15; **6**.11^{2}; **10**.29; **12**.22; **14**.20
2 Cor **1**.24; **2**.17; **3**.5; **4**.2, 16^{2}; **5**.16; **11**.1, 6^{2}; **12**.16
Gal **4**.8
Eph **5**.24, 27
Phil **2**.17; **3**.8
1 Tim **2**.12; **6**.4
2 Tim **4**.16
Tit **1**.15
Heb **3**.16
1 Jn **2**.27

ALLACHOTHEN ἀλλαχόθεν
another way, by

ALLACHOU ἀλλαχοῦ
on

ALLASSŌ ἀλλάσσω
change (5)
exchange

ALLĒGOREŌ ἀλληγορέω
allegory (*subst. pass. part.*)

ALLĒLŌN ἀλλήλων
§conflicting 1
each other (8)
§exchange 3
§mutual
one another (83)
others
themselves (3)
yourselves (2)

ALLOGENĒS ἀλλογενής
foreigner (*subst.*)

ALLOPHYLOS ἀλλόφυλος
nation, one of another

ALLOS ἄλλος
another (57)+
another man's
else (*neg.*) (3)
more (*pl.*) (5)
nothing (*subst. neut. neg.*)
one (3)
other (76)
some (*pl.*) (2)
IDIOMATICALLY
another, one *a* (1; Gr. 2); only *a;* some *a, b*

ALLŌS ἄλλως
[*otherwise*]
IDIOMATICALLY: not *a*

ALLOTRIEPISKOPOS
ἀλλοτριεπίσκοπος
mischief-maker

ALLOTRIOS ἀλλότριος
another man's (2)
another, of
another's (2)
foreign (2)
other (3)
others, belonging to
own, not his
stranger (*subst.*) (2)

ALOAŌ ἀλοάω
thresh
tread out grain (2)

ALOĒ ἀλόη
aloes

ALOGOS ἄλογος
irrational (2)
unreasonable

ALŌPĒX ἀλώπηξ
fox (3)

ALPHA ἄλφα
alpha (3)

ALYPOS ἄλυπος
anxious, less (*comp.*)

ALYSITELĒS ἀλυσιτελής
advantage, of no

AMACHOS ἄμαχος
quarrelsome, not
IDIOMATICALLY
quarreling *a*

AMAŌ ἀμάω
mow

AMARANTINOS ἀμαράντινος
unfading

AMARANTOS ἀμάραντος
unfading

AMARTYROS ἀμάρτυρος
witness, without

AMATHĒS ἀμαθής
ignorant

AMELEŌ ἀμελέω
heed, pay no
light of, make
neglect (2)

AMEMPTOS ἄμεμπτος
blameless (3)
faultless
unblamable

AMEMPTŌS ἀμέμπτως
§blameless (2)

AMĒN ἀμήν
amen (31)+
truly (99)
AMERIMNOS ἀμέριμνος
anxieties, free from
trouble, out of
AMETAKINĒTOS ἀμετακίνητος
immovable
AMETAMELĒTOS ἀμεταμέλητος
irrevocable
regret, that brings no
AMETANOĒTOS ἀμετανόητος
impenitent
AMETATHETOS ἀμετάθετος
unchangeable
unchangeable character, the (*subst. neut.*)
AMETHYSTOS ἀμέθυστος
amethyst
AMĒTŌR ἀμήτωρ
mother, without
AMETROS ἄμετρος
[*immeasurable*]
IDIOMATICALLY
limit, beyond ***a, b***
AMIANTOS ἀμίαντος
undefiled (3)
unstained
AMMOS ἄμμος
sand (5)
AMNOS ἀμνός
lamb (4)
AMOIBĒ ἀμοιβή
return, some (*pl.*)
AMŌMĒTOS ἀμώμητος
blemish, without
AMŌMON ἄμωμον
spice
AMŌMOS ἄμωμος
blameless (2)
blemish, without (5)
spotless
AMPELŌN ἀμπελών
vineyard (23)
AMPELOS ἄμπελος
grapevine
vine (7)
vintage
AMPELOURGOS ἀμπελουργός
vinedresser
AMPHIAZŌ ἀμφιάζω
clothe
AMPHIBALLŌ ἀμφιβάλλω
cast a net
AMPHIBLĒSTRON ἀμφίβληστρον
net
AMPHIENNYMI ἀμφιέννυμι
clothe (3)
AMPHODON ἄμφοδον
open street
AMPHOTEROI ἀμφότεροι
all of them (*subst. pl.*)
all, them (*subst. acc. pl.*)
both (12)
AMYNOMAI ἀμύνομαι
defend
AN ἄν
[*This particle is translated into English only in relation to other words or whole clauses.*]
§any, if 1
§*any one* 3 (Lk **20**.18)+
§*any one, if* 1 (7)
§as soon as 1
§*before* 12[a] (4)
§but only
§can
§*he who* 1[b] (4)
§however
§if 1[a] (3)
§once
§one, the 1[a] (2)
§should (5)
§till 1[b]; 2[a] (11)
§until 1[b]; 3[b] (4)
§whatever 2[a] (6); 3[c] (2); 3[e]; 4[b] (4)
§whenever 1; 2 (2)
§wherever 1[b] (3); 2
§whoever 1[a] (29); 2[a] (2)
§would 1 (35); 2[a]
IDIOMATICALLY
OR NOT TRANSLATED
Mk **6**.56
Lk **1**.62; **2**.26, 35; **6**.11; **9**.46; **12**.8; **15**.26
Jn **13**.20
Acts **2**.39, 45; **3**.19, 23; **4**.35; **5**.24; **7**.3; **8**.31; **10**.17; **15**.17; **17**.18; **26**.29
Rom **3**.4; **9**.15[2], 29; **10**.13; **15**.24
1 Cor **7**.5; **11**.34
2 Cor **10**.9
ANA ἀνά (+*acc.*)
§*among* 8[a]
§between 2[c]
each 1 (2); 2[a]
§each of them (2)
§midst 1[b]
§through 6
§two by two
IDIOMATICALLY
each ***a, b***
NOT TRANSLATED
Lk **9**.3
ANABAINŌ ἀναβαίνω
ascend (14)
climb in
climb up
come (2)
come up (7)
§conceive
get into (2)
go
go aboard
go up (42)
grow up (4)
march up
rise (5)
ANABALLŌ ἀναβάλλω
put off (*mid.*)
ANABATHMOS ἀναβαθμός
step (2)
ANABIBAZŌ ἀναβιβάζω
draw
ANABLEPŌ ἀναβλέπω
look up (8)
receive one's sight (14)
regain one's sight (3)
ANABLEPSIS ἀνάβλεψις
recovering of sight
ANABOAŌ ἀναβοάω
cry
ANABOLĒ ἀναβολή
delay
ANACHŌREŌ ἀναχωρέω
depart (5)
go aside
withdraw (8)
ANACHYSIS ἀνάχυσις
§wild
ANADECHOMAI ἀναδέχομαι
receive (2)
ANADEIKNYMI ἀναδείκνυμι
appoint
show
ANADEIXIS ἀνάδειξις
manifestation
ANADIDŌMI ἀναδίδωμι
deliver
ANAGAION ἀνάγαιον
upper room (2)
ANAGGELLŌ ἀναγγέλλω
announce
declare (7)
divulge
proclaim
show
tell (2)
ANAGENNAŌ ἀναγεννάω
bear anew (2)
ANAGINŌSKŌ ἀναγινώσκω
read (30)
reader (*subst. part.*) (2)
ANAGKAIOS ἀναγκαῖος
close
indispensable
necessary (5)
urgent
ANAGKASTŌS ἀναγκαστῶς
constraint, by
ANAGKAZŌ ἀναγκάζω
compel (5)
force
make (3)
ANAGKĒ ἀνάγκη
compulsion (2)
distress (3)
hardship (2)
§must (+*inf.*) (3)
§necessarily
§necessary, be (+*inf.*) (2)
§necessary, find (+*inf.*)
necessity (2)
need
§(obliged, be)
ANAGNŌSIS ἀνάγνωσις
§read
reading (2)
ANAGŌ ἀνάγω
bring again
bring out
bring up (3)
lead up
offer
put to sea (*mid. or pass.*) (3)
sail (*mid. or pass.*)
set out (*mid. or pass.*)
set sail (*mid. or pass.*) (9)
take
take up
ANAIDEIA ἀναίδεια
importunity
ANAIREŌ ἀναιρέω
abolish
adopt (*mid.*)
death, put to (4)
kill (16)
slay (2)

ANAIRESIS ἀναίρεσις
death

ANAITIOS ἀναίτιος
guiltless (2)

ANAKAINIZŌ ἀνακαινίζω
restore

ANAKAINOŌ ἀνακαινόω
renew (2)

ANAKAINŌSIS ἀνακαίνωσις
renewal (2)

ANAKALYPTŌ ἀνακαλύπτω
unlifted (*pass. part. neg.*)
unveil

ANAKAMPTŌ ἀνακάμπτω
return (4)

ANAKATHIZŌ ἀνακαθίζω
sit up (2)

ANAKEIMAI ἀνάκειμαι
guest (*subst. part.*) (3)
lie
seated, be
sit at table (6)
table, at (*part.*) (2)
table, be at

ANAKEPHALAIOŌ ἀνακεφαλαιόω
sum up
unite (*mid.*)

ANAKLINŌ ἀνακλίνω
lay
sit at table (*pass.*) (2)
sit at table, have s.
sit down (*pass.*) (2)

ANAKRAZŌ ἀνακράζω
cry out (5)

ANAKRINŌ ἀνακρίνω
call to account
discern
examine (7)
judge (5)
question, raise a (2)

ANAKRISIS ἀνάκρισις
§examine

ANAKYLIŌ ἀνακυλίω
roll back

ANAKYPTŌ ἀνακύπτω
look up (2)
stand up
straighten oneself

ANALAMBANŌ ἀναλαμβάνω
get
take (3)
take aboard
take on board
take up (7)

ANALĒMPSIS ἀνάλημψις
§receive up

ANALISKŌ ἀναλίσκω (ἀναλόω)
consume (2)

ANALOGIA ἀναλογία
proportion

ANALOGIZOMAI ἀναλογίζομαι
consider

ANALOS ἄναλος
[*without salt, tasteless*]
§saltness, lose

ANALYŌ ἀναλύω
come home
depart

ANALYSIS ἀνάλυσις
departure

ANAMARTĒTOS ἀναμάρτητος
sin, without

ANAMENŌ ἀναμένω
wait for

ANAMIMNĒSKŌ ἀναμιμνήσκω
recall (*pass.*)
remember (*pass.*) (3)
remind (2)

ANAMNĒSIS ἀνάμνησις
remembrance (3)
reminder

ANANEOŌ ἀνανεόω
renewed, be (*pass.*)

ANANĒPHŌ ἀνανήφω
escape

ANANTIRRĒTOS ἀναντίρρητος
contradicted, not to be

ANANTIRRĒTŌS ἀναντιρρήτως
objection, without

ANAPAUŌ ἀναπαύω
ease, take one's (*mid.*)
refresh (3)
rest (*mid.*) (4)
rest, give
rest, set at
rest, take (*mid.*) (2)

ANAPAUSIS ἀνάπαυσις
§cease
rest (4)

ANAPĒDAŌ ἀναπηδάω
spring up

ANAPEITHŌ ἀναπείθω
persuade

ANAPEMPŌ ἀναπέμπω
send
send back (3)
send over

ANAPĒROS ἀνάπηρος
maimed (2)

ANAPHAINŌ ἀναφαίνω
appear (*pass.*)
sight of, come in

ANAPHERŌ ἀναφέρω
bear (2)
carry up †
lead up (2)
offer (3)
offer up (2)

ANAPHŌNEŌ ἀναφωνέω
exclaim

ANAPIPTŌ ἀναπίπτω
lie (2)
sit
sit at table (2)
sit down (5)
sit down at table
IDIOMATICALLY
place *a*

ANAPLĒROŌ ἀναπληρόω
complete
fill up the measure of
fulfil (2)
in (*part.*)
make up

ANAPOLOGĒTOS ἀναπολόγητος
§excuse, have no
excuse, without

ANAPSYCHŌ ἀναψύχω
refresh

ANAPSYXIS ἀνάψυξις
refreshing

ANAPTŌ ἀνάπτω
kindle
set ablaze

ANARITHMĒTOS ἀναρίθμητος
innumerable

ANASEIŌ ἀνασείω
stir up (2)

ANASKEUAZŌ ἀνασκευάζω
unsettle

ANASPAŌ ἀνασπάω
draw up
pull out

ANASTASIS ἀνάστασις
resurrection (39)
§rise
§rise again to life
rising

ANASTATOŌ ἀναστατόω
stir up a revolt
turn upside down
unsettle

ANASTAUROŌ ἀνασταυρόω
crucify

ANASTENAZŌ ἀναστενάζω
sigh deeply

ANASTREPHŌ ἀναστρέφω
(abide)
act (*pass.*)
behave (*pass.*) (2)
conduct oneself (*pass.*)
live (*pass.*) (2)
return (2)
treated (*pass. part.*)

ANASTROPHĒ ἀναστροφή
behavior (3)
conduct (3)
life (4)
life, manner of
ways
NOT TRANSLATED
2 Pet **2**.7

ANATASSOMAI ἀνατάσσομαι
compile

ANATELLŌ ἀνατέλλω
dawn
descend
rise (6)
rise, make

ANATHALLŌ ἀναθάλλω
revive

ANATHEMA ἀνάθεμα
§accursed (3)
§accursed and cut off
§cursed
oath

ANATHĒMA ἀνάθημα
offering

ANATHEMATIZŌ ἀναθεματίζω
bind by an oath (2)
§bind strictly by an oath
curse on oneself, invoke a

ANATHEŌREŌ ἀναθεωρέω
consider
observe

ANATITHĒMI ἀνατίθημι
lay before (*mid.*) (2)

ANATOLĒ ἀνατολή
day
(dayspring †)
east (*sg. or pl.*) (8) +
rising

ANATREPHŌ ἀνατρέφω
bring up (3)

ANATREPŌ ἀνατρέπω
overturn
upset (2)

ANAXIOS ἀνάξιος
incompetent

ANAXIŌS ἀναξίως
unworthy manner, in an

ANAZAŌ ἀναζάω
alive again, be
revive

ANAZĒTEŌ ἀναζητέω
look for
seek (2)

ANAZŌNNYMI ἀναζώννυμι
gird up

ANAZŌPYREŌ ἀναζωπυρέω
rekindle

ANDRAPODISTĒS ἀνδραποδιστής
kidnaper

ANDRIZOMAI ἀνδρίζομαι
courageous, be

ANDROPHONOS ἀνδροφόνος
manslayer

ANECHŌ ἀνέχω
bear it (*mid.*)
bear with (*mid.*) (8)
endure (*mid.*) (3)
forbear (*mid.*) (2)
submit (*mid.*)

ANEGKLĒTOS ἀνέγκλητος
blameless (3)
guiltless
irreproachable

ANEKDIĒGĒTOS ἀνεκδιήγητος
inexpressible

ANEKLALĒTOS ἀνεκλάλητος
unutterable

ANEKLEIPTOS ἀνέκλειπτος
§fail, that does not

ANĒKŌ ἀνήκω
fitting, be (*impers.*) (2)
required, what is (*subst. part. neut.*)

ANEKTOS ἀνεκτός
tolerable, more (*comp.*) (5)

ANELEĒMŌN ἀνελεήμων
ruthless

ANELEOS ἀνέλεος
mercy, without

ANĒMEROS ἀνήμερος
fierce

ANEMIZŌ ἀνεμίζω
wind, be driven by the (*pass.*)

ANEMOS ἄνεμος
§gale
wind (30)

ANENDEKTOS ἀνένδεκτος
sure (*neg.*)

ANEPAISCHYNTOS ἀνεπαίσχυντος
ashamed, having no need to be

ANEPILĒMPTOS ἀνεπίλημπτος
reproach, above
reproach, free from
reproach, without

ANEPSIOS ἀνεψιός
cousin

ANĒR ἀνήρ
fellow
husband (53)
man (135)
manhood
§married, be
sir (*voc.*)
NOT TRANSLATED
Lk **17**.12; **24**.19
Acts **1**.16; **2**.29, 37; **3**.14; **7**.2; **8**.27; **10**.28; **13**.6, 15, 26, 38; **15**.7, 13; **19**.7; **22**.1, 3; **23**.1, 6; **25**.24; **28**.17
1 Cor **7**.13

ANERCHOMAI ἀνέρχομαι
go up (3)

ANESIS ἄνεσις
liberty
rest (3)
IDIOMATICALLY
ease *a*

ANETAZŌ ἀνετάζω
examine (2)

ANĒTHON ἄνηθον
dill

ANEU ἄνευ
§ungrudgingly 1
without (2)

ANEURISKŌ ἀνευρίσκω
find
seek out

ANEUTHETOS ἀνεύθετος
suitable, not

ANEXERAUNĒTOS ἀνεξεραύνητος
unsearchable

ANEXICHNIASTOS ἀνεξιχνίαστος
inscrutable
unsearchable

ANEXIKAKOS ἀνεξίκακος
forbearing

ANIĒMI ἀνίημι
fail
forbear
loosen
unfasten

ANIPTOS ἄνιπτος
unwashed (2)

ANISTĒMI ἀνίστημι
arise (17)
get up (5)
§leave
lift
raise (3)
raise up (10)
rise (49) +
rise again (3)
rise up (5)
stand
stand up (11)

ANŌ ἄνω
above (5)
up
upward
IDIOMATICALLY
brim *a*
NOT TRANSLATED
Jn **11**.41

ANOCHĒ ἀνοχή
forbearance (2)

ANOĒTOS ἀνόητος
foolish (5)
senseless

ANOIA ἄνοια
folly
fury

ANOIGŌ ἀνοίγω
open (78)

ANOIKODOMEŌ ἀνοικοδομέω
rebuild (2)

ANOIXIS ἄνοιξις
opening

ANOMIA ἀνομία
§evildoer (2)
iniquity (5)
lawlessness (5)
misdeed
wickedness

ANOMOS ἄνομος
law, outside the (3)
law, without
lawless (4)
transgressor (*subst.*) +

ANOMŌS ἀνόμως
law, without the (2)

ANŌPHELĒS ἀνωφελής
unprofitable
uselessness (*subst. neut.*)

ANORTHOŌ ἀνορθόω
lift and strengthen (+*two objects*)
set up
straight, make

ANOSIOS ἀνόσιος
unholy (2)

ANŌTERIKOS ἀνωτερικός
upper

ANŌTEROS ἀνώτερος
above (*neut.*)
higher (*neut.*)

ANŌTHEN ἄνωθεν
above, from (5)†
anew (2)
once more
time, for a long
time past, for some
IDIOMATICALLY: top *a* (2), *b*

ANTAGŌNIZOMAI ἀνταγωνίζομαι
struggle

ANTALLAGMA ἀντάλλαγμα
return for, s. in (+*gen.*) (2)

ANTANAPLĒROŌ ἀνταναπληρόω
complete

ANTAPODIDŌMI ἀνταποδίδωμι
render
repay (6)

ANTAPODOMA ἀνταπόδομα
§repaid, be
retribution

ANTAPODOSIS ἀνταπόδοσις
reward

ANTAPOKRINOMAI ἀνταποκρίνομαι
answer back
reply

ANTECHŌ ἀντέχω
devoted to, be (*mid.*) (2)
help (*mid.*)
hold firm (*mid.*)

ANTEIPON ἀντεῖπον
contradict
say in opposition

ANTHISTĒMI ἀνθίστημι
oppose (4)
resist (6)
withstand (4)

ANTHOMOLOGEOMAI ἀνθομολογέομαι
thanks, give

ANTHOS ἄνθος
flower (4)
ANTHRAKIA ἀνθρακιά
charcoal fire (2)
ANTHRAX ἄνθραξ
coal
ANTHRŌPARESKOS ἀνθρωπάρεσκος
men-pleaser (*subst.*) (2)
ANTHRŌPINOS ἀνθρώπινος
human (4)
human terms, in (*neut.*)
§humankind
man, that is common to
(men, ordained for †)
ANTHRŌPOKTONOS ἀνθρωποκτόνος
murderer (3)
ANTHRŌPOS ἄνθρωπος
any one
child
§human (12)
human being
man (487)+
mankind (*pl.*) (5)
§nature (4)
one (3)
§other
people (*pl.*) (4)
person (4)
self (2)
IDIOMATICALLY
humanly *a*
NOT TRANSLATED
Mt **11.**19; **13.**28, 52; **18.**23; **20.**1; **21.**33; **22.**2
Mk **7.**15; **11.**2
Lk **6.**26; **7.**34; **19.**12, 30
Acts **4.**9, 17; **21.**39
Rom **12.**17, 18
1 Cor **2.**11; **7.**7
Gal **2.**6
Jude .4
ANTHYPATOS ἀνθύπατος
proconsul (5)
ANTI ἀντί (+*gen.*)
§because 8 (4)
for (12)
for a reason
instead
instead of
place of, in
§therefore
upon
ANTIBALLŌ ἀντιβάλλω
hold
ANTICHRISTOS ἀντίχριστος
antichrist (5)
ANTIDIATITHĒMI ἀντιδιατίθημι
opponent (*subst. mid. part.*)
ANTIDIKOS ἀντίδικος
accuser (3)
adversary (2)
ANTIKALEŌ ἀντικαλέω
invite in return
ANTIKATHISTĒMI ἀντικαθίστημι
resist
ANTIKEIMAI ἀντίκειμαι
adversary (*subst. part.*) (3)
contrary, be
enemy (*subst. part.*)
opponent (*subst. part.*)
oppose
opposed, be

ANTIKRYS ἄντικρυς
opposite
ANTILAMBANŌ ἀντιλαμβάνω
benefit (*mid.*)
help (*mid.*) (2)
ANTILEGŌ ἀντιλέγω
contradict (2)
contrary (*part.*)
object
refractory, be
set oneself against
speak against (2)
ANTILĒMPSIS ἀντίλημψις
§helper
ANTILOGIA ἀντιλογία
dispute (2)
hostility
rebellion
ANTILOIDOREŌ ἀντιλοιδορέω
revile in return
ANTILYTRON ἀντίλυτρον
ransom
ANTIMETREŌ ἀντιμετρέω
measure, get back a (*pass.*)
ANTIMISTHIA ἀντιμισθία
penalty, due
IDIOMATICALLY
return *a*
ANTIPARERCHOMAI
ἀντιπαρέρχομαι
pass by on the other side (2)
ANTIPERA ἀντιπέρα
opposite
ANTIPIPTŌ ἀντιπίπτω
resist
ANTISTRATEUOMAI
ἀντιστρατεύομαι
war with, at (*part.*)
ANTITASSŌ ἀντιτάσσω
oppose (*mid.*) (3)
resist (*mid.*) (2)
ANTITHESIS ἀντίθεσις
contradiction
ANTITYPOS ἀντίτυπος
copy (*subst.*)
corresponds to, which
ANTLĒMA ἄντλημα
draw with, s. to
ANTLEŌ ἀντλέω
draw (3)
draw out
ANTOPHTHALMEŌ ἀντοφθαλμέω
face
ANYDROS ἄνυδρος
waterless (4)
ANYPOKRITOS ἀνυπόκριτος
genuine (2)
insincerity, without
sincere (3)
ANYPOTAKTOS ἀνυπότακτος
control, outside s.'s
disobedient
insubordinate (2)
AORATOS ἀόρατος
invisible (4)
invisible nature (*subst. neut. pl.*)
APAGCHŌ ἀπάγχω
hang oneself (*mid.*)
APAGGELLŌ ἀπαγγέλλω
declare (3)
proclaim (4)

report (7)
say
tell (29)
word, bring
APAGŌ ἀπάγω
bring
death, put to
lead (5)
lead astray
lead away (6)
take +
APAIDEUTOS ἀπαίδευτος
senseless
APAIRŌ ἀπαίρω
take away (3)
APAITEŌ ἀπαιτέω
ask again
require
APALGEŌ ἀπαλγέω
callous, become
APALLASSŌ ἀπαλλάσσω
deliver
leave (*pass.*)
settle (*pass.*)
APALLOTRIOŌ ἀπαλλοτριόω
alienated, be (*pass.*) (2)
estranged, be (*pass.*)
APANTAŌ ἀπαντάω
meet (2)
APANTĒSIS ἀπάντησις
§meet (3)
APARABATOS ἀπαράβατος
§permanently
APARASKEUASTOS ἀπαρασκεύαστος
ready, not
APARCHĒ ἀπαρχή
first convert (2)+
first fruits (6)
APARNEOMAI ἀπαρνέομαι
deny (11)
APARTISMOS ἀπαρτισμός
[*completion*]
IDIOMATICALLY
complete *a*
APASPAZOMAI ἀπασπάζομαι
farewell, bid
APATAŌ ἀπατάω
deceive (3)
APATĒ ἀπάτη
deceit
deceitful (*gen.*)
deceitfulness
deception
delight (2)
dissipation
APATŌR ἀπάτωρ
father, without
APAUGASMA ἀπαύγασμα
§reflect
APECHŌ ἀπέχω
abstain (*mid.*) (5)
abstinence (*mid. inf.*)
distant, be
enough, be (*impers.*)
far, be (3)
have back
receive (4)
receive payment
IDIOMATICALLY
distance *a*
NOT TRANSLATED
Lk **24.**13

APEILĒ ἀπειλή
threat (2)
threatening
APEILEŌ ἀπειλέω
threaten
warn
APEIMI I ἄπειμι
absent (*part.*) (3)
absent, be (2)
away, be (2)
APEIMI II ἄπειμι
go
APEIPON ἀπεῖπον
renounce (*mid.*)
APEIRASTOS ἀπείραστος
tempted, not to be
APEIROS ἄπειρος
unskilled
APEITHEIA ἀπείθεια
disobedience (6) +
APEITHEŌ ἀπειθέω
disbelieve
disobedient (*part.*)
disobedient, be (4)
disobey
obey, not (5)
unbeliever (*subst. part.*)
unbelieving (*part.*)
APEITHĒS ἀπειθής
disobedient (6)
APEKDECHOMAI ἀπεκδέχομαι
await
wait, eagerly
wait for (6)
APEKDYOMAI ἀπεκδύομαι
disarm
put off
APEKDYSIS ἀπέκδυσις
putting off
APELAUNŌ ἀπελαύνω
drive
APELEGMOS ἀπελεγμός
disrepute
APELEUTHEROS ἀπελεύθερος
freedman
APELPIZŌ ἀπελπίζω
(despair of †)
expect in return
APENANTI ἀπέναντι
against
before
opposite
presence of, in the
APERANTOS ἀπέραντος
endless
APERCHOMAI ἀπέρχομαι
come
depart (13) +
§follow
go (54)
go away (27)
go back (2)
go off (2)
go on (2)
go over
go up
leave (3)
pass (2)
pass away (2)
spread
IDIOMATICALLY
draw *a*, *b*; (go home *a*); indulge *b*

APERISPASTŌS ἀπερισπάστως
undivided
APERITMĒTOS ἀπερίτμητος
uncircumcised
APHAIREŌ ἀφαιρέω
cut off (3)
take away (7)
APHANĒS ἀφανής
hidden
APHANISMOS ἀφανισμός
§vanish away
APHANIZŌ ἀφανίζω
consume (2)
disfigure
perish (*pass.*)
vanish (*pass.*)
APHANTOS ἄφαντος
[*invisible, hidden*]
§vanish
APHEDRŌN ἀφεδρών
[*toilet, latrine*]
NOT TRANSLATED
Mt **15**.17
Mk **7**.19
APHEIDIA ἀφειδία
severity
APHELOTĒS ἀφελότης
generous (+*gen.*)
APHESIS ἄφεσις
forgiveness (15)
release
IDIOMATICALLY
liberty *a*
APHIĒMI ἀφίημι
abandon
allow (3)
§consent
divorce (3)
forgive (47) +
forsake (4)
give up
leave (53) +
let (12)
let alone (5)
let s. be so
let go
let s. have
neglect (2)
permit (3)
refuse (*neg.*)
tolerate
§utter
wait (*imper.*)
yield
APHIKNEOMAI ἀφικνέομαι
known, be
APHILAGATHOS ἀφιλάγαθος
hater of good (*subst.*)
APHILARGYROS ἀφιλάργυρος
love of money, free from
lover of money, no (*subst.*)
APHISTĒMI ἀφίστημι
depart (5)
draw away
fall away (2)
keep away
leave (2)
withdraw (3)
APHIXIS ἄφιξις
departure
APHNŌ ἄφνω
suddenly (3)

APHOBŌS ἀφόβως
boldly
§ease, at
fear, without (2)
APHOMOIOŌ ἀφομοιόω
resemble (*perf. pass.*)
APHŌNOS ἄφωνος
dumb (3)
meaning, without
APHORAŌ ἀφοράω
look
see
APHORIZŌ ἀφορίζω
exclude
separate (5)
set apart (3)
take with one
APHORMĒ ἀφορμή
cause
claim (2)
occasion
opportunity (3)
APHRIZŌ ἀφρίζω
foam (2)
APHRŌN ἄφρων
fool (*subst.*) (6)
foolish (5)
APHROS ἀφρός
[*foam*]
§foam
APHROSYNĒ ἀφροσύνη
§fool (2)
foolishness (2)
APHTHARSIA ἀφθαρσία
immortality (2)
§imperishable
imperishable, the (3)
§undying
APHTHARTOS ἄφθαρτος
immortal (2)
imperishable (5) +
APHTHORIA ἀφθορία
integrity
APHYPNOŌ ἀφυπνόω
asleep, fall
APHYSTEREŌ ἀφυστερέω
keep back
APISTEŌ ἀπιστέω
believe, not (4)
disbelieve (2)
faithless, be
unfaithful, be
APISTIA ἀπιστία
distrust
faithlessness
unbelief (8)
unbelieving
APISTOS ἄπιστος
faithless (5)
incredible
unbeliever (*subst.*) (12)
unbelieving (4)
unfaithful
APO ἀπό (+*gen.*)
account of, on
against (2)
§ago
at
because of (3)
before
§*belong* (2)
by (23)

for (15)
from (406) +†
in (9)
of (64)
§*off* (2)
§*on* (10)
out of (4)
since (3)
since, ever (2)
through
to (2)
with (11)
IDIOMATICALLY
OR NOT TRANSLATED
Mt **1**.42; **2**.16; **3**.8[2]; **5**.29, 30; **7**.28; **8**.34; **9**.22; **10**.28, 46; **15**.27, 28; **17**.18; **18**.8, 9; **20**.20; **23**.33, 39; **24**.1; **26**.29, 58, 64
Mk **7**.17; **8**.3; **11**.13; **12**.38; **14**.54
Lk **1**.48; **4**.38, 42; **5**.10, 13; **9**.5, 39; **12**.4, 52; **13**.7, 25; **14**.18; **16**.23; **23**.49; **24**.21, 27, 31
Jn **13**.19; **14**.7
Acts **2**.17, 18; **5**.41; **7**.45; **12**.10, 20; **13**.13; **16**.33, 39; **18**.2; **19**.12; **20**.18; **21**.21, 23; **24**.11
Rom **11**.25; **15**.15; **16**.17
1 Cor **1**.30; **10**.14
2 Cor **8**.10; **9**.2; **12**.8
Gal **1**.6; **3**.2
Phil **4**.15
Col **1**.26
1 Tim **3**.7
2 Tim **1**.3
Heb **12**.15
Jas **5**.4
Rev **14**.13; **16**.18; **18**.10, 15, 17

APOBAINŌ ἀποβαίνω
get out
go out
turn out
IDIOMATICALLY
time *a*

APOBALLŌ ἀποβάλλω
throw away
throw off

APOBLEPŌ ἀποβλέπω
look to

APOBLĒTOS ἀπόβλητος
rejected

APOBOLĒ ἀποβολή
loss
rejection

APOCHŌREŌ ἀποχωρέω
depart
leave (2)

APOCHŌRIZŌ ἀποχωρίζω
separate (*pass.*)
vanish (*pass.*)

APOCHRĒSIS ἀπόχρησις
§use

APODECHOMAI ἀποδέχομαι
accept
receive (3)
welcome (3)

APODEIKNYMI ἀποδείκνυμι
attest
exhibit
proclaim
prove

APODEIXIS ἀπόδειξις
demonstration

APODEKATEUŌ ἀποδεκατεύω
tithes of, give

APODEKATOŌ ἀποδεκατόω
tithe (2)
tithes from, take

APODEKTOS ἀπόδεκτος
acceptable (2)

APODĒMEŌ ἀποδημέω
go away
go into another country (3)
go on a journey
journey, take one's

APODĒMOS ἀπόδημος
§going on a journey

APODIDŌMI ἀποδίδωμι
award
give (6)
give back (2)
§justify
pay (11)
payment, make
perform
render (7)
repay (5)
requite
restore
return
reward (3)
sell (*mid.*) (3)
turn in
yield (2)
IDIOMATICALLY
make *b*

APODIORIZŌ ἀποδιορίζω
set up divisions

APODOCHĒ ἀποδοχή
acceptance (2)

APODOKIMAZŌ ἀποδοκιμάζω
reject (8)
rejected (*perf. pass. part.*)

APOGINOMAI ἀπογίνομαι
die

APOGRAPHĒ ἀπογραφή
census
enrollment

APOGRAPHŌ ἀπογράφω
enroll (4)

APOKALYPSIS ἀποκάλυψις
§reveal (3)
revealing (2)
revelation (13)

APOKALYPTŌ ἀποκαλύπτω
reveal (25)
revelation, make a

APOKARADOKIA ἀποκαραδοκία
expectation, eager
longing, eager

APOKATALLASSŌ ἀποκαταλλάσσω
reconcile (3)

APOKATASTASIS ἀποκατάστασις
establishing

APOKATHISTĒMI ἀποκαθίστημι
(ἀποκαθιστάνω)
restore (8)

APOKEIMAI ἀπόκειμαι
appointed, be
laid away (*part.*)
laid up (*part.*)
laid up, be

APOKEPHALIZŌ ἀποκεφαλίζω
behead (4)

APOKLEIŌ ἀποκλείω
shut

APOKOPTŌ ἀποκόπτω
cut away
cut off (4)
mutilate (*mid.*)

APOKRIMA ἀπόκριμα
sentence

APOKRINOMAI ἀποκρίνομαι
address (2)
answer (174)
answer, give
answer, make (7)
declare
reply (12) +
say (4)
NOT TRANSLATED
always in combination with LEGŌ, EIPON, *or* PHĒMI:
Mt **11**.25; **15**.15; **17**.4; **22**.1; **26**.25, 33; **27**.21; **28**.5
Mk **9**.5; **10**.24, 51; **11**.14; **12**.35; **14**.48; **15**.12
Lk **1**.35, 60; **8**.21; **13**.14; **14**.3; **17**.17, 37; **22**.51; **23**.40
Jn **2**.18; **3**.9; **4**.13; **5**.19
Acts **8**.34; **25**.9

APOKRISIS ἀπόκρισις
answer (4)

APOKRYPHOS ἀπόκρυφος
hidden (3)

APOKRYPTŌ ἀποκρύπτω
hidden (*perf. pass. part.*) (3)
hide

APOKTEINŌ
ἀποκτείνω (ἀποκτέννω)
death, put to (5)
end, bring to an
kill (63)
slay (4)
IDIOMATICALLY
strike dead *a*

APOKYEŌ ἀποκυέω
bring forth (2)

APOKYLIŌ ἀποκυλίω
roll away (2)
roll back

APOLAMBANŌ ἀπολαμβάνω
receive (6)
receive again
take aside (*mid.*)
win

APOLAUSIS ἀπόλαυσις
§enjoy
pleasure

APŌLEIA ἀπώλεια
§destroyed, be
destruction (9)
destructive (*gen.*)
perdition (4)
§perish
waste (2)

APOLEIPŌ ἀπολείπω
leave (4)
remain (*pass.*) (3)

APOLLYMI ἀπόλλυμι
death, put to
destroy (26) +
lose (33) +
perish (*mid.*) (28)
perishable (*mid. part.*)
ruin of, cause the

APOLLYŌN ἀπολλύων
(destroyer †)

APOLOGEOMAI ἀπολογέομαι
answer (2)
defend oneself
defense, make a
defense, make one's (4)
defense, say in one's
excuse

APOLOGIA ἀπολογία
clear oneself, eagerness to
defense (7)

APOLOUŌ ἀπολούω
wash away (*mid.*)
washed, be (*mid.*)

APOLYŌ ἀπολύω
depart (*mid.*)
dismiss (5)
divorce (10)
divorced woman (*subst. perf. pass. part. fem.*) (2)+
forgive (2)
free
free, set
let depart
let go (6)
liberty, set at
put away (2)
release (22)+
send away (9)
send off (3)

APOLYTRŌSIS ἀπολύτρωσις
§redeem
redemption (7)
release
IDIOMATICALLY
acquire *a*

APOMASSŌ ἀπομάσσω
wipe off against (*mid.*)

APONEMŌ ἀπονέμω
bestow

APONIPTŌ ἀπονίπτω
wash

APOPHERŌ ἀποφέρω
carry (2)
carry away (3)
lead away

APOPHEUGŌ ἀποφεύγω
escape
escape from (2)

APOPHORTIZOMAI ἀποφορτίζομαι
unload

APOPHTHEGGOMAI ἀποφθέγγομαι
address
speak
utterance (*inf.*)

APOPIPTŌ ἀποπίπτω
fall from

APOPLANAŌ ἀποπλανάω
lead astray
wander away (*pass.*)

APOPLEŌ ἀποπλέω
sail (4)

APOPNIGŌ ἀποπνίγω
choke (2)
drown

APOPSYCHŌ ἀποψύχω
faint

APOREŌ ἀπορέω
loss, be at a (*mid.*)
perplexed, be (*act. or mid.*) (4)
uncertain, be (*mid.*)

APORIA ἀπορία
perplexity

APORIPTŌ ἀπορίπτω
throw oneself overboard

APORPHANIZŌ ἀπορφανίζω
bereft, be (*pass.*)

APOSKIASMA ἀποσκίασμα
shadow

APOSPAŌ ἀποσπάω
draw
draw away
part (*pass.*)
withdraw (*pass.*)

APOSTASIA ἀποστασία
§forsake
rebellion

APOSTASION ἀποστάσιον
certificate of divorce
divorce (2)

APOSTEGAZŌ ἀποστεγάζω
§remove

APOSTELLŌ ἀποστέλλω
put in
send (117)
send away
send forth
send off
send out (8)
send round
IDIOMATICALLY
set *c*

APOSTEREŌ ἀποστερέω
bereft, be (*pass.*)
defraud (3)
refuse

APOSTOLĒ ἀποστολή
apostleship (3)
mission

APOSTOLOS ἀπόστολος
apostle (76)+
messenger (2)
sent, one who is

APOSTOMATIZŌ ἀποστοματίζω
provoke to speak

APOSTREPHŌ ἀποστρέφω
banish
pervert
put back
refuse (*aor. pass.*)
reject (*mid.*) (2)
turn away (2)
turn from

APOSTYGEŌ ἀποστυγέω
hate

APOSYNAGŌGOS ἀποσυνάγωγος
synagogue, put out of the (3)

APOTASSŌ ἀποτάσσω
farewell, say (*mid.*)
leave, take (*mid.*) (4)
renounce (*mid.*)

APOTELEŌ ἀποτελέω
full-grown, be (*aor. pass.*)
perform

APOTHĒKĒ ἀποθήκη
barn (4)
granary (2)

APŌTHEŌ ἀπωθέω
reject (*mid.*) (3)
thrust aside (*mid.*) (2)
thrust from one (*mid.*)

APOTHĒSAURIZŌ ἀποθησαυρίζω
lay up

APOTHESIS ἀπόθεσις
putting off
removal

APOTHLIBŌ ἀποθλίβω
press upon

APOTHNĒSKŌ ἀποθνήσκω
dead, be (*aor.*) (10)
§death (2)
die (97)
§killed, be
mortal (*part.*)
perish

APOTINASSŌ ἀποτινάσσω
shake off (2)

APOTINŌ ἀποτίνω
repay

APOTITHĒMI ἀποτίθημι
cast off (*mid.*)
lay aside (*mid.*)
lay down (*mid.*)
put (*mid.*)
put away (*mid.*) (4)
put off (*mid.*)

APOTOLMAŌ ἀποτολμάω
bold, be

APOTOMIA ἀποτομία
severity (2)

APOTOMŌS ἀποτόμως
§severe
sharply

APOTREPŌ ἀποτρέπω
avoid (*mid.*)

APOUSIA ἀπουσία
absence

APROSITOS ἀπρόσιτος
unapproachable

APROSKOPOS ἀπρόσκοπος
blameless
clear
§offense, give no

APROSŌPOLĒMPTŌS
ἀπροσωπολήμπτως
impartially

APSEUDĒS ἀψευδής
lies, who never (*attr.*)

APSINTHOS ἄψινθος (ἀψίνθιον)
wormwood (2)

APSYCHOS ἄψυχος
lifeless

APTAISTOS ἄπταιστος
[*without stumbling, infallible*]
IDIOMATICALLY
falling *a*

ARA I ἀρά
curses

ARA II ἄρα
§accordingly
case, in that
§possible
so (7)
so then (8)
then (20)
therefore (2)
§thus
IDIOMATICALLY
hope *a;* see *a;* true *a*
NOT TRANSLATED
Mt **18**.1
Lk **22**.23
Acts **12**.18
1 Cor **7**.14
2 Cor **1**.17

ARA III ἄρα
then
NOT TRANSLATED
in direct questions:
Lk **18**.8
Acts **8**.30

ARAPHOS ἄραφος
seam, without

ARCHAGGELOS ἀρχάγγελος
archangel (2)

ARCHAIOS ἀρχαῖος
ancient (3)
early (3)
old (3)
old, man of (*subst.*) (2)

ARCHĒ ἀρχή
(all, at [*acc.*]†)
authority
beginning (36)
corner (2)
elementary (*gen.*)
first (5)
position
principalities (*pl.*) (5)
rule (3)
ruler (2)

ARCHĒGOS ἀρχηγός
author
leader
pioneer (2)

ARCHIERATIKOS ἀρχιερατικός
high-priestly

ARCHIEREUS ἀρχιερεύς
chief priest (64)
high priest (57)
§high-priesthood

ARCHIPOIMĒN ἀρχιποίμην
chief shepherd

ARCHISYNAGŌGOS ἀρχισυνάγωγος
ruler (2)
ruler of the synagogue (7)

ARCHITEKTŌN ἀρχιτέκτων
master builder

ARCHITELŌNĒS ἀρχιτελώνης
chief tax collector

ARCHITRIKLINOS ἀρχιτρίκλινος
steward of the feast (3)

ARCHŌ ἄρχω
begin (*mid.*) (83)
rule (2)
NOT TRANSLATED
Lk **23**.5

ARCHŌN ἄρχων
authority (3)
magistrate
prince (5)
ruler (28)

ARĒN ἀρήν
lamb

ARESKEIA ἀρεσκεία
[*desire to please*]
§pleasing

ARESKŌ ἀρέσκω
displease (*neg.*)
please (15)
satisfy

ARESTOS ἀρεστός
§please
pleases, what (*neut. pl.*)
pleasing, what is (*neut. pl.*)
right

ARETĒ ἀρετή
excellence (2)
virtue (2)
wonderful deeds (*pl.*)

ARGEŌ ἀργέω
idle, be

ARGOS ἀργός
barren
careless
idle (2)
idler (*subst.*) (2)
ineffective
lazy

ARGYRION ἀργύριον
money (9)
silver (7)
silver, piece of (5)

ARGYROKOPOS ἀργυροκόπος
silversmith

ARGYROS ἄργυρος
silver (4)

ARGYROUS ἀργυροῦς
silver
silver, of (2)

ARISTAŌ ἀριστάω
breakfast, finished (*aor.*)
breakfast, have
dine

ARISTEROS ἀριστερός
left
§left hand (3)

ARISTON ἄριστον
dinner (3)

ARITHMEŌ ἀριθμέω
number (3)

ARITHMOS ἀριθμός
number (17)
§numbering

ARKEŌ ἀρκέω
content (*pass. part.*)
content, be (*pass.*) (3)
enough, be
satisfy
sufficient, be
IDIOMATICALLY
enough *a*

ARKETOS ἀρκετός
enough
§suffice
sufficient

ARKOS ἄρκος
bear

ARNEOMAI ἀρνέομαι
deny (29)
disown
refuse (2)
renounce

ARNION ἀρνίον
lamb (30)

ARŌMA ἄρωμα
spice (4)

AROTRIAŌ ἀροτριάω
plow (2)

AROTRON ἄροτρον
plow

ARRABŌN ἀρραβών
guarantee (3)

ARRĒTOS ἄρρητος
told, that cannot be (*attr.*)

ARRŌSTOS ἄρρωστος
ill
sick (4)

ARSĒN ἄρσην
male (6)
men (*subst. pl.*) (3)

ARSENOKOITĒS ἀρσενοκοίτης
§sexual perverts
sodomite

ARTEMŌN ἀρτέμων
foresail

ARTI ἄρτι
§again (2)
§henceforth (2)
§hereafter
§hitherto 1 (2)
just
now (23)
once, at
present (*attr.*)
§still (3)

ARTIGENNĒTOS ἀρτιγέννητος
newborn

ARTIOS ἄρτιος
complete

ARTOS ἄρτος
bread (*sg. or pl.*) (67)+
§dine 2
loaf (23)
loaf of bread
IDIOMATICALLY
living *a*
NOT TRANSLATED
Mt **15**.2
Mk **3**.20; **7**.2, 5

ARTYŌ ἀρτύω
saltness, restore
season (2)

ASALEUTOS ἀσάλευτος
immovable
shaken, that cannot be

ASBESTOS ἄσβεστος
unquenchable (3)

ASCHĒMŌN ἀσχήμων
unpresentable

ASCHĒMONEŌ ἀσχημονέω
behave properly, not
rude, be

ASCHĒMOSYNĒ ἀσχημοσύνη
shameless acts
IDIOMATICALLY
expose *a*

ASEBEIA ἀσέβεια
irreligion
ungodliness (4)
ungodly (*gen.*)

ASEBEŌ ἀσεβέω
ungodly, be
ungodly way, commit in such an

ASEBĒS ἀσεβής
impious
ungodly (8)

ASELGEIA ἀσέλγεια
§licentious
licentiousness (9)

ASĒMOS ἄσημος
mean

ASITIA ἀσιτία
§food, without

ASITOS ἄσιτος
food, without

ASKEŌ ἀσκέω
pains, take

ASKOS ἀσκός
skin (7)
wineskin (5)

ASMENŌS ἀσμένως
gladly
ASOPHOS ἄσοφος
unwise
ASŌTIA ἀσωτία
debauchery
profligacy
profligate (*gen.*)
ASŌTŌS ἀσώτως
§loose
ASPASMOS ἀσπασμός
greeting (6)
salutation (4)
ASPAZOMAI ἀσπάζομαι
greet (44)
greetings, give one's
greetings, send (8)
leave, take
salute (4)
welcome
ASPHALEIA ἀσφάλεια
§securely
security
truth
ASPHALĒS ἀσφαλής
definite
facts (*subst. neut.*)
reason, the real (*subst. neut.*)
safe
sure
ASPHALIZŌ ἀσφαλίζω
fasten (*mid.*)
secure, make (*mid.*) (3)
ASPHALŌS ἀσφαλῶς
assuredly
guard, under
safely
ASPILOS ἄσπιλος
spot, without (2)
unstained (2)
ASPIS ἀσπίς
asp
ASPONDOS ἄσπονδος
implacable
ASSARION ἀσσάριον
penny (2)
ASSON ἆσσον
close
ASTATEŌ ἀστατέω
homeless, be
ASTEIOS ἀστεῖος
beautiful (2)
ASTĒR ἀστήρ
star (24)
ASTĒRIKTOS ἀστήρικτος
unstable
unsteady
ASTHENEIA ἀσθένεια
ailment (2)
disease
illness
infirmity (5)
limitations
weakness (13)
Idiomatically
ill, be *a*
ASTHENĒMA ἀσθένημα
failing
ASTHENEŌ ἀσθενέω
diseased, be
ill (*part.*)
ill, be (7)
invalid (*subst. part.*)
sick (*part.*) (5)
sick, be (3)
sick, fall
weak (*part.*) (4)
weak, be (8)
weaken
weakened, be +
ASTHENĒS ἀσθενής
§cripple
sick (5)
weak (14)
weak, what is (*subst. neut.*)
weaker (*comp.*) (2)
weakness (*subst. neut.*) (2)
ASTOCHEŌ ἀστοχέω
miss the mark
swerve (2)
ASTORGOS ἄστοργος
heartless
inhuman
ASTRAPĒ ἀστραπή
lightning (4)
lightning, flash of (4)
ray
ASTRAPTŌ ἀστράπτω
dazzling (*part.*)
flash
ASTRON ἄστρον
star (4)
ASYMPHŌNOS ἀσύμφωνος
[*not harmonious*]
§disagree
ASYNETOS ἀσύνετος
foolish (2)
senseless
understanding, without (2)
ASYNTHETOS ἀσύνθετος
faithless
ATAKTEŌ ἀτακτέω
idle, be
ATAKTOS ἄτακτος
idler (*subst.*)
ATAKTŌS ἀτάκτως
§idleness (2)
ATEKNOS ἄτεκνος
§children, have no
children, without
ATENIZŌ ἀτενίζω
fixed, be
gaze (3)
gaze at
gaze, direct one's
look at
look closely at
look intently (3)
see
stare at (2)
ATER ἄτερ
absence of, in the
no, with
ATHANASIA ἀθανασία
immortality (3)
ATHEMITOS ἀθέμιτος
lawless
unlawful
ATHEOS ἄθεος
God, without
ATHESMOS ἄθεσμος
lawless
wicked
ATHETEŌ ἀθετέω
annul
break one's word to
disregard (2)
nullify
reject (7)
§rejecting, have a way of
thwart
violate (2)
ATHETĒSIS ἀθέτησις
§put away
§set aside
ATHLEŌ ἀθλέω
compete
Idiomatically
athlete *a*
ATHLĒSIS ἄθλησις
struggle
ATHŌOS ἀθῷος
innocent (2)
ATHROIZŌ ἀθροίζω
gather together
ATHYMEŌ ἀθυμέω
discouraged, become
ATIMAZŌ ἀτιμάζω
dishonor (4)
dishonor, suffer (*pass.*)
shamefully, treat (2)
ATIMIA ἀτιμία
§degrading
dishonor (2)
dishonorable (*gen.*)
ignoble use
menial use
shame
ATIMOS ἄτιμος
disrepute, held in
honor, without (2)
honorable, less (*comp.*)
ATMIS ἀτμίς
mist
vapor
ATOMOS ἄτομος
moment (*subst.*)
ATOPOS ἄτοπος
misfortune (*subst.*)
wicked
wrong (2)
AUCHEŌ αὐχέω
boast
AUCHMĒROS αὐχμηρός
dark
AUGAZŌ αὐγάζω
see
AUGĒ αὐγή
daybreak
AULĒ αὐλή
court (2)
courtyard (5)
fold
palace (3)
§sheepfold
AULEŌ αὐλέω
pipe (2)
Idiomatically
play *a*
AULĒTĒS αὐλητής
flute player (2)
AULIZOMAI αὐλίζομαι
lodge (2)
AULOS αὐλός
flute

AURION αὔριον
day, next
§morrow (2)
tomorrow (11)

AUSTĒROS αὐστηρός
severe (2)

AUTARKEIA αὐτάρκεια
contentment
enough

AUTARKĒS αὐτάρκης
content

AUTHADĒS αὐθάδης
arrogant
wilful

AUTHAIRETOS αὐθαίρετος
accord, of one's own
free will, of one's own

AUTHENTEŌ αὐθεντέω
authority over, have

AUTOCHEIR αὐτόχειρ
hand, with one's own

AUTOKATAKRITOS αὐτοκατάκριτος
self-condemned

AUTOMATOS αὐτόματος
itself, of
own accord, of its

AUTOPHŌROS αὐτόφωρος
[*in the act*]
IDIOMATICALLY
act *a*

AUTOPTĒS αὐτόπτης
eyewitness

AUTOS αὐτός
A common pronoun (*e.g.*: self; he, she, it). *It is not analyzed in this Concordance.*

AUTOU αὐτοῦ
here (2)
there (2)

AUXANŌ αὐξάνω (αὔξω)
grow (*act. or pass.*) (15)
growth, give (2)
increase (*act. or pass.*) (6)

AUXĒSIS αὔξησις
growth (2)

AXINĒ ἀξίνη
axe (2)

AXIOŌ ἀξιόω
best, think
deserve
desire
§presume
worthy, consider
worthy, count
worthy, make

AXIOS ἄξιος
advisable
befits, that (2)
§deserve (5)
deserves, for which one
deserves, what (*subst.*)
deserving (3)
fitting
reward, due (*subst. pl.*)
unworthy (*neg.*)
worth comparing
worthy (23)
IDIOMATICALLY
due *a*

AXIŌS ἀξίως
befits, as (2)
worthy (+*gen.*) (4)

AZYMOS ἄζυμος
unleavened
unleavened bread (*subst.*) (8)

B

BAION βάϊον
branch

BALLANTION βαλλάντιον
purse (4)

BALLŌ βάλλω
bring (2)
cast (16)
contribute (3)
fall (*pass.*)
invest
lay +
lie (*pass.*) (5)
place (3)
pour (4)
put (19)
put in (6)
put into
put on
scatter
shed
sow
§spring
strike
swing (2)
throw (46)
throw down (6)

BAPTISMA βάπτισμα
baptism (20)

BAPTISMOS βαπτισμός
ablution (2)
washing

BAPTISTĒS βαπτιστής
Baptist (12)

BAPTIZŌ βαπτίζω
baptize (72)+†
baptizer (*subst. part.*) (3)
wash (*pass.*)

BAPTŌ βάπτω
dip (4)

BARBAROS βάρβαρος
barbarian (*subst.*) (2)
foreigner (*subst.*) (2)
native (*subst.*) (2)

BAREŌ βαρέω
anxiety, with (*pres. pass. part.*)
burden
crush
heavy (*perf. pass. part.*) (2)
weigh down

BAREŌS βαρέως
[*with difficulty*]
§heavy (2)

BAROS βάρος
burden (4)
weight
IDIOMATICALLY
demands *a*

BARYS βαρύς
burdensome
fierce
heavy
serious
weightier (*comp.*)
weighty

BARYTIMOS βαρύτιμος
expensive, very

BASANISMOS βασανισμός
torment (4)
torture (2)

BASANISTĒS βασανιστής
jailer

BASANIZŌ βασανίζω
anguish, in (*pres. pass. part.*)
beat
distress, in (*pass. part.*)
painfully (*pass. part.*)
torment (6)
torture
vex

BASANOS βάσανος
pain
torment (*pl.*) (2)

BASILEIA βασιλεία
dominion
kingdom (156)+
kingship (3)
royal power (2)

BASILEIOS βασίλειος
king's court (*subst.*)
royal

BASILEUŌ βασιλεύω
king (*subst. part.*)
king, become a
reign (19)

BASILEUS βασιλεύς
emperor (2)
king (113)

BASILIKOS βασιλικός
king's
official (*subst.*) (2)
royal (2)

BASILISSA βασίλισσα
queen (4)

BASIS βάσις
foot

BASKAINŌ βασκαίνω
bewitch

BASTAZŌ βαστάζω
bear (13)
bear up
bearer (*subst. part.*)
carry (9)
support
take
take up

BATHMOS βαθμός
standing

BATHOS βάθος
deep
depth (5)
depths (*pl.*)
§extreme

BATHYNŌ βαθύνω
§deep

BATHYS βαθύς
deep (3)
early

BATOS I βάτος
bramble bush
bush (4)

BATOS II βάτος
measure

BATRACHOS βάτραχος
frog

BATTALOGEŌ βατταλογέω
heap up empty phrases

BDELYGMA βδέλυγμα
abomination (4)
sacrilege (2)

BDELYKTOS βδελυκτός
detestable

BDELYSSOMAI βδελύσσομαι
abhor
polluted (*perf. pass. part.*)

BEBAIOŌ βεβαιόω
attest
confirm (3)
establish (2)
strengthen
sustain

BEBAIOS βέβαιος
§confirm
§effect, take
firm +
guaranteed
steadfast
sure, made more (*comp.*)
unshaken
valid

BEBAIŌSIS βεβαίωσις
confirmation (2)

BEBĒLOŌ βεβηλόω
profane (2)

BEBĒLOS βέβηλος
godless (3)
irreligious
profane

BELONĒ βελόνη
needle

BELOS βέλος
dart

BELTIŌN βελτίων
well (*neut.*)

BĒMA βῆμα
judgment seat (4)
length
throne
tribunal (6)

BĒRYLLOS βήρυλλος
beryl

BIA βία
surf
violence (2) +

BIAIOS βίαιος
mighty

BIASTĒS βιαστής
violence, man of

BIAZŌ βιάζω
violence, suffer (*pass.*)
(violently, come [*mid.*]†)
violently, enter (*mid.*)

BIBLARIDION βιβλαρίδιον
scroll, little (3)

BIBLION βιβλίον
book (23)
certificate (2)
scroll (9)

BIBLOS βίβλος
book (10)

BIBRŌSKŌ βιβρώσκω
eat

BIOŌ βιόω
live

BIOS βίος
civilian (*gen.*)
goods
life (3)
living (4) +

BIŌSIS βίωσις
life, manner of

BIŌTIKOS βιωτικός
life, matters pertaining to this (*neut. pl.*)
life, of this
NOT TRANSLATED
1 Cor **6**.4

BLABEROS βλαβερός
hurtful

BLAPTŌ βλάπτω
harm, do
hurt

BLASPHĒMEŌ βλασφημέω
abuse
blaspheme (9)
blasphemer (*subst. part.*)
§blasphemy
curse (3)
defame
denounce
deride (2)
discredit
rail at
revile (8)
§slanderously
speak evil of
speak of s. as evil
utter blasphemy (2)

BLASPHĒMIA βλασφημία
blasphemous (*gen.*) (3)
blasphemy (8)
reviling (*gen.*)
slander (6)

BLASPHĒMOS βλάσφημος
abusive
§blaspheme
blasphemous
reviling

BLASTANŌ βλαστάνω (βλαστάω)
bring forth
bud
come up
sprout

BLEMMA βλέμμα
§sees, what one

BLEPŌ βλέπω
behold (2)
beware (*imper.*) (3)
care, take (*imper.*) (3)
consider (*imper.*) (2)
gaze at
heed, take (*imper.*) (10)
look (7)
look at (2)
look into (2)
look out for (3)
look to (*imper.*)
regard (2)
see (83) +
§see, can
see in
see to it (*imper.*)
sight (*inf.*)
sight, be without (*neg. periphr.*)
unseen (*pass. part. neg.*) (3)
IDIOMATICALLY
indeed *b* (2), *c*

BLĒTEOS βλητέος
put, must be

BOAŌ βοάω
cry (10) +
shout (2)

BOĒ βοή
cry

BOĒTHEIA βοήθεια
§help
IDIOMATICALLY
measures, take *a*

BOĒTHEŌ βοηθέω
help (7)
help of s., come to the

BOĒTHOS βοηθός
helper (*subst.*)

BOLĒ βολή
throw

BOLIZŌ βολίζω
sound (2)

BŌMOS βωμός
altar

BORBOROS βόρβορος
mire

BORRAS βορρᾶς
north (2)

BOSKŌ βόσκω
feed (6)
herdsman (*subst. part.*) (3)

BOTANĒ βοτάνη
vegetation

BOTHYNOS βόθυνος
pit (3)

BOTRYS βότρυς
cluster

BOULĒ βουλή
§advise
counsel (3)
plan (4)
purpose (4)

BOULĒMA βούλημα
likes to do, what s. (*gen.*)
purpose
will

BOULEUŌ βουλεύω
counsel, take (*mid.*) (2)
plan (*mid.*) (2)
plans, make (*mid.*)
NOT TRANSLATED
2 Cor **1**.17

BOULEUTĒS βουλευτής
member of the council (2)

BOULOMAI βούλομαι
choose (2)
desire (7)
direct
glad, be
intend (2)
like
refuse (*neg.*)
resolve
want (6)
will (2)
will have (2)
will, of one's own (*pred. part.*)
willing, be
wish (9)

BOUNOS βουνός
hill (2)

BOUS βοῦς
ox (8)

BRABEION βραβεῖον
prize (2)
BRABEUŌ βραβεύω
rule
BRACHIŌN βραχίων
arm (3)
BRACHYS βραχύς
§briefly
little (5)
while, for a (*neut.*)
BRADYNŌ βραδύνω
delayed, be
slow about s., be
BRADYPLOEŌ βραδυπλοέω
sail slowly
BRADYS βραδύς
slow (3)
BRADYTĒS βραδύτης
slowness
BRECHŌ βρέχω
§fall
rain (3)
rain, send
wet (2)
BREPHOS βρέφος
babe (5)
§childhood
infant (2)
BROCHĒ βροχή
rain (2)
BROCHOS βρόχος
restraint
BRŌMA βρῶμα
eats, what one (2)
food (*sg. or pl.*) (15)
BRONTĒ βροντή
peal of thunder (4)
thunder (7)
thunderpeal
BRŌSIMOS βρώσιμος
§eat
BRŌSIS βρῶσις
food (8)
meal
rust (2)
(worm †)
BRYCHŌ βρύχω
grind
BRYGMOS βρυγμός
§gnash
BRYŌ βρύω
pour forth
BYRSEUS βυρσεύς
tanner (3)
BYSSINOS βύσσινος
linen, fine (*subst.*) (5)
BYSSOS βύσσος
linen, fine
BYTHIZŌ βυθίζω
plunge
sink (*pass.*)
BYTHOS βυθός
[*depth*]
IDIOMATICALLY
sea *a*

C

CHAIRŌ χαίρω
farewell (*imper.*)
glad, be (14)
§greet
greeting (*pres. inf.*) (4)
hail (*imper.*) (6)
joyfully (*part.*)
rejoice (47)
IDIOMATICALLY
feel *c*
CHALAŌ χαλάω
let down (4)
lower (3)
CHALAZA χάλαζα
hail (3)
hailstone
CHALEPOS χαλεπός
fierce
stress, of
CHALINAGŌGEŌ χαλιναγωγέω
bridle (2)
CHALINOS χαλινός
bit
bridle
CHALKĒDŌN χαλκηδών
agate
CHALKEUS χαλκεύς
coppersmith
CHALKION χαλκίον
vessel of bronze
CHALKOLIBANON χαλκολίβανον
burnished bronze (2)
CHALKOS χαλκός
bronze
copper
gong
money (2)
CHALKOUS χαλκοῦς
bronze
CHAMAI χαμαί
ground, on the
ground, to the
CHARA χαρά
joy (54)
§joyfully (2)
§overjoyed, be
pleasant (*gen.*)
pleasure
IDIOMATICALLY
greatly *a*
CHARAGMA χάραγμα
mark (7)
representation
CHARAKTĒR χαρακτήρ
stamp, very
CHARAX χάραξ
bank
CHARIN χάριν
because of
for
§gain
§reason, for a (2)
§therefore
§why (2)
NOT TRANSLATED
1 Tim **5**.14
CHARIS χάρις
blessing
credit (3)
favor (10) +
gift (2)
grace (119) +
§gracious (2)
gracious work (3)
§grateful
§thank (3)
thankfulness (2)
thanks (6)
IDIOMATICALLY
approval *a*; approved *a*
CHARISMA χάρισμα
blessing
gift (10)
gift, free (3)
§healer
special gift
spiritual gift
CHARITOŌ χαριτόω
§bestow, freely
favored one (*subst. perf. pass. part.*)
CHARIZOMAI χαρίζομαι
bestow (3)
forgive (12)
give (2)
give up (2)
grant (4)
CHARTĒS χάρτης
paper
CHASMA χάσμα
chasm
CHEILOS χεῖλος
lip (6)
§seashore
CHEIMARROS χείμαρρος
valley
CHEIMAZŌ χειμάζω
storm-tossed, be (*pass.*)
CHEIMŌN χειμών
§stormy
tempest
winter (4)
CHEIR χείρ
§arrest 1 (2)
hand (170) +
NOT TRANSLATED
Acts **15**.23
Gal **3**.19
Rev **19**.2
CHEIRAGŌGEŌ χειραγωγέω
lead by the hand (2)
CHEIRAGŌGOS χειραγωγός
lead s. by the hand, people to (*pl.*)
CHEIROGRAPHON χειρόγραφον
bond
CHEIRŌN χείρων
worse (11)
CHEIROPOIĒTOS χειροποίητος
made by hands
made by man
made with hands (4)
CHEIROTONEŌ χειροτονέω
appoint (2)
CHĒRA χήρα
widow (26) +
CHEROUB χερούβ
cherub
CHILIARCHOS χιλίαρχος
captain (2)
(chief captain)
general
officer
tribune (17)
CHILIAS χιλιάς
thousand (23)
CHILIOI χίλιοι
thousand (11)

CHIŌN χιών
snow (2)
CHITŌN χιτών
coat (2)
garment (2)
shirt
tunic (6)
CHLAMYS χλαμύς
robe (2)
CHLEUAZŌ χλευάζω
mock
CHLIAROS χλιαρός
lukewarm
CHLŌROS χλωρός
green (3)
pale
CHOIKOS χοϊκός
dust, of (4)
CHOINIX χοῖνιξ
quart (2)
CHOIROS χοῖρος
swine (12)
CHOLAŌ χολάω
angry, be
CHOLĒ χολή
gall (2)
CHŌLOS χωλός
cripple (*subst.*)
lame (13)
CHŌRA χώρα
country (16)
field (2)
land (2)
neighborhood
region (7)
CHORĒGEŌ χορηγέω
supply (2)
CHŌREŌ χωρέω
contain
find a place
hold
open one's heart
pass
reach
receive (3)
room, be
CHŌRION χωρίον
field (4)
land (4)
place (2)
CHŌRIS χωρίς
apart from (12)
besides (2)
beyond
by itself
deal with, not to
independent of
out of
separated from
without (20)
NOT TRANSLATED
1 Cor **11**.11
CHŌRIZŌ χωρίζω
asunder, put (2)
depart (*pass.*)
leave (*pass.*) (2)
part
separate (5)
NOT TRANSLATED
1 Cor **7**.11, 15
CHOROS χορός
dancing

CHŌROS χῶρος
(northwest †)
southeast
CHORTASMA χόρτασμα
food
CHORTAZŌ χορτάζω
facing plenty (*inf.*)
feed (5)
fill (2)
gorge
satisfy (7)
CHORTOS χόρτος
blade
grass (12)
hay
plants
CHOUS χοῦς
dust (2)
CHRAOMAI χράομαι
avail oneself of the opportunity (*imper.*)
§be (2)
deal
treat
use (2)
use of, make (2)†
§vacillate
IDIOMATICALLY
take measures *a*
CHRĒ χρή
ought (*impers.*)
CHREIA χρεία
§dependent, be
duty
fits the occasion, as (*gen.*)
necessity
need (41)†
§needful
§require
IDIOMATICALLY
help *a;* need *a*
CHRĒMA χρῆμα
money (*sg. or pl.*) (4)
riches (*pl.*) (2)+
CHRĒMATISMOS χρηματισμός
reply, God's
CHRĒMATIZŌ χρηματίζω
called, be (*pass.*) (2)
direct
instruct
reveal
warn (4)
CHREOPHEILETĒS χρεοφειλέτης
debtor (2)
CHRĒSIMOS χρήσιμος
[*useful*]
IDIOMATICALLY
good *b*
CHRĒSIS χρῆσις
relations (2)
CHRĒSTEUOMAI χρηστεύομαι
kind, be
CHRĒSTOLOGIA χρηστολογία
fair words
CHRĒSTOS χρηστός
§(better)
easy
good (2)
kind (2)
§kindness (2)

CHRĒSTOTĒS χρηστότης
good
goodness
kindness (8)
CHRĒZŌ χρῄζω
need (4)
require
CHRIŌ χρίω
anoint (4)
commission
CHRISMA χρῖσμα
§anointed, be
anointing (2)
CHRISTIANOS Χριστιανός
Christian (3)
CHRISTOS χριστός
anointed
Christ (*subst.*) (528)+†
CHRONIZŌ χρονίζω
delay (*art. inf.*)
delayed, be (3)
tarry
CHRONOS χρόνος
§afterward
age (3)
delay
§long 6[a]
§long as, as 2[a] (2)
§long, how
§long, so 1[a]
§longer 1[a] (3)
period
time (32)
§while
while, for a (*acc.*) (4)
IDIOMATICALLY
during *a;* old *a*
NOT TRANSLATED
Acts **13**.18
CHRONOTRIBEŌ χρονοτριβέω
spend time
CHRŌS χρώς
body
CHRYSION χρυσίον
gold (13)
CHRYSODAKTYLIOS χρυσοδακτύλιος
gold rings, with
CHRYSOLITHOS χρυσόλιθος
chrysolite
CHRYSOŌ χρυσόω
bedeck (2)
CHRYSOPRASOS χρυσόπρασος
chrysoprase
CHRYSOS χρυσός
gold (9)
CHRYSOUS χρυσοῦς
gold, of (3)
golden (15)

D

DAIMŌN δαίμων
demon
DAIMONIŌDĒS δαιμονιώδης
devilish
DAIMONION δαιμόνιον
demon (61)
demonic (*gen. pl.*)
divinity

DAIMONIZOMAI δαιμονίζομαι
demon, one who has a (*subst. part.*)
demoniac (*subst. part.*) (7)
possessed by a demon, be
possessed with demons, one who is (*subst. part.*) (4)

DAKNŌ δάκνω
bite

DAKRYŌ δακρύω
weep

DAKRYON δάκρυον
tear (10)+

DAKTYLIOS δακτύλιος
ring

DAKTYLOS δάκτυλος
finger (9)

DAMALIS δάμαλις
heifer

DAMAZŌ δαμάζω
subdue
tame (3)

DANEION δάνειον
debt

DANEISTĒS δανειστής
creditor

DANEIZŌ δανείζω
borrow (*mid.*)
lend (3)

DAPANAŌ δαπανάω
spend (4)
IDIOMATICALLY
pay expenses *a*

DAPANĒ δαπάνη
cost

DE δέ
A connecting particle commonly translated but (*when some contrast is implied*) *or* and. *It is not analyzed in this Concordance.*

DĒ δή
come
indeed
so
therefore
NOT TRANSLATED
Lk **2**.15; **13**.2

DECHOMAI δέχομαι
accept (6)
receive (42)
refuse (*neg.*)
take (4)
take up
welcome
welcome, give

DEĒSIS δέησις
§pray
prayer (13)
supplication (5)

DEI δεῖ
be
doomed, be
§due
fitting, be
have (6)
must (59)
necessary, be (3)
ought (25)
right, have a
should (4)

DEIGMA δεῖγμα
example

DEIGMATIZŌ δειγματίζω
example, make an
shame, put to

DEIKNYMI δείκνυμι (δεικνύω)
manifest
show (31)+

DEILIA δειλία
timidity

DEILIAŌ δειλιάω
afraid, be

DEILOS δειλός
afraid (2)
cowardly

DEINA δεῖνα
certain one

DEINŌS δεινῶς
hard
§terrible

DEIPNEŌ δειπνέω
eat
§supper (3)

DEIPNON δεῖπνον
banquet (5)
feast (3)
meal
supper (7)

DEISIDAIMŌN δεισιδαίμων
religious, very (*comp.*)

DEISIDAIMONIA δεισιδαιμονία
superstition

DEKA δέκα
§eighteen
§(sixteen)
ten (24)

DEKAOKTŌ δεκαοκτώ
eighteen (2)

DEKAPENTE δεκαπέντε
§two
fifteen (2)

DEKATESSARES δεκατέσσαρες
fourteen (5)

DEKATOŌ δεκατόω
tithes, pay (*pass.*)
tithes, receive

DEKATOS δέκατος
tenth (4)+
tithe (*subst. fem.*) (3)

DEKTOS δεκτός
acceptable (5)

DELEAZŌ δελεάζω
entice (3)

DĒLOŌ δηλόω
disclose
indicate (3)
known, make
report
show

DĒLOS δῆλος
§betray
(certain)
evident
plain

DĒMĒGOREŌ δημηγορέω
oration, make an

DĒMIOURGOS δημιουργός
maker

DĒMOS δῆμος
crowd
people (3)

DĒMOSIOS δημόσιος
common
public, in (*fem. dat.*) (2)
publicly (*fem. dat.*)

DĒNARION δηνάριον
coin (3)
denarius (13)

DENDRON δένδρον
tree (25)

DEŌ δέω
bind (33)
bonds, in (*perf. pass. part.*)
fetter
imprisoned, be (*pass.*)
prison, be in (*perf. pass.*)
prison, in (*perf. pass. part.*)
tie (4)

DEOMAI δέομαι
ask
beg (7)
beseech (4)
pray (10)

DEOS δέος
awe

DĒPOU δήπου
surely

DERMA δέρμα
skin

DERMATINOS δερμάτινος
leather (2)

DERŌ δέρω
beat (11)
beating, receive a (*pass.*) (2)
strike (2)

DESMĒ δέσμη
bundle

DESMEUŌ δεσμεύω
bind (3)

DESMIOS δέσμιος
prison, one who is in
prisoner (15)

DESMOPHYLAX δεσμοφύλαξ
jailer (3)

DESMOS δεσμός
bond (2)
chain (3)
fetter (3)
imprisonment (*pl.*) (9)
NOT TRANSLATED
Mk **7**.35

DESMŌTĒRION δεσμωτήριον
prison (4)

DESMŌTĒS δεσμώτης
prisoner (2)

DESPOTĒS δεσπότης
lord
master (6)
master of the house
sovereign lord (2)

DEURO δεῦρο
come (7)
go
IDIOMATICALLY
far *a*

DEUTE δεῦτε
come (10)
§follow (2)

DEUTERAIOS δευτεραῖος
second day, on the (*pl.*)

DEUTEROPRŌTOS δευτερόπρωτος
(second first)

DEUTEROS δεύτερος
afterward (*neut.*+*art.*)
double
more, once (*neut.*)
second (40)
§twice

DEXIOLABOS δεξιολάβος
spearman

DEXIOS δεξιός
right (15)
§right hand (37)
§right side (2)

DIA διά
account of, on (+*acc.* 8)+
account, on s.'s (+*acc.* 2)
§*after* (+*gen.* 3)
among (+*gen.*)
at (+*gen.*; +*acc.*)
§avoid, to (+*acc.*)
because (+*acc.* 25)
because of (+*gen.*; +*acc.* 42)
before (+*gen.*)
benefit, for s.'s (+*acc.*)
by (+*gen.* 129; +*acc.* 9)†
by means of (+*gen.*)+
by way of (+*gen.*)
consideration for, out of (+*acc.*)
due to (+*acc.*)
during (+*gen.*)
fear of, for (+*acc.*)
for (+*gen.*; +*acc.* 37)
for s.'s sake (+*acc.* 26)
for the sake of (+*acc.* 15)
from (+*gen.* 2; +*acc.* 2)
ground of, on the (+*acc.* 2)
in (+*gen.* 15; +*acc.* 2)
of (+*gen.*)
on (+*gen.*; +*acc.*)
out of (+*acc.* 3)
over (+*gen.*; +*acc.* 2)
§*reason why, the* (+*acc.*) 1 (3)
since (+*acc.* 4)
§*so* (+*acc.*) 8[b] (3)
§taking (+*gen.*)
§*then* (+*acc.*) 9[c]
§*thereby* (+*gen.*) 1[b]
§*therefore* (+*acc.*) 1 (2); 11 (33)+
through (+*gen.* 157; +*acc.* 2)
§*thus* (+*gen.*) 4[b]
under (+*gen.*)
under the leadership of (+*gen.*)
view of, in (+*acc.*)
§*why* (+*acc.*) 1 (2); 9; 12[a] (26)
§*why, that is* (+*acc.*) 1; 3 (6)
§*why, this is* (+*acc.*) 1[a] (5)
with (+*gen.* 13)
IDIOMATICALLY
OR NOT TRANSLATED
with compound words (+*gen.*):
among
Acts **9**.32
through
Mt **12**.43
Mk **2**.23; **10**.25; **11**.16
Lk **4**.30; **6**.1; **11**.24
Jn **4**.4
1 Cor **10**.1
throughout
Acts **13**.49
+*genitive:*
Mt **8**.28; **18**.10
Mk **5**.5
Lk **5**.5; **24**.53
Jn **19**.23
Acts **2**.25; **10**.2; **15**.23; **24**.16
Rom **2**.27; **3**.27[2]; **4**.11; **5**.16, 18[2]; **11**.10; **14**.20
2 Cor **1**.11, 16, 19[2], 20; **4**.15; **5**.10
2 Th **3**.16
2 Tim **4**.17
Heb **2**.15; **7**.21; **9**.6, 12; **13**.15, 22
1 Pet **5**.12
2 Jn .12
Rev **1**.1
+*accusative:*
Lk **17**.11
Acts **28**.2
2 Cor **13**.10
2 Tim **1**.6
Heb **10**.2
1 Pet **2**.19

DIABAINŌ διαβαίνω
come over
cross
pass

DIABALLŌ διαβάλλω
charges, bring

DIABEBAIOOMAI διαβεβαιόομαι
assertions, make
insist

DIABLEPŌ διαβλέπω
look intently
see clearly (2)

DIABOLOS διάβολος
devil (*subst.*) (34)
slanderer (*subst.*) (3)†

DIACHEIRIZŌ διαχειρίζω
kill (*mid.*) (2)

DIACHLEUAZŌ διαχλευάζω
mock

DIACHŌRIZŌ διαχωρίζω
part (*pass.*)

DIADECHOMAI διαδέχομαι
turn, in (*part.*)

DIADĒMA διάδημα
diadem (3)

DIADIDŌMI διαδίδωμι
distribute (3)
divide

DIADOCHOS διάδοχος
§succeed

DIAGGELLŌ διαγγέλλω
notice, give
proclaim (2)

DIAGINOMAI διαγίνομαι
lose
pass (2)

DIAGINŌSKŌ διαγινώσκω
decide
determine

DIAGNŌSIS διάγνωσις
decision

DIAGŌ διάγω
lead
pass one's days

DIAGOGGYZŌ διαγογγύζω
murmur (2)

DIAGRĒGOREŌ διαγρηγορέω
waken

DIAIREŌ διαιρέω
apportion
divide

DIAIRESIS διαίρεσις
variety (3)

DIAKATELEGCHOMAI
διακατελέγχομαι
confute

DIAKATHAIRŌ διακαθαίρω
clear

DIAKATHARIZŌ διακαθαρίζω
clear

DIAKŌLYŌ διακωλύω
prevent

DIAKONEŌ διακονέω
administer
aid, with (*part.*)
carry on
deliver
§do
employ
helper (*subst. part.*)
minister (5)
provide
serve (20)
serve as deacon (2)
service, render (2)

DIAKONIA διακονία
dispensation (4)
distribution
ministry (12)
mission
offering
relief (2)
rendering
§serve (2)
service (7)
serving (3)

DIAKONOS διάκονος
agent
attendant
deacon (3)
deaconess (*fem.*)
minister (8)
servant (16)

DIAKOSIOI διακόσιοι
§hundred, a
two hundred (7)

DIAKOUŌ διακούω
hear

DIAKRINŌ διακρίνω
contend (*mid.*)
criticize (*mid.*)
decide
different in, see s.
discern
distinction, make a (2)
distinctions, make (*pass.*)
doubt (*mid. or aor. pass.*) (6)
interpret
judge
waver, make one (*pass.*)
weigh
IDIOMATICALLY
hesitation *a*

DIAKRISIS διάκρισις
dispute
§distinguish
distinguish, ability to

DIALALEŌ διαλαλέω
discuss
talk about

DIALEGOMAI διαλέγομαι
address
argue (7)
discuss
dispute (2)
talk (2)

DIALEIPŌ διαλείπω
cease

DIALEKTOS διάλεκτος
language (6)

DIALLASSŌ διαλλάσσω
reconcile
DIALOGISMOS διαλογισμός
argument
opinion
quarreling
questioning (3)
thinking (*pl.*)
thought (7)
DIALOGIZOMAI διαλογίζομαι
argue (2)
consider in one's mind
discuss (5)
question (6)
say
think
DIALYŌ διαλύω
disperse
DIAMACHOMAI διαμάχομαι
contend
DIAMARTYROMAI διαμαρτύρομαι
charge (3)
testify (10)
warn
IDIOMATICALLY
forewarn, solemnly *a*
DIAMENŌ διαμένω
continue (2)
preserved, be
remain (2)
DIAMERISMOS διαμερισμός
division
DIAMERIZŌ διαμερίζω
distribute (2)
divide (8)
part
DIANEMŌ διανέμω
spread (*pass.*)
DIANEUŌ διανεύω
make signs
DIANOĒMA διανόημα
thought
DIANOIA διάνοια
imagination
mind (9)
understanding (2)
DIANOIGŌ διανοίγω
explain
open (7)
DIANYKTEREUŌ διανυκτερεύω
continue all night
DIANYŌ διανύω
finish
DIAPARATRIBĒ διαπαρατριβή
wrangling (*pl.*)
DIAPERAŌ διαπεράω
cross (2)
cross again
cross over (3)
DIAPHĒMIZŌ διαφημίζω
spread (2)
spread s.'s fame
DIAPHERŌ διαφέρω
better, be
carry through
differ
difference, make a
drift
excellent, what is (*subst. part. neut. pl.*) (2)
spread (*pass.*)
value, be of more (5)

DIAPHEUGŌ διαφεύγω
escape
DIAPHOROS διάφορος
§differs, that
excellent, more (*comp.*) (2)
various (*pl.*)
DIAPHTHEIRŌ διαφθείρω
depraved (*perf. pass. part.*)
destroy (3)
destroyer (*subst. part.*)
waste away (*pass.*)
DIAPHTHORA διαφθορά
corruption (6)
DIAPHYLASSŌ διαφυλάσσω
guard
DIAPLEŌ διαπλέω
sail across
DIAPONEOMAI διαπονέομαι
annoyed
annoyed, be
DIAPOREŌ διαπορέω
perplexed, be (3)
perplexed, be much
DIAPOREUOMAI διαπορεύομαι
go by
go on one's way through (2)
go through
pass
DIAPRAGMATEUOMAI
διαπραγματεύομαι
gain by trading
DIAPRIŌ διαπρίω
enraged, be (*pass.*) (2)
DIARĒGNYMI διαρήγνυμι
(διαρρήγνυμι, διαρήσσω)
break (2)
tear (3)
DIARPAZŌ διαρπάζω
plunder (3)
DIASAPHEŌ διασαφέω
explain
report
DIASEIŌ διασείω
rob by violence
DIASKORPIZŌ διασκορπίζω
scatter (4)
scatter abroad
squander
waste
winnow (2)
DIASŌZŌ διασῴζω
escape (*pass.*) (3)
heal
safely, bring one
save (2)
well, make
DIASPAŌ διασπάω
tear in pieces
wrench apart
DIASPEIRŌ διασπείρω
scatter (3)
DIASPORA διασπορά
dispersion (3)
DIASTELLŌ διαστέλλω
caution (*mid.*)
charge (*mid.*) (4)
instructions, give (*mid.*)
order given (*subst. pass. part. neut.*)
DIASTĒMA διάστημα
interval

DIASTOLĒ διαστολή
§distinct
distinction (2)
DIASTREPHŌ διαστρέφω
crooked, make
perverse (*perf. pass. part.*) (4)
pervert
turn away
DIATAGĒ διαταγή
§appoint
§delivered
DIATAGMA διάταγμα
edict
DIATARASSŌ διαταράσσω
troubled, be greatly (*pass.*)
DIATASSŌ διατάσσω
appoint
arrange
command (4)
direct (4)
directions, give
instruct
instructions (*subst. perf. pass. part.*)
ordain
orders, give
§rule
DIATELEŌ διατελέω
continue
DIATĒREŌ διατηρέω
keep (2)
DIATHĒKĒ διαθήκη
covenant (30)†
will (3)
DIATITHĒMI διατίθημι
assign (*mid.*) (2)
give (*mid.*)
make (*mid.*) (4)
DIATRIBŌ διατρίβω
remain (6)
stay (3)
DIATROPHĒ διατροφή
food
DIAUGAZŌ διαυγάζω
dawn
DIAUGĒS διαυγής
transparent
DIAZŌNNYMI διαζώννυμι
gird (2)
put on
DICHAZŌ διχάζω
§set
DICHOSTASIA διχοστασία
dissension (2)
DICHOTOMEŌ διχοτομέω
(cut in pieces†)
punish (2)
DIDACHĒ διδαχή
doctrine (4)
instruction
lesson
§taught
teaching (23)
DIDAKTIKOS διδακτικός
teacher, apt (*subst.*) (2)
DIDAKTOS διδακτός
taught (3)
DIDASKALIA διδασκαλία
doctrine (10)
instruction
teaching (10)

DIDASKALOS διδάσκαλος
teacher (59)
DIDASKŌ διδάσκω
direct
teach (96)
DIDŌMI δίδωμι
allow (6)
assign
§bear
bring forth (2)
§cast
§command 4[a] (2)
commit
give (334)
give over (2)
give up (2)
grant (21)
§hold
impart
inflict
§instrument 2
§leave
let (2)
make (3)
§mark 1[a]
mingle
offer (3)
pay (3)
permit
put (9)
§put in the way
§reward 5[a]
set
show (4)
§strike with one's hand 1 (2)
§utter
§venture
yield
IDIOMATICALLY
drain *a;* gift *b;* have *d;* make *a*
NOT TRANSLATED
Mk **12**.15
DIDRACHMON δίδραχμον
half-shekel tax
tax
DIDYMOS δίδυμος
twin (3)
DIEGEIRŌ διεγείρω
arouse (2)
awaken (*pass.*) (2)
rise
waken
DIĒGEOMAI διηγέομαι
declare (2)
describe (2)
tell (4)
DIĒGĒSIS διήγησις
narrative
DIĒNEKĒS διηνεκής
[*continuous*]
IDIOMATICALLY
all *c, d* (=time *c*); continually *a;* ever, for *i*
DIENTHYMEOMAI διενθυμέομαι
ponder
DIERCHOMAI διέρχομαι
come (2)
cross
go
go about (2)
go abroad
go across (2)
go here and there
go over
go through (8)
pass (2)
pass along (2)
pass on (2)
pass through (13)
pierce through
spread
travel
IDIOMATICALLY
visit *a*
DIERMĒNEUŌ διερμηνεύω
interpret (5)
§mean
DIERMĒNEUTĒS διερμηνευτής
interpret, one to
DIERŌTAŌ διερωτάω
inquiry for, make
DIETĒS διετής
two years old
DIETIA διετία
two years (2)
DIEXODOS διέξοδος
[*outlet, passage*]
IDIOMATICALLY
thoroughfare *a*
DIIKNEOMAI διϊκνέομαι
pierce
DIISCHYRIZOMAI διϊσχυρίζομαι
insist (2)
DIISTĒMI διΐστημι
§interval
part
NOT TRANSLATED
Acts **27**.28
DIKAIOKRISIA δικαιοκρισία
righteous judgment
DIKAIŌMA δικαίωμα
decree
judgment
justification
ordinance
precept
regulation (2)
requirement, just
righteous deed
righteousness, act of
DIKAIOŌ δικαιόω
acquit
free (3)
justify (34)†
(righteous, reckon †)
vindicate
DIKAIOS δίκαιος
innocent (2)
just (17)
§justly (*subst. neut.*)
right (7)
righteous (49)+
sincere
upright (2)
DIKAIŌS δικαίως
justly (2)
§righteous
§upright
IDIOMATICALLY
right *a*
DIKAIŌSIS δικαίωσις
acquittal
justification
DIKAIOSYNĒ δικαιοσύνη
(benevolence †)
justice (3)
justification
§justify (2)
piety
right (4)
right, what is (2)
righteousness (76)†
NOT TRANSLATED
Rom **3**.26; **9**.30
DIKASTĒS δικαστής
judge (2)
DIKĒ δίκη
justice
punishment (2)
DIKTYON δίκτυον
net (12)
DILOGOS δίλογος
double-tongued
DIO διό
accordingly
consequently
reason why, this is the
so (11)
then
therefore (35)
why, that is (2)
DIODEUŌ διοδεύω
go on through
pass through
DIŌGMOS διωγμός
persecution (10)
DIŌKŌ διώκω
aim at (2)
aim, make s. one's
follow
persecute (30)
persecutor (*subst. part.*)
practice
press on (2)
pursue (5)
seek
strive for
DIŌKTĒS διώκτης
§persecute
DIOPER διόπερ
therefore (2)
DIOPETĒS διοπετής
§sacred stone that fell from the sky
DIORTHŌMA διόρθωμα
reform
DIORTHŌSIS διόρθωσις
reformation
DIORYSSŌ διορύσσω
break in (2)
break into (2)
DIOTI διότι
because (12)
for (9)
since
therefore (2)
DIPLOŌ διπλόω
repay
DIPLOUS διπλοῦς
double (3)
twice as much (*comp.*)
DIPSAŌ διψάω
thirst (9)
thirsty (*part.*) (3)
thirsty, be (4)
DIPSOS δίψος
thirst
DIPSYCHOS δίψυχος
double mind, man of (*subst.*)
double-minded

DIS *δίς*
twice (4)
IDIOMATICALLY
again *a, b*

DISCHILIOI *δισχίλιοι*
two thousand

DISMYRIAS *δισμυριάς*
twice ten thousand

DISTAZŌ *διστάζω*
doubt (2)

DISTOMOS *δίστομος*
two-edged (3)

DITHALASSOS *διθάλασσος*
§shoal

DIYLIZŌ *διϋλίζω*
strain

DOCHĒ *δοχή*
feast (2)

DŌDEKA *δώδεκα*
twelve (74)+

DŌDEKAPHYLON *δωδεκάφυλον*
twelve tribes

DŌDEKATOS *δωδέκατος*
twelfth

DOGMA *δόγμα*
decision
decree (2)
legal demand
ordinance

DOGMATIZŌ *δογματίζω*
regulations, submit to (*pass.*)

DOKEŌ *δοκέω*
§convinced, be
disposed, be
expect
imagine
judged, be
§judgment
pleasure (*subst. neut. part.*)
presume
regarded, be
repute, one who is of (*subst. part.*) (2)
reputed, one who is (*subst. part.*) (2)
seem (5)
seem good (4)+
suppose (6)
supposed to, be
think (32)
§unexpected (*neg.*)

DOKIMASIA *δοκιμασία*
test

DOKIMAZŌ *δοκιμάζω*
accredit
approve (4)
examine (2)
fit, see
interpret (2)
learn, try to
prove (2)
test (9)

DOKIMĒ *δοκιμή*
character (2)
proof
test (3)
worth

DOKIMION *δοκίμιον*
genuineness
testing

DOKIMOS *δόκιμος*
accepted
approved (3)
genuine
§test, stand the
test, to have met the

DOKOS *δοκός*
log (6)

DOLIOŌ *δολιόω*
deceive

DOLIOS *δόλιος*
deceitful

DOLOŌ *δολόω*
tamper with

DOLOS *δόλος*
deceit (3)
guile (6)
stealth (2)

DOMA *δόμα*
gift (4)

DŌMA *δῶμα*
housetop (6)
roof

DŌREA *δωρεά*
gift (9)
gift, free (2)

DŌREAN *δωρεάν*
cause, without a
cost, without
gift, as a
pay, without
paying, without (2)
payment, without
price, without
purpose, to no

DŌRĒMA *δώρημα*
gift
gift, free

DŌREOMAI *δωρέομαι*
grant (3)

DŌRON *δῶρον*
gift (15)
given to God (2)
(offering †)
present
NOT TRANSLATED
Lk **21**.4

DOSIS *δόσις*
endowment
giving

DOTĒS *δότης*
giver

DOULAGŌGEŌ *δουλαγωγέω*
subdue

DOULĒ *δούλη*
handmaid
handmaiden
maidservant

DOULEIA *δουλεία*
bondage (2)
slavery (3)

DOULEUŌ *δουλεύω*
bondage, be in (2)
enslaved, be
servant, be a
serve (17)
service, render
slave, be a (2)
slavery, be in

DOULOŌ *δουλόω*
bound, be (*pass.*)
enslave (2)
slave, become a (*pass.*) (4)
slave, make a

DOULOS I *δοῦλος*
[*slavish, servile*]
NOT TRANSLATED
Rom **6**.19[2]

DOULOS II *δοῦλος*
manservant
servant (84)
slave (38)†
§slavery

DOXA *δόξα*
§another
brightness (2)
glorification
glorious (*gen.*) (8)
glorious ones (*subst. pl.*) (2)
glory (137)+
honor (2)
praise (4)
pride
splendor (8)

DOXAZŌ *δοξάζω*
exalt (2)
glorify (47)
glory, give
honor (2)
magnify
praise (5)
splendor, have (*pass.*) (2)
triumph (*pass.*)

DRACHMĒ *δραχμή*
coin (2)
silver coin

DRAKŌN *δράκων*
dragon (13)

DRASSOMAI *δράσσομαι*
catch

DREPANON *δρέπανον*
sickle (8)

DROMOS *δρόμος*
course (2)
race

DYNAMAI *δύναμαι*
able, be (38)
can (100)
§cannot (57)
§enable
may (+*inf.*) (2)
might (+*inf.*) (3)
§possible
ready, be (2)
unable, be (*neg.*) (3)
IDIOMATICALLY
enough *c;* strength *a*

DYNAMIS *δύναμις*
ability
meaning
means (2)
might
§mightily
mighty (*gen.*)
mighty work (13)
miracle (6)
§miracles, worker of
power (88)+
raging (*gen.*)
strength, full
§unbearably
wealth

DYNAMOŌ *δυναμόω*
strength, win (*pass.*)
strengthen

DYNASTĒS *δυνάστης*
mighty, the (*pl.*)
minister
sovereign

DYNATEŌ δυνατέω
able, be (2)
powerful, be

DYNATOS δυνατός
able (6)
authority, man of (*subst.*)
can (+*inf.*)
mighty (3)
possible (13)
power (*subst.*)
§power, have (2)
powerful
strong (3)
versed, well

DYNŌ δύνω
set
§sundown, at

DYO δύο
§both 2
§forty-two (2)
§(seventy-two)
§twenty
two (127)+
§two by two (Gr. 2)

DYSBASTAKTOS δυσβάστακτος
hard to bear (2)

DYSENTERION δυσεντέριον
dysentery

DYSERMĒNEUTOS δυσερμήνευτος
hard to explain

DYSIS δύσις
(west)

DYSKOLOS δύσκολος
hard

DYSKOLŌS δυσκόλως
§hard (3)

DYSMĒ δυσμή
west (*pl.*) (5)

DYSNOĒTOS δυσνόητος
hard to understand

DYSPHĒMEŌ δυσφημέω
slander

DYSPHĒMIA δυσφημία
ill repute

E

E ε′
(fifth)

Ē ἤ
and (3)
either (4)
except
nor (+*neg.*) (3)
or (265)+
than (36)
what
IDIOMATICALLY
OR NOT TRANSLATED
Mt **1.**18; **5.**18; **26.**53
Mk **6.**56; **13.**35; **14.**30
Lk **2.**26
Acts **7.**2; **17.**21; **25.**16
Rom **6.**3; **7.**1; **9.**21; **11.**2
1 Cor **5.**11[2]; **6.**2, 9, 19; **7.**16; **9.**8, 10; **10.**22; **14.**6, 7
2 Cor **1.**13, 17; **11.**7; **13.**5
1 Th **2.**19

EA ἔα
ah!
(let one alone †)

EAN ἐάν
§*any one who* 3 (3)
§anything 4[a]
for one to
§*he who* 1[a] (2)
if (210)
if, even (2)
provided
that
though (2)
§whatever 2[b] (12)+; 3[a] (2); 3[b] (3); 4[a, c]; 6[a]
when (8)
§whenever 3
§wherever 1[a] (6); 3
whether (2)
§*whoever* 1[b] (14); 1[d]; 2[b]
NOT TRANSLATED
Mt **11.**6, 27; **15.**5; **22.**9
Mk **6.**10; **7.**11
Lk **4.**6
Jn **21.**25
Acts **7.**7
Rom **15.**24
1 Cor **6.**18; **11.**25, 26; **16.**2, 3
2 Cor **3.**16
Gal **5.**17
1 Th **2.**8
2 Tim **2.**5
3 Jn .5
Rev **3.**19; **11.**6

EAN MĒ ἐὰν μή
but
except (2)
unless (31)
without
NOT TRANSLATED
Mk **10.**30
Rev **13.**15

EANPER ἐάνπερ
if
if only

EAŌ ἐάω
allow (4)
leave (2)
let (4)
IDIOMATICALLY
more *a*

ĒCHEŌ ἠχέω
noisy (*part.*)

ECHIDNA ἔχιδνα
viper (5)

ECHŌ ἔχω
able, be (2)
§be (50)+
§be under
bear (4)
belong to (*pass.*)
bring
§can (3)
§cannot
§cease 1
come to
come upon
consider
derive
devoid of (*neg. part.*)
§endure patiently 1[b]
engaged in, be
§enjoy
§follow
§following day, the (*part.*)
get (3)
have (489)+
have to do with
hold (19)+
§honor 3
§hope 1[a]
in (*part.*) (2)
incur
keep (4)
§leaf 1[a]
§live 9
live with
§living 3
§long 3
maintain
§married, be 1
meet
§must (+*inf.*) 1[a]
§need 2[a, b] (19)
next (*part.*) (2)
§(obliged, be 1)
obtain (2)
possess (2)
possessed, be
possessed by, be (2)
§reap
receive (2)
recognize
§remember 4[b] (2)
§require 3
§share 6[a]
§sick 4 (2)
§stand 9
§stand in
§strive 1
suffer
(take [*imper.*]†)
§thank 1 (3)
§uncircumcised 1[a]
use
wear (2)
with (*part.*) (28)
§without (*neg. part.*) 5[a] (4)
§work 9
IDIOMATICALLY
able, be *a;* can *b;* child *c;* conceive *a, b;* day *c;* eat *b;* effect *a;* find *a;* mend *a;* present *b;* recover *a*
NOT TRANSLATED
Jn **19.**10
Acts **1.**12
1 Cor **7.**2; **8.**10; **14.**26[4]
Tit **1.**6
Rev **9.**3, 8

ĒCHOS I ἦχος
reports
sound (2)

ĒCHOS II ἦχος
roaring

ECHTHES ἐχθές
yesterday (3)

ECHTHRA ἔχθρα
enmity (3)
hostile (*pred.*)
hostility (2)

ECHTHROS ἐχθρός
enemy (*subst.*) (28)
foe (*subst.*) (3)
hostile

EDAPHIZŌ ἐδαφίζω
dash to the ground

EDAPHOS ἔδαφος
ground

ĒDĒ ἤδη
about
already (30)
just

now (18)
time, by this (2)
IDIOMATICALLY
soon as, as *a* (2), *c*
NOT TRANSLATED
Mk **6**.35; **15**.42
Lk **7**.6
Jn **4**.51; **5**.6
1 Cor **6**.7

EGCHRIŌ ἐγχρίω
anoint

EGEIRŌ ἐγείρω
§afflict 2
arise (*pass or act. imper.*) (11)
awake (*imper.*)
come (*imper.*) (2)
lift out
lift up (3)
raise (64)
raise up (13)
rise (*pass. or act. imper.*) (40)+
rise up (*pass.*)
wake (5)

EGERSIS ἔγερσις
resurrection

EGGIZŌ ἐγγίζω
approach (2)
come near (6)
come up
draw near (21)
hand, be at (*perf.*) (11)
IDIOMATICALLY
nearly *a*

EGGRAPHŌ ἐγγράφω
write
write in
write on

EGGYOS ἔγγυος
surety (*subst.*)

EGGYS ἐγγύς
hand, at (7)
near (22)
nearer (*comp.*)
ready

EGKAINIA ἐγκαίνια
feast of the Dedication

EGKAINIZŌ ἐγκαινίζω
open
ratify

EGKAKEŌ ἐγκακέω
lose heart (4)
weary, be
weary, grow

EGKALEŌ ἐγκαλέω
§accusation
accuse (3)
charge
charge, bring a
charges against, bring

EGKATALEIPŌ ἐγκαταλείπω
abandon (2)
desert (2)
forsake (4)
leave
neglect

EGKATHETOS ἐγκάθετος
spy (*subst.*)

EGKATOIKEŌ ἐγκατοικέω
live among

EGKAUCHAOMAI ἐγκαυχάομαι
boast of

EGKENTRIZŌ ἐγκεντρίζω
graft (6)

EGKLĒMA ἔγκλημα
charge laid against one
§charged

EGKOMBOOMAI ἐγκομβόομαι
clothe oneself

EGKOPĒ ἐγκοπή
obstacle

EGKOPTŌ ἐγκόπτω
detain
hinder (4)

EGKRATEIA ἐγκράτεια
self-control (4)

EGKRATĒS ἐγκρατής
self-controlled

EGKRATEUOMAI ἐγκρατεύομαι
self-control, exercise (2)

EGKRINŌ ἐγκρίνω
class

EGKRYPTŌ ἐγκρύπτω
hide

EGKYOS ἔγκυος
child, with

EGŌ ἐγώ
I (420)†
me (741)+
mine (17)
my (515)+
myself
IDIOMATICALLY
OR NOT TRANSLATED
Lk **11**.6
Acts **21**.17; **24**.11; **26**.5
Rom **7**.21; **15**.16
2 Tim **4**.17
2 Pet **1**.17
Rev **7**.14; **22**.12

EI εἰ
§although
§as
§assuming that (2)
chance that, on the
§except perhaps 1
for
if (318)+
§never (3)
§no
§only
§order to, in
§perhaps 4[a]
§provided that
since (2)
§so that
that (7)
though (13)
§unless 3 (2)
when
whether (17)
whether, to see (2)
§while
IDIOMATICALLY
hope *a;* would *a, b*
NOT TRANSLATED
Mt **12**.10; **19**.3
Mk **10**.2
Lk **6**.9; **22**.49
Acts **1**.6; **7**.1; **19**.2
Rom **8**.9
2 Cor **11**.20[4]
1 Tim **1**.10; **5**.10[4]
Heb **3**.11; **4**.3; **5**.1

EI MĒ εἰ μή
but (27)
else
except (33)+
only (6)
only, but (5)
then
unless (4)
§until 4
IDIOMATICALLY
only *a*
NOT TRANSLATED
1 Cor **10**.13

EI MĒN εἰ μήν
[*surely, certainly*]
IDIOMATICALLY
surely *c*

EIDEA εἰδέα
appearance

EIDŌLEION εἰδωλεῖον
idol's temple

EIDŌLOLATRĒS εἰδωλολάτρης
idolater (7)

EIDŌLOLATRIA εἰδωλολατρία
idolatry (3)
worship of idols

EIDŌLON εἴδωλον
idol (11)

EIDŌLOTHYTOS εἰδωλόθυτος
offered to an idol (5)
sacrificed to an idol (4)

EIDON εἶδον
behold
§consider
look (8)
look at (3)
note
perceive (6)
see (317)+
IDIOMATICALLY
surely *b*
NOT TRANSLATED
Acts **11**.6

EIDOS εἶδος
appearance
form (3)
sight

EIKĒ εἰκῇ
(cause, without)
reason, without
vain, in (5)

EIKŌ εἴκω
yield

EIKŌN εἰκών
form
image (16)
likeness (5)

EIKOSI εἴκοσι
§three
twenty (3)
§twenty-four (6)
§twenty-three

EILIKRINEIA εἰλικρίνεια
sincerity (3)

EILIKRINĒS εἰλικρινής
pure
sincere

EIMI εἰμί
alive, be
as (*inf.*)
be (2140)+
become (7)
being, have one's
§belong (18)
§come (16)
§consist in

§consist of
§correspond to
§count (2)
dwell
exist (5)
§fall
follow
happen
§hold
keep
live (4)
made, be
§make (3)
mean (10)
must be (7)
§own
prove
§rely
remain (3)
§rest (2)
side
stand (2)
take place
IDIOMATICALLY
OR NOT TRANSLATED
have a (27)
Mt **1**.23; **5**.25^{2}; **7**.29; **8**.12; **13**.21, 42, 50; **19**.22; **20**.15; **22**.13; **23**.30; **24**.51; **25**.30; **26**.66; **27**.33
Mk **1**.22; **2**.4; **4**.17; **5**.25, 41; **8**.1; **9**.21, 39, 41; **10**.22; **11**.23, 24; **14**.56, 59, 64; **15**.22, 26, 34, 46
Lk **1**.22; **2**.33; **3**.5; **5**.16, 17, 29; **6**.12, 43; **8**.43; **9**.30; **13**.16, 28; **14**.10; **19**.17; **20**.28; **23**.8, 15, 19, 51, 55; **24**.32
Jn **1**.41; **4**.9^{2}, 37; **6**.63; **7**.4, 36; **9**.8, 40; **10**.6, 40; **11**.39; **14**.10; **16**.18; **17**.5, 23; **18**.26; **19**.19; **20**.19
Acts **1**.14; **2**.12, 42; **3**.10; **4**.36; **5**.17; **8**.13, 16, 20, 27; **9**.28; **10**.34; **11**.22; **12**.3; **13**.1, 47; **14**.7; **16**.12, 21; **17**.20; **18**.24; **19**.36^{2}; **20**.16; **21**.33; **22**.19; **24**.11; **27**.2; **28**.17, 22, 25
Rom **1**.6, 32; **2**.11, 25; **3**.11^{2}, 12^{2}; **4**.11, 13, 17; **6**.11; **9**.26; **11**.17; **12**.3; **14**.14; **16**.1, 11, 19
1 Cor **1**.30; **3**.13; **4**.17; **7**.19, 29^{2}; **9**.16^{2}; **10**.6, 28; **11**.16; **12**.12, 23; **14**.15, 26; **16**.4
2 Cor **1**.7, 9, 14, 17, 24; **3**.8; **4**.7; **5**.9; **7**.11, 15; **8**.22; **9**.12; **10**.11; **11**.16; **12**.13, 16; **13**.5^{2}, 6, 7
Gal **1**.23; **2**.11; **3**.20
Eph **6**.12
Phil **3**.8
Col **2**.8, 10, 22; **3**.14, 20
1 Th **2**.6
2 Th **2**.9
1 Tim **1**.13, 20; **4**.15^{2}
2 Tim **1**.15
Tit **2**.4, 9; **3**.2
Phm .9, 12
Heb **1**.3; **2**.13; **4**.2; **7**.21(20); **9**.5; **11**.4; **12**.11, 21
Jas **1**.13; **5**.15
2 Pet **2**.11
1 Jn **5**.8
Rev **5**.11, 13; **9**.8; **13**.18; **21**.12, 21; **22**.12

EIŌTHA εἴωθα
accustomed, be
custom (*subst. perf. part.*) (2)
custom, be one's

EIPER εἴπερ
although
fact, if in
if
provided
since indeed

EIPON εἶπον
§after (*part.*)
ask (2)
bid (2)
call
command (5)
declare (3)
§insult 3
§make
order
reply
say (726)+†
speak (17)
tell (64)+
tell people (*imper.*)
§use
utter (2)
what is it (*imper.*)
IDIOMATICALLY
tell *a*
NOT TRANSLATED
Mt **3**.15; **4**.4; **11**.4; **12**.39, 48; **13**.11, 37; **14**.28; **15**.3, 4, 13, 24, 26, 28; **16**.2, 16, 17; **17**.11, 17; **19**.4; **20**.13, 22; **21**.21, 24, 29, 30; **22**.29; **24**.2, 4; **25**.12, 26; **26**.23; 66; **27**.25
Mk **6**.37; **10**.3
Lk **1**.19, 42; **4**.8, 12; **5**.5, 22, 31; **6**.3; **7**.22, 43; **9**.19, 20, 41, 49; **10**.27, 30, 41; **11**.7; **13**.2, 15; **15**.29; **16**.24; **17**.20; **19**.40; **20**.3, 39; **22**.51; **24**.18
Jn **1**.25, 48, 50; **2**.19; **3**.3, 10, 27; **4**.10, 17; **6**.26, 29, 43; **7**.16, 21, 52; **8**.14, 39, 48; **9**.20, 30, 36; **12**.30, 38; **13**.7, 21; **14**.23; **18**.30; **20**.28
Acts **4**.19; **5**.29; **8**.24, 37; **19**.15

EIRĒNĒ εἰρήνη
§friendly
peace (89)+
NOT TRANSLATED
Acts **7**.26

EIRĒNEUŌ εἰρηνεύω
peace, be at (2)
peace, live in
peaceably, live

EIRĒNIKOS εἰρηνικός
peaceable
peaceful

EIRĒNOPOIEŌ εἰρηνοποιέω
make peace

EIRĒNOPOIOS εἰρηνοποιός
peacemaker (*subst.*)

EIS εἰς (+*acc.*)
about
against (19)
among (16)
as (17)
at (40)†
before (3)
by
concerning (2)
dealing with, in (3)
for (144)†
in (159)
into (332)
of
on (38)
order, in (3)
over
so as
throughout (3)
to (485)+
toward (7)
until (10)
unto (2)
upon (6)
with (3)
IDIOMATICALLY
OR NOT TRANSLATED
Mt **5**.20; **6**.[13‡; **7**.21; **8**.5, 14, 34; **9**.6, 7, 26, 28; **10**.5^{2}, 11, 12, 18, 27, 41^{2}, 42; **12**.4, 9, 29; **14**.31; **15**.17; **16**.5; **17**.1, 25; **18**.3, 8, 9; **19**.1, 5, 17, 23, 24; **20**.19; **21**.10, 12, 19, 23, 42, 46; **22**.16; **24**.38; **25**.1, 6; **26**.2, 8; **27**.7, 31; **28**.1
Mk **1**.21, 29, 38, 45; **2**.11, 26; **3**.1, 3, 19(20), 27, 29; **4**.8; **5**.12, 13, 19, 26; **6**.8, 10, 56^{2}; **7**.17, 19^{3}, 24, 30; **8**.26; **9**.2, 25, 28, 43, 45, 47; **10**.8, 15, 23, 24, 25; **11**.2, 11, 14, 15; **12**.10, 14; **13**.9; **14**.4, 55; **15**.34; **16**.5
Lk **1**.9, 33, 40, 50, 55; **3**.5^{2}; **4**.38; **5**.17†‡, 24, 25; **6**.4, 6, 8; **7**.1, 44; **8**.30, 32, 33; **9**.4, 34, 52, 62; **10**.5, 8, 10, 38; **11**.49; **13**.9, 11, 19; **14**.28; **15**.6; **16**.16; **17**.12, 27; **18**.5, 17, 24, 25; **19**.4, 45; **20**.17; **21**.4, 13, 21; **22**.3, 10^{2}; **24**.20
Jn **3**.5; **4**.14; **6**.22, 51, 58, 66; **8**.35^{2}, 51, 52; **10**.1, 28; **11**.26; **12**.13, 34; **13**.8; **14**.16; **17**.23; **18**.1, 6, 15, 28, 33; **19**.9; **20**.4, 8, 14, 19, 26; **21**.11
Acts **2**.39; **3**.2, 8; **4**.11, 30; **5**.21; **7**.19, 26, 53; **8**.20; **9**.6, 17; **10**.24; **11**.8, 12, 29; **13**.22, 42, 47^{2}; **14**.20, 22; **19**.8; **21**.6^{2}, 8; **22**.13; **23**.16; **25**.23; **26**.24; **27**.6, 12, 41; **28**.15
Rom **1**.5, 11, 20, 25; **3**.25, 26; **4**.11^{2}, 16, 18; **5**.16^{2}, 18^{2}; **6**.12, 16^{3}, 19, 22; **7**.4, 5, 10^{2}; **8**.21; **9**.5, 31; **10**.1, 4, 10^{2}; **11**.9^{4}, 11, 36; **12**.2, 3, 10; **13**.4, 6, 14; **14**.19; **15**.13, 16, 18; **16**.19^{2}, 26, 27
1 Cor **4**.3; **6**.16; **8**.10, 13; **9**.18; **10**.6; **11**.22, 33, 34; **14**.22, 36; **15**.45^{2}
2 Cor **1**.4, 5, 11; **2**.9, 12; **3**.13; **4**.4, 17; **6**.18^{2}; **7**.3, 10; **8**.4, 6, 14^{2}, 23, 24; **9**.8, 9, 13; **10**.5, 13, 14, 15^{2}, 16^{2}; **11**.10, 31; **12**.6; **13**.2
Gal **1**.5; **3**.17; **5**.10
Eph **1**.5^{2}, 12, 18; **2**.15; **4**.16, 19; **5**.2, 31, 32; **6**.18, 22
Phil **1**.10, 12, 23; **2**.16; **3**.11; **4**.15, 16, 20
Col **1**.10, 12; **2**.2^{2}, 22
1 Th **2**.12, [16†; **3**.2, 3, 5, 10, 13; **4**.9, 10, 17; **5**.9
2 Th **1**.5, 11; **2**.2, 6, 10, 11, 13, 14; **3**.9
1 Tim **1**.17; **4**.3, 10; **6**.17
2 Tim **2**.25, 26; **4**.18
Tit **3**.14
Phm .5
Heb **1**.5^{2}, 8, 14; **2**.17; **3**.5, 11, 18; **4**.1, 3^{2}, 5, 6, 10, 11, 16; **5**.6; **6**.8, 20; **7**.3, 14, 17, 21, 24, 25^{2}, 28; **8**.3, 10^{2}; **9**.14, 15, 25, 26, 28^{2}; **10**.1, 12, 14, 19, 24, 39^{2}; **11**.3, 11; **12**.10; **13**.8, 21^{2}

Jas **1**.18, 19[2]; **3**.3; **5**.3, 4
1 Pet **1**.8, 10, 11, 25; **2**.5, 7, 8, 9†, 14; **4**.2, 6, 11; **5**.11
2 Pet **2**.12, 22; **3**.9
1 Jn **2**.17; **3**.8; **5**.8
2 Jn .2
Jude .13, 25
Rev **1**.6, 18; **4**.9, 10; **5**.13; **7**.12; **8**.11; **10**.6; **11**.15; **13**.3, 6, 10; **14**.11; **15**.7, 8; **19**.3; **20**.10; **21**.27; **22**.5, 14

EISAGŌ εἰσάγω
bring in (4)
bring into (7)

EISAKOUŌ εἰσακούω
hear (4)
listen

EISDECHOMAI εἰσδέχομαι
welcome

EISEIMI εἴσειμι
go in
go into (3)

EISERCHOMAI εἰσέρχομαι
arise
come (3)
come in (15)
come into (4)
come to (3)
enter (121)
enter into (13)
get in
go (6)
go in (13)
go in among
go into (6)
go to
reach
§return 10
§visit (2)

EISKALEOMAI εἰσκαλέομαι
call in

EISODOS εἴσοδος
coming
§enter
entrance
visit
welcome

EISPĒDAŌ εἰσπηδάω
rush in

EISPHERŌ εἰσφέρω
bring (2)
bring in (2)
bring into (2)
lead into (2)

EISPOREUOMAI εἰσπορεύομαι
come (2)
enter (9)
enter in
go in (2)
go into (4)

EISTRECHŌ εἰστρέχω
run

EITA εἶτα (εἶτεν)
besides this
then (14)

EITE εἴτε
as for (5)
either
if (9)
or (29)
such as
whether (14)

NOT TRANSLATED
Rom **12**.7, 8
1 Cor **8**.5; **12**.13[2]
2 Cor **5**.10

EK ἐκ (ἐξ) (+*gen.*)
according to
after
against
among (4)
among, from (6)
at (26)
based on (4)
basis of, on the
because of (4)
between (2)
by (52)†
§following (2)
for (9)
from (313)
ground of, on the
in (8)
matter of, as a
means of, by
of (237)+
off
on (11)
out from (2)
out of (98)+†
through (6)
to (2)
under
upon
with (19)+
IDIOMATICALLY
OR NOT TRANSLATED
Mt **13**.49; **15**.18; **17**.9; **19**.12
Mk **1**.29; **6**.51; **7**.29; **9**.9; **13**.15; **14**.72; **15**.39
Lk **11**.13, 54; **23**.7, 8
Jn **1**.44; **3**.31; **6**.11; **7**.42; **9**.32; **10**.26; **11**.1; **16**.14, 15; **18**.3
Acts **6**.9; **10**.15; **11**.2, 9; **15**.2; **18**.1; **19**.34; **23**.34; **26**.23
Rom **2**.8, 27; **3**.26; **4**.12, 16[3]; **11**.1; **12**.18; **16**.10, 11
1 Cor **1**.30; **12**.15, 16, 27; **13**.9[2], 10
2 Cor **1**.11; **2**.2; **4**.7; **5**.2; **6**.17; **9**.7
Gal **1**.15; **2**.12, 15; **3**.10, 12
Eph **2**.8
Col **2**.14; **3**.23
1 Th **2**.3
1 Tim **1**.5; **6**.4
2 Tim **2**.8
Tit **1**.10; **2**.8
Heb **2**.11; **3**.16; **7**.5, 6, 12; **9**.28
Jas **4**.1
1 Pet **2**.12
2 Pet **2**.8
1 Jn **5**.1[2]
Rev **9**.2[3]; **14**.8, 10; **15**.2[3]; **16**.11; **17**.11; **18**.3†‡; **19**.2

EKBAINŌ ἐκβαίνω
go out

EKBALLŌ ἐκβάλλω
bring
bring forth (2)
bring out (2)
cast (2)
cast out (46)
drive out (6)
(evacuate †)
leave out
pass on
pluck out
put out (2)
put outside (3)
send away
send out (3)
take out (7)
throw
throw out
thrust out

EKBASIS ἔκβασις
escape, way of
outcome

EKBOLĒ ἐκβολή
[*jettisoning*]
IDIOMATICALLY
throw cargo overboard *a*

EKCHEŌ ἐκχέω (ἐκχύννω)
abandon
gush out
pour (8)
pour out (10)
shed (5)
spill (2)

EKCHŌREŌ ἐκχωρέω
depart

EKDAPANAŌ ἐκδαπανάω
spend

EKDECHOMAI ἐκδέχομαι
expect
look forward to
wait
wait for (3)+

EKDĒLOS ἔκδηλος
plain

EKDĒMEŌ ἐκδημέω
away, be
away from, be (2)

EKDIDŌMI ἐκδίδωμι
let out (*mid.*) (4)

EKDIĒGEOMAI ἐκδιηγέομαι
declare
report

EKDIKEŌ ἐκδικέω
avenge (3)
punish
vindicate (2)

EKDIKĒSIS ἐκδίκησις
§avenge
§punish
punishment
vengeance (4)
§vindicate (2)

EKDIKOS ἔκδικος
avenger (*subst.*)
IDIOMATICALLY
execute *a*

EKDIŌKŌ ἐκδιώκω
drive out

EKDOCHĒ ἐκδοχή
prospect

EKDOTOS ἔκδοτος
delivered up

EKDYŌ ἐκδύω
strip (4)
unclothed, be (*pass.*)

EKEI ἐκεῖ
§bystander 1 (+*art.*); 2[a]
there (87)
which, in
yonder
NOT TRANSLATED
Lk **21**.2
Rom **9**.26
Rev **12**.6, 14

EKEINOS ἐκεῖνος
he (49)
himself
one
other, the
same (2)
she (4)
that (145)
that same (2)
that way (*gen.*)
they (19)
this (6)
very (*adj.*)
what (*neut. sg.*)
IDIOMATICALLY
OR NOT TRANSLATED
Mt **9.**22; **15.**28; **17.**18
Mk **6.**55
Jn **1.**33; **5.**11; **12.**48
Acts **1.**19
Rom **14.**14
1 Cor **10.**28

EKEISE ἐκεῖσε
there (2)

EKEITHEN ἐκεῖθεν
away
from there (17)
§place
there (3)
IDIOMATICALLY
side, on either *b*
NOT TRANSLATED
Mt **5.**26
Mk **6.**11
Lk **12.**59
Jn **4.**43

EKGONOS ἔκγονος
grandchild (*subst.*)

EKKAIŌ ἐκκαίω
consumed, be (*pass.*)

EKKATHAIRŌ ἐκκαθαίρω
cleanse out
purify

EKKENTEŌ ἐκκεντέω
pierce (2)

EKKLAŌ ἐκκλάω
break off (3)

EKKLEIŌ ἐκκλείω
exclude
shut out

EKKLĒSIA ἐκκλησία
assembly (4)
church (108)
congregation (2)

EKKLINŌ ἐκκλίνω
avoid
turn aside
turn away

EKKOLYMBAŌ ἐκκολυμβάω
swim away

EKKOMIZŌ ἐκκομίζω
carry out

EKKOPTŌ ἐκκόπτω
cut down (5)
cut from
cut off (3)
undermine

EKKREMANNYMI ἐκκρεμάννυμι
hang upon (*mid.*)

EKLALEŌ ἐκλαλέω
tell

EKLAMPŌ ἐκλάμπω
shine

EKLANTHANOMAI ἐκλανθάνομαι
forget

EKLEGOMAI ἐκλέγομαι
choice, make
choose (21)

EKLEIPŌ ἐκλείπω
(eclipsed, be †)
end
fail (3)

EKLEKTOS ἐκλεκτός
chosen (8)
elect (13)
eminent

EKLOGĒ ἐκλογή
§choose
§chosen (2)
elect (*pl.*)
election (3)

EKLYŌ ἐκλύω
courage, lose (*pass.*)
faint (*pass.*) (2)
heart, lose (*pass.*)
IDIOMATICALLY
fainthearted *a*

EKMASSŌ ἐκμάσσω
wipe (5)

EKMYKTĒRIZŌ ἐκμυκτηρίζω
scoff at (2)

EKNĒPHŌ ἐκνήφω
[*become sober*]
IDIOMATICALLY
mind *a*

EKNEUŌ ἐκνεύω
withdraw

EKPALAI ἔκπαλαι
ago, long
old, from of

EKPĒDAŌ ἐκπηδάω
rush out

EKPEIRAZŌ ἐκπειράζω
tempt (2)
test, put to the (2)

EKPEMPŌ ἐκπέμπω
send away
send out

EKPERISSŌS ἐκπερισσῶς
vehemently

EKPETANNYMI ἐκπετάννυμι
hold out

EKPHERŌ ἐκφέρω
bear
bring
carry out (4)
lead out
take out

EKPHEUGŌ ἐκφεύγω
escape (7)
flee out of

EKPHOBEŌ ἐκφοβέω
frighten

EKPHOBOS ἔκφοβος
afraid, exceedingly
IDIOMATICALLY
fear *a*

EKPHYŌ ἐκφύω
put forth (2)

EKPIPTŌ ἐκπίπτω
fail
fall (2)
fall away
fall off
go
lose
run on (3)

EKPLEŌ ἐκπλέω
sail
sail away (2)

EKPLĒROŌ ἐκπληρόω
fulfil

EKPLĒRŌSIS ἐκπλήρωσις
§fulfil

EKPLĒSSŌ ἐκπλήσσω
astonished, be (*pass.*) (13)

EKPNEŌ ἐκπνέω
breathe one's last (3)

EKPOREUOMAI ἐκπορεύομαι
come forth
come from (2)
come out (2) +
come out of (6)
(evacuated, be †)
flow from
go
go abroad
go out (6)
issue (5)
leave (2)
pass on
pour from
proceed from (2)
proceed out of
set out

EKPORNEUŌ ἐκπορνεύω
immorally, act

EKPSYCHŌ ἐκψύχω
die (3)

EKPTYŌ ἐκπτύω
despise

EKRIZOŌ ἐκριζόω
root up (3)
uproot

EKSTASIS ἔκστασις
amazement (3)
astonishment
trance (3)

EKSTREPHŌ ἐκστρέφω
pervert

EKTARASSŌ ἐκταράσσω
disturb

EKTEINŌ ἐκτείνω
lay
lay out
reach out
stretch out (13)

EKTELEŌ ἐκτελέω
finish (2)

EKTENEIA ἐκτένεια
§earnestly

EKTENĒS ἐκτενής
unfailing (*acc.*)

EKTENŌS ἐκτενῶς
§earnest
earnestly
(earnestly, more [*comp.*])

EKTHAMBEŌ ἐκθαμβέω
amaze (2)
amazed, be greatly (*pass.*)
distressed, be greatly (*pass.*)

EKTHAMBOS ἔκθαμβος
astounded

EKTHAUMAZŌ ἐκθαυμάζω
amazed, be

EKTHETOS ἔκθετος
[*sent away, exposed*]
§expose
EKTINASSŌ ἐκτινάσσω
shake off (3)
shake out
EKTITHĒMI ἐκτίθημι
explain
expose
expound (2)
EKTOS ἐκτός
but
§except 4[b]
out of (*prep.*)
outside (2)
§unless 2[a] (2)
IDIOMATICALLY
excepted *a*
EKTREPHŌ ἐκτρέφω
bring up
nourish
EKTREPŌ ἐκτρέπω
avoid (*pass.*)
joint, put out of (*pass.*)
stray (*pass.*)
wander (*pass.*)
wander away (*pass.*)
EKTRŌMA ἔκτρωμα
untimely born, one
EKZĒTEŌ ἐκζητέω
require (2)
search
seek (3)
seek for
EKZĒTĒSIS ἐκζήτησις
speculation
ELACHISTOS ἐλάχιστος
least (7)
little, very (3)
small a thing as that, as (*subst. neut.*)
small, very (2)
trivial
ELAIA ἐλαία
olive (10)
olive tree (3)
ELAION ἔλαιον
oil (11)
ELAIŌN ἐλαιών
Olivet (3)
ELAPHRIA ἐλαφρία
[*levity, vacillation*]
§vacillate
ELAPHROS ἐλαφρός
light
slight
ELASSŌN ἐλάσσων
inferior
less
poor
younger
ELATTONEŌ ἐλαττονέω
lack, have
ELATTOŌ ἐλαττόω
decrease (*pass.*)
lower, make (2)
ELAUNŌ ἐλαύνω
drive (3)
headway, make
row
ELEEINOS ἐλεεινός
pitiable
pitied, most to be (*comp.*)

ELEĒMŌN ἐλεήμων
merciful (2)
ELEĒMOSYNĒ ἐλεημοσύνη
alms (*sg. or pl.*) (12)
charity
ELEEŌ ἐλεέω
mercy, do acts of
mercy, obtain (*pass.*)
mercy on, have (17)
mercy, receive (*pass.*) (6)
mercy upon, have (3)
IDIOMATICALLY
mercy *a, b, c*
ELEGCHŌ ἐλέγχω
confute
convict (4)†
convince (3)
expose (3)
punish
rebuke (2)
reprove (3)
tell s. his fault
ELEGCHOS ἔλεγχος
conviction
ELEGMOS ἐλεγμός
reproof
ELEGXIS ἔλεγξις
[*reproof, rebuke*]
§rebuke
ELEOS ἔλεος
mercy (27)
ELEPHANTINOS ἐλεφάντινος
ivory, of
ELEUSIS ἔλευσις
coming
ELEUTHERIA ἐλευθερία
freedom (7)
liberty (4)
ELEUTHEROŌ ἐλευθερόω
free, make (2)
free, set (5)
ELEUTHEROS ἐλεύθερος
free (22)
IDIOMATICALLY
freedom *a*
ĒLI ἠλί
Eli (2)
ELLOGEŌ ἐλλογέω (ἐλλογάω)
account, charge to one's
count
ELŌI ἐλωΐ
Eloi (2)
ELPIS ἐλπίς
hope (53)
ELPIZŌ ἐλπίζω
expect
hope (23)
hope set, have one's
hope, set one's (5)
hoped for, s. (*subst. pass. part.*)
EMAUTOU ἐμαυτοῦ
me (3)
§my (2)
§my own (10)
myself (18)
myself, I
§presume 1
IDIOMATICALLY
refrain *b*
NOT TRANSLATED
Phil **3.**13

EMBAINŌ ἐμβαίνω
board, go on
get into (16)
(step in)
EMBALLŌ ἐμβάλλω
cast
EMBAPTŌ ἐμβάπτω
dip (2)
EMBATEUŌ ἐμβατεύω
stand on, take one's
EMBIBAZŌ ἐμβιβάζω
put on board
EMBLEPŌ ἐμβλέπω
look at (8)
look upon
see (2)
EMBRIMAOMAI ἐμβριμάομαι
moved, be deeply
moved, deeply (*part.*)
reproach
sternly charge (2)
EMEŌ ἐμέω
spew
EMMAINOMAI ἐμμαίνομαι
§fury (*part.*)
EMMENŌ ἐμμένω
abide
continue (2)
live
EMOS ἐμός
belongs to me, what (*subst. neut. pl.*)
§*I*
me, of (3)
mine (7)
mine, of
mine, what is (*subst. neut. sg. or pl.*) (3)
my (48)
my own (9)
my own, of
my own, what is (*subst. neut.*)
IDIOMATICALLY
me *a*
EMPAIGMONĒ ἐμπαιγμονή
scoffing
EMPAIGMOS ἐμπαιγμός
mocking
EMPAIKTĒS ἐμπαίκτης
scoffer (2)
EMPAIZŌ ἐμπαίζω
mock (12)
trick
EMPERIPATEŌ ἐμπεριπατέω
move among
EMPHANĒS ἐμφανής
manifest
§show
EMPHANIZŌ ἐμφανίζω
appear (*pass.*) (2)
case before, lay one's
clear, make it
inform (2)
information, give
manifest (2)
notice, give
EMPHOBOS ἔμφοβος
alarmed
frightened (2)
terrified
terror, in
EMPHYSAŌ ἐμφυσάω
breathe on

EMPHYTOS ἔμφυτος
implanted
EMPIMPLĒMI ἐμπίμπλημι (ἐμπιμπλάω)
eat one's fill (*pass.*)
enjoy company (*pass.*)
fill
full, be (*pass.*)
satisfy
EMPIMPRĒMI ἐμπίμπρημι
burn
EMPIPTŌ ἐμπίπτω
fall (7)
EMPLEKŌ ἐμπλέκω
entangled, be (*pass.*)
entangled, get (*pass.*)
EMPLOKĒ ἐμπλοκή
braiding
EMPNEŌ ἐμπνέω
breathe
EMPOREUOMAI ἐμπορεύομαι
exploit
trade
EMPORIA ἐμπορία
business
EMPORION ἐμπόριον
trade
EMPOROS ἔμπορος
merchant (5)
EMPROSTHEN ἔμπροσθεν
against
ahead (2)
at (2)
before (37)†
front, in
front of, in
NOT TRANSLATED
Mt **11**.26; **18**.14
Lk **10**.21; **19**.4
EMPTYŌ ἐμπτύω
spit (6)
EN ἐν (+*dat.*)
about (3)
§*across*
§*after* (2)
along
among (113)+
§*as* (17)
at (137)+
because of (4)
§*before* (6)
besides (2)
by (131)+†
by way of (2)
close to
during (5)
for (19)
from
in (1628)+†
into (6)+
means of, by (2)
midst of, in the
of (13)+
on (92)
out of
over (2)
through (21)
throughout (3)
§*thus* 4[a]
to (29)
under (6)
upon (3)
§*when* (18)
§*while* (13)
with (151)
within (15)
IDIOMATICALLY OR NOT TRANSLATED
Mt **1**.18, 23; **4**.23; **5**.13, 25; **7**.2; **10**.32[2]; **11**.20; **13**.1; **22**.16, 23; **24**.19, 48; **25**.4; **26**.31, 34
Mk **2**.19, 23; **4**.20[3], 24, 30; **5**.25; **6**.47, 48, 51; **9**.29, 41, 50; **13**.17
Lk **1**.8, 21; **2**.27, 36, 46; **4**.18; **5**.34; **7**.11, 25, 37; **8**.1, 7, 22, 43; **10**.31; **11**.1; **12**.8[2], 45; **14**.34; **17**.11; **18**.8; **19**.13, 30, 42; **20**.1; **21**.6, 21, 23; **22**.27; **23**.7, 9, 12, 14, 29, 31; **24**.13, 18, 36
Jn **2**.31; **4**.31, 37, 52, 53; **5**.5, 7, 9, 28; **9**.14, 30; **11**.38; **15**.2; **16**.29; **18**.20; **19**.41; **21**.3
Acts **1**.15; **2**.8, 41, 46; **5**.23; **7**.14; **9**.38; **10**.17; **12**.7; **13**.15; **15**.36; **16**.33; **17**.23; **18**.9; **20**.22, 26; **22**.18; **24**.16, 18; **25**.4; **26**.29[2]; **27**.21
Rom **1**.6, 12[2], 28; **2**.17, 28[3], 29[2]; **8**.3, 15, 23; **13**.9; **14**.18, 21; **16**.20
1 Cor **1**.10; **2**.3, 7; **4**.4; **5**.8; **7**.18, 20, 24; **8**.4, 7; **9**.15; **13**.12; **14**.6[4]; **15**.3, 42[2]
2 Cor **1**.6, 9; **2**.1, 14; **3**.11; **4**.2; **5**.2; **6**.4[2], 5[6], 6[5], 7[2]; **7**.9, 14, 16; **8**.22; **9**.4, 8; **10**.6; **11**.17, 21[2], 23[2], 25, 27; **12**.10[3]; **13**.5
Gal **3**.19; **4**.14; **5**.14; **6**.6
Eph **1**.10; **2**.15, 16; **3**.3, 12; **4**.16, 19; **5**.18; **6**.19, 20
Phil **1**.20, 30[2]; **4**.12
Col **1**.21, 29; **2**.1, 15, 16[2], 23; **3**.17, 20; **4**.5, 6
1 Th **1**.8, **2**.5 *var om.*, 6(7), 7; **4**.10; **5**.3
1 Tim **2**.12, 14; **3**.4; **4**.12, 14
2 Tim **1**.5; **4**.2, 5
Tit **1**.6
Phm .6
Heb **2**.18; **3**.9, 12; **6**.17; **9**.4, 23; **10**.32; **11**.19, 37; **13**.9
Jas **2**.1
1 Pet **1**.6, 14; **3**.2, 16; **4**.4, 13, 19; **5**.2
2 Pet **1**.5[2], 6[3], 7[2]; **2**.7; **3**.10, 16
1 Jn **5**.6
2 Jn .4, 6
3 Jn .3, 4
Rev **1**.1, 3, 9; **2**.1, 23; **4**.6; **5**.6[2], 13; **11**.1, 11; **12**.2, 12; **13**.12; **18**.19; **19**.14; **22**.6
ENAGKALIZOMAI ἐναγκαλίζομαι
take in one's arms (2)
ENALIOS ἐνάλιος
sea creature (*subst.*)
ENANTI ἔναντι
before (2)
ENANTION ἐναντίον
before (4)
presence of, in the
ENANTIOS ἐναντίος
against (4)
§facing
opposes, who (*attr.*+*dat.*)
§opposing, in
IDIOMATICALLY
opponent *a*
ENARCHOMAI ἐνάρχομαι
begin (2)
ENATOS ἔνατος
ninth (10)
ENDECHOMAI ἐνδέχομαι
cannot be, it (*impers.*+*neg.*)
ENDEĒS ἐνδεής
needy
ENDEIGMA ἔνδειγμα
evidence
ENDEIKNYMI ἐνδείκνυμι
display (*mid.*)
do
show (*mid.*) (8)
ENDEIXIS ἔνδειξις
omen, clear
proof
§prove
§show
ENDĒMEŌ ἐνδημέω
home, be at (3)
ENDIDYSKŌ ἐνδιδύσκω
clothe in
clothed in, be (*mid.*)
ENDIKOS ἔνδικος
just (2)
ENDŌMĒSIS ἐνδώμησις
§built, be
ENDOXAZOMAI ἐνδοξάζομαι
glorified, be (2)
ENDOXOS ἔνδοξος
glorious
§gorgeously
honor, held in
splendor, in
ENDYMA ἔνδυμα
clothing (4)
garment (3)
raiment
ENDYNAMOŌ ἐνδυναμόω
strength, give (2)
strength, increase in (*pass.*)
strengthen
strong, be (*pass.*) (2)
strong, grow (*pass.*)
ENDYNŌ ἐνδύνω
way into, make one's
ENDYŌ ἐνδύω
arrayed (*perf. mid. part.*)
clothed (*mid. part.*)
clothed, be (*mid.*) (2)
§garment 2[a]
put on (*act. or mid.*) (21)
robed (*mid. part.*)
wear (*mid.*)
ENDYSIS ἔνδυσις
wearing
ENECHŌ ἐνέχω
grudge against, have a
press
submit (*pass.*)
ENEDRA ἐνέδρα
ambush (2)
ENEDREUŌ ἐνεδρεύω
ambush, lie in
wait, lie in
ENEILEŌ ἐνειλέω
wrap
ENEIMI ἔνειμι
be within
ENENĒKONTA ἐνενήκοντα
[*ninety*]
§ninety-nine (4)

ENEOS ἐνεός
speechless
ENERGEIA ἐνέργεια
activity
energy
power
§strong
§work
working (3)
ENERGĒMA ἐνέργημα
working (*pl.*) (2)
ENERGEŌ ἐνεργέω
accomplish (2)
(effective, make †)
effects, in its (*pass. part.*)
§experience
inspire (3)
work (5)
work in, be at (8)
work within, be at
ENERGĒS ἐνεργής
active
effective work, for
§promote
ENEULOGEŌ ἐνευλογέω
bless
bless in
ENI ἔνι
be, there (*there is*) (6)
ENIAUTOS ἐνιαυτός
year (11)
§yearly
IDIOMATICALLY
year *a, b*
ENISCHYŌ ἐνισχύω
strengthen +
ENISTĒMI ἐνίστημι
come (*act. or mid.*) (2)
(impending [*perf. part.*]†)
present (*perf. part.*) (5)
ENNEA ἐννέα
nine
§ninety-nine (4)
ENNEUŌ ἐννεύω
make signs
ENNOIA ἔννοια
intention
thought
ENNOMOS ἔννομος
law, under the
regular
ENNYCHOS ἔννυχος
§day, before
ENOCHLEŌ ἐνοχλέω
trouble
trouble, cause
ENOCHOS ἔνοχος
§deserve (2)
guilty (3)
liable (4)
subject to (+*gen.*)
ENOIKEŌ ἐνοικέω
dwell in (3)
dwell within (2)
live in
ENŌPION ἐνώπιον
before (53)
presence, in s.'s (3)
presence of, in the (14)
sight, in s.'s (4)
sight of, in the (13)
to
NOT TRANSLATED
Lk **4**.7
Acts **6**.5
Rom **14**.26
1 Jn **3**.22
Rev **15**.4; **16**.19
ENORKIZŌ ἐνορκίζω
adjure
ENŌTIZOMAI ἐνωτίζομαι
ear to, give
ENTALMA ἔνταλμα
precept (3)
ENTAPHIASMOS ἐνταφιασμός
burial
burying
ENTAPHIAZŌ ἐνταφιάζω
§burial
burial, prepare for
ENTELLŌ ἐντέλλω
charge, give (*mid.*) (2)
command (*mid.*) (11)
commandment, give (*mid.*)
directions, give (*mid.*)
ENTEUTHEN ἐντεῦθεν
away
from here (2)
from the world
hence
§here
IDIOMATICALLY
side, on either *a* (1; Gr. 2), *b*
NOT TRANSLATED
Jas **4**.1
ENTEUXIS ἔντευξις
intercession
prayer
ENTHADE ἐνθάδε
here (7)
there
ENTHEN ἔνθεν
from here (2)
ENTHYMEOMAI ἐνθυμέομαι
consider
think
ENTHYMĒSIS ἐνθύμησις
imagination
thought (3)
ENTIMOS ἔντιμος
dear
eminent
§honor
precious (2)
(valuable †)
ENTOLĒ ἐντολή
charge
command (7)
commandment (57)+
instruction
order
requirement
ENTOPIOS ἐντόπιος
people there (*subst. pl.*)
ENTOS ἐντός
inside
midst of, in the
(within †)
ENTREPHŌ ἐντρέφω
nourish
ENTREPŌ ἐντρέπω
ashamed, be (*pass.*)
ashamed, make
regard (*pass.*) (2)
respect (*pass.*) (4)
shame, put to
ENTROMOS ἔντρομος
§tremble (2)
trembling
ENTROPĒ ἐντροπή
shame (2)
ENTRYPHAŌ ἐντρυφάω
revel
ENTYGCHANŌ ἐντυγχάνω
intercede (2)
intercession, make
petition
plead
ENTYLISSŌ ἐντυλίσσω
roll up
wrap (2)
ENTYPOŌ ἐντυπόω
carve
ENYBRIZŌ ἐνυβρίζω
outrage
ENYPNIAZOMAI ἐνυπνιάζομαι
dream
dreaming, in one's (*part.*)
ENYPNION ἐνύπνιον
dream
EOIKA ἔοικα
like, be (2)
EPAGGELIA ἐπαγγελία
promise (45)
§promised (2)
promised, what is (4)
NOT TRANSLATED
1 Jn **2**.25
EPAGGELLOMAI ἐπαγγέλλομαι
profess (2)
promise (11)
promise, make a (2)
EPAGGELMA ἐπάγγελμα
promise (2)
EPAGŌ ἐπάγω
bring upon (3)
EPAGŌNIZOMAI ἐπαγωνίζομαι
contend
EPAINEŌ ἐπαινέω
commend (4)
praise
NOT TRANSLATED
1 Cor **11**.22
EPAINOS ἔπαινος
approval
commendation
§famous
praise (8)
EPAIRŌ ἐπαίρω
airs, put on (*pass.*)
hoist
lift (2)
lift up (12)
§obstacle (*pass. part.*)
raise (2)
EPAISCHYNOMAI ἐπαισχύνομαι
ashamed, be (6)
ashamed of, be (5)
EPAITEŌ ἐπαιτέω
beg (2)
EPAKOLOUTHEŌ ἐπακολουθέω
appear later
attend
devote oneself
follow in

EPAKOUŌ ἐπακούω
listen to

EPAKROAOMAI ἐπακροάομαι
listen to

EPAN ἐπάν
when (3)

EPANAGKES ἐπάναγκες
necessary things (*subst. neut. pl.*)

EPANAGŌ ἐπανάγω
put out (2)
return

EPANAMIMNĒSKŌ ἐπαναμιμνήσκω
§reminder

EPANAPAUOMAI ἐπαναπαύομαι
rely upon
rest upon

EPANERCHOMAI ἐπανέρχομαι
come back
return

EPANISTĒMI ἐπανίστημι
rise against (*mid.*) (2)

EPANŌ ἐπάνω
above (2)
more than (2)
on (3)
over (7)
§rider 1[b]
thereon
upon (3)

EPANORTHŌSIS ἐπανόρθωσις
correction

EPAPHRIZŌ ἐπαφρίζω
cast up the foam of

EPARATOS ἐπάρατος
accursed

EPARCHEIA ἐπαρχεία
province (2)

EPARCHEIOS ἐπάρχειος
§(province)

EPARKEŌ ἐπαρκέω
assist (2)
relieve

EPATHROIZŌ ἐπαθροίζω
increase (*pass.*)

EPAULIS ἔπαυλις
habitation

EPAURION ἐπαύριον
§following day, on the (2)
§morrow, on the (5)
§next day (8)
§next day, on the (2)

EPECHŌ ἐπέχω
attention upon, fix one's
heed, take
hold fast
mark
stay

EPEGEIRŌ ἐπεγείρω
stir up (2)

EPEI ἐπεί
because (3)
for then
otherwise (6)
since (16)

EPEIDĒ ἐπειδή
after
as
because
for (3)
since (3)
when

EPEIDĒPER ἐπειδήπερ
inasmuch as

EPEIDON ἐπεῖδον
look on
look upon

EPEIMI ἔπειμι
following (*part.*) (2)
§following day, on the
§following day, the (2)

EPEIPER ἐπείπερ
since

EPEISAGŌGĒ ἐπεισαγωγή
§introduce

EPEISERCHOMAI ἐπεισέρχομαι
come upon

EPEITA ἔπειτα
then (15)

EPEKEINA ἐπέκεινα
beyond

EPEKTEINOMAI ἐπεκτείνομαι
strain forward

EPENDYOMAI ἐπενδύομαι
clothed, be further
put on

EPENDYTĒS ἐπενδύτης
clothes

ĒPER ἤπερ
than

EPERCHOMAI ἐπέρχομαι
assail
come
come on
come there
come upon (5)

EPĒREAZŌ ἐπηρεάζω
abuse
revile

EPERŌTAŌ ἐπερωτάω
ask (44)
ask a question (10)
question (2)

EPERŌTĒMA ἐπερώτημα
appeal

EPHALLOMAI ἐφάλλομαι
leap

EPHAPAX ἐφάπαξ
once for all (4)
one time, at

EPHĒMERIA ἐφημερία
division (2)

EPHĒMEROS ἐφήμερος
daily

EPHEURETĒS ἐφευρετής
inventor

EPHIKNEOMAI ἐφικνέομαι
reach (2)

EPHISTĒMI ἐφίστημι
appear (2)
arrive
attack
come
come up (2)
come upon (5)
go
stand (2)
stand by (4)
urgent, be
IDIOMATICALLY
begin *a*

EPHPHATHA ἐφφαθά
ephphatha

EPI ἐπί
about (+*dat.* 3; +*acc.* 2; +*gen.* 2)
above (+*gen.*; +*dat.*)
account of, on (+*acc.*)
after (+*acc.*; +*dat.*)
against (+*dat.* 5; +*acc.* 37)
among (+*acc.*)
at (+*gen.* 6; +*dat.* 36; +*acc.* 12)
because of (+*dat.* 2)
before (+*gen.* 13; +*acc.* 11)+
beside (+*dat.*; +*acc.*)
besides (+*dat.*)
by (+*gen.* 4; +*dat.* 6)
charge of, in (+*gen.*)
close to (+*acc.* 2)
concerning (+*dat.*)
for (+*dat.* 12; +*acc.* 24)†
from (+*dat.* 2)
in (+*gen.* 17; +*dat.* 39; +*acc.* 12)+
into (+*acc.* 5)
of (+*dat.* 3; +*acc.* 4)
on (+*gen.* 113; +*dat.* 19; +*acc.* 122)+
over (+*gen.* 12; +*dat.* 16; +*acc.* 30)+
§*then* (+*dat.*) 9[a]
throughout (+*acc.*)
to (+*gen.* 4; +*dat.* 3; +*acc.* 67)+†
toward (+*acc.* 5)
under (+*gen.*; +*dat.*)
upon (+*gen.* 21; +*dat.* 8; +*acc.* 80)+
when (+*dat.*; +*gen.*)
with (+*dat.* 8; +*acc.* 3)
IDIOMATICALLY
OR NOT TRANSLATED
+*genitive:*
Mt **21**.7; **28**.14
Mk **12**.14, 32; **14**.51
Lk **3**.2; **4**.25; **20**.21, 37; **22**.59
Acts **4**.27; **9**.33; **10**.34; **11**.28; **12**.20
1 Cor **6**.1
2 Cor **10**.7
Col **3**.5
Rev **7**.1; **9**.17; **10**.5; **13**.14; **21**.16
+*dative:*
Lk **24**.25
Acts **7**.33; **21**.24
Rom **5**.12, 14
2 Cor **5**.4; **9**.6[2]
Phil **3**.9, 12; **4**.10
2 Tim **2**.14
+*accusative:*
Mt **9**.15; **13**.48; **22**.34; **25**.40, 45; **26**.50†
Lk **1**.48; **4**.36; **10**.35; **11**.17; **15**.20; **17**.35; **23**.48
Jn **1**.33; **9**.6; **18**.4
Acts **1**.15; **2**.18, 44; **4**.17, 26; **5**.18; **10**.10, 16; **11**.10; **15**.17[2]; **20**.9, 11, 37; **24**.4; **28**.6
Rom **4**.5; **7**.1; **11**.13
1 Cor **2**.9; **7**.5, 39; **11**.20; **14**.23
Gal **4**.1
2 Th **2**.1
2 Tim **2**.14, 16; **3**.9
Jas **2**.7
2 Pet **1**.13
Rev **6**.2, 4, 5; **7**.16; **13**.16; **18**.17; **19**.18; **22**.5

EPIBAINŌ ἐπιβαίνω
come into
embark in
go aboard
go on
mount
set foot

EPIBALLŌ ἐπιβάλλω
§arrest (2)
beat
break down
fall to
lay on (7)
lay upon (2)
put on
put to
put upon
throw on

EPIBAREŌ ἐπιβαρέω
burden (2)
severely, put it too

EPIBIBAZŌ ἐπιβιβάζω
set on
set upon
IDIOMATICALLY
ride *a*

EPIBLĒMA ἐπίβλημα
piece (4)

EPIBLEPŌ ἐπιβλέπω
attention to, pay
look upon
regard

EPIBOULĒ ἐπιβουλή
plot (4)

EPICHEIREŌ ἐπιχειρέω
seek
undertake (2)

EPICHEŌ ἐπιχέω
pour on

EPICHORĒGEŌ ἐπιχορηγέω
nourish
provide
supplement
supply (2)

EPICHORĒGIA ἐπιχορηγία
help
supplied, with which it is (*gen.*)

EPICHRIŌ ἐπιχρίω
anoint (2)

EPIDECHOMAI ἐπιδέχομαι
acknowledge authority
welcome

EPIDEIKNYMI ἐπιδείκνυμι
point out
show (6)

EPIDĒMEŌ ἐπιδημέω
live
visitor (*subst. part.*)

EPIDIATASSOMAI ἐπιδιατάσσομαι
add to

EPIDIDŌMI ἐπιδίδωμι
deliver
give (7)+
give way

EPIDIORTHOŌ ἐπιδιορθόω
amend (*mid.*)

EPIDYŌ ἐπιδύω
go down

EPIEIKEIA ἐπιείκεια
gentleness
kindness

EPIEIKĒS ἐπιεικής
forbearance (*subst. neut.*)
gentle (4)

EPIGAMBREUŌ ἐπιγαμβρεύω
marry

EPIGEIOS ἐπίγειος
earth, on
earthly (4)
terrestrial (2)

EPIGINOMAI ἐπιγίνομαι
spring up

EPIGINŌSKŌ ἐπιγινώσκω
acknowledge
ascertain
find out
know (14)
known, well (*pass. part.*)
learn (4)
perceive (4)
realize (2)
recognition to, give
recognize (9)
understand (4)
understand fully (2)

EPIGNŌSIS ἐπίγνωσις
§enlightened
§know, come to
knowledge (17)
IDIOMATICALLY
acknowledge *a*

EPIGRAPHĒ ἐπιγραφή
inscription (5)

EPIGRAPHŌ ἐπιγράφω
inscribe
§inscription
§read (*pluperf. pass. periphr.*)
write on (2)

EPIKALEŌ ἐπικαλέω
appeal to (*mid.*) (6)
call (8)
call on (*mid.*) (4)
call upon (*mid.*) (5)
(called [*pass. part.*])
invoke
invoke as (*mid.*)
name was, whose other (*pass. part. attr.*) (2)
pray (*mid.*)
surname (2)

EPIKALYMMA ἐπικάλυμμα
pretext

EPIKALYPTŌ ἐπικαλύπτω
cover

EPIKATARATOS ἐπικατάρατος
cursed (2)

EPIKATHIZŌ ἐπικαθίζω
sit

EPIKEIMAI ἐπίκειμαι
imposed (*part.*)
laid upon, be
lie on (2)
lie upon
press upon
urgent, be

EPIKELLŌ ἐπικέλλω
run aground

EPIKOURIA ἐπικουρία
help

EPIKRINŌ ἐπικρίνω
sentence, give

EPILAMBANOMAI ἐπιλαμβάνομαι
arrest
catch (2)
concerned, be
seize (4)
take (6)
take hold of (4)
NOT TRANSLATED
Heb **2.16**

EPILANTHANOMAI ἐπιλανθάνομαι
forget (5)
neglect (2)
overlook

EPILEGŌ ἐπιλέγω
called (*pass. part.*)
choose (*mid.*)

EPILEICHŌ ἐπιλείχω
lick

EPILEIPŌ ἐπιλείπω
fail

EPILĒSMONĒ ἐπιλησμονή
forgets, that (*gen.*)

EPILOIPOS ἐπίλοιπος
§rest

EPILYŌ ἐπιλύω
explain
settle

EPILYSIS ἐπίλυσις
interpretation

EPIMARTYREŌ ἐπιμαρτυρέω
declare

EPIMELEIA ἐπιμέλεια
[*attention, care*]
§cared for, be

EPIMELEOMAI ἐπιμελέομαι
care for
care of, take (2)

EPIMELŌS ἐπιμελῶς
diligently

EPIMENŌ ἐπιμένω
continue (5)
hold to
persist
remain (3)+
spend
stay (5)

EPINEUŌ ἐπινεύω
decline (*neg.*)

EPINOIA ἐπίνοια
intent

EPIORKEŌ ἐπιορκέω
swear falsely

EPIORKOS ἐπίορκος
perjurer (*subst.*)

ĒPIOS ἤπιος
gentle
kindly

EPIOUSIOS ἐπιούσιος
daily (2)
(morrow, for the †)

EPIPHAINŌ ἐπιφαίνω
appear (*act. or aor. pass.*)
light, give

EPIPHANEIA ἐπιφάνεια
appearing (6)

EPIPHANĒS ἐπιφανής
manifest

EPIPHAUSKŌ ἐπιφαύσκω
light, give

EPIPHERŌ ἐπιφέρω
inflict
pronounce

EPIPHŌNEŌ ἐπιφωνέω
shout out (4)

EPIPHŌSKŌ ἐπιφώσκω
begin
dawn (*subst. part.*)

EPIPIPTŌ ἐπιπίπτω
bend over

§embrace (2)
fall on (5)
fall upon (2)
press upon

EPIPLĒSSŌ ἐπιπλήσσω
rebuke

EPIPOREUOMAI ἐπιπορεύομαι
come

EPIPOTHEŌ ἐπιποθέω
long (4)
long for (3)
yearn for
yearn over

EPIPOTHĒSIS ἐπιπόθησις
longing (2)

EPIPOTHĒTOS ἐπιπόθητος
longs for, whom one (*subst. appos.*)

EPIPOTHIA ἐπιποθία
[*longing, desire*]
§long

EPIRAPTŌ ἐπιράπτω
sew

EPIRIPTŌ ἐπιρίπτω
cast on
throw on

EPISCHYŌ ἐπισχύω
urgent, be

EPISĒMOS ἐπίσημος
note, man of (*subst.*)
notorious

EPISITISMOS ἐπισιτισμός
provisions

EPISKĒNOŌ ἐπισκηνόω
rest upon

EPISKEPTOMAI ἐπισκέπτομαι
care
dawn upon
pick out
visit (8)+†

EPISKEUAZOMAI ἐπισκευάζομαι
make ready

EPISKIAZŌ ἐπισκιάζω
fall on
overshadow (4)

EPISKOPĒ ἐπισκοπή
office
office of bishop
visitation (2)

EPISKOPEŌ ἐπισκοπέω
(oversight, exercise)
see to it

EPISKOPOS ἐπίσκοπος
bishop (3)
guardian
overseer †

EPISŌREUŌ ἐπισωρεύω
accumulate

EPISPAOMAI ἐπισπάομαι
remove the marks of circumcision

EPISPEIRŌ ἐπισπείρω
sow

EPISPHALĒS ἐπισφαλής
dangerous

EPISTAMAI ἐπίσταμαι
know (12)
realize
understand

EPISTASIS ἐπίστασις
pressure
§stir up

EPISTATĒS ἐπιστάτης
master (7)

EPISTELLŌ ἐπιστέλλω
send a letter
write (2)

EPISTĒMŌN ἐπιστήμων
understanding

EPISTĒRIZŌ ἐπιστηρίζω
strengthen (3)

EPISTOLĒ ἐπιστολή
letter (24)

EPISTOMIZŌ ἐπιστομίζω
silence

EPISTREPHŌ ἐπιστρέφω
bring back (2)
return (*act. or aor. pass.*) (6)
turn (*act. or aor. pass.*) (22)
turn about (*pass.*)
turn again (3)
turn back (2)

EPISTROPHĒ ἐπιστροφή
conversion

EPISYNAGŌ ἐπισυνάγω
gather (3)
gather together (5)

EPISYNAGŌGĒ ἐπισυναγωγή
assembling
§meet

EPISYNTRECHŌ ἐπισυντρέχω
running together, come

EPITAGĒ ἐπιταγή
authority
command (6)

EPITASSŌ ἐπιτάσσω
command (9)
orders, give

EPITĒDEIOS ἐπιτήδειος
needed

EPITELEŌ ἐπιτελέω
complete (4)
completion, bring to
end
erect
perfect, make
perform
require of

EPITHANATIOS ἐπιθανάτιος
sentenced to death

EPITHESIS ἐπίθεσις
§lay upon
laying on (3)

EPITHYMEŌ ἐπιθυμέω
covet (3)
desire (7)
long (3)
gladly, would (*imperf.+inf.*)
§lustfully
NOT TRANSLATED
1 Cor **10.6**

EPITHYMĒTĒS ἐπιθυμητής
§desire

EPITHYMIA ἐπιθυμία
covet, what it is to
covetousness
desire (11)
§earnestly
impulse
liking
§long for
lust (6)
passion (15)

EPITIMAŌ ἐπιτιμάω
charge (2)
charge, strictly
order (2)
rebuke (25)

EPITIMIA ἐπιτιμία
punishment

EPITITHĒMI ἐπιτίθημι
add to (2)
attack (*mid.*)
§beat 5
inflict
lay on (15)
lay upon (8)
put on (6)
put on board (*mid.*)
put upon
§surname (+*dat.*) (2)

EPITREPŌ ἐπιτρέπω
allow (3)
leave, give (5)
let (5)
§permission, have
permit (4)

EPITROPĒ ἐπιτροπή
commission

EPITROPOS ἐπίτροπος
guardian
steward (2)

EPITYGCHANŌ ἐπιτυγχάνω
obtain (4)
receive

EPIZĒTEŌ ἐπιζητέω
seek (13)

EPOIKODOMEŌ ἐποικοδομέω
build on (2)
build up
build up on
build upon (3)

EPONOMAZŌ ἐπονομάζω
call oneself (*pass.*)

EPOPTĒS ἐπόπτης
eyewitness

EPOPTEUŌ ἐποπτεύω
see (2)

EPOS ἔπος
[*word, speech*]
NOT TRANSLATED
Heb **7.9**

EPOURANIOS ἐπουράνιος
celestial (2)
heaven, in
heaven, of (3)
heavenly (13)

ERAUNAŌ ἐραυνάω
inquire
search (5)

ERCHOMAI ἔρχομαι
§accompany
alight
appear (2)
arrive (2)
§befall
brought in, be
come (548)+
come back (3)
come by
§enter (7)
§fall
§gather about
go (51)
go back
go on

§grow
next (*pres. part.*)
pass
§reach (3)
return (2)
serve
start
§visit (3)
§visit, make a

EREIDŌ ἐρείδω
stick

ERĒMIA ἐρημία
desert (3)
wilderness

ERĒMOŌ ἐρημόω
desolate (*perf. pass. part.*)
waste, lay (4)

ERĒMOS ἔρημος
§country
desert (*subst. fem.*) (2)
desolate (3)
lonely (8)
wilderness (*subst. fem.*) (34)

ĒREMOS ἤρεμος
quiet

ERĒMŌSIS ἐρήμωσις
desolating (*gen.*) (2)
desolation

ERETHIZŌ ἐρεθίζω
provoke
stir up

EREUGOMAI ἐρεύγομαι
utter

ERGASIA ἐργασία
business (2)
effort
gain (2)
§practice

ERGATĒS ἐργάτης
§evil-worker
laborer (11)
worker
workman (3)

ERGAZOMAI ἐργάζομαι
commit
do (9)
§employed, be
enforce
§evildoer 2[a]
labor
produce
service, render
trade
work (15)
work, do (5)
work for
work, perform
working for a living, refrain from (*neg.*)
IDIOMATICALLY
trade *a*

ERGON ἔργον
§act
conduct
deed (39)
§do (7)
doing (2)
effect
labor (2)
(occupation †)
§require
task
thing (2)
undertaking
§well-doing
work (105)+
workmanship
NOT TRANSLATED
Jn **10**.32
1 Cor **5**.2
2 Tim **4**.18
3 Jn .10

ERION ἔριον
wool (2)

ERIPHION ἐρίφιον
goat

ERIPHOS ἔριφος
goat
kid

ERIS ἔρις
dissension (2)
quarreling (*sg. or pl.*) (3)
rivalry
strife (3)

ERITHEIA ἐριθεία
§factious
partisanship
selfish ambition (2)
selfishness (*sg. or pl.*) (3)

ERIZŌ ἐρίζω
wrangle

ERŌ ἐρῶ
add
ask
bid
call
cry
§make
quote
say (53)
say about
speak (20)
tell (12)
NOT TRANSLATED
Mt **25**.40; **26**.75
Lk **13**.25

ERŌTAŌ ἐρωτάω
ask (42)
beg (6)
beseech (4)
pray (8)
question (2)
NOT TRANSLATED
Jn **12**.21

ERYTHROS ἐρυθρός
red (2)

ESCHATOS ἔσχατος
end (2)
finally (*neut.*)
last (45)
latter
lowest (2)
uttermost parts (*subst.*)

ESCHATŌS ἐσχάτως
[*to the extreme, finally*]
IDIOMATICALLY
death *a* (=point *a*)

ESŌ ἔσω
in the house
inmost
inner (2)
inside (4)
IDIOMATICALLY
right into *a*

ESOPTRON ἔσοπτρον
mirror (2)

ESŌTEROS ἐσώτερος
inner (2)

ESŌTHEN ἔσωθεν
inside (3)
inwardly
within (5)
within, from (3)

ESTHĒS ἐσθής
apparel (3)
clothing (3)
robe (2)

ESTHIŌ ἐσθίω (ἔσθω)
abstain (*neg.*) (4)
consume
devour
§dine
eat (143)
food (*inf.*) (4)
food from, get one's
get
IDIOMATICALLY
earn *a*
NOT TRANSLATED
1 Cor **8**.8

ETHELOTHRĒSKIA ἐθελοθρησκία
rigor of devotion

ETHIZŌ ἐθίζω
custom (*subst. perf. pass. part.*)

ETHNARCHĒS ἐθνάρχης
governor

ETHNIKOS ἐθνικός
Gentile (3)
heathen

ETHNIKŌS ἐθνικῶς
Gentile, like a

ETHNOS ἔθνος
Gentile (89)
heathen (2)
nation (69)+
pagan (2)

ETHOS ἔθος
custom (11)
habit

ĒTHOS ἦθος
morals (*pl.*)

ETI ἔτι
§again
even (4)
further (2)
further, any (*interrog.*)
longer (8)
more (15)
more, any (+*neg.*) (3)
§moreover (2)
§never 6[c]
still (41)+
yes
yet (10)
IDIOMATICALLY
other *a*
NOT TRANSLATED
Lk **9**.42
Phil **1**.9

ĒTOI ἤτοι
[*either*]
§*either* 1[a]

ETOS ἔτος
year (48)
NOT TRANSLATED
Lk **2**.37

EU εὖ
§good
well (2)
well done (3)
EUAGGELION εὐαγγέλιον
gospel (76)+
EUAGGELISTĒS εὐαγγελιστής
evangelist (3)
EUAGGELIZŌ εὐαγγελίζω
announce
bring good news (*mid.*) (6)
good news comes to one (*pass.*)
preach (*mid.*) (15)
preach a gospel (*mid.*) (2)
preach good news (*mid.*) (7)
preach the good news (*mid.*) (3)
preach the gospel (*mid.*) (15)
§proclaim
receive the good news (*pass.*)
tell good news (*mid.*)
IDIOMATICALLY
good news *a*
NOT TRANSLATED
1 Cor **15**.2
EUARESTEŌ εὐαρεστέω
please (2)
§pleasing to s., be
EUARESTOS εὐάρεστος
acceptable (3)
§please (2)
pleasing (3)
§satisfaction, give
EUARESTŌS εὐαρέστως
§acceptable
EUCHARISTEŌ εὐχαριστέω
thank (9)+
thankful, be
thanks, give (28)
EUCHARISTIA εὐχαριστία
gratitude
thanks
thanksgiving (13)
EUCHARISTOS εὐχάριστος
thankful
EUCHĒ εὐχή
prayer
vow (2)
EUCHOMAI εὔχομαι
pray (4)
wish
§would (*aor. opt.*)
EUCHRĒSTOS εὔχρηστος
useful (3)
EUDIA εὐδία
fair weather
EUDOKEŌ εὐδοκέω
content, be
§good pleasure, it is one's
pleased, be (5)
pleased, be well (6)
§pleases one, it
pleasure, have (2)
pleasure in, take (2)
ready, be
willing, be
would (+*inf.*)
EUDOKIA εὐδοκία
desire
good pleasure
good will +
gracious will (2)
pleased, with whom one is (*gen.*)
purpose (2)
resolve
(well-pleasing [*pred.*]†)
EUERGESIA εὐεργεσία
good deed
service
EUERGETEŌ εὐεργετέω
good, do
EUERGETĒS εὐεργέτης
benefactor
EUGENĒS εὐγενής
noble
noble birth, of
§nobleman
EUKAIREŌ εὐκαιρέω
leisure, have
opportunity, have
spend one's time
EUKAIRIA εὐκαιρία
opportunity (2)
EUKAIROS εὔκαιρος
[*well-timed, suitable*]
§opportunity
§time of need, in
EUKAIRŌS εὐκαίρως
season, in
IDIOMATICALLY
opportunity *a*
EUKOPOS εὔκοπος
easier (*comp.*) (7)
EULABEIA εὐλάβεια
godly fear
reverence
EULABEOMAI εὐλαβέομαι
heed, take
EULABĒS εὐλαβής
devout (4)
EULOGEŌ εὐλογέω
bless (29)+
blessed (*pass. part.*) (10)+
blessings, invoke
IDIOMATICALLY
surely *c*
EULOGĒTOS εὐλογητός
blessed (8)
EULOGIA εὐλογία
blessing (11)
§bountifully (2)
flattering words
gift
gift, willing
EUMETADOTOS εὐμετάδοτος
liberal
EUNOEŌ εὐνοέω
friends, make
EUNOIA εὔνοια
good will
EUNOUCHIZŌ εὐνουχίζω
eunuch, make a (2)
EUNOUCHOS εὐνοῦχος
eunuch (8)
EUŌDIA εὐωδία
aroma
fragrant (*gen.*)
IDIOMATICALLY
fragrant *a*
EUODOŌ εὐοδόω
prosper (*pass.*)
succeed in (*pass.*)
well with one, go (*pass.*)
well with one, it is (*pass.*)
EUŌNYMOS εὐώνυμος
left (4)
§left hand (5)
EUPAREDROS εὐπάρεδρος
devotion (*subst.*)
EUPEITHĒS εὐπειθής
reason, open to
EUPERISTATOS εὐπερίστατος
clings so closely, which
EUPHĒMIA εὐφημία
good repute
EUPHĒMOS εὔφημος
gracious
EUPHOREŌ εὐφορέω
bring forth plentifully
EUPHRAINŌ εὐφραίνω
feast (*pass.*)
glad, be (*pass.*)
glad, make
merry, be (*pass.*)
merry, make (*pass.*) (5)
rejoice (*pass.*) (5)
EUPHROSYNĒ εὐφροσύνη
gladness (2)
EUPOIIA εὐποιΐα
§good, to do
EUPOREŌ εὐπορέω
[*prosper*]
IDIOMATICALLY
ability *a*
EUPORIA εὐπορία
wealth
EUPREPEIA εὐπρέπεια
beauty
EUPROSDEKTOS εὐπρόσδεκτος
acceptable (5)
EUPROSŌPEŌ εὐπροσωπέω
good showing, make a
EUPSYCHEŌ εὐψυχέω
cheered, be
EURAKYLŌN εὐρακύλων
northeaster
EURYCHŌROS εὐρύχωρος
easy
EUSCHĒMŌN εὐσχήμων
good order (*subst. neut.*)
high standing, of (2)
presentable, more
respected
EUSCHĒMONŌS εὐσχημόνως
becomingly
decently
IDIOMATICALLY
respect *a*
EUSCHĒMOSYNĒ εὐσχημοσύνη
modesty
EUSEBEIA εὐσέβεια
godliness (11)
§godly
piety
religion (2)
EUSEBEŌ εὐσεβέω
religious duty (*inf.*)
worship
EUSEBĒS εὐσεβής
devout (2)
godly
EUSEBŌS εὐσεβῶς
§godly (2)

EUSĒMOS εὔσημος
intelligible
EUSPLAGCHNOS εὔσπλαγχνος
§tender heart, have a
tenderhearted
EUTHEŌS εὐθέως
immediately (17)
instantly
once, at (12)
soon
NOT TRANSLATED
Gal **1**.16
EUTHETOS εὔθετος
fit (2)
useful
EUTHYDROMEŌ εὐθυδρομέω
direct voyage, make a
straight course, by a (*part.*)
EUTHYMEŌ εὐθυμέω
cheerful, be
heart, take (2)
EUTHYMOS εὔθυμος
encouraged
EUTHYMŌS εὐθύμως
cheerfully
EUTHYNŌ εὐθύνω
pilot (*subst. part.*)
straight, make
EUTHYS I εὐθύς
right (2)
straight (6)
EUTHYS II εὐθύς
immediately (44)
once, at (7)
IDIOMATICALLY
as soon as *b*
EUTHYTĒS εὐθύτης
righteous (*gen.*)
EUTONŌS εὐτόνως
powerfully
vehemently
EUTRAPELIA εὐτραπελία
levity
EXAGGELLŌ ἐξαγγέλλω
declare
(report)
EXAGŌ ἐξάγω
bring out (2)
lead out (8)
take out (2)
EXAGORAZŌ ἐξαγοράζω
most of, make the (*mid.*) (2)
redeem (2)
EXAIPHNĒS ἐξαίφνης
suddenly (5)
EXAIREŌ ἐξαιρέω
deliver (*mid.*) (3)
pluck out (2)
rescue (*mid.*) (3)
EXAIRŌ ἐξαίρω
drive out
EXAITEŌ ἐξαιτέω
demand to have (*mid.*)
EXAKOLOUTHEŌ ἐξακολουθέω
follow (3)
EXALEIPHŌ ἐξαλείφω
blot out (2)
cancel
wipe away (2)
EXALLOMAI ἐξάλλομαι
leap up

EXANASTASIS ἐξανάστασις
resurrection
EXANATELLŌ ἐξανατέλλω
spring up (2)
EXANISTĒMI ἐξανίστημι
raise up (2)
rise up
EXAPATAŌ ἐξαπατάω
deceive (6)
EXAPINA ἐξάπινα
suddenly
EXAPOREŌ ἐξαπορέω
despair (*pass.*)
despair, be driven to (*pass.*)
EXAPOSTELLŌ ἐξαποστέλλω
send (5)
send away (4)
send forth (2)
send off (2)
(send out)
EXARTIZŌ ἐξαρτίζω
§end
equip
EXASTRAPTŌ ἐξαστράπτω
dazzling (*part.*)
EXAUTĒS ἐξαυτῆς
just
moment, at that very
once, at (4)
EXĒCHEŌ ἐξηχέω
sound forth (*pass.*)
EXEGEIRŌ ἐξεγείρω
raise up (2)
EXĒGEOMAI ἐξηγέομαι
known, make
relate (4)
tell
EXEIMI ἔξειμι
depart (2)
go out
make
EXELKŌ ἐξέλκω
lure
EXERAMA ἐξέραμα
vomit
EXERAUNAŌ ἐξεραυνάω
inquire
EXERCHOMAI ἐξέρχομαι
§accompany
come (11)
come forth
come forward
come from (3)
come out (26)+
come out from (2)
come out of (20)
depart (12)
depart from (4)
§descend
driven out, be
escape from
flow from
get out (2)
get out of (2)
go (11)
go ashore (2)
go away (6)
go forth (6)
go off
go on (5)
go out (77)
issue from

leave (8)
originate
proceed from (2)
§return 11
set out (2)
spread (2)
spread abroad
step out
IDIOMATICALLY
get *a*
EXESTI ἔξεστι
§allow
lawful, be (27)
§may (3)+
EXETAZŌ ἐξετάζω
ask
find out
search
EXISCHYŌ ἐξισχύω
power, have
EXISTĒMI ἐξίστημι (ἐξιστάνω, ἐξιστάω)
amaze (10)
amazed, be (*aor.* = *intrans.*) (3)
astound
beside oneself, be (2)
§overcome, be
EXŌ ἔξω
away (2)
away from
foreign
forth
out (11)
out of (2)
outer
outside (18)+
outsider (*subst.*) (3)
NOT TRANSLATED
Mt **10**.14; **21**.17, 39; **26**.75
Mk **8**.23; **11**.19; **12**.8; **14**.68
Lk **4**.29; **13**.28; **20**.15; **22**.62
Jn **6**.37; **9**.34, 35; **12**.31; **18**.29; **19**.4, 5
Acts **7**.58; **9**.40
EXOCHĒ ἐξοχή
§prominent
EXODOS ἔξοδος
departure (2)
exodus
EXOLETHREUŌ ἐξολεθρεύω
destroy
EXOMOLOGEŌ ἐξομολογέω
agree
confess (*mid.*) (5)†
praise (*mid.*)
praise, give (*mid.*)
thank (*mid.*) (2)
EXORKISTĒS ἐξορκιστής
exorcist
EXORKIZŌ ἐξορκίζω
adjure
EXORYSSŌ ἐξορύσσω
opening, make an
pluck out
EXŌTEROS ἐξώτερος
outer (3)
EXŌTHEN ἔξωθεν
out
outside (6)
outside, from
outsider (*subst.*)
outward (*attr.*)

outwardly (2)
without

EXŌTHEŌ ἐξωθέω
bring ashore
thrust out

EXOUDENEŌ ἐξουδενέω
contempt, treat with

EXOUSIA ἐξουσία
authority (57)
§authority, one who is in
§charge
control
disposal
dominion
jurisdiction (2)
liberty
power (26)
right (9)
rightful claim
§veil

EXOUSIAZŌ ἐξουσιάζω
authority over, one in (*subst. part.*)
enslave
rule (2)

EXOUTHENEŌ ἐξουθενέω
account, of no (*pass. part.*)
contempt, treat with
despise (6)
esteem least
reject
scorn

EXYPNIZŌ ἐξυπνίζω
awake out of sleep

EXYPNOS ἔξυπνος
[*awake*]
§wake

G

GAGGRAINA γάγγραινα
gangrene

GALA γάλα
milk (5)

GALĒNĒ γαλήνη
calm (3)

GAMEŌ γαμέω
marriage (*inf.*)
married (*part.*) (3)
marry (24)+

GAMISKŌ γαμίσκω
marriage, give in

GAMIZŌ γαμίζω
marriage, give in (5)
marriage, refrain from (*neg.*)
marry

GAMOS γάμος
marriage (5)
marriage feast (7)
wedding (3)

GAR γάρ
and (3)
§*as for*
because (8)+
but (3)
for (892)+
indeed (9)
now (2)
since (7)
then
though (3)
thus
why (6)
yet (2)
IDIOMATICALLY
OR NOT TRANSLATED
Mt **5**.29, 30; **24**.37; **26**.12
Mk **5**.42; **16**.4
Lk **10**.42; **12**.58; **14**.14; **22**.71
Jn **5**.22; **7**.1, 41; **8**.42; **12**.8; **13**.29
Acts **4**.34; **8**.31; **16**.37; **19**.35; **27**.34
Rom **1**.16, 20, 26; **2**.12, 14, 25; **3**.2, 3; **4**.9, 13, 14; **5**.13, 17; **6**.10, 20, 21; **7**.5, 7, 8, 14, 15, 18; **8**.6, 7, 18, 22; **10**.2, 5, 11, 12; **11**.1, 25, 30; **13**.4, 9; **14**.7, 8, 15, 18; **15**.24, 27
1 Cor **2**.10; **4**.4; **6**.20; **7**.16; **8**.11; **9**.10, 16; **10**.1; **11**.5, 9, 22; **12**.8; **14**.8; **16**.7
2 Cor **2**.10; **8**.10, 13; **9**.1; **10**.12, 14; **11**.2, 5
Gal **1**.10; **2**.6; **4**.24
Eph **5**.5
Phil **2**.20, 21
2 Tim **2**.11
Phm .15
Heb **3**.16; **7**.18, 21(20), 27; **8**.5; **12**.3
1 Pet **3**.5; **4**.3
2 Pet **1**.11; **3**.5
Rev **9**.19

GASTĒR γαστήρ
glutton
womb
IDIOMATICALLY
child *a, b* (3), *c, d;* conceive *a*

GAZA γάζα
treasure

GAZOPHYLAKEION γαζοφυλακεῖον
treasury (5)

GE γέ
yea
yet (4)
IDIOMATICALLY
OR NOT TRANSLATED
Mt **6**.1; **7**.20; **9**.17; **17**.26
Lk **5**.36, 37; **10**.6; **13**.9; **14**.32; **19**.42; **24**.21
Jn **4**.2
Acts **8**.30; **17**.27
Rom **5**.6; **8**.32; **9**.20; **10**.18
1 Cor **4**.8; **6**.3; **9**.2
2 Cor **5**.3; **11**.16
Gal **3**.4
Eph **3**.2; **4**.21
Phil **3**.8
Col **1**.23

GĒ γῆ
§ashore
district (2)
earth (168)†
ground (18)+
land (45)
soil (10)
IDIOMATICALLY
earthly *a*
NOT TRANSLATED
Acts **10**.12; **11**.6
Rev **13**.14

GEENNA γέεννα
hell (12)

GEITŌN γείτων
neighbor (4)

GELAŌ γελάω
laugh (2)

GELŌS γέλως
laughter

GEMIZŌ γεμίζω
fill (8)+

GEMŌ γέμω
full (*part.*) (6)
full, be (5)

GENEA γενεά
generation (43)
(man †)

GENEALOGEŌ γενεαλογέω
genealogy, have a (*pass.*)

GENEALOGIA γενεαλογία
genealogy (2)

GENĒMA γένημα
fruit (3)
harvest (*pl.*)

GENESIA γενέσια
birthday (2)

GENESIS γένεσις
birth (2)†
genealogy
natural (*gen.*)
nature

GENETĒ γενετή
birth

GENNAŌ γεννάω
bear (2)
bear children
beget (3)+
birth to, give
born (*pass. part.*) (3)
born, be (*pass.*) (36)
breed
child (*subst. perf. pass. part.*)
child, be a (*perf. pass.*)
conceived, be (*pass.*)
delivered of, be
father, become s.'s (2)
father of, be the (39)
father of, become the (2)
parent (*subst. part.*)
IDIOMATICALLY
birth *a;* native *a*

GENNĒMA γέννημα
brood (*pl.*) (4)

GENNĒTOS γεννητός
born (2)

GENOS γένος
birth
different (*gen. pl.*)
family (3)
kind (2)+
kinds, various (*pl.*) (2)
§native (3)
offspring (3)
people (3)
race (2)

GEŌRGEŌ γεωργέω
cultivate

GEŌRGION γεώργιον
field

GEŌRGOS γεωργός
farmer (2)
tenant (15)
vinedresser
NOT TRANSLATED
Mk **12**.2

GĒRAS γῆρας
old age

GĒRASKŌ γηράσκω
old, be
old, grow

GERŌN γέρων
old (*pred.*)

GEROUSIA γερουσία
senate

GEUOMAI γεύομαι
eat (2)
taste (13)

GINOMAI γίνομαι
accomplished, be
§amazed, be 5
appear
arise (16)
arrive (3)
§associate with 2
be (184)+†
become (101)
befall (2)
begin
§behavior is, one's
belong (+*dat.*)
§betray 3
born (*part.*) (2)
born, be (2)
§bring (2)
§certainly not (2)
come (58)
come to (2)
come to pass (5)
continue
§dawn
§determine 2
§die 5 (2)
§dismal, look 1
§do (2)
§doing, be s.'s (2)
done (*part.*) (4)
done, be (27)
§draw
during (*gen. absol.*)
§enraged, be 2
§examine 2
§experience
§fall (2)
§far be it
fare
finished, be (*aor.*)
follow
§gain
granted, be
happen (18)+
§have (3)
§held, be
introduced, be
§join in imitating 1
live (2)
§lose saltness
made (*part.*) (2)
made, be (17)
§make (2)
§means, by no (*neg. opt.*) (10)
§murder 2
§murmur 2
§never (*neg. opt.*) 3[a]
§obey 3
occur (2)
§offense, give no 1
§participate 2
past, be (*perf.*)
performed (*part.*)
performed, be (3)
§proclaim
§produce
§promise 1[b]
§promote 1
prove (5)
prove to be
§rank (2)
§receive
§repaid, be 1
§reward 4
§run together 1
§secure 1
§set
§set aside 1
§share 10; 12[a] (2)
§speak
spent (*part.*)
§split, be
started (*part.*)
§supply
§(swell up 2 †)
take place (33)
§test, stand the 1[a]
§thunder 1[a]
§tremble 1 (2)
turn
§vanish 2
§wake 2
§weep 3[b]
work (wrought, be)
IDIOMATICALLY
break *a;* forbid, God *b;* grow *a;* have *b;* have to *a;* make *a;* marry *a;* secure *a;* use *b*
NOT TRANSLATED
Mt **7**.28; **8**.16; **9**.10; **11**.1; **13**.53; **18**.13; **19**.1; **26**.1
Mk **1**.9, 32; **2**.15, 23; **4**.4; **6**.2; **9**.7
Lk **1**.8, 23, 41, 59; **2**.1, 6, 15, 46; **3**.21; **5**.1, 17; **6**.1, 6, 12; **7**.11; **8**.1, 22; **9**.28, 33, 37, 51; **11**.14, 27; **14**.1; **16**.22; **17**.11, 14; **18**.35; **19**.15, 29; **20**.1; **24**.4, 15, 30, 51
Acts **2**.6; **4**.5; **5**.7; **9**.3, 23, 37, 43; **10**.4, 25; **11**.26; **14**.1; **16**.16; **19**.1, 34; **21**.1, 5; **22**.6, 17; **28**.17
Phil **3**.6
Heb **5**.12; **7**.26
Rev **3**.2; **16**.18

GINŌSKŌ γινώσκω
aware of (*aor. part.*) (4)
aware of, being (*aor. part.*)
comprehend
decide
feel
find out (3)
grasp
know (164)
§knowledge
learn (8)
perceive (8)
regard (2)
see
shown, be
sure, may be (3)
understand (17)
IDIOMATICALLY
have *c;* news *a;* sure, be *a*
NOT TRANSLATED
1 Cor **2**.8

GLEUKOS γλεῦκος
wine, new

GLŌSSA γλῶσσα
speech
tongue (49)

GLŌSSOKOMON γλωσσόκομον
money box (2)

GLYKYS γλυκύς
fresh (2)
sweet (2)

GNAPHEUS γναφεύς
fuller

GNĒSIOS γνήσιος
genuine
true (3)

GNĒSIŌS γνησίως
genuinely

GNŌMĒ γνώμη
advice
consent
§determine
judgment (2)
mind (2)
opinion
purpose

GNOPHOS γνόφος
darkness

GNŌRIZŌ γνωρίζω
know, want s. to
know, would have s.
known, make (16)
known, make oneself (*pass.*)
proclaim
remind, would
tell (3)
tell, can
understand, want s. to

GNŌSIS γνῶσις
§considerately
knowing
knowledge (27)

GNŌSTĒS γνώστης
[*one who knows*]
§familiar

GNŌSTOS γνωστός
acquaintance (*subst.*) (2)
§know
known (11)
notable

GOĒS γόης
impostor

GOGGYSMOS γογγυσμός
grumbling
§murmur
muttering
§ungrudgingly

GOGGYSTĒS γογγυστής
grumbler

GOGGYZŌ γογγύζω
grumble (2)
murmur (4)
mutter
NOT TRANSLATED
1 Cor **10**.10

GOMOS γόμος
cargo (3)

GONEUS γονεύς
parent (20)

GŌNIA γωνία
corner (9)

GONY γόνυ
knee (6)
§kneel down (6)

GONYPETEŌ γονυπετέω
kneel
kneel before (3)

GRAMMA γράμμα
bill (*pl.*) (2)
learning (*pl.*)

letter (3) + †
§literal
writing (2)
written code (4)
IDIOMATICALLY
learning *a*

GRAMMATEUS γραμματεύς
clerk, town
scribe (62) +

GRAŌDĒS γραώδης
silly

GRAPHĒ γραφή
scripture (49) +
writing

GRAPHŌ γράφω
describe (2)
inscribe (2)
§read (*pluperf. pass. periphr.*)
read, which (*perf. pass. part.*)
scripture (*subst. perf. pass. part.*)
write (181)
write down
writer (*subst. aor. part.*)
IDIOMATICALLY
letter *a*

GRAPTOS γραπτός
written

GRĒGOREŌ γρηγορέω
alert, be
awake (4)
awake, keep†
wake
watch (12) +
watchful, be (3)

GYMNASIA γυμνασία
training

GYMNAZŌ γυμνάζω
train (4)

GYMNITEUŌ γυμνιτεύω
ill-clad, be

GYMNOS γυμνός
bare
ill-clad
naked (10)
open
stripped
IDIOMATICALLY
body *a*

GYMNOTĒS γυμνότης
exposure
nakedness (2)

GYNAIKARION γυναικάριον
weak woman

GYNAIKEIOS γυναικεῖος
woman (*subst.*)

GYNĒ γυνή
bride
§marriage
widow
wife (83)
woman (129) +

H

HADĒS ᾅδης
death
Hades (9)

HADROTĒS ἁδρότης
liberal gift

HAGIASMOS ἁγιασμός
holiness (4)
sanctification (5)
sanctified by (+*gen.*)

HAGIAZŌ ἁγιάζω
consecrate (7)
hallow (2)
holy, be (*pass.*)
reverence
sacred, make (2)
sanctify (15)

HAGIOS ἅγιος
holiness, of
holy (166) +
saint (*subst.*) (62)
sanctuary (*subst. neut. sg. or pl.*) (6)

HAGIŌSYNĒ ἁγιωσύνη
holiness (3)

HAGIOTĒS ἁγιότης
holiness (2)

HAGNEIA ἁγνεία
purity (2)

HAGNISMOS ἁγνισμός
purification

HAGNIZŌ ἁγνίζω
purified (*perf. pass. part.*)
purify (6)

HAGNOS ἁγνός
chaste (2)
guiltless
pure (5)

HAGNŌS ἁγνῶς
sincerely

HAGNOTĒS ἁγνότης
pure devotion
purity

HAIMA αἷμα
blood (95) +
§hemorrhage

HAIMATEKCHYSIA αἱματεκχυσία
shedding of blood, the

HAIMORROEŌ αἱμορροέω
hemorrhage, suffer from a

HAIREŌ αἱρέω
choose (*mid.*) (3)

HAIRESIS αἵρεσις
faction
heresy
party (4)
sect (3)

HAIRETIKOS αἱρετικός
factious

HAIRETIZŌ αἱρετίζω
choose

HALAS ἅλας
salt (8)

HALIEUŌ ἁλιεύω
fish

HALIEUS ἁλιεύς
fisher (2)
fisherman (3)

HALIZŌ ἁλίζω
salt +
§saltness, restore

HALLĒLOUIA ἀλληλουϊά
hallelujah (4)

HALLOMAI ἅλλομαι
leap
spring up
well up

HALŌN ἅλων
threshing floor (2)

HALŌSIS ἅλωσις
§caught, to be

HALS ἅλς
(salt)

HALYKOS ἁλυκός
salt

HALYSIS ἅλυσις
chain (11)

HAMA ἅμα
along with (*prep.*)
besides that
same time, at the (3)
together (2)
IDIOMATICALLY
early in the morning *a*
NOT TRANSLATED
Col 4.3

HAMARTANŌ ἁμαρτάνω
§commit
offend
sin (39)
sinful, be
wrong, do

HAMARTĒMA ἁμάρτημα
sin (4)

HAMARTIA ἁμαρτία
guilt (2)
sin (168) +
sinful (*gen.*) (3)
IDIOMATICALLY
(sin offering *a* †)

HAMARTŌLOS ἁμαρτωλός
sinful (4)
sinner (*subst.*) (43)

HAPALOS ἁπαλός
tender (2)

HAPAS ἅπας
all (25)
everything (*neut. pl.*) (2)
none (*neg.*)
perfect (*attr.*)
whole (3)

HAPAX ἅπαξ
once (7)
once for all (4)
IDIOMATICALLY
again *b*; once more *a, b*

HAPHĒ ἁφή
joint (2)

HAPLŌS ἁπλῶς
generously

HAPLOTĒS ἁπλότης
generosity (2)
liberality (2)
sincere devotion
singleness (2)

HAPLOUS ἁπλοῦς
sound (2)

HAPTŌ ἅπτω
handle (*mid.*)
hold (*mid.*)
kindle
light (3)
touch (*mid.*) (33)

HARMA ἅρμα
chariot (4)

HARMOS ἁρμός
joint

HARMOZŌ ἁρμόζω
betroth (*mid.*)

HARPAGĒ ἁρπαγή
extortion (2)
plundering

HARPAGMOS ἁρπαγμός
grasped, a thing to be

HARPAX ἅρπαξ
extortioner (*subst.*)
ravenous
robber (*subst.*) (3)

HARPAZŌ ἁρπάζω
catch up (5)
plunder
snatch (4)
snatch away
take by force (3)

HEAUTOU ἑαυτοῦ (αὑτοῦ)
§aside
each other (2)
her (*fem.*) (2)
her own (*fem.*)
herself (*fem.*) (4)
him
himself (92)
his (15)
his own (20)†
§inwardly (2)
itself (10)
one another (17)+
oneself (2)
our
our own
ourselves (15)
own, its
§spring 1
their (11)
their own (13)
them (6)
themselves (34)+
they (2)
us
§venture 1
you (5)
your own (3)
yours (*gen.*)
yourselves (36)
IDIOMATICALLY
feel *a;* (go home *a*); he *a;* under, be *a*
NOT TRANSLATED
Mt **18**.31
Mk **6**.51
Lk **12**.1; **19**.12; **20**.20
Jn **11**.33, 38
Acts **5**.35
Rom **12**.16; **13**.2
2 Cor **10**.7; **13**.5
Heb **10**.25
Rev **6**.15; **10**.3

HEBDOMĒKONTA ἑβδομήκοντα
seventy (3)
§seventy-five
§seventy-six
§(seventy-two)

HEBDOMĒKONTAKIS
ἑβδομηκοντάκις
seventy times
§(seventy-seven †)

HEBDOMOS ἕβδομος
seventh (9)

HĒDEŌS ἡδέως
gladly (5)

HĒDONĒ ἡδονή
passion (2)
pleasure (3)

HEDRAIŌMA ἑδραίωμα
bulwark

HEDRAIOS ἑδραῖος
§firmly
steadfast (2)

HĒDYOSMON ἡδύοσμον
mint (2)

HĒGEMŌN ἡγεμών
governor (19)
ruler

HĒGEMONEUŌ ἡγεμονεύω
governor, be (2)

HĒGEMONIA ἡγεμονία
reign

HĒGEOMAI ἡγέομαι
consider (2)
count (9)
esteem
governor (*subst. part.*)
judge
leader (*subst. part.*) (4)
leading (*part.*)
look on
§profane 3
regard
ruler (*subst. part.*)
think (4)
IDIOMATICALLY: chief *a*

HEIS εἷς
a, an (13)
§alike
alone (3)
anything (*neut.*+*neg.*)
§each 2[a]
equal
first (*attr.*)
man, a
none (*neg.*)
§once
one (261)+
one fact (*neut.*)
one man (11)+
one point (*neut.*)
one thing (*neut.*) (4)
one thing I do (*neut.*)
single (9)
IDIOMATICALLY
agree *a;* each *b* (1; Gr. 2); first *a* (7); individually *a;* one *a, b, d;* one another *b* (1; Gr. 2)
NOT TRANSLATED
1 Cor **11**.5
Eph **4**.7, 16; **5**.33

HEKASTOS ἕκαστος
all (+*pl. vb.*)
any one (*subst.*)
each (32)
each kind of
each man (*subst.*) (4)
each of them (*subst.*)
each of us (*subst.*)
each of you (*subst.*)
each one (*subst.*) (12)
each person (*subst.*)
each woman (*subst. fem.*)
every (6)
every man (*subst.*) (4)
every one (*subst.*) (11)
he
IDIOMATICALLY
another *a;* one *a, b*
NOT TRANSLATED
Phil **2**.4

HEKASTOTE ἑκάστοτε
at any time

HEKATON ἑκατόν
hundred, a (13)+
hundredfold, a (4)

HEKATONTAETĒS ἑκατονταετής
hundred years old, a

HEKATONTAPLASIŌN
ἑκατονταπλασίων
hundredfold, a (*neut. pl.*) (3)

HEKATONTARCHĒS ἑκατοντάρχης
(ἑκατόνταρχος)
centurion (20)

HĒKŌ ἥκω
come (24)
come forth

HEKŌN ἑκών
will, of one's own (2)

HEKOUSIOS ἑκούσιος
free will (*subst.*)

HEKOUSIŌS ἑκουσίως
deliberately
willingly

HEKTOS ἕκτος
sixth (14)

HĒLIKIA ἡλικία
span of life (2)
stature (3)†
(years †)
IDIOMATICALLY
age *b* (2), *c*

HĒLIKOS ἡλίκος
how great
§how greatly
small

HĒLIOS ἥλιος
sun (29)+
§sundown, at
§sun's light
NOT TRANSLATED
Rev **16**.12

HELISSŌ ἑλίσσω
roll up (2)

HELKŌ ἕλκω (ἑλκύω)
drag (3)
draw (3)
haul (2)

HELKOŌ ἑλκόω
sores, be full of (*pass.*)

HELKOS ἕλκος
sore (3)

HĒLOS ἧλος
nail (2)

HĒMEIS ἡμεῖς
I (2)
me
my (2)
our (300)+
ourselves
us (358)+
we (181)
IDIOMATICALLY
OR NOT TRANSLATED
Acts **27**.2
1 Cor **10**.6
2 Cor **1**.14
Col **2**.14
2 Th **3**.9
Heb **12**.1, 9

HĒMERA ἡμέρα
§always 3[b]
court

§daily (9)
day (361)
daytime
§midday, at
§opportunity
§recently
time (*pl.*) (5)
year (2)
IDIOMATICALLY
age *a;* day, every *a* (1; Gr. 2); today *a*
NOT TRANSLATED
Lk **2**.43

HĒMETEROS ἡμέτερος
our (5)+
our own
ours (*subst.*)

HĒMIŌRON ἡμίωρον
half an hour

HĒMISYS ἥμισυς
half (5)

HĒMITHANĒS ἡμιθανής
half dead

HENDEKA ἕνδεκα
eleven (6)

HENDEKATOS ἑνδέκατος
eleventh (3)

HENEKA ἕνεκα (ἕνεκεν, εἵνεκεν)
account of, on (3)
account, on s.'s
§because
because of (2)
for
order that, in
§reason, for a (3)
sake, for s.'s (11)
sake of, for the (2)
§why

HĒNIKA ἡνίκα
when
§whenever

HENOTĒS ἑνότης
unity (2)

HEORTAZŌ ἑορτάζω
celebrate the festival

HEORTĒ ἑορτή
feast (23)
festival +
NOT TRANSLATED
Jn **7**.2

HEŌS ἕως
before (5)
even (2)
even to (4)
far as, as (6)
§fully 4
§hitherto (2)
§how long (7)
many as, as
§still 2 (3)
till (29)
to (28)+
to, down (2)
to, up
until (42)
§when
while (6)
IDIOMATICALLY
brim *a;* more *a;* right into *a*
NOT TRANSLATED
Mt **18**.22[2]
1 Cor **4**.13

HEPTA ἑπτά
seven (87)
§(seventy-seven †)
IDIOMATICALLY
seventh *a*

HEPTAKIS ἑπτάκις
seven times (4)

HEPTAKISCHILIOI ἑπτακισχίλιοι
seven thousand

HERMĒNEIA ἑρμηνεία
interpretation (2)

HERMĒNEUŌ ἑρμηνεύω
mean (*pass.*) (2)
translation, by (*pass. part.*)

HERPETON ἑρπετόν
reptile (4)

HESPERA ἑσπέρα
evening (3)

HĒSSŌN ἥσσων
less
worse

HĒSYCHAZŌ ἡσυχάζω
cease
live quietly
rest
silenced, be
silent, be

HĒSYCHIA ἡσυχία
§quiet, be
quietness
silence
§silent, keep

HĒSYCHIOS ἡσύχιος
gentle
peaceable

HETAIROS ἑταῖρος
friend (3)
playmate

HETERODIDASKALEŌ
ἑτεροδιδασκαλέω
teach a different doctrine
teach otherwise

HETEROGLŌSSOS ἑτερόγλωσσος
strange tongues, men of (*subst. pl.*)

HETEROS ἕτερος
altered
another (35)
brother (*subst.*)
different (3)
else (3)
else, some one (*subst. indef.*)
§except
foreigner (*subst.*)
he
neighbor, one's (*subst.*) (3)
next
§next day (2)
§one
other (38)+
some (3)
unnatural

HETERŌS ἑτέρως
§otherwise

HETEROZYGEŌ ἑτεροζυγέω
mismated (*part.*)

HETOIMASIA ἑτοιμασία
equipment

HETOIMAZŌ ἑτοιμάζω
arrayed (*perf. pass. part.*)
(hold)
prepare (29)
ready (*perf. pass. part.*)
ready, get
ready, hold
ready, make (7)

HETOIMOS ἕτοιμος
already done, work (*subst. neut. pl.*)
here
prepared
ready (14)

HETOIMŌS ἑτοίμως
§ready
§ready, be (2)

HĒTTAOMAI ἡττάομαι
less favored in, be
§overcome
overpowered, be

HĒTTĒMA ἥττημα
defeat
failure

HEURISKŌ εὑρίσκω
§be
come upon (3)
find (164)
(gain)
get
prove (*pass.*)
redound (*pass.*)
secure (*mid.*)
work on the same terms (*pass.*)
IDIOMATICALLY
charge *b*

HEX ἕξ
§forty-six
§seventy-six
six (10)
§(sixteen)
§sixty-six

HEXAKOSIOI ἑξακόσιοι
six hundred (2)

HEXĒKONTA ἑξήκοντα
§seven
sixty (5)+
§sixtyfold (2)
§sixty-six

HEXĒS ἑξῆς
§afterward, soon
next
§next day (2)+
§next day, on the

HEXIS ἕξις
practice

HIDRŌS ἱδρώς
(sweat)

HIERATEIA ἱερατεία
priesthood
priestly office

HIERATEUMA ἱεράτευμα
priesthood (2)

HIERATEUŌ ἱερατεύω
serve as priest

HIEREUS ἱερεύς
priest (31)

HIERON ἱερόν
temple (71)

HIEROPREPĒS ἱεροπρεπής
reverent

HIEROS ἱερός
sacred +
temple service (*subst. neut. pl.*)

HIEROSYLEŌ ἱεροσυλέω
rob temples

HIEROSYLOS ἱερόσυλος
sacrilegious (*pred.*)

HIERŌSYNĒ ἱερωσύνη
priesthood (3)

HIEROTHYTOS ἱερόθυτος
offered in sacrifice

HIEROURGEŌ ἱερουργέω
priestly service, in (*part.*+*acc.*)

HIKANOŌ ἱκανόω
competent, make
qualify

HIKANOS ἱκανός
able
competent
considerable
enough (2)
great (2)
large (4)
long (6)
many (7)
much
number, a (*subst.*)
number of, a
§satisfy
security (*subst. neut.*)
some
sufficient
unfit (*neg.*)
worthy (5)
IDIOMATICALLY
length *a*
NOT TRANSLATED
Mt **28**.12
Acts **20**.37

HIKANOTĒS ἱκανότης
competence

HIKETĒRIA ἱκετηρία
supplication

HILAROS ἱλαρός
cheerful

HILAROTĒS ἱλαρότης
cheerfulness

HILASKOMAI ἱλάσκομαι
expiation, make
merciful, be

HILASMOS ἱλασμός
expiation (2)

HILASTĒRION ἱλαστήριον
expiation
mercy seat

HILEŌS ἵλεως
merciful
IDIOMATICALLY
forbid, God *a*

HIMAS ἱμάς
thong (4)

HIMATION ἱμάτιον
cloak (*sg. or pl.*)
clothes (*pl.*) (3)+
clothing (2)
coat
garment (42)+
mantle (5)
robe (5)

HIMATISMOS ἱματισμός
apparel
§appareled, be
attire
clothing
raiment

HIMATIZŌ ἱματίζω
clothe (2)

HINA ἵνα
how (2)
keep from, to (*neg.*) (5)
lest (*neg.*) (20)
must (*as imper.*) (2)
nor (*neg.*)
or (*neg.*) (3)
order to, in (10)
order to prevent from, in (*neg.*)
otherwise (*neg.*)
prevent from, to (*neg.*)
rather than (*neg.*)
since his aim is
so, and
so that (102)
that (278)†
that, in order (20)
that, see (*as imper.*) (3)
when (2)
IDIOMATICALLY
would *c*
NOT TRANSLATED
Mk **9**.30
Jn **11**.37
Rom **7**.13
2 Cor **1**.17
Phil **1**.10; **2**.2
Col **4**.16
1 Th **4**.1
1 Jn **1**.9

as imperative:
Mt **20**.23; **26**.63
Mk **5**.12, 23; **10**.51; **12**.15; **14**.49
Lk **18**.41
Jn **1**.22; **12**.7
1 Cor **1**.31; **5**.2; **7**.29
Gal **2**.10
Eph **5**.33
Heb **13**.17

as infinitive:
Mt **1**.22; **2**.15; **4**.3; **8**.8; **10**.25; **12**.16, 17; **14**.15; **16**.20; **17**.27; **18**.6; **19**.16; **20**.31; **21**.4; **26**.16; **27**.20, 26, 32; **28**.10
Mk **3**.9, 12, 14[2]; **4**.21, 22[2]; **5**.10; **6**.8, 25, 36, 41; **7**.26, 32, 36; **8**.6, 22, 30; **9**.9, 18, 22; **10**.17, 35, 37, 48; **11**.16, 28; **12**.2, 13; **13**.34; **14**.12; **15**.11, 15, 20, 21
Lk **4**.3; **6**.34; **7**.6, 36; **8**.31, 32; **9**.12, 40; **10**.40; **16**.24, 27; **18**.39; **19**.4
Jn **1**.7, 8, 19, 27; **2**.25; **3**.17; **4**.8, 34, 47; **5**.7, 36, 40; **6**.7, 15, 28, 38; **7**.32; **8**.59; **10**.10, 31; **11**.11, 19, 31, 52, 55; **12**.9, 10, 20, 23, 47[2]; **13**.1, 2; **14**.16; **15**.17, 25; **16**.30; **17**.2, 4, 24; **18**.9, 32, 37; **19**.16, 24, 28
Acts **9**.21; **16**.30, 36; **17**.15; **19**.4; **22**.5, 24; **23**.24; **24**.4; **27**.42
Rom **5**.20; **11**.11
1 Cor **1**.27[2], 28; **7**.35; **9**.15, 25; **13**.3†‡; **14**.5, 12, 13; **16**.12[2], 16
2 Cor **1**.9; **2**.4[2], 5; **4**.7; **9**.4, 5; **12**.7
Phil **2**.30
1 Th **5**.4
2 Th **3**.9, 12
1 Tim **5**.21
2 Tim **4**.17
Tit **2**.12, 14; **3**.14
Phm .19
Heb **5**.1; **9**.25
Jas **4**.3
1 Jn **3**.5, 8; **5**.20
3 Jn .4
Rev **2**.21; **3**.9, 18; **6**.2, 11; **8**.3, 6; **9**.4, 5[2], 15; **12**.6, 15; **13**.12, 13, 15, 16; **16**.12; **19**.8, 15, 18; **21**.15, 23

HINATI ἱνατί
why (6)

HIPPEUS ἱππεύς
horseman (2)

HIPPIKOS ἱππικός
cavalry (*subst. neut.*)

HIPPOS ἵππος
horse (17)

HISTĒMI ἵστημι (ἱστάνω)
bystander (*subst. perf. part.*) (2)
cease (*2 aor.*)
come forward (*aor. pass.*)
confirm
establish (2)
established, be (*perf.*)
fix
hold s. against
pay
place (2)
present
put (3)
put forward
remain (*perf.*)
rest (*pass.*)
set (6)
set up
set up, be (*perf.*)
stand (108)+
stand fast (*2 aor.*)
stand firm (*perf.*)
stand still (2)
stand up (3)
stop (*2 aor., aor. pass.*) (4)
sustain
uphold (2)
IDIOMATICALLY
have to do with *a*
NOT TRANSLATED
Lk **5**.1

HISTOREŌ ἱστορέω
visit

HO ὁ
The definite article (the) *is not analyzed in this Concordance.*

HODE ὅδε
such and such (*attr.*)
thus (*neut. pl.*)
NOT TRANSLATED
Lk **10**.39
Rev **2**.1, 8, 12, 18; **8**.1, 7, 14

HŌDE ὧδε
here (53)+
hither (2)
this place
IDIOMATICALLY
this *a, b*
NOT TRANSLATED
Lk **14**.21
1 Cor **4**.2

HODĒGEŌ ὁδηγέω
guide (3)
lead (2)

HODĒGOS ὁδηγός
guide (5)

HODEUŌ ὁδεύω
journey

HODOIPOREŌ ὁδοιπορέω
journey, be on one's

HODOIPORIA ὁδοιπορία
journey (2)

HODOS ὁδός
§go
highway
journey (7)
path (8)
road (14)
§roadside (3)
street
toward (*acc. as prep.*)
way (62)
wayside
IDIOMATICALLY
among a; thoroughfare *a*

HOIOS οἷος
as (3) (Mk **9**.3; 1 Cor **15**.48[2])
such as (3)
what (5)
what kind of man
which
IDIOMATICALLY
as though *a*

HOIOSDĒPOTOUN οἱοσδηποτοῦν
(whatever)

HOLOKAUTŌMA ὁλοκαύτωμα
burnt offering (2)
whole burnt offering

HOLOKLĒRIA ὁλοκληρία
perfect health

HOLOKLĒROS ὁλόκληρος
complete
sound

HOLOS ὅλος
all (49)+
§all over
full
§throughout
§utter
whole (52)
§wholly
IDIOMATICALLY
bottom *c*

HOLŌS ὅλως
actually
all, at (3)

HOLOTELĒS ὁλοτελής
§wholly

HOMEIROMAI ὁμείρομαι
affectionately desirous, be

HOMICHLĒ ὁμίχλη
mist

HOMILEŌ ὁμιλέω
converse (2)
talk (2)

HOMILIA ὁμιλία
company (*pl.*)

HOMOIŌMA ὁμοίωμα
§like
likeness (2)
§resembling
IDIOMATICALLY
appearance *a;* like *b*

HOMOIOŌ ὁμοιόω
compare (9)
like, be (*pass.*) (3)
like, be made (*pass.*) (2)
likeness of, in the (*pass. part.*)

HOMOIOPATHĒS ὁμοιοπαθής
like nature with, of (2)

HOMOIOS ὅμοιος
as
like (43)
§likewise

HOMOIŌS ὁμοίως
like manner, in (3)
likewise (16)
same way, in the (2)
so (10)

HOMOIŌSIS ὁμοίωσις
likeness

HOMOIOTĒS ὁμοιότης
likeness
IDIOMATICALLY
as a

HOMOLOGEŌ ὁμολογέω
acknowledge (8)
admit
confess (12)
§confession 1[a]
declare
grant
profess
promise

HOMOLOGIA ὁμολογία
acknowledging
confession (5)

HOMOLOGOUMENŌS
ὁμολογουμένως
§confesses, one

HOMOPHRŌN ὁμόφρων
§unity of spirit, have

HOMŌS ὅμως
even (2)
§nevertheless 2

HOMOTECHNOS ὁμότεχνος
same trade, of the

HOMOTHYMADON ὁμοθυμαδόν
accord, to one
accord, with one (2)
body, in a
together (6)
§united

HOMOU ὁμοῦ
§both
together (3)

HOPLIZŌ ὁπλίζω
arm

HOPLON ὅπλον
armor (*pl.*)
instrument (2)
weapon (3)

HOPOIOS ὁποῖος
what (2)
what, like
what sort of
NOT TRANSLATED
Acts **26**.29

HOPŌS ὅπως
how (3)
order that, in
so that (13)
that (21)
NOT TRANSLATED
Mt **8**.17, 34; **9**.38; **13**.35
Mk **3**.6
Lk **7**.3; **10**.2; **11**.37
Acts **9**.24; **23**.15, 20, 23; **25**.3
Rom **9**.17
Gal **1**.4

HOPOU ὅπου
§*above*
here
there
where (65)+
whereas
wherever (10)
which, on (2)
while

HŌRA ὥρα
hour (92)+
§instantly (3)
moment (2)
time (2)
while (3)
IDIOMATICALLY
day *a;* short *a*
NOT TRANSLATED
Mk **6**.35; **11**.11

HŌRAIOS ὡραῖος
beautiful (4)

HORAMA ὅραμα
sight
vision (10)

HORAŌ ὁράω
appear (*pass.*) (22)+
heed, take (*imper.*) (3)
look
must (*imper.*) (2)
see (80)+
see to it (*imper.*) (3)
§vision
IDIOMATICALLY
look *a*

HORASIS ὅρασις
vision (2)
IDIOMATICALLY
appear *a;* look *b*

HORATOS ὁρατός
visible

HORION ὅριον
district (*pl.*)
neighborhood (*pl.*) (2)
region (*pl.*) (8)
territory (*pl.*)

HORIZŌ ὁρίζω
appoint
definite (*pass. part.*)
designate
determine (3)
ordain
set

HORKIZŌ ὁρκίζω
adjure (2)

HORKŌMOSIA ὁρκωμοσία
oath (4)

HORKOS ὅρκος
oath (9)
sworn, what one has (*pl.*)

HORMAŌ ὁρμάω
rush (5)

HORMĒ ὁρμή
attempt
will

HORMĒMA ὅρμημα
violence

HOROTHESIA ὁροθεσία
boundary

HOS ὅς
§*another* (10)
§any, if
§*any one* (2)+
§*any one, if* (7)
any one who (4)
§*as* (2)
§*because* (8)

§before 15[a]
§*case, in*
§*case, in one*
§*ever since* 1[a]
he (78)†
he that (2)
he who (20)
I
it (11)
nothing (+*neg.*)
one (11)
one man
one, the (3)
one who (3)
one who, the (3)
§*other*
she (2)
she who
§*since* (3)†
§*some* (12)
some who (2)
such
such as
that (85)
that which (5)†
§*then, and*
they (26)
this (25)
those which
those who (10)
§*thus* (2)
§*till* (9)
§*until* 1[a, b] (6); 3[a] (8); 5[a]
we
what (128)+
whatever (22)+
§*when* 8; 10 (19)
§*when once*
§whenever (2)
§*where* (7)
§(*whereby* †)
which (279)+†
§*while* (5)
who (308)+†
who, the man
whoever (49)
whose
§*why*
yours
IDIOMATICALLY
OR NOT TRANSLATED
Mt **2**.9; **7**.2[2]; **11**.16; **12**.36; **18**.19[2]; **21**.24, [44‡; **23**.37; **24**.38, 44, 50
Mk **4**.24; **15**.23
Lk **1**.26, 61; **2**.20; **5**.29; **6**.38; **7**.32, 45, 47; **8**.41, 47; **9**.43; **12**.3, 20, 24, 40, 46; **13**.7, 34; **17**.27; **23**.14, 41; **24**.13
Jn **6**.13; **7**.3, 31, 36; **16**.18
Acts **1**.11; **7**.28, 40; **8**.27[2]; **9**.36; **10**.21[2]; **11**.30; **13**.6, 41; **14**.9; **15**.11; **17**.23; **22**.24; **24**.18; **25**.11, 18; **26**.2, 10; **27**.25[2], 33, 44[2]
Rom **1**.6, 27; **2**.1, 6, 23; **3**.30; **4**.16, 18; **6**.10[2]; **7**.15[3], 19[3]; **8**.3; **9**.4, 5[2]; **12**.3; **16**.7
1 Cor **2**.16; **4**.17[2]; **10**.13; **12**.28; **15**.1, 9
2 Cor **1**.10, 17; **4**.4; **5**.4; **10**.13; **11**.4[3], 12; **12**.6, 13
Gal **1**.7; **2**.20; **5**.17, 21
Eph **1**.10; **3**.4, 7; **5**.18
Phil **4**.10
Col **1**.6, 9; **2**.18; **3**.25
2 Th **2**.9
1 Tim **1**.15, 19
2 Tim **1**.6, 11, 12; **3**.8
Tit **1**.13; **3**.5
Phm .21
Heb **2**.11, 13; **3**.13; **5**.7; **6**.17; **8**.3; **9**.9; **11**.29
1 Pet **2**.8[2]; **4**.4
2 Pet **3**.1
1 Jn **1**.5; **3**.17; **4**.16; **5**.15
Rev **5**.13; **18**.6; **20**.8; **21**.12

HŌS ὡς
about (19)+
according to
§*after* (2)
§*appears to be, what*
as (231)+
as if (3)
§as soon as
as though (7)
§*be*
by way of
effect, to the
§*for*
how (18)
§*however*
just as (5)
like (105)
§*looks like, what*
purporting to be
referring (2)
§*seem*
§seems to be, what (3)
since (2)†
something like
that (3)
though
when (52)
where
while (7)
IDIOMATICALLY
OR NOT TRANSLATED
Mt **21**.26
Mk **9**.21
Lk **9**.52
Acts **8**.32; **20**.24; **27**.30, [37‡
Rom **4**.17; **9**.29
1 Cor **7**.17[2]; **9**.26
2 Cor **5**.19, 20; **7**.15; **10**.2, 9; **11**.21; **13**.7
Phil **2**.8
1 Th **2**.4
Phm .9, 14
Heb **7**.9
1 Pet **4**.15
2 Pet **1**.3
Rev **2**.24; **4**.7

HOSAKIS ὁσάκις
as often as (3)

HŌSAN ὡσάν
[*as if, as it were*]
NOT TRANSLATED
2 Cor **10**.9

HŌSANNA ὡσαννά
hosanna (6)

HŌSAUTŌS ὡσαύτως
also
likewise (9)
same, the (4)
same way, in the
so (2)

HŌSEI ὡσεί
about (13)
as
as of
like (5)+
§seem 3

HOSIOS ὅσιος
holy (8)

HOSIŌS ὁσίως
§holy

HOSIOTĒS ὁσιότης
holiness (2)

HOSOS ὅσος
all (*pl.*) (2)
all that (*neut. pl.*) (5)
all who (*pl.*) (13)
as (6)
every one who (*pl.*)
how much (*neut. pl.*) (6)
§long as, as (4)
many as, as (*pl.*) (6)
more, the (*neut.*)
much as, as
same as, the
that (11)
those who (5)
what (*neut. pl.*) (6)
whatever (*neut. pl.*) (24)
§wherever
which
§while 1
who (6)
IDIOMATICALLY
during *a;* inasmuch as *a;* just as *a;* more, all the *a;* while *a* (1; Gr. 2)
NOT TRANSLATED
Mk **6**.30; **12**.44
Heb **7**.20

HŌSPER ὥσπερ
as (28)
even as
just as (4)
like (3)

HŌSPEREI ὡσπερεί
as

HŌSTE ὥστε
for
hence
likewise
so (11)
so as (3)
so that (39)
so then (2)
that (6)
therefore (13)
thus (2)
NOT TRANSLATED
Mt **10**.1; **15**.33; **27**.1
Gal **4**.16

HOSTIS ὅστις
any one, if (2)
every one who (2)
he who
she, and
§since
that (7)
that, and
they, and
they, for (2)
this (3)
this, and
those who
§till 2[c]
§until 3[c] (3)
what (*neut.*) (2)
whatever (*neut.*) (7)
whenever (*neut.*)
which (20)
§while 4[a]
who (55)
who, a man

whoever (8)
(why [*neut.*]†)
IDIOMATICALLY
as b
NOT TRANSLATED
Lk **9.30**
Jn **21.25**
Acts **5.16**; **9.35**; **12.10**; **16.16**; **17.10**; **21.4**; **23.14**, 21, 33; **24.1**; **28.18**
Rom **1.25**, 32; **2.15**; **9.4**; **16.7**
2 Cor **8.10**
Gal **4.24**; **5.19**
Eph **4.19**
Col **2.23**
2 Th **1.9**
Tit **1.11**
Heb **2.3**; **8.5**; **9.2**; **10.8**
Jas **4.14**

HOTAN ὅταν
§*after* (2)
long as, as
§until
when (110)
whenever (4)
IDIOMATICALLY
as soon as *a* (2), *c*
NOT TRANSLATED
Rev **10.7**

HOTE ὅτε
§*at* (2)
long as, as
when (95)
while (+*imperf.*) (2)
NOT TRANSLATED
Mk **8.20**

HOTHEN ὅθεν
consequently
from there
from which (2)
hence (3)
so that
therefore (3)
where (3)
wherefore

HOTI ὅτι
and
as
because (155)†
for (262)+
ground that, on the
how (13)
if
in that
since (9)
that (558)+†
§***that, as for the fact***
§***that, the fact*** (2)
IDIOMATICALLY
OR NOT TRANSLATED
Mt **2.23**; **3.9**; **4.6**; **5.20**; **6.26**, 29; **7.23**; **8.11**; **9.18**; **10.7**; **12.6**, 36; **13.11**, 17; **14.26**; **16.7**, 18, 28; **18.13**, 19; **19.8**, 9, 23, 28; **20.10**, 15; **21.3**, 16, 31, 43; **24.34**, 47; **25.24**; **26.21**, 34, 72, 74, 75; **27.43**, 47; **28.13**
Mk **1.15**, 37, 40; **2.12**, 17; **3.11**, 21, 22², 28; **4.21**; **5.23**, 28, 35; **6.4**, 14, 15², 18, 35, 49, 55; **7.6**, 20; **8.4**, 16, 24, 28²; **9.1**, 26, 31; **10.33**; **11.17**, 23; **12.6**, 7, 26, 29, 43; **13.6**, 30; **14.14**, 18, 25, 27, 30, 58², 69, 71, 72
Lk **1.25**, 61; **2.23**; **3.8**; **4.4**, 10, 11, 12, 21, 24, 41, 43; **5.26**, 36; **7.4**, 16², 43; **8.49**; **9.22**; **10.12**; **12.24**, 37, 44, 54, 55; **13.14**; **14.24**, 30; **15.2**, 7, 27; **17.10**; **18.8**, 29, 37; **19.7**, 9, 31, 34, 42; **20.5**; **21.3**, 32; **22.16**, 61; **23.5**; **24.34**, 46
Jn **1.20**, 32, 50; **3.11**, 28; **4.17**, 21, 35, 37, 39, 42, 52; **5.24**, 25; **6.14**, 42; **7.12**, 40; **8.33**, 34, 55; **9.8**, 9², 11, 17, 19, 23, 30, 41; **10.34**, 36, 41; **11.31**; **13.11**, 21, 33; **14.28**; **15.25**; **16.19**, 20; **17.24**; **18.9**; **19.21**; **20.15**, 18; **21.12**
Acts **2.13**; **3.10**, 22; **5.23**, 25; **6.11**; **9.20**, 27; **11.3**; **13.34**; **15.1**, 5; **16.36**; **17.6**; **18.13**; **19.21**; **23.5**, 20; **24.11**, 21; **25.8**; **26.31**; **28.25**
Rom **3.2**, 8, 10; **4.17**, 23; **8.36**; **9.6**, 12, 17; **11.25**; **14.11**
1 Cor **1.26**; **6.7**; **14.21**; **15.12**, 27, 50
2 Cor **1.13**, 18, 23; **5.19**; **6.16**; **11.10**, 21; **13.6**
Gal **1.20**, 23; **3.10**
2 Th **2.4**; **3.7**, 10
2 Tim **1.5**
Phm .19, 22
Heb **7.17**; **8.10**; **10.8**; **11.18**
Jas **1.13**
1 Pet **1.16**; **2.3**
1 Jn **1.6**, 8, 10; **2.4**; **4.20**; **5.8**(7)
2 Jn .4
3 Jn .12
Jude .18
Rev **2.6**, 14; **3.1**², 15, 17; **15.4**; **16.5**, 21; **18.7**, 10, 17, 19, 23; **19.2**
Also variant to: Mk **6.23**

HOU οὗ
there
where (20)
§wherever
which, to (2)

HOUTOS οὗτος
he (25)
§***here*** (2)
it (4)
one (5)
present
§***reason why, the*** (3)
same, the (3)
§***so*** (7)
such (4)
that (50)
§***then*** (3)
§***there***
§***thereby*** (2)
§***therefore*** (33)+
they (11)
this (1021)+
thus (*neut.*) (15)
§***what*** (3)
who
§***why***
§***why, that is*** (6)
§***why, this is*** (8)
IDIOMATICALLY
OR NOT TRANSLATED
Mt **5.19**; **10.22**; **13.38**; **18.4**; **21.42**; **24.13**; **25.46**; **26.12**, 13, 23; **27.58**
Mk **3.35**; **4.18**; **6.16**; **12.10**, 40, 44; **13.11**, 13; **14.4**, 9
Lk **1.32**; **2.36**; **6.3**; **7.12**, 44, 45, 46; **8.14**, 15, 41, 42; **9.24**, 48; **17.8**; **18.4**; **19.42**; **20.17**, 28, 47; **21.4**²; **23.7**, 22, 35, 48, 51; **24.21**
Jn **1.2**, 7. 41; **3.26**, 32; **4.47**; **5.14**; **6.46**, 71; **7.18**, 36; **8.26**; **9.9**; **11.37**; **12.16**; **13.7**; **15.5**; **16.18**; **17.11**; **18.21**; **21.23**
Acts **1.5**; **3.6**, 10; **7.19**, 36; **9.15**, 20, 22, 36; **10.6**, 32, 36, 42; **13.7**; **14.9**; **16.3**, 17; **17.24**; **18.25**, 26; **21.23**, 38; **24.8**; **25.11**, 25; **27.34**
Rom **2.3**, 14; **6.6**; **7.10**, 15², 16, 20; **8.9**, 14, 30³; **9.6**, 17; **11.7**, 31; **14.13**; **15.28**
1 Cor **5.3**; **6.13**; **7.12**, 13, 20, 26, 29; **8.3**; **11.17**; **12.15**, 16; **15.54**; **16.17**
2 Cor **2.1**, 3; **5.14**; **7.11**; **8.20**; **9.4**; **10.7**, 11; **12.14**; **13.10**
Gal **2.10**; **3.7**; **5.17**, 21
Phil **1.6**, 9; **3.7**; **4.9**
1 Tim **3.10**
2 Tim **1.12**, 15; **2.2**, 21
Phm .12
Heb **3.3**; **4.8**; **7.4**; **9.23**; **10.12**, 33²; **11.12**
Jas **1.23**, 25; **3.2**
1 Pet **1.11**; **2.7**, 19, 20
1 Jn **3.8**
2 Jn .9
3 Jn .5
Jude .7
Rev **1.19**; **9.12**; **11.6**; **17.14**, 16

HOUTŌS οὕτως (οὕτω)
as it is
as one is (2)
effect, to this
like this (4)
only
so (124)
so, even (2)
so, just (2)
§such (5)
§*that*
that, can it be (*interrog.*)
that how, is (*interrog.*)
then (2)
§this (2)
this is how (2)
thus (21)
way, in the
way, in this (4)
way, it is the
IDIOMATICALLY
another *b* (1; Gr. 2); match *a;* one *c*
NOT TRANSLATED
Mk **4.26**; **9.3**
Lk **24.24**
Jn **4.6**; **12.50**; **14.31**; **15.4**
Acts **1.11**; **24.14**; **27.25**
Rom **5.15**, 21; **6.4**; **10.6**
1 Cor **7.17**, 36; **9.26**²
2 Cor **1.7**; **8.6**; **9.5**
Eph **5.33**
1 Th **5.2**
Heb **5.3**
1 Pet **2.15**
1 Jn **2.6**
Rev **16.18**

HUIOS υἱός
child (2)
descendant
foal
§guest, wedding 1 (3)
§Israelite 1ª (4)
son (363)+
NOT TRANSLATED
Acts **5.21**; **10.36**

HUIOTHESIA υἱοθεσία
adoption as sons (2)
§son
sonship (2)
HYAKINTHINOS ὑακίνθινος
sapphire
HYAKINTHOS ὑάκινθος
jacinth
HYALINOS ὑάλινος
glass (3)
HYALOS ὕαλος
glass (2)
HYBRIS ὕβρις
injury (2)
insult
HYBRISTĒS ὑβριστής
insolent (*pred.*)
§insult
HYBRIZŌ ὑβρίζω
molest
reproach
treat shamefully (3)
HYDŌR ὕδωρ
water (75)+
waves
HYDRIA ὑδρία
jar (2)
water jar
HYDRŌPIKOS ὑδρωπικός
dropsy, who has
HYDROPOTEŌ ὑδροποτέω
drink water
HYETOS ὑετός
rain (5)
HYGIAINŌ ὑγιαίνω
health, be in
safe and sound (*part.*)
sound (*part.*) (7)
sound, be
well, be (2)
HYGIĒS ὑγιής
§heal (2)
healed (3)+
sound
well (3)
whole (2)
HYGROS ὑγρός
green
HYLĒ ὕλη
forest
HYMEIS ὑμεῖς
you (1396)+†
you yourselves
your (354)+
your own (5)
yours (12)
yours, of
yourselves (19)
IDIOMATICALLY
OR NOT TRANSLATED
Mt **6**.9; **7**.12; **13**.18; **16**.11; **23**.32, 38; **28**.5
Mk **6**.31; **13**.9, 23
Lk **9**.44; **12**.29, 36; **13**.35; **24**.49
Jn **5**.42
Acts **8**.24
Rom **1**.6, 12; **15**.15
1 Cor **1**.11, 30; **15**.2; **16**.19, 20
2 Cor **6**.13
Gal **4**.11; **5**.10
Eph **2**.1; **4**.22; **6**.5
Col **3**.8; **4**.16
1 Th **2**.12
2 Th **2**.2; **3**.13
Heb **12**.3
1 Pet **1**.18; **2**.12; **4**.1
2 Pet **3**.8
1 Jn **2**.12
HYMETEROS ὑμέτερος
your (5)
your own (*subst. neut.*)
yours (*pred. or subst.*) (2)
IDIOMATICALLY
you *b* (3)
HYMNEŌ ὑμνέω
praise
sing a hymn (3)
HYMNOS ὕμνος
hymn (2)
HYPAGŌ ὑπάγω
begone (*imper.*)
get (*imper.*) (2)
go (69)
go away (4)
go one's way (3)
HYPAKOĒ ὑπακοή
obedience (12)
§obedient (2)
§obey
HYPAKOUŌ ὑπακούω
answer
obedient, be (2)
obedient, become
obey (17)
HYPANDROS ὕπανδρος
married
HYPANTAŌ ὑπαντάω
meet (9)
meet, go to
HYPANTĒSIS ὑπάντησις
§meet (3)
HYPARCHŌ ὑπάρχω
be (39)
belong to
goods (*subst. neut. pl.*) (3)
§have (3)
live
means (*subst. neut. pl.*)
possess (+*dat.*) (2)
possession (*subst. neut.*) (4)
property (*subst. neut. pl.*) (2)
IDIOMATICALLY
give *a*
NOT TRANSLATED
Acts **3**.2; **7**.55
Gal **2**.14
HYPARXIS ὕπαρξις
goods (*pl.*)
possession
HYPECHŌ ὑπέχω
undergo
HYPEIKŌ ὑπείκω
submit
HYPĒKOOS ὑπήκοος
obedient (2)
§obey
HYPENANTIOS ὑπεναντίος
adversary (*subst.*)
NOT TRANSLATED
Col **2**.14
HYPER ὑπέρ
about (+*gen.* 5)
above (+*acc.* 4)
behalf of, on (+*gen.* 5)
behalf, on s.'s (+*gen.* 8)
better (*adv.*)
beyond (+*acc.* 2)
concerning (+*gen.* 2)
favor of, in (+*gen.*)
for (+*gen.* 85)+
in (+*gen.* 3)
more than (+*acc.* 5)
of (+*gen.* 3)
over (+*gen.*, +*acc.*)
sake, for s.'s (+*gen.* 5)
sake of, for the (+*gen.* 8)
than (*after comp.*+*acc.* 3)
IDIOMATICALLY
OR NOT TRANSLATED
+*genitive:*
Rom **15**.8
2 Cor **1**.11; **8**.23
Col **4**.12
+*accusative:*
Acts **26**.13
1 Cor **4**.6
2 Cor **1**.8
Eph **3**.20
HYPERAIROMAI ὑπεραίρομαι
elated, be too (2)
exalt oneself
HYPERAKMOS ὑπέρακμος
[*of strong passions*]
IDIOMATICALLY
passion *a* (=strong *a; cf.* B.3.a.1)
HYPERANŌ ὑπεράνω
above
above, far (2)
HYPERAUXANŌ ὑπεραυξάνω
grow abundantly
HYPERBAINŌ ὑπερβαίνω
transgress
HYPERBALLŌ ὑπερβάλλω
immeasurable (*part.*) (2)
surpass (3)
HYPERBALLONTŌS ὑπερβαλλόντως
§countless
HYPERBOLĒ ὑπερβολή
abundance
§beyond measure
§more excellent
§transcendent
§utterly
§violently
IDIOMATICALLY: comparison, beyond all *a* (1; Gr. 2)
HYPERECHŌ ὑπερέχω
better than (*part.*)
governing (*part.*)
pass
supreme (*part.*)
surpassing worth (*subst. part. neut.*)
HYPEREIDON ὑπερεῖδον
overlook
HYPEREKCHYNNŌ ὑπερεκχύννω
run over (*pass.*)
HYPEREKEINA ὑπερέκεινα
beyond
HYPEREKPERISSŌS ὑπερεκπερισσῶς
highly, very
HYPEREKPERISSOU ὑπερεκπερισσοῦ
abundantly, far more earnestly
HYPEREKTEINŌ ὑπερεκτείνω
overextend

HYPERENTYGCHANŌ ὑπερεντυγχάνω
intercede
HYPERĒPHANIA ὑπερηφανία
pride
HYPERĒPHANOS ὑπερήφανος
arrogant
haughty
proud (3)
HYPĒRETEŌ ὑπηρετέω
attend to needs
minister
serve
HYPĒRETĒS ὑπηρέτης
§assist
attendant
guard (4)
minister
officer (10)
servant (2)
§serve
HYPERLIAN ὑπερλίαν
superlative (*attr.*) (2)
HYPERNIKAŌ ὑπερνικάω
conqueror, be more than
HYPEROCHĒ ὑπεροχή
high position
§lofty
HYPEROGKOS ὑπέρογκος
boast, loud (*subst. neut.*)
IDIOMATICALLY
loud-mouthed *a*
HYPERŌON ὑπερῷον
upper chamber
upper room (3)
HYPERPERISSEUŌ ὑπερπερισσεύω
abound all the more
§overjoyed, be 1
HYPERPERISSŌS ὑπερπερισσῶς
beyond measure
HYPERPHRONEŌ ὑπερφρονέω
think more highly of oneself
HYPERPLEONAZŌ ὑπερπλεονάζω
overflow
HYPERYPSOŌ ὑπερυψόω
highly exalt
HYPHAINŌ ὑφαίνω
(weave)
HYPHANTOS ὑφαντός
woven
HYPNOS ὕπνος
sleep (6)
HYPO ὑπό
at (+*acc.*)
at s.'s hands (+*gen.*)
at the hands of (+*gen.*)
by (+*gen.* 140)
from (+*gen.* 6)
in (+*acc.* 2)
of (+*gen.* 2)
to (+*acc.* 2)
under (+*gen.*; +*acc.* 43)
with (+*gen.*)
IDIOMATICALLY
OR NOT TRANSLATED
+*genitive:*
Mt **1**.22; **2**.15
Mk **5**.4
Lk **2**.18
Acts **17**.19; **22**.30; **26**.2; **27**.11
Rom **3**.21
2 Cor **1**.16; **2**.11; **8**.19, 20
Eph **5**.12
Phil **3**.12
+*accusative:*
Lk **17**.24[2]
Jas **2**.3
HYPOBALLŌ ὑποβάλλω
secretly instigate
HYPOCHŌREŌ ὑποχωρέω
withdraw (2)
HYPODECHOMAI ὑποδέχομαι
receive (4)
HYPODEIGMA ὑπόδειγμα
copy (2)
example (3)
sort
HYPODEIKNYMI ὑποδείκνυμι
show (3)
warn (3)
HYPODĒMA ὑπόδημα
sandal (8)
shoe (2)
HYPODEŌ ὑποδέω
put on (*mid.*)
shoe (*mid.*)
wear (*mid.*)
HYPODIKOS ὑπόδικος
accountable
HYPOGRAMMOS ὑπογραμμός
example
HYPOKATŌ ὑποκάτω
on
under (10)
HYPOKRINOMAI ὑποκρίνομαι
pretend
HYPOKRISIS ὑπόκρισις
hypocrisy (3)
insincerity (2)
pretensions
HYPOKRITĒS ὑποκριτής
hypocrite (17)+
HYPOLAMBANŌ ὑπολαμβάνω
reply
support
suppose (2)
take
HYPOLEIMMA ὑπόλειμμα
remnant
HYPOLEIPŌ ὑπολείπω
left, be (*pass.*)
HYPOLĒNION ὑπολήνιον
pit
HYPOLIMPANŌ ὑπολιμπάνω
leave
HYPOMENŌ ὑπομένω
endure (11)
patient, be
patiently, take s. (2)
remain
stay behind
steadfast, be
HYPOMIMNĒSKŌ ὑπομιμνήσκω
bring to remembrance
bring up
remember (*pass.*)
remind (4)
HYPOMNĒSIS ὑπόμνησις
§reminded, be
reminder (2)
HYPOMONĒ ὑπομονή
endurance (8)
endurance, patient (4)
§endure patiently (2)
patience (4)
perseverance
steadfastness (13)
HYPONOEŌ ὑπονοέω
suppose (2)
suspect
HYPONOIA ὑπόνοια
suspicion
HYPOPHERŌ ὑποφέρω
endure (3)
HYPŌPIAZŌ ὑπωπιάζω
pommel
wear out
HYPOPLEŌ ὑποπλέω
sail under the lee of (2)
HYPOPNEŌ ὑποπνέω
blow gently
HYPOPODION ὑποπόδιον
§foot
footstool (2)
stool (4)
HYPOSTASIS ὑπόστασις
assurance
confidence (2)
§confident, be
nature
HYPOSTELLŌ ὑποστέλλω
draw back
shrink back (*mid.*)
shrink from (*mid.*) (2)
HYPOSTOLĒ ὑποστολή
§shrink back, those who
HYPOSTREPHŌ ὑποστρέφω
return (33)
turn back (2)
HYPOSTRŌNNYŌ ὑποστρωννύω
spread
HYPOTAGĒ ὑποταγή
obedience
submission
§submissive
submissiveness
HYPOTASSŌ ὑποτάσσω
obedient, be (*pass.*)
put in subjection (4)
put under (3)
subject (20)
submissive, be (*pass.*) (6)
submit (*pass.*) (2)
submit oneself (*pass.*)
subordinate, be (*pass.*)
HYPOTITHĒMI ὑποτίθημι
put before (*mid.*)
risk
HYPOTRECHŌ ὑποτρέχω
run under the lee of
HYPOTYPŌSIS ὑποτύπωσις
example
pattern
HYPOZŌNNYMI ὑποζώννυμι
undergird
HYPOZYGION ὑποζύγιον
ass (2)
HYPSĒLOPHRONEŌ ὑψηλοφρονέω
haughty, be
HYPSĒLOS ὑψηλός
exalted
exalted above (*comp.*+*gen.*)
§haughty, be
high (6)

§proud, become
uplifted

HYPSISTOS ὕψιστος
high, most (9)
highest (4)

HYPSŌMA ὕψωμα
height
§proud

HYPSOŌ ὑψόω
exalt (14)
great, make s.
lift up (5)

HYPSOS ὕψος
exaltation
height (2)
§high, from on (2)
§high, on

HYS ὗς
sow

HYSSŌPOS ὕσσωπος
hyssop (2)

HYSTERĒMA ὑστέρημα
absence
lacking, what is (*pl.*) (2)
need
poverty
want (3)
NOT TRANSLATED: Phil **2**.30

HYSTEREŌ ὑστερέω
destitute (*pass. part.*)
fail
fail to obtain
fall short of (*pass.*)
give out
inferior (*pass. part.*)
inferior to, be (2)
lack (4)
want (*inf.*)
want, be in (*pass.*) (2)
worse off, be (*pass.*)

HYSTERĒSIS ὑστέρησις
poverty
want

HYSTEROS ὕστερος
after (*neut.*+*gen.*)
afterward (*neut.*) (8)
last, at (*neut.*)
later (2)

I

IAMA ἴαμα
§healer
healing (2)

IAOMAI ἰάομαι
cure
heal (25)

IASIS ἴασις
cure
§heal
healing

IASPIS ἴασπις
jasper (4)

IATROS ἰατρός
physician (6)+

ICHNOS ἴχνος
example (*pl.*)
step (2)

ICHTHYDION ἰχθύδιον
fish, small (2)

ICHTHYS ἰχθύς
fish (20)

IDE ἴδε
ah
behold (7)
here (6)
look (6)
now
see (5)
NOT TRANSLATED
Mk **26**.65
Jn **11**.3; **18**.21

IDIOS ἴδιος
§apart (4)
§aside
due
her own (*fem.*) (2)
his (11)
his friends (*subst. masc. pl.*)
his home (*subst. neut. pl.*)
his own (39)
his own home (*subst. neut. pl.*) (2)
his own nature (*subst. pl.*)
his own people (*subst. pl.*)
his relatives (*subst. masc. pl.*)
§individually
its own (3)
one's own (2 Pet **1**.20)
our home (*subst. neut. pl.*)
our own (2)
§privately (9)
proper (3)
their (6)
their friends (*subst. pl.*)
their own (8)
their proper
whose
whose own
your (2)
your own (3)
your own affairs (*subst. neut. pl.*)
IDIOMATICALLY
himself *a;* home *a;* themselves, by *a;* yourselves *a*

IDIŌTĒS ἰδιώτης
common (*attr.*)
(gifts, he that is without †)
outsider (3)
unskilled (*pred.*)

IDOU ἰδού
behold (131)
hark
here (6)
lo (27)
look (3)
now (2)
see (3)
see here is
NOT TRANSLATED
Mt **7**.4; **12**.[47‡; **13**.3; **17**.5; **23**.34; **26**.47
Mk **3**.32; **4**.3; **14**.41
Lk **5**.12; **8**.41; **13**.11, 16; **19**.2; **22**.47; **24**.13
Jn **4**.35; **16**.32
Acts **2**.7; **5**.25; **10**.21; **11**.11; **13**.25; **16**.1
Gal **1**.20
Heb **8**.8
Jas **3**.5

IKMAS ἰκμάς
moisture

IOS ἰός
poison
rust
venom

IŌTA ἰῶτα
iota

IOUDAIZŌ ἰουδαΐζω
Jew, live like a

IRIS ἶρις
rainbow (2)

ISAGGELOS ἰσάγγελος
equal to an angel

ISCHYŌ ἰσχύω
able, be (7)
avail, be of
can (9)
defeated, be (*neg.*)
force, be in
good, be
manage
§overpower
power, have
prevail
strength to, have the
strong enough, be
well, be (2)

ISCHYROS ἰσχυρός
great
loud
mightier (*comp.*) (3)
mighty (8)
strong (12)+
stronger (*comp.*) (3)

ISCHYS ἰσχύς
great (*gen.*)
might (5)
strength (4)

ISOPSYCHOS ἰσόψυχος
[*of like mind*]
IDIOMATICALLY
like *c*

ISOS ἴσος
§agree (2)
equal (3)
§equality
much, as (*neut. pl.*)
same

ISŌS ἴσως
may be, it

ISOTĒS ἰσότης
equality (2)
§fairly

ISOTIMOS ἰσότιμος
equal standing, of

K

KAGŌ κἀγώ
and I (40)
but I (2)
even so I
I (14)
I also (13)
I, if
I myself (4)
I too (3)
so I (5)
then I

KAI καί
The most common New Testament conjunction, providing connection (and) *as well as explanation and emphasis*

(*e.g.*: even, indeed). *It is not analyzed in this Concordance.*

KAINOS καινός
fresh (3)
new (39)+

KAINOTĒS καινότης
new life
newness

KAIŌ καίω
blaze (2)
burn (9)
light

KAIPER καίπερ
although
though (4)

KAIROS καιρός
age (2)
opportunity (3)
period
season (9)
(season, certain)
time (62)
time, appointed
time, due
time, full
time, opportune
time, proper (2)
time, right
while

KAITOI καίτοι
although
yet

KAITOIGE καίτοιγε
although

KAKEI κἀκεῖ
and there (7)
there
there too
with s., and

KAKEINOS κἀκεῖνος
and he (4)
and they (3)
and this
but they
even the other
he also (3)
other, the (2)
they (3)
they also (2)
NOT TRANSLATED
Jn **6**.57; **14**.12

KAKEITHEN κἀκεῖθεν
and there
from there (8)
then

KAKIA κακία
evil (2)
malice (6)
trouble
wickedness (2)

KAKOĒTHEIA κακοήθεια
malignity

KAKOLOGEŌ κακολογέω
speak evil of (4)

KAKOŌ κακόω
force
harm (2)
ill-treat
poison
§violent

KAKOPATHEIA κακοπάθεια
suffering

KAKOPATHEŌ κακοπαθέω
suffer (2)
suffering, endure

KAKOPOIEŌ κακοποιέω
evil, do
harm, do (2)
wrong, do

KAKOPOIOS κακοποιός
wrong, one who does (*subst.*)
wrongdoer (*subst.*) (2)

KAKOS κακός
bad (2)
evil (32)
§evildoer
§evil-worker
foul
harm (*subst.*) (3)
§resentful, be
wicked
wretch (*subst.*)
wrong (6)
§wrongdoer

KAKŌS κακῶς
§evil
§miserable
severely
§sick (2)
§sick, be (8)
terribly
wrongly (2)

KAKŌSIS κάκωσις
ill-treatment

KAKOUCHEŌ κακουχέω
ill-treat (2)

KAKOURGOS κακοῦργος
criminal (*subst.*) (4)

KALAMĒ καλάμη
straw

KALAMOS κάλαμος
measuring rod
pen
reed (8)
rod (2)

KALEŌ καλέω
call (121)
give
host (*subst. part.*)
invite (18)
known as (*pass. part.*)
name (2)
named (*pass. part.*) (2)
summon
IDIOMATICALLY
name s. after *a*

KALLIELAIOS καλλιέλαιος
cultivated olive tree

KALODIDASKALOS καλοδιδάσκαλος
§teach what is good

KALOPOIEŌ καλοποιέω
well-doing (*part.*)

KALOS καλός
beautiful (2)
§better (8)
clear
excellent
fair (*See also* FAIR HAVENS)
fine
good (61)
§goodness
honest
honorable (2)†
noble (3)
right (6)
§truth
well (*pred.*) (8)
§well-doing
NOT TRANSLATED
1 Cor **7**.26; **9**.15

KALŌS καλῶς
§fine
§good (2)
honorably
please
readily
§right (3)
§right, be
right, you are
rightly
§true, that is
well (20)
IDIOMATICALLY
good *a;* kind *a, b;* recover *a*

KALYMMA κάλυμμα
veil (4)

KALYPTŌ καλύπτω
cover (5)
swamp
veil (2)

KAMĒLOS κάμηλος
camel (6)

KAMINOS κάμινος
furnace (4)

KAMMYŌ καμμύω
close (2)

KAMNŌ κάμνω
sick (*part.*)
weary, grow

KAMPTŌ κάμπτω
bow (4)

KAN κἄν
and if (6)
even (2)
even if (5)
if (3)
least, at
§*or*
though
though, even

KANŌN κανών
field (2)
§limits
rule

KAPĒLEUŌ καπηλεύω
peddler (*subst. part.*)

KAPNOS καπνός
smoke (13)

KARDIA καρδία
heart (148)+
mind (4)
steadfast (*gen.*)
IDIOMATICALLY
himself *b, c*
NOT TRANSLATED
Acts **7**.54

KARDIOGNŌSTĒS καρδιογνώστης
knows the heart, one who (2)

KARPHOS κάρφος
speck (6)

KARPOPHOREŌ καρποφορέω
bear fruit (6)
bring forth fruit
produce

KARPOPHOROS καρποφόρος
fruitful

KARPOS καρπός
crops (*pl.*) (2)
fruit (51)
§fruitful
grain (5)
harvest (2)
§raised, what has been
return (2)
§yield 8[a]
IDIOMATICALLY
descendants *a*

KARTEREŌ καρτερέω
endure

KATA κατά
about (+*acc.* 5)
accord with, in (+*acc.* 2)
accordance with, in (+*acc.* 4)
according to (+*acc.* 80)+†
§*accords with, which* (+*acc.* 2)
after (+*acc.* 8)
after the likeness of (+*acc.*)
against (+*gen.* 47)
along (+*acc.*)
among (+*acc.*)
as (+*acc.* 3)
as it is (+*acc.*)
as to (+*acc.* 3)
(as s. would have [+*acc.*])
at (+*gen.*; +*acc.* 4)+†
§*authority, with s.'s* (+*acc.*)
§*belonging to* (+*acc.*)
§*belongs to, which* (+*acc.*)
by (+*gen.* 4; +*acc.* 25)
by way of (+*acc.*)
§*deserves, as s.* (+*acc.*)
down (+*gen.* 3)
following (+*acc.* 2)
for (+*acc.* 5)
from (+*acc.* 2)
§*further, to* (+*acc.*)
in (+*acc.* 41)
in the way of (+*acc.*)
just as (+*acc.*)
§*laid down by* (+*acc.*)
like (+*acc.* 4)
of (+*gen.*; +*acc.* 4)
off (+*acc.* 3)
on (+*gen.*; +*acc.* 7)
opposite (+*acc.*)
over (+*gen.*)
regards, as (+*acc.* 2)
§suit, to (+*acc.*)
through (+*gen.*; +*acc.*)
throughout (+*gen.* 4; +*acc.* 3)
to (+*gen.* 2; +*acc.* 4)
toward (+*acc.* 2)
under (+*acc.*)
upon (+*gen.*)
virtue of, in (+*acc.* 3)
with (+*acc.* 2)
IDIOMATICALLY
OR NOT TRANSLATED
+*genitive:*
Acts **16**.22; **19**.16; **25**.3; **27**.14
1 Cor **11**.4
2 Cor **8**.2
+*accusative:*
Mt **14**.13, 23; **17**.1, 19; **20**.17; **23**.3; **24**.3, 7; **26**.55
Mk **4**.10, 34; **6**.31, 32; **7**.33; **9**.2, 28; **13**.3, 8; **14**.19, 49
Lk **1**.18; **2**.41; **4**.16; **6**.23, 26; **8**.1, 4; **9**.6, 10, 18, 23; **10**.23, 33; **11**.3; **13**.22; **16**.19; **17**.30; **19**.47; **21**.11; **22**.22, 39, 53
Jn **21**.25
Acts **2**.46[2], 47; **3**.2; **5**.42; **8**.3; **13**.23, 27; **14**.1, 23; **15**.11, 21[2]; **16**.5; **17**.2, 11, 17, 28; **18**.4, 14, 15; **19**.9, 20; **20**.20, 23; **21**.19; **22**.19; **23**.19; **24**.22; **25**.14, 16, 23; **26**.3; **27**.2, 12[2], 25
Rom **1**.15; **2**.2; **3**.5; **4**.18; **7**.13; **9**.3; **10**.2; **11**.5, 21, 24[2]; **12**.5; **14**.22
1 Cor **3**.3; **7**.6; **9**.8; **10**.18; **12**.31; **14**.27, 31; **15**.31, 32
2 Cor **1**.8, 17; **4**.13, 17; **5**.16[2]; **7**.9, 10, 11; **8**.8; **10**.1, 2, 3, 7, 13, 15; **11**.15, 28; **13**.10
Gal **1**.11†, 13; **2**.2; **3**.1, 15
Eph **1**.15; **4**.16, 22; **5**.33; **6**.5, 21
Phil **1**.12; **2**.3
Col **3**.22; **4**.7
2 Tim **2**.8
Tit **1**.5, 9
Phm .14
Heb **2**.17; **3**.3, 13; **4**.15[2]; **7**.20, 22, 27; **9**.9, 25; **10**.1, 3, 11; **11**.7
1 Pet **1**.2; **3**.7
2 Pet **3**.3
2 Jn .6
3 Jn .15
Jude .16, 18
Rev **4**.8; **22**.2

KATABAINŌ καταβαίνω
come down (38)
descend (14)
drop
fall (2)
(fall down)
get out of
go down (21)+
step down

KATABALLŌ καταβάλλω
lay (*mid.*)
strike down

KATABAREŌ καταβαρέω
burden

KATABARYNŌ καταβαρύνω
heavy, be (*pass.*)

KATABASIS κατάβασις
descent

KATABIBAZŌ καταβιβάζω
bring down (2)

KATABOLĒ καταβολή
foundation (10)
IDIOMATICALLY
conceive *c*

KATABRABEUŌ καταβραβεύω
disqualify

KATACHEŌ καταχέω
pour
pour over

KATACHRAOMAI καταχράομαι
dealings with, have
use of, make full

KATACHTHONIOS καταχθόνιος
earth, under the

KATADĒLOS κατάδηλος
evident

KATADEŌ καταδέω
bind up

KATADIKAZŌ καταδικάζω
condemn (5)

KATADIKĒ καταδίκη
sentence

KATADIŌKŌ καταδιώκω
pursue

KATADOULOŌ καταδουλόω
bondage, bring into
slaves of, make

KATADYNASTEUŌ καταδυναστεύω
oppress (2)

KATAGELAŌ καταγελάω
laugh at (3)

KATAGGELEUS καταγγελεύς
preacher

KATAGGELLŌ καταγγέλλω
advocate
proclaim (17)

KATAGINŌSKŌ καταγινώσκω
condemn (2)
condemned, stand (*pluperf. pass. periphr.*)

KATAGNYMI κατάγνυμι
break (4)

KATAGŌ κατάγω
bring
bring down (6)
put in (*pass.*) (2)

KATAGŌNIZOMAI καταγωνίζομαι
conquer

KATAGRAPHŌ καταγράφω
write

KATAISCHYNŌ καταισχύνω
disappoint
dishonor (2)
humiliate (2)
shame (2)
shame, put to (6)

KATAKAIŌ κατακαίω
burn (9)
burn up (4)

KATAKALYPTŌ κατακαλύπτω
cover (*mid.*)
veil oneself (*mid.*)
veil, wear a (*mid.*)

KATAKAUCHAOMAI κατακαυχάομαι
boast (2)
boast over
triumph over

KATAKEIMAI κατάκειμαι
§bedridden, be
lie (6)
sit at table (3)
table, at (*pass. part.*)
table, be at

KATAKLAŌ κατακλάω
break (2)

KATAKLEIŌ κατακλείω
shut up (2)

KATAKLĒRONOMEŌ κατακληρονομέω
inheritance, give s. as an

KATAKLINŌ κατακλίνω
place at table, take one's (*pass.*)
sit down
sit down, make s. (2)
table, be at (*pass.*)

KATAKLYSMOS κατακλυσμός
flood (4)

KATAKLYZŌ κατακλύζω
deluge

KATAKOLOUTHEŌ κατακολουθέω
follow (2)

KATAKOPTŌ κατακόπτω
bruise

KATAKRĒMNIZŌ κατακρημνίζω
throw down headlong

KATAKRIMA *κατάκριμα*
condemnation (3)
KATAKRINŌ *κατακρίνω*
condemn (18)
KATAKRISIS *κατάκρισις*
§condemn
condemnation
KATAKYPTŌ *κατακύπτω*
bend down
KATAKYRIEUŌ *κατακυριεύω*
domineer
lord it over (2)
master
KATALALEŌ *καταλαλέω*
abuse
speak against
speak evil against (3)
KATALALIA *καταλαλιά*
slander (2)
KATALALOS *κατάλαλος*
slanderer (*subst.*)
KATALAMBANŌ *καταλαμβάνω*
attain
catch (2)
comprehend (*mid.*)
find (*mid.*)
obtain
overcome
overtake
own, make s. his
own, make s. my (2)
perceive (*mid.*) (2)
seize
surprise
KATALEGŌ *καταλέγω*
enroll
KATALEIPŌ *καταλείπω*
forsake
give up
keep
leave (19)
leave behind
remain (*mid.*)
KATALITHAZŌ *καταλιθάζω*
stone
KATALLAGĒ *καταλλαγή*
reconciliation (4)
KATALLASSŌ *καταλλάσσω*
reconcile (6)
KATALOIPOS *κατάλοιπος*
rest (*subst.*)
KATALYMA *κατάλυμα*
guest room (2)
inn
KATALYŌ *καταλύω*
abolish (2)
destroy (7)
fail (*pass.*)
guest, be the
lodge
overthrow
tear down
throw down (3)
KATAMANTHANŌ *καταμανθάνω*
consider
KATAMARTYREŌ *καταμαρτυρέω*
testify against (3)
KATAMENŌ *καταμένω*
stay (2)
KATANALISKŌ *καταναλίσκω*
consume

KATANARKAŌ *καταναρκάω*
burden (2)
burden, be a
KATANEUŌ *κατανεύω*
beckon
KATANOEŌ *κατανοέω*
consider (5)
look (2)
notice (3)
observe (3)
perceive
KATANTAŌ *καταντάω*
arrive (3)
attain (3)
come (5)
reach (2)
KATANYSSOMAI *κατανύσσομαι*
cut, be
KATANYXIS *κατάνυξις*
stupor
KATAPATEŌ *καταπατέω*
spurn
trample
tread under foot (2)
tread upon
KATAPAUŌ *καταπαύω*
cease
rest
rest, give
restrain
KATAPAUSIS *κατάπαυσις*
rest (9)
KATAPETASMA *καταπέτασμα*
curtain (6)
KATAPHERŌ *καταφέρω*
bring against
cast against
overcome, be (*pass.*)
sink (*pass.*)
KATAPHEUGŌ *καταφεύγω*
flee
flee for refuge
KATAPHILEŌ *καταφιλέω*
kiss (6)
KATAPHRONEŌ *καταφρονέω*
despise (7)
disrespectful, be
presume upon
KATAPHRONĒTĒS *καταφρονητής*
scoffer
KATAPHTHEIRŌ *καταφθείρω*
corrupt (*perf. pass. part.*)
KATAPINŌ *καταπίνω*
devour
drown
overwhelm
swallow (2)
swallow up (2)
KATAPIPTŌ *καταπίπτω*
fall (2)
fall down
KATAPLEŌ *καταπλέω*
arrive
KATAPONEŌ *καταπονέω*
distress
oppressed (*part.*)
KATAPONTIZŌ *καταποντίζω*
drowned, be (*pass.*)
sink (*pass.*)
KATAPSYCHŌ *καταψύχω*
cool

KATARA *κατάρα*
accursed (*gen.*)
curse (3)
cursed, being
cursing
KATARAOMAI *καταράομαι*
curse (5)
KATARGEŌ *καταργέω*
abolish (2)
destroy (6)
discharge (2)
doomed to pass away, be (*pass.*)
fade (*pass.*) (2)
fade away (*pass.*)
give up
nothing, bring to
nullify
overthrow
pass away (*pass.*) (3)
remove
severed, be (*pass.*)
take away
use up
void, be (*pass.*)
void, make
KATARITHMEŌ *καταριθμέω*
number
KATARTISIS *κατάρτισις*
improvement
KATARTISMOS *καταρτισμός*
§equip
KATARTIZŌ *καταρτίζω*
bring (*mid.*)
create
equip
make
mend (2)
mend one's ways (*pass.*)
prepare (*mid.*)
restore (2)
supply
teach
unite
KATASCHESIS *κατάσχεσις*
§dispossess
possession
KATASEIŌ *κατασείω*
motion (4)
KATASKAPTŌ *κατασκάπτω*
demolish
KATASKĒNOŌ *κατασκηνόω*
dwell
nests, make (3)
KATASKĒNŌSIS *κατασκήνωσις*
nest (2)
KATASKEUAZŌ *κατασκευάζω*
build (2)
builder (*subst. part.*) (2)
construct
preparations, make
prepare (5)
KATASKIAZŌ *κατασκιάζω*
overshadow
KATASKOPEŌ *κατασκοπέω*
spy out
KATASKOPOS *κατάσκοπος*
spy
KATASOPHIZOMAI *κατασοφίζομαι*
deal craftily with
KATASPHAZŌ *κατασφάζω*
slay

KATASPHRAGIZŌ κατασφραγίζω
sealed (*perf. pass. part.*)

KATASTELLŌ καταστέλλω
quiet (2)

KATASTĒMA κατάστημα
behavior

KATASTOLĒ καταστολή
apparel

KATASTRĒNIAŌ καταστρηνιάω
wanton against, grow

KATASTREPHŌ καταστρέφω
overturn (2)
ruin (*subst. perf. pass. part.*)

KATASTRŌNNYMI καταστρώννυμι
overthrow

KATASTROPHĒ καταστροφή
extinction
§ruin

KATASYRŌ κατασύρω
drag

KATATHEMA κατάθεμα
§accursed

KATATHEMATIZŌ καταθεματίζω
curse on oneself, invoke a

KATATITHĒMI κατατίθημι
§do (2)
(lay)

KATATOMĒ κατατομή
§mutilate the flesh, those who

KATATRECHŌ κατατρέχω
run down

KATAXIOŌ καταξιόω
accounted worthy, be (*pass.*)
counted worthy, be (*pass.*)
worthy, be made (*pass.*)

KATĒCHEŌ κατηχέω
inform
instruct (3)
teach (2)
tell (2)

KATECHŌ κατέχω
captive, hold
(have)
have goods
hold
hold fast (5)
keep (2)
maintain
make for
possess
restrain (2)
suppress
take

KATĒGŌR κατήγωρ
accuser

KATĒGOREŌ κατηγορέω
accusation against (*inf.*)
accusation, make an
accuse (14)
accused (*subst. pass. part.*)
bring a charge
bring charges
bring charges against
bring up against
IDIOMATICALLY
charge *a, c*

KATĒGORIA κατηγορία
accusation
charge (2)

KATĒGOROS κατήγορος
accuser (4)+

KATEIDŌLOS κατείδωλος
idols, full of

KATENANTI κατέναντι
before
opposite (5)
presence of, in the
sight of, in the (2)

KATENŌPION κατενώπιον
before (2)
before the presence of

KATĒPHEIA κατήφεια
dejection

KATEPHISTAMAI κατεφίσταμαι
attack upon, make an

KATERCHOMAI κατέρχομαι
arrive
come
come down (6)
go down (6)
land

KATERGAZOMAI κατεργάζομαι
§action
bring
commit
do (7)
perform
prepare (2)
produce (5)
work (3)
work out

KATESTHIŌ κατεσθίω (κατέσθω)
consume (3)
devour (8)+
eat (2)
prey upon

KATEULOGEŌ κατευλογέω
bless

KATEUTHYNŌ κατευθύνω
direct (2)
guide

KATEXOUSIAZŌ κατεξουσιάζω
authority over, exercise (2)

KATHA καθά
as

KATHAIREŌ καθαιρέω
depose
destroy (2)
pull down
put down
take down (4)

KATHAIRESIS καθαίρεσις
§destroy
destroying
tearing down

KATHAIRŌ καθαίρω
prune

KATHAPER καθάπερ
as (9)
for
just as (2)
like (2)
so
IDIOMATICALLY
match *a*
NOT TRANSLATED
2 Cor **3**.18

KATHAPTŌ καθάπτω
fasten on

KATHARISMOS καθαρισμός
§cleansed, that one was
cleansing (2)
purification (3)
purifying

KATHARIZŌ καθαρίζω
clean, be (*pass.*) (3)
clean, declare
clean, make (4)
cleanse (19)
purify (4)

KATHAROS καθαρός
clean (8)
clear (3)
innocent (2)
pure (13)

KATHAROTĒS καθαρότης
purification

KATHEDRA καθέδρα
seat (3)

KATHĒGĒTĒS καθηγητής
master (2)

KATHĒKŌ καθήκω
§ought
IDIOMATICALLY
improper *a*

KATHĒMAI κάθημαι
business, at one's (*part.*)
dwell (2)
§rider (*subst. part.*) (6)
seat, have a (*imper.*)
seated (*part.*) (7)
seated, be (10)
sit (59)
sit by (2)
sit down (3)

KATHĒMERINOS καθημερινός
daily

KATHEUDŌ καθεύδω
asleep (*part.*) (2)
asleep, be (2)
sleep (17)
sleeper (*subst. part.*)

KATHEXĒS καθεξῆς
§afterward, soon
afterward, those who came (*subst. pl.*)
order, in
orderly
place to place, from

KATHEZOMAI καθέζομαι
sit (6)
sit down

KATHIĒMI καθίημι
let down (4)

KATHISTĒMI καθίστημι (καθιστάνω)
appoint (4)
appoint to act
conduct
keep from being (*neg.*)
make (7)
set (6)+
NOT TRANSLATED
Jas **3**.6

KATHIZŌ καθίζω
lay before
rest
seat, take one's (4)
seated, be (*aor. or perf.*) (3)
set
sit (15)
sit down (18)
sit, make s.
stay (2)

KATHO καθό
according to (2)

as
far as, in so

KATHOLOU καθόλου
all, at (*neg.*)

KATHOPLIZŌ καθοπλίζω
armed, fully (*mid. part.*)

KATHORAŌ καθοράω
perceive

KATHŌS καθώς
as (131)
as well as (2)
even as (11)
for
how
just as (16)
like
since (2)
so (2)
such as
thus
way in which, in the same
§what
IDIOMATICALLY
according to *a; by a*
NOT TRANSLATED
Rom **3**.8
Phil **1**.7
1 Th **1**.5
Heb **4**.7
3 Jn .2

KATHŌSPER καθώσπερ
just as

KATHOTI καθότι
as (2)
because (3)
since

KATIOŌ κατιόω
rust (*pass.*)

KATISCHYŌ κατισχύω
prevail against (2)
strength, have

KATŌ κάτω
below (2)
beneath
down (4)
IDIOMATICALLY
bottom *a, b*

KATOIKEŌ κατοικέω
dwell (22)
dweller (*subst. part.*) (2)
inhabitant (*subst. part.*) (3)
live (12)
resident (*subst. part.*) (4)
NOT TRANSLATED
Rev **13**.14

KATOIKĒSIS κατοίκησις
[*dwelling, abode*]
§live

KATOIKĒTĒRION κατοικητήριον
dwelling place (2)

KATOIKIA κατοικία
habitation

KATOIKIZŌ κατοικίζω
dwell, make to

KATOPTRIZŌ κατοπτρίζω
behold (*mid.*)
(reflect †)

KATŌTERŌ κατωτέρω
under

KATŌTEROS κατώτερος
lower

KAUCHAOMAI καυχάομαι
boast (28)
glory (3)+
pride, express
pride oneself
rejoice (3)

KAUCHĒMA καύχημα
boast about, something to
boast, one's reason to
boasting (2)
boasting, ground for (2)
glory, cause to
pride
§proud, be (3)

KAUCHĒSIS καύχησις
boast (2)
boastful (*gen.*)
boasting (5)
pride (2)
proud, reason to be

KAUMA καῦμα
heat
scorching heat

KAUMATIZŌ καυματίζω
scorch (4)

KAUSIS καῦσις
§burn

KAUSŌN καύσων
scorching heat (3)

KAUSOŌ καυσόω
fire, with (*pass. part.*) (2)

KAUSTĒRIAZŌ καυστηριάζω
sear

KEIMAI κεῖμαι
laid, be (4)
laid down, be
laid up (*part.*)
lie (9)
§power of, be in the
put, be
set (*part.*)
set, be
stand (3)
there (*part.*)
IDIOMATICALLY
lot *a*

KEIRIA κειρία
bandage

KEIRŌ κείρω
cut
cut off one's hair (*mid.*)
shear
shearer (*subst. part.*)

KELEUŌ κελεύω
bid
command (10)+
order (12)
orders, give (2)

KELEUSMA κέλευσμα
command, cry of

KĒMOŌ κημόω
muzzle

KENODOXIA κενοδοξία
conceit

KENODOXOS κενόδοξος
[*conceited*]
IDIOMATICALLY
self-conceit *a*

KENOŌ κενόω
deprive
empty (2)
null, be (*perf. pass.*)
vain, prove (*pass.*)

KENOPHŌNIA κενοφωνία
chatter (2)

KENOS κενός
empty (3)
empty-handed (3)
shallow
vain
vain, in (*pred.*) (10)

KENŌS κενῶς
vain, in

KĒNSOS κῆνσος
tax
taxes (2)
tribute

KENTRON κέντρον
goad
sting (3)

KENTYRIŌN κεντυρίων
centurion (3)

KEPHALAION κεφάλαιον
point
sum

KEPHALĒ κεφαλή
§hair
head (74)

KEPHALIOŌ κεφαλιόω
wound in the head

KEPHALIS κεφαλίς
roll

KĒPOS κῆπος
garden (5)

KĒPOUROS κηπουρός
gardener

KERAIA κεραία
dot (2)

KERAMEUS κεραμεύς
potter (3)

KERAMIKOS κεραμικός
earthen

KERAMION κεράμιον
jar (2)

KERAMOS κέραμος
tile

KERANNYMI κεράννυμι
mix (2)
pour

KERAS κέρας
horn (11)

KERATION κεράτιον
pod

KERDAINŌ κερδαίνω
gain (6)
incur
make (4)
win (6)

KERDOS κέρδος
gain (3)

KERMA κέρμα
coin

KERMATISTĒS κερματιστής
money-changer

KĒRYGMA κήρυγμα
message (2)
preaches, what one
preaching (5)
(proclamation)

KĒRYSSŌ κηρύσσω
preach (49)

preacher (*subst. part.*)
proclaim (10)
talk

KĒRYX *κῆρυξ*
herald
preacher (2)

KĒTOS *κῆτος*
whale

KIBŌTOS *κιβωτός*
ark (6)

KICHRĒMI *κίχρημι*
lend

KINDYNEUŌ *κινδυνεύω*
danger, be in (2)
danger, there is
peril, be in

KINDYNOS *κίνδυνος*
danger (8)
peril

KINEŌ *κινέω*
§agitator (*subst. part.*)
arouse
move (2)
remove (2)
wag (2)

KINĒSIS *κίνησις*
(moving)

KINNAMŌMON *κιννάμωμον*
cinnamon

KITHARA *κιθάρα*
harp (4)

KITHARIZŌ *κιθαρίζω*
play
IDIOMATICALLY
play *a*

KITHARŌDOS *κιθαρῳδός*
harper (2)

KLADOS *κλάδος*
branch (11)

KLAIŌ *κλαίω*
mourn (2)
tears, with (*part.*)
weep (37)

KLAŌ *κλάω*
break (14)+

KLASIS *κλάσις*
breaking (2)

KLASMA *κλάσμα*
broken piece (7)
fragment (2)

KLAUTHMOS *κλαυθμός*
wailing
§weep (8)

KLEIŌ *κλείω*
close
locked (*perf. pass. part.*)
shut (13)
shut up

KLEIS *κλείς*
key (6)

KLĒMA *κλῆμα*
branch (4)

KLEMMA *κλέμμα*
theft

KLEOS *κλέος*
credit

KLEPTĒS *κλέπτης*
thief (16)

KLEPTŌ *κλέπτω*
steal (10)
steal away (2)
thief (*subst. part.*)

KLĒRONOMEŌ *κληρονομέω*
§heritage, have a
inherit (14)
obtain (3)

KLĒRONOMIA *κληρονομία*
inheritance (14)

KLĒRONOMOS *κληρονόμος*
heir (14)
§inherit

KLĒROŌ *κληρόω*
appoint

KLĒROS *κλῆρος*
charge, those in one's (*pl.*)
inheritance
lot (3)
lots (4)
place
share

KLĒSIS *κλῆσις*
call (8)
calling (2)
state

KLĒTOS *κλητός*
called (10)

KLIBANOS *κλίβανος*
oven (2)

KLIMA *κλίμα*
region (3)

KLINARION *κλινάριον*
bed

KLINĒ *κλίνη*
bed (7)+
sickbed

KLINIDION *κλινίδιον*
bed (2)

KLINŌ *κλίνω*
bow (2)
flight, put to
lay (2)
spent, be far (*perf.*)
wear away

KLISIA *κλισία*
company

KLOPĒ *κλοπή*
theft (2)

KLYDŌN *κλύδων*
wave
IDIOMATICALLY
raging *a*

KLYDŌNIZOMAI *κλυδωνίζομαι*
tossed to and fro (*part.*)

KNĒTHŌ *κνήθω*
itch (*pass.*)

KODRANTĒS *κοδράντης*
penny (2)

KOILIA *κοιλία*
§appetites
belly (2)+
heart
stomach (6)
womb (8)
IDIOMATICALLY
bear *a;* birth *a, b, c*

KOIMAŌ *κοιμάω*
asleep, be (*pass.*) (2)
asleep, fall (*pass.*) (11)
die (*pass.*) (2)
sleep (*pass.*) (3)

KOIMĒSIS *κοίμησις*
rest, taking

KOINŌNEŌ *κοινωνέω*
contribute to
participate in
partnership with, enter into
share (5)

KOINŌNIA *κοινωνία*
(communion †)
contribution (2)
fellowship (9)
participation (3)†
partnership
§share what one has, to
sharing
taking part
IDIOMATICALLY
share *a*

KOINŌNIKOS *κοινωνικός*
generous

KOINŌNOS *κοινωνός*
partaker (2)
partner (6)
§share
§take part

KOINOŌ *κοινόω*
common, call (2)
defile (12)

KOINOS *κοινός*
common (5)
common, in (*neut. pl.*) (2)
defiled (2)
§profane
unclean (4)

KOITĒ *κοίτη*
bed
bed, marriage
§debauchery (*pl.*)
IDIOMATICALLY
conceive *b*

KOITŌN *κοιτών*
[*bedroom*]
§chamberlain

KOKKINOS *κόκκινος*
scarlet (6)

KOKKOS *κόκκος*
grain (6)
kernel

KOLAKEIA *κολακεία*
flattery

KOLAPHIZŌ *κολαφίζω*
beat
buffet
harass
strike (2)

KOLASIS *κόλασις*
punishment (2)

KOLAZŌ *κολάζω*
punish
punishment, under (*pres. pass. part.*)

KOLLAŌ *κολλάω*
associate (*pass.*)
cling (*pass.*)
heaped, be (*pass.*)
hold fast (*pass.*)
join (5)
join oneself (*pass.*) (2)
united, be (*pass.*)

KOLLOURION *κολλούριον*
salve

KOLLYBISTĒS *κολλυβιστής*
money-changer (3)

KOLOBOŌ κολοβόω
shorten (4)
KŌLON κῶλον
body
KOLŌNIA κολωνία
colony
KOLPOS κόλπος
bay
bosom (3)
breast
lap
KOLYMBAŌ κολυμβάω
swim
KOLYMBĒTHRA κολυμβήθρα
pool (3)+
KŌLYŌ κωλύω
forbid (9)
hinder (5)
keep from
prevent (4)
restrain
stop
withhold
withstand
KOMAŌ κομάω
hair, have long
hair, wear long
KOMĒ κόμη
hair
KŌMĒ κώμη
village (27)
KOMIZŌ κομίζω
bring
obtain (*mid.*) (2)
paid back, be (*mid.*)
receive (*mid.*) (6)
receive back (*mid.*)
KŌMOPOLIS κωμόπολις
town
KŌMOS κῶμος
carousing (*pl.*)
reveling (*pl.*)
revels (*pl.*)
KOMPSOTERON κομψότερον
[*well, better*]
IDIOMATICALLY
mend *a*
KONIAŌ κονιάω
whitewashed (*perf. pass. part.*) (2)
KONIORTOS κονιορτός
dust (5)
KŌNŌPS κώνωψ
gnat
KOPAZŌ κοπάζω
cease (3)
KOPĒ κοπή
slaughter
KOPETOS κοπετός
lamentation
KOPHINOS κόφινος
basket (6)
KŌPHOS κωφός
deaf (5)
dumb (9)
KOPIAŌ κοπιάω
hard-working (*part.*)
labor (9)
laborer (*subst. part.*)
toil (6)
wearied as one is (*perf. part.*)
weary, grow
work (3)
worker (*subst. part.*)
KOPOS κόπος
§bother (2)
labor (11)
toil (2)
§trouble (3)
KOPRIA κοπρία
dunghill
KOPRION κόπριον
manure
KOPTŌ κόπτω
bewail (*mid.*) (2)
cut (2)
mourn (*mid.*) (2)
wail (*mid.*) (2)
KORASION κοράσιον
girl (8)
KORAX κόραξ
raven
KORBAN κορβᾶν
corban
KORBANAS κορβανᾶς
treasury
KORENNYMI κορέννυμι
filled (*perf. pass. part.*)
IDIOMATICALLY
enough *b*
KOROS κόρος
measure
KOSMEŌ κοσμέω
adorn (7)
order, put in (2)
trim
KOSMIKOS κοσμικός
earthly
worldly
KOSMIOS κόσμιος
dignified
seemly
KOSMOKRATŌR κοσμοκράτωρ
world ruler
KOSMOS κόσμος
adorning
universe (3)
world (178)
worldly (*gen.*) (3)
NOT TRANSLATED
1 Cor 8.4
KOUM κοῦμ
cumi
KOUPHIZŌ κουφίζω
lighten
KOUSTŌDIA κουστωδία
guard (3)
KRABATTOS κράβαττος
§bedridden, be
pallet (10)
KRAIPALĒ κραιπάλη
dissipation
KRANION κρανίον
skull (4)
KRASPEDON κράσπεδον
fringe (5)
KRATAIOŌ κραταιόω
strengthened, be (*pass.*)
strong, be (*pass.*)
strong, become (*pass.*) (2)
KRATAIOS κραταιός
mighty
KRATEŌ κρατέω
arrest (4)
cling
hold (4)
hold back
hold fast (6)
hold of, lay
hold of, take
hold to
keep (2)
observe (2)
obtain
retain (2)
seize (16)
take (5)
KRATISTOS κράτιστος
excellency, his (*subst.*)
excellent, most (*voc.*) (3)
KRATOS κράτος
dominion (5)
might (3)
§mightily
power
strength (2)
KRAUGAZŌ κραυγάζω
cry (3)
cry aloud
cry out (5)
KRAUGĒ κραυγή
clamor (2)
cry (3)
crying
KRAZŌ κράζω
call (3)
call out (3)
cry (11)+
cry aloud
cry out (32)+
proclaim (2)
shout (3)
KREAS κρέας
meat (2)
KREISSŌN κρείσσων (κρείττων)
better (16)
more graciously (*neut.*)
superior (2)
KREMANNYMI κρεμάννυμι
depend (*mid.*)
fasten
hang (*act. or mid.*) (5)
KRĒMNOS κρημνός
steep bank (3)
KRIMA κρίμα
§condemn (2)
condemnation (8)+
§judged, be
judgment (15)
lawsuit
KRINŌ κρίνω
condemn (8)
convinced, because one is (*part.*)
decide (7)
determine (2)
esteem (2)
judge (69)+
§judgment (2)
judgment is, one's
judgment, pass (6)
judgment, pronounce (2)
law, go to (*pass.*) (2)
§pronounce
§reach
sue (*pass.*)
think

trial, be on (*pass.*) (2)
trial, on (*pass. part.*)
try (3)
IDIOMATICALLY
give *b;* mind *b;* trial *a*

KRINON κρίνον
lily (2)

KRISIS κρίσις
condemnation
judgment (40)
justice (5)
IDIOMATICALLY
sentence *a*

KRITĒRION κριτήριον
case (2)
court (*pl.*)

KRITĒS κριτής
judge (19)

KRITHĒ κριθή
barley

KRITHINOS κρίθινος
barley (2)

KRITIKOS κριτικός
discerning

KROUŌ κρούω
knock (9)

KRYPHAIOS κρυφαῖος
secret (2)

KRYPHĒ κρυφῇ
secret, in

KRYPTĒ κρύπτη
cellar

KRYPTŌ κρύπτω
cover up
hidden (*perf. pass. part.*) (2)
hide (15)
secretly (*perf. pass. part.*)

KRYPTOS κρυπτός
hidden (4)
§inwardly
private
secret (9)
§secretly
underhanded

KRYSTALLIZŌ κρυσταλλίζω
clear as crystal (*part.*)

KRYSTALLOS κρύσταλλος
crystal (2)

KTAOMAI κτάομαι
buy (2)
(control †)
gain
get
obtain
take (2)

KTĒMA κτῆμα
possession (3)
property, piece of

KTĒNOS κτῆνος
animal
beast
cattle (*pl.*)
mount

KTĒTŌR κτήτωρ
possessor

KTISIS κτίσις
creation (15)
creature (3)†
institution

KTISMA κτίσμα
§created
creature (2)
creature, living

KTISTĒS κτίστης
creator

KTIZŌ κτίζω
create (12)
creator (*subst. part.*) (2)

KYBEIA κυβεία
cunning

KYBERNĒSIS κυβέρνησις
§administrator

KYBERNĒTĒS κυβερνήτης
captain
shipmaster

KYKLEUŌ κυκλεύω
surround

KYKLŌ κύκλῳ
§*among*
around
round (2)
round about (2)
side, on each
NOT TRANSLATED
Mk **3**.34

KYKLOŌ κυκλόω
encircle
gather about
gather round
surround

KYKLOTHEN κυκλόθεν
round (2)
round, all

KYLIŌ κυλίω
roll about (*pass.*)

KYLISMOS κυλισμός
§wallow

KYLLOS κυλλός
maimed (4)

KYMA κῦμα
wave (4)

KYMBALON κύμβαλον
cymbal

KYMINON κύμινον
cummin

KYNARION κυνάριον
dog (4)

KYŌN κύων
dog (5)

KYPTŌ κύπτω
bend
stoop down

KYRIA κυρία
lady (2)

KYRIAKOS κυριακός
lord's (2)

KYRIEUŌ κυριεύω
binding on, be
dominion over, have (2)
lord (*subst. part.*)
lord, be
lord it over
lordship over, exercise

KYRIOS κύριος
lord (648)+
master (44)
men (*voc. pl.*)
owner (9)
sir (*voc.*) (14)

KYRIOTĒS κυριότης
authority (2)
dominion (2)

KYROŌ κυρόω
ratify
reaffirm

L

LACHANON λάχανον
herb
shrub (2)
vegetable

LAGCHANŌ λαγχάνω
allotted, be
lot, fall to one by
lots, cast
obtain

LAILAPS λαῖλαψ
storm (3)

LAKAŌ λακάω
burst open

LAKTIZŌ λακτίζω
kick

LALEŌ λαλέω
address (2)
bring
declare (8)
impart (3)
§lie 7[a]
mean
preach
present
say (50)
sound (2)
speak (193)+
speaker (*subst. part.*) (2)
talk (8)†
teach
tell (16)
utter (5)
IDIOMATICALLY
boaster *a*
NOT TRANSLATED
Jn **7**.46

LALIA λαλιά
accent
§say
words

LAMA λαμά
lama

LAMBANŌ λαμβάνω
accept (2)
advantage of, take
better of, get the
bring (3)
by (*part.*)
choose
collector (*subst.*)
find (2)
gather (2)
get (3)
have
§incur
obtain
overtake
procure
receive (119)+
seize (4)
share
take (97)+
IDIOMATICALLY
gift *a;* show *a, c*
in combination with other words:
attempt 2; command 4[b]; edify 2[b];

first 1[a]; forget 3; judged, be 2; reminded, be 1; succeed 1; suffer 5
NOT TRANSLATED
Jn **13**.4, 26
Acts **3**.3

LAMPAS λαμπάς
lamp (5)
light
torch (3)

LAMPŌ λάμπω
light, give
light up
shine (5)

LAMPROS λαμπρός
bright (5)
fine (2)
gorgeous
splendor (*subst. pl.*)

LAMPRŌS λαμπρῶς
sumptuously

LAMPROTĒS λαμπρότης
[*brilliance, brightness*]
§brighter

LANTHANŌ λανθάνω
escape one's notice
hid, be
hidden, be
§ignore (2)
§unawares

LAOS λαός
people (142)

LARYGX λάρυγξ
throat

LATHRA λάθρᾳ
quietly (2)
secretly (2)

LATOMEŌ λατομέω
hew (2)

LATREIA λατρεία
ritual duty
service
worship (3)

LATREUŌ λατρεύω
serve (10)
worship (8)
worship, offer
worshiper (*subst. part.*) (2)

LAXEUTOS λαξευτός
rock-hewn

LEGIŌN λεγιών
legion (4)

LEGŌ λέγω
§address
affirm
§agree
aloud (*part.*)
ask (6)
be (*pass.*)
bid (2)
call (46)
§complain
cry (5)
declare (2)
give (2)
hold
§implore
mean (12)
§named (*pass. inf.*)
preach
pronounce
§repeat 1
reply
§right, be 1
say (953)+
sing (2)
so-called (*pass. part.*) (2)
speak (30)
state
tell (109)
IDIOMATICALLY
example *a;* word *a, b;* words *b* (7)
NOT TRANSLATED
Mt **1**.22; **2**.15, 17; **3**.2; **4**.14; **8**.17, 29, 31; **9**.27, 30; **10**.5; **11**.17; **12**.10, 17; **13**.35; **14**.30; **15**.22; **16**.13; **17**.9, 10; **18**.29; **19**.3; **20**.30, 31; **21**.9, 15, 25; **22**.32; **23**.2; **25**.9, 37, 44, 45; **26**.39, 42; **27**.11, 23, 46; **28**.18
Mk **1**.24; **3**.11, 33; **5**.12; **7**.28; **8**.27, 28, 29; **9**.11, 19; **11**.22, 31, 33; **14**.60, 61; **15**.2, 4, 9
Lk **1**.63; **3**.10, 11, 14, 16; **4**.36, 41; **5**.12; **7**.32, 39; **9**.18, 38; **11**.45; **12**.17; **13**.8; **15**.3; **18**.18, 38; **20**.2, 5, 14, 21; **21**.7; **22**.42, 64; **23**.3, 18, 21; **24**.7
Jn **1**.15, 26, 32; **7**.28, 37; **9**.2, 19; **12**.23; **16**.29; **18**.40; **19**.6, 12; **21**.19
Acts **1**.6; **5**.23; **7**.59; **8**.26; **11**.4; **14**.15; **15**.13; **16**.17, 28; **19**.28; **20**.23; **22**.26; **23**.9, 12; **26**.32; **28**.26
Rom **11**.4
Heb **2**.6; **12**.26
2 Jn .11
Rev **6**.10; **7**.10; **14**.18; **17**.1; **18**.2, 18, 19; **19**.17

LEIMMA λεῖμμα
remnant

LEIOS λεῖος
smooth

LEIPŌ λείπω
defective (*part.*)
lack (*pass.*) (4)
lack, in (*pass. part.*)

LEITOURGEŌ λειτουργέω
service, at one's (*part.*)
service, be of
worship

LEITOURGIA λειτουργία
ministry
offering
service (3)
worship, used in (*gen.*)

LEITOURGIKOS λειτουργικός
ministering

LEITOURGOS λειτουργός
minister (4)
servant

LEMA λεμά
lama

LĒMPSIS λῆμψις
receiving

LĒNOS ληνός
wine press (5)

LENTION λέντιον
towel (2)

LEŌN λέων
lion (9)

LEPIS λεπίς
scale

LEPRA λέπρα
leprosy (4)

LEPROS λεπρός
leper (*subst.*) (9)

LEPTOS λεπτός
§copper (*subst. neut.*)
§copper coin (*subst. neut.*) (2)

LĒROS λῆρος
idle tale

LĒSTĒS λῃστής
robber (15)

LĒTHĒ λήθη
[*forgetfulness*]
§forget

LEUKAINŌ λευκαίνω
bleach
white, make

LEUKOS λευκός
white (25)

LIAN λίαν
§furious
great while, a
greatly (3)
intensely
so
strongly
utterly
very (3)

LIBANOS λίβανος
frankincense (2)

LIBANŌTOS λιβανωτός
censer (2)

LIBERTINOS Λιβερτῖνος
freedman

LIKŌMA λικμάω
crush +

LIMĒN λιμήν
harbor (2)
haven (*See* HAVENS, FAIR)

LIMNĒ λίμνη
lake (11)

LIMOS λιμός
famine (10)
hunger (2)

LINON λίνον
linen
wick

LIPAROS λιπαρός
dainties (*subst. neut. pl.*)

LIPS λίψ
northeast
(southwest †)

LITHAZŌ λιθάζω
stone (9)

LITHINOS λίθινος
stone (3)

LITHOBOLEŌ λιθοβολέω
stone (7)

LITHOS λίθος
§another (4)
§jewel (5)
§millstone 1
stone (46)+
NOT TRANSLATED
Rev **4**.3

LITHOSTRŌTOS λιθόστρωτος
pavement (*subst.*)

LITRA λίτρα
pound (2)

LOGCHĒ λόγχη
spear +

LOGEIA λογεία
contribution (2)

LOGIKOS λογικός
spiritual (2)

LOGION λόγιον
oracle (3)
word (*pl.*)

LOGIOS λόγιος
eloquent

LOGISMOS λογισμός
argument
thought

LOGIZOMAI λογίζομαι
charge
claim
consider (4)
count (3)
hold
reason
reckon (15)+
regard (4)
§resentful, be
suppose
suspect
think (3)
think about
understand (2)
IDIOMATICALLY
remind *a*

LOGOMACHEŌ λογομαχέω
dispute about words

LOGOMACHIA λογομαχία
dispute about words

LOGOS λόγος
account (5)
accounts (2)
appearance
book
complaint
conversation (*pl.*)
credit
doctrine
eloquent (*gen.*)
ground
§justify
matter (3)
message (6)
news (2)
preaching (2)
§question (3)
report (2)
retort
§say (3)
saying (18)
says, what one (4)
sentence (2)
speaking
speech (9)
story
talk (6)
teaching
terms
utterance (4)
§why
word (228)+
IDIOMATICALLY
account *a;* do *b;* mean *a;* message, speak a *a;* reason *a;* speaker *a;* value *a*
NOT TRANSLATED
Mt **19**.22
Mk **5**.36; **8**.32
Lk **1**.4; **23**.9
Jn **4**.39
Acts **20**.2
Rom **9**.9
Phil **4**.15

LOIDOREŌ λοιδορέω
revile (4)

LOIDORIA λοιδορία
§revile
reviling (2)

LOIDOROS λοίδορος
reviler (2)

LOIMOS λοιμός
pestilence
pestilent fellow

LOIPOS λοιπός
beyond that (*neut.*)
finally (*neut.*) (6)
§henceforth (2)
last, at (*neut.*)
moreover (*neut.*)
now on, from (*neut.*)
other (15)
remains, what (*subst. neut. pl.*)
§rest (22)
rest of mankind (*subst. pl.*)
rest of the people (*subst. pl.*)
still (*neut.*) (2)
then (*neut.*)

LOUŌ λούω
bathe (*mid.*)
wash (4)

LOUTRON λουτρόν
washing (2)

LYCHNIA λυχνία
lampstand (8)
stand (4)

LYCHNOS λύχνος
lamp (14)

LYKOS λύκος
wolf (6)

LYMAINŌ λυμαίνω
ravage (*mid.*)

LYŌ λύω
break (6)
break down
destroy (2)
dissolve (3)
free
free, be (*perf. pass.*)
loose (8)
relax
release (3)
take off
unbind (2)
untie (13)

LYPĒ λύπη
grief (2)
pain (*sg. or pl.*) (2)
§painful (2)
§reluctantly
sorrow (9)

LYPEŌ λυπέω
distressed, be (*pass.*) (2)
grief (*aor. pass. inf.*)
grief, feel (*pass.*)
grieve (6)
injure
pain
pain, cause (3)
sorrowful (*pass. part.*) (3)
sorrowful, be (*pass*) (4)
sorry, be (*pass.*)
sorry, make
suffer (*pass.*)
NOT TRANSLATED
2 Cor **2**.5

LYSIS λύσις
§free, to be

LYSITELEŌ λυσιτελέω
better, be (*impers.*)

LYTRON λύτρον
ransom (2)

LYTROŌ λυτρόω
ransomed, be (*pass.*)
redeem (*mid.*) (2)

LYTRŌSIS λύτρωσις
§redeem
redemption (2)

LYTRŌTĒS λυτρωτής
deliverer

M

MACHAIRA μάχαιρα
sword (29)

MACHĒ μάχη
fighting (2)
quarrel (2)

MACHOMAI μάχομαι
dispute
fight
quarrel
quarrelsome, be

MAGEIA μαγεία
magic

MAGEUŌ μαγεύω
magic, practice

MAGOS μάγος
magician (2)
wise man (4)

MAINOMAI μαίνομαι
mad, be (5)

MAKARIOS μακάριος
blessed (47)
fortunate
happier (*comp.*)
happy

MAKARISMOS μακαρισμός
blessing (2)
satisfaction one feels

MAKARIZŌ μακαρίζω
blessed, call
happy, call

MAKELLON μάκελλον
meat market

MAKRAN μακράν
distance, at some
far (4)
far away
far off (3)
IDIOMATICALLY
distance *a*

MAKROCHRONIOS μακροχρόνιος
[*long-lived*]
§long, live

MAKROS μακρός
far (2)
long (2)+

MAKROTHEN μακρόθεν
afar, from (3)
distance, at a (4)
distance, in the
far off (5)
§long way, a

MAKROTHYMEŌ μακροθυμέω
delay long
forbearing, be
patience, have (2)
patient, be (5)
patiently, endure

MAKROTHYMIA μακροθυμία
forbearance (2)
patience (12)

MAKROTHYMŌS μακροθύμως
patiently

MALAKIA μαλακία
infirmity (3)

MALAKOS μαλακός
§sexual perverts
soft
soft raiment (*subst. pl.*) (2)

MALISTA μάλιστα
above all
especially (10)
most of all

MALLON μᾶλλον
§better 3[a]
better, all the
§contrary, on the
especially
§far
greater
instead (3)†
more (28)
more, all the (5)
more, so much the
more, still (2)
more than ever
more, the (2)
rather (21)
really
yes
yet
IDIOMATICALLY
all *a, b, e;* less *a;* more, all the *a;* more and more, do so *a, b*
NOT TRANSLATED
Mk **6**.26; **7**.36
Lk **12**.24
1 Cor **7**.21
Phil **1**.23

MAMMĒ μάμμη
grandmother

MAMŌNAS μαμωνᾶς
mammon (4)

MANIA μανία
[*madness, eccentricity*]
IDIOMATICALLY
mad *a*

MANNA μάννα
manna (4)

MANTEUOMAI μαντεύομαι
soothsaying, by (*part.*)

MANTHANŌ μανθάνω
know
learn (20)
listen
study
taught, be
IDIOMATICALLY
ask *a*

MARAINŌ μαραίνω
fade away (*pass.*)

MARANATHA μαράνα θᾶ
Lord come, our

MARGARITĒS μαργαρίτης
pearl (9)

MARMAROS μάρμαρος
marble

MARTYREŌ μαρτυρέω
approval, receive (*pass.*) (2)
attest
attested, be well (*pass.*)
attested, well (*pass. part.*)
§bear (2)
repute, of good (*pass. part.*)
speak well of (4)
testify (14)
§testimony
testimony, have (*pass.*)
testimony, in one's (*part.*)
warn
witness (4)
witness, be a
witness, bear (40)
IDIOMATICALLY
testimony *a*

MARTYRIA μαρτυρία
testimony (34)
witness (2)
IDIOMATICALLY
thought *a*

MARTYRION μαρτύριον
evidence
proof (3)
§testify
testifying
testimony (9)
§testimony, bear 3[a] (3)
witness (2)

MARTYROMAI μαρτύρομαι
charge
testify (4)

MARTYS μάρτυς
martyr
witness (33)
§witness, bear

MASAOMAI μασάομαι
gnaw

MASTIGOŌ μαστιγόω
chastise
flog
scourge (5)

MASTIX μάστιξ
disease (3)
plague
scourging (2)

MASTIZŌ μαστίζω
scourge

MASTOS μαστός
breast (*sg. or pl.*) (3)

MATAIOLOGIA ματαιολογία
vain discussion

MATAIOLOGOS ματαιολόγος
empty talker (*subst.*)

MATAIOŌ ματαιόω
futile, become (*pass.*)

MATAIOS μάταιος
futile (4)
vain (2)

MATAIOTĒS ματαιότης
folly
futility (2)

MATĒN μάτην
vain, in (2)

MATHĒTĒS μαθητής
disciple (262)

MATHĒTEUŌ μαθητεύω
disciple, be a (*pass.*)
disciples, make (2)
trained, be (*pass.*)

MATHĒTRIA μαθήτρια
disciple

MĒ μή (*See also* EI MĒ)
§*against*
§avoid
but
§cannot (2)
§except
§fail
fear that, for
instead of
lest (10)
§neither (3)
never (12)
no (80)
§none (5)
§*nor* (3)
not (522)
§nothing (6)
§nowhere
or (6)
§refrain (2)
§refuse
§*that* 14 (3); 15
§unable
§without (13)
§*As the negative in:*
abstain 2 (Rom **14**.3[2], 6a)
beware 3[a]
cannot 2[a] (2)
devoid of 1
disobey 3
displease 1
far be it 1
keep from, to 1 (5)
lack 3
lest 1 (20)
no 13 (1 Cor **1**.29; Eph **4**.29)
no means, by 1 (10)
no one 5 (1 Cor **16**.11)
nor 2
not, certainly 1 (2)
nothing 9 (Mk **8**.1); 10 (Jn **5**.14; **6**.12)
or 3 (3)
otherwise 3
prevent from, in order to 2
prevent from, to 2
rather than 2
sure 1
unable, be 1[a] (2)
unlifted 1
unseen 1 (2)
unwilling, be 1[a]
IDIOMATICALLY
forbid, God *b;* improper *a;* keep from *b, c*
NOT TRANSLATED
in questions:
Mt **7**.9, 10; **9**.15; **11**.23
Mk **2**.19
Lk **5**.34; **10**.15; **11**.11; **17**.9; **22**.35
Jn **3**.4; **4**.12, 33; **6**.67; **7**.31, 35, 41, 47, 48, 51, 52; **8**.53; **9**.27, 40; **10**.21; **21**.5
Acts **7**.28, 42
Rom **3**.3, 5; **9**.20; **10**.18, 19
1 Cor **1**.13; **9**.4, 5, 8, 9; **10**.22; **12**.29[4], 30[3]
2 Cor **3**.1; **12**.17
Jas **2**.14; **3**.12
other:
Lk **4**.42; **22**.34

Acts **5**.26; **10**.47; **14**.18; **20**.27; **23**.10; **27**.17
2 Cor **12**.21
Gal **4**.11; **5**.7
1 Pet **3**.6

MECHRI μέχρι (μέχρις)
§about
§before
far as, as
point of, to the
to (3)+
until (7)
unto
IDIOMATICALLY
nearly *a;* wear *a*

MĒDAMŌS μηδαμῶς
no (2)

MĒDE μηδέ
even (+*neg.*)
neither (2)
no, and
none, and
nor (18)
not (11)
not even (4)
§*nothing, and*
or (16)
§refuse, and
NOT TRANSLATED
1 Cor **5**.8

MĒDEIS μηδείς
any (+*neg.*) (3)
any one (+*neg.*) (3)
anything (*neut.*+*neg.*) (2)
no (16)
§no . . . anything (*neut.*)
no man +
no one (30)
nobody
none (2)
§*not* (2)
not any
not in the least (*neut.*)
nothing (*neut.*) (21)
§*without* (*neut.*) (3)
NOT TRANSLATED
2 Cor **13**.7

MĒDEPŌ μηδέπω
§yet, as

MĒDEPOTE μηδέποτε
never

MEGALEIOS μεγαλεῖος
mighty work (*subst. neut.*)

MEGALEIOTĒS μεγαλειότης
magnificence
majesty (2)

MEGALOPREPĒS μεγαλοπρεπής
majestic

MEGALŌS μεγάλως
greatly

MEGALŌSYNĒ μεγαλωσύνη
majesty (3)

MEGALYNŌ μεγαλύνω
enlarge greatly
extol (2)
honor
honor, hold in high
long, make
magnify
IDIOMATICALLY
great *a*

MEGAS μέγας
fearful
fierce
§gale 1
great (126)+
greatest (2)
grown up
haughty
heavy
high (2)
large (5)
long
loud (42)
much, too (*interrog.*)
profound
strange
strong
wide
IDIOMATICALLY
fill *b, c;* greatly *b*
NOT TRANSLATED
Mk **5**.42
Rev **16**.18

MEGETHOS μέγεθος
greatness

MEGISTAN μεγιστάν
courtier
great man (2)

MEGISTOS μέγιστος
great, very

MEIGNYMI μείγνυμι (μειγνύω)
mingle (3)
mix

MEIZŌN μείζων
elder
greater (33)
greatest (10)
higher
larger
more
more, the (*neut.*)

MĒKETI μηκέτι
again (+*neg.*) (2)
any longer (+*neg.*)
any more (+*neg.*)
never again
no longer (12)
no more (4)
not again

MĒKOS μῆκος
length (3)

MĒKYNŌ μηκύνω
grow (*pass.*)

MELAS μέλας
black (3)
ink (*subst. neut.*) (3)

MELEI μέλει
[*it is a care* (*impers.*)]
§attention, pay
§care (7)
§concerned, be
§mind (*imper.*)

MELETAŌ μελετάω
imagine
practice

MELI μέλι
honey (4)

MELLŌ μέλλω
about, be (+*inf.*) (21)
almost, be (+*inf.*)
be (+*inf.*) (29)
come, things to (*subst. part. neut. pl.*)
come, to (*attr. part.*) (7)+
come, w. is to (*subst. part.*) (4)
future (*part.*) (4)
going, be (+*inf.*) (2)
intend (7)
point, be at the (+*inf.*) (3)
should (+*inf.*) (3)
wait
would (+*inf.*)
IDIOMATICALLY
expect *a;* next *a*
+inf. as the future tense:
Mt **17**.12; **24**.6
Lk **21**.36; **22**.23
Jn **6**.6; **14**.22
Acts **11**.28; **17**.31; **23**.3; **24**.15; **26**.23; **27**.10
Rom **4**.24; **8**.13
Rev **3**.16
NOT TRANSLATED
Lk **24**.31
Acts **5**.35; **13**.34; **19**.27; **27**.30
Rev **3**.10; **10**.7

MELOS μέλος
member (27)
organ (2)
part (2)
NOT TRANSLATED
1 Cor **12**.26[2]
Col **3**.5

MĒLŌTĒ μηλωτή
skin of sheep

MEMBRANA μεμβράνα
parchment

MEMPHOMAI μέμφομαι
fault, find (2)

MEMPSIMOIROS μεμψίμοιρος
malcontent

MEN μέν
although
indeed (6)
not only
on the one hand
sometimes
NOT TRANSLATED
Mt **3**.11; **9**.37; **10**.13; **13**.4, 8, 23, 32; **16**.3, 14; **17**.11; **20**.23; **21**.35; **22**.5, 8; **23**.27, 28; **25**.15, 33; **26**.24
Mk **4**.4; **9**.12; **12**.5; **14**.21; **16**.19
Lk **3**.16, 18; **8**.5; **10**.2; **11**.48; **13**.9; **22**.22; **23**.33, 56
Jn **7**.12; **10**.41; **11**.6; **16**.9, 22; **19**.25(24), 32; **20**.30
Acts **1**.1, 5, 6, 18; **2**.41; **3**.13, 21, 22; **4**.16; **5**.41; **8**.4, 25; **9**.7, 31; **11**.16, 19; **12**.5; **13**.4, 36; **14**.3, 4; **15**.3, 30; **16**.5; **17**.12, 17, 30, 32; **18**.14; **19**.15, 32, 38; **21**.39; **22**.9; **23**.18, 22, 31; **25**.4, 11; **26**.4, 9; **27**.21, 41, 44; **28**.5, 22, 24
Rom **1**.8; **2**.7; **3**.2; **5**.16; **6**.11; **7**.12, 25; **8**.17; **9**.21; **10**.1; **11**.13, 22, 28; **14**.2, 5
1 Cor **1**.12, 18, 23; **2**.15; **3**.4; **5**.3; **6**.4, 7; **7**.7; **9**.24, 25; **11**.7, 14, 18, 21; **12**.8, 20, 28; **14**.17; **15**.39, 40
2 Cor **2**.16; **9**.1; **10**.1, 10; **11**.4; **12**.1, 12
Gal **4**.8, 23, 24
Eph **4**.11
Phil **1**.15, 16; **2**.23; **3**.1, 13
1 Th **2**.18
2 Tim **1**.10; **2**.20; **4**.4
Heb **1**.7; **3**.5; **7**.2, 5, 8, 11, 20, 23; **8**.4; **9**.1, 6, 23; **10**.11; **11**.15; **12**.9, 10, 11

Jas **3**.17
1 Pet **1**.20; **2**.4; **3**.18; **4**.6
Jude .8, 10, 22

MĒN I (*See* EI MĒN)

MĒN II *μήν*
month (18)

MENŌ *μένω*
abide (43)
alive, be
await
continue (10)
dwell (2)
endure (2)
lasting (*part.*)
live
permanent (*part.*)
remain (30)+
rest
stay (22)
still, be
survive
wait

MENOUN *μενοῦν*
rather

MENOUNGE *μενοῦνγε*
indeed (2)
NOT TRANSLATED
Rom **9**.20

MENTOI *μέντοι*
but (3)
§nevertheless
really
yet (3)

MĒNYŌ *μηνύω*
disclose
inform
know, let one
show

MĒPŌ *μήπω*
not yet (2)

MĒPOTE *μήποτε*
be that, can it (*interrog.*)
lest (18)
not
perhaps (2)
perhaps, whether
NOT TRANSLATED
Acts **5**.39

MERIMNA *μέριμνα*
anxiety (2)
cares (*sg. or pl.*) (4)

MERIMNAŌ *μεριμνάω*
anxiety, have
anxious, be (17)
care, have

MERIS *μερίς*
district
part
portion
§share
IDIOMATICALLY
common *a*

MERISMOS *μερισμός*
division
IDIOMATICALLY
distributed *a*

MERISTĒS *μεριστής*
divider

MERIZŌ *μερίζω*
apportion (2)
assign (2)
divide (*act. or mid.*) (10)

MEROS *μέρος*
case (2)
country (*pl.*)
district (*pl.*) (4)
§imperfect (3)
§individually
§little
lot
part (13)
partly (*acc.*)
party
piece
§regard to, with
share (3)
side (*pl.*)
trade
IDIOMATICALLY
detail *a;* some *c, d;* turn, in *a*
NOT TRANSLATED
Mt **24**.51
Lk **12**.46
Jn **19**.23

MĒROS *μηρός*
thigh

MESĒMBRIA *μεσημβρία*
noon †
south

MESITĒS *μεσίτης*
intermediary (2)
§mediate
mediator (3)

MESITEUŌ *μεσιτεύω*
interpose

MESONYKTION *μεσονύκτιον*
midnight (4)

MESOŌ *μεσόω*
§middle

MESOS *μέσος*
among (16)
§aside
§*before* (2)
§between (4)
§*from* (3)
§here (2)
§inside
§midday, at
middle (*subst.*) (3)
middle, in the
§midnight (2)
midst (*subst.*) (17)+
§out on +
§round
§through
two, in (*neut.*)
§way

MESOTOICHON *μεσότοιχον*
dividing wall

MESOURANĒMA *μεσουράνημα*
midheaven (3)

MESSIAS *Μεσσίας*
Messiah (2)

MESTOŌ *μεστόω*
fill

MESTOS *μεστός*
full (9)

META *μετά*
after (+*acc.* 85)+
§*afterward* (+*acc.* 6)
against (+*gen.* 6)
along with (+*gen.* 2)
among (+*gen.* 4)
§*before* (+*acc.* 2)
behind (+*acc.*)
§hereafter (+*acc.*)
in (+*gen.* 3)
§*later* (+*acc.* 3)
§*later than* (+*acc.*)
near (+*gen.*)
on (+*gen.*) (4)
§*soon* (+*acc.*)
§subsequent (+*acc., attr.*)
§*then* (+*acc.*) 9[b], 13
to (+*gen.* 10)
upon (+*gen.*)
with (+*gen.* 314)+
without (*neg.*+*gen.* 2)
IDIOMATICALLY
OR NOT TRANSLATED
+*genitive:*
Mt **27**.66
Mk **5**.37
Lk **9**.39
Jn **3**.25; **16**.19
Acts **2**.29; **24**.18; **28**.31
2 Cor **8**.4
1 Tim **2**.9; **3**.4; **4**.14
Heb **10**.14; **11**.31; **13**.17
Rev **6**.8; **14**.13; **22**.12
+*accusative:*
Rev **9**.12

METABAINŌ *μεταβαίνω*
depart
go
go on (3)
leave (3)
move (2)
pass (2)

METABALLŌ *μεταβάλλω*
change one's mind (*mid.*)

METADIDŌMI *μεταδίδωμι*
contribute
give
impart
share (2)

METAGŌ *μετάγω*
guide (2)

METAIRŌ *μεταίρω*
go away (2)

METAKALEŌ *μετακαλέω*
ask for (*mid.*)
call to one (*mid.*) (2)
summon (*mid.*)

METAKINEŌ *μετακινέω*
shift (*mid.*)

METALAMBANŌ *μεταλαμβάνω*
have
partake
receive
share
share, have a
take (2)

METALĒMPSIS *μετάλημψις*
§receive

METALLASSŌ *μεταλλάσσω*
exchange (2)

METAMELOMAI *μεταμέλομαι*
change one's mind
regret (2)
repent (3)

METAMORPHOŌ *μεταμορφόω*
changed, be (*pass.*)
transfigured, be (*pass.*) (2)
transformed, be (*pass.*)

METANOEŌ *μετανοέω*
repent (34)

METANOIA μετάνοια
§repent (2)
repentance (19)
repenting

METAPEMPŌ μεταπέμπω
bring (*mid.*) (2)
send for (*mid.*) (6)
sent, have s. (*mid.*)

METASCHĒMATIZŌ μετασχηματίζω
apply
change
disguise oneself (*mid.*) (3)

METASTREPHŌ μεταστρέφω
pervert
turn

METATHESIS μετάθεσις
change
removal
IDIOMATICALLY
take *a*

METATITHĒMI μετατίθημι
carry back
change
§desert (*mid.*)
pervert
take
take up

METATREPŌ μετατρέπω
turn

METAXY μεταξύ
between (6)
§conflicting
§meanwhile
next (*attr.*)

MĒTE μήτε
either (4)
neither (5)
no
no, and
nor (10)
not
not, and
or (11)

METECHŌ μετέχω
belong to
live on
partake (4)
share (2)

METEŌRIZOMAI μετεωρίζομαι
anxious mind, be of

METEPEITA μετέπειτα
afterward

MĒTĒR μήτηρ
mother (78) +
IDIOMATICALLY
bear *a;* birth *a, b, c*

METHĒ μέθη
drunkenness (3)

METHERMĒNEUŌ μεθερμηνεύω
§mean (7)
meaning of, be the (*pass.*)

METHISTĒMI μεθίστημι (μεθιστάνω)
put out
remove (2)
transfer
turn away

METHODEIA μεθοδεία
wiles (*sg. or pl.*) (2)

METHYŌ μεθύω
drunk (*part.*)
drunk, be (3)
drunken (*part.*)

METHYSKŌ μεθύσκω
drink freely (*pass.*)
drunk, become (*pass.*)
drunk, get (*pass.*) (3)

METHYSOS μέθυσος
drunkard (2)

MĒTI μήτι
[*interrog. particle expecting a negative reply*]
§except perhaps
§unless (2)
NOT TRANSLATED
in questions:
Mt **7**.16; **12**.23; **26**.22, 25
Mk **4**.21; **14**.19
Lk **6**.39
Jn **4**.29; **8**.22; **18**.35
Acts **10**.47
2 Cor **1**.17; **12**.18
Jas **3**.11

MĒTIGE μήτιγε
how much more

METOCHĒ μετοχή
partnership

METOCHOS μέτοχος
comrade (*subst.*)
partaker (*subst.*)
§participate
partner (*subst.*)
§share
§shares, who

METOIKESIA μετοικεσία
deportation (4)

METOIKIZŌ μετοικίζω
remove (2)

METŌPON μέτωπον
forehead (8)

MĒTRA μήτρα
womb (2)

METREŌ μετρέω
measure (6)
IDIOMATICALLY
measure, get *a;* measure, give *a, b*

METRĒTĒS μετρητής
§gallon

METRIOPATHEŌ μετριοπαθέω
deal gently

METRIŌS μετρίως
little, a

MĒTROLŌAS μητρολῴας
murderer of mother

METRON μέτρον
§limits
measure (10)
§measuring
§properly
NOT TRANSLATED
1 Cor **10**.13

MIAINŌ μιαίνω
corrupt (2)
defile (3)

MIASMA μίασμα
defilement

MIASMOS μιασμός
defiling (*gen.*)

MIGMA μίγμα
mixture

MIKROS μικρός
least (5)
little (15)
little, a (*neut.*) (2)
little farther, a (*neut.*) (2)
little while, a (*neut.*) (12)
small (7)
smallest (*comp.*) (2)
younger

MILION μίλιον
mile

MIMEOMAI μιμέομαι
imitate (4)

MIMĒTĒS μιμητής
imitator (6)

MIMNĒSKOMAI μιμνήσκομαι
mindful, be
remember (21)
remembrance, in (*pass. inf.*)

MISEŌ μισέω
hate (39)
hateful (*perf. mid. part.*)

MISTHAPODOSIA μισθαποδοσία
retribution
reward (2)

MISTHAPODOTĒS μισθαποδότης
[*rewarder*]
§reward

MISTHIOS μίσθιος
hired servant (2) +

MISTHŌMA μίσθωμα
expense
(hired dwelling †)

MISTHOŌ μισθόω
hire (*mid.*) (2)

MISTHOS μισθός
gain (2)
recompense
reward (18)
wages (7)
IDIOMATICALLY
for *a*

MISTHŌTOS μισθωτός
hired servant
hireling (2)

MNA μνᾶ
pound (9)

MNEIA μνεία
§mention (2)
§remember (4)
remembrance

MNĒMA μνῆμα
tomb (9) +

MNĒMĒ μνήμη
[*remembrance, memory*]
§recall

MNĒMEION μνημεῖον
grave
monument
tomb (37) +

MNĒMONEUŌ μνημονεύω
mention, make
remember (19)
think of

MNĒMOSYNON μνημόσυνον
memorial
memory (2)

MNĒSTEUŌ μνηστεύω
betrothed, be (*pass.*) (3)

MOCHTHOS μόχθος
hardship
toil (2)

MODIOS μόδιος
bushel (3)

MOGILALOS μογιλάλος
impediment in his speech, a man who has an (*subst.*)
MOICHALIS μοιχαλίς
adulteress (2)
adulterous (*attr.*) (3)
§adultery
unfaithful creature
MOICHAŌ μοιχάω
adultery, commit (*pass.*) (4)+
MOICHEIA μοιχεία
adultery (3)
MOICHEUŌ μοιχεύω
§adulteress (*pass. inf.*)
adultery, commit (13)+
IDIOMATICALLY
adultery *a*
MOICHOS μοιχός
adulterer (2)
adulterous (*pl.*)
MOLIS μόλις
difficulty, with (3)
hardly (2)
scarcely (2)
MŌLŌPS μώλωψ
wound
MOLYNŌ μολύνω
defile (2)
soil
MOLYSMOS μολυσμός
defilement
MŌMAOMAI μωμάομαι
blame
fault, find
MŌMOS μῶμος
blemish
MOMPHĒ μομφή
complaint
MONĒ μονή
home
room
MONOGENĒS μονογενής
only (9)
MONOŌ μονόω
left all alone, be (*pass.*)
MONOPHTHALMOS μονόφθαλμος
one eye, with (2)
MONOS μόνος
alone (24)
even (*neut.*)
§himself, by
merely (*neut.*)
only (81)
§themselves, by +
IDIOMATICALLY
any *a*; more *b*
NOT TRANSLATED
Mk **6.8**
Acts **11.19**
MŌRAINŌ μωραίνω
fool, become a (*pass.*)
foolish, make
loses its taste, s. (*pass.*) (2)
MŌRIA μωρία
folly (5)
MŌROLOGIA μωρολογία
silly talk
MŌROS μωρός
fool (*subst.*) (4)
foolish (5)
foolishness (*subst. neut.*)
stupid (2)

MORPHĒ μορφή
form (3)
MORPHOŌ μορφόω
form
MORPHŌSIS μόρφωσις
embodiment
form
MOSCHOPOIEŌ μοσχοποιέω
calf, make a
MOSCHOS μόσχος
calf (5)
ox
MOUSIKOS μουσικός
minstrel (*subst.*)
MYELOS μυελός
marrow
MYEŌ μυέω
learn the secret of (*pass.*)
MYKAOMAI μυκάομαι
roar
MYKTĒRIZŌ μυκτηρίζω
mock
MYLIKOS μυλικός
[*for a mill*]
§millstone
MYLINOS μύλινος
millstone (*subst.*)
MYLOS μύλος
mill
millstone (3)
MYŌPAZŌ μυωπάζω
shortsighted, be
MYRIAS μυριάς
innumerable (*pl.*+*gen.*)
myriad (3)
ten thousand
thousands (3)
MYRIOI μύριοι
ten thousand (2)
MYRIOS μυρίος
countless
MYRIZŌ μυρίζω
anoint
MYRON μύρον
myrrh
ointment (13)
MYSTĒRION μυστήριον
mystery (23)+
secret (4)+
MYTHOS μῦθος
myth (5)

N

NAI ναί
and
even so
indeed
surely
yea (3)
yes (25; Gr. 27)
NOT TRANSLATED
Mt **5.37**
2 Cor **1.17**
Jas **5.12**
NAOS ναός
sanctuary
shrine (2)
temple (42)

NARDOS νάρδος
nard (2)
NAUAGEŌ ναυαγέω
shipwreck, make
shipwrecked, be
NAUKLĒROS ναύκληρος
owner of a ship
NAUS ναῦς
vessel
NAUTĒS ναύτης
sailor (3)
NĒ νή
by
NEANIAS νεανίας
young man (3)
NEANISKOS νεανίσκος
young man (11)
NEKROŌ νεκρόω
dead, as good as (*perf. pass. part.*) (2)
death, put to
NEKROS νεκρός
corpse (*subst.*)
dead (123)
§death (*subst. pl.*) (2)
§die (2)
NEKRŌSIS νέκρωσις
barrenness
death
NEŌKOROS νεωκόρος
temple keeper
NEOMĒNIA νεομηνία
new moon
NEOPHYTOS νεόφυτος
recent convert (*subst.*)
NEOS νέος
new (11)
young (3)
younger (*comp.*) (8)
youngest (*comp.*)
NEŌTERIKOS νεωτερικός
youthful
NEOTĒS νεότης
youth (4)
NĒPHALIOS νηφάλιος
temperate (3)
NEPHELĒ νεφέλη
cloud (25)
NĒPHŌ νήφω
sober, be (4)
sober, keep
steady, be
NEPHOS νέφος
cloud
NEPHROS νεφρός
mind
NĒPIAZŌ νηπιάζω
babe, be a
NĒPIOS νήπιος
babe (*subst.*) (4)+
child (*subst.*) (9)
childish
NĒSION νησίον
island, small
NĒSOS νῆσος
island (9)
NĒSTEIA νηστεία
fast
fasting (2)+

§food, without
hunger
NĒSTEUŌ *νηστεύω*
fast (20)
NĒSTIS *νῆστις*
hungry (2)
NĒTHŌ *νήθω*
spin (2)
NEUŌ *νεύω*
beckon
motion
NIKAŌ *νικάω*
conquer (17)
overcome (10)
prevail
NIKĒ *νίκη*
victory
NIKOS *νῖκος*
victory (4)
NIPTĒR *νιπτήρ*
basin
NIPTŌ *νίπτω*
wash (*act. or mid.*) (17)
NOĒMA *νόημα*
design
mind (3)
thought (2)
NOEŌ *νοέω*
perceive (5)
see (2)
think
think over
understand (4)
IDIOMATICALLY
clearly *a*
NOMĒ *νομή*
pasture
IDIOMATICALLY
eat *b*
NOMIKOS *νομικός*
§law, over the
lawyer (*subst.*) (8)
NOMIMŌS *νομίμως*
lawfully
rules, according to the
NOMISMA *νόμισμα*
money
NOMIZŌ *νομίζω*
imagine
suppose (7)
think (7)
NOMODIDASKALOS *νομοδιδάσκαλος*
teacher of the law (3)
NOMOS *νόμος*
law (191)+
§legal
principle (2)
NOMOTHESIA *νομοθεσία*
law, giving of the·
NOMOTHETEŌ *νομοθετέω*
enacted, be (*pass.*)
receive the law (*pass.*)
NOMOTHETĒS *νομοθέτης*
lawgiver
NOSĒMA *νόσημα*
(disease)
NOSEŌ *νοσέω*
morbid craving, have a
NOSOS *νόσος*
disease (11)
NOSPHIZŌ *νοσφίζω*
keep back (*mid.*) (2)
pilfer (*mid.*)
NOSSIA *νοσσιά*
brood
NOSSION *νοσσίον*
brood (*pl.*)
NOSSOS *νοσσός*
§young
NOTHOS *νόθος*
illegitimate children (*subst. pl.*)
NŌTHROS *νωθρός*
dull
sluggish
NOTOS *νότος*
south (7)
NŌTOS *νῶτος*
back
NOUNECHŌS *νουνεχῶς*
wisely
NOUS *νοῦς*
mind (22)
understanding (2)
NOUTHESIA *νουθεσία*
admonishing
instruction (2)
NOUTHETEŌ *νουθετέω*
admonish (5)
instruct
warn (2)
NYCHTHĒMERON *νυχθήμερον*
night and a day, a
NYMPHĒ *νύμφη*
bride (5)+
daughter-in-law (3)
NYMPHIOS *νυμφίος*
bridegroom (16)
NYMPHŌN *νυμφών*
§wedding guest (3)
wedding hall
NYN *νῦν*
as it is (8)
§henceforth (3)
just
now (116)+†
§now on, from (4)
present (*attr.*) (7)
rather
this (*attr.*) (2)
yet
IDIOMATICALLY
present *a, b*
NOT TRANSLATED
Jn **18**.30
2 Cor **5**.16
NYNI *νυνί*
as it is
fact, in
now (13)
present, at
§so
§so then
NYSSŌ *νύσσω*
pierce +
NYSTAZŌ *νυστάζω*
asleep, be
slumber
NYX *νύξ*
§midnight (2)
night (59)

O

Ō I *Ω*
omega (3)
Ō II *ὦ*
O (12)
NOT TRANSLATED
Acts **13**.10; **27**.21
Rom **9**.20
1 Tim **6**.11
Jas **2**.20
OCHLEŌ *ὀχλέω*
afflicted (*pass. part.*)
OCHLOPOIEŌ *ὀχλοποιέω*
gather a crowd
OCHLOS *ὄχλος*
company (3)
company of people (2)
crowd (104)
many
multitude (31)
people (29)
throng (4)
OCHYRŌMA *ὀχύρωμα*
stronghold
ŌDĒ *ᾠδή*
song (6)
ŌDIN *ὠδίν*
birth-pangs (2)
pang
travail
ŌDINŌ *ὠδίνω*
pangs of birth, in one's (*part. fem.*)
travail, be in
travail with, be in
ODOUS *ὀδούς*
tooth (12)
ODYNAŌ *ὀδυνάω*
anguish, be in (*pass.*) (2)
anxiously (*pass. part.*)
sorrow (*pass.*)
ODYNĒ *ὀδύνη*
anguish
pang
ODYRMOS *ὀδυρμός*
lamentation
mourning
OGDOĒKONTA *ὀγδοήκοντα*
eighty
§eighty-four
OGDOOS *ὄγδοος*
eighth (4)
IDIOMATICALLY
seven other *a*
OGKOS *ὄγκος*
weight
OIDA *οἶδα*
acquainted with, be
aware, be
can
§have
informed, be
know (302)+†
knowledge, have
perceive
regard
respect
see
§sure, be
understand (6)
NOT TRANSLATED
2 Cor **12**.2

OIKEIOS οἰκεῖος
family, one's own (*subst. pl.*)
household, member of the (*subst.*)
household, one who is of the (*subst.*)

OIKĒMA οἴκημα
cell

OIKEŌ οἰκέω
dwell (6)
live (2)

OIKETEIA οἰκετεία
household

OIKĒTĒRION οἰκητήριον
dwelling (2)

OIKETĒS οἰκέτης
servant (4)

OIKIA οἰκία
home (3)
house (84) +
household (4)
IDIOMATICALLY
house *a* (2; Gr. 1); live *c*
NOT TRANSLATED
Lk **22**.11

OIKIAKOS οἰκιακός
household, those of a (*pl.*) (2)

OIKODESPOTEŌ οἰκοδεσποτέω
rule one's household

OIKODESPOTĒS οἰκοδεσπότης
householder (11)
master of the house

OIKODOMĒ οἰκοδομή
building (5)
building up (4)
edification
§edify (2)
edifying
structure
§upbuild
upbuilding (3)

OIKODOMEŌ οἰκοδομέω
build (32)
builder (*subst. part.*) (4)
edify (3)
encourage

OIKODOMOS οἰκοδόμος
builder

OIKONOMEŌ οἰκονομέω
steward, be

OIKONOMIA οἰκονομία
commission
office
(order †)
plan (2)
stewardship (4)†
training

OIKONOMOS οἰκονόμος
steward (8)
treasurer
trustee

OIKOS οἶκος
family (2)
home (20)
house (71)
household (15)
sanctuary
IDIOMATICALLY
house *b* (2; Gr. 1), *c* (2; Gr. 1);
household *a* (1; Gr. 2)

OIKOUMENĒ οἰκουμένη
world (15)

OIKOURGOS οἰκουργός
domestic

OIKTIRMŌN οἰκτίρμων
merciful (3)

OIKTIRMOS οἰκτιρμός
§compassion
mercy (3)
sympathy

OIKTIRŌ οἰκτίρω
compassion, have
compassion on, have

OINOPHLYGIA οἰνοφλυγία
drunkenness (*pl.*)

OINOPOTĒS οἰνοπότης
drunkard (2)

OINOS οἶνος
drink
wine (31)
NOT TRANSLATED
Rev **16**.19; **19**.15

OIOMAI οἴομαι
suppose (2)
think

OKNEŌ ὀκνέω
delay, without (*neg. part.*)

OKNĒROS ὀκνηρός
§flag
irksome
slothful

OKTAĒMEROS ὀκταήμερος
eighth day, on the

OKTŌ ὀκτώ
eight (6)
§eighteen
§thirty-eight

OLETHROS ὄλεθρος
destruction (3)
ruin

OLIGOPISTIA ὀλιγοπιστία
little faith

OLIGOPISTOS ὀλιγόπιστος
little faith, of (5)

OLIGOPSYCHOS ὀλιγόψυχος
fainthearted

OLIGŌREŌ ὀλιγωρέω
regard lightly

OLIGOS ὀλίγος
§briefly (2)
few (13) +
light
little (10)
little, a (*neut.*)
little farther, a (*neut.*)
little while, a (*neut.*) (2)
little while, for a (*neut.*)
short (4)
small (3)
§some
while, a (*neut.*)

OLIGŌS ὀλίγως
barely

OLOLYZŌ ὀλολύζω
howl

OLOTHREUŌ ὀλοθρεύω
destroyer (*subst. part.*)

OLOTHREUTĒS ὀλοθρευτής
destroyer

OLYNTHOS ὄλυνθος
winter fruit

OMBROS ὄμβρος
shower

OMMA ὄμμα
eye (2)

OMNYŌ ὀμνύω
swear (25)
vow

ŌMOS ὦμος
shoulder (2)

ONAR ὄναρ
dream (6)

ONARION ὀνάριον
ass, young

ONEIDISMOS ὀνειδισμός
abuse (3)
reproach (2)

ONEIDIZŌ ὀνειδίζω
reproach (3)
(reproach, suffer [*pass.*])
revile (4)
upbraid (2)

ONEIDOS ὄνειδος
reproach

ŌNEOMAI ὠνέομαι
buy

ONIKOS ὀνικός
§great (2)

ONINĒMI ὀνίνημι
benefit, want some (*aor. mid. opt.*)

ONOMA ὄνομα
name (179)
§named 1[a]; 3 (33)
person
§surname
IDIOMATICALLY
called *a;* every *a;* name s. after *a;*
sake, for s.'s *a, b*
NOT TRANSLATED
Mt **10**.41[2], 42
Jn **15**.21
Acts **15**.26
3 Jn .7
Rev **11**.13

ONOMAZŌ ὀνομάζω
name (7) +
name of, bear the (*pass.*)
pronounce

ONOS ὄνος
ass (5) +

ONTŌS ὄντως
certainly
indeed (4)
real (*attr.*) (4)
really

ŌON ᾠόν
egg

OPĒ ὀπή
cave
opening

OPHEILĒ ὀφειλή
conjugal rights
debt
dues (*pl.*)

OPHEILĒMA ὀφείλημα
debt
§due

OPHEILETĒS ὀφειλέτης
bound (*pred.*)
debt, in (*pred.*)
debtor (2)
obligation, under (*pred.*)
offender
owes, one who

OPHEILŌ ὀφείλω
bound, be (5)
debt (*subst. pass. part. neut.*) (2)
have (+*inf.*) (2)
indebted, be
need
ought (14)
owe (7)
should (+*inf.*) (2)
IDIOMATICALLY
duty *b*

ŌPHELEIA ὠφέλεια
advantage
value

ŌPHELEŌ ὠφελέω
advantage, be of
avail, be of
benefit (3)
better, be (*pass.*)
gain (*act. or pass.*) (4)
profit (3)
value, be of
IDIOMATICALLY
do *a*

ŌPHELIMOS ὠφέλιμος
profitable (2)
value, of (2)

OPHELON ὄφελον
wish (2)
would that (2)

OPHELOS ὄφελος
§gain
profit (2)

OPHIS ὄφις
serpent (14)

OPHRYS ὀφρῦς
brow

OPHTHALMODOULIA
ὀφθαλμοδουλία
eyeservice (2)

OPHTHALMOS ὀφθαλμός
§envy 3
eye (97)†
sight (*pl.*)
IDIOMATICALLY
begrudge *a*

OPISŌ ὀπίσω
after (16)
back (6)
behind (5)
§follow 2; 3 (2)
§round
IDIOMATICALLY
follow *a;* indulge *a, b*
NOT TRANSLATED
Mt **10.**38

OPISTHEN ὄπισθεν
after
back, on the
behind (5)

OPŌRA ὀπώρα
fruit

OPSARION ὀψάριον
fish (5)

OPSE ὀψέ
after (+*gen.*)
§evening
evening, in the
late

OPSIMOS ὄψιμος
§late rain

OPSIOS ὄψιος
evening (*subst. fem.*) (14)

OPSIS ὄψις
appearances
face (2)

OPSŌNION ὀψώνιον
expense
support
wages (*pl.*) (2)

OPTANOMAI ὀπτάνομαι
appear

OPTASIA ὀπτασία
vision (4)

OPTOS ὀπτός
broiled

ORCHEOMAI ὀρχέομαι
dance (4)

OREGŌ ὀρέγω
aspire (*mid.*)
crave (*mid.*)
desire (*mid.*)

OREINOS ὀρεινός
§hill country (2)

OREXIS ὄρεξις
passion

ORGĒ ὀργή
anger (7)
wrath (29)

ORGILOS ὀργίλος
quick-tempered

ORGIZŌ ὀργίζω
anger, in (*pass. part.*) (2)
angry, be (*pass.*) (5)
rage (*pass.*)

ORGUIA ὀργυιά
fathom (2)

ORNEON ὄρνεον
bird (3)

ORNIS ὄρνις
hen (2)

OROS ὄρος
hill (2)
hillside (2)
mount (18)
mountain (41)†

ORPHANOS ὀρφανός
desolate
orphan (*subst.*)

ORTHOPODEŌ ὀρθοποδέω
straightforward, be

ORTHOS ὀρθός
straight
upright

ORTHŌS ὀρθῶς
plainly
right
rightly (2)

ORTHOTOMEŌ ὀρθοτομέω
rightly handle

ORTHRINOS ὀρθρινός
§early in the morning

ORTHRIZŌ ὀρθρίζω
[*be awake before dawn*]
IDIOMATICALLY
early in the morning *b*

ORTHROS ὄρθρος
dawn, at (*gen.*)
daybreak
early in the morning (*gen.*)

ŌRYOMAI ὠρύομαι
roar

ORYSSŌ ὀρύσσω
dig (3)

OSMĒ ὀσμή
fragrance (4)
§offering
IDIOMATICALLY
fragrant *a*

OSPHRĒSIS ὄσφρησις
sense of smell

OSPHYS ὀσφῦς (ὀσφύς)
§descend
loins (*sg. or pl.*) (3)
waist (2)
IDIOMATICALLY
descendants *a*
NOT TRANSLATED
1 Pet **1.**13

OSTEON ὀστέον (ὀστοῦν)
bone (3)
burial (*pl.*)

OSTRAKINOS ὀστράκινος
earthen
§earthenware

ŌTARION ὠτάριον
ear (2)

OTHONĒ ὀθόνη
sheet (2)

OTHONION ὀθόνιον
linen cloth (4)+

ŌTION ὠτίον
ear (3)

OU οὐ (οὐκ, οὐχ)
§*before*
§*cannot* (5)
§*except*
§fail (3)
§*from* (2)
instead of
§less, any (2)
§*neither* (17)
never (13)+
no (173)
no more
§*no one* (4)
§*none* (7)
§*nor* (7)
not (1136)+
§*nothing* (7)
§*or*
§*rather than* (2)
§refuse (3)
§*than*
§*without* (4)
§*As the negative in:*
abstain 2 (Rom **14.**6b)
any more 1 (Rev **21.**4)
before 17[b]
cannot 2 (50); 3
cannot be, it 1
decline 1
defeated, be 1
extraordinary 1
few, a 1
keep from being 1
know 1 (2)
never 1 (Mk **3.**29)
no 13 (Mt **12.**25; **24.**22; Mk **13.**20; Rom **3.**20; Eph **5.**5; 2 Pet **1.**20; 1 Jn **2.**21; **3.**15)
no one 4 (5)
none 1; 7 (Jn **16.**30)

nor 1 (Jn **9**.21)
nothing 1; 2; 8[a]; 9 (Mt **15**.32; Mk **8**.2); 10 (Acts **25**.26; 1 Cor **2**.2)+
nothing at all 1
nowhere 2 (3)
only 2[a] (5)
refuse 1; 5; 6; 13 (7)
§*soon* 2
unable, be 1[b]
understand 1
understanding, be without 1
unexpected 1
unfit 2
unusual 1
unwilling, be 1[b]
unworthy 2
without 7 (2)
yet, ever 1
IDIOMATICALLY
imply *a;* more *b;* only *a*
NOT TRANSLATED
in questions:
Mk **14**.60; **15**.4
other:
Mt **22**.16
Mk **3**.27; **5**.37; **6**.5; **12**.14; **14**.61
Lk **4**.2
Jn **5**.19, 30; **8**.15; **9**.33; **12**.19; **14**.30; **15**.5; **16**.23, 24; **18**.9
Acts **4**.12; **8**.39; **19**.40; **26**.26
1 Cor **6**.5; **13**.4, 5[2]
2 Cor **12**.2
1 Jn **2**.22

OU MĒ οὐ μή
never (26)†
no (9)
no means, by
not (58)
§nothing 8[b]
NOT TRANSLATED
Lk **10**.19
Heb **13**.5

OUA οὐά
aha

OUAI οὐαί
alas (9)
woe (37)+

OUCHI οὐχί
§instead of
no (6)
not (46)
not so

OUDAMŌS οὐδαμῶς
no means, by

OUDE οὐδέ
and (+*neg.*)
§cannot 2[c] (3)
even (3)
neither (12)+
never even
no 10 (7); 13 (1 Jn **2**.23)
no, and (2)
nor (48)
not (19)
not, and
not, but
not even (18)
not, no
not, then . . . (2)
or (22)
NOT TRANSLATED
Jn **5**.29
Rev **7**.16

OUDEIS οὐδείς (οὐθείς)
any (+*neg.*) (3)
any man (+*neg.*)
any one (+*neg.*) (6)
anything (+*neg.*) (5)
neither . . . anything
no (39)
no . . . any one
no . . . anything
no man (11)
no one (84)+
none (18)
not (*attr.*)
§not any (2)
not any one
not anything
§not at all (2)
not one
nothing (53)
nothing at all (*neut.*+*neg.*)
NOT TRANSLATED
1 Cor **7**.19

OUDEPŌ οὐδέπω
ever (+*neg.*)
not, as yet
not yet (2)

OUDEPOTE οὐδέποτε
never (14)
no . . . ever
nothing . . . ever

OUKETI οὐκέτι
after that
again (+*neg.*) (2)+
any more (+*neg.*) (3)
never again
no longer (29)
no more (8)
now . . . not
IDIOMATICALLY
further *a;* refrain *a*

OUKOUN οὐκοῦν
so (*interrog.*)

OUN οὖν
accordingly
and
but (4)
hence
however
now (18)
so (121)
§so then 1 (7); 4 (2)
then (128)
therefore (92)
thus (4)
IDIOMATICALLY
OR NOT TRANSLATED
Mt **3**.8; **6**.8; **12**.12; **13**.40; **18**.4, 31
Lk **3**.8; **13**.14; **14**.34; **21**.7
Jn **1**.39; **4**.9, 53; **5**.[4‡, 18, 19; **6**.14, 19, 34, 60, 67; **7**.6, 11, 15, 35, 40, 47; **8**.5‡, 12, 21, 24, 25, 38; **9**.8, 10, 15, 16, 18, 20, 25, 26; **10**.39; **11**.12, 14, 16, 20, 21, 31, 33, 56; **12**.1, 2, 3, 7, 9, 17, 29, 34, 35; **13**.6, 12, 26, 27, 31; **16**.17, 18; **18**.6, 7, 11, 17, 25, 27, 31, 33, 37, 39, 40; **19**.1, 6, 8, 13, 20, 23, 26, 30, 31, 40; **20**.8, 11, 19, 21; **21**.5, 7[2], 9, 15, 21, 23
Acts **17**.30; **25**.4; **26**.4, 9
Rom **4**.9; **11**.5, 19
1 Cor **6**.7; **7**.26; **9**.25; **11**.20; **14**.15; **16**.18
2 Cor **1**.17; **3**.12; **7**.1; **12**.9
Gal **3**.5; **4**.15
Phil **3**.15
Jas **4**.17
Rev **3**.3, 19

OUPŌ οὔπω
ever (+*neg.*)
ever yet (+*neg.*)
not
not yet (21)+
yet not, as

OURA οὐρά
tail (5)

OURANIOS οὐράνιος
heaven, who is in
heavenly (8)

OURANOS οὐρανός
air (9)
heaven (*sg. or pl.*) (250)+
§heavenly (3)
sky (9)
IDIOMATICALLY
other *c*

OURANOTHEN οὐρανόθεν
heaven, from (2)

OUS οὖς
ear (33)+
hearing (*pl.*)
IDIOMATICALLY
whisper *a, b*

OUSIA οὐσία
property (2)

OUTE οὔτε
§either (4)
neither (19)+
§no (2)
no, and
no more
§none, and
nor (39)+
not (3)
§nothing
or (13)
§refuse
whether
IDIOMATICALLY
never *a* (2)
NOT TRANSLATED
1 Cor **6**.9

OUTHEIS (*See* OUDEIS)

OXOS ὄξος
vinegar (6)

OXYS ὀξύς
sharp (6)
swift
NOT TRANSLATED
Rev **14**.18

OZŌ ὄζω
odor, be an

P

PACHYNŌ παχύνω
dull, grow (*pass.*) (2)

PAGIDEUŌ παγιδεύω
entangle

PAGIS παγίς
snare (5)

PAIDAGŌGOS παιδαγωγός
custodian (2)
guide

PAIDARION παιδάριον
lad
PAIDEIA παιδεία
discipline (5)
training
PAIDEUŌ παιδεύω
chasten (2)
chastise (2)
correct
discipline (3)
educate
instruct
learn (*pass.*)
punish
train
PAIDEUTĒS παιδευτής
corrector
§discipline
PAIDION παιδίον
child (51)
NOT TRANSLATED
Mk **5**.41
PAIDIOTHEN παιδιόθεν
childhood, from
PAIDISKĒ παιδίσκη
maid (6)
maidservant
slave (5)
slave girl
PAIŌ παίω
sting
strike (4)
PAIS παῖς
boy (3)
child (3)†
lad
male child
manservant
servant (14)
son
PAIZŌ παίζω
dance
PALAI πάλαι
along, all
long ago (3)
old
old, of
(some time)
PALAIOŌ παλαιόω
obsolete, become (*pass.*)
obsolete, treat as
old, grow (*pass.*) (2)
PALAIOS παλαιός
old (19)
PALAIOTĒS παλαιότης
old code
PALĒ πάλη
§contend
PALIGGENESIA παλιγγενεσία
new world
regeneration
PALIN πάλιν
again (122)
§another
back (4)
further
more, once 1[a]; 3 (2)
§repeat
§return (2)
yet
IDIOMATICALLY
remind *a*; resume *a*

NOT TRANSLATED
Mt **26**.44
Jn **4**.54; **21**.16
Acts **18**.21
PAMPLĒTHEI παμπληθεί
together
PANDOCHEION πανδοχεῖον
inn
PANDOCHEUS πανδοχεύς
innkeeper
PANĒGYRIS πανήγυρις
festal gathering
PANOIKEI πανοικεί
household, with all one's
PANOPLIA πανοπλία
armor
whole armor (2)
PANOURGIA πανουργία
craftiness (3)
cunning (2)
PANOURGOS πανοῦργος
crafty
PANTACHĒ πανταχῇ
everywhere
PANTACHOU πανταχοῦ
everywhere (7)
PANTĒ πάντῃ
every way, in
PANTELĒS παντελής
[*complete, perfect*]
§fully
IDIOMATICALLY
time *b*
PANTOKRATŌR παντοκράτωρ
almighty (10)
PANTŌS πάντως
all, at (+*neg.*) (3)
all means, by
certainly
doubt, no
doubtless
entirely
PANTOTE πάντοτε
always (40)
IDIOMATICALLY
anybody *a*
PANTOTHEN πάντοθεν
all sides, on
every quarter, from
every side, on
PARA παρά
along (+*acc.* 7)
among (+*dat.* 4)
at (+*acc.* 9)+
before (+*dat.* 4)
beside (+*acc.* 4)
beyond (+*acc.* 2)
by (+*gen.* 2; +*dat.* 2; +*acc.* 5)
by s.'s side (+*dat.*)
contrary to (+*acc.* 3)
from (+*gen.* 59; +*dat.*)
§*less* (+*acc.*)
of (+*gen.* 4)
on s.'s part (+*dat.*)
opposition to, in (+*acc.*)
past (+*acc.*)
rather than (+*acc.* 2)
§than (+*acc.* 10)
with (+*gen.*; +*dat.* 28)+
§worse than (+*acc.* 2)

IDIOMATICALLY
OR NOT TRANSLATED
+*genitive:*
Mt **21**.42
Mk **3**.21; **5**.26; **12**.11
Lk **10**.7
Jn **1**.40; **4**.52; **7**.51
Acts **9**.2; **10**.22
Rom **11**.27
2 Th **3**.8
Jas **1**.5
+*dative:*
Lk **19**.7
Jn **17**.5
Rom **2**.11; **12**.16
1 Cor **16**.2
2 Cor **1**.17
2 Th **1**.6
1 Pet **2**.4, 20
+*accusative:*
Mt **20**.30
Mk **10**.46
Lk **18**.35
Acts **10**.6, 32; **16**.13
Rom **1**.26; **4**.18; **14**.5
1 Cor **12**.15, 16
PARABAINŌ παραβαίνω
transgress (2)
turn aside
PARABALLŌ παραβάλλω
touch
PARABASIS παράβασις
breaking
transgression (5)
§transgressor
PARABATĒS παραβάτης
§break
breaks, one who
transgressor (3)
PARABIAZOMAI παραβιάζομαι
constrain
prevail upon
PARABOLĒ παραβολή
§figuratively speaking
lesson (2)
parable (45)
proverb
§symbolic
PARABOLEUOMAI παραβολεύομαι
risk
PARACHEIMASIA παραχειμασία
§winter in
PARACHEIMAZŌ παραχειμάζω
winter (2)
winter, spend the (2)
PARACHRĒMA παραχρῆμα
immediately (14)
once, at (4)
PARADECHOMAI παραδέχομαι
accept (3)
admit
receive
welcome
PARADEIGMATIZŌ παραδειγματίζω
contempt, hold up to
PARADEISOS παράδεισος
paradise (3)
PARADIDŌMI παραδίδωμι
arrest (2)
betray (30)
betrayer (*subst. part.*) (5)
commend (2)

commit (3)
death, put to
deliver (38)
deliver up (16)
entrust
give
give over
give up (9)
hand on
hand over (6)
ripe, be
risk
trust

PARADOSIS παράδοσις
tradition (13)

PARADOXOS παράδοξος
strange things (*subst. neut. pl.*)

PARAGGELIA παραγγελία
charge (3)
instruction
IDIOMATICALLY
strictly *a*

PARAGGELLŌ παραγγέλλω
charge (16)
charge, give
command (11)
command, give
§instructions
order
(tell)

PARAGINOMAI παραγίνομαι
appear
arrive (6)
come (27)
go
present, be
take s.'s part (+*dat.*)

PARAGŌ παράγω
pass along
pass away (*act. or pass.*) (3)
pass by (2)
pass on (3)
passer-by (*subst. part.*)

PARAINEŌ παραινέω
advise
bid

PARAITEOMAI παραιτέομαι
ask for
entreat
escape, seek to
excused (*perf. pass. part.*) (2)
excuses, make
nothing to do with, have (3)
refuse (3)

PARAKALEŌ παρακαλέω
apologize to
appeal (9)
appeal, heed an (*pass. imper.*)
appeal, make an
ask
beg (15)
beseech (14)
comfort (15)
conciliate, try to
console
encourage (6)
encouragement, give
entreat (6)
exhort (19)
§exhortation
instruction, give
invite (2)
urge (13)
NOT TRANSLATED: 1 Cor **16.**15

PARAKALYPTŌ παρακαλύπτω
conceal

PARAKATHEZOMAI παρακαθέζομαι
sit

PARAKEIMAI παράκειμαι
lie at hand
IDIOMATICALLY
can *a*

PARAKLĒSIS παράκλησις
appeal (2)
comfort (12)
consolation (2)
§earnestly
encouragement (6)
exhortation (5)
preaching

PARAKLĒTOS παράκλητος
advocate
counselor (4)

PARAKOĒ παρακοή
disobedience (3)

PARAKOLOUTHEŌ παρακολουθέω
accompany
follow (2)
observe

PARAKOUŌ παρακούω
ignore
(overhear †)
refuse to listen (2)

PARAKYPTŌ παρακύπτω
look (2)
(stoop and look)
stoop to look (2)

PARALAMBANŌ παραλαμβάνω
bring (2)
learn
receive (12)
take (26)+
take with one (7)
§tradition

PARALEGOMAI παραλέγομαι
coast along
sail along

PARALIOS παράλιος
seacoast (*subst.*)

PARALLAGĒ παραλλαγή
variation

PARALOGIZOMAI παραλογίζομαι
deceive
delude

PARALYŌ παραλύω
paralyze (4)
weak (*perf. pass. part.*)

PARALYTIKOS παραλυτικός
paralytic (*subst.*) (9)
paralyzed

PARAMENŌ παραμένω
continue (2)
persevere

PARAMYTHEOMAI παραμυθέομαι
console (2)
encourage (2)

PARAMYTHIA παραμυθία
consolation

PARAMYTHION παραμύθιον
incentive

PARANOMEŌ παρανομέω
contrary to the law (*part.*)

PARANOMIA παρανομία
transgression

PARAPHERŌ παραφέρω
carry along
lead away
remove (2)

PARAPHRONEŌ παραφρονέω
madman, like a (*pred. part.*)

PARAPHRONIA παραφρονία
madness

PARAPIKRAINŌ παραπικραίνω
rebellious, be

PARAPIKRASMOS παραπικρασμός
rebellion (2)

PARAPIPTŌ παραπίπτω
commit apostasy

PARAPLEŌ παραπλέω
sail past

PARAPLĒSIOS παραπλήσιος
near (*neut.*)

PARAPLĒSIŌS παραπλησίως
likewise

PARAPOREUOMAI παραπορεύομαι
go
pass
pass by (3)

PARAPTŌMA παράπτωμα
trespass (20)+

PARARREŌ παραρρέω
drift away

PARASĒMOS παράσημος
[*distinguished, marked*]
IDIOMATICALLY
figurehead *a*

PARASKEUAZŌ παρασκευάζω
prepare
ready, be (*perf. mid.*) (2)
ready, get (*mid.*)

PARASKEUĒ παρασκευή
Preparation, day of (6)

PARATEINŌ παρατείνω
prolong

PARATĒREŌ παρατηρέω
observe (*mid.*)
watch (*act. or mid.*) (5)

PARATĒRĒSIS παρατήρησις
signs to be observed

PARATHALASSIOS παραθαλάσσιος
sea, by the

PARATHĒKĒ παραθήκη
entrusted, what has been (3)†
(entrusts, what s. †)

PARATHEŌREŌ παραθεωρέω
neglect

PARATITHĒMI παρατίθημι
commend (*mid.*)
commit (*mid.*) (4)
entrust (*mid.*) (2)
prove (*mid.*)
put before (2)
set before (9)

PARATYGCHANŌ παρατυγχάνω
chance to be there

PARAUTIKA παραυτίκα
§momentary

PARAZĒLOŌ παραζηλόω
jealous, make (3)
provoke to jealousy

PARDALIS πάρδαλις
leopard

PARECHŌ παρέχω
§be
§bother 1 (2)
bring (2)
do (*mid.*)
furnish
give
offer
promote
show (2)
§treat (*mid.*)
§trouble 3 (3)
PAREDREUŌ παρεδρεύω
serve
PARĒGORIA παρηγορία
comfort
PAREIMI πάρειμι
be
come (5)†
come, be to
§coming
§have (2)
here, be (3)
here present, be
§lack (*neg.*)
moment (*subst. part. neut.*)
present (*part.*)
present, be (7)
PAREISAGŌ παρεισάγω
secretly bring in
PAREISAKTOS παρείσακτος
secretly brought in
PAREISDYNŌ παρεισδύνω
admission, secretly gain
PAREISERCHOMAI παρεισέρχομαι
come in
slip in
PAREISPHERŌ παρεισφέρω
[*apply, bring to bear*]
IDIOMATICALLY: effort *a*
PAREKTOS παρεκτός
except
except for
§other things
PAREMBALLŌ παρεμβάλλω
cast up
PAREMBOLĒ παρεμβολή
army
barracks (6)
camp (3)
PARENOCHLEŌ παρενοχλέω
trouble
PAREPIDĒMOS παρεπίδημος
exile (*subst.*) (3)
PARERCHOMAI παρέρχομαι
come (2)+
disobey
go by
neglect
over be (*aor.*)
pass (5)
pass away (14)
pass by (3)
past (*perf. part. attr.*)
PARESIS πάρεσις
§pass over
PARIĒMI παρίημι
droop (*pass.*)
neglect
PARISTĒMI παρίστημι (παριστάνω)
bring
bystander (*subst. part.*) (3)
come
commend
help
present (10)
prove
provide
send
set oneself in array
stand (3)
stand before (*act. or mid.*) (2)
stand beside
stand by (8)
stand near
yield (5)
PARODOS πάροδος
passing
PAROICHOMAI παροίχομαι
past (*perf. pass. part.*)
PAROIKEŌ παροικέω
sojourn
visitor (*subst. part.*)
PAROIKIA παροικία
exile
stay
PAROIKOS πάροικος
alien (*subst.*) (2)
exile (*subst.*)
sojourner (*subst.*)
PAROIMIA παροιμία
figure (4)
proverb
PAROINOS πάροινος
drunkard (*subst.*) (2)
PAROMOIAZŌ παρομοιάζω
like, be
PAROMOIOS παρόμοιος
such
PAROPSIS παροψίς
plate (2)
PARORGISMOS παροργισμός
anger
PARORGIZŌ παροργίζω
angry, make
provoke to anger
PAROTRYNŌ παροτρύνω
incite
PAROUSIA παρουσία
coming (22)
presence (2)
PAROXYNŌ παροξύνω
irritable, be (*pass.*)
provoke
PAROXYSMOS παροξυσμός
contention, sharp
§stir up
PARRĒSIA παρρησία
§bold, be (2)
§boldly
boldness (4)
confidence (10)
§confidently
courage
§openly (6)
plainly (*dat.*) (5)
§public
PARRĒSIAZOMAI παρρησιάζομαι
courage, have
declare boldly
freely (*part.*)
preach boldly (2)
speak boldly (3)
speak out boldly
PARTHENIA παρθενία
virginity
PARTHENOS παρθένος
[*maiden, girl, virgin*]
betrothed (3)
bride
chaste (*pred.*)
girl (2)
maiden (3)
§unmarried (2)
virgin (3)
PAS πᾶς
all (844)+
all kinds of (3)
all manner of
§always (5)
any (18)
any one (5)
anything (*subst. neut.*) (7)
§constantly
§continually (3)
entire
every (142)+†
every one (61)
everything (*neut.*) (65)
§everywhere (2)
full (4)
§fully (2)
great
men (*subst. pl.*)
no (+*neg.*) (11)
no one (+*neg.*) (5)
nothing (*neut.*+*neg.*) (2)
perfect (2)
§quite
§unfailing
§universe
§very
whatever (+*subst. part. neut.*) (6)
§whoever (7)
whole (19)
IDIOMATICALLY
ever, for *j*; lifelong *a*; whoever *a*
NOT TRANSLATED
Mt **7**.12; **21**.22; **23**.3
Mk **5**.5; **11**.24
Acts **2**.21; **3**.22; **5**.23; **13**.10
2 Cor **9**.8
Col **3**.17
2 Th **1**.3
Heb **2**.9; **7**.7
1 Jn **4**.7
Jude .25
Rev **18**.17, 22
PASCHA πάσχα
paschal lamb
Passover (28)
PASCHŌ πάσχω
experience
passion (*art. inf.*)
suffer (39)+
PATASSŌ πατάσσω
smite (3)
strike (7)
PATEŌ πατέω
trample
tread (3)
tread down
PATĒR πατήρ
ancestor
father (407)+
forefather (2)
parent
patriarch (2)

PATHĒMA πάθημα
passions (*pl.*) (2)
suffering (14)

PATHĒTOS παθητός
§suffer, must

PATHOS πάθος
passion (3)

PATRIA πατριά
family (2)
lineage

PATRIARCHĒS πατριάρχης
patriarch (4)

PATRIKOS πατρικός
fathers, of one's

PATRIS πατρίς
country
country, one's own (6)
homeland

PATROLŌAS πατρολῴας
murderer of father

PATRŌOS πατρῷος
fathers, of one's (3)

PATROPARADOTOS πατροπαράδοτος
inherited from one's father

PAUŌ παύω
cease (*mid.*) (12)
keep
stop (*mid.*) (2)

PĒCHYS πῆχυς
cubit (3)
§yard

PĒDALION πηδάλιον
rudder (2)

PEDĒ πέδη
fetter (3)

PEDINOS πεδινός
level

PĒGANON πήγανον
rue

PĒGĒ πηγή
fountain (4)
§hemorrhage 1
spring (4)
well (2)

PĒGNYMI πήγνυμι
set up

PEINAŌ πεινάω
hunger (6)
hunger, facing (*inf.*)
hungry (*part.*) (3)
hungry, be (13)

PEIRA πεῖρα
[*trial, attempt*]
§attempt
§suffer

PEIRAŌ πειράω
try (*mid.*)

PEIRASMOS πειρασμός
§prove
temptation (11)
testing
trial (8)

PEIRAZŌ πειράζω
attempt (2)
examine
tempt (15)+
tempter (*subst. part.*) (2)
test (13)
test, put to the
trial of, make
try (2)
NOT TRANSLATED
1 Cor **7**.5

PEISMONĒ πεισμονή
persuasion

PEITHARCHEŌ πειθαρχέω
listen
obedient, be
obey (2)

PEITHŌ πείθω
advice, take (*pass.*)
attention to, pay (*pass.*)
confidence, have (*perf.*) (2)
confidence, have reason for (*perf.*)
confidence, put (*perf.*)
confident (*perf. part.*)
confident, be (*perf.*)
confident, make
convince (4)
convinced (*perf. part.*)
favor of, seek the
follow (*pass.*) (2)
obey (*pass.*) (4)
persuade (10)
plead
reassure
rely (*perf. periphr.*)
satisfied, be (*perf. pass.*)
satisfy
sure, be (6)
sure, feel (2)
think
trust (*perf. or pluperf.*) (4)+
trust, put one's (*fut. perf. periphr.*)
urge
yield (*pass.*)

PEITHOS πειθός
plausible

PELAGOS πέλαγος
depth
sea

PELEKIZŌ πελεκίζω
behead

PĒLIKOS πηλίκος
great, how
large, what

PĒLOS πηλός
clay (6)

PEMPŌ πέμπω
§exchange
put in (2)
send (76)

PEMPTOS πέμπτος
fifth (4)

PENĒS πένης
poor (*pl.*)

PENICHROS πενιχρός
poor

PENTAKIS πεντάκις
five times

PENTAKISCHILIOI πεντακισχίλιοι
five thousand (6)

PENTAKOSIOI πεντακόσιοι
five hundred (2)

PENTE πέντε
§fifty
five (35)
§seventy-five
§three

PENTEKAIDEKATOS πεντεκαιδέκατος
fifteenth

PENTĒKONTA πεντήκοντα
fifty (6)
§fifty-three

PENTĒKOSTĒ πεντηκοστή
Pentecost (3)

PENTHEŌ πενθέω
mourn (10)

PENTHERA πενθερά
mother-in-law (6)

PENTHEROS πενθερός
father-in-law

PENTHOS πένθος
mourning (5)

PEPOITHĒSIS πεποίθησις
confidence (4)
confidence, reason for
§sure, be

PĒRA πήρα
bag (6)

PERAITERŌ περαιτέρω
further

PERAN πέραν
across (4)
beyond (6)
other side of, on the (*prep.*) (2)
other side of, to the (*prep.*)
other side, the (*subst. neut.*) (10)

PERAS πέρας
end (3)
final (*pred.*)

PERI περί
about (+*gen.* 66; +*acc.* 18)+
against (+*gen.*)
around (+*acc.* 3)
(*as* [+*gen.*]†)
at (+*gen.* 5)
concerning (+*gen.* 28)
for (+*gen.* 58; +*acc.* 2)
for, as (+*gen.* 4)
from (+*acc.*)
in (+*gen.*)
of (+*gen.* 67; +*acc.*)
on (+*gen.* 2)
over (+*gen.*)
regard to, with (+*gen.*)
regarding (+*gen.*)
regards, as (+*acc.*)
respect to, with (+*gen.* 2)
round (+*acc.* 3)
§*surrounding* (+*acc.*)
to (+*gen.* 18)
to, as (+*gen.* 2)
upon (+*gen.*)
with (+*gen.*; +*acc.*)+
IDIOMATICALLY
OR NOT TRANSLATED
+*genitive:*
Mk **5**.16
Lk **2**.17
Jn **5**.36; **7**.17; **9**.18; **11**.13; **16**.19; **18**.19
Acts **7**.52; **10**.19; **15**.6; **19**.40³; **22**.10; **23**.15; **24**.10, 13, 21; **25**.18, 20
Rom **8**.[3†
1 Cor **7**.37
Eph **6**.22
Phil **2**.19
Col **4**.8
2 Tim **1**.3
Heb **5**.3; **6**.9; **10**.6, 8; **11**.20; **13**.11
3 Jn .2

+*accusative:*
Acts **13**.13; **19**.25; **28**.7
Phil **2**.23
2 Tim **3**.8
Tit **2**.7
Rev **15**.6

PERIAGŌ περιάγω
accompanied by, be
go about (4)
traverse

PERIAIREŌ περιαιρέω
abandon
cast off
remove
take away

PERIAPTŌ περιάπτω
kindle

PERIASTRAPTŌ περιαστράπτω
flash
shine

PERIBALLŌ περιβάλλω
array (5)
clad in
clad in, be (2)
clothe (10)
dress
wear (*pass.*)
with (*perf. pass. part.*)
wrap s. around
wrap s. in (*pass.*)

PERIBLEPŌ περιβλέπω
look around (3)
look around at
look around on (2)
look round at

PERIBOLAION περιβόλαιον
covering
mantle

PERICHŌROS περίχωρος
§region
§region about (2)
§surrounding country (4)
§surrounding region (2)

PERIDEŌ περιδέω
wrap

PERIECHŌ περιέχω
stand
IDIOMATICALLY
astonished, be *a*

PERIERCHOMAI περιέρχομαι
circuit, make a
gad about
go about
itinerant (*part.*)

PERIERGAZOMAI περιεργάζομαι
busybody, be a

PERIERGOS περίεργος
busybody (*subst.*)
magic arts (*subst. pl.*)

PERIISTĒMI περιίστημι
avoid (*mid.*) (2)
stand about
stand by (*perf.*)

PERIKALYPTŌ περικαλύπτω
blindfold
cover (2)

PERIKATHARMA περικάθαρμα
refuse (*pl.*)

PERIKEIMAI περίκειμαι
beset with, be
bound with, be
hung round, be (2)
surround

PERIKEPHALAIA περικεφαλαία
helmet (2)

PERIKRATĒS περικρατής
[*having power*]
§secure

PERIKRYBŌ περικρύβω
hide

PERIKYKLOŌ περικυκλόω
surround

PERILAMPŌ περιλάμπω
shine around
shine round

PERILEIPOMAI περιλείπομαι
left, be (2)

PERILYPOS περίλυπος
sad
sorrowful, very (2)
sorry, exceedingly

PERIMENŌ περιμένω
wait for

PERIOCHĒ περιοχή
passage

PERIOIKEŌ περιοικέω
neighbor (*subst. part.*)

PERIOIKOS περίοικος
neighbor (*subst.*)

PERIOUSIOS περιούσιος
own, of one's

PERIPATEŌ περιπατέω
act (2)
adherent (*subst. part.*)
behave
conduct oneself (2)
§do (2)
§follow (5)
go
go about (6)
lead a life (4)
live (9)
observe (+*dat.*)
§practice
prowl around
walk (58)
IDIOMATICALLY
command *a*

PERIPEIRŌ περιπείρω
pierce

PERIPHERŌ περιφέρω
bring
carry (2)

PERIPHRONEŌ περιφρονέω
disregard

PERIPIPTŌ περιπίπτω
fall among (+*dat.*)
meet (+*dat.*)
§strike

PERIPOIEŌ περιποιέω
gain (*mid.*) (2)
obtain (*mid.*)

PERIPOIĒSIS περιποίησις
§keep
§obtain (2)
IDIOMATICALLY
own *a;* possession *a*

PERIPSĒMA περίψημα
offscouring

PERIRĒGNYMI περιρήγνυμι
tear off

PERISPAŌ περισπάω
distracted, be (*pass.*)

PERISSEIA περισσεία
abundance (2)
§greatly
rank growth

PERISSEUMA περίσσευμα
abundance (4)
§left over

PERISSEUŌ περισσεύω
abound (8)†
abundance (*subst. part. or inf.*) (4)
abundance, have (*pass.*) (2)
abundance, provide in (2)
§abundantly, share (2)
§ample, have
better off, be
enough and to spare, have
exceed (2)
excel (3)
increase (2)
lavish
leave
left over (*part.*) (4)
overflow (2)
IDIOMATICALLY
more *c;* more and more, do so *a, b*

PERISSOS περισσός
abundantly (*neut.*)
advantage (*subst. neut.*)
more (*neut.*)
more, anything (*subst. neut.*)
superfluous
§utterly 2[a]

PERISSŌS περισσῶς
exceedingly
more, all the (2)
§raging

PERISSOTEROS περισσότερος
excessive
greater (5)+
§harder (*neut.*)
more (*neut.*) (3)
more convincingly (*neut.*)
more than (*neut.*) (2)
more than, much (*neut.*)
§zealously, more (*neut.*)
IDIOMATICALLY
much, too *a*

PERISSOTERŌS περισσοτέρως
§abundant
closer, the
earnestly, the more
extremely, so
greater, far
more, all the
more, far
more, much
more, still 1[a]; 2
more, the (2)

PERISTERA περιστερά
dove (5)
pigeon (5)

PERITEMNŌ περιτέμνω
circumcise (13)
circumcision, receive (*pass.*) (3)
circumcision, seek (*pass.*)

PERITHESIS περίθεσις
decoration

PERITITHĒMI περιτίθημι
invest
put on (4)
put upon
set around (2)

PERITOMĒ *περιτομή*
§circumcised (13)
circumcision (23)

PERITRECHŌ *περιτρέχω*
run about

PERITREPŌ *περιτρέπω*
turn

PERIX *πέριξ*
around

PERIZŌNNYMI *περιζώννυμι* (*περιζωννύω*)
gird (*act. or mid.*) (5)
§with (*perf. pass. part.*)

PERPEREUOMAI *περπερεύομαι*
boastful, be

PERYSI *πέρυσι*
§year ago, a
year, last

PETEINON *πετεινόν*
bird (14)

PETOMAI *πέτομαι*
fly (5)

PETRA *πέτρα*
rock (15)+

PETRŌDĒS *πετρώδης*
rocky ground (*subst. sg. or pl.*) (4)

PEZĒ *πεζῇ*
foot, on (2)

PEZEUŌ *πεζεύω*
go by land

PHAGOS *φάγος*
glutton (2)

PHAILONĒS *φαιλόνης*
cloak

PHAINŌ *φαίνω*
appear (*pass.*) (14)
§seem (*pass.*)
seen, be (*pass.*) (4)
shine (10)
shown, be (*pass.*)
IDIOMATICALLY
decision *a*

PHANEROŌ *φανερόω*
appear (*pass.*) (11)
clear, make
disclose (2)
known, be (*pass.*) (2)
manifest (9)
manifest, make (7)
open
plain, be (*pass.*)
plain, make
reveal (6)
seen, be (*pass.*)
seen, be clearly (*pass.*)
show (3)
spread
visible, become (*pass.*) (2)

PHANEROS *φανερός*
disclosed
external
known (5)
light (*subst.*) (2)
manifest (3)
§outwardly
plain (2)
recognized
§see
seen

PHANERŌS *φανερῶς*
clearly
openly
publicly

PHANERŌSIS *φανέρωσις*
manifestation
open statement

PHANOS *φανός*
lantern

PHANTASIA *φαντασία*
pomp

PHANTASMA *φάντασμα*
ghost (2)

PHANTAZŌ *φαντάζω*
sight (*subst. pass. part. neut.*)

PHARAGX *φάραγξ*
valley

PHARMAKEIA *φαρμακεία*
sorcery (3)

PHARMAKOS *φάρμακος*
sorcerer (2)

PHASIS *φάσις*
word

PHASKŌ *φάσκω*
affirm
assert
claim

PHATNĒ *φάτνη*
manger (4)

PHAULOS *φαῦλος*
bad
evil (4)
vile

PHEGGOS *φέγγος*
light (2)+

PHEIDOMAI *φείδομαι*
refrain from
spare (9)

PHEIDOMENŌS *φειδομένως*
sparingly (2)

PHĒMĒ *φήμη*
report (2)

PHĒMI *φημί*
answer
charge
imply
mean
say (58)
tell
written, as it is (*indef.*)
NOT TRANSLATED
Mt **8.8**
Lk **23.3**

PHERŌ *φέρω*
bear (12)+
bring (34)
carry (2)
come (*pass.*) (2)
drive (2)
endure (2)
establish
go on
lead
move
pronounce
put (2)
§rush
take (3)
uphold
yield

PHEUGŌ *φεύγω*
escape (3)
flee (20)
fly
run away
shun (4)

PHIALĒ *φιάλη*
bowl (12)

PHILADELPHIA *φιλαδελφία*
brotherly affection (3)
brotherly love
love of the brethren (2)

PHILADELPHOS *φιλάδελφος*
§love of the brethren, have

PHILAGATHOS *φιλάγαθος*
lover of goodness (*subst.*)

PHILANDROS *φίλανδρος*
§love one's husband

PHILANTHRŌPIA *φιλανθρωπία*
kindness
loving kindness

PHILANTHRŌPŌS *φιλανθρώπως*
kindly

PHILARGYRIA *φιλαργυρία*
love of money

PHILARGYROS *φιλάργυρος*
lover of money (*subst.*) (2)

PHILAUTOS *φίλαυτος*
lover of self (*subst.*)

PHILĒDONOS *φιλήδονος*
lover of pleasure (*subst.*)

PHILĒMA *φίλημα*
kiss (7)

PHILEŌ *φιλέω*
kiss (3)
love (22)

PHILIA *φιλία*
friendship

PHILONEIKIA *φιλονεικία*
dispute

PHILONEIKOS *φιλόνεικος*
contentious

PHILOPHRONŌS *θιλοφρόνως*
hospitably

PHILOPRŌTEUŌ *φιλοπρωτεύω*
like to put oneself first

PHILOS *φίλος*
friend (*subst.*) (29)

PHILOSOPHIA *φιλοσοφία*
philosophy

PHILOSOPHOS *φιλόσοφος*
philosopher

PHILOSTORGOS *φιλόστοργος*
[*affectionate, devoted*]
§love

PHILOTEKNOS *φιλότεκνος*
§love one's children

PHILOTHEOS *φιλόθεος*
lover of God (*subst.*)

PHILOTIMEOMAI *φιλοτιμέομαι*
aim, make it one's
ambition, make it one's
aspire

PHILOXENIA *φιλοξενία*
hospitality (2)

PHILOXENOS *φιλόξενος*
hospitable (2)
§practice hospitality

PHIMOŌ *φιμόω*
muzzle
silence
silence, put to
silent, be (*pass.*) (2)
speechless, be (*pass.*)
still, be (*pass.*)

PHLOGIZŌ φλογίζω
set on fire (2)

PHLOX φλόξ
flame (6)
flaming (*gen.*)

PHLYAREŌ φλυαρέω
prate

PHLYAROS φλύαρος
gossip (*subst.*)

PHOBEŌ φοβέω
afraid, be (*pass.*) (36)
§awe, be filled with (*pass.*) (3)
awe, stand in (*pass.*)
fear (*pass.*) (50)
§fear, be filled with (*pass.*)
frightened, be (*pass.*)
§God-fearing (*pass. part.*)
respect (*pass.*)
terrify

PHOBEROS φοβερός
fearful (2)
terrifying

PHOBĒTRON φόβητρον
terror

PHOBOS φόβος
alarm
awe (2)
fear (37)
respect (3)
reverence (2)
§reverent
terror

PHOINIX φοῖνιξ
palm branch
palm tree

PHŌLEOS φωλεός
hole (2)

PHŌNĒ φωνή
blast
call (2)
cry (2)
§instrument
language (2)
noise (2)
sound (10)
tone
utterance
voice (115)
NOT TRANSLATED
Acts **24**.21
Rev **10**.3

PHŌNEŌ φωνέω
call (25)
call out (2)
crow (11)+
cry (3)
invite

PHONEUŌ φονεύω
kill (10)
murder (2)

PHONEUS φονεύς
§murder
murderer (6)

PHONOS φόνος
§killed, be
murder (8)+

PHOREŌ φορέω
bear (3)
wear (3)

PHORON φόρον
forum (*See* FORUM OF APPIUS)

PHOROS φόρος
taxes (*sg. or pl.*) (3)
tribute (2)

PHORTION φορτίον
burden (4)
cargo
load

PHORTIZŌ φορτίζω
laden, be heavy (*perf. pass.*)
load

PHŌS φῶς
fire
light (71)
NOT TRANSLATED
Rev **22**.5

PHŌSPHOROS φωσφόρος
morning star (*subst.*)

PHŌSTĒR φωστήρ
light
radiance

PHŌTEINOS φωτεινός
bright (2)
light, full of (3)

PHŌTISMOS φωτισμός
light (2)

PHŌTIZŌ φωτίζω
bright, make
enlighten (4)
light, be (2)
light, bring to (2)
light, give
see, make

PHRAGELLION φραγέλλιον
whip

PHRAGELLOŌ φραγελλόω
scourge (2)

PHRAGMOS φραγμός
hedge (3)
NOT TRANSLATED
Eph **2**.14

PHRASSŌ φράσσω
silence
stop (2)

PHRAZŌ φράζω
explain

PHREAR φρέαρ
shaft (4)
well (3)

PHRĒN φρήν
thinking (*pl.*) (2)

PHRENAPATAŌ φρεναπατάω
deceive

PHRENAPATĒS φρεναπάτης
deceiver

PHRISSŌ φρίσσω
shudder

PHRONĒMA φρόνημα
mind
mind on, to set the (+*gen.*) (2)
mind that is set on (+*gen.*)

PHRONEŌ φρονέω
§agree (2)
concern (*inf.*)
concerned, be
feel
§haughty, be
mind, be of a (2)
mind, have a
mind on, set one's (3)
minded, be (2)
observe (2)
§proud, become
think (3)
§view
§view, take a
IDIOMATICALLY
live *a*, *b;* side *a* (2)

PHRONĒSIS φρόνησις
insight
wisdom

PHRONIMOS φρόνιμος
§conceited
sensible
shrewd, more (*comp.*)
wise (11)

PHRONIMŌS φρονίμως
§shrewdness

PHRONTIZŌ φροντίζω
careful, be

PHROUREŌ φρουρέω
confine
guard (2)
keep

PHRYASSŌ φρυάσσω
rage

PHRYGANON φρύγανον
stick

PHTHANŌ φθάνω
attain
come (3)
come, be the first to
precede (*pass.*)
§succeed in fulfilling

PHTHARTOS φθαρτός
mortal
perishable (5)

PHTHEGGOMAI φθέγγομαι
speak (2)
utter

PHTHEIRŌ φθείρω
astray, lead
corrupt (3)
destroy (4)
ruin

PHTHINOPŌRINOS φθινοπωρινός
§autumn, in late

PHTHOGGOS φθόγγος
note
voice

PHTHONEŌ φθονέω
§envy

PHTHONOS φθόνος
envy (8)
§jealously

PHTHORA φθορά
corruption (3)
decay
destruction
§kill
§perish
§perishable
perishable, the

PHYGĒ φυγή
flight

PHYLAKĒ φυλακή
guard
haunt (2)
imprisonment (3)
part of the night
prison (35)
watch (4)

PHYLAKIZŌ φυλακίζω
imprison

PHYLAKTĒRION φυλακτήριον
phylactery

PHYLASSŌ φυλάσσω
abstain from (*mid.*)
beware (*mid.*) (3)
guard (9)
keep (11)
keep under guard
observance, for (*inf.*)
observance, in (*part.*)
observe (*act. or mid.*) (3)
preserve

PHYLAX φύλαξ
sentry (3)

PHYLĒ φυλή
tribe (31)

PHYLLON φύλλον
leaf (6)

PHYŌ φύω
grow (*pass.*)
grow up (*pass.*)
spring

PHYRAMA φύραμα
lump (5)

PHYSIKOS φυσικός
instinct, creature of (*subst. neut.*)
natural (2)

PHYSIKŌS φυσικῶς
instinct, by

PHYSIOŌ φυσιόω
arrogant (*perf. pass. part.*)
arrogant, be (*pass.*) (3)
puff up (3)

PHYSIŌSIS φυσίωσις
conceit

PHYSIS φύσις
birth
§humankind 1
kind
§natural (2)
nature (7)
§physically
§unnatural

PHYTEIA φυτεία
plant

PHYTEUŌ φυτεύω
plant (11)

PIAZŌ πιάζω
arrest (6)
capture
catch (2)
seize (2)
take

PIEZŌ πιέζω
press down

PIKRAINŌ πικραίνω
bitter, make (2)
bitter to, be
harsh, be (*pass.*)

PIKRIA πικρία
bitterness (4)

PIKROS πικρός
bitter
brackish (*subst. neut.*)

PIKRŌS πικρῶς
bitterly (2)

PIMPLĒMI πίμπλημι
come (*pass.*) (3)
end
fill (18)
fulfil (*pass.*)
IDIOMATICALLY
end *b*

PIMPRĒMI πίμπρημι
swell up

PINAKIDION πινακίδιον
writing tablet

PINAX πίναξ
dish
platter (4)

PINŌ πίνω
drink (73)+

PIOTĒS πιότης
(rich [*gen.*]†)
richness

PIPRASKŌ πιπράσκω
sell (9)

PIPTŌ πίπτω
end
fall (67)+
fall down (14)
§strike
void, become
IDIOMATICALLY
fallen *a* (4)

PISTEUŌ πιστεύω
believe (220)+
believer (*subst. part.*) (8)
entrust (7)
faith, have (4)
trust (2)

PISTIKOS πιστικός
pure (2)

PISTIS πίστις
assurance
belief
faith (236)+
faithfulness (2)
fidelity
pledge

PISTOŌ πιστόω
believe, firmly (*pass.*)

PISTOS πιστός
believer (*subst.*) (6)
believes, one who (*subst.*) (2)
believing (2)
(believing man [*subst.*])
believing woman (*subst.*)
§confidence, have (*subst.*)
faith, who had (*attr.*)
faithful (42)
loyal
sure (6)
sure blessings (*subst. neut. pl.*)
trustworthy (4)

PITHANOLOGIA πιθανολογία
beguiling speech

PLANAŌ πλανάω
astray, go (*pass.*) (5)
astray, lead (10)
beguile
deceive (14)
deceiver (*subst. part.*) (2)
stray (*pass.*)
wander (*pass.*) (2)
wayward (*pass. part.*)
wrong, be (*pass.*) (3)

PLANĒ πλάνη
deceitful (*gen.*)
delusion
error (7)
fraud

PLANĒTĒS πλανήτης
§wandering

PLANOS πλάνος
deceitful
deceiver (*subst.*) (2)
impostor (*subst.*) (2)

PLASMA πλάσμα
molded, what is

PLASSŌ πλάσσω
form
molder (*subst. part.*)

PLASTOS πλαστός
false

PLATEIA πλατεῖα
street (9)

PLATOS πλάτος
breadth (3)
broad (+*gen.*)

PLATYNŌ πλατύνω
broad, make
wide, be (*perf. pass.*)
widen (*pass.*)

PLATYS πλατύς
wide

PLAX πλάξ
table
tablet (2)

PLĒGĒ πληγή
§beat
beating (*sg. or pl.*) (3)
blow
plague (13)
wound (3)
§wounded, be

PLEGMA πλέγμα
braided hair (*pl.*)

PLEIŌN πλείων
§exceed
§further (2)
great numbers, in (*pl.*)
greater (5)
longer
majority (*subst. pl.*) (2)
many (4)
many in number (*pl.*)
many things (*subst. neut. pl.*)
more (10)
more and more (2)
more, as much
more than (13)
more, the (*subst.*)
most (*pl.*) (3)
most of them (*subst. pl.*) (2)
some (2)
§very far
IDIOMATICALLY
longer, still *a*
NOT TRANSLATED
Mt 5.20

PLEISTOS πλεῖστος
large, very
most (2)
most, at (*subst. neut.*)

PLEKŌ πλέκω
plait (3)

PLĒKTĒS πλήκτης
violent (*pred.*) (2)

PLĒMMYRA πλήμμυρα
flood

PLĒN πλήν
but (14)
except (2)
however
instead

nevertheless (7)
only (3)
only, but
than (+*neg. and comp.*)
yet

PLEŌ πλέω
sail (5)
seafaring man (*subst. part.*)

PLEONAZŌ πλεονάζω
abound (2)
extend
increase (5)
over, have

PLEONEKTEŌ πλεονεκτέω
advantage of, take (3)
advantage over, gain the
(defraud †)
wrong

PLEONEKTĒS πλεονέκτης
covetous, one who is
greed, guilty of (*pred.*)
greedy, the (*pl.*) (2)

PLEONEXIA πλεονεξία
coveting
covetousness (4)
exaction
greed (3)
§greedy

PLĒRĒS πλήρης
§enraged, be 2
full (15)

PLĒRŌMA πλήρωμα
everything
fulfilling
§full (2)
full inclusion
full number
fulness (8)
patch (2)
IDIOMATICALLY
fully *b*

PLĒROŌ πληρόω
accomplish
complete (5)
elapse (*pass.*)
end
fill (19)
fill up
filled (*pass. part.*)
finish
fulfil (41)+
full, be (*pass.*) (4)
full, make
fully, come
fully known, make
fulness of life, come to (*pass. periphr.*)
pass (*pass.*) (2)
perfect (*perf. pass. part.*)
supply
IDIOMATICALLY
after a; fully *a;* old *a*

PLĒROPHOREŌ πληροφορέω
accomplish
assured, fully (*perf. pass. part.*)
convinced, be fully (*pass.*)
convinced, fully (*part.*)
fulfil
IDIOMATICALLY
fully *c*

PLĒROPHORIA πληροφορία
assurance, full (2)
§assured
conviction

PLĒSION πλησίον
near (*prep.*)
neighbor (*subst.*) (16)

PLĒSMONĒ πλησμονή
§(indulge †)
indulgence

PLĒSSŌ πλήσσω
strike

PLĒTHOS πλῆθος
assembly (2)
body
§bundle
company (3)
congregation (2)
many
mob
multitude (13)
people (4)
quantity
shoal
IDIOMATICALLY
many as, as *a*

PLĒTHYNŌ πληθύνω
increase
multiply (*act. or pass.*) (10)
NOT TRANSLATED
Heb **6**.14

PLEURA πλευρά
side (5)+

PLOIARION πλοιάριον
boat (4)+

PLOION πλοῖον
boat (46)+
ship (22)

PLOOS πλόος
voyage (3)

PLOUSIOS πλούσιος
rich (28)

PLOUSIŌS πλουσίως
richly (4)

PLOUTEŌ πλουτέω
prosper
rich (*part.*) (2)
rich, be (3)
rich, become (2)
rich, grow (2)
riches, bestow one's
wealth, gain

PLOUTIZŌ πλουτίζω
enrich (2)
rich, make

PLOUTOS πλοῦτος
riches (18)
wealth (4)

PLYNŌ πλύνω
wash (3)

PNEŌ πνέω
blow (6)
wind (*subst. part.*)

PNEUMA πνεῦμα
breath (3)
mind (2)
spirit (371)+
§spiritual
wind (2)

PNEUMATIKOS πνευματικός
spirit, those who possess the (*subst. pl.*)
spiritual (22)†
supernatural (3)

PNEUMATIKŌS πνευματικῶς
allegorically
spiritually

PNIGŌ πνίγω
drown
IDIOMATICALLY
throat *a*

PNIKTOS πνικτός
strangled (3)

PNOĒ πνοή
breath
wind

PODĒRĒS ποδήρης
robe, long (*subst.*)

POIĒMA ποίημα
made, things that have been (*pl.*)
workmanship

POIEŌ ποιέω
account
act (4)
appoint (2)+
§*be* (5)
bear (12)+
bring
carry out
§cause (2)
commit (9)
create (2)
deal (*mid.*)
do (327)+
execute (3)
exercise (2)
follow
give (9)
guilty of, be
§have (*imper.*)
hold
keep (5)
live according to
make (*act. or mid.*) (102)+
obey
offer (*mid.*)
perform (4)
plan
practice (7)
produce
provide (2)
put
put forth
realize
show (3)+
spend (4)
§task
treat (2)+
with (*part.*)
work (6)
yield (4)
IDIOMATICALLY
claim *a;* conduct *a;* duty *b;* keep from *a;* mean *b;* put *a;* sweep away *a;* throw cargo overboard *a*
in combination with other words:
avenge 2; betray 1; confirm 2; evildoer 2[b], 3; expose 1; heal 2 (2); journey 4; mention 1 (2); recall 2; redeem 5; remember 4[a] (2); satisfy 5; stir up 3; vindicate 3 (2); well-doing 3
NOT TRANSLATED
Mt **23**.3
Lk **16**.8
2 Cor **8**.11

POIĒSIS ποίησις
doing

POIĒTĒS ποιητής
doer (5)
poet

POIKILOS ποικίλος
diverse
varied
various (8)

POIMAINŌ ποιμαίνω
care for
govern
keep sheep
look after
rule (3)
shepherd, be a
tend (3)

POIMĒN ποιμήν
pastor
shepherd (17)

POIMNĒ ποίμνη
flock (4)
NOT TRANSLATED
1 Cor **9.**7

POIMNION ποίμνιον
flock (5)

POIOS ποῖος
§way
what (25)
what kind of
(what manner of)
which (4)
NOT TRANSLATED
1 Pet **1.**11

POLEMEŌ πολεμέω
fight (3)
war
war, make (2)
war, wage

POLEMOS πόλεμος
battle (5)
war (13)

PŌLEŌ πωλέω
dealer (*subst. part.*)
sell (21)

POLIS πόλις
city (137)
town (24)
IDIOMATICALLY
town *a*

POLITARCHĒS πολιτάρχης
city authority (2)

POLITEIA πολιτεία
citizenship
commonwealth

POLITĒS πολίτης
citizen (3)
fellow

POLITEUMA πολίτευμα
commonwealth

POLITEUOMAI πολιτεύομαι
§life is, one's manner of live

POLLAKIS πολλάκις
§frequent
§many
often (13)
repeatedly (3)

POLLAPLASIŌN πολλαπλασίων
(manifold)
manifold more

PŌLOS πῶλος
colt (12)

POLYLOGIA πολυλογία
many words

POLYMERŌS πολυμερῶς
many ways, in

POLYPOIKILOS πολυποίκιλος
manifold

POLYS πολύς
ample
§contrary, on the
eagerly (*neut. pl.*)
§earnestly 5
enough
§far 3 (2)
few, a (*neg. pl.*)
freely (*neut. pl.*)
full
great (57)+
greatly (*neut.*)
hard (4)
hearty
large (5)
late (2)
§liberally
long (4)
loud
loudly (*neut. pl.*)
many (195)
§more, all the 1[a] (2)
most men (*subst. pl.*)
most of them (*subst. pl.*)
much (50)+
§multitude 1[a] (2)
often, so (*subst. neut. pl.*)
plentiful (2)
quite (*neut.*)
severe (2)
§soon (*neg.*)
strictly (*neut. pl.*) (2)
strongly (*neut. pl.*)
terribly (*neut. pl.*)
than ever (+*comp.*)
§very
violent
NOT TRANSLATED
Mk **5.**23
Tit **2.**3

POLYSPLAGCHNOS πολύσπλαγχνος
compassionate

POLYTELĒS πολυτελής
costly
costly, very
precious, very

POLYTIMOS πολύτιμος
costly
precious
value, of great

POLYTROPŌS πολυτρόπως
various ways, in

POMA πόμα
drink (2)

PONĒRIA πονηρία
evil (2)
malice
wickedness (4)

PONĒROS πονηρός
bad
base
§envy
evil (64)†
selfish
sound, not (2)
vicious
wicked (6)

IDIOMATICALLY
begrudge *a*

PONOS πόνος
anguish
pain (2)
§work

PŌPOTE πώποτε
ever (3)
never (+*neg.*) (3)

POREIA πορεία
§journey
pursuit

POREUOMAI πορεύομαι
§accompany (2)
depart (2)
§follow (3)
go (114)
go away (4)
go on
go on one's journey
go on one's way (3)
go one's way (3)
journey (4)
journey, make one's
§leave (2)
living (*perf. part.*)
§ride
set (*part.*)
walk (4)
§way, on one's
IDIOMATICALLY
get *a;* indulge *a;* way *a*
NOT TRANSLATED
Mk **16.**12
Acts **20.**1

PORISMOS πορισμός
gain
gain, means of

PORNĒ πόρνη
harlot (10)
prostitute (2)

PORNEIA πορνεία
fornication (*sg. or pl.*) (9)
immorality (7)
impure (*gen.*) (2)
unchastity (6)
NOT TRANSLATED
1 Cor **5.**1

PORNEUŌ πορνεύω
fornication, commit (3)
immoral man (*subst. part.*)
immorality, indulge in
immorality, practice (2)
NOT TRANSLATED
1 Cor **10.**8

PORNOS πόρνος
fornicator (3)
immoral (*pred.*)
immoral man
immoral person
immoral, the (*pl.*) (3)
immorality, guilty of (*pred.*)

PŌROŌ πωρόω
harden (5)

PŌRŌSIS πώρωσις
hardening
hardness (2)

PORPHYRA πορφύρα
purple (2)
purple cloak (2)

PORPHYROPŌLIS πορφυρόπωλις
purple, seller of

PORPHYROUS πορφυροῦς
purple (4)
PORRŌ πόρρω
§far (2)
further (*comp.*)
way off, a great
PORRŌTHEN πόρρωθεν
afar, from
distance, at a
PORTHEŌ πορθέω
destroy (2)
havoc of, make
PŌS I πῶς
how (94)+
way to, a (+*subj.*)
what (2)
what, with
IDIOMATICALLY
way *b*
NOT TRANSLATED
Mk **4**.40; **12**.41; **14**.11
Rom **8**.32
2 Cor **3**.8
PŌS II πώς
§lest 2[a] (2)
§*or* 5[a]
§order to, in
perhaps (2)
possible, if
somehow (5)
NOT TRANSLATED
2 Cor **11**.3
Gal **4**.11
POSAKIS ποσάκις
how often (3)
POSIS πόσις
drink (3)
POSOS πόσος
how great
§how long
how many (11)
how much (13)
what
POTAMOPHORĒTOS ποταμοφόρητος
[*carried away by a river*]
IDIOMATICALLY
flood *a*
POTAMOS ποταμός
flood (2)
river (12)
§riverside
stream (2)
POTAPOS ποταπός
what
what sort of (4)
what wonderful (2)
POTE I πότε
§how long (7)
when (11)
NOT TRANSLATED: Lk **12**.36
POTE II ποτέ
ever (4)
former
formerly (3)
length, at
never (*neg.*) (2)
once (13)
time, at one
when
IDIOMATICALLY
last *a*
NOT TRANSLATED
Lk **22**.32
1 Cor **9**.7
Gal **2**.6
POTĒRION ποτήριον
cup (31)
POTERON πότερον
whether
POTHEN πόθεν
how (5)
what causes (2)
what, from
whence (6)
where (5)
where, from (9)
why
POTIZŌ ποτίζω
drink, give (4)
drink, give s. to (3)
drink, make to (2)
feed
give
water (4)
POTOS πότος
carousing
POU I ποῦ
nowhere (*neg.*) (3)
what becomes of
what has become of
where (40)
whither (3)
POU II πού
about
somewhere (2)
§*that*
POUS πούς
foot (89)+
leg
NOT TRANSLATED
Mt **5**.35
Acts **7**.49
PRAGMA πρᾶγμα
§anything 4[a]
(business †)
deed
grievance
matter (2)
practice
realities (*pl.*)
thing (3)
NOT TRANSLATED
Rom **16**.2
PRAGMATEIA πραγματεία
pursuit
PRAGMATEUOMAI πραγματεύομαι
trade
PRAITŌRION πραιτώριον
praetorian guard
praetorium (7)
PRAKTŌR πράκτωρ
officer (2)
PRASIA πρασιά
[*garden plot*]
IDIOMATICALLY
group *a* (1; Gr. 2)
PRASSŌ πράσσω
act (2)
collect (2)
commit
§deed
do (25)
§harm 3[a]
mind
obey
perform
practice (3)
§wrongdoer
PRAXIS πρᾶξις
deed (2)
done, what s. has
function
practice (2)
PRAYPATHEIA πραϋπάθεια
gentleness
PRAYS πραΰς
gentle
humble
meek
quiet
PRAYTĒS πραΰτης (πραότης)
courtesy
gentleness (5)
meekness (5)
PRĒNĒS πρηνής
headlong
§(swell up †)
PREPŌ πρέπω
befit (2)
fitting, be (4)
proper, be
PRESBEIA πρεσβεία
embassy (2)
PRESBEUŌ πρεσβεύω
ambassador, be an (2)
PRESBYTERION πρεσβυτέριον
elders, assembly of
elders, council of (2)
PRESBYTEROS πρεσβύτερος
elder (61)
eldest
old man
old, man of
older man
older woman
PRESBYTĒS πρεσβύτης
ambassador
old man †
older man
PRESBYTIS πρεσβῦτις
older woman
PRIN πρίν
before (13)
PRIZŌ πρίζω
saw in two
PRO πρό (+*gen.*)
above (2)
§ago (3)
§ahead of (2)
at (2)
before (36)
front of, in
§recently 1
PROAGŌ προάγω
bring before
bring out (3)
former (*part.*)
front, be in
go ahead
go before (10)
point (2)
walk ahead
PROAIREŌ προαιρέω
[*determine, decide*]
IDIOMATICALLY
make up *a*
PROAITIAOMAI προαιτιάομαι
charge, already

PROAKOUŌ προακούω
hear before
PROAMARTANŌ προαμαρτάνω
sin before (2)
PROAULION προαύλιον
(fore-court †)
gateway
PROBAINŌ προβαίνω
advanced (*perf. part.*) (2)
go on (2)
IDIOMATICALLY
age *a*
PROBALLŌ προβάλλω
come out in leaf
put forward
PROBATIKOS προβατικός
§sheep gate
PROBATION προβάτιον
sheep (2)
PROBATON πρόβατον
sheep (36)
§sheepfold
PROBIBAZŌ προβιβάζω
prompt
PROBLEPŌ προβλέπω
foresee (*mid.*)
PROCHEIRIZŌ προχειρίζω
appoint (*mid.*) (3)
PROCHEIROTONEŌ προχειροτονέω
choose
PRODĒLOS πρόδηλος
conspicuous (2)
evident
PRODIDŌMI προδίδωμι
give a gift
PRODOTĒS προδότης
§betray (+*gen.*)
traitor
treacherous (*pred.*)
PRODROMOS πρόδρομος
forerunner (*subst.*)
PROECHŌ προέχω
better off, be any (*mid. interrog.*)
(disadvantage, be at a [*pass.*]†)
PROĒGEOMAI προηγέομαι
outdo
PROEIDON προεῖδον
foresee (2)
PROEIPON προεῖπον
predict
§prediction (2)
say before (2)
speak beforehand
tell beforehand (2)
warn
warn before
IDIOMATICALLY
forewarn, solemnly *a;* quote *a*
PROELPIZŌ προελπίζω
hope, first
PROENARCHOMAI προενάρχομαι
begin
beginning, already make a
PROEPAGGELLŌ προεπαγγέλλω
promise (*mid.*)
promise beforehand (*mid.*)
PROERCHOMAI προέρχομαι
get there ahead of
go (3)
go ahead
go on (2)
lead
pass on through
PROETOIMAZŌ προετοιμάζω
prepare beforehand (2)
PROEUAGGELIZOMAI προευαγγελίζομαι
preach the gospel beforehand
PROGINOMAI προγίνομαι
former (*perf. part.*)
PROGINŌSKŌ προγινώσκω
destine
foreknow (2)
know
know beforehand
PROGNŌSIS πρόγνωσις
§destined
foreknowledge
PROGONOS πρόγονος
father (*subst.*)
parent (*subst.*)
PROGRAPHŌ προγράφω
designated, be (*pass.*)
publicly portray
write
write in former days
PRŌI πρωΐ
early (4)
morning
morning, in the (5)
IDIOMATICALLY
early in the morning *a;* morning *a*
PRŌIA πρωΐα
morning
IDIOMATICALLY
day *b*
PROIMOS πρόϊμος
§early rain
PRŌINOS πρωϊνός
morning (2)
PROISTĒMI προΐστημι
aid, give (*mid.*)
apply oneself to (*mid.*) (2)
(enter [*mid.*]†)
manage (*act. or mid.*) (3)
over, be (*mid.*)
rule
PROKALEŌ προκαλέω
provoke (*mid.*)
PROKATAGGELLŌ προκαταγγέλλω
announce beforehand
foretell
PROKATARTIZŌ προκαταρτίζω
arrange in advance
PROKEIMAI πρόκειμαι
serve as
set before (3)
there, be
PROKĒRYSSŌ προκηρύσσω
preach before
PROKOPĒ προκοπή
§advance
progress (2)
PROKOPTŌ προκόπτω
advance
far gone, be (*aor.*)
get
go on
increase
lead people
PROKRIMA πρόκριμα
favor
PROKYROŌ προκυρόω
ratify previously
PROLAMBANŌ προλαμβάνω
§beforehand
go ahead with
overtake
PROLEGŌ προλέγω
tell beforehand
warn (2)
PROMARTYROMAI προμαρτύρομαι
predict
PROMELETAŌ προμελετάω
meditate beforehand
PROMERIMNAŌ προμεριμνάω
anxious beforehand, be
PRONOEŌ προνοέω
aim at
provide
thought for, take (*mid.*)
PRONOIA πρόνοια
provision (2)
PROORAŌ προοράω
see before (*mid.*)
see previously
PROORIZŌ προορίζω
decree
destine
destined (*part.*)
predestine (3)
PROPASCHŌ προπάσχω
suffer, already
PROPATŌR προπάτωρ
forefather
PROPEMPŌ προπέμπω
bring
bring on one's way
send one on his journey
send one on his way (2)
speed one on his journey (2)
speed one on his way (2)
PROPETĒS προπετής
rash
reckless
PROPHASIS πρόφασις
cloak
excuse
pretense (4)+
PROPHERŌ προφέρω
produce (2)
PROPHĒTEIA προφητεία
prophecy (14)
prophesying (2)
prophetic powers
prophetic utterance (2)
PROPHĒTĒS προφήτης
prophet (144)
PROPHĒTEUŌ προφητεύω
§prophecy
prophesy (27)
PROPHĒTIKOS προφητικός
prophetic (2)
PROPHĒTIS προφῆτις
prophetess (2)
PROPHTHANŌ προφθάνω
§speak first
PROPOREUOMAI προπορεύομαι
go before (2)
PRŌRA πρῷρα
bow (2)

PROS πρός
about (+*acc.* 6)
according to (+*acc.* 2)
against (+*acc.* 21)
among (+*acc.* 6)
at (+*dat.* 4; +*acc.* 15)
before (+*acc.* 6)
beside (+*acc.* 2)
for (+*acc.* 38)
§give (+*acc.*)
in (+*acc.* 10)
of (+*acc.* 4)
on (+*dat.*)
order, in (+*acc.*)
round (+*dat.*)
§*some* (+*acc.*) 5
to (+*acc.* 445)
toward (+*acc.* 9)
unto (+*acc.*)
with (+*acc.* 50)
IDIOMATICALLY
OR NOT TRANSLATED
+*genitive:*
Acts **27.**34
+*dative:*
Jn **20.**11
+*accusative:*
Mt **5.**28; **13.**30; **23.**5, 34; **25.**39
Mk **13.**22
Lk **2.**18, 20; **4.**4; **5.**22, 31, 36; **6.**3; **11.**6; **12.**3, 16; **14.**32; **15.**3; **18.**1; **20.**3, 9; **22.**23; **24.**[12‡, 18, 50
Jn **4.**47; **13.**28
Acts **3.**12, 19, 22; **4.**19; **11.**2; **16.**40; **17.**2; **19.**2; **23.**22; **25.**16; **26.**9; **27.**12; **28.**8, 10
Rom **3.**26; **15.**2
1 Cor **7.**35; **16.**5, 12
2 Cor **1.**16; **2.**1; **3.**13; **5.**12; **7.**3; **10.**4; **11.**8; **13.**7
Eph **3.**4; **6.**11
Col **2.**[23†
1 Th **2.**9; **4.**12
2 Th **3.**2
1 Tim **4.**8
Heb **2.**17; **5.**1, 14; **7.**21; **9.**20
Jas **4.**5
1 Pet **3.**15; **4.**12
2 Pet **1.**3
1 Jn **5.**16[3], 17
2 Jn .12

PROSABBATON προσάββατον
sabbath, the day before the

PROSAGŌ προσάγω
bring
bring to (3)
near

PROSAGŌGĒ προσαγωγή
access (3)

PROSAGOREUŌ προσαγορεύω
designate

PROSAITEŌ προσαιτέω
beg

PROSAITĒS προσαίτης
beggar (2)

PROSANABAINŌ προσαναβαίνω
go up

PROSANALISKŌ προσαναλίσκω
(προσαναλόω)
(spend)

PROSANAPLĒROŌ προσαναπληρόω
supply (2)

PROSANATITHĒMI προσανατίθημι
add (*mid.*)
confer (*mid.*)

PROSAPEILEŌ προσαπειλέω
threaten, further

PROSCHYSIS πρόσχυσις
[*pouring out, sprinkling*]
§sprinkle

PROSDAPANAŌ προσδαπανάω
spend more

PROSDECHOMAI προσδέχομαι
accept (3)
await
look for (4)
receive (3)
wait for (3)

PROSDEOMAI προσδέομαι
need

PROSDOKAŌ προσδοκάω
expect (4)
expectation, be in
look for (3)
suspense, in (*part.*)
wait (2)
wait for (5)

PROSDOKIA προσδοκία
expecting, what s. is (+*gen.*)
foreboding

PROSEAŌ προσεάω
allow to go on

PROSECHŌ προσέχω
addicted (*part.*)
attend to
attention, pay (2)
beware (8)
§care what one does, take heed, give (6)
heed, take (3)
occupy oneself with
serve

PROSEGGIZŌ προσεγγίζω
near, get

PROSĒLOŌ προσηλόω
nail

PROSĒLYTOS προσήλυτος
convert
proselyte (3)

PROSERCHOMAI προσέρχομαι
agree
come (21)
come forward to (6)
come to (20)
come up (17)
draw near (3)
draw near to (3)
go (3)
go to (7)
go to see
go up
go up to (2)
visit

PROSERGAZOMAI προσεργάζομαι
make more

PROSEUCHĒ προσευχή
prayer (35)+
IDIOMATICALLY
fervently *a*

PROSEUCHOMAI προσεύχομαι
pray (79)+
§prayer (3)
§prayer, keep the hour of
prayers, make (2)+

PROSKAIROS πρόσκαιρος
§endure (2)
fleeting
transient

PROSKALEŌ προσκαλέω
call (*mid.*) (6)
call for (*mid.*)
call in (*mid.*)
call to one (*mid.*) (16)
summon (*mid.*) (5)

PROSKARTEREŌ προσκαρτερέω
attend (2)
constant, be
continue
continue steadfastly
devote oneself (3)
ready, have
wait on

PROSKARTERĒSIS προσκαρτέρησις
perseverance

PROSKEPHALION προσκεφάλαιον
cushion

PROSKLĒROŌ προσκληρόω
join (*pass.*)

PROSKLINŌ προσκλίνω
join (*pass.*)

PROSKLISIS πρόσκλισις
partiality

PROSKOLLAŌ προσκολλάω
joined, be (*pass.*) (2)

PROSKOMMA πρόσκομμα
stumble, that will make men (*gen.*) (2)
stumbling (*gen.*)
stumbling block (2)
IDIOMATICALLY
fall *a*

PROSKOPĒ προσκοπή
obstacle

PROSKOPTŌ προσκόπτω
beat against
strike (2)
stumble (5)

PROSKYLIŌ προσκυλίω
roll (2)

PROSKYNEŌ προσκυνέω
bow down
bow in worship
§homage
kneel before (4)
worship (50)+
worshiper (*subst.*)
IDIOMATICALLY
knee *a*

PROSKYNĒTĒS προσκυνητής
worshiper

PROSLALEŌ προσλαλέω
speak to
speak with

PROSLAMBANŌ προσλαμβάνω
eat (*mid.*)
receive (*mid.*)
take (*mid.*) (5)
welcome (*mid.*) (5)

PROSLĒMPSIS πρόσλημψις
acceptance

PROSMENŌ προσμένω
be with (2)
continue (2)
remain
remain faithful
stay

PROSOCHTHIZŌ προσοχθίζω
provoked, be (2)
PROSOPHEILŌ προσοφείλω
owe
PROSŌPOLĒMPSIA προσωπολημψία
partiality (4)
PROSŌPOLĒMPTEŌ προσωπολημπτέω
partiality, show
PROSŌPOLĒMPTĒS προσωπολήμπτης
§partiality, show
PROSŌPON πρόσωπον
§ahead of (2)
appearance (2)
§*before* (3)
countenance
face (43)
person
§position (3)
presence (9)
IDIOMATICALLY
eye *a;* face *a;* flatter *a;* partiality, show *a, b;* sight *a*
NOT TRANSLATED
2 Cor **1**.11; **3**.7
Jas **1**.11
Rev **12**.14
PROSORMIZŌ προσορμίζω
moor to the shore (*pass.*)
PROSPĒGNYMI προσπήγνυμι
crucify
PROSPEINOS πρόσπεινος
hungry
PROSPHAGION προσφάγιον
fish
PROSPHATOS πρόσφατος
new
PROSPHATŌS προσφάτως
lately
PROSPHERŌ προσφέρω
bring
bring to (12)
hold s. to
offer (25)
offer up (3)
offering, make an
present
treat (*pass.*+*dat.*)
PROSPHILĒS προσφιλής
lovely
PROSPHŌNEŌ προσφωνέω
address (2)
call (2)
call to (2)
speak to
PROSPHORA προσφορά
offering (9)
PROSPIPTŌ προσπίπτω
beat upon
fall down at (2)
fall down before (5)
PROSPOIEŌ προσποιέω
appear (*mid.*)
PROSPOREUOMAI προσπορεύομαι
come forward to
PROSPSAUŌ προσψαύω
touch
PROSRĒSSŌ προσρήσσω
break against (2)
PROSTASSŌ προστάσσω
allotted (*perf. pass. part.*)
command (6)
PROSTATIS προστάτις
helper
PROSTITHĒMI προστίθημι
add (8)
give still more
increase
lay
proceed (2)
well, be s. as (*pass.*+*dat.*) (2)
IDIOMATICALLY
further *b*
NOT TRANSLATED
Lk **20**.11, 12
PROSTRECHŌ προστρέχω
run to
run up (2)
PROTEINŌ προτείνω
tie up
PROTEROS πρότερος
before (*neut.*) (3)
first (*neut.*) (2)
first, at (*neut.*)
former (3)
formerly (*neut.*) (2)
PRŌTEUŌ πρωτεύω
pre-eminent (*part.*)
PROTHESIS πρόθεσις
aim in life
presence (4)
purpose (7)
PROTHESMIA προθεσμία
set, the date
PROTHYMIA προθυμία
eagerness
good will
readiness (3)
PROTHYMOS πρόθυμος
eager
willing (2)
PROTHYMŌS προθύμως
eagerly
PROTITHĒMI προτίθημι
intend
put forward
set forth
PRŌTOKATHEDRIA πρωτοκαθεδρία
best seat (4)
PRŌTOKLISIA πρωτοκλισία
place of honor (5)
PRŌTOS πρῶτος
before (+*gen.*) (3)
§begin
begin with, to (*neut.*)
best
chief
first (132)+
foremost (2)
former
leader (*subst.*)
leading (4)
§once
outer (3)
principal (2)
IDIOMATICALLY
first *b*
PRŌTŌS πρώτως
first time, for the
PRŌTOSTATĒS πρωτοστάτης
ringleader
PRŌTOTOKIA πρωτοτόκια
birthright
PRŌTOTOKOS πρωτότοκος
first-born (8)
PROTRECHŌ προτρέχω
§outrun
run on ahead
PROTREPŌ προτρέπω
encourage (*mid.*)
PROYPARCHŌ προϋπάρχω
be before this
§previously
PRYMNA πρύμνα
stern (3)
PSALLŌ ψάλλω
melody, make
sing (3)
sing praise
PSALMOS ψαλμός
hymn
psalm (6)
PSĒLAPHAŌ ψηλαφάω
feel after
handle
touch (2)
PSĒPHIZŌ ψηφίζω
count
reckon
PSĒPHOS ψῆφος
stone (2)
vote
PSEUDADELPHOS ψευδάδελφος
false brother (2)
PSEUDAPOSTOLOS ψευδαπόστολος
false apostle
PSEUDĒS ψευδής
false (2)
liar (*subst.*)
PSEUDOCHRISTOS ψευδόχριστος
false Christ (2)
PSEUDODIDASKALOS ψευδοδιδάσκαλος
false teacher
PSEUDOLOGOS ψευδολόγος
liar (*subst.*)
PSEUDOMAI ψεύδομαι
false, be
false, prove
falsely (*part.*)
lie (9)
PSEUDOMARTYREŌ ψευδομαρτυρέω
false witness, bear (5)
PSEUDOMARTYRIA ψευδομαρτυρία
false testimony
false witness
PSEUDOMARTYS ψευδόμαρτυς
false witness
§misrepresent
PSEUDŌNYMOS ψευδώνυμος
falsely called
PSEUDOPROPHĒTĒS ψευδοπροφήτης
false prophet (11)
PSEUDOS ψεῦδος
false, what is
falsehood (3)
lie (5)
pretended (*gen.*)
PSEUSMA ψεῦσμα
falsehood

PSEUSTĒS ψεύστης
§false
liar (9)
PSICHION ψιχίον
crumb (2)
PSITHYRISMOS ψιθυρισμός
gossip
PSITHYRISTĒS ψιθυριστής
gossip
PSŌCHŌ ψώχω
rub
PSŌMION ψωμίον
morsel (4)
PSŌMIZŌ ψωμίζω
feed
give away
PSYCHĒ ψυχή
being, a (2)
heart
§heartily
life (43)+
§living
mind (3)
person (3)
self
soul (42)
IDIOMATICALLY
fainthearted *a;* suspense, keep in *a;* thing *a*
NOT TRANSLATED
2 Cor **1**.23
PSYCHIKOS ψυχικός
(natural†)
physical (3)
unspiritual (2)
worldly people (*subst. pl.*)
PSYCHŌ ψύχω
cold, grow (*pass.*)
PSYCHOS ψῦχος
cold (3)
PSYCHROS ψυχρός
cold (3)
§cold water
PTAIŌ πταίω
fail
fall
mistake, make a (2)
stumble
PTĒNOS πτηνός
bird (*subst.*)
PTERNA πτέρνα
heel
PTERYGION πτερύγιον
pinnacle (2)
PTERYX πτέρυξ
wing (5)
PTŌCHEIA πτωχεία
poverty (3)
PTŌCHEUŌ πτωχεύω
poor, become
PTŌCHOS πτωχός
beggarly
poor (33)
PTOEŌ πτοέω
startle
terrify
PTOĒSIS πτόησις
[*fear, terror*]
§terrify 1
PTŌMA πτῶμα
body (4)
dead body (2)
NOT TRANSLATED
Rev **11**.9
PTŌSIS πτῶσις
fall (2)
PTYŌ πτύω
spit (3)
PTYON πτύον
winnowing fork (2)
PTYRŌ πτύρω
frightened (*part.*)
PTYSMA πτύσμα
spittle
PTYSSŌ πτύσσω
close
PYGMĒ πυγμή
[*fist* (?)]
NOT TRANSLATED
Mk **7**.3 (*See RSV footnote*)
PYKNOS πυκνός
frequent
often (2)+
PYKTEUŌ πυκτεύω
box
PYLĒ πύλη
gate (9)
§power
PYLŌN πυλών
gate (16)
gateway
porch
PYNTHANOMAI πυνθάνομαι
ask (5)
inquire (5)
learn
PYR πῦρ
burning (*gen.*)
fire (70)+
PYRA πυρά
fire (2)
PYRESSŌ πυρέσσω
fever, with a (*part.*) (2)
PYRETOS πυρετός
fever (6)
PYRGOS πύργος
tower (4)
PYRINOS πύρινος
color of fire, the
PYROŌ πυρόω
aflame, be (*pass.*)
flaming (*perf. pass. part.*)
indignant, be (*pass.*)
kindled, be (*pass.*)
refined (*perf. pass. part.*) (2)
PYRŌSIS πύρωσις
burning (2)
fiery ordeal
PYRRAZŌ πυρράζω
red, be (2)
PYRROS πυρρός
red
red, bright
PYTHŌN πύθων
divination, spirit of

R

RHABBI ῥαββί
master (5)
rabbi (10)†
RHABBOUNI ῥαββουνί
master
(rabbi†)
rabboni
RHABDIZŌ ῥαβδίζω
beat with rods (2)
RHABDOS ῥάβδος
rod (5)
scepter (2)
staff (5)
RHABDOUCHOS ῥαβδοῦχος
police (*pl.*) (2)
RHADIOURGĒMA ῥᾳδιούργημα
crime
RHADIOURGIA ῥᾳδιουργία
villainy
RHAKA ῥακά
[*fool!* (*Heb. expression of contempt*)]
§insult
RHAKOS ῥάκος
cloth (2)
RHANTISMOS ῥαντισμός
sprinkled (*gen.*)
sprinkling
RHANTIZŌ ῥαντίζω
purify (*mid.*)
sprinkle (2)+
sprinkle clean (*mid.*)
§sprinkling
RHAPHIS ῥαφίς
needle (2)
RHAPISMA ῥάπισμα
blow
§strike with one's hand (2)
RHAPIZŌ ῥαπίζω
slap
strike
RHEDĒ ῥέδη
chariot
RHĒGMA ῥῆγμα
ruin
RHĒGNYMI ῥήγνυμι (ῥήσσω)
attack
break forth
burst (3)
dash down
tear
RHĒMA ῥῆμα
charge (2)
message (*pl.*)
§nothing (*neg.*) 8[a]
preaching
§prediction 1 (2)
§say (2)
saying (11)
statement
thing (7)
word (37)
NOT TRANSLATED
Mk **14**.72
Acts **10**.44; **26**.25
RHEŌ ῥέω
flow
RHĒTŌR ῥήτωρ
spokesman
RHĒTŌS ῥητῶς
expressly
RHIPĒ ῥιπή
twinkling
RHIPIZŌ ῥιπίζω
toss

RHIPTŌ *ῥίπτω (ῥιπτέω)*
cast
cast out
helpless, be (*perf. pass.*)
let out
put
throw down (2)
wave
RHIZA *ῥίζα*
root (16)+
RHIZOŌ *ῥιζόω*
rooted (*perf. pass. part.*)
rooted, being (*perf. pass. part.*)
RHOIZĒDON *ῥοιζηδόν*
loud noise, with a
RHOMPHAIA *ῥομφαία*
sword (7)
RHŌNNYMI *ῥώννυμι*
farewell (*pass. imper.*)
RHYMĒ *ῥύμη*
lane
street (3)
RHYOMAI *ῥύομαι*
deliver (11)
deliverer (*subst. part.*)
rescue (5)
RHYPAINŌ *ῥυπαίνω*
filthy, be (*pass.*)
RHYPARIA *ῥυπαρία*
filthiness
RHYPAROS *ῥυπαρός*
filthy
shabby
RHYPOS *ῥύπος*
dirt
RHYSIS *ῥύσις*
flow (3)
RHYTIS *ῥυτίς*
wrinkle

S

SABACHTHANI *σαβαχθάνι*
sabachthani (2)
SABAŌTH *Σαβαώθ*
hosts (2)
SABBATISMOS *σαββατισμός*
sabbath rest
SABBATON *σάββατον*
sabbath (58)†
week (10)
SAGĒNĒ *σαγήνη*
net
SAINŌ *σαίνω*
moved, be (*pass.*)
SAKKOS *σάκκος*
sackcloth (4)
SALEUŌ *σαλεύω*
shake (14)
stir up
SALOS *σάλος*
waves
SALPIGX *σάλπιγξ*
bugle
trumpet (8)
trumpet call
trumpet, sound of the
SALPISTĒS *σαλπιστής*
trumpeter
SALPIZŌ *σαλπίζω*
§blow (2)
blow one's trumpet (7)
sound a trumpet (3)
SANDALION *σανδάλιον*
sandal (2)
SANIS *σανίς*
plank
SAPPHIROS *σάπφιρος*
sapphire
SAPROS *σαπρός*
bad (7)
evil
SARDION *σάρδιον*
carnelian (2)
SARDONYX *σαρδόνυξ*
onyx
SARGANĒ *σαργάνη*
basket
SARKIKOS *σαρκικός*
earthly
flesh, of the (3)
material (2)
worldly
SARKINOS *σάρκινος*
bodily
carnal
flesh, of the
human
SAROŌ *σαρόω*
sweep (3)
SARX *σάρξ*
bodily (*gen.*)
body (6)
condition
§earthly (3)
flesh (110)
human being (4)
natural (*gen.*)
§physical
§race
sensuous (*gen.*)
world
§worldly (2)
§worldly fashion, in a
§worldly man, like a
§worldly standards, according to
§worldly things, of
IDIOMATICALLY
fellow Jews *a;* human *a* (2); lust *a, b;* one *e;* people *a*
NOT TRANSLATED
1 Cor **15.**39[3]
Col **2.**1
SATANAS *σατανᾶς (σατάν)*
Satan (36)
SATON *σάτον*
measure (2)
SBENNYMI *σβέννυμι*
go out (*pass.*)
quench (5)+
SCHEDON *σχεδόν*
almost (3)
SCHĒMA *σχῆμα*
form (2)
SCHISMA *σχίσμα*
discord
dissension
division (4)
tear (2)
SCHIZŌ *σχίζω*
divide (2)
open
split
tear (7)
SCHOINION *σχοινίον*
cord
rope
SCHOLAZŌ *σχολάζω*
devote oneself
empty (*part.*)
SCHOLĒ *σχολή*
hall
SEAUTOU *σεαυτοῦ*
self, your own
you
yourself (36)
IDIOMATICALLY
thy *a;* you *a* (2); your *a, b*
SEBASMA *σέβασμα*
worship, object of (2)
SEBASTOS *σεβαστός*
Augustan
emperor (*subst.*) (2)
SEBAZOMAI *σεβάζομαι*
worship
SEBŌ *σέβω*
devout (*mid. part.*) (4)
worship (*mid.*) (4)
worshiper (*subst. mid. part.*) (2)
SEIŌ *σείω*
shake (3)
stir
tremble (*pass.*)
SEISMOS *σεισμός*
earthquake (13)
storm
SELĒNĒ *σελήνη*
moon (9)
SELĒNIAZOMAI *σεληνιάζομαι*
epileptic, an (*subst. part.*)
epileptic, be an
SĒMAINŌ *σημαίνω*
foretell
indicate
known, make
show (3)
SĒMEION *σημεῖον*
mark
portent (3)
sign (73)
SĒMEIOŌ *σημειόω*
note (*mid.*)
SĒMERON *σήμερον*
day, this (13)
today (27)+
IDIOMATICALLY
very *a, b*
SEMIDALIS *σεμίδαλις*
flour, fine
SEMNOS *σεμνός*
honorable
serious (3)
SEMNOTĒS *σεμνότης*
gravity
§respectful (2)
SĒPŌ *σήπω*
rot
SĒS *σής*
moth (3)
SĒTOBRŌTOS *σητόβρωτος*
moth-eaten

SIAGŌN σιαγών
cheek (2)
SIDĒROS σίδηρος
iron
SIDĒROUS σιδηροῦς
iron (5)
SIGAŌ σιγάω
finish speaking (*aor.*)
secret, keep
silence, keep (4)
silent, be (4)
SIGĒ σιγή
hush
silence
SIKARIOS σικάριος
assassin
SIKERA σίκερα
strong drink
SIMIKINTHION σιμικίνθιον
apron
SINAPI σίναπι
mustard (5)
SINDŌN σινδών
linen cloth (2)
linen shroud (4)
SINIAZŌ σινιάζω
sift
SIŌPAŌ σιωπάω
peace (*imper.*)
silent, be (9)
SIRIKOS σιρικός
silk (*subst. neut.*)
SIROS σιρός
pit
SITEUTOS σιτευτός
fatted (3)
SITION σιτίον
grain (*pl.*)
SITISTOS σιτιστός
fat calf (*subst. neut.*)
SITOMETRION σιτομέτριον
portion of food
SITOS σῖτος
grain (2)
wheat (12)
SKANDALIZŌ σκανδαλίζω
fall away (*pass.*) (9)
fall, cause to
fall, make to
falling, be a cause of s.'s
offend
offense, give
§offense, take (5)
sin, cause s. to (10)
(stumble †)
(upset, be [*pass.*])
SKANDALON σκάνδαλον
difficulty
fall, that will make one (*gen.*) (2)
hindrance (2)
pitfall
sin, cause of
stumbling block (3)
stumbling, cause for
temptation (2)
temptation to sin (2)
SKAPHĒ σκάφη
boat (3)
SKAPTŌ σκάπτω
dig (3)
SKELOS σκέλος
leg (3)
SKĒNĒ σκηνή
booth (3)
dwelling (3)
habitation
(tabernacle †)
tent (13)
SKĒNŌMA σκήνωμα
body (2)
habitation
SKĒNOŌ σκηνόω
dwell (4)
shelter
SKĒNOPĒGIA σκηνοπηγία
feast of Tabernacles
SKĒNOPOIOS σκηνοποιός
tentmaker
SKĒNOS σκῆνος
tent (2)
SKEPASMA σκέπασμα
clothing
SKEUĒ σκευή
tackle
SKEUOS σκεῦος
anything (+*neg.*)
article (2)
(body †)
bowl
gear
goods (*pl.*) (3)
instrument
pot
§sex
§something (2)
thing
vessel (8)
wife
SKIA σκιά
shade
shadow (6)
SKIRTAŌ σκιρτάω
leap (3)
SKLĒROKARDIA σκληροκαρδία
hardness of heart (3)
SKLĒROS σκληρός
hard (2)
harsh
§hurt
strong
SKLĒROTĒS σκληρότης
§hard
SKLĒROTRACHĒLOS σκληροτράχηλος
stiff-necked
SKLĒRYNŌ σκληρύνω
harden (5)
stubborn, be (*pass.*)
SKŌLĒKOBRŌTOS σκωληκόβρωτος
eaten by worms
SKŌLĒX σκώληξ
worm +
SKOLIOS σκολιός
crooked (3)
overbearing
SKOLOPS σκόλοψ
thorn
SKOPEŌ σκοπέω
careful, be
look to (3)
mark
note, take
SKOPOS σκοπός
goal
SKORPIOS σκορπίος
scorpion (5)
SKORPIZŌ σκορπίζω
scatter (4)
scatter abroad
SKOTEINOS σκοτεινός
dark
darkness, full of (2)
SKOTIA σκοτία
dark (4)
darkness (13)
SKOTIZŌ σκοτίζω
darken (5) +
SKOTOŌ σκοτόω
darken (2)
darkness, in (*perf. pass. part.*)
SKOTOS σκότος
darkness (30)
SKYBALON σκύβαλον
refuse
SKYLLŌ σκύλλω
harass
trouble (2)
trouble oneself (*pass.*)
SKYLON σκῦλον
spoil (*pl.*)
SKYTHRŌPOS σκυθρωπός
§dismal, look
sad, looking
SMARAGDINOS σμαράγδινος
emerald
SMARAGDOS σμάραγδος
emerald
SMYRNA σμύρνα
myrrh (2)
SMYRNIZŌ σμυρνίζω
myrrh, mingled with (*perf. pass. part.*)
SŌMA σῶμα
bodily (*gen.*) (2)
body (138)
slave
substance
SŌMATIKOS σωματικός
bodily (2)
SŌMATIKŌS σωματικῶς
bodily
SOPHIA σοφία
wisdom (50)
§wisely
SOPHIZŌ σοφίζω
cleverly devised (*perf. pass. part.*)
instruct
SOPHOS σοφός
skilled
wise (18)
wiser (*comp.*)
SŌPHRŌN σώφρων
§master of oneself
sensible (3)
SŌPHRONEŌ σωφρονέω
control oneself
keep sane
right mind, be in one's
right mind, in one's (*pass. part.*) (2)
sober judgment (*inf.*)
SŌPHRONISMOS σωφρονισμός
self-control

SŌPHRONIZŌ σωφρονίζω
train
SŌPHRONŌS σωφρόνως
§sober
SŌPHROSYNĒ σωφροσύνη
modesty
§sensibly
§sober
SŌREUŌ σωρεύω
burden
heap
SOROS σορός
bier
SOS σός
thine (*pred.* 3; *subst. neut.* 2)
thy
you, what belongs to (*subst. neut.*)
your (14)
your goods (*subst. neut. pl.*)
your own (2)
yours (*pred. or subst.*) (2)
yours, what is (*subst. neut.*)
SŌTĒR σωτήρ
savior (24)
SŌTĒRIA σωτηρία
deliverance (2)
salvation (36)+
§save (4)
saving
strength
IDIOMATICALLY
save *a*
SŌTĒRIOS σωτήριος
§salvation (5)
SOUDARION σουδάριον
cloth
handkerchief
napkin (2)
SŌZŌ σῴζω
heal (2)
recover (*pass.*)
save (90)+
well, be (*pass.*)
well, make (12)
SPAŌ σπάω
draw (*mid.*) (2)
SPARASSŌ σπαράσσω
convulse (3)
SPARGANOŌ σπαργανόω
wrap in swaddling cloths (2)
SPATALAŌ σπαταλάω
pleasure, live in
self-indulgent, be
SPEIRA σπεῖρα
band of soldiers (2)
battalion (2)
cohort (3)
SPEIRŌ σπείρω
sow (44)
sower (*subst. part.*) (7)
NOT TRANSLATED
1 Cor 9.37
SPEKOULATŌR σπεκουλάτωρ
soldier of the guard
SPĒLAION σπήλαιον
cave (2)
den (4)
SPENDŌ σπένδω
pour as a libation
sacrificed, be on the point of being (*pass.*)
SPERMA σπέρμα
children (*pl.*) (8)
§descendant
descendants (11)
§descended (3)
nature
offspring (6)†
posterity (5)
seed (8)
IDIOMATICALLY
conceive *c*
SPERMOLOGOS σπερμολόγος
babbler (*subst.*)
SPEUDŌ σπεύδω
(desire, earnestly †)
haste, make (3)
haste, with (*part.*)
hasten (2)
SPHAGĒ σφαγή
slaughter (2)
slaughtered, to be (*gen.*)
SPHAGION σφάγιον
slain beast
SPHAZŌ σφάζω
murder (2)
slay (7)
IDIOMATICALLY
wound *a*
SPHODRA σφόδρα
exceedingly
greatly (4)
so
very (3)
IDIOMATICALLY
fill *a* (2)
SPHODRŌS σφοδρῶς
violently
SPHRAGIS σφραγίς
seal (16)
SPHRAGIZŌ σφραγίζω
§deliver (*mid.*)
seal (9)
seal, set one's (2)
seal up (2)
seal upon, put one's
SPHYDRON σφυδρόν
ankle
SPILAS σπιλάς
blemish
(reef †)
SPILOŌ σπιλόω
spot
stain
SPILOS σπίλος
blot
spot
SPLAGCHNIZOMAI σπλαγχνίζομαι
compassion, have (3)
compassion on, have (5)
pity, have
pity, in (*part.*)
pity, moved with (*part.*)
pity, out of (*part.*)
SPLAGCHNON σπλάγχνον
affection (*pl.*) (3)
bowels (*pl.*)
§compassion 1
heart (*pl.*) (5)
§tender
SPODOS σποδός
ashes (3)
SPOGGOS σπόγγος
sponge (3)
SPORA σπορά
seed
SPORIMOS σπόριμος
grainfield (*subst.*) (3)
SPOROS σπόρος
resources
seed (4)
SPOUDAIOS σπουδαῖος
earnest
earnest, more (*comp.*)
earnest, very (*comp.*)
SPOUDAIŌS σπουδαίως
§eager, the more (*comp.*)
eagerly
earnestly
IDIOMATICALLY
best *a*
SPOUDAZŌ σπουδάζω
best, do one's (4)
eager (*part.*)
eager, be
endeavor eagerly
see to it
strive
zealous, be (2)
SPOUDĒ σπουδή
earnest care
earnestness (4)
haste (2)
zeal (3)
IDIOMATICALLY
eager *a;* effort *a*
SPYRIS σπυρίς
basket (5)
STACHYS στάχυς
ear (2)
head of grain (3)
STADION στάδιον
furlong
§mile (3)
race
stadium (2)+
STAMNOS στάμνος
urn
STAPHYLĒ σταφυλή
grapes (*sg. or pl.*) (3)
STASIASTĒS στασιαστής
rebel
STASIS στάσις
§agitator 1
dissension (3)
insurrection (3)
rioting
§stand
STATĒR στατήρ
shekel
STAUROŌ σταυρόω
crucify (46)
STAUROS σταυρός
cross (27)
STEGĒ στέγη
roof (3)
STEGŌ στέγω
bear
bear, can (+*neg.*) (2)
endure
STEIROS στεῖρος
barren (4)

STĒKŌ στήκω
stand (4)
stand fast (2)
stand firm (4)

STELLŌ στέλλω
keep away (*mid.*)
IDIOMATICALLY
intend *a*

STEMMA στέμμα
garland

STENAGMOS στεναγμός
groaning
sigh

STENAZŌ στενάζω
groan (2)
grumble
sadly (*part.*)
sigh (2)

STENOCHŌREŌ στενοχωρέω
crush
restrict (2)

STENOCHŌRIA στενοχωρία
calamity (2)
distress (2)

STENOS στενός
narrow (3)

STEPHANOŌ στεφανόω
crown (3)

STEPHANOS στέφανος
crown (17)
wreath

STEREŌMA στερέωμα
firmness

STEREOŌ στερεόω
strengthen
strong, make (2)

STEREOS στερεός
firm (2)
solid (2)

STĒRIGMOS στηριγμός
stability

STĒRIZŌ στηρίζω
establish (6)
fix
set
strengthen (6)

STĒTHOS στῆθος
breast (5)

STHENOŌ σθενόω
strengthen

STIBAS στιβάς
leafy branch

STIGMA στίγμα
mark

STIGMĒ στιγμή
moment

STILBŌ στίλβω
glistening (*part.*)

STOA στοά
portico (4)

STOICHEION στοιχεῖον
element (2)
elemental spirit (4)
principle

STOICHEŌ στοιχέω
follow (+*dat.*)
hold true
live
walk (2)

STOLĒ στολή
robe (7)
robe, long (2)

STOMA στόμα
edge (2)
§evidence (2)
§face (4)
lips (5)
mouth (62)
§voice
IDIOMATICALLY
loud-mouthed *a;* say *a*

STOMACHOS στόμαχος
stomach

STRATĒGOS στρατηγός
captain (3)
magistrate (5)
officer (2)

STRATEIA στρατεία
warfare (2)

STRATEUMA στράτευμα
army (3)
soldiers (*sg. or pl.*) (3)
troops (*pl.*) (2)

STRATEUOMAI στρατεύομαι
soldier (*subst. part.*)
soldier on service (*subst. part.*)
soldier, serve as a
§wage
war, be at
war, carry on a
war, wage

STRATIA στρατιά
host (2)

STRATIŌTĒS στρατιώτης
soldier (26)

STRATOLOGEŌ στρατολογέω
enlist

STRATOPEDON στρατόπεδον
army

STREBLOŌ στρεβλόω
twist

STRĒNIAŌ στρηνιάω
wanton, be
wanton, play the

STRĒNOS στρῆνος
wantonness

STREPHŌ στρέφω
bring back
turn (*act. or aor. pass.*) (20)

STRŌNNYŌ στρωννύω (στρώννυμι)
furnished (*perf. pass. part.*) (2)
make
spread (3)

STROUTHION στρουθίον
sparrow (4)

STYGĒTOS στυγητός
hated

STYGNAZŌ στυγνάζω
countenance falls, one's
threaten

STYLOS στῦλος
pillar (4)

SY σύ
as for you (3)
thee (41)†
(*thine*)
thou (24)
thy (80)+
you (559)+
your (302)+†
your own (7)
yours
yours, of (2)
yourself (3)
IDIOMATICALLY
OR NOT TRANSLATED
Mt **5**.29, 30; **6**.6; **9**.6; **16**.22; **18**.8, 9; **20**.15†; **22**.16; **26**.18; **27**.19
Mk **1**.24; **2**.11; **5**.19; **6**.22; **12**.14
Lk **4**.34; **5**.24; **10**.37
Jn **18**.30; **21**.22
Acts **1**.24; **4**.24; **5**.3; **8**.34; **23**.21
1 Cor **7**.21
Phm .19
Jas **2**.3[2]
3 Jn .13

SYGCHAIRŌ συγχαίρω
rejoice
rejoice together
rejoice with (5)

SYGCHEŌ συγχέω (συγχύννω)
bewildered, be (*pass.*)
confound
confusion, be in (*pass.*) (2)
stir up

SYGCHRAOMAI συγχράομαι
dealings with, have

SYGCHYSIS σύγχυσις
confusion

SYGGENEIA συγγένεια
kindred (3)

SYGGENĒS συγγενής
kin (*subst. pl.*)
kinsfolk (*subst. pl.*) (2)
kinsman (*subst.*) (8)

SYGGENIS συγγενίς
kinswoman

SYGGNŌMĒ συγγνώμη
concession

SYGKAKOPATHEŌ συγκακοπαθέω
suffering, share in (2)

SYGKAKOUCHEOMAI
συγκακουχέομαι
ill-treatment, share

SYGKALEŌ συγκαλέω
call together (*act. or mid.*) (8)

SYGKALYPTŌ συγκαλύπτω
cover up

SYGKAMPTŌ συγκάμπτω
bend

SYGKATABAINŌ συγκαταβαίνω
go down with

SYGKATAPSĒPHIZOMAI
συγκαταψηφίζομαι
enrolled with, be

SYGKATATHESIS συγκατάθεσις
agreement

SYGKATATITHĒMI συγκατατίθημι
consent (*mid.*)

SYGKATHĒMAI συγκάθημαι
sit with (2)

SYGKATHIZŌ συγκαθίζω
sit down together
sit with

SYGKERANNYMI συγκεράννυμι
compose
meet with
(unite)

SYGKINEŌ συγκινέω
stir up

SYGKLEIŌ συγκλείω
consign (2)
enclose
keep under restraint

SYGKLĒRONOMOS συγκληρονόμος
fellow heir (*subst.*) (2)
heir with (*subst.*)
joint heir (*subst.*)

SYGKOINŌNEŌ συγκοινωνέω
share
take part (2)

SYGKOINŌNOS συγκοινωνός
partaker with
§share (3)

SYGKOMIZŌ συγκομίζω
bury

SYGKRINŌ συγκρίνω
compare (2)†
interpret

SYGKYPTŌ συγκύπτω
bent over, be

SYGKYRIA συγκυρία
chance

SYKAMINOS συκάμινος
sycamine tree

SYKĒ συκῆ
fig tree (16)

SYKOMOREA συκομορέα
sycamore tree

SYKON σῦκον
fig (4)

SYKOPHANTEŌ συκοφαντέω
defraud
rob by false accusation

SYLAGŌGEŌ συλαγωγέω
prey of, make a

SYLAŌ συλάω
rob

SYLLALEŌ συλλαλέω
confer (2)
say
talk (3)

SYLLAMBANŌ συλλαμβάνω
arrest (2)
capture (2)
conceive (5)
help (*mid.*) (2)
seize (*act. or mid.*) (4)
take

SYLLEGŌ συλλέγω
gather (7)
sort

SYLLOGIZOMAI συλλογίζομαι
discuss

SYLLYPEŌ συλλυπέω
grieved (*pass. part.*)

SYMBAINŌ συμβαίνω
§actually
befall
happen (6)

SYMBALLŌ συμβάλλω
confer
encounter
help (*mid.*)
meet (2)
ponder

SYMBASILEUŌ συμβασιλεύω
reign with
share the rule with

SYMBIBAZŌ συμβιβάζω
conclude
instruct
knit together (*pass. part.*) (2)
knit together, be (*pass.*)
prompt
prove

SYMBOULEUŌ συμβουλεύω
counsel
counsel, give
counsel together, take (*mid.*)
plot (*mid.*)

SYMBOULION συμβούλιον
consultation
council
counsel (6)

SYMBOULOS σύμβουλος
counselor

SYMMARTYREŌ συμμαρτυρέω
witness, also bear
witness, bear
witness with, bear

SYMMATHĒTĒS συμμαθητής
fellow disciple

SYMMERIZOMAI συμμερίζομαι
share

SYMMETOCHOS συμμέτοχος
§associate with
partaker (*subst.*)

SYMMIMĒTĒS συμμιμητής
§join in imitating

SYMMORPHIZŌ συμμορφίζω
like s., become (*pass.*)

SYMMORPHOS σύμμορφος
conformed
like (+*dat.*)

SYMPARAGINOMAI συμπαραγίνομαι
assemble

SYMPARAKALEŌ συμπαρακαλέω
encouraged, be mutually (*pass.*)

SYMPARALAMBANŌ συμπαραλαμβάνω
bring with one
take along with one
take with one (2)

SYMPAREIMI συμπάρειμι
present with, be

SYMPASCHŌ συμπάσχω
suffer together
suffer with

SYMPATHEŌ συμπαθέω
compassion on, have
sympathize

SYMPATHĒS συμπαθής
§sympathy, have

SYMPEMPŌ συμπέμπω
send
send with

SYMPERILAMBANŌ συμπεριλαμβάνω
embrace

SYMPHĒMI σύμφημι
agree

SYMPHERŌ συμφέρω
advantage, it is to s.'s (*impers.*+*dat.*)
best for s., it is (*impers.*+*dat.*)
better, it is (*impers.*) (3)
bring together
expedient, it is (*impers.*) (3)
good, one's (*subst. part. neut.*)
good, the common (*subst. part. neut.*)
helpful, be (2)
profitable, what is (*subst. part. neut.*)
IDIOMATICALLY
gain *a*

SYMPHŌNEŌ συμφωνέω
agree (5)
match (+*dat.*)

SYMPHŌNĒSIS συμφώνησις
accord

SYMPHŌNIA συμφωνία
music

SYMPHŌNOS σύμφωνος
agreement (*subst.*)

SYMPHOROS σύμφορος
advantage (*subst. neut.*)
benefit (*subst. neut.*)

SYMPHYLETĒS συμφυλέτης
countryman

SYMPHYŌ συμφύω
grow with (*pass.*)

SYMPHYTOS σύμφυτος
united

SYMPINŌ συμπίνω
drink with

SYMPIPTŌ συμπίπτω
fall

SYMPLĒROŌ συμπληρόω
come (*pass.*)
draw near (*pass.*)
fill with water (*pass.*)

SYMPNIGŌ συμπνίγω
choke (4)
press round

SYMPOLITĒS συμπολίτης
fellow citizen

SYMPOREUOMAI συμπορεύομαι
accompany
gather
go with (2)

SYMPOSION συμπόσιον
[*party, group*]
IDIOMATICALLY
company *a* (1; Gr. 2)

SYMPRESBYTEROS συμπρεσβύτερος
fellow elder

SYMPSĒPHIZŌ συμψηφίζω
count

SYMPSYCHOS σύμψυχος
full accord, in

SYN σύν (+*dat.*)
§accompany 1; 2; 4 (2)
along with (3)
and
beside
besides
by
together with (4)
with (112)+
IDIOMATICALLY
OR NOT TRANSLATED
Acts **27**.2

SYNAGŌ συνάγω
assemble (5)
come together (*pass.*)
gather (29)
gather together (14)
gather up (2)
(guest, be the [*pass.*]†)
meet (*pass.*) (2)
return (*pass.*)

store (2)
welcome (3)

SYNAGŌGĒ συναγωγή
assembly
synagogue (55)

SYNAGŌNIZOMAI συναγωνίζομαι
strive together with

SYNAICHMALŌTOS συναιχμάλωτος
fellow prisoner (3)

SYNAIRŌ συναίρω
reckon
§settle (2)

SYNAKOLOUTHEŌ συνακολουθέω
follow (3)

SYNALIZŌ συναλίζω
(eat with †)
stay with (*pass.*)

SYNALLASSŌ συναλλάσσω
reconcile

SYNANABAINŌ συναναβαίνω
come up with (2)

SYNANAKEIMAI συνανάκειμαι
guest (*subst. part.*) (2)
sit at table with (2)
sit down with
sit with
table with, be at

SYNANAMEIGNYMI συναναμείγνυμι
associate with (*pass.*) (2)
do with, have to (*pass.*)

SYNANAPAUOMAI συναναπαύομαι
refreshed in s.'s company, be (+*dat.*)

SYNANTAŌ συναντάω
befall, what shall (*subst. part. neut. pl.*)
meet (5)

SYNANTILAMBANOMAI συναντιλαμβάνομαι
help (2)

SYNAPAGŌ συναπάγω
associate with (*pass.*)
carried away by, be (*pass.*)
carried away with, be (*pass.*)
(give oneself [*pass.*]†)

SYNAPOLLYMI συναπόλλυμι
perish with (*mid.*)

SYNAPOSTELLŌ συναποστέλλω
send with

SYNAPOTHNĒSKŌ συναποθνήσκω
die together
die with (2)

SYNARMOLOGEŌ συναρμολογέω
join together (2)

SYNARPAZŌ συναρπάζω
catch
drag with one
seize (2)

SYNATHLEŌ συναθλέω
labor side by side with
strive side by side with

SYNATHROIZŌ συναθροίζω
gather together (2)

SYNAUXANŌ συναυξάνω
grow together (*pass.*)

SYNDEŌ συνδέω
prison with, in (*pass. part.*)

SYNDESMOS σύνδεσμος
§bind together
bond (2)
ligament

SYNDOULOS σύνδουλος
fellow servant (10)

SYNDOXAZŌ συνδοξάζω
glorified with, be (*pass.*)

SYNDROMĒ συνδρομή
§run together

SYNECHŌ συνέχω
afflicted (*pass. part.*)
constrained, be (*pass.*)
control
hard pressed, be (*pass.*)
hem in
hold
ill, be (*pass.*)
occupied with, be (*pass.*)
seize
sick (*pass. part.*)
stop
surround

SYNĒDOMAI συνήδομαι
delight

SYNEDRION συνέδριον
council (22)

SYNEGEIRŌ συνεγείρω
raise up with
raise with (2)

SYNEIDĒSIS συνείδησις
conscience (27)
consciousness
§mindful
scruples

SYNEIDON συνεῖδον
learn of
realize

SYNEIMI I σύνειμι
be with (2)

SYNEIMI II σύνειμι
come together

SYNEISERCHOMAI συνεισέρχομαι
enter with (2)

SYNEKDĒMOS συνέκδημος
companion in travel
§travel

SYNEKLEKTOS συνεκλεκτός
chosen, likewise

SYNĒLIKIŌTĒS συνηλικιώτης
age, s. of one's own

SYNEPHISTĒMI συνεφίστημι
[*rise together* (*pass., 2 aor.*)]
IDIOMATICALLY
join in attacking *a*

SYNEPIMARTYREŌ συνεπιμαρτυρέω
witness, also bear

SYNEPITITHEMAI συνεπιτίθεμαι
join in the charge

SYNEPOMAI συνέπομαι
accompany

SYNERCHOMAI συνέρχομαι
accompany (2)
assemble (2)
assembled, be
come together (12)
come with (3)
gather (4)
go with (4)
meet (2)

SYNERGEŌ συνεργέω
active along with, be
fellow worker (*subst. part.*)
work with (3)

SYNERGOS συνεργός
fellow worker (11)
§work with

SYNESIS σύνεσις
cleverness
insight
understanding (5)

SYNESTHIŌ συνεσθίω
eat with (5)

SYNĒTHEIA συνήθεια
accustomed, being (*dat.*)
custom
practice

SYNETOS συνετός
clever
intelligence, of
understanding (2)

SYNEUDOKEŌ συνευδοκέω
approve (2)
consent (4)

SYNEUŌCHEOMAI συνευωχέομαι
carouse (2)

SYNIĒMI συνίημι (συνίω)
understand (25)
understanding, be without (*neg.*)

SYNISTĒMI συνίστημι (συνιστάνω, συνιστάω)
commend (9)
formed (*perf. part.*)
hold together (*perf.*)
prove (2)
serve to show
show
stand with

SYNOCHĒ συνοχή
anguish
distress

SYNODEUŌ συνοδεύω
travel with

SYNODIA συνοδία
company

SYNŌDINŌ συνωδίνω
§travail together

SYNOIDA σύνοιδα
aware of, be
§knowledge

SYNOIKEŌ συνοικέω
live with

SYNOIKODOMEŌ συνοικοδομέω
built, be (*pass.*)

SYNOMILEŌ συνομιλέω
talk with

SYNOMOREŌ συνομορέω
next door to, be

SYNŌMOSIA συνωμοσία
conspiracy

SYNTASSŌ συντάσσω
direct (3)

SYNTELEIA συντέλεια
close (5)
end

SYNTELEŌ συντελέω
accomplish
complete
end (2)
establish
rigor, with (*part.*)

SYNTEMNŌ συντέμνω
dispatch, with (*part.*)

SYNTĒREŌ συντηρέω
keep

keep safe
preserve

SYNTHAPTŌ συνθάπτω
bury with (2)

SYNTHLAŌ συνθλάω
break to pieces +

SYNTHLIBŌ συνθλίβω
press around
throng about

SYNTHRYPTŌ συνθρύπτω
break

SYNTITHĒMI συντίθημι
agree (*mid.*) (2)
engage (*mid.*)

SYNTOMŌS συντόμως
briefly +

SYNTRECHŌ συντρέχω
join
run
run together

SYNTRIBŌ συντρίβω
break (2)
break in pieces (2)
bruised (*perf. pass. part.*)
crush
shatter

SYNTRIMMA σύντριμμα
ruin

SYNTROPHOS σύντροφος
member of the court (*subst.*)

SYNTYGCHANŌ συντυγχάνω
reach

SYNYPOKRINOMAI συνυποκρίνομαι
act insincerely with

SYNYPOURGEŌ συνυπουργέω
help

SYRŌ σύρω
drag (4)
sweep

SYSCHĒMATIZŌ συσχηματίζω
conform to (2)

SYSPARASSŌ συσπαράσσω
convulse (2)

SYSSĒMON σύσσημον
sign

SYSSŌMOS σύσσωμος
member of the same body (*subst.*)

SYSTATIKOS συστατικός
recommendation, of

SYSTAUROŌ συσταυρόω
crucify with (5)

SYSTELLŌ συστέλλω
grow very short (*pass.*)
wrap up

SYSTENAZŌ συστενάζω
groan together

SYSTOICHEŌ συστοιχέω
correspond to

SYSTRATIŌTĒS συστρατιώτης
fellow soldier (2)

SYSTREPHŌ συστρέφω
gather (2)

SYSTROPHĒ συστροφή
commotion
plot

SYZAŌ συζάω
live together
live with (2)

SYZĒTEŌ συζητέω
argue (2)
discuss
discuss together
dispute (3)
question (3)

SYZĒTĒSIS συζήτησις
(dispute)

SYZĒTĒTĒS συζητητής
debater

SYZEUGNYMI συζεύγνυμι
join together (2)

SYZŌOPOIEŌ συζωοποιέω
alive together with, make s. (2)

SYZYGOS σύζυγος
yokefellow

T

TABERNĒ ταβέρνη
tavern (*See* TAVERNS, THREE)

TACHA τάχα
perhaps (2)

TACHEŌS ταχέως
§hasty
quickly (5)
shortly
soon (3)
soon as possible (*superl.*)

TACHINOS ταχινός
soon (*pred.*)
swift

TACHION τάχιον
§outrun 1[a]
quickly
soon +
sooner, the

TACHOS τάχος
[*swiftness, speed*]
§quickly (2)
§shortly
§soon (4)
§speedily

TACHYS ταχύς
quick
quickly (*neut.*) (5)
soon (*neut.*) (6)
soon after (*neut.*)

TAGMA τάγμα
order

TAKTOS τακτός
appointed

TALAIPŌREŌ ταλαιπωρέω
wretched, be

TALAIPŌRIA ταλαιπωρία
misery (2)

TALAIPŌROS ταλαίπωρος
wretched (2)

TALANTIAIOS ταλαντιαῖος
heavy as a hundredweight

TALANTON τάλαντον
talent (15)

TALITHA ταλιθά
talitha

TAMEION ταμεῖον
room
room, inner
room, private
storehouse

TAPEINOŌ ταπεινόω
abase (2)
humble (11)
low, bring

TAPEINOPHRŌN ταπεινόφρων
§humble mind, have a

TAPEINOPHROSYNĒ ταπεινοφροσύνη
humility (3)
lowliness (2)
self-abasement (2)

TAPEINOS ταπεινός
downcast
humble (3)
(humble tasks [*subst. neut. pl.*]†)
low degree, of
lowly (3)

TAPEINŌSIS ταπείνωσις
humiliation (2)
low estate
lowly (*gen.*)

TAPHĒ ταφή
§bury

TAPHOS τάφος
grave
sepulchre (4)
tomb (2)

TARACHĒ ταραχή
(troubling)

TARACHOS τάραχος
stir (2)

TARASSŌ ταράσσω
disturb
incite
terrify (2)
trouble (13) +

TARTAROŌ ταρταρόω
cast into hell

TASSŌ τάσσω
appoint (3)
devote
direct (*mid.*)
institute
ordain
set

TAUROS ταῦρος
bull (2)
ox (2)

TAXIS τάξις
good order
order (7)
IDIOMATICALLY
duty *a*

TE τέ
also (2)
and (86)
both (27)
but (4)
even
§*not only*
or
then (5)
with
IDIOMATICALLY
OR NOT TRANSLATED
Mt **27**.48
Lk **15**.2; **21**.11; **23**.12
Jn **4**.42; **6**.18
Acts **1**.1, 8, 13, 15; **2**.9, 10; **5**.24; **8**.25; **9**.2, 15, 24; **10**.22; **12**.12; **13**.1[2]; **14**.12, 21; **15**.6, 9, 39; **17**.4, 10, 14; **18**.4, 5, 26; **20**.3, 11, 35; **21**.12, 25, 28, 37; **24**.3;

25.23; **26**.3, 16, 20, 22; **27**.1, 3, 8, 21, 43
Rom **1**.16, 20, 26, 27; **2**.9, 10; **7**.7; **10**.12; **14**.8
1 Cor **1**.30; **4**.21
2 Cor **12**.12
Heb **1**.3; **2**.4, 11; **4**.12; **5**.1, 7, 14; **6**.2, 4, 19; **8**.3; **9**.2, 9; **10**.33; **11**.32
Jas **3**.7[2]

TECHNĒ τέχνη
art
craft
trade

TECHNITĒS τεχνίτης
builder
craftsman (3)

TEICHOS τεῖχος
wall (9)

TEKMĒRION τεκμήριον
proof

TEKNION τεκνίον
child, little (9)

TEKNOGONEŌ τεκνογονέω
bear children

TEKNOGONIA τεκνογονία
bearing children
(birth of the child †)

TEKNON τέκνον
child (88) +
son (10)

TEKNOTROPHEŌ τεκνοτροφέω
bring up children

TĒKŌ τήκω
melt (*pass.*)

TEKTŌN τέκτων
carpenter (2)

TĒLAUGŌS τηλαυγῶς
clearly

TELEIOŌ τελειόω
accomplish (4)
complete
end
finish one's course (*pass.*)
fulfil
perfect (6)
perfect, be (*perf. pass.*)
perfect, make (7)
§perfectly (*perf. pass. part.*)

TELEIOS τέλειος
full
mature (7)
perfect (10)
perfect, more (*comp.*)

TELEIŌS τελείως
fully

TELEIŌSIS τελείωσις
fulfilment
perfection

TELEIOTĒS τελειότης
maturity
perfect harmony

TELEIŌTĒS τελειωτής
perfecter

TELEŌ τελέω
accomplish (2)
end (5)
finish (9)
fulfil (5)
go through
gratify
keep
pay (2)
perfect, make
perform

TELESPHOREŌ τελεσφορέω
fruit matures, one's

TELEUTAŌ τελευτάω
dead (*perf. part.*)
death (*inf.*)
die (8) +
end of one's life, at the (*part.*)

TELEUTĒ τελευτή
death

TĒLIKOUTOS τηλικοῦτος
great, so (2)
great, such a
IDIOMATICALLY
peril *a*

TELŌNĒS τελώνης
tax collector (21)

TELŌNION τελώνιον
tax office (3)

TELOS τέλος
aim
§continual
end (29) +
§finally
fulfilment
§fully
outcome
purpose
revenue (2)
toll
IDIOMATICALLY
(completely *a* †); (ever, for *k* †); last *b*

TEPHROŌ τεφρόω
turn to ashes

TERAS τέρας
wonder (16)

TĒREŌ τηρέω
disobey (*neg.*)
guard (2)
hold
keep (56)
keep in custody (2)
keep watch over (2)
maintain
observe (2)
reserve (2)
IDIOMATICALLY
refrain from *b* (2)

TĒRĒSIS τήρησις
custody
keeping
prison

TESSARAKONTA τεσσαράκοντα
forty (15)
§forty-four (4)
§forty-six
§forty-two (2)

TESSARAKONTAETĒS
τεσσαρακονταετής
forty years (2)

TESSARES τέσσαρες
§eighty-four
§forty-four (4)
four (30)
§twenty-four (6)

TESSARESKAIDEKATOS
τεσσαρεσκαιδέκατος
fourteenth (2)

TETARTAIOS τεταρταῖος
§four days

TETARTOS τέταρτος
fourth (9)
IDIOMATICALLY
four *b*

TETRADION τετράδιον
squad

TETRAGŌNOS τετράγωνος
foursquare

TETRAKISCHILIOI τετρακισχίλιοι
four thousand (5)

TETRAKOSIOI τετρακόσιοι
four hundred (4)

TETRAMĒNOS τετράμηνος
four months (*subst. fem.*)

TETRAPLOUS τετραπλοῦς
fourfold

TETRAPOUS τετράπους
animal (*subst.*) (3)

TETRARCHEŌ τετραρχέω
tetrarch, be (3)

TETRARCHĒS τετράρχης
tetrarch (4)

THALASSA θάλασσα
sea (88) +
§seashore
§seaside (2)

THALPŌ θάλπω
care of, take
cherish

THAMBEŌ θαμβέω
amazed, be (*pass.*) (3)

THAMBOS θάμβος
§amazed, be
wonder
IDIOMATICALLY
astonished, be *a*

THANASIMOS θανάσιμος
deadly

THANATĒPHOROS θανατηφόρος
deadly

THANATOŌ θανατόω
death, have s. put to (2)
death, put to (6)
die (*pass.*)
kill (2)

THANATOS θάνατος
§deadly
death (105)
§die (2)
mortal (7)
pestilence (2)
IDIOMATICALLY
dead, strike *a;* surely *a*

THAPTŌ θάπτω
bury (11)

THARREŌ θαρρέω (θαρσέω)
bold, be
boldness, show
cheer, be of good
confidence, have
confidently (*part.*)
courage, be of good (2)
courage, take
heart, take (5)

THARSOS θάρσος
courage

THAUMA θαῦμα
wonder

IDIOMATICALLY
greatly *b*

THAUMASIOS θαυμάσιος
wonderful

THAUMASTOS θαυμαστός
marvel (*subst.*)
marvelous (3)
wonderful (2)

THAUMAZŌ θαυμάζω
astonished, be (2)
marvel (*act., fut. pass.*) (24)
wonder (13)
wonder at +
IDIOMATICALLY
flatter *a;* wonder *a*

THEA θεά
goddess

THEAOMAI θεάομαι
behold (3)
look at
look upon
see (17)

THEATRIZŌ θεατρίζω
publicly expose

THEATRON θέατρον
spectacle
theater (2)

THEIŌDĒS θειώδης
color of sulphur, the

THEION θεῖον
sulphur (7)

THEIOS θεῖος
Deity (*subst. neut.*)
divine (2)

THEIOTĒS θειότης
deity

THĒKĒ θήκη
sheath

THĒLAZŌ θηλάζω
suck
suck, give (3)
suckling (*subst. part.*)

THELĒMA θέλημα
desire (2)
impulse
will (59)

THELĒSIS θέλησις
will

THELŌ θέλω
choose (5)
decide
deliberately (*part.*)
desire (31)
disposed, be
glad, be
insist
like (3)
mean (3)
please (2)
prefer
refuse (*neg.*) (7)
unwilling, be (*neg.*) (2)
want (51)
will (64) +
will, be one's (4)
will have (3)
willing, be (3)
wish (20)
IDIOMATICALLY
be *c;* let *a;* would *a*

THĒLYS θῆλυς
female (3)
woman (*subst. fem.*) (2)

THEMELION θεμέλιον
foundation

THEMELIOŌ θεμελιόω
found (2) +
ground
(settle)
stable (*perf. pass. part.*)

THEMELIOS θεμέλιος (θεμέλιον)
foundation (14)
NOT TRANSLATED
Rev **21.19**

THEODIDAKTOS θεοδίδακτος
taught by God

THEOMACHOS θεομάχος
opposing God

THEOPNEUSTOS θεόπνευστος
inspired by God

THEŌREŌ θεωρέω
behold (2)
look on (2)
perceive (3)
see (48)
§sight
watch (2)

THEŌRIA θεωρία
sight

THEOS θεός
divine (*gen. or dat.*) (5)
God (1300) +
goddess (*fem.*)
§God-fearing
§godly (4)
NOT TRANSLATED
Rom **8.28**

THEOSEBEIA θεοσέβεια
religion

THEOSEBĒS θεοσεβής
worshiper of God (*subst.*)

THEOSTYGĒS θεοστυγής
hater of God (*subst.*)

THEOTĒS θεότης
deity

THĒRA θήρα
trap

THERAPEIA θεραπεία
healing (2)
household

THERAPEUŌ θεραπεύω
cure (6)
heal (36)
serve

THERAPŌN θεράπων
servant

THĒREUŌ θηρεύω
catch

THĒRIOMACHEŌ θηριομαχέω
fight with beasts

THĒRION θηρίον
beast (40)
beast of prey
beast, wild (2)
creature (2)

THERISMOS θερισμός
harvest (13)

THERISTĒS θεριστής
reaper (2)

THERIZŌ θερίζω
harvester (*subst. part.*)
reap (19)
reaper (*subst. part.*)

THERMAINŌ θερμαίνω
warm oneself (*mid.*) (5)
warmed, be (*mid.*)

THERMĒ θέρμη
heat

THEROS θέρος
summer (3)

THĒSAURIZŌ θησαυρίζω
lay up (3)
lay up treasure (2)
store up (3)†

THĒSAUROS θησαυρός
treasure (17)

THIGGANŌ θιγγάνω
touch (3)

THLIBŌ θλίβω
afflict (5)
afflicted (*pass. part.*) (2)
affliction, suffer (*pass.*)
crush
hard (*perf. pass. part.*)

THLIPSIS θλῖψις
§afflict
affliction (19)
anguish
persecution
§suffer
suffering (2)
tribulation (17)
trouble
troubles
IDIOMATICALLY
burden *a*

THNĒSKŌ θνήσκω
dead (*perf. part.*)
dead, be (*perf.*) (7)
die

THNĒTOS θνητός
mortal (6)

THŌRAX θώραξ
breastplate (4)
scale

THORYBAZŌ θορυβάζω
troubled, be (*pass.*)

THORYBEŌ θορυβέω
alarmed, be (*pass.*)
tumult, make a (*pass.*) (2)
uproar, set in an

THORYBOS θόρυβος
riot
tumult (4)
uproar (2)

THRAUŌ θραύω
oppressed (*perf. pass. part.*)

THREMMA θρέμμα
cattle

THRĒNEŌ θρηνέω
lament (2)
wail (2)

THRĒSKEIA θρησκεία
religion (3)
worship

THRĒSKOS θρησκός
religious

THRIAMBEUŌ θριαμβεύω
triumph, lead in
triumph over

THRIX θρίξ
hair (15)
THROEŌ θροέω
alarmed, be (*pass.*) (2)
excited, be (*pass.*)
THROMBOS θρόμβος
(drop)
THRONOS θρόνος
throne (62)
THYELLA θύελλα
tempest
THYGATĒR θυγάτηρ
daughter (28)
THYGATRION θυγάτριον
daughter, little (2)
THYINOS θύϊνος
scented
THYMIAMA θυμίαμα
incense (6)
THYMIAŌ θυμιάω
incense, burn
THYMIATĒRION θυμιατήριον
altar of incense
THYMOMACHEŌ θυμομαχέω
angry, be
THYMOŌ θυμόω
rage, be in a (*pass.*)
THYMOS θυμός
anger (3)
§enraged, be
fury (3)
passion (2)
wrath (9)
THYŌ θύω
kill (7)
sacrifice (3)
sacrifice, offer (3)
THYRA θύρα
door (35)
gate (4)
THYREOS θυρεός
shield
THYRIS θυρίς
window (2)
THYRŌROS θυρωρός
door, maid who keeps the (*fem.*)
door, who keeps the (*appos.*)
doorkeeper
gatekeeper
THYSIA θυσία
sacrifice (27)+
§sacrificial
THYSIASTĒRION θυσιαστήριον
altar (22)
§sacrificial offerings
TIKTŌ τίκτω
bear (9)
birth to, give (2)
bring forth (3)
delivered, be (2)
delivery (*inf.*)
travail, be in
TILLŌ τίλλω
pluck (3)
TIMAŌ τιμάω
honor (18)†
§present
IDIOMATICALLY
price *a;* set *a*
NOT TRANSLATED
Mt **27**.9

TIMĒ τιμή
beauty
gift
honor (26)†
money
noble use
precious (*pred.*)
price (3)
proceeds (*sg. or pl.*) (3)
sum
value (2)
TIMIOS τίμιος
costly (*superl.*)
honor, held in (2)
§jewel (4)
precious (5)
rare, most (*superl.*)
TIMIOTĒS τιμιότης
wealth
TIMŌREŌ τιμωρέω
punish (2)
TIMŌRIA τιμωρία
punishment
TINŌ τίνω
suffer
TIS I τίς
any
anything
each
how (9)
how great
how is it? (3)
nothing (+*neg.*) (3)
something (2)
what (261)+†
what about
what person (2)
which (23)
who (140)
why (104)
IDIOMATICALLY
OR NOT TRANSLATED
Lk **12**.49; **17**.8
1 Cor **15**.2
TIS II τὶς
all, at (*neut.*) (2)
any (34)
any man (10)+
any one (85)
any thing (2)
anything (35)
certain (6)
certain man (2)
certain person (3)
every one
it (3)
kind of, a
§*little, a* (*neut.*)
man, a (20)
matter of, a
none (+*neg.*) (5)
nothing (+*neg.*) (5)+
one (33)
one, no (+*neg.*) (18)
one thing (*neut.*) (2)
other (2)
person, a
§*piece*
several (*pl.*)
some (109)
some men (*pl.*)
some one (13)+
some people (*pl.*)
some persons (*pl.*)
some things (*pl.*)

somebody (2)
something (16)
somewhat
§still
§such as
what (2)
whatever (2)
whoever (3)
(*Note:* TIS II *is translated twice in* Phm .18.)
IDIOMATICALLY
OR NOT TRANSLATED
Mt **18**.12
Mk **11**.5; **14**.47, 51; **15**.21
Lk **1**.5; **7**.2, 19; **8**.27; **10**.25, 30, 31, 33, 38[2]; **11**.27, 36; **12**.4, 15, 16; **14**.1, 2, 16; **15**.11; **16**.1, 19, 20; **17**.12; **18**.2, 18, 35; **19**.12; **21**.2; **22**.50, 56, 59; **23**.19
Jn **4**.46; **7**.4; **11**.49
Acts **3**.2; **5**.1, 34; **8**.9; **9**.10, 33, 36; **10**.1, 6, 11; **11**.5; **14**.8; **16**.1, 9, 16; **17**.21; **18**.2, 24; **19**.14; **20**.9; **21**.10, 16; **23**.23; **25**.14; **27**.8, 16, 27, 39; **28**.3, 19
1 Cor **4**.2, 5; **9**.12; **14**.24
2 Cor **2**.10; **11**.1, 16, 20[4]
Col **2**.23
1 Th **5**.15
1 Tim **1**.10; **5**.4
2 Tim **2**.5
Heb **2**.6, 7, 9; **10**.27; **12**.15
TITHĒMI τίθημι (τιθέω)
§advise 1
appoint (*act. or mid.*) (6)
arrange (*mid.*)
contrive (*mid.*)
destine (*act. or mid.*) (2)
entrust (*mid.*)
fix (*mid.*)
§kneel down 1 (6)
lay (32)+
lay aside
lay down (11)
lay up (*mid.*)
make (*act. or mid.*) (8)
place
put (*act. or mid.*) (19)
resolve (*mid.*)
serve
set (2)
settle
sink, let s. (*mid. imper.*)
IDIOMATICALLY
use *a*
NOT TRANSLATED
Mk **4**.21
TITLOS τίτλος
title (2)
TOICHOS τοῖχος
wall
TOIGAROUN τοιγαροῦν
therefore (2)
TOINYN τοίνυν
then
therefore
well
TOIOSDE τοιόσδε
[*such as this*]
NOT TRANSLATED
2 Pet **1**.17
TOIOUTOS τοιοῦτος
he (*subst.*)
kind, of a
other, no (*neg.*)

so (2)
such (39)
that
this (4)
§thus
what
IDIOMATICALLY
like *a*
NOT TRANSLATED
Mk **13**.19
2 Cor **2**.7; **10**.11; **12**.2
Phm .9

TOKOS τόκος
interest (2)

TOLMAŌ τολμάω
bold, be
courage, take
dare (10)
presume
§show
venture (2)

TOLMĒROTERŌS τολμηροτέρως
boldly, very

TOLMĒTĒS τολμητής
bold (*appos.*)

TOMOS τομός
sharper (*comp.*)

TOPAZION τοπάζιον
topaz

TOPOS τόπος
chance
§country 3
§everywhere (2)
§leave 9
mark
opportunity (2)
place (79)
port
position
§rock 2
room (2)
§shoal 1
IDIOMATICALLY
occasion *a*
NOT TRANSLATED
Rev **18**.17

TOSOUTOS τοσοῦτος
all this
enough
great, so (2)
long, so (2)
many (*pl.*)
many, so (*pl.*) (4)
many, these (*pl.*)
measure of, a like
much, as
much, so (2)
such (2)
IDIOMATICALLY
all *e*
NOT TRANSLATED
Heb **7**.22

TOTE τότε
formerly
moment, that
then (150)
time, at that
time, that (2)
NOT TRANSLATED
Mt **27**.3
Jn **11**.6
1 Cor **16**.2

TOUNANTION τοὐναντίον
contrary, on the (2)
NOT TRANSLATED
2 Cor **2**.7

TOUNOMA τοὔνομα
[= τὸ ὄνομα (*the*) *name*]
§named

TOXON τόξον
bow

TRACHĒLIZŌ τραχηλίζω
bare, be laid (*pass.*)

TRACHĒLOS τράχηλος
§embrace (2)
neck (5)

TRACHYS τραχύς
§rock
rough

TRAGOS τράγος
goat (4)

TRAPEZA τράπεζα
bank
§food
table (13)

TRAPEZITĒS τραπεζίτης
banker

TRAUMA τραῦμα
wound

TRAUMATIZŌ τραυματίζω
wound (2)

TRECHŌ τρέχω
compete
exertion (*subst. part.*)
run (14) +
runner (*subst. part.*)
rush
speed on

TREIS τρεῖς
§fifty-three
§thirty
three (65) (*See also* THREE TAVERNS)
§twenty-three

TRĒMA τρῆμα
eye (2)

TREMŌ τρέμω
afraid, be
tremble (2)

TREPHŌ τρέφω
bring up
fatten
feed (3)
food, depend on for (*pass.*)
nourish (2)
suck, give

TRIAKONTA τριάκοντα
§four
thirty (7)
§thirty-eight
§thirtyfold (2)

TRIAKOSIOI τριακόσιοι
three hundred (2)

TRIBOLOS τρίβολος
thistle (2)

TRIBOS τρίβος
path (3)

TRICHINOS τρίχινος
[*of hair*]
NOT TRANSLATED
Rev **6**.12

TRIETIA τριετία
three years

TRIMĒNOS τρίμηνος
three months (*subst. fem.*)

TRIS τρίς
three times (12)

TRISCHILIOI τρισχίλιοι
three thousand

TRISTEGON τρίστεγον
third story

TRITOS τρίτος
third (49)
third time, the (*neut.*) (7)

TRIZŌ τρίζω
grind

TROCHIA τροχια
path

TROCHOS τροχος
cycle
(wheel †)

TRŌGŌ τρώγω
eat (6)

TROMOS τρόμος
trembling (5)

TROPĒ τροπή
change
(turning †)

TROPHĒ τροφή
food (15)
IDIOMATICALLY
eat *a*

TROPHOPHOREŌ τροφοφορέω
(care for)

TROPHOS τροφός
nurse

TROPOPHOREŌ τροποφορέω
bear with

TROPOS τρόπος
as (*acc.*) (6)
§just as
life
§likewise (*acc.*)
way (4)
way as, in the same (*acc.*)

TRYBLION τρύβλιον
dish (2)

TRYGAŌ τρυγάω
gather (2)
pick

TRYGŌN τρυγών
turtledove

TRYMALIA τρυμαλιά
eye

TRYPHAŌ τρυφάω
live in luxury

TRYPHĒ τρυφή
luxury
§revel

TYGCHANŌ τυγχάνω
attain
§cared for, be
§doubtless
enjoy
extraordinary (*neg. part.*)
have
obtain (2)
§perhaps (2)
§rise again to life 1
unusual (*neg. part.*)

TYMPANIZŌ τυμπανίζω
torture

TYPHLOŌ τυφλόω
blind (3)

TYPHLOS τυφλός
blind (49)
TYPHŌ τύφω
smolder (*pass.*)
TYPHŌNIKOS τυφωνικός
tempestuous
TYPHOOMAI τυφόομαι
puffed up with conceit, be (2)
swollen with conceit, be
TYPIKŌS τυπικῶς
warning, as a
TYPOS τύπος
example (5)
figure
model
pattern (2)
print
standard
type
warning
IDIOMATICALLY
effect *a*
TYPTŌ τύπτω
beat (6)
strike (6)
wound

X

XENIA ξενία
guest room
lodging
XENIZŌ ξενίζω
entertain (2)
lodge (*pass.*) (4)
strange (*pass. part.*)
surprised, be (*mid.*) (2)
IDIOMATICALLY
guest *a*
XENODOCHEŌ ξενοδοχέω
show hospitality
XENOS ξένος
foreign
foreigner (*subst.*)
host (*subst.*)
strange (2)
stranger (*subst.*) (9)
XĒRAINŌ ξηραίνω
cease (*pass.*)
dry up
rigid, become (*pass.*)
ripe, be fully (*pass.*)
wither (6)
wither away (*pass.*) (3)
withered (*perf. pass. part.*)
withered away (*perf. pass. part.*)
XĒROS ξηρός
dry (2)
land (*subst. fem.*)
paralyzed
withered (4)
XESTĒS ξέστης
pot
XYLINOS ξύλινος
wood, of (2)
XYLON ξύλον
club (5)
stocks
tree (10)
wood (4)
XYRAŌ ξυράω (ξυρέω, ξύρω)
shave (*mid.*) (3)

Z

ZAŌ ζάω
alive (*part.*) (5)
alive, be (12)
life (*art. inf.*) (2)
life, come to (*aor.*) (3)
life, man who has been brought to (*subst. part.*)
live (113)
live a life (2)
IDIOMATICALLY
life *a;* lifelong *a*
ZĒLEUŌ ζηλεύω
zealous, be
ZĒLOŌ ζηλόω
covet
desire, earnestly (3)
jealous (*part.*)
jealous, be (2)
much of, make (3)
IDIOMATICALLY
feel *b*
ZĒLOS ζῆλος
fury
jealousy (9)
zeal (6)
ZĒLŌTĒS ζηλωτής
eager (*pred.*)
Zealot (2)
zealous (*pred.*) (5)
ZĒMIA ζημία
loss (4)
ZĒMIOŌ ζημιόω
forfeit (*pass.*) (3)
loss, suffer (*pass.*) (3)
ZEŌ ζέω
aglow, be
fervent, be
ZESTOS ζεστός
hot (3)
ZĒTĒMA ζήτημα
controversy
dispute, point of
question (3)
ZĒTEŌ ζητέω
ask (3)+
desire
endeavor, in one's (*part.*)
inquire
insist
look after
look for (5)
require (2)
search for (3)
§search of, in (2)
seek (87)
strive
try (6)
wish
IDIOMATICALLY
be *b*
ZĒTĒSIS ζήτησις
controversy (3)
debate (2)
discussion
question
ZEUGOS ζεῦγος
pair
yoke
ZEUKTĒRIA ζευκτηρία
rope
ZIZANION ζιζάνιον
weed (8)
ZŌĒ ζωή
alive (*pred.*)
life (132)
lifetime
living (*gen.*) (2)
ZŌGREŌ ζωγρέω
capture
catch
ZŌNĒ ζώνη
belt (2)
girdle (6)
ZŌNNYMI ζώννυμι (ζωννύω)
dress oneself (*mid.*)
gird (2)
ZŌOGONEŌ ζῳογονέω
alive, keep
life, give
preserve
ZŌON ζῷον
animal (3)
living creature (20)
ZŌOPOIEŌ ζῳοποιέω
alive, make (3)
life, come to (*pass.*)
life, give (6)
life-giving (*part.*)
ZOPHOS ζόφος
gloom
nether gloom (4)
ZYGOS ζυγός
balance
yoke (5)
ZYMĒ ζύμη
leaven (13)
ZYMOŌ ζυμόω
leaven (4)

APPENDIX I

NOTES ON THE ANALYSIS OF THE RSV NEW TESTAMENT

The following notes will enable the user of the Concordance to understand the analysis upon which it is based in many special cases. Fortunately, in the vast majority of cases no comment is needed. Occasionally, however, the observing user will notice that the form of the Greek translated on the **subtitle** line is different from that of the English of the **title**. This is especially evident with regard to parts of speech. For example, under the word KNOWLEDGE is a Greek word meaning "know."

It is the purpose of these notes to interpret a broad range of questions relating to the subtitle lines. Most persons will be content with the knowledge that such matters are merely the usual evidence of translation from one language to another, and they will have no interest in the notes that follow. Others, however, curious to see drawn together briefly in one place common examples of the translator's art, may find some of these notes useful. These Notes on Analysis are designed to be understood by those who have not studied Greek—although they may need to consult their English dictionaries if they have forgotten certain grammatical terms. The notes may acquaint students of the Greek New Testament, who for instructional purposes have been limited to so-called "literal translation," with acceptable possibilities of translation more favorable to English idiom.

These notes fall into two parts. **Part One: English Paraphrase** has been arranged in outline form. References to it, which appear on subtitle lines, are letter-number combinations —e.g.: [A.1.b.2]. Part One deals with questions of paraphrase, illustrating the practice of the translators in typical situations. Letter-number references to Part One are also given as needed on the technical lines. A single bracketed reference at the right margin on the technical line applies to all notes on that line. When it is obvious that two Greek words are being translated by a single English word, the pertinent reference—B.3.b.4—may be omitted.

The notes in **Part Two: Grammatical Terms** deal with translation, sometimes paraphrase, in traditional terms of grammar and syntax. References to Part Two are given in parentheses on the subtitle line, between the Greek word and its transliteration, and they pertain only to formal matters—e.g.: (gen.), the genitive case.

Illustrations use the RSV text in every instance, except that the first sentence or phrase represents a literal translation of the Greek—to the extent necessary for illustration. The second sentence or phrase (followed by the Scripture reference) is entirely the RSV translation. The italicized words bear in particular on the point being illustrated.

PART ONE: ENGLISH PARAPHRASE

The following notes are arranged in a progression from the simple to the more complex. This applies generally both to the sections and to the notes within each section.

A. PARTS OF SPEECH. Frequently the part of speech, or function, of a word is affected in the course of translation while its meaning in the sentence is not appreciably altered. Thus in one instance what would be rendered literally "to be *false witnesses* of God" is translated with greater clarity by the RSV "to be *misrepresenting* God" (1 Cor 15.15). What would be rendered literally "with *speed*" is translated by the RSV in better English idiom "*quickly*" (Acts 22.18). Changes of this sort through translation usually require other adjustments in the sentence. Such adjustments represent other types of paraphrase or translation that are taken up at appropriate places elsewhere in these notes.

A.1. NOUNS. **A noun may be translated by another part of speech.**

A.1.a. A noun may be translated as a **verb,** when modified (cf. A.6.a.3; B.3.a).

they show the *work* of the law written
they show that what the law *requires* is written (Rom 2.15)

as he is *mediator* of a better covenant
as the covenant he *mediates* is better (Heb 8.6)

the *material* of its wall was jasper
the wall was *built* of jasper (Rev 21.18)

A.1.b. A noun may be translated as an **adjective** (including the participle) when (**1**) modifying (gen., dat.) or modified; (**2**) used with an appositive; (**3**) in a compound relationship (such as hendiadys); or (**4**) a predicate noun. (**5**) A noun may exchange functions with its modifier (cf. 1). (For nouns in prepositional phrases, see B.1.)

1. the scepter of *righteousness*
the *righteous* scepter (Heb 1.8)

every *creature* of God
everything *created* by God (1 Tim 4.4)

2. they took up *what-was-left-over* of the broken pieces, twelve baskets full
they took up twelve baskets full of the broken pieces *left over* (Mt 14.20)

he who talked to me had a *measure,* a rod of gold
he who talked to me had a *measuring* rod of gold (Rev 21.15)

3. by your *hardness* and impenitent heart
by your *hard* and impenitent heart (Rom 2.5)

sacrifice and offering
sacrificial offering (Phil 2.17)

4. which is a *parable* for the present age
which is *symbolic* for the present age (Heb 9.9)

[it] is a *dishonor* to him
[it] is *degrading* to him (1 Cor 11.14)

5. with *gladness and generosity* of heart
with *glad and generous* hearts (Acts 2.46)

receive the *promise* of the eternal inheritance
receive the *promised* eternal inheritance (Heb 9.15)

God sends upon them a *power* of delusion
God sends upon them a *strong* delusion (2 Th 2.11)

in the *likeness* of his death
in a death *like* his (Rom 6.5)

A.1.c. A noun may be translated as an **adverb** (**1**) to suit the translation of the verb; and (**2**) to express nouns cognate with the verb.

1. show your slaves *justice and fairness*
treat your slaves *justly and fairly* (Col 4.1)

2. the friend . . rejoices with *joy*
the friend . . rejoices *greatly* (Jn 3.29)

Elijah . . prayed in *prayer*
Elijah . . prayed *fervently* (Jas 5.17)

A.1.d. A noun may be translated as an **infinitive** or infinitive clause in corresponding functions (object, modification, etc.).

those who do such things are worthy of *death*
those who do such things deserve *to die* (Rom 1.32)

to appoint you a *witness*
to appoint you *to . . bear witness* (Acts 26.16)

you teach . . the Jews . . *apostasy* from Moses
you teach . . the Jews . . *to forsake* Moses (Acts 21.21)

the days . . of his *ascension*
the days . . for him *to be received up* (Lk 9.51)

A.1.e. A noun may be expressed by a **clause** or **phrase.**

he . . has raised up a horn of salvation for us . . , *salvation* from our enemies
he . . has raised up a horn of salvation for us . . , *that we should be saved* from our enemies (Lk 1.68–71)

God may . . grant them *repentance*
God may . . grant *that they will repent* (2 Tim 2.25)

as there was a great *lack-of-food*
as they had been long *without food* (Acts 27.21)

A.1.f. A noun may combine with a modifier or other word to form another **noun;** weights and measures are reconciled by adjustment of modifying numbers (cf. A.3.c.1).

earthen vessels
vessels . . of earthenware (2 Tim 2.20)

suitable day
opportunity (Mk 6.21)

twenty-five or thirty stadia
three or four miles (Jn 6.19)

A.1.g. A noun may be expressed by a **pronoun,** especially when its repetition would be awkward English style.

here a stone will not be left upon a *stone*
there will not be left here one stone upon *another* (Mk 13.2)

from the ends of the heavens to their *ends*
from one end of heaven to the *other* (Mt 24.31)

A.2. PRONOUNS. **A pronoun may be translated by another part of speech.**

A.2.a. A pronoun may be replaced by the **noun** referent. This change reflects an editorial decision to assure clarity.

for a proof to *them*
for a proof to *the people* (Mt 8.4)

Christ was faithful over *his* house
Christ was faithful over *God's* house (Heb 3.6)

A.2.b. There may be an exchange between types of pronouns to suit clarity and English idiom.

to *those* it has not been given
to *them* it has not been given (Mt 13.11)

the Jerusalem above is free, *who* is our mother
the Jerusalem above is free, and *she* is our mother (Gal 4.26)

they . . do not have *anything* to eat
they . . have *nothing* to eat (Mt 15.32)

whomever I shall kiss
the one I shall kiss (Mt 26.48)

A.2.c. A pronoun may be translated as an **adverb** (cf. A.3.b.3).

While he was speaking *these things* to them
While he was *thus* speaking to them (Mt 9.18)

A.3. ADJECTIVES (INCLUDING PARTICIPLES). **An adjective may be translated by another part of speech.**

A.3.a. An adjective may be translated by a corresponding **noun** (**1**) when it is a substantive in the Greek; (**2**) when it is translated as a modifier; (**3**) when it is a restatement of the predicate adjective (cf. B.3.a.1, 2); or (**4**) when it exchanges functions with the word it modifies (cf. A.1.b.5).

1. I shall not be a *foolish* [one]
I shall not be a *fool* (2 Cor 12.6)

2. they went through the . . *Galatian* region
they went through the region of . . *Galatia* (Acts 16.6)

3. all of you, [be] . . *sympathetic*
all of you, have . . *sympathy* (1 Pet 3.8)

4. guard the *true* tradition
guard the *truth* that has been entrusted to you (2 Tim 1.14)

have tasted the *good* word of God
have tasted the *goodness* of the word of God (Heb 6.5)

A.3.b. An adjective may be expressed by an **adverb** or adverbial phrase (**1**) as a result of rephrasing, especially when the word it modifies assumes a different function, or part of speech, in English; (**2**) when the noun that would ordinarily support it is wanting or implied; or (**3**) when predicative (a construction that cannot be duplicated in English).

1. those in *gorgeous* apparel
those who are *gorgeously* appareled (Lk 7.25)

gave *many* alms
gave alms *liberally* (Acts 10.2)

that they may become *perfected* into one
that they may become *perfectly* one (Jn 17.23)

2. if then your whole body is full of light, . . [the] *whole* [body] will be bright
if then your whole body is full of light, . . it will be *wholly* bright (Lk 11.36)

3. lest . . that day come upon you *sudden*
lest . . that day come upon you *suddenly* (Lk 21.34)

A.3.c. Numbers are often subject to change—as when the English expresses the sum of the Greek numbers used; or (**1**) when a number is translated with reference to a different unit of measure; or (**2**) when sets of numbers are combined.

1. *twenty-five or thirty* stadia
three or four miles (Jn 6.19)

two hundred cubits
a hundred yards (Jn 21.8)

two or three measures
twenty or thirty gallons (Jn 2.6)

2. *five* myriads
fifty thousand (Acts 19.19)

A.3.d. A variety of constructions that perform the function of an adjective may translate adjectives: (**1**) **prepositional phrases;** (**2**) **infinitives;** (**3**) **clauses.**

1. fruitless *autumnal* trees
fruitless trees *in late autumn* (Jude .12)

a letter *judging* that they should abstain
a letter *with our judgment* that they should abstain (Acts 21.25)

2. have you anything . . *edible*
have you anything . . *to eat* (Lk 24.41)

3. a man . . *disabled* in his feet
a man . . *who could not use* his feet (Acts 14.8)

A.3.e. The predicate adjective (**1**) may be rendered as a **verb** when combined with "to be" (cf. A.6.a.3; B.3.a.1, 2); (**2**) may be rendered as a verb even when "to be" is only implied.

1. we are not *worthless*
we *have* not *failed* (2 Cor 13.6)

2. [be] *devoted* to one another
love one another (Rom 12.10)

A.3.f. English idiom may require a different **degree** of the adjective.

it is *good* for you to enter life maimed
it is *better* for you to enter life maimed (Mt 18.8)

A.4. ADVERBS. **An adverb may be translated by another part of speech.**

A.4.a. An adverb will be expressed by an **adjective** or a **demonstrative pronoun** when, as a result of rephrasing, the word it modifies assumes a different function, or part of speech, in English, or when it is moved to modify another word.

to live *soberly, uprightly, and devoutly*
to live *sober, upright, and godly* lives (Tit 2.12)

held that John was *really* a prophet
held that John was a *real* prophet (Mk 11.32)

thus I direct in all the churches
this is my rule in all the churches (1 Cor 7.17)

more *eagerly* I send him
I am the more *eager* to send him (Phil 2.28)

A.4.b. An adverb may be translated by a **prepositional phrase.**

will come [at midnight . . or] *early*
will come [at midnight . . or] *in the morning* (Mk 13.35)

A.4.c. A negative in the Greek may be variously expressed in English translation.

you do *not* have something to draw with
you have *nothing* to draw with (Jn 4.11)

be anxious about *nothing*
have *no* anxiety about anything (Phil 4.6)

you are *without* excuse
you have *no* excuse (Rom 2.1)

events *not as yet* seen
events *as yet un*seen (Heb 11.7)

acted that this man *not* die
kept this man *from* dying (Jn 11.37)

neither does he himself welcome the brethren
he *refuses* himself to welcome the brethren (3 Jn .10)

A.4.d. The meaning of an adverb may be expressed by a **noun.**

when it became *late*
when *evening* came (Mk 11.19)

until you leave *thence*
until you leave the *place* (Mk 6.10)

A.4.e. Adverbs may be variously adapted to English idiom in particular contexts, as by combining with other words or expanding.

the dispensation . . must *much more* exceed
the dispensation . . must *far* exceed (2 Cor 3.9)

going on *thence* he saw
going on *from there* he saw (Mt 4.21)

A.5. CONJUNCTIONS. **Conjunctions and other particles are variously translated for clarity or emphasis.**

if *then* the dead are not raised
if *it is true that* the dead are not raised (1 Cor 15.15)

This adaptation includes their (**a**) combining among themselves or with other words; and (**b**) adaptation to or expression of the context.

a. *therefore then*
accordingly (Rom 7.3)

b. *that somehow* I may make my fellow Jews jealous
in order to make my fellow Jews jealous (Rom 11.14)

A.6. VERBS. Of all parts of speech, **verbs are open to the widest range of translation possibilities.**

A.6.a. Many possibilities extend beyond the verb itself in their effect and often embrace other words in its restatement. Here follow instances in which the verb changes or causes other words to change function, or part of speech. (**1**) The number of English words used to translate the Greek verb can affect the translation of related words. (**2**) A common form of paraphrase is the introduction of "to be" into the translation, shifting the substance of the Greek verb to an English noun, adjective, or prepositional phrase. (**3**) Conversely, the Greek "to be" or "to become," explicit or implied, with predicate noun or adjective or prepositional phrase, may be embraced by the English verb or clause (cf. B.3.a.1, 2; B.3.b.2). (**4**) Likewise, other Greek words combine naturally in English translation.

The verb itself may be modified in use: (**5**) The Greek verb may be adapted to English idiom with respect to other words in its context, yielding a meaning not otherwise appropriate to the Greek (cf. B.2.d). (**6**) But when a verb engages a cognate or is repeated, it tends to provide for the translation little more than a verbal indicator not otherwise adequate to define the Greek, or the cognate may be wholly absorbed by the translated verb. (**7**) When other words suffice, the verb may retire in the interest of economy of words.

1. he will *cruelly* annihilate those wretches
he will put those wretches to a *miserable* death (Mt 21.41)

exceedingly infuriated against them, I persecuted
in *raging* fury against them, I persecuted (Acts 26.11)

whoever stands *firm* in his heart
whoever is *firmly* established in his heart (1 Cor 7.37)

2. we *prophesy* imperfectly
our *prophecy* is imperfect (1 Cor 13.9)

what does it *seem* to you
what is your *judgment* (Mt 26.66)

3. unless indeed you *are counterfeit*
unless indeed you *fail to meet the test* (2 Cor 13.5)

if you can *become free*
if you can *gain your freedom* (1 Cor 7.21)

4. *have need* to
must (Lk 14.18)

have in remembrance
acknowledge (Rom 1.28)

5. *be offenseless*
give no offense (1 Cor 10.32)

have a pattern
follow the pattern (2 Tim 1.13)

As day was about to *happen*
As day was about to *dawn* (Acts 27.33)

becoming headlong
falling headlong (Acts 1.18)

6. God *has judged* the judgment
God *has given* judgment (Rev 18.20)

not *being afraid* of any *terror*
let nothing *terrify* you (1 Pet 3.6)

serving the saints, as you still *serve*
serving the saints, as you still *do* (Heb 6.10)

7. and *after saying* this he said to him
and *after* this he said to him (Jn 21.19)

and *answering* Jesus again spoke to them
and again Jesus spoke to them (Mt 22.1)

A.6.b. Verbs in nonindicative moods, especially infinitives and participles, may be translated into English by a part of speech directly appropriate to their function in a sentence.

thresh in hope *to share* in the crop
thresh in hope *of a share* in the crop (1 Cor 9.10)

as is the custom of the Jews *to bury*
as is the *burial* custom of the Jews (Jn 19.40)

gods have come . . *being like* men
gods have come . . *in the likeness of* men (Acts 14.11)

Peter said *replying*
Peter said *in reply* (Mt 19.27)

A.6.c. The rephrasing of a verb may embrace other parts of the sentence as well, especially modifiers. The substance of these words may be variously redistributed in the English translation. (**1**) The verb and other words may apparently exchange parts of speech, or functions. (**2**) A compound verb may be expressed complexly. (**3**) The significance of a verb is subtly altered (as from active to passive) when in translation the subject of the verb is transposed with another element in the clause, or the verb changes from personal to impersonal, or the reverse (cf. A.6.e).

1. he *drew near* death
he *nearly* died (Phil 2.30)

kneeling down they *venerated* him
they knelt down *in homage to* him (Mk 15.19)

2. whatever you *pray and ask*
whatever you *ask in prayer* (Mk 11.24)

3. the sufferings of Christ *abound* for us
we *share abundantly* in Christ's sufferings (2 Cor 1.5)

so that your cause to glory may *abound* in Christ Jesus
so that . . you may *have ample* cause to glory in Christ Jesus (Phil 1.26)

[what] also has not *come upon* the heart of man
nor the heart of man [has] *conceived* (1 Cor 2.9)

A.6.d. Verbs may be translated as **nouns.**

whatever you *do*
whatever your *task* (Col 3.23)

we *know* imperfectly
our *knowledge* is imperfect (1 Cor 13.9)

I *judge*
my *judgment* is (Acts 15.19)

A.6.e. Beyond the possibility of translation by another part of speech, which it shares with other words, the verb may change in other ways to aid the translator. Some of these possibilities affect other words, some do not. Note especially translation moving between personal and impersonal; definite and indefinite (cf. A.6.c); active and passive; passive and indefinite.

it *is permitted* to you
you *have permission* (Acts 26.1)

there will *be weeping*
there men will *weep* (Mt 8.12)

he *blasphemes*
it *is blasphemy* (Mk 2.7)

if they *were able*
if *possible* (Acts 27.39)

lest . . there *be a repayment* to you
lest . . you *be repaid* (Lk 14.12)

when there *has been an examination*
after we *have examined* him (Acts 25.26)

Felix *received a successor*, Porcius Festus
Felix *was succeeded by* Porcius Festus (Acts 24.27)

B. WORD GROUPS may be paraphrased as a whole.

B.1. PREPOSITIONAL PHRASES.

B.1.a. A prepositional phrase may be paraphrased as verb, noun, adjective, or adverb (**1**) by a word (perhaps modified); (**2**) by an infinitive, clause, or participial phrase; or (**3**) by coordination with another part of the sentence. Like predicate nominatives and adjectives, prepositional phrases (**4**) may combine in translation with "to be" (explicit or implied); or (**5**) may otherwise adapt to English idiom.

1. what is *in part* will pass away
the *imperfect* will pass away (1 Cor 13.10)

I say . . as *in foolishness*
I say . . as a *fool* (2 Cor 11.17)

the sufferings of Christ abound *for us*
we share abundantly in Christ's sufferings (2 Cor 1.5)

2. give the enemy no occasion *for reviling*
give the enemy no occasion *to revile* us (1 Tim 5.14)

it convulses him *with foaming*
it convulses him *till he foams* (Lk 9.39)

hence, *in a figure*, he did receive him back
hence, *figuratively speaking*, he did receive him back (Heb 11.19)

a death has occurred *for redemption*
a death has occurred *which redeems* them (Heb 9.15)

3. to the exiles . . chosen *according to the foreknowledge* of God the Father
to the exiles . . chosen and *destined* by God the Father (1 Pet 1.2)

he confesses with his lips *unto salvation*
he confesses with his lips *and so is saved* (Rom 10.10)

4. disputing about words, [which is] *to the ruin* of the hearers
disputing about words, which . . *ruins* the hearers (2 Tim 2.14)

5. *before* fourteen years
fourteen years *ago* (2 Cor 12.2)

B.1.b. Even when a prepositional phrase is translated by another prepositional phrase, there may be paraphrase and mutual influence among the words in the context.

when he ascended *unto a high place*
when he ascended *on high* (Eph 4.8)

the crowd stood up together *against them*
the crowd joined *in attacking* them (Acts 16.22)

might become sinful *to excess*
might become sinful *beyond measure* (Rom 7.13)

B.2. CLAUSES may be translated in many ways.

B.2.a. A clause may be translated by (**1**) a word (often modified) that performs a corresponding syntactical function; (**2**) a prepositional phrase.

1. the soldiers, according to *what was commanded* them, took Paul
the soldiers, according to their *instructions,* took Paul (Acts 23.31)

every one who looks at a woman *to desire her*
every one who looks at a woman *lustfully* (Mt 5.28)

2. the master commended the dishonest steward *because he acted shrewdly*
the master commended the dishonest steward *for his shrewdness* (Lk 16.8)

"I found also an altar *on which was inscribed* 'To an unknown god
"I found also an altar *with this inscription,* 'To an unknown god (Acts 17.23)

B.2.b. A complex clause may often be more effectively expressed by (**1**) a compound English structure of two or more clauses; or (**2**) breaking into shorter sentences.

1. God is faithful, *who* will not let you be tempted
God is faithful, *and* he will not let you be tempted (1 Cor 10.13)

I am suffering *to the point of* fetters
I am suffering *and* wearing fetters (2 Tim 2.9)

2. who is the head of all rule and authority, *in whom* also you were circumcised
who is the head of all rule and authority. *In him* also you were circumcised (Col. 2.10–11)

B.2.c. Conversely, some compound sentences are better expressed by complex structure.

and they went up into heaven in a cloud *and their foes saw them*
and *in the sight of their foes* they went up to heaven in a cloud (Rev 11.12)

I John, your brother *and partner* in the tribulation
I John, your brother, *who share with you* . . the tribulation (Rev 1.9)

Moses said, "*I am frightened and trembling*
Moses said, "*I tremble with fear* (Heb 12.21)

B.2.d. A Greek clause may be restated within the potential of English idiom. (**1**) While communicating the substance of the Greek clause, the English words do not individually correspond to particular Greek words, even in cases where corresponding parts of speech survive. (**2**) Adding or omitting "to be" (or "to become") is a common factor in these restatements (cf. A.6.a.2, 3; B.3.a.1, 2). (**3**) Greek phrasing may be reversed or shifted in English.

1. so that . . I have *accomplished* the gospel
so that . . I have *fully preached* the gospel (Rom 15.19)

that they might *experience a better resurrection*
that they might *rise again to a better life* (Heb 11.35)

it is sown in destruction
what is sown is perishable (1 Cor 15.42)

he sought *how he might betray him opportunely*
he sought *an opportunity to betray him* (Mk 14.11)

does he not leave . . and *going, seek* the one
does he not leave . . and *go in search of* the one (Mt 18.12)

2. do not *think high things*
do not *become proud* (Rom 11.20)

you *have patient endurance*
you *are enduring patiently* (Rev 2.3)

there *was amazement* upon all
they *were* all *amazed* (Lk 4.36)

Pilate gave sentence that their demand *should be*
Pilate gave sentence their their demand *should be granted* (Lk 23.24)

Moses, when he *became large*
Moses, when he *was grown up* (Heb 11.24)

3. *questioning nothing*
without raising any question (1 Cor 10.25)

often *in hunger*
often *without food* (2 Cor 11.27)

all who are *slaves under the yoke*
all who are *under the yoke of slavery* (1 Tim 6.1)

you were *wholly* born in sin
you were born in *utter* sin (Jn 9.34)

B.3. WORDS USED IN COMBINATIONS. The Greek uses certain words in combinations that may be restated in English, varying with the context.

B.3.a. This includes such verbs in Greek as (**1**) be (cf. A.3.a.3; A.6.a.3); (**2**) become, happen; (**3**) do, make; (**4**) give; (**5**) have; (**6**) receive; (**7**) think.

1. we *are fellow workers* for your joy
we *work with* you for your joy (2 Cor 1.24)

they . . *are temporary*
they . . *endure for a while* (Mk 4.17)

2. when you fast, do not *become dismal looking*
when you fast, do not *look dismal* (Mt 6.16)

but if the salt *has become saltless*
but if the salt *has lost its saltness* (Mk 9.50)

he *became of the opinion*
he *determined* (Acts 20.3)

be offenseless
give no offense (1 Cor 10.32)

he *became invisible* to them
he *vanished out of* their *sight* (Lk 24.31)

3. the man who *made* me *healthy*
the man who *healed* me (Jn 5.11)

God gave them up to a base mind, *to do things that are not proper*
God gave them up to a base mind and *to improper conduct* (Rom 1.28)

4. as the Father *has given* me *commandment*
as the Father *has commanded* me (Jn 14.31)

begged him not to *present himself* at the theater
begged him not to *venture* into the theater (Acts 19.31)

5. to know how great *a struggle I have* for you
to know how greatly *I strive* for you (Col. 2.1)

I *have need* to go out and see it
I *must* go out and see it (Lk 14.18)

6. so that the church may *receive edification*
so that the church may *be edified* (1 Cor 14.5)

7. I entreat S. to *think the same thing*
I entreat S. to *agree* (Phil 4.2)

do not *think of high things*
do not *be haughty* (Rom 12.16)

B.3.b. Other combinations that may be restated in English are (**1**) prepositional phrases; (**2**) elliptical expressions and expressions in which "to be" is implied; (**3**) impersonal, indefinite, and similar expressions; (**4**) simple paraphrase and combinations for economy of words; (**5**) series; (**6**) emphasis and pleonasm; (**7**) redundancy; (**8**) short common expressions.

1. *of a truth*
truly (Mk 12.14); *certainly* (Lk 22.59)

according to the flesh
from a human point of view (2 Cor 5.16); *earthly* (Col. 3.22); *in worldly fashion* (2 Cor 10.2)

from myself
on my own authority (Jn 5.30); *of my own accord* (Jn 7.28)

2. *on the next*
on the next day (Acts 25.17); *next day* (Acts 27.18)

when [the hour] *became late*
when evening came (Mt 14.23)

who is *at the right*
who is *at the right hand* (Rom 8.34)

they all *with one* [mind? voice?] began
they all *alike* began (Lk 14.18)

by his own [?]
by himself (Mt 14.23); *apart* (Lk 9.10); *privately* (Mk 13.3)

then as one man's trespass [was] *unto condemnation* for all men
then as one man's trespass *led to condemnation* for all men (Rom 5.18)

3. *it is necessary for s. to*
s. must (Mt 16.21); *s. has to* (Lk 22.7); *s. should* (Acts 27.21)

it is lawful for s. to
s. is allowed to (Mt 20.15)

whoever
he who (Mt 5.19); *the one* (Mt 26.48); *if any one* (Mt 23.16)

into whatever town you enter
whenever you enter a town (Lk 10.8)

whatever you ask
if you ask *anything* (Jn 16.23)

4. all *slaves* who are under the yoke
all who are under the yoke of *slavery* (1 Tim 6.1)

when first I have enjoyed
once I have enjoyed (Rom 15.24)

some of them have come *from far off*
some of them have come *a long way* (Mk 8.3)

he was *about to die*
he was *at the point of death* (Jn 4.47)

5. but the glory of the celestial is *different*, and the glory of the terrestrial is *different*
but the glory of the celestial is *one*, and the glory of the terrestrial is *another*
(1 Cor 15.40)

and not in this age *and not* in the age to come
not .. *either* in this age *or* in the age to come
(Mt 12.32)

6. (Additional words underlie the following):
spirit of divination (Acts 16.16); *utterly* (Mk 6.51)

7. how you ought to live . . , just as you are *living*
how you ought to live . . , just as you are *doing*
(1 Th 4.1)

you must no longer live as the Gentiles *live*
you must no longer live as the Gentiles *do*
(Eph 4.17)

8. *let it not be*
far be it (Gal 6.14); *God forbid* (Lk 20.16); *certainly not* (Gal 3.21); *by no means* (Rom 3.6); *never* (1 Cor 6.15)

C. Stylistic devices. The New Testament and its translations show the influence of various stylistic devices common to Greek, although some reflect Semitic style.

C.1. Euphemism.

let us conduct ourselves becomingly . . , not in .. *beds* and licentiousness
let us conduct ourselves becomingly . . , not in .. *debauchery* and licentiousness (Rom 13.13)

it enters .. his stomach, and so passes on *into the latrine*
it enters .. his stomach, and so passes on
(Mk 7.19)

C.2. Metonymy and synecdoche.

to make my *flesh* jealous, and thus save some
to make my *fellow Jews* jealous, and thus save some (Rom 11.14)

by the *mouth* of two or three witnesses
by the *evidence* of two or three witnesses
(2 Cor 13.1)

to witness against *my soul*
to witness against *me* (2 Cor 1.23)

he *prepared a table*
he *set food before them* (Acts 16.34)

C.3. Semitic style, some of which is strictly translated and has become acceptable English.

seeing you shall see but never perceive
you shall *indeed* see but never perceive
(Mt 13.14)

[may this happen to me] *if* a sign shall be given to this generation
no sign shall be given to this generation
(Mk 8.12)

do not fear the fear of them
have no fear of them (1 Pet 3.14)

C.4. Expressions common to the Septuagint.

a fragrant *smell*
a fragrant *offering* (Phil 4.18)

C.5. Other un-English idioms and technical terms.

son of the bridal chamber
wedding guest (Mt 9.15)

D. The element of uncertainty. Some analysis is based upon uncertain understanding of Greek words or syntax by the RSV translators, or upon a corrupt text.

D.1. Some words or phrases are doubtful or, in a given context, uncertain or ambiguous, and the translators provide their best interpretation, usually with a footnote.

a death has occurred which redeems them .. under the first covenant.[u] For where a will[u] is involved
[u]The Greek word here used means both *covenant* and *will*
(Heb 9.15–16)

that is why a woman ought to have a veil[r] on her head
[r]Greek *authority* (the veil being a symbol of this)
(1 Cor 11.10)

a harbor .. looking northeast and southeast[a]
[a]Or *southwest and northwest*
(Acts 27.12)

the city of the Ephesians is temple keeper . . of what has fallen from the sky
the city of the Ephesians is temple keeper . . of the sacred stone that fell from the sky[s]
[s]The meaning of the Greek is uncertain
(Acts 19.35)

D.2. A "corrupt text" in the Greek may mean that the translation based upon the best manuscript evidence is nevertheless unclear or at variance with the clear meaning of the passage. Analysis in this case will lead to an inappropriate association of Greek and English words.

four days ago *until* this hour
four days ago *about* this hour (Acts 10.30)

and *in the midst of* the throne, and on each side of the throne, are four living creatures
and *round* the throne, on each side of the throne, are four living creatures (Rev 4.6)

PART TWO: GRAMMATICAL TERMS

Part One has dealt with matters of grammar and syntax from a purely descriptive perspective that may be grasped by the English reader. Thus, letter-number combinations are used in referring to Part One.

Part Two consists of notes on a number of grammatical concepts that are either well known or easy to understand, and whose terminology is used both on the subtitle lines and in the Index-Lexicon. The purpose of this Part is not to provide a layman's Greek grammar, but to identify and illustrate a few grammatical terms within the limited range in which they have actually been used in the Concordance.

CASE. The cases in Greek, beyond their usual functions of signaling the subject, object, etc., serve other functions that, when translated into English, often require rephrasing and a change of the part of speech or the usual meaning of the Greek word. Some common instances follow.

The **genitive** is the case of the modifier (among many other functions). Use of the genitive case accounts for many nouns being translated as adjectives:

the judge *of unrighteousness*
the *unrighteous* judge (Lk 18.6)

The **dative** is the case of the indirect object (among many other functions). The dative case can affect meaning in its expression of manner:

he said this *with openness*
he said this *plainly* (Mk 8.32)

The **accusative** is the case of the direct object (among many other functions). It may indicate an adverbial function (manner, extent, etc.):

the end [acc.], all of you, have unity
finally, all of you, have unity (1 Pet 3.8)

GENDER. Gender (**masculine, feminine, neuter**) influences meaning in some obvious ways:

Phoebe, a *deacon* [fem.]
Phoebe, a *deaconess* (Rom 16.1)

However, the neuter is often used to express the adverbial sense:

that you might have him back *eternal* [neut.]
that you might have him back *for ever* (Phm .15)

NUMBER. Number (**singular, plural**) is noted only when the English differs from the Greek. The meanings rest upon the singular unless otherwise indicated.

TENSE. Indication of tense (**present, future, aorist,** etc.) is rarely needed in this work. The tense most commonly noted is the **perfect,** which in Greek indicates the present result of a completed past action—i.e., a state or condition previously established.

those who sought the child's life *have died*
those who sought the child's life *are dead* (Mt 2.20)

Other tenses that are not self-evident may be ignored by persons unacquainted with Greek.

VOICE. Voice will ordinarily not be of interest to the non-Greek-reading user of the Concordance. References to voice (**active, middle, passive**) cannot be excluded, however, because of the nature of Greek lexicography. Greek verbs ending in -OMAI are middle or passive; the meanings of other verbs are based on the active voice unless otherwise indicated. A deponent verb has the middle or passive form but otherwise functions as an active verb.

MOOD. All verb meanings are based on the **indicative** mood unless otherwise noted. Mood is indicated especially in the case of the **participle.** The participle is a verbal adjective, as in English, the common form of the verb that is translated as an adjective. Like the adjective, it is easily used as a noun in Greek as well as in English (see discussion of "substantive," below). In its predicative use—as contrasted with the adjectival (attributive) and noun (substantive) uses—the participle serves an adverbial function and is commonly translated by a phrase or clause having this function.

The **infinitive** is noted primarily where it serves (as it may in English) as a noun.

The **imperative** is noted where it accounts for some idiomatic usage.

> *take away* this man [imper.]
> *away with* this man (Lk 23.18)
>
> *see* the scribes [imper.]
> *beware of* the scribes (Mk 12.38)

PERSON. Verbs are ordinarily defined in forms applicable to the first, second, or third person. There are instances (marked "impersonal" or "indefinite") that will alert the reader to an exception.

OTHER. The term **substantive** is used often and indicates that a particular word (usually adjective, participle, or infinitive) is used as a noun (including the possibilities in A.1, above). If the substantive is placed in the neuter gender, it may take on an abstract or general character ("good" in the neuter may mean "goodness," "the good," or [pl.] "goods"). The English word "thing/things" is a common clue to a neuter substantive in the Greek.

Other terminology used in this book will, for the most part, be intelligible to the reader or may be ignored.

APPENDIX II

FORMER READINGS OF THE RSV NEW TESTAMENT

The Revised Standard Version of the New Testament was published Feb. 11, 1946. Republication with the RSV Old Testament (Sept. 30, 1952) afforded the opportunity to make about eighty changes in the New Testament text and notes. Further changes in about the same number and also of an editorial nature, or in the interest of consistency, clarity, or accuracy, were authorized by the Standard Bible Committee in June (9–16), 1959. For the Second Edition of the RSV (March 15, 1971), about two hundred additional changes were made to keep the version abreast of textual and linguistic scholarship and to make further clarifications. In 1965 there was authorized a Catholic Edition, prepared by the Catholic Biblical Association of Great Britain. It differed in about sixty instances from the current regular edition; about a third of these changes were later adopted in the Second Edition.

In this Appendix are recorded all readings of the RSV New Testament that have been superseded on one of the occasions just mentioned or that remain peculiar to the Catholic Edition. After each reading is a capital letter indicating the latest date when that reading was used. The matter changed in the text is italicized. (When a reading contains no italics, the subsequent change will be found to be an addition.) Changes in the footnotes are not marked, since they use italics on their own part and alternation of type could prove confusing. There is no entry when the only change has been the addition of a note.

A = 1946 **B** = 1952 **C** = 1959 **CE** = Catholic Edition, 1965

Mt 1.19 Joseph . . resolved to *send her away* quietly **CE**

2. 6 " 'And *thou* Bethlehem . . *art* by no means least . . ; for from *thee* shall come a ruler **A**

6. 2 "I say to you, they *have* their reward **C**

6. 5 "I say to you, they *have* their reward **C**

6.16 "I say to you, they *have* their reward **C**

7. 9 "if his son asks him for *a loaf* **B**

10. 8 "You received without *pay* **C**

10.25 "If they have called the master of the house *Beelzebub*[z] **A**

[z]Greek *Beelzebul* **A**

12. 1 they began to pluck *ears* of grain **C**

12.24 "It is only by *Beelzebub*[h] **A**

[h]Greek *Beelzebul* **A**

12.27 "if I cast out demons by *Beelzebub*[h] **A**

[h]Greek *Beelzebul* **A**

12.46 his *brethren* stood outside **CE**

12.47 [g]Other ancient authorities insert verse 47, . . "*your brethren are standing outside* **CE**

12.48 "who are my *brethren?* **CE**

12.49 "Here are my mother and my *brethren*! **CE**

13.33 "leaven . . in three measures of *meal* **C**

13.55 "his *brethren* James and Joseph **CE**

14.23 he went up *into the hills* by himself **C**

15.27 "crumbs . . from their *master's* table **C**

15.29 he went up *into the hills* **C**

Mt 17.20 " 'Move *hence to yonder place* **C**

18. 8 "cut it off and throw it *from you* **C**

18. 9 "pluck it out and throw it *from you* **C**

18.12 "does he not leave the ninety-nine on the *hills* **C**

19. 5 " 'the two shall become one[i] **C**

[i]Greek *one flesh* **C**

19. 6 "So they are no longer two but one[i] **C**

[i]Greek *one flesh* **C**

19. 6 "let *no* man put asunder **C**

19. 9 "whoever divorces his wife, except for unchastity,[j] and marries another, commits adultery*; and he who marries a divorced woman, commits adultery*[k] **CE**

[k]Other ancient authorities omit *and he who marries a divorced woman, commits adultery* **CE**

19.11 "Not all men can receive this *precept* **C**

19.21 "go, sell . . and give *it* to the poor **A**

21. 9 "Blessed *be* he who comes **B**

21.44 "*And he who falls on this stone will be broken to pieces; but when it falls on any one, it will crush him*[q] **CE**

[q]Other . . authorities omit verse 44 **CE**

23.39 " 'Blessed *be* he who comes **B**

24. 8 "the beginning of the *sufferings* **C**

Mt 25.17 "So *too,* he who had the two talents **B**
25.18 "he who had received the one talent, went **B**
26. 7 a woman . . with an alabaster *jar* **C**
26.13 "what *this woman* has done will be told **A**
26.18 "Go into the city to *such a* one **C**
26.59 sought false *witness* against Jesus, that they might put him to death **A**
26.60 though many witnesses came forward **A**
27.11 Jesus said *to him,* "You have said so **C**
27.24 "I am innocent of this *righteous* man's blood[l] **CE**
[l]Other ancient authorities omit *righteous* or *man's* **CE**
27.32 As they *were marching* out **C**
27.54 "Truly this was *a* son of God! **B**
27.60 he rolled a great stone to the *entrance* of the tomb **A**
27.61 *And* Mary Magdalene and the other Mary were there, sitting opposite the *tomb* **A**
27.64 "order the *tomb* to be made secure **A**
27.66 they went and made the *tomb* secure **A**

Mk 1.36 those who were with him *followed* him **C**
1.41 *And being* moved with pity **A**
2.23 disciples began to pluck *ears* of grain **C**
3.13 And he went up *into the hills* **C**
3.21 And when his *friends* heard it, they went out to seize him, for *they said,* "He is beside himself **C**
3.22 "He is possessed by *Beelzebub*[k] **A**
[k]Greek *Beelzebul* **A**
3.31 his mother and his *brethren* came **CE**
3.32 "your *brethren*[l] are outside **CE**
3.33 "Who are my mother and my *brethren*? **CE**
3.34 "Here are my mother and my *brethren*! **CE**
4.36 they took him with them, *just as he was, in the boat* **C**
5.42 the girl got up and walked*; for* she was twelve years *old. And immediately they were* overcome with amazement **C**
6.29 When *the* disciples heard of it **A**
6.34 As he *landed* he saw a great throng **C**
6.46 he went *into the hills* to pray **C**
6.48 they were *distressed in rowing,* for the wind was against them **C**
7.22 "licentiousness, *an evil eye,* slander **A**
7.26 a Syrophoenician by *race* **A**
7.31 *Soon after this* he returned **A**
9. 1 "before they see the kingdom of God *come* with power **C**
9.28 when he had *gone home* **A**
9.29 "not . . by anything but prayer *and fasting*[j] **CE**
[j]Other ancient authorities omit *and fasting* **CE**
10. 8 " 'and the two shall become one.'[q] So they are no longer two but one.[q] **C**
[q]Greek *one flesh* **C**
10.21 "go, sell *all that* you have, and give *it* to the poor **A**
10.24 "how hard it is *for those who trust in riches*[r] **CE**
[r]Other ancient authorities omit *for those who trust in riches* **CE**
11. 9 "Blessed *be* he who comes **B**
11.10 "Blessed *be* the kingdom of our father David **B**
11.24 "believe that you *receive* it, and *you will* **C**
13. 8 "but the beginning of the *sufferings* **C**
13.33 "Take heed, watch *and pray*[a]
[a]Other . . authorities omit *and pray* **CE**
14. 3 an alabaster *jar* of ointment **C**
14. 3 she broke the *jar* and poured **C**
14.20 "dipping bread *in* the *same* dish with me **C**
14.44 "seize him and lead him away *safely* **C**
14.62 "Son of man *sitting* at the right hand **C**
14.63 the high priest tore his *mantle* **C**
15. 6 one prisoner *whom* they asked **C**
15.39 "Truly this man was *a son* of God! **B**
16. 4 was rolled back*; for* it was very large **C**

Mk 16. 8 [k]Other texts and versions add as 16.9–20 the following passage:
9 *Now when he rose early on the first day*
of the week, he appeared first to Mary Mag-
dalene, from whom he had cast out seven
demons. 10*She went and told those who had*
been with him, as they mourned and wept.
11*But when they heard that he was alive and*
had been seen by her, they would not believe it.
12 *After this he appeared in another form*
to two of them, as they were walking into the
country. 13*And they went back and told the*
rest, but they did not believe them.
14 *Afterward he appeared to the eleven*
themselves as they sat at table; and he up-
braided them for their unbelief and hardness
of heart, because they had not believed those
who saw him after he had risen. 15*And he said*
to them, "Go into all the world and preach the
gospel to the whole creation. 16*He who be-*
lieves and is baptized will be saved; but he
who does not believe will be condemned.
17*And these signs will accompany those who*
believe: in my name they will cast out
demons; they will speak in new tongues;
18*they will pick up serpents, and if they drink*
any deadly thing, it will not hurt them; they
will lay their hands on the sick, and they will
recover."
19 *So then the Lord Jesus, after he had*
spoken to them, was taken up into heaven,
and sat down at the right hand of God. 20*And*
they went forth and preached everywhere,
while the Lord worked with them and con-
firmed the message by the signs that attended
it. Amen.

Other ancient authorities add after verse 8 the following: *But they reported briefly to Peter and those with him all that they had been told. And after this, Jesus himself sent out by means of them, from east to west, the sacred and imperishable proclamation of eternal salvation* **C**
16.20 [k]Other ancient authorities omit verses 9–20. Some ancient authorities conclude Mark instead with the following: *But they reported briefly to Peter and those with him all that they had been told. And after this, Jesus himself sent out by means of them, from east to west, the sacred and imperishable proclamation of eternal salvation* **CE**

Lk 1.28 "Hail, *full of grace,*[b2] the Lord is with you![c] **CE**
[b2]Or *O favored one* **CE**
1.34 Mary said . . "How *can* this be **C**
3.29 the son of *Jesus,* the son of Eliezer **B**
3.30 the son of *Symeon,* the son of *Judas,* the son of Joseph **B**
6. 1 his disciples . . ate some *ears* of grain **C**
6.12 he went out *into the hills* to pray **C**
6.16 [u]Or *brother* **B**
6.29 "from him who takes away your *cloak* do not withhold your *coat as well* **C**
6.30 "of him who takes away your goods, do not ask them again **B**
7.25 "A man clothed in soft *raiment*? **C**
7.36 he went . . , and *sat* at table **C**
7.37 she learned that he was *sitting* at table **C**
8.19 his *brethren* came to him **CE**
8.20 "your *brethren* are standing outside **CE**
8.21 "my *brethren* are those who hear the word **CE**
8.43 a woman who had had a flow of blood for twelve years *and had spent all her living upon physicians*[b] **CE**
[b]Other ancient authorities omit *and had spent all her living upon physicians* **CE**
8.45 Peter *and those who were with him*[g] said **A**

[g]Some ancient authorities omit *and those who were with him* **A**

Lk 8.51 the father and mother of the *maiden* **A**
9.32 were heavy with sleep *but kept awake, and* they saw his glory **C**
11.15 "He casts out demons by *Beelzebub*[r] **A**
[r]Greek *Beelzebul* **A**
11.16 others, to *try* him, sought . . a sign **A**
11.17 "and *house falls upon house* **C**
11.18 "you say that I cast out demons by *Beelzebub* **A**
11.19 "if I cast out demons by *Beelzebub* **A**
11.43 "*For* you love the best *seats* in synagogues **A**
12. 3 "Whatever you have said in the dark **C**
12.39 "he *would have been awake and*[q] **C**
[q]Other ancient authorities omit *would have been awake and* **C**
12.40 "coming *at an hour you do not expect* **C**
12.44 "I *tell you,* he will set him over all **C**
13.21 "like leaven . . in three measures of *meal* **C**
13.35 " 'Blessed *be* he who comes **B**
14. 5 "Which of you, having *an ass*[s] **C**
[s]Other ancient authorities read *a son* **C**
15. 7 "*Even* so, . . there will be more joy **B**
15.10 "*Even* so, I tell you, there is joy **B**
16. 8 "The master commended the dishonest steward for his *prudence*; for the sons of this world[w] are *wiser in* their own generation **C**
17.29 "fire and *brimstone* rained from heaven **C**
17.34 "there will be two *men* in one bed **C**
19.10 "to seek and to save *that which was* lost **A**
19.12 "to receive *kingly power*[d] **C**
[d]Greek *a kingdom* **C**
19.15 "having received the *kingly power*[d] **C**
[d]Greek *a kingdom* **C**
19.38 "Blessed *be* the King who comes **B**
22. 4 with the chief priests and *captains* **C**
22.16 "I tell you I shall *never* eat it *again*[o] **A**
[o]Some ancient authorities omit *again* **A**
22.19 "This is my body[j] **C**
[j]Other ancient authorities add *which is given for you. Do this in remembrance of me." [20]And likewise the cup after supper, saying, "This cup which is poured out for you is the new covenant in my blood* **C**
22.29 "*as my Father appointed a kingdom for me, so do I appoint for you* [30]that you may eat and drink **C**
22.43–44 *And there appeared to him an angel from heaven, strengthening him. [44]And being in an agony he prayed more earnestly; and his sweat became like great drops of blood falling down upon the ground*[l] **C**
[l]Other ancient authorities omit verses 43 and 44 **C**
22.52 Jesus said to the . . *captains* of the temple **C**
23.42 "when you come *in your kingly power*[p] **C**
[p]Greek *kingdom* **C**
24. 5 "*He is not here, but has risen*[u] **CE**
[u]Other ancient authorities omit *He is not here, but has risen* **CE**
24.12 *But Peter rose and ran to the tomb; stooping and looking in, he saw the linen cloths by themselves; and he went home wondering at what had happened*[v] **CE**
[v]Other ancient authorities omit verse 12 **CE**
24.13 [w]Greek *sixty-stadia* **B**
24.28 they drew near to the village to which they were going; *and* he *made as though he would go* further **A**
24.36 Jesus . . stood among them, *and said to them, "Peace to you*[x] **CE**
[x]Other ancient authorities omit *and said to them, "Peace to you* **CE**
24.40 *And when he had said this, he showed them his hands and his feet*[y] **CE**
[y]Other . . authorities omit verse 40 **CE**

Lk 24.51 While he blessed them, he parted from them[a] **C**
[a]Other ancient authorities add *and was carried up into heaven* **C**
24.52 they *worshiped him, and*[b] returned to Jerusalem **CE**
[b]Other ancient authorities omit *worshiped him, and* **CE**

Jn 1.42 "called Cephas" (which means *Rock*[b]) **A**
[b]Greek *Peter* **A**
2. 3 When the wine *failed* **C**
2. 6 jars . . holding *two or three measures*[c] **A**
[c]That is, about twenty or thirty gallons **A**
2.12 with his mother and his *brethren* **CE**
2.23 they saw *his* signs which he did **B**
5. 2 in Jerusalem by the *sheep gate* a pool **B**
5.18 he . . also called God his Father **C**
6. 3 Jesus went up *into the hills* **C**
6.15 Jesus withdrew again to the *hills* **C**
6.28 "to be doing the *work* of God **B**
6.64 who it was that *should* betray him **C**
6.67 "*Will you also* go away? **C**
7. 3 So his *brethren* said to him **CE**
7. 5 even his *brethren* did not believe **CE**
7. 8 "I am not[o] going up to *the* feast **B**
7.10 after his *brethren* had gone up **CE**
7.52 [r]Other ancient authorities add 7.53–8.11 either here or at the end of this gospel or after Luke 21.38, with variations of the text:
8 *[53]They went each to his own house, [1]but Jesus went to the Mount of Olives. [2]Early in the morning he came again to the temple; all the people came to him, and he sat down and taught them. [3]The scribes and the Pharisees brought a woman who had been caught in adultery, and placing her in the midst [4]they said to him, "Teacher, this woman has been caught in the act of adultery. [5]Now in the law Moses commanded us to stone such. What do you say about her?" [6]This they said to test him, that they might have some charge to bring against him. Jesus bent down and wrote with his finger on the ground. [7]And as they continued to ask him, he stood up and said to them, "Let him who is without sin among you be the first to throw a stone at her." [8]And once more he bent down and wrote with his finger on the ground. [9]But when they heard it, they went away, one by one, beginning with the eldest, and Jesus was left alone with the woman standing before him. [10]Jesus looked up and said to her, "Woman, where are they? Has no one condemned you?" [11]She said, "No one, Lord." And Jesus said, "Neither do I condemn you; go, and do not sin again* **C**
8.31 "you are my disciples **A**
8.53 "*Whom* do you *make yourself* to be? **A**
10.33 "*We stone you for no* good work **C**
11.50 and *not* that the whole nation *should perish* **A**
12. 2 *but* Lazarus was one of those at table **B**
12.13 "Blessed *be* he who comes **B**
12.27 "what shall I say, 'Father, save me from this hour'? **B**
13.10 "you are clean, but not *all* of you **C**
16. 8 "he will convince the world *of* sin and *of* righteousness and *of* judgment **C**
16. 9 "*of* sin, because they do not believe **C**
16.10 "*of* righteousness, because I go **C**
16.11 "*of* judgment, because the ruler . . is judged **C**
16.23 "you will ask *me no questions* **B**
17. 2 "*so that he might* give eternal life **A**
17.11 "keep them in thy name which thou hast given me **B**

Jn 17.12 "thy name which thou hast given me **B**
17.17 "*Consecrate* them in the truth **A**
17.20 "for those who *are to* believe **B**
19. 4 "*Behold,* I am bringing him out **C**
19. 5 Pilate said . . "*Here is* the man! **C**
19.14 the day of Preparation *for* the Passover **B**
19.14 He said to the Jews, "*Here is* your King! **C**
19.23 four parts, one for each soldier. But *his* tunic was without seam **B**
19.25 *but* standing by the cross of Jesus **B**
19.26 "Woman, behold your son! **B**
19.27 "Behold your mother! **B**
20. 6 and *he* went into the tomb **B**

Acts 1.14 together . . with his *brethren* **CE**
8. 3 But Saul *laid waste* the church **C**
8.27 a minister of *Candace the queen* of the Ethiopians **C**
9.36 Tabitha, which means Dorcas *or Gazelle* **C**
9.39 weeping, and showing *coats* and garments **C**
10.12 animals and reptiles and *wild* birds **A**
11. 6 "I observed . . reptiles and *wild* birds **A**
11.12 "go with them *without hesitation* **B**
13. 1 Barnabas, *Symeon* who was called Niger **C**
13. 6 [l]Greek *magus* (as in Matthew 2.1) **B**
15. 4 "*Symeon* has related **C**
15.25 "seemed good to us *in assembly* **C**
17.28 " 'In him we live and move and *are* **A**
20.25 "among whom I have gone *about* preaching **C**
20.28 "obtained *for himself* with his own blood[v] **A**
20.28 "the Holy Spirit has made you *guardians, to feed* the church of *the Lord*[v] which he obtained with *his own* blood[w] **C**
[v]Other ancient authorities read *of God* **C**
[w]Or *with the blood of his Own* **C**
20.32 "among all those who are *consecrated* **A**
23.17 "*Bring* this young man to the tribune **C**
26.18 " 'those who are *consecrated* by faith **A**

Rom 1. 4 designated[a2] Son of God in power **CE**
[a2]Or *constituted* **CE**
1. 5 to bring about obedience *to the* faith **B**
1. 5 to bring about *the* obedience *of faith* **C**
1. 5 his name among all the *Gentiles* **A**
3.20 no human being will be justified in his sight by works of the law since through the law comes knowledge of sin **B**
3.30 he will justify . . the uncircumcised *because of* their faith **B**
5. 5 the Holy Spirit *who* has been given to us **CE**
5. 6 While we were *yet helpless* **C**
8. 9 if the Spirit of God *really* dwells in you **C**
8.11 through his Spirit *who* dwells in you **CE**
9. 5 of their race . . is the *Christ, who is God over all, blessed for ever.*[n] Amen **CE**
[n]Or *Christ. God who is over all be blessed for ever* **CE**
9. 7 but, "*Your descendants will be reckoned through Isaac* **A**
9.20 But, who are you, a man, to answer back **B**
10.16 they have not all *heeded* the gospel **C**
11. 9 "Let their *feast* become a snare **C**
11.11 through their *transgression* salvation has come **A**
11.12 if their *transgression* means riches **A**
11.28 but as regards *his* election **A**
14.16 do not let *what is* good *to you* be spoken of as evil **C**
14.17 the kingdom of God *does not mean* food **C**
15.16 acceptable, *consecrated* by the Holy Spirit **A**
16.26 to bring about obedience *to the* faith **B**

1 Cor 1. 2 to those *consecrated* in Christ Jesus **A**
1.30 our righteousness and *consecration* **A**
2. 4 in demonstration of the Spirit and power **C**
3. 9 For we are fellow *workmen* for God[f] **B**
3. 9 we are fellow workers *for God*[f] **C**
[f]Greek *God's fellow workers* **C**
3. 9 [f]Or *fellow workers for God* **CE**
3.10 the *commission* of God given to me **C**
3.12 precious stones, wood, hay, *stubble* **C**
4. 5 disclose the *purpose of men's hearts* **A**
4. 6 learn by us *to live according to scripture* **C**
5. 6 a little leaven *ferments* the whole lump *of dough* **B**
5. 7 that you may be *fresh dough* **B**
5.13 God judges those outside. Drive out the wicked person from among you **B**
6. 9 nor adulterers, nor *homosexuals*[j] **C**
[j]Two Greek words are rendered by this expression **C**
6.11 you were washed, you were *consecrated* **A**
6.16 "The two shall become one[k] **C**
[k]Greek *one flesh* **C**
7.26 in view of the *impending*[m] distress **C**
[m]Or *present* **C**
7.32 I want you to be free from *all* anxieties **A**
7.34 to be *consecrated* in body and spirit **A**
7.36 and *if* it has to be, let him do *what he will, he does not sin;* let them marry **A**
9. 5 [n]Greek *woman, sister* **CE**
9. 5 the *brethren* of the Lord and Cephas **CE**
10.17 Because there is one *loaf* **B**
10.18 Consider the *practice* of Israel **C**
11.24 "my body which is *broken*[o] *for* you **A**
[o]Many ancient authorities omit *broken*; a few read *given* **A**
12.24 But God has so *adjusted* the body **C**
13. 8 as for *prophecy, it* will pass away **B**
15.18 those also who have *died* in Christ **A**
15.19 If *in* this life we *who are in Christ have only hope*[y] **B**
[y]Or *If in this life only we have hoped in Christ* **B**
16. 2 put something aside and *save* **A**
16.12 it was not at all *God's* will *for him to go*[b] now **B**
[b]Or *his will to go* **B**
16.19 the church *that meets* in their house **A**

2 Cor 1.10 he delivered us from *such a deadly* peril **A**
2. 3 I might not *be pained by* those **C**
3. 5 Not that we are *sufficient* of ourselves . . ; our *sufficiency* is from God **C**
3. 6 Who has *qualified us* to be ministers **C**
3. 8 *why should* not the dispensation **B**
4. 1 Therefore, *being engaged in this service* by the mercy of God[e] **A**
5.19 that is, *God was in Christ* reconciling[h] **C**
[h]Or *in Christ God was reconciling* **C**
12.11 For I *am* not at all inferior **C**

Gal 1.11 [b]Greek *according to* (or *after*) *man* **B**
3. 4 Did you *suffer* so many things in vain? **A**
3. 8 "In *thee* shall all the nations be blessed **B**
4.27 "O barren one *that dost* not bear **C**
4.27 "*thou* who *art* not in travail **C**
4.27 "the *desolate hath more children than she who hath a husband* **C**
5. 8 not from him who *called* you **C**
5. 9 A little *yeast* leavens the whole lump **B**
5.19 *immorality*, impurity, licentiousness **C**
6.15 neither *is* circumcision *anything* **A**

Eph 1.14 *who* is the guarantee of our inheritance **CE**
1.15 [c]Other ancient authorities omit *and your love* **B**
2.20 Jesus himself being the *chief* cornerstone **B**
4.12 *for the equipment of the saints,* for the work of ministry **C**
5. 3 But *immorality* and all impurity **C**
5. 5 that no *immoral* or impure man **C**
5.26 that he might *consecrate* her **A**
5.27 that the church *might be presented before him* in splendor **B**
5.31 "the two shall become one **C**
5.32 This *is a great* mystery, and *I take it to mean* Christ and the church **C**

Eph 5.32 This *is a great* mystery, and *I mean in reference to* Christ and the church **CE**
6.16 *above* all taking the shield of faith **C**
Phil 1. 7 I hold you *all* in my heart *as* partakers **A**
2. 5 Have this mind . . , which *you have* in Christ Jesus **C**
2. 5 Have this mind . . , which *was* in Christ Jesus **CE**
3.17 mark those who live as you have an example **A**
Col 1.24 what *remains of* Christ's afflictions **A**
2. 9 in him *dwells the whole fulness of deity* bodily **A**
3. 5 *immorality*, impurity, passion **C**
3. 6 wrath of God is coming *upon the sons of disobedience*[f] **A**
[f]Some ancient authorities omit *upon the sons of disobedience*, and read *in which* **A**
3. 7 *among whom you also* once walked, when you lived in *these things* **A**
3. 8 now put *away also all these:* anger, wrath **A**
3.16 richly, *as you* teach . . and *as you* sing psalms **C**
1 Th 4. 3 the will of God, your *consecration* **A**
4. 3 that you abstain from *immorality* **C**
4. 4 how to take a wife . . in *consecration* and honor **A**
4. 4 how to *control his own body* in holiness **CE**
4. 7 but in *consecration* **A**
5.13 Be at peace among yourselves[c2] **CE**
[c2]Or *with them* **CE**
5.14 brethren, admonish the *idle* **C**
2 Th 2.13 through *consecration* by the Spirit[c] **A**
1 Tim 3. 2 above reproach, *married only once*,[e] temperate **B**
[e]Greek *the husband of one wife* **B**
3.12 Let deacons be *married only once*[g] **B**
[g]Greek *husbands of one wife* **B**
4.14 when the elders laid their hands upon you **C**
5. 9 or *who* has been married more than once **A**
5. 9 Let *no one* be enrolled *as a widow who is under* sixty years of age, *or has been married more than once*[k] **B**
[k]Greek *the wife of one husband* **B**
2 Tim 1. 8 but *take your share of* suffering for the gospel **C**
1.12 I know whom I have believed and I am sure **B**
2. 3 *Take your share of* suffering **C**
2. 9 and wearing fetters, like a criminal **B**
2.10 may obtain *the* salvation *which* in Christ Jesus *goes* with eternal glory **C**
3. 8 men of corrupt *minds* and *rejected as regards the* faith **A**
4.17 strength to proclaim the *word* fully **C**
Tit 1. 6 *men who are* blameless, *married only once*,[b] *whose* children are believers **B**
[b]Greek *the husband of one wife* **B**
Phm .11 [b]The name Onesimus means *useful* or (verse 20) *beneficial* **B**
Heb 2. 8 in putting everything in subjection to *man* **B**
3. 6 if we hold fast[g] our confidence and pride in our hope **B**
[g]Other ancient authorities insert *firm to the end* **B**
3.15 While it is *still* "today," when you hear his voice, do not harden your hearts as in the rebellion **A**
4. 2 [h]Other manuscripts read *they were not united in faith with those who heard* **B**
4.15 tempted as we are, yet without *sinning* **C**
6. 1 let us leave the elementary *doctrines* of Christ **C**
10.10 by that will we have been *consecrated* **A**
10.14 for all time those who are *consecrated* **A**
Heb 10.29 the blood of the covenant by which he was *consecrated* **A**
11. 4 Abel offered[z] a more acceptable sacrifice **A**
[z]Many ancient authorities add *to God* **A**
11.18 "Through Isaac shall your *posterity* be named **A**
11.19 hence *he did receive him back and this was a symbol* **CE**
12.14 Strive for peace . . and for the *consecration* **A**
13.12 in order to *consecrate* the people **A**
13.13 outside the camp, *bearing* abuse *for him* **C**
Jas 1. 1 To the twelve tribes in the *dispersion* **B**
1. 5 let him ask God who gives to all men **B**
2. 7 who blaspheme *that* honorable name *by which you are called* **C**
2.13 without mercy to one who has shown no mercy; mercy triumphs over judgment **A**
2.20 Do you want to be shown, you *foolish fellow*, that faith apart from works is barren? **C**
1 Pet 1. 1 To the exiles of the *dispersion* **B**
3. 3 decoration of gold, and wearing of *robes* **C**
4. 7 The end of all things is at hand; keep sane **A**
4.19 entrust their souls to a faithful *creator* **B**
2 Pet 1. 1 *Simon* Peter, a servant and apostle **C**
1 Jn 3.10 it may be seen . . who are the children of the devil: *no one who does not do right is of God, nor any one* who does not love his brother **A**
3.14 He who does not love *remains* in death **C**
5.12 he who has not the Son has not life **B**
2 Jn . 9 he who abides in the doctrine *of Christ* has both **B**
3 Jn . 2 that you may *keep well, as I know* it is well with your soul **A**
Rev 1.13 clothed with a long robe and a golden girdle **A**
8. 5 peals of thunder, *loud noises*, flashes **C**
9. 6 death *flies* from them **B**
9. 9–10 with horses rushing into battle*;* [10]*they* have tails like scorpions **B**
11. 5 thus he is doomed to *die* **A**
11.19 flashes of lightning, *loud noises*, peals **C**
13.15 those who *will* not worship the image **B**
14. 9 another angel, a third, followed, saying **B**
14.10 "tormented with fire and *brimstone* **C**
16.14 they are *devil* spirits **A**
16.17 and a *great* voice came out of the temple **C**
16.18 lightning, *loud noises*, peals of thunder **C**
17. 9 "seven heads are seven *hills* **C**
19. 1 the *mighty* voice of a great multitude **C**
19. 3 The smoke *of* her goes up for ever and ever **A**
19.20 lake of fire that burns with *brimstone* **C**
20. 4 They came to life *again*, and reigned **B**
20. 5 The rest . . did not come to life *again* **B**
20.10 the lake of fire and *brimstone* **C**
21. 3 I heard a *great* voice from the throne **C**
21. 6 I will give *water without price* from the fountain of the water of life **C**
21. 8 the lake that burns with fire and *brimstone* **C**

NOTE: Footnotes providing an absolute evaluation of ancient coins were abandoned after 1959 in favor of relative evaluation in terms of the wages of a laborer.

The denarius was worth about twenty cents **C** Mt **18.28**[a]; **20.2**[m]; Mk **6.37**[u]; **14.5**[b]; Lk **10.35**[i]; Jn **6.7**[l]; **12.5**[b]; Rev **6.6**[a]

The drachma, rendered here by *silver coin*, was about sixteen cents **C** Lk **15.8**[t]

The mina, rendered here by *pound*, was equal to about twenty dollars **C** Lk **19.13**[e]

This talent was probably worth about a thousand dollars **C** Mt **18.24**[f]; **25.15**[d]

MAPS

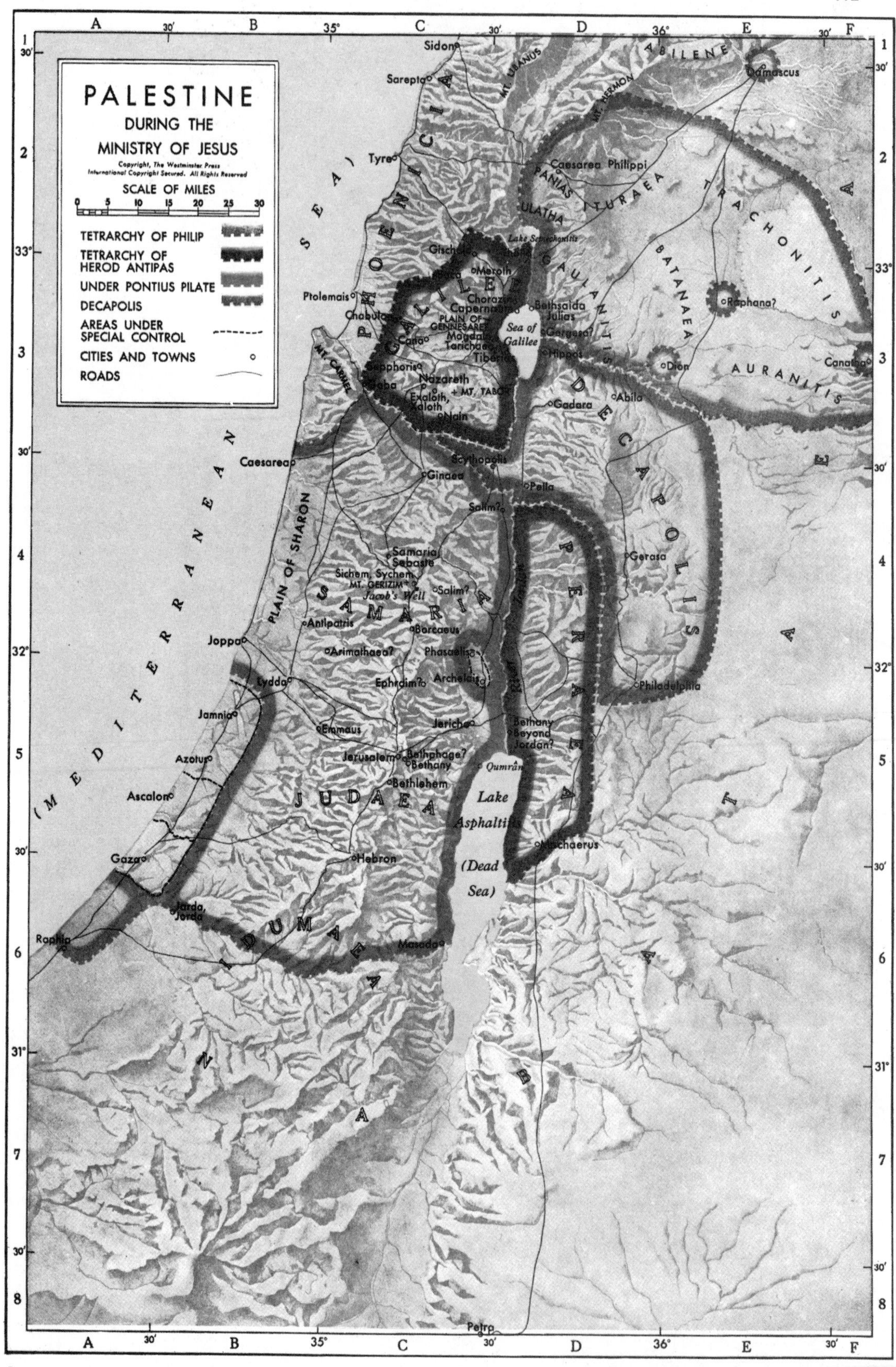

Cartography By G. A. Barrois and Hal & Jean Arbo

Edited By G. Ernest Wright and Floyd V. Filson

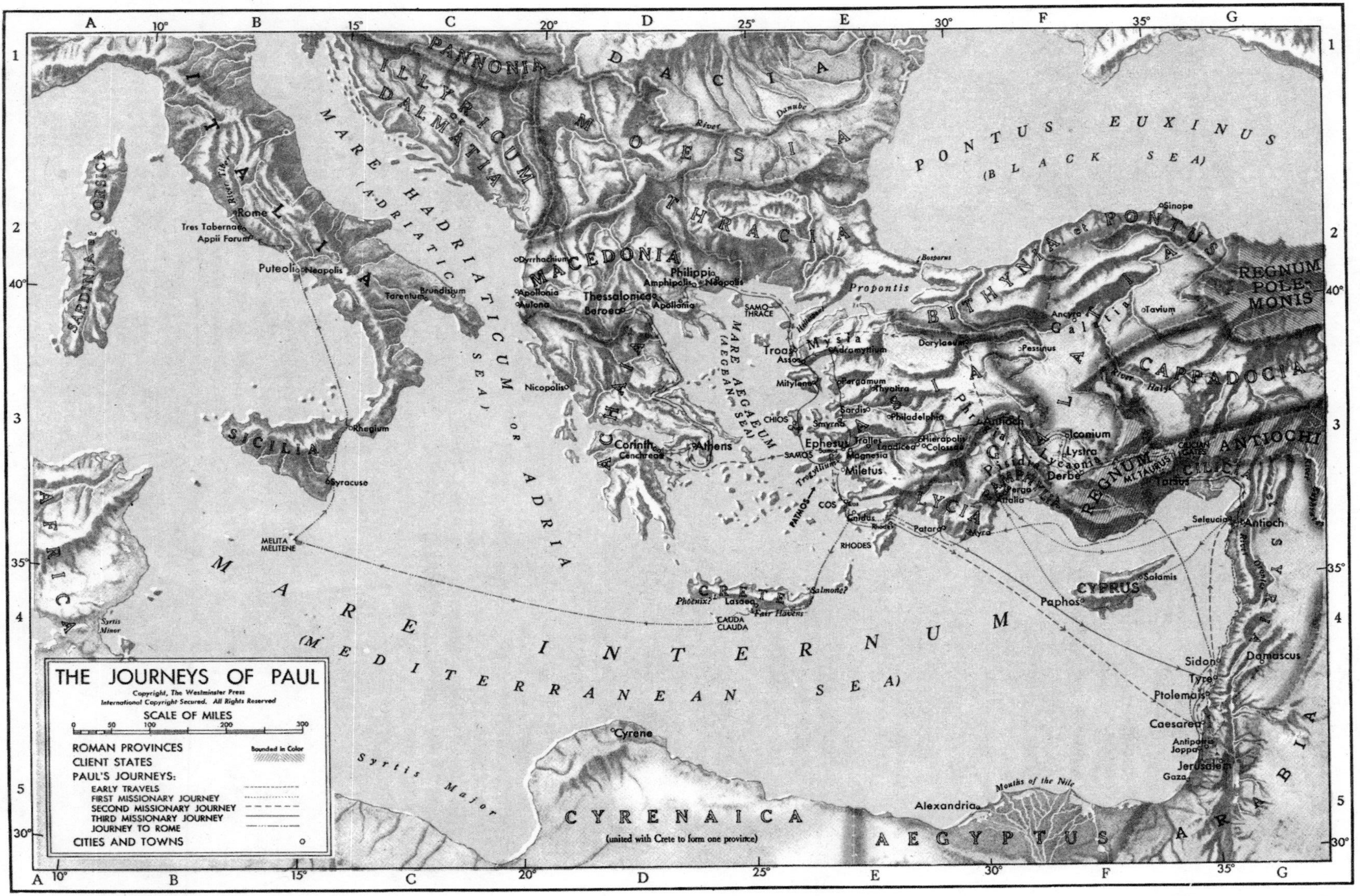

Cartography By Hal & Jean Arbo

Edited By G. Ernest Wright and Floyd V. Filson